Time-Saver Standards for
Landscape Architecture

DESIGN AND CONSTRUCTION DATA

COEDITORS

Charles W. Harris

Nicholas T. Dines

ASSISTANT EDITOR

Gary M. Fishbeck

CONSULTING EDITOR

Albert Fein

WITH A FOREWORD BY

Hideo Sasaki

McGraw-Hill Book Company

New York St. Louis San Francisco Auckland Bogotá
Hamburg London Madrid Mexico Milan
Montreal New Delhi Panama Paris São Paulo
Singapore Sydney Tokyo Toronto

Library of Congress Cataloging-in-Publication Data

Time-saver standards for landscape architecture.

Includes bibliographies and index.
1. Landscape architecture—Standards—Handbooks, manuals, etc. 2. Construction industry—Standards—Handbooks, manuals, etc. 3. Landscape architecture—Handbooks, manuals, etc. 4. Building—Handbooks, manuals, etc. I. Harris, Charles W. (Charles Ward) II. Dines, Nicholas T.
SB475.9.S72T55 1988 712'.0218 87-22817
ISBN 0-07-026725-1

1 2 3 4 5 6 7 8 9 0 HAL/HAL 8 9 3 2 1 0 9 8

ISBN 0-07-026725-1

The editors for this book were Nadine Post and Jim Bessent, the designers were Mark E. Safran and Naomi Auerbach, and the production supervisor was Richard A. Ausburn. It was set in Optima by University Graphics, Inc.

Printed and bound by Arcata Graphics/Halliday.

Contents

division 900: Details and Devices

Division Editors: Nicholas T. Dines and Gary M. Fishbeck
Technical Coordinator and Detailer: Chien-Cheng Wu, *Anthony Guzzardo & Associates*

Foreword

The publication of this handbook represents an historic event for the profession of landscape architecture. By scope and organization it provides a broad practical definition of what landscape architecture is as an applied art and science. The data and standards it contains demonstrate how and where the profession interconnects with the efforts of many specialists from different sciences and technologies. In this way it is a book for the future as much as it is for the present; it recognizes the need for more interdependence between the various professions as specific tasks become larger and more complicated.

The initial idea for this handbook was conceived by Jeremy Robinson, formerly a senior editor at McGraw-Hill, who saw the growing national and international importance of landscape architecture and the need for such a handbook on design and construction data. It would be not only for landscape architects but also for architects, planners, engineers, conservationists, land developers, landscape contractors, and others who are concerned with our natural environment and how it is modified. Dr. Albert Fein, a consulting editor for landscape and landscape architecture at McGraw-Hill, brought the concept to Professor Charles Harris of the Harvard Graduate School of Design. Professor Harris has spent most of his career teaching landscape architecture with an early and continuing interest in land planning, design, and development. This book is a natural outgrowth of his long-standing interest in landscape construction, which was first influenced by Professor Otto Schaeffer of the University of Illinois and later by Professor Walter L. Chambers of the Harvard Graduate School of Design. Harris enlisted the help of Professor Nicholas T. Dines of the Department of Landscape Architecture and Regional Planning, University of Massachusetts in organizing, compiling, and editing material for the handbook.

Two basic abilities were needed for the successful completion of this handbook. They were the ability to persuade a large number of practitioners and academics to contribute and/or review material for the various sections and the ability to organize this massive amount of information into a useful overall format. The task took longer and much more personal effort and funds than the editors planned. Because both editors are teachers, they should be pleased that this handbook will provide a way to continue their "teaching" long after they have ended their present academic careers.

Hideo Sasaki
Lafayette, California

Preface

Time-Saver Standards for Landscape Architecture: Design and Construction Data is a book about building on the land, a comprehensive process which involves several elements: (1) interaction with existing natural and cultural systems, (2) dependence upon both site-specific and equipment-specific design and construction techniques, and (3) the use of a wide range of materials and devices.

The book covers some 50 topics, each comprising a separate section and grouped into 9 divisions. They are linked together by a system of cross references. For example, when the topic of a section requires showing a variety of alternatives for one detail, such as a curb, the reader is shown only a few generic types within the section. Additional examples are covered under the appropriate heading in Division 900: Details and Devices.

The topics represented within this handbook are but a small portion of the potential range of topics that deserve treatment. Several other topics have already been identified and some have even received preliminary work, but for reasons of space, time, and other factors, they could not make it into this edition. Readers are invited to suggest topics and contributors for possible inclusion in later editions.

A dual system of measurements, U.S. standard and metric, has been included for many sections, but not all. The metric data, where shown, has been subordinated to the U.S. units.

Many of the standards shown in this book are considered to be minimal. The reader is urged to consider using more optimal standards for specific situations. Contributors were asked to include both "low-tech" and "high-tech" standards and data. It is expected that the reader will adapt the data as necessary for a specific application. References have been cited at the end of most sections from which more detailed data may be obtained. The reader is reminded that the data shown in this book cannot be considered a substitute for informed judgment based on careful consideration of all aspects of a specific problem. In all cases where public health and safety are involved, an authority on that problem should be consulted.

Charles W. Harris

Professor of Landscape Architecture, Emeritus
Harvard University, Cambridge, Massachusetts

Nicholas T. Dines

Professor of Landscape Architecture and Regional Planning
University of Massachusetts, Amherst, Massachusetts

Acknowledgments

Many individuals and organizations worked with the editors to assemble, edit, and prepare the material contained in this handbook. Others reviewed various drafts, and still others at McGraw-Hill refined the material for printing.

The contributors, technical writers, and reviewers who helped prepare the material for a section are shown at the beginning of that section. These individuals, often with their firm's, institution's, or agency's support, gave many years of effort to generating the substantive parts of the handbook. The contributors and technical writers were either known experts on the topic of their section or agreed to assemble useful material on that topic. The reviewers were selected because they too were experts or experienced professional practitioners with regard to a specific topic.

In addition to the vast amount of time and energy that went into preparing the substantive parts of this handbook, the entire project could not have been accomplished without the cooperation and support of our respective academic institutions as well as foundations, professional firms, commercial organizations, banks, and numerous individuals. Although neither Harvard University nor its Graduate School of Design had any formal ties or obligations to any aspect of the project, it could not have been completed without the cooperation and indirect support of the Design School. Special thanks go to Dean Gerald M. McCue, Associate Deans Polly Price, Kate Rooney, and J. Alden Brown and their support staff for allowing the project to be based within the school.

A large number of faculty, staff, and students in our two institutions contributed to the project. Some of these are acknowledged elsewhere in specific sections of the handbook. The editors want specifically to acknowledge the following individuals or groups:

- Gary M. Fishbeck, Assistant Editor, for his role in processing the final manuscript to give it overall continuity, plus his work on several sections as contributor and/or technical writer.
- Tess Canfield, Tobias Dayman, Daniel Bubly, Gary Bye, Robert Sykes, Gregg Bleam, Herbert Nolan, Alan Fujimori, John W. Burkholder, and Krisan Osterby-Benson, for their work on outlines, drafts, and final manuscripts for various sections.
- Chien-Cheng Wu, for generously donating his time assembling and contributing material to create Division 900.
- Thomas Oslund, for developing the techniques for making drawings on the MacIntosh computer, and Joseph Cloud, for almost single-handedly executing and laser-printing the computer drawings.
- The following people assisted with research or were graphic artists for many of the figures in the handbook. Among students, both U.S. and international, at

Harvard's Graduate School of Design are Laura C. Burnett, Raveevarn Choksombatchai (Thailand), Diane H. Dierkes, Kristanta Dewara (Indonesia), Douglas R. Findlay, Joanna Fong, Molly D. Gerard, Mark S. Goldschmidt, Nancy M. Green, Walter R. Havener, Vandee Jearkjirm (Thailand), Do Kyong Kim (South Korea), Jeffrey S. Lakey, Craig S. McGlynn, Just C. Moller, Leticia D'Aquino Morris, Sharon J. Murphy, Michael H. Nihan, Gregory J. Osband, Judith E. Otto, Laurel S. Raines, Nor Ain H. M. Rejab (Malaysia), Sara C. Robertson, Stuart H. Sacks, Gary M. Schiff, Elizabeth Shreeve, Austin K. Smith, Cynthia W. Smith, Kenneth W. Smith, Susan C. Stainback, and Bhakorn Vanuptikul (Thailand). Among the local graphic artists and employees of local design offices are John H. Coley, Samuel R. Coplan, Peter A. Davis, Jean E. Garbier, Steve Garbier, Carolynn S. Leaman, Kejoo Park (South Korea), Michael F. McGoldrick, and Camilo A. Santana.

- Rodney A. Cobi and Charles Burger for their input into the handbook, especially Division 800.
- Marla Abrams, Patty VanNess, and several others for their help with typing and general secretarial support.

Special thanks are in order for the firms of Sasaki Associates, Inc. of Watertown and The Architects' Collaborative of Cambridge. David Hirzel, Kenneth Bassett, and Maurice Freedman of the Sasaki office reviewed some material and gave us free access to the large pool of professional people in their office who reviewed or prepared material. Laurence Zuelke of The Architects' Collaborative did the same thing.

This handbook was funded in part by grants from The National Endowment for the Arts, The Hubbard Educational Trust (Boston, Massachusetts), and Harvard University through gifts made to a special account set up for this handbook project.

Jeremy Robinson, during his tenure at McGraw-Hill, suggested the idea of this handbook to Dr. Albert Fein, formerly consulting editor on landscape and landscape architecture for McGraw-Hill. It was to create a *Time-Saver Standards for Landscape Architecture* to parallel the other well-known books in the McGraw-Hill Time-Saver Series. The co-editors initially worked under the supervision of Joan Zseleczky, formerly a senior editor at McGraw-Hill, and also with Nadine Post, the current editor.

In addition, we wish to acknowledge James Bessent, for his efforts coordinating the flow of material, and Mark Safran and Naomi Auerbach for the design and layout of the handbook.

As every author or editor soon learns, the demands of producing a book begin to take over their lives in subtle but powerful ways. We recognize the special friendship and support we have received from Hideo Sasaki and Albert Fein with regard to this particular project and to our professional lives in general.

Finally, we want to thank our many friends and our families who allowed us to see this project through. We dedicate this book to our parents, wives, and children.

Charles W. Harris and Nicholas T. Dines

About the Editors

Charles Ward Harris, FASLA, is a professor of landscape architecture, emeritus, at Harvard University where he teaches the process of land development. He was department chairman for ten years and recently changed his status from full-time to part-time to resume private practice and research related to environmentally sensitive, socially needed, and financially sound land planning, design, and development.

Professor Harris has taught landscape architecture at both the University of Illinois (Urbana) and Harvard University. He has over 30 years of teaching experience and has also worked in the professional offices of John and Phillip Simonds (Pittsburgh), Hideo Sasaki and Peter Walker (Watertown), and The Architect's Collaborative (Cambridge and Rome, Italy) under the leadership of Walter Gropius and some of his associates. He also had a practice in Cambridge with two partners for six years and formed an international association of university and professional practitioners to do work overseas. He worked on large-scale planning, design, and development projects in various parts of the Middle East and North and Central America.

Professor Harris holds two bachelors' degrees from the University of Illinois: one in landscape architecture and one in landscape operations (landscape construction and contracting). He also earned a Master of Education degree from Harvard University. He lives in Watertown, Massachusetts.

Nicholas T. Dines, ASLA, is an associate professor of landscape architecture at the University of Massachusetts in Amherst where he teaches courses in landscape architecture construction technology, studio design, design theory, and drawing. He has been the Master of Landscape Architecture graduate program director for seven years and for five years was a visiting professor of landscape architecture at the Harvard University School of Design where he taught courses in landscape construction.

A graduate of Michigan State University and the Harvard University Graduate School of Design, Professor Dines has over 22 years of professional design and construction experience, including public and private works in the Mediterranean region. As a member of the American Society of Landscape Architects, he has conducted national seminars on energy-efficient site planning and has collaborated on instructional films about landscape construction and design drawing. Professor Dines is currently working with colleagues at the University of Massachusetts exploring aspects of spatial design theory and computer applications to design and construction drawing. He lives in Williamsburg, Massachusetts.

section 110: Construction Documents

CREDITS

Section Editor: Nicholas T. Dines
Illustrations for Figures 110-1 through 110-14 supplied by Sasaki Associates, Inc., Watertown, Massachusetts. These have been coordinated by Nancy Leask, Heather Ryan, Tom Ryan, and others within the office.

Reviewers:

Tom Ryan
Sasaki Associates, Inc.
Watertown, Massachusetts

Nelson Hammer
The Architect's Collaborative, Inc.
Cambridge, Massachusetts

CONTENTS

1.0 INTRODUCTION

1.1 General

The production of landscape construction drawings (which, together with the specifications, constitute *construction,* or *contract, documents*) culminates a systematic design process and begins the site development implementation or construction phase of project administration.

1.2 Planning, Design, and Construction Process

The use of a systematic planning and design process is an essential prerequisite for preparing landscape construction documents (drawings and specifications) for a project. The five major phases of the planning, design, and construction process are

PHASE 1: Project initiation
PHASE 2: Project or master planning
- Diagnostic investigation
- Analysis
- Planning/design concepts (schematic planning and design)
- Design development
- Construction documents
- Preconstruction and bidding

PHASE 3: Construction and supervision
PHASE 4: Assigning or marketing
PHASE 5: Management and operations

Table 110-1 outlines each of these phases and lists some of the major steps or considerations involved in each phase.

1.3 Example Project: Planning-Design-Construction Documents

The following drawings and related materials have been assembled by Sasaki Associates, Inc., of Watertown, Massachusetts, and represent the scope of work most generally associated with site planning projects. Although the figures pertain to a specific case study, they can serve as a general model for other similar projects (Figures 110-1 through 110-15).

TABLE 110-1
Planning Design Construction Process

Phase	*Activity*	*Description*
One	Project initiation: Initiation of a public or private project may occur in a variety of ways.	Some of the major steps or considerations are: ▪ Form and organize project development team. ▪ Draft preliminary goals, objectives, and program. ▪ Identify and perhaps secure possible site(s).
Two (project or master planning)	Diagnostic investigation: Collection and evaluation of readily available data via an initial investigation of the opportunities and constraints of a proposed project is done to determine whether to continue the process.	Some of the major steps or considerations are: ▪ Organize project planning process and form team of participants. ▪ Survey literature, area, and site data, maps, photos, etc. ▪ Collect data on policies, legislation, programs, and plans related to the project. ▪ Identify critical issues and policies. ▪ Prepare initial development program and strategies. ▪ Execute preliminary planning and design concepts. ▪ Perform initial pro forma and cash flow analyses. ▪ Explore financial and ownership strategies. ▪ Make informal contacts with approval agencies, etc. ▪ Decide to go ahead, modify, or drop project.
	Analysis: Purpose is to examine all information available, research any missing information, and put all data into a form for use during the course of the project.	Some of the major steps or considerations are: ▪ Plan the inventory process. ▪ Prepare base maps. ▪ Do a demand study and market analysis. ▪ Perform physical area, site inventory, and analysis. ▪ Analyze cultural, political, and social factors. ▪ Determine approval requirements and consequent strategies.
	Planning/design concepts (schematic planning and design): The objective is to determine whether a project is feasible based on the needs of the client or users and the physical, economic, political, and legal aspects of the proposed project.	Some of the major steps or considerations are: ▪ Define program and alternatives. ▪ Establish design criteria and standards. ▪ Do conceptual or schematic plans. ▪ Develop prototypical design studies. ▪ Establish square footages, number of units, etc. ▪ Test feasibility of important design elements. ▪ Analyze impact of each use concept. ▪ Test market reaction to various concepts. ▪ Refine earlier cost estimates (based on above). ▪ Refine projections of cash flow. ▪ Determine public response to concepts. ▪ Seek preliminary approvals for final concept. ▪ Obtain preliminary commitments for financing.
	Technical documents: Final approvals are contingent upon refinement of the schematic plans into design development documents (DD), and then into construction documents (CD).	Design development includes the following major steps or considerations: ▪ Prepare site, building, and engineering plans. ▪ Evaluate design for marketing purposes. ▪ Assess legal and community planning implications. ▪ Make economic analysis to confirm costs. ▪ Perform sensitivity analysis of major assumptions.

(*Continued*)

Phase	Activity	Description
		Construction documents include the following types of drawings (letter symbols are used as prefixes to page numbers in order to differentiate the various disciplines): ■ L or SD: Landscape or site ■ IL: Interior landscape ■ A or AD: Architectural ■ C or CE: Civil engineering ■ S or SE: Structural engineering ■ M or ME: Mechanical engineering ■ E or EE: Electrical engineering Final public approval comes as a result of submission of some or all of the above documents as required for each project.
	Preconstruction: The management of the construction process should be planned carefully to ensure a well-organized construction process and maximum control of quality and cost.	Some of the major steps or considerations are: ■ Organize the construction management process. ■ Prepare preconstruction schedules (CPM, PERT, etc.) ■ Meet with potential bidders. ■ Solicit bids within a predetermined process. ■ Negotiate contracts with selected bidder(s). ■ Award contracts. ■ If required, do final closing on property. ■ Start construction financing.
Three	Construction and supervision: Contractors needed to complete specified tasks and project manager needed to coordinate the work.	Some of the major steps or considerations are: ■ To construct, supervise, and coordinate, including administration, scheduling, reporting, recording, inspection, and cost control, etc. ■ To accept plans, including approving completed work and payments to contractors.
Four	Assigning or marketing: If not determined before the project starts, finding users or "buyers" is normally started in parallel with earlier phases and is completed as soon as possible.	Some of the major steps or considerations are: ■ Develop assignment or sales strategy. ■ Prepare promotion or advertising material. ■ Initiate program for assignments or sales. ■ Review marketing and market continuously.
Five	Management and operations: This phase should be started while the project is being designed	Some of the major steps or considerations are: ■ Establish management team. ■ Prepare management and operations plan. ■ Provide for necessary staff budgets, facilities, equipment, and materials, etc.

The project example shown is the product of a team effort of designers and other professionals (listed below) working very closely with the owners to create a new corporate headquarters for the firm of TRW, Inc.

The program required that a 450,000-ft^2 office building be sited and built on a 100-acre mature estate. The site analysis indicated that the building could maximize landscape views and minimize flooding hazards and avoid poor soils by being sited on the hilltops. In addition, a design analysis indicated that surface parking or a freestanding parking structure would obscure the best features and views of the site. The solution adopted placed all parking beneath the building, thereby ensuring that each office had a view of the exterior landscape or into the large interior atrium.

After completion of the preliminary concept studies for the site and building, an *early action program* was created. This called for the transplanting of trees, shrubs, and large areas of ground cover where the new buildings and roads were to be placed. An on-site nursery was to be established to hold the plants that could not be transplanted immediately. To protect the remaining plant material and other landscape elements, erosion control measures and protective fences were to be installed. Having decided to take such extensive and costly measures to save and enhance the existing landscape, it was decided to make a videotape in which the owner, construction manager, and design team would explain the intent, methods, and rules for protecting the site. Every tradesperson working on the site was required to view this videotape prior to starting work.

The illustrations (Figures 110-1 through 110-15) represent only a very small sample of the types and numbers of documents used to design and build this project. Some were prepared only for study purposes, while others were part of the contract documents. Some of the examples shown are a small portion of larger plans, which were reduced to fit the limited space of this handbook.

Consultant Credits:

Owner:	TRW, Inc. Lyndhurst, Ohio
Architect:	Lohan Associates Chicago, Illinois
Landscape Architect:	Sasaki Associates, Inc. Watertown, Massachusetts
Civil Engineer:	Bevins Consultants, Inc. Chicago, Illinois
Forester:	Urban Forest Management Prairie View, Illinois
Lighting Designer:	Howard Brandston Lighting Design, Inc. New York, New York
Interior Design:	Interspace, Inc. Philadelphia, Pennsylvania
Construction Manager:	Gilbane Building Company Cleveland, Ohio
Soils:	Herron Consultants, Inc. Cleveland, Ohio
Mechanical Engineer:	Environmental Systems Design, Inc. Chicago, Illinois
Structural Engineer:	GCE of Illinois, Inc. Chicago, Illinois

Figure 110-1 Site prior to Development. The photograph shows the existing estate grounds selected as the site for the new corporate headquarters of TRW, Inc.

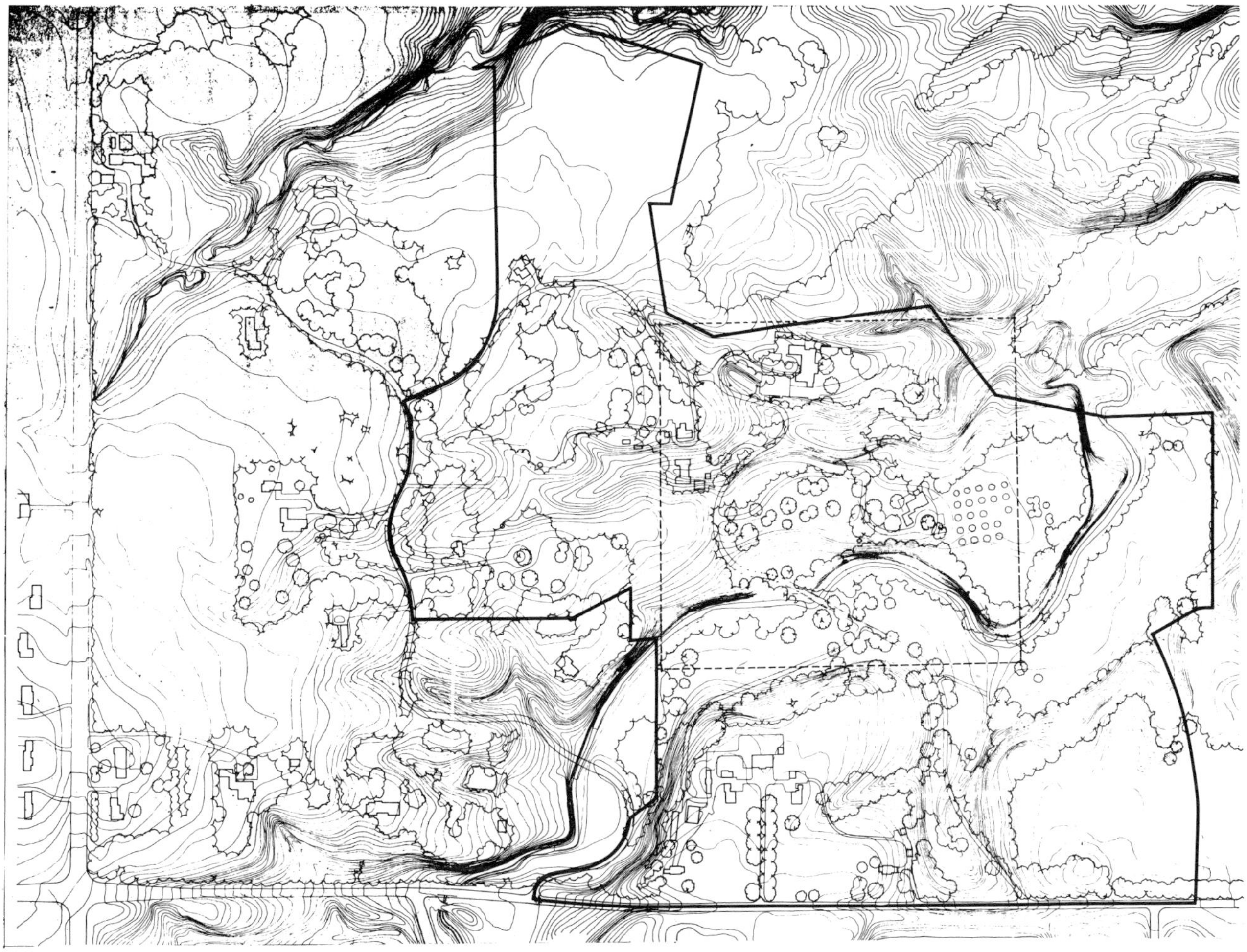

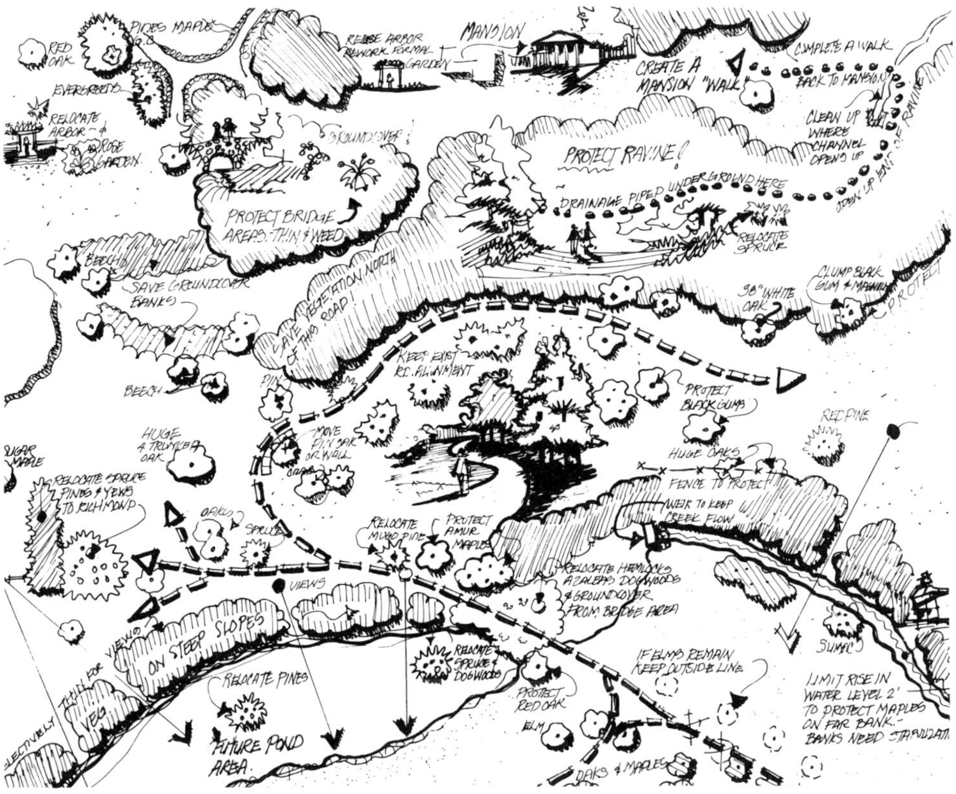
RED OAK
EVERGREENS
RELOCATE ARBOR & ROSE GARDEN
MANSION
CREATE A MANSION "WALK"
COMPLETE A WALK BACK TO MANSION
CLEAN UP WHERE CHANNEL OPENS UP
PROTECT RAVINE!
DRAINAGE PIPED UNDERGROUND HERE
GROUNDCOVER
PROTECT BRIDGE AREAS: THIN & WEED
RELOCATE SPRUCE
BEECH
SAVE GROUNDCOVER BANKS
SAVE VEGETATION NORTH OF THIS ROAD
CLUMP BLACK GUM & MAGNOLIA
38" WHITE OAK
PROTECT BLACK GUMS
RED PINE
HUGE OAKS
FENCE TO PROTECT
WEIR TO KEEP CREEK FLOW
SUGAR MAPLE
RELOCATE SPRUCE PINES & YEWS TO RICHMOND
OAKS
PROTECT AMUR MAPLES
VIEWS
ON STEEP SLOPES
SUMAC
IF ELMS REMAIN KEEP OUTSIDE LINE
RELOCATE PINES
PROTECT RED OAK
ELM
FUTURE POND AREA
OAKS & MAPLES

Figure 110-2 (*Above*) Survey and Base Plan. The base plan shows some of the existing natural features, such as topography, significant vegetation, waterbodies and channels, roads, drives, structures, and utilities. This information was obtained from aerial photos, surveys, and on-site investigations. (The dashed box shows the location for Figures 110-3, 110-5, and others.)

Figure 110-3 (*Left*) Landscape Assessment. A site inventory and analysis was conducted to determine the opportunities and constraints of the site as well as its relationships to the surrounding area. The drawing shown is one of several that were prepared to assess the various qualities of the TRW, Inc., site.

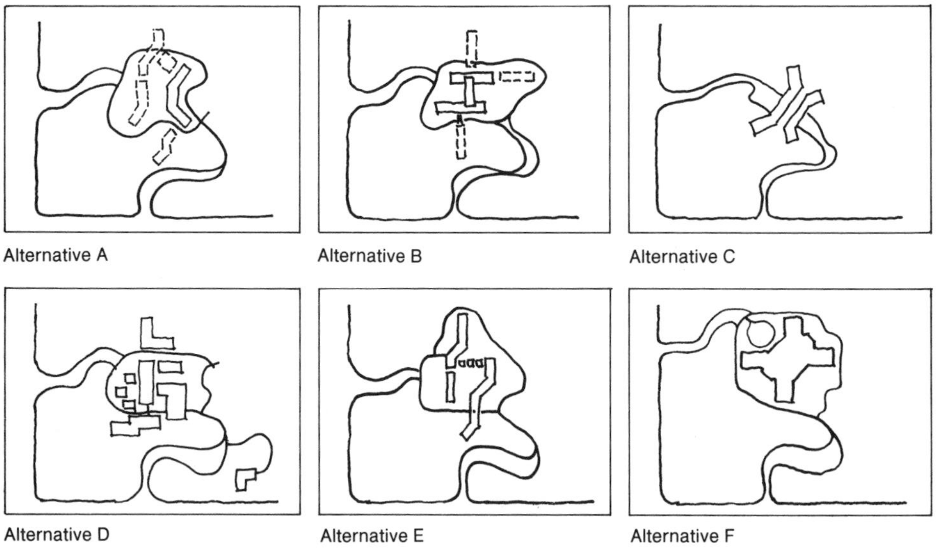
Alternative A
Alternative B
Alternative C
Alternative D
Alternative E
Alternative F

Figure 110-4 Site and Building Concept Studies. The building space-planning and massing studies evolved concurrently with the site planning studies. Various alternatives were studied, and alternative *F* was selected.

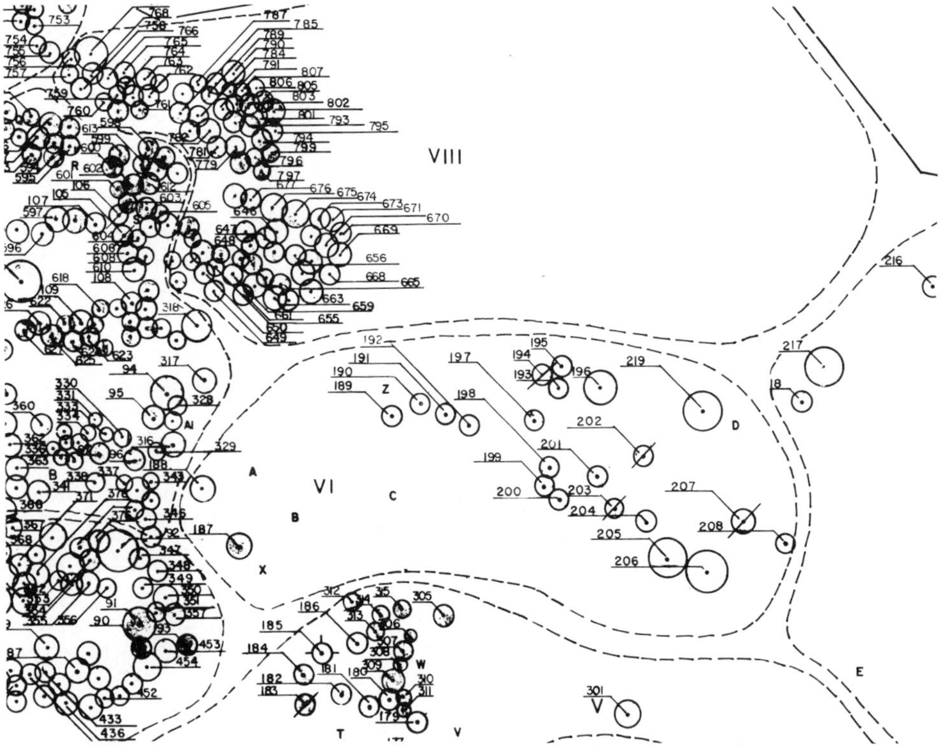
VIII
VI

Figure 110-5 Horticultural Survey. Based upon the site and building concept studies, an intensive on-site survey was completed to identify and tag existing vegetation that was to be saved. These data were recorded in a field survey manual and on survey drawings. (See dashed box in middle of Figure 110-2.)

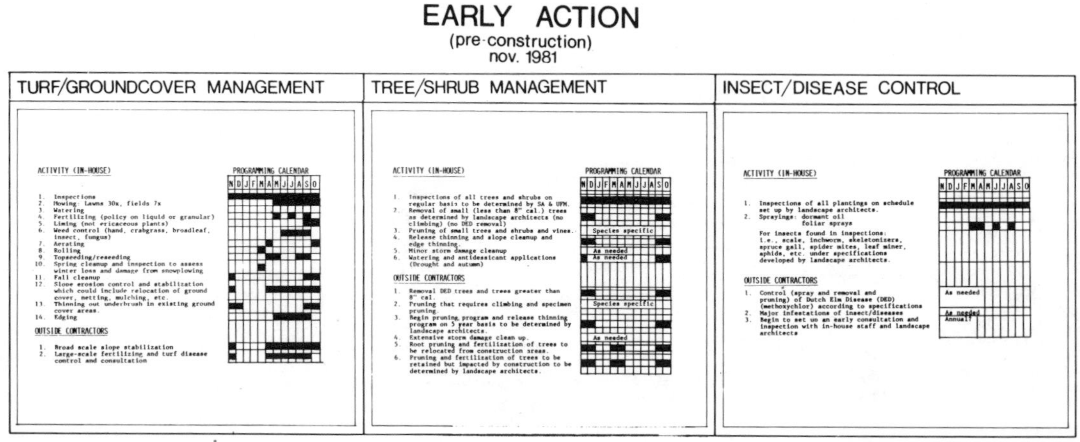
EARLY ACTION
(pre-construction)
nov. 1981
TURF/GROUNDCOVER MANAGEMENT
TREE/SHRUB MANAGEMENT
INSECT/DISEASE CONTROL

Figure 110-6 (*Below*) Early Action Program. An early action program was created to help save and enhance the existing landscape, especially the woodlands. The early action schedule and plan (plan not shown) preceded all construction activity. The schedule identified existing turf, ground-cover, shrub, and tree management issues, including insect and disease problems, transplantation out of development areas, extensive pruning, and the personnel and equipment required to carry out the schedule. The *Yield To The Trees* logo was given to every worker on the site after they had viewed a videotape produced by the owner to explain the rules and methods of construction to protect the site.

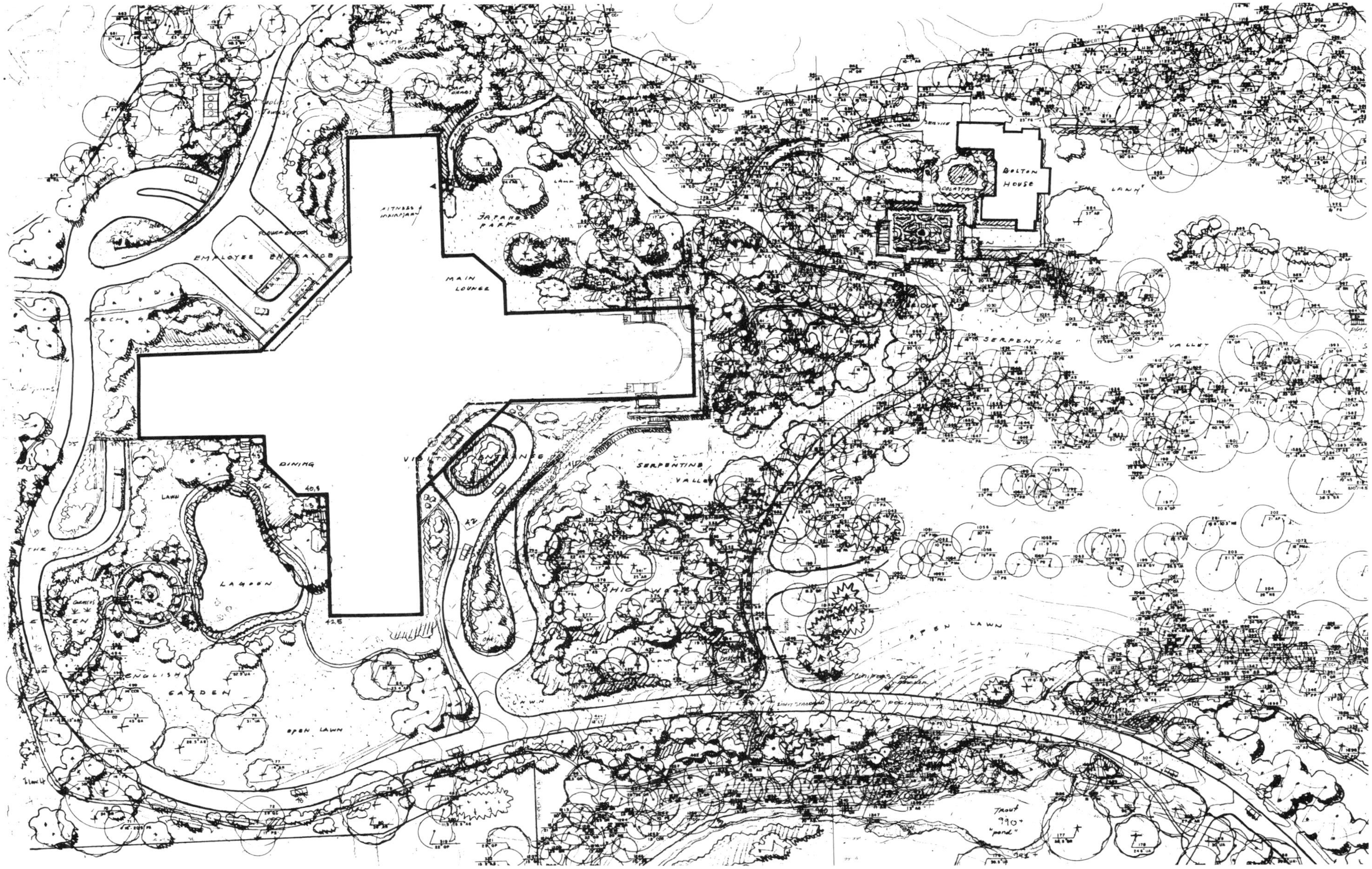
BOLTON HOUSE
SERPENTINE
VALLEY
OPEN LAWN
JAPANESE PARK
MAIN LOUNGE
FITNESS & INFIRMARY
EMPLOYEE ENTRANCE
DINING
LAGOON
ENGLISH GARDEN
OPEN LAWN
LAWN
SERPENTINE VALLEY
TROUT "pond"

Figure 110-7 Schematic Design Plan. The schematic plan shows in more detail the location of the proposed elements of the site. In the example shown, the plan was drawn over the horticultural survey plan. In this way the designer was able to utilize horticultural information when making site planning decisions.

TREES IN BACKGROUND
42.33
Skylight
DINING
38.5
POND
WATER EL: 37.5
B. SECTION AT BUILDING
PATH
38.5

Figure 110-8 (*Above*) Schematic Sections. Sections and sketches (sketches not shown) of selected parts of the schematic plan were drawn to determine the general validity of the grading scheme, planting plan, and other aspects of the proposed development. The above illustration is a section from building edge to pond edge.

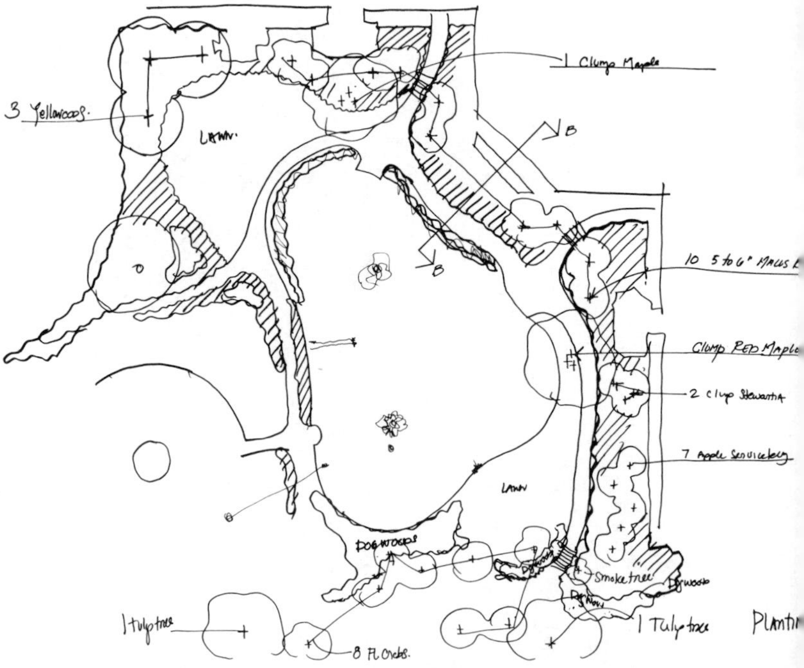
1 Clump Maple
3 Yellowwoods
LAWN
B
10 5 to 6" Malus
Clump Red Maple
2 clump Stewartia
7 Apple Serviceberry
LAWN
Dogwoods
Smoketree
Dogwood
1 Tulip tree
1 Tulip tree
Plantin

Figure 110-9 (*Above right*) Schematic Sketch Plan for the Pond Area. The schematic sketch plan establishes the rough character of the proposed landscape for the pond area. This plan also includes the labeling of plants.

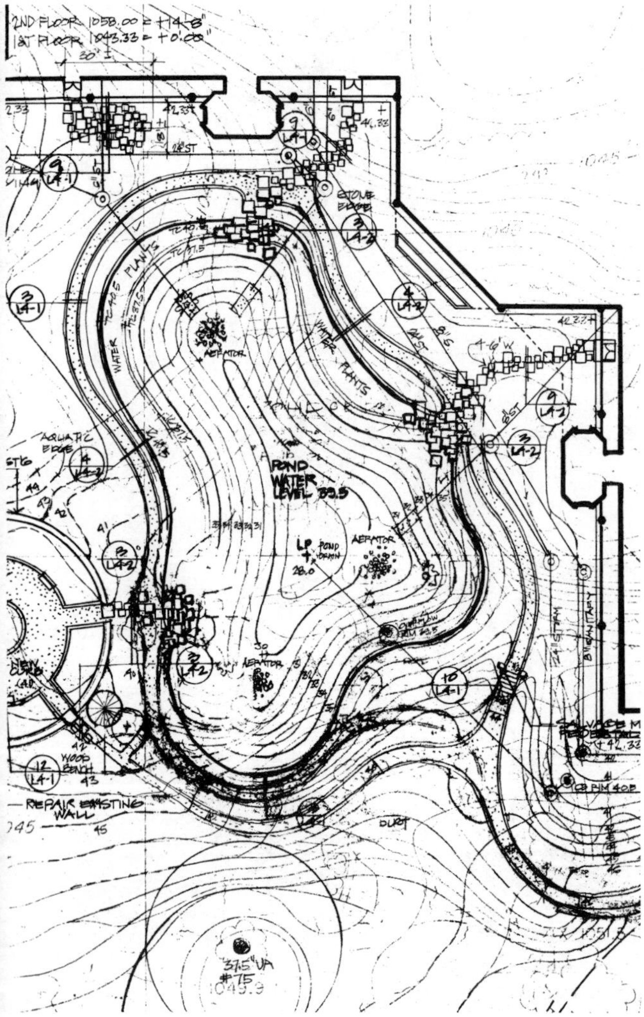
POND
WATER
LEVEL 33.5
AERATOR
AQUATIC EDGE
WOOD BENCH
REPAIR EXISTING WALL

Figure 110-10 (*Left*) Design Development Phase. In the design development phase, design concepts were translated into plans showing the scope of all improvements and the specific intent of the design. The above illustration shows grading, storm drainage, and constructed elements for the pond area.

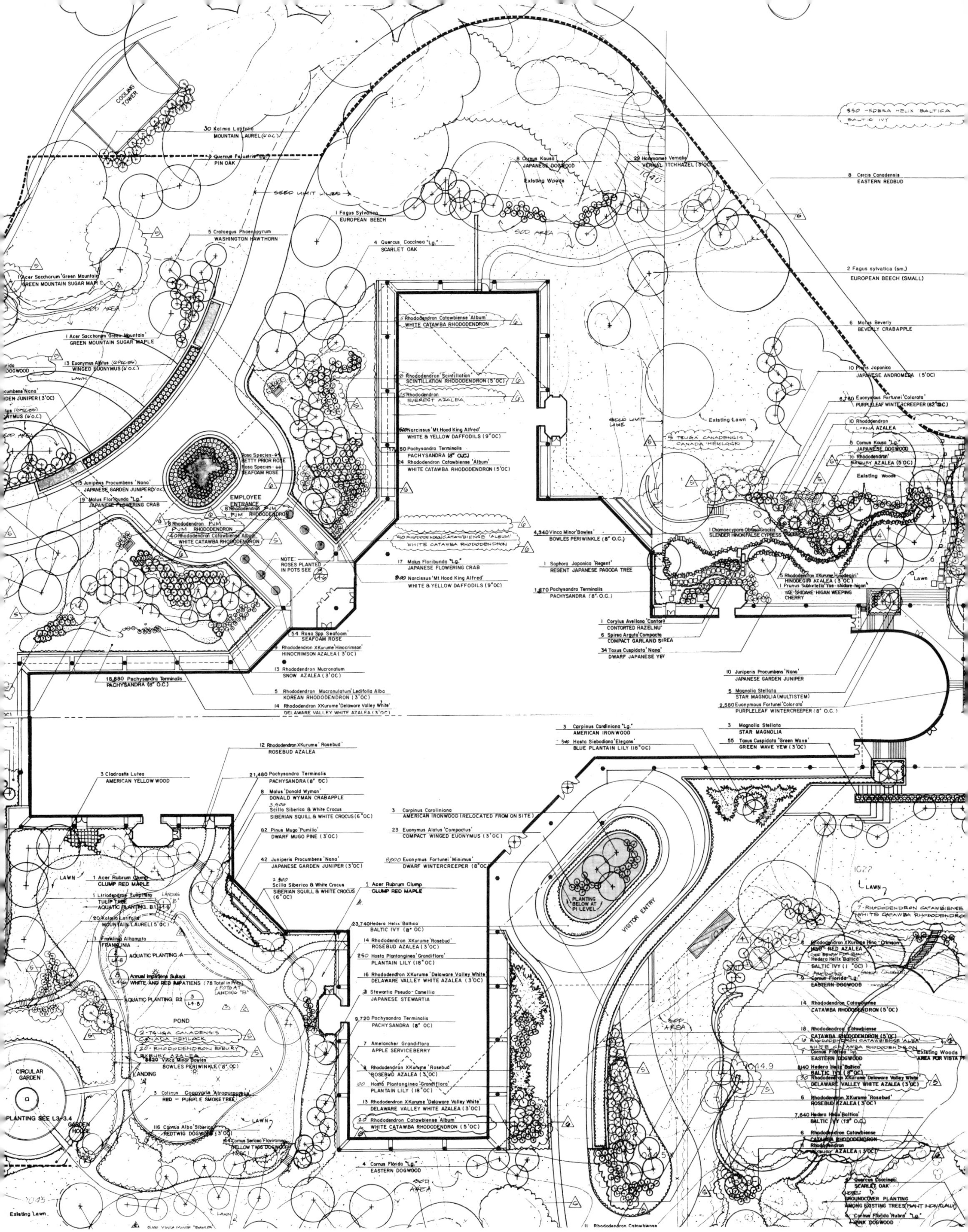
COOLING TOWER
30 Kalmia Latifolia
MOUNTAIN LAUREL (6' OC)
3 Quercus Palustris
PIN OAK
SEED LIMIT LINES
5 Crataegus Phaenopyrum
WASHINGTON HAWTHORN
1 Acer Saccharum 'Green Mountain'
GREEN MOUNTAIN SUGAR MAPLE
SOD AREA
1 Acer Saccharum 'Green Mountain'
GREEN MOUNTAIN SUGAR MAPLE
13 Euonymus Alatus
WINGED EUONYMUS (6' O.C.)
LAWN
Rosa Species
BETTY PRIOR ROSE
Rosa Species
SEAFOAM ROSE
15 Juniperus Procumbens 'Nana'
JAPANESE GARDEN JUNIPER (3' OC)
19 Malus Floribunda 'Lg.'
JAPANESE FLOWERING CRAB
EMPLOYEE ENTRANCE
8 Rhododendron PJM
PJM RHODODENDRON
40 Rhododendron Catawbiense 'Album'
WHITE CATAWBA RHODODENDRON
NOTE: ROSES PLANTED IN POTS SEE
1 Fagus Sylvatica
EUROPEAN BEECH
4 Quercus Coccinea 'Lg.'
SCARLET OAK
8 Cornus Kousa
JAPANESE DOGWOOD
Existing Woods
29 Hamamelis Vernalis
VERNAL WITCHHAZEL (5' OC)
SOD AREA
Rhododendron Catawbiense 'Album'
WHITE CATAWBA RHODODENDRON
Rhododendron 'Scintillation'
SCINTILLATION RHODODENDRON (5' OC)
Rhododendron
EVEREST AZALEA
Narcissus 'Mt. Hood King Alfred'
WHITE & YELLOW DAFFODILS (9" OC)
Pachysandra Terminalis
PACHYSANDRA
24 Rhododendron Catawbiense 'Album'
WHITE CATAWBA RHODODENDRON (5' OC)
40 Rhododendron Catawbiense 'Album'
WHITE CATAWBA RHODODENDRON
17 Malus Floribunda 'Lg.'
JAPANESE FLOWERING CRAB
Narcissus 'Mt. Hood King Alfred'
WHITE & YELLOW DAFFODILS (9" OC)
54 Rosa Spp. Seafoam
SEAFOAM ROSE
Rhododendron X Kurume 'Hinocrimson'
HINOCRIMSON AZALEA (3' OC)
13 Rhododendron Mucronatum
SNOW AZALEA (3' OC)
18,880 Pachysandra Terminalis
PACHYSANDRA (8" O.C.)
5 Rhododendron Mucronulatum 'Ledifolia Alba'
KOREAN RHODODENDRON (3' OC)
14 Rhododendron X Kurume 'Delaware Valley White'
DELAWARE VALLEY WHITE AZALEA (3' OC)
$50 HEDERA HELIX BALTICA
BALTIC IVY
8 Cercis Canadensis
EASTERN REDBUD
2 Fagus sylvatica (sm.)
EUROPEAN BEECH (SMALL)
6 Malus Beverly
BEVERLY CRABAPPLE
10 Pieris Japonica
JAPANESE ANDROMEDA (5' OC)
6,760 Euonymus Fortunei 'Colorata'
PURPLELEAF WINTERCREEPER (8" OC)
10 Rhododendron
LORNA AZALEA
6 Cornus Kousa 'Lg.'
JAPANESE DOGWOOD
16 Rhododendron
EXBURY AZALEA (5' OC)
Existing Woods
SEED LIMIT LINE
Existing Lawn
5 TSUGA CANADENSIS
CANADA HEMLOCK
4,340 Vinca Minor 'Bowles'
BOWLES PERIWINKLE (8" O.C.)
1 Sophora Japonica 'Regent'
REGENT JAPANESE PAGODA TREE
1,870 Pachysandra Terminalis
PACHYSANDRA (8" O.C.)
1 Chamaecyparis Obtusa 'Gracilis'
SLENDER HINOKI FALSE CYPRESS
5 Rhododendron X Kurume 'Hinodegiri'
HINODEGIRI AZALEA (3' OC)
1 Prunus Subhirtella 'Yae-shidare-higan'
YAE-SHIDARE-HIGAN WEEPING CHERRY
Lawn
1 Corylus Avellana 'Contorta'
CONTORTED HAZELNUT
6 Spirea Arguta 'Compacta'
COMPACT GARLAND SPIREA
34 Taxus Cuspidata 'Nana'
DWARF JAPANESE YEW
10 Juniperus Procumbens 'Nana'
JAPANESE GARDEN JUNIPER
5 Magnolia Stellata
STAR MAGNOLIA (MULTISTEM)
2,580 Euonymus Fortunei 'Colorata'
PURPLELEAF WINTERCREEPER (8" O.C.)
3 Carpinus Caroliniana 'Lg.'
AMERICAN IRONWOOD
Hosta Sieboldiana 'Elegans'
BLUE PLANTAIN LILY (18" OC)
3 Magnolia Stellata
STAR MAGNOLIA
55 Taxus Cuspidata 'Green Wave'
GREEN WAVE YEW (3' OC)
12 Rhododendron X Kurume 'Rosebud'
ROSEBUD AZALEA
3 Cladrastis Lutea
AMERICAN YELLOW WOOD
21,480 Pachysandra Terminalis
PACHYSANDRA (8" OC)
8 Malus 'Donald Wyman'
DONALD WYMAN CRABAPPLE
Scilla Siberica & White Crocus
SIBERIAN SQUILL & WHITE CROCUS (6" OC)
82 Pinus Mugo 'Pumilio'
DWARF MUGO PINE (3' OC)
42 Juniperis Procumbens 'Nana'
JAPANESE GARDEN JUNIPER (3' OC)
Scilla Siberica & White Crocus
SIBERIAN SQUILL & WHITE CROCUS (6" OC)
3 Carpinus Caroliniana
AMERICAN IRONWOOD (RELOCATED FROM ON SITE)
23 Euonymus Alatus 'Compactus'
COMPACT WINGED EUONYMUS (3' OC)
8,000 Euonymus Fortunei 'Minimus'
DWARF WINTERCREEPER (8" OC)
1 Acer Rubrum Clump
CLUMP RED MAPLE
PLANTING BELOW AT P1 LEVEL
VISITOR ENTRY
LAWN
1 Acer Rubrum Clump
CLUMP RED MAPLE
1 Liriodendron Tulipifera
TULIP TREE
AQUATIC PLANTING
20 Kalmia Latifolia
MOUNTAIN LAUREL (5' OC)
3 Franklinia Alatamaha
FRANKLINIA
AQUATIC PLANTING A
Annual Impatiens Sultani
WHITE AND RED IMPATIENS (78 Total in Pots)
AQUATIC PLANTING B2
POND
2 TSUGA CANADENSIS
CANADA HEMLOCK
20 RHODODENDRON EXBURY
EXBURY AZALEA
Vinca Minor 'Bowles'
BOWLES PERIWINKLE (8" OC)
LANDING
CIRCULAR GARDEN
PLANTING SEE L3-3.4
3 Cotinus Coggygria 'Atropurpureus'
RED - PURPLE SMOKE TREE
GARDEN HOUSE
116 Cornus Alba 'Siberica'
REDTWIG DOGWOOD (3' OC)
14 Cornus Sericea 'Flaviramea'
YELLOW TWIG DOGWOOD
LAWN
Existing Lawn
23,740 Hedera Helix 'Baltica'
BALTIC IVY (8" OC)
14 Rhododendron X Kurume 'Rosebud'
ROSEBUD AZALEA (3' OC)
250 Hosta Plantaginea 'Grandiflora'
PLANTAIN LILY (18" OC)
16 Rhododendron X Kurume 'Delaware Valley White'
DELAWARE VALLEY WHITE AZALEA (3' OC)
3 Stewartia Pseudo-Camellia
JAPANESE STEWARTIA
9,720 Pachysandra Terminalis
PACHYSANDRA (8" OC)
7 Amelanchier Grandiflora
APPLE SERVICEBERRY
8 Rhododendron X Kurume 'Rosebud'
ROSEBUD AZALEA (3' OC)
100 Hosta Plantaginea 'Grandiflora'
PLANTAIN LILY (18" OC)
13 Rhododendron X Kurume 'Delaware Valley White'
DELAWARE VALLEY WHITE AZALEA (3' OC)
20 Rhododendron Catawbiense 'Album'
WHITE CATAWBA RHODODENDRON (5' OC)
4 Cornus Florida 'Lg.'
EASTERN DOGWOOD
SOD AREA
LAWN
7 RHODODENDRON CATAWBIENSE
WHITE CATAWBA RHODODENDRON
Rhododendron X Kurume 'Hino-Crimson'
HINO-RED AZALEA
Hedera Helix Baltica
BALTIC IVY
Cornus Florida 'Lg.'
EASTERN DOGWOOD
14 Rhododendron Catawbiense
CATAWBA RHODODENDRON (5' OC)
18 Rhododendron Catawbiense
CATAWBA RHODODENDRON (5' OC)
Cornus Florida
EASTERN DOGWOOD
Existing Woods
AREA FOR VISTA
8,140 Hedera Helix 'Baltica'
BALTIC IVY (8" OC)
30 Rhododendron X Kurume 'Delaware Valley White'
DELAWARE VALLEY WHITE AZALEA (3' OC)
6 Rhododendron X Kurume 'Rosebud'
ROSEBUD AZALEA (3' OC)
7,840 Hedera Helix 'Baltica'
BALTIC IVY (12" O.C.)
6 Rhododendron Catawbiense
CATAWBA RHODODENDRON
Rhododendron
EXBURY AZALEA (3' OC)
Quercus Coccinea
SCARLET OAK
GROUNDCOVER PLANTING AMONG EXISTING TREES
Cornus Florida 'Rubra' 'Lg.'
PINK DOGWOOD
11 Rhododendron Catawbiense
SOD AREA

Figure 110-11 Construction Document Phase. The construction document phase involves the drafting of various technical drawings and specifications needed to construct the project. The above illustration shows the planting plan for the project, with a background reference of the proposed grading and layout for the area.

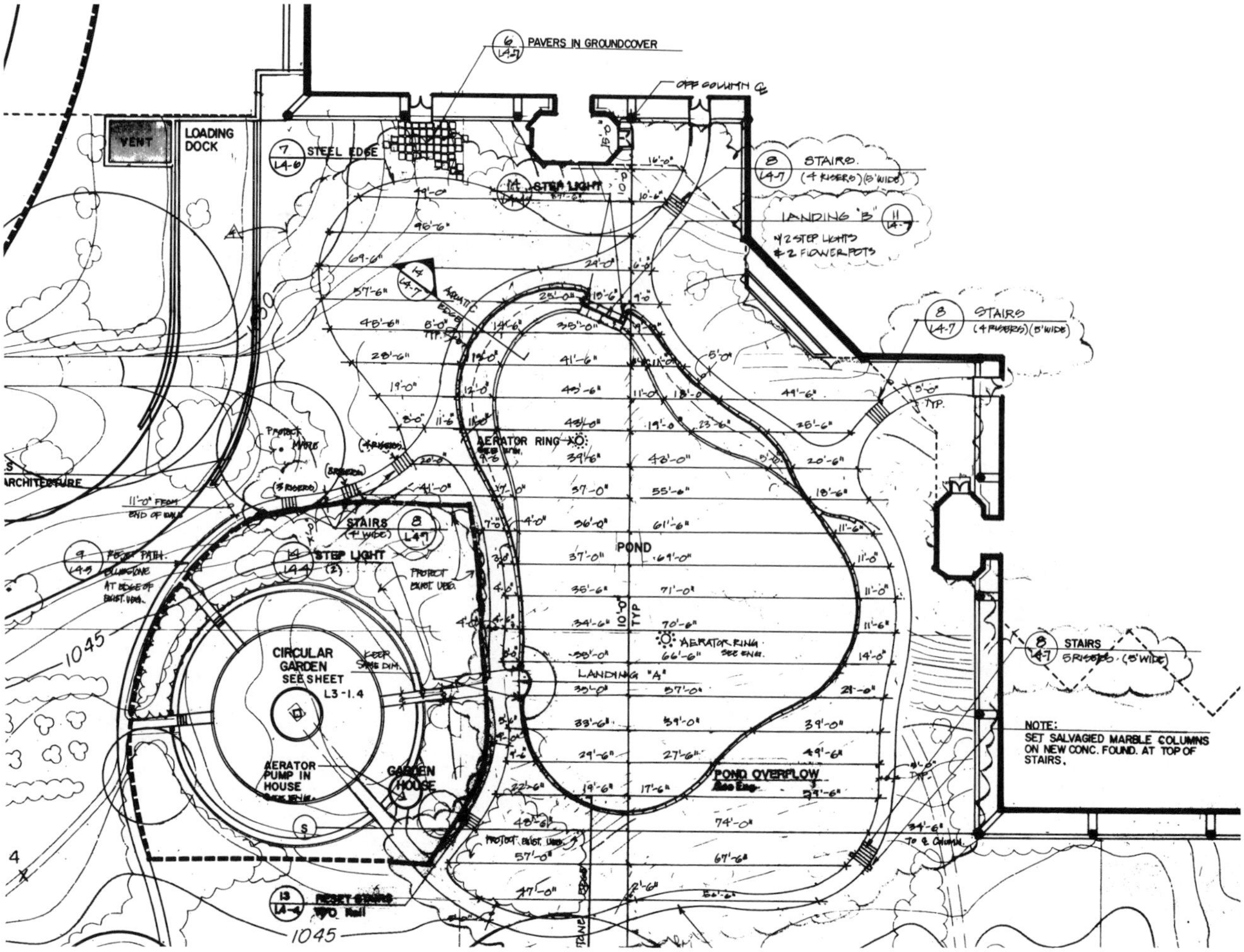
PAVERS IN GROUNDCOVER
LOADING DOCK
VENT
STEEL EDGE
STEP LIGHT
STAIRS (4 RISERS)(8' WIDE)
LANDING "B"
12 STEP LIGHTS
2 FLOWER POTS
STAIRS (4 RISERS)(5' WIDE)
AERATOR RING
POND
STAIRS (4' WIDE)
STEP LIGHT
CIRCULAR GARDEN SEE SHEET L3-1.4
AERATOR PUMP IN HOUSE
GARDEN HOUSE
LANDING "A"
AERATOR RING
POND OVERFLOW
STAIRS
NOTE:
SET SALVAGED MARBLE COLUMNS ON NEW CONC. FOUND. AT TOP OF STAIRS.
1045

Figure 110-12 (*Above*) Layout and Materials Plan. This figure shows the layout plan for the pond area. The precise locations of all proposed elements are shown, with identification of all materials to be used.

Figure 110-13 (*Left and below*) Construction Details. Construction details are used to provide vertical information (sections, elevations, perspectives, etc.) or plan details unsuitable for general plans or specifications. The examples show some of the details for the pond.

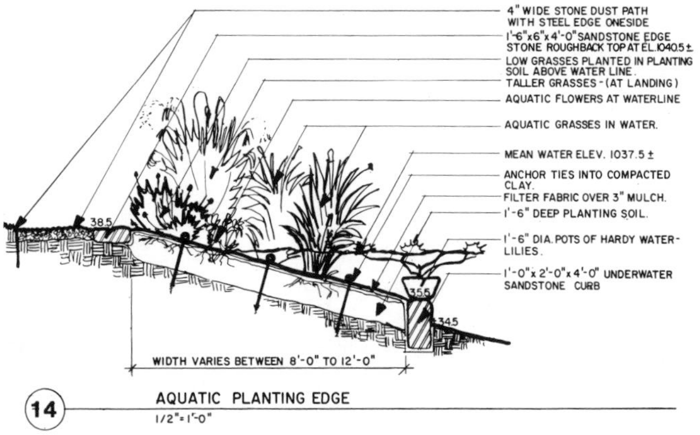
4" WIDE STONE DUST PATH WITH STEEL EDGE ONESIDE
1'-6"x6"x4'-0" SANDSTONE EDGE STONE ROUGHBACK TOP AT EL. 1040.5 ±
LOW GRASSES PLANTED IN PLANTING SOIL ABOVE WATER LINE.
TALLER GRASSES - (AT LANDING)
AQUATIC FLOWERS AT WATERLINE
AQUATIC GRASSES IN WATER.
MEAN WATER ELEV. 1037.5 ±
ANCHOR TIES INTO COMPACTED CLAY.
FILTER FABRIC OVER 3" MULCH.
1'-6" DEEP PLANTING SOIL.
1'-6" DIA. POTS OF HARDY WATER-LILIES.
1'-0"x 2'-0"x 4'-0" UNDERWATER SANDSTONE CURB
WIDTH VARIES BETWEEN 8'-0" TO 12'-0"
14 AQUATIC PLANTING EDGE
1/2"=1'-0"

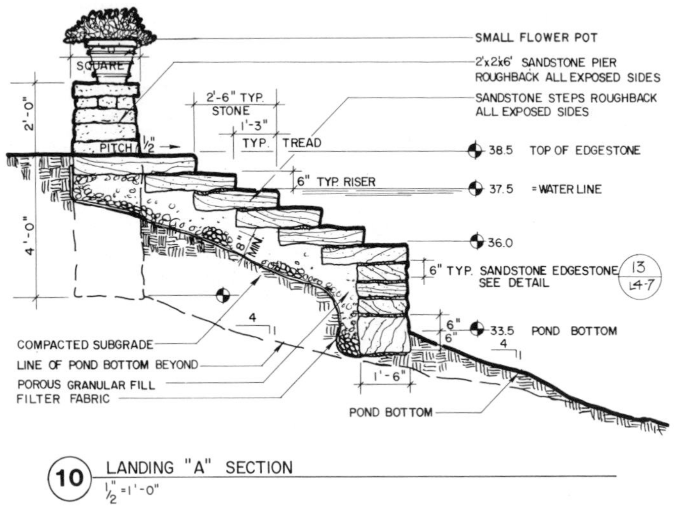
SMALL FLOWER POT
2'x2'x6' SANDSTONE PIER ROUGHBACK ALL EXPOSED SIDES
SANDSTONE STEPS ROUGHBACK ALL EXPOSED SIDES
SQUARE
2'-6" TYP. STONE
1'-3" TYP. TREAD
PITCH 1/2"
38.5 TOP OF EDGESTONE
6" TYP RISER
37.5 =WATER LINE
36.0
6" TYP. SANDSTONE EDGESTONE SEE DETAIL
33.5 POND BOTTOM
COMPACTED SUBGRADE
LINE OF POND BOTTOM BEYOND
POROUS GRANULAR FILL
FILTER FABRIC
POND BOTTOM
10 LANDING "A" SECTION
1/2"=1'-0"

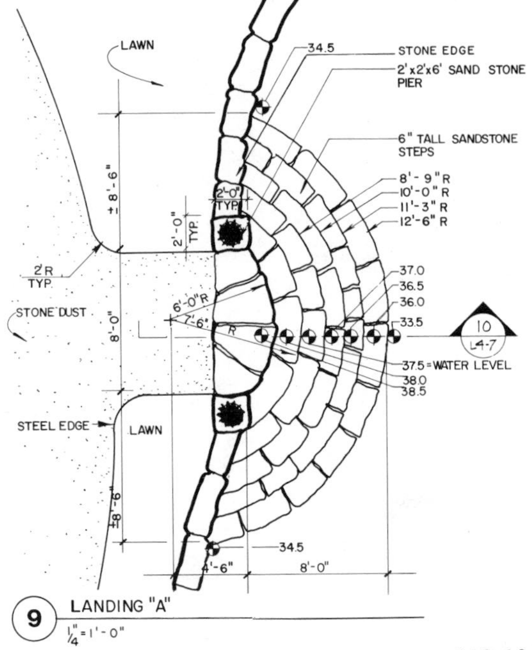
LAWN
STONE EDGE
2'x2'x6' SAND STONE PIER
6" TALL SANDSTONE STEPS
8'-9"R
10'-0"R
11'-3"R
12'-6"R
37.0
36.5
36.0
33.5
37.5=WATER LEVEL
38.0
38.5
2'R TYP.
STONE DUST
STEEL EDGE
LAWN
34.5
8'-0"
9 LANDING "A"
1/4"=1'-0"

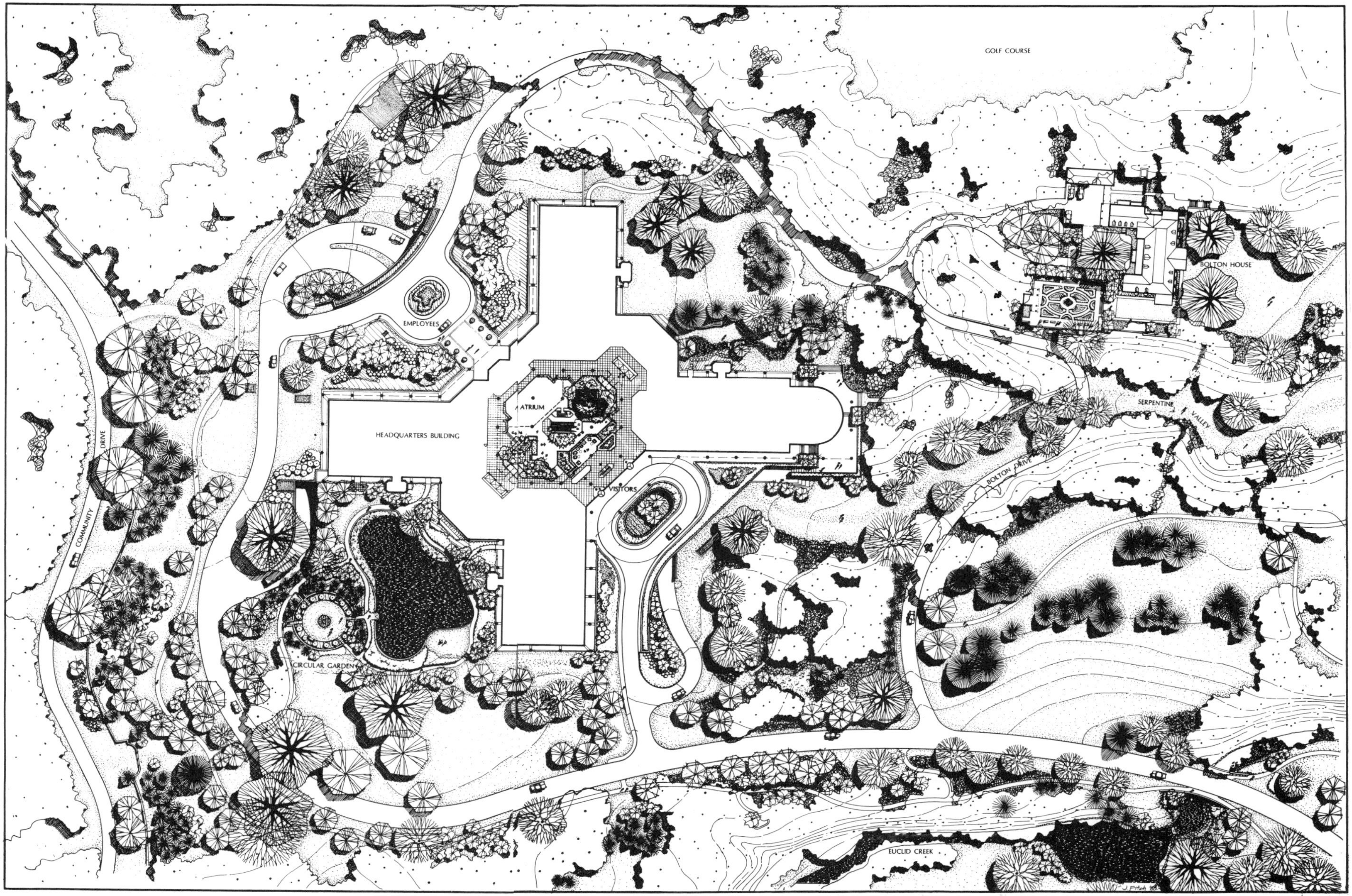
GOLF COURSE
BOLTON HOUSE
SERPENTINE VALLEY
BOLTON DRIVE
EMPLOYEES
ATRIUM
HEADQUARTERS BUILDING
VISITORS
CIRCULAR GARDEN
COMMUNITY DRIVE
EUCLID CREEK

Figure 110-14 Illustrative Site Plan. Illustrative plans and models are often prepared early in the process as an aid to design and as a way to help convey qualities about the project to the client, who may have difficulty understanding construction documents.

Figure 110-15 Site After Development. The photograph shows a view of the completed pond area for the project.

2.0 CONSTRUCTION DOCUMENTS

2.1 Purpose

In essence, *construction documents* are graphic and verbal instructions to a contractor for the purpose of bidding and constructing a proposed design. Drawings are drawn to scale so that a contractor can readily assess the spatial relationships of proposed objects to each other and to existing known points. Specifications include detailed descriptions of (1) general conditions, (2) special provisions, (3) materials, (4) quantities, and (5) information on installation. (Refer to 3.0 Specifications in this section for more information on specifications.)

Legal Responsibilities:

As formal legal contract documents, construction drawings must be accurate. Discrepancies between the proposed work and the existing conditions, or between the construction drawings and the specifications, should be kept to an absolute minimum.

Cost Estimates:

Construction drawings, together with the specifications, are used by contractors to estimate costs for bidding purposes. The specifications spell out in detail the type and quantity of materials to be used, the procedures for fabrication, and the application of products and materials. Construction drawings provide the contractor with information concerning linear and areal dimensions, volumes, and the location of proposed elements (structures, trees, etc.). The drawings should be coordinated with the specifications so that the contractor has enough information to construct the project from the data shown.

2.2 Construction Operations Represented by Drawings

In actual practice, the information on each drawing is translated by the contractor into various operations, involving equipment and personnel. In effect, each drawing represents various types of operations in the field. The drawings are therefore organized by construction activity or operation. Several different operations are normally carried out simultaneously during the construction of a project. Project construction is not a linear process; it more resembles a network of simultaneous activities.

The actual construction activities associated with site construction (as briefly discussed below) are:

1. Preliminary surveying
2. Tree protection, temporary conditions, erosion control, and transplanting
3. Clearing, grubbing, and demolition
4. Topsoil stripping and stockpiling
5. Rough grading
6. Finish grading
7. Installation of site improvements
8. Planting and seeding

Preliminary Surveying:

The contractor verifies the major dimensions, roadway geometry, property boundaries, construction limit line, stockpiling areas, and other horizontal measurements.

Tree Protection, Temporary Conditions, Erosion Control, and Transplanting:

All trees so designated on the drawings are wrapped or enclosed according to the specifications to protect them from root or bark damage. Some trees may be temporarily transplanted to avoid construction damage. Erosion control measures are employed to prevent silting of streams and drains and are usually regulated by Environmental Protection Agency specifications.

Clearing, Grubbing, and Demolition:

All trees, shrubs, rock outcrops, slabs, structures, and utility lines within the project area that are to be abandoned or moved are designated on the drawings for removal by the contractor.

Topsoil Stripping and Stockpiling:

The contractor removes all topsoil within the grading limits and stockpiles the soil in whatever areas will be convenient for future respreading at the completion of the project.

Rough Grading:

By blasting, trenching, backfilling, and cutting and filling to the proposed new subgrade, the contractor prepares all subgrade surfaces to receive foundation footings and subbase material for below- and on-grade structures. Trenching for utility lines also occurs at this stage. The top elevations of manholes and drains are preliminarily set without final brick course shims or rims.

At the completion of the rough grading, all exterior surfaces are cut or filled to specified rough-grade tolerances [± 6 to 12 in (15 to 30 cm)]. They are then ready for final grading prior to placing the topsoil and the wearing surfaces (concrete, asphalt, brick, etc.).

Finish Grading:

The project is staked out and resurveyed to establish the finished geometry and the elevations of walks, roads, and other edges. The paved areas are then graded to finer tolerances, and base material is installed. Topsoil is spread over the rough grades in the planted areas to within a tolerance of ± 1 to 3 in (25 to 76 mm).

Installation of Site Improvements:

The contractor installs fixtures, benches, pavements, steps, trash receptacles, planters, equipment, etc., and finish amenities.

Planting and Seeding:

The contractor plants trees, shrubs, and other plant materials; mulches and edges beds; and harrows, rakes, conditions, fertilizes, and seeds or sods lawn areas.

2.3 Drawing Organization

The contractor must fully understand the total package of information presented and understand how the information is organized before any single operation can occur. So that information can remain clear and unconfusing, it is separated into the following set of drawings:

1. Cover or index sheet
2. Existing conditions and demolition plan(s)
3. Site preparation plan(s)
4. Layout and materials plan(s)
5. Grading and drainage plan(s)
6. Planting plan and details
7. Plan enlargements
8. Site details, sections, elevations, etc.
9. Road profiles and sections
10. Utility plan(s)

Multiple sheets of each drawing may be required for large, complicated projects, depending on the project area, drawing scale, and sheet size.

Cover or Index Sheet:

The cover sheet displays the project title, its sponsor, the consultants' names, an index to drawings by title and sheet number, a project location map, and sometimes a graphic key to the drawing symbols.

Existing Conditions and Demolition Plan:

An existing conditions plan is normally a reproduction of a registered survey plan for the site, drawn to or spliced into the standard sheet size of the working drawing set. It is this sheet that forms the basis for the horizontal controls presented in the layout plan and the vertical controls shown on the grading plan. This plan shows the property boundary line lengths and bearings, the total acres, the topographic configuration illustrated with contours and significant spot elevations, all existing structures, the vegetation (by type and size), utilities, easements, adjacent roads, a geodetic or DPW survey grid at 500- or 1000-ft (50- or 100-m) stations, a location map, and, in some cases, borings (see Figure 110-2).

The scale, date, and north arrow—which are required in all plan drawings—are of particular importance to the existing conditions plan. The date of the survey should be current enough to ensure that the survey is not out of date. The north arrow should be labeled as true or magnetic north, since discrepancies between the two can vary by as much as 20 degrees or more, depending on geographic location. This plan often shows the items to be demolished, removed, relocated, or transplanted.

Site Preparation Plan:

This sheet illustrates the proposed development (in a line drawing only) and indicates the location of stockpiling areas, trees to be removed and thinned, limit of the work line, employee parking and construction road access, erosion control methods, concrete truck washout areas, staging areas, storage areas, stockpile areas, trees to be protected, and location of dewatering trenches or construction siltation ponds, etc.

Layout and Materials Plan:

The layout plan shows the proposed development superimposed on the existing conditions plan (see Figure 110-12). The proposed design is located horizontally on the ground by using bearings and distances, station offsets, and coordinate points. Materials are identified, and keys to details and blowup plans are indicated. It is from this drawing that quantities of materials are calculated by the contractor.

Grading and Drainage Plan:

The grading plan enables the contractor to establish vertical controls for the location of all site and building elements, based on their relationship to existing, identifiable elevations, or bench marks (see Figure 110-10). Elevational information is normally provided by both spot elevations and contour lines.

Surface drainage is an integral part of a grading plan. The locations and rim elevations of structures accepting storm runoff should be indicated on the grading plan even if complete subsurface utility information is provided on a separate site utility plan, since this information is basic to the site grading. If a separate site utility plan is not provided, the invert elevations and pipe sizes, types, and locations should also be included.

Care should be taken to coordinate the grading plan with building elevation drawings, finish floor elevations, and all utility drawings in order to avoid below-grade conflicts. The limit of grading is usually indicated by the no-cut/no-fill line.

TABLE 110-2
Construction Specifications Institute: Detail File Index,* Division 2—Sitework

02200	EARTHWORK
02270	SLOPE PROTECTION
	Slope erosion control
02350	PILES, CAISSONS, AND COFFERDAMS
02360	PILE
02370	CAISSON
02380	COFFERDAM
02400	DRAINAGE
02401	DEWATERING
	French drain
	Relief well
	Sand drain
	Well point
02410	SUBDRAINAGE
	Trench drain
02411	FOUNDATION DRAIN
	Drain tile
	Footing drain cleanout
02412	UNDERSLAB DRAIN
02420	SURFACE RUNOFF COLLECTION
	Area drain
	Storm drain
02430	DRAINAGE STRUCTURE
	Drain fitting
	Drain pipe
02431	CATCH BASIN
	Catch basin cover
	Catch basin frame
02432	CURB INLET
02434	CULVERT
02435	SPLASH BLOCK
	Splash block drain bed
02440	SITE IMPROVEMENTS
02443	FOUNTAIN
02444	CHAIN LINK FENCE
	Chain link gate
02445	WIRE FENCE
	Wire gate
02446	WOOD FENCE
	Wood gate
	Yard screen
02447	METAL FENCE
02448	FLAGPOLE BASE
02449	MASONRY FENCE
02451	GUARDRAIL
	Bollard
	Collapsible bollard
	Pipe stanchion
02452	SIGN
	Bulletin board
	Direction map
	Information kiosk
02453	TRAFFIC SIGNAL
	Pavement traffic detector
	Traffic signal box
02454	CULVERT PIPE UNDERPASS
02455	PARKING BARRIER
	Lift gate
	Tire stop
02456	PARKING BUMPER
	Precast bumper
	Timber bumper
02457	BICYCLE RACK
	Bicycle locker
02458	HANDICAPPED RAMP
02459	TRAFFIC DIVIDER
	Traffic island
02460	PLAY EQUIPMENT
02463	PLAY STRUCTURE
	Jungle gym
	Railroad tie structure
	Rubble structure
	Sculpture
02471	SEAT
	Bench
	Stools
02472	TABLE
	Game table
	Picnic table
02475	TRASH RECEPTOR
02476	NEWS RACK
02477	SHELTER
	Bus stop shelter
	Gazebo
	Parking attendant shed
	Tea house
02478	OUTDOOR COOKING/BBQ/FIRE PIT
02479	OUTDOOR DRINKING FOUNTAIN
02480	LANDSCAPING
02491	TREE PLANTING
	Tree grate
	Tree guying
02492	SHRUB PLANTING
02495	AGGREGATE BED
	Bed curb
	Border board
02496	WOOD CHIP BED
	Bed curb
	Border board
02500	PAVING AND SURFACING
02506	WOOD PLANK WALK
02511	CRUSHED STONE PAVING
02512	ROCK PAVING
02513	ASPHALTIC CONCRETE PAVING
02514	BRICK PAVING
	Brick roadway
	Brick walkway
	Expansion joint
	Tile paving
02515	CONCRETE PAVING
	Concrete apron
	Concrete drive
	Concrete ramp
	Concrete roadway
	Expansion joint
02516	ASPHALT BLOCK PAVING
	Asphalt paving, heavy-duty
	Asphalt paving, light-duty
	Asphalt speed control bump
	Edge of asphalt
02517	STONE PAVING
02518	CONCRETE BLOCK PAVING
02519	GRAVEL SURFACING
	Border board
	Curb
02520	SHREDDED BARK SURFACING
	Border board
	Curb
02525	GRANITE CURB
02526	PRECAST CONCRETE CURB
02527	ASPHALT CONCRETE CURB
02528	CONCRETE CURB
	Curb expansion joint
02529	CONCRETE WALK
02530	SPORTS PAVING
02550	HIGHWAY PAVING
	Expansion joint
02577	PAVEMENT MARKING
	Direction and crosswalk marking
	Handicapped symbols
	Highway marking
	Parking stripes
02600	PIPED UTILITY MATERIALS AND METHODS
02601	MANHOLE
	Utility cleanout
02644	HYDRANT
02700	PIPED UTILITIES
02721	STORM SEWERAGE
02722	SANITARY SEWERAGE
02730	WATER WELL
02742	GREASE INTERCEPTOR
02743	SEPTIC TANK
02745	DISTRIBUTION BOX
02800	POWER AND COMMUNICATION UTILITIES
02801	TOWER
02802	POLE

* Most numbers in this index are not individual detail file numbers. Instead they represent categories or sections within the detail file. The final individual detail numbers will have further subdivisions or suffix numbers depending on what special condition they show, sizes or types of components, scale of drawing, and sequence of selection of the detail for inclusion in the file.

Source: Fred A. Stitt, *Systems Graphics,* McGraw-Hill, New York, 1984, pp. 188–189.

Planting Plan and Details:

Planting plans must accurately show the locations of all proposed plant materials (differentiated graphically from existing plant materials to remain), their names, their sizes, and any other characteristics that will assist the designer in specifying the precise type of specimen required (see Figure 110-11). A plant list indicating the quantity, botanical name (including genus, species, and variety), common name, size (height, spread, caliper, etc.), spacing, and special requirements (multistem, first branch height, etc.) is normally included on the plan. (Refer to Section 550: Plants and Planting, for more information.)

Landscape contractors will use the plant list to determine the quantities for each variety unless directed to do otherwise. A note on the drawing or a clause in the specifications should state that the plan shall take precedence over the list in the event of a discrepancy.

Plan Enlargements:

Plan enlargements are used as needed to show detail design layouts in courtyards or entrances, etc. They can show dimensions, grading, material pattern, planting, etc.

For construction purposes, the scales of these blowups are typically 1⁄16″ = 1′-0″ (approximately 1:200), 1⁄8″ = 1′-0″ (approximately 1:100), 1″ = 20′-0″ (approximately 1:200), and 1″ = 10′-0″ (approximately 1:100).

Road Profiles and Sections:

Road profiles show a profile section along the roadway centerline and designate finish and existing grades at 50- to 100-ft (10- to 25–50-m) stations along that line. The horizontal (*H*) scale is usually the same as that of the plan, and the vertical (*V*) scale is exaggerated at least 4:1 but more commonly 10:1 [1″ = 50′*H* (1:500) and 1″ = 5′ *V* (1:50)]. The profile sheet shows the location and length of:

1. All vertical parabolic curves
2. Horizontal curves by symbol
3. Superelevation
4. High and low points
5. Top of curb
6. Bottom of gutter lines

Site Details, Sections, Elevations, etc.:

The site details convey specific methods of construction to the contractor. The manner in which this is achieved is often through sections, usually drawn to a scale of from 1⁄2″ = 1′-0″ to 1 1⁄2″ = 1′-0″ (1:10 to 1:20). Though not necessary, it is helpful to group details of like subjects together, such as pavements, walls, and stairs. Besides helping to locate details, this shows more vividly the differences between similar sections. (Refer to Division 900: Details and Devices, for more information on construction details.)

As with the accompanying plans, the details work in concert with the specifications to provide complete data to the contractor. The information supplied by the specifications should not be included in the details (see Figure 110-13).

Utility Plan:

Depending on the scale and complexity, the number of drawings under this general heading will vary with each project.

Typical items included on utility plans and details include:

1. *Stormwater drainage:* surface and conduit system
2. *Subdrainage:* tile fields, footings, etc.
3. *Sewerage:* sanitary sewer and septic systems
4. *Water distribution:* drinking, irrigation, fountains, and fire control
5. *Electrical layout:* lighting and outlets
6. *Buried cables:* telephone, electrical, optic, cable TV, etc.
7. *Special waste drains:* chemical/acid, petroleum, etc.
8. *Steam and heat lines:* pipes, expansion joints, and heat cables
9. *Fuel lines:* natural gas and petroleum

In practice, utility plans are most often drawn on halftone grading plans so that existing conditions, horizontal layout, and vertical dimensions are shown. Utility plans must be coordinated with other drawings in order to avoid conflicts with major plantings or important hard-surfaced areas (future maintenance requirements), to avoid conflicts with other buried utilities, and to ensure sufficient cover.

3.0 SPECIFICATIONS

The importance of well-written specifications for a design project cannot be overemphasized. The specifications present detailed information on the materials required, the fabrication procedures, and the application of products and materials. They establish the scope of the work and clearly spell out the criteria for altering the scope (change orders, deletions, etc.). The drawings establish the dimensions and identify the materials to be used, and the specifications establish the procedural and performance standards required to construct the design as shown on the drawings.

A major source of general construction specifications is the Construction Specifications Institute (CSI). Division 2 (Sitework) is reproduced in Table 110-2 to show the general headings. Note that Division 2, as presently constituted, requires additional subsections to accommodate typical landscape construction documents; nevertheless, it serves as a useful point of departure.

4.0 CHECKLIST FOR SITE PLANS

The checklist in Table 110-3 can serve as a useful tool for preparing site construction drawings and for preplanning their content. This checklist may not apply to all projects because of scale, complexity, or type of professional practice. It is most applicable to medium- and larger-scale projects.

TABLE 110-3
Checklist for Site Plans*

Survey

General Reference Data

[ ] Drawing title and scale (beneath drawing or on title block)

[ ] Arrows showing compass north, true north, and/or reference north

[ ] Property address: Street___ City___ County___ State___ Country (if foreign)___

[ ] Owner's name___ Address___ (If not shown on title block)

[ ] Property legal description: Lot___ Block___ Tract___ Subdivision___ Map book___

[ ] Lot and block numbers of adjacent properties

[ ] Surveyor's name___ Address___ Phone number___ Registration number___

[ ] Survey date

[ ] Approval/authorization (public agencies)___

Property Data

[ ] Property boundary lines___ Dimensions___ Directions of property lines shown in degrees, minutes, and seconds___

[ ] Monument___ Benchmark___ Reference points___ Stakes___ Reference datum___

(Continued)

TABLE 110-3
Checklist for Site Plans* (*Continued*)

[ ] Contour lines with grade elevations

[ ] ± Notes on elevation points if grades are both above and below datum point

[ ] On-site and adjacent easements___ Rights-of-way___ (Show identities and dimensions)

[ ] Required front, rear, and side setback lines___ Dimensions to property line___

[ ] Adjacent streets or roads: Names___ Width dimensions___ Elevation points at street centerlines___ Elevation points at sides___ Concrete traffic islands___

[ ] Adjacent streets or roads: Total rights-of-way___ Easements for road widening___

[ ] Street storm mains___ Basins___ Direction and elevation points of drain slopes___ Invert elevations___

[ ] Street sewer hookup___ Sewer manhole___ Elevation point at top of manhole___ Elevation point at sewer invert___ Direction of flow___

[ ] Street gas and electric manholes___ Electrical vaults___ Other utilities in street or adjacent to street___

[ ] Sidewalk: Lifts___ Vaults___ Vault skylights___ Vault gratings___ Tunnels___ Chute and fuel pipe inlets___ Meter boxes___

[ ] Existing curbs and walkways adjacent to property___ Dimensions and elevation points___

[ ] Curb elevation points shown at extensions of property lines

[ ] Traffic lights___ Signs___ Parking meters___ Fire alarm boxes___ Police call boxes___

[ ] Fire hydrants

[ ] Existing sidewalk trees or shrubs

[ ] Existing power pole(s)

[ ] Gas main and hookup location

[ ] Street water main and hookup location___ Existing water meter location___

[ ] Overhead or buried cable on or adjacent to property

[ ] Existing buildings on adjacent property within 5 ft of property line___ Known future adjacent construction___

[ ] Adjacent building footings and foundation walls at property line

[ ] Existing on-site paving, curbs, and walkways: Dimensions___ Materials___ Elevation points___

[ ] Existing on-site structures: Identity___ Size___ Floor elevation points___

[ ] Existing fences and walls: Materials___ Heights___

[ ] Existing underground structures___ Foundations___ Holes and trenches___

[ ] Existing buried or surface trash

[ ] Existing on-site utilities___ Sewers___ Tunnels___ Drain pipes___

[ ] Utilities easements

[ ] Existing on-site or adjacent drainage culverts___ Riprap___

[ ] Existing springs or wells

[ ] Existing ponds___ Creeks___ Streams___ Overflow areas___

[ ] High-water table___ Standing water___ Marsh___ Quicksand___

[ ] Rock outcrops___ Rock elevation points___

[ ] Existing trees (Trees with trunks of less than 6-in diameter are not usually noted. Landscape architect may want smaller trees identified for removal and transplanting.): Identities___ Trunk sizes___ Approximate foliage area___

[ ] Existing major shrubs___ Undergrowth___ Ground cover areas___

Site work

GENERAL REFERENCE DATA

[ ] Legal setback lines

[ ] Site photos (sometimes printed on site plan transparency print and keyed to site plan drawing)

[ ] Legends of site plan symbols and materials indications

[ ] Landscape consultant's name___ Address___ Phone number___

[ ] Civil engineer's name___ Address___ Phone number___ Registration number___

[ ] Soils engineer's name___ Address___ Phone number___ Registration number___

[ ] Test-boring contractor's name___ Address___ Phone number___

[ ] Soil test lab's name___ Address___ Phone number___

[ ] Small-scale location or vicinity map showing neighboring streets and nearest major highway access

[ ] Note requiring bidders to visit site and verify conditions before submitting bids

[ ] Percolation test plan___ Soils test-boring schedule and profile___

[ ] Work not in contract

[ ] Drawing title and scale

[ ] Arrows showing compass north and reference north

[ ] Property size in square feet or acres

[ ] Contract limit lines

[ ] Location and size dimensions of constructed components___ Construction notes___ Detail keys___ Drawing cross-references___ Specification references___

Demolition and Repair

[ ] Existing fences and walls: Which to retain___ Which to repair___ Which to remove___

[ ] Existing structures: Which to retain___ Which to repair___ Which to relocate___ Which to demolish___

[ ] Existing paving, walks, steps, and curbs: Which to retain___ Which to repair___ Which to remove___

[ ] Existing on-site utilities, sewers, and drains: Which to retain___ Which to use___ Which to remove___

[ ] Existing trees, shrubs, and undergrowth: Which to retain___ Which to remove___ Which to relocate and store for transplanting___

[ ] Areas for clearing and grubbing___ Existing trash to be removed___ Stumps to be removed___

[ ] Rock outcrops to retain___ Rock to be removed___

Grading, Construction, and Drainage

[ ] Existing and new site contours___ Existing and new finish grades___ Elevation points___

[ ] New benchmark and/or boundary markers

[ ] Existing holes and trenches: Which to retain___ Which to fill in___

[ ] New fill___ Note on soil compaction___

[ ] Cut and fill profile (may be on separate drawing)

[ ] New building and related structures___ Overall exterior wall dimensions___ Dimensions to property lines___ Outline of future building additions___

[ ] New building finish floor elevation at ground floor or basement

[ ] New finish grade elevations at building corners___ Grade slope at building line___

[ ] Foundation or basement excavation limit lines

[ ] Retaining walls or wells for existing trees affected by changes in finish grade: Material___ Dimensions___ Elevation points___ Note___ Detail keys___

[ ] New fences, gates, and walls: Materials___ Heights___ Dimensions___ Footing lines___ Drains___ Detail keys___

[ ] New surface and subsurface soil drainage: Materials___ Sizes___ Slopes___ Depths___

[ ] New riprap___ Culverts___ Storm drains___ Head walls___

[ ] Dry wells: Sizes___ Depths___

[ ] Building perimeter foundation drain tile___ Slope and direction of drain to dry well or storm sewer___

Paving, Walkways, and Parking

[ ] New public curbs and street driveway entries

[ ] Driveways: Materials___ Dimensions___ Centerline elevation points___ Drainage slopes___ Drains___

[ ] Existing and new grade elevations at paving, noted at centerlines and sides of driveways

[ ] Driveway and parking area grades (normally a minimum of 0.5%, with a maximum of 5% at crowns)

[ ] Exterior parking located minimum 5 ft from walls and other structures___ Parking located outside tree drip lines___ Parking located clear of icicle or roof snow drop lines___

[ ] Pavement and walkway ice-melting equipment

[ ] Pavement humps___ Dips___ Warning signs to slow through traffic___

[ ] Cross-sectional diagrams through roadways or driveways

[ ] Restricted access roadways___ Lockable posts or chain barriers at restricted access___

[ ] Painted parking lines___ Traffic control lines or markers___ Arrows and signs painted on pavement___

[ ] Parking bumpers___ Traffic control curbs___

(Continued)

TABLE 110-3
Checklist for Site Plans* *(Continued)*

[ ] Vehicular curbs, bumpers, or guard railings at vulnerable areas: Walls___ Ledges___ Walkways___ Trees___ Standards___ Columns___

[ ] Wide-space parking for handicapped___ Ramps from parking area to adjacent sidewalks___

[ ] Construction joints in concrete paving___

[ ] New walks and steps: Materials___ Dimensions___ Notes___ Elevation points___ Direction of slopes___ Riser number and heights___

[ ] Handrails at steps over three risers

[ ] Three risers minimum at any point along walks or ramps

[ ] Rough, nonskid surfaces at exterior walks, steps, and landings___ Sloping walk or ramp handrails___ (Maximum slope for walkway without handrails is 1 in 8)

[ ] Pipe sleeves at pavement fencing and handrail posts

[ ] Walkway low points sloped to drain

[ ] Exterior stair treads sloped to drain___ Side gutters at ramps___ Identification numbers at exterior stairs___ Metal tread nosings at concrete steps___

[ ] Concrete walkway construction joints

[ ] Paved terraces___ Patios___ Off-the-ground decks___

[ ] Openings or gratings at trees in paved areas for watering space

[ ] Synthetic grass or turf

[ ] Sidewalk vaults___ Sidewalk paving glass for underground rooms___ Sidewalk elevator___ Fuel delivery access___

[ ] Sidewalk plaques specifying property ownership and limits on public use

[ ] Manholes___ Gratings___ Cleanouts___ Meter boxes___

[ ] Bicycle and paraplegic ramps adjacent to walkway steps and at curbs

PLANTING

[ ] Existing trees, shrubs, and undergrowth: Which to retain___ Which to remove___ Which to relocate and store for transplanting___

[ ] Trees to be wrapped___ Tree guards for protection during construction___

[ ] New topsoil storage area___ Excavation loam storage area___

[ ] Temporary erosion control

[ ] New landscape areas with landscape legend and keys to identify tree, plant, and lawn types

[ ] Slopes and drainage for lawn and ground cover areas___ All pockets and standing water areas filled or provided with drainage___

[ ] Planting beds___ Bark___ Gravel___ Curbs or border boards at beds___

[ ] Root feeding pipes

[ ] Landscape irrigation and/or sprinkler system: Autotimer___ Valves___ Hose bibbs and hydrants___ Sprinkler head locations___ (May be shown on separate plumbing plan)

[ ] Decorative yard lighting and timer switch (May be shown on electrical drawings)

APPURTENANCES AND SITE FURNITURE (These are often combined with the landscape plan)

[ ] New ponds, pools, fountains, materials___ Utilities___

[ ] New planters___ Plant tubs___ Planter drains___

[ ] Sculpture pedestals or support slabs

[ ] Direction signs___ Location map stands___ Directory plaques___ Bulletin boards___ Kiosks___

[ ] Walkway and parking light standards and pedestals

[ ] Benches

[ ] Trash receptacles___

[ ] Pergolas___ Lattices___

[ ] Drinking fountains___ Paraplegic fountains___ Children's fountains___ Pet fountains___

[ ] Bicycle racks___ Pram racks___

[ ] Newspaper racks___

[ ] Public phones___ Emergency phones___ Low phone for paraplegics___ Fire alarm boxes___

[ ] Public mailbox___ Cluster mailboxes___ Mail slot for paraplegics___

[ ] Flagpoles

[ ] Bus or shuttle stop: Bench___ Shelter___ Waste receptacle(s)___

[ ] Walkway canopies___ Wind screens___

[ ] Turnstiles

[ ] Information or guard booth

[ ] Paid parking: Ticket dispenser___ Automatic gate___ Tire spike barrier___

[ ] Maintenance yard___ Gasoline tank inlet, valve, and pump___

[ ] Trash enclosures___ Incinerator yard enclosure___

[ ] Playground equipment___ Fenced play yard___

UTILITIES

[ ] New water supply main___ New water meter___ Water meter and shutoff box and cover___

[ ] Fire hydrants___ Hose bibbs___ Standpipes___

[ ] New sewer main___ Vent and cleanout___ Direction of slope___ Elevation points___

[ ] New gas main___ Gas meter___ Shutoff valve at building (provide a conspicuous location for shutoff, with an identifying sign)___

[ ] New buried or overhead electric cable___ Phone cable___ TV cable___

[ ] New power poles (Overhead cables to clear walks and driveways as required by building authority)

[ ] All utility trenches: Minimum and maximum depth limits___ Trenching located to avoid damage to tree roots and neighboring structures___

[ ] Excavation warning signs/plaques along routes of buried utility lines

[ ] Length of mains

[ ] Exterior electric outlets and lights at building and at auxiliary structures

[ ] Fuel oil or liquified gas storage tank___ Fuel line to building___ Vent___ Gauge box___ Fill box___ Manhole___

[ ] Package sewage treatment tank and housing: Size___ Location___ Construction notes___ Detail keys___

CONSTRUCTION WORK SITE PLAN

[ ] Erosion control___ Temporary retaining walls___ Shoring___ Temporary drainage___

[ ] Job sign and temporary fence: Design and details

[ ] Construction shed___ Barriers___ Gates___ Toilets___

[ ] Testing area___ Samples storage area___

[ ] Material and equipment storage areas___ Platforms___

[ ] Temporary roads___ Walkways___

[ ] Topsoil stockpile area

[ ] Plant storage yard___ Greenhouse___

[ ] Construction power pole and meter

[ ] Site illumination

[ ] Security guard's shanty

[ ] Construction water supply hydrants___ Temporary hose bibbs___

[ ] Bridges for protection of paving, walks, and curbs from construction equipment and trucks

[ ] Trash and debris storage

[ ] Soil test-boring plan___ Test pits___

* This checklist can serve as a useful tool when preparing construction drawings as well as a guide when checking for comprehensiveness, especially on medium- to large-scale projects.

Source: Fred A. Stitt, *Systems Graphics,* McGraw-Hill, New York, 1984, pp. 212–216.

REFERENCES

Chambers, Walter L. "Contracts and Specifications for Landscape Architects," *Landscape Architecture Quarterly,* July 1956, p. 294.

Lynch, Kevin, and Gary Hack. *Site Planning,* 3d ed., MIT Press, Cambridge, MA, 1984.

Parker, Harry. *Simplified Site Engineering for Architects and Builders,* Wiley, New York, 1954.

Ramsey/Sleeper, Robert T. Packard, AIA (ed.). *Architectural Graphic Standards,* 7th ed., Wiley, New York, 1981.

Stitt, Fred A. *Systems Graphics,* McGraw-Hill, New York, 1984. ■

section 130: Computer-Aided Design and Drafting

CREDITS

Contributor:

Mark C. Gionet
Winter Park, Florida

Reviewers:

Carl Steinitz
Department of Landscape Architecture
Harvard University
Cambridge, Massachusetts

C. Dana Tomlin
Department of Landscape Architecture
Harvard University
Cambridge, Massachusetts

CONTENTS

1.0 INTRODUCTION

The use of computers in design offices has become widespread and now affects all aspects of landscape architectural practice. Computers are being used for bookkeeping and correspondence, land use and resource inventories, various kinds of analyses, land use allocation problems, site engineering tasks, and the production of working drawings. Much of this work can now be accomplished with microcomputers, which are readily affordable by any size firm.

A complete appraisal of the ever-increasing number and variety of computer applications useful in design and planning is impossible in the space of this text. However, this section can provide a general overview of computer technology and of various applications useful in the process of site planning and design. It is important to remain aware of current advances in the state of computer technology and to take advantage of the opportunities that computers have to offer to professional design practice.

Readers should understand that several of the other sections in this handbook refer to particular aspects of landscape architectural practice that commonly involve the use of computers. All aspects of site engineering, for instance, are amenable to the use of computers as a tool to resolve problems and expedite decision making. Several programs are available for use in road alignments, earthwork calculations, grading and drainage problems, and the calculations involved in bridge or deck construction. Readers should also keep in mind that all of the processes and techniques given in various sections of this handbook are amenable to the use of computers, even though their use may not be mentioned in every section.

Technical terms can be found in the Glossary at the end of this section.

2.0 BASIC COMPONENTS OF COMPUTER SYSTEMS

Modern digital computer systems typically have five main components: (1) input device(s), (2) a central processing unit (CPU), (3) internal memory, (4) auxiliary memory, and (5) output device(s). The relationships between these components are diagramed in Figure 130-1.

For detailed information on various components of computer systems, readers are urged to refer to Bruce MacDougall's *Microcomputers in Landscape Architecture,* listed in the References at the end of this section.

A typical computer-aided drafting system is shown in Figure 130-2.

2.1 Input Devices

Text is easily input on most computers with a keyboard and can be edited with word processing software to produce reports (Figure 130-1).

Map information (i.e., spatial data) can

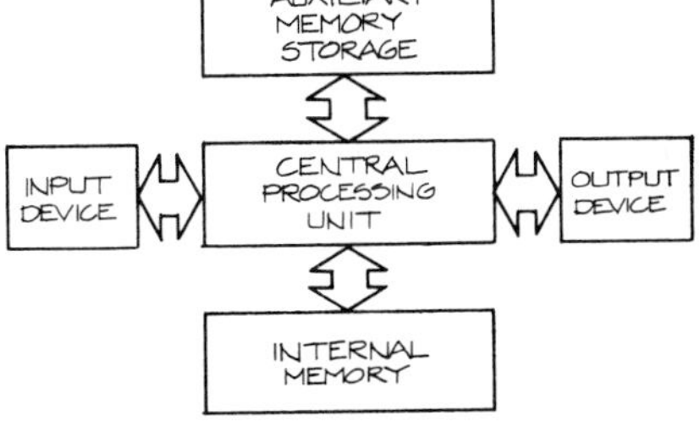
AUXILIARY MEMORY STORAGE
INPUT DEVICE
CENTRAL PROCESSING UNIT
OUTPUT DEVICE
INTERNAL MEMORY

Figure 130-1 The main components of a computing system.

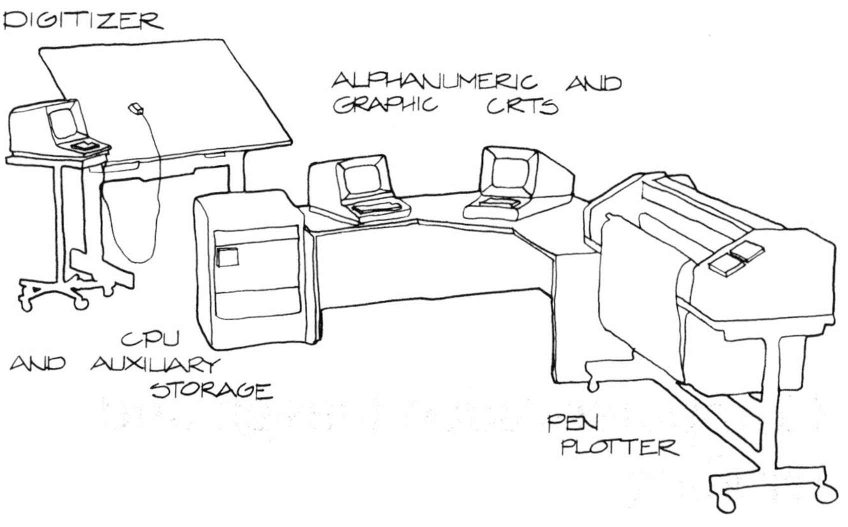
DIGITIZER
ALPHANUMERIC AND GRAPHIC CRTS
CPU AND AUXILIARY STORAGE
PEN PLOTTER

Figure 130-2 Typical computer-aided drafting system.

be traced with a digitizing stylus, thereby recording the boundaries of polygons or the extent of various spatial data. Polygonal data require more sophisticated software to process, although they can be significantly more accurate than gridded data.

Other means for inputting data include optical scanning digitizers, video digitizers, and line following devices mounted on plotters. These methods of input can often be employed through a service bureau. Alternatively, some utilities, corporations, and government agencies maintain large data bases which may contain data specific to a particular site. Data from these bases can often be purchased in tape format or accessed through time-sharing facilities. Table 130-1 describes common forms of data entry.

2.2 Data Storage

Data storage can be met with a number of hardware options. Criteria for selection include: (1) the amount of information to be stored, (2) its expected useful life span, (3) the required ease of access and transportation, and (4) any necessary compatibility with already-computerized data. Offices will often find it advantageous to share data storage among many computer users, especially when each user requires access to the same site-specific data base. This can be accomplished with an operating system which supports shared peripheral devices. Table 130-2 describes common storage devices.

2.3 Graphic Display

Computer graphic display alternatives have expanded in scope and availability since the first gray scale maps were produced by overstriking alphanumeric characters. A wide range of media and hardware options are now available. Graphic software packages are widely marketed, and numerous books and journals carry program listings which allow designers to display a variety of plans, sections, and perspective views.

Graphic displays refer to either *soft copy* [i.e., images produced on a video display terminal (VDT)] or *hard copy* (i.e., images printed or plotted on paper film or other permanent medium). Regarding the quality of hard-copy graphic displays, it is important to differentiate between poor-quality graphics (useful during the continued refinement of a design concept) and the high-quality graphics suitable for presentation to clients and review agencies, for brochures, and the like. Display alternatives for both informal and formal graphic presentations are shown in Tables 130-3 and 130-4. Brief technical descriptions of soft-copy and hard-copy technologies follow.

Soft-Copy Technology:

Most microcomputer display systems are based on raster-scan video displays (Table 130-3). These create images by tracing a succession of horizontal lines on a screen. Graphic images are built up of pixels (picture elements), which are created by dividing the video image into a rectangular grid of screen locations which can be turned on or off. Screen images can be monochrome or colored.

Vector displays are slightly more expensive (Table 130-3). An electron gun directs a beam between two points on a phosphor-coated screen to produce a line. A direct view storage tube (DVST) retains the image for a longer period of time without having to redraw it. Vector technology eliminates the stair-stepping effect created when diagonal lines are drawn on raster displays. A disadvantage is that only monochrome or very limited color displays are currently possible. Motion is also very difficult to depict.

Hard-Copy Technology:

Hard-copy alternatives are generally categorized as either impact or nonimpact technologies.

Impact devices produce images by striking a ribbon against paper or film. Dot matrix printers, available with black or multicolored ribbons, are most commonly used. They are suitable for easy reproductions of raster images or for text which need not have the crisp quality of print wheel copy. Formed letter printers print symbols in the manner that typewriters do, while dot matrix printers strike various combinations of pins within a matrix against the ribbon (Table 130-4).

Line drawings are typically produced by pen plotters (Table 130-4). Pens on flatbed plotters are mounted on a mechanical arm; the arm moves on one axis, and the pen moves perpendicularly along the arm. Drum plotters move the drafting surface along one axis beneath the pen while they move the pen on the perpendicular axis. The line quality can be changed by selecting a different pen. Pen plotters are available in a wide variety of sizes, pen capacities, and pen types.

Ink jet plotters spray fine jets of ink at prescribed locations and can replicate the many color combinations available on high-quality color monitors (Table 130-4). Electrostatic plotters employ electronic charges to produce images on sensitized media (Table 130-4). Direct photo plotting on film is another available technology.

Special camera units have been designed to photograph raster displays. These cameras compensate for screen warp, refresh rate, and other variables that affect reproduction quality. New film technologies also make possible a very clear reproduction of screen images.

3.0 COMPUTERS AND DESIGN PROCESSES

Figure 130-3 identifies major tasks in the typical process of site planning. In each of these areas, computer-aided design (CAD) techniques have been developed and marketed as software packages or as combined hardware and software systems. Many of these products have been designed especially for the professions of architecture, civil engineering, and cartogra-

TABLE 130-1
Common Methods of Data Entry

Device	*Data type*	*Landscape architectural use*	*Selection criteria*
Keyboard 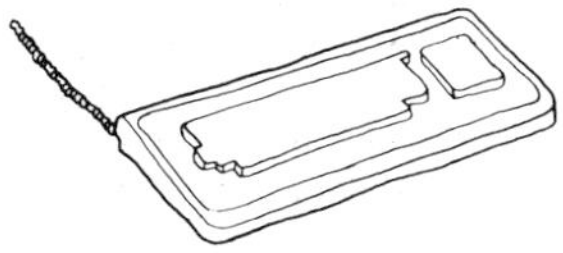	Alphanumeric	■ Encode textual data ■ Encode numeric data and perform arithmetic operations ■ Select functions	■ Number of keys ■ User-definable function buttons
Joystick, trackball, mouse 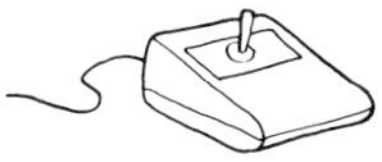	Cursor movement	■ Move cursor to select objects or options displayed on screen ■ Identify location in plan view ■ Move object or draw line ■ Scroll screen (trackball)	■ Resolution ■ Accuracy ■ Required software ■ Working area required
2-D digitizer or bit pad 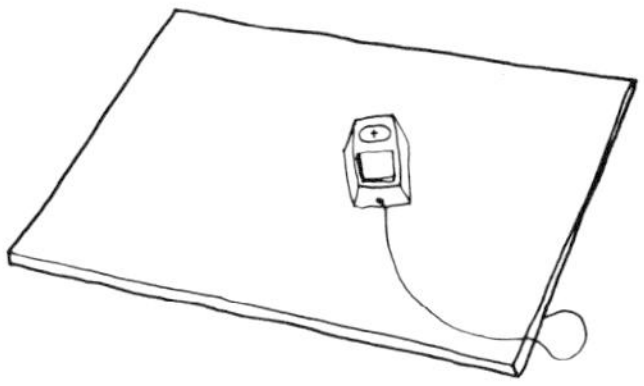	2-D graphic information	■ Trace and encode planimetric data ■ Draw and encode sketch or section information ■ Edit screen displays	■ Resolution ■ Accuracy ■ Software ■ Working area ■ Cursor control buttons ■ Data format ■ Interface type
Automatic scanning digitizers 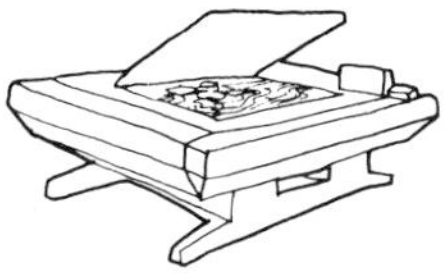	2-D graphic data	■ Digitize large numbers of drawings ■ Fast, highly accurate digitizing of complicated plans	■ Cost ■ Effective area ■ Accuracy ■ Resolution ■ Repeatability ■ Required software ■ Required additional hardware
Video digitizers 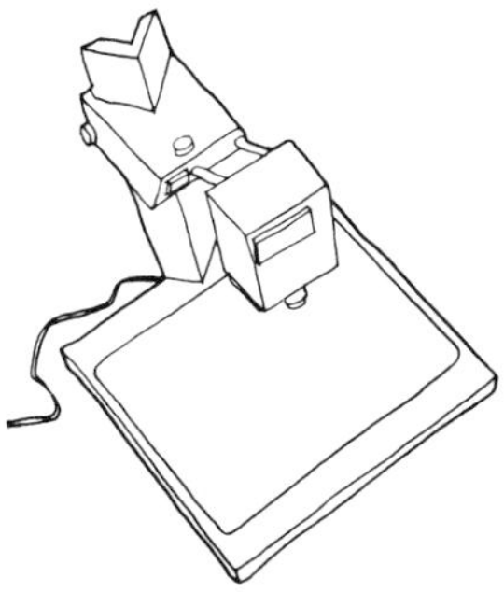	2-D graphic data and video images	■ Digitize data other than line drawings ■ Encode gray levels of aerial photographic images	■ Cost ■ Working area ■ Resolution ■ Accuracy ■ Repeatability ■ Color recognition
3-D digitizer 	3-D graphic data	■ Digitize 3-D physical models of proposed designs for testing and display	■ Accuracy ■ Resolution ■ Repeatability ■ Working area required ■ Software
External data sources	All types of data	■ LANDSAT imagery from EROS ■ Coastal zone data from NOAA ■ DTM tapes taken from USGS maps ■ Utility location data	■ Disk or tape format ■ Telephone transmission requirements ■ Cost ■ Required software and hardware

TABLE 130-2
Data Storage Options

Device	*Description*	*Selection criteria*
Floppy disk 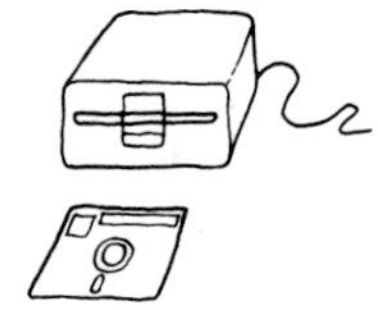	■ Disk drives are available with most microcomputers and some more powerful systems	■ Physical size ■ Capacity ■ Density and formatting ■ Required operating system to effectively access ■ Required interface
Winchester hard disk 	■ Built into housing, physically not removable for transport ■ High-speed access to large quantities of data	■ All of the above
Tape cartridges 	■ Available for many microcomputers ■ More advanced units used for backup storage	■ All of the above
Large reel-to-reel tape and freestanding disk drives 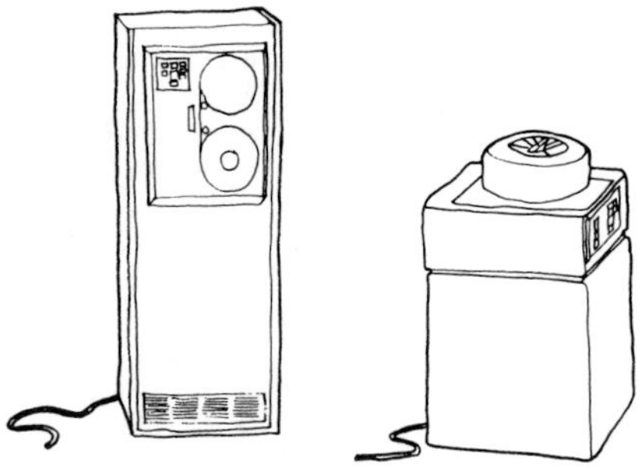	■ Used by larger CAD systems ■ Require minicomputer or mainframe to drive	■ All of the above ■ Physical space occupied by units

TABLE 130-3
Soft Copy Options

Device	*Landscape architectural use*	*Selection criteria*
Vector display 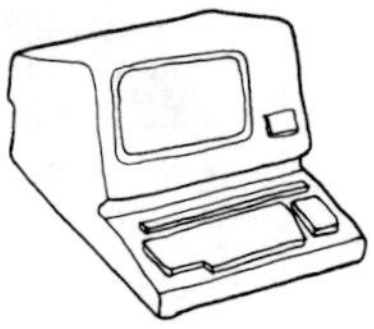	■ Line drawings such as alignments, profiles, and contour plans	■ Resolution (addressable points) ■ Local intelligence ■ Number of screens of graphic memory available ■ Ergonomic features
Raster display 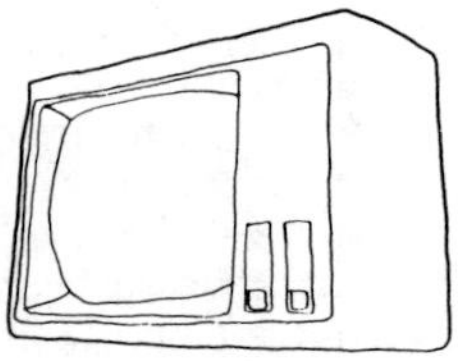	■ Lower resolution is multipurpose ■ Higher resolution and additional color for renderings and discriminating wide range of mapped data values	■ Resolution (pixels) ■ Local intelligence ■ Number of screens of graphic memory ■ Colors ■ Ergonomic features

TABLE 130-4
Hard Copy Options

Device	*Description/output media*	*Landscape architectural use*	*Selection criteria*
Print wheel printer 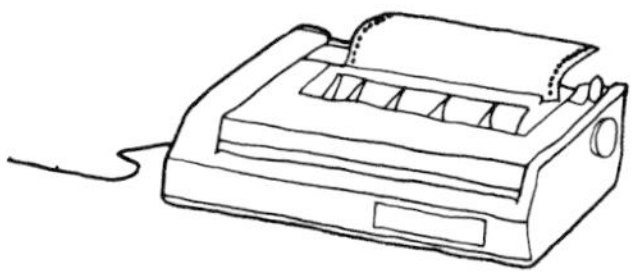	High-quality text	■ Correspondence ■ Proposal writing	■ Speed ■ Available type fonts ■ Interface
Dot matrix printer 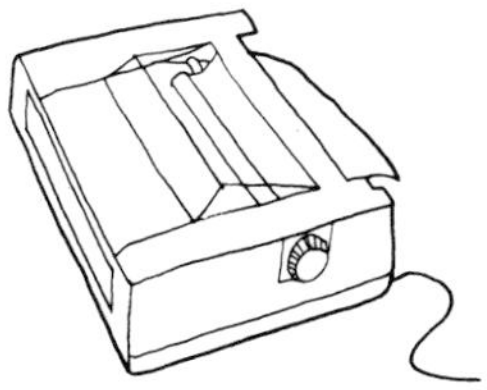	Lower-quality text and quick copy graphics	■ All other text writing ■ Quick hard copy of graphics screen displays	■ Speed ■ Resolution (matrix dimensions) ■ Colors ■ Interface ■ Local hardware-based intelligence
Pen plotters 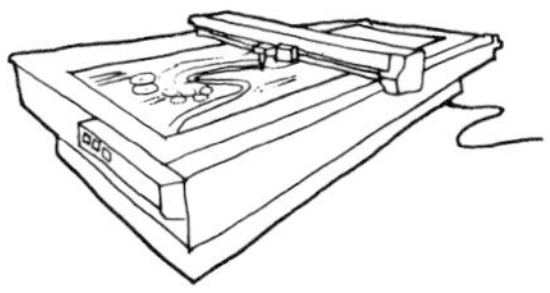	Ballpoint, felt-tip, and gravity-fed pens on paper, Mylar, and other media	■ Plotting of design drawings ■ Plotting of contract documents ■ Colored plotting of charts, simple plans	■ Speed ■ Paper size ■ Repeatability ■ Accuracy ■ Resolution (size of pen steps) ■ Local intelligence including predefined symbols or alphanumeric characters ■ Pen ■ Color availability ■ Interfaces
Electrostatic plotters 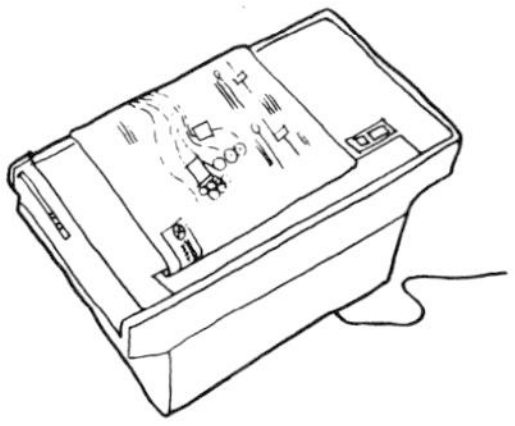	Charge reacts with special paper or Mylar to produce graphic or alphanumeric image	■ Same as pen plotter	■ Same as pen plotters with the exception of color availability or pen type
Ink jet plotter 	Spray fine jets of ink on any media	■ High-quality color renderings	■ Same as above ■ Available colors

phy. Some systems are generic in nature and can be used by many disciplines, including landscape architecture (2-D drafting systems fall into this category).

Consequently, one of the most critical decisions that professionals will make as they begin to computerize office tasks involves software selection. Potential implementers of CAD systems are advised by many computer consultants first to locate the software that best meets their design needs and then to build the remainder of the system with whatever hardware can accommodate the particular software.

3.1 Base Information

Once having identified the major problems to be solved in a site planning project, one typically needs to collect and record a large quantity of site-specific information. The initial requirement is usually a site survey that includes descriptions of topographic, boundary, cultural, and structural features. This survey is usually supplemented with other data, including local soil types and characteristics, extent of vegetative cover, subsurface geology, and factors such as views, ambient sound levels, and existing circulation patterns. Many if not all of these data have traditionally been recorded in the form of two-dimensional maps.

Spatial Data:

Much site-specific information is spatial in nature and is usually represented graphically. The development of spatial data bases for site planning projects requires only that designers describe the spatial data geometrically. Spatial data are commonly represented in the form of points, lines, and polygons. Examples of landscape design elements represented in this fashion are shown in Table 130-5.

Alternatively, the spatial features of a site can be described by dividing the site into a matrix of rectangular (or hexagonal) cells. Each of these cells is then assigned a value corresponding to the type, level, or intensity of a characteristic being mapped. The operation of LANDSAT and other digital imagery, for example, is based on the assignment of quantitative values to individual cells, i.e., small rectangular parcels of land. (In the case of LANDSAT, the values represent the relative degree of light reflectivity.) Because of the regularity of such a matrix, actual locational descriptions of each cell need not be explicitly stored. Cell locations can be calculated from the cell size, spacing, and orientation of the matrix.

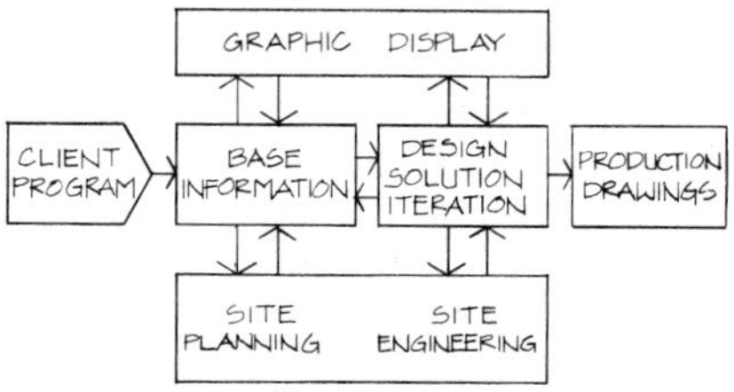
GRAPHIC DISPLAY
CLIENT PROGRAM
BASE INFORMATION
DESIGN SOLUTION ITERATION
PRODUCTION DRAWINGS
SITE PLANNING
SITE ENGINEERING

Figure 130-3 Major tasks in the process of computer-aided design.

Textual Data:

Much of the information generated during the process of design can be represented in the form of text. This may include the client's program and the field notes, correspondence, cost estimates, specifications, related planning studies, and other documents.

3.2 Site Planning

Computer-aided techniques for site planning (i.e., land use allocation and the siting

TABLE 130-5
Landscape Architectural Design Elements

Points	*Lines*	*Polygons*
	Landform	
 PROPOSED ELEVATION 101.50 Spot grade	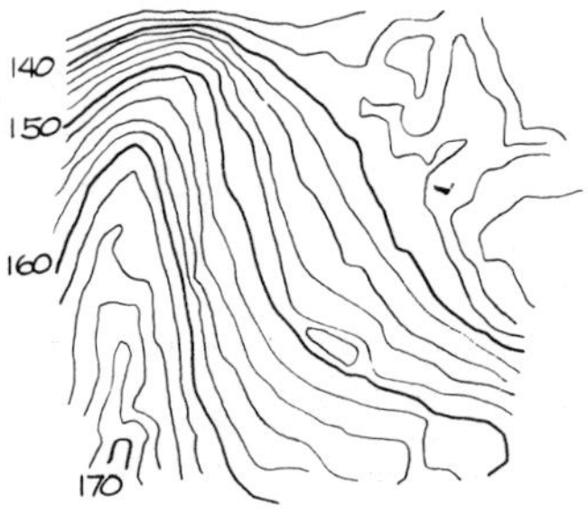 140 150 160 170 Contours	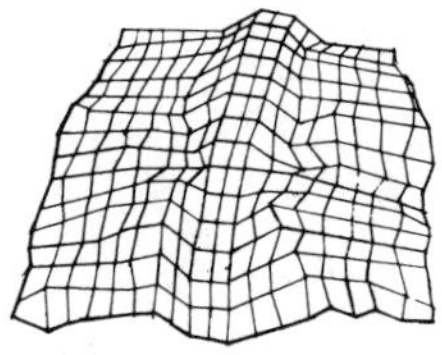 Mesh drawing
	Plant materials	
 10" CAL. MAPLE Survey location	 Line drawing (wire frame representation)	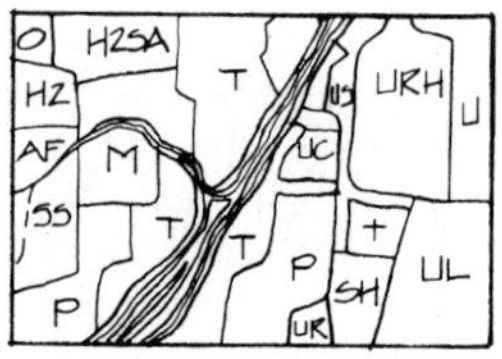 Land cover map
	Structure	
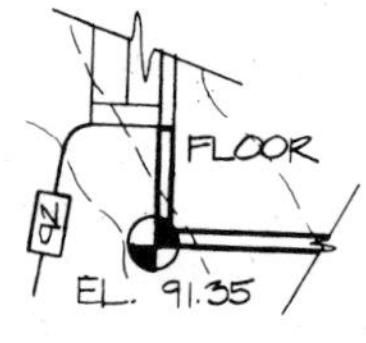 FLOOR EL. 91.35 Corner of building	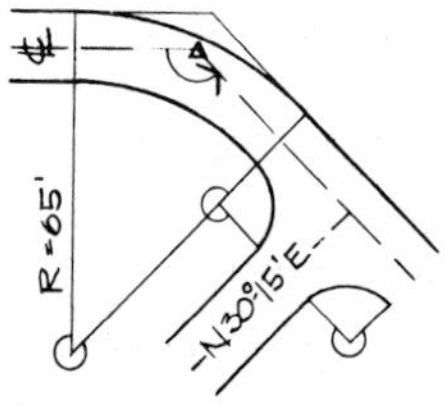 R=65' Construction baseline	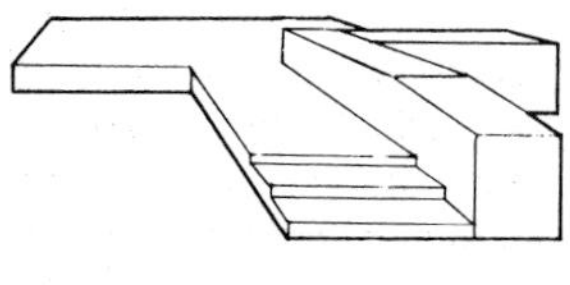 Faces of structure

of various design elements) are derived from larger computer-aided land planning or geographic information system (GIS) applications. The techniques involve basic calculations on a sitewide data base. The results are typically numeric or boolean (true or false) values associated with a particular spatial location or grid cell, or attributes describing some polygonal area. This information is typically displayed in map format. Designers can determine the occurrence, co-occurrence, or absence of certain spatial data and then construct composite maps focusing on areas of interest.

This overlay process is used principally to locate programmatic design elements. Sets of criteria are assembled comprising preferred site characteristics—such as acceptable soils, buildable slopes, or advantageous solar orientations. Software programs then facilitate the process of determining which areas of the site satisfy these criteria or, alternatively, whether or not any specific location is acceptable in terms of prescribed criteria. Other features of typical planning software include the capability to add weight to the more important criteria of a set and the capability to determine minimum distances between certain features either in terms of travel time or physical distance. Table 130-6 describes common characteristics of typical site planning software.

Successful use of computer-aided site planning processes depends on the existence of a thorough and well-structured data base. A data base should be accessible by programs designed to accomplish tasks such as those described in Table 130-6. Tablet digitizers and high-resolution color monitors are important peripheral devices that will facilitate easy mapping and recognition of spatial data.

A number of dedicated GIS and image processing systems have become commercially available. These are built around microcomputers for stand-alone use, or feature microprocessor-based image processing separate from tasks assigned to the host computer. Although these systems are more cost-effective when used for large-scale landscape planning projects or for correcting, coloring, and displaying LANDSAT images, they can be employed to solve problems at the project scale.

TABLE 130-6
Site Planning Software

Task	*Description*
	Calculations
Area calculation and measurement	■ Measure size of given polygon ■ Compute distance from one feature or polygon to another
Contouring	■ Produce contour plans from gridded or irregularly spaced data ■ Draw axonometric or perspective contoured views
Slope; aspect; intensity of sun	■ Calculate slope, aspect, and insolation at given locations
Visibility; areas seen	■ Produce maps showing areas visible from a location ■ Determine from what vantage points a feature is visible
Runoff patterns and watershed areas	■ Graphically show direction of flow ■ Calculate Q for various rainfall intensities, areas, and covers
	*Data manipulation**
Data retrieval	■ Locate area of interest (window) and specify size, shape, and other attributes
Map generalization	■ Assemble single map from multiple sources by scaling and generalizing data
Map abstraction	■ Convert irregular spatial data to gridded data, calculate centroids, reclassify polygons, create proximal maps
Map sheet manipulation	■ Change scale or projection or rotate coordinates
Buffer generation	■ Create new polygons representing areas of interest or shared properties as in highway corridors or parcels suitable for development
Polygon overlay and dissolve	■ Create composite maps and data combining polygons of similar characteristics into separate polygons

*For a more thorough explanation, see Jack Dangermond, "Software Components Commonly Used in Geographic Information Systems," delivered at Harvard Computer Graphics Week, Cambridge, 1982.

3.3 Design Idea Definition

Computer-assisted design definition (i.e., graphic expression of an idea) begins with, or moves rapidly into, the manipulation of three-dimensional representations. After a design has been laid out and the necessary data have been inputted, quick displays of plan, section, and perspective views can be generated. Where numeric precision is required for constructability, computers can be used to link complex representations to mathematical descriptions. For example, some systems allow users to create horizontal alignments by specifying only a few coordinate points. A series of curves are then automatically filled in between the points. A designer can choose a pleasing curve form, and the computer program will then calculate its geometry.

The interactive definition, scaling, manipulation, and display of representations require sophisticated data bases and methods to describe the actual representations. Four general approaches to design representation input are useful in site planning and design processes. These are: (1) definition of 3-D form by individual coordinate points, (2) definition of 3-D form by successive sections, (3) 2-D to 3-D transformations, and (4) volume modeling.

Three-dimensional representations or layouts can be described by specifying a sufficient number of points with *X*, *Y*, and *Z* coordinates to approximate what is to be represented. The modeling of sections begins with a defined baseline to which sections or offset distances are added at specified station points. Two- to three-dimensional transformations require user-defined two-dimensional representations as bases. Based on selected criteria, the third dimension is *extruded* from the two-dimensional representation. This technique has been used to define landforms in surface mining and other landscape reclamation projects (Mallary and Ferraro). The modeling of volume involves certain operations or predefined *legal* objects to create more complex representations. A set of rules identifies both the legal objects and the operations involved. Table 130-7 describes these four approaches.

3.4 Site Engineering

Site engineering tasks include typical calculations and tests performed on design data or site analysis information. These tasks are either descriptive or prescriptive; they either precisely describe or measure some characteristic of a design idea, or they test a design idea against a set of quantifiable criteria. Most site engineering software was originally designed for applications in civil engineering.

Architectural programs are another major source of site engineering software,

TABLE 130-7
Methods of Design Definition

Method	*Input*	*Software*	*Landscape architectural use*
Individual points 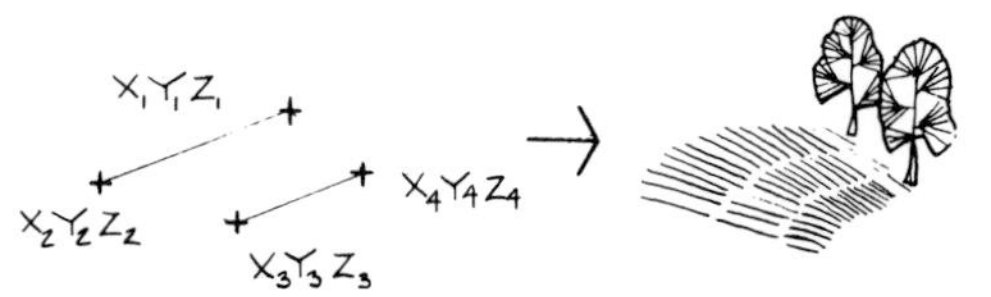 $X_1Y_1Z_1$ $X_2Y_2Z_2$ $X_3Y_3Z_3$ $X_4Y_4Z_4$	■ Keyed in ■ Stored file of points ■ 2-D or 3-D digitizer ■ Output from other application program	■ Ability to translate coordinate pairs or triples into edge, face, or volume descriptions	■ Create profiles ■ Place design elements on site ■ Construct complex surfaces or structural forms ■ Edit models developed with other methods
Sectional modeling 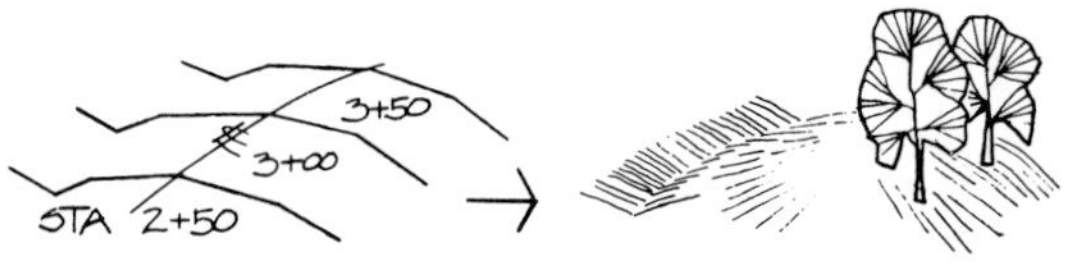 3+50 3+00 STA 2+50	■ Keyed in ■ Stored file of sections ■ Digitizer ■ Output from application programs	■ Combine and store horizontal and vertical layout ■ Assign information to specified sections	■ Road alignment design ■ Earth dam design ■ Design of linear forms ■ Layout of construction baseline
2-D to 3-D transformation 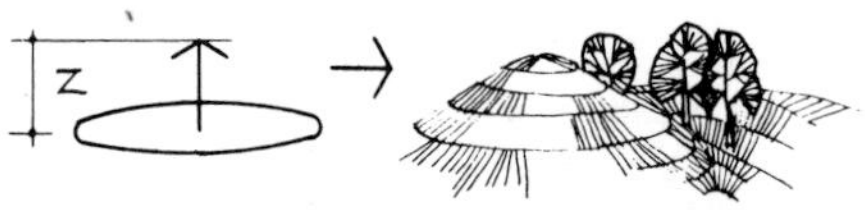 Z	■ Base form defined using technique from above ■ Keyed-in commands from which to extrude	■ Definitions of criteria and rules for extruding in any of three dimensions	■ Shaping large landforms ■ Design for reclaimed lands
Volume modeling 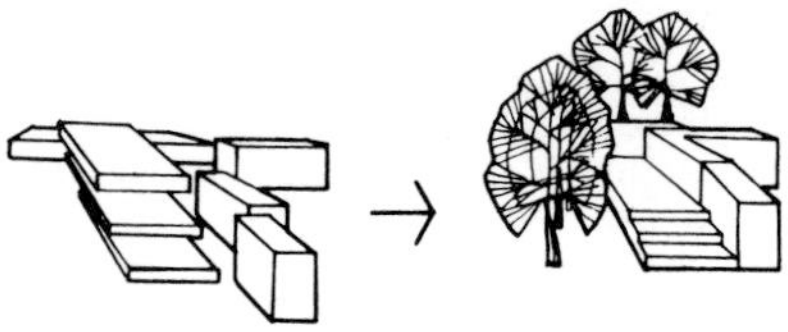	■ Keyed-in commands ■ Digitizer, trackball, mouse, etc., used to move objects on screen	■ Library of legal objects represented as constructions (made up of other objects) or representations (made up of faces, etc.) ■ Defined operations including intersection, union, difference, and tweaking (moving one face with automatic adjustment of other faces)	■ Design of wall, terraces ■ Design of mechanical, drainage, or other structural components

TABLE 130-8
Site Engineering Software

Task	*Software characteristics*
Surveying	■ Accepts field notes ■ Field control
Road alignment	■ Street stationing ■ Profiles of pavement and storm drainage
Cut and/or fill	■ Average end method ■ Borrow pit method ■ Hauling estimates ■ Quantities for estimating programs
Runoff	■ Calculate *Q* ■ Calculate erosion
Quantity takeoff	■ Quantities of all materials used or work performed in site construction ■ Tied to cost estimating system
Plant list	■ Choose plant by identifying criteria ■ Identify criteria to output appropriate plants
Storm drainage pipe and swale sizing	■ Input site area, layout measurements, and runoff characteristics ■ Determine appropriate sizes and spacing of drainage structures
Retaining wall design	■ Perform graphic test and tests for horizontal sliding, crushing, and overturning ■ Detail rebars
Wooden structure design	■ Calculate live and dead loads ■ Size beams and other structural members

particularly for the design of structural elements in the landscape. Landscape architects have developed some site engineering software specifically for landscape applications. These programs include plant specification systems which identify certain species, given a set of characteristics, or which identify various characteristics, given a particular species.

Site engineering tasks are an integral part of the site planning process. Site engineering must readily accept input from other programs, and the output must be suitable for graphic display. Table 130-8 lists various types of site engineering software available for landscape architectural use.

Computer systems vary in their ability to carry out arithmetic operations with *floating point numbers* (real numbers with significant digits to the right of the decimal point). A computer's precision with respect to these operations requires thorough investigation prior to lease or purchase. Many site engineering tasks (i.e., wall, pavement, or drainage design) carry the risk of significant liability if incorrect calculations result in flaws or failures after construction.

3.5 Production

Computer-assisted production of contract documents may provide the most straightforward cost savings of all CAD approaches to site planning and design processes. Presentation-quality graphics and color transparencies are also available. Timesavings from computer-assisted production will vary depending on a firm's experience with computer technology and on the level of computer integration in the office practice. It is more cost-effective to use existing computer-based design data to produce construction drawings than it is to manually digitize design development drawings produced without computer assistance, and then edit them to finish the construction documents.

Computer-assisted drafting systems typically employ a library of standard details, symbols, lines, labels, etc. Representations of these symbols are arranged on a menu mounted on a digitizer tablet or displayed on a CRT. The designer chooses a symbol by touching a digitizer stylus to the appropriate selection, and the symbol is displayed on a screen. It can then be scaled, moved, rotated, or labeled and other symbols or labels added.

If previously developed design data are used, the designer may call up a plan view from memory, scale it, position it on the screen, and make it a permanent part of the construction drawing. When the drawing is complete, it can be plotted on any reproducible medium. Changes to the drawing are made by editing the computer disk or tape-based description of the drawing or by manually changing the already-plotted film or paper reproducible.

GLOSSARY

Addressable point: The smallest single location that a CRT beam can be directed at on a vector display unit.

Algorithm: A set of procedures which will produce a solution to a given problem.

ASCII: American Standard Code for Information Interchange. A code for the representation of alphanumeric characters and symbols as bits.

Assembler: Computer language which is particular to a certain machine and its architecture or microprocessor. Assembly programs are lengthy, but they generally run faster.

Basic: Refers to a simple and commonly used programming language (beginner's all-purpose symbolic code). It is less efficient than other high-level programming languages.

Bit: The smallest unit of computerized data, having the value of either 1 or 0.

Byte: A group of bits representing a number or other data item.

CAD: Computer-aided design.

Compiler: A computer program which takes programs written in a higher-level language and translates them into the machine language particular to the computer. Often this requires more than one pass or run-through.

Core system: A package of subroutines developed by the Association for Computing Machinery's Special Interest Group on Graphics (ACM SIGGRAPH). It is standardized and device independent, allowing software written for it to be transported from one machine environment to another.

CPU: Central processing unit. That part of the computer containing all of the control circuitry and processing capabilities.

Cursor: A symbol used to indicate a particular location on a screen. It can be controlled by keyboard keys, joysticks, data tablets, or other graphic input devices, or it may be moved by means of programming techniques.

Data tablet: A graphic input device which reports the coordinate location of a stylus as the stylus is traced across its surface.

Digital terrain model (DTM): The representation of topography as a matrix of elevation values.

Digitizer: Any one of many available types of hardware for encoding 2-D or 3-D data into a format usable by computers.

Direct view storage tube (DVST): A vector graphics display unit with the ability to maintain an image for a lengthy period of time without redrawing it.

Disk: A type of data storage medium.

Drum plotter: A pen plotter in which the drafting surface is moved over a drum while the pen moves across it.

EBCDIC: Extended binary-coded decimal interchange code. The IBM convention for representing alphanumeric characteristics and symbols as bits.

Electrostatic plotter: A plotter which produces images on sensitized paper with electrostatic charges.

EPROM: Erasable programmable read-only memory. A chip which can be programmed to perform certain tasks and erased for reprogramming if necessary.

Firmware: Programs encoded on EPROMs, PROMs, or ROMs.

Floating point: A method used to store very large or very small real numbers.

Floppy disk: A flexible, transportable disk used for data storage.

Fortran: Formula translator. A widely used, sophisticated programming language. Much software for engineering and graphics is written in Fortran.

Hard copy: Copies of computer-generated images which can be separated from the machine.

Hard disk: A hard, usually nontransportable medium used to store data. Hard disks have greater capacity than floppy disks.

Hardware: The computer itself or any of its related peripheral input or output devices.

Intelligent: An adjective applied to peripherals or terminals which are equipped with firmware which performs functions which would otherwise be accomplished by the CPU of the host computer.

Interpreter: A program which interprets a program written in a higher-level language into machine language. Interpreted programs generally run slower than compiled ones.

Joystick: A lever which can be moved to provide coordinate input to the display device.

***K*:** The number 1024 (2^{10}), although sometimes *K* is used to refer to 1000.

Light pen: A hand-held device which detects light within an area when held against a VDT.

***M*:** Used to represent 1 million.

Machine language: The language employed by the microprocessor of a given computer to perform an operation.

Microprocessor: A computer chip which contains the circuitry necessary to manipulate data.

Modem: Modulator-demodulator. A device used to translate computerized data into a form which can be transmitted across telephone lines and to decode data at the receiving end.

Mouse: A graphic input device which is moved across a surface to generate coordinate data.

Pascal: A very popular and powerful programming language named after the French mathematician who developed it.

Pixel: Picture element. The smallest addressable display element on a raster display. Pixels are typically rectangular.

Plotter: An output device which produces an image on paper or film by moving a pen across it.

PROM: Programmable read-only memory. A ROM which can be programmed to perform a particular task.

RAM: Random-access memory. Internal memory used during the processing of data.

Raster: Used to describe TV-like display units which produce images from a rectangular matrix of pixels.

ROM: Read-only memory. A chip onto which data have been encoded permanently. ROMs are used to store operating systems, interpreters, and other frequently used data.

Scanning digitizer: A digitizer which employs optical laser technology to encode a plan or other document as a raster image.

Software: Computer programs.

Track ball: A half-exposed ball which is rotated to move a cursor on a screen.

VDT: Video display terminal. Any terminal used to display imagery.

Video digitizer: A digitizer based on a video camera. It creates a digital image of the source data; the image can then be manipulated.

REFERENCES

Chasen, S. H., and J. W. Dow. *The Guide for the Evaluation and Implementation of CAD/CAM Systems,* CAD/CAM Decisions, Atlanta and Marietta, GA, 1979.

Focuses on implementation of large systems; management principles are useful for all computerization scenarios.

Dangermond, Jack. "Software Components Commonly Used in Geographic Information Systems," *Harvard Computer Graphics Week,* Cambridge, MA, 1982.

This paper outlines useful and necessary characteristics of GIS software and systems.

MacDougall, E. Bruce. *Microcomputers in Landscape Architecture,* Elsevier North Holland, New York, 1983.

Detailed introductory text on all aspects of computer use in landscape architecture.

Mallary, Robert, and Michael Ferraro. "'ECO-SITE': An Application of Computer-Aided Design to the Composition of Landforms for Reclamation," *Computer Graphics* 11, Summer 1977.

An example of CAD techniques applied to a large-scale landscape design and construction problem.

Mitchell, William J. *Computer-Aided Architectural Design,* Petrocelli/Charter, New York, 1977.

A thorough text on the field, including information on sitework. Particular emphasis is given to modeling spatial allocation problems and to the construction of integrated data bases.

Newman, William M., and Robert F. Sproull. *Principles of Interactive Computer Graphics,* 2d ed., McGraw-Hill, New York, 1979.

The classic work on the subject, containing explanations of many common algorithms and techniques.

Pickholtz, Andrew. "Interactive 3-D Graphics for the Apple II," *BYTE* vol. 7, November 1982.

Introduction and programs for perspective transformations. Useful for microcomputers other than the Apple.

Yen, Elizabeth H. "A Graphics Glossary," *Computer Graphics* vol. 15, July 1981.

A complete glossary of common and technical terms used in discussing graphics, hardware, software, and systems.

Additional References

Program listings of software useful to landscape architects are often given in *Landscape Architecture Magazine, Civil Engineering,* and the popular microcomputer journals. Software is usually advertised in the professional journals above and in *Engineering News-Record.*

Program listings can also be found in *BYTE.* Descriptions of algorithms are often published in *Computer Graphics and Image Processing* and in *Computer Graphics and Computer-Aided Design. Computer Graphics World* often reviews various computer systems. ■

section 210: Spatial Standards

CREDITS

Section Editors: Gary M. Fishbeck and Charles W. Harris
Contributor for Famous Outdoor Spaces: William A. Mann
Graphic Assistance: Kristanta Dewara and Mandi Moreland
Sources of other graphics shown in Source Notes.

Technical Advisers:

Arnold H. Vollmer
Vollmer Associates
New York, New York

Berry Pell
Sasaki Associates, Inc.
Watertown, Massachusetts

CONTENTS

1.0 INTRODUCTION

1.1 General

This section is designed to assist the reader in gaining easy access to a body of data related to spatial and physical standards which can be used during preliminary stages of project planning and design. They can also serve as a point of reference or datum from which the reader can decide to make deviations for special reasons and/or conditions.

1.2 Use of Spatial Standards

There are two major points of caution that should be considered in using these standards. The first is that all "standards" should be put into some real-world context. For instance, what part of the world or in what types of climate might these be used? Most of the standards included in this section have been drawn from experiences in North America and may have to be modified for use in some other part of the world.

The second caution relates to our use of the terms "averages," "minimums," and "maximums." Typically, minimums are shown to identify what are considered crucial limits. Only in rare cases and for good reasons would the reader be expected to use the minimums or less. Averages seek to allow more optimum space or greater safety and comfort of the users.

Use of these standards beyond the preliminary stages of project planning and design should not be done unless each standard has been verified as appropriate for a specific site or user's needs.

1.3 Organization of Section

The data in this section have been grouped by very general types or categories. In several instances only the "more typical" types are shown and the reader is expected to seek out data for the "less typical" types. As in all handbooks, some of the standards shown here eventually will become dated or will need to be replaced by more recent standards.

Some standards are not covered in this section but are covered in another section of this handbook according to the specific topic for which it might be needed. For instance, most of the "typical" spatial standards and layouts for outdoor recreation are contained in Section 520: Recreation and Athletic Facilities.

The last subsection, or group of figures, in this section is devoted to a series of plans of some famous landscapes and places. All are drawn to similar scales. The generosity of William A. Mann of the University of Georgia, author of *Space and Time in Landscape Architectural History,* made possible the inclusion of these plans in this section. Only a few of the plans in this book have been included here. The reader is urged to refer to the original book for more complete coverage of these famous landscapes and spaces.

1.4 Sources of Spatial Standards

The editors are very grateful to the authors and their publishers, listed in the Source Notes at the end of this book, who gave permission for extensive copying or adapting of most of the data contained in this section.

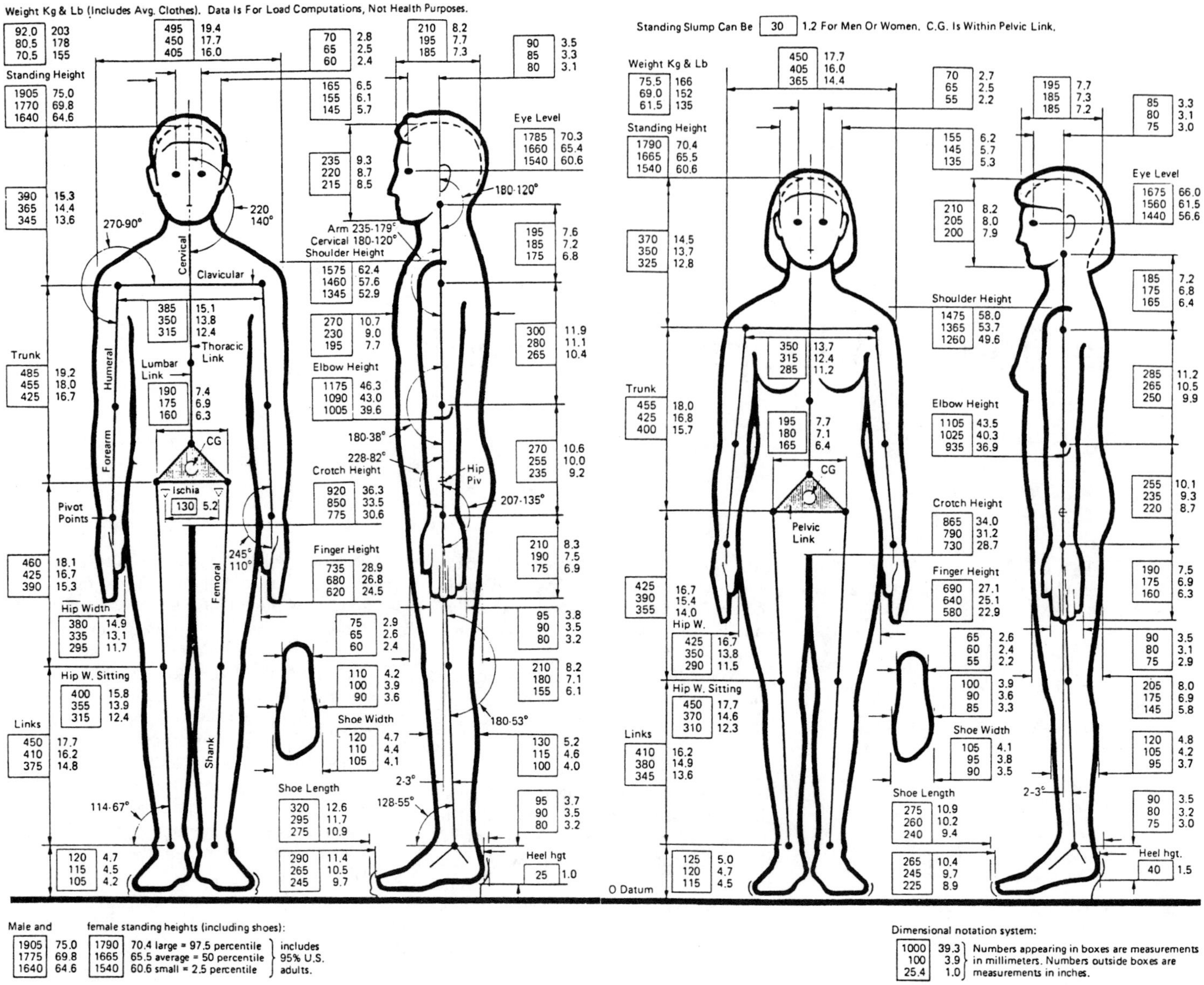
Weight Kg & Lb (Includes Avg. Clothes). Data Is For Load Computations, Not Health Purposes.
92.0 203
80.5 178
70.5 155
Standing Height
1905 75.0
1770 69.8
1640 64.6
495 19.4
450 17.7
405 16.0
70 2.8
65 2.5
60 2.4
210 8.2
195 7.7
185 7.3
90 3.5
85 3.3
80 3.1
165 6.5
155 6.1
145 5.7
Eye Level
1785 70.3
1660 65.4
1540 60.6
235 9.3
220 8.7
215 8.5
180-120°
390 15.3
365 14.4
345 13.6
270-90°
220
140°
Arm 235-179°
Cervical 180-120°
Shoulder Height
195 7.6
185 7.2
175 6.8
Cervical
Clavicular
1575 62.4
1460 57.6
1345 52.9
385 15.1
350 13.8
315 12.4
Thoracic Link
270 10.7
230 9.0
195 7.7
300 11.9
280 11.1
265 10.4
Trunk
485 19.2
455 18.0
425 16.7
Humeral
Lumbar Link
190 7.4
175 6.9
160 6.3
Elbow Height
1175 46.3
1090 43.0
1005 39.6
Forearm
CG
180-38°
228-82°
Crotch Height
270 10.6
255 10.0
235 9.2
Hip Piv
Ischia
130 5.2
920 36.3
850 33.5
775 30.6
207-135°
Pivot Points
245°
110°
Finger Height
210 8.3
190 7.5
175 6.9
460 18.1
425 16.7
390 15.3
Femoral
735 28.9
680 26.8
620 24.5
Hip Width
380 14.9
335 13.1
295 11.7
75 2.9
65 2.6
60 2.4
95 3.8
90 3.5
80 3.2
Hip W. Sitting
400 15.8
355 13.9
315 12.4
110 4.2
100 3.9
90 3.6
210 8.2
180 7.1
155 6.1
Links
450 17.7
410 16.2
375 14.8
Shank
Shoe Width
120 4.7
110 4.4
105 4.1
180-53°
130 5.2
115 4.6
100 4.0
2-3°
Shoe Length
114-67°
128-55°
320 12.6
295 11.7
275 10.9
95 3.7
90 3.5
80 3.2
120 4.7
115 4.5
105 4.2
290 11.4
265 10.5
245 9.7
Heel hgt
25 1.0
O Datum
Standing Slump Can Be 30 1.2 For Men Or Women. C.G. Is Within Pelvic Link.
Weight Kg & Lb
75.5 166
69.0 152
61.5 135
450 17.7
405 16.0
365 14.4
70 2.7
65 2.5
55 2.2
195 7.7
185 7.3
185 7.2
85 3.3
80 3.1
75 3.0
Standing Height
1790 70.4
1665 65.5
1540 60.6
155 6.2
145 5.7
135 5.3
Eye Level
1675 66.0
1560 61.5
1440 56.6
210 8.2
205 8.0
200 7.9
370 14.5
350 13.7
325 12.8
185 7.2
175 6.8
165 6.4
Shoulder Height
1475 58.0
1365 53.7
1260 49.6
350 13.7
315 12.4
285 11.2
285 11.2
265 10.5
250 9.9
Trunk
455 18.0
425 16.8
400 15.7
Elbow Height
195 7.7
180 7.1
165 6.4
1105 43.5
1025 40.3
935 36.9
CG
255 10.1
235 9.3
220 8.7
Crotch Height
Pelvic Link
865 34.0
790 31.2
730 28.7
Finger Height
190 7.5
175 6.9
160 6.3
425 16.7
390 15.4
355 14.0
690 27.1
640 25.1
580 22.9
Hip W.
425 16.7
350 13.8
290 11.5
65 2.6
60 2.4
55 2.2
90 3.5
80 3.1
75 2.9
Hip W. Sitting
450 17.7
370 14.6
310 12.3
100 3.9
90 3.6
85 3.3
205 8.0
175 6.9
145 5.8
Shoe Width
Links
410 16.2
380 14.9
345 13.6
105 4.1
95 3.8
90 3.5
120 4.8
105 4.2
95 3.7
Shoe Length
2-3°
275 10.9
260 10.2
240 9.4
90 3.5
80 3.2
75 3.0
Heel hgt.
40 1.5
125 5.0
120 4.7
115 4.5
265 10.4
245 9.7
225 8.9
Male and female standing heights (including shoes):
1905 75.0
1775 69.8
1640 64.6
1790 70.4 large = 97.5 percentile
1665 65.5 average = 50 percentile
1540 60.6 small = 2.5 percentile
includes 95% U.S. adults.
Dimensional notation system:
1000 39.3
100 3.9
25.4 1.0
Numbers appearing in boxes are measurements in millimeters. Numbers outside boxes are measurements in inches.

Introduction to Anthropometric Data

The anthropometric drawings show three values for each measurement: The top figure is for the large person, or 97.5 percentile; the middle figure, the average person, or 50 percentile; and the lower figure, the small person, or 2.5 percentile. The chosen extreme percentiles thus include 95 percent. The remaining 5 percent include some who learn to adapt and others, not adequately represented, who are excluded to keep designs for the majority from becoming too complex and expensive. Space and access charts are designed to accept the 97.5 percentile large man and will cover all adults except a few giants. Therefore, use the 97.5 percentile to determine space envelopes, the 2.5 percentile to determine the maximum "kinetopsheres" or reach areas by hand or foot, and the 50 percentile to establish control and display heights. To accommodate both men and women, it is useful at times to add a dimension of the large man to the corresponding dimension of the small woman and divide by 2 to obtain data for the average adult. This is the way height standards evolve. Youth data are for combined sex. Although girls and boys do not grow at the same rate, differences are small when compared with size variations.

Pivot point and link systems make it easy to construct articulating templates and manikins. Links are simplified bones. The spine is shown as a single link; since it can flex, pivot points may be added. All human joints are not simple pivots, though it is convenient to assume so. Some move in complicated patterns like the roving shoulder. Reaches shown are easy and comfortable; additional reach is possible by bending and rotating the trunk and by extending the shoulder. Stooping to reach low is better than stretching to reach high. The dynamic body may need 10 percent more space than the static posture allows. Shoes have been included in all measurements; allowance may need to be made for heavy clothing. Sight lines and angles of vision given in one place or another apply to all persons.

Millimeters have been chosen to avoid use of decimals. Rounding to 5 mm aids mental retention while being within the tolerance of most human measurements.

Figure 210-1 Standing adult dimensions.

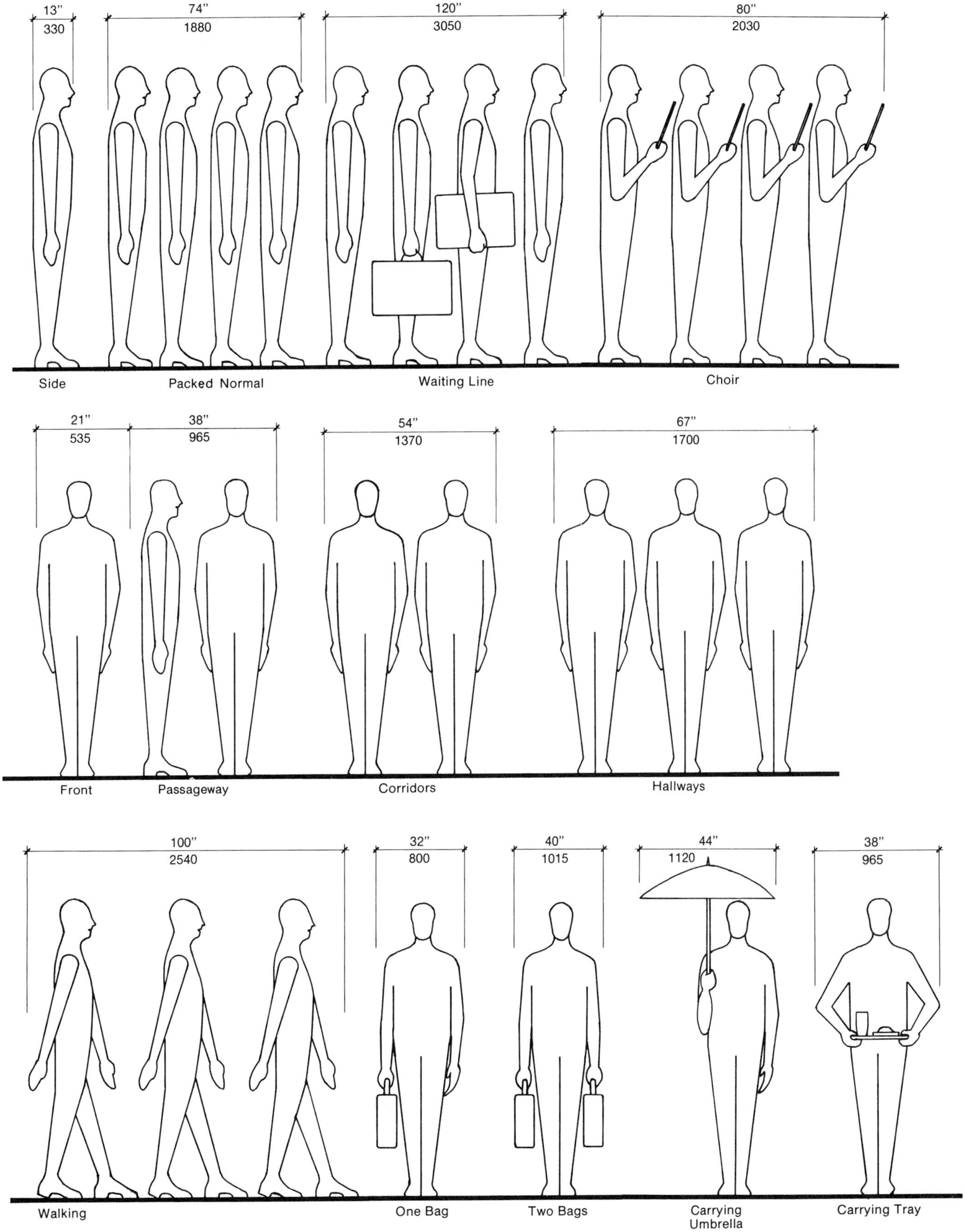

13"
330
74"
1880
120"
3050
80"
2030
Side
Packed Normal
Waiting Line
Choir
21"
535
38"
965
54"
1370
67"
1700
Front
Passageway
Corridors
Hallways
100"
2540
32"
800
40"
1015
44"
1120
38"
965
Walking
One Bag
Two Bags
Carrying Umbrella
Carrying Tray

Figure 210-2 Queuing and standing width dimensions.

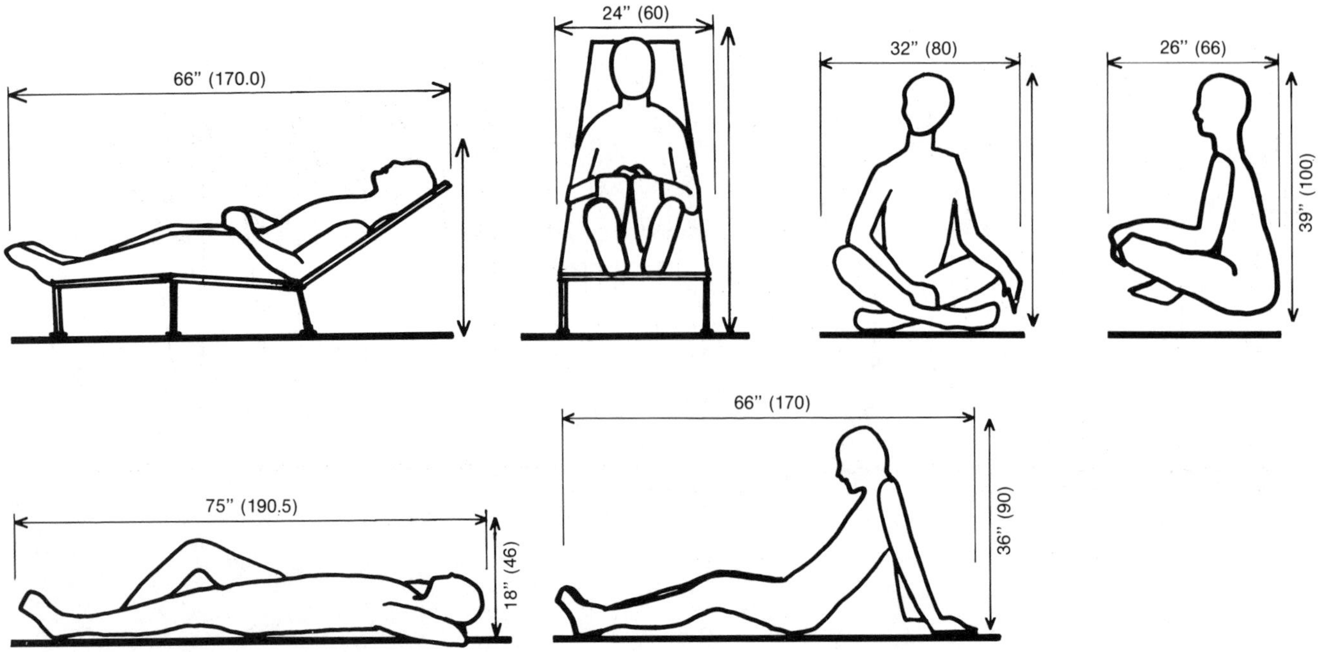
66" (170.0)
24" (60)
32" (80)
26" (66)
39" (100)
75" (190.5)
18" (46)
66" (170)
36" (90)

Figure 210-3 Active positions of adults.

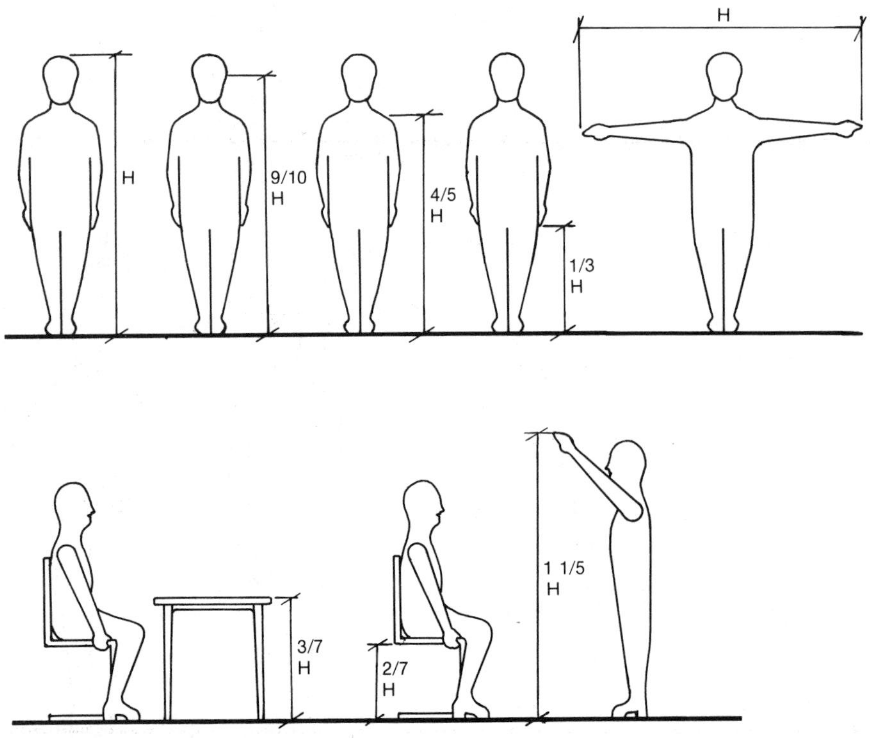
H
H
9/10 H
4/5 H
1/3 H
3/7 H
2/7 H
1 1/5 H

Figure 210-4 Physical proportions of children.

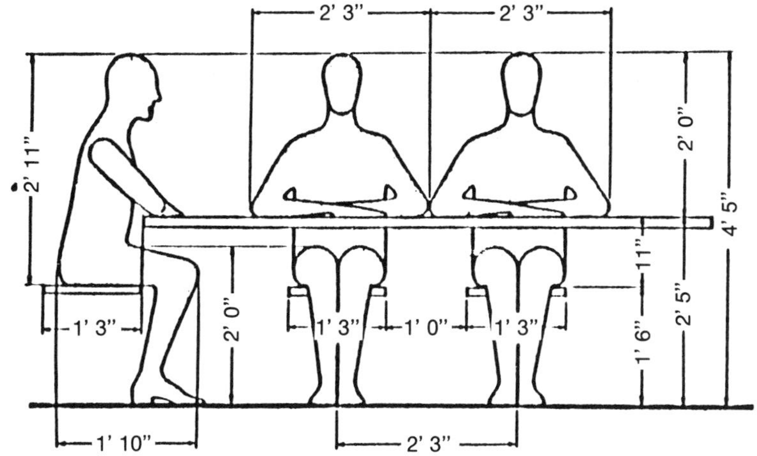
2' 3"
2' 3"
2' 11"
2' 0"
4' 5"
11"
2' 5"
1' 3"
1' 3"
1' 0"
1' 3"
2' 0"
1' 6"
1' 10"
2' 3"

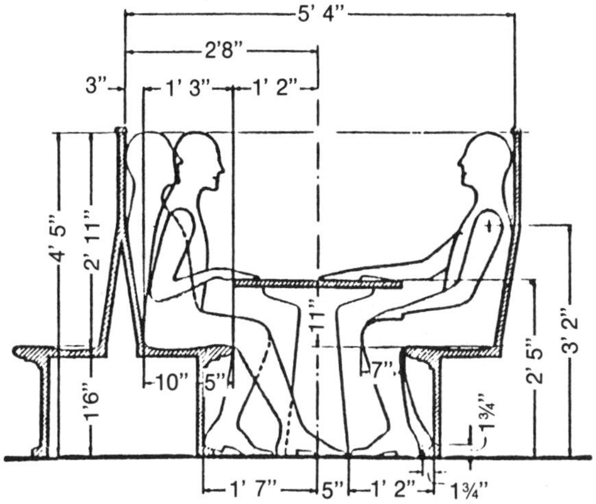
5' 4"
2'8"
3"
1' 3"
1' 2"
4' 5"
2' 11"
11"
1'6"
10"
5"
7"
1¾"
2' 5"
3' 2"
1' 7"
5"
1' 2"
1¾"

Height of tabletops shown is 2 ft 5 in.; some authorities prefer 2 ft 6 in., or sometimes 2 ft 6½ in.

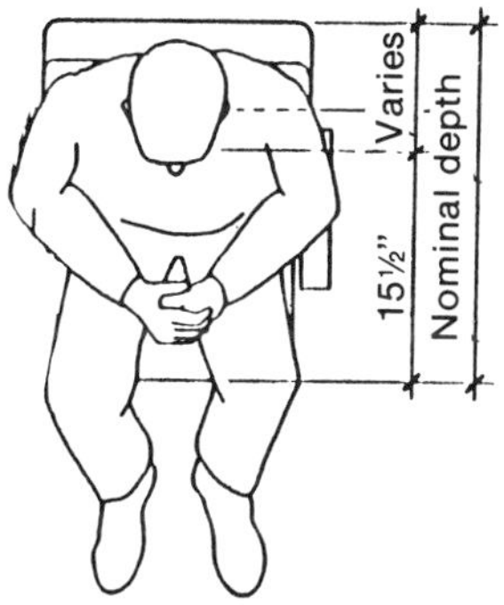
Varies
Nominal depth
15½"

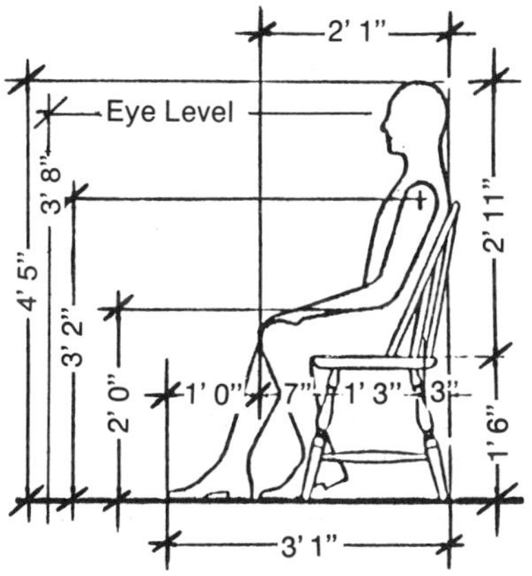
2' 1"
Eye Level
3' 8"
4' 5"
3' 2"
2' 0"
2' 11"
1' 0"
7"
1' 3"
3"
1' 6"
3' 1"

Circle (a)		Square (a, b)		Rectangular (a, b)		
Persons	a	Persons	a&b	Persons	a	b
2	2-3'	2	2-3'	—	—	—
4	3-4'	4	3-4'	4	2' 6"	5'
6	4-5'	6	4-5'	6-8	3'	7'
8	5-6'	8	5-6'	8-10	3' 6"	8'
10	6-7'	10	6-7'	10-12	4'	10'

Figure 210-5 Seating data by sizes and shapes of tables.

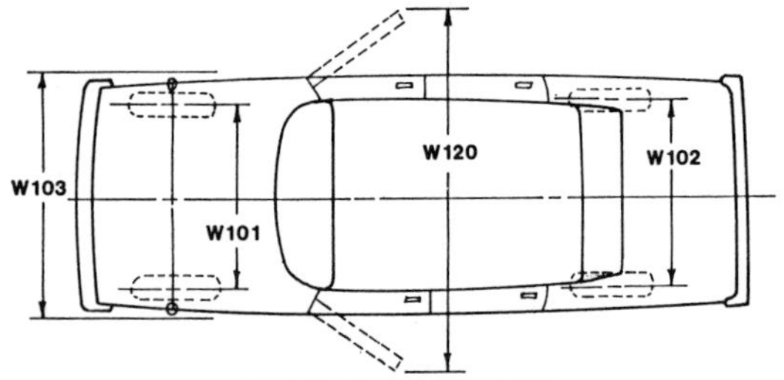
W103
W101
W120
W102
EXTERIOR WIDTH DIMENSIONS

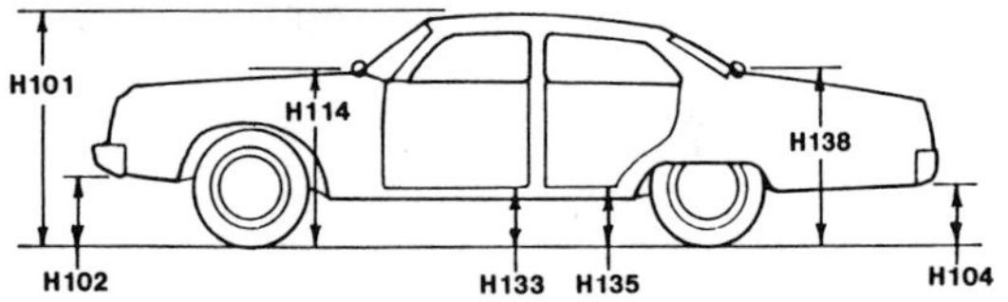
H101
H114
H138
H102
H133
H135
H104
EXTERIOR HEIGHT DIMENSIONS

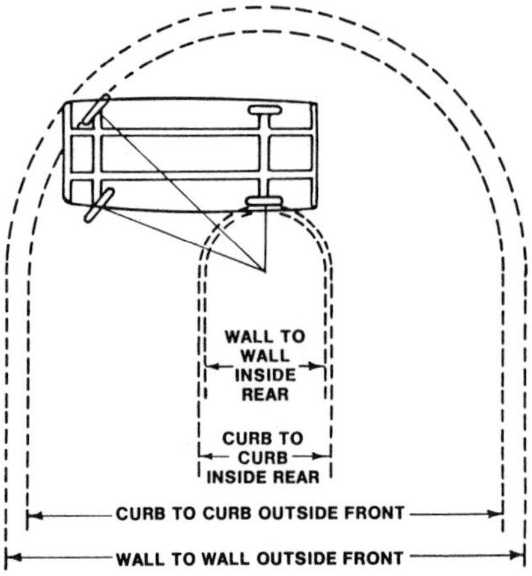
WALL TO WALL INSIDE REAR
CURB TO CURB INSIDE REAR
CURB TO CURB OUTSIDE FRONT
WALL TO WALL OUTSIDE FRONT
TURNING DIAMETER DIMENSIONS

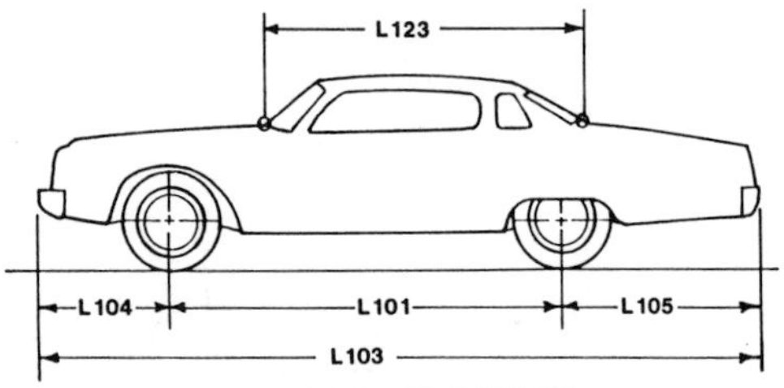
L123
L104
L101
L105
L103
EXTERIOR LENGTH DIMENSIONS

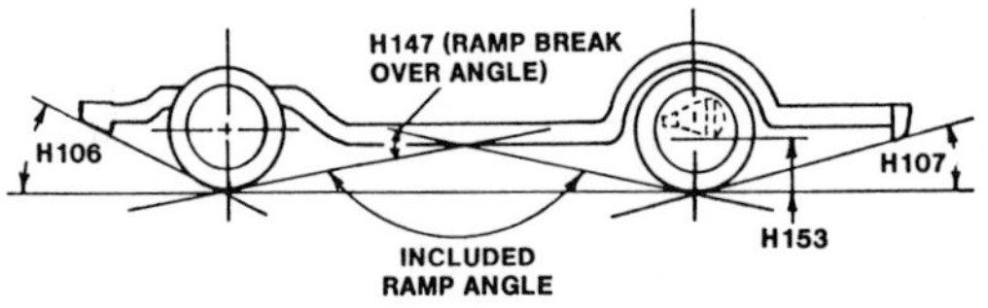
H147 (RAMP BREAK OVER ANGLE)
H106
H107
INCLUDED RAMP ANGLE
H153
GROUND CLEARANCE DIMENSIONS

STANDARD AUTOMOBILE DIMENSIONS (1983 U.S. Passenger Cars)

Overall Dimensions, in.

	Wheelbase L101	Overall length L102	Overall width W103	Overall width, doors open W120	Overall height H101	Minimum running ground clearance H153
Smallest	89.4	153.4	61.8	120.0	46.7	3.05
Largest	121.5	221.4	79.3	169.5	59.5	6.68*

Front of Car Dimensions, in.

	Height			Length		
	Bottom of front bumper to ground H102	Bottom of front door to ground H133	Cowl at rear to ground H114	Upper structure L123	Overhang, front L104	Width tread W101
Smallest	5.2	8.9	33.5	59.1	31.0	51.2
Largest	22.1	19.1	41.2	128.4	46.6	62.2

Rear of Car Dimensions, in.

	Bottom of rear bumper to ground H104	Axle differential to ground H153	Deck at rear window to ground H138	Bottom of rear door to ground H135	Overhang, rear L105	Tread W102
Smallest	8.46	3.5	30.8	8.3	28.7	51.2
Largest	18.29*	14.7	45.0	19.1	58.6	64.1

Angles of Approach and Departure, Ramp Breakover Angle, and Turning Diameter

	Angle of approach (degrees) H106	Angle of departure (degrees) H107	Ramp breakover angle (degrees) H147	Turning diameter (ft) Outside front Wall/wall	Turning diameter (ft) Outside front Curb/curb	Turning diameter (ft) Inside rear Wall/wall	Turning diameter (ft) Inside rear Curb/curb
Smallest	8.4	9.1	5.38	10.8	10.0	16.3	15.9
Largest	29.48*	34.8	23.8	45.3	42.9	25.1	24.9

*Curb height

Figure 210-6 Passenger cars (1983 U.S. models).

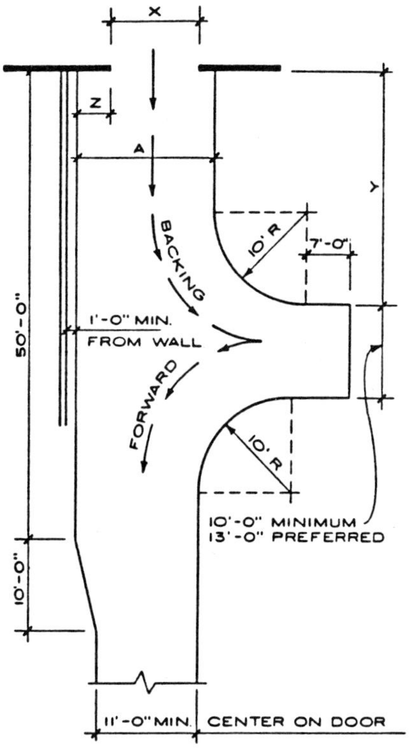
X
Z
A
Y
BACKING
10' R
7'-0"
1'-0" MIN.
FROM WALL
FORWARD
10' R
50'-0"
10'-0"
10'-0" MINIMUM
13'-0" PREFERRED
11'-0" MIN.
CENTER ON DOOR

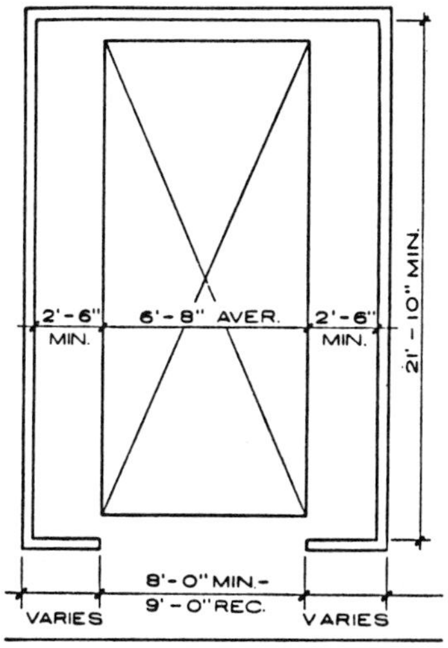
2'-6"
MIN.
6'-8" AVER.
2'-6"
MIN.
21'-10" MIN.
8'-0" MIN.-
9'-0" REC.
VARIES
VARIES

ONE-CAR GARAGE

STRAIGHT IN BACK OUT

X	9'-0"	10'-0"	12'-0"	16'-0"
Y	26'-0"	25'-0"	23'-6"	24'-0"
Z	3'-4"	3'-1"	2'-0"	3'-0"
A	14'-4"	14'-5"	14'-8"	20'-0"

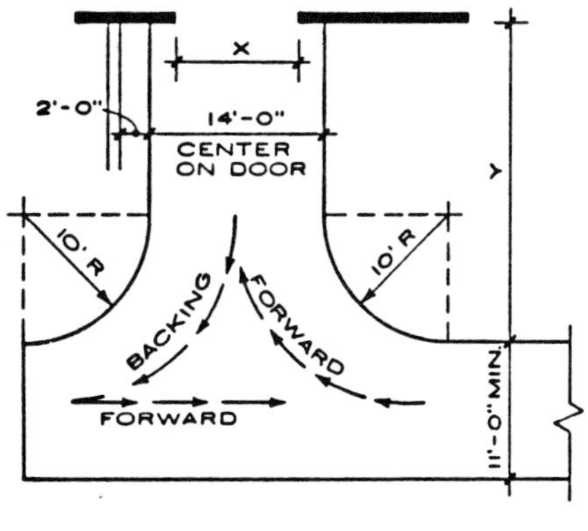
X
2'-0"
14'-0"
CENTER
ON DOOR
Y
10' R
10' R
BACKING
FORWARD
FORWARD
11'-0" MIN.

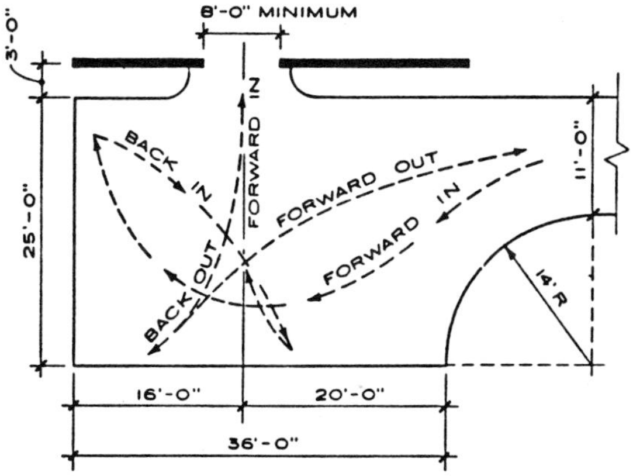
8'-0" MINIMUM
3'-0"
BACK IN
FORWARD IN
FORWARD OUT
FORWARD IN
BACK OUT
25'-0"
11'-0"
14' R
16'-0"
20'-0"
36'-0"

NOTE

Three maneuver entrance for single car garage. Employ only when space limitations demand use. Dimensioned for large car.

Figure 210-7 Private driveways and garages.

RECOMMENDED RANGE OF STALL WIDTHS (SW)

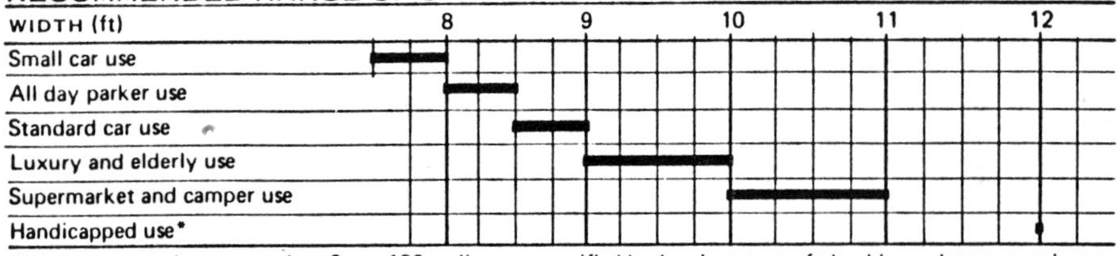
WIDTH (ft)
8
9
10
11
12
Small car use
All day parker use
Standard car use
Luxury and elderly use
Supermarket and camper use
Handicapped use*

*Minimum requirements = 1 or 2 per 100 stalls or as specified by local, state, or federal law; place convenient to destination.

ANGLED PARKING DIMENSIONS (Some are shown for interior parking.)

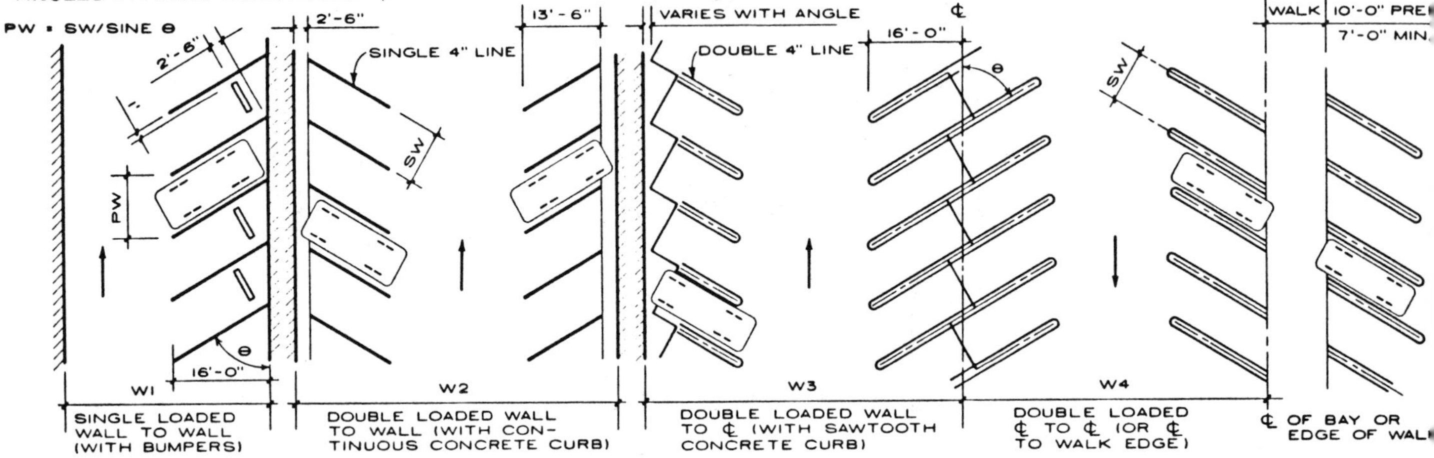
PW = SW/SINE θ
2'-6"
2'-6"
SINGLE 4" LINE
SW
PW
θ
16'-0"
W1
SINGLE LOADED WALL TO WALL (WITH BUMPERS)
13'-6"
W2
DOUBLE LOADED WALL TO WALL (WITH CONTINUOUS CONCRETE CURB)
VARIES WITH ANGLE
DOUBLE 4" LINE
W3
DOUBLE LOADED WALL TO ℄ (WITH SAWTOOTH CONCRETE CURB)
℄
16'-0"
θ
W4
DOUBLE LOADED ℄ TO ℄ (OR ℄ TO WALK EDGE)
SW
WALK
10'-0" PRE
7'-0" MIN
℄ OF BAY OR EDGE OF WAL

PARKING DIMENSIONS (FEET AND INCHES)

	SW	W	θ ANGLE OF PARK 45°	50°	55°	60°	65°	70°	75°	80°	85°	90°
Group I: small cars	8'·0"	1	25'·9"	26'·6"	27'·2"	29'·4"	31'·9"	34'·0"	36'·2"	38'·2"	40'·0"	41'·9
		2	40'·10"	42'·0"	43'·1"	45'·8"	48'·2"	50'·6"	52'·7"	54'·4"	55'·11"	57'·2
		3	38'·9"	40'·2"	41'·5"	44'·2"	47'·0"	49'·6"	51'·10"	53'·10"	55'·8"	57'·2
		4	36'·8"	38'·3"	39'·9"	42'·9"	45'·9"	48'·6"	51'·1"	53'·4"	55'·5"	57'·2
Group II: standard cars	8'·6"	1	32'·0"	32'·11"	34'·2"	36'·2"	38'·5"	41'·0"	43'·6"	45'·6"	46'·11"	48'·0
		2	49'·10"	51'·9"	53'·10"	56'·0"	58'·4"	60'·2"	62'·0"	63'·6"	64'·9"	66'·0
		3	47'·8"	49'·4"	51'·6"	54'·0"	56'·6"	59'·0"	61'·2"	63'·0"	64'·6"	66'·0
		4	45'·2"	46'·10"	49'·0"	51'·8"	54'·6"	57'·10"	60'·0"	62'·6"	64'·3"	66'·0
	9'·0"	1	32'·0"	32'·9"	34'·0"	35'·4"	37'·6"	39'·8"	42'·0"	44'·4"	46'·2"	48'·
		2	49'·4"	51'·0"	53'·2"	55'·6"	57'·10"	60'·0"	61'·10"	63'·4"	64'·9"	66'·
		3	46'·4"	48'·10"	51'·4"	53'·10"	56'·0"	58'·8"	61'·0"	63'·0"	64'·6"	66'·
		4	44'·8"	46'·6"	49'·0"	51'·6"	54'·0"	57'·0"	59'·8"	62'·0"	64'·2"	66'·
	9'·6"	1	32'·0"	32'·8"	34'·0"	35'·0"	36'·10"	38'·10"	41'·6"	43'·8"	46'·0"	48'·
		2	49'·2"	50'·6"	51'·10"	53'·6"	55'·4"	58'·0"	60'·6"	62'·8"	64'·6"	65'·
		3	47'·0"	48'·2"	49'·10"	51'·6"	53'·11"	57'·0"	59'·8"	62'·0"	64'·3"	65'·
		4	44'·8"	45'·10"	47'·6"	49'·10"	52'·6"	55'·9"	58'·9"	61'·6"	63'·10"	65'·
Group III: large cars	9'·0"	1	32'·7"	33'·0"	34'·0"	35'·11"	38'·3"	40'·11"	43'·6"	45'·5"	46'·9"	48'·
		2	50'·2"	51'·2"	53'·3"	55'·4"	58'·0"	60'·4"	62'·9"	64'·3"	65'·5"	66'·
		3	47'·9"	49'·1"	52'·3"	53'·8"	56'·2"	59'·2"	61'·11"	63'·9"	65'·2"	66'·
		4	45'·5"	46'·11"	49'·0"	51'·8"	54'·9"	58'·0"	61'·0"	63'·2"	64'·10"	66'·
	9'·6"	1	32'·4"	32'·8"	33'·10"	34'·11"	37'·2"	39'·11"	42'·5"	45'·0"	46'·6"	48'·
		2	49'·11"	50'·11"	52'·2"	54'·0"	56'·6"	59'·3"	61'·9"	63'·4"	64'·8"	66'·
		3	47'·7"	48'·9"	50'·2"	52'·4"	55'·1"	58'·4"	60'·11"	62'·10"	64'·6"	66'·
		4	45'·3"	46'·8"	48'·5"	50'·8"	53'·8"	57'·0"	59'·10"	62'·2"	64'·1"	66'·
	10'·0"	1	32'·4"	32'·8"	33'·10"	34'·11"	37'·2"	39'·11"	42'·5"	45'·0"	46'·6"	48'·
		2	49'·11"	50'·11"	52'·2"	54'·0"	56'·6"	59'·3"	61'·9"	63'·4"	64'·8"	66'·
		3	47'·7"	48'·9"	50'·2"	52'·4"	55'·1"	58'·4"	60'·11"	62'·10"	64'·6"	66'·
		4	45'·3"	46'·8"	48'·5"	50'·8"	53'·8"	57'·0"	59'·10"	62'·2"	64'·1"	66'·

NOTE: θ angles greater than 70° have aisle widths wide enough for two-way travel.

Figure 210-8 Parking area layouts for passenger cars.

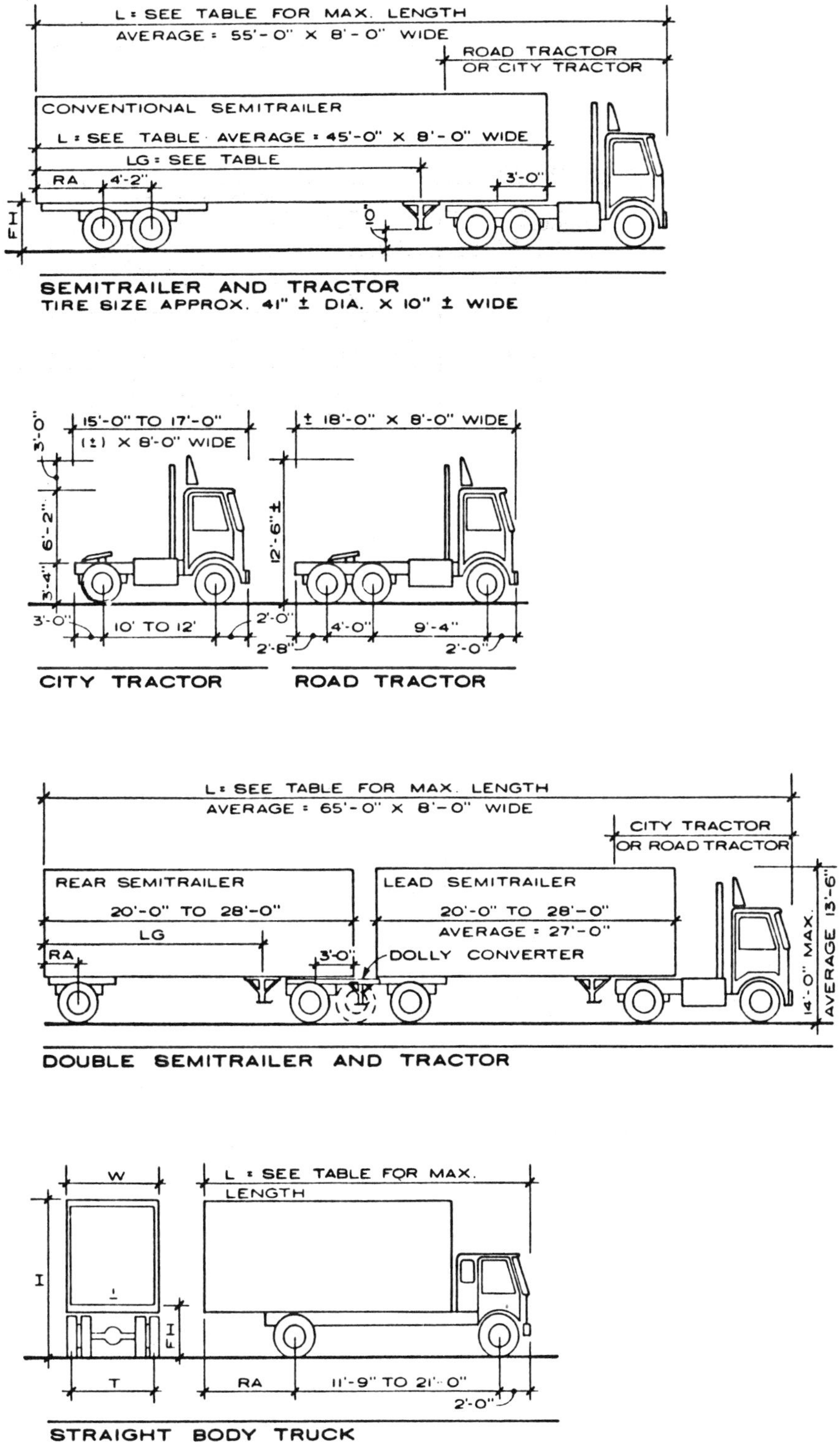
L = SEE TABLE FOR MAX. LENGTH
AVERAGE = 55'-0" X 8'-0" WIDE
ROAD TRACTOR
OR CITY TRACTOR
CONVENTIONAL SEMITRAILER
L = SEE TABLE AVERAGE = 45'-0" X 8'-0" WIDE
LG = SEE TABLE
RA
4'-2"
3'-0"
FH
10"
SEMITRAILER AND TRACTOR
TIRE SIZE APPROX. 41" ± DIA. X 10" ± WIDE
15'-0" TO 17'-0"
(±) X 8'-0" WIDE
3'-0"
6'-2"
3'-4"
3'-0"
10' TO 12'
2'-0"
2'-8"
CITY TRACTOR
± 18'-0" X 8'-0" WIDE
12'-6" ±
4'-0"
9'-4"
2'-0"
ROAD TRACTOR
L = SEE TABLE FOR MAX. LENGTH
AVERAGE = 65'-0" X 8'-0" WIDE
CITY TRACTOR
OR ROAD TRACTOR
REAR SEMITRAILER
20'-0" TO 28'-0"
LG
RA
3'-0"
LEAD SEMITRAILER
20'-0" TO 28'-0"
AVERAGE = 27'-0"
DOLLY CONVERTER
14'-0" MAX.
AVERAGE 13'-6"
DOUBLE SEMITRAILER AND TRACTOR
W
I
T
FH
L = SEE TABLE FOR MAX.
LENGTH
RA
11'-9" TO 21'-0"
2'-0"
STRAIGHT BODY TRUCK

Figure 210-9 Large vehicle dimensions.

Large vehicle dimensions

VEHICLE	(L) LENGTH	(W) WIDTH	(OR) OVERHANG REAR
Intercity bus	45'-0"	9'-0"	10'-1"
City bus	40'-0"	8'-6"	6'-6"
School bus	39'-6"	8'-0"	12'-8"
Ambulance	20'-10¼"	6'-11"	5'-4"
Paramedic van	18'-0"	6'-7"	5'-2"
Hearse	20'-10¼"	6'-11"	5'-4"
Airport limousine	22'-5¾"	6'-4"	3'-11"
Trash truck	28'-2"	8'-0"	6'-0"
U.P.S. truck	23'-2"	7'-7"	8'-2"
Fire truck	31'-4"	8'-1"	10'-0"

*Exact sizes of large vehicles may vary.

Average dimensions of vehicles

	TYPE OF VEHICLES			
	DOUBLE SEMITRAILER	CONVENTIONAL SEMITRAILER	STRAIGHT BODY TRUCK	VAN DELIVERY
Length (L)	65'-0"	55'-0"	17'-0" to 35'-0"	15'-0" to 20'-0"
Width (W)	8'-0"	8'-0"	8'-0"	7'-0"
Height (H)	13'-6"	13'-6"	13'-6"	7'-0"
Floor Height (FH)	4'-0" to 4'-6"	4'-0" to 4'-4"	3'-0" to 4'-0"	2'-0" to 2'-8"
Track (T)	6'-6"	6'-6"	5'-10"	5'-0" to 5'4"
Rear Axle (RA)	3'-0" to 4'-0"	4'-0" to 12'-0"	2'-3" to 12'-0"	–

Average semitrailer dimensions

LENGTH OF VEHICLE (L)	FLOOR HEIGHT (FH)	VEHICLE HEIGHT (H)
55'-0" semitrailer	4'-0" to 4'-6"	14'-0"
37'-0" semitrailer	4'-0" to 4'-2"	13'-6"
25'-0" straight body	3'-8" to 4'-2"	13'-6"
18'-0" van	2'-0" to 2'-8"	7'-0"

NOTE: Refer to other pages for truck and trailer sizes.

Space requirements
for tractor-trailers

	LENGTH (L)			
	27'-0"	40'-0"	45'-0"	REFRIG. 40'-0"
Floor height (FH)	4'-2"	4'-2"	4'-2"	4'-9"
Rear axle (RA)	3'-0"	5'-2"	5'-10"	4'-5"
Landing gear (LG)	19'-0"	30'-0"	34'-6"	29'-5"
Cubic feet (CU)	1564±	2327±	2620±	2113±

Figure 210-10 Space requirements for tractor-trailors.

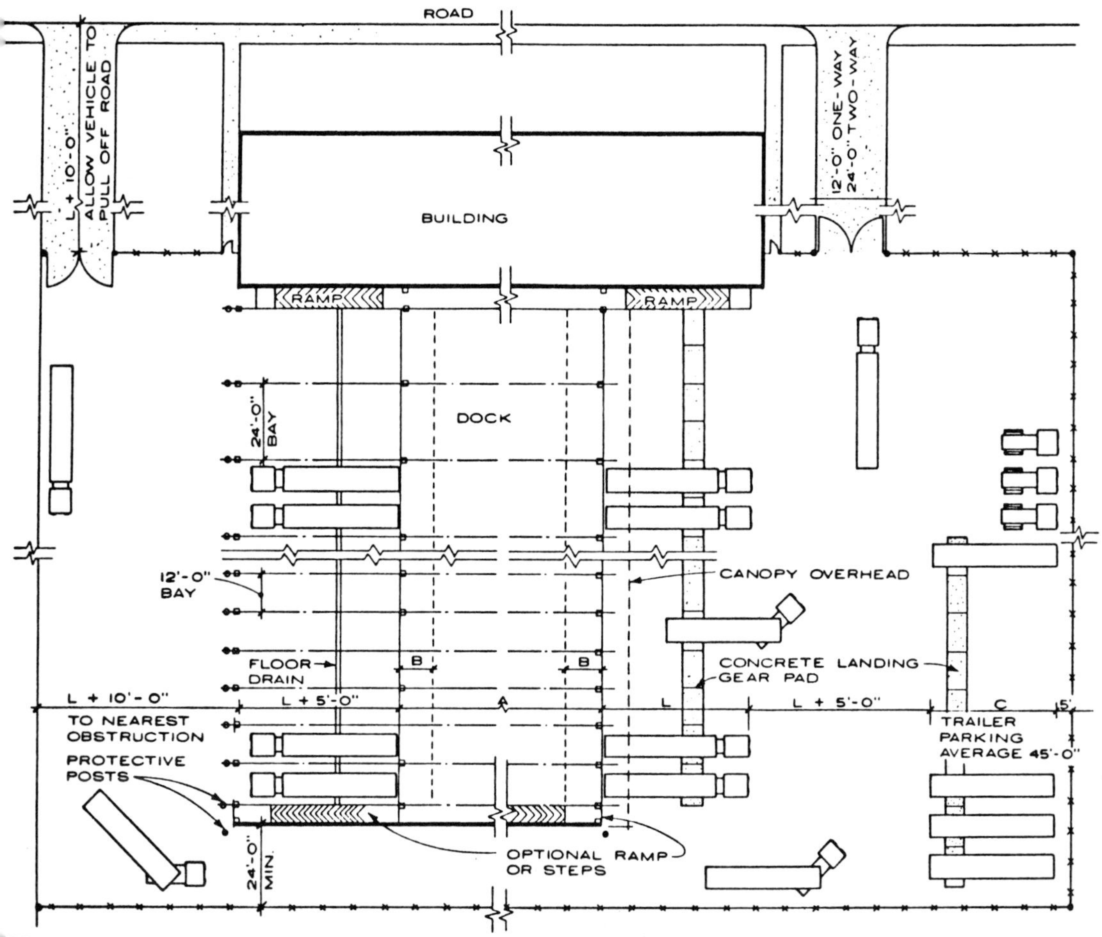
ROAD
L + 10'-0"
ALLOW VEHICLE TO PULL OFF ROAD
12'-0" ONE-WAY
24'-0" TWO-WAY
BUILDING
RAMP
RAMP
24'-0" BAY
DOCK
12'-0" BAY
CANOPY OVERHEAD
FLOOR DRAIN
B
B
CONCRETE LANDING GEAR PAD
L + 10'-0"
L + 5'-0"
A
L
L + 5'-0"
C
5'
TO NEAREST OBSTRUCTION
TRAILER PARKING AVERAGE 45'-0"
PROTECTIVE POSTS
OPTIONAL RAMP OR STEPS
24'-0" MIN.

TYPICAL PLAN OF CLOSED DOCK
DOUBLE DOOR (PREFERRED) 22'-0" WIDE x 14'-6" HIGH. SINGLE DOOR (OPTIONAL) 12'-0" WIDE X 14'-6" HIGH

TYPICAL PLAN OF OPEN DOCK
SINGLE DOOR (PREFERRED) 9'-0" WIDE X 10'-0" HIGH. DOUBLE DOOR (OPTIONAL) 20'-0" WIDE X 10'-0" HIGH

NOTES

1. Allow for off-street employee and/or driver parking.
2. Entrances and exits should be of reinforced concrete when excessive twisting and turning of vehicles are expected.
3. Average gate (swing or slide) 30'-0" wide for two-way traffic. People gate 5'-0" wide with concrete walkway 4'-0" to 6'-0" wide.
4. For yard security use a 6'-0" high chain link fence with barbed wire on top.
5. It is desirable to provide on-site fueling facilities for road units as they leave the yard.
6. Provide general yard lighting from fixtures mounted on building or on 24'-0" high minimum poles at fence line. Mercury vapor or high pressure sodium preferred.
7. Tractor parking requires 12'-0" wide x 20'-0" long slot minimum. Provide motor heater outlets for diesel engines in cold climates.
8. Trailer parking requires 12'-0" wide slot minimum. Provide 10'-0" wide concrete pad for landing gear. Score concrete at 12'-0" o.c. to aid in correct spotting of trailer.
9. 4'-0" wide minimum concrete ramp from dock to grade. 3 to 15% slope (10% average) score surface for traction.
10. Vehicles should circulate in a counterclockwise direction, making left hand turns, permitting driver to see rear of unit when backing into dock.
11. Double trailers are backed into dock separately.

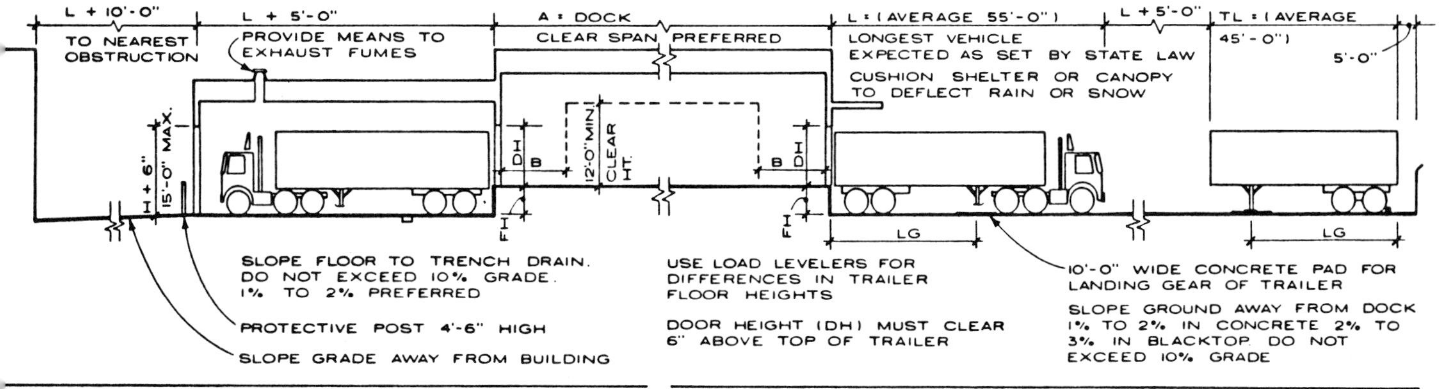
L + 10'-0"
TO NEAREST OBSTRUCTION
L + 5'-0"
PROVIDE MEANS TO EXHAUST FUMES
A = DOCK
CLEAR SPAN PREFERRED
L = (AVERAGE 55'-0")
LONGEST VEHICLE EXPECTED AS SET BY STATE LAW
L + 5'-0"
TL = (AVERAGE 45'-0")
5'-0"
CUSHION SHELTER OR CANOPY TO DEFLECT RAIN OR SNOW
H + 6"
15'-0" MAX.
DH
B
12'-0" MIN. CLEAR HT.
B
DH
FH
FH
LG
LG
SLOPE FLOOR TO TRENCH DRAIN. DO NOT EXCEED 10% GRADE. 1% TO 2% PREFERRED
PROTECTIVE POST 4'-6" HIGH
SLOPE GRADE AWAY FROM BUILDING
USE LOAD LEVELERS FOR DIFFERENCES IN TRAILER FLOOR HEIGHTS
DOOR HEIGHT (DH) MUST CLEAR 6" ABOVE TOP OF TRAILER
10'-0" WIDE CONCRETE PAD FOR LANDING GEAR OF TRAILER
SLOPE GROUND AWAY FROM DOCK 1% TO 2% IN CONCRETE 2% TO 3% IN BLACKTOP. DO NOT EXCEED 10% GRADE

TYPICAL SECTION OF CLOSED DOCK

TYPICAL SECTION OF OPEN DOCK

AVERAGE WIDTHS OF DOCKS

TYPE OF OPERATION	TWO-WHEEL HAND TRUCK	FOUR-WHEEL HAND TRUCK	FORKLIFT TRUCK	DRAGLINE	AUTO SPUR DRAGLINE
Dock width (A)	50'-0"	60'-0"	60'-0" to 70'-0"	80'-0"	120'-0" to 140'-0"
Work aisle (B)	6'-0"	10'-0"	15'-0"	10'-0" to 15'-0"	10'-0" to 15'-0"

Figure 210-11 Loading dock dimensions.

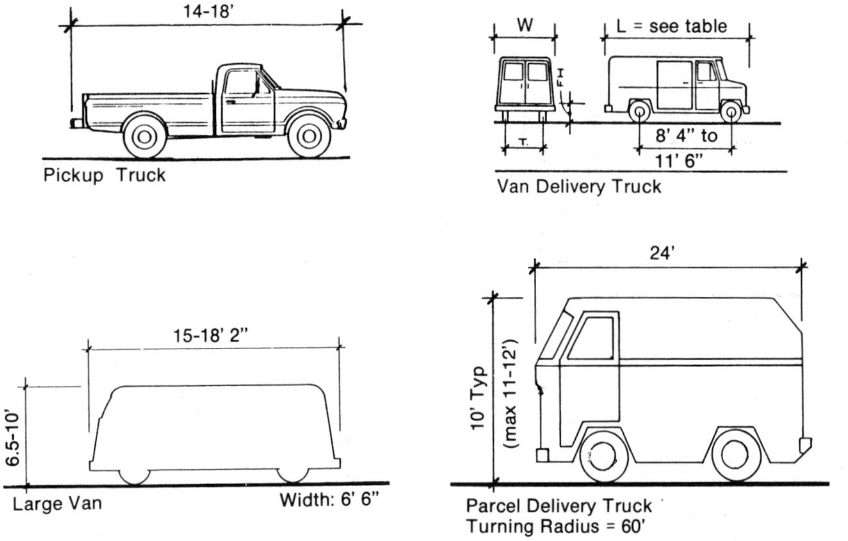
14-18'
Pickup Truck
W
L = see table
FH
T
8' 4" to
11' 6"
Van Delivery Truck
24'
15-18' 2"
6.5-10'
Large Van
Width: 6' 6"
10' Typ
(max 11-12')
Parcel Delivery Truck
Turning Radius = 60'

Figure 210-12 Small trucks.

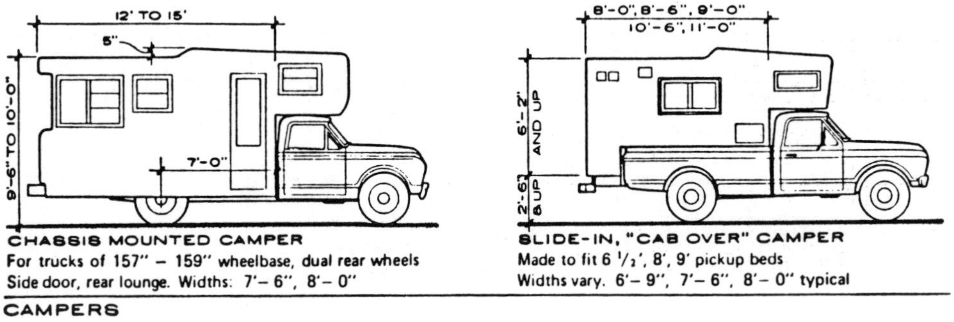
12' TO 15'
5"
9'-6" TO 10'-0"
7'-0"
CHASSIS MOUNTED CAMPER
For trucks of 157" – 159" wheelbase, dual rear wheels
Side door, rear lounge. Widths: 7'– 6", 8'– 0"
8'-0", 8'-6", 9'-0"
10'-6", 11'-0"
6'-2" AND UP
2'-6" & UP
SLIDE-IN, "CAB OVER" CAMPER
Made to fit 6 1/2', 8', 9' pickup beds
Widths vary. 6'– 9", 7'– 6", 8'– 0" typical
CAMPERS

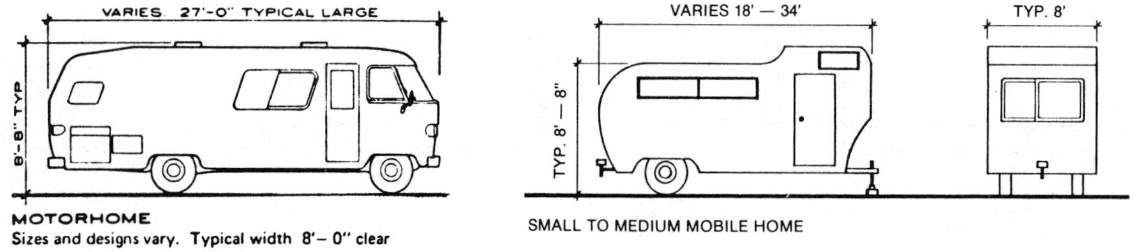
VARIES 27'-0" TYPICAL LARGE
9'-8" TYP
MOTORHOME
Sizes and designs vary. Typical width 8'– 0" clear
VARIES 18' — 34'
TYP. 8' — 8"
TYP. 8'
SMALL TO MEDIUM MOBILE HOME

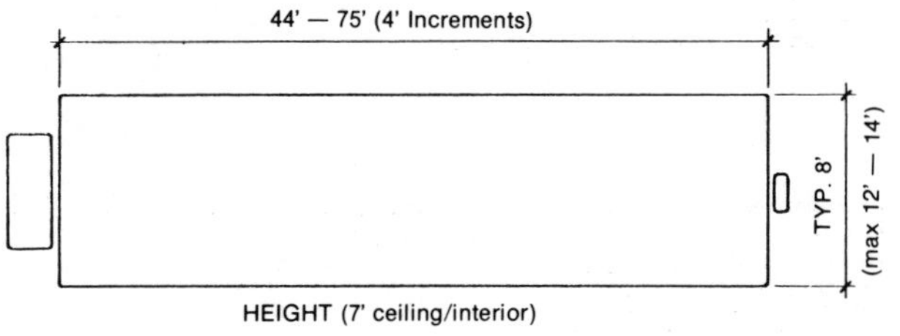
44' — 75' (4' Increments)
TYP. 8'
(max 12' — 14')
HEIGHT (7' ceiling/interior)

LARGE MOBILE HOME OR TRAILER

Office Units
(Construction sites)

Length, ft	*Width, ft*
36	12
36	14

Figure 210-13 Recreational vehicles and trailers.

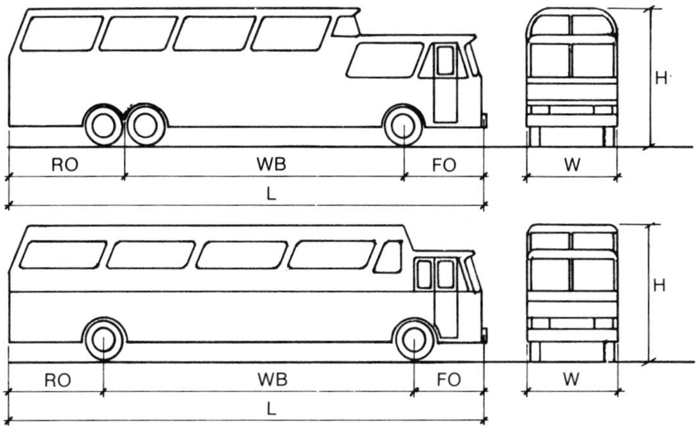
H
RO
WB
FO
W
L
H
RO
WB
FO
W
L

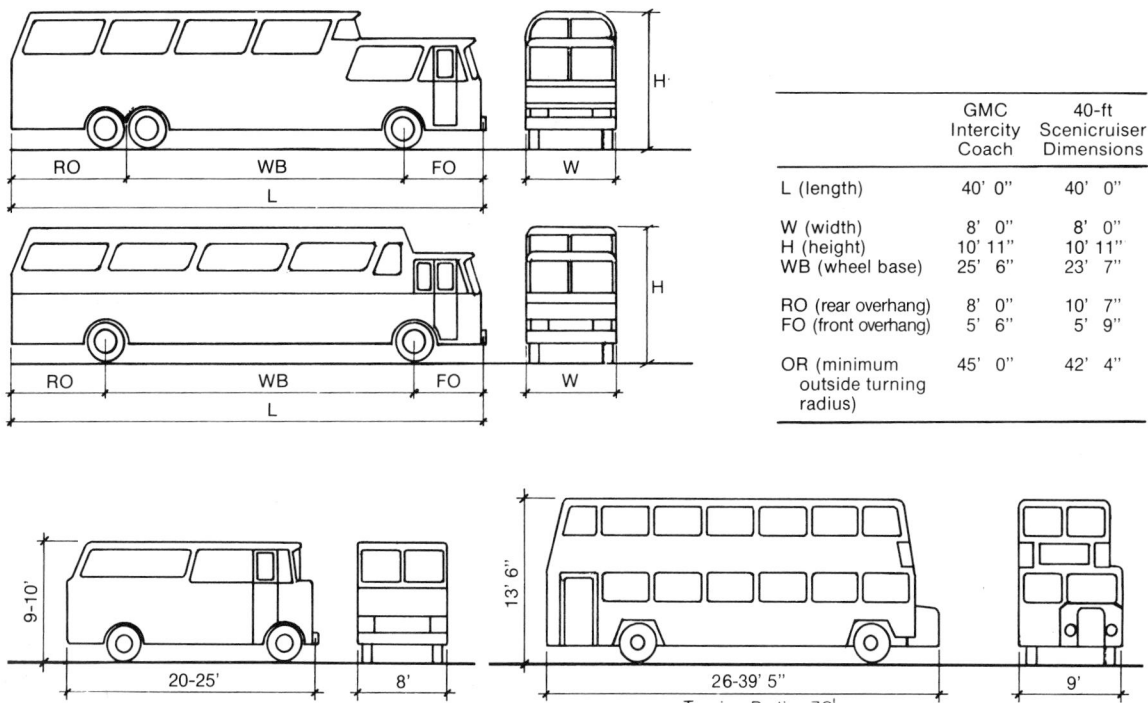

	GMC Intercity Coach	40-ft Scenicruiser Dimensions
L (length)	40' 0"	40' 0"
W (width)	8' 0"	8' 0"
H (height)	10' 11"	10' 11"
WB (wheel base)	25' 6"	23' 7"
RO (rear overhang)	8' 0"	10' 7"
FO (front overhang)	5' 6"	5' 9"
OR (minimum outside turning radius)	45' 0"	42' 4"

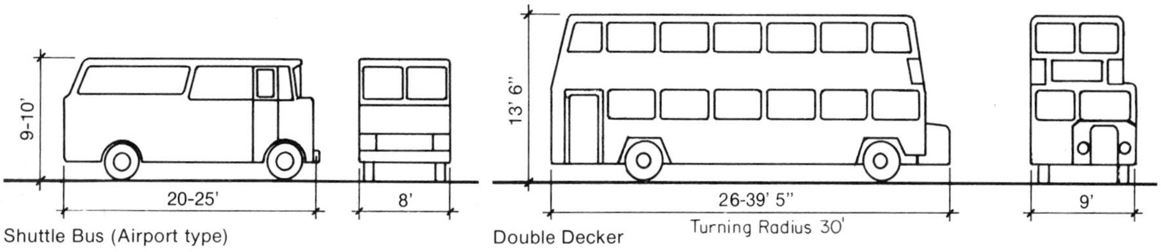
9-10'
20-25'
8'
Shuttle Bus (Airport type)
13' 6"
26-39' 5"
Turning Radius 30'
9'
Double Decker

Figure 210-14 Buses.

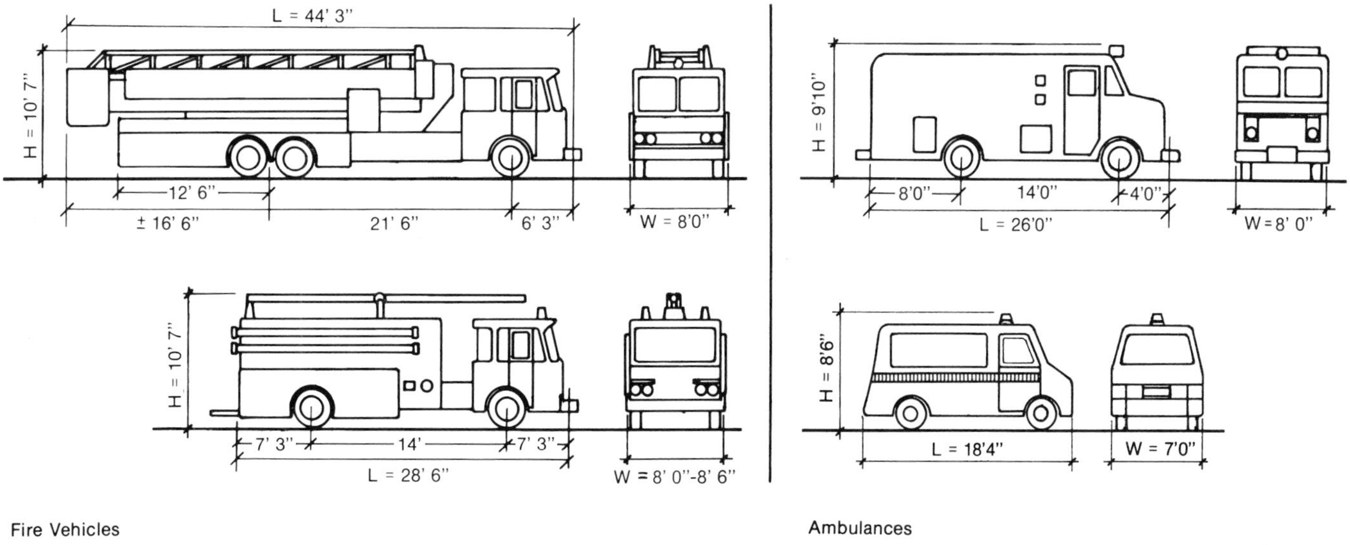
L = 44' 3"
H = 10' 7"
12' 6"
± 16' 6"
21' 6"
6' 3"
W = 8'0"
H = 10' 7"
7' 3"
14'
7' 3"
L = 28' 6"
W = 8' 0"-8' 6"
Fire Vehicles
H = 9'10"
8'0"
14'0"
4'0"
L = 26'0"
W = 8' 0"
H = 8'6"
L = 18'4"
W = 7'0"
Ambulances

Figure 210-15 Emergency and service vehicles.

Miscellaneous trucks.

	Item	Maximum length	Maximum width	Maximum height	Minimum turning radius
	Collection truck	26' 1"	8' 6"	10' 7"	34'
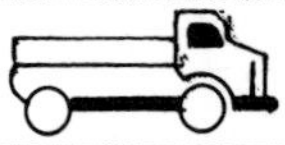	Bulk collection truck	27' 8"	8' 6"	9' 0"	34'
	Detachable container and hauling unit	29' 10"	8' 0"	13' 1"	29'
	Concrete mixer	30' 0"	8' 6"	10' 6"	34'

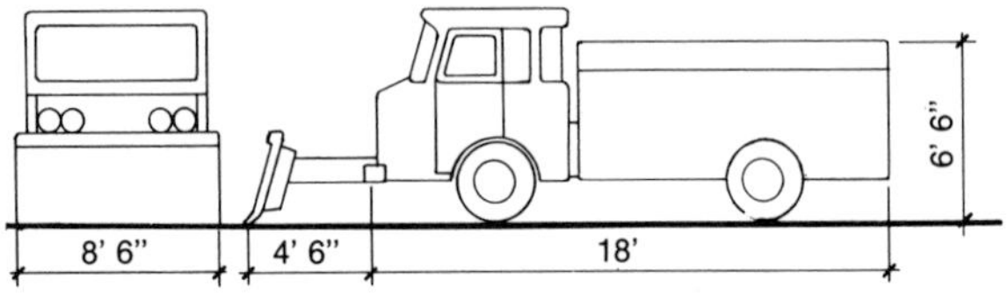
8' 6"
4' 6"
18'
6' 6"

Snow plow.

Tree spade and mover.

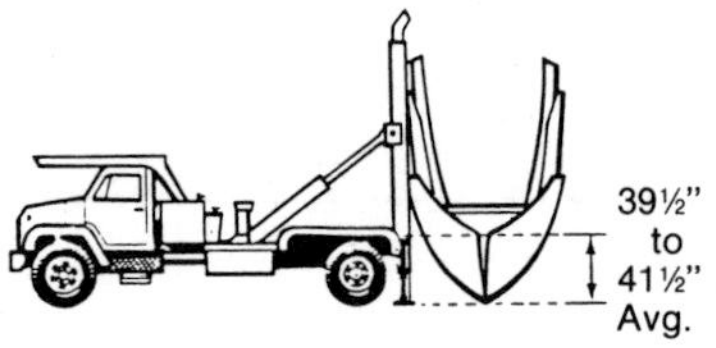
39½"
to
41½"
Avg.

12-13.5'

Tree spade table.

Specification	Model 55	Model 65	Model 80	Model 90
*Nominal tree trunk diameter	5-6"	6-7"	8-10"	10-12"
Weight of transplanter	8,500 lbs.	10,000 lbs.	13,000 lbs.	15,800 lbs.
**Height closed for transporting (approx.) (A)	11' 10"	12' 2"	13' 4½"	13' 6"
Width closed for transporting	7' 11¾"	7' 11¾"	8' 5¾"	8' 5¾"
Root ball width (approx.) (hydraulically adjustable)	55"	65"	80"	90"
Root ball depth (hydraulically adjustable)	48"	53"	54"	60"
Root ball weight (approx.)	3,500 lbs.	4,750 lbs.	8,500 lbs.	11,000 lbs.

**Dependent upon truck chassis frame height.

Figure 210-16 Miscellaneous vehicles.

GOLF CARTS GASOLINE OR ELECTRIC POWER

3 WHEELS		4 WHEELS
46 3/4"	Overall Height	47 1/8"
10 3/4"	Floorboard Height	11 1/4"
27 3/4"	Seat Height	28 1/4"
102"	Length	102"
47"	Width	47"
68"	Wheel Base	68 3/4"
–	Front Wheel Tread	34"
34 5/8"	Rear Wheel Tread	34 5/8"
4 5/8"	Ground Clearance	4 5/8"
19'–6"	Clearance Circle	24'–0"

Lawn and garden tractors	
Length	72"
Overall width	38' - 44"
Turning radius	36"
Rear blades	48", 60", 72", 84", 96" widths
Earth augers	maximum drill depths: 42", 45" drill diameters: 4' - 24"

Power mowers (cutting widths)	
Flail mower	62", 74" 88"
Side mower	5', 6', 9'
Rear mounted	5', 7', 9'
Rotary cutter	48", 60", 72", 84", 120", 144", 180"

Landscape rakers	
Widths	72", 96"

Dozer Blades (for moving earth or snow)	
Widths	54", 60", 72"
Degrees turn	15 to 30' (right or left)

Note: The data shown above is considered typical, but some manufacturers make machines that have significantly different dimensions.

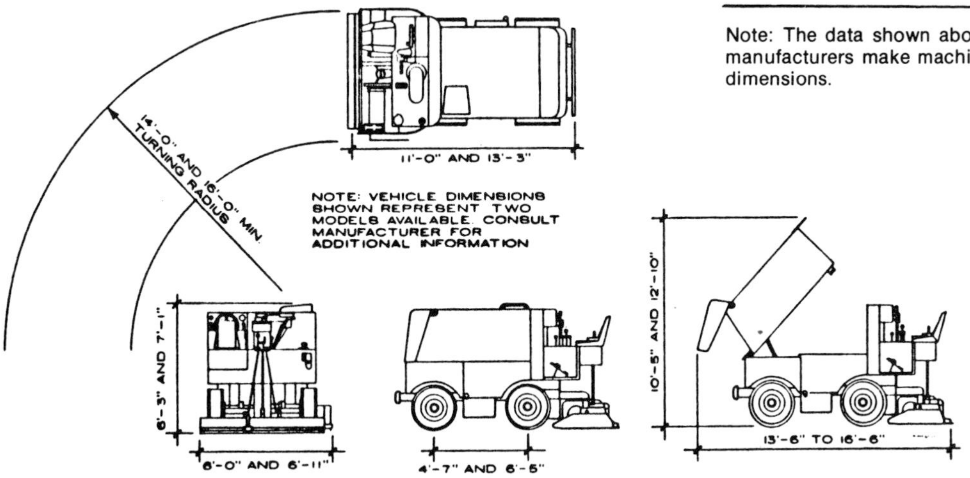
14'-0" AND 16'-0" MIN. TURNING RADIUS
11'-0" AND 13'-3"
NOTE: VEHICLE DIMENSIONS SHOWN REPRESENT TWO MODELS AVAILABLE. CONSULT MANUFACTURER FOR ADDITIONAL INFORMATION
6'-3" AND 7'-1"
6'-0" AND 6'-11"
4'-7" AND 6'-5"
10'-5" AND 12'-10"
13'-6" TO 16'-6"

ZAMBONI ICE RESURFACER

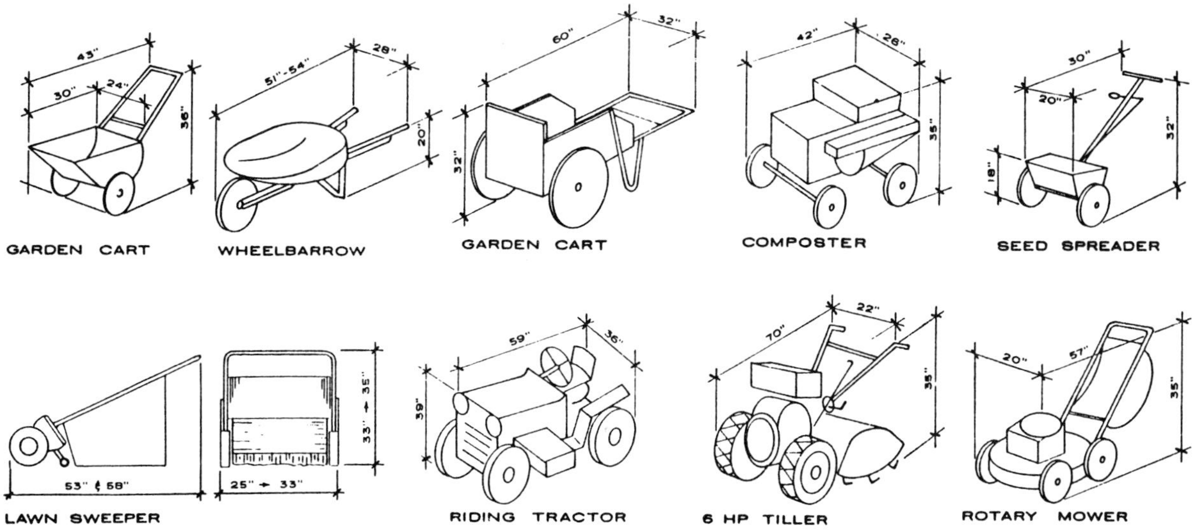
43"
30"
24"
36"
GARDEN CART
51"-54"
28"
20"
WHEELBARROW
60"
32"
32"
GARDEN CART
42"
26"
35"
COMPOSTER
30"
20"
32"
18"
SEED SPREADER
53" ¢ 58"
25" + 33"
33" + 35"
LAWN SWEEPER
59"
36"
39"
RIDING TRACTOR
22"
70"
35"
6 HP TILLER
20"
57"
35"
ROTARY MOWER

GARDEN EQUIPMENT

Figure 210-17 Garden equipment and vehicles.

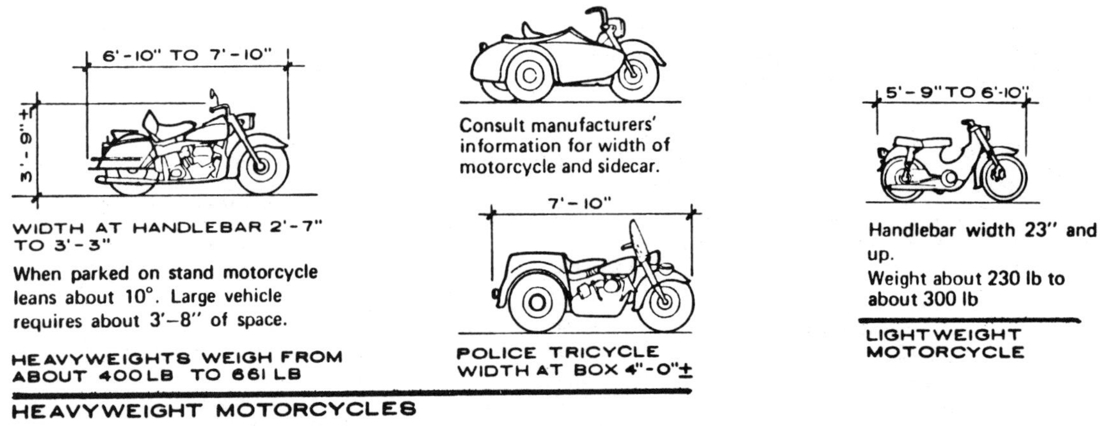
6'-10" TO 7'-10"
3'-9"±
WIDTH AT HANDLEBAR 2'-7" TO 3'-3"
When parked on stand motorcycle leans about 10°. Large vehicle requires about 3'–8" of space.
HEAVYWEIGHTS WEIGH FROM ABOUT 400 LB TO 661 LB
HEAVYWEIGHT MOTORCYCLES
Consult manufacturers' information for width of motorcycle and sidecar.
7'-10"
POLICE TRICYCLE
WIDTH AT BOX 4'-0"±
5'-9" TO 6'-10"
Handlebar width 23" and up.
Weight about 230 lb to about 300 lb
LIGHTWEIGHT MOTORCYCLE

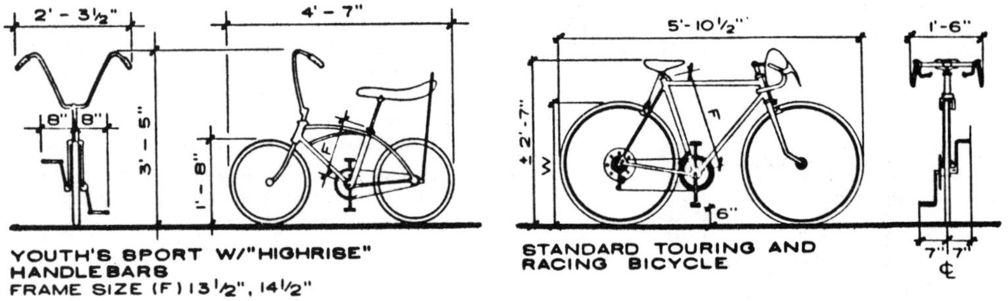
2'-3½"
8" 8"
4'-7"
3'-5"
1'-8"
YOUTH'S SPORT W/"HIGHRISE" HANDLEBARS
FRAME SIZE (F) 13½", 14½"
5'-10½"
±2'-7"
W
F
6"
STANDARD TOURING AND RACING BICYCLE
1'-6"
7" 7"
℄

BICYCLE SIZES

FRAME SIZE "W"	FRAME SIZE "F"
16"	12"
20"	13"
24"	16" boys 15" girls
26"	18", 19", 21", 23"
27"	19", 21", 23"

Figure 210-18 Bicycles and motorcycles.

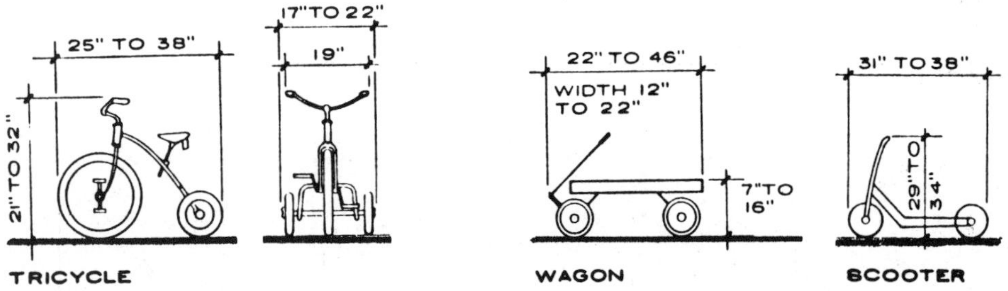
25" TO 38"
21" TO 32"
17" TO 22"
19"
TRICYCLE
22" TO 46"
WIDTH 12" TO 22"
7" TO 16"
WAGON
31" TO 38"
29" TO 34"
SCOOTER

Figure 210-19 Children's wheeled play equipment.

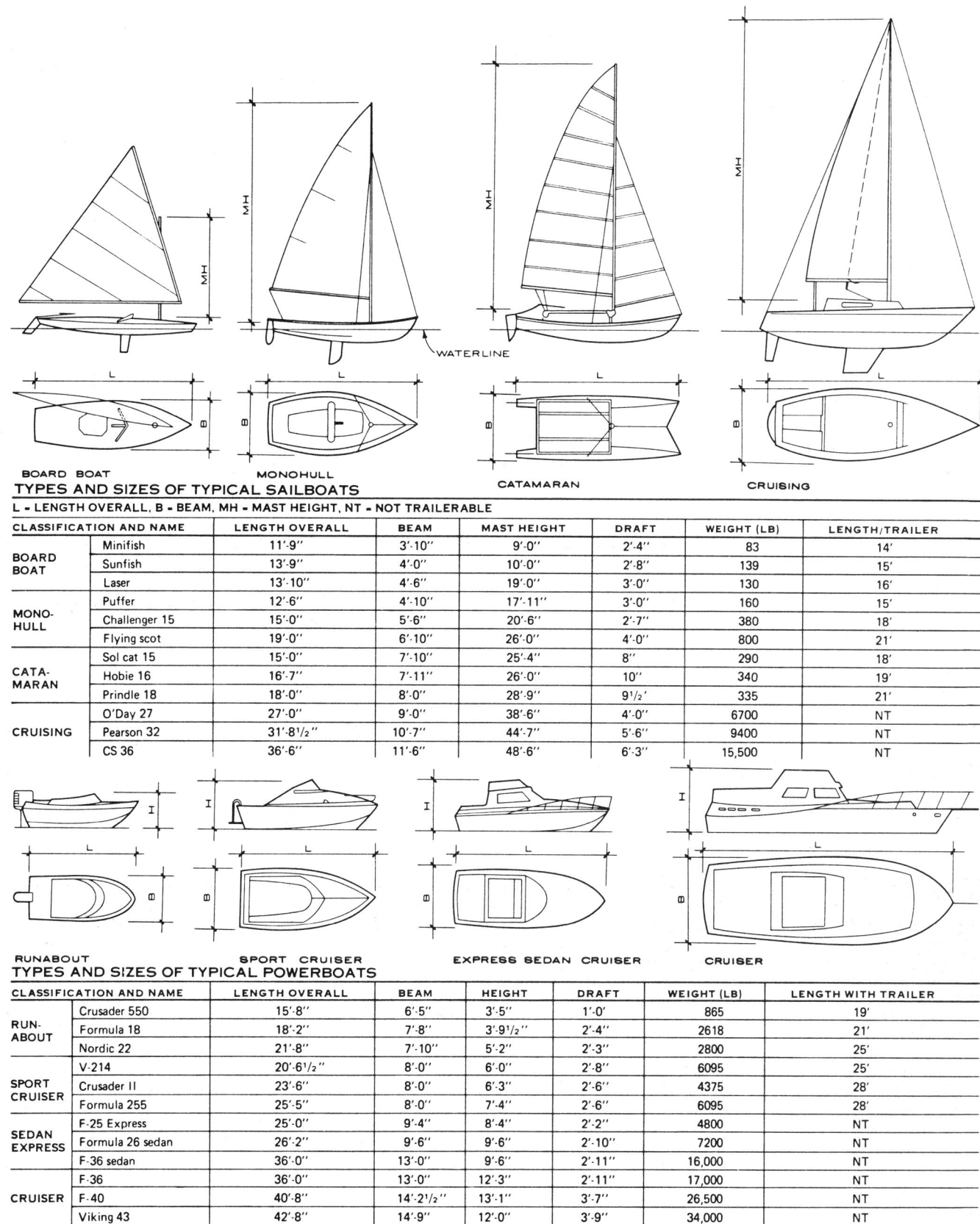

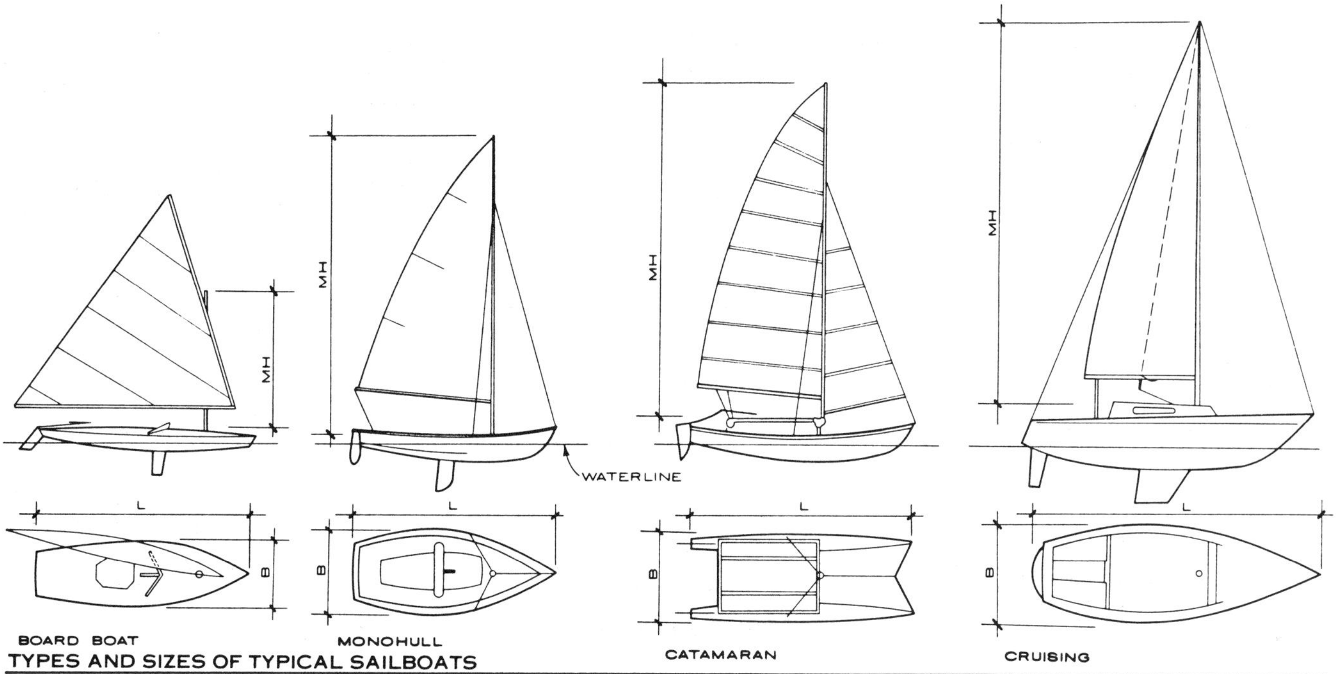
MH
WATERLINE
L
B
BOARD BOAT
MONOHULL
CATAMARAN
CRUISING

TYPES AND SIZES OF TYPICAL SAILBOATS

L - LENGTH OVERALL, B - BEAM, MH - MAST HEIGHT, NT - NOT TRAILERABLE

CLASSIFICATION AND NAME		LENGTH OVERALL	BEAM	MAST HEIGHT	DRAFT	WEIGHT (LB)	LENGTH/TRAILER
BOARD BOAT	Minifish	11′-9″	3′-10″	9′-0″	2′-4″	83	14′
	Sunfish	13′-9″	4′-0″	10′-0″	2′-8″	139	15′
	Laser	13′-10″	4′-6″	19′-0″	3′-0″	130	16′
MONO-HULL	Puffer	12′-6″	4′-10″	17′-11″	3′-0″	160	15′
	Challenger 15	15′-0″	5′-6″	20′-6″	2′-7″	380	18′
	Flying scot	19′-0″	6′-10″	26′-0″	4′-0″	800	21′
CATA-MARAN	Sol cat 15	15′-0″	7′-10″	25′-4″	8″	290	18′
	Hobie 16	16′-7″	7′-11″	26′-0″	10″	340	19′
	Prindle 18	18′-0″	8′-0″	28′-9″	9 1/2′	335	21′
CRUISING	O'Day 27	27′-0″	9′-0″	38′-6″	4′-0″	6700	NT
	Pearson 32	31′-8 1/2″	10′-7″	44′-7″	5′-6″	9400	NT
	CS 36	36′-6″	11′-6″	48′-6″	6′-3″	15,500	NT

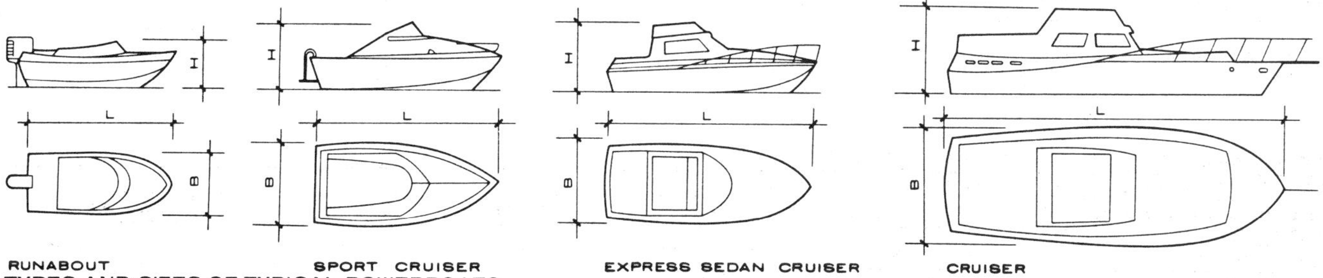
H
L
B
RUNABOUT
SPORT CRUISER
EXPRESS SEDAN CRUISER
CRUISER

TYPES AND SIZES OF TYPICAL POWERBOATS

CLASSIFICATION AND NAME		LENGTH OVERALL	BEAM	HEIGHT	DRAFT	WEIGHT (LB)	LENGTH WITH TRAILER
RUN-ABOUT	Crusader 550	15′-8″	6′-5″	3′-5″	1′-0′	865	19′
	Formula 18	18′-2″	7′-8″	3′-9 1/2″	2′-4″	2618	21′
	Nordic 22	21′-8″	7′-10″	5′-2″	2′-3″	2800	25′
SPORT CRUISER	V-214	20′-6 1/2″	8′-0″	6′-0″	2′-8″	6095	25′
	Crusader II	23′-6″	8′-0″	6′-3″	2′-6″	4375	28′
	Formula 255	25′-5″	8′-0″	7′-4″	2′-6″	6095	28′
SEDAN EXPRESS	F-25 Express	25′-0″	9′-4″	8′-4″	2′-2″	4800	NT
	Formula 26 sedan	26′-2″	9′-6″	9′-6″	2′-10″	7200	NT
	F-36 sedan	36′-0″	13′-0″	9′-6″	2′-11″	16,000	NT
CRUISER	F-36	36′-0″	13′-0″	12′-3″	2′-11″	17,000	NT
	F-40	40′-8″	14′-2 1/2″	13′-1″	3′-7″	26,500	NT
	Viking 43	42′-8″	14′-9″	12′-0″	3′-9″	34,000	NT

David B. Richards; Rossetti Associates/Architects Planners; Detroit, Michigan

Figure 210-20 Sailboats and power boats.

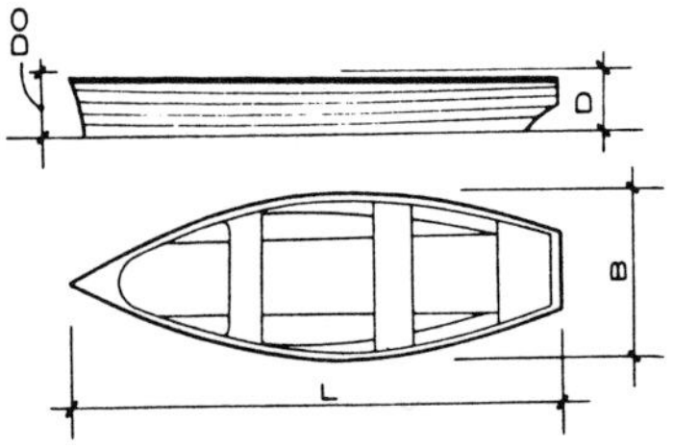
D
DO
L
B

ROWBOAT

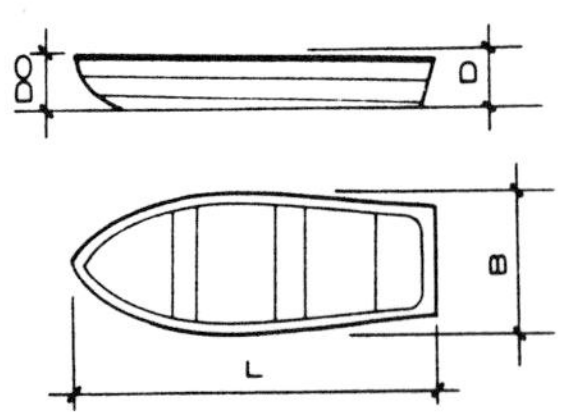
DO
D
B
L

DINGHY OR TENDER

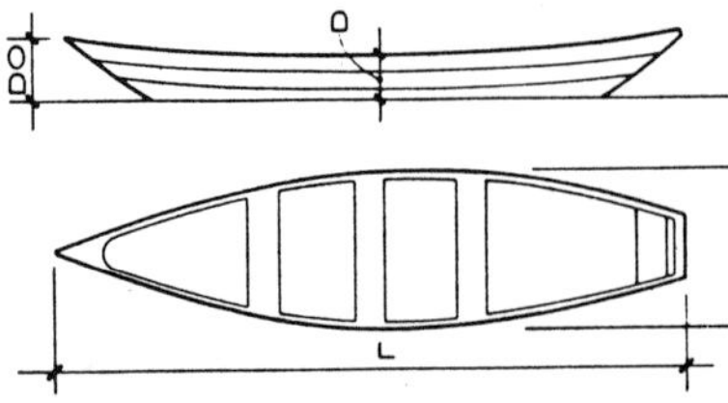
D
DO
B
L

DORY

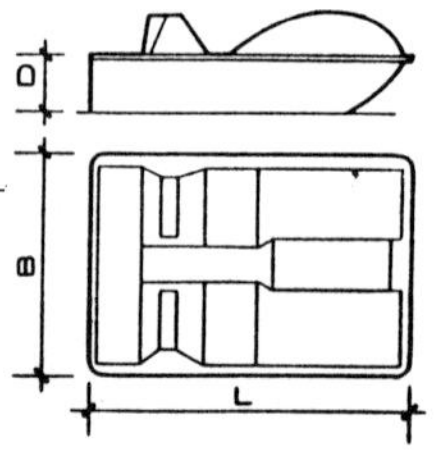
D
B
L

PEDAL BOAT

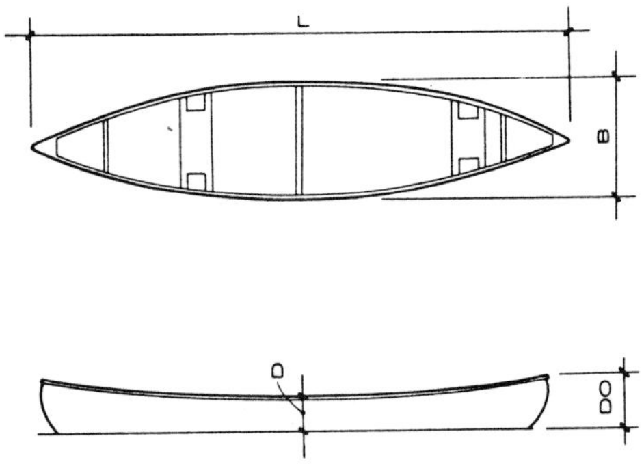
L
B
D
DO

CANOE

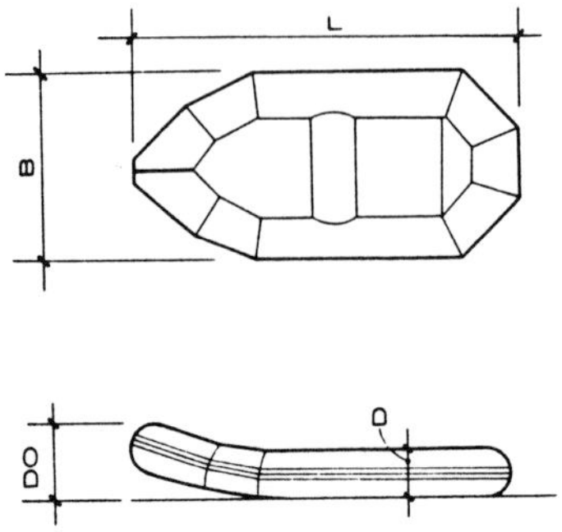
L
B
D
DO

INFLATABLE BOAT

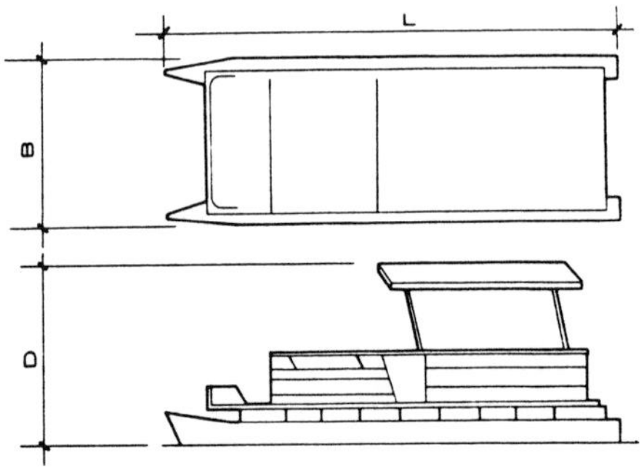
L
B
D

PONTOON BOAT

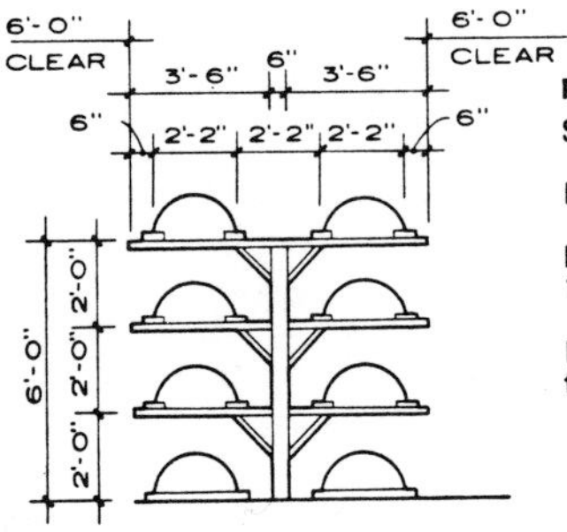
6'-0"
CLEAR
3'-6"
6"
3'-6"
6'-0"
CLEAR
6"
2'-2"
2'-2"
2'-2"
6"
6'-0"
2'-0"
2'-0"
2'-0"

RACKS

RACK SPACING

Single and double: 2 racks 8'-0" apart.

Four-oared: 3 racks 8'-0" apart.

Eight-oared: 3 racks 18'-0" apart or 4 racks 12'-0" apart.

Racks are 6'-0" high for daily use, higher for long term storage.

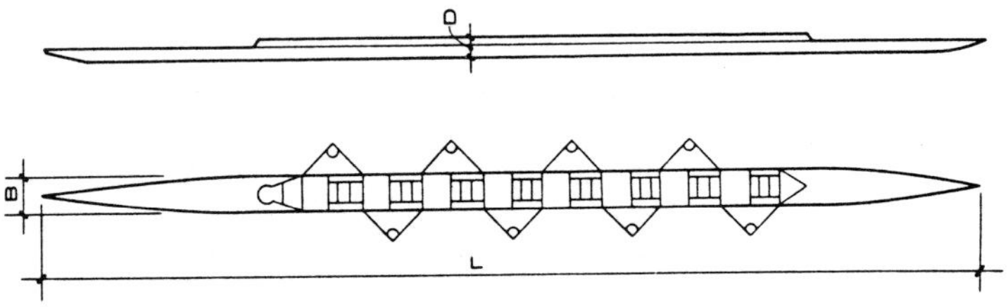
D
B
L

RACING SHELL OR GIG RACING

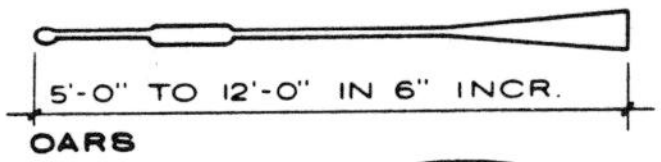
5'-0" TO 12'-0" IN 6" INCR.

OARS

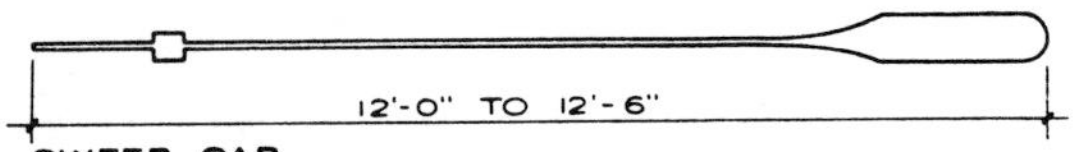
12'-0" TO 12'-6"

SWEEP OAR

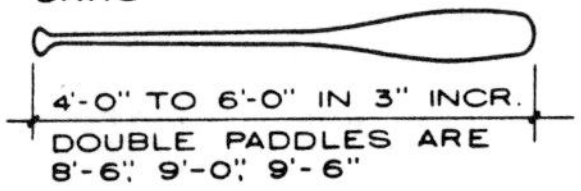
4'-0" TO 6'-0" IN 3" INCR.
DOUBLE PADDLES ARE
8'-6", 9'-0", 9'-6"

PADDLES

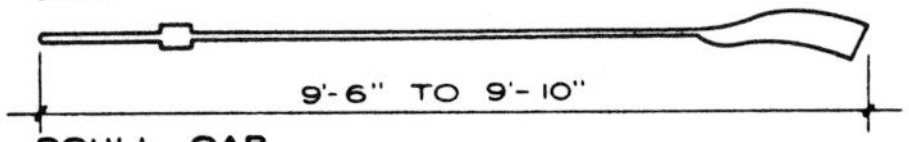
9'-6" TO 9'-10"

SCULL OAR

NOTE

Many of the boats above, except pedal boats, pontoon boats, and racing shells, may be fitted with sails.

Design boat house with ceiling height to allow storage of oars on end.

TYPES AND SIZES OF TYPICAL SMALL BOATS

LO - LENGTH OVERALL, B - BEAM, D - DEPTH, DO - DEPTH OVERALL

CLASSIFICATION AND TYPE		LENGTH OVERALL	BEAM	DEPTH	DEPTH OVERALL	WEIGHT (LB)
Rowboats (many types and designs)		6'-5" to 18'-0"	3'-11" to 5'-5"	1'-2" to 1'-8"	2'-0" ±	50 to 270
DINGHY OR TENDER		6'-1" to 14'-0"	2'-10" to 5'-5"	1'-6" to 1'-8"	1'-6" to 1'-8"	40 to 155
DORY	Lifesaving	18'-0" ±	4'-6" ±	1'-8" ±	1'-11" ±	275
	Fisherman	12'-0" to 16'-0"	3'-6" to 5'-8"	1'-6" to 1'-8"	1'-6" to 1'-10"	64 to 320
PEDAL BOAT		7'-2" to 10'-4"	5'-1" to 5'-4"	1'-11"		115 to 140
INFLATABLE CANOE	One-man	9'-0" to 15'-0"	2'-10" to 3'-0"	1'-0" ±	2'-0" to 2'-4"	44 to 85
	Standard	12'-0" to 17'-0"	3'-0" to 3'-8"	1'-2"	1'-4"	55 to 79
	Fisherman	16'-0" to 18'-0"	3'-5" to 3'-7"	1'-0" to 1'-1"	2'-0" to 2'-4"	70 ±
	War	23'-0" to 35'-0"	3'-8"	1'-3"	2'-3"	225
	Dinghy	8'-2" to 12'-8"	4'-0" to 5'-6"	1'-0" to 1'-4"	1'-6" to 1'-10"	56 to 119
	Riverboat	13'-9" to 18'-0"	6'-10" to 8'-0"	1'-6" to 1'-9"	2'-0" to 2'-8"	99 to 154
PONTOON BOAT		20'-0" to 28'-0"	8'-0"	7'-8"		1015 to 1155
SHELL OR GIG	Single racing	25'-0" to 28'-0"	1'-2"	6½"	10½"	30
	Double racing	29'-0" to 33'-0"	1'-4"	7"	11"	60
	Four-oared	40'-0" to 42'-0"	1'-9"	8½"	1'-0½"	120
	Eight-oared	56'-0" to 62'-0"	2'-0" to 2'-4"	1'-4"	1'-2" to 1'-8"	270

David B. Richards; Rossetti Associates/Architects Planners; Detroit, Michigan

Figure 210-21 Small boats.

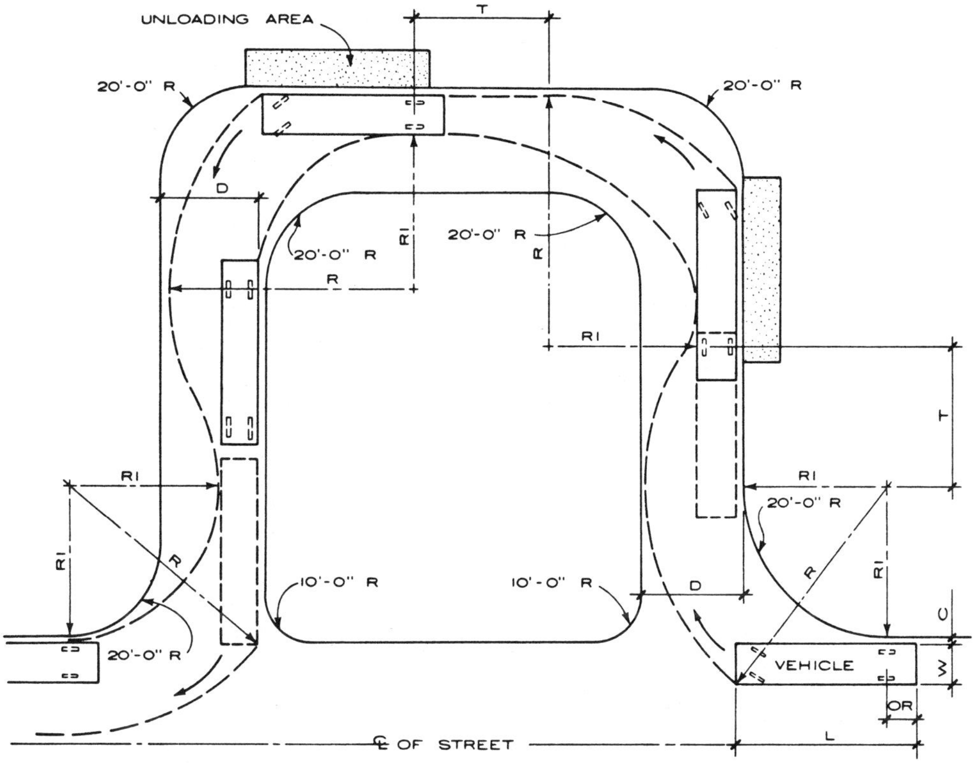

UNLOADING AREA
T
20'-0" R
20'-0" R
D
R1
20'-0" R
20'-0" R
R
R
R1
T
R1
20'-0" R
R1
R
R
R1
10'-0" R
10'-0" R
D
C
20'-0" R
VEHICLE
W
OR
L
℄ OF STREET

"U" DRIVE AND VEHICLE TURNING DIMENSIONS

VEHICLE	R	R1	T	D	C
Small car	19'-10"	10'-9"	12'-0"	10'-0'	6"
Compact car	21'-6"	11'-10"	15'-0"	10'-10"	7"
Standard car	22'-5"	12'-7"	15'-0"	11'-2"	8"
Large car	23'-0"	12'-7"	15'-0"	12'-0"	9"
Intercity bus*	55'-0"	33'-0"	30'-0"	22'-6"	1'-0"
City bus	53'-6"	33'-0"	30'-0"	22'-6"	1'-0"
School bus	43'-6"	26'-0"	30'-0"	19'-5"	1'-0"
Ambulance	30'-0"	18'-9"	25'-0"	13'-3"	1'-0"
Paramedic van	25'-0"	14'-0"	25'-0"	13'-0"	1'-0"
Hearse	30'-0"	18'-9"	20'-0"	13'-3"	1'-0"
Airport limousine	28'-3"	15'-1 1/2"	20'-0"	15'-1 1/2"	1'-0"
Trash truck†	32'-0"	18'-0"	20'-0"	16'-0"	1'-0"
U.P.S. truck	28'-0"	16'-0"	20'-0"	14'-0"	1'-0"
Fire truck	48'-0"	34'-4'	30'-0"	15'-8"	1'-0"

*Headroom = 14'.
†Headroom = 15'.

William T. Mahan, AIA; Santa Barbara, California

GENERAL NOTES

The "U" drive shown in the table and figure illustrates a procedure for determining the configuration of a drive based upon the vehicle's dimensions and turning radii. The T (tangent) dimensions given here are approximate minimums only and may vary with the driver's ability and speed of the vehicle.

Figure 210-22 Turning radii of motor vehicles.

Figure 210-22 *(Continued)*

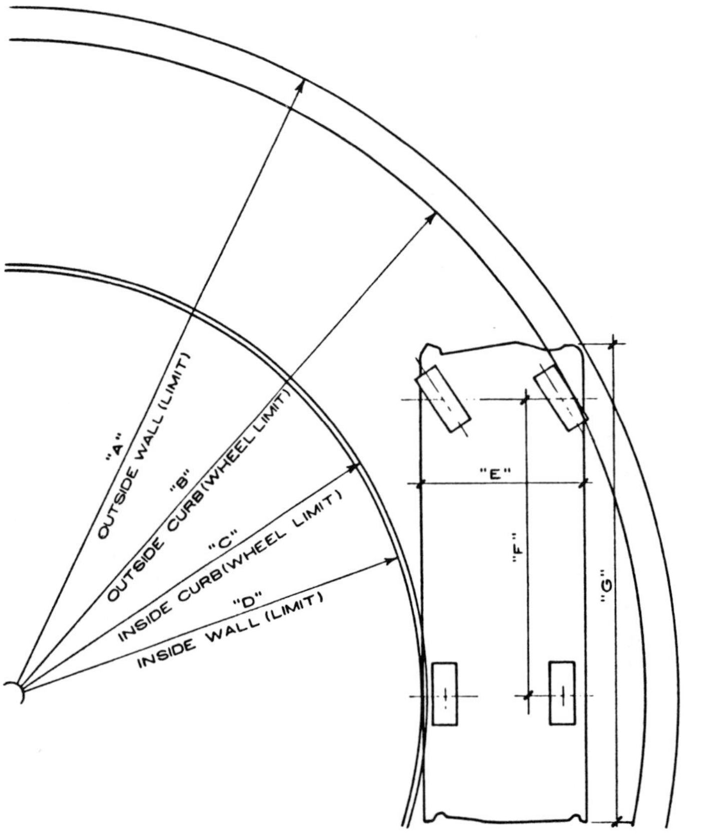
"A" OUTSIDE WALL (LIMIT)
"B" OUTSIDE CURB (WHEEL LIMIT)
"C" INSIDE CURB (WHEEL LIMIT)
"D" INSIDE WALL (LIMIT)
"E"
"F"
"G"

AMBULANCES AND HEARSES
DIMENSIONS AND TURNING RADII

MAKE OF CAR	"A"	"B"	"C"	"D"	"E"	"F"	"G"
Cadillac	30'-0"	28'-6"	18'-11 1/2"	18'-9"	6'-11"	13'-0"	20'-10 1/4"
Dodge	23'-4"	21'-9"	13'-4 1/2"	12'-10 3/4"	6'-8"		18'-4"

AIRPORT LIMOUSINE

Checker	28'-3"				6'-4"	15'-9"	22'-5 3/4"

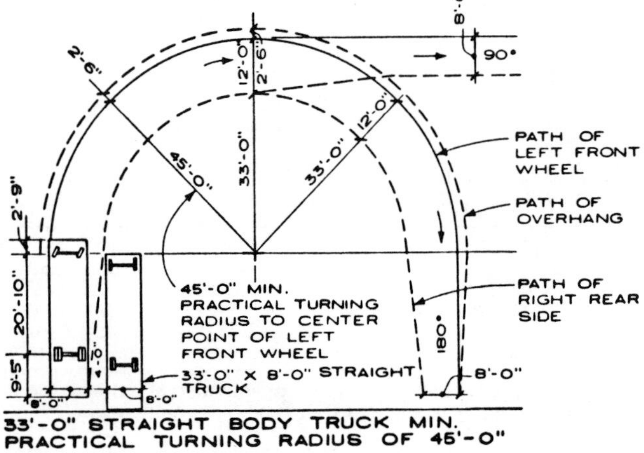
2'-6"
12'-0"
2'-6"
8'-0"
90°
45'-0"
33'-0"
33'-0"
12'-0"
PATH OF LEFT FRONT WHEEL
PATH OF OVERHANG
2'-9"
20'-10"
9'-5"
8'-0"
4'-0"
45'-0" MIN. PRACTICAL TURNING RADIUS TO CENTER POINT OF LEFT FRONT WHEEL
PATH OF RIGHT REAR SIDE
180°
33'-0" X 8'-0" STRAIGHT TRUCK
8'-0"
8'-0"

33'-0" STRAIGHT BODY TRUCK MIN. PRACTICAL TURNING RADIUS OF 45'-0"

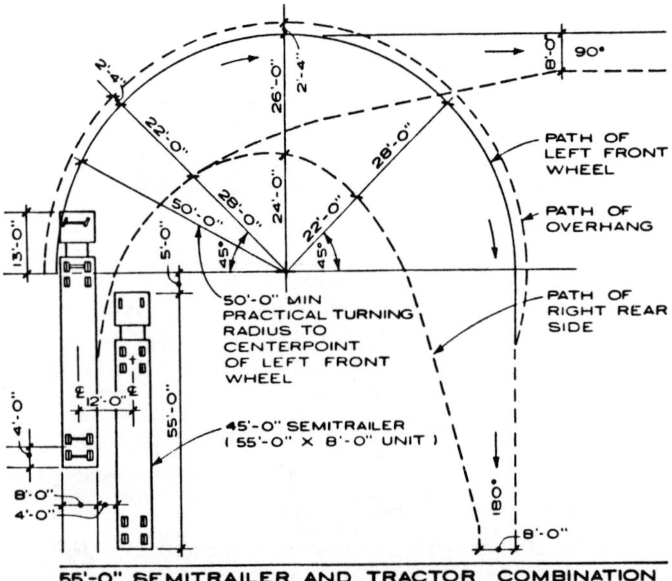
2'-4"
26'-0"
2'-4"
8'-0"
90°
22'-0"
28'-0"
28'-0"
24'-0"
22'-0"
50'-0"
45°
45°
PATH OF LEFT FRONT WHEEL
PATH OF OVERHANG
13'-0"
5'-0"
50'-0" MIN PRACTICAL TURNING RADIUS TO CENTERPOINT OF LEFT FRONT WHEEL
PATH OF RIGHT REAR SIDE
12'-0"
55'-0"
4'-0"
45'-0" SEMITRAILER (55'-0" X 8'-0" UNIT)
8'-0"
4'-0"
180°
8'-0"

55'-0" SEMITRAILER AND TRACTOR COMBINATION MIN. PRACTICAL TURNING RADIUS OF 50'-0"

Robert H. Lorenz, AIA; Preston Trucking Company, Inc.; Preston, Maryland
The Operations Council, American Trucking Association; Washington, D.C.

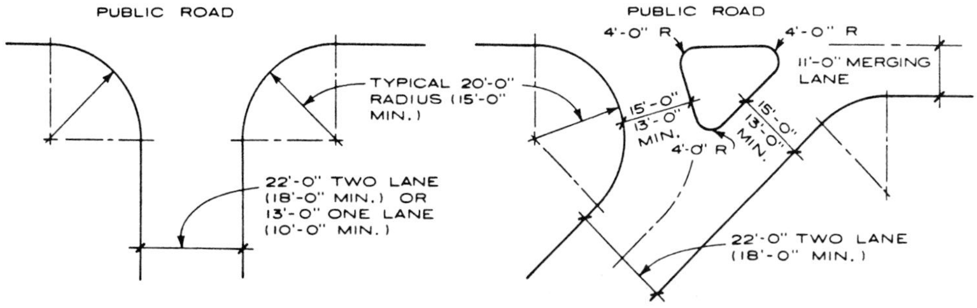
PUBLIC ROAD
PUBLIC ROAD
TYPICAL 20'-0" RADIUS (15'-0" MIN.)
22'-0" TWO LANE (18'-0" MIN.) OR 13'-0" ONE LANE (10'-0" MIN.)
4'-0" R
4'-0" R
11'-0" MERGING LANE
15'-0" 13'-0" MIN.
15'-0" 13'-0" MIN.
4'-0' R
22'-0" TWO LANE (18'-0" MIN.)

PRIVATE ROADS INTERSECTING PUBLIC ROADS

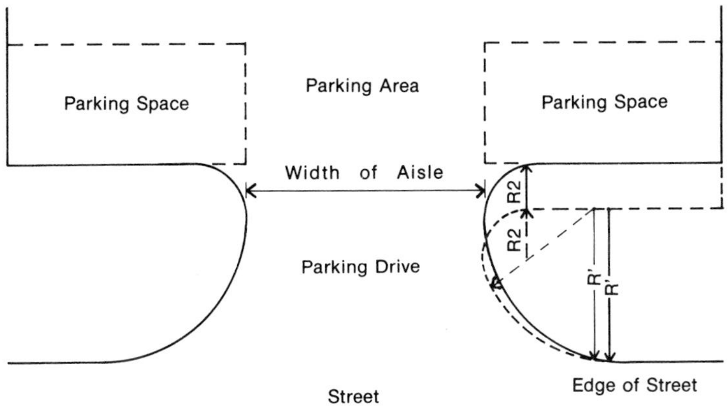
Parking Space
Parking Area
Parking Space
Width of Aisle
Parking Drive
R2
R2
R'
R'
Street
Edge of Street

Procedure for determining entrance or exit radii for parking areas

Step 1: Establish the desired minimum radii from street into the parking area (typically 12–15′ radius).
Step 2: Determine desired minimum radii from parking drive into nearest parking space (typically 3–5′ radius).
Step 3: If the total of these two radii is less than the distance from the street edge to the outer edge of the nearest parking space, then construct a compound curve, where the two curves share the same radius lines as shown in the figure.

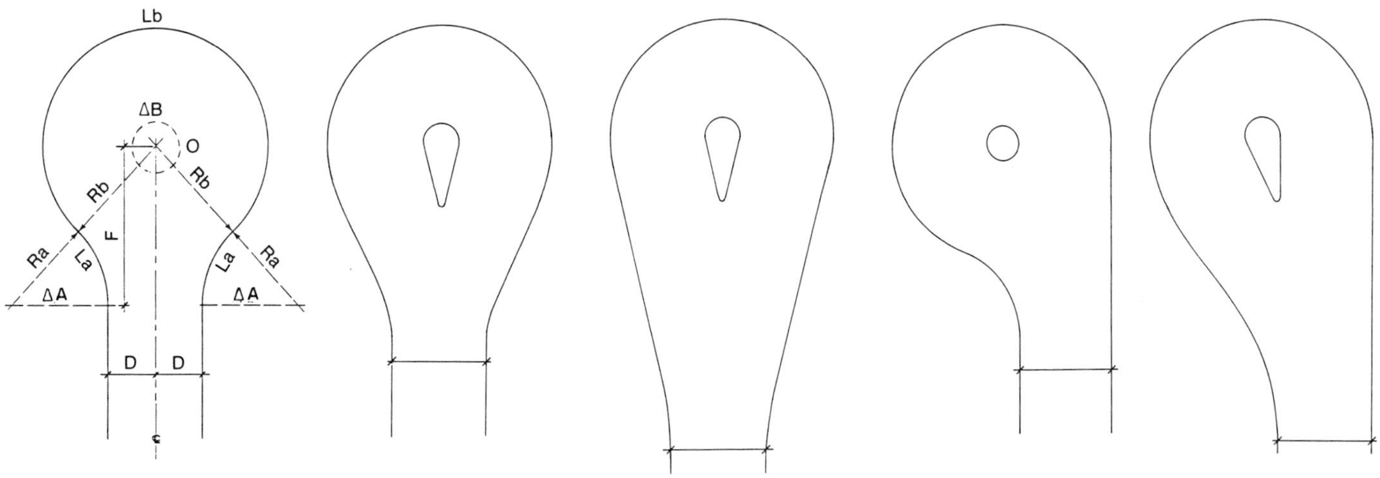
Lb
ΔB
O
Rb
Rb
Ra
La
F
La
Ra
ΔA
ΔA
D
D

CUL-DE-SAC

	SMALL	LARGE
O	16′-0″	22′-0″
F	50′-11″	87′-3″
A	46.71°	35.58°
B	273.42°	251.15°
Ra	32′-0″	100′-0″
Rb	38′-0″	50′-0″
La	26′-1″	61′-8″
Lb	181′-4″	219′-2″

Notes: (1) R values for vehicles intended to use these cul-de-sacs should not exceed Rb. (2) O values are the radii for optional inner circles or islands. (3) D values are the required widths of each travel lane at the beginning of the cul-de-sac or loop. (4) If parking is permitted along the outer edge of the cul-de-sac, then make the radii for the remaining inner lane adequate for other vehicles to turn around.

Figure 210-23 Curb radii and turnarounds.

GENERAL NOTES: Community Facilities Based Upon Population

The area standards shown below were compiled or derived from selected existing communities in North America. They offer some extremely "general standards" which can be used for a specific community or situation if checked against professional experience and coupled with a careful study of comparable communities and/or projects.

The data shown is based upon a single use of a specific surface. If multiple sport uses are planned for an area, then the number of areas needed for these sports can often be reduced.

Due to the growing interest in active sports and physical exercise on the part of all segments of a population, these standards may need to be increased by 25 to 50% for a specific situation and cross-section of the user population.

AREA SPACE STANDARDS (based upon population)

Sport	Facilities per 1000 population	Notes
Multicourt	Minimum 1 + 1/2000-light 25–50%	1½ mile maximum radius
Handball	Minimum 1 + 1/5000-10,000	
"	1/10,000	
Volleyball	1/2000 to 1/3–4000	communities 10,000+
Shuffleboard	Minimum 1–2 + 1/2000-light 25%	communities over 500
Basketball	1 goal/500	communities under 3000
"	1 goal/1000 + one full court	communities over 3000
"	1 acre/5000 persons	
Croquet	1/2000-light 25%	
Horsehoe	Minimum 2 + 1/2000-light 25–50%	community over 500
Softball	Minimum 1 + 1/3000-light 50%	community over 1000
Little league	1/10,000	
	Minimum 1 + 1/4000-light 25%	
Baseball	1/3000	
"	Minimum 1 + 1/6000-light 50%	community over 1500
"	1/30,000	
"	1/6000	community 1 mile maximum radius
Football soccer	Minimum 1 + 1/5-15,000	
"	Minimum 1 + 1/8000 for football	
"	2 acres/1000	
"	1/80,000	
Tennis	Minimum 1 + 1/2000-light 50–76%	community-⅔ miles radius
"	1/10,000	
"	1/2000	
"	1500 ft^2/player	
"	1 acre/5000	
Athletic field	Approximate 20 acres	
	1/50,000-lighted	1–2 miles or 20 minutes
	accommodate 200 people/acre	

PARKING RATIOS FOR OUTDOOR SPORTS FACILITIES

Sport	Suggested minimum parking for normal use
Archery	1/target
Badminton	2/court
Baseball	15+/diamond-player
Baseball	20/diamond-spectator
Bowling, lawn	2/green lane
Croquet	2/court
Golf	8/green
Golf	1/practice tee
Football, touch	10/field
Horseshoes	1/court
Trap shooting	2/range
Shuffleboard	2/court
Softball	15/diamond
Tennis, deck	2/court
Tennis, lawn	2/court
Volleyball	6/court

Figure 210-24 Area space standards and parking ratios for outdoor sport facilities.

Type of equipment or area	Area per unit, ft^2	Capacity in number of users	Suggested number to be included
	Apparatus		
Slide	450	6	1†
Horizontal bars	180	4	3†
Horizontal ladders	375	8	2†
Traveling rings	625	6	1
Giant stride	1,225	6	1
Small junglegym	180	10	1
Low swing	150	1	4*
High swing	250	1	6*
Balance beam	100	4	1
See-saw	100	2	4
Medium junglegym	500	20	1
	Misc. equipment and areas		
Open space for games (ages 6–10)	10,000	80	1*
Wading pool	3,000	40	1*
Handcraft, quiet games	1,600	30	1*
Outdoor theater	2,000	30	1
Sand box	300	15	2
Shelter house	2,500	30	1‡
	Special sports areas		
Soccer field	36,000	22	1
Playground baseball	20,000	20	2
Volleyball court	2,800	20	1
Basketball court	3,750	16	1
Jumping pits	1,200	12	1
Paddle tennis courts	1,800	4	2§
Handball courts	1,050	4	2
Tether tennis courts	400	2	2§
Horseshoe courts	600	4	2
Tennis courts	7,200	4	2§
Straightaway track	7,200	10	1§
Landscaping	(a)6,000		
Paths, circulation, etc.	(a)7,000		

*Minimum desirable.
†One or all of these units may be omitted if playground is not used in conjunction with a school.
‡May be omitted if sanitary facilities are supplied elsewhere.
§May be omitted if space if limited.
Source: From *Architectural Systems Community Planning.*

Figure 210-25 Area requirements for playgrounds and sports areas.

Type of development	Neighborhood population				
	1000 persons, 275 families	2000 persons, 550 families	3000 persons, 825 families	4000 persons, 1100 families	5000 persons, 1375 families
	One- or Two-Family Development†				
Area in component uses					
Acres in school site	1.20	1.20	1.50	1.80	2.20
Acres in playground	2.75	3.25	4.00	5.00	6.00
Acres in park	1.50	2.00	2.50	3.00	3.50
Acres in shopping center	0.80	1.20	2.20	2.60	3.00
Acres in general community facilities‡	0.38	0.76	1.20	1.50	1.90
Aggregate area					
Acres: total	6.63	8.41	11.40	13.90	16.60
Acres per 1000 persons	6.63	4.20	3.80	3.47	3.32
Square feet per family	1050	670	600	550	530
	Multifamily Development§				
Area in component uses					
Acres in school site	1.20	1.20	1.50	1.80	2.20
Acres in playground	2.75	3.25	4.00	5.00	6.00
Acres in park	2.00	3.00	4.00	5.00	6.00
Acres in shopping center	0.80	1.20	2.20	2.60	3.00
Acres in general community facilities‡	0.38	0.76	1.20	1.50	1.90
Aggregate area					
Acres: total	7.13	9.41	12.90	15.90	19.10
Acres per 1000 persons	7.13	4.70	4.30	3.97	3.82
Square feet per family	1130	745	680	630	610

Note: This table combines the recommended or assumed values.
†With private lot area of less than ¼ acre per family (for private lots of ¼ acre or more park area may be omitted).
‡Allowance for indoor social and cultural facilities (church, assembly hall, etc.) or separate health center, nursery school, etc.
§Or other development predominantly without private yards.
Source: Adapted from *Architectural Systems Community Planning*

Figure 210-26 Land area requirements for neighborhood community facilities.

Use of site and/or building	Minimum number of parking spaces required*
Residential	
Single family homes	2.0/dwelling unit
Multifamily:	
Efficiency	1.0/dwelling unit
One and two bedrooms	1.5/dwelling unit
Three and more apartments	2.0/dwelling unit
Dormitories, sororities, fraternities	0.5/units
Hotels and motels	1.0/dwelling unit
Commercial	
Offices and banks	3.0/1000 s.f. GFA
Business and professional services	3.3/1000 s.f. GFA
Commercial recreational facilities	8.0/1000 s.f. GFA
Bowling alleys	4.0/alley
Regional shopping centers	4.5/1000 s.f. GFA
Community shopping centers	5.0/1000 s.f. GFA
Neighborhood centers	6.0/1000 s.f. GFH
Restaurants	0.3/seat
Educational	
Elementary and junior high schools	1.0/teacher and staff
High schools and colleges	1.0/2–5 students
Medical	
Medical and dental offices	1.0/200 s.f. GFA
Hospitals	1.0/2–3 bed
Convalescent & nursing homes	1.0/3 bed
Public Building	
Auditoriums, theaters, stadiums	1.0/4 seats
Museums and libraries	1.0/300 s.f. GFA
Public utilities and offices	1.0/two employees
Recreation	
Beaches	1.0/100 s.f.
Swimming pools	1.0/30 s.f.
Athletic fields and courts	1.0/3000 s.f.
Golf courses	1.0/acre
Industrial	
Industrial manufacturing	1.0/2–5 employees
Churches	
Churches	1.0/4 seats

*The data was derived from existing conditions in North America. Special conditions including local codes and requirements may be quite different and should be used where appropriate. Study of comparable types of land uses nearby or in other similar situations is recommended. Access to and from the site/building via public transportation will affect significantly the number of parking spaces needed for most types of uses.

Figure 210-27 Parking spaces needed for various land uses.

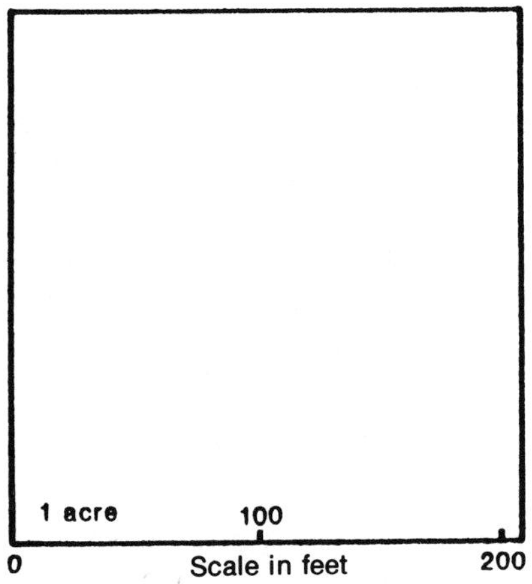
1 acre
100
0
Scale in feet
200

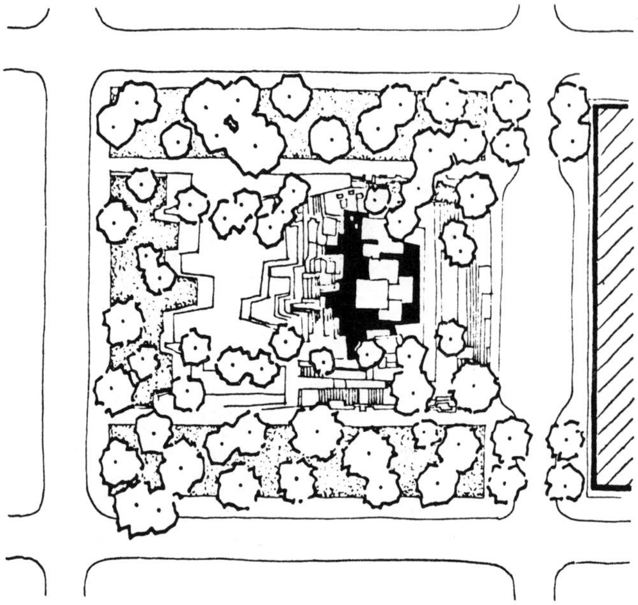

Auditorium Forecourt Plaza, Portland, Oregon

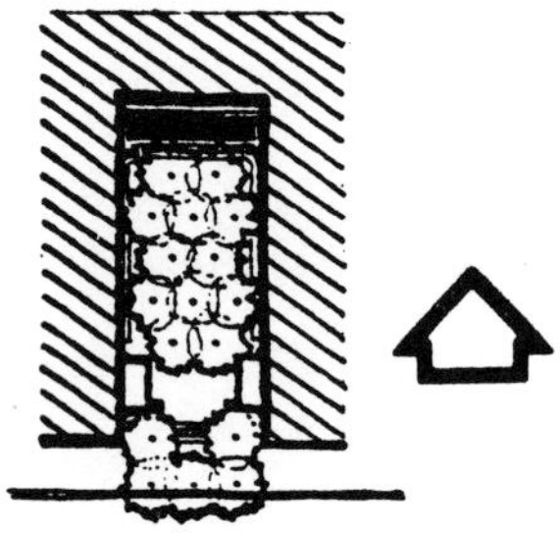

Paley Park, New York, New York

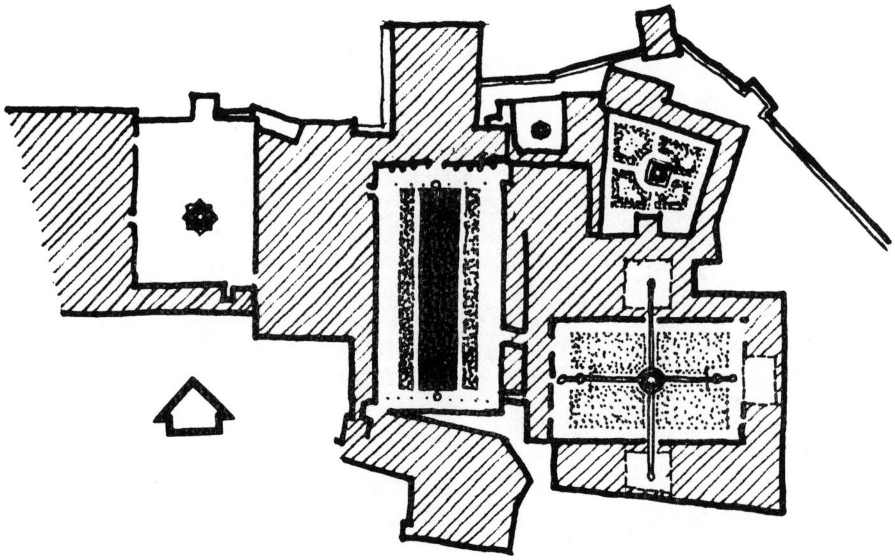

Court of the Lions and Court of the Myrtles, the Alhambra, Granada, Spain

Figure 210-28 Famous outdoor spaces (drawn to the same scale as the *acre square* by William A. Mann).

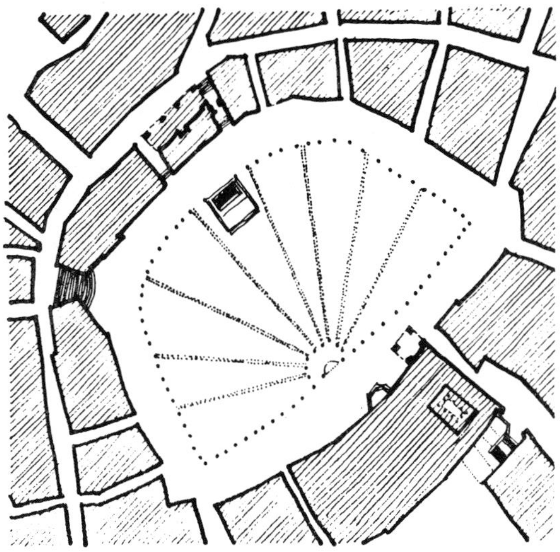

Piazza del Campo, Siena, Italy

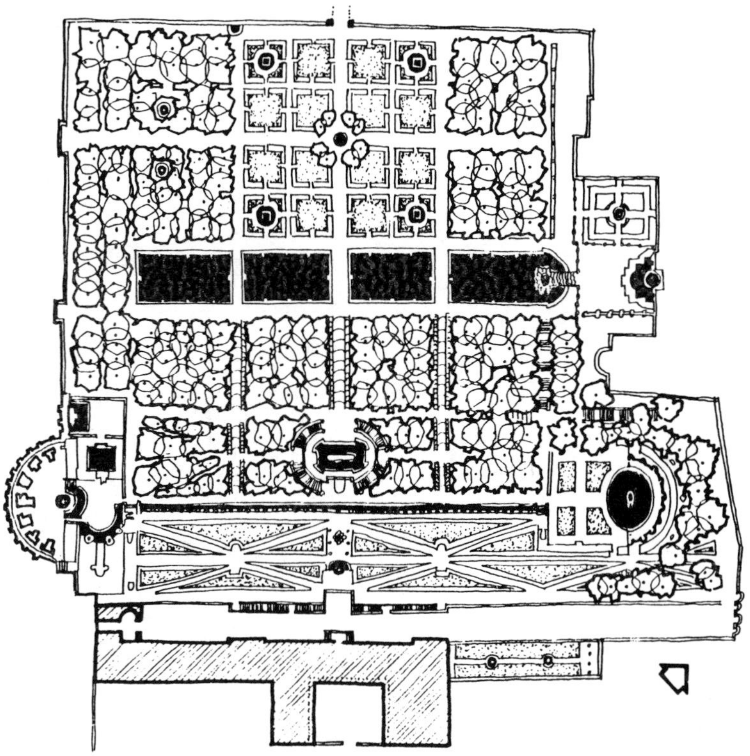

Villa d'Este, Tivoli, Italy

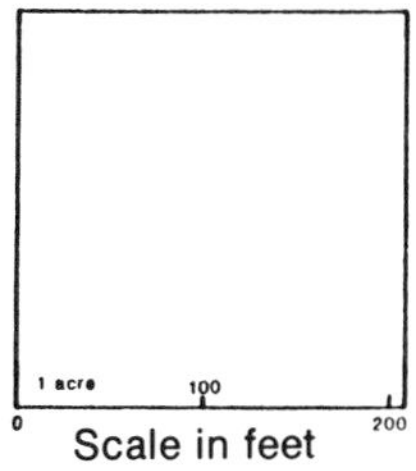
1 acre
0
100
200
Scale in feet

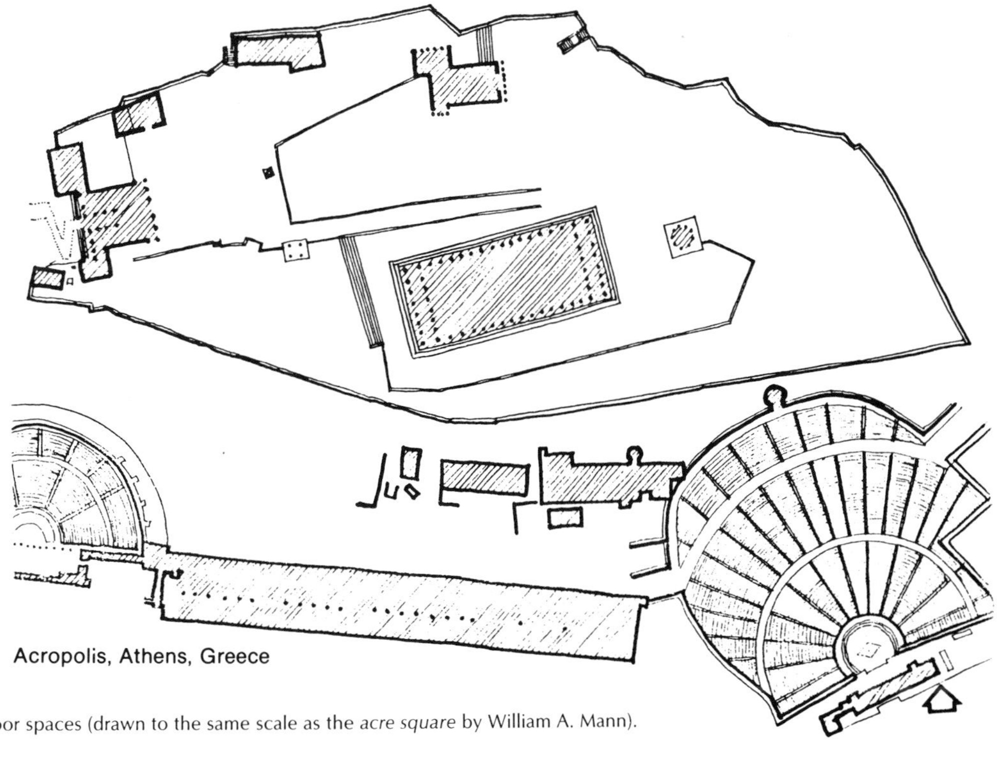

Acropolis, Athens, Greece

Figure 210-29 Famous outdoor spaces (drawn to the same scale as the *acre square* by William A. Mann).

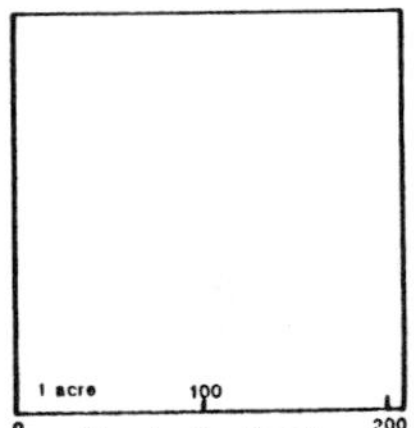
1 acre
0
100
200

Scale in feet

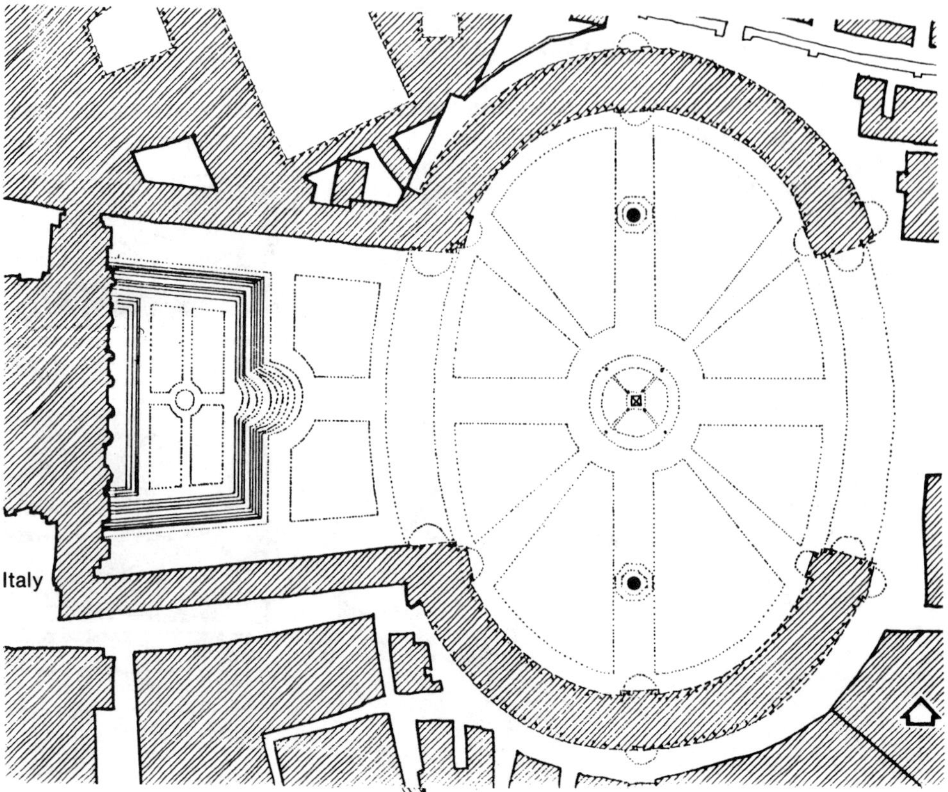

Piazza di San Pietro, Vatican City, Rome, Italy

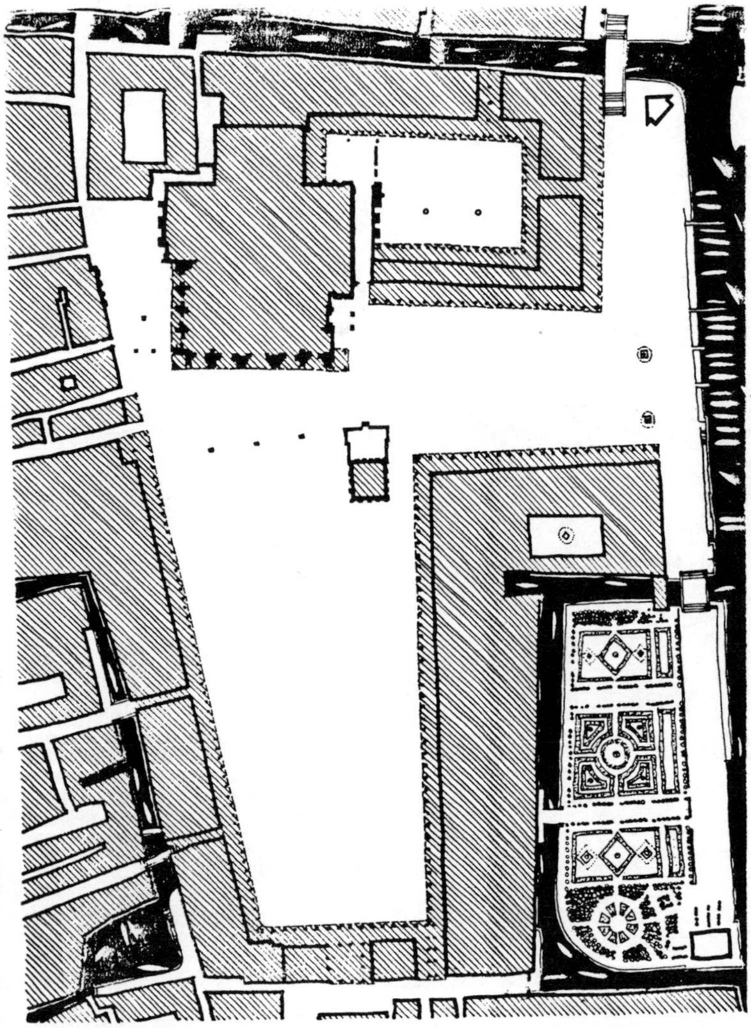

Piazza San Marco, Venice, Italy

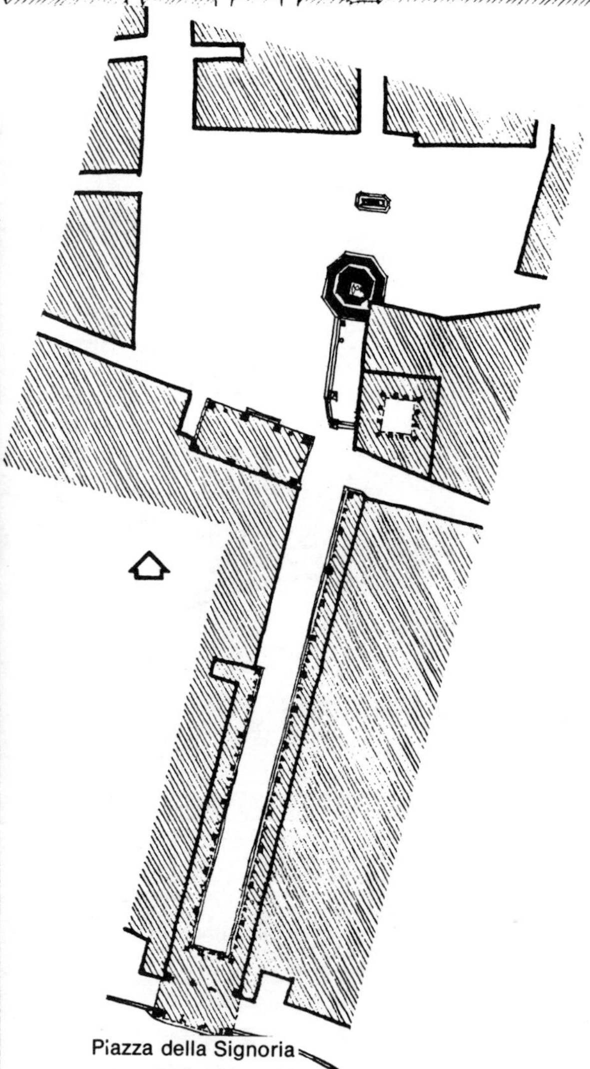

Piazza della Signoria (with Uffizi courtyard), Florence, Italy

Figure 210-30 Famous outdoor spaces (drawn to the same scale as the *acre square* by William A. Mann).

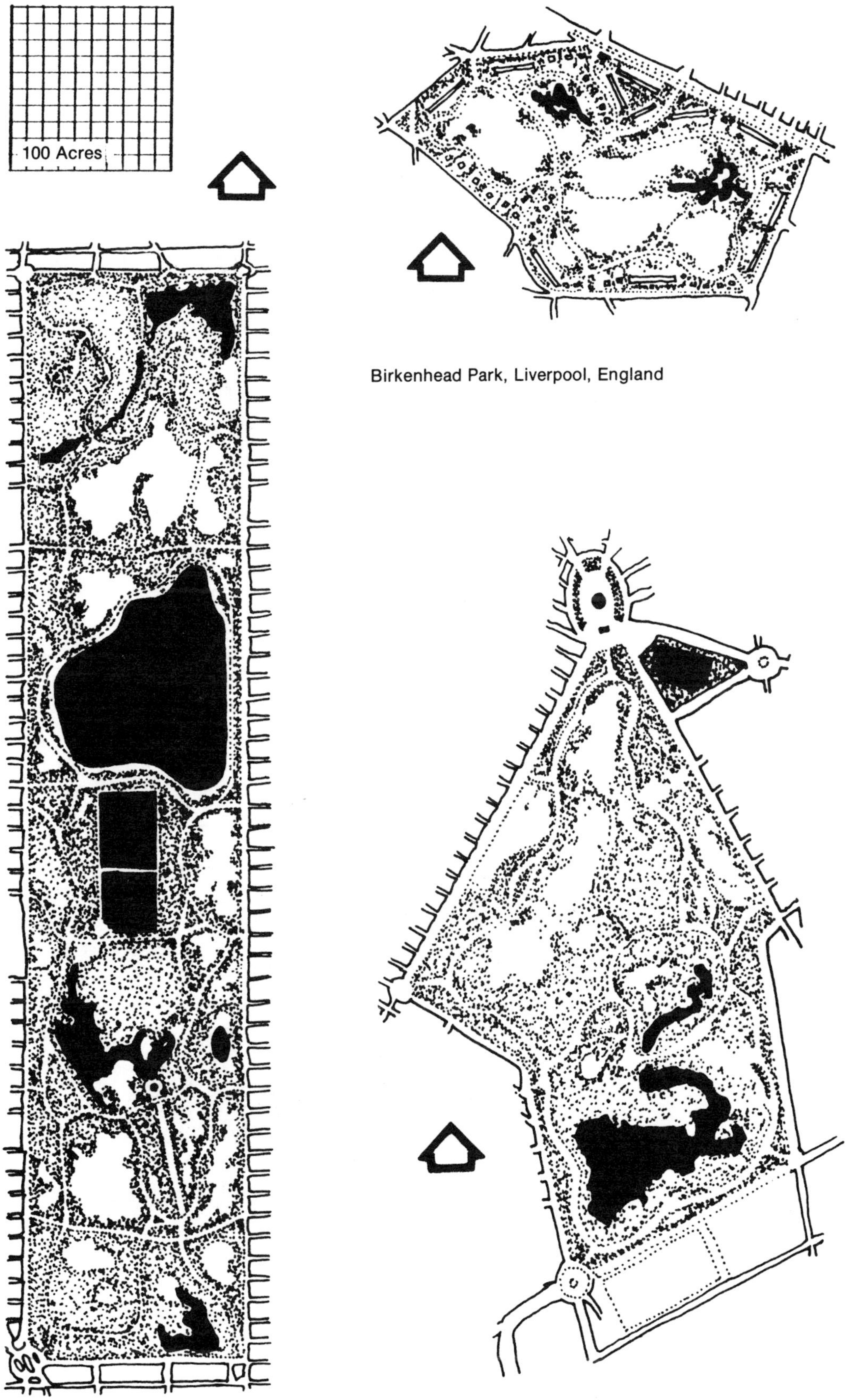
100 Acres
Birkenhead Park, Liverpool, England
Central Park, New York
Prospect Park, Brooklyn, New York

Figure 210-31 Famous outdoor spaces (drawn to the same scale as the 100 *acre square* by William A. Mann).

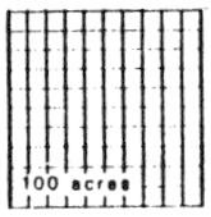
100 acres

100 Acres

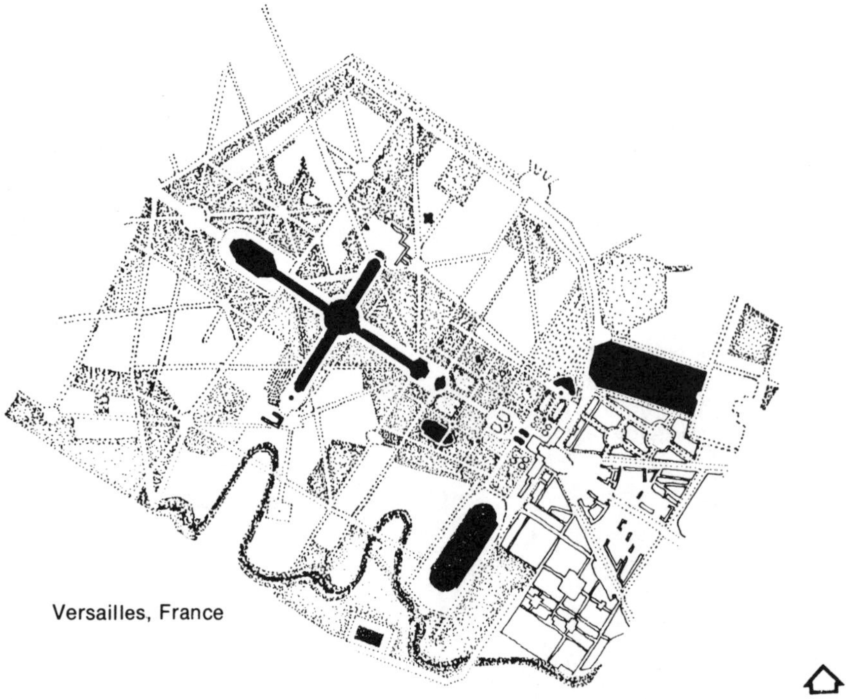

Versailles, France

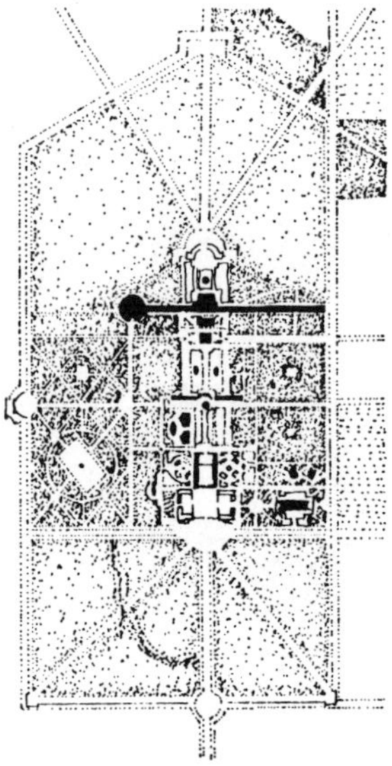

Vaux-le-Vicomte, Melun, France

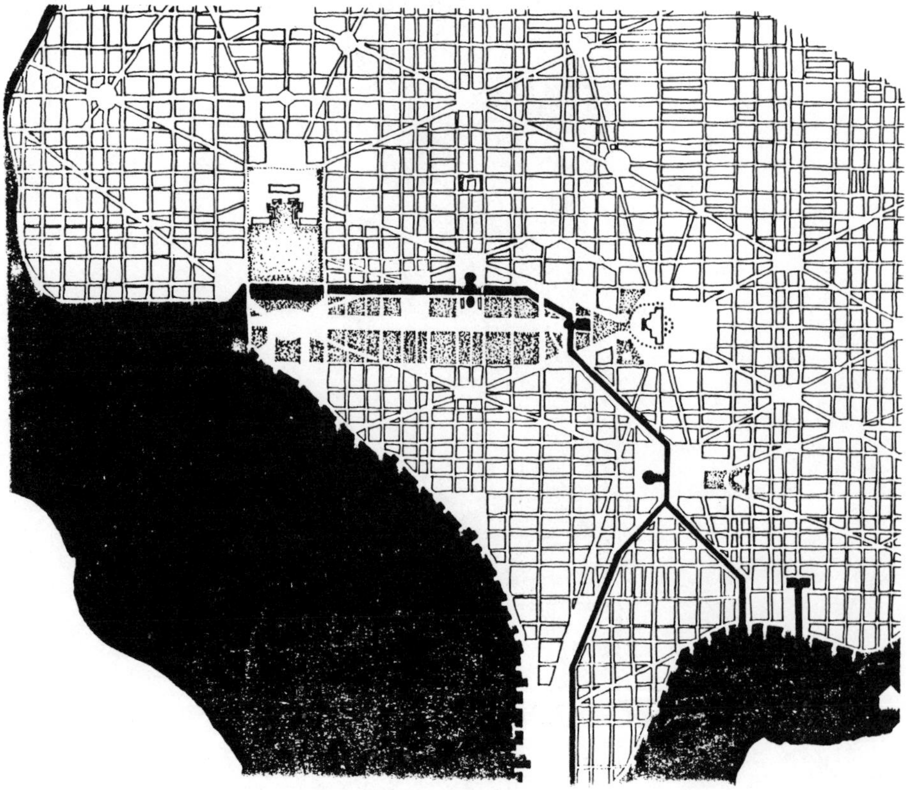

The National Capital Plan, Washington, D.C.

Figure 210-32 Famous outdoor spaces (drawn to the same scale as the 100 *acre square* by William A. Mann).

section 240: Outdoor Accessibility

CREDITS

Contributor:

Gary M. Fishbeck
Sasaki Associates, Inc.
Watertown, Massachusetts

Graphics:

Laura Burnett
SWA Group
Laguna Beach, California

Reviewers:

John P. S. Salmen, AIA
National Center for a Barrier-Free Environment
Washington, D.C.

Jay L. Jorgensen
Fairfax County Park Authority
Annandale, Virginia

CONTENTS

1.0 INTRODUCTION

Most publications on accessibility have focused on architecture rather than on outdoor environments. This section fills that gap by focusing on problems of accessibility in outdoor environments, including parks, playgrounds, gardens, wilderness areas, beaches, and common urban environments.

The information here has been prepared as a complement to two well-known publications on accessibility, the *Uniform Federal Accessibility Standards* (UFAS) and *ANSI A117.1* (The American National Standards Institute).

The *Uniform Federal Accessibility Standards* (1984) were developed to minimize the difference between the standards previously used by four federal agencies (the General Services Administration, the Department of Housing and Urban Development, the Department of Defense, and the U.S. Postal Service), and between those standards and the access standards recommended for facilities that are not federally funded or constructed.

The ANSI standards *(A117.1-1986)*, entitled, "Specifications for Making Buildings and Facilities Accessible to, and Usable by, Physically Handicapped People," has generally been accepted by the private sector. Most state governments (U.S.) have adopted *ANSI 117.1* as published or in modified form.

The UFAS standards (1984) are reprinted in their entirety in the appendix to this handbook. *ANSI 117.1* can be acquired by contacting the American National Standards Institute in New York.

With few exceptions, information included in UFAS is not repeated here, and vice versa. The UFAS standards includes architectural and transportation guidelines as well as a large amount of basic information useful for formulating minimum dimensional criteria for almost any situation. Section 240, here, includes landscape architectural guidelines as well as a discussion of important concepts in accessible design; this section also includes specific design recommendations for various outdoor situations. Cross-references to UFAS, as well as ANSI A117.1, Section 241 are sometimes given for further information on a topic.

The design recommendations given in this section are based on a number of important design concepts and principles related to accessibility, as well as on a specific knowledge about the effects of various types of impairment as they relate to environmental design.

2.0 IMPORTANT DESIGN CONCEPTS

A number of important concepts related to accessibility have emerged recently which are important to understand prior to reviewing the guidelines outlined in this section.

2.1 Temporarily Able-Bodied

As a designer, it is better to embrace the attitude that the *majority* of the population is *temporarily able-bodied* (TAB) than it is to embrace the attitude that a *minority* of the population is handicapped. Full physical ability is a temporary condition, meaning that all people become handicapped in one way or another periodically in life. Whether it be a full armload of groceries, or a brief spell of dizziness or fatigue, or a sprained ankle, or pregnancy, or high heel shoes, or the normal consequences of aging, all people occasionally encounter difficulty negotiating environment. Consequently, environment could be designed to reflect this attitude by incorporating all design elements into a functionally and aesthetically integral package, rather than designing environment primarily for life's periods of unhampered physical ability, with discrete design details added on for those who are handicapped.

2.2 Pedestrian Accessible Network

Extensive *pedestrian accessible networks* are absolutely necessary if handicapped individuals can expect to move around from place to place (Figure 240-1). Design details for handicapped access are of minimal value if the connections between parts are incomplete. Accessibility should be coordinated not only within projects but also between projects, by analyzing and responding to the context of the site in question. Coordination should exist between parking areas, curb ramps, paved areas, rest areas with adequate seating, lighting, signage, building entries, and interiors. Continuous accessibility should exist between buildings and within buildings, between parking areas and corresponding destinations, and between alternative destinations. Pedestrian circulation systems should include loops rather than dead ends.

2.3 Graduated Difficulty of Access

A system of *graduated difficulty of access* is an idea most applicable to the design and management of outdoor recreational facilities, and is especially relevant to hiking and camping areas. In outdoor recreational areas, the design of two distinctly different types of facilities, i.e., one for those with handicaps and another for able-bodied individuals, is not recommended. A better alternative is to provide a wide variety of trail types, each characterized by a *degree of difficulty* to negotiate. By providing a diversity of trail types (with varying surfaces, widths, slopes, cross-slopes, lengths, edges, number of rest stops, etc.), a wider spectrum of opportunity with diverse experiences can be provided that will accommodate or challenge all people regardless of their abilities. A good system of signage enables one to choose for oneself the type of experience or degree of challenge desired. In this regard, it is not necessary that all facilities be totally accessible. Some may be difficult to negotiate even for the fittest of individuals. The main objective is to provide greater diversity in trail types, based on an understanding of the wide variation of ability in people. Such a system does not compromise the recreational experience for anyone, and it also has the advantage of not always segregating the able-bodied from those who are not.

3.0 TYPES OF IMPAIRMENT

Misconceptions about various physical and learning impairments are common, and improper assumptions are often made about the abilities of individuals with such impairments. Such assumptions influence design decisions.

People with physical or learning impairments should not be viewed together as a single group, mainly because abilities vary considerably among individuals even within a particular disability group. Overgeneralizations usually lead to design solutions which either inadequately address the needs of individuals meant to be accommodated, or compromise the aesthetics of a site plan to an unnecessary extent. The diversity of ability among those who are handicapped must be understood, and a means devised to accommodate this diversity. For the most part, such diversity can be addressed by careful provision of a few systems, primarily addressing the needs of those with visual impairments and those with mobility impairments.

Visual and mobility impairments are the two conditions that are the easiest to design for in terms of accessibility. Individuals with hearing, manual, and learning impairments surely have need for accommodation, but the design ramifications for these groups are less clearly defined. In most cases, these groups can be accommodated by devices designed for visually impaired and mobility-impaired individuals. In some instances, however, specific devices are necessary to accommodate these other groups. Experience has found that employment of the guidelines presented here in this section will usually provide at least basic accommodation.

Typical categories of impairment include visual impairments, mobility impairments, hearing impairments, manual impairments, and learning impairments. Combinations commonly occur, especially as individuals get older.

3.1 Visual Impairments

Of the 6.4 million U.S. citizens (1981) who are visually impaired, only 27 percent are severely impaired (legally blind), and only 6½ percent have no usable vision at all. The large majority of those who are visually impaired have limited vision which is actively used for orientation and negotiation. Of the 27 percent who are severely impaired, 10 percent (i.e., less than 3 percent of the total U.S. population) can read braille.

Most visual impairments are associated with aging. Incidences of congenital blindness are relatively small in number. Ninety percent of those visually impaired are over the age of 45, and 65 percent are over the age of 65. As a function of age, most of those who are visually impaired also have the disadvantage of limited balance, stamina, reaction time, and general agility.

Ninety-six percent of those who are visually impaired become blind during adulthood and consequently understand the way urban environments are typically structured. Time to adapt to the gradually worsening condition of visual impairment usually existed. Such individuals learn to rely upon the other senses of smell, hearing, and touch. Those with limited vision learn how best to use what remains of their vision. Simple perception of light, for example, helps one discriminate between night and day, sunlight and shadow, or the four cardinal directions.

To a practiced ear, the echo in a space can indicate the approximate size of the space and the location of walls or openings. The direction and location of auto traffic can also be determined from audible cues.

The sense of smell can be used to identify landmarks such as restaurants, canals, and petrol stations, and these landmarks can aid orientation through complex envi-

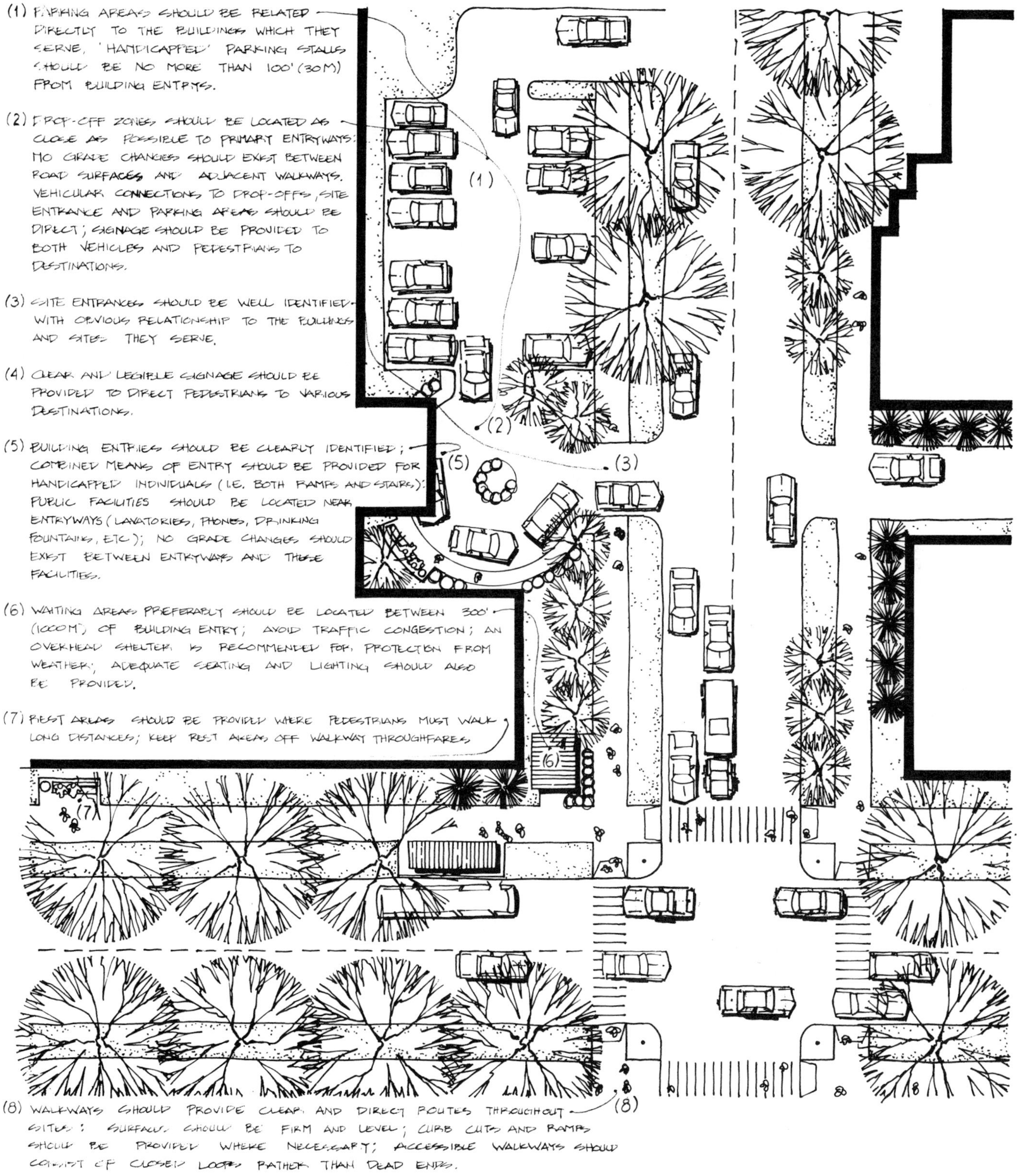
(1) PARKING AREAS SHOULD BE RELATED DIRECTLY TO THE BUILDINGS WHICH THEY SERVE. 'HANDICAPPED' PARKING STALLS SHOULD BE NO MORE THAN 100' (30M) FROM BUILDING ENTRYS.
(2) DROP-OFF ZONES SHOULD BE LOCATED AS CLOSE AS POSSIBLE TO PRIMARY ENTRYWAYS; NO GRADE CHANGES SHOULD EXIST BETWEEN ROAD SURFACES AND ADJACENT WALKWAYS. VEHICULAR CONNECTIONS TO DROP-OFFS, SITE ENTRANCE AND PARKING AREAS SHOULD BE DIRECT; SIGNAGE SHOULD BE PROVIDED TO BOTH VEHICLES AND PEDESTRIANS TO DESTINATIONS.
(3) SITE ENTRANCES SHOULD BE WELL IDENTIFIED WITH OBVIOUS RELATIONSHIP TO THE BUILDINGS AND SITES THEY SERVE.
(4) CLEAR AND LEGIBLE SIGNAGE SHOULD BE PROVIDED TO DIRECT PEDESTRIANS TO VARIOUS DESTINATIONS.
(5) BUILDING ENTRIES SHOULD BE CLEARLY IDENTIFIED; COMBINED MEANS OF ENTRY SHOULD BE PROVIDED FOR HANDICAPPED INDIVIDUALS (I.E. BOTH RAMPS AND STAIRS); PUBLIC FACILITIES SHOULD BE LOCATED NEAR ENTRYWAYS (LAVATORIES, PHONES, DRINKING FOUNTAINS, ETC); NO GRADE CHANGES SHOULD EXIST BETWEEN ENTRYWAYS AND THESE FACILITIES.
(6) WAITING AREAS PREFERABLY SHOULD BE LOCATED BETWEEN 300' (100M) OF BUILDING ENTRY; AVOID TRAFFIC CONGESTION; AN OVERHEAD SHELTER IS RECOMMENDED FOR PROTECTION FROM WEATHER; ADEQUATE SEATING AND LIGHTING SHOULD ALSO BE PROVIDED.
(7) REST AREAS SHOULD BE PROVIDED WHERE PEDESTRIANS MUST WALK LONG DISTANCES; KEEP REST AREAS OFF WALKWAY THROUGHFARES.
(1)
(2)
(3)
(5)
(6)
(7)
(8)
(8) WALKWAYS SHOULD PROVIDE CLEAR AND DIRECT ROUTES THROUGHOUT SITES; SURFACES SHOULD BE FIRM AND LEVEL; CURB CUTS AND RAMPS SHOULD BE PROVIDED WHERE NECESSARY; ACCESSIBLE WALKWAYS SHOULD CONSIST OF CLOSED LOOPS RATHER THAN DEAD ENDS.

Figure 240-1 Pedestrian accessible network. A pedestrian accessible network ensures that all people will have uninterrupted access to facilities.

ronment. Characteristic odors and fragrances can be remembered and cognitively mapped.

The perception of wind or drafts against the skin can help identify street corners, tunnels, subway entrances, or narrow passages, as well as help determine spatial form to some extent. Heat or cold can be perceived and can indicate the direction of the sun and the presence of street gratings, exhaust fans, or a doorway. Differences in paving materials can provide tactile cues which can aid negotiation and identify hazards.

A sense of balance helps identify topo-

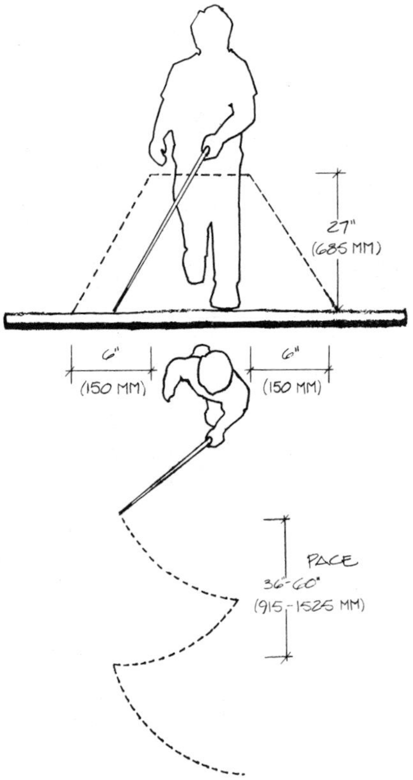
27"
(685 MM)
6"
(150 MM)
6"
(150 MM)
PACE
36"-60"
(915-1525 MM)

Figure 240-2 Cane technique. The Typhlo cane is primarily used by those with limited vision and will detect objects only within a specific range. Objects should not protrude into pedestrian pathways above a 27-in (686-mm) height.

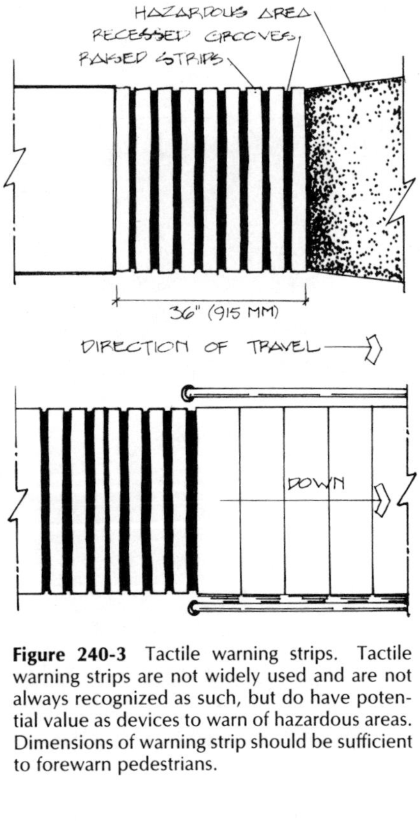
HAZARDOUS AREA
RECESSED GROOVES
RAISED STRIPS
36" (915 MM)
DIRECTION OF TRAVEL
DOWN

Figure 240-3 Tactile warning strips. Tactile warning strips are not widely used and are not always recognized as such, but do have potential value as devices to warn of hazardous areas. Dimensions of warning strip should be sufficient to forewarn pedestrians.

graphic gradients, the beginning or end of a ramp, the approximate width of a crowned road, drainage structure, and the like.

Most individuals with impaired vision require no mobility aids, relying instead on their limited vision and various environmental cues. Others employ a variety of aids. Many travel by holding onto the arm or shoulder of a sighted person.

Many visually impaired individuals use a long cane (i.e., the *Typhlo* or *Hoover* cane) (Figure 240-2). Most users will swing the cane systematically from side to side, sweeping an area they feel comfortable with. Others simply hold the cane motionless, outstretched at an angle in front of them. In either case, the angle of the cane does not always detect protruding objects at a height greater than about 27 in (670 mm). Railings, for instance, should have a second rail lower than 27 in (670 mm) for easier detection. Overhanging branches are not easily detected.

Dog guides are occasionally used, but not as commonly as canes. The disadvantages include care for the dog, temperamental incompatability between dog and owner, a faster walking pace, and less information gathered about the texture of the ground. Dog guides are best for those who are completely blind, because opposite reaction to sudden stimuli is less likely.

Electronic travel aids are not as common as canes or dog guides but are available. Devices which employ lasers or sonic signals detect obstacles in the immediate vicinity of the user. Their disadvantages include their unusual appearance, their high expense, and the difficulty of learning how to operate them.

3.2 Mobility Impairments

Impaired mobility can include a wide variety of conditions, ranging from temporary injury and the normal effects of aging to severe disability and the dependent use of a wheelchair. Variation in mobility impairments spans a wide spectrum, making generalizations difficult to formulate. Individual abilities vary considerably.

Impaired mobility generally refers to an impaired function of the legs, but it can also refer to limited stamina, poor balance, a heart condition, and the like. Those with limited use of their legs find it difficult to use stairs and ramps, especially if no handrailings are present. Handrailings are absolutely necessary on all ramps and stairways. Careful design of ramps, landings, stairways, stair nosings, and tread-riser ratios is important, as is the choice of surface materials. Walkway surfaces should not constitute a potential hazard in themselves.

Those who are dependent on wheelchairs for mobility find a formidable barrier in any kind of level change. For some individuals, even a properly designed ramp may be a problem. Accessibility for wheelchair users also implies adequate dimensioning of spaces, routes, and doorways, and proper placement of street furniture. *Kinetospheres,* or reach limitations, are also important determinants. The concept of a pedestrian accessible network is especially relevant to those who use wheelchairs.

3.3 Hearing Impairments

Individuals with hearing impairments (assuming that their vision and mobility are not also affected) encounter problems that center around information and warning communication. Vision must be relied upon almost exclusively for informational needs. Problems occur with the use of sound alarms—automobile horns or fire alarms, for example. Alarms that are accompanied by flashing lights afford the greatest protection against hazard, if the lights are readily perceived. Clear signage and other visual cues for directional information are especially important to individuals with hearing impairments because many cannot rely on verbal communication.

3.4 Manual Impairments

Manual impairments generally refer to dysfunctions of arms or hands. An impairment can be temporary, as with a bone fracture or sprain; or circumstantial, as with a full armload of groceries; or permanent, as in paralysis or amputation. Elderly people characteristically have manual difficulty as a function of reduced strength in arms and hands.

Operating controls such as those found on elevators, vending machines, doorways, or gates often present a problem. Push plates and pull bars on gates or doors are easier to use. Buttons or large swing knobs are preferable to small twisting or dialing mechanisms. Mechanisms that require twisting or some degree of strength to operate are often a hindrance. Equipment that can be operated with a closed fist will accommodate most people.

3.5 Learning Impairments

Individuals with learning difficulties are a group requiring consideration for several reasons. Many individuals have difficulty with orientation and route memory as a function of cognitive mapping difficulty. Landmarks or parts of a route may be remembered, but interconnections often are not. Directional signage is helpful. Illiteracy is a problem which can be overcome by the use of graphic symbolization. Graphic symbols can also minimize the hazards to those with learning difficulties by calling out crosswalks, the edges of traffic, dangerous and restricted areas, and

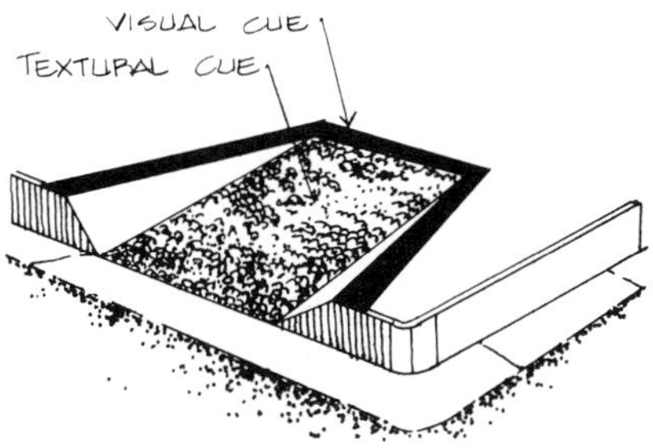
VISUAL CUE
TEXTURAL CUE

Figure 240-4 Components for visual and textural cueing. Both visual and textural cues can be employed to forewarn handicapped pedestrians of hazardous areas.

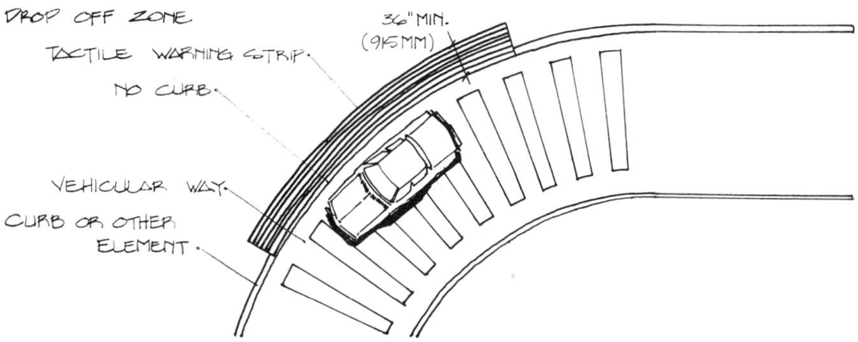
DROP OFF ZONE
TACTILE WARNING STRIP
NO CURB
36" MIN. (915 MM)
VEHICULAR WAY
CURB OR OTHER ELEMENT

Figure 240-5 Tactile warning at hazardous vehicular areas. Visual and/or textural cues can be used to forewarn motorists of pedestrian areas, and vice-versa.

the like. Graphic symbolization (banded crosswalks, for example) can stimulate memory in those with learning difficulties and minimize forgetful behavior.

It must be stressed that a primary motivation of most handicapped individuals is a desire for greater independence. Only by understanding the many variables of human ability and then minimizing environmental barriers can designers meet this desire for greater independence.

4.0 DESIGN DETAILS

4.1 Walkways and Paved Surfaces

General:

Closed networks of pedestrian accessible routes rather than discontiguous units of accessible design are essential, and they should include periodic places to stop and rest.

In pavements, irregularities should be minimized. The widths of expansion and contraction joints in concrete walks should be minimal, preferably under ½ in (12 mm). Sawed joints are recommended where use by handicapped people is frequent.

All walkways should be maintained and adequately lighted for safety and accessibility. (Refer to UFAS sections 4.2 Space Allowances and Reach Ranges, 4.4 Protruding Objects, and 4.5 Ground and Floor Surfaces for more information.)

Tactile Warning Strips:

Tactile warning strips that warn of danger can be useful on walkway surfaces (Figures 240-3 through 240-5). They can be used to warn visually impaired pedestrians of abrupt grade changes, vehicular areas, potentially dangerous exits, pools or water fountains, and the like.

Note that tactile warning strips are not yet in wide use and are not always recognized as such by visually impaired pedestrians, especially at the first interception. A higher level of standardization and education will be required if such devices are to become practical and effective.

Although tactile warning strips are not common, in many cases they can contribute to greater safety for those with visual impairments; they are known to be effective for habitual users of a space. The widely varying nature of walkway surfaces commonly used makes standardization difficult, but the standardization of textured warning surfaces within any one site or facility can be easily accomplished.

Textural contrasts should be strong but should not constitute a safety hazard in themselves. Color contrasts, if utilized, should also be strong. Contrast in tone is the important criterion. State regulations should be checked.

Tactile warning strips are recommended at both the top and bottom of stairways (Figure 240-3). The extent of the strip should be adequate to forewarn the user.

Tactile warning strips are recommended in front of doors that lead to potentially hazardous areas. Textured door knobs or handles are also beneficial. However, such warnings should not be used at emergency exits, as they can discourage use of the exit during real emergencies.

Tactile warning strips at curb ramps and street crossings are also recommended, as they can sometimes prevent visually impaired individuals from inadvertently walking into vehicular traffic (Figures 240-4 and 240-5).

Pathways for recreational use are especially amenable to visual and textural cues. (Refer to 5.0 Accessible Recreation in this section and to Figure 240-40 for more information.)

Street furniture, including trees, should be located within a defined zone along the outer edge of walkways, leaving a clear path without obstruction. A linear tactile warning strip can define this zone. [Refer to ANSI 1117.1 (1986) sections 4.7.7 and 4.27 for more information on tactile warnings.]

4.2 Outdoor Stairs and Landings

Stairways:

Stairways constitute the most formidable barrier and safety hazard for those with physical impairments. Forty-four percent of all accidents by severely visually impaired individuals occur at level changes (U.S. Federal Highway Administration, May 1980). Walkways should be designed to accommodate the greatest diversity of people in any type of level change.

Stairs should include at least two steps for safety reasons and always be easily visible. Handrailings are necessary on all stairs and landings. (Refer to 4.4 Handrailings in this section for more information.)

Additional Recommendations:

1. Locate unexpected level changes, such as descending stairways, out of the main line of traffic (Figure 240-6). Both visual and textural warning cues are recom-

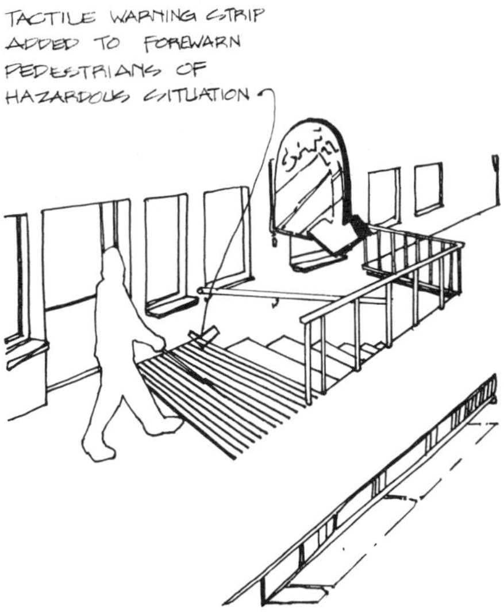
TACTILE WARNING STRIP ADDED TO FOREWARN PEDESTRIANS OF HAZARDOUS SITUATION

Figure 240-6 Unexpected level changes. Unexpected level changes are hazardous and should not occur in the main line of pedestrian walkways. Existing situations can be modified to forewarn unsuspecting pedestrians.

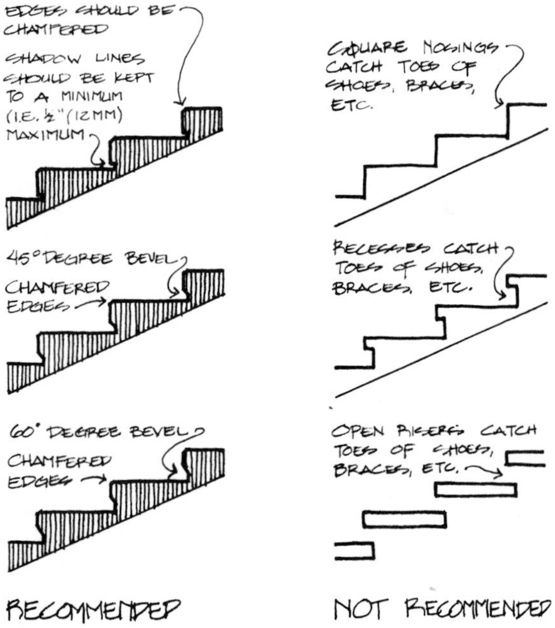
EDGES SHOULD BE CHAMFERED
SHADOW LINES SHOULD BE KEPT TO A MINIMUM (I.E. ½" (12MM) MAXIMUM
SQUARE NOSINGS CATCH TOES OF SHOES, BRACES, ETC.
45° DEGREE BEVEL
CHAMFERED EDGES
RECESSES CATCH TOES OF SHOES, BRACES, ETC.
60° DEGREE BEVEL
CHAMFERED EDGES
OPEN RISERS CATCH TOES OF SHOES, BRACES, ETC.
RECOMMENDED
NOT RECOMMENDED

Figure 240-7 Outdoor step types. Steps should be designed to safely accommodate those who will use them. Careful attention to nosing and shadowline details is especially important.

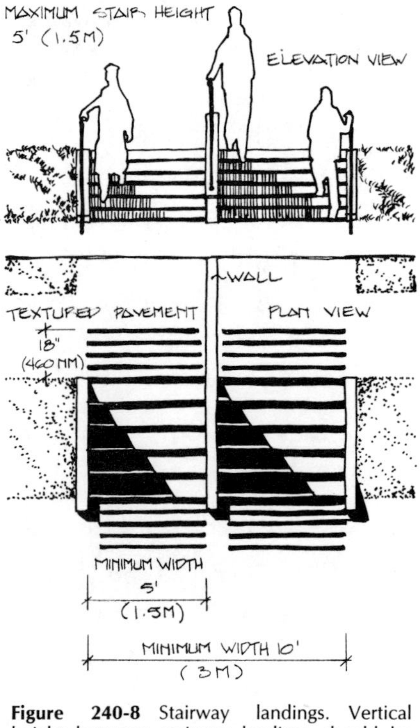
MAXIMUM STAIR HEIGHT 5' (1.5M)
ELEVATION VIEW
WALL
TEXTURED PAVEMENT
PLAN VIEW
18" (460 MM)
MINIMUM WIDTH 5' (1.5M)
MINIMUM WIDTH 10' (3M)

Figure 240-8 Stairway landings. Vertical height between stairway landings should be minimized to accommodate individuals with limited strength. Note that minimum widths do not include the thickness of walls.

mended at the top and bottom of all stairways. (Refer to 4.1 Walkways and Paved Surfaces in this section for more information.)

2. The nose of each step should be easy to see and not obscured by confusing surface patterns. Treads should be visually distinct from one another.

3. Open treads and shadow line recesses can cause tripping and should be used with discretion (Figure 240-7).

4. Refer to UFAS section 4.9 Stairs for more information on stairs and handrailings.

Landings:

Outdoor landings to stairways should be adequately dimensioned to allow room for the convenient movement of people, especially for those who need assistance negotiating stairways. The maximum height between landings should be 5 ft (1.5 m) for visual coherence and psychological invitation between adjacent levels. Lower heights are preferred (Figure 240-8).

Public lobbies should contain the following items as close to entryways as possible:

1. Accessible public telephones
2. Accessible rest room facilities
3. Accessible drinking fountains
4. Waiting area with appropriate seating
5. Informational and directional signage
6. Elevators and escalators

Additional Recommendations:

1. Maintain and provide adequate lighting for all stairs and landings. (Refer to 4.10 Outdoor Lighting in this section for more information.)

2. Handrailings are necessary on all stairs and landings. (Refer to 4.4 Handrailings in this section for more information.)

3. Refer to UFAS section 4.9 Stairs for more information on stairs and handrailings.

4.3 Outdoor Ramps

Ramps are crucial for those who use wheelchairs but may not be easier to negotiate than stairs for others. Both means of access should be provided whenever possible.

Additional Recommendations:

1. Provide visual and textural cues at the top and bottom of all ramps. (Refer to 4.1 Walkways and Paved Surfaces in this section for more information.)

2. Design ramps to carry a minimum live load of 100 pounds per square foot (psf) (474 kg/m^2).

3. For open ramps, provide low curbs [at least 2 in (50 mm) high] along the edges of ramps and landings for stopping, detection by cane, etc.

4. Maintain and provide adequate lighting at all ramps and landings. (Refer to 4.10 Outdoor Lighting in this section and Section 540: Outdoor Lighting, for more information.)

5. Note that 12:1 ramps are only acceptable when enclosed and protected; 20:1 ramps are more appropriate for the outdoors. (Figure 240-9)

6. Refer to UFAS sections 4.7 Curb Ramps and 4.8 Ramps for more information on ramp slopes, ramp widths, and surfacing.

4.4 Handrailings

Handrailings are important for normal reasons of safety, for the physical support of individuals with mobility impairments, and for guidance of those with visual impairments. Steps, ramps, soft ground, and irregular paving surfaces are formidable barriers for those with mobility impairments if no handrailings are present. For those with visual impairments, handrailings aid both orientation and cognitive mapping of environment. *Handrailings* can be thought of as including any linear device which serves to aid mobility and/or orientation.

In recreational settings, ropes with periodic knots have often been used as *orienteering* devices enabling the visually impaired to enjoy environments otherwise disorienting and previously inaccessible.

(Refer to 5.0 Accessible Recreation in this section for more information.)

Additional Recommendations:

1. Specify handrailings that are easy to grip and comfortable to handle (Figure 240-10).
2. Below the top rail of handrailings, provide a second rail at a height of 27 in (670 mm) or lower for detection by cane users, children, etc.
3. Eliminate sharp or protruding ends or edges from handrailings, fastening devices, and the like.
4. Physical strength is one-sided for many individuals. Always provide both left and right handrails, or a central handrailing. On exceptionally wide stairways, intermediate handrailings should be provided at 10 to 20 ft (2–6 m) intervals.
5. Refer to UFAS section 4.9 Stairs for more information on handrailings.

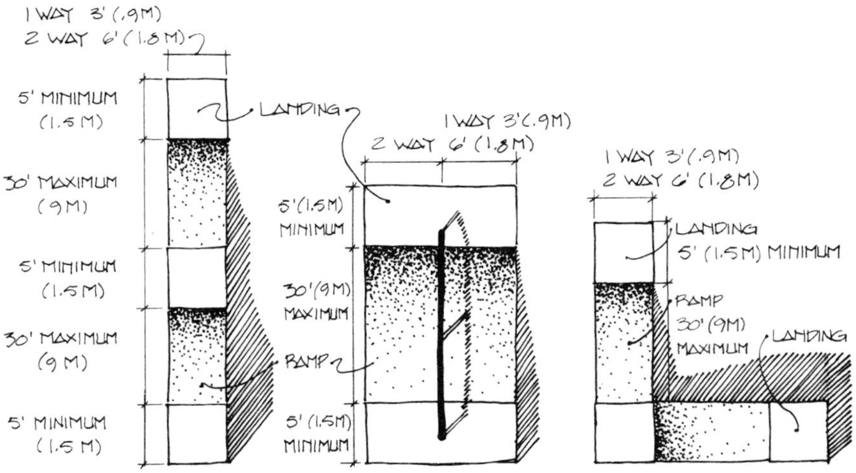

1 WAY 3' (.9M)
2 WAY 6' (1.8M)
5' MINIMUM (1.5 M)
30' MAXIMUM (9M)
5' MINIMUM (1.5M)
30' MAXIMUM (9 M)
5' MINIMUM (1.5 M)
LANDING
RAMP
5'(1.5M) MINIMUM
30'(9M) MAXIMUM
5'(1.5M) MINIMUM
1 WAY 3'(.9M)
2 WAY 6' (1.8M)
1 WAY 3'(.9M)
2 WAY 6' (1.8M)
LANDING
5' (1.5M) MINIMUM
RAMP
30' (9M) MAXIMUM
LANDING

Figure 240-9 Typical ramp configurations. Regardless of the ramp configuration, all inclines and landings should be sufficiently dimensioned.

4.5 Walls, Benches, and Outdoor Seating

Walls, benches, and other forms of outdoor seating are important outdoor elements for all people. Reasons to sit vary widely, and readily available places to sit are often crucial. It is important to recognize the diversity of need among individuals.

The detailing of outdoor seating for accommodation of handicapped individuals is often overlooked in environmental design. Elderly people, for example, require arm rests when getting into or out of a seated position. Heel space is also necessary to make rising from a seated position easier (Figures 240-11 and 240-12). Wheelchair users often desire places to stop and rest and places to set packages.

Walls with or without handrailings can aid negotiation, providing both physical and psychological support for people. For the elderly, a wall height of 18 to 22 in (450 to 550 mm) for seating is preferable to lower heights because lower heights require greater strength to use and sometimes become a hazard if not seen. Wall heights of 24 to 36 in (600 to 1000 mm) provide a surface to lean against in a half-sitting position. This is sometimes preferred by those with limited strength. This height is also good for wheelchair users to set packages on.

Additional Recommendations:

1. Outdoor seating should be maintained and kept free of dirt and debris.
2. Seat surfaces should be pitched to shed water.
3. Weep holes should not drain out on to walking surfaces where wetness or ice may constitute a hazard.
4. Refer to UFAS section 4.32 Seating, Ta-

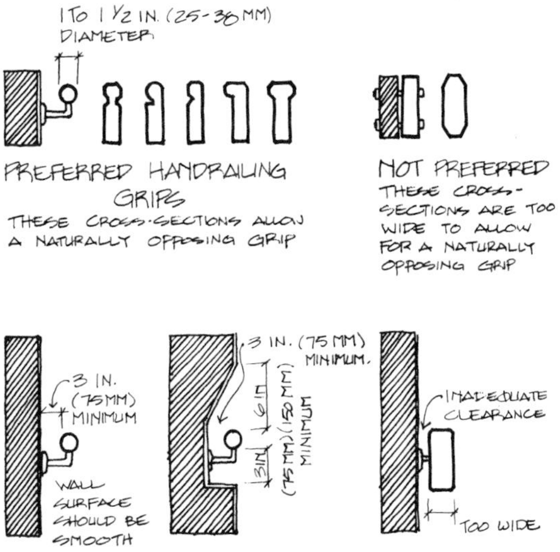

1 TO 1 1/2 IN. (25-38 MM) DIAMETER
PREFERRED HANDRAILING GRIPS
THESE CROSS-SECTIONS ALLOW A NATURALLY OPPOSING GRIP
NOT PREFERRED
THESE CROSS-SECTIONS ARE TOO WIDE TO ALLOW FOR A NATURALLY OPPOSING GRIP
3 IN. (75MM) MINIMUM
WALL SURFACE SHOULD BE SMOOTH
3 IN. (75 MM) MINIMUM.
6 IN (150 MM) MINIMUM
3 IN (75 MM)
INADEQUATE CLEARANCE
TOO WIDE

Figure 240-10 Handrailing cross sections. The cross section of a handrailing should be designed to allow a firm, prehensile grasp.

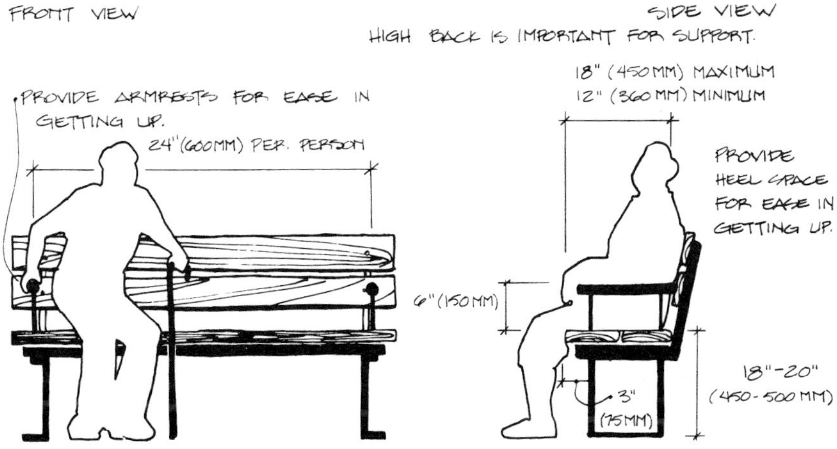

FRONT VIEW
SIDE VIEW
HIGH BACK IS IMPORTANT FOR SUPPORT.
18" (450MM) MAXIMUM
12" (360 MM) MINIMUM
PROVIDE ARMRESTS FOR EASE IN GETTING UP.
24"(600MM) PER. PERSON
PROVIDE HEEL SPACE FOR EASE IN GETTING UP.
6"(150MM)
18"-20" (450-500MM)
3" (75MM)

Figure 240-11 Typical bench requirements. Benches should be designed to facilitate individuals with limited strength. Armrests and adequate heelspace are especially important details.

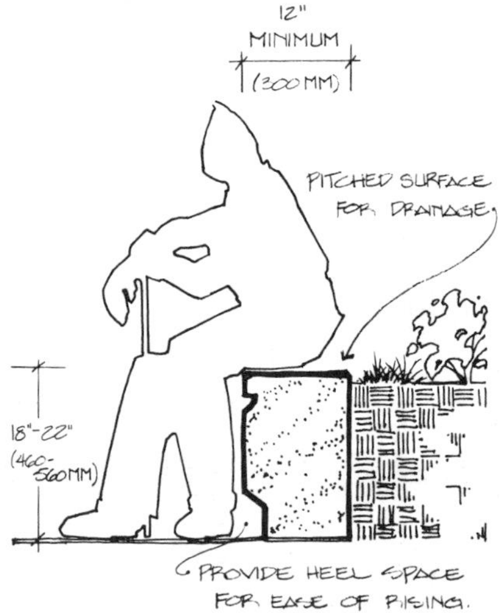
12"
MINIMUM
(300 MM)
PITCHED SURFACE
FOR DRAINAGE
18"-22"
(460-560MM)
PROVIDE HEEL SPACE
FOR EASE OF RISING.

Figure 240-12 Typical seating wall requirements. Although wall heights can vary, all should be designed to facilitate use by a wide range of user types.

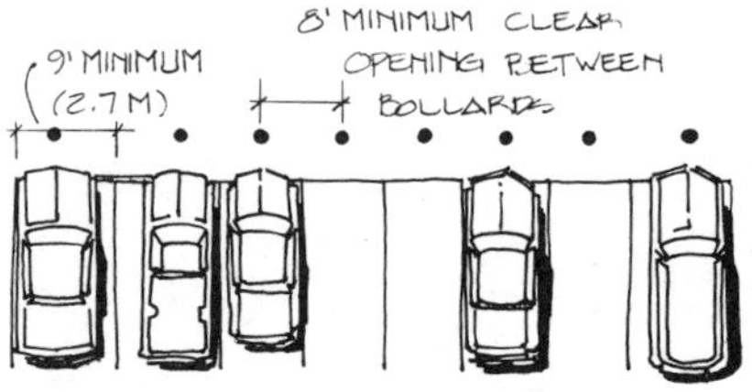
9' MINIMUM
(2.7 M)
8' MINIMUM CLEAR
OPENING BETWEEN
BOLLARDS

Figure 240-13 Bollard placement. Bollards should be placed to minimize obstruction to pedestrian flow, including transverse flow from parking areas.

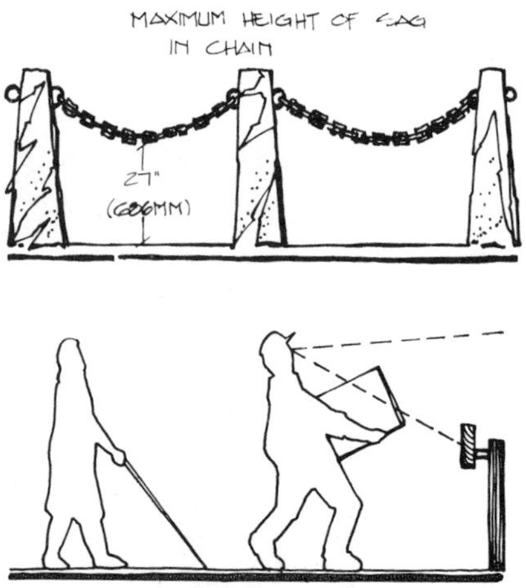
MAXIMUM HEIGHT OF SAG
IN CHAIN
27"
(686MM)

Figure 240-14 Chain barriers and guardrails. Chain barriers can be very hazardous and should be used only with a high degree of discretion. Chains that sag below 27 inches (686 mm) in height are detectable by cane but are often unseen by others, especially the elderly. Guardrails must be high enough to be easily seen, but rail must be detectable within a 27-in (686-mm) clear maximum height range.

bles, and Work Surfaces for more information on wheelchair clearances, table heights, etc.

4.6 Walkway Furnishings and Street Crossings

Walkway Furnishings:

Walkways should be designed to accommodate a wide diversity of people, including those with visual and mobility impairments. Walkway furnishings should be carefully organized for safety and easier negotiation for those with visual impairments. Furnishings should be easily detectable by cane, either in themselves or by way of a hazard strip. A hazard strip (linear textured surface) can be used to separate walkway furnishings from clear walking space. (Refer to 4.1 Walkways and Paved Surfaces in this section for more information on tactile warning strips.)

Bollards, or post barriers, should not be placed in the main line of pedestrian travel and should be centered on parking stalls, when applicable, to allow free pedestrian travel to and from parking areas (Figure 240-13). The same principle applies to trees, light standards, parking meters, and the like.

Chain barriers can be hazardous to pedestrians, bicyclists, and motorcyclists since these barriers are difficult to see, especially when lower than 32 in (790 mm) in height, and especially at night (Figure 240-14). Chains at a height of 27 in (670 mm) or less are more easily detected by visually impaired cane users. Discretion should be used when designing chain barriers, and a means should be devised to increase their detection by all people.

Guardrails are also potentially hazardous if improperly designed. They should be constructed high enough to be easily seen but should also be designed for easy detection by those who are visually impaired (Figure 240-14).

Additional Recommendations:

1. Provide ample seating along walkways with places to stop and rest and places to set packages.
2. Provide trash receptacles that are easy to use by those who are handicapped (Figure 240-15). Open-top varieties are easiest to use but allow snow and rain to collect. Semiopen tops prevent entry of snow and rain and are relatively easy to use. Hinged-door varieties prevent entry of snow and rain, but their operation is difficult for some people.
3. For information on drinking fountains, refer to UFAS section 4.15 Drinking Fountains and Water Coolers.
4. For information on telephones, refer to UFAS section 4.31 Telephones.
5. Refer to UFAS section 4.4 Protruding Objects for more information.

Street Crossings:

1. Provide visual and textural cues to advertise the location of crosswalks. [Refer to 4.1 Walkways and Paved Surfaces in this section and ANSI A117.1 (1986) sections 4.7.7 and 4.27 for more information on tactile warnings.]
2. Provide crosswalk widths that are as wide or wider than adjacent sidewalks.

4.7 Parking and Passenger Loading Zones

The number of handicapped parking spaces necessary per parking lot depends on the frequency of need. Some facilities require a greater than normal number, but always at least one accessible parking space per lot. The Uniform Federal Accessibility Standard for accessible parking spaces (see Table in section 4.1 of UFAS) was derived from many state and local building codes. This reference table represents an adequate minimum for most types of facilities.

Additional Recommendations:

1. Passenger loading zones should be adequately dimensioned to allow room for doors, movement of wheelchairs, etc.
2. Provide clear signage for handicapped parking spaces and loading zones.
3. Consult state and local building codes.
4. Refer to UFAS section 4.6 Parking and

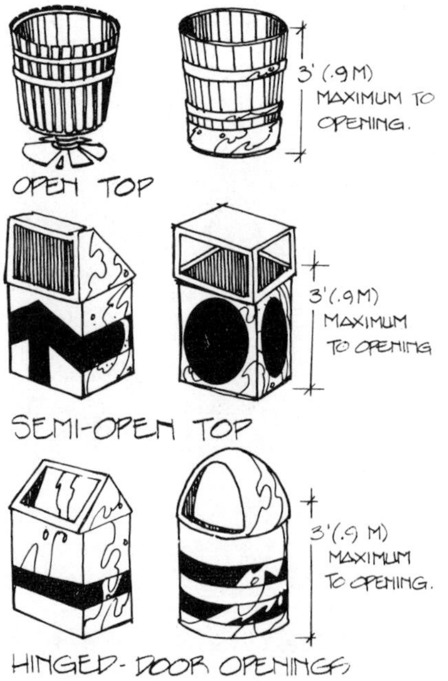
3' (.9 M)
MAXIMUM TO
OPENING.
OPEN TOP
3' (.9 M)
MAXIMUM
TO OPENING
SEMI-OPEN TOP
3' (.9 M)
MAXIMUM
TO OPENING.
HINGED-DOOR OPENINGS

Figure 240-15 Trash receptacles. Trash receptacle designs have various advantages and disadvantages depending on the climate and situation, including ease of use and exclusion of rain or snow.

Passenger Loading Zones for more information.

4.8 Bus Shelters and Lifts

All bus shelters should have an unobstructed view of arriving vehicular traffic for both standing and seated individuals. The drop-off zone should be part of an extensive pedestrian accessible network.

The street adjacent to accessible bus stops should not have a high crown which would cause the bus lift to tilt, and the curb upon which the lift descends should be low enough to allow full deployment of the lift. A maximum curb height of 8 in (190 mm) allows for the operation of standard lifts (Figure 240.16).

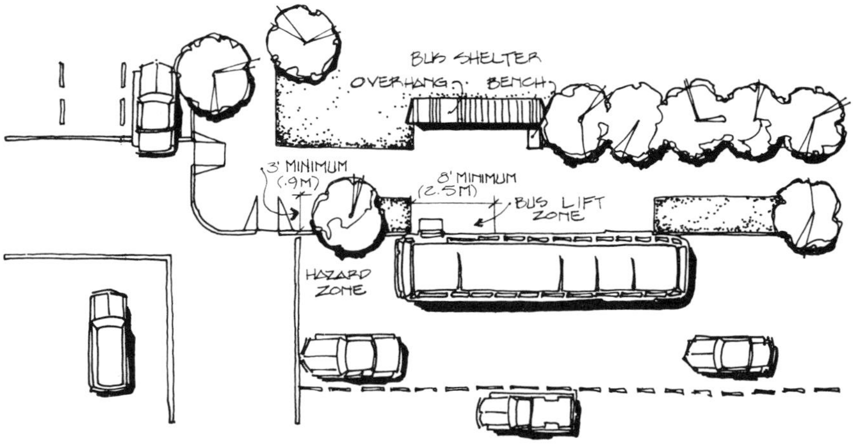
BUS SHELTER
OVERHANG
BENCH
3' MINIMUM (.9M)
8' MINIMUM (2.5M)
BUS LIFT ZONE
HAZARD ZONE

Figure 240-16 Accessible bus stop. Bus stops should be part of an accessible pedestrian network and include an area designed for deployment of a lift. A clear view of approaching buses should be maintained.

Additional Recommendations:

1. Eliminate obstructions such as newspaper boxes, benches, planters, tree gratings, mailboxes, guy wires, or sprinkler heads from the lift area to allow full deployment of the lift.

2. Refer to UFAS sections 4.6 Parking and Passenger Loading Zones and 4.11 Platform Lifts for more information.

4.9 Outdoor Plantings and Gardens

Plantings:

Plants can effectively be used to control the movement of pedestrians through public spaces and to keep unwary individuals away from hazardous areas.

Individuals with visual impairments can be greatly helped by careful placement of plant materials. Visual cues such as strong contrasts or the use of strikingly silhouetted forms can aid orientation for those with limited vision. Tactile cues are also useful for those who are visually impaired.

Plantings along public walkways should not constitute a potential hazard or nuisance. Species with branches that characteristically break under ice or snow, produce excessive litter, droop down over walkways, produce dangerous thorns, or produce poisonous or slippery fruits should be used with discretion (Table 240-1, page 240-10).

Microclimate control is especially important for elderly and handicapped people. Plant materials can be used to mitigate the discomforting effects of wind, glare, reflection, temperature, and humidity (Figure 240-17). Plantings along walkways can be designed to control snow drifting and to encourage the clearing of snow from walkway surfaces by directing and modifying the wind flow. (Refer to Olgyay, *Design With Climate,* listed in the References at the end of this section.)

Elderly people typically have the visual problem of diminished depth perception and a slower adjustment to abrupt changes in light. With careful planting or other means, harsh transitions between areas of bright sunlight and deep shade can be softened (Figure 240-18).

WINDS DIVERTED
SHADE FROM DIRECT AND REFLECTED SUNLIGHT

Figure 240-17 Microclimatic comfort. Microclimate control is especially important for elderly people, who are adversely affected by bright light, glare, cold drafts, and excessive heat. On warm, sunny days, for instance, a lightly shaded area without windiness is a preferred environment.

Speech is often difficult to hear, especially by the elderly, who have trouble segregating simultaneous sounds. Unwanted noise sources near outdoor conversation areas should be buffered wherever possible (Figure 240-19). Refer to Section 570: Sound Control in this handbook for more information.

Gardens:

Gardens are an important source of enjoyment for all people and should be designed with consideration for all, including those with visual and mobility impairments.

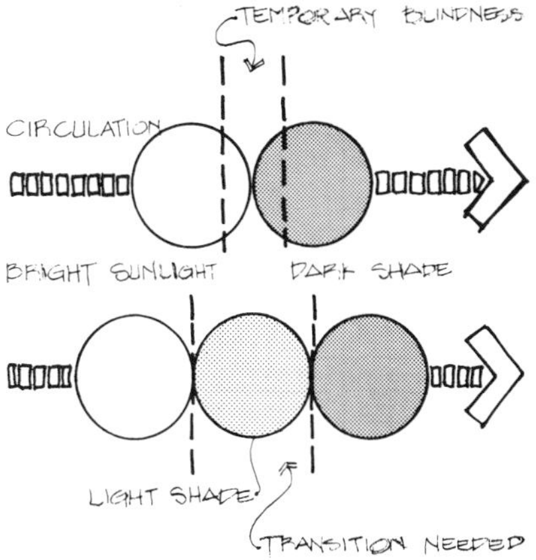
TEMPORARY BLINDNESS
CIRCULATION
BRIGHT SUNLIGHT
DARK SHADE
LIGHT SHADE
TRANSITION NEEDED

Figure 240-18 Transition between dark and sunlit areas. As a function of aging, visual response to abrupt changes in light intensity becomes slower. Careful choice and placement of trees, arbors, trelliswork, and similar devices can soften the transition between darkly shaded and brightly sunlit areas.

TABLE 240-1
Hazardous and Noxious Plant Species

Hazard/nuisance	*Species*	*Comments*
Poisonous plants 	Holly, yew, privet, laurel, rhododendron	Children may be tempted to sample bright-colored berries or leaves.
Debris:		
Fruits and nuts 	Crab apple, plum, cherry, oak, chestnut, hickory, walnut	Long, straplike rods, berries, cones, and nuts can be slippery or difficult to walk on. They are easily tracked into buildings and can stain clothing if sat upon.
Cones 	Pines, spruce, fir, larch, hemlock	Cones, while having many decorative uses, can cause problems for pedestrians and small-wheeled vehicles on walkway surfaces.
Seed pods 	Sweetgum, sycamore, London plane tree, honey locust, maple	Pods create unsure footing for pedestrians and hinder the movements of small-wheeled vehicles.
Branch breakage 	Birch, silver maple, box elder, horse chestnut, poplar, willow, tulip tree, elm	Branch debris is difficult to walk on or to push small-wheeled vehicles over. Large branches can cause extensive damage to items on which they might happen to fall, such as cars, small wood-frame structures, etc.
Drooping branches 	Birch willow, fin oak, beech, magnolia	Branches can drop below minimum clearances on walkways or streets causing facial or eye injuries to pedestrians and hazards for motorists.
Shallow roots 	Willow, red maple, silver maple, beech, cottonwood, poplar varieties	Surface root systems can cause walks to heave and break apart, and pedestrians may trip and fall. Uneven or broken surfaces can be extremely difficult for small-wheeled vehicles.
Odor 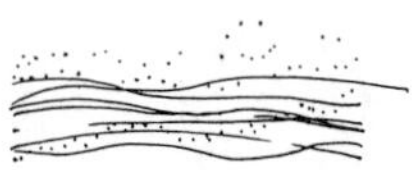	Siebold viburnum, female ginkgo	Foul-smelling odors not only degrade the aesthetic appeal of an area but also tend to make some people nauseous.
Thorns and spikes 	Barberry, quince, hawthorne, locust, holly, rose varieties, privet	Plants with thorns or spikes can be painful and dangerous to brush against or fall into. Leaves, twigs, and branches that fall to the ground can also be hazardous to people in light footwear or walking barefoot.
Insects and pests 	Fruit trees (crab apple, cherry, plum, etc.), mountain laurel	Because of the severe reaction certain people have to insect bites and stings, the location of plant materials which attract these pests are not recommended for areas near walks and sitting areas.

Source: Gary Robinette, ed., *Barrier Free Site Design,* Van Nostrand Reinhold, New York, 1985.

100' (30 M) OF DENSE VEGETATION IS MOST EFFECTIVE IF NO EARTH BERM IS PROVIDED
DENSE UNDERGROWTH
EARTH BERM

Figure 240-19 Noise buffer for easier outdoor conversation. As a function of aging, elderly people often lose their ability to clearly segregate simultaneous sounds. Outdoor conversation areas should be buffered from interfering noise whenever possible.

OPPORTUNITIES TO EXPLORE, DISCOVER, THE GARDEN.
INCENTIVE TO EXERCISE
PROVIDE TACTILE EXPERIENCES.

Figure 240-20 Gardens for elderly and handicapped people. Gardens and gardening can provide pleasure as well as incentive to exercise for people with disabilities and others who would benefit from higher levels of physical activity.

Suitably paved walking surfaces are necessary in gardens used by elderly or physically handicapped individuals (Figure 240-20). Safe opportunities to leave paved surfaces should also be provided where applicable. A sufficient number of places to sit and rest is very important.

Gardens as well as gardening can serve as an incentive, offering a challenge to exercise for elderly and handicapped individuals (Figure 240-20). Gardens provide excellent opportunities for personal growth and accomplishment. A pleasingly tactile environment is important in this regard. Opportunities to pick fruits, smell flowers, pull weeds, etc., should be provided. Raised platforms for potting, raised planting beds for nonstooping access, and horticultural opportunities at aboveground levels (e.g., berry picking from shrubs, dwarf fruit tree culture, upright flowering plants, and tall vegetables) should also be provided (Figure 240-20). Gardens which attract songbirds and other forms of wildlife are greatly enjoyed by all people.

Understanding the kinetospheres, or reach abilities, of elderly people and of people with limited abilities (especially wheelchair users) is important when designing gardens for use and maintenance by those who are handicapped. This is especially important in greenhouses, which offer year-round opportunities for gardening (Figure 240-21). Suitable space for maneuvering, proper levels for work surfaces, accessible tool storage, watering facilities, and adequate floor drainage should be provided. Proper maintenance of the facilities is necessary for safety and continued accessibility. (Refer to UFAS section 4.2 Space Allowances and Reach Ranges for dimensional criteria.)

4.10 Outdoor Lighting

Lighting is especially important in places potentially hazardous to elderly and handicapped people. Lighting schemes should be designed with fixtures and locations responsive to the more sensitive needs of those who are handicapped. Higher levels of illumination or a greater distribution of fixtures is beneficial to those with limited vision.

Many lighting standards are based on the eye level of the average standing adult. Wheelchair users have an eye level of approximately 3 ft 8 in (1190 mm). Posts and light standards should not be placed where they may present a potential hazard to handicapped pedestrians. Glare is a problem that is especially troublesome to elderly people and should be mitigated whenever possible.

Additional Recommendations:

1. Refer to Section 540: Outdoor Lighting, for detailed information on lamp characteristics, fixtures, and applications. Also consult lighting fixture manufacturers.

2. Refer to UFAS section 4.4 Protruding Objects for more information.

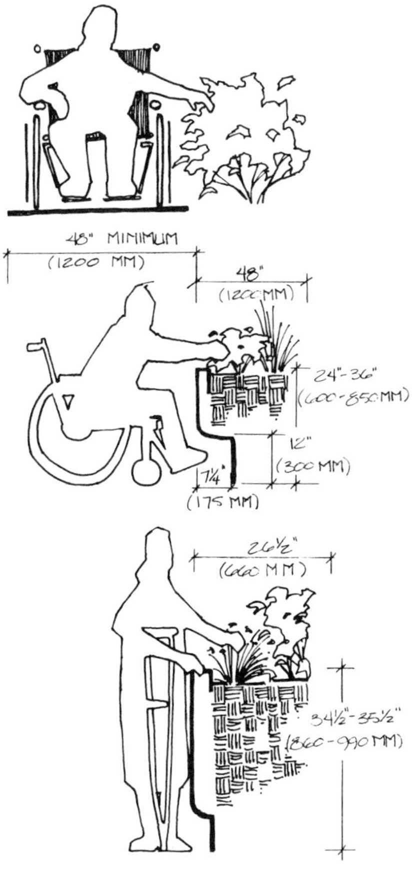
48" MINIMUM
(1200 MM)
48"
(1200 MM)
24"-36"
(600-850MM)
12"
(300 MM)
7¼"
(175 MM)
26½"
(660 MM)
34½"-35½"
(860-990 MM)

Figure 240-21 Raised plantings for individuals with reach limitations. Opportunities for individuals with reach limitations are important, especially for those requiring mobility aids.

4.11 Signage

Signage is a crucial aid to negotiation for all people. Essential functions include place identity, notice of accessibility, warnings, and directional information. All information must be clear and precise. Placement, scale, and graphic style are important.

Signage should be readily observable by all people, including those who are visually handicapped. Braille and raised or recessed letters are readable by the blind or partially sighted. Raised or routed letters are preferable to braille because only 10 percent of the blind population in the United States (1 percent of the total population) is able to read braille. Cassette tapes or audible tones are other possibilities with distinct advantages over written information, except for those with impaired hearing. Traffic signals and kiosks are especially amenable to audible signalization.

Braille strips can be added to the edges of signs that are reachable and located for that purpose. (Refer to UFAS section 4.30 Signage for dimensional criteria.)

Graphic symbols transmit messages quickly, but only if their meaning is readily understood. Symbols should not be too abstract, nor should they be the only means of communication, because they have no applicability for the blind.

Readability in signage is a function of comprehension, tone contrasts, character height, and character proportion. Design criteria for literal signage have been developed to facilitate easier readability. Table 240-2 illustrates the Canadian system for determining character height, based on reading distance for pedestrians.

Signage with a matt finish and color contrast between characters and background is most readable. A dark background with light letters is the easiest to read. (Refer to UFAS section 4.30 Signage for dimensional criteria, tone contrasts, symbols of accessibility, etc.)

TABLE 240-2
Character Height (Canadian System)

*Character × height, in (mm)**	*Reading distance, ft (m)*	*Traffic speed, mph (K/hr)*
0.20 (5)	10 (3.0)	Pedestrian
0.24 (6)	12 (3.7)	
0.32 (8)	16 (4.9)	
0.40 (10)	20 (6.2)	
0.48 (12)	24 (7.4)	
0.60 (15)	30 (9.2)	
0.80 (20)	40 (12.3)	
1.00 (25)	50 (15.4)	
1.20 (30)	60 (18.5)	
1.60 (40)	80 (24.6)	Vehicular
2.00 (50)	100 (30.0)	10–20 (3–6)
2.40 (60)	120 (37.0)	10–20 (3–6)
3.20 (80)	160 (49.3)	20–30 (6–9)
4.00 (100)	200 (61.6)	20–30 (6–9)
4.80 (120)	240 (73.9)	40–60 (12–19)
6.00 (150)	300 (92.4)	40–60 (12–19)
8.00 (200)	400 (123.2)	40–60 (12–19)

* Note: Character × height refers to the height of the lowercase "x" character in a particular font or typeface.

International Symbols:

The *international symbol of access* is widely used and recognized. It identifies where provisions have been made for handicapped access (Figure 240-22). Additionally, a standardized set of pictographs has been developed by a committee of the American Institute of Graphic Arts for the U.S. Department of Transportation. This system, called *Symbol Signs,* is also recognized internationally (Figure 240-23).

Placement of Signage:

Placement of signage is important. Signage for sighted people is most easily seen at approximately eye level, but areas frequented often by wheelchair users may warrant placing signage at a lower level. Reading distance determines where it should be placed (see Table 240-2). Signs should not be obscured or confused with other graphics and should be easily recognized for what they represent. Signage intended for those with visual impairments should be well lit and/or located for easy access and touch (Figure 240-24).

Site-related areas requiring signage include public lavatories, handicapped parking areas, vehicular and pedestrian circulation routes, accessible points of buildings and facilities, and accessible rest stops.

Many situations require a system of sequential signs. Hospitals, college campuses, and other institutions should have posted signs, visual and textural cues, and pavement markings where applicable. Access to buildings or facilities with only one or two accessible entrances (or exits) should be clearly marked with sequential signage.

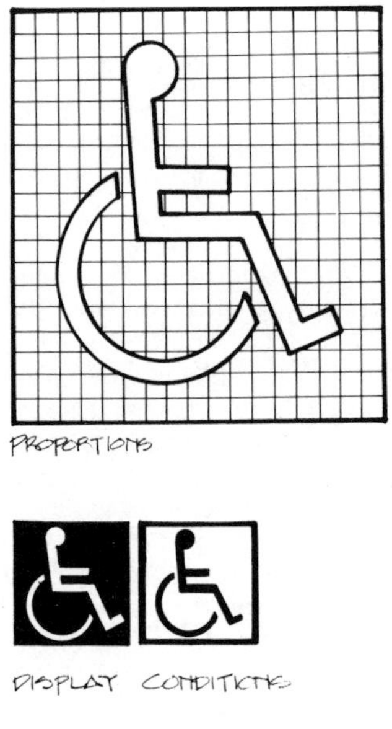
PROPORTIONS
DISPLAY CONDITIONS

Figure 240-22 International symbol of accessibility.

5.0 ACCESSIBLE RECREATION

Accessible recreation is an important aspect of accessible design. All people, regardless of their abilities, should be given ample opportunity to enjoy and recreate within environments free of barriers. Often, facilities are designed inadequately to accommodate individuals with physical or mental limitations or are designed to provide only minimal access.

A common argument against accessible design of recreational areas is the claim that accessibility destroys the natural character of landscape and consequently impairs the quality of the experience for those who are using the site. This argument stems from too coarse an understanding of human abilities. It is too often assumed that handicapped individuals are either bound to wheelchairs or blind. Most individuals with physical or mental impairments can negotiate and enjoy the same environments enjoyed by the remainder of the population. Individuals who are completely blind can also negotiate and enjoy a diverse range of recreational opportunities, provided that some environmental or personal assistance is available.

It is also too often assumed that the desire for exciting, challenging, adventurous recreational opportunities is somewhat less intense in handicapped individuals than it is in the able-bodied. This assumption apparently stems from a belief that people with handicaps find the normal, everyday environment quite formidable enough. But the fact is that handicapped individuals vary as widely as do the able-bodied in their abilities and desires to meet new challenges.

The solution to the problem of access in recreational areas rests with (1) the understanding that all people, including those who are handicapped, strongly desire and rightly deserve high-quality recreational experiences and (2) the understanding that there is a wide range of ability in the handicapped population and that the natural character of landscape need not always be compromised in recreational design. In some instances, to be sure, the natural character of landscape would be compromised by accessible design, but all recreational areas need not become totally barrier-free. Accessible design in recreation areas requires a diversity of quality expe-

I
II
III
IV
P

Public Services I
1 Telephone
2 Mail
3 Currency Exchange
4 Cashier
5 First Aid
6 Lost and Found
7 Coat Check
8 Baggage Lockers
9 Escalator
10 Stairs
11 Elevator
12 Toilets, Men
13 Toilets, Women
14 Toilets
15 Nursery
16 Drinking Fountain
17 Waiting Room
18 Information
19 Hotel Information
20 Air Transportation
21 Heliport
22 Taxi
23 Bus
24 Ground Transportation
25 Rail Transportation
26 Water Transportation

Concessions II
27 Car Rental
28 Restaurant
29 Coffee Shop
30 Bar
31 Shops
32 Barber Shop/Beauty Salon
33 Barber Shop
34 Beauty Salon

Processing Activities III
35 Ticket Purchase
36 Baggage Check-in
37 Baggage Claim
38 Customs
39 Immigration
40 Departing Flights
41 Arriving Flights

Regulations IV
42 Smoking
43 No Smoking
44 Parking
45 No Parking
46 No Dogs
47 No Entry
48 Exit
49 Fire Extinguisher
50 Litter Disposal

Figure 240-23 (*Above*) Pictographs. These symbol signs are recognized internationally as substitutes for literal signage and are especially useful for those who are illiterate in either their own language or a foreign language.

Figure 240-24 (*Below*) Placement of outdoor signage. Accessible signage refers to graphic information that is accessible to everyone regardless of mobility impairment, and also includes accommodation for those with visual impairments and learning impairments.

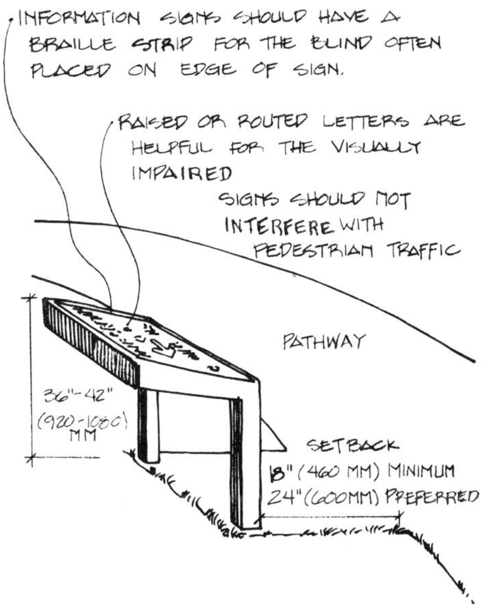
INFORMATION SIGNS SHOULD HAVE A BRAILLE STRIP FOR THE BLIND OFTEN PLACED ON EDGE OF SIGN.
RAISED OR ROUTED LETTERS ARE HELPFUL FOR THE VISUALLY IMPAIRED
SIGNS SHOULD NOT INTERFERE WITH PEDESTRIAN TRAFFIC
PATHWAY
36"-42" (920-1080) MM
SETBACK
18" (460 MM) MINIMUM
24" (600MM) PREFERRED

rience, not an absolute standardization of all facilities.

Faced with the seeming incompatibility between accessible design and a natural landscape experience, in 1979 the Minnesota Department of Natural Resources (MDNR) devised a comprehensive scheme for accommodating all types of people, regardless of their abilities, in a statewide recreational model. Recognizing both the considerable landscape diversity in the state and the widely varying physical abilities among all people, handicapped or not, the MDNR worked to "provide recreational opportunities for all persons in the state . . . providing diverse physical access and program availability in as many areas as is possible which have the most potential for utilization by all persons, including persons with disabilities." One of the consequences of this objective was a systematic approach to trail planning in the state (see Table 240-3 and Figure 240-25).

Some handicapped groups are best accommodated by specific design criteria. For instance, it is preferable to provide audible information for those with visual impairments, visual information for those with hearing impairments, and eye level information for those who use wheelchairs. Going beyond regulated standards, it is important to establish processes which allow and encourage people with handicaps to explore their capabilities fully—i.e., processes that provide a wide spectrum of opportunities.

Recreational areas and programs vary greatly; standardization of facilities is therefore difficult because of the diversity of people involved. The process must involve a positive attitude and awareness, the minimization of physical barriers, the

TABLE 240-3
Trail Planning Classifications

Class of trail	*I*	*II*	*III*	*IV*	*V*
Approximate length of trail	0–¼ mi	¼–1 mi	1–3 mi	3–10 mi	Over 10 mi
Rest stop spacing and types (use natural materials whenever possible for benches, shelters, etc.)	100–150 ft benches, shelter, interpretation	200–300 ft benches,* shelter, interpretation	500–600 ft natural benches occasionally, interpretation	Rest area or interpretation every 1 mi	None unless unique interpretation
Width of trail	1-way: 4 ft 2-way: 6 ft	1-way: 3–4 ft 2-way: 4–5 ft	3–4 ft	2–3 ft	Undefined
Shoulder of trail	1½ ft grass; slight slope toward trail	Clear understory brush to 1 ft from trail; gradual slope either direction	Clear understory brush to 1 ft from trail; no abrupt dropoffs adjacent	Clear understory brush to ½ ft from trail	Undefined
Slope of trail	1:50	1:20 with 5 ft level space at 100 ft intervals	1:12 with 5 ft level space at 30 ft intervals	1:8 with occasional level space when possible	Steps or natural
Cross slope	None	1:50 for maximum of 30 ft and varied from one side of trail to other	1:25 for maximum of 50 ft, vary from side to side	1:20	Undefined
Surface of trail	Concrete, asphalt	Asphalt, perpendicular wood planking, very fine crushed rock solidly packed	Firm surface, well-compacted	Bound woodchips, class 5 gravel mixture coarse	Sandy, rough unbound wood chips, rocks
Trail edge (rails, curbs, etc.; use natural materials whenever possible)	Curbs used where necessary for safety; 3-ft (1-m) high rails for safety or for resting along lineal slope where necessary	Gradual ramping; rails for resting along lineal slope and to provide safety on cross slope or hazard area	Compacted earth, level with trail edge; definite texture change. Rails for holding slope at steepest grade and for safety	Texture change with immediate drop to natural terrain from trail edge; rails used to guard hazard	Nothing

* Benches refers either to the commercial type or a big log or boulders suitable for sitting.

Source: From the Minnesota Department of Natural Resources.

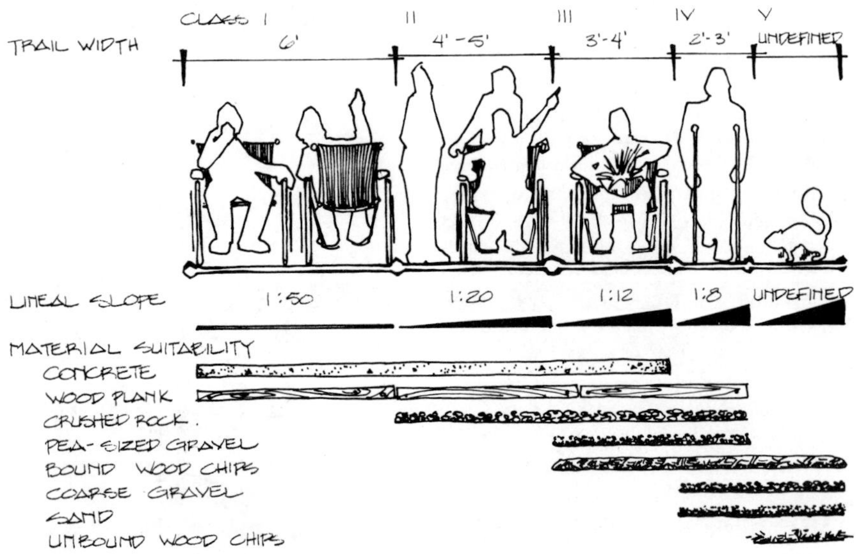
CLASS I
II
III
IV
V
TRAIL WIDTH
6'
4'-5'
3'-4'
2'-3'
UNDEFINED
LINEAL SLOPE
1:50
1:20
1:12
1:8
UNDEFINED
MATERIAL SUITABILITY
CONCRETE
WOOD PLANK
CRUSHED ROCK
PEA-SIZED GRAVEL
BOUND WOOD CHIPS
COARSE GRAVEL
SAND
UNBOUND WOOD CHIPS

Figure 240-25 Trail classification system. This recreation trail classification system was developed by the Minnesota Department of Natural Resources as part of a comprehensive scheme to accommodate all types of people in a statewide recreation model. The five trail classifications represent "graduated difficulty" in terms of accessibility.

development of programs, and the involvement of many participants. Design standards and concepts must be considered in relation to each recreational facility, program, and participant. Designers must come to understand the needs and abilities of people with handicaps and must study the full range of possibilities at any recreational facility. Only after such understanding is it possible to program within the limits of the facility.

Despite the inherent problems of standardization, a systematic approach to facility and program development would most likely facilitate higher-quality developments. Regardless of the facility or part thereof, quality is necessary to realize the purpose intended. Designing a facility with varying degrees of accessibility is a good approach because it allows all individuals to explore the full range of their abilities.

5.1 Hiking Trails

General:

The two primary objectives of the hiking experience—the physical negotiation of landscape and the enjoyment of natural beauty—should be met in a diverse way for all potential users of a trail system. A realistic challenge for those with mobility impairments and a high-quality sensory experience for those with visual impairments should not be overlooked.

The greatest diversity of people can be accommodated not by a simple, dual system of trails (that is, one for handicapped individuals and one for the able-bodied) but rather by providing a wider range of opportunity—a wider variety of trail types and challenges to choose from. Such a system also minimizes social segregation between user groups.

Signage:

Signage should be compatible with the type of trail for which it is intended. In terms of extent, prominance, style, and message, signage should reflect the character of the particular trail experience. All potentially hazardous areas should be clearly marked, and in many cases include a means for safeguarding visitors.

Trail Planning Classification System:

Table 240-3 and Figure 240-25 illustrate a trail planning classification system and accompanying guidelines for a varying degree of accessibility in trail types. This system is an example of what can be done to provide quality recreational opportunities for all people without compromising the natural landscape experience for most, if any at all.

5.2 Interpretive Trails

General:

Design solutions for interpretive experiences should not only provide physical accessibility but also facilitate full enjoyment and comprehension of the environment by the greatest diversity of people. A system of graduated difficulty of access is an excellent way of providing healthy challenges and a diversity of experience for people with varying interests and abilities.

Signage:

A comprehensive system of signs along interpretive trails is crucial. Essential messages *at the beginning of the trail system* should include:

1. A map in raised relief accompanied by raised or routed letters of all trails and their respective lengths

2. A difficulty-of-access classification (or comparable description) for each trail

3. A general description of each trail, including its emphasis, character, and main features

4. A description of locations where users can expect to find additional signs along each trail

5. The meaning of special signals such as textural changes on trails, etc.

Essential messages *along the trails* should include:

1. Locations of special areas for rest, comfort, special features, danger, etc.

2. Descriptions of events and places, special features, things to view, touch, smell, or hear, etc.

Signage should accommodate both those with visual impairments and the sighted population. Raised or recessed letters are preferable to braille. Prerecorded messages can be either locally activated or contained in continuously worn headsets activated within a specified range.

Orienting devices such as high rope lines, textural cues, and barriers are beneficial and can ensure a reasonable level of safety. Knotted ropes or other periodic cues can both call out features and also serve as distance meters.

5.3 Outdoor Camping and Picnicking

Camping:

A variety of outdoor camping facilities should be provided to accommodate people with varying abilities. A degree of *remoteness* is typically characteristic of the camping experience and can be maintained by allotting suitable acreages for each facility. Potable water and comfort facilities should be provided within a reasonable distance of each facility. Medical accommodation of some kind should also be readily available. A diversity of recreational opportunities at or near the camping site itself, such as swimming, fishing, and remote hiking, is beneficial.

Campsites should not be located near potentially hazardous areas. Hazardous obstructions and items—such as deadfalls, low-hanging branches, holes in the ground, poisonous plants, or thorns—should not exist near campsites. High-use areas—such as shelters, comfort stations, swimming pools, beaches, campsites, and food areas—should be located on relatively level ground that is easy to negotiate (Figures 240-26 and 240-27).

The unique experience of camping may suggest using a different type of signage system than that used for interpretive trail systems.

Picnicking:

Opportunities for picnicking should accommodate all types of people, regardless of their abilities. Ground surfaces at picnic sites should be relatively level, free of obstructions, and appropriate in both their surfacing and size for wheelchairs.

Picnic tables, work surfaces, and the like should be raised to accommodate wheelchairs. A clear space of 29 in (715 mm) minimum under tables is necessary. Table tops should have a maximum height of 34 in (840 mm). Potable water and comfort facilities should be located within a reasonable distance of picnic areas.

Cooking Facilities:

Fireplaces and grills should be raised 18 to 24 in (450 to 600 mm) off the ground for easier use by seated individuals (Figure 240-28). Grills are preferable to fireplaces because of fire control and the convenience of their grating. The top of the unit should be no more than 30 in (740 mm) high. Rotating grills are most accessible for those in wheelchairs. Placement on a hard, level ground surface is necessary.

Water faucets and drinking fountains should be 3 to 4 ft (1 to 1.2 m) in height and easily operable. (Refer to UFAS sections 4.15 Drinking Fountains and Water Coolers and 4.27 Controls and Operating Mechanisms for more information on economic considerations of facility design.) Placement of fixtures on a hard, relatively level ground surface is recommended. Adequate drainage is important.

5.4 Swimming Facilities

Swimming Pools:

The advantages of pools over beaches include the control they afford over water

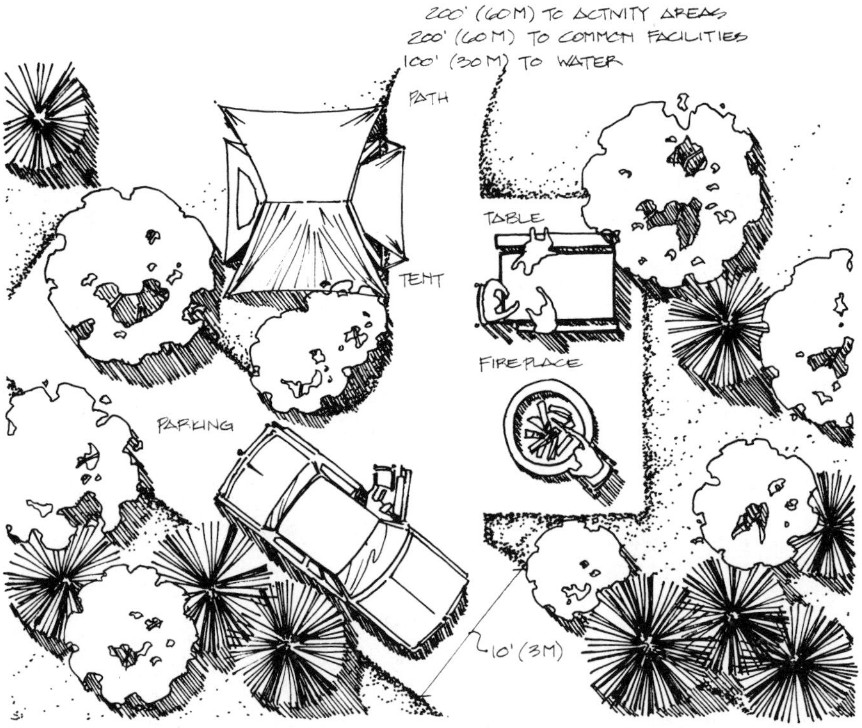
200' (60M) TO ACTIVITY AREAS
200' (60M) TO COMMON FACILITIES
100' (30M) TO WATER
PATH
TABLE
TENT
FIREPLACE
PARKING
10' (3M)

Figure 240-26 Typical accessible campsite (plan view). Campsites should be organized to provide varying degrees of challenge and remoteness.

WALKS AT 4'(1.2M) MINIMUM WIDTH
CAMPSITE FREE OF POISONOUS PLANTS
FIREPLACE LOCATED DOWNWIND OF TABLE, TENT AND TREES
18"-24" (.46-.6M)
6"(150 MM)

Figure 240-27 Typical accessible campsite.

EXTRAWIDE BACKS AND ARMS ALLOW ADDITIONAL SPACE FOR UTENSILS, PLATES, ETC.
18" (460 MM) MINIMUM GRATE HEIGHT
24"-30" (610-760MM)

Figure 240-28 Typical accessible fireplace and grill. Ground surfaces around campsites and fireplaces should be stabilized and free-draining.

depth, water temperature, and sanitation. The disadvantages of pools include their questionable environmental ambience and their hard and slippery edges and surfaces, high noise levels, and size limitations. Swimming pools should be designed to accommodate a wide variety of people.

Additional Recommendations:

1. A pool coping at sitting height, with grab bars, will allow easier access to the water for many individuals. The water level should not be too far below the coping.

2. A ramp descending into the water, with handrails on both sides at a height of 36 in (890 mm), should be provided at the shallow end of the pool. The ramp should have a curb edging and a nonslip surface.

3. A staircase descending into the water, also with handrails, should be provided at the shallow end of the pool. *Tiered transfer platforms* are recommended (Figure 240-29).

4. Underwater seating is necessary for resting and for those with limited mobility. The seating should be easily identifiable and should be isolated from swimmers jumping into the water from above.

5. Mechanical lifts and swings are commercially available for raising and lowering individuals into the water.

6. A deep pool should not be specified unless diving is an objective. Floats and markings should warn swimmers of increasing water depth.

7. No sharp or protruding objects should exist anywhere, and all corners should be rounded. All paving near the pool should have a nonslip surface. Figure 240-30 shows an indoor pool designed according to the above-mentioned recommendations.

Beaches:

The advantages of beaches over swimming pools include their gradual water depth, their lack of slippery surfaces or hard edges, and the psychological benefit of an outdoor, natural environment. Waves, sunlight, breezes, wildlife, fragrance, spaciousness, and the general ambience of the out-of-doors are qualities of incalculably beneficial value. Ideally, access to both a swimming pool and a nearby beach could accommodate the needs of all individuals and allow for diversity and flexibility in programming.

Additional Recommendations:

1. Accessibility to the beach from parking lots, shelters, camping grounds, picnic areas, and other points of origin should be provided. A network of accessible routes is necessary if handicapped individuals are to enjoy a wide range of recreational opportunities independently or with minimal assistance.

2. Beach gradients into the water should be 10 percent maximally. Drop-offs, abrupt bottom changes, bottom irregularities, obstructions, and sharp objects should not exist in the water or on the beach. Ramps, stairways, and boardwalks at the water's edge and leading into the water are important for many individuals (Figure 240-31). Connected floating buoys should be used to delineate the extent of the swimming area and to discourage entry to deeper water (Figure 240-32).

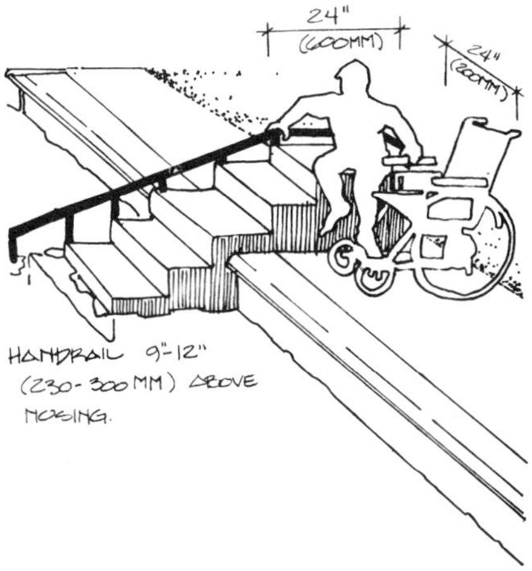
24" (600MM)
24" (600MM)
HANDRAIL 9"-12" (230-300 MM) ABOVE NOSING.

Figure 240-29 Tiered transfer platform for pools. Tiered transfer platforms allow easy entry into the pool from wheelchairs.

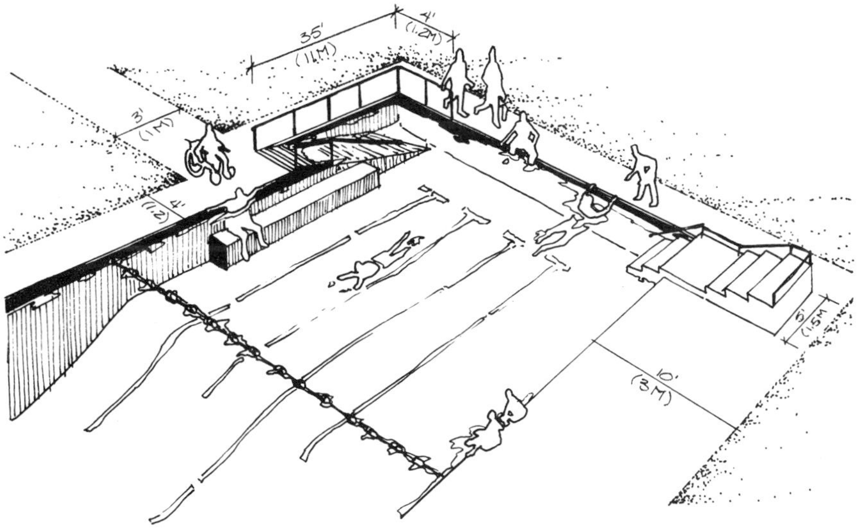
35' (11M)
4' (1.2M)
3' (1M)
4' (1.2)
5' (1.5M)
10' (3M)

Figure 240-30 General considerations for pool swimming. Note that a variety of means for entering the pool should be provided.

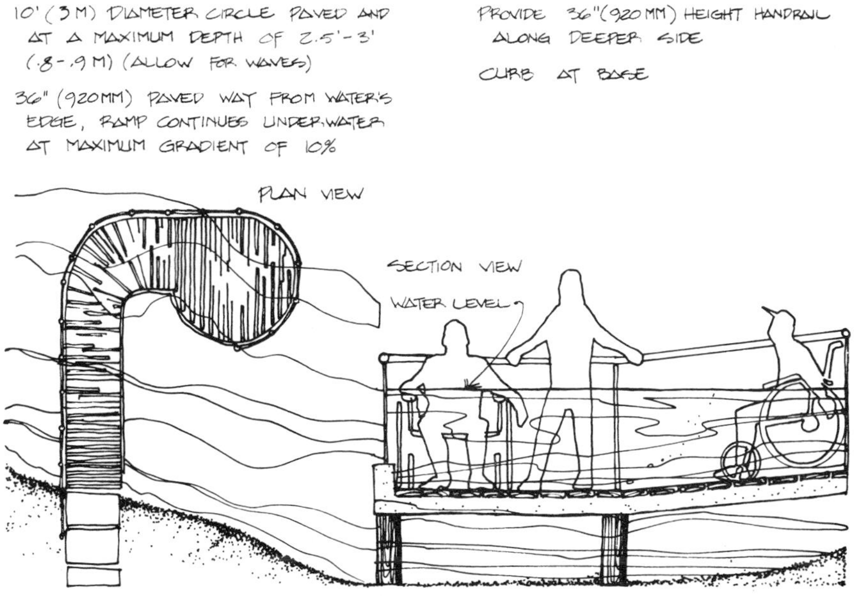
10' (3 M) DIAMETER CIRCLE PAVED AND AT A MAXIMUM DEPTH OF 2.5'-3' (.8-.9 M) (ALLOW FOR WAVES)
36" (920MM) PAVED WAY FROM WATER'S EDGE, RAMP CONTINUES UNDERWATER AT MAXIMUM GRADIENT OF 10%
PROVIDE 36"(920 MM) HEIGHT HANDRAIL ALONG DEEPER SIDE
CURB AT BASE
PLAN VIEW
SECTION VIEW
WATER LEVEL

Figure 240-31 Underwater ramp for beach swimming. The length of a ramped walk should be adjusted to the slope of the particular lake profile (10 percent maximum gradient), and should consider the size of anticipated waves.

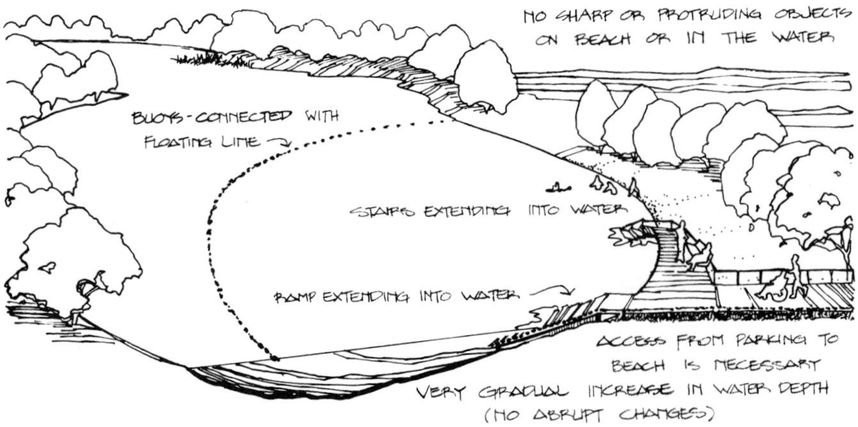
NO SHARP OR PROTRUDING OBJECTS ON BEACH OR IN THE WATER
BUOYS - CONNECTED WITH FLOATING LINE
STAIRS EXTENDING INTO WATER
RAMP EXTENDING INTO WATER
ACCESS FROM PARKING TO BEACH IS NECESSARY
VERY GRADUAL INCREASE IN WATER DEPTH (NO ABRUPT CHANGES)

Figure 240-32 General considerations for beach swimming.

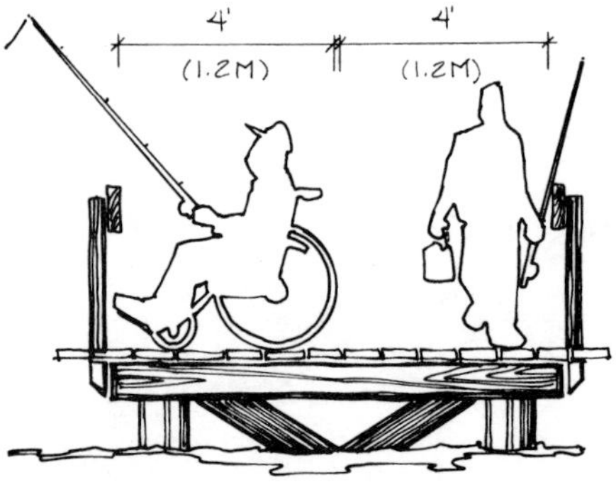
4'
(1.2M)
4'
(1.2M)

Figure 240-33 Accessible fishing docks and piers. The width of a fishing dock or pier should allow the free movement of pedestrians when wheelchairs are perpendicular to the side railing.

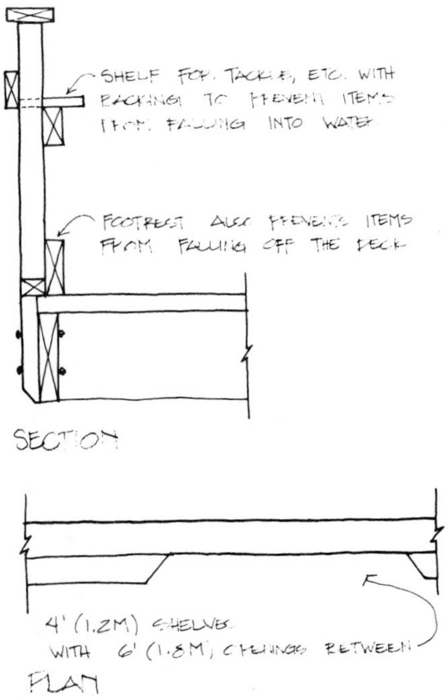
SHELF FOR TACKLE, ETC. WITH BACKING TO PREVENT ITEMS FROM FALLING INTO WATER
FOOTREST ALSO PREVENTS ITEMS FROM FALLING OFF THE DECK
SECTION
4' (1.2M) SHELVES WITH 6' (1.8M) OPENINGS BETWEEN
PLAN

Figure 240-34 Handrailing detail for a fishing dock or pier. Handrailings to accommodate wheelchair users should have a number of important features.

5.5 Fishing and Boating

Fishing:

Accessible networks leading to fishing waters are necessary, including access to fishing piers, docks, and boarding areas. Floating piers have the advantage of closeness to the water level but are often unstable, especially for those who use wheelchairs.

Additional Recommendations:

1. Fishing piers should be stable and of sufficient dimension to accommodate those who use wheelchairs (Figure 240-33). (Refer to UFAS section 4.2 Space Allowances and Reach Ranges, and 4.5 Ground and Floor Surfaces for more information.)

2. Handrailings on both sides of a dock or pier are recommended at a 36-in (890-mm) height and should include lower rails for additional safety.

3. Shelves at a height sufficient for wheelchairs are good for accommodating fishing gear, etc. Edging or footrails on docks and piers provide an added measure of safety and prevent items from falling into the water (Figure 240-34).

Boating:

Boarding a boat or small yacht is difficult, especially if the craft is small and buoyant. Railings are absolutely necessary and should extend beyond the edge or end of the dock, providing support to individuals even while aboard craft (Figure 240-35). Devices to stabilize the craft while individuals are boarding are very helpful. Supportive devices (grab bars, etc.) on the craft itself are also essential. However, railings or grab bars should not indiscriminately be *added* to a previously unequipped small craft, as the balance in its design may be adversely affected.

Heavy, wide-bottomed boats with a low center of gravity offer the greatest stability and safety. Pontoons and platform boats are ideal. Narrow, buoyant boats such as canoes are easy to capsize and especially difficult to board. Boarding on the beach and then shoving off is advisable.

Dock heights within 18 to 24 in (450 to 600 mm) of the water level allow easier access to boats than do greater heights. Tide fluctuation may have to be accommodated by means of ramps, stable floating platforms, and the like (Figure 240-36).

5.6 Spectator Areas

Spectator areas should be accessible by hard-surfaced ramps and safe stairways (Figure 240-37). (Refer to UFAS sections 4.8 Ramps and 4.9 Stairs for more information.)

Additional Recommendations:

1. Provide a choice in seating areas to whatever extent possible, including areas for extended legs and wheelchairs. Programming 2 percent of the total seating capacity for such use is normally adequate. Locate these areas near access ramps to minimize the need for negotiating through a crowd.

2. Protect special seating areas from excessive sun, wind, and rain to whatever extent possible.

3. Refer to UFAS section 4.33 Assembly Areas for more information on dimensional criteria, surfaces, access, etc.

5.7 Parks and Playgrounds

Parks and playgrounds should be accessible from adjacent communities and include a continuous *pedestrian accessible network* throughout. Hard surfaces to accommodate wheelchairs should be provided both to and within the parks and play areas in order to facilitate their use not only by handicapped children but also by handicapped parents. Accessible routes should be multifunctional to discourage social segregation between handicapped and able-bodied children. A system of graduated difficulty of access within the park or playground can provide a diversity of experiences and a healthy challenge to individuals as long as outright inaccessibility to focal areas does not exist.

The design should minimize the likelihood that able-bodied children would ostracize those with physical or learning impairments. Apparent differences in ability between children should not be emphasized in physical design solutions. Common playground apparatus and facilities are often adequate for handicapped individuals with or without some modification (Figure 240-38). Social interaction between groups is important.

Both structured play facilities and opportunities for creative, imaginative, nonstructured play are important features of a

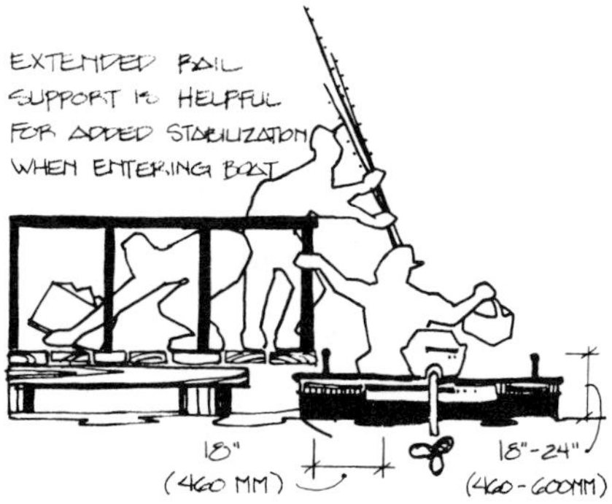
EXTENDED RAIL SUPPORT IS HELPFUL FOR ADDED STABILIZATION WHEN ENTERING BOAT
18" (460 MM)
18"-24" (460-600MM)

Figure 240-35 (*Above*) Boat access. Devices which provide support both on the dock and in the craft itself are of crucial importance. Dock heights should be within 18 to 24 in (460 to 610 mm) of the water to facilitate easier transference of people and gear from the boat to the dock.

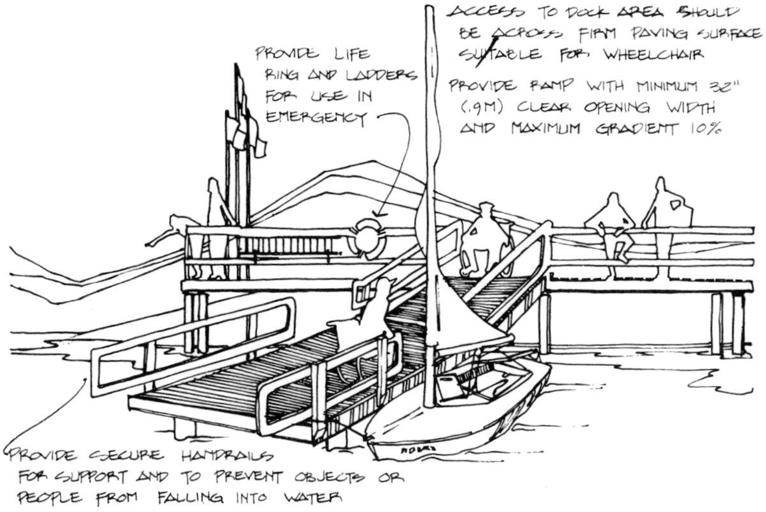
PROVIDE LIFE RING AND LADDERS FOR USE IN EMERGENCY
ACCESS TO DOCK AREA SHOULD BE ACROSS FIRM PAVING SURFACE SUITABLE FOR WHEELCHAIR
PROVIDE RAMP WITH MINIMUM 32" (.9M) CLEAR OPENING WIDTH AND MAXIMUM GRADIENT 10%
PROVIDE SECURE HANDRAILS FOR SUPPORT AND TO PREVENT OBJECTS OR PEOPLE FROM FALLING INTO WATER

Figure 240-36 (*Top right*) General considerations for boat launching areas. Boat launching areas for handicapped individuals require a variety of considerations and devices.

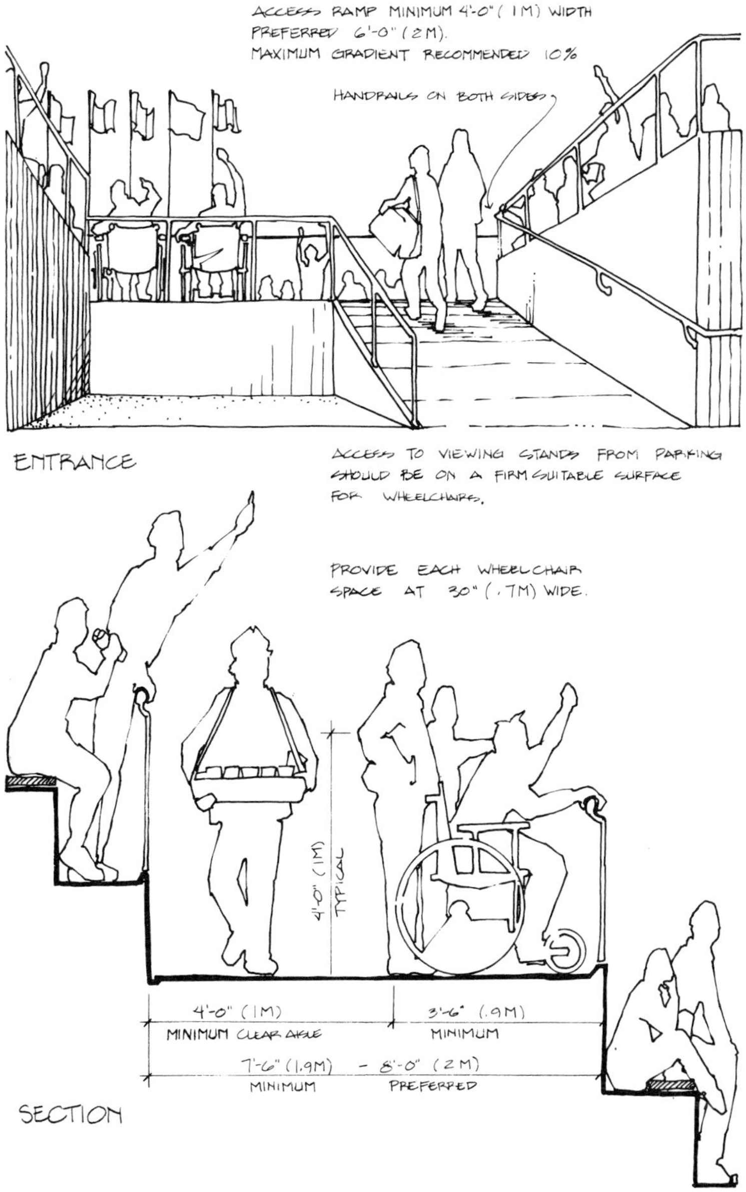
ACCESS RAMP MINIMUM 4'-0" (1M) WIDTH PREFERRED 6'-0" (2M). MAXIMUM GRADIENT RECOMMENDED 10%
HANDRAILS ON BOTH SIDES
ENTRANCE
ACCESS TO VIEWING STANDS FROM PARKING SHOULD BE ON A FIRM SUITABLE SURFACE FOR WHEELCHAIRS.
PROVIDE EACH WHEELCHAIR SPACE AT 30" (.7M) WIDE.
4'-0" (1M) TYPICAL
4'-0" (1M) MINIMUM CLEAR AISLE
3'-6" (.9M) MINIMUM
7'-6" (1.9M) MINIMUM
- 8'-0" (2M) PREFERRED
SECTION

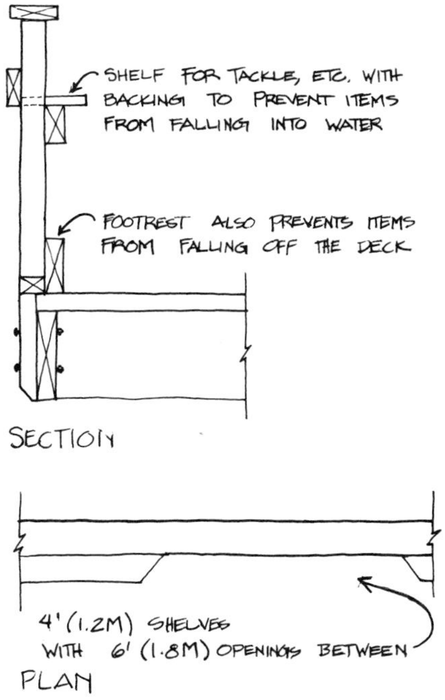
SHELF FOR TACKLE, ETC. WITH BACKING TO PREVENT ITEMS FROM FALLING INTO WATER
FOOTREST ALSO PREVENTS ITEMS FROM FALLING OFF THE DECK
SECTION
4' (1.2M) SHELVES WITH 6' (1.8M) OPENINGS BETWEEN
PLAN

Figure 240-37 (*Bottom*) General considerations for accessible spectator stands. Space for wheelchair users should be located near entrance ramps to minimize maneuvering through crowds. Access aisles should be maintained behind wheelchair users.

play environment (Figure 240-39). Preferences for these two types of play vary among individuals, some responding more positively to one type of play than to another. A diversity of opportunity for meaningful experiences should be provided within both types of play.

Opportunities for manipulation of environment are both mentally stimulating and important for motor skill development. Diversity within the opportunities to manipulate environment should be provided to accommodate all levels of ability and need.

The physical organization of a park or playground should be readily comprehensible by those with visual impairments who rely on cognitive mapping for orientation.

Adult supervision of play areas is usually necessary. Its extent varies according to user abilities, user numbers, and the type of facility.

5.8 Jogging Paths

Jogging paths and trails should be made safe for all types of users. Where bicyclists, walkers, roller skaters, and skateboarders will also use a pathway, an adequate means of separation or cooperation between user groups is advisable.

Signage is important and should accommodate those who are sighted, those with limited vision, and also those who are blind. Textural and visual cues on ground surfaces are helpful. Textured path edges, especially at turning points, also aid negotiation. A brightly colored or contrasting center stripe helps those with limited vision stay on course and can also serve to separate various functions (Figure 240-40).

Access for wheelchair users should be clearly understood so that an understanding exists between all user groups. Path dimensions depend on type of use.

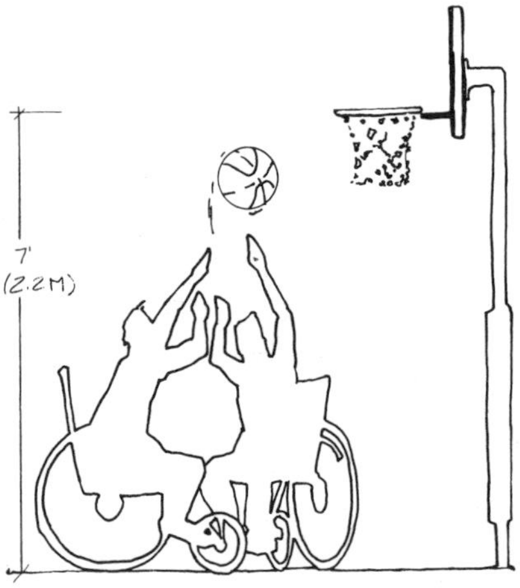
7'
(2.2M)

Figure 240-38 Accessible basketball. Basketball hoops lowered to 7 ft (2.13 m) from the standard 10-ft (3.04-m) height allow wheelchair users and young children greater enjoyment of the game.

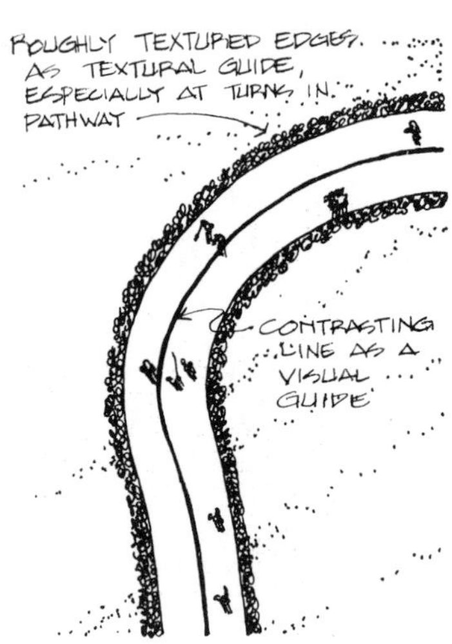
ROUGHLY TEXTURED EDGES AS TEXTURAL GUIDE, ESPECIALLY AT TURNS IN PATHWAY
CONTRASTING LINE AS A VISUAL GUIDE

Figure 240-40 Jogging path for use by individuals with visual impairments. Textural and visual cues along jogging paths, especially at turns in the pathway, can aid those with visual limitations.

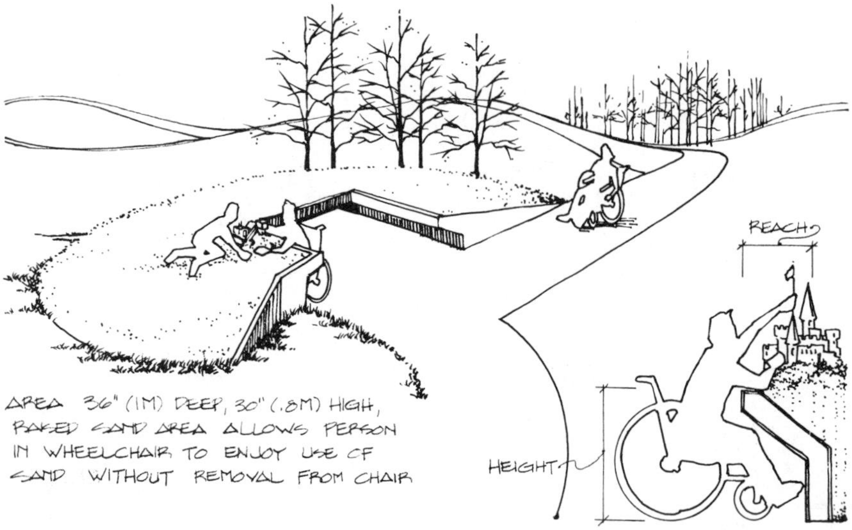
REACH
AREA 36" (1M) DEEP, 30" (.8M) HIGH, RAISED SAND AREA ALLOWS PERSON IN WHEELCHAIR TO ENJOY USE OF SAND WITHOUT REMOVAL FROM CHAIR
HEIGHT

Figure 240-39 Accessible sand area. Elevated areas containing sand or water allow access by wheelchair users.

AGENCIES AND ORGANIZATIONS

U.S. Federal Government

Architectural and Transportation Barriers Compliance Board
U.S. Department of Health, Education and Welfare
Washington, D.C.

U.S. Heritage Conservation and Recreation Service
Department of the Interior
Washington, D.C.

United States Library of Congress
Reference Section, Division for the Blind and Physically Handicapped
Washington, D.C.

U.S. National Park Service
Office of Special Programs and Populations
Department of the Interior
Washington, D.C.

Private

American Camping Association
Martinsville, Indiana

American Coalition of Citizens with Disabilities
Washington, D.C.

American Foundation for the Blind
New York, New York

American National Standards Institute (ANSI)
New York, New York

Access Recreation
3308 Valley Drive
Alexandria, Virginia

National Center for a Barrier-Free Environment
Washington, D.C.

Pedestrian Research Laboratory
Georgia Institute of Technology
College of Architecture
Atlanta, Georgia

Vinland National Center
Lorretto, Minnesota

International

Canadian Rehabilitation Council for the Disabled
Toronto, Ontario
Canada

ICTA Information Center
Swedish Central Committee for Rehabilitation (SUCR)
Fack, S-161-03
Bromma 3
Sweden

Rehabilitation International, USA
New York, New York

REFERENCES

U.S. Publications

American Foundation for the Blind, compiled by John Duncan, Calasha Gish, Mary Ellen Mulholland, and Alex Towsend. *Environmental Modifications for the Visually Impaired: Handbook,* New York, 1982.

American Foundation for the Blind, edited by Richard L. Welsh and Bruce B. Blasch, "Environmental Modifications" by Kent Wardell, in *Foundations of Orientation and Mobility,* New York, 1980, pp. 477–526.

American National Standards Institute. *Specifications for Making Buildings and Facilities Accessible to and Usable by Physically Handicapped People,* A117.1-1986, New York.

National Center for a Barrier Free Environment. *Access Information Bulletins.*

Olgyay, Victor. *Design With Climate,* Princeton University Press, Princeton, NJ, 1963.

U.S. Architectural and Transportation Barriers Compliance Board (ATBCB), in joint cooperation with the General Services Administration, the Department of Defense, the Department of Housing and Urban Development, and the U.S. Postal Service. *Uniform Federal Accessibility Standards,* 1984.

U.S. Federal Highway Administration, John Templer et al. *Development of Priority Accessible Networks: An Implementation Manual,* Superintendent of Documents, U.S. Government Printing Office, Washington, DC, January 1980. 224 pp. illus.

U.S. Federal Highway Association. *Provisions for Elderly and Handicapped Pedestrians,* vol. 2: *Hazards, Barriers, Problems and the Law,* U.S. Department of Transportation, Washington, DC, May 1980.

U.S. Heritage Conservation and Recreation Service. *A Guide to Designing Accessible Outdoor Recreation Facilities,* Department of the Interior, Lake Central Region, January 1980.

International Publications

British Standard Code of Practice, CP 96. *Access for the Disabled to Buildings,* pt. 1: *General Recommendations,* London, 1967.

Insight (Australian Federation of Blind Citizens), F. R. Hilsher, *Traffic Signal Facilities for Blind Pedestrians,* New South Wales, Australia, February 1977.

International Centre on Technical Aids, Housing, and Transportation; and the Netherlands Society for Rehabilitation. *Architectural Facilities for the Disabled,* Bromma, Sweden, 1973. ■

section 252: Natural Hazards: Earthquakes

CREDITS

Section Editor: Charles W. Harris
Technical Writer: Tess Canfield

Reviewers:

Gilbert F. White and Staff
Natural Hazards Research and Applications Information Center
University of Colorado
Boulder, Colorado

W. J. Kockelman
Office of Earthquakes, Volcanoes and Engineering
United States Geological Survey
Menlo Park, California

Tuncer B. Edil, Prof.
Department of Civil and Environmental Engineering
University of Wisconsin—Madison
Madison, Wisconsin

Daniel L. Schodek, Prof.
Harvard University Graduate School of Design
Department of Architecture
Cambridge, Massachusetts

CONTENTS

1.0 INTRODUCTION

The occurrence of a major earthquake creates such primary hazards as surface rupturing and displacement (occurring along a fault), ground shaking, earthquake-induced ground failures, and seiching (oscillation of water surface). Secondary hazards include landslides, floods, subsidence, and tsunamis (large sea waves). (Refer to Sections 253 through 255: Natural Hazards, for information on these types of hazards.)

Fire often follows earthquake damage, as utilities are damaged and fire-fighting equipment is either destroyed or unable to travel through debris-filled streets and roadways. Tectonic subsidence and uplift can have long-lasting ecological and physical effects.

2.0 CAUSES OF EARTHQUAKES

2.1 Theory of Plate Tectonics

Since 1967, the theory of plate tectonics has been used to explain the occurrence of earthquakes. The earth's crust and upper mantle are thought to be composed of a mosaic of 50- to 60-mile-thick (80- to 100-km-thick) rigid plates which move slowly and continuously over the interior of the earth (Figure 252-1). This movement results in pressure, separation, or sliding at plate edges. Velocities range from extremely slow to about 5 in (130 mm) per year. As these plates move, strain accumulates, eventually causing faults along plate boundaries to slip abruptly. The resultant release of stress, which usually occurs within a few cubic kilometers of the earth's crust, is called an earthquake.

Figure 252-1 shows the major tectonic plates of the world, and Figure 252-2 shows the worldwide distribution of earthquakes occurring in 1970.

Most earthquakes occur in tectonically active plate boundary regions, and these are referred to as *plate-edge earthquakes.* Other types of earthquakes also occur. However, the theory of plate tectonics does not adequately explain *intraplate earthquakes,* which occur within plates rather than along plate edges.

2.2 Elastic Rebound Theory

Both plate-edge earthquakes and intraplate earthquakes conform to elastic rebound theory, which supposes that differential displacements within the earth's crust create elastic strains greater than the

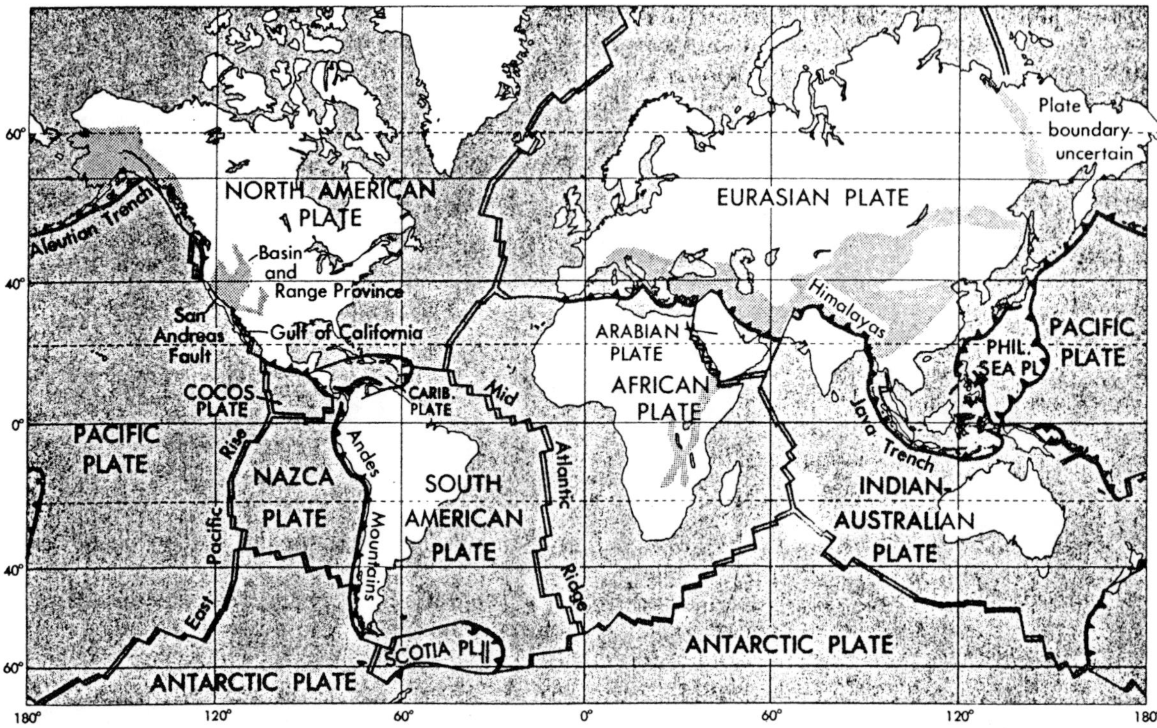
Plate boundary uncertain
NORTH AMERICAN PLATE
EURASIAN PLATE
Aleutian Trench
Basin and Range Province
San Andreas Fault
Gulf of California
Himalayas
ARABIAN PLATE
AFRICAN PLATE
PACIFIC PLATE
PHIL. SEA PL
COCOS PLATE
CARIB PLATE
Mid Atlantic Ridge
PACIFIC PLATE
NAZCA PLATE
Andes Mountains
SOUTH AMERICAN PLATE
Java Trench
INDIAN-AUSTRALIAN PLATE
East Pacific Rise
SCOTIA PL
ANTARCTIC PLATE
ANTARCTIC PLATE

Figure 252-1 Major tectonic plates of the world. The double line indicates a zone of spreading from which plates are moving apart. Lines with barbs indicate a zone where one plate is sliding beneath another. A single line indicates a strike-slip fault along which plates are sliding past one another.

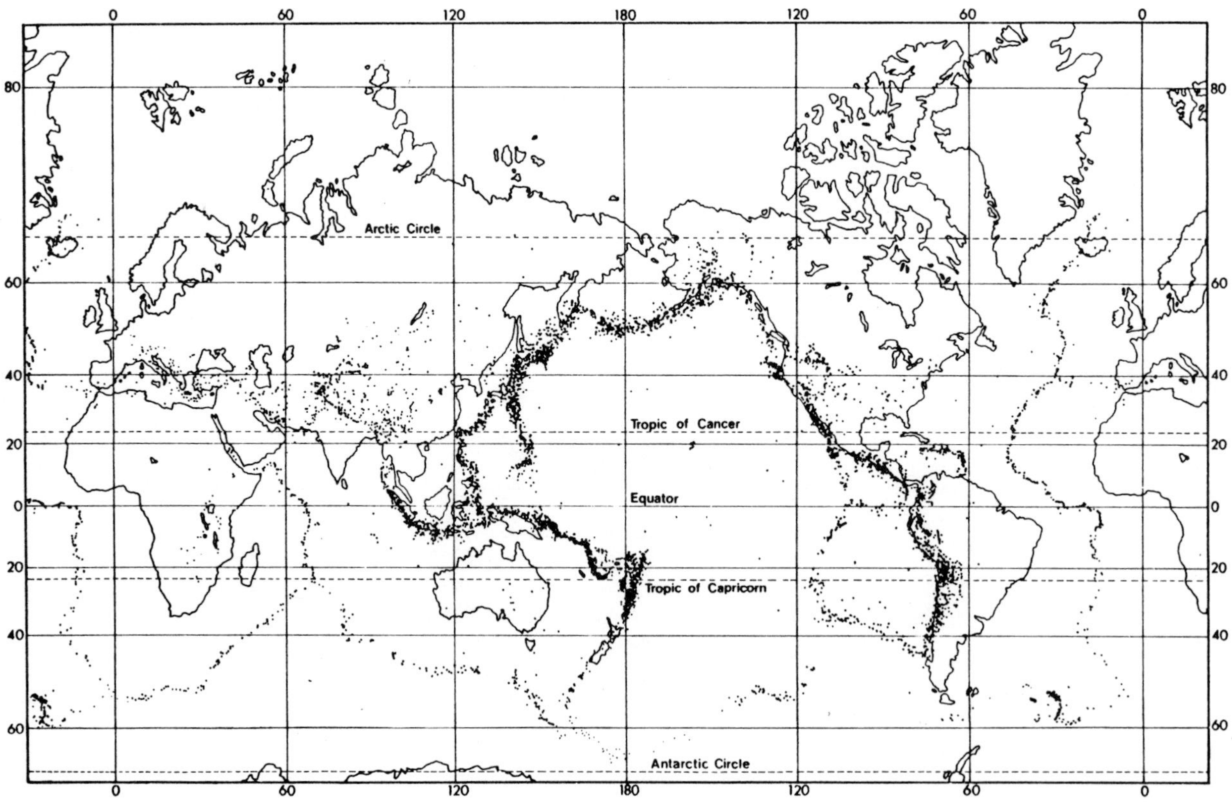
Arctic Circle
Tropic of Cancer
Equator
Tropic of Capricorn
Antarctic Circle

Figure 252-2 Seismicity map of the world. The dots indicate the distribution of seismic events in the mid-20th century (after Bavazangi and Dorman).

rock can endure. Ruptures (faults) then occur, and the rock rebounds along the fault until the strain is partly or completely relieved. The focus of an earthquake is the point at which the rupture suddenly begins. The rupture then spreads in all directions along the fault surface in a series of erratic movements due to variations in the strength of rocks along the rupture. The fault or rupture typically moves at a velocity of 1.25 to 1.85 mi/s (2 to 3 km/s) in irregular steps lasting fractions of a second each. Ground shaking that occurs away from the fault is created by wave vibrations originating at the fault.

2.3 Other Causes

Other causes of earthquakes include volcanic activity, underground nuclear explosions, injection of waste liquid into susceptible rock strata, and in some cases, the weight of newly constructed large dams and reservoirs.

3.0 MEASUREMENT

Two types of measurement are commonly used to assess the relative magnitude of earthquakes. These are described below.

3.1 Intensity

Intensity is a subjective measure of the effects of an earthquake; it describes the degree of shaking at a specified place. The most widely used intensity scale is the *modified Mercalli scale (MM)* (Table 252-1). Other scales in international use are correlated in Table 252-2.

3.2 Magnitude

Magnitude is a quantitative measure of the size of an earthquake, independent of the place of observation. It is calculated from amplitude measurements and is expressed in decimal numbers on a logarithmic scale. The most commonly used magnitude scale is the *Richter scale* (M). Figure 252-3 shows energy release equivalents of Richter scale magnitudes and illustrates the magnitude of several well-known earthquakes.

TABLE 252-1
Modified Mercalli Intensity Scale

I. Not felt except for a very few under exceptionally favorable circumstances.
II. Felt by persons at rest, on upper floors, or favorably placed.
III. Felt indoors; hanging objects swing; vibration similar to passing of light trucks; duration may be estimated; may not be recognized as an earthquake.
IV. Hanging objects swing; vibration similar to passing of heavy trucks, or sensation of a jolt similar to a heavy ball striking the walls; standing motor cars rock; windows, dishes, and doors rattle; glasses clink and crockery clashes; in the upper range of IV wooden walls and frames creak.
V. Felt outdoors; direction may be estimated; sleepers wakened, liquids disturbed, some spilled; small unstable objects displaced or upset; doors swing, close, or open; shutters and pictures move; pendulum clocks stop, start, or change rate.
VI. Felt by all; many frightened and run outdoors; walking unsteady; windows, dishes and glassware broken; knick-knacks, books, etc., fall from shelves and pictures from walls; furniture moved or overturned; weak plaster and masonry D* cracked; small bells ring (church or school); trees and bushes shaken (visibly, or heard to rustle).
VII. Difficult to stand; noticed by drivers of motor cars; hanging objects quiver; furniture breaks; damage to masonry D, including cracks; weak chimneys break at roof line; fall of plaster, loose bricks, stones, tiles, cornices (also unbraced parapets and architectural ornaments); some cracks in masonry C*; waves on ponds; water turbid with mud; small slides and caving in along sand or gravel banks; large bells ring; concrete irrigation ditches damaged.
VIII. Steering of motor cars affected; damage to masonry C or partial collapse; some damage to masonry B*; none to masonry A*; fall of stucco and some masonry walls; twisting and fall of chimneys, factory stacks, monuments, towers and elevated tanks; frame houses moved on foundations if not bolted down; loose panel walls thrown out; decayed piling broken off; branches broken from trees; changes in flow or temperature of springs and wells; cracks in wet ground and on steep slopes.
IX. General panic; masonry D destroyed; masonry C heavily damaged, sometimes with complete collapse; masonry B seriously damaged; general damage to foundations; frame structures, if not bolted, shifted off foundations; frames racked; serious damage to reservoirs; underground pipes broken; conspicuous cracks in ground; in alluviated areas sand and mud ejected, earthquake fountains and sand craters appear
X. Most masonry and frame structures destroyed with their foundations; some well-built wooden structures and bridges destroyed; serious damage to dams, dikes, and embankments; large landslides; water thrown on banks of canals, rivers, lakes, etc.; sand and mud shifted horizontally on beaches and flat land; rails bend slightly.
XI. Rails bent greatly; underground pipelines completely out of service
XII. Damage nearly total; large rock masses displaced; lines of sight and level distorted; objects thrown into the air

* Masonry A, B, C, and D as used in MM Scale above:
Masonry A: Good workmanship, mortar, and design; reinforced, especially laterally, and bound together by using steel, concrete, etc.; designed to resist lateral forces.
Masonry B: Good workmanship and mortar; reinforced, but not designed in detail to resist lateral forces.
Masonry C: Ordinary workmanship and mortar; no extreme weaknesses like failing to tie in at corners, but neither reinforced nor designed against horizontal forces.
Masonry D: Weak materials, such as adobe; poor mortar; low standards of workmanship; weak horizontally.

TABLE 252-2
Conversion Table for Seismic Intensity Scales

Rossi–Forel scale, 1873	*Mercalli–Cancani–Sieberg European scale, 1917*	*Modified Mercalli scale (MM), 1931*	*Richter scale, 1935*	*Japanese scale, 1950*	*Scale of the USSR Academy of Sciences' Institute of Geophysics, 1952*	*MSK seismic scale, 1964*
1	1	1	1	0	1	1
2	2	2	2	1	2	2
3	3	3	3	2	3	3
4	4	4	4	2–3	4	4
5–6	5	5	5	3	5	5
7	6	6	6	4	6	6
8	7	7	7	4–5	7	7
9	8	8	8	5	8	8
10	9	9	9	5–6	9	9
10	10	10		6	10	10
10	11	11		7	11	11
10	12	12		7	12	12

Source: Compiled by Medvedev, Sponheuer, and Karnik, *Disaster Prevention and Mitigation,* vol. 5, United Nations, 1978.

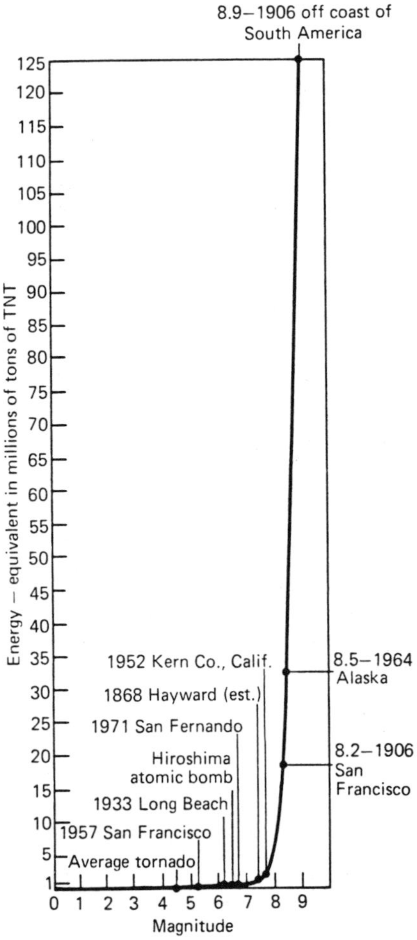
8.9–1906 off coast of South America
Energy – equivalent in millions of tons of TNT
125
120
115
110
105
100
95
90
85
80
75
70
65
60
55
50
45
40
35
30
25
20
15
10
5
1
1952 Kern Co., Calif.
1868 Hayward (est.)
1971 San Fernando
Hiroshima atomic bomb
1933 Long Beach
1957 San Francisco
Average tornado
8.5–1964 Alaska
8.2–1906 San Francisco
0 1 2 3 4 5 6 7 8 9
Magnitude

Figure 252-3 Richter magnitude scale. This graph shows the amount of energy released by earthquakes of different magnitudes.

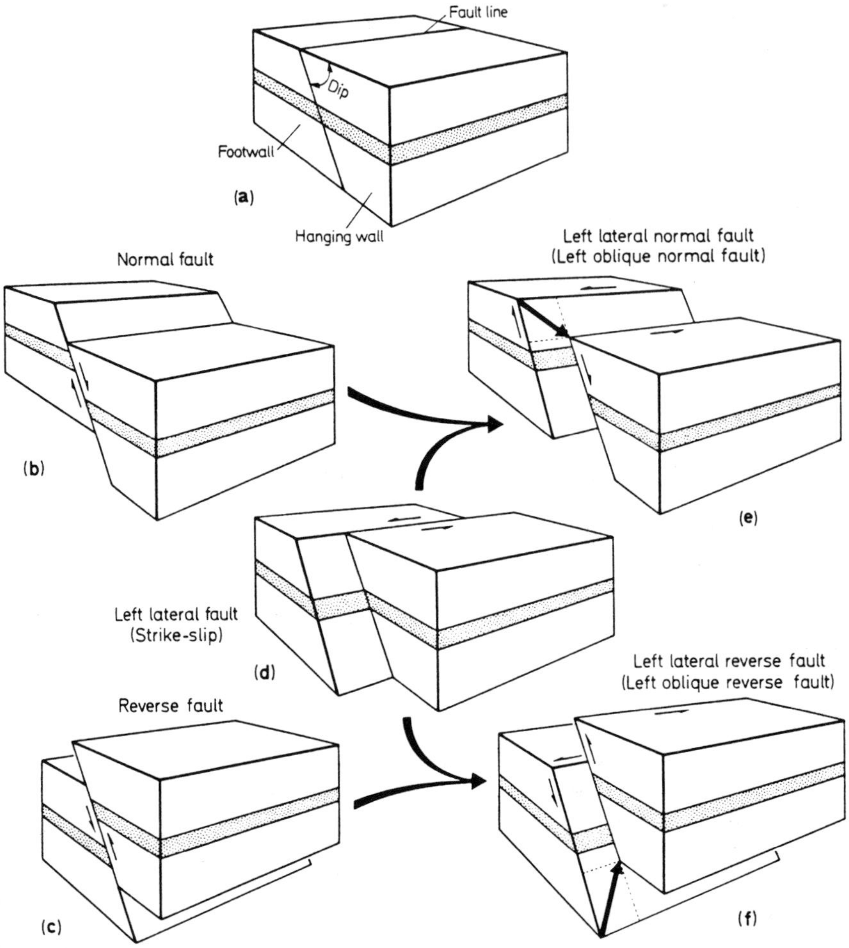
Fault line
Dip
Footwall
(a)
Hanging wall
Normal fault
(b)
Left lateral normal fault
(Left oblique normal fault)
(e)
Left lateral fault
(Strike-slip)
(d)
Reverse fault
(c)
Left lateral reverse fault
(Left oblique reverse fault)
(f)

Figure 252-4 Types of faults: (*a*) names of components, (*b*) normal fault, (*c*) reverse fault, (*d*) left-lateral strike-slip fault, (*e*) left-lateral normal fault, and (*f*) left-lateral reverse fault.

4.0 EFFECTS OF EARTHQUAKES

4.1 Primary and Secondary Effects

Earthquakes cause destruction of property and death or injury to people and the environment. As noted earlier, primary effects of earthquakes (those caused by the earthquake vibrations themselves) include fault displacement and ground shaking. Secondary effects are the result of other processes which are initiated by the earthquake vibrations, such as ground failures of various kinds.

4.2 Fault Displacement

A *fault* is a fracture along which differential movement of rocks has occurred. *Fault displacement* is defined as the differential movement of two sides of a fault at the earth's surface. Displacement can occur as the result either of a sudden rupture during an earthquake or of slow differential slippage, referred to as *tectonic creep*. Geological hazards will vary depending on the type of fault involved. Classification of fault type is based on the geometry and direction of relative slippage. Figure 252-4 diagrammatically illustrates various fault types and gives the names of their components.

Most major faults do not consist of a single break line but include parallel and interleaved breaks in a zone of considerable width.

Classification of Faults:

Most known faults which appear on geological maps are inactive and are not considered potentially hazardous. Most geologists consider a fault active if it has moved during the past 11,000 years (Holocene Epoch). Faults that have moved during the past 3 million years (Quarternary Period, during which most of the present day landscape has been produced) can be classified as possibly active. Faults which have not moved in the past 3 million years are generally classified as inactive. Figure 252-5 shows a classification of faults in southern California used in the *San Francisco Bay Region Study, 1970-76* to help assess potential sources of damage to structures.

Active Faults: Active fault zones can be identified by the presence of geomorphically young fault-produced features. Scarps, sag ponds, offset stream courses, and linear ridges indicate active strike-slip faults having a predominantly horizontal motion (Figures 252-6 and 252-7).

Estimated Age of Displacement:

The estimation of the age of soils on opposite sides of a fault can help to establish a relative age for the displacement. Radiocarbon dating may be required in some types of geologic material.

Predicting Future Fault Rupture Location:

Predicting the location of future fault rupture is difficult. Most geologists expect the next rupture to occur on or near the place where the last rupture occurred, especially

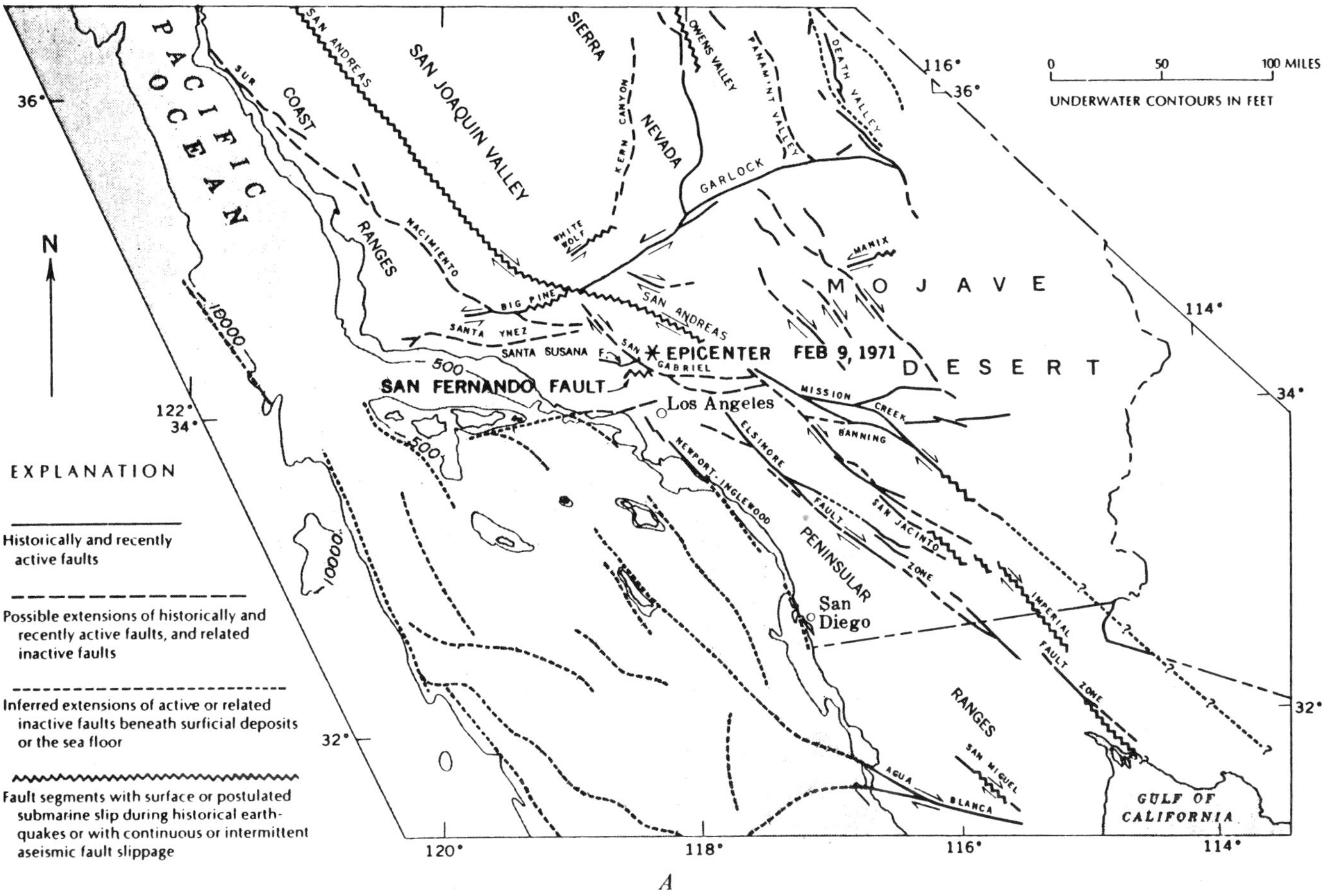
PACIFIC OCEAN
SAN ANDREAS
SAN JOAQUIN VALLEY
SIERRA NEVADA
OWENS VALLEY
DEATH VALLEY
KERN CANYON
GARLOCK
SUR
COAST RANGES
NACIMIENTO
WHITE WOLF
BIG PINE
SANTA YNEZ
SANTA SUSANA F.
SAN GABRIEL
EPICENTER FEB 9, 1971
SAN FERNANDO FAULT
MOJAVE DESERT
MANIX
MISSION CREEK
BANNING
Los Angeles
NEWPORT-INGLEWOOD
ELSINORE FAULT
SAN JACINTO ZONE
PENINSULAR RANGES
IMPERIAL FAULT ZONE
San Diego
SAN MIGUEL
AGUA BLANCA
GULF OF CALIFORNIA
0 50 100 MILES
UNDERWATER CONTOURS IN FEET
N
EXPLANATION
Historically and recently active faults
Possible extensions of historically and recently active faults, and related inactive faults
Inferred extensions of active or related inactive faults beneath surficial deposits or the sea floor
Fault segments with surface or postulated submarine slip during historical earthquakes or with continuous or intermittent aseismic fault slippage
36°
34°
32°
122°
120°
118°
116°
114°
500
10000
A

Figure 252-5 Major historically and geologically recent active faults in southern California.

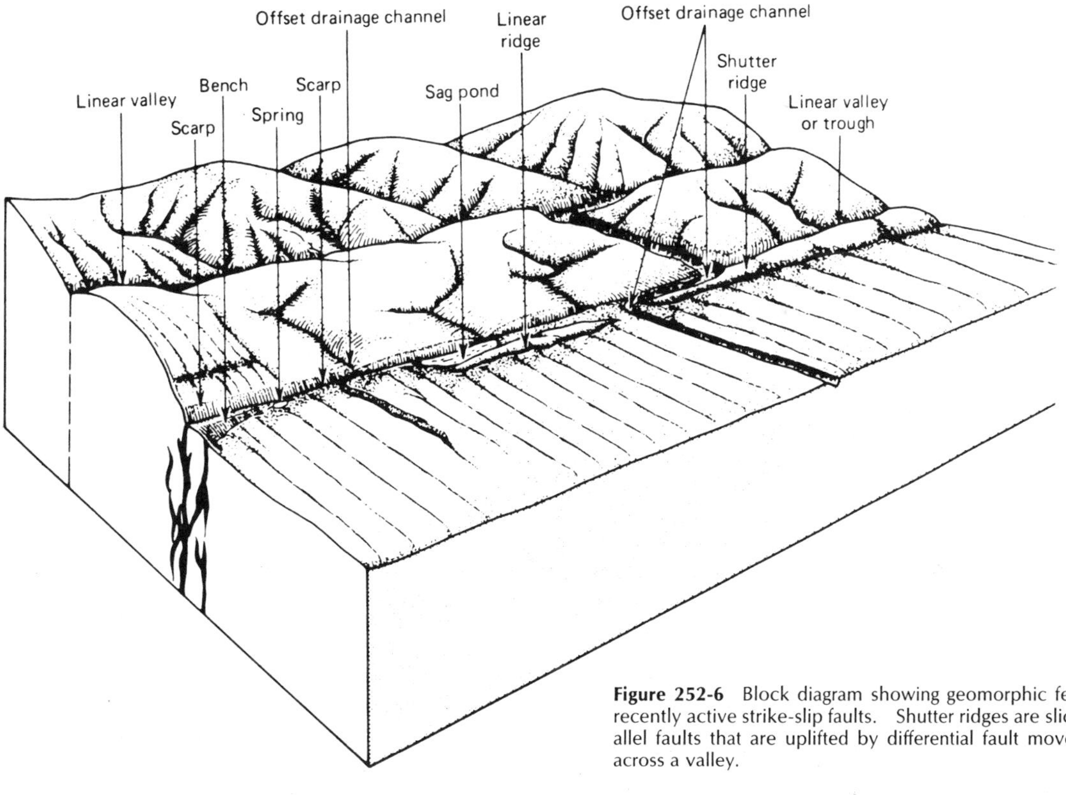
Offset drainage channel
Linear ridge
Offset drainage channel
Shutter ridge
Linear valley or trough
Linear valley
Bench
Scarp
Scarp
Spring
Sag pond

Figure 252-6 Block diagram showing geomorphic features developed along recently active strike-slip faults. Shutter ridges are slices of rock between parallel faults that are uplifted by differential fault movement to form a barrier across a valley.

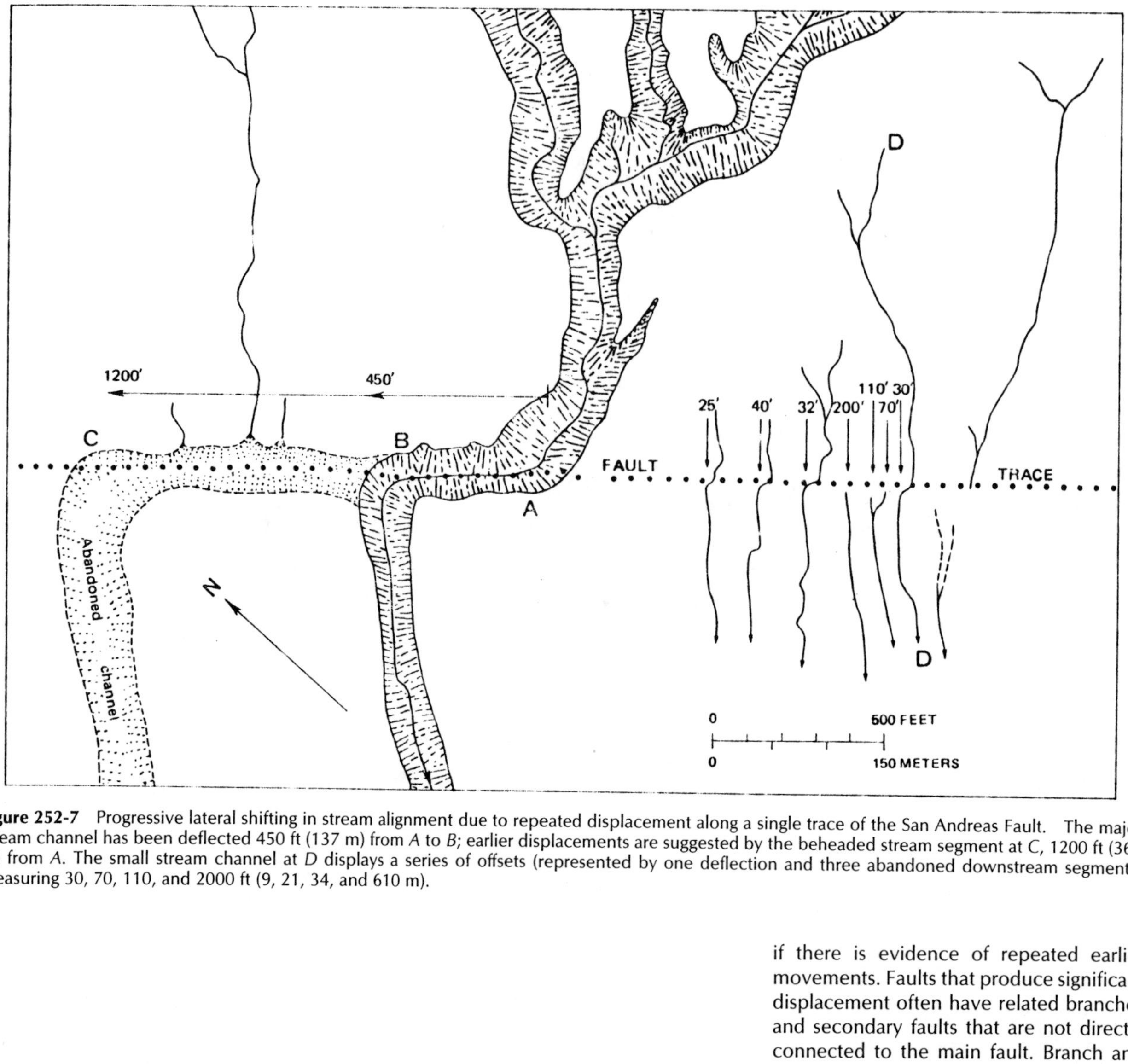
1200'
450'
C
B
A
FAULT
TRACE
D
25'
40'
32'
200'
110' 30'
70'
Abandoned channel
N
0
600 FEET
0
150 METERS

Figure 252-7 Progressive lateral shifting in stream alignment due to repeated displacement along a single trace of the San Andreas Fault. The major stream channel has been deflected 450 ft (137 m) from *A* to *B*; earlier displacements are suggested by the beheaded stream segment at *C*, 1200 ft (366 m) from *A*. The small stream channel at *D* displays a series of offsets (represented by one deflection and three abandoned downstream segments) measuring 30, 70, 110, and 2000 ft (9, 21, 34, and 610 m).

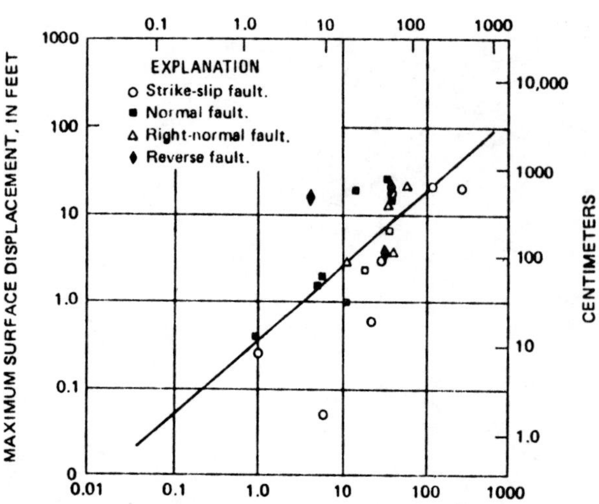
KILOMETERS
0.1
1.0
10
100
1000
EXPLANATION
Strike-slip fault.
Normal fault.
Right-normal fault.
Reverse fault.
MAXIMUM SURFACE DISPLACEMENT, IN FEET
1000
100
10
1.0
0.1
0
10,000
1000
100
10
1.0
CENTIMETERS
0.01
0.1
1.0
10
100
1000
LENGTH OF SURFACE RUPTURE, IN MILES

Figure 252-8 Logarithmic plot relating maximum amount of surface displacement to the length of surface rupture on the main fault trace. Plotted points record known historical surface faulting that has accompanied various earthquakes in the continental United States and adjacent parts of Mexico.

if there is evidence of repeated earlier movements. Faults that produce significant displacement often have related branches and secondary faults that are not directly connected to the main fault. Branch and secondary faults are usually subject to only a fraction of the displacement experienced along the main fault trace.

Fault Creep: The amount of displacement caused by a fault rupture is related, generally, to the length of the fault (Figure 252-8). However, not all surface fault displacement is rapid and related to earthquake activity. Extremely slow movement, referred to as *fault creep,* results in the plastic deformation of materials in the fault zone.

Both rupture and fault creep pose hazards to built structures.

4.3 Effect on Structures

Fault rupture at the surface may or may not be produced by a given earthquake. If a surface rupture does occur, it may be very limited or it may extend over several hundred miles. Figure 252-9 illustrates zones of surface rupture in the San Francisco Bay region. The displacement which occurs along a fault rupture is very rapid. It may be horizontal, vertical, or both, and it can vary from a few inches to several feet in length.

Damage to structures astride a ruptured fault is usually severe, since few structures can tolerate the stresses created by the unequal movement of the two sides of the fault. Damage caused by fault rupture occurs only in a narrow zone.

Fault creep is also damaging to structures which lie across a fault. It can cause slow displacement and deformation of buildings, streets, underground utilities, and other structures. The amount of slippage can range from minute fractions of an inch (a few millimeters) to perhaps ½ in (a centimeter or so) per year.

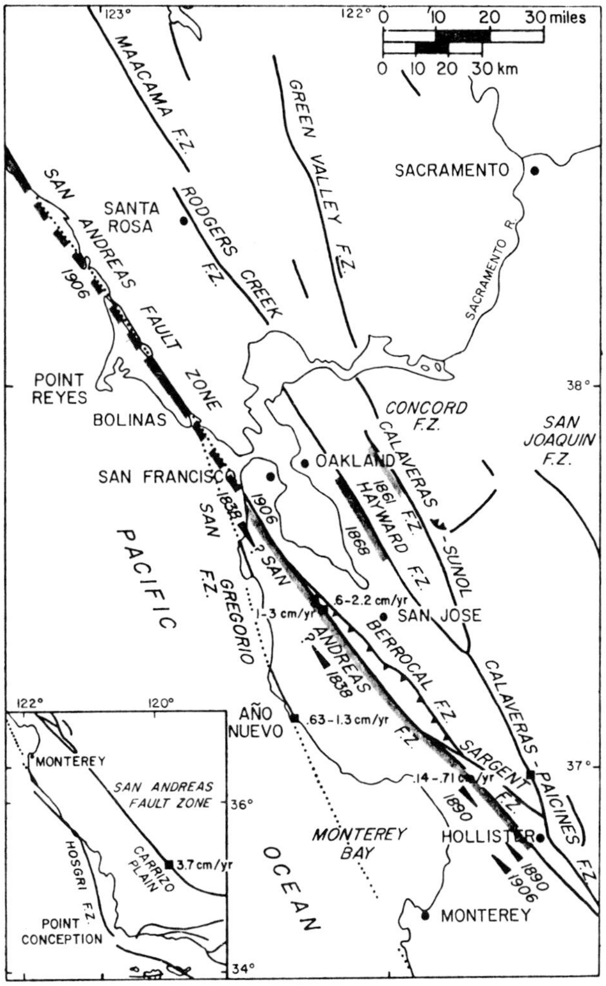

123°
122°
0 10 20 30 miles
0 10 20 30 km
MAACAMA F.Z.
GREEN VALLEY F.Z.
SACRAMENTO
SACRAMENTO R.
SANTA ROSA
RODGERS CREEK F.Z.
SAN ANDREAS FAULT ZONE
1906
POINT REYES
BOLINAS
CONCORD F.Z.
SAN JOAQUIN F.Z.
38°
OAKLAND
CALAVERAS F.Z.
1861 HAYWARD F.Z.
1868
SUNOL
SAN FRANCISCO
1838
SAN GREGORIO F.Z.
PACIFIC OCEAN
.6-2.2 cm/yr
1-3 cm/yr
SAN JOSE
BERROCAL F.Z.
SAN ANDREAS
AÑO NUEVO
.63-1.3 cm/yr
SARGENT F.Z.
37°
.14-.71 cm/yr
1890
CALAVERAS-PAICINES F.Z.
MONTEREY BAY
HOLLISTER
MONTEREY
122°
120°
MONTEREY
SAN ANDREAS FAULT ZONE
36°
CARRIZO PLAIN
3.7 cm/yr
HOSGRI F.Z.
POINT CONCEPTION
34°

Figure 252-9 Principal recently active faults in San Francisco Bay region. Map shows zones of surface rupture associated with historical earthquakes. Squares denote locally determined rates of geologic offset.

4.4 Ground Shaking

Ground shaking refers to the vibration of the ground occurring during an earthquake. It affects much larger areas than does fault displacement and is responsible for most earthquake damage to structures.

The frequency and amplitude of the vibrations produced on the surface (and hence the severity of the shaking caused by an earthquake) depend upon the amount of mechanical energy released at the focus, the distance to and depth of the focus, and the structural properties of soil and bedrock at the location in question.

The focus of an earthquake (the point directly below the epicenter at which the fault ruptures) can be as deep as 430 mi (700 km) below the surface, but most seismic energy (over 75 percent) is released by earthquakes whose foci are less than 38 mi (60 km) deep. These shallow focus earthquakes are the major cause of earthquake damage.

Types of Seismic Waves:

From the focus of an earthquake, mechanical energy is propagated in the form of *waves* which radiate in all directions. *Body waves* are of two types: *compressional* (or *P*) and *shear* (or *S*) waves. *P* waves travel approximately 15,000 mph (24,000 km/h) and are the first indication that an earthquake has occurred at locations away from the fault rupture. The arrival of *P* waves is felt as a sudden thud. *P* waves cause vertical movement of buildings and other built structures. The slower and more destructive *S* waves cause buildings to vibrate from side to side.

When the released mechanical energy of the waves arrives at the surface, it creates *surface waves* of two types, referred to as *Rayleigh waves* and *Love waves*. These waves are of lower frequencies than *S* and *P* waves and are more inclined to cause tall buildings to vibrate. Because amplitudes of low-frequency vibrations decay less rapidly than do those of high-frequency vibrations (as distance from the focus increases), tall buildings located at relatively great distances away from the focus [e.g., 60 mi (100 km)] can be damaged.

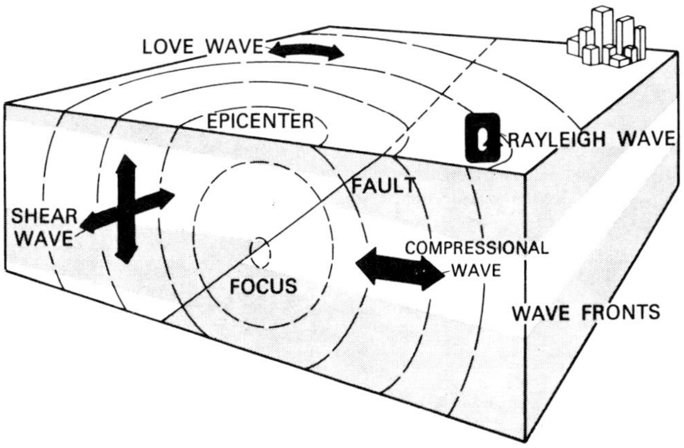

LOVE WAVE
EPICENTER
RAYLEIGH WAVE
FAULT
SHEAR WAVE
COMPRESSIONAL WAVE
FOCUS
WAVE FRONTS

Figure 252-10 Directions of vibration caused by body and surface seismic waves generated during an earthquake. When a fault ruptures, seismic waves are propagated in all directions, causing the ground to vibrate at frequencies ranging from about 0.1 to 30 Hz.

Figure 252-10 diagrammatically illustrates body and surface seismic waves, and Figure 252-11 shows the patterns of ground motion caused by each of the four types of seismic waves.

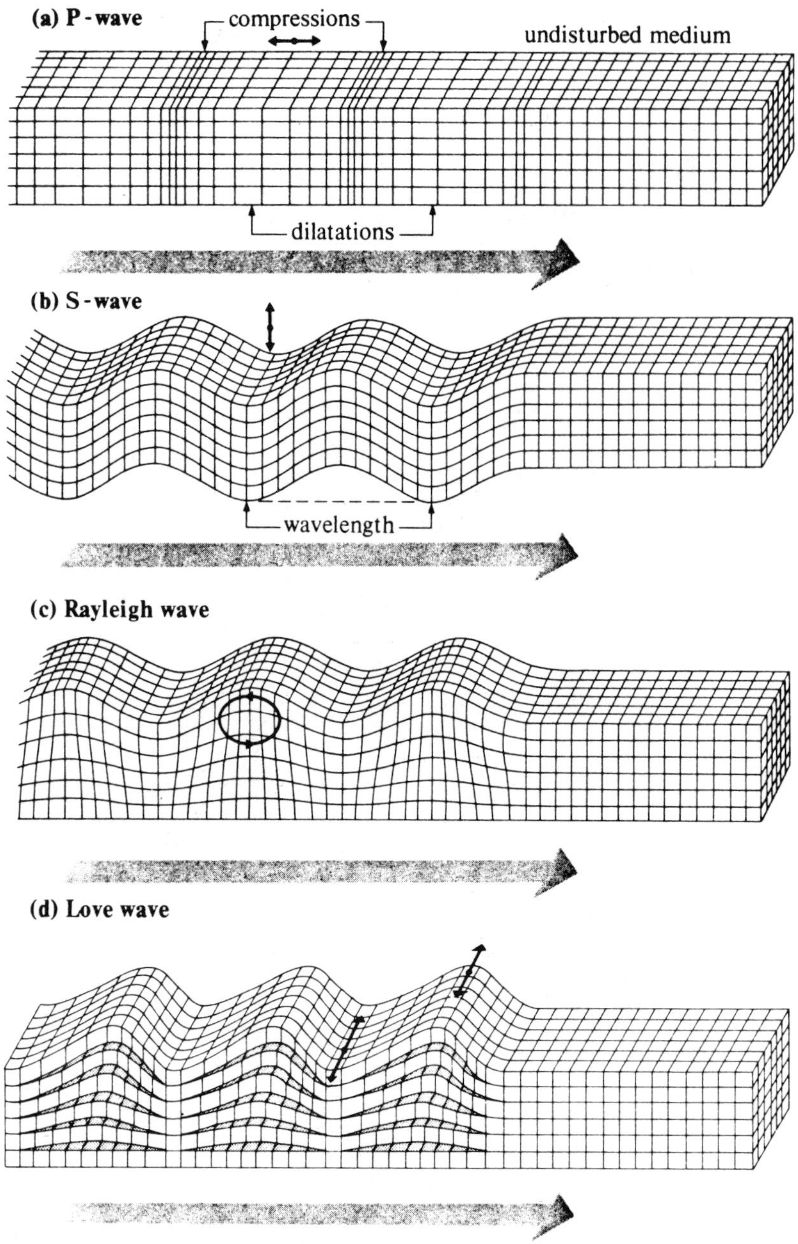
(a) P-wave
compressions
undisturbed medium
dilatations
(b) S-wave
wavelength
(c) Rayleigh wave
(d) Love wave

Figure 252-11 Types of seismic waves. In *P waves,* particles oscillate to and fro along the direction of propagation of the wave. In *S waves,* particle motion is transverse. The particle motion of *Rayleigh waves* is more complex, but near the surface is a backward vertical ellipse. In *Love waves,* particle motion is transverse and horizontal. In both Rayleigh and Love waves, particle motion decreases with depth from the surface.

Measurement of Acceleration:

An important indication of the ability of an earthquake to cause damage is the amount of acceleration of ground shaking. Measured by an instrument called an accelerograph, ground acceleration is expressed as a percentage of the force of gravity. Shaking in excess of 10 percent of gravity can cause significant damage to buildings.

Figure 252-12 is a map of peak horizontal ground acceleration (in percentages of the acceleration of gravity) expected within a 50-year period in the coterminous United States underlain by rock. There is a 10 percent probability that these values will be exceeded within a 50-year period.

Shaking of a given site is often amplified by local geologic conditions. The frequency and amplitude of seismic waves are altered by the material through which they pass. This amplification of shaking intensity, particularly in areas of deep alluvium or silt and mud, accounts for severe damage at relatively long distances away from the focus of an earthquake. Sites closer to the focus will experience relatively less severe shaking if hard bedrock is at the surface.

Because of the effects of the earth's materials on the behavior of seismic waves, each earthquake causes unique combinations of intensity, direction, and type of vibration.

Table 252-3 shows a general classification of different geologic responses to earthquakes. This can provide useful guidance in selecting sites for structures, since vibration damage is partly controlled by the characteristics of the ground on which a structure is located. For instance, the shaking amplitudes of an earthquake in Japan, occurring in unconsolidated, water-saturated material, were 10 times greater than those in bedrock.

4.5 Earthquake-Induced Ground Failures

Ground failures are the direct result of earthquake shaking on vulnerable geological materials. Liquefaction is a physical process which results in several types of earthquake-caused ground failures; it is not itself a type of ground failure.

Liquefaction:

Liquefaction causes three particularly damaging types of ground failure: lateral spreads, flow failures, and loss of bearing strength. It also contributes to ground settlement and can cause sand boils, which result from the action of subsurface water carrying sediments to the surface from a pressurized liquified zone below.

Liquefaction causes soil deposits to lose strength temporarily and behave as viscous fluids rather than as solids. It occurs when seismic shear waves pass through a saturated granular soil layer (usually sands and silts), causing some of the void spaces to collapse. If drainage is restricted, rapid increases in pore water pressure can occur when the pressure is approximately equal to the pressure caused by the weight of the overlying soil. The affected soil layer behaves like a fluid rather than a solid for a short period of time.

Liquefaction does not occur in gravel or clay soils. For liquefaction to occur, liquefiable materials must be within about 100 ft (30 m) of the surface and subject to strong ground-shaking forces. The liquefaction potential of a soil has been estimated based on relative density (Table 252-4, page 252-14), standard penetration resistance (Figure 252-13), and particle size distribution (Figure 252-14). Because these three criteria may yield conflicting results for a given site, professional advice is necessary in order to determine the true liquefaction potential of a soil.

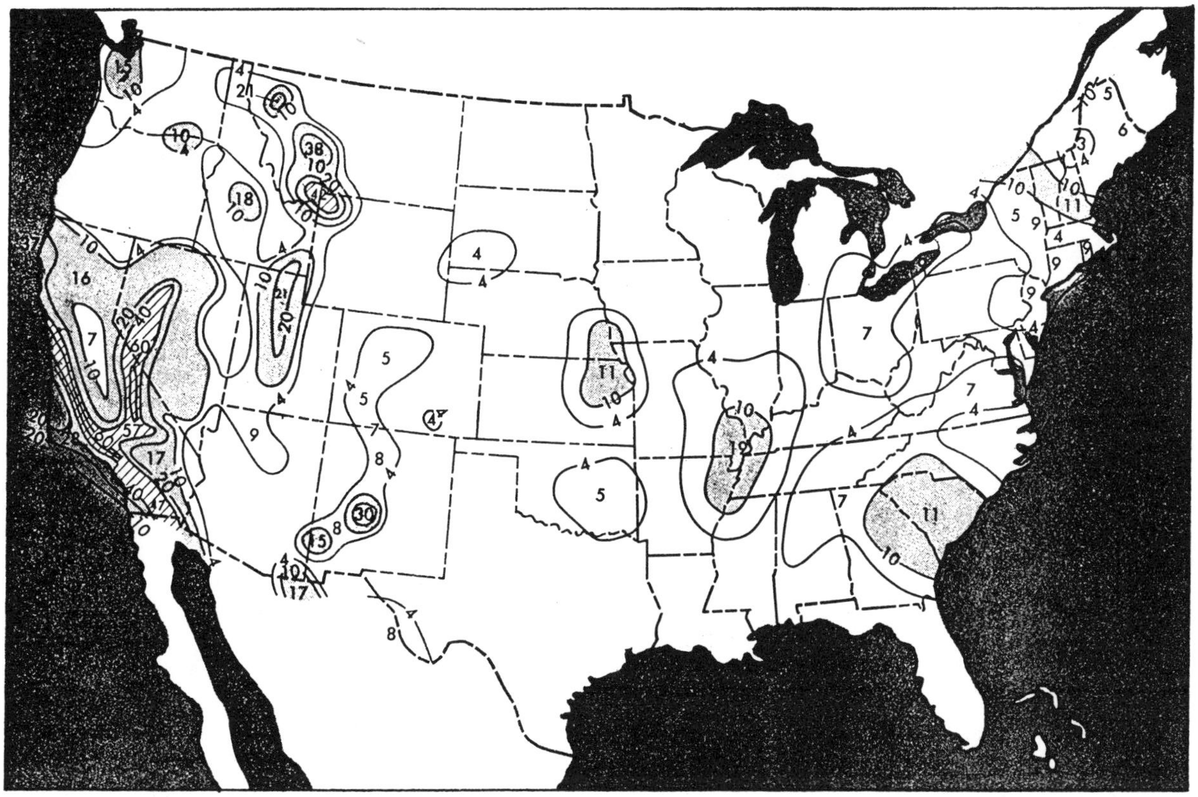

Figure 252-12 Peak horizontal ground acceleration expected at sites in the coterminous United States underlain by rock in a 50-year period (from Algermissen and Perkins, 1976). This map represents the ground-shaking hazard in terms of the peak amplitude of horizontal acceleration, one characteristic of the strength of the seismic shaking. Locations having the same value of peak acceleration are connected with a contour line. Values shown on each contour and on the map are percentages of the acceleration of gravity. There is a 10 percent probability that these values will be exceeded in a 50-year period. This map takes into account the relative differences in rate of seismic activity in the eastern and western United States. Areas where peak acceleration exceeds 10 percent of the acceleration of gravity are shaded. The largest values shown, along the California coast, are 80 percent of gravity.

Lateral Spreads:

Lateral spreads refer to the generally horizontal movement of large blocks of soil as a result of the liquefaction of a subsurface layer. The movement occurs in response to earthquake-generated ground shaking. Lateral spreads usually develop on relatively flat slopes (i.e., 1 to 7 percent). Horizontal movements are often as much as 10 to 15 ft (3 to 5 m), but under a long duration of shaking on favorable slopes, the movement may be as great as 100 to 150 ft (30 to 45 m). Lateral spreads usually break up internally, causing fissures and scarps at the surface.

Floodplain deposits are particularly vulnerable to lateral spreading toward river channels. The disruption caused by lateral spreading usually includes (1) damage to bridges by displacement of their abutments and (2) damage to underground utilities.

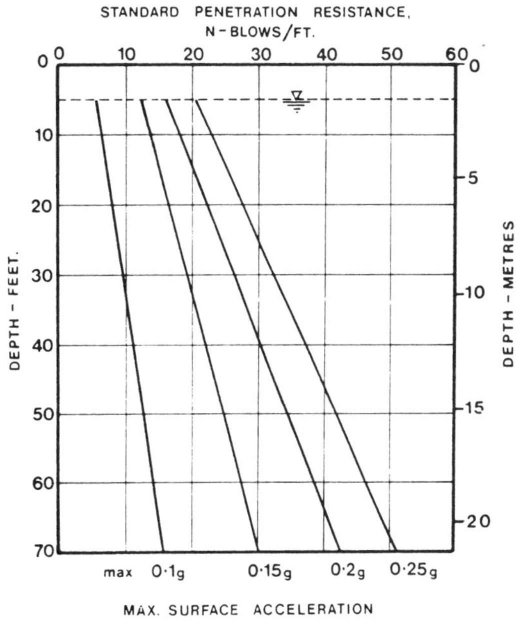
STANDARD PENETRATION RESISTANCE, N-BLOWS/FT.
0 10 20 30 40 50 60
DEPTH - FEET
0 10 20 30 40 50 60 70
DEPTH - METRES
0 5 10 15 20
max 0·1g 0·15g 0·2g 0·25g
MAX. SURFACE ACCELERATION

Figure 252-13 Standard penetration resistance values above which liquefaction is unlikely to occur under any conditions.

Flow Failures:

Flow failures are the most catastrophic type of ground failure caused by liquefac-

TABLE 252-3
Typical Engineering–Geologic Conditions That Determine the Size of the Correction to Seismic Intensity*

	Type geologic section	Engineering geologic condition	Degree of seismic hazard		
			General appraisal	*Increase in the seismic intensity*	*Deviation from the average intensity*
1	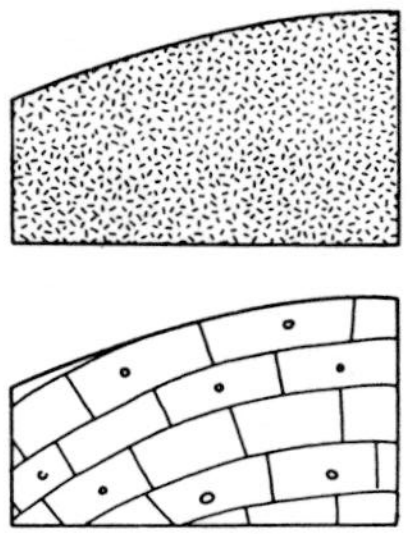	Massively crystalline and the most compact schistose and layered hard and semihard rocks of great thickness, unweathered and unfractured, magmatic crystalline and compact structures, e.g., granite and basalt, sedimentary rocks, thickly layered, e.g., conglomerate, sandstone, and limestone; metamorphic rocks, e.g., gneiss and quartzite.	The safest in seismic behavior; not subjected to permanent deformation (except for earthquakes above intensity 10–11).	0	Decreased by 1–2 units.
2		Less compact layered and schistose and also porous hard and semihard rocks of great thickness, gently lying or contorted by shallow folds, without signs of fault dislocations, unweathered and unfractured, volcanic tuffs and tufaceous sandstones, micaceous and argillaceous schists; thin-bedded sandstones; marls; porous rocks—such as calcareous tufa, chalk, tripoli; soft rocks such as gypsum.	Also safe in seismic behavior, but less so than case 1; these rocks, now subject to permanent deformation, can develop fissures.	0.7–1.1	Decreased by 1 unit.
3	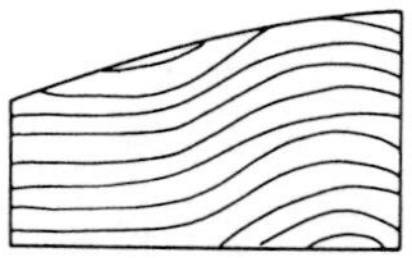	Thick (not less than 10 m) layers of dry argillaceous rocks, gently dipping or folded.	Safe under dry conditions, but when wet, the rocks become dangerous and are subject to permanent dislocation in proportion to the degree of wetness.	1.2–1.6	Unchanged.
4	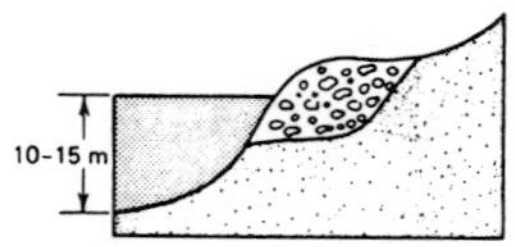 10-15 m	Thick (not less than 10–15 m) layers of compactly deposited granular rocks: sandstone, gritstone, and boulder gravel.	Can be seismically hazardous because of low seismic stability, subject to compaction and unequal settling; sudden sags on saturated, weakly compacted sands are possible.	1.2–1.8	Unchanged or increased by 1 unit on layered strata.
5	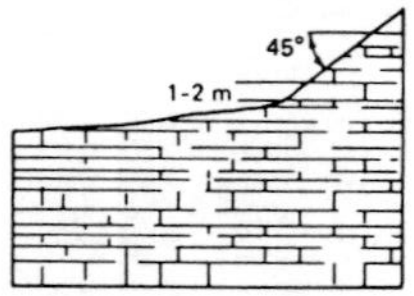 45° 1-2 m	Interbedded layers (1–2 m thick) of unconsolidated (argillaceous or sandy) and hard or semihard rocks—alternating bands of clay or sand with sandstone, limestone, or other sedimentary rock; total thickness of the series is large.	Seismic hazard not great; behavior is worse on steep slopes (steeper than 45°), where local reflected waves can arise; respond more strongly to shaking than layered, massive, homogeneous rocks.	1.0–2.0	Unchanged or increased by 1 unit on layered strata.

6 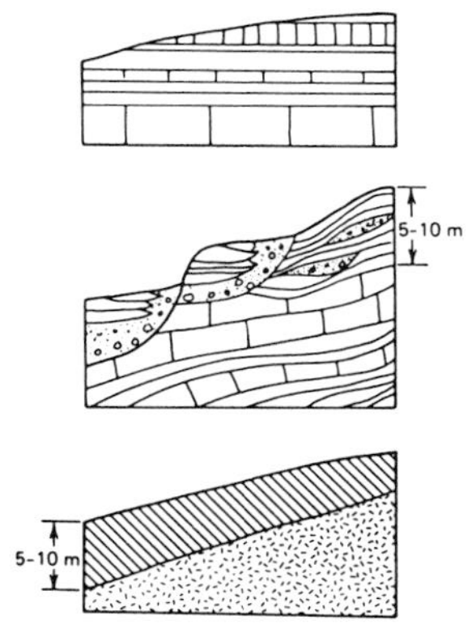5-10 m 5-10 m	Layers 5–10 m thick of dry homogeneous argillaceous or sandy gravelly formations of various origins (marine, lacustrine, glacial, alluvial, proluvial, diluvial with or without thin (less than 1 m) bands of hard or semihard rock (sandstones, limestones); also similar rocks with sharp facies variations.	Not strongly hazardous seismically, the greater the difference in physical properties of contiguous layers, the greater the hazard.	1.0–2.0	Unchanged or increased by 1 unit when the rocks are saturated at a depth not greater than 5 m.
7 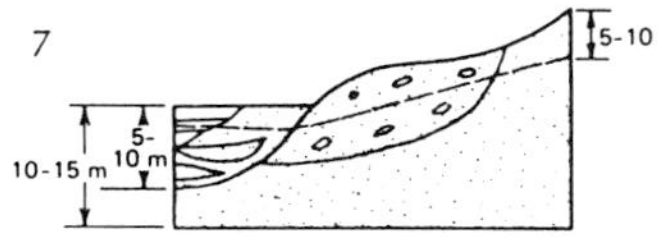5-10 5-10 m 10-15 m	Rather thick unconsolidated formations (clay, sand, gravel) saturated at depths greater than 5 m.	Not strongly hazardous seismically, since saturation at depths greater than 5 m does not strengthen seismic effects.	2.0–2.5	Unchanged or increased by 1 unit when the rocks are saturated at a depth of 5 m.
8 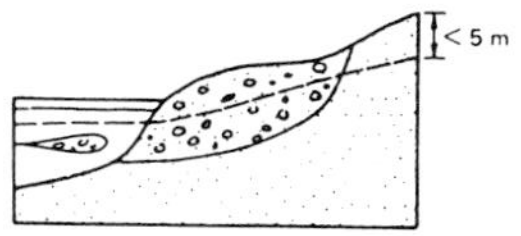< 5 m	Rather thick unconsolidated formations (clay, sand, gravel), but saturated at depths shallower than 5 m (in some places saturated to depths of only 1–3 m).	Argillaceous types and peat bogs are seismically more hazardous than sands, grits, and bouldery gravels; seismic stability of rewetted argillaceous rock types (including loess) is greatly reduced.	1.6–2.4	Increased by 1 unit.
9 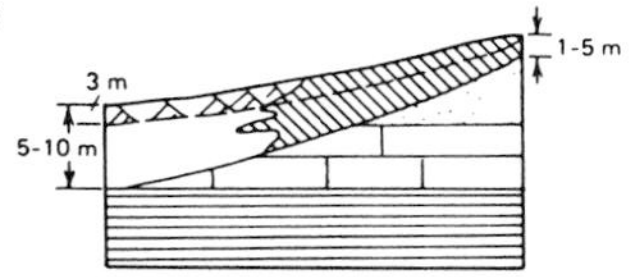1-5 m 3 m 5-10 m	Less thick (5–10 m) unconsolidated formations (clay, sand, gravel) saturated almost to the surface of the earth (1–3 m).	More hazardous seismically than section 8.	1.6–2.8	Increased by 1–2 units.
10 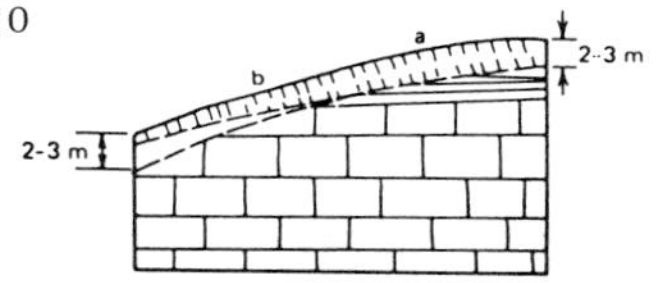a b 2-3 m 2-3 m	Eluviated hard, semihard, or argillaceous rocks in the dry (*a*) or saturated (*b*) state, converted into rubbly or disintegrated loamy formations.	Just as hazardous seismically as section 9, particularly in loosely bedded large fragments.	1.6–2.9	Increased by 1–2 units.
11 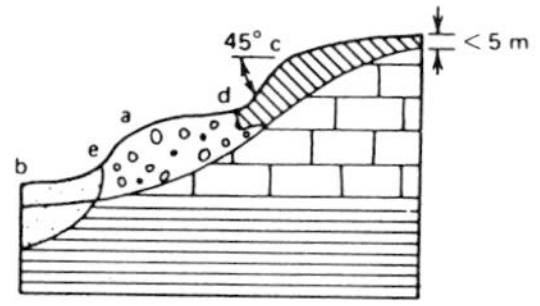45° c < 5 m d a e b	Layers (less than 5 m thick) of unconsolidated formations (diluvial and alluvial argillaceous loams, sandy loams, sands, gravels) lying on compact rock (*a, b, c*). Also contact of diluvial, alluvial (*d*, e) and other types of Quartenary formations.	Just as hazardous seismically as section 10, particularly on steep slopes; the seismic effect becomes stronger the larger the difference in physical properties of the overlying formations and the underlying rocks that are in contact.	2.3–3.0	Increased by 1–2 units.

TABLE 252-3 *(Continued)*

	Type geologic section	Engineering geologic condition	Degree of seismic hazard		
			General appraisal	*Increase in the seismic intensity*	*Deviation from the average intensity*
12	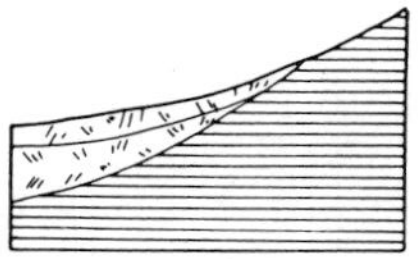	Continually wet or swampy argillaceous formations, such as muddy, sandy, or coarsely broken accumulations on seashores, lake and river banks, river courses, low islands, and turfs that are saturated to the surface of the earth.	Very hazardous seismically, not only on slopes but also on level parts of the region; dilute argillaceous rocks and swamp rocks have a very low seismic stability and may flatten.	2.3–3.9	Increased by 1–2 units (on saturated peat soils).
13	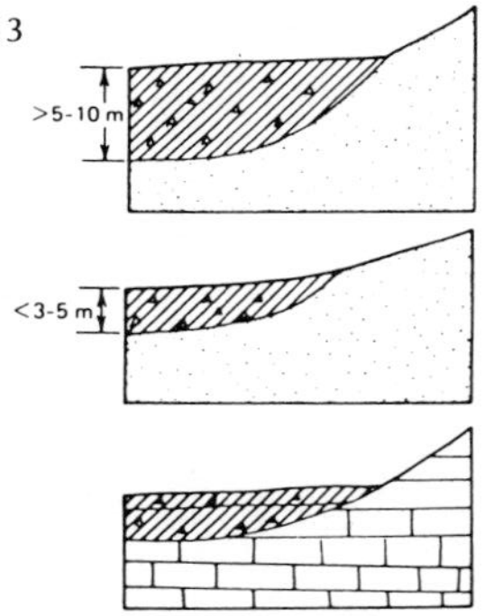>5-10 m <3-5 m	Layers of filled mineral ground and various man-made materials, such as structural debris, that are either (*a*) thicker than 5–10 m; (*b*) thinner than 3–5 m; or (*c*) saturated.	Very hazardous seismically, especially on slopes and in fills that are loosely bedded and may undergo strong, unequal settling (sections *b* and *c* are always hazardous).	2.3–3.9	Increased by 1–2 units.
14	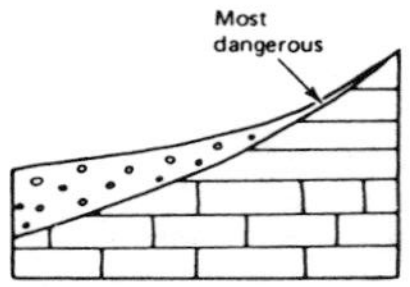Most dangerous	Unstable bedded gravitating formations; hillside waste (talus) of finely broken material and large angular fragments of different thicknesses.	Very harzardous seismically, especially on steep slopes and also in regions undergoing solufluction.	2.0–3.9	Increased 1–2 units.
15	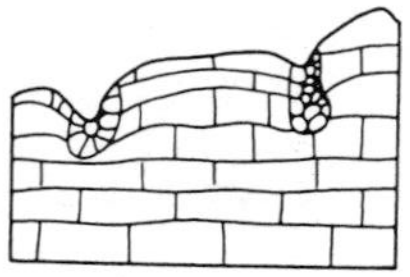	Karst carbonate, hard and semihard rocks, strongly deformed but with the phenomena of settling and caving in not yet completed; here also can be classified rocks that have been disrupted by mining.	Very hazardous seismically on active karst because of unequal settling; on old karst, seismic islands can occur.	2.0–4.0	Intensity unchanged or increased by 1–2 units.
16	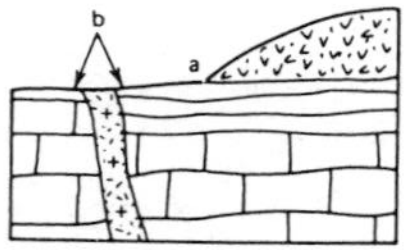b a	Contacts of intrusive and extrusive rocks with metamorphic or sedimentary rocks; e.g., contacts of basaltic lava flows with clays (*a*) and other rocks, and contacts of intrusive rocks with their enclosing rocks (*b*).	Sometimes very hazardous seismically, especially at contacts between rocks with sharply different physical properties.	1.0–4.0	Intensity unchanged or increased by 1 unit.

17	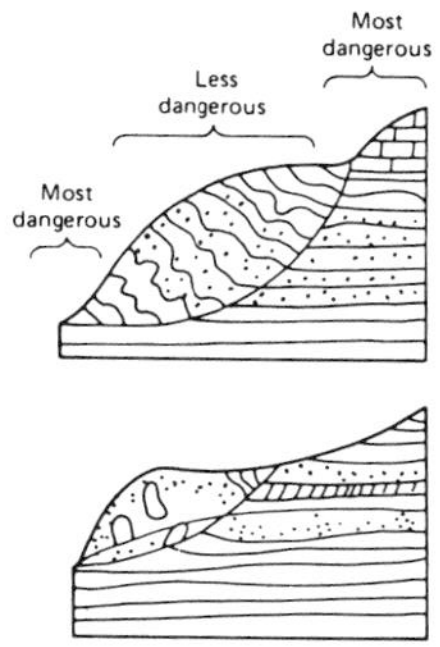 Most dangerous Less dangerous Most dangerous	Old, dry, arrested landslides and earthflows of diverse rocks (*a*); active earthflows of various types, with different thicknesses of the sliding material, and saturated (*b*).	Old, dry large earthflows are relatively safe, but active, wet earthflows are very hazardous, for earthquakes can cause them to move; the breakaway line and sectors located on it are the most hazardous.	1.0–4.0	Intensity unchanged (on old earthflows) or increased by 1–2 units (on active earthflows).
18	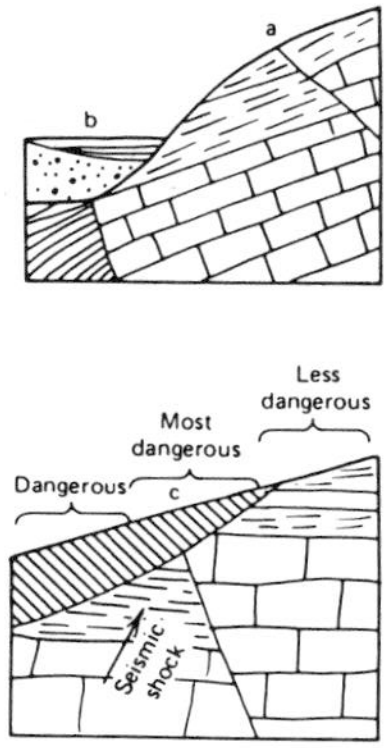 a b Less dangerous Most dangerous Dangerous c Seismic shock	Hard (stony), semihard, or soft (nonstony) rocks broken by fissures due to faults and offsets, or a whole zone of fractures, cropping out at the earth's surface (*a*) or covered by unconsolidated formations (*b*, saturated, *c*, dry).	Extremely hazardous seismically, but deep zones of fractures and faults can decrease the seismic effect on the other side of these disturbances in relation to the direction of arrival of the seismic shock (*c*). Thick, uncompacted mantling formations are capable of mitigating the seismic effect on faults; but thin, especially saturated, mantling formations increase the seismic effect, being badly cracked, and having settled.	3.0–4.0	Increased by 2 units

* Granite is taken as the standard rock (O).

Source: USGS Bulletin 1279, "Use of Seismic Intensity Data to Predict the Effects of Earthquakes and Underground Nuclear Explosions in Various Geologic Settings;" and John E. Costa and Victor R. Baker, *Surficial Geology Building with the Earth,* Wiley, New York, 1981.

TABLE 252-4
Liquefaction Potential Related to Relative Density D_r of Soil

Maximum ground surface acceleration	*Liquefaction very likely*	*Liquefaction depends on soil type and earthquake magnitude*	*Liquefaction very unlikely*
0.10 g	$D_r < 33\%$	$33\% < D_r < 54\%$	$D_r > 54\%$
0.15 g	$D_r < 48\%$	$48\% < D_r < 73\%$	$D_r > 73\%$
0.20 g	$D_r < 60\%$	$60\% < D_r < 85\%$	$D_r > 85\%$
0.25 g	$D_r < 70\%$	$70\% < D_r < 92\%$	$D_r > 92\%$

Source: After H. B. Seed and I. M. Idriss, "Simplified Procedure for Evaluating Soil Liquefaction Potential," *Journal Soil Mechanics and Foundation Division*, ASCE97, SM9, 1249–1273, September 1971.

tion. Liquefied soil or blocks of intact material are transported on a layer of liquefied soil. The flows may be very large [e.g., 1 mi^2 (1.6 km^2)] and may move many feet (meters) or even miles (kilometers) at velocities reaching tens of miles (kilometers) per hour. Flow failures usually occur in loose saturated sands or silts on slopes greater than 6 or 7 percent.

Flows can originate either underwater or on land masses. Underwater flows can generate large sea waves (tsunamis) which in turn cause additional damage to inhabited coastal areas.

Loss of Bearing Strength:

A loss of bearing strength of liquefied soil poses a significant hazard to large built structures. Major deformations can occur within the soil, causing large buildings to settle and tip.

Liquefaction-caused bearing failures are particularly damaging when a layer of saturated cohesionless material extends from near the ground surface to a depth approximately equal to the width of the building that is subjected to shaking.

5.0 STRATEGIES TO REDUCE EARTHQUAKE LOSSES

5.1 Evaluating Seismic Hazards and Risk

In planning for seismic safety, seismic risk must be evaluated. Seismic risk differs from seismic hazard in that *seismic risk* is the exposure of individuals and objects to potential injury or damage from seismic hazards, whereas *seismic hazards* are the physical effects of tectonic activity such as ground shaking and soil failures. At present, little can be done to modify earthquake hazards, but much can be done to reduce seismic risk.

Estimations of both earthquake hazards and risk are based on the predicted location, duration, and intensity of future earthquakes. The prediction of earthquakes is at present receiving a great deal of attention in many countries, and significant progress has been made in recent years.

Risk evaluation at a more detailed level requires an evaluation of the seismic hazards and assessment of the degree of exposure of individuals and structures to those hazards. Figure 252-15 shows the basic procedure commonly used in evaluating seismic risk.

Regional seismicity is assessed on the basis of a geological investigation of fault zones. Individual hazards are then assessed.

5.2 The Design Earthquake

The *design earthquake* is a hypothetical event which is used as the basis for assess-

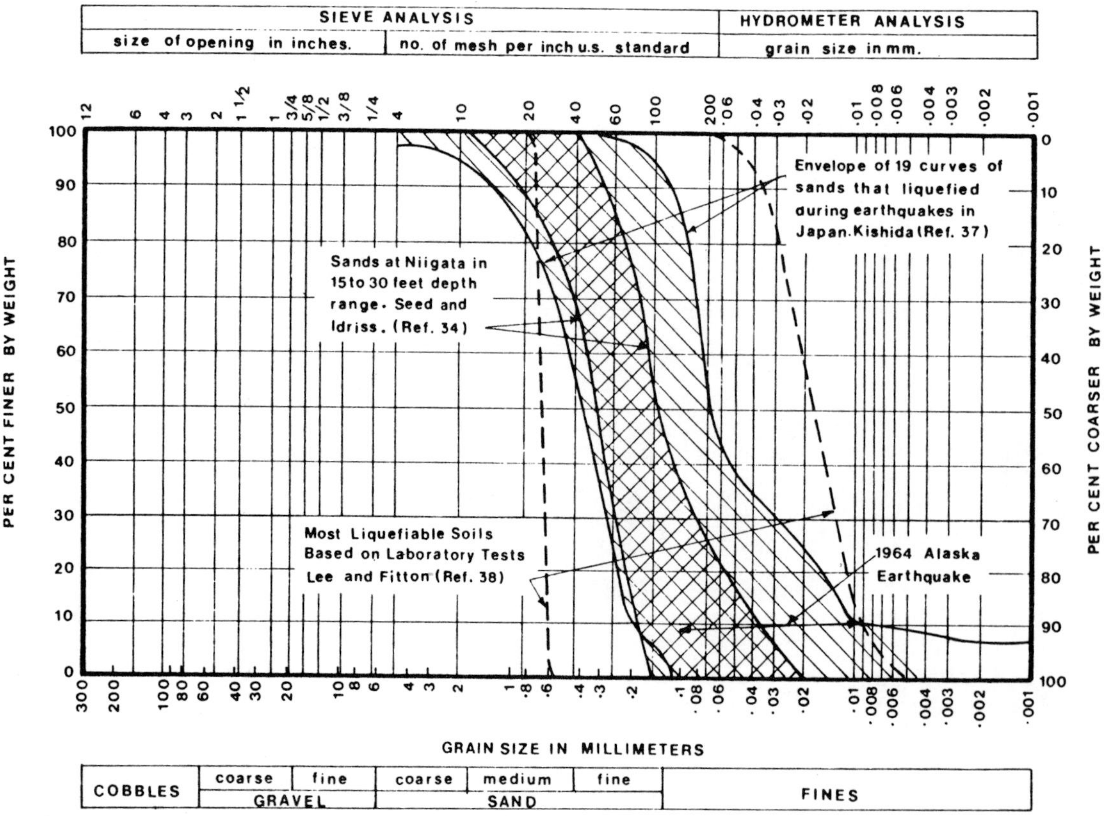

SIEVE ANALYSIS
HYDROMETER ANALYSIS
size of opening in inches.
no. of mesh per inch u.s. standard
grain size in mm.
PER CENT FINER BY WEIGHT
PER CENT COARSER BY WEIGHT
Envelope of 19 curves of sands that liquefied during earthquakes in Japan. Kishida (Ref. 37)
Sands at Niigata in 15 to 30 feet depth range. Seed and Idriss. (Ref. 34)
Most Liquefiable Soils Based on Laboratory Tests Lee and Fitton (Ref. 38)
1964 Alaska Earthquake
GRAIN SIZE IN MILLIMETERS
COBBLES
coarse
fine
GRAVEL
coarse
medium
fine
SAND
FINES

Figure 252-14 Liquefaction potential related to particle size.

ing seismic hazards. The design earthquake can be defined based on:

1. The geologically determined rate of slip and the historical records of ground deformation

2. The seismic history of the fault and the surrounding tectonic regime

3. Geologic evaluation of the tectonic setting

4. The empirically derived relationship between the magnitude of earthquakes and the fault length or other parameters

The design earthquake establishes the expected maximum magnitude and location, which is then used to estimate the extent and severity of the various seismic hazards. If the expected frequency of occurrence is very low, the expected magnitude of the design earthquake is sometimes reduced. The design earthquake is usually the maximum event expected on the largest fault affecting the area. It may represent a single large earthquake or a series of earthquakes of different magnitudes.

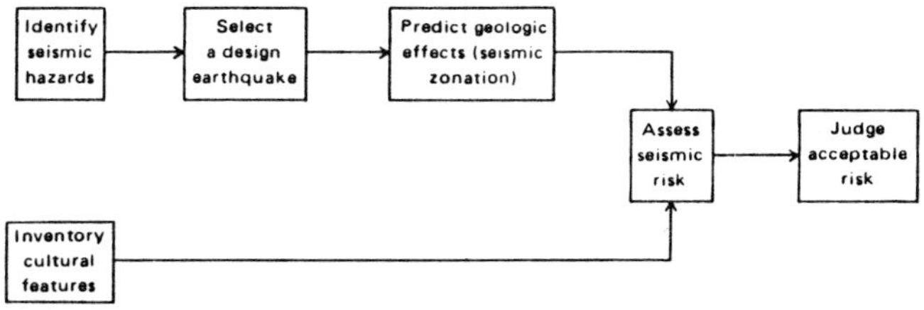
Identify seismic hazards
Select a design earthquake
Predict geologic effects (seismic zonation)
Assess seismic risk
Judge acceptable risk
Inventory cultural features

Figure 252-15 Steps in evaluating seismic risk.

Seismic Zonation:

Seismic zonation predicts the effects of the design earthquake on seismic hazards. Since the hazards are closely related to the geologic conditions, the accuracy of the evaluation depends on the level of detail and the accuracy of the basic geologic mapping. Seismic zonation is the delineation of geographical areas with different potentials for the surface faulting, ground shaking, flooding, liquefaction, and landsliding which result from the design earthquake (Figure 252-16). Individual maps can be prepared for individual seismic hazards, and a composite map of hazard zones can be prepared by evaluating the severity of each hazard.

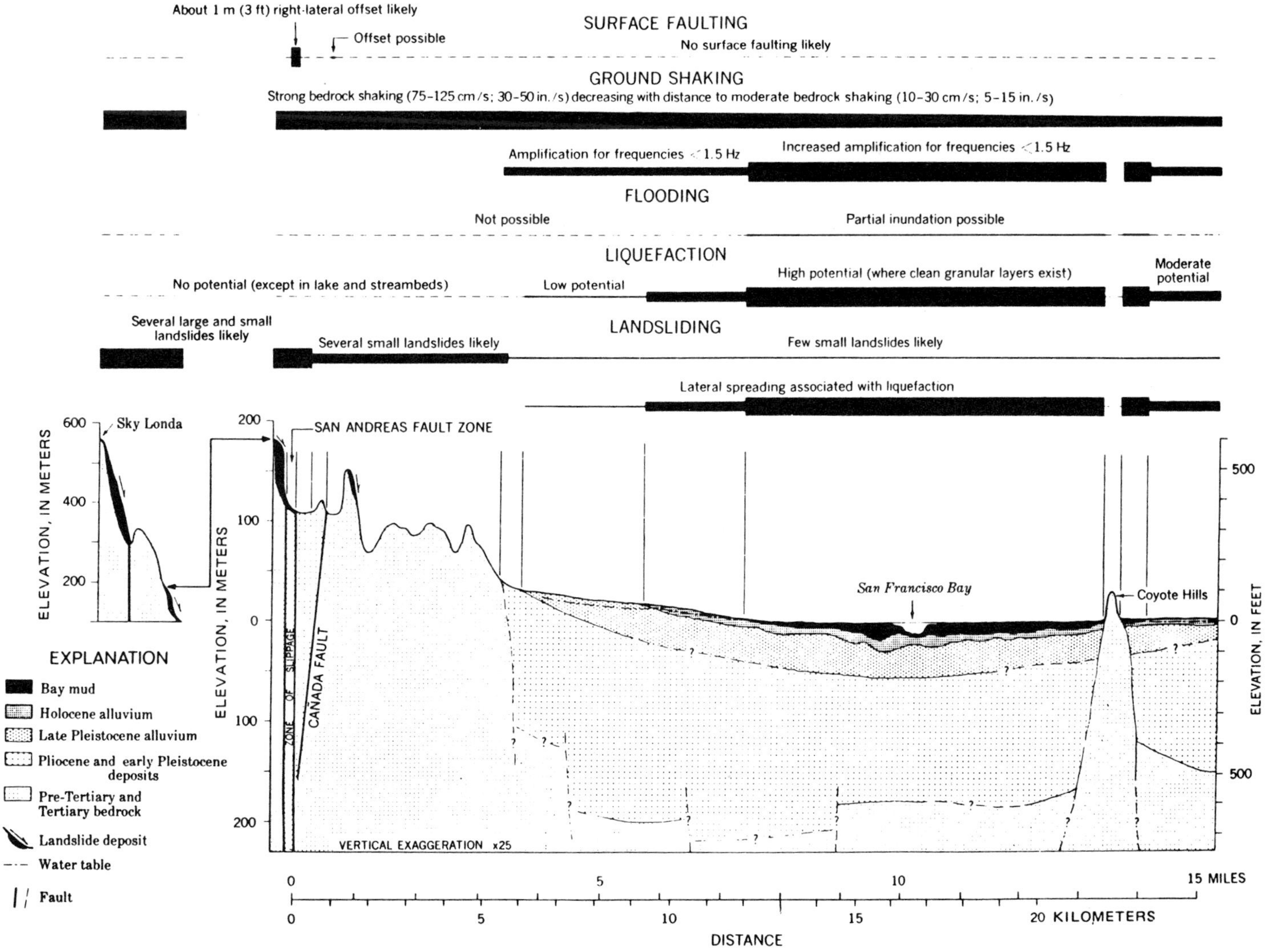
About 1 m (3 ft) right-lateral offset likely
Offset possible
SURFACE FAULTING
No surface faulting likely
GROUND SHAKING
Strong bedrock shaking (75–125 cm/s; 30–50 in./s) decreasing with distance to moderate bedrock shaking (10–30 cm/s; 5–15 in./s)
Amplification for frequencies < 1.5 Hz
Increased amplification for frequencies < 1.5 Hz
FLOODING
Not possible
Partial inundation possible
LIQUEFACTION
No potential (except in lake and streambeds)
Low potential
High potential (where clean granular layers exist)
Moderate potential
Several large and small landslides likely
LANDSLIDING
Several small landslides likely
Few small landslides likely
Lateral spreading associated with liquefaction
Sky Londa
SAN ANDREAS FAULT ZONE
ZONE OF SLIPPAGE
CANADA FAULT
San Francisco Bay
Coyote Hills
ELEVATION, IN METERS
ELEVATION, IN FEET
VERTICAL EXAGGERATION x25
EXPLANATION
Bay mud
Holocene alluvium
Late Pleistocene alluvium
Pliocene and early Pleistocene deposits
Pre-Tertiary and Tertiary bedrock
Landslide deposit
Water table
Fault
15 MILES
20 KILOMETERS
DISTANCE

Figure 252-16 Predicted geologic effects of a postulated earthquake (magnitude 6.5) on the San Andreas Fault. The severity of each earthquake effect is indicated qualitatively by thickness of underlining and is quantified to the extent permitted by the current state of the art of seismic zonation on a regional scale. The severity of the predicted earthquake effects generally depends on the type of underlying geologic material.

Evaluation of Land Uses and Structure Occupancies:

The next step in risk assessment is an evaluation of the vulnerability of various land uses and structure occupancies to earthquake damage. An inventory of uses and structures when related to seismic hazard maps can be used to estimate the risk to structures and people associated with the design earthquake.

Regulation Based on Seismic Risk:

The regulation of land to reduce seismic risk varies in terms of the legal framework of the locality. For instance, the state of California requires all city and county plans to include a seismic element. Subdivision regulations, zoning ordinances, and building codes may require special geological studies in identified risk zones.

Table 252-5 lists those countries in which earthquakes may be a design consideration. It also provides a seismic risk rating and shows whether or not building codes exist for the country as of 1977.

TABLE 252-5
Seismicity and Codes of Various Countries

Countries with earthquakes[a]	*Codes in IAEE publication*[b]	*Also has code*[c]	*Seismic risk rating*[d]	*Maximum base shear coefficient α = a/g*[e]	*Comments*[f]
Afghanistan			High		
Albania			High		
Algeria	1955(F)[g]		Medium	0.175	Code average
Argentina	post-1965(S)		High	0.120	Code average
Australia			Low		
Austria	pre-1966(G)		Low	0.005	Code meaningless, α too low
Bangladesh			High		
Bolivia			Medium		
Bulgaria	1964		Medium	0.32 approximately	Code average
Burma			High		Based on U.S.A., α too small
Canada	1970		Medium in parts	(0.033 Shear) (0.017 Framed)	
Caribbean Islands		1972 (draft)			Based on U.S.A.
Chile	1972(S)		High	(0.144 Shear) (0.096 Ductile)	Code average
China			High in parts		
Colombia			High		
Congo Republic			Low		
Costa Rica			High		Code average
Cuba	1964		Low	(0.10 Shear) (0.08 Framed)	
Cyprus			High		
Dominican Republic			High		
Ecuador			High		
El Salvador	1966		High	(0.24 Shear) (0.12 Framed)	Code average
France	1967		Medium in parts	0.22 approximately	Code average
Germany	1957(G)		Low	0.10	No detail, but α fairly safe
Ghana			Low		
Gibraltar			Low		
Greece	1959		High	0.16	Not very good
Guatemala			High		
Haiti			Medium		
Honduras			High		
India	1970		High in parts	0.12	Code above average
Indonesia		1970	High in parts	0.15	Code below average
Iran	Post-1955		High	0.10	Code not official
Iraq			High		
Israel	Proposed		Low	0.04	Code gives forces only

[a] List of most countries where earthquakes may be a design consideration.

[b] List of those countries whose code is published. The date of each individual code is given where known. Some of these codes are published in their original language only, and this is indicated by letters as follows: (F) = French; (G) = German; (S) = Spanish; (Y) = Yugoslavian.

[c] Other countries known to have codes. No doubt there will always be omissions in this column, as each year more countries are adopting codes.

[d] This column gives a broad indication of the seismic risk in each country; the terms low, medium, and high should not be taken too literally. It is interesting to observe that there are 20 or so countries with medium to high seismic risk which have not formally adopted an earthquake code.

[e] This column gives a rough comparison of the horizontal seismic forces assumed by the various national codes. Values are given for the base shear coefficient $\alpha = V/G + Q$, where V is the seismic base shear, G is the dead load of the structure, and Q is the live load on the structure. α has been calculated for steel or reinforced concrete buildings in each case and is the highest value imposed by each code, i.e., it is for the highest risk zone, with the worst foundation conditions, and for the most valued public buildings (if such differentiations are made).

5.3 Design Strategies for Individual Hazards

Fault Displacement:

Since the areas affected by surface fault rupture and tectonic creep are narrow and since movement can cause severe damage, avoidance of active fault zones for construction of all types is also recommended.

Roads, underground utilities, and other structures which cross active fault traces create continual maintenance problems wherever the fault is subject to tectonic creep. Should a large sudden movement on the fault occur, serious disruption is highly likely. Essential facilities (such as hospitals) whose services must cross fault zones should be equipped with on-site emergency services. In some cases, alternative service networks can be provided which do not cross active fault traces.

Ground Shaking:

Ground shaking causes the most wide-

Countries with earthquakes[a]	*Codes in IAEE publication*[b]	*Also has code*[c]	*Seismic risk rating*[d]	*Maximum base shear coefficient* $\alpha = a/g^e$	*Comments*[f]
Italy	1962		High	0.10	Code poor
Jamaica		See Caribbean	Medium		
Japan	1951–1968		High	0.20	Code above average
Jordan			Low		
Lebanon			Low		
Libya			Medium		
Malawi			Low		
Mexico	1966		High	(0.312 Shear) (0.156 Framed)	Code average, α for Acapulco
Morocco			Medium		
Mozambique			Low		
Nepal			High		
New Guinea			High		
New Zealand	1965		High	0.16	Code average
Nicaragua			High		
Panama			High		
Peru	1968		High	(0.16 Shear) (0.08 Framed)	Code average, α values for T = 0.1[h]
Philippines	1972		High	(0.16 Shear) (0.08 Framed)	Code average, α values for T = 0.1[h]
Portugal	1961		Medium	0.15	Code below average
Rhodesia			Low		
Rumania	Pre-1968		Medium	0.30 approximately	Code average
Spain	1968(S)		Medium	0.40	Code above average
Syria			Medium		
Taiwan			High		
Tanzania			Low		
Tunisia			Medium		
Turkey	1968		High	0.108	Code average
Uganda			Low		
U.S.A.	1970	High in parts		(0.133 Shear) (0.067 Framed)	Code average
U.S.S.R.	1970		High in parts	0.250 (5 storeys)	Code above average
Venezuela	1967		Medium	(0.110 Shear) (0.085 Framed)	Code average
Yugoslavia	1964(Y)		High	0.50 approximately	Code average
Zambia			Low		

Numerical comparisons should not be made too literally as many other code features vary from country to country, e.g., seismic design stresses. Also a few codes, such as those of Bulgaria and Russia, use dynamic rather than static analysis, and only an approximate maximum value of α can be given.

[f] A broad indication of the value of each code to the designer is given. Some of the codes are very bad, either because they give unsafe criteria or because they give too little guidance. Even the best codes are at fault to some extent in either or both of these respects, and the conscientious designer may wish to do better. For example, the designer may see fit to increase the seismic coefficients, or to use larger gaps between adjacent buildings. In this column, 'Code average' means that the code concerned should be used with caution, and some knowledgeable evaluation of the code should be obtained to identify its strengths and weaknesses.

[g] Superseded by 1967 French Code.

[h] T = fundamental period of vibration of the structure, in seconds.

Source: D. J. Dowrick, *Earthquake Resistant Design,* John Wiley & Sons, Ltd., Chicester, England, 1977.

spread damage from earthquakes. The second factor contributing to structural damage is that the initial shock reaching a site causes the peak ground acceleration which results in severe damage to structures; since the local geology of a site can amplify seismic waves, site selection is very important. The third factor is resonance, which is affected by an earthquake's duration and magnitude.

The duration of shaking is an important factor contributing to failure in structures, soils, and slopes. A long duration of strong shaking can cause materials to behave inelastically (i.e., become permanently deformed) and can increase the damaging effects of resonance.

The magnitude of an earthquake affects its duration much more than it affects its peak acceleration. Greater magnitudes are indicative of greater lengths of fault rupture. Seismic waves are progressively emitted along the fault as it ruptures, resulting in a prolongation of shaking at a particular site as seismic waves from along the fault rupture arrive.

Most damage occurs during the first moments of an earthquake. However, tall buildings are particularly vulnerable to the subsequent effects of resonance. Earthquakes produce wave vibrations over a wide range of frequencies, and structures respond to these vibrations by vibrating at various frequencies, depending on the shape, size, and composition of the structure. If a building vibrates with the same frequency as the earthquake waves striking it, resonant motion is established, and increased damage is caused as the vibrations of the structure are reinforced. The rate of vibration is called the *fundamental period.* The effect of a similarity of fundamental

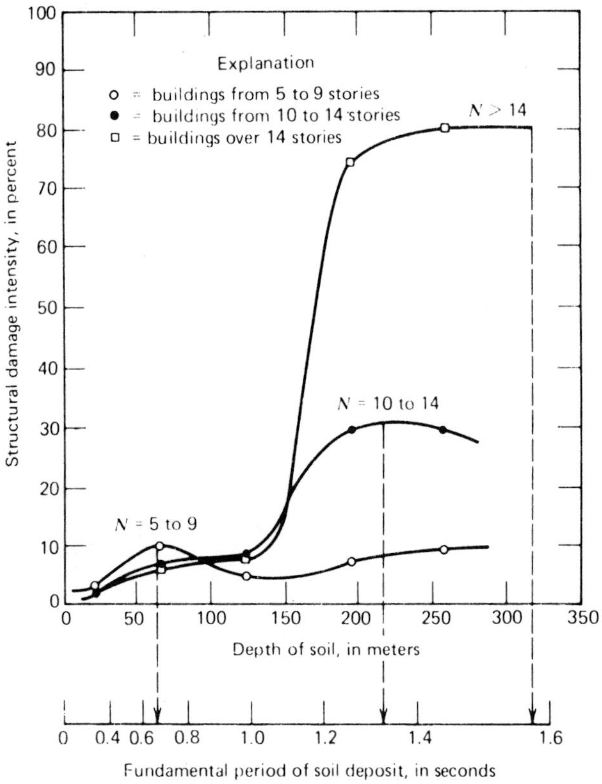
Structural damage intensity, in percent
Explanation
o = buildings from 5 to 9 stories
• = buildings from 10 to 14 stories
□ = buildings over 14 stories
N > 14
N = 10 to 14
N = 5 to 9
0
10
20
30
40
50
60
70
80
90
100
0
50
100
150
200
250
300
350
Depth of soil, in meters
0
0.4
0.6
0.8
1.0
1.2
1.4
1.6
Fundamental period of soil deposit, in seconds

Figure 252-17 Structural damage intensity for different-height buildings related to depth of soil and computed fundamental period of soil deposit. N = number of stories. Where the fundamental period of a soil deposit is short (between 0.6 and 0.8 s) the greatest damage will occur to buildings from five to nine stories tall. With longer soil periods, the damage intensity to higher structures increases.

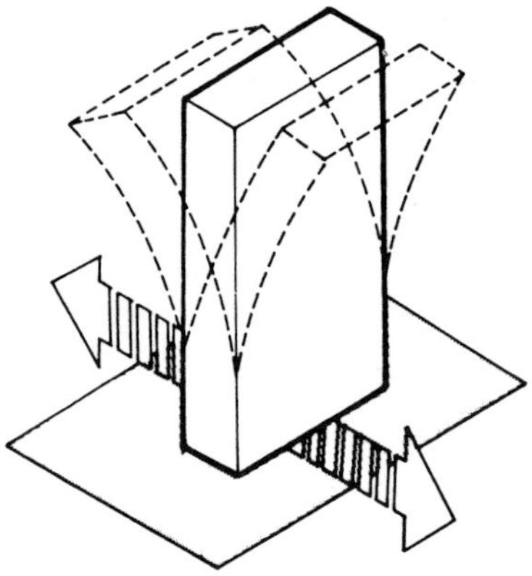

Figure 252-18 Pendulum action. The building acts like a pendulum with respect to the ground.

Figure 252-19 Effects of cyclic reversals of ground acceleration. At the same time that the upper part of a structure begins to move to catch up with the initial displacement, the ground motion reverses itself.

Figure 252-20 Torsion effect on a building plan. Building on left shows rotation of the mass of an east-west wing relative to the mass of a north-south wing. The drawing on the right shows a *regular* plan building with asymmetrical stiffening. In a rectangular building with a very stiff off-center core area and with the remainder of the structure flexible, torsion will develop in the flexible portion around the stiffer core.

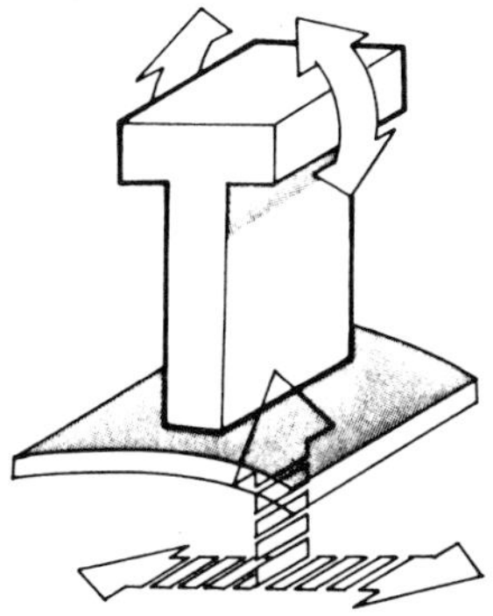

Figure 252-21 Oblique view of vertical torsion effect. Where the upper stories of a tall structure have a greater floor area than those below, torsional problems can result because of vertical accelerations.

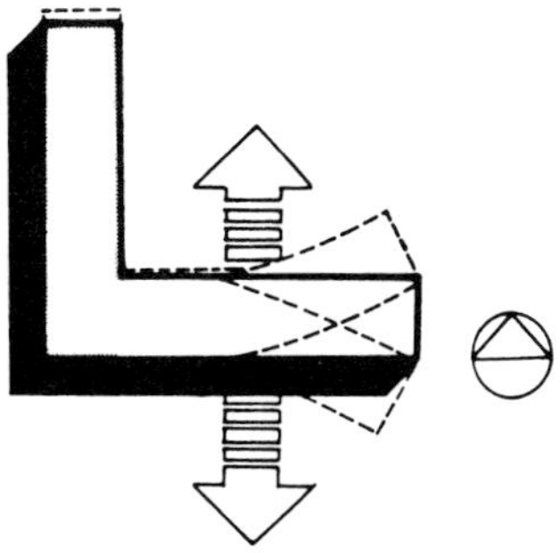

Figure 252-22 Stiffness of a structure related to building plan. The north-south wing of an L-shaped building will be relatively stiffer if its long axis is parallel to the earthquake motion. The east-west is shallow in the direction of the earthquake motion, and unless designed to have adequate capacity to absorb and dissipate the forces, it can suffer greater damage.

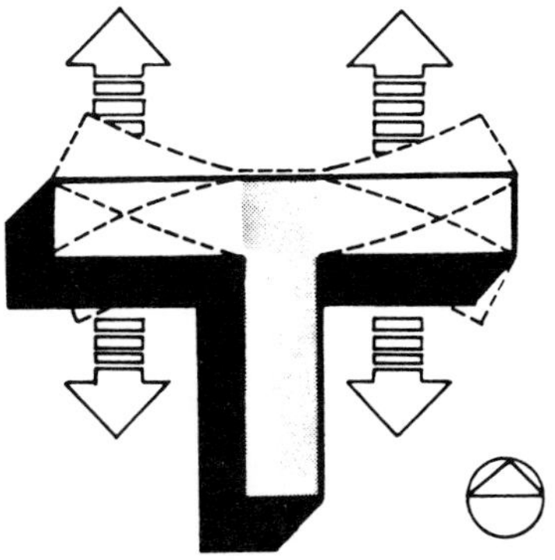

Figure 252-23 Stiffness of a structure related to building plan. The north-south wing of a T-shaped building will be relatively stiffer if its long axis is parallel to earthquake motion. The east-west wing is shallow in the direction of the earthquake motion, and unless designed to have adequate capacity to absorb and dissipate the forces, it can suffer greater damage.

period between a building and the ground shaking on a site can be compared to the effect of pushing on a flexible flagpole at a regular tempo which works with the response of the pole (its fundamental period) to increase its swaying.

Adjacent structures with different characteristics may also vibrate at their own frequencies, causing severe damage as structures vibrating out of phase strike each other.

Taller buildings have longer fundamental periods and are thus subject to greater damage if sited on deep soils with long fundamental periods. Figure 252-17 relates the depth of a soil and the computed fundamental period of a soil to the intensity of structural damage.

Figures 252-18 and 252-19 show the complex effects which earthquake vibrations have on buildings. Earthquake vibrations cause the ground to oscillate in all directions, creating more or less random motions of varying frequencies. Torsional effects of ground and shaking are shown in Figures 252-20 and 252-21. Torsional effects are difficult to assess and can be very destructive.

Selection of a good structural form in regions subject to earthquakes is of major importance, since most earthquake losses (both of life and property) result from the structural failure of buildings.

The plan shape of a building can have significant influence on its ability to withstand the effects of ground shaking. Figures 252-22 and 252-23 illustrate some of the problems caused by complex plan shapes.

Figure 252-24 shows recommended plan and elevation shapes. Square or nearly square plans are preferred, and stiff elements (such as stair towers) should be placed symmetrically within the building envelope. If a square plan is not satisfactory for architectural reasons, movement gaps of at least 4 in (100 mm) in width should be used to divide a long building.

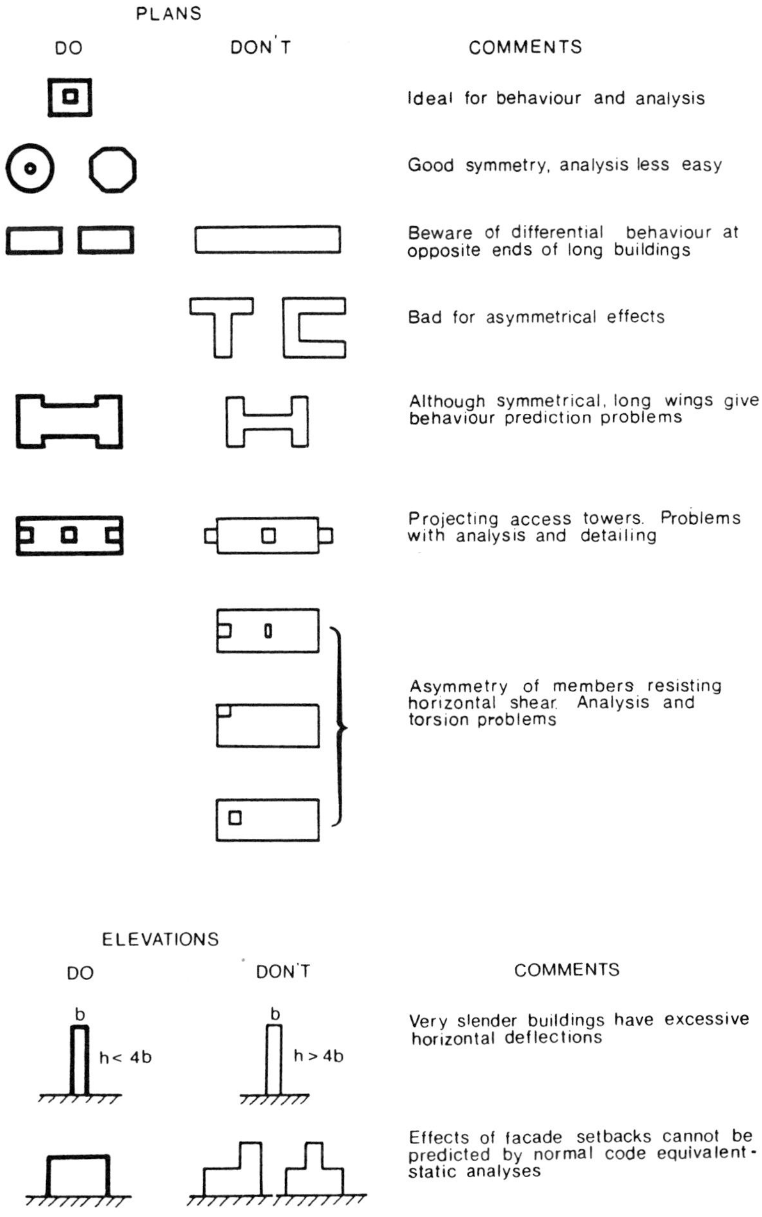

PLANS
DO
DON'T
COMMENTS
Ideal for behaviour and analysis
Good symmetry, analysis less easy
Beware of differential behaviour at opposite ends of long buildings
Bad for asymmetrical effects
Although symmetrical, long wings give behaviour prediction problems
Projecting access towers. Problems with analysis and detailing
Asymmetry of members resisting horizontal shear. Analysis and torsion problems
ELEVATIONS
DO
DON'T
COMMENTS
b
h< 4b
b
h > 4b
Very slender buildings have excessive horizontal deflections
Effects of facade setbacks cannot be predicted by normal code equivalent-static analyses

Figure 252-24 Simple rules for plan layouts and elevation shapes of aseismic buildings. These rules should be broken only with dynamic analysis and careful detailing.

TABLE 252-6
Seismic Coefficients for Earth-Retaining Structures

	Seismic coefficient α = (a/g)		
*Importance category**	*Zone†* A	*Zone†* B	*Zone†* C
1	0.24	0.18	0.12
2	0.17	0.13	0.09

* 1: Major retaining walls supporting important structures or services where failure would have disastrous consequences, such as cutting vital services or causing serious loss of life. 2: Free-standing structures at least 20 ft (6 m) high, not in locations as in category 1, but where replacement would be difficult or costly and other consequences would be serious. 3: For less important structures than above, no specific provision for earthquake loading need be made.

† New Zealand Seismic Zones. Zone *A* represents moderately high seismic risk on a world scale, the maximum design earthquake being of magnitude 7.8, approximately.

Source: D. J. Dowrick, *Earthquake Resistant Design,* John Wiley & Sons, Ltd., Chicester, England, 1977.

Detailing of these gaps is difficult, since they must allow free movement and be wide enough to prevent adjacent sections of the building from striking each other.

It is interesting to note that relatively few failures of retaining walls in earthquakes have been reported. Apparently, retaining walls (which are adequately designed for static earth pressures) will be able to withstand moderate earthquakes without failure. Table 252-6 shows the New Zealand Ministry of Works importance classification for earth retaining structures, along with recommended seismic coefficients for those structures which warrant seismic consideration in design.

Earthquake-Induced Ground Failures:

Since the liquefaction potential can be estimated based on detailed geological investigations, and since the subsequent types of ground failure likely to occur can also be estimated, the locations of potential ground failure can be identified. Avoidance of such sites is preferable. If avoidance is impossible, then the use of deep foundations or pilings may be necessary in areas subject to settlement or to loss of bearing strength.

In all instances, consultation with a professional engineer is recommended for both the identification of potential ground failures and the construction of foundations.

REFERENCES

Arnold, Christopher, and Robert Reitherman. *Building Configuration and Seismic Design,* Wiley, New York, 1982.

Bolt, B. A., et al. *Geological Hazards,* 2d ed., Springer-Verlag, New York, 1975.

Botsai, Elmer E., et al. *Architects and Earthquakes,* AIA Research Corporation, Washington, DC, 1977.

Dowrick, D. J. *Earthquake Resistant Design: A Manual for Engineers and Architects,* Wiley, New York, 1977.

Nichols, D. R., and J. M. Bachanan-Banks. *Seismic Hazards and Land Use Planning,* Geological Survey Circular 690, Washington, DC, 1974.

Weigel, Robert. L. *Earthquake Engineering,* Prentice-Hall, Englewood Cliffs, NJ, 1970.

section 253: Natural Hazards: Landslides and Snow Avalanches

CREDITS

Section Editor: Charles W. Harris
Technical Writer: Tess Canfield

Reviewers:

Professor Tuncer B. Edil
Department of Civil and Environmental Engineering
University of Wisconsin—Madison
Madison, Wisconsin

James E. Hough
James E. Hough and Associates
Cincinnati, Ohio

Jack D. Ives
International Mountain Society
Boulder, Colorado

CONTENTS

1.0 INTRODUCTION

This section deals with the hazards of landslides and snow avalanches. *Landslides* are defined as the downward and outward mass movement of rock, soil, artificial fill, or a combination of these materials. Slope movement results from the action of gravity and climate on geologic materials. Slope processes can be separated into two broad groups. In *mass movement,* debris begins to move as a coherent unit. In *particle movement,* particles move as individuals, with little or no relation to other particles. The distinction between these two categories is often difficult; however, erosional processes caused by rain, waves, currents, groundwater, and winds are generally considered to be particle movements. (Refer to Sections 320: Grading Techniques and 330: Site Drainage, for more information.)

Snow avalanches are defined as the rapid downward movement of a mass of snow, originating on steep slopes, often carrying ice, rock, and debris which contribute to its potential destructiveness.

2.0 LANDSLIDES

2.1 Types of Landslides

In the United States, the most widely used classification of landslide types is based on the predominant type of mass movement which occurs. The six classifications are given in Table 253-1. Table 253-2 shows a rate of movement scale for landslides. Figure 253-1 shows the anatomy of a complex landslide.

2.2 Causes of Landslides

Landslides are caused when the strength of a mass of soil and/or rock that makes up a slope is less than the downhill pull of gravitational force upon it. Normally, most slopes are stable, but the balance of forces can be shifted either by increasing the weight on a slope or by decreasing its resistance to sliding. Landslides often accompany flooding or heavy rains. Unusually wet conditions will increase the weight of the slope and decrease the friction between soil particles. Erosion and/or cuts at the base of a slope can cause weakening and sliding. Earthquakes are an important cause of landslides.

Landslides can also be caused by human activity. Construction, removal of protective vegetation, or activities which cause vibration in the soil (blasting, heavy equipment, etc.) can upset the balance of forces acting on a slope. Common human activities which increase the potential for landslides include:

1. The placement of earth and other heavy fill materials on a slope, which increases the downward force acting on the slope

2. The construction of roads, buildings and other types of structures, which in-

TABLE 253-1
Classification of Landslides

<table>
<tr><th></th><th>Type of movement</th><th>Rate</th><th>Description</th></tr>
<tr><td>Falls</td><td></td><td>Extremely rapid</td><td>Material travels most of the distance through the air.</td></tr>
<tr><td>Topples</td><td>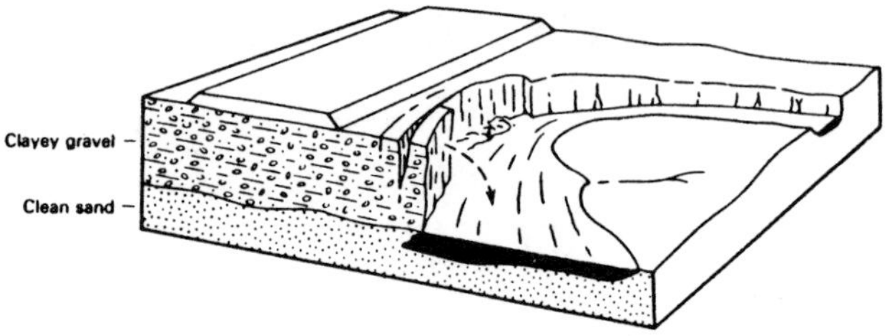
Clayey gravel
Clean sand</td><td>Rapid</td><td>Material tilts forward over a pivot point, resulting in a fall or slide.</td></tr>
<tr><td>Slides</td><td>ROCK SLUMP
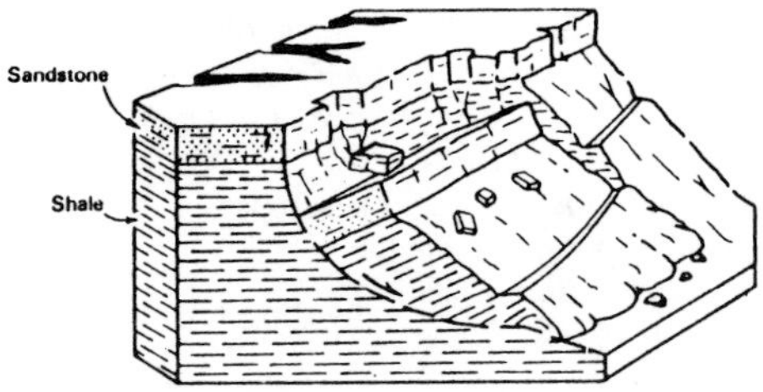
Sandstone
Shale
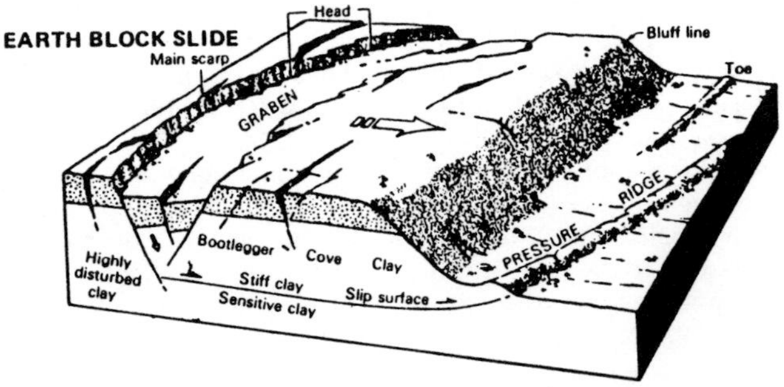
EARTH BLOCK SLIDE
Head
Bluff line
Main scarp
GRABEN
Toe
RIDGE
PRESSURE
Bootlegger
Cove
Clay
Highly disturbed clay
Stiff clay
Sensitive clay
Slip surface</td><td>Extremely slow to moderate

Very slow to rapid</td><td>Rotational (slumps): concave surface of rupture. Material moves along one or more identifiable surfaces.
Translational (slides): generally planar or undulating surface of rupture. Frequently these are caused by structural weaknesses related to faults, bedding planes, etc.</td></tr>
</table>

Source: D. J. Varnes, "Slope Movement Types and Processes," in *Landslides: Analysis and Control,* Special Report 176, Transportation Research Board, National Academy of Sciences, Washington, D.C., 1978.

Type of movement	*Rate*	*Description*
Lateral spreads 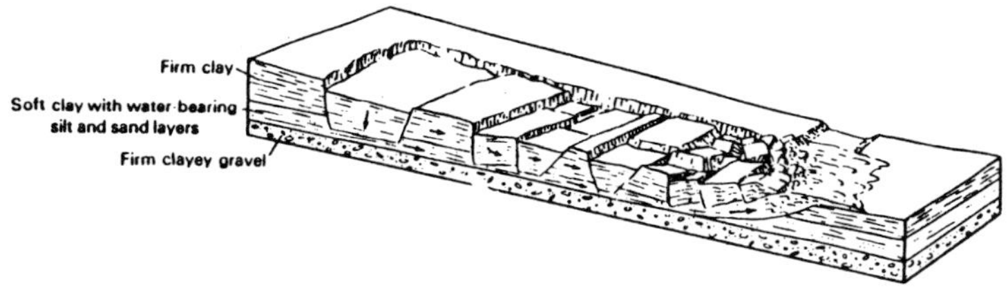 Firm clay Soft clay with water-bearing silt and sand layers Firm clayey gravel	Very rapid to slow	Material in a fractured mass moves laterally, often as a result of liquefaction or plastic flow in subadjacent material.
Flows EARTH FLOW 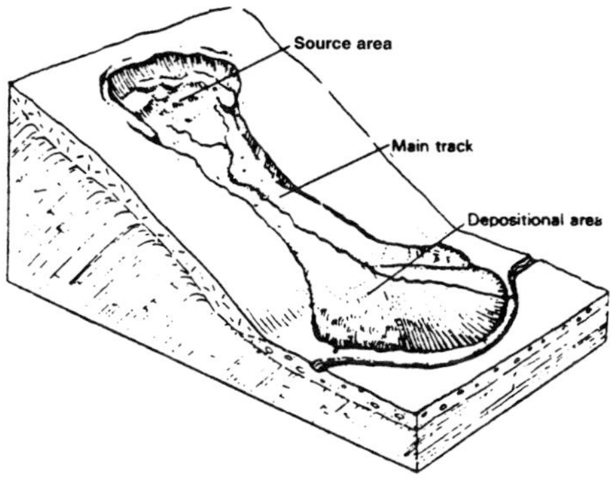 Source area Main track Depositional area	Extremely rapid to extremely slow	Material moves as a viscous fluid.
SOIL CREEP 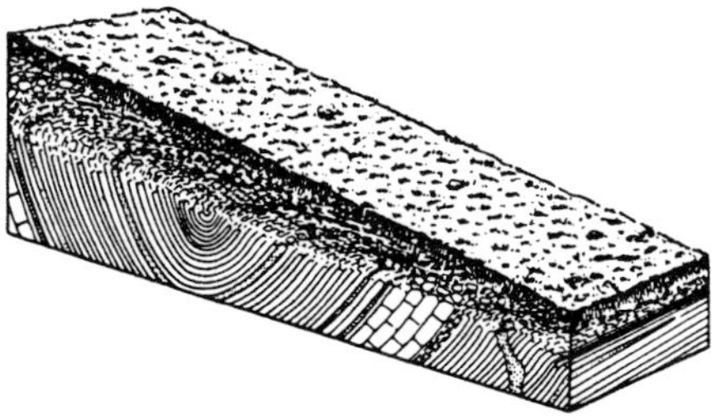	Extremely slow	Material moves downslope at imperceptible rates, usually as a result of soil particle movement.
Complex	—	Movement is a combination of two or more of the above types.

TABLE 253-2
Rate of Movement Scale

ft/sec	Approximate ranges of rates of movement
10^{2}	Extremely rapid
10	10 ft/s (3 m/s)
1	Very rapid
10^{-1}	
10^{-2}	1 ft/min (0.3 m/min)
10^{-3}	Rapid
10^{-4}	5 ft/d (1.5 m/d)
10^{-5}	Moderate
	5 ft/mo (1.5 m/mo)
10^{-6}	Slow
10^{-7}	5 ft/yr (1.5 m/yr)
	Very slow
10^{-8}	1 ft/5 yr (0.06 m/yr)
10^{-9}	Extremely slow

Source: D. J. Varnes, "Slope Movement Types and Processes," in *Landslides: Analysis and Control,* Special Report 176, Transportation Research Board, National Academy of Sciences, Washington, D.C., 1978.

TABLE 253-3
Factors Contributing to Instability of Earth Slopes (After Varnes, 1958)

Factors that contribute to high shear stress	*Factors that contribute to low shear strength*
1. Removal of lateral support *a.* Erosion—bank cutting by streams and rivers *b.* Human agencies—cuts, canals, pits, etc. 2. Surcharge *a.* Natural agencies—weight of snow, ice, and rainwater *b.* Human agencies, fills, buildings, etc. 3. Transitory earth stresses—earthquakes 4. Regional tilting 5. Removal of underlying support *a.* Subaerial weathering—solutioning by groundwater *b.* Subterranean erosion—piping *c.* Human agencies—mining 6. Lateral pressures *a.* Water in vertical cracks *b.* Freezing water in cracks *c.* Swelling *d.* Root wedging	1. Initial state *a.* Composition—inherently weak materials *b.* Texture—loose soils, metastable grain structures *c.* Gross structure—faults, jointing, bedding, planes, varving, etc. 2. Changes due to weathering and other physicochemical reations *a.* Frost action and thermal expansion *b.* Hydration of clay minerals *c.* Drying and cracking *d.* Leaching 3. Changes in intergranular forces due to pore water *a.* Buoyancy in saturated state *b.* Loss in capillary tension upon saturation *c.* Seepage pressure of percolating groundwater 4. Changes in structure *a.* Fissuring of preconsolidated clays due to release of lateral restraint *b.* Grain structure collapse upon disturbance

Source: Donald H. Gray and Andrew T. Leiser, *Biotechnical Slope Protection and Erosion Control,* Van Nostrand Reinhold, New York, 1982.

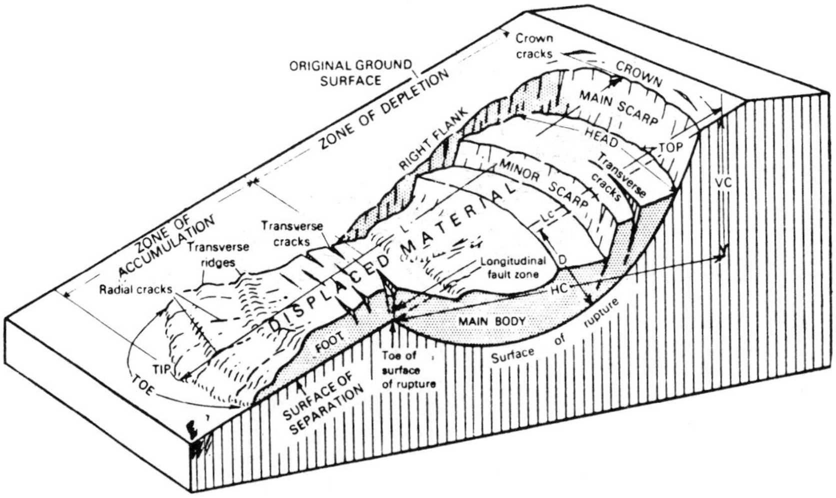
Crown cracks
CROWN
ORIGINAL GROUND SURFACE
ZONE OF DEPLETION
MAIN SCARP
RIGHT FLANK
HEAD
TOP
Transverse cracks
MINOR SCARP
VC
DISPLACED MATERIAL
ZONE OF ACCUMULATION
Transverse ridges
Transverse cracks
Radial cracks
Longitudinal fault zone
HC
MAIN BODY
FOOT
TIP
TOE
SURFACE OF SEPARATION
Toe of surface of rupture
Surface of rupture

Figure 253-1 Anatomy of a complex landslide.

MAIN SCARP—A steep surface on the undisturbed ground around the periphery of the slide, caused by the movement of slide material away from undisturbed ground. The projection of the scarp surface under the displaced material becomes the surface of rupture.

MINOR SCARP—A steep surface on the displaced material produced by differential movements within the sliding mass.

HEAD—The upper parts of the slide material along the contact between the displaced material and the main scarp.

TOP—The highest point of contact between the displaced material and the main scarp.

TOE OF SURFACE OF RUPTURE—The intersection (sometimes buried) between the lower part of the surface of rupture and the original ground surface.

TOE—The margin of displaced material most distant from the main scarp.

TIP—The point on the toe most distant from the top of the slide.

FOOT—That portion of the displaced material that lies downslope from the toe of the surface of rupture.

MAIN BODY—That part of the displaced material that overlies the surface of rupture between the main scarp and toe of the surface of rupture.

FLANK—The side of the landslide.

CROWN—The material that is still in place, practically undisplaced and adjacent to the highest parts of the main scarp.

ORIGINAL GROUND SURFACE—The slope that existed before the movement which is being considered took place. If this is the surface of an older landslide, that fact should be stated.

LEFT AND RIGHT—Compass directions are preferable in describing a slide, but if right and left are used they refer to the slide as viewed from the crown.

SURFACE OF SEPARATION—The surface separating displaced material from stable material but not known to have been a surface on which failure occurred.

DISPLACED MATERIAL—The material that has moved away from its original position on the slope. It may be in a deformed or undeformed state.

ZONE OF DEPLETION—The area within which the displaced material lies below the original ground surface.

ZONE OF ACCUMULATION—The area within which the displaced material lies above the original ground surface.

creases both the load and the water infiltration

3. The use of on-site sewage disposal systems, the construction of ponds, and the use of sprinkler systems, all of which increase the infiltration of water into a slope and increase its tendency to slide

4. The grading of a site which results in undercutting the toe of a vulnerable slope

Table 253-3 outlines the causes of earth slope instability, both human-caused and naturally occurring. Table 253-4 describes geologic conditions which indicate high susceptibility to landslides.

TABLE 253-4
Conditions Susceptible to Sliding

Condition	*Description*
Saturated cohesive, clayey soils	Sloped areas of cohesive, clayey soils are susceptible to sliding because of an increase in weight due to the absorbed water.
Loose, granular materials with low shear strength	Loose, granular materials readily absorb moisture, thus increasing their weight and causing slides, slumps, and flows.
Interbedded sedimentary rock parallel to hillslopes	Interbedded sedimentary rock with joints parallel to valley walls are susceptible to sliding due to the increased weight of the water. Bedding planes or joints are lubricated by water, which causes slippage.
Highly foliated metamorphic rock	Foliations parallel to valley walls cause conditions similar to those for interbedded sedimentary rocks. The occurrence of minerals such as micas and serpentine increases the slipperiness of a slope.
Rotten or decomposed igneous or metamorphic rock	Rotten, loose, granular rock debris is susceptible to increases in moisture content and can create potential sliding conditions.
Fractures and faults	When fractures or faults parallel or intercept a slope, and there is no lateral support, or when seepage lubricates rock surfaces, there is an increased danger of sliding.
Interbedded materials of differing resistance or permeability	Interbedded materials with differences in their resistance to weathering result in the deterioration of the softer materials, thereby allowing water to accumulate in the elevated rock layers. Conditions such as limestones over shale or clay, sandstone underlaid by an impervious stratum, and lava flows over tuff can result in the development of cliffs and overhangs and conditions susceptible to falls.
Seepage of water along hillsides	The appearance of seepage water along hillslopes may indicate the development of high pore or hydrostatic pressures, especially if the water is found near the toe of the slope.
Colluvial soils	These and other soils formed by earlier mass-wasting indicate previously unstable conditions which may still exist.
Water and land edges after rapid decreases in water level	The recession of flood waters or the lowering of reservior levels can create temporary unstable conditions along the land edges.
Borrowed fills	Fill areas are susceptible to slumping or sliding if hydrostatic pressures build up, if seepage occurs under the fill, or if the fill is placed on a soil of high volume change. Such fills should be anchored and well-drained.
Coastal slopes and river banks	Coastal slopes and river banks are subject to erosive action of waves and currents.

Source: Adapted from Douglas S. Way, *Terrain Analysis: A Guide to Site Selection Using Aerial Photographic Interpretation,* Douglas S. Way, Columbus, Ohio, 1978.

2.3 Estimation of Landslide Hazard

Figure 253-2 is a landslide susceptibility map developed by the U.S. Geological Survey; the map is based on both the physical conditions which make landslides possible (bedrock geology, soils, slopes, and pattern of rainfall) and on recorded occurrences of landslides. This map for the United States and similar maps for other parts of the world are useful for ascertaining a generalized view of the landslide potential of a region and for helping alert the reader to areas that may require further investigation. These generalized maps, however, are not meant to be used to determine the potential for landslides on a particular site, even on a very large site.

In the United States, more-detailed maps of landslide hazards have been prepared by the U.S. Geological Survey for areas where the problems have been most severe. District offices maintain lists of available maps. State geological survey units or mining regulation agencies may also provide landslide hazard maps. Soil survey maps can be useful as an interim source of information until more precise studies are available.

In many areas of the United States and elsewhere in the world, such detailed information on landslide hazards is not available. A preliminary investigation of a site by a knowledgeable person or geological engineer, particularly by aerial photo analyses, can give good indications as to whether more comprehensive geotechnical investigations are required.

Certain combinations of surface disturbances can signify former landslides or areas of high landslide potential. These key features are described in Table 253-5.

Aerial photographs can reveal the distribution of former landslides in an area. Zones of previous sliding activity are evident on aerial photographs by characteristic crescent-shaped scarps and hummocky topography. It is more difficult to identify areas that have a potential for future landsliding. Because the key features in such cases are rather small, large-scale photographs (greater than 1:9600) are most useful. Surface evidence is often either hidden by vegetation or is so subtle that only direct field observation will reveal the need for more thorough studies.

As part of the geotechnical investigation of a site in an area thought to be potentially hazardous, the presence of unstable materials should be determined by investigation of surface and subsurface features. Surface investigations should include hydrologic aspects of the site, such as seepage zones and the groundwater's depth and seasonal fluctuations. Borings may be necessary to provide information on the vertical stratification of soils. The compactness of granular soils and the consistency of cohesive soils should also be ascertained. The investigation should be conducted by a geotechnical engineer, who should also assess both the short- and long-term stability of the site and the possible effects of any development on adjoining areas.

2.4 Landslide Loss Prevention and Reduction

Because landslide-prone areas often offer spectacular views, they are frequently sought for all kinds of land development. Both the regulation of future development and the protection of existing develop-

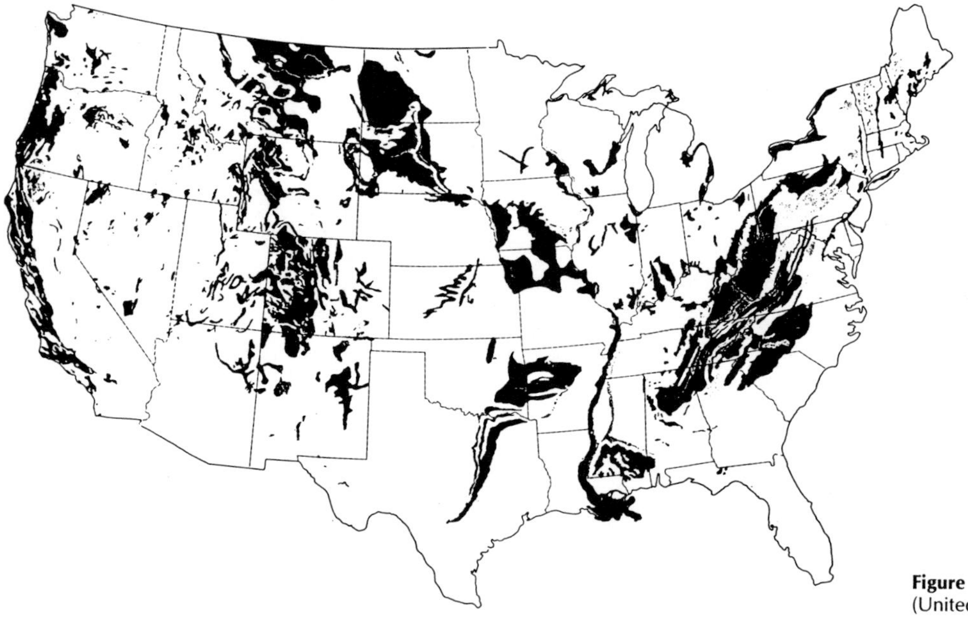

Figure 253-2 Landslide susceptibility map (United States).

TABLE 253-5
Features Indicating Landslides or Areas with High Landslide Potential

Feature	*Significance*
Structural damage	Road settlement or uplift; broken pipes or power lines; spalling or cracking of concrete structures; closure of expansion joints in bridge plates or rigid pavement; loss of alignment; leaking pools; doors or windows that jam.
Hummocky, dissected topography	Common feature in old and active progressive slides (slides with many individual components). Slide mass is prone to gullying.
Abrupt change in slope	May indicate either an old landslide area or a change in the erosion characteristics of underlying material. Portion with low slope angle is generally weaker and often has higher water content.
Scarps and cracks	Definite indication of an active or recently active landslide. Age of scarp can usually be estimated by the amount of vegetation established upon it. Width of cracks may be monitored to estimate relative rates of movement.
Grabens or "stair step" topography	Indication of progressive failure. Complex or nested series of rotational slides can also cause surface of slope to appear stepped or tiered.
Lobate slope forms	Indication of former earth flow or solifluction area.
Hillside ponds	Local catchments or depressions formed as result of (4) above act as infiltration source which can exacerbate or accelerate landsliding.
Hillside seeps	Common in landslide masses. Area with high landslide potential. Can usually be identifed by associated presence of denser or phreatophyte vegetation (cattails, equisetum, alder, etc.) in vicinity of seep.
Incongruent vegetation	Patches or areas of much younger or very different vegetation (e.g., alder thickets); may indicate recent landslides or unstable ground.
"Jackstrawed" trees	Leaning or canted trees on a slope are indicators of previous episodes of slope movement or soil creep.
Bedding planes and joints dipping downslope	Potential surface of sliding for translational slope movements.
Accumulation of debris in valleys and stream channels	Accumulations of soil materials in these areas indicate previous sliding and slumping, commonly associated with stream undermining of embankments.
Light tones along upper edges of hillsides or cliffs	These tones, especially when linear, may indicate the formation of subsurface cracks; these facilitate drainage and cause the lighter tone. The appearance of these tones may precede the occurrence of actual breaks and scarps in the land surface.
Changes in tone along upper areas of cliffs or embankments	Changes in tone near edges of embankments may indicate moisture differences in the subsoil, reflecting moisture accumulation and the development of hydrostatic water pressures.

Source: Adapted from Donald H. Gray and Andrew T. Leiser, *Biotechnical Slope Protection and Erosion Control,* Van Nostrand Reinhold Company, New York, 1982; and Douglas S. Way, *Terrain Analysis: A Guide to Site Selection Using Aerial Photographic Interpretation,* Douglas S. Way, Columbus, Ohio, 1978.

ment are important in reducing landslide hazards.

Regulation:

The regulation of future development can be achieved by zoning, subdivision, and sanitary regulations and by special regulations for hillsides identified as landslide-prone areas. Zoning can restrict intensive development and/or prohibit land uses that would be vulnerable to landslide damage. Subdivision regulations can require that landslide hazard areas be identified and reserved for open-space uses. The siting of roads and bridges should avoid such hazardous areas. If alternative locations cannot be found for roads or bridges, then they should be designed to require minimal cuts and fills and should be able to withstand expected landslide conditions. Regulations can restrict the use of on-site water-based sanitary disposal systems which could trigger landslides by wetting vulnerable areas. Hillside and slide-prone area regulations can limit densities, prohibit certain uses, such as the storage of hazardous materials, and restrict activities that could trigger sliding, such as off-road vehicles. Regulations can also establish certain grading practices and call for the preservation of existing vegetation.

Protection:

The protection of existing development is a complex problem because corrective measures are difficult to standardize. Four responses to landslide hazard include:

1. Do nothing and accept possible losses.

2. Avoid or eliminate the problem by (a) moving off the hazardous part of a site, (b) bridging over or tunneling under the area, and (c) completely or partially removing the unstable material.

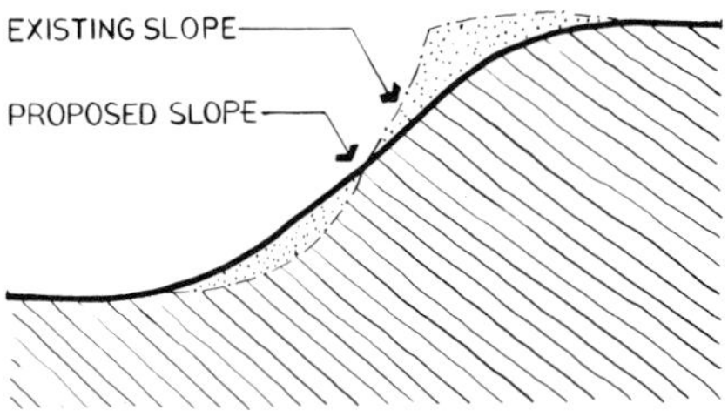
EXISTING SLOPE
PROPOSED SLOPE

Figure 253-3 Flattening a slope.

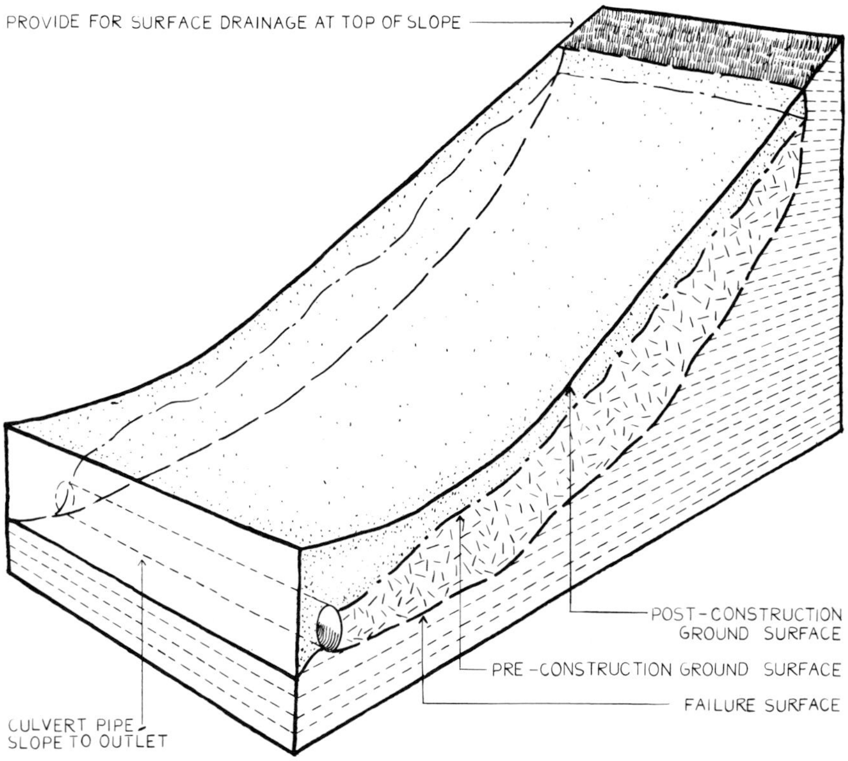
PROVIDE FOR SURFACE DRAINAGE AT TOP OF SLOPE
POST-CONSTRUCTION GROUND SURFACE
PRE-CONSTRUCTION GROUND SURFACE
FAILURE SURFACE
CULVERT PIPE SLOPE TO OUTLET

Figure 253-4 Grading with toe loading.

3. Provisionally maintain the facility by (a) rebuilding periodically, as needed, and (b) periodically excavating encroaching material.

4. Mitigate the hazard by (a) reducing the causal forces or (b) increasing the resistance forces.

Due to the complex dynamics of geological materials, each landslide and corrective slope design will be unique. Experts in geotechnical engineering and geology should be consulted.

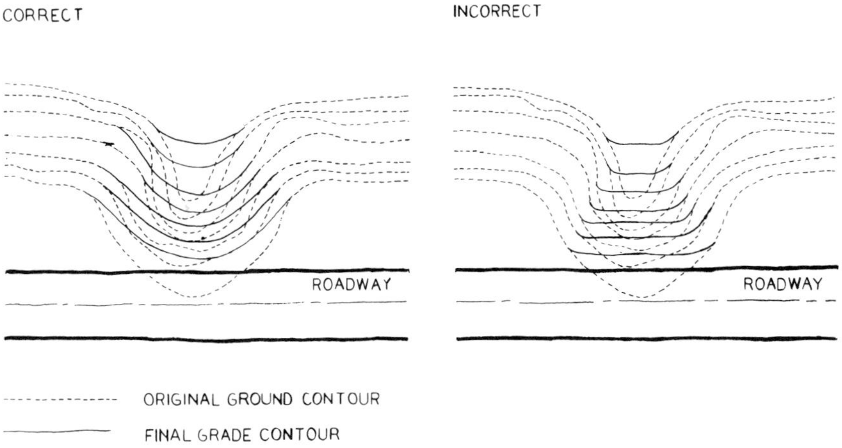
CORRECT
INCORRECT
ROADWAY
ROADWAY
ORIGINAL GROUND CONTOUR
FINAL GRADE CONTOUR

Figure 253-5 Rounding cut slopes.

Prevention and Correction:

Table 253-6 (page 253-8) describes a range of useful methods for the prevention and correction of landslides. They are categorized under: *Excavation,* which reduces shearing stresses; *Drainage,* which both reduces shearing stresses and increases shear resistance; *Restraining structures,* which increase shearing resistance; and *Miscellaneous methods,* which primarily increase resistance to shearing.

Excavation: Excavation can be one of the least expensive methods for stabilizing a slope. By unloading the head of a potential slide mass and depositing the material at the toe of the slope, either temporarily or permanently, the driving force is reduced and the resistance increased. It is extremely important to round off the slope at the head and toe. Where the sliding mass is shallow, the entire mass may have to be removed. See Figures 253-3 to 253-5.

Drainage: Drainage is essential for the control of all types of landslide hazards; a correct drainage practice will reduce the shear stresses and increase the shear resistance. Streams, springs, and surface runoff entering the top of a vulnerable area should be diverted. In most cases, drainage of the subsurface can be beneficial. At large construction sites, the pumping of groundwater (dewatering) can temporarily reduce hazards, but this approach offers no long-term benefits. A combination of regrading and improved drainage can be useful in repairing a failed slope. See Figures 253-6 to 253-8.

Vegetation: Vegetation can be a very powerful and relatively inexpensive method for the control of some landslide hazards. The physical binding action of deep roots can help anchor earth volumes prone to sliding. Deep-rooted plants also reduce the weight of water loading a slope. For slopes subject to toe erosion by waves and/or currents, a combination of vegetation and structural measures at the toe is the essential first step in landslide control.

Note, however, that plants can directly or indirectly contribute to slope failures

TABLE 253-6
Method for the Prevention and Correction of Landslides

Method of treatment	Frequency of successful use* Fall	Slide	Flow	Position of treatment of landslide	Applications and limitations
Excavation					
Removal of head	N	1	N	Top and head	Deep masses of cohesive material
Flattening of slopes	1	1	1	Above road or structure	Bedrock; also extensive masses of cohesive material where little material is removed at toe
Benching of slopes	1	1	1	Above road or structure	
Removal of all unstable material	2	2	2	Entire slide	Relatively small shallow masses of moving material
Lighweight fill				Head	May be unavailable and costly; cinders, slag, encapsulated sawdust, expanded shale, and sea shells have been used.
Drainage					
Surface					
Surface ditches	1	1	1	Above crown	Essential for all types
Slope treatment	3	3	3	Surface of moving mass	Rock facing or pervious blanket to control seepage
Regrading surface	1	1	1	Surface of moving mass	Beneficial for all types
Sealing cracks	2	2	2	Entire crown to toe	Beneficial for all types
Sealing joint planes and fissures	3	3	N	Entire crown to toe	Applicable to rock formations
Subdrainage					
Horizontal drains	N	2	2	Located to intercept and remove subsurface water	Deep extensive soil mass where ground water exists
Drainage trenches	N	1	3	—	Relatively shallow soil mass with ground water present
Tunnels	N	3	N	—	Deep extensive soil mass with some permeability
Vertical drain wells	N	3	3	—	Deep slide mass, ground water in various strata or lenses
Continuous siphon	N	2	3	—	Used principally as outlet for trenches or drain wells
Restraining structures					
Buttresses at foot					
Rock fill	N	1	1	Toe and foot	Bedrock or firm soil at reasonable depth
Earth fill	N	1	1	Toe and foot	Counterweight at toe provides additional resistance
Crib or retaining walls	3	3	3	Foot	Relatively small moving mass or where removal of support is neglible
Reinforced earth	N		N	Toe and foot	Can be constructed easily and quickly
Vidal-type system					
Geotextile					
Piling					
Fixed at slip surface	N	3	N	Foot	Shearing resistance at slip surface increased by force required to shear or bend piles
Not fixed at slip surface	N	3	N	Foot	
Dowels in rock	3	3	N	Above road or structure	Rock layers fixed together with dowels
Tie-rodding slopes	3	3	N	Above road or structure	Weak slope retained by barrier, which in turn is anchored to solid formation
Rock bolts and anchors			N	Head to foot	Used to reinforce the surface and near-surface rock. Advantages of prestressing: (1) no movement has to occur before anchor develops its full capacity, (2) each anchor is in effect test-loaded at installation.
Passive					
Prestressed					
Tendons and cable anchors			N	Head to foot	Longer than bolts; used to control large failure blocks
Anchor beams			N	Head to foot	Used to distribute the support of rock bolts and anchors
Anchor cable nets		N	N	Head to foot	Used to restrain masses of small loose blocks as large as 1.5–2.5 m (5–8 ft)
Cable lashings		N	N	Head to foot	Used to restrain large blocks by tying with individual cable strands anchored to slope
Beam and cable walls		N	N	Head to foot	Used to prevent smaller blocks of rock from falling out of slope; will reach as high as 20 m (60 ft)
Shotcrete		N	N	Head to foot	Mortar and coarse aggregate projected by air-jet onto thoroughly scaled rock surface; prevents weathering and spalling and provides surface reinforcement
Miscellaneous methods					
Hardening of slide mass					
Cementation or chemical treatment					
At foot	3	3	3	Toe and foot	Noncohesive soils
Entire slide mass	N	3	N	Entire slide mass	Noncohesive soils
Freezing	N	3	3	Entire	To prevent movement temporarily in relatively large moving mass
Heating	N			Entire	High temperatures cause a permanent drying of the cut slope; experimental
Electro-osmosis	N	3	3	Entire	Effects hardening of soil by reducing moisture content
Blasting	N	3	N	Lower half of landslide	Relatively shallow cohesive mass underlaid by bedrock Slip surface disrupted; blasting may also permit water to drain out of slide mass.

TABLE 253-6 (*Continued*)

Method of treatment	*Frequency of successful use** Fall	Slide	Flow	*Position of treatment of landslide*	*Applications and limitations*
Vegetation	N			Entire	Deep-rooted woody vegetation (trees and shrubs) may help to stabilize shallow landslides. Can be used with gabions, crib walls, welded wire walls, etc.
Compaction and densification				—	
Partial removal of slide at toe	N	N	N	Foot and toe	Temporary expedient only; usually decreases stability of slide
Protection methods (used to prevent damage from rock falls: sloped ditches and shaped berms		N	N	Head to midslope	Used to intercept rock falls and in some instances divert them laterally into disposal areas. Design so as not to over-steepen upper slope and to facilitate removal of material
Wire mesh covers		N	N	Head to foot	Pinned to slope to prevent small loose rocks from falling, or draped over rock face to guide falling rocks to ditch or foot
Wire mesh catchnets and fenches	N	N		Near foot	Used to intercept and slow down bouncing rocks as large as 0.6–1 m (2–3 ft); must be flexible, unlike standard wire fences; often used in conjunction with shaped ditches
Catchwalls	N	N		Foot	Used to form a rigid barrier to stop rolling or bouncing rocks as large as 1.5–2 m (5–6 ft); serves to increase the storage capacity of ditch; made of concrete, rails, box gabions, etc.
Rocksheds and tunnels		N		Head to foot	Allows material to pass overhead; expensive but effective, with low maintenance
Warning systems (alerts people to the occurrence of a slope failure in a remote area) Electric fences and wires				Foot	Falling rock of sufficient size breaks wire, triggering a warning signal.

* 1, frequently; 2, occasionally; 3, rarely; N, not applicable

Source: Adapted from Transportation Research Board, *Landslides and Engineering Practice,* Special Reports Nos. 29 (1958) and 176 (1978); and Douglas S. Way, *Terrain Analysis: A Guide to Site Selection Using Aerial Photographic Interpretation,* Douglas S. Way, Columbus, Ohio, 1978.

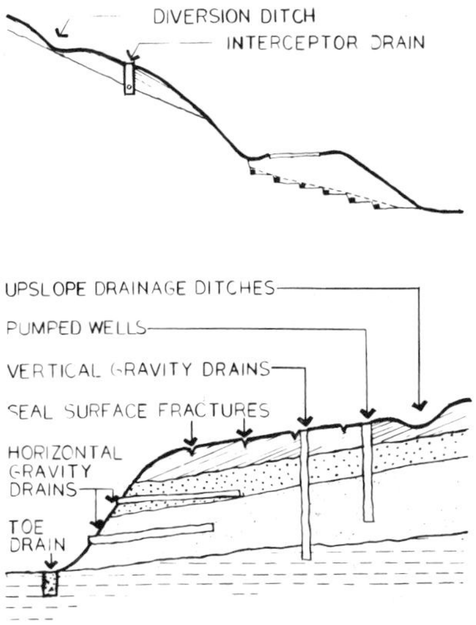
DIVERSION DITCH
INTERCEPTOR DRAIN
UPSLOPE DRAINAGE DITCHES
PUMPED WELLS
VERTICAL GRAVITY DRAINS
SEAL SURFACE FRACTURES
HORIZONTAL GRAVITY DRAINS
TOE DRAIN

Figure 253-6 Surface drainage of slope by diversion ditch and interceptor drain.

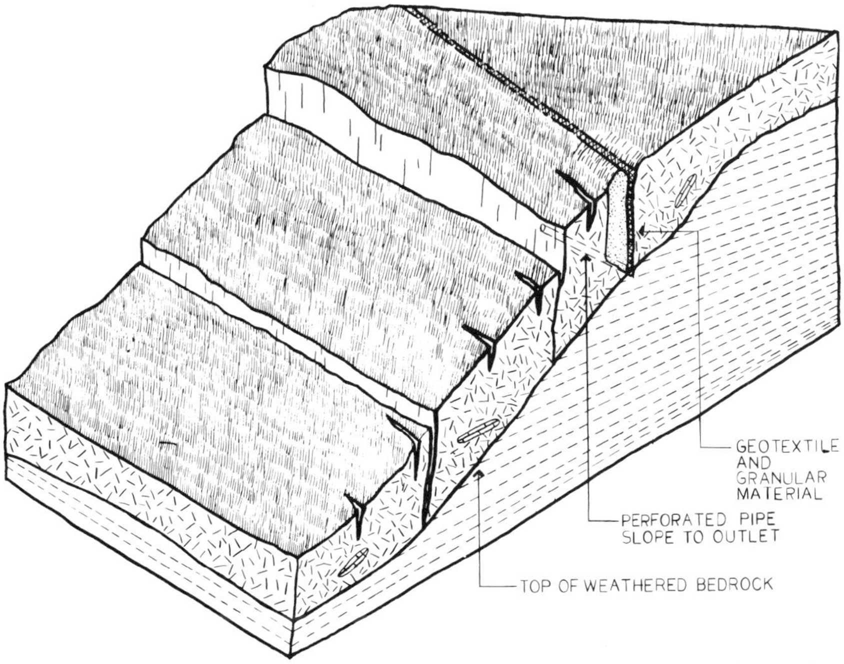
GEOTEXTILE AND GRANULAR MATERIAL
PERFORATED PIPE SLOPE TO OUTLET
TOP OF WEATHERED BEDROCK

Figure 253-7 Subsurface interceptor trench drain and surface-runoff diversion ditch.

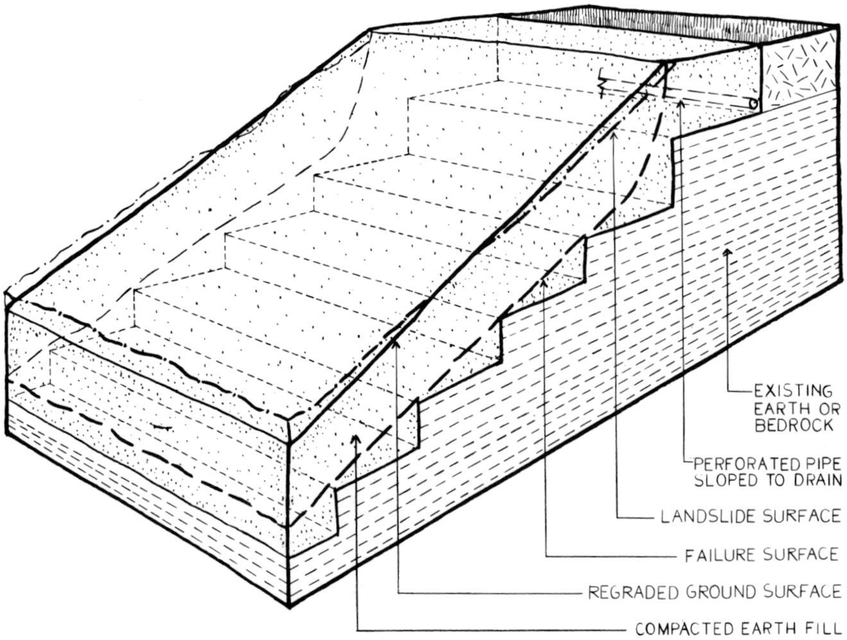
EXISTING
EARTH OR
BEDROCK
PERFORATED PIPE
SLOPED TO DRAIN
LANDSLIDE SURFACE
FAILURE SURFACE
REGRADED GROUND SURFACE
COMPACTED EARTH FILL

Figure 253-8 Regrading with subsurface drain.

under some conditions. On rocky slopes, root wedging and windthrow can precipitate failures. Large trees also add weight to a slope, the effect of which must be assessed on a case-by-case basis. Shallow-rooted plant materials are generally not as beneficial as deep-rooted ones for reducing the potential for deep-seated soil movements, but they are essential in mitigating surface erosion. Caution must be exercised when installing new plantings on unstable slopes, since watering can increase the landslide potential.

Restraining Structures: Restraining structures should be considered a last resort. They are often expensive and should be employed only when there are no other alternatives.

When rock falling onto an area creates a hazard, the use of restraining cables or nets or walls may be the only feasible solution. Table 253-7 gives design criteria for rock catchment ditches, which are useful where space permits. Various net and wall combinations are shown in Figures 253-9 to 253-10.

Walls for landslide restraint can range from relatively low, strong dikes designed to divert potential mudflows around existing development, to various types of retaining walls designed to prevent future movement of a slope. In areas of known landslide hazard, the design of retaining structures should be made adequate to carry the potential extra load. (Refer to Section 410: Retaining Walls, for information on construction of these structures.)

Other devices useful for the reduction of landslide hazard include:

1. Live wooden crib walls (Figure 253-11 and see Section 410: Retaining Walls, for more data)
2. Drilled (not driven) caisson walls (Figure 253-12)
3. Earth buttresses (Figure 253-13)
4. Reinforced earth wall buttresses (Figure 253-14 and see Section 410: Retaining Walls, for more data)

Both the determination of landslide potential and the design and implementation of corrective measures require careful engineering investigation, and consultation with experts in the field of geotechnical engineering and engineering geology.

TABLE 253-7
Rock Trajectory for Various Slope Angles and Design Criteria for Shaped Ditches

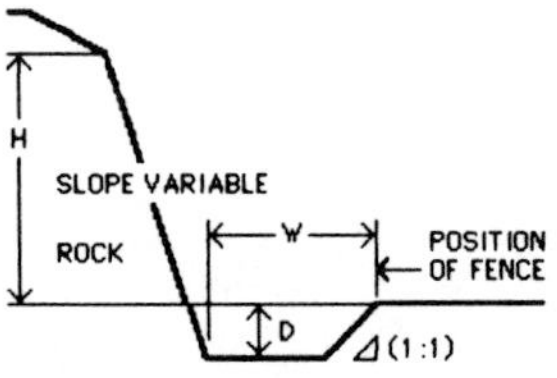
H
SLOPE VARIABLE
ROCK
W
POSITION
OF FENCE
D
(1:1)

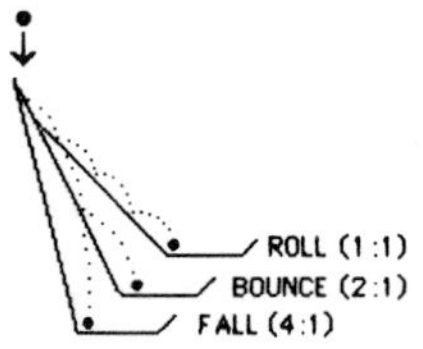
ROLL (1:1)
BOUNCE (2:1)
FALL (4:1)

Angle	*Height* (H), *ft (m)*	*Fallout area width* (W), *ft (m)*	*Ditch depth* (D), *ft (m)*
Near vertical	16–32 (5–10)	12 (3.7)	3 (1.0)
	32–65 (10–20)	15 (4.6)	4 (1.2)
	>65 (>20)	20 (6.1)	4 (1.2)
0.25 or 0.3:1	16–32 (5–10)	12 (3.7)	3 (1.0)
	32–65 (10–20)	15 (4.6)	4 (1.2)
	65–100 (20–30)	20 (6.1)	6 (1.8)*
	>100 (>30)	25 (7.6)	6 (1.8)*
0.5:1	16–32 (5–10)	12 (3.7)	4 (1.2)
	32–65 (10–20)	15 (4.6)	6 (1.8)*
	65–100 (20–30)	20 (6.1)	6 (1.8)*
	>100 (>30)	25 (7.6)	9 (2.7)*
0.75:1	0–32 (0–10)	12 (3.7)	3 (1.0)
	32–65 (10–20)	15 (4.6)	4 (1.2)
	>65 (>20)	15 (4.6)	6 (1.8)*
1:1	0–32 (0–10)	12 (3.7)	3 (1.0)
	32–65 (10–20)	12 (3.7)	5 (1.5)*
	>65 (>20)	15 (4.6)	6 (1.8)*

* May be 4 ft (1.2 m) if catch fence is used.

Source: Adapted from Douglas R. Piteau and F. Lionel Peckover, *Landslides: Analysis and Control*, Special Report 176, Transportation Research Board, National Academy of Sciences, Washington, D.C., 1978.

3.0 SNOW AVALANCHES

3.1 Causes and Types of Snow Avalanches

Avalanches, which are common to mountainous or hilly terrain that receives heavy snowfall, may occur wherever snow is deposited on slopes steeper than about 20 degrees. The most serious avalanches

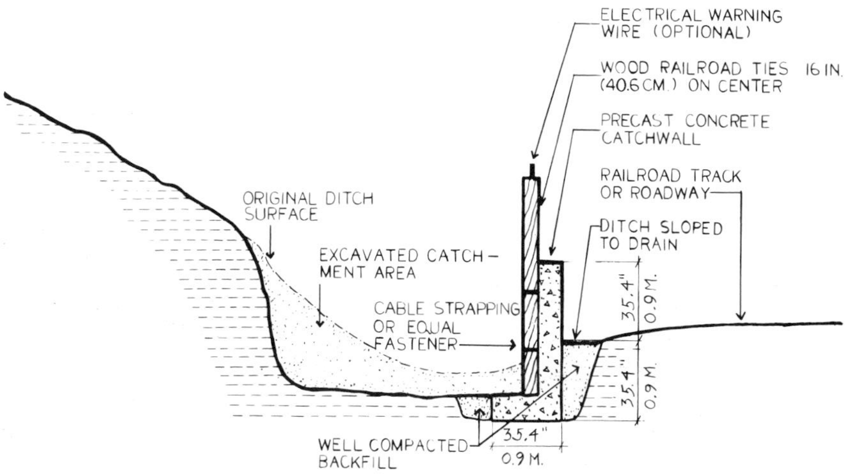

ELECTRICAL WARNING WIRE (OPTIONAL)
WOOD RAILROAD TIES 16 IN. (40.6 CM.) ON CENTER
PRECAST CONCRETE CATCHWALL
RAILROAD TRACK OR ROADWAY
DITCH SLOPED TO DRAIN
ORIGINAL DITCH SURFACE
EXCAVATED CATCHMENT AREA
CABLE STRAPPING OR EQUAL FASTENER
35.4" 0.9 M.
35.4" 0.9 M.
WELL COMPACTED BACKFILL
35.4" 0.9 M.

Figure 253-9 Precast concrete wall.

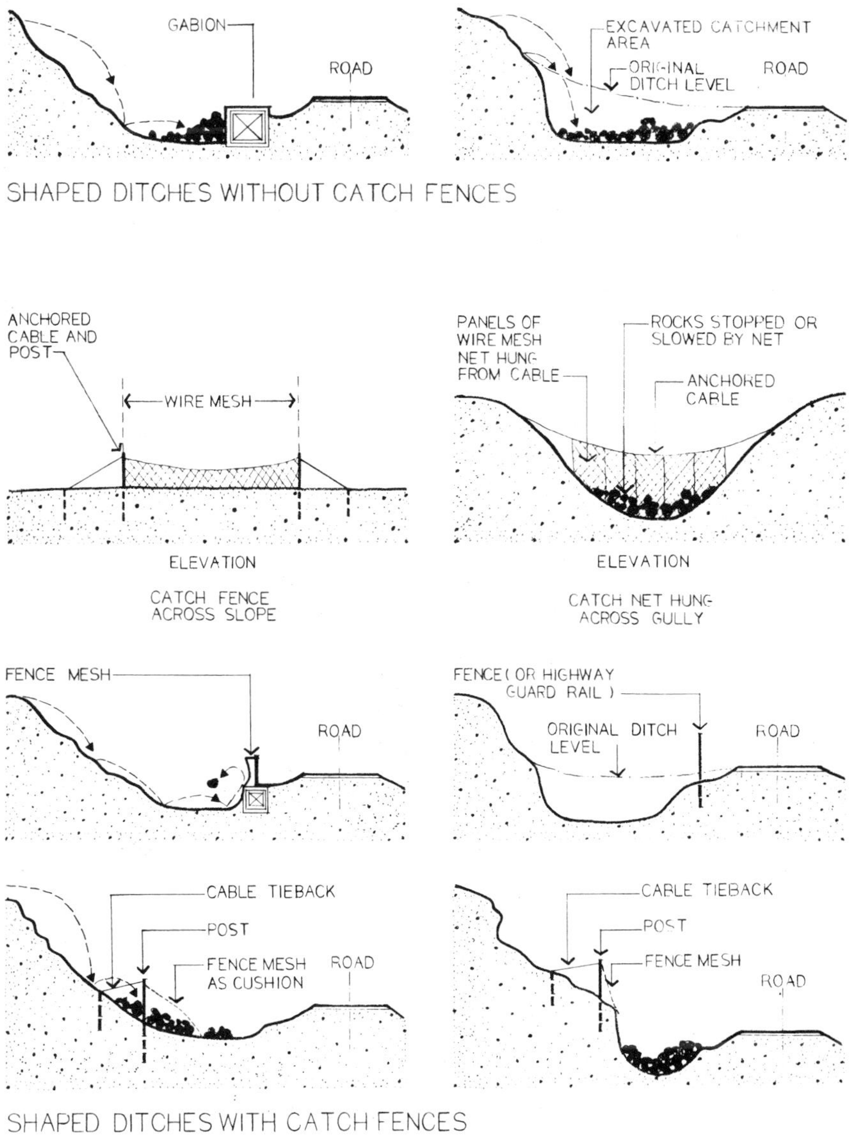

GABION
ROAD
EXCAVATED CATCHMENT AREA
ORIGINAL DITCH LEVEL
ROAD
SHAPED DITCHES WITHOUT CATCH FENCES
ANCHORED CABLE AND POST
WIRE MESH
ELEVATION
CATCH FENCE ACROSS SLOPE
PANELS OF WIRE MESH NET HUNG FROM CABLE
ROCKS STOPPED OR SLOWED BY NET
ANCHORED CABLE
ELEVATION
CATCH NET HUNG ACROSS GULLY
FENCE MESH
ROAD
FENCE (OR HIGHWAY GUARD RAIL)
ORIGINAL DITCH LEVEL
ROAD
CABLE TIEBACK
POST
FENCE MESH AS CUSHION
ROAD
CABLE TIEBACK
POST
FENCE MESH
ROAD
SHAPED DITCHES WITH CATCH FENCES

Figure 253-10 Shaped ditches and catch fences.

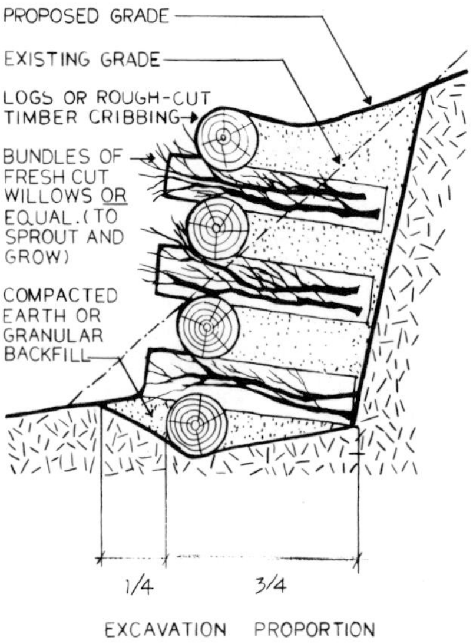
PROPOSED GRADE
EXISTING GRADE
LOGS OR ROUGH-CUT TIMBER CRIBBING
BUNDLES OF FRESH CUT WILLOWS OR EQUAL. (TO SPROUT AND GROW)
COMPACTED EARTH OR GRANULAR BACKFILL
1/4
3/4
EXCAVATION PROPORTION

Figure 253-11 Diagram of a live wooden cribwall.

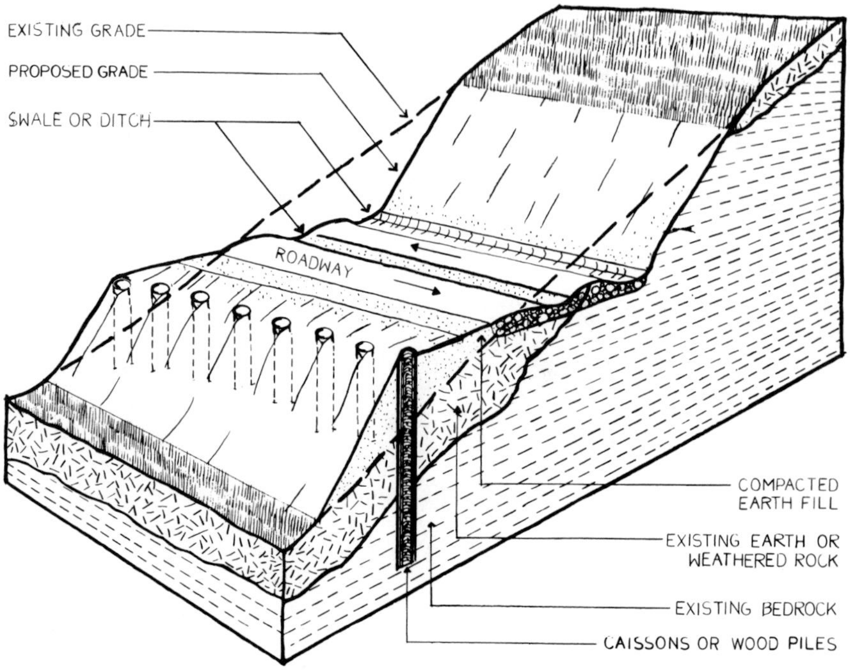
EXISTING GRADE
PROPOSED GRADE
SWALE OR DITCH
ROADWAY
COMPACTED EARTH FILL
EXISTING EARTH OR WEATHERED ROCK
EXISTING BEDROCK
CAISSONS OR WOOD PILES

Figure 253-12 Drilled caisson wall relying on soil arching.

occur on slopes of 30 to 45 degreees because slopes steeper than this generally do not accumulate much snow. Snow will remain on a slope only if its shearing strength at all depths exceeds the shearing stress developed by the weight of the snow and the angle of the slope (see Figure 253-15).

Table 253-8 gives a classification system for avalanches and describes conditions for their occurrence.

Secondary avalanches (those which occur after snowfall) result from internal changes in the snow mass. *Destructive metamorphism* occurs when snow particles break down into smaller units, resulting in a denser, more-stable snow mass. *Constructive metamorphism* occurs when snow particles grow larger by sublimation, resulting in a layer of snow at some depth below the surface (*depth hoar*) which contains voids between rounded particles of ice. Depth hoar possesses virtually no resistance to shearing. Because of inadequate internal stability, cracking may take place on the edges of a large area of snow, usually at slope convexities where steepness increases. The snow mass tears away as a unit, breaking up as it moves down the slope.

If a snow mass containing dense strata breaks loose, the destructive power of the avalanche is increased. The most destructive type of avalanche is referred to as a *climax avalanche*. When a considerable depth of snow has accumulated, and as

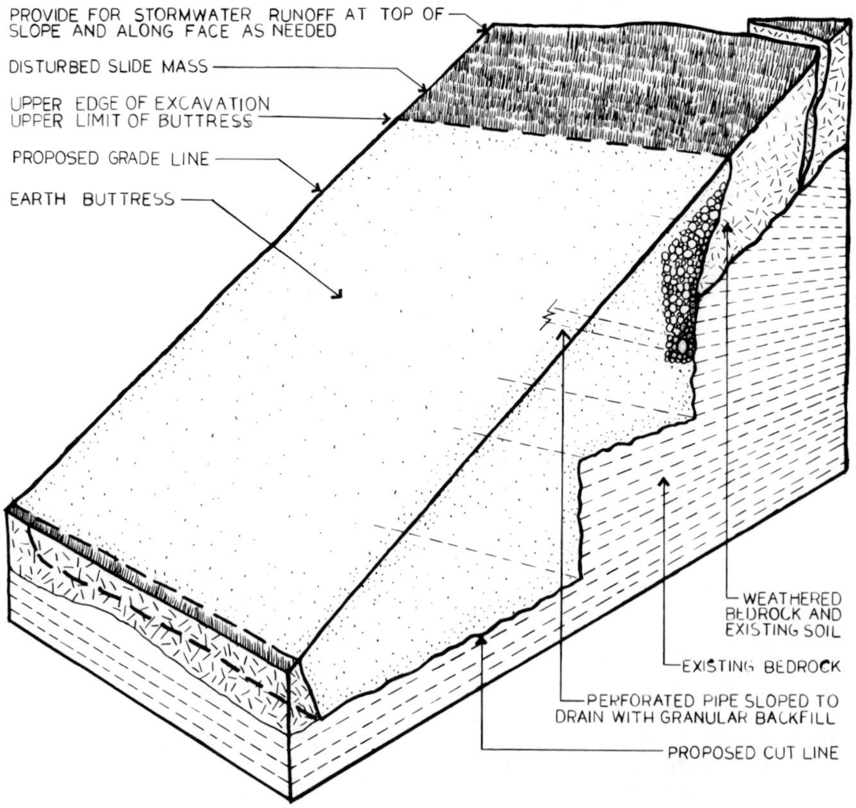
PROVIDE FOR STORMWATER RUNOFF AT TOP OF SLOPE AND ALONG FACE AS NEEDED
DISTURBED SLIDE MASS
UPPER EDGE OF EXCAVATION
UPPER LIMIT OF BUTTRESS
PROPOSED GRADE LINE
EARTH BUTTRESS
WEATHERED BEDROCK AND EXISTING SOIL
EXISTING BEDROCK
PERFORATED PIPE SLOPED TO DRAIN WITH GRANULAR BACKFILL
PROPOSED CUT LINE

Figure 253-13 Earth buttress with subsurface drain.

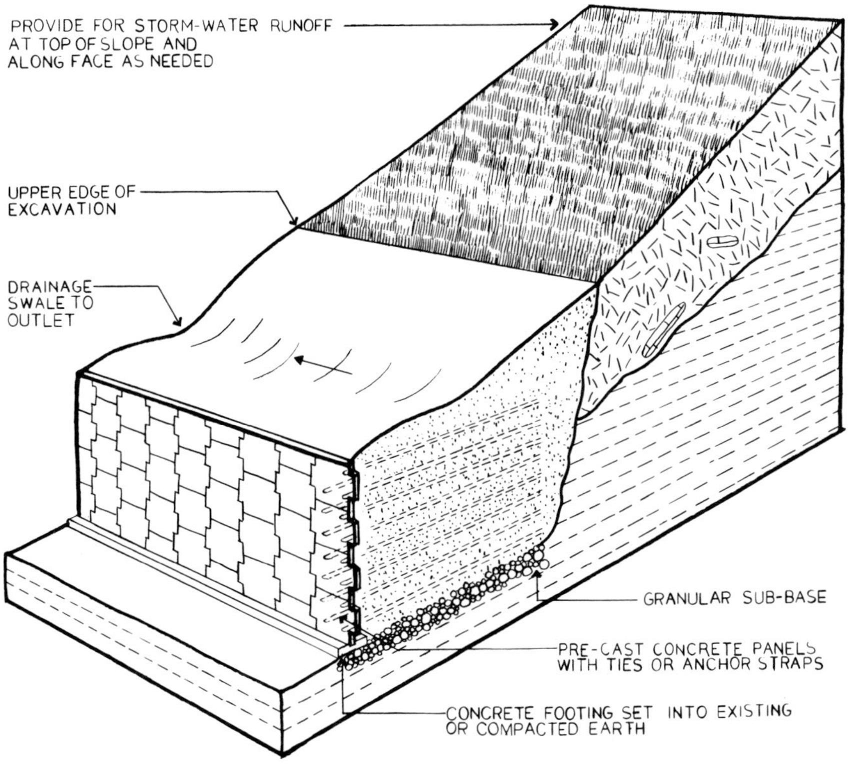
PROVIDE FOR STORM-WATER RUNOFF
AT TOP OF SLOPE AND
ALONG FACE AS NEEDED
UPPER EDGE OF
EXCAVATION
DRAINAGE
SWALE TO
OUTLET
GRANULAR SUB-BASE
PRE-CAST CONCRETE PANELS
WITH TIES OR ANCHOR STRAPS
CONCRETE FOOTING SET INTO EXISTING
OR COMPACTED EARTH

Figure 253-14 Reinforced earth wall and buttress.

TABLE 253-8
Classification of Avalanches

Snow type	*Conditions for occurrence*	*Scale*	*Characteristics*
	*Primary movement**		
Dry	Slope steeper than friction angle of snow	Small	Surface runs of snow
	Secondary movement†		
New snow on crust	External trigger	Small to intermediate	Snow block debris
Crusted surface	Settling of underlying snow	Intermediate	Large slabs
Wet surface layer	Solar radiation, warm wind, rain	Small	Wet mass, slow
Depth hoar	Constructive metamorphism	Intermediate to large	Large blocks, entire layer
Wet snow	Warm weather, weak base	Intermediate to very large	Large blocks, slow to medium velocity

* During snowfall. *Source:* B.A. Bolt et al., *Geological Hazards,* Springer-Verlag, New York, 1975.
† After snowfall.

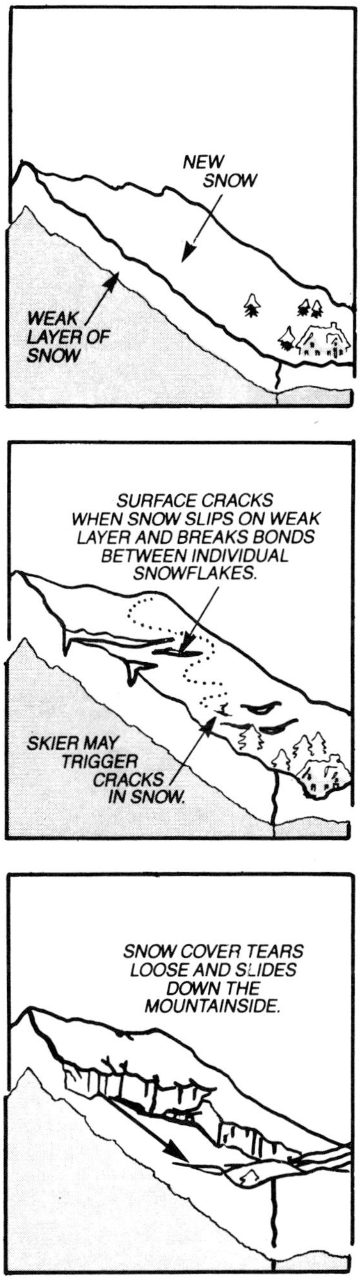
NEW
SNOW
WEAK
LAYER OF
SNOW
SURFACE CRACKS
WHEN SNOW SLIPS ON WEAK
LAYER AND BREAKS BONDS
BETWEEN INDIVIDUAL
SNOWFLAKES.
SKIER MAY
TRIGGER
CRACKS
IN SNOW.
SNOW COVER TEARS
LOOSE AND SLIDES
DOWN THE
MOUNTAINSIDE.

Figure 253-15 Anatomy of an avalanche.

solar radiation increases at the end of winter, the entire depth of snow down to soil or bedrock can break loose and move. Climax avalanches are relatively rare.

Small avalanches, or *sluffs,* are far more numerous. They may be only 40 to 50 yd (30 to 45 m) wide and run downwards only 120 yd (110 m), but they can deposit snow up to depths of 8 ft (2.5 m). Victims caught in these avalanches have been found buried 3 to 4 ft (1 to 1.2 m) deep in hard-packed snow. The survival rate is low unless a victim is recovered within 10 to 15 minutes.

Potentially destructive avalanches travel at high rates of speed. Average velocities observed at the Snow Research Station in Japan ranged from 40 to 60 km/h (25 to 38 mph), however, speeds of 200 to 300 km/h (125 to 185 mph) have been observed. Velocity is a function of the shearing strength and density of snow, the angle of slope, and the length of the avalanche path. Many avalanches carry significant amounts of rock, soil, and vegetative debris, which makes them more destructive as they travel down a slope.

3.2 Estimation of Avalanche Hazard

The combination of weather and topography significantly influences the potential occurrence, the frequency, and the type of avalanche in a given region. Local knowledge of weather conditions and the history of previous avalanching is invaluable when estimating hazards. The complex temperature and structural changes which occur in a snowmass make the prediction of avalanches on a given slope extremely difficult.

Since avalanches tend to occur in known locations (determined primarily by weather conditions, topography, and aspect), high-risk areas can be mapped. The technique of mapping avalanche hazard is well developed in the European Alps and is starting to be done in the United States and other parts of the world.

Figure 253-16 shows a part of an avalanche hazard map developed for a portion of the Colorado Rockies by M. Plam. Three types of avalanche hazard are shown:

1. Active avalanches on confined paths having a large starting zone, a track, and a well-developed run-out zone

2. Active avalanches on unconfined slopes (steeper than 30 degrees) having either no vegetation or sparse coniferous vegetation

3. Potential avalanches on timbered slopes (steeper than 30 degrees) where removal of forest cover would promote avalanches

Figure 253-17 shows the microzonation of avalanches and the estimated impact pressures on a village in Colorado.

3.3 Avalanche Loss Prevention and Reduction

Avoidance of known avalanche hazard areas when siting roads, power lines, and other facilities is the best way to minimize economic losses. It is also important to control logging operations and fires on avalanche-prone slopes.

When avoidance of a hazard area is not feasible, several strategies have been developed to reduce hazards. In ski areas, slopes and weather conditions are monitored, and occasionally small avalanches are intentionally triggered at times when the slopes are not in use.

Figures 253-18 and 253-19 show several devices used to control different parts of an avalanche-prone slope. Additionally, layer or strip terraces can be used to roughen smooth, steep slopes in order to hold the snow cover better. These horizontal terraces are usually 100 ft (30 m) wide and 300 ft (100 m) apart. Square miniberms arranged in a checkerboard pattern are also used for the same purpose. These

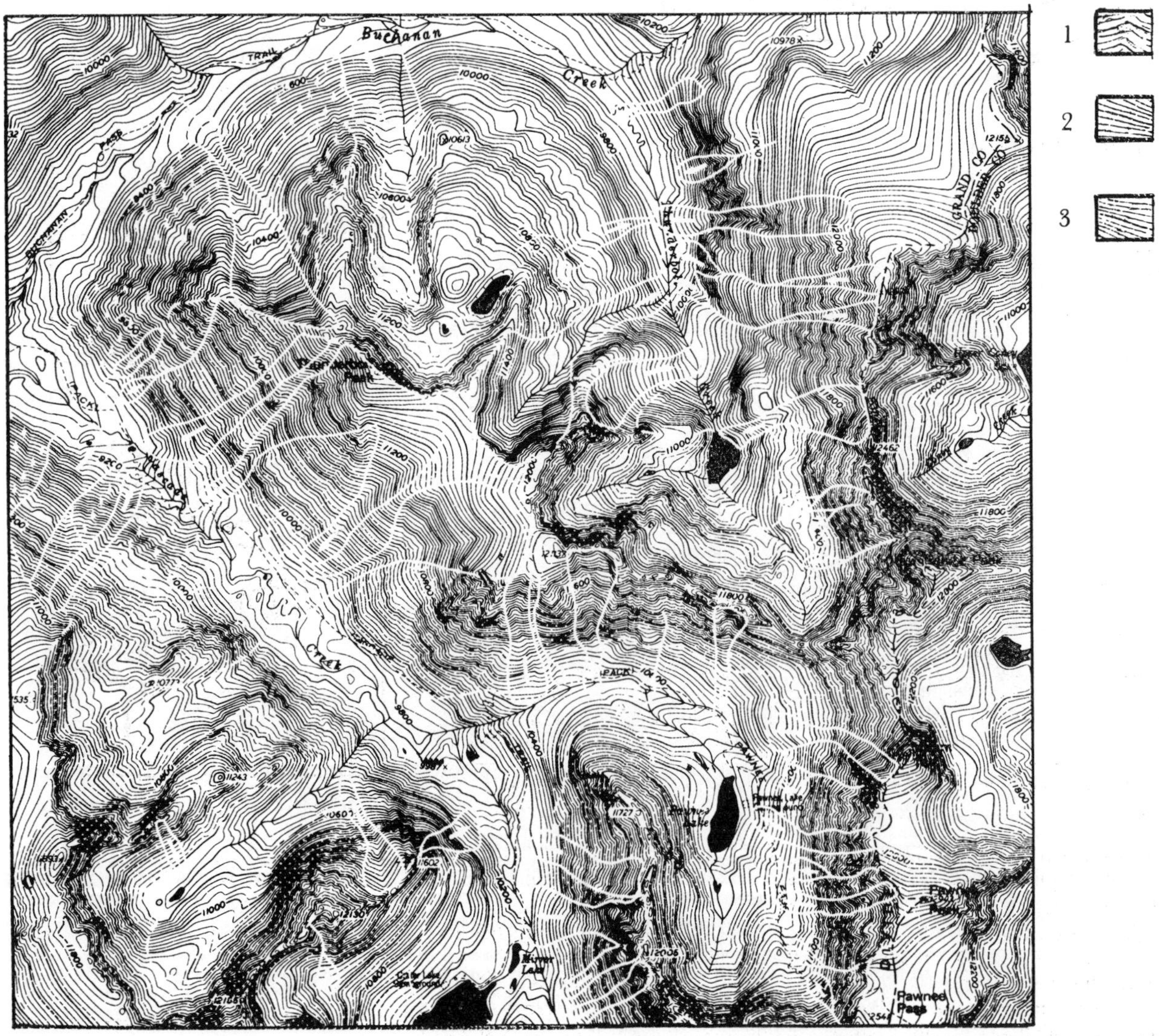
Buchanan
Creek
TRAIL
GRAND CO
BOULDER CO
Pawnee Pass
1
2
3

Figure 253-16 Section of avalanche hazard map. This map was drawn by M. Plam, using a 1: 24,000-scale U.S. Geological Survey topographic map as a base. Three types of areas are shown: (1) active avalanche, confirmed paths; (2) active avalanche, unconfirmed paths; and (3) potential avalanche slopes.

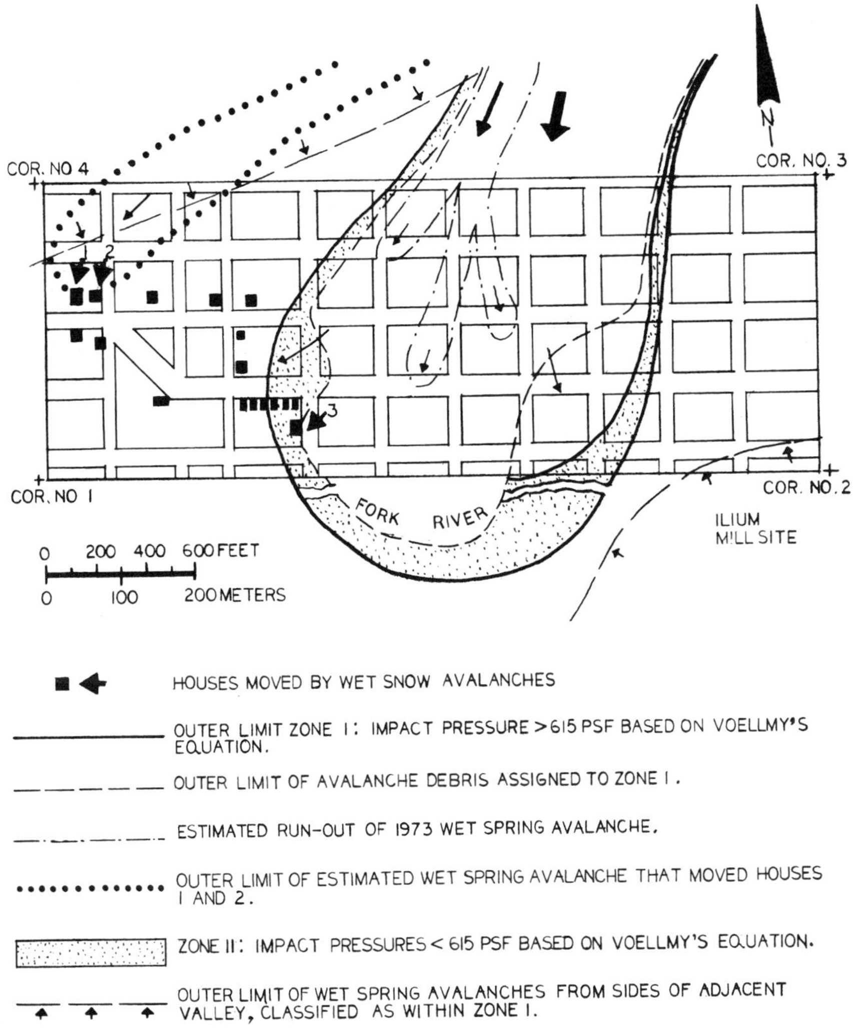
COR. NO 4
COR. NO. 3
COR. NO 1
COR. NO. 2
N
1
2
3
FORK RIVER
ILIUM MILL SITE
0 200 400 600 FEET
0 100 200 METERS
HOUSES MOVED BY WET SNOW AVALANCHES
OUTER LIMIT ZONE I: IMPACT PRESSURE >615 PSF BASED ON VOELLMY'S EQUATION.
OUTER LIMIT OF AVALANCHE DEBRIS ASSIGNED TO ZONE I.
ESTIMATED RUN-OUT OF 1973 WET SPRING AVALANCHE.
OUTER LIMIT OF ESTIMATED WET SPRING AVALANCHE THAT MOVED HOUSES 1 AND 2.
ZONE II: IMPACT PRESSURES < 615 PSF BASED ON VOELLMY'S EQUATION.
OUTER LIMIT OF WET SPRING AVALANCHES FROM SIDES OF ADJACENT VALLEY, CLASSIFIED AS WITHIN ZONE I.

Figure 253-17 Avalanche microzonation.

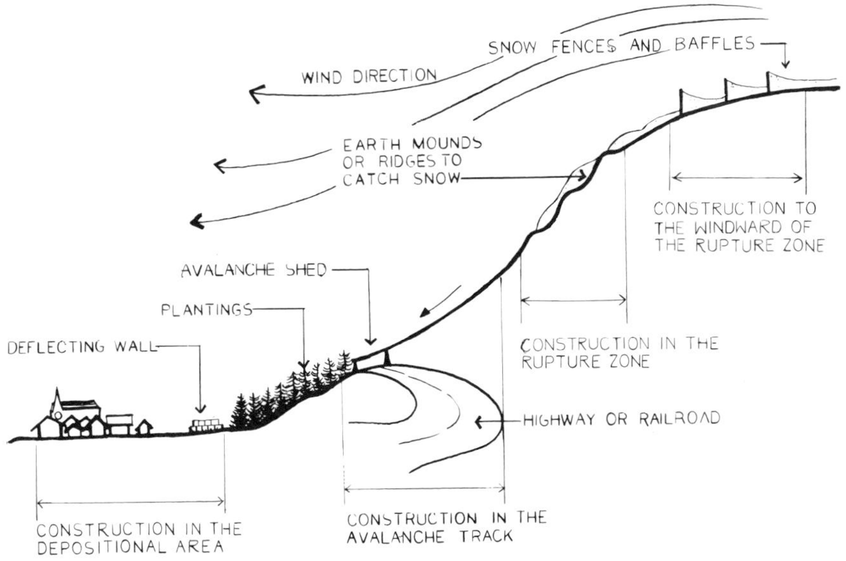
SNOW FENCES AND BAFFLES
WIND DIRECTION
EARTH MOUNDS OR RIDGES TO CATCH SNOW
CONSTRUCTION TO THE WINDWARD OF THE RUPTURE ZONE
AVALANCHE SHED
PLANTINGS
DEFLECTING WALL
CONSTRUCTION IN THE RUPTURE ZONE
HIGHWAY OR RAILROAD
CONSTRUCTION IN THE DEPOSITIONAL AREA
CONSTRUCTION IN THE AVALANCHE TRACK

Figure 253-18 Avalanche control structures. A number of different types of structures can be built in the rupture zone, path, and depositional site of an avalanche.

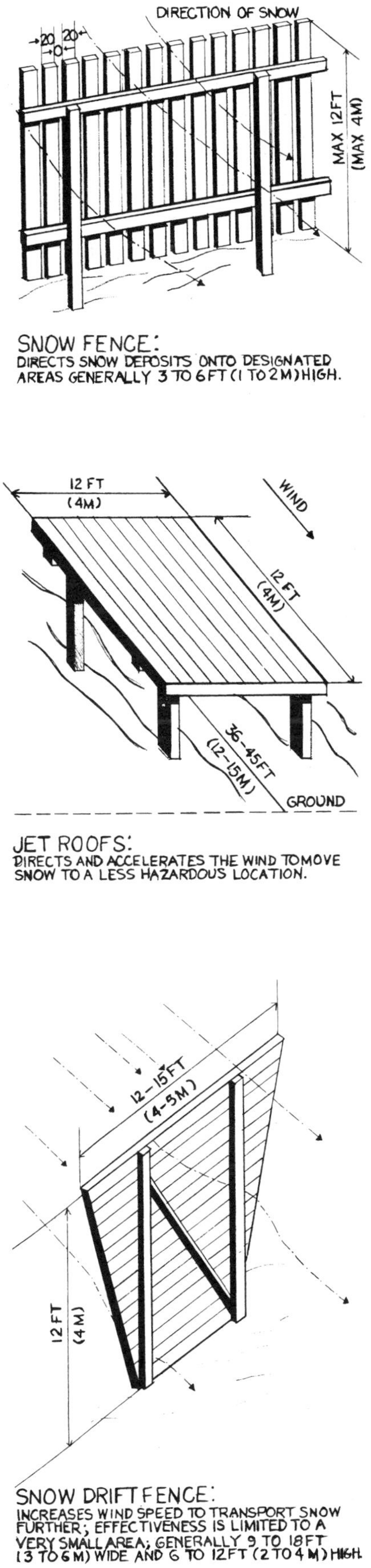
DIRECTION OF SNOW
20 20
0
MAX 12FT (MAX 4M)
SNOW FENCE:
DIRECTS SNOW DEPOSITS ONTO DESIGNATED AREAS GENERALLY 3 TO 6FT (1 TO 2M) HIGH.
12 FT (4M)
WIND
12 FT (4M)
36-45FT (12-15M)
GROUND
JET ROOFS:
DIRECTS AND ACCELERATES THE WIND TO MOVE SNOW TO A LESS HAZARDOUS LOCATION.
12-15FT (4-5M)
12 FT (4M)
SNOW DRIFT FENCE:
INCREASES WIND SPEED TO TRANSPORT SNOW FURTHER; EFFECTIVENESS IS LIMITED TO A VERY SMALL AREA; GENERALLY 9 TO 18FT (3 TO 6M) WIDE AND 6 TO 12FT (2 TO 4 M) HIGH.

Figure 253-19 Snow fences and deflecting structures.

berms are approximately 3 ft (1 m) square in size and are placed 3 to 5 ft (1 to 1.5 m) apart. These areas are often reforested to provide additional surface roughness.

Although expensive, tunnels or avalanche sheds can be cost-effective when full protection is essential. Braking and deflection structures, which usually consist of heavy masonry deflecting walls or inclined permeable steel braking barriers, can be useful in the depositional area when developed areas need protection. Large-scale deflecting systems for altering the flow direction of avalanches should be designed only by specialists. They are expensive and require continual maintenance but offer maximum protection to large areas and fixed installations.

REFERENCES

Landslides

Erly, D., and W. J. Kockelman. *Reducing Landslide Hazards: A Guide for Planners,* Planning Advisory Service Report Number 359, American Planning Association, Chicago, 1981.

Gray, Donald H., and Andrew T. Leiser. *Biotechnical Slope Protection: Economic Methods for Earth Support and Erosion Control,* Van Nostrand Reinhold, New York, 1982.

Hough, James E. *Key to Mitigation of Failed Soil Slopes,* Geological Society of America (unpublished field trip handout), Cincinnati, OH, November 1981.

A. W. Martin Associates, Inc. *Review of Construction Methods for Use in Landslide Prone Areas,* National Technical Information Service (PB-261 574), Washington, DC, 1975.

Royster, D. L. "Landslide Remedial Measures," *Bulletin of the Association of Engineering Geologists,* vol. 16, no. 2, Spring 1979, pp. 302–252.

Schuster, Robert L., and Raymond J. Krizek (eds.). *Landslides: Analysis and Control,* Special Report 176, National Academy of Sciences, Transportation Research Board, Washington, DC, 1978.

USGS. *Goals and Tasks of the Landslide Part of a Ground Failure Hazards Reduction Program,* U.S. Geological Survey Circular 880, 1982.

Avalanches

Bolt, B. A., W. L. Horn, G. A. MacDonald, and R. F. Scott. *Geological Hazards,* Springer-Verlag, New York, 1975.

"Colorado Snow-Avalanche Area Studies and Guidelines for Avalanche-Hazard Planning," Colorado Geological Survey Special Publication 7, Department of Natural Resources, Denver, 1979, 123 pp.

de Coulon, M. "Lawinschultz in der Schweiz," Davos, 1972, translated as "Avalanche Protection in Switzerland," General Technical Report RM-9, USDA Forest Service, Rocky Mountain Forest and Range Experiment Station, March 1975, 168 pp.

Mears, Arthur I. "Guidelines and Methods for Detailed Snow Avalanche Hazard Investigations in Colorado," Colorado Geological Survey Bulletin 38, Department of Natural Resources, State of Colorado, Denver, 1976, 125 pp.

Perla, R. I., and M. Martinelli. *Avalanche Handbook,* Forest Service Agriculture Handbook 489, U.S. Department of Agriculture, 1961.

Symposium on Snow in Motion, *Journal of Glaciology,* vol. 26, no. 94, 1980, p. 527.

U.S. Forest Service, *Snow Avalanche Handbook,* no. 194, U.S. Government Printing Office, Washington, DC, 1961. ■

section 254: Natural Hazards: Land Subsidence

CREDITS

Section Editor: Charles W. Harris
Technical Writer: Tess Canfield

Reviewers:

James E. Hough
James E. Hough and Associates
Cincinnati, Ohio

Gilbert White, Susan Tubbesing, Jacquelyn L. Monday, and Sarah Nathe
Natural Hazards Research and Applications Information Center
University of Colorado
Boulder, Colorado

Richard Zoino
Goldberg-Zoino and Associates
Newton, Massachusetts

CONTENTS

1.0 GENERAL CONSIDERATIONS

Land subsidence is defined as any displacement of a generally level ground surface resulting from surface or subsurface causes. This section deals with subsidence resulting from the alteration of surface or internal loading, the removal of subsurface materials, and other causes. Causes not addressed in this section include tectonic activity, landslides, and expansive soils. (Refer to Sections 252: Natural Hazards: Earthquakes, 253: Natural Hazards: Landslides and Snow Avalanches, and 255: Natural Hazards: Expansive Soils, for additional information.)

Land subsidence and displacement can occur at a wide range of speeds and extend over areas ranging from a few square feet to thousands of acres. Detection of subsidence hazards can be difficult, because the processes which cause it can operate for long periods without visible effects. The first indications of subsidence may be changes noticed by railway survey crews or unusually high road maintenance demands. The precise amount of subsidence and its distribution must be determined by the use of surveying and leveling networks. Detailed understanding of a particular subsidence basin depends upon the correlation of historical survey information from various sources with current survey information. Unless the historical data are very accurate, considerable uncertainty is likely.

The effect of land subsidence on a structure is dependent on the relationship between the dimensions of the structure and the size of the area which is subsiding. A subsidence basin of several miles or kilometers in diameter will have little effect on small structures within the subsiding area. It may, however, have serious effects on larger structures, such as canals, large bridges, roadways, railways, and drainage systems.

Subsidence occurring over relatively small areas, and on time scales approximating the lifetime of built structures, have the highest potential for causing major damage.

Subsidence can lead to increased risk from other hazards, particularly increased flood risk and increased rates of coastal erosion. Surface drainage patterns can be altered, creating unforeseen problems.

To estimate the degree of hazard resulting from subsidence, the physical mechanism, the magnitude of displacement, and the time over which movement takes place must be known.

Geological and geophysical information is essential in order to estimate the subsidence hazard. Information on some types of subsidence is available from government sources; in the United States, information can be obtained from the U.S. Geological Survey, state surveys, other geologic-related agencies of states and communities, geology departments of local colleges and universities, and private consultants. Because subsidence can be caused by many combinations of either natural processes or human intervention, potential hazards must be identified on the basis of a site-by-site evaluation. City or county engineers, consulting engineers, engineering geologists, and geologists may be sources of the types of site-specific information needed. Mine development plans on file with federal, state, or local agencies and local mining firms may indicate areas of past, present, or future underground openings. In regions of karst terrain or where mine plans do not exist, it may be necessary to undertake geophysical exploration and drilling programs to ensure that a site is free of caverns, cavities, or mine openings.

Restriction of human activities in areas identified as being susceptible to subsidence is the best overall strategy for reducing hazards and potential losses. Land use controls and zoning can help protect property and lives by directing intensive activities away from hazardous areas and by promoting nonintensive uses. Land use planning and zoning can aid in directing future activities, such as coal mining, away from areas where severe hazards would result, or can require the use of mining methods which will reduce future hazards.

2.0 SUBSIDENCE CAUSED BY SURFACE OR INTERNAL LOADING

2.1 Description

Surface loading causes compaction of compressible materials. Both the amount of compression and the time over which it will occur must be investigated. The total amount of compression that will occur under the anticipated load is calculated based on the compressibility of the soil layer, its thickness, and the magnitude of the load to be placed upon it. The calculation of how the compression of the soil layer develops with time is complex and, if the compressible material is saturated, depends upon the movement of water in the soil. The rate at which drainage can take place depends on the permeability of the soil and on the availability of drainage boundaries. Free-draining granular soils will settle very quickly. Clays and silts of low permeability will allow water to escape very slowly, and settlement may take months or years. The process of slow, gradual compaction is called *consolidation*.

2.2 Causes

The effects of loading on the earth's surface are observable around the borders of natural or artificial lakes, where the crust readjusts to the load imposed by the weight of the water. With suitable soil conditions, even the load caused by buildings or engineering structures can cause subsidence over an area 2 to 3 times greater than their own dimension.

Inadequately compacted areas of artificial fill material are subject to subsidence. Old refuse dumps, spoil heaps, and filled land should be regarded as potentially hazardous. Filled land, even if properly placed and compacted, can be subject to subsidence if it lies over a mud layer, which can compress under a load or flow out from beneath the filled area.

2.3 Mitigation

Laboratory testing of soil samples can be used to predict the total settlement and the behavior of the soil based on anticipated loadings.

Where settlement caused by the weight of material on the ground surface is anticipated, analyses are performed to ensure that the design of the structure can withstand forces resulting from differential settlement. If the total settlement is expected to be more than a few inches or centimeters, precautionary measures are taken. The structure can be founded on piles which carry its weight to a noncompressible stratum. Another approach is to design the structure with a deep basement, so that the weight of the excavated material is equal to the weight of the building. The result of this approach is analogous to a ship floating in water; thus, the term *floating foundations*. In some cases, a load equal to the weight of the building, usually in the form of an earth fill, is applied to the site in advance of construction. When the anticipated settlement has occurred, the weight is removed and construction is begun.

3.0 SUBSIDENCE CAUSED BY REMOVAL OF SUBSURFACE MATERIALS

The removal of subsurface materials as a result of natural processes or of human intervention can cause major subsidence.

Natural processes which remove subsurface materials include subterranean solution withdrawal and volcanic activity. Underground mining and solution mining result in similar hazards created by the existence of underground voids and cavities.

The removal of water, oil, and gas generally does not create large subsurface voids, but causes widespread lowering of surface levels.

3.1 Subterranean Solution Withdrawal and Volcanic Activity

Subsurface deposits of limestone and other carbonate rocks are subject to solution in groundwater, particularly in hot, humid climates. Underground voids called *solution cavities* are created as mineral material is carried away dissolved in groundwater. Where the cavities are shallow or the overlying material is weak, collapsing areas result in surfaces sinkholes and depressions.

Figure 254-1 illustrates the formation of sinkholes. The characteristic pockmarked topography resulting from the widespread presence of limestone in a humid climate is called *karst topography*. Figure 254-2 shows the general distribution of karst and pseudokarst topography in the United States.

Volcanic activity can also cause a similar effect. Lava flows which cool and solidify at the surface, leaving a flowing stream of molten material below, can result in a hollow structure if the molten material flows away and is not replaced by later flows. These voids are generally created in the form of shallow tunnels, called *lava tubes*, and overlying areas are subject to collapse.

Figure 254-3 shows areas of solution caves and other caves and areas where lava tubes are common. Subsurface cavities may be located by electrical, seismic, or gravimetric methods or by direct boring of test holes. Ground surfaces adjacent to but not directly over subsurface cavities may also be subject to subsidence. The width of this area varies, depending upon local conditions.

3.2 Removal of Water, Oil, and Gas

The removal of water, oil, and gas, the extraction of materials by solution mining, and the removal of solid materials by mining are responsible for the largest surface displacements caused by human activity.

The most noticeable effects are caused by the removal of water, oil, and gas at various depths. Generally, water is removed from shallower layers of fairly compressible materials, and gas and oil are removed from deeper layers of less compressible material.

The amount of subsidence depends on the amount of material removed, the depth of the layer from which it is extracted, and the stiffness or rigidity of the overlying soil materials.

When, for example, water is withdrawn from a well, the water level is lowered, reducing the pore pressure and allowing the soil material above to compress the water bearing strata. If a single well is used, a dish-shaped depression results. If a large well field is operated, widespread vertical displacement can occur, resulting in severe damage to utilities and large structures and disrupting surface drainage patterns.

Engineering methods can be used to reduce the subsidence hazards resulting from the withdrawal of water, oil, or gas. In areas where the withdrawal of groundwater by wells is causing subsidence, the de-

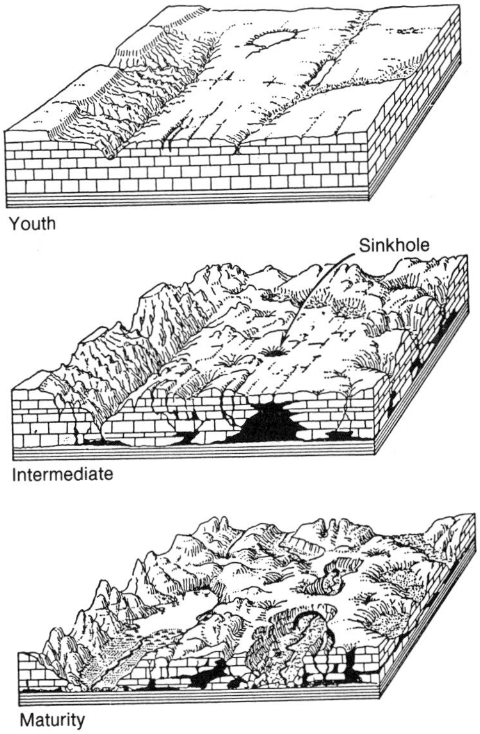
Youth
Sinkhole
Intermediate
Maturity

Figure 254-1 Sinkhole Formation. Sinkholes are formed when ground collapses into subsurface cavities. Illustration shows the formation of karst topography from relative youth to maturity.

Figure 254-2 Areas of karst topography in the United States.

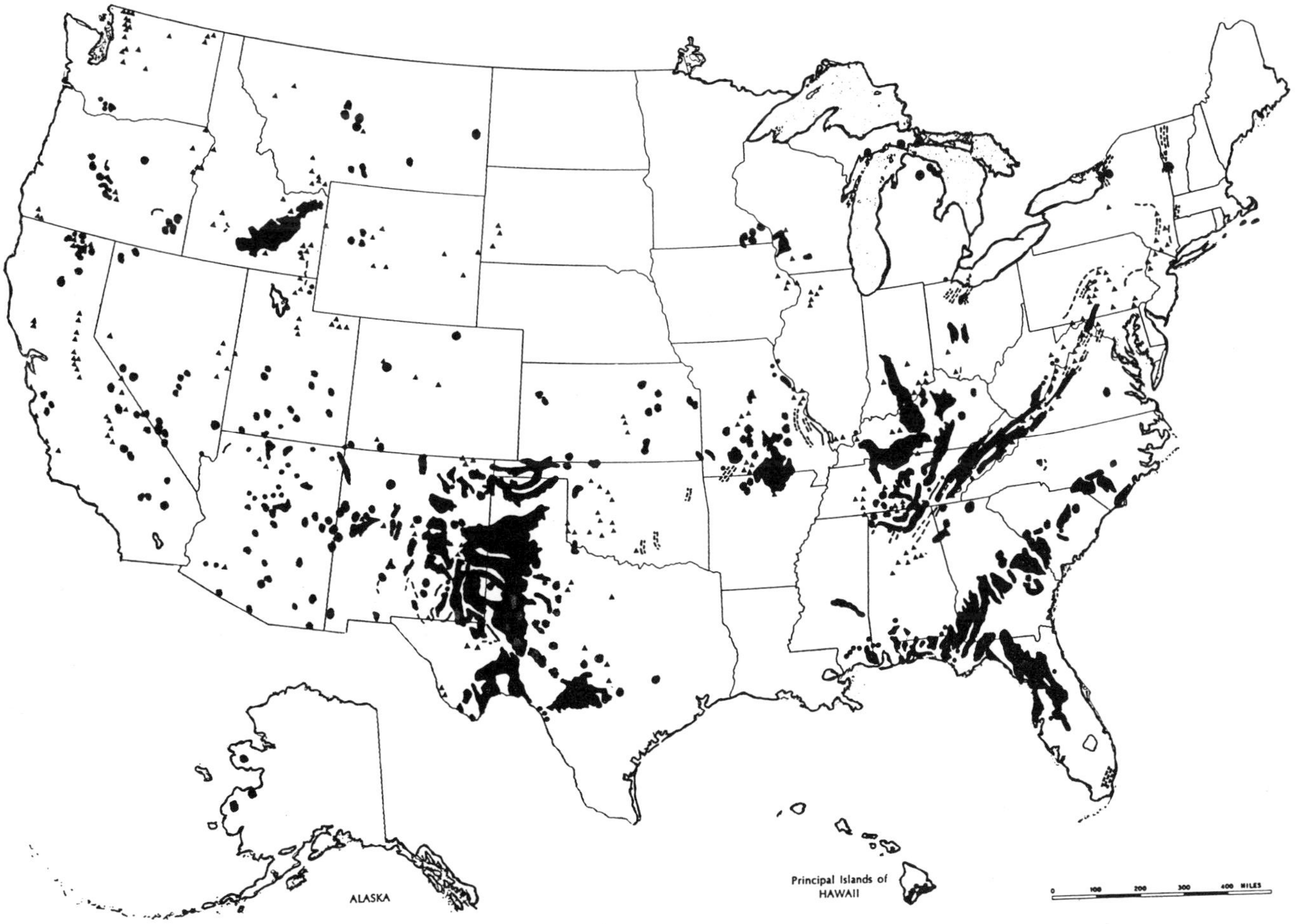
ALASKA
Principal Islands of HAWAII
0 100 200 300 400 MILES

■ ● ▲ Karst and pseudokarst terrain

=== Limestone ledges outside of areas of other karst types

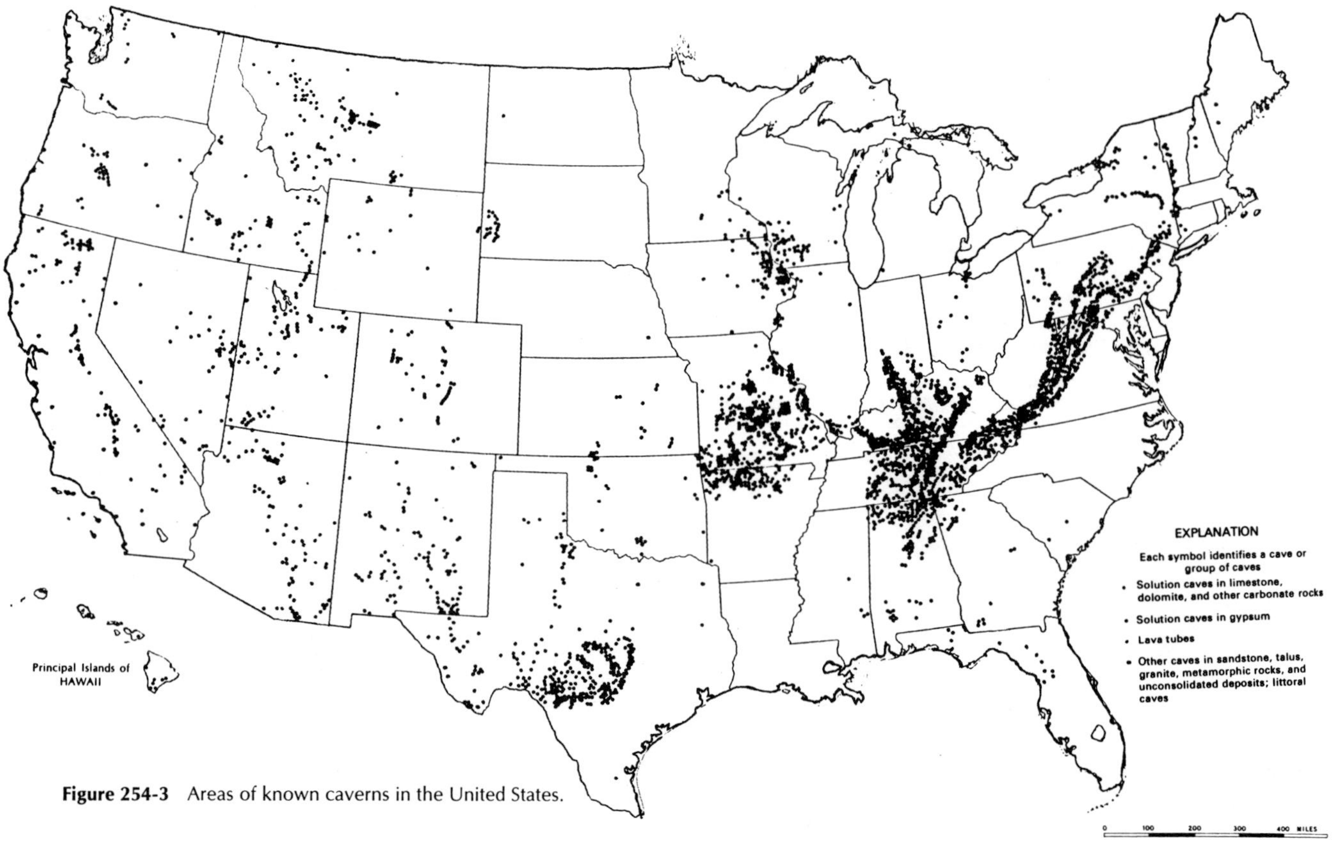
Principal Islands of HAWAII
EXPLANATION
Each symbol identifies a cave or group of caves
Solution caves in limestone, dolomite, and other carbonate rocks
Solution caves in gypsum
Lava tubes
Other caves in sandstone, talus, granite, metamorphic rocks, and unconsolidated deposits; littoral caves
0 100 200 300 400 MILES

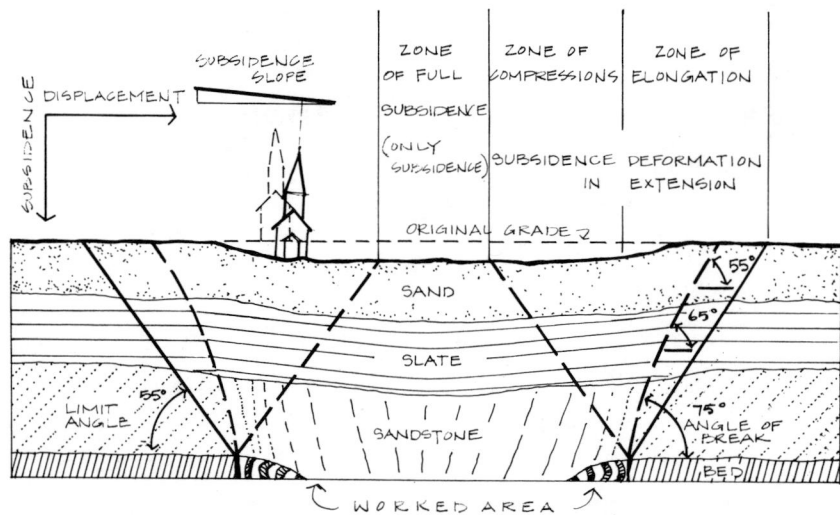

Figure 254-3 Areas of known caverns in the United States.

velopment of a water supply system based on surface water may be necessary.

Subsidence caused by the withdrawal of oil, gas, or water has been reduced or stopped by the addition of imported water to subsurface sediments, replacing the material that was withdrawn.

3.3 Underground Mining

Underground mining of solid materials, particularly shallow coal workings, is a significant cause of subsidence hazard. Construction of a tunnel close to the surface generally results in surface settlement. If the material into which the tunnel is driven is weak or inadequately supported, a process called *caving* or *stopping* can occur, in which rock in the roof collapses, leaving a void above it. Repeated caving results in the void migrating upward, eventually resulting in the formation of a sinkhole at the surface. Figure 254-4 shows the effect of the collapse of a relatively deep mine.

Figure 254-5 shows the general locations of coalfields in the United States. In regions where coal is present, subsidence resulting from previous mining activities should be regarded as a potential hazard. If abandoned mine workings are located on a site, several engineering methods have been developed to overcome the problem. It is always expensive, however, and some methods involve considerable uncertainty. Avoidance of such a site is preferred.

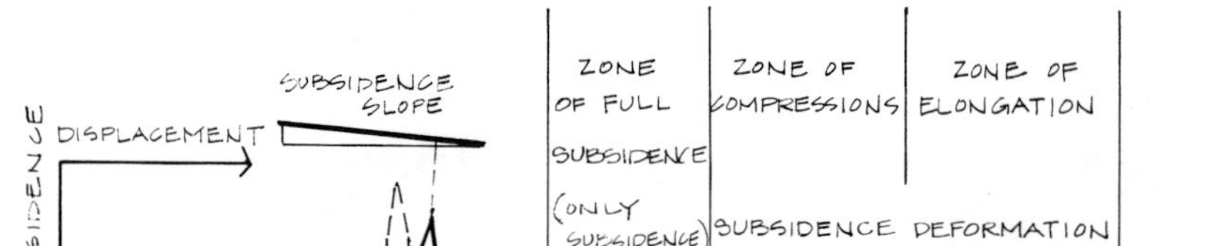
SUBSIDENCE SLOPE
DISPLACEMENT
SUBSIDENCE
ZONE OF FULL SUBSIDENCE
(ONLY SUBSIDENCE)
ZONE OF COMPRESSIONS
SUBSIDENCE IN
ZONE OF ELONGATION
DEFORMATION IN EXTENSION
ORIGINAL GRADE
55°
SAND
65°
SLATE
LIMIT ANGLE
55°
SANDSTONE
75°
ANGLE OF BREAK
BED
WORKED AREA

Figure 254-4 Subsidence Due to Mine Collapse. The *limit angle* is defined by the line joining the edge of the collapsed area underground to the edge of the area of surface sinking. The *angles of break* will vary depending upon the geological characteristics of the rock formations.

Calculation of anticipated subsidence resulting from tunneling or mining is particularly difficult because of the limited knowledge of conditions at the time of tunneling (which affects stresses in the surrounding materials), the material properties involved, and complex spatial considerations. Often, records of mining operations are absent, and identification of exact tunnel locations is difficult.

Old coal mine workings are frequently of the type referred to as *pillar and stall* or *room and pillar*. As the coal is removed, roughly rectangular pillars of coal are left at intervals to support the roof of the workings, creating an underground maze of voids and solids. In cases where future subsidence must be prevented, shallow workings can be grouted with an injection of cement slurry. Grouting is very expensive and can be ineffective if water is present underground; it can also be difficult to control the flow of grout and to verify that the grouting operation has been successful. Backfilling with waste materials has also been attempted, but this is even less certain than grouting and can introduce contaminants into the groundwater.

Figure 254-6 illustrates a modern

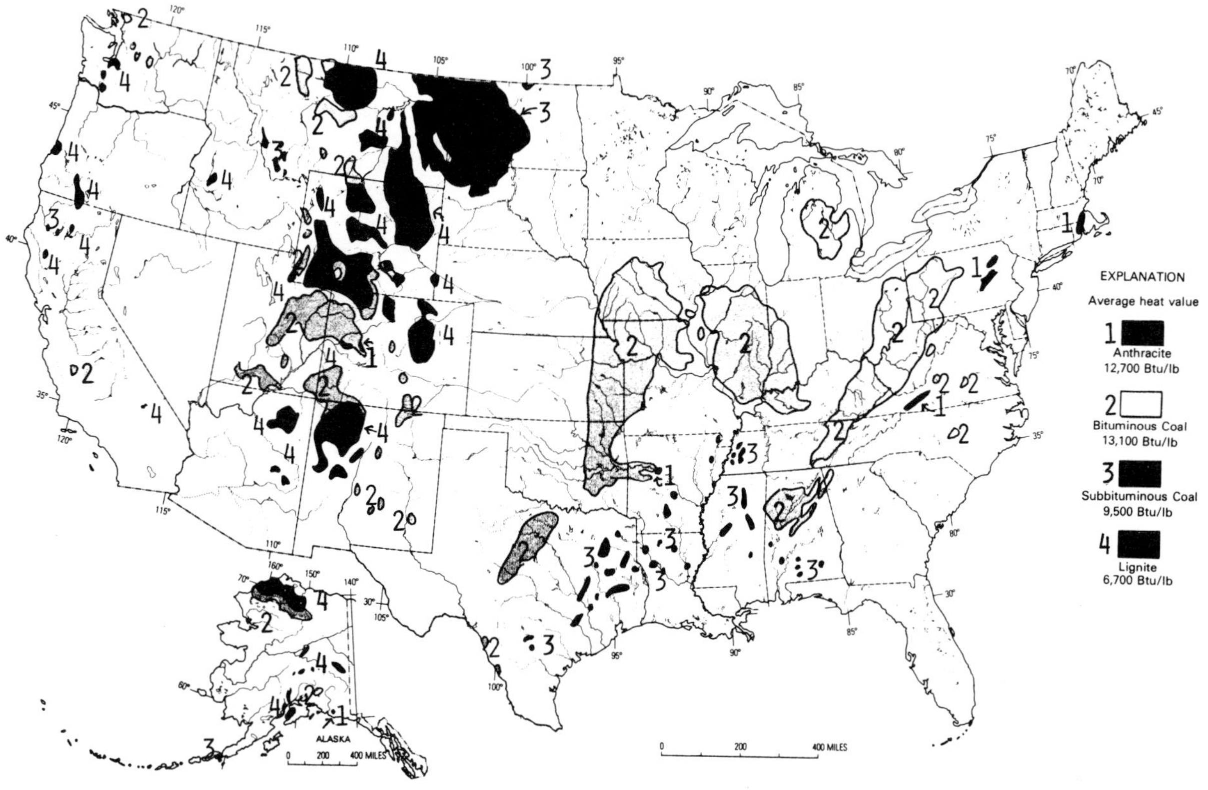
EXPLANATION
Average heat value
1 Anthracite 12,700 Btu/lb
2 Bituminous Coal 13,100 Btu/lb
3 Subbituminous Coal 9,500 Btu/lb
4 Lignite 6,700 Btu/lb
ALASKA
0 200 400 MILES

Figure 254-5 Location of coalfields in the United States.

method for injecting a slurry of water and sand or other material, using a hydrostatic pumping technique which allows a more complete filling of voids and which can require only a single injection well for an area of up to 3 acres (1.2 ha). (Grouting may require injection points only a few yards or meters apart.)

3.4 Solution Mining

The removal of subsurface materials by solution mining can cause a serious subsidence hazard, made particularly difficult to manage because of the difficulty of locating the limits of the affected area. *Solution mining* is the removal of water soluble materials such as salt, gypsum, or potash from beneath the surface by an injection of water which dissolves the material. The solution is then pumped to the surface and the water is evaporated, leaving the desired material. The resulting subsurface voids can be very large and are subject to collapse, much like the naturally occurring cavities in limestone regions.

3.5 Piping

Piping is the term used to describe subsurface drainage conduits occurring in relatively insoluble soils as a result of the passage of sediment-laden water. Piping occurs in relatively weak, incoherent soil layers, such as loess, tuff, volcanic ash, fine-grained alluvium or colluvium, and some rocks (claystone, mudstone, and siltstone). Water moving through saturated layers toward either a naturally occurring or constructed free face carries with it some sediment in suspension. As the water removes material, drainage is directed to the more permeable area, resulting in the formation of a small hole on the free face, which, as drainage continues, expands into the cliff, ultimately causing substantial un-

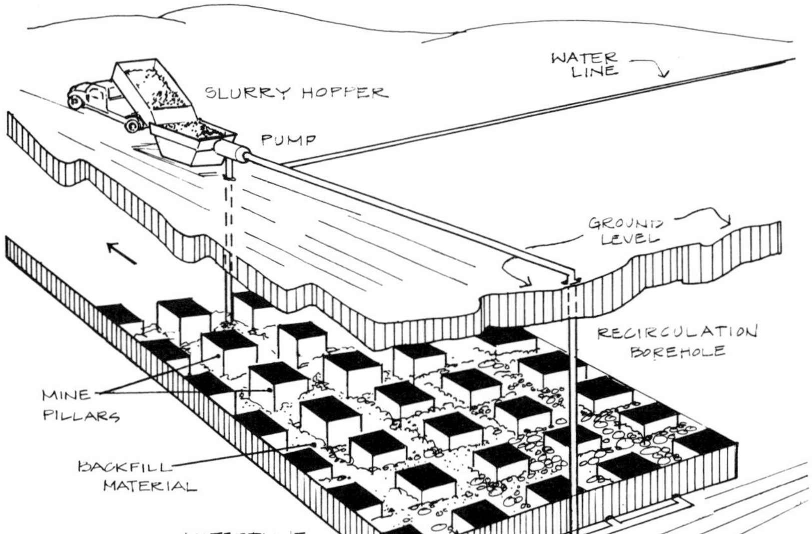
WATER LINE
SLURRY HOPPER
PUMP
GROUND LEVEL
RECIRCULATION BOREHOLE
MINE PILLARS
BACKFILL MATERIAL
WATERTIGHT BULKHEAD
PUMP

Figure 254-6 Hydraulic Backfilling of an Abandoned Coal Mine. Filling an abandoned mine provides support for the ground surface and is also a way to dispose of spoil or waste material left over from a mining operation. Mixing the material into a slurry or liquid form provides better filling than does dry placement.

derground voids. Collapse and subsidence may occur, in some cases, creating a pseudokarst topography. Figure 254-7 shows highway damage resulting from piping in the southwestern United States.

Piping is classified into three types, based on its mode of origin:

1. *Desiccation, with stress cracks:* soils which become dry and cracked are subjected to rainfall which enters the cracks and travels to a free face, forming drainage conduits.

2. *Entrainment:* occurs when dewatered building foundations or a rise in water level behind or under dams or levees causes changes in hydraulic head pressures and subsequent subsurface channeling. Entrainment of water and saturated materials to downgradient outflow points can result in sand boils, mud volcanoes, and a collapse of sediment and overlying structures.

3. *Variable permeability subsidence:* occurs when sufficient hydraulic head exists to move sediment-laden water through a stratum to the face of a gully or embankment. The conduits formed in this way grow from the outlet back into the cliff face.

Where possible, construction should be avoided in areas where piping is likely. If construction is unavoidable, the careful design of drainage systems to avoid a concentration of runoff in vulnerable areas is essential. Runoff should be conveyed in closed culverts to points away from vulnerable structures.

4.0 OTHER CAUSES

4.1 Permafrost

Subsidence is also a hazard in regions of permafrost or where large masses of underground ice exist. At temperatures below freezing, large blocks of ice are in effect *arctic rocks;* thawing decreases their support of the overlying soils and results in subsidence. When permafrost is disturbed or subjected to warming, it is a cause of surface subsidence; soil particles formerly held together by ice are freed, resulting in subsidence as free-flowing water accumulates at the surface or drains away, leaving lowered levels of saturated soils. Disturbed areas can turn into mud-filled depressions which expand with each season's thaw. Winter effects include heaving and the formation of ridges and ice dikes as water trapped between the permanently frozen strata and the recently frozen surface expands upon freezing, forcing the surface upward. Subsidence will then occur during the spring thaw.

Figure 254-8 shows areas in the northern hemisphere of continuous permafrost (where the entire seasonally thawing layer refreezes each winter) and of discontinuous permafrost (where the seasonal thaw layer does not totally refreeze to the depth of the permanently frozen layer).

Figure 254-9 gives a block diagram of permafrost morphology.

A number of engineering strategies have been developed to overcome the difficulties encountered in permafrost regions. *Granular frozen permafrost,* in which soil grains are in contact with each other and excess ice is not present, normally causes few serious engineering difficulties. *Hard frozen permafrost,* in which some water remains unfrozen, does cause serious difficulties; in these conditions, the usual approach is either to thaw the area and remove the excess water or to maintain the permafrost in its natural thermal condition. Preservation of permafrost can be achieved by ensuring that no additional heat is introduced into the ground. Construction may be carried out on an insulating pad of gravel over the site or may be raised on thermally isolated pilings.

Preservation of existing vegetation in permafrost regions is particularly important, since its removal will allow direct sun to heat the surface and cause increased seasonal thawing.

4.2 Collapsing Soils and Hydrocompactive Soils

Collapsing soils are those which rely on a water soluble mineral cement to maintain

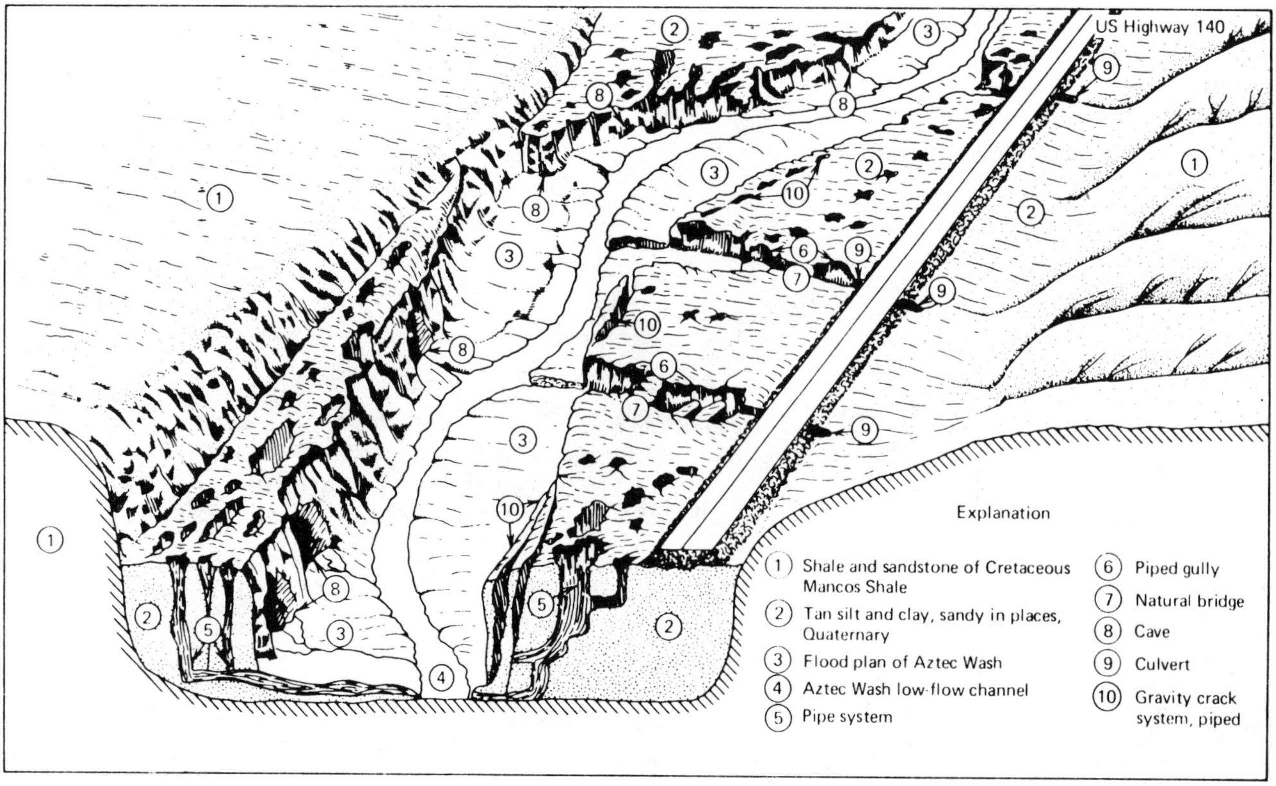
US Highway 140
Explanation
1 Shale and sandstone of Cretaceous Mancos Shale
2 Tan silt and clay, sandy in places, Quaternary
3 Flood plan of Aztec Wash
4 Aztec Wash low-flow channel
5 Pipe system
6 Piped gully
7 Natural bridge
8 Cave
9 Culvert
10 Gravity crack system, piped

Figure 254-7 Structural failure of highways (western United States) caused by piping of valley fill.

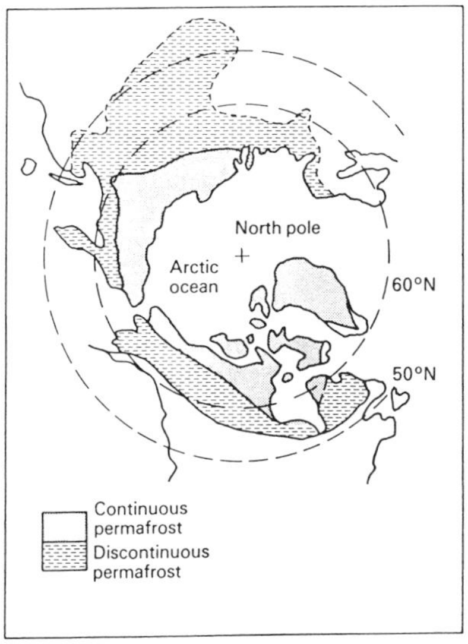
North pole
Arctic ocean
60°N
50°N
Continuous permafrost
Discontinuous permafrost

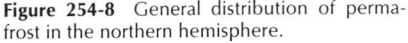

Figure 254-8 General distribution of permafrost in the northern hemisphere.

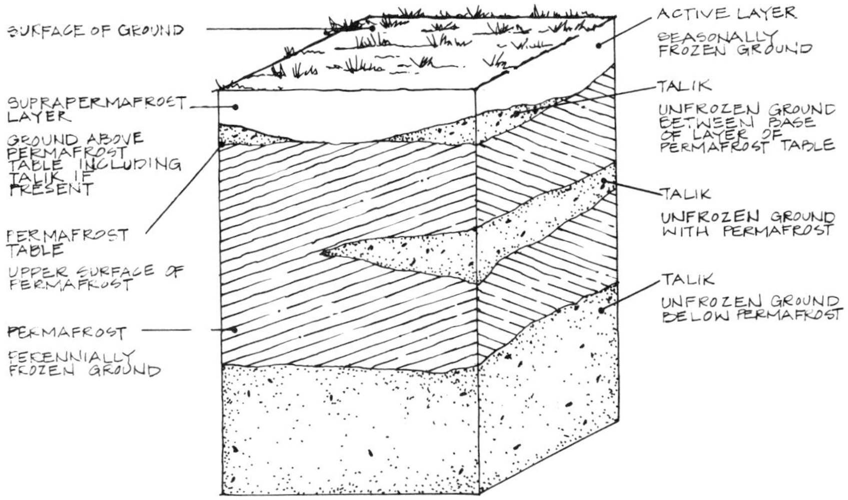
SURFACE OF GROUND
SUPRAPERMAFROST LAYER
GROUND ABOVE PERMAFROST TABLE INCLUDING TALIK IF PRESENT
PERMAFROST TABLE
UPPER SURFACE OF PERMAFROST
PERMAFROST
PERENNIALLY FROZEN GROUND
ACTIVE LAYER
SEASONALLY FROZEN GROUND
TALIK
UNFROZEN GROUND BETWEEN BASE OF LAYER OF PERMAFROST TABLE
TALIK
UNFROZEN GROUND WITH PERMAFROST
TALIK
UNFROZEN GROUND BELOW PERMAFROST

Figure 254-9 Block diagram of permafrost morphology.

their strength. When wet, the mineral cement dissolves and these soils collapse, leaving a bumpy terrain. Loess and some other soils of a loose, open structure are subject to this type of subsidence.

A similar effect is observed in hydrocompactive soils. In arid regions, alluvial fan deposits and soils which were originally deposited as a result of mudflows or mudslides and have a loose structure containing a relatively large quantity of air can form hydrocompactive soils. Wetting causes a reorientation of the soil particles and can result in significant subsidence [4.5 m (15 ft) in California after the introduction of irrigation water].

In regions where hydrocompactive soils or collapsing soils are common, site-specific geologic reports which assess potential subsidence should be required.

These soils should be avoided for most types of development. When avoidance is impossible, the usual engineering approach is to precompact the area by the addition of water. Maintenance of existing structures depends on strict management of surface water.

4.3 Organic Soils

Highly compressible organic soils respond to the withdrawal of water by significant subsidence. The drainage of marshes for agricultural purposes and the dewatering of peat bogs has resulted in widespread subsidence, usually resulting from the combined effects of drying, oxidation, and wind erosion.

Organic soils should be avoided for most construction purposes. When unavoidable, the usual approach is either to dump solid fill material on the site until settlement ceases or to replace the soft material with suitable fill.

REFERENCES

Bell, F. G. *Site Investigation in Areas of Mining Subsidence,* Newnes-Butterworth's, London, 1975.

Bolt, B. A., et al. *Geological Hazards,* Springer-Verlag, New York, 1975.

Costa, John E., and Victor R. Baker. *Surficial Geology: Building with the Earth,* Wiley, New York, 1981.

Keller, Edward A. *Environmental Geology,* 2d ed., Charles E. Merrill, Columbus, OH, 1979.

National Coal Board, Mining Department (UK). *Subsidence Engineer's Handbook,* London, 1975. ■

section 255: Natural Hazards: Expansive Soils

CREDITS

Section Editor: Charles W. Harris
Technical Writer: Tess Canfield

Special Consultants:

Richard Myrick and H. Rowland Jackson
Myrick-Newman-Dahlberg Partnership
Dallas, Texas

Patrick Buckley
Yandell and Hiller
Dallas, Texas

Reviewers:

Ernest L. Buckley, Dean
School of Engineering
South Dakota State University
Brookings, South Dakota

James E. Hough
James E. Hough and Associates
Cincinnati, Ohio

Susan Tubbesing, Jacquelyn L. Monday, Sarah Nathe, Gilbert White, and Staff
Natural Hazards Research and Applications Information Center
University of Colorado
Boulder, Colorado

CONTENTS

1.0 CAUSES

Soils and soft rocks which shrink or swell as a result of changes in moisture content are commonly known as *expansive soils.* Expansive soils are usually clays, but some types of shales also exhibit shrinking and swelling. Aluminum silicate minerals of volcanic origin decompose to form expansive clays of the smectite group, the best known of which is montmorillonite.

Pure montmorillonite may swell up to 15 times its dry volume, but most natural soils contain other materials that swell less, so few natural soils swell to more than 1½ times their original volume (Figure 255-1).

Three conditions must be met for expansive soils to become a hazard:

1. The soil must contain a mineral component which is subject to significant swelling.

2. The soil must experience changes in moisture content.

3. The soil strata containing the expansive material must be sufficiently thick to exert significant movement.

Volume increases of 3 percent or more are potentially damaging and are generally considered to require specially designed foundations. In the United States, 60 percent of new houses built on expansive clays suffer minor damage, but 10 percent will suffer major damage. Property damage caused by expansive soils exceeds the damage from floods, hurricanes, tornadoes, and earthquakes combined. Also affected are roads, bridges, pipelines, and other rigid structures which rest on or pass through expansive soils.

Expansive soils become a problem when construction takes place because of the pressure changes which occur as a result of uneven moisture distribution throughout the soil. Small buildings, bridges, and roads impose relatively negligible loads on an expansive soil in comparison to its swelling pressures, which may exceed 10,000 psf (479,000 Pa).

The problem created by expansive soils is the differential movement it causes under the structure itself. Seasonal changes in moisture and water-table levels cause expansive soil to move under natural conditions. This zone of seasonal change can extend to a depth of about 7 ft (2 m). Once an area is covered by a road or structure, normal seasonal change and drying (desiccation) are usually prevented. Desiccation and wetting still occur around the perimeter but gradually decrease toward the center. A characteristic *doming* of soil under the structure occurs as the soil shrinks at the perimeter, causing downwarping. *Cupping* results from wetting formerly dry areas at the perimeter (Figure 255-2). More commonly, the pattern of soil expansion is asymmetrical, related to leaking water or sewer connections, shade patterns created by the structure itself, surface runoff from an adjacent slope collecting against a building or roadway, or a number of other causes (Figure 255-3).

Two forms of heaving exist, superimposed on each other. These are general heave and seasonal heave (Figure 255-4).

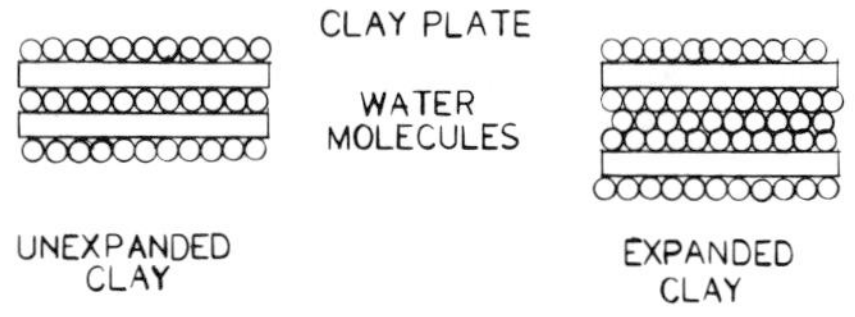
CLAY PLATE
WATER MOLECULES
UNEXPANDED CLAY
EXPANDED CLAY

Figure 255-1 Diagram of a Montmorillonite Clay Particle. Note that water is incorporated within the clay structure itself.

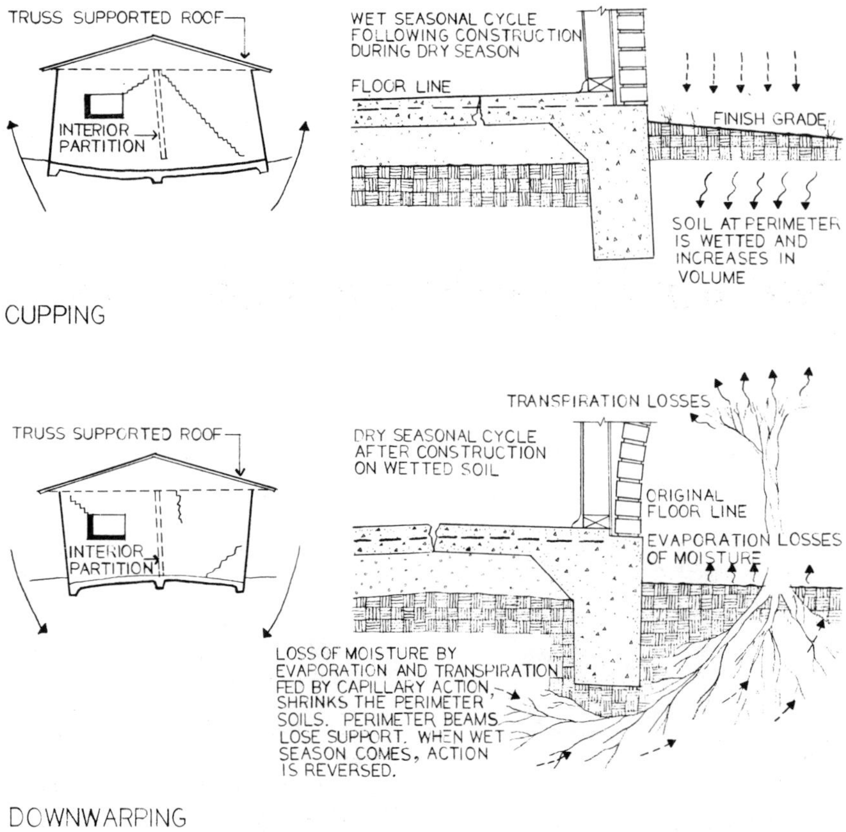
TRUSS SUPPORTED ROOF
INTERIOR PARTITION
WET SEASONAL CYCLE FOLLOWING CONSTRUCTION DURING DRY SEASON
FLOOR LINE
FINISH GRADE
SOIL AT PERIMETER IS WETTED AND INCREASES IN VOLUME
CUPPING
TRUSS SUPPORTED ROOF
INTERIOR PARTITION
TRANSPIRATION LOSSES
DRY SEASONAL CYCLE AFTER CONSTRUCTION ON WETTED SOIL
ORIGINAL FLOOR LINE
EVAPORATION LOSSES OF MOISTURE
LOSS OF MOISTURE BY EVAPORATION AND TRANSPIRATION FED BY CAPILLARY ACTION, SHRINKS THE PERIMETER SOILS. PERIMETER BEAMS LOSE SUPPORT. WHEN WET SEASON COMES, ACTION IS REVERSED.
DOWNWARPING

Figure 255-2 Heaving Patterns Beneath Structures. With slab-on-ground foundations, the characteristics of expansive clay problems depend on the seasonal cycle.

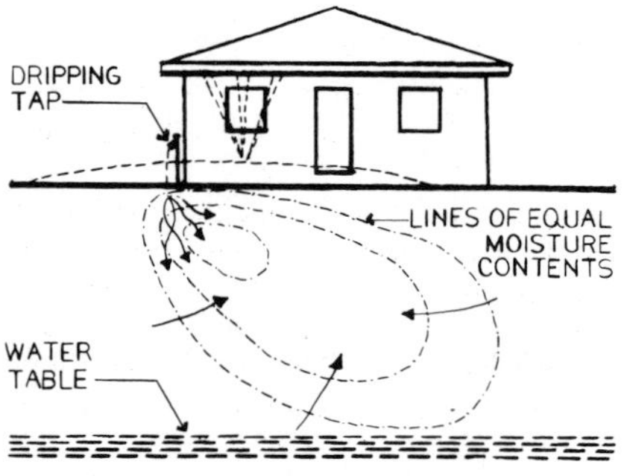
DRIPPING TAP
LINES OF EQUAL MOISTURE CONTENTS
WATER TABLE

Figure 255-3 Distorted Heaving Pattern. Expanded soil is indicated by the concentric dashed lines.

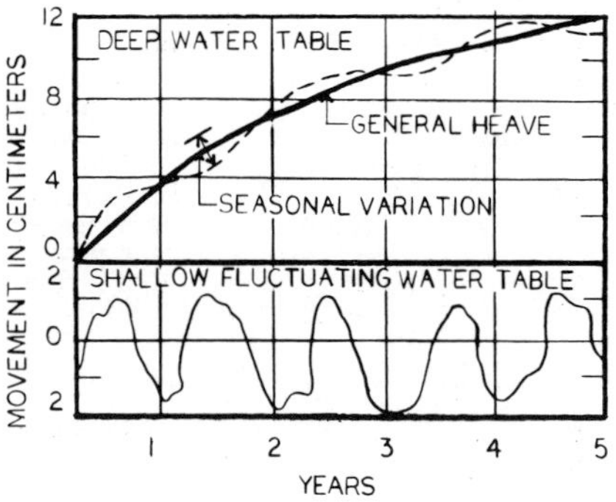
DEEP WATER TABLE
GENERAL HEAVE
SEASONAL VARIATION
SHALLOW FLUCTUATING WATER TABLE
MOVEMENT IN CENTIMETERS
12
8
4
0
2
0
2
1
2
3
4
5
YEARS

Figure 255-4 Relationship between the Extent of Soil Heave and Time. Note the effect of the depth of the water table.

2.0 ESTIMATION OF HAZARD

Figure 255-5 shows a generalized map of expansive soil hazards in the United States. Small local deposits are not shown, and careful site investigation is required if there is reason to suspect the presence of expansive soils.

Professional geotechnical engineers or engineering geologists should be consulted for positive identification, but a combination of several signs may suggest the presence of expansive soils: (1) the soft, puffy, *popcorn* appearance of clay soil when dry; (2) soil that is very sticky when wet; (3) the presence of substantial open cracks in dry clay soil; and (4) soil that is very highly plastic and weak when wet but rock hard when dry. Existing structures in the vicinity should be inspected for signs of damage which could indicate expansive soils.

The soil plasticity index (Figure 255-6, and further described in Section 810: Soils and Aggregates) is a first indicator of expansivity as a problem; when related to the percentage of clay in a sample, it can be used to estimate the severity of the problem. Experience in the United States reveals that the plasticity index (PI) indicates expansivity as follows:

PI	*Expansivity*
0–14	Noncritical
14–25	Marginal
25–40	Critical
Over 40	Highly critical

However, the plasticity index alone does not adequately define the expansive potential of a soil profile. A thorough understanding of the soil structure and depth of the active zone is necessary in order to predict the expansive potential of a given site. Prior to selecting a foundation design, consideration must be given to geologic, groundwater, and soil conditions at each building site.

For major projects, laboratory testing can give a precise estimate of expansion potential. Several test methods have been developed to estimate heave on a particular site.

3.0 LOSS PREVENTION AND REDUCTION

Some techniques for reducing damage caused by expansive soils are outlined in this section. If hazardous sites cannot be avoided, then the development of a comprehensive approach based on several techniques tailored to particular site conditions is recommended.

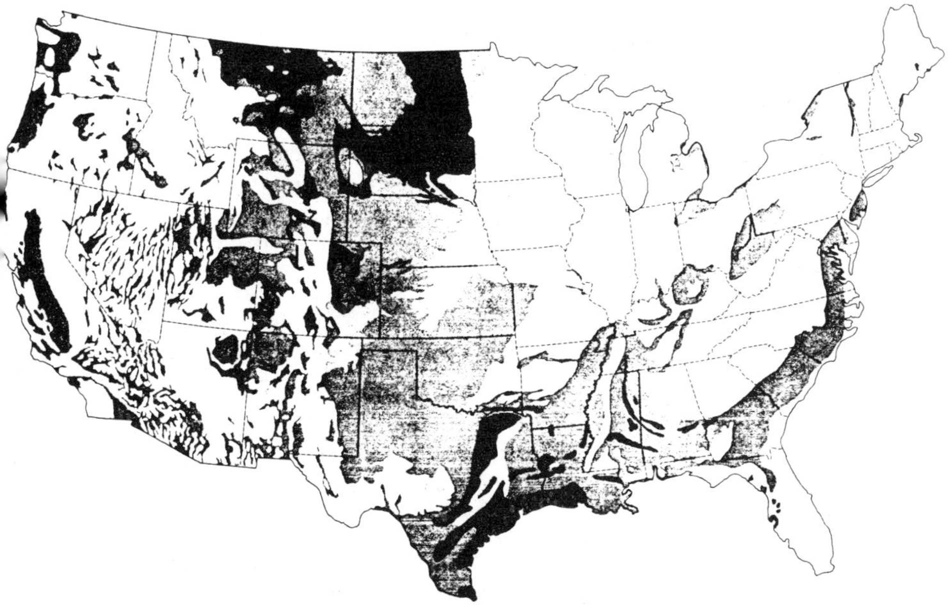

Figure 255-5 Generalized Map of Expansive Soils in the United States. Expansive soils are most abundant in areas colored black; they are common in areas colored gray.

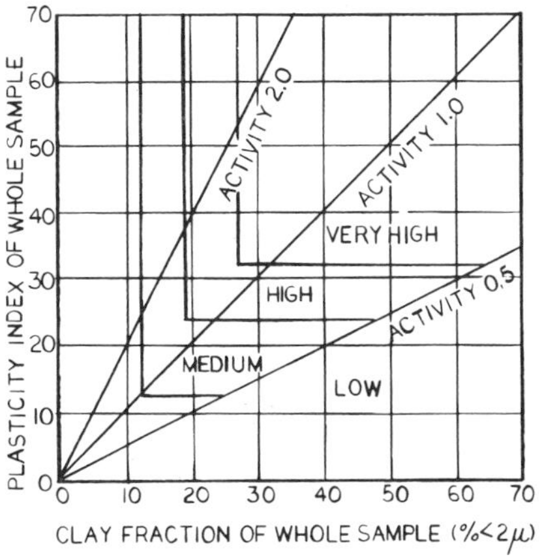
PLASTICITY INDEX OF WHOLE SAMPLE
0
10
20
30
40
50
60
70
CLAY FRACTION OF WHOLE SAMPLE (%<2μ)
ACTIVITY 2.0
ACTIVITY 1.0
ACTIVITY 0.5
VERY HIGH
HIGH
MEDIUM
LOW

Figure 255-6 Plasticity index versus soil composition as an indicator of the severity of soil expansivity.

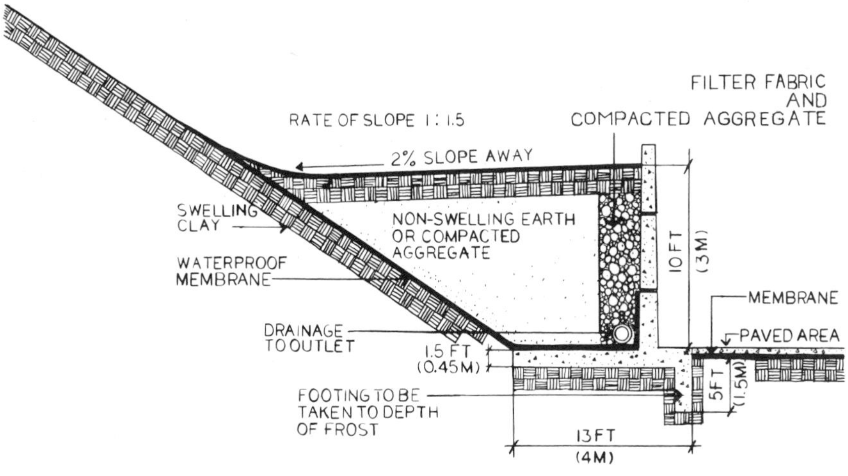
FILTER FABRIC AND COMPACTED AGGREGATE
RATE OF SLOPE 1 : 1.5
2% SLOPE AWAY
SWELLING CLAY
WATERPROOF MEMBRANE
NON-SWELLING EARTH OR COMPACTED AGGREGATE
10 FT (3M)
MEMBRANE
DRAINAGE TO OUTLET
PAVED AREA
1.5 FT (0.45M)
FOOTING TO BE TAKEN TO DEPTH OF FROST
5 FT (1.5M)
13 FT (4M)

Figure 255-7 Design of retaining wall in swelling clay soil.

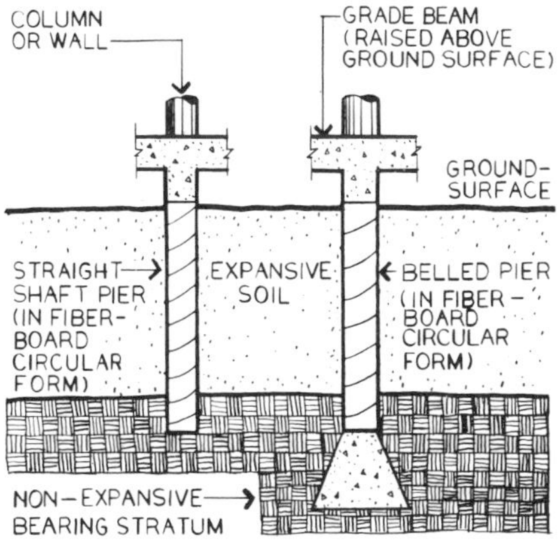
COLUMN OR WALL
GRADE BEAM (RAISED ABOVE GROUND SURFACE)
GROUND-SURFACE
STRAIGHT SHAFT PIER (IN FIBER-BOARD CIRCULAR FORM)
EXPANSIVE SOIL
BELLED PIER (IN FIBER-BOARD CIRCULAR FORM)
NON-EXPANSIVE BEARING STRATUM

Figure 255-8 Two types of machine-drilled piers.

3.1 Avoidance of Hazardous Sites

The best method to prevent loss from expansive soils is simply to find an alternative construction site. If this is impossible, strategies for coping with expansive soils are described below.

3.2 Isolation from Expansive Soils

In areas where expansive soils are unavoidable, damage can be prevented by isolating structures from the stresses caused by the shrinking and swelling of the soil.

In areas where the stratum of expandable soil is relatively shallow, it may be feasible to excavate and replace it with nonexpansive fill. If the stratum is deep, it may be effective to excavate a greater than normal depth of soil, backfill with nonswelling material, and immediately cover it to prevent drying.

Expansive soils also create horizontal stresses when confined by vertical structures such as basement walls or retaining walls. Figure 255-7 shows the recommended practice for construction of large retaining walls in areas of expansive soils. Removing the expansive material from behind the wall, replacing it with nonswelling material, and installing waterproof membranes will control changes in soil moisture behind the wall.

Where excavation of expansive soils is not feasible, the intended structure may be placed on piers, which effectively isolate it from the effects of unequal movement (Figure 255-8). Piers are encased in fiberboard circular forms which isolate the pier from uplift forces. Piers may be preferable to pilings because the heave and vibration associated with pile driving can be avoided.

Pier or pile foundations should be designed by a qualified engineer, since improper design can result in serious failures in buildings and other large structures (Figure 255-9). Piers or piles are subject to upward forces produced by expansive soils. These forces must be resisted by the load

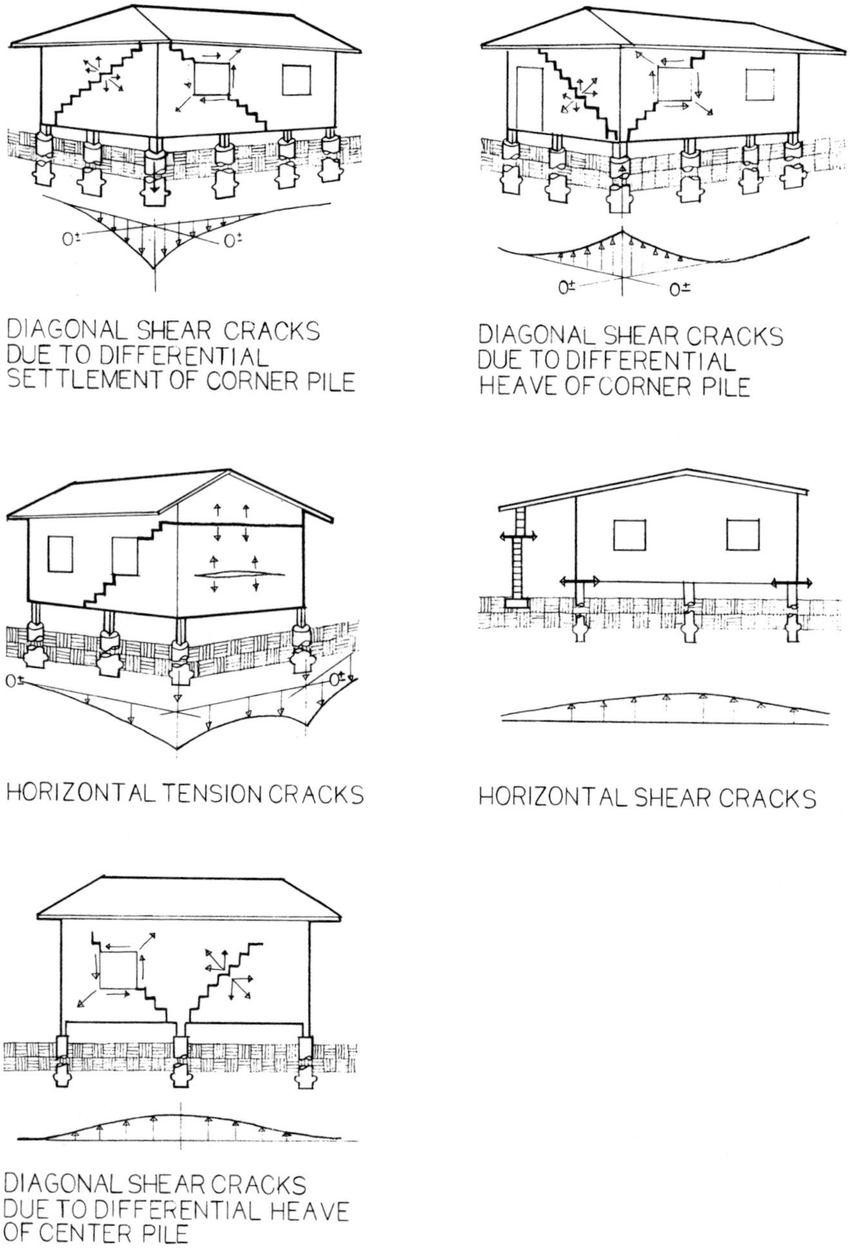
DIAGONAL SHEAR CRACKS
DUE TO DIFFERENTIAL
SETTLEMENT OF CORNER PILE
DIAGONAL SHEAR CRACKS
DUE TO DIFFERENTIAL
HEAVE OF CORNER PILE
HORIZONTAL TENSION CRACKS
HORIZONTAL SHEAR CRACKS
DIAGONAL SHEAR CRACKS
DUE TO DIFFERENTIAL HEAVE
OF CENTER PILE

Figure 255-9 Failures of buildings caused by movement of pile foundations.

on the pier or pile—as well as by the restraining force of the foot of the bellied pier, if that design is chosen.

3.3 Flexibility in Design

The design of structures to accommodate the heaving by expansive soils includes the use of floating slabs in basements (Figure 255-10) and the provision of clear space under slabs on-grade.

Figure 255-11 shows two types of fiberboard void forms, which are available in various depths, usually 4, 6, and 8 in (100, 150, and 200 mm). These forms are strong enough to support the weight of fresh concrete placed over them, but under pressure from expanding soil below are weak enough to crush and allow the soil to move freely. Figure 255-12 shows a typical use of void forms to isolate a concrete slab from expansive soil. Since the slab is not supported on soil, it must be designed to span from pier to pier under gravity (down) loads. The size of void required is based on the estimated vertical rise of the soil beneath the structure.

Another approach uses rigid elements joined by flexible ones (brick masonry walls with steel panels at intervals, for example) which can accommodate movement. Elements which bridge from a rigid protected structure to the ground surface (the entry steps of a house built on piles, for example) should be isolated from the main structure by use of a flexible filler to absorb movement, thereby protecting the structure from damage (Figure 255-13).

Undergound utilities are also subject to disruption from expansive soils. Drainage and water connections are particularly important because, should they fail, the leakage introduced into sensitive soils compounds the problem. Figure 255-14 shows an approach to making drainage connections.

3.4 Soil Treatments to Reduce Volume Change Potential

Compaction:

The compaction of expansive soils may reduce the permeability of the material; it can slow the subsequent expansion of soils which have a low to moderate expansion potential. It is most effective on granular, noncohesive soils. In some cases, compaction at high degrees of saturation is accompanied by changes in soil structure, which in turn affect swelling characteristics. A kneading compaction to a moderate density, as by a sheepsfoot roller under wetter than optimum conditions, can lead to less swell and less swell pressure. The excavation and recompaction of existing soil prior to its use as subgrade may be necessary.

Compaction should be done with cau-

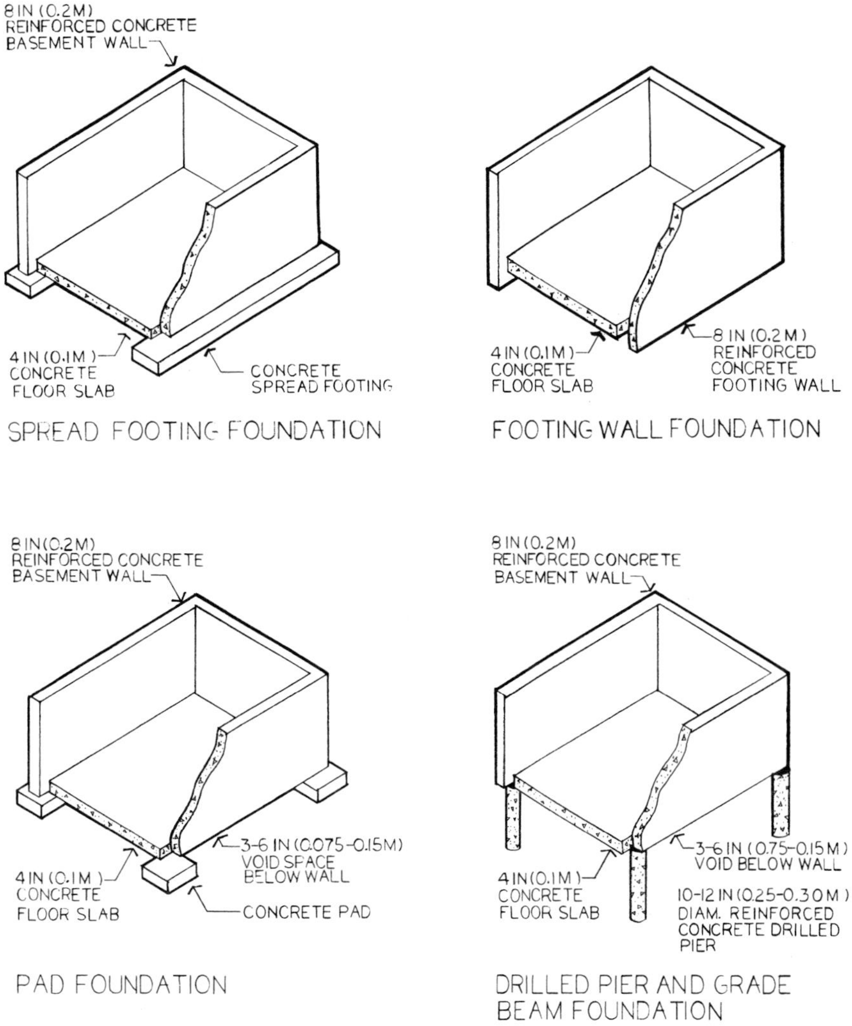
8 IN (0.2M)
REINFORCED CONCRETE
BASEMENT WALL
4 IN (0.1M)
CONCRETE
FLOOR SLAB
CONCRETE
SPREAD FOOTING
SPREAD FOOTING FOUNDATION
4 IN (0.1M)
CONCRETE
FLOOR SLAB
8 IN (0.2M)
REINFORCED
CONCRETE
FOOTING WALL
FOOTING WALL FOUNDATION
8 IN (0.2M)
REINFORCED CONCRETE
BASEMENT WALL
4 IN (0.1M)
CONCRETE
FLOOR SLAB
3-6 IN (0.075-0.15M)
VOID SPACE
BELOW WALL
CONCRETE PAD
PAD FOUNDATION
8 IN (0.2M)
REINFORCED CONCRETE
BASEMENT WALL
4 IN (0.1M)
CONCRETE
FLOOR SLAB
3-6 IN (0.75-0.15M)
VOID BELOW WALL
10-12 IN (0.25-0.30M)
DIAM. REINFORCED
CONCRETE DRILLED
PIER
DRILLED PIER AND GRADE
BEAM FOUNDATION

Figure 255-10 Four Alternative Designs for Residential Basements. In all cases a floating floor slab may be used; otherwise, an air space of several inches is left beneath to permit soil swell.

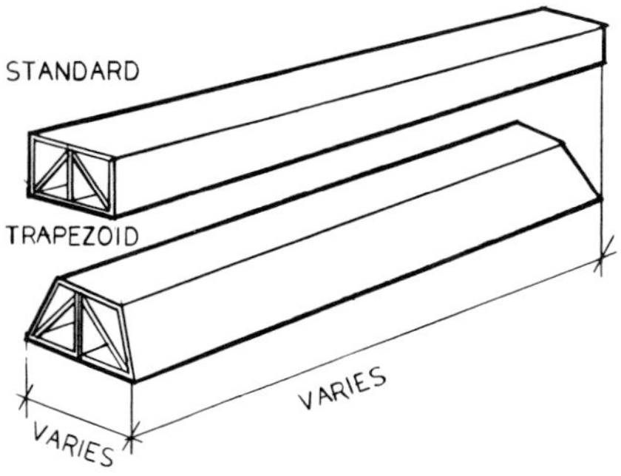
STANDARD
TRAPEZOID
VARIES
VARIES

Figure 255-11 Typical folded fiberboard void forms.

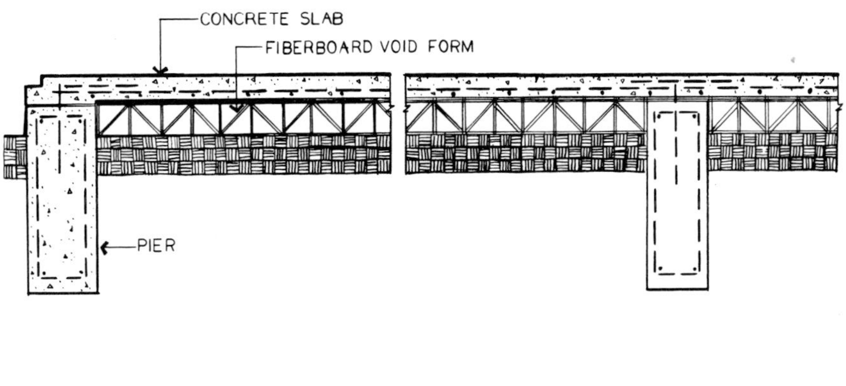
CONCRETE SLAB
FIBERBOARD VOID FORM
PIER

Figure 255-12 Detail of fiberboard void forms used to provide space for soil expansion below concrete slab.

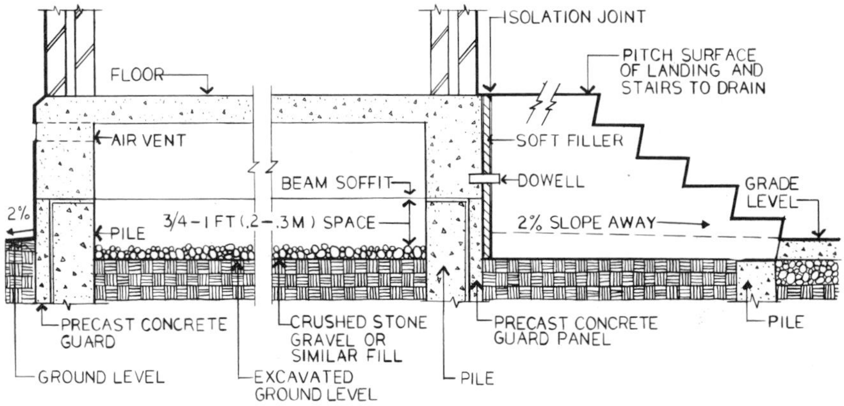
ISOLATION JOINT
PITCH SURFACE OF LANDING AND STAIRS TO DRAIN
FLOOR
AIR VENT
SOFT FILLER
BEAM SOFFIT
DOWELL
GRADE LEVEL
2%
PILE
3/4 – 1 FT (.2 – .3 M) SPACE
2% SLOPE AWAY
PRECAST CONCRETE GUARD
CRUSHED STONE GRAVEL OR SIMILAR FILL
PRECAST CONCRETE GUARD PANEL
PILE
GROUND LEVEL
EXCAVATED GROUND LEVEL
PILE

Figure 255-13 Detail of grade beam on piled foundation.

tion, however, since the overcompaction of very active soils can result in *rebound,* which will exaggerate the swelling effects. Laboratory tests to determine the effects of compaction should be based on the soil structure as found on the site.

Prewetting:

The prewetting of a site prior to construction either by ponding or spraying has been successful in controlling expansivity. Wetting is intended to bring the moisture content of the soil to the level expected at equilibrium after completion of construction. This requires a knowledge of the swelling characteristics of the soil and the distribution and magnitude of the loadings to be applied.

This method has several drawbacks. To allow the wetting to penetrate to a depth of 4 to 5 ft (1.2 to 1.5 m), a period of 30 days is typically required. When the wetting has been completed, the site may be so soft and sticky that construction equipment cannot function effectively. Soil strength may be reduced to the extent that the addition of lime to the upper foot or so is necessary to create a suitable working platform. Although wetting is a slow process, drying can be very rapid under some weather conditions. To prevent drying, complete the construction and seal the prewetted soil mass as quickly as possible. Later drying of the site may cause shrinkage.

Heat Treatment:

Heating expansive clays to 392 degrees F (±200 degrees C) may significantly reduce their ability to swell or shrink. One thousand degrees C (1830 degrees F) causes soil to fuse, but the cost of this method may seldom be justified.

Chemical Additives:

The application of hydrated lime or other chemicals has been successful in controlling soil expansivity. Studies have shown that the ionic character of water has a major effect on volume change. The addition of chemicals for control of expansivity is summarized in Table 255-1.

3.5 Drainage and Control of Surface Runoff

Techniques for managing the amount of moisture change in expansive soils include the provision of vertical moisture barriers to isolate the soil under a structure from the surrounding soil. The moisture barrier may be one of two types. One uses impermeable material (e.g., low-grade concrete at three sacks of cement per cubic yard, or ground rubber tires in an asphalt emulsion binder) which stops the movement of water. The other uses crushed rock to create a capillary barrier. Since most of the movement of water through clay is by capillary action, breaking the contact between masses of expansive soil stops moisture change at least for the short term. Capillary barriers may be less desirable than impermeable barriers in areas where trees exist, since the long-term effect of tree roots on capillary barriers is not yet known.

After installation of the moisture barrier, the supporting soil is prewetted to bring its moisture content up to 1 to 2 percent above the plastic limit. Construction should proceed quickly, to prevent loss of soil moisture. See Figure 255-15.

Other techniques which can reduce soil movement include the provision of downspouts and drain blocks so that roof runoff is carried well away from the structure [at least 5 ft (1.5 m) but preferably more]. The provision of a wide paved area around a structure is frequently recommended, but this usually succeeds only in reducing the differential movement by spreading it over a larger area. Sites on the tops of mounds, either natural or artificial, are preferable to sites on slopes because positive surface drainage away from the structure in all directions is easier to achieve.

Although often recommended, the use of slab-on-grade subdrains must be carefully considered. Unless outfalls and trenches can be protected from surcharged conditions, foundation drains can sometimes introduce backflow into the areas they are designed to keep dry. An alternative approach recommended by the U.S. Federal Housing Administration is the use of impervious backfill at the building perimeter and proper control of surface runoff and roof water.

3.6 Management of Vegetation

Vegetation is an important consideration when planning construction on sites with expansive soils. Plant root activity causes desiccation of the soil, particularly during dry seasons of the year, resulting in shrinkage of the soil, which is only partially offset by the plant's shading of the soil. Artificial irrigation of planting can cause expansion of the soil.

The Royal Botanic Garden, Kew, Tree Root Survey (1971–1979) has reported the following experience of damage to buildings on shrinkable clays caused by the activity of tree roots. The survey reports experience in the humid climate of Great Britain and includes the extreme drought of 1975–1976, which caused extensive soil shrinkage and damage to structures. The study is based on 3000 reports of damage, chiefly from London and the south of England, mostly in urban situations. Table 255-2 summarizes the findings of the survey.

Existing mature trees whose root systems are not actively expanding may cause relatively less damage than newly planted or young trees in active growth. Soils under paving or structures tend to become wetter than surrounding soil because of capillary action. Thus, they will attract tree roots.

Based upon the findings of the Kew survey and consultation with American landscape architects experienced in dealing with expansive soils, the following actions

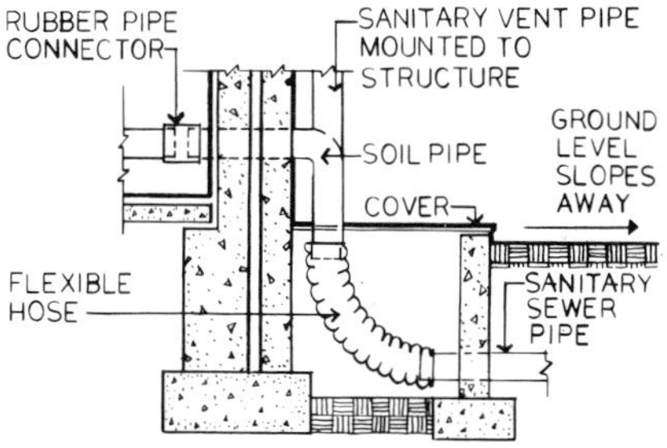
RUBBER PIPE CONNECTOR
SANITARY VENT PIPE MOUNTED TO STRUCTURE
GROUND LEVEL SLOPES AWAY
SOIL PIPE
COVER
FLEXIBLE HOSE
SANITARY SEWER PIPE

Figure 255-14 Typical flexible drainage connection.

TABLE 255-1
Methods for Volume Change Control Using Additives

Method or additive	*Effects on soil*	*Method of applicaton*	*Comments*
Lime treatment	Reduce or eliminate swelling by ion exchange, flocculation, cementation, alteration of clay minerals	▪ Remove, mix, replace, or mix in place	▪ Only suitable for shallow depths ▪ Mixing difficult in highly plastic clays ▪ Delay between initial addition of lime and final mixing and placement improves ease of handling and compaction ▪ 2–6% lime usually required
		▪ Deep-plow	▪ Treat depths to 36 in (1 m) ▪ Can use conventional equipment ▪ Requires careful quality control
		▪ Lime slurry injection; lime piles	▪ Controversial, very sensitive to initial moisture conditions ▪ Limited by slow lime diffusion rate ▪ May not be effective in dry, fissured material or accepted if soil is wet
		▪ Mixing in place: piles and walls	▪ Not yet investigated ▪ Might be suitable in highly plastic soils for treatment to large depth ▪ Could use dry lime, lime mortar, or slurry
Cement treatment	Reduce or eliminate swelling by cementation, ion exchange, and alteration of clay minerals	▪ Remove, mix, replace; plant mix	▪ Cement may be less effective than lime in highly plastic clays ▪ Mixing difficult in highly plastic clays ▪ Reduction in swelling noticeable for cement contents >4–6%
		▪ Mixing in place	▪ No excavation and backfilling required ▪ Has been used for construction of piles and walls ▪ Better, more economical equipment needed
Chemicals: hydroxides, chlorides, phosphoric acid, carbonates, sulfates, lignins, siliconates, asphalts, quaternary ammonium chloride Proprietary: "compaction aids"	Various effects have been measured or hypothesized, including reduced plasticity, improved compaction, reduced swell, waterproofing, preservation of soil structure, increased strength, increased or decreased permeability.	▪ Usually remove, mix, and replace or mix in place ▪ In some instances spraying or injection is used ▪ Electro-osmosis may be useful in special cases ▪ Diffusion may be effective	▪ Problems of mixing or injection may be significant ▪ No chemical additives for control of volume change appear to be available that are effective, permanent, and economically competitive with lime or cement when large volumes of soil must be treated ▪ Calcium chloride may be effective at least temporarily in soils with expanding lattice clays. It may be useful in soils with a high sulfate content ▪ A number of proprietary formulations have been marketed. The beneficial effects of these materials have not generally been documented

Source: Modified from James K. Mitchell and Lufti Rand, *Control of Volume Changes in Expansive Earth Materials,* vol. 2: *Proceedings: Expansive Clays and Shales in Highway Design and Construction,* FHA.

TABLE 255-2
The Effect of Tree Roots on Buildings in Expansive Soils

Species	Number of reports of damage	Percentage on clay soils, %	Urban mature height in clay soils, ft (m)	Maximum distance to damage, ft (m)	90% damage within, ft (m)	Rooting habit	Remarks
			Broadleaves				
Malus	61	96	25–30 (8–10)	33 (10)	26 (8)	Shallow but locally deep	
Pyrus	19	96	40 (12)	33 (10)	26 (8)	Shallow but locally deep	
Fraxinus excelsior	145	+99	75 (23)	70 (21)	42 (13)	Deep	
Fraxinus ornus	145	+99	45 (14)	70 (21)	42 (13)	Deep	
Fagus	23	100	60 (20)	50 (15)	38 (11)	Shallow	Scarce on clay soils
Betula	35	100	35–45 (11–14)	33 (10)	26 (8)	Shallow	
Prunus	114	100	20–40 (6–12)	36 (11)	26 (7.5)	Shallow to medium deep	
Ulmus	70	100	55–80 (17–25)	80 (25)	61 (19)	Deep	
Robinia	20	100	55–60 (18–20)	40 (12.4)	34 (10.5)		
Crateuqus	65	+99	30 (10)	38 (11.5)	28 (8.7)	Moderately deep	
Aesculus	63	+98	55–80 (16–25)	75 (23)	44 (15)	Shallow to moderately deep	
Tilia	238	100	55–78 (16–24)	65 (20)	36 (11)	Moderately deep	
Quercus	293	100	55–75 (16–23)	96 (30)	55 (18)	Deep	Highest return of reported damage
Platanus	327	100	80–100 (25–30)	50 (15)	33 (10)	Moderately deep	
Populus	191	+99	80–95 (25–28)	100 (30)	65 (20)	Deep	Second highest return of reported damage
Sorbus	32	96	25–40 (8–12)	38 (11)	30 (9.5)		
Acer	135	99	30–78 (10–24)	65 (20)	40 (12)	Deep	
Salix	124	100	50–(<15, rarely) 60–80 (20–25)	130 (40)	55 (18)	Moderately deep	Largest root spreads reported in survey
Alnus	1	100	55–65 (17–20)	13 (4)			
Sambucus nigra	13	100	20–23 (6–7)	26 (8)			
Ficus carica	3	100	20 (6)	16 (5)			
Carylus avellana	1	100	30 (10)	10 (3)			
Leix aquifoliom	2	100	40–45 (12–14)	10 (3)			
Carpinus betulus	8	100	40–55 (12–18)	60 (17)			
Laburnum	7	89	23–29 (7–9)	22 (7)			
Syringa vulgaris	9	89	23–26 (7–8)	22 (7)			
Gleditsia tricanthos	1	100	43–55 (13–16)	44 (15)			
Magnolia soulongeana	2	100	16–23 (5–7)	16 (5)			
Sophara japonica	1	100	45–55 (14–16)	10 (3)			
Ailanthus	2	100	55–66 (18–22)	10 (3)			
Juglans regia	3	100	40–50 (12–15)	26 (8)			
			Conifers				
Cypress *(cupressus cupressaceae)*	31	100	50–80 (15–25)	65 (20)			
Firs *(Abies)*	1	100	50–60 (15–20)	6 (2)			
Monkey puzzle *(Araucaria)*	2	100	50–55 (15–18+)	10 (3)			
Pines *(Pinus)*	5	100	60–95 (20–29)	20 (8)			
Redwoods *(Sequoia)*	1	100	55–75 (17–23)	3 (1)			
Yew *(Taxus)*	1	100	25–40 (8–12)	16 (5)			

Note: The proportion of conifers in relation to all trees reported to have damaged buildings is very low.

Source: U.K. damage reports contained in D. F. Cutler and I. B. K. Richardson, *Tree Roots and Buildings,* Construction Press, London and New York, 1981; reproduced with permission of the controller, Her Britannic Majesty's Stationery Office, and the Trustees, Royal Botanic Gardens, Kew, England.

are suggested to reduce possible damage caused by vegetation.

Good maintenance and frequent and copious watering of vegetation to prevent excessive soil desiccation may be the best protection for structural elements.

Where possible, avoid building within the root zone of existing trees or within the area into which the roots will grow during the expected life of the structure. Depending upon the species and the site conditions, avoid construction within a zone approximately equal to the mature height of an existing tree.

If construction must take place within an active or potential root zone, one of the three following techniques may be appropriate:

1. Prewet the soil prior to construction, and maintain a constant high moisture level through artificial irrigation.

2. Keep the soil as dry as possible so that roots are not encouraged to develop in the critical area.

3. Construct a subterranean impervious barrier similar to that shown in Figure 255.14 to prevent tree roots from penetrating vulnerable areas.

If none of the above methods is feasible, then large existing trees that could cause major damage should be considered for removal.

It should be noted that in many parts of the world existing vegetation is considered so valuable that it is undesirable to remove it unless absolutely necessary. Some professionals would rather risk some minor damage to landscape construction (such as retaining walls, steps, or paving) than remove existing trees or not plant proposed trees on a site with expansive soils. They also say that allowing expansive soil to dry out and shrink is far more dangerous than the swelling when it becomes wet.

When building on a site formerly occupied by trees, a careful assessment should be made as to whether the moisture level of the soil at the time of the removal of the trees will be maintained during and after construction. If this cannot be assured, then the cleared and regraded site should be allowed to reestablish its new moisture level, which might take as long as a year, or other measures should be taken to protect the existing or proposed construction.

New planting in expansive soils can be accomplished in several ways. Where the planting is well away from structures, the activity of roots will have little effect. Attention should be paid to drainage patterns, so that excess water from artificial irrigation is not directed toward vulnerable areas. Where the planting of trees near buildings is desired, the use of above- or below-grade tubs or impervious barriers can isolate the roots from the surrounding soil. Although this solution may create other problems, such as restricted growth and high maintenance demands, it may be the only acceptable solution in extreme circumstances.

Local experience is particularly important in devising an appropriate strategy for the management of vegetation on sites with expansive soils. Consultation with individuals familiar with local conditions and practice is essential. The general information supplied in this section should be modified and supplemented as appropriate for specific site conditions.

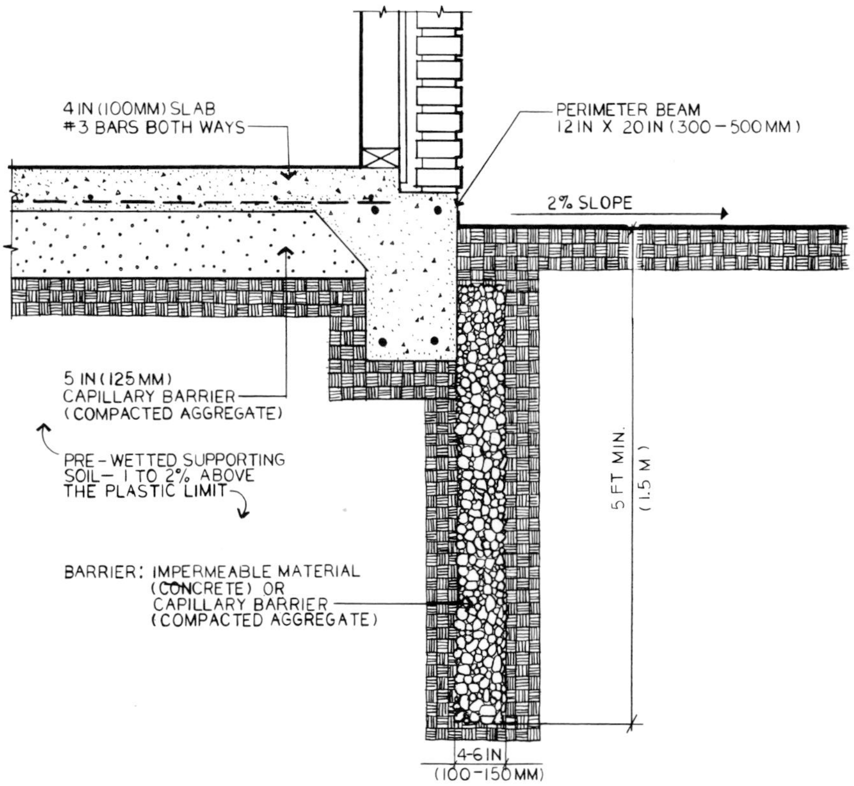
4 IN (100MM) SLAB
#3 BARS BOTH WAYS
PERIMETER BEAM
12 IN X 20 IN (300 – 500 MM)
2% SLOPE
5 IN (125 MM)
CAPILLARY BARRIER
(COMPACTED AGGREGATE)
PRE-WETTED SUPPORTING SOIL— 1 TO 2% ABOVE THE PLASTIC LIMIT
BARRIER: IMPERMEABLE MATERIAL (CONCRETE) OR CAPILLARY BARRIER (COMPACTED AGGREGATE)
5 FT MIN. (1.5 M)
4-6 IN (100-150 MM)

Figure 255-15 Detail Showing Stabilization of Expansive Clay Foundation Soil. Expansive clay foundation soils can be stabilized by prewetting and by installing a barrier that prevents the loss of moisture from the zone of seasonal change at the perimeter.

REFERENCES

Chen, H. F. *Foundations on Expansive Clays,* Elsevier Scientific Publishing, New York, 1975.

Cutler, D. F., and I. B. K. Richardson. *Tree Roots and Buildings,* Construction Press, London and New York, 1981.

Holty, Wesley, G., and Stephen S. Hart. *Home Construction on Shrinking and Swelling Soils,* American Society of Civil Engineers, New York, 1978.

Jochim, Candace L. *Home Landscaping and Maintenance on Swelling Soil,* Colorado Geological Survey Special Publication 14, Denver, 1979.

Lamb, Donald R., and Steven J. Hanna. *Proceedings of Workshop on Expansive Clays and Shales in Highway Design and Construction,* vols. 1 and 2, Federal Highway Administration, U.S. Goverment Printing Office, May 1973.

Proceedings of First International Conference on Expansive Soils, vol. 1: *Moisture Equilibria and Moisture Changes in Soils Beneath Covered Areas,* and vol. 2: *Engineering Effects of Moisture Changes in Soils,* Austin, TX, 1965.

Proceedings of Second International Conference on Expansive Soils, Austin, TX, 1969.

Proceedings of Third International Conference on Expansive Soils, Haifa, Israel, 1973.

Proceedings of Fourth International Conference on Expansive Soils, Denver, CO, 1980. ■

section 320: Grading Techniques

CREDITS

Contributor:

Scruggs and Hammond, Inc.
Landscape Architects-Planning Consultants
Lexington, Kentucky

Persons in Charge:

D. Lyle Aten
John Dudley Scruggs

Graphic Designer: Douglas L. Sharp

Reviewers/Advisors:

Horst Schach, Chairman
Department of Landscape Architecture
University of Kentucky
Lexington, Kentucky

David M. DuTot
The Delta Group, Landscape Architects
Philadelphia, Pennsylvania

Eugene West
L. E. Gregg & Associates, Consulting Engineers
Lexington, Kentucky

CONTENTS

1.0 INTRODUCTION

1.1 Importance of Grading

Landscape architects and other designers must ensure that grading becomes an integral part of the design process, on a par with the location of buildings, circulation patterns, and the recognition and use of all landscape qualities. Indeed, in many cases the grading scheme is a primary determinant in the total design.

1.2 Functional and Aesthetic Reasons for Grading

Grading may be done for a number of functional and/or aesthetic reasons. Figures 320-1 through 320-9 show a range of typical examples.

2.0 STANDARDS

2.1 Abbreviations on Grading Plans

Landscape architects, engineers, and architects who do grading plans, as well as the contractor who does the actual grading, should all understand a common terminology. Table 320-1 shows abbreviations that are commonly used on grading plans.

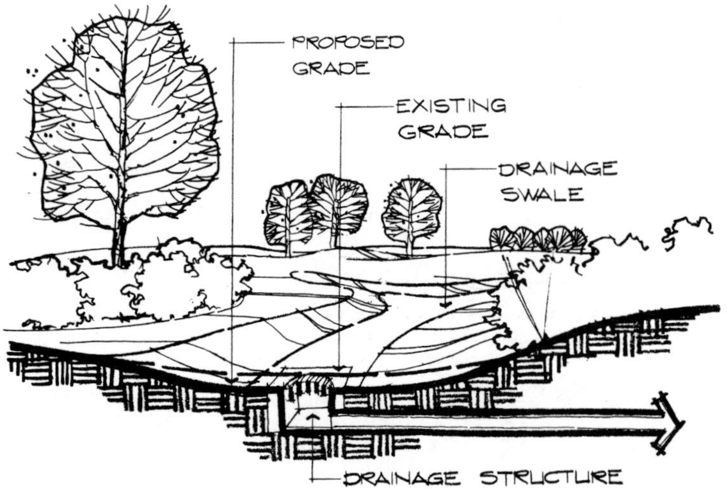
PROPOSED
GRADE
EXISTING
GRADE
DRAINAGE
SWALE
DRAINAGE STRUCTURE

Figure 320-1 Grading for Drainage. Surface drainage can be achieved by pitching surfaces to natural drainage features and systems.

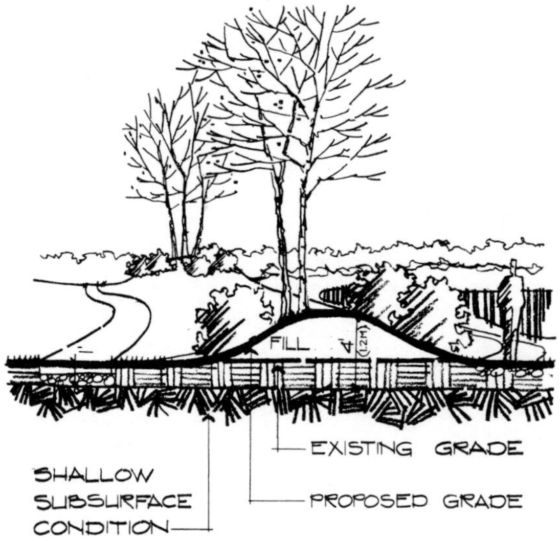
FILL
4' (1.2M)
EXISTING GRADE
SHALLOW
SUBSURFACE
CONDITION
PROPOSED GRADE

Figure 320-2 Grading to Create Berms. Berms can be created for noise and wind barriers or for additional soil depth above unfavorable subgrade conditions, such as a high groundwater table.

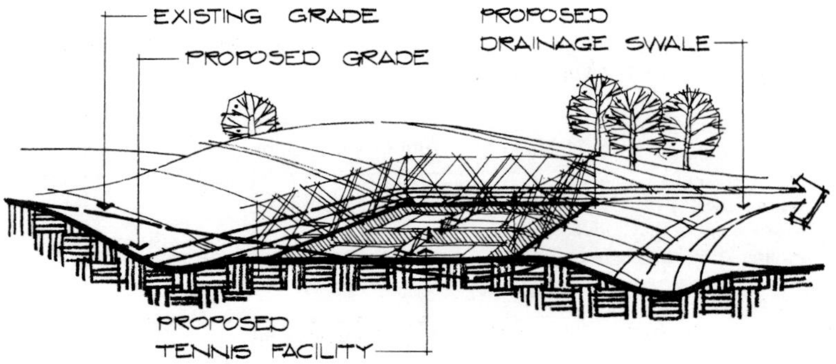
EXISTING GRADE
PROPOSED GRADE
PROPOSED
DRAINAGE SWALE
PROPOSED
TENNIS FACILITY

Figure 320-3 Grading to Create Level Areas. Relatively flat gradients are needed for sports fields, outdoor terraces, and sometimes for areas near buildings.

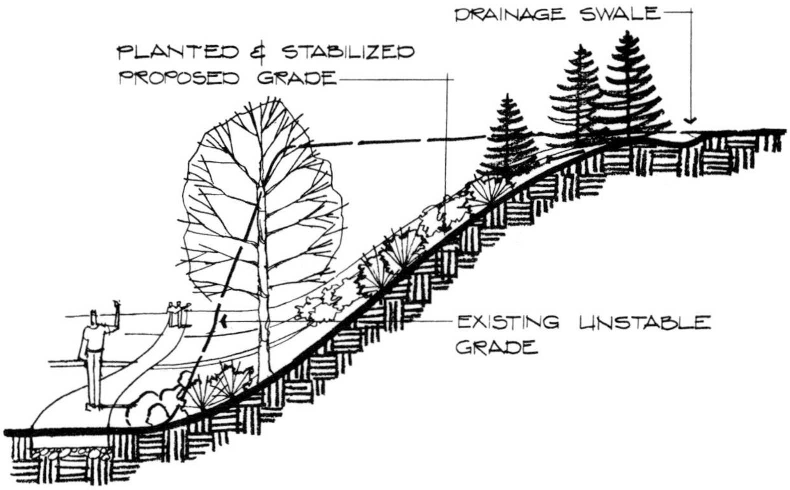
DRAINAGE SWALE
PLANTED & STABILIZED
PROPOSED GRADE
EXISTING UNSTABLE
GRADE

Figure 320-4 Grading to Modify Existing Landforms. Deep gullies, narrow ridges, or steep slopes can be modified to create more useful and attractive landforms.

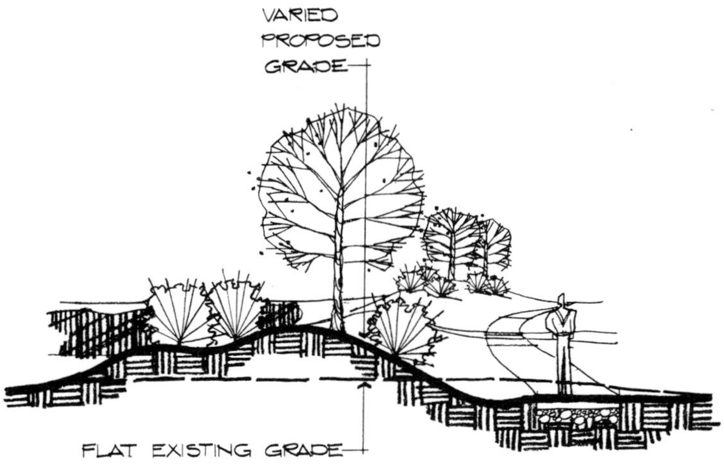
VARIED
PROPOSED
GRADE
FLAT EXISTING GRADE

Figure 320-5 Grading for Increased Site Interest. Grading can help emphasize a site's topography or add interest to an otherwise flat site.

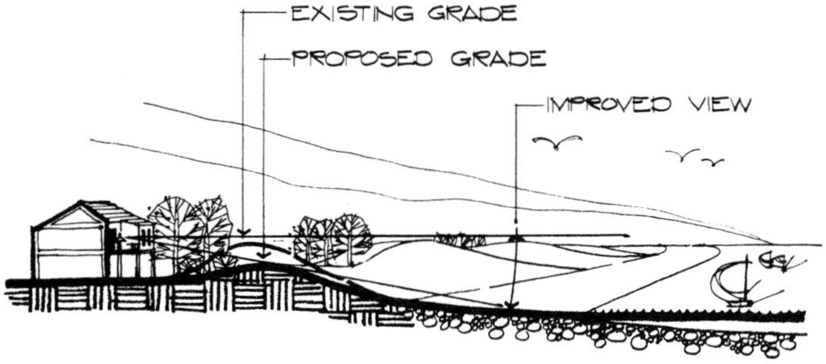
EXISTING GRADE
PROPOSED GRADE
IMPROVED VIEW

Figure 320-6 Grading related to good views.

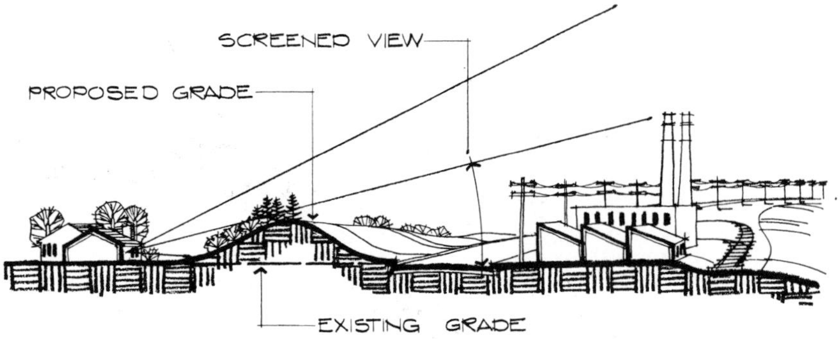
SCREENED VIEW
PROPOSED GRADE
EXISTING GRADE

Figure 320-7 Grading related to bad views.

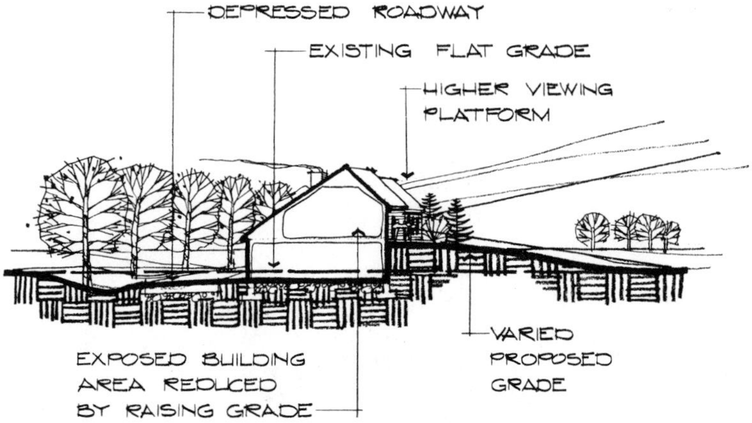
DEPRESSED ROADWAY
EXISTING FLAT GRADE
HIGHER VIEWING PLATFORM
EXPOSED BUILDING AREA REDUCED BY RAISING GRADE
VARIED PROPOSED GRADE

Figure 320-8 Grading to fit structures to sites.

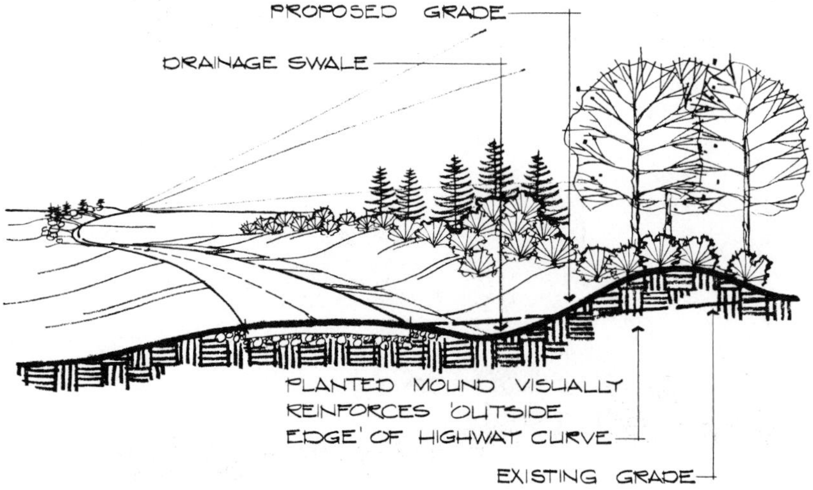
PROPOSED GRADE
DRAINAGE SWALE
PLANTED MOUND VISUALLY REINFORCES 'OUTSIDE EDGE' OF HIGHWAY CURVE
EXISTING GRADE

Figure 320-9 Grading to emphasize or control circulation.

TABLE 320-1
Grading Abbreviations

Abbreviation	*Meaning*
CI	Contour interval
TC	Top of curb
BC	Bottom of curb (include spot elevation)
TW	Top of wall (include spot elevation)
BW	Bottom of wall (include spot elevation)
HP	High point (include spot elevation)
LP	Low point (include spot elevation)
TS	Top of steps (include spot elevation)
BS	Bottom of steps (include spot elevation)
IE	Invert elevation (include spot elevation)
RE	Rim elevation
DI	Drain inlet (needs RE and IE)
SD	Storm drain (needs RE and IE)
MH	Manhole (needs RE and IE)
CB	Catch basin (needs RE and IE)
PL	Property line
ROW	Right of way

2.2 Methods of Expressing Slope

Slope is expressed either in terms of a percentage, a proportional ratio, or a degree of slope. Each of these is explained and illustrated below.

Percentage (of Slope):

Percentage of slope is expressed as the number of feet rise in 100 ft of horizontal distance, typically referred to as *rise/run*. If the slope rises 2 ft in 100 ft, it is considered a 2 percent slope. The percentage of slope can be calculated by the following formula:

$$G = \frac{D}{L} \times 100$$

where D = vertical rise, ft(m)
L = horizontal distance, ft(m)
G = gradient, %

Figure 320-10 shows an example problem where part *a* is the longitudinal or centerline profile of a proposed roadway and part *b* is the same roadway shown in plan. The actual calculations for the example are:

Elevation of point B	=	158.62 ft
Elevation of point A	=	155.72 ft
Vertical difference D	=	2.90 ft
Horizontal difference L	=	116.00 ft

Therefore:

$$G = \frac{D}{L} \times 100$$

$$= \frac{2.9}{116} \times 100$$

$$= 2.5\%$$

It is common practice to indicate the direction and rate of slope by use of an arrow, which always points down the slope.

Proportion (of Slope):

Slope can be expressed as a ratio of the horizontal distance to the vertical rise, such as three to one (3:1). The ratio method is used typically for slopes 4:1 or steeper.

Degree (of Slope):

Slope is expressed in degrees (e.g., a 30-degree slope) only on large-scale earthmoving projects such as strip-mining and other extractive operations.

Spot Elevations:

Spot elevations are used to establish limits of slope, to locate contour lines, and to provide detail for establishing control points that cannot be obtained via contour lines.

On an accurately drawn contour plan, the elevation of any point may be determined by interpolation. The contour interval (C.I.) for the plan in Figure 320-11 is 1 ft. Point A lies about 7⁄10 the distance from contour 53 to contour 54; thus, A has an approximate elevation of 53.7. Interpolation assumes, of course, that slopes are uniform, which in many cases they are not. Understandably, interpolated figures are approximations and should not be relied on as much as surveyed figures for crucial measurements.

2.3 Making a Contour Map

Field Survey:

All corners of a grid are marked on the ground with temporary stakes; the elevations of each corner are taken with a transit or level and the elevation data is plotted on a gridded plan of the site (Figure 320-12). Normally, the elevations of critical high or low points that fall between the corners are also located on the plan. Contour lines can then be plotted.

Plotting Contours:

Once all spot elevations have been determined, even-foot contours can be located and plotted on a map, as shown in Figure 320-13. Often this can be done by eye,

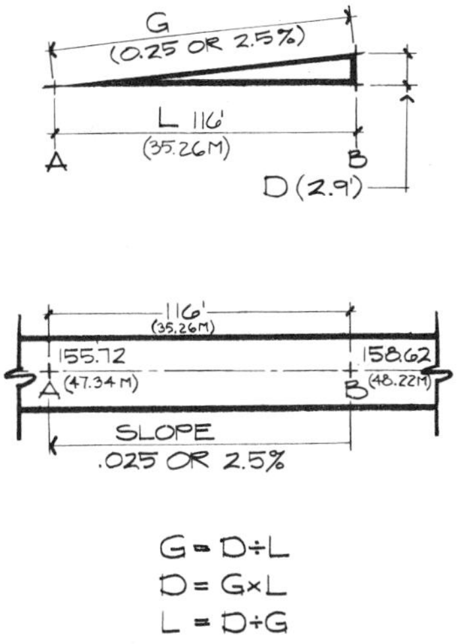
G
(0.25 OR 2.5%)
L 116'
(35.26M)
A
B
D (2.9')
116'
(35.26M)
155.72
(47.34 M)
158.62
(48.22M)
SLOPE
.025 OR 2.5%
G = D÷L
D = G×L
L = D÷G

Figure 320-10 Figuring slopes as percent.

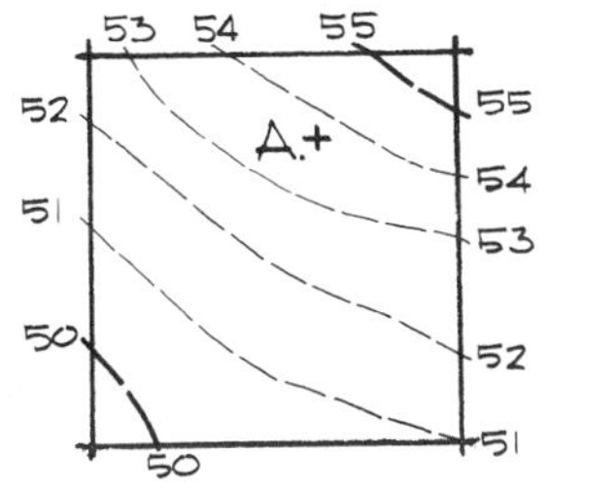
53 54 55
52
A+
55
54
51
53
50
52
50
51

Figure 320-11 Spot elevation by interpolation (1-foot contour interval).

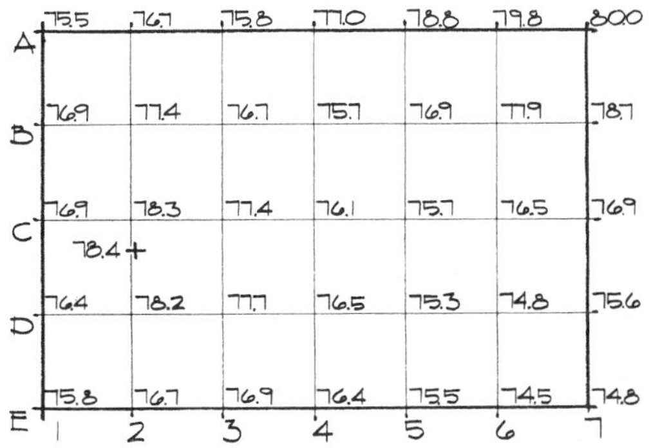
75.5 76.7 75.8 77.0 78.8 79.8 80.0
76.9 77.4 76.7 75.7 76.9 77.9 78.7
76.9 78.3 77.4 76.1 75.7 76.5 76.9
78.4+
76.4 78.2 77.7 76.5 75.3 74.8 75.6
75.8 76.7 76.9 76.4 75.5 74.5 74.8
A
B
C
D
E
1 2 3 4 5 6 7

Figure 320-12 Transit survey grid.

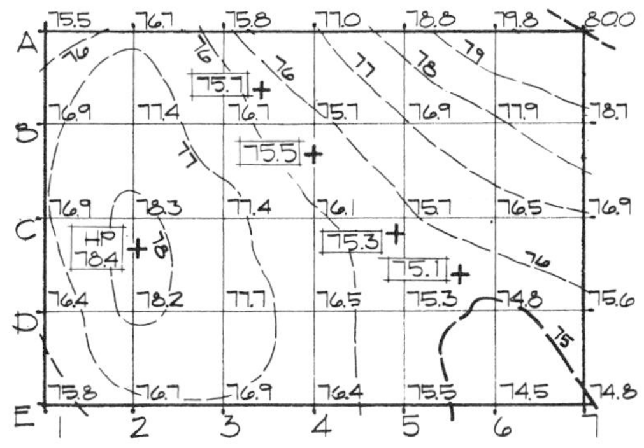
75.5 76.7 75.8 77.0 78.8 79.8 80.0
75.7+
76.9 77.4 76.7 75.7 76.9 77.9 78.7
75.5+
76.9 78.3 77.4 76.1 75.7 76.5 76.9
HP
78.4+
75.3+
75.1+
76.4 78.2 77.7 76.5 75.3 74.8 75.6
75.8 76.7 76.9 76.4 75.5 74.5 74.8
A
B
C
D
E
1 2 3 4 5 6 7

Figure 320-13 Contours interpolated from grid.

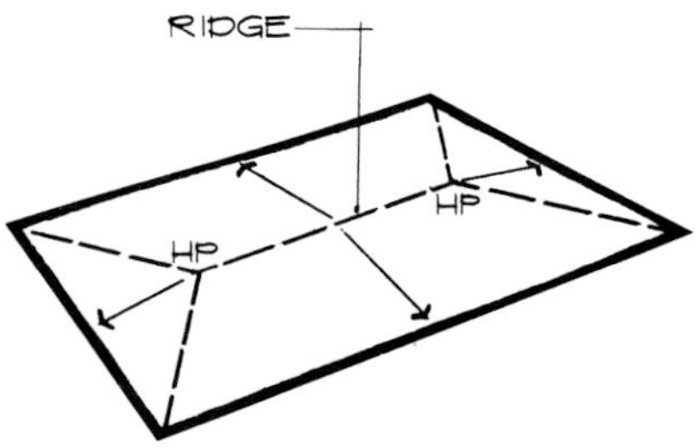
RIDGE
HP
HP

Figure 320-14 Perimeter edge level—drain from ridge line to all edges.

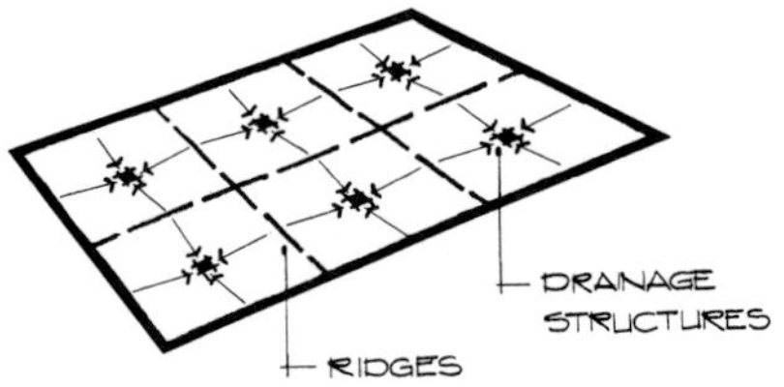
DRAINAGE STRUCTURES
RIDGES

Figure 320-18 Perimeter edge level—all slopes to drain inlets at the same gradient.

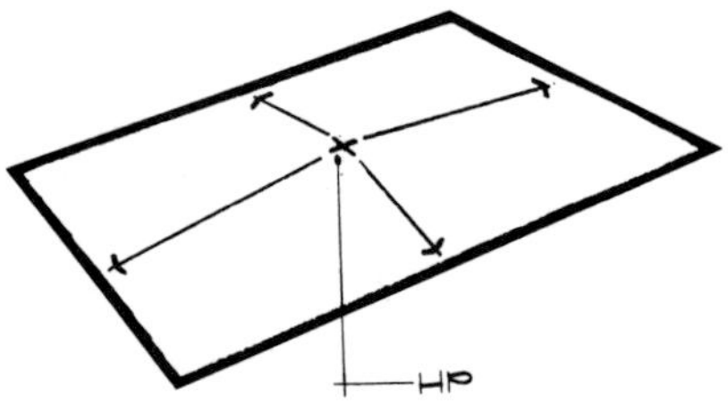
HP

Figure 320-15 Perimeter edge level—drain from single high point.

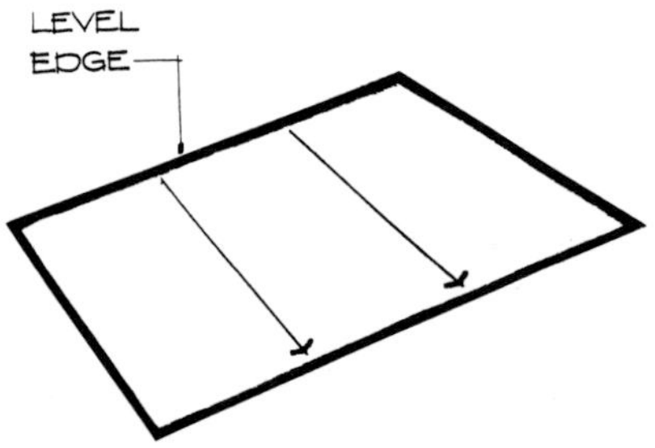
LEVEL EDGE

Figure 320-19 Perimeter edge level—slope away at uniform gradient.

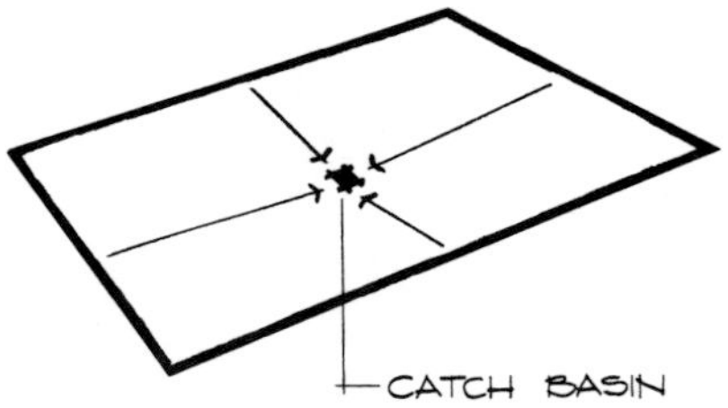
CATCH BASIN

Figure 320-16 Perimeter edge level—slope to center drain inlet.

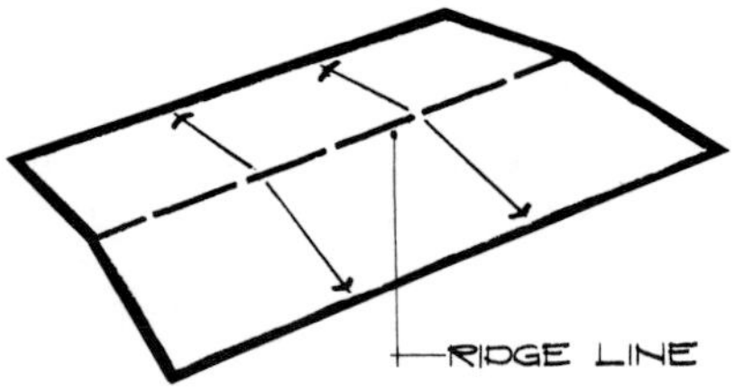
RIDGE LINE

Figure 320-20 Two perimeter edges level—slope from ridge line.

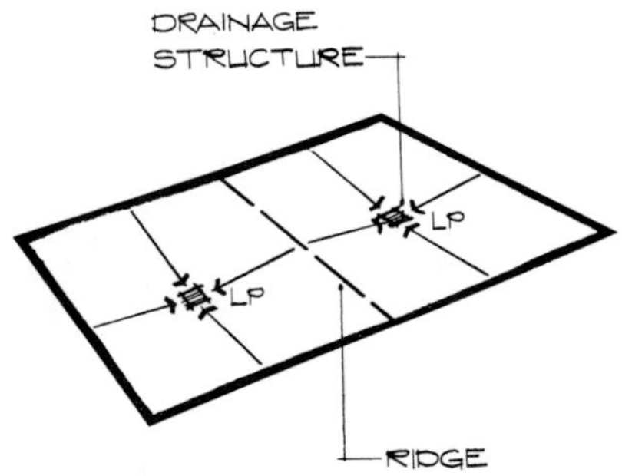
DRAINAGE STRUCTURE
LP
LP
RIDGE

Figure 320-17 Perimeter edge level—all slopes to drain inlets at the same gradient.

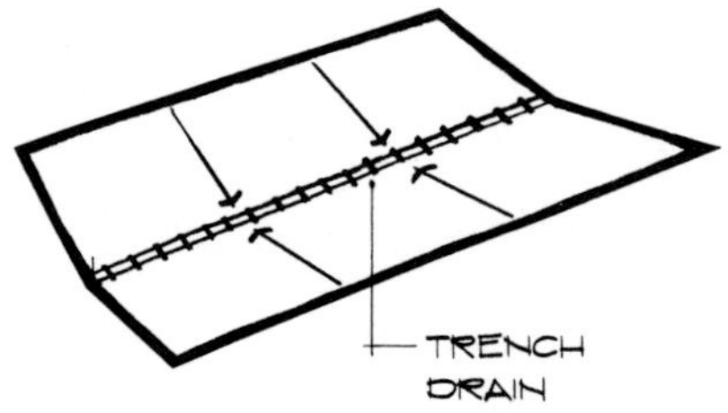
TRENCH DRAIN

Figure 320-21 Two perimeter edges level—minimum slopes to trench drain.

since few contour maps require great precision.

3.0 GRADING CONCEPTS

3.1 Schematic Grading Alternatives for a Defined Area

In the open landscape, slopes of less than about 2 percent appear flat to the human eye. However, in areas adjacent to built structures, such as around buildings, even the slightest slope becomes noticeable because of the relationship to mortar joints, roof lines, and other level architectural features.

Perimeter Edge Level:

Figures 320-14 through 320-19 schematically illustrate alternative methods for manipulating a surface for drainage while allowing at least one peripheral edge to remain level.

Two Perimeter Edges Level:

Figures 320-20 and 320-21 schematically illustrate drainage schemes applicable when two perimeter edges need to be level.

Entire Area Level:

In a few circumstances, such as for rooftop landscapes or enclosed courtyards, the entire surface of the enclosed area must be level. Figures 320-22 and 320-23 illustrate two ways that an area can remain level and still drain properly by the use of porous surface material, such as sand/gravel, or by the use of individually elevated pavers. In each case there must be an adequate drainage system beneath the pavers to carry off the required rainfall effectively. For more data related to drainage of rooftops and the like, refer to Section 610: Roof and Deck Landscapes.

3.2 Schematic Grading Alternatives for Open Areas

When surrounding buildings do not fully enclose an area to be graded and there is sufficient peripheral space for transition to surrounding areas, then there are several ways to solve the grading problem. Such a wide range of alternatives gives the designer the opportunity to resolve aesthetic objectives while solving the engineering problems involved. Figures 320-24 through 320-26 show schematic alternatives for grading open areas; these alternatives are especially applicable to relatively flat surfaces, such as tennis courts and other types of game courts.

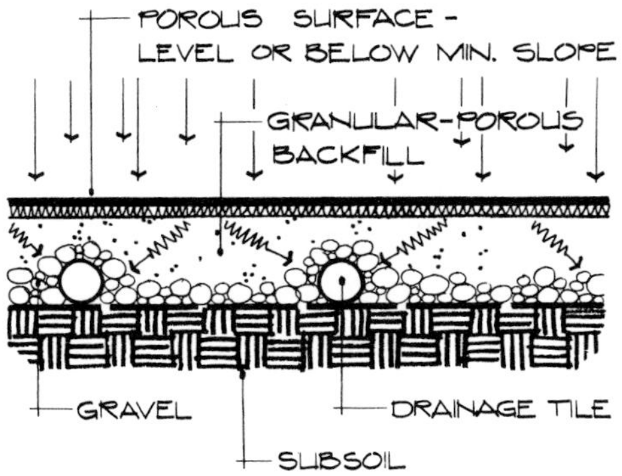
POROUS SURFACE -
LEVEL OR BELOW MIN. SLOPE
GRANULAR-POROUS
BACKFILL
GRAVEL
DRAINAGE TILE
SUBSOIL

Figure 320-22 *Level* surface with porous paving.

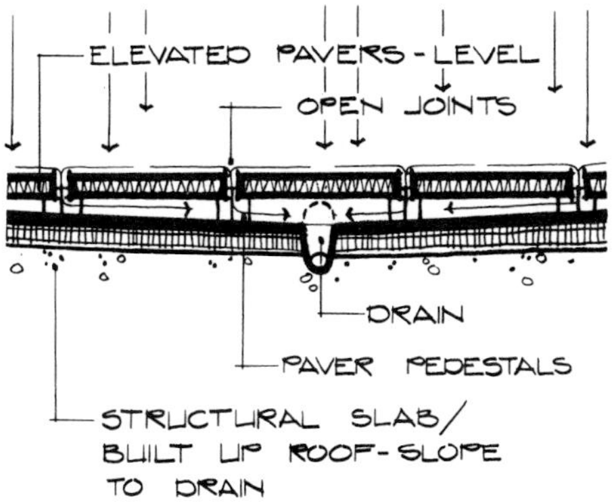
ELEVATED PAVERS - LEVEL
OPEN JOINTS
DRAIN
PAVER PEDESTALS
STRUCTURAL SLAB/
BUILT UP ROOF- SLOPE
TO DRAIN

Figure 320-23 *Level* surface with elevated pavers.

3.3 Preparing a Site Grading Plan

Grading of a site should be thought of as a systematic process that begins with the analysis and understanding of the existing site and ends with an overall detailed grading plan. Figures 320-27 through 320-31 help illustrate this procedure.

Site Analysis:

Study the general lay of the land by using topographic maps and site visits.

1. Determine high points, low points, ridges, and valleys.

2. Note natural drainage systems and directions of flow that exist on the site.

Site Use Concept:

Determine how existing landforms would affect proposed use areas, such as building locations, roads, parking areas, walkways, plazas, and lawn areas.

Schematic Grading Plan:

Define general use areas, set building floor areas by spot elevations, and diagram drainage flow by slope arrows toward the direction of flow. This will help in the following ways:

1. Developing a general landform concept.

2. Locating swales and surface water flow.

3. Locating drainage receptacles.

4. Calculating water runoff for various areas.

5. Defining an area that could be altered (raised or lowered) with limited impact on drainage or existing trees. This area could be used to help balance any surplus cut or fill.

Grading by Spot Elevations:

Grade by spot elevations and form preliminary contouring, using the following steps in the order shown (always strive to keep disturbed areas as small as possible):

1. Set tentative gradients and spot grades on roads, walks, and swales. Establish critical spot elevations.

2. Set the building grade circuit, i.e., floor elevation, steps, walls, terraces, etc.

3. Draw in preliminary contours at 5- or 10-ft (1- or 2-m) intervals, depending upon the scale of the project and topographic change. Make certain that all gradients and slopes are within the maximum/minimum criteria for a particular use, i.e., lawn, roadway, terrace, and cut slope or embankment.

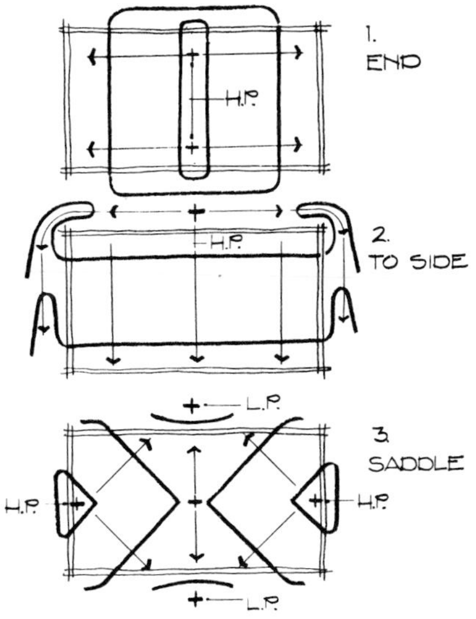
1.
END
H.P.
2.
TO SIDE
H.P.
3.
SADDLE
L.P.
H.P.
H.P.
L.P.

Figure 320-24 Examples of basic area grading.

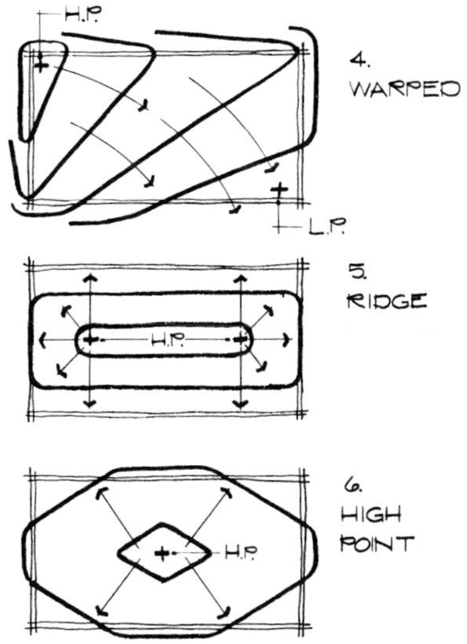
H.P.
4.
WARPED
L.P.
5.
RIDGE
H.P.
6.
HIGH
POINT
H.P.

Figure 320-25 Examples of basic area grading.

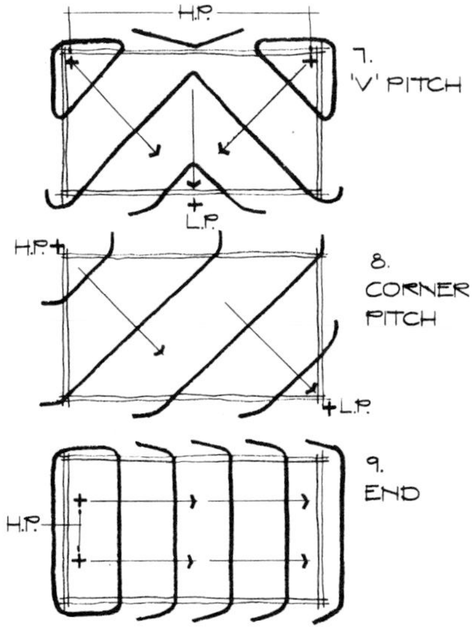
H.P.
7.
'V' PITCH
L.P.
H.P.
8.
CORNER
PITCH
L.P.
9.
END
H.P.

Figure 320-26 Examples of basic area grading.

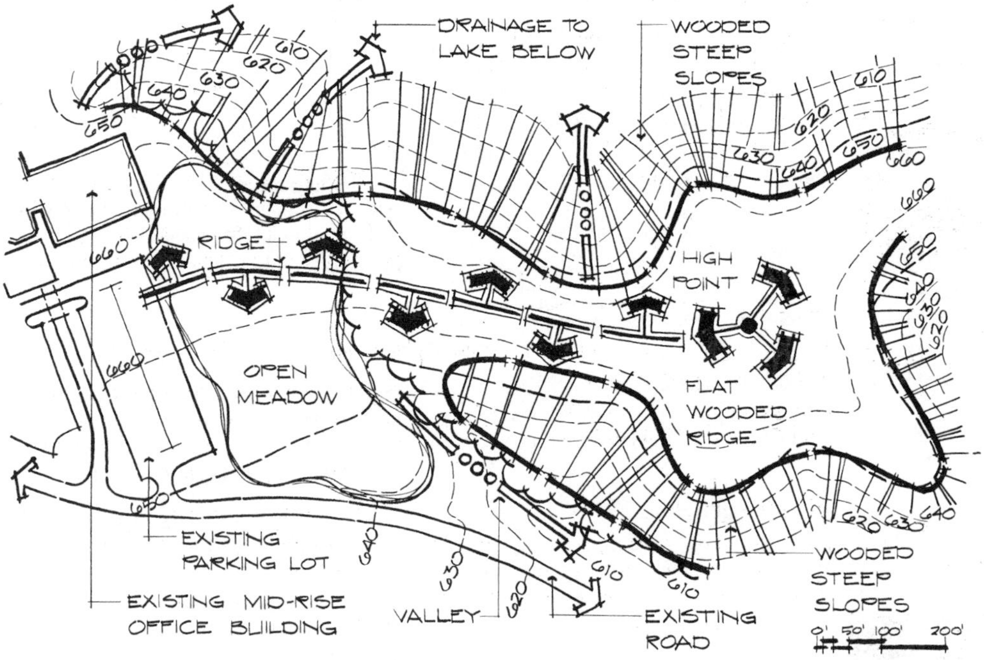
DRAINAGE TO
LAKE BELOW
WOODED
STEEP
SLOPES
RIDGE
HIGH
POINT
OPEN
MEADOW
FLAT
WOODED
RIDGE
EXISTING
PARKING LOT
EXISTING MID-RISE
OFFICE BUILDING
VALLEY
EXISTING
ROAD
WOODED
STEEP
SLOPES
0' 50' 100' 200'

Figure 320-27 Site analysis (example).

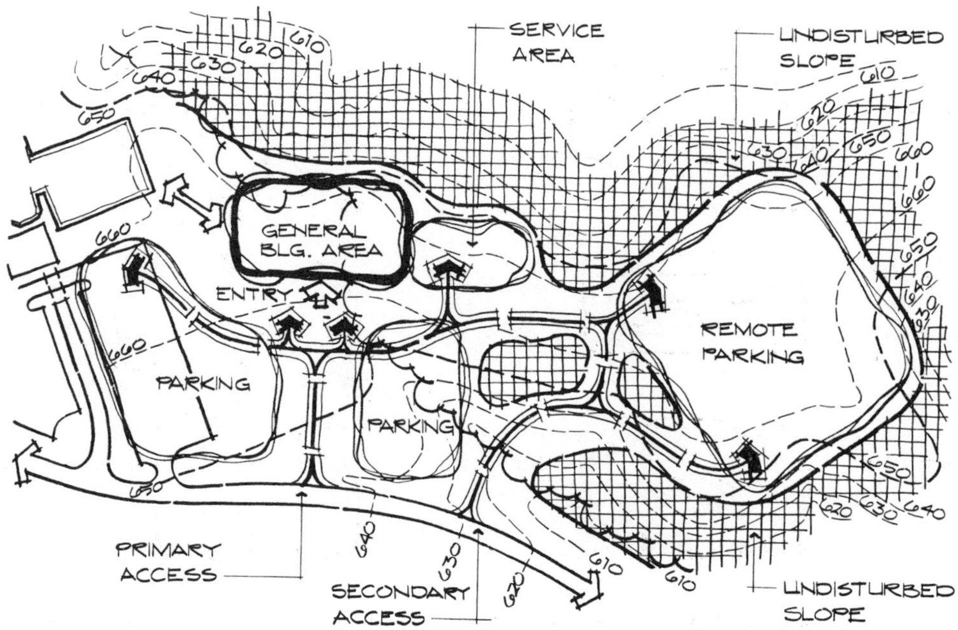
SERVICE
AREA
UNDISTURBED
SLOPE
GENERAL
BLG. AREA
ENTRY
REMOTE
PARKING
PARKING
PARKING
PRIMARY
ACCESS
SECONDARY
ACCESS
UNDISTURBED
SLOPE

Figure 320-28 Site use concept (example).

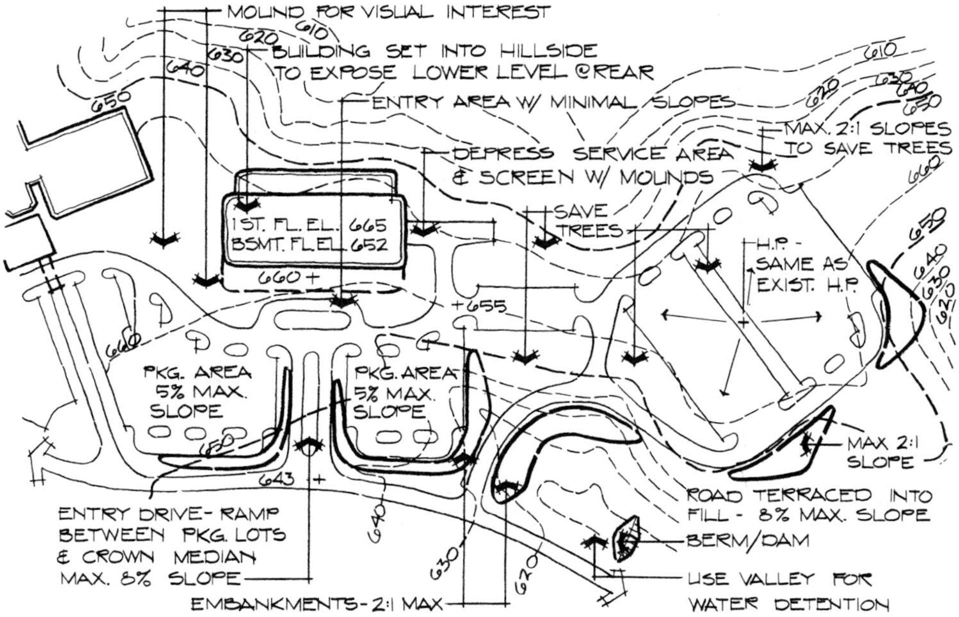
MOUND FOR VISUAL INTEREST
BUILDING SET INTO HILLSIDE TO EXPOSE LOWER LEVEL @REAR
ENTRY AREA W/ MINIMAL SLOPES
MAX. 2:1 SLOPES TO SAVE TREES
DEPRESS SERVICE AREA & SCREEN W/ MOUNDS
SAVE TREES
1ST. FL. EL. 665
BSMT. FL. EL. 652
660 +
+655
H.P. - SAME AS EXIST. H.P.
PKG. AREA 5% MAX. SLOPE
PKG. AREA 5% MAX. SLOPE
MAX 2:1 SLOPE
643 +
ROAD TERRACED INTO FILL - 8% MAX. SLOPE
ENTRY DRIVE- RAMP BETWEEN PKG. LOTS & CROWN MEDIAN MAX. 8% SLOPE
BERM/DAM
USE VALLEY FOR WATER DETENTION
EMBANKMENTS- 2:1 MAX

Figure 320-29 Schematic grading plan (example).

Grade by Spot Elevations — Schematic Diagram

Consider land form, circulation,and structures together in determining proposed grades.

1. Determine beginning grade at existing road.
2. Determine spot elevation at building unit (limited cut/fill) or other critical tie-in areas, i.e.,parking, etc.
3. Determine the percentage of slope by measuring distance and rise or fall between points. Gradient must be compatible to criteria for use intended.
4. Set grades adjacent to structure in keeping with architectural character and functional requirements of building.
5. Determine parking areas or lawn areas as relates to slope criteria (parking area slope and embankment slope).
6. Determine storm water retention and sedimentation basins.

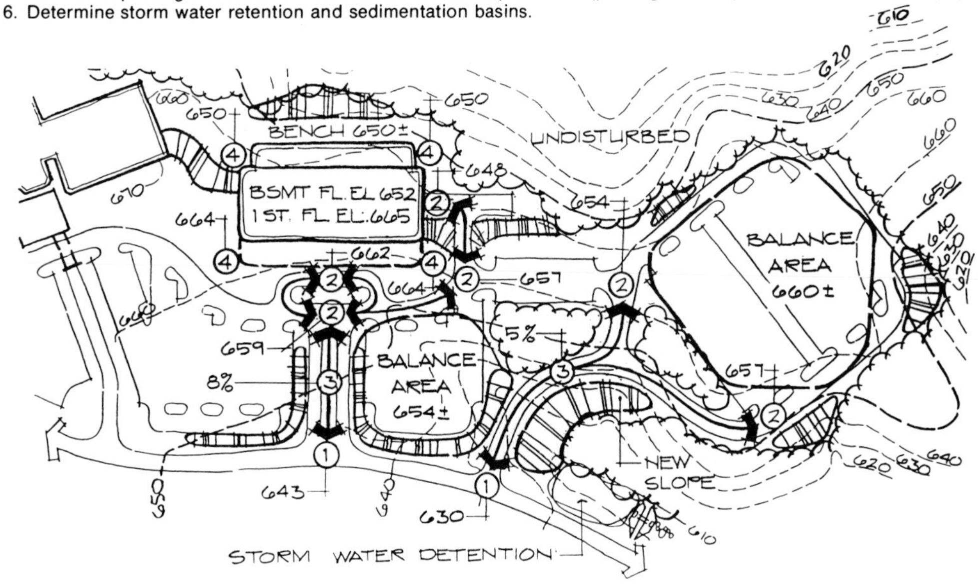
BENCH 650±
UNDISTURBED
BSMT FL. EL 652
1ST. FL. EL. 665
664
662
648
654
657
664
BALANCE AREA 660±
5%
659
8%
BALANCE AREA 654±
657
NEW SLOPE
643
630
STORM WATER DETENTION

Figure 320-30 Grade by spot elevations (example).

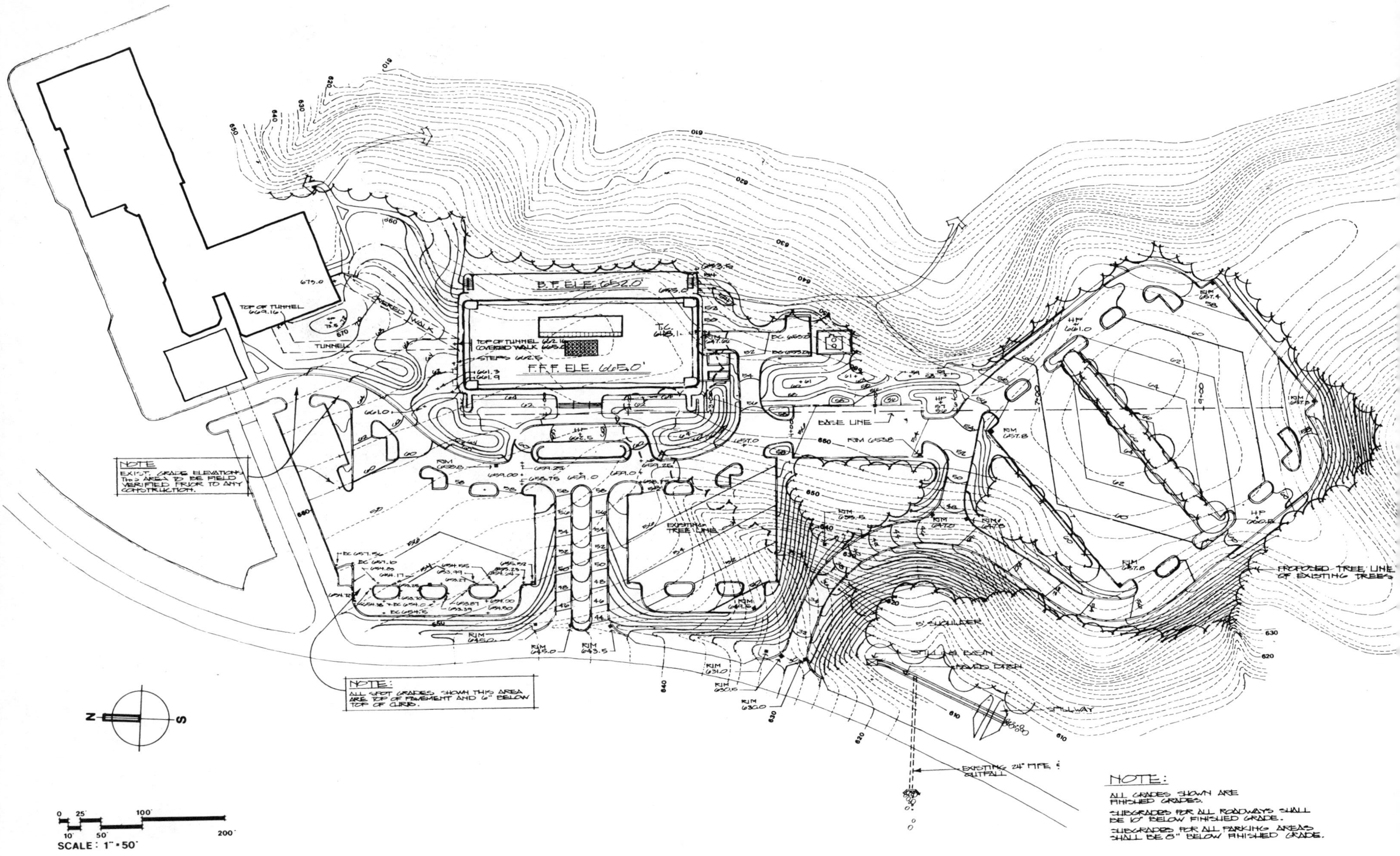

NOTE:
ALL GRADES SHOWN ARE FINISHED GRADES.
SUBGRADES FOR ALL ROADWAYS SHALL BE 10" BELOW FINISHED GRADE.
SUBGRADES FOR ALL PARKING AREAS SHALL BE 8" BELOW FINISHED GRADE.
NOTE:
ALL SPOT GRADES SHOWN THIS AREA ARE TOP OF PAVEMENT AND 6" BELOW TOP OF CURB.
NOTE
EXIST. GRADE ELEVATIONS THIS AREA TO BE FIELD VERIFIED PRIOR TO ANY CONSTRUCTION.
B.F.F. ELE. 652.0'
F.F.F. ELE. 665.0'
TUNNEL
COVERED WALK
BASE LINE
EXISTING TREE LINE
PROPOSED TREE LINE OF EXISTING TREES
5' SHOULDER
STILLING BASIN
PAVED DITCH
SPILLWAY
EXISTING 24" PIPE & OUTFALL
N
S
SCALE: 1" = 50'

Figure 320-31 Final grading plan (example).

4. Complete all contour alterations within the property line or project limits.

Preliminary Cut-and-Fill Calculations

Do preliminary calculations (if needed) to determine whether there is a balance between the amount of earth to be cut out and the amount of earth needed for fill.

Final Grading Plan:

1. Prepare final road profiles.
2. Indicate changes in direction or rate of slopes.
3. Show spot elevations for all critical points—including manholes, inverts, and drainage structures—for tops and bottoms of all walls, steps, and curbs at intersections and/or other critical points.
4. Draw proposed contours and complete the final grading plan.
5. Based upon the proposed grading plan, do an estimate of the amount of cut and fill and, if needed, adjust the amount of one or both to make them balance.

TABLE 320-2
Recommended Gradients: General

Types of areas	*Maximum, %*	*Minimum, %*	*Preferred, %*
Streets, driveways, and parking areas			
Crown of improved streets	3	1	2
Crown of unimproved streets	3	2	2.5
Slope of shoulders	15	1	2–3
Longitudinal slope of streets	20	0.5	1–10
Longitudinal slope of driveways	20	0.25	1–10
Longitudinal slope of parking areas	5	0.25	2–3
Cross slope of parking area	10	0.5	1–3
Concrete walks			
Longitudinal slope of sidewalks	10	0.5	1–5
Cross slope of sidewalks	4	1	2
Approaches, platforms, etc.	8	0.5	2
Service areas	10	0.5	2–3
Terrace and sitting areas			
Concrete	2	0.5	1
Flagstone, slate, brick	2	0.75	1
Lawn areas			
Recreation, games, etc. (noncompetitive)	5	1	2–3
Grassed athletic fields	2	0.5	1
Lawns and grass areas	25	1	5–10
Berms and mounds	20	5	10
Mowed slopes	25 (3:1)	—	20
Unmowed grass banks	Angle of repose		25
Planted slopes and beds	10	0.5	3–5

4.0 GRADING CRITERIA

4.1 General Landscape Elements

Recommended Gradients:

Grading of outdoor areas is done primarily to control the runoff of surface water. Essentially, all surfaces should have some slope, or pitch, for proper drainage. Owing to the difficulties of installation and to imperfections during the repair of surfaces, it is better to use the *preferred* rather than the *minimum* gradients shown in Table 320-2. Figure 320-32 is an example of typical gradients used for small structures, such as residences.

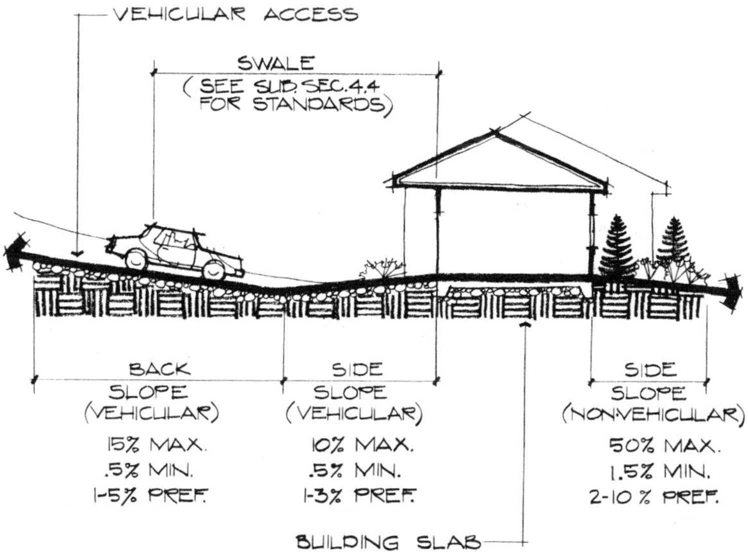

VEHICULAR ACCESS
SWALE
(SEE SUB. SEC. 4.4 FOR STANDARDS)
BACK SLOPE (VEHICULAR)
15% MAX.
.5% MIN.
1-5% PREF.
SIDE SLOPE (VEHICULAR)
10% MAX.
.5% MIN.
1-3% PREF.
SIDE SLOPE (NONVEHICULAR)
50% MAX.
1.5% MIN.
2-10 % PREF.
BUILDING SLAB

Figure 320-32 Standards for grading around a typical building.

Earth Fill against Buildings:

Earth fill against buildings may be desirable for insulation or aesthetic reasons. A precaution, however, is that soil and related moisture may cause decay and/or promote the growth of insects that may damage or destroy some of the materials used in the construction of the building.

The exterior surfacing and structural system of a building determine the height to which fill may be brought up against a structure. Figures 320-33 through 320-38 are representative examples.

4.2 Athletic Fields

Recommended Gradients for Outdoor Sports:

Table 320.3 shows recommended gradients for outdoor sports areas and playing surfaces.

Baseball and Softball:

The construction of playing fields usually involves a combination of turf and dirt surfaces. Use minimum gradients for these surfaces unless subdrains are introduced or other special drainage provisions are made.

The expected skill levels of players and the rules of appropriate sport organizations, such as the National Collegiate Athletic Association (NCAA) in the United States typically determine the standards for grading. Figures 320-39 through 320-42 show typical alternatives.

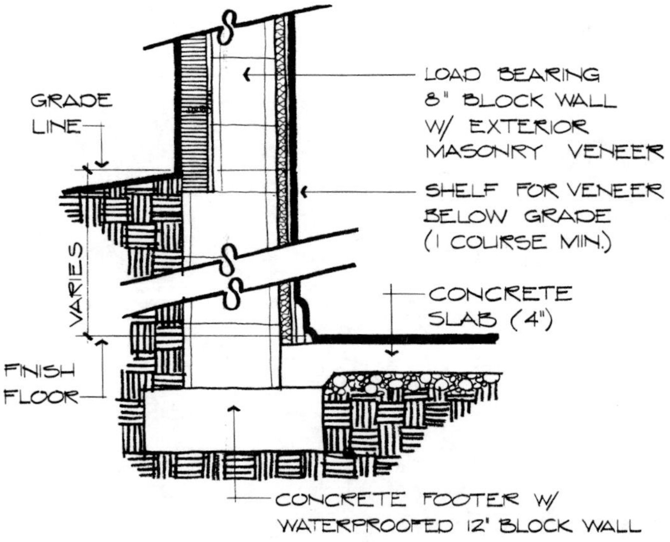
GRADE LINE
LOAD BEARING 8" BLOCK WALL W/ EXTERIOR MASONRY VENEER
SHELF FOR VENEER BELOW GRADE (1 COURSE MIN.)
VARIES
CONCRETE SLAB (4")
FINISH FLOOR
CONCRETE FOOTER W/ WATERPROOFED 12' BLOCK WALL

Figure 320-33 Typical masonry veneer-type exterior wall.

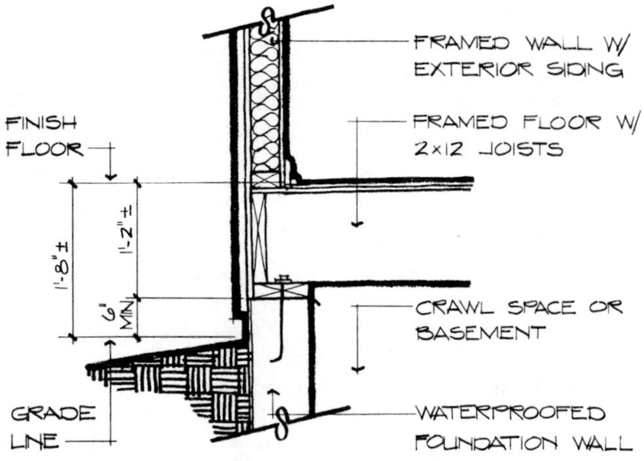
FRAMED WALL W/ EXTERIOR SIDING
FRAMED FLOOR W/ 2×12 JOISTS
FINISH FLOOR
1'-8"±
1'-2"±
6" MIN.
CRAWL SPACE OR BASEMENT
GRADE LINE
WATERPROOFED FOUNDATION WALL

Figure 320-36 Typical wood-framed and -sided wall with crawl space or basement.

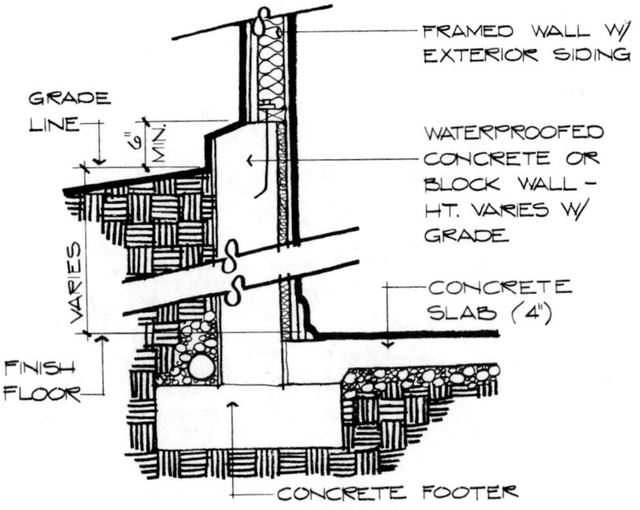
FRAMED WALL W/ EXTERIOR SIDING
GRADE LINE
6" MIN.
WATERPROOFED CONCRETE OR BLOCK WALL - HT. VARIES W/ GRADE
VARIES
CONCRETE SLAB (4")
FINISH FLOOR
CONCRETE FOOTER

Figure 320-34 Typical wood-framed wall with exterior siding set into a slope.

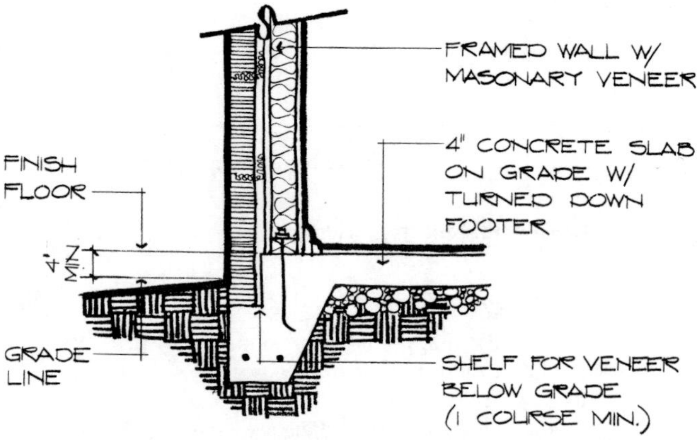
FRAMED WALL W/ MASONARY VENEER
4" CONCRETE SLAB ON GRADE W/ TURNED DOWN FOOTER
FINISH FLOOR
4" MIN.
GRADE LINE
SHELF FOR VENEER BELOW GRADE (1 COURSE MIN.)

Figure 320-37 Typical slab construction with masonry exterior wall.

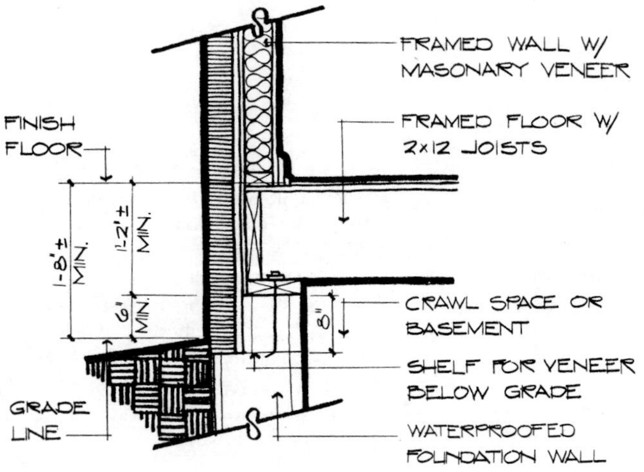
FRAMED WALL W/ MASONARY VENEER
FINISH FLOOR
FRAMED FLOOR W/ 2×12 JOISTS
1'-8"± MIN.
1'-2"± MIN.
6" MIN.
8"
CRAWL SPACE OR BASEMENT
SHELF FOR VENEER BELOW GRADE
GRADE LINE
WATERPROOFED FOUNDATION WALL

Figure 320-35 Typical veneered wall with crawl space or basement.

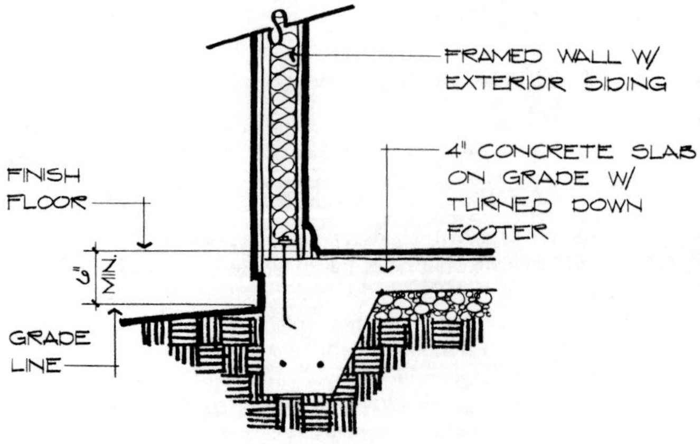
FRAMED WALL W/ EXTERIOR SIDING
4" CONCRETE SLAB ON GRADE W/ TURNED DOWN FOOTER
FINISH FLOOR
6" MIN.
GRADE LINE

Figure 320-38 Typical slab construction with frame wall and siding.

TABLE 320-3
Recommended Gradients: Sports

Play area	*Gradient, %*
Archery	1.5–2 (cross slope)
Turf	1 (along length)
Aerial darts	Same as tennis
Badminton	
Concrete	1.25–1.5
Asphalt	1.5
Clay	1.5
Grasstex or equal	0.8–1
Synthetic turf	0.8–1
Baseball	
Skinned infield	1–1.25
Infield turf	1.25–1
Mound	See Figure 320-39
Outfield turf	1.25–1.5
Synthetic turf infield/outfield	0.5
Batting area—clay, earth, etc.	0.5–0.8
Bocci	0.5 (along length)
Basketball	
Concrete	1–1.5
Asphalt	1.25–1.5
Grasstex or equal	0.8–1
Bicycle	
Little effort	0–3
Medium effort	8
Walk bike	20
Bowling (lawn)	
Turf	0–0.25
Curling	Level
Croquet	
Sand, clay, or equal	0–0.25
Deck tennis	Same as tennis
Field hockey	Same as football
Football	
Turf	1.5–2 to sides
Synthetic turf	0.5–1
Fencing	Level
Handball court	0.5–1
Horseshoe (longitudinal ridge level)	1.5–2 to sides
Lacrosse	Same as football
Paddle tennis	Same as tennis
Quoits	Level
Quoitennis	Same as tennis
Roller skating, recreational	
Linear straightaway, concrete	1–1.25 (pitch to side)
Curved	2–4 (bank)
Running track, straightaway	
Clay or soil surface	0.5–1 (to drain)
Synthetic surface	0.5–0.8 (to drain)
Running track, straight with circular ends	
Clay or soil surface	0.5–0.8 (to curb) 0.3–1 (100–300 mm) (superelevation)
Synthetic surface	0.5–0.8 (to curb) 0.3–1 (100–300 mm) (superelevation)
Shuffleboard	Level
Skeetshoot, general area	1.5–2
Soccer	Same as football
Softball	Same as football
Speedball	Same as football
Tennis courts	
Concrete	0.5–1 (cross slope) 0.4–0.5 (end to end)
Asphalt, rolled on base	1
Clay and grass	0.9–1
Synthetic surface	0.5–0.8
Synthetic turf	0.5–0.8
Tetherball	1–2 (from poled)
Track-field events	
Shot put, turf area	1 (axial crown)
Hammer throw, turf area	Same
Javelin, turf area	Same
High jump	Essentially level
Long jump	Essentially level
Pole vault	Essentially level

Note: Refer to rules published by NCAA and USLYA for more information.

Source: From Jot D. Carpenter, *Handbook of Landscape Architectural Construction*, Landscape Architecture Foundation, Washington, D.C., 1976.

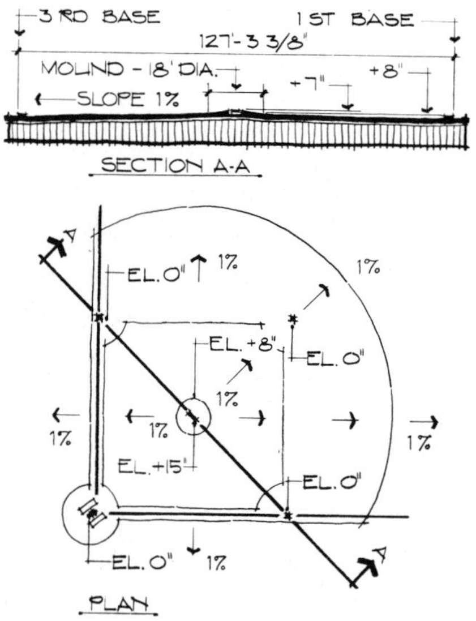
3 RD BASE
1 ST BASE
127'-3 3/8"
MOUND - 18' DIA.
+8"
+7"
SLOPE 1%
SECTION A-A
EL. 0"
1%
EL. +8"
EL. 0"
1%
1%
1%
1%
EL. +15"
EL. 0"
EL. 0"
1%
PLAN

Figure 320-39 Typical baseball infield grading.

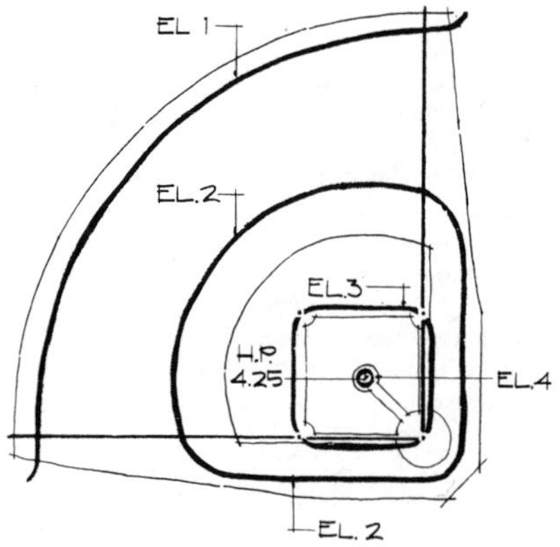
EL 1
EL.2
EL.3
H.P
4.25
EL.4
EL. 2

Figure 320-40 Alternative grading pattern for baseball field.

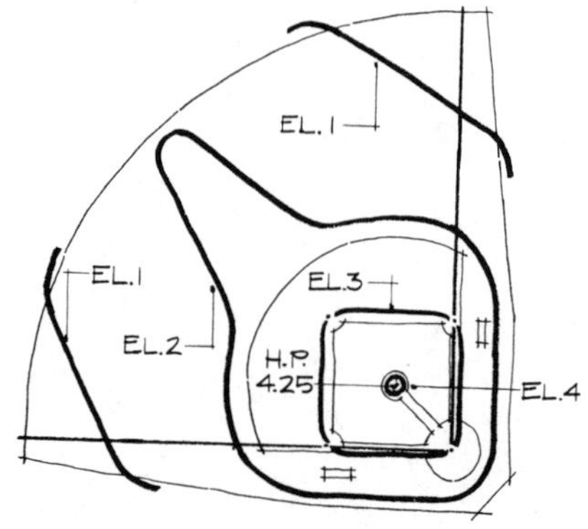
EL. 1
EL. 1
EL. 3
EL. 2
H.P.
4.25
EL. 4

Figure 320-41 Alternative grading pattern for baseball field.

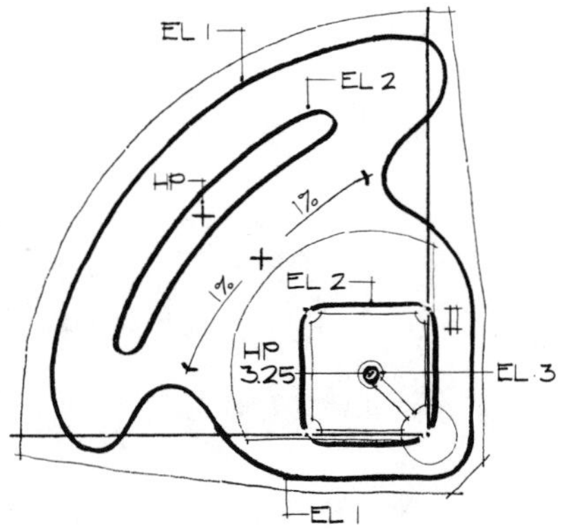
EL 1
EL 2
HP
1%
1%
EL 2
HP
3.25
EL. 3
EL 1

Figure 320-42 Alternative grading pattern for baseball field.

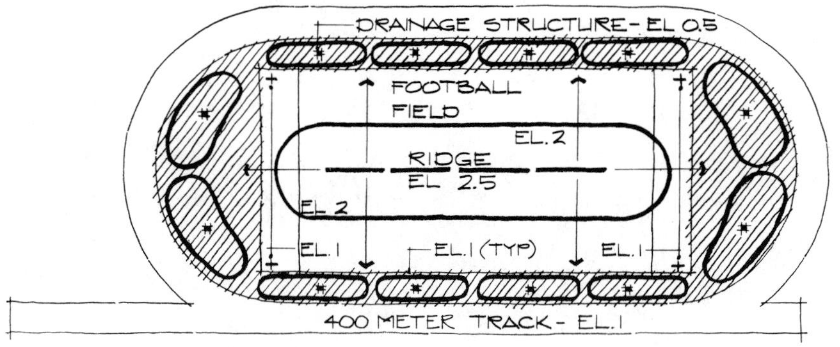
DRAINAGE STRUCTURE - EL 0.5
FOOTBALL
FIELD
EL. 2
RIDGE
EL 2.5
EL 2
EL. 1
EL. 1 (TYP)
EL. 1
400 METER TRACK - EL. 1

Figure 320-43 Schematic grading for football/soccer/field hockey.

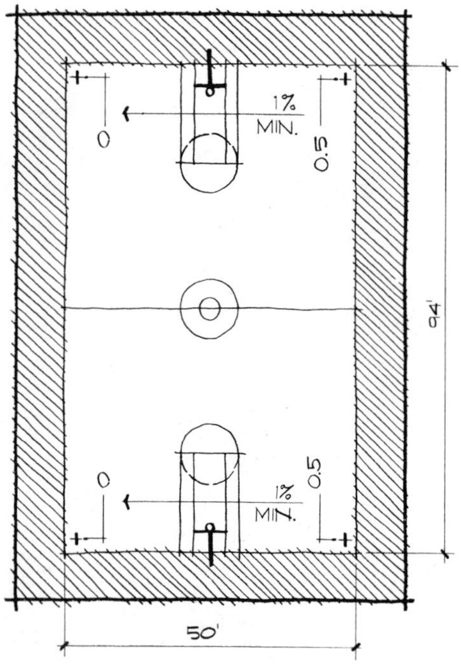
1%
MIN.
0
0.5
94'
0
1%
MIN.
0.5
50'

Figure 320-44 Schematic grading for outdoor basketball court.

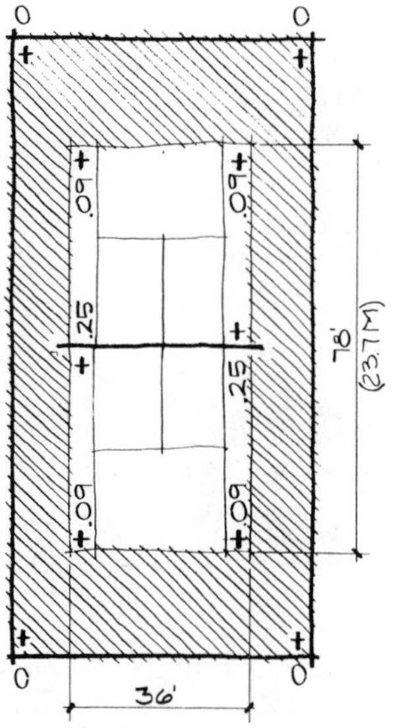
0
0
.09
.09
.25
.25
.25
.09
.09
78'
(23.7M)
0
0
36'

Figure 320-45 Schematic grading for outdoor tennis court.

Football/Soccer/Field Hockey:

Turf football fields require a crowned surface sloping from the center of the field to a drainage system beyond the sidelines (Figure 320-43). Soccer and field hockey can have a 1 percent slope in one direction or can be played on a football field.

Court Games:

Most court games should have a relatively flat surface, with no perceptible swales or ridges (except at the net line for tennis courts) (Figures 320-44 and 320-45).

4.3 Roadways

Grading and Alignment:

In the United States, the principles and criteria for the design of major urban and rural highways have been established by the American Association of State Highway and Transportation Officials (AASHTO). The standards for streets and local access roads in residential, institutional, commercial, and industrial areas are determined by local city or county standards.

Roadway design consists of two major phases: (1) alignment of the road—giving it horizontal and vertical direction—and (2) grading the adjacent landscape to the road edge. The designer of a roadway should go beyond merely satisfying the engineering requirements and see the user as choreographed through the landscape.

During the grading phase of the roadway, the designer should consider the following:

1. Remove extra soils to expose potential vistas (Figure 320-46).

2. Use roadside mounds to screen undesirable views (Figure 320-47).

3. Improve the soil adjacent to a road to enhance the growth of plants (Figure 320-48).

4. Blend the slopes with the existing terrain (Figure 320-49).

Criteria for Road Design:

1. For *cut side* of section, see Figure 320-50 and Table 320-4.

2. For *fill side* of section, see Figure 320-51 and Table 320-4.

4.4 Details and Special Conditions

Several typical elements found in a landscape involve special grading. Some of the most common ones are discussed below.

Swales and Ditches:

Typically, *swales* are shallow, have a parabolic cross section, and are sometimes very wide, while *ditches* are deeper and have a narrower geometric configuration (Figure 320-52).

Empirical data related to the hydraulic properties of ditches can be found in Section 330: Site Drainage. Swales are commonly used in grading to move water gently from one part of the site to another. Their function is to collect and divert the flow of surface runoff away from critical parts of a site. At their terminus, swales must either spread the channelized water to make it sheet drainage or empty the water into a ditch, stream, or underground drainage system. Figure 320-53 illustrates the use of a swale to divert water away from a building site.

During the design process, it helps to show graphically the direction of the swale. The slope of the channel determines the velocity of flow and consequently the erosive potential. Since the side slopes of the swale do not affect this rate of flow, they may be much steeper and respond to other design criteria.

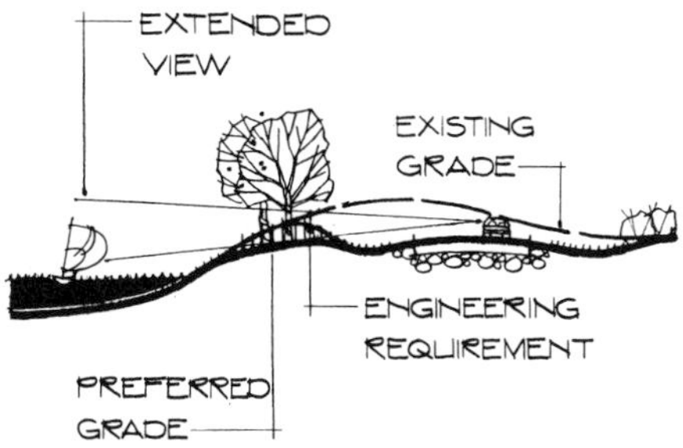
EXTENDED VIEW
EXISTING GRADE
ENGINEERING REQUIREMENT
PREFERRED GRADE

Figure 320-46 Grading to expose vista.

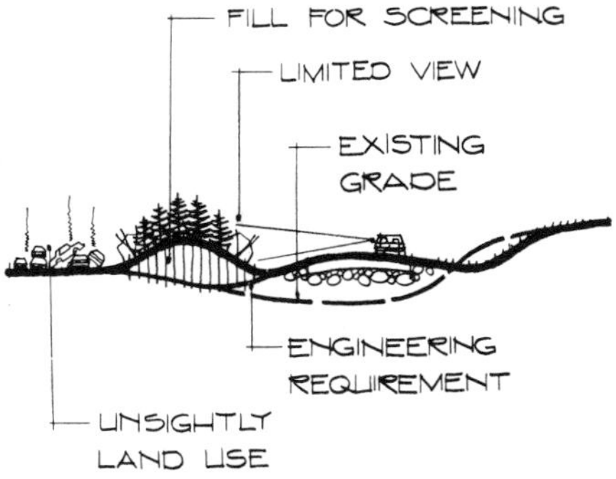
FILL FOR SCREENING
LIMITED VIEW
EXISTING GRADE
ENGINEERING REQUIREMENT
UNSIGHTLY LAND USE

Figure 320-47 Grading to screen undesirable view.

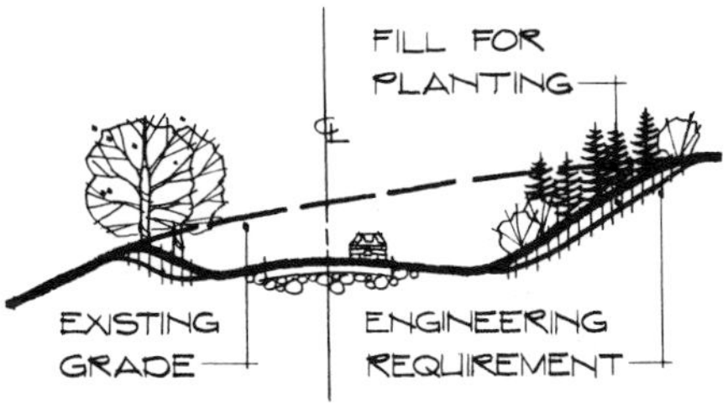
FILL FOR PLANTING
EXISTING GRADE
ENGINEERING REQUIREMENT

Figure 320-48 Grading to facilitate better plant growth.

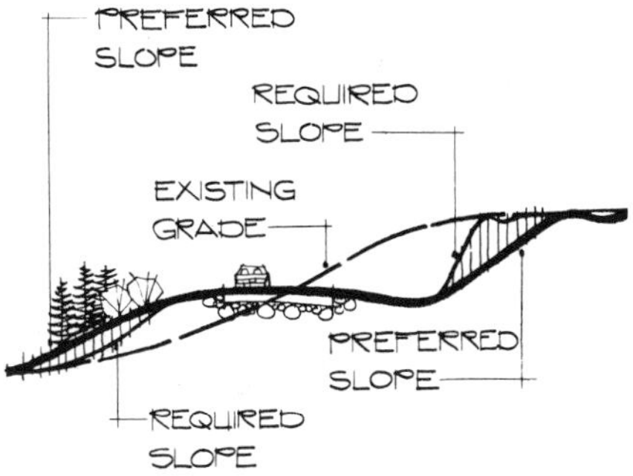
PREFERRED SLOPE
REQUIRED SLOPE
EXISTING GRADE
PREFERRED SLOPE
REQUIRED SLOPE

Figure 320-49 Grading to blend slopes with existing terrain.

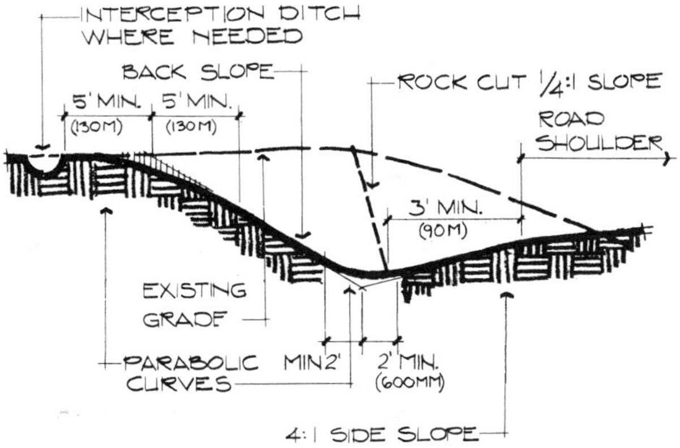
INTERCEPTION DITCH WHERE NEEDED
BACK SLOPE
5' MIN. (130M)
5' MIN. (130M)
ROCK CUT 1/4:1 SLOPE
ROAD SHOULDER
3' MIN. (90M)
EXISTING GRADE
PARABOLIC CURVES
MIN 2'
2' MIN. (600MM)
4:1 SIDE SLOPE

Figure 320-50 Cut side of cross section through road.

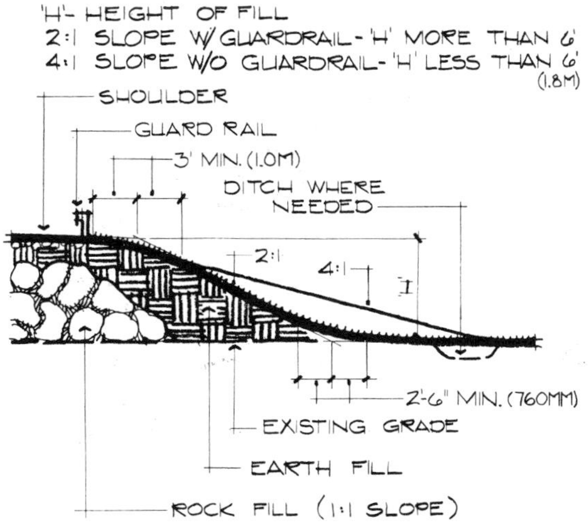
'H'- HEIGHT OF FILL
2:1 SLOPE W/GUARDRAIL-'H' MORE THAN 6'
4:1 SLOPE W/O GUARDRAIL-'H' LESS THAN 6' (1.8M)
SHOULDER
GUARD RAIL
3' MIN. (1.0M)
DITCH WHERE NEEDED
2:1
4:1
H
2'-6" MIN. (760MM)
EXISTING GRADE
EARTH FILL
ROCK FILL (1:1 SLOPE)

Figure 320-51 Fill side of cross section through road.

TABLE 320-4
Spatial Standards for Roads

Pavement widths	
Single-lane road	10–14 ft (3–4.3 m)
Two-lane road	20–24 ft (6–7.3 m)
Four-lane road	20–24 ft (6–7.3 m) either direction
Pavement crown	
Natural soil	½ in : 1 ft 0 in (12 mm : 300 mm)
Gravel, crushed stone	⅜–½ in : 1 ft 0 in (9–12 mm : 300 mm)
Intermediate-type bituminous	¼–⅜ in : 1 ft 0 in (6–9 mm : 300 mm)
High-type bituminous	⅛–¼ in : 1 ft 0 in (3–6 mm : 300 mm)
Concrete	1/10–3/16 in : 1 ft 0 in (2.5–4 mm : 300 mm)
Brick or stone	¼ in : 1 ft 0 in (6 mm : 300 mm)
Shoulders	
Minimum width	1 ft 0 in (300 mm)
Minimum desirable width	2 ft 0 in (600 mm)
Preferred width	8 ft 0 in–10 ft 0 in (2.4–3 m)
Slope	½ in : 1 ft 0 in (12 mm : 300 mm) (approximately 4%)
Side slopes	
Slope	4 : 1
Back slopes	
Earth, minimum	1½ : 1
Earth, preferred	2 : 1 or 3 : 1
Ledge rock, minimum	¼ : 1
Shale	½ : 1
Fill slopes	
Earth, minimum	2 : 1
Earth, preferred	4 : 1
Ditches	
Minimum depth	1–2 ft below shoulder elevation
Maximum inslope	3 : 1 (300–600 mm)

Source: From Public Roads Administration, American Association of State Highway Officials, State Highway Departments.

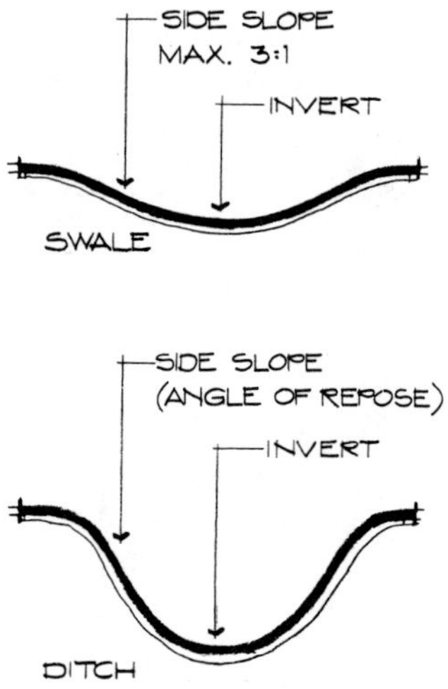
SIDE SLOPE
MAX. 3:1
INVERT
SWALE
SIDE SLOPE
(ANGLE OF REPOSE)
INVERT
DITCH

Figure 320-52 Swale and ditch cross sections.

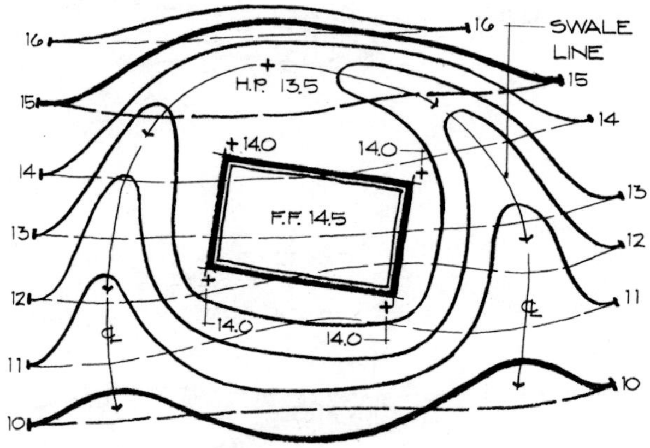
SWALE
LINE
H.P. 13.5
+14.0
14.0
F.F. 14.5
14.0
14.0

Figure 320-53 Swales to Divert Water around Building. Note that the channel widens and the slope diminishes as the swale approaches existing grade.

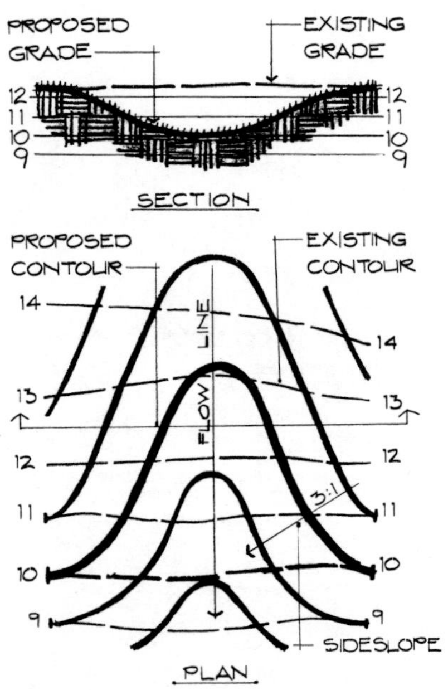
PROPOSED
GRADE
EXISTING
GRADE
SECTION
PROPOSED
CONTOUR
EXISTING
CONTOUR
FLOW LINE
3:1
SIDESLOPE
PLAN

Figure 320-54 Typical grass swale grading.

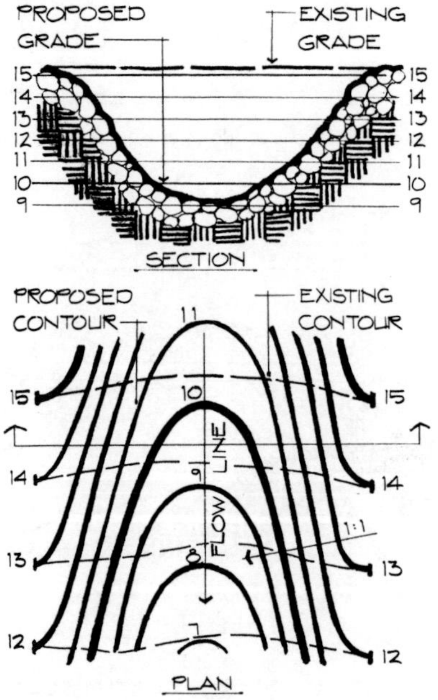
PROPOSED
GRADE
EXISTING
GRADE
SECTION
PROPOSED
CONTOUR
EXISTING
CONTOUR
FLOW LINE
1:1
PLAN

Figure 320-55 Typical ditch grading.

Grass swales (Figure 320-54) tend not to erode if velocities do not exceed 4 feet per second (fps) (1.2 m/s) for established bluegrass turf or 6 fps (1.8 m/s) for established tall fescue turf. Spreading grasses, such as *Bermuda* or *St. Augsten,* exhibit similar resistance to erosion. The durability of grasses will vary considerably throughout various climatic regions. In the United States, regional Soil Conservation Service offices can be consulted about which native grasses to use for erosion control.

If velocities exceed 6 fps (1.8 m/s), then some form of nonvegetative material should be used to construct the swale, such as gravel, crushed stone, or riprap (Figure 320-55).

Drainage Channels with Unprotected Soil:

Table 320-5 gives the velocities which will not erode *aged* drainage channels.

1. *Aging* means allowing time to increase the density and stability of the channel bed material through the deposit of silt in the interstices and the cementation of the soil by colloids. New channels may be safely operated at less than maximum design velocities by the use of typical erosion control measures, including temporary check structures.

2. Velocities should be reduced for depths of flow under 6 in (150 mm) and for water which may transport abrasive materials.

TABLE 320-5
Erodibility of Drainage Channels with Unprotected Soils

Material of channel bed	Velocity	
	Shallow ditch, ft/s (m/s)	*Deep canal, ft/s(m/s)*
Fine sand or silt, noncolloidal	0.50–1.50 (0.15–0.45)	1.50–2.50 (0.45–0.76)
Coarse sand or sandy loam, noncolloidal	1.00–1.50 (0.30–0.45)	1.75–2.50 (0.53–0.76)
Silty or sand loam, noncolloidal	1.00–1.75 (0.30–0.53)	2.00–3.00 (0.60–0.90)
Clayey loam or sandy clay, noncolloidal	1.50–2.00 (0.45–0.60)	2.25–3.50 (0.68–1.05)
Fine gravel	2.00–2.50 (0.60–0.76)	2.50–5.00 (0.76–1.50)
Colloidal clay or noncolloidal gravelly loam	2.00–3.00 (0.60–1.0)	3.00–5.00 (1.00–1.50)

Culverts and Headwalls:

The grading scheme and the design of the headwall for a culvert must be totally integrated. Figure 320-56 illustrates how a headwall and wings serve as a retaining wall to allow full exposure of the culvert pipe.

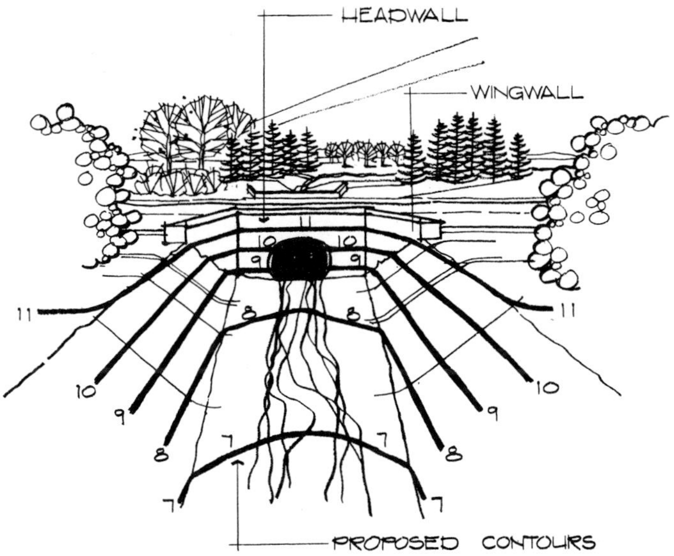
HEADWALL
WINGWALL
11
10
9
8
7
PROPOSED CONTOURS

Figure 320-56 Grading of a typical head wall.

Slopes and Berms:

The angle of slopes should be considered in regard to aesthetic, drainage, and maintenance needs.

Figure 320-57 shows how steep slopes used for earth berms or mounds can be graded, using the following rules of thumb:

1. Provide for nonerosive drainage at the tops and bottoms of slopes.

2. Grade the tops of banks to be smoothly convex and the toes smoothly concave.

3. Grade the slopes to blend in with the surrounding landscape.

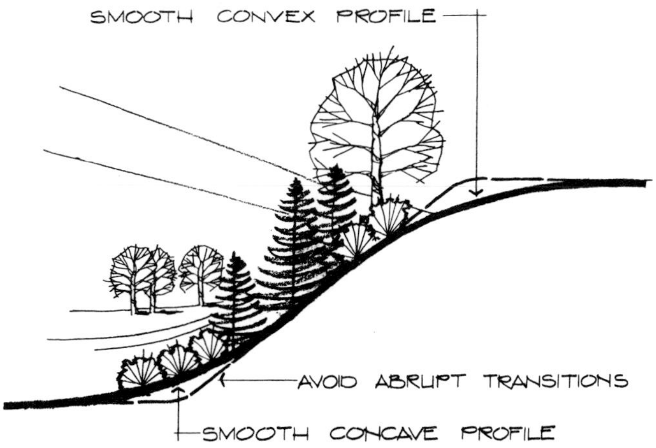
SMOOTH CONVEX PROFILE
AVOID ABRUPT TRANSITIONS
SMOOTH CONCAVE PROFILE

Figure 320-57 Grading criteria for slopes.

Stairs and Ramps:

Standards for outdoor stairs and ramps are discussed more fully in Section 240: Access and Egress: Outdoor Standards. Stairs and ramps should be designed as an integral part of any overall grading plan (Figure 320-58).

Existing Trees:

Grading around existing trees should be managed with great care, using one or more of the following techniques:

1. Figure 320-59 shows how to avoid grading, cutting, or filling above the root zone of a tree. For most species this means staying outside the drip line of the tree. Also, the weight of the grading equipment driven over the root zone will tear root hairs and compact the soil, thereby restricting vital water and air from flowing to and being assimilated by the roots.

2. If filling around an existing tree cannot be avoided, then a way must be found to protect the tree. Figures 320-60 and 320-61 illustrate a typical way to accomplish this. This technique permits adequate flow of air and water to the roots of the tree.

3. Figure 320-62 shows another way to create a flat area and at the same time protect existing trees. This is done by constructing a deck with minimum footings around a tree; the deck's layout can be adjusted to the specific site conditions. When buildings or other such structures are involved, as shown in Figure 320-62, it is better to use lightweight footings with crawl spaces rather than on-grade slabs with compacted subgrades.

Figure 320-63 shows how grade beams and piers can be used to support walls and other structures without having to cut the major roots of existing trees.

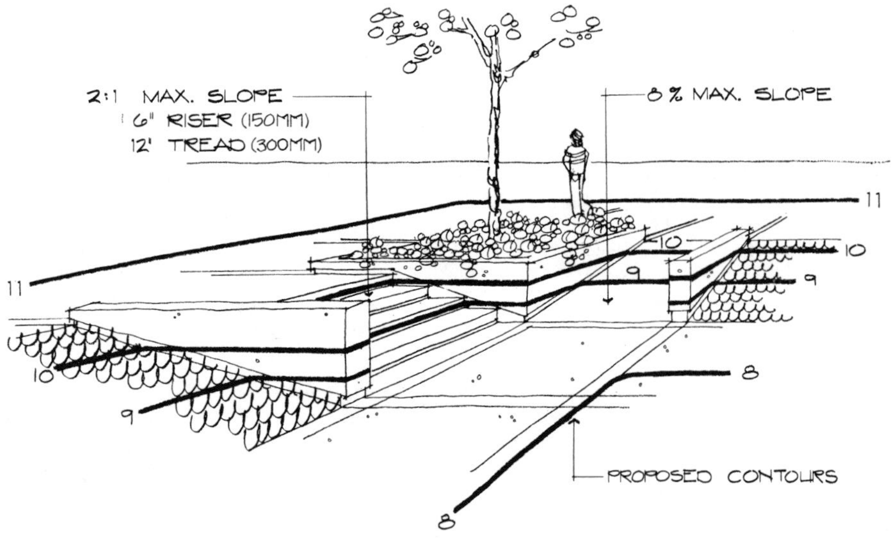
2:1 MAX. SLOPE
6" RISER (150MM)
12' TREAD (300MM)
8 % MAX. SLOPE
11
10
9
8
PROPOSED CONTOURS

Figure 320-58 Grading of Stairs and Ramps. Note that tread/riser ratios greater than 2:1 are advisable whenever possible.

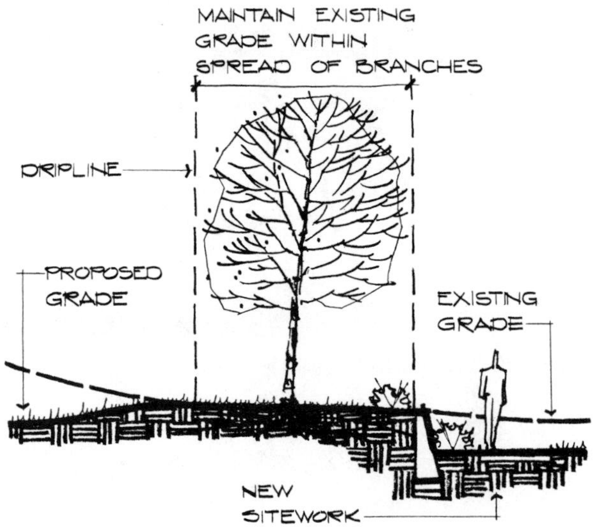
MAINTAIN EXISTING GRADE WITHIN SPREAD OF BRANCHES
DRIPLINE
PROPOSED GRADE
EXISTING GRADE
NEW SITEWORK

Figure 320-59 Grading near existing trees.

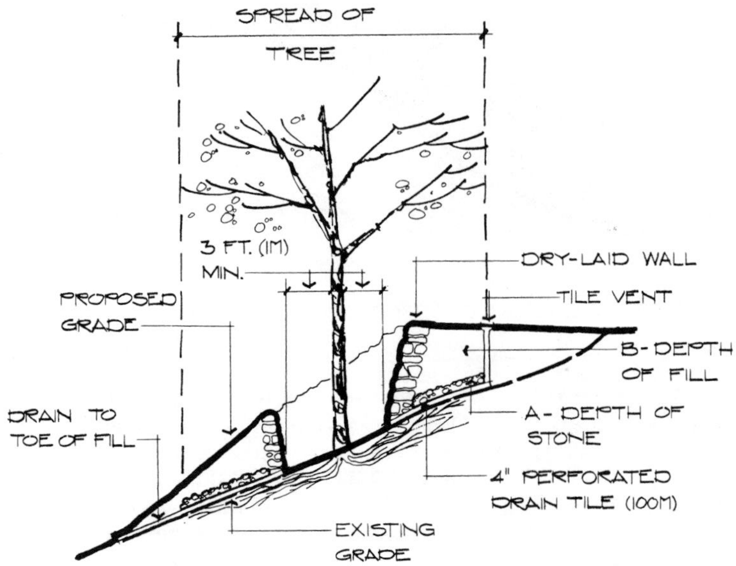
SPREAD OF TREE
3 FT. (1M) MIN.
DRY-LAID WALL
TILE VENT
PROPOSED GRADE
B- DEPTH OF FILL
DRAIN TO TOE OF FILL
A- DEPTH OF STONE
4" PERFORATED DRAIN TILE (100M)
EXISTING GRADE

Figure 320-60 Retaining wall and drainage for existing tree in area of fill (section).

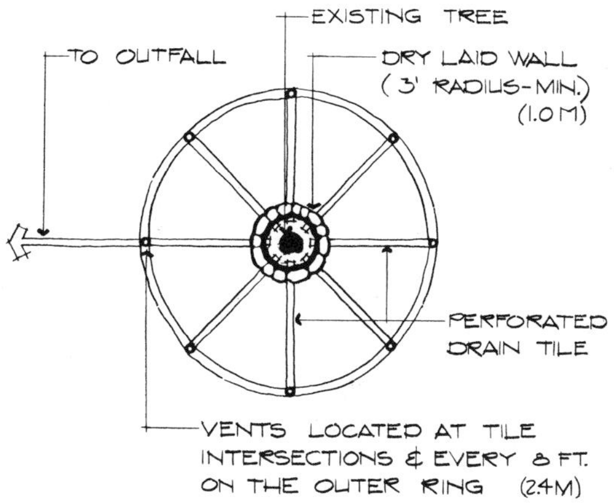
EXISTING TREE
TO OUTFALL
DRY LAID WALL
(3' RADIUS-MIN.)
(1.0 M)
PERFORATED
DRAIN TILE
VENTS LOCATED AT TILE
INTERSECTIONS & EVERY 8 FT.
ON THE OUTER RING (2.4M)

Figure 320-61 Retaining wall and drainage for existing tree in area of fill (plan).

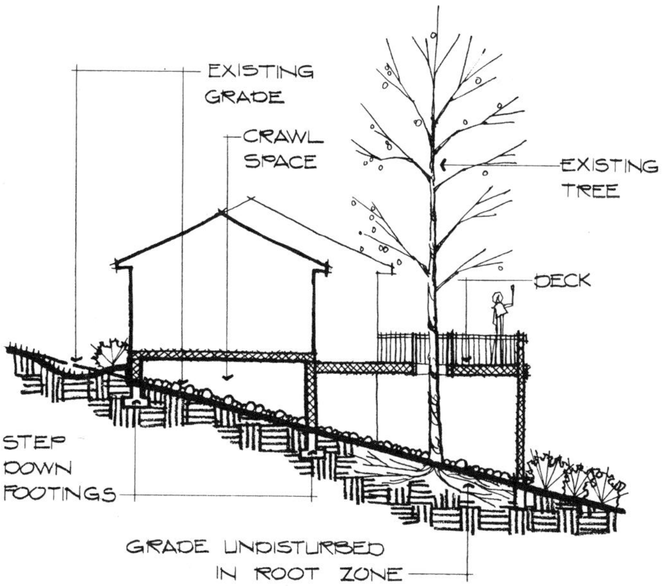
EXISTING
GRADE
CRAWL
SPACE
EXISTING
TREE
DECK
STEP
DOWN
FOOTINGS
GRADE UNDISTURBED
IN ROOT ZONE

Figure 320-62 Crawl space and decking near existing trees.

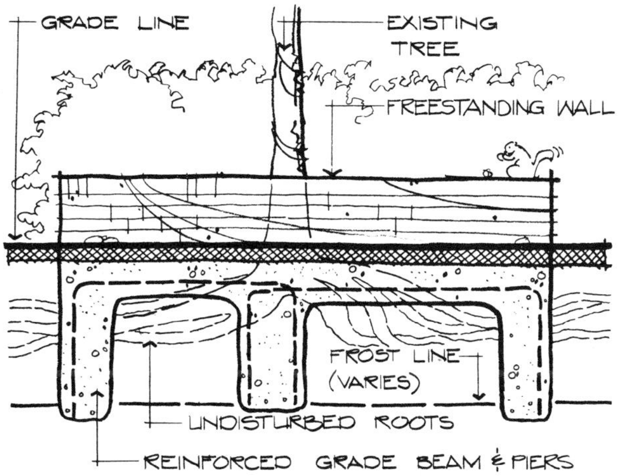
GRADE LINE
EXISTING
TREE
FREESTANDING WALL
FROST LINE
(VARIES)
UNDISTURBED ROOTS
REINFORCED GRADE BEAM & PIERS

Figure 320-63 Grade beam method of tree root protection.

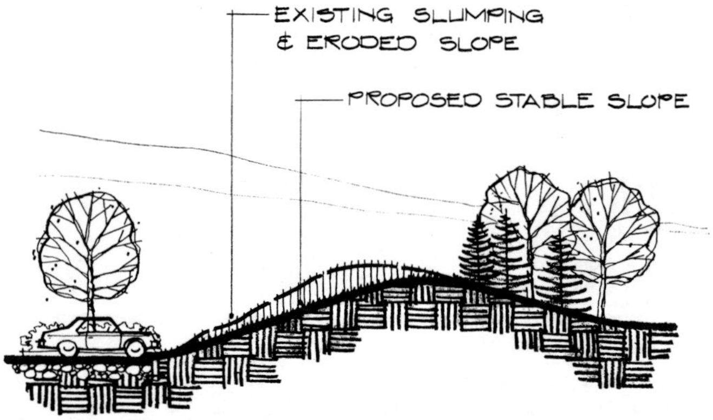
EXISTING SLUMPING
& ERODED SLOPE
PROPOSED STABLE SLOPE

Figure 320-64 Erosion control by reducing gradient of slopes.

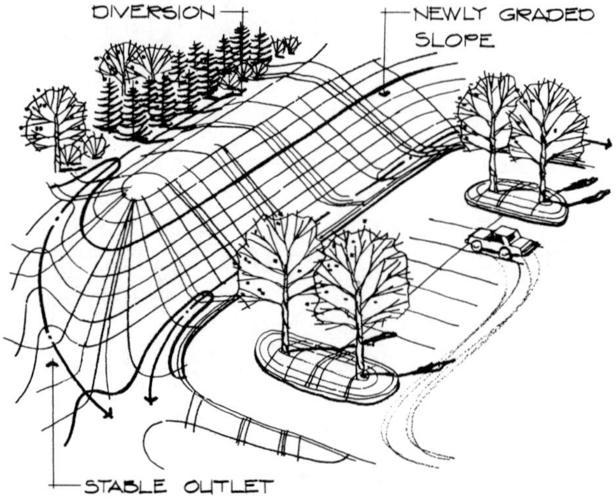
DIVERSION
NEWLY GRADED
SLOPE
STABLE OUTLET

Figure 320-65 Grading to divert runoff.

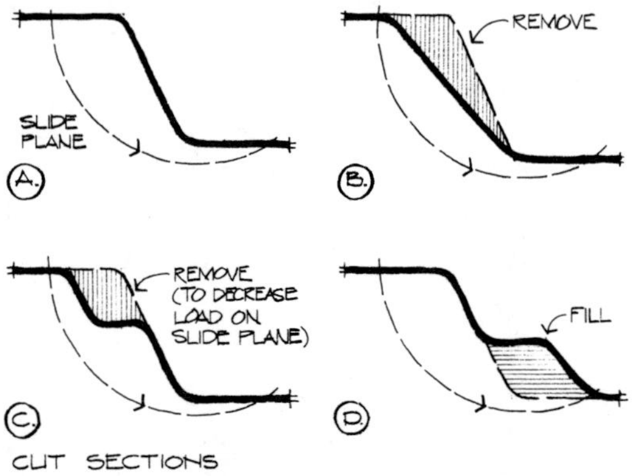
SLIDE
PLANE
A.
REMOVE
B.
REMOVE
(TO DECREASE
LOAD ON
SLIDE PLANE)
C.
FILL
D.
CUT SECTIONS

Figure 320-66 Stabilization techniques for cuts on hillsides.

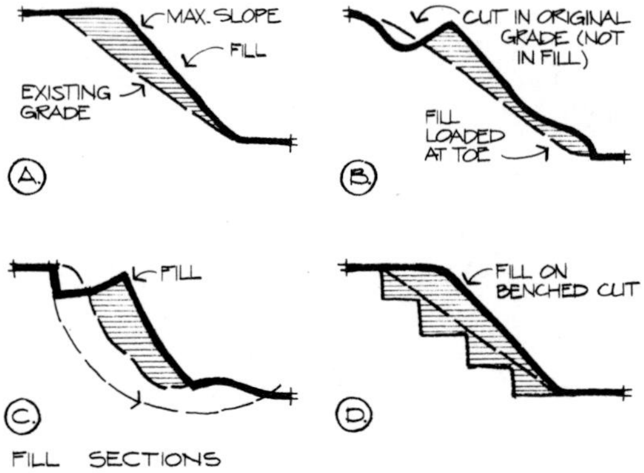
MAX. SLOPE
FILL
EXISTING
GRADE
A.
CUT IN ORIGINAL
GRADE (NOT
IN FILL)
FILL
LOADED
AT TOE
B.
FILL
C.
FILL ON
BENCHED CUT
D.
FILL SECTIONS

Figure 320-67 Stabilization techniques for fills on hillsides.

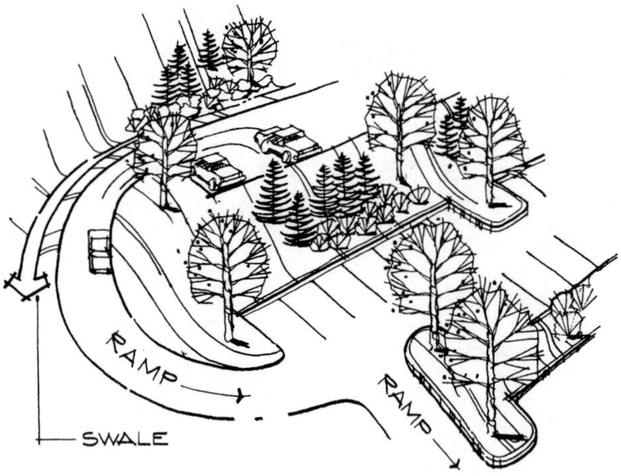
RAMP
RAMP
SWALE

Figure 320-68 Example of a stepped-down parking area.

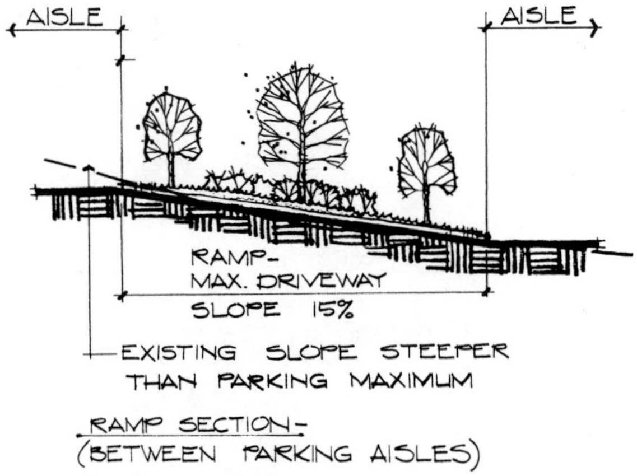
AISLE
AISLE
RAMP-
MAX. DRIVEWAY
SLOPE 15%
EXISTING SLOPE STEEPER
THAN PARKING MAXIMUM
RAMP SECTION-
(BETWEEN PARKING AISLES)

Figure 320-69 Example of a ramp section between parking aisles.

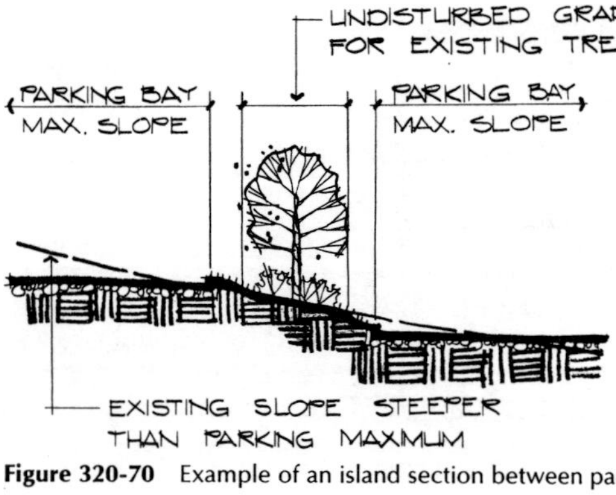
UNDISTURBED GRADE
FOR EXISTING TREE
PARKING BAY
MAX. SLOPE
PARKING BAY
MAX. SLOPE
EXISTING SLOPE STEEPER
THAN PARKING MAXIMUM

Figure 320-70 Example of an island section between parking bays.

Erosion Control by Grading:

Most erosion is caused by flowing water. The size and shape of a watershed, the porosity of its soils, and the length and gradient of its slopes and channels are key determinants controlling the volume and velocity of runoff and the consequent risk of erosion. Several site grading techniques can be employed to limit the size, shape, length, and gradient of these slopes and channels, thereby reducing the volume and velocity of runoff.

Gradients can be reduced by extending the length of a slope. This uses more land, but it does reduce the amount of erosion and the potential slumping of hillsides (Figure 320-64).

Used singly or in combination, diversion swales, ditches, and dikes can intercept and divert runoff from the face of a slope (Figure 320-65).

Soil Slippage: Several factors may cause soil masses altered by either cutting or filling to slide. The most common causes are improper cuts or fills and insufficient attention to surface and subsurface drainage characteristics. (In some regions where there are unstable soils there may be local standards that have to be met, including the use of vegetative or mechanical anchors.) Figures 320-66 and 320-67 illustrate alternatives for grading to stabilize cut-and-fill banks.

Grading for Porous Paved Surfaces:

The use of gravel, crushed stone, porous asphalt, or other types of *porous* paving does allow either flatter or steeper gradients than bare soil, but their use may not justify radical changes from the grading and drainage standards normally used in a region.

In the case of some artificial turf systems, an extremely porous subbase may be used so that water will immediately penetrate the surface. This water must then be carried away by a subsurface drainage system of an appropriate capacity. Using such a system allows play surfaces to be graded flat.

Parking Areas:

Grading of Parking Areas: The minimum and maximum gradients required for vehicular access and parking areas are often the major determinants for the grading plan of a site. Figure 320-68 illustrates how a parking lot can be stepped down a steep slope.

As shown in Table 320-2, the recommended maximum cross slope for a parking area is 10 percent. The steeper transitional area between bays can be taken up by a planting bay and a ramp (maximum 15 percent slope) (Figures 320-69 and 320-70).

Figure 320-71 shows how in extreme circumstances single-loaded parking bays may be used to fit steep sites. Similarly, a combination of ramps and segmented parking bays may be used to achieve a grading solution on a slope with existing vegetation (Figure 320-72).

Runoff Control from Parking Areas: More and more municipalities require that increased stormwater runoff, due to paving and to roofs of buildings, should be contained within a site. The manner in which this is achieved is usually determined during the grading process. Quantities of water can be calculated with the data provided in Section 330: Site Drainage.

Figure 320-73 illustrates the alternative of using an overflow parking area as a retention basin when a separate retention basin cannot be fitted into the scheme.

Figures 320-74 through 320-76 illustrate how swales may be filled with a porous material, such as rock, to give a level appearance and yet act as multiple retention basins between parking bays. This method, in addition to controlling runoff, serves to recharge the groundwater and increase the moisture content of surrounding soils.

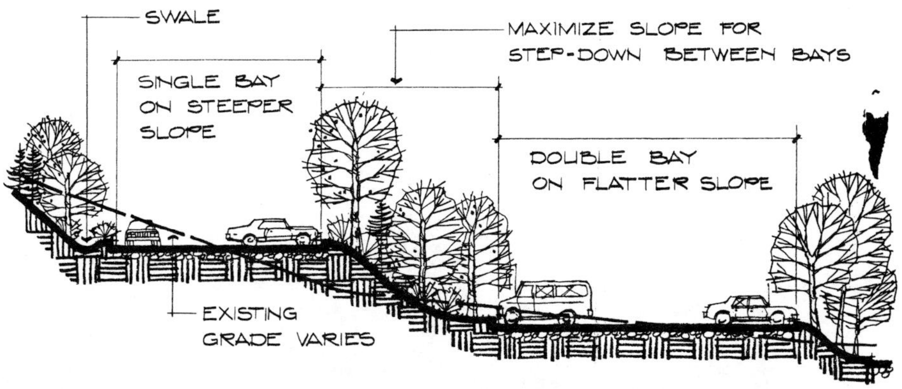

SWALE
MAXIMIZE SLOPE FOR STEP-DOWN BETWEEN BAYS
SINGLE BAY ON STEEPER SLOPE
DOUBLE BAY ON FLATTER SLOPE
EXISTING GRADE VARIES

Figure 320-71 Combined single and double parking bays to adapt to steep slope.

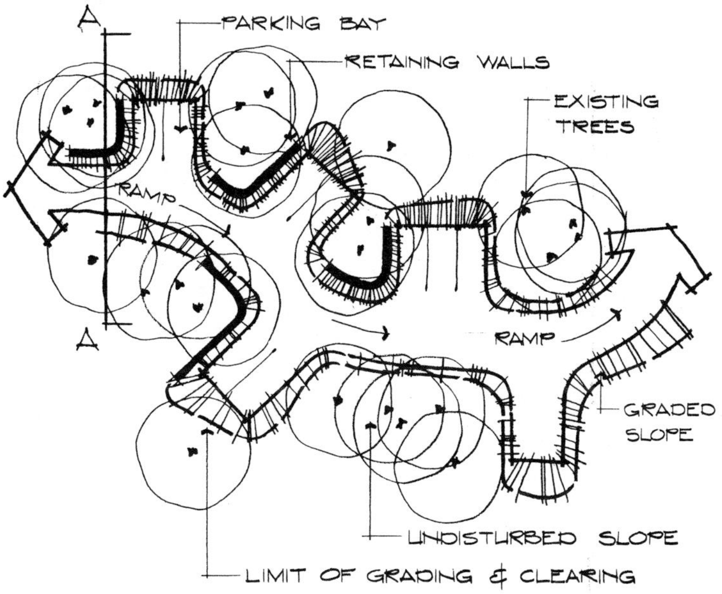

A
PARKING BAY
RETAINING WALLS
EXISTING TREES
RAMP
RAMP
A
GRADED SLOPE
UNDISTURBED SLOPE
LIMIT OF GRADING & CLEARING

Figure 320-72 Segmented parking with walls and ramps to save existing trees.

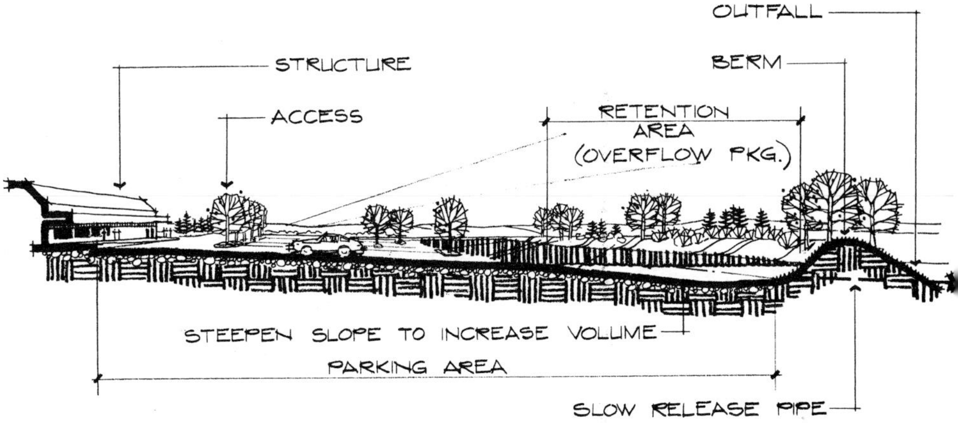

OUTFALL
STRUCTURE
BERM
ACCESS
RETENTION AREA (OVERFLOW PKG.)
STEEPEN SLOPE TO INCREASE VOLUME
PARKING AREA
SLOW RELEASE PIPE

Figure 320-73 Overflow parking area used to retain stormwater.

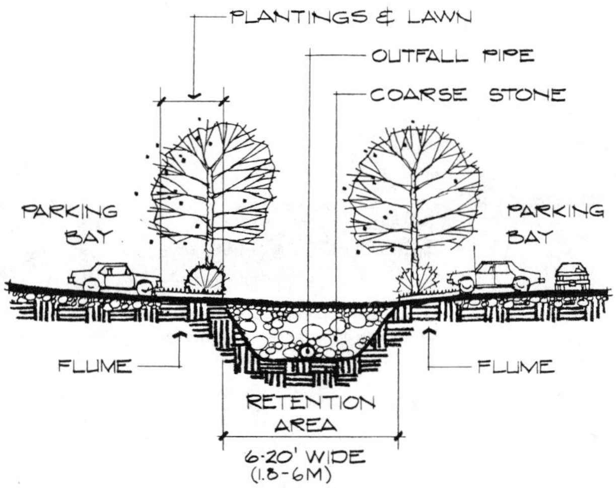
PLANTINGS & LAWN
OUTFALL PIPE
COARSE STONE
PARKING BAY
PARKING BAY
FLUME
FLUME
RETENTION AREA
6-20' WIDE (1.8-6M)

Figure 320-74 Porous-fill stormwater retention area between parking bays (section).

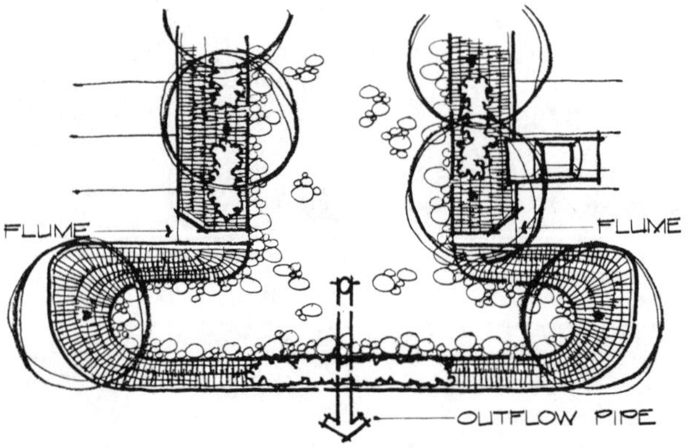
FLUME
FLUME
OUTFLOW PIPE

Figure 320-75 Porous-fill retention area between parking bays (plan).

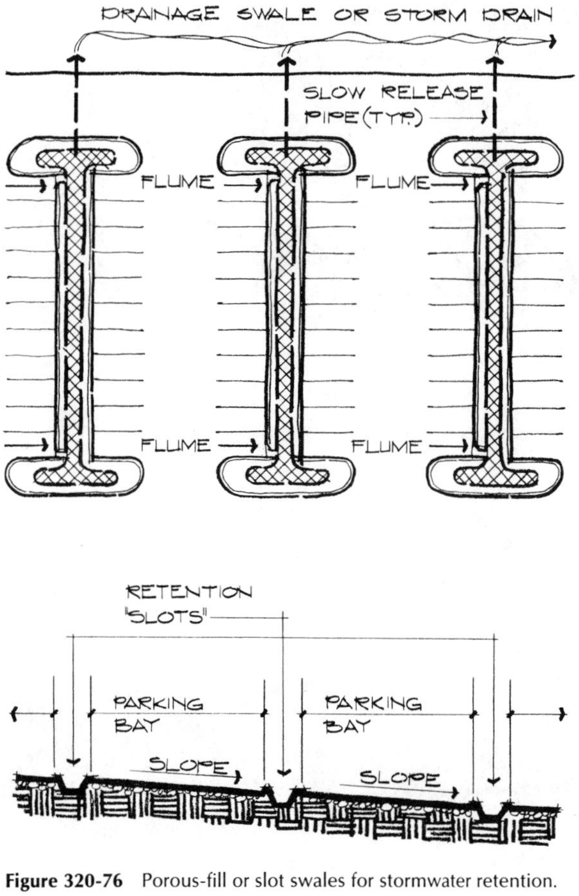
DRAINAGE SWALE OR STORM DRAIN
SLOW RELEASE PIPE (TYP)
FLUME
FLUME
FLUME
FLUME
RETENTION "SLOTS"
PARKING BAY
PARKING BAY
SLOPE
SLOPE

Figure 320-76 Porous-fill or slot swales for stormwater retention.

5.0 EARTHWORK PROCESSES

5.1 Grading As Part of a Sequential Design Process

Although circumstances may vary from site to site, most grading operations proceed according to the following steps.

Preparation of the Site:

Clearing, Grubbing, and Removal: Remove designated trees and other types of vegetation from an area to be graded. Note that in some cases it is recommended that all existing plant material to be removed should be chopped and mixed with topsoil. This technique often proves to be an excellent way to help reestablish a similar type of vegetative cover. Sod should be removed or broken up by disks to prevent lumping during reuse.

Topsoil Stripping:

1. Strip to a specified depth determined by evaluation of the soil. This depth may vary from 3 in to 2 ft (70 to 600 mm).

2. Stockpile the stripped topsoil in locations outside of the no-cut/no-fill limits of the project and nearest to where it will be used later.

Excavation and Preparation of Subgrade:

1. Cut to the elevations indicated on the grade stakes set by the engineer or surveyor. Cutting and filling can be conducted simultaneously. The fill portion must be compacted according to predetermined construction standards.

2. Fill for planted areas should be compacted only enough to retain 30 percent minimum porosity.

3. Fill material must be put down in 6- to 8-in (150- to 200-mm) layers. Compact and test each layer to conform with specified densities.

4. Topsoil is added last to bring the grades to the levels and slopes shown on the grading plans.

5.2 Earth and Rock-Moving Equipment

There are many types of equipment that can be used to do grading. Table 320-6 shows some of the more common types and describes their characteristics, including typical uses.

5.3 Information on Soil and Rock Material

The initial site design and the eventual grading plan should be prepared based upon knowledge of the composition and other characteristics of the soil and/or rock to be moved. This data can be obtained in a variety of ways, depending upon the level of detail needed.

Sources of Information:

General soil data in the United States is published by the U.S. Department of Agriculture (USDA) and the Soil Conservation Service (SCS) for most states, on a county-by-county basis.

Specific information on soils can be obtained by borings or test pits at selected places on a site. These soil profiles can be analyzed to determine their effect on design and/or construction costs.

Data on depth to bedrock can be obtained by rod soundings for small-scale projects or by borings made by power augers.

Typical Soil Profile:

Figure 320-77 illustrates a typical soil profile for the central United States. Similar data can be found for other parts of the United States via the Soil Conservation Service, local university or state agricultural departments, and other local sources of information. In other countries there are often similar sources of generalized soil data.

TABLE 320-6
Earth and Rock-Moving Equipment

Machine	*Characteristics*	*Use*
Bulldozer	Front-fitted rectangular blade can be raised or lowered	Push earth or rock. Limited capacity over large distances
Angledozer	Same principle as for a bulldozer	Push earth aside to left or right rather than ahead
Sideboom dozer	Cantilevered blade on side of machine adjustable in vertical plane	Trim slopes to an even batter
Grader	Curved section steel blade rotates in horizontal or vertical positions	Excavate shallow cuts. Cannot operate on vertical sites
Ripper-scarifier	Steel teeth, or tines, mounted on a frame	Break up or scarify hard, compacted earth
Face shovel	Operates at its own level. Open-type bucket or dipper is filled by driving it into material being excavated	Excavate clay, chalk, and loosened rock
Skimmer	Similar to face shovel, with more restricted movement and lower output. Will produce accurate finished level	Shallow digging
Backshovel or dragshovel	Working stroke is toward the machine. Excavates at a level below that of the machine's tracks	Ideal for use in confined spaces
Trencher or digger	Alternative to the backshovel	Excavating narrow, vertical-sided trenches
Dragline	Excavating bucket filled by dragging it toward the machine. Excavates at a level below that of the machine's tracks	Excavating in soft materials and swampy sites

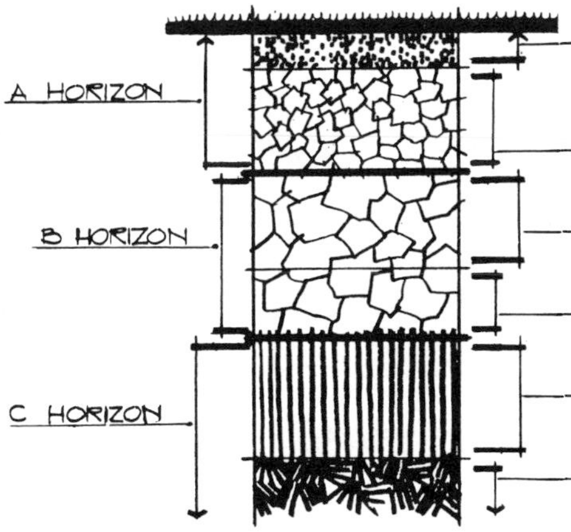
A HORIZON
B HORIZON
C HORIZON

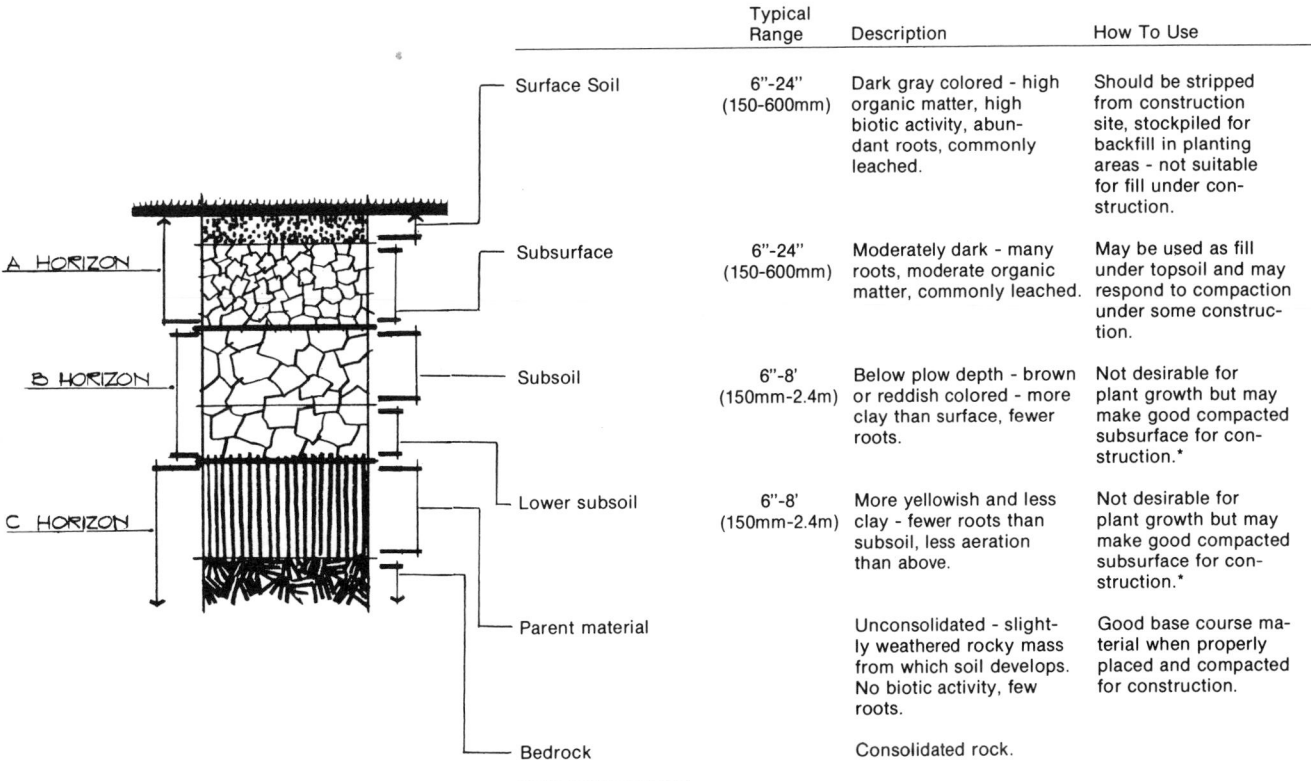

	Typical Range	Description	How To Use
Surface Soil	6"-24" (150-600mm)	Dark gray colored - high organic matter, high biotic activity, abundant roots, commonly leached.	Should be stripped from construction site, stockpiled for backfill in planting areas - not suitable for fill under construction.
Subsurface	6"-24" (150-600mm)	Moderately dark - many roots, moderate organic matter, commonly leached.	May be used as fill under topsoil and may respond to compaction under some construction.
Subsoil	6"-8' (150mm-2.4m)	Below plow depth - brown or reddish colored - more clay than surface, fewer roots.	Not desirable for plant growth but may make good compacted subsurface for construction.*
Lower subsoil	6"-8' (150mm-2.4m)	More yellowish and less clay - fewer roots than subsoil, less aeration than above.	Not desirable for plant growth but may make good compacted subsurface for construction.*
Parent material		Unconsolidated - slightly weathered rocky mass from which soil develops. No biotic activity, few roots.	Good base course material when properly placed and compacted for construction.
Bedrock		Consolidated rock.	

*Depends upon soil quality and type of construction anticipated.

Figure 320-77 Typical Soil Profile. A *soil horizon* is a significant layer of soil that has distinct characteristics produced by soil-forming processes.

Rock in Relation to Grading:

Rock is generally considered to be any material which requires blasting before it can be dug or moved by most machines.

In preparing a grading plan that involves rock, the most useful data includes: (1) the amount of soil cover or depth of earth to rock, (2) how much of the top layer rock is loose and can be easily broken, (3) how much of the rock will have to be blasted, and (4) the basic type of rock. As a general rule of thumb, the cost of blasting and moving rock is typically 7 to 10 times more expensive than moving dry, deep, moderately cohesive soil.

Classifications of Rock: Rock is typically classified into three major groups. Only a brief description of each is included here.

Igneous: Igneous rock is solidified from a molten state, either at or beneath the surface of the earth. It is crystalline, typically not exhibiting a grain. Thus, it breaks irregularly depending on its composition.

Sedimentary: Sedimentary rock is made from the sedimentation of soil, plant, and animal remains that have hardened as a result of pressure, time, and the deposition of natural cements, typically at ocean depths. It will fracture along the planes of sedimentation.

Metamorphic: Metamorphic rock consists of previously igneous or sedimentary rock that has been altered by extreme heat and pressure, either at great depths or along tectonic fault lines, etc. It often exhibits some veining or foliation, which may fracture naturally as well as during blasting and excavation.

Swell and Shrinkage:

When soil or rock is dug or blasted out of its original position, it breaks into particles or chunks, which creates more spaces and adds to its bulk. This increase in volume is called *swell.* When soil is placed in a new location with nominal compaction, these voids are filled and some shrinkage occurs. Rock, on the other hand, swells. Compaction will not compress rock excavation to its original volume. Table 320-7 shows a guide to help estimate the amount of shrink or swell involved with different types of materials.

Weights of Soil and Rock Material:

Table 320-8 shows typical weights for a range of materials based upon the material in place and after being excavated.

5.4 Estimating Cut and Fill

General Considerations:

Techniques for estimating earthwork quantities are only approximations. This is true for several reasons: (1) spot grades from field surveys are typically accurate

TABLE 320-7
Estimating Shrink and Swell

Material	*After excavation during transport or stockpile*	*Borrow yard**	*Amount produced by 1 yd, replaced with only moderate compaction*
Sand	1.11 yd^3 (0.83 m^3) 111% swell	1 yd^3 (0.75 m^3)	0.88 yd^3 (0.66 m^3) 12% shrink
Common earth	1.25 yd^3 (0.94 m^3) 125% swell	1 yd^3 (0.75 m^3)	0.82 yd^3 (0.60 m^3) 18% shrink
Clay	1.43 yd^3 (1.00 m^3) 143% swell	1 yd^3 (0.75 m^3)	0.87 yd^3 (0.65 m^3) 13% shrink
Shot rock	1.67 yd^3 (1.30 m^3) 167% swell	1 yd^3 (0.75 m^3)	
Gravel, loose		1 yd^3 (0.75 m^3)	0.89 yd^3 (0.67 m^3) 11% shrink

* Materials used for compacted subbase will exhibit higher shrinkage levels under the appropriate moisture conditions and compaction technique.

TABLE 320-8
Weights of Soil and Rock Materials

Material	*Weight in bank, lb/yd³ (kg/m³)*	*Loose weight, lb/yd³ (kg/m³)*
Clay		
Dry	2300 (1044)	1840 (835)
Light	2800 (1271)	2160 (981)
Dense, tough, or wet	3000 (1362)	2250 (1021)
Earth		
Dry	2800 (1271)	2240 (1017)
Wet	3370 (1530)	2700 (1256)
With sand and gravel	3100 (1407)	2640 (1198)
Earth and rock mixture, such as unclassified excavation	2500–3000 (1135–1362)	1920–2310 (872–1048)
Gravel		
Dry	3250 (1475)	2900 (1317)
Wet	3600 (1634)	3200 (1453)
Loam	2700 (1226)	2240 (1017)
Rock, hard, well-blasted	4000 (1816)	2680 (1216)
Sand		
Dry	3250 (1475)	2900 (1317)
Wet	3600 (1634)	3200 (1453)
Sandstone	4140 (1880)	2980–2610 (1353–1185)

Source: Herbert L. Nichols, Jr., *Moving the Earth,* D. Van Nostrand Company, Princeton, New Jersey, 1955.

TABLE 320-9
Corrections for an Imbalance of Cut or Fill

Imbalance area	*Volume for changes in elevation, yd³ (m³)*						
	3 in (76 mm)	*6 in (150 mm)*	*9 in (230 mm)*	*12 in (300 mm)*	*18 in (450 mm)*	*24 in (600 mm)*
1 acre (0.405 ha)	403 (139)	806 (608)	1209 (913)	1613 (1218)	2420 (1827)	3226 (2436)
20,000 ft^2 (1860 m^2)	185 (140)	370 (279)	555 (419)	740 (559)	1110 (838)	1480 (1117)
10,000 ft^2 (930 m^2)	93 (70)	185 (140)	277 (209)	370 (279)	555 (419)	740 (559)
5,000 ft^2 (465 m^2)	46 (35)	92 (69)	139 (104)	185 (140)	277 (209)	370 (279)
4,000 ft^2 (372 m^2)	37 (28)	74 (56)	111 (84)	148 (112)	252 (190)	296 (223)
3,000 ft^2 (279 m^2)	28 (21)	56 (42)	84 (63)	112 (85)	167 (126)	225 (170)
2,000 ft^2 (186 m^2)	19 (14)	38 (29)	47 (35)	76 (57)	111 (84)	148 (112)
1,000 ft^2 (93 m^2)	9 (7)	19 (14)	28 (21)	37 (28)	57 (43)	76 (57)

only to 0.1 ft (30 mm), (2) contours shown on survey maps are legally accurate only to one-half of the contour interval, and (3) the amount of swell or shrinkage cannot be determined with any high degree of precision.

Not all estimates of cut and fill need to involve the same degree of accuracy. For instance, in the early stages of a site plan it may be important to know in only general terms whether there can be a balance of cut and fill.

Corrections at Early Design Stages:

After preparing a preliminary site and related grading plan, it is easy to see whether there would be a serious imbalance of cut or fill. Often an imbalance can be corrected by raising or lowering noncritical areas of a site design or even by raising or lowering the finish grades for an entire site.

Table 320-9 provides a quick estimate of the amount of raising and/or lowering required to correct an imbalance of cut and fill, once the amount of such imbalance is known.

Examples of calculations (U.S. customary system):

Volume of 1 acre changed 12 in. in elevation $= \dfrac{(43{,}560\ \text{ft}^2)(1\ \text{ft})}{27} = 1600\ \text{yd}^3$

Volume of an area 100 ft × 100 ft changed 12 in. in elevation $= \dfrac{(100)(100)(1)}{27} = 370\ \text{yd}^3$

Examples of calculations (metric):

Volume of 1 hectare changed 30 centimeters (cm) in elevation $= \dfrac{10{,}000\ \text{m}^2 \times 0.30}{1} = 3000\ \text{m}^3$

Volume of an area 10 m × 10 m changed 30 cm in elevation $= \dfrac{10 \times 10 \times 0.30}{1} = 30\ \text{m}^3$

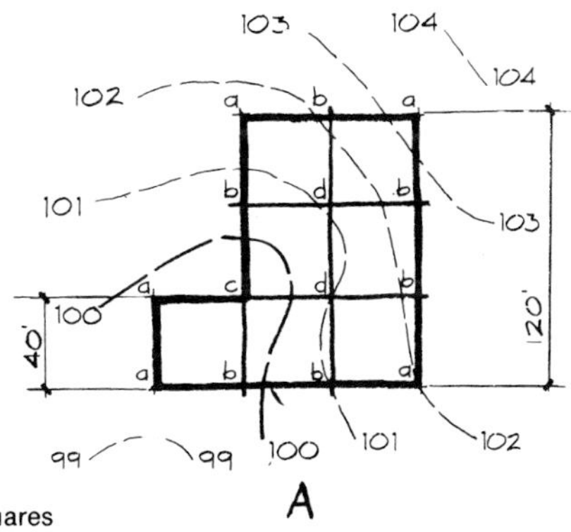

103
104
104
102
a
b
a
101
b
d
b
103
a
c
d
b
100
40'
120'
a
b
b
a
99
99
100
101
102
A

The area to be graded is divided into squares and the corners of the squares are labeled a,b, c, and d, depending on the number of squares each corner pertains to. The bottom of the excavation is to be at elevation 95.00. Figure B shows the existing elevations of the earth surface obtained by interpolating between the contours. Figure C shows the depth of cut at each of the corners, obtained as follows:

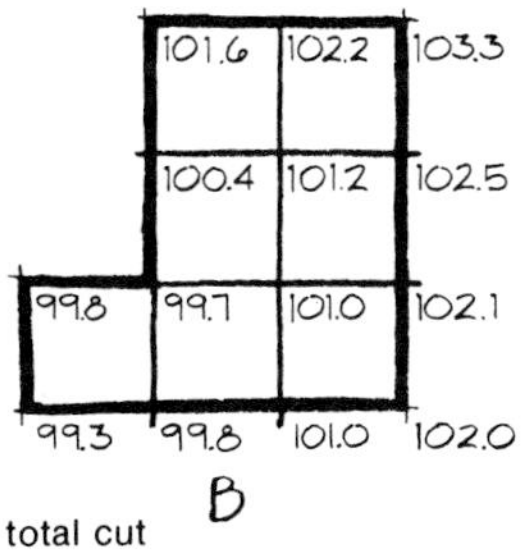

101.6
102.2
103.3
100.4
101.2
102.5
99.8
99.7
101.0
102.1
99.3
99.8
101.0
102.0
B

'a' Corners

101.6	103.3	99.8	99.3	102.0	
-95.0	-95.0	-95.0	-95.0	-95.0	
6.6	8.3	4.8	4.3	7.0	= 31.0 total cut

'b' Corners

102.2	200.4	102.5	102.1	99.8	101.0	
-95.0	-95.0	-95.0	-95.0	-95.0	-95.0	
7.2	5.4	7.5	7.1	4.8	6.0	= 38.0 total cut

'c' Corners

99.7	
-95.0	
4.7	= 4.7 total cut

'd' Corners

101.2	101.0	
-95.0	-95.0	
6.2	6.0	= 12.2 total cut

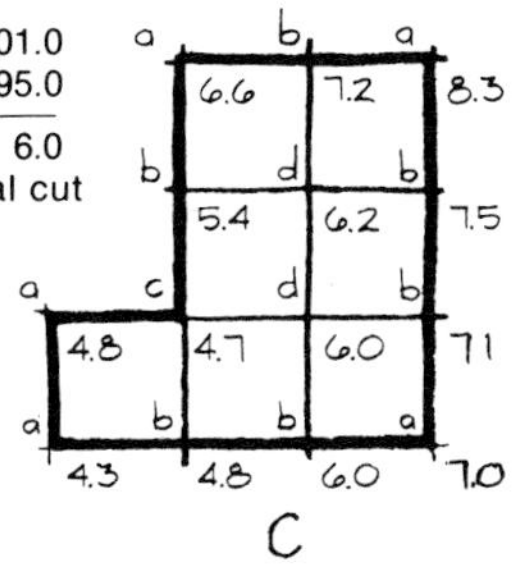

a
b
a
6.6
7.2
8.3
b
d
b
5.4
6.2
7.5
a
c
d
b
4.8
4.7
6.0
7.1
a
b
b
a
4.3
4.8
6.0
7.0
C

Then, using the formula

$$\text{Volume} = \frac{a + 2b + 3c + 4d}{4} \times A$$

where A = a40 x 40 ft. square, or 1,600 sq. ft. Then

$$\text{Volume} = \frac{31.0 + 2\ (38.0) + 3\ (4.7 + 4\ (12.2)}{4} \times 1600$$

$$= \frac{31.0 + 76.0 + 14.1 + 48.8}{4} \times 1600$$

$$= \frac{169.9}{4} \times 1600 = 67{,}960 \text{ cu. ft.}$$

$$\frac{67{,}960}{27} = 2{,}517 \text{ cu. yd.}$$

Figure 320-78 *Grid method* for estimating earth volume.

Estimating Required Grading Quantities:

Three methods are commonly used to prepare estimates of the quantities of grading needed. Each one is briefly discussed below on the assumption that the reader is already familiar with these general methods but needs to be reminded of the general procedures and formulas needed:

Grid or Borrow Pit Method:

The grid method is relatively simple, quick, and easy to use. It is useful for estimating the excavation of buildings, etc. This method provides a considerable degree of accuracy (Figure 320-78).

Average End-Area Method:

The average end-area method is commonly used to estimate volumes on linear elements, such as roads and highways. Cross sections are taken at 50- to 100-ft intervals perpendicular to the centerline. The simplest average end-area procedure is to average square-foot areas, multiply by the distance between them, and then, assuming that this results in a cubic-foot figure, divide by 27 to convert to cubic yards.

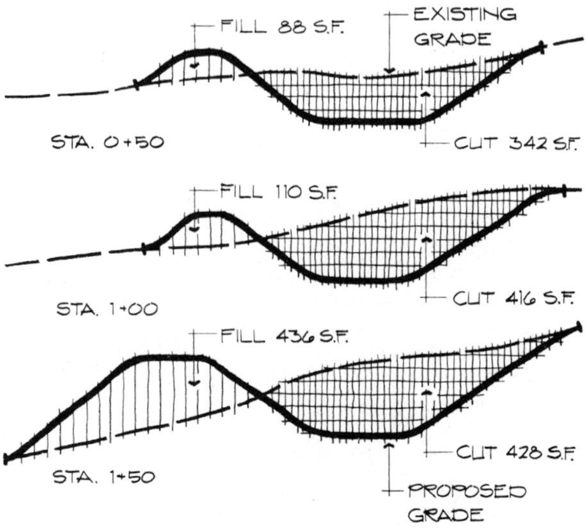
FILL 88 S.F.
EXISTING GRADE
STA. 0+50
CUT 342 S.F.
FILL 110 S.F.
STA. 1+00
CUT 416 S.F.
FILL 436 S.F.
STA. 1+50
CUT 428 S.F.
PROPOSED GRADE

Figure 320-79 Average End-Area Method for Estimating Earth Volume (Sample Problem). *Note:* Calculate taper to existing grade Station 0 to Station 50, and last station to the end of grading, by averaging.

Sample Problem (Figure 320-79):

Stations

$$0+00 \text{ to } 0+50: \frac{0+342}{2} \times 50 = 8550 \text{ ft}^3 \qquad \frac{0+88}{2} \times 50 = 2200 \text{ ft}^3$$

$$0+50 \text{ to } 1+00: \frac{342+416}{2} \times 50 = 18{,}950 \text{ ft}^3 \qquad \frac{88+110}{2} \times 50 = 4950 \text{ ft}^3$$

$$1+00 \text{ to } 1+50: \frac{416+428}{2} \times 50 = 21{,}100 \text{ ft}^3 \qquad \frac{110+436}{2} \times 50 = 13{,}650 \text{ ft}^3$$

$$1+50 \text{ to } 1+60: \frac{428+0}{2} \times 50 = 2140 \text{ ft}^3 \qquad \frac{436+0}{2} \times 10 = 2180 \text{ ft}^3$$

$$= \frac{50{,}740 \text{ ft}^3}{27} \qquad = \frac{22{,}980 \text{ ft}^3}{27}$$

$$= 1879 \text{ yd}^3 \qquad = 851 \text{ yd}^3$$

Contour Method:

This method, when combined with the summary sheet (Table 320-10), provides the following information:

1. Total area stripped
2. Topsoil stripped
3. Topsoil replaced (including shrinkage)
4. Subsoil removed
5. Subsoil replaced (including shrinkage)
6. Total area and volume of hardscape
7. Area for planting

This method is widely used by landscape architects because it is felt to be most accurate for making final adjustments to the grading and for preparing cost estimates. The step-by-step process for using the contour method is outlined below.

Step 1: Delineate the no-cut/no-fill zone throughout the entire project (Figure 320-80).

Step 2: Measure the total surface area of each cut or fill separately and enter this square-foot (square-meter) area on the appropriate line.

Step 3: With knowledge of the soil horizon, determine how much topsoil is to be stripped. Calculate the cubic-yard (cubic-meter) volume separately for each cut or fill area. Enter these figures in the summary chart on the appropriate *Cut* and *Fill* lines of Table 320-10.

Step 4: With a planimeter, measure the hardscape areas in the cut zone and the fill zone and enter the square-foot (square-meter) measurements under column *R* in the respective *Cut* and *Fill* lines.

Step 5: Calculate the volumes in cubic

TABLE 320-10
Planimeter Tabulation Form and Summary Sheet

Horizontal Scale ____________
Vertical Scale ____________
Contour Interval ____________

	Contour Number	First Reading	Second Reading	Corrected Reading	Area in ft^2
FILL					
CUT					

A = AREA of contour planes measured with planimeter

$$\frac{A_1}{3} + \frac{A_1 + A_2}{2} + \frac{A_2 + A_3}{2} + \text{Additional As Needed} + \frac{\text{A of last Reading}}{3} \times \frac{\text{Square of Scale}}{27} = \text{Volume } yd^3$$

Enter Total Area of All Cut ____________ Fill ____________
(Do not add above section areas - this is a separate planimeter reading)

SUMMARY

Areas	C yd^3	SC yd^3	F yd^3	SF yd^3	TS yd^3	R yd^3	R areas ft^2	TR yd^3	S ft^2
Cut			(shaded)	(shaded)					
Fill	(shaded)	(shaded)							
Sub. Total									
Shrinkage									
Total									

C = Cut
F = Fill
R = Roads, Sidewalks, etc.
S = Seeded Areas
SC = Subsoil Cut - C + R + TR - TS
SF = Subsoil Fill - F + TS - TR - R
TR = Topsoil Replaced

SOURCE: From Horst Schach, Department of Landscape Architecture, University of Kentucky, Lexington, Kentucky, 1983.

yards (cubic meters) for the portions in the cut and the fill zones and enter these volumes under *R* areas in the summary chart at the appropriate *Cut* and *Fill* lines.

Step 6: Subtract the *area* (under *R* areas) of the hardscape from the total area; this is done separately for the cut and the fill areas. Enter the resulting square feet (square meters) in column *S* (seeded area) at the lines appropriate for cut and fill (Figure 320-81).

Step 7: Determine the thickness to which the topsoil is to be replaced and calculate separately the required volumes for the cut and the fill areas found in Step 6. Enter the cubic-yard (cubic-meter) volumes in column TR (topsoil replaced) on the appropriate lines for cut and fill.

Step 8: Complete the upper chart of the work sheet. Coloring or shading the area between each existing and proposed contour line will aid in making the planimeter reading. In essence, this creates a visual section of each contour, thereby allowing the use of the average end-area formula to calculate gross volume.

Step 9: Calculate the gross cut and gross fill separately by using the formula below the chart. Enter the cubic yards (cubic meters) for the cut area under C (cut) on the *Cut* line. Enter the cubic-yard (cubic-meter) fill under *F* (fill) on the *Fill* line.

Step 10: Using the formula SC = $-C + R +$ TR $-$ TS, calculate the subsoil cut. Enter the cubic-yard (cubic-meter) cut in column SC (subsoil cut).

Step 11: Using the formula SF = $-F +$ TS $-$ TR $-R$, calculate the subsoil fill. Enter the cubic yards (cubic meters) under

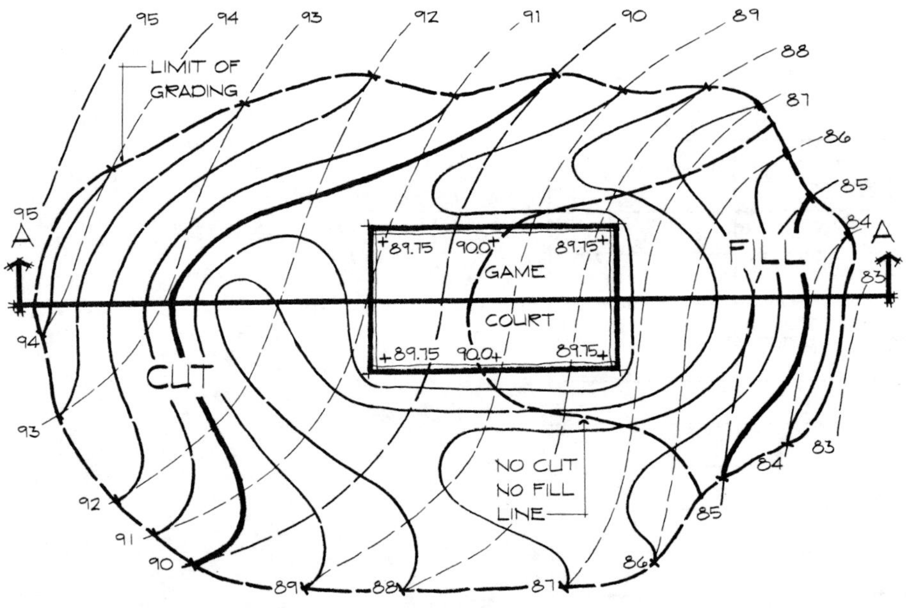
LIMIT OF GRADING
GAME
COURT
CUT
FILL
NO CUT NO FILL LINE
A
A

Figure 320-80 *Contour plan method* for estimating earth volume.

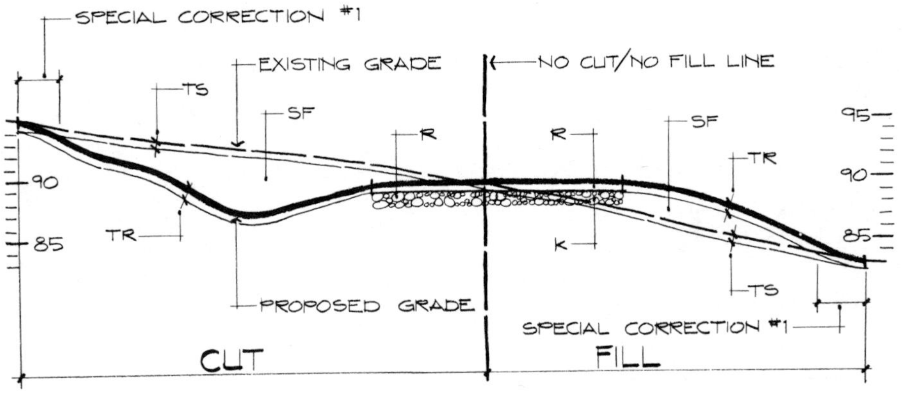
SPECIAL CORRECTION #1
EXISTING GRADE
NO CUT/NO FILL LINE
PROPOSED GRADE
CUT
FILL

Figure 320-81 Section for contour method.

column SF (subsoil fill) on the *Fill* line. (A negative answer can be interpreted as an indication that additional subsoil may need to be removed in order to make room for hardscape materials.)

Step 12: Complete the summary chart by adding the columns vertically and incorporating shrinkage factors where appropriate.

REFERENCES

Munson, Albe E. *Construction Design for Landscape Architects,* McGraw-Hill, New York, 1974.

Parker and MacGuire. *Simplified Site Engineering for Architects and Builders,* Wiley, New York, 1952.

Untermann, Richard K. *Grade Easy,* ASLA Foundation, Washington, DC, 1974.

Weddle, Arnold. *Techniques of Landscape Architecture,* Heinemann, London, 1979. ■

section 330: Site Drainage

CREDITS

Contributor:

Denise M. Dittmar
Denise M. Dittmar Landscape Architect
Plano, Texas

Reviewers:

James R. Robin
James Robin Landscape Architect
Excelsior, Minnesota

Nicholas T. Dines
University of Massachusetts/Amherst
Amherst, Massachusetts

CONTENTS

1.0 INTRODUCTION

1.1 General

Land development invariably alters the drainage pattern of preexisting landscapes. The effects are both local and off-site, sometimes adversely affecting downstream waters and land uses. It is commonly accepted practice that development should have a minimal impact on off-site drainage and that on-site drainage will respect or emulate natural drainage patterns whenever possible.

It is important that site drainage be perceived as a part of design rather than as a discrete aspect of site engineering, only functionally related to the concept of a design scheme. Strategies for the drainage of a site should be formulated during the process of design and strongly reinforce the spatial, visual, and functional concepts of the design. In this regard, all aspects of site engineering should be learned well enough to be employed integrally during the creative processes of design.

In most cases, any site drainage problem can be solved in a variety of ways. In recent years, a *soft* approach to the engineering of site drainage, with its accompanying advantages, has gained acceptance as a viable means for solving drainage problems. The "soft approach" typically means a minimum amount of engineering techniques and devices to achieve control and better use of runoff waters. The major advantages of a soft approach to site drainage problems include an improved match between design intent and constructed results and, in many cases, significant cost savings in both the short and the long term. When designed in conjunction with natural drainage techniques, conventional storm systems have been designed for smaller amounts of stormwater, thus freeing up money useful for other purposes. Designers should continually remain aware of the advances being made in various techniques of site drainage.

1.2 Functions of Site Drainage

Prevention of Flooding:

Conventional methods of drainage often attempt to remove runoff water as quickly as possible from a site, thus often causing problems of flooding both on- and off-site. Natural means of delay or interception by vegetation, temporary ponds, and infiltration can be used to minimize unnecessary concentrations of water, which can destroy both natural and built environments.

A primary purpose of site drainage is to prevent flooding or water damage to buildings and high-use areas by persistent water. Drainage is directed away from these areas and from circulation and other use areas for reasons of safety and usability, particularly in northern climates, where ice on pavements can be hazardous. Consequently, site planning often involves the direction of runoff to low areas, sometimes intentionally creating ponds or wetland areas. Low-use areas, such as recreational fields, can be programmed to accept temporary flooding.

The on-site delay of runoff is an effective technique for preventing flash flooding downstream and the sweep of pollutants into water systems. Although the runoff quantities may be greater after development, if released in a controlled manner over time, their impacts will be less. Many public agencies require that the rate of runoff after the land is developed should not exceed the prior runoff of the site.

Prevention of Erosion:

Erosion is a serious problem. It can undermine structures and paved areas, degrade the environmental and aesthetic attractions of planted areas, and clog downstream areas with excess sediment. Stream banks which have developed flash flood characteristics as a result of new grading should be protected by planting and other means of stabilization. Sediment at the source should be retained by means of sediment traps, sedimentation ponds, vegetative cover, and proper grading.

Minimization of Soil Swelling and Frost Heave:

Proper drainage techniques can prevent or minimize soil swelling and frost heave in certain subgrades and under paved or built structures. Infiltration can be drained away from these areas by the use of aggregate base courses, underdrains, and gravel. Soils of a site have to be analyzed for their drainage characteristics to determine which measures might be taken to solve existing problems.

Maintenance of High Water Quality:

The adverse impact of new development on natural hydrologic systems should be minimized as much as possible. Water tables should not be unduly influenced by drainage practices, and streams, lakes, and groundwater should be maintained as high as their normal levels.

Changes in drainage patterns can alter the amount of water available to plants by making some soils too wet or others too dry.

Sedimentation in streams should be minimized because it decreases flow capacity, increases the rate of flow moving downstream, and decreases the health of the stream by covering aquatic plants, covering fish spawning beds, and changing water depths.

Pollution of water by organic pollutants should be minimized. Nutrients from lawn fertilization and from an accumulation of decaying plants (e.g., lawn cuttings) can cause high concentrations of phosphorus and nitrogen in the water, resulting in algae blooms; these blooms degrade the quality of fish habitats and impact on other organisms necessary for stream health. Buffers between fertilized areas and streams can be used to minimize the problem. Areas of sandy soils with shallow underground water sources are susceptible to contamination by nitrogen from fertilization as well as from septic systems and leaky sewer pipes.

Sources such as parking lots and roads contribute toxic materials such as zinc, lead, manganese, and cadmium to waters, and these eventually accumulate in the food chain. Petroleum substances kill aquatic organisms by cutting off oxygen supplies. Chlorides from road salt also kill organisms and fish and cause water discoloration, gas formation, and unpleasant odors. Asbestos dust from brake linings is also washed into waters from roads and parking lots.

Strategies to handle such pollution problems include the use of vegetated buffer zones and of wetlands populated by plants which have the ability to remove organic as well as toxic substances from the water. Street cleaning removes dust and other particulates from paved surfaces before they reach the water system. Some atmospheric pollutants and airborne particulates can be trapped by trees and shrubs. Methods to counter pollution are most effective in combination with each other.

Groundwater Recharge:

Areas of aquifer recharge should be preserved in land development areas. Depletion of groundwater inhibits natural cleansing of water, dries up wells, drastically alters vegetation, and occasionally results in subsidence of the land. The promotion of recharge not only helps preserve the existing environment pattern, but facilitates easier management of runoff.

Protection of Wildlife Habitat:

An environmental benefit of preserving existing drainage patterns is the protection of wildlife habitat. Natural habitats are being adversely altered or destroyed by indiscriminate, poorly designed developments. Minimal disturbance of wildlife habitat should be part of any site development.

Creation of Amenity:

Natural habitats are a precious resource which should become or remain part of both city and regional parks. The creation of water bodies and other natural areas, for example, can become a visual amenity in built environments as well as provide other positive opportunities for design.

2.0 DESIGN CONSIDERATIONS

Drainage systems must respond to natural features and conditions, including climate, topography, soils, geology, hydrology, and vegetation, mainly because these factors determine the runoff characteristics of the site. Social factors such as land use, density of development, size of the site, and whether or not the drainage system will be part of a larger system must also be evaluated. Functional criteria have to be formulated for each land use, etc.

Table 330-1 illustrates the various factors that contribute to increasing amounts of runoff. Each of these factors is further discussed below.

2.1 Natural Features

Climate:

A climatic region is usually described in terms of temperature, moisture, and vegetation. World distribution of climatic types is shown in Figure 330-1.

Rainfall amounts per year in any one region will vary, but the type of rainfall must be described fully in order to understand

TABLE 330-1
Factors that Contribute to Increasing Amounts of Runoff

Gradient of increasing runoff →				
Duration of Storm:	1 hour			24 hours
Intensity of Storm:	2 years		10 years	100 years
Climate:	arid	temperate	semiarid	subtropical
Soil Texture:	sand		silt	clay
Topography:	flat		rolling	hilly
Land Use:	undeveloped land		medium density development	high density development

the characteristics of resultant runoff. In the temperate Pacific northwestern United States, for example, the amount of rainfall is high over time, but it is released continually in small showers. Runoff in natural areas of this region is usually minimal because of the interception of rainfall by plants and the ability of the soil to absorb water. By contrast, the arid southwestern region of the United States has infrequent rainfall, but when storms do occur, they produce large amounts of runoff with little infiltration.

The design of site drainage systems will vary in different climatic regions not only because of runoff quantity, but also because of other climatic factors, such as humidity and the consequent rate of evaporation.

Soil and Topography:

Runoff is affected by soil texture and topography, including watershed characteristics.

Where infiltration is low to begin with, development will have a smaller impact on runoff than it would have on more-pervious areas. Consequently, in more-impervious areas, fewer measures (such as runoff detention) have to be taken to meet pre-development rates.

Since site design usually affects a watershed, the site's location within the watershed will influence drainage design decisions. Therefore, site planning should be coordinated within a comprehensive watershed strategy. Lower lands, for instance, accept water from higher ground in addition to receiving rainfall directly.

Regional public agencies often set up watershed policies to influence site planning solutions. For example, lower lands are often made to discharge runoff without delay, while upland areas are designed to discharge runoff at controlled, reduced rates. By the time the water from upstream reaches the bottom of the watershed, that water can be sent on with no flooding. It has been found, however, that problems result when *all* sites contribute in a delayed manner. Comprehensive strategies must therefore be formulated.

Bedrock and Water Table:

The depth to bedrock and the level of the water table also influence design strategies for site drainage. Infiltration is typically greater, the greater the depth to bedrock or to the water table. Surface ponding and delay techniques are two possible strategies to use when a site is limited by shallow depths to bedrock or water table.

2.2 Social Factors

Land Use:

Certain land uses significantly increase the runoff on a site. The amount of impervious surface becomes greater with increased urbanization, thereby reducing infiltration and the intercepting action of vegetation. Greater densities therefore require more complex strategies and greater investments in site drainage.

Because dense urban areas have little land for the detention or infiltration of water, drainage techniques that require little space have to be considered. One technique to delay runoff is to use vegetation, whether in the form of street trees, parks, or rooftop gardens.

Site Size:

Site size influences the extent to which a drainage system can be shared by more than one site. A planned unit development often has one or more detention or recharge areas for all units on the site. These areas will be located in the lowest portion of the development and make use of natural drainage patterns to direct runoff to them.

2.3 Functional Criteria

Functional criteria have to be established for all land uses, surfaces, etc., including percolation rates, minimum and maximum slopes for drainage away from buildings and walkways, drainage times, and the like. Ordinances often exist which have to be adhered to in land development projects.

3.0 DESIGN PROCEDURE

Three major steps taken prior to any drainage calculations are: (1) site analysis, (2) determination of performance criteria, and (3) selection of management techniques. Figure 330-2 illustrates the design procedure flow chart.

3.1 Site Analysis

General:

The design of site drainage systems involves the gathering of certain types of information as determinants in the decision-making process. If a site is large and/or complex, such information is best represented in map form.

Site Determinants:

Soils: In the United States, information about soil types is usually available from a county soil conservation service survey. These surveys have soils mapped on aerial photos with complete descriptions about soil type, drainage characteristics, average depth to water table, and depth to bedrock. They also include descriptions of the geology of the region. The accuracy of all such surveys should be field-verified. A soil report done by a soil scientist is often necessary as part of the development process. Test pits can verify information about the seasonal levels of a water table.

Land Cover: Land cover conditions should be mapped, since they are required for runoff calculations. Vegetated areas and types should be noted, as well as any paved or roofed surfaces.

Drainage Patterns: Natural drainage patterns should be mapped by marking swale directions and watershed divides on a plan. Areas of standing water should be noted.

It is important to determine whether or not a site or part of a site lies within a

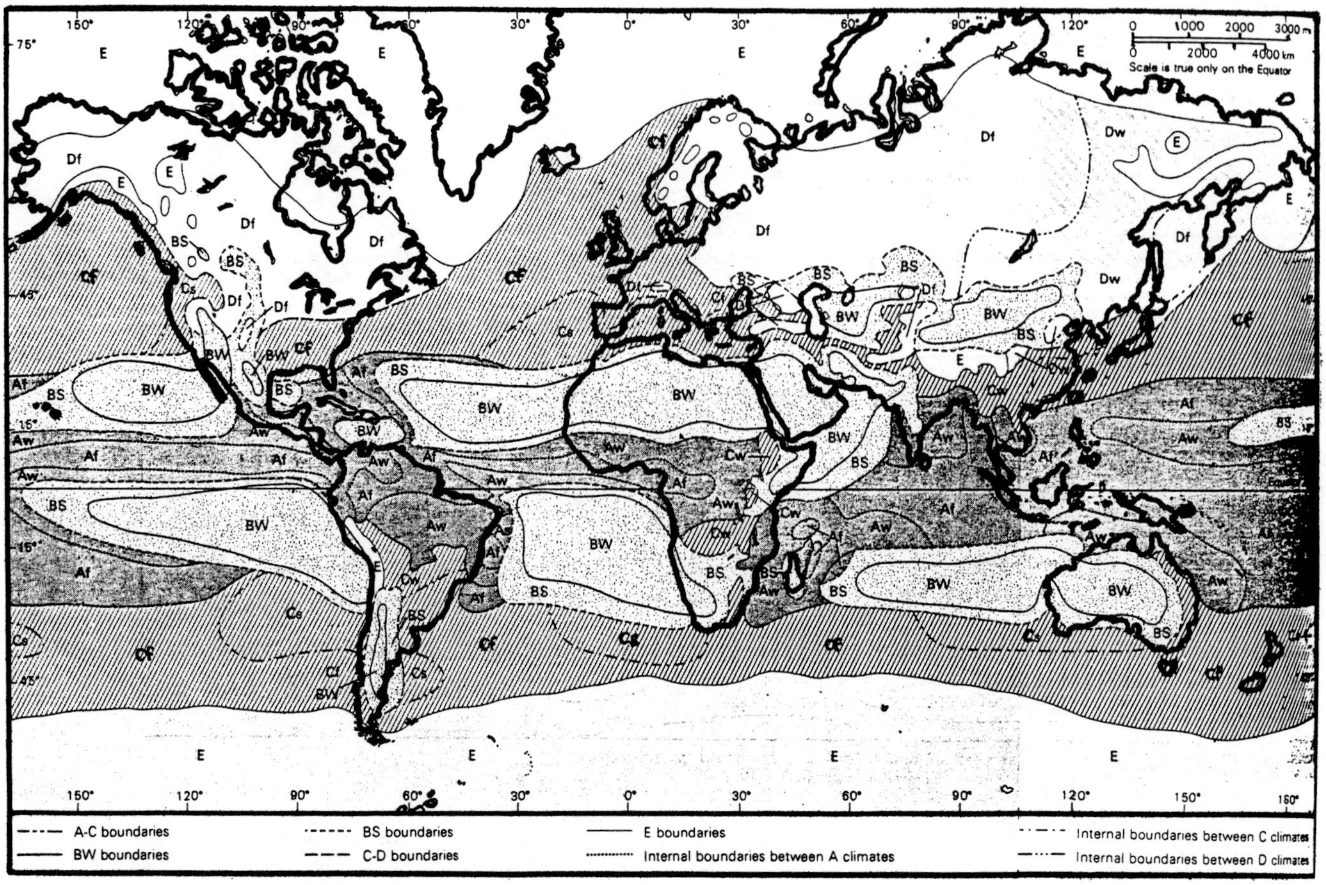
0 1000 2000 3000 mi
0 2000 4000 km
Scale is true only on the Equator
A-C boundaries
BW boundaries
BS boundaries
C-D boundaries
E boundaries
Internal boundaries between A climates
Internal boundaries between C climates
Internal boundaries between D climates

Figure 330-1 World distribution of climatic types (Koppen system).

In this system, A stands for equatorial and tropical rain climates, B for the dry climates of the arid zone, C for temperate climates of the mainly broad-leafed forest zone, D for the colder temperate forest climates, and E for treeless polar climates. The boundaries and subdivisions have been defined by climate values that appear to limit the characteristic species of vegetation. The notation is as follows:

A average temperature of every month above 18° C (64° F).

B average rainfall for the year (R) is
- (a) less than $2T + 28$ where summer is the rainiest season
- (b) less than $2T + 14$ where the rainfall is fairly uniform throughout the year
- (c) less than $2T$ where winter is the rainiest season.

In these formulas T is the average temperature over the year in ° C.

C average temperature of the coldest month in the range 18° C (64° F) to −3° C (27° F); warmest month in no case below 10° C (50° F).

D average temperature of the coldest month below −3° C (27° F); warmest month in no case below 10° C (50° F).

E average temperature of every month below 10° C (50° F).

s dry season in summer.
w dry season in winter.
f all seasons moist.

Af—the driest month must have 60 millimetres (2.4 inches) or more of rain.

Aw—the driest month has less than 60 millimetres rain and the year's total rainfall fails to make up for the deficiency.

(**Af** produces rain forest; **Aw** produces savanna, a vegetation that is largely grassland with a few trees.)

BS—the average yearly rainfall (R) exceeds $T + 14$ in areas with summer rainfall, is between this figure and $T + 7$ where the rains are spread over the year, and is between this value and $R = T$ in areas with mainly winter rainfall.

(The **S** stands for steppe or savanna; these climates produce grassland or bush.)

BW—in these climates R is less than $T + 14$ where summer is the rain season, under $T + 7$ where the rains are spread over the year, and less than T where winter is the rain season.

(The **W** stands for desert wastes.)

Cs—in these climates the wettest month comes in winter and has over three times the rainfall of the driest (summer) month.

Cw—in these climates the wettest month comes in summer and has more than ten times the rainfall of the driest (winter) month.

Cs climates produce broad-leafed evergreen forest; **Cw** produces the evergreen forests of the mountain heights in the **Aw** zone and hardly occurs anywhere else.)

Dw—the wettest month comes in summer and provides more than ten times the water equivalent of the total downput of rain and snow in the driest (winter) month. The milder **D** climates go with deciduous, broad-leafed forest, the colder **D** climates with needle-tree forest. **D** climates are only found in the great continents of the northern hemisphere.

floodplain. Insurance flood maps or regional water authorities usually have flood line information. There will usually be restrictions on development (in terms of type, special precautions, etc.) if the site lies completely or partially within a floodplain. Appropriate city or government agencies should be contacted to find out what information is necessary and what strategies are acceptable to these agencies.

Topography: Topographic analyses can be done by mapping the steepness of slopes. Mapping these characteristics in conjunction wtih the aforementioned information will help determine the design type and layout of a drainage system on a site.

3.2 Performance Criteria

The agencies responsible for approval of storm drainage design usually have specific requirements for project performance. Requirements include detention/retention criteria, where discharge may be directed, which design storm to use in a swale or storm pipe, and specifications for drainage structures. A design storm is typically the expected peak intensity, duration, and frequency of rainfall or snowfall, as for instance a 10, 20, or 100 year storm in a particular region. Typically, local agencies are responsible for coordinating a watershed management plan for a region with the implications for development within it.

Submittal of a plan to a government agency usually requires a drainage and grading plan, calculations showing runoff amounts and rates, and detention/retention amounts. The materials to be used and the location of structures also have to be specified. The use of nonconventional construction techniques, such as a trench drain, may be acceptable if proper documentation is provided. Often government agencies advocate the use of alternative management techniques if the result would be a healthier watershed.

3.3 Selection of Management Techniques

Designers usually have a number of alternatives at their disposal when deciding on management techniques for a site. A range of techniques has been developed for slowing runoff, providing detention or retention, and encouraging infiltration or recharge. When runoff leaves the site, it will conform to the method prevailing in any particular region or neighborhood; typically, this is as an underground storm sewer system or as an overland discharge system to a swale or stream.

Site analyses and performance criteria will provide the information necessary to help determine the management technique(s) most appropriate for the proposed development. Table 330-2 is a decision tree for use in determining possible solutions to any given situation. Higher densities of development will limit choices because land will not be available for space consuming techniques. In medium- to low-density developments, natural factors influence drainage strategies.

4.0 DRAINAGE TECHNIQUES AND DEVICES

The techniques described here will be presented in order of closeness to the source of runoff. Those listed first intercept rainfall and immediately deal with the resultant runoff. The later techniques accept runoff from distant areas of the site to be managed at a common collection point. Devices required for more conventional techniques are described last.

4.1 Rooftop Systems

In urban settings, the roofs of buildings (particularly flat roofs) provide an opportunity to detain and even eliminate runoff that would normally be quickly discharged. Roofs designed for high snow loads can sometimes accommodate the added weight of detained water. Maintenance of rooftop systems is very important to ensure that drains do not become clogged and that roof membranes do not remain submerged or become saturated.

Garden Rooftop:

Figure 330-3 illustrates soil beds and the drainage from plantings on a flat roof. Underdrainage is required to discharge excess runoff, once the soil is saturated. The advantages of plantings are direct interception of rainfall, soil infiltration, and loss of water due to evapotranspiration.

Rooftop Delay:

A delay of runoff is achieved by using structural means to impede immediate runoff on flat or sloped roofs. On a flat roof, discharge is controlled for a design storm but a floodway is provided for larger-storm runoff, once capacity is reached (Figure 330-4). Roof roughness (i.e., ripples or gravel on a flat roof) is another technique which can be useful for small design storms. On a sloped roof, small fin dams can be used (Figure 330-5).

4.2 Trench Drain

Trench drains can be used to intercept sheet runoff near the source (Figure 330-6). These drains can be used in high- to low-density developments. The higher densities and less well-drained soils will require an underdrain. Well-drained medium-density sites may be able to absorb a greater degree of runoff, allowing the top of the drain to act as a swale for the larger design storms. The depth to bedrock and water table should be greater than 3½ ft (1.1 m).

A trench drain is typically constructed with a base layer of crushed stone which may or may not surround a perforated pipe serving as an underdrain. It is then covered with coarse sand and finished with a surface of pavers, gravel, grass, or a grate. A longitudinal fall along the surface lets the drain act as an infiltration swale.

The advantages of trench drains include: (1) possible recharge to the groundwater, (2) reduction in later system size, and (3) an increased amount of available soil moisture for plants in paved areas. Cost considerations include: (1) high maintenance of the surface (to prevent clogging by debris), (2) possible pollution of groundwater by substances from paved surfaces, and (3) a possibly higher cost of materials than for a straight conventional system.

Trench drains are most useful near paved surfaces or at the edge of gutterless

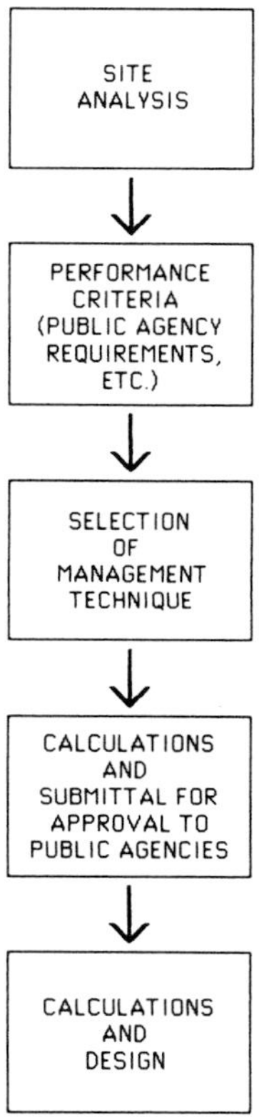
SITE ANALYSIS
PERFORMANCE CRITERIA (PUBLIC AGENCY REQUIREMENTS, ETC.)
SELECTION OF MANAGEMENT TECHNIQUE
CALCULATIONS AND SUBMITTAL FOR APPROVAL TO PUBLIC AGENCIES
CALCULATIONS AND DESIGN

Figure 330-2 Design procedure flowchart.

TABLE 330-2
Decision Tree for the Selection of Management Techniques

Development site (Residential) (Industrial) (Commercial) (Institutional)

High to medium density urban-suburban little/no open space

LOCATON	DRAINAGE TECHNIQUES
basement	roor
roof	cistern
paved surfaces	trench drain porous paving parking storage

Medium to low density suburban-rural larger open space

SOIL TYPE	BEDROCK AND WATER TABLE	TOPOGRAPHY	DRAINAGE TECHNIQUES	
well drained	low	flat	trench drain porous pavement vegetation seepage area tile and pipe	seepage pit seepage basin well pond sedimentation basin
		rolling	trench drain vegetation tile seepage pit	seepage basin well pond sedimentation basin
		steep	trench drain vegetation well	pond sedimentation basin
	high	flat	porous pavement vegetation	pond sedimentation basin
		rolling/steep	vegetation pond	sedimentation basin
moderately well drained	low	flat	porous pavement vegetation tile and pipe seepage area	seepage basin well pond sedimentation basin
		rolling	vegetation tile and pipe seepage basin	well pond sedimentation basin
		steep	vegetation well	pond sedimentation basin
	high	flat	porous pavement vegetation	pond sedimentation basin
		rolling/steep	vegetation pond	pond sedimentation basin
somewhat poorly to poorly drained	low	any	vegetation well	pond sedimentation basin
	high	any	vegetation	pond sedimentation basin

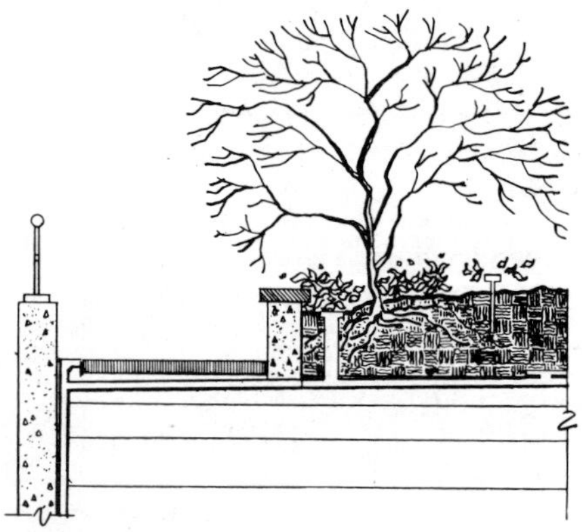

Figure 330-3 Section of rooftop drain.

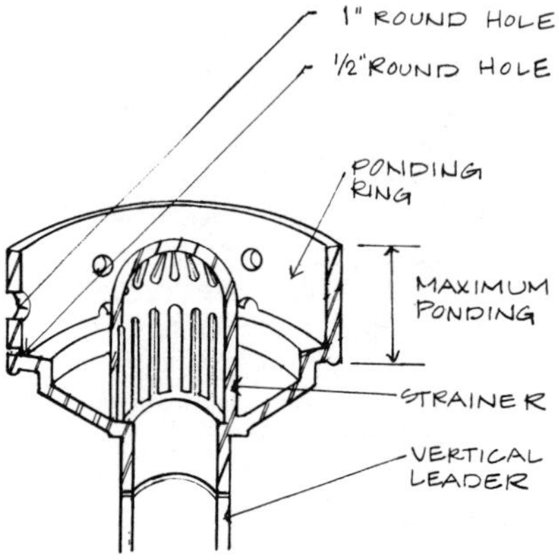
1" ROUND HOLE
1/2" ROUND HOLE
PONDING RING
MAXIMUM PONDING
STRAINER
VERTICAL LEADER

Figure 330-4 Typical rooftop delay control device.

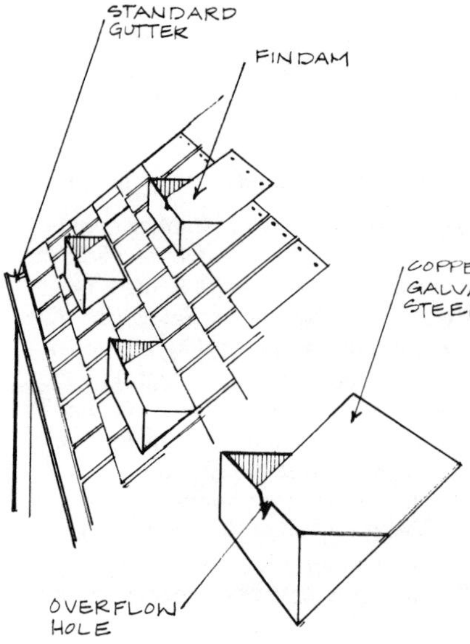
STANDARD GUTTER
FIN DAM
COPPER OR GALVANIZED STEEL
OVERFLOW HOLE

Figure 330-5 Typical fin dam.

roofs. They can be used near playing fields or other areas that generate runoff and have too little room for a detention pond.

4.3 Porous Paving

While development will increase the amount of paving and thus the amount of runoff, the impact may be diminished if that surface is not totally impervious. There are various paving techniques that permit infiltration and affect runoff at the source (Figure 330-7).

Gravel:

Gravel surfaces will slow runoff by virtue of their rough texture and by infiltration. Gravel is useful for driveways, small sitting areas, and walkways.

Modular Paving:

Infiltration is possible when pavers are unmortared and set on a sand or gravel base course or on risers. Possible frost heaving would necessitate periodic resetting of the pavers or a more efficient subdrainage system.

Asphalt Porous Paving:

Porous asphalt paving is a very versatile material, consisting of a pervious asphalt covering and a specially designed crushed stone bed, permitting infiltration and underdrainage. Runoff may be intercepted at the source or directed to this surface after concentration for detention and recharge. Sites using this technique may be high- to low-density and include driveways, parking lots, minor roads, and basketball courts. The depth to bedrock and water table should be greater than 3½ ft (1.1 m). Well-drained soils are appropriate; moderately well drained soils may require an underdrain.

The advantages of porous paving include: (1) recharge, (2) minimal use or elimination of a conventional system, (3) improved soil moisture for vegetation near paved surfaces, and (4) moderate cost. The disadvantages include: (1) the necessity for maintenance to remove debris and sediment which would clog pores and (2) the inability of asphalt paving to function efficiently under certain freezing and melting conditions, thus causing surface ponding.

4.4 Vegetation

Plant material is useful in stormwater management in several ways.

Woody Vegetated Strips:

The use of floodplain or wetland trees and shrubs in or at the edge of depressions and

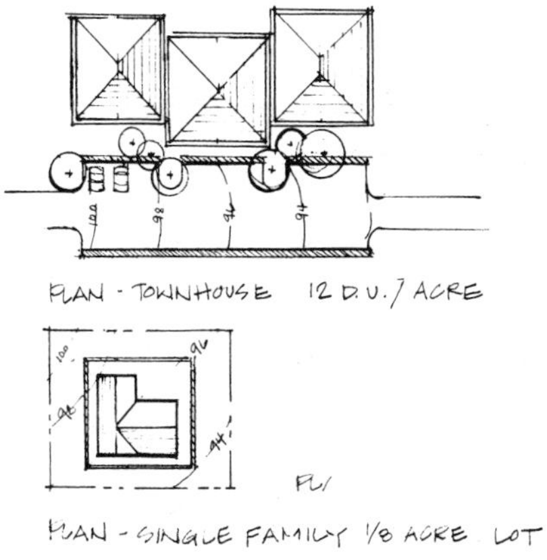
PLAN - TOWNHOUSE 12 D.U./ACRE
PLAN - SINGLE FAMILY 1/8 ACRE LOT

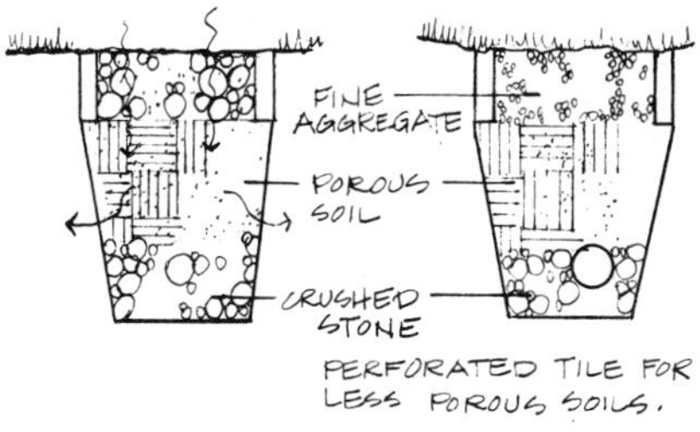
FINE AGGREGATE
POROUS SOIL
CRUSHED STONE
PERFORATED TILE FOR LESS POROUS SOILS.

Figure 330-6 Typical trench drain.

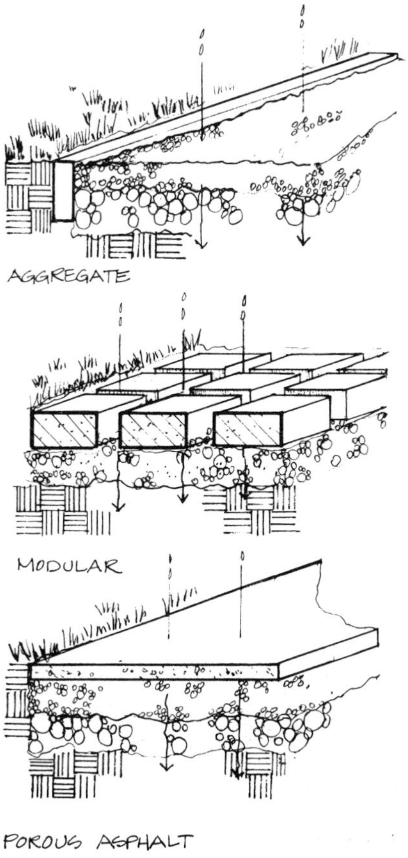
AGGREGATE
MODULAR
POROUS ASPHALT

Figure 330-7 Types of porous paving.

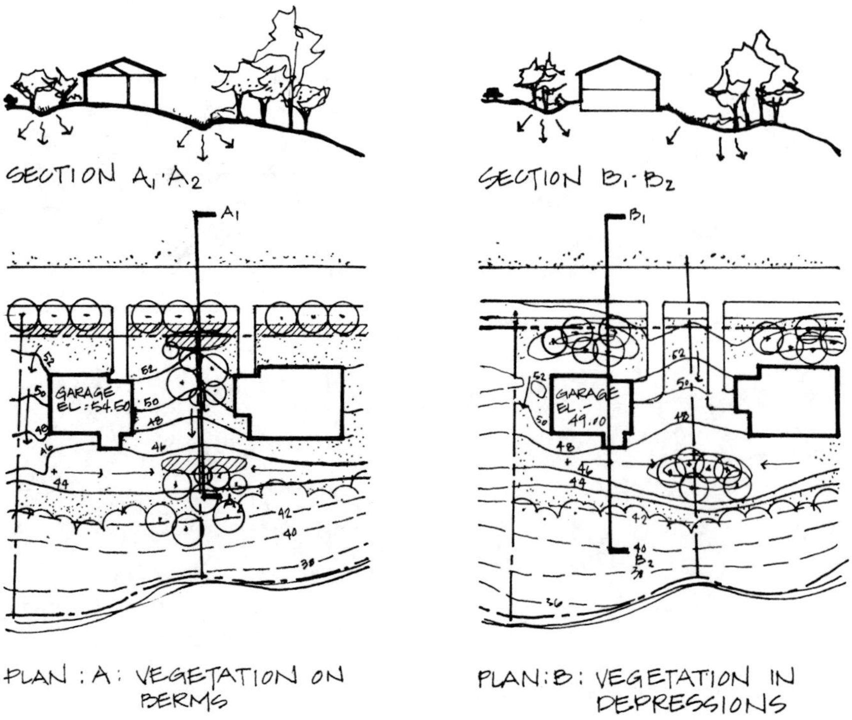
SECTION A1-A2
SECTION B1-B2
GARAGE EL: 54.50
GARAGE EL 49.00
PLAN: A: VEGETATION ON BERMS
PLAN: B: VEGETATION IN DEPRESSIONS

Figure 330-8 Woody vegetated strips.

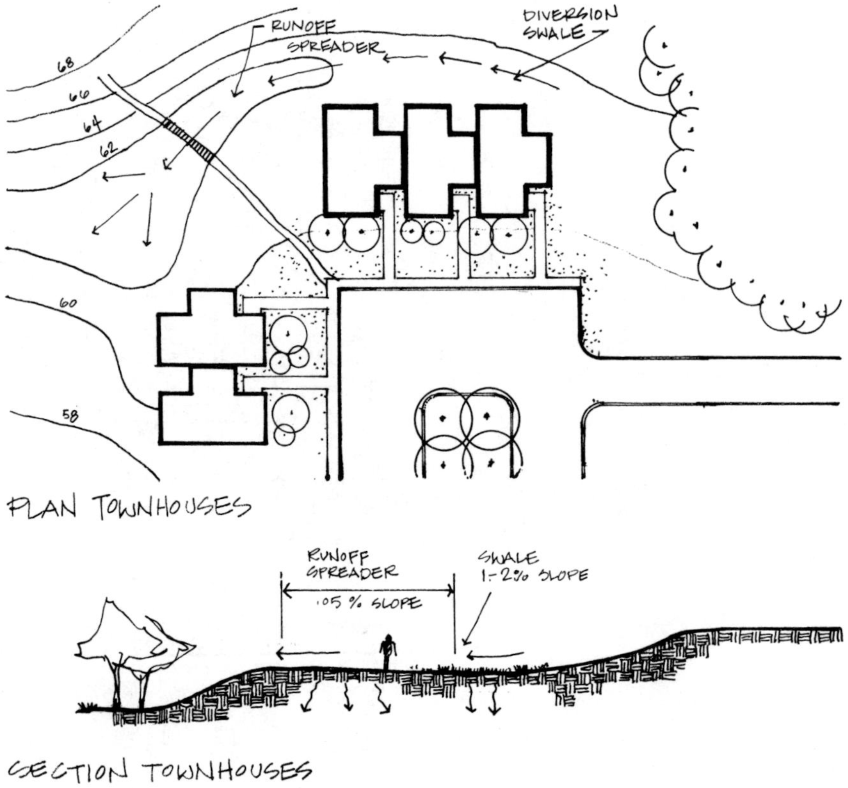
RUNOFF SPREADER
DIVERSION SWALE
PLAN TOWNHOUSES
RUNOFF SPREADER
SWALE 1-2% SLOPE
.05 % SLOPE
SECTION TOWNHOUSES

Figure 330-9 Runoff spreader.

swales can impede runoff and facilitate a greater degree of infiltration. Figure 330-8 shows examples of a single-family residential property without a conventional storm sewer. The series of swales, depressions, berms, and plantings are part of a system which can extend over an entire development.

Planting on berms, where stormwater would enter or leave as in a floodway, allows the planting to slow the runoff and act as a filter. Planting in depressions or swales also slows runoff. Plants also stabilize the area being inundated against erosion and improve the environmental quality of an area by providing wildlife habitat and filters for sediment.

Grass Areas/Swales:

Grass areas through which drainage is directed will slow runoff and facilitate a greater degree of infiltration. The choice of grasses with a high degree of roughness will increase the delay effect.

A low-velocity swale outlet can be specially designed to convert preconcentrated runoff to sheet flow. The *spreader* should have a shallow slope where water will slow and soak into the ground (Figure 330-9). Soils should be highly to moderately well drained and not highly erodible.

The length of the spreader can be calculated by estimating the inflowing quantity of runoff (*Q*) in terms of cubic feet per second or cubic meters per second by using Table 330-3. The lip of the spreader, over which water will flow, may have to be protected by fiberglass matting running the length of the spreader, as shown in Figure 330-10. The lip level must be graded to ensure sheet flow.

Another infiltration inducing area is a terrace, which is often covered with grass and periodically mowed. A *terrace* is an earth embankment forming a channel and ridge which is constructed across-slope (Figure 330-11). It serves as a diversion or swale impoundment for sheet flow coming downslope. In highly permeable soils with low to moderate rainfall [not to exceed 25 to 30 in (65 to 75 cm) per year] the terrace channel and ridge may be level to impound runoff for infiltration. In other situations the channel has a gradient to transport a larger portion of the runoff to an outlet. These channels are designed like swales (Figure 330-11).

Figure 330-11 illustrates a diversion terrace and a level spreader dispersing runoff to a woodland area.

Seepage Area:

A major vegetated area, often lawn, can accept runoff from other areas and temporarily impound it until considerable recharge occurs. As in other methods, a

TABLE 330-3
Spreader Length Chart

Designed Q, ft³/s	*Minimum length, L/ft*
less than 10	15
11–20	20
21–30	26
31–40	36
41–50	44

Source: From J. Toby Tourbier and Richard Westmacott, *Water Resources Protection Technology*, Urban Land Institute, Washington, D.C., 1981.

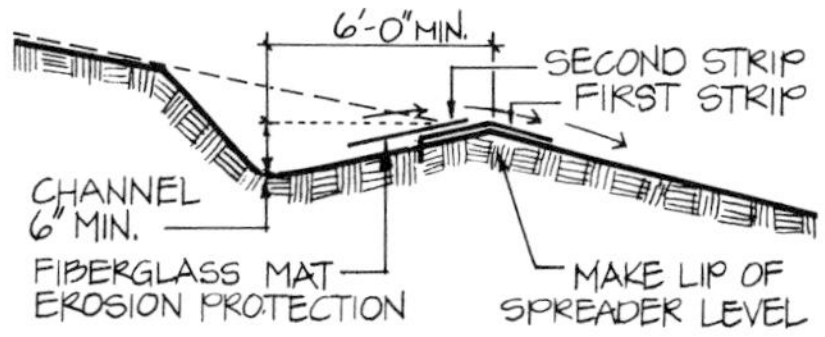
6'-0" MIN.
SECOND STRIP
FIRST STRIP
CHANNEL
6" MIN.
FIBERGLASS MAT
EROSION PROTECTION
MAKE LIP OF
SPREADER LEVEL

Figure 330-10 Construction of a level spreader.

DIVERSION TERRACE
COMPACTED EARTH SPREADER BERM, SEEDED AND MOWN
LEVEL LIP OF SPREADER ON UNDISTURBED GROUND.
SPREADER IN CUT ONLY

Figure 330-11 Terrace and level spreader.

floodway for runoff from excessively intense storms is also designed as part of the scheme.

Ideally, the seepage area is part of an open-space system in a recreational facility or medium-density site. The soil must be well-drained, with the bedrock and water table at least 5 ft (1.5 m) below the surface. Underdrainage may be required. Figure 330-12 shows the design of a wetland depression in a single-family development. The seepage area and overland swales replace a conventional storm sewer system.

Maintenance is required to remove sediment prior to discharge by filter berms, sediment traps, or basins. The system has the ability to be multiuse (such as a playing field), but other uses may cause compaction and thus reduce infiltration. Continued maintenance is then necessary in order to maintain adequate porosity. The second function cannot be in use after a rainfall.

4.5 Concentrated Underground Infiltration

Techniques are available which accept concentrated runoff and, by means of an underground system, discharge it directly into subsoil or bedrock. For such methods to work, the subsoil must be well-drained or the bedrock highly permeable. In these methods, the advantage of filtration through topsoil is not present.

Tile Field:

An underground field of perforated pipes (i.e., tiles) can be used to infiltrate water directly into subsoil. Abandoned septic systems have been converted for such purposes. Tile fields are typically covered with lawn or shallow-rooted plants. Figure 330-13 shows the layout of a typical field; the water enters a sedimentation basin before being discharged into the system. If sediment were allowed into the tile system, it would eventually clog the system and render it ineffective.

The topography for tile fields should be fairly flat, with the bedrock and water table at least 5 ft (1.5 m) below the surface. Well-drained soils are ideal, but moderately well drained soils are adequate if the trenches are gravel-filled (Figure 330-13).

Maintenance is required to prevent siltation, although tiles can be wrapped with filter fabric to minimize the problem. Tile fields have the advantage of promoting groundwater recharge.

Perforated Corrugated Steel Pipe:

PCS pipe can be used in an underground large-diameter pipe network through which runoff from large areas is sent for recharge and detention. Soils should be highly to moderately well drained, with the bedrock and water table at least 5 ft (1.5 m) below the pipe limit. The use of PCS pipe is particularly appropriate in an aquifer recharge area, with careful monitoring of water quality. The disadvantages and advantages are the same as with the tile drain system.

Cistern:

The underground containment of stormwater runoff can allow either reuse of the water or slow discharge. Cisterns have the greatest application in arid regions. Water is often used for residential irrigation and fire safety. Cisterns are also useful in high-density areas with underground storage space for temporary retention. Sediment should be removed prior to storage.

Seepage Pit:

A seepage pit consists of a deep, crushed stone bed, over which concentrated runoff is directed and allowed to recharge. Figure 330-14 shows an example where drains from the roof and parking lot of a buiding are directed across the surface of a recharge area. Water for the design storm will infiltrate while larger discharges continue along the floodway swale. The crushed stone berm allows seepage overflow before capacity is reached during intense storms in order to have the maximum benefit in reducing flood peaks. A filter blanket around the crushed stone minimizes chances of clogging. Alternatively, a sediment trap can be used.

Seepage pits are typically less than 10 ft (3 m) deep and must be located on well-drained soils, with the bedrock and water table no less than 40 in (1 m) from the bottom of the pit. Slopes should not exceed 20 percent. Seepage pits are advantageous on sites with limited surface detention capacity. Maintenance or periodic replacement of the silt-removal system is necessary for the continued effectiveness of a seepage pit.

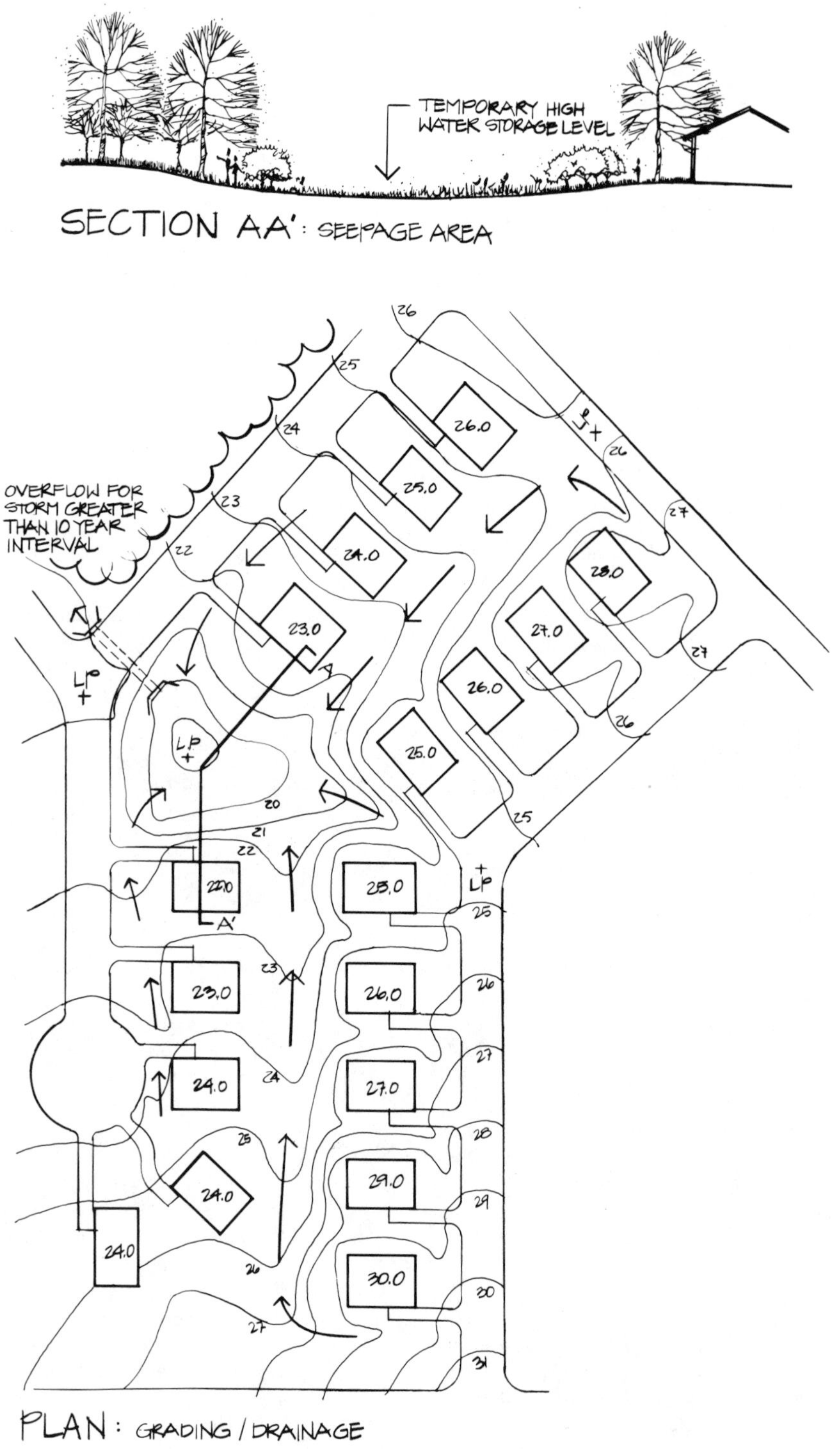
TEMPORARY HIGH WATER STORAGE LEVEL
SECTION AA': SEEPAGE AREA
OVERFLOW FOR STORM GREATER THAN 10 YEAR INTERVAL
LP
A
A'
PLAN: GRADING / DRAINAGE

Figure 330-12 Design of a seepage area. Ten-year design storm, temperate climate, sandy soil, calculated using the *rational formula*.

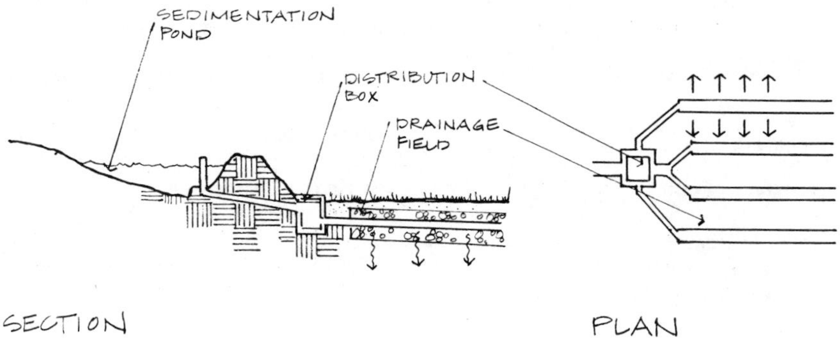
SEDIMENTATION POND
DISTRIBUTION BOX
DRAINAGE FIELD
SECTION
PLAN

Figure 330-13 Tile field.

Wells and Shafts:

Under suitable conditions, a vertical shaft into the subsurface of the ground can allow direct recharge from concentrated runoff. The bedrock and water table must not be shallow, however. This technique is useful when impervious or poorly drained soils or strata exist over porous strata. Filters may have to be installed at the top of the well to minimize clogging. Wells are usually less than 3 ft (1 m) in diameter, and shafts are larger in diameter. Shafts may be backfilled with porous material for filtering purposes.

Small-diameter shallow holes have shown promise as recharge devices. Because their installation costs are low, holes can be easily rebored or new holes dug if they fail.

Induced Infiltration by Groundwater Extraction:

This technique is useful where groundwater quality is high and surface water quality is low, as is the case in many river valleys. The result of pumping groundwater close to the recharge point is that a cone of depression in the water table induces infiltration from the ground surface (Figure 330-15). This infiltration of surface water improves its water quality so that it is suitable for human use.

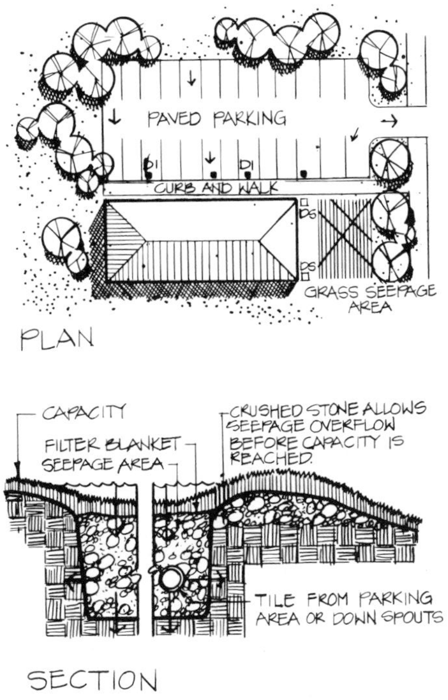
PAVED PARKING
DI
DI
CURB AND WALK
DS
DS
GRASS SEEPAGE AREA
PLAN
CAPACITY
FILTER BLANKET
SEEPAGE AREA
CRUSHED STONE ALLOWS SEEPAGE OVERFLOW BEFORE CAPACITY IS REACHED
TILE FROM PARKING AREA OR DOWN SPOUTS
SECTION

Figure 330-14 Typical seepage pit.

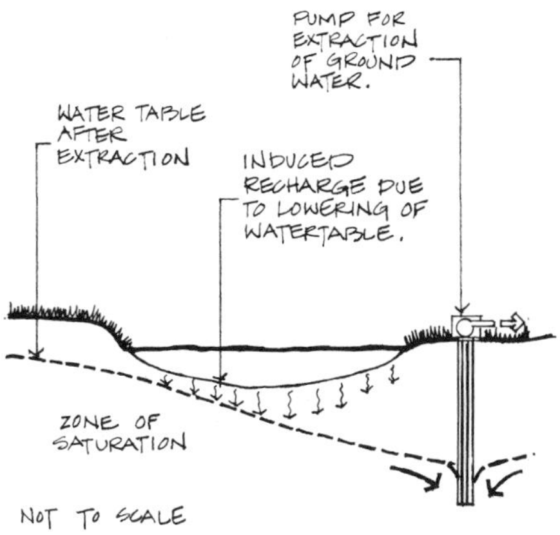
PUMP FOR EXTRACTION OF GROUND WATER.
WATER TABLE AFTER EXTRACTION
INDUCED RECHARGE DUE TO LOWERING OF WATERTABLE.
ZONE OF SATURATION
NOT TO SCALE

Figure 330-15 Induced infiltration by groundwater extraction.

4.6 Ponding

Concentrated runoff, directed to a holding pond or facility, can be impounded temporarily until infiltration or a slow rate of release is achieved. Detention is designed for a particular storm intensity or runoff rate, and all systems have emergency floodways.

Seepage Basin:

Seepage basins differ from seepage areas in that they hold a permanent body of water. Basins have regions which become impounded during rainfall, allowing infiltration for design storms.

Soils must be highly to moderately well drained, with the bedrock and water table at least 48 in (1.2 m) below the surface. These basins are principally used in aquifer recharge areas.

With the recharge regions surrounding it, these permanent ponds can function as a recreational amenity for nearby communities. Figure 330-16 shows a pond and basin as a part of a residential development.

Little or no conventional sewer system is required when using this technique. Sediment must be removed prior to entry and adequate porosity maintained by boring seep holes in the recharge area.

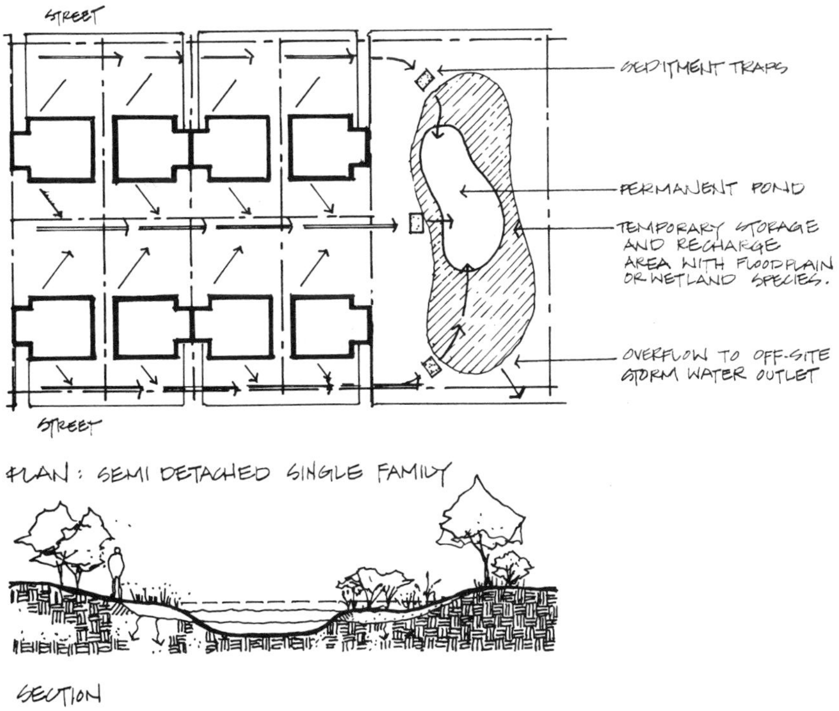
STREET
SEDIMENT TRAPS
PERMANENT POND
TEMPORARY STORAGE AND RECHARGE AREA WITH FLOODPLAIN OR WETLAND SPECIES.
OVERFLOW TO OFF-SITE STORM WATER OUTLET
STREET
PLAN : SEMI DETACHED SINGLE FAMILY
SECTION

Figure 330-16 Design of a typical seepage basin. Runoff calculations by *rational formula.*

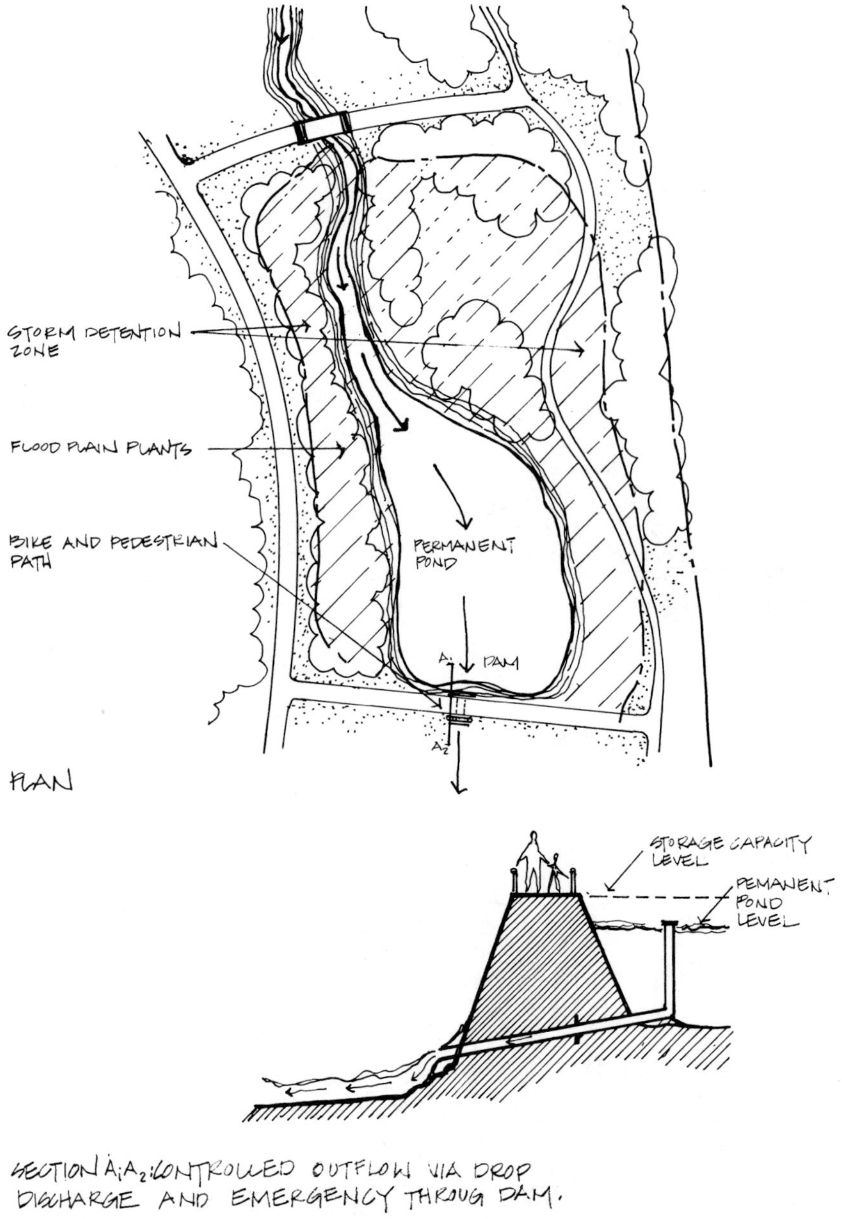
STORM DETENTION ZONE
FLOOD PLAIN PLANTS
BIKE AND PEDESTRIAN PATH
PERMANENT POND
DAM
PLAN
STORAGE CAPACITY LEVEL
PERMANENT POND LEVEL
SECTION A1A2: CONTROLLED OUTFLOW VIA DROP DISCHARGE AND EMERGENCY THROUG DAM.

Figure 330-17 Design of a typical detention pond.

Detention Pond:

Concentrated runoff can be directed to a pond where it is stored temporarily by means of a limited outflow device. A permanent pond with a design storm detention zone is often used for this purpose (Figure 330-17). The pond is usually located on a drainage way and can be part of an open-space system.

Detention ponds offer opportunities for fishing, boating, and skating, and their shores can become picnic and hiking sites. The shores may become temporarily inundated after heavy rainfalls. Detention ponds can function as habitat for wildlife, although mosquito control, eutrophication, and concerns of safety may require careful monitoring. Siltation of detention ponds should be minimized upstream by some means (e.g., a sedimentation pond). Periodic dredging of the pond may be necessary.

Sedimentation Pond:

The primary purpose of a sedimentation pond is to accept and impound concentrated runoff so that sediments can settle out of the water (Figure 330-18). Ponds are usually located along drainage ways and (in the sequence of flow) are used prior to other systems, such as detention ponds or seepage basins. The periodic removal of collected debris and sediment is usually necessary. Sedimentation ponds may be ecologically poor in comparison with detention ponds because aquatic organisms are overcome by sediment.

Paved Storage:

An impervious paved area can be used to accumulate or receive runoff, impound it temporarily, and then release it by means of a limited outflow device. Figure 330-19 shows the allowed detention in a parking lot. The depth of water is never permitted to be greater than 8 in (200 mm); otherwise, damage to automobiles and hazards to pedestrians could result.

The multipurpose use of a paved area can increase its value. Stormwater sewer systems can be downsized to accept a design storm only, resulting in cost savings. Maintenance is necessary to keep inlets clear of debris, and paved surfaces may require periodic cleaning. Outlets must be designed to allow for the collection and trapping of floatage, such as petroleum products.

4.7 Drainage Structures

Drainage structures are used to direct and aid the flow of stormwater in a concentrated form.

Head Walls and End Walls:

Head walls and end walls are used as retaining walls and transition areas between natural channel flow and a pipe or culvert. Figure 330-20 shows the position of each type relative to flow. The head wall must make the transition from a rough, natural channel to a smooth, closed channel with a minimum of head loss. End walls are outlets of piped flow and, in discharging to a natural channel, function to slow downstream velocity and thereby limit channel scour. The head-wall size depends on the pipe size.

Inlet Structures:

Surface runoff can be collected and transferred to undergound pipes by means of inlets (Figure 330-21). The bottoms of the inlets differentiate them into two types. A *drop inlet* has a smooth bottom, permitting immediate flow into the pipe. A *catch basin* has a sediment basin at the structure's bottom which collects heavy sediment material before it can enter the pipe; periodic maintenance is required.

Calculations for the sizing of inlet openings, critical for control of design storms, are explained in 5.4 Design of Storm Pipes in this section.

Access Structures:

Access structures, such as manholes and cleanouts, are devices which allow access for the maintenance of undergound pipes (Figure 330-22).

Manholes allow a person to enter a structure; typically, they have a diameter of 4 ft (1.2 m) at the base. Manholes are constructed of masonry units or precast units.

Cleanouts typically consist of a pipe riser connected to the line by a Y fitting. These permit visual inspection of the pipe or access by cleaning equipment.

Piping:

Drainage pipes are manufactured in a variety of materials, which can vary for different sizes. The choice of materials will be based on local code regulations, pipe size, function, availability, and price. Common materials are listed below. Sizing calculations are shown in 5.3 Design of Open Channels in this section.

Clay Pipe: Typical diameters of 6 to 12 in (150 to 300 mm). Can be perforated.

1. *Tile:* the weakest pipe, but can be used for subdrainage and minor drainage systems

2. *Vitrified clay pipe (VCP):* a glazed clay material that resists chemical damage

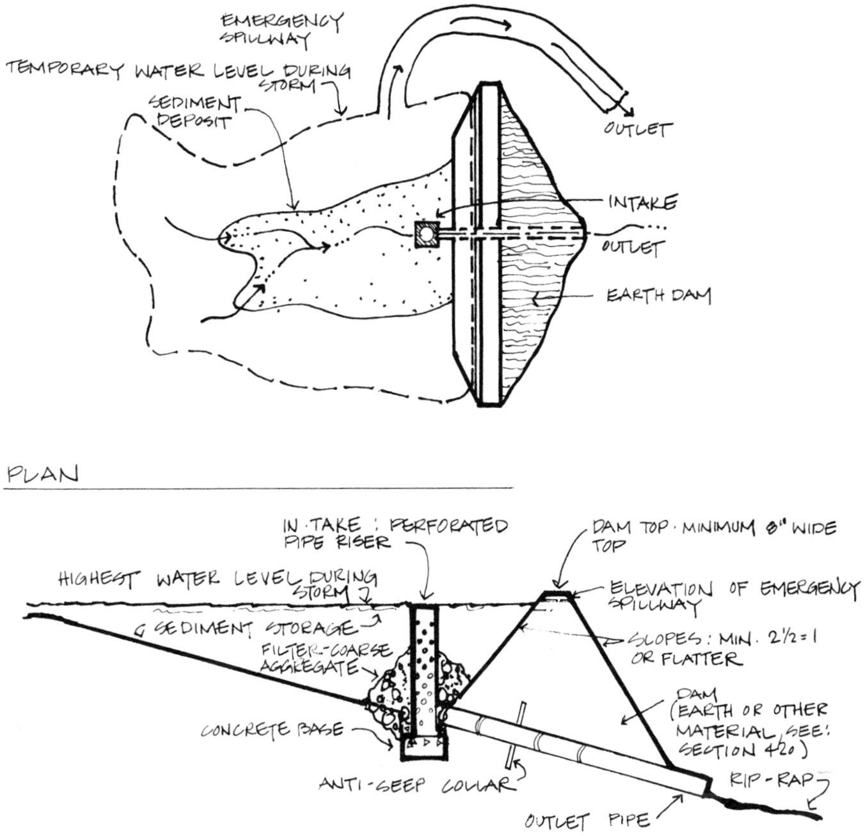
EMERGENCY SPILLWAY
TEMPORARY WATER LEVEL DURING STORM
SEDIMENT DEPOSIT
OUTLET
INTAKE
OUTLET
EARTH DAM
PLAN
IN·TAKE: PERFORATED PIPE RISER
DAM TOP · MINIMUM 8" WIDE TOP
HIGHEST WATER LEVEL DURING STORM
ELEVATION OF EMERGENCY SPILLWAY
SEDIMENT STORAGE
FILTER-COARSE AGGREGATE
SLOPES: MIN. 2½=1 OR FLATTER
DAM (EARTH OR OTHER MATERIAL, SEE: SECTION 420)
CONCRETE BASE
ANTI-SEEP COLLAR
RIP-RAP
OUTLET PIPE

Figure 330-18 Design of a typical sedimentation pond.

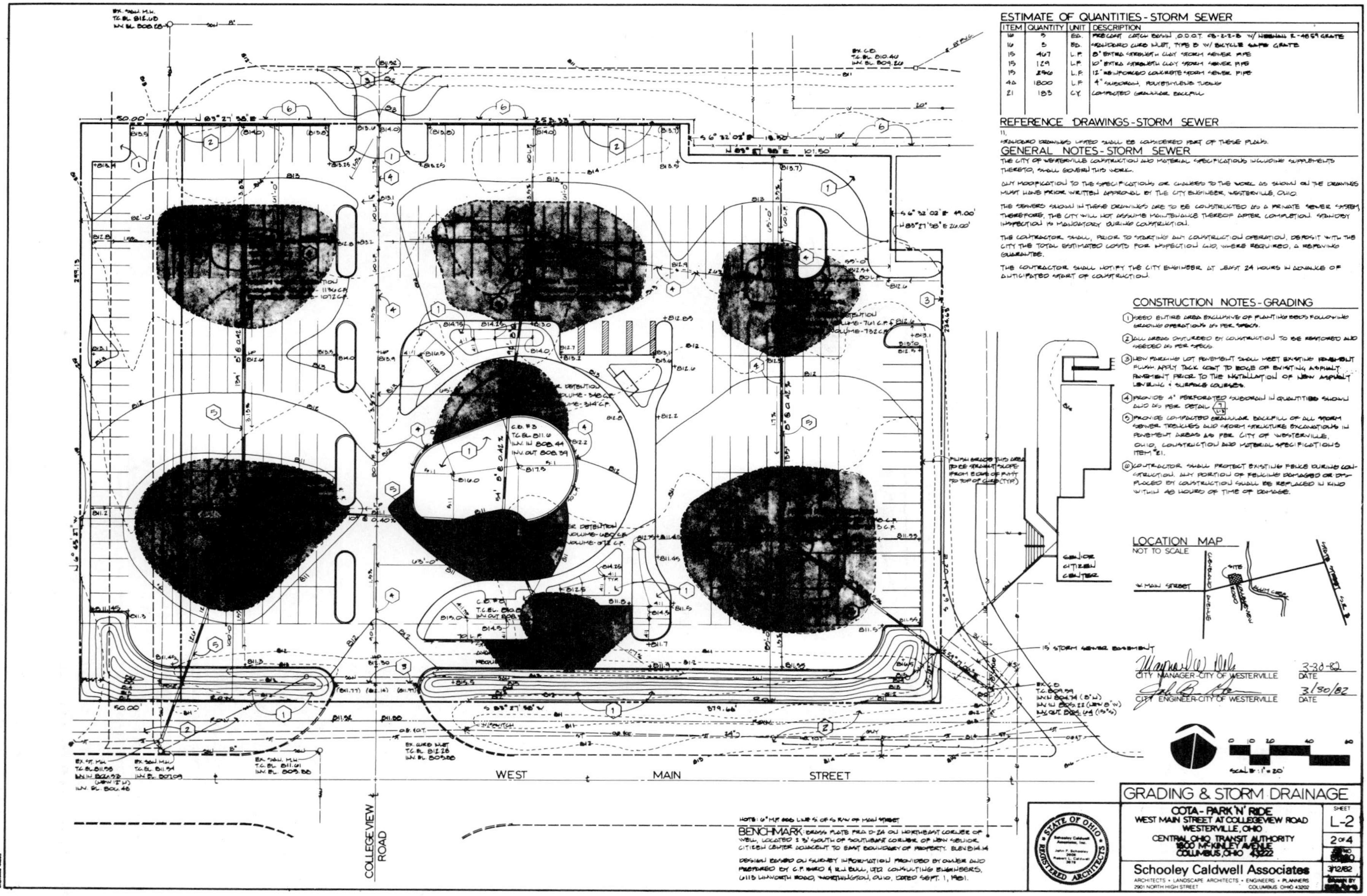
ESTIMATE OF QUANTITIES - STORM SEWER
ITEM
QUANTITY
UNIT
DESCRIPTION
REFERENCE DRAWINGS - STORM SEWER
GENERAL NOTES - STORM SEWER
CONSTRUCTION NOTES - GRADING
LOCATION MAP
NOT TO SCALE
CITY MANAGER-CITY OF WESTERVILLE
CITY ENGINEER-CITY OF WESTERVILLE
DATE
WEST
MAIN
STREET
COLLEGEVIEW ROAD
BENCHMARK
GRADING & STORM DRAINAGE
COTA - PARK 'N' RIDE
WEST MAIN STREET AT COLLEGEVIEW ROAD
WESTERVILLE, OHIO
CENTRAL OHIO TRANSIT AUTHORITY
1600 McKINLEY AVENUE
COLUMBUS, OHIO 43222
SHEET
L-2
2 OF 4
Schooley Caldwell Associates
ARCHITECTS • LANDSCAPE ARCHITECTS • ENGINEERS • PLANNERS
2901 NORTH HIGH STREET
COLUMBUS OHIO 43202
STATE OF OHIO
REGISTERED ARCHITECTS

Figure 330-19 Paved storage design. Gray areas show detention. Standard catch basins are used.

Plastic Pipe: Typical diameters of 6 to 10 in (150 to 250 mm). Can be perforated.

1. *PVC (polyvinyl chloride):* available in solid (smaller sizes) or truss (stronger for larger sizes) wall pipe

2. *ABS (acrylonitrile butadiene):* solid or truss wall pipe

Concrete Pipe: Variable diameters, depending on type.

1. *Plain concrete pipe:* up to 10 in (250 mm) in diameter

2. *Reinforced concrete pipe (RCP):* 12-in (300-mm) and larger diameters are typical; often specified under areas where surface pressures are applied

Corrugated Steel Pipe (CSP): Diameters of 10 in (250 mm) and greater. Can be perforated. Often used for culvert construction. The pipe must be laid on a uniform surface and backfilled properly to prevent crushing.

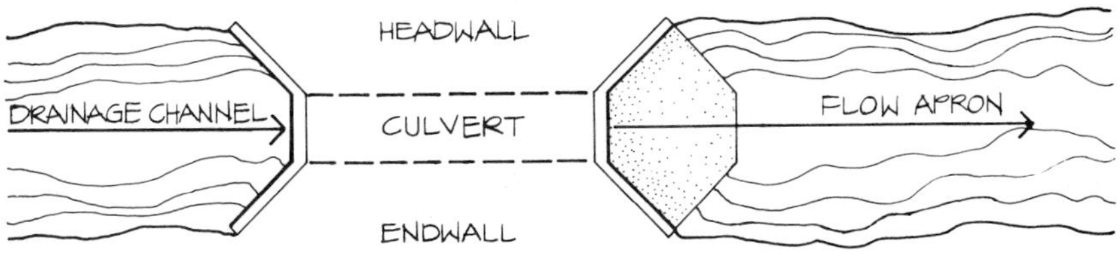
HEADWALL
DRAINAGE CHANNEL
CULVERT
FLOW APRON
ENDWALL

Figure 330-20 Typical head-wall/end-wall design.

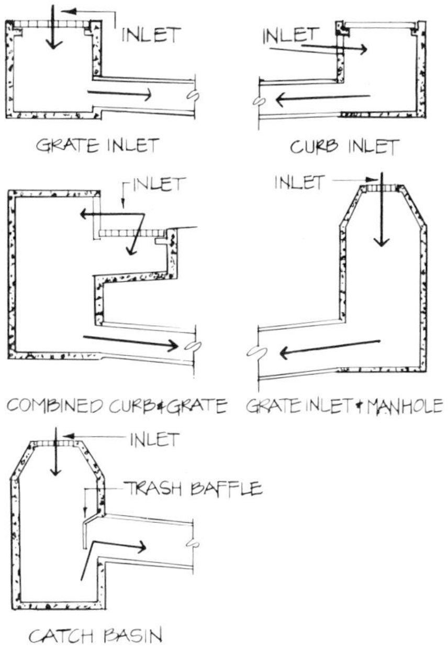
INLET
GRATE INLET
INLET
CURB INLET
INLET
COMBINED CURB&GRATE
INLET
GRATE INLET&MANHOLE
INLET
TRASH BAFFLE
CATCH BASIN

Figure 330-21 Typical drainage inlet structures.

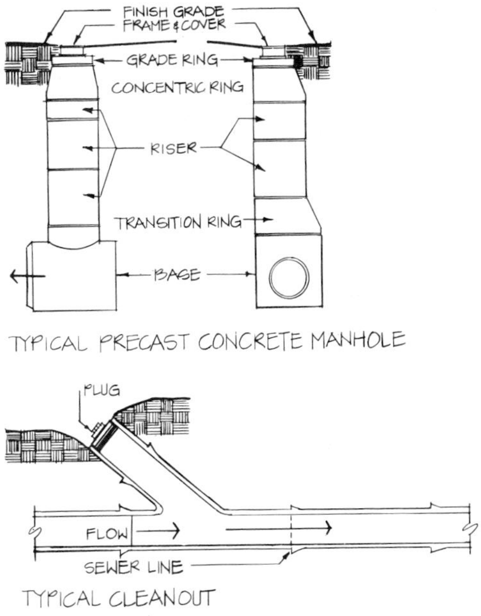
FINISH GRADE
FRAME&COVER
GRADE RING
CONCENTRIC RING
RISER
TRANSITION RING
BASE
TYPICAL PRECAST CONCRETE MANHOLE
PLUG
FLOW
SEWER LINE
TYPICAL CLEANOUT

Figure 330-22 Typical manhole and cleanout structures (precast).

Underdrain:

Subsurface drainage refers to movement of water below the surface of the ground Water movement is slower than on the surface but still follows the same principles of movement toward lower areas in lateral as well as vertical directions. Lateral movement results either when more-impervious layers or the water table is reached.

Figure 330-23 shows groundwater movement toward an underdrain located in a low area. If the drain were not present, soils in the low area would quickly become saturated and the groundwater would become surface water, resulting in ponding. The subdrainage system becomes most valuable in areas where the soil has poor drainage or the water table has to be lowered because it is too close to the surface for certain land uses. In addition, three particular conditions which typically require subdrainage are: (1) frost heave–prone areas (2) a perched water table (because of a hardpan or a fine-particle soil layer on top of a more-coarse layer), and (3) expansive soils.

Subdrains consist of a trench, porous backfill, and perforated pipe (Figure 330-24). Water fills the void space in the porous backfill and is then taken through perforations in the pipe. The pipe is sloped to transport the water away. This acts as a sponge, drawing water laterally through the soil toward the porous backfill and the pipe. Because water is infiltrating through soil, this system is much slower than surface drainage.

The pipe depth and spacing of a subdrainage field are discussed in 5.6 Underdrain Design in this section.

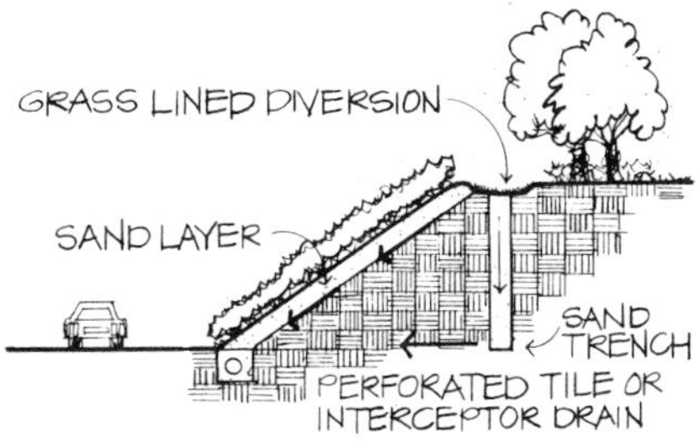
GRASS LINED DIVERSION
SAND LAYER
SAND TRENCH
PERFORATED TILE OR INTERCEPTOR DRAIN

Figure 330-23 Groundwater movement toward underdrain.

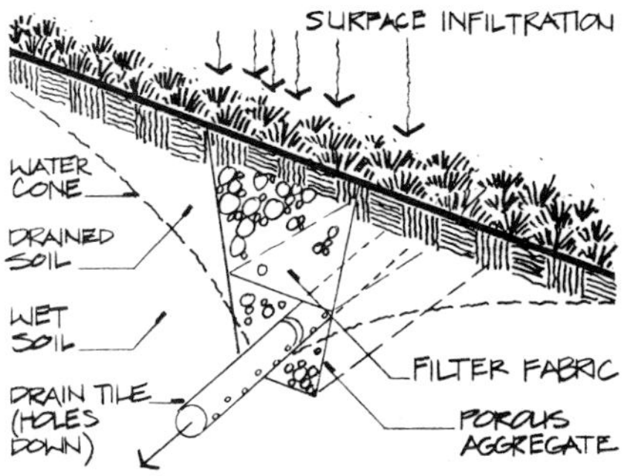
SURFACE INFILTRATION
WATER CONE
DRAINED SOIL
WET SOIL
DRAIN TILE (HOLES DOWN)
FILTER FABRIC
POROUS AGGREGATE

Figure 330-24 Typical underdrain section.

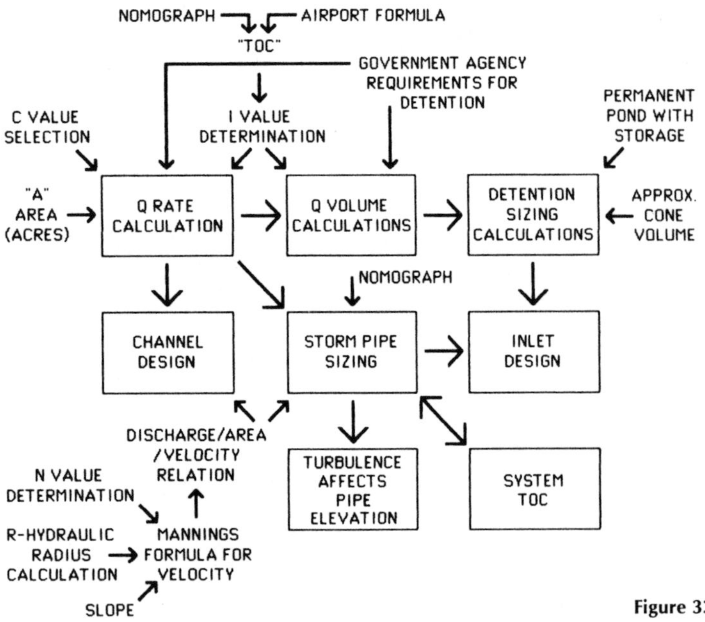

NOMOGRAPH
AIRPORT FORMULA
"TOC"
GOVERNMENT AGENCY REQUIREMENTS FOR DETENTION
C VALUE SELECTION
I VALUE DETERMINATION
PERMANENT POND WITH STORAGE
"A" AREA (ACRES)
Q RATE CALCULATION
Q VOLUME CALCULATIONS
DETENTION SIZING CALCULATIONS
APPROX. CONE VOLUME
NOMOGRAPH
CHANNEL DESIGN
STORM PIPE SIZING
INLET DESIGN
DISCHARGE/AREA /VELOCITY RELATION
N VALUE DETERMINATION
TURBULENCE AFFECTS PIPE ELEVATION
SYSTEM TOC
R-HYDRAULIC RADIUS CALCULATION
MANNINGS FORMULA FOR VELOCITY
SLOPE

Figure 330-25 Site drainage calculations flowchart.

TABLE 330-4
Values of C (Runoff Coefficients) for Various Surfaces

Surfaces	Value proposed	
	Minimum	*Maximum*
Roofs, slag to metal	0.90	1.00
Pavements		
Concrete or asphalt	0.90	1.00
Bituminous macadam, open and closed type	0.70	0.90
Gravel, from clean and loose to clayey and compact	0.25	0.70
Railroad yards	0.10	0.30
Earth surfaces		
Sand, from uniform grain size, no fines, to well-graded, some clay or silt		
Bare	0.15	0.50
Light vegetation	0.10	0.40
Dense vegetation	0.05	0.30
Loam, from sandy or gravelly to clayey		
Bare	0.20	0.60
Light vegetation	0.10	0.45
Dense vegetation	0.05	0.35
Gravel, from clean gravel and gravel sand mixtures, no silt or clay to high clay or silt content		
Bare	0.25	0.65
Light vegetation	0.15	0.50
Dense vegetation	0.10	0.40
Clay, from coarse sandy or silty to pure colloidal clays		
Bare	0.30	0.75
Light vegetation	0.20	0.60
Dense vegetation	0.15	0.50
Commercial site areas		
City, business areas	0.60	0.75
City, dense residential areas; vary as to soil and vegetation	0.50	0.65
Suburban residential areas; vary as to soil and vegetation	0.35	0.55
Rural districts; vary as to soil and vegetation	0.10	0.25
Parks, golf courses, etc.; vary as to soil and vegetation	0.10	0.35
Lawns (sandy soil)		
2% slopes (flat)	0.05	0.10
2% to 7% slopes	0.10	0.15
Greater than 7% slopes	0.15	0.20
Lawns (heavy soil)		
2% slopes (flat)	0.13	0.17
2% to 7% slopes	0.18	0.22
Greater than 7% slopes	0.25	0.35

Note: Values of C for earth surfaces are further varied by degree of saturation, compaction, surface irregularity, and slope; by character of subsoil; and by presence of frost or glazed snow or ice.

Source: From Water Pollution Control Federation *Design and Construction of Sanitary and Storm Sewers,* 1967, and from Elwin E. Seelye, *Design: Data Book for Civil Engineers,* 3d ed., Wiley, New York, 1960.

5.0 CALCULATIONS

Years of study and of gathering empirical evidence in the field have made it possible to quantify the relationships between natural factors and drainage. These are expressed in formulas, tables, and charts which approximate the relationships and often facilitate more than one way of meeting an objective. As more data are collected, complex computer simulation models become possible.

The methods presented in this section are sufficient for use in most cases. Figure 330-25 illustrates a process for calculations.

5.1 Calculation of Runoff Rate *(Q)*

One of the most important pieces of information is the calculation of runoff rate Q. The *new development* rate is necessary to size the system being designed, and the *predevelopment* rate is necessary to find the difference between the two (i.e., that runoff which should be retained on the site).

The most widely used formula for calculating *Q* for small watersheds is the *rational method.* The Soil Conservation Service has stated that this method is applicable for use on parcels 0.01 acres (40.5 m^2) to 5 square miles [3200 acres (1295 ha)] in size in nonurbanized areas, and up to 10 acres (4 ha) in size in urbanized areas. However, many civil engineers have found the method to be adequate only for parcels under ½ mile square (130 ha) in size. The formula is based on two assumptions: (1) that rainfall will occur at a uniform intensity for a time equal to the *time of concentration* of the watershed (the time required for all areas to contribute to runoff) and (2) that rainfall will occur at a uniform intensity over the entire watershed (which is usually true in small watersheds).

The formula for the rational method is:

$$Q = CiA$$

where Q = peak runoff rate, cfs
C = coefficient of runoff (C value)
i = rainfall intensity, in/hour (for a given storm frequency and duration)
A = watershed area, acres

Another way to calculate Q is the SCS (U.S. Soil Conservation Service) Runoff Curve Number method, in which the parameters of hydrologic soil group, cover type, treatment, hydrologic condition, and antecedent runoff conditions are considered in the calculations. (See US/SCS Technical Release #55, 1986.)

C Value:

The C value is a unitless number which represents the composite resistance of surface conditions (i.e., vegetation, soils, impervious surfaces, slopes, etc.) to flows. It is the most ambiguous and subjective parameter; the designer chooses it by evaluating existing or proposed cover conditions.

Table 330-4 lists approximate C values compiled from various sources. Often a government agency will have its own recommended C values.

When applied to the formula, a C value adds the factor of resistance to the calculation of runoff rates. Thus, the closer to 1 a C value is, the more impervious the surface, and thus the higher the runoff rate Q will be.

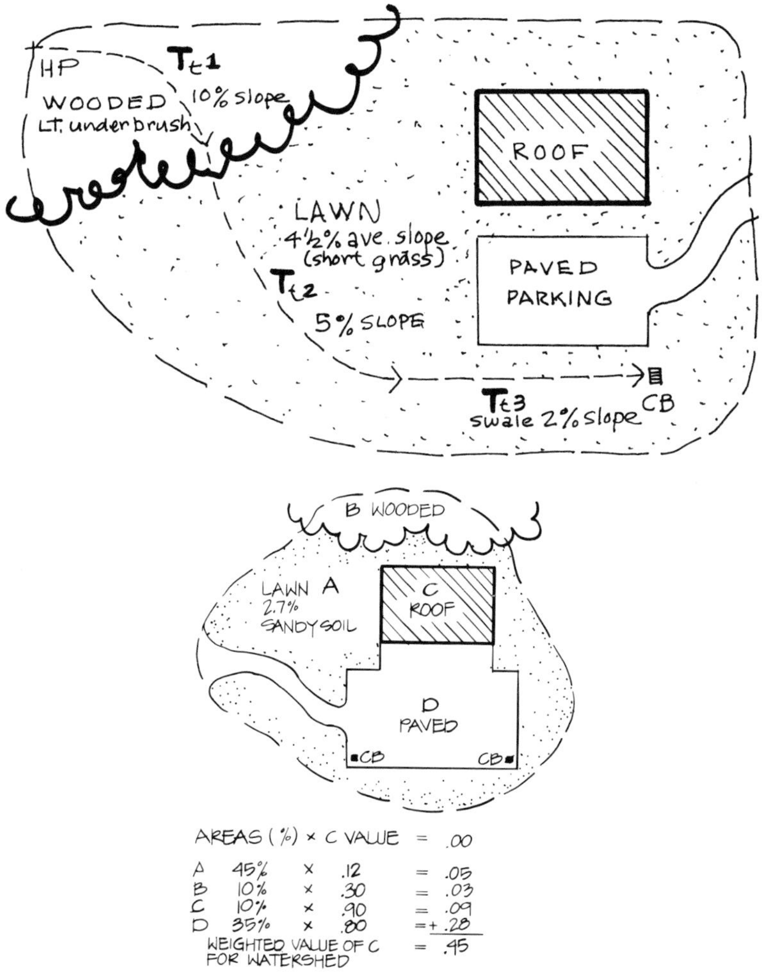
HP
T_{t1}
WOODED
10% slope
LT. underbrush
ROOF
LAWN
4½% ave. slope (short grass)
T_{t2}
5% SLOPE
PAVED PARKING
T_{t3}
swale 2% slope
CB
B WOODED
LAWN A
2.7%
SANDY SOIL
C
ROOF
D
PAVED
CB
CB
AREAS (%) × C VALUE = .00
A 45% × .12 = .05
B 10% × .30 = .03
C 10% × .90 = .09
D 35% × .80 =+ .28
WEIGHTED VALUE OF C FOR WATERSHED = .45

Figure 330-26 Watershed A—Example.

Weighted C Values:

A watershed will often contain more than one type of surface, as shown in the example of watershed A in Figure 330-26. The first step is to divide that watershed into regions of one type and find the area of each region. Planimeters are useful to calculate a percentage of the total for each region to be figured. The C values for each region are now chosen by using the available data and a recommended chart. Each C value is multiplied by the percent (%) area, the C values are then summed, and a weighted C value for the watershed is determined as shown in Figure 330-26.

i Value:

The i value is based on data gathered by the U.S. Weather Service for a particular storm frequency and duration. The storm frequency to be used is related to the proposed intensity of development and the type of drainage system. Local government agencies usually have their own requirements. A typical range is shown in Table 330-5. It follows that the larger the number of years of recurrence, the greater the rainfall or storm, and thus ultimately the higher the runoff rate Q.

Duration, another parameter for finding i, is determined by the *time of concentration* (TOC) for the watershed. The time of concentration is the time it takes for *all* areas in the watershed to contribute to the outlet. Thus, the outlet should have maximum runoff at that time.

Calculating TOC: There has been considerable debate concerning the accuracy of various methods used to calculate TOC. This section will use the method adopted by the U.S. Soil Conservation Service (SCS) and shown below.

Runoff can travel overland as sheet flow, shallow concentrated flow, or channel flow. Runoff can encounter changes in rate of slope and/or various conditions of channel roughness. TOC should be determined based upon the travel time (Tt) for each type and segment of the flow. Thus,

$$TOC = Tt^1 + Tt^2 + \ldots Tt\,m$$

where TOC = time of concentration, hour
Tt = travel time, hour
m = number of flow segments

For *sheet flow* of less than 300 ft, Manning's kinematic solution may be used to find Tt.

$$Tt = \frac{0.007(nL)^{0.8}}{(P_2)^{0.5}\, S^{0.4}}$$

where Tt = travel time, hour
n = Manning's roughness coefficient (see Table 330-7)
L = flow length (ft)
P_2 = 2-year, 24-hour rainfall (in)
S = slope of hydraulic gradeline or land slope (ft/ft)

NOTE: P_2 rainfall depth can be obtained from the National Weather Service Map for the USA (see Figure 330-27).

For *shallow concentrated flows,* the definition of travel time as a ratio of flow

TABLE 330-5
Tables of Recommended Design Storms

System	*Duration, yrs*
Initial drainage system	
Storm sewer system	10
Grass swale	10
Major drainage system	
Roadway low point	25
Storage volume	100 for permanent, 10 for temporary
Outlet discharge, pipe spillway	2, 10, 25, 50, 100—all shall not exceed existing conditions
Emergency spillway	100
Diversions, open channels, stream culverts	Refer to local ordinances
Initial drainage system	
Residential	
Inlets, sewers	2–5
Low points, outfalls	10–15
Commercial	
Inlets, sewers	10–15
Industrial	2–15
Major drainage system	
Low-density (basements may flood)	25
Medium density (living quarters may flood)	50
High-density (buildings' proximity may aggravate flood conditions by increasing depth and velocity)	100
Commercial	25–100

Source: Dahlem and Schwartz, *Regional Standards and Criteria for Stormwater Management TR-11,* DVRPC, 1974. Also, DER, PA *Stormwater Management Guidelines,* 1980.

2-YEAR 24-HOUR RAINFALL (INCHES)
(j)

Figure 330-27 2-year, 24-hour rainfall (inches).

length to velocity will help find Tt.

where *Tt* = travel time, hour
L = flow length, ft
V = average velocity (ft/sec) (use Figure 330-28.)

NOTE: If the land has been tilled across slope, flow may not follow the slope of the watershed.

Open channels are assumed where channels are visible on aerial photographs or where blue lines appear on USGS quadrangle sheets.

The same formula to find *Tt* for shallow concentrated flow may be used for open channels. *V* is found in Manning's formula (see 5.3 Design of Open Channels in this section).

In Figure 330-26, TOC is calculated by finding the travel times for segments in sheet flow and shallow concentrated flows and adding them up at the end.

Determining i: When the frequency and duration are known, *i* can be determined by referencing a local rainfall intensity chart. Figure 330-29 is a typical chart for the region monitored by the Columbus station (Ohio). Local government agencies (i.e., storm sewer departments) have these charts.

The total runoff rate *Q* can be calculated for the example, as shown in Figure 330-26. The *i* value has been selected from the rainfall intensity chart based on a 10-year storm frequency and a duration equal to the TOC of 13.5 minutes.

Figure 330-26 shows postdevelopment *Q*. If predevelopment *Q* is known, then the increase in rate may be found.

Q (postdevelopment) − *Q* (predevelopment) = *Q* increase in rate

The difference in these two values for *Q* yields an amount which may be necessary for the calculation of detention. The value of postdevelopment *Q* is also necessary for the sizing of storm systems being designed.

Often, postdevelopment sites are made up of several small watersheds (Figure 330-30). *Q* values have to be found for each of these miniwatersheds in order to size the pipes required for that system. (Sizing calculations are explained in 5.3 Design of Open Channels in this section.) The sum of all *Q* values yields the postdevelopment *Q* required for the calculation of detention for the entire site.

5.2 Calculation of Volumes for Detention

Runoff *rates* can be transformed into runoff *volumes* for the purpose of sizing storage areas for detention or retention. Since the *Q* rate was based on a TOC in minutes, the following formula yields a *Q* volume:

Q(TOC)(60) = *Q* volume

where *Q* = runoff rate, cfs
TOC = time of concentration, minutes
Quol. = runoff volume, ft^3
60 = number of seconds per minute

However, while the TOC is useful for determining when the peak flows occur, it does not represent the maximum detention volume required. To find the required volume, a range of time should be chosen and all calculations carried through. A standard computation chart (as shown in Table 330-6) keeps the calculations orderly, and it is often required for submittal to local government agencies.

In the example shown (Table 330-6a), to calculate the *Q Volume Developed, i* values are found on the rainfall chart, using a range of times rather than the TOC. On the other hand the *Q Volume Allowable* (Table 330-6*b*) is based on the *Q* runoff rate calculated by using the TOC for that site. In this example (Table 330-6*b*) the local government agency has determined that the 6-year developed design storm rate may be discharged but that the detention must be designed for 10-year storm volumes.

In the example shown (Table 330-6c), the maximum storage for a 10-year storm is reached after 10 minutes. The resultant site design will have storm pipes or outflow devices which are specified to release water at the rate of 34.0 cfs (*6-year Q Allowable*). To hold 8700 ft^3 of water, a storage area (such as a detention pond) will be necessary; in addition, a floodway for runoff exceeding the 10-year design storm must be provided.

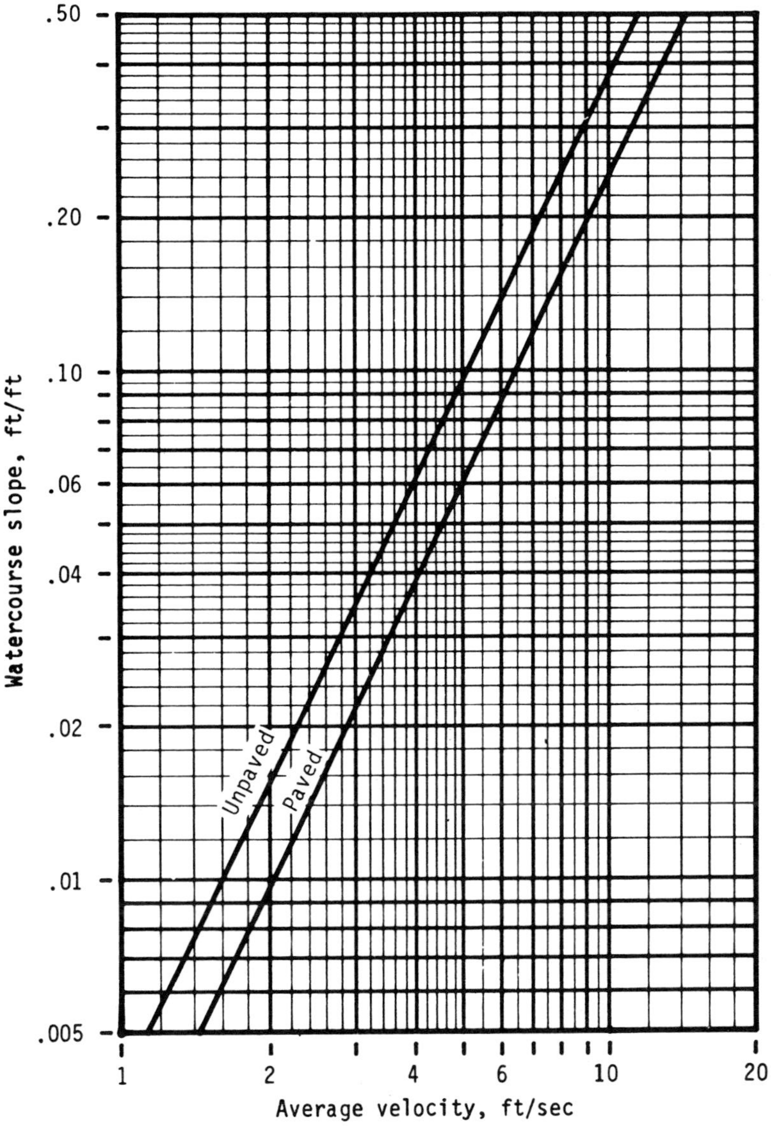
.50
.20
.10
.06
.04
.02
.01
.005
Watercourse slope, ft/ft
Unpaved
Paved
1
2
4
6
10
20
Average velocity, ft/sec

Figure 330-28 Average velocities for estimating travel.

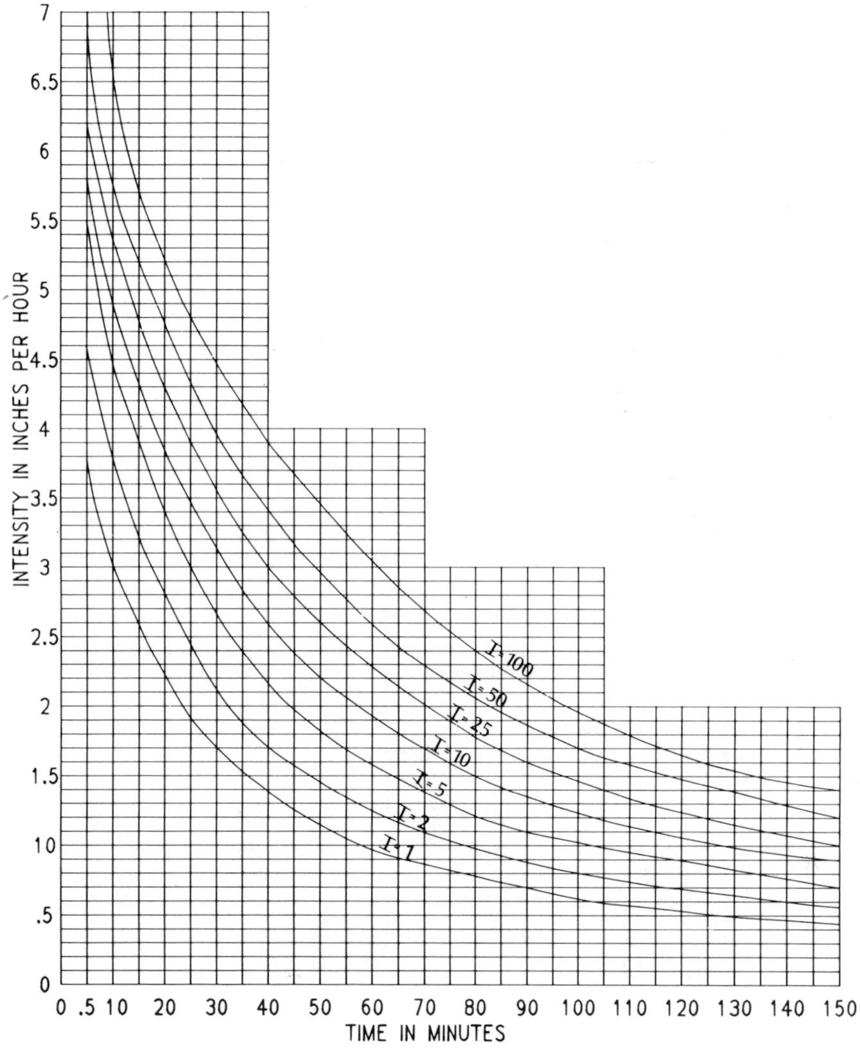
INTENSITY IN INCHES PER HOUR
7
6.5
6
5.5
5
4.5
4
3.5
3
2.5
2
1.5
10
.5
0
I=100
I=50
I=25
I=10
I=5
I=2
I=1
0 .5 10 20 30 40 50 60 70 80 90 100 110 120 130 140 150
TIME IN MINUTES

Figure 330-29 Rainfall frequency curves (Columbus, Ohio).

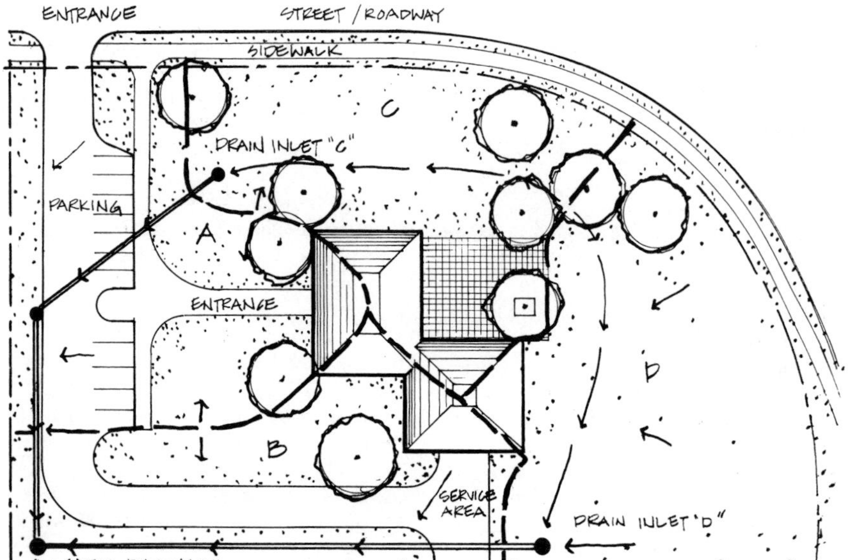
ENTRANCE
STREET / ROADWAY
SIDEWALK
C
DRAIN INLET "C"
PARKING
A
ENTRANCE
D
B
SERVICE AREA
DRAIN INLET 'D"
CATCH BASIN 'B"

Figure 330-30 Example of postdevelopment miniwatersheds.

Detention Pond/Area Sizing:

There are a number of rule-of-thumb methods to calculate pond storage.

Permanent Ponds: If a pond is to be permanent and have the capacity for extra storage during runoff from rainfall, a system such as is shown in Figure 330-31 is used. The outlet is sized to let out *Q Allowable*. The area above the outlet, to the top of the *dam*, is the detention area. The depth is calculated by:

$$D = \frac{2V}{A_{perm} + A_{high}}$$

or

$$V = \frac{A_{perm} + A_{high}}{2}(D)$$

where V = volume to be retained
D = depth of water between permanent and high water levels
A_{perm} = area of permanent water level
A_{high} = area of high water level

By trial and error, D and A_{high} should be adjusted up or down until V matches the required volume.

Temporary Ponds: A temporary pond can be calculated from the following formula:

$V = \frac{1}{3}$ (surface area)(maximum water depth)

Figure 330-32 illustrates the use of this approximation of cone volume. Either the surface area or the maximum water depth may be varied until a suitable design is reached. This method is most useful in parking lot ponding where the detention is conelike.

5.3 Design of Open Channels

The *rational formula* for runoff calculations pertains to sheet flow. When water enters a swale, ditch, or channel, there are hydraulic characteristics which affect the fluid behavior of water and thus the ability of the drainage system to function efficiently.

A *drainage channel* is defined as any drainage course that is open to the atmosphere. This includes open swales and ditches as well as a pipe flowing *partially* full. Thus, the hydraulic characteristics and laws described for swales also apply to pipes that are not full. Drainage channels with constant slopes and cross sections will have uniform flow. *Uniform flow* means that the slope of the water surface is the same as the channel slope. The rate of discharge from the channel is directly related to the cross-sectional area of the channel and the velocity of the flow. This is ex-

TABLE 330-6
Watershed B—Example of Q Volume Calculations

a. Find *Q volume developed* for 10-year storm where C = .50 and A = 20

Minutes	*Seconds*	*CxA*	*i*	*Q volume, ft³*
5	300	10	6.00	18,000
10	600	10	4.85	29,100
15	900	10	4.30	38,700
20	1200	10	3.85	46,200

b. Find *Q volume allowable* as set by local authority for 6-year storm at TOC = 20 minutes.

Q rate allowable = C i A
= .50 × 3.40 × 20
= 34.0 cfs

Minutes	*Seconds*	*Q rate cfs*	*Q volume, ft³*
5	300	34.0	10,200
10	600	34.0	20,400
15	900	34.0	30,600
20	1200	34.0	40,800

c. Find Q volume detention required, ft³

Minutes	*Q volume developed*	*Q volume allowable*	*Q volume detention*
5	18,000	10,200	7800
10	29,100	20,400	8700
15	38,700	30,600	8100
20	46,200	40,800	5400

Conclusion: 8700 ft³ is the maximum storage required for 10-year storm volumes.

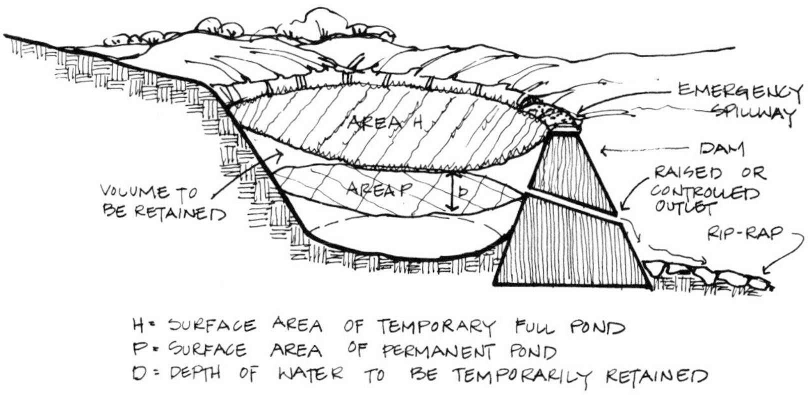
EMERGENCY SPILLWAY
AREA H
DAM
RAISED OR CONTROLLED OUTLET
VOLUME TO BE RETAINED
AREA P
D
RIP-RAP
H = SURFACE AREA OF TEMPORARY FULL POND
P = SURFACE AREA OF PERMANENT POND
D = DEPTH OF WATER TO BE TEMPORARILY RETAINED

Figure 330-31 Calculation of permanent detention pond storage.

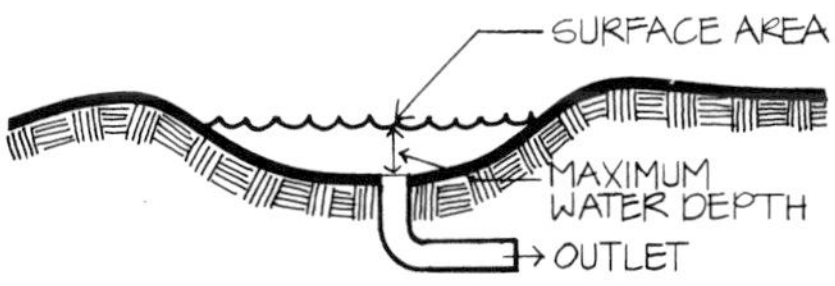
SURFACE AREA
MAXIMUM WATER DEPTH
OUTLET

Figure 330-32 Calculation of temporary detention pond storage.

TABLE 330-7
Table of *N*-Values (To be used with Manning's formula)

Surface description	*n**
Smooth surfaces (concrete, asphalt, gravel, or bare soil)	0.011
Fallow (no residue)	0.05
Cultivated soils	
Residue cover ≤20%	0.06
Residue cover >20%	0.17
Grass	
Short grass prairie	0.15
Dense grasses†	0.24
Bermudagrass	0.41
Range (natural)	0.13
Woods‡	
Light underbrush	0.40
Dense underbrush	0.80

* The *n* values are a composite of information compiled by Engman (1986).

† Includes species such as weeping lovegrass, bluegrass, buffalo grass, blue grama grass, and native grass mixtures.

‡ When selecting *n*, consider cover to a height of about 0.1 ft. This is the only part of the plant cover that will obstruct sheet flow.

Source: Soil Conservation Service, TRSS 1986 (210-VI-TR-55, 2d ed., June 1986).

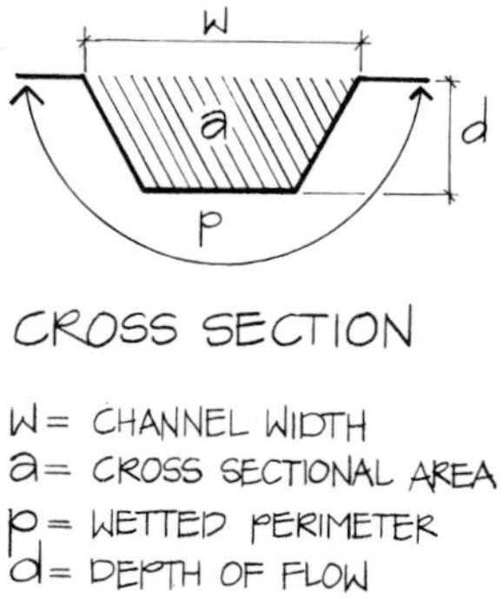
W
a
d
P
CROSS SECTION
W= CHANNEL WIDTH
a= CROSS SECTIONAL AREA
P= WETTED PERIMETER
d= DEPTH OF FLOW

Figure 330-33 Components of hydraulic radius.

pressed by the formula:

$$Q = Va$$

where Q = discharge rate, cfs
V = mean velocity, fps
a = cross-sectional area of the channel, ft^2

The velocity of water in a channel is important because it is directly related to the discharge rate and thus to the volume of water in a system. But velocity is also important because it determines the acceptable design of a channel in terms of slope, size, and surface material. The most commonly used empirical expression for velocity is *Manning's formula:*

$$V = \frac{1.486}{n} R^{0.667} S^{0.500}$$

where V = mean velocity, fps
n = friction coefficient between water and containing surface
S = mean gradient of channel, %
R = hydraulic radius, ft

Velocity V is related to channel erosion, scour, and sedimentation. High velocities cause accelerated rates of erosion and scour. In pipes, excessive scour will result in the weakening and eventual failure of pipe joints or other structures. Severe erosion in swales is the result of unacceptably high velocities. Sedimentation is caused when velocities are too low, whereby particles in the water settle out. This will build up and block proper channel flow. Acceptable channel velocities fall in the following ranges:

2 to 4 fps for turf channels

2 to 8 fps for paved or piped channels

n-Value: This determination for swales offers the most difficulty in using Manning's formula with accuracy. It can vary in different seasons and vary with time as vegetation changes. Also, swale bottoms sometimes vary along their lengths. Typical n values are shown in Table 330-7.

R-Value: The R value, or hydraulic radius, is the ratio between the cross-sectional area and the wetted perimeter, expressed in the formula:

$$R = \frac{a}{p}$$

where R = hydraulic radius, ft
a = cross-sectional area, ft^2
p = wetted perimeter, ft

Figure 330-33 graphically illustrates a and p.

The hydraulic efficiency of a channel to be designed depends on n, S, and R. Designing a channel involves a process of trial and error and includes the following steps:

1. Q is given. A and V values are approximated, using acceptable limits.

2. A cross section is selected. (Typical cross sections and their hydraulic properties are illustrated in Figure 330-34.)

3. The size and velocity are tested for acceptability.

4. The dimensions are readjusted or new cross sections are selected as required.

An alternative method is to use Manning's formula reorganized with a Q instead of V:

$$aR^{2/3} = \frac{nQ}{1.486S^{0.5}}$$

where a = cross-sectional area, ft^2
R = hydraulic radius, ft
n = friction coefficient between water and containing surface
Q = runoff rate, cfs
S = mean gradient of channel, %

Trial tests of cross sections against this product can reduce the number of computations necessary to determine the best section. It is important to test the velocity of each channel by using the following formula:

$$V = \frac{Q}{a}$$

5.4 Design of Storm Pipes

Channel design and pipe design are very similar, but there are differences in their hydraulic properties. As a typical channel becomes full, the hydraulic properties continue to increase, as shown in Figure 330-35. However, a circular pipe reaches its maximum velocity at about 82 percent of its depth and its greatest discharge at 93 percent of its depth; this is illustrated in Figure 330-36. The example in the illustration shows how a velocity may be found for a pipe not flowing full when the velocity of a pipe flowing full is known.

In general, Manning's formula may be used for storm pipe calculations. Figure 330-37 is a nomograph for circular pipes based on Manning's formula for various n values.

Water Turbulence:

Turbulence is created when water either moves from a surface channel to an underground pipe, or passes through a drain inlet or into a manhole, or otherwise changes slope, channel material, or direction of flow. Uniform flow is disrupted, resulting in a loss of energy and a decrease in velocity.

Figure 330-38 illustrates water turbulence and its consequences. The water level increases at the pipe entrance but under the influence of gravity begins to decrease, with a subsequent increase in velocity farther down the pipe. A new balance is eventually reached and uniform flow results.

The design implication of water turbulence and the resulting head loss is that in order to match the hydraulic surfaces (water levels) of meeting pipes, invert elevations will have to be adjusted at these points (i.e., inverts and manholes). An accepted method to compensate for head loss involves dropping the invert of the outgoing pipe. Figure 330-39 shows suggested allowances for head loss under three conditions.

TYPE SECTION	WIDTH W	BASE b	DEPTH d	AREA a	WETTED PERIMETER P	HYDRAULIC RADIUS A/P
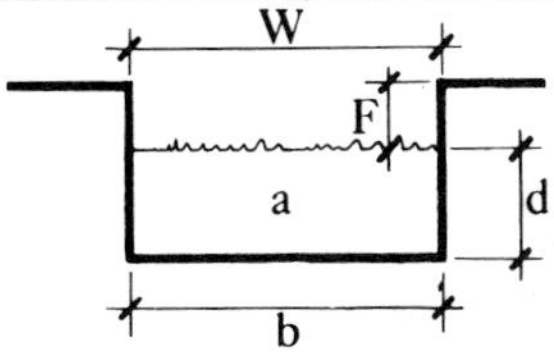W F a d b RECTANGULAR	b or $\frac{a}{d}$	W or $\frac{a}{d}$	$\frac{a}{b}$	wd	W+ 2 d	$\frac{d}{\frac{1 + 2d}{W}}$
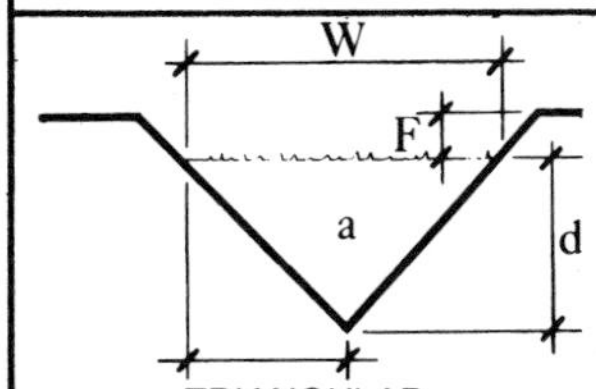W F a d TRIANGULAR	2e		$\frac{a}{e}$	ed	$e\sqrt{e^2 + d^2}$	$\frac{ed}{2\sqrt{e^2 + d^2}}$
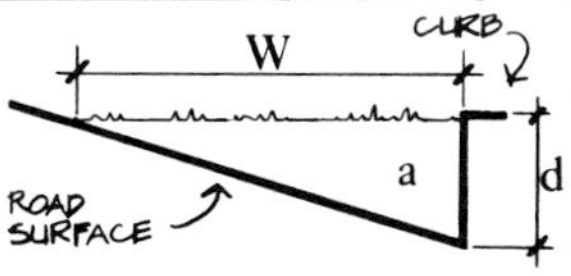W CURB a d ROAD SURFACE TRIANGULAR Curb & Gutter	$\frac{2a}{d}$		$\frac{2a}{W}$	$\frac{Wd}{2}$	$d + \sqrt{d^2 + W^2}$	$\frac{2\ Wd}{d + \sqrt{e^2 + W^2}}$
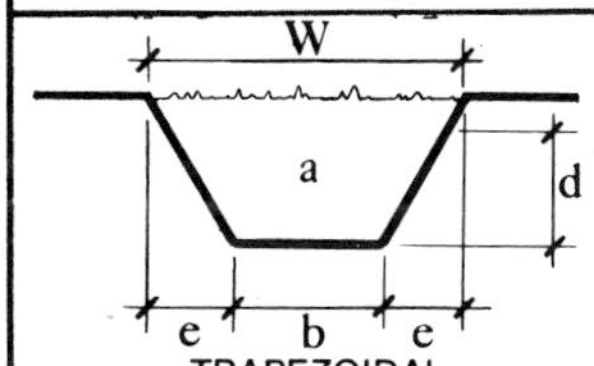W a d e b e TRAPEZOIDAL Even Sides	b + 2e	W-2e	$\frac{a}{b + e}$	d(b + e)	$b + 2\sqrt{e^2 + d^2}$	$\frac{d\ (b + e)}{b + 2\ \sqrt{e^2 + d^2}}$
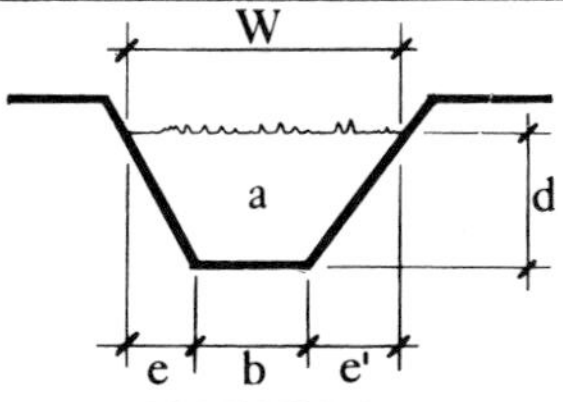W a d e b e' TRAPEZOIDAL Uneven Sides	b + e +e'	W-(e +e'	$\frac{a}{b + \left(\frac{e+ e}{2}\right)}$	$d\left(b + \frac{e + e'}{2}\right)$	$b + \sqrt{e^2 + d^2} + \sqrt{e^2 + d^2}$	$\frac{d\left(b + \frac{e + e'}{2}\right)}{b + \sqrt{e^2 + d^2} + \sqrt{e^2 + d^2}}$
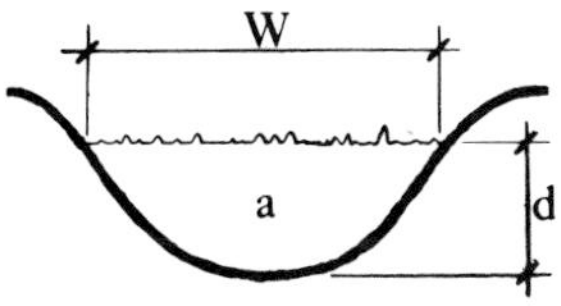W a d PARABOLIC	$\frac{a}{0.67d}$		$\frac{a}{0.67W}$	0.67 Wd	$W + \left(\frac{8d^2}{3W}\right)$	$\frac{a}{W + \left(\frac{8d^2}{3W}\right)}$

NOTE: 0.3' to 0.5' Recommended Freeboard (F)

Figure 330-34 Hydraulic properties of typical sections.

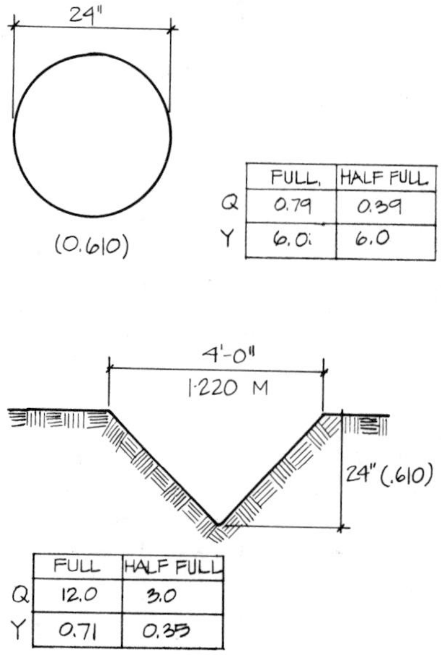
24"
(0.610)
FULL
HALF FULL
Q 0.79 0.39
Y 6.0 6.0
4'-0"
1.220 M
24" (.610)
FULL
HALF FULL
Q 12.0 3.0
Y 0.71 0.35

Figure 330-35 Characteristics of circular pipe versus triangular section.

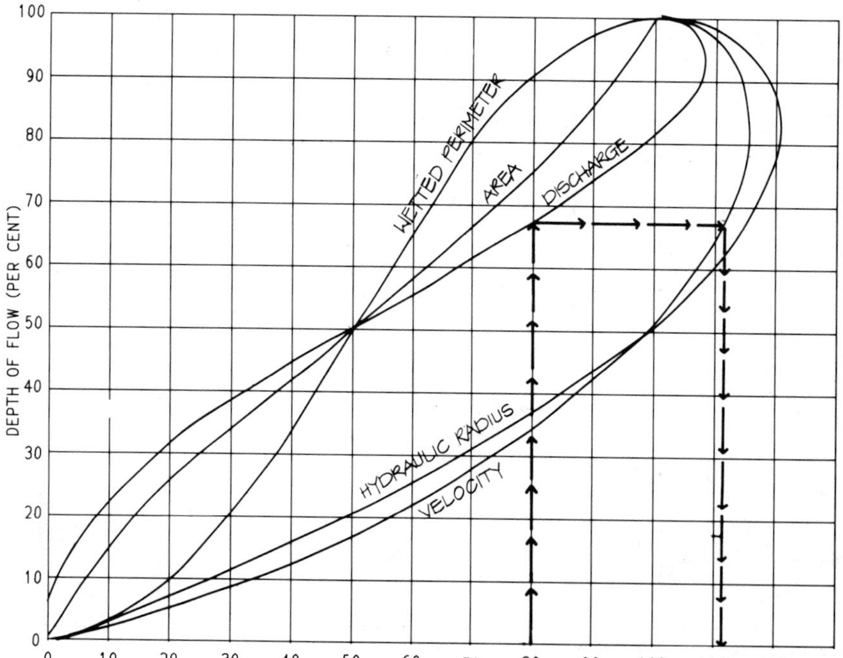
DEPTH OF FLOW (PER CENT)
100
90
80
70
60
50
40
30
20
10
0
WETTED PERIMETER
AREA
DISCHARGE
HYDRAULIC RADIUS
VELOCITY
0 10 20 30 40 50 60 70 80 90 100 110 120
HYDRAULIC ELEMENTS
PER CENT OF VALUE FOR FULL SECTION (APPROXIMATE)

Figure 330-36 Hydraulic properties of circular section.

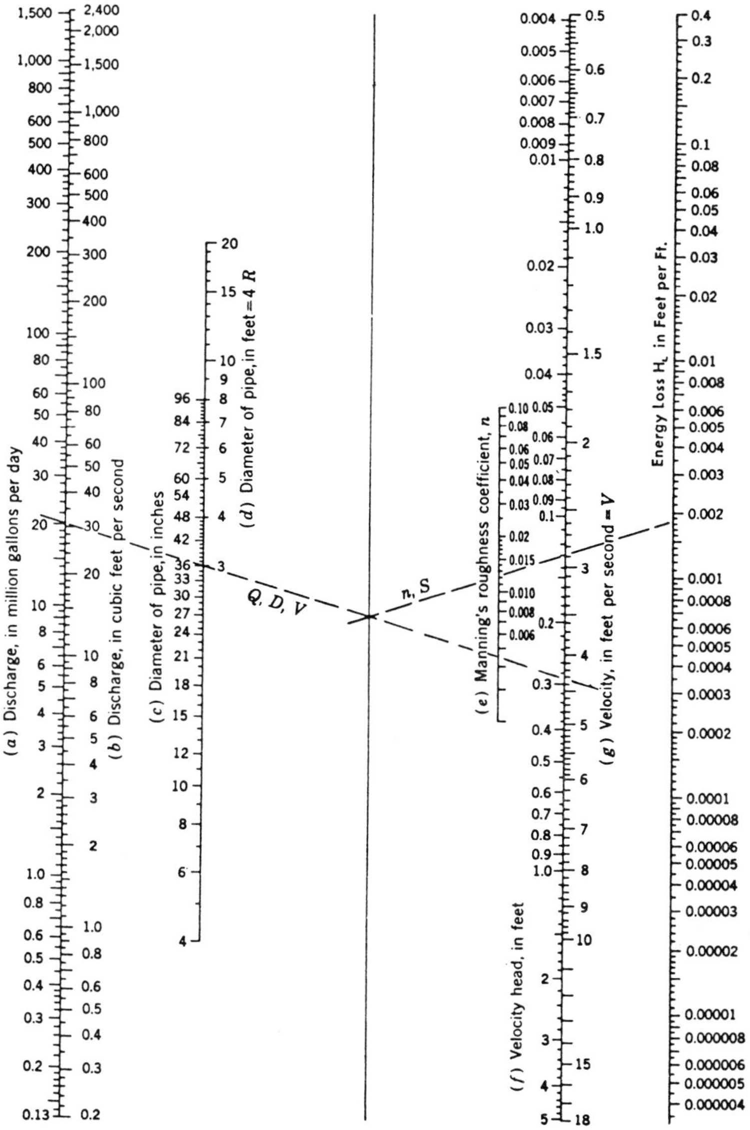
(a) Discharge, in million gallons per day
(b) Discharge, in cubic feet per second
(c) Diameter of pipe, in inches
(d) Diameter of pipe, in feet = 4 R
Q, D, V
n, S
(e) Manning's roughness coefficient, n
(f) Velocity head, in feet
(g) Velocity, in feet per second = V
Energy Loss H_L in Feet per Ft.

(*f*) Velocity Head is the height of water above entrance (ponding) that will keep the pipe flowing full.

Note: When using this chart for culvert design and the pipe projects beyond the embankment on the upstream side multiply charted values by 1.9; when the pipe is beveled to conform to embankment slope multiply by 1.7; when headwalls are present and have square inlet edges or if prefabricated end sections are used multiply by 1.5; when headwalls are constructed with rounded inlet edges use charted values.

Figure 330-37 Nomograph for computing circular drains.

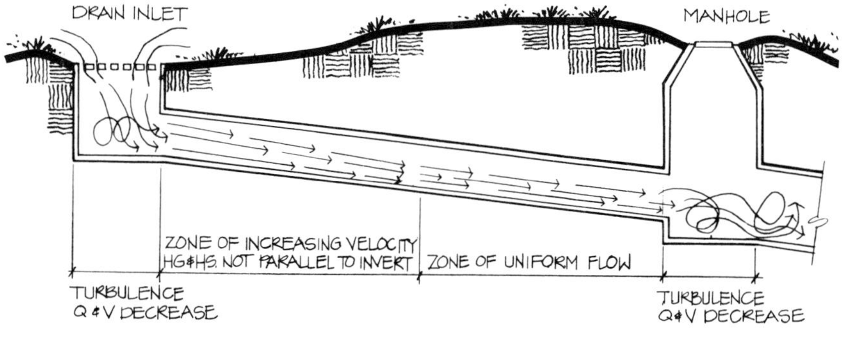
DRAIN INLET
MANHOLE
ZONE OF INCREASING VELOCITY
HG&HS NOT PARALLEL TO INVERT
ZONE OF UNIFORM FLOW
TURBULENCE
Q & V DECREASE
TURBULENCE
Q & V DECREASE

Figure 330-38 Water turbulence and its consequences.

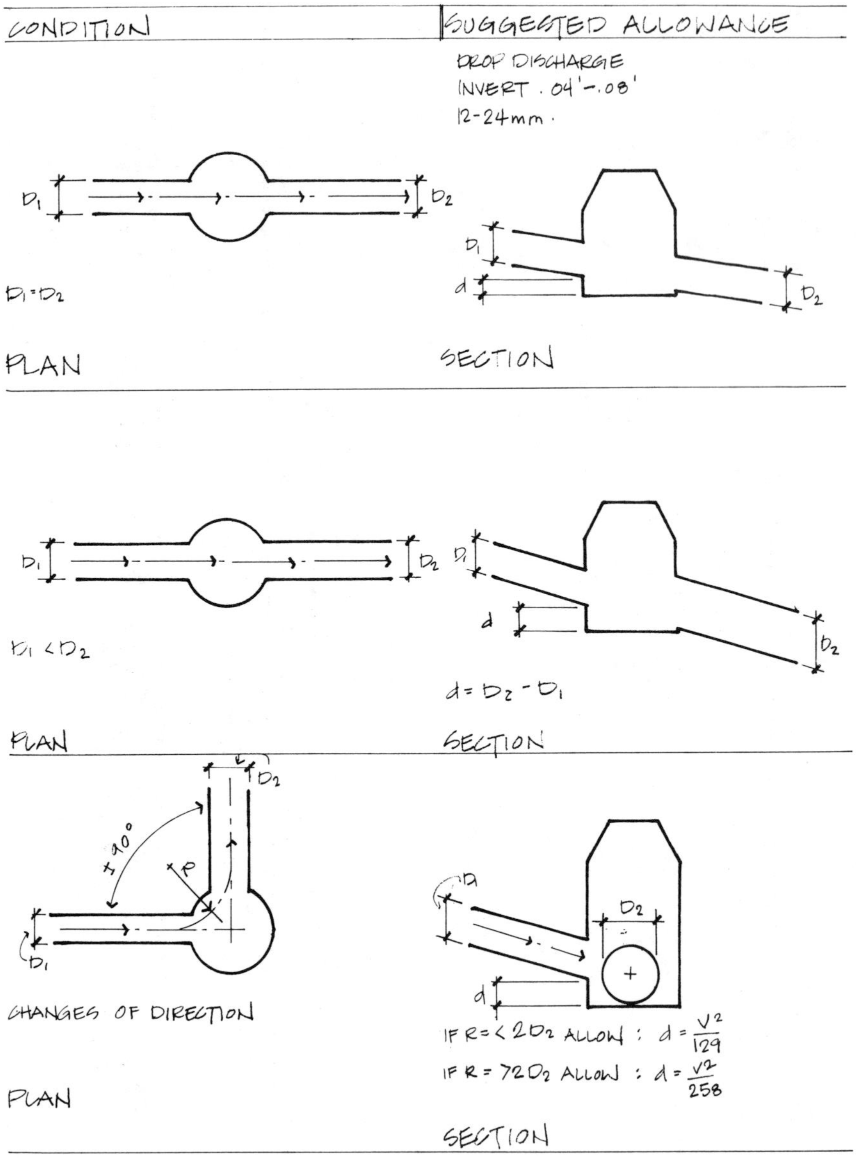
CONDITION
SUGGESTED ALLOWANCE
DROP DISCHARGE
INVERT .04'–.08'
12-24mm.
D1
D2
D1=D2
d
PLAN
SECTION
D1<D2
d=D2-D1
PLAN
SECTION
D2
±90°
R
D1
CHANGES OF DIRECTION
IF R=<2D2 ALLOW : d = V²/129
IF R = 72D2 ALLOW : d = V²/258
PLAN
SECTION

Figure 330-39 Suggested allowances for head loss.

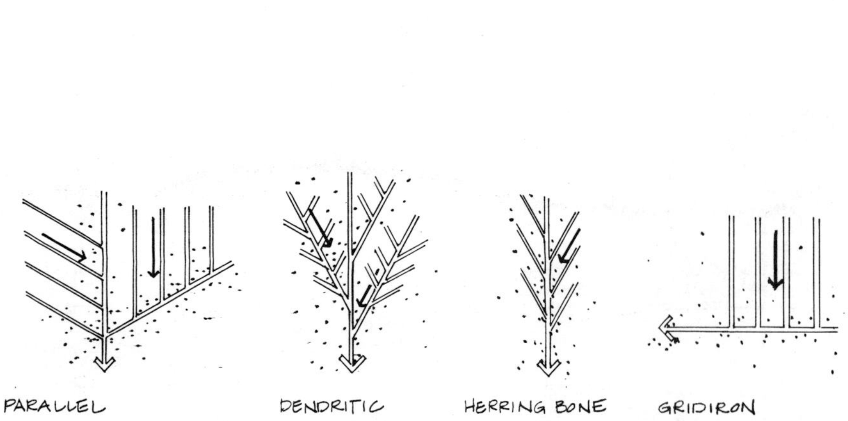
PARALLEL
DENDRITIC
HERRING BONE
GRIDIRON

Figure 330-40 Typical subdrainage layouts.

TABLE 330-8
Recommended Depths and Spacing of Subdrains by Soil Type

Soil character	*Silt*		*Clay*	*Depth, ft (m)*	*Spacing OC, ft (m)*
Sand with >20% fine	0–15%		0–10%	5 (1.5)	200 (60)
gravel and sand		<20% total			
Sandy loam with >20%	10–35%		5–15%		
fine gravel and sand	>20%		<50%	4 (1.2)	120 (36)
Fine sandy loam with	10–35%		—	3.5 (1)	100 (30)
<20% fine gravel	>20%		<50%		
and sand					
Loam	0–55%		15–25%	4 (1.2)	75 (22)
		>50%			
Clay loam	25–50%		25–35%	3 (0.9)	45 (14)
		>50%			
Clay	—		35–100%	3 (0.9)	25 (8)
		>60%			

Source: Jot D. Carpenter, ed. *Handbook of Landscape Architectural Construction,* Landscape Architecture Foundation, McLean, Virgina, 1976.

5.5 Inlet Design

The design of inlet grates is based on structural (i.e., loading) and hydraulic considerations. Manufacturers of standard cast-iron grates provide orifice and structural data. Computations are based on a standard *orifice formula* modified by a factor to represent potential clogging (Seelye):

$$Q = 0.66CA(64.4h)^{0.5}$$

where Q = design rate at inlet, cfs
C = orifice coefficient (0.6 for square-edge openings, 0.8 for round-edge openings)
A = net area of opening, ft^2
h = allowable depth of water over inlet, ft

The three significant variables, Q, A, and h, can be balanced as necessary for the design. Usually, Q and h are assumed and A is to be found, although each may be adjustable.

5.6 Underdrainage Design

The pipe size used for most subdrainage systems is usually 4 in. in diameter because it takes more time for surface storm water to soak through the ground and reach the drain tiles.

Subdrainage slopes should conform to the natural ground, with a minimum slope of 0.001 ft/ft, although slopes less than 0.005 ft/ft are difficult to construct. The minimum slope required will vary with the pipe size and the interior surface of the pipe. Larger pipe diameters, as well as smooth interior surfaces (low friction factor), require less slope. A slope of 0.012 ft/ft is common with 4-in pipe. Lines should be self-cleaning (i.e., have enough velocity to carry all sediment out of the line); a velocity of 2 fps is usually adequate. Subdrain velocities that are too fast may create vacuum pressures which would draw in fine soil particles.

The layout of a drain tile system should fit the topography and could be any one of several types (Figure 330-40).

Pipe depth is determined by the depth to which the water table should be dropped. To prevent frost heave damage to the system, the pipes must be below the frost line. The deeper the pipe, the more efficiently it will function, because the natural head generated will force water into the drain.

Spacing of lines is determined relative to soil texture. Table 330-8 gives the recommended depths and spacing of subdrains by soil type. Finer soils are more adhesive and are compensated for by closer spacing of the underdrains.

REFERENCES

Carpenter, Jot D., ed., *The Handbook of Landscape Architectural Construction,* American Society of Landscape Architecture Foundation, McLean, Virginia, 1976.

Dunne, Thomas, and Luna B. Leopold. *Water in Environmental Planning,* W.H. Freeman, San Francisco, 1978.

Landphair, Harlow C., and Fred Klatt, Jr. *Landscape Architectural Construction,* Elsevier, New York, 1979.

Lynch, Kevin, and Gary Hack. *Site Planning,* 3d ed., MIT Press, Cambridge, MA, 1984.

Michigan Soil Erosion and Sedimentation Control Guidebook, Michigan Department of Natural Resources, Lansing, MI, 1978.

Seelye, Elwyn, E. *Design,* 3d ed., Wiley, New York, 1966.

Soil Conservation Service. *National Engineering Handbook,* sect. 4: *Hydrology,* U.S. Department of Agriculture, 1972.

———. *Urban Hydrology for Small Watersheds,* Technical Release 55, U.S. Department of Agriculture, 1986.

Tourbier, J. Toby, and Richard Westmacott. *Water Resources Protection Technology: A Handbook of Measures to Protect Water Resources in Land Development,* Urban Land Institute, Washington, DC, 1981. ■

section 340: Pedestrian Circulation

CREDITS

Section Editor:

Gary M. Fishbeck
Sasaki Associates
Watertown, Massachusetts

Research Assistants:

Tobias Dayman and Diane Brown

Reviewer:

Roger B. Martin
Martin-Pitz, Inc.
Minneapolis, Minnesota

Note on Steps and Ramps:

Some data on Steps and Ramps were compiled by Robert LaRocca and Steven Brosnan of *Robert LaRocca & Associates, San Francisco, California,* and reviewed by David Arbegast of *Arbegast, Newton & Griffith, Berkeley, California,* and Richard Vignolo, *Landscape Architect, San Francisco, California.*

CONTENTS

1.0 INTRODUCTION

Pedestrian circulation is not easily discussed in specific terms because of the large differences in purpose between various types of systems. Most urban pedestrian circulation systems, for example, are typically perceived and utilized as a functional device more than as media for aesthetic experiences, a characteristic typical of park systems and other recreational open spaces. Moreover, because pedestrian circulation is an integral part of any particular design scheme, it is difficult to discuss the subject removed from the context in which it plays a role.

Consequently, the usefulness of this section in the handbook is limited to a "general" discussion of various aspects of pedestrian circulation. Specific situations may require research beyond the scope of this section and decisions based on professional judgment.

1.1 General

Generally speaking, pedestrian circulation systems fall into two broad categories: (1) those where the basic structure of a system already exists and (2) those where no circulation currently exists.

With existing systems, projects typically involve aesthetic enhancement of the system by provision of various amenities, improved views, conveniences, imageability, and the like. This type of work involves improvement of the "pedestrian experience" as much or more than it involves improvement of the functional aspects of the system.

In the case of new systems, the system must first be laid out according to proposed origin and destination points and must have adequate width to accommodate expected loads of pedestrian traffic during peak periods of use. As part of this process, aesthetic aspects of the proposed system are studied and carefully integrated with the functional aspects of the system.

Additional information on various aspects of pedestrian circulation can be found in other sections of this handbook, including 210: Spatial Standards; 240: Outdoor Accessibility; 510: Site Furniture and Features; and 540: Outdoor Lighting.

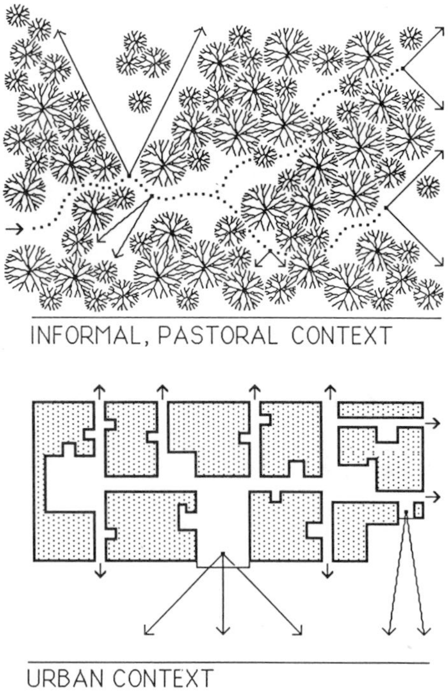
INFORMAL, PASTORAL CONTEXT
URBAN CONTEXT

Figure 340-1 Spatial modulation. Modulation of space can occur both vertically and horizontally.

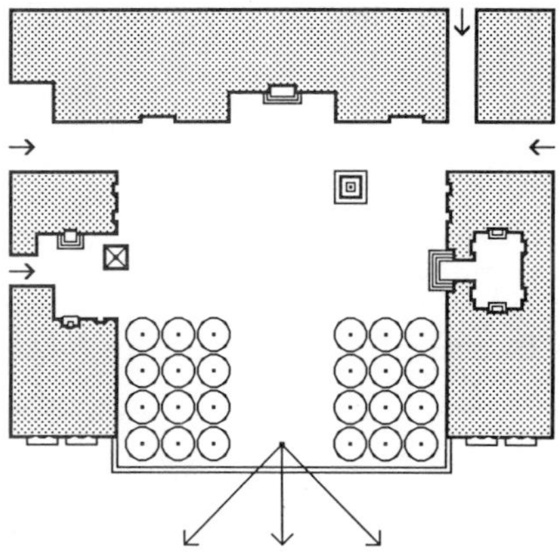

Figure 340-2 Hierarchical ordering of outdoor space. Note the relationships between primary, secondary, and tertiary spaces.

1.2 The Pedestrian Experience

Convenience:

The functional aspect of a pedestrian system is, of course, of primary importance, and the quality of this functional aspect is measured in terms of the "convenience" offered by the system. In addition to the obvious requirement of connecting all origin and destination points with walkways of adequate width, the two factors of *orientation* and *negotiation* play an important role.

In terms of orientation, landmark features and visual cues such as walkway width (e.g., wider walkways suggesting greater importance), formality (e.g., curvilinear walkways suggesting a more relaxing experience), paving material (e.g., expensive or highly articulated materials suggesting greater importance), and the presence and quality of ancillary features (the nature of which may suggest the predominant purpose of the walkway), can suggest purpose and expected behavior to the pedestrians using the system.

If carefully designed, visual cues (including signage) can aid the pedestrian in terms of way-finding and in terms of general orientation within a larger environmental context. This is especially important in complex environments.

Negotiation refers to the relative ease of moving from one destination to another. Pedestrian density (including conflicts at intersections and potential gathering spots) obviously plays an important role in this regard, but other aspects, such as physical obstructions (i.e., trash receptacles, light fixtures, flag poles, parking meters, water hydrants, telephones, benches, etc.); the presence of water or ice on the walkway; the nuisance of excessive litter; seed and fruit droppings from overhanging vegetation; excessive wind problems; etc., also contribute to relative difficulty in terms of negotiation.

Pathways should be accessible to all types of pedestrians, and sometimes on a selective basis to emergency vehicles such as police cars, ambulances, and firefighting equipment.

Amenities:

The purpose of any pedestrian circulation system is the connection it offers between various natural or cultural amenities, including the attraction of human activity. Social interaction, both passive and active, is extremely important and in many cases is the primary determinant regarding enjoyment of a place.

Because the activity of watching other people is universally appealing, spaces to gather with ample opportunities to sit are crucial to the success of most places, especially those in urban contexts.

Recent observations suggest that the availability of food and the activity of eating is a strong stimulus which attracts significant numbers of people to a place. For this reason, vendors are now often encouraged to operate in pedestrianized environments.

Spatial Considerations:

It is well known that the human environments most appreciated are those characterized by a relatively strong degree of spatial enclosure. In this regard, it is important to remain cognizant not only of weak spatial structures in outdoor environment but also of the differences between transitional space and nodal space.

For this reason, and because movement through an environment is a visual-spatial sequential experience, the "modulation" of transitional space and the "hierarchical ordering" of nodal space have become design principles of paramount importance.

Figures 340-1 and 340-2 illustrate these two principles in general terms.

Sensory Stimuli and Related Considerations:

Aesthetic aspects of pedestrian circulation refer to the myriad sensory and intellectual "experiences" enjoyed by pedestrians when moving through various environments. Designers should remain cognizant of the many environmental factors that contribute to the experiential enjoyment of outdoor places and should seek to provide a richness of experience and a depth of meaning to all who potentially may enjoy participation in designed or managed environments.

Table 340-1 is a checklist of various sensory stimuli, some of which are related to pleasant experiences and others of which relate to experiences of an unpleasant nature, and thus, are normally avoided or mitigated. Obviously, a checklist of this sort cannot be comprehensive, but it does provide a starting point for assessment of existing or proposed pedestrian environments from a sensory point of view.

2.0 PHYSICAL CHARACTERISTICS OF THE PEDESTRIAN

Basic information on the pedestrian is useful in those instances in design where spatial standards do not exist or where existing spatial standards are inapplicable. In such instances, reference can be made to physical characteristics of the human figure itself in order to make rational decisions about required dimensions of organized space and other details of a proposed pedestrian environment.

2.1 Dimensional Criteria

Human Dimensions and Activity:

Figure 340-3 illustrates approximate dimensions of human figures in various activity positions. (See Section 210: Spatial Standards, for more data.) Use of this information will, of course, depend on the purpose for which it is being used. Also,

TABLE 340-1
Common Sensory Stimuli in Pedestrian Environments

Sensory category	*Examples of common stimuli*
Tactile	Temperature
	Humidity
	Wind and breezes
	Precipitation
	Benches and seatwalls
	Sittable ground surfaces
	Bars, knobs, and handles
	Handrailings and armrests
	Telephones, vending and banking machines
	Textures under foot
	Vegetation within reach
	Water
	Architectural facades
	Food and drink
	Human contact
Auditory	Normal traffic noise
	Excessive truck traffic
	Underground rumblings
	Air traffic
	Distant highway noise
	Echo
	Conversation
	Play activity
	Music and song
	Professional and amateur entertainment
	Wind
	Water
	Wildlife
	Bells, chimes, and whistles
	Wind-blown flags and fabrics
	Movable furniture
	Vendors
	Machinery
	Heating, ventilation, and cooling systems
	Foot traffic on various pavements
Visual	Spatial perception (form, scale, etc.)
	Form of objects
	Proportion and scale of objects
	Social activity
	Vehicular activity
	Prominent landforms
	Vegetation
	Water features
	Miscellaneous natural features
	Sun and shadow
	Rain, snow, fog, mist
	Smoke
	Litter
	Signage
	Storefront advertisements
	Window displays
	Posted bills
	Billboards
	Walls and fences
	Street furniture and features
	Overhead wires and cables
	Architecture
	Vegetation
	Wildlife
	Overall character of a place
	Sites under construction
	Surface textures
	Color compositions
	Tonal contrasts
	Diurnal change
	Seasonal change
	Moonlight
	Night-lighting
	Glare and albedo
	Viewsheds from important vantage points
	General order
	Overall congruencies
Olfactory	Vehicular emissions
	Industrial odors
	Odorous smoke
	Fresh air
	Fragrant vegetation
	Restaurant doorways
	Outdoor cafes
	Odorous litter and debris
	Refuse areas
	Exhaust fans

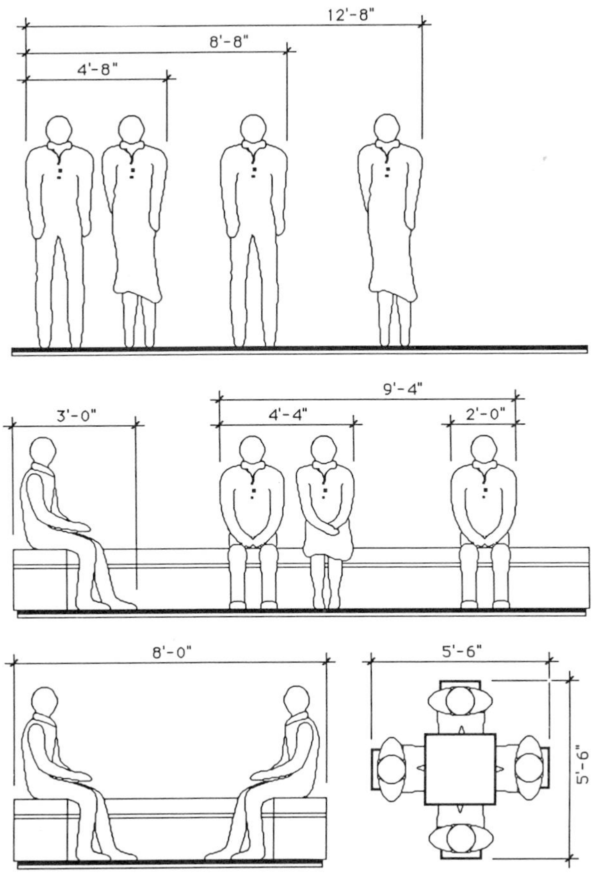
12'-8"
8'-8"
4'-8"
9'-4"
3'-0"
4'-4"
2'-0"
8'-0"
5'-6"
5'-6"

Figure 340-3 Human dimensions in various activity positions. These dimensions are approximate average spatial requirements which are used primarily as an aid to professional judgment, rather than as standard criteria.

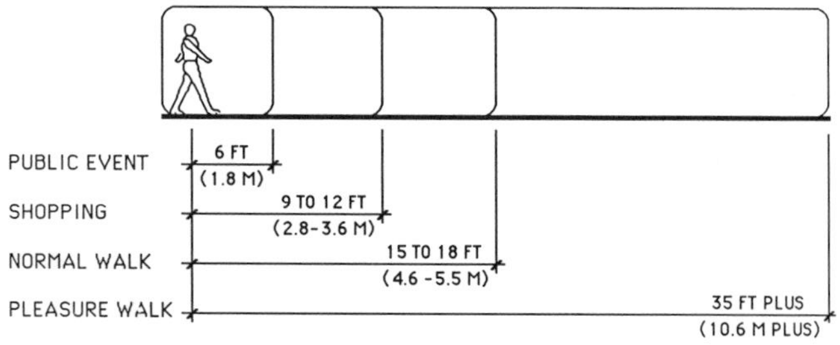
PUBLIC EVENT
SHOPPING
NORMAL WALK
PLEASURE WALK
6 FT
(1.8 M)
9 TO 12 FT
(2.8-3.6 M)
15 TO 18 FT
(4.6 -5.5 M)
35 FT PLUS
(10.6 M PLUS)

Figure 340-4 Forward spatial bubbles.

spatial requirements differ in various regions of the United States (and other cultures as well) as a function of accustomed densities of people, heritage, social and environmental values, and so forth.

Forward Spatial Bubbles:

Figure 340-4 illustrates forward spatial bubbles (i.e., the extent of unobstructed forward vision while walking) held to be psychologically comfortable for the average pedestrian under various circumstances. As mentioned earlier, degree of psychological comfort (in terms of spatial requirements) will differ across various regions of the United States and between various cultures.

This information on spatial bubbles is useful when calculating how much clear space is necessary to accommodate expected numbers of people in various situations, if the intent is to maintain a reasonable degree of psychological comfort for those involved.

Use of a mathematical formula to determine minimum walkway widths requires that a decision be made on an acceptable spatial bubble for each walkway being considered (refer to 3.1 in this section for use of this formula).

2.2 Movement Criteria

Walking Rates:

Table 340-2 shows average walking rates of adult pedestrians, expressed in various units of measurement.

The average walking rate of a pedestrian will decrease when pedestrian density on a walkway increases and/or the clear space ahead of the pedestrian becomes less than approximately 15 ft (5 m). Pedestrian walking rates are not significantly affected by grade changes of 6 percent or less, but intersections, stairways, escalators, and turnstiles will slow down average walking rates.

Refer to 3.1 in this section for information on calculating minimum walkway widths based on pedestrian walking rates.

Acceptable Walking Distances:

Figure 340-5 illustrates the average range of walking distances that people (in the United States) are typically willing to walk (e.g., between activities or from parking areas to activities). Acceptable distances will vary from these averages depending on the purpose of the trip, cultural differences in various regions of the United States, climatic conditions, etc., but these averages do give a rough idea of the kind of behavior to expect from pedestrians in situations involving parking lots, trips within communities, and the like.

Pedestrian Density Criteria:

Figures 340-6 and 340-7 show pedestrian flow volume, speed, and density for walkways and stairways. This information can be used as a visual guide for estimating existing or proposed pedestrian traffic volumes and speed and for determining minimum walkway widths by use of the mathematical formula given in 3.1 of this section.

2.3 Visual Criteria

Eye Levels and Cone of Vision:

The eye level of an average adult in a standing position and a sitting position is illustrated in Figure 340-8. Pedestrians will focus most of their attention at eye level and below during normal perception of their surroundings.

The human cone of vision (i.e., the fixed eye) is approximately 30 degrees vertically and 60 degrees horizontally, with angles of acute vision somewhat less than this, as illustrated in Figure 340-9.

Eye levels and cones of vision are especially important in terms of the placement and orientation of pedestrian signage.

Visual Perception:

Sense of Spatial Enclosure: An external enclosure is most comfortable when its vertical planes are one-half to one-third as high as the width of the space enclosed. If the ratio falls below one-fourth, the space begins to lack a sense of enclosure (Figure 340-10).

Social Communication: For a variety of reasons, the scale and form of a space will influence pedestrian behavior and the type of social communication that may occur within that space. Important in this regard are the physical distances that bring into close proximity, or separate, people who are using the space at any given moment. Settings meant to be conducive to active social communication, or settings meant to allow a certain degree of privacy, for example, each require careful thought as to

TABLE 340-2
Average Walking Rates of Adult Pedestrians

Type	*Ft/min*	*M/min*	*Km/min*
Average adult	260	72	4.3
Elderly (75 yrs)	215	67	4
Bunching	200	61	3.7
Stairways (going down)	152	46	2.8
Stairways (going up)	113	34	2

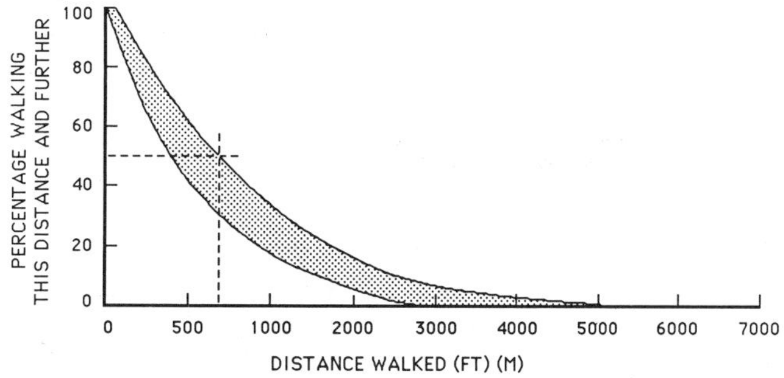
PERCENTAGE WALKING
THIS DISTANCE AND FURTHER
100
80
60
40
20
0
0
500
1000
2000
3000
4000
5000
6000
7000
DISTANCE WALKED (FT) (M)

Figure 340-5 Range of acceptable walking distances (U.S. cities). Most people are not willing to walk distances greater than about 700 ft (220 m).

Average Flow Volume: 7 PFM* or less
Average Speed: 260 ft/min
Average Pedestrian Area Occupancy: 36 ft^2./person or greater

Description: Virtually unrestricted choice of speed; minimum maneuvering to pass; crossing and reverse movements unrestricted; flow approximately 25% of maximum capacity.

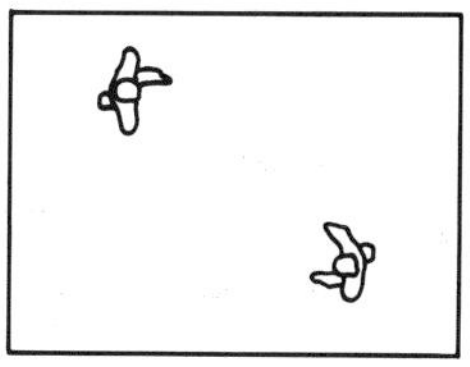

Average Flow Volume: 7–10 PFM
Average Speed: 250–260 ft/min
Average Pedestrian Area Occupancy: 25–35 ft^2./person

Description: Normal walking speeds only occasionally restricted; some occasional interference in passing; crossing and reverse movements possible with occasional conflict; flow approximately 35% of maximum capacity.

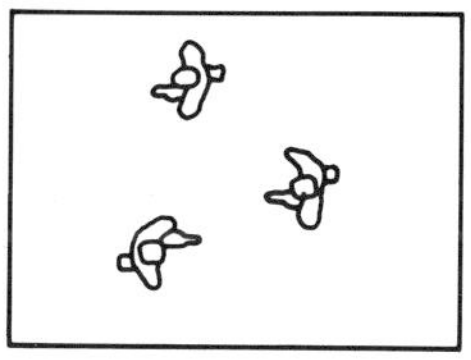

Average Flow Volume: 10–15 PFM
Average Speed: 230–250 ft/min
Average Pedestrian Area Occupancy: 15–25 ft^2./person

Description: Walking speeds partially restricted; passing restricted but possible with maneuvering; crossing and reverse movements restricted and require significant maneuvering to avoid conflict; flow reasonably fluid and about 40–65% of maximum capacity.

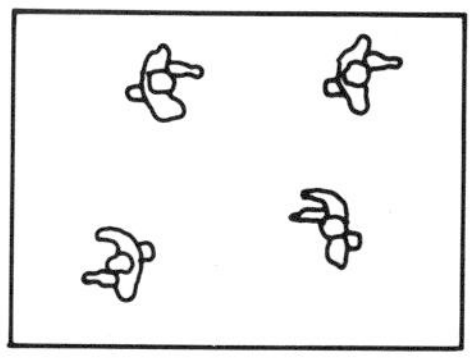

Average Flow Volume: 15–20 PFM
Average Speed: 200–230 ft/min
Average Pedestrian Area Occupancy: 10–15 ft^2./person

Description: Walking speeds restricted and reduced; passing rarely possible without conflict; crossing and reverse movements severely restricted with multiple conflicts; some probability of momentary flow stoppages when critical densities might be intermittently reached; flow approximately 65–80% of maximum capacity.

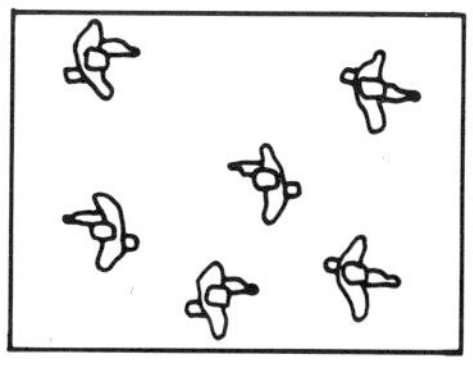

Average Flow Volume: 20–25 PFM
Average Speed: 110–200 ft/min
Average Pedestrian Area Occupancy: 5–10 ft^2./person

Description: Walking speeds restricted and frequently reduced to shuffling; frequent adjustment of gait required; passing impossible without conflict; crossings and reverse movements severely restricted with unavoidable conflicts; flows attain maximum capacity under pressure, but with frequent stoppages and interruptions of flow.

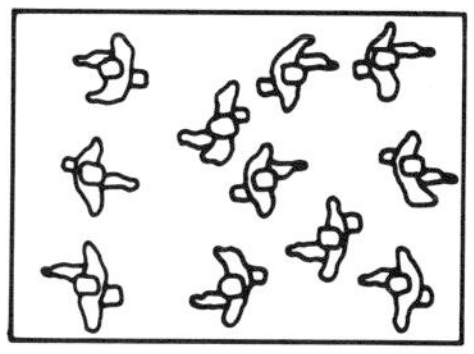

Average Flow Volume: 25 PFM or more
Average Speed: 0–110 ft/min
Average Pedestrian Area Occupancy: 5 ft^2./person or less

Description: Walking speed reduced to shuffling; passing impossible; crossing and reverse movements impossible; physical contact frequent and unavoidable; flow sporadic and on the verge of complete breakdown and stoppage.

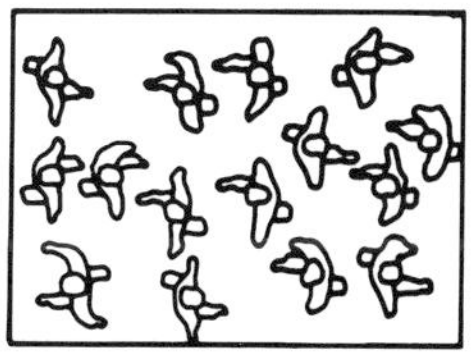

*PFM = pedestrians per foot width of walkway, per minute.

Figure 340-6 Average flow volume, speed, and density (walkways).

Average Flow Volume: 5 PFM* or less
Average Speed: 125 ft/min or more
Average Pedestrian Area Occupancy: 20 ft^2./person

Description: Unrestricted choice of speed; relatively free to pass; no serious difficulties with reverse traffic movements; flow approximately 30% of maximum capacity.

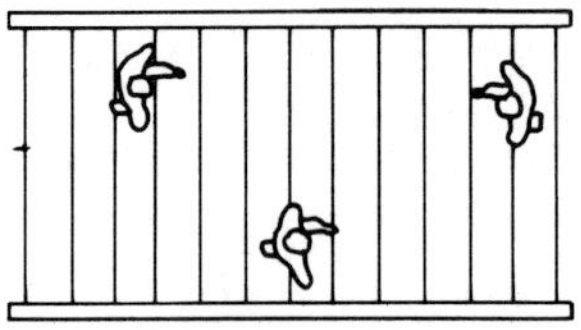

Average Flow Volume: 5–7 PFM
Average Speed: 120–125 ft/min
Average Pedestrian Area Occupancy: 15–20 ft^2./person

Description: Restricted choice of speed; passing encounters interference; reverse flows create occasional conflicts; flow approximately 34% of maximum capacity.

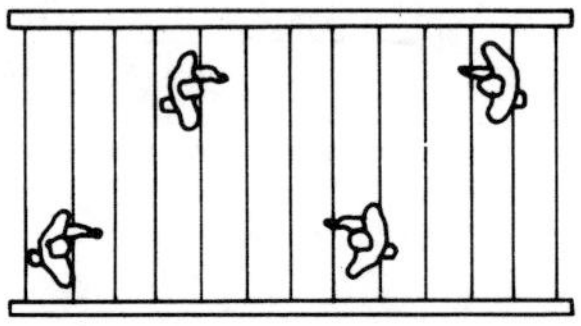

Average Flow Volume: 7–10 PFM
Average Speed: 115–120 ft/min
Average Pedestrian Area Occupancy: 10–15 ft^2./person

Description: Speeds partially restricted; passing restricted; reverse flows partially restricted; flow approximately 50% of maximum capacity.

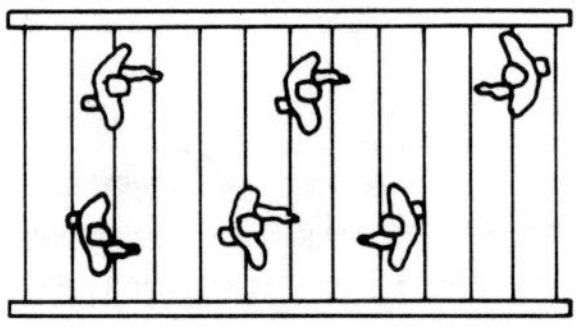

Average Flow Volume: 10–13 PFM
Average Speed: 105–115 ft/min
Average Pedestrian Area Occupancy: 7–10 ft^2./person

Description: Speeds restricted; passing virtually impossible; reverse flows severely restricted; flows approximately 50–65% of maximum capacity.

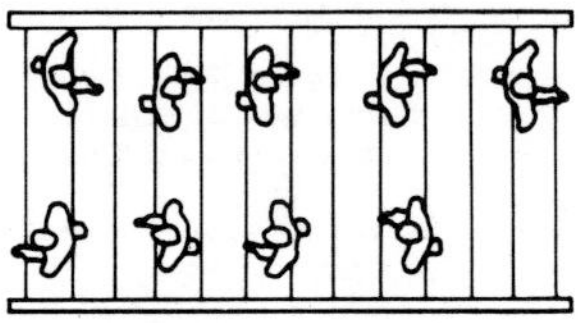

Average Flow Volume: 13–17 PFM
Average Speed: 85–115 ft/min
Average Pedestrian Area Occupancy: 4–7 ft^2./person

Description: Speeds severely restricted; passing impossible; reverse traffic flows severely restricted; intermittent stoppages of flow likely to occur; flows approximately 65–86% of maximum capacity.

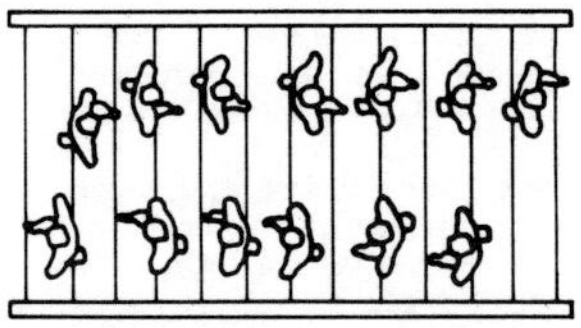

Average Flow Volume: 17 PFM or greater
Average Speed: 0–85 ft/min
Average Pedestrian Area Occupancy: 4 ft^2./person or less

Description: Speed severely restricted; flow subject to complete breakdown with many stoppages; passing as well as reverse flows impossible.

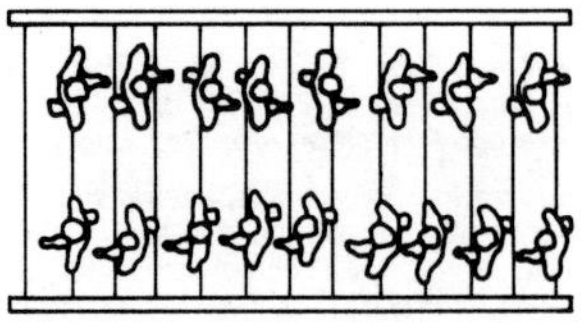

*PFM = pedestrians per foot width of stairway, per minute.

Figure 340-7 Average flow volume, speed, and density (stairways).

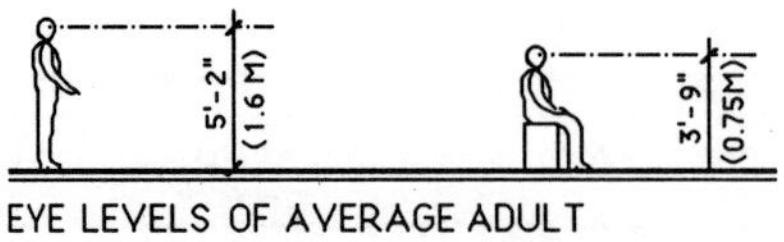
5'-2"
(1.6 M)
3'-9"
(0.75M)
EYE LEVELS OF AVERAGE ADULT

Figure 340-8 Eye levels of an average adult.

the degree of eye contact possible, and probable, within the scale and layout of the setting.

In this regard, it is helpful to possess a general understanding of the capabilities and limitations of normal human vision in terms of social communication. Several examples are illustrated in Figure 340-11.

3.0 SPATIAL STANDARDS

3.1 Pathway Width and Slope Criteria

General Considerations:

Widths of pedestrian pathways vary depending on the purpose of the pathway and the existing or expected intensity of use. As a general rule of thumb, a 24 in (600 mm) width for each pedestrian is necessary, which suggests a minimum pathway width of 4 ft (1.2 m) for public walkways. When pedestrian flows are significant and greater precision required in the determination of walkway width, minimum acceptable widths of a pathway can be calculated using the formula given below.

It is important to remember that pedestrians as a group typically do not use the entire width of most walkways. The edge of a walkway adjacent to a curbed roadway (i.e., 30 in (0.75 m) from the street edge) is avoided by pedestrians, as is the edge of a walkway along a building facade [i.e., 18 to 30 in (0.50 to 0.75 m)]. These edges are used only under conditions of high pedestrian density.

The presence of street furniture and features such as fire hydrants, trees, parking meters, telephones, trash receptacles, fountains, sculpture, and kiosks also reduces the effective width of a pathway.

Calculation of Walkway Width (by Formula):

Minimum width for a pedestrian pathway can be determined by mathematical calculation as a function of expected pedestrian volume, acceptable density, and desirable rate of movement. The number of pedestrians (volume) passing a stationary point on a pathway is expressed by unit measurements of time, such as "pedestrians per minute" or "pedestrians per hour." Density refers to personal buffer zones, expressed in terms of square feet per pedestrian. Given these criteria, pathway widths can be calculated using the *standard flow theory* shown below.*

* Charles F. Scheffey, Director, Office of Research, *A Pedestrian Planning Procedure Manual,* vols. II and III, Report no. FHWA-RD-79-46, Virginia National Technical Information Service, November 1978.

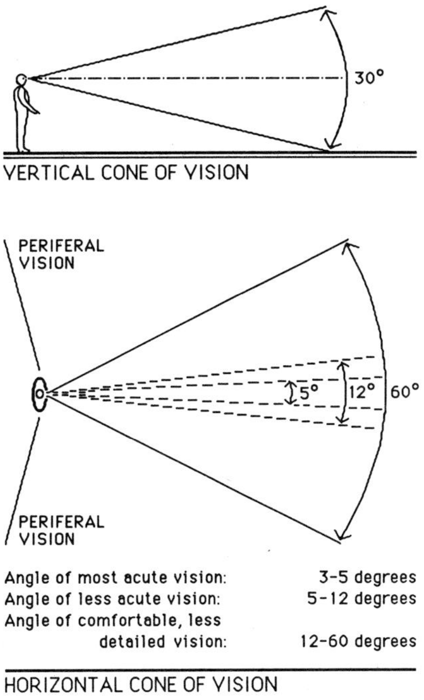
30°
VERTICAL CONE OF VISION
PERIFERAL VISION
5°
12°
60°
PERIFERAL VISION
Angle of most acute vision: 3-5 degrees
Angle of less acute vision: 5-12 degrees
Angle of comfortable, less detailed vision: 12-60 degrees
HORIZONTAL CONE OF VISION

Figure 340-9 Normal cone of vision.

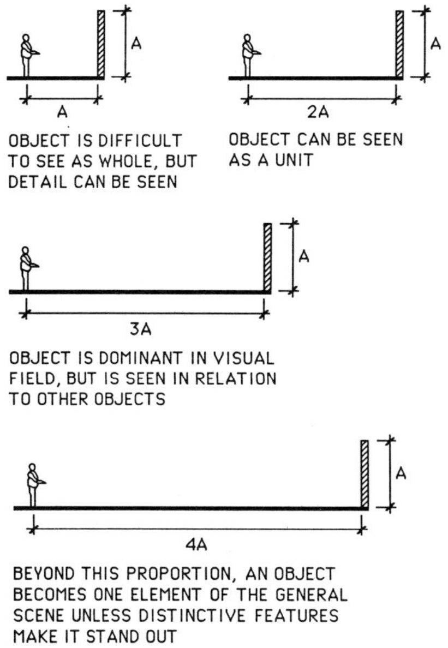
A
A
OBJECT IS DIFFICULT TO SEE AS WHOLE, BUT DETAIL CAN BE SEEN
A
2A
OBJECT CAN BE SEEN AS A UNIT
A
3A
OBJECT IS DOMINANT IN VISUAL FIELD, BUT IS SEEN IN RELATION TO OTHER OBJECTS
A
4A
BEYOND THIS PROPORTION, AN OBJECT BECOMES ONE ELEMENT OF THE GENERAL SCENE UNLESS DISTINCTIVE FEATURES MAKE IT STAND OUT

Figure 340-10 Sense of spatial enclosure outdoors.

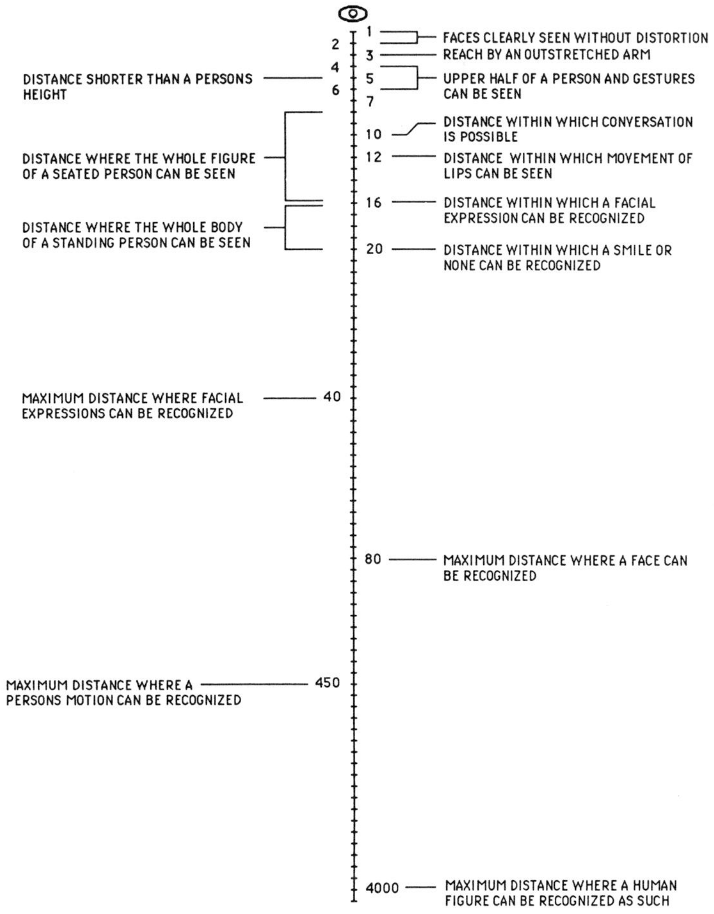
1 FACES CLEARLY SEEN WITHOUT DISTORTION
3 REACH BY AN OUTSTRETCHED ARM
DISTANCE SHORTER THAN A PERSONS HEIGHT 2 4 6
5 7 UPPER HALF OF A PERSON AND GESTURES CAN BE SEEN
10 DISTANCE WITHIN WHICH CONVERSATION IS POSSIBLE
DISTANCE WHERE THE WHOLE FIGURE OF A SEATED PERSON CAN BE SEEN
12 DISTANCE WITHIN WHICH MOVEMENT OF LIPS CAN BE SEEN
16 DISTANCE WITHIN WHICH A FACIAL EXPRESSION CAN BE RECOGNIZED
DISTANCE WHERE THE WHOLE BODY OF A STANDING PERSON CAN BE SEEN
20 DISTANCE WITHIN WHICH A SMILE OR NONE CAN BE RECOGNIZED
MAXIMUM DISTANCE WHERE FACIAL EXPRESSIONS CAN BE RECOGNIZED 40
80 MAXIMUM DISTANCE WHERE A FACE CAN BE RECOGNIZED
MAXIMUM DISTANCE WHERE A PERSONS MOTION CAN BE RECOGNIZED 450
4000 MAXIMUM DISTANCE WHERE A HUMAN FIGURE CAN BE RECOGNIZED AS SUCH

Figure 340-11 Inherent capabilities of human vision in terms of social communication (not to scale).

In this formula, pedestrian volume (*V*) refers to the number of pedestrians that are expected to pass any one point on the pathway each minute. (Refer to Figures 340-6 and 340-7 for information on pedestrian flow volumes.) Space modules (*M*) typically range from a minimum of 5 ft² per person to 35 ft² or greater. (Refer to Figure 340-4 for information on space modules.) Walking speed (*S*) typically averages about 260 ft/min, but of course can vary significantly depending on the predominant activities in the area, the types of pedestrians, etc. (Refer to Table 340-2 for information on walking speeds.)

Expected loads of pedestrian traffic are determined through observation of similar projects in other areas, formal studies, and professional judgment.

$$\text{Pathway Width} = \frac{V(M)}{S}$$

where V = volume, pedestrians/minute
M = space module, ft²/pedestrian
S = walking speed, ft/minute

Example calculation: Given: Volume of pedestrians = 200/minute, minimum space module desired = 18 ft²/pedestrian, pedestrian walking speed (normal) = 260 ft/minute

$$\frac{200 \times 18}{260} = \frac{3600}{260} = 13.3 \text{ ft}$$

In this example, the walkway width would have to be at least 13.3 ft (4.2 m) wide to accommodate the given flow of pedestrians.

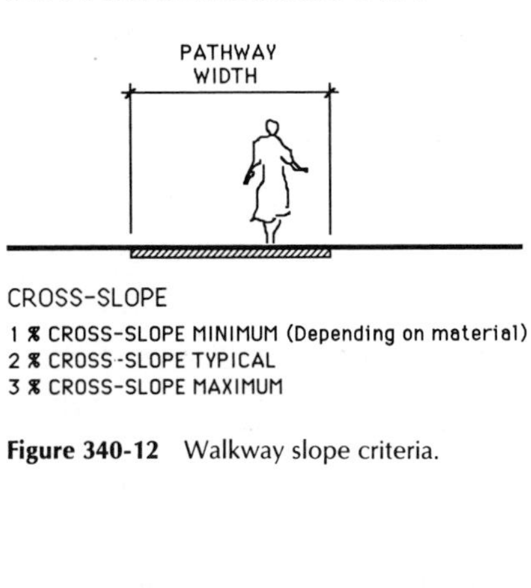
LONGITUDINAL SLOPE
0 TO 3 % SLOPES PREFERRED
5 % SLOPES MAXIMUM
5 TO 10 % SLOPES POSSIBLE IF CLIMATIC CONDITIONS PERMIT
5 TO 8 % SLOPES ARE CONSIDERED RAMPS
PATHWAY WIDTH
CROSS-SLOPE
1 % CROSS-SLOPE MINIMUM (Depending on material)
2 % CROSS-SLOPE TYPICAL
3 % CROSS-SLOPE MAXIMUM

Figure 340-12 Walkway slope criteria.

Note that this formula can yield answers suggesting very narrow walkway widths when light pedestrian traffic loads are calculated. Such answers imply that a common walkway width of 4 or 5 ft (1.2 or 1.6 m) would be adequate to accommodate the expected traffic load.

It is important to note that this formula does not take into account the spatial requirements of street furniture, social gathering places, minimal use of walkway edges, and the like. If such features or circumstances are involved, then adjustments have to be made to the overall width of the pathway. Moreover, this formula yields *minimum* (functional) walkway widths, not *optimal* widths based on aesthetic criteria. Very often, walkway widths are designed to be much greater than necessary for reasons of scale, proportion, etc.

Consequently, this formula is more often used as a check against a proposed design scheme rather than as a rigid method for determining walkway widths.

Walkway Slope Criteria:

Figure 340-12 provides longitudinal and cross-slope criteria for walkways under various circumstances. Longitudinal slope criteria are based on user abilities and design objectives, and cross-slope criteria are based on the need for positive drainage (depending on paving material). Porous paving, for instance, does not require as much of a cross-slope for drainage as does a nonporous paving material.

3.2 Stairways

Widths:

Minimum width for public stairways should be 60 in (1.5 m). Minimum width for private stairways should be 42 in (1.1 m).

Tread-Riser Ratios:

For ease of ascent or descent, and for safety reasons, tread-riser ratios are always held constant within any particular stairway or set of stairways. On rare occasions riser heights in stairways will vary (e.g., stairways built obliquely into a slope, as in plazas, etc.), but these are hazardous and should be avoided whenever possible. On very gentle slopes of 0.5 to perhaps 2.0 percent, a stairway can be built to slope with the grade rather than remain level, in order to keep the bottom riser at a constant dimension. In addition, or alternatively, the bottom of stairway grade (B.S.) can be warped to maintain a constant along the edge of the bottom tread.

Occasionally, tread widths also vary for aesthetic reasons (again in plazas and the like), and this is generally found to be acceptable as long as it is understood that ascending or descending such stairways (typically referred to as terraced plazas) is often cumbersome. This is generally acceptable because terraced plazas are typically used as informal gathering places rather than as purely utilitarian transitional spaces.

RISER	TREAD
4.00	18.00-19.00
4.25	17.50-18.50
4.50	17.00-18.00
4.75	16.50-17.50
5.00	16.00-17.00
5.25	15.50-16.50
5.50	15.00-16.00
5.75	14.50-15.50
6.00	14.00-15.00
6.25	13.50-14.50
6.50	13.00-14.00
6.75	12.50-13.50
7.00	12.00-13.00
7.25	11.50-12.50
7.50	11.00-12.00

Figure 340-13 Quick reference chart of typical tread-risers ratios for outdoor stairways. Check state codes where applicable.

In dimensionally unconstrained situations, employing a tread-riser ratio is up to the discretion of the designer. Choice of a ratio will depend on the kinesthetic effect desired by the designer, and on appearance.

In dimensionally constrained situations (i.e., where the elevations of both the top and the bottom of a stairway, or a set of stairways, are given), an appropriate tread-riser ratio has to be determined that will allow a given number of steps (including landings if necessary) to be "fit" into the space.

Figure 340-13 is a quick-reference chart of typical tread-riser ratios for outdoor stairways. As an alternative to tread-riser charts, the following formula is commonly used to determine acceptable tread-riser ratios for outdoor stairways, especially when fractions of an inch are involved.

$$2R + T = 26 \text{ to } 27 \text{ in } (650 \text{ to } 675 \text{ mm})$$

where R = riser
T = tread

Additional Considerations:

1. Outdoor stairways should be made easier to ascend and descend than interior stairways. People tend to move at greater rates outdoors than they do indoors.

2. Inherent to a particular tread-riser ratio is the ease at which the stairway can be ascended or descended, and consequently, the sense of rhythm to be enjoyed by the pedestrian. Ideally, the kinesthetic character of a stairway should be congruent with the character of the environment in which the stairway is a part.

3. Single steps in a walkway are very dangerous and should never be specified. At least two steps, but preferably three, should be specified, and their presence should be announced conspicuously with railings, plantings, lighting, and the like.

4. Risers for outdoor stairways should be a minimum of 4.5 in (112 mm) and a maximum of 7 in (175 mm).

5. Treads should be pitched downgrade 2 percent for drainage.

Nosing and Shadow Line Profiles: Shadow lines are often included in steps for aesthetic reasons, used mainly to give a "refined" look to a stairway. They can, however, be hazardous if large enough to catch the toes of pedestrians. Nosings can also catch toes unless they are rounded.

Figure 340-14 shows various nosing and shadow line profiles, some of which are potentially hazardous and therefore not recommended, particularly in public areas and in areas frequented by handicapped individuals. (Refer to Section 240: Outdoor Accessibility, for more information.)

Height between Landings:

Height between stairway landings is an important criterion for psychological reasons as well as for reasons of human endurance. Although many building codes state maximum heights of 12 ft (3.8 m), lesser heights are recommended.

In terms of environmental psychology, it is known that abrupt changes in ground levels, even as little as 1 to 1½ ft (0.3 to 0.5 m) can decrease incentive to proceed. Changes of 6 ft (1.8 m) or more are found to be strongly discouraging. For this reason, heights between stair landings are best designed so that an adult of average height standing on one landing can see the ground plane of the next higher landing, i.e., 5 ft (1.6 m) or less (Figure 340-15). Conversely, in conjunction with other design elements, height between landings is sometimes made to be greater than 5 ft (1.6 m) to effectively control sightlines.

In terms of human endurance, it should be remembered that elderly and handicapped individuals use stairways, and their abilities are more limited than the average, physically healthy adult. For this reason, all changes in elevation should be designed with an understanding of the diversity of

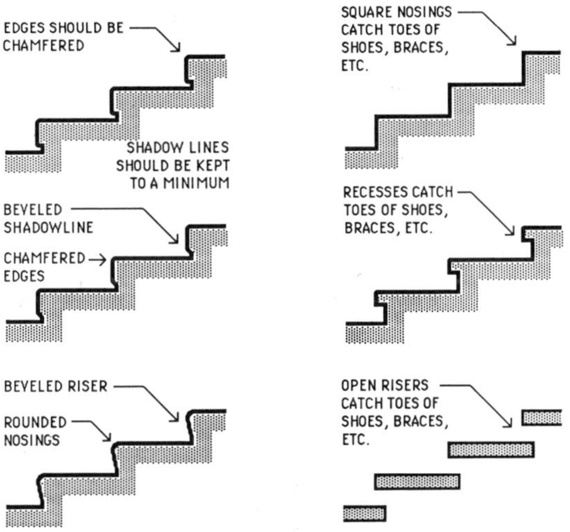
EDGES SHOULD BE CHAMFERED
SHADOW LINES SHOULD BE KEPT TO A MINIMUM
BEVELED SHADOWLINE
CHAMFERED EDGES
BEVELED RISER
ROUNDED NOSINGS
SQUARE NOSINGS CATCH TOES OF SHOES, BRACES, ETC.
RECESSES CATCH TOES OF SHOES, BRACES, ETC.
OPEN RISERS CATCH TOES OF SHOES, BRACES, ETC.
THESE PROFILES ARE CONSIDERED RELATIVELY SAFE
THESE PROFILES CAN BE HAZARDOUS

Figure 340-14 Typical nosing and shadow line profiles. Check state codes where applicable.

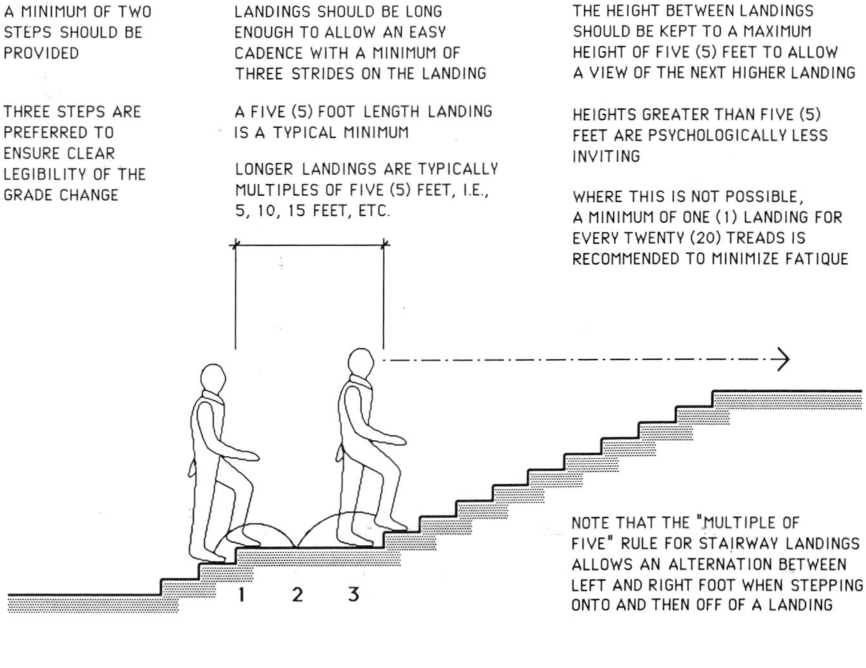
A MINIMUM OF TWO STEPS SHOULD BE PROVIDED
THREE STEPS ARE PREFERRED TO ENSURE CLEAR LEGIBILITY OF THE GRADE CHANGE
LANDINGS SHOULD BE LONG ENOUGH TO ALLOW AN EASY CADENCE WITH A MINIMUM OF THREE STRIDES ON THE LANDING
A FIVE (5) FOOT LENGTH LANDING IS A TYPICAL MINIMUM
LONGER LANDINGS ARE TYPICALLY MULTIPLES OF FIVE (5) FEET, I.E., 5, 10, 15 FEET, ETC.
THE HEIGHT BETWEEN LANDINGS SHOULD BE KEPT TO A MAXIMUM HEIGHT OF FIVE (5) FEET TO ALLOW A VIEW OF THE NEXT HIGHER LANDING
HEIGHTS GREATER THAN FIVE (5) FEET ARE PSYCHOLOGICALLY LESS INVITING
WHERE THIS IS NOT POSSIBLE, A MINIMUM OF ONE (1) LANDING FOR EVERY TWENTY (20) TREADS IS RECOMMENDED TO MINIMIZE FATIQUE
NOTE THAT THE "MULTIPLE OF FIVE" RULE FOR STAIRWAY LANDINGS ALLOWS AN ALTERNATION BETWEEN LEFT AND RIGHT FOOT WHEN STEPPING ONTO AND THEN OFF OF A LANDING
1 2 3

Figure 340-15 Stairway height and landing proportions. Check state codes where applicable.

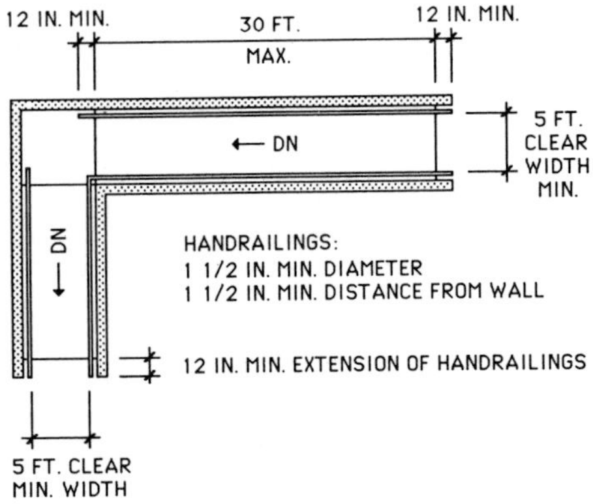
12 IN. MIN.
30 FT.
MAX.
12 IN. MIN.
5 FT.
CLEAR
WIDTH
MIN.
← DN
DN ↓
HANDRAILINGS:
1 1/2 IN. MIN. DIAMETER
1 1/2 IN. MIN. DISTANCE FROM WALL
12 IN. MIN. EXTENSION OF HANDRAILINGS
5 FT. CLEAR
MIN. WIDTH

Figure 340-16 Dimensional criteria for two-way handicap ramp. Minimum clear width for one-way travel is 36 in (900 mm). Check state codes where applicable.

human ability that exists among members of the population. (Refer to Section 240: Outdoor Accessibility, for more information on the abilities of elderly and handicapped individuals.)

Figure 340-15 summarizes several important considerations for the design of outdoor stairways and landings.

3.3 Ramps

Widths:

Ramp widths are determined according to type and intensity of use. One-way travel requires a minimum width of 3 ft (900 mm) clear, whereas two-way travel requires a clear minimum width of 5 ft (1500 mm) (Figure 340-16). If turns occur at landings, adequate space for maneuvering wheelchairs must be provided. (Refer to the Uniform Federal Accessibility Standards (UFAS) in the Appendix of this handbook for a comprehensive compilation of dimensional criteria and to state and local codes, many of which have been adopted in whole or in part from ANSI Standards.)

Slope Criteria:

Ramp slopes should be no greater than 12:1 (8.33 percent) (Figure 340-12). Curb cuts are an exception, 8:1 (12 percent) being acceptable if the running distance is less than 3 ft (1 m).

Distance between Landings:

Landings should be provided within every 30 ft (9 m) or less of ramp length (Figure 340-16).

3.4 Seating Criteria

Benches should be designed to ensure greatest comfort for the individual. Figure 340-17 illustrates preferred height and the seating angle for outdoor benches.

Seat walls are typically 16 to 18 in wide and between 14 and 18 in (400 to 450 mm) in height, 16 in (400 mm) being most preferred. Refer to Section 931: Seating Walls, in this handbook for examples of seating wall details.

3.5 Handrailings

Handrailings, the cross-section of which should allow a secure and comfortable grip

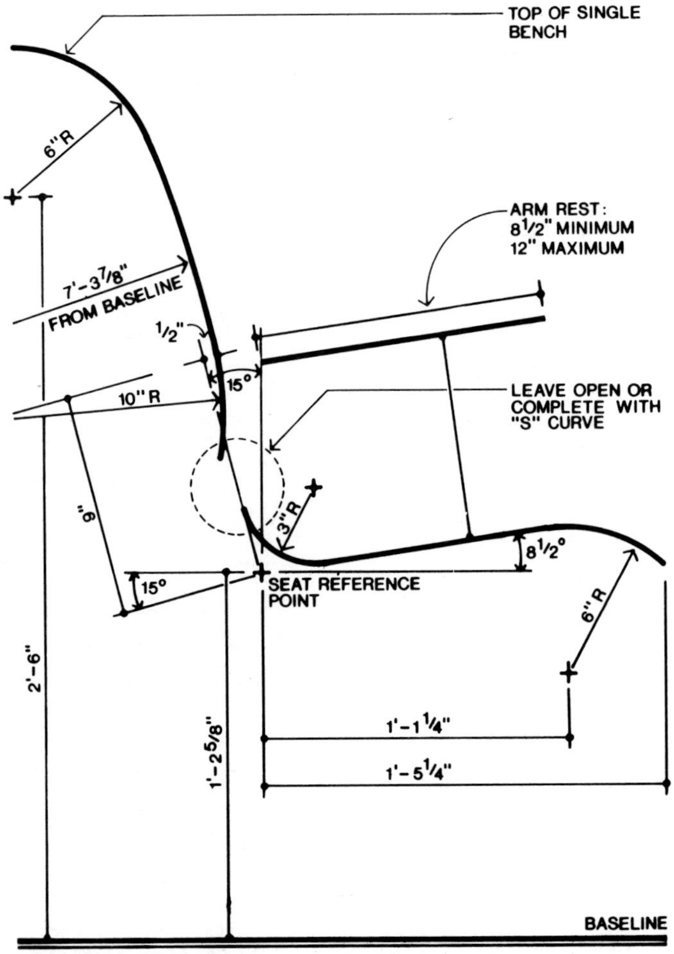
TOP OF SINGLE
BENCH
6"R
7'-3 7/8"
FROM BASELINE
1/2"
10"R
15°
ARM REST:
8 1/2" MINIMUM
12" MAXIMUM
LEAVE OPEN OR
COMPLETE WITH
"S" CURVE
3"R
8"
15°
8 1/2°
SEAT REFERENCE
POINT
6"R
2'-6"
1'-2 5/8"
1'-1 1/4"
1'-5 1/4"
BASELINE

Figure 340-17 Preferred height and seating angle for outdoor benches. Dimensions shown are for optional double- and single-bench contour.

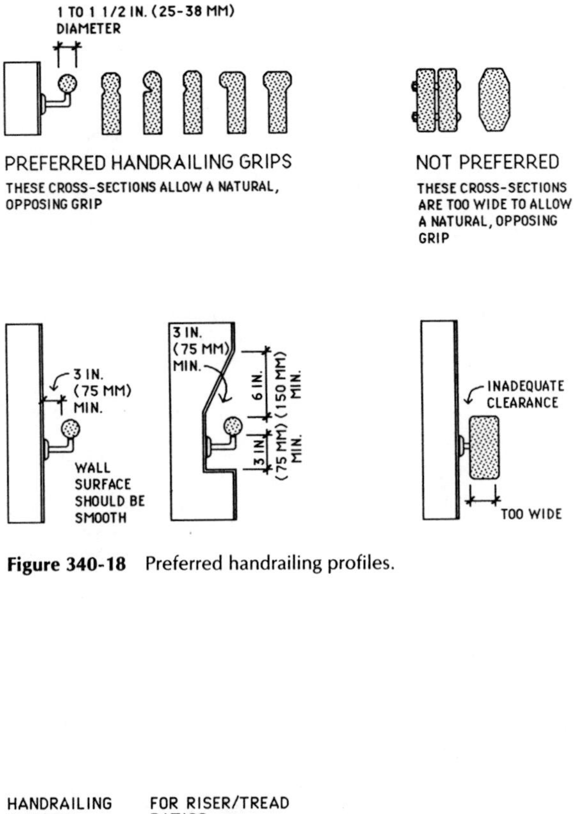
1 TO 1 1/2 IN. (25-38 MM)
DIAMETER
PREFERRED HANDRAILING GRIPS
THESE CROSS-SECTIONS ALLOW A NATURAL, OPPOSING GRIP
NOT PREFERRED
THESE CROSS-SECTIONS ARE TOO WIDE TO ALLOW A NATURAL, OPPOSING GRIP
3 IN.
(75 MM)
MIN.
WALL
SURFACE
SHOULD BE
SMOOTH
3 IN.
(75 MM)
MIN.
6 IN.
(150 MM)
MIN.
3 IN.
(75 MM)
MIN.
INADEQUATE
CLEARANCE
TOO WIDE

Figure 340-18 Preferred handrailing profiles.

HANDRAILING HEIGHTS	FOR RISER/TREAD RATIOS
2'-9"	6.00/14.00 to 7.00/13.00
2'-10"	5.00/16.00 to 6.00/13.50

Handrailing Heights For Ramps: 2'-8" to 2'-10"

Figure 340-19 Handrailing heights for exterior stairs and ramps.

for maximim support, are important on all stairways and ramps. (Figure 340-18).

Handrailing heights for outdoor stairways and ramps typically range from 30 to 34 in (750 to 850 mm) (Figure 340-19). Municipal codes should always be checked to ensure conformance of proposed heights. The ends of railings should extend beyond the top and bottom step by 12 to 18 in (300 to 450 mm) and should be rounded off or turned under for safety reasons. This detail is especially important for individuals with impaired vision. (Refer to ANSI or UFAS standards for more information.)

Additional Considerations:

1. Handrailings on both sides of a stairway or ramp are important because some people have one-sided strength.

2. Extra-wide stairways should have center railings for greater convenience. Handrailings should be no more than 20 ft (6 m) apart.

3. Railings should continue across intermediate landings.

4. Railings should be capable of supporting 250 lbs (114 kg) of weight.

5. Handrailings for children, at a lower height than that specified for adults, are sometimes advisable and are also useful on ramps for individuals who use wheelchairs.

3.6 Pedestrian Signage

Design and placement of signs for use by pedestrians involves consideration of visual field, scale of letters, proportion of letters, and tonal contrast between letters and background (Figures 340-20 and 340-21).

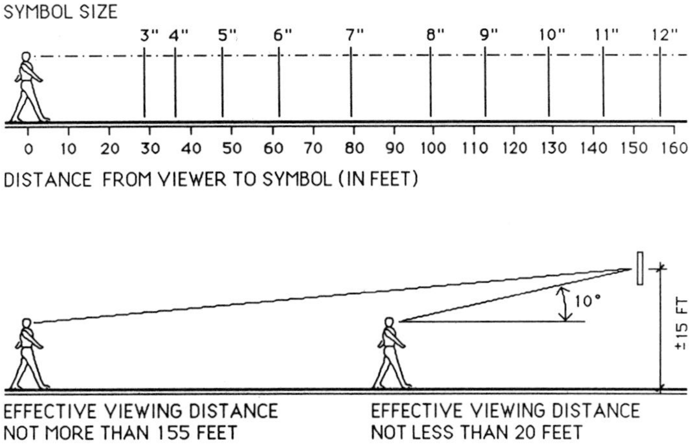
SYMBOL SIZE
3" 4" 5" 6" 7" 8" 9" 10" 11" 12"
0 10 20 30 40 50 60 70 80 90 100 110 120 130 140 150 160
DISTANCE FROM VIEWER TO SYMBOL (IN FEET)
10°
±15 FT
EFFECTIVE VIEWING DISTANCE NOT MORE THAN 155 FEET
EFFECTIVE VIEWING DISTANCE NOT LESS THAN 20 FEET

Figure 340-20 Pedestrian signage criteria.

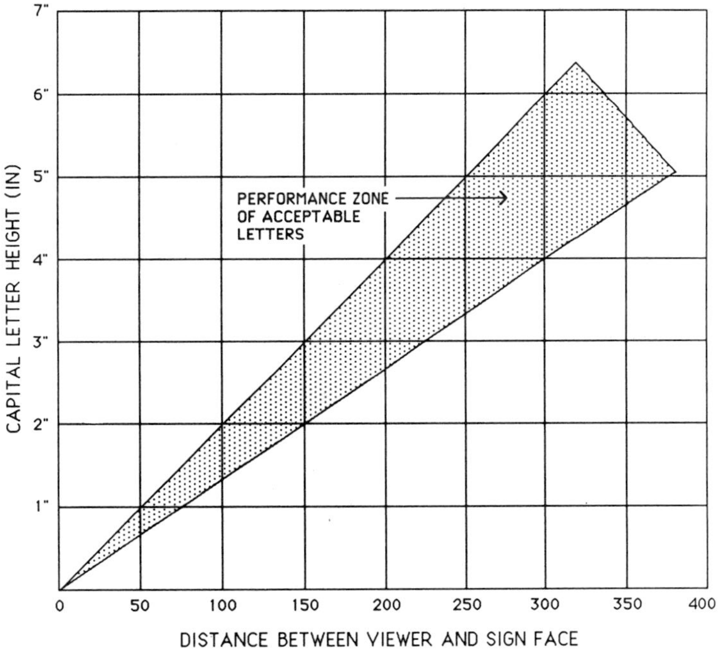
7"
6"
5"
4"
3"
2"
1"
CAPITAL LETTER HEIGHT (IN)
PERFORMANCE ZONE OF ACCEPTABLE LETTERS
0 50 100 150 200 250 300 350 400
DISTANCE BETWEEN VIEWER AND SIGN FACE

Figure 340-21 Minimum legibility for capital letter height for pedestrian signage. Under normal daylight conditions with an angular distortion of 0 degrees, approximately 50 ft/in of capital letter height can be taken as a guideline for minimal legibility.

REFERENCES

Cullen, Gordon. *The Concise Townscape,* Van Nostrand Reinhold, New York, 1961.

Fruin, J. J. *Pedestrian Planning and Design,* Metropolitan Association of Urban Designers and Environmental Planners (MAUDEP), Inc., New York, 1971.

Lynch, Kevin. *The Image of the City,* Harvard University Press, Cambridge, 1960.

——— and Gary Hack. *Site Planning,* 3d ed., The MIT Press, Cambridge, 1984.

Pushkarev, Boris, with Jeffrey M. Zupan. *Urban Space for Pedestrians,* The MIT Press, Cambridge, 1975.

Ramsey, C. G. and H. R. Sleeper. *Architectural Graphic Standards,* 7th ed., Robert T. Packard, ed., Wiley, New York, 1981.

Rudofsky, Bernard. *Streets for People,* Doubleday, New York, 1964.

Untermann, R. K. *Pedestrian Circulation,* The American Society of Landscape Architects, Washington, D.C., 1974.

Whyte, William H. *The Social Life of Small Urban Places,* The Conservation Foundation, Washington, D.C., 1980. ■

section 341: Bicycle Circulation

CREDITS

Contributor:

Edward Macleod and Terrance Reckord
Edward Macleod and Associates
Seattle, Washington

Technical Assistant: Linda Sullivan

Reviewers:

Richard Lemieux
Bicycle Programs Manager, U.S. Department of Transportation
Washington, D.C.

Richard Utterman
Department of Landscape Architecture
University of Washington
Seattle, Washington

CONTENTS

1.0 INTRODUCTION

The recently increased use of bicycles in the United States makes it imperative to design bicycle systems with fewer conflicts between such systems and other modes of travel.

Such improved systems are normally found in the form of a *bikeway,* defined as "any road, path, or way, which in some manner is specifically designated as being open to bicycle travel, regardless of whether such facilities are designated for the exclusive use of bicycles or are to be shared with other modes of transportation" (American Association of State Highway and Transportation Officials).

To design quality bicycle facilities, an understanding of bicyclists and their objectives is important.

2.0 TYPES OF USERS

2.1 Bicyclists

Bicyclists fall into two major categories:

1. The recreational bicyclist, who uses the bicycle for pleasure or exercise

2. The pragmatic bicyclist, who uses the bicycle for transportation to school, to work, or to shop

Because most bicyclists use a bicycle for both pragmatic and recreational reasons, the bicycle path must be designed to accord with a corridor's existing characteristics rather than to accord with narrowly defined user traits or purposes.

Since bicyclists vary in skill and experience, the emphasis must be on establishing minimum standards which accommodate a full range of user types while optimizing safety for all.

2.2 Moped Riders

The use of motorized bicycles, called mopeds, is increasing. Their use and classification as bicycles has become recognized by most local laws in the United States. A typical moped weighs approximately 100 lb (45 kg) and is approximately 70 in (1.8 m) in length. When parking a moped, the user must be able to guide it from either the left or right side.

3.0 PRIMARY TYPES OF BIKEWAYS

The American Association of State Highway and Transportation Officials (AASHTO) classifies three primary types of bikeways. These are described below.

SEPARATED RIGHT-OF-WAY

Figure 341-1 Bicycle path (Class I).

PAVEMENT MARKING
BIKE LANE
DESIGNATED RIGHT-OF-WAY

Figure 341-2 Bicycle lane (Class II).

PAVEMENT MARKING
BIKE ROUTE
SHARED RIGHT-OF-WAY

Figure 341-3 Shared roadway (Class III).

3.1 Bicycle Path (Class I)

This type of bikeway refers to a completely separated right-of-way for the primary use of bicycles (Figure 341-1).

3.2 Bicycle Lane (Class II)

This type of bikeway refers to a portion of a roadway which has been designated by striping, signing, and pavement markings for preferential or exclusive use by bicyclists (Figure 341-2).

3.3 Shared Roadway (Class III)

This type of bikeway refers to a right-of-way designated by signs or permanent markings as a bicycle route, but which is also shared with pedestrians and motorists (Figure 341-3).

4.0 ROUTE SELECTION AND PLANNING

The selection and planning of a bikeway route depends on a combination of five factors: (1) bicycle traffic generators, (2) scenic and recreational amenities, (3) terrain, (4) adequate space, and (5) negative factors.

4.1 Bicycle Traffic Generators

An estimated range of 3 to 6 mi (4.8 to 9.7 km) covers most recreational and pragmatic bicycle trips, and these can be identified with a specific traffic generator. Generators include:

1. Schools
2. Parks and recreational facilities
3. Community activity centers
4. Employment concentrations
5. Shopping and commercial centers

NOTE: For all types of trips in urban areas of up to 5 mi (8 km), the bicycle and the motor vehicle require about the same travel time.

4.2 Scenic and Recreational Amenities

The value of a bikeway as an amenity is enhanced by close proximity and connection to parks or other scenic and recreational attractions. All else being equal, the most varied and attractive routes will be used the most.

4.3 Terrain

Bicyclists will avoid steep grades. Studies indicate that if gradients exceed 5 percent there will be a sharp drop in the length of uphill grade that bicyclists will tolerate. Figure 341-4 illustrates commonly accepted maximum uphill grades (based on length of grade).

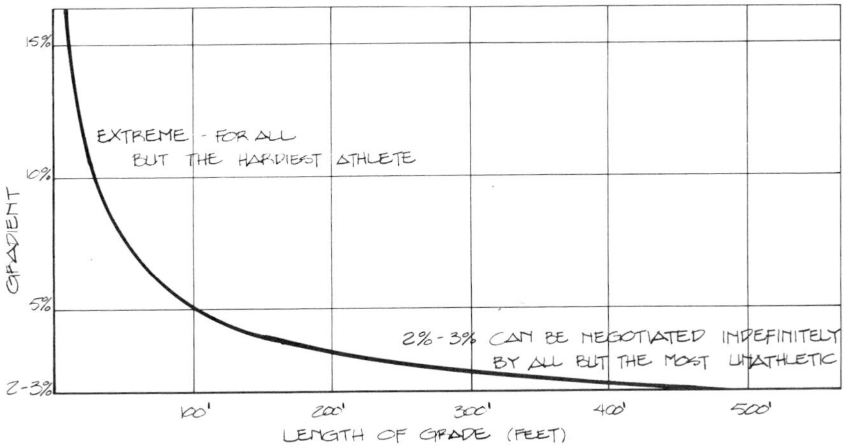

15%
10%
5%
2-3%
GRADIENT
EXTREME - FOR ALL BUT THE HARDIEST ATHLETE
2%-3% CAN BE NEGOTIATED INDEFINITELY BY ALL BUT THE MOST UNATHLETIC
100'
200'
300'
400'
500'
LENGTH OF GRADE (FEET)

Figure 341-4 Maximum Uphill Grades. The length of uphill grade that bicyclists will normally tolerate drops sharply when the gradient reaches 5 percent.

4.4 Width of Bikeways

Factors to consider when determining widths for bikeways must include:

1. The spatial dimensions of bicyclist and bicycle
2. Maneuvering space required for balancing
3. Additional clearances required to avoid obstacles (Figure 341-5)

NOTE: Designers should assume that in almost all cases two-way travel will occur on bicycle paths, regardless of design intentions. Appropriate widths should be provided.

4.5 Negative Factors

Factors that negatively influence the selection of a route for a bikeway include elevated embankments, freeways and their interchanges, busy arterials, and areas with frequent periods of adverse weather conditions.

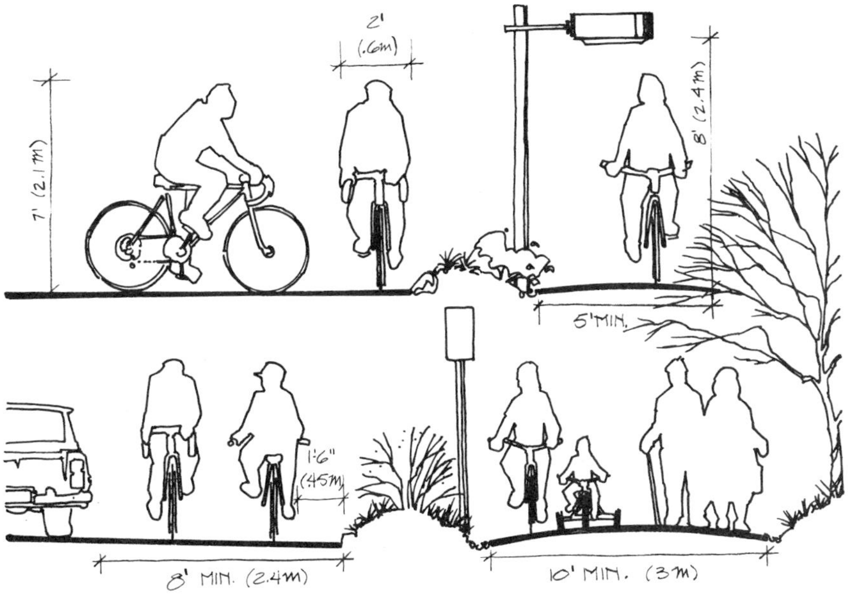

2' (.6m)
7' (2.1m)
8' (2.4m)
5' MIN.
1'6" (.45m)
8' MIN. (2.4m)
10' MIN. (3m)

Figure 341-5 Widths of bikeways.

5.0 DESIGN CRITERIA

Minimum levels of safety can be provided by carefully considering bicycle speed, sight/stopping distances, curve radii, intersection design, surfacing, and protection from hazards.

5.1 Bicycle Speed

Design speed is a term referring to the speed for which a bicycle path is designed. A design speed should be chosen that is at least as fast as the preferred speed of the faster bicyclists. In general, a minimum design speed of 20 mph (32 km/h) should be used. However, when downhill grades exceed 4 percent or where strong tail winds often exist, a higher minimum design speed of 30 mph (48 km/h) is advisable. On unpaved surfaces, a lower minimum design speed of 17 mph (24 km/h) can be used.

5.2 Sight/Stopping Distance

Sight/stopping distance is the physical distance required for a bicyclist to see an obstruction and come to a complete stop. Figure 341-6 shows minimum sight/stopping distances for various design speeds and grades based on a total perception and brake reaction time of 2.5 seconds and a

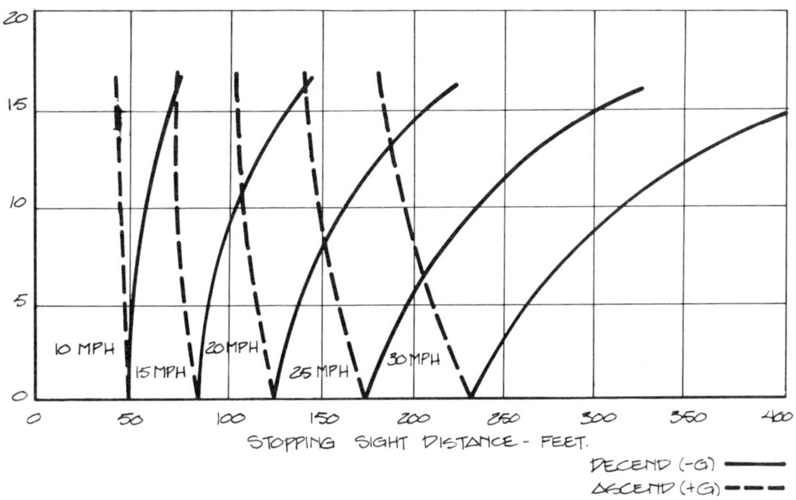

20
15
10
5
0
10 MPH
15 MPH
20 MPH
25 MPH
30 MPH
0
50
100
150
200
250
300
350
400
STOPPING SIGHT DISTANCE - FEET
DECEND (-G)
ASCEND (+G)

Figure 341-6 Minimum sight/stopping distances.

coefficient of friction of 0.25, to account for the poor wet-surface braking characteristics of most bicycles.

Figure 341-7 is used to select the minimum length of vertical curve necessary to provide minimum sight/stopping distances at various speeds on crests. The eye height of the average bicyclist is assumed to be 4½ ft (1.4 m) and the height of the perceived object is assumed to be zero.

Figure 341-8 shows the minimum clearance that should be used for line-of-sight obstructions on horizontal curves. The desired lateral clearance is obtained by entering Figure 341-8 with the sight/stopping distance from Figure 341-6 and the proposed horizontal radius of curvature.

NOTE: To avoid head-on bicycle accidents, lateral clearances on horizontal curves should be calculated based on the sum of the sight/stopping distances for bicyclists traveling in opposite direction around the curve. Where this is not possible, consideration should be given to widening the path through the curve, installing a yellow center stripe, and installing a *CURVE AHEAD* warning sign.

5.3 Curve Radii

General:

The design speed chosen determines the appropriate curve radii. If bikeways are part of a motor vehicle roadway, then no changes in radii are needed. If separate facilities are planned, then the curves should be designed to allow unbraked turns at a prescribed design speed.

Minimum Curve Radii for Unbraked Turns:

Minimum curve radii for unbraked turns are based on the bicycle speed, the rate of superelevation, and the coefficient of friction between bicycle tire and pavement. Table 341-1 gives minimum curve radii for unbraked turns on paved bicycle paths, assuming a superelevation rate of 0.02 ft/ft (0.006 m/m), the minimum required for adequate drainage of the surface.

Minimum curve radii for bikeways with greater rates of superelevation can be derived from the following formula. Superelevation rates should not exceed a maximum of 0.05 ft/ft (0.015 m/m).

$$R = \frac{V^2}{15(e + f)}$$

where R = minimum radius of curvature, ft

V = design speed, mph

e = superelevation, ft/ft (varies from 0.02 to 0.05 ft/ft (0.006 to 0.015 m/m))

f = coefficient of friction (varies from 0.17 to 0.27)

NOTE: This formula is for paved surfaces only. Friction factors for unpaved surfaces would be considerably less than (i.e., less than half of) those for paved surfaces.

Avoid short-radius curves when curves occur at the bottom of a long grade. Widening the bikeway at short-radius curves is recommended to compensate for the increased operating space required by a bicyclist leaning through a curve (Figure 341-9).

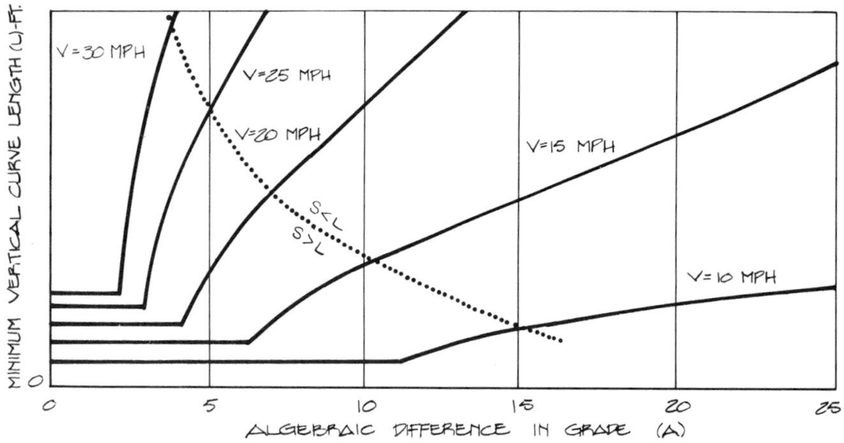
MINIMUM VERTICAL CURVE LENGTH (L)-FT.
V=30 MPH
V=25 MPH
V=20 MPH
V=15 MPH
V=10 MPH
S<L
S>L
0
5
10
15
20
25
ALGEBRAIC DIFFERENCE IN GRADE (A)

Figure 341-7 Sight/stopping distances for crest vertical curves.

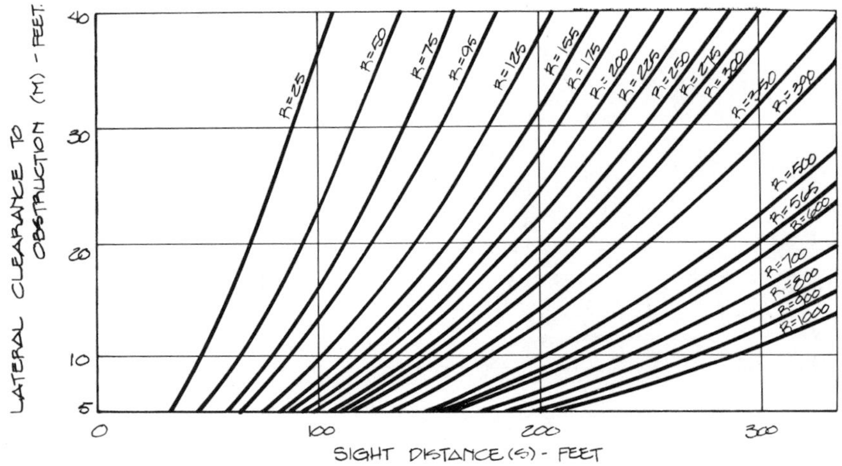
LATERAL CLEARANCE TO OBSTRUCTION (M) - FEET
40
30
20
10
5
R=25
R=50
R=75
R=95
R=125
R=155
R=175
R=200
R=225
R=250
R=275
R=300
R=350
R=390
R=500
R=565
R=600
R=700
R=800
R=900
R=1000
0
100
200
300
SIGHT DISTANCE (S) - FEET

Figure 341-8 Lateral clearances on horizontal curves.

5.4 Intersections

Conflicts at Intersections:

A large share of bicycle-related accidents occurs at intersections of streets and bikeways because of the confused comingling of bicycles, motor vehicles, and pedestrians. Major problems occur from the following conditions:

1. Bicyclists turning left across traffic
2. Bicyclists crossing an intersection when

TABLE 341-1
Minimum Curve Radii for Paved Bicycle Paths

*Design speed—V, mph**	*Friction factor—f†*	*Design radius—R, ft‡*
20	0.27	95
25	0.25	155
30	0.22	250
35	0.19	390
40	0.17	565

* 1 mph = ⅝ km/hr.
† e = 2%.
‡ 1 ft = 0.3 m.
Source: From AASHTO, Guide for the Development of New Bicycle Facilities, 1981.

vehicular traffic is entering from or turning to the right

The types of problems encountered in these two situations vary with the type, or class, of the bikeway. Intersection problems are nonexistent with bicycle paths (Class I) by virtue of their complete separation from vehicular traffic. The intersection problems of a bicycle lane (Class II) and of a shared roadway (Class III) are similar. Bicycle lanes (Class II) represent the most complex set of intersection problems because both of the above-listed problems are involved and solutions to conflicts between motorists and bicyclists are expected, given the obvious demarcation of their separate domains.

Conflict points and solutions for each problem are described below.

SUPERELEVATION: MAXIMUM .05% FEET PER FOOT

Figure 341-9 Superelevation and Curve Widening. These two devices help bicyclists negotiate small-radii curves.

Bicyclists Turning Left across Traffic:

Although there are several ways for bicyclists to turn left across vehicular traffic, each one poses serious hazards to the rider. Figure 341-10 illustrates the many intersection conflict points that exist when a bicyclist turns left across traffic.

Path *A* in Figure 341-10 shows the bicyclist leaving the bikeway lane on the far right and, like a motor vehicle, moving to the center lane position to execute a left turn. This alternative accepts the established desires of bicyclists to be treated as vehicle operators rather than as pedestrians, but it exposes the bicyclists to sideswipes and to the failure of automobiles going in either direction to yield the right-of-way. Many bicyclists nevertheless choose this alternative unless a different route is mandated.

Path *B* in Figure 341-10 shows the bicyclist crossing the intersection in the right lane and, when traffic allows, executing a 90-degree left turn across the street. This alternative is considered contrary to the established desires of bicyclists to be treated as vehicle operators rather than as pedestrians, and it may be slightly confusing to motorists because the bicyclist is behaving neither like a motorist nor like a pedestrian. This solution presents several hazards from through-traveling vehicles as well as from vehicles turning in front of the bicyclist. A less confusing system is one that calls for the bicyclist to walk the bike across both streets, precisely like a pedestrian, but some bicyclists may object to such an inconvenience.

Path *C* in Figure 341-10 shows the bicyclist weaving across the approach street and, at the first gap in the traffic, proceeding wrong-way through the intersection. This approach is not really considered an acceptable alternative because it is very dangerous. It should be discouraged or prevented whenever possible.

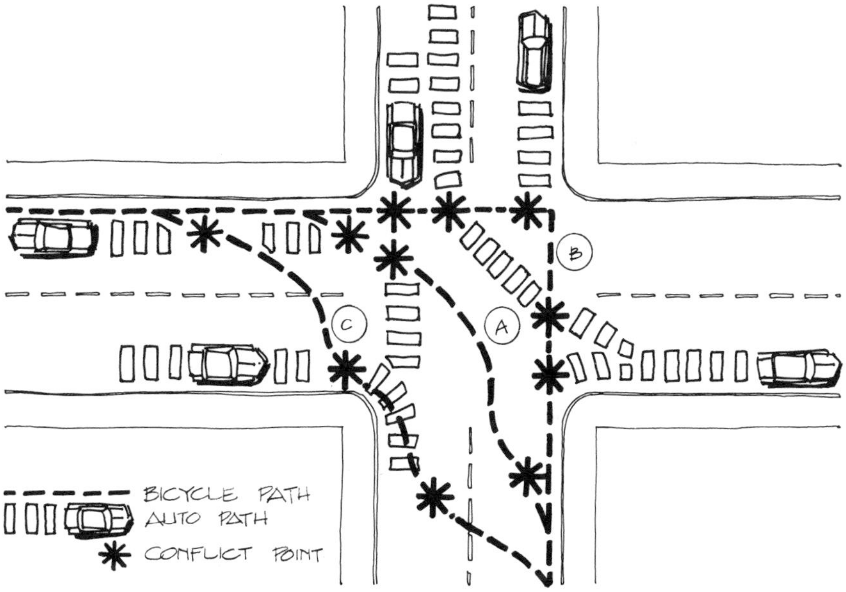
A
B
C
BICYCLE PATH
AUTO PATH
CONFLICT POINT

Figure 341-10 Intersection conflict points for left-turning bicyclists.

Figures 341-11, 341-12, and 341-13 illustrate three common solutions to the problem of left-turning bicyclists.

Vehicular Traffic Entering from or Turning to the Right:

For Class II and Class III bikeways, a serious problem exists for bicyclists where there are designated vehicular right-turn lanes which force motor vehicles into the bikeway. Many motorists do not see bicyclists coming from the rear either because they are preoccupied with other motor vehicles or because of the blind spot to the right rear of most automobiles. Also, most motorists are not accustomed to looking for bicyclists on roadways, and some are simply reluctant to grant the right-of-way to bicyclists. Figures 341-14 and 341-15 show intersection conflict points for this situation.

If the auto traffic on cross-streets is moderate to heavy, a possible, albeit marginal, solution to the problem is to make the right-turn lanes extra wide to give bicyclists the opportunity to maneuver around the turning vehicles (Figure 341-16). This kind of *open-field* approach is re-

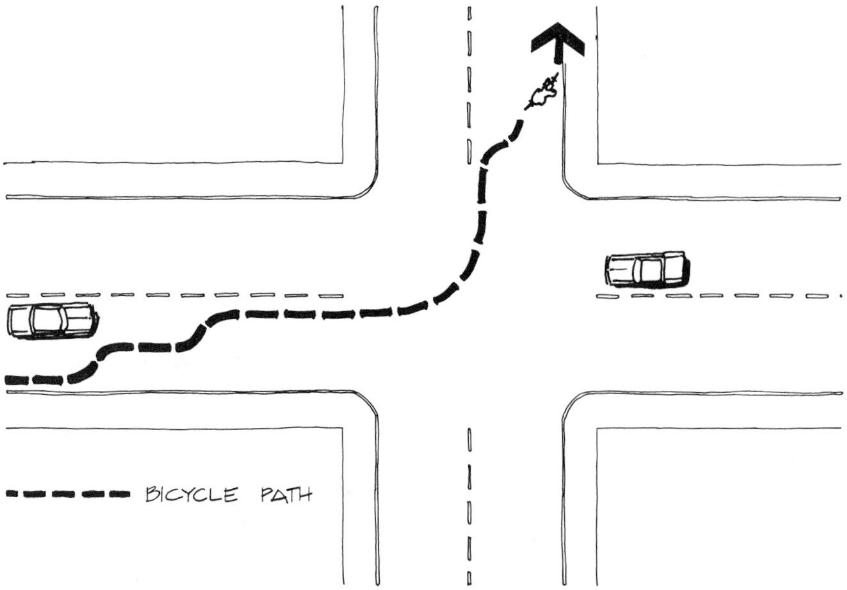
BICYCLE PATH

Figure 341-11 Problem of Left-Turning Bicyclists. If auto traffic is moderate to heavy, bicyclists can turn left, flowing with the traffic.

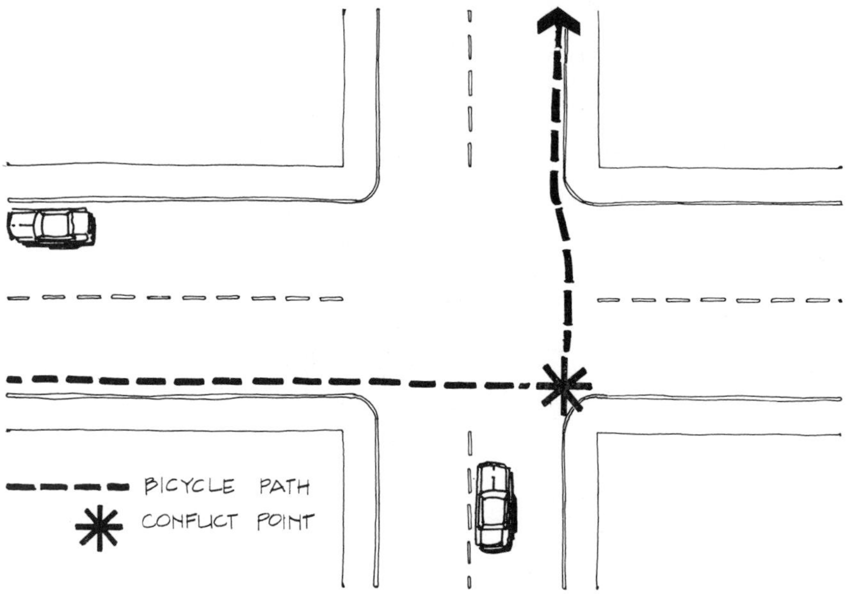
BICYCLE PATH
CONFLICT POINT

Figure 341-12 Problem of Left-Turning Bicyclists. When auto traffic is moderate to heavy, bicyclists often stop at far corner and wait for a break in traffic.

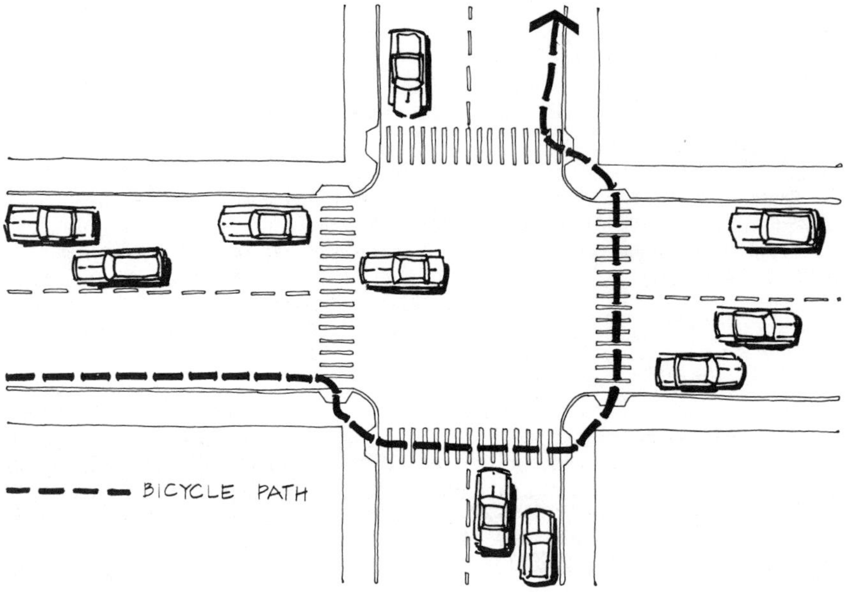
BICYCLE PATH

Figure 341-13 Problem of Left-Turning Bicyclists. If auto traffic is very heavy, it may be advisable to encourage bicyclists to walk their bicycles with pedestrian circulation.

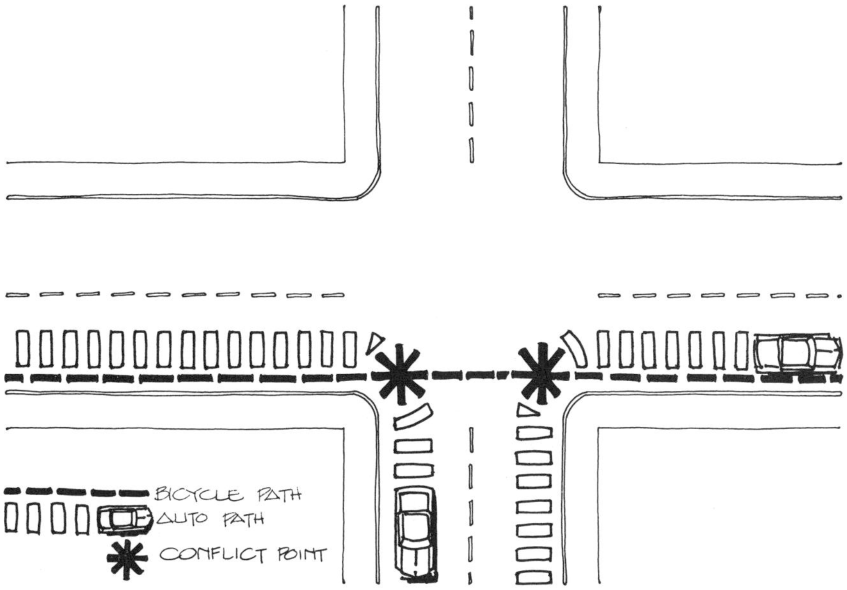
BICYCLE PATH
AUTO PATH
CONFLICT POINT

Figure 341-14 Intersection conflict points when vehicular traffic is entering from or turning right.

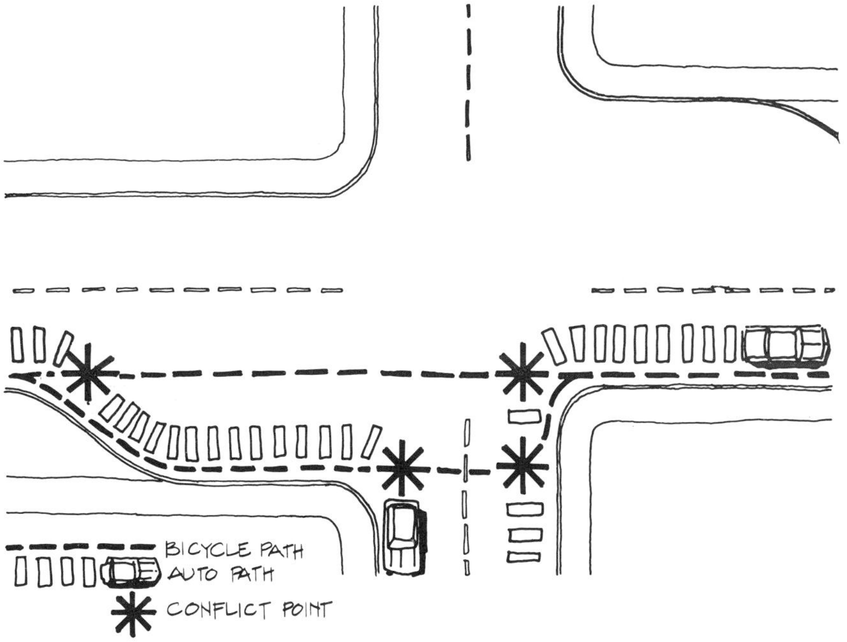
BICYCLE PATH
AUTO PATH
CONFLICT POINT

Figure 341-15 Intersection conflict points when vehicular traffic is entering from or turning right (indented right-turn lanes).

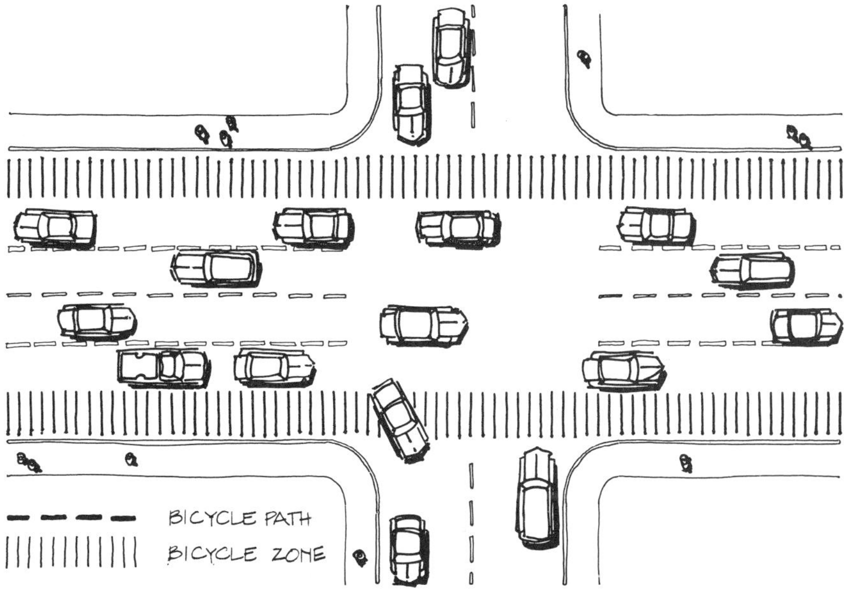
BICYCLE PATH
BICYCLE ZONE

Figure 341-16 Problem of Entering or Right-Turning Auto Traffic. One alternative is to widen the right lane to give bicyclists the opportunity to maneuver around right-turning auto traffic.

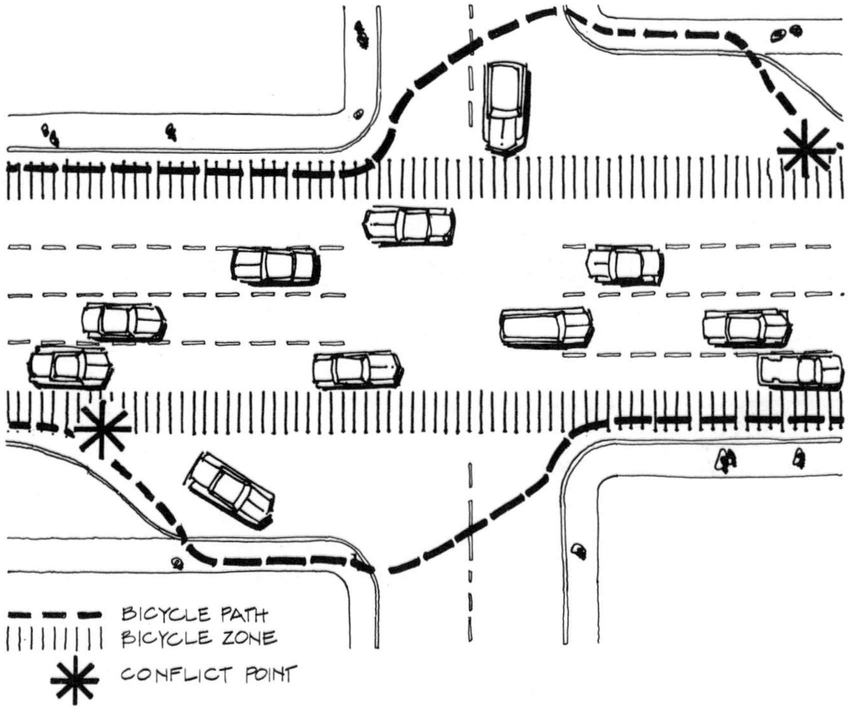
BICYCLE PATH
BICYCLE ZONE
CONFLICT POINT

Figure 341-17 Problem of Entering or Right-Turning Auto Traffic. In this instance, it is primarily the responsibility of the bicyclist to understand the inherent danger at the major conflict point.

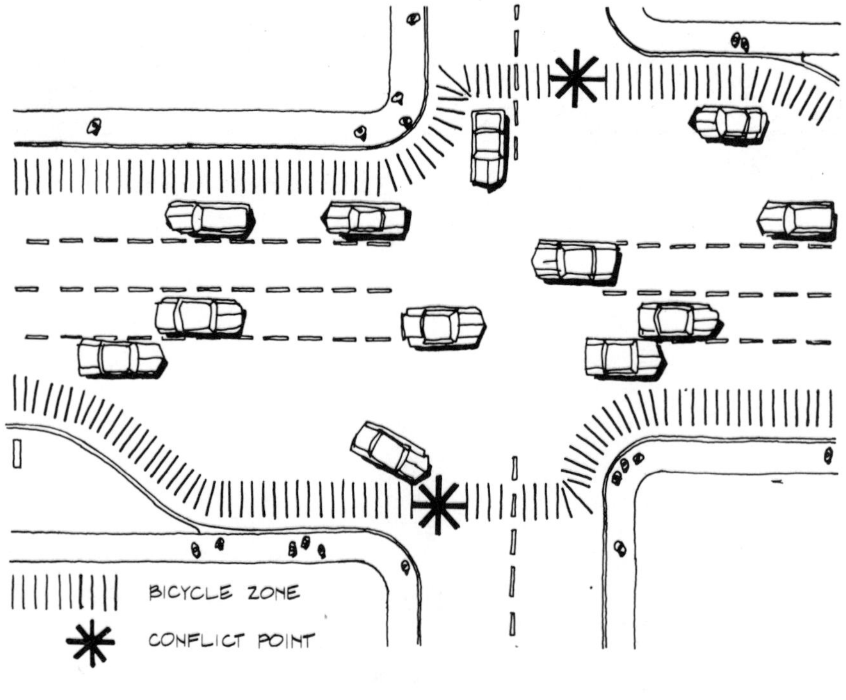
BICYCLE ZONE
CONFLICT POINT

Figure 341-18 Problem of Entering or Right-Turning Auto Traffic. This alternative usually requires that the bicyclist stop at the major conflict point and wait for a break in right-turning traffic.

plete with user uncertainty and inherent danger. In all cases, signs should be used to alert right-turning motorists to bicyclists on their right. Figures 341-17 and 341-18 show possible solutions to the problem for roadways with indented right-turn lanes.

If the auto traffic on cross-streets is light, the bikeway lanes might better continue straight through the intersection, as shown in Figure 341-19.

Midblock Crossings:

If Class I or Class II bikeways have to cross a roadway with relatively light traffic at midblock, an *at-grade* crossing might be used. It should be made to intersect the roadway as close to a right angle as possible so that the bicyclists will be able to see the oncoming traffic in both directions (Figure 341-20). If these bikeways have to cross more heavily traveled roadways, then overpasses or underpasses should be used.

Freeway Ramp Crossings:

Where bikeways follow highways or freeways with off ramps, bicyclists should be encouraged to cross these intersections early enough to be easily seen by exiting vehicles (Figure 341-21).

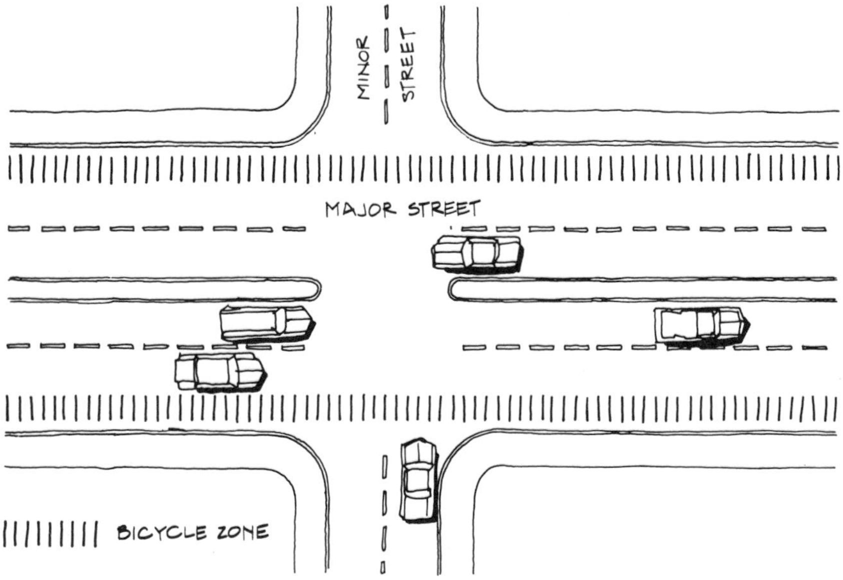
MINOR STREET
MAJOR STREET
BICYCLE ZONE

Figure 341-19 Problem of Entering or Right-Turning Auto Traffic. If auto traffic is light, bicycle traffic can continue straight through the intersection.

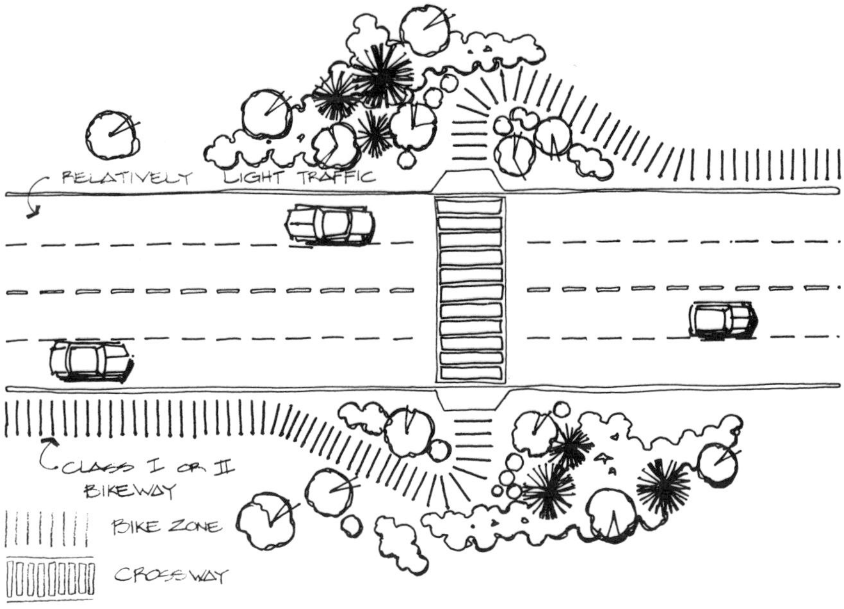
RELATIVELY LIGHT TRAFFIC
CLASS I OR II BIKEWAY
BIKE ZONE
CROSSWAY

Figure 341-20 Midblock Intersection. Where at midblock a bikeway intersects a roadway with relatively light traffic, and an overpass or underpass is not possible, the bikeway should cross the roadway at a right angle.

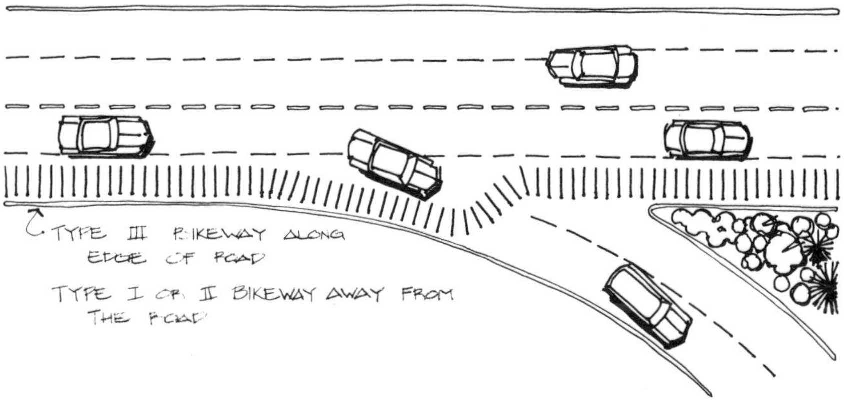
TYPE III BIKEWAY ALONG EDGE OF ROAD
TYPE I OR II BIKEWAY AWAY FROM THE ROAD

Figure 341-21 Freeway Ramp Crossings. Bikeways should cross freeway ramps early enough to be seen by right-turning traffic.

APPROACH WIDTH OR WIDER
4'-6"
(1.4M)

Figure 341-22 Underpass and overpass.

8% MAX.
3' MIN.
(0.9m)

Figure 341-23 Curb ramp.

Underpasses and Overpasses:

Ramp grades for either underpasses or overpasses should be no steeper than 6 to 8 percent. The approach to the underpass or overpass should be visually obvious and should provide the easiest and safest alternative to crossing the roadway (Figure 341-22).

Curb Ramps:

If a bikeway encounters a roadway with curbs, a ramped curb should be provided (Figure 341-23). These structures also permit crossings by wheelchairs, baby carriages, etc. The maximum running grade should not be greater than 1:12, or about 8 percent. (Refer to Section 240: Access and Egress: Outdoor Standards, and Section 241: Access and Egress: Architectural and Transportation Guidelines, for more information.)

6.0 DESIGN ELEMENTS

6.1 Barriers and Separators

Bikeways which share or are immediately adjacent to a roadway can be delineated in several ways. Each of these is described below.

Bikeway Plantings:

Plantings between bikeway and roadway can prevent screen headlight glare and accidental crossovers and can improve the aesthetic quality of a bikeway. The disadvantages of plantings include the consumption of a substantial amount of space and possible confusion at intersections where the planted strip must be broken. Trees planted in a row between the two modes of transportation provide a visual, psychological, and limited physical barrier and take up less space than heavy shrub massings.

Painted Lines:

For bicycle lanes (Class II), the simplest and least expensive bikeway delineation is the painted line. It can continue through intersections, allow bicyclists to leave the lane to make left turns, and permit automobiles to enter driveways. A disadvantage of painted lines is the lack of a physical barrier or tactile warning to prevent the encroachment of motor vehicles. Paint that will not become slippery when wet should be specified.

Traffic Buttons:

Raised and reflectorized traffic buttons are sometimes used to delineate bike lanes, either alone or in combination with painted lines. This method provides a visual and tactile warning to the motorists while still allowing lane changes and access to driveways. However, some bicyclists feel that the buttons are dangerous and make left turns difficult.

6.2 Paving and Surfacing

Class II and Class III bikeways share the pavement of an existing roadway, so that construction considerations are specific to vehicular traffic. However, if a street or shoulder is widened or a separate Class I bikeway is constructed, the pavement should be a smooth, nonslick surface and have a thickness capable of supporting normal-size maintenance vehicles.

This section does not include detailed information about the construction of pavements for bicycle routes. However, the following notes on various pavement materials are offered as a general overview, and references to other appropriate sections are given.

Asphalt:

Hot-mix asphalt is the most popular paving material used for bikeways. (Refer to Section 820: Asphalt, for more information.)

Concrete:

Concrete is the second most frequently used paving material for bikeways. The finish should be lightly textured to prevent slipperiness when wet. Unless sawed joints are used, conventional contraction and construction joints in the pavement cause rhythmic bumps which are annoying to some riders. (Refer to Section 830: Concrete, for more information.)

Soil Cement:

Soil cement is a material that is occasionally used for bikeways, although it will deteriorate much sooner than either asphalt or concrete. If deterioration occurs, a seal coat of bituminous asphalt or asphaltic concrete can be applied. (Refer to Sections 810: Soils and Aggregates, 820: Asphalt, and 830: Concrete, for more information.)

Stone Chip Aggregate:

Stone chip aggregate is a material that gives the most suitable results when the bikeway is to be used primarily for recreational purposes. This material creates fewer drainage problems than the other types of paving, although it does require some kind of edging (e.g., wood, metal, or plastic) to keep it from raveling on the edges. (Refer to Section 810: Soils and Aggregates, for more information.)

Stabilized Earth:

Stabilized earth is perhaps the least expensive way to create a *paved* surface for a bikeway. However, it is also the least durable and requires the most maintenance to keep it in good condition. (Refer to Sections 810: Soils and Aggregates, and 440: Surfacing and Paving, for more information.)

6.3 Drainage of Bikeway Surfaces

Bikeway surfaces should be pitched at least 2 percent (depending on the texture and composition of the surfacing material) to provide positive drainage. (Refer to Sections 320: Grading Techniques, and 330: Site Drainage, for more information.)

If continuous curbing is used, then these should be interrupted intermittently to allow for drainage of the bikeway and any adjacent hard surfaces. If the curbs are not interrupted, then surface drain inlets should be provided. Drainage grates with slots running parallel to the line of bicycle travel can catch bicycle wheels, damaging rims and causing accidents (Figure 341-24). Some communities solve the problem by temporarily welding transverse bars over existing grates, but snowplows may destroy these. Transverse (or angled) bar or honeycomb grates are preferred. Because most bicyclists will avoid riding over almost any type of grate, drainage grates narrow the effective width of a bikeway and may cause riders to swerve into traffic or other bicyclists. For this reason and wherever possible, drains should be designed and located to minimize danger to bicyclists.

6.4 Information Systems

Nearly all signs and markings placed on public streets and highways for the benefit of the motorist also apply to the bicyclist.

Traffic Control Devices:

In the United States, basic principles governing the design and use of traffic control devices are set forth in the 1983 *Manual on Uniform Traffic Control Devices* (MUTCD) (pt. 9: *Bicycle Facilities*), produced by the U.S. Department of Transportation. This source identifies five basic requirements that a traffic control device should meet to be effective; it should:

1. Fulfill a need
2. Command attention
3. Convey a clear, simple meaning
4. Command respect of road users
5. Provide adequate time for response

Standards of design, placement, operation maintenance, and uniformity have been carefully developed to meet these requirements. Care should be taken not to employ a special treatment when a standard treatment will serve the purpose.

NOTE: In the United States, the MUTCD can often be found in local and state highway engineering offices.

Types of Signage:

Signs are categorized into three basic types: (1) regulatory, (2) warning, and (3) guide.

Regulatory Signs: These signs inform users of traffic laws and regulations governing movements, parking, speeds, etc., and indicate rules that would otherwise not be apparent, such as *MOTOR VEHICLES PROHIBITED, NO PARKING,* or *BICYCLES ONLY.*

Warning Signs: Warning signs call the user's attention to potentially hazardous conditions and should be placed sufficiently in advance of the hazard to allow for responsive action. The *BIKE-X-ING* warning, for example, is used to alert motorists to places where a bikeway crosses an otherwise uncontrolled street or roadway. Other examples include *BUMP, PAVEMENT ENDS, DIP, ROAD NARROWS,* and *NARROW BRIDGE.*

Guide Signs: Guide signs provide roadside information to orient and assist users geographically. Typically, guide signs are of most use to bicyclists who are unfamiliar with the layout of an area or facility. Standard guide signs include the *BIKE ROUTE* sign, supplementary plates such as BEGIN or *END,* and directional plates with a variety of arrow designations.

Placement of Signs:

Guide signs, such as *BIKE ROUTE* and supplemental plates, should be placed where a route begins, ends, changes direction, or intersects with other bikeways. If distances are great between major decision points, some intermediate guide signs should be provided to reassure bicyclists of their position. Signs warning motorists that bicyclists may be encountered, and vice versa, should be provided where a bikeway intersects a road or sidewalk, at the beginning and end of a bikeway, and at points

Figure 341-24 Hazards of drainage grates.

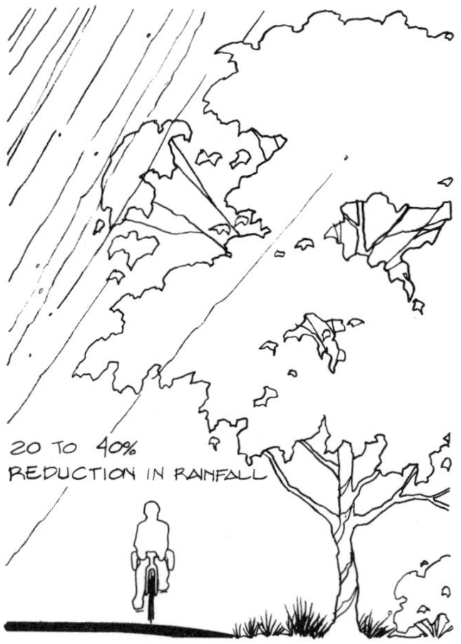
20 TO 40%
REDUCTION IN RAINFALL

Figure 341-25 Convenience to Bicyclists. Tree canopies can reduce the amount of rainfall reaching the bicyclist.

where large numbers of bicyclists may be expected (e.g., schools and parks).

Signs erected at the roadside should be mounted with the lower edge of the sign no less than 5 ft (1.5 m) above the pavement on rural roadways, and 7 ft (2.1 m) above the pavement in residential, business, and commercial districts and on expressways. However, these heights respond to the motorist's field of vision. Because the bicyclist's field of vision is lower, signs on roadways which include bicycle lanes should be placed at a lower level. Signs on isolated bicycle routes can be mounted 4 to 5 ft (1.2 to 1.5 m) above the pavement, and signs along roadways that are intended specifically for bicyclists may be mounted at a lower height.

Care should be taken to place signs—particularly those at the lower heights—where they will not be obscured by other common elements such as parked cars, vegetation, and the like. Bicycle-oriented warning signs should be positioned far enough in advance of the condition to allow time for perception and response, based upon design speeds and sight/stopping distances (Figure 341-6). Placement should be such that a safe horizontal distance of 1½ ft (0.5 m) is maintained between the edge of the bikeway surface and the nearest projection of the sign.

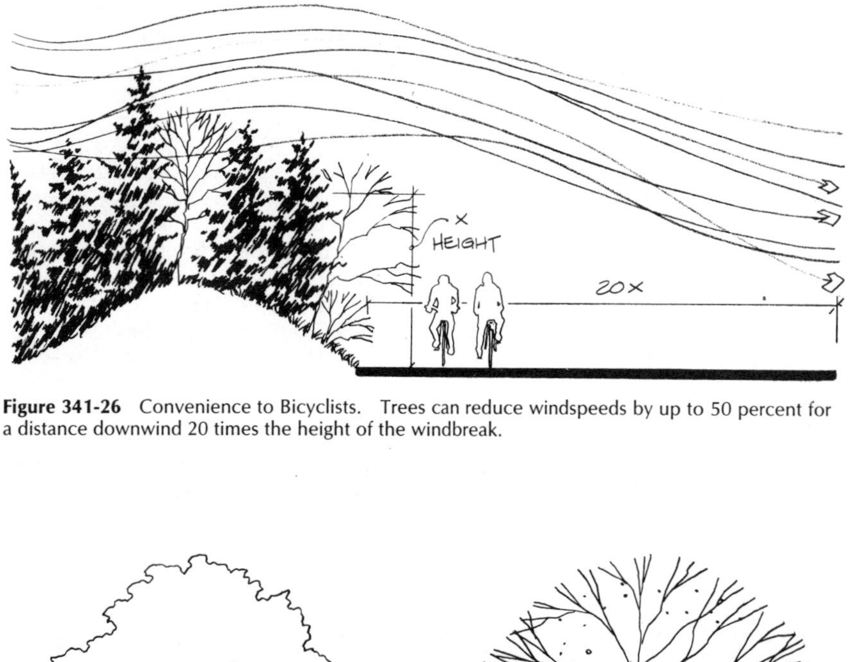
X
HEIGHT
20X

Figure 341-26 Convenience to Bicyclists. Trees can reduce windspeeds by up to 50 percent for a distance downwind 20 times the height of the windbreak.

Pavement Markings:

Pavement markings are used to reinforce signage by providing additional information. They are particularly useful for bikeways since they, more than signs, are directly in the bicyclist's normal zone of vision. Striping and message stencils are the most common forms of pavement markings.

Bicycle lanes are normally delineated by a solid, painted line 4 or 6 in (100 or 150 mm) wide between the bicycle lane and the roadway. White is the standard color for bicycle lane-related pavement markings. Some experimentation has been done with other colors in attempts to increase recognition, but the National Advisory Committee on Uniform Traffic Control Devices recently concluded that other colors had poor visibility characteristics and were unacceptable for bicycle lane markings. Additional cross-striping *(zebra striping)* is often used to increase visibility at intersections.

Stenciled message markings are normally white, with a minimum letter and arrow height of 4 ft (1.2 m), and include such messages as *STOP, YIELD, PED-X-ING, SLOW, RR X-ING,* and *BIKE LANE,* supplemented with an arrow indicating the direction of travel. *BIKE LANE* or *BIKE ONLY* messages should be placed at the beginning of a bikeway, at intersections with roadways and other facilities, at midpoints on long blocks, and downstream of major driveways. Because painted pavements can reduce friction, making stopping more difficult and increasing the dangers of sideslip, care should be taken to avoid placing pavement markings at critical stopping points and to limit markings to those necessary. In areas where snow is a problem, such pavement markings are sometimes less visible, thereby reducing their effectiveness.

SUMMER SHADE
WINTER WARMTH

Figure 341-27 Convenience to Bicyclists. Deciduous trees provide shade in summer and allow light through in winter.

7.0 COMFORT AND CONVENIENCE

Plant materials and site furnishings can enhance the experience of those using the bikeway. The need for storage lockers, comfort stations, lighting, picnic facilities, and shelter from the elements depends upon the length of the bikeway, the time necessary to travel on it, the type of user, and the extent to which such facilities exist nearby.

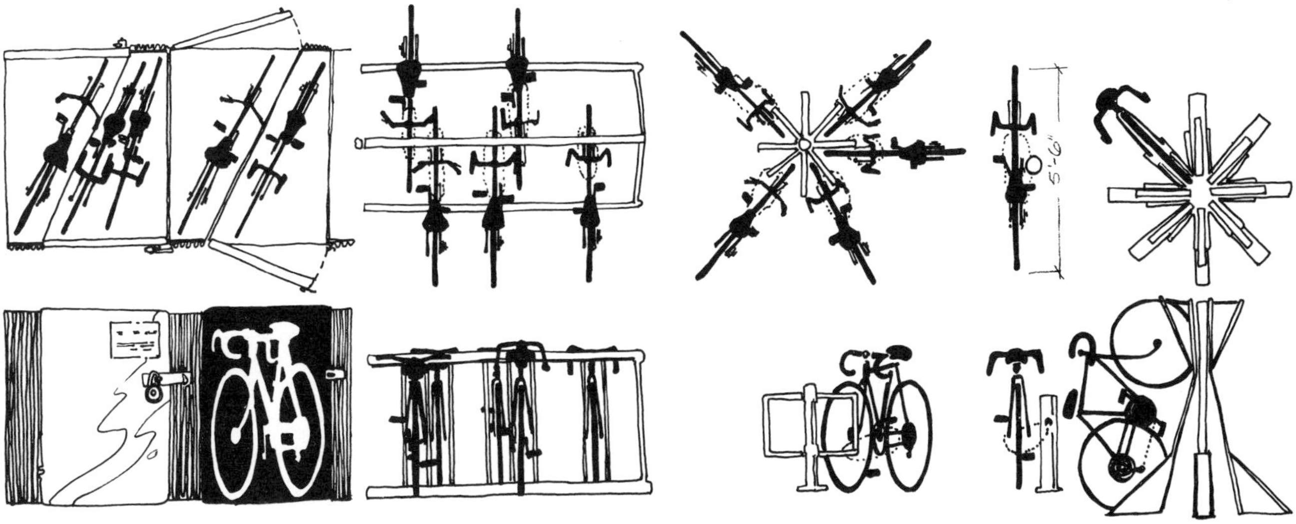
5'-6"

Figure 341-28 Storage lockers and racks.

7.1 Bikeway Plantings

Plants can reduce headlight glare and traffic dust when used to provide a visual and physical barrier between bicycle and motor vehicle traffic. Plant materials can also mitigate the discomforts of weather. A canopy of deciduous and coniferous trees over a bikeway, for instance, can reduce the amount of rainfall reaching bicyclists by as much as 20 to 40 percent (Figure 341-25).

Dense planting of trees in a row, perpendicular to prevailing winds and parallel to the bikeway, can reduce wind speeds by 50 percent for a distance downwind of from 10 to 20 times the height of the windbreak (Figure 341-26).

Extremes of heat and cold can also be modified by careful selection and use of plant materials. Deciduous trees can provide shade from the sun in the warm seasons, allow sunlight to penetrate to the ground in the cool seasons, and minimize diurnal temperature changes by trapping heat and reducing its loss through radiation to the atmosphere (Figure 341-27). Plant massings can also alter snow drifting patterns and melting rates through microclimate modification. (Refer to Sections 260: Climate and Energy, and 550: Plants and Planting, for more information on microclimate control.)

7.2 Site Furnishings

Racks and Locking Devices for Bicycles:

Three primary methods for parking bicycles and protecting them from theft are: (1) to enclose the bicycle in a locker, cabinet, or other lockable space; (2) to make the bicycle inoperable by weaving a chain and lock through the frame and wheels; and (3) to lock the bicycle to a rack, post, or other stationary object. The first and third methods are most effective (Figure 341-28). Coin-operated lockers effectively prevent thefts and relieve the bicyclist of the need to carry heavy chains and locks, but they are space consuming and expensive to install. Devices which provide lateral support only at one wheel leave the bicycle vulnerable to damage.

Bicycle racks and parking facilities should be located as close to destinations as possible without interfering with pedestrian traffic. Storage facilities too far away [more than 50 ft (15 m)] encourage the bicyclist to attach the bicycle to the nearest tree, lightpole, or parking meter. Locate storage facilities where there is visual supervision, lighting, and shelter from inclement weather.

Fixtures for Bicycle Routes:

Depending upon the character, scale, and anticipated use of a bikeway, such elements as shelters, benches, tables, grills, rest rooms, trash receptacles, bulletin boards, telephones, and drinking fountains may be provided.

Installation and maintenance costs are a major determining factor, especially with water and toilet facilities. Simple rest stops where bicyclists can pull off the bikeway and rest or enjoy a fine view are obviously much less expensive, and they can add much to the attractiveness of a recreational facility.

Bikeway Lighting:

Bikeway lighting requirements vary from 0.6 footcandles (fc) [6 lux (lx)] in parks and similar areas, to 1.0 fc (10 lx) in commercial areas, to 2.0 fc (20 lx) at intersections with heavily trafficked streets. Commercial areas with existing illumination require no additional lighting. The positioning of new luminaires should be such that bicyclists are backlighted against approaching traffic. (Refer to Section 540: Outdoor Lighting, for more information.)

REFERENCES

American Association of State Highway and Transportation Officials (AASHTO). *Guide for the Development of New Bicycle Facilities,* Washington, DC, 1981.

Maryland Department of Transportation. *A Bikeway Criteria Digest: The ABCD's of Bikeways,* U.S. Department of Transportation, Washington, DC, 1977.

Mayer, Richard W. *Landscape Architectural Technical Information Series,* vol. 1, no. 1: *Bicycle Planning and Design,* Landscape Architecture Foundation, Washington, DC, 1978.

Smith, D. T., Jr. *Safety and Locational Criteria for Bicycle Facilities, User Manual,* vol. 1: *Bicycle Facility Locational Criteria,* and vol. 2: *Design and Safety Criteria,* U.S. Department of Transportation, Washington, DC, 1976.

U.S. Department of Transportation. *Manual on Uniform Traffic Control Devices* (MUTCD), *Bicycle Facilities,* U.S. Superintendent of Documents, Washington, DC, 1983. ■

section 342: Vehicular Circulation

CREDITS

Contributor:

Robert Zolomij
Land Design Collaborative
Evanston, Illinois

Reviewers:

Nicholas T. Dines
University of Massachusetts/Amherst
Amherst, Massachusetts

Glen Erickson
Barton-Ashman Associates, Inc.
Evanston, Illinois

Charles W. Harris
Harvard University Graduate School of Design
Department of Landscape Architecture
Cambridge, Massachusetts

CONTENTS

1.0 Introduction

1.1 General

The automobile has become a basic unit in site planning and design, and often sets the scale and pattern of future development. As a result, the integration of vehicular circulation in the site planning process is critical in order to satisfy its functions.

Vehicular circulation on a site accommodates one or more of the following purposes (Figure 342-1):

1. To provide access to land uses and buildings

2. To provide linkage between land uses

3. To provide for the movement of goods and people

1.2 Classification of Vehicular Circulation Systems

Roadway systems are grouped into a number of different classifications for administrative, planning, and design purposes. Classifications are usually based on traffic volumes, speed, general design requirements, and maintenance requirements.

In the most basic classification system for design work, highways and streets are typically grouped into the following four categories (Figure 342-2). Table 342-1 lists criteria for vehicular system classification.

1. *Freeway systems* (including expressways and parkways): these systems allow rapid and efficient movement of large volumes of through-traffic between and across urban areas. They have limited access with grade-separated interchanges.

2. *Major arterial systems:* these systems allow through-traffic movement between and across urban areas with direct access to abutting properties. They are subject to control of entrances, exits, and curb use.

3. *Collector street systems:* these systems allow traffic movement between major arterials and local streets, with direct access to abutting properties. Traffic control is usually provided by stop signs on the side streets.

4. *Local street systems:* these systems allow local traffic movement and direct access to abutting land.

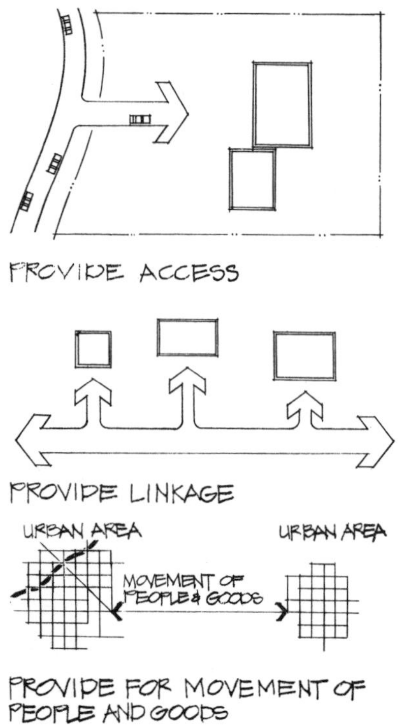
PROVIDE ACCESS
PROVIDE LINKAGE
URBAN AREA
URBAN AREA
MOVEMENT OF PEOPLE & GOODS
PROVIDE FOR MOVEMENT OF PEOPLE AND GOODS

Figure 342-1 Purposes of vehicular site circulation.

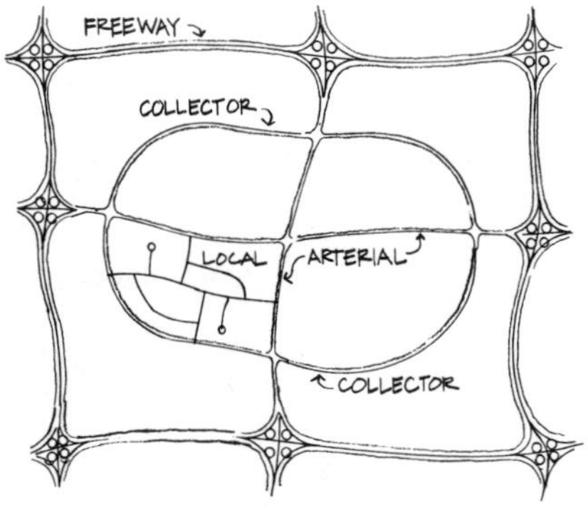
FREEWAY
COLLECTOR
LOCAL
ARTERIAL
COLLECTOR

Figure 342-2 Typical vehicular classification system.

Parkways are a very important type of recreational circulation route, facilitating the efficient movement of large volumes of through-traffic through areas of high scenic quality. They usually disallow commercial vehicles, such as trucks and buses.

On-site drives and roads refer to vehicular access routes *within* a site; they represent a category of classification finer than that of the local street system.

Most of this section will focus on the design and construction of on-site roads and parkways, although design standards, techniques of layout, and methods of construction apply to all categories of vehicular circulation. Design and construction measures appropriate to each category will depend upon the local practices and requirements set by controlling public authorities.

1.3 Circulation Patterns

Various roadway patterns are commonly used to lay out a vehicular circulation system (Table 342-2).

1.4 Basic Design Guidelines and Principles

The design of vehicular circulation systems involves both aesthetic judgment and sound engineering practice. A well-designed roadway should possess internal harmony (i.e., the driver should be able to see smooth lines ahead and have a clear vision of the landscape) and should also possess external harmony (i.e., to the eye of an onlooker a roadway should fit into its surroundings). These objectives require that the designer visualize the three-dimensional aspects of all elements of a roadway, including the various combinations of horizontal and vertical curves, of cuts merging smoothly with fills, and of side slopes blending well with the terrain.

A roadway, however, is primarily a transportation medium. It must be designed and built to facilitate the safe movement of vehicles. To achieve this objective, the design of a roadway must incorporate criteria of strength, safety, and uniformity.

The following are general design guidelines and principles to consider when designing vehicular circulation systems at any scale:

1. The *location* of a roadway should be based on a survey of all determinants. These include but are not limited to:

- **a.** Present and proposed land uses and traffic ways
- **b.** Areas where redevelopment or change is desirable
- **c.** Existing and planned transportation facilities
- **d.** Traffic "desire lines"
- **e.** Topographic features
- **f.** Ecological factors
- **g.** Historical factors
- **h.** Permanent areas and features to remain
- **i.** Scenic opportunities
- **j.** Social, economic, and political structures
- **k.** Safety
- **l.** Acquisition and development costs
- **m.** Operation and maintenance costs

2. The location and design of a roadway must include consideration of its effect on contiguous uses in terms of noise and fumes. (Refer to Section 660: Sound Control, for more information.)

3. The location of a roadway must be responsive to natural forces and features.

4. A roadway should be so aligned and constructed as to preserve and accentuate the best qualities of the landscape.

5. The vertical and horizontal alignment of

TABLE 342-1
Criteria for Vehicle System Classification

Classification	*Principal service function*	*Typical trip lengths, mi*	*Elements linked by facility*	*Desirable spacing, mi*
Freeway	Through movement exclusively	3	CBD major generators	1–3
Arterial	Through movement, some land access	1	CBD secondary generators	1
Collector	Through movement and land access	1	Local areas	½
Local	Land access	½	Individual land sites	

TABLE 342-2
Typical Roadway Patterns

Grid pattern

Advantages
- Simplicity, regularity
- Ease of layout (engineering)
- Convenient access
- Good orientation, easy to follow
- Good on level land
- Suitable for complex distributed flow

Disadvantages
- Visual monotony
- Disregard of topography
- Vulnerability to through traffic
- Lack of difference between heavily and lightly traveled ways

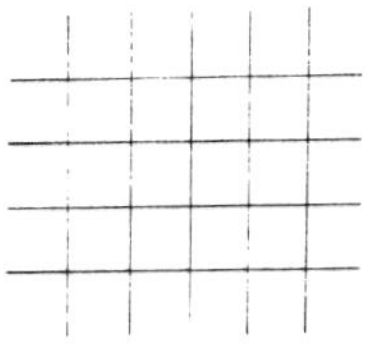

Radial pattern

Advantages
- Good direct line of travel

Disadvantages
- Not good when neither origin nor destination are related to center
- Difficult for service
- Causes problems in local flow and creates difficult building sites

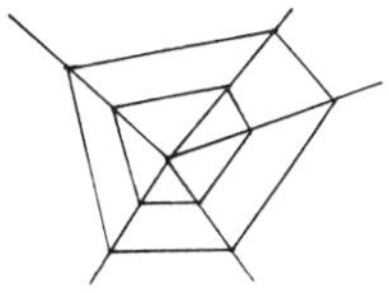

Classic pattern

Advantages
- Favors the specialization of major vs. minor arteries
- Makes the intersection problem manageable by distributing instead of concentrating at center

Disadvantages
- Very sensitive to interruptions at single point

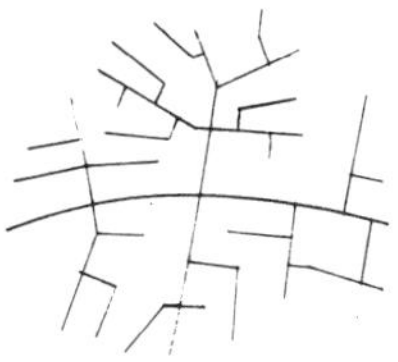

Linear system

Advantages
- Flow primarily between two points
- Typically found along railroads, canals, highways

Disadvantages
- Lack of focus

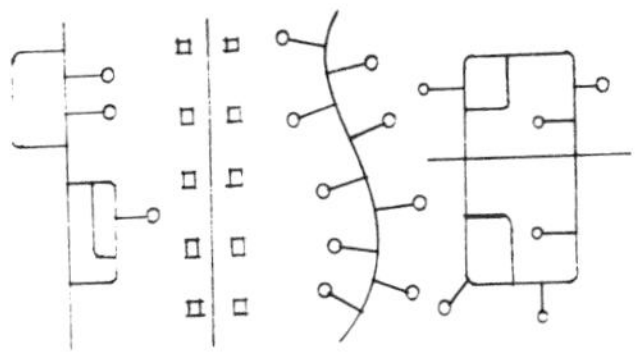

TABLE 342-3
Summary of Minimum Design Standards for Urban Streets

	Principal arterial			*Collector streets*		*Local streets*	
Design elements	*Freeways and expressways*	*Other*	*Minor arterials*	*Single-family residential areas*	*Other*	*Single-family residential areas*	*Other*
Design speed, mph	60	40	30	30	30	20	20
Number of traffic lanes	4 up	4 up	4–6	2	4	2	2–4
Width of traffic lanes, ft	12	12	12	12	12	10	11
Width of curb parking lane or shoulder, ft	12	10	10	10	10	8	10
Width of right-of-way, ft	120 up	120 up	100–120	60	80	50–60	60–80

a roadway should be carefully coordinated.

6. A roadway should provide for a variety of visual experiences.

7. Where used as an approach or entry, a road, by its location and design, should respond to interesting views.

2.0 DESIGN CONTROLS

2.1 General Roadway Standards

Table 342-3 is a comparative summary of design standards for arterial, collector, and local streets. Tables 342-4 and 342-5 give standards for collector and local streets based on terrain and development density.

2.2 Driver Characteristics

Because the driver is a major part of the transportation system, human limitations and behavior must be understood and

TABLE 342-4
Collector Street Design Standards for Low, Medium, and High Development Densities

	Ordinary terrain			*Rolling terrain*			*Hilly terrain*		
	Low	*Medium*	*High*	*Low*	*Medium*	*High*	*Low*	*Medium*	*High*
Right-of-way, ft	70	70	70	70	70	70	70	70	70
Pavement width	36	36	40	36	36	40	36	36	40
Type of curb		vertical face			vertical face			vertical face	
Sidewalk width, ft	5	5	5	5	5	5	5	5	5
Sidewalk distance from curb face, ft	10	10	10	10	10	10	10	10	10
Minimum sight distance	250	250	250	20	20	20	150	150	150
Maximum grade, %	4	4	4	8	8	8	12	12	12
Minimum spacing along major traffic route, ft	1300	1300	1300	1300	1300	1300	1300	1300	1300
Design speed, mph	35	35	35	30	30	30	25	25	25
Minimum centerline radius, ft	350	350	350	230	230	230	150	150	150

TABLE 342-5
Local Street Design Standards for Low, Medium, and High Development Densities

	Ordinary terrain			*Rolling terrain*			*Hilly terrain*		
	Low	*Med*	*High*	*Low*	*Med*	*High*	*Low*	*Med*	*High*
Right-of-way width, ft	60	60	60	60	60	60	50	60	60
Pavement width	22–27	32	36	22–27	34	36	27	34	36
Type of curb*	O/R	V	V	V	V	V	V	V	V
Sidewalk width, ft	0	5	5	0	5	5	0	5	5
Sidewalk distance from curb face	—	6	6	—	6	6	—	6	6
Minimum sight distance, ft	20	20	20	150	150	150	110	110	110
Maximum grade, %	4	4	4	8	8	8	15	15	15
Maximum cul-de-sac length, ft	1000	500	500	1000	500	500	1000	500	500
Minimum cul-de-sac radius (right-of-way)	50	50	50	50	50	50	50	50	50
Design speed, mph	30	30	30	25	25	25	20	20	20
Minimum centerline radius, ft	250	250	250	175	175	175	110	110	110

* V = vertical; R = roll curb; O = none.

taken into account when designing vehicular circulation systems. Design success is dependent upon a thorough understanding of user characteristics. An understanding not only of average human physical and mental limitations but also of the range of user performance is important for sound judgment in the design of traffic controls and operating measures.

Reaction to External Stimuli:

The process of reaction to stimuli involves a series of events which are inherently related to human physical factors:

1. *Perception:* involves seeing the stimuli along with other perceived objects

2. *Identification:* involves the identification and understanding of the stimuli

3. *Judgment:* involves the decision-making process

4. *Reaction:* involves the physical execution of the decision

The total time required to perceive and react to a stimulus is the sum of the above four factors, referred to as PIJR.

Visual Factors in Perception and Identification:

Visual Acuity: Visual acuity refers to the field of clearest vision. The most acute vision is limited to a narrow cone of 3 to 5 degrees; however, sight is fairly clear within a cone of 10 to 12 degrees (Figure 342-3).

Peripheral Vision: Peripheral vision refers to the field of view within which an individual can see objects, but without clear detail or color. The field of normal peripheral vision in humans varies from 120 to 180 degrees (Figure 342-4).

Depth Perception: Depth perception refers to the ability to estimate distance and speed.

Glare Vision and Recovery: Glare recovery time (i.e., the time required to recover from the effects of glare after a light source has passed), is approximately 6 or more seconds when moving from light to dark areas and about 3 seconds when moving from dark to light areas.

Color Vision: Generally, full color vision is not of great importance in driving because most people who are color blind learn to compensate. In general, the eye is most sensitive to black and white or black and yellow combinations.

Total Driver Response Time:

Total driver response time (PIJR) increases with the number of choices and the complexity of the judgment required. PIJR times are used to determine safe stopping distances, safe approach speeds at intersections, and the length of the yellow interval used for traffic signals.

The American Association of State Highway and Transportation Officials (AASHTO) recommends that a minimum PIJR time of no less than 2.5 seconds be used to determine safe stopping distances for all ranges of speed, and that a minimum PIJR time of 2.0 seconds be used for intersection sight distances. Wherever possible, greater PIJR times should be used.

Variability of Drivers:

The variability of drivers and their attitudes with respect to age, sex, attentiveness, knowledge, skill of driving, nervousness, and impatience are important factors and must be taken into account when establishing design criteria. Design values are normally based on satisfying the needs of the 85th percentile drivers, with minor consideration given to the variability of the 15th percentile who represent poorer drivers.

Behavior of Drivers:

A sense of reason will govern the behavior of most drivers, but neither drivers nor pedestrians will react consistently to controls and regulations that seem unreasonable. This phenomenon must be taken into consideration when establishing regulations and controls.

Effect of Climate on Drivers:

Various climatic factors such as patterns of wind movement, temperature, precipitation, and sun angle can affect the driver's perception of the road and the driver's consequent behavior.

Visual information increases in direct proportion to the amount of light reflected on the object. Consequently, climatic conditions can obscure the driver's perception. Rain, fog, and mist at night create the greatest visual problems. Such climatic effects create difficulty in determining the size of the object in front of the vehicle, its distance ahead, and the speed at which that object is moving.

Low sun angles in morning or late afternoon can cause nearly total dissolution of the driver's visual field. The result is momentary blindness and an inability to discern information readily. Whenever possible, roads should be aligned to minimize such problems.

2.3 Vehicular Characteristics

The physical characteristics of vehicles using a roadway will determine the geometric design and construction of the roadway. For general design use, major class groupings should be determined and representative-size vehicles established within each class.

A *design vehicle* is a representative motor vehicle the weight, dimensions, and operating characteristics of which are used to establish highway design controls to accommodate vehicles of a designated type. For purposes of geometric design, the design vehicle should be one with dimensions and a minimum turning radius larger than those of almost all vehicles in its class.

Design Vehicle Types and Sizes:

Five design vehicle types are commonly used in determining geometric design and construction of roads. Table 342-6 lists the five types and their dimensional design characteristics.

Operating Characteristics:

Three operating characteristics that influence roadway design are turning radius, acceleration, and braking distance.

Turning Radii: Turning radii for the five design vehicle types are illustrated in Figures 342-5 through 342-9.

Acceleration: Acceleration data are used to determine:

1. The time required to cross an intersection from a stationary position

2. The distance required to pass another vehicle

3. The gap acceptance

The rate of acceleration of passenger vehicles is from 4 to 6 mph per second (6.4 to 9.7 km/h per second), which is equal to 6 to 9 fps (1.8 to 2.7 m/s). The rate of acceleration for trucks is from 1½ to 2 mph per second (2.4 to 3.2 km/h per second), or 2 to 3 fps (0.6 to 0.9 m/s).

Braking Distance: The braking ability of a motor vehicle and the forward-friction factor between tires and a pavement determine the slowing and stopping abilities of the vehicle.

For relatively level roadways, the following formula is used to determine braking distance:

$$S = \frac{V^2}{30F}$$

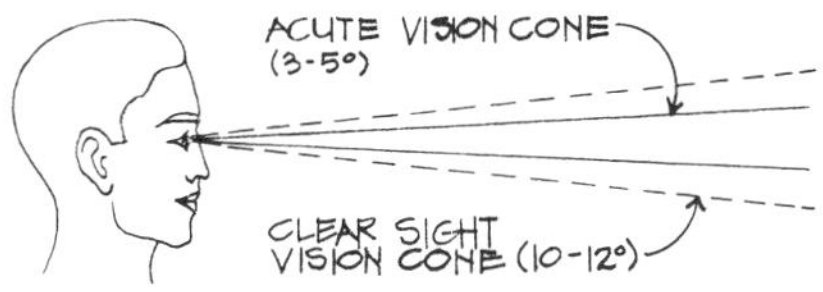
ACUTE VISION CONE
(3-5°)
CLEAR SIGHT
VISION CONE (10-12°)

Figure 342-3 Visual acuity cone.

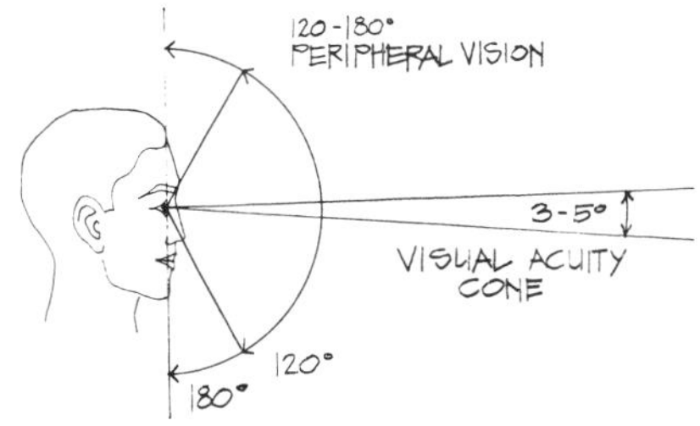
120-180°
PERIPHERAL VISION
3-5°
VISUAL ACUITY
CONE
120°
180°

Figure 342-4 Peripheral vision.

TABLE 342-6
Design Vehicle Types and Sizes

Dimensions	*Passenger vehicle (P), ft*	*Single-unit truck or bus (SU), ft*	*Semi-trailer combinations (WB-40), ft*	*Semi-trailer combination (WB-50), ft*	*Bus (B-40), ft*
Wheelbase	11.0	20.0	13 + 27 = 40	20 + 30 = 50	24.0
Front overhang	3.0	4.0	6.0	3.0	7.0
Rear overhang	5.0	6.0	6.0	2.0	9.0
Overall length	19.0	30.0	50.0	55.0	40.0
Overall width	7.0	8.5	8.5	8.5	8.5
Height	5.5	12.0	13.5	13.5	9.5

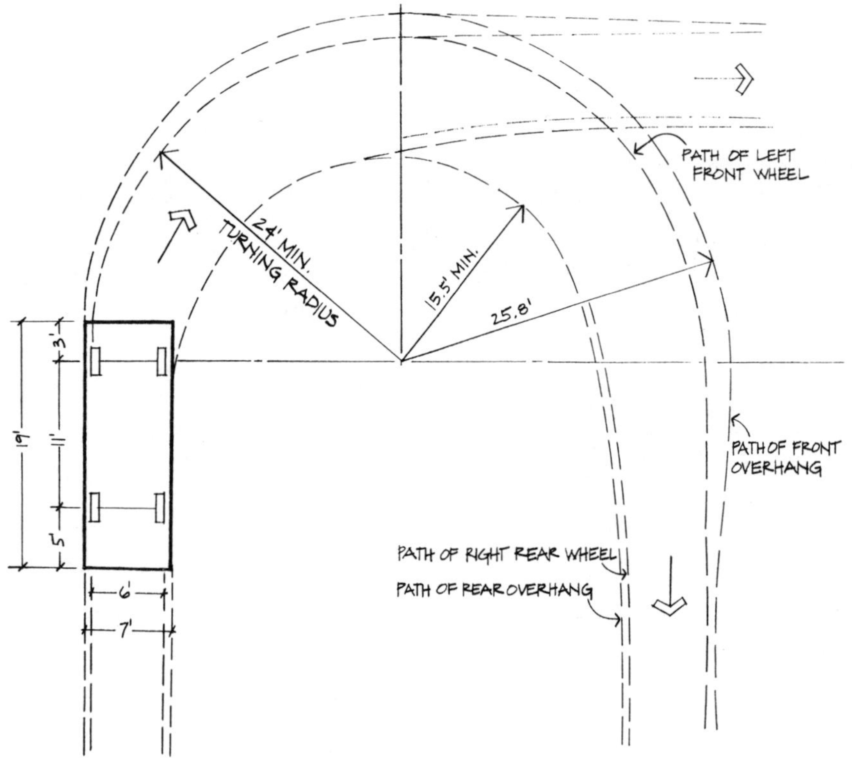
PATH OF LEFT FRONT WHEEL
24' MIN. TURNING RADIUS
15.5' MIN.
25.8'
3'
11'
19'
5'
6'
7'
PATH OF FRONT OVERHANG
PATH OF RIGHT REAR WHEEL
PATH OF REAR OVERHANG

Figure 342-5 Turning radius: passenger design vehicle. Values are based on speeds less than 10 mph (16 km/h). *(Courtesy of AASHTO.)*

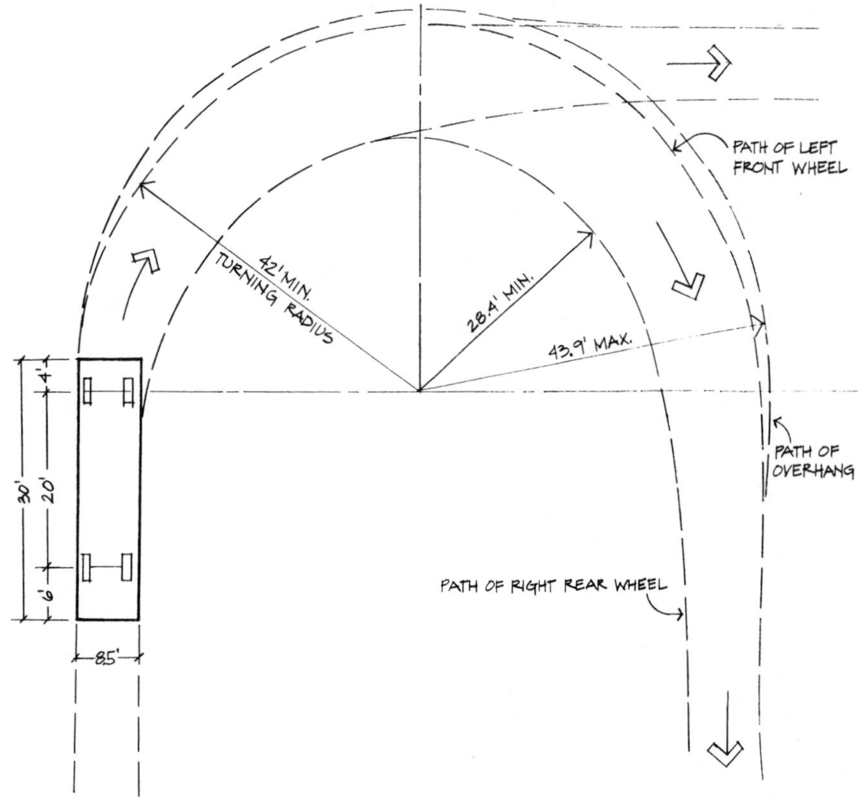
PATH OF LEFT FRONT WHEEL
42' MIN. TURNING RADIUS
28.4' MIN.
43.9' MAX.
4'
20'
30'
6'
8.5'
PATH OF OVERHANG
PATH OF RIGHT REAR WHEEL

Figure 342-6 Turning radius: single-unit design vehicle. Values are based on speeds less than 10 mph (16 km/h). *(Courtesy of AASHTO.)*

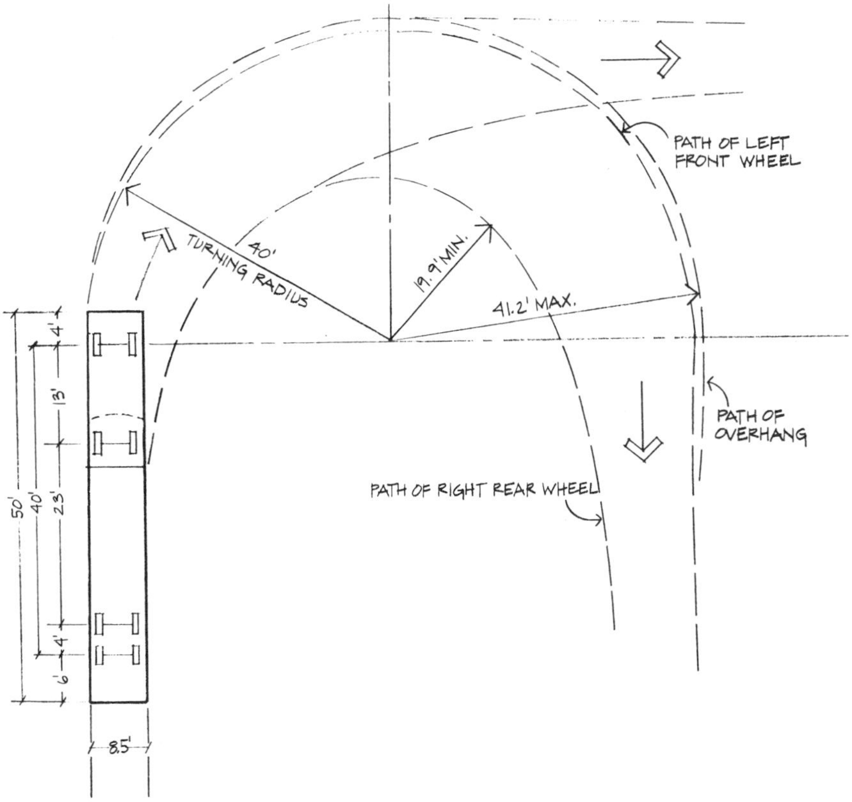
PATH OF LEFT FRONT WHEEL
40'
TURNING RADIUS
19.9' MIN.
41.2' MAX.
PATH OF OVERHANG
PATH OF RIGHT REAR WHEEL
4'
13'
23'
40'
50'
4'
6'
8.5'

Figure 342-7 Turning radius: truck-combination design vehicle (40-ft wheelbase). Values are based on speeds less than 10 mph (16 km/h). *(Courtesy of AASHTO.)*

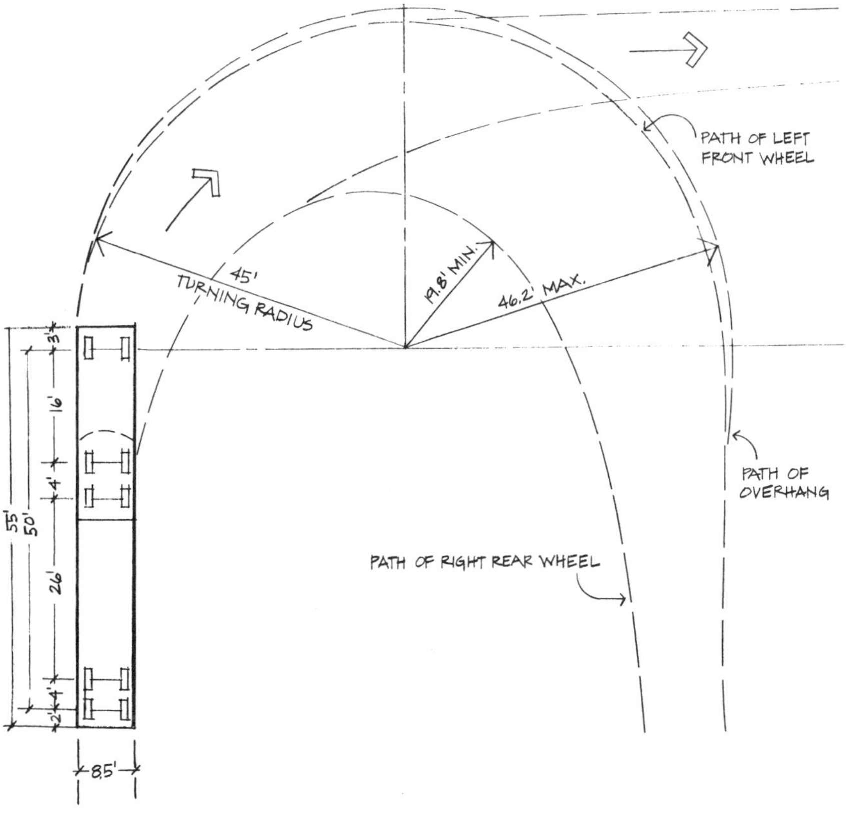
PATH OF LEFT FRONT WHEEL
45'
TURNING RADIUS
19.8' MIN.
46.2' MAX.
PATH OF OVERHANG
PATH OF RIGHT REAR WHEEL
3'
16'
4'
26'
4'
2'
50'
55'
8.5'

Figure 342-8 Turning radius: truck-combination design vehicle (50-ft wheelbase). Values are based on speeds less than 10 mph (16 km/h). *(Courtesy of AASHTO.)*

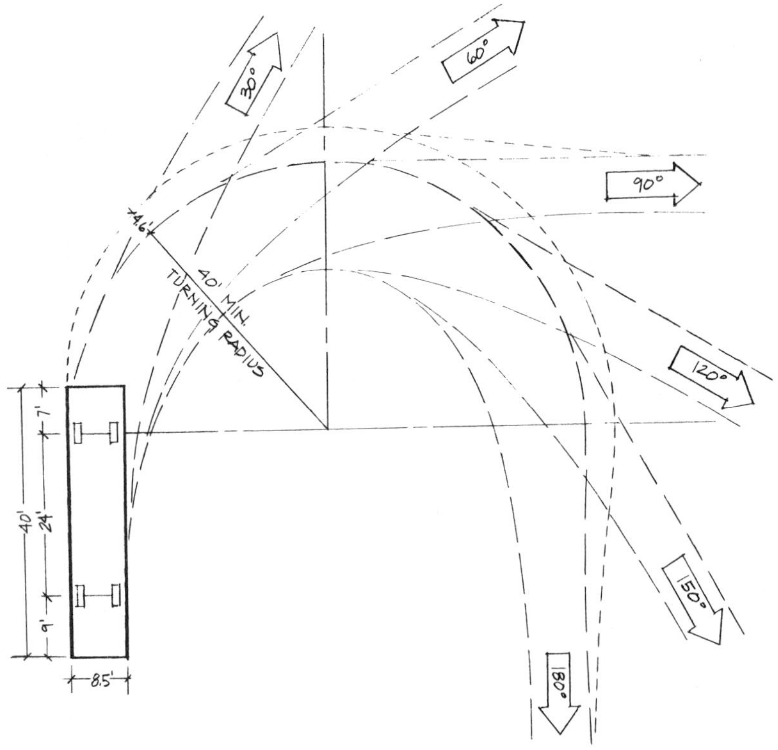

30°
60°
90°
120°
150°
180°
46'
40' MIN. TURNING RADIUS
7'
24'
9'
40'
8.5'

Figure 342-9 Turning radius: bus design vehicle (24-ft wheelbase). Values are based on speeds less than 10 mph (16 km/h).

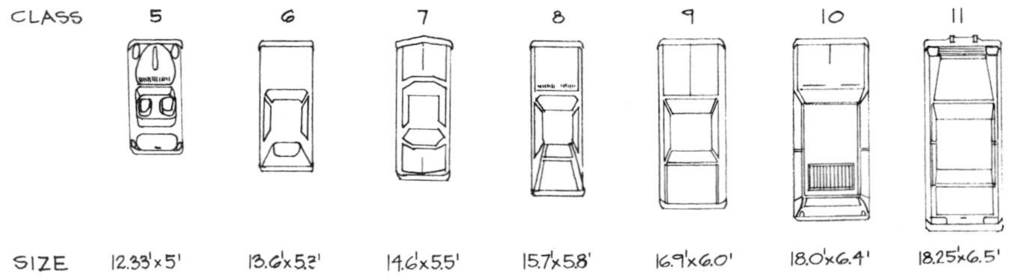

CLASS
5
6
7
8
9
10
11
SIZE
12.33'x5'
13.6'x5.3'
14.6'x5.5'
15.7'x5.8'
16.9'x6.0'
18.0'x6.4'
18.25'x6.5'

Figure 342-10 Average class size of automobiles (1983 models).

TABLE 342-7
Safe Coefficients of Friction *(F)*

Design speed, mph	*Assumed speed for conditions, mph*	*Safe coefficient of friction (F)*
30	28	0.36
40	36	0.33
50	44	0.31
60	52	0.30
65	55	0.30
70	58	0.29

where S = the braking distance or skidding distance, ft
V = the initial speed, mph
F = the coefficient of forward friction (Table 342-7)

Trends in Automobile Sizes:

Figure 342-10 illustrates the typical class sizes of private passenger vehicles. An analysis of the dimensions of automobiles for the model years 1980 through 1983 shows a clear trend to more models each year in size Class 8 or smaller.

Table 342-8 shows the trends, both for individual size classes and for the combination of Classes 5 to 8 and 9 to 11. There appears to be a movement away from the extremes of the two smallest (Classes 5 and 6) and the three largest (Classes 9, 10, and 11).

2.4 Design Speed (by Roadway Types)

The value of a road is often judged by the convenience, safety, and economy by which it transports goods and people. The speed adopted by a driver depends upon four general circumstances:

1. The physical characteristics of a road and its surroundings

2. The weather conditions

3. The presence of other vehicles

4. The speed limitations, either legal or by control devices

While any one of these may govern, the effects of these circumstances are almost always combined. An approximately uniform speed is generally the aim of most drivers. Provision should be made for a speed which satisfies most drivers. The speed chosen for design should be that typically used by drivers under favorable weather conditions.

Design speed is a speed determined for the design and correlation of the physical features of a road that influence vehicle operation. It is the maximum safe speed that can be maintained over a specific section of a road when conditions are sufficiently favorable that the design features of the road govern.

Suggested design speeds for roads of various classifications are given in Table 342-9.

The selection of a design speed should be done with great care and on the premise that, once selected, all pertinent geometric design will be related to the value selected.

2.5 Sight Distance

The design of a safe and efficient vehicular circulation system depends upon the ability of the driver to see ahead while moving along a roadway.

Criteria for Measuring Sight Distance:

1. *Height of eye:* the eye height of the average driver in a passenger vehicle is 3 ft 9 in (1150 mm) above the road surface (Figure 342-11).

2. *Height of object:* an object height of 6 in (152 mm) is customarily assumed for measuring stopping distances for crest vertical curves (Figure 342-12).

For passing sight distances, the object height is 4½ ft (1.37 m), which is generally the current passenger vehicle body height above the pavement.

Sight/Stopping Distance:

Sight distance is the length of road ahead visible to the driver. The minimum sight distance available on any stretch of road should be sufficient to enable a vehicle traveling at or near the design speed to stop before reaching an object in its path.

The minimum sight/stopping distance is a function of two elements. The first is the distance traveled after the obstruction comes into view but before the driver applies the brakes. During this period of perception and reaction, the vehicle travels at its initial velocity. The second distance is traversed while the driver brakes the vehicle to a stop (Figure 342-13).

Perception and Brake Reaction Time: The formula for determining the perception and brake reaction time is:

$$PR = 1.47(t)(V)$$

where PR = perception and reaction distance, ft

TABLE 342-8
Trends by Class (1980–1983)

Size class	1980 No.	1980 %	1981 No.	1981 %	1982 No.	1982 %	1983 No.	1983 %
5	3	3.1	2	2.1	2	2.0	2	1.9
6	14	14.6	18	19.1	18	18.0	18	17.0
7	25	26.0	23	24.5	29	29.0	30	28.3
8	15	15.6	16	17.1	21	21.0	27	25.5
9	23	24.0	19	20.2	19	19.0	18	17.0
10	9	9.4	10	10.6	9	9.0	9	8.5
11	7	7.3	6	6.4	2	2.0	2	1.8
	96	100.0	94	100.0	100	100.0	106	100.0
5–8		59.3		62.8		70.0		72.7
9–11		40.7		37.2		30.0		27.3

Source: From Barton-Aschman Associates, Inc.

TABLE 342-9
Design Speeds (by Roadway Types)

Highway type	*Design speed, mph*
Interstate rural	55
Rural highways	55
Flat terrace	55
Rolling terrain	50–55
Rough terrain	30–50
Urban interstate	
Through areas of concentrated development	50 (minimum)
Through areas of moderate development	40–55
Urban expressways	40 (minimum)
Through areas of concentrated development	30 (minimum)
Through areas of moderate development	30–50
Minor residential streets	25
Access roads—recreational developments	15–25
Drives—site access roads	10–20

Note: The selection of the design speed should be done with great care on the premise that once selected, all pertinent geometric design should be related to the value selected.

3'-9"

Figure 342-11 Average vehicle eye height.

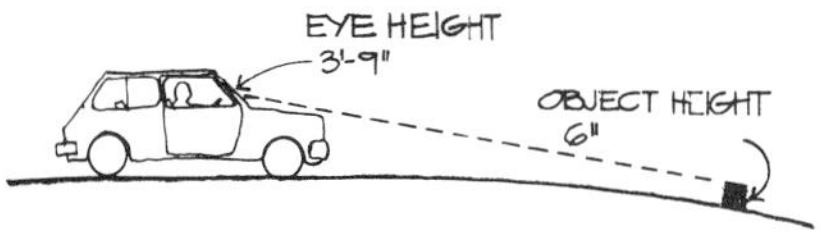
EYE HEIGHT
3'-9"
OBJECT HEIGHT
6"

Figure 342-12 Assumed object height for crest vertical curves.

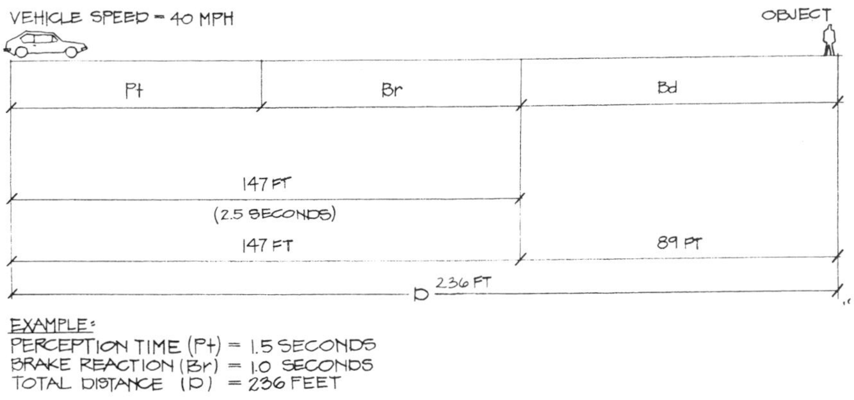
VEHICLE SPEED = 40 MPH
OBJECT
Pt
Br
Bd
147 FT
(2.5 SECONDS)
147 FT
89 FT
D
236 FT
EXAMPLE:
PERCEPTION TIME (Pt) = 1.5 SECONDS
BRAKE REACTION (Br) = 1.0 SECONDS
TOTAL DISTANCE (D) = 236 FEET

Figure 342-13 Components of sight/stopping distance.

TABLE 342-10
Sighting to Stopping—Minimum Distance

Design speed, mph	Assumed speed for condition, mph	Perception and brake reaction: Time, sec	Perception and brake reaction: Distance, ft	Coefficient of friction (F)	Braking distance on level, ft	Sight/stopping distance: Computed	Sight/stopping distance: Rounded for design, ft
			Design criteria—wet pavements				
30	28	2.5	103	0.36	73	176	200
40	36	2.5	132	0.33	131	263	275
50	44	2.5	161	0.31	208	369	350
60	52	2.5	191	0.30	300	491	475
65	55	2.5	202	0.30	336	538	550
			Comparative values—dry pavements				
30	30	2.5	110	0.62	48	158	
40	40	2.5	147	0.60	89	236	
50	50	2.5	183	0.58	144	327	
60	60	2.5	220	0.56	214	434	
65	65	2.5	238	0.56	251	489	

t = perception plus reaction time, seconds (2.5 seconds)
V = initial speed, mph

Example (Figure 342-13): Given that the initial speed = 40 mph,

$$PR = 1.47(t)(V)$$
$$= 1.47(2.50)(40)$$
$$= 147 \text{ ft}$$

Braking Distance: Once the driver has perceived and reacted to an obstruction, the approximate braking distance of a vehicle on a *level* roadway can be determined by use of the following formula:

$$d = \frac{V^2}{30f}$$

where d = braking distance, ft
V = initial speed, mph
f = coefficient of friction between tires and pavement

As in the same example (Figure 342-13), the braking distance for a speed of 40 mph would be as follows:

V = 40 mph

f = 0.60

$$d = \frac{40^2}{30(0.60)}$$
$$= \frac{1600}{18}$$
$$= 89 \text{ ft}$$

Total Stopping Distance: The formula for determining the total distance (D) required to stop the vehicle is therefore (Figure 342-13):

$$D = 1.47(t)(V) + \frac{V^2}{30f}$$
$$= 1.47(2.5)(40) + \frac{40^2}{(30)(0.60)}$$
$$= 147 + 89$$
$$= 236 \text{ ft}$$

For some design speeds, Table 342-10 gives for both wet and dry pavements the recommended minimums regarding actual initial speeds, perception and brake reaction times, and coefficients of friction.

Effects of Grades on Stopping: The design values given for minimum sight/stopping distances in Table 342-10 assume a braking distance on a *level* roadway. If the vehicle is traveling uphill, the braking distance is decreased. Conversely, if the vehicle is traveling downhill, the braking distance is increased. When a highway is on a grade, the braking distance is expressed by the formula:

$$D = \frac{V^2}{30(f \pm G)}$$

where G = grade of the road (uphill grades are +, downhill grades are −)

Example: Given that V = 4 mph and that G = −10%,

$$D = 1.47(t)(V) + \frac{V^2}{30(f \pm G)}$$
$$= 1.47(2.5)(40) + \frac{40^2}{30(0.60 - 0.10)}$$
$$= 147 + 107$$
$$= 254 \text{ ft}$$

Variations Due to Vehicle Type: Minimum sight/stopping distances derived from the above formula reflect passenger car operation only. Trucks, especially the larger and heavier units, require a longer stopping distance for a given speed than do passenger vehicles. However, two factors tend to counteract the need for additional braking distance for trucks. First, the truck operator is able to see substantially farther because of a higher position in the vehicle. Second, in many cases, trucks may be traveling more slowly than passenger vehicles.

Passing Sight Distance:

It is often necessary on two-lane roads to provide an opportunity to pass slow moving vehicles. Table 342-11 gives the minimum sight distance ahead that must be clear to permit safe passing.

TABLE 342-11
Recommended Design Values for Passing Sight Distance for Two-Lane Highways

	Design speed, mph 30	40	50	60	70
Assumed speeds					
Passed vehicle, mph	26	34	41	47	54
Passing vehicle, mph	36	44	51	57	64
Passing sight distance, ft	1100	1500	1800	2100	2500

Source: Courtesy of AASHTO.

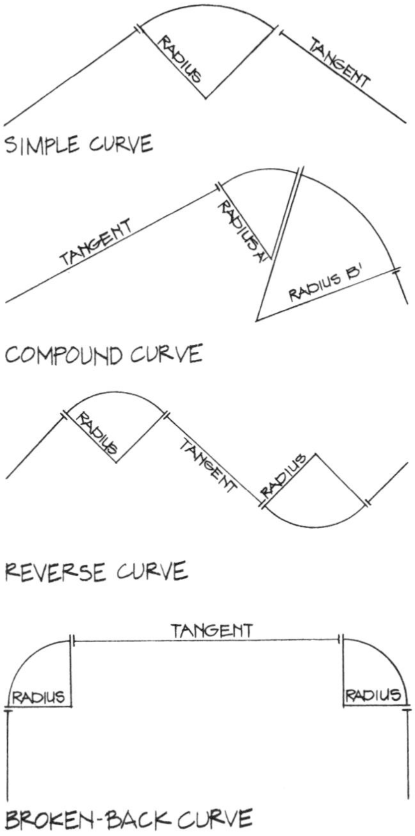
RADIUS
TANGENT
SIMPLE CURVE
TANGENT
RADIUS A'
RADIUS B'
COMPOUND CURVE
RADIUS
TANGENT
RADIUS
REVERSE CURVE
TANGENT
RADIUS
RADIUS
BROKEN-BACK CURVE

Figure 342-14 Classification of circular curves.

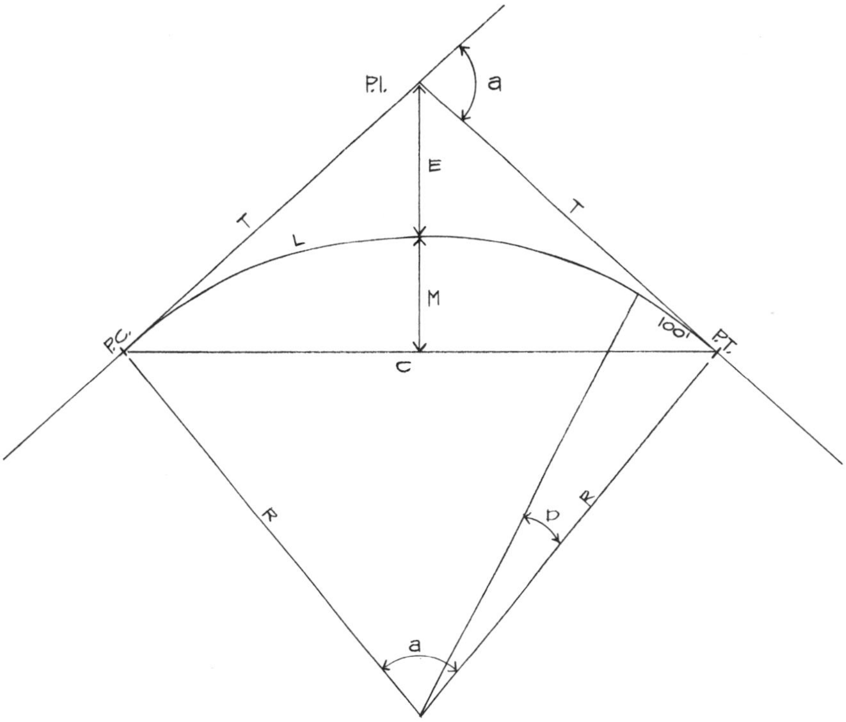
P.I.
a
E
T
T
L
M
P.C.
C
100'
P.T.
R
D
R
a

P.C. (point of curvature): the beginning of the curve in the direction of stationing

P.T. (point of tangency): the end of the curve in the direction of stationing

P.I. (point of intersection): point where the tangents, if extended, will intersect

a (delta, intersection angle, central angle): the angle deflection between the tangents, also equal to the angle between radii

T (tangent distance): horizontal distance between P.C. to P.I. and P.T. to P.I. (They are always equal.)

R (radius): radius of curve

L (length of curve): computed (actual) length of curve (arc) from P.C. to P.T.

C (long chord): distance measured along a straight line (shortest distance) between P.C. and P.T.

E (external distance): distance from the P.I. to the center of the curve

M (middle ordinate): distance from the center of the curve to the center of the long chord

D (degree of curvature): the angle at the center subtended by an arc of 100 ft which corresponds to a radius of 5729.58 ft for a central angle of 1 degree

Figure 342-15 Geometric components of a circular curve (horizontal alignment).

3.0 ROADWAY DESIGN ELEMENTS

3.1 Horizontal Alignment

General Design Criteria for Horizontal Alignment:

In addition to the specific design controls described in 2.0 Design Controls of this section, a number of general design criteria should be considered when developing the horizontal alignment for a roadway:

1. Alignment should be as direct as possible, but respectful of topography and other critical natural or cultural features.

2. Longer curves are preferred to those which satisfy minimum radii.

3. Abrupt changes from straight lines to sharp curves should be avoided.

4. Sharp compound and broken-back curves should be avoided (see Figure 342-14).

5. Abrupt reversal in alignment (i.e., *S curves*) without transitional tangents should be avoided.

Components of Horizontal Alignment:

Horizontal alignment is generally composed of two geometric components (see Figure 342-14):

1. Straight lines (tangents)

2. Circular curves (arcs)

Tangents: Tangents are the most common element of horizontal alignment. They are the shortest distance between two points and the easiest to lay out. Characteristics of tangents include the following:

1. They can provide clear orientation.

2. They are predictable and tend to encourage excessive speeds.

3. They are justifiable in flat terrain, but in rolling terrain they can be aesthetically uninteresting, monotonous, and fatiguing.

Circular Curves (Arcs): Circular curves are constructed from parts of circles rather than parabolas (as in vertical curves). Several common classifications of circular curves are illustrated in Figure 342-14. Figure 342-15 illustrates the geometric components of a circular curve.

Calculation of Circular Curves:

Formulas necessary to calculate the components of circular curves are as follows:

$$D = \frac{5729.58}{R} \quad \text{or} \quad D = \frac{100a}{L}$$

$$L = \frac{100a}{D} \quad \text{or} \quad L = \frac{(\pi)(R)a}{180}$$

$$R = \frac{5729.58}{D}$$

$$T = R \tan \frac{a}{2}$$

$$C = 2R \sin \frac{a}{2}$$

$$E = T \tan \frac{a}{4}$$

$$M = R\left(1 - \cos \frac{a}{2}\right)$$

where a = angle
$\pi = 3.14$

Sample circular curve calculation: Given are two tangents with bearings N50E and S30E. A curve with a 1000-ft (330-m) radius is desired (Figure 342-16).

Superelevation:

Superelevation refers to the cross slope of a road from the outside edge to the inside

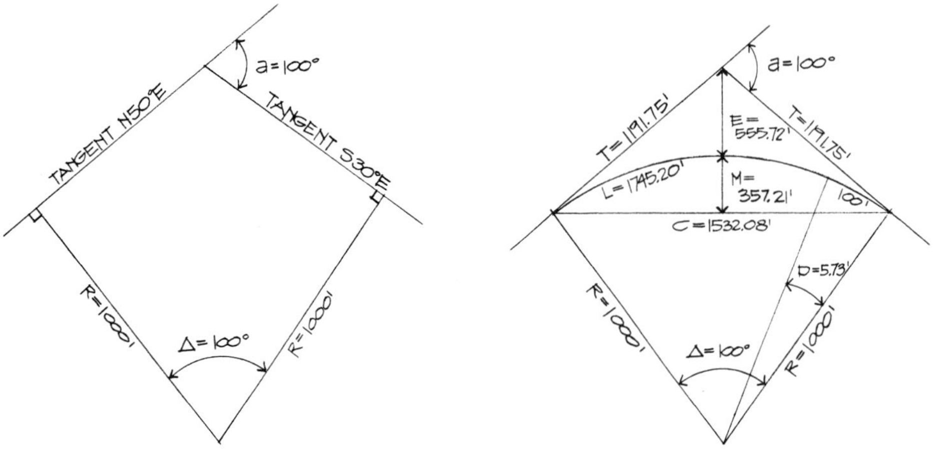
a=100°
TANGENT N50°E
TANGENT S30°E
R=1000'
Δ=100°
R=1000'
a=100°
T=1191.75'
E=555.72'
T=1191.75'
L=1745.20'
M=357.21'
100'
C=1532.08'
D=5.73°
R=1000'
Δ=100°
R=1000'

a = 100 degrees

$$D = \frac{5729.58 \text{ ft}}{R} = \frac{5729.58 \text{ ft}}{1000 \text{ ft}} = 5.73$$

$$L = \frac{100a}{D} = \frac{100 * 100}{5.73} = 1745.20 \text{ ft}$$

$$T = R \tan\frac{a}{2} = 1000 * \tan\frac{100 \text{ degrees}}{2} = 1000 * \tan 50 \text{ degrees}$$
$$= 1000 * 1.19175$$
$$= 1191.75 \text{ ft}$$

$$C = 2\,R \sin\frac{a}{2} = 2 * 1000 * \sin\frac{100 \text{ degrees}}{2}$$
$$= 2000 * \sin 50 \text{ degrees}$$
$$= 2000 * .76604$$
$$= 1532.08 \text{ ft}$$

$$E = T \tan\frac{a}{4} = 1191.75 * \tan\frac{100 \text{ degrees}}{4}$$
$$= 1191.75 * \tan 25 \text{ degrees}$$
$$= 1191.75 * .46631$$
$$= 555.72 \text{ ft}$$

$$M = R\left(1 - \cos\frac{a}{2}\right) = 1000\left(1 - \cos\frac{100 \text{ degrees}}{2}\right)$$
$$= 1000 * (1 - \cos 50 \text{ degrees})$$
$$= 1000 * (1 - .64279)$$
$$= 1000 * .35721$$
$$= 357.21 \text{ ft}$$

Figure 342-16 Calculation of circular curves.

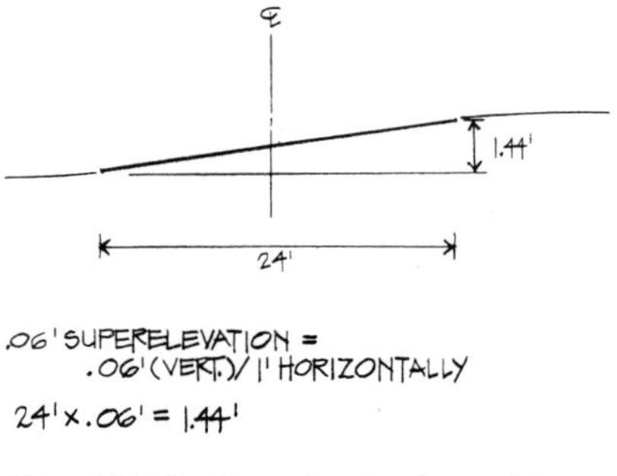
℄
1.44'
24'
.06' SUPERELEVATION =
.06' (VERT.)/ 1' HORIZONTALLY
24' x .06' = 1.44'

Figure 342-17 Superelevation (example).

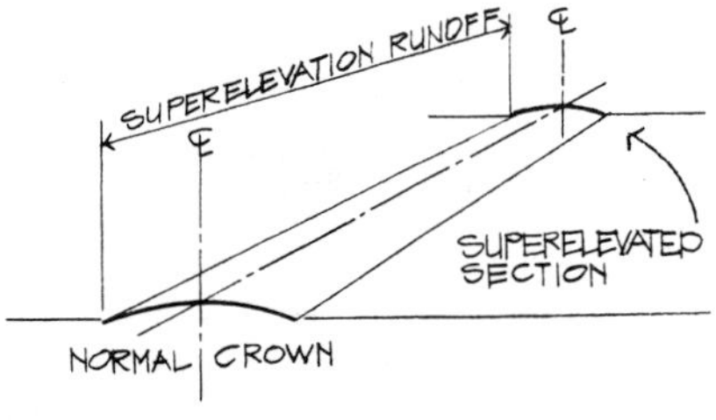
SUPERELEVATION RUNOFF
℄
℄
SUPERELEVATED SECTION
NORMAL CROWN

Figure 342-18 Superelevation runoff.

TABLE 342-12
Maximum Rates of Superelevation *(E)*

Surface	*Rate of (E)*
Urban streets and expressways (with snow and ice)	0.06
Rural roads (with snow and ice)	0.08
Urban expressways	0.10
Rural roads	0.12

TABLE 342-13
Maximum Coefficient of Side Friction *(F)*

Design speed	*Coefficient* (F)
10	0.18
15	0.18
20	0.17
25	0.17
30	0.16
35	0.16
40	0.15
45	0.15
50	0.14
55	0.14
60	0.13
65	0.13

edge measured in feet or meters (vertically) per foot or meter (horizontally). Superelevation is necessary on higher-speed curves to counteract centrifugal force and to provide a safe coefficient of friction between tires and a roadway surface (Figure 342-17).

Maximum Rates of Superelevation: The maximum rate of superelevation on a roadway is controlled by several factors (Table 342-12):

1. Regional climatic conditions
2. Terrain conditions
3. Type of area (e.g., rural versus urban)
4. Frequency and speed of vehicles

Maximum Degree of Curvature: The maximum degree of curvature, or the minimum radius, is a limiting value for a given design speed. It can be determined from the maximum rate of superelevation and the maximum side-friction factor. The minimum safe radius (R) can be calculated directly by use of the following formula:

$$R = \frac{v^2}{15(e + f)} \quad \text{or} \quad R = \frac{85{,}900\,(e + f)}{v^2}$$

where e = rate of roadway superelevation, ft/ft
f = maximum coefficient of side friction (Table 342-13)
v = vehicle speed, mph
R = radius of curve, ft

Table 342-14 lists the maximum degree of curvature and the minimum radius for designated design speeds.

Superelevation Runoff: Superelevation runoff is the length of roadway required to provide a transition from the normal road crown to a fully superelevated section or vice versa (Figure 342-18).

Table 342-15 lists minimum superelevation runoff lengths for various design speeds and superelevation rates.

Superelevation Location and Runoff: In general, superelevation runoff is assumed to run into the tangent. Figure 342-19 shows that from 60 to 80 percent of the length of runoff should be located on the tangent.

Pavement Widening on Curves:

Often, on two-lane roadways, a wider roadway cross-section is desirable on sharp curves for the following reasons (Figure 342-20):

1. Tendency for drivers to shy away from the pavement edge

TABLE 342-14
Maximum Degree of Curvature and Minimum Radius for Limiting Values of *E* and *F*

Design speed, mph	*Max,* E	*Max,* F	*Total,* E *and* F	*Minimum radius*	*Maximum degree of curve*	*Maximum degree of curvature**
20	.06	.17	.23	116	49.39	49.0
25	.06	.17	.23	131	31.61	31.5
30	.06	.16	.22	273	20.99	21.0
35	.06	.16	.22	371	15.43	15.5
40	.06	.15	.21	508	11.27	11.5
45	.06	.15	.21	643	8.91	9.0
50	.06	.14	.20	824	6.95	7.0
55	.06	.14	.20	1004	5.68	5.5
60	.06	.13	.19	1265	4.53	4.5
65	.06	.13	.19	1484	3.86	4.0
20	.08	17	.25	107	53.69	53.5
25	.08	.17	.25	167	34.36	34.5
30	.08	.17	.24	250	22.91	23.0
35	.08	.16	.24	340	16.83	17.0
40	.08	.15	.23	464	12.35	12.5
45	.08	.15	.23	587	9.76	10.0
50	.08	.14	.22	756	7.56	7.5
55	.08	.14	.22	917	6.25	6.5
60	.08	.13	.21	1144	5.01	5.0
65	.08	.13	.21	1342	4.27	4.5
20	.10	.17	.27	99	57.98	58.0
25	.10	.17	.27	154	37.11	37.0
30	.10	.16	.26	231	24.82	25.0
35	.10	.16	.26	314	18.23	18.0
40	.10	.15	.25	427	13.42	13.5
45	.10	.15	.25	541	10.60	10.5
50	.10	.14	.24	694	8.25	8.5
55	.10	.14	.24	840	6.82	7.0
60	.10	.13	.23	1044	5.47	5.5
65	.10	.13	.23	1224	4.68	4.5
20	.12	.17	.29	92	62.27	62.5
25	.12	.17	.29	144	39.85	40.0
30	.12	.16	.28	214	26.72	26.5
35	.12	.16	.28	292	19.63	19.5
40	.12	.15	.27	395	14.50	14.5
45	.12	.15	.27	500	11.45	11.5
50	.12	.14	.26	642	8.93	9.0
55	.12	.14	.26	776	7.38	7.5
60	.12	.13	.25	960	5.97	6.0
65	.12	.13	.25	1128	5.08	5.0

* Numbers rounded-off.

TABLE 342-15
Lengths Required for Superelevation Runoff (Two-Lane Pavements)

Superelevation rate, ft/ft	*Length of runoff (L), ft, for design speed, mph*									
	20	25	30	35	40	45	50	55	60	65
	12-ft lanes									
0.02	75	90	100	115	125	140	150	165	175	190
0.04	75	90	100	115	125	140	150	165	175	190
0.06	85	100	110	120	125	140	150	165	175	190
0.08	120	135	145	160	170	180	190	205	215	230
0.10	150	165	180	195	210	225	240	255	270	290
0.12	180	200	215	235	250	250	290	310	325	345
	10-ft lanes									
0.02	75	90	100	115	125	140	150	165	175	190
0.04	75	90	100	115	125	140	150	165	175	190
0.06	75	90	100	115	125	140	150	165	175	190
0.08	100	110	120	130	140	150	160	170	180	190
0.10	125	140	150	165	175	170	200	215	225	240
0.12	150	165	180	195	210	225	240	255	270	290

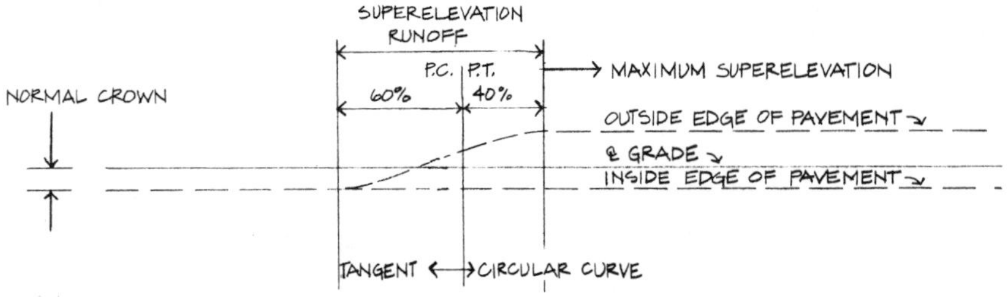
SUPERELEVATION RUNOFF
P.C. | P.T.
60% | 40%
MAXIMUM SUPERELEVATION
NORMAL CROWN
OUTSIDE EDGE OF PAVEMENT
℄ GRADE
INSIDE EDGE OF PAVEMENT
TANGENT ↔ CIRCULAR CURVE

Figure 342-19 Superelevation location and runoff.

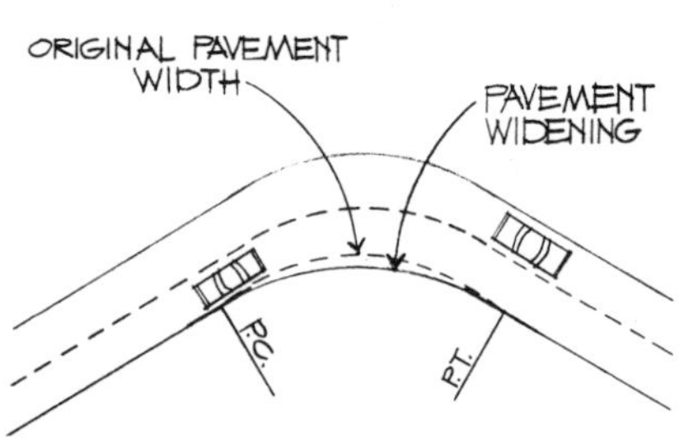
ORIGINAL PAVEMENT WIDTH
PAVEMENT WIDENING
P.C.
P.T.

Figure 342-20 Pavement widening on curves.

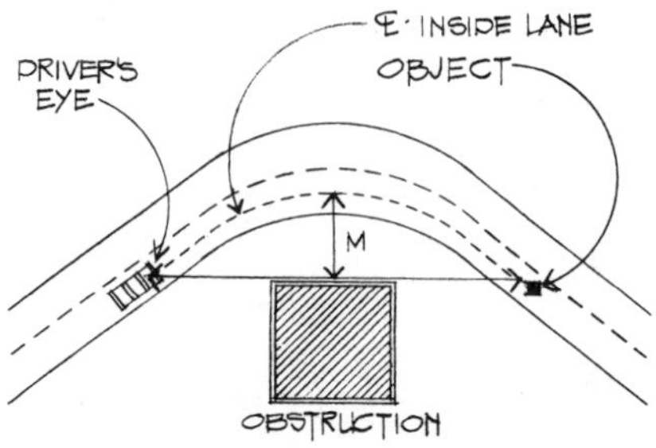
DRIVER'S EYE
℄ · INSIDE LANE
OBJECT
M
OBSTRUCTION

Figure 342-21 Sight distance on horizontal curve.

TABLE 342-16
Pavement Widening Values (Two-Lane Roads)

Degree of curve	24-ft lane design speed,				22-ft lane design speed,				20-ft lane design speed,			
	30	*40*	*50*	*60*	*30*	*40*	*50*	*60*	*30*	*40*	*50*	*60*
1	0.0	0.0	0.0	0.0	0.5	0.5	0.5	1.0	1.5	1.5	1.5	2.0
2	0.0	0.0	0.0	0.5	1.0	1.0	1.0	1.5	2.0	2.0	2.0	2.5
3	0.0	0.0	0.5	0.5	1.0	1.0	1.5	1.5	2.0	2.0	2.5	2.5
4	0.0	0.5	0.5	1.0	1.0	1.5	1.5	2.0	2.0	2.5	2.5	3.0
5	0.5	0.5	1.0	1.0	1.5	1.5	2.0	2.0	2.0	2.5	3.0	3.0
6	0.5	1.0	1.0	1.5	1.5	2.0	2.0	2.5	2.5	3.0	3.0	3.5
7	0.5	1.0	1.5		1.5	2.0	2.5		2.5	3.0	3.5	
8	1.0	1.0	1.5		2.0	2.0	2.5		3.0	3.0	3.5	
9	1.0	1.5	2.0		2.0	2.5	3.0		3.0	3.5	4.0	
10–11	1.0	1.5			2.0	2.5			3.0	3.5		
12–14.5	1.5	2.0			2.5	3.0			3.5	4.0		
15–18	2.0				3.0				4.0			
19–21	2.5				3.5				4.5			
22–25	3.0				4.0				5.0			
26–26.5	3.5				4.5				5.5			

Source: AASHTO, *A Policy on Geometric Design of Rural Highways,* 1965.

2. Increased transverse vehicle width because the front and rear wheels do not track
3. Added width because of the slanted position of the front of the vehicle relative to the roadway centerline

Table 342-16 gives pavement widening values for two-lane roadways.

Sight Distance on Curves:

As a vehicle travels around a horizontal curve, any obstruction near the inside edge of the road will block the driver's view ahead (Figure 342-21). Any particular combination of the sharpness of the curve with the position of an obstruction establishes a *horizontal sight distance,* which is the greatest distance at which a driver can see an object lying in the roadway. If the design is to provide safe operation, this horizontal sight distance must equal or exceed the safe stopping distances for each design speed (Table 342-17).

3.2 Vertical Alignment

Components of Vertical Alignment:

The vertical plane, or profile, of a road or drive is essentially made up of two geometric components (Figure 342-22):

1. Inclined straight lines (i.e., tangent grades)
2. Vertical curves

Grades: Maximum grades for roads vary considerably, depending upon terrain, speed, capacity, and use of the road. Table 342-18 shows the relationship between maximum grades and design speeds for major roadways. Maximum grades for roadways of a secondary nature may be about 2 percent steeper. In extreme cases, steeper grades for relatively short lengths may be considered.

Vertical Curves: Vertical curves are constructed from parts of parabolas rather than circles, and connect two different grades

TABLE 342-17
Sighting to Stopping Distance on Horizontal Curve (ft): M—Middle Ordinate

Design speed	Sight/ stopping distance	Degree of curve																				
		1	*2*	*3*	*4*	*5*	*6*	*7*	*8*	*9*	*10*	*11*	*12*	*13*	*14*	*15*	*16*	*17*	*18*	*19*	*20*	*21*
30	200	—	—	—	—	—	5	6	7	8	9	10	11	11	12	13	14	15	16	16	17	18
40	300	—	—	6	8	10	12	14	15	18	20	21	23	25	27	29	31	33	35	—	—	—
50	450	—	8	13	18	22	27	31	35	—	—	—	—	—	—	—	—	—	—	—	—	—
60	650	8	19	28	—	—	—	—	—	—	—	—	—	—	—	—	—	—	—	—	—	—

TABLE 342-18
Relation of Maximum Grades to Design Speed (Main Highways)

	Design speed, mph					
Type of topography	*30*	*40*	*50*	*60*	*65*	*70*
Flat	6	5	4	3	3	3
Rolling	7	6	5	4	4	4

Source: AASHTO, *A Policy on Geometric Design of Rural Highways,* 1965.

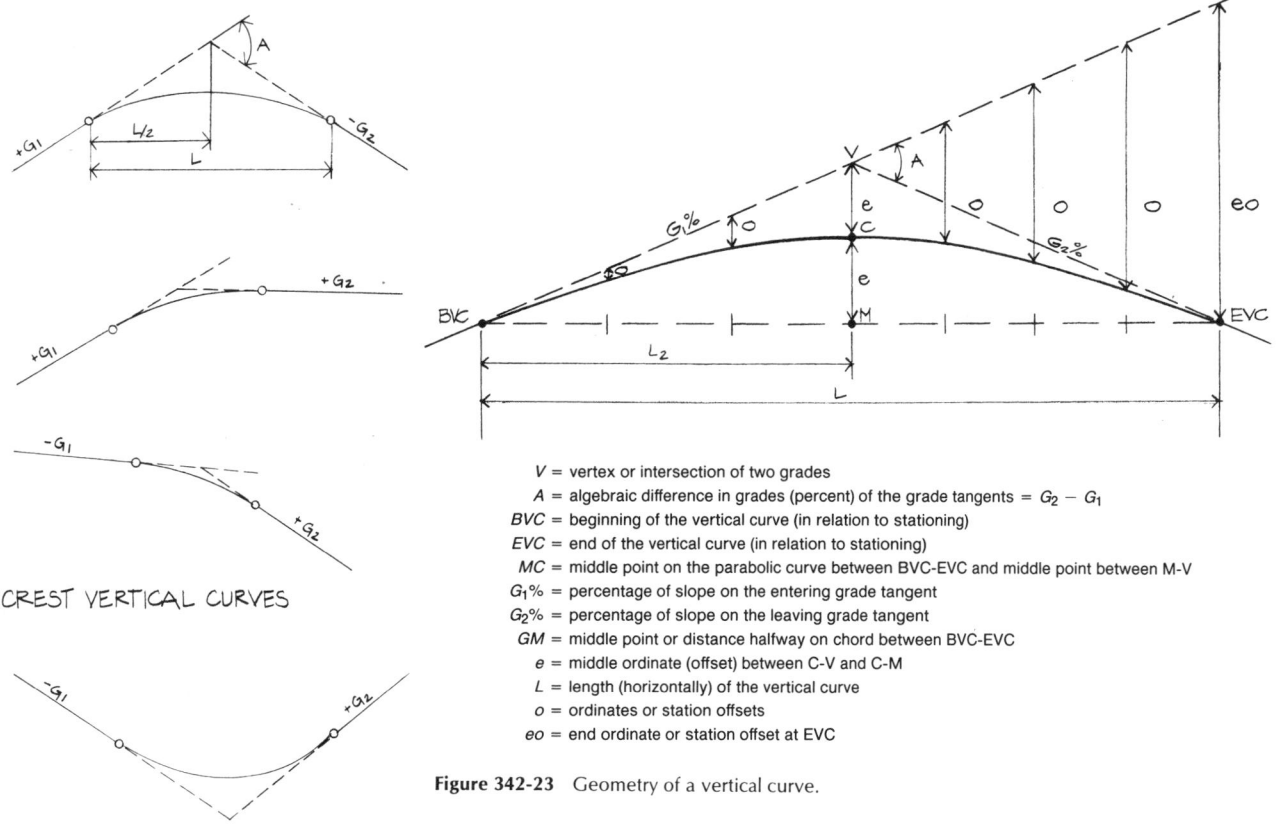

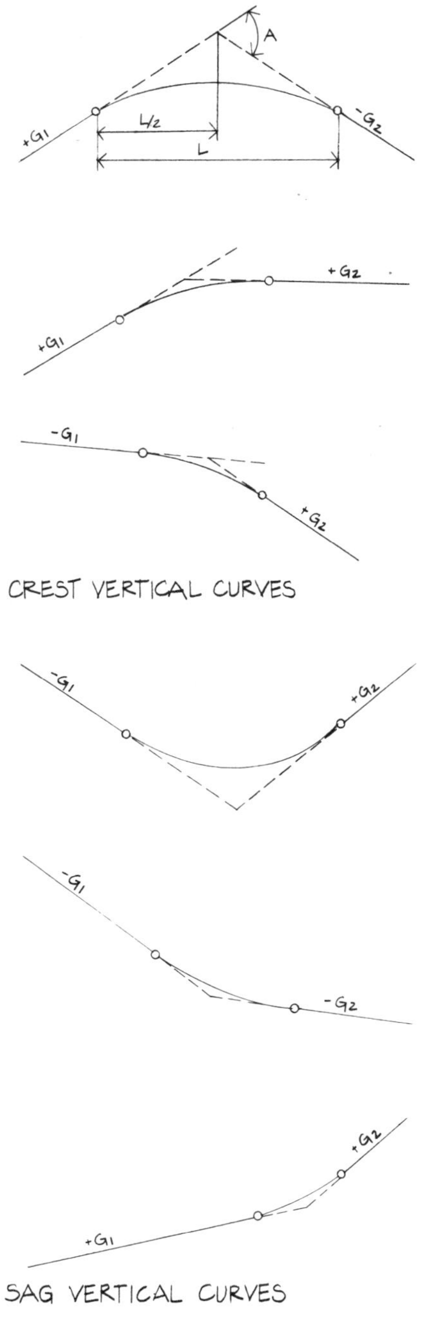
A
L/2
L
+G1
-G2
+G2
+G1
-G1
+G2
CREST VERTICAL CURVES
-G1
+G2
-G1
-G2
+G2
+G1
SAG VERTICAL CURVES

Figure 342-22 Components of vertical curves.

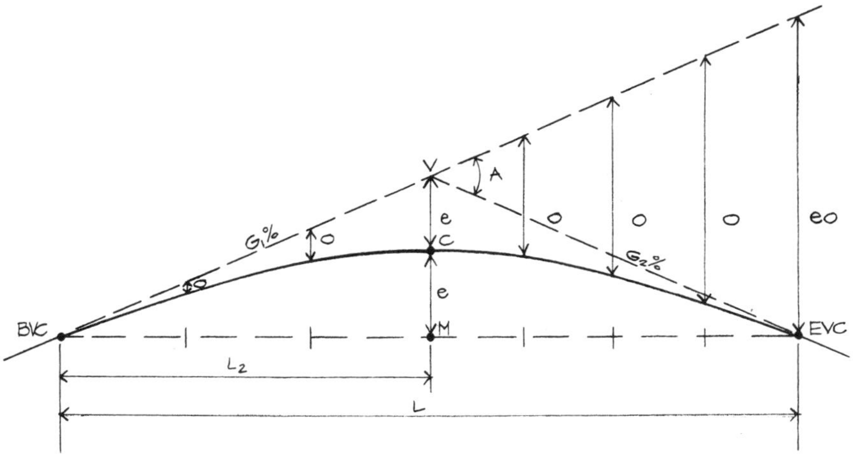
V
A
e
C
e
M
G1%
G2%
o
eo
BVC
EVC
L2
L

V = vertex or intersection of two grades
A = algebraic difference in grades (percent) of the grade tangents = $G_2 - G_1$
BVC = beginning of the vertical curve (in relation to stationing)
EVC = end of the vertical curve (in relation to stationing)
MC = middle point on the parabolic curve between BVC-EVC and middle point between M-V
$G_1\%$ = percentage of slope on the entering grade tangent
$G_2\%$ = percentage of slope on the leaving grade tangent
GM = middle point or distance halfway on chord between BVC-EVC
e = middle ordinate (offset) between C-V and C-M
L = length (horizontally) of the vertical curve
o = ordinates or station offsets
eo = end ordinate or station offset at EVC

Figure 342-23 Geometry of a vertical curve.

or tangents. Figure 342-22 shows the various types of vertical curves. Figure 342-23 illustrates the geometry of a vertical curve.

Calculation of Symmetrical Vertical Curves:

Calculations for a symmetrical vertical curve are shown below and basically involve a five-step process.

Step 1 (Figure 342-24):

1. Locate and determine the length of the vertical curve—the stations (lengths) of BVC and EVC (beginning and end of vertical curve). (Refer to information later in this section for determining the minimum lengths of crest or sag vertical curves.)

2. Determine the algebraic difference (A) of the grade tangents:

$$A = g_2 - g_1$$
$$= -7 - (+4)$$
$$= -11\%$$

Step 2 (Figure 342-25): Determine the elevations along the grade tangents at each 50-ft station.

Step 3 (Figure 342-26): Determine the middle ordinate (e) [middle ordinate (e) is equivalent to ⅛ the algebraic difference (A) times the length of the parabola in stations]:

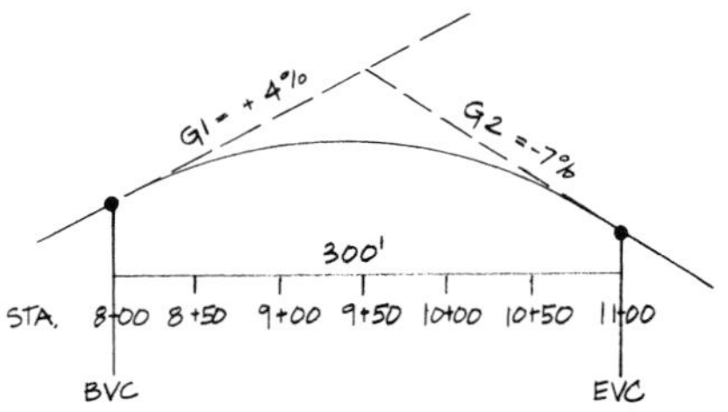
G1 = + 4%
G2 = -7%
300'
STA. 8+00 8+50 9+00 9+50 10+00 10+50 11+00
BVC
EVC

Figure 342-24 Calculation of symmetrical vertical curve (example problem).

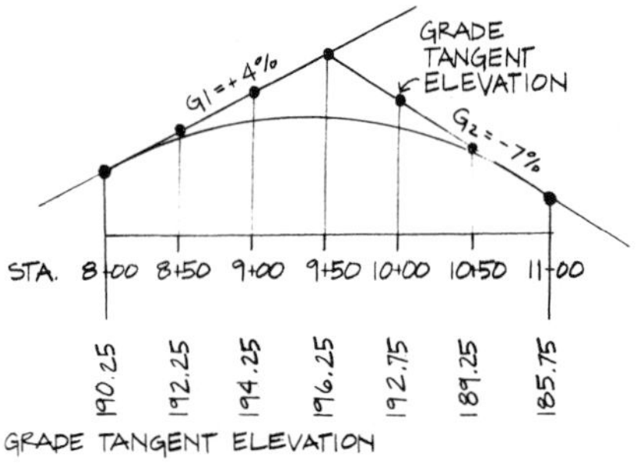
GRADE
TANGENT
ELEVATION
G1 = + 4%
G2 = -7%
STA. 8+00 8+50 9+00 9+50 10+00 10+50 11+00
190.25
192.25
194.25
196.25
192.75
189.25
185.75
GRADE TANGENT ELEVATION

Figure 342-25 Calculation of symmetrical vertical curve (example problem).

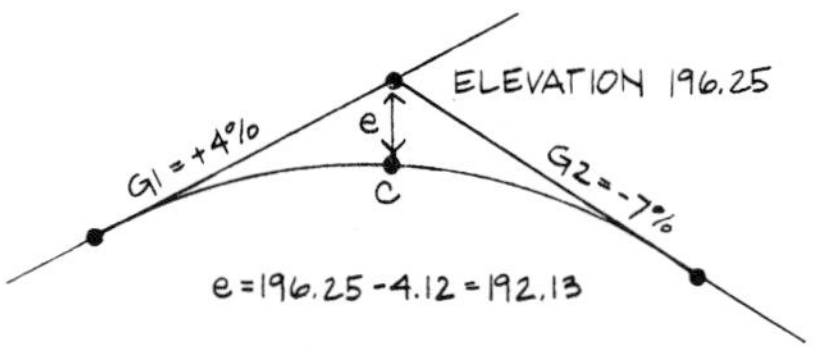
ELEVATION 196.25
G1 = +4%
G2 = -7%
e
C
e = 196.25 - 4.12 = 192.13

Figure 342-26 Calculation of symmetrical vertical curve (example problem).

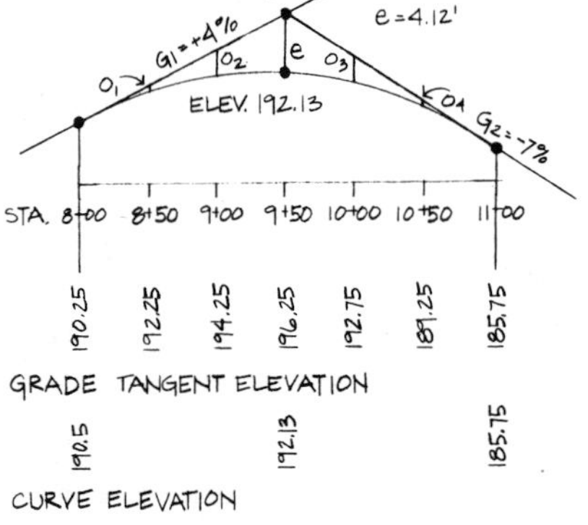
ELEV. 196.25
e = 4.12'
G1 = +4%
G2 = -7%
ELEV. 192.13
STA. 8+00 8+50 9+00 9+50 10+00 10+50 11+00
190.25
192.25
194.25
196.25
192.75
189.25
185.75
GRADE TANGENT ELEVATION
190.5
192.13
185.75
CURVE ELEVATION

Figure 342-27 Calculation of symmetrical vertical curve: Middle ordinate (e) method (example problem).

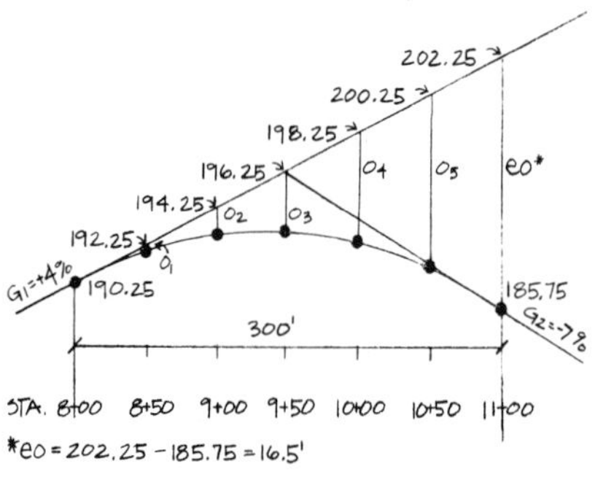
202.25
200.25
198.25
196.25
194.25
192.25
190.25
185.75
G1 = +4%
G2 = -7%
eo*
300'
STA. 8+00 8+50 9+00 9+50 10+00 10+50 11+00
*eo = 202.25 - 185.75 = 16.5'

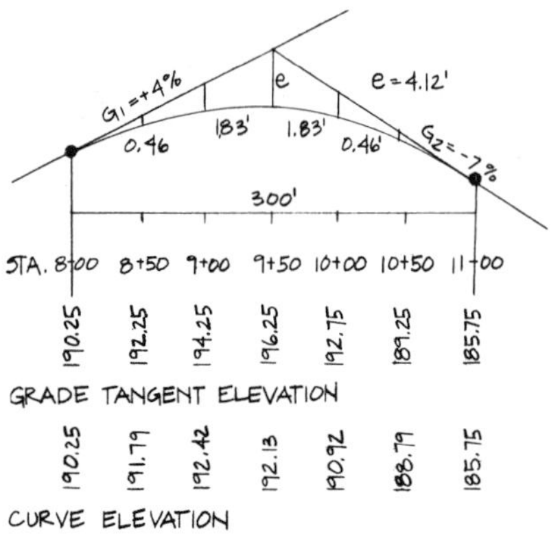
G1 = +4%
G2 = -7%
e = 4.12'
0.46
1.83'
1.83'
0.46'
300'
STA. 8+00 8+50 9+00 9+50 10+00 10+50 11+00
190.25
192.25
194.25
196.25
192.75
189.25
185.75
GRADE TANGENT ELEVATION
190.25
191.79
192.42
192.13
190.92
188.79
185.75
CURVE ELEVATION

Figure 342-28 Calculation of symmetrical vertical curve: End ordinate (eo) method (example problem).

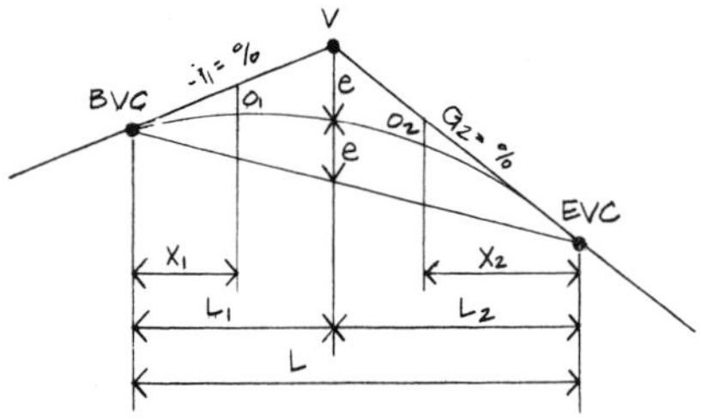
V
BVC
EVC
X1
X2
L1
L2
L

Figure 342-29 Unsymmetrical vertical curve.

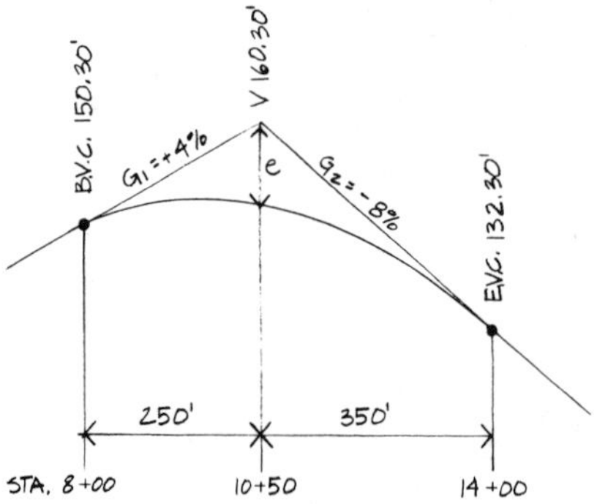
BVC. 150.30'
V 160.30'
EVC. 132.30'
G1 = +4%
G2 = -8%
e
250'
350'
STA. 8+00
10+50
14+00

Figure 342-30 Calculation of unsymmetrical vertical curve (example problem).

$$e = \tfrac{1}{8}(g_2 - g_1)L/100$$

$$= \tfrac{1}{8}[-7 - (+4)]^{300}/_{100}$$

$$= {}^{11}/_{8} \times 3$$

$$= 4.12 \text{ ft}$$

Step 4: Find the elevations on the curve at intermediate stations. Either of two methods may be employed (see below).

NOTE: Elevations on the vertical curve (offsets) are always determined at *even* 50- or 100-ft stations, although the curve may not necessarily begin or end at a 50- or 100-ft station. It is not necessary to adjust the curve to start and end on a station, although it does sometimes simplify the calculations.

First method [middle ordinate (e) method]: The middle ordinate method for determining elevations on the curve involves the use of the middle ordinate (e) as determined in step 3 above. The formula for the middle ordinate (e) method is:

$$0 = e\left(\frac{\text{distance to station from BVC or EVC}}{L/2}\right)^2$$

Example (Figures 342-27 and 342-28):

0_1 (station 8 + 50) $= 4.12(^{50}/_{150})^2$

$= 4.12(0.111)$

$= 0.46$ ft

0_2 (station 9 + 00) $= 4.12(^{100}/_{150})^2$

$= 4.12(0.444)$

$= 1.83$ ft

0_3 (station 10 + 00) $= 4.12\,(^{100}/_{150})^2$

$= 4.12(0.444)$

$= 1.83$ ft

0_4 (station 10 + 50) $= 4.12\,(^{50}/_{150})^2$

$= 4.12(0.111)$

$= 0.46$ ft

Data for the above curve can be recorded using the form shown in Table 342-19.

Second method [end ordinate (eo) method]: Alternatively, the end ordinate method can be used to determine elevations on a vertical curve at intermediate stations (Figure 342-29).

1. Determine station grades along g_1 grade tangent. [Note that offset (*eo*) is equal to 4 times the middle ordinate (e) as previously calculated.]

2. Determine offsets at stations from the g_1 grade tangent using the following formula:

$$0 = eo\left(\frac{\text{distance from BVC to station}}{L}\right)^2$$

Example:

$$O_1 = 16.5(^{50}/_{300})^2$$
$$= 16.5 \times 0.027$$
$$= 0.46 \text{ ft}$$
$$O_2 = 16.5(^{100}/_{300})^2$$
$$= 16.5 \times 0.111$$
$$= 1.83 \text{ ft}$$
$$O_3(e) = 16.5(^{150}/_{300})^2$$
$$= 16.5 \times 0.25$$
$$= 4.12 \text{ ft}$$
$$O_4 = 16.5(^{200}/_{800})^2$$
$$= 16.5 \times 0.44$$
$$= 7.33 \text{ ft}$$
$$O_5 = 16.5(^{250}/_{300})^2$$
$$= 16.5 \times 0.69$$
$$= 11.46 \text{ ft}$$

Data for the above curve can be recorded using the form shown in Table 342-20.

Step 5:

1. Calculate the horizontal distance from the BVC to the high or low point on the profile of a vertical curve:

$$X = \frac{L(g_1)}{A}$$

where X = distance from the BVC to the high or low point
L = length of vertical curve
g_1 = entering grade
A = algebraic difference

Using the previous example's problem, the results are as follows:

$$X = \frac{L(g_1)}{A}$$
$$= \frac{300(4)}{11}$$
$$= 109.09 \text{ ft}$$

Thus, the high point is located 109.09 ft from BVC, or at station 9 + 09.09.

2. Determine the elevation of the high point on the vertical curve by calculating the grade tangent elevation at station 9+ 09.09:

$^4/_{100} \times 109.09 = 4.36$ ft

190.25 (BVC elevation) + 4.36 = 194.61

3. Determine the offset from the grade tangent to the curve at the high-point station (9 + 09.09) by using either of the two previously shown methods:

e Method	eo Method
$O_{hp} = e\left(\frac{109.09}{150}\right)^2$	$O_{hp} = eo\left(\frac{109.09}{300}\right)^2$
= 4.12(0.53)	= 16.5(4.13)
= 2.18	= 2.18

Thus, the grade tangent elevation is: (9 + 09.09) − offset (high point) = high-point elevation on vertical curve: 194.61 − 2.18 = 192.43 ft at station 9 + 09.09.

Calculation of Unsymmetrical Vertical Curves:

Sometimes an unsymmetrical vertical curve, rather than a symmetrical (or equal-tangent) curve, may more closely fit certain requirements of the terrain. The terminology applied to the unsymmetrical curve also applies to the symmetrical curve, except that the middle point (M) on the chord and the middle point (C) on the parabolic curve are not located midway between the BVC and EVC (Figure 342-30).

Calculations for determining elevations along an unsymmetrical vertical curve are as follows (Figure 342-31):

Step 1: Determine the algebraic difference (A) of the grade tangents:

$$A = g_2 - g_1$$
$$= -8 - (+4) = -12$$

Step 2: Determine the middle ordinate (e):

TABLE 342-19
Vertical Curve Data Form: Middle Ordinate *(e)* Method (Example Problem Data)

Intersection station 9 + 50 Elevation 196.25 VC no. 2
Algebraic difference −7 − (+4) = −11 Curve length 300 ft
BVC station 8 + 00 Elevation 190.25
EVC station 11 + 00 Elevation 185.75
Middle ordinate *(e)* 1/8(−11)300/100 = 4.12 ft

	Station	*Distance from BVC or EVC*	*Tangent grade elevation*	*VC ordinate*	*VC elevation*
BVC	8 + 00	00.00	190.25	00.00	190.25
	8 + 50	50.00	192.25	00.46	191.79
	9 + 00	100.00	194.25	01.83	192.42
V	9 + 50	150.00	196.25	04.12	192.13
	10 + 00	100.00	192.75	01.83	190.92
	10 + 50	50.00	189.25	00.46	188.79
EVC	11 + 00	00.00	185.75	00.00	185.75

TABLE 342-20
Vertical Curve Data Form: End Ordinate *(eo)* Method (Example Problem Data)

Intersection station 9 + 50 Elevation 196.25 VC no. 2
Algebraic difference −7 − (+4) = −11 Curve length 300 ft
BVC Station 8 + 00 Elevation 190.25
EVC Station 11 + 00 Elevation 185.75
Elevation of entering grade at EVC station 202.25
End ordinate *(eo)* 16.50

	Station	*Distance from BVC*	*Tangent rise or drop from BVC, ft*	*Tangent grade elevation*	*VC ordinate*	*VC elevation*
BVC	8 + 00	00.00	0.0	190.25	00.00	190.25
	8 + 50	50.00	2.0	192.25	00.46	191.79
	9 + 00	100.00	4.0	194.25	01.83	192.42
V	9 + 50	150.00	6.0	196.25	04.12	192.13
	10 + 00	200.00	8.0	198.25	07.33	190.92
	10 + 50	250.00	10.0	200.25	11.46	188.79
EVC	11 + 00	300.00	12.0	202.25	16.50	185.75

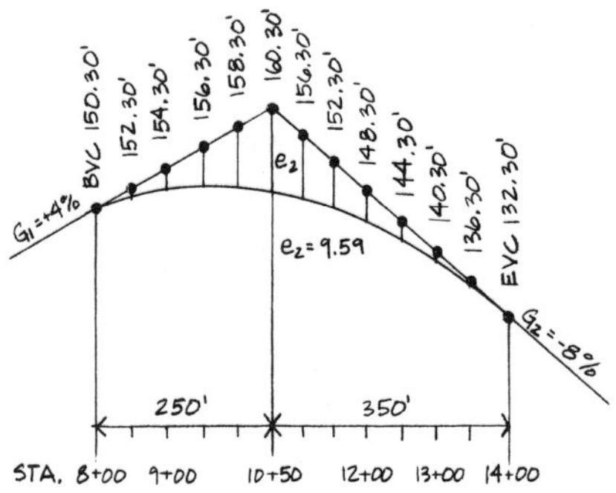
G1=+4%
BVC 150.30'
152.30'
154.30'
156.30'
158.30'
160.30'
156.30'
152.30'
148.30'
144.30'
140.30'
136.30'
EVC 132.30'
e2
e2=9.59
G2=-8%
250'
350'
STA. 8+00 9+00 10+50 12+00 13+00 14+00

Figure 342-31 Calculation of unsymmetrical vertical curve: Middle ordinate (e) method (example problem).

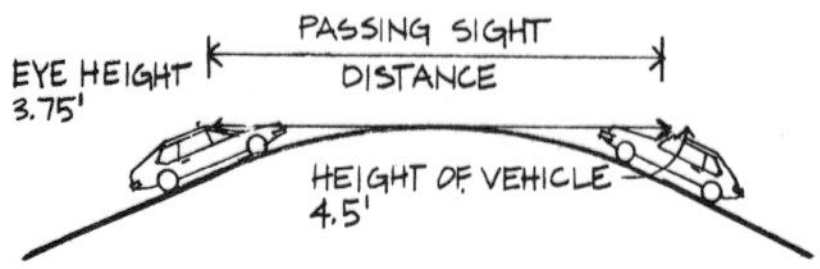
EYE HEIGHT
3.75'
PASSING SIGHT
DISTANCE
HEIGHT OF VEHICLE
4.5'

Figure 342-33 Passing sight distance on crest vertical curve.

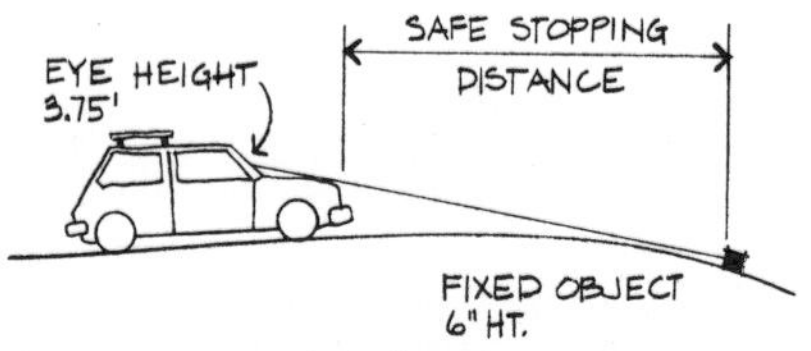
EYE HEIGHT
3.75'
SAFE STOPPING
DISTANCE
FIXED OBJECT
6" HT.

Figure 342-32 Sight/stopping distance on crest vertical curve.

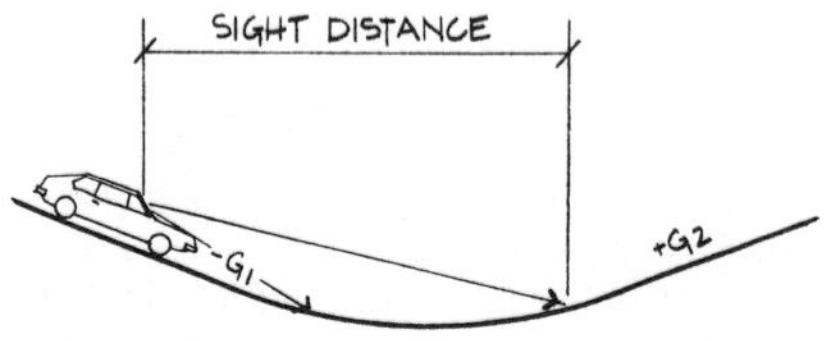
SIGHT DISTANCE
-G1
+G2

Figure 342-34 Headlight sight distance on sag vertical curve.

TABLE 342-21
Vertical Curve Data Form: Unsymmetrical Curve (Example Problem Data)

Intersection station 10 + 50 Elevation 160.30 VC no. 4
Algebraic difference −8 − (+4) = 12 Curve length 600 ft
BVC station −8 + 00 Elevation 150.30
EVC station 14 + 00 Elevation 132.30

Middle ordinate $(e)\ \dfrac{250 \times 350}{2(250 + 350)} \times 12/100 = 9.59$ ft

	Station	Distance from BVC or EVC	Tangent grade elevation	VC ordinate	VC elevation
BVC	8 + 00	0	150.30	0.00	150.30
	8 + 50	50	152.30	0.38	151.42
	9 + 00	100	154.30	1.53	152.77
	9 + 50	150	156.30	3.45	152.85
	10 + 00	200	158.30	6.14	152.16
V	10 + 50	250–350	160.30	9.59	150.71
	11 + 00	300	156.30	7.00	149.30
	11 + 50	250	152.30	4.89	147.41
	12 + 00	200	148.30	3.16	145.14
	12 + 50	150	144.30	1.73	142.57
	13 + 00	100	140.30	0.77	139.53
	13 + 50	50	136.30	0.19	136.11
EVC	14 + 00	0	132.30	0.00	132.30

$$e = \frac{l_1 - l_2}{2(l_1 + l_2)} \times A/100$$

$$= \frac{250 \times 350}{2(250 + 350)} \times 12/100$$

$$= \frac{87{,}500}{1200} \times 0.12$$

$$= 72.92 \times 0.12$$

$$= 9.59 \text{ ft}$$

Step 3: Determine the grade tangent elevations at the 50- and 100-ft stations.

Step 4: Calculate the offsets at the 50- and 100-ft stations:

$$0(8 + 50) = 9.59(50/250)^2 = 9.59(0.04) = 0.38 \text{ ft}$$

$$0(9 + 00) = 9.59(100/250)^2 = 9.59(0.16) = 1.53 \text{ ft}$$

$$0(9 + 50) = 9.59(150/250)^2 = 9.59(0.36) = 3.45 \text{ ft}$$

$$0(10 + 00) = 9.59(200/250)^2 = 9.59(0.64) = 6.14 \text{ ft}$$

$$0(11 + 00) = 9.59(300/350)^2 = 9.59(0.73) = 7.00 \text{ ft}$$

$$0(11 + 50) = 9.59(250/350)^2 = 9.59(0.51) = 4.89 \text{ ft}$$

$$0(12 + 00) = 9.59(200/350)^2 = 9.59(0.33) = 3.16 \text{ ft}$$

$$0(12 + 50) = 9.59(150/350)^2 = 9.59(0.18) = 1.73 \text{ ft}$$

TABLE 342-22
Vertical Curve Lengths *(L)* Necessary to Obtain a Required Sight/Stopping Distance

Design speed	Sight/ stopping distance	Algebraic difference, %														
		1	2	3	4	5	6	7	8	9	10	11	12	13	14	15
20	110	—	—	—	—	—	—	20	45	65	80	93	104	113	121	130
25	150	—	—	—	—	20	67	100	125	144	161	177	193	209	225	241
30	200	—	—	—	51	120	[illegible]	200	229	257	286	315	343	372	401	429
35	250	—	—	34	150	220	268	313	358	402	447	492	536	581	626	671
40	300	64	129	193	258	321	386	451	515	579	644	708	773	837	901	966
45	375	101	201	302	402	503	604	704	805	905	1006	1106	1207	1308	1408	1509
50	450	145	290	435	579	724	869	1014	1159	1304	1448	1593	1738	1883	2028	2173
50	550	216	432	649	866	1084	1298	1515	1731	1947	2164	2380	2597	2813	3029	3246

$$0(13 + 00) = 9.59(^{100}/_{350})^2$$
$$= 9.59(0.08)$$
$$= 0.77 \text{ ft}$$
$$0(13 + 50) = 9.59(^{50}/_{350})^2$$
$$= 9.59(0.02)$$
$$= 0.19 \text{ ft}$$

Data for the above unsymmetrical vertical curve can be recorded using the form shown in Table 342-21.

TABLE 342-23
Vertical Curve Lengths (*L*) Necessary to Obtain the Following Passing Sight Distances

Design speed	Passing sight distance	Algebraic difference, %									
		1	2	3	4	5	6	7	8	9	10
30	1100	—	550	1103	1471	1839	2207	2575	2942	3310	3678
40	1500	—	1355	2052	2736	3419	4103	4787	5471	6155	6839
50	1800	310	1970	2954	3939	4924	5909	6894	7878	8863	9848
60	2100	910	2681	4021	5361	6702	8043	9383	—	—	—
65	2300	1310	3216	4824	6432	8040	9647	—	—	—	—

Minimum Crest Vertical Curves:

On all crest vertical curves, the length of the curve should permit safe stopping distances (Figure 342-32).

Two basic formulas exist for determining the length of a vertical curve in terms of sight distance(s) and algebraic differences in grade:

When *S* is *less* than *L*:

$$L = \frac{AS^2}{100(\sqrt{2h_1} + \sqrt{2h_2})^2}$$

When *S* is *greater* than *L*:

$$L = 2S - \frac{200\,(\sqrt{2h_1} + \sqrt{2h_2})^2}{A}$$

where L = horizontal length of the vertical curve, ft
S = sight distance, ft
A = algebraic difference in grades, %
h_1 = height of eye above roadway surface, ft
h_2 = height of object above roadway surface, ft

Solutions to these equations based on criteria of eye height and fixed object height (see Figure 342-32) are given in Table 342-22, from which can be determined the minimum length of vertical curve necessary to match a required stopping sight distance for algebraic differences in grades up to 25 percent.

Passing Sight Distance on Vertical Curves:

Criteria used for determining passing sight distances on crest vertical curves are: a driver eye height of 45 in (1143 mm) and a height of 54 in (1372 mm) for an overcoming vehicle (Figure 342-33).

Equations that express the relationship between passing sight distance, algebraic difference in grades, and length of vertical curve are as follows:

When *S* is *less* than *L*:

$$L = \frac{ASp^2}{3290}$$

When *S* is *greater* than *L*:

$$L = 2Sp - \frac{3290}{A}$$

where Sp = passing sight distance, ft
A = algebraic difference in grades, %
L = minimum length of vertical curve, ft

Solutions to these equations based on the above criteria of eye height and vehicle height (Figure 342-33) are given in Table 342-23, from which can be found the minimum length of vertical curve necessary to match a required passing sight distance for algebraic differences in grades up to 10 percent.

Minimum Sag Vertical Curves:

Criteria that are critical for determining the minimum lengths of sag vertical curves include:

1. Headlight illumination
2. Rider comfort
3. Drainage control
4. General appearance

Headlight sight distance has been used as the major controlling factor. When a vehicle traverses a sag vertical curve at night, the portion of the highway illuminated, and therefore the sight distance, is dependent upon the position of the headlights and the direction of the light beam (Figure 342-34).

The following two formulas show the relationship between light beam distance, length of vertical curve, and algebraic difference:

When *S* is *less* than *L*:

$$L = \frac{AS^2}{400 + 3.55}$$

When *S* is *greater* than *L*:

$$L = 2S - \frac{400 + 3.55}{A}$$

where S = light beam distance, ft
A = algebraic difference in grades, %
L = length of sag vertical curve, ft

16	17	18	19	20	21	22	23	24	25
138	147	156	164	173	182	190	199	208	216
257	273	290	306	322	338	354	370	386	402
458	486	515	544	572	601	629	658	687	715
715	760	805	849	894	939	984	1028	1073	1118
1030	1094	1159	1223	1288	1352	1416	1481	1545	1609
1609	1710	1811	1911	2012	2112	2213	2314	2414	2515
2318	2462	2607	2752	2897	3042	3187	3332	3476	3621
3462	3678	3895	4111	4328	4544	4760	4977	5193	5409

TABLE 342-24
Minimum Sag Vertical Curve Lengths *(L)* Necessary to Obtain Light Beam Distance

Design speed	Sight/ stopping and light-beam distance	Algebraic difference, %															
		1	2	3	4	5	6	7	8	9	10	11	12	13	14	15	16
20	110	—	—	—	24	63	89	108	123	138	154	170	185	200	216	231	247
25	150	—	—	—	69	115	146	170	195	219	243	268	292	316	341	365	389
30	200	—	—	33	125	180	218	255	291	327	364	400	436	473	509	545	582
35	250	—	—	75	181	245	294	343	392	441	490	539	588	637	686	735	784
40	300	—	—	117	228	310	372	434	497	559	621	683	745	807	869	931	993
45	375	—	—	179	322	411	493	575	657	739	821	903	985	1068	1150	1232	1314
50	450	—	—	242	406	513	615	718	820	923	1025	1128	1230	1333	1435	1538	1641
55	550	—	—	325	519	651	781	911	1041	1171	1301	1431	1561	1691	1822	1952	2082
60	650	—	—	408	631	790	948	1106	1264	1421	1579	1737	1895	2053	2211	2369	2527

TABLE 342-25
Minimum Widths for Two-Lane Roads, ft

Design speed, mph	*ADT*, 50–250*	*ADT, 250–400*	*ADT, 400–750*	*DHV†, 200–400*	*DHV, over 400*
30	20	20	20	22	24
40	20	20	22	22	24
50	20	20	22	24	24
60	20	22	22	24	24
65	20	22	24	24	24
70	20	22	24	24	24

* ADT = average daily traffic.

† DHV = future design hourly volume.

TABLE 342-26
Recommended Pavement Widths (by Type of Use)

Use type	*Widths, ft*
Driveways (residentials)	7–10
Minor residential streets	
No parking	20–24
Parking on one side	26–28
One-way, parking on one side	18
Major residential streets	
No parking	24–16
Parking on one side	28–32
Streets with truck traffic	24–26
Recreational sites	
Heavy vegetation	18–22
Rough terrain	18–22
Scenic drives	20–24
Industrial areas	24 minimum (no parking)

TABLE 342-27
Recommended Cross-Slopes for Various Types of Pavements

Surface type	*Cross slope, in/ft*
High	1/8–1/4
Rigid (concrete)	
Asphaltic concrete	
Plant mix	
Intermediate	3/16–3/8
Plant mix	
Low	1/4–1/2
Road mix	
Macadam	
Surface treatment	
Untreated surface	

Solutions to these equations based on the above criteria are given in Table 342-24.

3.3 Cross-Sectional Elements

Pavement Widths:

The safety and comfort of the driver is influenced by the width and condition of the pavement surface. Because of upward trends in traffic volumes, vehicle speed, and width of trucks, two-lane roads have increased from early widths of 16 and 18 ft (4.9 and 5.5 m) to present widths of 22 to 26 ft (6.7 to 7.9 m). Lane widths of 10 to 13 ft (3 to 4 m) are now common. The determination of pavement width depends on many factors, including:

1. Density/intensity of land use

2. Parking (i.e., off-street versus on-street)

3. Whether alignment is smooth and continuous

4. Speed of traffic

5. Volume of traffic

6. Type of traffic (i.e., automobiles, trucks, buses, etc.)

7. Distance between edge of pavement and any obstructions along the roadside

Table 342-25 gives recommended minimum widths for two-lane roads based on traffic volumes and speed. Table 342-26 gives recommended ranges of pavement width based on use.

Pavement Crowns:

Pavements on tangents and on flat curves are crowned for positive drainage of water off the roadway surface (Figure 342-35). Table 342-27 gives recommended ranges of cross-slope for various types of pavement surfaces.

3.4 Intersection Design Elements

Types of Grade Intersections:

Figure 342-36 shows various types of grade intersections.

17	18	19	20
262	277	293	308
414	438	462	486
618	655	691	727
833	882	931	980
1055	1117	1179	1241
1396	1478	1560	1642
1743	1846	1948	2051
2212	2342	2472	2602
2685	2843	3000	3159

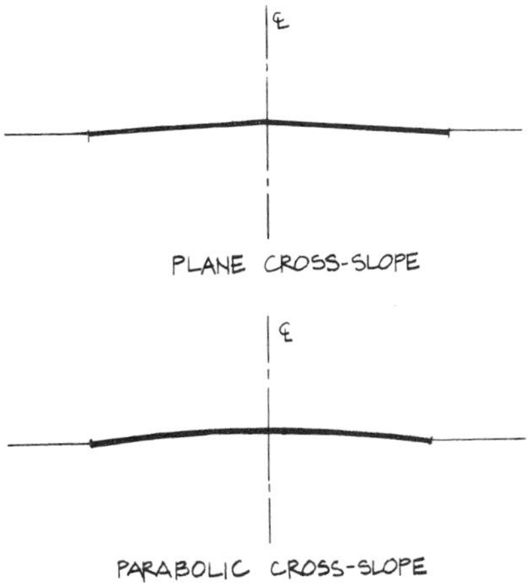

℄
PLANE CROSS-SLOPE
℄
PARABOLIC CROSS-SLOPE

Figure 342-35 Pavement crowns.

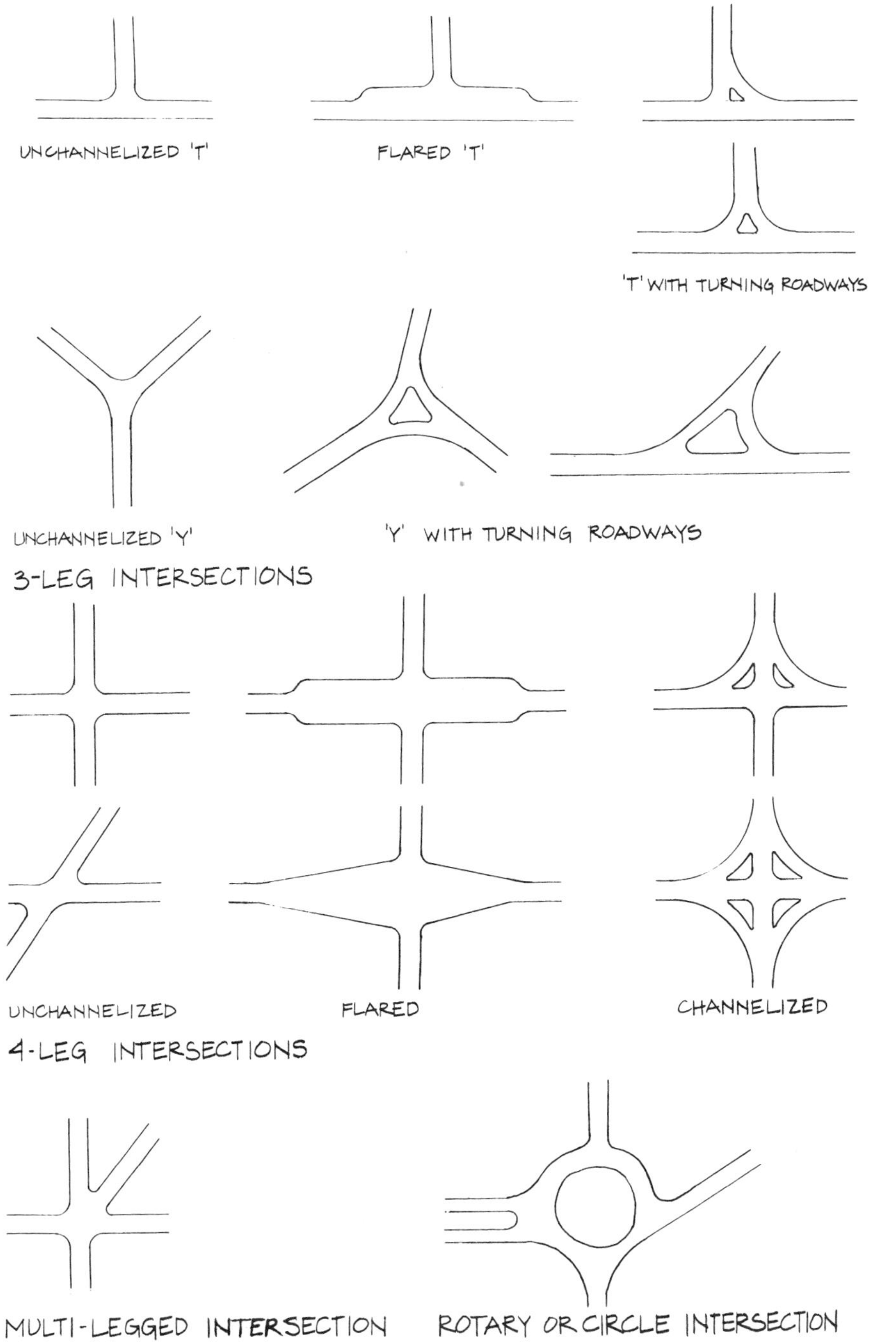

UNCHANNELIZED 'T'
FLARED 'T'
'T' WITH TURNING ROADWAYS
UNCHANNELIZED 'Y'
'Y' WITH TURNING ROADWAYS
3-LEG INTERSECTIONS
UNCHANNELIZED
FLARED
CHANNELIZED
4-LEG INTERSECTIONS
MULTI-LEGGED INTERSECTION
ROTARY OR CIRCLE INTERSECTION

Figure 342-36 Types of grade intersections.

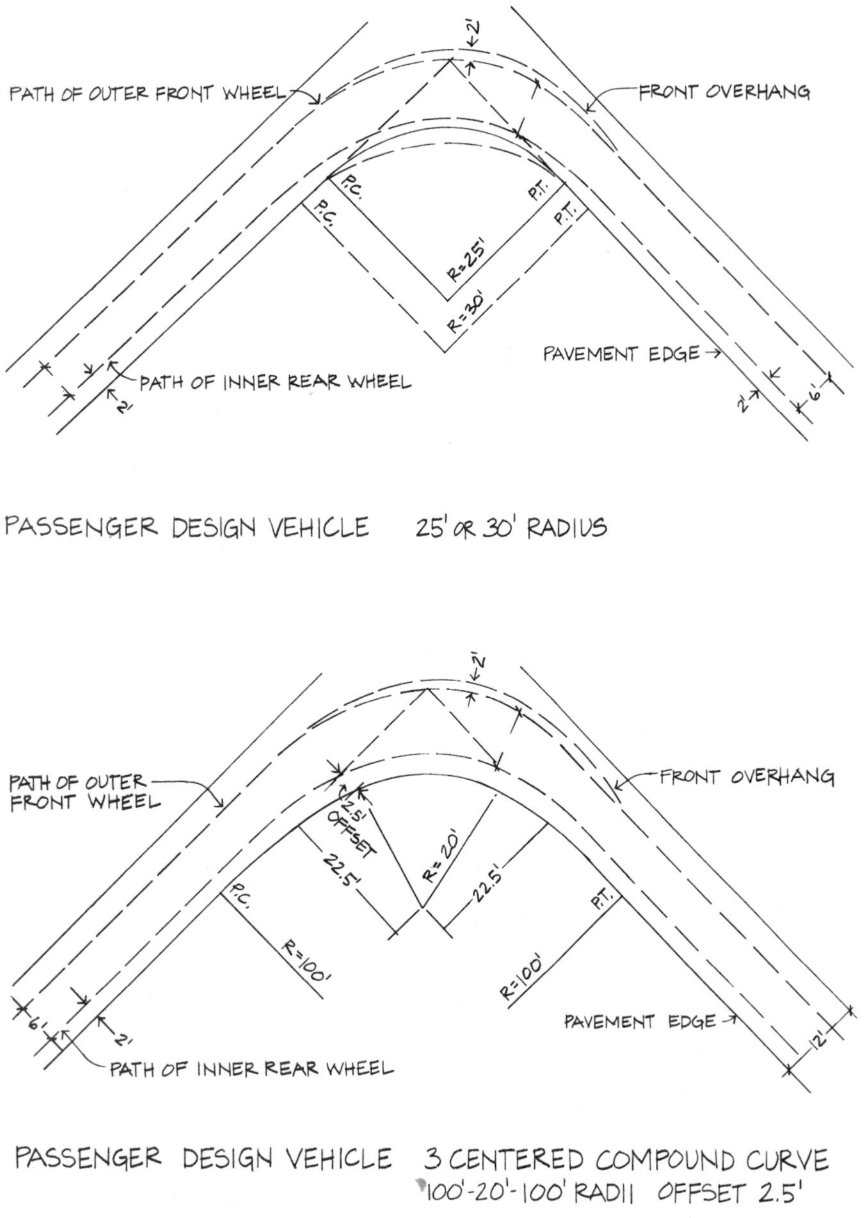
PATH OF OUTER FRONT WHEEL
FRONT OVERHANG
P.C.
P.T.
R=25'
R=30'
PAVEMENT EDGE
PATH OF INNER REAR WHEEL
2'
6'
PASSENGER DESIGN VEHICLE 25' OR 30' RADIUS
PATH OF OUTER FRONT WHEEL
FRONT OVERHANG
2.5' OFFSET
22.5'
R=20'
R=100'
PAVEMENT EDGE
12'
PATH OF INNER REAR WHEEL
PASSENGER DESIGN VEHICLE 3 CENTERED COMPOUND CURVE
100'-20'-100' RADII OFFSET 2.5'

Figure 342-37 Minimum curves: passenger vehicles.

Intersection Curves:

Minimum Radii for Sharpest Turns: When turning space is minimal, as at unchanneled intersections, the minimum turning radius of the design vehicle is the controlling factor in the design of the curve. Minimum curves for various design vehicles are illustrated in Figures 342-37 through 342-40. The paths indicated are the minimum attainable at low speed [i.e., less than 10 mph (16 km/h)], which are a little above the minimum paths of nearly all vehicles in each class and consequently account for minor variations in driver behavior.

Minimum Radius for Turning Speed: Figure 342-41 and Table 342-28 give design criteria for curves at various driving speeds.

Alignment and Profile at Intersections:

For safety reasons, horizontal alignment at intersections should be handled as shown in Figure 342-42. Figure 342-43 illustrates preferable grade criteria for intersections.

Sight Distances at Intersections:

It is important that sight lines are unobstructed along both roads of an intersection and across their corners for distances sufficient to allow drivers approaching the intersection simultaneously to see each other in time to prevent collision (Figure 342-44).

Uncontrolled Intersections: At uncontrolled intersections, drivers approaching an intersection must be able to recognize a hazard in sufficient time to slow down, to whatever extent is necessary, before reaching the intersection. For two roads of known design speeds, the minimum sight triangle (Figure 342-44) can be determined from Table 342-29.

Controlled Intersections on Minor Roads: At controlled intersections on minor roads, the driver of a stopped vehicle must be able to see enough of the crossroad to cross without danger of collision (Figure 342-45).

Table 342-30 provides the necessary distances needed along the highway from the intersection for various design vehicles.

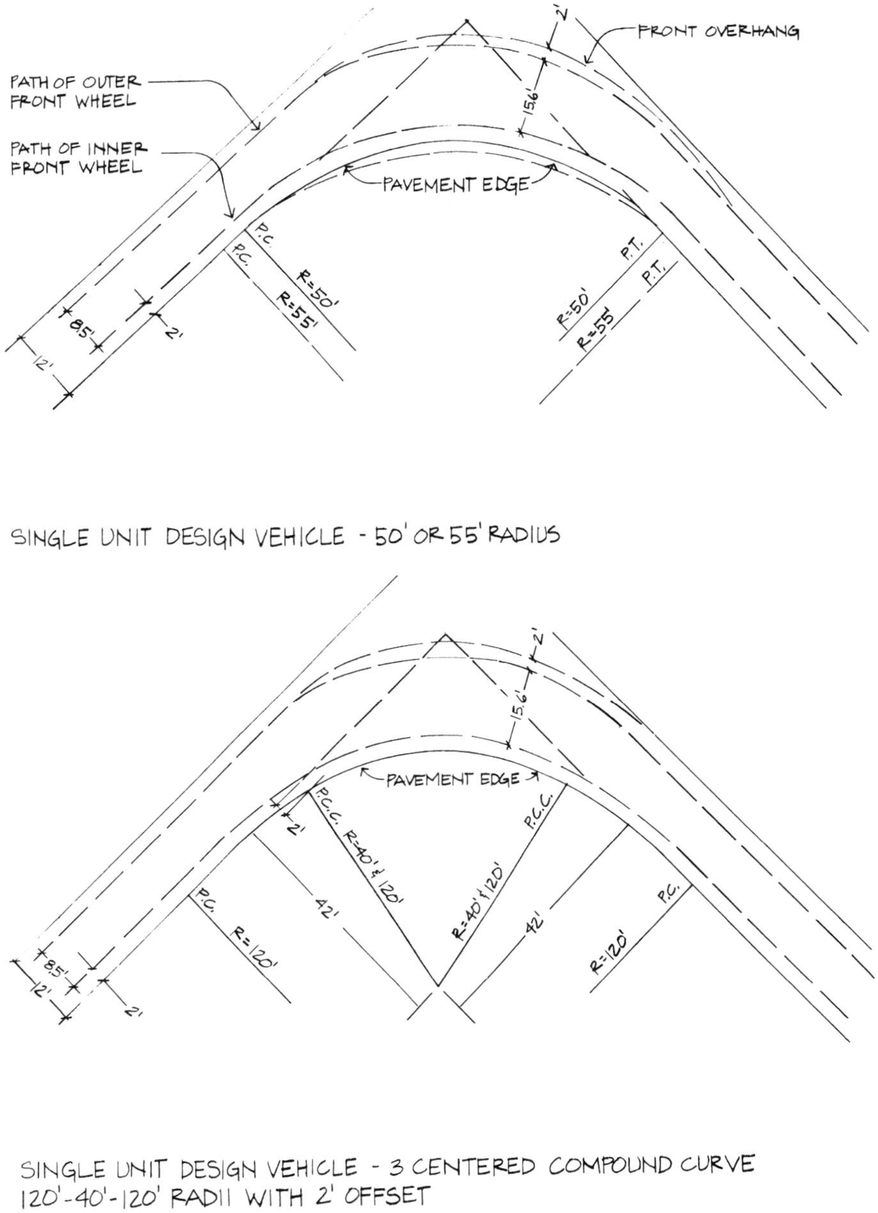
PATH OF OUTER FRONT WHEEL
PATH OF INNER FRONT WHEEL
FRONT OVERHANG
PAVEMENT EDGE
2'
15.6'
P.C.
R=50'
R=55'
P.T.
8.5'
12'
SINGLE UNIT DESIGN VEHICLE - 50' OR 55' RADIUS
PAVEMENT EDGE
P.C.C.
R=40' & 120'
42'
R=120'
SINGLE UNIT DESIGN VEHICLE - 3 CENTERED COMPOUND CURVE
120'-40'-120' RADII WITH 2' OFFSET

Figure 342-38 Minimum curves: single-unit vehicles.

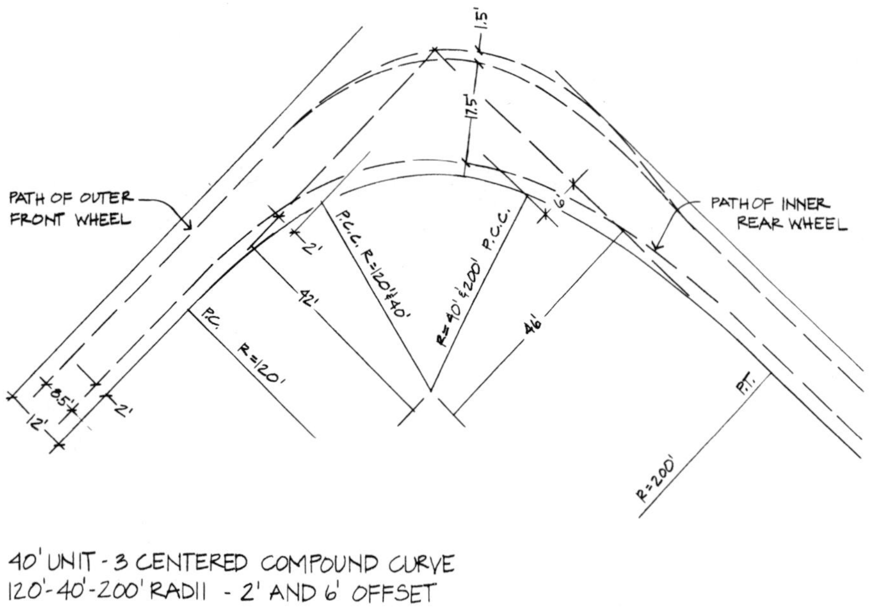
1.5'
17.5'
PATH OF OUTER FRONT WHEEL
PATH OF INNER REAR WHEEL
6'
2'
P.C.C. R=120'+40'
R=40'+200' P.C.C.
42'
46'
P.C.
R=120'
8.5'
12'
2'
P.T.
R=200'
40' UNIT - 3 CENTERED COMPOUND CURVE
120'-40'-200' RADII - 2' AND 6' OFFSET

Figure 342-39 Minimum curve: 40-ft design vehicle.

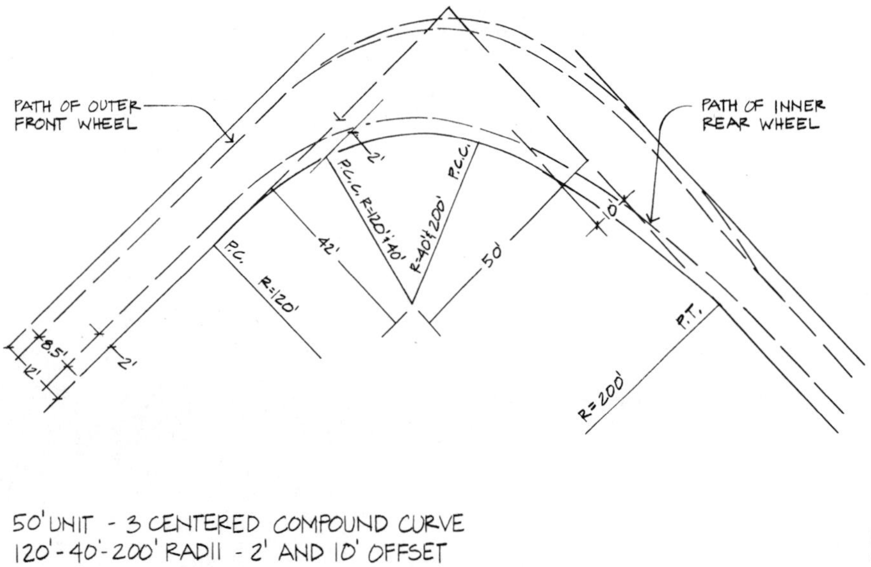
PATH OF OUTER FRONT WHEEL
PATH OF INNER REAR WHEEL
2'
P.C.C. R=120'+40'
R=40'+200' P.C.C.
10'
42'
50'
P.C.
R=120'
8.5'
12'
2'
P.T.
R=200'
50' UNIT - 3 CENTERED COMPOUND CURVE
120'-40'-200' RADII - 2' AND 10' OFFSET

Figure 342-40 Minimum curve: 50-ft design vehicle.

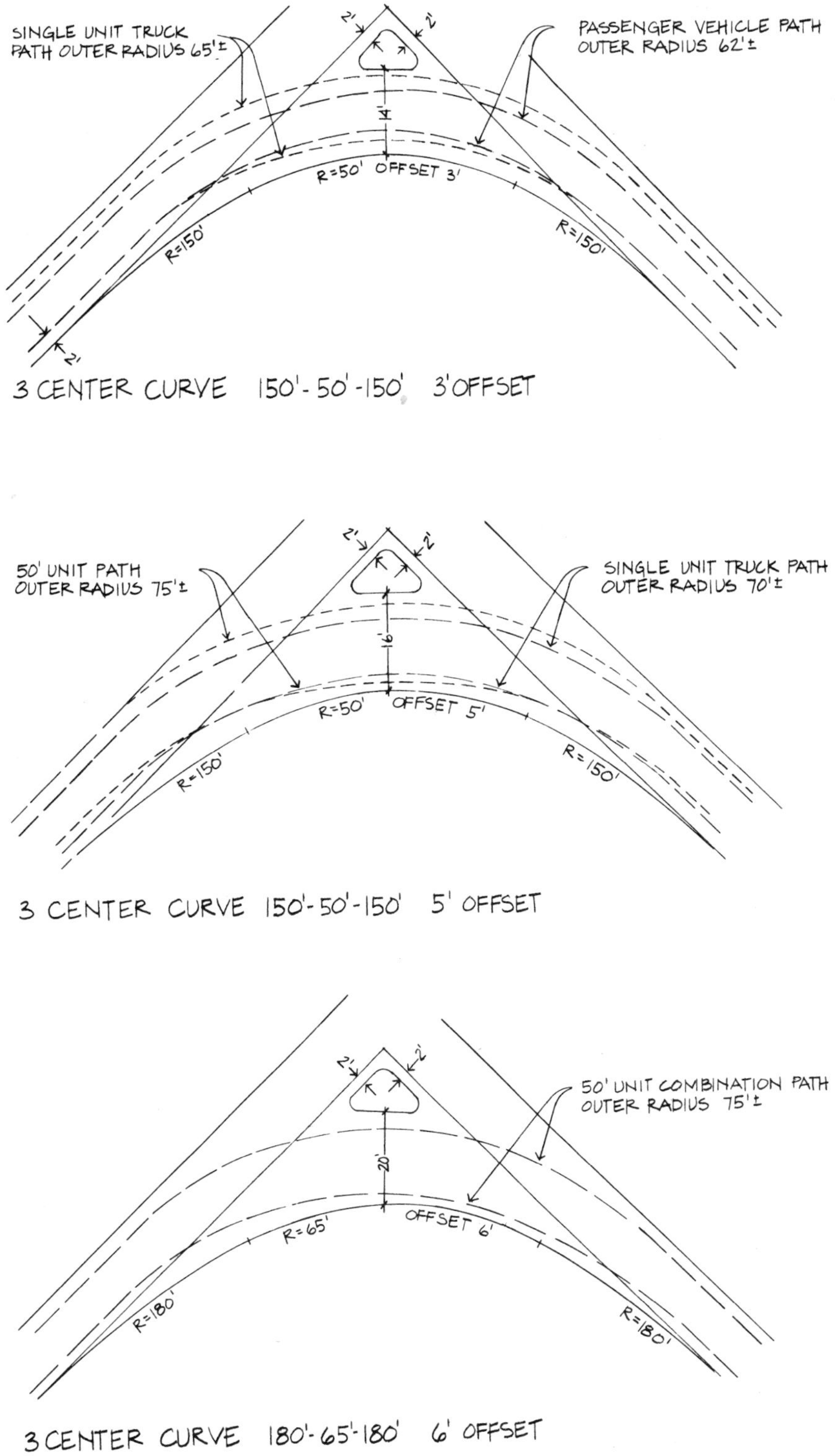
SINGLE UNIT TRUCK PATH OUTER RADIUS 65'±
PASSENGER VEHICLE PATH OUTER RADIUS 62'±
14'
R=50' OFFSET 3'
R=150'
R=150'
3 CENTER CURVE 150'-50'-150' 3'OFFSET
50' UNIT PATH OUTER RADIUS 75'±
SINGLE UNIT TRUCK PATH OUTER RADIUS 70'±
16'
R=50' OFFSET 5'
R=150'
R=150'
3 CENTER CURVE 150'-50'-150' 5' OFFSET
50' UNIT COMBINATION PATH OUTER RADIUS 75'±
20'
R=65' OFFSET 6'
R=180'
R=180'
3 CENTER CURVE 180'-65'-180' 6' OFFSET

Figure 342-41 Designs for turning roadways.

TABLE 342-28
Minimum Radii for Intersection Curves

Design (turning) speed *V*, mph*	15	20	25	30	35	40
Side friction factor, *F*	0.32	0.27	0.23	0.20	0.18	0.16
Assumed minimum superelevation, *E*	0.00	0.02	0.04	0.06	0.08	0.09
Total, *E* + *F*	0.32	0.29	0.27	0.26	0.26	0.25
Calculated minimum radius *R*, ft	47	92	154	231	314	426
Suggested curvature for design:						
Radius—maximum, ft	50	90	150	230	310	430
Degree of curve—maximum	—	64	38	25	18	13
Average running speed, mph	14	18	22	26	30	34

* For design speeds of more than 40 mph, use values for open highway conditions.

Source: Courtesy of AASHTO.

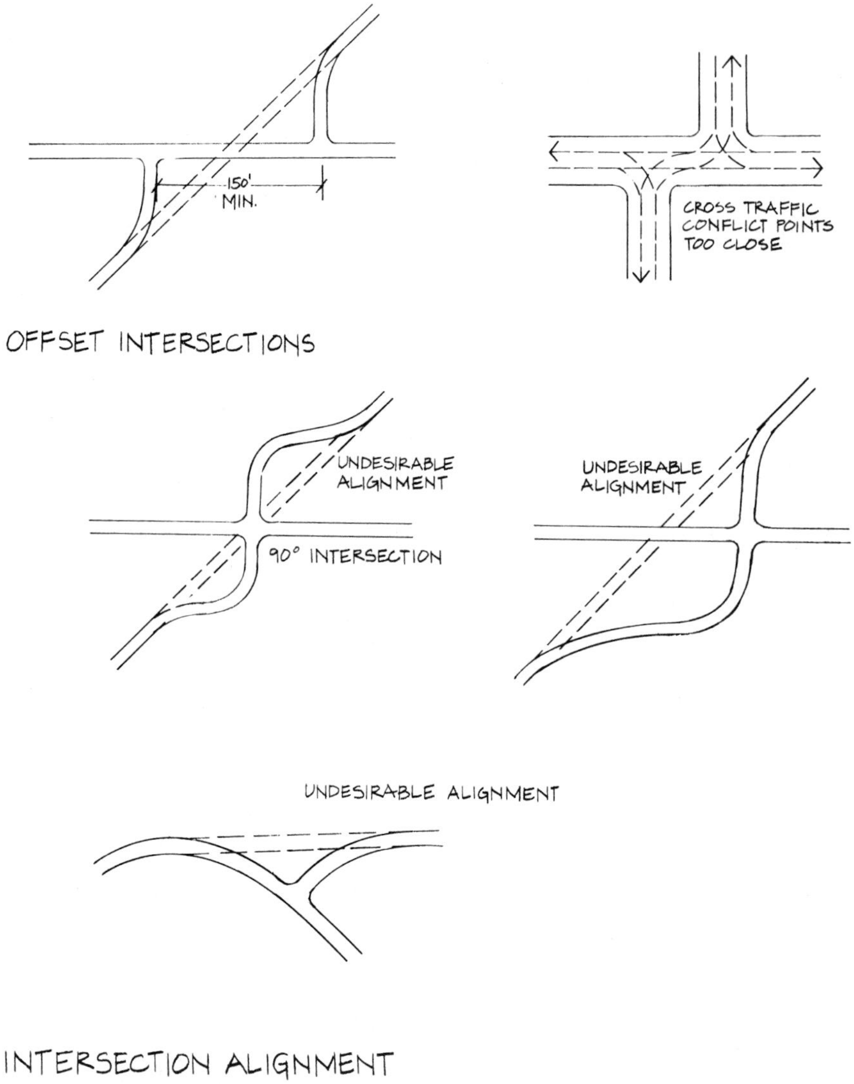
150'
MIN.
CROSS TRAFFIC
CONFLICT POINTS
TOO CLOSE
OFFSET INTERSECTIONS
UNDESIRABLE
ALIGNMENT
90° INTERSECTION
UNDESIRABLE
ALIGNMENT
UNDESIRABLE ALIGNMENT
INTERSECTION ALIGNMENT

Figure 342-42 Horizontal alignment at intersections.

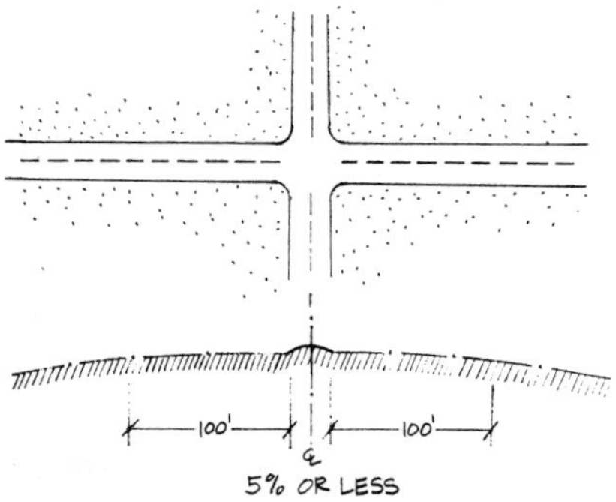
100'
100'
5% OR LESS

Figure 342-43 Intersection grades.

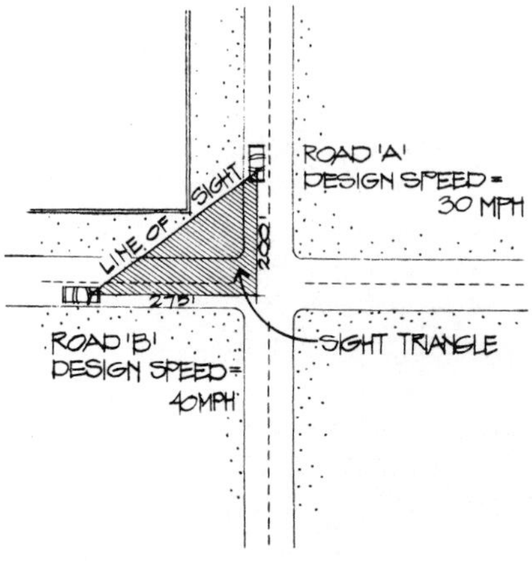
ROAD 'A'
DESIGN SPEED =
30 MPH
LINE OF SIGHT
ROAD 'B'
DESIGN SPEED =
40MPH
SIGHT TRIANGLE

Figure 342-44 Sight triangle at intersections.

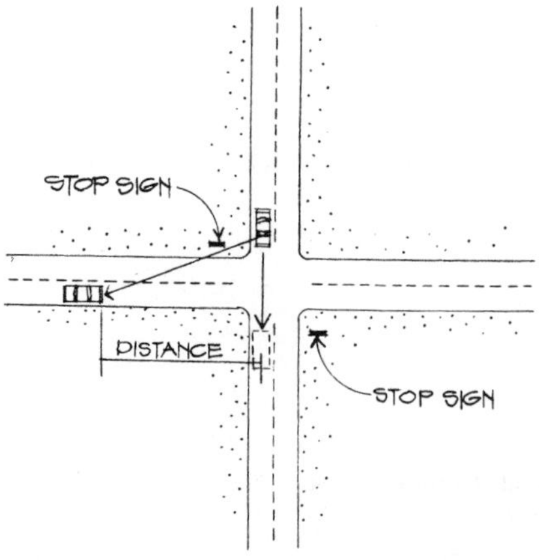
STOP SIGN
DISTANCE
STOP SIGN

Figure 342-45 Sight distance at controlled intersection.

TABLE 342-29
Intersection Safe Stopping Distances

Design speed, mph	*Safe stopping distance, ft*
30	200
40	275
50	350
60	475
70	600

TABLE 342-30
Minimum Sight Distances (in feet) Necessary along Highway from Intersection

	Major highway design speed				
Type of vehicle stopped	*30 mph*	*40 mph*	*50 mph*	*60 mph*	*70 mph*
Passenger vehicle					
Two-lane highway*	300	400	500	600	700
Four-lane highway	350	475	600	700	825
Single-unit vehicle					
Two-lane highway	400	550	675	800	950
Four-lane highway	475	625	775	925	1075
50-ft design vehicle					
Two-lane highway	525	700	875	1050	1225
Four-lane highway	600	775	975	1175	1375

* 12-ft lanes with level conditions.

4.0 PARKING

This Section 342: Vehicular Circulation, does not include detailed information on parking dimensions, lot sizes, handicapped parking standards, or truck loading and docking standards. Such information can be found in Sections 210: Spatial Standards, and 240: Outdoor Accessibility.

This section provides general information on site planning and the layout of parking areas.

4.1 Site Planning Considerations

Thorough consideration of all factors pertaining to parking should be given to the overall plan of any project at its inception in order to integrate the design of buildings and structures with parking areas and related improvements. Residential, commercial, industrial, institutional, recreational, and other types of projects all have particular requirements relative to parking and should be planned accordingly. When detailed parking layouts are developed simultaneously with building plans, oversights leading to inefficient control of traffic and similar errors of design can be avoided; otherwise, makeshift changes in construction or acceptance of unsatisfactory or compromise controls at a later date can lead to an unfortunate result.

The parking habits of users have a tremendous influence on standards. Urban drivers will usually accept narrower stalls than will drivers in rural or suburban areas. Activities like picnicking call for wider stalls to make the handling of bulky items in and out of cars easier. In shopping centers where carts are used, wider stalls are more desirable, as compared to all-day parking areas for office workers.

If experienced attendants are to park cars, aisles at least 4 ft narrower can be used for 90-degree parking. Designers should also be mindful of the fact that drivers typically will not park precisely in the center of the stall, nor will they always drive in all the way. If stalls are too narrow, drivers will ignore demarcation lines and lap over into adjoining stalls.

In any parking area, handicapped parking spaces or a passenger loading zone should be located as close as possible to the shortest accessible path of travel to buildings.

4.2 General Layout of Parking Areas

A major consideration in the design of any parking area is simplicity. Parking areas should not be complex or designed in such a manner as to test a driver's ability.

The three basic dimensions of any parking layout are: (1) the length and width of car stalls, (2) the width of aisles, and (3) the angle between car stall and aisle. Aisle width is related to stall width and angle of stalls. With a wider stall, it is possible to use a slightly narrower aisle. With the trend to smaller cars, dimensions for parking have generally decreased. The 9-ft (1.8-m) stall is most common, but the 8½-ft (2.6-m) stall is being used more frequently.

5.0 PAVEMENTS AND CURBS

This Section 342: Vehicular Circulation, does not include detailed information on the construction of various pavements and curbs. Specific information on the design and construction of these elements is included in Sections 820: Asphalt, and 830: Concrete. Division 900: Details and Devices, includes representative detail drawings of various pavements and curbs.

This section includes general information on pavements and curbs, including information on the advantages and disadvantages of various types of pavements.

5.1 Pavements: General Considerations

Pavements for vehicular use are generally divided into two main categories, i.e., rigid pavements and flexible pavements. The two vary in terms of construction methods, durability, and cost.

Rigid Pavements:

Rigid (i.e., concrete) pavements have a high compressive strength, which tends to distribute the load over a relatively wide area of soil.

The advantages of properly constructed rigid pavements include:

1. Low maintenance costs
2. Long life, with extreme durability
3. High value as a base for future resurfacing with asphalt
4. Load distribution over a wide area, therefore decreasing base and subgrade requirements
5. Ability to be placed directly on poor soils
6. No damage from oils and grease
7. Strong edges

The disadvantages of rigid pavements include:

1. High initial costs
2. Joints required for contraction and expansion
3. A generally rough riding quality
4. Expensive to repair

TABLE 342-31
Recommended Shoulder Widths

Type of highway	*Width of shoulder, ft*
Heavily traveled	10 ft minimum, 12 ft desirable
High-speed	
Low-type	4 ft minimum, 6–8 ft desirable
In difficult terrain	

TABLE 342-32
Recommended Shoulder Cross-Slopes

Type of surface	*Shoulder cross-slope* in/ft	ft/ft
No pavement edge curbs		
Bituminous	⅜–½	0.03–0.04
Gravel or crushed stone	½–¾	0.04–0.06
Turf	1	0.08
With shoulder curbs at pavement edge		
Bituminous	¼	0.02
Gravel or crushed stone	¼–½	0.02–0.04
Turf	⅜–½	0.03–0.04

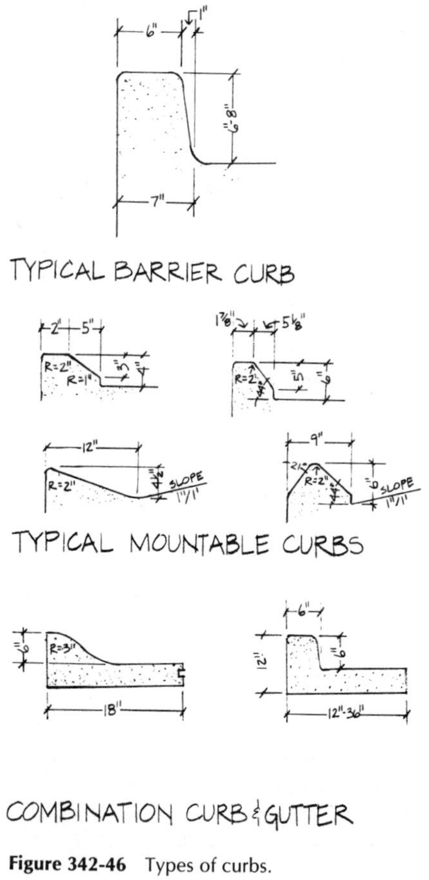
TYPICAL BARRIER CURB
TYPICAL MOUNTABLE CURBS
COMBINATION CURB & GUTTER

Figure 342-46 Types of curbs.

Rigid Pavement Design Considerations: To arrive at the proper design of rigid concrete pavements, the following factors must be considered:

1. Wheel loads
2. Subgrade (modulus of subgrade reaction)
3. Protected or unprotected corners
4. Uniform or thickened edge
5. Quality of concrete (flexural strength)

Pavement Subgrade: The subgrade soils must be of uniform material and density to provide satisfactory pavement performance. The supporting power of the subgrade is expressed as values of *K*, the modulus of subgrade reaction.

Protected or Unprotected Corners: Since joints are required for concrete paving because of expansion and contraction, the strength of the pavement will be lost between separate slabs. Protected corners are those at which provision is made for transferring at least 20 percent of the load across the intervening joints by means of aggregate interlock, dowels, or keys. Unprotected corners are those at which there is not adequate provision for load transference.

Pavement Joints: Joints are always necessary in rigid pavements (1) to permit expansion and contraction of the concrete due to temperature and moisture changes, (2) to relieve warping and curling stresses which result from temperature and moisture gradients within the slab, and (3) as a construction expedient to separate areas of concrete placed at different times.

The three basic types of joints used in rigid pavements are (1) *contraction* joints, which are used to provide controlled contraction cracking; (2) *construction* joints, which are provided to separate areas of concrete placed at different times; and (3) *expansion* joints, which are provided for the relief of forces resulting from thermal expansion of the pavement. Expansion joints also permit unrestrained differential horizontal movement of adjoining pavements and/or structures.

Flexible Pavements:

Flexible pavements consist of a series of layers, with the highest-quality materials at or near the surface. The strength of a flexible pavement is a result of building up thick layers and thereby distributing the load over the subgrade, rather than the surface material assuming the structural strengths as with rigid pavements.

The advantages of flexible pavements include:

1. Adaptability to stage construction
2. Availability of low-cost types which can be easily built
3. Ability to be easily opened and patched
4. A generally low initial cost
5. Easy repair of frost heave and settlement
6. Resistance to the formation of ice glaze

The disadvantages include:

1. Higher maintenance costs
2. Shorter life span under heavy use
3. Damage by oils and certain chemicals
4. Weak edges that may require curbs or edge devices

Principles of Flexible Pavement Design: The design of a flexible pavement employs the principle that a load of any magnitude may be dissipated by carrying it deep into the gound through successive layers of granular material. This is because the intensity of a load diminishes in geometrical proportion as it is transmitted downward from the surface, by virtue of spreading over an increasingly larger area. Because of this, materials with a progressively lower bearing value may be employed as the depth increases.

There are various methods employed to determine the thickness required for flexible pavements. Refer to Section 820· Asphalt, for a description of the thickness design procedure.

5.2 Shoulders: General Considerations

A *shoulder* is the portion of a roadway contiguous with the pavement for (1) accommodation of stopped vehicles in emergencies and (2) lateral support of base and surface courses.

Well-designed and properly maintained shoulders on roads, where appreciable volumes of traffic exist, may serve one or more of the following purposes:

1. Space is provided for stopping free of the traffic lane.
2. Space is provided for the occasional motorist who desires to stop to consult road maps, to rest, etc.
3. Space is provided to escape potential accidents or to reduce their severity.
4. Horizontal sight distance may be improved in cut sections and may thus reduce hazards.
5. The capacity of the highway may be improved, encouraging uniform speeds.
6. Space is provided for maintenance operations.
7. Stormwater can be discharged farther away from the pavement, and seepage adjacent to the pavement is minimized.

8. Structural support is given to the pavement, which is especially important for flexible pavements.

Shoulder Widths:

Shoulders should be designed wide enough to allow a stopped or disabled vehicle to pull entirely off the road (Table 342-31). Their surface treatment should sustain the weight of vehicles in all seasons. Most frequently, this can be accomplished by the use of well-drained soil mixed with aggregate that has been compacted and, where appropriate, seeded with grass or other types of low-growing ground cover.

Shoulder Cross Slopes:

Table 342-32 gives recommended cross-slopes for roadway shoulders.

5.3 Curbs: General Considerations

The type and location of curbing will affect driver behavior and, in turn, the safety and utility of a roadway. Curbs are used:

1. To control drainage

2. To act as a deterrent to vehicles leaving the pavement at hazardous points

3. To present a more finished appearance

4. To stabilize the road edge in flexible pavements.

Types of Curbs:

Two general classes of curbs are *barrier* and *mountable,* and each class includes numerous types (Figure 342-46). Each may be designed as a separate unit or integrated with the pavement. Barrier and mountable curbs may be designed with a gutter to form a combination curb-and-gutter section (Figure 342-46).

Barrier Curbs: Barrier curbs are relatively high and steep-faced, designed to restrict or at least to discourage vehicles from leaving the pavement. They are usually 6 in (150 mm) or more in height, with a sloping face not exceeding 1 in per 3 in (25 mm per 75 mm) of height.

Curbs used for pedestrian islands should be made with heights between 5 and 7 in (125 and 180 mm).

Mountable Curbs: Mountable curbs refer to curbs that can be mounted by automobile tires.

Curb Materials:

Concrete: Concrete is probably the most common material used for both barrier and mountable curbs. Concrete curbs are durable and relatively easy to construct.

Asphalt: Asphalt is frequently used for curbing, especially in parking areas where they can be curved for islands. They are economical, easy to construct, and available in a variety of cross sections.

Granite: Granite curbs are not as frequently used as asphalt or concrete in most parts of the world, but in areas where granite is quarried, it is commonly used and is often no more expensive than concrete. Granite curbs are far more durable than concrete.

REFERENCES

American Association of State Highway and Transportation Officials (AASHTO). *A Policy on Design of Urban Highways and Arterial Streets,* Washington, DC, 1973.

———. *A Policy on Design Standards for Stopping Sight Distance,* Washington, DC, 1971.

———. *A Policy on Geometric Design of Rural Highways,* Washington, DC, 1966.

Baker, Robert F. (ed.). *Handbook of Highway Engineering,* Van Nostrand Reinhold, New York, 1975.

Institute of Traffic Engineers. *Transportation and Traffic Engineering Handbook,* John E. Baerwald (ed.), Prentice-Hall, Englewood Cliffs, NJ, 1976.

Lynch, Kevin, and Gary Hack. *Site Planning,* 3d ed., MIT Press, Cambridge, MA, 1984.

Oglesby, Clarkson H., and R. Gary Hicks. *Highway Engineering,* 4th ed., Wiley, New York, 1982.

Pignatoro, Louis J. *Traffic Engineering: Theory and Practice,* Prentice-Hall, Englewood Cliffs, NJ, 1973.

Untermann, Richard K. *Principles and Practices of Grading, Drainage and Road Alignment: An Ecologic Approach,* Prentice-Hall, Reston, VA, 1978. ■

section 410: Retaining Walls

CREDITS

Contributor:

Domenico Annese, RLA, and Peter F. Martecchini, PE
Clarke & Rapuano, Inc.
New York, New York

Design Calculations: James M. Sousa

Drawings: Steven J. Malesardi

Reviewers:

Bradford G. Sears, RLA
Fayetteville, New York

Stephen Hamway
Sasaki Associates, Inc.
Dallas, Texas

CONTENTS

1.0 INTRODUCTION

Retaining walls and devices are commonly used in the landscape to create relatively level areas at different elevations. They are used where changes in elevation cannot be accomplished by grading because of limited horizontal distances, or where changes of grade must be accomplished with the least disturbance to topography and natural features.

This section provides typical designs and standards for retaining walls that can either be used as shown or can be modified by a designer who has technical knowledge of soil and structural mechanics. In this section, the designs and standards for retaining walls are limited to a maximum height of 10 ft (3 m), including depth to foundation. For retaining structures above 10 ft (3 m) in height, the number of variables affecting their design (soils, pressures, foundation, and construction materials) are assumed to be too complex to be solved with the formulas used in this section. When faced with greater size or complexity, one should secure the advice of a structural engineer.

2.0 SELECTION CRITERIA

2.1 Basic Categories of Retaining Structures

Retaining structures basically fall into two general categories: flexible construction and rigid construction.

Flexible Construction:

Flexible construction includes dry stone walls, bin walls, crib walls, gabion walls, and other types of walls that are not rigid structures. The base, or footing, for a flexible wall need not go below the frost line if the depth (*D*) has a suitable bearing, i.e., undisturbed ground or a compacted subbase. Typically, a setting bed of sand or compacted granular material is used to improve drainage and provide a level surface. The advantage of flexible construction is that it will tolerate a certain amount of differential settlement without being significantly affected.

Rigid Construction:

Rigid construction is used where any movement of the structure cannot be tolerated or when aesthetic considerations require it, such as in association with buildings or in formal landscape designs. Typically, rigid construction implies the use of concrete and masonry in a gravity wall or reinforced cantilevered wall type of construction.

2.2 Design Criteria

As mentioned, the designs and standards for retaining walls given in this section refer only to walls of a limited height. These criteria and others for this section are listed below:

Heights: All retaining walls and devices are for a maximum height (*H*) of 10 ft (3 m).

Loading: All walls will permit only a 2-ft (0.06-m) surcharge without danger of overturning except for timber crib walls which are at their limits.

Bearing: The maximum soil bearing pressure is assumed to be 1.5 tons/ft^2 (16,750 kg/m^2).

Depth: The foundation depth (*D*) should extend to 2 ft (0.6 m), to the frost line, or to ½*H*, whichever is the greatest.

Strength: The compressive strength of all concrete is assumed to be 2500 pounds per square inch (psi), and the tensile strength of the steel reinforcement is 24,000 pounds.

Joints: Expansion joints, when needed, should be put every 30 ft (10 m) or less.

NOTE: When structures have live loads, sloping backfills higher than 2 ft (0.6 m), or poor foundations, the reader is urged to seek the assistance of a structural engineer experienced with the design of retaining walls and/or to refer to the technical reference books listed at the end of this section.

3.0 ELEMENTS OF RETAINING STRUCTURES

Major elements or components that have to be considered in the design and engineering of most retaining structures are described below.

3.1 Foundations

The foundation for any retaining structure is of critical importance, playing a major role in the stability of the structure. The following considerations are important.

Properties of Soils:

Table 410-1 shows the Unified System of Soil Classification and the relevant properties of each soil type. More detailed information can normally be obtained in the United States from federal, state, or local government soil and geology maps. Specific data for any site should be obtained through field testing (see below).

Foundation Depths:

Figure 410-1 shows the average depth of frost penetration for the United States. Foundations for rigid retaining structures should be taken to the frost line. Foundations for flexible retaining structures need not be to frost line if they are built on a well-drained subbase with suitable bearing capacities. All foundations should be above the water table, but if this is impractical, then a structural engineer should be consulted to help determine what type of foundation is most appropriate. Where applicable, follow local building codes for

TABLE 410-1
Soil Types and Their Properties (Unified Soil Classification System)

Division	Symbols: Letter	Symbols: Color	Soil description	Value as a foundation material*	Frost action	Drainage
Gravel and gravelly soils	GW	Red	Well-graded gravel, or gravel-sand mixture, little or no fines	Excellent	None	Excellent
	GP	Red	Poorly graded gravel, or gravel-sand mixtures, little or no fines	Good	None	Excellent
	GM	Yellow	Silty gravels, gravel-sand-silt mixtures	Good	Slight	Poor
	GC	Yellow	Clayey-gravels, gravel-clay-sand mixtures	Good	Slight	Poor
Sand and sandy soils	SW	Red	Well-graded sands, or gravelly sands, little or no fines	Good	None	Excellent
	SP	Red	Poorly graded sands, or gravelly sands, little or no fines	Fair	None	Excellent
	SM	Yellow	Silty sands, sand-silt mixtures	Fair	Slight	Fair
	SC	Yellow	Clayey sands, sand-clay mixtures	Fair	Medium	Poor
Silts and clays LL <50†	ML	Green	Inorganic silts, rock flour, silty or clayey fine sands, or clayey silts with slight plasticity	Fair	Very high	Poor
	CL	Green	Inorganic clays of low to medium plasticity, gravelly clays, silty clays, lean clays	Fair	Medium	Impervious
	OL	Green	Organic silt-clays of low plasticity	Poor	High	Impervious
Silts and clays LL >50	MH	Blue	Inorganic silts, micaceous or diatomaceous fine sandy or silty soils, elastic silts	Poor	Very high	Poor
	CH	Blue	Inorganic clays of high plasticity, fat clays	Very poor	Medium	Impervious
	OH	Blue	Organic clays of medium to high plasticity, organic silts	Very poor	Medium	Impervious
Highly organic soils	Pt	Orange	Peat and other highly organic soils	Not suitable	Slight	Poor

* Consult soil engineers and local building codes for allowable soil-bearing capacities.

† LL indicates liquid limit.

Source: Douglas S. Way, *Terrain Analysis: A Guide to Site Selection Using Photographic Interpretation*, Douglas S. Way, Columbus, Ohio, 1972.

the minimum requirements for foundations and footings.

Field Testing:

Three methods commonly used in field testing are:

1. Probing with a steel bar driven by a hammer to determine the character of the soil and the depth to bedrock or other underground structure.

2. Digging test pits either by hand or mechanically to reveal the nature of the soil and height of the water table.

3. Boring by hand or with a powered rig to obtain samples of the soil. Borings made by powered rigs will provide solid cores, which are essential for determining the requirements of deep foundations. Normally, these are driven to a point where they will go no farther (i.e., to a *point of refusal*), meaning that they have hit bedrock or a hard-packed layer of earth.

Soil tests for retaining structures should be made to a depth of at least 4 ft (1.2 m) below the proposed finish grade at the bottom of the structure. The core boring method of testing is used when the depths are over 15 ft (4.6 m). When needed, laboratory analysis should be made of the samples to determine the types and characteristics of each sample.

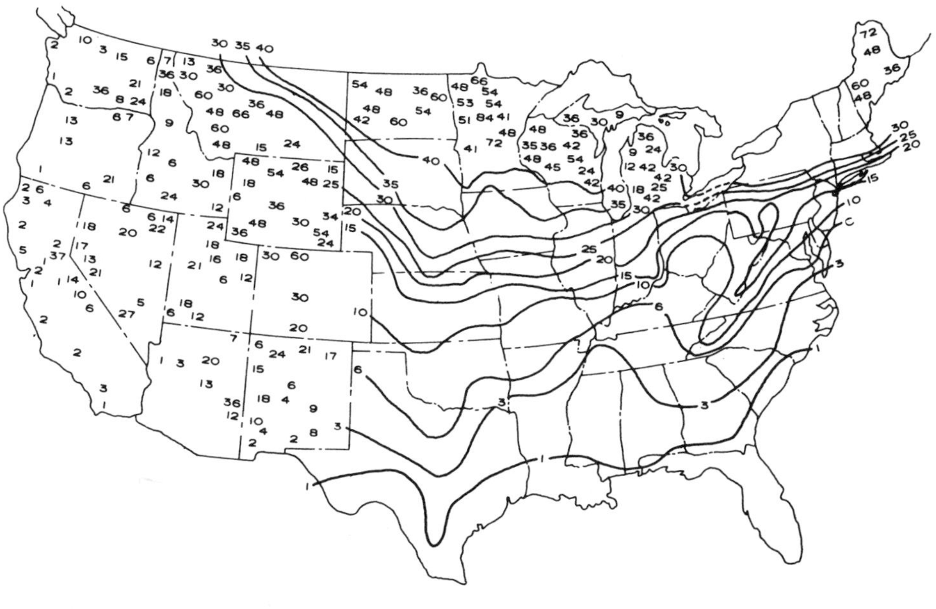

Figure 410-1 Average depth of frost penetration (inches).

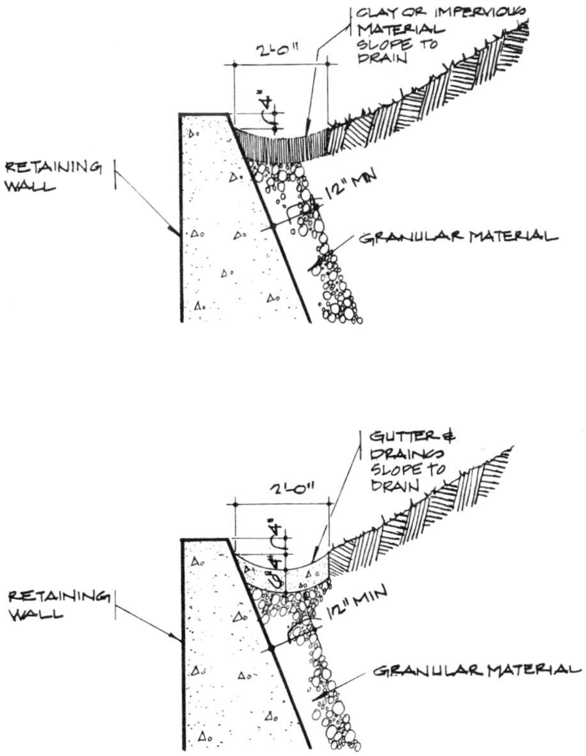
CLAY OR IMPERVIOUS MATERIAL SLOPE TO DRAIN
2'-0"
4"
RETAINING WALL
12" MIN
GRANULAR MATERIAL
GUTTER & DRAINS SLOPE TO DRAIN
2'-0"
4"
RETAINING WALL
12" MIN
GRANULAR MATERIAL

Figure 410-2 Drainage detail at toe of slope.

3.2 Subbase

Ideally, the foundation should rest on a subbase of undisturbed ground capable of supporting the estimated pressures of the proposed retaining structure. If the subbase has to be built up to a certain level, a compacted granular base should be provided. Granular subbase for *drainage* is not essential in rigid construction if back drainage is provided, but it is essential for flexible construction to minimize freeze/thaw action.

3.3 Drainage Devices

The leaning, bulging, or misalignment of retaining structures is often caused by the buildup of water pressure behind the structure and/or by freeze/thaw action in cold climates. Water can cause problems (1) when surface runoff gets behind the retaining structure via the top or toe of the wall and/or (2) when groundwater seeps through the soil behind or under the structure.

There are several ways to facilitate adequate drainage of retaining structures. Surface runoff should be directed away from both the top and base of the wall. It should also be blocked from penetrating down through the soil either by installing a clay seal under the sod or, where heavy concentrations of runoff exist, by constructing an impervious gutter or drainage channel behind the top of the wall (Figure 410-2). Water filtering down through the soil can be intercepted and taken away from the structure by the use of granular backfills connected to weep holes through the face of the structure or, if possible, by drainage tiles connected to outlets directed away from the structure. Clay tile, porous concrete, perforated plastic, or galvanized metal pipe should be used for this purpose. In the alignment of such devices, low points should not occur where water could be trapped behind the structure.

3.4 Batter in Wall Faces

Many types of walls have a vertical face but many others have either/or faces that are off vertical by various amounts. Such designed slopes are called *batters*. Both the back and/or the exposed face of a retaining wall can be battered. The face of the wall is sometimes battered when walls are very high to help overcome the optical illusion of the wall leaning forward. A batter also helps obscure deficiencies in the finishing of the wall's face. For flexible walls made of dry stone, for instance, a batter can obscure minor bulges and other movements. Also, a batter can increase the wall's stability and resistance to overturning.

A typical batter for walls of flexible construction is 6:1, but other ratios are often used. For rigid walls, particularly those with relatively smooth faces, a batter of no greater than 12:1 is recommended. When a wall appears to be an extension of a building, a batter is seldom used.

3.5 Face Treatment

Some materials used to construct retaining structures, such as poured concrete or masonry construction, permit the greatest variety of surface treatments (Figure 410-3). Crib, bin, and gabion types of retaining structures are more limited in their variety of surface treatments. (Refer to Division 800: Materials, in this handbook for various types of finishes.)

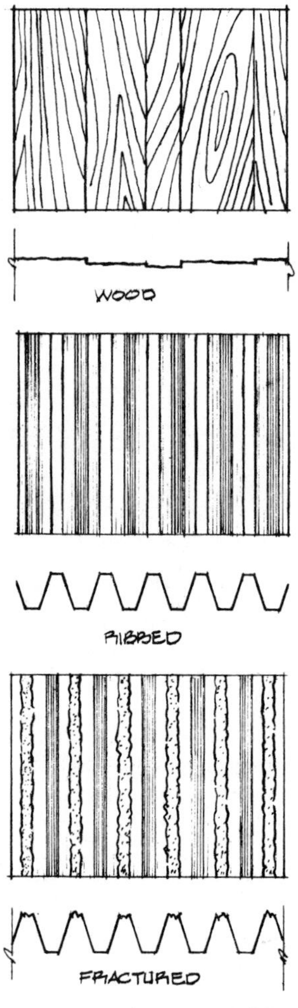
WOOD
RIBBED
FRACTURED

Figure 410-3 Typical concrete wall finishes.

3.6 Expansion and Construction Joints

The placement and spacing of expansion and construction joints should be considered as part of the overall design expression of the surface treatment of retaining walls. For rigid wall construction, these joints should normally be no farther than 30 ft (9 m) apart.

4.0 TYPES OF RETAINING WALLS

Three major types of structural solutions are gravity walls, cantilevered walls, and crib walls. Each one has several variations that may be considered, depending upon the criteria used for selection.

4.1 Gravity Walls

Gravity walls depend upon their mass (i.e., weight and volume) for stability (Figure 410-4). Regardless of their size, the ratio of the base width to height is approximately constant, varying from about 0.40 to 0.45 for a horizontally loaded wall. Gravity walls are constructed of concrete, stone masonry, or concrete faced with stone or brick. Gravity walls less than 5 ft (1.5 m) high are usually built vertically at the front and back or with a slight batter. In such cases, the base width should be at least $0.4H$.

Gravity walls built of stone laid without mortar, customarily called *dry stone* walls, are useful in many situations where the retained heights are low [less than 10 ft (3 m)], the stone is available on or near the site, and the economy of such construction is desired. For fill situations, a stone dike constructed simply by dumping is an inexpensive alternative to a laid-up dry stone wall.

4.2 Reinforced Concrete Cantilevered Wall

A cantilevered wall consists of a base and a stem, which are securely tied together by reinforcing rods extending from the base up through the stem (Figure 410-5). Reinforcing rods running laterally through the stem provide longitudinal reinforcement in the wall. The weight of the backfill on the base counteracts the forward pressure of the retained height and helps to keep the wall from overturning.

Reinforced concrete cantilevered construction is particularly useful for long lengths of wall where standard metal forms can be reused with great economy in construction. Liners can be used to achieve a variety of finishes and joint patterns in the face of the wall. A veneer of brick or stone can be applied to the wall shown in Figure 410-5 by using standard metal fasteners.

4.3 Reinforced Masonry and Concrete Cantilevered Wall

A two-wythe brick retaining wall is especially suitable for low-wall construction (Figure 410-6). It has the finished appearance of brick but the structural stability of a cantilevered wall. It can be laid up without any formwork, using only brick and grout.

The vertical reinforcement bars must be placed within about ½ in (12 mm) of the brick on the tension side (i.e., the retained earth side) so that the bars will be bonded to the grout. The vertical bars must extend the full height of the wall. The brick should be laid with full shoved head and bed mortar joints with no headers projecting into the grout (See Section 2413 of the Unified Building Code, Grouted Masonry). Brick should be laid up in successive tiers of about 8 in (200 mm) and the space then filled each time with grout (ASTM C270, Mortar for Unit Masonry, type M), followed by puddling with a grout stick. All joints behind the wall should be fully grouted. The work should be completed in one session, but if it is necessary to delay for more than an hour, the tiers should be brought to the same elevation with the grout 1 in (25 mm) below the top.

While Figure 410-6 shows a facing that is one brick wide laid up in running bond, the face can be two bricks wide, laid in other patterns. Solid concrete units or stone units may also be used.

4.4 Reinforced Concrete Block Cantilevered Wall

A concrete block retaining wall using a cantilever and grout design can be laid up without any framework (Figure 410-7). The vertical reinforcement bars must be placed within about ½ in (12 mm) of the inside face of the blocks on the tension side (i.e., the retained earth side) so that the bars will be bonded to the grout. The cells are filled with grout, which should be thoroughly puddled during pouring. If the work is stopped for more than an hour, a horizontal construction joint should be formed by stopping the blocks at the same elevation with the grout 1 in (25 mm) below the top.

Various architectural treatments in the face of the retaining wall can be achieved with split-face and split-rub concrete blocks. The blocks can be laid normal, running bond, or laid up with vertical joints the height of the wall.

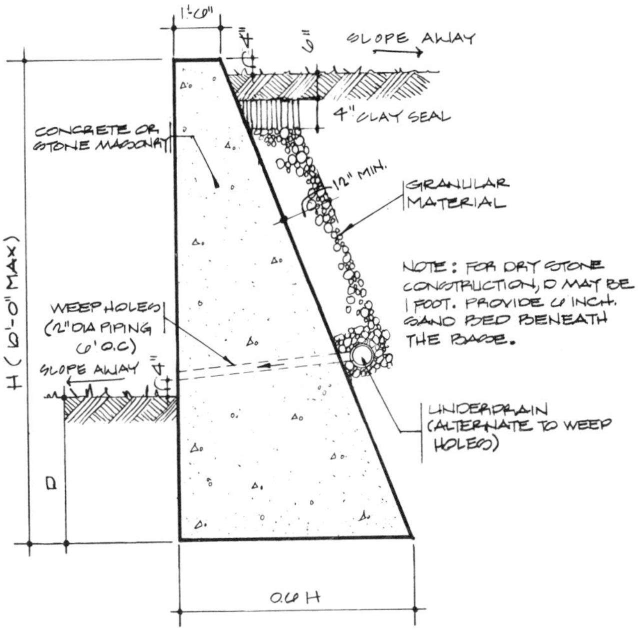
1'-0"
SLOPE AWAY
4" CLAY SEAL
CONCRETE OR STONE MASONRY
12" MIN.
GRANULAR MATERIAL
NOTE: FOR DRY STONE CONSTRUCTION, D MAY BE 1 FOOT. PROVIDE 6 INCH. SAND BED BENEATH THE BASE.
WEEP HOLES (2" DIA PIPING 6' O.C)
SLOPE AWAY
UNDERDRAIN (ALTERNATE TO WEEP HOLES)
H (10'-0" MAX)
D
0.6 H

Figure 410-4 Typical Concrete or Stone Masonry Gravity Wall. *D* = *H*/3, or 2 ft (0.6 m), or depth of frost, whichever is greatest. Use expansion joints at 90 ft (30 m) maximum. Do not use on soils having an allowable bearing pressure less than 1.5 tons/ft^2 (0.575 mPa).

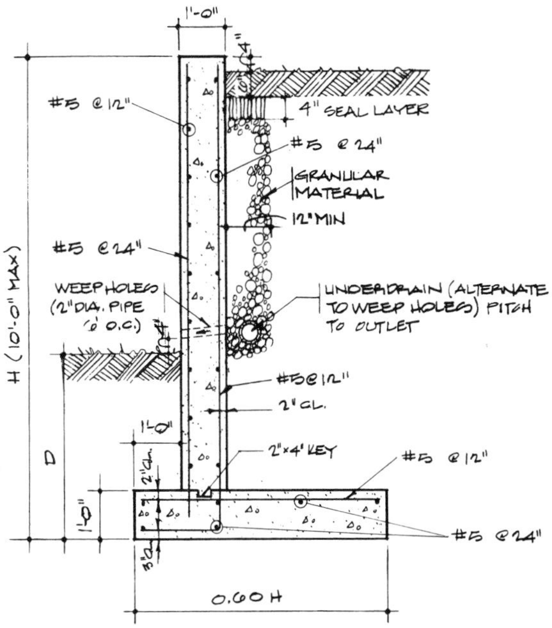
1'-0"
#5 @ 12"
4" SEAL LAYER
#5 @ 24"
GRANULAR MATERIAL
12" MIN
#5 @ 24"
WEEP HOLES (2" DIA. PIPE 6' O.C.)
UNDERDRAIN (ALTERNATE TO WEEP HOLES) PITCH TO OUTLET
#5 @ 12"
2" CL.
1'-0"
2"x4" KEY
#5 @ 12"
#5 @ 24"
H (10'-0" MAX)
D
1'-0"
3" CL.
0.60 H

Figure 410-5 Reinforced Concrete Cantilevered Wall. *D* = *H*/3, or 2 ft (0.6 m), or depth of frost, whichever is greatest. Use No. 4 reinforcement bars for H less than 6 ft (1.8 m). Use expansion joints at 90 ft (30 m) maximum. Do not use on soils having an allowable bearing pressure less than 1.5 tons/ft^2 (0.575 mPa).

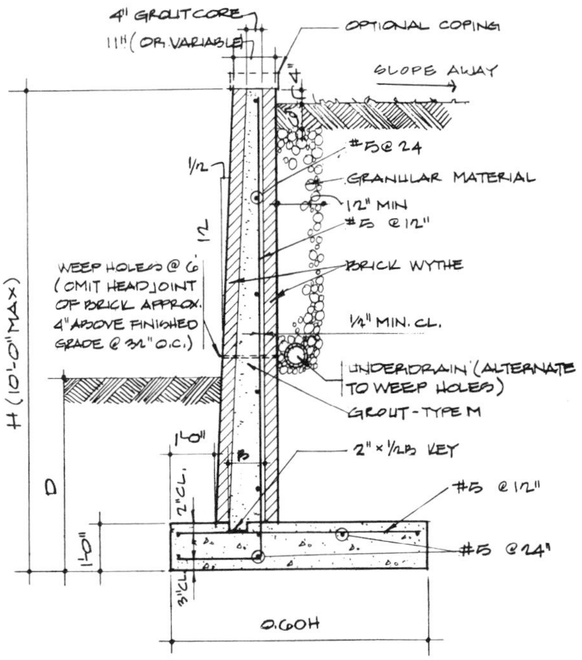
4" GROUT CORE
11" (OR VARIABLE)
OPTIONAL COPING
SLOPE AWAY
#5 @ 24
GRANULAR MATERIAL
12" MIN
#5 @ 12"
BRICK WYTHE
WEEP HOLES @ 6' (OMIT HEAD JOINT OF BRICK APPROX. 4" ABOVE FINISHED GRADE @ 32" O.C.)
1/2" MIN. CL.
UNDERDRAIN (ALTERNATE TO WEEP HOLES)
GROUT - TYPE M
1'-0"
2" x 1/2 B KEY
#5 @ 12"
#5 @ 24"
H (10'-0" MAX)
D
2" CL.
1'-0"
3" CL.
0.60H

Figure 410-6 Reinforced Masonry and Concrete Cantilevered Wall. *D* = *H*/3, or 2 ft (0.6 m), or depth of frost, whichever is greatest. Use No. 4 reinforcement bars for H less than 6 ft (1.8 m). Do not use on soils having an allowable bearing pressure less than 1.5 tons/ft^2 (0.575 mPa).

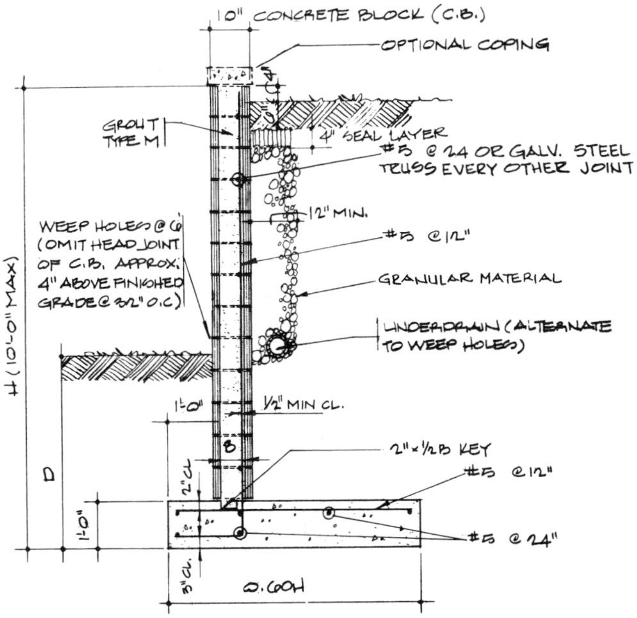
10" CONCRETE BLOCK (C.B.)
OPTIONAL COPING
GROUT TYPE M
4" SEAL LAYER
#5 @ 24 OR GALV. STEEL TRUSS EVERY OTHER JOINT
12" MIN.
WEEP HOLES @ 6' (OMIT HEAD JOINT OF C.B. APPROX. 4" ABOVE FINISHED GRADE @ 32" O.C.)
#5 @ 12"
GRANULAR MATERIAL
UNDERDRAIN (ALTERNATE TO WEEP HOLES)
1/2" MIN CL.
1'-0"
2"x 1/2 B KEY
#5 @ 12"
#5 @ 24"
H (10'-0" MAX)
D
2" CL.
1'-0"
3" CL.
0.60H

Figure 410-7 Reinforced Concrete Block Cantilevered Wall. *D* = *H*/3, or 2 ft (0.6 m), or depth of frost, whichever is greatest. Use No. 4 reinforcement bars for H less than 6 ft (1.8 m). Do not use on soils having an allowable bearing pressure less than 1.5 tons/ft^2 (0.575 mPa).

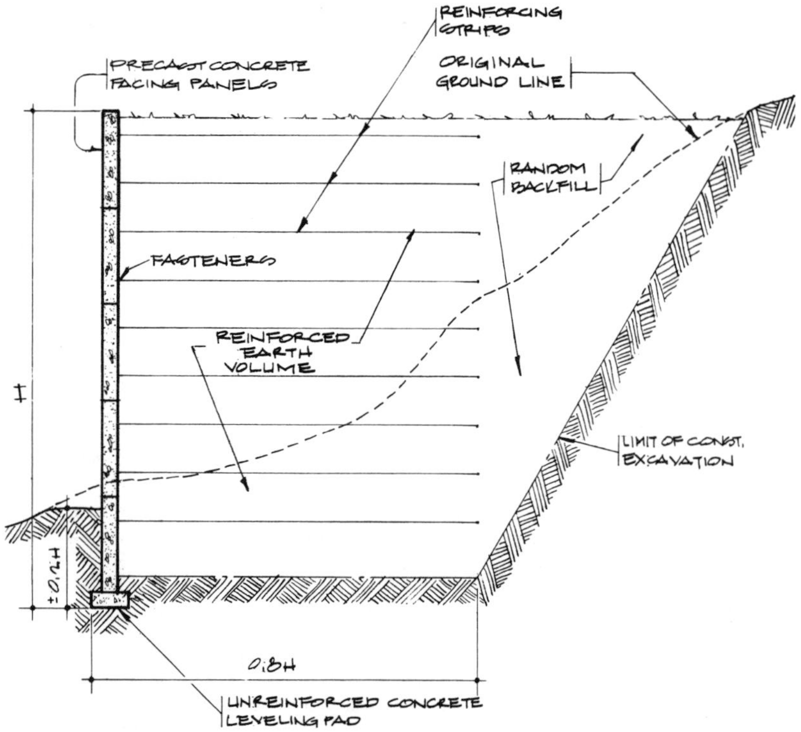
REINFORCING STRIPS
PRECAST CONCRETE FACING PANELS
ORIGINAL GROUND LINE
RANDOM BACKFILL
FASTENERS
REINFORCED EARTH VOLUME
LIMIT OF CONST. EXCAVATION
H
±0.2H
0.8H
UNREINFORCED CONCRETE LEVELING PAD

Figure 410-8 Earth Tieback Retaining Wall. Refer to manufacturer's literature for special details.

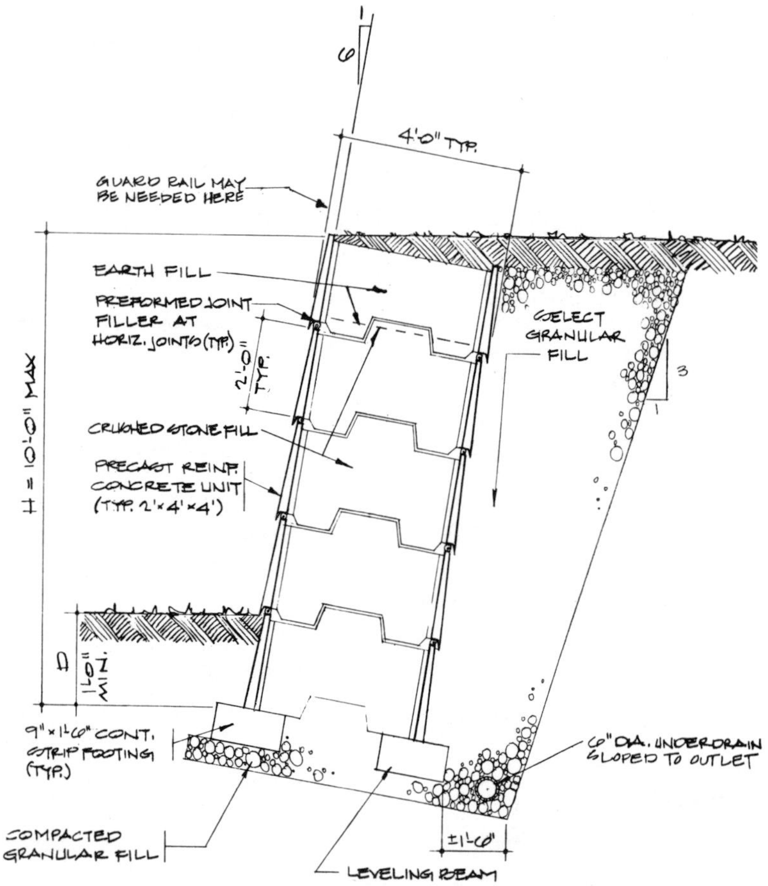
6
1
4'-0" TYP.
GUARD RAIL MAY BE NEEDED HERE
EARTH FILL
PREFORMED JOINT FILLER AT HORIZ. JOINTS (TYP.)
2'-0" TYP.
SELECT GRANULAR FILL
3
1
CRUSHED STONE FILL
PRECAST REINF. CONCRETE UNIT (TYP. 2'×4'×4')
H = 10'-0" MAX
D = 1'-0" MIN.
9"×1'-6" CONT. STRIP FOOTING (TYP.)
6" DIA. UNDERDRAIN SLOPED TO OUTLET
COMPACTED GRANULAR FILL
±1'-6"
LEVELING BEAM

Figure 410-9 Bin Wall. Refer to manufacturer's literature for special details.

4.5 Earth Tieback Retaining Wall

An earth tieback retaining wall consists of interlocking concrete facing panels and compacted cohesionless soil backfill reinforced with thin metallic strips bolted to the facing panels (Figure 410-8). This type of structure uses the construction principle of sheeting with tiebacks to deadmen, except that multiple strips (i.e., tiebacks) rely for anchorage on friction instead of deadmen. The strips, usually galvanized steel, absorb the tensile stresses within the backfill through friction with the soil and thereby hold the soil together in an integral gravity mass. The facing panels are not structural members; they can be cast in any kind of interlocking geometric design or finish.

Earth tieback construction begins with the casting of an unreinforced concrete leveling pad to support and align the first layer of facing panels (Figure 410-8). The leveling pad is cast on the prepared site at a depth below finished grade, depending on the soil conditions and wall height. The first row of facing panels is set and positioned on the leveling pad, followed by the first backfill lift of cohesionless soil (i.e., silt, sand, broken stone, etc.), which is spread and compacted. The first layer of reinforcing strips is placed on the backfill and bolted to the facing panels. Backfill is spread over the design and compacted. The process is repeated until the finished wall height is reached.

Earth tieback construction is particularly suitable for situations where fill is required or can be placed. Because it is flexible, it can withstand differential settlement on poor foundation soils. To ensure the strength and stability of the wall, the backfill must be protected from erosion. Polyester foam inserted into panel joints—or filtered cloth placed behind the joints—allows drainage to occur but keeps the soil lines from washing out.

4.6 Bin Wall

Bin walls (also known as cellular walls) are constructed of precast reinforced concrete interlocking modular units which are stacked and then filled with granular fill, i.e., crushed stone, gravel, etc. (Figure 410-9). A form of gravity wall, the bin wall depends on its mass for stability. The modules can be manufactured with a variety of concrete finishes (e.g., smooth, exposed aggregate, bush-hammered, or striated).

Figure 410-9 shows a typical section using 2-ft × 4-ft × 4-ft (0.6-m × 1.2-m × 1.2-m) units with earth fill placed to the front of the bin wall. Figure 410-10 shows the same section but with a concrete cap and fill placed up to the back of the bin wall. A continuous concrete strip footing along the front serves to align the modular units, and a leveling beam at the back is used to set the batter. While a batter of 6:1 is indicated in the figures, the bin wall could be built with either more batter or with a vertical face.

Bin walls are especially suitable for projects of heavy construction where special equipment, such as a crane, can be used to lift the units into place. They are also suitable where large scale or massiveness in the design expression is desired, as for instance at the edge of a vertical cut or toe of a slope that rises for a considerable distance. A bin wall is useful at the edge of a fill where there is not sufficient space for the slope of the fill to meet an existing grade, as might occur along a property line, for instance.

Since water can filter through the stone fill and joints of the stacked units, weep holes are not necessary in a bin wall. However, to avoid staining or a buildup of groundwater, an underdrain should be installed in the granular fill at the back of the bin wall.

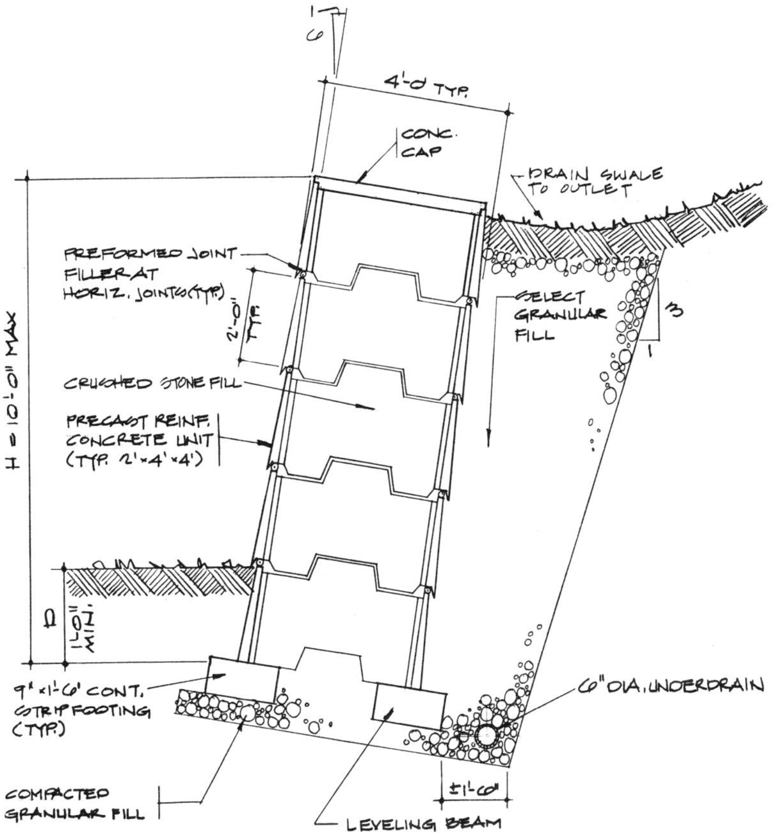
4'-0" TYP.
CONC. CAP
DRAIN SWALE TO OUTLET
PREFORMED JOINT FILLER AT HORIZ. JOINTS (TYP.)
2'-0" TYP.
SELECT GRANULAR FILL
CRUSHED STONE FILL
PRECAST REINF. CONCRETE UNIT (TYP. 2'×4'×4')
H = 10'-0" MAX
9"×1'-6" CONT. STRIP FOOTING (TYP.)
6" DIA. UNDERDRAIN
COMPACTED GRANULAR FILL
±1'-6"
LEVELING BEAM

Figure 410-10 Bin Wall with Concrete Cap. Refer to manufacturer's literature for special details.

4.7 Concrete Crib Wall

A concrete crib wall is constructed of precast reinforced concrete units laid up in interlocking stretchers and headers to form vertical bins which are filled with crushed stone or other granular material. They are a particularly utilitarian solution for retaining fills in situations where excavation is not necessary. Figure 410-11 shows a typical section using a concrete unit 4 ft (1.2 m) long (the smallest unit normally available). Reinforced projecting lugs on the headers are typically used to lock the headers and stretchers together.

Manufactured standard concrete units are designed for both open-face cribbing and closed-face cribbing. Figure 410-11 shows open-face cribbing. Backfilling should follow closely the erection of units, and the cribbing should not be laid up higher than 3 ft (1 m) above the backfilled portion.

Metal units made of galvanized steel are also available for crib walls. Weighing less than precast reinforced concrete units, they are easier to handle during construction.

4.8 Timber Crib Wall

Crib walls may be built of timber when the appearance of wood is desired in the landscape design (Figure 410-12). All timber units should be pressure-treated with a suitable preservative. New or used crushed railroad ties were commonly used in early crib wall construction and continue to be used. However, timber units cut to size and pressure-treated with copper salts or other nonbleeding preserva-

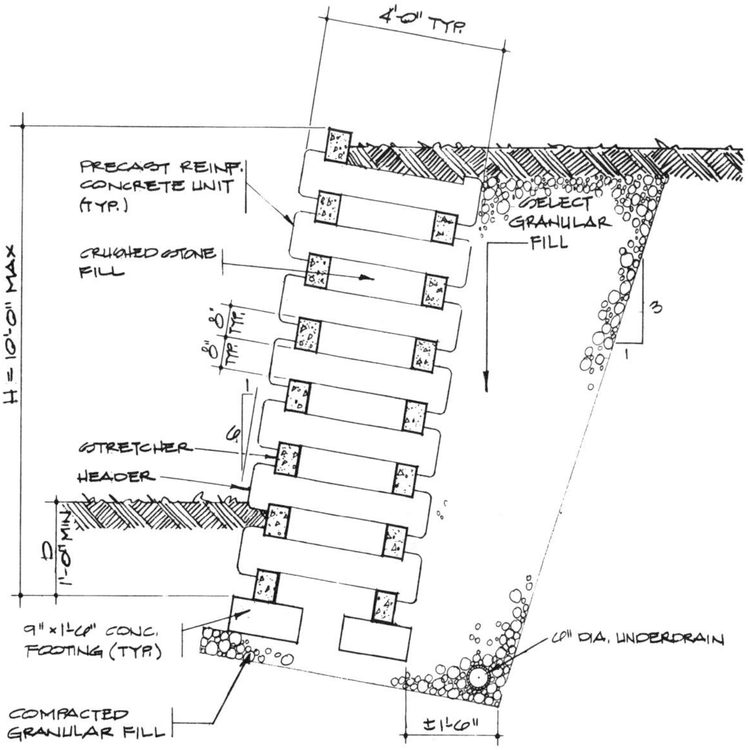
4'-0" TYP.
PRECAST REINF. CONCRETE UNIT (TYP.)
SELECT GRANULAR FILL
CRUSHED STONE FILL
H = 10'-0" MAX
STRETCHER
HEADER
1'-0" MIN.
9"×1'-6" CONC. FOOTING (TYP.)
6" DIA. UNDERDRAIN
COMPACTED GRANULAR FILL
±1'-6"

Figure 410-11 Concrete Crib Wall. Refer to manufacturer's literature for special details.

tives are preferred in current design practice.

4.9 Timber Wall

Typical sections for horizontal and vertical timber walls suitable for retained heights up to 3 ft (1 m) are shown in Figures 410-13 and 410-14. Since the timber wall's resistance to overturning depends upon one-half of its height being below finished grade, it is often not economical or practical to use this timber design for retained heights greater than 3 ft (1 m). The timber units in the horizontal wall can be of variable length but should be at least 5 ft (1.5 m) long. Low timber walls are especially useful for raised planting beds and boxes.

A timber wall of posts and planking is illustrated in Figure 410-15. Besides differing in appearance from the heavy timber walls shown in Figures 410-13 and 410-14, the planking in this design provides some economy in materials.

4.10 Gabion Walls

Gabions are rectangular baskets made of galvanized steel wire or polyvinyl-coated (PVC) wire hexagonal mesh which are filled with stone and tied together to form a wall (Figures 410-16 and 410-17). The baskets are manufactured in standard sizes usually 3 ft (1 m) wide in lengths of 6, 9, and 12 ft (1.8, 2.7, and 3.7 m) and heights of 1, 1½, and 3 ft (0.3, 0.5, and 1 m). Each gabion has a lid and is subdivided by diaphragms into 3-ft (1-m) cells. After being filled with stone, the lid is closed and laced to the top edges of the gabion. Each gabion is then laced to the adjacent gabions. A gabion wall with a battered face is shown in Figure 410-16. A stepped design is shown in Figure 410-17.

Gabion walls, being flexible, can adapt to ground settlement. Their permeability allows water to drain through, making gabions especially suitable along stream and river banks where variations in water depths occur between flood and dry weather conditions. Volunteer vegetation establishes itself quickly in gabions, softening the structure's appearance in the landscape while also adding durability.

4.11 Green Retaining Walls

Techniques have been developed in recent years that combine vegetation and structural elements in retaining sloped embankments and accommodating changes in elevation. A common system that uses precast concrete units interfilled with soil is illustrated in Figure 410-18. Designed as troughs to hold soil and moisture sufficiently for plant growth, the concrete units

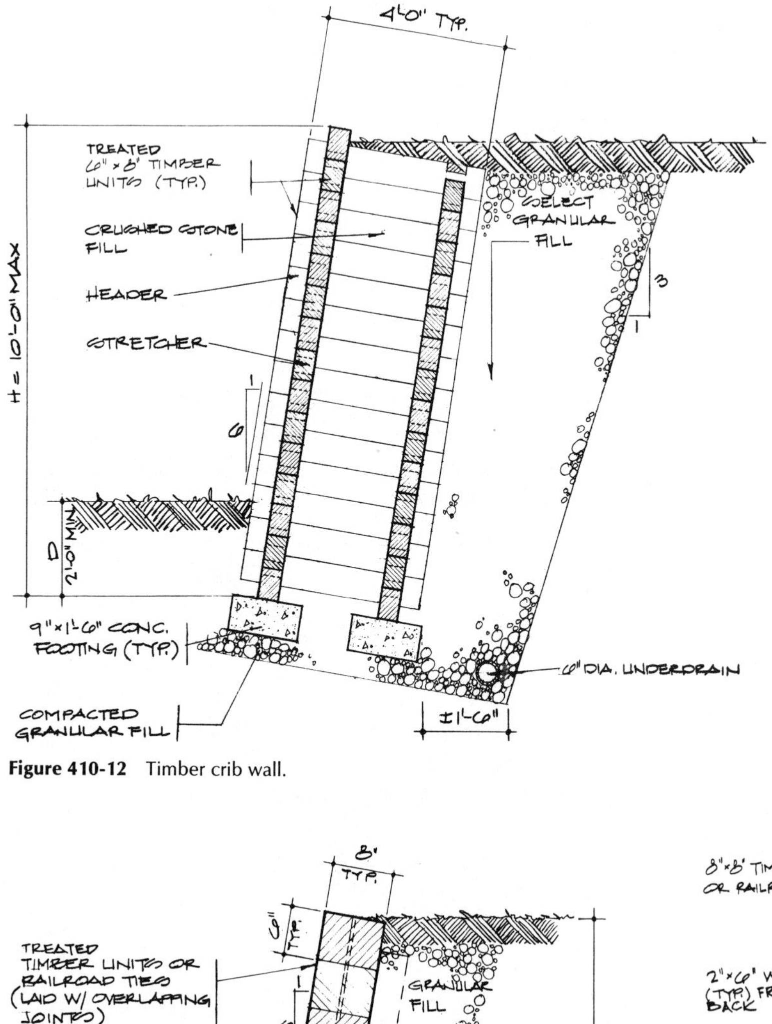
4'-0" TYP.
TREATED 6"x8' TIMBER UNITS (TYP.)
CRUSHED STONE FILL
HEADER
STRETCHER
H = 10'-0" MAX
D 2'-0" MIN.
SELECT GRANULAR FILL
6" DIA. UNDERDRAIN
9"x1'-6" CONC. FOOTING (TYP.)
COMPACTED GRANULAR FILL
±1'-6"

Figure 410-12 Timber crib wall.

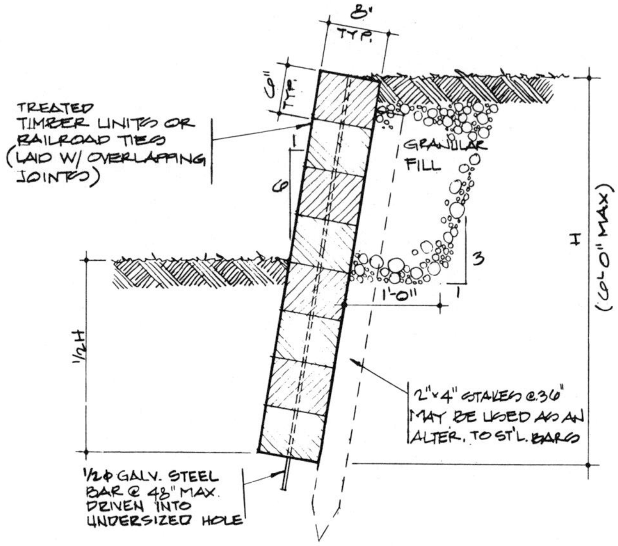
8" TYP.
6" TYP.
TREATED TIMBER UNITS OR RAILROAD TIES (LAID W/ OVERLAPPING JOINTS)
GRANULAR FILL
H (6'-0" MAX)
1'-0"
1/2H
2"x4" STAKES @36" MAY BE USED AS AN ALTER. TO ST'L. BARS
1/2ϕ GALV. STEEL BAR @ 48" MAX. DRIVEN INTO UNDERSIZED HOLE

Figure 410-13 Timber wall (horizontal).

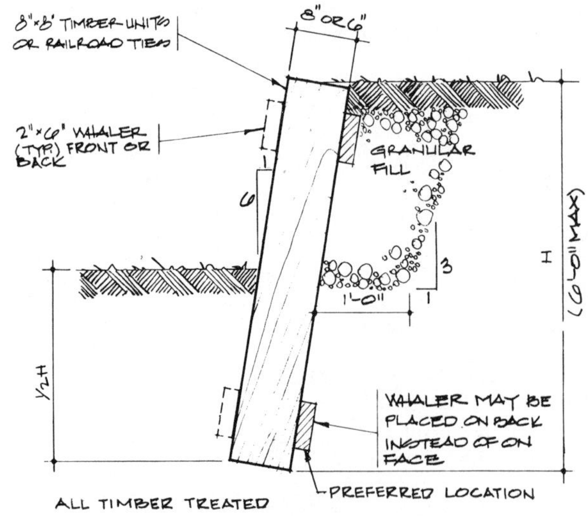
8"x8' TIMBER UNITS OR RAILROAD TIES
8" OR 6"
2"x6" WHALER (TYP.) FRONT OR BACK
GRANULAR FILL
H (6'-0" MAX)
1'-0"
1/2H
WHALER MAY BE PLACED ON BACK INSTEAD OF ON FACE
PREFERRED LOCATION
ALL TIMBER TREATED

Figure 410-14 Timber wall (vertical).

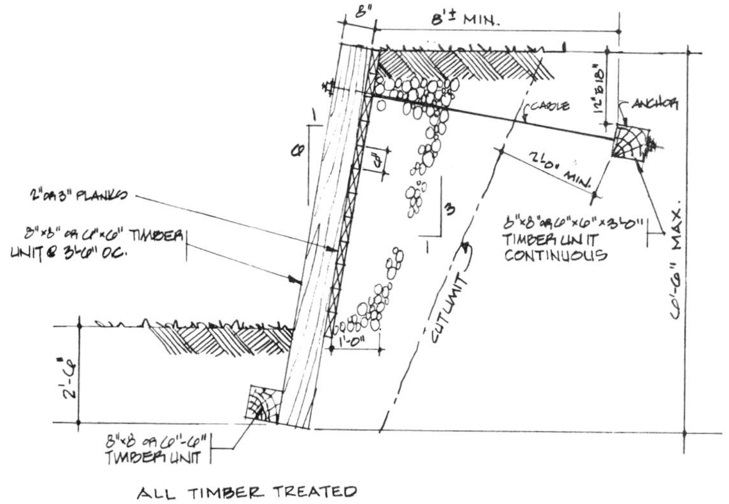

8"
8'± MIN.
CABLE
ANCHOR
12" ± 18"
2'-0" MIN.
2" OR 3" PLANKS
8"×8" OR 6"×6" TIMBER UNIT @ 3'-6" O.C.
8"×8" OR 6"×6"×3'-0" TIMBER UNIT CONTINUOUS
6'-6" MAX.
CUT LIMIT
1'-0"
2'-6"
8"×8" OR 6"-6" TIMBER UNIT
ALL TIMBER TREATED

Figure 410-15 Timber wall (planking).

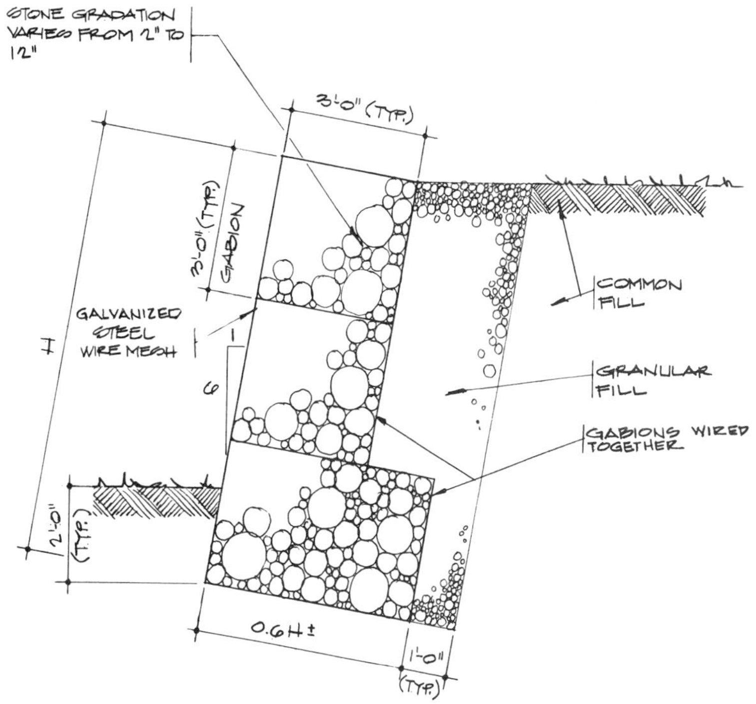

STONE GRADATION VARIES FROM 2" TO 12"
3'-0" (TYP.)
3'-0" (TYP.) GABION
GALVANIZED STEEL WIRE MESH
H
COMMON FILL
GRANULAR FILL
GABIONS WIRED TOGETHER
2'-0" (TYP.)
0.6H±
1'-0" (TYP.)

Figure 410-16 Gabion Wall. Refer to manufacturer's literature for special details.

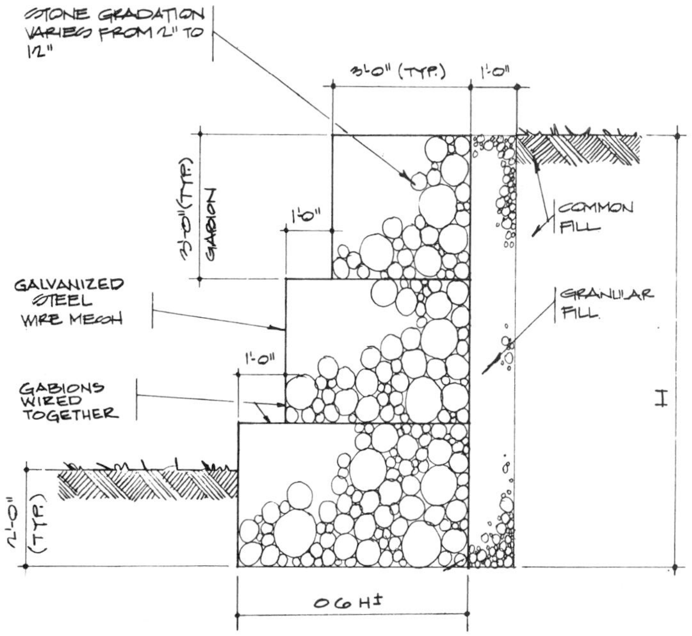

STONE GRADATION VARIES FROM 2" TO 12"
3'-0" (TYP.)
1'-0"
3'-0" (TYP.) GABION
1'-6"
COMMON FILL
GALVANIZED STEEL WIRE MESH
GRANULAR FILL
1'-0"
GABIONS WIRED TOGETHER
H
2'-0" (TYP.)
0.6 H±

Figure 410-17 Gabion Wall (Stepped Face). Refer to manufacturer's literature for special details.

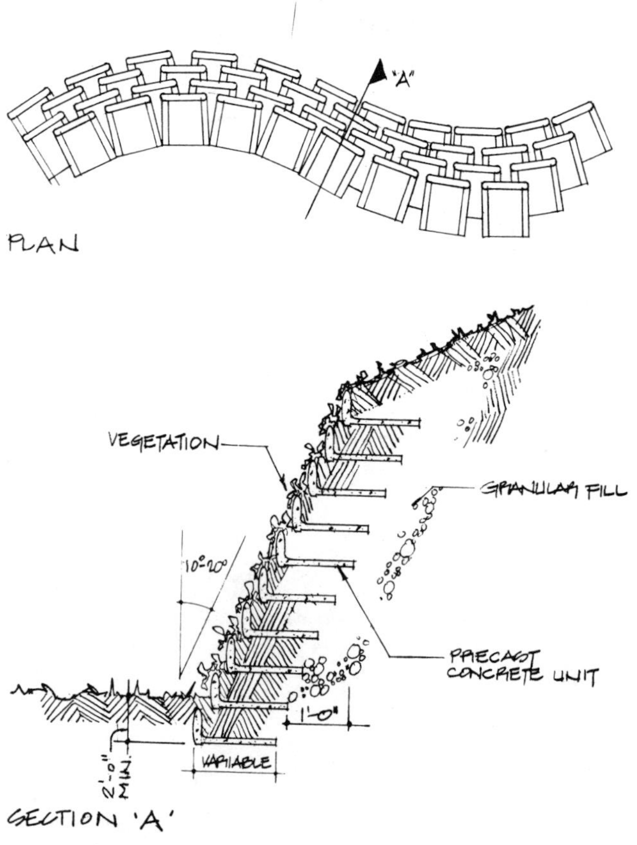
"A"
PLAN
VEGETATION
GRANULAR FILL
10°-20°
PRECAST CONCRETE UNIT
1'-0"
VARIABLE
SECTION 'A'

Figure 410-18 Green Retaining Wall. Refer to manufacturer's literature for special details.

are set in a staggered arrangement, each course resting on the units beneath and filled with soil. The units can be laid at angles of inclination between 70 and 25 degrees.

This type of flexible construction recalls the laying up of stones in the traditional rock garden. It is easily fitted to irregular slopes and accommodates a significant amount of settlement. The interstices in the face can be planted or be allowed to vegetate naturally. As with any flexible wall construction, analysis for sliding, bulging, and rupture should be made.

REFERENCES

"Building Code Requirements for Reinforced Concrete (ACI 318–77)," American Concrete Institute, Michigan, 1977.

Munson, Albe E. *Construction Design for Landscape Architects,* McGraw-Hill, New York, 1974.

Schneider, Robert R., and Walter L. Dickey. *Reinforced Masonry Design,* Prentice-Hall, Reston, VA, 1980.

Seelye, Elwyn E. *Design-Data Book for Civil Engineers,* Wiley, New York, 1957. ■

section 420: Small Dams

CREDITS

Section Editor: Charles W. Harris
Technical Writer: Krisan Osterby-Benson

Reviewers:

Alton P. Davis, Jr.
Charles T. Main, Inc.
Boston, Massachusetts

Varoujian Hagopian
Sasaki Associates, Inc.
Watertown, Massachusetts

Steve J. Poulos
Geotechnical Engineers, Inc.
Winchester, Massachusetts

Illustrations:

Samuel Coplon
Jeffrey Lakey
Michael McGoldrick
Kejoo Park

CONTENTS

1.0 INTRODUCTION

This section provides basic information on the selection and design of small gravity-type dams whose maximum net heads (headwater to tailwater) do not exceed 20 ft (6 m). It does not cover the calculation of runoff and other factors related to stormwater retention and management. Such information can be found in Section 330: Site Drainage, and Section 730: Stormwater Management and Water Resources Protection.

Because safety is an important factor in the design and construction of any type of dam, information and expertise gathered from local authorities is essential during the planning and construction stages of design. Even small dams should be carefully located and constructed so that failure will not result in serious accidents or damage to property.

2.0 PURPOSES OF DAMS

Dams are used to retain and/or retard the flow of water for many reasons, including irrigation, fire protection, mechanical or hydroelectric power, flood protection, the establishment of wildlife habitat, recreational opportunities, livestock needs, fish production, drainage structures, aquifer recharge, and the creation of visual landscape amenities.

Several sections in this handbook provide specific information on the purposes and construction of reservoirs. Section 330: Site Drainage, provides information on measures to mitigate the impact of large storms on stormwater systems. In this regard, dams can be used to retard stormwater flows, thereby lessening the need for high-capacity stormwater systems. Dams can also be used to retain water and spread it over large areas of land in order to: (1) increase infiltration, (2) serve as a sediment basin, and (3) minimize erosion from runoff. Retention ponds are also discussed in Section 730: Stormwater Management and Water Resources Protection.

Sections 710: Water Supply, and 740: Recreational Waterbodies, provide information on the design of ponds for wildlife habitat and for recreational uses. Section 750: Irrigation, briefly discusses the feasibility of water retention for irrigation purposes.

Occasionally, dams are constructed to serve several purposes. For multipurpose uses, the following considerations are important:

1. Whether there is an adequate amount of water to meet the requirements of all uses

2. Whether the various uses are compatible with each other in terms of water quality and periods of use

TABLE 420-1
Important Factors for the Analysis of Potential Dam Sites

Factors to be investigated	*Possible sources of information (U.S.A.)**
	Reconnaissance
Site configuration	U.S. Geological Survey (USGS) air photos
Evidence of good foundation	USGS surficial geology and bedrock maps
Available construction materials	USGS topographic surveys
	U.S. Department of Agriculture (USDA) soil surveys
	USGS surficial geology and bedrock maps
	Detailed site investigations
Available topographic maps	USGS topographic surveys
	State and county highway maps
Surficial geology	USGS surficial geology and bedrock maps
Subsurface geology	USGS topographic surveys
	USDA soil surveys
	USGS surficial geology and bedrock maps
Location of the source of construction materials	USGS topographic surveys
	USDA soil surveys
	USGS surficial geology and bedrock maps
Land required for the dam and reservoir	USDA soil conservation service (SCS) drainage area maps
	USGS topographic surveys
Flood-producing characteristics of the stream	USDA/SCS area maps
	USGS topographic surveys
	U.S. Weather Bureau rainfall maps (24-hr storm based on 10-, 25-, or 50-yr frequency)
	USDA/SCS hydrologic groupings of soils
	USDA/SCS runoff curve tables (calculated for land use and soil type)
	USDA/SCS runoff depth, in (for a given rainfall and runoff curve number)
	USDA/SCS Type I, II storm charts
Previous flood routing studies	Federal Emergency Management Area (FEMA) flood insurance maps and reports
Legal aspects and riparian rights	State laws
	Department of Public Works (DPW)
	Departments of conservation
	State boards of health
	Corps of Engineers (COE)†
Silt carried by stream	USGS water supply papers
	USGS river surveys
	USDA/SCS reports
Water quality	USGS water supply papers
	Health Education and Welfare (HEW) reports
	State board of health reports
Land use and ownership	U.S. Bureau of Land Management (BLM) public land surveys
	USDA Forest Service national forest maps
	County survey or engineer maps
	City or county recorder plats
	U.S. Bureau of Reclamation federal reclamation project maps

*Possible sources will vary from country to country. Only U.S. sources are shown here.

†Corps of Engineers, *Register of Dams in the USA.*

3.0 SELECTION OF DAM SITE

3.1 Investigation of Alternative Sites

As part of the process of selecting a dam site, it is usually necessary to make preliminary studies of several potential sites. Sites should be evaluated for their practicality, economic feasibility, and aesthetic opportunity.

In most site analyses, both a geotechnical engineer and a structural engineer are consulted. Table 420-1 lists the types of information required during the investigation of potential dam sites, and possible sources of this information.

3.2 Survey of Proposed Site

General:

Once the location for a dam has been determined, an engineering survey is required to lay out the dam, the spillway, and other features. Engineering surveys consist of centerline profiles of the dam and spillway, and topographic mapping to determine the ultimate extent and capacity of the proposed reservoir.

Extent and Capacity of Proposed Reservoir:

After establishing the normal full-water and possible high-water elevations of a proposed reservoir, the extent of the reservoir (i.e., surface area) at full capacity can be determined by using any one of three methods:

1. Ground topographic survey techniques

2. Aerial survey techniques

3. Measuring the width of the valley at the normal full-water elevation at regular intervals

The capacity of a proposed reservoir is determined by any one of four methods:

1. Planimeter method

2. Cross-sectional method

TABLE 420-2
Selection Criteria for Small Dams

	Earthfill	*Rockfill*	*Masonry*	*Timber*
		Site considerations		
Suitable topography	Low rolling plains	Low rolling plains	Narrow stream; high, rocky walls	Narrow stream; high, rocky walls
Stream diversion	Required during construction	Usually required	Minimal requirements	Minimal requirements
Foundation requirements	Least stringent; solid rock; gravel	Minimal settlement required; same as earth fill	Reasonably sound rock ideal; gravel	Suitable for unstable soils
Earthquake resistance	Very good	Excellent	Good	Good
Suitable materials on site	Fill materials may have to be borrowed; variety of materials suitable for zoned embankment	Local stone suitable; rock of all sizes used	Local stone may be suitable; carefully graded aggregate required	Local timber may be suitable
Visibility	Slopes are plantable (except with trees)	Highly visible	Free, natural forms possible	Beaver type is least visible
		Cost considerations		
Construction expense*				
Maintenance	Damaged by animals and woody plants; upstream slope inspection and repair required periodically	Upstream slope inspection and repair required periodically	Concrete spalls and other types of masonry damage may occur; periodic inspection and repair required	Considerable maintenance; periodic replacement is required
		Design considerations		
Crest width	Table 420-3	Table 420-3	4-ft (1.2-m) minimum	3-ft (1-m) minimum
Crest height (freeboard)	Table 420-4	Table 420-4	4 ft (1.2 m) above pond at design discharge	Normal maximum pond level
Maximum gradient of side slopes:				
Upstream	2.5 : 1	1.3 : 1 (hard rock); 1.5 : 1 (shales)	Vertical	2 : 1
Downstream	2 : 1 Table 420-5	1.3 : 1 (hard rock); 1.6 : 1 (shales)	0.7 : 1	1 : 1
Seepage control	Clay core required	Face slab required	None required	Timber planking required
Wave protection	Table 420-12	Face slab required	None required	Timber planking required
Spillway	Spillway generally located away from dam as a separate structure	Spillway generally located away from dam as a separate structure	Overflow crest may be incorporated inexpensively in design	All are overflow dams suitable for large drainage areas
Strength and stability	Easily eroded or destroyed if overtopped	Damaged or destroyed if overtopped	Relatively stable if overtopped	Never fails by overturning
Durability	Considered practically permanent	Considered practically permanent	Considered practically permanent	Short-lived unless continuously maintained (permanent if concrete ribbing is used)

*Optimal type of dam depends on relative cost of securing local borrow and/or construction materials.

3. Average depth method
4. Multiplying the surface area by 0.3 times the maximum water depth

4.0 TYPES OF DAMS AND SELECTION CRITERIA

This section describes the following types of small dams:

1. Embankment dams
   a. Earthfill embankment dams
   b. Diaphragm rockfill embankment dams
   c. Composite earthfill and rockfill embankment dams
2. Masonry dams
   a. Stone masonry dams
   b. Concrete dams
3. Timber or precast concrete cribbing dams
   a. Beaver-type dams
   b. Crib dams

Table 420-2 lists general selection criteria for small dams.

4.1 Earthfill Embankment Dams

Types of Earthfill Embankment Dams:

Covered in this section are three types of earthfill embankment dams that do not rely upon impervious internal cores (or walls) of concrete, timber, steel, or masonry as part of their construction (Figure 420-1). They do, however, depend upon the construction of carefully rolled and compacted earth fill to ensure proper retention of the water.

Homogeneous Earthfill Embankment Dams: A homogeneous earthfill dam consists of a single kind of material (exclusive of the slope protection) that is sufficiently impervious to function as an adequate water barrier. The side slopes must be relatively flat for stability. Some seepage through the dam typically occurs on the downstream slope if the reservoir level is maintained at or near full at all times. This weakens the downstream slope and may cause erosion of the dam. Consequently, homogeneous earthfill embankment dams are seldom recommended and should not be designed without consultation with an experienced geotechnical engineer. Modified homogeneous earthfill dams are designed to overcome seepage problems.

Modified Homogeneous Earthfill Embankment Dams: Modified homogeneous earthfill dams have largely replaced the use of homogeneous earthfill dams (Figure 420-1). Small amounts of carefully placed pervious materials can divert seepage to the downstream base of a dam rather than the slope itself, thereby minimizing the problem of erosion. Control is accomplished by using a large filtered-rock toe or by installing a filter drain (i.e., pipe). Filter pipes are best used in combination with a rockfill toe because of clogging problems.

Zoned Earthfill Embankment Dams: In zoned earthfill embankment dams, an impervious core is added and flanked on either side by pervious materials which enclose, support, and protect the core (Figure 420-1). Zoned embankment dams are the most reliable and commonly used type of earthfill embankment dam. The upstream zone provides stability against rapid drawdown and acts as a drain to control seepage. The extent of permeability increases progressively from the center out toward each slope. The width and slope of the zones are based on stability and seepage criteria.

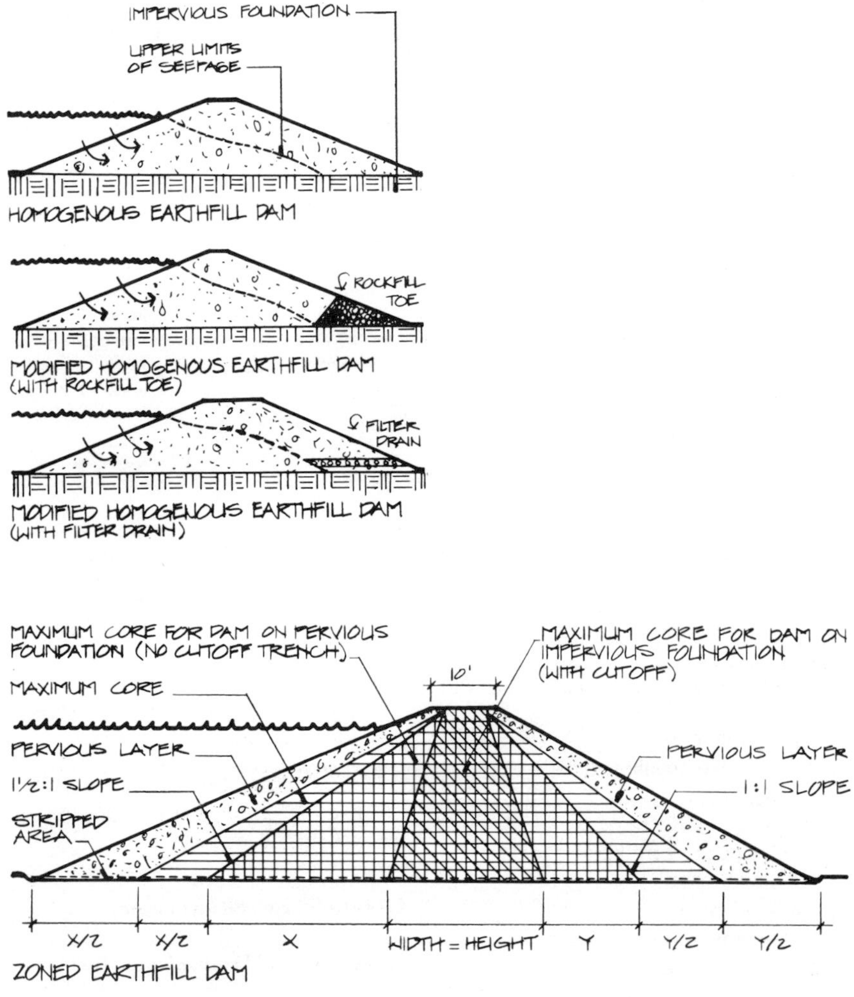
IMPERVIOUS FOUNDATION
UPPER LIMITS OF SEEPAGE
HOMOGENOUS EARTHFILL DAM
℄ ROCKFILL TOE
MODIFIED HOMOGENOUS EARTHFILL DAM (WITH ROCKFILL TOE)
℄ FILTER DRAIN
MODIFIED HOMOGENOUS EARTHFILL DAM (WITH FILTER DRAIN)
MAXIMUM CORE FOR DAM ON PERVIOUS FOUNDATION (NO CUTOFF TRENCH)
MAXIMUM CORE FOR DAM ON IMPERVIOUS FOUNDATION (WITH CUTOFF)
10'
MAXIMUM CORE
PERVIOUS LAYER
1½:1 SLOPE
STRIPPED AREA
PERVIOUS LAYER
1:1 SLOPE
X/2
X/2
X
WIDTH = HEIGHT
Y
Y/2
Y/2
ZONED EARTHFILL DAM

Figure 420-1 Types of earthfill embankment dams.

Foundations for Earthfill Embankment Dams:

The ideal foundation for all earthfill embankment dams consists of (or is underlain at a shallow depth by) a thick layer of relatively impervious material. If earthfill dams are constructed on coarse-textured (i.e., pervious) materials, they must be sealed with an impervious cutoff core or blanket. If they are constructed on fine-textured or unconsolidated materials, they require careful investigation and design to maintain stability. In such instances, an experienced engineer should be consulted. The side slopes of the dam must be flattened to reduce the unit load on the foundation.

Figures 420-2 and 420-3 show how to treat pervious foundations, and Figure 420-4 shows how to treat foundations that have an overlying impervious layer. Figure 420-5 shows construction over a saturated fine-grained foundation.

Top Width Dimensions:

Minimum top width dimensions for earthfill embankment dams are listed in Table 420-3. If the top will be used as a roadway, the width dimension should be at least 16 ft (4.9 m) and include shoulders to prevent raveling of the roadway edge.

Settlement Allowance:

Earthfill embankment dams should be built to allow for:

1 percent settlement on coarse-textured foundations

2 percent settlement on silty sandy gravel

5 percent settlement on clay foundations

A minimum camber of 12 in (300 mm) should be specified for well-compacted low dams.

Freeboard:

All earthfill embankment dams must be constructed high enough above the water line that wave action will not result in water flowing over the top of the dam (Table 420-4).

Side Slopes:

The degree of side slope on an earthfill embankment dam depends on the stability and strength of the fill and foundation material. The more stable the fill, the steeper can be the slopes (Table 420-5). Side

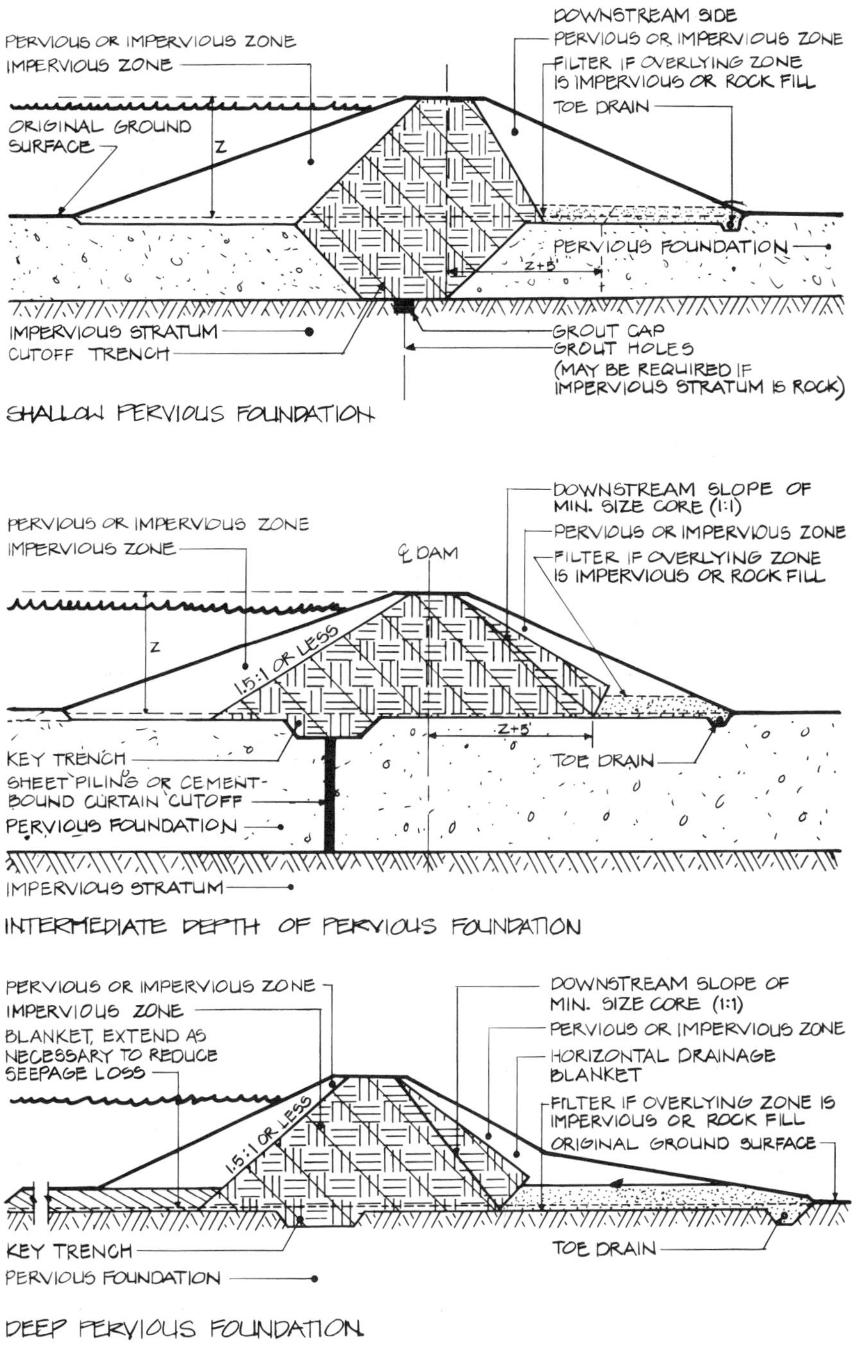
DOWNSTREAM SIDE
PERVIOUS OR IMPERVIOUS ZONE
PERVIOUS OR IMPERVIOUS ZONE
IMPERVIOUS ZONE
FILTER IF OVERLYING ZONE IS IMPERVIOUS OR ROCK FILL
TOE DRAIN
ORIGINAL GROUND SURFACE
Z
PERVIOUS FOUNDATION
Z+5'
IMPERVIOUS STRATUM
CUTOFF TRENCH
GROUT CAP
GROUT HOLES
(MAY BE REQUIRED IF IMPERVIOUS STRATUM IS ROCK)
SHALLOW PERVIOUS FOUNDATION
DOWNSTREAM SLOPE OF MIN. SIZE CORE (1:1)
PERVIOUS OR IMPERVIOUS ZONE
PERVIOUS OR IMPERVIOUS ZONE
IMPERVIOUS ZONE
℄ DAM
FILTER IF OVERLYING ZONE IS IMPERVIOUS OR ROCK FILL
Z
1.5:1 OR LESS
Z+5'
KEY TRENCH
TOE DRAIN
SHEET PILING OR CEMENT-BOUND CURTAIN CUTOFF
PERVIOUS FOUNDATION
IMPERVIOUS STRATUM
INTERMEDIATE DEPTH OF PERVIOUS FOUNDATION
PERVIOUS OR IMPERVIOUS ZONE
IMPERVIOUS ZONE
BLANKET, EXTEND AS NECESSARY TO REDUCE SEEPAGE LOSS
DOWNSTREAM SLOPE OF MIN. SIZE CORE (1:1)
PERVIOUS OR IMPERVIOUS ZONE
HORIZONTAL DRAINAGE BLANKET
FILTER IF OVERLYING ZONE IS IMPERVIOUS OR ROCK FILL
ORIGINAL GROUND SURFACE
1.5:1 OR LESS
KEY TRENCH
TOE DRAIN
PERVIOUS FOUNDATION
DEEP PERVIOUS FOUNDATION

Figure 420-2 Treatment of pervious foundations.

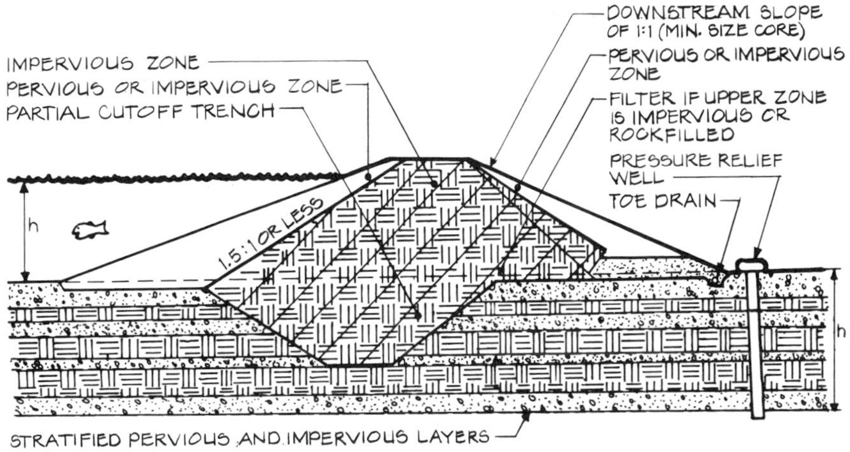
DOWNSTREAM SLOPE OF 1:1 (MIN. SIZE CORE)
IMPERVIOUS ZONE
PERVIOUS OR IMPERVIOUS ZONE
PERVIOUS OR IMPERVIOUS ZONE
PARTIAL CUTOFF TRENCH
FILTER IF UPPER ZONE IS IMPERVIOUS OR ROCKFILLED
PRESSURE RELIEF WELL
TOE DRAIN
h
1.5:1 OR LESS
h
STRATIFIED PERVIOUS AND IMPERVIOUS LAYERS

Figure 420-3 Alternative treatment of pervious foundations.

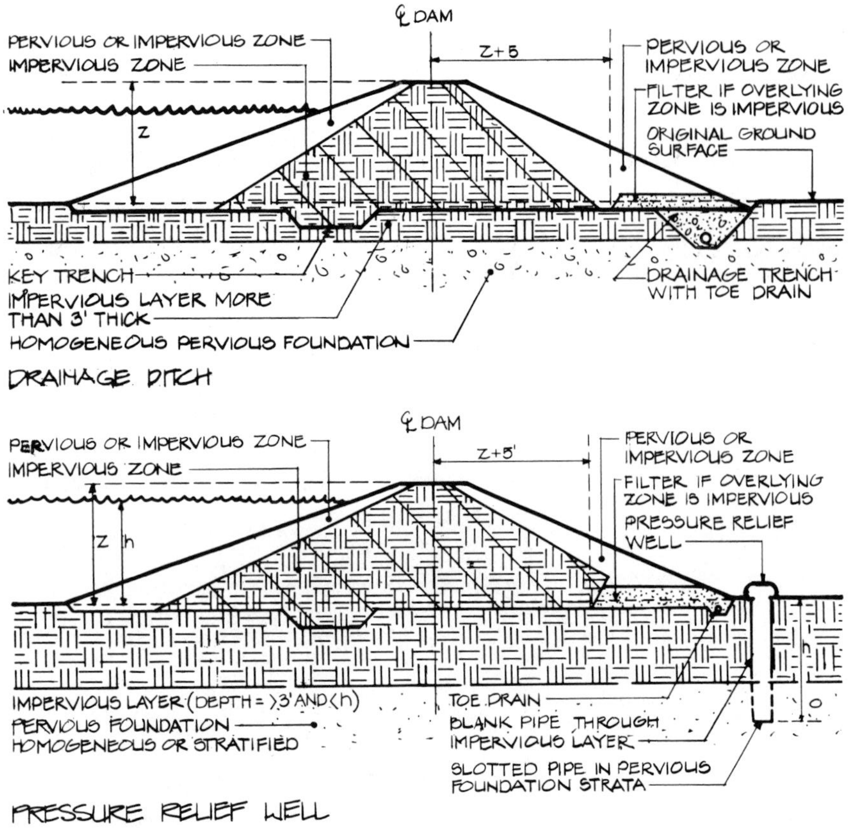
℄ DAM
PERVIOUS OR IMPERVIOUS ZONE
IMPERVIOUS ZONE
Z+5
PERVIOUS OR IMPERVIOUS ZONE
FILTER IF OVERLYING ZONE IS IMPERVIOUS
ORIGINAL GROUND SURFACE
Z
KEY TRENCH
IMPERVIOUS LAYER MORE THAN 3' THICK
HOMOGENEOUS PERVIOUS FOUNDATION
DRAINAGE TRENCH WITH TOE DRAIN
DRAINAGE DITCH
℄ DAM
PERVIOUS OR IMPERVIOUS ZONE
IMPERVIOUS ZONE
Z+5'
PERVIOUS OR IMPERVIOUS ZONE
FILTER IF OVERLYING ZONE IS IMPERVIOUS
PRESSURE RELIEF WELL
Z
h
IMPERVIOUS LAYER (DEPTH =)3' AND (h)
PERVIOUS FOUNDATION HOMOGENEOUS OR STRATIFIED
TOE DRAIN
BLANK PIPE THROUGH IMPERVIOUS LAYER
SLOTTED PIPE IN PERVIOUS FOUNDATION STRATA
PRESSURE RELIEF WELL

Figure 420-4 Treatment of foundations with overlying impervious layer.

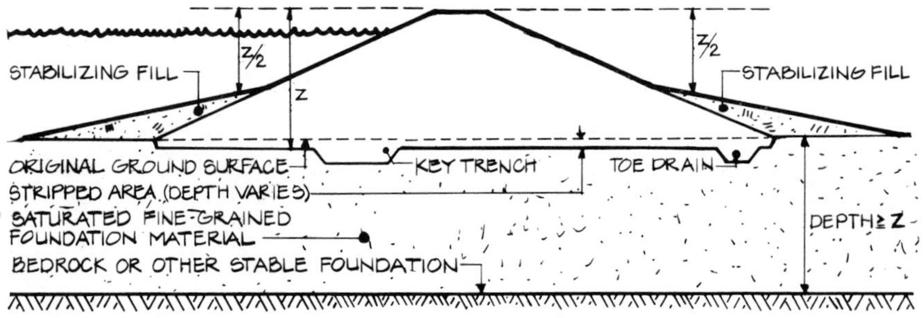
STABILIZING FILL
Z/2
Z
Z/2
STABILIZING FILL
ORIGINAL GROUND SURFACE
STRIPPED AREA (DEPTH VARIES)
SATURATED FINE-GRAINED FOUNDATION MATERIAL
BEDROCK OR OTHER STABLE FOUNDATION
KEY TRENCH
TOE DRAIN
DEPTH ≥ Z

Figure 420-5 Design of Earthfill Dam on Saturated Fine-Grained Foundation. The outside slope of both the upstream and the downstream stabilizing fills should be the same, but not greater than 3:1.

TABLE 420-3
Minimum Top (Crest) Width Dimensions for Earthfill Embankment Dams

Height of dam, ft (m)	*Minimum top width, ft (m)*
Under 10 (3.0)	6 (1.8)
11–14 (3.4–4.2)	8 (2.4)
15–19 (4.6–5.8)	10 (3.0)
20–24 (6.0–7.4)	12 (3.6)
25–34 (7.6–10.4)	14 (4.2)

Source: Soil Conservation Service, "Ponds—Planning, Design, Construction," *Agricultural Handbook Number 590,* USDA, June 1982.

TABLE 420-4
Minimum Freeboard (Crest Height) Requirements for Small Earth-fill Embankment Dams

Fetch, mi (km)	*Minimum freeboard, ft (m)*	*Recommended freeboard, ft (m)*
Less than 1 (1.6)	3 (0.9)	4 (1.2)
1.0 (1.6)	4 (1.2)	5 (1.5)
2.5 (4.0)	5 (1.5)	6 (1.8)
5.0 (8.0)	6 (1.8)	8 (2.4)
10.0 (16.0)	7 (2.1)	10 (3.0)

Source: U.S. Department of the Interior, Bureau of Reclamation, *Design of Small Dams,* 2d ed., U.S. Printing Office, Washington, D.C., 1973.

slopes can be contoured to blend in with surrounding landforms as long as good surface drainage is maintained.

4.2 Diaphragm Rockfill Embankment Dams

Description:

Diaphragm rockfill embankment dams consist of a rockfill core and a waterproof diaphragm on the reservoir side of a dam (Figure 420-6). Diaphragm rockfill dams have the following advantages:

1. They provide the greatest safety against downstream sliding.

2. Grouting may be done during rock placement.

3. There are fewer problems with uplift pressure.

4. The diaphragm can be placed after the embankment is constructed.

5. The diaphragm can be made accessible for periodic inspection and repair.

Construction Materials:

Selection of Materials: The type of rock used for the rockfill zone must not break down during hauling and placing, and it must resist disintegration under freeze/thaw and wetting/drying processes.

Most unweathered igneous and metamorphic rock works well. Some types of sedimentary rock are satisfactory, but most shales, siltstones, and mudstones are not. If these materials must be used, flatter slopes should be specified and allowances made for wastage.

Well-graded rock, from ½ ft^3 to 1 yd^3 (0.015 to 0.765 m^3) in size, should be used. Enough fines (the smallest particles) should be present to fill the voids. Flat, angular rocks do not work well.

Placement of Materials: Precautions must be taken to prevent the rockfill from settling and causing damage to the impervious membrane. This can happen at two stages:

1. During the *construction stage* if the rock material is not compacted sufficiently. Rockfill should be placed in layers 2 to 3 ft (0.6 to 0.9 m) thick. Each layer should be sluiced, using a volume of water equal to ¼ to 1 times the volume of rock. Sluicing should take place during compaction with heavy vibratory rollers [e.g., 10-ton (9-metric ton) 1400-rpm rollers].

2. During the *first filling stage,* owing to the weight of the water. Figure 420-7 illustrates the mathematics of settlement in a diaphragm rockfill dam.

TABLE 420-5
Recommended Side-Slope Gradients for Compacted Earthfill Embankment Dams

Fill material	Slope	
	Upstream	*Downstream*
Clayey sand, clayey gravel, sandy clay, silty sand, silty gravel	3:1	2:1
Silty clay, clayey silt	3:1	3:1

Source: Soil Conservation Service, "Ponds—Planning, Design, Construction," *Agriculture Handbook Number 590,* USDA, June 1982.

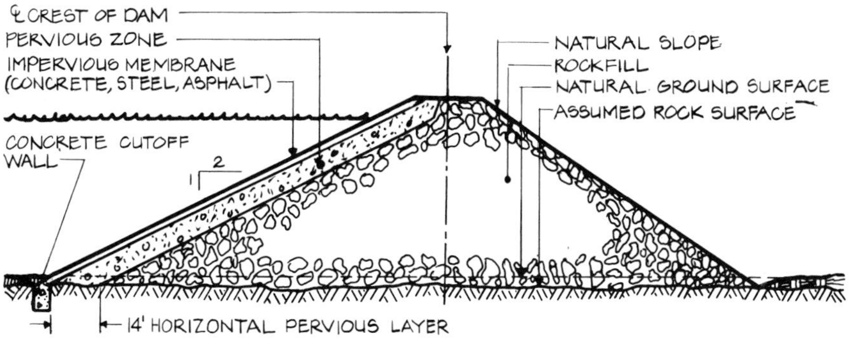
℄ CREST OF DAM
PERVIOUS ZONE
IMPERVIOUS MEMBRANE (CONCRETE, STEEL, ASPHALT)
CONCRETE CUTOFF WALL
2
1
NATURAL SLOPE
ROCKFILL
NATURAL GROUND SURFACE
ASSUMED ROCK SURFACE
14' HORIZONTAL PERVIOUS LAYER

Figure 420-6 Typical diaphragm rockfill embankment dam.

Foundations:

Diaphragm rockfill embankment dams require foundations that will exhibit little settlement or deformation. To achieve this, the dams should be constructed on:

1. Existing bedrock foundations

a. Consisting of existing hard, durable bedrock resistant to percolating water

b. Free from faults and shear zones

c. Clear of silt, clay, sand, and organic material

2. Sand and gravel foundations, including a cutoff constructed to bedrock

3. Deep, pervious soil foundations, including extensive grouting

Profile:

The downstream slope of a diaphragm rockfill embankment dam should be flatter than the natural angle of repose of the dumped rockfill. The upstream face should be slightly convex in order to close the contraction joints in the membrane.

The crest width, freeboard requirements, and other details are the same as for earthfill embankment dams. The freeboard, however, should be twice that for a riprap face because of the smoothness of the facing.

Facing:

A zone of graded sand and gravel, quarry fines, or rubble masonry is typically used as

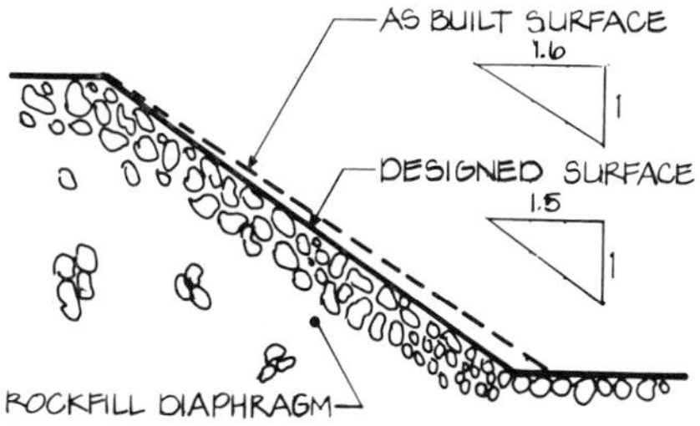
AS BUILT SURFACE
1.6
1
DESIGNED SURFACE
1.5
1
ROCKFILL DIAPHRAGM

Figure 420-7 Settlement of rockfill material in diaphragm rockfill dams.

a *base* for the facing of a diaphragm rockfill embankment dam. This zone should have a minimum horizontal width of 10 ft (3 m) and should be constructed in 12-in (305-mm) layers, wetted and then compacted by 10- to 20-ton (9- to 18-metric ton) vibrating rollers. Pervious well-graded material in sizes ranging from ¼ to 3 in (6 to 76 mm) with fines should be used for this base.

After placement, the zone can be dressed smooth to accept any type of facing. Cutback asphalt [1 gallon per 40 ft^2 (1 liter per m^2)] can be used to seal and to stabilize the surface against erosion prior to constructing the facing.

Typical Membranes:

Typical membranes (i.e., facings) for diaphragm rockfill embankment dams include:

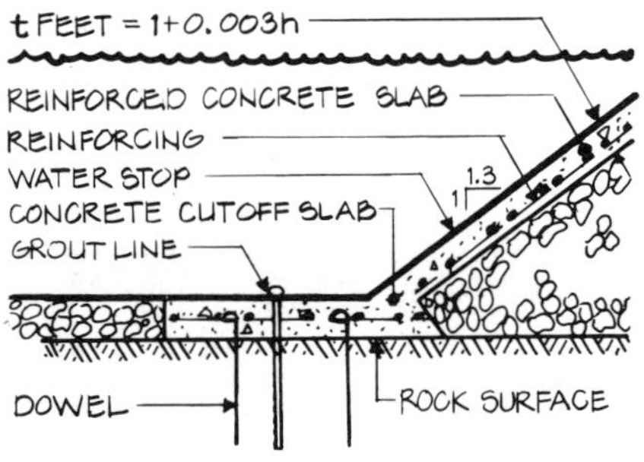
t FEET = 1+0.003h
REINFORCED CONCRETE SLAB
REINFORCING
WATER STOP
CONCRETE CUTOFF SLAB
GROUT LINE
1.3
1
DOWEL
ROCK SURFACE

Figure 420-8 Concrete facing and cutoff slab for diaphragm rockfill embankment dam.

1. Concrete (Figure 420-8) or rollcrete (concrete compacted when laid)
2. Asphalt (Figure 420-9)
3. Timber (Figure 420-10)
4. Steel (Figure 420-11)

4.3 Masonry Dams

Description:

Masonry dams are important because they can pass large flood flows over their crest without sustaining damage. Their construction costs may be higher than those of earthfill or rockfill embankment dams of comparable height and crest length, but their long-term durability is much greater. Figure 420-12 illustrates two types of masonry dams with overflow spillways.

Foundations:

A solid rock foundation is ideal for masonry dams, but a low dam can be built on a foundation of firm earth as long as the excavation is extended down to an impervious stratum with adequate bearing capacity. If a firm stratum is not present, piles must be used. The uplift pressure and buoyancy from tailwater must be considered when building on earth or poor rock foundations. Porous strata, or earth materials that become plastic when wet, are not suitable.

Nonoverflow Sections:

To determine the finished elevation at the top of a masonry dam, a minimum freeboard of 4 ft (1.2 m) above the maximum high-water surface in the reservoir is assumed. A profile based on the criteria outlined in Table 420-2 is assumed. The final design width of the base and the downstream slope are determined by stability analysis. (Refer to 5.0 Stability Analysis of Gravity Dams in this section for information on calculations.)

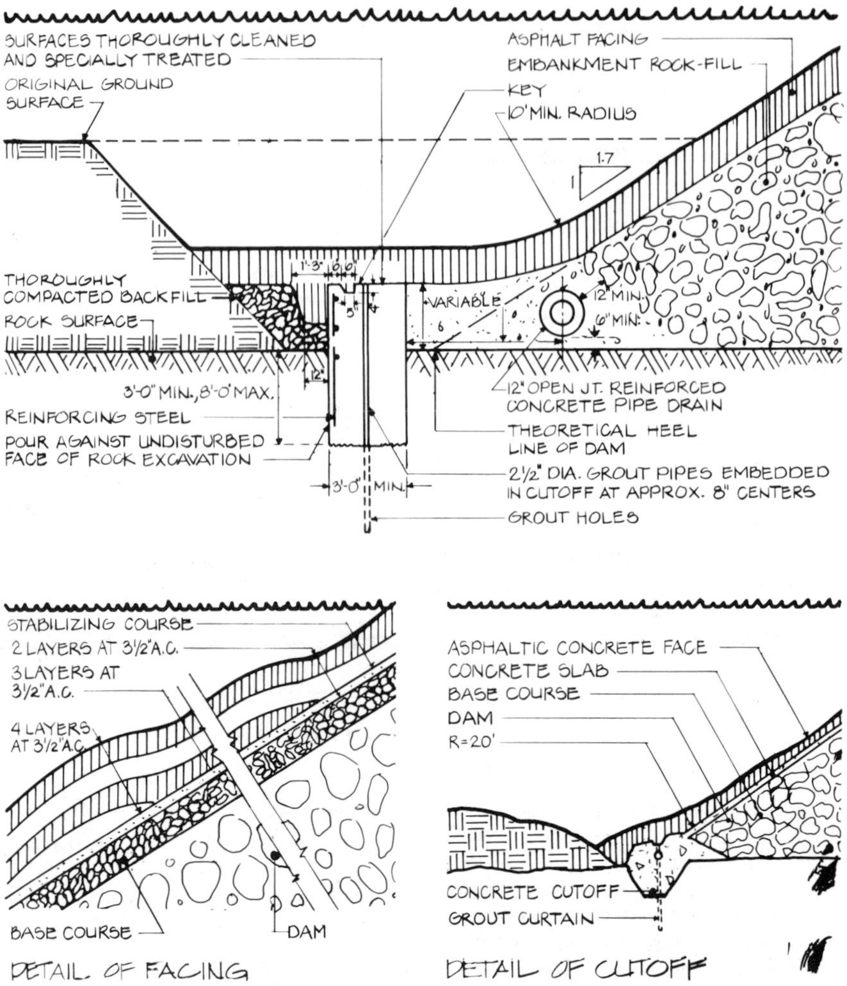
SURFACES THOROUGHLY CLEANED AND SPECIALLY TREATED
ORIGINAL GROUND SURFACE
ASPHALT FACING
EMBANKMENT ROCK-FILL
KEY
10' MIN. RADIUS
1.7
1
THOROUGHLY COMPACTED BACKFILL
ROCK SURFACE
VARIABLE
12" MIN.
6" MIN.
3'-0" MIN., 8'-0" MAX.
REINFORCING STEEL
POUR AGAINST UNDISTURBED FACE OF ROCK EXCAVATION
3'-0" MIN.
12" OPEN JT. REINFORCED CONCRETE PIPE DRAIN
THEORETICAL HEEL LINE OF DAM
2 1/2" DIA. GROUT PIPES EMBEDDED IN CUTOFF AT APPROX. 8" CENTERS
GROUT HOLES
STABILIZING COURSE
2 LAYERS AT 3 1/2" A.C.
3 LAYERS AT 3 1/2" A.C.
4 LAYERS AT 3 1/2" A.C.
BASE COURSE
DAM
DETAIL OF FACING
ASPHALTIC CONCRETE FACE
CONCRETE SLAB
BASE COURSE
DAM
R=20'
CONCRETE CUTOFF
GROUT CURTAIN
DETAIL OF CUTOFF

Figure 420-9 Asphalt facing and foundation cutoff for diaphragm rockfill embankment dam.

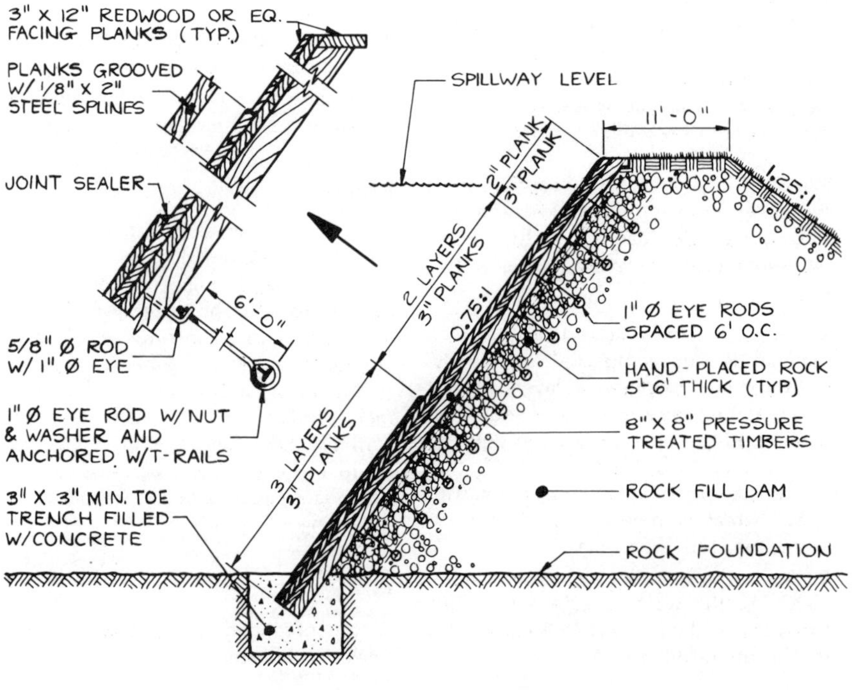
3" X 12" REDWOOD OR EQ. FACING PLANKS (TYP.)
PLANKS GROOVED W/ 1/8" X 2" STEEL SPLINES
JOINT SEALER
6'-0"
5/8" Ø ROD W/ 1" Ø EYE
1" Ø EYE ROD W/ NUT & WASHER AND ANCHORED W/T-RAILS
3" X 3" MIN. TOE TRENCH FILLED W/CONCRETE
SPILLWAY LEVEL
11'-0"
1.25:1
2" PLANK
3" PLANK
2 LAYERS 3" PLANKS
0.75:1
3 LAYERS 3" PLANKS
1" Ø EYE RODS SPACED 6' O.C.
HAND-PLACED ROCK 5'-6' THICK (TYP)
8" X 8" PRESSURE TREATED TIMBERS
ROCK FILL DAM
ROCK FOUNDATION

Figure 420-10 Timber facing for diaphragm rockfill embankment dam.

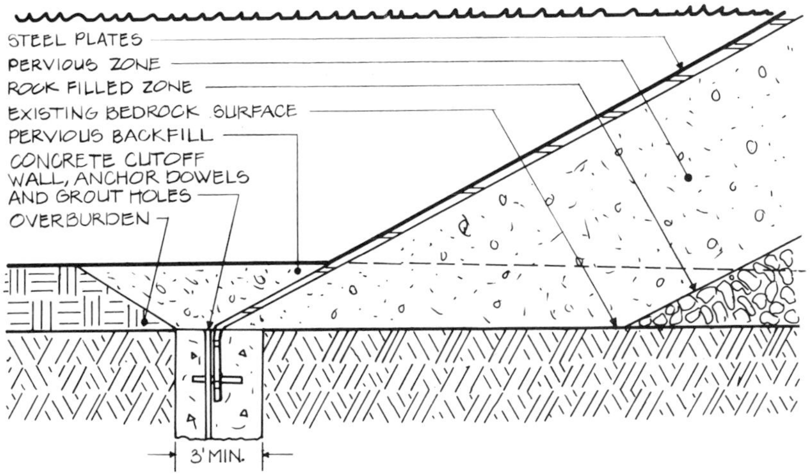
STEEL PLATES
PERVIOUS ZONE
ROCK FILLED ZONE
EXISTING BEDROCK SURFACE
PERVIOUS BACKFILL
CONCRETE CUTOFF WALL, ANCHOR DOWELS AND GROUT HOLES
OVERBURDEN
3' MIN.

Figure 420-11 Steel facing and cutoff wall for diaphragm rockfill embankment dam.

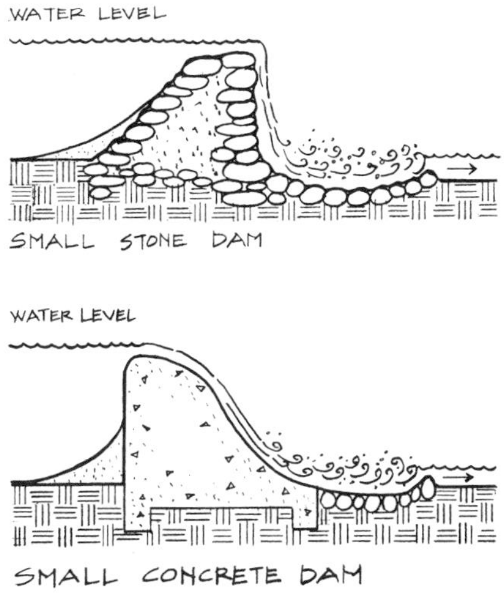
WATER LEVEL
SMALL STONE DAM
WATER LEVEL
SMALL CONCRETE DAM

Figure 420-12 Two types of masonry dams.

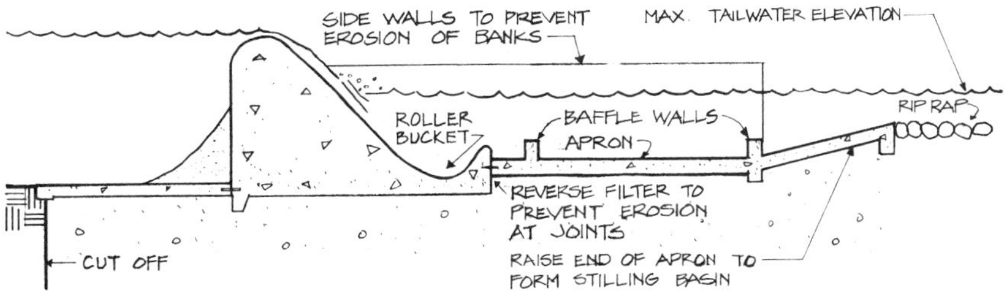
SIDE WALLS TO PREVENT EROSION OF BANKS
MAX. TAILWATER ELEVATION
RIP RAP
ROLLER BUCKET
BAFFLE WALLS
APRON
REVERSE FILTER TO PREVENT EROSION AT JOINTS
RAISE END OF APRON TO FORM STILLING BASIN
CUT OFF

Figure 420-13 Typical overflow section of a concrete dam.

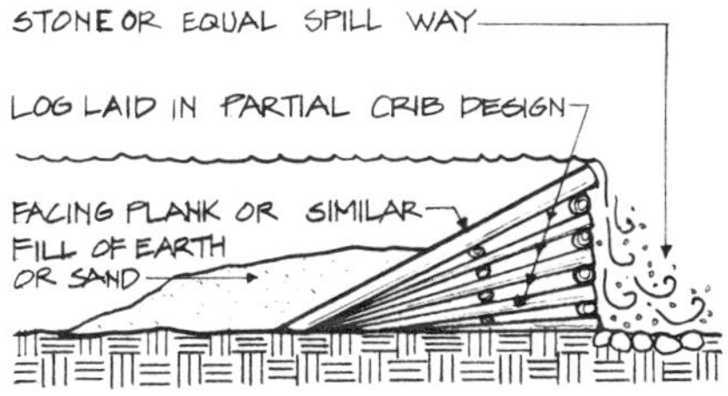
STONE OR EQUAL SPILL WAY
LOG LAID IN PARTIAL CRIB DESIGN
FACING PLANK OR SIMILAR
FILL OF EARTH OR SAND

Overflow Sections:

The lip of a masonry dam should be sloped in front and designed with a large section to resist ice pressure. Figure 420-13 shows a slight curve at the crest and base to approximate the natural curve of falling water. The stability of an overflow dam is determined by the same method as for a nonoverflow dam. Where a longitudinal contraction joint at the downstream toe is provided, only that portion of the dam upstream of the joint is used in the stability analysis. If an apron at the upstream face is used to reduce uplift and improve stability, it should also be accounted for in the calculations.

Wing Walls:

Wing walls function to join a masonry dam to the side banks of a stream and to prevent seepage of water around the ends of the dam. The length of the path of percolation along any line beneath or around the wing walls must not be less than the path beneath the dam. Wing walls should have a minimum thickness of 30 in (760 mm) and should have properly constructed footings. They should be high enough to confine the maximum flow within the banks of the stream.

Apron Walls:

The configuration of apron walls depends on the topography of the streambed. Washing must be prevented from occurring around the ends. A minimum thickness of 18 in (450 mm) is recommended for aprons, and they should be backfilled with porous material for drainage.

4.4 Timber or Precast Concrete Cribbing Dams

Of the many types of timber and precast concrete cribbing dams, two are described below. All timber dams must be kept wet to prevent dry rot. Most failures are due to leakage underneath the dam or to undermining by the overfall.

Beaver-Type Dams:

Beaver-type dams are typically very low. A profile can be constructed from the criteria outlined in Table 420-2. If logs are used, they should all be drift-pinned. Bottom timbers in the dam are sometimes anchored to bedrock. Longitudinal logs should be laid with their butts downstream. Voids should be filled with gravel and compacted impervious earth. Plank flooring should be carried from well under the upstream earth fill up to the crest (Figure 420-14).

Crib Dams:

Crib dams constructed of timber or precast concrete units have advantages in instances where a drainage area is large, or where an overflow dam is necessary, or where it is difficult to drain off the foundation. Crib dams are also an attractive alternative where rock fill is difficult to obtain economically (Figure 420-15).

Foundations for crib dams should be excavated to a minimum depth of 12 in (305 mm) or, if unstable soils exist, to a deeper, suitable foundation.

Abutments for crib dams should be keyed into the side banks of the streambed to prevent washing around the ends. Two rows of sheet piling should be driven to a depth at least the height of the dam *(H)* below the profile. The rows should be staggered to form a better seal against seepage. The piling at the downstream end of the apron can be of a constant thickness but should reach a minimum depth of 2½

TABLE 420-6
Forces Acting on Gravity Dams*

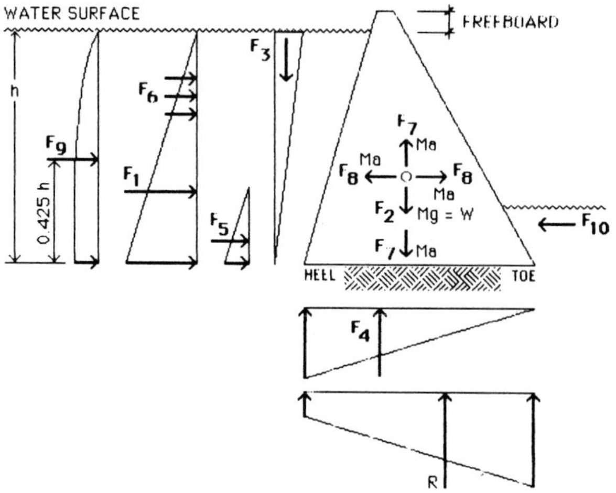
WATER SURFACE
FREEBOARD
h
0.425 h
F9
F6
F1
F5
F3
F7
Ma
F8
Ma
F8
Ma
F2
Mg = W
F7
Ma
F10
HEEL
TOE
F4
R

Force	Description	Formula	References
F_1	Water pressure: calculated for reservoir pressure (headwater); F_1 acts at ⅓ *h*	$32.2\ h^2$	Can be calculated by landscape architect for planning purposes
F_2	Weight of dam: F_2 acts at mass centroid of design section: $\frac{\text{total moment weight}}{\text{total mass weight}}$	 $= A\ (H \cdot M)$  $= A/2\ (H \cdot M)$	Can be calculated by landscape architect for planning purposes†
F_3	Weight of water on face of dam: added to weight of dam	 $= A/2\ (H \cdot W)$	Can be calculated by landscape architect for planning purposes†
F_4	Uplift pressure: subtracted from weight of dam	$\frac{d(F_1 + F_{10})}{2}$	Calculated by engineer based on foundation conditions
F_5	Silt pressure	Horizontal pressure = 20 psf Horizontal force = $10\ (h_1)^2$	Calculated by engineer where siltation is important
F_6	Ice pressure: F_6 acts 1 ft below the top of the reservoir.	= 1–2000 psf	Calculated by engineer
F_7 F_8 F_9	Vertical earthquake force Horizontal earthquake force (dam) Horizontal earthquake force (water) F_9 acts 0.425 *h* above the base	$0.555\ awh^2$	Calculated by engineer using: "ER 1110-2-1806, *Engineering and Design, Earthquake Design and Analysis for Corps of Engineers Projects,* May 16, 1983" (or equivalent source of data)
F_{10}	Water pressure: calculated for tailwater pressure F_{10} acts at ⅓ *h*	$32.2\ h^2$	Can be calculated by landscape architect for planning purposes
R	Resultant	Detailed analysis of all forces acting on the base of the dam	A simple analysis, can be done by landscape architect for planning purposes (Table 420-7)
f	Pressure at the toe, psf	$\frac{Rv}{A} = \frac{1 + 6e}{d}$	Calculated by engineer to determine maximum bearing stress of foundation at toe of dam

* A = area of base (ft²)
a = acceleration due to earthquake (fps)
d = full width of base from heel to toe
e = eccentricity (distance from centerline of base to point where line of force of resultant cuts base)
h = maximum depth of water (ft)
h_1 = maximum depth of silt (ft)
O = heel of the dam
R_v = weight or vertical component of the resultant (lb)
R_h = horizontal component of the resultant (lb)
T = toe of the dam
W = unit weight of water (62.4 pcf)
H = height of dam
M = unit weight of dam material
† Refer to the Appendix of this handbook for unit weights of materials.
Source: Adapted from Frederick S. Merritt, (ed.) *Standard Handbook for Civil Engineers,* McGraw-Hill, New York, 1976.

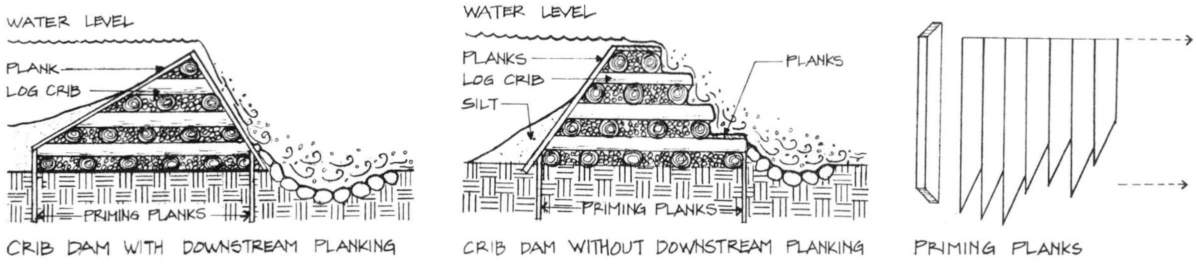
WATER LEVEL
PLANK
LOG CRIB
PRIMING PLANKS
CRIB DAM WITH DOWNSTREAM PLANKING
WATER LEVEL
PLANKS
LOG CRIB
SILT
PLANKS
PRIMING PLANKS
CRIB DAM WITHOUT DOWNSTREAM PLANKING
PRIMING PLANKS

Figure 420-15 Typical crib dams.

ft (0.75 m) to prevent undermining. A 1-in (25-mm) space should be provided between the planks to drain off accumulated water in the crib on the downstream side when the tailwater falls. Cribs, abutments, and the apron should be filled with gravel or small rocks.

Wood deck planking (upstream and downstream) must be tied to the timber or precast concrete cribbing to prevent floating and bonded ice from plucking at the deck. Periodic maintenance and the replacement of rotting timbers are necessary in order to ensure the long-term durability of the dam. In terms of maintenance requirements, precast concrete cribbing and planking have proved to be more economical than timber cribbing.

5.0 STABILITY ANALYSIS OF GRAVITY DAMS

5.1 Forces Acting on Gravity Dams

The various forces that act on gravity dams must be compensated for in the design of a cross section. Table 420-6 describes the forces acting on gravity dams.

5.2 Calculation of Stability

Any one of three processes can cause a gravity dam to fail, all of which should be checked during the design of the cross section. These processes are:

1. Overturning
2. Crushing (settlement at the toe)
3. Horizontal sliding

General Stability:

Prior to checking a cross section for either overturning, crushing, or horizontal sliding, the cross section should be checked for *general stability* by using the procedure outlined in Table 420-7, testing a 1-ft (305-mm) strip of the dam.

TABLE 420-7
General Stability Analysis of a Gravity Dam (Example Calculation)

Given | Analysis

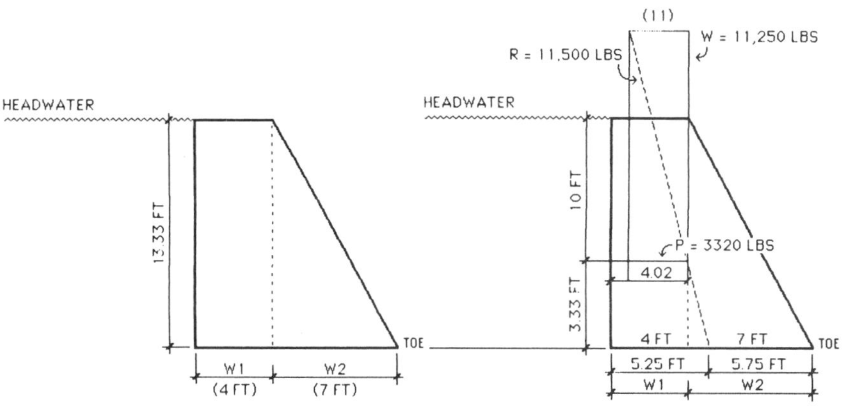
HEADWATER
13.33 FT
TOE
W1
(4 FT)
W2
(7 FT)
(11)
W = 11,250 LBS
R = 11,500 LBS
HEADWATER
10 FT
P = 3320 LBS
4.02
3.33 FT
4 FT
7 FT
TOE
5.25 FT
5.75 FT
W1
W2

Procedure

1 Calculate the weight of section W_1 (F_2 of Table 420-6). Example:

$$4(10)\,(1)\,(150) = 6{,}000 \text{ lb}$$

2 Calculate the weight of section W_2 (F_2 of Table 420-6). Example:

$$\frac{7}{2(10)(1)(150)} = 5{,}250 \text{ lb}$$

3 Add the weight of section W_1 to the weight of section W_2. This equals the total mass weight of the cross section ($F2$). Example:

$$6{,}000 + 5{,}250 = 11{,}250 \text{ lb}$$

4 Calculate the center of gravity of W_1 from point O. Example:

$$W_1/2 = 2$$

5 Calculate the center of gravity of W_2 from point O. Example:

$$W_1 + W_2/3 = 6.33$$

6 Multiply the weight of section W_1 by its arm. This yields its moment about point O. Example:

12,000

7 Multiply the weight of section W_2 by its arm. This yields its moment about point O. Example:

33,232

8 Add both moments. This yields the moment weight of the cross section. Example:

$$12{,}000 + 33{,}232 = 45{,}232$$

9 Divide the total moment weight of the cross section by the total mass weight of the cross section. This yields the mass centroid from point O. Example:

Arm of mass from O = 4.02

10 Calculate the pressure of retained water (P) and where it is acting on the dam (F_1 from Table 420-6). Example:

Water pressure (P) = 3,320 psf acting at 3.33 ft from O.

11 Construct a parallelogram of F_1 and F_2 and draw in the diagonal resultant. Extend the diagonal until it intersects the base. If the resultant cuts through the base "within the middle one-third," the dam is considered generally stable.

Source: Frederick S. Merritt, (ed.), *Standard Handbook for Civil Engineers,* Mc-Graw-Hill, New York, 1976.

TABLE 420-8
Approximate Bearing Capacities of Various Soils and Rock*

Material	*Ton/ft²*	*lb/ft²*	*t/m²*	*kg/m²*
Alluvial soil	½	1,000	4.5	4,500
Soft clay	1	2,000	9.5	9,500
Firm clay	2	4,000	19.5	19,000
Wet sand	2	4,000	19.5	19,000
Sand and clay mixed	2	4,000	19.5	19,000
Fine dry sand	3	6,000	29.0	29,000
Hard clay	4	8,000	39.0	38,500
Coarse dry sand	4	8,000	39.0	38,500
Gravel	6	12,000	58.5	58,000
Gravel and sand (well-cemented)	8	16,000	78.0	77,500
Hard pan or hard shale	10	20,000	97.5	97,000
Medium rock	20	40,000	195.0	194,500
Hard rock	80	160,000	780.0	779,000

* Tons = U.S. short tons (2000 lb), t = metric tons.

Source: Adapted from Albe E. Munson, *Construction Design for Landscape Architects*, McGraw-Hill, New York, 1974.

TABLE 420-9
Average Coefficients of Friction for Concrete on Various Foundation Beds

Foundation bed	*Coefficient of friction*
Rock (moderate)	0.7
Rock (hard angular)	1.0
Gravel	0.6
Dry clay	0.5
Sand	0.4
Wet clay	0.3

Source: Adapted from Albe E. Munson, *Construction Design for Landscape Architects*, McGraw-Hill, New York, 1974.

Overturning:

If a dam were to overturn, it would revolve about its toe (*T*). The force resisting overturning must be greater than the force tending to overturn the dam. To check a cross section for its tendency to overturn, divide the resisting force by the overturning force. A safety factor (quotient) of 2 or more is considered acceptable.

Example: Given that R_h = 4000 lb and its moment arm from T = 4 ft, and given that R_v (weight of dam) = 9500 lb and its moment arm from T = 3.83 ft, the overturning force is found by multiplying R_h by its moment arm from T:

$$4000(4) = 16{,}000 \text{ ft}\cdot\text{lb}$$

The resisting force is found by multiplying R_v by its moment arm from T:

$$9500(3.83) = 36{,}385 \text{ ft}\cdot\text{lb}$$

$$\frac{36{,}385}{16{,}000} = 2.27 \qquad \text{acceptable}$$

Therefore, the dam is not likely to overturn, given the above dimensions.

Crushing:

To eliminate the possibility of crushing, the toe pressure of the structure (*f*) (measured in psf) must be less than the bearing capacity of the soil (psf). Table 420-8 lists approximate bearing capacities of various types of soil and rock. This table can be used for lesser work, but more-important work requires test borings and load tests made on-site.

The pressure (*f*) at the toe of a cross section can be calculated from the following formula:

$$f = \frac{Rv}{A}\left(1 + \frac{6e}{d}\right)$$

where f = pressure at the toe, psf
R_v = downward force (weight or vertical component of the resultant), lb
A = area of base, ft² (meaning a 1-ft strip of the dam)
e = eccentricity (distance from centerline of base to point where line of force of resultant cuts base), ft
d = full width of base from heel to toe, ft

Example:

$$f = \frac{6000}{6}\left[1 + \frac{6(0.90)}{6}\right]$$

$$= 1000(1 + 0.9)$$

$$= 1900 \text{ psf}$$

Referring to Table 420-8, a dam of this design could not be built on alluvial soil and would not be recommended on soft clay, but it could be built on the other types of soil.

Horizontal Sliding:

The force tending to cause horizontal sliding of a gravity dam is the horizontal component of the resultant (R_h). The force tending to resist sliding is the vertical component of the resultant (R_v) (the weight of the dam) multiplied by the coefficient of friction between the dam material and the type of soil on which the structure will rest. (Refer to Table 420-9 for average coefficients of friction for concrete on various foundation beds.) A safety factor of 1.5 or more is considered acceptable.

Example: Given a dam with a triangular cross section on a gravel foundation bed, where R_h = 3125 lb and R_v = 6000 lb, the horizontal sliding force (R_h) = 3125 lb and the resisting force (R_v) (coefficient) = 6000(0.6) = 3600 lb. Thus, the safety factor is

$$\frac{3600}{3125} = 1.15 \qquad \text{not acceptable}$$

Other factors that help to resist horizontal sliding are: (1) deep construction into the ground to prevent underwashing of the footing, and (2) roughening the bottom of the excavation for the footing, thereby causing an increase of the coefficient of friction (Table 420-9).

6.0 DESIGN OF MAJOR COMPONENTS

6.1 Foundations

Foundations must be designed with six objectives in mind:

1. The provision of adequate bearing strength
2. The prevention of horizontal sliding
3. The prevention of excessive seepage
4. The prevention of piping in earth foundations
5. The prevention of scouring
6. The prevention of excessive differential settlement (earthfill and rockfill embankment dams)

(Refer to 4.0 Types of Dams and Selection Criteria in this section for design responses to various types of foundations.)

Types of Foundations:

The existing conditions of earth and rock at the site of the proposed dam influence the choice of a dam type. Foundation conditions that should be evaluated include the thickness, inclination, permeability, and existing faults and fissures of the load-bearing strata.

Five common types of foundations on which small gravity dams can be built include:

1. Solid rock foundations
   a. These offer few restrictions as to type of dam.
   b. Disintegrated rock is removed, and fractures are grouted to ensure long-term stability of the foundation.
2. Gravel foundations
   a. If well-compacted, gravel is suitable for earthfill, rockfill, and concrete gravity dams.
   b. Effective water cutoffs or seals are required in order to prevent or minimize water percolation.
3. Silt or fine-sand foundations
   a. These are suitable only for earthfill embankment and concrete gravity dams.
   b. Appropriate steps must be taken to prevent settlement, to prevent piping and percolation losses, and to protect the toe on the downstream side of the foundation from erosion.
4. Clay foundations
   a. These are suitable for earthfill embankment dams, but special design treatment is required.
   b. Field testing is required in order to determine the load-bearing capacity and consolidation characteristics of the foundation.
5. Nonuniform foundations. Special design treatment by experienced engineers is recommended.

Bearing Strength of Foundations:

All weathered material must be removed from the surface of rock foundations. Unless the rock is of unquestionable durability, its shear strength should be tested.

Consolidation and shear strength tests should be made on earth foundations to determine the expected degree of settlement and the required distribution of loading (to prevent cracking).

Sliding:

The surfaces of rock foundations must be cleaned to prevent sliding. On horizontally bedded shales with thin beds, the foundation should be designed by an experienced engineer. Where danger of sliding is present, the dam must be anchored by using a weighted upstream blanket or an asphalt or concrete cutoff (see Figures 420.8 and 420.11).

6.2 Drainage Problems

Seepage and piping is a pervasive problem in the design of dams. Several techniques are commonly employed to minimize seepage and piping through dams and/or their foundations.

Masonry or Timber Dams:

The amount of leakage that occurs through foundations depends on the type of foundation on which the dam is built.

On rock foundations, masonry dams typically have drilled drainage holes downstream to relieve uplift pressures on the base of the dam.

On earth foundations, both masonry and timber dams require:

1. A cutoff of concrete or sheet piling driven to rock or to an impervious stratum
2. An upstream blanket of earth or concrete
3. A heavy downstream apron to increase the length of the base of the dam
4. A combination of the above

The *Lane formula* is used to estimate the required length of the path of percolation under masonry dams to prevent piping (Table 420-10). The formula gives the ratio of the weighted creep distance to the net head on the dam. These ratios can be reduced to 80 percent of the values given, if filtered drains are properly used; or 70 percent of the values given, if a flow-net analysis is also made. However, the weighted creep ratio should never be less than 1.5.

Earthfill Embankment Dams:

For leakage control, earthfill embankment dams require:

1. A narrow cutoff trench filled with concrete, earth (with bentonite), impervious earth, slurry, or a line of sheet piling (see Figures 420.8 through 420.12)
2. An upstream filter blanket

6.3 Filter Drains

The design of all small dams on homogeneous pervious foundations should include the use of pervious shells, horizontal drainage blankets, toe drains, pressure-relief wells (see Figure 420-4), or combinations of these, if positive cutoff trenches are not provided (Figure 420-16). Filter drains of gravel or rock prevent piping by collecting the seepage and allowing it to flow away harmlessly. Filter drains are also used on homogeneous pervious foundations overlaid by thin impervious layers (see Figure 420.4).

Pervious Downstream Shells:

1. The weight of the shell must be adequate to stabilize the foundation.
2. Pressures must be relieved on the impervious layer.
3. Shells must be designed to prevent piping or must be replaced with a horizontal drainage blanket designed to meet filter requirements.

Horizontal Drainage Blankets:

1. Piping must be prevented.
2. Drainage trenches and pressure-relief walls can be used to reduce uplift and control seepage.
3. Blankets must have sufficient capacity to conduct the total amount of seepage from the embankment and foundation to the toe drains.
4. A minimum blanket thickness of 12 in (305 mm) is necessary to ensure continu-

TABLE 420-10
Recommended Creep Ratios (R)

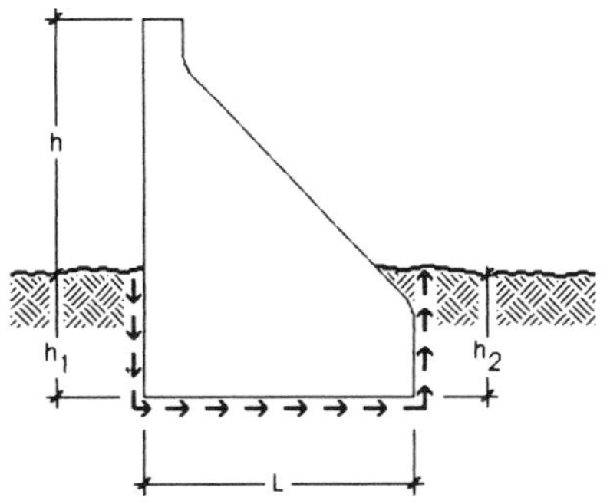
h
h1
h2
L

$$R = \frac{h_1 + h_2 + 1/3\,L}{h}$$

Material	R
Very fine sand and silt	8.5
Fine sand	7.0
Medium sand	6.0
Coarse sand	5.0
Fine gravel	4.0
Medium gravel	3.5
Coarse gravel including some cobbles	3.0
Boulders with some cobbles and gravel	2.5
Soft clay	3.0
Medium clay	2.0
Hard clay	1.8
Very hard clay or hardpan	1.6

Note: If R for a critical section is less than the tabular value, additional flow resistance should be inserted in design section. Limitations: The above R values, determined by the Lane formula, do not take into account (1) the importance of dam shape and (2) the fact that the line of creep may not follow the most direct path of seepage ($h_1 + L + h_2$).

Source: Adapted from Elwyn E. Seelye, *Design: Data Book for Civil Engineers,* vol. I, Wiley, New York, 1960, (from transactions of ASCE by E. W. Lane, 1935.)

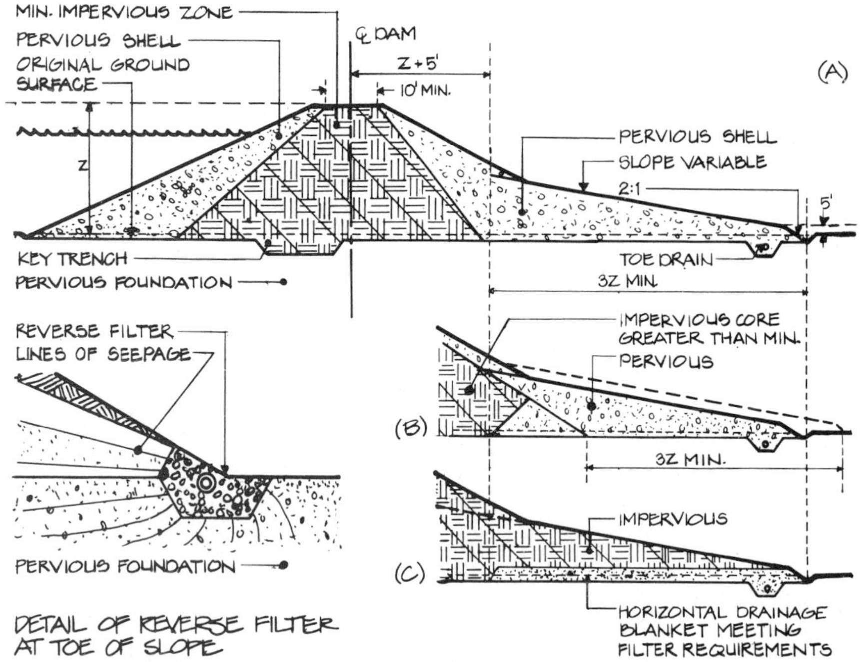
MIN. IMPERVIOUS ZONE
PERVIOUS SHELL
ORIGINAL GROUND SURFACE
℄ DAM
Z+5'
10' MIN.
(A)
Z
PERVIOUS SHELL
SLOPE VARIABLE
2:1
5'
KEY TRENCH
PERVIOUS FOUNDATION
TOE DRAIN
3Z MIN.
REVERSE FILTER
LINES OF SEEPAGE
IMPERVIOUS CORE GREATER THAN MIN.
PERVIOUS
(B)
3Z MIN.
PERVIOUS FOUNDATION
IMPERVIOUS
(C)
DETAIL OF REVERSE FILTER AT TOE OF SLOPE
HORIZONTAL DRAINAGE BLANKET MEETING FILTER REQUIREMENTS

Figure 420-16 Downstream Embankment Sections for Pervious Foundations. Horizontal drainage blankets meeting filter requirements may be required beneath pervious shells in sections (*A*) and (*B*) to prevent foundation piping. The enlarged toe-drain detail illustrates a reversed filter and drain below the ground level to carry off water and thereby stabilize the embankment by lowering the water table, where foundations are pervious.

ity; the thicker the layer, the greater the permissible deviation from the filter requirements given.

Toe Drains:

1. They are commonly installed with horizontal drainage blankets.

2. They are progressively increased in size; the smallest drains are laid along the abutment sections, and the largest drains are placed across the valley floor.

3. They collect seepage and lead it to an outfall pipe which discharges into a spillway, outlet works stilling basin, or river channel below the dam where it can be monitored.

4. Vitrified clay pipe, concrete tile, or perforated asphalt-bonded corrugated metal pipe is typically used.

5. Minimum depth of trench is 3 to 4 ft (0.9 to 1.2 m).

6. Minimum pipe diameter is 6 in (150 mm).

7. Pipes should be surrounded by aggregate which meets filter requirements; two-layer filters are often required.

Drainage Trenches:

1. They are used when pervious foundations are overlaid by a thin impervious layer (see Figure 420-4).

2. They relieve uplift pressures in the pervious stratum.

3. Typically, they are installed with toe drains.

4. They are not effective if the pervious foundation is stratified; more-effective drainage can be accomplished by pressure-relief wells (see Figure 420-3).

Filter Drain Requirements:

1. The gradation must be adequate to prevent foundation and embankment soil particles from entering the filter and clogging it.

2. The filter capacity must be adequate to handle the total seepage flow from the foundation and embankment.

3. The permeability must be adequate to ensure the discharge of seepage water at minimum uplift pressures.

4. The maximum particle size in the filter material should be 3 in (76 mm).

6.4 Cutoffs

Cutoffs prevent excessive seepage through a dam by joining the impervious stratum in the foundation with the base of the impervious element in the dam. A watertight seal must exist along the upstream contact of the impervious membrane with the foundation and abutments (see Figures 420-8 through 420-11).

Cutoff Trenches:

1. They require a minimum bottom width of 8 ft (2.4 m) and a maximum side slope of 1:1 (see Figures 420-2 and 420-3).

2. They are cut along the centerline of the dam and extend into the impervious layer.

3. They are filled and compacted with thin layers of clay or sandy clay material.

Cutoff Walls:

1. They are typically constructed of concrete (see Figures 420-9 and 420-11).

2. They should extend from the upstream toe at least 3 ft (0.9 m) into bedrock.

3. They may require a deeper wall and/or grouting.

4. They must provide support for the weight and thrust of the impervious membrane.

6.5 Surface Drainage

Surface erosion from runoff tends to develop along the contact line between the dam abutments and the side slopes of the streambed (Figure 420-17). Runoff can be controlled by constructing a gutter of cobbles, grouted riprap, concrete, asphalt, or dry-rock pavement.

Earth swales or open drains can be provided to control surface drainage. Discharge should be diverted from the toe drain away form the downstream toe of the embankment by the use of outfall drains or channels.

6.6 Spillway Requirements

Spillways are a vital component of dams, functioning to protect some types of dams from overtopping during flooding. The size, type, or location of a spillway will influence the choice of dam type. Runoff and streamflow characteristics determine spillway requirements. On streams with large flood potential, the spillway structure will dominate the dam configuration. The expense of constructing a large spillway may suggest the adoption of an overflow dam where the spillway and dam can be combined into one structure.

6.7 Spillways and Fish Ladders

Reservoirs require spillways in order to discharge flood flows without damage to the dam and to keep the reservoir's water surface below some predetermined level.

Important Considerations:

1. The safety of the dam from engineering, economic, and social points of view should be considered, and the probability of occurrence of a spillway design flood should be determined. Typically, a range of 0.1 to 0.01 chance per year is considered safe.

2. The magnitude of the design flood (in terms of peak flow and volume) that corresponds to the selected probability of occurrence should be determined. Note that there is a ceiling to the flood potential: *probable maximum flood* (PMF). In most cases, the magnitude of the PMF can be determined for any station on any river. Peak flow can be determined by extrapolating a flood frequency curve toward the ceiling of the PMF (Figure 420-18).

3. The conventional hydraulic design of the spillway and stilling basin should be based on the maximum reservoir level without wind. This design should be checked for a discharge resulting from maximum reservoir level, including full wind buildup.

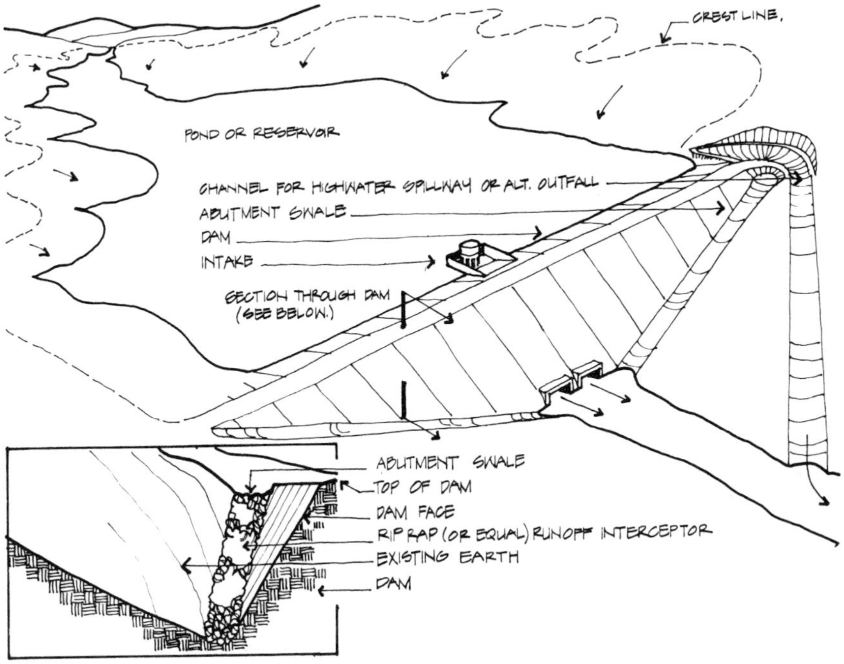
CREST LINE.
POND OR RESERVOIR
CHANNEL FOR HIGHWATER SPILLWAY OR ALT. OUTFALL
ABUTMENT SWALE
DAM
INTAKE
SECTION THROUGH DAM
(SEE BELOW.)
ABUTMENT SWALE
TOP OF DAM
DAM FACE
RIP RAP (OR EQUAL) RUNOFF INTERCEPTOR
EXISTING EARTH
DAM

Figure 420-17 Abutment contact protection.

Masonry Spillways:

Several types of masonry spillways are commonly used in dam construction, the most important of which are overflow spillways, chute spillways, side-channel spillways, drop-inlet spillways, and siphon spillways.

Overflow spillways refer to the flow of water over the crest of the dam (Figure 420-19). (Refer to 4.3 Masonry Dams in this section for information on overflow sections of masonry dams.)

Chute spillways are used with both earthfill and rockfill embankment dams where the topography allows the construction of a chute to carry the water away from the toe, thereby eliminating the danger of undermining. The side walls of the chute are designed as gravity, cantilever, retaining, or lining walls (Figure 420-20).

Side-channel spillways are used in narrow canyons where it is impossible to obtain sufficient crest length for overflow or chute spillways. The channel normally runs parallel to the river.

Drop-inlet spillways refer to vertical shaft inlets with a horizontal conduit extending through the dam to the base of the downstream face. Figure 420-21 illustrates a typical example of a drop-inlet spillway for a small dam.

Siphon spillways hold the water level of reservoirs within close limits. They are not suitable for handling large variations in flow. They are also relatively expensive because of the cost of the head (Figure 420-22).

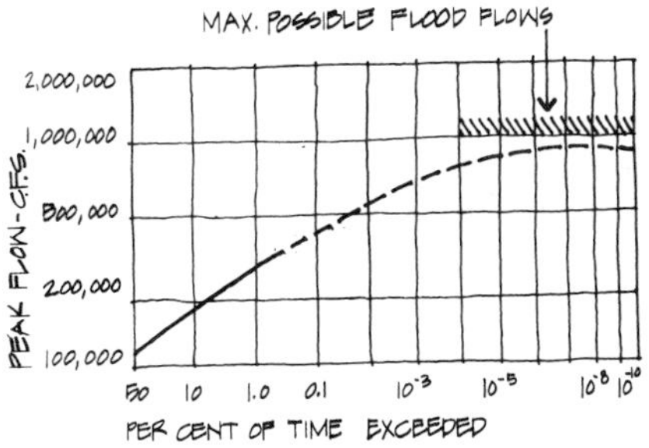
MAX. POSSIBLE FLOOD FLOWS
2,000,000
1,000,000
500,000
200,000
100,000
PEAK FLOW-C.F.S.
50 10 1.0 0.1 10⁻³ 10⁻⁵ 10⁻⁸ 10⁻¹⁰
PER CENT OF TIME EXCEEDED

Figure 420-18 Extrapolation of flood frequency curves.

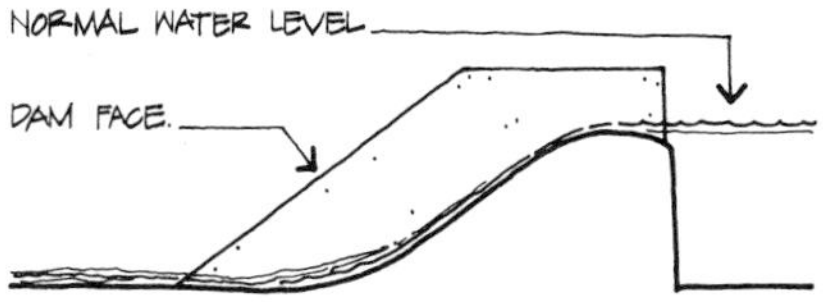
NORMAL WATER LEVEL
DAM FACE.

Figure 420-19 Typical overflow spillway.

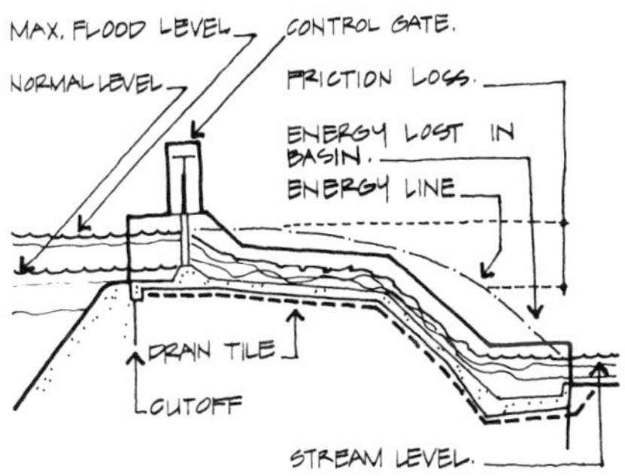
MAX. FLOOD LEVEL
CONTROL GATE.
NORMAL LEVEL
FRICTION LOSS.
ENERGY LOST IN BASIN.
ENERGY LINE
DRAIN TILE
CUTOFF
STREAM LEVEL.

Figure 420-20 Typical chute spillway.

Earth Spillways:

Earth spillways consist of three elements: an inlet channel, a level portion, and an outlet channel (Figure 420-23).

Permissible spillway velocities can be

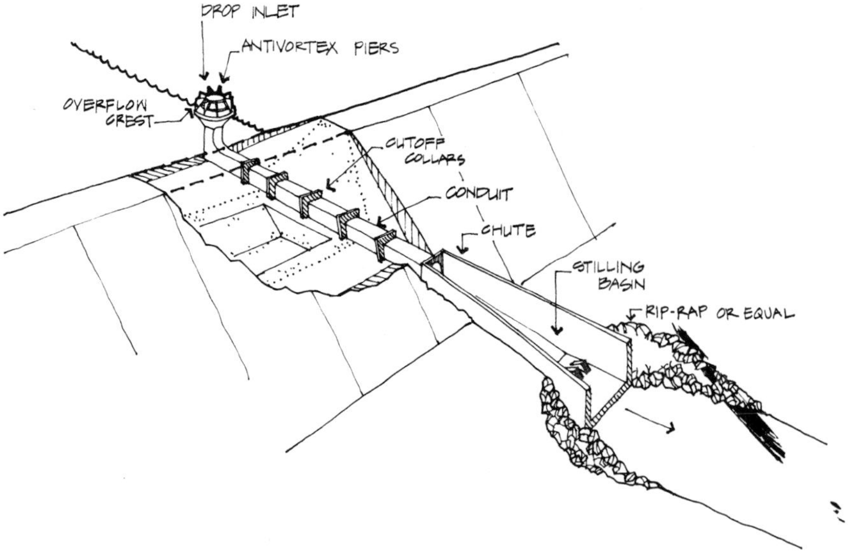
DROP INLET
ANTIVORTEX PIERS
OVERFLOW CREST
CUTOFF COLLARS
CONDUIT
CHUTE
STILLING BASIN
RIP-RAP OR EQUAL

Figure 420-21 Typical drop-inlet spillway for a small dam.

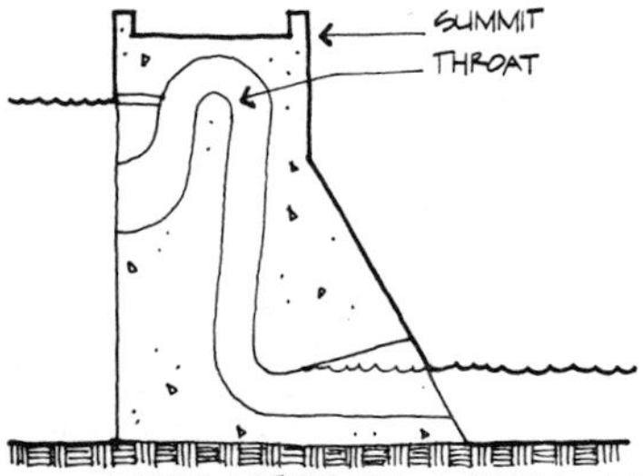
SUMMIT
THROAT

NEAR VERTICAL LOWER LEG WITH DIVERGING OUTLET

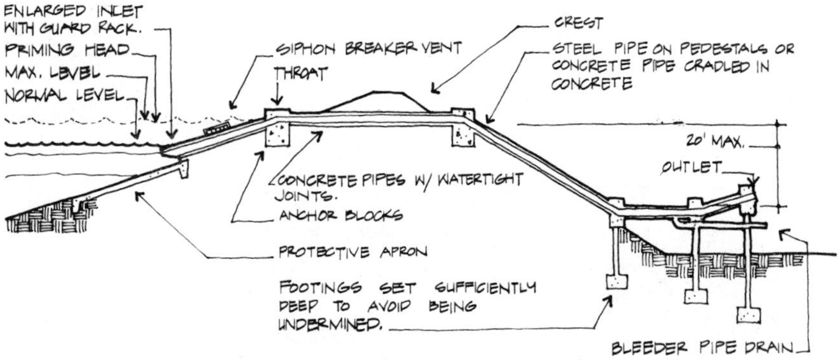
ENLARGED INLET WITH GUARD RACK.
PRIMING HEAD
MAX. LEVEL
NORMAL LEVEL
SIPHON BREAKER VENT
THROAT
CREST
STEEL PIPE ON PEDESTALS OR CONCRETE PIPE CRADLED IN CONCRETE
20' MAX.
OUTLET
CONCRETE PIPES W/ WATERTIGHT JOINTS.
ANCHOR BLOCKS
PROTECTIVE APRON
FOOTINGS SET SUFFICIENTLY DEEP TO AVOID BEING UNDERMINED.
BLEEDER PIPE DRAIN

Figure 420-22 Typical siphon spillway for a small dam.

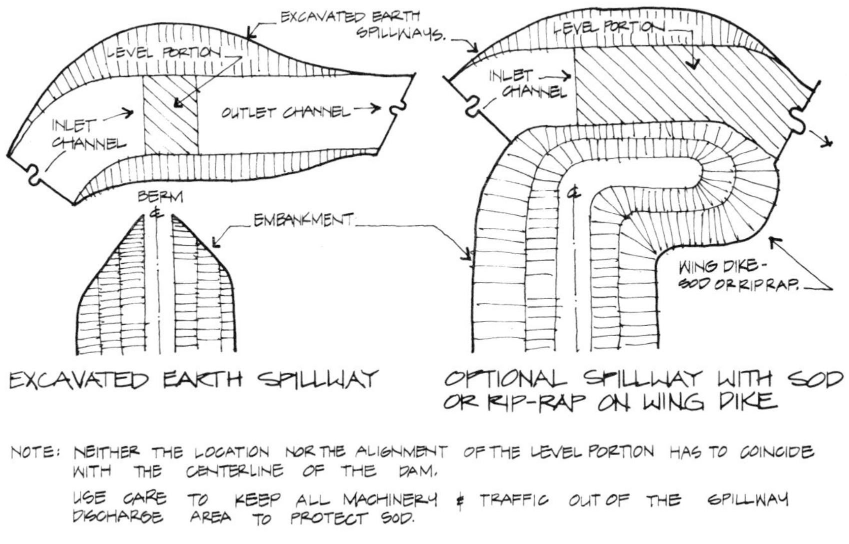
EXCAVATED EARTH SPILLWAYS.
LEVEL PORTION
INLET CHANNEL
OUTLET CHANNEL
BERM
EMBANKMENT
WING DIKE - SOD OR RIPRAP.
EXCAVATED EARTH SPILLWAY
OPTIONAL SPILLWAY WITH SOD OR RIP-RAP ON WING DIKE
NOTE: NEITHER THE LOCATION NOR THE ALIGNMENT OF THE LEVEL PORTION HAS TO COINCIDE WITH THE CENTERLINE OF THE DAM.
USE CARE TO KEEP ALL MACHINERY & TRAFFIC OUT OF THE SPILLWAY DISCHARGE AREA TO PROTECT SOD.

Figure 420-23 Typical earth spillways.

determined from three factors: the vegetation type (degree of retardance), the natural slope of the outlet channel, and the soil erodability factor (Table 420-11).

Earth spillways require regular maintenance, including the repair of erosion channels, the removal of brush and trees, and the clearance of trash from the inlet channel of the spillway.

TABLE 420-11
Permissible Velocities for Vegetated Spillways

	Permissible velocity, erosion-resistant soil,† ft/sec*		*Permissible velocity,* easily eroded soils,‡ ft/sec*	
	Slope of outlet channel			
	0–5%	*5–10%*	*0–5%*	*5–10%*
Vegetation				
Bermuda grass, bahiagrass	8	7	6	5
Buffalograss, Kentucky bluegrass, smooth brome, tall fescue, reed canarygrass	7	6	5	4
Sod-forming grass and legume mixtures	5	4	4	3
Lespedeza sericea, weeping lovegrass, yellow bluestem, native grass mixtures	3.5	3.5	2.5	2.5

* Increase values 10% when the anticipated average use of the spillway is not more frequent than once in 5 years, or 25% when the anticipated average use is not more frequent than once in 10 years.

† Those with a higher clay content and higher plasticity; typical soil textures are silty clay, sandy clay, and clay.

‡ Those with a high content of fine sand or silt and lower plasticity, or nonplastic; typical soil textures are fine sand, silt, sandy loam, and silty loam.

Source: "Ponds—Planning, Design, Construction," *Agriculture Handbook No. 590,* USDA Soil Conservation Service, June 1982.

Fish Ladders:

In the United States most local and state laws require that dams be constructed with a provision of some means for the safe passage of fish. Fish ladders, although built in a variety of configurations, essentially consist of an inclined trough with an average slope of 4:1 baffled to form stepped pools in which the water flows at a velocity against which the fish can easily swim. In the United States, specifications for fish ladders are typically furnished by state authorities. The nature and position of the entrance to a fish ladder constitute a critical design feature. The entrance to the lower end must be located in an eddy and in the path of migration. The minimum water depth should be approximately 3 ft (1 m) (Figure 420-24).

6.8 Outlets

Functions:

Dam outlets serve the following purposes:

1. To maintain downstream uses of water
2. To maintain a live stream
3. To abate stream pollution
4. To water domestic livestock
5. To allow the emptying of a reservoir for inspection, maintenance, or repair

Dam outlets are also used as service spillways when used in conjuction with bypass overflows or when used as flood control regulators.

The outlet works and their controls are designed to release water at prescribed rates, as determined by downstream requirements, flood control regulations, storage considerations, or legal requirements. Any pipe under a dam on an earth foundation must be properly bedded to prevent piping failure along the pipe. This detail should be approved by an experienced geotechnical engineer.

Types of Outlets:

Drop-inlet trickle tubes consist of a pipe barrel located under the dam, with a riser connected to the upstream end of the barrel (Figure 420-25). The diameter of the riser must be somewhat larger than the diameter of the barrel if the tube is to flow full. Since small-diameter pipe is easily clogged, pipe no smaller than 6 in (150 mm) in diameter should be used.

Drainpipes provide a means for both partial and complete drainage of reservoirs for safety and maintenance reasons. A suitable gate or other control device should be installed, and the drainpipe should be extended to the upstream toe of the dam (Figure 420-25).

6.9 Dam Facing

Upstream Slope Protection:

Upstream slopes of dams should be protected against wave action and burrowing animals. Common materials used for dam facings are listed in Table 420.12. Protective materials should be extended from the crest of the dam to 2 ft (0.6 m) below minimum water level plus the height of waves. They should be sized for wave action and terminated on a supporting berm (Figure 420-26). Upstream riprap should be protected with suitable filter/transition layers. (Refer to Section 880: Geotextiles, for more information on the use of fabrics for slope protection.)

Downstream Slope Protection:

No special surface treatment is required for downstream slopes if the downstream zone of an embankment consists of rock or cobble fill. Downstream slopes of dams with outer surfaces of earth, sand, or gravel should be protected against wind and water by a layer of rock, cobbles, or sod (see Table 420-12).

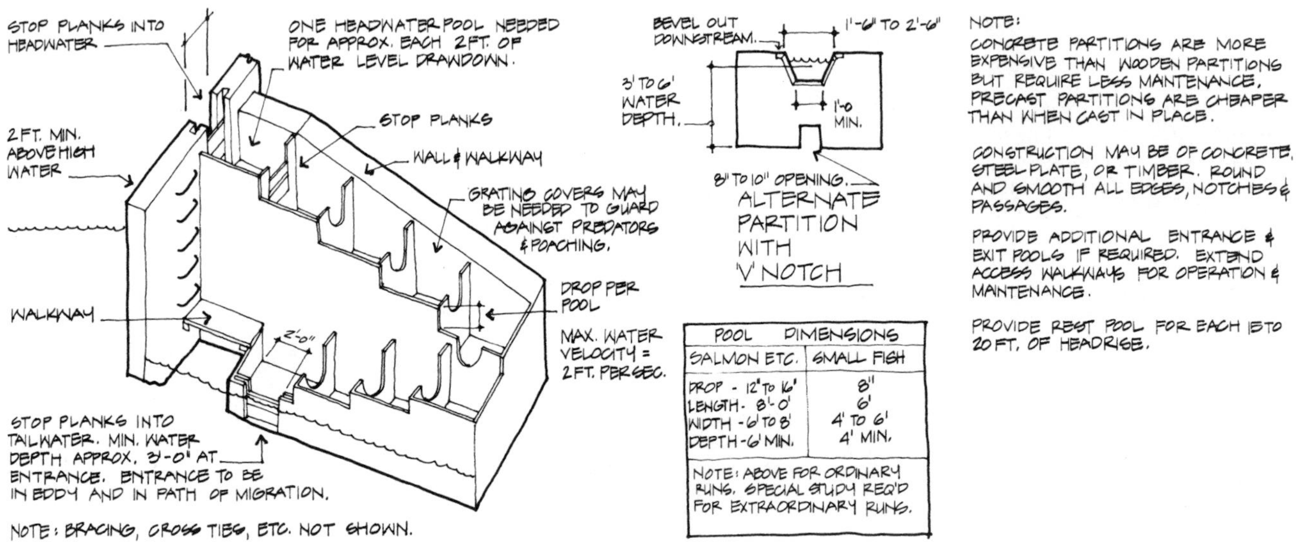
STOP PLANKS INTO HEADWATER
ONE HEADWATER POOL NEEDED FOR APPROX. EACH 2FT. OF WATER LEVEL DRAWDOWN.
2FT. MIN. ABOVE HIGH WATER
STOP PLANKS
WALL & WALKWAY
GRATING COVERS MAY BE NEEDED TO GUARD AGAINST PREDATORS & POACHING.
WALKWAY
DROP PER POOL
MAX. WATER VELOCITY = 2FT. PER SEC.
2'-0"
STOP PLANKS INTO TAILWATER. MIN. WATER DEPTH APPROX. 3'-0" AT ENTRANCE. ENTRANCE TO BE IN EDDY AND IN PATH OF MIGRATION.
NOTE: BRACING, CROSS TIES, ETC. NOT SHOWN.
BEVEL OUT DOWNSTREAM.
1'-6" TO 2'-6"
3' TO 6' WATER DEPTH.
1'-0 MIN.
8" TO 10" OPENING.
ALTERNATE PARTITION WITH 'V' NOTCH
POOL DIMENSIONS
SALMON ETC. | SMALL FISH
DROP - 12" TO 16" | 8"
LENGTH - 8'-0" | 6'
WIDTH - 6' TO 8' | 4' TO 6'
DEPTH - 6' MIN. | 4' MIN.
NOTE: ABOVE FOR ORDINARY RUNS. SPECIAL STUDY REQ'D FOR EXTRAORDINARY RUNS.
NOTE:
CONCRETE PARTITIONS ARE MORE EXPENSIVE THAN WOODEN PARTITIONS BUT REQUIRE LESS MAINTENANCE. PRECAST PARTITIONS ARE CHEAPER THAN WHEN CAST IN PLACE.
CONSTRUCTION MAY BE OF CONCRETE, STEEL PLATE, OR TIMBER. ROUND AND SMOOTH ALL EDGES, NOTCHES & PASSAGES.
PROVIDE ADDITIONAL ENTRANCE & EXIT POOLS IF REQUIRED. EXTEND ACCESS WALKWAYS FOR OPERATION & MAINTENANCE.
PROVIDE REST POOL FOR EACH 15 TO 20 FT. OF HEADRISE.

Figure 420-24 Typical pool-type fish ladder.

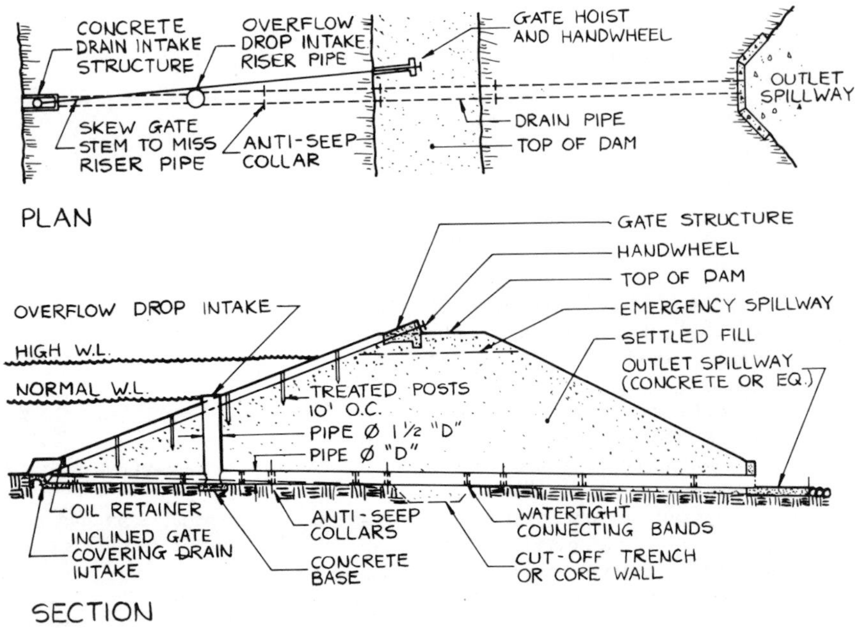
CONCRETE DRAIN INTAKE STRUCTURE
OVERFLOW DROP INTAKE RISER PIPE
GATE HOIST AND HANDWHEEL
OUTLET SPILLWAY
SKEW GATE STEM TO MISS RISER PIPE
ANTI-SEEP COLLAR
DRAIN PIPE
TOP OF DAM
PLAN
GATE STRUCTURE
HANDWHEEL
TOP OF DAM
OVERFLOW DROP INTAKE
EMERGENCY SPILLWAY
HIGH W.L.
SETTLED FILL
NORMAL W.L.
OUTLET SPILLWAY (CONCRETE OR EQ.)
TREATED POSTS 10' O.C.
PIPE Ø 1½ "D"
PIPE Ø "D"
OIL RETAINER
INCLINED GATE COVERING DRAIN INTAKE
ANTI-SEEP COLLARS
CONCRETE BASE
WATERTIGHT CONNECTING BANDS
CUT-OFF TRENCH OR CORE WALL
SECTION

Figure 420-25 Typical Drop-Inlet Trickle Tube with Drain Pipe. Trash racks and baffles at all intakes are not shown.

TABLE 420-12
Common Materials Used for Dam Face Protection

Type of material	*Slope*	*Depth placed*	*Considerations*
Riprap (dumped)	Upstream Downstream	18–36 in (460–920 mm)	Placed 4–6 in (100–150 mm) above elevation reached by normal spring flood Best type of protection for low ultimate cost
Riprap (handplaced)	Upstream Downstream	12 in (300 mm) minimum	Not suitable for areas with settling Relatively expensive
Concrete	Upstream Downstream	6 in (150 mm) minimum	Should extend from crest to below minimum water level Expensive Not suitable for areas with settling Laid monolithically or with few sealed joints Precast blocks suitable for less important structures Requires higher freeboard (sometimes wave wall)
Asphalt	Upstream Downstream	4-in (100-mm) layers minimum	Requires higher freeboard (sometimes wave wall)
Steel	Upstream		Expensive Seldom used
Sod	Downstream		Native grasses suitable Drainage berms required Fertilizer and uniform irrigation required to establish the sod
Reinforced earth	Upstream Downstream		Designed as complete dam structure
Rock cobbles	Downstream	3–12 in. (75–300 mm)	Suitable for arid regions
Soil cement	Upstream	3–10 ft (0.9–3 m) horizontal	May be used in lieu of riprap where rock of adequate size is not locally available
Grouted riprap	Upstream	6–12 in (150–300 mm)	Stone placed in a mortar bed and filled in with mortar Economical for small dams with cheap source of 6–12-in (150–300-mm) stone
Concrete injection mats	Upstream	6–8 in (150–205 mm)	Economical Easily installed Useful for small ponds and channels
Gabion mats	Upstream	6–12 in (150–300 mm)	Economical where only small stone sizes are available Used only for temporary structures

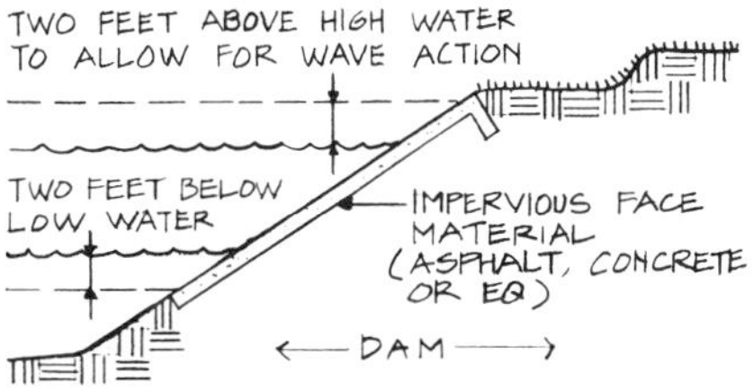
TWO FEET ABOVE HIGH WATER
TO ALLOW FOR WAVE ACTION
TWO FEET BELOW
LOW WATER
IMPERVIOUS FACE
MATERIAL
(ASPHALT, CONCRETE
OR EQ)
DAM

Figure 420-26 Slope Protection for Small Dams. The required minimum depth may be obtained by trenching.

REFERENCES

Abbett, Robert W. (ed.). *American Civil Engineering Practice,* vol. 2, Wiley, New York, 1956.

American Iron and Steel Institute. *Handbook of Steel Drainage and Highway Construction Products,* 2d ed., Washington, DC, 1971.

Golze, Alfred R. (ed.). *Handbook of Dam Engineering,* Van Nostrand Reinhold, New York, 1977.

Merritt, Frederick S. (ed.). *Standard Handbook for Civil Engineers,* 3d ed., McGraw-Hill, New York, 1983.

Munson, Albe E. *Construction Design for Landscape Architects,* McGraw-Hill, New York, 1974.

Seelye, Elwin E. *Design: Data Book for Civil Engineers,* vol. 1, Wiley, New York, 1960.

U.S. Department of Agriculture, Soil Conservation Service. *Ponds—Planning, Design, Construction,* Agriculture Handbook 590, Washington, DC, June 1982.

U.S. Department of the Interior, Bureau of Reclamation. *Design of Small Dams,* 2d ed., Washington, DC, 1973. ■

section 440: Surfacing and Paving

CREDITS

Section Editor: Nichols T. Dines
Consultant: Royston, Hanamoto, Alley & Abey
Mill Valley, California

Reviewers:

Robert Fager
Sasaki Associates, Inc.
Watertown, Massachusetts

Charles W. Harris
Harvard Graduate School of Design
Cambridge, Massachusetts

CONTENTS

1.0 INTRODUCTION

1.1 General

This section is supplemented by data contained in other sections of this handbook in Divisions 800: Materials, and 900: Details and Devices. Division 800 provides design and construction data on a variety of materials used for paving. Sections 820: Asphalt, and 830: Concrete, refer in considerable detail to the use of these two materials for paving. Division 900 includes many examples of typical paving details for a variety of uses; it also includes examples of related details, such as curbs and edges.

Names of agencies, organizations, and manufacturers of various products used for paving are listed at the end of respective sections in this handbook.

1.2 Definitions

Pavements are composite structures that bear the weight of various loads from pedestrian and vehicular circulation. Figure 440-1 illustrates the components of a typical pavement. The definition and function of each of these components are discussed below.

Subgrade:

The bearing capacity and the permeability of the subgrade are two factors that determine the total pavement thickness. Ultimately, the subgrade receives the pavement load and the moisture from infiltration. The *subgrade* is defined as either *undisturbed earth* or as *compacted controlled fill*. In either case, the subgrade must be sloped to drain infiltration water and must have sufficient bearing capacity to support the design load.

Base and Subbase:

The base consists of a graded aggregate foundation that transfers the load on the pavement to the subgrade in a controlled manner. The base also prevents upward migration of capillary water. Heavy-duty pavements usually require an additional layer of base material, called a *subbase*, which also consists of a clean but coarser-graded aggregate, such as crushed stone. (Refer to Division 900:Details and Devices, for specific examples of paving details.)

Pavement:

The pavement material receives the traffic wear, protects the base, and transfers received loads to the base structure. Pavements are classified as being either *flexible* or *rigid* and as either *monolithic* or *unit* (Figures 440-2 and 440-3).

Flexible pavements are somewhat resilient and distribute loads down through the subbase in a radiating manner, as shown in Figure 440-4. A thick base will distribute design loads over a greater subgrade area and prevent subgrade deformation. Flexible pavements are characterized by relatively thin wearing surfaces and relatively thick bases and subbases. (*Deep base* heavy-duty bituminous concrete pavements are an exception; under favorable circumstances, they are placed directly over a suitable subgrade.)

Bituminous concrete is an example of a flexible monolithic pavement. Brick placed on a sand setting bed is an example of a flexible unit pavement.

Rigid pavements (reinforced concrete slabs, or mortared paver units on a reinforced concrete base) are structurally different than flexible pavements (Figure 440-3). Figure 440-4 illustrates how loads are distributed internally within the rigid pavement and transferred to the subgrade over a broad area, in a manner similar to

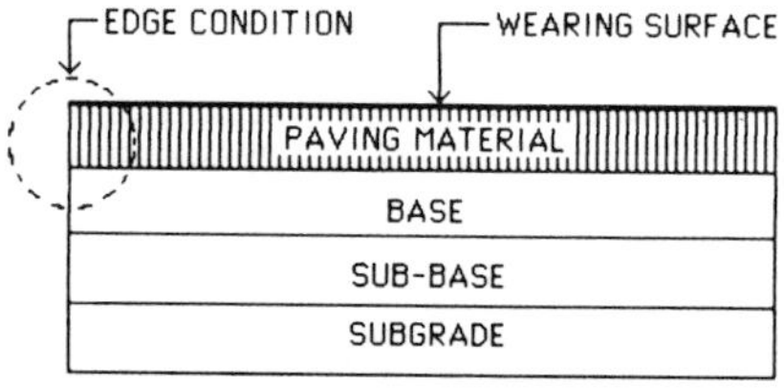
EDGE CONDITION
WEARING SURFACE
PAVING MATERIAL
BASE
SUB-BASE
SUBGRADE

Figure 440-1 Components of a typical pavement.

that found in spread footings used in retaining walls and the like.

Table 440-1 illustrates differences between flexible and rigid pavements in terms of the thicknesses required to support various loads. For rigid pavements, the subgrade condition has less effect on a pavement's thickness than it does for flexible pavements. Conversely, the thickness of flexible pavements is affected significantly by subgrade conditions. For example, in Table 440-1 note the differences in thicknesses required when an identical design load is to be supported by a gravel subgrade (which has a high bearing capacity) versus a poor subgrade condition, such as soft, expansive clay.

TABLE 440-1
Differences between Flexible and Rigid Pavements in Terms of Thicknesses Required

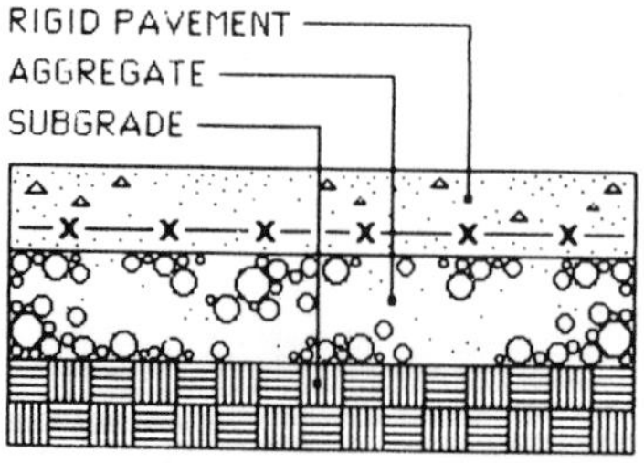
RIGID PAVEMENT
AGGREGATE
SUBGRADE

RIGID PAVEMENT THICKNESS (IN.)

Subgrade	4-Ton Wheel Load	6-Ton Wheel Load	8-Ton Wheel Load
Soft Clay	6.00	7.50	8.50
Sandy Clay	5.75	7.25	8.25
Gravel & Clay	5.50	7.00	8.00
Gravel	5.25	6.50	7.50

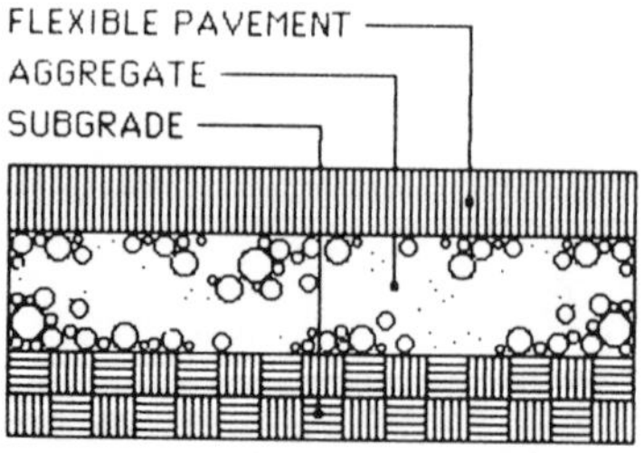
FLEXIBLE PAVEMENT
AGGREGATE
SUBGRADE

FLEXIBLE PAVEMENT THICKNESS (IN.)

Subgrade	4-Ton Wheel Load	6-Ton Wheel Load	8-Ton Wheel Load
Soft Clay	15.0	18.0	21.0
Sandy Clay	8.0	9.0	10.5
Gravel & Clay	5.5	6.5	8.0
Gravel	4.5	5.5	7.5

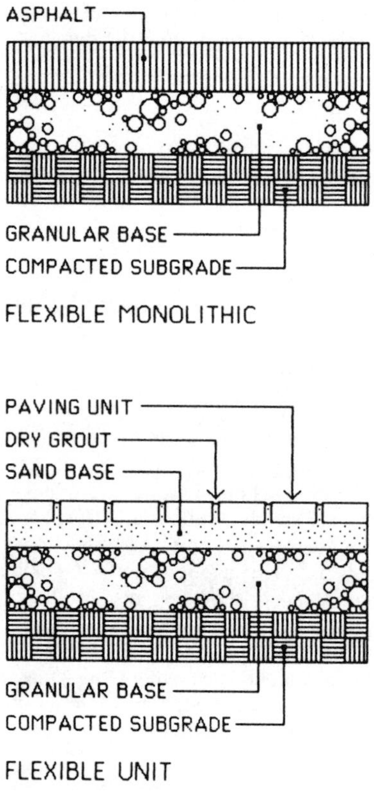
ASPHALT
GRANULAR BASE
COMPACTED SUBGRADE
FLEXIBLE MONOLITHIC
PAVING UNIT
DRY GROUT
SAND BASE
GRANULAR BASE
COMPACTED SUBGRADE
FLEXIBLE UNIT

Figure 440-2 Flexible Pavement Structure. Flexible pavements are somewhat resilient and do not distribute imposed loads over an area as broadly as do rigid pavements. Therefore, flexible pavements require thicker aggregate bases than do rigid pavements, given the same design load. Expansion joints are not generally necessary.

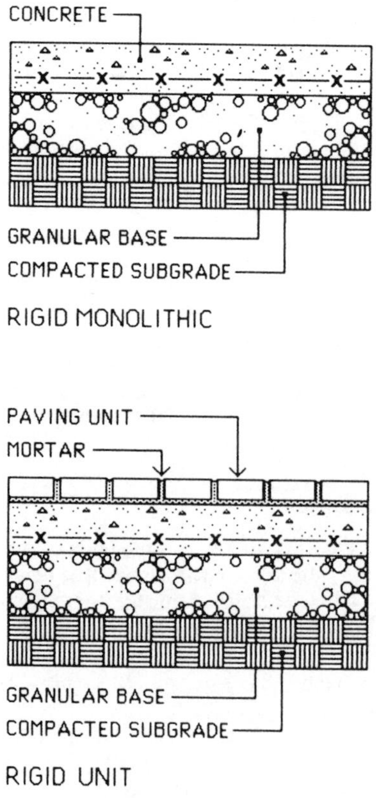
CONCRETE
GRANULAR BASE
COMPACTED SUBGRADE
RIGID MONOLITHIC
PAVING UNIT
MORTAR
GRANULAR BASE
COMPACTED SUBGRADE
RIGID UNIT

Figure 440-3 Rigid Pavement Structure. Note that aggregate bases do not need to be as thick as with flexible pavements, given the same design load. Expansion joints are necessary.

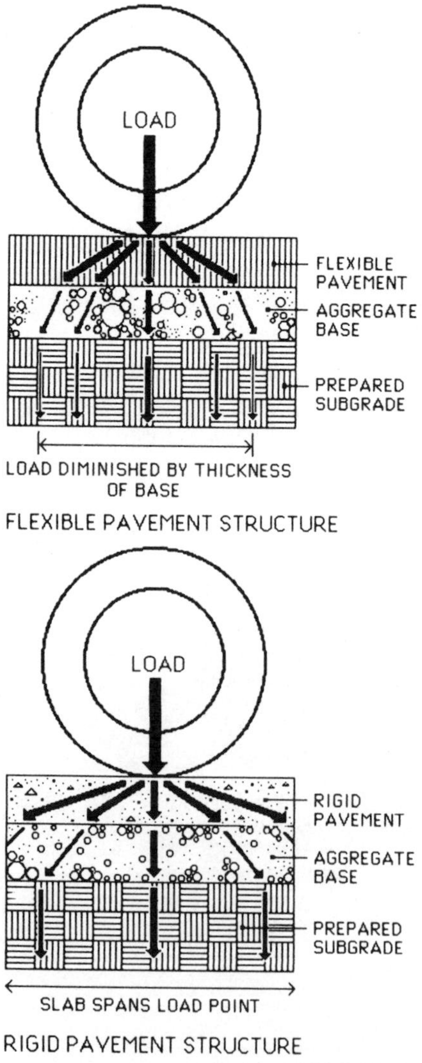
LOAD
FLEXIBLE PAVEMENT
AGGREGATE BASE
PREPARED SUBGRADE
LOAD DIMINISHED BY THICKNESS OF BASE
FLEXIBLE PAVEMENT STRUCTURE
LOAD
RIGID PAVEMENT
AGGREGATE BASE
PREPARED SUBGRADE
SLAB SPANS LOAD POINT
RIGID PAVEMENT STRUCTURE

Figure 440-4 Load Distribution through Pavements. Note that rigid pavements distribute the imposed load over a broader area than do flexible pavements.

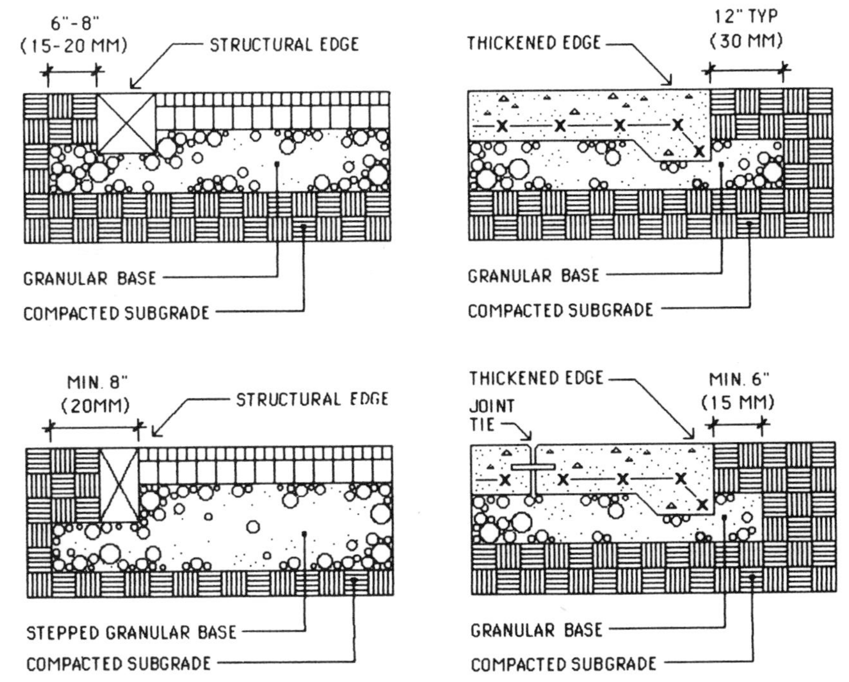

6"-8"
(15-20 MM)
STRUCTURAL EDGE
GRANULAR BASE
COMPACTED SUBGRADE
12" TYP
THICKENED EDGE
(30 MM)
GRANULAR BASE
COMPACTED SUBGRADE
MIN. 8"
(20MM)
STRUCTURAL EDGE
STEPPED GRANULAR BASE
COMPACTED SUBGRADE
THICKENED EDGE
MIN. 6"
JOINT
TIE
(15 MM)
GRANULAR BASE
COMPACTED SUBGRADE

Figure 440-5 Pavement Edge Reinforcement. Pavement edges (both perimeter and joints) require extra reinforcing to prevent breaking or crumbling.

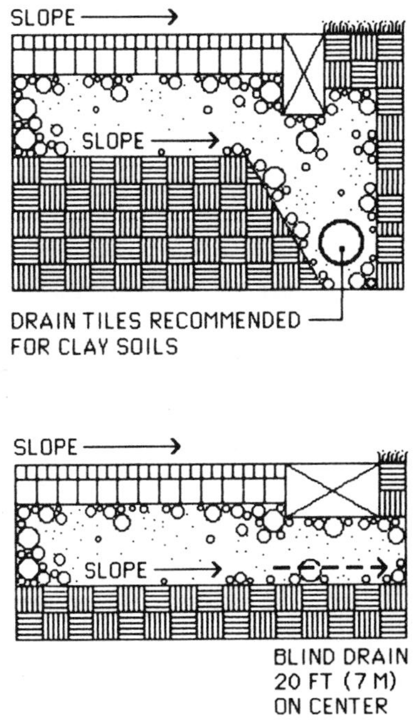

SLOPE
SLOPE
DRAIN TILES RECOMMENDED
FOR CLAY SOILS
SLOPE
SLOPE
BLIND DRAIN
20 FT (7 M)
ON CENTER

Figure 440-6 Edges for Expansive or Moist Soils. Note that the subgrade on these two details must be sloped for positive drainage.

Pavement Edge:

Pavement edges (both perimeters and joints) require extra reinforcing to prevent breaking or crumbling. This is accomplished in both rigid and flexible pavements by extending the subbase beyond the finished pavement edge (Figures 440-5 and 440-6). Additionally, flexible pavements may be edged with wood, steel, stone, or masonry curbs (raised or flush) for additional lateral support. Rigid pavements may be reinforced and thickened at the edge. (Refer to Division 900: Details and Devices, for several examples of paving details.)

Figure 440-6 illustrates special edge detailing for use in moist or expansive soils.

TABLE 440-2
Pavement Purpose and Design Loads

Description	*Static wheel load—highway, lb*	*Static wheel load—street or road, lb*
Heavy-duty, primary highways for freight, metropolitan districts	13,000–14,000	10,000–11,000
Medium traffic routes, uniform passenger and commercial vehicles	11,000–12,000	8,000–9,000
Lightly traveled primary route	10,000–11,000	
Secondary arterial and feeder routes serving main arterial system	9,000–10,000	
Streets and roads carrying little traffic, residential areas		5,000–6,000
Small park roads carrying light maintenance and passenger vehicles*		4,000–5,000
Large walkways in institutional settings*		2,000–4,000

* Extrapolated by author.

Source: Adapted from Elwyn E. Seelye, *Design: Data Book for Civil Engineers,* Wiley, New York, 1960.

2.0 PAVEMENT DESIGN CRITERIA

2.1 Function

The function of a pavement will determine its thickness, the material to be used (to some extent), and the area required.

Load-Bearing Ability:

Table 440-2 illustrates the range of wheel loads accommodated by various levels of use. Typical site scale developments require pavements that accommodate loads from 2000 to 6000 lb (900 to 2700 kg). In institutional or similar settings, careful consideration should be given to walkways that may serve as routes for emergency, maintenance, or other types of vehicles.

TABLE 440-3
Asphalt Pavement Thicknesses for Parking Areas

	Passenger cars		
Subgrade	*Bituminous surface, in*	*Base course, in**	*Subbase, in†*
Gravelly or sandy soils, well-drained	1–3	4	
Fine-grained soils, slight to nonplastic	2–3	4	
Fine-grained soils, plastic	2–3	4	4

* Base course assumed to have a CBR of at least 70.

† Subbase-bank-run aggregate: CBR 40–60.

Notes: (1) A 5-in concrete slab would accommodate up to 6000-lb wheel loads on all three soils. In fine-grained, plastic soils subject to frost, a granular base of 4 in would be required for drainage. (2) A 4-in concrete slab would accommodate up to 4000-lb wheel loads or all three soils, and would require a granular base in plastic soils.

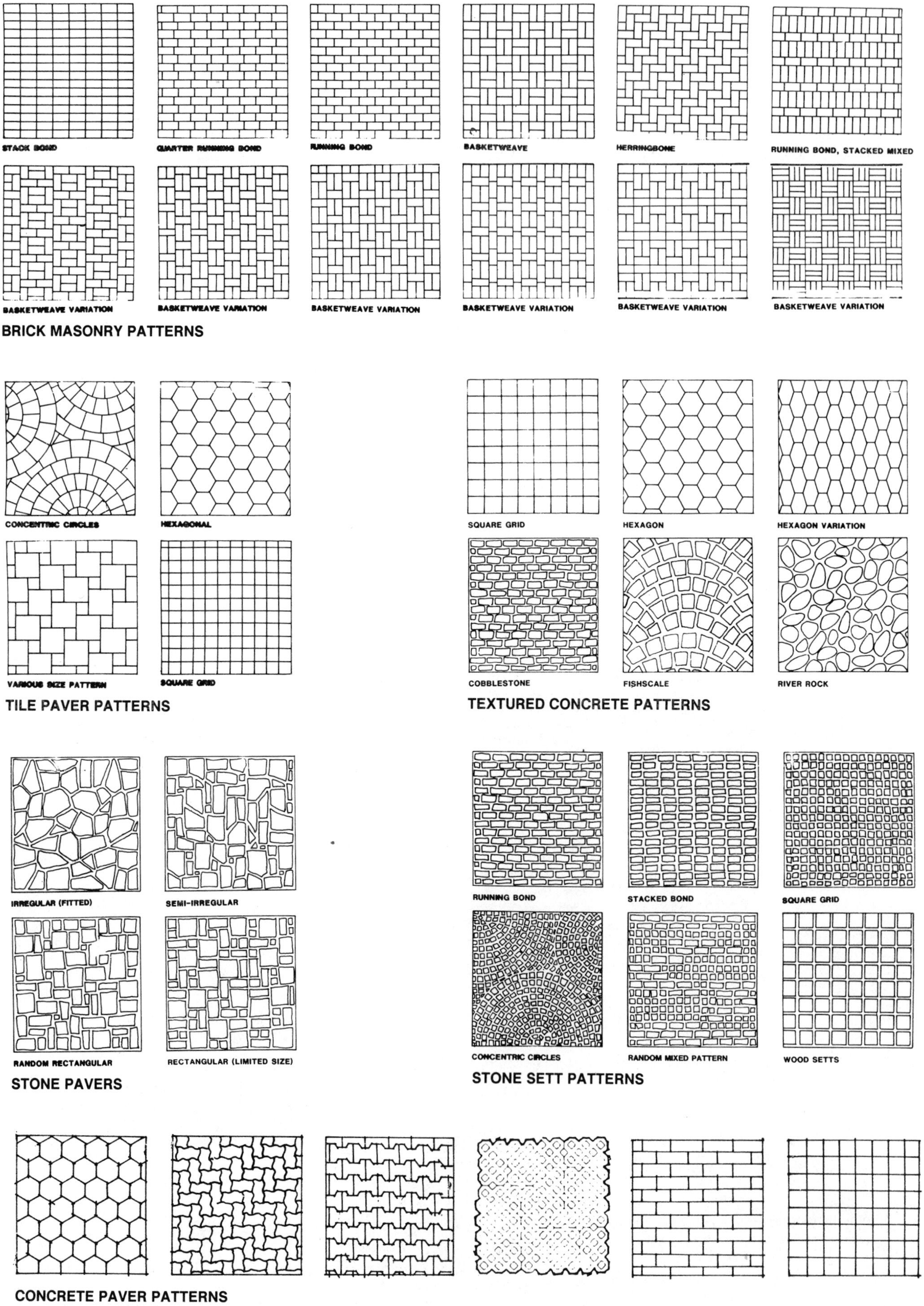
STACK BOND
QUARTER RUNNING BOND
RUNNING BOND
BASKETWEAVE
HERRINGBONE
RUNNING BOND, STACKED MIXED
BASKETWEAVE VARIATION
BASKETWEAVE VARIATION
BASKETWEAVE VARIATION
BASKETWEAVE VARIATION
BASKETWEAVE VARIATION
BASKETWEAVE VARIATION
BRICK MASONRY PATTERNS
CONCENTRIC CIRCLES
HEXAGONAL
VARIOUS SIZE PATTERN
SQUARE GRID
TILE PAVER PATTERNS
SQUARE GRID
HEXAGON
HEXAGON VARIATION
COBBLESTONE
FISHSCALE
RIVER ROCK
TEXTURED CONCRETE PATTERNS
IRREGULAR (FITTED)
SEMI-IRREGULAR
RANDOM RECTANGULAR
RECTANGULAR (LIMITED SIZE)
STONE PAVERS
RUNNING BOND
STACKED BOND
SQUARE GRID
CONCENTRIC CIRCLES
RANDOM MIXED PATTERN
WOOD SETTS
STONE SETT PATTERNS
CONCRETE PAVER PATTERNS

Figure 440-7 Typical pavement patterns.

Such walkways should be designed to support weights of at least 2000 to 4000 lb (900 to 1800 kg), with special attention given to edge reinforcement. Such loads can be supported by 1 to 3 in (25 to 76 mm) of bituminous concrete on 4- to 8-in (100- to 200-mm) bases, or by 4 in (100 mm) of reinforced concrete on a 4- to 6-in (100- to 150-mm) base.

Table 440-3 lists recommended thicknesses for bituminous parking areas.

Durability:

Several factors influence the durability of a paving material. These include climatic factors (such as precipitation and temperature), the quality of site preparation, the specific construction materials used, and the quality of skilled work involved. Pavements that are properly installed and constructed of high-quality materials can nevertheless wear out or disintegrate if subjected to unplanned extremes of heavy traffic or if improperly maintained. Pavement selection requires a careful analysis of all factors involved.

Safety:

Some pavements require high traction ratings, such as those used for access ramps or used in areas of icy conditions, while others require a smoother surface in order to prevent hazards to handicapped individuals or to facilitate the use of wheeled carts and the like. Highly textured pavements usually require steeper slopes for drainage (i.e., 2 percent minimum).

A pavement must fulfill its design purpose in all types of weather conditions that affect a particular site (i.e., significant snow or ice conditions requiring plowing equipment or chemical applications).

2.2 Aesthetics

In addition to issues of a purely subjective nature, it is important to remember that pavement color affects the degree to which heat and light are absorbed or reflected. Glare and heat absorption are qualities that require consideration in many instances.

The potential for achieving richly detailed patterns and earth-toned colors make unit pavers a very popular pavement type. Figure 440-7 illustrates several commonly used paving patterns.

2.3 Costs

Pavement costs must be analyzed on both a short-term and a long-term basis. Cost factors include initial installation, maintenance, durability, and repairability. For instance, a nonunit pavement that is difficult to repair is seldom a good choice in areas

TABLE 440-4
Pavement Checklist*

Type of paving	*Advantages*	*Disadvantages*
In-situ paving		
Concrete	▪ Relatively easy to install ▪ Available with several finishes, many colors, and various textures ▪ Durable surface ▪ Year-round and multiple usage ▪ Low lifetime maintenance costs ▪ Long-lasting ▪ Low heat absorbency ▪ Hard, nonresilient surface ▪ Adaptable to curvilinear forms	▪ Joints are required ▪ Some surfaces are aesthetically unappealing ▪ Can disintegrate if not properly installed ▪ Difficult to color evenly and permanently ▪ Light color is reflective and can cause glare ▪ Some types can deteriorate from deicing salts ▪ Relatively low tensile strength; can crack easily ▪ Low resiliency
Asphalt	▪ Low heat and light reflectivity ▪ Year-round and multiple use ▪ Durable ▪ Low maintenance costs ▪ Dust-free surface ▪ Resiliency can vary depending on mixture ▪ Water repellent surface ▪ Adaptable to curvilinear forms ▪ Can be made porous	▪ Will fray at edges if not supported ▪ Can soften in warm weather ▪ Soluble by gasoline, kerosene, and other petroleum solvents ▪ Susceptible to freeze damage if water penetrates the base
Synthetic surfacing systems (proprietary)	▪ Can be designed for a specific purpose (e.g., court games, track) ▪ Wide color range ▪ More resilient than concrete or asphalt ▪ Sometimes can be applied over old concrete or asphalt	▪ Specially trained labor may be required for installation and repair ▪ More costly than asphalt or concrete
Unit paving		
Brick	▪ Nonglare surface ▪ Nonskid surface ▪ Wide color range ▪ Good scale ▪ Easily repaired	▪ High installation cost ▪ Difficult to clean ▪ Can disintegrate in freezing weather ▪ Susceptible to differential settlement ▪ Efflorescence
Titles	▪ Polished indoor/outdoor appearance	▪ Suitable only for milder climates ▪ High installation cost
Adobe blocks	▪ Fast and easy installation ▪ Can last indefinitely if base contains an adequate amount of asphaltic stabilizer ▪ Rich color and texture	▪ Tend to crumble at the edges ▪ Store considerable amounts of heat ▪ Fragile; require level foundations (fracture easily) ▪ Dusty ▪ Suitable only for warm and nonhumid areas
Flagstones	▪ Very durable if properly installed ▪ Natural weathering qualities	▪ Moderately expensive to install ▪ Might seem cold, hard, or quarry-like in appearance ▪ Color and random pattern sometimes difficult to work with aesthetically ▪ Can become smooth and slippery when wet or worn

(Continued)

TABLE 440-4 *(Continued)*

Type of paving	*Advantages*	*Disadvantages*
Granite	■ Hard and dense ■ Very durable under extreme weathering conditions ■ Will support heavy traffic ■ Can be polished to a hard gloss surface that is durable and easily cleaned	■ Hard and dense; difficult to work with ■ Some types are subject to a high rate of chemical weathering ■ Relatively expensive
Limestone	■ Easy to work with ■ Rich color and texture	■ Susceptible to chemical weathering (especially in humid climates and urban environments)
Sandstone	■ Easy to work with ■ Durable	Same as limestone
Slate	■ Durable ■ Slow to weather ■ Range of colors	■ Relatively expensive ■ Can be slippery when wet
Molded units (synthetic)	■ Can be designed or selected for various purposes (i.e., firm, soft) ■ Short installation time ■ Easy installation, removal, and replacement usually without specialized labor ■ Wide color range	■ Subject to vandalism ■ Higher installation costs than asphalt or concrete
Soft paving		
Aggregates	■ Economical surfacing material ■ Range of colors	■ Requires replenishment every few years depending on amount of use ■ Potential for weeds ■ Requires edging
Organic materials	■ Relatively inexpensive ■ Compatible with natural surroundings ■ Quiet, comfortable walking surface	■ Suitable only for light traffic ■ Requires periodic replenishment or replacement
Turfgrass	■ Colorful ■ Nonabrasive ■ Dust-free ■ Good drainage characteristics ■ Quiet, comfortable walking surface ■ Ideal for many types of recreation ■ Relatively low installation costs	■ Difficult and expensive to maintain, especially in areas of heavy use
Turf blocks	■ Same as turf alone but has added stability to withstand light vehicular loads	■ Requires high levels of maintenance (frequent watering, etc.)
Artificial turf	■ Instant turf surface ■ Can be used sooner after rains without wet spots ■ Allows flat grading of playing surface ■ Available with built-in markings, etc. ■ No irrigation or maintenance problems as with natural turfgrass	■ Results in a higher number of player injuries (regarding field sports) ■ Results in faster and higher ball roll and bounce ■ Initial installation costs higher than natural turfgrass

* No one surface will meet the needs of all outdoor activities. Each activity has its own surface requirements that determine which types of materials are suitable.

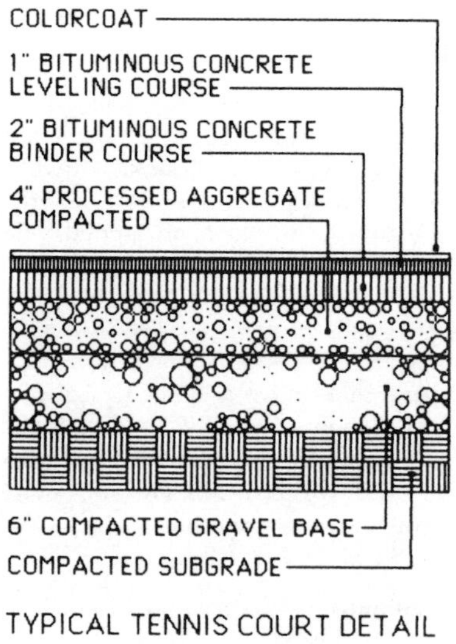
COLORCOAT
1" BITUMINOUS CONCRETE LEVELING COURSE
2" BITUMINOUS CONCRETE BINDER COURSE
4" PROCESSED AGGREGATE COMPACTED
6" COMPACTED GRAVEL BASE
COMPACTED SUBGRADE
TYPICAL TENNIS COURT DETAIL

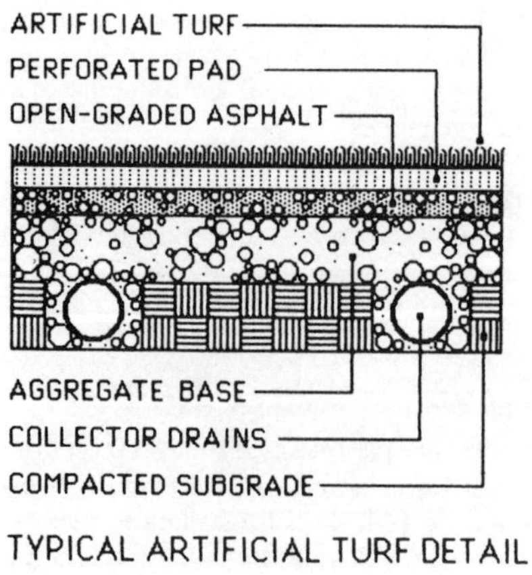
ARTIFICIAL TURF
PERFORATED PAD
OPEN-GRADED ASPHALT
AGGREGATE BASE
COLLECTOR DRAINS
COMPACTED SUBGRADE
TYPICAL ARTIFICIAL TURF DETAIL

Figure 440-8 Typical proprietary surface details.

TABLE 440-5
Proprietary Surfaces

Category of use generic names	*Comments on material and ranges of uses*	*Proprietary names and sources*
Synthetic emulsions		
Bonding agents	Specialized compounds used to bond one material to another, i.e., waterproof membrane to roof slab	There are too many trade names and manufacturers to attempt to list here.
Cushion coats	Special compounds of rubber granules, acrylic polymer with elastomers, and resin particles or fibers. Manufacturers recommend thickness or number of layers for various purposes.	Plexicushion (R) By Calif. Products Corp. Elasta Cushion (R) by Julicher Athletic Engineering & Constructors
Wearing or weathering surfaces	Special compounds put over cushion coat or other materials to improve resistance to wear and weathering. Typically, several layers are needed and finish color and texture are incorporated into these.	Cushion Court (R) by: Julicher Athletic Engineering & Constructors Flexipave by California Products Corp. Asitrak or Asitex (R) by Athletic Surfacing International Acrylo-Kote (R) by Koch Asphalt Co.
Striping, painting, or resurfacing	Special compounds or paints used by hand or machine to create striping or for adding color for other purposes	Plexicolor, Acrylic Line Paint or Acrylic Resurfacer (R) by Calif. Product Corp. Acrylo-line Paint (R) by Koch Asphalt Co.
Synthetic surfacing systems	A combination of synthetic materials placed in layers with each layer serving a distinct function to form a final specified surface	Asitrak (R) by Athletic Surfacing International Acrylic Surface by Koch Asphalt Co.
Preformed materials		
Artificial turf	Developed to provide a substitute for natural turf. It is generally made of nylon or other synthetics.	Astroturf (R) by Monsanto Co. All-pro Turf (R) by All-Pro Athetic Surfaces Courturf (R) by Julicher Ahtletic Engineering & Constructors
Artificial ice	A synthetic material used as an alternative to natural or refrigerated ice. For ice or roller skating, certain court games, dancing, etc.	Lenn-ice (R) by Julicher Athletic Engineering & Constructors
Synthetic units or sheets and rolls	Molded modular or sheet material used to create hard sufaces for court games, track, decks around pools, etc. Can be made porous to permit drainage.	Multideck (R) by Julicher Athletic Engineering & Constructors Duragrid (R) by Duragrid Inc. Sportan (R) by Sportan Surfaces Inc. Cal-track, Plexicourt, and Plex-tac (R) by Calif. Products Corp.

subject to damage, or where access to underground utilities, etc., may be required.

Long-term maintenance involves such cost considerations as repairability, specialized equipment (sweepers, washers, etc.), periodic cleanings, and coatings.

Table 440-4 lists the advantages and disadvantages of various types of pavement.

3.0 PROPRIETARY SURFACES

As noted at the beginning of this section, Divisions 800: Materials, and 900: Details and Devices, contain technical data on various materials and their application in pavement construction.

A number of proprietary surfaces not covered in either of these two divisions are briefly listed in Table 440-5, grouped according to categories of use. These materials are normally purchased in ready-mixed or manufactured form and sometimes have to be installed by licensed contractors. In this table, generic names have been used, followed by proprietary names. (Note that the use of these trade names and of the names of various manufacturers or distributors is only for the convenience of the reader. The use of these names does not constitute an endorsement of any product or service to the exclusion of others that may be equal or superior in quality.)

It should be noted that the variety of proprietary products available and the range of application to which these materials can be used will continue to expand in years to come. The reader is urged to keep abreast of these changes via trade journals and via the literature supplied by various manufacturers. See Figure 440-8 for some typical proprietary surface details.

REFERENCES

Callender, John (ed.). *Time-Saver Standards for Architectural Design Data,* 5th ed. McGraw-Hill, New York, 1974.

Carpenter, Jot. *Handbook of Landscape Architectural Construction,* Landscape Architecture Foundation, MacLean, 1976.

Church, Thomas. *Gardens Are for People,* Reinhold, New York, 1955.

Halprin, Lawrence. *Cities,* MIT Press, Cambridge, Mass., 1972.

Lynch, Kevin, and Gary Hack. *Site Planning,* 3d ed., MIT Press, Cambridge, Mass., 1984.

Ramsey/Sleeper. *Architectural Graphic Standards,* 7th ed., Robert T. Packard (ed.), Wiley, New York, 1981.

Walker, Theodore D. *Site Design and Construction Detailing,* PDA Publishers, West Lafayette, Ind., 1978. ■

section 450: Fences, Screens, and Walls

CREDITS

Contributor:

Don Hilderbrandt and Patrick Mullaly
Land Design/Research, Inc.
Columbia, Maryland

Assistants:

David R. Holden
Cynthia L. Riemer
Charles H. Shaw, Jr.
Anne Coward
Lori Flemm
Nancy Takahashi
Thomas W. Snyder
Mark Hilderbrandt

Reviewer:

Kenneth DeMay
Sasaki Associates, Inc.
Watertown, Massachusetts

CONTENTS

1.0 INTRODUCTION

1.1 General

Fences, screens, and walls are used for a variety of reasons, including visual privacy, the physical exclusion or control of people and animals, the modification of environmental factors such as noise, wind, and sunlight, and purely aesthetic reasons. The design of such barriers should respond not only to functional requirements but also to the aesthetic qualities of the site. Some of the major purposes of fences, screens, and walls are described below.

1.2 Major Purposes of Fences, Screens, and Walls

Privacy:

Privacy implies a degree of protection against visual and/or physical intrusion. The extent of privacy desired and its context will greatly influence the design and materials used for privacy barriers.

Obscuring or completely blocking views from adjacent land is a primary way to achieve a sense of privacy. The most effective privacy barrier is often a high, solid barrier as close as possible to the source of intrusion (Figure 450-1).

Safety and Security:

Barriers can discourage deliberate trespassing, keep people away from such potentially dangerous items as mechanical equipment, electric transformers, or swim-

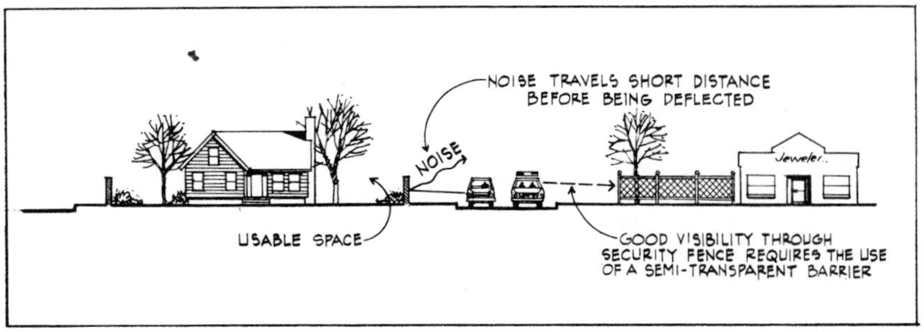
NOISE TRAVELS SHORT DISTANCE BEFORE BEING DEFLECTED
NOISE
USABLE SPACE
GOOD VISIBILITY THROUGH SECURITY FENCE REQUIRES THE USE OF A SEMI-TRANSPARENT BARRIER

Figure 450-1 Placement of privacy barriers.

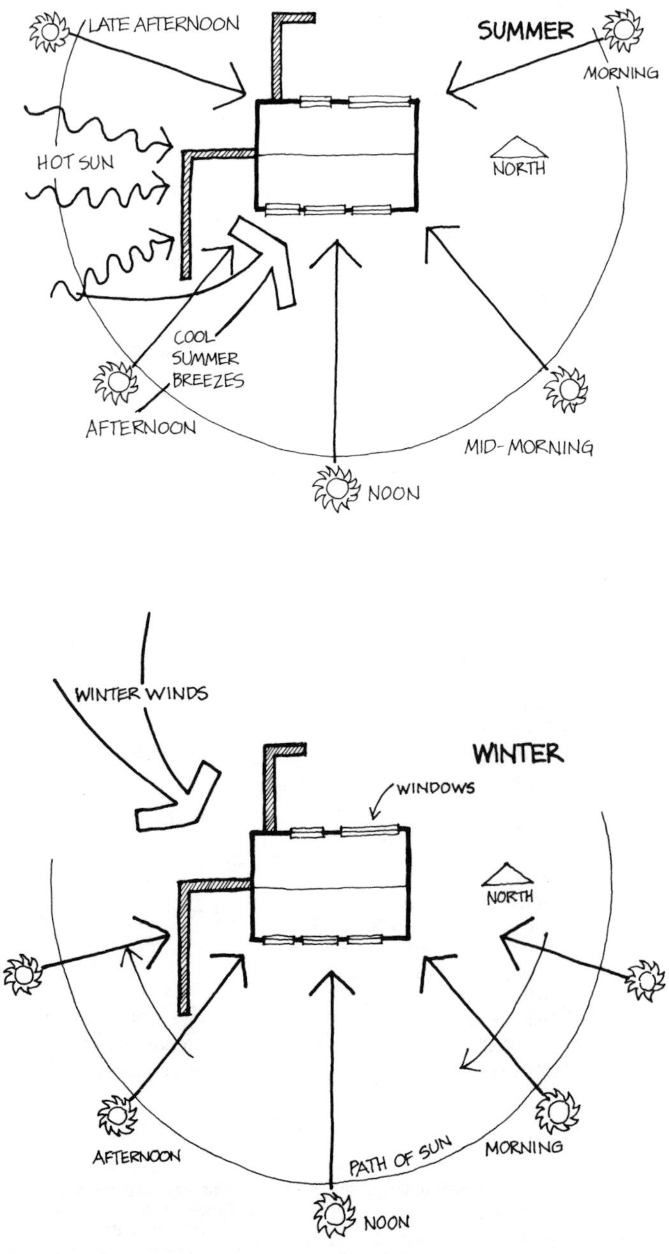
LATE AFTERNOON
SUMMER
MORNING
HOT SUN
NORTH
COOL SUMMER BREEZES
AFTERNOON
MID-MORNING
NOON
WINTER WINDS
WINTER
WINDOWS
NORTH
AFTERNOON
PATH OF SUN
MORNING
NOON

Figure 450-2 Barriers for Environmental Modification. Fences, screens, and walls can be used to alter microclimatic qualities of a space in several ways. Example here refers to the northern hemisphere.

ming pools, and keep children and/or animals in safe areas.

Transparent or semitransparent barriers are sometimes preferable to completely solid barriers because they permit supervision from either side by property owners, police, or security personnel. If solid barriers are used they should be truly impenetrable, because once inside, an intruder may be more protected than an owner.

Boundary Definition:

Defining boundaries to prevent or discourage trespassing is one of the most common uses of fences and walls.

Circulation Control:

Barriers can control and direct the movement of people, animals, or vehicles. Low walls can channel or direct pedestrian traffic, but walls should be designed to discourage unauthorized or unsafe shortcuts. It is often desirable to see over a wall or fence to know what is ahead or what may be approaching.

A gate or portal can be designed to be intentionally uninviting, implying *Stay Out,* or may simply be designed as a symbolic entryway, inviting people into a space.

Environmental Modification:

Barriers can reduce or eliminate unpleasant nuisances, such as heavy winds, noise, drifting snow, glare, and strong sunlight. Strategically placed windbreaks and shaded areas can reduce the energy required for heating and cooling (Figure 450-2). Snow fences can control drifting and thus mitigate snow removal problems. (Refer to Section 260: Climate and Energy, for specific information on modification of microclimate, etc.)

Aesthetics:

Often such structures as fences, screens, or walls can complement their architectural surroundings by extending the lines of a building out into the landscape. They can also be used to dramatize selected views, form backdrops for specific settings, or add interest to an otherwise featureless or monotonous landscape. In most cases, fences or walls should be visually attractive on both sides.

2.0 DESIGN CRITERIA

2.1 Meeting Stated Needs

The *purpose* of any particular barrier and the *degree of exclusion* necessary will largely determine the type, size, and materials needed. The following are considerations:

1. Whether the barrier is to be only an aesthetic feature or a practical boundary
2. Whether the barrier is to provide a strong sense of privacy or security
3. Whether the barrier is to be solid or allow some degree of visual accessibility
4. Whether the barrier is to be in harmony with other features
5. Whether areas near the barrier are to be planted
6. Whether to plant heavily or only for accent

The layout and purpose of fences, screens, and walls should be coordinated with both grading and planting plans. In many cases, planting and/or grading can accomplish the same purpose as a fence or wall, may be more economical to construct, and may require less long-term maintenance.

Site Context:

Design objectives for fences, screens, and walls are merely abstract concepts until they are related to the larger site context in which they must be achieved. For instance, security for a factory or a retail store would normally require far more elaborate solutions than security for a home. A solution would also be different in a city than it would be on a large suburban or rural site.

Off-Site Impacts:

Poorly styled or improperly built fences, screens, or walls can detract from the appearance of adjacent properties, become a nuisance for neighbors by blocking views, cut off desired local breezes, or create unwanted shade (Figure 450-3). Large walls can alter stormwater runoff patterns on neighboring sites and create annoying ponding or saturation problems. All potentially adverse off-site impacts need to be assessed during the design stages and certainly well before any construction begins.

Temporary Fences:

Barriers can be used temporarily until plants are mature enough to perform their intended function and/or until a later stage of construction is completed. Very short time spans seldom justify the use of expensive materials or construction detailing.

Design Expression:

Choosing a basic fence or wall type is only the first step in developing a successful design solution. Design elements and details which make up the barrier must also be carefully worked out and coordinated.

Compatibility: The design of a fence or wall should respond to its landscape context and adjacent architecture. Compatibility can be enhanced by using the same or similar materials and the same details and proportions of nearby buildings, streetscape elements, and plant materials.

Scale: Large barriers can be scaled down to relate to human scale by the use of textures and shadow lines and by the articulation of individual elements, such as posts, panels, rails, and caps (Figure 450-4).

Proportions: The relationship of the height to the width of panels, post sizing, etc., should be carefully managed to respond to the established design expression of major horizontal or vertical elements nearby (Figure 450-5).

Rhythm: The rhythmic use of such elements as posts, slats, or panels can affect the perceived size or scale of a barrier, especially with regard to perception from a moving vehicle.

Color: Lighter colors tend to call attention to the individual elements of a fence or wall, while darker colors appear to unify the appearance. The number of colors used in a barrier should be kept to a minimum.

Texture: The type of materials used and the kind of finish selected will affect the texture of the barrier. In this regard, both the distance between the barrier and the observer and the speed of the observer (i.e., in a moving vehicle) are major factors to consider.

2.2 Legal and Code Requirements

A proposed barrier or screen must comply with all relevant legal and building code requirements, including:

1. Rights of access
2. Health and safety
3. Design and aesthetic controls

Boundaries:

Before construction begins, property lines should be precisely determined to prevent possible legal disputes. If necessary, a boundary survey should be made by a registered surveyor.

Easements:

Utility and drainage easements across a site generally preclude using those areas

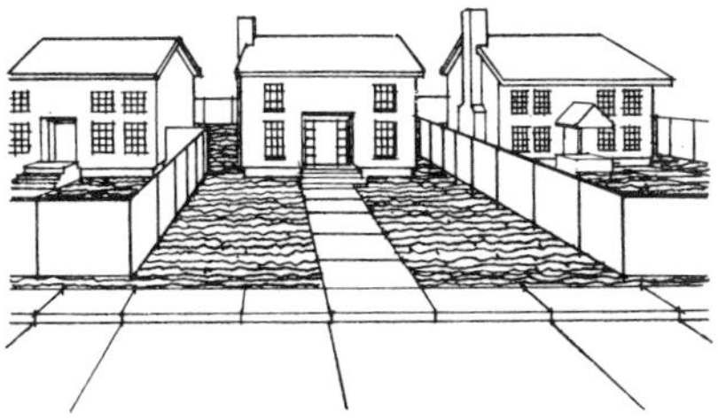

Figure 450-3 Problem of Off-Site Impacts. In this example, a residence is fenced in, contrary to desires.

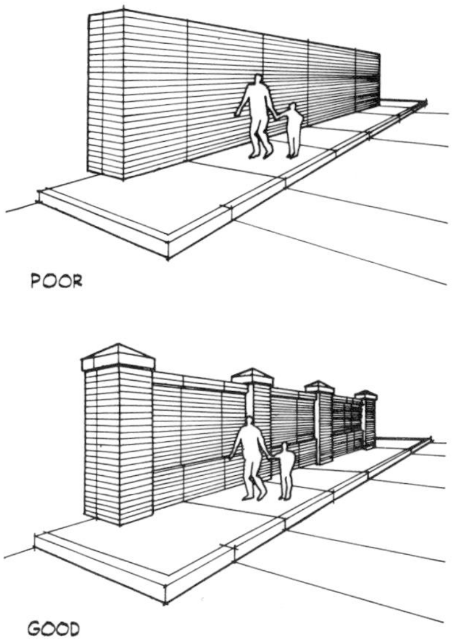
POOR
GOOD

Figure 450-4 Reduction of apparent scale of a wall by use of textures, shadow lines, and articulation of details.

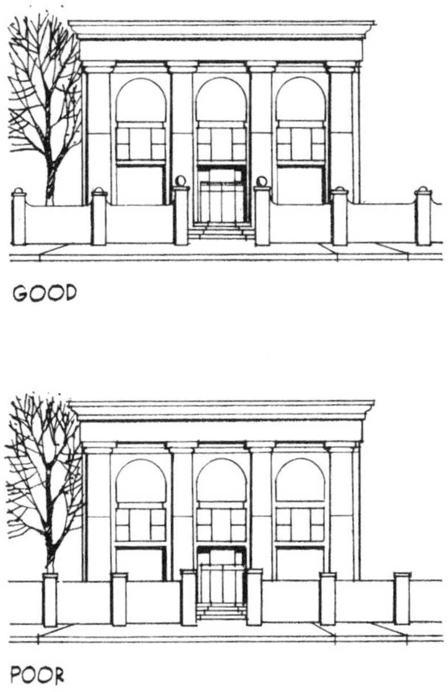
GOOD
POOR

Figure 450-5 Relationship between fence or wall and adjacent structures.

for permanent walls or fences, but nonpermanent or moveable features are usually permitted.

Fire Lanes and Police Surveillance:

Fire and police departments require readily identifiable, barrier-free access to certain types of sites. For instance, they require easy access to mid- or high-rise buildings and to buildings or areas where potentially hazardous materials are stored.

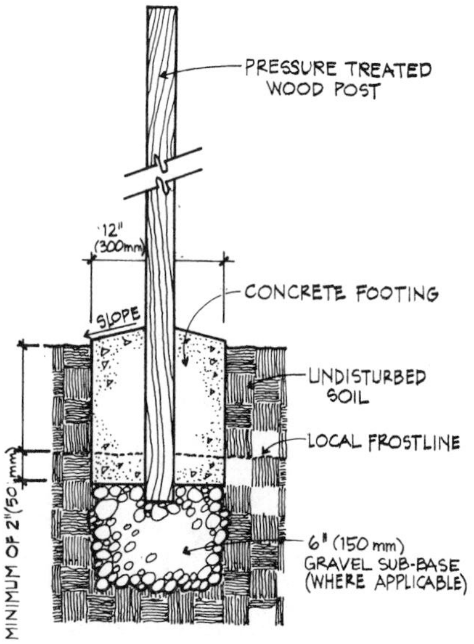
PRESSURE TREATED WOOD POST
12" (300mm)
CONCRETE FOOTING
SLOPE
UNDISTURBED SOIL
LOCAL FROSTLINE
MINIMUM OF 2" (50 mm)
6" (150 mm) GRAVEL SUB-BASE (WHERE APPLICABLE)

Figure 450-6 Typical post footing.

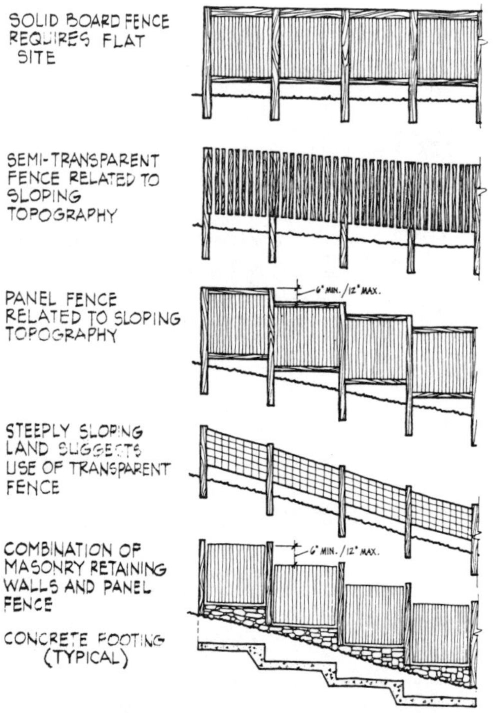
SOLID BOARD FENCE REQUIRES FLAT SITE
SEMI-TRANSPARENT FENCE RELATED TO SLOPING TOPOGRAPHY
PANEL FENCE RELATED TO SLOPING TOPOGRAPHY
6" MIN./12" MAX.
STEEPLY SLOPING LAND SUGGESTS USE OF TRANSPARENT FENCE
COMBINATION OF MASONRY RETAINING WALLS AND PANEL FENCE
6" MIN./12" MAX.
CONCRETE FOOTING (TYPICAL)

Figure 450-7 Methods for responding to terrain.

Permits and Codes:

In many jurisdictions, permits are required for fences and walls beyond a certain height or length. Design minimums or other performance standards for structural integrity, safety, or visual quality may also be included in local building codes. For instance, barriers are mandatory for site facilities such as swimming pool areas, which generally must be enclosed by a fence or wall of a specified height and type.

Design Controls and Covenants:

For purely aesthetic reasons, local legal or quasi-legal regulations may exercise control on the choice of materials and colors and even on the design expression and placement of fences, screens, and walls.

2.3 Feasibility

The feasibility of a proposed barrier should be studied based upon the following factors.

Costs:

Budget decisions about fences or walls should be based upon a careful assessment of both short-term and long-term costs.

As a general rule of thumb, the initial construction cost of building a fence will fall about halfway between the cost of a planted barrier and a masonry wall. However, fences cannot perform all the tasks which walls can, and their costs can vary greatly according to the type of material used, the amount of detailing involved, and the skill of the labor needed to build and maintain them. Furthermore, the long-term maintenance and replacement costs for brick or concrete are much less than for wooden fencing or screening.

Availability of Materials, Labor, and Equipment:

If a particular type of barrier is chosen, the necessary materials, labor, and equipment needed for construction should be readily available at the price estimated.

Time:

Some types of barriers require more time to construct than others, and this can be an especially important consideration on a large project where the construction deadline is short.

Maintenance Responsibility:

The feasibility and ultimate selection of a barrier design should take into consideration who will be responsible and have the funds to maintain the barrier properly over the expected life of the structure.

3.0 CONSTRUCTION METHODS AND DETAILS

The major components for all types of fences and walls, including gates, are presented below. For major structures (such as high masonry walls) in difficult soil conditions, a structural engineer or contractor familiar with local conditions and standard practices should be consulted.

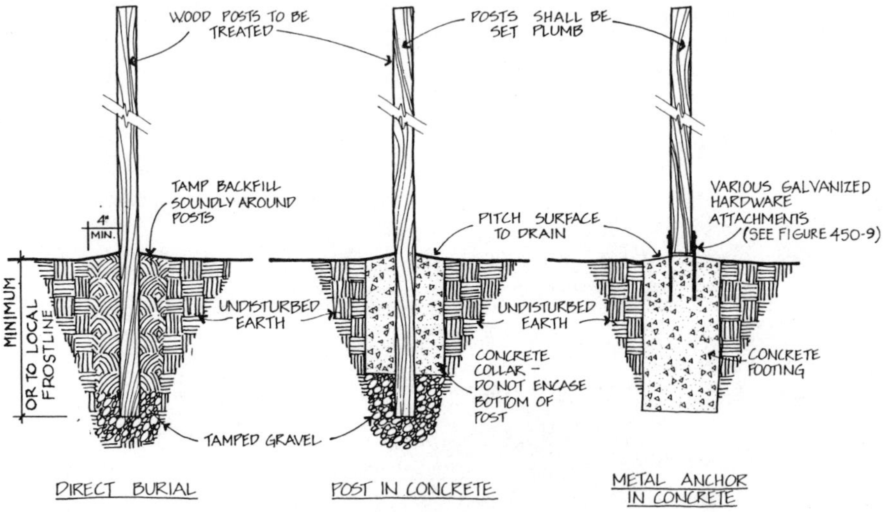
WOOD POSTS TO BE TREATED
POSTS SHALL BE SET PLUMB
TAMP BACKFILL SOUNDLY AROUND POSTS
4" MIN.
PITCH SURFACE TO DRAIN
VARIOUS GALVANIZED HARDWARE ATTACHMENTS (SEE FIGURE 450-9)
MINIMUM OR TO LOCAL FROSTLINE
UNDISTURBED EARTH
UNDISTURBED EARTH
CONCRETE COLLAR - DO NOT ENCASE BOTTOM OF POST
CONCRETE FOOTING
TAMPED GRAVEL
DIRECT BURIAL
POST IN CONCRETE
METAL ANCHOR IN CONCRETE

Figure 450-8 Typical post and footing details.

3.1 Footings and Foundations

Footing Depth:

The depth of a footing or foundation is based upon the following factors:

1. Structural stability (against storm winds, impact, abuse, etc.)
2. Weight of barrier
3. Depth of frostline (Figure 450-6)

The depth of the local frostline is the primary criterion regarding footing or foundation depth. The bottom of footings should be at least 2 in (50 mm) below the frostline to eliminate upward stresses on the structure (Figure 450-6). Natural stresses—such as heavy winds, soil creep on steep slopes, or expansive soils—may dictate even deeper footings or foundations.

Soil Conditions:

Extremely sandy, heavy clay, or very wet soil conditions require special considerations. In some cases the existing soil may have to be replaced.

Drainage:

In cold climates, freeze/thaw processes can cause heaving of posts, footings, and foundations. Periodic or persistent flooding of low spots can accelerate heaving as well as cause decay of wooden posts and damage to foundations.

Surface water should not be allowed to collect but should be drained away from the base of fences, screens, and walls.

Uneven Terrain:

Some types of fences and walls can run parallel to a sloping or rolling landscape, while others require some method of *stepping down.* It is generally easier to step down a fence than a wall (Figure 450-7).

Posts and Footings:

Wooden fence posts are typically 4 in × 4 in (100 mm × 100 mm) with 6-in × 6-in (150-mm × 150-mm) posts at corners for added stability and/or for structural reasons. Various methods are employed to set posts in the ground (Figure 450-8). In some cases it is better to fasten wood or metal posts to concrete footings with standard fastenings (Figure 450-9). Decay-resistant wood or wood preservatives should be used.

Masonry walls require continuous footings, which are generally horizontal slabs of reinforced concrete poured in place. The wall is then built upon these footings (Figure 450-10).

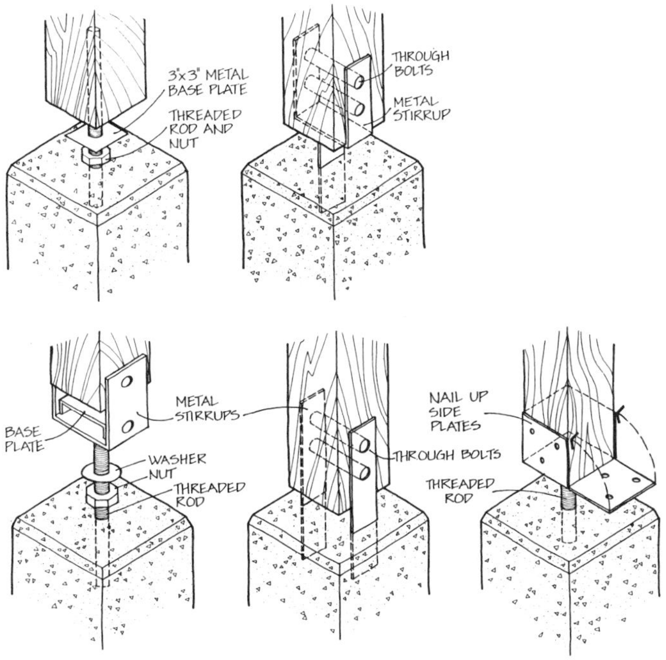
3"x3" METAL BASE PLATE
THREADED ROD AND NUT
THROUGH BOLTS
METAL STIRRUP
BASE PLATE
METAL STIRRUPS
WASHER NUT
THREADED ROD
THROUGH BOLTS
NAIL UP SIDE PLATES
THREADED ROD

Figure 450-9 Typical post-to-footing connections.

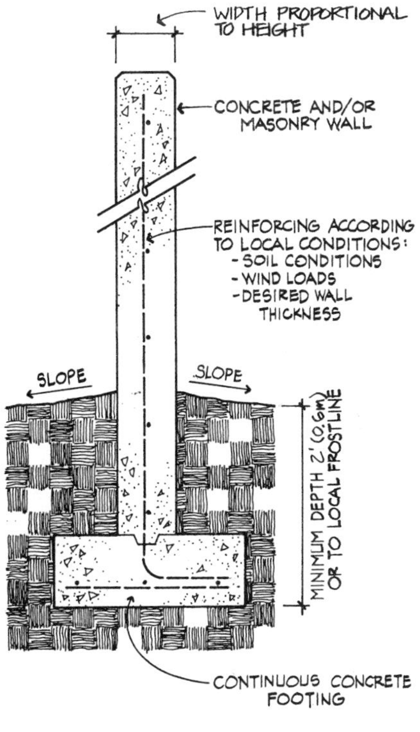
WIDTH PROPORTIONAL TO HEIGHT
CONCRETE AND/OR MASONRY WALL
REINFORCING ACCORDING TO LOCAL CONDITIONS:
- SOIL CONDITIONS
- WIND LOADS
- DESIRED WALL THICKNESS
SLOPE
SLOPE
MINIMUM DEPTH 2' (0.6m) OR TO LOCAL FROSTLINE
CONTINUOUS CONCRETE FOOTING

Figure 450-10 Continuous-footing construction.

3.2 Wooden Fences and Screens

Structural Framework:

Horizontal rails attached to posts make a basic structural frame for supporting pickets, plywood panels, or other wooden fencings (Figure 450-11). Caps can be added for visual appeal and/or to keep water off of the tops of posts or other structural elements (Figure 450-12).

Wood Preservatives and Finishes:

Chemical preservatives are typically used to prolong the life of a wooden fence or screen, particularly its posts. If pressure-treated, the wood fibers should be saturated with the preservative. Preservative can also be painted on or soaked into the wood.

Vertical facing members should never touch the ground. In some cases, drainage

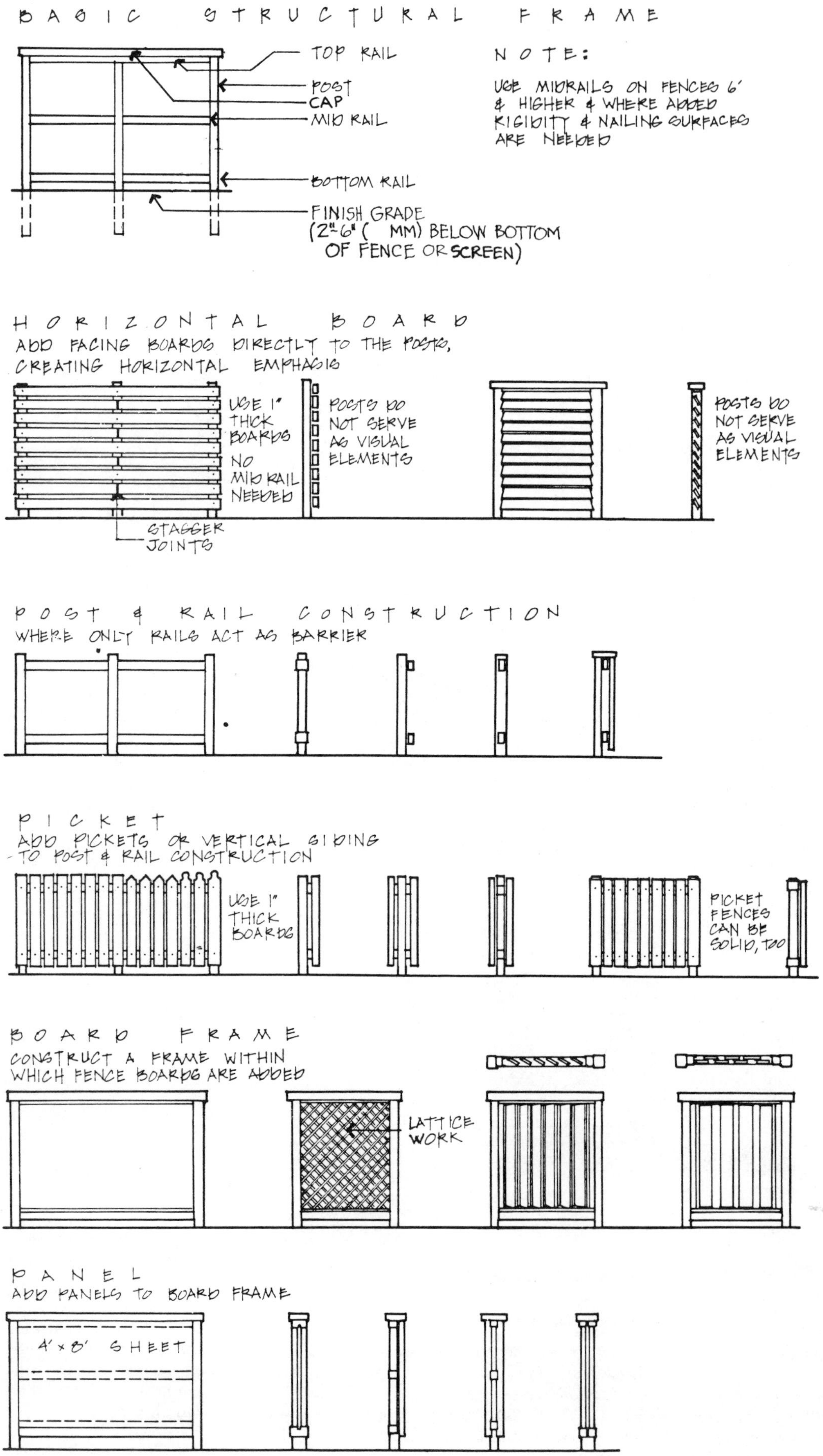
BASIC STRUCTURAL FRAME
TOP RAIL
POST
CAP
MID RAIL
BOTTOM RAIL
FINISH GRADE (2"-6" (MM) BELOW BOTTOM OF FENCE OR SCREEN)
NOTE:
USE MIDRAILS ON FENCES 6' & HIGHER & WHERE ADDED RIGIDITY & NAILING SURFACES ARE NEEDED
HORIZONTAL BOARD
ADD FACING BOARDS DIRECTLY TO THE POSTS, CREATING HORIZONTAL EMPHASIS
USE 1" THICK BOARDS
NO MID RAIL NEEDED
STAGGER JOINTS
POSTS DO NOT SERVE AS VISUAL ELEMENTS
POSTS DO NOT SERVE AS VISUAL ELEMENTS
POST & RAIL CONSTRUCTION
WHERE ONLY RAILS ACT AS BARRIER
PICKET
ADD PICKETS OR VERTICAL SIDING TO POST & RAIL CONSTRUCTION
USE 1" THICK BOARDS
PICKET FENCES CAN BE SOLID, TOO
BOARD FRAME
CONSTRUCT A FRAME WITHIN WHICH FENCE BOARDS ARE ADDED
LATTICE WORK
PANEL
ADD PANELS TO BOARD FRAME
4' x 8' SHEET

Figure 450-11 Various types of fence construction.

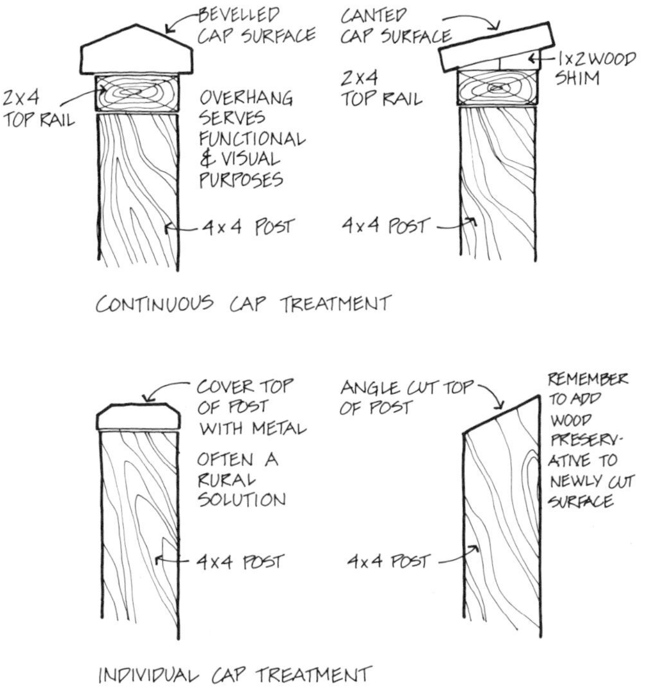
BEVELLED CAP SURFACE
CANTED CAP SURFACE
2x4 TOP RAIL
OVERHANG SERVES FUNCTIONAL & VISUAL PURPOSES
2x4 TOP RAIL
1x2 WOOD SHIM
4x4 POST
4x4 POST
CONTINUOUS CAP TREATMENT
COVER TOP OF POST WITH METAL
OFTEN A RURAL SOLUTION
ANGLE CUT TOP OF POST
REMEMBER TO ADD WOOD PRESERVATIVE TO NEWLY CUT SURFACE
4x4 POST
4x4 POST
INDIVIDUAL CAP TREATMENT

Figure 450-12 Typical cap details.

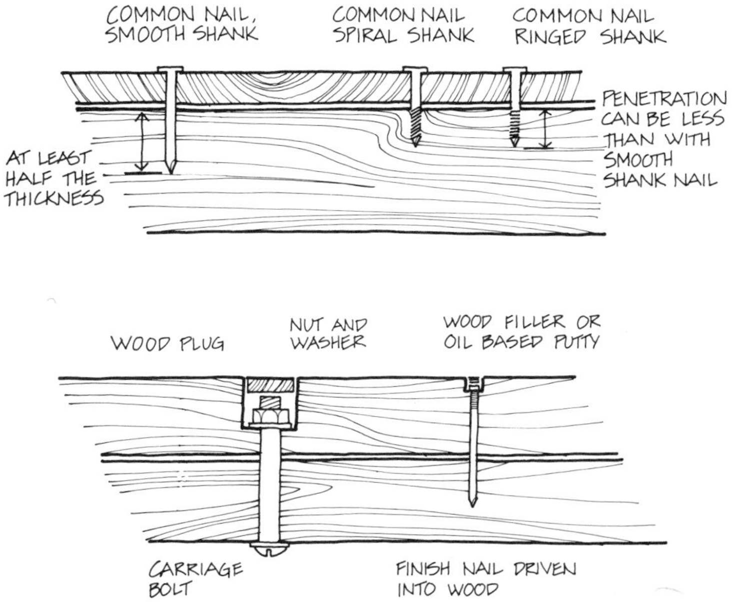
COMMON NAIL, SMOOTH SHANK
COMMON NAIL SPIRAL SHANK
COMMON NAIL RINGED SHANK
PENETRATION CAN BE LESS THAN WITH SMOOTH SHANK NAIL
AT LEAST HALF THE THICKNESS
WOOD PLUG
NUT AND WASHER
WOOD FILLER OR OIL BASED PUTTY
CARRIAGE BOLT
FINISH NAIL DRIVEN INTO WOOD

Figure 450-14 Fastening techniques for wood fences and screens.

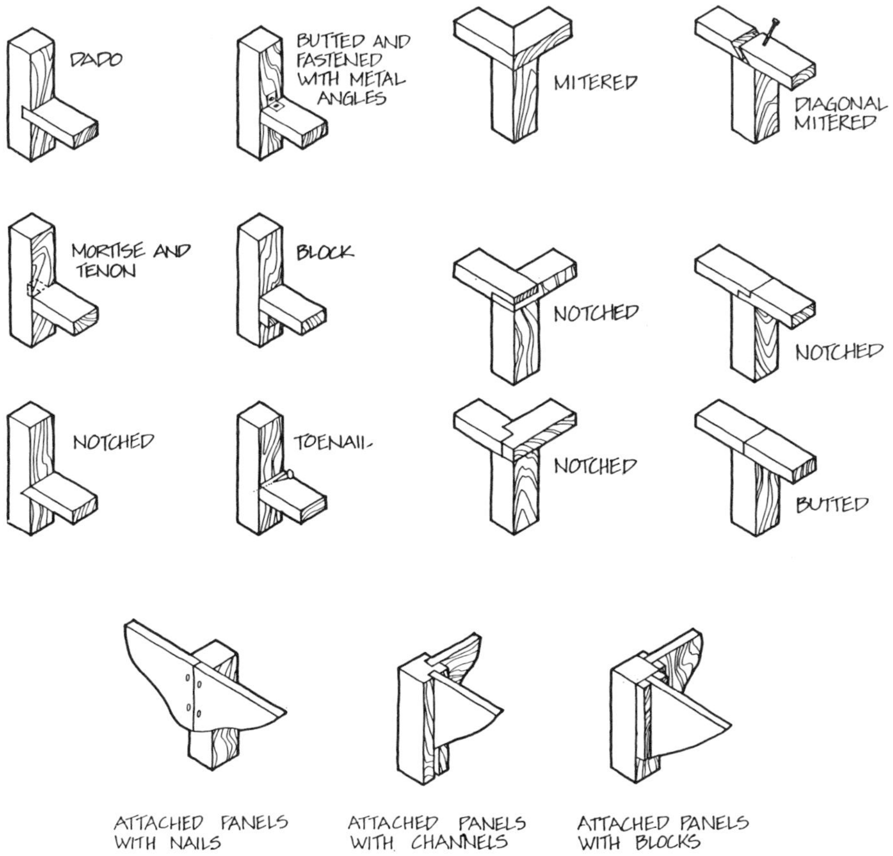
DADO
BUTTED AND FASTENED WITH METAL ANGLES
MITERED
DIAGONAL MITERED
MORTISE AND TENON
BLOCK
NOTCHED
NOTCHED
NOTCHED
TOENAIL
NOTCHED
BUTTED
ATTACHED PANELS WITH NAILS
ATTACHED PANELS WITH CHANNELS
ATTACHED PANELS WITH BLOCKS

Figure 450-13 Typical Joining Techniques for Wood Fences and Screens. Details that trap moisture should not be used in humid climates.

holes can be drilled in the supporting rails to prevent them from trapping water.

Wind Control:

A slat fence will only reduce wind velocity, whereas a solid fence will give wind protection on the side away from the wind for a distance equal to the height of the fence. A louver fence will reduce the velocity and alter the direction of the wind. A baffle at the top of the fence angled 45 degrees into the prevailing wind gives the greatest protection closest to the fence. A 45-degree baffle angled away from the wind directs the wind over the fence and creates a wider calm pocket on the lee side of the fence. (Refer to Section 260: Climate and Energy, for more information.)

Joining and Fastening:

Figure 450-13 shows several ways to join together members of wooden fences or screens. The technique chosen and the quality of the hardware used will affect the visual appeal and the structural integrity of the fence.

Hot-dipped galvanized or aluminum fastenings can be used to prevent the corrosion or discoloring of materials and finishes. Screws and bolts provide the firmest connections and may be needed to guarantee a strong supporting framework. Wood screws can be used to join pieces 1 in (25 mm) thick or less, but *lag bolts,* which come in a range of sizes, should be used to join more substantial wooden members.

Normally, nails should penetrate at least half the thickness of the receiving member of wood, and shanked nails should be used to prevent eventual loosening of the nail (Figure 450-14).

Countersunk bolt and screw fastenings are less susceptible to corrosion or vandalism when hidden by wooden plugs. Cover countersunk nails with a non-oily filler if the wood is to be stained or left in its natural state. Use oil-base putty if the wood will be painted. Wood fillers may need tinting to match the tone of the wood.

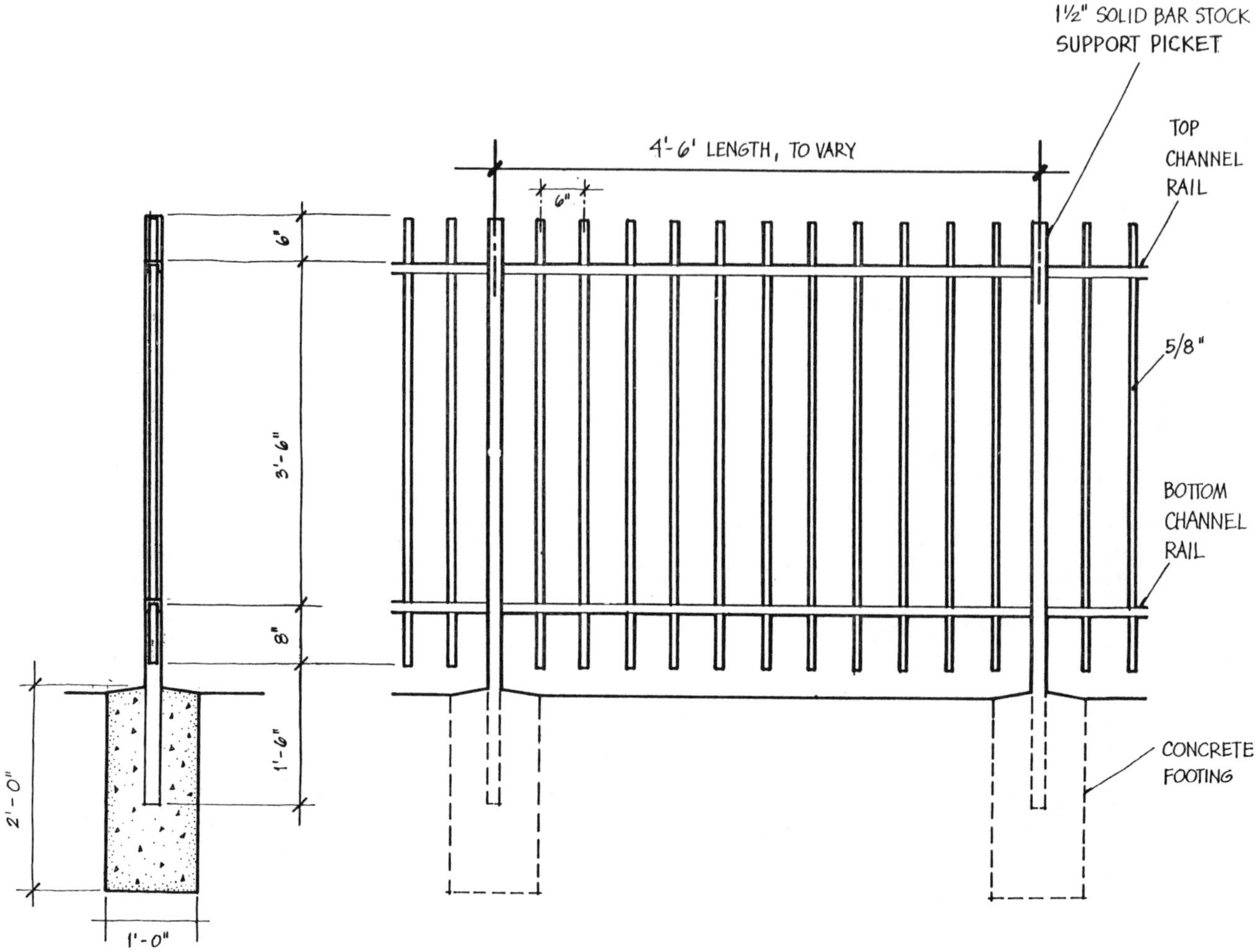
1½" SOLID BAR STOCK
SUPPORT PICKET
4'-6' LENGTH, TO VARY
6"
TOP
CHANNEL
RAIL
5/8"
BOTTOM
CHANNEL
RAIL
CONCRETE
FOOTING
6"
3'-6"
8"
1'-6"
2'-0"
1'-0"

Figure 450-15 Typical metal picket fence construction.

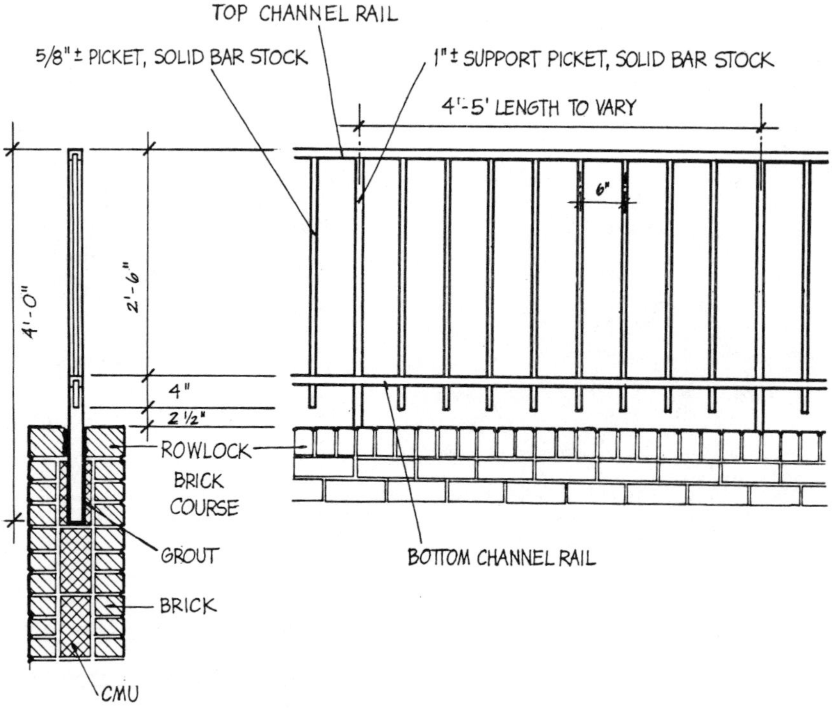
TOP CHANNEL RAIL
5/8" ± PICKET, SOLID BAR STOCK
1" ± SUPPORT PICKET, SOLID BAR STOCK
4'-5' LENGTH TO VARY
6"
4'-0"
2'-6"
4"
2½"
ROWLOCK
BRICK
COURSE
GROUT
BRICK
CMU
BOTTOM CHANNEL RAIL

Figure 450-16 Closed-picket metal fencing on masonry wall.

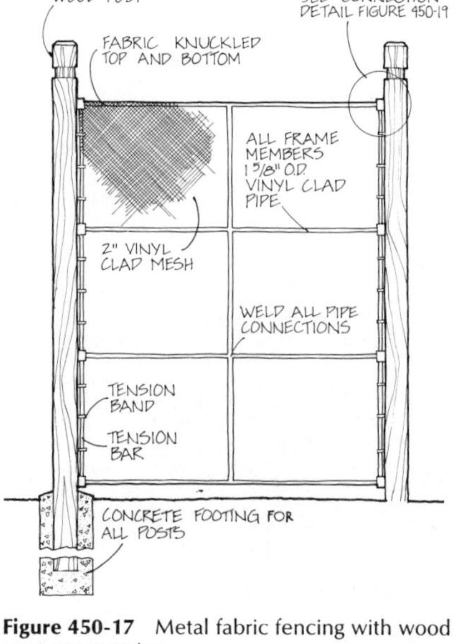
WOOD POST
SEE CONNECTION
DETAIL FIGURE 450-19
FABRIC KNUCKLED
TOP AND BOTTOM
ALL FRAME
MEMBERS
1 5/8" O.D.
VINYL CLAD
PIPE
2" VINYL
CLAD MESH
WELD ALL PIPE
CONNECTIONS
TENSION
BAND
TENSION
BAR
CONCRETE FOOTING FOR
ALL POSTS

Figure 450-17 Metal fabric fencing with wood post construction.

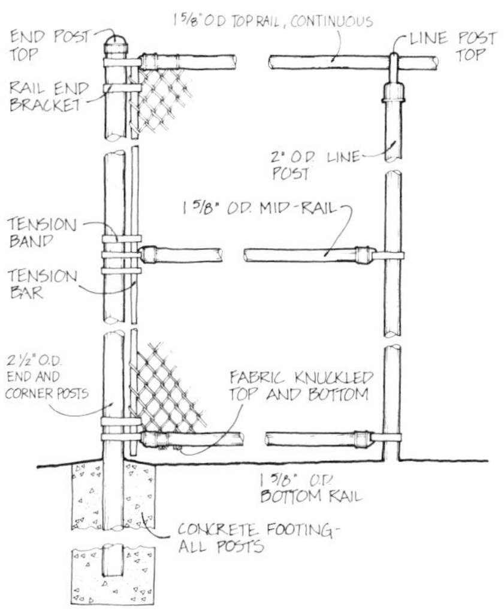
END POST TOP
1 5/8" O.D. TOP RAIL, CONTINUOUS
LINE POST TOP
RAIL END BRACKET
2" O.D. LINE POST
1 5/8" O.D. MID-RAIL
TENSION BAND
TENSION BAR
2 1/2" O.D. END AND CORNER POSTS
FABRIC KNUCKLED TOP AND BOTTOM
1 5/8" O.D. BOTTOM RAIL
CONCRETE FOOTING-ALL POSTS

Figure 450-18 Typical chain link fencing.

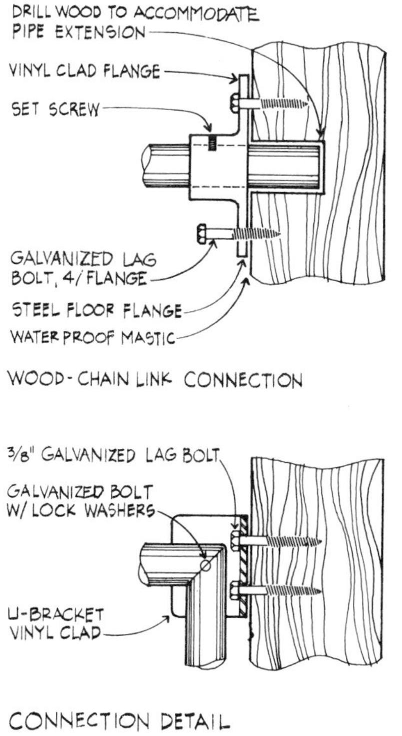
DRILL WOOD TO ACCOMMODATE PIPE EXTENSION
VINYL CLAD FLANGE
SET SCREW
GALVANIZED LAG BOLT, 4/FLANGE
STEEL FLOOR FLANGE
WATERPROOF MASTIC
WOOD-CHAIN LINK CONNECTION
3/8" GALVANIZED LAG BOLT
GALVANIZED BOLT W/ LOCK WASHERS
U-BRACKET VINYL CLAD
CONNECTION DETAIL

Figure 450-19 Chain link-to-wood frame connection details.

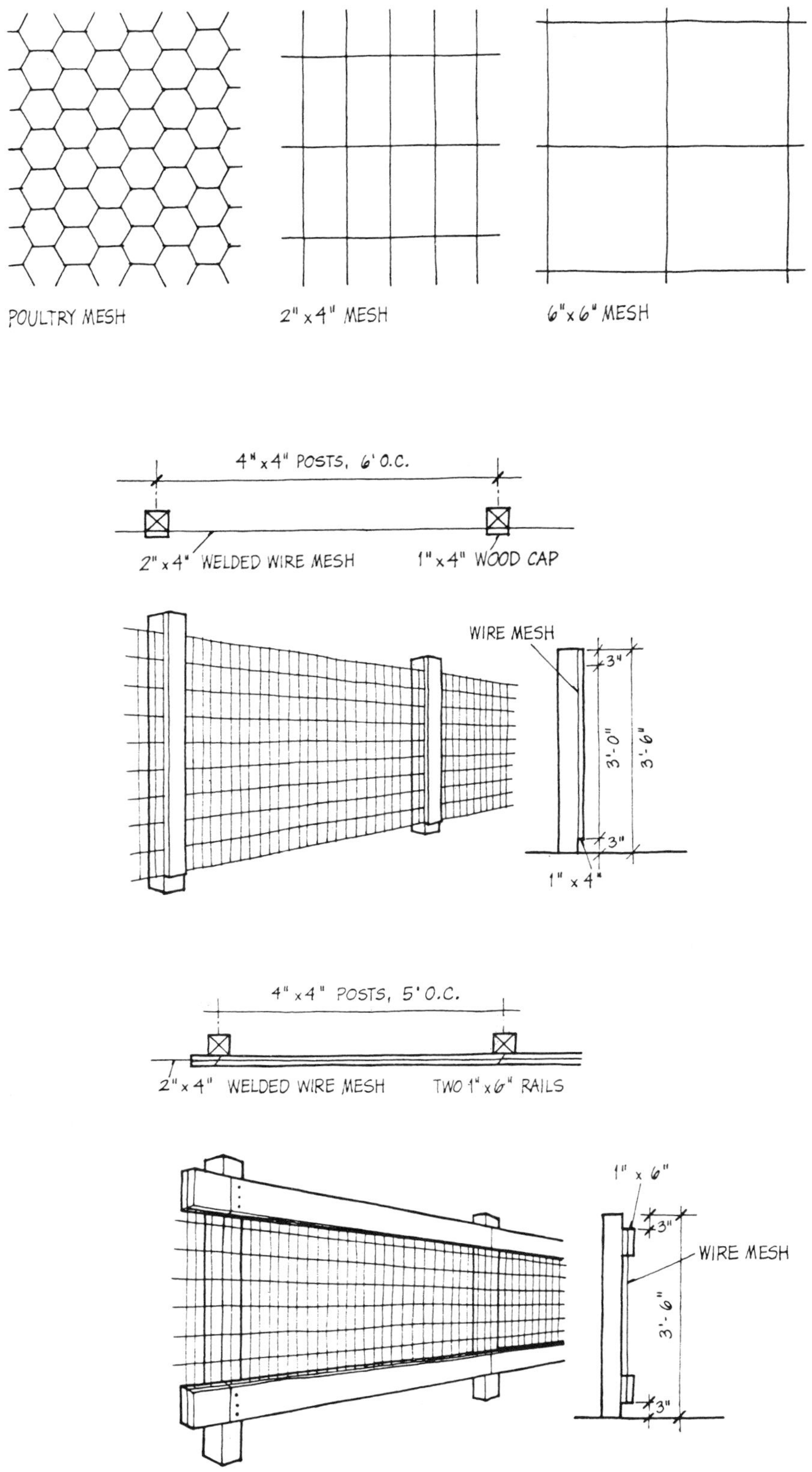
POULTRY MESH
2" x 4" MESH
6" x 6" MESH
4" x 4" POSTS, 6' O.C.
2" x 4" WELDED WIRE MESH
1" x 4" WOOD CAP
WIRE MESH
3"
3'-0"
3'-6"
3"
1" x 4"
4" x 4" POSTS, 5' O.C.
2" x 4" WELDED WIRE MESH
TWO 1" x 6" RAILS
1" x 6"
3"
WIRE MESH
3'-6"
3"

Figure 450-20 Types and application of metal fabrics.

3.3 Metal Barriers

Metal Picket Fences:

Posts can be made of 1- or 2-in (25-mm or 50-mm) square or round tempered steel tubing set in concrete footings (Figures 450-15 and 450-16).

Metal Fabric Fencing:

Metal fabric fencing is typically stretched between posts set in concrete. As with other fences, corner posts are normally larger and set deeper than inner posts. Metal picket and metal fabric fences can be combined with other types of fences and walls. Chain link fabric is usually stretched between metal posts of a 2-in (50-mm) diameter, but it can also be mounted on wooden posts (Figures 450-17 through 450-19).

Metal fabric fencing was originally used for agricultural and security purposes, but this material can be used attractively in other applications as well (Figure 450-20).

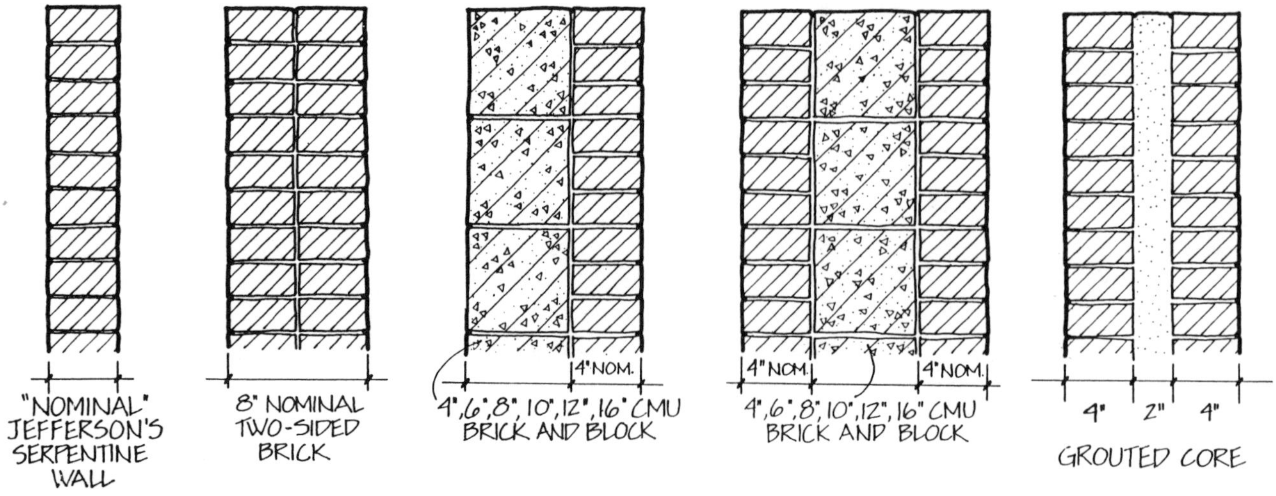
"NOMINAL" JEFFERSON'S SERPENTINE WALL
8" NOMINAL TWO-SIDED BRICK
4"NOM.
4",6",8",10",12",16" CMU BRICK AND BLOCK
4"NOM.
4"NOM.
4",6",8",10",12",16" CMU BRICK AND BLOCK
4" 2" 4"
GROUTED CORE

Figure 450-21 Typical brick wall construction.

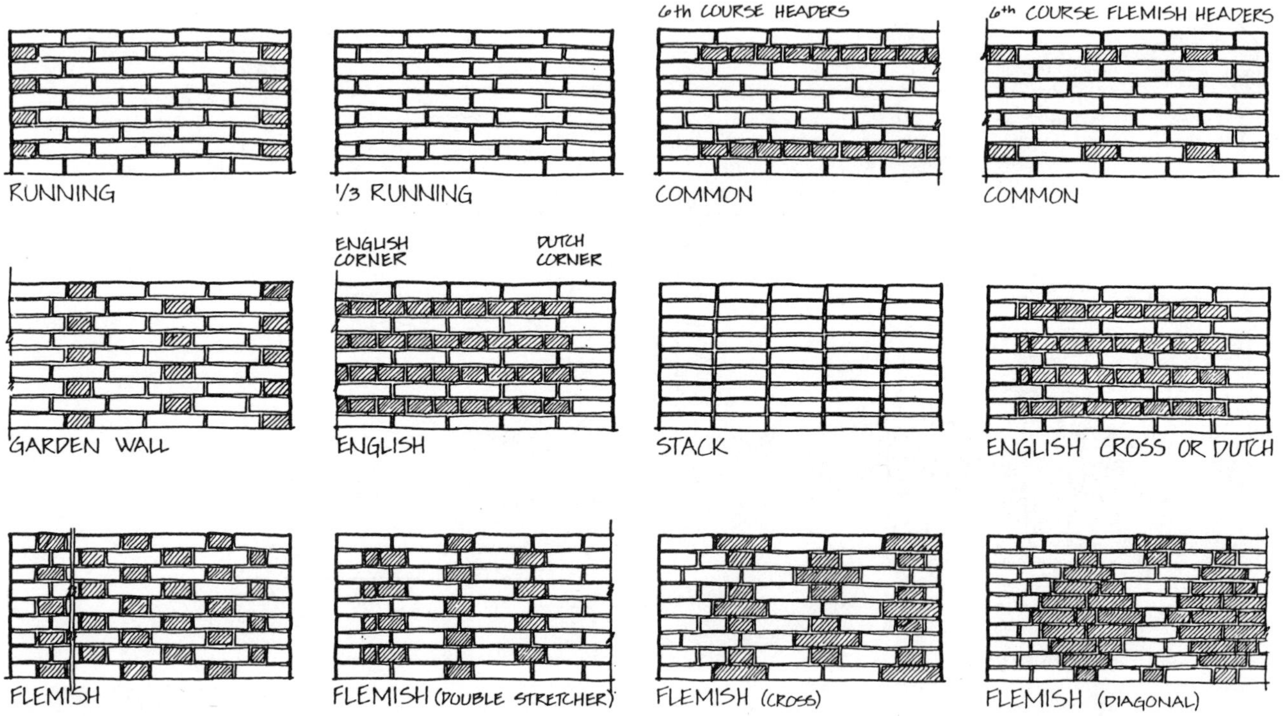
6th COURSE HEADERS
6th COURSE FLEMISH HEADERS
RUNNING
1/3 RUNNING
COMMON
COMMON
ENGLISH CORNER
DUTCH CORNER
GARDEN WALL
ENGLISH
STACK
ENGLISH CROSS OR DUTCH
FLEMISH
FLEMISH (DOUBLE STRETCHER)
FLEMISH (CROSS)
FLEMISH (DIAGONAL)

Figure 450-22 Common brickwork patterns.

Various-colored vinyl coatings are available.

3.4 Brick and Concrete Block Walls

Freestanding masonry walls can be made of brick and/or concrete block (Figure 450-21). Tile or stucco can be added. Concrete block is normally less expensive than brick, and it is available in standard and special sizes and shapes. Often, hollow concrete blocks are used to add thickness or to provide a structure that can be faced on one or both sides with brick, tile, or other material.

Brickwork Patterns:

Figure 450-22 shows some of the more common *bonds* used in bricklaying. Because the ends of walls are often visible, they are usually designed with a running bond pattern or an end-wall pier or column.

Moisture Control:

The top surfaces of walls should be pitched to drain, and caps should be extended beyond the wall to shed water away from the wall face. Joints on horizontal surfaces should be sealed to prevent seepage and possible damage to the joint.

Brick Cap Units:

Caps can be made from standard bricks or from bricks cut on the site, and they can be set in a pattern different from the wall bond. Prefabricated caps are also available. There are also special brick cap units for the ends and corners of walls. Alternatively, caps for masonry walls can be of wood, precast concrete, or cut stone (Figure 450-23).

Reinforcement:

Truss design reinforcement is laid horizontally within the mortar bed between every third or fourth course. It helps resist lateral displacement in walls over 2 ft (600 mm) high (Figure 450-24).

For freestanding walls above 4 ft (1200 mm) high, there should be bar reinforcement running vertically, either in the mortar between the brick or in the open cells of concrete blocks (Figure 450-25).

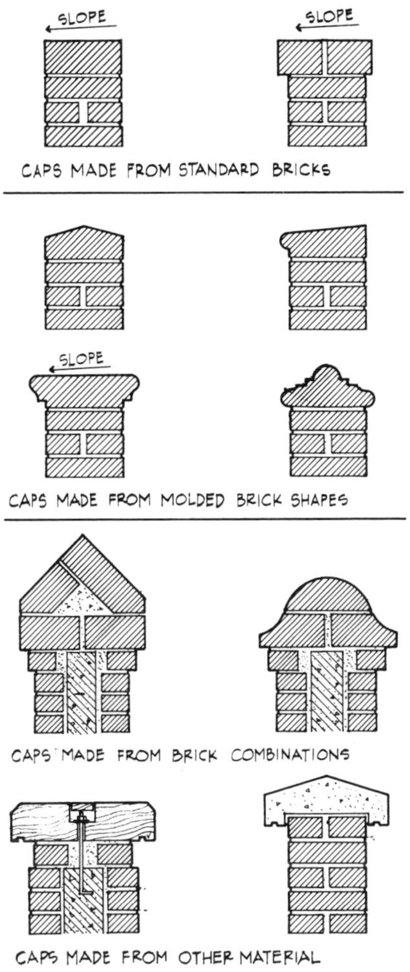
SLOPE
SLOPE
CAPS MADE FROM STANDARD BRICKS
SLOPE
CAPS MADE FROM MOLDED BRICK SHAPES
CAPS MADE FROM BRICK COMBINATIONS
CAPS MADE FROM OTHER MATERIAL

Figure 450-23 Typical caps for masonry walls.

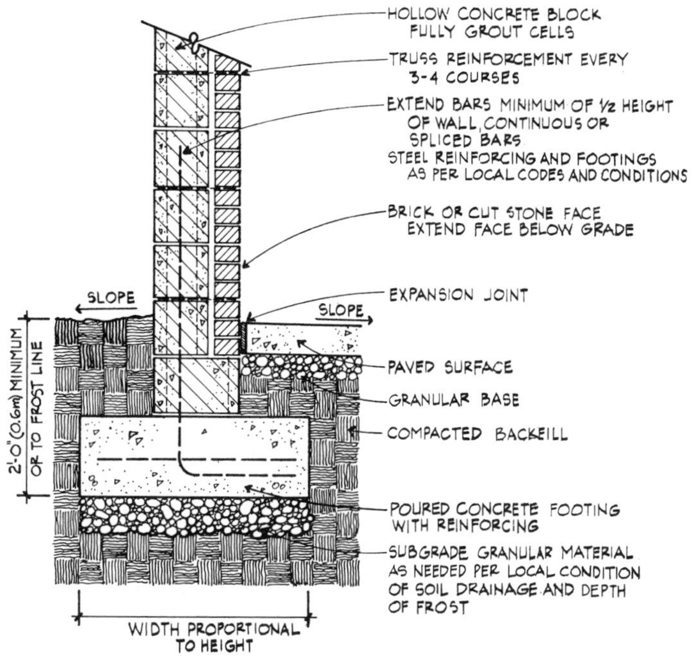
HOLLOW CONCRETE BLOCK FULLY GROUT CELLS
TRUSS REINFORCEMENT EVERY 3-4 COURSES
EXTEND BARS MINIMUM OF ½ HEIGHT OF WALL, CONTINUOUS OR SPLICED BARS
STEEL REINFORCING AND FOOTINGS AS PER LOCAL CODES AND CONDITIONS
BRICK OR CUT STONE FACE EXTEND FACE BELOW GRADE
EXPANSION JOINT
SLOPE
SLOPE
2'-0" (0.6m) MINIMUM OR TO FROST LINE
PAVED SURFACE
GRANULAR BASE
COMPACTED BACKFILL
POURED CONCRETE FOOTING WITH REINFORCING
SUBGRADE GRANULAR MATERIAL AS NEEDED PER LOCAL CONDITION OF SOIL DRAINAGE AND DEPTH OF FROST
WIDTH PROPORTIONAL TO HEIGHT

Figure 450-25 Reinforcement for masonry walls.

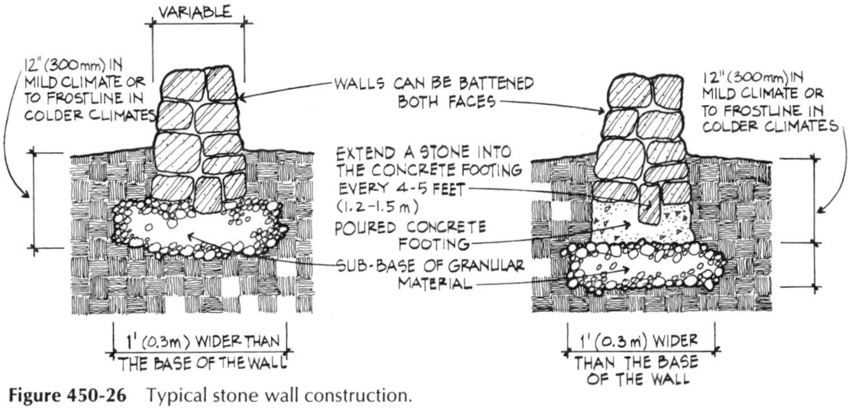
VARIABLE
12" (300mm) IN MILD CLIMATE OR TO FROSTLINE IN COLDER CLIMATES
WALLS CAN BE BATTENED BOTH FACES
EXTEND A STONE INTO THE CONCRETE FOOTING EVERY 4-5 FEET (1.2-1.5 m)
POURED CONCRETE FOOTING
SUB-BASE OF GRANULAR MATERIAL
12" (300mm) IN MILD CLIMATE OR TO FROSTLINE IN COLDER CLIMATES
1' (0.3m) WIDER THAN THE BASE OF THE WALL
1' (0.3 m) WIDER THAN THE BASE OF THE WALL

Figure 450-26 Typical stone wall construction.

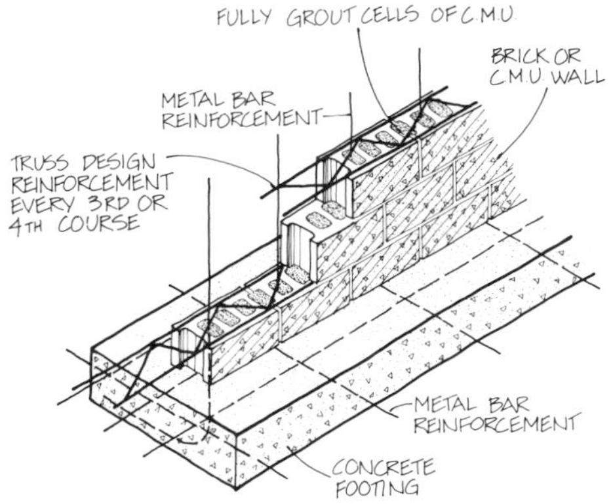
FULLY GROUT CELLS OF C.M.U.
BRICK OR C.M.U. WALL
METAL BAR REINFORCEMENT
TRUSS DESIGN REINFORCEMENT EVERY 3RD OR 4TH COURSE
METAL BAR REINFORCEMENT
CONCRETE FOOTING

Figure 450-24 Reinforcement for masonry walls.

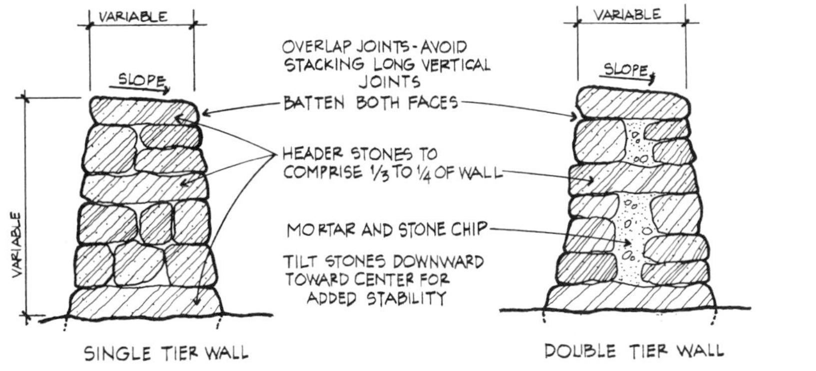
VARIABLE
VARIABLE
SLOPE
SLOPE
OVERLAP JOINTS-AVOID STACKING LONG VERTICAL JOINTS
BATTEN BOTH FACES
HEADER STONES TO COMPRISE ⅓ TO ¼ OF WALL
MORTAR AND STONE CHIP
TILT STONES DOWNWARD TOWARD CENTER FOR ADDED STABILITY
VARIABLE
SINGLE TIER WALL
DOUBLE TIER WALL

Figure 450-27 Typical stone wall construction.

3.5 Stone Walls

Two basic methods of stone wall construction are *dry wall* and *mortar-laid*. Dry stone walls have no mortar, the stones are irregular in shape, and the stones are laid flat. Mortar-laid stone walls have continuous footings (and therefore are stronger and can be higher) and require fewer stones than dry walls (Figures 450-26, 450-27, and 450-28).

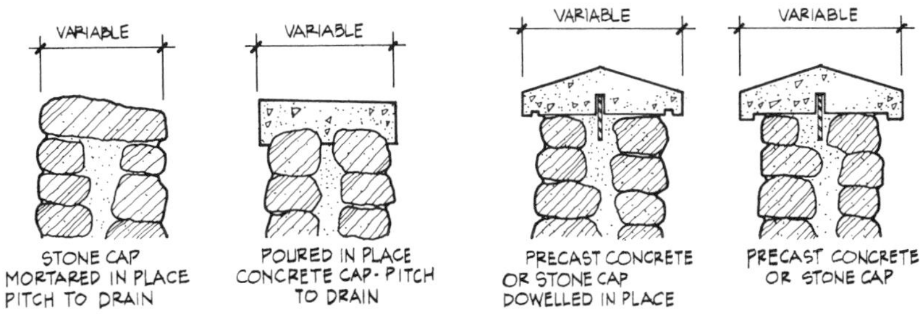
VARIABLE
VARIABLE
VARIABLE
VARIABLE
STONE CAP MORTARED IN PLACE PITCH TO DRAIN
POURED IN PLACE CONCRETE CAP-PITCH TO DRAIN
PRECAST CONCRETE OR STONE CAP DOWELLED IN PLACE
PRECAST CONCRETE OR STONE CAP

Figure 450-28 Caps for stone walls.

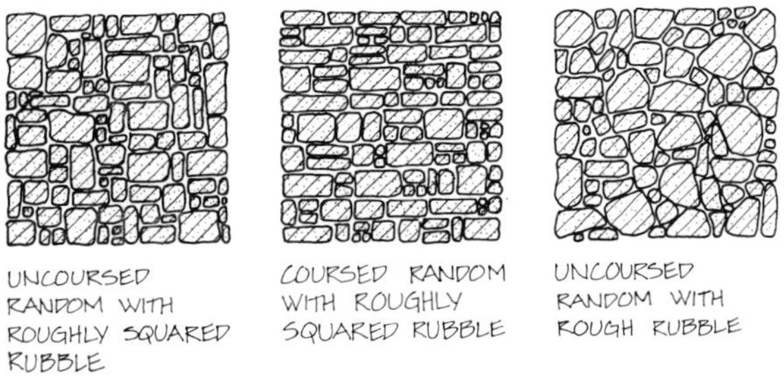
UNCOURSED RANDOM WITH ROUGHLY SQUARED RUBBLE
COURSED RANDOM WITH ROUGHLY SQUARED RUBBLE
UNCOURSED RANDOM WITH ROUGH RUBBLE

Figure 450-29 Random Rubble Masonry Patterns. Units are squared and dressed by stone masons in the field.

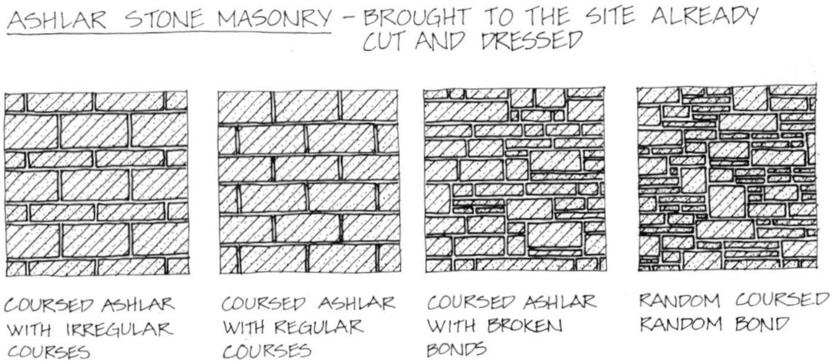
ASHLAR STONE MASONRY – BROUGHT TO THE SITE ALREADY CUT AND DRESSED
COURSED ASHLAR WITH IRREGULAR COURSES
COURSED ASHLAR WITH REGULAR COURSES
COURSED ASHLAR WITH BROKEN BONDS
RANDOM COURSED RANDOM BOND

Figure 450-30 Ashlar Stone Masonry Patterns. Units are precut and dressed before delivery to the site.

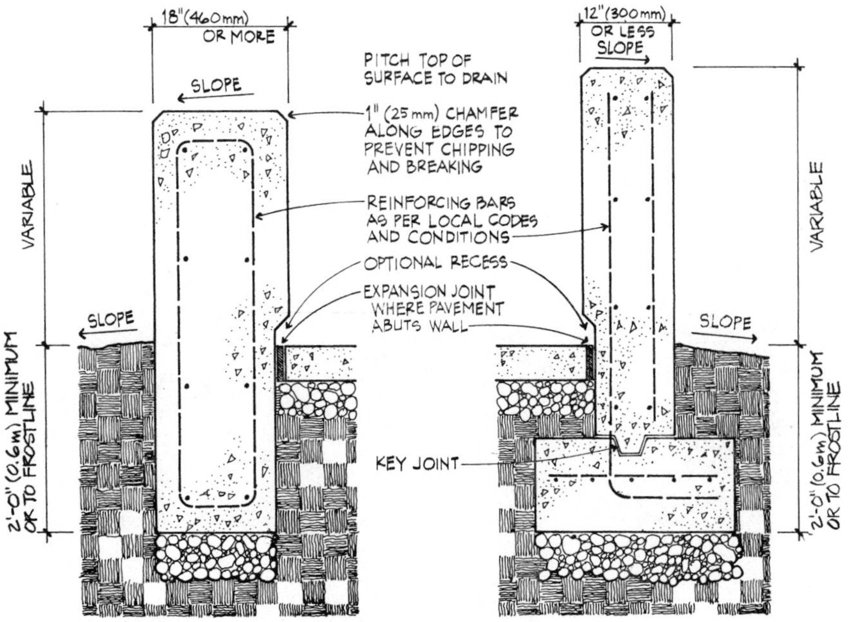
18"(460mm) OR MORE
SLOPE
PITCH TOP OF SURFACE TO DRAIN
1" (25 mm) CHAMFER ALONG EDGES TO PREVENT CHIPPING AND BREAKING
REINFORCING BARS AS PER LOCAL CODES AND CONDITIONS
OPTIONAL RECESS
EXPANSION JOINT WHERE PAVEMENT ABUTS WALL
KEY JOINT
12"(300mm) OR LESS
SLOPE
VARIABLE
SLOPE
SLOPE
2'-0" (0.6m) MINIMUM OR TO FROSTLINE
VARIABLE
2'-0" (0.6m) MINIMUM OR TO FROSTLINE

Figure 450-31 Typical poured concrete wall construction.

Stonework Patterns:

Two basic stonework patterns used in wall construction are *random rubble* and *ashlar* (Figures 450-29 and 450-30). Stones for a wall should be similar in size, or, if in a variety of shapes and sizes, should be evenly distributed to give a balanced appearance to the wall.

Mortar Mix:

Refer to Section 830: Concrete, for a recommended mortar mixture. Stone must be free of dirt and thoroughly wetted before being set.

3.6 Poured Concrete Walls

Poured concrete walls require the same type of footing as other masonry walls, with key joints to lock the footing to the wall above. Concrete walls also require formwork and vertical and horizontal reinforcing bars to provide stability. A typical reinforcing bar pattern for a poured concrete wall is shown in Figure 450-31. For walls over 6 ft (2 m) in height, a structural engineer should be consulted to determine loads and structural specifications.

3.7 Miscellaneous Barrier Materials

Panels for fences and screens can be constructed of any number of materials, especially if the fence or screen is going to serve either a temporary or special need. Figure 450-32 shows Plexiglas and canvas being used, but such materials are subject to abuse or vandalism and may therefore require a higher degree of maintenance. The durability of a material is another factor and may imply a shorter useful life.

3.8 Gates

Gate posts are usually larger [e.g., at least 6 in × 6 in (150 mm × 150 mm)] and taller than the posts used for the remainder of the fence (which are often the same size as the corner posts). They should always be installed deeper, and often with concrete footings (Figure 450-33).

Sagging is the main structural problem with most gates; therefore, the gate should be as light as possible and have diagonal bracing. A plywood panel makes a sag-free gate (Figure 450-34).

Bolts and wood screws instead of nails should be specified for gate construction. Typical gate hardware is shown in Figure 450-35.

3.9 Connections to Buildings or Other Structures

The point, or juncture, where a barrier joins another structure is a detail crucial to

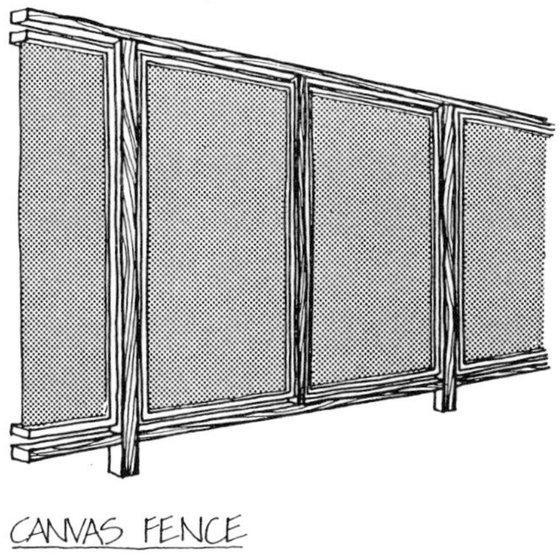
CANVAS FENCE

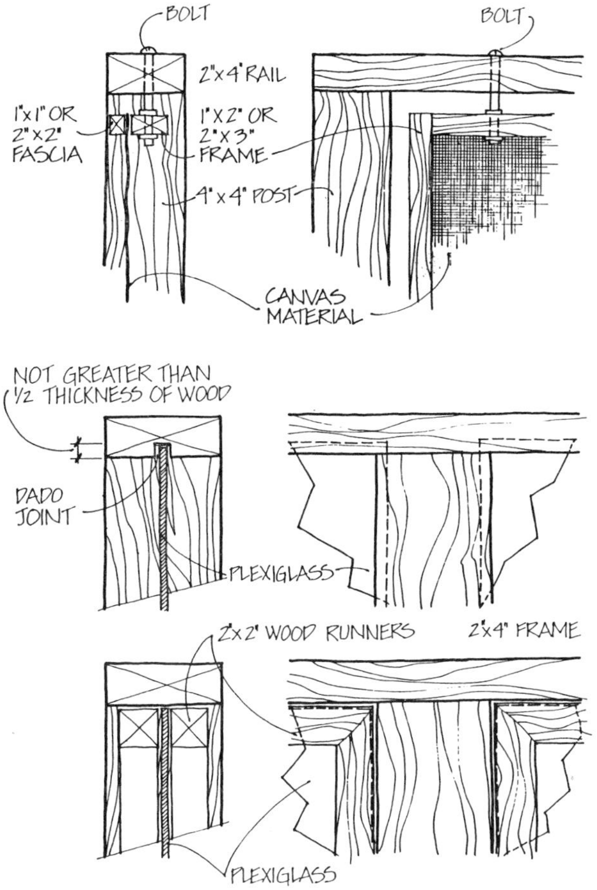
BOLT
BOLT
2"x4" RAIL
1"x1" OR
2"x2"
FASCIA
1"x2" OR
2"x3"
FRAME
4"x4" POST
CANVAS
MATERIAL
NOT GREATER THAN
1/2 THICKNESS OF WOOD
DADO
JOINT
PLEXIGLASS
2"x2" WOOD RUNNERS
2"x4" FRAME
PLEXIGLASS

Figure 450-32 Alternative materials for fence or screen panels.

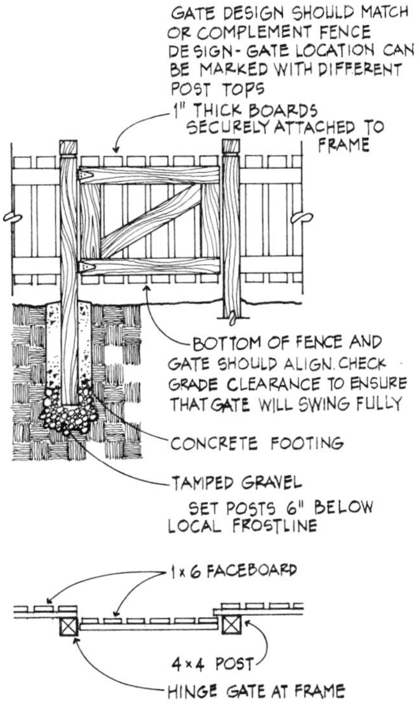
GATE DESIGN SHOULD MATCH
OR COMPLEMENT FENCE
DESIGN - GATE LOCATION CAN
BE MARKED WITH DIFFERENT
POST TOPS
1" THICK BOARDS
SECURELY ATTACHED TO
FRAME
BOTTOM OF FENCE AND
GATE SHOULD ALIGN. CHECK
GRADE CLEARANCE TO ENSURE
THAT GATE WILL SWING FULLY
CONCRETE FOOTING
TAMPED GRAVEL
SET POSTS 6" BELOW
LOCAL FROSTLINE
1 x 6 FACEBOARD
4 x 4 POST
HINGE GATE AT FRAME

Figure 450-33 Typical gate and gatepost construction.

2 x 4 WOOD BRACE
STEEL ROD OR
WIRE W/ TURNBUCKLE
PLYWOOD PANEL

Figure 450-34 Common bracing techniques for wood gates.

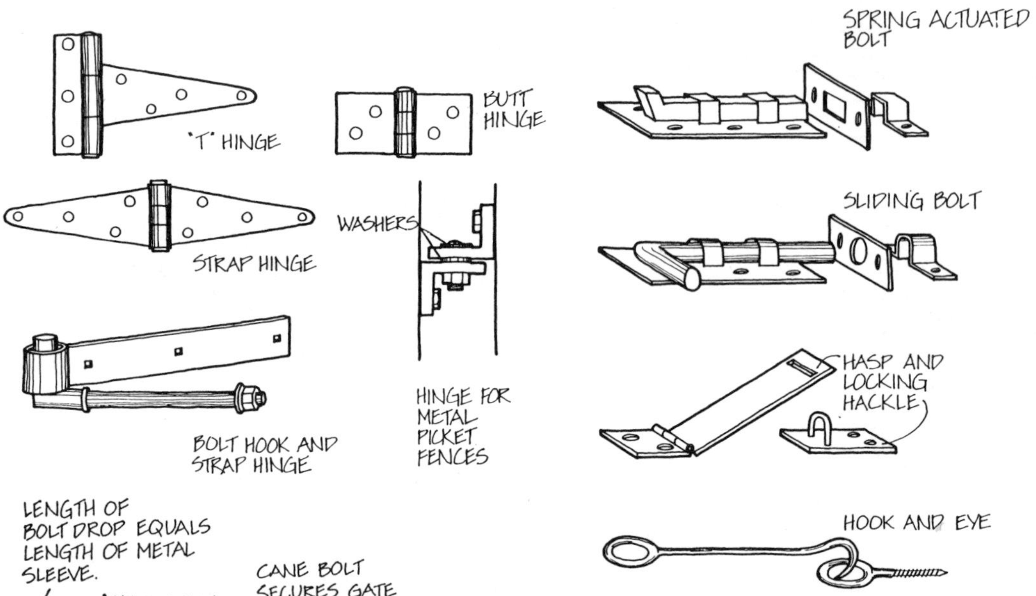
SPRING ACTUATED BOLT
'T' HINGE
BUTT HINGE
SLIDING BOLT
STRAP HINGE
WASHERS
BOLT HOOK AND STRAP HINGE
HINGE FOR METAL PICKET FENCES
HASP AND LOCKING HACKLE
HOOK AND EYE

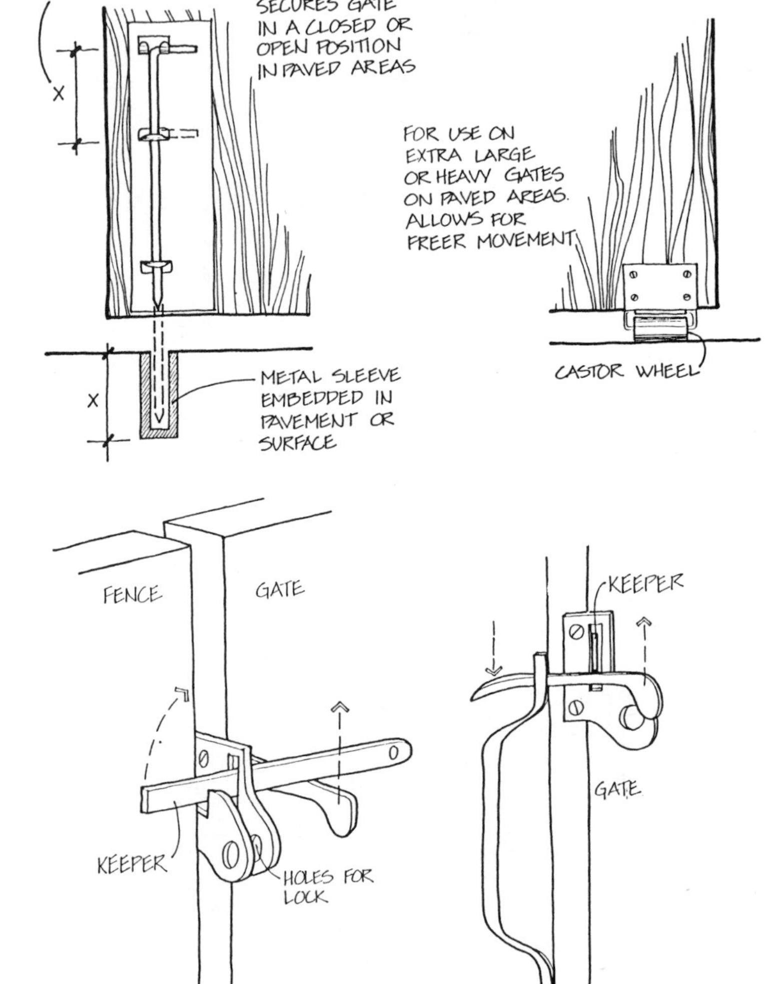
LENGTH OF BOLT DROP EQUALS LENGTH OF METAL SLEEVE.
CANE BOLT SECURES GATE IN A CLOSED OR OPEN POSITION IN PAVED AREAS
X
FOR USE ON EXTRA LARGE OR HEAVY GATES ON PAVED AREAS. ALLOWS FOR FREER MOVEMENT
X
METAL SLEEVE EMBEDDED IN PAVEMENT OR SURFACE
CASTOR WHEEL
FENCE
GATE
KEEPER
KEEPER
HOLES FOR LOCK
GATE

Figure 450-35 Common Gate Hardware. Galvanized metal hardware is often used to prevent rusting and consequent staining of wood.

good appearance and structural integrity (Figures 450-36, 450-37, and 450-38). If needed, a gate is often located at this point to solve the problem.

3.10 Maintenance around the Base of Walls and Fences

A fence or wall on a paved surface has few maintenance problems, but if set on mowed grass, then a mowing or maintenance strip along the base of the structure might be considered. Alternatively, a low-maintenance ground cover can be substituted for the lawn (Figure 450-39).

If there is a danger of vehicles coming in contact with a fence, screen, or wall, then curbs, car stops, or other such device should be used for protection (Figure 450-40).

3.11 Reproducing Historic Styles

Accurate reproductions of earlier barrier styles are sometimes needed in historic landscape restoration. (Refer to Section 630: Historic Landscapes, for more information.) In most cases, however, exact reproductions are unnecessary. Generally, an historic appearance can be suggested by careful detailing of the elements—such as the caps, pilasters, pickets, posts, or finials—as well as by choosing materials that have strong historical connotations simply because of their past widespread use (e.g., stone, brick, or iron or wooden picket) (Figure 450-41).

REFERENCES

Walker, Theordore D. *Site Design and Construction Detailing,* PDA Publishers, West Lafayette, IN, 1978. ■

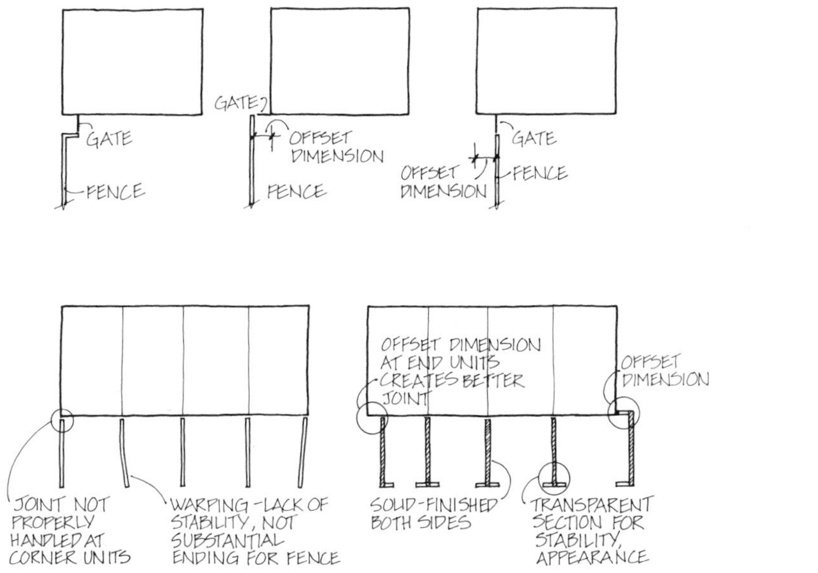
GATE
FENCE
GATE
OFFSET DIMENSION
FENCE
GATE
OFFSET DIMENSION
FENCE
OFFSET DIMENSION AT END UNITS CREATES BETTER JOINT
OFFSET DIMENSION
JOINT NOT PROPERLY HANDLED AT CORNER UNITS
WARPING - LACK OF STABILITY, NOT SUBSTANTIAL ENDING FOR FENCE
SOLID-FINISHED BOTH SIDES
TRANSPARENT SECTION FOR STABILITY, APPEARANCE

Figure 450-36 Aesthetic considerations for connections between walls or fences and buildings.

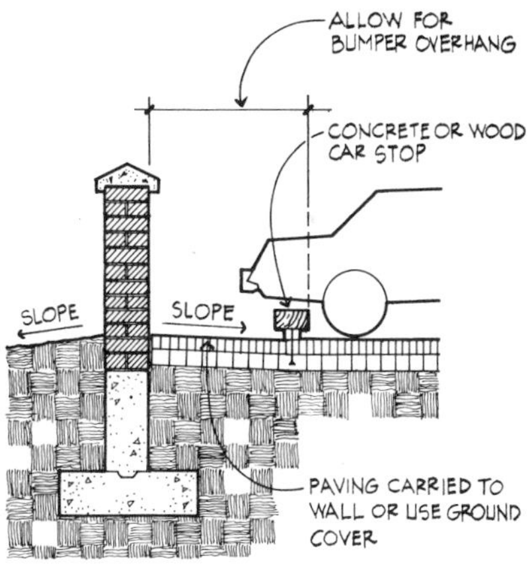
ALLOW FOR BUMPER OVERHANG
CONCRETE OR WOOD CAR STOP
SLOPE
SLOPE
PAVING CARRIED TO WALL OR USE GROUND COVER

Figure 450-40 Car stop for protection of walls or fences.

SOLID SECTION
TRANSPARENT TRELLIS WORK
OPEN FRAME-WORK EXTENDED AROUND CORNER

Figure 450-37 Offset details for connections between walls or fences and buildings.

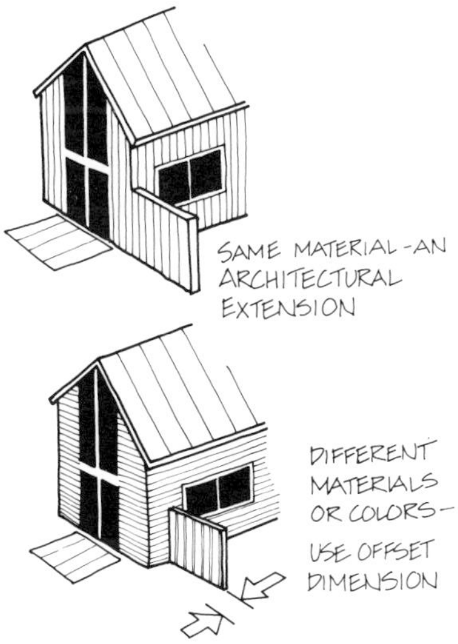
SAME MATERIAL - AN ARCHITECTURAL EXTENSION
DIFFERENT MATERIALS OR COLORS - USE OFFSET DIMENSION

Figure 450-38 Aesthetic considerations for building/wall extension.

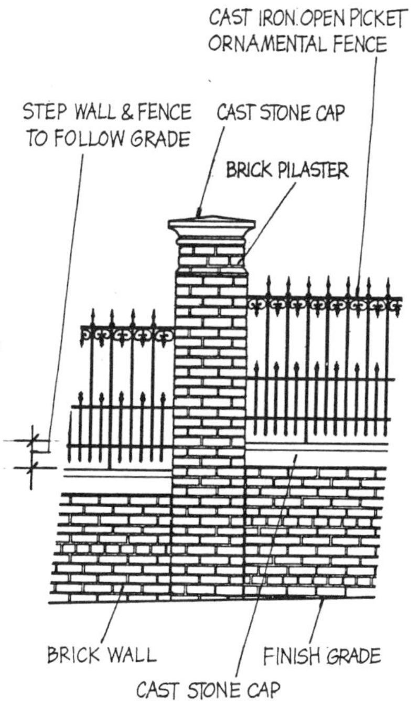
CAST IRON OPEN PICKET ORNAMENTAL FENCE
STEP WALL & FENCE TO FOLLOW GRADE
CAST STONE CAP
BRICK PILASTER
BRICK WALL
FINISH GRADE
CAST STONE CAP

Figure 450-41 Representative example of historic detailing. (Otterbein Church, Baltimore, Maryland, c. 1850.)

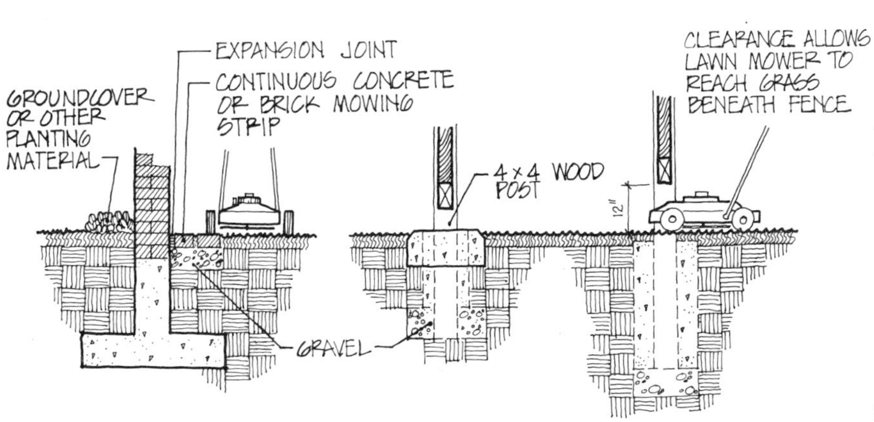
EXPANSION JOINT
CONTINUOUS CONCRETE OR BRICK MOWING STRIP
GROUNDCOVER OR OTHER PLANTING MATERIAL
GRAVEL
4×4 WOOD POST
CLEARANCE ALLOWS LAWN MOWER TO REACH GRASS BENEATH FENCE
12"

Figure 450-39 Low-maintenance techniques for the base of walls and fences.

section 460: Wood Decks and Boardwalks

CREDITS

Contributor: Gary M. Fishbeck
Sasaki Associates, Inc.
Watertown, Massachusetts

Graphics:

John Copley
Copley Fleming Associates, Inc.
Boston, Massachusetts

Reviewers:

J. Brooks Breeden
Department of Landscape Architecture
School of Architecture
Ohio State University
Columbus, Ohio

Olin Fralick
Marvin & Associates, Inc.
Walterboro, South Carolina

Thomas and Heather Ryan
Sasaki Associates, Inc.
Watertown, Massachusetts

CONTENTS

1.0 INTRODUCTION

1.1 General

This section focuses on fundamental principles and techniques of wood deck and boardwalk construction; it is organized to reflect logical steps in the process of designing a wood deck and/or boardwalk. Each of the major structural components of a deck is described, and information on sizing methodology is given. Construction details for various types of connections, including steps, railings, and the like are given at the end of the section.

1.2 Preliminary Considerations

Several important factors require consideration at the outset of wood deck or boardwalk design, including selection of framing method, selection of materials, methodology for sizing wood members, and considerations of maintenance. These factors will determine the appearance and relative costs of a deck or boardwalk, as well as the stiffness (i.e., extent of deflection) of the structure.

Selection of Framing Method:

Two methods of framing are commonly employed in deck or boardwalk construction: platform framing and plank-and-beam framing. Each of these methods has advantages and disadvantages, depending on the objectives of the designer. The choice of one method over another is usually based on a combination of cost comparisons and/or aesthetic preference. Sometimes the choice of a framing method is a matter of regional bias. Cost differences between these two framing methods will differ, but the many variables involved make comparisons difficult. Comparative costs have to be calculated on a project-by-project basis.

The manner in which a structure is

framed will affect its finished appearance, its initial cost, and sometimes its long-term maintenance costs.

Selection of Materials:

The type and species of lumber chosen for a deck or boardwalk will affect its finished appearance, initial cost, and short- and long-term maintenance costs. Some species are resistant to the detrimental effects of insects and decay, while others require protection with chemical preservatives. If a wood is to be stained, various aesthetic characteristics will result, depending on the species and grade of lumber used.

The choice of hardware is also, to some extent, a matter of aesthetic preference. For example, corrosion of metals is typically avoided, but the effects of corrosion can be used to aesthetic advantage.

Methodology for Sizing Wood Members:

Wood members can be sized according to their *strength in bending* or by their *deflection,* depending on how stiff a deck or boardwalk is desired. Sizing wood members according to their strength in bending will typically produce a deck that is less stiff than one sized for its deflection because wood members can deflect considerably and still be within acceptable limits of safety. Generally speaking, the cost of a stiffer deck will be higher than the cost of a less-stiff deck because of the greater number (or greater dimensions) of wood members involved.

Maintenance:

Maintenance costs are an important part of wood deck and boardwalk design. Especially in humid climates, the main problem to overcome is wood decay. This is largely accomplished by minimizing the incidence of infiltrating moisture, especially at points of connection. Moisture trapping can be avoided, or at least minimized, by the proper use of spacers, flashing, caulking, decktapes, and appropriate joinery. Plank-and-beam framing has an advantage over platform framing in this regard, for it has fewer potential moisture traps and less total area of wood surface requiring protection.

Design details for wood decks and boardwalks should be suitable for outdoor use. Many details that are typical for indoor situations are not suitable for use out-of-doors, including tongue-and-groove decking, tightly mitred corners, and the like. The use of such details can result in accelerated deterioration of the wood structure because of their tendency to trap moisture. Some forms of framing hardware (joist hangers, angle irons, plates, etc.) have the disadvantage of trapping moisture unless carefully detailed.

Exposed wood structures should be made to drain freely, not collecting water or trapping moisture, and should be minimally exposed to contact with plant materials and moist soils.

Special preservative treatments and/or finishes are an important part of maintaining a deck or boardwalk. Most woods require some kind of chemical protection, especially in humid climates. Termites are also a problem in certain regions and may require special flashing and/or chemical treatments.

The appearance of the wood is affected by the choice of preservative or finish. Some woods (e.g., cedar and redwood) turn an attractive gray color if left unprotected over time. A sealant can be used to halt the weathering process at any desired point in the color change.

2.0 PRINCIPLES OF CONSTRUCTION

2.1 Framing Methods

Platform Framing:

Platform framing is a beam-and-joist method of construction (Figure 460-1). Few beams are necessary because joists carry the load over a wide area. Joists typically are of a nominal thickness of 2 in (50 mm) and essentially function as closely spaced beams. The spacing of joists is determined by (1) the load-carrying ability of the joists themselves (a function of their cross-sectional dimension and length of span) and (2) the maximum allowable decking spans, which depend on the cross-sectional dimensions of the decking material and on the species of lumber used. Different species of wood have different inherent strengths.

Platform framing results in a deeper (thicker) deck profile than does plank-and-beam framing because of the inclusion of joists.

Plank-and-Beam Framing:

Plank-and-beam framing refers to a beam-and-decking method of construction (Figure 460-2). No joists are used because the beams are spaced close enough together to function like joists. The decking material always has an actual thickness of 1 in (25 mm) or more. The spacing of beams is related to the maximum allowable decking spans, the cross-sectional dimension of the beams employed, and the maximum allowable beam spans.

A major advantage of plank-and-beam framing over platform framing is its shallow profile, which gives it a simple and clean appearance. It is commonly employed in boardwalk construction.

2.2 Basic Components

The main difference between platform framing and plank-and-beam framing is that platform framing has joists. The other members are essentially the same in both systems. Thus, descriptions of the various components apply to both methods of framing.

Decking:

Decking refers to the surface walked upon. It is supported directly by either joists or beams, depending on the framing method employed. The allowable span of the decking material determines the maximum spacing of the joists—or, in the case of plank-and-beam framing, the maximum spacing of the beams.

Decking is usually laid flat but can be laid on edge. The appearance or finish of the decking, as well as the railings, benches, planters, etc., is usually far more important than is the appearance of other wood members because all are in clear view of the users of the deck. For this reason, the type of wood used for decking is sometimes different, i.e., of better quality or appearance, than the type used for the underlying support members of the deck.

Important Reminders:

1. Decking material should be greater than 1 in (nominal thickness) unless noticeable deflection is acceptable. An actual thickness of 1 in or greater is often used, but 2-in (nominal) material is most common. Plank-and-beam framing typically requires 2-in (nominal thickness) or greater decking material and wider planks than those used in platform framing.

2. The use of square-edge planks with $\frac{3}{16}$- to $\frac{1}{4}$-in (5.0 to 6.5 mm) spacing between planks is preferable to tongue-and-groove planks because of better drainage. Tongue-and-groove planks allow longer spans but they tend to trap moisture and promote rotting in humid climates.

3. Decking wider than 6 in is not recommended because of its propensity to warp.

4. Decking should be laid with the *bark side* up to avoid cupping of the decking material and consequent drainage problems.

Joists:

Joists are used only in platform framing and function to support decking material of relatively short spans. They also function to distribute imposed loads over a wider area. They are typically spaced close together [i.e., 16 to 24 in (400 to 600 mm) apart] because of the limited span of decking members. Bridging is sometimes used between joists to minimize lateral movement, especially if joist spans are long. Stress patterns and types of failure are the same in joists as they are in beams. When fastening joists or beams, especially with bolts, care must be exercised to prevent weakening of the member along the line of maximum shear (see Figure 460-3).

Important Reminders:

1. Lumber classified as *dimension* (NFPA) should be specified for joists. Joists must be so oriented that the cross section's longitudinal axis is vertical (i.e., narrow dimension up).

2. Ideally, joists should be supported on each end by a beam, a ledger, or metal hangers, but nailing directly to a facer is sometimes adequate for small decks with light loading requirements.

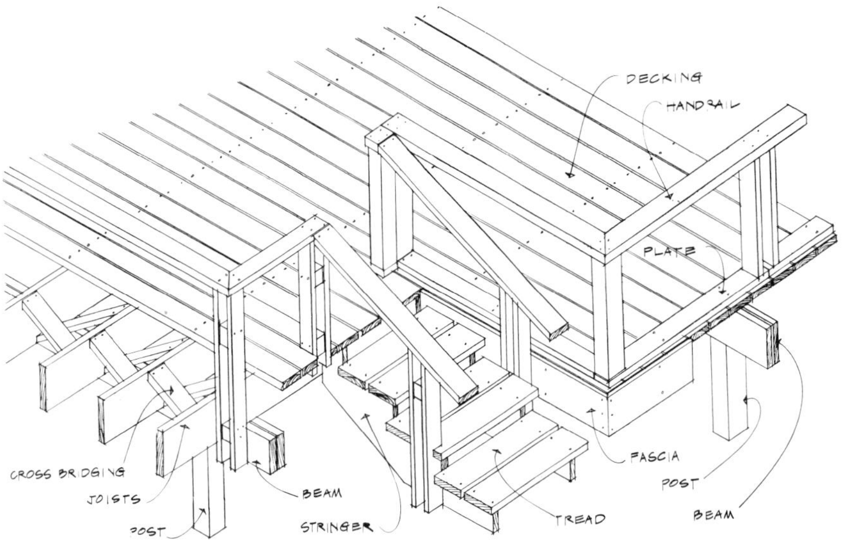
DECKING
HANDRAIL
PLATE
CROSS BRIDGING
JOISTS
POST
BEAM
STRINGER
TREAD
FASCIA
POST
BEAM

Figure 460-1 Typical platform framing.

Beams:

Beams function to support the weight of joists and decking, transferring the load to posts or directly to a foundation. Their spacing is directly related to the allowable span of the members which they are directly supporting, be they joists or decking. Typically, beams are spaced 6 to 8 ft (1.8 to 2.4 m) apart in plank-and-beam framing and 8 to 16 ft (2.4 to 4.9 m) apart in platform framing. Their required cross-sectional dimension is directly related to the length of their allowable span, given any particular loading requirement.

Common types of beams include:

1. *Simple beam:* rests on a support at each end

2. *Cantilevered beam:* supported at one end only

3. *Overhanging beam:* projects beyond one or both supports

4. *Continuous beam:* rests on three or more supports

5. *Fixed beam:* fixed at both ends

The formulas for calculating either the strength in bending or the deflection of a beam depend on the type of beam involved and on the way that the load is distributed (see Tables 460-12 and 460-13).

Figure 460-3 illustrates stress patterns and the line of maximum shear in beams.

Important Reminders:

1. Lumber classified as *beams and stringers* (NFPA) graded for strength in bending should be specified for beams.

2. Beams must be so oriented that the cross section's longitudinal axis is vertical.

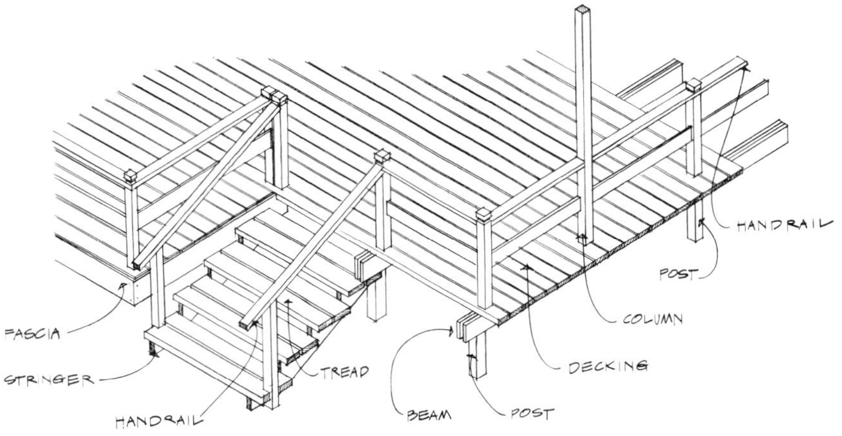
HANDRAIL
POST
COLUMN
DECKING
FASCIA
STRINGER
TREAD
HANDRAIL
BEAM
POST

Figure 460-2 Typical plank-and-beam framing.

3. Effective spans (i.e., the spacing *between* supporting members) rather than center-to-center spans are used in sizing calculations.

4. Steel and concrete beams are less commonly used in deck or boardwalk construction except under unusual loading conditions, in exceptionally long spans, or in very large deck systems.

Posts:

Posts carry the weight of the entire deck structure to the foundation. Vertical supporting members are commonly used in one way or another to control the finished elevation of a deck or boardwalk. Vertical members are not a necessary part of the construction if the deck or boardwalk is to lie close to the ground. Beams or joists can rest directly on foundations. Where posts are used, their spacing is directly related to the allowable span of the beams they are supporting.

Important Reminders:

1. Lumber classified as *post and timbers* (NFPA) graded to carry longitudinal load should be specified for posts.

2. Wood posts of approximately square cross-section have the least propensity to twist or warp.

3. Wood posts should be sized to resist buckling and, under unusually heavy loading conditions, to resist crushing. The cross-sectional dimension of a post sized

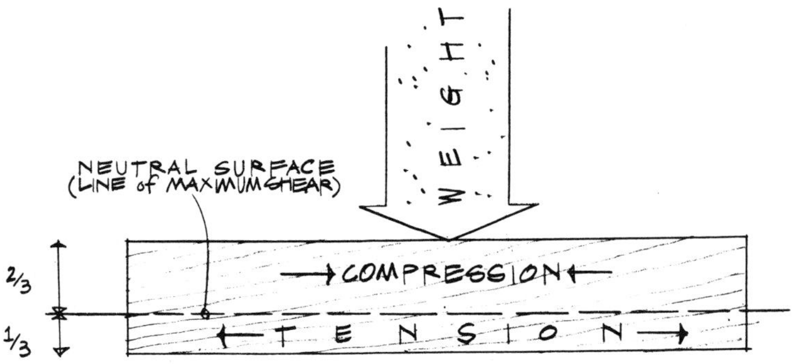
WEIGHT
NEUTRAL SURFACE (LINE of MAXIMUM SHEAR)
2/3
1/3
COMPRESSION
TENSION

Figure 460-3 Line of maximum shear. Extensive bolting along the line of maximum shear will weaken the beam.

for aesthetic reasons usually exceeds that necessary for strength reasons.

4. Posts extended up through the deck or boardwalk can also serve as a railing component.

5. Various types of post-to-pier connections are possible. Choices often depend on climate. Avoid wicking or moisture entrapment by specifying a clearance or some sort of barrier between the pier and post.

6. Steel or masonry columns are usually not tested for bearing strength except under extremely heavy loading conditions.

7. Minimize moisture infiltration at the exposed top end of wood posts by angle cutting, capping, or covering.

Footings:

Footings anchor a deck or boardwalk to the ground, supporting its weight and its expected live loading. In colder climates, footings must extend below the line of maximum frost penetration to prevent movement caused by freeze/thaw processes, but small freestanding decks and light structures can tolerate marginal soil movement and do not necessarily require footings below the frost line. If attached to stabilized structures, however, decks must also be stabilized. (Refer to Section 810: Soils and Aggregates, for information on the properties of various soils, including the bearing capacities of common soil types.)

Important Reminders:

1. Expansive clay soils, unstable organic soils, and deep fills require pier-and-beam foundations.

2. The footing size required depends on the weight to be supported and on the load-bearing capacity of the soil, although the weight of most decks and light structures rarely exceeds the bearing capacity of most soils, especially if the footing is twice the cross-sectional area of the pier. Avoid using a narrow pier without a footing, as spearing may result.

3. Reinforcing is necessary in larger footings and piers to prevent failure of the concrete, especially in colder climates.

4. Humid climates require different footing types and post connections than arid climates because of moisture trapping problems. In humid climates, avoid the possibility of wicking (i.e., capillary absorption of water), moisture entrapment, and unnecessary contact between wood posts and moisture-bearing materials such as soil, masonry, or concrete.

5. Protect footings from the possibility of washouts, i.e., soil erosion around the footing.

Bracing and Blocking:

Bracing and blocking help stabilize the deck or boardwalk by limiting lateral movement of the structure. The use of bracing should be considered on all vertical supportive members exceeding 5 ft (1.5 m) in height, and it is especially important at corners of the structure. Freestanding structures require more support than those supported by adjacent structures. Blocking is more common in platform framing than it is in plank-and-beam framing. It is less important for small decks but becomes very important for large decks, especially when long joist spans are used.

Important Reminders:

1. Methods of fastening are important in bracing details. Moisture trapping should be avoided and connections should not be weakened by inappropriate or excessive bolting, nailing, etc.

2. For short lengths of bracing (i.e., less than 8 ft (2.4 mm), 2 × 4s are commonly used, while 2 × 6s are common for longer lengths.

3. Several bracing techniques are commonly used, some being stronger than others, but the technique used is largely a matter of aesthetic preference.

Stairs and Railings:

The need for stairs and/or railings on a deck or boardwalk depends on its height above ground level. They become increasingly necessary with greater elevations above ground. Stairs essentially function as a means of level change. Thus, their purpose can sometimes be accomplished by other means, such as regrading, terraced decking, or ramps. Boardwalks can undulate vertically with the ground plane and less often require steps, terracing, or railings. Low-profile decks and boardwalks may not require either steps or railings, but elevated decks usually require both.

Stairs, ramps, railings, and other such features contribute significantly to the overall appearance (i.e., attractiveness) of the finished deck or boardwalk and therefore require careful attention to design detail.

Important Reminders:

1. Local building codes should be checked for safety requirements pertaining to tread/riser ratios, railing heights, rail spacing, etc. (Refer to Section 240: Outdoor Accessibility, and the Uniform Federal Accessibility Standards (UFAS) for information on handicapped access requirements.)

2. Tread/riser ratios are a function of the difference between the top of stair elevation and the bottom of stair elevation or, if unconstrained conditions exist, are determined according to a particular mood, character, or kinesthetic rhythm that the designer wishes to convey. Normally, outdoor stairs are less steep than indoor stairs, and are generally more pleasant, safer, and easier to negotiate. Tread/riser ratios of 15:6 and 17:5 are common. Lower ratios (e.g., 19:4) become cumbersome to negotiate.

3. Level changes can be accomplished in a variety of ways. Investigate alternatives such as regrading, successive platforms, and ramps.

4. Construction techniques for stair and railing connections vary widely. The design is often determined by the extent of durability and safety necessary. Nails sometimes are not strong enough for railing-to-deck connections. Details that incorporate bolts or lag bolts are preferred.

5. Benches can often serve as safety barriers on low decks.

3.0 DESIGN PROCESS

As in all design, the design of a deck or boardwalk necessarily involves an orderly

TABLE 460-1
Relative Comparison of Various Qualities of Wood Used in Deck Construction

	Douglas fir—larch	*Southern pine*	*Hemlock fir**	*Soft pines†*	*Western red cedar*	*Redwood*	*Spruce*	*Cypress*
Hardness	Fair	Fair	Poor	Poor	Poor	Fair	Poor	Fair
Warp resistance	Fair	Fair	Fair	Good	Good	Good	Fair	Fair
Ease of working	Poor	Fair	Fair	Good	Good	Fair	Fair	Fair
Paint-holding	Poor	Poor	Poor	Good	Good	Good	Fair	Good
Stain acceptance‡	Fair	Fair	Fair	Fair	Good	Good	Fair	Fair
Nail-holding	Good	Good	Poor	Poor	Poor	Fair	Fair	Fair
Heartwood decay resistance	Fair	Fair	Poor	Poor	Good	Good	Poor	Good
Proportion of heartwood	Good	Poor	Poor	Fair	Good	Good	Poor	Good
Bending strength	Good	Good	Fair	Poor	Poor	Fair	Fair	Fair
Stiffness	Good	Good	Good	Poor	Poor	Fair	Fair	Fair
Strength as a post	Good	Good	Fair	Poor	Fair	Good	Fair	Fair
Freedom from pitch	Fair	Poor	Good	Fair	Good	Good	Good	Good

* Includes West Coast and eastern hemlocks.

† Includes western and northeastern pines.

‡ Categories refer to semitransparent oil base stain.

Source: C. G. Ramsey and H. R. Sleeper, *Architectural Graphic Standards,* 7th ed., Robert T. Packard, ed., Wiley, New York, 1981, p. 332.

process of decision-making. Basic steps in the process include:

1. *Program requirements:* program requirements should be clarified, the proposed uses for the structure well-understood, the size requirements determined, etc.

2. *Schematic design:* the form of the deck or boardwalk, spatial organization, general decisions of scale, expected circulation patterns, and argumentation supporting such decisions should be formulated. A fairly good idea of how the structure will be constructed is also necessary at this point. In the process of design, it is common that one repeatedly return to earlier stages in the process to change (i.e., adjust) decisions made earlier, as a consequence of clarifying intentions and more precisely resolving design details.

3. *Rough layout and framing plan:* a final layout and framing plan cannot be determined until sizing calculations are made for all structural members in the wood deck or boardwalk. Calculations, of course, cannot begin until a rough framing plan is first laid out. Sizing calculations will then further refine the rough framing plan (i.e., by precisely determining the spans of all horizontal members and the size and location of all posts and footings).

4. *Sizing wood members and refinement of layout:* when sizing wood members, it is always necessary to proceed from top to bottom, i.e., from decking calculations to joist calculations to beams and lastly to post calculations. (Refer to 5.0 Sizing Wood Members in this section for a comprehensive explanation of all sizing calculations.)

5. *Details and auxiliary features:* features such as steps, railings, benches, tubs, and planters are usually not inherent parts of the structural framing of a wood deck or boardwalk, but they do have to be included in the determination of loading if they are of considerable weight. Methods of attachment are important and sometimes become part of the framing plan itself.

6. *Evaluation:* all design should be evaluated periodically in the process of design to ensure that all objectives are met.

NOTE: It is good practice to have the final design and engineering of all except minor residential-type decks and boardwalks checked by a structural engineer.

4.0 MATERIALS

4.1 Wood

Tables 460-1 and 460-2 provide comparative information on various species of wood commonly used for deck construction. Information on decay resistance and the grading of lumber is given below. (Refer to Section 850: Wood, for a comprehensive explanation of wood and wood products suitable for use out-of-doors.)

Decay Resistance:

Decay resistance is a very important consideration in wood deck and boardwalk design. Not all woods are suitable for use out-of-doors. Some species (e.g., California redwood) are naturally resistant to decay, but no species of wood, regardless of its inherent natural resistance, will last indefinitely without preventative maintenance of some kind. Because the effects of climate vary from region to region, the type of treatment necessary will also vary. (Refer to Section 850: Wood, for a comprehensive discussion of wood preservatives.)

Lumber Grades:

Careful attention to quality and the selection of *grade* designations are important for many reasons in wood deck construction. Costs vary between species and grades, appearances vary, and relative resistance to decay also varies, not only between species but also between heartwood and sapwood within the same species. Heartwood typically has greater natural resistance to decay than sapwood but is usually more expensive. Appearance is largely a subjective matter, but sapwood, containing more knots than heartwood, may be weak as a result of too many knots. Knots also accept stains and paints poorly. (Refer to Section 850: Wood, for a detailed explanation of the four regional classification systems used in the United States.)

4.2 Hardware

Various types of metal hardware are typically used in deck and boardwalk construction, primarily as a means of fastening wood members together. Representative examples of each are described below.

Anchors, Hangers, and Plates:

Various types of anchors, hangers, and plates are used to facilitate easy and strong

TABLE 460-2
Table for Selection of Decking Lumber

Species	*Growing range*	*Characteristics*	*Color*	*Average weight, lb/ft³*	*Recommended finishes and preservatives*
Western red cedar	Pacific northwest	Durable; resistant to decay and termites; high resistance to checking, weathering, and warping; free from resins; moderately soft; moderate nail-holding ability, very easy workability	Heartwood: reddish brown, light yellow Sapwood: almost pure white	23	No exterior finish required; can be treated with water preservatives, bleaches, stains, or blister-resistant paints; good finish-holding ability
Southern yellow pine (longleaf, slash, shortleaf, loblolly)	Southeastern United States and Gulf states	High resistance to decay and termites when pressure-treated with preservatives; heavy, hard, and resinous; very strong and stiff; high resistance to blemishes and scars; moderate warp resistance; good nail-holding ability; moderately easy workability	Heartwood: reddish brown to orange Sapwood: cream to light yellow	36–43	Should be pressure-treated with preservatives for maximum durability, especially in moist situations and humid climates; moderate to poor paint-holding ability
Redwood	Pacific Northwest (coastal)	Durable; natural resistance to decay, disease, and termites; resistant to checking and warping; free from pitch, resins, and oils; moderately hard, strong, and stiff; medium nail-holding ability; good finish-holding ability; easy workability	Heartwood: cherry to deep red Sapwood: cream to nearly white	28	No exterior finish required; no preservatives required for heartwood, including in-ground use; can be treated with water-repellent preservatives; bleaches, or light-bodied pigment stains; can be painted; good finish-holding ability
Douglas fir-western larch	Western United States (Rocky Mountains and coast ranges)	Heartwood is moderately decay-resistant; moderate resistance to cupping and twisting; resinous; moderately hard; very heavy, strong, and stiff; good nail-holding ability; moderately difficult workability	Heartwood: orange red, reddish brown Sapwood: yellowish white	33–38	Preservative treatment recommended for exterior use; average stain-holding ability; moderate to poor paint-holding ability

TABLE 460-2 *(Continued)*

Species	*Growing range*	*Characteristics*	*Color*	*Average weight, lb/ft³*	*Recommended finishes and preservatives*
Eastern white, northern and western pine	Eastern and Northern Pine: Alantic states and Great Lakes states Western Pine: Idaho, western states	Very light and soft with poor resistance to decay and termites; warp resistance high; moderate nail-holding ability; easy workability	Heartwood: cream, light reddish, orange, or light brown Sapwood: nearly white	25–28	Should be pressure-treated with preservatives for maximum durability. Accepts paints and stains well
Eastern and western hemlock (hem-fir)	Eastern hemlock: Northeastern United States and Appalachian range Western hemlock: Idaho, Montana, and Pacific	Poor durability; fairly strong and stiff; nonresinous; resistant to checking, warping, and weathering; poor nail-holding ability; western hemlock moderately easy to work, eastern hemlock more difficult	Heartwood: reddish brown Sapwood: cream	29	Should be well-treated with preservatives; accepts most oil or water-base preservatives and finishes; poor paint-holding ability
Spruce (Engelmann, eastern)	Engelmann: Cascade and Rocky Mountain ranges Eastern (Red, White, and Black): Maine through Great Lakes states, Canada	Poor decay resistance; warp, split, and splinter resistant; nonresinous; lightweight; moderately strong and stiff; good nail-holding ability; easy workability	Heartwood and sapwood: nearly white to pale yellowish-brown	24	Preservative treatment recommended; will accept most preservatives and finishes; good paint-holding ability

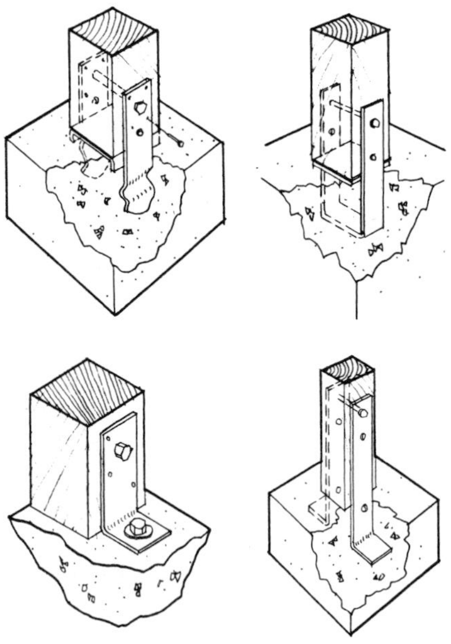

Figure 460-4 Typical post anchors.

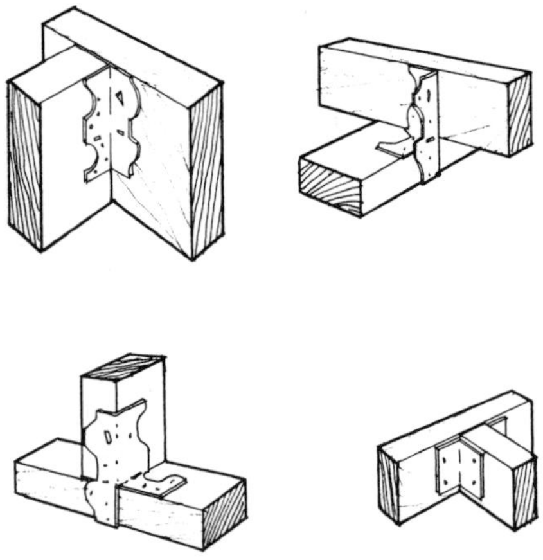

Figure 460-5 Typical framing anchors.

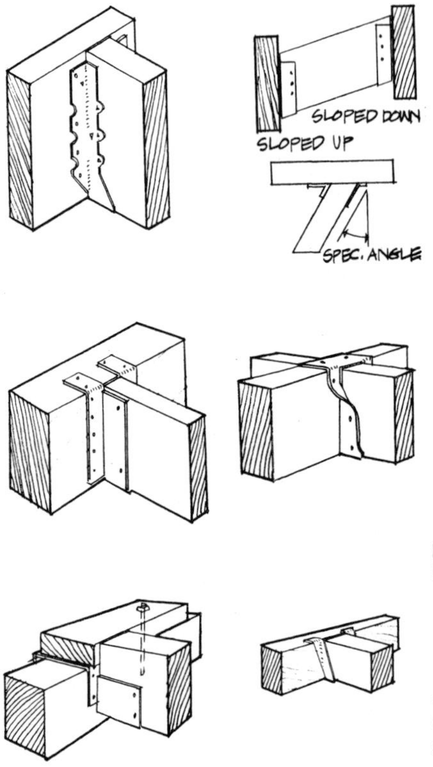
SLOPED DOWN
SLOPED UP
SPEC. ANGLE

Figure 460-6 Typical joist hangers and girder hangers.

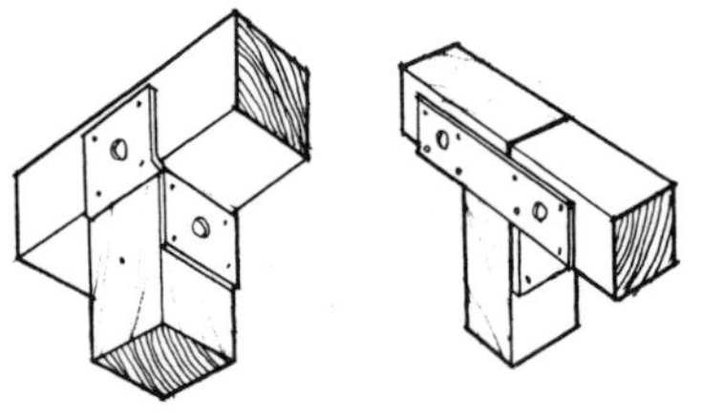

Figure 460-7 Typical post cap and tie plate.

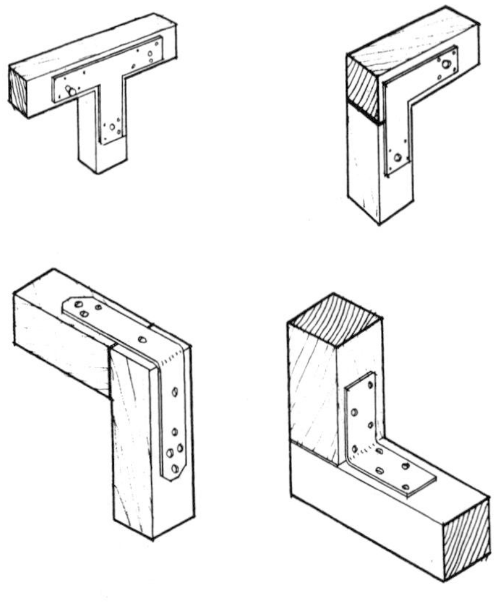

Figure 460-8 Typical metal straps and brackets.

connections between various wood members and between wood members and concrete foundations (Figures 460-4 through 460-8.)

Nails:

Figure 460-9 illustrates those types of nails that are commonly used in wood deck and boardwalk construction. (Refer to Section 860: Metals, for a comprehensive description of several other types of nails.)

Important Reminders:

1. The dimensions, shape, and surface of a nail affect its holding power. Normally, a nail 2½ times as long as the thickness of the board nailed should be used. Hot-dipped galvanized, zinc-coated, cement-coated, ring, and spiral nails also resist withdrawal.

2. Nails with heads (e.g., common) should be used for structural framing. Finish nails are only used in nonstructural situations where appearance is important. Driving the nail at a slight angle will improve its holding power.

3. Nails may tend to pull out under heavy loading conditions. Bolts or lag bolts should be used in such instances.

4. Aluminum, stainless-steel, and hot-dipped galvanized nails resist rusting and consequent staining of wood.

5. Nails are available in zinc, brass, monel, copper, aluminum, iron, steel, stainless steel, copper bearing steel, and muntz metal. Coatings include tin, copper, cement, brass-plated, zinc, nickel, chrome, cadmium, etched acid, and parkerized.

Wood Screws:

Figure 460-10 illustrates those types of screws that are commonly used in wood deck and boardwalk construction. (Refer to Section 860: Metals, for a comprehensive description of several other types of screws.)

Important Reminders:

1. A screw should be long enough to embed more than one-half of its length into the base.

2. Clearance and pilot holes facilitate the installation of screws and will prevent splitting of the wood member.

3. Flathead screws may be flush or countersunk. Washers under the head are recommended for roundheaded screws, especially with softer woods. These can also be countersunk.

Bolts:

Figure 460-11 illustrates those types of bolts that are commonly used in wood deck and boardwalk construction. (Refer to Section 860: Metals, for a comprehensive description of several other types of bolts.)

Important Reminders:

1. Bolts should be long enough to permit a washer under both the head and the nut and allow at least 3⁄16 in (5 mm) to protrude beyond the nut. Carriage bolts are used with metal plates with a square hole to prevent the bolt from turning while being tightened.

2. A hole 1⁄16-in greater than the diameter of the bolt should be drilled for a snug fit. Washers at both ends of bolts are recommended.

3. Lag bolts require a washer under the head. The threaded end of a lag bolt should never be exposed. Pilot holes facilitate the installation of the lag bolt and will prevent splitting of the wood member.

4.3 Masonry

Although this section on deck and boardwalk construction focuses on the use of wood as a material, it should be noted that in many instances other materials offer advantages. For instance, concrete and other types of masonry materials (such as brick and stone) can be used to build the support system or be used for other components of a deck or boardwalk. Some of these nonwood materials are much stronger and more durable than wood in certain climates, and they can offer many aesthetic advantages as well.

4.4 Other Materials

Plant Materials:

In addition to the use of plants for defining outdoor space and for providing character to a setting, plant materials can be used with low decks and boardwalks to define edges and to help prevent users from accidentally walking or falling off the structure. Plant materials can also provide screening and windbreaks that might otherwise have to be constructed and maintained at much greater expense.

Metals:

In addition to hardware, metal products such as tubing can be used for such structures as railings, foot rests, arbors, overhead canopies, planters, and the like. Members such as I-beams and metal columns can be substituted for wooden beams and posts, respectively.

Plastics:

The wide variety of plastics available make this material ideal for many situations. Used for railings, arbors, overhead canopies, tubs, planters, and the like, plastics offer durability, light weight, and innumerable colors. As construction materials, plastics have yet to be used to their fullest potential.

Fabrics:

Fabrics are ideal for such structures as screens, overhead canopies, and miscellaneous decorative elements. The many colors available, especially in the lightweight synthetic fabrics, are advantageous for use as overhead canopies, roofs of gazebos, and the like. Fabrics can also be used as a part of railings for added privacy.

5.0 SIZING WOOD MEMBERS

Joists, beams, and posts should be sized by use of formulas, although tables for this purpose are readily available. Many designers feel comfortable relying exclusively on tabular data for their sizing determinations if the deck is simple or not unusually large—but in most situations it is best to double-check sizing decisions with formulas, if for no other reason than as a second assurance that the deck or boardwalk is safe. Tables have their greatest value as expedient means for tentative decision-making during preliminary design stages. Formulas can then be used to check the final scheme for adequacy. Tabular data should never be relied upon exclusively in final design decisions where large or complex deck systems are involved.

It is necessary to proceed from top to bottom when sizing wood members for a deck, i.e., from decking calculations to joist calculations to beams and lastly to post calculations. Figure 460-12 shows the interrelationships between decking spans, joist spans, and beam spans.

5.1 Span Tables

Tables 460-4 through 460-6 provide a quick means for determining *maximum allowable spans* for decking, joists, and beams based on their cross-sectional dimensions, the species of lumber used, and in the case of joists and beams, their spacing. Table 460-8 shows post sizes and corresponding *maximum allowable heights* based on the cross-sectional dimensions and the species of lumber used.

Note that these tables are based on a uniform live loading of 40 psf, a common figure for residential decks, and that the dimensions in these tables represent *maximum allowable* spans, sizes, or heights. Margins of safety are a normal precaution and are always recommended. Also, stiffer decks are nearly always preferred and are more likely to be used.

Table 460-3 classifies various species of wood according to their inherent strength characteristics. It is used in conjunction with the span tables, Tables 460-4 through 460-7.

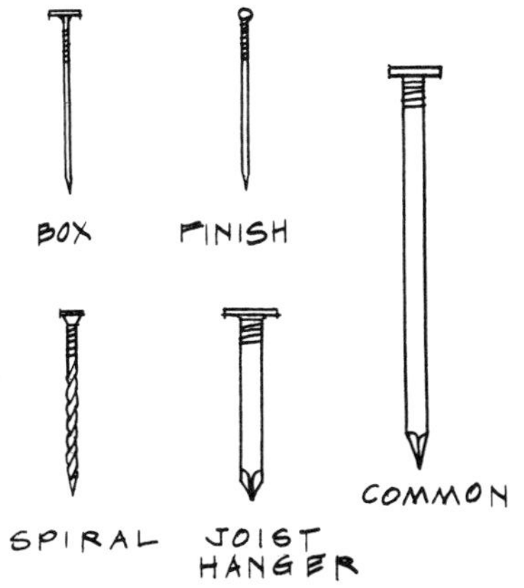
BOX
FINISH
SPIRAL
JOIST HANGER
COMMON

Figure 460-9 Nails commonly used in wood deck construction.

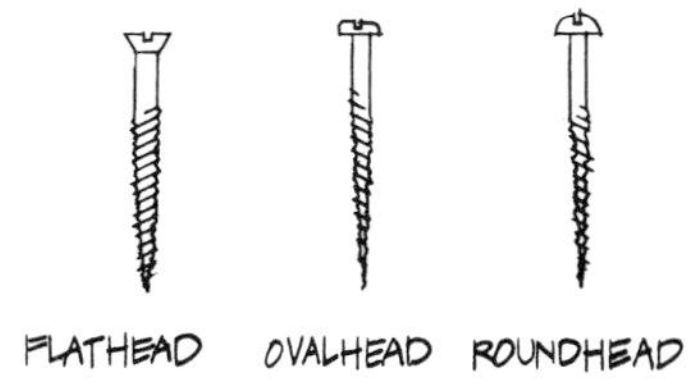
FLATHEAD
OVALHEAD
ROUNDHEAD

Figure 460-10 Wood screws commonly used in wood deck construction.

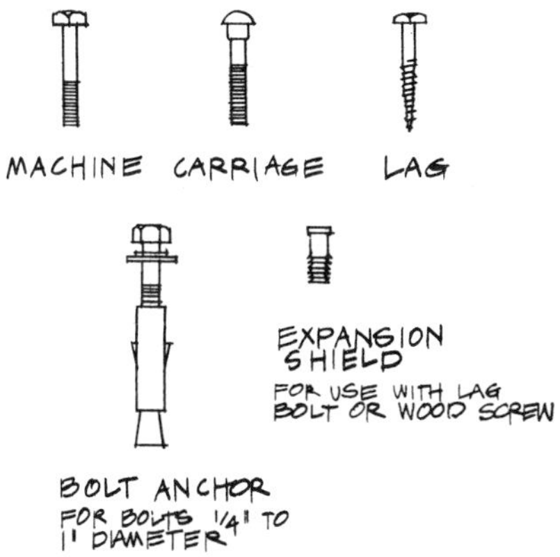
MACHINE
CARRIAGE
LAG
EXPANSION SHIELD
FOR USE WITH LAG BOLT OR WOOD SCREW
BOLT ANCHOR
FOR BOLTS 1/4" TO 1" DIAMETER

Figure 460-11 Bolts commonly used in wood deck construction.

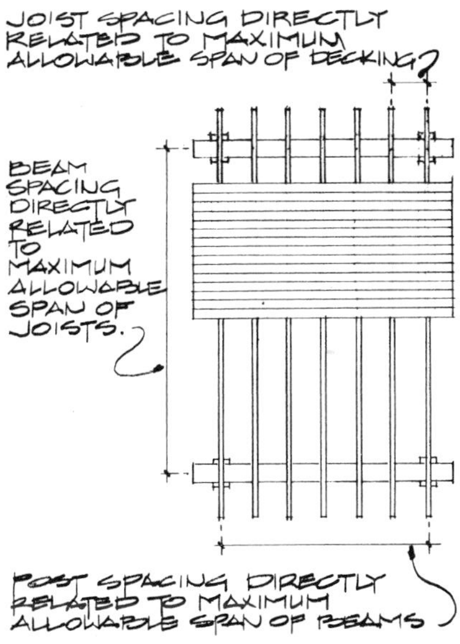
JOIST SPACING DIRECTLY RELATED TO MAXIMUM ALLOWABLE SPAN OF DECKING
BEAM SPACING DIRECTLY RELATED TO MAXIMUM ALLOWABLE SPAN OF JOISTS.
POST SPACING DIRECTLY RELATED TO MAXIMUM ALLOWABLE SPAN OF BEAMS

Figure 460-12 Decking, joist, and beam span relationships.

TABLE 460-3
Strength Groupings of Common Softwood Species*

Strength group	*Species*
High	Douglas fir
	Hemlock, western
	Larch, western
	Pine:
	Loblolly†
	Longleaf†
	Pitch
	Slash
	Shortleaf
	Virginia
	Spruce:
	Canadian coastal
	Coast Sitka
Moderate	Cedar, western red
	Cypress
	Douglas fir (south)
	Fir:
	Subalpine
	White
	Hemlock:
	Eastern
	Western
	Pine:
	Eastern white
	Lodgepole
	Ponderosa
	Red
	Sugar
	Western white
	Redwood, California
	Spruce:
	Eastern
	Engelmann
	Sitka
	Tamarack
Low	Cedar, northern white

* No. 1 or better.

† Also known as southern pine.

Source: Adapted from *U.S. Department of Agriculture Construction Guides for Exposed Wood Decks,* U.S.D.A. Handbook No. 432, 1972.

TABLE 460-5
Maximum Allowable Spans for Joists

Joist material	*Strength group*	*Maximum allowable span*
	16-in joist spacings	
2 × 6	High	9′9″
	Moderate	8′7″
	Low	7′9″
2 × 8	High	12′10″
	Moderate	11′4″
	Low	10′2″
2 × 10	High	16′5″
	Moderate	14′6″
	Low	13′0″
	24-in joist spacings	
2 × 6	High	7′11″
	Moderate	7′0″
	Low	6′2″
2 × 8	High	10′6″
	Moderate	9′3″
	Low	8′1″
2 × 10	High	13′4″
	Moderate	11′10″
	Low	10′4″
	32-in joist spacings	
2 × 6	High	6′2″
	Moderate	5′8″
	Low	5′0″
2 × 8	High	8′1″
	Moderate	7′6″
	Low	6′8″
2 × 10	High	10′4″
	Moderate	9′6″
	Low	8′6″

Source: Adapted from *U. S. Department of Agriculture Construction Guides for Exposed Wood Decks,* U.S.D.A. Handbook No. 432, 1972.

TABLE 460-4
Maximum Allowable Spans for Decking*

Decking material	*Strength group*	*Maximum allowable span, in*
2 × 2, 2 × 4, 2 × 6, 2 × 8, 2 × 10, 2 × 12 (laid flat)	High	64
	Moderate	57
	Low	51
2 × 3 (laid on edge)	High	108
	Moderate	96
	Low	86
2 × 4 (laid on edge)	High	152
	Moderate	134
	Low	120

* Span for diagonal decking should be measured on diagonal, not joist spacing.

Source: Adapted from *U. S. Department of Agriculture Construction Guides for Exposed Wood Decks,* U.S.D.A. Handbook No. 432, 1972.

5.2 Sizing by Formulas (Decking, Joists, and Beams)

Sizing decisions for horizontal members in a deck structure are based on the *strength in bending* of the members. However, since a wood member can be well within the limits of safety but still deflect considerably, members are also often checked for deflection (and adjusted if necessary) if a stiffer deck is desired. This is especially true for decking members. Stiffness is a desirable trait of most decks and boardwalks, mainly for psychological reasons.

If the deflection is not meant to be noticeable, the extent of deflection should be limited to 1/200th the span of the members in question. If joinery to a fixed structure (e.g., stucco) might be damaged by the deflection of a deck, then the deflection should be kept to 1/360th of the span of the members in question.

Sizing Decking, Joists, and Beams:

Sizing the horizontal members of a proposed deck or boardwalk, whether it be for decking, joists, or beams, refers to a determination of adequate *cross-sectional* dimensions, given a span and particular species of lumber. A horizontal member is sized by performing calculations to determine the required *section modulus* of the member in question (see Table 460-12).

Sizing wood members for a deck or boardwalk is always carried out from top to bottom, i.e., beginning with the decking and then proceeding with the joists, beams, and posts. However, it should be noted that the sizing procedure is not entirely linear because factors such as aesthetics, spatial constraints, and psychological considerations typically make it necessary (during the process) to go back and adjust the initial sizing decisions until a point is reached at which the entire structure conforms to the intentions of the designer. The members of a deck or boardwalk are never sized by relying exclusively on strength considerations. It should also be noted that because the dimensions of various members in a wood deck are based (to some extent) on reasons of appearance, the result is a deck that is often stronger than absolutely necessary.

The following procedure is used to determine adequate section moduli for decking, joists, and beams:

1. Determine the *maximum bending moment (M)* (ft-lb). (Refer to Table 460-10 for the applicable formula. Convert ft-lb to in-lb by multiplying by 12.)

2. Determine the *extreme fiber stress in bending (fb)* (psi). (Refer to Table 460-11 for the applicable value.)

3. Compute the *required section modulus*

TABLE 460-6
Maximum Allowable Spans for Beams*

<table>
<tr><th rowspan="2">Beam size, in</th><th colspan="9">Spacing between beams, ft</th></tr>
<tr><th>4</th><th>5</th><th>6</th><th>7</th><th>8</th><th>9</th><th>10</th><th>11</th><th>12</th></tr>
<tr><td></td><td colspan="9">Species group: high</td></tr>
<tr><td>4 × 6</td><td colspan="3">Up to 6′ spans →</td><td></td><td></td><td></td><td></td><td></td><td></td></tr>
<tr><td>3 × 8</td><td colspan="2">Up to 8′ →</td><td>Up to 7′ →</td><td colspan="3">Up to 6′ spans →</td><td></td><td></td><td></td></tr>
<tr><td>4 × 8</td><td>Up to 10′ →</td><td>Up to 9′ →</td><td>Up to 8′ →</td><td colspan="2">Up to 7′ →</td><td colspan="3">Up to 6′ spans →</td><td></td></tr>
<tr><td>3 × 10</td><td>Up to 11′ →</td><td>Up to 10′ →</td><td>Up to 9′ →</td><td colspan="2">Up to 8′ →</td><td colspan="2">Up to 7′ →</td><td colspan="2">Up to 6′ →</td></tr>
<tr><td>4 × 10</td><td>Up to 12′ →</td><td>Up to 11′ →</td><td>Up to 10′ →</td><td colspan="2">Up to 9′ →</td><td colspan="2">Up to 8′ →</td><td colspan="2">Up to 7′ →</td></tr>
<tr><td>3 × 12</td><td></td><td>Up to 12′ →</td><td>Up to 11′ →</td><td>Up to 10′ →</td><td colspan="2">Up to 9′ →</td><td colspan="3">Up to 8′ spans →</td></tr>
<tr><td>4 × 12</td><td></td><td></td><td colspan="2">Up to 12′ →</td><td>Up to 11′ →</td><td colspan="2">Up to 10′ →</td><td colspan="2">Up to 9′ →</td></tr>
<tr><td>6 × 10</td><td></td><td></td><td></td><td></td><td>Up to 12′ →</td><td>Up to 11′ →</td><td colspan="3">Up to 10′ spans →</td></tr>
<tr><td>6 × 12</td><td></td><td></td><td></td><td></td><td></td><td colspan="4">Up to 12′ spans →</td></tr>
<tr><td></td><td colspan="9">Species group: moderate</td></tr>
<tr><td>4 × 6</td><td colspan="2">Up to 6′ →</td><td></td><td></td><td></td><td></td><td></td><td></td><td></td></tr>
<tr><td>3 × 8</td><td colspan="2">Up to 7′ →</td><td colspan="2">Up to 6′ →</td><td></td><td></td><td></td><td></td><td></td></tr>
<tr><td>4 × 8</td><td>Up to 9′ →</td><td>Up to 8′ →</td><td colspan="2">Up to 7′ →</td><td colspan="2">Up to 6′ →</td><td></td><td></td><td></td></tr>
<tr><td>3 × 10</td><td>Up to 10′ →</td><td>Up to 9′ →</td><td>Up to 8′ →</td><td colspan="2">Up to 7′ →</td><td colspan="3">Up to 6′ spans →</td><td></td></tr>
<tr><td>4 × 10</td><td>Up to 11′ →</td><td>Up to 10′ →</td><td>Up to 9′ →</td><td colspan="2">Up to 8′ →</td><td colspan="3">Up to 7′ spans →</td><td>Up to 6′</td></tr>
<tr><td>3 × 12</td><td>Up to 12′ →</td><td>Up to 11′ →</td><td>Up to 10′ →</td><td>Up to 9′ →</td><td colspan="2">Up to 8′ →</td><td colspan="3">Up to 7′ →</td></tr>
<tr><td>4 × 12</td><td></td><td>Up to 12′ →</td><td>Up to 11′ →</td><td colspan="2">Up to 10′ →</td><td colspan="2">Up to 9′ →</td><td colspan="2">Up to 8′ →</td></tr>
<tr><td>6 × 10</td><td></td><td></td><td>Up to 12′ →</td><td>Up to 11′ →</td><td colspan="2">Up to 10′ →</td><td colspan="3">Up to 9′ spans →</td></tr>
<tr><td>6 × 12</td><td></td><td></td><td></td><td colspan="3">Up to 12′ spans →</td><td colspan="2">Up to 11′ →</td><td>Up to 10′</td></tr>
<tr><td></td><td colspan="9">Species group: low</td></tr>
<tr><td>4 × 6</td><td>Up to 6′ →</td><td></td><td></td><td></td><td></td><td></td><td></td><td></td><td></td></tr>
<tr><td>3 × 8</td><td>Up to 7′ →</td><td>Up to 6′ →</td><td></td><td></td><td></td><td></td><td></td><td></td><td></td></tr>
<tr><td>4 × 8</td><td>Up to 8′ →</td><td>Up to 7′ →</td><td colspan="2">Up to 6′ →</td><td></td><td></td><td></td><td></td><td></td></tr>
<tr><td>3 × 10</td><td>Up to 9′ →</td><td>Up to 8′ →</td><td>Up to 7′ →</td><td colspan="3">Up to 6′ spans →</td><td></td><td></td><td></td></tr>
<tr><td>4 × 10</td><td>Up to 10′ →</td><td>Up to 9′ →</td><td colspan="2">Up to 8′ →</td><td colspan="2">Up to 7′ →</td><td colspan="3">Up to 6′ spans →</td></tr>
<tr><td>3 × 12</td><td>Up to 11′ →</td><td>Up to 10′ →</td><td>Up to 9′ →</td><td>Up to 8′ →</td><td colspan="3">Up to 7′ spans →</td><td colspan="2">Up to 6′ →</td></tr>
<tr><td>4 × 12</td><td>Up to 12′ →</td><td>Up to 11′ →</td><td>Up to 10′ →</td><td colspan="2">Up to 9′ →</td><td colspan="2">Up to 8′ →</td><td colspan="2">Up to 7′ →</td></tr>
<tr><td>6 × 10</td><td></td><td>Up to 12′ →</td><td>Up to 11′ →</td><td>Up to 10′ →</td><td colspan="2">Up to 9′ →</td><td colspan="3">Up to 8′ spans →</td></tr>
<tr><td>6 × 12</td><td></td><td></td><td colspan="2">Up to 12′ →</td><td colspan="2">Up to 11′ →</td><td colspan="2">Up to 10′ →</td><td>Up to 8′</td></tr>
</table>

* Beams are assumed to be on edge, spans are center to center distances between posts or supports, and based on 40 p.s.f. deck live load plus 10 p.s.f. dead load, using grade No. 2 or better; No. 2, medium grain southern pine.

† Group 1—Douglas fir-larch and southern pine; Group 2—Hem-fir and Douglas-fir south; Group 3—Westen pines and cedars, redwood, and spruces.

Source: Adapted from *U. S. Department of Agriculture Construction Guides for Exposed Wood Decks,* U.S.D.A. Handbook No. 432, 1972.

TABLE 460-7
Recommended Live-Loads for Decking

Surface	*Load, lb/ft²*
Residential decks, light-duty	40
Public decks, heavy-duty	80–100
Foot bridges	100
Light vehicular bridges	200–300

Note: Data are for evenly distributed live loads. The higher numbers are intended for northern areas subject to snow loading.

Source: Adapted from *U. S. Department of Agriculture Construction Guides for Exposed Wood Decks,* U.S.D.A. Handbook No. 432, 1972.

TABLE 460-8
Maximum Allowable Post Heights*

Post size, in	*Load area = beam spacing × post spacing, ft²*									
	36	*48*	*60*	*72*	*84*	*96*	*108*	*120*	*132*	*144*
					Species group: high					
4 × 4	Up to 12′ heights →				Up to 10′ heights →			Up to 8′ heights →		
4 × 6					Up to 12′ heights →				Up to 10′ →	
6 × 6									Up to 12′ heights →	
					Species group: moderate					
4 × 4	Up to 12′ →		Up to 10′ →			Up to 8′ heights →				
4 × 6			Up to 12′ →			Up to 10′ heights →				
6 × 6						Up to 12′ heights →				
					Species group: low					
4 × 4	Up to 12′ →	Up to 10′ →		Up to 8′ →			Up to 6′ heights →			
4 × 6		Up to 12′ →		Up to 10′ →			Up to 8′ heights →			
6 × 6				Up to 12′ heights →						

* Based on 40 p.s.f. deck live load plus 10 p.s.f. dead load. Grade Standard and Better for 4 × 4 inch posts and No. 1 and Better for larger sizes.

Source: Adapted from *U.S. Department of Agriculture Construction Guides for Exposed Wood Decks,* U.S.D.A. Handbook No. 432, 1972.

TABLE 460-9
Moduli of Elasticity

*Species and commercial grade**	*Size classification*	*Modulus of elasticity*
Balsam fir, eastern spruce		
Select structural		1,200,000
No. 1	2–4″ thick	1,200,000
No. 2	2–4″ wide	1,100,000
No. 3		900,000
Stud		900,000
Construction	2–4″ thick	900,000
Standard	4″ wide	900,000
Utility		900,000
Select structural	2–4″ thick	1,200,000
No. 1	5″ and wider	1,200,000
No. 2		1,100,000
No. 3		900,000
Stud		900,000
California redwood		
Select decking†	Decking	1,400,000
Select decking	2″ thick	1,100,000
Commercial decking	6″ and wider	1,000,000
Douglas fir-larch		
Select structural	2–4″ thick	1,800,000
No. 1	2–4″ wide	1,800,000
No. 2		1,700,000
No. 3		1,500,000
Appearance		1,800,000
Stud		1,500,000
Construction	2–4″ thick	1,500,000
Standard	4″ wide	1,500,000
Utility		1,500,000
Dense select structural	2–4″ thick	1,900,000
Select structural	5″ and wider	1,800,000
Dense No. 1		1,900,000
No. 1		1,800,000
Dense No. 2		1,700,000
No. 2		1,700,000
No. 3		1,500,000
Appearance		1,800,000
Stud		1,500,000
Dense select structural	Beams and stringers	1,700,000
Selected structural		1,600,000
Dense No. 1		1,700,000
No. 1		1,600,000
Dense select structural	Posts and timbers	1,700,000
Select structural		1,600,000
Dense No. 1		1,700,000
No. 1		1,600,000
Selected decking	Decking	1,600,000
Commercial decking		1,700,000
Selected decking	Decking	1,900,000
Commercial decking		1,700,000
Engelmann spruce-alpine fir (Engelmann spruce-lodgepole pine)		
Select structural	2–4″ thick	1,300,000
No. 1	2–4″ wide	1,300,000
No. 2		1,100,000
No. 3		1,000,000
Appearance		1,300,000
Stud		1,000,000
Construction	2–4″ thick	1,000,000
Standard	4″ wide	1,000,000
Utility		1,000,000
Select structural	2–4″ thick	1,300,000
No. 1	5″ and wider	1,300,000
No. 2		1,100,000
No. 3		1,000,000
Appearance		1,300,000
Stud		1,000,000
Select structural	Beams and stringers	1,100,000
No. 1		1,100,000
Engelmann spruce-alpine fir (Engelmann spruce-lodgepole pine) (Continued)		
Select structural	Posts and timbers	1,100,000
No. 1		1,100,000
Selected decking	Decking	1,300,000
Commercial decking		1,100,000
Selected decking	Decking	1,300,000
Commercial decking		1,200,000
Spruce-pine-fir		
Select structural	2–4″ thick	1,500,000
No. 1	2–4″ wide	1,500,000
No. 2		1,300,000
No. 3		1,200,000
Appearance		1,500,000
Stud		1,200,000
Construction	2–4″ thick	1,200,000
Standard	4″ wide	1,200,000
Utility		1,200,000
Select structural	2–4″ thick	1,500,000
No. 1	5″ and wider	1,500,000
No. 2		1,300,000
No. 3		1,200,000
Appearance		1,500,000
Stud		1,200,000
Select	Decking	1,500,000
Commercial		1,300,000
Western cedar		
Selected decking	Decking	1,100,000
Commercial decking		1,000,000
Selected decking	Decking	1,100,000
Commercial decking		1,000,000
Western hemlock		
Select structural	2–4″ thick	1,600,000
No. 1	2–4″ wide	1,600,000
No. 2		1,400,000
No. 3		1,300,000
Appearance		1,600,000
Stud		1,300,000
Construction	2–4″ thick	1,300,000
Standard	4″ wide	1,300,000
Utility		1,300,000
Select structural	2–4″ thick	1,600,000
No. 1	5″ and wider	1,600,000
No. 2		1,400,000
No. 3		1,300,000
Appearance		1,600,000
Stud		1,300,000
Select structural	Beams and stringers	1,400,000
No. 1		1,400,000
Select structural	Posts and timbers	1,400,000
No. 1		1,400,000
Select dex	Decking	1,600,000
Commercial dex		1,400,000
Selected decking	Decking	1,600,000
Commercial decking		1,400,000
Selected decking	Decking	1,700,000
Commercial decking		1,500,000
White woods (western woods)		
Select structural	2–4″ thick	1,100,000
No. 1	2–4″ wide	1,100,000
No. 2		1,000,000
No. 3		900,000
Appearance		1,100,000

(continued)

TABLE 460-9 *(Continued)*

*Species and commercial grade**	*Size classification*	*Modulus of elasticity*
White woods (western woods) (Continued)		
Stud		900,000
Construction	2–4″ thick	900,000
Standard	4″ wide	900,000
Utility		900,000
Select structural	2–4″ thick	1,100,000
No. 1	5″ and wider	1,100,000
No. 2		1,000,000
No. 3		900,000
Appearance		1,100,000
Stud		900,000
Select structural	Beams and	1,000,000
No. 1	stringers	1,000,000
Select structural	Posts and	1,000,000
No. 1	timbers	1,000,000
Selected decking	Decking	1,100,000
Commercial decking		1,000,000
Selected decking	Decking	1,100,000
Commercial decking		1,000,000
Southern pine‡		
Select structural	2–4″ thick	1,800,000
No. 1	2–4″ wide	1,200,000
No. 2		1,600,000
No. 3		1,500,000
Stud		1,500,000
Construction	2–4″ thick	1,500,000
Standard	4″ wide	1,500,000
Utility		1,500,000
Select structural	2–4″ thick	1,800,000
Dense select structural	5″ and wider	1,900,000
No. 1		1,800,000
No. 1 dense		1,900,000
No. 2		1,600,000
No. 2 dense		1,700,000
No. 3		1,500,000
No. 3 dense		1,500,000
Stud		1,500,000
Dense standard decking	2–4″ thick	1,900,000
Select decking	2″ and wider	1,600,000
Dense select decking	Decking	1,700,000
Commercial decking		1,600,000
Dense commercial decking		1,700,000

*Species and commercial grade**	*Size classification*	*Modulus of elasticity*
Southern pine‡		
Select structural	2–4″ thick	1,700,000
No. 1	2–4″ wide	1,700,000
No. 2		1,600,000
No. 3		1,400,000
Stud		1,400,000
Construction	2–4″ thick	1,400,000
Standard	4″ wide	1,400,000
Utility		1,400,000
Select structural	2–4″ thick	1,700,000
Dense select structural	5″ and wider	1,800,000
No. 1		1,700,000
No. 1 dense		1,800,000
No. 2		1,600,000
No. 2 dense		1,600,000
No. 3		1,400,000
No. 3 dense		1,500,000
Stud		1,400,000
Dense standard decking	2–4″ thick	1,800,000
Select decking	2″ and wider	1,600,000
Dense select decking	Decking	1,600,000
Commercial decking		1,600,000
Dense commercial decking		1,600,000
Southern pine¶		
Select structural	2½–4″ thick	1,500,000
No. 1	2½–4″ wide	1,500,000
No. 2		1,400,000
No. 3		1,200,000
Stud		1,200,000
Construction	2½–4″ thick	1,200,000
Standard	4″ wide	1,200,000
Utility		1,200,000
Select structural	2½–4″ thick	1,500,000
Dense select structural	5″ and wider	1,600,000
No. 1		1,500,000
No. 1 dense		1,600,000
No. 2		1,400,000
No. 2 dense		1,400,000
No. 3		1,200,000
No. 3 dense		1,300,000
Stud		1,200,000
Dense standard decking	2½–4″ thick	1,600,000

* Surfaced dry or surfaced green. Used at 19% maximum moisture content.

† Close grain.

‡ Surfaced at 15% maximum moisture content, K. D. Used at 15%.

§ Surfaced dry. Used at 19% maximum moisture content.

¶ Surfaced green. Used at any condition.

Source: Adapted from C. G. Ramsey and H. R. Sleeper, *Architectural Graphic Standards,* 7th ed., Robert T. Packard (ed.), Wiley, New York, 1980, as prepared by the National Forest Products Association, Washington, D.C.

TABLE 460-9 *(Continued)*

Species and commercial grade*	Size classification	Modulus of elasticity
Sourthern pine¶ (Continued)		
Select decking	2″ and wider	1,400,000
Dense select decking	Decking	1,400,000
Commercial decking		1,400,000
Dense commercial decking		1,400,000
No. 1 SR	5″ and thicker	1,500,000
No. 1 dense SR		1,600,000
No. 2 SR		1,400,000
No. 2 dense SR		1,400,000
Hem-fir		
Select structural	2–4″ thick	1,500,000
No. 1	2–4″ wide	1,500,000
No. 2		1,400,000
No. 3		1,200,000
Appearance		1,500,000
Stud		1,200,000
Construction	2–4″ thick	1,200,000
Standard	4″ wide	1,200,000
Utility		1,200,000
Select structural	2–4″ thick	1,500,000
No. 1	5″ and wider	1,500,000
No. 2		1,400,000
No. 3		1,200,000
Appearance		1,500,000
Stud		1,200,000
Select structural	Beams and stringers	1,300,000
No. 1		1,300,000
Select structural	Posts and timbers	1,300,000
No. 1		1,300,000
Selected decking	Decking	1,500,000
Commercial decking		1,400,000
Selected decking	Decking	1,600,000
Commercial decking		1,400,000
Idaho white pine		
Selected decking	Decking	1,400,000
Commercial decking		1,300,000
Selected decking	Decking	1,500,000
Commercial decking		1,400,000

Species and commercial grade*	Size classification	Modulus of elasticity
Northern pine		
Select structural	2–4″ thick	1,400,000
No. 1	2–4″ wide	1,400,000
No. 2		1,300,000
No. 3		1,100,000
Appearance		1,400,000
Stud		1,100,000
Construction	2–4″ thick	1,100,000
Standard	4″ wide	1,100,000
Utility		1,100,000
Select structural	2–4″ thick	1,400,000
No. 1	5″ and wider	1,400,000
No. 2		1,300,000
No. 3		1,100,000
Appearance		1,400,000
Stud		1,100,000
Ponderosa pine-sugar pine (ponderosa pine, lodgepole pine)		
Select structural	2–4″ thick	1,200,000
No. 1	2–4″ wide	1,200,000
No. 2		1,100,000
No. 3		1,000,000
Appearance		1,200,000
Stud		1,000,000
Construction	2–4″ thick	1,000,000
Standard	4″ wide	1,000,000
Utility		1,000,000
Select structural	2–4″ thick	1,200,000
No. 1	5″ and wider	1,200,000
No. 2		1,100,000
No. 3		1,000,000
Appearance		1,200,000
Stud		1,000,000
Selected decking	Decking	1,200,000
Commercial decking		1,200,000
Selected decking	Decking	1,300,000
Commercial decking		1,100,000

TABLE 460-10
Maximum Bending Moment (M)

1. Uniformly distributed load:

$$M = \frac{wl^2}{8}$$

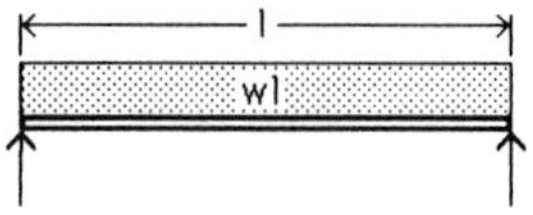
l
wl

2. Load increasing uniformly to one end:

$$M = 0.1283Wl$$

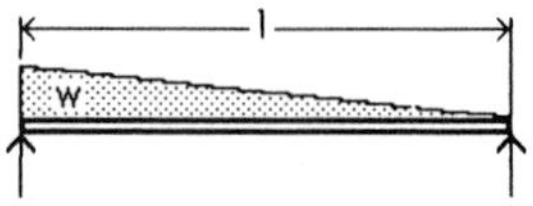
l
W

3. Load increasing uniformly to the center:

$$M = \frac{Wl}{6}$$

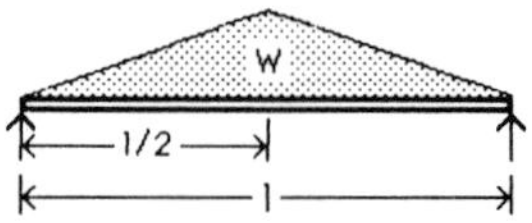
W
l/2
l

4. Uniform load partially distributed:

$$M = R_1\left(a + \frac{R_1}{2w}\right)$$

$$R_1 = \frac{wb}{2l}(2c + b)$$

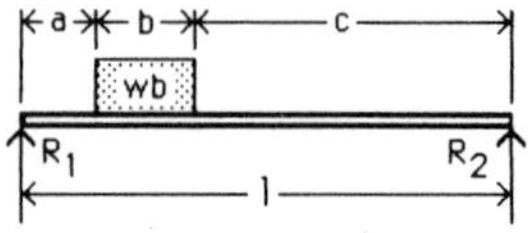
a
b
c
wb
R1
R2
l

5. Uniform load partially distributed at one end:

$$M = \frac{(R_1)^2}{2w}$$

$$R_1 = \frac{wa}{2l}(2l - a)$$

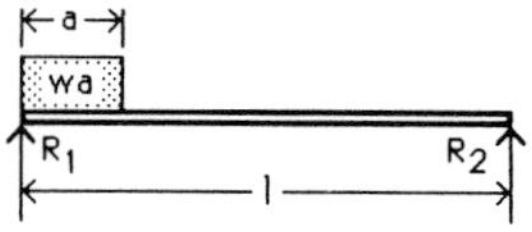
a
wa
R1
R2
l

6. Uniform load partially distributed at each end:

$$M = \begin{cases} \dfrac{(R_1)^2}{2w_1} & \text{when } R_1 < w_1a \\ \dfrac{(R_2)^2}{2w_2} & \text{when } R_2 < w_2c \end{cases}$$

$$R_1 = \frac{w_1a(2l - a) + w_2c^2}{2l}$$

$$R_2 = \frac{w_2c(2l - c) + w_1a^2}{2l}$$

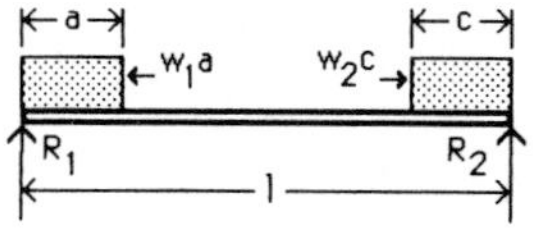
a
w1a
w2c
c
R1
R2
l

7. Concentrated load at center:

$$M = \frac{Pl}{4}$$

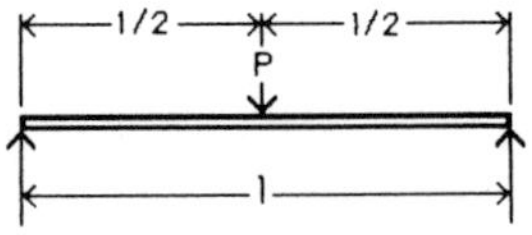
l/2
l/2
P
l

8. Concentrated load at any point:

$$M = \frac{Pab}{l}$$

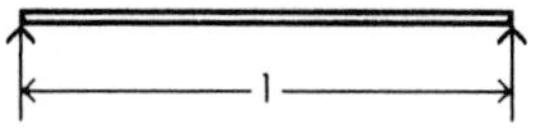
l

9. Two equal concentrated loads symmetrically placed:

$$M = Pa$$

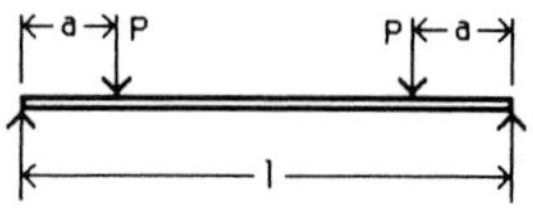
a
P
P
a
l

10. Two equal concentrated loads unsymmetrically placed:

$M_1 = R_1a$ when $a > b$
$M_2 = R_2b$ when $a < b$

$$R_1 = \frac{P}{l}(l - a + b)$$

$$R_2 = \frac{P}{l}(l - b + a)$$

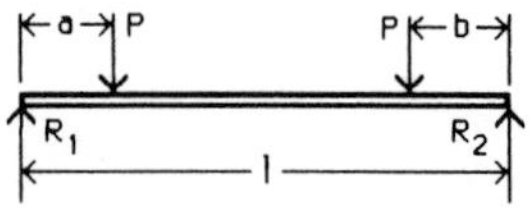
a
P
P
b
R1
R2
l

11. Two unequal concentrated loads unsymmetrically placed:

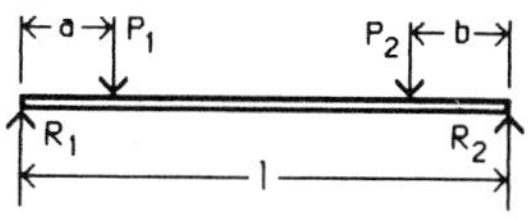
a
P_1
P_2
b
R_1
R_2
l

$$M_1 = R_1 a \quad \text{when } R_1 < P_1$$
$$M_2 = R_2 b \quad \text{when } R_2 < P_2$$
$$R_1 = \frac{P_1(l - a) + P_2 b}{l}$$
$$R_2 = \frac{P_1 a + P_2(l - b)}{l}$$

Maximum bending moments for beams fixed at one end, supported at other

12. Uniformly distributed load:

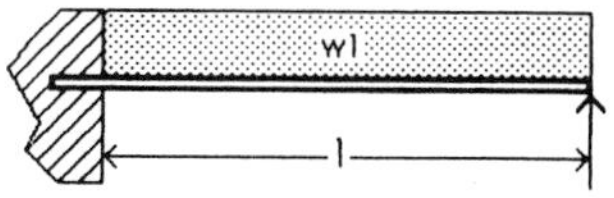
wl
l

$$M = \frac{wl^2}{8}$$

13. Concentrated load at center:

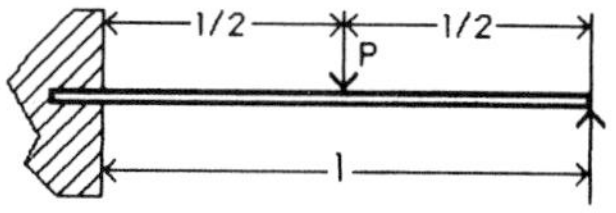
l/2
l/2
P
l

$$M = \frac{3Pl}{16}$$

14. Concentrated load at any point:

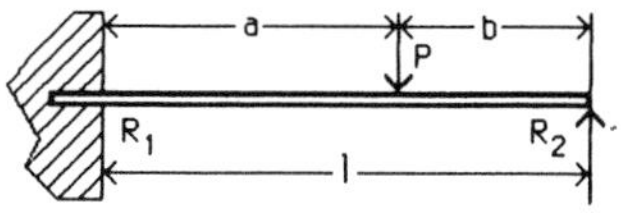
a
b
P
R_1
R_2
l

$$M = R_2 b$$
$$R_2 = \frac{Pa^2}{2l^3}(b + 2l)$$

Maximum bending moments for beams fixed at both ends

15. Uniformly distributed load:

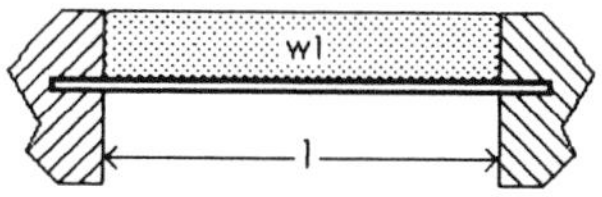
wl
l

$$M = \frac{wl^2}{12}$$

16. Concentrated load at center:

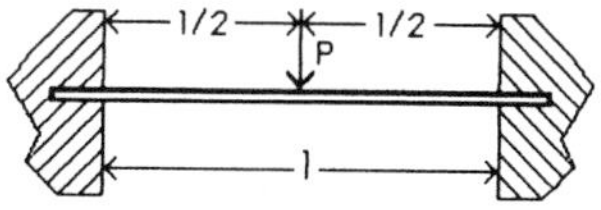
l/2
l/2
P
l

$$M = \frac{Pl}{8}$$

17. Concentrated load at any point:

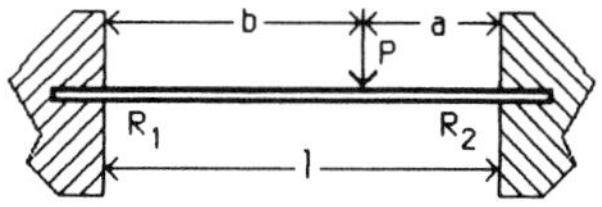
b
a
P
R_1
R_2
l

$$M = \begin{cases} \dfrac{Pab^2}{l^2} & \text{when } a < b \\[2ex] \dfrac{Pa^2 b}{l^2} & \text{when } a > b \end{cases}$$

Maximum bending moments for cantilevered beams

18. Beam fixed at one end, free but guided at the other—uniformly distributed load:

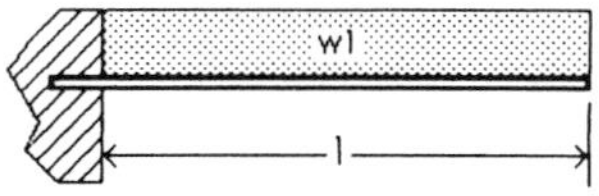
wl
l

$$M = \frac{wl^2}{3}$$

19. Beam fixed at one end, free but guided at the other—concentrated load at guided end:

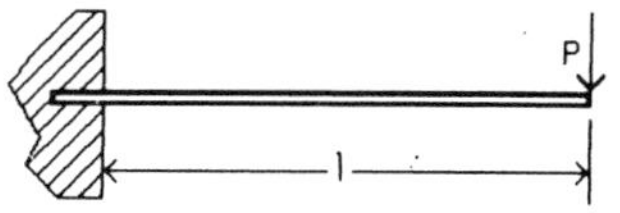
P
l

$$M = \frac{Pl}{2}$$

20. Uniformly distributed load:

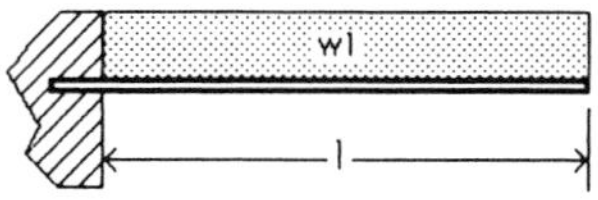
wl
l

$$M = \frac{wl^2}{2}$$

(Continued)

21. Load increasing uniformly to the fixed end:

$$M = \frac{Wl}{3}$$

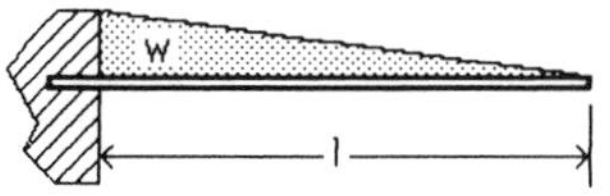
W
l

22. Concentrated load at any point:

$$M = Pb$$

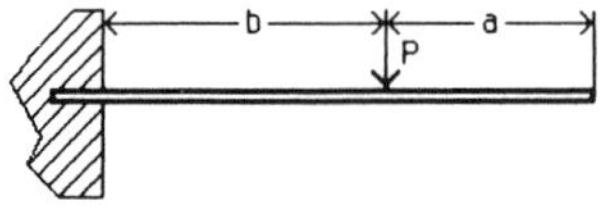
b
a
P

23. Concentrated load at free end:

$$M = Pl$$

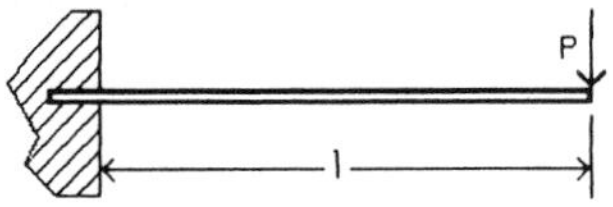
P
l

Maximum bending moments for beams overhanging one support

24. Uniformly distributed load:

$$M_1 = \frac{w}{8l^2}(l + a)^2(l - a)^2$$

$$M_2 = \frac{wa^2}{2} \quad \text{at } R_2$$

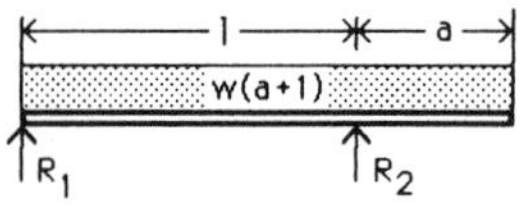
l
a
w(a+l)
R1
R2

25. Uniformly distributed load on overhang:

$$M = \frac{wa^2}{2}$$

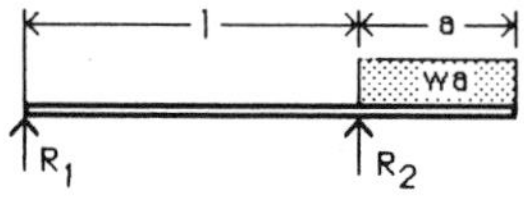
l
a
wa
R1
R2

26. Concentrated load at end of overhang:

$$M = Pa$$

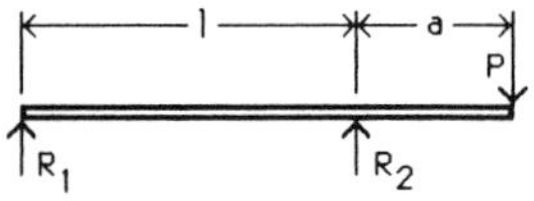
l
a
P
R1
R2

27. Uniformly distributed load between supports:

$$M = \frac{wl^2}{8}$$

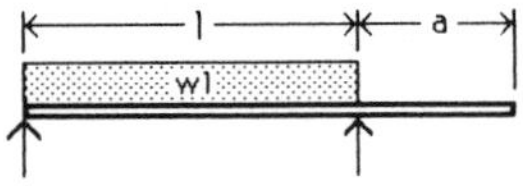
l
a
wl

28. Concentrated load at any point between supports:

$$M = \frac{Pab}{l}$$

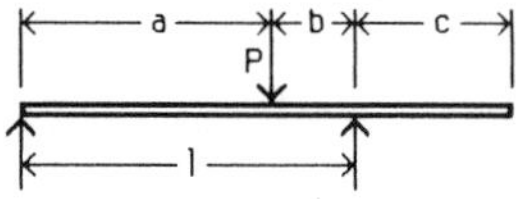
a
b
c
P
l

Maximum bending moments for continuous beams

29. Two equal spans—uniform load on one span:

$$M = \frac{49}{512}wl^2$$

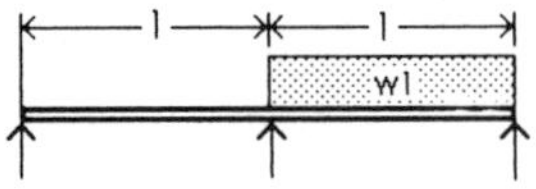
l
l
wl

30. Two equal spans—concentrated load at center of one span:

$$M = \frac{13}{64}Pl$$

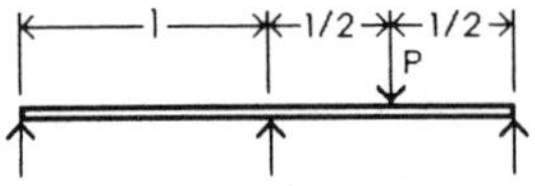
l
l/2
l/2
P

31. Two equal spans—concentrated load at any point:

$$M = \frac{Pab}{4l^2}[4l^2 - b(l + b)]$$

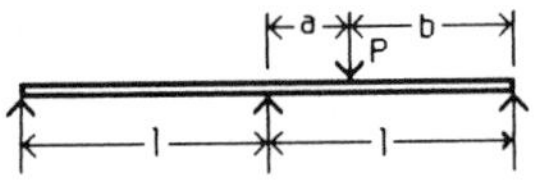
a
b
P
l
l

NOTE: Where two *M*'s are given, either *M* could be the maximum depending on the situation. *M* = maximum bending moment (in/lb^2); *w* = weight per linear foot supported (live + dead) plus beam itself for whatever area (width available) (lb) (See Table 460-12); *l* = length between supports (ft); *W* = total weight (equivalent to *wl*); *R* = reaction (lb); *P* = concentrated load (lb).

Source: Albe E. Munson, *Construction Design for Landscape Architects,* McGraw-Hill, New York, 1974, pp. 146–149.

TABLE 460-11
Allowable Extreme Fiber Stress in Bending (*fb*)

Species	*Classification*	*Grade*	*fb, psi*
Cedar, western	2–4 in thick 6 in and wider	Select structural	1250
		No. 1	1050
		No. 2	875
		No. 3	525
	Beams and stringers	Select structural	1100
		No. 1	900
	Posts and timbers	Select structural	1050
		No. 1	850
	Decking	Selected decking	1400*
		Commercial decking	1200*
Douglas fir, larch, West Coast	2–4 in thick 6 in and wider	Dense select structural	2100
		Select structural	1800
		Dense No. 1	1800
		No. 1	1500
		Dense No. 2	1450
		No. 2	1250
		No. 3	725
	Beams and stringers	Dense select structural	1900
		Select structural	1600
		Dense No. 1	1550
		No. 1	1300
	Posts and timbers	Dense select structural	1750
		Select structural	1500
		Dense No. 1	1400
		No. 1	1200
	Decking	Select dex	2000*
		Commercial dex	1650*
Douglas fir, inland	2–4 in thick 6 in and wider	Select structural	1700
		No. 1	1450
		No. 2	1200
		No. 3	700
	Beams and stringers	Select structural	1550
		No. 1	1300
	Posts and timbers	Select structural	1400
		No. 1	1150
	Decking	Selected decking	1900*
		Commercial decking	1600*
Hemlock, mountain, West Coast	2–4 in thick 6 in and wider	Select structural	1500
		No. 1	1250
		No. 2	1050
		No. 3	625
	Beams and stringers	Select structural	1350
		No. 1	1100
	Posts and timbers	Select structural	1250
		No. 1	1000
	Decking	Select dex	1650*
		Commercial dex	1400*
Hemlock, tamarack, eastern	2–4 in thick 6 in and wider	Select structural	1550
		No. 1	1300
		No. 2	1050
		No. 3	625
	Beams and stringers	Select structural	1400
		No. 1	1150
	Posts and timbers	Select structural	1300
		No. 1	1050
	Decking	Select	1700*
		Commercial	1250*
Pine, red, Canada	2–4 in thick 6 in and wider	Select structural	1200
		No. 1	1000
		No. 2	825
		No. 3	500
	Beams and stringers	Select structural	1050
		No. 1 structural	875
	Posts and timbers	Select structural	1000

(Continued)

TABLE 460-11 *(Continued)*

Species	*Classification*	*Grade*	*fb, psi*
		No. 1 structural	800
	Wall and roof plank	Select	1350
		Commercial	1100
Pine, southern	2–4 in thick 6 in and wider	Dense select structural	2100
		Select structural	1800
		No. 1 dense	1800
		No. 1	1500
		No. 2 dense	1450
		No. 2 medium grain	1250
		No. 2	1050
		No. 3 dense	850
		No. 3	725
	5 in and thicker	Dense structural 65	1650
		No. 1 dense SR	1500
		No. 1 SR	1300
		No. 2 dense SR	1300
		No. 2 SR	1100
Pine, western, sugar, ponderosa, lodgepole	2–4 in thick 6 in and wider	Select structural	1200
		No. 1	1050
		No. 2	850
		No. 3	500
	Beams and stringers	Select structural	1100
		No. 1	925
	Posts and timbers	Select structural	1000
		No. 1	825
	Decking	Selected decking	1350*
		Commercial decking	1150*
Redwood, California	2–4 in thick 6 in and wider	Selected structural	1750
		Select structural open grain	1400
		No. 1	1500
		No. 1 open grain	1150
		No. 2	1200
		No. 2 open grain	950
		No. 3	700
		No. 3 open grain	550
	5 × 5 in and larger	Clear heart structural	1850
		Clear structural	1850
		Select structural	1400
		No. 1	1200
		No. 2	975
		No. 3	550
Spruce, eastern	2–4 in thick 6 in and wider	Select structural	1300
		No. 1	1100
		No. 2	900
		No. 3	525
	Beams and stringers	Select structural	1150
		No. 1	950
	Posts and timbers	Select structural	1100
		No. 1	875
	Decking	Select	1450*
		Commercial	1200*
Spruce, Sitka, Canadian coastal	2–4 in thick 6 in and wider	Select structural	1300
		No. 1	1100
		No. 2	900
		No. 3	525
	Beams and stringers	Select structural	1150
		No. 1 structural	950
	Posts and timbers	Select structural	1100
		No. 1 structural	875
	Decking	Select	1450*
		Commercial	1200*

* Allowable unit stresses for repetitive-member use. For individual-member use, 87% of value shown is applicable.

Source: Albe E. Munson, *Construction Design for Landscape Architects,* McGraw-Hill, New York, 1974.

(S) (in^3). (Compute S by using the *flexure formula:* $S = M/f$.)

4. Refer to Table 460-12 to determine members with adequate section moduli. (A member selected must have a section modulus equal to or greater than the required section modulus.)

Example: Figure 460-13 shows the general layout of a simple 16 × 24 ft platform-framed residential deck attached to a fixed structure along one edge. The joists are supported along the outside edge (with no significant overhang) by a continuous beam supported by three equally spaced 4-ft posts. A uniformly distributed live load of 40 psf is assumed.

Sizing the Decking: For aesthetic reasons, assume that 2 × 4 in decking is desirable. The first task is to determine an acceptable spacing of the joists, or in other words, to find out the length that 2 × 4 in decking can safely span (or acceptably deflect). Obviously, the equation used for *maximum bending moment* (see below) can be solved for the unknown variable l (to determine the *maximum allowable span* of a 2 × 4 in member). But instead, knowing that wide joist spacings usually require a deep joist dimension (i.e., resulting in a thick deck profile), a joist spacing of 18 in is tested with the expectation that a shallower deck solution can be found (e.g., using 2 × 8 or 2 × 10 joists).

Maximum bending moment (M) for the decking (Table 460-10, case 1):

$$M = \frac{wl^2}{8} = \frac{45(1.5)^2}{8} = \frac{101.3}{8}$$

$$= 12.7 \text{ ft-lb, or } 151.9 \text{ in-lb}$$

where w is the load on each square foot of deck, i.e., a 40-lb live load (from Table 460-7) plus 4.7 lb, the weight of the decking itself (from Table 460-12) rounded off to 5 psf; l is the span between joists, i.e., 1.5 ft. Although the *effective* span is slightly less than 1.5 ft, the longer dimension is chosen to provide an extra margin of safety.

Extreme fiber stress in bending (fb) for western cedar (decking) (Table 460-11):

1400

Required section modulus:

$$S = \frac{M}{fb} = \frac{151.9}{1400} = 0.02 \text{ in}^3$$

Members with *acceptable section moduli* (Table 460-12, S_{y-y}) include:

1 × 4 (0.3 in^3) and greater

(Note that the stress modulus S_{y-y} is used when the members will be laid flat and that

TABLE 460-12†
Section Moduli

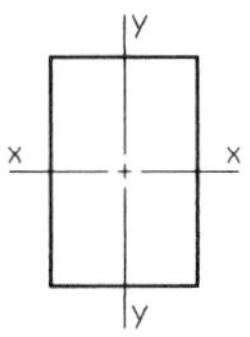
y
x
x
y

Nominal size, in	American standard dressed size, in	Area of section, sq in	Pounds* per linear foot	Section modulus, in^3	
				S_{x-x}	S_{y-y}
1 × 4	¾ × 3½	2.63	0.7	1.5	0.3
1 × 6	¾ × 5½	4.13	1.1	3.8	0.5
1 × 8	¾ × 7¼	5.44	1.5	6.6	0.7
1 × 10	¾ × 9¼	6.94	1.9	10.7	0.9
1 × 12	¾ × 11¼	8.44	2.3	15.8	1.1
2 × 3	1½ × 2½	3.75	1.0	1.5	0.7
2 × 4	1½ × 3½	5.25	1.5	3.1	1.3
2 × 6	1½ × 5½	8.25	2.3	7.6	2.1
2 × 8	1½ × 7¼	10.88	3.0	13.1	2.7
2 × 10	1½ × 9¼	13.88	3.8	21.4	3.5
2 × 12	1½ × 11¼	16.88	4.7	31.6	4.2
2 × 14	1½ × 13¼	19.88	5.5	43.9	5.0
3 × 4	2½ × 3½	8.75	2.4	5.1	3.6
3 × 6	2½ × 5½	13.75	3.8	12.6	5.7
3 × 8	2½ × 7¼	18.13	5.0	21.9	7.6
3 × 10	2½ × 9¼	23.13	6.4	35.7	9.6
3 × 12	2½ × 11¼	28.13	8.4	52.7	7.8
3 × 14	2½ × 13¼	33.13	9.2	73.2	13.8
3 × 16	2½ × 15¼	38.13	10.6	96.9	15.9
4 × 4	3½ × 3½	12.2	3.4	7.1	7.1
4 × 6	3½ × 5½	19.2	5.3	17.7	11.2
4 × 8	3½ × 7¼	25.38	7.0	30.7	14.8
4 × 10	3½ × 9¼	32.38	8.9	49.9	18.9
4 × 12	3½ × 11¼	39.38	10.9	73.8	23.0
4 × 14	3½ × 13¼	46.38	12.9	102.4	27.1
4 × 16	3½ × 15¼	53.38	14.8	135.7	31.1
6 × 6	5½ × 5½	30.3	8.4	27.7	27.7
6 × 8	5½ × 7½	41.3	11.5	51.6	37.8
6 × 10	5½ × 9½	52.3	14.5	82.7	47.9
6 × 12	5½ × 11½	63.3	17.6	121.2	58
6 × 14	5½ × 13½	74.3	20.6	167.1	68.1
6 × 16	5½ × 15½	85.3	23.7	220.2	78.1
6 × 18	5½ × 17½	96.3	26.7	280.7	88.2
8 × 8	7½ × 7½	56.3	15.6	70.3	70.3
8 × 10	7½ × 9½	71.3	19.8	112.8	89.1
8 × 12	7½ × 11½	86.3	24.0	165.3	107.8
8 × 14	7½ × 13½	101.3	28.1	228	127
8 × 16	7½ × 15½	116.3	32.3	300	145
8 × 18	7½ × 17½	131.3	36.5	383	164
8 × 20	7½ × 19½	146.3	40.6	475	183
10 × 10	9½ × 9½	90.3	25.0	143	143
10 × 12	9½ × 11½	109	30.3	209	173
10 × 14	9½ × 13½	128	35.6	289	203
10 × 16	9½ × 15½	147	40.9	380	233
10 × 18	9½ × 17½	166	46.2	485	263
10 × 20	9½ × 19½	185	51.5	602	293
10 × 24	9½ × 23½	223	62.0	874	353
12 × 12	11½ × 11½	132	36.7	253	253
12 × 14	11½ × 13½	155	43.1	349	298
12 × 16	11½ × 15½	178	49.5	460	342
12 × 18	11½ × 17½	201	55.9	587	386
12 × 20	11½ × 19½	224	62.3	729	430
12 × 22	11½ × 21½	247	68.7	886	474
12 × 24	11½ × 23½	270	75.0	1,058	518
14 × 14	13½ × 13½	182	50.6	410	410
14 × 16	13½ × 15½	209	58.1	541	471
14 × 18	13½ × 17½	236	65.6	689	532
14 × 20	13½ × 19½	263	73.1	856	592
14 × 24	13½ × 23½	317	88.1	1,243	714

* Based on 40 pcf.

† A member selected should have a width no less than one-third its depth to prevent lateral bending, unless the member will be braced by decking, etc.

Source: Albe E. Munson, *Construction Design for Landscape Architects*, McGraw-Hill, New York, 1974, p. 154.

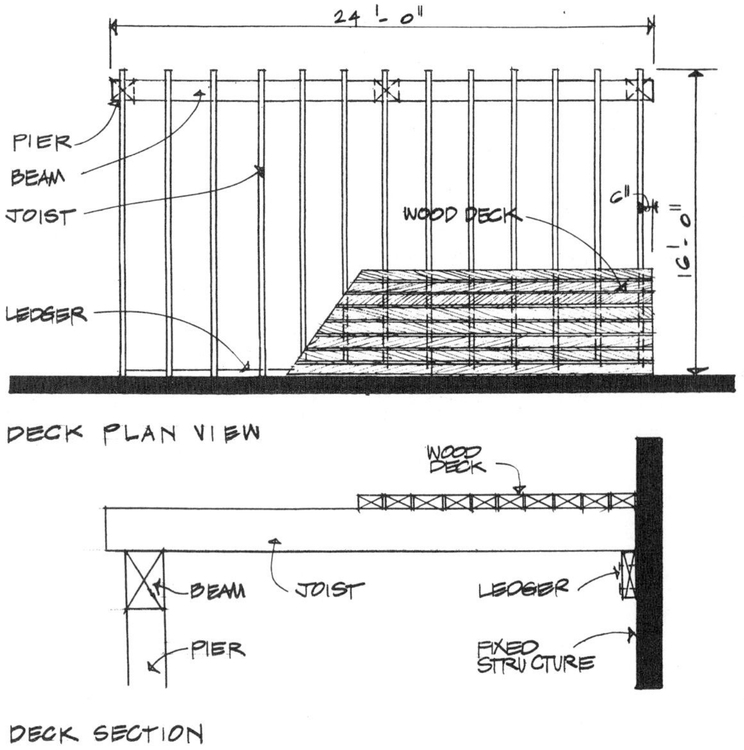
24'-0"
PIER
BEAM
JOIST
WOOD DECK
6"
16'-0"
LEDGER
DECK PLAN VIEW
WOOD DECK
BEAM
JOIST
LEDGER
PIER
FIXED STRUCTURE
DECK SECTION

Figure 460-13 Example problem: sizing members for a wood deck.

the stress modulus *Sx-x* is used when the members will be laid on-edge.)

Obviously, an 18-in joist spacing is acceptable for the 2 × 4 in decking. (Actually, the joists could be spaced nearly 5 ft apart and still be within safety limits; the extent of deflection, however, might be greater than desirable for psychological reasons.)

NOTE: The extent of deflection of the 2 × 4 in decking material (over the 18-in span) could be checked at this point in the process, but this is better postponed in the event that the joist spacing is changed as a result of subsequent calculations. For example, if the joist spacing becomes significantly closer than 18 in, it may become entirely unnecessary to check the deflection of the decking material.

Sizing the Joists: To determine the size of the *joists* in this example (16-ft span, 18 in on center), follow the same procedure used in sizing the decking:

Maximum bending moment (*M*) for the joists (Table 460-10, case 12):

$$M = \frac{wl^2}{8} = \frac{72(16)^2}{8} = \frac{18{,}432}{8}$$

$$= 2304 \text{ ft-lb, or } 27{,}648 \text{ in-lb}$$

An inner joist is chosen as representative since each inner joist supports a greater weight than either of the two outer joists. Each lineal foot of the joist will be carrying the live load, 1.5 square feet of decking, and its own weight. This equals 60 lb (the live load) (i.e., 40 × 1.5), plus 7 lb (the weight of the decking) (i.e., 1.5 × 4.7, from Table 460-12), plus an estimated 3.8 lb (the unit weight of the joist itself, using a 2 × 10 in member as an approximation, Table 460-12). Therefore, *w* equals 72 lb.

The span *l* between supports is 16 ft. Although the effective span is slightly less than 16 ft, the longer dimension is chosen to provide an extra margin of safety.

Extreme fiber stress (fb) for western cedar (No. 1) (Table 460-11):

1050

Required section modulus:

$$S = \frac{M}{fb} = \frac{27{,}648}{1050} = 26.33 \text{ in}^3$$

Members with *acceptable section moduli* (Table 460-12, S_{x-x}) include:

2 × 12 (31.6 in³) and greater

(Note that the stress modulus S_{x-x} is used for members that are vertically oriented, such as joists, beams, and stringers. The stress modulus S_{y-y} is used for members, such as decking, that will be laid flat.)

Although widths of members are less than one-third their depths, they have a greater tendency to twist. This can be minimized because the joists will be braced by the decking. Nevertheless, if 2 × 12 in joists are used, it would be wise to employ blocking to minimize the potential for lateral bending.

NOTE: At this point in the process, a decision might be made to resort to narrower joist spacing to yield a deck with a thinner profile (e.g., using 2 × 8 or 2 × 10 joists). Joists with a 12-in spacing are therefore tested:

$$M = \frac{48.5(16)^2}{8} = \frac{12{,}416}{8}$$

$$= 1552 \text{ ft-lb, or } 18{,}624 \text{ in-lb}$$

where *w* equals 40 (the live load), plus 4.7 lb (the weight of the decking), plus an estimated 3.8 lb (the unit weight of the joist itself).

$$S = \frac{18{,}624}{1050} = 17.74$$

Therefore, with a 12-in joist spacing, 2 × 10 in joists are acceptable (Table 460-12). Note that at this joist spacing, the possibility of excessive deflection of decking material is no longer an issue. Hence, the deflection does not have to be tested.

Sizing the Beam: Lastly, the size of the beam must be determined. Follow the same procedure used above.

Maximum bending moment (*M*) for the beam (Table 460-10, case 1):

$$M = \frac{wl^2}{8} = \frac{185(12)^2}{8} = \frac{26{,}640}{8}$$

$$= 3330 \text{ ft-lb, or } 39{,}960 \text{ in-lb}$$

Each lineal foot of the beam carries the live load, one joist, 16 square feet of decking, and its own weight. This equals 40 lb (the live load), plus 62 lb (the weight of one joist) (i.e., 16 × 3.8 = 60.8, or 62 rounded off, from Table 460-12), plus 76 lb (the weight of the decking) (i.e., 4.7 × 16 = 75.2, or 76 rounded off), plus an estimated 7 lb (the unit lineal weight of the beam itself) (using a 4 × 8 in member as an approximation, Table 460-12). Therefore, *w* equals 185 lb.

The span *l* between supports is 12 ft. Although the *effective* span is slightly less than 12 ft, the longer dimension is chosen to provide an extra margin of safety.

Extreme fiber stress (*fb*) for western cedar (select structural) (Table 460-11):

1100

Required section modulus:

$$S = \frac{M}{fb} = \frac{39{,}960}{1100} = 36.33 \text{ in}^3$$

Members with *acceptable section moduli* (Table 460-12, S_{x-x}) include:

2 × 14 (43.9 in^3)

3 × 10 (35.7 in^3)

3 × 12 (52.7 in^3)

3 × 14 (73.2 in^3)

3 × 16 (96.9 in^3)

4 × 8 (30.7 in^3)

and greater

The member selected should have a width no less than one-third its depth in order to prevent lateral bending, unless the member will be braced by decking, blocking, etc. Therefore, a 4 × 8 member would be acceptable.

It should be noted that built-up beams can be employed in a deck or boardwalk structure, but the above formulas would not directly apply. Refer to 6.0 Construction Details, in this section for information on built-up members and the principles governing their use.

TABLE 460-13
Deflection Formulas*

Uniformly distributed load:

$$D = \frac{5WL^3}{384EI}$$

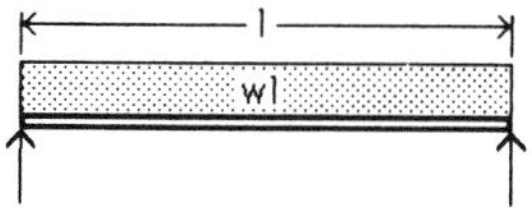
l
wl

Uniformly distributed load:

$$D = \frac{WL^3}{8EI}$$

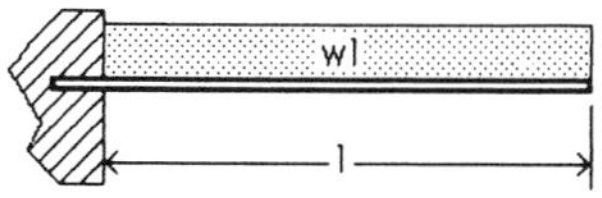
wl
l

Concentrated load at free end:

$$D = \frac{PL^3}{3EI}$$

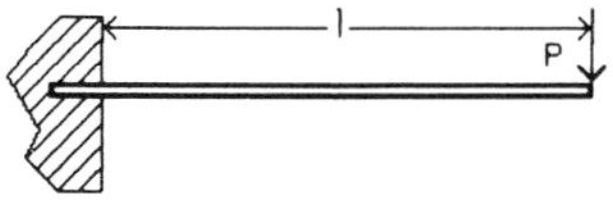
l
P

Two equal concentrated loads symmetrically placed:

$$D = \frac{23PL^3}{648EI}$$

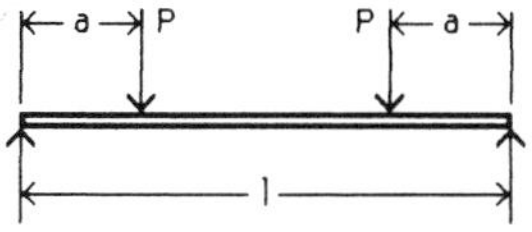
a
P
P
a
l

Concentrated load at center:

$$D = \frac{PL^3}{48EI}$$

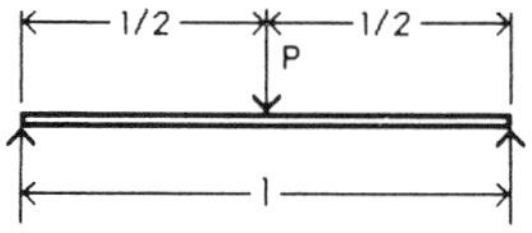
l/2
l/2
P
l

*D = deflection (in)
E = modulus of elasticity (refer to Table 460-9 for E values)
I = moment of inertia (in^4), calculated using the formula
$I = bd^3/12$
where
b = the width of the beam
d = the depth of the beam
W = uniformly distributed load (lb)
L = span of beam (in)
P = concentrated load (lb)

Checking the Extent of Deflection:

To check the extent of deflection for the decking used in the above example, the following formula (for center-point load) can be used (Table 460-13):

$$D = \frac{PL^3}{48EI}$$

where D = deflection
P = concentrated load (lb/ft^2)
L = span (in)
E = modulus of elasticity (Refer to Table 460-9 for E values.)
I = moment of inertia (in^4) (The moment of inertia is calculated from the formula $I = bd^3/12$, where b = the width of the beam, and d = the depth of the beam.)

NOTE: A deflection of 1/360th the effective span is rigid enough for most deck structures. A deflection of 1/200th should be considered the lowest limit, to avoid noticeable deflection.

Example (2 × 4 decking):

$$D = \frac{PL^3}{48EI} = \frac{250(12)^3}{48(1{,}400{,}000)(0.984)}$$

$$= \frac{250(1728)}{48(1{,}377{,}600)}$$

$$= \frac{432{,}000}{66{,}124{,}800} = 0.0065, \text{ or } 0.01 \text{ in}$$

($I = bd^3/12 = 3.5(1.5)^3/12 = 11.813/12$

$= 0.984$ in)

In other words, the deflection of the 2 × 4 in decking would be 0.01 in over the 72-in span, or about 1/7200th the length of the span. Since a maximum deflection of 1/200th the length of the span is recommended, 1/7200th would be acceptable and would result in a relatively stiff deck.

5.3 Sizing by Formulas (Posts)

Posts can be tested for two possible failures, *buckling* and *crushing*. Crushing is rarely a problem in wood deck or boardwalk construction because the loads are usually light. Testing for buckling alone is sufficient in most cases.

Testing for Buckling:

The ability of a post to resist buckling is determined by comparing its inherent unit strength to the actual unit force (load) applied to it. The inherent strength of a post is a function of its unsupported height, its cross-sectional dimensions, and its modulus of elasticity.

The procedure involves four steps:

1. Choose a post size.

2. Calculate the *maximum allowable unit stress (fc)* of the post (i.e., the maximum allowable compressive axial load parallel to the grain).

3. Calculate the *actual unit stress (f)* on the post.

4. Compare *fc* and *f*. The post is adequately sized if *fc* is greater than *f* (i.e., it will not buckle).

The formulas for *fc* and *f* are:

$$fc = \frac{0.3E}{L^2/d}$$

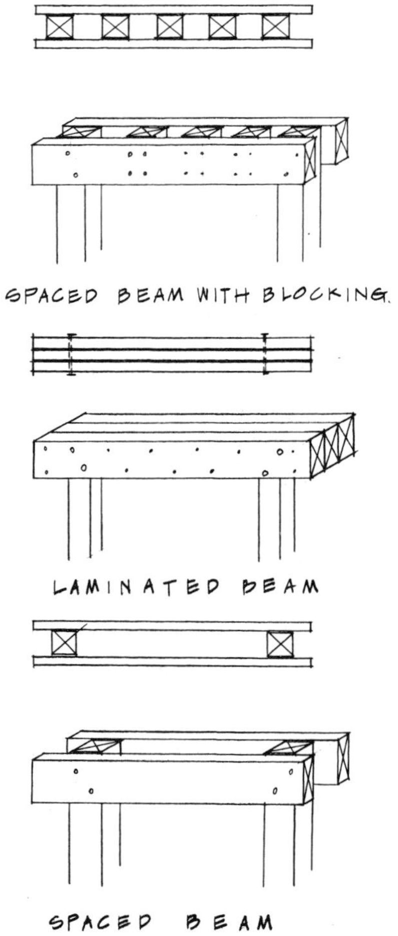
SPACED BEAM WITH BLOCKING
LAMINATED BEAM
SPACED BEAM

Figure 460-14 Built-up beam assemblies.

where fc = maximum allowable unit stress (psi)
E = modulus of elasticity (psi) (Table 460-9)
L = unsupported length of post (in)
d = actual dimension of the least side of the cross-section (in)

$$f = \frac{P}{A}$$

where f = actual unit stress (psi)
P = total axial load (lb)
A = actual (not nominal) area of the post's cross-section (in²)

Example: Referring to Figure 460-13, note that the central post of the deck supports part of the weight of the continuous beam and about 128 ft² of decking (8 × 16 ft). Three 4 × 4 in posts are proposed, each 4 ft in height.

Maximum allowable unit stress *(fc)* of the post:

$$fc = \frac{0.3E}{L^2/d} = \frac{0.3(1{,}600{,}000)}{(48)^2/3.5} = \frac{480{,}000}{658.29} = 729.2 \text{ psi}$$

Actual unit stress *(f)* on the post:

$$f = \frac{P}{A} = \frac{2040}{(3.5)^2} = \frac{2040}{12.25} = 166.5 \text{ psi}$$

where P equals the weight of the beam supported by the post in question (i.e., 5 lb per lineal foot × 16 ft = 80 lb), plus the weight of the decking supported by the post in question [i.e., 5 lb per square foot × 192 ft (12 × 16 ft) = 960 lb], plus the live loading [i.e., 1000 lb (ten people standing on the deck)]. Therefore, fc is greater than f, and the posts will not buckle.

As in all calculations, it is advisable to leave a reasonable margin of safety between the two figures fc and f. Local building codes should always be checked for specific requirements.

Testing for Crushing:

To test the posts (in the above example) for *crushing,* which is more likely with a short post than with a long post, compare the *actual unit stress (f)* (calculated above) with the values for *compression parallel to the grain (Fc)* given in Tables 850-10 and 850-11 in Section 850: Wood. If Fc is greater than f, the post will not fail by crushing.

5.4 Sizing Built-Up Members

Built-Up Beams:

The strength in bending and the extent of deflection between built-up and solid beams are different and cannot be easily compared. Therefore, the formulas given for solid do not apply to built-up beams. However, a precise determination of strength in bending or of deflection in a built-up beam is unnecessary in most instances. Reasonable estimations are adequate and are possible with a basic understanding of a few principles, related to the manner in which built-up beams are constructed. Below are the characteristics of built-up beams that need to be considered when estimating their strengths relative to solid beams.

Spaced Beams: If it has no internal blocking, a spaced beam functions essentially as two independent joists and only achieves increased supportive strength by virtue of close spacing (Figure 460-14). Lateral movement is not reduced.

A spaced beam with internal blocking significantly reduces lateral movement and begins to function as an equivalently sized solid beam (Figure 460-14). Both the strength in bending and the deflection of a spaced beam depend on the amount of internal blocking included. A spaced beam is never as strong as a solid beam.

Laminated Beams: The strength and extent of deflection in a laminated beam depend on the method of lamination. The more the lateral movement in a laminated beam is reduced, the greater its strength and the less its deflection. Strongly glued members can surpass the strength of an equivalently sized solid beam.

The effectiveness of nailing or bolting as a means of lamination depends on the extent and pattern of fastening. Extensive nailing or bolting effectively minimizes lateral movement and tends to make the laminated beam function like a solid beam. However, an overly excessive number of nails or bolts can weaken the beam, especially if located along the line of maximum shear line (see Figure 460-14 for the proper extent and pattern of fastening). Nails should be driven from both sides and should extend nearly through the entire width of the beam. Waterproof glue can provide added strength.

Each wood species has inherent strength characteristics which also should be considered. Also, the *actual* dimensions of a built-up beam constructed of dressed lumber should be recognized as being different than those of an equivalently sized solid beam.

Built-Up Posts:

As mentioned in 5.3 Sizing by Formulas (Posts) of this section, buckling rather than crushing is the more common problem in most wood deck construction. Since buckling is a function of relative slenderness in posts, decreasing the slenderness ratio brings about increasingly greater resistance to buckling, assuming a solid post.

As with built-up beams, standard formulas do not directly apply to built-up posts. The slenderness ratio, as an indication of strength, is less meaningful in the case of a hollow post. As in any vertical member, resistance to lateral movement (buckling) and resistance to crushing are the primary concerns.

Since resistance to buckling is usually the crucial criterion, this is the quality to design for. Built-up posts can achieve this quite easily. Great rigidity can be achieved from built-up posts assembled with members in opposition to one another (i.e., square or triangular cross-section) (Figure 460-15). Built-up posts assembled with all their members parallel to one another have a greater propensity to move laterally and hence are not as resistant to buckling.

Bracing also helps restrict lateral movement and the likelihood of buckling. Bracing should be used on vertical supports exceeding 5 ft (1.5 m) in height.

In all instances, the means and quality of fastening are important components of ultimate strength, as are the grade and species of lumber used.

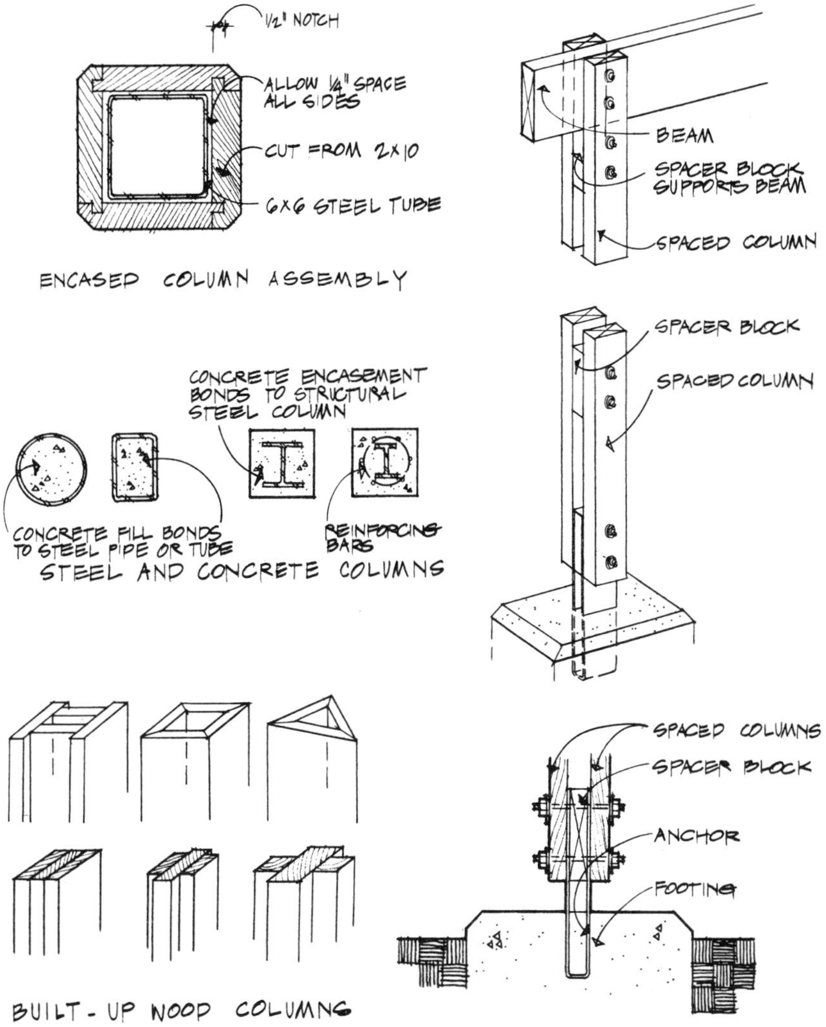
1/2" NOTCH
ALLOW 1/4" SPACE ALL SIDES
CUT FROM 2X10
6X6 STEEL TUBE
ENCASED COLUMN ASSEMBLY
BEAM
SPACER BLOCK SUPPORTS BEAM
SPACED COLUMN
SPACER BLOCK
SPACED COLUMN
CONCRETE ENCASEMENT BONDS TO STRUCTURAL STEEL COLUMN
CONCRETE FILL BONDS TO STEEL PIPE OR TUBE
REINFORCING BARS
STEEL AND CONCRETE COLUMNS
SPACED COLUMNS
SPACER BLOCK
ANCHOR
FOOTING
BUILT-UP WOOD COLUMNS

Figure 460-15 Built-up posts and columns.

6.0 CONSTRUCTION DETAILS

In addition to the various details shown earlier in this section, Figures 460-16 through 460-31 illustrate several other details and principles commonly used in wood deck and boardwalk construction.

GLOSSARY

Bending moment *M*: The stress resulting from the forces acting on the beam and the reaction of the supports. The bending moment at any section in the beam is the sum of the moments on either side of the section. Expressed in inch-pounds (in-lb).

Deflection *D*: The tendency of a member to deform when placed under a load; present in all structures regardless of the material or magnitude of the load. Common acceptable limits of deflection range from 1/200th to 1/360th the effective span of the member in question. Expressed in inches (in).

Extreme fiber stress in bending (*fb*): A measure of inherent strength in a species and grade of lumber. Expressed in pounds per square inch (psi).

Loading (*P*): *Dead load* is the weight of the materials in the structure, including permanently attached fixtures and equipment. *Live load* is the weight of the people using the structure, the moveable furniture and equipment, snow, water, ice, and wind. Expressed in pounds per square foot (psf).

Modulus of elasticity *E*: A measure of how much a material deforms in relation to the load applied.

Moment: The tendency of a force to cause rotation about an axis. Moment is the product of a force and a distance.

Moment arm: The perpendicular distance from the line of action of a force to the point being acted on.

Moment of inertia *I*: An abstract measure described as the sum of all the products of all infinitely small areas times the square of their distance from the neutral surface of the beam. Expressed as in^4.

Section modulus (*S*): The ratio of the moment of inertia to the distance of the most remote fiber in the beam. Expressed in cubic inches (in^3).

Span versus effective span (*L*): *Span* refers to center-to-center measurement. *Effective span* refers to the distance measured between supports.

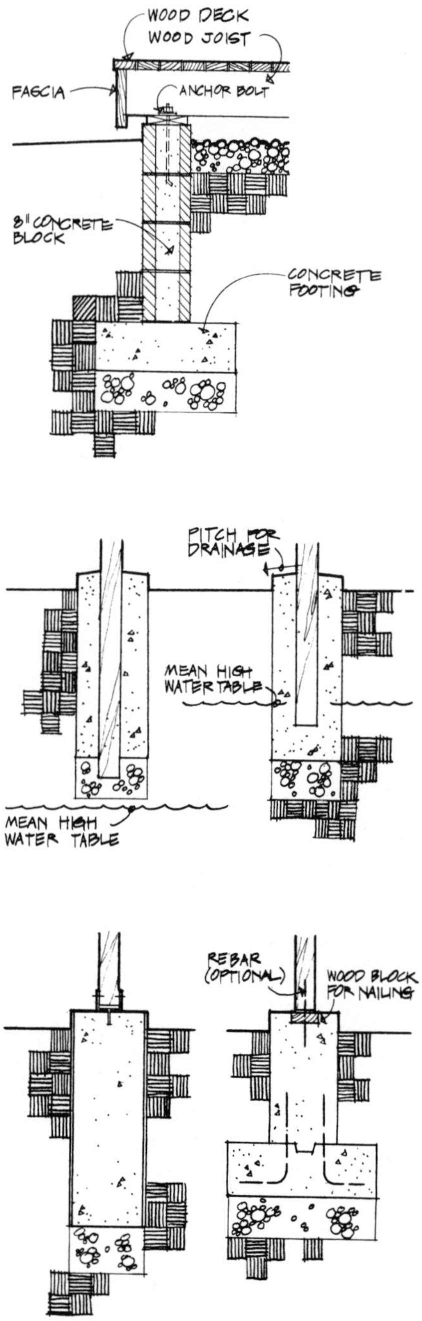
WOOD DECK
WOOD JOIST
FASCIA
ANCHOR BOLT
8" CONCRETE BLOCK
CONCRETE FOOTING
PITCH FOR DRAINAGE
MEAN HIGH WATER TABLE
MEAN HIGH WATER TABLE
REBAR (OPTIONAL)
WOOD BLOCK FOR NAILING

Figure 460-16 Footings and piers.

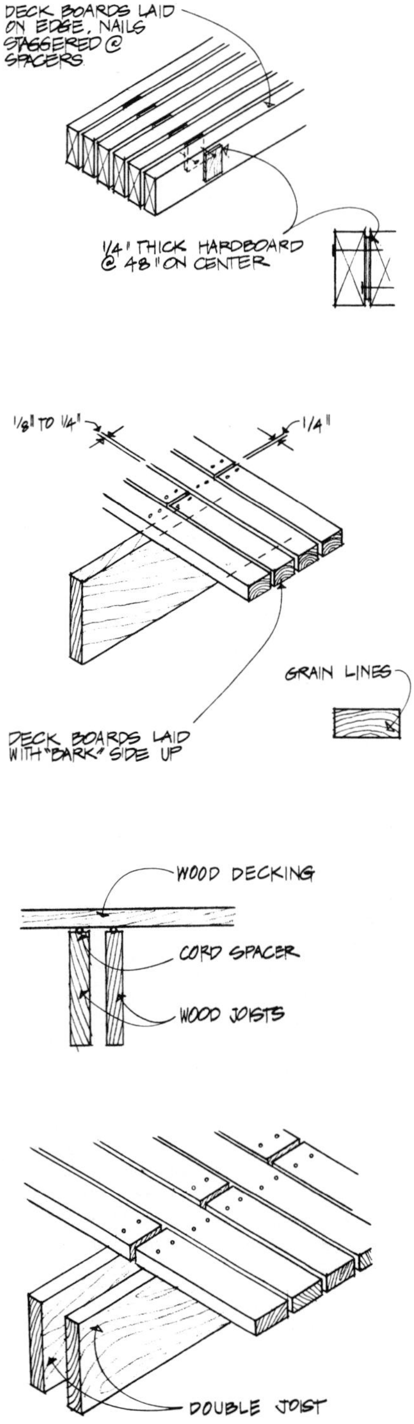
DECK BOARDS LAID ON EDGE, NAILS STAGGERED @ SPACERS
1/4" THICK HARDBOARD @ 48" ON CENTER
1/8" TO 1/4"
1/4"
GRAIN LINES
DECK BOARDS LAID WITH "BARK" SIDE UP
WOOD DECKING
CORD SPACER
WOOD JOISTS
DOUBLE JOIST

Figure 460-17 Decking details.

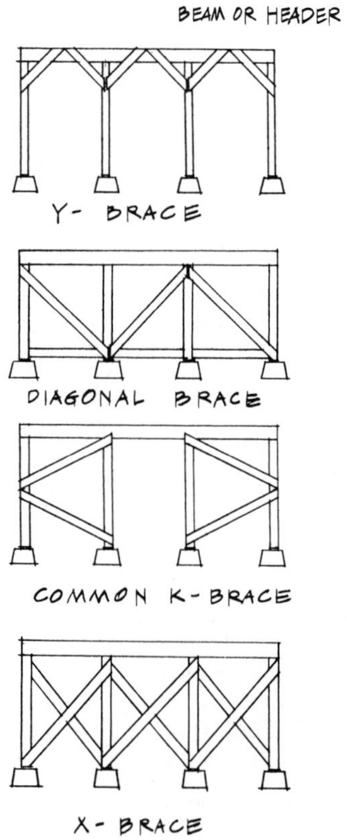
BEAM OR HEADER
Y- BRACE
DIAGONAL BRACE
COMMON K-BRACE
X- BRACE

Figure 460-18 Typical bracing systems.

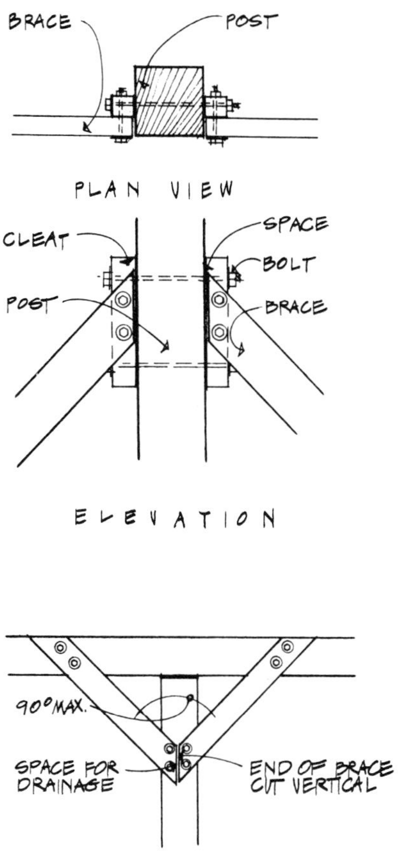
BRACE
POST
PLAN VIEW
CLEAT
SPACE
BOLT
POST
BRACE
ELEVATION
90°MAX.
SPACE FOR DRAINAGE
END OF BRACE CUT VERTICAL

Figure 460-19 Bracing details.

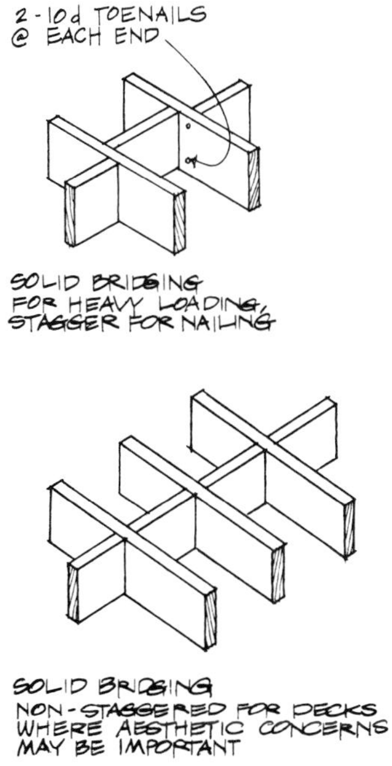
2-10d TOENAILS @ EACH END
SOLID BRIDGING FOR HEAVY LOADING, STAGGER FOR NAILING
SOLID BRIDGING NON-STAGGERED FOR DECKS WHERE AESTHETIC CONCERNS MAY BE IMPORTANT

Figure 460-20 Bridging details.

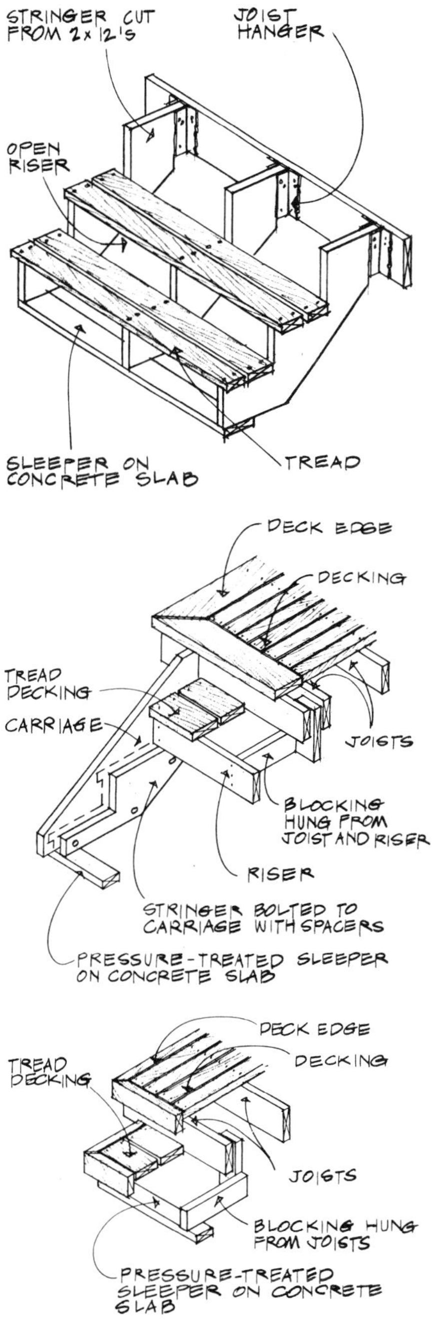
STRINGER CUT FROM 2x12'S
JOIST HANGER
OPEN RISER
SLEEPER ON CONCRETE SLAB
TREAD
DECK EDGE
DECKING
TREAD DECKING
CARRIAGE
JOISTS
BLOCKING HUNG FROM JOIST AND RISER
RISER
STRINGER BOLTED TO CARRIAGE WITH SPACERS
PRESSURE-TREATED SLEEPER ON CONCRETE SLAB
DECK EDGE
DECKING
TREAD DECKING
JOISTS
BLOCKING HUNG FROM JOISTS
PRESSURE-TREATED SLEEPER ON CONCRETE SLAB

Figure 460-21 Typical stair details.

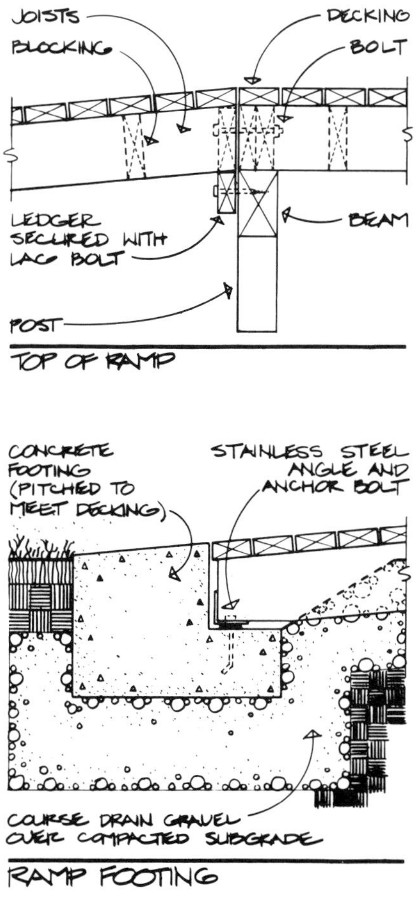
JOISTS
DECKING
BLOCKING
BOLT
LEDGER SECURED WITH LAG BOLT
BEAM
POST
TOP OF RAMP
CONCRETE FOOTING (PITCHED TO MEET DECKING)
STAINLESS STEEL ANGLE AND ANCHOR BOLT
COURSE DRAIN GRAVEL OVER COMPACTED SUBGRADE
RAMP FOOTING

Figure 460-22 Typical ramp assemblies.

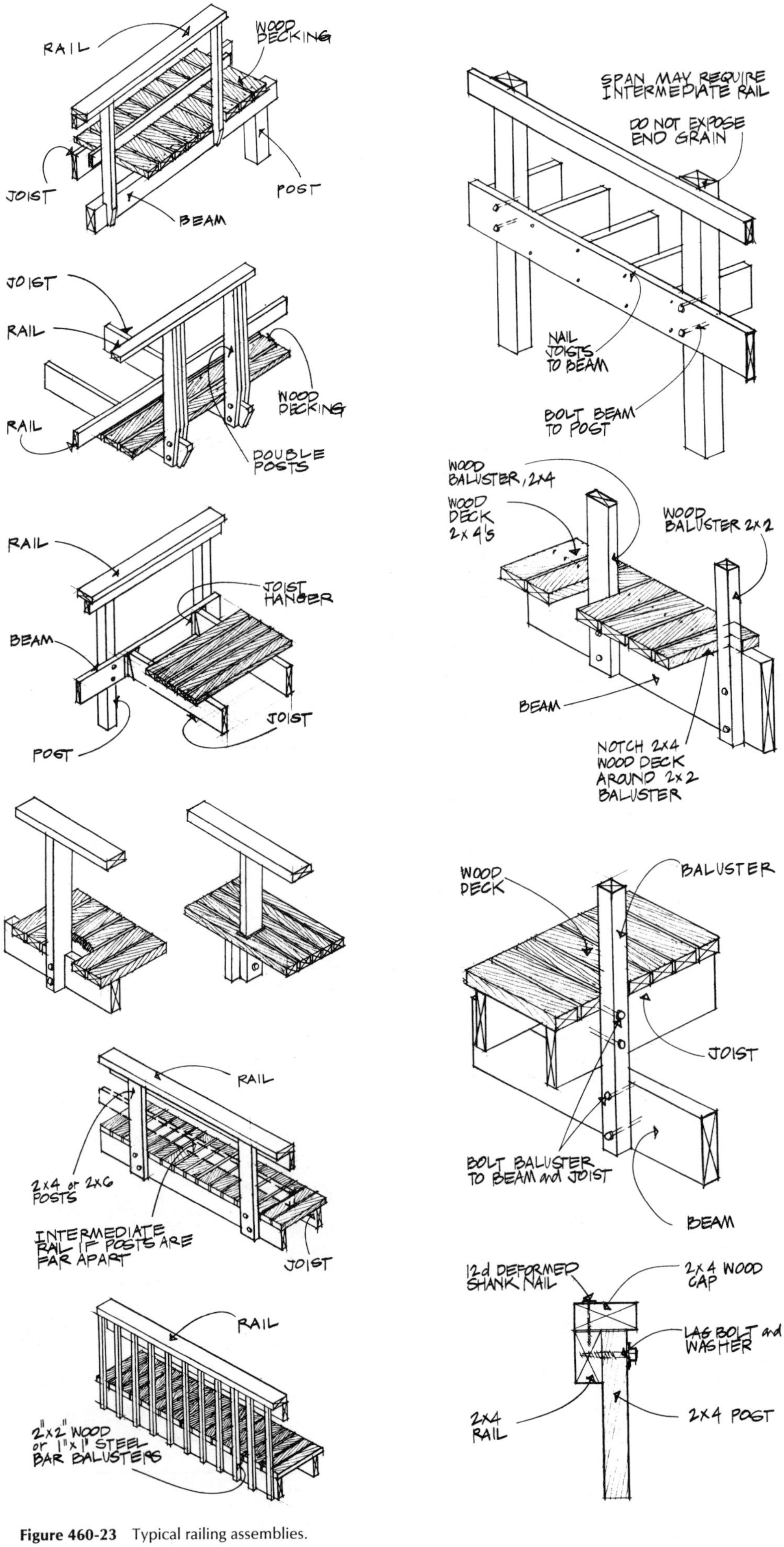
RAIL
WOOD DECKING
JOIST
POST
BEAM
JOIST
RAIL
RAIL
WOOD DECKING
DOUBLE POSTS
RAIL
JOIST HANGER
BEAM
JOIST
POST
RAIL
2x4 or 2x6 POSTS
INTERMEDIATE RAIL IF POSTS ARE FAR APART
JOIST
RAIL
2"x2" WOOD or 1"x1" STEEL BAR BALUSTERS
SPAN MAY REQUIRE INTERMEDIATE RAIL
DO NOT EXPOSE END GRAIN
NAIL JOISTS TO BEAM
BOLT BEAM TO POST
WOOD BALUSTER, 2x4
WOOD DECK 2x4's
WOOD BALUSTER 2x2
BEAM
NOTCH 2x4 WOOD DECK AROUND 2x2 BALUSTER
WOOD DECK
BALUSTER
JOIST
BOLT BALUSTER TO BEAM and JOIST
BEAM
12d DEFORMED SHANK NAIL
2x4 WOOD CAP
LAG BOLT and WASHER
2x4 RAIL
2x4 POST

Figure 460-23 Typical railing assemblies.

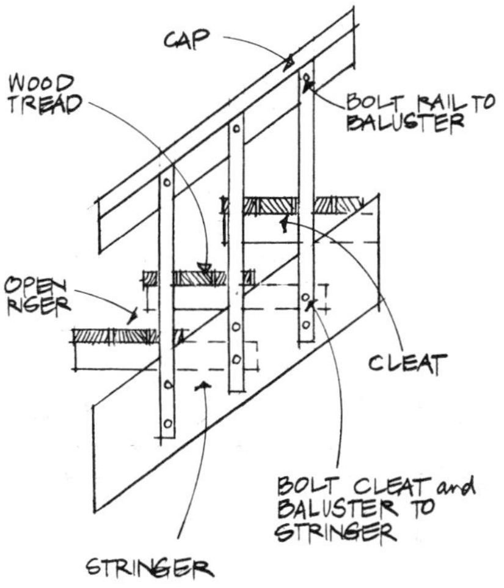
CAP
WOOD TREAD
BOLT RAIL TO BALUSTER
OPEN RISER
CLEAT
BOLT CLEAT and BALUSTER TO STRINGER
STRINGER

Figure 460-24 Stair to railing details.

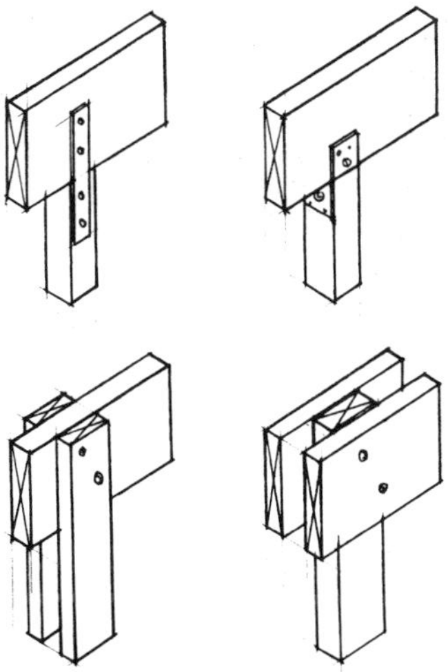

Figure 460-25 Beam to post connections.

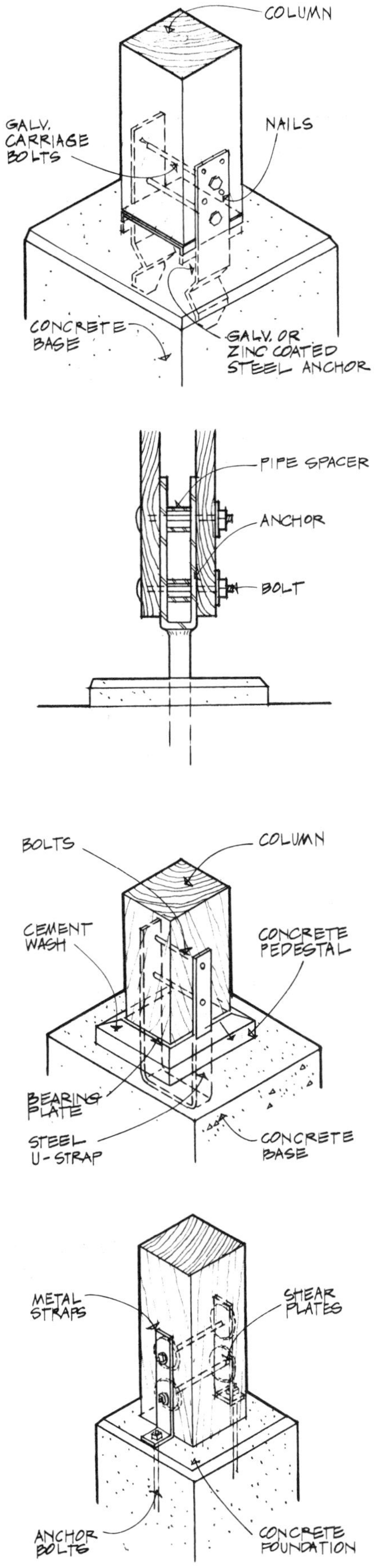
COLUMN
GALV. CARRIAGE BOLTS
NAILS
CONCRETE BASE
GALV. OR ZINC COATED STEEL ANCHOR
PIPE SPACER
ANCHOR
BOLT
BOLTS
COLUMN
CEMENT WASH
CONCRETE PEDESTAL
BEARING PLATE
STEEL U-STRAP
CONCRETE BASE
METAL STRAPS
SHEAR PLATES
ANCHOR BOLTS
CONCRETE FOUNDATION

Figure 460-26 Post to pier connections.

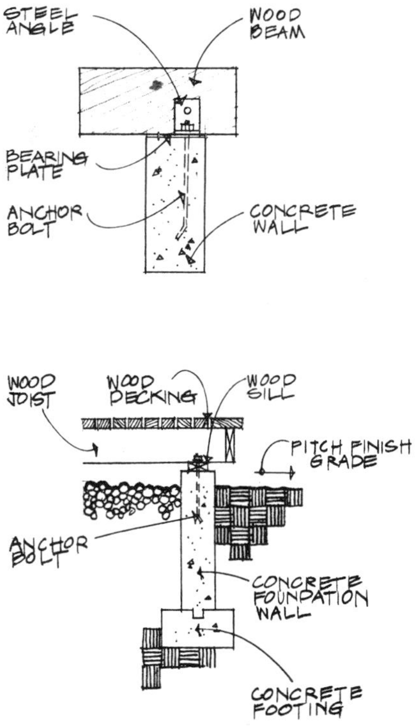
STEEL ANGLE
WOOD BEAM
BEARING PLATE
ANCHOR BOLT
CONCRETE WALL
WOOD JOIST
WOOD DECKING
WOOD SILL
PITCH FINISH GRADE
ANCHOR BOLT
CONCRETE FOUNDATION WALL
CONCRETE FOOTING

Figure 460-27 Beam to pier connections.

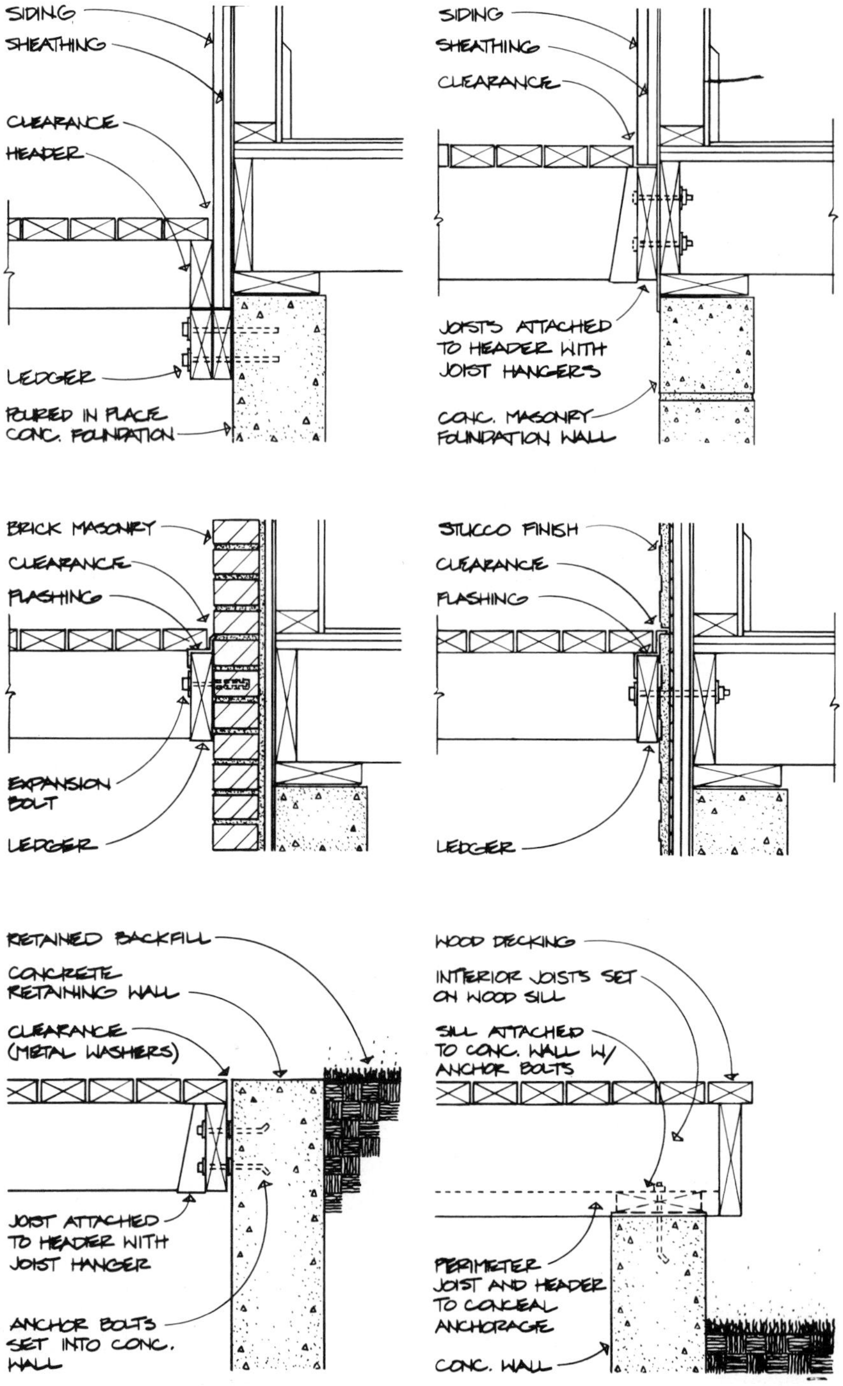
SIDING
SHEATHING
CLEARANCE
HEADER
LEDGER
POURED IN PLACE CONC. FOUNDATION
SIDING
SHEATHING
CLEARANCE
JOISTS ATTACHED TO HEADER WITH JOIST HANGERS
CONC. MASONRY FOUNDATION WALL
BRICK MASONRY
CLEARANCE
FLASHING
EXPANSION BOLT
LEDGER
STUCCO FINISH
CLEARANCE
FLASHING
LEDGER
RETAINED BACKFILL
CONCRETE RETAINING WALL
CLEARANCE (METAL WASHERS)
JOIST ATTACHED TO HEADER WITH JOIST HANGER
ANCHOR BOLTS SET INTO CONC. WALL
WOOD DECKING
INTERIOR JOISTS SET ON WOOD SILL
SILL ATTACHED TO CONC. WALL W/ ANCHOR BOLTS
PERIMETER JOIST AND HEADER TO CONCEAL ANCHORAGE
CONC. WALL

Figure 460-28 Anchorage to fixed structures.

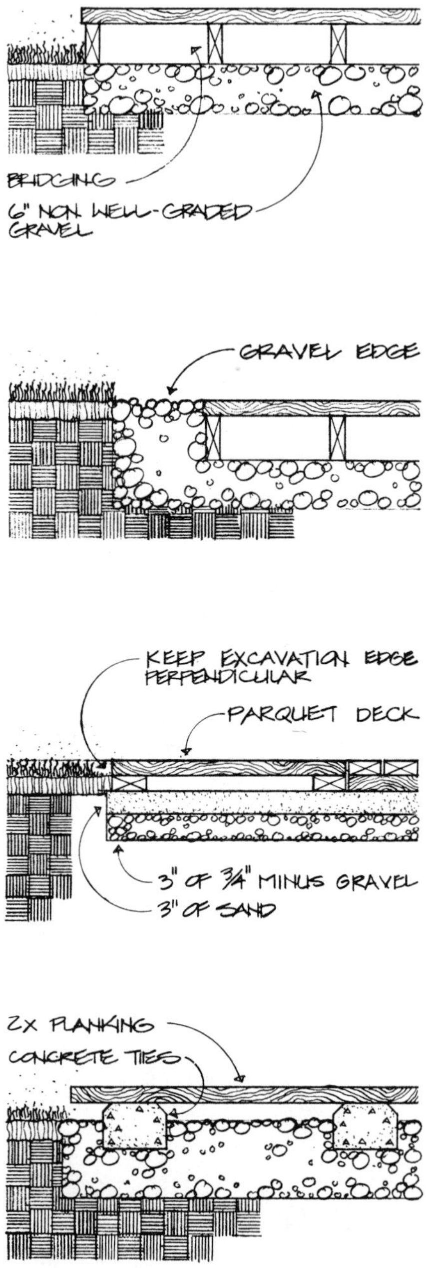
BRIDGING
6" NON WELL-GRADED GRAVEL
GRAVEL EDGE
KEEP EXCAVATION EDGE PERPENDICULAR
PARQUET DECK
3" OF 3/4" MINUS GRAVEL
3" OF SAND
2X PLANKING
CONCRETE TIES

Figure 460-29 Low profile decks on grade.

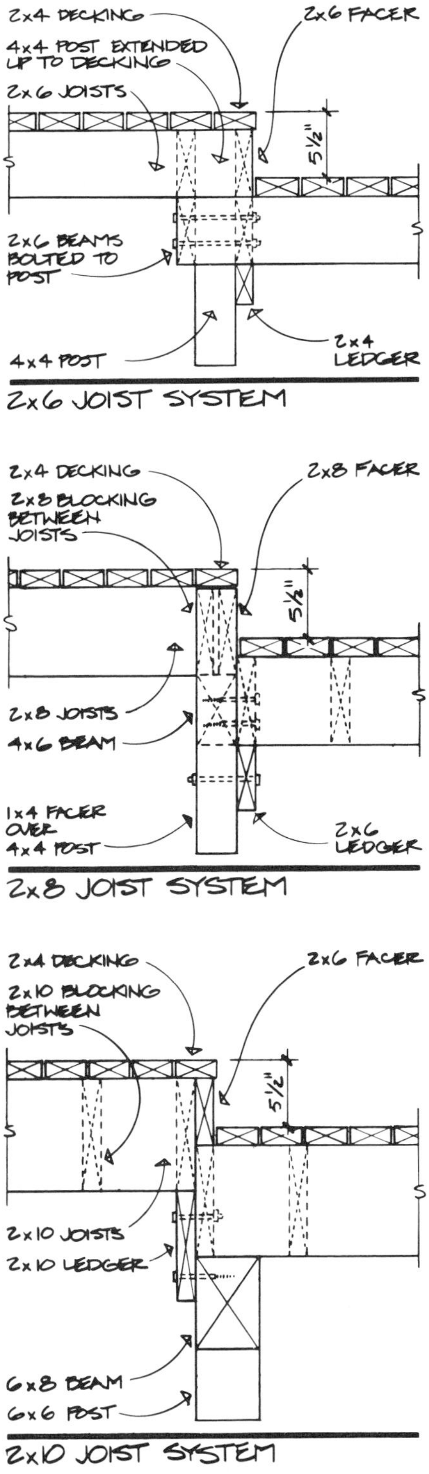
2x4 DECKING
2x6 FACER
4x4 POST EXTENDED UP TO DECKING
2x6 JOISTS
5½"
2x6 BEAMS BOLTED TO POST
4x4 POST
2x4 LEDGER
2x6 JOIST SYSTEM
2x4 DECKING
2x8 FACER
2x8 BLOCKING BETWEEN JOISTS
5½"
2x8 JOISTS
4x6 BEAM
1x4 FACER OVER 4x4 POST
2x6 LEDGER
2x8 JOIST SYSTEM
2x4 DECKING
2x6 FACER
2x10 BLOCKING BETWEEN JOISTS
5½"
2x10 JOISTS
2x10 LEDGER
6x8 BEAM
6x6 POST
2x10 JOIST SYSTEM

Figure 460-30 Level change in decking.

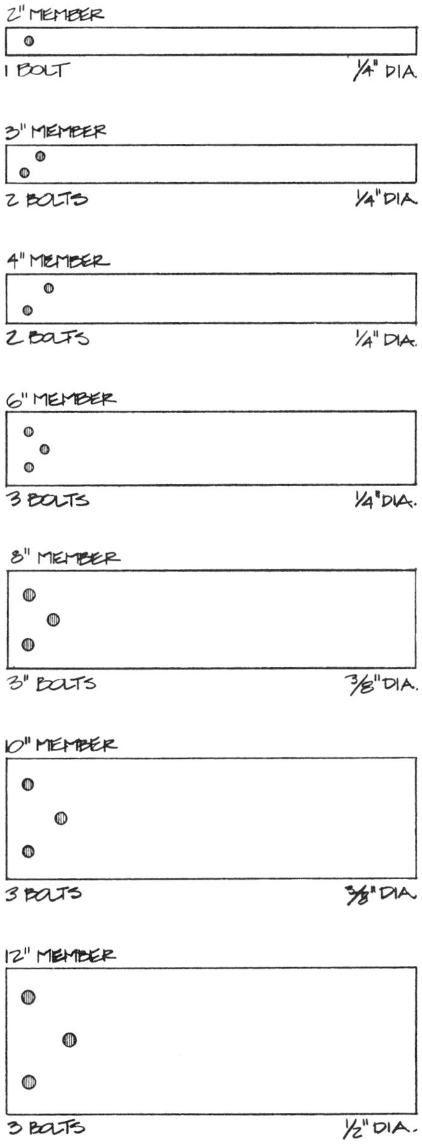
2" MEMBER
1 BOLT
¼" DIA.
3" MEMBER
2 BOLTS
¼"DIA.
4" MEMBER
2 BOLTS
¼" DIA.
6" MEMBER
3 BOLTS
¼"DIA.
8" MEMBER
3" BOLTS
⅜"DIA.
10" MEMBER
3 BOLTS
⅜"DIA.
12" MEMBER
3 BOLTS
½" DIA.

Figure 460-31 Guide to bolt/lag spacing.

AGENCIES AND ORGANIZATIONS

California Redwood Association (CRA)
San Francisco, California

National Building Code (NBC)
c/o American Insurance Association
New York, New York

National Fire Protection Association (NFPA)
Boston, Massachusetts

National Forest Products Association (NFPA)
Washington, D.C.

Southern Building Code
Congress International
Birmingham, Alabama

Uniform Building Code
c/o International Conference of Building Officials
Whittier, California

Western Wood Products Association
Portland, Oregon

REFERENCES

American Standards Association. *The American Standard Building Code Requirements for Minimum Design Loads in Buildings and Other Structures,* The Association, New York, 1955 (or latest edition).

Landphair, H. C., and Fred Klatt, Jr. *Landscape Architecture Construction,* Elsevier, North Holland, New York, 1980 (or latest edition).

Munson, Albe E. *Construction Design for Landscape Architects,* McGraw-Hill, New York, 1974.

National Forest Products Association (NFPA). *National Design Specification for Wood Construction,* April 1973 (or latest edition).

C. G. Ramsey and H. R. Sleeper. *Architectural Graphic Standards,* 7th ed., Robert T. Packard, ed., Wiley, New York, 1981.

Timber Engineering Company. *Timber Design and Construction Handbook,* McGraw-Hill, New York, 1956.

Walker, Theodore D. *Site Design and Construction Detailing,* 2d ed., PDA Publishers, Mesa, Arizona, 1978. ■

section 470: Pedestrian Bridges

CREDITS

Section Editor: Charles W. Harris
Technical Writer: Tess Canfield
Research Assistant: Gary Schiff
Selected Graphics: Jeffrey Lakey

Reviewers:

Hans Willian Hagen, P.E.
LeMessurier Associates, Inc.
Cambridge, Massachusetts

Stephen E. Hamwey, P.E.
Sasaki Associates, Inc.
Watertown, Massachusetts

Anthony Hunt
Anthony Hunt Associates
London, England

Henry H. Liede
Kane, Liede & Ratyna, P.C.
Pleasantville, New York

ACKNOWLEDGEMENT

The material contained in this section was derived primarily from *Footbridges in the Countryside—Design and Construction* with the permission of the Countryside Commission for Scotland.

The commission's officer for the project was Michael Beese. The consultant architects were Reiach & Hall, and the consulting engineers were Blyth and Blyth, with both of the Edinburgh partners, John Spencely and David Small, in charge of the project.

CONTENTS

1.0 INTRODUCTION

Bridges are special structures which allow the easy movement of vehicles, people, and animals over such features as water and steep topography or over such built obstacles as major roadways. Bridges can enhance the scenic character of a site and can create new observation points from which fine views may be seen.

In almost all cases, the design of bridges requires the assistance of structural and/or civil engineers. All dimensions included in this section are for guidance only and for indicating the scale of parts.

2.0 GENERAL DESIGN GUIDELINES

2.1 User Definitions

Design determinants for bridges are based on user characteristics and site characteristics. Types of users may include:

1. People as individuals or in small or large groups (the latter related to spectators or tourists, etc.).

2. People using wheelchairs, bicycles, or other nonmotorized vehicles.

3. People on horseback and using a range of motorized vehicles (motor bikes, motorcycles, power mowers, and in some instances single cars or lightweight trucks, cattle, etc.).

Any of the above types of users may use a bridge in accordance to or contrary to the designer's intention.

2.2 Spatial Standards

Spatial standards for bridges to serve bicyclists, pedestrians, and those who are handicapped are given in Table 470-1. Bridges to serve riders on horseback should be at least 4 ft (2.1 m) wide for single passage crossing.

If a bridge is to be built, then consideration must be given to what may pass underneath. Statutory considerations involving clearances and safety measures apply to roads, rails, and water courses used by canoeists, people fishing or sailing boats, or commercial traffic. Where streams are involved in cold climatic zones, ice floes can create serious problems if not accounted for in design.

2.3 User Safety

General:

The principal hazard to users of bridges is falling from the bridge or its approach paths. Depending upon the expected users and types of dangers, provisions could range from no handrails over shallow streams to shoulder-high rails with infills of mesh, etc., over deep gorges.

Considerations for handicapped users should include appropriate design of the approaches to the bridge. Landings and platforms, rest areas, handrailings, and walking surfaces are all elements that should be checked for compliance with local codes. (Refer to Section 240: Access and Egress: Outdoor Standards, for more information.)

Landings, Rest Areas, and Handrailings:

Level landings or platforms should be provided at the top and bottom of ramp runs. Where ramp grades exceed 1:16 (6.25 percent), intermediate landings should occur no more than 40 ft (12 m) apart. The landing should have a clear width at least equal to the width of the largest ramp leading to it. The minimum landing depth should be 5 ft (1.5 m).

Places to sit or rest are particularly beneficial on very long bridges. They can also function as vantage points for scenic views.

Handrailings that are easily grasped should extend continuously along the en-

TABLE 470-1
Spatial Standards for Bridges for Use by Bicyclists, Pedestrians, and Handicapped Individuals

	Bicycle		*Pedestrian*		*Handicapped*	
Geometric element	*Maximum or minimum*	*Desirable*	*Maximum or minimum*	*Desirable*	*Maximum or minimum*	*Desirable*
Clear width						
One-lane	1.06 m minimum (3.5 ft)	1.22 m or more (4.0 ft)	0.91 m minimum (3.0 ft)	1.22 m or more (4.0 ft)	0.91 m minimum (3.0 ft)	1.22 m or more (4.0 ft)
Two-lanes	2.13 m minimum (7.0 ft)	2.43 m or more (8.0 ft)	1.80 m minimum (6.0 ft)	2.13 m or more (7.0 ft)	1.22 m minimum (4.0 ft)	1.67 m or more (5.5 ft) (to pass two wheelchairs)
More than two lanes*						
Clearance						
Vertical unobstructed height	2.53 m minimum (8.3 ft)	2.89 m (9.5 ft)	2.13 m minimum (7.0 ft)	2.43 m (8.0 ft)	Same as pedestrian	Same as pedestrian
Lateral clearance to obstructions	0.30 m minimum (1.0 ft)	0.61 m (2.0 ft)	0.30 m minimum (1.0 ft)	0.46 m or more (1.5 ft)	Same as pedestrian	Same as pedestrian
Grades	10% for maximum distances of 15.20 m (50 ft) or less	5% for maximum distances of 91.20 m (300 ft) or less	15% maximum	5%	8.33% maximum [length of single run is 9.12 m (30 ft)]	5% or less
Cross slope	2% minimum on curves	Calculated from superelevation formulas	6% maximum	5% or less	2% maximum	1% or less
Design speed (bicycles)	16.09 k/h minimum (10 mph)	24.14 k/h (15 mph) 32.19 k/h on long down grades (20 mph)	Not applicable	Not applicable	Not applicable	Not applicable
Radius of curvature (bicycles)	4.6 m minimum (15 ft)	Calculate from appropriate formulas (see Table 470-3).	Not applicable	Not applicable	Not applicable	Not applicable
Sight distance	Varies with grade and speed. Calculate from appropriate formulas (see Table 470-4).		Provide significant sight distance at curves and turns to avoid collision	Provide significant sight distance at curves and turns to avoid collision	Provide significant sight distance at curves and turns to avoid collision	Provide significant sight distance at curves and turns to avoid collision

* Where volumes of all types of user groups are heavy, widths should be calculated by using level of service concepts.
Source: DeLeuw, Cather & Company, Inc., Boston, Massachusetts.

tire length of the bridge, on both sides, including approach ramps.

Decking and Surface Treatments:

The choice of decking and surface treatments for bridges is very important. Nonslip surfaces are crucial. Wood decking is acceptable if the joints are no more than ½ in (12 mm) wide (preferably less). Slip-resistant metal checkerplates, walkway gratings, or traction strips are often used.

3.0 BRIDGE CONSTRUCTION

3.1 Site Selection

Selection Criteria:

Site factors to consider when deciding on the precise location for a bridge include the following:

1. Which area requires the shortest span?

2. Which area has the best foundation conditions?

3. Which area is closest to the line of the existing footpath?

4. Which area has the fewest obstacles in the way of the bridge and/or its approaches?

5. Which area allows the most clearance from flooding?

6. Which area is easiest to reach with equipment, labor, and materials?

7. Which area has the fewest hazards to make safe, such as precipices, steep paths, or exposure to strong winds?

8. Which location would users prefer and enjoy the most? For instance, are there pools beneath for looking at fish, whitewater rapids in sight, or exceptional views from each side of the bridge and approaches?

Site Survey:

Once the location for a bridge is determined, the site must be surveyed to obtain necessary information for the bridge design, its foundations, and approaches. The following information is necessary:

1. Longitudinal cross section across the gap, extending at least 10 ft (3 m) beyond each end, on the centerline of the bridge.

2. Lateral cross sections extending at least 10 ft (3 m) on either side of the centerline and showing elevations of the side of the gap (i.e., river bank, etc.).

3. Plan of the area encompassed by the sections.

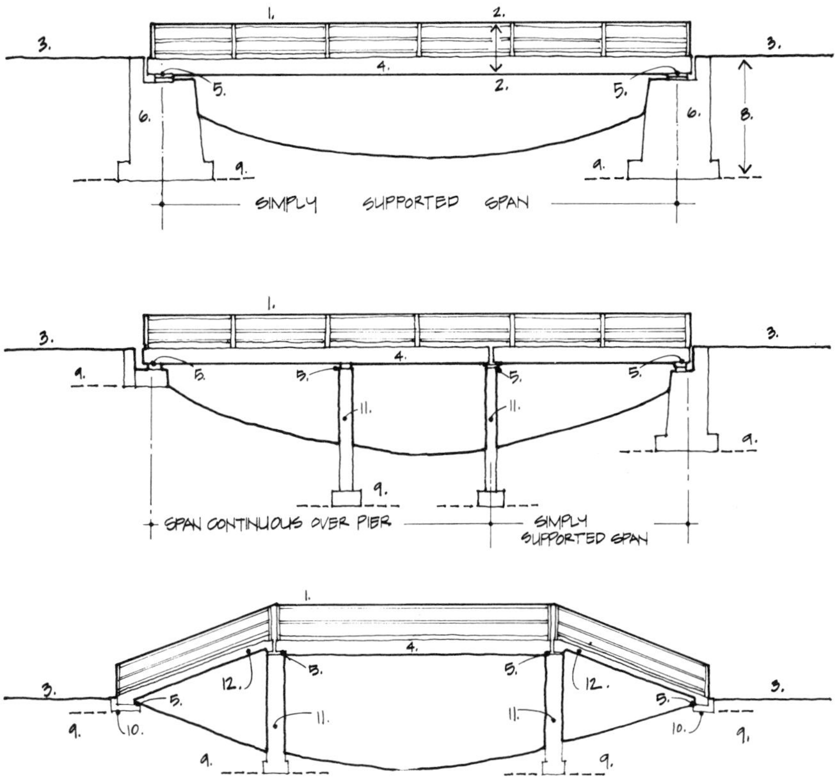
SIMPLY SUPPORTED SPAN
SPAN CONTINUOUS OVER PIER
SIMPLY SUPPORTED SPAN

Figure 470-1 Basic Components of a Bridge. (1) Handrail, (2) superstructure, (3) approach path, (4) main beam, (5) bridge bearing, (6) abutment, (7) end dam, (8) substructure, (9) bearing strata, (10) end seat, (11) pier, (12) approach ramp.

4. Spot elevations taken every 3 ft (1 m) and at significant points (assumed foundation positions, abrupt changes in level, etc.).

5. Positions of obstacles, such as trees. (In the case of trees, their botanical names, their girth, and in some cases their branch height and exposed root systems should be noted.)

6. The ground on which foundations are likely to be built. This can vary from a simple site inspection, which may reveal stable outcrops of rock in which to construct the foundations, to using rotary drill techniques. In most cases a geological engineer should be employed to direct the site investigation and to interpret the results. (Whatever type of investigation is conducted, a careful record must be kept—locating the sample point, describing the materials encountered, and recording the results of any tests carried out.)

7. A record of potential problems (e.g., width, gradient, obstructions, and ground conditions) where access for equipment, laborers, and materials may be difficult.

8. A more specific survey of a particular point may be necessary during the detailed design stage after a bridge type has been selected.

3.2 Selection of Footbridge Type

Basic Components:

Figure 470-1 illustrates the basic components of simple footbridges.

Selection Chart:

There are many factors that require consideration when selecting a bridge type. Table 470-2 illustrates 16 structural forms and describes the materials, foundation conditions, and spans for which they are suitable.

Additional Considerations:

In addition to the design considerations given in Table 470-2, the following points should be kept in mind when selecting a bridge type.

Clearance: The clearance required will determine the construction depth available between the deck and the underside of the bridge. The bridge can be raised by using approach ramps but usually at increased costs. Table 470-3 lists some typical requirements for clearance and the resulting lengths of ramps based upon 8 and 10 percent gradients.

TABLE 470-2
Bridge Selection Chart

Key to Classifications

Key #	*Comparative costs (CC)*	*Maintenance classification (MC)*	*Life classification (LC)*	*Design and erection classification (DEC)*
1	Lowest cost	Every five years	Over 30 years	S—Standard design may be used
2	Low costs	Paint/preservative every three years	20-30 years	C—Design by structural engineer
3	Medium costs	Repair decking and handrailing every two years	10-20 years	V—Can be erected by voluntary unskilled labor with skilled supervisor
4	High costs	Repairs required every year	5-10 years	F—Can be erected by voluntary unskilled labor with skilled supervisor using prefabricated parts made by a subcontractor
5	Highest costs	Regular attention throughout year	Up to five years	P—Must be erected by a contractor

Notes: The classification is based upon typical comparative costs, assuming built by a contractor, site with easy access, and simple foundations.

It is assumed all footbridges are well built using sound materials.

Annual inspection and good regular maintenance is required for all structures.

In all cases the construction of the footbridge should be carried out in accordance with the construction plans and specifications.

Bridge diagram	*Material*	*Span range*	*CC*	*MC*	*LC*	*DEC*	*Notes*
	Simply supported beam or slab						
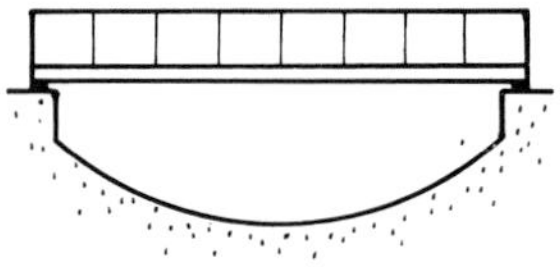	Timber:						■ This is the simplest footbridge for short spans. Where there are poor foundation conditions, some settlement at abutments can be tolerated. ■ Beams can be shaped and cambered. Transport problems due to length.
	Log beams	Up to 10	2	4	5	SV	
	Sawn beams	Up to 10	2	3	4	SV	
	Laminated timber beams	8 to 25	5	3	3	CF	
	Steel beams:						■ Steel requires good paint specifications.
	Timber deck	5 to 15	3	3	3	SF	
	Concrete deck	5 to 15	4	2	2	CP	
	Concrete:						■ Can be shaped for aesthetic effect. Centering required.
	In situ reinforced slab	Up to 10	5	1	1	CP	■ Heavy sections for transport and erection. Factory made.
	Precast reinforced or pretensioned beams	Up to 20	5	1	1	CP	
	Continuous beam or slab						
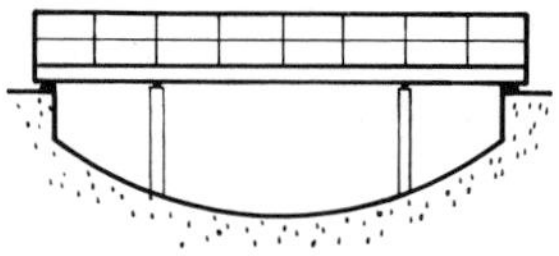							■ Economical with regard to main structural members; requires sound foundations because settlement can overstress the super-structure. The span range is given for the center span. Side spans can be up to approximately two-thirds of the center span.
	Laminated timber beams	8 to 25	5	3	3	CP	■ Beams can be shaped and cambered. Transport of long lengths difficult. Site splices required.
	Steel beams:						
	Timber deck	8 to 19	3	3	3	CF	■ Steel beams can be transported in short lengths and spliced at site.
	Concrete deck	8 to 19	4	2	2	CP	■ Steel beams can be transported in short lengths and spliced at site.
	Concrete:						
	In situ reinforced slab or beam	6 to 20	5	1	1	CP	■ Can be shaped; centering required.
	In situ or precast sections pretensioned	10 to 25	5	1	1	CP	■ Heavy sections for transport and erection.

TABLE 470-2 *(Continued)*

Bridge diagram	*Material*	*Span range*	*CC*	*MC*	*LC*	*DEC*	*Notes*
	Cantilever and suspended span (beam or slab)						
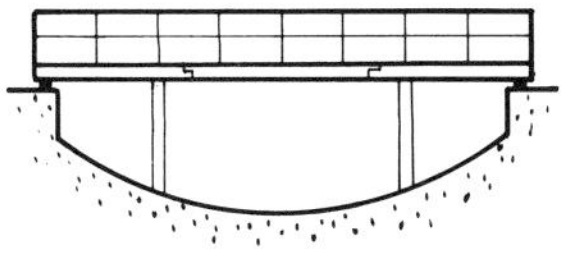							■ Has the same advantages as a continuous span but can tolerate some settlement of the supports; may cause uplift problems at the abutments, especially with short side spans. The span lengths are given for the pier to pier distances. The length of the suspended span should be approximately 0.6 of this. Side spans can be up to the length of the suspended span. ■ Beams can be shaped and cambered. Transport of long lengths difficult. Site splices required.
	Steel beams:						
	Timber deck	8 to 19	3	3	3	CF	■ Steel beams can be transported in short lengths and spliced at site.
	Concrete deck	8 to 19	4	2	2	CP	■ Steel beams can be transported in short lengths and spliced at site.
	Concrete:						
	In situ beam and slab	6 to 20	5	1	1	CP	■ Can be shaped; centering required.
	Precast beam and slab	10 to 25	5	1	1	CP	■ Heavy sections for transport and erection.
	Trussed beam						
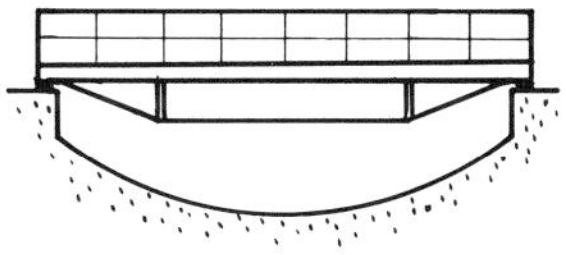	Steel beams and rod or wire rope tension member; timber or precast concrete deck	10 to 20	3	3	1	CP	■ Requires ample clearance below the tension member to prevent damage. By forming a truss, it allows use of a slender main member. ■ Requires skilled fabrication of struts and anchorage points.
	Lattice girder (through-type or Warren truss)						
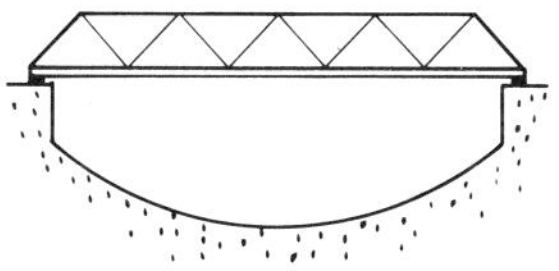							■ Allows minimum construction depth below deck level. The structural girder members act as handrailing. Top flanges of the girders should be braced with raking supports or overhead frames. Horizontal bracing for wind may be required. The small structural members are more susceptible to accidental damage than beam-type footbridges. Girders can be transported to the site in small sections and assembled.
	Timber: sawn sections	5 to 15	5	4	3	CF/P	■ Skill required in fabrication and erection.
	Steel:						
	Angles	10 to 25	1	3	2	CF/P	■ "F" for smaller spans.
	Rectangular hollow sections	10 to 25	1	3	2	CF/P	
	Tubes	10 to 25	1	3	2	CF/P	
	Aluminum (standard design by British Aluminum Co., Ltd.)	8.75 to 30	5	3	1	CP	■ These require good paint specifications.
	Bow string girder						
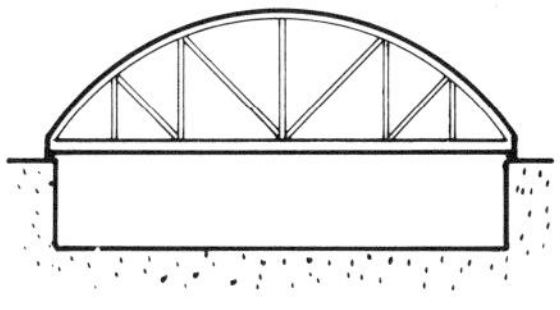							■ An economical solution for longer spans where the top cords can be braced together above head height of the user. Horizontal wind bracing may be required. Girders can be transported to the site in small sections.
	Timber: sawn sections	15 to 30	5	4	3	CP	
	Steel (all sections, including RHS and tubes)	15 to 30	2	3	2	CP	
	Three-pinned arch						
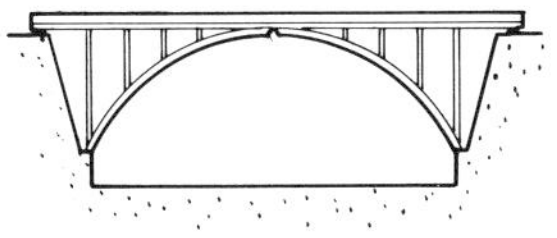							■ Requires good foundation conditions with little settlement. Preformed arch members can be transported to site in half-span lengths. Best suited for longer spans where appearance is important. Complex erection procedure.
	Laminated timber	15 to 30	5	3	2	CP	■ Arch ribs can be transported in half-span lengths.
	Steel	15 to 30	5	3	1	CP	■ Arch ribs can be transported in short sections.
	Concrete: In situ and precast	15 to 30	1	1	1	CP	■ Requires in situ centering. Precast units are long, heavy, and difficult to transport.

(continued)

TABLE 470-2 *(Continued)*

Bridge diagram	*Material*	*Span range*	*CC*	*MC*	*LC*	*DEC*	*Notes*
		Suspension					
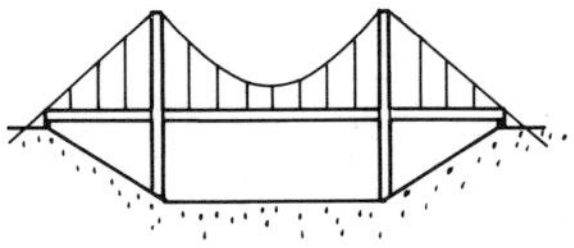	Cables						▪ The span range shown refers to the main span only. This type is good for long spans over water or deep ravines where intermediate piers are not possible. Sometimes used for shorter spans for aesthetic reasons. Wind bracing is sometimes required and the width of the walkway may be determined by structural stability considerations. Cable anchorage points should be firm and safe from accidents or vandalism. The design and erection is complex and requires a trained structural engineer and expert construction supervision. ▪ High risk of corrosion at cable and suspender anchorage points, which requires good construction detailing and regular inspection.
	Galvanized high-tensile steel wire ropes						
	Suspenders						
	Galvanized high-tensile wire ropes or steel rods						
	Deck structure and towers:						
	Timber: sawn structure	15 to 35	3	4	3	CF/P	▪ "F" for shorter spans.
	Steel: timber deck	20 to 60	3	3	2	CP	▪ Lattice girders can also act as handrails.

Source: Countryside Commission for Scotland.

Accessibility: The difficulty of transporting the main structural members to the site may eliminate certain types of bridges which require long, heavy members. The difficulty of getting earthmoving equipment to both sides of the site may limit the amount of foundation and approach path work which can be done and thus influence the type of bridge.

Vandalism: In areas of risk from vandalism, certain types of bridges that have parts which can be easily detached or broken should be avoided.

Resources Available: Bridges in rural or remote areas may have to be constructed with low-skilled labor and locally available materials.

Planning, Design, and Engineering Knowledge: Local codes or ordinances usually require the use of a registered engineer for detailed bridge design. In the absence of such professional assistance, it may be necessary to restrict the choice of bridge types to familiar designs with minor spans of 30 ft (9 m) or less.

Fitting the Bridge to a Site: A bridge is essentially a continuation of a path. Therefore, it should tie in well with the overall design of the landscape. When a bridge has to be set higher than the original ground level on either side, then access ramps will be necessary. Table 470-3 shows typical lengths of ramps for pedestrian bridges.

Because people tend to slow down, linger, and sometimes congregate at a footbridge, approach paths should be widened to facilitate easy pedestrian flow.

TABLE 470-3
Typical Ramp Lengths for Pedestrian Bridges

Description of structure	*Required vertical clearance, m (ft)*	*Elevation change, m (ft)*	*Approximate length of one approach ramp**	
			8% Grade, m (ft)	*10% Grade, m (ft)*
Bridge over highway	5.2 (17)	5.8–6.4 (19–21) ascent	76 (250)	61 (200)
Bridge over road or street	4.6 (15)	5.2–5.8 (17–19) ascent	68 (225)	55 (180)
Bridge over railroad	7.0 (23)	8.2–9.2 (27–30) ascent	109 (360)	86 (285)
Bridge over electrified railroad	8.0 (26)	9.2–10 (30–33) ascent	122 (400)	95 (315)

* Landings are not considered, but if they are used, the approach ramp should be lengthened.

Source: DeLeuw, Cather & Company, Inc., Boston, Massachusetts.

3.3 Selection of Main Structural Members

When a bridge type has been selected, the size and form of the main structural members may be determined in one of the following three ways:

1 *Typical bridge designs:* for spans under 30 ft (9 m) where no site difficulties exist, a typical footbridge may be built. (Refer to 4.0 Typical Designs for Short-Span Footbridges in this section for more information.)

2. *Prefabricated bridge designs:* specialist suppliers offer a range of standard bridge types, either in kit form or completed and ready to place in position. Commonly available bridge types in the United States include:

- **a.** Laminated timber beams
- **b.** Hardwood beams and made-up girders
- **c.** Steel lattice girders
- **d.** Aluminum lattice girders
- **e.** Precast concrete beams

(Refer to 5.0 Typical Designs for Prefabricated Bridges in this section for more information.)

3. *Special designs:* custom-made bridge structures may be designed by experienced engineers, especially for spans exceeding 30 ft (9 m).

NOTE: The conceptual design of substructures (foundations, etc.) should be done in parallel with the design of the bridge deck and approaches. Decisions related to span arrangement affect: (1) the number, loading, and size of foundations; (2) the zones of soil providing support; and (3) the relative difficulties of construction of different types of foundations.

Design loads on a particular foundation might be adjusted by a change in the length of spans or the form of deck construction.

3.4 Loadings on the Bridge's Superstructure

Types of Loading:

Various loads which a bridge's superstructure must support include (Figure 470-2):

1. *Dead Load:* the weight of the bridge materials themselves
2. *Live load:*
   a. The weight of people, together with any dynamic effect from their movement
   b. Wind pressure on the bridge structure, or suction or pressure on the bridge deck
   c. Accumulation of snow and ice
   d. Flooding via water pressure acting on the bridge structure or transmitted to the bridge structure from floating debris and ice

Design Loading:

The design loading should be determined based on anticipated use (pedestrians and small vehicles, emergency vehicles, etc.).

When estimating loadings, consideration must be given to exceptional conditions which may cause extreme stresses on the structure. For example, if a bridge spans a stream on which boat races may occur, spectator crowding on the bridge (first on the upstream side, and then shifting to the downstream side) could cause twisting and extreme load conditions. If the bridge is on a ceremonial route, where large numbers of people walk in step, concentrated rhythmic impacts could cause excessive vibration and consequent failure. Extreme conditions may result when the bridge is opened or dedicated and is subjected to heavy crowd loadings.

User Loads for Rural Footbridges:

Most footbridges in rural areas will rarely be wider than 3 to 5 ft (1 to 1.5 m) and will rarely be subjected to large crowds or other extraordinary loads. An exception may be the existence of a spectacular gorge or waterfall which can be reached by passengers from tour buses. Table 470-4

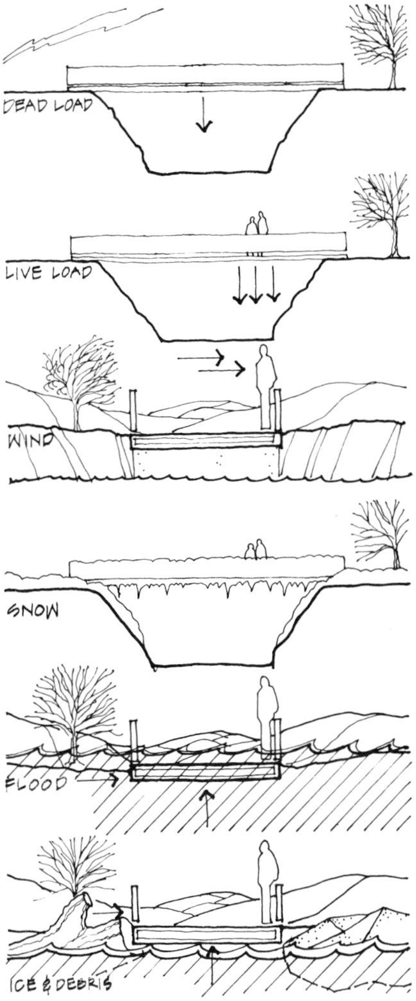
DEAD LOAD
LIVE LOAD
WIND
SNOW
FLOOD
ICE & DEBRIS

Figure 470-2 Types of bridge loading.

TABLE 470-4
Loads for Narrow Footbridges in Rural Areas*

Member	*Load type*	Loading: *Uniformly distributed*	Loading: *Point load*	*Remarks*
Main beams	Pedestrian normal crowd Horse and rider, cattle or sheep	 2.3 KN/m² 3.2 KN/m² 2.3 KN/m²		For wider footbridges and urban sites, use appropriate loading standards.
Short-span members	Pedestrian normal crowd Sheep Horse and rider Cattle	The greater: either 3.2 KN/m² or 1.62 KN on a 75-mm square up to a 1900 span. Thereafter 1.69 KN/m run of member. 3.2 KN/m² or 8.12 KN on a 75-mm square 3.2 KN/m² or 6.12 KN on a 120-mm square		All short-span members may carry crowd loading. Individual timber deck boards may carry point or line load.
Handrail (horizontal load)	Pedestrian normal crowd Horse and rider, cattle	0.74 KN/m, 1000 mm above deck 1.4 KN/m, 1100 mm above deck 1.3 KN/m, 1250 mm above deck		
All members	Snow	0.4 KN/m²		
Unloaded footbridge	Wind: 40m/sec (horizontal load)	1.4 KN/m²		Permissible stresses increased by 25%.
Loaded footbridge	Wind: 28 m/sec (horizontal load)	0.7 KN/m²		

*Width of footbridge is 800–1700 mm.
Source: Adapted from Reiach Hall Blyth Partnership, preparers, *Footbridges in the Countryside*, the Countryside Commission for Scotland, Perth, 1981.

shows loadings for narrow bridges based upon likely uses in rural areas.

Pedestrian Loading:

1. *Main beams and girders:* a uniformly distributed live load (UDLL) over the whole span is equivalent to that shown for normal and crowd loading (Figure 470-3).

2. *Deck members:* where the deck is made of small individual units, such as deck boards, the entire weight concentrated on one foot should be assumed: e.g., total weight 246 lb (112 kg) on a 3-in (75-mm) square, including an impact factor of 1.250, or a line of people each weighing 200 lb (90 kg) at 2-ft (650-mm) centers along the member with an impact factor of 1.000 (Figure 470-3).

Horse and Rider Loading:

1. *Main beams and girders:* horses and riders in single file at spacings of $1\frac{1}{2}$ horse lengths with an impact factor of 1.300.

2. *Deck members:* where the deck is of small individual units, such as deck boards, the full weight of a trotting animal resting on one hoof should be assumed. For a horse, this load will be on a 7-in (175-mm) square with an impact factor of 1.250.

Deflections:

The deflection of the individual structural members and the main beams and girders under full loading should be limited to $\frac{1}{240}$th of the span. Where possible, structures should be built with a precamber at least equal to the dead load deflection (Figure 470-4). The aesthetic appearance of a footbridge is improved by making this precamber substantial. Use $\frac{1}{8}$ in/ft (10 mm/m) of total span to $\frac{7}{16}$ in/ft (35 mm/

TABLE 470-5
Loading on Substructures and Foundations*

Loading	*Comment*
Dead load	*a.* Self weight of substructure *b.* Weight of fill supported by foundation *c.* Dead load and superimposed load of superstructure
Earth pressure	Continuously acting on completed substructure but likely to fluctuate in intensity with substructure movement, vibration, water table, etc.
Differential settlement	Differential settlement of embankment relative to substructure transfers load to substructure and foundations. Differential movements of supports of indeterminate bridge change reactions.
Hydraulic	Piers in rivers are subjected to lateral forces from change of direction of water flow. Forces increase in times of flood.
Flood	Drawdown condition following flooding of embankment. Also, flooding of retaining wall drainage membrane from behind or above.
Creep and shrinkage	Creep and shrinkage movements of superstructure can affect reactions and thrusts on substructure.
Temperature	Temperature changes in superstructure can alter reactions and thrusts or apply displacement to supports (which can in turn alter earth pressures). Temperature changes in parts of substructures and ground affect the forces and differential movement between them.
Traffic on bridge	Detailed information is included in various bridge-design standards for loading from: *a.* Vertical gravitational load incorporating impact allowance *b.* Centrifugal load acting radially *c.* Longitudinal loads, which can act toward or away from substructure
Traffic on abutment	Live load surcharges to represent vertical traffic loading are given in standards for bridge design. Horizontal loads due to braking and traction can act on substructure through fill and pavement.
Wind	Detailed information on wind loads on superstructure and piers is included in the standards listed above.
Impact	Piers may be vulnerable to impact from vehicles, trains, and river craft. Standards provide guidance for piers alongside highways. Massive abutments and foundations are much less vulnerable and not likely to fail, although some displacement can occur from severe impact.
Exceptional	Snow, ice packs, earthquake, etc.
Construction	Combinations of any of the above loads can be critical for incomplete substructures during stages of construction together with loads due to temporary works, stored materials, moving loads, and possibly also accompanied by reduction of support.

* This table lists various design loadings for substructures. The loadings are not considered to act all at the same time, and various combinations are identified during design.

Source: Building Research Establishment.

TABLE 470-6
Permissible Bearing Pressure

Material	*Permissible bearing pressure on ground, KN/per m²*	*Tons/ft²*
Hard rock	2150	21
Shale and soft rock	1075	11
Compact sand or gravel and hard compact clay	430	4
Firm sand, sandy clay, and ordinary fairly dry boulder clay	215	2
Wet or loose sand and soft clay	105	1
Unconsolidated fill, alluvial soil peat	Varies up to 25	Up to 0.25

Note: This table should be used for preliminary estimations only.

Source: Adapted from Reiach Hall Blyth Partnership, preparers, *Footbridges in the Countryside,* the Countryside Commission for Scotland, Perth, 1981.

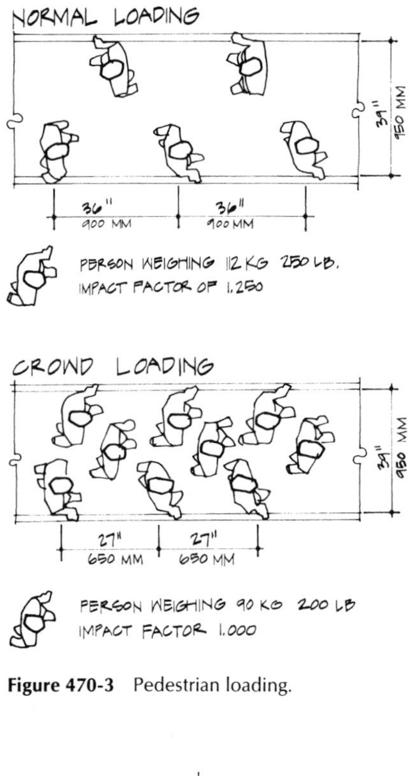
NORMAL LOADING
39"
950 MM
36"
900 MM
36"
900 MM
PERSON WEIGHING 112 KG 250 LB.
IMPACT FACTOR OF 1.250
CROWD LOADING
39"
950 MM
27"
650 MM
27"
650 MM
PERSON WEIGHING 90 KG 200 LB
IMPACT FACTOR 1.000

Figure 470-3 Pedestrian loading.

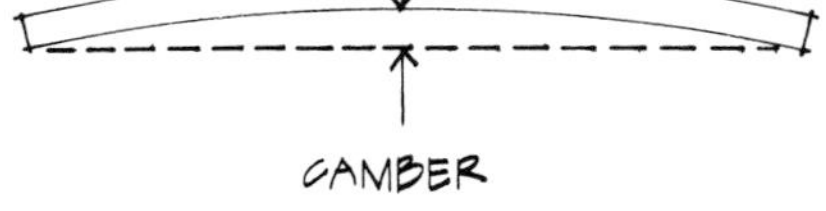
CAMBER

Figure 470-4 Camber. Where possible, structures should be built with a precamber at least equal to the dead load deflection.

TABLE 470-7
General Guide to Choice of Foundation

Ground	*Footings preferred*	*Piles preferred*
Stiff clay, medium-dense dry sand, or gravel	Footings are most often appropriate for footbridges for reasons of cost, reliability, and ease of construction.	Piles may have to be used where very heavy concentrated loads have to be transmitted to ground.
Firm clays, loose dry gravels, or sand and gravel	Some designers prefer to use footings with bearing pressures as low as 100–150 kN/m^2 if significant settlement is expected during or soon after construction.	Piles are often the preferred solution because settlement of a pile group is often as much as one-half or one-third of that of a footing and takes place rapidly.
Stiff stratum at moderate depth with deep water table	Shallow spread footings supported on mass concrete or granular fill which forms a firm stratum are sometimes less expensive than deep footings.	
High water table in permeable ground		Driven or cased bored piles are typically used, but installation can be difficult.
Stiff ground overlying soft ground, e. g., gravel over clay	Shallow footings can be designed to make use of load-spreading quality of the stiff ground.	Use of piles can create driving or boring problems and by concentrating the load above or in the clay can cause larger settlements.
Soft silty clays, peat, and uncompacted fills	Spread footings can be used on fill if the ground can be consolidated in advance by use of a surcharge.	Piles are usually preferred. Measures sometimes have to be taken to prevent damage from lateral loading due to adjacent embankment.
Interbedded sand and silt layers	Excavation can be hindered by water in layers, but installation of bored piles has also given many problems.	
Loose sands increasing in strength with depth	Improving the strength of existing sand often is cheaper than using piles, but it is difficult to predict and monitor these special techniques. Therefore, piles are sometimes preferred.	Driven piles compact the sand and provide high load capacity with minimum settlement. (Note: single size sands can be impossible to compact.)
Chalk	Use footings unless chalk is deeper than the spread footings. Even soft chalk consolidates quickly under a load (usually during construction).	If upper surface is at unpredictable depths due to swallow holes, piles may be better because they can be driven to different depths without delays in the contract. Chalk softens during driving or boring but recovers some strength during following weeks; therefore delay testing test piles at different depths to determine the optimum.
Unpredictable and impenetrable ground, such as boulders or rock with clay matrix	Excavation for footings or installation of piles can be very difficult, with predictions of movement unreliable. Shallow footings can be the more economical.	Steel H piles have been driven either to deep firm stratum or to sufficient depths to mobilize adequate friction.
Compacted fill	Well-compacted, suitable, or selected fill is generally as good as, if not better than, natural deposits of the same material.	
Steeply dipping rock substratum	Mass concrete fill can grip stepped interfaces where piles might glance off.	If stratum is very deep, then precast concrete piles with rock shoes or use steel piles.
Over rivers and estuaries		Piles are usually preferred irrespective of ground conditions.

Source: Adapted from Building Research Establishment.

m). The top end of this range results in a deck gradient of about 1:15, which is reasonable for pedestrian traffic.

Dynamic Deflection: Long-span footbridges [over 65 ft (20 m)] should be checked for their response to dynamic loading and to excitation by wind. The design should avoid the use of structures whose primary natural frequency coincides with the pace frequency of pedestrians (i.e., approximately 2.0 cycles per second). The calculation of the vibration frequency of a structure is complex and requires consultation with an experienced engineer.

Footbridges found to be susceptible to vibration can be dampened in a variety of ways, including the use of rubber bearings, or of side guys for suspension bridges.

3.5 Substructures (Foundations)

Substructures are the parts of the bridge which transmit loads from the bridge span to the ground. Substructures include abutments, end seats, and piers.

Loading on Substructures:

Table 470-5 lists various design loadings for bridge substructures.

Foundations and Soil Bearing Capacity:

The applied load from the substructure must be resisted by the ground to prevent failure and excessive settlement (Table 470-6). In almost all cases, engineering advice is required when estimating soil bearing capacity.

Soft clay and materials of low bearing capacity and high water content are likely to compress under load and result in rapid short-term or slower long-term settlement. Within limits, such settlement may not be serious for a footbridge of a short to medium span. For longer continuous-beam-type bridges, such settlement could cause

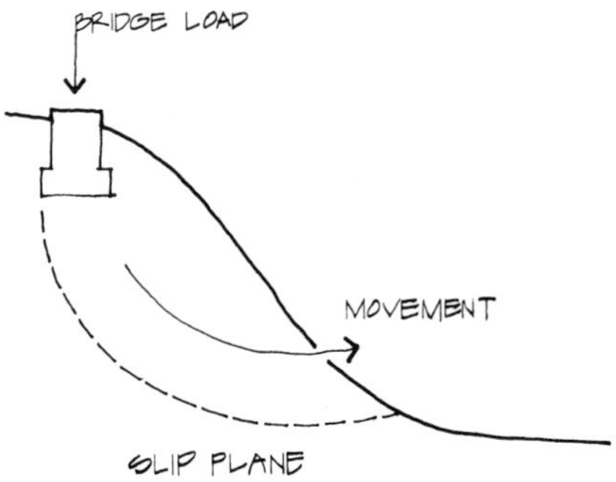
BRIDGE LOAD
MOVEMENT
SLIP PLANE

Figure 470-5 Ground Failure at Bridge Foundation. Abutments sited on steeply sloping ground may fail when an entire section of the bank slips.

TABLE 470-8
Open Abutments

Type, use, and comment	Sketch
Bank seats: Often used in cut areas and less common in fill areas. Bank seats are simple economic structures of semimass or reinforced concrete. Ideal for bridges where there is firm undisturbed ground. The exposed bearing shelf is more economical than the buried type because of the reduced length of deck, but the front edge of the footing should be kept back from the slope face because of erosion, frost action, and because the fill on a slope is not well compacted. Wing walls are constructed as cantilevers or on footings.	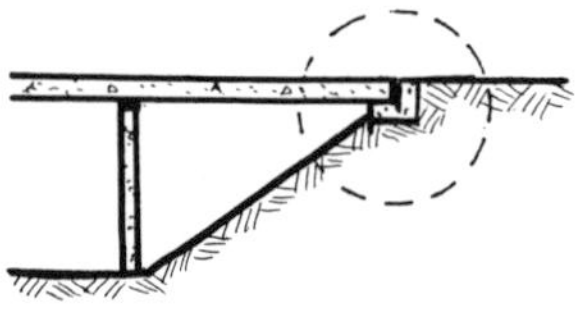 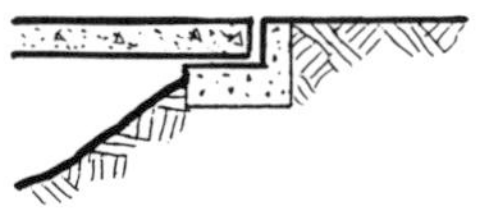 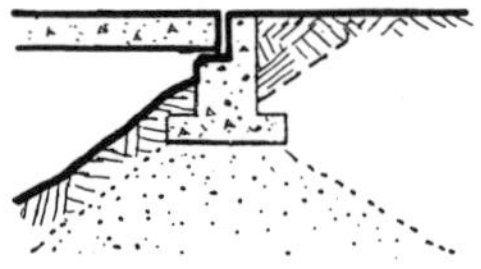
Bank seats on piles: Used occasionally. Bank seats are placed on piles when the ground or fill is not strong enough.	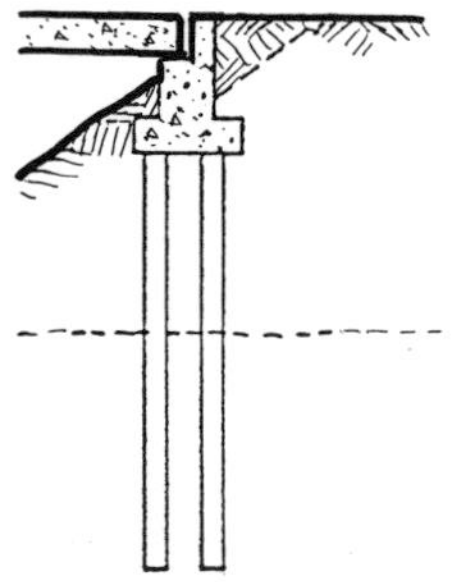

Source: Modified from Building Research Establishment.

high stresses within the bridge beams.

The bearing capacity of poor soils, such as peat and soft clay, can be improved by spreading the imposed load. High-tensile plastic fiber sheets which allow the passage of moisture but not of soil material are now commonly used. (Refer to Section 880: Geotextiles, for more information on these types of materials.)

The overall stability of the foundation should be considered. For example, abutments sited on steeply sloping ground may fail when an entire section of the bank begins slipping (Figure 470-5).

The management of water in excavations is difficult and carries considerable risk. Many materials, especially sand, become unstable when subjected to porewater flow, which is the direct result of pumping water from a hole. These operations should only be undertaken by experienced contractors under the direction of an experienced geotechnical engineer.

Choice of Foundation (Footings or Piles):

Engineering advice is important for all but the simplest of structures when selecting an appropriate foundation design. Spread footings are usually preferable to piles because they are less expensive and generally pose less risk in terms of encountering unforeseen and expensive technical and contractual problems during construction.

Table 470-7 lists some of the ground conditions and construction considerations for which footings or piles have been found to be advantageous. For sites with variable bearing qualities of the strata, designers may have to work through a range of types, depths, and sizes of foundation to identify the most acceptable economic solution.

Types of Abutments:

Open Abutments: Open abutments, with the end spans of the deck bearing on seatings at the tops of embankments, are often preferable to and can look better than a retaining wall type of abutment (Table 470-8). The cost of the end span, pier, and end support of a narrow bridge is likely to be less than that of a closed abutment with wing walls and a retained fill. For a wide bridge, the cost of wing walls is relatively less significant, and the closed abutment is then likely to be more economical.

Open abutments are particularly suitable where the ground is not firm enough to support the heavy weight of a closed abutment, or where horizontal forces must be kept to a minimum. Since the bank seat settles with the embankment, the problems of settlement of backfill behind the abutment are minimal.

Wall Abutments: Various types of wall abutments are described in Table 470-9.

Strutted, Portal, and Box Structures: Strutted, portal, and box structures are described in Table 470-10.

Wing Walls:

The cost of wing walls can be a significant part of the total cost of a substructure, particularly for narrow bridges (Table 470-11). They can also have a negative effect on the aesthetic appearance of the bridge and result in only a marginal cost saving. The choice of geometry is usually controlled by the topography of the site, construction restrictions, and the construction sequence. If possible, it is advantageous to design the wing walls so that a contractor can construct them before constructing the deck. Wing walls often can be structurally independent of the abutment, in which case the joints between them need to be designed to permit significant movement, with provisions made to hide minor tilts.

TABLE 470-9
Wall Abutments

Type, use, and comment	*Sketch*
Mass or gravity type: Common usage for walls up to 6–9 ft (2–3 m). Rare above 18 ft (6 m). Mass concrete without reinforcement provides a simple form of construction but the large quantity of concrete is relatively expensive. Lack of reinforcement may make it ideal for a small contract with little or no other steel used in the construction. Low strength concrete can be used with less heat due to hydration and less cracking problems.	
Semimass: Common usage. A combination of mass concrete and minimum reinforcement.	
Reinforced T Most common form of construction. Minimum width of base can be achieved if heel is larger than the toe. Complicated reinforcement details make construction slower than semimass.	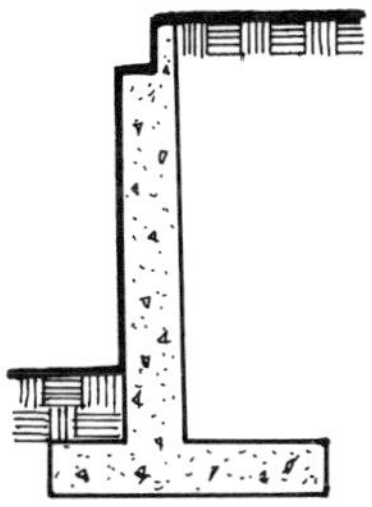
Counterfort: Seldom used except for very tall walls. The complicated construction of counterforts and much formwork make this uneconomic for walls less than 10–12 m (30–35 ft) in height. Compaction of fill between counterforts is difficult and not always satisfactory.	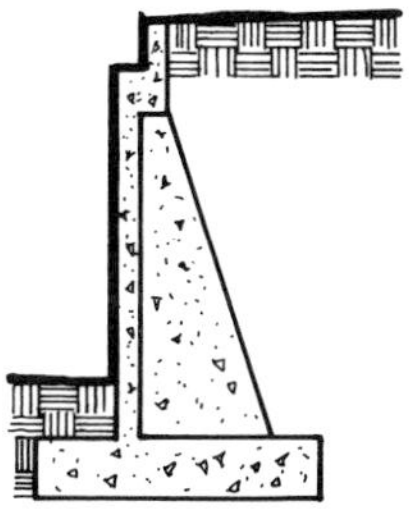
Abutment on fill: Used only when appropriate. A deep foundation can often be achieved more economically by placing a small abutment on fill than by constructing a large abutment. In difficult ground conditions fill can be selfcompacting, such as by mass concrete, and placed without workmen entering the excavations. Speed and simplicity of construction more than compensate for the cost of large quantities of material.	
Reinforced earth Reinforced earth may be appropriate where filled embankments are behind the abutments, but are not appropriate in cut areas. These types of structures have a large tolerance for movement and are ideal for sites with poor ground near the surface (but not if poor stratum is deep because circular slip is not resisted by ties). A batter to the front face is desirable. Be sure to assess the corrosion life of ties and fittings and the possibility of erosion through gaps in some types of facing.	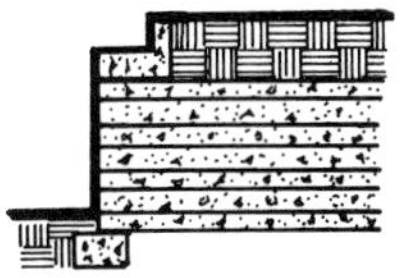

(continued)

TABLE 470-9 *(Continued)*

Type, use, and comment	*Sketch*
Diaphragm (contiguous bored pile or sheet pile) wall: Used for special situations only. These forms of structure are convenient for construction from ground level, when their high cost is compensated for by the speed of construction and lack of temporary works. They usually require some form of facing after excavation. The piles can be in line or staggered to increase the wall thickness and provide a tolerance for variation in pile size. Diaphragm walling may be economic for large or repetitive works. It can be constructed with precast elements with adequate drainage behind it. Steel sheet piling may not be suitable for permanent works with a long design life. Economy is particularly evident when they are good for temporary cofferdams.	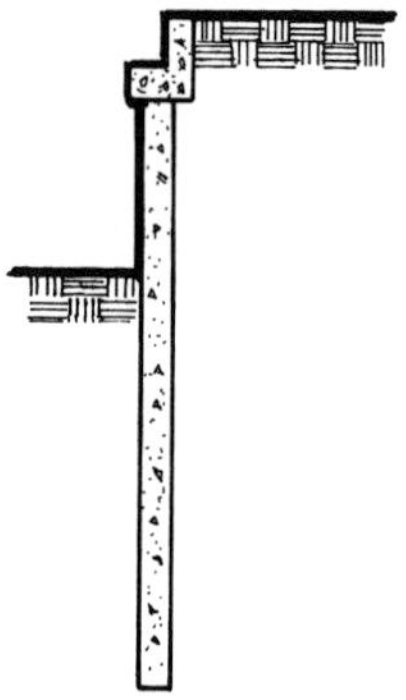 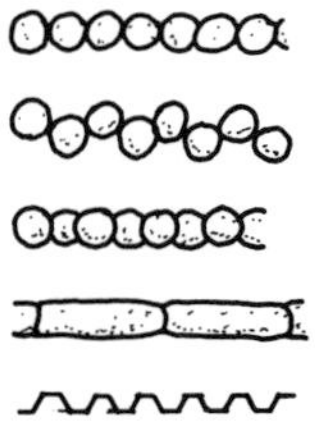
Anchors and ties Ground anchors are practical for abutments if the existing soil is not cohesive or where there is a low water table. When ties are used for deadman anchors, provision should be made for settlement of wall and fill. Allow the movement needed to mobolize the anchor resistance. Anchors and ties, like ground struts used for reinforced earth, can be damaged during excavation when services are performed at a later date.	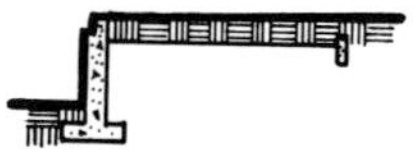 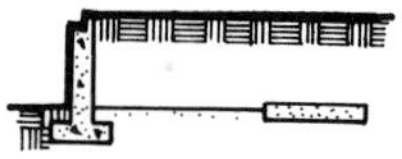 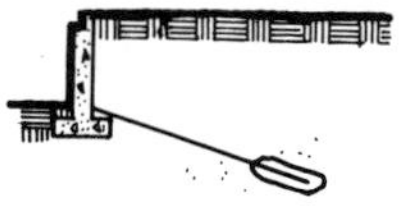

Source: Modified from Building Research Establishment.

TABLE 470-10
Strutted, Portal, and Box Structures

Type, use, and comment	Sketch
Strutted or vertical beam abutments: Often used for small bridges, but seldom used for spans exceeding 60 ft (20 m) Many small bridges of spans up to 15 m (45 ft) use the deck and structure of the bridge as a strut to the top of abutments. This allows the foundations to be narrower and simpler than for freestanding cantilever walls. Usually the walls are monolithic with the footings. Strutting of abutments is not recommended for skews greater than 20°, although the effect of the skew depends on the length-width ratio.	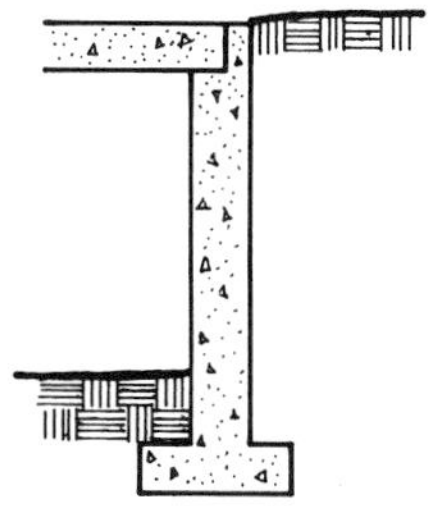
	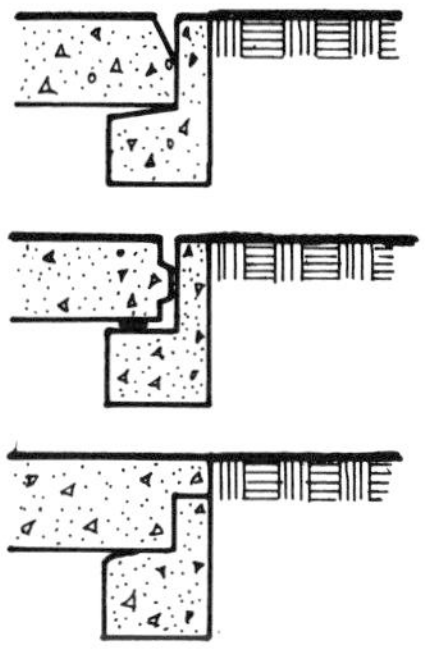
Portal frames: This type is occasionally used. Portal frames are used for the same advantage as strutted abutments, but for much longer spans. It is possible to use a more slender deck than for a simple supported span. The portal frames are generally more expensive, and their foundations have to resist horizontal movement to prevent overstressing the top corners of the portal.	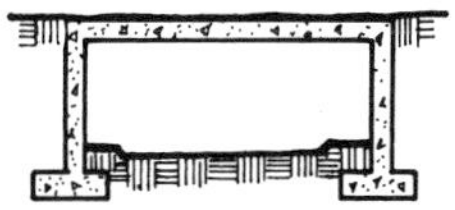

Source: Modified from Building Research Establishment.

TABLE 470-11
Wing Walls

Type, use, and comment	*Sketch*
Wing walls parallel to abutment: Wing walls parallel to the abutment face are not as economic as angled walls but are usually simpler to build. They are often designed monolithic with abutment. For bridges constructed on existing embankments, they cause less disturbance.	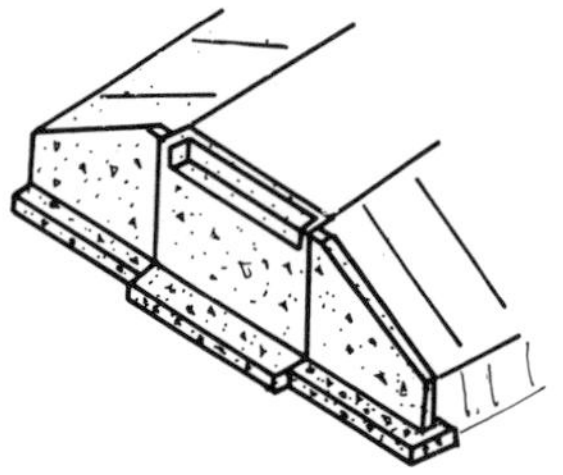
Wing walls at angle to abutment face: These are generally the most economic as far as materials used.	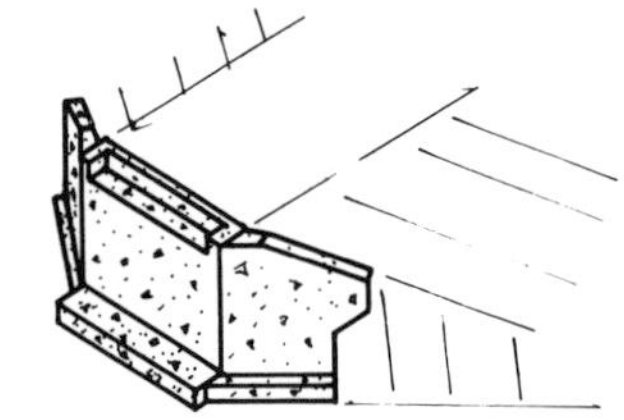
Wing walls parallel to the bridge: Less economic than angled walls, but continue line of deck and provide support for parapets. Such wing walls may not be appropriate when they or their excavations impinge on adjacent structures, services, or traffic diversion. Proper compaction of backfill in the corners is seldom achieved, and forming of exposed edges of abutments requires special care.	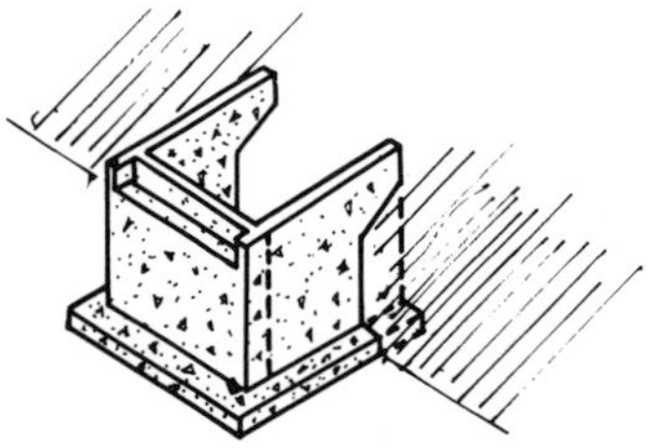
Cantilever wing walls parallel to over-road: Commonly used with sloping abutments An abutment with large cantilever wing walls looks similar, when complete, to the abutment with wing walls on footings parallel to the bridge. It has the advantage of having the whole structure supported on a single footing, which can settle as a single body, but it also has the same problems during construction as the one above. Reinforced earth or sheet piling can sometimes be used for wing walls to a concrete abutment.	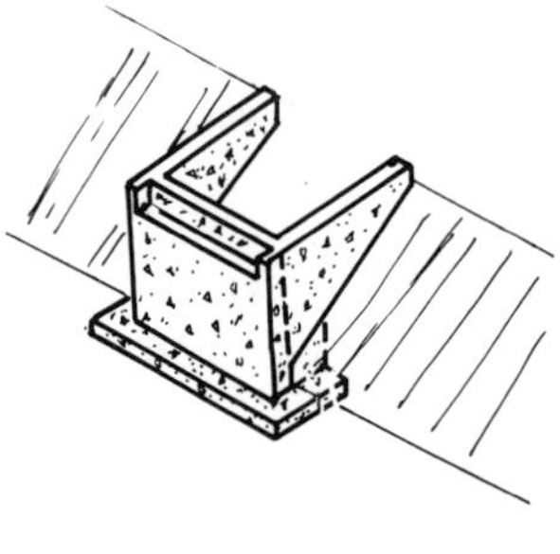
Crib walls Crib walling is suitable for wing wall construction. (It is not considered suitable for abutments.) Its appearance makes it more acceptable in rural than in urban situations.	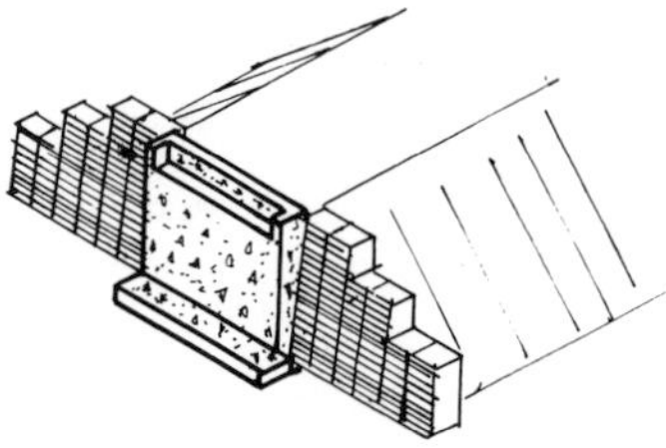

Source: Modified from Building Research Establishment.

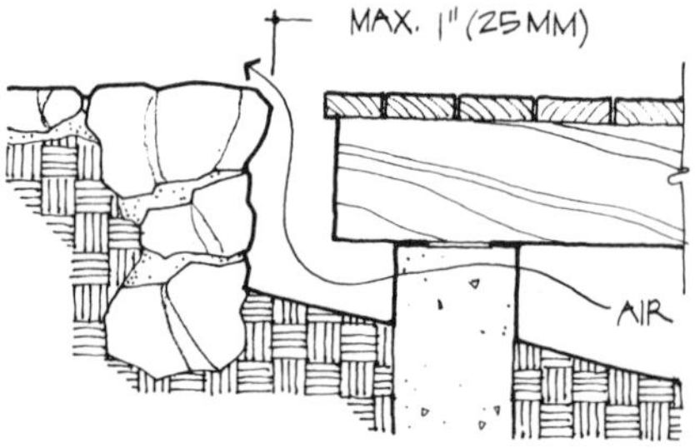
MAX. 1" (25MM)
AIR

Figure 470-6 Air space at beam end.

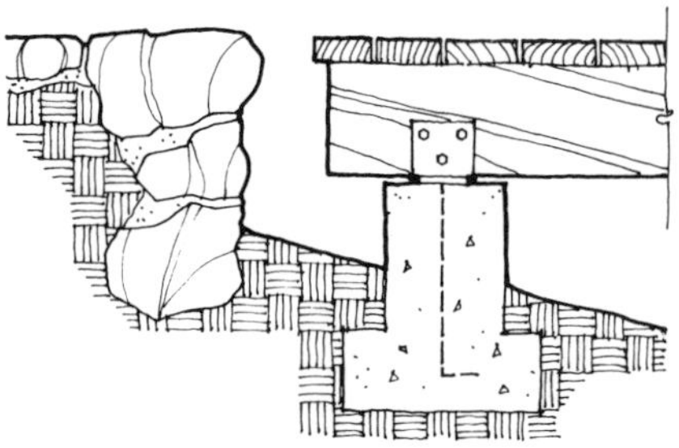

Figure 470-7 Beam bolted to abutment.

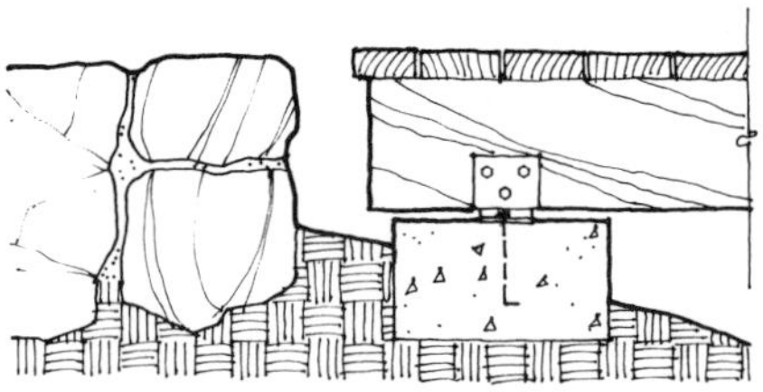

Figure 470-8 Typical bank seat.

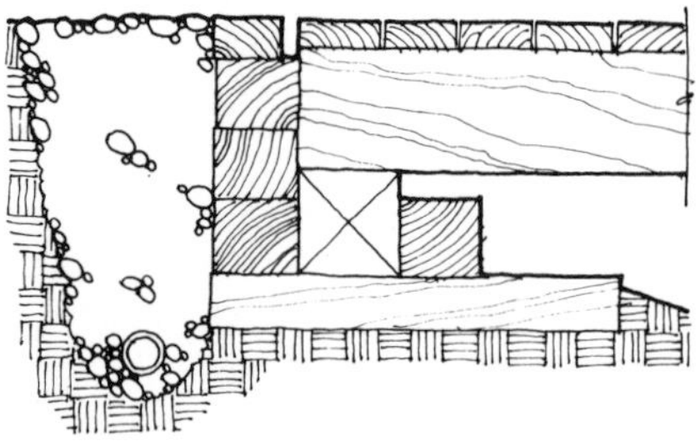

Figure 470-9 Typical timber bank seat.

Differences in settlement between the abutment and the wing walls can be due largely to the greater pressure on the abutment.

Simple Abutments for Footbridges:

Sophisticated abutments are not necessary for narrow footbridges. All abutments should provide adequate air space and drainage at the bearing area (Figure 470-6).

Footbridges may have to be bolted or clamped to the abutments to hold them in place during flooding or while vibrating under live loads (Figure 470-7).

The simplest abutment is a *bank seat*, where the bridge superstructure meets the ground at its natural level on a stable area of suitable bearing capacity. In such cases, a concrete strip foundation is adequate (Figure 470-8).

Timber bank seats can be used but will have a limited life. Timber must be treated with some type of wood preservative, and a tile drain is necessary (Figure 470-9).

Where the bridge deck level is above the natural ground level, a mass abutment can be constructed. The fill used to ramp the footpath can be allowed to spill naturally around it. Where abutments are set on steep slopes, it may be necessary to retain the fill for the footpath by widening the abutment or providing wingwalls (Figures 470-10 and 470-11).

Figures 470-12 and 470-13 show typical small abutments suitable for narrow footbridges. If high abutments [over 10 ft (3 m)] are required or if the soil has poor bearing capacity, then more sophisticated solutions, using reinforced concrete or piled foundations, can be adopted. In all these cases, an experienced engineer should be consulted.

Piers:

Piers are used to break up long spans. They should be adopted only where they can be located easily on sound foundations. Piers in waterways are difficult to construct and are subject to abnormal conditions from flooding. Expert advice should be sought before such a solution is adopted.

Piers can be used to limit the size of abutments and to avoid forming embankments for footpaths by using them to support the main span and an approach ramp (Figure 470-14).

The top of a pier must be wide enough to accommodate bearings and beam ends. If the spans are simply supported, two bearings will be necessary, but for a continuous beam only one bearing need be specified (Figure 470-15).

Bridge superstructures exert longitudinal forces from expansion, wind, and traction, which have an overturning effect on piers (Figure 470-16).

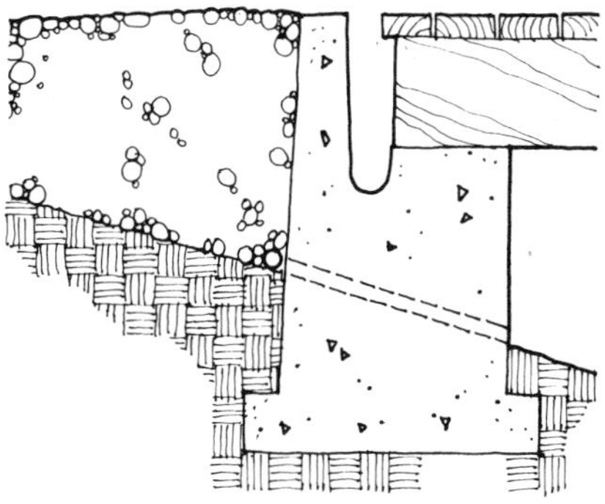

Figure 470-10 Typical mass abutment.

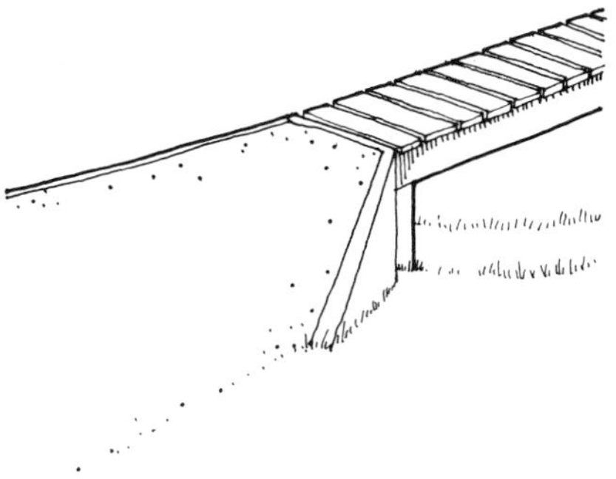

Figure 470-11 Typical mass abutment with wing walls.

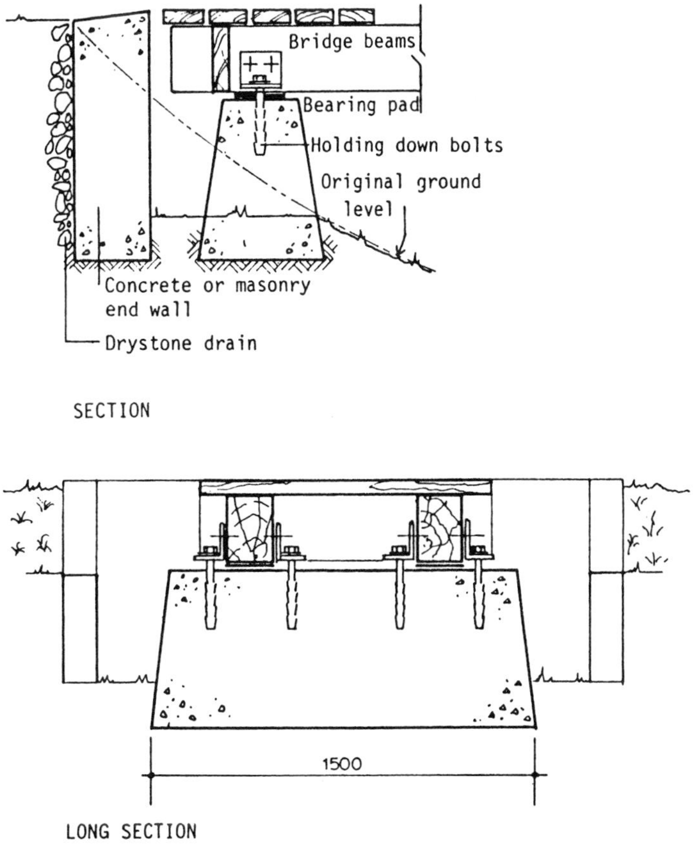
Bridge beams
Bearing pad
Holding down bolts
Original ground level
Concrete or masonry end wall
Drystone drain
SECTION
1500
LONG SECTION

Figure 470-12 Typical Small-Abutment (End-Seat) Detail. Backfilling should be well compacted and water should be led away from the abutment.

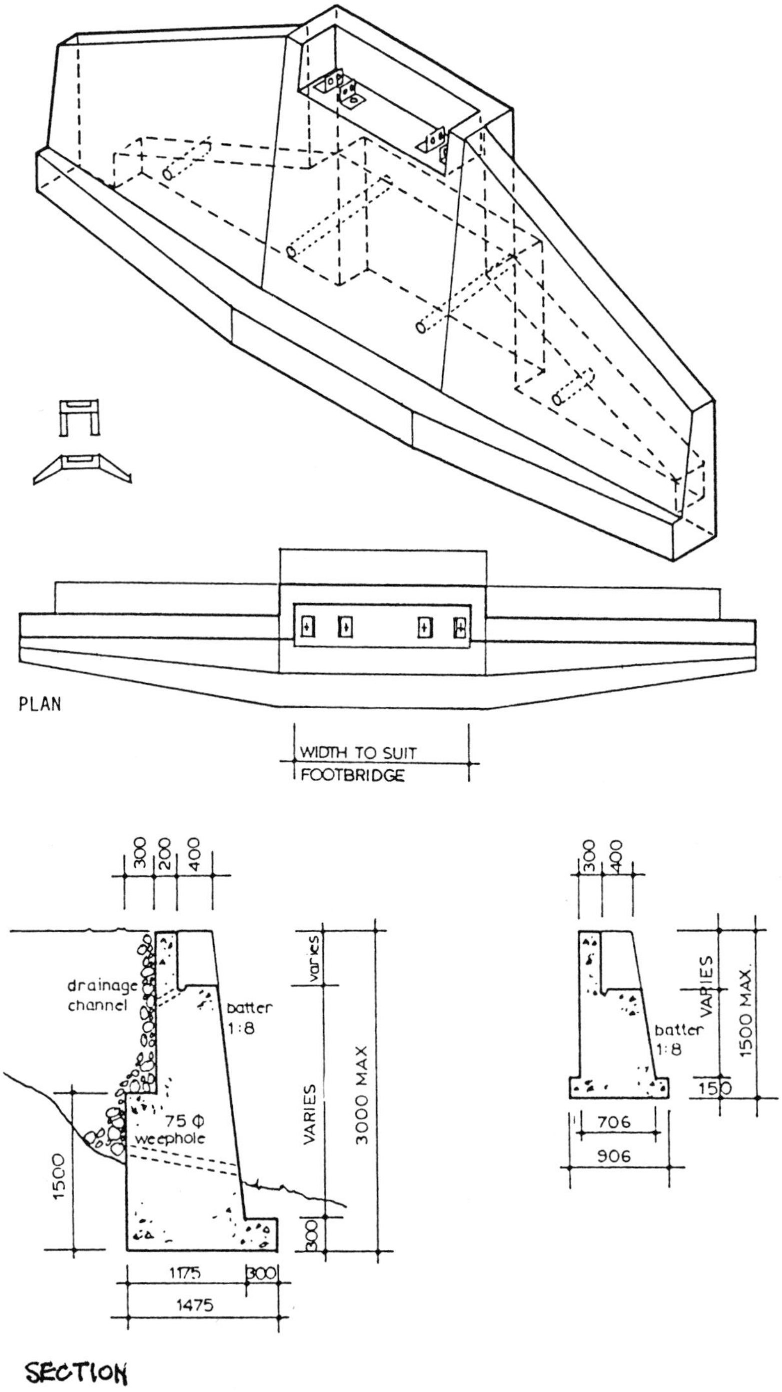
PLAN
WIDTH TO SUIT
FOOTBRIDGE
300
200
400
drainage channel
batter 1:8
75 Φ weephole
varies
VARIES
3000 MAX
1500
300
1175
300
1475
SECTION
300
400
VARIES
1500 MAX.
batter 1:8
150
706
906

Figure 470-13 Typical mass-concrete abutment and wing walls.

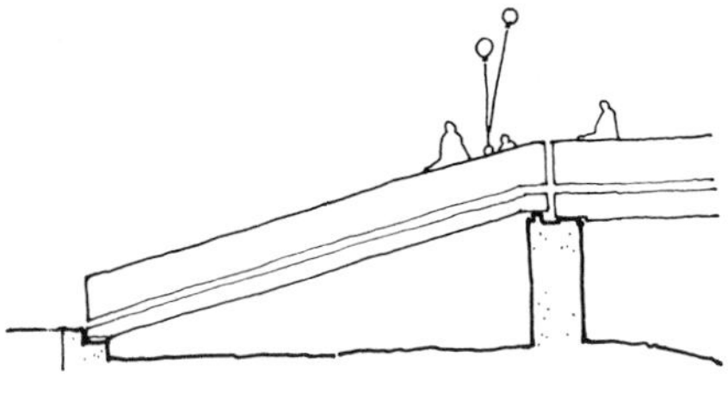

Figure 470-14 Pier supporting access ramp.

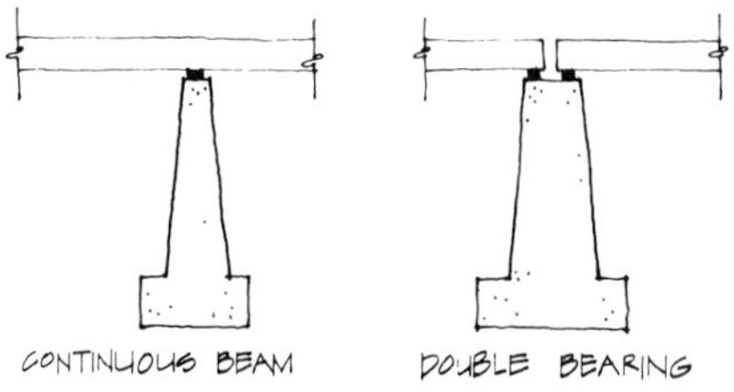
CONTINUOUS BEAM
DOUBLE BEARING

Figure 470-15 Single and Double Bearing Piers. The top of a pier must be wide enough to accommodate bearings and beam ends.

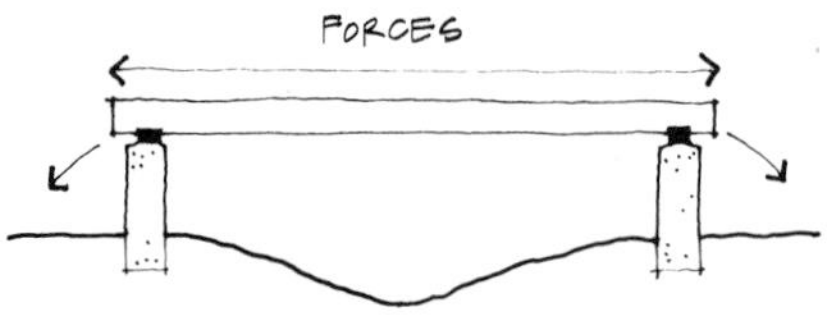
FORCES

Figure 470-16 Effect of Superstructure Expansion on Piers. Piers must be constructed to counteract overturning effects due to longitudinal forces such as bridge expansion, wind, and traction.

The simplest piers to construct, and the most economical, are those that are vertical with a uniform rectangular or circular cross section. Typical pier details are shown in Figures 470-17 and 470-18.

When foundations must be prepared underwater, a cofferdam is necessary to keep out the water while the footing is being placed. When the water is deep or the current swift, these cofferdams are very expensive, and the construction of each one is a separate problem which should not be attempted except under the direction of an experienced engineer.

Excavation Shape and Shear Keys:

The foundation for an abutment should be level. Sliding must be resisted by friction under the base or by passive resistance in front of the toe. Often a wider base is needed to prevent sliding than for bearing or to prevent overturning. For this reason, some designers dimension the base for bearing and provide additional resistance to sliding by using a shear key or by inclining the footing (Figures 470-19 and 470-20). To minimize ground softening, some designers give the footing a small cross fall to improve drainage.

The process of constructing a shear key frequently loosens the subbase. Also, rainwater can cause a softening of the soil. Therefore, when shear keys are used, they should be excavated and concreted in one continuous process.

Three typical locations for shear keys are (Figure 470-19):

1. *Front shear keys:* they have to be far enough below ground level to avoid softening due to frost action and to reduce the risk of later scouring or excavations in front of the toe.

2. *Middle shear keys:* they are usually easier to excavate and do not cause complications in the formation of the abutment.

3. *Rear or back shear keys:* they gain additional lateral resistance from the ground because of the increased vertical compression of the abutment and toe. The excavation for a rear shear key normally causes less disturbance of the supporting soil but causes more excavation on the retained side.

Inclined Footing:

A footing with an inclined bottom has a simpler cross section than one with a shear key, but the excavation and construction of this inclined footing can be more expensive than a shear key (Figure 470-20).

Drainage:

In climates with considerable rainfall, adequate drainage is necessary behind the abutment to prevent the buildup of water pressure and the saturation of the soil behind the abutment.

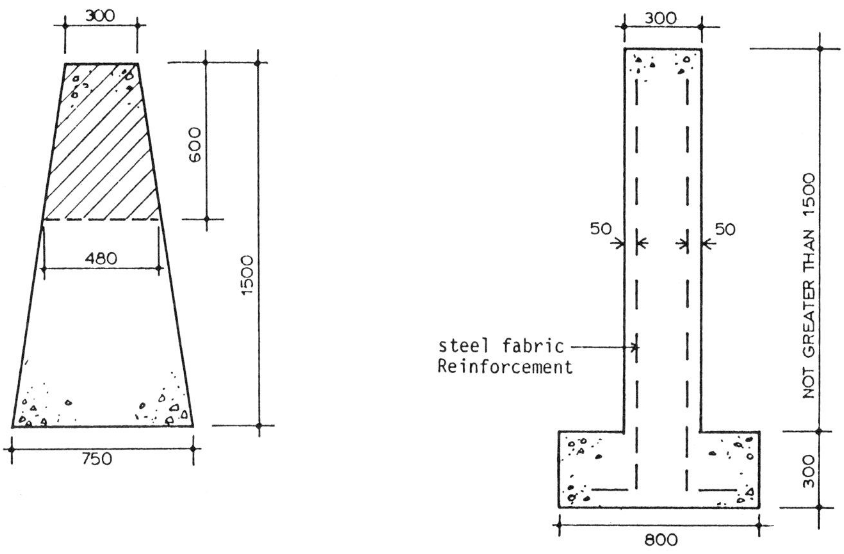
300
600
480
1500
750
300
50
50
steel fabric
Reinforcement
NOT GREATER THAN 1500
300
800

Figure 470-17 Typical Support Piers for Timber Beam Bridges (Span under 10 Meters Fixed at Both Ends). Smaller piers use top of section (as shown with cross-hatching).

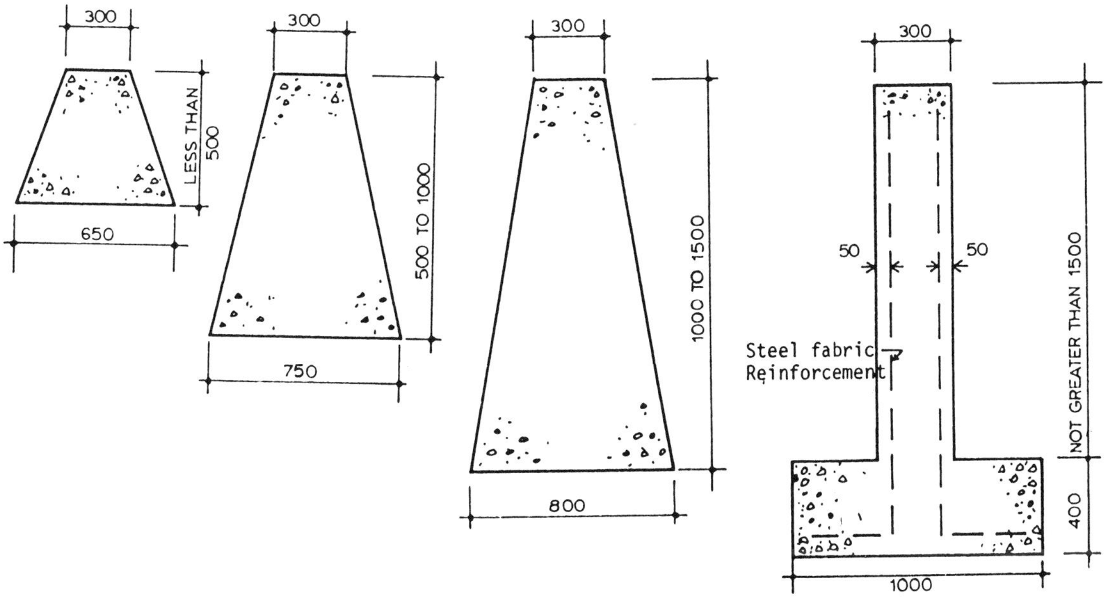
300
LESS THAN 500
650
300
500 TO 1000
750
300
1000 TO 1500
800
300
50
50
Steel fabric
Reinforcement
NOT GREATER THAN 1500
400
1000

Figure 470-18 Typical support piers for steel beam bridges (Span under 10 meters fixed at one end).

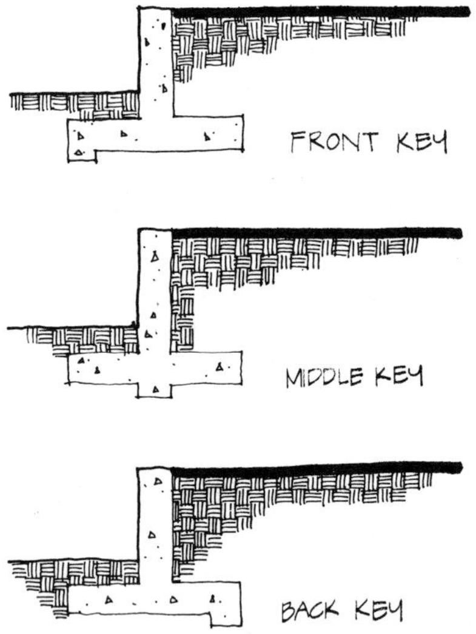
FRONT KEY
MIDDLE KEY
BACK KEY

Figure 470-19 Position of shear keys.

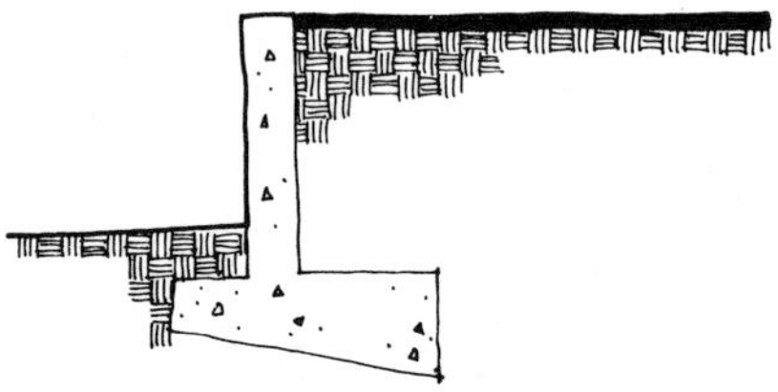

Figure 470-20 Footing with inclined base.

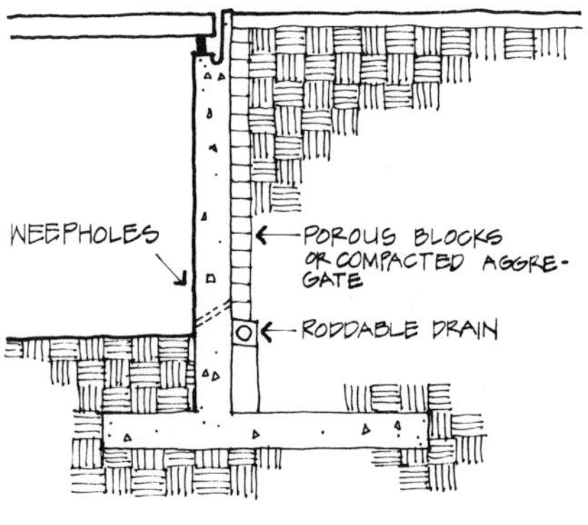
WEEPHOLES
POROUS BLOCKS OR COMPACTED AGGREGATE
RODDABLE DRAIN

Figure 470-21 Typical drainage system behind wall abutment (for wet climates).

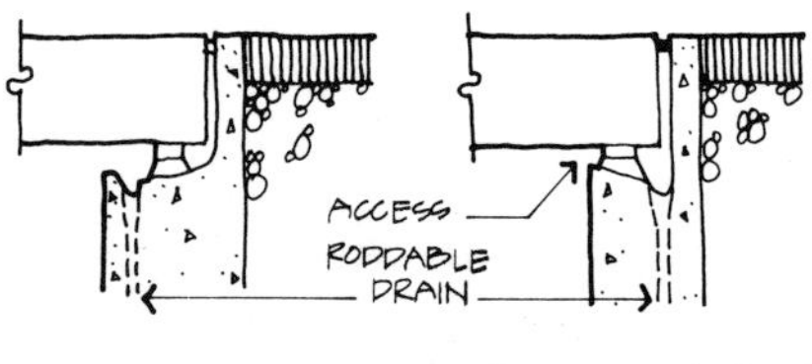
ACCESS
RODDABLE DRAIN

Figure 470-22 Drainage of Bearing Shelves. The channel along the top of the bearing shelf should be accessible for cleaning.

The drainage system requires an outlet, must be testable, and has to be easily maintainable. Figure 470-21 shows uses of a porous block or equivalent porous material through which the water can drain to a pipe that can be cleared by rods. Weep holes are often specified to allow drainage in case of pipe blockage.

NOTE: A dry stone wall 18 in (450 mm) wide or wider may be equally as good as or better than a concrete abutment in regions where local rock and skilled labor are available.

Bearing Shelves:

If bearing shelves are used, then they require drainage (Figure 470-22). A channel along the top of the bearing shelf should be accessible for cleaning. Placing the channel in front of the bearings makes it simpler to clean.

Protective Coatings:

The back faces of concrete abutments can be given some form of protective coating to inhibit corrosion of the reinforcing in the concrete.

Groundwater:

Groundwater affects the performance of bridge substructures by:

1. Reducing the bearing capacity of substrata.

2. Increasing lateral pressures caused by flooding or a perched water table.

3. Frost heaving of light structures.

4. Reducing the stability of earth slopes supporting bank seats or abutments (horizontal and vertical boreholes for drainage can help stabilize a bankslope in shales, mudstones, etc.).

Levels of groundwater in test boreholes should be recorded at the time of construction. Permanent standpipes or piezometers are necessary if groundwater is, or is thought to be, a serious problem.

In regions where there are very large seasonal and yearly variations in the groundwater level, it is important to record the standpipe levels regularly and for as long a time as possible.

Flood Damage and Scour:

Floods and flood debris can sometimes pose a greater threat during bridge construction than afterwards. During the design stage, it is important to obtain information on flood frequencies and to make this information available to bidders and contractors.

Floods may cause damage to a bridge when there is:

1. Insufficient waterway *at the bridge site,* thereby causing flooding and/or high water velocities and a resulting scour of the streambed and banks, which may undermine the abutments

2. Insufficient waterway *downstream* of the bridge, causing flooding of the area

3. Insufficient waterway *upstream* of the bridge site, causing a damming effect which could be released suddenly and carry the bridge away

Types of damage to a bridge caused by these three problems include:

1. Scour of the streambed and banks, which may undermine abutments

2. Floating debris and ice wedging against the bridge structure, creating stress and possible structural failures

3. High flows and/or backing up of the river, which can cause the structure to float off its bearings and be carried away

Avoiding Flood Damage: Flood damage can be avoided either by (1) specifying longer spans to allow the largest recorded flood to pass safely or (2) setting the bridge high enough to allow passage of the highest flows and to provide clearance for floating branches and other debris. Areas upstream of the bridge should be inspected to determine what can be carried downstream during a flood.

Scour: Scour is one of the most frequent causes of failure in bridges over streams. The dangers of scour around abutments and piers can be minimized when:

1. The abutments are kept behind the natural bank line so they do not become an obstruction.

2. The foundations are set well below the lowest level of the scour.

3. The face of the abutment is made rough, to reduce the speed of the water flow and the resulting scour at the abutment.

4. The piers, if used, are streamlined to cause fewer eddies.

5. The sheet piling, if used for cofferdams, is left in place for scour protection.

6. Scour protection techniques (gabions, riprap, etc.) are used to slow down the flow and provide resistance to scouring.

If scour protection devices and techniques are necessary, they should extend far enough upstream and downstream that the stream cannot erode behind them. Often the scour protection device is turned back into the stream bank in order to protect the ends from scouring.

Common techniques of scour protection include:

1. *Riprapping:* stones or precast concrete

units are laid on a bed of smaller stone or gravel (Figure 470-23). The profile of the riprapping should divert the water flow smoothly around the abutment without any obstruction. Once the riprapping has been damaged, the damaged area can enlarge very quickly and cause a complete breakdown.

2. *Stone-filled wire gabions:* gabions are galvanized wire cages filled with cobbles (Figure 470-23). They must be installed strictly in accordance with the manufacturer's instructions. Since a large amount of stone filling is required, gabions are best suited for areas where this can be obtained locally. (Refer to Section 410: Retaining Walls, for more information on gabions.)

3. *Revetments:* wood or precast concrete can be used to create a wall (revetment), which is then filled with stone and/or gravel. Various techniques are employed in the construction of revetments. Figure 470-23 shows one technique using wood. Concrete cribbing is also used and generally has a longer life, although it may be more expensive to construct. (Concrete cribbing is described briefly in Section 410: Retaining Walls.)

4. *Interlocking steel sheet piling:* steel sheet piling may be advantageous in particularly difficult situations where ground conditions are very poor (Figure 470-23). This technique usually requires installation by an experienced contractor.

Bearings:

When superstructures rest on abutments and piers, the load is transferred through some form of bearing device which allows the bridge to expand and contract under temperature or moisture changes. Bearings also let the ends of the beam flex slightly as they are loaded and unloaded (see Figure 470-12).

Timber Footbridges: Timber structures expand in relatively small amounts and do not need special expansion bearings unless the spans are over 100 ft (30 m). Glass-fiber-reinforced bituminous felt, lead, or rubber pads can be used as bearings. Because timber bridges are relatively lightweight, vibration from heavy use may move the bridge off its bearings, or flooding may float it away. Therefore, most wood bridges should be held down by bolts or stainless-steel straps. (See Figures 470-33 and 470-34.)

Steel and Concrete Footbridges: Structures made of steel or concrete may be mounted on glass-fiber-reinforced bituminous felt, lead, or rubber pads for spans up to about 30 ft (10 m). Because a steel footbridge is relatively lightweight, a positive method of holding it down should be incorporated in the bearings. Recent experience shows that prefabricated bearings with stainless steel sliding on a pad of fluorocarbon provides very low friction forces for both steel and concrete bridges.

3.6 Decking, Handrailings, and Fastenings

Decking:

Decking is the travel or wear surface of the bridge. Four materials commonly used for the surfacing, or decking, of a footbridge are:

1. *Wood:* wood decking is lightweight, strong, and easily worked and repaired, but it requires regular inspection and maintenance.

2. *Precast concrete slabs:* precast slabs are either laid with open joints or are grouted together to form a homogeneous slab.

3. *Poured-in-place concrete slabs:* poured-in-place concrete slabs require formwork or the use of proprietary metal trough sheeting.

4. *Metal:* metal decking requires delivery to the site in finished pieces, is generally used under special circumstances, and is typically made of galvanized steel or aluminum formed into planks, checkerplates, or open-mesh flooring.

Where wood is readily available and relatively inexpensive, it is a commonly used material not only for the decking but for the entire superstructure of the footbridge.

Timber Decking: The size of the boards used for decking depends on:

1. The span between supports
2. The loading
3. The width of the individual boards and the spacing between boards
4. The grade of timber used
5. The additional thickness allowed for wear

Boards should not be less than 4 in (100 mm) wide in order to provide adequate strength against loads applied individually to a single board from a pedestrian foot or animal hoof.

All timber decking should be laid with spacing between the individual boards unless there are compelling reasons why this is unacceptable. The spacing should be no less than ¼ in (6 mm) in order to allow air to circulate around the boards, thereby minimizing decay, and also to allow dirt and debris to pass through the decking. Spacing also facilitates removal and replacement of any damaged boards and provides extra grip when boards are wet and slippery (Figure 470-24).

Because the top surfaces of timber decks wear over time, deck boards should be thicker than required purely for strength. Softwood decking should be no less than 2 in (50 mm) thick and hardwood 1½ in (36 mm) thick.

Algae growing on a timber deck can make it slippery when wet or damp. An antifungicidal treatment and good ventilation will minimize the problem. A nonslip surface can be achieved with epoxy sprays spread with some type of granular material (sand, etc.).

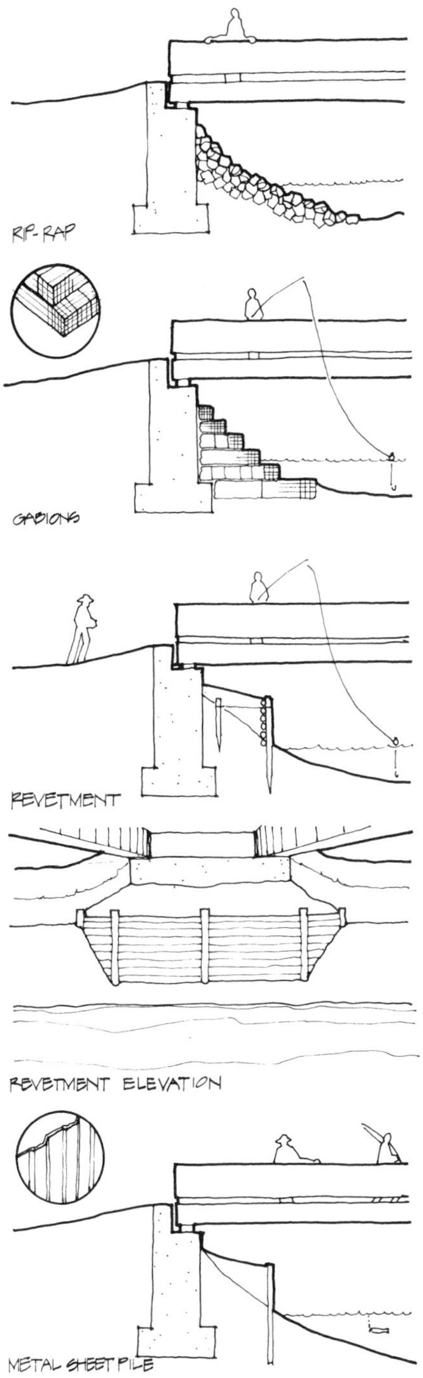
RIP-RAP
GABIONS
REVETMENT
REVETMENT ELEVATION
METAL SHEET PILE

Figure 470-23 Scour protection devices for narrow footbridges.

1/4" MINIMUM (6 MM)
5/8" MAX W/HEELS (16MM)
1" SUITS REMOTE AREAS (25MM)

Figure 470-24 Deck Board Spacing. Spacing of deck boards allows air to circulate, allows dirt and debris to pass through, and provides traction when boards are wet and slippery.

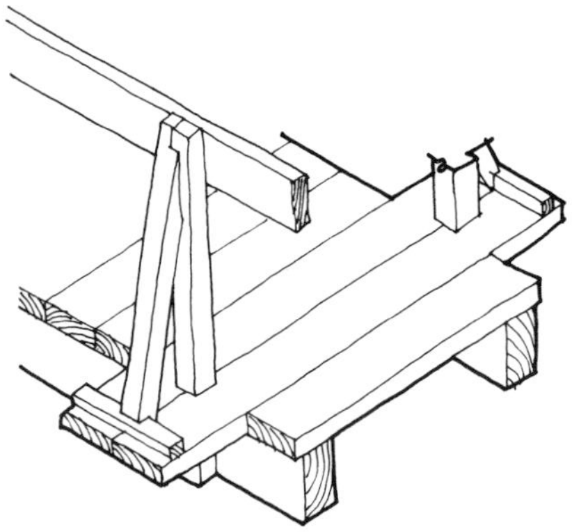

Figure 470-25 Simple handrail supported on deck boards.

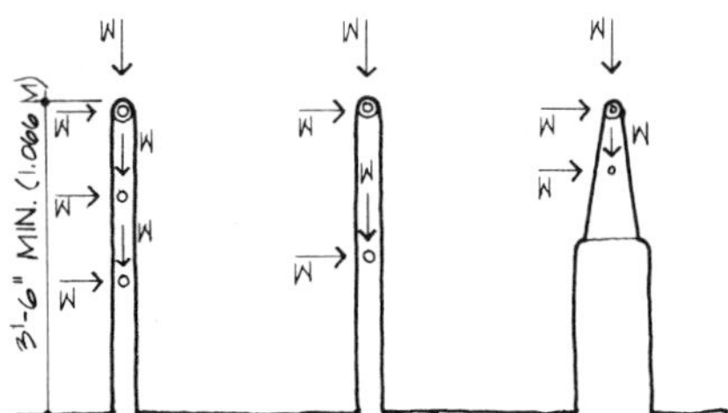
W
3'-6" MIN. (1.066 M)
WALKWAY SURFACE

Figure 470-26 AASHTO Standards for Pedestrian Railings on Highway Bridges. The minimum design loading for a pedestrian railing shall be w = 50 lb per lineal foot (74.5 kg/m) acting simultaneously transversely and vertically on each longitudinal member. Rail members located more than 5 ft (1.524 m) above the walkway are excluded from these requirements. Posts shall be designed for a transverse load of wl acting at the center of gravity of the upper rail, or for high rails, at 5 ft (1.524 m) maximum above the walkway.

To prevent cupping, all decking boards should be placed heart-side down and should be screwed or nailed to bearers with galvanized screws or nails.

The use of prefabricated wood deck panels in short lengths will facilitate removal of the decking for maintenance. Because the boards are mounted on stringers, the contact area with the main beams, where moisture can be trapped, is minimized.

Handrailings:

Handrailings are typically required on both sides of a footbridge, but for remote or low-risk bridges one handrailing or perhaps no handrailings may be appropriate. Pedestrians must feel safe where obvious dangers exist.

If handrailings are provided, they must be strong enough to support people leaning or sitting on them. It would be better to provide no handrailings than to provide weak ones.

The simplest handrailing is a single horizontal rail mounted at waist height. Single rails can be used in low-risk situations or in remote areas. The addition of midrailings and a bottom railing reduces the risk of accidentally falling or rolling off the bridge. The space betweeen the top railing and the deck can be infilled with vertical members for the same reasons.

In certain situations involving young children or animals, the risk of falling off may be so great that a more impenetrable barrier is required. For footbridges over major roads and railways, unclimbable or even solid parapets are advisable.

Handrailing Dimensions: Local or national building codes often govern handrailing height and dimensions. These should be consulted. In the absence of codes, the following guidelines are suggested:

1. For simple pedestrian footbridges in rural areas, a height of 33 to 36 in (840 to 910 mm) is recommended. If the drop from the bridge is particularly hazardous, or if bicyclists are expected to use the bridge, then the handrailing height should be increased to 54 in (1370 mm).

2. Normally, three horizontal rails are sufficient. The spacing between the bottom railing and the decking should be no greater than 4 in (100 mm).

3. Handrailing posts can be attached to the bridge deck or to the supporting structure below. A common solution is to extend the deck members adjacent to the post and provide diagonal braces to the top of it (Figure 470-25). Figure 470-26 shows the standards for pedestrian railings developed by AASHTO, 12th ed., 1977.

Figures 470-27 and 470-28 show typical handrailing details.

Materials for Handrailings: For rural footbridges, pressure-treated softwood is typically used for handrailings. Galvanized steel or aluminum handrailings are also common and can be fabricated from a variety of cross sections, the most common being round tube.

Fastenings:

Every hole, split, and joint in any part of the bridge structure has the potential of encouraging fungal decay and/or rust. Good design, detailing, and workmanship are essential if these problems are to be avoided or at least minimized. Cutting and fitting at joints requires skilled labor. If skilled labor is not available, then simpler, more watertight fastening systems might be used.

Metal fasteners for use with timber include nails (including large spikes), screws, lag screws, bolts and washers, timber connectors, metal gussets and cleats, hangers, glands, and straps. All metal used in timber fastenings should be protected against corrosion. Hot-dip galvanizing or electroplating in zinc and cadmium are common techniques used to protect metals from corrosion. Holes for fastenings should be predrilled to prevent splitting of wood.

Bolts: Holes for bolts should be drilled not more than $\frac{1}{16}$ in (1.6 mm) larger than the bolt diameter. The bolt should be long enough to permit a washer under both the head and nut and allow at least $\frac{3}{16}$ in (5 mm) to protrude beyond the nut. Because of the risk of crushing the timber near the bolt, the washers should be larger than those typically used with the same-diameter bolt in steelwork.

Nails: Minimum spacing and edge distances for nailing are shown in Figure 470-29. Nails should penetrate the main member of a joint by no less than $\frac{1}{2}$ the nail length for softwoods and $\frac{2}{3}$ths the nail length for hardwoods.

Wood Screws: Predrill the hole for the shank equal to the shank diameter, and make the hole for the threaded portion no more than 0.9 times the diameter at the root of the thread adjacent to the shank. Figure 470-30 gives minimum spacing and edge distances for screws.

Timber Connectors: Timber connectors greatly enhance the strength of a bolted joint by spreading the load concentration outside the bolt hole into the timber. Three types of timber connectors are (Figure 470-31):

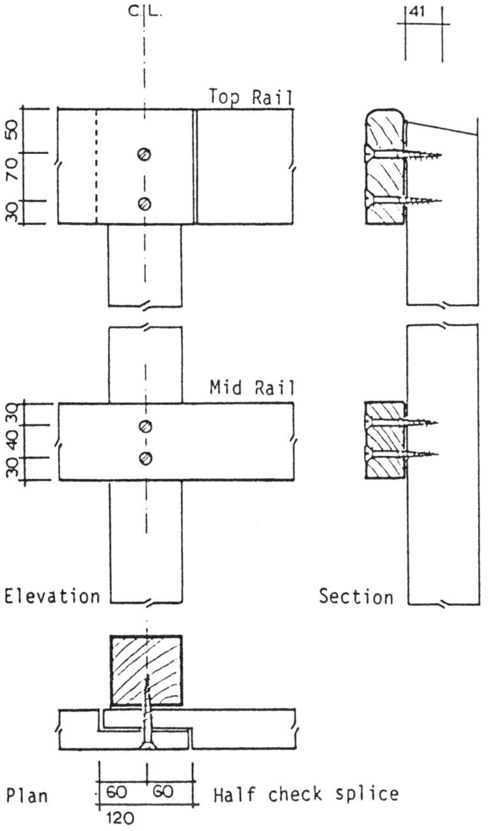
C L.
41
Top Rail
50
70
30
Mid Rail
30
40
30
Elevation
Section
Plan
60
60
120
Half check splice

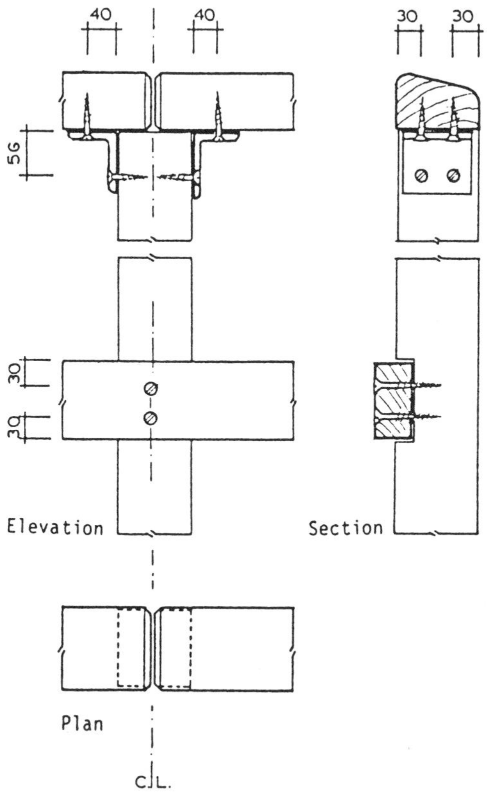
40
40
30
30
56
30
30
Elevation
Section
Plan
C L.

FIXED TO FACE OF POST

Galvanised steel counter-sunk screws to be No.12 (5.6 dia) penetrating the post not less than 41 mm.

Predrilled holes.

SPLICE JOINT

Only one rail to be spliced at any one post.

Treat all cut edges with preservative.

TOP RAIL OVER POST

76x64x6.2mm galvanised steel angles drilled and countersunk for screws. Screws No 12 x 50 long for normal loading or No 16 x 63 long for crowd loading.

Predrilled holes.

MID RAIL

half checked into post. Fixed with 2 No 12 screws penetrating the post not less than 41mm.

BUTT JOINT

top rail over the post. Cut ends treated with preservative.

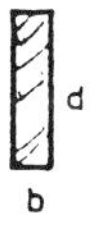
d
b

TABLE OF SPANS between posts

Timber size bxd	Loading	Timber Grades				
		GS S2	GS S1	SS S2	SS S1	Keruing M50
50x75	Normal Crowd	1400 1000	1500 1100	1500 1250	1600 1300	1750 1400
50x100	Normal Crowd	1600 1200	1700 1300	1700 1300	1800 1400	1900 1500
50x150	Normal Crowd	1800 1500	2000 1600	1900 1500	2000 1600	2250 1800
75x50	Normal Crowd	1900 1350	2100 1500	2100 1600	2300 1800	2500 1900
75x75	Normal Crowd	2200 1600	2400 1800	2300 1900	2500 2000	2700 2200

Figure 470-27 Typical handrailing details.

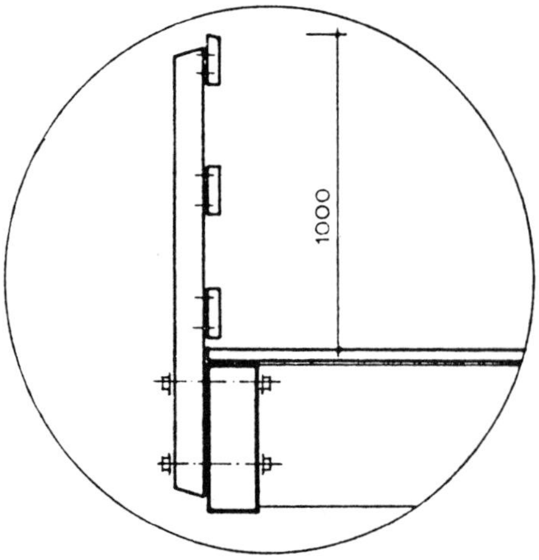
1000

THROUGH BOLTED

12 to 20mm dia. mild steel bolts with 76 sq x 6th washers. Main beam should be not less than 400 deep and restrained against rotation by adequate cross bracing.
Suitable for laminated timber beam applications.

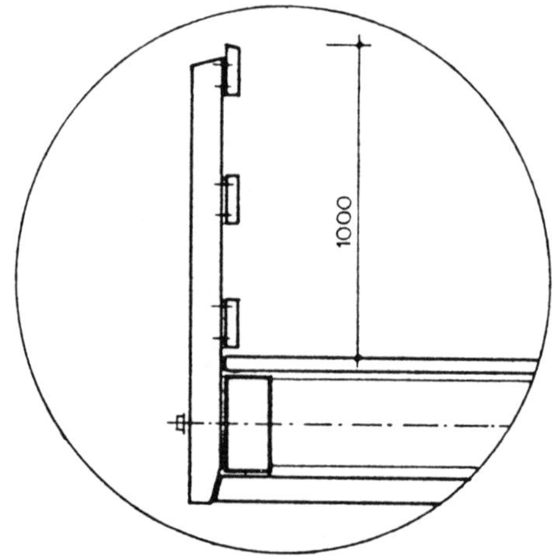
1000

THROUGH-BOLTED AND FRAMED

20mm dia. mild steel tie rod through whole width of structure with 76sq x 6th washers.
Bottom strut added below main beams.
Main beams not less than 150 deep and strutted apart.
Suitable for small span timber footbridges with transverse decking.

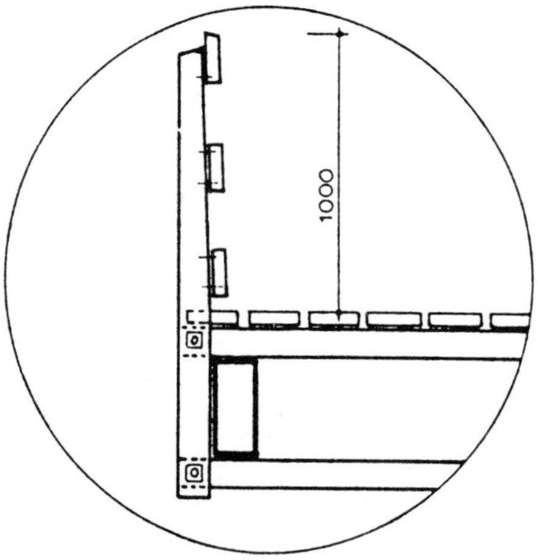
1000

FRAMED

Post framed to deck transom and member below main beams. Main beams should not be less than 200 deep. Suitable for footbridges with long-itudinal deck boarding.

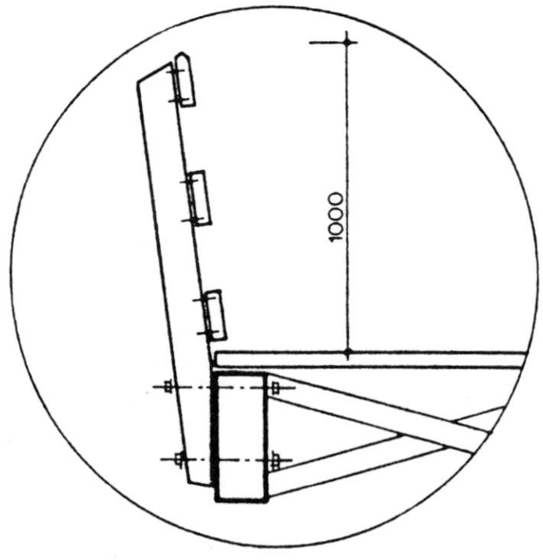
1000

THROUGH-BOLTED INCLINED

Tapered base to post gives outward slope for appearance and additional width at waist height.
A larger post may be required due to reduction in section.

Figure 470-28 Typical cantilevered handrailings.

CANTILEVERED HANDRAIL POSTS

section sizes are given
as d x b mm

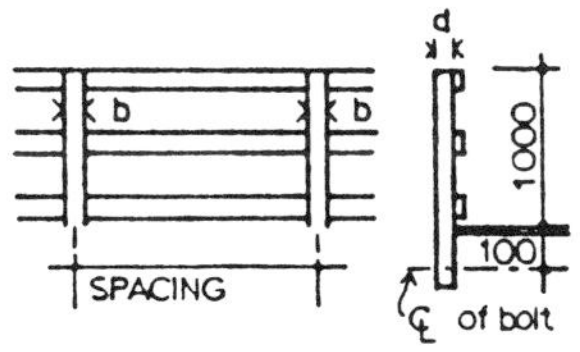
d
b
b
1000
100
SPACING
℄ of bolt

TABLE OF SIZES

SPACING Ss	Timber Grade GS Douglas Fir or Larch		Timber Grade SS Douglas Fir or Larch		Hardwood Keruing M50	
	Normal loading	Crowd loading	Normal loading	Crowd loading	Normal loading	Crowd loading
1000	100x75	120x100	100x75	100x100	100x75	100x100
1250	100x100	150x100	100x75	120x100	100x75	100x100
1500	100x100	150x100	100x100	120x100	100x75	120x100
1750	120x100	150x100	100x100	150x100	100x100	120x100
2000	120x100	150x150	100x100	150x100	100x100	150x100
2250	150x100	150x150	120x100	150x100	100x100	150x100
2500	150x100	150x150	120x100	150x100	120x100	150x100

Table allows for one 22mm dia. hole in post.

TIMBER HANDRAILS

size given is b x d mm

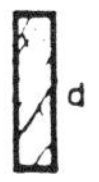
d
b

TABLE OF SPANS

Timber size bxd	Loading	Timber Grades				
		GS S2	GS S1	SS S2	SS S1	Keruing M50
50x75	Normal	1400	1500	1500	1600	1750
	Crowd	1000	1100	1250	1300	1400
50x100	Normal	1600	1700	1700	1800	1900
	Crowd	1200	1300	1300	1400	1500
50x150	Normal	1800	2000	1900	2000	2250
	Crowd	1500	1600	1500	1600	1800
75x50	Normal	1900	2100	2100	2300	2500
	Crowd	1350	1500	1600	1800	1900
75x75	Normal	2200	2400	2300	2500	2700
	Crowd	1600	1800	1900	2000	2200

1. *Toothed plate* connectors are square or round, single-sided or double-sided, and available in sizes ranging from 1½ to 3 in (38 to 75 mm) in diameter. They are suitable for softwoods only. The connector is placed between the members to be joined, and the teeth are embedded into the timber when the bolt is tightened.

2. *Split ring* and *shear plate* connectors require very accurate layout of the holes and require special tools for cutting the grooves necessary in the timber faces. They can be used with both hardwoods and softwoods.

3. *Hangers, bent bolts,* and *straps* can be used in various forms in timber fabrication.

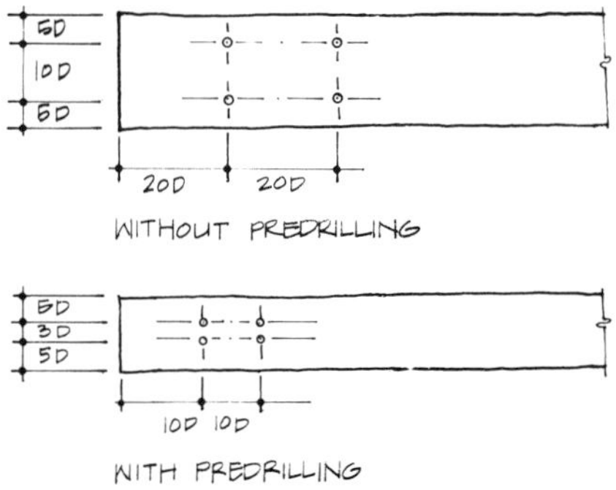
5D
10D
5D
20D
20D
WITHOUT PREDRILLING
5D
3D
5D
10D 10D
WITH PREDRILLING

Figure 470-29 Minimum spacing and edge distances for nails.

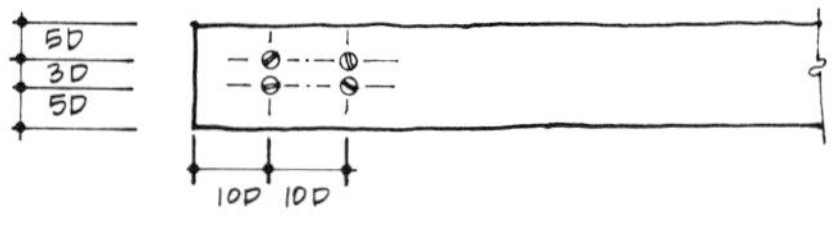
5D
3D
5D
10D 10D

Figure 470-30 Minimum spacing and edge distances for wood screws.

They are made of steel and are normally galvanized or painted with a zinc-rich paint. Most standard joist hangers and clips fabricated for interior use are insufficiently strong to be satisfactory for external use.

In some instances, the clamping action of a bent bolt is sufficiently strong to hold members together. A bent bolt has the advantage of not involving cuts or drilled holes in the timber, thereby minimizing the likelihood of fungal decay and rust. Some metal fittings (such as bent bolts) can be arranged to accommodate variations in timber sizes.

4.0 TYPICAL DESIGNS FOR SHORT-SPAN FOOTBRIDGES

This subsection includes drawings and accompanying technical information on five types of wood and metal footbridges as developed and used by the Countryside Commission for Scotland.

Because of the complexity involved in converting the data shown from Scottish to American standards, the editors have decided to leave most of the data as shown in the 1981 publication, *Footbridges in the Countryside—Design and Construction.*

Figures 470-32 to 470-37 show representative designs for footbridges for spans under 30 ft (9 m) where the loading is limited to *Pedestrian—normal* (see Table 470-4). Where the tabular data in Figures 470-32 through 470-37 indicate spans greater than 30 ft (9 m), an experienced bridge designer should be consulted.

4.1 Log Footbridge

For a log footbridge (Figure 470-32), natural logs are often used when timber can be cut at or near the footbridge site. Natural log footbridges may have a relatively short (8- to 10-year) lifespan, depending on the durability of the logs and the wetness of the local climate. The most decay-resistant species of timber should be selected.

4.2 Sawn Timber Footbridge

The main beams of a sawn timber footbridge (Figure 470-33) should be of high-quality wood and should be pressure-treated with an appropriate wood preservative to provide long life. Sawn timber is lighter and easier to handle than natural logs, and such bridges have a better life than log bridges, typically ranging from 15 to 20 years.

4.3 Galloway Timber Footbridge

The Forestry Commission (United Kingdom) staff and the Royal Engineers in Scotland developed this design (Figure 470-34) with the following aims:

1. The main beams would not be penetrated by bolt holes or other fasteners after preservative treatment.

2. The bridge would be demountable to permit periodic maintenance and easy replacement of damaged sections.

3. Skilled site work would not be required.

These aims have been achieved by using bent bolts to bind the bridge parts together so that friction between the faces would replace bolted connections. The bent bolts could be loosened to allow parts to be removed for maintenance or repair. The problem of fastening handrail posts has been solved by using a prefabricated H frame which is made off-site. The bridge is assembled by unskilled laborers on-site from a kit of parts. Care must be taken regarding the following:

1. The abutment clamp rods must be set in position to the correct elevation and held by a jig while the abutment is constructed.

2. The H frames do not have to fit tightly to the sides of the beams, but they should be set to the best straight line possible so that the handrailing is straight.

3. The abutment, frame, and deck clamps must be properly tightened to ensure interaction of the bridge members. Tightness should be checked as a regular maintenance item.

4.4 Galloway Steel Footbridge

The British Army developed this design (Figure 470-35) from the Galloway timber

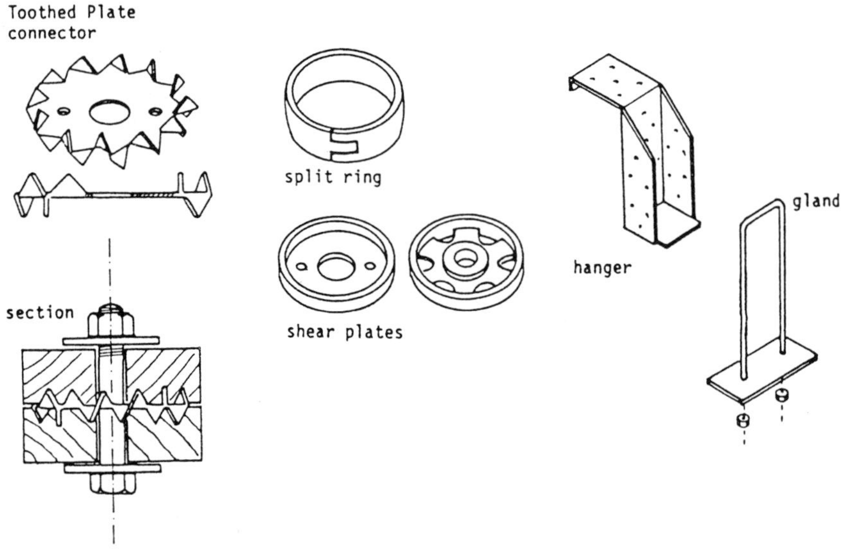
Toothed Plate
connector
split ring
shear plates
section
hanger
gland

Figure 470-31 Types of timber connectors.

LOGS: Form a 38-mm-wide surface on top of logs for decking. Notch sides to minimum depth to allow handrail posts to be erected in a straight line. Soak all cut areas with wood preservative.

LOG END SEATING: Notch bottom of logs no more than one-third of nominal diameter to form level bearing. Place 12-mm-thick rubber or felt bearing pads between logs and abutment. Secure ends of logs with abutment clamps recessed 20 mm into top of log. Soak all cut areas in log with wood preservative. Make a gap of 20 mm to a maximum of 25 mm between ends of logs/decking and masonry end.

ABUTMENT CLAMP: Use three steel straps (6 × 60 × 1160) bent to fit log size. Drill holes 25 mm in diameter for three steel rods 20 mm in diameter (nominal) threaded on one end and cast 300 mm deep into concrete abutment for two-log bridge. For three-log bridge, use a 6 × 60 × 1500 strap and four rods 20 mm in diameter (nominal).

DECKING: Use 50 × 150 mm boards laid flat with 20 mm gaps. Approximately every 1000 to 1275 mm, extend two boards and notch to hold handrails. Use either two 12 × 90 mm (nominal) wood screws or three 8 gauge × 100 mm (nominal) nails placed into predrilled holes. Fasten toe board (50 × 70 mm) to alternate deck boards with one 12 × 90 mm (nominal) screw or one 8 gauge × 90 mm (nominal) nail in a predrilled hole.

HANDRAILS: Fix 75 × 75 posts approximately 1000 to 1275 mm apart with two 12 × 175 mm (nominal) coach screws into predrilled holes. Use 3 × 50 mm washers. Fasten top rails (50 × 75 mm) and middle rails (50 × 75 mm), if used, to posts with two 12 × 90 mm (nominal) steel screws in predrilled holes. Half-notch joints in rails at posts. In some instances, depending on degree of hazard and types of users involved, handrails can be left off on one or both sides. For wide bridges, a middle rail may be required.

RAKERS (SIDE BRACES): Rakers should be 75 × 75 mm, fastened to posts with 12 × 140 mm bolts. Use two 3 × 50 mm washers. Fasten raker to extended deck boards with one 12 × 140 mm (nominal) coach screw in a predrilled hole.

SPECIFICATIONS

LOGS: Logs should be Douglas fir, larch, or Scotch pine, and should be straight without excessive taper (10 mm/meter taper is acceptable). Remove bark and seal cut ends. Logs should be rejected if they have knots larger than 100 mm in diameter, signs of decay or other serious defects, severe checking, or fissures (total depth of all fissures not to exceed one-third the diameter of the log at any point).

SAWN TIMBER: Decking and handrails to be of softwood Grade GS or MGS Species 1.

PRESERVATIVE TREATMENT: Decking should be pressure impregnated with wood preservative to 100 kg/m^3. Handrails should be pressure impregnated with wood preservative.

METALWORK: Mild steel to have galvanized finish. Bolts and threaded rods to be electroplated with zinc. Wood screws to be galvanized with slotted countersunk heads and dipped in linseed oil before fixing.

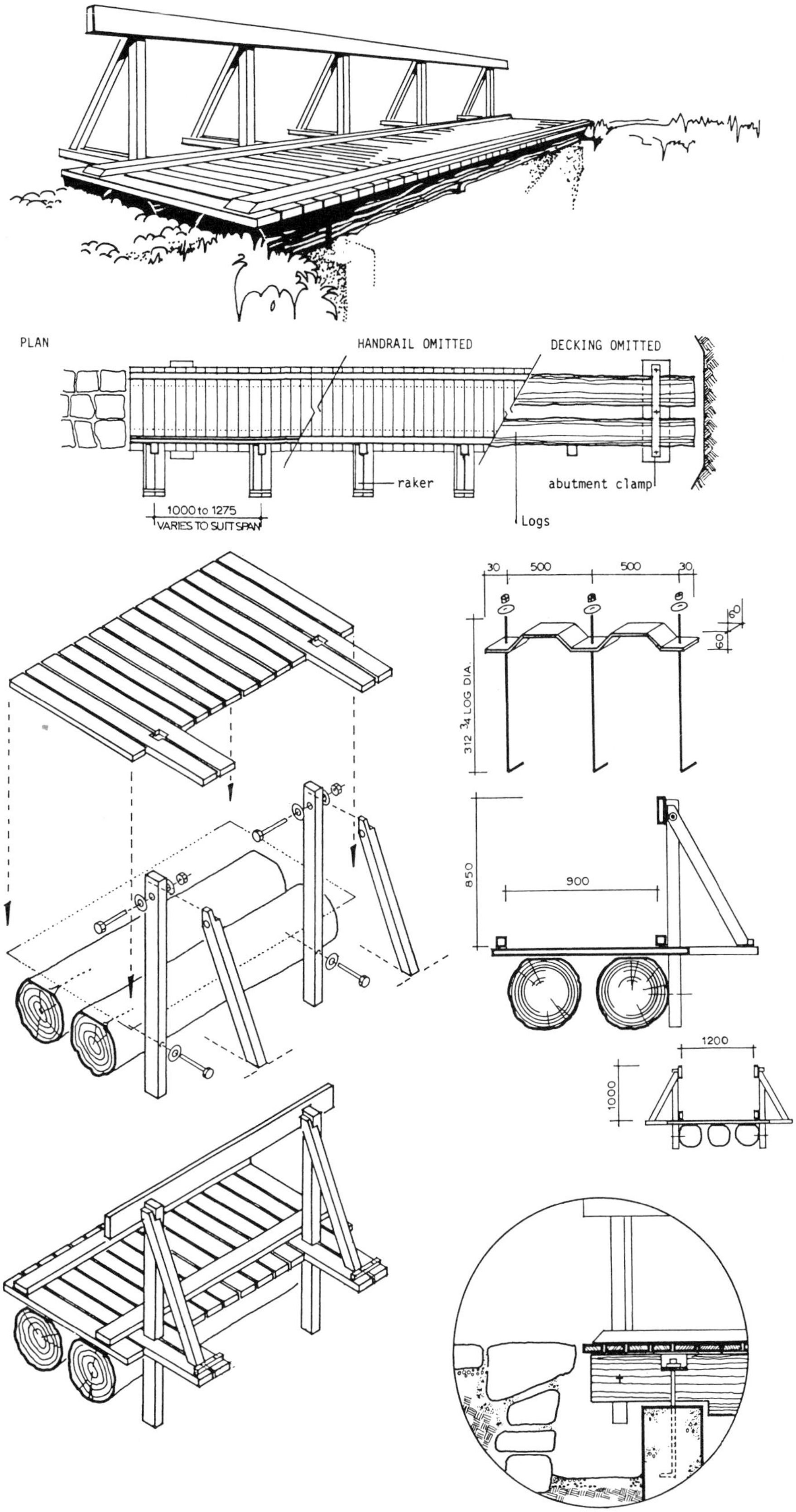
PLAN
HANDRAIL OMITTED
DECKING OMITTED
raker
abutment clamp
Logs
1000 to 1275
VARIES TO SUIT SPAN
30
500
500
30
60
60
312 ¾ LOG DIA.
850
900
1200
1000

Log Size	*Span C/C Bearing*	
Average diameter	*2-log, 900-mm-wide deck*	*3-log, 1200-mm-wide deck*
250 mm	5m	5.5 m
300 mm	6.7 m	7 m
350 mm	8 m	8.5 m
400 mm	9.75 m	10 m

Figure 470-32 Log footbridge.

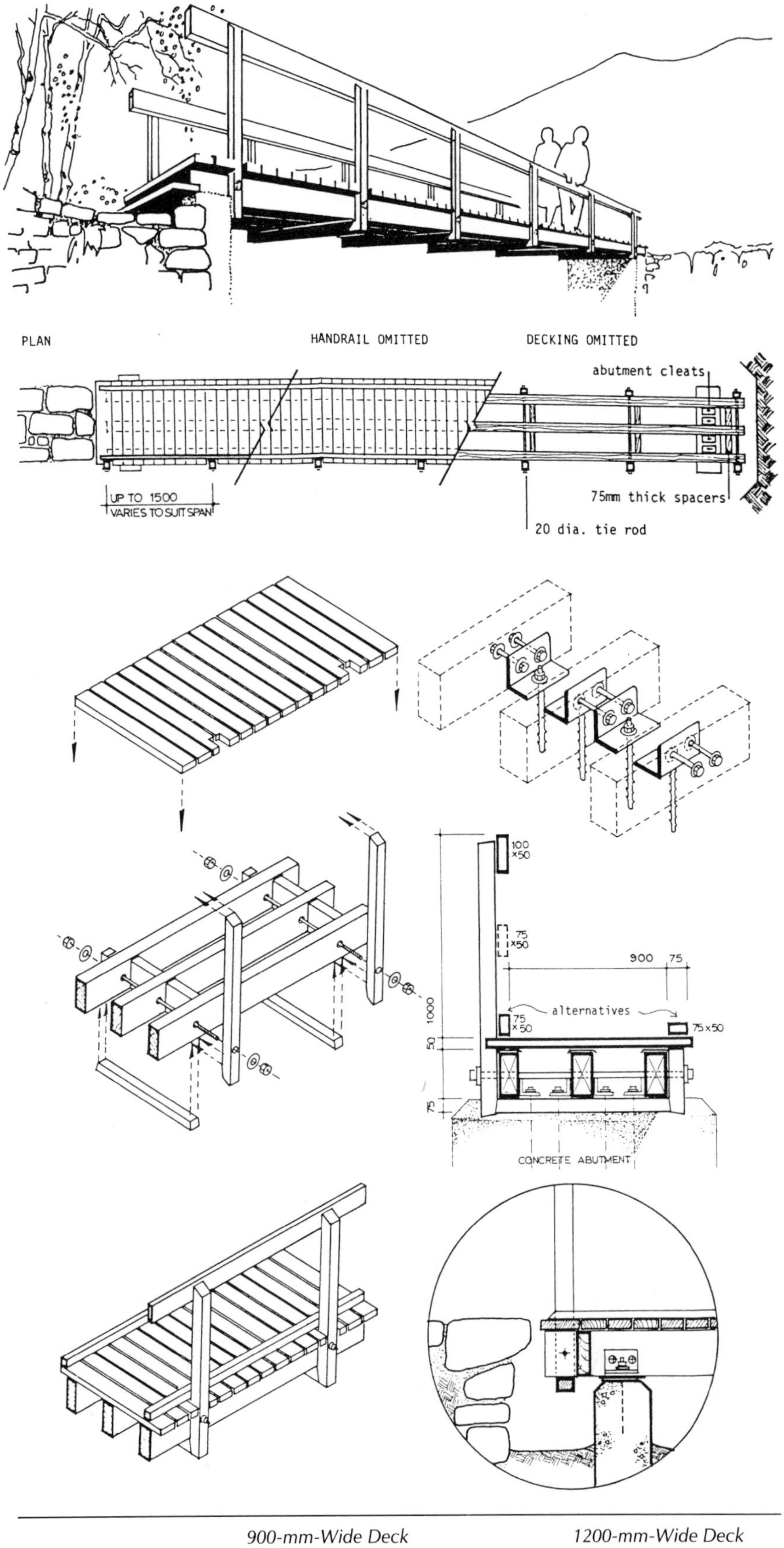
PLAN
HANDRAIL OMITTED
DECKING OMITTED
abutment cleats
UP TO 1500
VARIES TO SUIT SPAN
75mm thick spacers
20 dia. tie rod
100 x50
75 x50
900
75
alternatives
75 x50
75x50
1000
50
75
CONCRETE ABUTMENT

Beam Size	*900-mm-Wide Deck* No. of Beams	Span	*1200-mm-Wide Deck* No. of beams	Span
150 × 75 mm	3	3.0 m	3	2.75 m
200 × 100 mm	3	4.5 m	3	4.0 m
250 × 150 mm	3	6.5 m	3	5.75 m
250 × 200 mm	3	6.25 m	3	7.5 m
300 × 225 mm	2		3	
350 × 250 mm	2		3	

(Adapted from CSS as prepared by Reiach Hall Blyth Partnership.)

BEAM END SEATING: Concrete end seat made with 1:1 ½:3 mix. Masonry end abutment to provide gap of 20 mm to a maximum of 25 mm between timber deck and timber beam ends.

SAWN TIMBER BEAMS: Sawn timber beams are to be of the sizes and number shown in the table. Beams are to be drilled with holes 25 mm in diameter to match handrail centers for steel tie-rods 20 mm in diameter threaded 50 mm at each end with washers 76 mm in diameter × 6 mm thick. Place bitumen felt strip (20 mm wider than the beams between beam and decking.) Spacers (75 mm thick and full depth) are to be placed to one side of each handrail post, fastened with 8 gauge × 100 mm nails (for 200 mm deep beam or No. 12 for over 200 mm), driven at an angle into predrilled holes.

ABUTMENT CLEATS (ANGLE IRONS): Cleats are to be used to clamp beams to concrete abutment. Sizes of cleats vary with beam size: (a) beam sizes up to 200 × 100 mm require 89 × 89 × 6.3 mm galvanized angles, 110 mm long, with two holes for a bolt 12 mm in diameter (for beams) and one hole (25 mm in diameter) for a galvanized bolt 12 mm in diameter × 250 mm long into abutment; or (b) for beam sizes 250 × 150 mm and above, cleats should be 152 × 102 × 9.5 mm, 160 mm long, with two holes for bolts 20 mm in diameter (beams) and one hole 30 mm in diameter for a galvanized bolt 20 mm in diameter × 35 mm long into abutment. Place 12-mm-thick bearing pads under each beam.

DECKING: Decking boards (150 × 50 mm) are to be laid with 20-mm gaps. Boards are to be fastened to each beam with two No. 8 gauge × 100 mm nails in predrilled holes. Handrail posts are to be centered on a gap between boards, cut to a tight fit. Toe board (75 × 50 mm) is to be fastened to alternate deck boards with one nail, No. 8 gauge × 90 mm.

HANDRAILS: Top rails (100 × 50 mm), middle rails, and toe rails (if fitted, 75 × 50 mm) are to be continuous and fastened to each post with two galvanized screws No. 12 × 90 mm long set into predrilled holes. Joints in rails are to be half-notched at a post, and only one rail is to be joined at any one post.

SPECIFICATIONS

TIMBER: Beams are to be softwood Grade GS or MGS Species S1 or S2 (Douglas fir, larch, or Scotch pine). Decking, handrails, and posts are to be softwood Grade GS or MGS Species 1 only (Douglas fir or larch).

PRESERVATIVE TREATMENT: Beams and decking are to be pressure impregnated with a wood preservative to 100 kg/m^3. Handrailings and posts are to be treated to 5.3 kg/m^3. All cuts are to be treated with wood preservative.

BEARING PADS AND FELT STRIPS: Bearing pads are to be 12-mm-thick rubber or glass fiber reinforced bitumen felt. Felt strips under the decking are to be the same.

METALWORK: All steel, wood screws, and nails are to have a galvanized finish. Bolts and threaded rods are to be electroplated with zinc. Screws are to be dipped in linseed oil before use.

Figure 470-33 Sawn timber footbridge.

H-FRAME: Jig should be built to a high standard. Posts are to be 100 × 120 mm tapered to 100 × 70 mm × length (beam depth + 1300 mm). Crosspiece is to be 100 × 100 × 1140 mm long tenoned through posts 100 × 50 mm. Tenon is to be wedged and glued (according to manufacturer's instructions). Joints are to be secured after glue has cured with bolts and nuts 20 mm in diameter × 135 mm with washers 64 mm in diameter × 5 mm thick. Bottom rails (150 × 50 × 1140) are to be drilled after tightening frame-clamp and then bolted as above.

METALWORK: Abutment Clamp—(50 × 6 × 1050) steel strap with holes 25 mm in diameter for rods 20 mm in diameter and threaded 50 mm on ends. Frame Clamp—(40 × 6 × 276) steel strap with two slotted holes for two No. 12 mm diameter rods (inside dimensions as shown) and threaded 60 mm on ends. Decking Clamp—(40 × 6 × 180) steel strap with two slotted holes for U-bolt 12 mm in diameter with inside dimensions as shown.

DECKING: Prefabricated sections are to be lengths required to match H-frame spacing. Three bearers (200 × 50 × 900) long (nominal). Six deck boards (150 × 50) (nominal) with 20 mm gaps. Fasten prefabricated sections with two 12 × 90 mm (nominal) steel countersunk screws through each bearer via predrilled holes, or use three nails (No. 8 gauge × 100 mm) with round heads set into predrilled holes.

HANDRAILS: Use two or three rails (150 × 50) in continuous lengths. Fasten with two 12 × 90 mm steel countersunk screws into each post via predrilled holes. Only one rail is to be joined at any one post. Bottom rail, if used, is to be fastened on one side only using bolts 20 mm in diameter × 205 mm with cup-heads and square necks, and with 64 × 5 mm thick washers. The other side is to be fastened with screws.

Span	*No. of Beams*	*Timber Size*
Up to 6.5 m	2	250 × 200 mm
6.5 to 8 m	2	300 × 225 mm
350 mm	2	350 × 250 mm

SPECIFICATIONS

TIMBER: Decking and handrails of softwood Grade GS or MGS Species 1 or 2. Main beams are to be of softwood Grade GS or MGS Species (Douglas fir, larch, or Scotch pine).

PRESERVATIVE TREATMENT: Decking and main beams are to be pressure impregnated with wood preservative to 100 kg/m^3. Handrailings and posts are to be pressure treated with wood preservative. All cuts should be treated with wood preservative.

BEARING PADS AND FELT: (Same as for Sawn Timber Bridge shown in Figure 470-33).

METALWORK: (Same as for Sawn Timber Bridge shown in Figure 470-33).

(Adapted from CCS prepared by Reiach Hall Blyth Partnership based upon a design developed by the Forestry Commission in association with the staff of the C.R.E. of Scotland.)

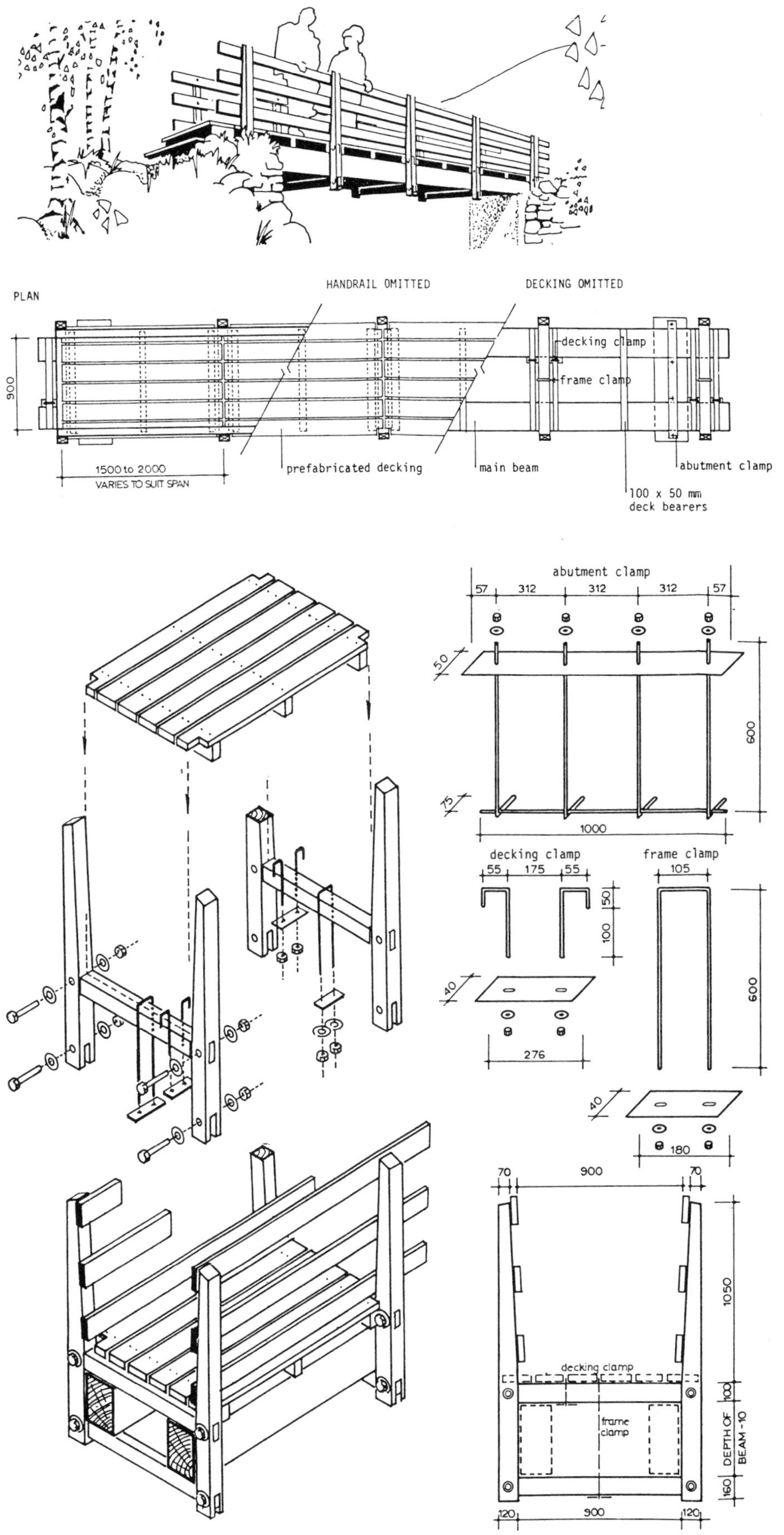

PLAN
HANDRAIL OMITTED
DECKING OMITTED
decking clamp
frame clamp
900
1500 to 2000
VARIES TO SUIT SPAN
prefabricated decking
main beam
abutment clamp
100 x 50 mm
deck bearers
abutment clamp
57
312
312
312
57
50
600
75
1000
decking clamp
55
175
55
150
100
40
276
frame clamp
105
600
40
180
70
900
70
1050
decking clamp
frame clamp
100
DEPTH OF BEAM -10
160
120
900
120

Figure 470-34 Galloway timber footbridge.

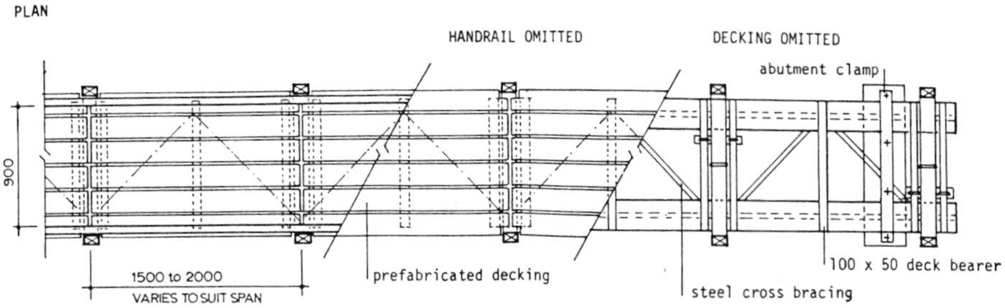
PLAN
HANDRAIL OMITTED
DECKING OMITTED
abutment clamp
900
1500 to 2000
VARIES TO SUIT SPAN
prefabricated decking
100 x 50 deck bearer
steel cross bracing

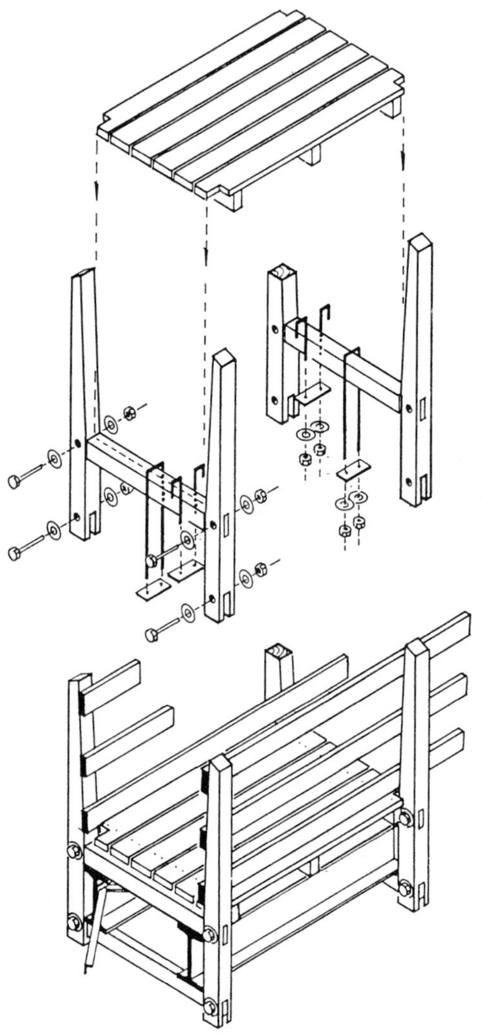

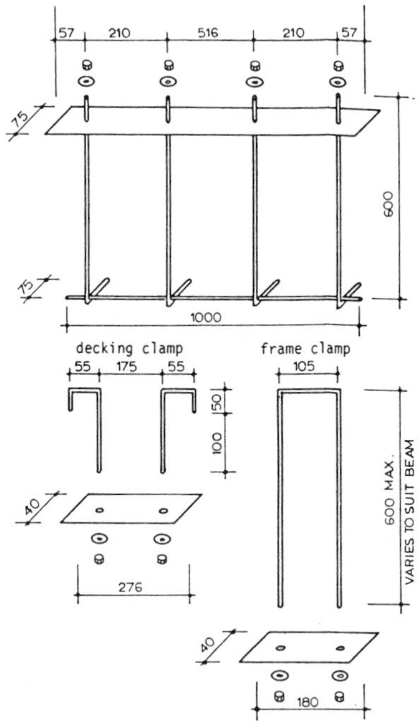
57
210
516
210
57
75
600
75
1000
decking clamp
55
175
55
150
100
40
276
frame clamp
105
600 MAX.
VARIES TO SUIT BEAM
40
180

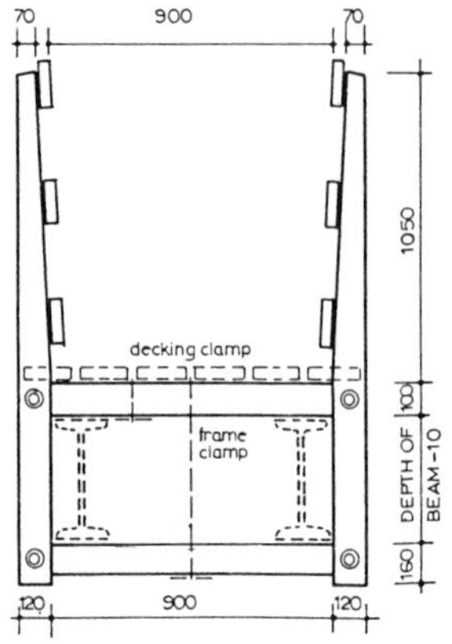
70
900
70
1050
decking clamp
frame clamp
100
DEPTH OF BEAM -10
160
120
900
120

H-FRAME: Jig should be built to high standards in same way as described for Galloway Timber Footbridge (Figure 470-34).

METALWORK: Abutment Clamp—(75 × 6 × 1050) steel strap made as for Galloway Timber Footbridge (Figure 470-34). Frame and Decking Clamps made in the same way with dimensions same as for Galloway Timber Footbridge (Figure 470-34).

DIAGONAL BRACING: 60 × 60 × 6 mm angle is to be bolted to underside of beam's top flange with a single bolt. Bracing is to be arranged to fit cross bearer centers (see plan).

DECKING: Prefabricated sections are to be made in same way and dimensions as for Galloway Timber Footbridge (Figure 470-34).

HANDRAILS: Made in the same way and dimensions as for Galloway Timber Footbridge (Figure 470-34).

SPECIFICATIONS

STEEL: Steel shall be Grade 43 as in BSS 4360. Rolled sections shall be in accordance with BSS 4: Part 1. Fabrication shall be in accordance with BS 449.

PAINTING STEEL: Wire brush to remove loose rust and mill scale. Degrease and apply two coats of zinc chromate primer and two coats of micaceous iron oxide pigmented oleo-resinous paint (or equal) to a minimum dry film thickness of 150 microns. Alternatively, use a factory applied coating of similar or better quality. After erection, touch up all paint work to full specifications, especially at bolted connections.

TIMBER: Decking, handrails, and posts to be made of softwood Grade GS or MGS Special 1 or 2.

PRESERVATIVE TREATMENT: Decking to be pressure impregnated with wood preservative to 100 kg/m^3. Handrailing and posts are to be pressure treated with wood preservative. All cuts should be treated with wood preservative.

BEARING PADS AND FELT: (Same as for Sawn Timber Bridge, Figure 470-33).

METALWORK: (Same treatment as for Sawn Timber Bridge, Figure 470-33).

(This footbridge is based upon a design developed by the Forestry Commission in association with the staff of C.R.E. of Scotland, adapted by Reiach Hall Blyth Partnership for CCS.)

Universal Beam Size (d × b × weight)	*Simply Supported Span*	*Cantilever Length*	*Single Bolt Connection*
203 × 133 × 25 kg/m	8.75 m	1.8 m	12 diameter
254 × 146 × 31 kg/m	10.75 m	2.2 m	12 diameter
305 × 171 × 45 kg/m	13.25 m	2.7 m	16 diameter
365 × 171 × 45 kg/m	14.75 m	3.0 m	16 diameter

Figure 470-35 Galloway steel footbridge.

BEARINGS: Steel beams should be fastened in position at one bearing end and allowed to move (expand and contract) at the other end. For spans up to 6250 mm, the anchor rods should be 12 mm in diameter × 275 mm long with 50 mm threaded, and the other end cast or grouted 200 mm into the concrete abutment. For spans greater than 6250 mm, the anchor rods should be 20 mm in diameter × 375 mm long and cast 300 mm into concrete or as above.

Beams should have two holes (17 mm or 25 mm in diameter) (nominal) at fixed ends and slotted (17 mm wide and 37 mm long or 25 mm × 50 mm) at free end. Beams should be seated on 12-mm-thick rubber pads cut to size.

BRACING: To counteract side bucking of long slender steel beams, horizontal braces are used to form a lattice (as shown), or steel diaphragms are connected to main beams at regular intervals. Wood decking will provide more stability if the decking members are continuous and rigidly fixed to the steel beams (see typical cross-section).

DECKING AND HANDRAILS: Fasten nailing strip (150 × 50) to steel beams using bolts 10 mm in diameter with cup heads countersunk into timber at 300 mm on center and placed at alternate sides of the flange. Nailing strip should stop at each transom position. Deck boards (150 × 50 × 1500 long) are laid with 20 m gaps and fastened with two 12 × 90 mm (nominal) steel countersunk screws in predrilled holes at each end. Transom (100 × 100 × 2250) at each handrail post is to be bolted to the outside flange of each joint with two cup-head bolts 10 mm (nominal) in diameter and washer plate 50 × 100 × 5 thick. Handrail posts (100 × 75 × 1025) are to be installed at approximately 1500 mm centers. Rakers (braces) (75 × 75) are to be half-notched to transom and to post. Use the following bolts: (a) raker to post—16 mm in diameter × 145 mm with washers placed 36 mm from outside edge of post, (b) raker to transom—16 mm × 170 mm with washers placed same as above, and (c) post to transom—16 × 210 mm with washers placed same as above.

HANDRAILS: Handrails (100 × 50) are to be in continuous lengths fastened to each post with two 12 × 90 mm (nominal) steel countersunk screws in predrilled holes. Joints are to be half-notched at a post, and only one rail is to be jointed at any one post.

Span (m)	*Universal Beam Section*
Up to 6.25	152 × 89 × 17.09 kg/m
6.25 to 8.50	203 × 133 × 25.00 kg/m
8.50 to 10.40	254 × 146 × 31.00 kg/m
10.40 to 12.75	305 × 165 × 40.00 kg/m
12.75 to 14.20	365 × 171 × 45.00 kg/m
14.20 to 16.00	406 × 178 × 54.00 kg/m

SPECIFICATIONS

STEEL: (Same as for Galloway Steel Footbridge, Figure 470-35).

PAINTING STEEL: (Same as above).

TIMBER: (Same as for Galloway Steel Footbridge, Figure 470-35).

METALWORK: (Same as for Sawn Timber Footbridge, Figure 470-33).

(Adapted from design prepared by Reiach Hall Blyth Partnership for CSS.)

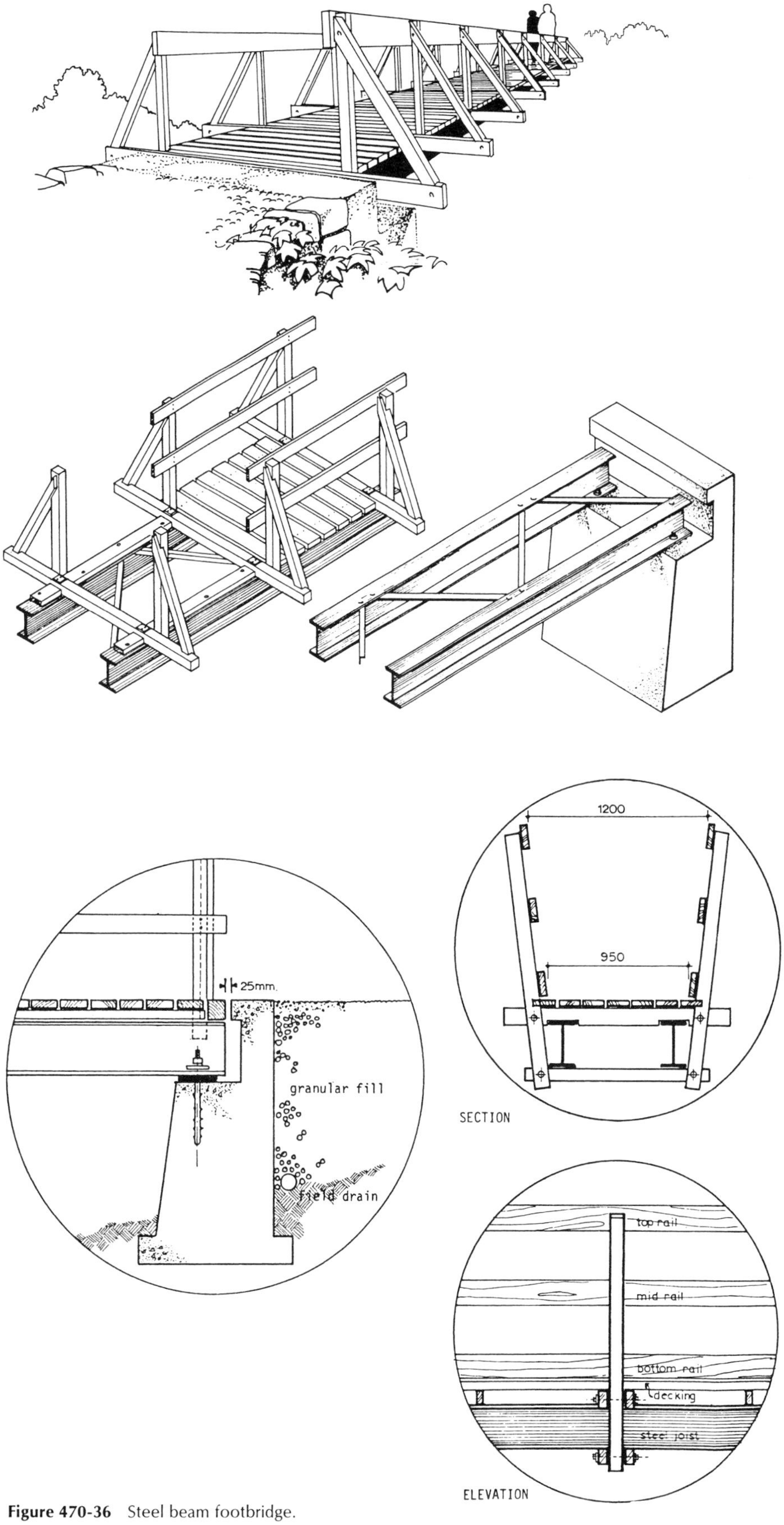
25mm.
granular fill
field drain
1200
950
SECTION
top rail
mid rail
bottom rail
decking
steel joist
ELEVATION

Figure 470-36 Steel beam footbridge.

CABLE TOWERS: Cable towers should be constructed of steel or reinforced concrete with appropriate cable-saddle at the top.

HANGERS: Hangers should be of galvanized rope or steel rods, and cable clamps should be used to grip the cable to prevent slippage and consequent distortion of the frame. Rod hangers should be "pin-ended" to avoid high bending stresses.

ANCHORS: Three methods of anchorage include: (1) mass concrete blocks, (2) anchors grouted and in some way fastened to existing rock, and (3) buried large timbers or logs. Careful attention to the detailing and treatment of the ends of the cables and fittings is required to minimize corrosion.

CABLES: Cables are to be of galvanized high tensile steel wire rope. 25 mm (nominal) in diameter is suitable for shorter spans. Larger cables for major structures have to be ordered to an exact length with socketed ends. Cable clamps should grip the cable to prevent slippage but not weaken it through distortion. The sag to span ratio of the main cables should be between 1:8 and 1:11. The back or anchor side should be placed at the same angle as the cable on the span side of the towers.

DECKING: Spans of 15 to 20 m for footbridges frequently have timber decking and handrails, as shown. The decking material should be laid to stagger any joints. Decking must incorporate horizontal bracing to control wind swaying and to help control oscillations caused by the rhythms of pedestrian traffic.

HANDRAILS: If the drop from the bridge is hazardous, handrails should be installed 1.2 m high with wire mesh as infill.

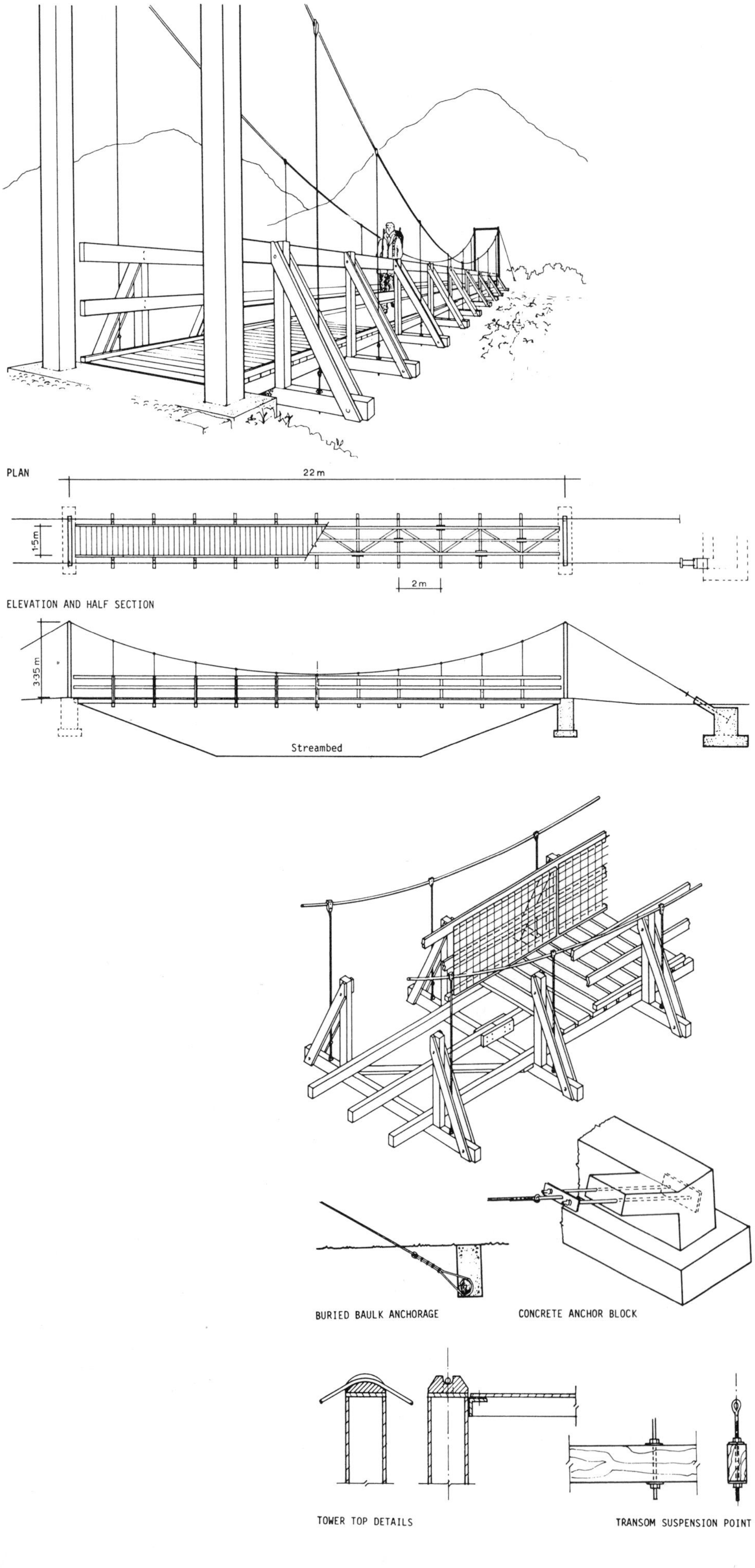
PLAN
22 m
1·5 m
2 m
ELEVATION AND HALF SECTION
3·35 m
Streambed
BURIED BAULK ANCHORAGE
CONCRETE ANCHOR BLOCK
TOWER TOP DETAILS
TRANSOM SUSPENSION POINT

Figure 470-37 Suspension footbridge.

footbridge. The steel beams extend the useful span and are lighter than timber. Horizontal bracing is required between the steel beams because they are less stiff in this direction than timber. A good paint specification and regular maintenance are required to extend the life of the steelwork. The longer spans should not be attempted without engineering advice.

4.5 Steel Beam Footbridge

Two suggested cross sections for steel beam structures are shown in Figure 470-36. The life of the structure will depend on the quality of the maintenance protecting it from corrosion.

4.6 Suspension Bridge

Suspension bridges (Figure 470-37) are used when (a) streams have fluctuating water levels, (b) the currents are very rapid, (c) conditions for foundations, particularly intermediate piers, are impractical, and (d) sites are remote so that small pieces needed for a suspension bridge can be carried in. Where large crowds are not expected low technology solutions are possible for footbridges of 49 to 66 ft (15 to 20 m).

The sizes of all members of a suspension bridge must be determined by an experienced designer or engineer who will also check the method of erection. This should be done under the guidance of a competent construction supervisor. Erection of a suspension bridge is hazardous. Safe working procedures must be formulated and used by experienced personnel using correct equipment.

4.7 Concrete or Masonry Arch Footbridges

In addition to the five types of wood and metal bridges developed and used by the Countryside Commission of Scotland, there are several bridge types that could be constructed from poured-in-place concrete or various kinds of masonry construction. Figure 470-38 shows two variations, one using concrete and one using stone. In the latter example, other types of masonry (such as brick or precast concrete) could be used as the structural material or as a facing material for a poured concrete footbridge.

As with other types of footbridges, concrete or masonry arch bridges require solid foundations. Most concrete or masonry arch bridges require the advice of a structural engineer to ensure compliance with safe design and construction standards.

If rough stone or rubble masonry is used to construct the arch, then the stones should be roughly squared and laid in port-

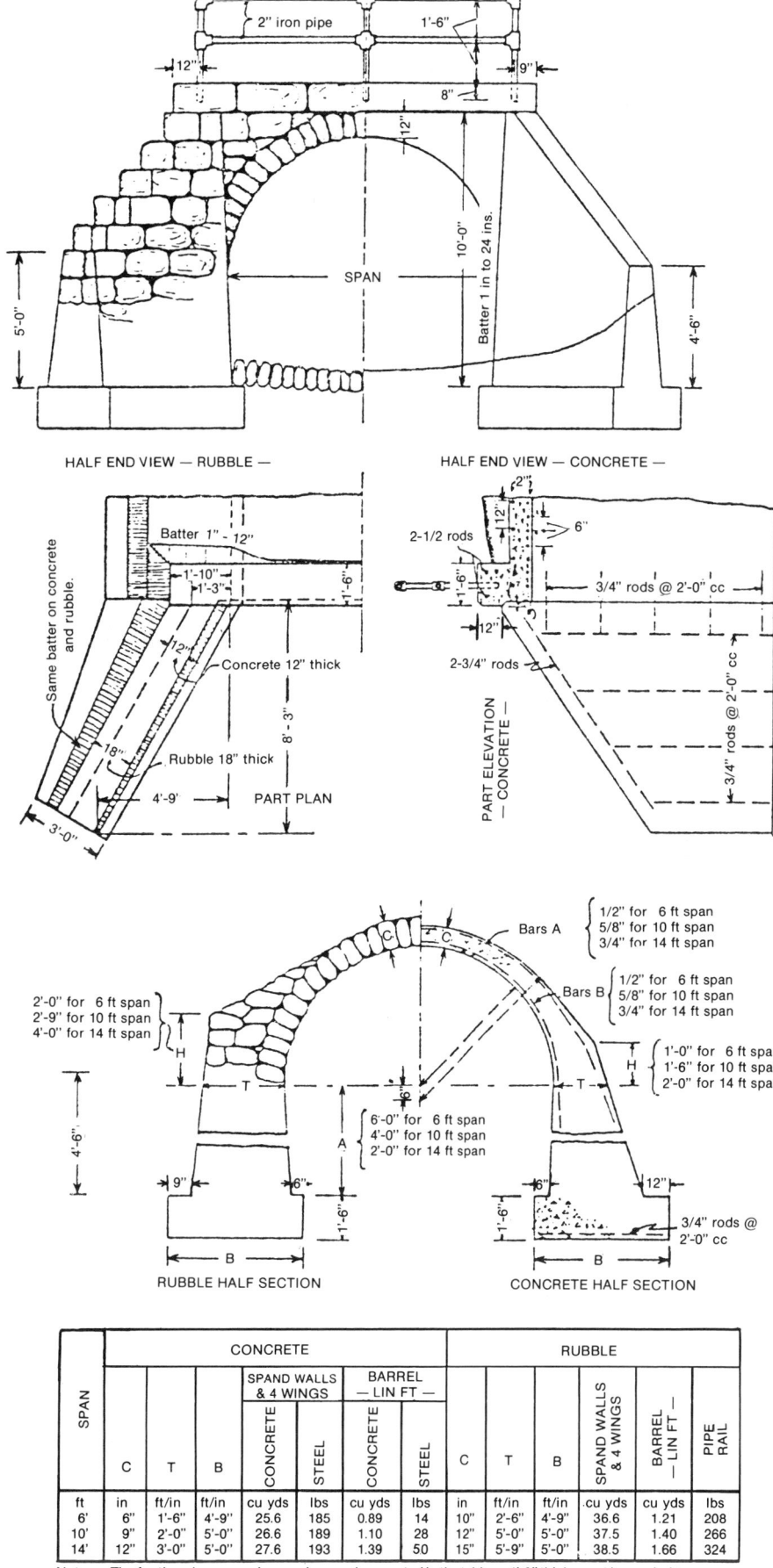

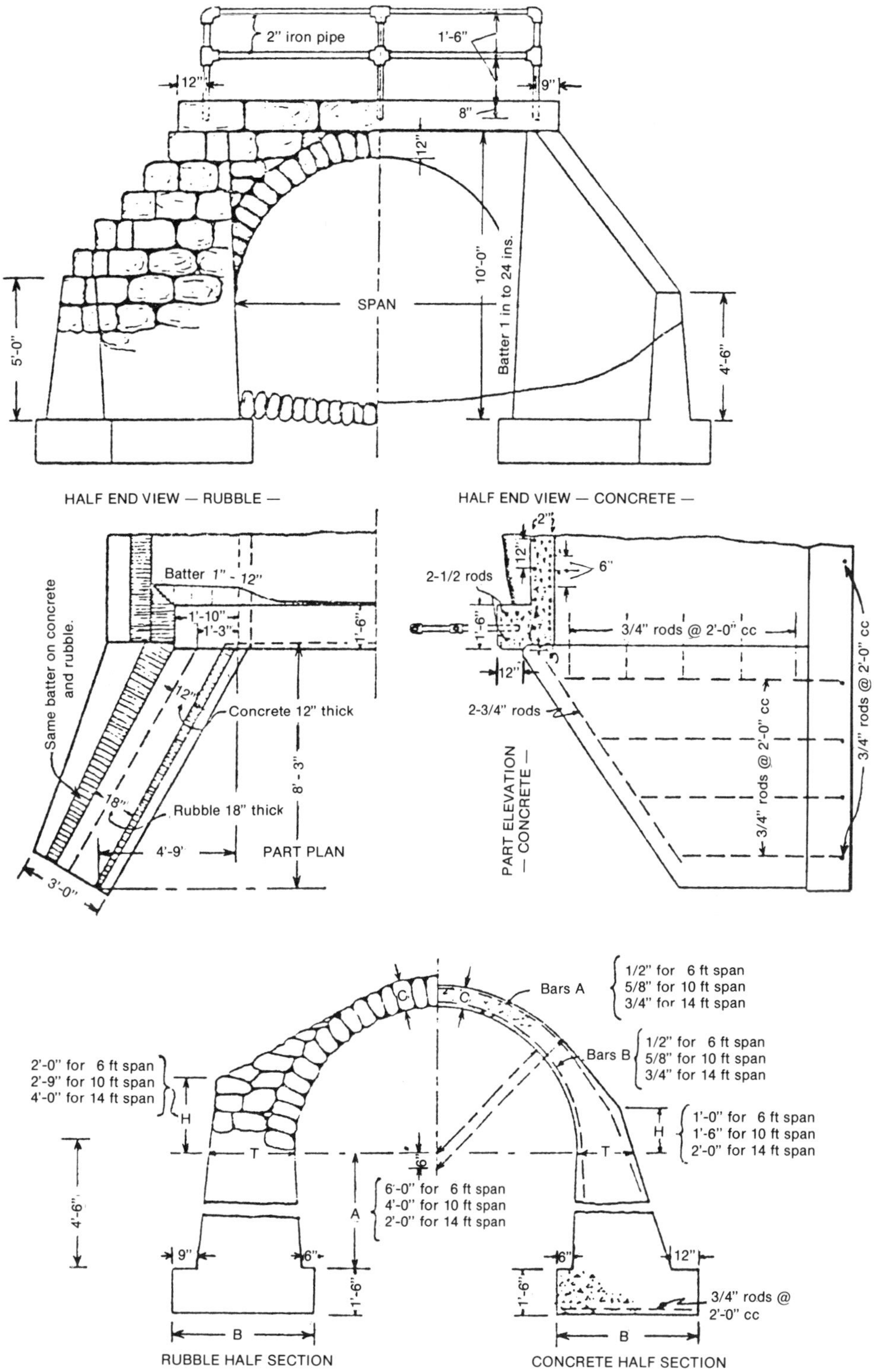

2" iron pipe
1'-6"
12"
9"
8"
12"
10'-0"
Batter 1 in to 24 ins.
SPAN
5'-0"
4'-6"
HALF END VIEW — RUBBLE —
HALF END VIEW — CONCRETE —
Same batter on concrete and rubble.
Batter 1" - 12"
1'-10"
1'-3"
1'-6"
12"
Concrete 12" thick
8'-3"
18"
Rubble 18" thick
4'-9'
PART PLAN
3'-0"
2"
2-1/2 rods
12"
6"
1'-6"
3/4" rods @ 2'-0" cc
12"
2-3/4" rods
PART ELEVATION — CONCRETE —
3/4" rods @ 2'-0" cc
3/4" rods @ 2'-0" cc
Bars A
1/2" for 6 ft span
5/8" for 10 ft span
3/4" for 14 ft span
Bars B
1/2" for 6 ft span
5/8" for 10 ft span
3/4" for 14 ft span
2'-0" for 6 ft span
2'-9" for 10 ft span
4'-0" for 14 ft span
H
1'-0" for 6 ft span
1'-6" for 10 ft span
2'-0" for 14 ft span
T
C
6"
6'-0" for 6 ft span
4'-0" for 10 ft span
2'-0" for 14 ft span
A
4'-6"
9"
6"
12"
1'-6"
3/4" rods @ 2'-0" cc
B
RUBBLE HALF SECTION
CONCRETE HALF SECTION

SPAN	CONCRETE							RUBBLE					
				SPAND WALLS & 4 WINGS		BARREL — LIN FT —							
	C	T	B	CONCRETE	STEEL	CONCRETE	STEEL	C	T	B	SPAND WALLS & 4 WINGS	BARREL — LIN FT —	PIPE RAIL
ft	in	ft/in	ft/in	cu yds	lbs	cu yds	lbs	in	ft/in	ft/in	cu yds	cu yds	lbs
6'	6"	1'-6"	4'-9"	25.6	185	0.89	14	10"	2'-6"	4'-9"	36.6	1.21	208
10'	9"	2'-0"	5'-0"	26.6	189	1.10	28	12"	5'-0"	5'-0"	37.5	1.40	266
14'	12"	3'-0"	5'-0"	27.6	193	1.39	50	15"	5'-9"	5'-0"	38.5	1.66	324

Note: — The footing shown as plus or minus and computed in the table as 1'-6" thick, must be carried to a solid foundation.

Figure 470-38 Concrete or masonry arch footbridge.

land cement mortar. The stones must be hard, durable, and reasonably flat. Not more than one-third of the stone should be less than 1 ft (300 mm) thick, and no stone should be less than 6 in (150 mm) thick and have a bed area of less than 1 ft (300 mm) square. Walls must be laid using large, flat, selected stone in the bottom and having at least one-fifth of the wall surface made of face headers. All of the spaces in the heart of the wall should be filled with suitable stones or spalls which are thoroughly bedded in cement mortar. The outer arch ring should be made of full-size stones that have been rough-dressed to create smoother abutting inner surfaces. They should be laid simultaneously from both ends, with mortar joints not exceeding 1 in (25 mm) in thickness.

Arch centers should not be struck until directed by the designer. The tops of the face walls should be finished with cope-stones no less than 6 in (150 mm) thick and 1½ ft (450 mm) wide, with a length of at least 1½ times the breadth.

Dry rubble masonry can be used, but it should meet all of the other requirements for rough-stone or rubble masonry. Only flat stones at least twice as wide as thick should be used. Generally, the larger stones should be placed in the lower part of the wall, although different sizes can be more evenly distributed over the wall face.

If the wall is sloped, then the stones should be placed at right angles to the slope and every stone must extend the full depth of the wall.

5.0 TYPICAL DESIGNS FOR PREFABRICATED BRIDGES

Manufactured prefabricated bridges can offer advantages in sites where access is easy, where long spans are necessary, where minimal costs are required, or where skilled labor is unavailable.

Flat-span and arch-span types of bridges are available in the United States for spans ranging from 10 to 160 ft (3 to 50 m). Lengths over 65 ft (20 m) are fabricated in sections to be bolted together in the field. Carbon-steel or self-weathering-steel bridge structures finished with wooden decking and handrailings are also available. Loadings are designed in accordance with AASHTO specifications. Optional handrailings 54 in (1370 mm) high are available when use by bicyclists is anticipated.

The same careful consideration of foundation and abutment design is required for prefabricated bridges as for site-built bridges because manufacturers provide only bridge superstructures.

Table 470-12 gives the sizes of prefabricated bridges currently available in the United States.

TABLE 470-12
Size Ranges of Prefabricated Bridges

Type	Span, m (ft)	Inside width, m (ft)	Truss height, m (ft)
Low-profile bridge (steel)	3–32 (10–105)	1.2–3 (4–10)	1.2 (4)
High-profile bridge (steel)	3–32 (10–105)	1.2–3 (4–10)	2.4 (8)
Aluminum box truss pedestrian bridge	18–34.5 (60–113)	—	—
Steel arch bridge	3–30.5 (10–100) in 1.5 m (5 ft) increments	1.2 (4) 1.8 (6) 2.4 (8) 3.0 (10)	—
Steel through truss	22–51.2 (72–168) in 2.4 m (8 ft) increments	1.8 (6) 2.4 (8)	2.4 (8)

6.0 PROBLEMS AND METHODS OF ERECTING BRIDGES

Every site will present its own distinctive problems in the erection of a bridge. Five of the most common areas of difficulty are discussed below.

6.1 Access to the Site

Normally, the most difficult items to transport to a site are the bridge beams. A typical 30-ft (9-m) beam will weigh approximately 625 lb (279 kg) in steel and 945 lb (422 kg) in timber. Where access is particularly difficult, it may be necessary to design main structural members with small pieces that can be assembled at the bridge site.

6.2 Working Areas

If the bridge's structural elements have to be assembled at the site before being placed across a gap, then a suitable level area is required. Until they are braced together, some members are so flexible that it is often better to erect the entire bridge on the bank before lifting it into place.

6.3 Lifting into Place

The most difficult task in erecting a footbridge is placing the main structural members into position. The method used to place these members will depend on their length, weight, and stability and on the nature of the equipment which can be brought to the site. This has to be anticipated at the beginning of the design stage. This information will often determine the choice of bridge type, especially if the span is over 20 ft (7 m) or where temporary supports across the gap are impractical. Common methods of placing the main structural beams across a gap are described below.

Cranes:

If access is good, a mobile crane of suitable capacity and working radius can be used. The cost of this method should be determined before disregarding other more labor-intensive methods of erection.

Shear Legs and Spars:

Shear legs and spars may be used for moving beams into position with chain blocks fastened to dead-end anchorages lifting the load, thereby allowing controlled lifting either by a sheaved pulley section with rope or by using other types of pulling devices (Figure 470-39). Although loads are typically not large, a knowledge of rigging blocks, pulley sheaves, and guy ropes is essential for anyone attempting this method of erection.

Temporary Supports:

Where temporary supports can be provided in the gap, the structural members may be rolled into position (Figure 470-39). The supports should be well-braced so that they will not be knocked over. Structural members can be lowered onto the bearing either by the use of relatively short shear legs and chain blocks or by staged jacking with hydraulic or screw jacks, using packing in front and on the bearing.

Cantilevering:

Beams can be cantilevered over the gap by using one of the other beams (Figure 470-39). Care must be taken to keep the system suitably counterweighted. Once the beam is over the bearings, it can be picked up with shear legs and chain blocks or progressively jacked until it sits on the bearings, as described above. The remainder of the beams can be rolled over the top of the first beam.

Lattice Girders:

Building lattice girders in place, using temporary supports to form the correct profile, is another method of erection (Figure 470-39). This allows both girders to be erected and the cross-bracing to be inserted so that they are stable at all times.

Where temporary supports cannot be constructed, a temporary tower and cable support may be used, but the sophistication of such a method requires it to be under the control of an experienced engineer.

6.4 Dangerous Working Conditions

There are inherent risks to those involved in bridge erection. Accidents can be avoided only by adopting safe working methods which are carefully supervised. While some of the risks are those encountered on any building site, working on long, heavy bridge members before the bracing, decking, and handrailing are installed increases the probability of accidents.

7.0 MAINTENANCE OF BRIDGES

All bridges deteriorate over time as a result of constant use and of decay. Therefore, all bridges need periodic inspections and repair. The following procedures should be adopted to ensure longer life of the bridge.

7.1 Maintenance in Design

Provide for maintenance in design by:

1. Ensuring that the main beams can be inspected along their entire length and especially where they rest on piers and end seats

2. Ensuring that secondary elements (decking, handrailings, etc.) can be removed and replaced without undue difficulty

3. Ensuring that inspections are easy to carry out, including the provision of anchor points for harnesses and/or of platforms for ladders or scaffolds

4. Ensuring that design assumptions are recorded and that design drawings and specifications are kept secure

7.2 Maintenance in Construction

Provide for maintenance in construction by:

1. Ensuring that the bridge is built to design standards and specifications

2. Ensuring that variations are recorded and that an accurate set of as-built drawings is produced, including a simplified plan and elevation for inspection purposes

3. Taking a set of photographs, so that construction work, particularly that which will be hidden, is recorded, and so that progressive deterioration can be assessed by comparison with the original condition.

7.3 Maintenance in Use

Provide for maintenance in use by:

1. Briefing maintenance staff on standards and procedures

2. Maintaining a record file for each bridge

3. Inspecting each bridge and its approaches annually, preparing a bridge inspection report, and ensuring that maintenance recommendations are implemented

Sensible *housekeeping* measures include cleaning vegetation and soil from timber decking, maintaining free air space around beam ends, and tightening loose fastenings. Wood preservative should be reapplied every 3 years, and metal paint every 5 years. Rust spots should be cleaned every year, coated with antirust primer, and touched up.

7.4 Inspection

Points to look for during inspection are:

1. Scouring of riverbed and bridge foundations

2. Damage to banks and adjacent land

3. Unsafe trees close to the bridge

4. Muddy or worn footpaths, steps, and ramps

5. Decay of timbers, especially at holes, cracks, and ends

6. Water and moisture traps on horizontal surfaces and joints

7. Loose bolts, screws, nails, posts, and handrailings

8. Metal corrosion

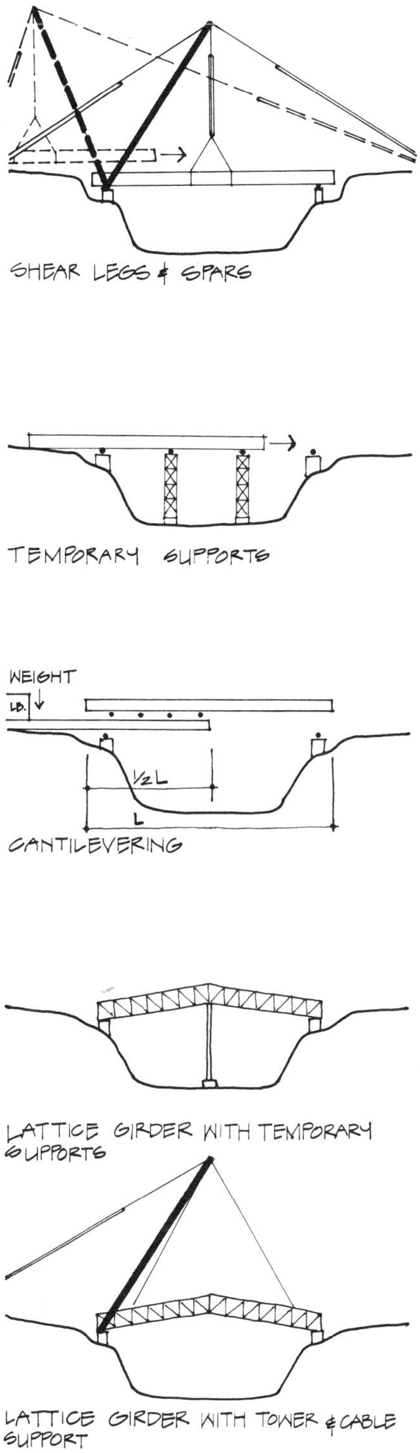
SHEAR LEGS & SPARS
TEMPORARY SUPPORTS
WEIGHT
LB.
½L
L
CANTILEVERING
LATTICE GIRDER WITH TEMPORARY SUPPORTS
LATTICE GIRDER WITH TOWER & CABLE SUPPORT

Figure 470-39 Methods of Bridge Erection. The method used to place members will depend on their length, weight, and stability and on the nature of the equipment which can be brought to the site.

REFERENCES

American Association of State Highway and Transportation Officials (AASHTO). *Standards for Highway Bridges,* 12th ed., Washington, DC, 1977.

DeLeuw Cather, et al. *Effective Treatment of Over and Undercrossings for Use by Bicyclists, Pedestrians and the Handicapped,* FHWA-RD-79-70, U.S. Federal Highway Administration, Washington, DC, January 1981.

Hamberg, E. C. *Bridge Foundations and Substructures,* Building Research Establishment, Department of the Environment, HMSO, London, 1979.

Reiach Hall Blyth Partnership. *Footbridges in the Countryside—Design and Construction.* Countryside Commission for Scotland, Perth, Scotland, 1981.

The source from which most of the data in Section 470 was taken. ■

section 510: Site Furniture and Features

CREDITS

Contributor:

Ilse Jones and G. H. Lee
Jones & Jones, Inc.
Seattle, Washington
Portland, Oregon

Reviewers:

Kenneth Demay
Sasaki Associates, Inc.
Watertown, Massachusetts

Nicholas T. Dines
University of Massachusetts
Amherst, Massachusetts

CONTENTS

1.0 INTRODUCTION

1.1 General

Elements placed in a landscape or streetscape for comfort, convenience, information, circulation control, protection, and user enjoyment are collectively referred to as *site furniture* (Figure 510-1). Benches, bollards, signage, lighting, tree grates, and utility boxes are but a few examples. Their design and placement require careful consideration, involving several factors, each of which is described in this section.

Many of the same types of furnishings are also used for similar reasons in special landscapes, such as interiors or roof decks. (Refer to Sections 620: Interior Landscapes, and 610: Roof and Deck Landscapes, for more information.)

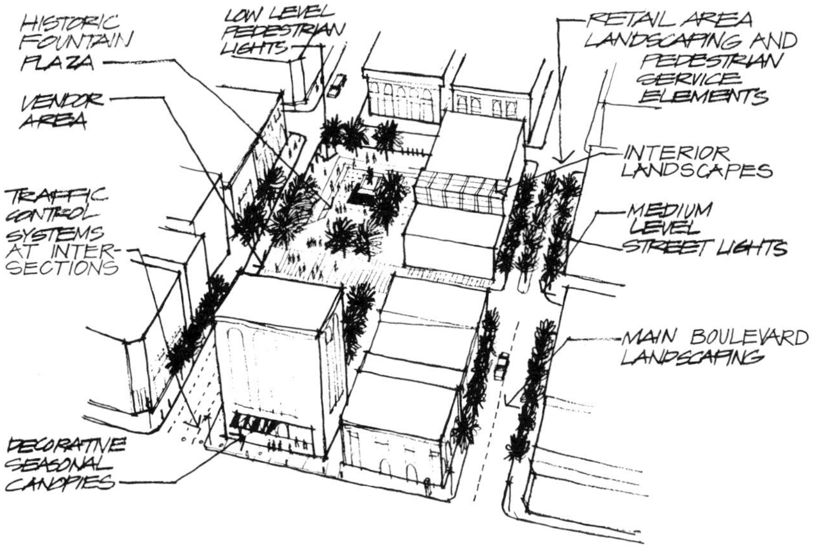

HISTORIC FOUNTAIN PLAZA
LOW LEVEL PEDESTRIAN LIGHTS
RETAIL AREA LANDSCAPING AND PEDESTRIAN SERVICE ELEMENTS
VENDOR AREA
INTERIOR LANDSCAPES
TRAFFIC CONTROL SYSTEMS AT INTERSECTIONS
MEDIUM LEVEL STREET LIGHTS
MAIN BOULEVARD LANDSCAPING
DECORATIVE SEASONAL CANOPIES

Figure 510-1 The context of site furniture.

1.2 Design Objectives

Appropriateness:

Appropriateness is a major objective in the design and placement of site furniture elements. It is important to respond to the character of a site as well as its existing and proposed functions (Figures 510-2 and 510-3).

Response to Setting:

Design should respond to the essential identity or inherent character of a place. Successful, lasting design will flow out of its setting, continually responding to the needs of its users, meeting functional requirements, and adapting to the environmental stresses affecting it.

LODGE 4
INFORMAL CHARACTER WITH "ROUGH" SITE FURNITURE AND FEATURES

Figure 510-2 Site context: Informal character.

2.0 DESIGN DETERMINANTS

Settings should be analyzed in terms of both cultural and physical factors.
Cultural factors include:

1. Social context
2. Political context

Physical factors include:

1. Climate
2. Natural physiography
3. The existing built environment

Each of these factors is described below.

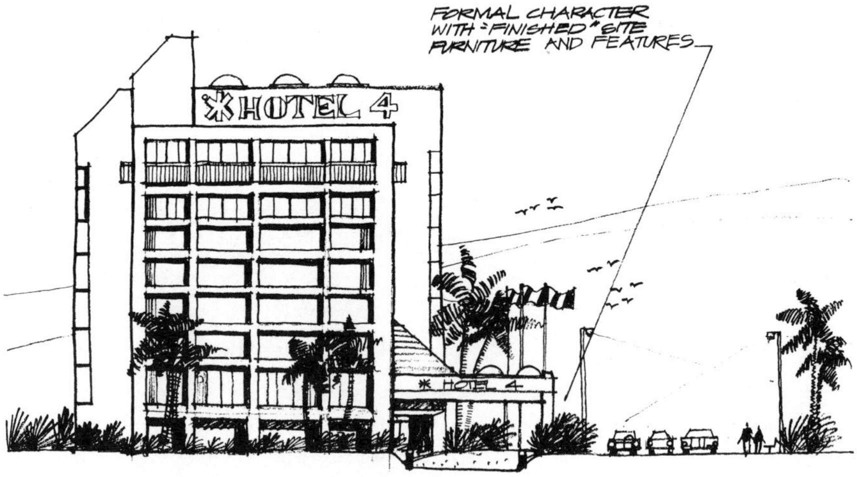
FORMAL CHARACTER WITH "FINISHED" SITE FURNITURE AND FEATURES
HOTEL 4
HOTEL 4

Figure 510-3 Site contact: Formal character.

2.1 Cultural Factors

Social Context:

Attention to both the existing and proposed large-scale social setting will indicate who is currently using the site and who will likely use the site in the future. The manner in which the site is being used requires careful investigation (Figure 510-4).

The traditions and habits of particular user groups provide a basis for unique design departures that can enliven the setting as a whole, while at the same time serving specific needs. This can be reflected in terms of both site organization as a whole and the design of individual elements themselves.

Inattention to the cultural habits and desires of particular groups and the use of improper elements can foster negative reaction in a neighborhood. The use of themes or vernacular forms which have no local cultural root seldom contribute to the evolving identity of a place.

Some ethnic groups, for instance, have need for special types of site furniture appropriate to particular activities. Finding what is needed is not only a basic responsibility of the designer, but often opens up an opportunity to explore new design ideas.

LITTLE HAVANA
ENTERING LITTLE ITALY
COLONIAL HILL CEMETERY
SUNSET
HISTORIC
CHINATOWN
PLAYGROUND
R.I.P. JOE
RIP JILL

Figure 510-4 Diversity of social settings.

Political Context:

Design ideas will evolve from thoughtful examination of the natural, built, and social setting, but a complex and contradicting array of administrative, operational, regulatory, and legal issues can compromise a design (Figure 510-5). Designing solely to meet these regulations often produces nothing of present or enduring value. This is particularly true regarding the design and placement of furniture in public spaces where a great number of functional, visual, and regulatory factors coincide.

The nature of the setting, whether a public square or a corporate courtyard, implies major differences in the choice of design elements. Public streets and spaces are susceptible to incidences of vandalism, and are also periodically *abandoned* by revenue-starved local governments. Lastly, issues of long-term maintenance, public safety, and circulation control require careful consideration.

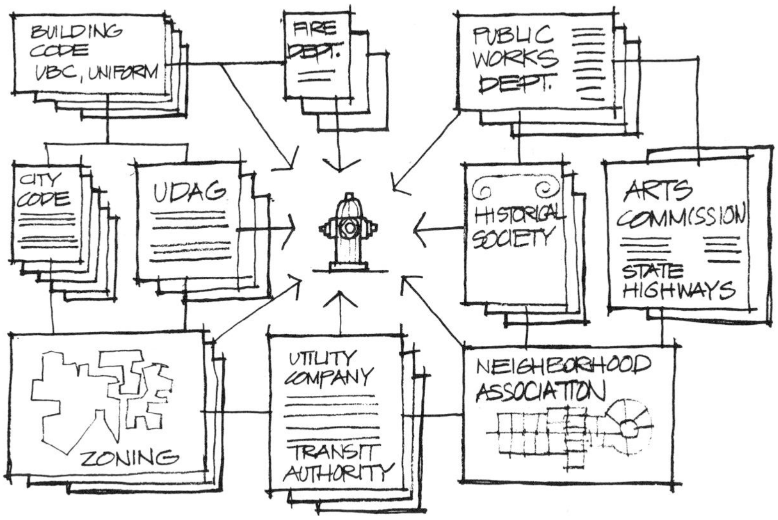
BUILDING CODE UBC, UNIFORM
FIRE DEPT.
PUBLIC WORKS DEPT.
CITY CODE
UDAG
HISTORICAL SOCIETY
ARTS COMMISSION
STATE HIGHWAYS
ZONING
UTILITY COMPANY
TRANSIT AUTHORITY
NEIGHBORHOOD ASSOCIATION

Figure 510-5 Diversity of regulatory standards.

2.2 Physical Factors

Climate:

Different climates and/or dramatic seasonal changes can significantly influence the design of site furniture and the consequent comfort of the users. Figure 510-6 shows typical climate factors. Designs appropriate to Florida in July are usually not appropriate to Ontario in January. A thorough understanding of the consequences of seasonal variation, including both advantages and disadvantages, is an essential prerequisite for the design of site furnishings.

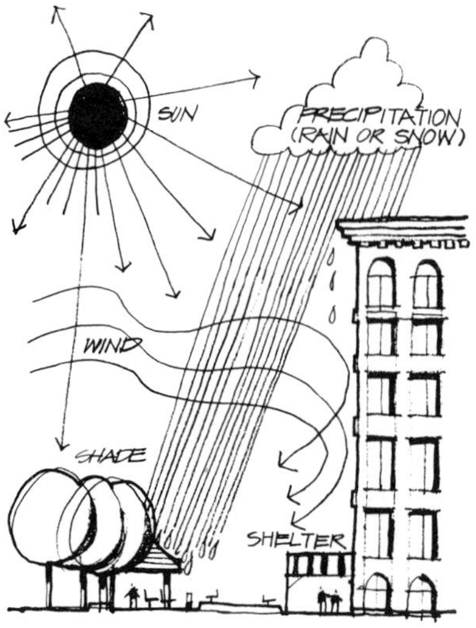
SUN
PRECIPITATION
(RAIN OR SNOW)
WIND
SHADE
SHELTER

Figure 510-6 Climatic factors.

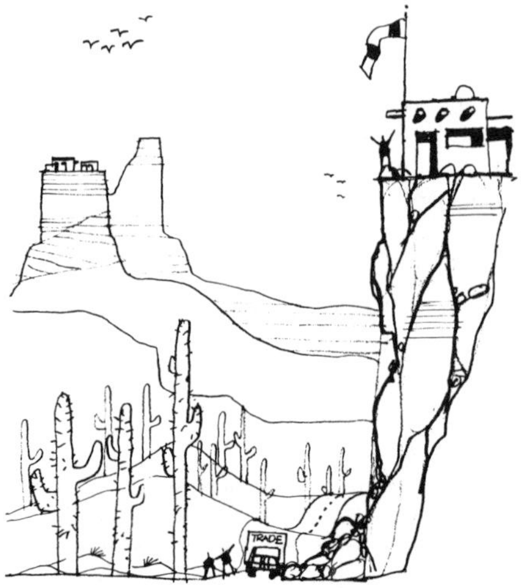
TRADE

Figure 510-7 Physiographic factors.

Physiography:

There are distinctive qualities about all parts of the world's landscapes that require careful consideration when designing and placing site furniture. Particular landforms, vegetation, and other qualities which give an area its special regional or local character should be responded to in a congruent manner (Figure 510-7). For instance, in the United States the building vernacular of the Rocky Mountains is distinctly different from that of the Appalachian Highlands. Special attention should be given to examining local landscapes and materials before translating program requirements into built elements.

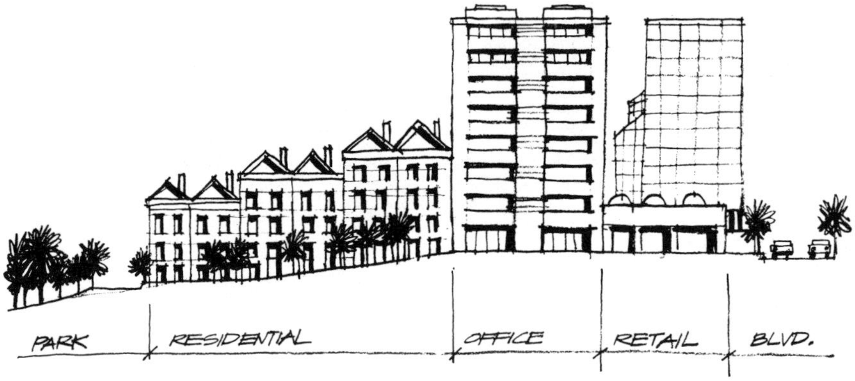
PARK
RESIDENTIAL
OFFICE
RETAIL
BLVD.

Figure 510-8 Built environment.

Built Environment:

Site furnishings can strengthen the link between a development and its surroundings, can personalize the setting, and can enhance the positive aspects of the surrounding built landscape.

A careful inventory of the existing built environment should precede decisions of scale, pattern, color, sequence, age, quality, materials, and construction detailing. Figure 510-8 illustrates the typical mix of uses and settings to which furnishing systems must relate.

Furniture elements should reflect the character of the built environment, be internally integrated between themselves, and not promote a cluttered appearance. In any streetscape, for instance, effective site furniture design and placement can resolve a chaotic scene of light standards, parking meters, mailboxes, newspaper stands, and trash receptacles. There should be a balance between the visual importance of individual furniture elements and their compatibility within the visual context of the setting. It is important to incorporate the vistas, views, and visual composition of the entire site.

2.3 Environmental Factors

Individual site furniture elements should meet several environmental criteria (Figure 510-9). These are described below.

Temperature:

Heat: The climate of a particular area is a key consideration when trying to determine whether permanent, partial, or temporary shade and glare reduction measures are needed. Furniture elements, such as permanent benches, should not be placed near extensive areas of paving or wall surfaces which reflect or radiate excessive amounts of heat, unless adequately buffered by shade, etc.

Benches, handles, and handrails exposed to full sunlight should be nonmetallic and/or light in color to remain comfortable to the touch.

Cold: In regions subject to cool weather, site furniture should be placed to take advantage of natural *sun traps,* thereby extending the usefulness of the site. Materials which absorb and radiate heat are advantageous in cold climates. Darkly colored, smoothly textured materials will inhibit snow and ice accumulation.

Furniture should be designed to minimize water or ice accumulation. For some elements of furniture it may be necessary periodically to shut down service on the site or totally remove the furniture. Such factors should be considered when selecting each item. Consult with manufacturers to determine the all-weather value of various products.

Materials used in cold climates should not become brittle when cold, especially in locations where they may be stressed by normal use. Most cast metals and some kinds of plastics should be carefully analyzed before being used in cold climates. Fasteners and joints should also be able to withstand stresses caused by expansion and contraction of the materials.

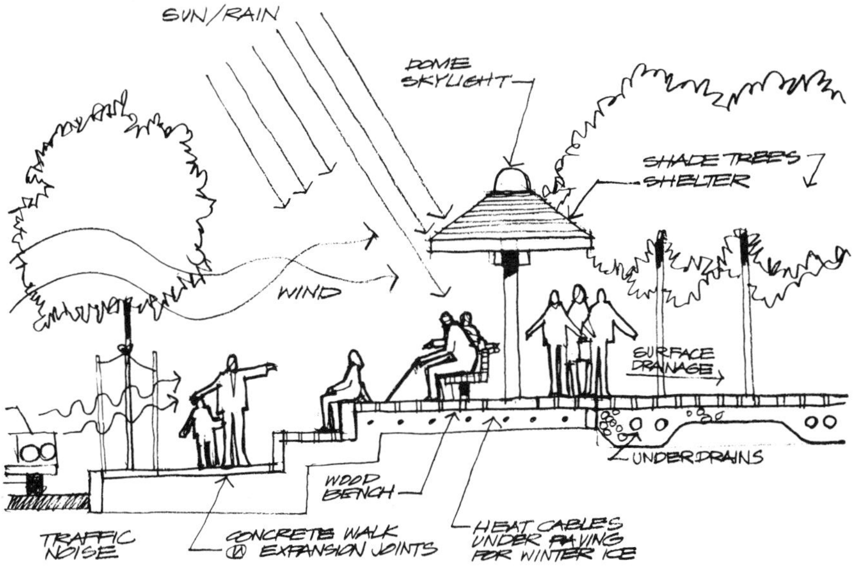
SUN/RAIN
DOME SKYLIGHT
SHADE TREES
SHELTER
WIND
SURFACE DRAINAGE
UNDERDRAINS
WOOD BENCH
TRAFFIC NOISE
CONCRETE WALK @ EXPANSION JOINTS
HEAT CABLES UNDER PAVING FOR WINTER ICE

Figure 510-9 Environmental factors.

48" - 72"
(1.2 - 1.8m)
± 24"
(0.6m) CLR
± 20"
(0.5m) CLR
VARIES
± 36" - 60"
PASSENGER AUTO (0.9-1.5m)
JOE
± 6' AVER.
(1.8m)
± 5'6" AVER.
(1.7m)
VARIES

Figure 510-10 Human dimensions.

Precipitation:

Rain: In regions subject to rain and/or snowfall, some of the site furniture used for sitting should be placed in sheltered locations.

Benches should drain well; they could be constructed of nonabsorptive materials to promote rapid drying. They should also be located to take advantage of the warming effects of sunlight. In humid climates, it is essential that all materials be naturally decay- and fungus-resistant, or specially treated to minimize mildew, rot, and consequent staining.

Snow: Logical placement of site furniture in areas of high snowfall will depend on the methods to be used for snow removal. Areas where snow is trapped or stockpiled should be identified before locating furniture so that furniture can be designed and located to avoid damage from snow removal equipment. Maneuvering space and clearances should be provided so that major pedestrian ways can remain open to all essential access points.

Adequate drainage is essential for carrying off snowmelt and preventing ice formation. Furniture should be located where winter sunlight can help to melt the snow.

Wind:

In areas subject to strong prevailing winds, site furniture (benches, tables, etc.) should be located to minimize any negative gusting impacts upon users. Patterns of snow drifting should be studied to minimize its accumulation on furniture.

In warm climates, furniture can be located to take advantage of natural cooling breezes. Trees can provide shade and, to some extent, control the movement of air.

Light:

Site furniture should take advantage of the quality and character of light available on the site.

Wherever possible, minimize the glare from light fixtures and intense sunlight. Recognizing that light conditions change both daily and seasonally, locate furniture and especially outdoor signs in such a way as to minimize the glare from them caused by low sun angles on wet, frosted, or otherwise reflective surfaces.

Noise:

The sounds of songbirds, children, street performers, and the like can be so pleasant that site furniture may be focused toward the source. Reciprocally, undesirable sounds can be blocked. Sound barrier walls, earth mounds, and other techniques of noise control should be considered. (Refer to Section 660: Sound Control, for more information.)

2.4 Operational Factors

Human Body Dimensions and Movement:

The physical dimensions and movement characteristics of the human body are essential determinants for the design of all types of site furniture. These common denominators set all working distances and operational dimensions in the design of furniture components and their aggregate layout. Figure 510-10 illustrates basic human dimensions used for design applications. Sections 210: Spatial Standards, and 340: Pedestrian Circulation, include additional information on human dimensions and movement.

Regulatory Standards:

Site furniture must also stand up to a host of regulatory standards imposed by municipal, state, and federal governments. Nowhere are these more profuse (and contradictory) than in urban public rights-of-way, where the greatest number of jurisdictional domains overlap. For example, typical standards deal with required light intensities for pedestrians and vehicles, light fixture mounting heights, the proximity of trees to utility poles and underground utilities, traffic signalization, signage and control systems, intersection setbacks, wheelchair ramp gradients and placement, the height of mailboxes, the width of vehicular lanes, turning radii, curbside usage, and even the size of garbage cans (Figure 510-11).

These regulations require careful scrutiny rather than slavish adherence in order to achieve a quality result. The designer must understand the purpose and rationale for the regulation, and then be able to interpret its most appropriate application and be prepared to negotiate creatively.

The vast number of off-the-shelf components available are subject to the same regulatory criteria. In some cases, they may be neither adaptable nor appropriate.

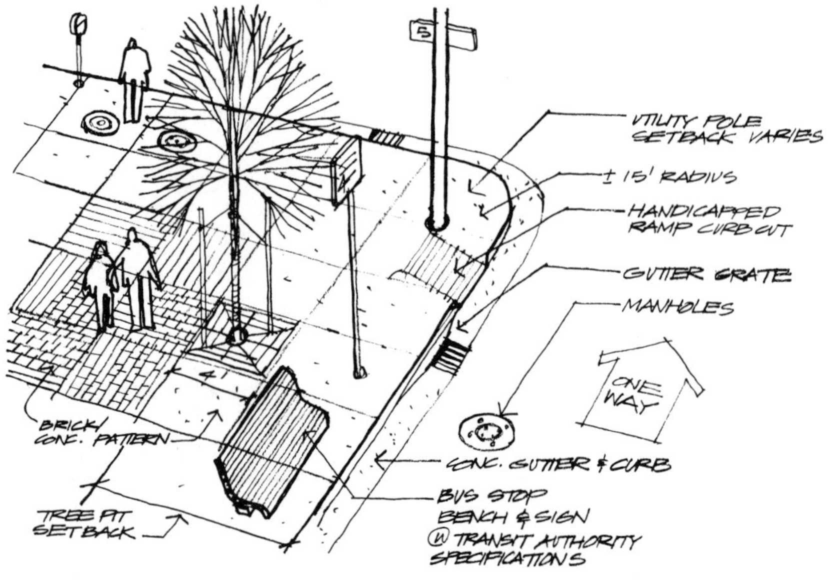
UTILITY POLE SETBACK VARIES
± 15' RADIUS
HANDICAPPED RAMP CURB CUT
GUTTER GRATE
MANHOLES
ONE WAY
CONC. GUTTER & CURB
BUS STOP BENCH & SIGN @ TRANSIT AUTHORITY SPECIFICATIONS
BRICK/CONC. PATTERN
TREE PIT SETBACK

Figure 510-11 Regulatory standards.

3.0 DESIGN CONSIDERATIONS

3.1 Selection Process

Figure 510-12 illustrates how site furniture and features can be selected by careful evaluation of stated site objectives and use criteria.

These objectives and needs are matched with a range of alternatives, such as whether to select the elements from existing ready-made sources, make modifications to such manufactured designs, or develop a new design.

Key factors in the process of either selecting ready-made or custom designing elements are: (1) availability of each unit, (2) maintenance requirements, (3) initial and lifetime costs, and (4) whether the solution will be consistent with the overall design of the project.

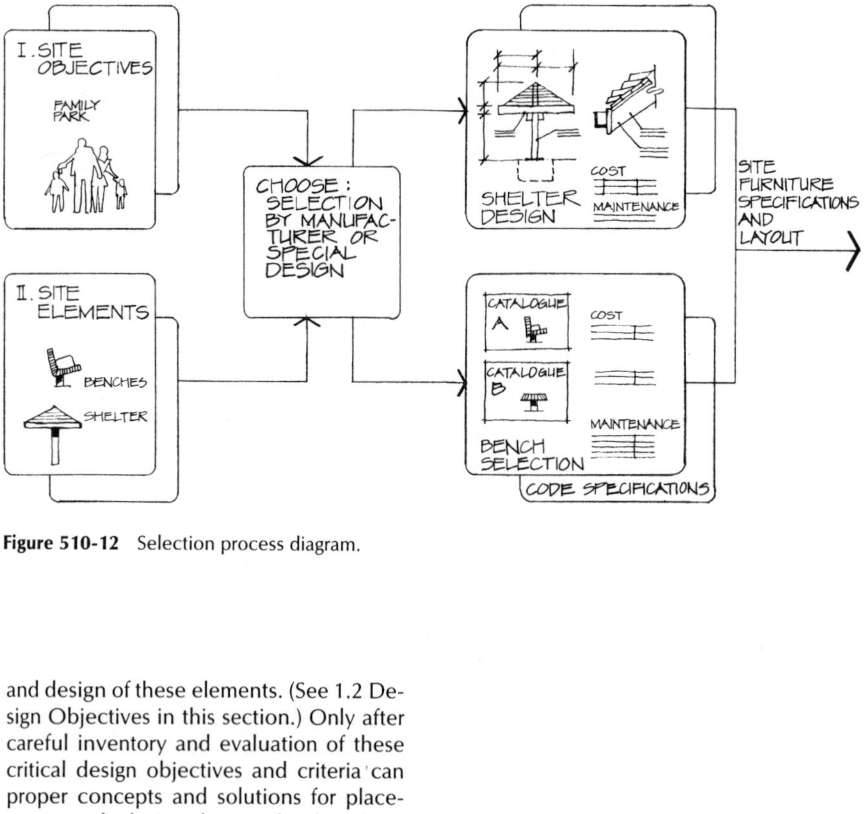
I. SITE OBJECTIVES
FAMILY PARK
II. SITE ELEMENTS
BENCHES
SHELTER
CHOOSE: SELECTION BY MANUFACTURER OR SPECIAL DESIGN
COST
MAINTENANCE
SHELTER DESIGN
CATALOGUE A
CATALOGUE B
BENCH SELECTION
CODE SPECIFICATIONS
SITE FURNITURE SPECIFICATIONS AND LAYOUT

Figure 510-12 Selection process diagram.

3.2 Design Elements

The categories of design elements summarized in Figures 510-13 through 510-21 illustrate a range of designs, materials, and uses of site furniture for various purposes. These figures show basic components of each element, along with generic examples. To aid the designer further, diagrams and notes illustrating site concepts are included.

Appropriateness is the key to the siting and design of these elements. (See 1.2 Design Objectives in this section.) Only after careful inventory and evaluation of these critical design objectives and criteria can proper concepts and solutions for placement and design be made for these elements.

REFERENCES

Halprin, Lawrence. *Cities,* MIT Press, Cambridge, MA, 1972. ■

SEATING

SEATING

Principles of design should emphasize:

1. Comfort.
2. Simplicity of form.
3. Simplicity of detail.
4. Ease of maintenance.
5. Durability of finish.
6. Resistance to vandalism.

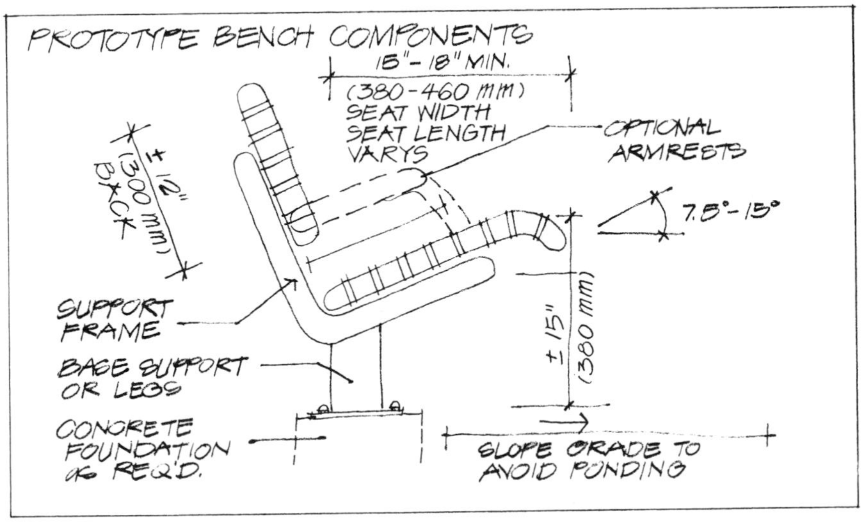
PROTOTYPE BENCH COMPONENTS
15"-18" MIN.
(380-460 mm)
SEAT WIDTH
SEAT LENGTH VARYS
OPTIONAL ARMRESTS
± 12" (300 mm) BACK
7.5°-15°
SUPPORT FRAME
BASE SUPPORT OR LEGS
± 15" (380 mm)
CONCRETE FOUNDATION AS REQ'D.
SLOPE GRADE TO AVOID PONDING

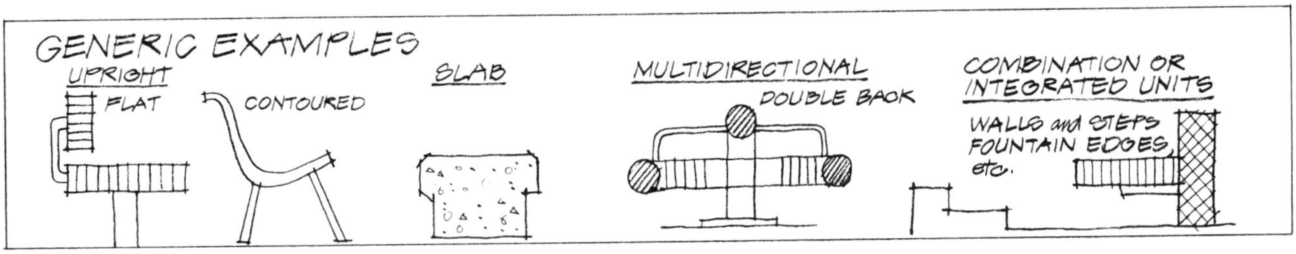
GENERIC EXAMPLES
UPRIGHT
FLAT
CONTOURED
SLAB
MULTIDIRECTIONAL
DOUBLE BACK
COMBINATION OR INTEGRATED UNITS
WALLS and STEPS FOUNTAIN EDGES, etc.

SITE OBJECTIVES

Seating should be sited so as to:

1. Be sheltered from wind.
2. Take advantage of site views.
3. Be situated back of circulation paths.
4. Provide a variety of options for pedestrians, such as:
   - Sunlight
   - Shade
   - Quietude
   - Activity
   - Formality
   - Informality

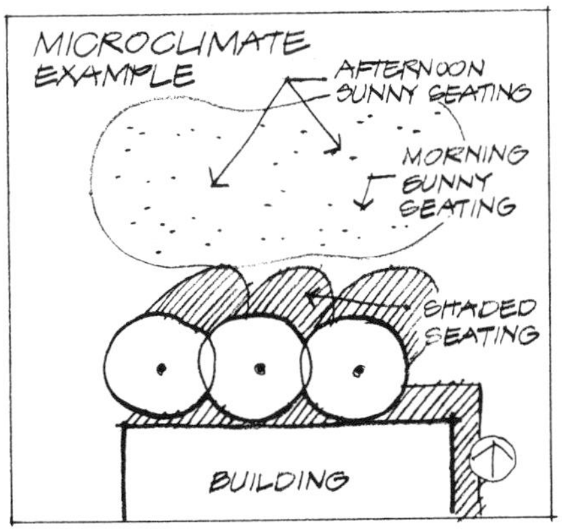
MICROCLIMATE EXAMPLE
AFTERNOON SUNNY SEATING
MORNING SUNNY SEATING
SHADED SEATING
BUILDING

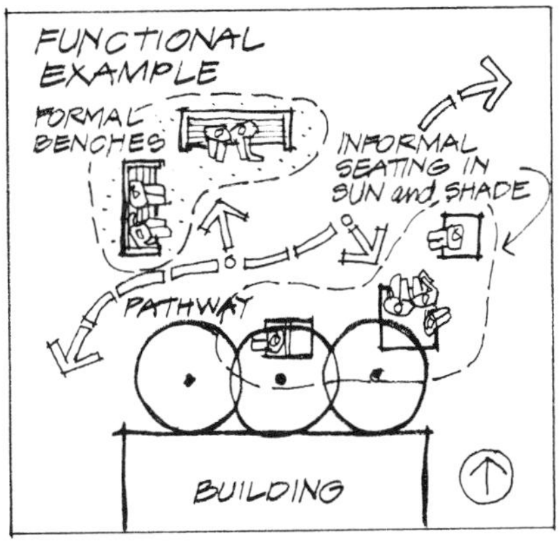
FUNCTIONAL EXAMPLE
FORMAL BENCHES
INFORMAL SEATING IN SUN and SHADE
PATHWAY
BUILDING

CONTEXT

Seating elements are important elements of an environment and should be designed to be compatible with all other elements of the site. Seating elements include:

1. Benches
2. Stoops
3. Ledges
4. Seat walls
5. Steps

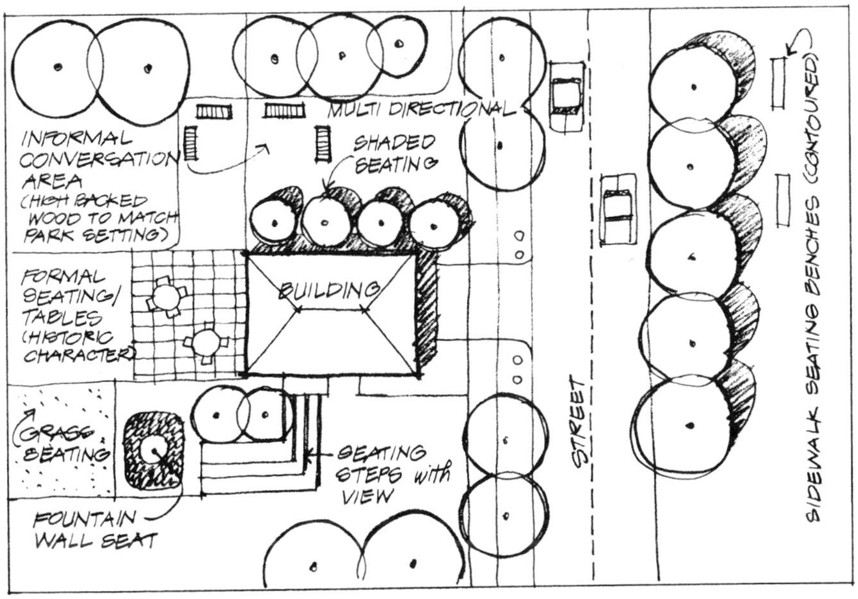
MULTI DIRECTIONAL
INFORMAL CONVERSATION AREA (HIGH BACKED WOOD TO MATCH PARK SETTING)
SHADED SEATING
FORMAL SEATING/ TABLES (HISTORIC CHARACTER)
BUILDING
GRASS SEATING
SEATING STEPS with VIEW
FOUNTAIN WALL SEAT
STREET
SIDEWALK SEATING BENCHES (CONTOURED)

Figure 510-13 Seating.

SHELTER

SHELTERS

Shelters diversify the use of a site by accommodating elements that require weather protection, such as:

1. Graphic displays
2. TV monitors

Types of shelters range from very modest structures, such as picnic shelters, to very elaborate structures, such as bandstands.

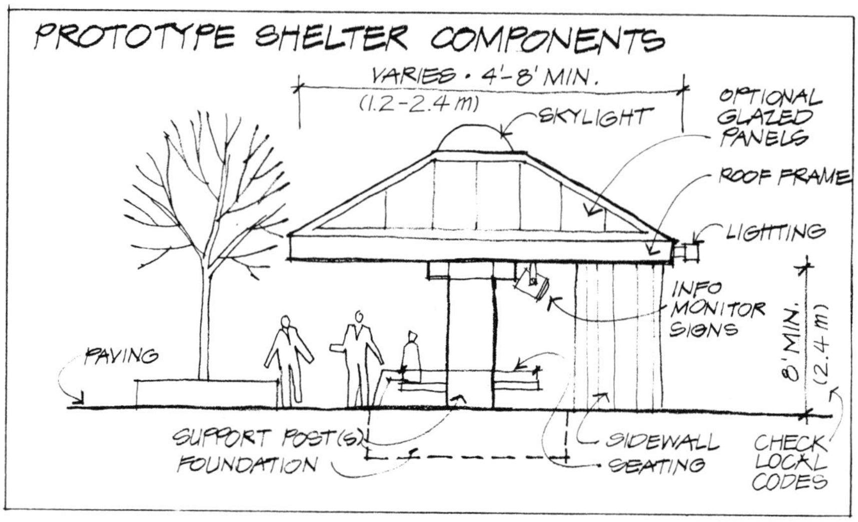

PROTOTYPE SHELTER COMPONENTS
VARIES • 4'-8' MIN.
(1.2-2.4 m)
SKYLIGHT
OPTIONAL GLAZED PANELS
ROOF FRAME
LIGHTING
INFO MONITOR SIGNS
8' MIN.
(2.4 m)
PAVING
SUPPORT POST(S)
FOUNDATION
SIDEWALL
SEATING
CHECK LOCAL CODES

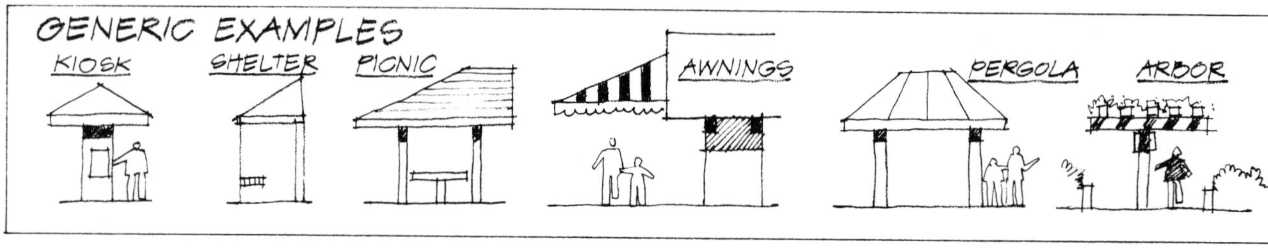

GENERIC EXAMPLES
KIOSK
SHELTER
PICNIC
AWNINGS
PERGOLA
ARBOR

SITE OBJECTIVES

Shelters provide:

1. Protection against inclement weather.
2. A focal point for site activities.
3. Transitional areas between outdoors and indoors.

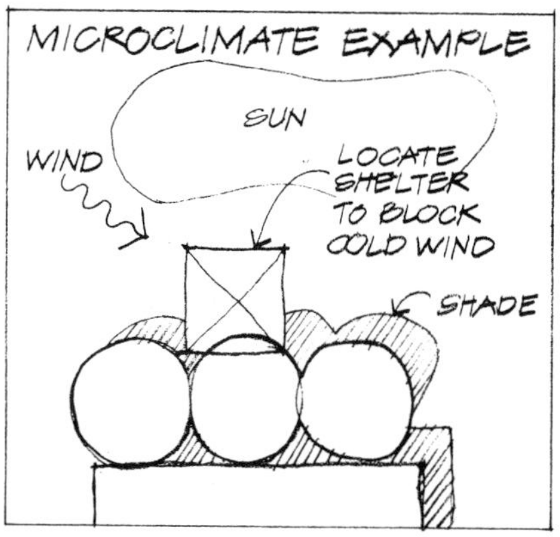

MICROCLIMATE EXAMPLE
SUN
WIND
LOCATE SHELTER TO BLOCK COLD WIND
SHADE

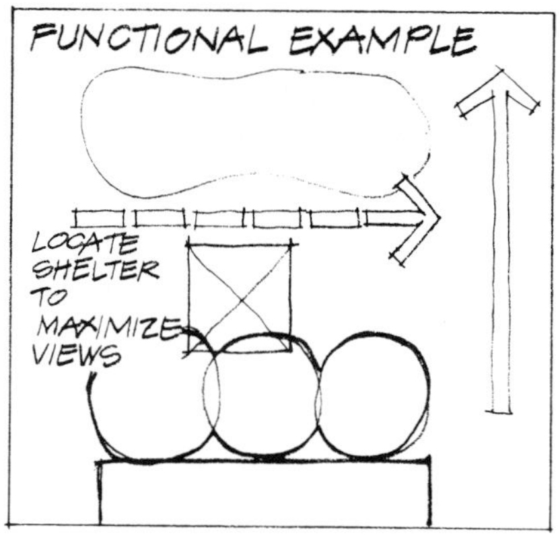

FUNCTIONAL EXAMPLE
LOCATE SHELTER TO MAXIMIZE VIEWS

CONTEXT

Shelters are often major elements of a site. They can be used as a visual reference to the historical or cultural character of a place. The choice of an appropriate design idiom should reflect an understanding of the social and cultural forces that have given the place its unique identity.

Because shelters often serve as focal points of a site, they should be:

1. Readily visible.
2. Easily accessible.
3. Sited to take advantage of views.
4. Sited adjacent to major pedestrian routes.

Figure 510-14 Shelter.

CONVENIENCE ELEMENTS

CONVENIENCE ELEMENTS

Convenience elements should be:

1. Easily recognizable.
2. Sited to reduce clutter.
3. Placed to facilitate easy access.

General zones are defined by access requirements.

ZONES

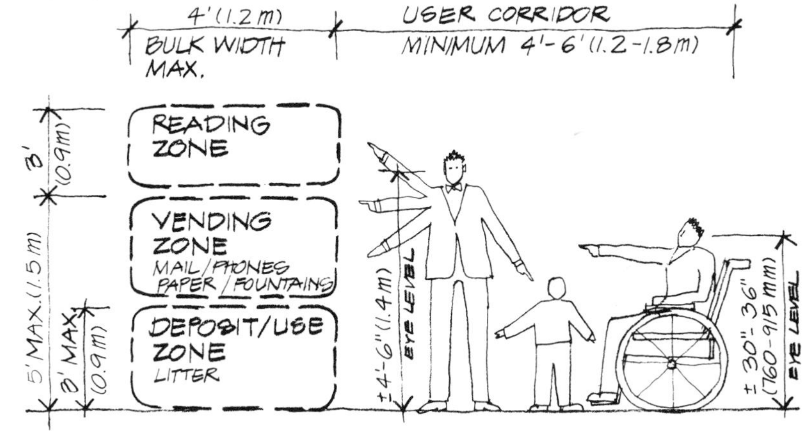
4' (1.2 m)
BULK WIDTH MAX.
USER CORRIDOR
MINIMUM 4'-6' (1.2-1.8 m)
READING ZONE
VENDING ZONE
MAIL/PHONES
PAPER/FOUNTAINS
DEPOSIT/USE ZONE
LITTER
3' (0.9 m)
5' MAX. (1.5 m)
3' MAX. (0.9 m)
± 4'-6" (1.4 m)
EYE LEVEL
± 30"-36" (760-915 mm)
EYE LEVEL

GENERIC EXAMPLES

DRINKING FOUNTAINS

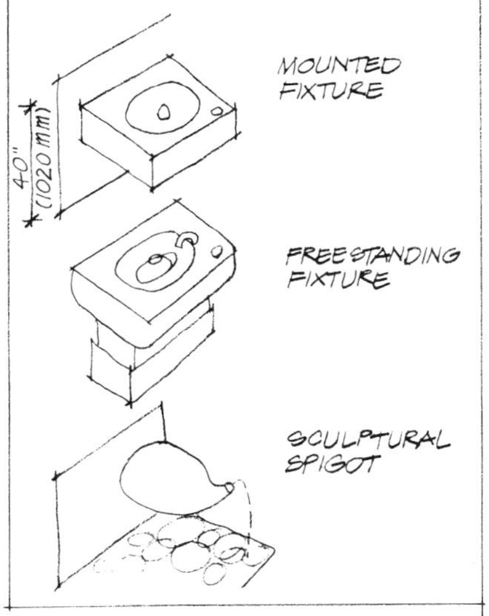
MOUNTED FIXTURE
40" (1020 mm)
FREESTANDING FIXTURE
SCULPTURAL SPIGOT

BIKE RACKS

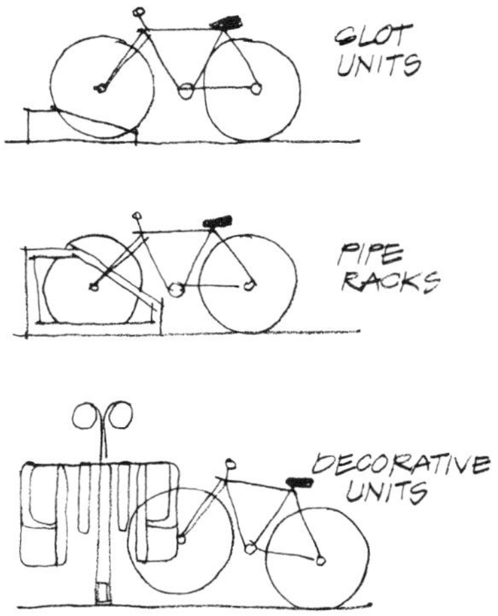
SLOT UNITS
PIPE RACKS
DECORATIVE UNITS

TRASH RECEPTACLES

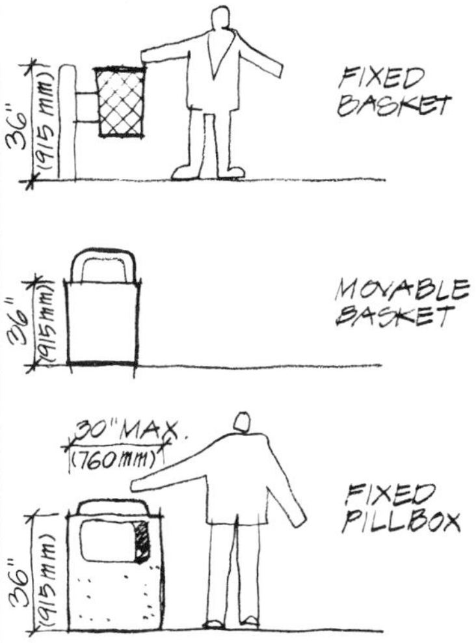
36" (915 mm)
FIXED BASKET
36" (915 mm)
MOVABLE BASKET
30" MAX. (760 mm)
36" (915 mm)
FIXED PILLBOX

CONTEXT

Consolidation of various convenience elements into a single larger structure can enhance the visual character of a site and provide a readily indentifiable feature within a busy streetscape. Convenience elements include:

1. Newspaper vendors
2. Telephones
3. Information stands
4. Mail deposit boxes

CONVENIENCE ELEMENTS WITHIN KIOSK

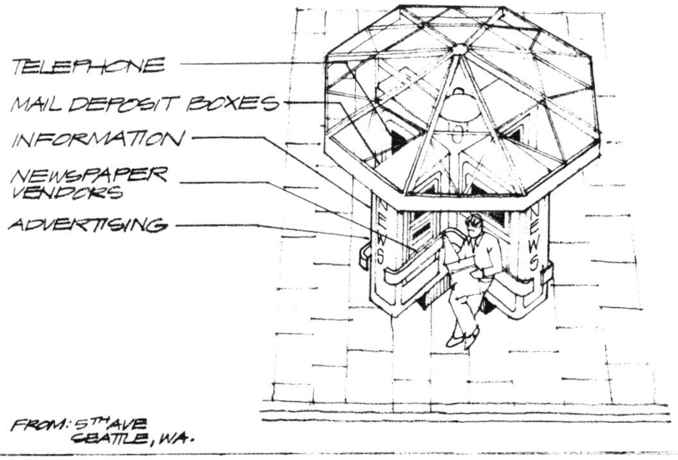
TELEPHONE
MAIL DEPOSIT BOXES
INFORMATION
NEWSPAPER VENDORS
ADVERTISING
NEWS
NEWS
FROM: 5TH AVE SEATTLE, WA.

Figure 510-15 Convenience elements.

INFORMATION

INFORMATION

Outdoor information can be grouped into four categories:

1. Directional
2. Locational
3. Identification
4. Display

The information should be formatted and placed within easy view of either the pedestrian or the motorist.

The primary mode of transportation, whether pedestrian or vehicular, will determine the optimum location and size of signs.

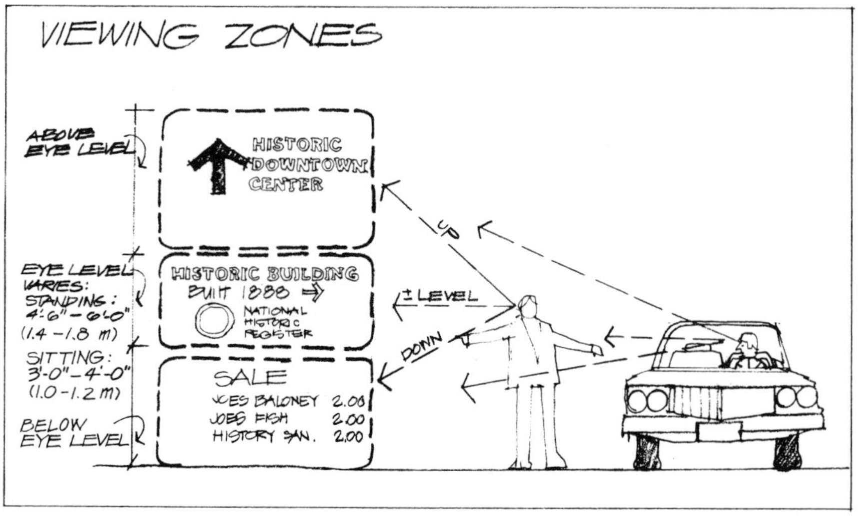

VIEWING ZONES
ABOVE EYE LEVEL
HISTORIC DOWNTOWN CENTER
EYE LEVEL VARIES:
STANDING: 4'-6"–6'-0" (1.4–1.8 m)
SITTING: 3'-0"–4'-0" (1.0–1.2 m)
BELOW EYE LEVEL
HISTORIC BUILDING BUILT 1888
NATIONAL HISTORIC REGISTER
SALE
JOES BALONEY 2.00
JOES FISH 2.00
HISTORY SAN. 2.00
UP
± LEVEL
DOWN

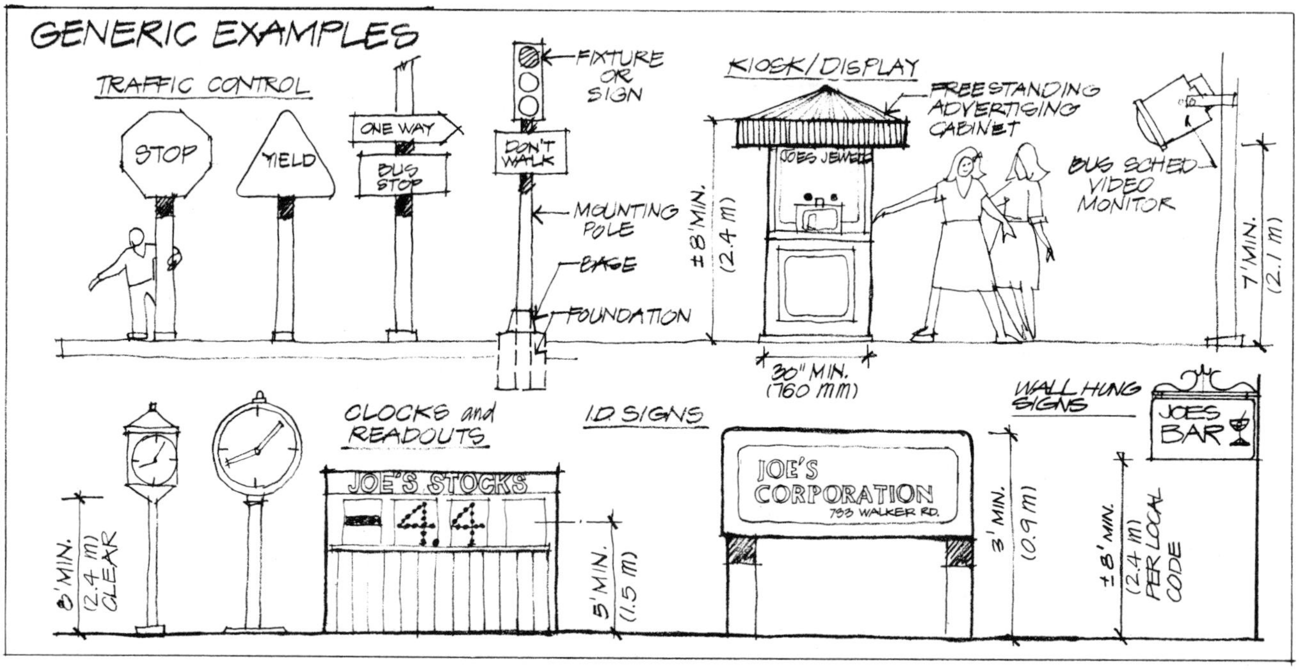

GENERIC EXAMPLES
TRAFFIC CONTROL
STOP
YIELD
ONE WAY
BUS STOP
FIXTURE OR SIGN
DON'T WALK
MOUNTING POLE
BASE
FOUNDATION
KIOSK/DISPLAY
FREESTANDING ADVERTISING CABINET
BUS SCHED. VIDEO MONITOR
±8' MIN. (2.4 m)
7' MIN. (2.1 m)
30" MIN. (760 mm)
CLOCKS and READOUTS
JOE'S STOCKS
8' MIN. (2.4 m) CLEAR
5' MIN. (1.5 m)
I.D. SIGNS
JOE'S CORPORATION
783 WALKER RD.
3' MIN. (0.9 m)
WALL HUNG SIGNS
JOES BAR
±8' MIN. (2.4 m) PER LOCAL CODE

CONTEXT

Because of its brief viewing time, signage aimed at vehicular traffic requires an especially clear hierarchy of lettering.

Sites such as industrial parks and suburban office centers, where circulation is exclusively vehicular, are places that require signage for:

1. Identification of the area
2. Directions within the compound
3. Identification of individual facilities within the compound

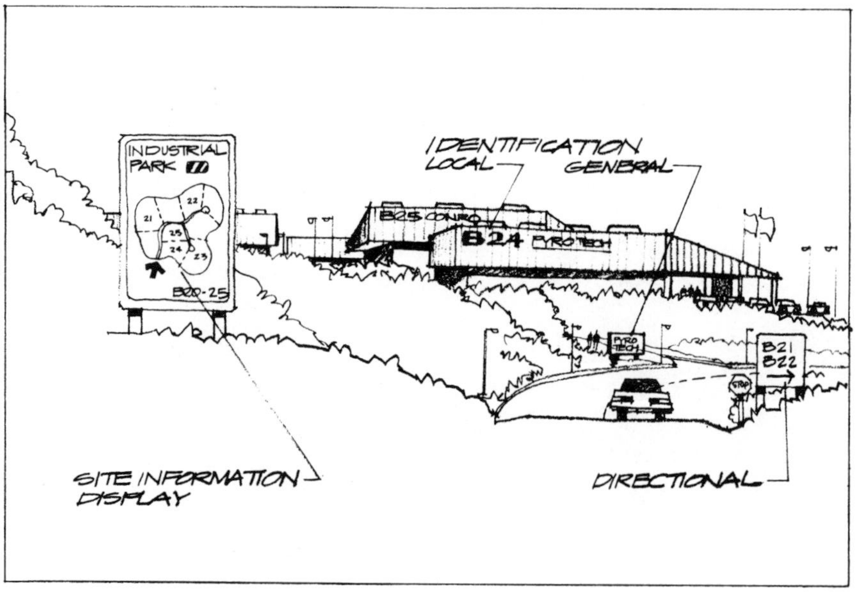

INDUSTRIAL PARK
IDENTIFICATION
LOCAL
GENERAL
B24
SITE INFORMATION DISPLAY
DIRECTIONAL

Figure 510-16 Information.

LIGHTING

LIGHTING

The height of light standards is the single factor that most directly determines the quality of the light and the consequent ambience of the site.

Exterior lighting can be generally categorized as:

1. Decorative lighting
2. Vehicular use lighting
3. General site lighting
4. Pedestrian use lighting
5. Feature lighting

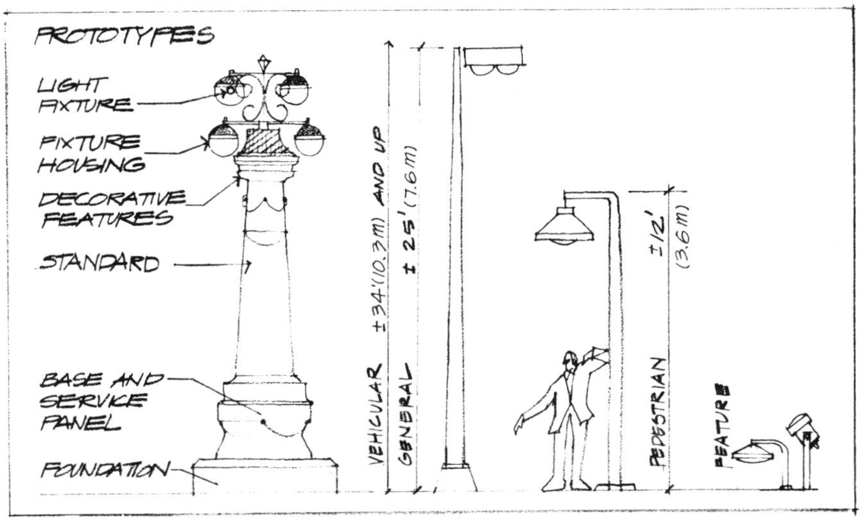
PROTOTYPES
LIGHT FIXTURE
FIXTURE HOUSING
DECORATIVE FEATURES
STANDARD
BASE AND SERVICE PANEL
FOUNDATION
VEHICULAR ±34'(10.3m) AND UP
GENERAL ± 25'(7.6m)
PEDESTRIAN ± 12' (3.6m)
FEATURE

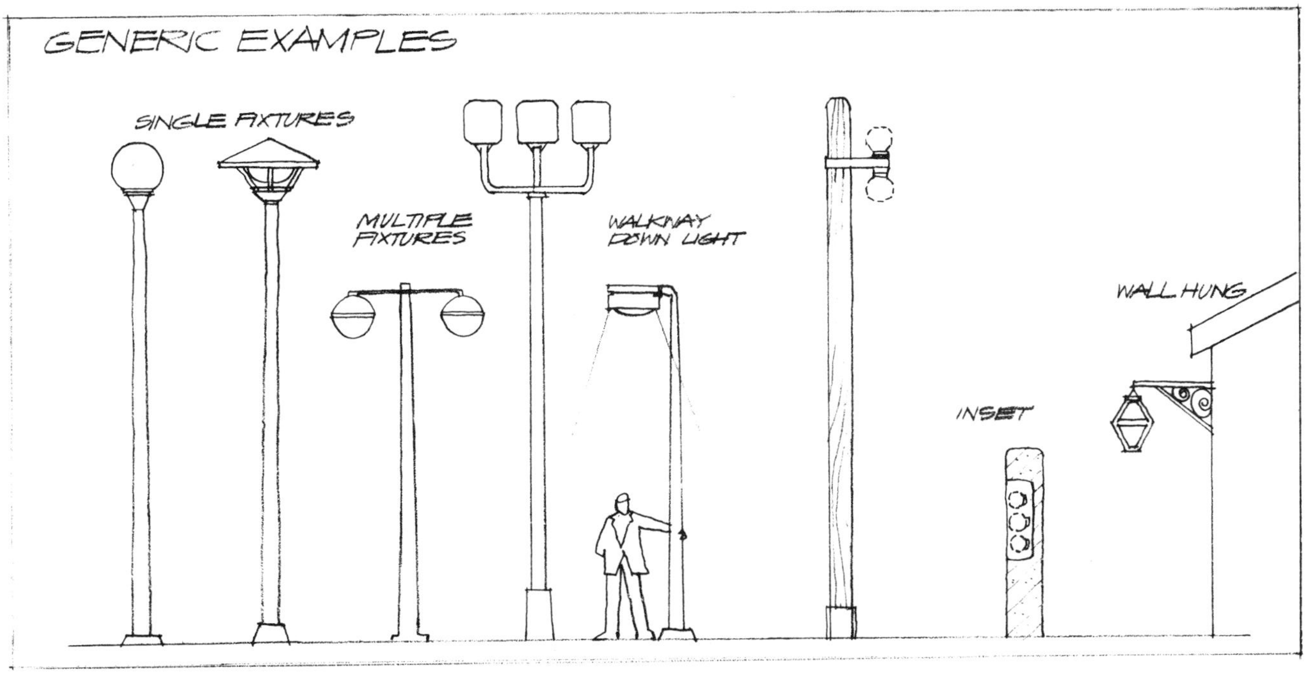
GENERIC EXAMPLES
SINGLE FIXTURES
MULTIPLE FIXTURES
WALKWAY DOWN LIGHT
INSET
WALL HUNG

CONTEXT

Lighting must be functionally appropriate and properly scaled to both the pedestrian and the vehicular precincts of the site. For pedestrian area lighting, the light source should be relatively low to the ground in order to remain in scale with the human body and to provide light beneath the canopy of street trees. Uniform area illumination is not always desirable.

Vehicular light standards on roadways must have much greater height than those for pedestrians and must illuminate the road more uniformly.

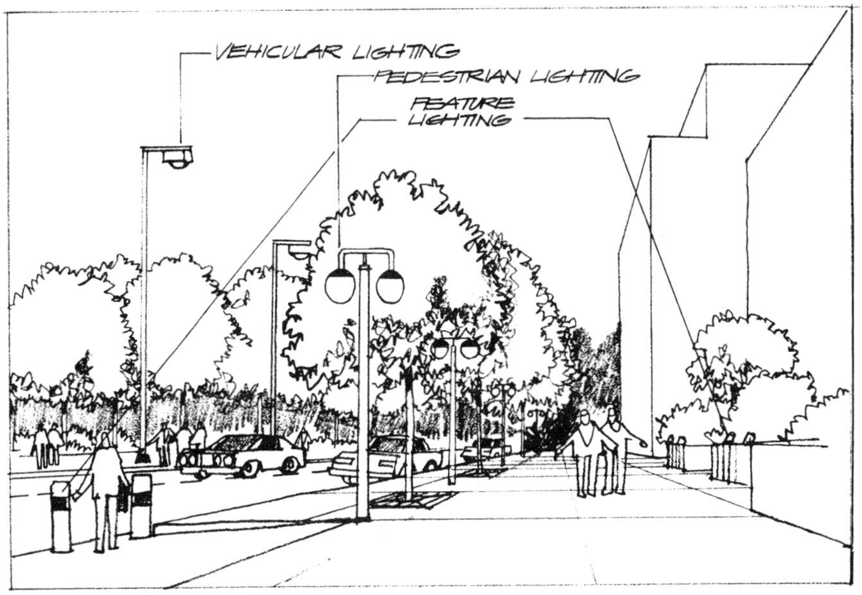
VEHICULAR LIGHTING
PEDESTRIAN LIGHTING
FEATURE LIGHTING

Figure 510-17 Lighting.

TRAFFIC CONTROL AND PROTECTION

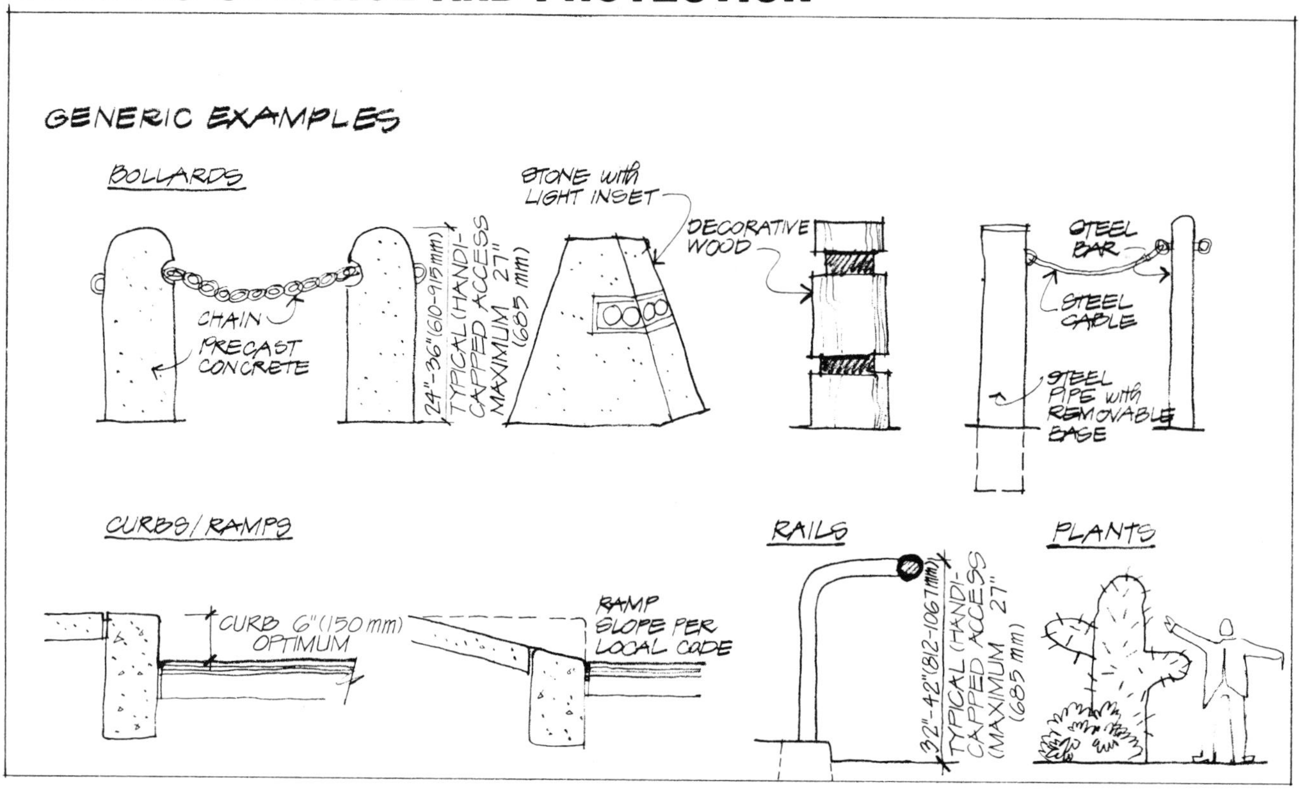
GENERIC EXAMPLES
BOLLARDS
CHAIN
PRECAST CONCRETE
24"-36" (610-915 mm) TYPICAL (HANDI-CAPPED ACCESS MAXIMUM 27" (685 mm))
STONE with LIGHT INSET
DECORATIVE WOOD
STEEL BAR
STEEL CABLE
STEEL PIPE with REMOVABLE BASE
CURBS/RAMPS
CURB 6" (150 mm) OPTIMUM
RAMP SLOPE PER LOCAL CODE
RAILS
32"-42" (812-1067 mm) TYPICAL (HANDI-CAPPED ACCESS MAXIMUM 27" (685 mm))
PLANTS

TRAFFIC CONTROL AND PROTECTION

A variety of elements are used to meet the general objectives of traffic control and protection.

Elements to warn both pedestrians and motorists of each other's presence include:
(1) Paving material changes; (2) Bollards; (3) Grade changes

Elements to preclude pedestrian entry include: (1) Railings; (2) Kick rails; (3) Walls; (4) Hedges

Elements to preclude vehicular entry include: (1) Steep banks; (2) Planted areas; (3) Steps; (4) Guard railings

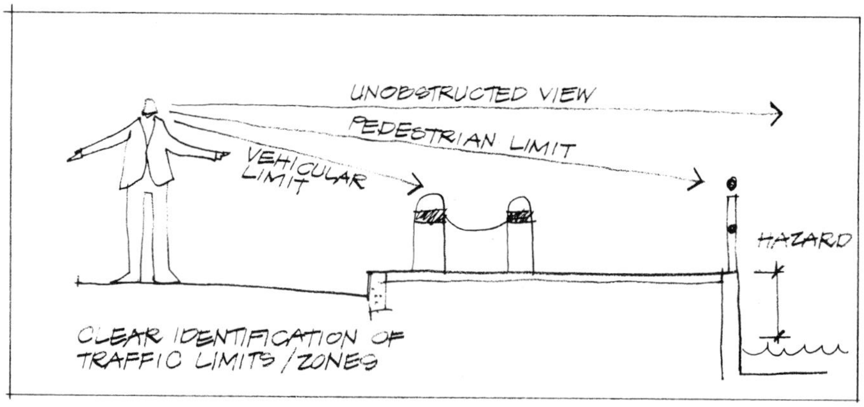
UNOBSTRUCTED VIEW
PEDESTRIAN LIMIT
VEHICULAR LIMIT
HAZARD
CLEAR IDENTIFICATION OF TRAFFIC LIMITS/ZONES

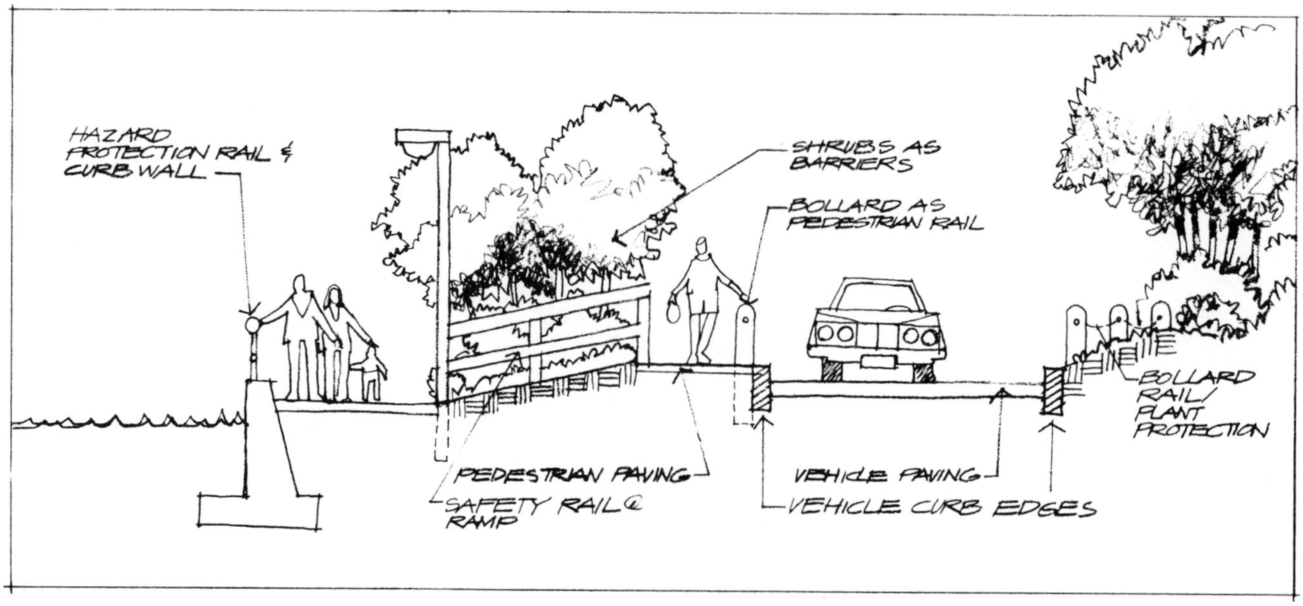
HAZARD PROTECTION RAIL & CURB WALL
SHRUBS AS BARRIERS
BOLLARD AS PEDESTRIAN RAIL
BOLLARD RAIL/ PLANT PROTECTION
PEDESTRIAN PAVING
SAFETY RAIL @ RAMP
VEHICLE PAVING
VEHICLE CURB EDGES

Figure 510-18 Traffic control and protection.

UTILITIES

SURFACE UTILITY ELEMENTS

The urban floor contains underground utility systems and vault structures that often restrict the placement of site furniture features.

Access to these utilities and structures is provided by means of metal covers and grates, which in themselves are a feature of the urban floor.

Many utility fixtures, such as fire hydrants and traffic signalization controls, can be spatially constraining.

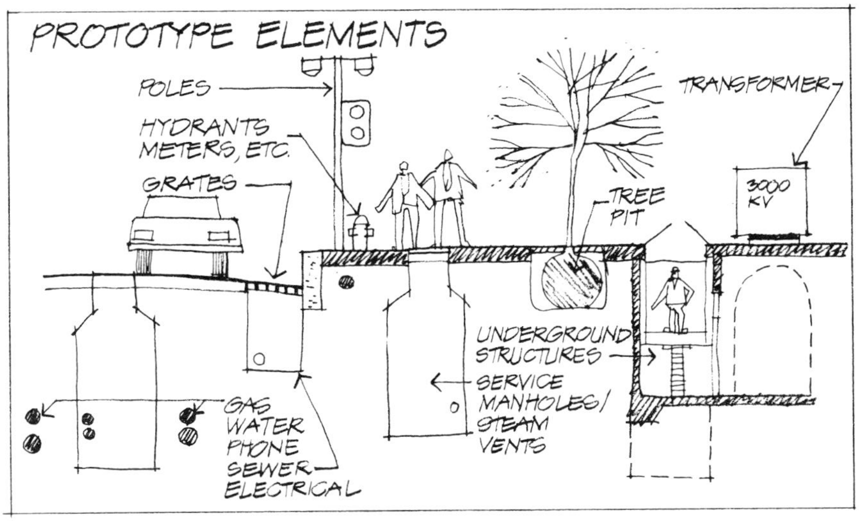

PROTOTYPE ELEMENTS
POLES
HYDRANTS METERS, ETC.
GRATES
TRANSFORMER
3000 KV
TREE PIT
UNDERGROUND STRUCTURES
SERVICE MANHOLES/ STEAM VENTS
GAS WATER PHONE SEWER ELECTRICAL

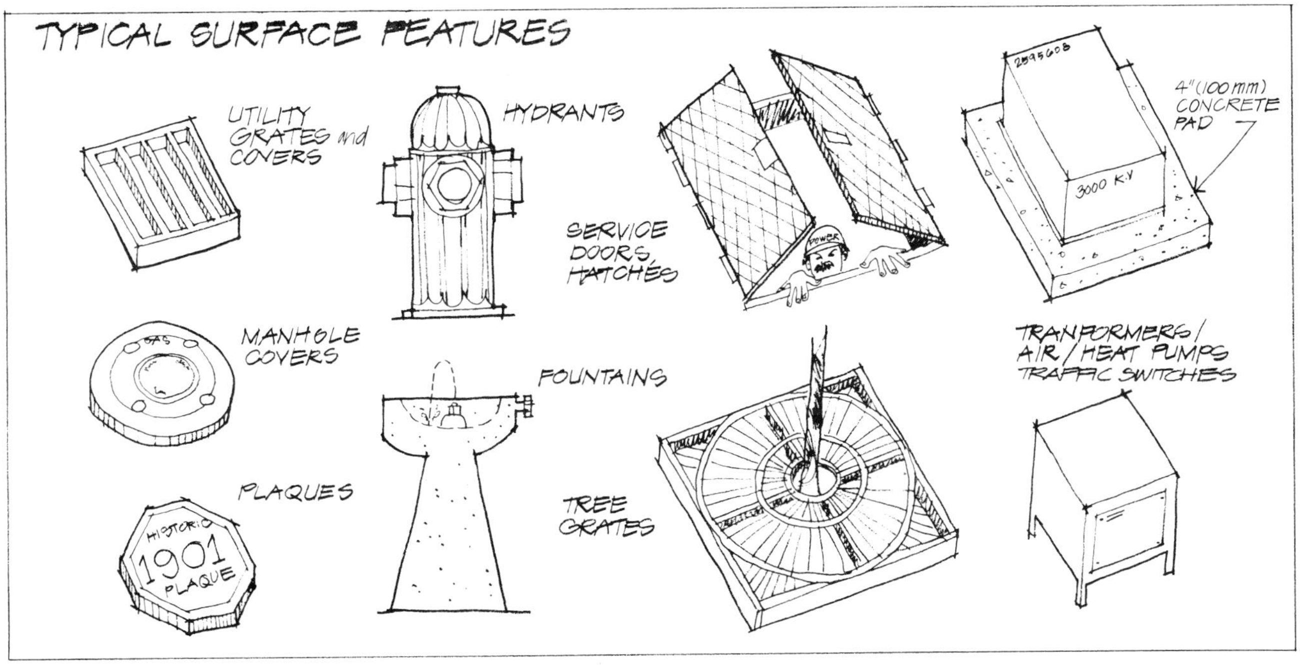

TYPICAL SURFACE FEATURES
UTILITY GRATES and COVERS
HYDRANTS
SERVICE DOORS, HATCHES
4" (100 mm) CONCRETE PAD
3000 K.V
MANHOLE COVERS
FOUNTAINS
TRANFORMERS/ AIR/HEAT PUMPS TRAFFIC SWITCHES
PLAQUES
HISTORIC 1901 PLAQUE
TREE GRATES

CONTEXT

Ideally, the heavily used pedestrian core should be kept relatively free from utility covers. Where this is not possible, utility covers can be incorporated as part of the total floor pattern.

Gratings and cover plates are available in many attractive patterns. The custom design of decorative covers can commemorate past events or themes that are of particular local significance.

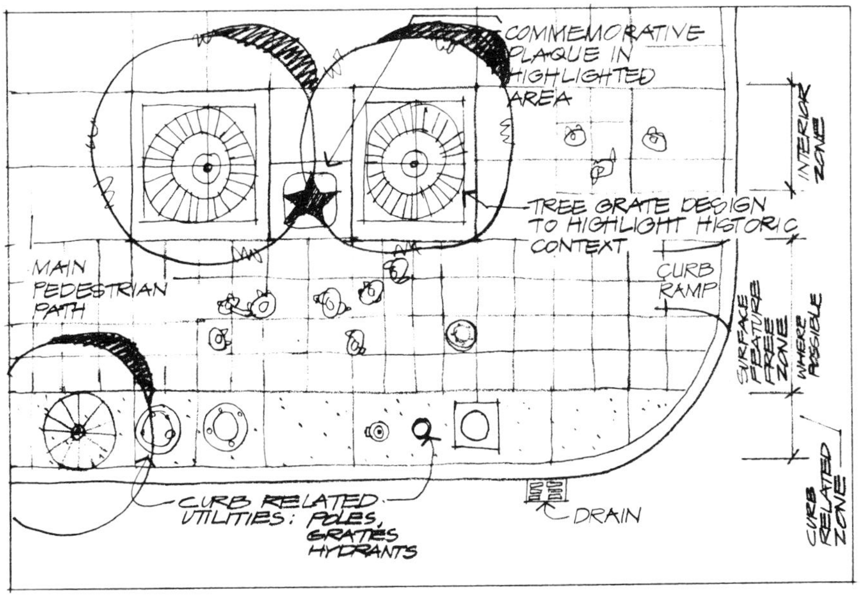

COMMEMORATIVE PLAQUE IN HIGHLIGHTED AREA
INTERIOR ZONE
TREE GRATE DESIGN TO HIGHLIGHT HISTORIC CONTEXT
MAIN PEDESTRIAN PATH
CURB RAMP
SURFACE FEATURE FREE ZONE
WHERE POSSIBLE
CURB RELATED UTILITIES: POLES, GRATES HYDRANTS
DRAIN
CURB RELATED ZONE

Figure 510-19 Utilities.

SEASONAL ELEMENTS

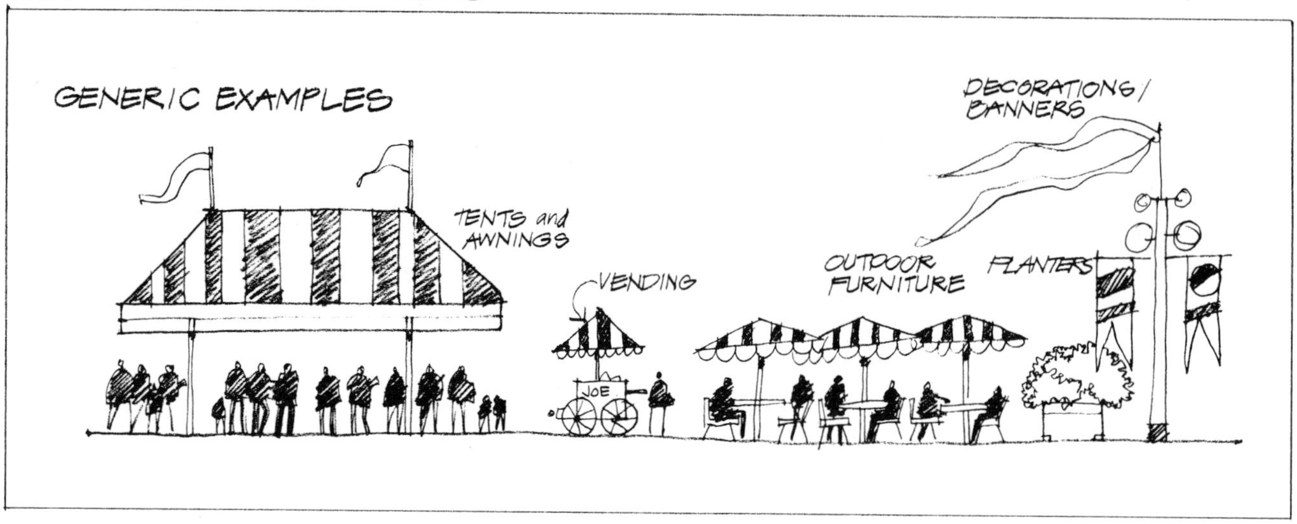
GENERIC EXAMPLES
DECORATIONS/ BANNERS
TENTS and AWNINGS
VENDING
OUTDOOR FURNITURE
PLANTERS
JOE

SEASONAL ELEMENTS

Seasonal elements can significantly enliven a place. Their appearance signals an event. These elements include:

1. Temporary structures
2. Vending wagons
3. Outdoor furniture
4. Planting tubs

Seasonal elements:

1. Require a flexible site layout.
2. Work well when they augment established year-round facilities.
3. Should be sited to conform to the basic circulation structure of the site.
4. Should be readily visible and accessible.

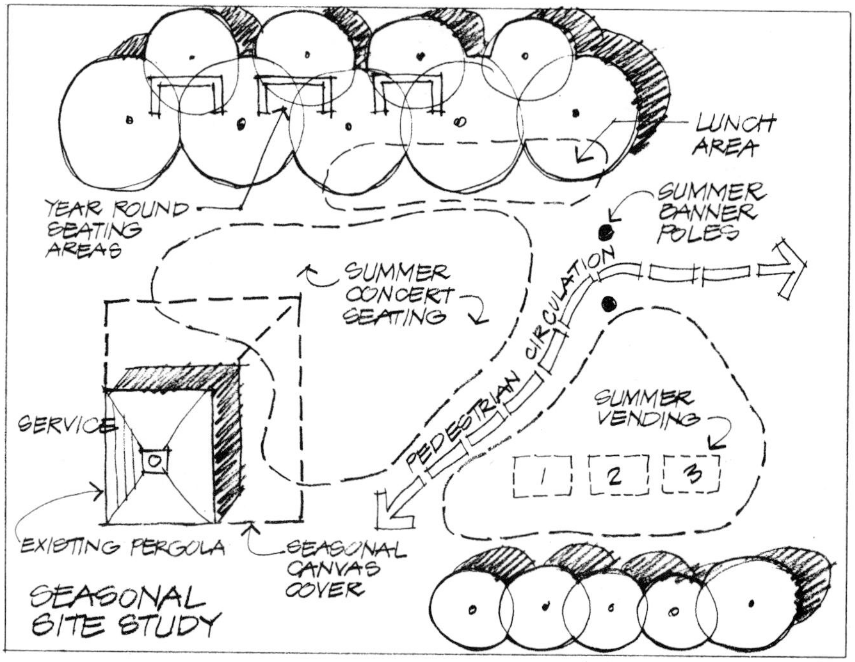
LUNCH AREA
YEAR ROUND SEATING AREAS
SUMMER BANNER POLES
SUMMER CONCERT SEATING
PEDESTRIAN CIRCULATION
SERVICE
SUMMER VENDING
1
2
3
EXISTING PERGOLA
SEASONAL CANVAS COVER
SEASONAL SITE STUDY

Figure 510-20 Seasonal elements.

SPECIAL FEATURES

SPECIAL FEATURES

Special features are unique site elements that can be used to commemorate significant cultural and social events for the community. They present a unique opportunity for the designer to incorporate:

1. Indigenous materials.
2. Local historical resources.
3. Local cultural resources.

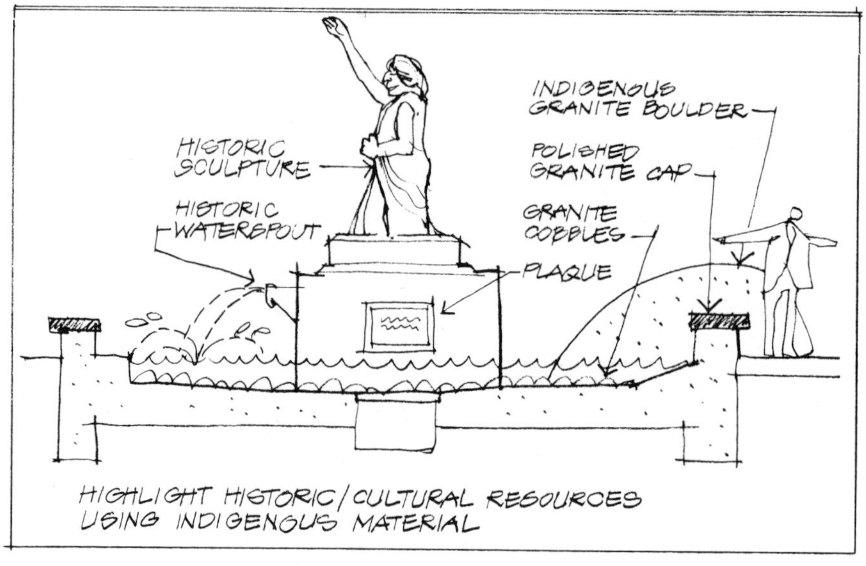
INDIGENOUS GRANITE BOULDER
HISTORIC SCULPTURE
POLISHED GRANITE CAP
HISTORIC WATERSPOUT
GRANITE COBBLES
PLAQUE
HIGHLIGHT HISTORIC/CULTURAL RESOURCES USING INDIGENOUS MATERIAL

Figure 510-21 Special features.

section 520: Recreational and Athletic Facilities

CREDITS

Contributors:

James D. Mertes, Ph.D.
Department of Park Administration and Landscape Architecture
Texas Tech University
Lubbock, Texas

Kay Hutmacher
Department of Park Administration and Landscape Architecture
Texas Tech University
Lubbock, Texas
currently with Katherine S. Hutmacher, ASLA
Fresno, California

Gene Schrickel, Terry Cheek, and Victor Baxter
Schrickel, Rollins and Associates
Arlington, Texas

Research Assistants:

Robert B. Ruth
E. Brian Bristow

Reviewers:

Albert J. Rutledge, Professor and Chairman
Department of Landscape Architecture
Iowa State University
Ames, Iowa

Monty L. Christiansen, Associate Professor
Department of Recreation and Parks
Pennsylvania State University
University Park, Pennsylvania

ACKNOWLEDGEMENT

The authors would like to acknowledge the aid and insight provided by Mr. Ernie Ralston, landscape architect, Marshall, Maklin, Monaghan Limited, Edmonton, Alberta; and Mr. Garrett Gill, Department of Park Administration and Landscape Architecture, Texas Tech University, Lubbock, Texas, and David Gill Corporation (golf course architect), St. Charles, Illinois.

CONTENTS

1.0 INTRODUCTION

The standards for play, recreational, and athletic facilities in this section represent the state of the art as developed by agencies, organizations, manufacturers, and various interest groups.

By definition, *recreation* represents any rational human activity that results in a pleasurable response, at any time or place or circumstance, with attendant enriching physical, intellectual, or emotional benefits, within the constraints of individual morality and/or social acceptability (Doell and Twardzik, *Elements of Park and Recreation Administration*). Participation in recreational and athletic activities involves virtually every age group and segment of society from children to senior citizens, including those who are infirm, incarcerated, or physically and/or mentally handicapped. Physical activities go beyond exercise and athletic programs for youth and professional teams to embrace every interest, physical stature, and level of skill. A vast, almost endless array of new activities, equipment, and instructional programs are constantly appearing.

1.1 Trends in Recreational Orientation

In North America, several changes are occurring within the national recreation participation profile. First is the reduction in travel to distant recreational and tourism destinations, with the emphasis shifting to an increased use of city, county, and regional parks. Family-oriented activities within the home community are on the increase.

The introduction of new equipment and activities has resulted in a greater popularization of sports activities among all groups and ages. Activities such as jogging and weight training, for example, are now popular among both men and women.

A 1973–1979 study of the popularity of participation in sports in the United States revealed some interesting trends in activity popularity. Table 520-1 shows the shifts in the top 30 sports.

TABLE 520-1
1979 Popularity of Participation Sports (Top 30 Rankings)

Activity	*1973*	*1976*	*1979*
Swimming	1	1	1
Bicycling	2	2	2
Camping	4	4	3
Fishing	3	3	4
Bowling	5	5	5
Boating (other than sailing)	8	7	6
Jogging, running*	—	—	7
Tennis	12	9	8
Pool, billiards	7	6	9
Softball	9	10	10
Table tennis	6	8	11
Roller skating	—	—	12
Basketball	11	11	13
Hunting	13	13	14
Ice skating	10	12	15
Water skiing	17	17	16
Golf	14	14	17
Snow skiing	20	18	18
Baseball	15	15	19
Football	16	16	20
Racquetball†	—	24	21
Motorbiking, motorcycling	18	19	22
Sailing	21	21	23
Snowmobiling	19	20	24
Soccer*	—	—	25
Handball†	—	23	26
Archery	22	22	27
Paddle tennis†	—	26	28
Ice hockey	23	25	29
Platform tennis†	—	27	30

* Not measured in 1973 and 1976.

† Not measured in 1973.

Source: R. J. Halstenrud, "Trends in Participation Sports during the Decade of the 70's," in *Proceedings: 1980 National Outdoor Recreation Trends Symposium,* Vol. II. U.S. Department of Agriculture, 1980.

1.2 Standards

The standards for recreational and athletic facilities are expressed in many ways. This section describes the *design* standards established for many activities. These standards are compiled from numerous sources and range from rigid dimensions to suggestions derived from experience. Adherence to standards assures the user of continuity in his experience, regardless of location. Conversely, the designer needs to be sensitive to necessary adjustments in the standards as demanded by the local conditions, budget, and clientele.

1.3 General Concepts in Facility Design

The purpose of this section is to provide standards for the development of outdoor recreational facilities. In all facility design it is important to consider the following factors as they relate to *all* types of recreational facilities.

Safety and Security:

User safety and security should be paramount concerns of the designer and administrator. Ultimately, user satisfaction with a facility is related to how safe and secure the users feel. Safety concerns will be addressed for each activity. Strategies for discouraging vandalism and increasing security must be incorporated into the planning, design, construction, operation, and maintenance of a facility. (Site security is treated as a special topic under Section 230: Safety and Security.)

Provision for Elderly and Handicapped Users:

Any persons with temporary or permanent limitations on their motor activity or sense perceptions should be able to gain access to recreational facilities. The primary concerns of the designer with regard to handicapped users are access, mobility, and safety. (Refer to Sections 240 and 241 for more information.)

The References at the end of this section provide more detailed information on design modifications of specialized recreational facilities.

Maintenance and Operations:

The daily operations and maintenance of facilities are critical to user satisfaction. The maintenance administration can be centralized or decentralized, depending upon the size, character, location, and use level of the facilities.

Maintenance facilities usually include: administrative headquarters, shop and covered storage, open-air or bulk storage, garage and/or service parking, and sometimes greenhouses and nursery space. These areas are best located out of view but should remain easily accessible by motor vehicles. Operations facilities may in some instances have an interpretive and/or educational value, as for example the kitchen and veterinary facilities in a zoo. In this case, controlled public access may be sought or at least permitted.

Parking:

Standards for parking vary with each type of activity. A common average in North America is 2.5 to 3 persons per automobile. Parking areas for facilities that attract large crowds (such as sports stadiums) can be designed to accommodate other activities, such as basketball or tennis, and these areas can be used for overflow parking.

Signage:

Signage should be coordinated to provide essential information and a design unity to an area. As illustrated by Figure 520-1, there are three categories of signs:

1. *Identification:* these signs are used for entrances and for identifying individual facilities within an area.

2. *Directional:* these signs channel the flow of visitors/users. They should be simple and placed in locations appropriate to the speed of the user.

3. *Regulatory:* these include regulations of speed, and other rules and regulations as needed. This information should be presented in a positive way.

WHITE WATER STATE PARK
ENTRANCE SIGN
• BEACH
• LODGE
DIRECTIONAL SIGN
YIELD
REGULATORY SIGN

Figure 520-1 Three major types of signs.

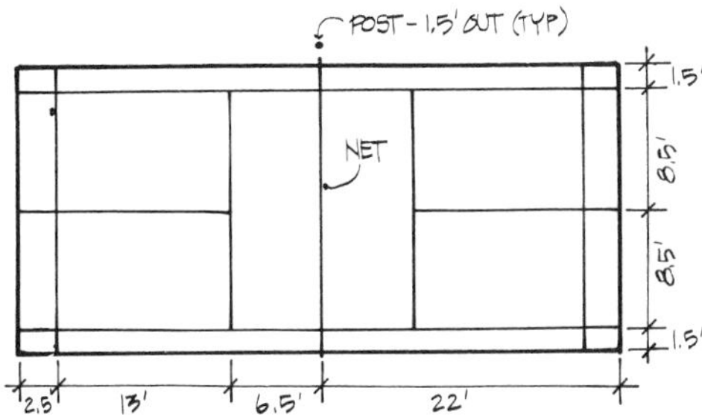
POST - 1.5' OUT (TYP)
NET
1.5'
8.5'
8.5'
1.5'
2.5'
13'
6.5'
22'

Figure 520-2 Badminton.

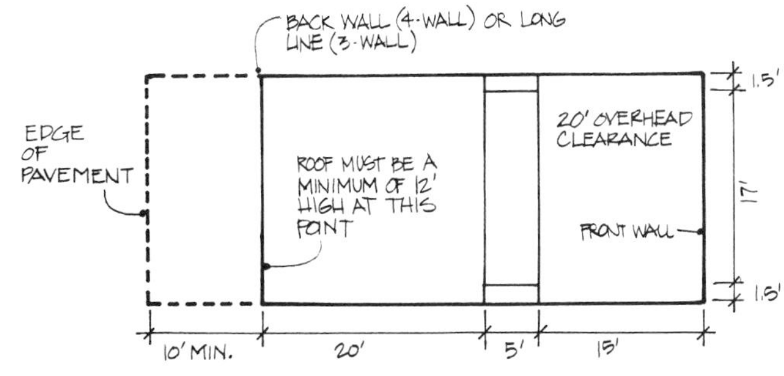
BACK WALL (4-WALL) OR LONG LINE (3-WALL)
EDGE OF PAVEMENT
ROOF MUST BE A MINIMUM OF 12' HIGH AT THIS POINT
20' OVERHEAD CLEARANCE
FRONT WALL
1.5'
17'
1.5'
10' MIN.
20'
5'
15'

Figure 520-3 Handball/racquetball.

2.0 COURT GAMES

2.1 General

Court games are sports played primarily on hard surfaces rather than on turf. The standards for courts vary, depending on whether competition is under the auspices of international, national, collegiate, or high school societies. Two organizations mentioned most extensively in this section are the International Amateur Athletic Federation (IAAF) and the National Collegiate Athletic Association (NCAA). For competition-quality court design, contact the organization setting the rules and standards. Major organizations in the United States are listed at the end of this section under Sports Organizations.

2.2 Basic Dimensions

Some facilities are provided primarily for popular enjoyment; therefore, their dimensions can be changed to fit the site, clientele, and/or budget. The standards shown in Figures 520-2 through 520-10 and Table 520-2 should thus be considered *desirable* rather than mandatory.

3.0 FIELD SPORTS

Field sports include any activities preferably played on soft (turf) surfaces. Much as for court games, the standards for field sports are to be considered *desirable*. Dimensions for quality fields should be verified with the governing organization. In

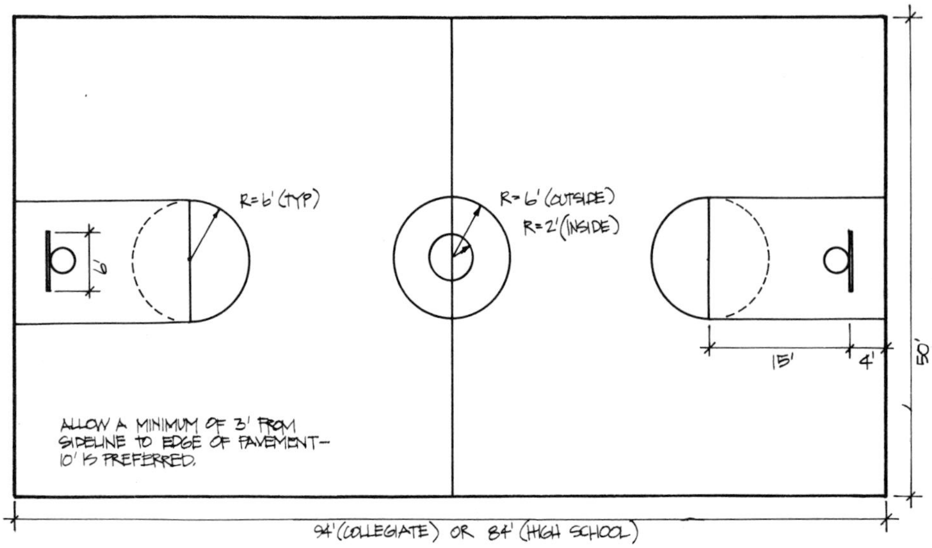

R=6' (TYP)
6'
R=6' (OUTSIDE)
R=2' (INSIDE)
15'
4'
50'
ALLOW A MINIMUM OF 3' FROM SIDELINE TO EDGE OF PAVEMENT—10' IS PREFERRED.
94' (COLLEGIATE) OR 84' (HIGH SCHOOL)

Figure 520-4 Basketball.

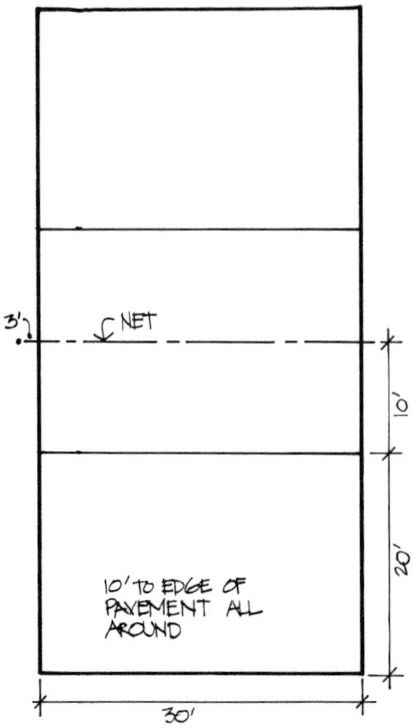

3'
℄ NET
10'
20'
10' TO EDGE OF PAVEMENT ALL AROUND
30'

NOTE: UNLESS OTHERWISE SPECIFIED, THE LAYOUT AND DIMENSIONS OF ALL COURTS ARE SYMMETRICAL AROUND THE CENTER LINES.

Figure 520-5 Volleyball.

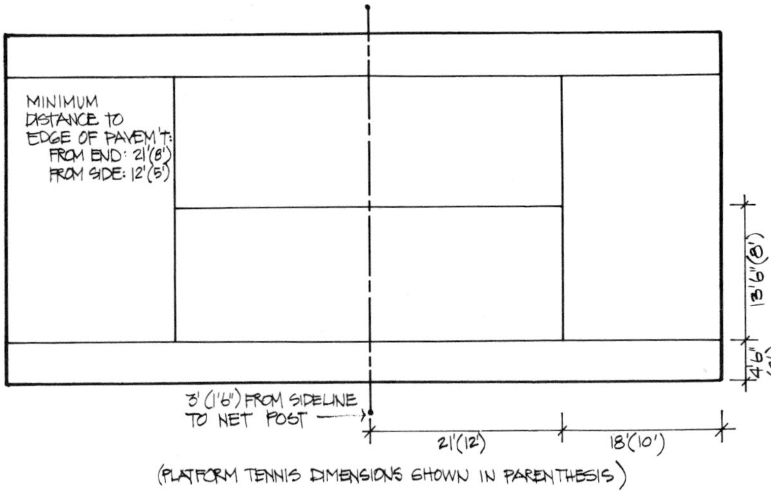

MINIMUM DISTANCE TO EDGE OF PAVEM'T:
FROM END: 21' (8')
FROM SIDE: 12' (5')
13'6" (8')
4'6" (2')
3' (1'6") FROM SIDELINE TO NET POST
21' (12')
18' (10')
(PLATFORM TENNIS DIMENSIONS SHOWN IN PARENTHESIS)

TENNIS NOTES:
TENNIS COURTS ARE OFTEN CONSTRUCTED IN BANKS OF 2+. ALLOW 10' (12' PREFERRED) BETWEEN COURTS.

LIGHTS SHOULD BE LOCATED A MINIMUM OF 12' FROM PLAY LINES. IN BATTERIES OF COURTS, NOT SEPARATED BY 24' POLES, SHOULD BE AT BACK FENCE AND NET LINE. ARRANGEMENT OF POLES DEPENDS ON TYPE AND SIZE OF LIGHT SOURCE.

Figure 520-6 Tennis.

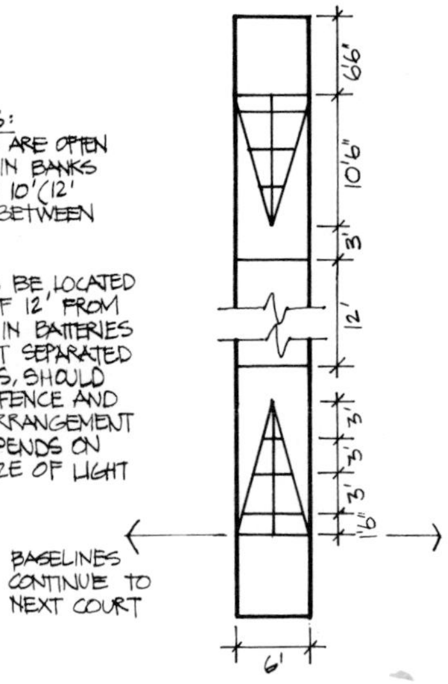

6'6"
10'6"
3'
12'
3'
3'
3'
1'6"
BASELINES CONTINUE TO NEXT COURT
6'

Figure 520-7 Shuffleboard.

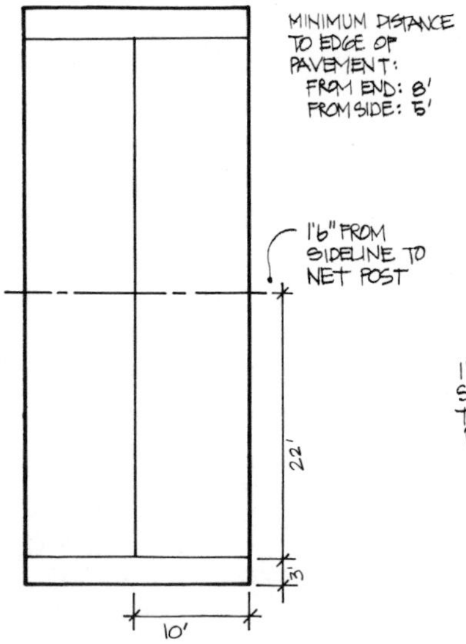

MINIMUM DISTANCE TO EDGE OF PAVEMENT:
FROM END: 8'
FROM SIDE: 5'
1'6" FROM SIDELINE TO NET POST
22'
3'
10'

Figure 520-8 Paddle tennis.

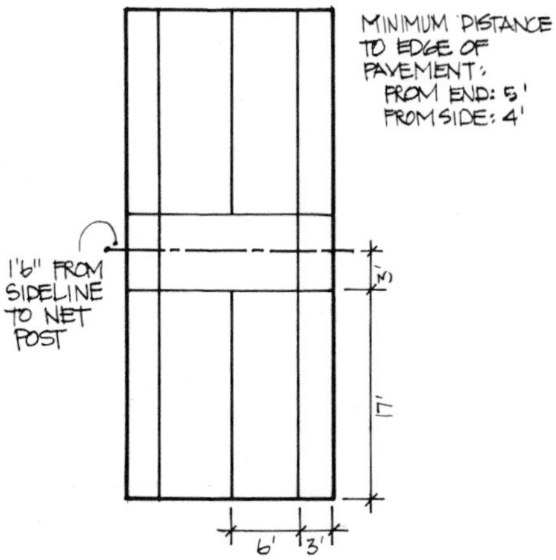

MINIMUM DISTANCE TO EDGE OF PAVEMENT:
FROM END: 5'
FROM SIDE: 4'
1'6" FROM SIDELINE TO NET POST
3'
17'
6'
3'

Figure 520-9 Deck tennis.

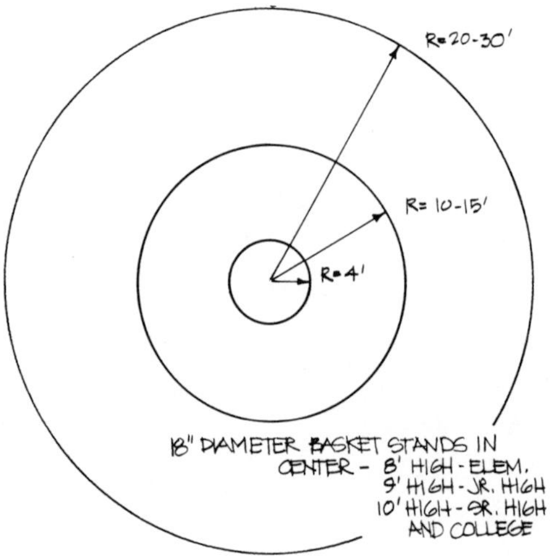

R=20-30'
R=10-15'
R=4'
18" DIAMETER BASKET STANDS IN CENTER - 8' HIGH - ELEM. 9' HIGH - JR. HIGH 10' HIGH - SR. HIGH AND COLLEGE

Figure 520-10 Goal-in.

TABLE 520-2
Court Games

Sport	Use area required including clear zones, ft	Court dimensions, ft	Orientation	Surface
Badminton				
Doubles	5-ft clear zones between courts and at end.	20 ft × 44 ft	Competition play is usually indoors. Outdoor courts long axis north-south.	Any hard surface or turf; drain as in tennis.
Singles	Same as doubles.	17 ft × 44 ft		(Same)
Basketball				
High school	104 ft × 70 ft.	84 ft × 50 ft	North-south.	Concrete, drain end to end at 1 in per 10 ft.
College	114 ft × 70 ft.	94 ft × 50 ft	(Same)	(Same)
International	18 m × 30 m.	14 m × 26 m	(Same)	(Same)
Goal-hi	60 ft × 60 ft to 80 ft × 80 ft.	Circle—40 ft to 60 ft in diameter	Optional.	Asphalt or synthetic; drain to edges.
Handball				
One wall	34 ft × 20 ft × 16-ft high.	34 ft × 20 ft × 16-ft high	Can be added to exteriors of gym or may be free standing.	Any hard surface; drain from front to rear.
Three or four walls	40 ft × 20 ft × 20-ft high.	40 ft × 20 ft × 20-ft high	Competition play normally indoors.	(Same)
Racquetball	See handball—same court is used.			
Shuffleboard	52 ft × 10 ft, including 4 ft between courts.	52 ft × 6 ft	Long axis north-south.	Hard/smooth concrete without expansion joints. Alley depressed and drained with catch basins.
Tennis	60 ft × 120 ft for one doubles court. Multiples can be designed with 10 to 12 ft between courts.	36 ft × 78 ft	Long axis north-south is OK; long axis 22 degrees west of north and east of south is better in southern latitudes.	Many, including concrete, clay, asphalt, and turf. Drain side to side (preferred) or end to end at 0.8 to 1% (nonporous) or 0.003 to 0.004% (porous). Never allow high point at net.
Deck	26 ft × 50 ft (doubles) (needs a 10-ft fence).	18 ft × 40 ft	Long axis north-south.	Asphalt or concrete; drain side to side at 1 in per 10 ft.
Paddle	37 ft × 80 ft (needs an 8-ft fence).	20 ft × 50 ft	Long axis north-south.	Same as deck tennis.
Platform	30 ft × 60 ft (needs a 12-ft fence).	20 ft × 44	Long axis north-south.	Raised level wood or aluminum platform; ¼-in spacing between 6-in decking.
Volleyball	50 ft × 80 ft preferred; 42 ft × 72 ft OK.	30 ft × 60 ft	Long axis north-south.	Asphalt, sand, clay mix, turf (ropes are used for marking sand and turf); drain at 1 in per 10 ft.

some cases—soccer, for instance, where precise standards have not been established—a range of dimensions is shown. Adequate surface and subsurface drainage will make the difference between the success or failure of a facility. The type of turf used should be sturdy and nonstoloniferous if shoes with cleats are to be used. Where temporary bleachers are to be used, allow a width of 20 to 30 yd (18 to 27 m) between the sidelines and the playing fields (Figure 520-11 and Table 520-3).

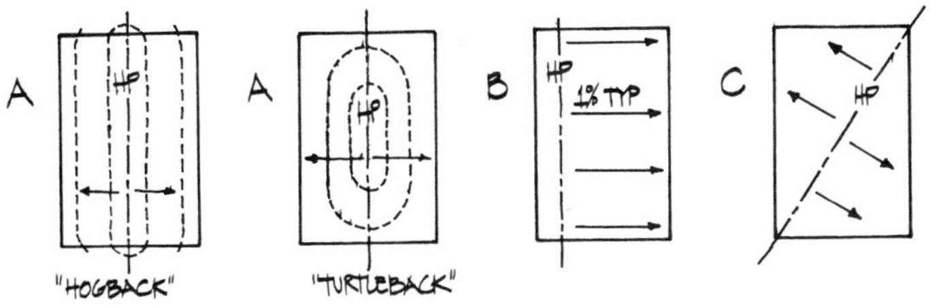

A
HP
A
HP
B
HP
1% TYP
C
HP
"HOGBACK"
"TURTLEBACK"

Figure 520-11 Drainage alternatives for fields.

4.0 TRACK AND FIELD

4.1 General

The design of combined track and field facilities depends upon the age group and class of athletes using the facilities. Although specific guidelines are established by governing agencies, in terms of lane marking and the execution of individual events, there are few specifics in terms of overall track/field layouts. The dimensions and specifications presented here are only guidelines and should be checked against the standards established by the appropriate governing organization.

4.2 Basic Dimensions

According to the standards published in the United States by the NCAA, a championship track shall be at least 400 m in length, with uniform straights and curves. The track width should be a minimum of six lanes, although tracks for large meets often have eight lanes and a few tracks

TABLE 520-3
Field Sports

Sport	*Use area required*	*Playing area*	*Orientation*	*Drainage*	*Comments*
Bocce	19 ft to 25 ft 6 in × 82–101 ft	13 ft to 19 ft 6 in × 78–92 ft	North-south preferred but not critical	Drain in any direction at 1%	10- to 12-in wooden boards used at end and side as backstops
Bowling (lawn)	130 ft × 130 ft	19- to 21-ft × 120-ft alleys		Dead level—use underdrainage	Alleys grouped in banks of six
Cricket	Size varies, but area generally oval with no part of boundary closer than 75 yds to pitch	No official size for field, but pitch is 66 ft × 10 ft			
Croquet	45 ft × 75 ft	40 ft × 70 ft (smaller size is appropriate for nonregulation play	Orient so that bleachers do not face sun	Drain as in A† at a maximum slope of 2%	
Fieldball	Identical to soccer field	Identical to soccer field	Identical to soccer field	Identical to soccer field	
Field hockey					
Women	*	300 ft × 150 ft	Same as football	Same as football	
Men	*	300 ft × 180 ft	Same as football	Same as football	
Flag or touch football	44 yds × 104 yds	40 yds × 100 yds (includes two 10-yd end zones)	Same as football	Same as football	
Football	Minimum 172 ft × 372 ft	160 ft × 360 ft (including two 10-yd end zones)	Long axis, northwest to southeast, or north-south for longer season	Drain as in A; B or C† are permitted but not preferred; provide adequate underdrainage	
Horseshoes	20 ft × 70 ft	10 ft × 50 ft	Long axis, north-south	Drain as in "A;" two end pegs must have identical elevation	
Lacrosse					
Women		Boundaries set by referee; minimum width 150 ft, length 360–410 ft	Same as football	Same as football	
Men	200 ft × 350 ft with fence; 220 ft × 370 ft without fence	Prefer 180 ft × 330 ft, but can be played on football field	Same as football	Same as football	
Polo	Play area includes safety area	300 yds × 160 yds if boarded; 300 yds × 200 yds if not			
Quoits	Allow 5–10 ft at side and back boundaries	54–72 ft × about 10 ft	Same as horseshoes	Same as horseshoes	
Rogue	40 ft × 70 ft	30 ft × 60 ft	Same as croquet	Dead level; use underground drainage	Surface is packed earth
Rugby (league-professional)	*	110 yds × 60 yds plus 6–12 yds at each end for ingoal	Same as football	Same as football	
(union-amateur)	*	110 yds × 60 yds plus 25 yds at each end for ingoal	Same as football	Same as football	
Soccer	10 yds on all sides free of obstructions	55–75 yds × 100–120 yds (75 yds × 120 yds for championship)	North-south, except south of 38th parallel where long axis may approach 20 degrees west of north	Same as football	There are no official standards for soccer—size varies even among Olympic sites
Speedball					
Women	*	60 yds × 100 yds	Same as football	Same as football	
Men	*	53⅓ × 120 yds	Same as football	Same as football	

* When not specified, no standard exists; 10 yds is recommended on all sides.

† See Figure 520-11.

have more. The lane width varies from 36 to 48 in (0.9 to 1.2 m). Many high schools have 36-in (0.9-m) lanes, especially for practice tracks. On world class tracks, 48-in (1.2-m) lanes are preferred, but the most common lane width is 42 in (1.07 m).

4.3 Orientation

Orientation is not as vital a concern in track layout as it is for field events. A north-south orientation along the length of the straightway is preferred. Factors such as space constraints, grading, and prevailing winds often alter the orientation slightly.

4.4 Grading Requirements

Longitudinal slopes for tracks, runways, and landing areas for field events should not exceed a maximum of 0.1 percent (1:1000). Transverse slopes should be no more than 1 percent (1:100) or, for high schools, 2 percent (2:100). The slope should be pitched toward the inside of the track. Within the circles for throwing events there should be a slope of no more than 0.1 percent (1:1000) in the throwing direction.

4.5 Construction Materials

Tracks should be constructed of materials that will create a uniform, smooth, safe, and comfortable running surface. Construction methods tend to vary according to local construction practices and in response to specific soil conditions.

4.6 Typical Synthetic Track Construction

Inside Curb:

Both the NCAA and the IAFF require a curb 2 in (50 mm) high along the inner edge of an oval track. The NCAA requires a curb 6 in (150 mm) wide. The allowable minimum curb width is 2 in (50 mm) for the IAFF and 6 in (150 mm) for the NCAA. Often, a removable aluminum curb is used; American and world records will not be accepted without this inside curb.

Field Events:

Field events may be located on the interior of the track to conserve space. Throwing events may be moved outside the track to allow for a warm-up area, to accommodate a synthetic turf football field, or to provide for additional safety.

There is no prescribed arrangement for the various facilities. They should be arranged to reflect the opportunities and constraints created by soil conditions, prevailing winds, and safety considerations. Sample arrangements are shown in Figures 520-12 through 520-32.

Figure 520-12 Comparative field sizes of common field sports.

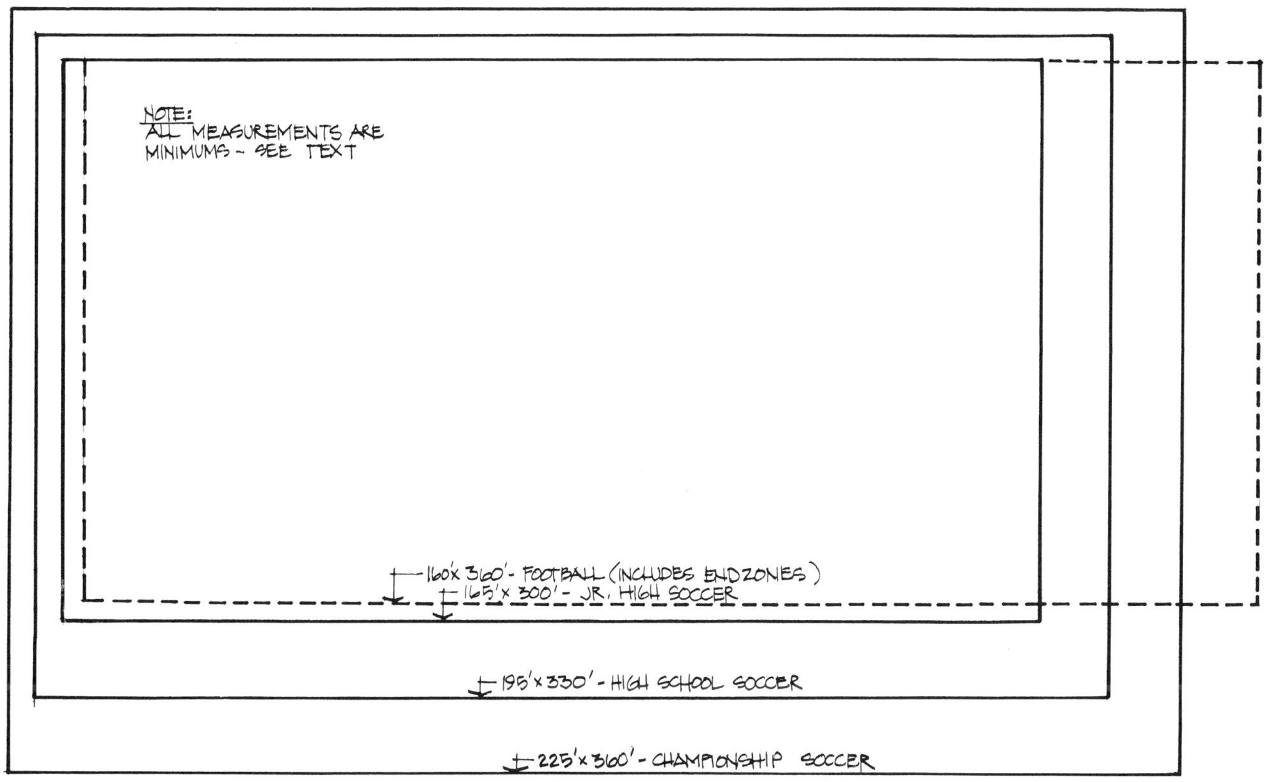
NOTE:
ALL MEASUREMENTS ARE MINIMUMS - SEE TEXT
160'x 360' - FOOTBALL (INCLUDES ENDZONES)
165'x 300' - JR. HIGH SOCCER
195'x 330' - HIGH SCHOOL SOCCER
225'x 360' - CHAMPIONSHIP SOCCER

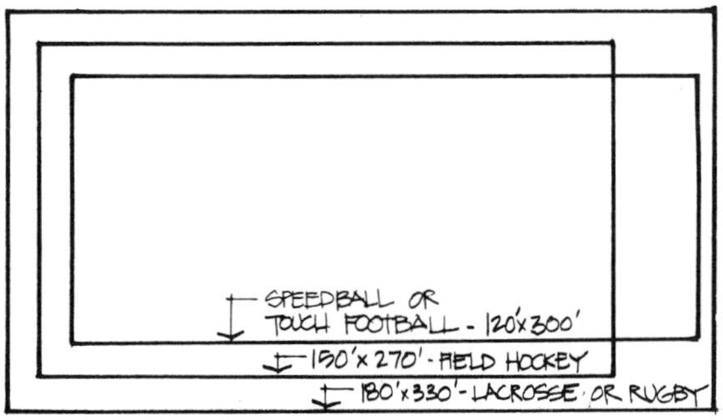
SPEEDBALL OR
TOUCH FOOTBALL - 120'x300'
150'x270' - FIELD HOCKEY
180'x330' - LACROSSE OR RUGBY

Figure 520-13 Typical field sizes.

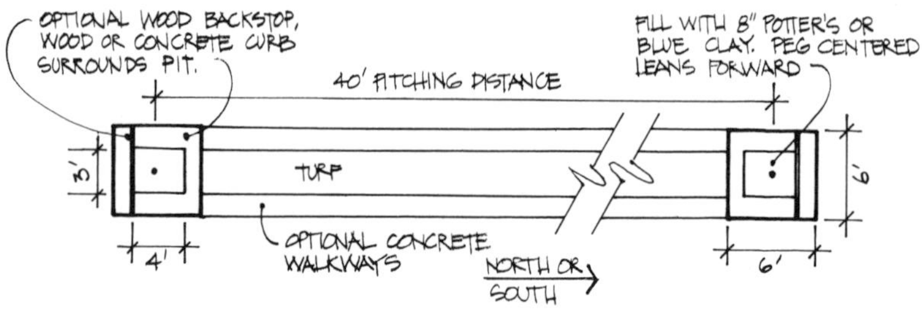
OPTIONAL WOOD BACKSTOP,
WOOD OR CONCRETE CURB
SURROUNDS PIT.
FILL WITH 8" POTTER'S OR
BLUE CLAY. PEG CENTERED
LEANS FORWARD
40' PITCHING DISTANCE
3'
TURF
6'
4'
OPTIONAL CONCRETE
WALKWAYS
NORTH OR
SOUTH
6'

Figure 520-14 Horseshoes.

54' TO 72'
QUOITS IS PLAYED LIKE HORSESHOES
BUT WITH A METAL 'QUOIT,' OR RING
4" DIAMETER WHITE
CIRCLE AROUND PEG

Figure 520-15 Quoits.

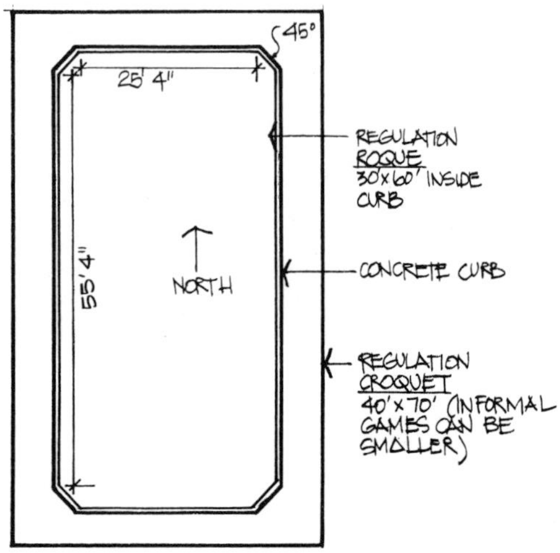
45°
25' 4"
REGULATION
ROQUE
30'x60' INSIDE
CURB
55' 4"
NORTH
CONCRETE CURB
REGULATION
CROQUET
40'x70' (INFORMAL
GAMES CAN BE
SMALLER)

Figure 520-16 Roque/croquet.

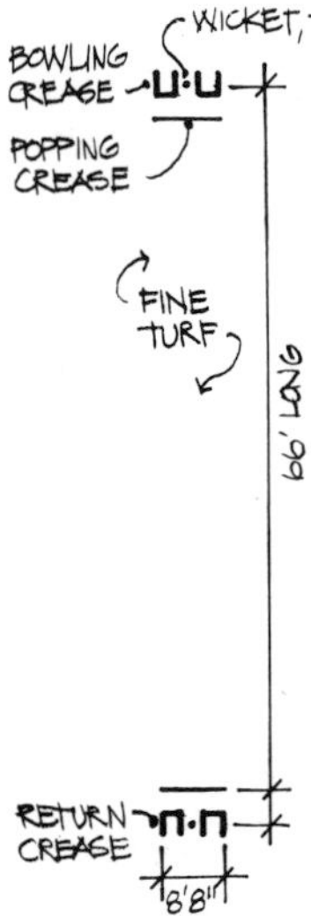
WICKET, TYP.
BOWLING
CREASE
POPPING
CREASE
FINE
TURF
66' LONG
RETURN
CREASE
8'8"

Figure 520-17 Cricket pitch.

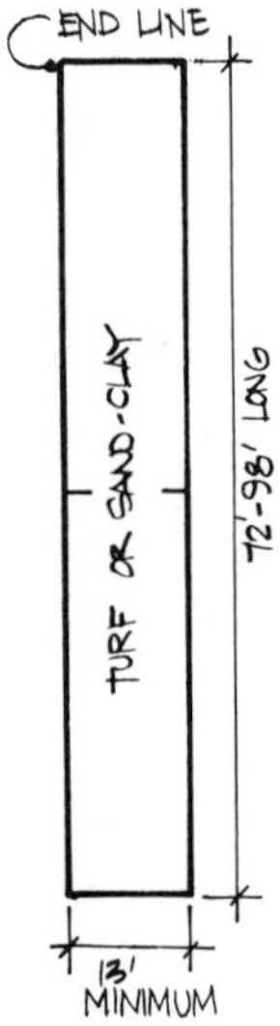
END LINE
TURF OR SAND-CLAY
72'-98' LONG
13'
MINIMUM

Figure 520-18 Bocce.

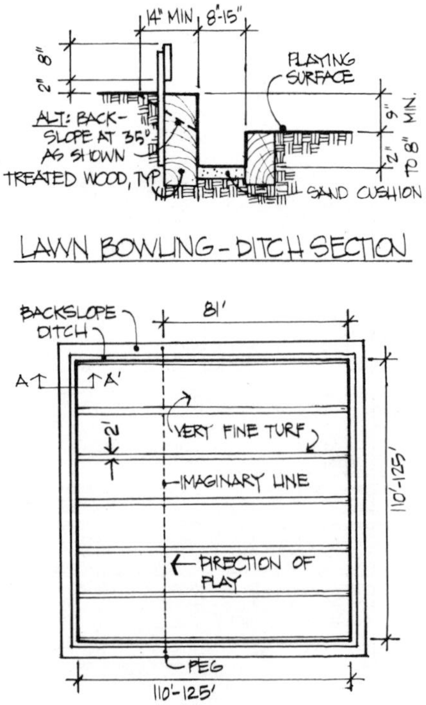
14" MIN
8"-15"
2' 8"
PLAYING
SURFACE
ALT: BACK-
SLOPE AT 35°
AS SHOWN
TREATED WOOD, TYP.
9" MIN.
2" TO 8"
SAND CUSHION
LAWN BOWLING - DITCH SECTION
BACKSLOPE
DITCH
81'
A
A'
2'
VERY FINE TURF
IMAGINARY LINE
DIRECTION OF
PLAY
110'-125'
PEG
110'-125'

Figure 520-19 Lawn bowling.

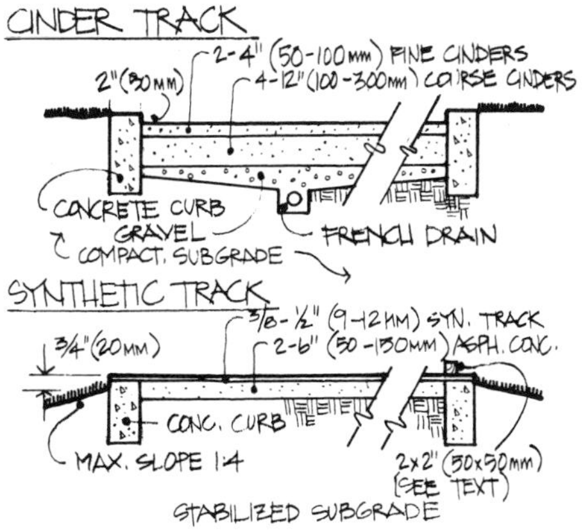

CINDER TRACK
2-4" (50-100mm) FINE CINDERS
2" (50MM)
4-12" (100-300mm) COARSE CINDERS
CONCRETE CURB
GRAVEL
COMPACT. SUBGRADE
FRENCH DRAIN
SYNTHETIC TRACK
3/8-1/2" (9-12MM) SYN. TRACK
3/4" (20MM)
2-6" (50-150MM) ASPH. CONC.
CONC. CURB
MAX. SLOPE 1:4
2x2" (50x50mm) (SEE TEXT)
STABILIZED SUBGRADE

Figure 520-20 Typical track sections.

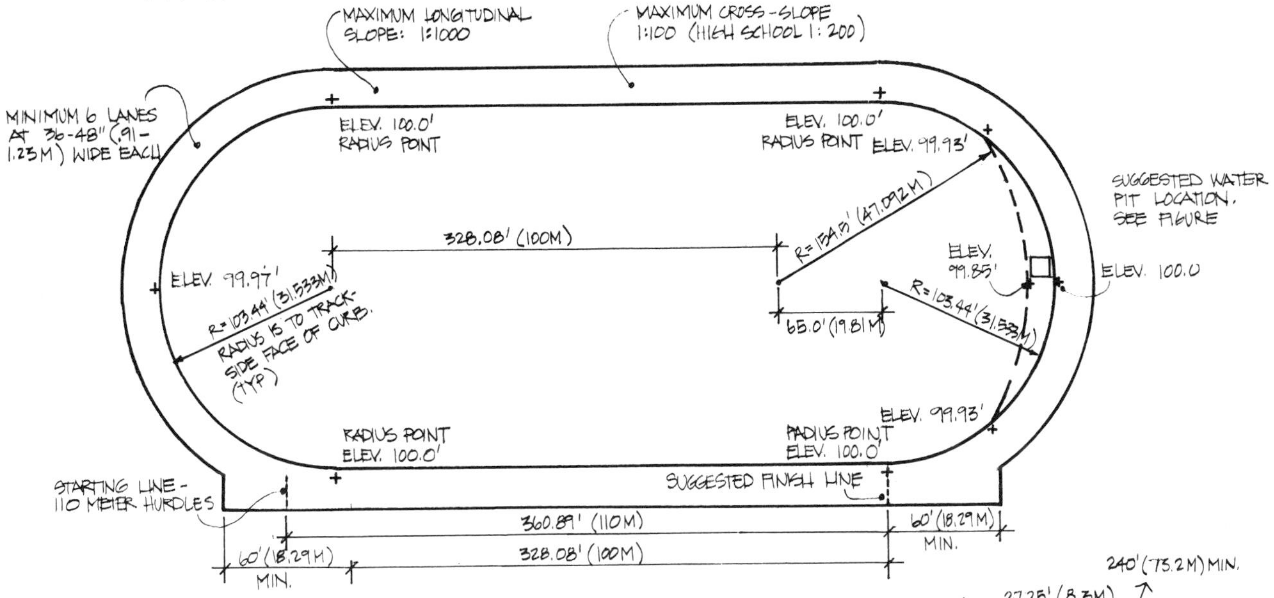

MAXIMUM LONGITUDINAL SLOPE: 1:1000
MAXIMUM CROSS-SLOPE 1:100 (HIGH SCHOOL 1:200)
MINIMUM 6 LANES AT 36-48" (.91-1.23M) WIDE EACH
ELEV. 100.0' RADIUS POINT
ELEV. 100.0' RADIUS POINT
ELEV. 99.93'
SUGGESTED WATER PIT LOCATION. SEE FIGURE
R=154.5' (47.092M)
328.08' (100M)
ELEV. 99.85'
ELEV. 100.0
ELEV. 99.97'
R=103.44' (31.533M) RADIUS IS TO TRACK-SIDE FACE OF CURB. (TYP)
R=103.44' (31.533M)
65.0' (19.81M)
ELEV. 99.93'
RADIUS POINT ELEV. 100.0'
RADIUS POINT ELEV. 100.0'
STARTING LINE - 110 METER HURDLES
SUGGESTED FINISH LINE
360.89' (110M)
60' (18.29M) MIN.
60' (18.29M) MIN.
328.08' (100M)

Figure 520-21 Basic layout: 400-meter track.

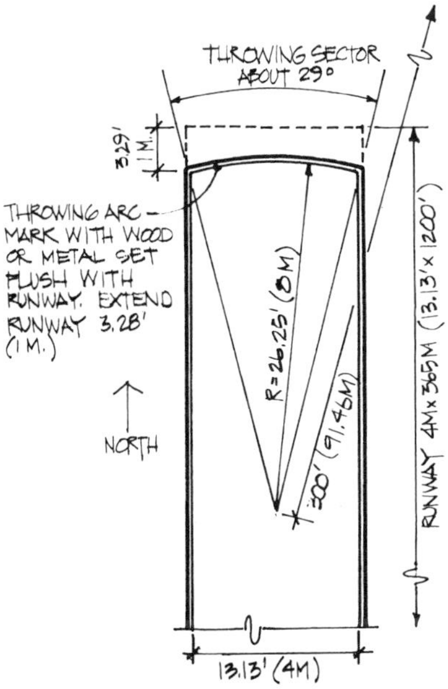

THROWING SECTOR ABOUT 29°
3.28' 1M.
THROWING ARC - MARK WITH WOOD OR METAL SET FLUSH WITH RUNWAY. EXTEND RUNWAY 3.28' (1M.)
R=26.25' (8M)
300' (91.46M)
RUNWAY 4M x 365M (13.13' x 1200')
NORTH
13.13' (4M)

Figure 520-22 Javelin.

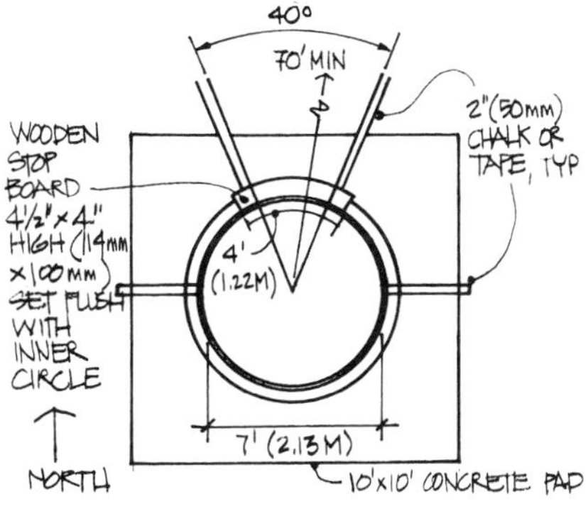

40°
70' MIN
WOODEN STOP BOARD 4½" x 4" HIGH (114mm x 100mm) SET FLUSH WITH INNER CIRCLE
2" (50mm) CHALK OR TAPE, TYP
4' (1.22M)
7' (2.13M)
NORTH
10'x10' CONCRETE PAD

Figure 520-23 Shot put.

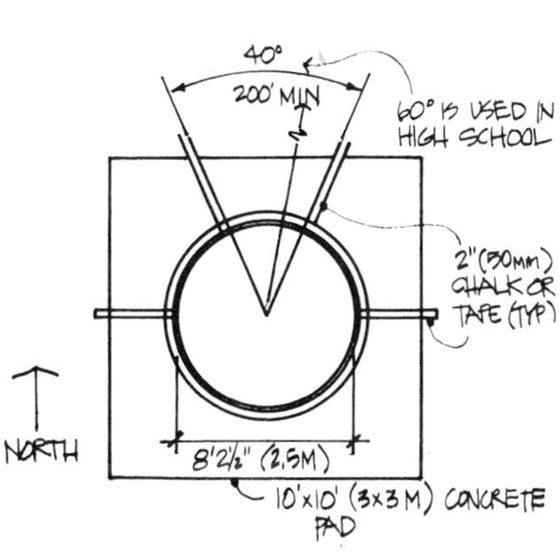

40°
200' MIN
60° IS USED IN HIGH SCHOOL
2" (50mm) CHALK OR TAPE (TYP)
NORTH
8'2½" (2.5M)
10'x10' (3x3 M) CONCRETE PAD

Figure 520-24 Discus.

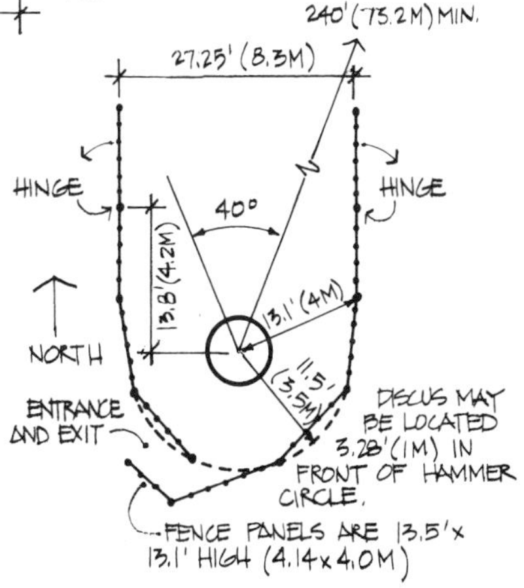

240' (73.2M) MIN.
27.25' (8.3M)
HINGE
HINGE
40°
13.8' (4.2M)
13.1' (4M)
11.5' (3.5M)
NORTH
ENTRANCE AND EXIT
DISCUS MAY BE LOCATED 3.28' (1M) IN FRONT OF HAMMER CIRCLE.
FENCE PANELS ARE 13.5' x 13.1' HIGH (4.14 x 4.0M)

Figure 520-25 Hammer throw.

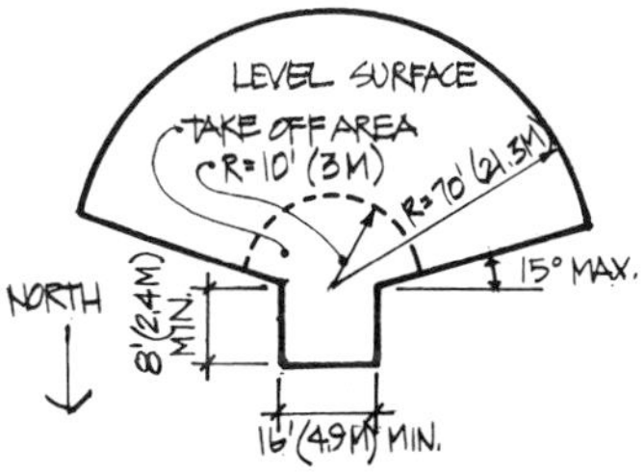

LEVEL SURFACE
TAKE OFF AREA R=10' (3M)
R=70' (21.3M)
15° MAX.
NORTH
8' (2.4M) MIN.
16' (4.9M) MIN.

Figure 520-26 High jump.

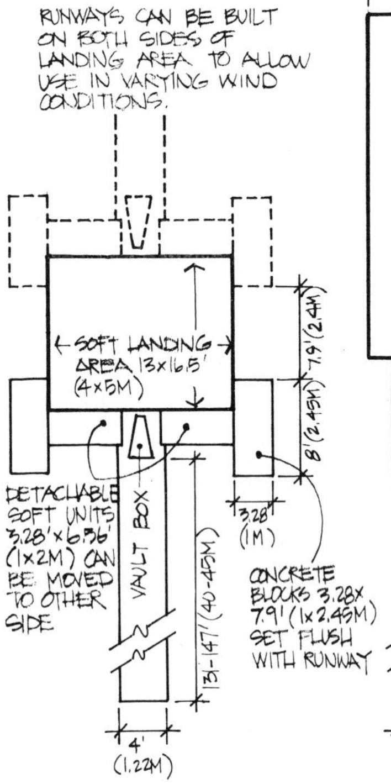
RUNWAYS CAN BE BUILT ON BOTH SIDES OF LANDING AREA TO ALLOW USE IN VARYING WIND CONDITIONS.
SOFT LANDING AREA 13x16.5' (4x5M)
7.9' (2.4M)
8' (2.45M)
DETACHABLE SOFT UNITS 3.28'x6.56' (1x2M) CAN BE MOVED TO OTHER SIDE
VAULT BOX
3.28' (1M)
131-147' (40-45M)
CONCRETE BLOCKS 3.28x7.9' (1x2.45M) SET FLUSH WITH RUNWAY
4' (1.22M)

Figure 520-27 Pole vault.

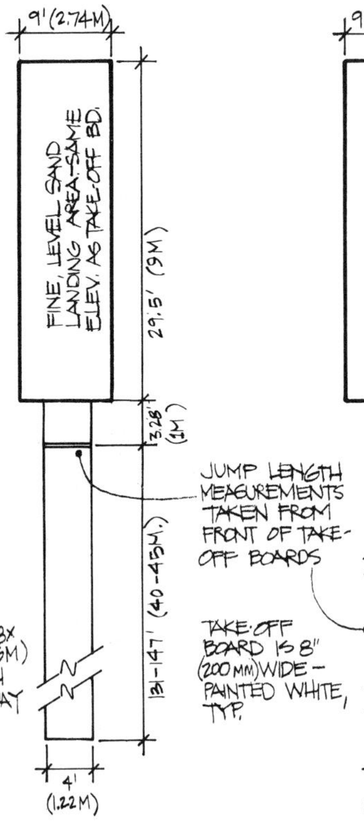
9' (2.74M)
FINE, LEVEL SAND LANDING AREA-SAME ELEV. AS TAKE-OFF BD.
29.5' (9M)
3.28' (1M)
131-147' (40-45M)
JUMP LENGTH MEASUREMENTS TAKEN FROM FRONT OF TAKE-OFF BOARDS
TAKE-OFF BOARD IS 8" (200 MM) WIDE—PAINTED WHITE, TYP.
4' (1.22M)

Figure 520-28 Long jump.

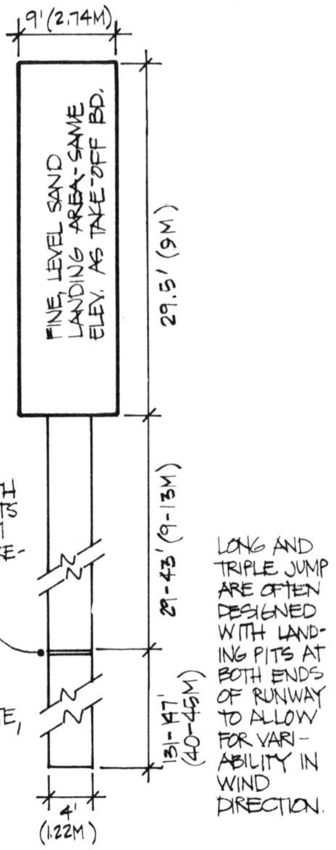
9' (2.74M)
FINE, LEVEL SAND LANDING AREA-SAME ELEV. AS TAKE-OFF BD.
29.5' (9M)
29-43' (9-13M)
131-147' (40-45M)
LONG AND TRIPLE JUMP ARE OFTEN DESIGNED WITH LANDING PITS AT BOTH ENDS OF RUNWAY TO ALLOW FOR VARIABILITY IN WIND DIRECTION.
4' (1.22M)

Figure 520-29 Triple jump.

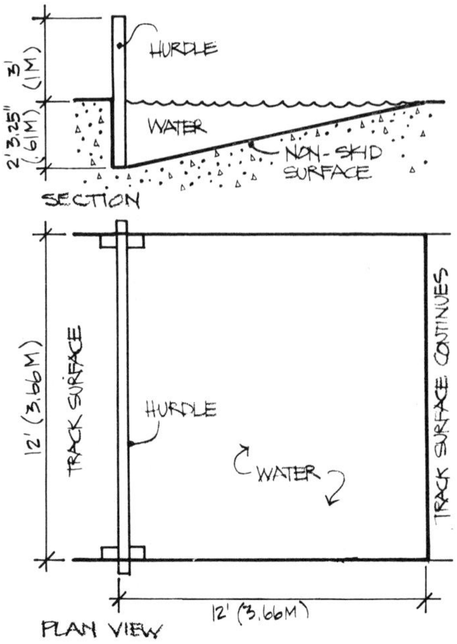
HURDLE
3' (1M)
2' 3.25" (.61M)
WATER
NON-SKID SURFACE
SECTION
12' (3.66M)
TRACK SURFACE
HURDLE
WATER
TRACK SURFACE CONTINUES
12' (3.66M)
PLAN VIEW

Figure 520-30 Water jump.

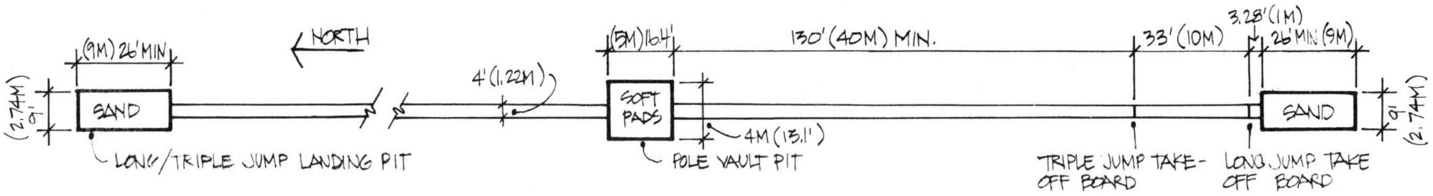
(9M) 26' MIN
NORTH
(2.74M) 9'
SAND
4' (1.22M)
(5M) 16.4'
SOFT PADS
130' (40M) MIN.
4M (13.1')
33' (10M)
3.28' (1M)
26' MIN (9M)
SAND
9' (2.74M)
LONG/TRIPLE JUMP LANDING PIT
POLE VAULT PIT
TRIPLE JUMP TAKE-OFF BOARD
LONG JUMP TAKE OFF BOARD

Figure 520-31 Combined long jump, triple jump, and pole vault.

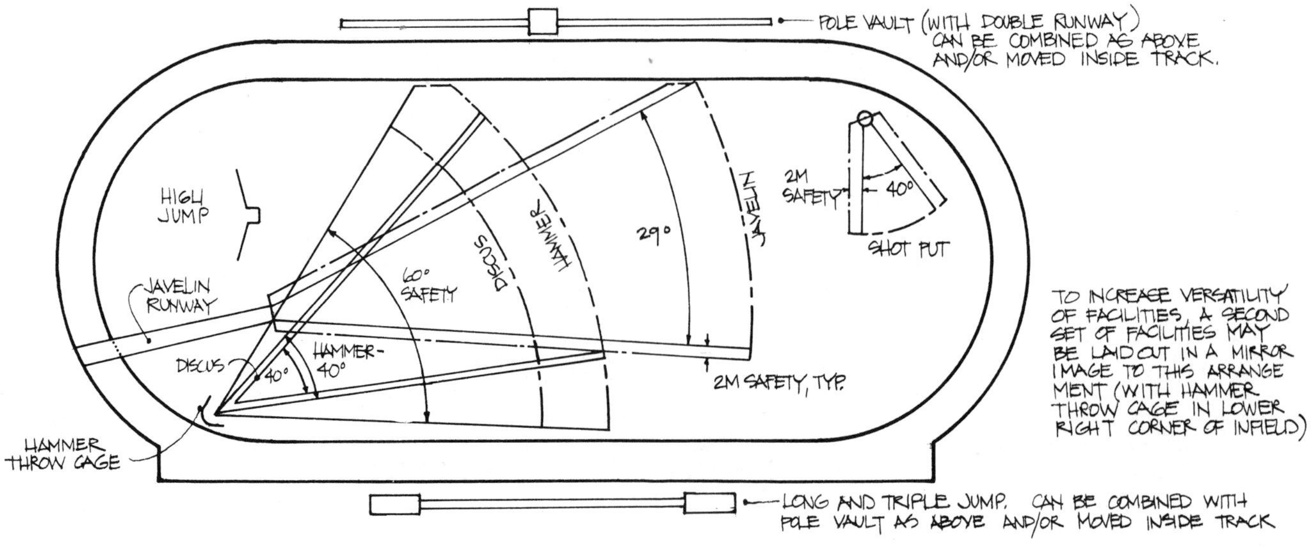
POLE VAULT (WITH DOUBLE RUNWAY) CAN BE COMBINED AS ABOVE AND/OR MOVED INSIDE TRACK.
HIGH JUMP
JAVELIN RUNWAY
60° SAFETY
DISCUS
HAMMER
29°
JAVELIN
2M SAFETY
40°
SHOT PUT
DISCUS
40°
HAMMER-40°
2M SAFETY, TYP.
HAMMER THROW CAGE
TO INCREASE VERSATILITY OF FACILITIES, A SECOND SET OF FACILITIES MAY BE LAID OUT IN A MIRROR IMAGE TO THIS ARRANGEMENT (WITH HAMMER THROW CAGE IN LOWER RIGHT CORNER OF INFIELD)
LONG AND TRIPLE JUMP. CAN BE COMBINED WITH POLE VAULT AS ABOVE AND/OR MOVED INSIDE TRACK

Figure 520-32 Schematic arrangement of infield.

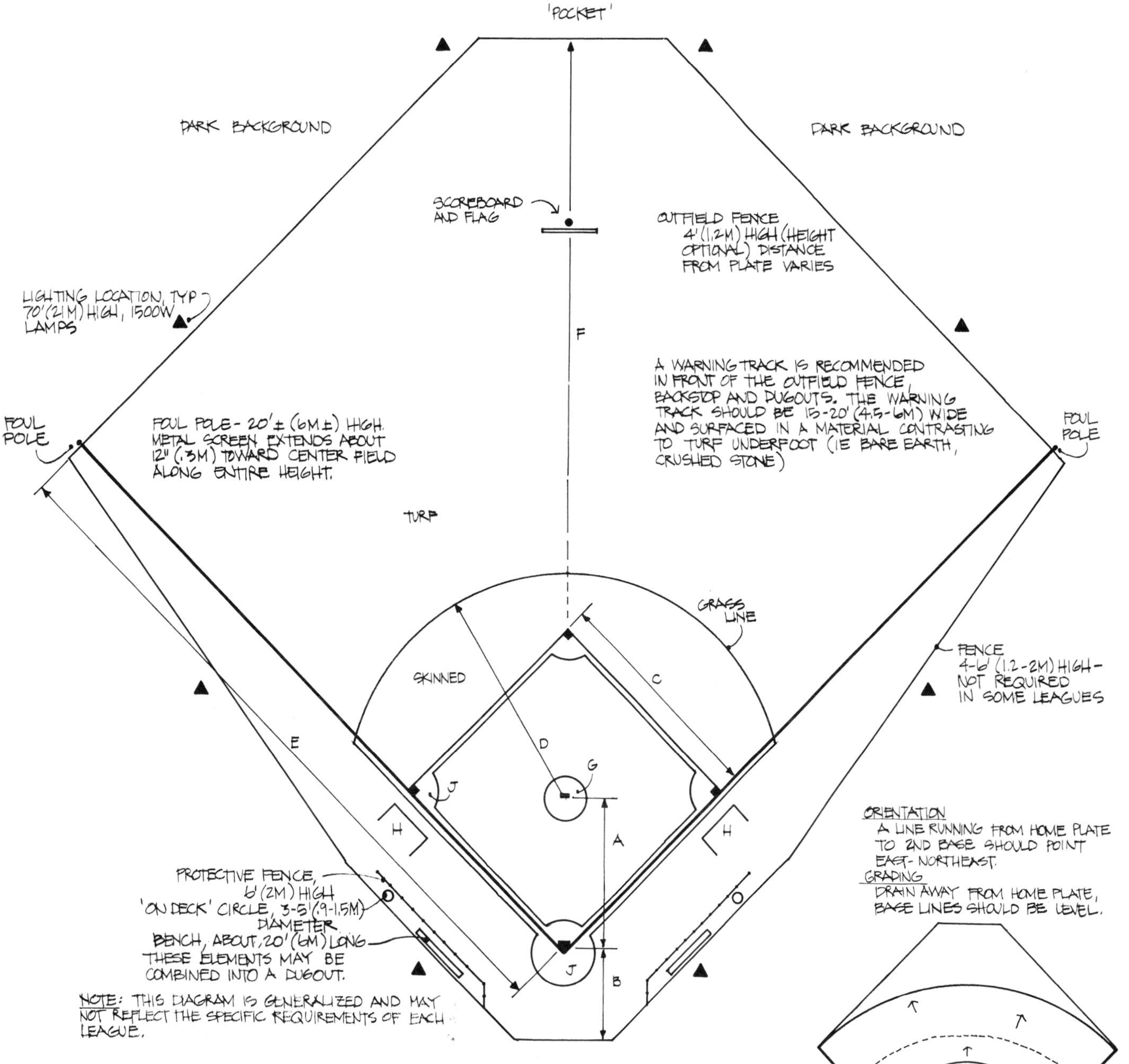

'POCKET'
DARK BACKGROUND
DARK BACKGROUND
SCOREBOARD AND FLAG
OUTFIELD FENCE 4'(1.2M) HIGH (HEIGHT OPTIONAL) DISTANCE FROM PLATE VARIES
LIGHTING LOCATION, TYP 70'(21M) HIGH, 1500W LAMPS
F
A WARNING TRACK IS RECOMMENDED IN FRONT OF THE OUTFIELD FENCE, BACKSTOP AND DUGOUTS. THE WARNING TRACK SHOULD BE 15-20'(4.5-6M) WIDE AND SURFACED IN A MATERIAL CONTRASTING TO TURF UNDERFOOT (IE BARE EARTH, CRUSHED STONE)
FOUL POLE
FOUL POLE - 20'± (6M±) HIGH. METAL SCREEN EXTENDS ABOUT 12" (.3M) TOWARD CENTER FIELD ALONG ENTIRE HEIGHT.
FOUL POLE
TURF
GRASS LINE
SKINNED
C
FENCE 4-6' (1.2-2M) HIGH - NOT REQUIRED IN SOME LEAGUES
E
D
G
J
H
H
A
ORIENTATION
A LINE RUNNING FROM HOME PLATE TO 2ND BASE SHOULD POINT EAST-NORTHEAST.
GRADING
DRAIN AWAY FROM HOME PLATE, BASE LINES SHOULD BE LEVEL.
PROTECTIVE FENCE, 6'(2M) HIGH
'ON DECK' CIRCLE, 3-5'(.9-1.5M) DIAMETER
BENCH, ABOUT 20'(6M) LONG
THESE ELEMENTS MAY BE COMBINED INTO A DUGOUT.
J
B
NOTE: THIS DIAGRAM IS GENERALIZED AND MAY NOT REFLECT THE SPECIFIC REQUIREMENTS OF EACH LEAGUE.

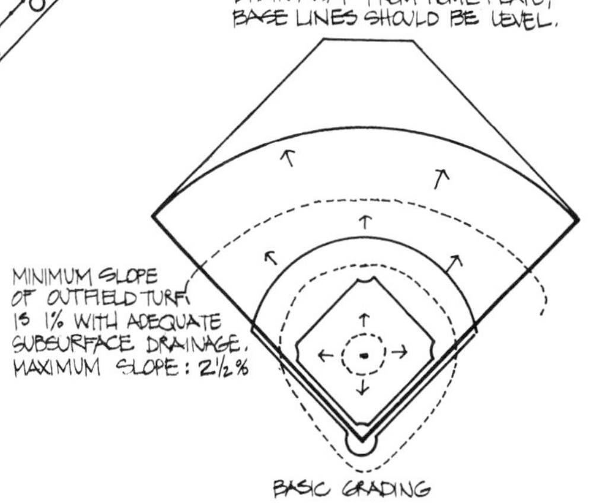

MINIMUM SLOPE OF OUTFIELD TURF IS 1% WITH ADEQUATE SUBSURFACE DRAINAGE. MAXIMUM SLOPE: 2½%
BASIC GRADING

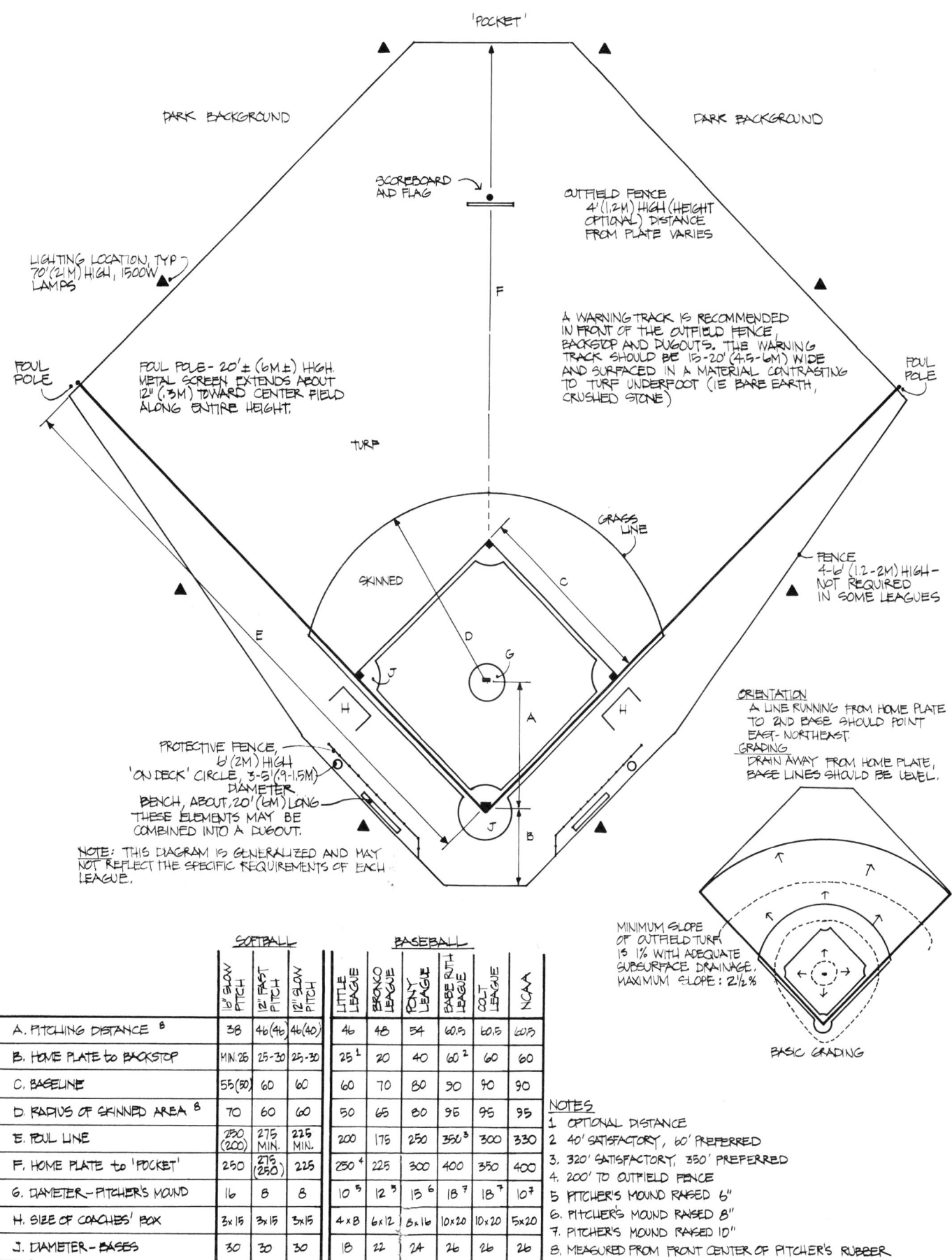

	SOFTBALL			BASEBALL					
	16" SLOW PITCH	12" FAST PITCH	12" SLOW PITCH	LITTLE LEAGUE	BRONCO LEAGUE	PONY LEAGUE	BABE RUTH LEAGUE	COLT LEAGUE	NCAA
A. PITCHING DISTANCE [8]	38	46(46)	46(40)	46	48	54	60.5	60.5	60.5
B. HOME PLATE to BACKSTOP	MIN. 25	25-30	25-30	25 [1]	20	40	60 [2]	60	60
C. BASELINE	55(50)	60	60	60	70	80	90	90	90
D. RADIUS OF SKINNED AREA [8]	70	60	60	50	65	80	95	95	95
E. FOUL LINE	250 (200)	275 MIN.	225 MIN.	200	175	250	350 [3]	300	330
F. HOME PLATE to 'POCKET'	250	275 (250)	225	250 [4]	225	300	400	350	400
G. DIAMETER - PITCHER'S MOUND	16	8	8	10 [5]	12 [5]	15 [6]	18 [7]	18 [7]	10 [7]
H. SIZE OF COACHES' BOX	3x15	3x15	3x15	4x8	6x12	8x16	10x20	10x20	5x20
J. DIAMETER - BASES	30	30	30	18	22	24	26	26	26

ALL MEASUREMENTS ARE IN FEET. WOMEN'S DIMENSIONS, IF DIFFERENT, ARE IN PARENTHESIS.

NOTES
1. OPTIONAL DISTANCE
2. 40' SATISFACTORY, 60' PREFERRED
3. 320' SATISFACTORY, 350' PREFERRED
4. 200' TO OUTFIELD FENCE
5. PITCHER'S MOUND RAISED 6"
6. PITCHER'S MOUND RAISED 8"
7. PITCHER'S MOUND RAISED 10"
8. MEASURED FROM FRONT CENTER OF PITCHER'S RUBBER

Figure 520-33 Softball/baseball layout.

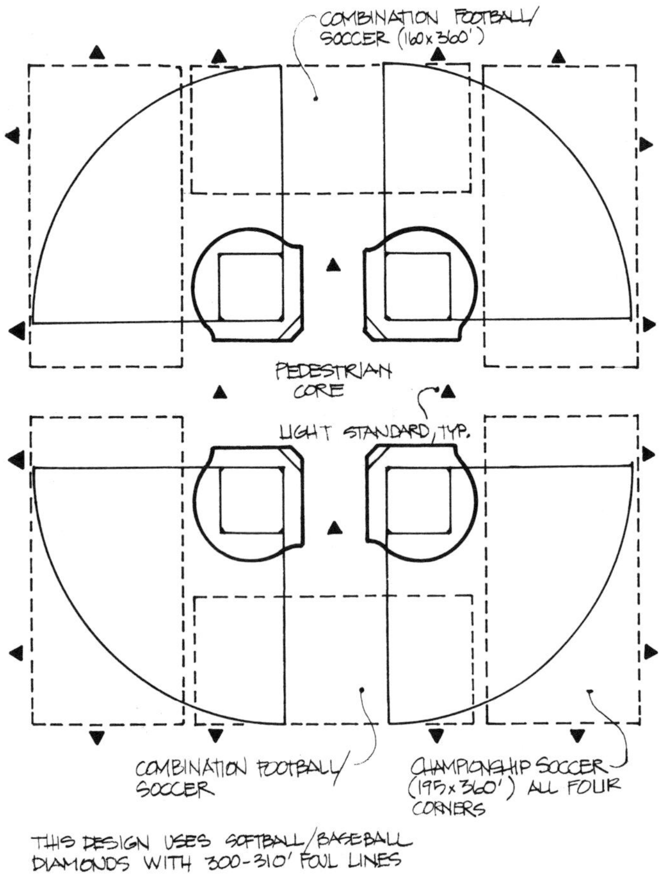
COMBINATION FOOTBALL/ SOCCER (160x360')
PEDESTRIAN CORE
LIGHT STANDARD, TYP.
COMBINATION FOOTBALL/ SOCCER
CHAMPIONSHIP SOCCER (195x360') ALL FOUR CORNERS
THIS DESIGN USES SOFTBALL/BASEBALL DIAMONDS WITH 300-310' FOUL LINES

Figure 520-34 Schematic sports complex.

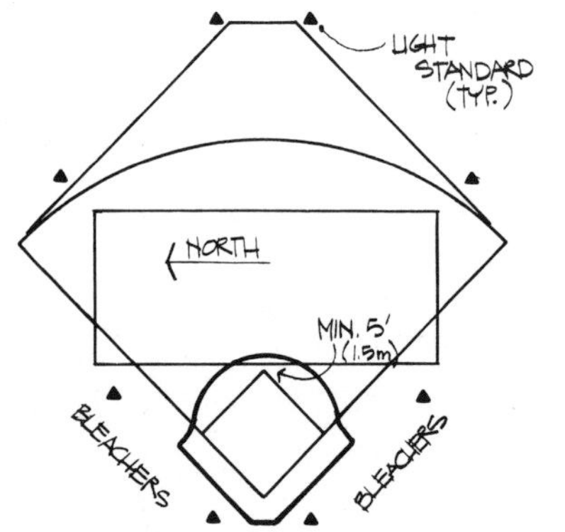
LIGHT STANDARD (TYP.)
NORTH
MIN. 5' (1.5m)
BLEACHERS
BLEACHERS

Figure 520-35 Baseball/football complex (baseball primary).

5.0 MULTIPURPOSE ATHLETIC FIELD COMPLEXES

5.1 General

Athletic complexes can take the form of *cloverleafs,* or *fourplexes,* where the home plates of the ball diamonds (softball/baseball) are near a central core and football/soccer fields overlap the outfields, as shown in Figure 520-34.

Advantages of Multipurpose Complexes:

The advantages of multipurpose complexes are that they can use the same parking lot for separate sports, as well as use the same irrigation and lighting systems; that they can use single rather than separate tracts of land; that they can share restrooms, concessions, and other common support facilities; and that they allow for concentrated and more cost-effective maintenance. In addition, a centralized administration can help to schedule league and tournament play.

Disadvantages of Multipurpose Complexes:

The disadvantages of multipurpose complexes are that the amount of traffic, noise, and night lighting involved may disturb nearby residential areas and that the outfield lights create an excessive amount of glare. Other disadvantages include the need for portable outfield fences during championship or tournament ball games and for portable goals during football or soccer play. Also, a greater potential exists for scheduling conflicts when all four sports have demands for fields when the seasons lap over into one another; furthermore, not all fields will enjoy optimum orientation.

The parking requirements for a fourplex complex (as shown in Figure 520-34) when games are scheduled 5 minutes apart is approximately 250 cars.

5.2 Design Considerations

Ball fields need adequate spacing so that foul balls are not a hazard and so that noise and confusion are reduced. An optimum distance between the foul lines of adjacent ball diamonds is 120 to 140 ft (36 to 42 m). A complex capable of accommodating four diamonds, each with 300-ft (90-m)-long foul lines, will occupy a space approximately 800 ft × 800 ft (240 m × 240 m). That space, plus parking and buffer areas, will occupy approximately 18 to 20 acres [7 to 8 hectares (ha)] of relatively level land (more if sloping or hilly). Figures 520-33 through 520-35 show two basic grading concepts that can be used in this type of complex: one that uses a high spot at the center with water draining off toward all edges, and the other that uses a plane with a uniform slope across the complex. As always, local site conditions will dictate the final solution.

6.0 WATER-BASED FACILITIES

6.1 Docks

Two courtesy docks are needed for each launching facility (Figure 520-36). The minimum width of all docks is 6 ft (2 m), not counting the finger walkways between slips; these walkways can be as narrow as 2½ ft (0.75 m) if they are less than 20 ft (6 m) long. Floating docks are preferred to stationary ones when the water height fluctuates more than 1½ ft (0.45 m). At least one comfort station should be located within 400 ft (122 m) of the dock, and the fire codes relating to dock areas should be consulted.

A service dock or float is necessary to supply fuel to outgoing boats. Locate fuel storage tanks underground and above the high-water line as specified by local and National Fire Protection Association (NFPA) codes. Dumps, comfort stations, and other permanent structures should also be constructed above the 100-year flood line or should be floodproofed.

6.2 Launch Facilities

Launch lanes should be at least 15 ft (4.5 m) wide in a multiple-lane facility; the lane in a single-lane facility should be 18 ft (5.5 m) wide. (See Figure 540-37.) The prepared surface should be finished with a cross-scored pattern. The ramp grade should be no steeper than 12 to 15 percent. The lowest end of the ramp should extend into the water to a point where it will be at least 4 ft (1.2 m) below the lowest water elevation in order to protect the base of the ramp from wave action. The backing up of a vehicle should be limited to 200 ft (60 m), and the maneuvering area should be at least 80 ft (24 m), and preferably 100 ft (30 m), in diameter.

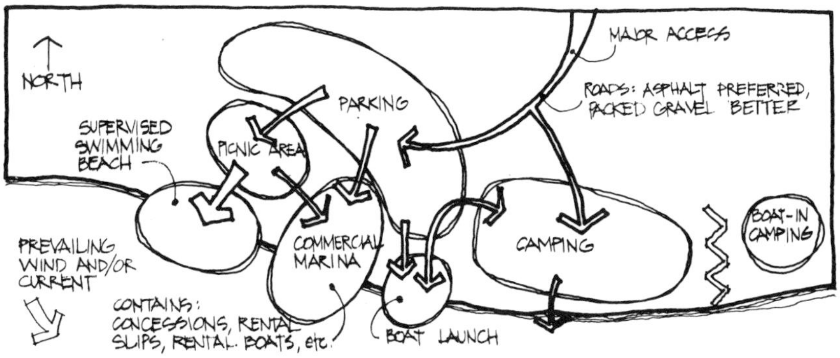
NORTH
MAJOR ACCESS
ROADS: ASPHALT PREFERRED, PACKED GRAVEL BETTER
PARKING
SUPERVISED SWIMMING BEACH
PICNIC AREA
BOAT-IN CAMPING
CAMPING
COMMERCIAL MARINA
PREVAILING WIND AND/OR CURRENT
CONTAINS: CONCESSIONS, RENTAL SLIPS, RENTAL BOATS, etc.
BOAT LAUNCH

Figure 520-36 Schematic marina layout.

6.3 Swimming Beaches

General:

Good swimming beaches should be protected from boats, fuel spillage, and organic pollutants, and water should circulate through the area. Ideally, the beach should face the full or at least the afternoon sun. It should have a cross-sectional slope of 4 to 10 percent (based upon local health codes) and consist of sand or a soil mixture having sandy qualities.

Spatial Standards:

Lookout towers should be provided every 300 ft (90 m). A swimming area of 50 ft^2 (4.6 m^2) should be allowed for each bather. Ladders should be provided on all docks within and adjacent to swim areas. Docks should be a minimum of 18 in (0.45 m) above water level (Figure 520-38).

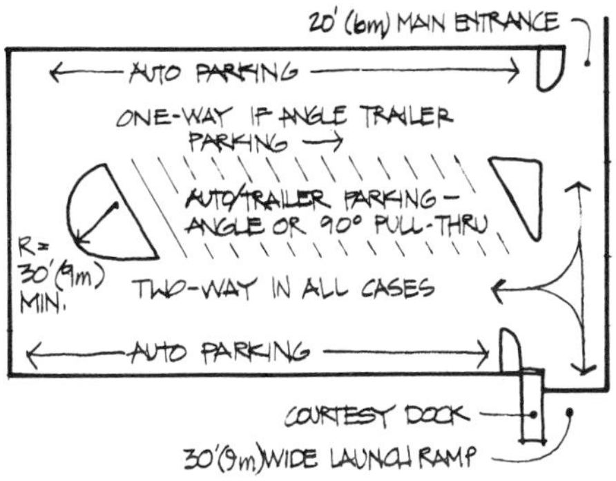
20' (6m) MAIN ENTRANCE
AUTO PARKING
ONE-WAY IF ANGLE TRAILER PARKING
AUTO/TRAILER PARKING - ANGLE OR 90° PULL-THRU
R= 30'(9m) MIN.
TWO-WAY IN ALL CASES
AUTO PARKING
COURTESY DOCK
30'(9m)WIDE LAUNCH RAMP

Figure 520-37 Boat launch/parking diagram.

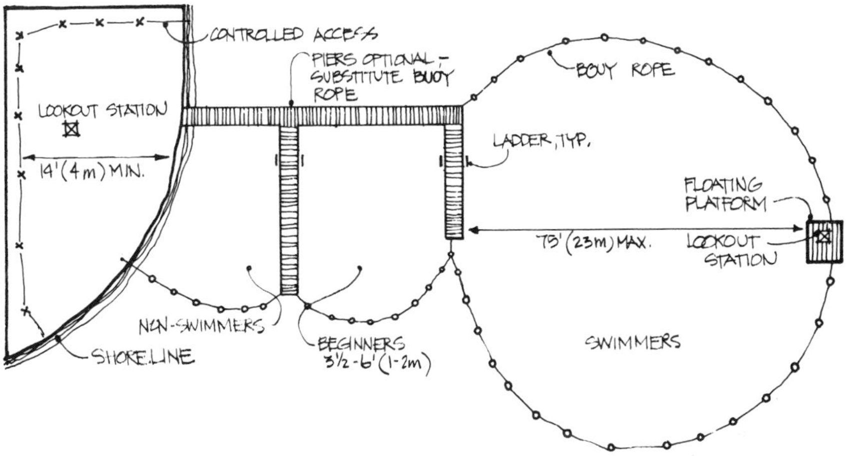
CONTROLLED ACCESS
PIERS OPTIONAL - SUBSTITUTE BUOY ROPE
BOUY ROPE
LOOKOUT STATION
14'(4m) MIN.
LADDER, TYP.
FLOATING PLATFORM
75'(23m) MAX.
LOOKOUT STATION
NON-SWIMMERS
BEGINNERS 3½-6'(1-2m)
SWIMMERS
SHORE LINE

Figure 520-38 Schematic diagram (lake swimming).

6.4 Swimming Pools

General:

Swimming pools can be made in a variety of shapes, from free-form to T or L shapes, but the basic design of all public and semipublic pools should be checked against local health codes.

Spatial Standards:

The following standards are considered typical for swimming pools:

1. Recreational pools are sized to allow 10 ft^2 (0.93 m^2) of water surface for every wader, or nonswimmer, expected and 27 ft^2 (2.5 m^2) of surface for every swimmer.

2. The area for nonswimmers should be less than 5 ft (1.5 m) deep.

3. More and more public pools have 80 percent of the water area devoted to nonswimmers (Figure 520-39).

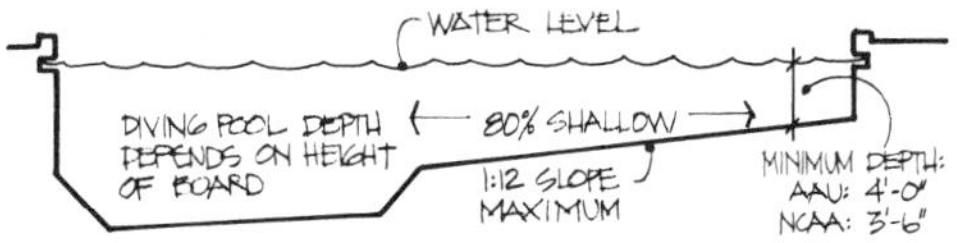
WATER LEVEL
DIVING POOL DEPTH DEPENDS ON HEIGHT OF BOARD
80% SHALLOW
1:12 SLOPE MAXIMUM
MINIMUM DEPTH: AAU: 4'-0" NCAA: 3'-6"

Figure 520-39 Schematic pool section.

4. An extra 300 ft^2 (27.9 m^2) should be added for each diving board.

5. Twenty-five yards (actually 75 ft 1½ in to accommodate timing equipment) is the minimum length for interscholastic or intercollegiate competition in the United States. In 1973 the NCAA agreed that in all U.S. indoor competition events, pools will remain 25 yd (23 m) in length. A 50-m (55-yd) pool is preferred outdoors, with 25 yd the second choice. International competition requires a 50-m length.

6. Lanes should be 7 ft (2.1 m) wide between the centerlines, which should be marked with lane stripes 10 in (250 mm) wide. Add 18 in (0.45 m) to each of the outside lanes.

7. The deck space around recreational pools should be at least equal to the water surface because generally only one-third of the swimmers will be in the pool at any one time. A 3:1 to 4:1 ratio between deck and water surface provides the most functional arrangement.

8. Official standards for water polo depend on the standard-setting agency (Figure 520-40).

Wading Pools:

Wading pools can be placed in the same complex as competition-size pools, but they should be separated and fenced for safety. Fountains or sprays can be added. Shaded seating should be provided for parents or other supervisors.

6.5 Fishing

The following guidelines highlight some key concerns when establishing a natural or constructed fishing pond:

1. A surface area of 1 acre (0.4 ha) is sufficient; a commercial sporting operation can be maintained if the surface area is at least 10 acres (4 ha).

2. Areas less than 3 ft (1 m) deep will encourage the growth of aquatic plants. These plants are considered undesirable because they provide breeding and protection areas for some smaller species of fish, which may lead to overcrowding for the desirable species. Six feet (2 m) is a good average depth.

3. Increase the depths in arid areas where evaporation is a problem or in areas where ice forms.

4. The water supply should have a low amount of silt. If drainpipes are installed, they should be wide enough to allow the fish to pass through unharmed.

5. Along some areas of the shoreline, allow at least 6 ft (2 m) of unobstructed space between the water edge and any dense vegetation. For casting, allow 6 ft (2 m) between each person fishing.

6. A gently sloping shoreline is the least prone to erosion and the safest in terms of people accidentally falling.

7. An access point for a truck is necessary for the stocking and fertilization of a fishing pond.

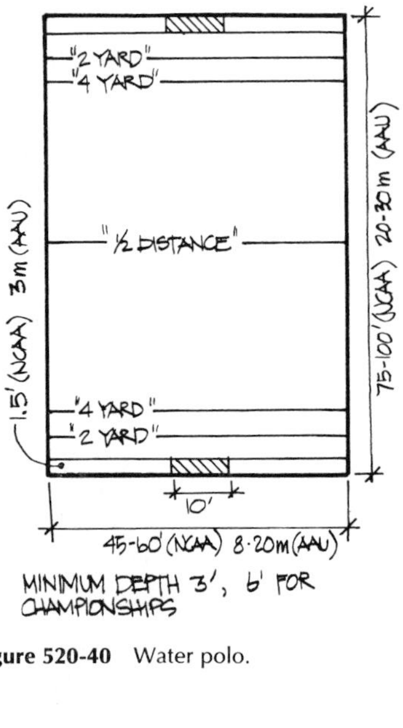

"2 YARD"
"4 YARD"
"½ DISTANCE"
"4 YARD"
"2 YARD"
1.5' (NCAA) 3m (AAU)
75-100' (NCAA) 20-30m (AAU)
10'
45-60' (NCAA) 8-20m (AAU)
MINIMUM DEPTH 3', 6' FOR CHAMPIONSHIPS

Figure 520-40 Water polo.

6.6 Handicapped Swimming, Fishing, and Boating

More complete and comprehensive information on the design of water-based facilities for the handicapped is found in Section 240: Access and Egress: Outdoor Standards.

Swimming Pools:

Swimming pools need entry ramps at a slope of 1:12 or less. Two handrails 2½ to 3 ft (0.75 to 1 m) high and 3 ft (1 m) apart should be provided. In a natural setting, provide a paved (or at least a stabilized) surface between the bathhouse and the water.

Beaches:

At beaches, the path should terminate in a 6-ft × 6-ft (2-m × 2-m) paved area and should provide a handrail approximately 32 in (0.8 m) high that extends into the water to a depth of 2½ ft (0.75 m). The beach gradient should be no steeper than 1:12.

Fishing and Boating:

Docks provide access to boating and fishing for those who are handicapped. These docks should be at least 8 ft (2.5 m) wide, with the boards laid perpendicular to the direction of travel and with the open joints no greater than ½ in (12 mm) wide. At least one side of the dock should have a railing that will support a 300-lb (136-kg) individual during loading and unloading. Fishing rails should have a shelf for bait and tackle that is 8 to 12 in (200 to 250 mm) wide and 30 in (0.75 m) above the dock surface. The top rail should be 36 in (1 m) high and slope at 30 degrees toward the user as an arm-and-pole rest. Provide a kick plate to prevent wheelchair foot pedals from going off piers.

6.7 Waterskiing

The lake size should be 8 to 15 acres (3.25 to 6 ha) per boat. The higher figure should be used where considerable powerboat traffic is anticipated. If many boats are involved, then a proportionate number of piers, docks, etc., should be added.

6.8 Crew

International crew races are set at 2000, 1500, and 1000 m and require at least an additional 820-ft (250-m) distance beyond the finish line. Races require a water body with no moving water, no bridges, and no prevailing crosswinds. A uniform depth of at least 10 ft (3 m) is required. The course consists of six parallel lanes and one return lane, each a minimum of 41 ft (12.5 m) wide. Although natural areas such as rivers have been used, recent Olympic races have been held in artificial ponds.

7.0 WINTER SPORTS ACTIVITIES

7.1 Snowmobiling

Snowmobiles are often used on terrain and trail systems similar to cross-country skiing (although they are usually considered incompatible with most forms of nonmotorized winter recreation). Snowmobiles are often used on existing snow-covered fire lanes, trails, and rural roads extending out from a central lodge facility (Figure 520-41). Grades in excess of 12 percent, as well as trails cut into steep side slopes, should be avoided. Ice-covered lakes and ponds are often traversed.

Snowmobiling is often a group sport. Groups gather to race and tour. Racing facilities include *tracks,* generally 1 to 2 mi (1.6 to 3.2 km) in length over wooded terrain, and *sprints*—50-yd to ½-mi (45- to 800-m) strips with a run-out of approximately 1/16 mi (100 m). Cross-country races and tours may involve several hundred participants racing against a clock and are generally 25 to 100 mi (40 to 160 km) in length. Starting areas need to be large enough to accommodate the potentially large number of entrants; an open meadow is often used.

7.2 Cross-Country (Nordic) Skiing

The design of cross-country facilities should reflect the skier's desire to be isolated from other activities, and it should include the following:

1. Adequate separation from such conflicting uses as snowmobiling and downhill (alpine) skiing

2. A variety of terrains, from flat open meadows to steeper grades

3. Relatively *avalanche-safe* terrain

7.3 Downhill (Alpine) Skiing

General:

Precise design criteria and standards for downhill ski areas cannot be established

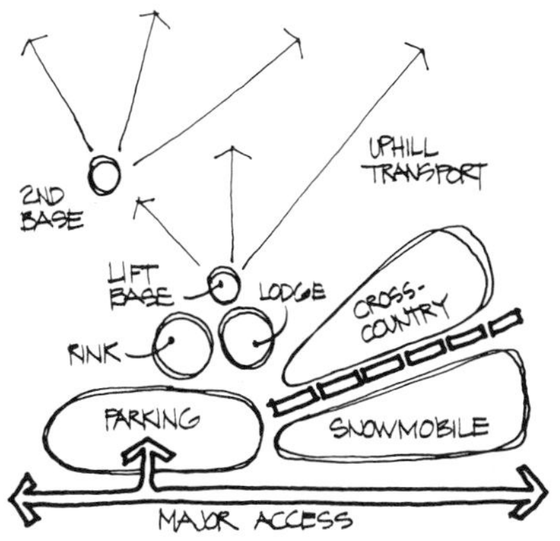
UPHILL TRANSPORT
2ND BASE
LIFT BASE
LODGE
RINK
CROSS-COUNTRY
PARKING
SNOWMOBILE
MAJOR ACCESS

Figure 520-41 Schematic winter sports area.

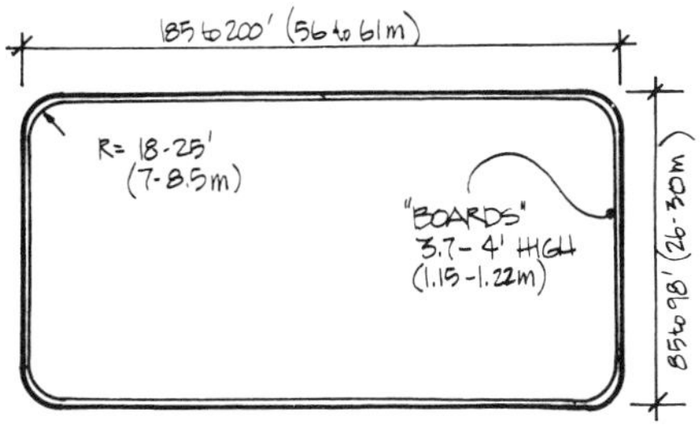
185 to 200' (56 to 61m)
R= 18-25' (7-8.5m)
"BOARDS" 3.7-4' HIGH (1.15-1.22m)
85 to 98' (26-30m)

Figure 520-42 Ice hockey.

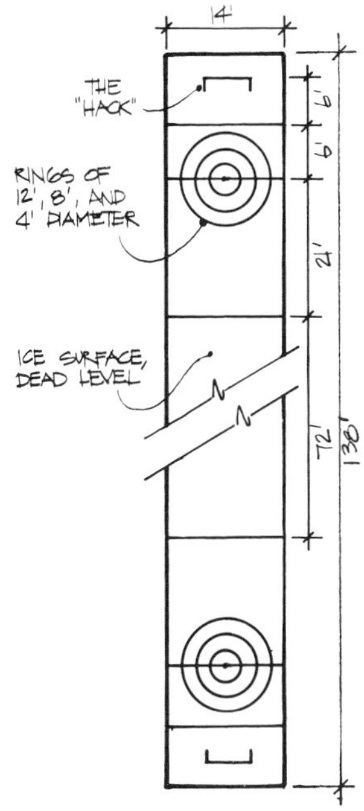
14'
THE "HACK"
RINGS OF 12', 8', AND 4' DIAMETER
ICE SURFACE, DEAD LEVEL
6'
6'
21'
72'
138'

Figure 520-43 Curling.

because each development is influenced by the physiographic character and the opportunities afforded by (1) the site and its topography and (2) the characteristics of the targeted market area. Computer technology is often used to simulate the development of ski areas.

Major Considerations:

Major considerations in the planning and design of downhill skiing facilities include the following:

1. If steep slopes separate the base from the more gentle slopes, a second base or staging area may be desired. Also, multiple bases can reduce congestion around the lodge and excessive wear on the snow.

2. Facilities such as water tanks (with their distribution lines) and sanitary facilities (with their pipelines) should be located away from the trails and out of view of skiers. If feasible, utilities should be installed during the first phase at the ultimate size and capacity required.

3. Existing and potential wind patterns should be analyzed before locating runs, particularly runs through dense timber. Adverse wind patterns can cause a slowdown or stoppage of lifts, can scour snow from previously well-packed slopes, and can decrease comfort and safety. Timber is best cleared in small increments, with a constant evaluation of changes in wind pattern. Leave the edges of timber lines *feathered* to appear more natural and to reduce abrupt changes in wind patterns.

4. Avoid areas that are avalanche-prone, since the prediction and prevention of avalanches is not a reliable science.

5. North facing slopes are preferred because they allow a longer skiing season.

6. Surface drainage should not be directed across the slopes but into channels away from them in order to avoid the problems of icing and of melting snow.

7. Environmental protection and management should be a major consideration in the planning, design, construction, and operation of the facility. Fragile mountain ecosystems can be impacted adversely by poorly planned ski developments. Because ski areas are often at the headwaters of a watershed, they generally have thin soil layers, short growing seasons, and a high degree of off-site visibility.

8. Roads should be as narrow as possible, switch back only where skiing will not occur, and carry runoff water in buried culverts rather than in ditches when control is necessary. If feasible, all roads for the final development should be planned and constructed during the first phase.

7.4 Ice Skating

Competition hockey generally takes place on an indoor rink (Figure 540-42). *Free skating* can be done indoors or outdoors; it requires a solid ice surface and a space relatively free from obstructions. Natural ice is normally swept regularly to remove leaves and other obstructions. Low walls or railings are optional but do offer support for the beginner and a container for ice made by flooding. The size of the area depends on the type of sport to be played on the surface. *Speed skating* is done normally on a race track but can be done more informally on a long stretch of frozen river. European-style tracks are 400 m (437 yd) in length and double-laned. Each lane is 5 m (5½ yd) wide. *Curling* is an ice-surface sport played on a court (Figure 540-43).

7.5 Ice Boating

Ice boating takes place on frozen lakes or rivers. Race courses can be 12 mi (19 km) or more long and should meet the requirement for sailing both with the wind and into it.

7.6 Toboggan, Bobsled, and Luge

Toboggan, bobsled, and luge courses are highly site-specific and are generally associated with Winter Olympic sites. A course is typically 1093 yd (1000 m) in length, and contains both sharp and gentle curves. The average gradient is about 11 percent (a range of 8½ to 15 percent is common). Straightways should be 6½ ft (2 m) wide and curves should be 10 to 22 ft (3 to 6 m) wide; when banked perpendicularly, curves can be as much as 30 ft (9 m) wide. Banked walls are plastered with an ice-snow mixture and may even be finished with a template to meet precise engineering specifications.

8.0 SPECIAL COURSES AND AREAS

8.1 Golf

Golf course design is too complex to be detailed in this section; however, some of the major considerations and variations are summarized below.

The Site:

Gently rolling terrain provides both a better playing course and a visually more interesting course. Positive drainage is essential, and therefore sandy soils are preferred. High-quality water will be required for irrigation at rates of approximately 2 in per week for greens and tees, and 1 to 1½ in per week for fairways, the latter depending on the geographic region. Visual connections between tees, landing areas, and greens are essential.

The Course:

Regulation 18-hole courses have pars ranging from 68 to 72. They can be laid out in one of five basic configurations, their required areas ranging from 140 to 175 acres (57 to 71 ha) (Figure 520-44). The configuration chosen will depend upon the character of the site, the program elements, and such determinants as adjacent housing. Figure 520-45 shows the layout of a typical hole.

The Variations:

There are numerous variations of a regulation 18-hole course which offer alternatives in terms of site size, duration of play, etc. These variations include:

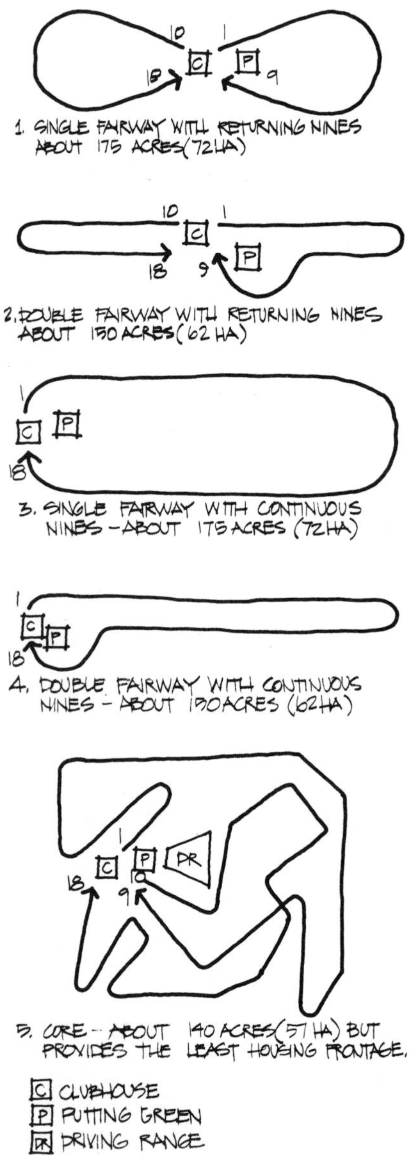
10
1
18
C
P
9
1. SINGLE FAIRWAY WITH RETURNING NINES ABOUT 175 ACRES (72 HA)
2. DOUBLE FAIRWAY WITH RETURNING NINES ABOUT 150 ACRES (62 HA)
3. SINGLE FAIRWAY WITH CONTINUOUS NINES - ABOUT 175 ACRES (72 HA)
4. DOUBLE FAIRWAY WITH CONTINUOUS NINES - ABOUT 150 ACRES (62 HA)
PR
5. CORE - ABOUT 140 ACRES (57 HA) BUT PROVIDES THE LEAST HOUSING FRONTAGE.
C CLUBHOUSE
P PUTTING GREEN
DR DRIVING RANGE

Figure 520-44 Typical golf course arrangements.

1. Thirty-six holes: any combination of the basic configuration.

2. Twenty-seven holes: three returning 9s are preferred; continuous 18 and one returning 9 is permitted.

3. Nine-hole regulation with multiple tees (2 shots taken to each green for a total of 18 shots).

4. Eighteen-hole *executive, pitch 'n' putt, par 3,* or other short courses. These courses are generally 3000 to 4000 yd (2740 to 3660 m) in length with a par of 56 to 60. They require areas of approximately 45 to 60 acres (18 to 24 ha) and use full-size greens to distribute wear.

8.2 Equestrian Facilities

Site Criteria:

Equestrian facilities should be located where they will be 500 ft (150 m) downwind from other public activity centers. Drainage must be positive and controlled both on- and off-site. Runoff must be retained on-site or properly treated before release into storm sewers or natural drainages. The spacing between buildings will be regulated by local fire codes, but usually at least a 15-ft (4.5-m) fire lane is required. Boarding and rental stables should be separated by at least 100 ft (30 m). Horse trails should be an average of 3 to 6 ft (1 to 2 m) wide, 10 ft (3 m) wide for passing, and be clear of overhanging limbs to a height of 12 ft (3.5 m). Grades should not exceed 5 percent, although 10 percent for short distances is permissible. (See Figure 520-46.)

Design Criteria:

1. *Pasture:* 2 acres (0.8 ha) per horse (zoning ordinances vary)

2. *Staff office and apartment:* 226 ft² (21 m²) per staff member

3. *Treatment stalls:* 12 ft × 17 ft (3.5 m × 5 m), 1 per 30 horses

4. *Quarantine stalls:* 12 ft × 12 ft (3.5 m × 3.5 m), 1 per 30 horses

5. *Rental or boarding stalls:* 12 ft × 12 ft × 14 ft (3.5 m × 3.5 m to 3.5 × 4 m), 1 per horse

6. *Hay storage (for 40 horses):* 825 ft² (77 m²)

7. *Grain storage (for 40 horses):* 200 ft² (18.5 m²)

8. *Bedding storage (for 40 horses):* 400 ft² (37 m²)

8.3 Roller Skating

With the advent of plastic wheels, outdoor roller skating is now possible on most hard surfaces whether they are generally flat or steeply sloping. Roller skating should be separated from other modes of travel.

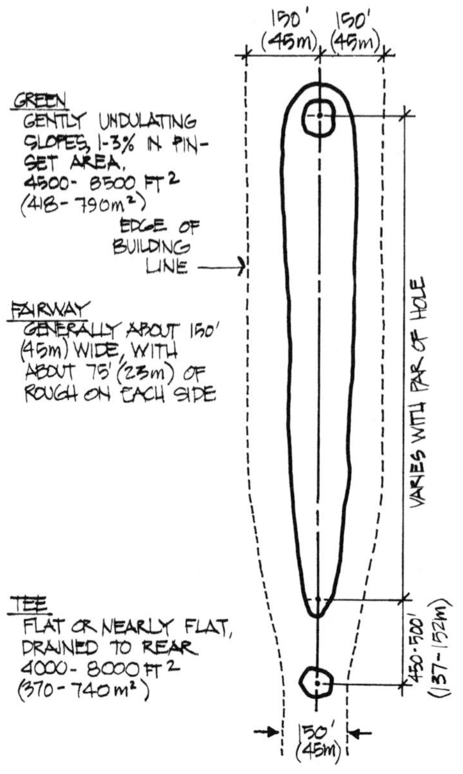
150' (45m)
150' (45m)
GREEN
GENTLY UNDULATING SLOPES, 1-3% IN PIN-SET AREA.
4500- 8500 FT²
(418- 790m²)
EDGE OF BUILDING LINE
FAIRWAY
GENERALLY ABOUT 150' (45m) WIDE, WITH ABOUT 75' (23m) OF ROUGH ON EACH SIDE
VARIES WITH PAR OF HOLE
TEE
FLAT OR NEARLY FLAT, DRAINED TO REAR
4000- 8000 FT²
(370- 740 m²)
450-500' (137-152m)
150' (45m)

Figure 520-45 Typical golf hole.

8.4 Skateboard Parks

Park designs vary, although they usually range from ½ to 5 acres (0.1 to 2 ha) in size. Surfaces should be made of a smooth, fluid, nonjointed material such as shotcrete or fiberglass. Features in a skateboard park include:

1. *Freestyle areas:* about 80 ft × 40 ft (24 m × 12 m), with slightly banked walls.

2. *Slalom run:* about 100 ft (30 m) long, dropping 10 to 15 ft (3 to 4.5 m), with slightly banked walls.

3. *Snake run:* curved channel, with walls 8 to 12 ft (2.4 to 3.5 m) high.

4. *Bowls and pools:* depths from 7 to 12 ft (2.1 to 3.5 m). Pools should include a slight overhanging lip around the edge.

5. *Half pipe:* literally a half pipe with no flat area; variable length; diameter usually around 22 ft (6.7 m). Some walls rise beyond vertical.

6. *Full pipe:* literally a full pipe with no flat spot.

8.5 Jogging Paths

Jogging requires only a path, preferably of crushed stone or a similar resilient material, that is well-drained and has a minimum width of 4 ft (1.2 m). The stone used will depend on local availability but should be smaller than ½ in (12 mm) in diameter and angular enough to pack to a firm surface. Paths should be a minimum of 1 mi (0.62 km) in length and should be arranged in some variation of a figure eight to allow shorter runs and a greater variety of routes. Official marathons are 26 mi 385 yd (4.22 km) long and are generally run on existing paved or dirt roads.

8.6 Exercise Courses

Exercise trails are jogging routes with exercise stations located periodically along the path. The stations can be as close together as 50 yd (46 m) or as far apart as 400 yd (365 m), depending on the total length of the track; 150 to 200 yd (135 to 180 m) apart seems to be a good average. Proprietary tracks are available from several firms complete with stations, signs, and installation guidelines. Some firms offer courses specifically designed for handicapped participants.

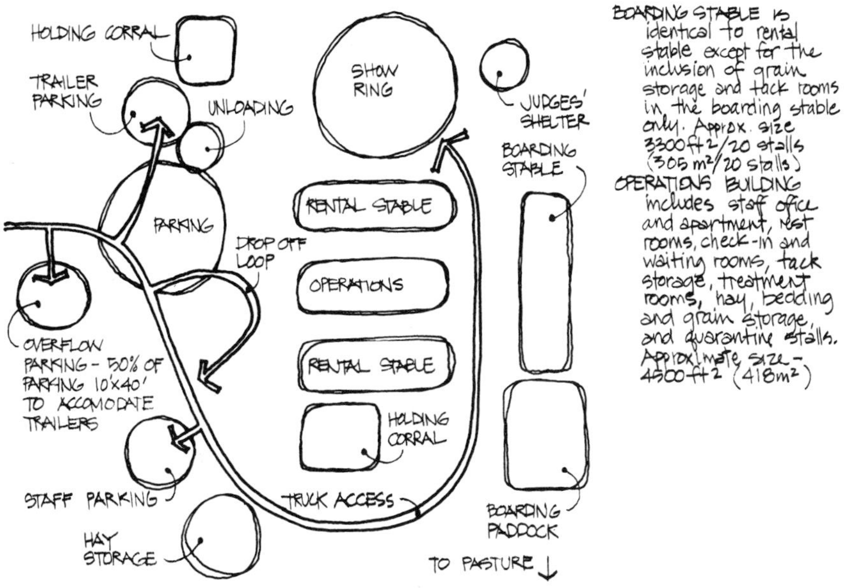
HOLDING CORRAL
TRAILER PARKING
UNLOADING
SHOW RING
JUDGES' SHELTER
BOARDING STABLE
PARKING
DROP OFF LOOP
RENTAL STABLE
OPERATIONS
RENTAL STABLE
HOLDING CORRAL
OVERFLOW PARKING - 50% OF PARKING 10'x40' TO ACCOMODATE TRAILERS
STAFF PARKING
TRUCK ACCESS
HAY STORAGE
BOARDING PADDOCK
TO PASTURE
BOARDING STABLE IS identical to rental stable except for the inclusion of grain storage and tack rooms in the boarding stable only. Approx. size 3300 ft2/20 stalls (305 m2/20 stalls)
OPERATIONS BUILDING includes staff office and apartment, rest rooms, check-in and waiting rooms, tack storage, treatment rooms, hay, bedding and grain storage, and quarantine stalls. Approximate size - 4500 ft2 (418m2)

Figure 520-46 Schematic riding stable layout.

9.0 CAMPING AND PICNICKING

9.1 Organized Camping

Definitions:

Organized camping is defined by the American Camping Association (ACA) as "A sustained experience which provides a creative recreational and educational opportunity in group living in the out-of-doors. It utilizes trained leadership and resources of the natural surroundings to contribute to each camper's mental, physical, social and spiritual growth."

Design:

Organized camp design can be inwardly focused toward a campfire ring or some other feature, such as a swimming pool, or outwardly focused toward a lake or river. Most are located in a forested setting, with good breeze orientation and readily available potable water.

Spatial Standards:

Although camps vary in size and configuration, a camp for 75 to 100 campers averages approximately 35 to 40 acres (14 to 16.5 ha) in size.

1. *A central core:* service area garage, staff and help quarters, central washhouse, infirmary, dining lodge, administration building, and nature study center.

2. *Units:* organized in groups of six 4-bed tents or cabins, plus counselor accommodations, a bathroom, and a central core. Units of this size occupy roughly 2 acres (0.8 ha).

ACA Standards:

The ACA has established standards by which they evaluate camps seeking accreditation. These standards address camp administration, personnel programs, and specific programs for persons with special needs, as well as site conditions (Figure 520-47). Contact the ACA for complete standards.

9.2 Trailers

The cross section of a trailer pad should be level across the width of the trailer. A slight slope along its length is permissible, with a slope toward the rear preferred. Trailers load on the passenger side; utility connections are on the driver's side (Figures 520-48 and 520-49).

Camping is feasible for handicapped individuals. The major design adaptation required for those who are handicapped is the provision of paved surfaces between campsites and other features, such as water, comfort stations, and parking.

9.3 Individual Campsites

Family-size sites should be 14 ft × 16 ft (4.2 m × 4.9 m), with a soft tent pad within this area. Campfire rings should be raised 2 ft (0.6 m) and seating should be provided within 3 ft (1 m) of the fire. Push lids on trash cans are preferred, and these lids

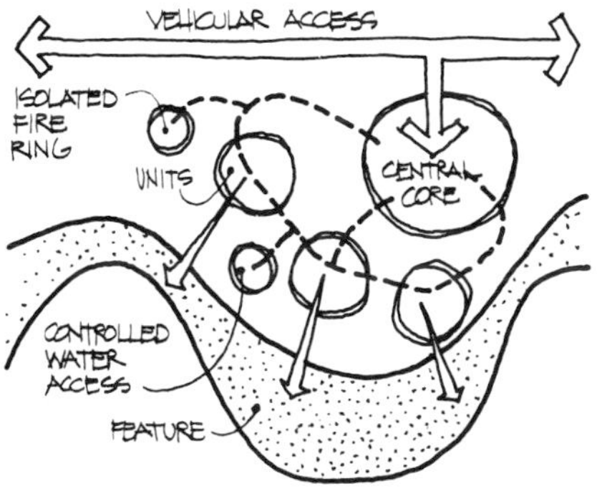
VEHICULAR ACCESS
ISOLATED FIRE RING
UNITS
CENTRAL CORE
CONTROLLED WATER ACCESS
FEATURE

Figure 520-47 Outwardly focused camp.

should be 40 in (1 m) from the ground. Trails should be designed without obstructions to a height of 7½ ft (2.3 m).

9.4 Picnic Areas

Picnic areas are generally designed in clusters of 10 to 100 units with 35 ft (10.7 m) between units. (A *unit* consists of a table with benches, a grill, and a trash receptacle.) A maximum density of 20 units per gross acre is desired, with a buffer strip of 200 ft (60 m) between picnicking and other activities. Comfort stations should be provided and placed at least 50 ft (15 m) away, but no further than 400 ft (122 m) away from any unit, and drinking fountains should be within 100 ft (30 m) of the units. Centralized parking at 1 space per 1.5 tables is required, with several tables within 400 ft (122 m) of the parking area.

Handicapped persons can be easily accommodated by providing paved access to facilities and by making minor modifica-

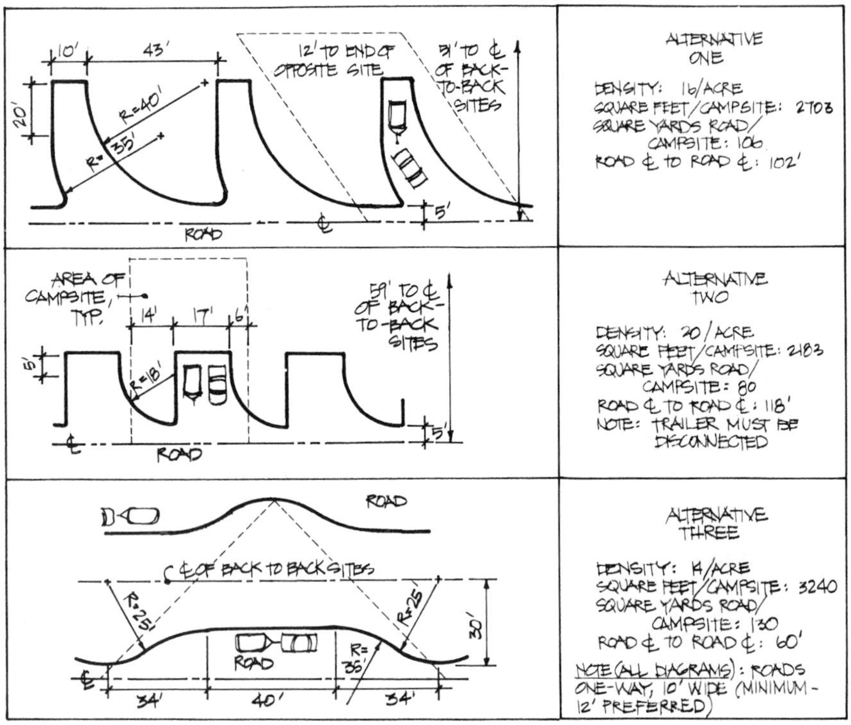
ALTERNATIVE ONE
DENSITY: 16/ACRE
SQUARE FEET/CAMPSITE: 2708
SQUARE YARDS ROAD/CAMPSITE: 106
ROAD ℄ TO ROAD ℄: 102'
ALTERNATIVE TWO
DENSITY: 20/ACRE
SQUARE FEET/CAMPSITE: 2183
SQUARE YARDS ROAD/CAMPSITE: 80
ROAD ℄ TO ROAD ℄: 118'
NOTE: TRAILER MUST BE DISCONNECTED
ALTERNATIVE THREE
DENSITY: 14/ACRE
SQUARE FEET/CAMPSITE: 3240
SQUARE YARDS ROAD/CAMPSITE: 130
ROAD ℄ TO ROAD ℄: 60'
NOTE (ALL DIAGRAMS): ROADS ONE-WAY, 10' WIDE (MINIMUM - 12' PREFERRED)
12' TO END OF OPPOSITE SITE
31' TO ℄ OF BACK-TO-BACK SITES
AREA OF CAMPSITE, TYP.
59' TO ℄ OF BACK-TO-BACK SITES
℄ OF BACK TO BACK SITES
ROAD

Figure 520-48 Sample motor camping layouts.

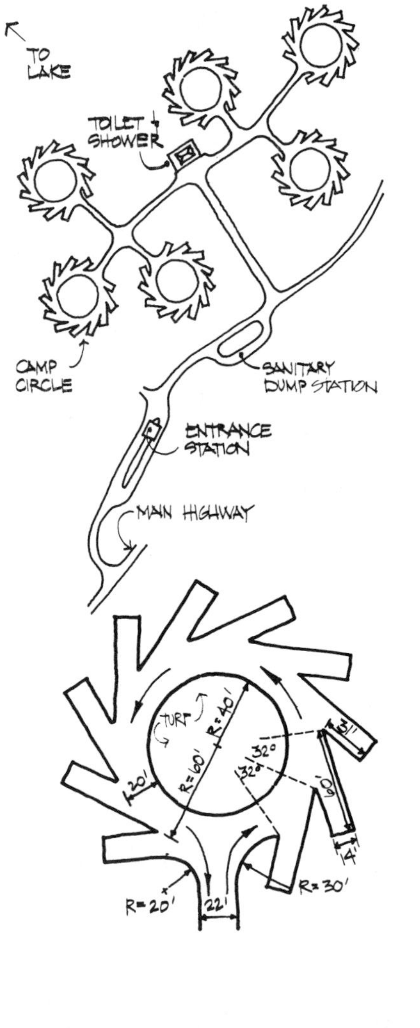
TO LAKE
TOILET + SHOWER
CAMP CIRCLE
SANITARY DUMP STATION
ENTRANCE STATION
MAIN HIGHWAY
TURF
R=40'
R=60'
R=20'
R=30'
32°
22'
20'
80'

Figure 520-49 Rosette trailer parking layout.

tions to site furnishings. Allow 8 ft (2.4 m) between tables used by wheelchairs and a clear space 30 in (0.8 m) high and 24 in (0.6 m) deep under the table to allow a wheelchair to slide under. Grills should be 30 in (0.8 m) tall at their top, rotate 360 degrees, and be provided with a utility shelf for cooking tools. Grills on adjustable supports offer flexibility for many user groups. Keep plant material back 3 ft (1 m) and cleared to a height of 7½ ft (2.3 m).

10.0 RANGE SPORTS

10.1 Rifle and Pistol Range

General Information:

1. Targets can be placed at varying distances from the firing line (staggered butt range) or can be aligned on a single line with firing positions staggered (butt-in-line range).

2. Consideration should be given to problems that may result from the noise, particularly downwind of a range. Refer to Section 660: Sound Control, for various ways this problem may be treated.

3. Existing hillsides or built-up berms should be used behind and to the sides of the target area for safety reasons (Figures 520-50 through 520-52).

Range Distances:

1. *Small-bore rifle:* 50 ft, 50 yd, 50 m*, 100 yd

2. *High-power rifle:* 100 yd, 200 yd, 300 yd,* 300 m(I†), 500 to 600 yd, 800 to 900 yd, 1000 yd

3. *Metallic silhouette:*

- **a.** Small-bore rifle: 40 m, 60 m, 77 m, 100 m
- **b.** High-power rifle: 200 m, 300 m, 385 m, 500 m
- **c.** Pistol: 50 m, 100 m, 150 m, 700 m
- **d.** Pistol shoot range: 25 m, 50 m, 75 m, 100 m

4. *Outdoor pistol:* 25 yd, 25 m(I†), 50 yd, 50 m(I†)

5. *Pistol (police combat course):* 7 yd, 15 yd, 25 yd, 50 yd

6. *International running boar:* 50 m

10.2 Archery

1. The distance to the target should be 300 ft (91 m) for men and 180 ft (55 m) for women.

---

* competition distance.

† I = international distance.

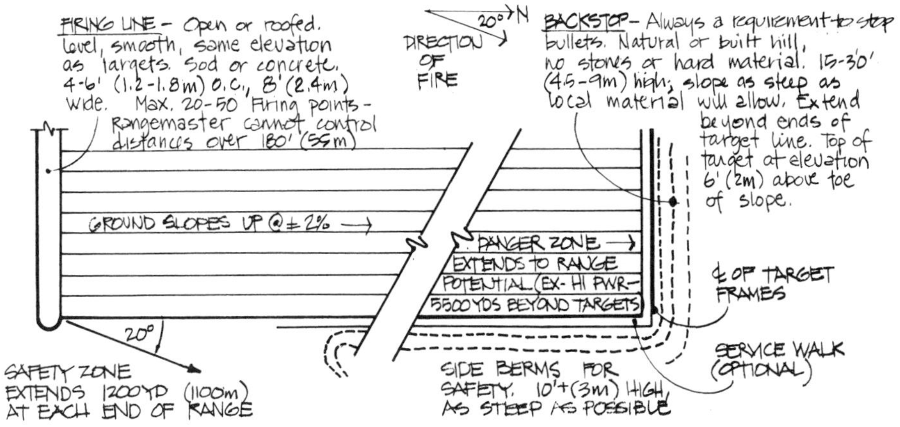
FIRING LINE - Open or roofed. Level, smooth, same elevation as targets. Sod or concrete. 4-6' (1.2-1.8m) O.C., 8' (2.4m) wide. Max. 20-50 firing points - Rangemaster cannot control distances over 180' (55m)
DIRECTION OF FIRE
20° N
BACKSTOP - Always a requirement to stop bullets. Natural or built hill, no stones or hard material. 15-30' (4.5-9m) high; slope as steep as local material will allow. Extend beyond ends of target line. Top of target at elevation 6' (2m) above toe of slope.
GROUND SLOPES UP @ ± 2% →
DANGER ZONE → EXTENDS TO RANGE POTENTIAL (EX-HI PWR-5500 YDS BEYOND TARGETS)
℄ OF TARGET FRAMES
20°
SAFETY ZONE EXTENDS 1200YD (1100m) AT EACH END OF RANGE
SIDE BERMS FOR SAFETY. 10'+(3m) HIGH, AS STEEP AS POSSIBLE
SERVICE WALK (OPTIONAL)

Figure 520-50 Basic rifle/pistol range layout.

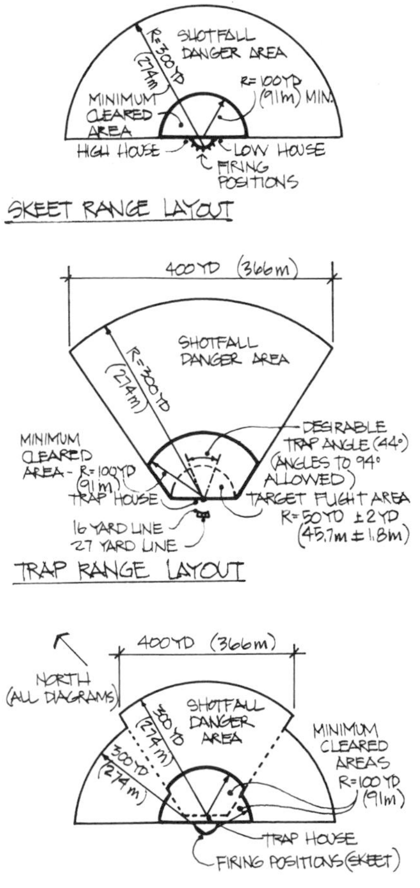
SHOTFALL DANGER AREA
R=300YD (274m)
R=100YD (91m) MIN.
MINIMUM CLEARED AREA
HIGH HOUSE
LOW HOUSE
FIRING POSITIONS
SKEET RANGE LAYOUT
400YD (366m)
SHOTFALL DANGER AREA
R=300YD (274m)
MINIMUM CLEARED AREA - R=100YD (91m)
DESIRABLE TRAP ANGLE (44°) (ANGLES TO 94° ALLOWED)
TRAP HOUSE
TARGET FLIGHT AREA R=50YD ±2YD (45.7m ± 1.8m)
16 YARD LINE
27 YARD LINE
TRAP RANGE LAYOUT
NORTH (ALL DIAGRAMS)
400YD (366m)
SHOTFALL DANGER AREA
300YD (274m)
MINIMUM CLEARED AREAS R=100YD (91m)
TRAP HOUSE
FIRING POSITIONS (SKEET)

Figure 520-51 Combination skeet and trap range layouts.

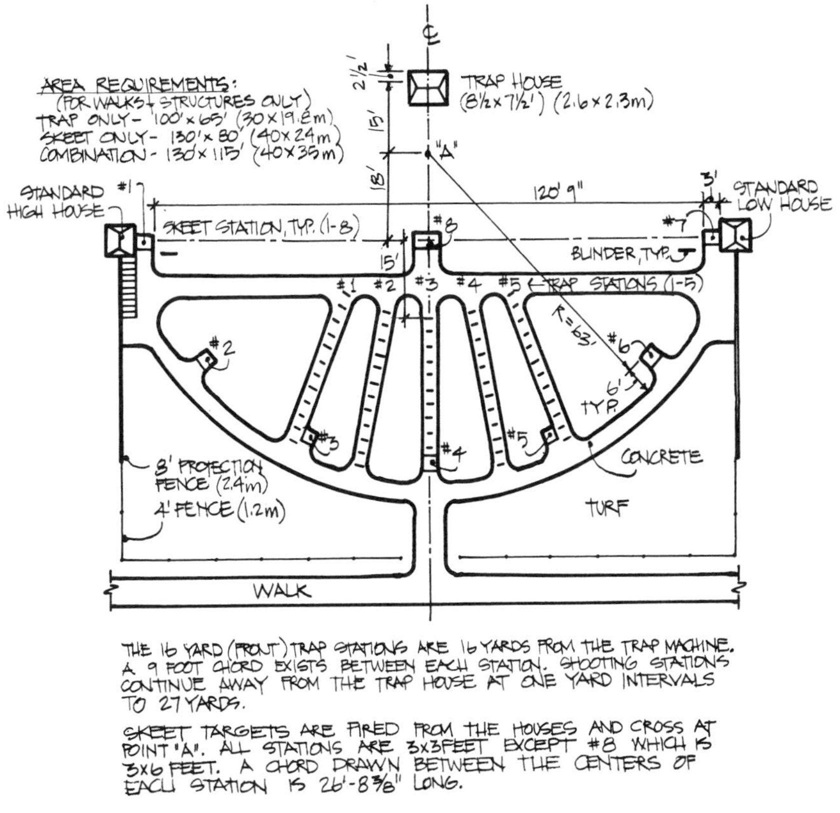
℄
2½'
15'
18'
TRAP HOUSE (8½x7½') (2.6x2.3m)
"A"
AREA REQUIREMENTS: (FOR WALKS & STRUCTURES ONLY)
TRAP ONLY - 100'x65' (30x19.8m)
SKEET ONLY - 130'x80' (40x24m)
COMBINATION - 130'x115' (40x35m)
STANDARD HIGH HOUSE
#1
120' 9"
3'
STANDARD LOW HOUSE
SKEET STATION, TYP. (1-8)
#8
#7
15'
BLINDER, TYP.
#1 #2 #3 #4 #5 TRAP STATIONS (1-5)
R=63'
#2
#6
6' TYP.
#3
#4
#5
8' PROTECTION FENCE (2.4m)
4' FENCE (1.2m)
CONCRETE
TURF
WALK
THE 16 YARD (FRONT) TRAP STATIONS ARE 16 YARDS FROM THE TRAP MACHINE. A 9 FOOT CHORD EXISTS BETWEEN EACH STATION. SHOOTING STATIONS CONTINUE AWAY FROM THE TRAP HOUSE AT ONE YARD INTERVALS TO 27 YARDS.
SKEET TARGETS ARE FIRED FROM THE HOUSES AND CROSS AT POINT "A". ALL STATIONS ARE 3X3FEET EXCEPT #8 WHICH IS 3X6 FEET. A CHORD DRAWN BETWEEN THE CENTERS OF EACH STATION IS 26'-8⅜" LONG.

Figure 520-52 Combination skeet and trap range.

2. Targets should be 16 to 20 ft (4.9 to 6 m) on-center, with the bullseye 4 to 4½ ft (1.2 to 1.4 m) off the ground.

3. The archer and the target should be at approximately the same elevation, the range should be free from hard obstructions, and the site should be sheltered from wind.

4. For visual reasons, the archer should face within 45 degrees of north in the northern hemisphere; the preferred background for a target is a natural or built-up embankment or tall, dense vegetation.

5. Existing hillsides or built-up berms should be used both behind and to the sides of the target area for safety reasons.

10.3 Driving Range (Golf)

Figure 520-53 illustrates a typical driving range for golf.

11.0 SPECTATOR FACILITIES

11.1 Council Rings

The diameter of council rings is normally not very large, because beyond about 15 to 20 ft (4.5 to 6 m) eye contact between participants is lost. Allow at least 20 in (0.5 m) of bench space per person. If the area has a natural bowl shape, this

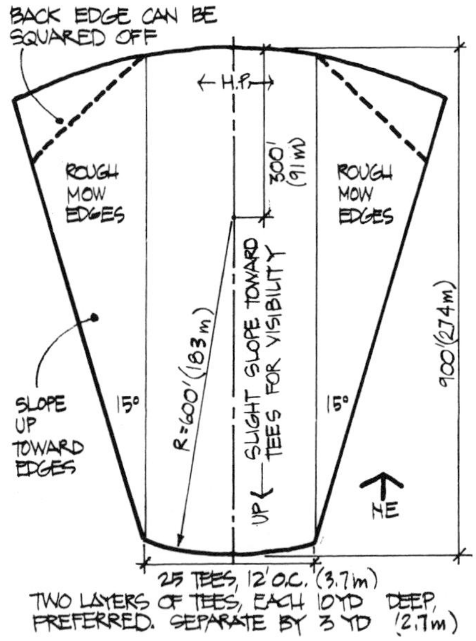
BACK EDGE CAN BE SQUARED OFF
H.P.
ROUGH MOW EDGES
ROUGH MOW EDGES
300' (91 m)
SLOPE UP TOWARD EDGES
15°
15°
R=600' (183 m)
UP ← SLIGHT SLOPE TOWARD TEES FOR VISIBILITY
900' (274 m)
NE
25 TEES, 12' O.C. (3.7 m)
TWO LAYERS OF TEES, EACH 10 YD DEEP, PREFERRED. SEPARATE BY 3 YD (2.7 m)

Figure 520-53 Driving range (golf).

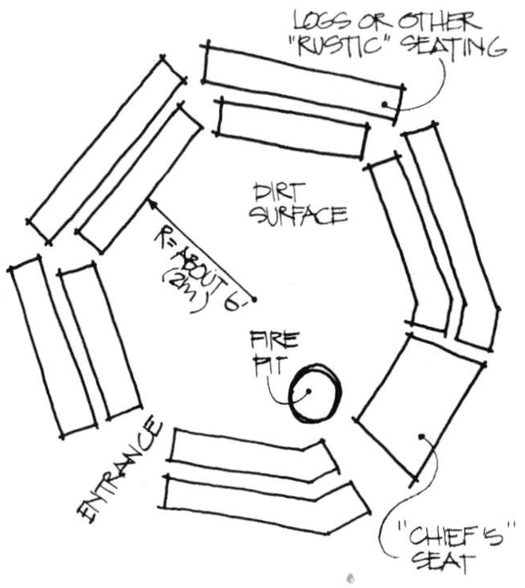
LOGS OR OTHER "RUSTIC" SEATING
DIRT SURFACE
R= ABOUT 6' (2m)
FIRE PIT
ENTRANCE
"CHIEF'S" SEAT

Figure 520-54 Council ring.

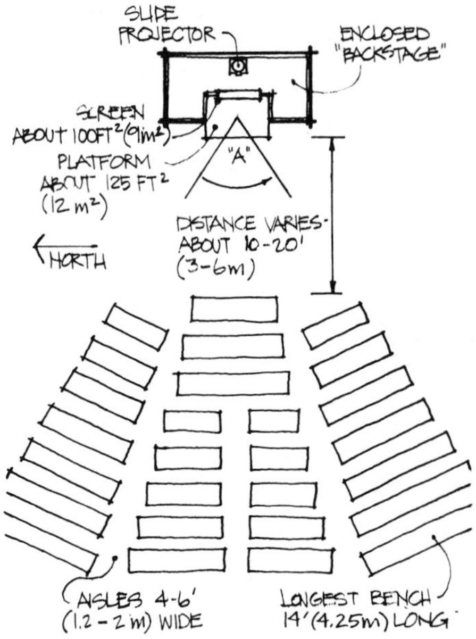
SLIDE PROJECTOR
ENCLOSED "BACKSTAGE"
SCREEN ABOUT 100FT² (9m²)
PLATFORM ABOUT 125 FT² (12 m²)
"A"
NORTH
DISTANCE VARIES· ABOUT 10-20' (3-6m)
AISLES 4-6' (1.2-2 m) WIDE
LONGEST BENCH 14' (4.25m) LONG

Figure 520-55 Interpretive amphitheater.

allows better viewing for more people (Figure 520-54).

A fire ring is optional, but if included it should be at least 6 ft (2 m) in diameter and 5 ft (1.5 m) from the nearest seated audience. The leader's spot should have a dark background and face the direction of the setting sun.

11.2 Amphitheaters

Small Amphitheaters:

Small amphitheaters, usually designed for campgrounds, consist of seats, a small stage or podium, nighttime lighting, and sometimes a public-address system and provision for showing slides and films (Figure 520-55). There should also be ramps and associated special design facilities for those who are handicapped. Where possible, the amphitheater should be built into a naturally existing or graded bowl and should face away from late afternoon sun. In addition, the following design guidelines can be used:

1. Aisles should be at least 5 ft (1.5 m) wide, with a maximum space of 30 ft (9 m) between aisles.

2. The backstage area can be enclosed, and where needed it can be used to set up and store slide and film equipment for rear-projection screens.

3. The platform is usually about 18 in (0.45 m) off the ground and a minimum of 125 ft^2 (11.6 m^2) in size.

4. Angle *A* varies to as wide as 120 degrees, but more often it ranges between 60 and 90 degrees.

Major Outdoor Theaters:

Major outdoor theaters are usually characterized by professional theater lighting, curtains, orchestra facilities, and elaborate sound systems. Some have wooden or metal seats with backs. The seating area may be concrete, with step lights. Ticket sales areas, restrooms, backstage areas, concession areas, and adequate parking are all necessary.

These facilities pose many more complex design, construction, and operations issues than the basic interpretive or small amphitheaters. Persons interested in facilities of this magnitude should consult the appropriate major reference books and go visit and study successful projects. In the United States the following are considered good examples: Wolf Trap Farm Park Amphitheater (Vienna, Virginia), Starlight Theater (Kansas City, Missouri), Concord Pavilion (Concord, California), Hollywood Bowl (Hollywood, California), and Red Rock Amphitheater (Denver, Colorado).

11.3 Sports Stadiums

General:

Spectator sight lines are the principal design consideration in stadium design. The seating capacity can be increased by making the seating either longer or higher. In general, longer, lower seating is less expensive but has fewer seats that are considered prime (Figure 520-56).

Spatial Standards:

Seats can be mounted to either the tread or the riser (Figure 520-57). Treads should never be less than 22 in (0.55 m) wide; 26 in (0.66 m) is preferred. A tread width of 30 in (0.76 m) should be used for benches with backs and 32 in (0.81 m) used for chair-type seating.

Provision for those who are physically handicapped is important and requires special consideration. Refer to Sections 240 and 241: Access and Egress, for more information. Some of the major considerations follow.

Spaces for wheelchairs should be 48 in (1.2 m) deep and 34 in (0.87 m) wide. Seats for persons using crutches or braces should be 24 in (0.6 m) wide, with 28 in (0.71 m) of clear space in front. Spaces for wheelchairs and persons with crutches should be accessible by a level floor or ramp (such as at the front or rear of the stadium). The handicapped-spectator area should be recessed to allow for free circulation.

There are several important variables that have to be known to determine the amount of parking that is needed for a sports stadium. In the United States the following standards are often used, although each case may have some special feature.

For stadiums near mass transportation, such as New York City's Yankee Stadium, or for stadiums on university campuses where students, faculty, and many guests are within walking distance, there may be very little need for on-site parking. As a rule of thumb, if people do come by car they come at a rate of three passengers per car. For peak crowds, such as at football games, many people will normally come by chartered or special buses. A stadium with a seating capacity of 50,000 people should have spaces for about 100 buses.

There will be a need for special parking spaces for people who are physically handicapped. The parking spaces should be 13 ft (4 m) wide, and there should be about 1 space for every 50 standard parking spaces; this number should be determined based upon local needs. A drop-off zone should be provided within 50 ft (15 m) of an entrance where those who are physically handicapped can gain access to the stadium.

12.0 SPECIAL AREAS

The activities listed below are normally accommodated by providing enough open space to set up temporary facilities during special events.

12.1 Dancing

When folk or square dancing is done outdoors, it requires a flat and unobstructed area of about 50 ft × 100 ft (15 m × 30 m). Hardwood is the preferred surface for dancing, but smooth concrete or other types of hard paving can be used. In some situations, a covered pavilion with a band platform, special lighting, and amplification equipment is more desirable.

12.2 Boxing

The boxing surface should be no more than 4 ft (1.2 m) off the ground and 16 ft × 24 ft (5 m × 8 m) in size within the ropes, plus 2 ft (0.6 m) around all edges. The surface should be padded with 1 in (25 mm) of a stiff cushioning material covered with canvas and laced outside the apron of the ring (Figure 520-58).

12.3 Wrestling

For international competition, the mat is 39 ft 3 in × 39 ft 3 in (12 m × 12 m) square with an inner circle of 9 ft 6 in (9 m) in diameter (Figure 520-59).

The platform may be raised 1.1 m off the floor in international competition, but under NCAA rules, it must not be raised.

12.4 Table Games

Checkers:

A minimum table size is 2 ft × 2 ft (0.6 m × 0.6 m). It should have seating for two, plus enough gathering space for onlookers.

Table Tennis (Ping-Pong):

A regulation-size table top is 5 ft × 9 ft (1.5 m × 2.7 m) wide and 2½ ft (0.75 m) high, and a small table for children (or when used as a picnic table) is 4 ft × 8 ft (1.2 m × 2.4 m) wide and 2½ ft (0.75 m) high. Allow 6 ft (1.8 m) of unobstructed space between tables or adjacent facilities/structures. This dimension also serves the needs for access by those who are handicapped.

13.0 TOT LOTS AND PLAYGROUNDS

13.1 General

Many experts advocate a play environment for children that provides opportunities for development of motor skills, make-believe, building, competitions, and quiet, solitary activities. Activities that are linked together so that many children can use them simultaneously are generally preferred to isolated apparatus. Safety both within and outside of the playground is important, but an overemphasis on safety measures can sometimes lower the quality of the play environment (Frost; Rutledge).

Safety Measures:

Safety measures are dealt with extensively in *A Handbook for Public Playground Safety* by the U.S. Consumer Product Safety Commission. General concerns include the following:

1. Hard surfaces are more expensive to install but less expensive to maintain. They are not generally recommended because they do not cushion falls as well as soft materials, such as sand, pea gravel, bark chips, and rubber.

2. After determining the *use zone* of each piece of equipment (by calculating, for instance, the fullest arc of the swing plus jump-off space), allow 8 ft (2.5 m) between pieces of equipment and between pieces of equipment and walls, fences, etc.

3. Avoid visual barriers that could hide potential collisions.

Dimensions:

Provide seating for supervisors, and storage for loose apparatus, maintenance equipment, etc. Tot lots generally average about 2400 to 5000 ft^2 (225 to 465 m^2) in size. More complex playgrounds, including areas for paved courts, shelter, a wading pool, etc., average 2½ to 10 acres (1 to 4 ha) in size.

13.2 Adventure Playgrounds

Creative, junk, or *adventure* playgrounds are generally fenced areas which offer children a variety of junk building supplies with which to assemble forts, play equipment, etc. Concerns about this kind of playground revolve around safety and visual impact. Boundary screening is important, and generally the child will have a safer and more educational experience under the eye of a supervisor/helper who can watch, check out tools, and offer help to builders.

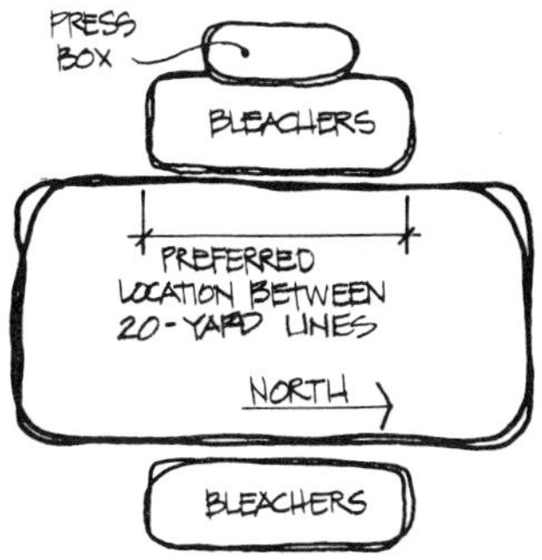
PRESS BOX
BLEACHERS
PREFERRED LOCATION BETWEEN 20-YARD LINES
NORTH
BLEACHERS

Figure 520-56 Schematic sports stadium.

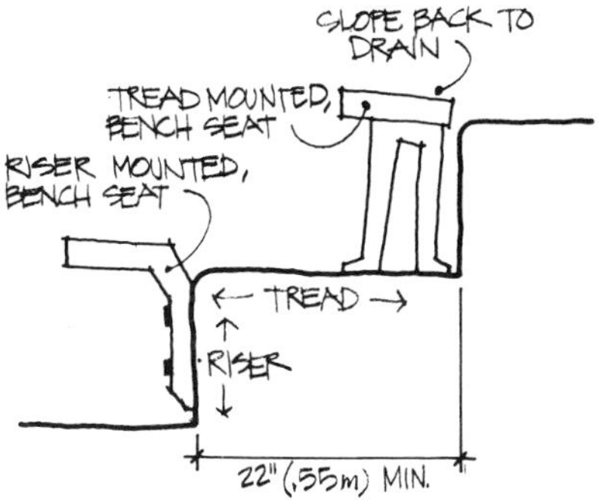
SLOPE BACK TO DRAIN
TREAD MOUNTED, BENCH SEAT
RISER MOUNTED, BENCH SEAT
TREAD
RISER
22" (.55m) MIN.

Figure 520-57 Stadium seating.

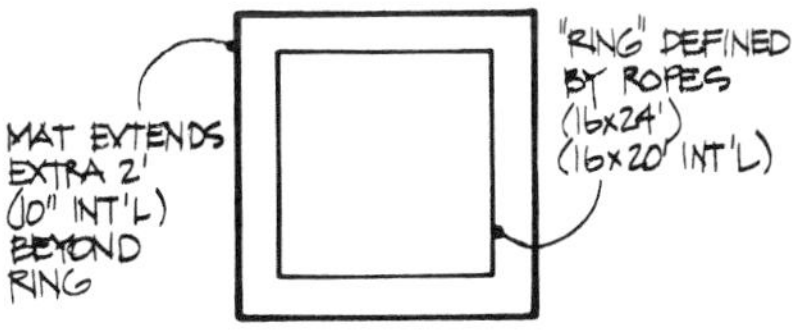
MAT EXTENDS EXTRA 2' (60" INT'L) BEYOND RING
"RING" DEFINED BY ROPES (16x24') (16x20' INT'L)

Figure 520-58 Boxing layout.

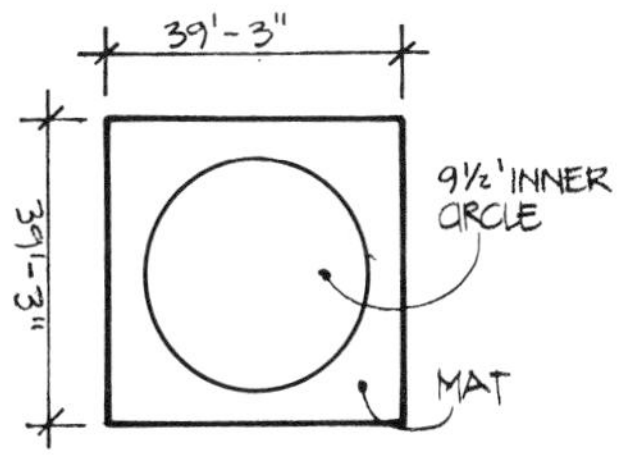
39'-3"
39'-3"
9½' INNER CIRCLE
MAT

Figure 520-59 Wrestling layout.

13.3 Nature Trails

Nature trails are paths along which are placed interpretive stations to explain the surroundings. These paths can be made accessible to those who are blind by adding braille strips or raised letters to the interpretive plaques, using textured surfaces on the ground plane to identify the interpretive stations, and providing low curbs to help define the pathway. If the path is to accommodate those with mobility handicaps, it should have a minimum width of 7 ft (2.1 m), a maximum grade of 8 percent, and a firm surface. The adjacent vegetation should not overhang the path at a height less than 7½ ft (2.3 m). The trail may also be delineated with ropes running through rings on 36-in (1-m) posts, and knots can be used to call attention to upcoming interpretive stations [U.S. Department of Housing and Urban Development (HUD)]. (Refer to Sections 240 and 241: Access and Egress, for more information.)

SPORTS ORGANIZATIONS

There are many organizations and companies in the United States and around the world that provide guidelines for the planning, design, construction, operation, and maintenance of both competition- and noncompetition-level athletic facilities. The list shown below includes only U.S.-based organizations. In other parts of the world these guidelines may not apply; they should therefore be checked against local customs and practices. Specific postal addresses should be rechecked before attempting to make any contact.

Badminton

U.S. Badminton Association
P. O. Box 237
Swartz Creek, MI 48473

Baseball, Babe Ruth League

Babe Ruth League, Inc.
P. O. Box 5000
Trenton, NJ 08638

Baseball, Little League

Little League Baseball, Inc.
P. O. Box 3485
Williamsport, PA 17701

Bocce, Croquet, Deck Tennis, Horseshoes, Shuffleboard

General Sport Craft Co., Ltd.
140 Woodbine Street
Bergenfield, NJ 07621

Camping

American Camping Association
Bradford Woods
Martinsville, IN 46151

Croquet

See Bocce

Exercise Courses

The Gamefield Concept
2088 Union Street, Suite One
San Francisco, CA 94123

Parcourse, Ltd.
3701 Buchanan Street
San Francisco, CA 94123

Football, Junior League

Pop Warner Football
1315 Walnut Street Building, Suite 606
Philadelphia, PA 19107

Golf

U.S. Golf Association
Far Hills, NJ 07931

Handball

U.S. Handball Association
4101 Dempster Street
Skokie, IL 60076

Hockey

Amateur Hockey Association of the U.S.
2997 Broadmoor Valley Road
Colorado Springs, CO 80906

Ice Skating

Ice Skating Institute of America
1000 Skokie Boulevard
Wilmette, IL 60091

Platform Tennis

American Platform Tennis Association, Inc.
P. O. Box 901
Upper Montclair, NJ 07043

Paddle Tennis

U.S. Paddle Tennis Association, Inc.
189 Seeley Street
Brooklyn, NY 11218

Racquetball

U.S. Racquetball Association
4101 Dempster Street
Skokie, IL 60076

Rifle and Pistol Ranges

National Rifle Association of America
1600 Rhode Island Ave., N.W.
Washington, DC 20036

Roller Skating

U.S. Amateur Confederation of Roller Skating
P. O. Box 83067
Lincoln, NE 68501

Roque

American Roque League, Inc.
4205 Briar Creek Lane
Dallas, TX 75214

Shuffleboard

American Shuffleboard Leagues, Inc.
210 Paterson Plank Road
Union City NJ 07087

Skeet

National Skeet Shooters Association
P. O. Box 28188
San Antonio, TX 78228

Winchester-Western
Recreational Shooting & Marksmanship Department
275 Winchester Avenue
New Haven, CT 06504

Skiing

U.S. Ski Association
P. O. Box 100
Park City, UT 84060

Softball

Amateur Softball Association
2801 North East 50th
Oklahoma City, OK 73111

Special Olympics

Special Olympics, Inc.
1701 K Street, N.W.
Suite 203
Washington, DC 20006

Speed Skating

Amateur Skating Union of the U.S.
4423 West Deming Place
Chicago, IL 60639

Tennis

U.S. Lawn Tennis Association
51 East 42nd Street
New York, NY 10017

U.S. Tennis Association
Education & Research Center
739 Alexander Road
Princeton, NJ 08540

Trapshooting

Amateur Trapshooting Association
601 W. National Road
Vandalia, OH 45377

Remington Arms Co., Inc.
Bridgeport, CT 06602

General

International Amateur Athletic Federation (IAAF)
162 Upper Richmond Road
Putney, London SW152SL, England

National Collegiate Athletic Association (NCAA)
NCAA Publishing Department
P. O. Box 1906
Mission, KS 66226

National Federation of State High School Athletic Associations
11724 Plaza Circle
P. O. Box 20626
Kansas City, MO 64195

Amateur Athletic Union of the U.S.
3400 West 86th Street
Indianapolis, IN 46268

American Alliance for Health, Physical Education and Dance
Division of Girls' and Women's Sports
1900 Association Drive
Reston, VA 22091

REFERENCES

Arlott, John (ed). *The Oxford Companion to Sports and Games,* Oxford University Press, New York, 1975.

Bennett, George W. *Management of Lakes and Ponds,* 2d ed., Van Nostrand Reinhold, New York, 1970.

Cuddon, J. A. *The International Dictionary of Sports and Games,* Schocken Books, New York, 1979.

Davidson, Ben. *The Skateboard Book,* Grosset and Dunlap, New York, 1979.

Diagram Group. *The Official World Encyclopedia of Sports and Games,* Ruth Midgley (ed.), Paddington Press, New York, 1979.

Doell, C. E., and L. F. Twardzik. *Elements of Park and Recreation Administration,* Burgess, Minneapolis, MN, 1979.

Frost, Reuben B. (vol. ed.). *Encyclopedia of Physical Education,* vol. 1: *Fitness and Sports,* Addison-Wesley, Reading, MA, 1977.

Gabrielsen, M. Alexander (ed.). *Swimming Pools—A Guide to Their Planning, Design and Operation, A Project of the Council for National Cooperation in Aquatics,* 3d ed., Hoffman, Ft. Lauderdale, FL, 1975.

Gardiner, Fredric M. *Wings on the Ice,* Yachting Publishing Corporation, New York, 1938.

Jones, Rees L., and Guy L. Rando. *Golf Course Developments, Technical Bulletin 70,* Urban Land Institute, Washington, DC, 1974.

Malo, John W. *Snowmobiling—The Guide,* Macmillan, New York, 1971.

Menke, Frank G., and Peter Palmer. *The Encyclopedia of Sports,* A. S. Barnes, New York, 1978.

Patterson, George R. (ed.). *AAU Boxing Rules,* Amateur Athletic Union of the United States, New York, 1969.

Putnam, Harold (ed.). *The Dartmouth Book of Winter Sports,* A. S. Barnes, New York, 1939.

Rutledge, Albert J. *Anatomy of a Park,* McGraw-Hill, New York, 1971.

Tourbier, J., and R. Westmacott. *Lakes and Ponds,* Urban Land Institute, Washington, DC, 1976.

Urban Research and Development Corporation. *Recreation Carrying Capacity Handbook—Methods and Techniques for Planning Design and Management,* prepared for the Chief Engineers, U.S. Army, Washington, DC, 1980.

Webster's Sports Dictionary, Merriam-Webster, Springfield, MA, 1976. ■

section 530: Pools and Fountains

CREDITS

Contributor:

Richard Chaix
CMS Collaborative
Carmel, California

Illustrations:

Rick Briggs
Environmental Planning Consultants
Cape Meares, Oregon

Reviewers:

Angela Danadjieva
Danadjieva and Koenig Associates
Tiburon, California

Edward Janelli, Senior Landscape Architect
Department of Public Works
City of San Francisco, California

E. Byron McCulley
Amphion Environmental, Inc.
Oakland, California

Kevin Shanley
The SWA Group
Houston, Texas

CONTENTS

1.0 HISTORY

Contemporary water displays rely heavily on historic precedent, with elements usually abstracted to satisfy broader design and environmental constraints.

1.1 Middle East

The use of water in decorative applications dates from the development of irrigation techniques in desert climates, particularly in the Middle East. Because water was such a scarce and valuable commodity in arid lands, it seldom was used exclusively for decorative purposes. Instead, some of the water and the systems needed for irrigation were turned into decorative features in the gardens, via channels, pools, and fountains, before being used for non-decorative purposes. Mesopotamian and Egyptian displays tended to be simple geometric pools and channels and often contained aquatic plants. Due to Islamic religious sanctions against standing water and the representation of living things, Persian designs emphasized the moving water itself, leading to the development of pressurized displays.

1.2 Europe

Islamic technology was transported to Europe during the Moslem conquest of Spain in the eighth century, eventually influencing the use of water in Italy and the rest of Western Europe.

The earliest use of water for decorative applications in Europe had the same utilitarian origins as in the Middle East. During the Italian Renaissance, water began to be applied as a purely decorative element, first as a single basin adorned with statuary, and ultimately as the more complex gravity-powered displays in the hilly areas north of Rome, exemplified by the sixteenth century Villa D'Este. Later European installations included the fountains at Versailles in France and the canals and lakes of seventeenth- and eighteenth-century England.

1.3 China and Japan

Concurrent with this development in the Middle East and Europe, the use of water as a garden element was also developing in China, and later, with the spread of Buddhism, in Japan. Here the use was more symbolic, an idealization of natural forms with strict rules of composition and a closely defined relationship with other landscape elements.

2.0 PURPOSE OF WATER DISPLAYS

2.1 Aesthetic Reasons

A designer usually incorporates water into a space as a visual element. The aesthetic qualities of water, however, reach far beyond the visual aspect. The human species is psychologically drawn to water as a primal element and sustainer of life. The sound of water and the coolness associated with being near or touching water are equally a part of our emotional response to water in the environment.

Visual:

Water can function as a focal point within a space or as a means of creating and maintaining a sense of continuity within a space. A water display can strongly temper the character of a space. A sense of calm and serenity is created by a quiet stream or pool, while excitement and drama can be achieved by swiftly moving, densely massed, or strongly vertical displays. The level of formality will be influenced by the forms of the pools and displays, and the mood further defined or reinforced by appropriate lighting.

Psychological:

It is an essential aspect of human behavior to be drawn toward a riverbank, lake edge, or seashore. We either live near water or convey it to where we live, using canals or pipelines. Our food supply likewise depends upon water for growth and sustenance.

Auditory:

The intensity and frequency of the sound generated by a water display can be used to convey a sense of calm or excitement, and can also mask unpleasant or distracting ambient noise.

Cooling Effects:

Airborne spray and evaporation from water displays cause a cooling effect. Since this cooling is a function of total water surface area, droplets and sprays from active, aerated displays are particularly effective.

2.2 Functional Reasons

Pools also may be introduced or used secondarily for the following functional reasons:

Recreation:

Pools may be designed for wading, swimming, fishing, boating, or just water play, as with *participatory* water displays.

Circulation Control:

Pools may be used to direct or interrupt traffic patterns for reasons of safety or security or simply to promote an orderly progression through a space.

Utilitarian:

Practical applications for water displays include their use as a fire fighting or irrigation reservoir, as a retention pond for site drainage, or as a means for cooling air and/or mechanical equipment.

3.0 WATER

3.1 Quantification

Three units of measure are used to define water used for a display.

Capacity:

The volume of water in a system is usually expressed in gallons (gal) or liters (L).

When designing a water display, it is useful to know that 1 gal (3.75 L) of water is equal to 0.134 ft^3 (0.04 m^3) or, reciprocally, 1 ft^3 (0.04 m^3) is equal to 7.48 gal (23.56 L).

Flowrate:

The amount of water flowing through or circulating within a system is expressed as a volume per unit time, usually gallons per minute (gpm) or cubic meters per second (m^3/s). *Flowrate* is perhaps best understood by this comparison: a garden hose discharges about 7 gpm (26.2 Lpm), a fire hose about 150 gpm (562 Lpm), and a sheared-off fire hydrant about 1000 gpm (3750 Lpm).

Pressure:

Whether gravity is employed or a pump is used, the pressure is usually expressed in terms of pounds per square inch (psi) or feet of water column, which is more commonly called *feet of head.* The relationship—and for that matter, the concept—is probably best understood as the weight of a column of water over a unit area. Consider that 1 ft^3 of water weighs 62.4 lb. If the weight of a column of water 1 ft high is distributed over a base area of 1 ft^2, it will exert a pressure of 62.4 pounds per square foot (psf), or 0.43 psi. Reciprocally, 1 psi is equal to 2.31 feet of head. These are convenient numbers to remember when selecting valves, fittings, and piping, some of which are related in feet of head, others in psi.

3.2 Water Quality

The quality of the water in a pool or fountain is determined by the nature of the supply and the extent of filtration, chemical treatment, and/or biological balance.

Supply:

The most common source of supply is the piped domestic water system. Alternative sources include wells, springs, streams, and other natural bodies of water.

Domestic water is usually filtered and chemically treated and is suitable as delivered. Water from a well, spring, or stream can include excessive minerals and organic nutrients and may require chemical treatment.

Chemical Treatment:

Chlorination levels in the range of 1 to 2 parts per million (ppm) should be maintained as a minimum. Occasional superchlorination or shock treatment with an algacide may be required for algae control. Other chemicals may have to be added to mitigate concentrations of minerals, particularly calcium and iron. The need for any treatment beyond the maintenance of chlorine residual is generally empirically determined and should be administered only after consultation with water treatment specialists and after consideration of its compatibility with pool piping, hardware, and finishes and with governmental standards regulating overflow or effluents from the drain systems.

Biological Balance:

Even static water may be kept fresh by promoting biological balance through the use of fish and aquatic plants. In order for plants to grow, they need to photosynthesize carbon dioxide in the presence of light. This releases oxygen into the water and starves out lower plants such as algae by virtue of competition. The oxygen promotes water clarity and sustains the fish. The fish in turn fertilize the plants, keep down pests, and provide some of the carbon dioxide for photosynthesis.

4.0 WATER EFFECTS

4.1 Classification and Description

Table 530-1 provides a framework for discussion of water effects. These effects are typically grouped into two basic categories: (1) still water and (2) moving water (Figures 530-1 through 530-5).

Still Water:

The container defines the form assumed by the water. The finish of the underwater surfaces and the condition of the water at the surface influence the ultimate effect. If the pool finish is dark, an undisturbed surface will function as a *reflector,* while a disturbed surface is a *texture.* If the pool finish is light-colored and/or patterned, the undisturbed surface will function as a *window,* while a disturbed surface will act as a *modifier,* imparting a dynamic quality to the submerged surface. A light, unpatterned finish will emphasize water clarity.

Moving Water:

There are two subcategories within this classification. *Falling water* refers to water moving solely under the influence of gravity, while *spouting water* refers to water discharged or displaced under pressure, countering or complementing gravitational movement. This latter category includes waves and spouts (jets) of water. The wave effect, while a viable alternative visually and mechanically, has not been widely applied because of the excessive energy requirements and the considerable bulk of the activating mechanisms. Falling water may be further categorized as free-falling, flowing, or cascading.

TABLE 530-1
Water Effect Classification

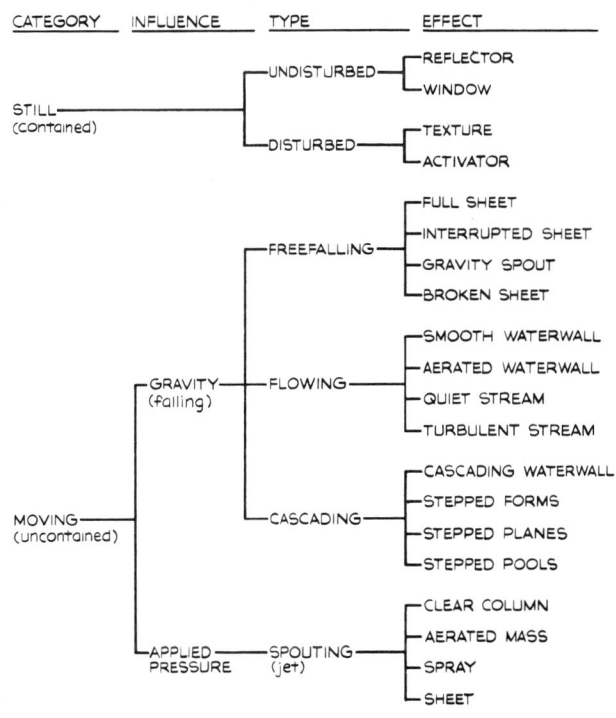

CATEGORY	INFLUENCE	TYPE	EFFECT
STILL (contained)		UNDISTURBED	REFLECTOR
			WINDOW
		DISTURBED	TEXTURE
			ACTIVATOR
MOVING (uncontained)	GRAVITY (falling)	FREEFALLING	FULL SHEET
			INTERRUPTED SHEET
			GRAVITY SPOUT
			BROKEN SHEET
		FLOWING	SMOOTH WATERWALL
			AERATED WATERWALL
			QUIET STREAM
			TURBULENT STREAM
		CASCADING	CASCADING WATERWALL
			STEPPED FORMS
			STEPPED PLANES
			STEPPED POOLS
	APPLIED PRESSURE	SPOUTING (jet)	CLEAR COLUMN
			AERATED MASS
			SPRAY
			SHEET

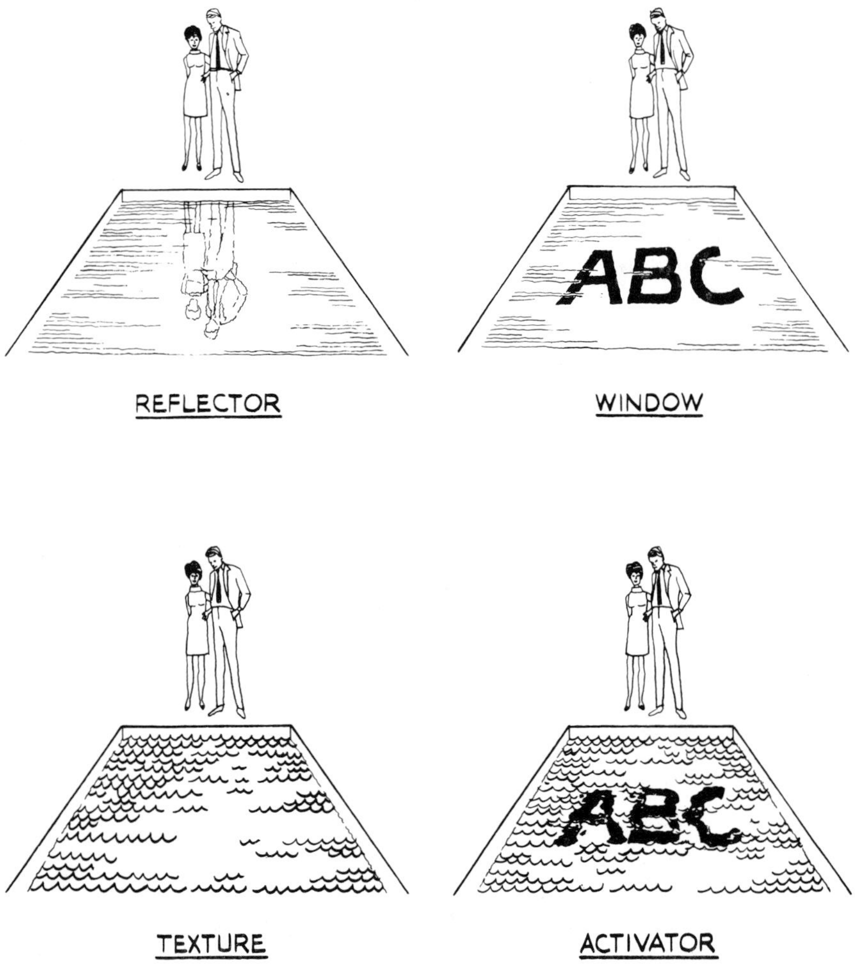
REFLECTOR
WINDOW
ABC
TEXTURE
ACTIVATOR
ABC

Figure 530-1 Still-water effects.

Free-Falling Water: Free-falling water moves vertically without contacting any surfaces and is most often expressed as a *full sheet* (Figure 530-2). If the flowrate is decreased, a rainlike *broken sheet* is produced. Other variations include obstructing the weir periodically to form an *interrupted sheet* or supplying water behind an orifice to form a *gravity spout.*

Flowing water is, by contrast, constantly in contact with the container. If the flow is vertically oriented, the effect is a waterwall (Figure 530-3). If the plane is smooth, the resultant *smooth waterwall* will derive only subtle highlights from the moving water. A textured plane will entrain air and generate an *aerated waterwall.* If the flow is horizontally oriented, the effect is a stream. A flat container of uniform width will create a *quiet stream* similar to a body of still water. A *turbulent stream* is derived by increasing the flowrate and/or manipulating the sides of the container.

Cascading water is a combination of flowing and falling water. A *cascading waterwall* differs from a smooth or aerated waterwall in the sense that water moves over a texture comprised of projecting forms of sufficient dimension to divert the flow laterally or to cause it to spring free of the vertical surface, thereby resulting in a pattern of free-falling water, flowing water, and dry areas. A *stepped-form* cascade directs water over an irregularly stepped structure which may vary from a random array of natural stone to a precise, geometric, often sculptural element. A *stepped-plane* cascade, typified by the waterstair, provides a controlled, more architectural display, varying from highly aerated to predominantly clear as the dimensions of the *tread* increase. *Stepped pools* provide more control and give a more formal appearance with less aeration than other cascading displays (Figure 530-4).

Spouting Water: Spouting water relies on externally applied force to direct water through an orifice or nozzle and, working with gravity, forms a jet of some configuration. A *clear-column* effect is a straight, clear, vertical jet complemented by veiling peripheral fallback. An *aerated mass* is a strong, turbulent, whitewater jet produced by combining air and/or pool water with the primary stream, using a venturi to accomplish the induction. This effect comprises three basic profiles and assumes one of three forms: hemispherical, conical, or columnar. *Sprays* derive their form using droplets rather than a stream or sheet. They are available in planar forms similar to irrigation heads or in solid form from near planar description to solid cones of 120 degrees overall spread. *Sheet* effects are generated by forcing the water through a fine, linear orifice to generate such forms as *mushrooms, morning glories, fans,* and *dandelions* (Figure 530-5).

4.2 Characteristics of Various Effects

Table 530-2 lists characteristics for each type of display, or effect. It should be realized that these evaluations are both generalized and subjective and that a particular characteristic for any display can be reinforced. As an example, an increased flowrate will improve the visibility, sound level, and wind stability but adversely affect the splash pattern and energy efficiency of a display.

Characteristics are subjectively rated on a scale of 1 to 4: poor or nominal, fair or low, good or moderate, and excellent or substantial.

A *nominal* sound level is barely perceptible against the ambient level at an urban plaza or shopping mall. A *moderate* sound level is one that ranges up to 75 decibels (dB), or roughly the level of sound within the cabin of a commercial jet plane. At the extreme, large free-falling displays may generate sound levels as high as 90 dB. Obviously, such levels are not appropriate for interior spaces or for areas where people might want to converse.

A *nominal* splash might affect a 2-ft (600-mm) radius, while the *substantial* classification ranges to a radius of 10 ft (3 m).

Unless the systems do not require motors to operate them, an energy budget must be considered. A small, moderately active system may require a pump of 5 to 10 (4.9 to 9.8 metric) horsepower (hp). At a large scale, with considerable activity, the pumping horsepower might range to 400 hp (398 metric hp) or more. While the former example would cost $3000 to $6000 annually to operate (based on 10 U.S. cents per kilowatt hour, 16 hours daily operation, 365 days a year), the 400-hp system, using the same criteria, would cost $235,000 (U.S.) annually to operate.

Visibility and wind stability are subject to even more variables; accordingly, the ratings should be considered as relative, understanding that considerable overlap may accrue to combinations of these variables.

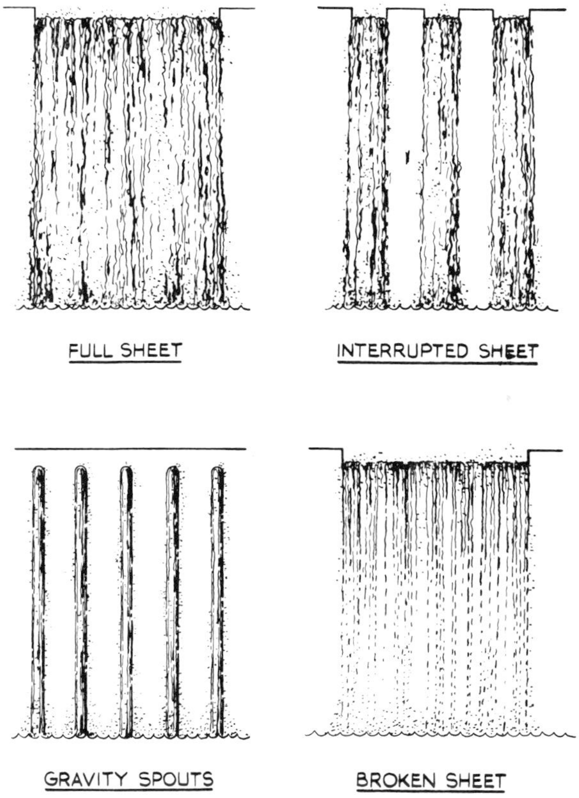
FULL SHEET
INTERRUPTED SHEET
GRAVITY SPOUTS
BROKEN SHEET

Figure 530-2 Free-falling water effects.

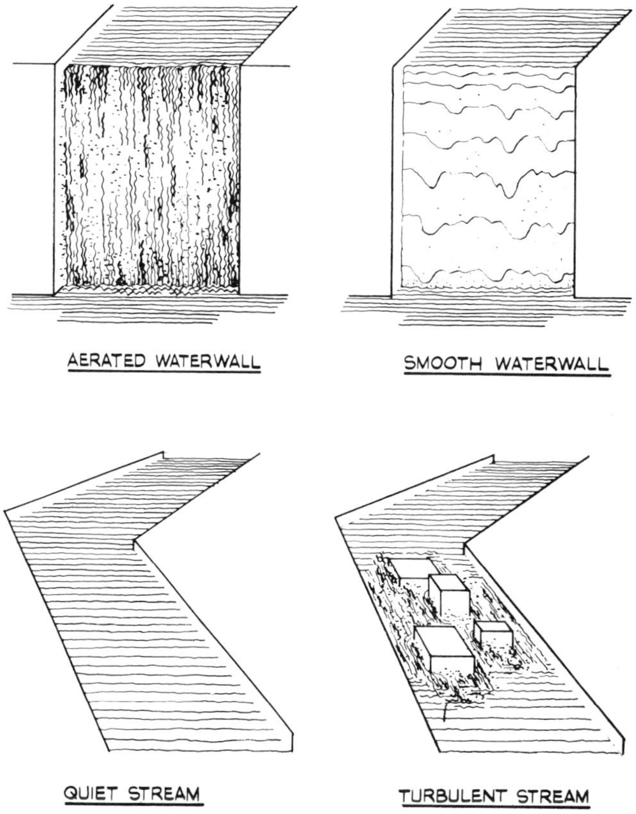
AERATED WATERWALL
SMOOTH WATERWALL
QUIET STREAM
TURBULENT STREAM

Figure 530-3 Flowing water effects.

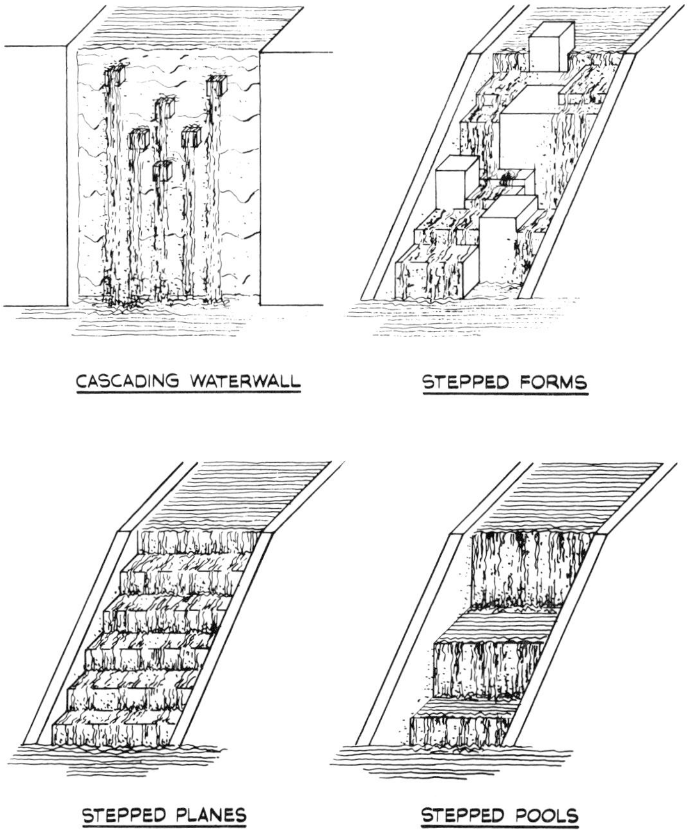
CASCADING WATERWALL
STEPPED FORMS
STEPPED PLANES
STEPPED POOLS

Figure 530-4 Cascading water effects.

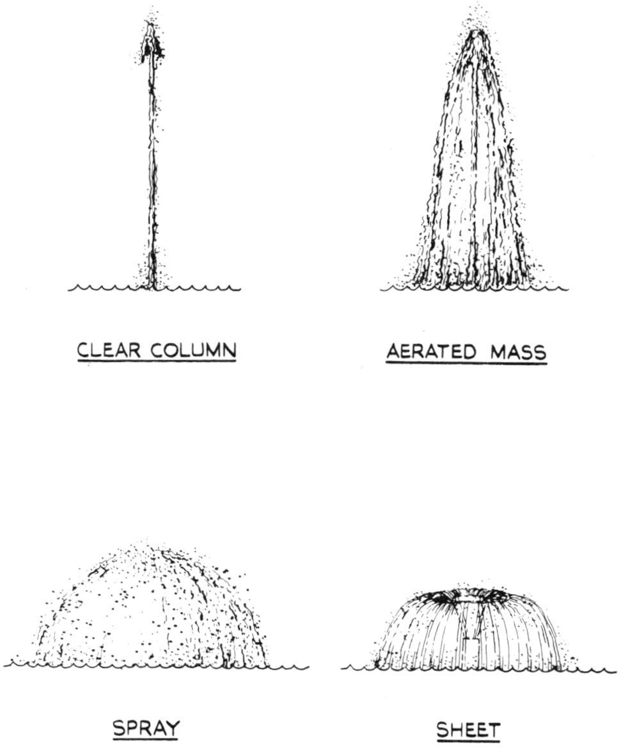
CLEAR COLUMN
AERATED MASS
SPRAY
SHEET

Figure 530-5 Spouting water effects.

TABLE 530-2
Water Effect Characteristics

TYPE OR EFFECT	VISIBILITY	SOUND LEVEL	SPLASH	WIND STABILITY	ENERGY EFFICIENCY
STILL UNDISTURBED	FAIR	NONE	NONE	EXCELLENT	EXCELLENT
STILL DISTURBED	FAIR	NOMINAL	NONE	EXCELLENT	EXCELLENT
FULL SHEET TO 4' HIGH	GOOD	MODERATE	MODERATE	GOOD	POOR
FULL SHEET OVER 4' HIGH	GOOD	SUB-STANTIAL	SUB-STANTIAL	FAIR	POOR
INTERRUPTED SHEET, SPOUTS	GOOD	MODERATE	SUB-STANTIAL	GOOD	GOOD
BROKEN SHEET	FAIR	LOW	MODERATE	FAIR	FAIR
SMOOTH WATERWALL	FAIR	NOMINAL	NONE	EXCELLENT	EXCELLENT
AERATED WATERWALL	EXCELLENT	MODERATE	MODERATE	GOOD	GOOD
QUIET STREAM	FAIR	NOMINAL	NONE	EXCELLENT	EXCELLENT
TURBULENT STREAM	GOOD	LOW	NOMINAL	EXCELLENT	EXCELLENT
CASCADING WATERWALL	GOOD	MODERATE	SUB-STANTIAL	GOOD	GOOD
STEPPED FORMS, PLANES	EXCELLENT	MODERATE	MODERATE	GOOD	GOOD
STEPPED POOLS	GOOD	MODERATE	MODERATE	EXCELLENT	GOOD
CLEAR COLUMN	GOOD	MODERATE	SUB-STANTIAL	POOR	FAIR
AERATED MASS	EXCELLENT	MODERATE	MODERATE	GOOD	GOOD
SPRAY	GOOD	LOW	NOMINAL	POOR	EXCELLENT
SPOUTING SHEET	GOOD	LOW	NOMINAL	FAIR	GOOD

4.3 Applications

Still water is a consideration in virtually any pool or fountain design, even in those that are not intended primarily as still or reflective pools. Most designs using moving water incorporate still areas as a complementary element, and attention should be given to the appearance and function of all pools when the display system is not operating. As a primary element, still water may be used in quiet, passive areas to reinforce a sense of tranquility, or in active areas to impart a sense of formality.

Free-falling displays and steep cascades can provide a high level of activity, visibility, and sound in a limited area. For falls of 3 ft (1 m) or less, a free-falling full sheet, an interrupted sheet, or spouts are generally preferable. For greater heights, an interrupted sheet, spouts, a waterwall, or a cascade will provide a display of equal or greater visibility while affording considerable energy savings, less splash, greater wind stability, and a sound quality more appropriate to confined or interior spaces. At even greater heights, free-falls are appropriate for installations which are to be seen through or viewed from both sides, or in situations requiring a higher level of sound.

Smooth waterwalls and broken sheets have limited application. A broken sheet is generally a complementary or secondary element. A smooth waterwall is limited to close viewing, except for very large area applications, and does not generate any significant sound. In some installations the sound level can be increased by free-falling a short distance below the smooth waterwall.

Flatter cascades and streams are used to provide a sense of continuity to architectural and/or landscape elements and to direct or interrupt traffic patterns.

Spouting water provides verticality and sound in a flat pool and a sense of source or beginning to free-falling, flowing, or cascading displays. In groupings, jets can be organized to provide dynamic, sculptural compositions. Jets are also used functionally in lakes and ponds to improve water quality through aeration.

4.4 Design

General:

Still-water effects are a function of container configuration, color, and material, of the influence of wind or mechanically generated activity at the water surface, and of the siting of the pool in relation to vertical elements in the immediate environment.

The container may convey a sense of formality by virtue of a regular geometric configuration or by the use of a cut, polished stone for edge material. Conversely, a free-form container with an edge of plant material or natural stone appears quite informal. If the pool is nonreflective, the bottom materials may be articulated in a sculptural fashion or as a mural with carefully designed patterns of tile, pavers, or cobbles. A finer texture (smaller units) will make better use of surface rippling and reflected sunlight.

Reflectivity is generated by dark container surfaces or opaque water, which absorb rather than reflect light in conjunction with an undisturbed water surface. The pool must be sited to reflect the desired vertical elements at logical observer positions, as illustrated in Figure 530-6. Opaque water can be achieved by using dyes or allowing the controlled growth of algae and plants in a biologically balanced system. A disturbed surface may be generated by prevailing winds or can be introduced mechanically by employing small, closely spaced jets, aimed horizontally, near the surface of the water.

Design Criteria for Various Effects:

Free-Falling Sheet and Waterwall: Figure 530-7 shows design criteria for a free-falling sheet. This detail is appropriate for all free-falling and cascading effects except gravity spouts and cascading waterwalls. Figure 530-8 shows criteria for waterwalls. The back-battered weir is used for a number of reasons. Concrete can be finished to the front (downstream) form, which can be leveled using instruments, generally resulting in an acceptable ± ⅛-in (3-mm) tolerance along the entire weir. If tolerance cannot be maintained, high spots can readily be ground level along the ridge created by the sloped configuration. When the fountain is off, the water occupies the entire horizontal plane, generally resulting in a more desirable relationship with the container. The slope also moderates the sudden increase in velocity that causes water to draw down sharply at the back edge of a flat weir, interrupting the continuity of the horizontal plane. The color of the weir and vertical surfaces should be as dark as possible to facilitate perception of the water movement by virtue of contrast and reflection from the sheet itself. The knife-edge weir used for free-falling water causes the sheet to break free of the structure and may easily be roughened to cause striations at the back of the sheet to increase visibility. The radius used for the waterwall weir works in conjunction with the back batter to direct the water onto the waterwall.

Waterstair: Figure 530-9 shows specific criteria for a waterstair. These criteria gen-

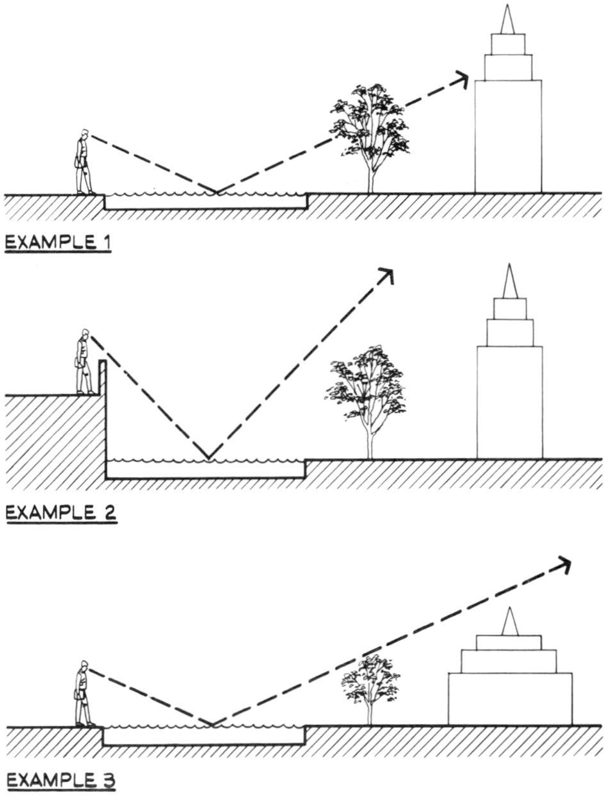
EXAMPLE 1
EXAMPLE 2
EXAMPLE 3

Figure 530-6 Still-water design.

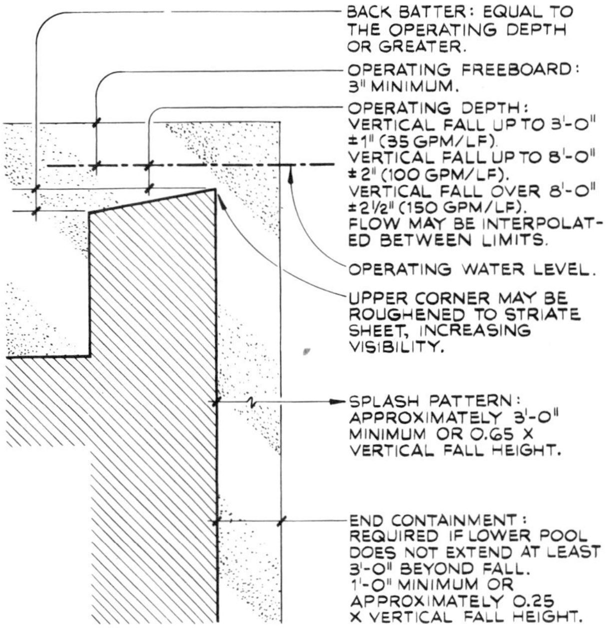
BACK BATTER: EQUAL TO THE OPERATING DEPTH OR GREATER.
OPERATING FREEBOARD: 3" MINIMUM.
OPERATING DEPTH: VERTICAL FALL UP TO 3'-0" ±1" (35 GPM/LF). VERTICAL FALL UP TO 8'-0" ±2" (100 GPM/LF). VERTICAL FALL OVER 8'-0" ±2½" (150 GPM/LF). FLOW MAY BE INTERPOLATED BETWEEN LIMITS.
OPERATING WATER LEVEL.
UPPER CORNER MAY BE ROUGHENED TO STRIATE SHEET, INCREASING VISIBILITY.
SPLASH PATTERN: APPROXIMATELY 3'-0" MINIMUM OR 0.65 X VERTICAL FALL HEIGHT.
END CONTAINMENT: REQUIRED IF LOWER POOL DOES NOT EXTEND AT LEAST 3'-0" BEYOND FALL. 1'-0" MINIMUM OR APPROXIMATELY 0.25 X VERTICAL FALL HEIGHT.

Figure 530-7 Free-falling or cascading sheet design. (No scale)

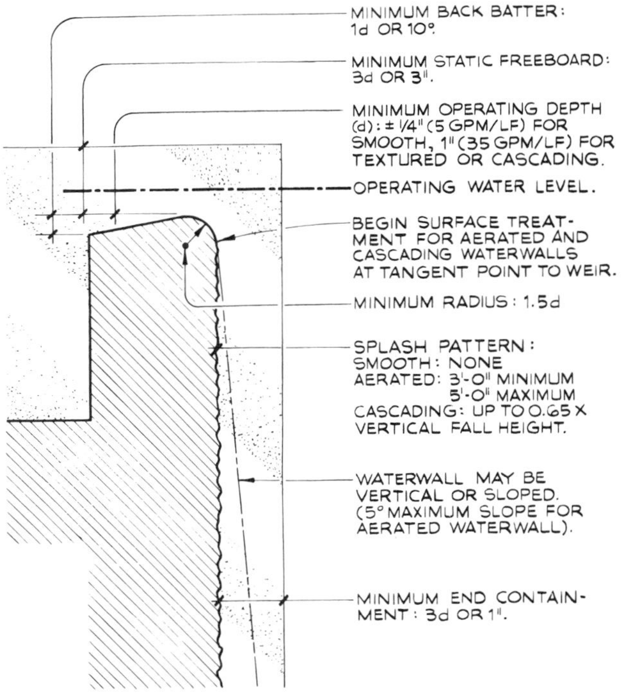
MINIMUM BACK BATTER: 1d OR 10°.
MINIMUM STATIC FREEBOARD: 3d OR 3".
MINIMUM OPERATING DEPTH (d): ± 1/4" (5 GPM/LF) FOR SMOOTH, 1" (35 GPM/LF) FOR TEXTURED OR CASCADING.
OPERATING WATER LEVEL.
BEGIN SURFACE TREATMENT FOR AERATED AND CASCADING WATERWALLS AT TANGENT POINT TO WEIR.
MINIMUM RADIUS: 1.5d
SPLASH PATTERN: SMOOTH: NONE AERATED: 3'-0" MINIMUM 5'-0" MAXIMUM CASCADING: UP TO 0.65 X VERTICAL FALL HEIGHT.
WATERWALL MAY BE VERTICAL OR SLOPED. (5° MAXIMUM SLOPE FOR AERATED WATERWALL).
MINIMUM END CONTAINMENT: 3d OR 1".

Figure 530-8 Waterwall design (smooth-textured or cascading). (No scale)

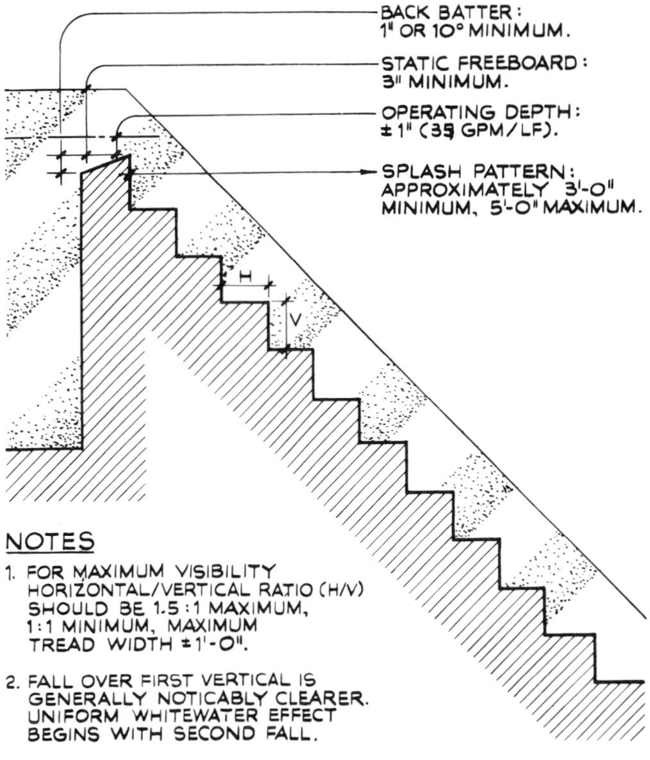
BACK BATTER: 1" OR 10° MINIMUM.
STATIC FREEBOARD: 3" MINIMUM.
OPERATING DEPTH: ± 1" (35 GPM/LF).
SPLASH PATTERN: APPROXIMATELY 3'-0" MINIMUM, 5'-0" MAXIMUM.
H
V
NOTES
1. FOR MAXIMUM VISIBILITY HORIZONTAL/VERTICAL RATIO (H/V) SHOULD BE 1.5:1 MAXIMUM, 1:1 MINIMUM, MAXIMUM TREAD WIDTH ±1'-0".
2. FALL OVER FIRST VERTICAL IS GENERALLY NOTICABLY CLEARER. UNIFORM WHITEWATER EFFECT BEGINS WITH SECOND FALL.

Figure 530-9 Waterstair cascade design (stepped planes). (No scale) erally apply to all stepped-form or stepped-plane cascades, except that the criteria for splash should be projected for the highest free-fall.

Streams, like still water, assume a form defined by the container. In addition, the level of activity is primarily determined by the container. Figure 530-10 shows five ways to increase the level of activity by virtue of increasing the velocity and/or introducing turbulence and, correspondingly, increasing the visibility and sound level in a stream.

The character of a waterwall as well as the flow requirement will be determined by the finish of the material over which the water flows. A very smooth surface such as glass, sheet metal, or polished stone achieves maximum visibility, using the surface tension of the material to create a standing wave effect with a very nominal flow. Too much flow will in fact substantially reduce the visibility. An intermediate texture such as troweled concrete or thermal-finish stone also reduces visibility by moderating the effect of surface tension. The minimum textural articulation required to generate an aerated waterwall is on the order of ¼ to ⅜ in (6.35 to 9.52 mm), and the transitions must be sufficiently abrupt to entrap air. The most common and predictable method to achieve this textural quality is exposed aggregate concrete, using carefully graded aggregate with the matrix retarded ¼ to ⅜ in (6.35 to 9.52 mm). Other methods include bush-hammered concrete or stone, corbelled brick or tile, and horizontal saw cuts with random areas broken out.

Finishes at joints in weirs and waterwall surfaces should be as nearly flush as practical to avoid localized streams breaking free of the wall and to avoid air pockets between the wall and the water.

There are several critical considerations in the design of spouting (jet) displays. For outdoor installations, the variability in wind velocity and direction is most readily accommodated by designing the pool/jet combination to provide a clear radius equal to the height of the jet to any point beyond the pool. If the immediate surroundings include a building or heavy pedestrian or vehicular traffic, a wind control system should be employed. Splash is usually a secondary consideration with outdoor displays, since the normal pattern is only 3 to 5 ft (1 to 1.5 m) and is more than adequately accommodated by the clearances required for height. For interior spaces and low jets, the splash pattern is the prime determinant of the jet placement/clearance requirement.

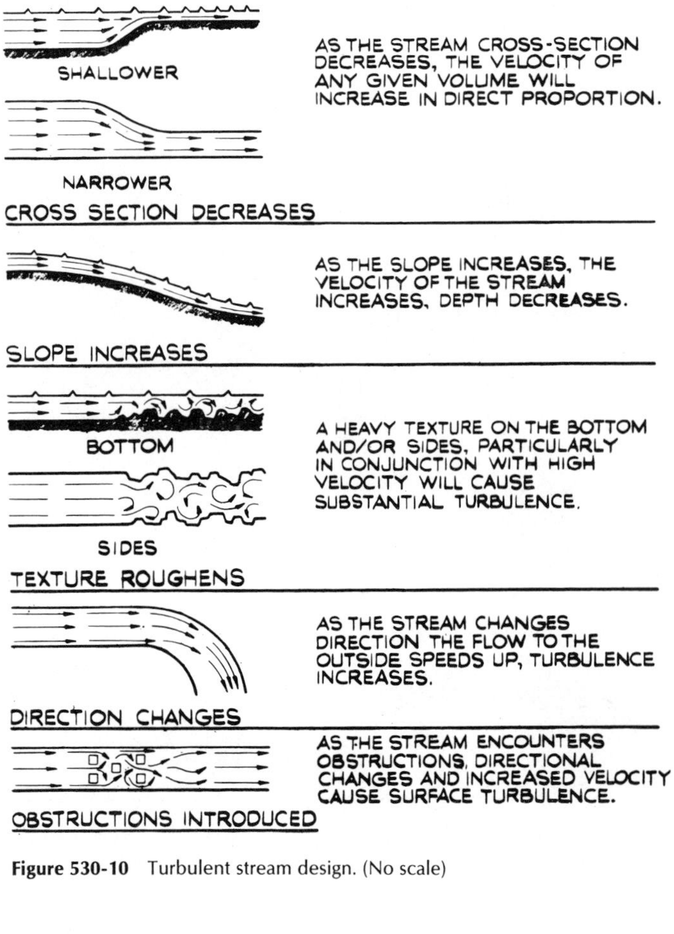
SHALLOWER
AS THE STREAM CROSS-SECTION DECREASES, THE VELOCITY OF ANY GIVEN VOLUME WILL INCREASE IN DIRECT PROPORTION.
NARROWER
CROSS SECTION DECREASES
AS THE SLOPE INCREASES, THE VELOCITY OF THE STREAM INCREASES, DEPTH DECREASES.
SLOPE INCREASES
BOTTOM
A HEAVY TEXTURE ON THE BOTTOM AND/OR SIDES, PARTICULARLY IN CONJUNCTION WITH HIGH VELOCITY WILL CAUSE SUBSTANTIAL TURBULENCE.
SIDES
TEXTURE ROUGHENS
AS THE STREAM CHANGES DIRECTION THE FLOW TO THE OUTSIDE SPEEDS UP, TURBULENCE INCREASES.
DIRECTION CHANGES
AS THE STREAM ENCOUNTERS OBSTRUCTIONS, DIRECTIONAL CHANGES AND INCREASED VELOCITY CAUSE SURFACE TURBULENCE.
OBSTRUCTIONS INTRODUCED

Figure 530-10 Turbulent stream design. (No scale)

Accommodations of Mechanical System:

Accommodations to be considered in the mechanical system include the following.

Adjustability: Most jets are oriented vertically, but arching and horizontal variations are used. For either application, adjustability is generally desirable. Adjustable swivel joints are available with a range of 15 to 20 degrees about the center through a full 360-degree arc. These swivels are available for supply pipe sizes from ⅛ in (3.18 mm) through 4 in (100 mm).

Multiple-Jet Display: Jets are often employed in groups. If a few loosely spaced jets are used, they are generally piped individually with a balancing valve for each to allow for varying heights and/or differences in pipe and fitting losses. For singly massed displays, a plenum arrangement, often called a *pod* or *cluster,* may be used. For closely massed groupings, depending upon the configuration, a *spray bar* or *spray ring* may be used. With these singly or closely massed groups, the flow is sufficiently balanced that balancing valves are only required if varying heights are desired.

Debris: A jet display is more readily affected by waterborne particulates and debris and variables in the pumping system than are other types of displays. They will require more day-to-day maintenance and more frequent repairs than still or falling water. Of utmost importance in the initial design are the selection (1) of a pump strainer with perforations smaller than the smallest jet orifice and (2) of a pump with characteristics that will afford a constant display throughout the normal range of strainer loading.

Surge Collar: Submerged jets, such as a cascade or bubbler, often generate wave patterns that periodically cause flooding. This exposes the submerged jet, thereby generating more waves which could exceed the confines of the pool, or at the very least causing a major change from the intended display. This can be countered by installing a perforated collar (i.e., a surge collar) with a diameter at least twice that of the jet, placing it concentrically around the jet at or slightly below water level.

Straightening Vanes: In situations where a single jet requires flowrates in excess of 1000 gpm (3750 Lpm), or where the installation of the jet precludes a clear vertical feed equal to 5 times or more the nominal diameter of the supply pipe, straightening vanes may be required. If the situation is marginal, merely provide for a retrofit.

4.5 Maximization of Water Effect

The transit time, volume, and readability should all be maximized to optimize the impact of any given flowrate, to minimize the cost, and to conserve energy, if a recirculating system is used.

Transit Time:

Transit time is probably the single most important factor in designing with water. The longer the water is kept in play (transit time), the greater will be the effect achieved at any given flowrate. For example, water is introduced to one end of a cascade 300 ft (90 m) long and 15 ft (4.56 m) high, then recirculated from the other end. If an average stream velocity of 2 fps (600 mm/s) is assumed, the water will take 2½ minutes to traverse the system. If 400 gpm (1500 Lpm) is recirculated, there will be 1000 gal (3750 L) of water in motion. In contrast, consider a sheet or spout of water free-falling 15 ft (4.56 m); under the influence of gravity this water will reach the lower pool in approximately 1 second. At this extreme, 60,000 gpm (225,000 Lpm) would have to be pumped to maintain the same 1000 gal (3750 L) in motion.

Air Entrainment:

White water is generated by creating sufficient turbulence in a sheet or stream to entrap air, or by artificially introducing air to the display. The entrained air provides additional volume for any given flowrate and further increases visibility by reflecting a much greater component of natural or artificial light. This technique is employed for most cascades and for aerating jets.

Readability:

Further impact is achieved by maximizing the surface area, optimizing the exposure to natural or artificial light, and using dark, contrasting materials in and around active water.

4.6 Optimization of Water Effect

The effect of a water display may be further optimized by graphic and model studies, observation of similar effects, prototype testing, and field adjustment of the completed system.

Graphic and Model Studies:

Graphic and model studies are an excellent way to study the scale and massing appropriate for the container, the integrated structures, and the immediate environment. These studies can further serve as a basis for quantifying the effects and for communicating with clients and other members of the design team. Figure 530-11 is a copy of an early sketch prepared by Angela Danadjieva for Ira's Fountain (Portland Auditorium Forecourt Fountain, Portland, Oregon), which served as a basis for the development of models and for early structural and hydraulic studies.

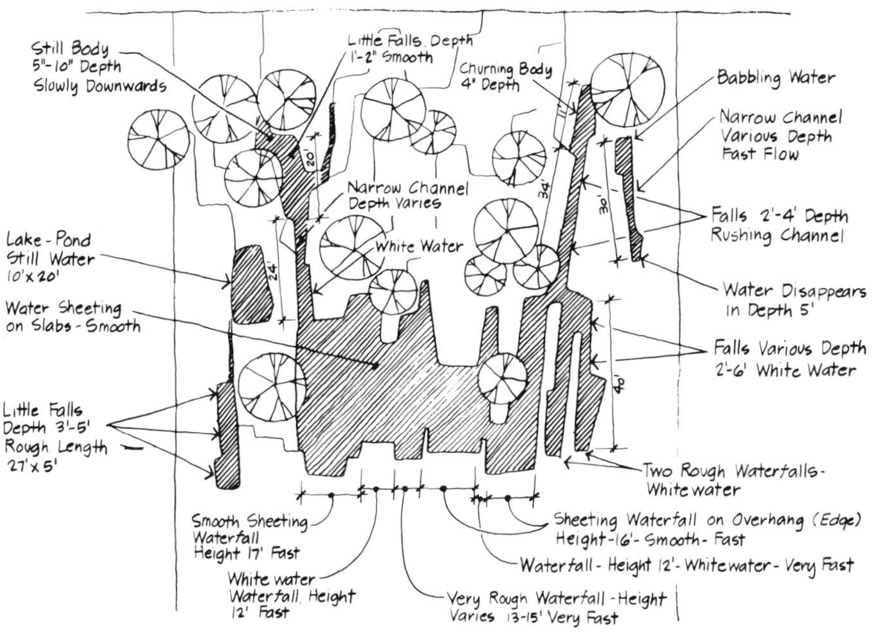
Still Body
5"-10" Depth
Slowly Downwards
Little Falls, Depth
1'-2" Smooth
Churning Body
4' Depth
Babbling Water
Narrow Channel
Various Depth
Fast Flow
Narrow Channel
Depth Varies
Falls 2'-4' Depth
Rushing Channel
Lake-Pond
Still Water
10'x20'
White Water
Water Disappears
In Depth 5'
Water Sheeting
on Slabs - Smooth
Falls Various Depth
2'-6' White Water
Little Falls
Depth 3'-5'
Rough Length
27'x5'
Two Rough Waterfalls-
White water
Smooth Sheeting
Waterfall
Height 17' Fast
Sheeting Waterfall on Overhang (Edge)
Height-16'- Smooth - Fast
Waterfall - Height 12' - Whitewater - Very Fast
White water
Waterfall, Height
12' Fast
Very Rough Waterfall - Height
Varies 13-15' Very Fast

Figure 530-11 Water effects sketch.

Observation of Precedent:

Observation of effects similar to those to be used will serve to confirm visual characteristics as well as sound levels, splash patterns, and the overall feel of the display.

Prototype Testing:

Hydraulic testing is used to determine the feasibility and design criteria for prototypical effects and/or to fine tune such items as weir configuration, splash containment, and waterwall textures. Tests may be conducted at the designer's office, on the construction site, or at an established testing facility, such as a manufacturer's test pool or a university hydraulics laboratory. The testing program should be witnessed and evaluated by the designer, consultants, and appropriate construction personnel.

Tests must generally be conducted at full scale, since hydraulic factors such as surface tension are constant or vary in a nonlinear fashion. For most testing, a single spout, a short length of weir, or a small area of waterwall surface is adequate for evaluation.

The construction of the test assembly, the variables to be evaluated, and the performance criteria should be carefully specified prior to testing in order that each item such as weir profiles, surface textures, waterwall joints, drip notches, pool depths, splash patterns, and jet heights can be evaluated as fully as possible. Where appropriate, two or three variations of each critical item should be tested.

Field Adjustment:

Field adjustment, including modifications where necessary, is extremely important, since each installation is a prototype and must finally be evaluated in place. This effort, as the culmination of close and difficult work collaboration, should include consultants and construction personnel as well as the designer.

5.0 CONTAINERS AND STRUCTURES

The pool may evolve in a number of ways. It can be a primary landscape form working with space and/or structures, an envelope-sized (or contorted) to contain a preconceived display element, an *amenity* to derive a density bonus for an expensive Manhattan parcel, or a filler to make use of an odd area on a plaza or mall or of the space under an escalator. It can even be a *nonpool,* that is, a display integrated into the paving or walls, with no visible reservoir.

Obviously, in addition to imposing constraints, each of these suggests a design direction. Other factors affecting the design approach include the environment, construction budget, appropriate materials, and governing codes.

5.1 Environment

Each of a number of contextual variables within the designed and natural environment dictates further design direction. Among these are scale, setting, climate, location, and surrounding materials.

Scale:

Because scale is perhaps the most important of the contextual variables, an aesthetically viable water display must in some way relate to the scale of its surroundings. This need not be the scale of the entire space, however. The water display often relates to a space that is a component of the larger space, as with a small fountain in a bosque of trees or on a dining terrace. Once this relationship is established, scale and proportion among the parts of the fountain itself are equally important. Displays should relate properly to the pool, and if the display includes structure, the water massing must be adequate and complementary in character.

Setting:

The configuration, edge condition, materials, and display itself will be influenced by the formality of the designed environment. A very formal setting will lead to strongly geometric shapes, hard edges, and more refined materials. Conversely, a naturalistic setting will direct the design toward more organic shapes, soft edges, and nonexpressed construction materials. Most of these matters will likewise be influenced by whether the pool is indoor or outdoor, urban or suburban, commercial, residential, or institutional.

Topography:

It is usually difficult from a design standpoint, and certainly expensive, to install a large reflecting pool on a steeply sloping site or a major fall on a flat site. A more viable solution, accepting the goal of reflectivity on the steep site and verticality on the flat site, might be a series of interconnected ponds or rectilinear trays for the former, and a massive composition of jets for the latter.

Climate:

Climatic variables are quite important considerations for an outdoor installation. Prevailing winds, sunshine frequency and orientation, and temperature extremes can offer direction as well as constraint. Long, hot summers suggest cooling displays, perhaps even a participatory design. Severe winters dictate a 4- to 6-month shutdown, necessitating that configurations, materials, display structures, and particularly hardware be carefully considered both with and without water. In many instances a nonpool, as mentioned earlier, is an excellent answer to protracted winter shutdown. Other wintertime solutions include a pool that doubles as a skating rink, and ice formations which complement display structures.

Support Medium:

A number of potential constraints must be investigated for pools, whether they are built above-structure or on-grade. An above-structure solution is generally the more difficult to work with, as there are usually very definitive limits to depth and weight, and waterproofing must be very carefully addressed. An on-grade installation requires considerably less attention to waterproofing, as minimal leakage does not usually present a problem. Soil stability must be carefully investigated, however, as even nominal differential settlement may have a substantial effect on the pool, particularly if it involves long weirs and waterwalls. If the soil is expansive, an underdrain system should be considered.

Surrounding Materials:

If the water display is used as a primary element rather than as a complement to the pool, it is often desirable to minimize the presence of the container and any support structure for the display by integrating it into the immediate surroundings. Continuity of material is probably the single most important element in accomplishing this end.

5.2 Construction Budget

Although construction budget considerations may be somewhat beyond the scope of this section, it should be recognized that a fountain is a very expensive element in the landscape. To proceed with any design without both the designer and the owner recognizing the potential costs may be a waste of time. To help broadly bracket these costs, a few examples are cited below:

The mid-1980s cost in the United States for a simple recirculating fountain of 100 ft^2 (9.3 m^2) or less, using a submersible system to generate a display of 100 gpm (375 Lpm) or less, would be on the order of $15,000 (1985 U.S.).

The mid-1980s cost for a fountain of about 1000 ft^2 (93 m^2), with recirculated water and a display flowrate of 300 to 1000 gpm (1125 to 3750 Lpm), would be on the order of $150,000 to $200,000 (1985 U.S.).

At the extreme, several fountains were constructed in the late 1960s and early 1970s at a cost exceeding $1 million (1985 U.S.) each.

5.3 Materials

There are a variety of materials appropriate for the construction of pools and displays. For installations seeking a *natural* appearance, the material may be native soil, if it is sufficiently impermeable, or a clay or flexible liner with nominal edge treatment. For the more formal and primarily urban installations, the choices could include concrete, stone, brick, and in the case of smaller installations, wood, metal, or fiberglass. (Refer to Division 800: Materials, for technical data about each of these materials.)

Native Soil and Clay:

Generally, these are used for large ponds, lakes, and reservoirs, and as such are somewhat beyond the scope of this discussion, offering geotechnical problems that must be expertly addressed on a project-by-project basis. Flexible liners are simply waterproofing membranes. (Refer to 5.5 Waterproofing in this section.)

Concrete:

Concrete is probably the most commonly used material for urban installations. It is durable, economical, reasonably waterproof, and amenable to a wide range of configurations, finishes, and construction techniques, including cast-in-place, precast, and sprayed (gunite).

Cast-in-place concrete can be enhanced by the addition of integral color or finished with a variety of textures, including exposed aggregate, bush hammering, or random formboard. Or it could be coated or veneered, using epoxy paint, tile, or stone.

Precast concrete may be used for display structures or for the pool itself where precise control of the configuration, dimension, or surface is required. The only drawback is that the joints between sections must be waterproofed in pools or bowls. And in the case of a weir or waterwall, where a depressed or raised joint might cause irregular flow, the joint must be both waterproof and flush.

Sprayed concrete, or *gunite* as it is commonly called, is generally used where a free form or naturalistic form is required, or on structures where the light weight of forms created by spraying gunite over wire mesh or expanded metal lath are an asset because of marginal load-bearing capacity.

Stone:

Widely used, stone imparts a richness and permanence difficult to achieve with concrete. Granite is by far the most common and appropriate stone for fountain use. Where possible, the stone should be dark to enhance the reading of moving water and the reflectivity of still water.

Stone may be expressed as cut, finished material in either monolithic or veneered form, or as naturally occurring boulders, slabs, or smaller stones. With cut material, polished finishes are generally best, since rough or honed finishes, particularly with dark stone, tend to read differently wet and dry, magnifying the presence of overspray and other misdirected water—which is virtually unreadable on a polished surface.

Brick:

Brick generally provides a finish intermediate to concrete and stone in terms of both cost and aesthetics. It integrates well with brick paving and structures and can be articulated to generate whitewater waterwalls or cascades. Brick generally requires sealing unless glazed, and, as with precast concrete, joints at weirs and waterwalls must be carefully controlled, generally flush.

Wood, Metal, and Fiberglass:

Used for smaller installations and structures within the pool, each of these materials offers inherent advantages. Wood absorbs water, sealing the joints as it expands, and is inexpensive and simple to construct. Metal, either cast or fabricated from sheets, is waterproof and offers a richness and permanence equivalent to that of stone. Suitable metals include bronze, brass, copper, and stainless steel. Fiberglass is waterproof and may be integrally colored or filled with ground or crushed stone for situations on a structure where, as with gunite, the light weight is required to accommodate a marginal load-bearing capacity. Fiberglass can also be used to resurface or repair existing pools.

5.4 Cross-Sectional Configuration

In addition to the shape of the water feature as seen in plan, there are several aspects of cross-sectional configuration that must be considered, including the relationship to plaza level and the edge conditions, depth, and freeboard.

Relationship to Plaza Level:

Both the rim and water level elevations are very important considerations. For instance, the more a rim is elevated, the more it tends to break up the visual continuity of the surrounding space and focus the viewer's attention on the pool itself. This often reduces the visual impact of the display and/or reflected images. On the positive side, the elevated rim may be used for seating and for keeping out dust and debris blown in from the surrounding plane. It can also serve as a barrier to prevent accidental walking or falling into the pool.

An elevated water level is often appropriate to provide a desired field of reflection. An at-grade water level, particularly with a still pool, will integrate the pool into the surrounding plane. A depressed water level will strengthen the impact of the display, much like the nonpool will.

Edge Conditions:

Figure 530-12 shows a number of typical edge conditions. A cantilevered inner edge is probably the detail used most often. It serves to contain the waves generated by the wind or the display and will conceal any stains caused by normal variations in the water level. Critical dimensions are shown in Figure 530-13.

The stepped recess, the wall, and the warped paving tend to integrate the pool with its immediate environment, minimizing its impact on the space and maximizing the impact of the display. The rounded edge and the trough detail allow the water level to be at or above plaza level, expressing the entire body of water as a dynamic display element.

Hard-planted edges (Figure 530-12) are accomplished by back-battering the pool edge in such a fashion that the planted plane can be carried up to the point of intersection with the plane of the pool wall. A *soft-planted* edge extends the plant material to the waterline and is often used in an earth-bottomed pool or in one having loosely set cobbles or sprayed concrete edges. It is usually employed in the construction of naturalistic streams, ponds, and lakes.

Depth, Freeboard, and Clearance from Displays:

Figure 530-13 shows the primary considerations for a pool with a single level or for the lower pool of a multilevel design. The freeboard for the upper pool's falling or cascading water is discussed for various displays in 4.0 Water Effects in this section.

Depth: The pool depth generally varies between 12 and 18 in (300 and 450 mm).

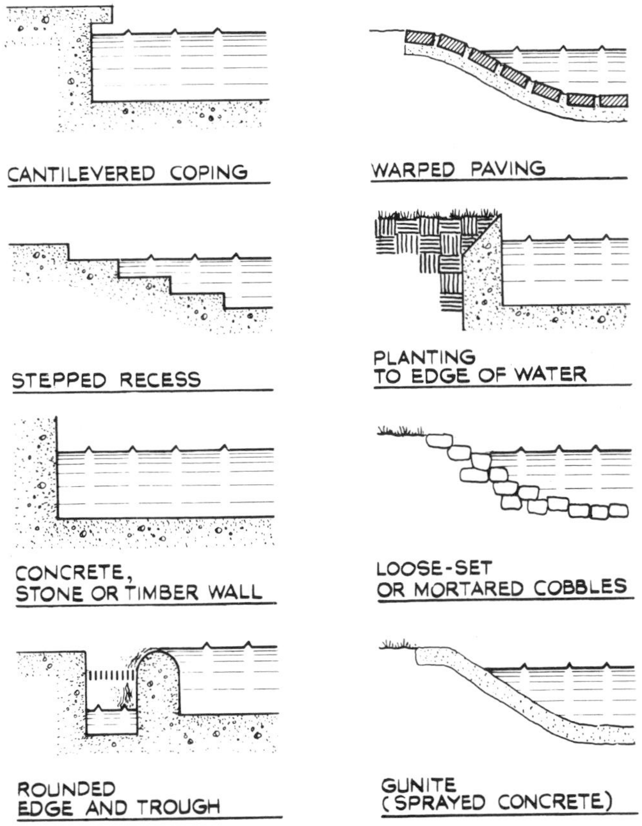
CANTILEVERED COPING
WARPED PAVING
STEPPED RECESS
PLANTING TO EDGE OF WATER
CONCRETE, STONE OR TIMBER WALL
LOOSE-SET OR MORTARED COBBLES
ROUNDED EDGE AND TROUGH
GUNITE (SPRAYED CONCRETE)

Figure 530-12 Edge conditions.

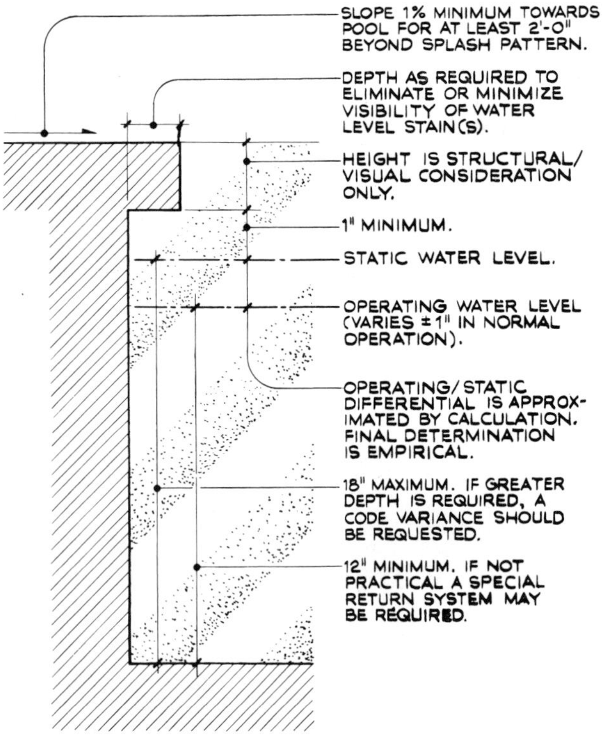
SLOPE 1% MINIMUM TOWARDS POOL FOR AT LEAST 2'-0" BEYOND SPLASH PATTERN.
DEPTH AS REQUIRED TO ELIMINATE OR MINIMIZE VISIBILITY OF WATER LEVEL STAIN(S).
HEIGHT IS STRUCTURAL/ VISUAL CONSIDERATION ONLY.
1" MINIMUM.
STATIC WATER LEVEL.
OPERATING WATER LEVEL (VARIES ± 1" IN NORMAL OPERATION).
OPERATING/STATIC DIFFERENTIAL IS APPROXIMATED BY CALCULATION. FINAL DETERMINATION IS EMPIRICAL.
18" MAXIMUM. IF GREATER DEPTH IS REQUIRED, A CODE VARIANCE SHOULD BE REQUESTED.
12" MINIMUM. IF NOT PRACTICAL A SPECIAL RETURN SYSTEM MAY BE REQUIRED.

Figure 530-13 Pool design. (No scale)

TABLE 530-3
Various Flowrates

FLOWRATE FOR RECTANGULAR WEIRS

DEPTH OVER WEIR	1/4"	1/2"	3/4"	1"	1 1/2"	2"	2 1/2"	3"	4"	5"	6"
GPM PER LINEAR FT.	4.5	13	23	36	65	101	141	185	285	399	524

FLOWRATE FOR SOLID STREAM JETS (GPM)

HEIGHT (FT.)	2	4	6	8	10	15	20	30	50	75	100
HEAD (FT.)	3	5	8	10	14	20	27	41	69	97	150
1/4" ORIFICE	2	2.8	3.4	4	5	6	-	-	-	-	-
3/8" ORIFICE	4	6	7	8	9	12	15	20	-	-	-
1/2" ORIFICE	7	11	12	15	19	22	26	33	-	-	-
3/4" ORIFICE	16	21	26	31	35	50	58	74	93	-	-
1" ORIFICE	37	46	50	56	60	82	106	127	167	199	238
1 1/2" ORIFICE	-	-	-	-	159	199	233	304	368	444	518
2" ORIFICE	-	-	-	-	309	357	410	526	650	780	938
3" ORIFICE	-	-	-	-	-	-	965	1220	1640	1750	1905

FLOWRATE FOR CASCADE TYPE AERATED STREAM JET

SIZE	HGT. (FT.)	2	4	6	8	10	12	15	20	25	30
3/4"	GPM	18	21	26	30	-	-	-	-	-	-
	HEAD	30	43	61	77	-	-	-	-	-	-
1 1/2"	GPM	28	32	40	46	50	56	67	-	-	-
	HEAD	15	27	37	50	60	70	83	-	-	-
3"	GPM	71	110	142	157	171	186	210	246	312	330
	HEAD	9	16	26	32	36	44	56	66	108	134

In the United States, 18 in (450 mm) is the maximum recommended depth because interpretation of the Uniform Building Code generally leads to the conclusion that anything of greater depth can be considered a swimming pool, as opposed to a wading pool. Twelve inches (300 mm) is generally the minimum depth required to provide for a satisfactory return system and to submerse wall-mounted and freestanding pool lights properly. Source pools usually need a minimum depth of 12 in (300 mm) for a jet or nonexpressed source. As the depth decreases in outdoor installations, algae growth is enhanced by increased heat and ultraviolet light. With a large pool or pond or lake, most jurisdictions will accept a gradual slope or steps to a deepened central area.

Freeboard: Freeboard requirements vary as a function of the edge condition. With a cantilevered or stepped edge, the freeboard need only be an inch or so below the cantilever or tread to allow for nominal fluctuations in water level. Adequate freeboard is inherent to the wall edge; the trough water level at the rounded edge should allow at least 6 in (150 mm) of freeboard, the hard-planted edge should have minimum freeboard of 3 in (75 mm), and the soft-planted edge made of loosely set cobbles, and gunite edges should extend to at least 6 in (150mm) above the highest water level.

When multiple levels are involved, the lower pool will have two different water levels—the static, or nonoperating, level and the operating level, which will be lower. The difference is due to the water that is built up behind the weirs, etc., during operation, which will ultimately reach the lower pool when the fountain is not operating. If the flowrate and weir lengths are known, this amount can be calculated by first determining the area of each pool and then determining the depth over the weir(s), using Table 530-3.

Clearance from Displays: Where possible, all displays (fountains, etc.) should be set back from the pool edge to a distance equal to or greater than the splash pattern or jet clearance, as described above in 4.0 Water Effects. Where pool edges are flush with the paving, an additional margin of safety should be obtained by sloping the pool rim and/or adjacent surfaces from a point at least 2 ft (600 mm) beyond the necessary clearance back toward the pool.

5.5 Waterproofing

Measures needed for waterproofing depend upon whether the pool is on-grade or on-structure above a functional area in a building.

On-Grade:

Unless there is a critical area immediately adjacent, or an unusual soil condition where even nominal leakage might present a problem (such as in areas of expansive soils), waterproofing is usually confined to the proper mixing and vibrating of the concrete in conjunction with waterstops at slab joints and pipe penetrations (Figure 530-14). Additional protection may be provided by plastering or tiling the surface or by coating the pool with an epoxy paint or elastomeric coating.

On-Structure:

Waterproofing is accomplished by coating the inside of the basic pool structure with a waterproof membrane, usually the fluid-applied types. Sometimes a hot-mopped felt membrane is used; in rarer instances, lead, copper, or stainless-steel liners with soldered or welded joints are used. Waterproofing should be protected from physical damage, terminated above the static water level, and run continuously behind waterwalls and weirs. Figure 530-15 shows typical pool and pipe penetration waterproofing.

6.0 OPERATING SYSTEMS

There are two basic ways commonly used to operate decorative pools and fountains. The oldest and in some cases still the most cost-effective and reliable method is to use natural sources of water and let the water flow through rather than be recirculated through the system. This is typically accomplished by the use of water from flowing streams, springs, or artesian wells, from gravity-operated irrigation systems, or from elevated water tanks and impoundments.

The second way is through the use of mechanical motors and pumps and typically involves recirculation of the water. This section covers only this second method of operation and provides data on two types of mechanical systems—the *submersible* pump (located within the pool and below the water) and the *remote* pump (located outside of the water and pool). Each of these two approaches is described below.

6.1 Submersible Systems

The submersible system is generally limited to installations of 100 ft^2 (9.3 m^2) or less in area that are drained, cleaned, and filled every few days in lieu of filtering. Other potential applications include larger, biologically balanced pools with minimal displays or temporary, portable, or seasonal displays. The primary concerns with

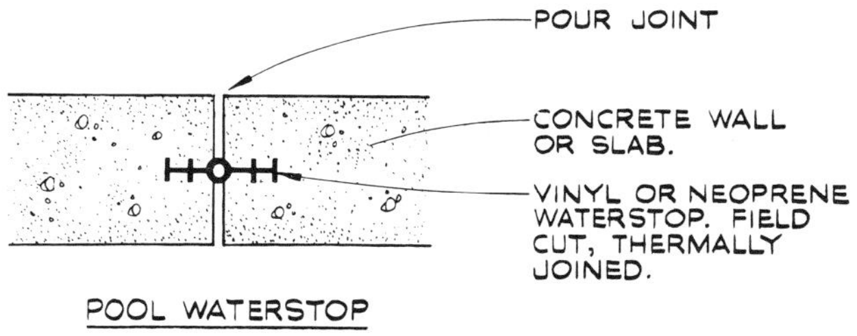
POUR JOINT
CONCRETE WALL OR SLAB.
VINYL OR NEOPRENE WATERSTOP. FIELD CUT, THERMALLY JOINED.
POOL WATERSTOP

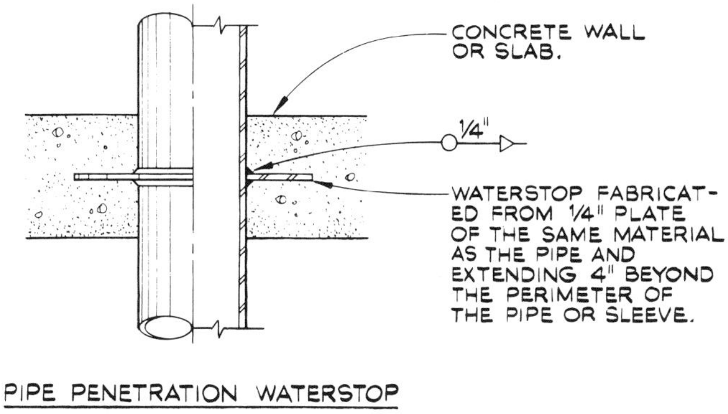
CONCRETE WALL OR SLAB.
1/4"
WATERSTOP FABRICATED FROM 1/4" PLATE OF THE SAME MATERIAL AS THE PIPE AND EXTENDING 4" BEYOND THE PERIMETER OF THE PIPE OR SLEEVE.
PIPE PENETRATION WATERSTOP

Figure 530-14 Waterproofing. (No scale)

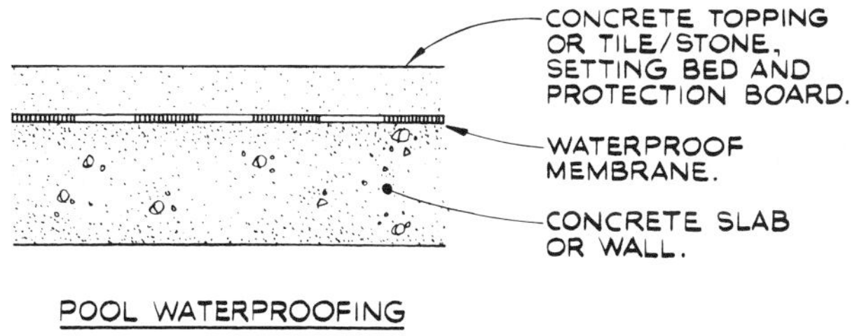
CONCRETE TOPPING OR TILE/STONE, SETTING BED AND PROTECTION BOARD.
WATERPROOF MEMBRANE.
CONCRETE SLAB OR WALL.
POOL WATERPROOFING

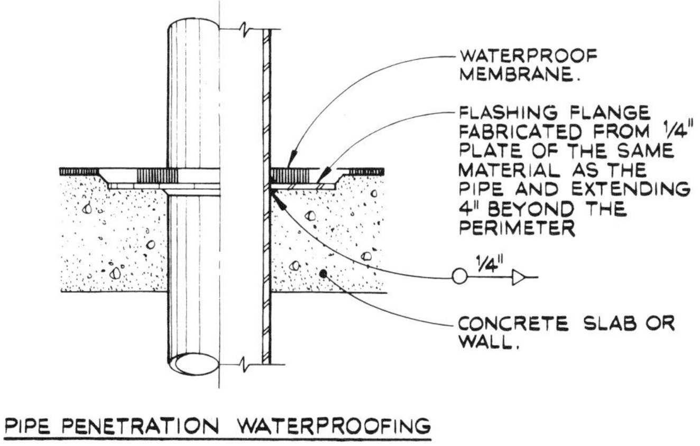
WATERPROOF MEMBRANE.
FLASHING FLANGE FABRICATED FROM 1/4" PLATE OF THE SAME MATERIAL AS THE PIPE AND EXTENDING 4" BEYOND THE PERIMETER
1/4"
CONCRETE SLAB OR WALL.
PIPE PENETRATION WATERPROOFING

Figure 530-15 Waterproofing. (No scale)

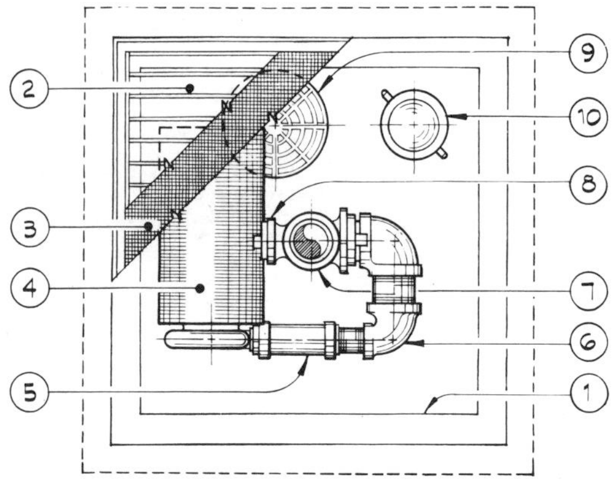

NOTES:

1. 2'-0" SQUARE X 1'-6" DEEP SUMP.
2. GRATING.
3. LEAF SCREEN.
4. DISPLAY PUMP. 100 GPM @ 20' TDH.
5. 1½" NEOPRENE HOSE AND CLAMPS.
6. 2½" X 1½" BRASS REDUCING ELL.
7. 2½" BRASS PIPING TO DISPLAY.
8. 2½" ALL BRONZE ADJUSTING COCK.
9. 4" DRAIN FITTING.
10. CAST BRONZE SUBMERSIBLE JUNCTION BOX.

Figure 530-16 Submersible fountain system. (No scale)

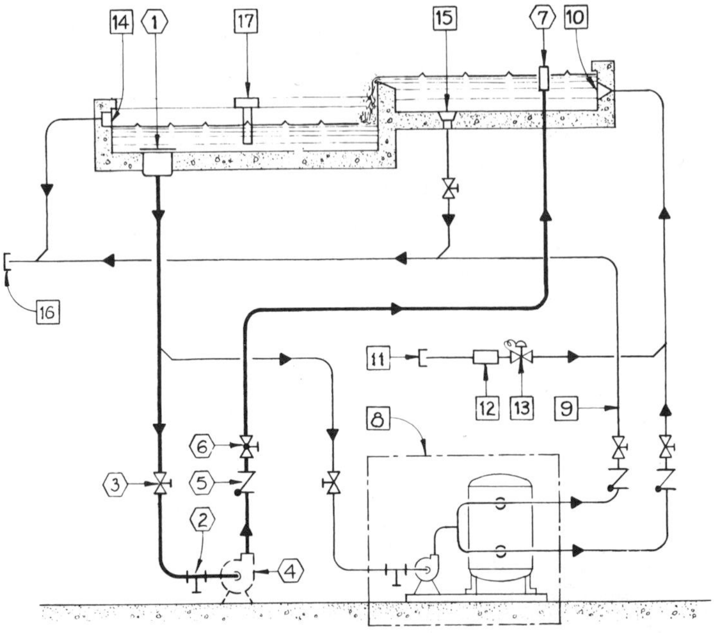

LEGEND

(arrow) ARROW INDICATES FLOW DIRECTION

(heavy line) ○ DISPLAY SYSTEM

(light line) □ SUPPORT SYSTEM; FILTER, FILL/MAKE-UP, OVERFLOW/DRAIN.

Figure 530-17 Schematic fountain diagram. (No scale)

submersible systems are maintenance and electrical safety. If the pool requires filtering rather than periodic draining, cleaning, and refilling, then a remote system should be used.

A typical submersible system is shown in Figure 530-16. Located in the floor of the pool, it comprises (1) a sump with a grating and large mesh screen to protect the pump and intercept larger debris and leaves; (2) a submersible pump with noncorrosive piping to the display, along with appropriate electrical connections; (3) a drain, which often has a standpipe extended to the surface to double as an overflow; and (4) a submersible junction box for the electrical connection. In the simplest of systems, the drain can be omitted and the pool simply siphon-drained. In a slightly more sophisticated system, a niche-mounted float valve can be installed, eliminating the need to top up the pool periodically. The same niche assembly can be purchased with an adjustable overflow standpipe to stabilize the water level further.

6.2 Remote Systems

Figure 530-17 illustrates the essential elements to consider in the design of a remote fountain system. The system, as shown, may appear complex; however, it comprises several modules, or subsystems, which are only marginally interrelated and which in their most basic form are quite simple and understandable. These subsystems include display, filtration, fill/makeup, and overflow/drain.

6.3 Equipment Space

The system design and the equipment selected will depend in great measure on the location and configuration of the equipment space. A number of interrelated considerations are required in order to optimize an equipment space; the most important of these are elevation, location, size, and configuration.

Elevation:

Elevation is the single most important consideration with regard to the equipment space. If at all possible, the floor elevation of the space should be at least 2 ft (600 mm) below the lowest water level in the pool in order to provide a flooded suction for the pump. If no viable space can be found, a vertical pump inserted into a large pipe or sump below the floor should be considered. If a pump is started automatically each day, any location above water level (suction lift) will be an ongoing maintenance headache, since the pump will periodically air-lock and must, at the very least, be protected with a flow switch or similar device.

Location:

If at all possible, the equipment space should be located within a building or a structure that has horizontal access for maintenance personnel and equipment removal. The location should be as close as possible to the pool—or to the lowest pool in a multilevel situation. Distances of 100 to 150 ft (15.2 to 30.4 m) are acceptable for an installation with piping of 6 to 8 in or smaller, but anything over 50 to 100 ft for large piping becomes quite expensive. If a subterranean vault with a vertical access hatch is used, there must be adequate provision for access, equipment removal, waterproofing, draining, and ventilation.

Size and Configuration:

The dimensions of the equipment space must be adequate to provide access to all equipment and valves. They must also provide for the code-required clearances around electrical equipment, as established by local building codes. Generally, a minimum size is 75 ft^2 (22.8 m^2), commonly ranging up to 400 ft^2 (121 m^2) for larger installations. The ideal configuration is broadly rectangular or square with no dimension less than 8 ft (2.4 m).

Accommodations:

A properly designed equipment space should have a floor drain and/or a sump pump to handle water from strainer cleaning, repairs, etc. It should be ventilated to maintain a reasonable temperature and to control humidity. It should also have minimal heating (if needed to prevent freezing), power outlets for movable lights and small tools, and overall electric lighting of 50 to 75 fc (538 to 807 lx) to facilitate routine maintenance.

6.4 Water Display System

The water display system comprises items 1 through 7 on Figure 530-17 (bold flow lines).

Item 1 is the return fitting, or return sump, used to return water from the pool to the display pump.

Item 2 is the line strainer, used to keep leaves and debris from clogging the pump. On larger installations this function is accomplished by screening at the sump.

Item 3 is a shutoff valve (usually a gate or butterfly type) to control the flow to the water supply fitting.

Item 4 is a display, or circulating, pump.

Item 5 is a check valve, necessary only in multilevel pools, to keep water in the higher pool(s) from draining back through the piping of the display system to the lowest pool.

Item 6 is a throttling valve (usually a globe or butterfly type) to control the flow to the supply fitting.

Item 7 is a supply fitting. This may provide a display effect by itself, as with a spouting (jet) display, or may be a concealed outlet to supply water for a weir, etc.

6.5 Support Systems

As a group, the *support systems* are subsystems used to help maintain the quality and level of the water in the pool and to facilitate cleaning.

Filter System:

Comprising items 8, 9, and 10 in Figure 530-17, the filter system uses a circulating pump, a line strainer, and shutoff, check, and throttling valves, just as the display system does. One of the most common systems returns the water to the pool through a filter medium consisting of fine silica sand supported on a base of heavier sand and gravel. This medium is contained in a steel or fiberglass tank. It is generally considered a permanent installation. Trapped particulates can be removed from the finer sand by reversing the flow through the medium (called *backwashing*) and discharging the effluent to the sanitary or stormwater drain system. The return water from the pool can be routed through the display return system or through a separate fitting.

Item 8 is the filter package, which includes the strainer, circulating pump, filter tank, and filter media.

Item 9 is the filter backwash line.

Item 10 is the supply (effluent) fitting for the filter system and is often used to add fill/makeup water. In a fountain with a nonexpressed source, this water may be returned through a display system supply fitting.

Fill/Makeup System:

Comprising items 11, 12, and 13, the system establishes the static water level (in conjunction with the overflow) and maintains the operating water level.

Item 11 is the water supply, usually connected to the domestic water system.

Item 12 is a backflow preventer, required by code when the supply is derived from the domestic water supply (in the absence of an air gap) to prevent back siphoning of potentially contaminated fountain water back into the domestic water supply. Generally installed in the equipment space, below-grade and/or below the pool's water level, it requires a reduced-pressure-type device.

Item 13 is a solenoid-actuated valve, used in conjunction with the water level controller to establish or maintain appropriate water levels. (Item 17 is the water level controller, which is discussed below in 9.6 Water Level Control.)

Overflow/Drain System:

Comprising items 14, 15, and 16, the overflow/drain system establishes the static water level (in conjunction with the fill system) and provides for draining of the pools, piping, and equipment both for cleaning and for shutting down the pool and fountain in climates where the water could freeze and thus cause problems.

Item 14 is the overflow fitting, used to remove excess water resulting from rainfall, irrigation runoff, or a malfunctioning fill/makeup system.

Item 15 is a drain fitting, used to remove water from the various pools to facilitate cleaning and equipment maintenance. Pools with return or supply fittings may be drained at the equipment room via the piping to these systems; they may be drained either at the primary fitting or through an auxiliary drain fitting installed at the low point in the pool. Each pool level in a multilevel installation requires a drain fitting.

Item 16 is the sewer or outlet connection. Most local health codes require that the effluent from a filter should be treated as any other sanitary waste. The overflow drainwater can be treated as any other onsite stormwater runoff.

7.0 EQUIPMENT AND PIPING SELECTION

Tables 530-3 through 530-6 have been included to reduce most required data to chart or nomograph form. Table 530-3 shows flowrates for weirs. Table 530-3 also includes charts showing flowrate and head requirements for solid-stream jets and for jets of the *geyser,* or *cascade,* type, which is the most commonly applied of the aerated types. Data for other aerated types and for sculpted jets may be derived from the manufacturer's data. Tables 530-4, 530-5, and 530-6 show data required to determine system head losses. These, in conjunction with other system head data, will enable the designer to select and determine the size of the pump.

7.1 Display Pump

There are three conditions that must be optimized in selecting a pump: (1) flowrate, (2) head, and (3) minimum net positive suction head. A typical pump selection curve is shown in Figure 530-18.

Flowrate:

Using Table 530-3 or the manufacturer's data for display nozzles, all requirements must be totalled. The required flow at any weir may be reduced by the amount that jets or other weirs contribute to the source of that weir.

Head:

The *head* is the total pressure required to accommodate the difference in elevation between the highest and lowest pools (static level differential), plus discharge head requirements for display jets taken from Table 530-3 or the manufacturer's data, plus total calculated head for entrance, exit, velocity head, pipe, fitting, valve, and strainer losses can be taken from Tables 530-3, 530-4, and 530-5.

NOTE: The requirements may be reduced if the jets are not located in the upper pool.

TABLE 530-4

Pipe Sizing and Head Loss Chart

(Expressed in feet of water per 100 feet length of pipe)

VELOCITY	2 F.P.S.		5 F.P.S.		7 F.P.S.		10 F.P.S.	
FUNCTION	• GRAVITY RETURN		• RETURN ≤ 3" • GRAVITY DRAIN		• RETURN > 3" • PRESSURE SUPPLY OR DRAIN ≤ 3"		• PRESSURE SUPPLY OR DRAIN > 3"	
SIZE	GPM	HD. LOSS	GPM	HD. LOSS	GPM	HD. LOSS	GPM	HD. LOSS
½"	2	7.4	5	38.3	7	70.5	10	134.8
¾"	3	5.9	8	28.6	12	50.2	17	95.1
1"	5	3.8	13	20.4	19	38.0	27	73.7
1¼"	10	2.9	23	14.6	32	27.1	46	53.1
1½"	13	2.2	32	12.2	44	23.3	63	44.0
2"	19	1.8	49	9.5	68	17.7	98	34.5
2½"	31	1.3	76	7.3	103	13.8	151	26.5
3"	44	1.1	110	6.0	152	11.0	220	21.5
4"	78	0.78	195	4.0	273	8.0	393	15.0
5"	125	0.60	308	3.3	428	6.1	612	11.8
6"	177	0.48	440	2.6	616	4.9	881	9.7
8"	315	0.34	780	1.8	1090	3.5	1560	6.7
10"	490	0.27	1240	1.4	1657	2.7	2450	5.2
12"	725	0.23	1760	1.2	2466	2.2	3550	4.2
14"	950	0.18	2400	0.99	3354	1.8	4761	3.6
16"	1250	0.15	3127	0.98	4387	1.6	6255	3.0
20"	1960	0.12	4900	0.65	6910	1.2	9850	2.3
24"	2830	0.09	7100	0.55	9970	0.97	14400	1.9
30"	4400	0.08	11022	0.40	15400	0.95	21500	1.4
VELOCITY HEAD	0.06		0.39		0.76		1.55	

TABLE 530-5

Head Loss Nomograph for Fittings and Valves

(Expressed in equivalent feet of pipe)

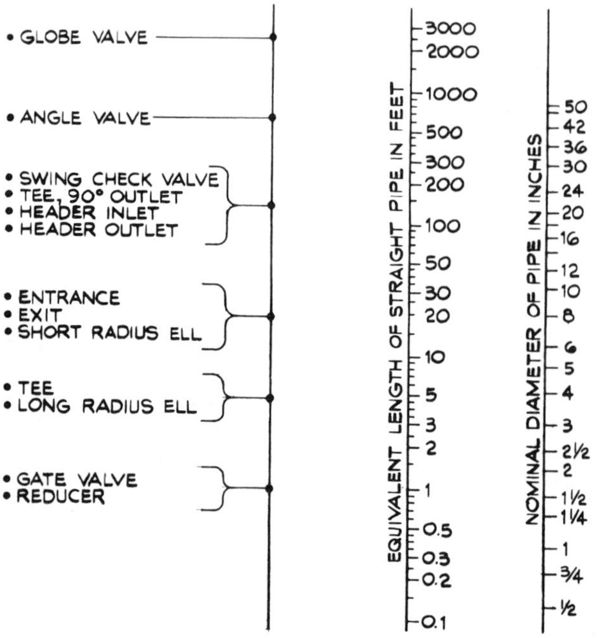
• GLOBE VALVE
• ANGLE VALVE
• SWING CHECK VALVE
• TEE, 90° OUTLET
• HEADER INLET
• HEADER OUTLET
• ENTRANCE
• EXIT
• SHORT RADIUS ELL
• TEE
• LONG RADIUS ELL
• GATE VALVE
• REDUCER
EQUIVALENT LENGTH OF STRAIGHT PIPE IN FEET
3000
2000
1000
500
300
200
100
50
30
20
10
5
3
2
1
0.5
0.3
0.2
0.1
NOMINAL DIAMETER OF PIPE IN INCHES
50
42
36
30
24
20
16
12
10
8
6
5
4
3
2½
2
1½
1¼
1
¾
½

TABLE 530-6

Head Loss Chart for Strainers and Valves

(Expressed in feet of water)

BUTTERFLY VALVE

V(fps)	3"	4"	6"	8"	10"	12"	14"	16"	20"	24"	30"	
5	-	-	-	-	-	-	-	-	-	.18	.17	
7	.53	.34	.57	.115	-	-	-	-	-	.35	.37	
10	1.31	1.06	1.38	.78	.69	.46	.57	.6	.5	.75	.70	

BASKET STRAINER

V(fps)	2"	2½"	3"	4"	6"	8"	10"	12"	14"	16"	20"	
5	2.35	1.73	1.5	1.1	.80	.64	.36	.25	.23	.23	-	
7	5.77	4.15	3.0	2.07	1.51	1.03	.64	.55	.46	.46	.46	
10	11.55	6.43	6.46	4.62	2.77	3.01	1.38	1.15	.80	.92	.87	

SILENT CHECK VALVE

V(fps)	2"	2½"	3"	4"	6"	8"	10"	12"	14"	16"	20"	24"
5	4.38	4.15	4.15	4.5	4.62	4.85	4.96	3.9	4.85	3.9	1.73	1.61
7	6.00	6.23	6.69	6.69	7.16	7.85	7.39	5.31	6.0	6.0	6.0	3.11
10	11.08	11.08	11.31	11.31	12.01	13.86	13.16	9.24	10.39	11.55	12.7	23.1+

DIAPHRAM VALVE - GLOBE

V(fps)	1"	1½"	2"	2½"	3"	4"	6"	8"	10"	12"	14"	16"
7	6.2	6.4	4.1	5.7	4.6	1.6	1.6	4.8	2.0	4.6	5.7	5.7
10	11.5	13.4	9.0	11.5	10.4	7.8	4.4	8.0	11.0	9.4	11.5	11.5
12	20.7	20.3	12.7	18.5	15.7	11.8	12.0	13.1	15.9	13.8	16.1	16.1

DIAPHRAM VALVE - ANGLE

V(fps)	1½"	2"	2½"	3"	4"	6"	8"	10"	12"	14"	16"	
7	5.5	3.2	3.2	2.3	2.3	-	2.8	-	2.3	2.8	2.3	
10	11.0	6.5	5.8	5.5	4.6	1.8	4.6	4.6	4.1	4.9	4.8	
12	16.1	8.3	9.5	7.4	6.7	7.2	7.8	6.5	6.2	7.2	7.0	

TABLE 530-7

High Rate Sand Filter Data

FILTER TANK DIAMETER	SAND BED AREA	POOL SIZE		FLOW RATE	
		3/1000	4/1000	15GPM	20GPM
1'-4"	1.4 SQ. FEET	465	350	21	28
1'-8"	2.2 SQ. FEET	730	550	33	44
2'-0"	3.1 SQ. FEET	1030	775	47	62
2'-6"	4.9 SQ. FEET	1630	1225	74	98
3'-0"	7.1 SQ. FEET	2366	1775	107	142
3'-6"	9.6 SQ. FEET	3200	2400	144	192
4'-0"	12.6 SQ. FEET	4200	3150	189	252
4'-6"	15.9 SQ. FEET	5300	3975	239	318
5'-0"	19.6 SQ. FEET	6530	4900	294	392
5'-6"	23.7 SQ. FEET	7900	5925	356	474
6'-0"	28.3 SQ. FEET	9430	7075	425	566
6'-6"	33.2 SQ. FEET	11,065	8300	498	664
7'-0"	38.5 SQ. FEET	12,830	9625	578	770
7'-6"	44.2 SQ. FEET	14,730	11,050	663	884
8'-0"	50.3 SQ. FEET	16,765	12,575	755	1006

Note: Filter tanks may be grouped to accommodate larger pools or equipment space configuration.

Net Positive Suction Head:

The *net positive suction head* (NPSH) is the resultant pressure available at the pump from atmospheric pressure after adding or deducting (1) the differential between the operating water level and the pump elevation, (2) all losses accruing to entrance conditions, (3) the friction losses through pipes, fittings, valves, and strainers on the suction side of the pump. Atmospheric pressure is 34.0 ft (10.4 m) at sea level, decreasing approximately 1.2 ft (0.365 m) with each 1000-ft (304-m) rise in elevation. If the NPSH is marginal, more definitive calculations should be made, using expanded-pipe sizing charts based on the particular materials used and the manufacturer's data for each component in the return system.

Pump Selection:

Refer to Figure 530-18. After determining the required flowrate and head plus the available NPSH, select the pump to satisfy these parameters and to maximize efficiency. In general, efficiencies of 70 to 90 percent (increasing with the flowrate) should be attainable. Finally, determine the pump manufacturer, the model, the suction and discharge sizes, and the motor horsepower and speed (rpm).

As a general rule, pumps up to 1000 to 1200 gpm (3750 to 4500 Lpm) are end-suction centrifugal types. Those ranging from 1000 to 5000 gpm (3750 to 18,750 Lpm) are more likely to be double-suction split-case types. Beyond 5000 gpm (18,750 Lpm), the pumps used are either the multiple split-case or the mixed-flow and propeller types. These are the same as those used to move large volumes of water in irrigation and wastewater applications. Pumps with low head requirements, i.e., 35 to 50 ft (10.6 to 15.2 m), will generally be of a lower speed, i.e., 1150 rpm or less, and/or have the smaller impeller diameters. As a final general consideration, if the equipment-space floor elevation is near or above the return pool's water level, a vertically mounted pump of the turbine, mixed-flow, or propeller type will greatly improve the suction conditions, allowing optimization of NPSH and submergence.

7.2 Fountain Filters

Refer to Table 530-7. Fountain filters are usually a high-rate sand-type unit, sized on the basis of pool area. Use 3 to 4 ft^2 (0.28 to 0.37 m^2) of filter area for each 1000 ft^2 (94 m^2) of pool area: 3 ft^2 (0.28 m^2) is adequate for indoor applications and 4 ft^2 (0.37 m^2) is appropriate for outdoor installations in an urban area. Diatomaceous earth and cartridge-type filters are sometimes used for fountain installations but are not recommended, given their greater maintenance requirements.

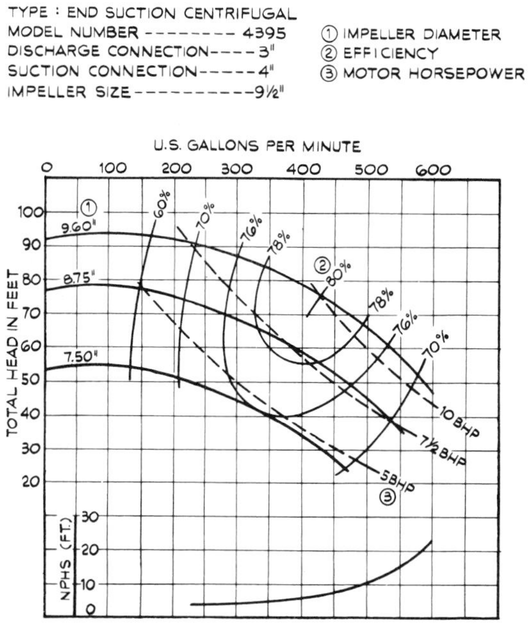
TYPE : END SUCTION CENTRIFUGAL
MODEL NUMBER -------- 4395
DISCHARGE CONNECTION---- 3"
SUCTION CONNECTION----- 4"
IMPELLER SIZE---------- 9½"
① IMPELLER DIAMETER
② EFFICIENCY
③ MOTOR HORSEPOWER
U.S. GALLONS PER MINUTE
TOTAL HEAD IN FEET
NPHS (FT.)
9.60"
8.75"
7.50"
60%
70%
76%
78%
80%
10 BHP
7½ BHP
5 BHP

Figure 530-18 Typical pump curve.

7.3 Filter Pump

For units 30 in (762 mm) or less in diameter, it is usually included as part of a prepiped unit. For larger units, select the pumps as follows.

Flowrate:

Refer to Table 530-7. The 15-gpm (56.2-Lpm) rate should be used unless the extra flow associated with the 20-gpm (75-Lpm) rate is required for display purposes.

Head:

The total head required has to accommodate (a) static level differential; (b) the total calculated for entrance, exit, velocity head, pipe, fitting, valve, and strainer (as taken from Tables 530-4, 530-5, and 530-6); and allowance for losses due to dirt and other particulates building up on the sand bed between backwashings. This allowance should be 35 ft (10.6 m) for units with manual backwash and 25 ft (7.6 m) for units with automatic backwash.

Net Positive Suction Head Selection:

The NPSH calculations and pump selection will be the same as for the display pump. (See 7.1 Display Pump in this section.)

7.4 Piping Materials

Piping materials are generally noncorrosive. Each material has particular advantages and limitations, particularly in light of economic considerations.

Polyvinyl Chloride:

Polyvinyl chloride (PVC) is noncorrosive and has low friction losses. Its limitations include its vulnerability to ultraviolet deterioration in exposed outdoor situations and its limited physical strength, leading to a variety of failures, particularly at fittings. Failure may be induced by differential settlement, physical damage, or vibration in the pumping system. Vibration is a particularly common problem for open fountain systems where either entrained air in the return system or operation at more or less than design flow (and hence lower efficiency) will cause the pump(s) to vibrate. PVC is appropriate for low-budget installations, for underground piping in planted areas where repairs can easily be made, or for carefully controlled circumstances where it may be embedded in concrete.

Copper:

Copper, also noncorrosive, has much better physical strength than PVC, particularly at fittings. Costs generally limit its application to sizes 3 in (76 mm) and smaller. Copper must be dielectrically isolated from adjacent steel piping and equipment to prevent galvanic action, which causes deterioration of the steel—particularly galvanized steel.

Red Brass:

Red brass has many of the same characteristics as copper but has greater physical strength, making it particularly useful for

TABLE 530-8
Sizing of Gravity Flow Piping

TYPE OF PIPING	SIZING	SIZED FOR MAXIMUM VELOCITY OF:
GRAVITY RETURN PIPING	SIZING IS CRITICAL & MUST BE CAREFULLY CALCULATED FOR LONG PIPING RUNS & MINIMAL SLOPES	2 fps (600 mm/sec.)
RETURN PIPING	3 IN. (76mm) & SMALLER 4 IN. (100mm) & LARGER	5 fps (1.5 m/sec.) 7 fps (2.1 m/sec.)
SUPPLY PIPING	3 IN. (76mm) & SMALLER 4 IN. (100mm) & LARGER	7 fps (2.1 m/sec.) 10 fps (3.04 m/sec.)
GRAVITY DRAWN AND OVERFLOW PIPING		5 fps (1.5 m/sec.)
PUMPED DRAIN PIPING	3 IN. (76mm) & SMALLER 4 IN. (100mm) & LARGER	7 fps (2.1 m/sec.) 10 fps (3.04 m/sec.)
FILL/MAKE-UP PIPING		10 fps (3.04 m/sec.)

exposed piping in the pool. In general, its high cost limits it to this application.

Steel:

Steel is probably the best overall material for any piping that is 3 to 4 in (76 to 100 mm) or larger in diameter. Because fountain water has a high oxygen content and because the system is not only open but often drained down for cleaning and winterization, the piping should be galvanized or epoxy-lined to prevent rust formation and staining. Note that galvanization may be impractical where the piping is threaded or in close proximity to fittings (or other hardware) made of brass or bronze.

Ductile or Cast Iron:

Ductile or cast iron is used in all sizes for the overflow/drain system. Generally, it is an economic alternative to steel for long runs at diameter sizes of 8 in (200 mm) or larger. It should be specified to be cement-lined, and for pressure systems it should have mechanical joints. Ductile iron may be welded for waterstops, shaped nipples, and other special fabrications, whereas cast iron cannot be.

7.5 Pipe Sizing

Table 530-8 shows maximum pipe sizes and corresponding velocities for any given function. Return piping size must be reviewed in light of NPSH requirements.

Sizing for gravity return, drain, and overflow piping is critical and must be carefully calculated, particularly for long piping runs and minimal slopes. Improper sizing may result in flooding and/or pump damage.

7.6 Fittings, Valves, and Strainers

This hardware is generally of the same material and size as the piping. Gate valves are suitable for shutoff only, while butterfly valves, globe valves, and ball valves and cocks may be used for shutoff or throttling. Diaphragm valves are used for sequencing, flow regulation, and other forms of automatic modulation. All strainers should be fitted with brass or stainless-steel baskets. Strainers over 8 in (200 mm) in diameter should be provided with either an integral cover lift or an auxiliary means to lift the cover.

7.7 Pool Hardware

Aside from underwater lighting, several basic items of hardware are required for pool operation, and several more are available to facilitate maintenance.

Return Fitting:

A fabricated fiberglass or metal sump is usually employed, with an antivortex cover plate to prevent any entrainment of air. For large installations, the return fitting may be a concrete sump formed in the pool floor, with a cover grate and leaf screen; a cover plate is not necessary, as the increased depth prevents vortexing or air entrainment.

Figure 530-19 shows a fabricated sump with an infill-type antivortex cover plate. The plate is designed to receive concrete or tile infill to match the pool bottom. Figure 530-20 shows a formed concrete sump in the pool floor. This type of sump is generally employed for flowrates in excess of 1000 gpm (3750 Lpm) where the fountain is on-grade. In a rectangular configuration, a sump can simply have more return elbows; for instance, a 2½-ft × 5-ft (0.9-m × 1.5-m) sump would have two 8-in (200-mm) return ells entering the long wall on quarter points. The sump may assume any irregular shape, which can be accommodated simply by discounting all sump area beyond the basic configuration.

Supply Fitting:

Either a nozzle (as discussed above in 4.0 Water Effects) or a nonexpressed source employing one or more fabricated sumps (as shown in Figure 530-19) is necessary. For larger nonexpressed sources, one or more formed concrete sumps may be used, as shown in Figure 530-21.

Fill/Makeup Fitting:

If the supply is nonexpressed, fill/makeup fittings may be routed via the supply fitting. If jets are used, then a separate fitting should be used (Figure 530-22).

Filter Systems Fittings: Main-drain (filter return), skimmer, *eyeball* supply, and vacuum fittings are all carryovers from swimming pool design and should be avoided if possible, as they will clutter the pool with hardware that is of questionable value and nearly impossible to conceal. The filter return may be via the main return sump in lieu of the main drain and skimmers. Supply to the pool may be via the fill/makeup fitting rather than eyeball supply fittings if effective circulation can be promoted via the display system.

Overflow Fitting:

Refer to Figure 530-22. Where possible, a submerged overflow strainer may be used in conjunction with an inverted trap. If the pool is elevated, a conventional sidewall fitting may be used unless the freeboard is inadequate, in which case a standpipe or a specially fabricated slot-type overflow may be used.

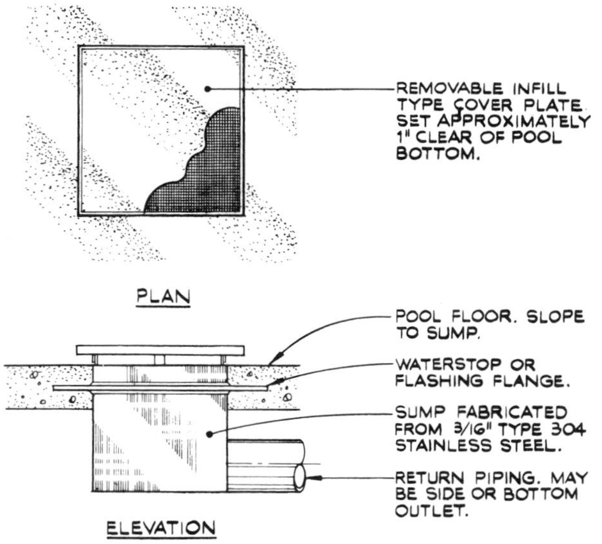
REMOVABLE INFILL TYPE COVER PLATE SET APPROXIMATELY 1" CLEAR OF POOL BOTTOM.
PLAN
POOL FLOOR. SLOPE TO SUMP.
WATERSTOP OR FLASHING FLANGE.
SUMP FABRICATED FROM 3/16" TYPE 304 STAINLESS STEEL.
RETURN PIPING. MAY BE SIDE OR BOTTOM OUTLET.
ELEVATION

MAXIMUM G.P.M.	SUMP SIZE	COVER PLATE SIZE	RETURN PIPE SIZE
200	8" X 8" X 8" DEEP	1'-2" SQUARE	4" Φ
300	1'-2" X 1'-2" X 1'-2" DEEP	1'-4" SQUARE	6" Φ
500	1'-2" X 1'-2" X 1'-4" DEEP	2'-0" SQUARE	8" Φ

Figure 530-19 Return/supply sump (No scale).

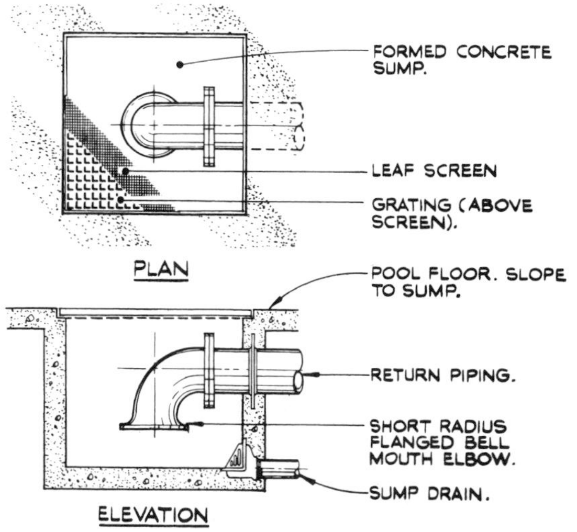
FORMED CONCRETE SUMP.
LEAF SCREEN
GRATING (ABOVE SCREEN).
PLAN
POOL FLOOR. SLOPE TO SUMP.
RETURN PIPING.
SHORT RADIUS FLANGED BELL MOUTH ELBOW.
SUMP DRAIN.
ELEVATION

MAXIMUM G.P.M.	MINIMUM SUMP SIZE	RETURN PIPE SIZE
1000	2'-6" X 2'-6" X 2'-6" DEEP	8" Φ
1750	3'-0" X 3'-0" X 3'-0" DEEP	10" Φ
2500	3'-6" X 3'-6" X 3'-6" DEEP	12" Φ
3250	4'-0" X 4'-0" X 4'-0" DEEP	14" Φ
4000	4'-6" X 4'-6" X 4'-6" DEEP	16" Φ
5500	5'-0" X 5'-0" X 5'-0" DEEP	18" Φ
7000	5'-6" X 5'-6" X 5'-6" DEEP	20" Φ

Figure 530-20 Return sump (No scale).

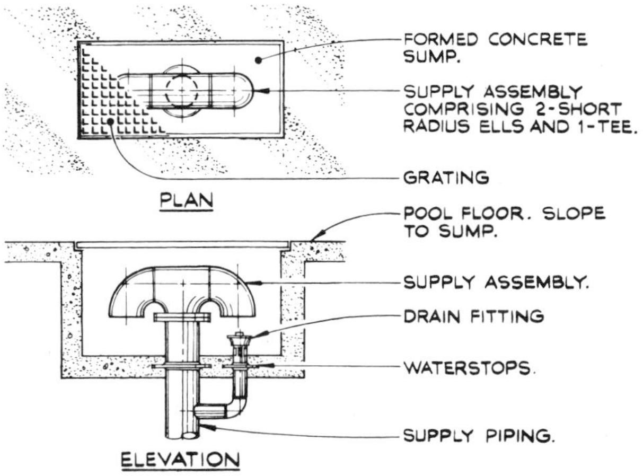
FORMED CONCRETE SUMP.
SUPPLY ASSEMBLY COMPRISING 2-SHORT RADIUS ELLS AND 1-TEE.
GRATING
PLAN
POOL FLOOR. SLOPE TO SUMP.
SUPPLY ASSEMBLY.
DRAIN FITTING
WATERSTOPS.
SUPPLY PIPING.
ELEVATION

MAXIMUM G.P.M.	MINIMUM SUMP SIZE	SUPPLY PIPE SIZE
150	2'-0" X 1'-0" X 1'-3" DEEP	3" Φ
400	2'-6" X 1'-3" X 1'-6" DEEP	4" Φ
900	3'-6" X 1'-6" X 2'-0" DEEP	6" Φ
1600	4'-6" X 2'-0" X 2'-6" DEEP	8" Φ
2500	6'-0" X 2'-6" X 3'-0" DEEP	10" Φ
3500	7'-0" X 3'-0" X 3'-6" DEEP	12" Φ
4750	8'-0" X 3'-6" X 4'-0" DEEP	14" Φ
6250	9'-0" X 4'-0" X 4'-6" DEEP	16" Φ

Figure 530-21 Return sump (No scale).

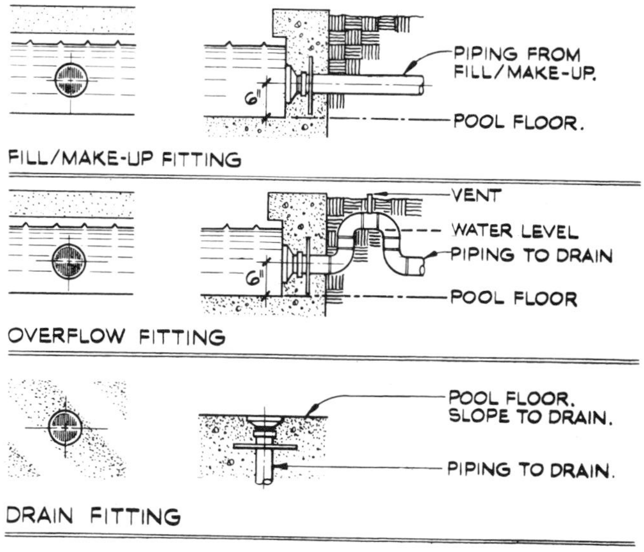
PIPING FROM FILL/MAKE-UP.
6"
POOL FLOOR.
FILL/MAKE-UP FITTING
VENT
WATER LEVEL
PIPING TO DRAIN
6"
POOL FLOOR
OVERFLOW FITTING
POOL FLOOR. SLOPE TO DRAIN.
PIPING TO DRAIN.
DRAIN FITTING

NOTES

1. IF POSSIBLE, ALL STRAINERS SHOULD BE THE SAME CONFIGURATION, DIMENSION AND SHAPE.
2. FOR CONCRETE FINISH POOLS, A ROUND STRAINER WILL ELIMINATE THE POSSIBILITY OF AN OUT-OF-SQUARE FITTING.
3. FOR TILE FINISH POOLS, AN 8" SQUARE STRAINER CAN VISUALLY BE INTEGRATED INTO THE TILE MODULE.
4. FOR STONE FINISH POOLS, A 7" ROUND STRAINER CAN BE FITTED IN A 8" CORE DRILL HOLE.

Figure 530-22 Pool fittings. (No scale)

Drain Fittings:

Refer to Figure 530-22. In general, each pool should have a drain at its lowest elevation. In the case of return or source pools, this may be via the return or sump, utilizing the fittings or drains shown in Figures 530-19, 530-20, or 530-21. For intermediate pools, a separate valved drain or solid-top drain may be used.

Finishes:

It is important that compatible finishes be selected, since the pool fittings may be provided by several suppliers and/or fabricators. Generally, either a brass/bronze or stainless-steel/nickel plate vernacular is used. This should include gratings and frames for the return/supply pumps, jets, and fill/makeup, overflow, and drain fittings, as well as for the lighting fixtures.

8.0 FOUNTAIN LIGHTING

Fountain lighting is typically thought of only in terms of underwater lighting; however, the use of daylighting (i.e., optimizing orientation relative to sunlight) as well as floodlighting has great potential and is considerably less costly than underwater lighting. Effective use of each of these alternatives is both an art and a science. Although a thorough discussion is beyond the scope of this section, a brief overview of the applications of each is appropriate. Information on colored lighting is not included here, as ample reference material is available from manufacturers and the applications are limited. (Refer to Section 540: Outdoor Lighting, for more information.)

8.1 Daylighting

Daylighting is a very important aspect of siting and display orientation, particularly with directional displays. Sunlight is especially effective on free-falling or formed jets, as it attractively reflects off the sheet surface, illuminating surface highlights. It also works well with whitewater displays such as textured waterwalls, waterstairs, cascading falls, and aerated jets. In the northern hemisphere, a southerly exposure is optimal. An easterly or westerly orientation affords morning or afternoon light. Northerly exposures generally offer little enhancement to the basic readability of the display; moreover, windborne spray and splash do not dry quickly, and so the cooling potential is minimized.

8.2 Floodlighting

The effects of floodlighting are very similar to those of daylighting, but floodlighting must be used very judiciously, as the distraction of visible sources often offsets the value of the lighting. If sources can be minimized, this can be a very effective and economical means of lighting. Floodlighting may also be used in combination with underwater lighting, affording a broader spectrum of effects with which to achieve the overall composition.

8.3 Underwater Lighting

Underwater lighting is potentially the most dramatic, as it renders a self-illuminated quality to display effects, particularly with regard to free-falling sheets and jets. The water acts like a lens, refracting and diffusing the light. Underwater lighting must, however, be used judiciously, as each fixture in place costs 3 to 5 times as much as a floodlight or typical open-air landscape fixture by virtue of the requirements for submersibility, corrosion resistance, and code-required safety provisions. Furthermore, the maintenance for underwater units is considerably more costly than for landscape units.

Underwater lighting may be used in two basic ways: *uplighting,* as used for a sheet or jet, and *pool lighting,* where the pool itself is lighted to delineate surrounding surfaces or to feature materials and/or textures. Uplighting is generally the more dramatic and practical of the two.

Pool lighting generally requires many more fixtures than uplighting, and because the inside surfaces of the pool need to be light-colored to reflect the light, this often compromises the pool's reflective capabilities during the day; it should be mentioned, too, that painting a pool a light color will give it an appearance more like a commercial swimming pool than an ornamental pool or fountain. Pool lighting also makes silt and debris considerably more visible, necessitating more frequent maintenance. Lastly, but perhaps of greatest importance, the lighting must be very well maintained, because the effect of having only one or two lamps burned out may be much worse than having no light at all.

8.4 Design Principles

Although nighttime lighting, whether floodlighting or underwater lighting, is generally used to accentuate only a part of the total fountain composition, it typically intensifies the nighttime presence of the illuminated pools or display elements (as compared to the daylight impact). With larger, more complex fountains, an intermediate lighting level is often introduced, subordinate to the focal elements while still strongly contrasting with the immediate surroundings. This typically requires the use of underwater lighting in lieu of, or in addition to, any floodlighting that may be used.

Once the basic composition is determined, the design criteria are fairly objective. Lighting intensity is based on *luminance,* i.e., surface brightness, measured in footlamberts rather than footcandles.

Human perception of light intensity is generally logarithmic in nature, requiring 10 times the brightness to double the intensity perceptually. Accordingly, the brightness of a primary display should average at least 10 times the surrounding ambient light level and 3 times the subordinated displays. The *uniformity ratio*—the maximum to minimum brightness for any display element—ideally should not exceed 3:1.

TABLE 530-9
Lighting

MINIMUM BEAM CANDLEPOWER REQUIREMENTS													
WATER EFFECT HEIGHT (IN FEET)	5	10	15	20	25	30	35	40	45	50			
CANDLEPOWER REQ'D. (IN THOUSANDS)	4	11	21	34	50	69	91	115	144	170			

BEAM CANDLEPOWER AVAILABLE FOR VARIOUS LAMPS													
WATTAGE ENVELOPE BEAM (1)	150 PAR SP (3)	150 PAR FL (3)	250 PAR SP (4)	250 PAR FL (4)	300 PAR NSP (3)	300 PAR MFL (3)	300 PAR WFL (3)	500 PAR NSP (4)	500 PAR MFL (4)	500 PAR WFL (4)	1000 PAR NSP (4)	1000 PAR MFL (4)	1000 PAR WFL (4)
CANDLEPOWER AVAILABLE (2) (IN THOUSANDS)	10.5	3.5	34	6	70	22	10	90	49	18	160	60	27

(1) NSP = NARROW SPOT, SP = SPOT, FL = FLOOD, MFL = MEDIUM FLOOD, WFL = WIDE FLOOD.

(2) CANDLEPOWER SHOWN IS INITIAL AVERAGE IN CENTRAL 5° CONE FOR SPOTS, CENTRAL 10° CONE FOR FLOODS.

(3) INCANDESCENT LAMPS, 2000 HOUR AVERAGE LIFE.

(4) TUNGSTEN HALOGEN LAMPS, 4000 HOUR AVERAGE LIFE.

Since water displays are generally highly reflective and localized, the use of relatively low-level light will effect the desired brightness. Careful selection of the type of lamp is the key to proper lighting and, as such, should precede the selection of the lighting fixture itself. For example, when lighting a narrow, vertical jet, a very narrow low-voltage 240-W spot lamp affords more light in the critical 5-degree central cone than does a 1000-W spotlight. In general, narrow-beam spotlights are used for lighting jets and wide-beam floodlights for falling water. In the interest of uniformity, a minimum of two fixtures should be used for jet displays and maximum spacing of 3 ft (1 m) on center used for waterfall uplights. Fixtures should be selected to accommodate (1) the type and orientation of the lamps, (2) the pool configuration and finish, (3) applicable codes, and (4) regular maintenance.

It should be noted that fountains are rarely overlighted, but the lighting for a single jet or waterfall need not be as complex as described above. Most suppliers of components offer relatively simple tabular data, such as that shown in Table 530-9.

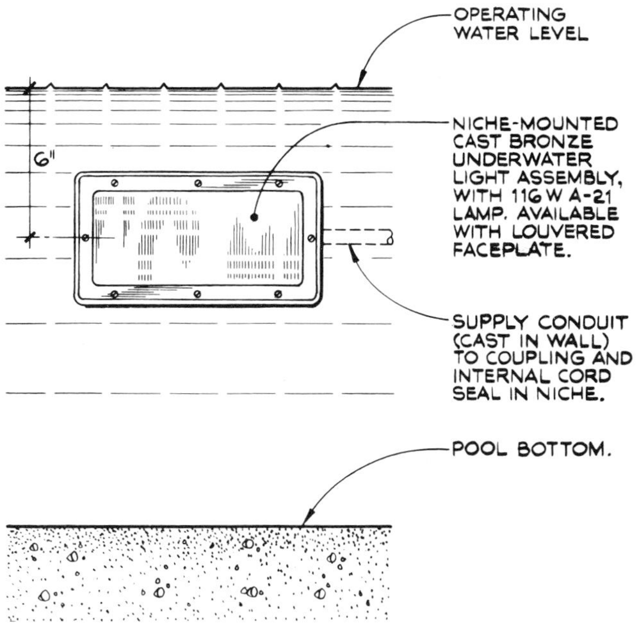
OPERATING WATER LEVEL
6"
NICHE-MOUNTED CAST BRONZE UNDERWATER LIGHT ASSEMBLY, WITH 116 W A-21 LAMP. AVAILABLE WITH LOUVERED FACEPLATE.
SUPPLY CONDUIT (CAST IN WALL) TO COUPLING AND INTERNAL CORD SEAL IN NICHE.
POOL BOTTOM.

Figure 530-23 Lighting. (No scale)

8.5 Installation

There are several critical considerations regarding the physical installation of underwater fixtures, including proper submersion, minimization of hardware, shielding the source from view, and accommodating code-mandated safety requirements.

Submersion:

Most underwater fixtures rely on submersion for cooling to prevent lamp and lens breakage. Minimum submersion is about 1 in (25 mm), with 2-in (50-mm) submersion commonly specified to accommodate wave action and water level variability. Any depth beyond this dimension should be minimized, as the light output is reduced by 10 percent for every 2 in of submergence.

Minimization of Hardware:

Underwater fixtures are inherently bulky, and the need for cords, junction boxes, and other related hardware compounds the problem. Figures 530-23, 530-24, and 530-25 show clear, typical details for the installation of underwater fixtures for the delineation and uplighting of sheets and jets; although these are only representative, they do show methods for concealing cords, conduits, and junction boxes and for minimizing the presence of the fixture itself. Among the several variations on typical fixture construction and installation detailed in these figures, the more important include the following.

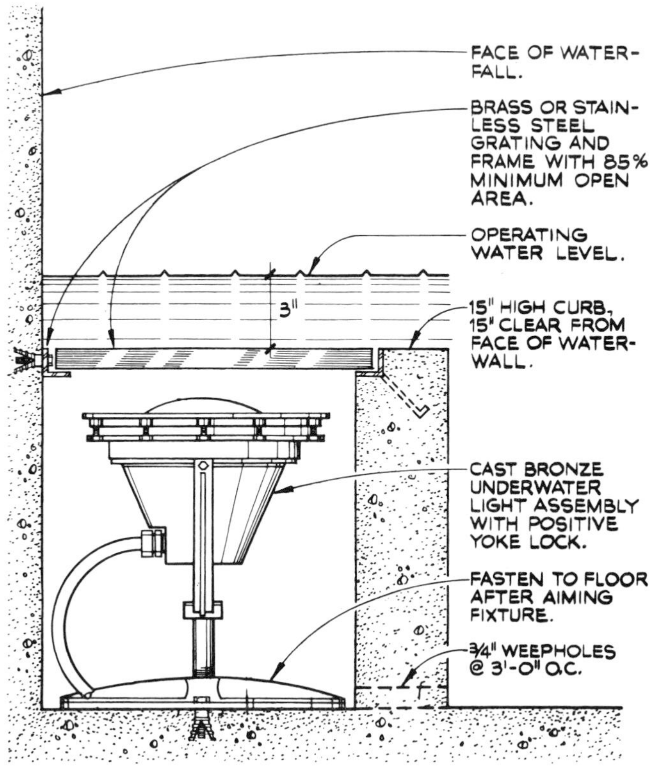
FACE OF WATER-FALL.
BRASS OR STAINLESS STEEL GRATING AND FRAME WITH 85% MINIMUM OPEN AREA.
OPERATING WATER LEVEL.
3"
15" HIGH CURB, 15" CLEAR FROM FACE OF WATER-WALL.
CAST BRONZE UNDERWATER LIGHT ASSEMBLY WITH POSITIVE YOKE LOCK.
FASTEN TO FLOOR AFTER AIMING FIXTURE.
3/4" WEEPHOLES @ 3'-0" O.C.

Figure 530-24 Lighting. (No scale)

Yoke Locks: Yoke locks should be specified for fixtures used to illuminate falling water from jets or waterfalls, particularly when vertical dimensions exceed 20 ft (6 m). Fixtures positioned by friction devices are inadequate for heavy falls or jets.

Bases: Bases should be secured to the pool floor to prevent any movement due to falling water or any dislocation that might occur in the course of normal pool maintenance.

Rock Guards: Rock guards are required by code for fixtures facing upward. A cast-bronze grid integrated with the lens door is

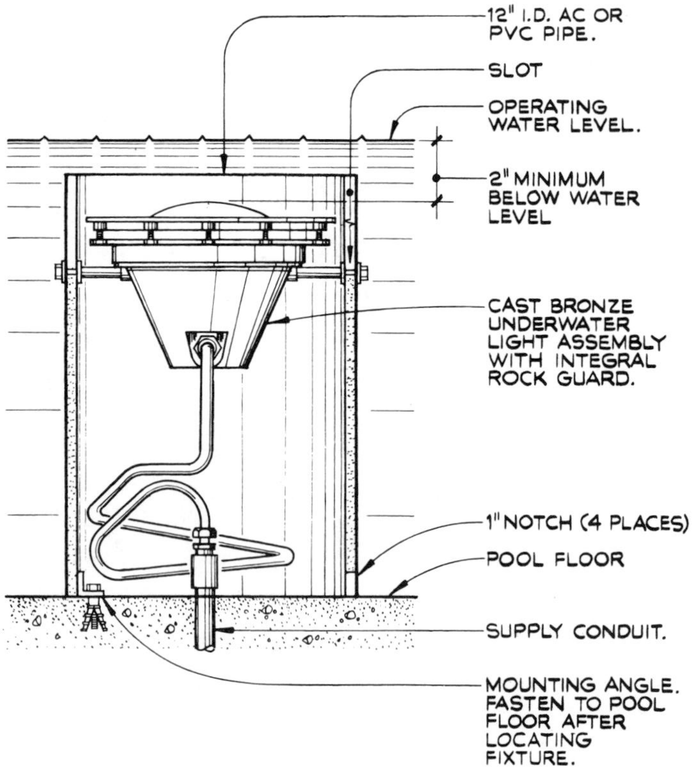
12" I.D. AC OR PVC PIPE.
SLOT
OPERATING WATER LEVEL.
2" MINIMUM BELOW WATER LEVEL
CAST BRONZE UNDERWATER LIGHT ASSEMBLY WITH INTEGRAL ROCK GUARD.
1" NOTCH (4 PLACES)
POOL FLOOR
SUPPLY CONDUIT.
MOUNTING ANGLE. FASTEN TO POOL FLOOR AFTER LOCATING FIXTURE.

Figure 530-25 Lighting. (No scale)

commonly used, but a protective grating (as shown in Figure 530-24) will serve the purpose just as well.

Flush-Mounted Fixtures: A flush-mounted fixture (as shown in Figure 520-23) cannot be embedded directly in concrete, but must be installed in a niche with sufficient length of cord to allow the fixture to be elevated to at least 2 ft (600 mm) above water level for relamping. Since the niche is a wet area, a cord seal, like that used at the fixture for the cord connection, should be used at the conduit entry to the niche to keep water out of the conduit system. This fixture, which employs the standard *A*-type lamp, should always be provided with the traffic signal version of this lamp, which affords an 8000-hour average lamp life rather than the 750-hour life of the household version.

Shielding the Source:

Figure 530-23 shows a fixture that can be fitted with an optional cast-bronze louver if the fixture falls within the line of sight from normal viewing positions. Figure 530-24 shows a fixture below a linear bar grate that, in itself, functions as a louver. In Figure 530-25, the mounting cylinder itself will afford some shielding. Other underwater fixtures have optional louvers that are integral with the lens door and double as the code-required rock guard.

Safety Requirements:

Article 680 of the U.S. National Electric Code (NEC) mandates several safety provisions, including corrosion-resistant conduits, positive grounding, and ground-fault current-interrupting circuit breakers, which trip instantaneously if current leakage to ground exceeds 5 mA (a fraction of the current level that might pose a lethal shock hazard). These provisions must be carefully studied and applied. Because of the somewhat subjective nature of the wording contained in the codes, it is often wise to review the provisions with the authority who will be responsible for inspection and approval of a particular installation.

9.0 CONTROLS

The fountain control system may be as simple as a single manual switch used to turn on or off a submersible pump, or as complex as a fully automatic system with hundreds of electromechanical devices responding to a controlling computer. The primary functions of an automatic control system are: (1) automating otherwise manual chores which may be aesthetic or practical in nature and (2) protecting equipment against damage or deterioration due to inoperative auxiliary equipment, inadequate maintenance, or variable external circumstances. Interestingly, as complex as these systems can become, variants and combinations of only a handful of control devices and a half-dozen or so basic subsystems are used to moderate, protect, and maintain the subsystems discussed above in 6.0 Operating Systems.

9.1 Control Devices

Selector Switch:

Selector switches are used to select, vary, bypass, or deenergize the automatic control devices in each subsystem.

Pilot Light:

Pilot lights are used, where appropriate, to show the status of each subsystem.

Motor Starter, Contactor, Relay:

These are magnetically operated or actuated switches. A motor starter, in addition, integrates a thermally operated switching device to protect the motor against a variety of potential malfunctions. When control power is applied to the coil of the actuating electromagnet, one or more contact pairs are simultaneously opened or closed. Removing the control power will reverse the contacts. A relay may have up to 12 sets of contacts, and each of these may be specified as closed or open in the normal (deenergized coil) mode. Each contact pair is then *normally open* or *normally closed.*

Time Delay Relay:

A time delay relay is similar to the relay described above, except that actuation is delayed by an auxiliary timing device. The delay may occur upon energization or deenergization, the length of delay may be adjusted, and instantaneous (nondelayed) contacts may be actuated by the same coil.

Time Switch:

A time switch is a clock-operated switch that may be preset to switch on and off at any desired time of day. If required, the device may be specified to switch several times during each day. Time switches used for lighting may be specified with an *astronomic dial* which corrects the *on* time for the time of year and the specific latitude.

Pressure Switch:

A pressure switch opens or closes upon change of pressure. It can be specified to operate on either increasing or decreasing pressure. If the desired actuation is at less than atmospheric pressure, a combination pressure-vacuum or vacuum switch must be specified.

Flow Switch:

A flow switch opens or closes when water is flowing in a pipe, and it reverses mode when the flow ceases.

Level Sensor:

A level sensor is a float- or probe-actuated device used to sense liquid level in a container and to cause a remote low-voltage relay to switch on and off as the level falls and rises. The minimum practical difference between the on and off levels is on the order of 1 in (25 mm).

Wind Sensor:

An anemometer (wind-driven generator) is used to sense wind velocity and to cause a remote relay to switch on or off as the velocity exceeds or falls below a preset velocity.

9.2 Pump Control

Refer to Figure 530-26. Power for the pump is routed through a motor starter. The coil is actuated by a time switch, set to switch the pump motor on and off at the desired times of day. Additional controls in the control circuit will prevent the motor from running if the shutdown system is energized or if the water level in the pool is too low. An auxiliary contact (interlock) in the motor starter is used to keep the makeup system from operating if the pool is drained or a low-water condition exists.

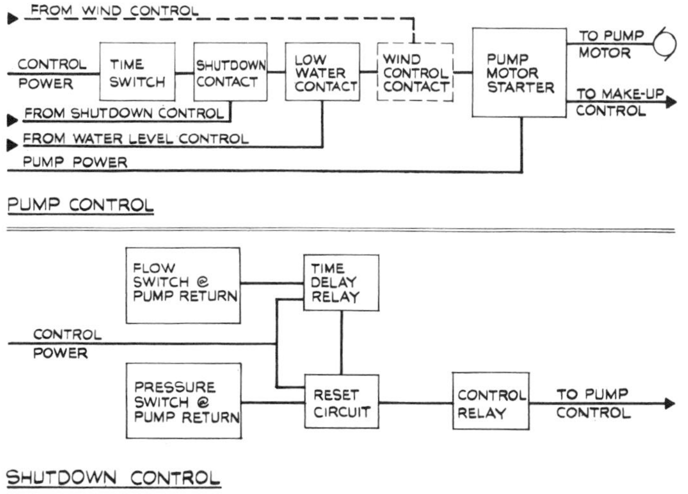
FROM WIND CONTROL
CONTROL POWER
TIME SWITCH
SHUTDOWN CONTACT
LOW WATER CONTACT
WIND CONTROL CONTACT
PUMP MOTOR STARTER
TO PUMP MOTOR
TO MAKE-UP CONTROL
FROM SHUTDOWN CONTROL
FROM WATER LEVEL CONTROL
PUMP POWER
PUMP CONTROL
FLOW SWITCH @ PUMP RETURN
TIME DELAY RELAY
CONTROL POWER
PRESSURE SWITCH @ PUMP RETURN
RESET CIRCUIT
CONTROL RELAY
TO PUMP CONTROL
SHUTDOWN CONTROL

Figure 530-26 Controls (pump control, shutdown control).

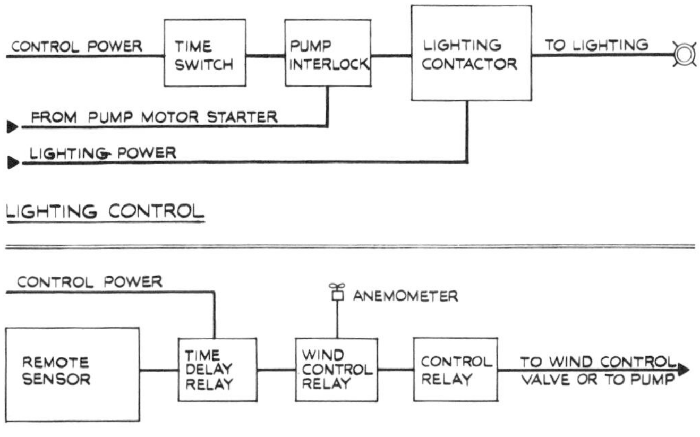
CONTROL POWER
TIME SWITCH
PUMP INTERLOCK
LIGHTING CONTACTOR
TO LIGHTING
FROM PUMP MOTOR STARTER
LIGHTING POWER
LIGHTING CONTROL
CONTROL POWER
ANEMOMETER
REMOTE SENSOR
TIME DELAY RELAY
WIND CONTROL RELAY
CONTROL RELAY
TO WIND CONTROL VALVE OR TO PUMP

Figure 530-27 Controls (lighting control, wind control).

9.3 Shutdown Control

Refer to Figure 530-26. This system is designed to keep the pump(s) from running if the return system is clogged or if the water is not flowing. A third shutdown circuit is included in the water level control. (See 9.6 Water Level Control in this section.)

Clogged Return:

Clogged returns are usually caused by a poorly maintained leaf screen or strainer. As the pump works harder to draw water, a low pressure or vacuum develops between the strainer and the pump. A properly installed pressure or pressure/vacuum switch on the return line will signal this condition.

No Flow:

This condition is caused by a loss of prime (air in the pump), a malfunctioning pump, or a closed valve or other obstruction in the supply piping. A time relay is incorporated in conjunction with the flow switch to allow the flow to become established on start-up.

The control relay is actuated on signal from the pressure/vacuum or flow switch, interrupting power to the pump control circuit. Once the pump is stopped, the system must be reset manually; otherwise, the system would try to restart as the flow diminishes and a full static head is re-established.

9.4 Lighting Control

Refer to Figure 530-27. This system is virtually identical to the pump control system, utilizing a lighting contactor, or heavy duty type of relay, in lieu of the motor starter. Power is routed through a lighting contactor, which is actuated by an astronomic dial time switch via an auxiliary contact in the display motor starter, ensuring that the lights will not operate if the display is off for any reason.

9.5 Wind Control

This system switches control power through a relay actuated by a wind-driven generator. An integral time delay ensures that the system is not triggered by momentary gusts. Often two relays are used, each with a different set point. When the lower velocity set point is reached, the first-stage control relay is actuated, throttling an automatic valve to reduce jet heights. When the higher velocity is reached, the second-stage control relay interrupts power to the pump and lights. A restart time delay is used to ensure that the pump does not exceed an allowable number of starts per hour or day, which could cause damage to the motor.

9.6 Water Level Control

Refer to Figures 530-17 (Item 13) and 530-28. This system switches control power through relays actuated by water level sensors, either probes or floats, which monitor

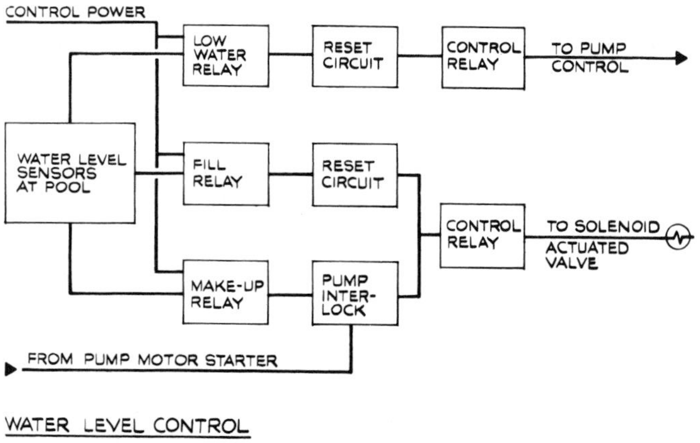
CONTROL POWER
LOW WATER RELAY
RESET CIRCUIT
CONTROL RELAY
TO PUMP CONTROL
WATER LEVEL SENSORS AT POOL
FILL RELAY
RESET CIRCUIT
CONTROL RELAY
TO SOLENOID ACTUATED VALVE
MAKE-UP RELAY
PUMP INTER-LOCK
FROM PUMP MOTOR STARTER
WATER LEVEL CONTROL

Figure 530-28 Controls (water level control).

the water level at the pool. The probe system is most commonly used, each function comprising two probes and a probe relay—although, with proper design, the fill and low-water functions can be combined. The fill and makeup systems utilize a common water level control relay which is used to actuate the solenoid-operated valve. The low-water shutdown system has a separate control relay which is used to interrupt power to the pumps and lights should the water in the pool fall below a preset minimum level.

9.7 Sequencing

The mechanics of controlling a sequenced fountain are sufficiently varied and complex, and the applications infrequent enough, that a detailed discussion here is probably not justified. It is appropriate to note, however, that there are four commonly used methods of controlling sequenced fountains. They are, in order of complexity:

1. A simple cam timer, of the type used to control traffic signals
2. A series of step switches and timing relays
3. Programmable solid-state logic modules
4. Computers of varying capacities

Each of these has a particular useful range. The cam timer, for instance, might control a relatively straightforward group of three or four jets. Intermediate systems could range to the latter methods, which might be used to deliver complex instructions to hundreds of jets and lights—while at the same time responding to environmental variables, such as wind, rain, and temperature—or used to provide a constantly modulated, or *fluid,* effect rather than a stepped effect.

REFERENCES

Much of the preceding material has been derived from the contributor's own experience and observations. The following material was, however, drawn upon heavily for the subsections 1.0, 2.0, and 5.0.

Alpern, Andrew (ed.). *Handbook of Specialty Elements in Landscape Architecture,* chap. 8: "Decorative Pools and Fountains," M. Paul Friedberg and Cynthia Rice, McGraw-Hill, New York, 1982.

Campbell, Craig S. *Water in Landscape Architecture,* Van Nostrand Reinhold, New York, 1978.

Carpenter, Jot (ed.). *Handbook of Landscape Architectural Construction,* chap. 13: "Water-Pools and Fountains," E. Byron McCully, The Landscape Architecture Foundation, Washington, D.C., 1976.

Weddle, A. E., *Landscape Techniques,* chap. 8: "Water," G. A. Jellicoe, Van Nostrand Reinhold, New York, 1979. ■

section 540: Outdoor Lighting

CREDITS

Contributor:

Michael Sardina
The SWA Group, Inc.
Boston, Massachusetts

Alan Fujimori
Sasaki Associates, Inc.
Watertown, Massachusetts

Reviewers:

Peter Coxe
William Lam Associates
Cambridge, Massachusetts

Kenneth E. Bassett
Sasaki Associates, Inc.
Watertown, Massachusetts

CONTENTS

1.0 INTRODUCTION

1.1 General

This section includes information useful for solving site lighting problems. Included are definitions of terms associated with lighting, general design principles, characteristics of various lamps, and recommended levels of illumination (industry standards) for various landscape uses. The information included here will help the designer focus on specific ideas about lighting and aid in the process of specifying fixtures for particular lighting projects.

1.2 Objectives of Outdoor Lighting

The purposes of outdoor lighting include: (1) improving the legibility of critical nodes, landmarks, and circulation and activity zones in the landscape; (2) facilitating the safe movement of pedestrians and vehicles, promoting a more secure environment, and minimizing the potential for personal harm and damage to property; and (3) helping to reveal the salient features of a site at a desired intensity of light in order to encourage nighttime use of a particular environment.

2.0 TERMINOLOGY

Lumen: A quantitative unit of measurement referring to the amount of light energy emitted by a light source, without regard to the effectiveness of its distribution.

Footcandle (fc): A quantitative unit of measurement referring to illumination incident at a single point. One footcandle is equal to one lumen uniformly distributed over an area of one square foot.

Lux (lx): The International Standard (SI) mea-

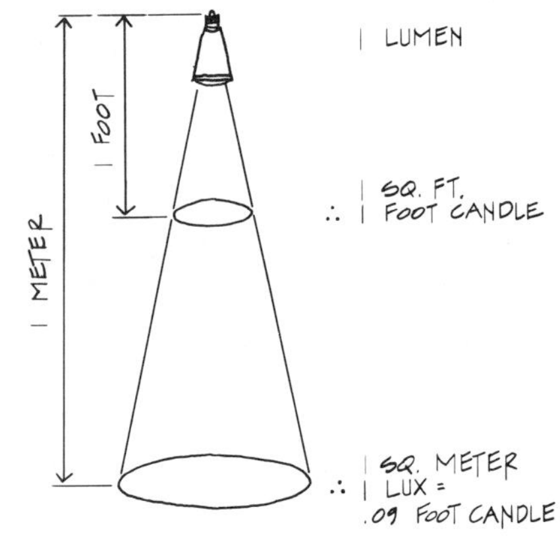
1 LUMEN
1 FOOT
1 METER
1 SQ. FT.
∴ 1 FOOT CANDLE
1 SQ. METER
∴ 1 LUX =
.09 FOOT CANDLE

Figure 540-1 Lighting terms.

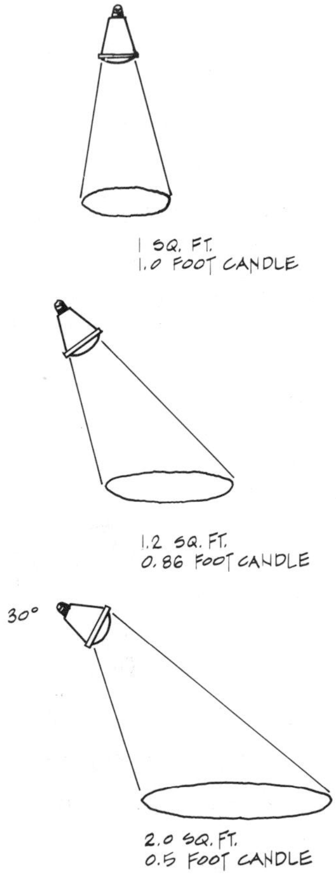
1 SQ. FT.
1.0 FOOT CANDLE
1.2 SQ. FT.
0.86 FOOT CANDLE
30°
2.0 SQ. FT.
0.5 FOOT CANDLE

Figure 540-2 Incident illumination.

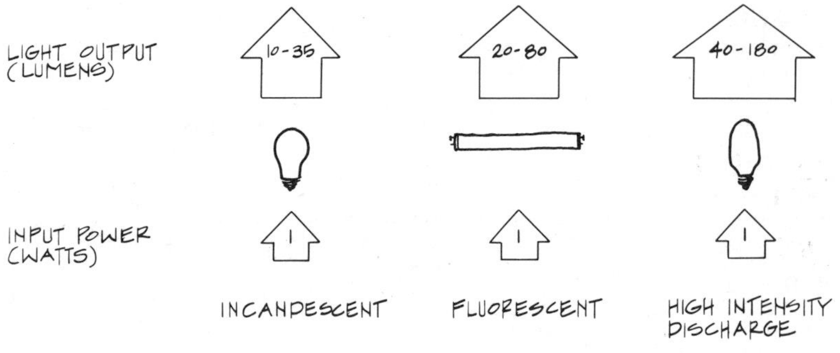
LIGHT OUTPUT
(LUMENS)
10-35
20-80
40-180
INPUT POWER
(WATTS)
1
1
1
INCANDESCENT
FLUORESCENT
HIGH INTENSITY
DISCHARGE

Figure 540-3 Lamp efficacy.

sure of illumination incident at a single point. It is equal to one lumen uniformly distributed over an area of one square meter (1 fc = 10.7 lx). (See Figure 540-1.)

Candela: The unit of intensity of a light source in a specific direction, often referred to as candlepower. One candela directed perpendicularly to a surface one foot away generates one footcandle of light.

Incident illumination: The amount of illumination incident on a surface varies with the intensity of the source in the direction of the surface, the distance between the source and surface, and the angle of incidence. (See Figure 540-2.)

Efficacy: A measure of how efficiently a lamp converts electric power (watts) into light energy (lumens) without regard to the effectiveness of its illumination. It should not be assumed that a lamp which has high efficacy will give better illumination than a less efficient lamp (Figure 540-3.)

Light depreciation: Lamp output (lumens) will depreciate over its effective life. Illumination will be reduced further due to an accumulation of dirt and grime on the lamp and fixture. Adjustments should be made to compensate for this depreciation when determining the average values of illumination maintained over time. A *maintenance* factor of 50 to 70 percent is common for outdoor applications. New installations are routinely designed to deliver 1½ to 2 times as much illumination as needed, to sustain this *maintained* output over the anticipated life of the lamp.

Color: Two measures used to describe the color characteristics of lamps are (1) the apparent color and (2) the color rendering index.

The *apparent color* of a light source is given by the *color temperature.* Figure 540-4 shows various index numbers used to rank sources on a scale that range from *warm* to *cool* in appearance. Preference for one or another is a matter of taste and usually varies with the context of the application and with the illumination level. Warm tones tend to be favored when illumination is low and cooler tones are preferred under high lighting levels.

The *color rendering index* (CRI) is a measurement of the degree to which object colors are faithfully rendered. This scale ranges from 0 to 100 and is a reasonable approximation of color rendering accuracy. CRI is completely independent of whether a light source casts the object in a warm or cool tone. For instance, deluxe high-pressure sodium lamps (warm tone) and metal halide lamps (cool tone) have a nearly identical CRI. Although people and objects appear distinctly different under each, both are considered to be fairly accurate when compared to a *perfect* source. The CRI graph shows the ranking of the major outdoor light sources (Figure 540-4). As a general guideline, a minimum CRI of 50 is suggested to attain a reasonably faithful or natural color rendition. Lamps ranked significantly below this are judged to cause visible distortions to appearance.

Glare: Glare is illumination that causes annoyance, discomfort, and sometimes a brief loss of vision. The measurement or quantification of glare is extremely difficult and tends to be a subjective matter. *Disability glare* impairs visibility and is primarily a physiological phenomenon; e.g., the nighttime glare from an oncoming vehicle's headlights can momentarily blind a driver's perception of the road ahead. *Discomfort glare* does not impair visibility but is primarily a psychological phenomenon or an annoyance which may produce fatigue if it continues over an extended period of time.

Cutoff light distribution: A term used in reference to the optical design of some fixture types. By the careful location of lamps and the use of carefully aligned reflectors, intense high-angle light can be effectively eliminated. Most designs severely restrict fixture intensities above 75 degrees from nadir, that is, within 15 degrees of horizontal (Figure 540-5).

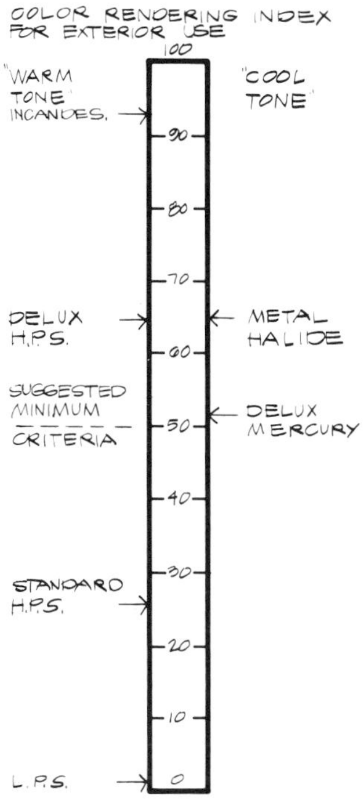
COLOR RENDERING INDEX FOR EXTERIOR USE
100
"WARM TONE" INCANDES.
"COOL TONE"
90
80
70
DELUX H.P.S.
METAL HALIDE
60
SUGGESTED MINIMUM CRITERIA
50
DELUX MERCURY
40
30
STANDARD H.P.S.
20
10
L.P.S.
0

Figure 540-4 Color rendering index.

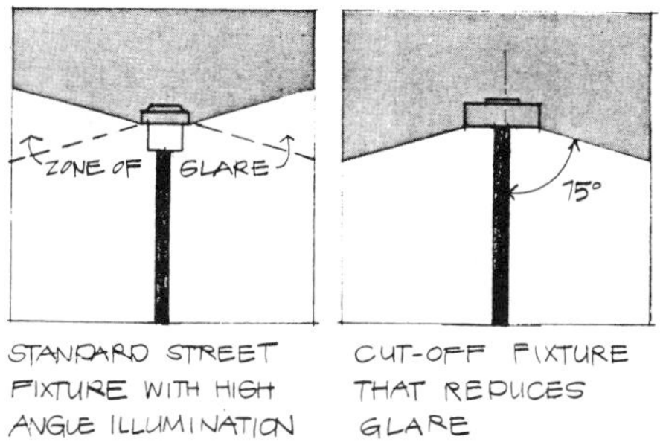
ZONE OF GLARE
75°
STANDARD STREET FIXTURE WITH HIGH ANGLE ILLUMINATION
CUT-OFF FIXTURE THAT REDUCES GLARE

Figure 540-5 Cutoff light distribution.

3.0 GENERAL DESIGN PRINCIPLES

3.1 Orientation

Lighting Hierarchy:

Driver and pedestrian orientation can be aided by providing a hierarchy of lighting effects that correspond to the different zones and uses of a site. For instance, subtle but recognizable distinctions can be made between major and minor roads, paths, and use areas by varying the distribution and brightness of the light and by varying the height, spacing, and color of the lamps (Figure 540-6).

Attaining high levels of illumination along circulation routes does not have to be a prime consideration in outdoor lighting. If a clear and consistent system is provided, low levels may be adequate for safe circulation. Once a modest illumination intensity has been provided, the degree of lighting uniformity will become a more important determinant than increased intensity.

Clear Lighting Patterns:

Clear optical guidance can be provided with the positive alignment of light fixtures positioned in consistent, recognizable, and unambiguous patterns. A staggered layout of road and pathway lights tends to obscure rather than reinforce the direction of the circulation alignment and the location of intersections (Figure 540-7).

3.2 Identification

Intersection Articulation:

Intersections, decision points, crossings, bus stops, steps, arrival points, etc., should be articulated in a manner that signals their presence, shape, and nature. The illumination pattern should serve as a visual cue to what conditions may lie ahead.

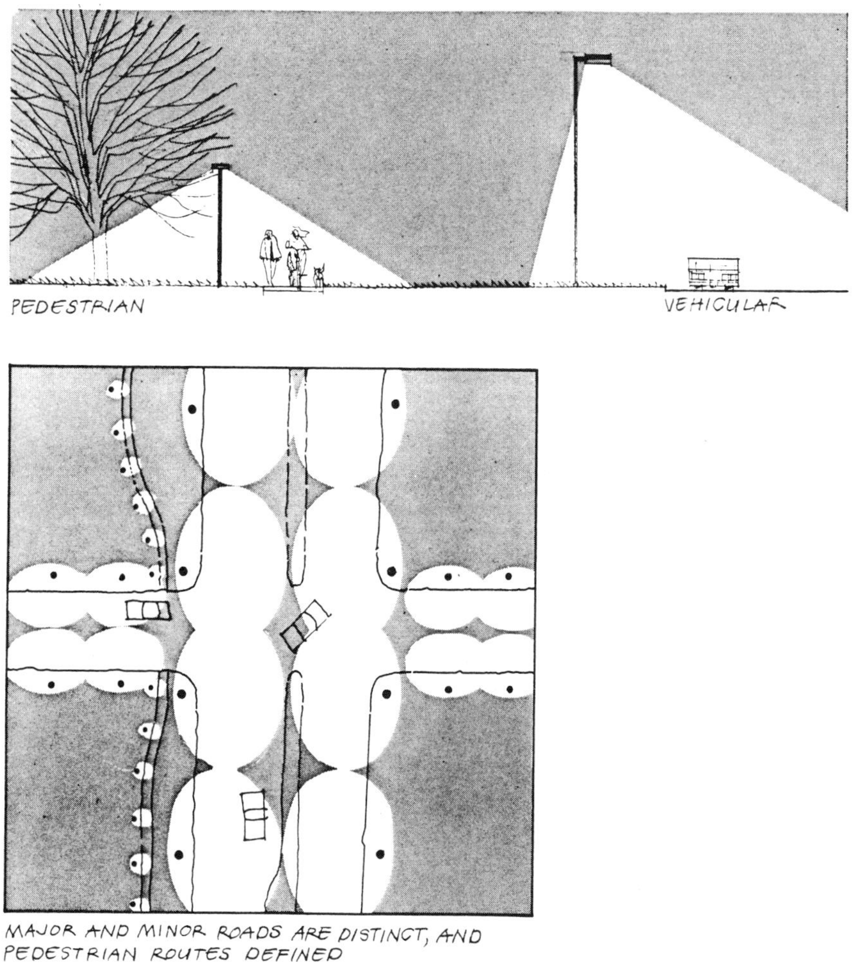
PEDESTRIAN
VEHICULAR
MAJOR AND MINOR ROADS ARE DISTINCT, AND PEDESTRIAN ROUTES DEFINED

Figure 540-6 Lighting hierarchy.

UNDESIRABLE
DESIRABLE

Figure 540-7 Clear lighting patterns.

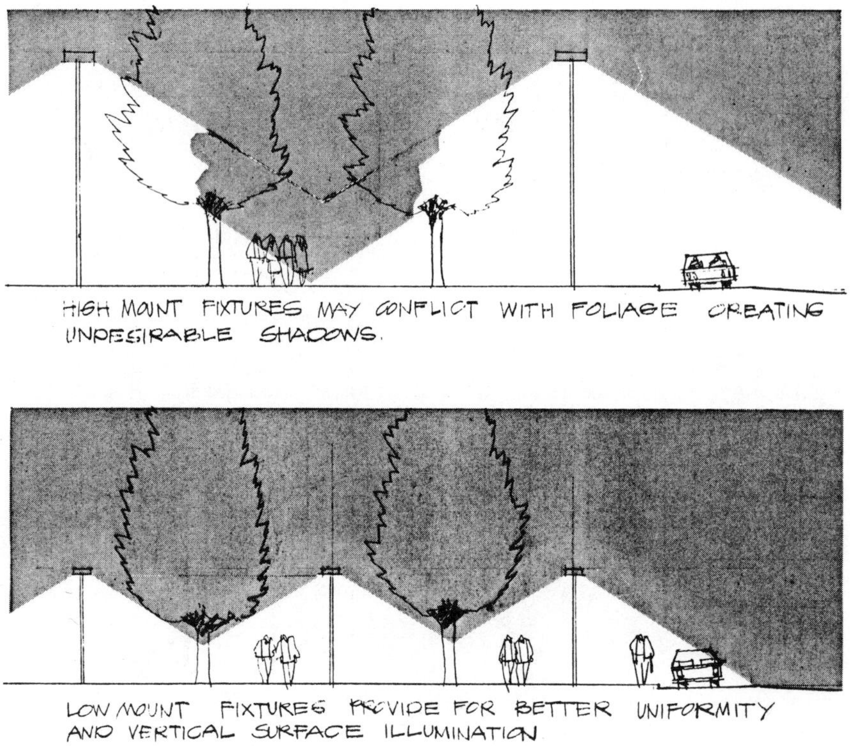
HIGH MOUNT FIXTURES MAY CONFLICT WITH FOLIAGE CREATING UNDESIRABLE SHADOWS.
LOW MOUNT FIXTURES PROVIDE FOR BETTER UNIFORMITY AND VERTICAL SURFACE ILLUMINATION

Figure 540-8 Luminaire mounting heights. Low mount fixtures provide for better uniformity and vertical surface illumination.

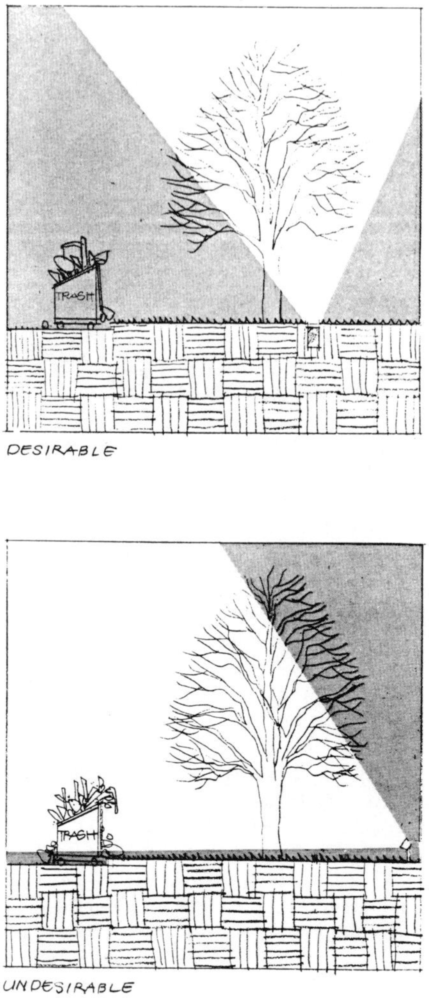
TRASH
DESIRABLE
TRASH
UNDESIRABLE

Figure 540-9 What to light versus what not to light.

Placement of Luminaires:

A luminaire spacing, height, and distribution pattern should be specified that avoids foliage shadows and gives good uniformity and vertical surface illumination. High fixture mounting, using wide spacing, may result in disruptions to the illumination pattern due to tree shadows [Figure 540-8 (top)]. Lower mounting heights and closer spacings between fixtures can create a more uniform distribution, and the pedestrian's sense of security is promoted by the uniformity of the light [Figure 540-8 (bottom)].

Deciding What to Light:

In some circumstances, it may be equally as important to determine what not to light as to determine what to light (Figure 540-9).

3.3 Safety

Poor lighting layout and design, as well as glare and underlighting, can create hazardous conditions. In addition to the above-stated principles, the following are important for safety reasons.

Glare:

Glare is a major inhibitor of good visibility and the most unpleasant aspect of visual discomfort. Disruptive glare can be produced by any scale of light fixture, including small lens-type step lights (Figure 540-10).

Glare is more of a problem when exposed light sources, such as lamps or lenses, can be seen directly. Luminaire location and mounting height, fixture type, and lamp intensity must be carefully selected to optimize light distribution and minimize glare.

Lower mounting lanterns may or may not have sharp cutoff optics. If high-angle illumination is appropriate in order to illuminate facades, trees, and other streetscape elements fully, then care must be taken to prevent the likelihood of glare. An outdoor mock-up at night is an excellent technique to use when deciding what light distribution pattern and intensity to use and whether or not there will be any likelihood of glare.

Large amounts of glare are caused when high-angled *cobra-head* types of lenses are used along roadways. Luminaires with sharp cutoffs effectively direct the light into a visually useful and comfortable pattern.

Underlighting:

Underlighting (i.e., insufficient lighting) is potentially hazardous if not enough light is provided to protect pedestrians and/or vehicles from potential injury and damage. Sufficient light is especially important at crosswalks where heavy pedestrian traffic is expected, such as near parks, ball fields, and other places which attract crowds of people, or where children cross streets to get home. Parking areas, access and egress points, loading areas, etc., should have adequate lighting to help protect drivers, passengers, and vehicles.

Note that overlighting an area can generate high amounts of glare, which in itself can create hazardous conditions. A careful balance of light intensities must be considered. Table 540-3 lists recommended levels of illumination as stated in the Illuminating Engineering Society's *IES Lighting Handbook*. Levels of lighting are related to types of use and other characteristics within use areas.

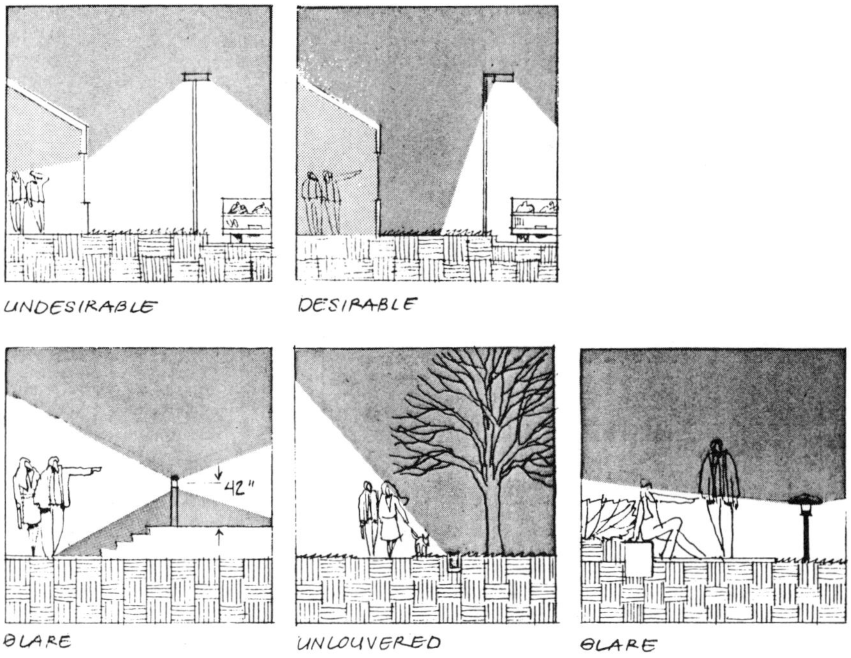
UNDESIRABLE
DESIRABLE
42"
GLARE
UNLOUVERED
GLARE

Figure 540-10 Glare.

3.4 Security

Darkness, together with unfamiliar surroundings, can incite strong feelings of insecurity. To provide a sense of security, possible hiding places and dense shadows should be minimized by the placement of appropriate light fixtures.

Walkway Lights:

Walkway lights should have enough peripheral distribution to illuminate the immediate surroundings. Vertical light distribution over walkway areas should cover or overlap at a height of 7 ft (2 m) so that visual recognition of other pedestrians is maintained (Figure 540-11). When the pedestrian's sense of security is a primary consideration, low mounting height with close spacing and a vertical illumination pattern may be the most effective approach.

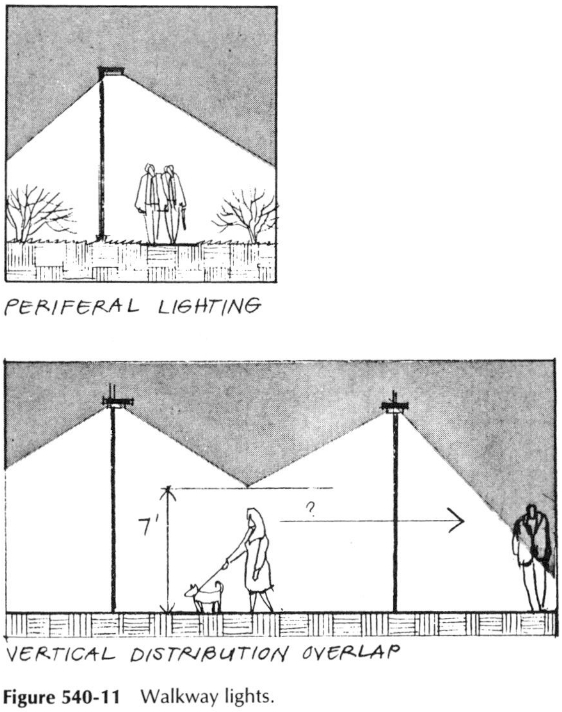
PERIFERAL LIGHTING
7'
?
VERTICAL DISTRIBUTION OVERLAP

Figure 540-11 Walkway lights.

Surveillance:

For surveillance needs, lighting requirements should permit the detection of suspicious movement rather than provide for the recognition of definitive details. For the same expenditure of light energy, it is often more effective to light backgrounds, thereby generating silhouettes, than to light the foreground (e.g., lighting the vertical face of a building instead of its horizontal foreground (Figure 540-12). It is also desirable to *highlight entrances* and to direct lighting away from points of surveillance.

UNDESIRABLE
DESIRABLE

Figure 540-12 Surveillance.

Vandalism:

The best way to reduce the vandalism of light fixtures is to use fixtures that are durable enough to withstand abuse, or to

UNIFORM LIGHTING
SINGLE POINT SOURCE
FORM & SHADE LIGHT
FILL LIGHTING
COMBINATION LIGHTING

Figure 540-13 Shape accentuation.

place them out of reach. An alternative solution may be to use hardware that is less expensive to replace.

3.5 Atmosphere and Character

A consistency of design expression can be achieved by identifying the common elements in a landscape that give it character, and then using similar approaches to their lighting. The clarity with which an object is perceived is influenced by its context.

Background:

Exterior spaces should have a well-defined sense of background. Background spaces should be illuminated as unobtrusively as possible to meet the functional needs of safe circulation and of protecting people and property. Whenever possible, these needs should be accommodated with peripheral lighting from the walkways, signage, entrances, and other elements relevant to the definition of the space.

Foreground:

Foreground spaces or objects can be major elements and should be treated accordingly. Foreground spaces should utilize local lighting which produces maximum focus, minimum distractions, and no glare. Objects of interest and activities can be brightly illuminated while the background produces only minimal distraction.

Illumination of Objects (Shape Accentuation):

The direction of the light source is important for perception of three-dimensional objects. The ability to perceive volumetric form is influenced by the gradient of light and shadow falling on the object. Uniformly distributed, diffused light results in poorly rendered shadows (Figure 540-13); one must then rely upon outline and color in order to perceive the shape and form of the object. Conversely, a single point source will produce maximum shadows but may also minimize the perception of details.

Usually, the best way to illuminate standing objects is with a combination of both types of lighting. One source should accentuate shape and form by contrasting the surface with sharp shadows while the other source provides fill-lighting for details.

Color Perception:

Differences in lamplight color are often used with great effect in public lighting to *color code* roadways or to clearly delineate one area from another. As the general illumination level rises in a given situation, preference usually shifts away from a warm appearance toward the cool range.

Accurate color rendition will aid recognition and improve the perception of outdoor environments. This is especially important at the pedestrian scale, where the color contrast of paving and landscape materials is often subtle.

4.0 LAMP CHARACTERISTICS AND LIGHT DISTRIBUTION

4.1 Lamp Characteristics

Selection of a lamp involves trade-offs between lamp size/optical control, efficacy, appearance, color temperature, color rendition, lamp life, costs, and maintenance (Table 540-1).

Incandescent Lamps:

Incandescent lamps have superior color rendition and a warm white appearance. The disadvantage of a short lamp life can be overcome by the use of a rugged traffic signal lamp rated at 8000 hours nominal life or by undervoltaging the circuits to extend the life. Incandescent lamps have the lowest efficacy of all the lamps. However, they are inexpensive and the small filament permits good optical control.

Fluorescent Lamps:

Although compact shapes are becoming more widely used, most flourescent lamps

TABLE 540-1
Summary of Lamp Characteristics*

Lamp	*Wattage range, ft*	*Efficacy, lumen/watt*†	*Average life, hrs*	*Apparent color*	*Color rendering*	*Initial cost of equipment*
Incandescent	10–1000	10–25	750–2000	Warm white	Best overall	Low
Fluorescent	15–215	40–80	7500–15,000	Warm to cool white	Good	Medium
Mercury vapor (deluxe white)	40–1000	25–60	24,000	Cool white	Good	Medium
Metal halide	175–1500	65–105	7500–20,000	Cool white	Very good	Medium to high
High-pressure sodium (STP)	35–1000	60–120	—	Yellowish	Poor	High
High-pressure sodium (deluxe color)	150–250	75–80	—	Warm white	Very good	High
Low-pressure sodium	18–180	70–150		Yellow-orange	Very poor	High

* Data current at time of writing. Technological improvements are anticipated to be centered on the metal halide and deluxe color high-pressure sodium lamp families.

† Includes ballast losses.

are long and linear, making optical control very difficult. They tend to produce glare unless they are well baffled. They have a good color rendition, whitish appearance, and superior life. Although they have good efficacy, their light output can be severely diminished by very cold weather.

Mercury Vapor Lamps (Deluxe White):

Mercury vapor (MV) lamps have good efficacy, excellent life, and a good cool white color. Strong in the blue-green end of the color spectrum, the lamp is popular for foliage lighting. The cost of the lamp and fixture is the lowest of the high-intensity discharge (HID) lamps. In general, it has a good combination of characteristics when no extremes are required.

Metal Halide Lamps:

Metal halide (MH) lamps offer superior optical control and color rendition. Their efficacy is substantially better than mercury vapor lamps but slightly poorer than high-pressure sodium lamps. The light appears cool white and has a shorter life than the other HIDs. The cost falls between that for mercury vapor and high-pressure sodium lamps. MH lamps are not currently available in low-wattage–low-light output sizes.

High-Pressure Sodium Lamps:

High-pressure sodium (HPS) lamps have excellent efficacy, superior optical control, superior life, and very low maintenance, which accounts for their popularity. The light tends to have a yellowish appearance and a mediocre color rendition of objects. It rarely enhances foliage colors because of deficiencies at the blue-green end of the color spectrum. If color is not an important consideration, this lamp can have broad application. The initial cost for the lamp and fixture is higher than for metal halide. HPS lamps and fixtures are available in a wide range of sizes.

High-Pressure Sodium Lamps (Deluxe Color):

These lamps provide excellent color rendition in a warm tone. Lamp life and operating efficacy were sacrificed to obtain improved color. The resulting characteristics are similar to those of metal halide lamps.

Low-Pressure Sodium Lamps:

These LPS lamps have the highest operating efficacy but depreciate considerably over their lifetime. A large arc tube results in poor optical control, but the lamp does have superior life. The light itself appears yellow-orange and has very poor color rendition properties. Colors in the landscape appear as shades of gray. The costs are comparable to those of high-pressure sodium lamps.

4.2 Light Distribution

Horizontal and Vertical Distribution:

Horizontal illumination is especially important along the ground plane where changes in grade occur. However, a considerable portion of the night environment is perceived through direct and silhouette lighting of vertical objects and surfaces. Both patterns should be carefully coordinated in developing a successful lighting scheme.

Illumination data for outdoor lighting fixtures are illustrated by the manufacturers' photometric charts. These charts illustrate the actual light patterns and intensity levels on horizontal and vertical planes. Three types of charts are commonly used. The two charts shown in Figures 540-14 and 540-15 consist of isolines that represent points of equal illumination, measured in footcandles. The difference between these two charts is that one is projected on a horizontal plane (Figure 540-14) and the other on a vertical plane (Figure 540-15). Each chart has some reference to a specific mounting height or layout position which will determine the fixture spacing. The horizontal photometric chart is used for walkway, road, and area lighting, and the vertical photometric chart is normally used for wall and signage applications.

A third type of photometric chart shows the distribution of candlepower, or intensity, in various directions, independent of any specific surface (Figure 540-16). The maximum value within any given point on the distribution curve can be converted into footcandles with the formula shown in Figure 540-16. This chart is used when de-

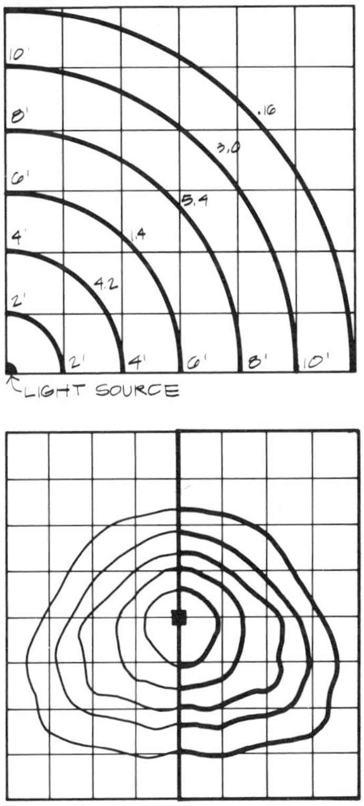
LIGHT SOURCE

Figure 540-14 Photometric chart: Horizontal distribution.

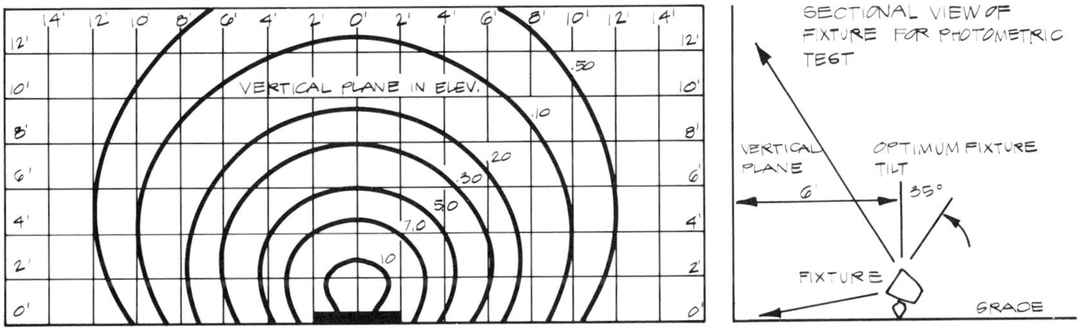
VERTICAL PLANE IN ELEV.
SECTIONAL VIEW OF FIXTURE FOR PHOTOMETRIC TEST
VERTICAL PLANE
OPTIMUM FIXTURE TILT
35°
FIXTURE
GRADE

Figure 540-15 Photometric chart: Vertical distribution.

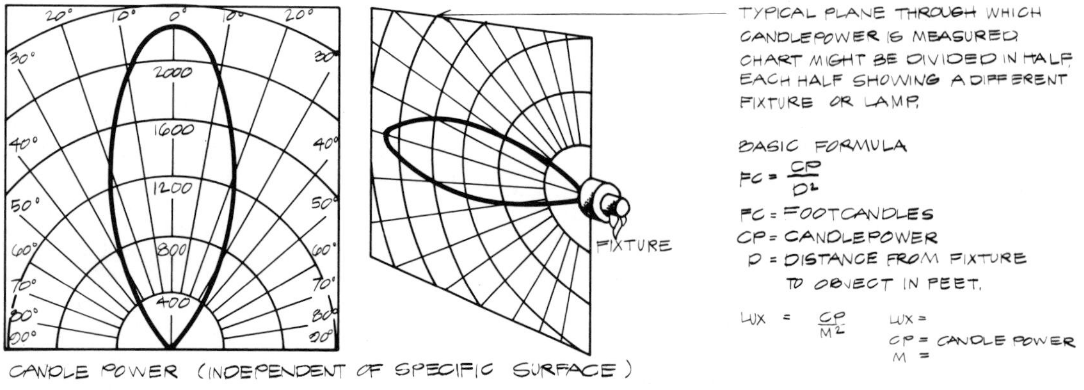
20°
10°
0°
10°
20°
30°
30°
2000
40°
1600
40°
1200
50°
50°
60°
800
60°
70°
400
70°
80°
80°
90°
90°
FIXTURE
CANDLE POWER (INDEPENDENT OF SPECIFIC SURFACE)
TYPICAL PLANE THROUGH WHICH
CANDLEPOWER IS MEASURED.
CHART MIGHT BE DIVIDED IN HALF,
EACH HALF SHOWING A DIFFERENT
FIXTURE OR LAMP.
BASIC FORMULA
FC = CP / D2
FC = FOOTCANDLES
CP = CANDLEPOWER
D = DISTANCE FROM FIXTURE
TO OBJECT IN FEET.
LUX = CP / M2
LUX =
CP = CANDLE POWER
M =

Figure 540-16 Photometric chart: Distribution of candlepower.

termining light intensity and the angle of distribution for accent lighting (uplighting of trees, floodlighting, etc.).

Basic Light Distribution Patterns:

Spread and Path Lights: These fixtures produce circular patterns of light that are symmetrical around the light center. The charts usually show no more than a typical quadrant (i.e., one-quarter of the light pattern) in order to provide maximum size and accuracy (see Figure 540-14). Curve values are in horizontal footcandles.

Whenever fixtures produce a light pattern that is symmetrical in two halves, only one half is reported, permitting maximum size and accuracy for the charts (see Figure 540-14).

Wall or Sign Lighters: These fixtures are nearly always used to light vertical surfaces. Therefore, photometrics are presented on a vertical plane with the fixture set at an optimum distance (which varies per fixture) and backlilt from the plane (see Figure 540-15). For a long wall or sign, the spacing from fixture to fixture can be determined by overlapping curves until the minimum acceptable light level between fixtures is established.

Accent Lights: Photometrics for adjustable accent lights, where the aiming angle and distance to lighted objects can vary, must be expressed in terms of the light output from the source rather than of the light falling upon the object. Candlepower is measured on a typical plane through the fixture and is charted in curve form (see Figure 540-16). Conversion to footcandles can be accomplished by formula.

Uniformity:

The uniformity of an illuminated field can be described with a ratio of light intensity values [in footcandles (lux)]. The *uniformity ratio* typically compares the average illumination with the minimum footcandle value of a particular field. A low ratio appears more evenly lit and very uniform. Conversely, the opposite is true for a high ratio where the two values are wide apart, resulting in a field that has distinct and contrasting values. Refer to Table 540-2 for a general description of different uniformity ratios.

Cutoff:

Recent improvements to many kinds of light fixtures have greatly reduced glare by restricting high-angle light to not more than 75 degrees above nadir (Figure 540-17). The following criteria are the general industry classifications of degrees of high-angle cutoff:

1. *Noncutoff:* unrestricted high-angle illumination

2. *Semicutoff:* not more than 5 percent of peak intensity radiating above 90 degrees and 20 percent of peak intensity above 80 degrees

3. *Cutoff:* not more than 2½ percent of peak intensity radiating above 90 degrees and 10 percent of peak intensity above 80 degrees

4.3 Categories of Light Fixtures

Various categories of light fixtures commonly used in outdoor lighting situations are described below (Figure 540-18).

Low-Level Landscape Lights:

Typical characteristics include:

1. Heights usually less than 6 ft (2 m) but sometimes up to 10 ft (3 m).

2. Lamps may be incandescent, fluorescent, mercury vapor, or high-pressure sodium.

3. Low-wattage capabilities, with limited intensities.

4. Substantial variety, with some sizes and shapes fitting within modules of finish materials (brick, etc.).

5. Finite light patterns, with directing capabilities.

6. Light sources are usually below eye level, so glare must be controlled.

7. Low maintenance requirements but high susceptibility to vandalism.

Intermediate-Height Landscape Lights:

Typical characteristics include:

1. Average heights of 10 to 15 ft (3 to 5 m).

TABLE 540-2
Uniformity Ratios

Uniformity ratio		
Average, fc (lux)	*Minimum, fc (lux)*	*Visual description of illuminated field*
2 (21.4)	1 (10.7)	Just a visible difference in light intensities
3 (32.3)*	1 (10.7)*	The high values of the field are twice as bright as the low values
4 (43.0)†	1 (10.7)†	—
10 (107.6)	1 (10.7)	Very distinct focal highlights; spotty

* Average and minimum uniformity ratios usually recommended for roads.

† Average and minimum uniformity ratios usually recommended for walkways.

2. Lamps can be incandescent, mercury vapor, metal halide, or high-pressure sodium.

3. Substantial variety of fixtures and respective lighting patterns.

4. Generally used in or around pedestrian pavements, and considered *pedestrian* in scale.

5. Lower fixture mounting heights are susceptible to vandalism.

Parking Lot and Roadway Lights:

Typical characteristics include:

1. Average heights of 20 to 50 ft (6 to 15.2 m).

2. Lamps can be mercury vapor, metal halide, or high-pressure sodium.

3. Used to light streets, parking lots, and recreational, commercial, and industrial areas.

High-Mast Lights:

Typical characteristics include:

1. Average heights of 60 to 100 ft (18 to 30 m).

2. Lamps can be mercury vapor, metal halide, or high-pressure sodium.

3. Used for large parking lots, highway interchanges, and recreational areas.

4. Fixtures must be lowered to be maintained.

4.4 Landscape Lighting Effects

Six lighting effects most frequently used in outdoor lighting situations are described below (Figures 540-19 through 540-25).

Uplighting:

Uplighting for Directional Viewing: When a lighted object can be seen from one direction only, above-grade accent lights can be used. To prevent glare, fixtures should be aimed away from observers and, if possible, concealed to keep the landscape uncluttered (Figure 540-19).

Uplighting for All-Around Viewing: If the lighted object can be seen from any direction, then well lights with louvers should be considered (Figure 540-20). With newly planted trees, place uplights as close as possible to the outside of the root ball.

Placing fixtures midway between trees is rarely satisfactory. The light typically misses the trunk and most foliage. It is particularly unsuccessful if trees are deciduous, especially during the winter stage.

Moonlighting:

The effect of moonlight filtering through the trees is another pleasing outdoor lighting technique. Up-and-down lighting is used to create this effect, which requires that fixtures be carefully placed in trees (Figure 540-21). Ground lighting is accented by shadows from leaves and branches.

Silhouette Lighting:

Trees and shrubs with interesting branching structure can be dramatically expressed when silhouetted against a wall or building facade. Such lighting also provides additional security near the building (Figure 540-22).

Spotlighting:

Special objects such as statues, sculpture, or specimen shrubs can be lighted with well-shielded fixtures using spot lamps (Figure 540-23). By mounting lights overhead in trees or nearby structures, glare and fixture distraction can be eliminated. If ground-mounted fixtures are used, they should be concealed with shrubbery.

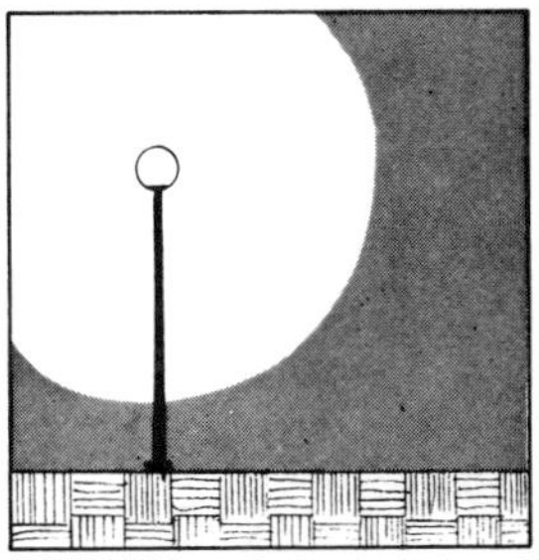
EXAMPLE OF NON CUT-OFF LIGHT

Figure 540-17 Cutoff.

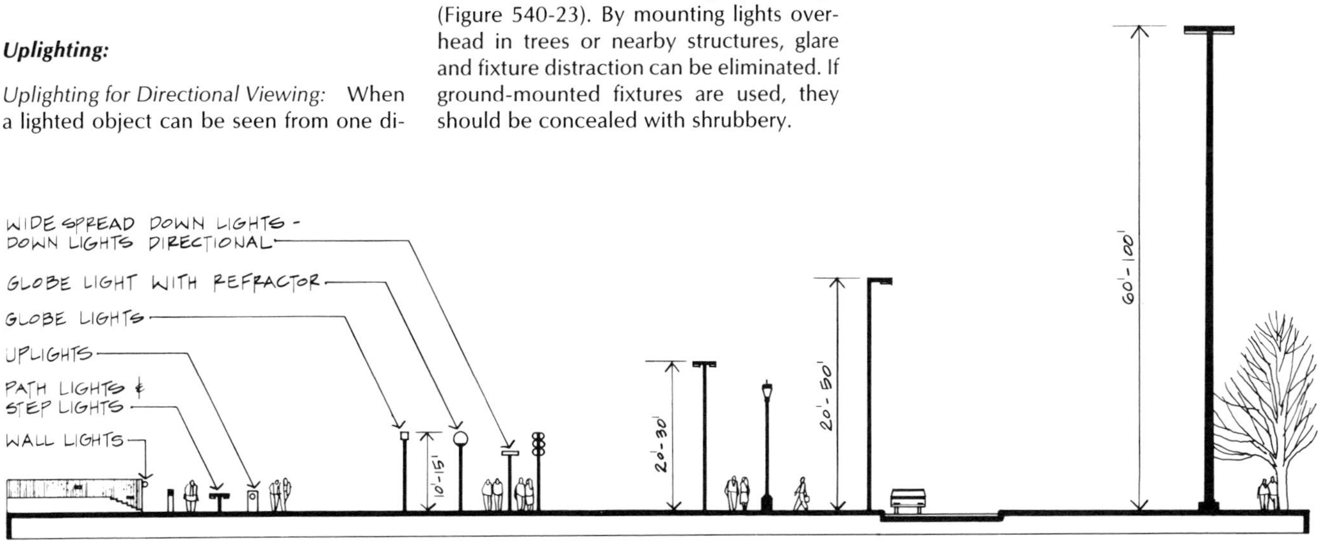
WIDE SPREAD DOWN LIGHTS - DOWN LIGHTS DIRECTIONAL
GLOBE LIGHT WITH REFRACTOR
GLOBE LIGHTS
UPLIGHTS
PATH LIGHTS & STEP LIGHTS
WALL LIGHTS
10'-15'
20'-30'
20'-50'
60'-100'
1. LOW-LEVEL LANDSCAPE LIGHTS-LOCALIZED
2. INTERMEDIATE-HEIGHT LANDSCAPE LIGHTS
3. PARKING LOT AND ROADWAY LIGHTS
4. HIGH MAST LIGHTS

Figure 540-18 Categories of light fixtures.

ABOVE GRADE ACCENT LIGHT

Figure 540-19 Uplighting (directional viewing).

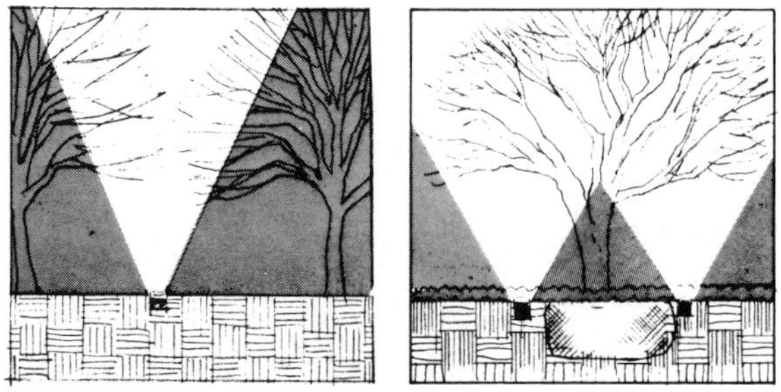
WELL LIGHTS WITH LOUVERS

Figure 540-20 Uplighting (all-around viewing).

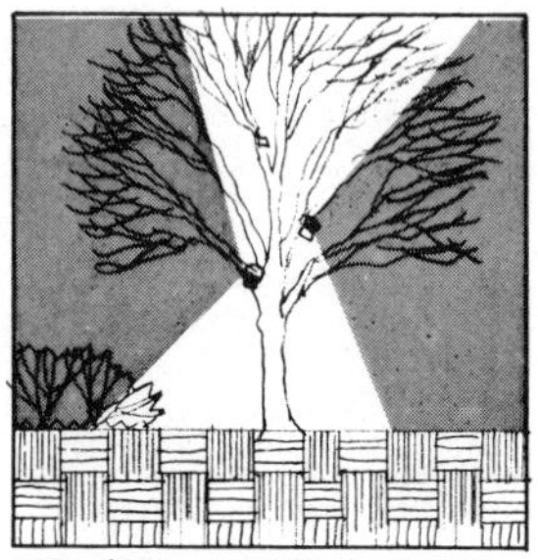
UP AND DOWN LIGHTS PLACED IN TREES

Figure 540-21 Moonlighting.

Figure 540-22 Silhouette lighting.

Figure 540-23 Spotlighting.

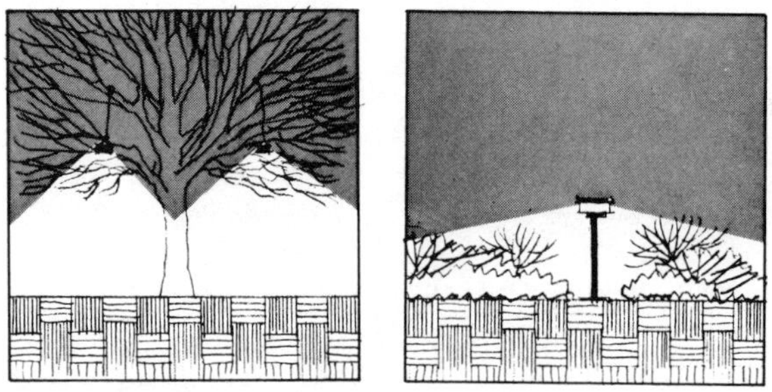

Figure 540-24 Spreadlighting.

Figure 540-25 Pathlighting.

Figure 540-26 Wall lights.

TABLE 540-3
Recommended Levels of Illumination

Area/activity	*Lux (lx)*	*Footcandles (fc)*
Outdoor facilities		
Building exterior		
Entry		
Active use	50	5.0
Locked or infrequent use	10	1.0
Vital locations or structures	50	5.0
Building surrounds	10	1.0
Building and monuments (floodlighted)		
Bright Surroundings		
Light surfaces	150	15.0
Medium light surfaces	200	20.0
Medium dark surfaces	300	30.0
Dark surfaces	500	50.0
Dark surroundings		
Light surfaces	50	5.0
Medium light surfaces	100	10.0
Medium dark surfaces	150	15.0
Dark surfaces	200	20.0
Bikeways		
Along roadside		
Commercial areas*	10	0.9
Intermediate areas*	6	0.6
Residential areas*	2	0.2
Distant from roadside	5	0.5
Bulletin and posterboards, signs		
Bright surroundings		
Light surfaces	500	500
Dark surfaces	1000	100.0
Dark surroundings		
Major Roads		
Commercial areas*	20	2.0
Intermediate areas*	15	1.4
Residential areas*	10	1.0
Collector roads		
Commercial areas*	13	1.2
Intermediate areas*	10	0.9
Residential areas*	6	0.6
Local Roads		
Commercial areas*	10	0.9
Intermediate areas*	6	0.6
Residential areas*	4	0.4
Walkways		
Along roadside		
Commercial areas*	10	0.9
Intermediate areas*	6	0.6
Residential areas*	2	0.2
Distant from roadside	5	0.5
Park walkways	5	0.5
Pedestrian tunnels	40	4.0
Pedestrian overpasses	3	0.3
Pedestrian stairways	6	0.3
Light surfaces	200	20.0
Dark surfaces	500	50.0
Gardens		
General lighting	5	0.5
Path, steps away from home	10	1.0
Backgrounds, fences, walls, trees, shrubbery	20	2.0
Flower beds, rock gardens	50	5.0
Trees, shrubs (when emphasized)	50	5.0
Focal points (large)	100	10.0
Focal points (small)	200	20.0
Loading and unloading platforms	200	20.0
Parking areas		
Self parking	10	1.0
Attendant parking	20	2.0
Piers		
Freight	200	2.0

(continued)

Table 540-3 (*Continued*)

Area/activity	*Lux (lx)*	*Footcandles (fc)*
Outdoor facilities		
Passenger	200	2.0
Active shipping area surrounding	50	5.0
Playgrounds	50	5.0
Roads		
Expressways	6	0.6
Commercial areas*	15	1.4
Intermediate areas*	13	1.2
Residential areas*	10	1.0
Badminton (outdoor)		
Recreational	100	10
Club	200	20
Baseball		
Recreational		
Infield	105	15
Outfield	100	10
Junior League (Class I and II)		
Infield	300	30
Outfield	200	20
Semipro and municipal league		
Infield	200	20
Outfield	150	15
On seats during game	20	2
On seats before and after game	50	5
Basketball (outdoor) recreational	100	10
Football		
Distance from nearest sideline to the farthest rows of spectators		
Class I (over 30,000 spectators) over 100 ft (30 m)	1000	100
Class II (10 to 15,000 spectators) 50 to 100 ft (15 to 30 m)	500	50
Class III (5 to 10,000 spectators) 30 to 50 ft (9 to 15 m)	300	30
Class IV (under 5000 spectators) under 30 ft (9 m)	200	20
Class V (no fixed seating facilities)	100	10
Handball and raquetball (outdoor)		
Recreational (two-court)	100	10
Club (two-court)	200	20
Hockey (outdoor)		
Recreational	100	10
Amateur	200	20
Horse shows		
Recreational	50	5
Tournament	100	10

* Areas are defined as follows:

Commercial areas: Dense business districts with heavy vehicular and pedestrian traffic throughout the day and night.

Intermediate areas: Moderately heavy pedestrian traffic during nights (libraries, recreation centers, large apartment complex, neighborhood retail stores).

Residential areas: Predominantly a residential area with light pedestrian traffic at night (single family, multifamily apartments).

Area/activity	Lux (lx)	Footcandles (fc)
Outdoor facilities		
Playgrounds	50	5
Shuffleboard		
Recreational	50	5
Skating		
Roller rink	100	10
Ice rink (outdoor)	50	5
Lagoon, pond, or flooded area	10	1
Ski slope	10	1
Soccer (see Football)		
Softball		
Slow pitch, recreational (6 pole)		
Infield	100	10
Outfield	70	7
Slow pitch, tournament		
Infield	200	20
Outfield	150	15
Recreational (6-pole)		
Infield	200	20
Outfield	150	15
Industrial League		
Infield	200	20
Outfield	150	15
Semiprofessional		
Infield	300	30
Outfield	200	20
Professional and championship		
Infield	500	50
Outfield	300	30
Swimming (outdoor)		
Recreational	100	10
Underwater 600 (60) lamp lux of surface area		
Exibitions	200	20
Tennis (outdoor)		
Recreational	200	20
Club	300	30
Tournament	500	50
Volleyball		
Recreational	100	10
Tournament	200	20

Source: Illuminating Engineering Society of North America, John E. Kaufman, (ed.). *IES Lighting Handbook,* Reference Volume and Application Volume, IES, New York, 1981.

Spreadlighting:

Spread lights produce circular patterns of illumination for general area lighting (Figure 540-24). They are effective for groundcovers, low shrubs, walks, and steps. However, to take full advantage of the light throw, fixtures should be kept to open areas so that shrubbery does not restrict light distribution. The overhead spread light provides additional height and throw. When used in eating or recreational areas, several fixtures should be used to soften shadows while creating a uniform lighting effect.

Pathlighting:

Path lights are essentially spread lights at a lower height (Figure 540-25). In areas where other landscape lighting is used, a high degree of light shielding is necessary for path lights. This prevents the glare which inhibits a full view of the surrounding landscape.

If no other outdoor lighting is used in the immediate area, less-shielded path lights may be acceptable. These fixtures illuminate the path and some of the surrounding landscape as well, but there remains the possibility that the glare will be disruptive.

5.0 RECOMMENDED LEVELS OF ILLUMINATION

The levels of illumination listed in Table 540-3 represent current standards in the lighting industry.

REFERENCES

Gloeilampenfabrieken, N. V. Philips. *Lighting Manual,* 2d ed., Lighting Design and Engineering Centre, Eindhoven, The Netherlands, 1975.

Illuminating Engineering Society of North America, John E. Kaufman (ed.). *IES Lighting Handbook,* Reference Volume and Application Volume, IES, New York, 1981.

Lam, William M. C. *Perception and Lighting as Formgivers for Architecture,* McGraw-Hill, New York, 1977 and *Sunlighting as Formgiver for Architecture*, Van Nostrand Reinhold, Princeton, NJ, 1986.

National Academy of Sciences. *Lighting, Visibility and Railroad-Highway Grade Crossings,* Transportation Research Record 628, Transportation Research Board, Washington, DC, 1977.

Sunset Books, Bob Horne (ed.). *Outdoor Lighting,* Lane Magazine and Book Company, Menlo Park, CA, 1969. ■

section 550: Plants and Planting

CREDITS

Contributor:

Michael Van Valkenburgh, Landscape Architect
Michael Van Valkenburgh Associates
Cambridge, Massachusetts

Graphics:

Bhakorn Vanuptikul

Reviewers:

Gary L. Koller
Arnold Arboretum, Harvard University
Jamaica Plain, Massachusetts

George E. Patton
George Patton, Inc.
Philadelphia, Pennsylvania

James H. Curtis
Costa Mesa, California

CONTENTS

1.0 INTRODUCTION

The main purpose of this section is to provide technical information on planting and plant-related technology. It is assumed that the reader has a working knowledge of plant materials and their uses or has sought such information elsewhere.

2.0 PLANTING PLANS, DETAILS, AND SPECIFICATIONS

Most proposals for site development require preparation of special plans and related documents to guide the work of installing plant materials. Planting plans, together with construction details for their installation, typically comprise part of a complete set of working drawings for project construction.

2.1 Planting Plans

General Information:

Planting plans should include common and botanical names of all plant materials, their proposed locations (as well as locations of existing plant material), their sizes, and quantities. Most of this information typically is shown in a schedule somewhere on the drawing(s). Plant size designations, including height, caliper, ball or pot size, etc., are typically referred to by national voluntary standards set up by the American Association of Nurserymen in their publication entitled *American Standard for Nursery Stock* or equivalent in other places in the world.

Notes on Planting Plans:

Shown below is a list of notes that are typically shown on planting plans and/or contained in related details and documents. Others needed for special circumstances are often added.

1. The contractor shall locate and verify the existence of all utilities prior to starting work.

2. The contractor shall supply all plant materials in quantities sufficient to complete the planting shown on all drawings.

3. All material shall conform to the guidelines established by the current *American Standard for Nursery Stock*, published by the American Association of Nurserymen or equivalent.

4. No plant shall be put into the ground before rough grading has been finished and approved by the project landscape architect or equal.

5. All plants shall bear the same relationship to finished grade as the plant's original grade before digging.

TABLE 550-1
Plant Spacing Chart

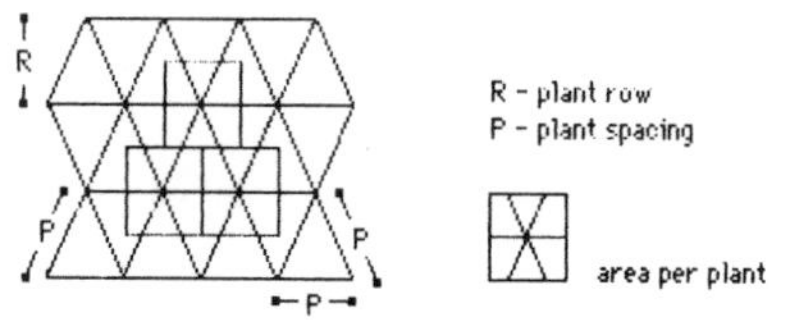
R
P
P
P
R - plant row
P - plant spacing
area per plant

$$\text{no. plants} = \frac{\text{area}}{\text{area per plant}}$$

Plant Spacing (On Center)				Area per Plant	
"P" (ft)	"P" (m)	"R" (ft)	"R" (m)	ft²	m²
.15	.50	.13	.43	.0195	.2150
.20	.67	.18	.58	.0360	.3886
.25	.83	.22	.72	.0550	.5976
.30	1.00	.26	.87	.0780	.8700
.38	1.25	.33	1.08	.1254	1.3500
.46	1.50	.40	1.30	.1840	1.9500
.61	2.00	.53	1.73	.3233	3.4600
.76	2.50	.66	2.17	.5016	5.4250
.91	3.00	.79	2.60	.7189	7.8000
1.00	3.28	.87	2.84	.8700	9.3152
1.22	4.00	1.06	3.46	1.2900	13.8400
1.25	4.10	1.08	3.55	1.3500	14.5550
1.50	4.92	1.30	4.27	1.9500	21.0084
1.52	5.00	1.32	4.33	2.0064	21.6500
1.75	5.74	1.52	4.97	2.660	28.5278
1.83	6.00	1.58	5.20	2.8914	31.2000
2.00	6.56	1.73	5.68	3.4600	37.2608
2.44	8.00	2.11	6.92	5.1484	55.3600
2.50	8.20	2.17	7.10	5.4250	58.2200
3.00	9.84	2.60	8.47	7.8000	86.3448
3.05	10.00	2.64	8.66	8.0520	86.6000
4.00	13.12	3.46	11.37	13.8400	149.1744
4.57	15.00	3.96	12.99	18.0972	194.8500
5.00	16.41	4.33	14.21	21.6500	233.1861
6.00	19.69	5.20	17.05	31.2000	335.7145
6.10	20.00	5.28	17.32	32.2080	346.4000
8.00	26.25	6.93	22.73	55.4400	596.6625
10.00	32.81	8.66	28.41	86.6000	932.1321
15.00	49.22	12.99	42.62	194.8500	2097.7564

*This chart is used when plants are to be spaced equidistant from each other as shown.

6. All plants shall be balled and wrapped or container grown as specified. No container grown stock will be accepted if it is root bound. All root wrapping material made of synthetics or plastics shall be removed at time of planting.

7. With container grown stock, the container shall be removed and the container ball shall be cut through the surface in two vertical locations.

8. The day prior to planting, the location of all trees and shrubs shall be staked for approval by the project landscape architect or equal.

9. All plant material shall be selected at the nurseries by the project landscape architect or equal.

10. At planting time, all plants shall be thinned by removing a balanced one-third of the vegetative material.

11. All plants shall be sprayed with an antidessicant within 24 hours after planting. In temperate zones, all plants shall be sprayed with an antidessicant at the beginning of their first winter.

12. All plants shall be installed as per details and the contract specifications.

13. All plants and stakes shall be set plumb unless otherwise specified.

14. The landscape contractor shall provide loam fill as per the contract specifications.

15. All plants shall be watered thoroughly twice during the first 24-hour period after planting. All plants shall then be watered weekly or more often, if necessary, during the first growing season.

16. The landscape contractor shall refer to the contract specifications for additional requirements.

17. The landscape contractor shall refer to the plant list for seasonal requirements and other restrictions related to the time of planting.

2.2 Plant Spacing Chart

Table 550-1 can be used as a general guide to plant spacing when placing plants in rows or large masses.

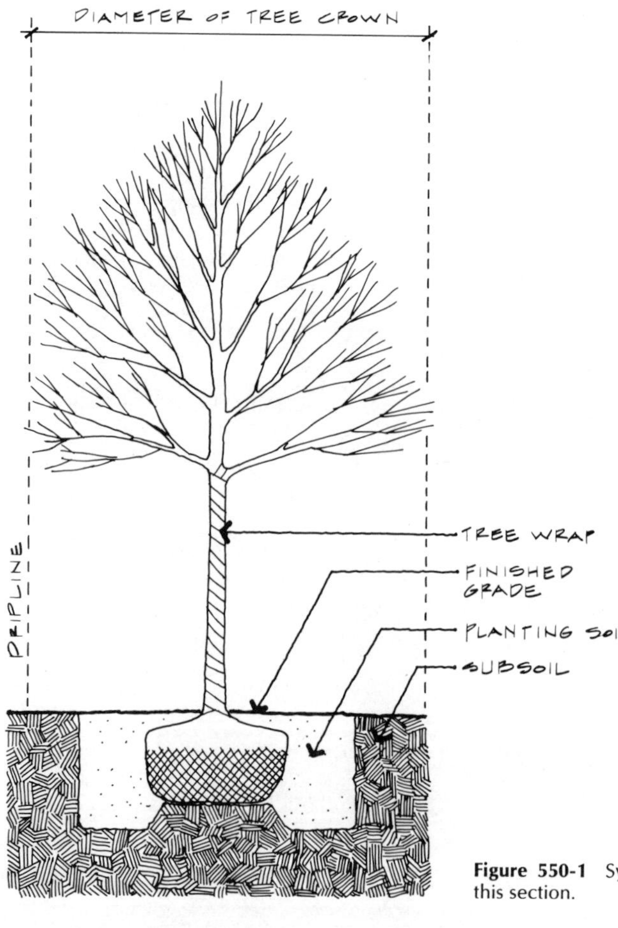
DIAMETER OF TREE CROWN
DRIPLINE
TREE WRAP
FINISHED GRADE
PLANTING SOIL
SUBSOIL

2.3 Planting Details

Figures 550-1 through 550-9 illustrate typical planting details for different situations and types of plants. Local practice may require minor variations on these details.

2.4 Protecting Plant Material

During Construction:

Existing plants and new plantings often need to be protected from physical injury and root zone compaction during periods of construction.

A common method for protecting existing plants during construction is to erect a barrier around the plant, enclosing an area as large as the root zone of the plant or plants to be protected. This prevents compaction of soil and other forms of damage to the existing roots and also prevents mechanical damage to the plant. Figures 550-10 and 550-11 illustrate various ways to protect plant materials during construction.

Permanent Protection:

Plant roots require a continual supply of air, which is normally maintained by air

Figure 550-1 Symbol key for figures in this section.

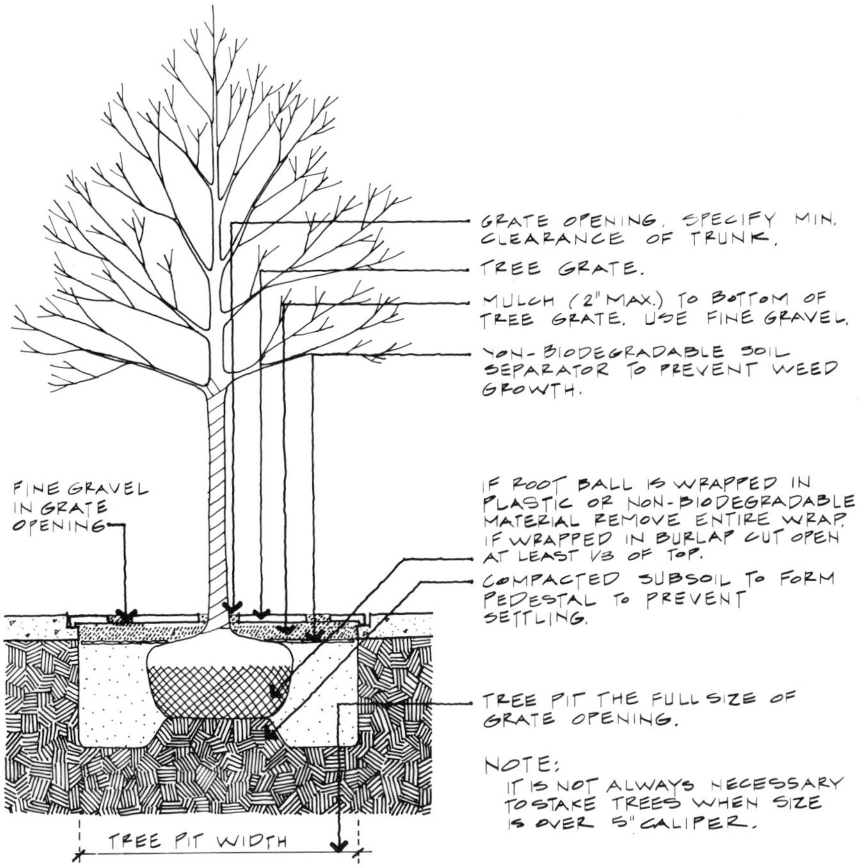
GRATE OPENING. SPECIFY MIN. CLEARANCE OF TRUNK.
TREE GRATE.
MULCH (2" MAX.) TO BOTTOM OF TREE GRATE. USE FINE GRAVEL.
NON-BIODEGRADABLE SOIL SEPARATOR TO PREVENT WEED GROWTH.
FINE GRAVEL IN GRATE OPENING
IF ROOT BALL IS WRAPPED IN PLASTIC OR NON-BIODEGRADABLE MATERIAL REMOVE ENTIRE WRAP. IF WRAPPED IN BURLAP CUT OPEN AT LEAST 1/3 OF TOP.
COMPACTED SUBSOIL TO FORM PEDESTAL TO PREVENT SETTLING.
TREE PIT THE FULL SIZE OF GRATE OPENING.
NOTE:
IT IS NOT ALWAYS NECESSARY TO STAKE TREES WHEN SIZE IS OVER 5" CALIPER.
TREE PIT WIDTH

Figure 550-2 Typical tree planting in pavement with grate (5-in caliper and larger). Tree stakes are not always necessary when caliper is 5 in or larger.

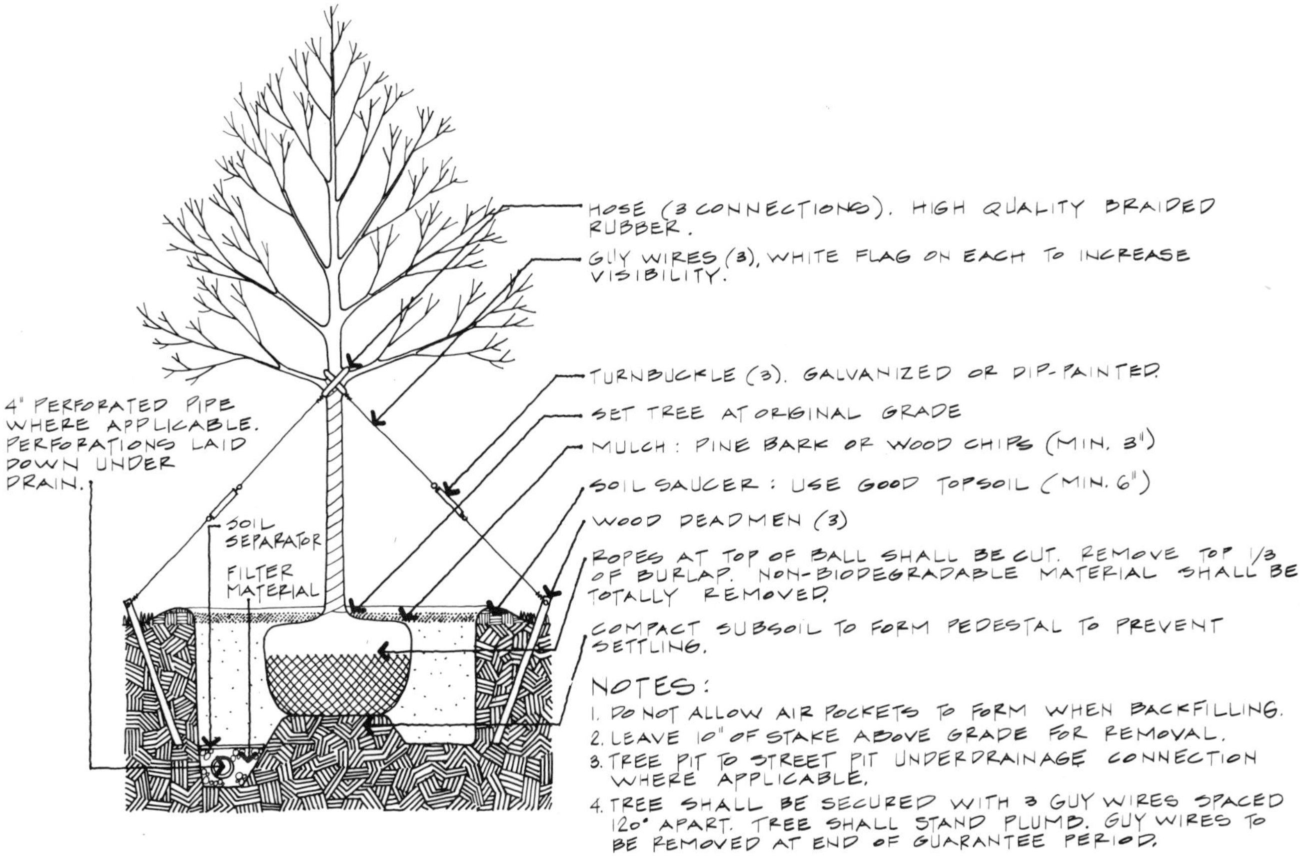
HOSE (3 CONNECTIONS). HIGH QUALITY BRAIDED RUBBER.
GUY WIRES (3), WHITE FLAG ON EACH TO INCREASE VISIBILITY.
TURNBUCKLE (3). GALVANIZED OR DIP-PAINTED.
SET TREE AT ORIGINAL GRADE
MULCH: PINE BARK OR WOOD CHIPS (MIN. 3")
SOIL SAUCER: USE GOOD TOPSOIL (MIN. 6")
WOOD DEADMEN (3)
ROPES AT TOP OF BALL SHALL BE CUT. REMOVE TOP 1/3 OF BURLAP. NON-BIODEGRADABLE MATERIAL SHALL BE TOTALLY REMOVED.
COMPACT SUBSOIL TO FORM PEDESTAL TO PREVENT SETTLING.
4" PERFORATED PIPE WHERE APPLICABLE. PERFORATIONS LAID DOWN UNDER DRAIN.
SOIL SEPARATOR
FILTER MATERIAL
NOTES:
1. DO NOT ALLOW AIR POCKETS TO FORM WHEN BACKFILLING.
2. LEAVE 10" OF STAKE ABOVE GRADE FOR REMOVAL.
3. TREE PIT TO STREET PIT UNDERDRAINAGE CONNECTION WHERE APPLICABLE.
4. TREE SHALL BE SECURED WITH 3 GUY WIRES SPACED 120° APART. TREE SHALL STAND PLUMB. GUY WIRES TO BE REMOVED AT END OF GUARANTEE PERIOD.

Figure 550-3 Typical tree planting and guying (12-ft height and larger).

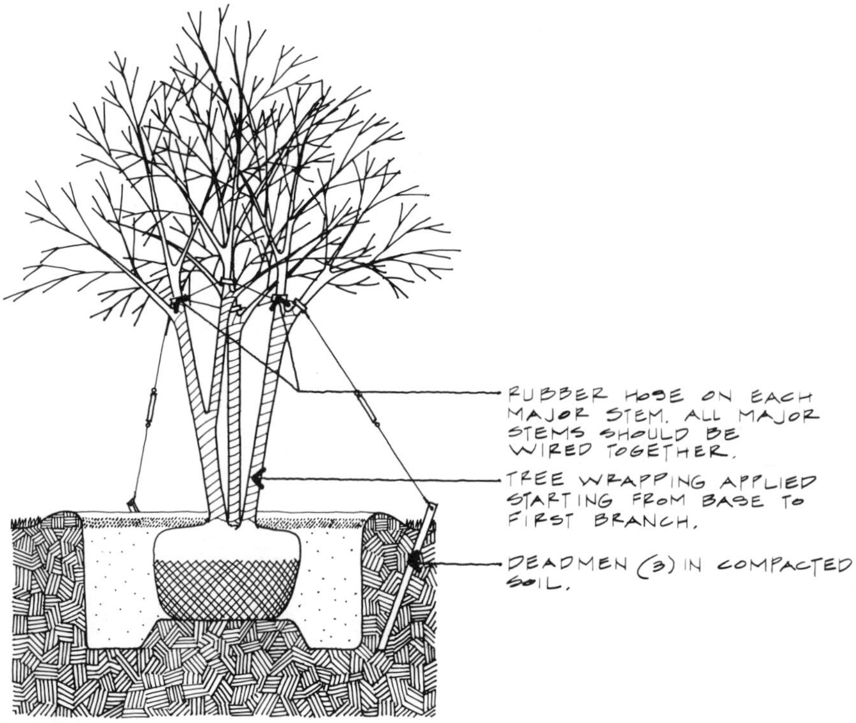
RUBBER HOSE ON EACH MAJOR STEM. ALL MAJOR STEMS SHOULD BE WIRED TOGETHER.
TREE WRAPPING APPLIED STARTING FROM BASE TO FIRST BRANCH.
DEADMEN (3) IN COMPACTED SOIL.

Figure 550-4 Typical multistem tree planting and guying.

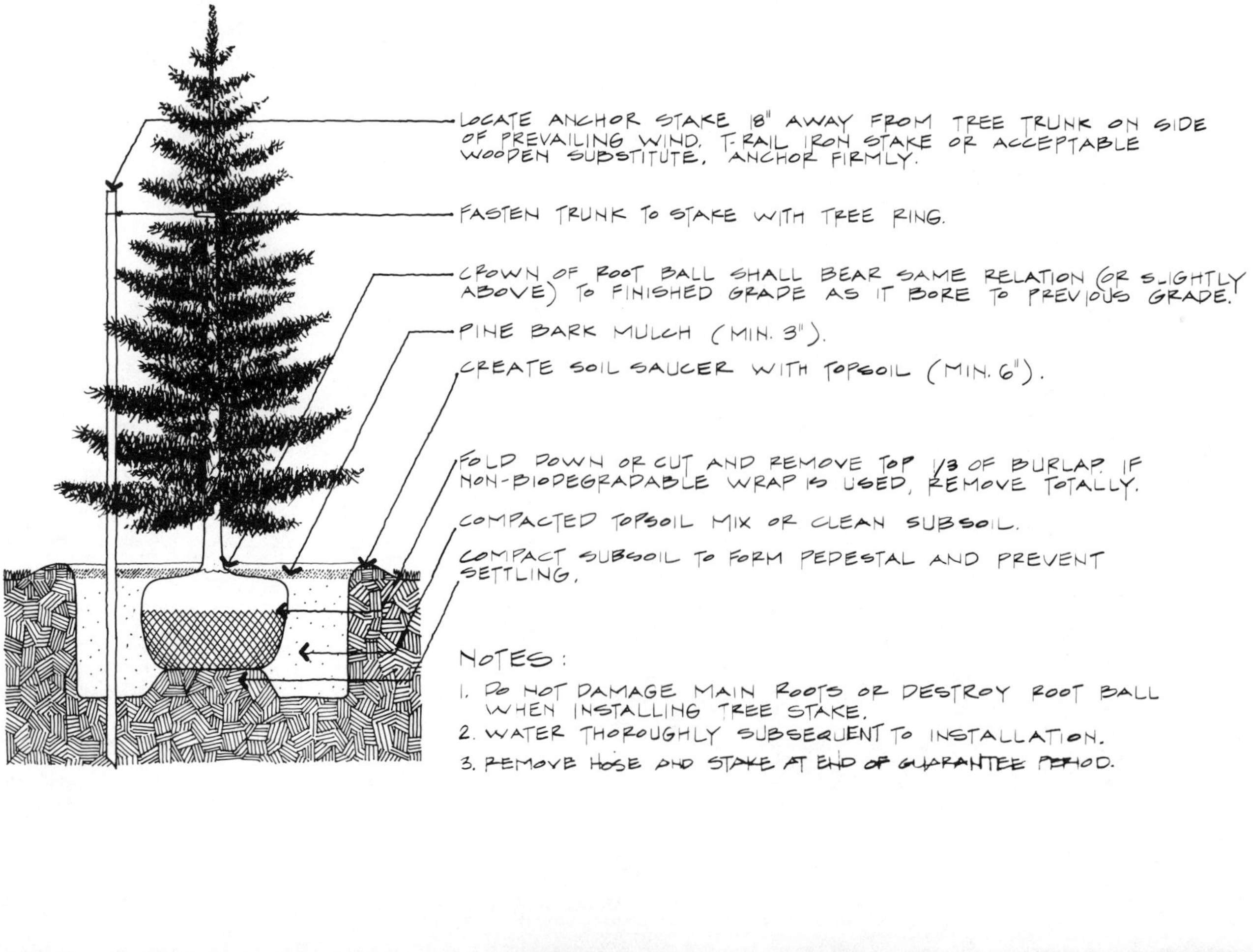
LOCATE ANCHOR STAKE 18" AWAY FROM TREE TRUNK ON SIDE OF PREVAILING WIND. T-RAIL IRON STAKE OR ACCEPTABLE WOODEN SUBSTITUTE. ANCHOR FIRMLY.
FASTEN TRUNK TO STAKE WITH TREE RING.
CROWN OF ROOT BALL SHALL BEAR SAME RELATION (OR SLIGHTLY ABOVE) TO FINISHED GRADE AS IT BORE TO PREVIOUS GRADE.
PINE BARK MULCH (MIN. 3").
CREATE SOIL SAUCER WITH TOPSOIL (MIN. 6").
FOLD DOWN OR CUT AND REMOVE TOP 1/3 OF BURLAP. IF NON-BIODEGRADABLE WRAP IS USED, REMOVE TOTALLY.
COMPACTED TOPSOIL MIX OR CLEAN SUBSOIL.
COMPACT SUBSOIL TO FORM PEDESTAL AND PREVENT SETTLING.
NOTES:
1. DO NOT DAMAGE MAIN ROOTS OR DESTROY ROOT BALL WHEN INSTALLING TREE STAKE.
2. WATER THOROUGHLY SUBSEQUENT TO INSTALLATION.
3. REMOVE HOSE AND STAKE AT END OF GUARANTEE PERIOD.

Figure 550-5 Typical coniferous tree planting (6-ft height and smaller).

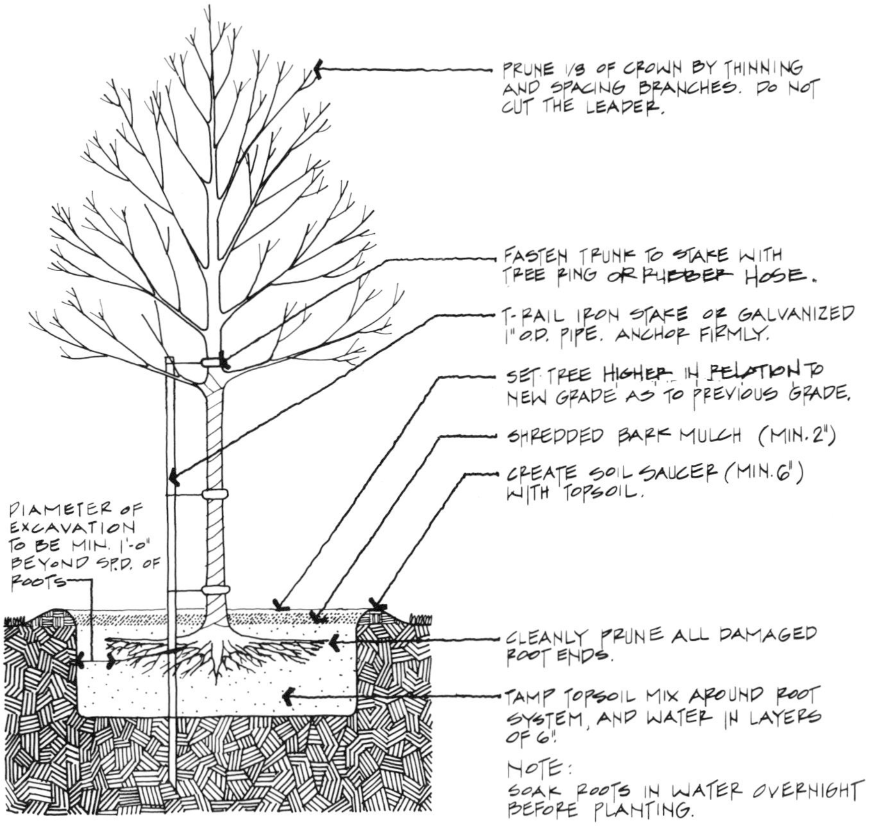
PRUNE 1/3 OF CROWN BY THINNING AND SPACING BRANCHES. DO NOT CUT THE LEADER.
FASTEN TRUNK TO STAKE WITH TREE RING OR RUBBER HOSE.
T-RAIL IRON STAKE OR GALVANIZED 1" O.D. PIPE. ANCHOR FIRMLY.
SET TREE HIGHER IN RELATION TO NEW GRADE AS TO PREVIOUS GRADE.
SHREDDED BARK MULCH (MIN. 2")
CREATE SOIL SAUCER (MIN. 6") WITH TOPSOIL.
DIAMETER OF EXCAVATION TO BE MIN. 1'-0" BEYOND SPD. OF ROOTS
CLEANLY PRUNE ALL DAMAGED ROOT ENDS.
TAMP TOPSOIL MIX AROUND ROOT SYSTEM, AND WATER IN LAYERS OF 6".
NOTE:
SOAK ROOTS IN WATER OVERNIGHT BEFORE PLANTING.

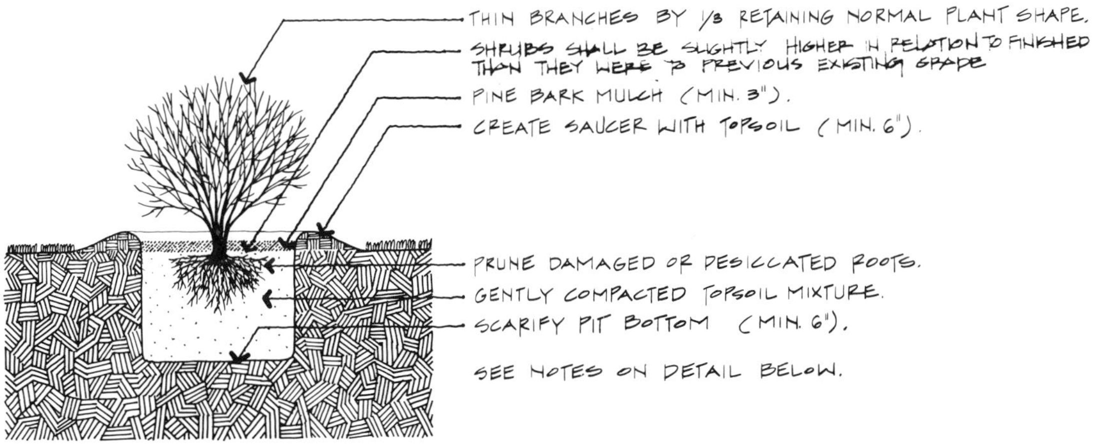
THIN BRANCHES BY 1/3 RETAINING NORMAL PLANT SHAPE.
SHRUBS SHALL BE SLIGHTLY HIGHER IN RELATION TO FINISHED THAN THEY WERE TO PREVIOUS EXISTING GRADE
PINE BARK MULCH (MIN. 3").
CREATE SAUCER WITH TOPSOIL (MIN. 6").
PRUNE DAMAGED OR DESICCATED ROOTS.
GENTLY COMPACTED TOPSOIL MIXTURE.
SCARIFY PIT BOTTOM (MIN. 6").
SEE NOTES ON DETAIL BELOW.

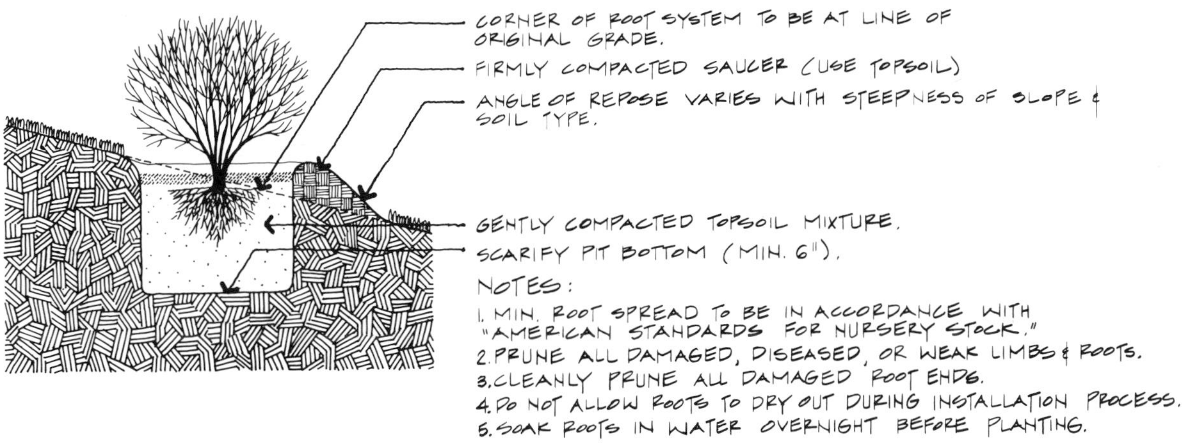
CORNER OF ROOT SYSTEM TO BE AT LINE OF ORIGINAL GRADE.
FIRMLY COMPACTED SAUCER (USE TOPSOIL)
ANGLE OF REPOSE VARIES WITH STEEPNESS OF SLOPE & SOIL TYPE.
GENTLY COMPACTED TOPSOIL MIXTURE.
SCARIFY PIT BOTTOM (MIN. 6").
NOTES:
1. MIN. ROOT SPREAD TO BE IN ACCORDANCE WITH "AMERICAN STANDARDS FOR NURSERY STOCK."
2. PRUNE ALL DAMAGED, DISEASED, OR WEAK LIMBS & ROOTS.
3. CLEANLY PRUNE ALL DAMAGED ROOT ENDS.
4. DO NOT ALLOW ROOTS TO DRY OUT DURING INSTALLATION PROCESS.
5. SOAK ROOTS IN WATER OVERNIGHT BEFORE PLANTING.

Figure 550-6 Typical deciduous tree planting (bare root) (10-ft height and smaller).

Figure 550-7 Typical shrub planting (bare root). Continuous trenches are often dug for hedge plantings.

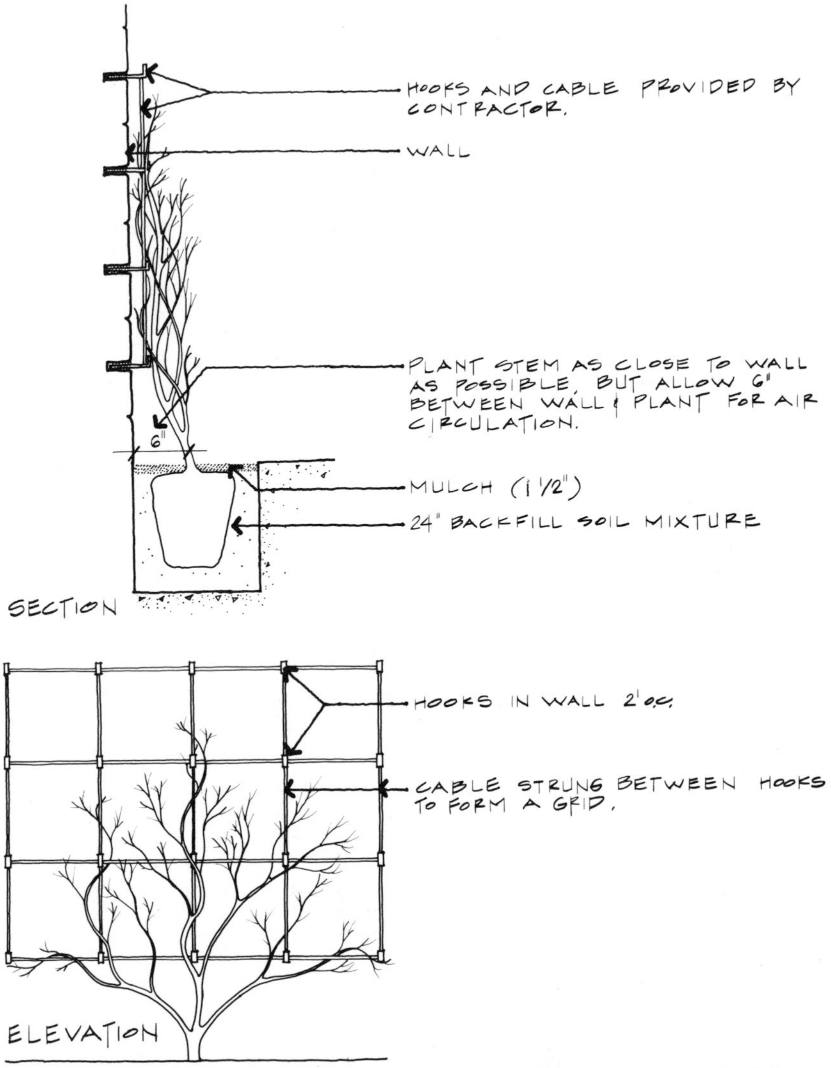
HOOKS AND CABLE PROVIDED BY CONTRACTOR.
WALL
PLANT STEM AS CLOSE TO WALL AS POSSIBLE, BUT ALLOW 6" BETWEEN WALL & PLANT FOR AIR CIRCULATION.
6"
MULCH (1 1/2")
24" BACKFILL SOIL MIXTURE
SECTION
HOOKS IN WALL 2' O.C.
CABLE STRUNG BETWEEN HOOKS TO FORM A GRID.
ELEVATION

Figure 550-8 Typical espalier planting (elevation). Hooks are fastened to wall 24 in on center, and cable is strung taut between hooks.

Figure 550-9 Typical bulb plantings. Spacing will vary depending on desired effect of plantings.

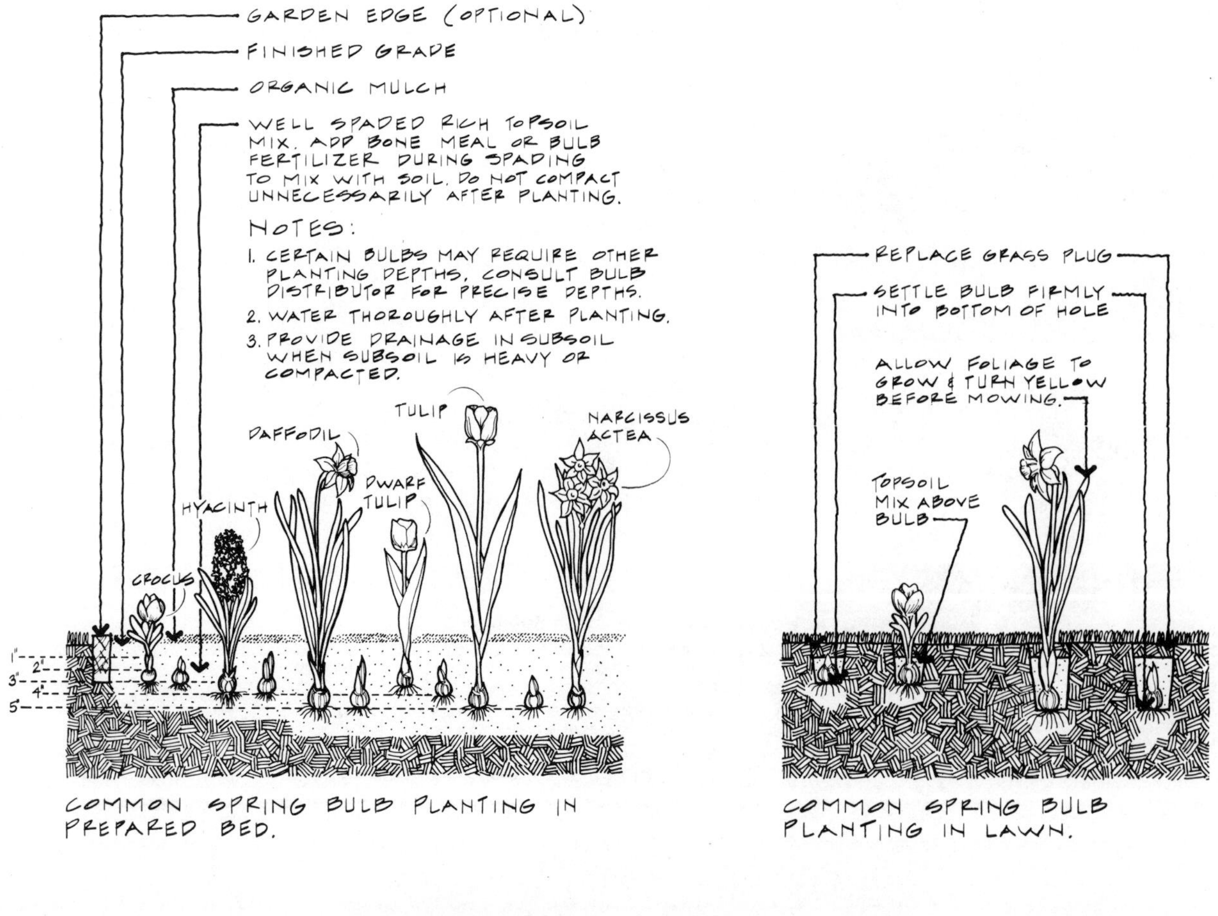
GARDEN EDGE (OPTIONAL)
FINISHED GRADE
ORGANIC MULCH
WELL SPADED RICH TOPSOIL MIX. ADD BONE MEAL OR BULB FERTILIZER DURING SPADING TO MIX WITH SOIL. DO NOT COMPACT UNNECESSARILY AFTER PLANTING.
NOTES:
1. CERTAIN BULBS MAY REQUIRE OTHER PLANTING DEPTHS. CONSULT BULB DISTRIBUTOR FOR PRECISE DEPTHS.
2. WATER THOROUGHLY AFTER PLANTING.
3. PROVIDE DRAINAGE IN SUBSOIL WHEN SUBSOIL IS HEAVY OR COMPACTED.
TULIP
NARCISSUS ACTEA
DAFFODIL
DWARF TULIP
HYACINTH
CROCUS
1"
2"
3"
4"
5"
COMMON SPRING BULB PLANTING IN PREPARED BED.
REPLACE GRASS PLUG
SETTLE BULB FIRMLY INTO BOTTOM OF HOLE
ALLOW FOLIAGE TO GROW & TURN YELLOW BEFORE MOWING.
TOPSOIL MIX ABOVE BULB
COMMON SPRING BULB PLANTING IN LAWN.

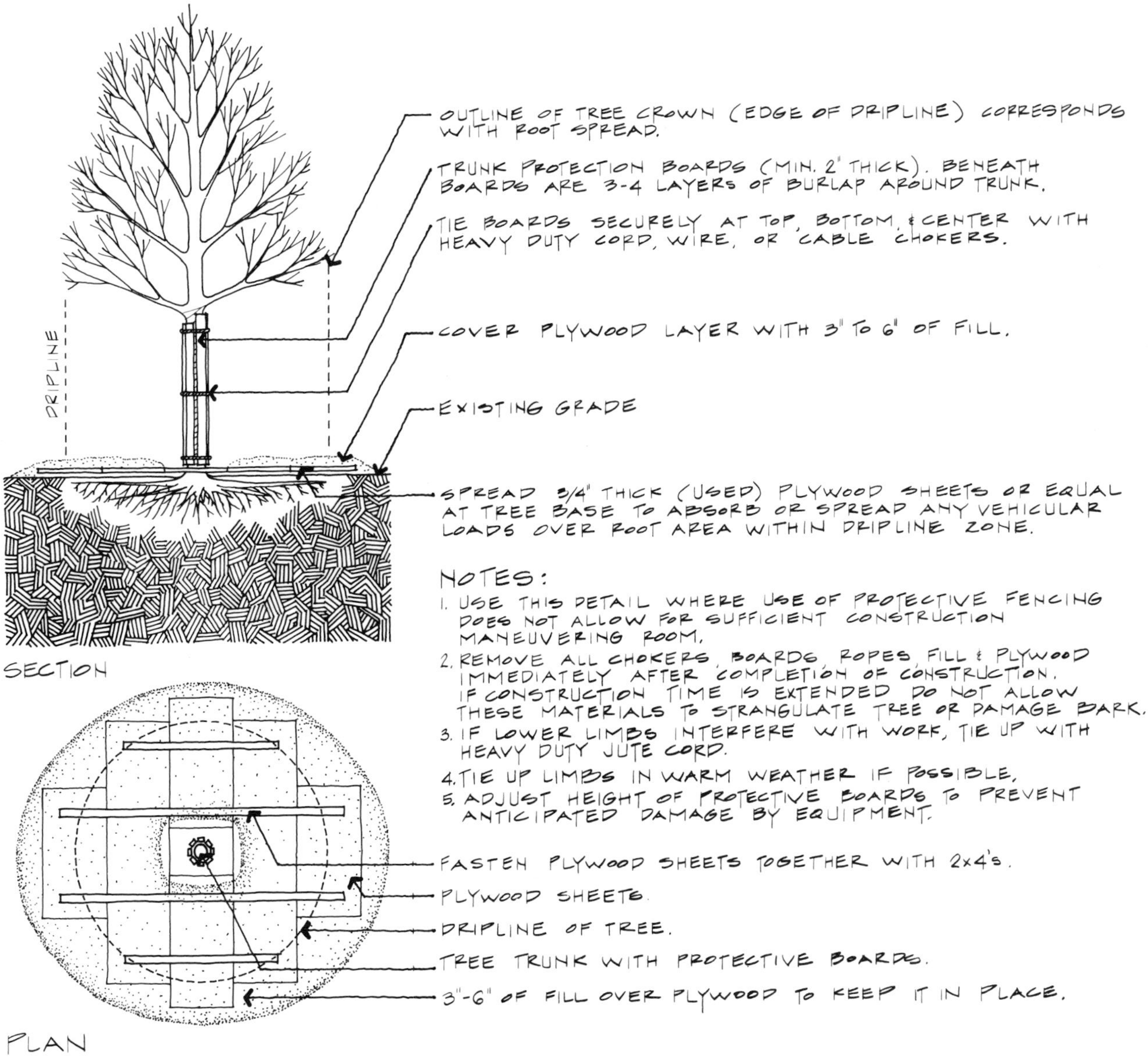
OUTLINE OF TREE CROWN (EDGE OF DRIPLINE) CORRESPONDS WITH ROOT SPREAD.
TRUNK PROTECTION BOARDS (MIN. 2" THICK). BENEATH BOARDS ARE 3-4 LAYERS OF BURLAP AROUND TRUNK.
TIE BOARDS SECURELY AT TOP, BOTTOM, & CENTER WITH HEAVY DUTY CORD, WIRE, OR CABLE CHOKERS.
COVER PLYWOOD LAYER WITH 3" TO 6" OF FILL.
EXISTING GRADE
SPREAD 3/4" THICK (USED) PLYWOOD SHEETS OR EQUAL AT TREE BASE TO ABSORB OR SPREAD ANY VEHICULAR LOADS OVER ROOT AREA WITHIN DRIPLINE ZONE.
DRIPLINE
SECTION
NOTES:
1. USE THIS DETAIL WHERE USE OF PROTECTIVE FENCING DOES NOT ALLOW FOR SUFFICIENT CONSTRUCTION MANEUVERING ROOM.
2. REMOVE ALL CHOKERS, BOARDS, ROPES, FILL & PLYWOOD IMMEDIATELY AFTER COMPLETION OF CONSTRUCTION. IF CONSTRUCTION TIME IS EXTENDED DO NOT ALLOW THESE MATERIALS TO STRANGULATE TREE OR DAMAGE BARK.
3. IF LOWER LIMBS INTERFERE WITH WORK, TIE UP WITH HEAVY DUTY JUTE CORD.
4. TIE UP LIMBS IN WARM WEATHER IF POSSIBLE.
5. ADJUST HEIGHT OF PROTECTIVE BOARDS TO PREVENT ANTICIPATED DAMAGE BY EQUIPMENT.
FASTEN PLYWOOD SHEETS TOGETHER WITH 2x4's.
PLYWOOD SHEETS.
DRIPLINE OF TREE.
TREE TRUNK WITH PROTECTIVE BOARDS.
3"-6" OF FILL OVER PLYWOOD TO KEEP IT IN PLACE.
PLAN

Figure 550-10 Protection of existing tree during construction.

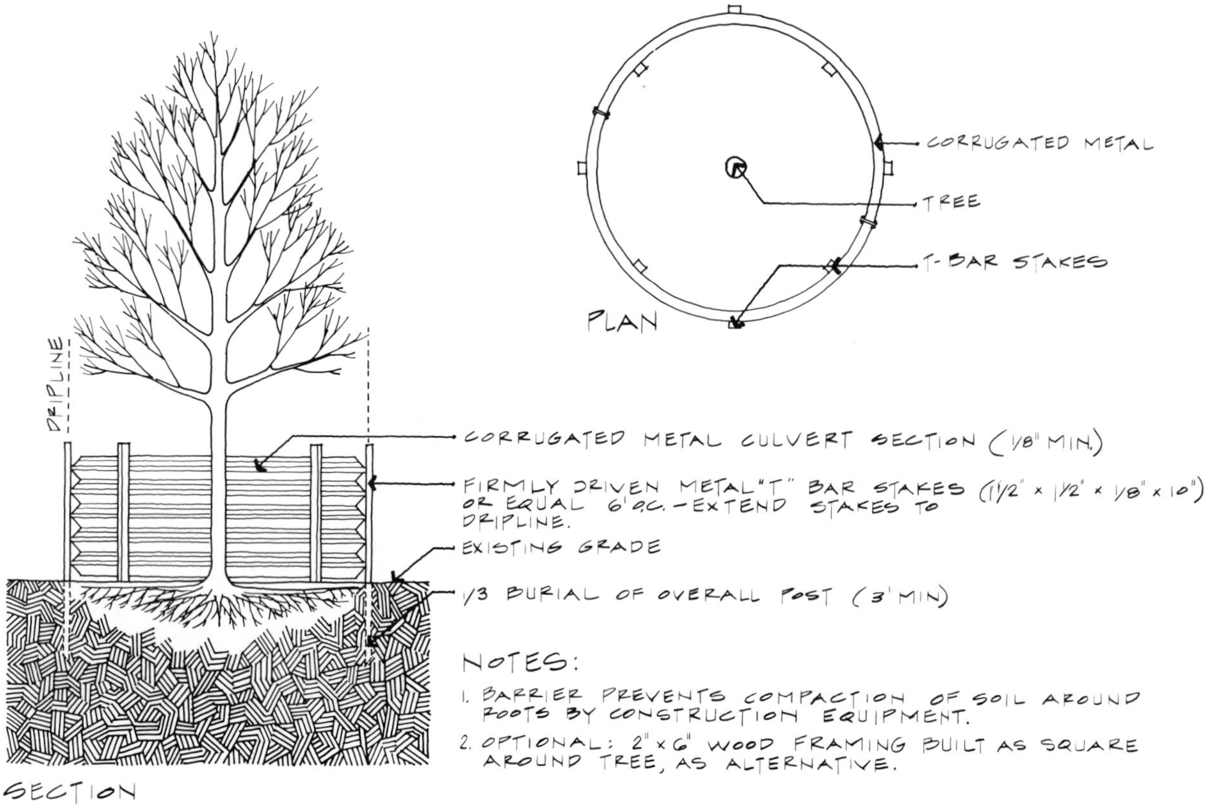

CORRUGATED METAL
TREE
T-BAR STAKES
PLAN
DRIPLINE
CORRUGATED METAL CULVERT SECTION (1/8" MIN.)
FIRMLY DRIVEN METAL "T" BAR STAKES (1 1/2" x 1/2" x 1/8" x 10") OR EQUAL 6' O.C. – EXTEND STAKES TO DRIPLINE.
EXISTING GRADE
1/3 BURIAL OF OVERALL POST (3' MIN)
NOTES:
1. BARRIER PREVENTS COMPACTION OF SOIL AROUND ROOTS BY CONSTRUCTION EQUIPMENT.
2. OPTIONAL: 2" x 6" WOOD FRAMING BUILT AS SQUARE AROUND TREE, AS ALTERNATIVE.
SECTION

Figure 550-11 Protection of existing tree during construction.

spaces (pores) in the soil surrounding the roots. Because of this need for air, as well as the need for water, the majority of a plant's root system lies within the top 18 in (0.5 m) of soil, regardless of the type or size of plant. Therefore, measures have to be taken to ensure that the root zone of a plant is neither compacted nor covered with a material that would restrict the amount of air or moisture reaching the root zone.

Various techniques can be used to prevent restriction of air and moisture to the root zone. Figures 550-12 and 550-13 illustrate techniques for raising and lowering grades around existing trees (or major plantings) when such grading is necessary. In Division 900 are illustrated a few techniques for restricting compaction of the root zone area in heavily trafficked areas such as pedestrian walkways and the like. These represent examples of tree grates and urban plantings.

2.5 Contract Specifications

Whenever possible, all contract specifications related to plants and planting should conform to current standardized practices used in building and site construction. In the United States, the Construction Specification Institute (CSI) has produced a widely accepted and used format. The CSI Format is a consistent, nationally unified system which consists of 16 Divisions ranging from General Requirements to Electrical. Division 2 is assigned to Site Work. Sections within Division 2 pertain to technical sections or basic units of work, such as Landscaping (02800). Table 550-2 is a checklist of the major items covered in the CSI Format related to plants and planting.

3.0 STANDARDS FOR NURSERY STOCK

A well-known set of standards has been developed by the American Association of Nurserymen to guarantee quality and to facilitate commerce in nursery stock. These are voluntary national standards subject to rules and approval by the American National Standards Institute (ANSI). Similar standards for other countries may be available and may differ in some ways from those developed by the AAN.

Table 550-3 was prepared for the AAN publication in cooperation with the Canadian Nursery Trades Association to facilitate nursery trade between the United States and Canada as well as with other countries that use the international metric system of measurement. Table 550-3 lists "rounded metric equivalents" as recommended for use in sizing nursery-grown plants.

REFERENCES

Plant Material

Bailer, Liberty Hyde, and Ethel Zoe. *Hortus Third,* MacMillan, New York, 1976.

den Ouden, P., in collaboration with B.K. Boom. *Manual of Cultivated Conifers Hardy in Cold and Warm Temperature Zones,* Martinus Nijoff, The Hague, 1978.

Dirr, Michael. *Manual of Woody Landscape Plants,* 3d ed., Stipes Publishing, Champaign, IL, 1983.

Wyman, Donald. *Wyman's Gardening Encyclopedia,* MacMillan, New York, 1972.

Plants and Climate

Geiger, Rudolf. *Climate Near the Ground,* Harvard University Press, Cambridge, MA, 1965.

Spirn, Anne Whiston. *The Granite Garden: Urban Nature and Human Design,* Basic Books, New York, 1984.

Plant Technology

American Association of Nurserymen. *American Standard for Nursery Stock,* Washington, DC, annual.

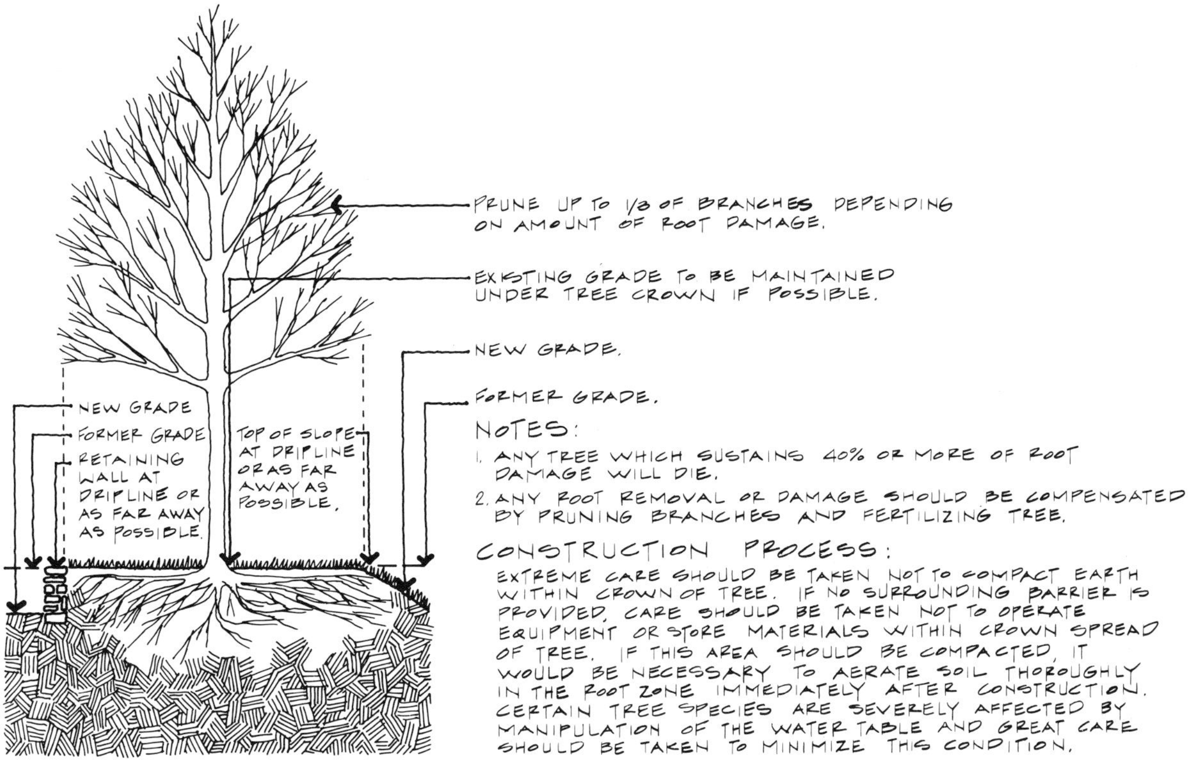
PRUNE UP TO 1/3 OF BRANCHES DEPENDING ON AMOUNT OF ROOT DAMAGE.
EXISTING GRADE TO BE MAINTAINED UNDER TREE CROWN IF POSSIBLE.
NEW GRADE.
FORMER GRADE.
NEW GRADE
FORMER GRADE
RETAINING WALL AT DRIPLINE OR AS FAR AWAY AS POSSIBLE.
TOP OF SLOPE AT DRIPLINE OR AS FAR AWAY AS POSSIBLE.
NOTES:
1. ANY TREE WHICH SUSTAINS 40% OR MORE OF ROOT DAMAGE WILL DIE.
2. ANY ROOT REMOVAL OR DAMAGE SHOULD BE COMPENSATED BY PRUNING BRANCHES AND FERTILIZING TREE.
CONSTRUCTION PROCESS:
EXTREME CARE SHOULD BE TAKEN NOT TO COMPACT EARTH WITHIN CROWN OF TREE. IF NO SURROUNDING BARRIER IS PROVIDED, CARE SHOULD BE TAKEN NOT TO OPERATE EQUIPMENT OR STORE MATERIALS WITHIN CROWN SPREAD OF TREE. IF THIS AREA SHOULD BE COMPACTED, IT WOULD BE NECESSARY TO AERATE SOIL THOROUGHLY IN THE ROOT ZONE IMMEDIATELY AFTER CONSTRUCTION. CERTAIN TREE SPECIES ARE SEVERELY AFFECTED BY MANIPULATION OF THE WATER TABLE AND GREAT CARE SHOULD BE TAKEN TO MINIMIZE THIS CONDITION.

Figure 550-12 Cutting or lowering a grade near an existing tree.

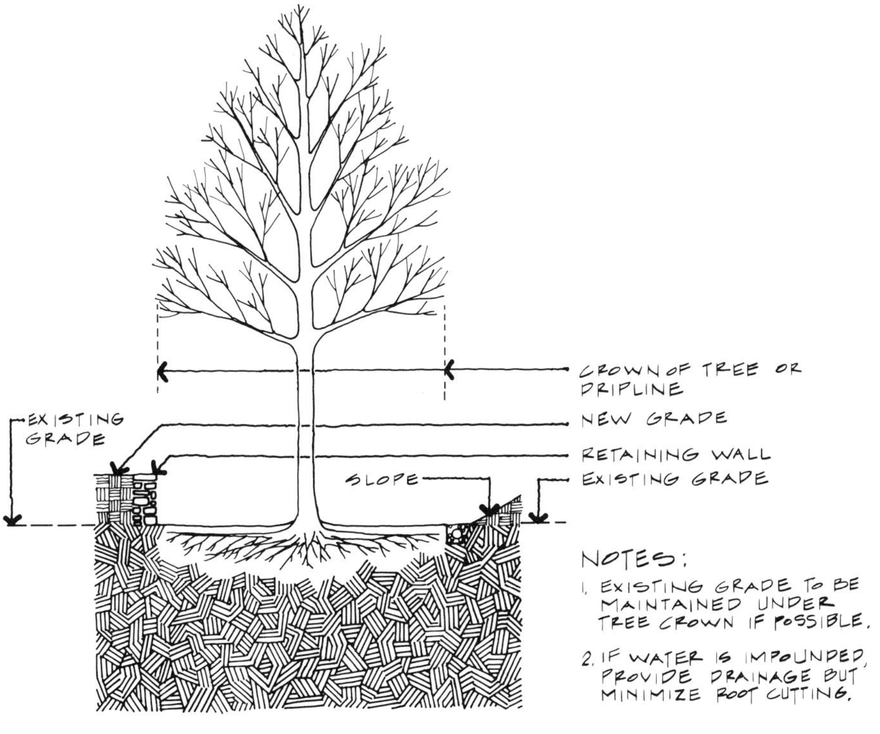
CROWN OF TREE OR DRIPLINE
EXISTING GRADE
NEW GRADE
RETAINING WALL
SLOPE
EXISTING GRADE
NOTES:
1. EXISTING GRADE TO BE MAINTAINED UNDER TREE CROWN IF POSSIBLE.
2. IF WATER IS IMPOUNDED, PROVIDE DRAINAGE BUT MINIMIZE ROOT CUTTING.

Figure 550-13 Filling or raising a grade near an existing tree.

TABLE 550-2
Checklist of CSI Specifications for Plants and Planting

DIVISION 2—SITEWORK: TREES AND SHRUBS
PART 1—GENERAL

1.01 Scope of work
- A. Plants and planting (trees, shrubs, ground cover)
- B. Lawns: seeding and/or sodding

1.02 Agency standards
- A. Nomenclature
  - 1. American Joint Committee on Horticultural Nomenclature, 1942 edition of *Standardized Plant Names*
  - 2. *American Standard for Nursery Stock,* 1980, American Association of Nurserymen

1.03 Contract conditions

1.04 Submittals
- A. Samples
  - 1. Tree stakes and tree-wrapping materials
  - 2. Mulch
  - 3. Soil separator
- B. Test reports
  - 1. Topsoil
    - *a.* mechanical analysis
    - *b.* percentage of organic content analysis
    - *c.* soil nutrient levels
    - *d.* soil pH
  - 2. Peat moss and soil amendments
    - *a.* loss of weight by ignition
    - *b.* moisture absorption capacity
- C. Certificates
  - 1. Manufactures labels for:
    - *a.* limestone
    - *b.* commercial fertilizer
    - *c.* aluminum sulfate
    - *d.* fungicide
  - 2. Certificates of inspection of plant material

1.05 Product delivery, storage, and handling
- A. Digging plant material
- B. Transportation of plant material
- C. Temporary storage
- D. Handling of plant materials
- E. Changes and substitutions

1.06 Job conditions
- A. Planting season
  - 1. deciduous trees, all shrubs, and ground covers
  - 2. evergreen trees
  - 3. seeding

1.07 Inspection, acceptance, and guarantee
- A. Acceptance
- B. Acceptance in part
- C. Guarantee period
- D. Replacements
- E. Final inspection and final acceptance

PART 2—MATERIALS

2.01 Plant materials
- A. Plant list
- B. Form
- C. Quality health
- D. Measurements
- E. Pruning
- F. Labels

2.02 Lawn seeding material
- A. Grass seed
- B. Grass seed mixture
- C. Mulch
- D. Fertilizer
- E. Ground surface stabilizer to prevent erosion during establishment period

2.03 Sod
- A. Composition
- B. Thickness of cut
- C. Strip size
- D. Strength of sod strips
- E. Moisture content
- F. Time limitations
- G. Thatch
- H. Diseases, nematodes, and insects
- I. Weeds

2.04 Topsoil
- A. Mechanical analysis
- B. Organic matter content
- C. pH Range
- D. Fertility

2.05 Peat moss

2.06 Limestone (if required)

2.07 Sand (if required)

2.08 Commercial fertilizer

2.09 Mulch

2.10 Guying material

2.11 Miscellaneous
- A. Tree paint
- B. Fungicide
- C. Soil separator

PART 3—EXECUTION

3.01 Spreading topsoil and finish grading

3.02 Staking and layout

3.03 Planting
- A. Time of planting
- B. Setting plants
- C. Backfilling of planting pits and planting beds
- D. Trees
- E. Shrubs
- F. Ground covers

3.04 Fungicide spraying

3.05 Wrapping

3.06 Staking and guying

3.07 Mulching

3.08 Watering

3.09 Pruning and repair
- A. Weather conditions
- B. Sowing
- C. Fertilizing
- D. Raking
- E. Mulching
- F. Watering

3.10 Seeding procedure
- A. Weather conditions
- B. Placement pattern
- C. Watering

3.11 Sodding procedures

PART 4—MAINTENANCE

4.01 Maintenance of planting
- A. Watering
- B. Weeding and mulching
- C. Fertilizing
- D. Removal of staking materials
- E. Pruning of shrubs and trees
- F. Mowing of lawn areas
- G. Care of ground covers

TABLE 550-3
Metric Equivalents for Sizing Nursery Plants*

Plants sized by height or spread		*Plants sized by caliper*	
English measure	*Recommended metric equivalent*	*English measure, in*	*Recommended metric equivalent, cm*
6 in	15 cm	⅜	1.0
8 in	20 cm	½	1.5
10 in	25 cm	¾	2.0
12 in	30 cm	1	2.5
15 in	40 cm	1¼	3.0
18 in	50 cm	1½	4.0
2 ft	60 cm	1¾	4.5
2½ ft	80 cm	2	5.0
3 ft	90 cm	2½	6.0
3½ ft	1.00 m	3	8.0
4 ft	1.25 m	3½	9.0
5 ft	1.50 m	4	10.0
6 ft	1.75 m	4½	11.0
7 ft	2.00 m	5	13.0
8 ft	2.50 m	5½	14.0
		6	15.0

* Metric equivalents have been rounded off.

Source: Prepared by the American Association of Nurserymen in cooperation with the Canadian Nursery Trades Association.

Briokell, Christopher. *Pruning,* Simon and Schuster, New York, 1979.

Pirone, P. O. *Tree Maintenance,* 4th ed., Oxford University Press, New York, 1976.

Design References

Arnold, Henry F. *Trees in Urban Design,* Van Nostrand Reinhold, New York, 1980.

Clouston, Brian (ed.). *Landscape Design with Plants,* Van Nostrand Reinhold, New York, 1979.

Fairbrother, Nan. *The Nature of Landscape Design,* Knopf, New York, 1974.

Hackett, Brian. *Planting Design,* Spon, London, 1979. ■

section 610: Roof and Deck Landscapes

CREDITS

Contributor:

Theodore Osmundson & Associates
Berkeley, California

Writer: Theodore Osmundson
Editor: Gordon Osmundson

Graphics:

Theodore Osmundson
April Potter

Advisor:

Ralph E. Wilcoxen
Berkeley, California

Reviewers:

Thomas Wirth
Sherborn, Massachusetts

William L. Clarke
EDAW
San Francisco, California

Fred H. Peterson
Soil & Plant Lab, Inc.
Santa Clara, California

CONTENTS

1.0 INTRODUCTION

The high cost of land in downtown and other urban areas has brought about a reappraisal of the usable space on the roofs of buildings. Flat space, whether at ground level above underground structures or on many levels above the street, is expensive to obtain. Consequently, the development and use of roof areas is rapidly becoming obligatory as an economic necessity.

Although aesthetic and social needs regarding roof and deck spaces have prevailed for centuries, most structures depend on economic justification to be built and maintained. Aesthetic justification is obvious from a superficial downward glance at the roofscape of our cities. The social justification is almost as obvious when comparison is made between undeveloped roof terraces and the public and commercially developed areas in the United States and Canada—such as Constitution Square in Hartford, Connecticut, the Golden Gateway Development in San Francisco, and even the very private roof garden for executive offices at Kaiser Resources, Ltd., in Vancouver, British Columbia. These and many other such roof and deck landscapes throughout the world provide outdoor areas for social interchange that are otherwise almost impossible to obtain in most densely developed cities.

There are important design and structural differences between ground level landscape development and rooftop developments. This section deals with the following special construction requirements:

1. Protection of the integrity of the roof and structure

2. Positive drainage

3. A long-term, lightweight planting medium

4. Adaptation to climate, winds, sun, and shade

5. Optimum irrigation

6. Selection of paving, structural materials, site furnishings, and water as a design element

7. Provision of water, electricity, and telephone

8. Public safety and security

9. Ease of maintenance

This section covers only new construction. Construction methods needed for existing or historic buildings are too complex and unique to each situation to be included here, although all of the above-listed construction requirements may be involved.

2.0 PROTECTION OF THE INTEGRITY OF THE ROOF AND STRUCTURE

The single most important consideration concerning rooftop landscape construction is protecting the integrity of the roof and structure beneath the garden. For this reason, there must be waterproofing of exceptional security, longevity, and protection from damage. It should be established at the outset that the roof structure and waterproofing is an integral part of the building; consequently, it is the building architect's responsibility to: (1) waterproof the roof, (2) protect the waterproofing from mechanical damage, and (3) insulate the roof for energy conservation. The landscape architect or designer of the roof landscape has no responsibility for the design and construction of these items. However, it is the rooftop designer's responsibility to protect the roof from damage, and as a general rule, this responsibility starts with the bottom of the subdrainage layer that is added to the finished roof.

2.1 Load Bearing Capacity

The maximum load bearing capacity of a roof is established by the structural engineer and must never be exceeded. Fortunately, if care is exercised in the selection and location of materials, this constraint can be overcome. In projected construction, the roof structure can usually be strengthened to accommodate heavier loads. Typically, a minimum additional dead load limit of 125 psf between columns is needed to accommodate the construction of a roof garden, although the loads above columns and at the bearing edges of a roof can be much greater. A structural engineer should always be consulted before beginning any type of roof or deck landscape design and construction.

2.2 Waterproofing

Waterproofing and protection against penetration of the waterproofing is another important factor in the design of a roof garden. A typical section through a roof consists of the structural framing or reinforced concrete slab, sometimes a sloping layer of thin concrete to provide drainage to roof drains, a layer of waterproofing material, a layer of insulation, and a layer of lightweight concrete to protect the insulation and the waterproof membrane. This final layer of lightweight concrete is sloped to carry off surface drainage.

There are a growing number of ways to create a waterproof membrane, but regardless of which material or method is used, a complete and long-lasting seal must be achieved before any additional materials can be put on top. At this stage, quality control and testing by the building architect is crucial to ensure the integrity of the roof, and thereby to prevent costly repairs if leaks occur under the finished roof or deck landscape. Although a properly installed waterproof membrane can last for the life of a building, a single leak may require the removal of the entire garden in order to find the leak.

Even small leaks in the membrane may create water-filled openings into which roots may penetrate. Over time, these roots can enlarge the openings, causing more and more hidden damage to the waterproof membrane and eventually to the roof and building below.

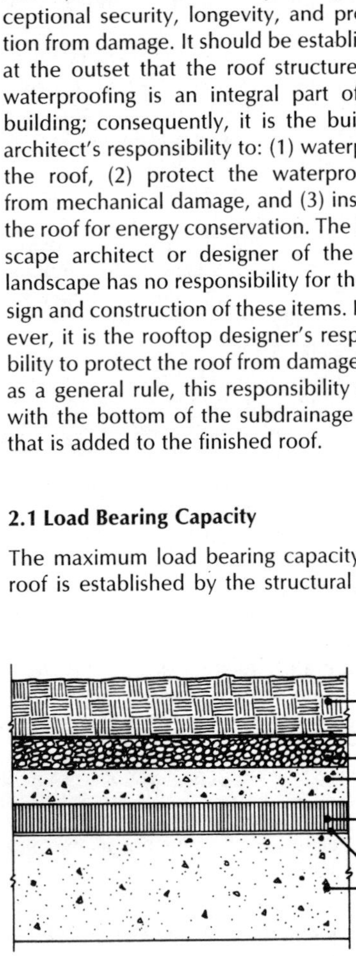
PLANTING MEDIUM
FILTER BLANKET
DRAINAGE MEDIUM
CONCRETE PROTECTIVE SLAB
INSULATION BOARD
WATERPROOF MEMBRANE
STRUCTURAL SLAB

Figure 610-1 Typical cross section through roof.

3.0 SPECIAL PROVISIONS

3.1 Drainage

Drainage for roof gardens must be just as effective in carrying off water as is the basic building roof. The best way to handle the drainage for the roof garden is through the same system used by the building. There is no need to duplicate or add a larger system unless the roof garden design requires this. Often, extra surface drains can be installed by connecting them to additional pipes laid on the roof surface, which in turn are connected to the building roof's drains. Roof drains, like all others used in the roof garden, should be designed to collect both surface and lateral subsurface drainage water.

The planting medium used on roofs allows almost immediate downward percolation of water. Because these soils are shallow and rest on a sealed surface, positive lateral drainage should be provided through the subsurface of the soil toward the drains.

Figure 610-1 illustrates a typical section through a roof planting. The structural slab is covered with a waterproof membrane, an insulation board, and a lightweight concrete protective slab sloped to drains. On top of this a lightweight drainage layer is added. To prevent the soil medium from entering and clogging the drainage medium, a rot-resistant filter layer of woven or nonwoven polypropylene fabric (filter blanket) is laid down before the planting medium. It is crucial that the planting medium contain no fine silts which will clog the filter blanket and block drainage. With this cross section, water can penetrate the soil layer, pass through the filter blanket into the drainage layer, and flow across the protective concrete slab into openings in the sides of the roof drain and out through the stormwater system. Any excess water will flow across the surface of the soil to the perforated upper surface of the same drains. This system has proved to be very effective even in areas of extremely heavy rainfall.

There are a number of drainage details that can be tied in with any typical rooftop landscape section. Figures 610-2 through 610-15 are provided with expanded legends to help explain these special purposes as well as their specific details. Any one or more of these can be adapted or combined to fit special circumstances.

Note that all concealed pipe and drains should be carefully recorded on an *as-built plan* of the roof garden. This is important not only to prevent possible damage due to later digging but also to provide easy access for cleaning and/or repairing these elements.

Whenever possible, provisions should be made for the periodic cleaning of

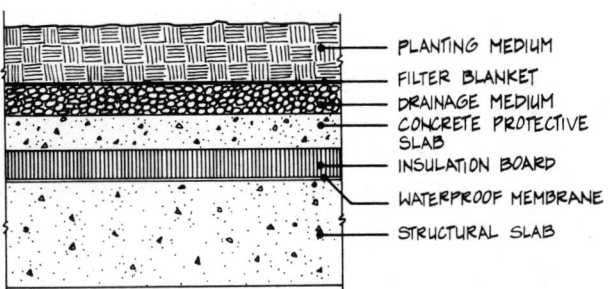

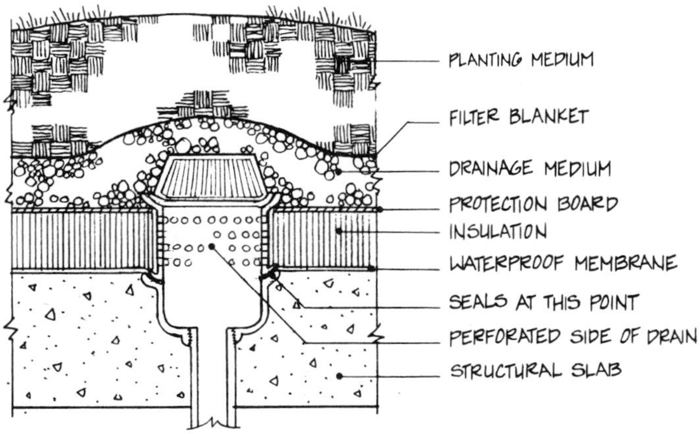
PLANTING MEDIUM
FILTER BLANKET
DRAINAGE MEDIUM
PROTECTION BOARD
INSULATION
WATERPROOF MEMBRANE
SEALS AT THIS POINT
PERFORATED SIDE OF DRAIN
STRUCTURAL SLAB

Figure 610-2 Roof Drain under Planting Area. Insulation layer placed directly on waterproof membrane with perforated protection board to prevent damage to insulation. Water reaching the insulation is carried off through the roof drain.

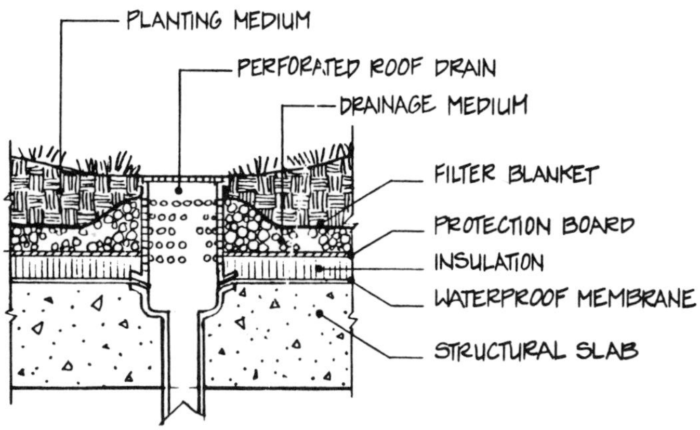
PLANTING MEDIUM
PERFORATED ROOF DRAIN
DRAINAGE MEDIUM
FILTER BLANKET
PROTECTION BOARD
INSULATION
WATERPROOF MEMBRANE
STRUCTURAL SLAB

Figure 610-3 Roof Drains for Flat Planted Surfaces. On flat planted surfaces, both surface and subsurface drainage is accomplished with perforated roof drain flush with planting medium. Filter blanket prevents seepage of planting medium into the draining layer.

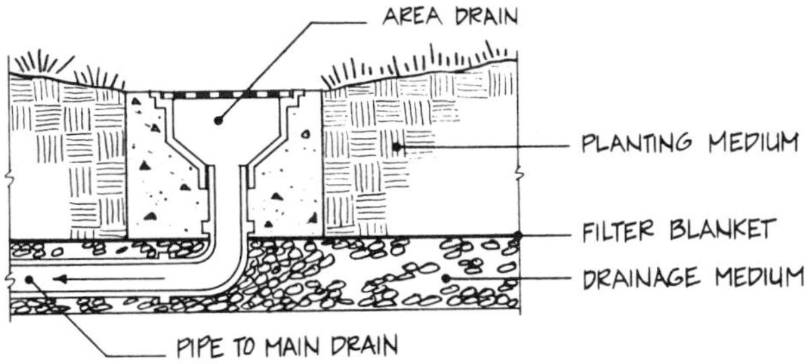
AREA DRAIN
PLANTING MEDIUM
FILTER BLANKET
DRAINAGE MEDIUM
PIPE TO MAIN DRAIN

Figure 610-4 Drains for Low Areas. When low places occur on the surface not near a major subsurface drain, a lateral pipe and drain can carry water quickly to the main drain.

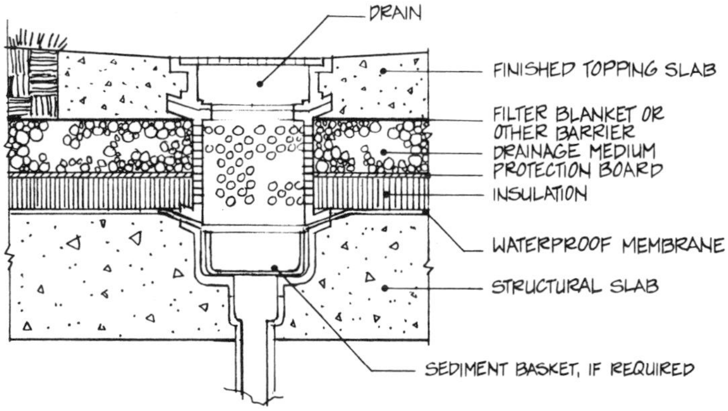
DRAIN
FINISHED TOPPING SLAB
FILTER BLANKET OR OTHER BARRIER
DRAINAGE MEDIUM
PROTECTION BOARD
INSULATION
WATERPROOF MEMBRANE
STRUCTURAL SLAB
SEDIMENT BASKET, IF REQUIRED

Figure 610-5 Drains for Paved Areas near Planting Beds. For drains in paving near an area of planting medium, topping slab is installed directly on the drainage medium after filter blanket is first placed to prevent loss of wet concrete into the drainage medium.

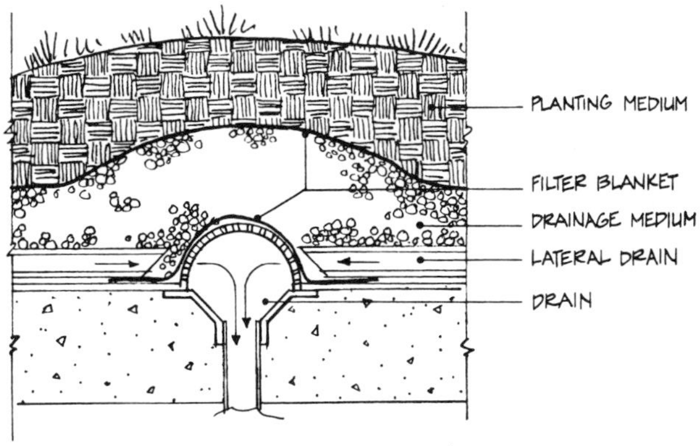
PLANTING MEDIUM
FILTER BLANKET
DRAINAGE MEDIUM
LATERAL DRAIN
DRAIN

Figure 610-6 Main Roof Drain under Planting. Main roof drain can be located under a thickened section of the drainage medium, which is protected by a filter blanket. A second filter blanket over the drain strainer and the ends of the lateral drain pipes prevents plugging of drain openings by planting medium.

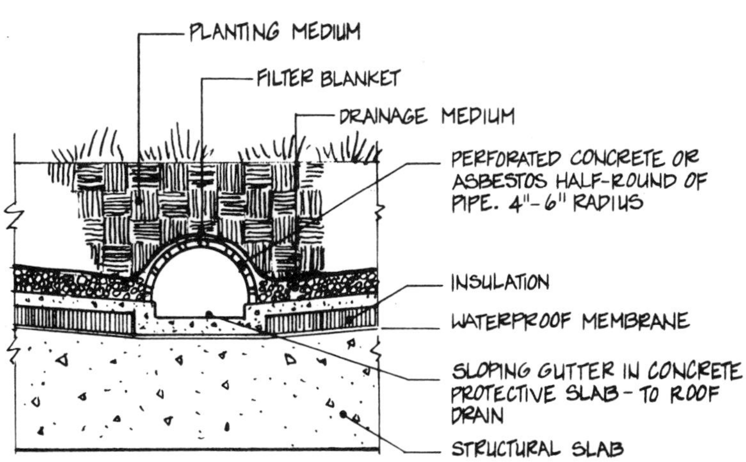
PLANTING MEDIUM
FILTER BLANKET
DRAINAGE MEDIUM
PERFORATED CONCRETE OR ASBESTOS HALF-ROUND OF PIPE. 4"-6" RADIUS
INSULATION
WATERPROOF MEMBRANE
SLOPING GUTTER IN CONCRETE PROTECTIVE SLAB-TO ROOF DRAIN
STRUCTURAL SLAB

Figure 610-7 Half-Round Drainage Channel under Planting. A sloping drainage channel formed in the concrete protective slab is covered with half-round perforated pipe in 2- to 3-ft (0.6 to 0.9m) lengths and a filter blanket.

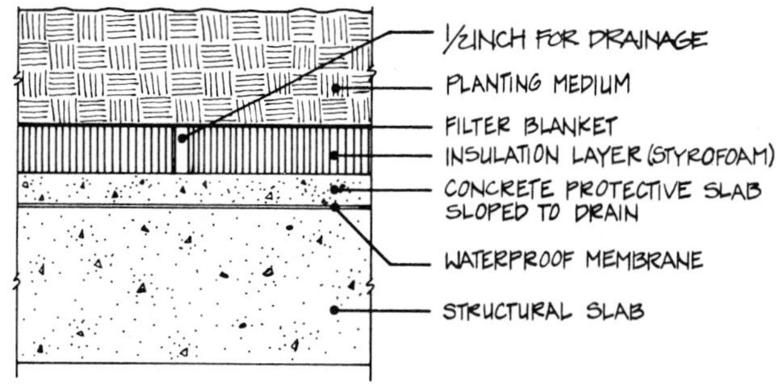
½INCH FOR DRAINAGE
PLANTING MEDIUM
FILTER BLANKET
INSULATION LAYER (STYROFOAM)
CONCRETE PROTECTIVE SLAB SLOPED TO DRAIN
WATERPROOF MEMBRANE
STRUCTURAL SLAB

Figure 610-8 Lightweight Drainage Techniques. In small areas where a lightweight drainage medium is needed, slope the protective slab to the roof drain, and cover with 4 ft × 4 ft × 2 in (1.22 m × 1.22 m × 50 mm) Styrofoam sheets. Sheets must be square with 2-in (50 mm) spaces between for adequate drainage. Cover with filter blanket.

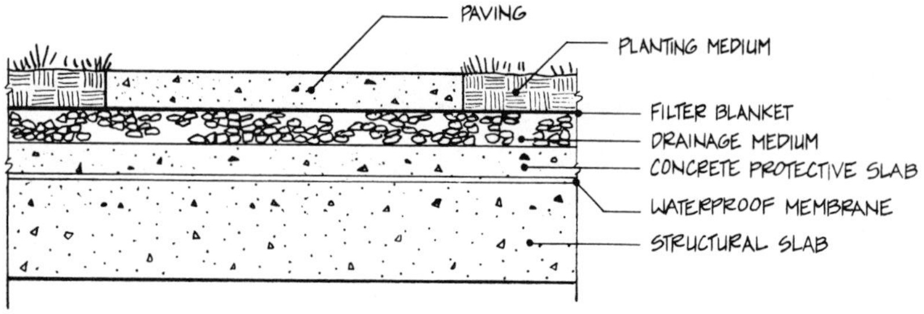
PAVING
PLANTING MEDIUM
FILTER BLANKET
DRAINAGE MEDIUM
CONCRETE PROTECTIVE SLAB
WATERPROOF MEMBRANE
STRUCTURAL SLAB

Figure 610-9 Subsurface Drainage under Paving. Paved area is placed directly on surface of the drainage medium to allow a continuous subsurface drainage layer sloped toward the roof drains. Filter blanket prevents wet concrete from penetrating drainage material. Drainpipe under the paving at intervals improves drainage.

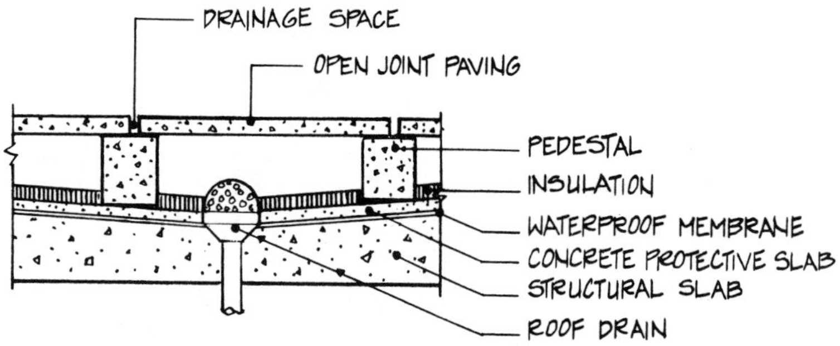
DRAINAGE SPACE
OPEN JOINT PAVING
PEDESTAL
INSULATION
WATERPROOF MEMBRANE
CONCRETE PROTECTIVE SLAB
STRUCTURAL SLAB
ROOF DRAIN

Figure 610-10 Subsurface Drainage for Paving on Pedestals. Pedestal-mounted, removable, open-joint paving provides positive drainage, adjustable heights, and easy access to the roof surface for cleaning or repair. Insulation is fitted between the pedestals.

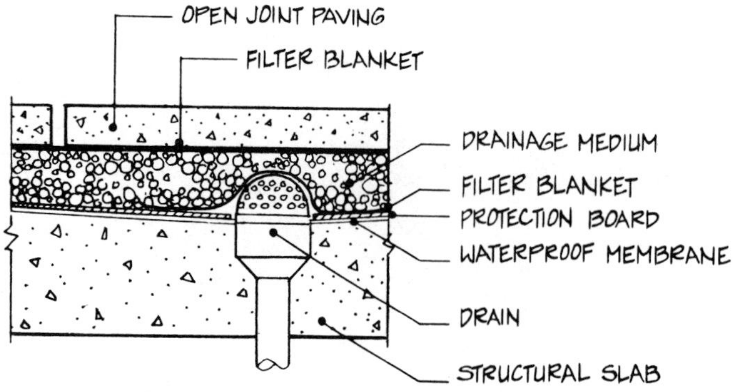
OPEN JOINT PAVING
FILTER BLANKET
DRAINAGE MEDIUM
FILTER BLANKET
PROTECTION BOARD
WATERPROOF MEMBRANE
DRAIN
STRUCTURAL SLAB

Figure 610-11 Subsurface Drainage under Paving on Grade. In open-joint paving without pedestals, where no insulation is needed, filter blanket is held to the protection board by mastic or hot tar at its outer edges to prevent seepage of silt into the drain, and the gravel drainage layer is compacted with a 400-lb (180-kg) roller.

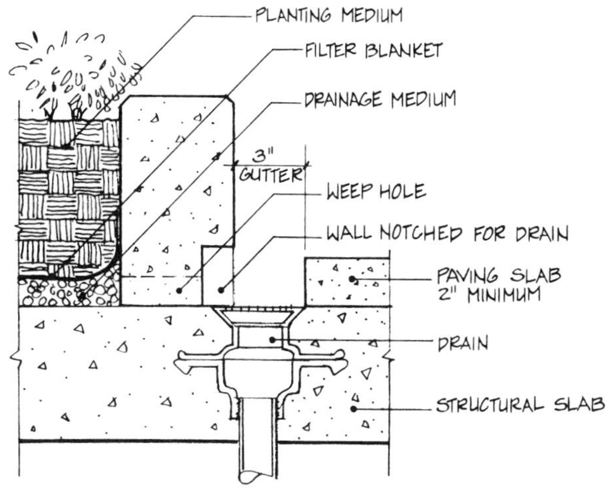
PLANTING MEDIUM
FILTER BLANKET
DRAINAGE MEDIUM
3" GUTTER
WEEP HOLE
WALL NOTCHED FOR DRAIN
PAVING SLAB 2" MINIMUM
DRAIN
STRUCTURAL SLAB

Figure 610-12 Weep Holes and Gutter to Roof Drain. Where a waterproof roof is not necessary, paving slab is poured directly onto the structural slab. Planting medium behind wall is drained through weep holes to an open gutter.

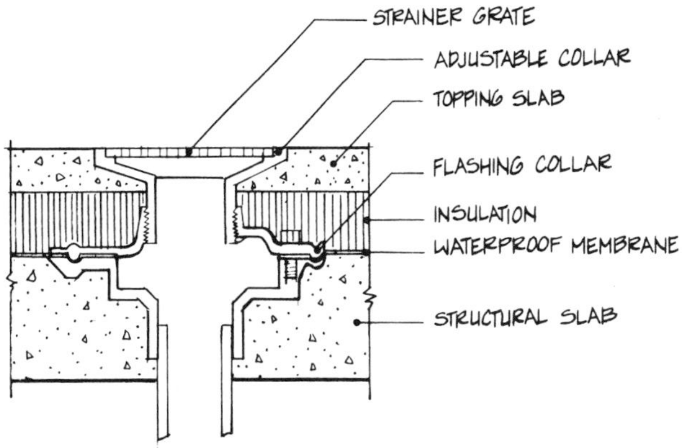
STRAINER GRATE
ADJUSTABLE COLLAR
TOPPING SLAB
FLASHING COLLAR
INSULATION
WATERPROOF MEMBRANE
STRUCTURAL SLAB

Figure 610-13 Roof Drain through Topping Slab. Basic method used to drain a roof which has a topping slab protecting the waterproof membrane. Insulation is optional. Common when roof plantings are held in pots or tubs only, or when the deck includes no plantings at all.

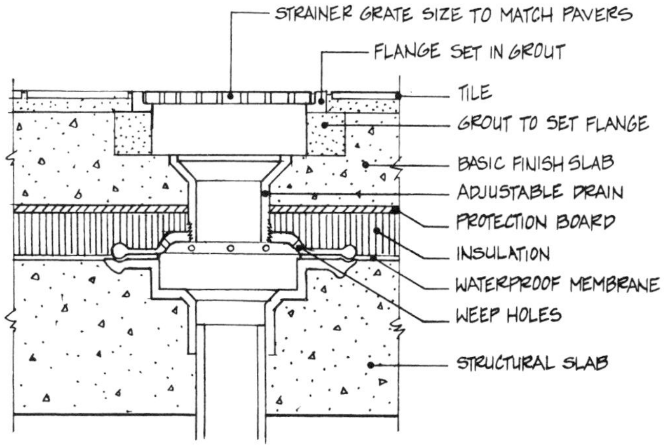
STRAINER GRATE SIZE TO MATCH PAVERS
FLANGE SET IN GROUT
TILE
GROUT TO SET FLANGE
BASIC FINISH SLAB
ADJUSTABLE DRAIN
PROTECTION BOARD
INSULATION
WATERPROOF MEMBRANE
WEEP HOLES
STRUCTURAL SLAB

Figure 610-14 Square Surface Drain. A typical round drain is installed with its grating below the top of the basic finish slab, to allow installation of a square grill on a square-patterned surface. The finish slab is formed with an indentation for the grout.

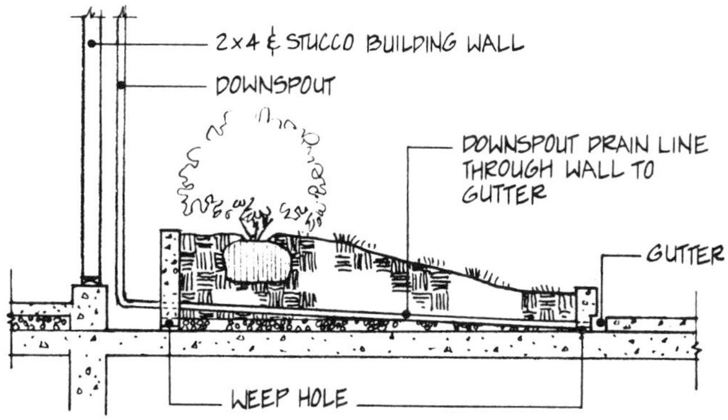
2×4 & STUCCO BUILDING WALL
DOWNSPOUT
DOWNSPOUT DRAIN LINE THROUGH WALL TO GUTTER
GUTTER
WEEP HOLE

Figure 610-15 Drainage through Raised Planting Bed. Raised planting areas can be separated from a porous building wall to protect it from soil dampness. Allow clearance for repairs. Downspouts are brought through the planting bed to a walkway gutter. The back space is drained by weep holes through the drainage medium to the front gutter and/or by slope to either end of the back space.

trapped sediment and the removal of roots growing into the drainage system.

3.2 Lightweight Planting Medium

The critical factors in the formulation of a suitable planting medium for roof garden planting are light weight, the ability to hold nutrients for plant growth, and the capability of developing a firm but easily drained soil structure. Ready-mixed soils are available commercially, but a suitable soil mixture can be prepared for each project following the given formula per cubic yard:

$\frac{1}{2}$ yd^3 fine sand (No. 10 or 18, with no silt)

$\frac{1}{2}$ yd^3 fir or pine bark

1 lb calcium nitrate

3 lb single superphosphate

1 lb sulfate of potash

7 lb dolomite lime

When this mix is too heavy, it may be lightened by substituting 3 parts expanded shale ⅜-in No. 8 screen and 3 parts expanded shale No. 10 (texture of fine sand) for the sand elements. Expanded shale is commonly used in place of gravel in lightweight concrete and is generally available from suppliers of concrete materials.

Fine Sand:

The fine sand used in soil mixes is of critical importance in terms both of the soil's drainage characteristics and of its ability to function without blocking the permeability of the filter blanket. Sand with the physical properties listed in Table 610-1 and with the chemical properties listed in Table 610-2 has been proved effective for roof garden soil mixes.

TABLE 610-1
Sieve Analysis for Sand*

Sieve size	*Weight (% passing)*
No. 4	100
No. 10	95–100
No. 18	90–100
No. 35	65–100
No. 60	0–50
No. 140	0–20
No. 270	0–7

*With no silt mixed in.

TABLE 610-2
Suitable Chemical Properties

Chemical property	*Permissible range*
Salinity (millisiemens per cm of saturation extract at 25° C)	Nil–3.0
Saturation extract concentration of boron	Nil–1.0
Adsorption ratio of sodium (SAR)	Nil–6.0

Soil Amendments:

Any soil amendments to be used in the soil mix should be tested by an approved laboratory for the minimal properties listed in Table 610-3.

Organic materials such as fertilizers—particularly nitrogen, but also other minerals which go into solution—will gradually dissolve and be leached away by watering. Local public water supplies may also lack calcium, magnesium, and sulphur. Thus, periodic replacement of these and other materials by surface application may be needed. At least once a year, soil tests should be made by a competent soils laboratory to determine deficiencies and to recommend additives.

TABLE 610-3
Minimal Properties of Soil Amendments

Physical properties:	*Percent passing*	*Sieve designation*
	95–100	6.35 mm, ¼-in mesh
	75–100	2.38 mm, No. 8, 8 mesh
	0–30	500, No. 35, 32 mesh
Source:	*Nitrogen content, dry weight basis, if nitrogen stabilized*	*Dry bulk density, lb/y³ (kg/m³)*
Redwood sawdust	0.40–0.60%	270–370 (159–218)
Redwood bark fiber	0.35–0.50%	250–350 (147–206)
Fir or cedar sawdust	0.56–0.84%	270–370 (159–218)
Fir or pine bark	0.80–1.20%	450–580 (265–341)
Hardwood bark	0.80–1.20%	450–500 (265–294)
Iron content	Minimum 0.08% dilute acid soluble iron based on dry weight if specified as, or claimed to be, iron treated.	
Soluble salts	Maximum 3.0 ms/cm at 25° C as determined in saturation extract.	
Organic content	Minimum 92% based on dry weight and determined by ash method.	
Mineralized	Other mineral fertilizers or chemical amendments may be specified for incorporation.	
Wettability	The air-dry product shall, when applied to a cup or small beaker of water at 70° F in the amount of 1 tsp, become completely wet in a period not exceeding 2 min. Any wetting agent added to accomplish this shall be guaranteed to be nonphytotoxic at rate used.	

Other Ways to Reduce Weight:

If optimum soil depths result in excessive weight on the structure, then lightweight soil mixes can be used. It should be remembered, however, that if the subsurface drainage system fails and the soil becomes saturated, the planting mix can reach a weight of about 120 pounds per cubic foot (pcf). If the roof cannot withstand a loading of this magnitude, then various ways must be used to create voids beneath the soil medium (Figures 610-16 through 610-18). The most common methods used include casting a false bottom or using large blocks of high-density Styrofoam, which is commonly sold in blocks 4 ft × 8 ft × 10 in thick.

Figure 610-19 shows how a roof structure can be designed to provide a recessed planting area over a column for a large tree.

Depths and Weights of Planting Medium and Plants:

Table 610-4 shows the minimum soil depths needed for different types of rooftop plantings, Table 610-5 shows typical dry and damp weights of various planting media, and Table 610-6 shows the weight of container- and field-grown plants.

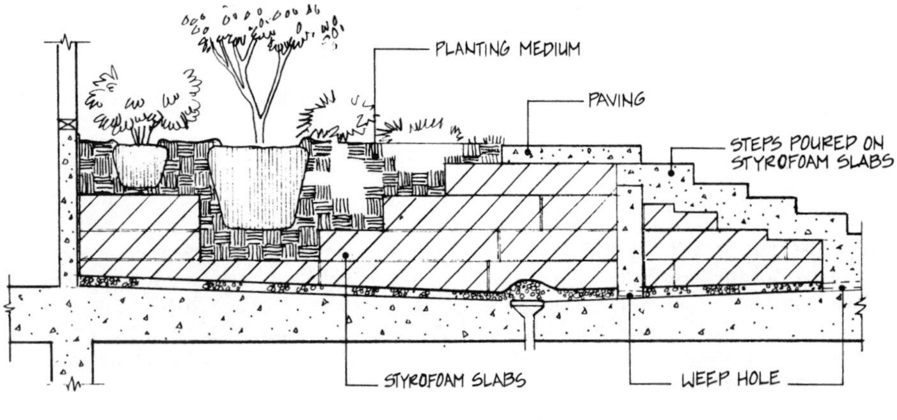
PLANTING MEDIUM
PAVING
STEPS POURED ON STYROFOAM SLABS
STYROFOAM SLABS
WEEP HOLE

Figure 610-16 Lightweight Alternative for Raising Planting Bed. Alternative method for raising a planting bed adjacent to a building wall. A concrete wall is carried 6 in (152 mm) above the finished grade of the planting level and waterproofed. The planting medium can include lightweight Styrofoam blocks for weight reduction.

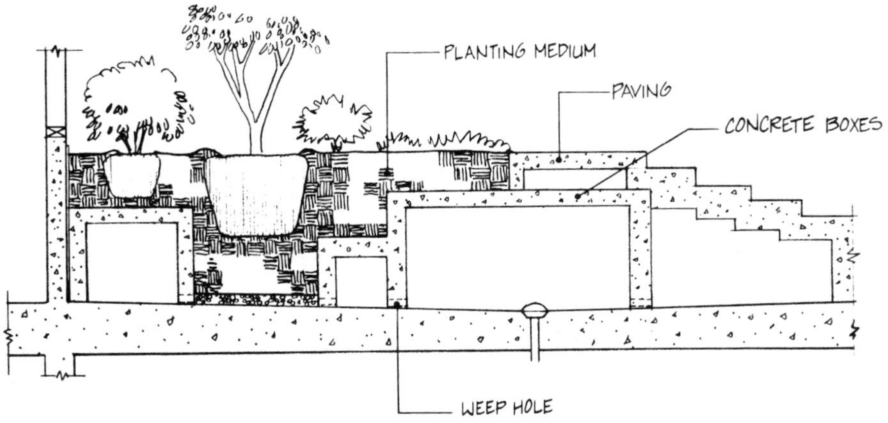
PLANTING MEDIUM
PAVING
CONCRETE BOXES
WEEP HOLE

Figure 610-17 Concrete Boxes Used to Raise Beds. Concrete boxes, instead of soil or Styrofoam, are used for lightweight structural strength.

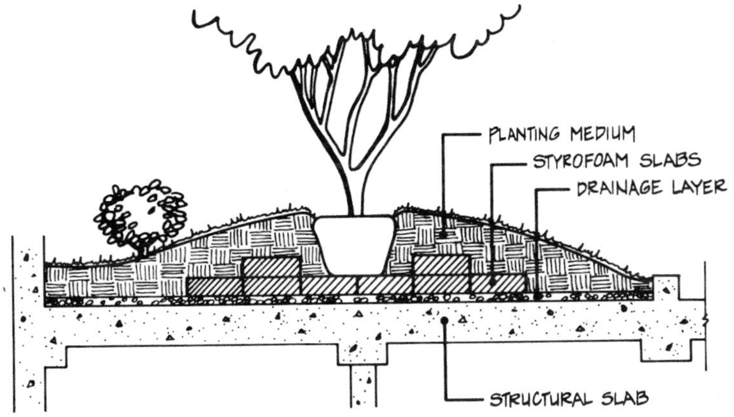
PLANTING MEDIUM
STYROFOAM SLABS
DRAINAGE LAYER
STRUCTURAL SLAB

Figure 610-18 Alternative Way to Reduce Weight of Planting Medium. Styrofoam blocks placed at suitable depths reduce the weight and mass of the planting medium.

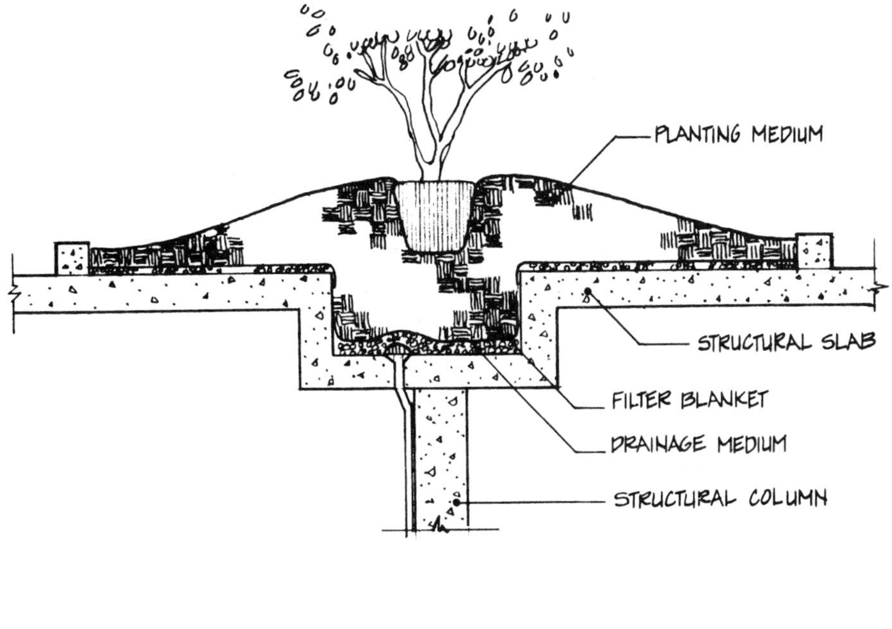
PLANTING MEDIUM
STRUCTURAL SLAB
FILTER BLANKET
DRAINAGE MEDIUM
STRUCTURAL COLUMN

Figure 610-19 Recessed Area for Large Plants. Roof structure is designed to provide a recessed planting area over a column for a large tree.

TABLE 610-4
Minimum Soil Depths

Planting	Minimum soil depths*
Lawns	8–12 in (200–300 mm)
Flowers and ground covers	10–12 in (260–300 mm)
Shrubs	24–30 in (600–750 mm)†
Small trees	30–42 in (750–1200 mm)
Large trees	5–6 ft (1.5–1.8 m)

* On filter blanket and drainage medium.

† Depending on ultimate shrub size.

TABLE 610-5
Weight of Planting Medium

Material	Dry		Damp	
	lb/ft³	(kg/m³)	lb/ft³	(kg/m³)
Fine sand	90.00	1446.42	120.00	1928.56
Cedar shavings with fertilizer	9.25	148.66	13.00	208.93
Peat moss	9.60	154.28	10.30	165.53
Red lava–5⁄16 in (8 mm) maximum	50.00	803.57	53.70	863.03
Redwood compost and shavings	14.80	237.86	22.20	356.78
Fir and pine bark humus	22.20	356.78	33.30	535.17
Perlite	6.50	104.46	32.40*	520.71*
Vermiculite				
Coarse	6.25	100.45		
Medium	5.75	92.41		
Fine	7.50	120.53		
Topsoil	76.00	1221.42	78.00	1253.56

* Applies to wet—not damp—perlite

TABLE 610-6
Weight of Container and Field-Grown Plants

Container size	Container grown in mushroom compost, lb (kg)	Field-grown, lb (kg)
15-gal (56-L) can	80 (36)	—
20-in (510-mm) box	200 (90)	400 (180)
24-in (610-mm) box	400 (180)	725 (325)
30-in (760-mm) box	800 (360)	1,500 (675)
36-in (900-mm) box	1,300 (585)	2,500 (1,125)
48-in (1220-mm) box	3,500 (1,575)	6,000 (2,700)
54-in (1370-mm) box	4,000 (1,800)	7,000 (3,150)
60-in (1520-mm) box	5,000 (2,250)	8,000 (3,600)
72-in (1830-mm) box	7,000 (3,150)	12,000 (5,400)
84-in (2130-mm) box	9,000 (4,050)	16,000 (7,200)
96-in (2440-mm) box	12,000 (5,400)	20,000 (9,000)
120-in (3050-mm) box	14,000 (6,300)	24,000 (10,800)

Note: All the above are shipping weights, including the box.

Figure 610-20 illustrates a method to change grades between an on-grade sidewalk and roof deck without using excessive depths of planting media.

Figure 610-21 shows one way to reduce weights for plants in containers.

3.3 Adaptation to Climate

Climate:

Wind, sun and shade, and extremes of temperature—as well as long dry or wet periods, snow loads, frost levels, and problems of frozen drains, irrigation piping, ponds, and water features—are all much greater problems for roof gardens than for gardens on the ground.

There are very few localities where no specialized accommodations to some aspect of climate are needed. The worst conditions are found in parts of the world where there are extremes of both hot and cold. In such climates, all piping must be drained completely or insulated against freezing prior to the onset of winter. There must be quick and positive surface and subsurface drainage to prevent flooding due to heavy rains. The weight of accumulated ice and snow must not exceed the weight limits of the roof's structural system.

Even in regions where these extremes of climate are less important, there can be temporary extremes caused by hurricanes, typhoons, tornadoes, or other types of storms.

Wind:

Tall plants, vertical structures (such as fences, walls, and light standards), and other similar elements must be designed or selected and installed to resist wind damage due to overturning or breaking. Plants are also subject to *flagging,* or lopsided growth, due to strong, persistent winds. More typically, even normal wind flow can also cause excessive drying of plant materials and soils and even high evaporation of ornamental and irrigation water.

Sun and Shade:

The planting must be selected in accordance with its adaptability to either sun or shade conditions, but in sunny areas the water requirements may be much greater because of more rapid drainage and evaporation. The creation of natural or artificial shade can reduce water loss and related damage. Human use and enjoyment of roof gardens varies considerably between sunny and shady areas, and this distinction should therefore be taken into account in the location and layout of any roof or deck landscape.

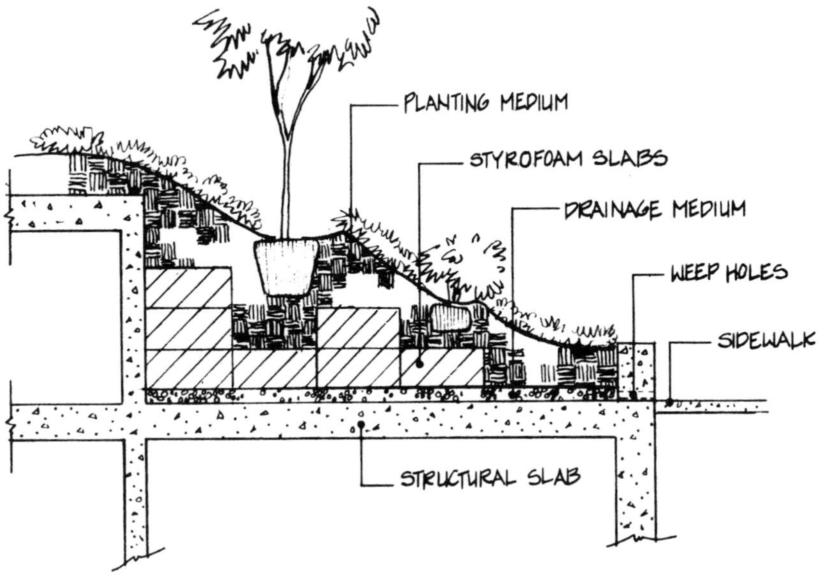
PLANTING MEDIUM
STYROFOAM SLABS
DRAINAGE MEDIUM
WEEP HOLES
SIDEWALK
STRUCTURAL SLAB

Figure 610-20 Lightweight Method for Changing Grades. Method to change grades between sidewalk and roof deck.

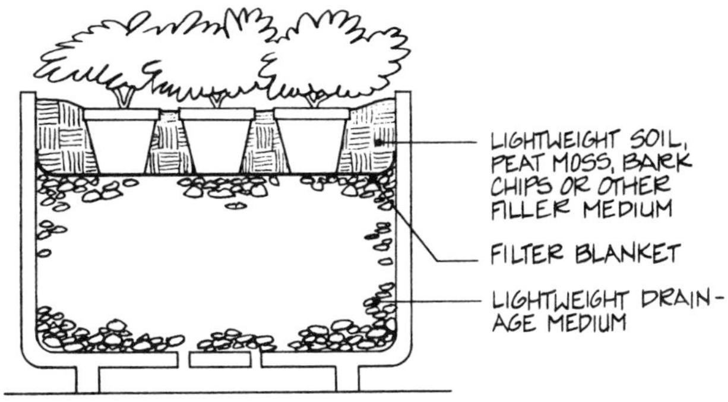
LIGHTWEIGHT SOIL, PEAT MOSS, BARK CHIPS OR OTHER FILLER MEDIUM
FILTER BLANKET
LIGHTWEIGHT DRAINAGE MEDIUM

Figure 610-21 Lightweight Plant Containers. Method for stringent weight restrictions. Plastic containers are substituted for clay, and lightweight drainage medium is substituted for soil. For planting directly in soil, 8 to 10 in (205 to 255 mm) of lightweight soil is placed on drainage medium covered with a filter blanket.

3.4 Irrigation

The relatively thin, well-drained soil mixtures typically used in roof gardens cannot provide plants with the subsurface water normally available to ground level plantings. As a result, care must be exercised to prevent the planting medium from drying out and causing damage to or even the loss of plant materials. For large roof or deck landscapes, hand watering is usually too labor-intensive and unreliable. In such cases an underground sprinkler or irrigation system with automatic controls is the most reliable and cost-effective method of watering plants and lawns on roofs. These systems can be made of plastic pipe and fittings, which are durable, lightweight, easy to install, and often the least expensive to install and operate.

Piping should be installed directly on top of the filter blanket. The riser heads should be temporarily capped and tested under pressure for leaks before the planting medium is added. Sprinkler controllers may be placed in a locked outdoor cabinet or placed in an adjacent inside room. Complete drainage of all the lines and fixtures should be provided in regions where freezing can occur. Access to a source of electrical power of 110 to 120 V ac (or equivalent appropriate level of power in non-United States locations) is required for the controller clock and step-down transformer. Close coordination with the building's electrical and mechanical engineers is required to ensure that all of the water, electrical, and drainage needs for the roof garden are provided and that the responsibility for this work is described in the building's construction specifications.

4.0 SELECTION OF MATERIALS AND METHODS OF ANCHORING

4.1 Structural Materials

The construction of light standards, walls, fences, wind screens, pergolas, curbs, steps, and other structural elements should all be considered in relationship to the structural limitations of the roof and its supports below. Again, the omnipresent factor of weight has a strong effect on which material is used. Aluminum light standards, lightweight concrete for paving, curbs and walls, and other strong but lightweight materials should be used whenever such elements are needed. All of these constructed elements need to be made of materials as lightweight as possible and to be anchored securely to the roof or other parts of the building. Tables 610-7 and 610-8 give typical weights for some of the common materials used in the construction of roof gardens.

4.2 Paving

The type and pattern of paving materials chosen are as important to the viewers from surrounding buildings as they are to the actual users of the roof garden. The color, tone, texture, and contrast of these materials can sometimes be greater than ordinarily found in a typical ground level landscape. For instance, the color and texture of concrete or brick as seen from above can strongly contrast with the planting and water surfaces, thereby creating

TABLE 610-7
Weight of Common Building Materials

Material	lb/ft³	*kg/m³*
Granite	170	2757
Marble	170	2757
Slate	160–180	2595–2919
Limestone	155	2514
Sandstone	145	2352
Shale	162	2627
Expanded shale	40–45	649–730
Field stone	95	1541
Gravel	120	1946
Pebbles	120	1946
Pumice	40	649
Concrete		
Lightweight	80–100	1298–1622
Precast	130	2108
Reinforced	150	2433
Concrete block: 8 in	50–60	811–973
Brickwork (average)	115	1865
Cast iron	450	7297
Steel	490	7945
Bronze	513	8318
Timber		
Hardwood (average)	45	730
Softwood (average)	35	568
Sand		
Dry	90–110	1460–1784
Wet	110–130	1784–2108
Sand and gravel: mixed	115	1865
Clay soil		
Compacted, dry	75–100	1216–1622
Compacted, wet	125	2027
Loam		
Dry	80	1298
Wet	120	1946
Special commercial soil: wet	110	1784
Topsoil		
Dry	80	1298
Wet	120	1946
Peat		
Dry	50	811
Wet	60	973
Humus		
Dry	35	568
Wet	82	1330
Water	62.428	1013
Flagstone and setting bed	25 lb/ft²	122 kg/m²
Tile and setting bed	15 to 73 lb/ft²	73 to 353 kg/m²

Source: A. E. Weddle, *Landscape Techniques,* Van Nostrand Reinhold, New York, 1983; C. G. Ramsey and H. R. Sleeper, *Architectural Graphic Standards,* 7th ed., Wiley, New York, 1981; Olwen C. Marlowe, *Outdoor Design,* Watson-Guptill, New York, 1977; American Institute of Steel Construction, Inc.

TABLE 610-8
Weight of Wood

	Green				*Dried to 12% moisture content*			
	lb/ft³	*kg/ft³*	*lb/fbm*	*kg/fbm*	*lb/ft³*	*kg/ft³*	*lb/fbm*	*kg/fbm*
Douglas fir	38	17	3.17	1.43	34	15	2.83	1.27
Redwood	52	23	4.33	1.95	28	13	2.33	1.05
Cedar, western red	27	12	2.25	1.01	23	10	1.92	0.86

* 1 ft³ = 12 board ft (fbm) of lumber.

Source: Courtesy of the California Redwood Association.

strong visual impressions. Materials should also be selected for their light weight and durability. Brick pavers, tiles, textured wood decking (where permitted by local codes), and colored or exposed aggregate concrete are all excellent choices for rooftop developments.

4.3 Methods of Anchoring

The structural elements, including light fixtures, need to be carefully anchored when used on rooftops. Figures 610-22 through 610-24 show ways that this can be done without penetrating the waterproof roofing or structural slab. Figures 610-25 and 610-26 illustrate ways to secure an element to a roof when such anchorage is mandatory. Normally, nothing should be tied to the structural slab without consulting with and gaining the approval of the building architect. Other techniques for anchoring elements are shown in Figures 610-27 through 610-29.

Unlike the chairs, benches, etc., in most on-grade public landscapes, rooftop furniture often does not need to be fixed in place but can be left to be moved as needed.

5.0 POOLS AND FOUNTAINS

5.1 General Considerations

The use of water and water effects can add greatly to the interest and enjoyment of roof deck areas. There are several factors to consider, however, regarding the weight of the water and its container, plus the dangers of possible leaks into the structure below. If it is known prior to the roof's structural design that a pool or fountain is to be used, then it can often be easily accommodated, although there may be considerable restraint in the amount of water that can be used. Where possible, the heaviest water elements should be located directly over columns. The illusion of greater water depth can be achieved by coloring the bottom and sides of the pool or basin dark gray or black. Satisfactory water effects can be achieved in depths as shallow as 4 to 16 in (100 to 400 mm). This is particularly true if the surface can be kept agitated so that visibility to the bottom is obscured. (Refer to Section 530: Pools and Fountains, for information on the design and detailing of these elements.)

On roofs where weight constraints are very stringent and the roof structure cannot be strengthened, a shallow pool can be created by using preformed shapes made from ¼-in (6-mm) fiberglass. A satisfactory water surface can be obtained with a very

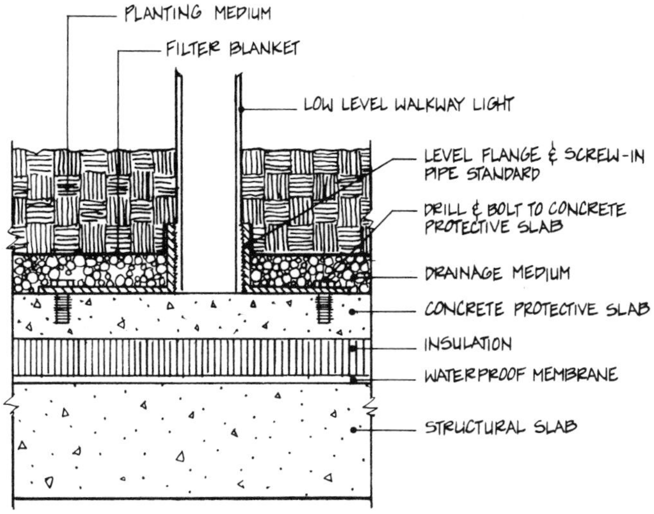
PLANTING MEDIUM
FILTER BLANKET
LOW LEVEL WALKWAY LIGHT
LEVEL FLANGE & SCREW-IN PIPE STANDARD
DRILL & BOLT TO CONCRETE PROTECTIVE SLAB
DRAINAGE MEDIUM
CONCRETE PROTECTIVE SLAB
INSULATION
WATERPROOF MEMBRANE
STRUCTURAL SLAB

Figure 610-22 Anchoring Light Standards to Protective Slabs. The base flange of low-level [(30- to 48-in) (760- to 1220-mm)] light standards can be anchored to the concrete protective slab by bolts either screwed into expansion shields set in drilled holes or fired into the slab by explosive cartridges.

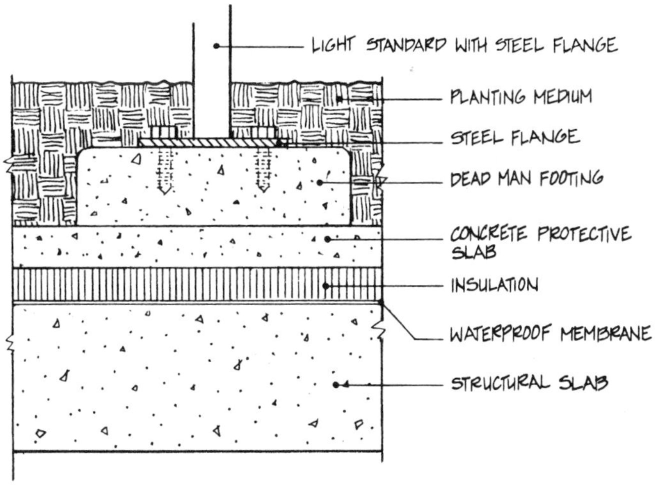
LIGHT STANDARD WITH STEEL FLANGE
PLANTING MEDIUM
STEEL FLANGE
DEAD MAN FOOTING
CONCRETE PROTECTIVE SLAB
INSULATION
WATERPROOF MEMBRANE
STRUCTURAL SLAB

Figure 610-23 Use of Deadmen as Anchors. Deadman footings can anchor light standards.

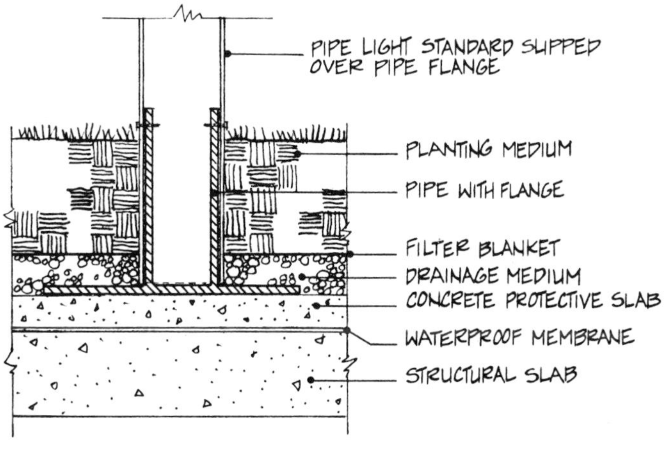
PIPE LIGHT STANDARD SLIPPED OVER PIPE FLANGE
PLANTING MEDIUM
PIPE WITH FLANGE
FILTER BLANKET
DRAINAGE MEDIUM
CONCRETE PROTECTIVE SLAB
WATERPROOF MEMBRANE
STRUCTURAL SLAB

Figure 610-24 Anchoring Low-Level Light Standards. A low-level light standard held in place by the weight of soil on the flange; best-suited for areas where vandalism is negligible.

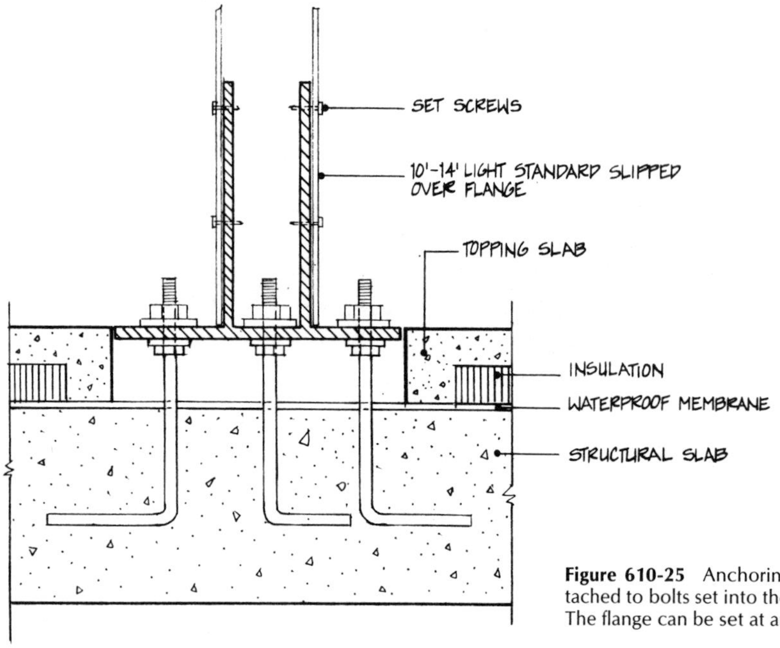
SET SCREWS
10'-14' LIGHT STANDARD SLIPPED OVER FLANGE
TOPPING SLAB
INSULATION
WATERPROOF MEMBRANE
STRUCTURAL SLAB

Figure 610-25 Anchoring Tall Light Standards. Tall, wind-resistant light standard attached to bolts set into the structural slab when poured. Bolts are sealed against leakage. The flange can be set at any desired grade. Also useful for shelters, benches, fences, etc.

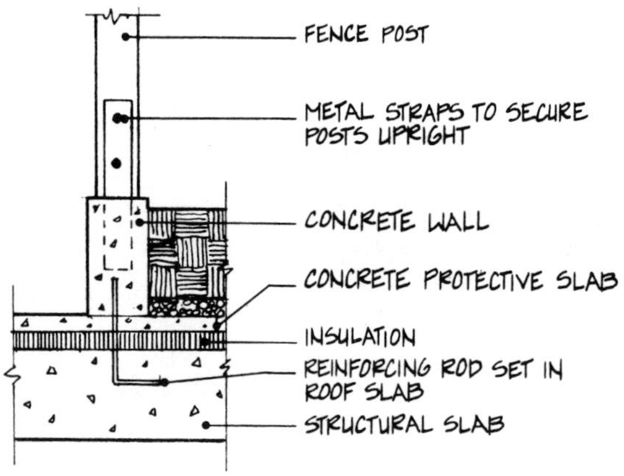
FENCE POST
METAL STRAPS TO SECURE POSTS UPRIGHT
CONCRETE WALL
CONCRETE PROTECTIVE SLAB
INSULATION
REINFORCING ROD SET IN ROOF SLAB
STRUCTURAL SLAB

Figure 610-26 Attaching Fences to Walls. Preferred attachment of fence to the top of a wall instead of directly to roof surface. Fittings should be durable and strong, or galvanized pipe posts can be substituted and placed when wall is poured.

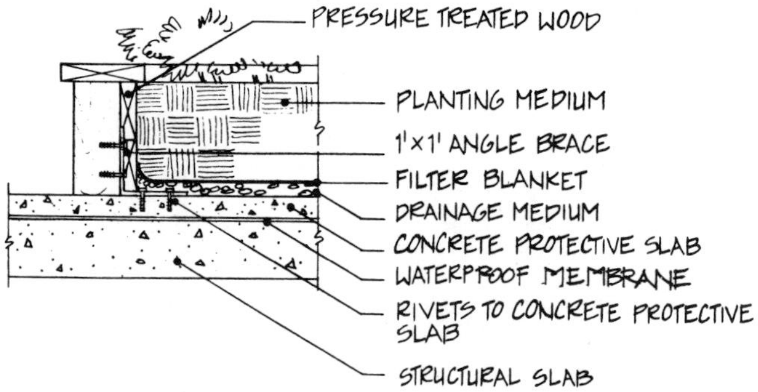
PRESSURE TREATED WOOD
PLANTING MEDIUM
1'x1' ANGLE BRACE
FILTER BLANKET
DRAINAGE MEDIUM
CONCRETE PROTECTIVE SLAB
WATERPROOF MEMBRANE
RIVETS TO CONCRETE PROTECTIVE SLAB
STRUCTURAL SLAB

Figure 610-27 Attaching Wood to Concrete Decks. Wood posts and planks of a garden, flower bed, or sandbox attached to concrete deck. Walls not over 2 ft (0.6 m) in height are braced with 1 ft × 1 ft × ¼ in (300 mm × 300 mm × 6.5 mm) galvanized angle braces. Small four-sided beds need only corner braces. Soil or rivets hold bed in place.

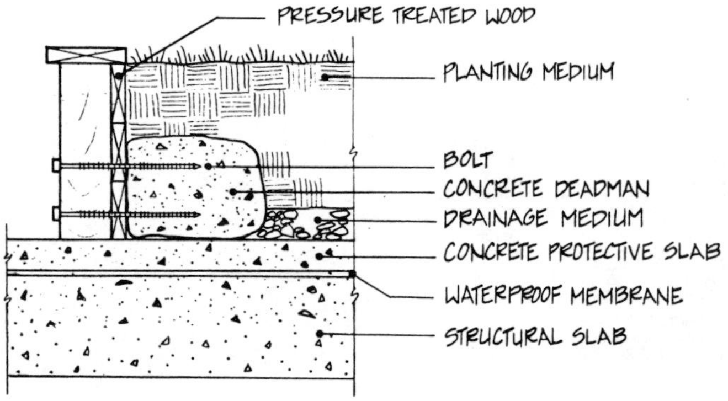
PRESSURE TREATED WOOD
PLANTING MEDIUM
BOLT
CONCRETE DEADMAN
DRAINAGE MEDIUM
CONCRETE PROTECTIVE SLAB
WATERPROOF MEMBRANE
STRUCTURAL SLAB

Figure 610-28 Use of Deadmen to Anchor Wood Structures. Alternative method for anchoring wood posts and plants to concrete deadmen.

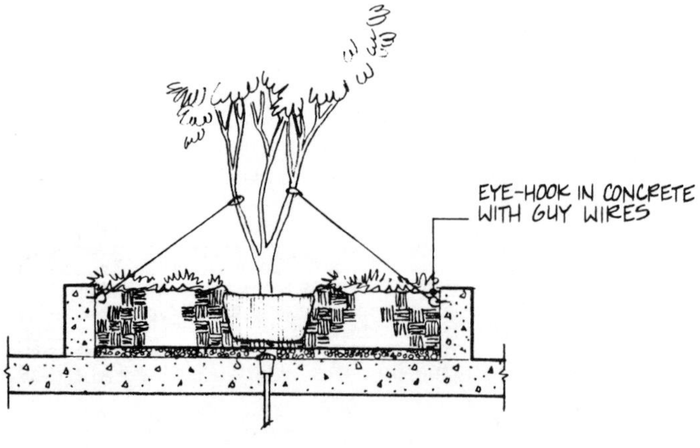
EYE-HOOK IN CONCRETE WITH GUY WIRES

Figure 610-29 Anchoring Large Plants and Trees. Method for securing guy wires to concrete beds. Galvanized eye-hook bolts are placed when the walls are constructed. Eye bolts can also be attached to masonry building surfaces. Waterproofing is necessary at attachment points.

shallow depth (Figure 610-30). This detail is often used in ponds to give them a natural appearance.

5.2 Waterproofing and Anchoring Pool Walls

Unless pool walls are properly anchored and sealed, they can cause serious leaks. Figures 610-31 through 610-33 illustrate three methods of achieving a positive, leakproof seal. In Figure 610-31, the pool bottom and wall are poured as an integral unit directly on the continuous waterproof membrane of the roof. The anchoring reinforcing rods may be placed when pouring the structural slab if recommended by the structural engineer. In Figure 610-32, a smaller core wall is poured and tied into the structural slab with preplaced rods. The waterproof membrane is then laid on the structural slab and brought over the core wall and down to the slab surface again in a continuous run. The pool bottom, as well as the balance of the wall, is then poured separately over the core wall. Because of the chance of cracking, this separate pour should be reinforced with wire mesh, and consultation with a structural engineer is recommended. The water surface elevation of the pool is established just below the height of the core wall.

Figure 610-33 is a variation of Figure 610-32. The core wall is poured on top of the finished protective slab. Inside the pool area, a waterproof membrane is placed and brought to the top of the core wall. The bottom and wall of the pool are then poured separately as a unit. In areas where freezing occurs in the winter, pools should be drained for the duration of the season to prevent damage to the waterproof structure. Figure 610-34 shows a variation where the pool is lined with tile.

6.0 PROVISION FOR UTILITIES

6.1 Electrical

A standard 110- to 120-volt ac electrical supply is sufficient for most roof garden uses, such as lighting, cooking, barbecuing, appliances, and fountain and irrigation controllers. Outdoor heaters, electrically powered mobile window washing machines, and occasionally fountain pumps may require 220 V ac. All electrical requirements should be met in accordance with the recommendations of an electrical engineer.

All electrical supply conduits should be enclosed in metal for protection from digging, given the shallow soil conditions, although low-voltage lighting may be supplied by flexible cable. The subsurface

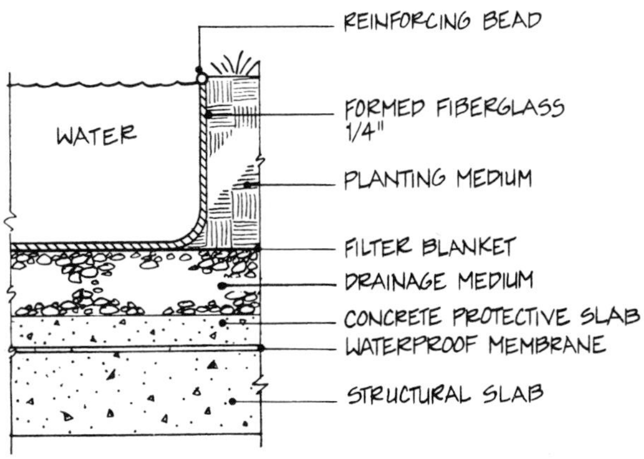
REINFORCING BEAD
WATER
FORMED FIBERGLASS 1/4"
PLANTING MEDIUM
FILTER BLANKET
DRAINAGE MEDIUM
CONCRETE PROTECTIVE SLAB
WATERPROOF MEMBRANE
STRUCTURAL SLAB

Figure 610-30 Fiberglass pool wall.

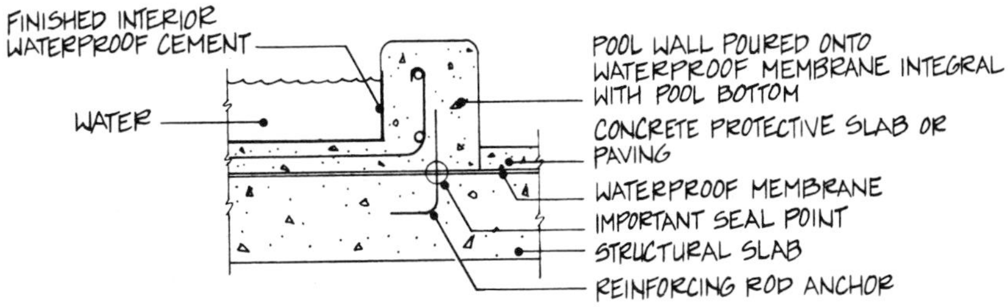
FINISHED INTERIOR WATERPROOF CEMENT
WATER
POOL WALL POURED ONTO WATERPROOF MEMBRANE INTEGRAL WITH POOL BOTTOM
CONCRETE PROTECTIVE SLAB OR PAVING
WATERPROOF MEMBRANE
IMPORTANT SEAL POINT
STRUCTURAL SLAB
REINFORCING ROD ANCHOR

Figure 610-31 Pool wall and bottom poured as one.

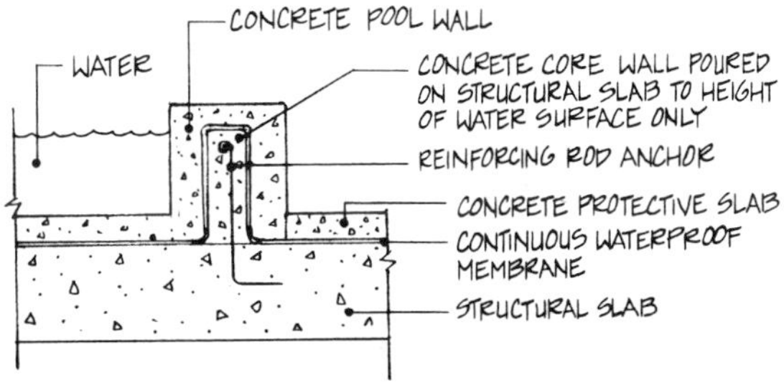
CONCRETE POOL WALL
WATER
CONCRETE CORE WALL POURED ON STRUCTURAL SLAB TO HEIGHT OF WATER SURFACE ONLY
REINFORCING ROD ANCHOR
CONCRETE PROTECTIVE SLAB
CONTINUOUS WATERPROOF MEMBRANE
STRUCTURAL SLAB

Figure 610-32 Pool wall tied to structural slab (alternative 1).

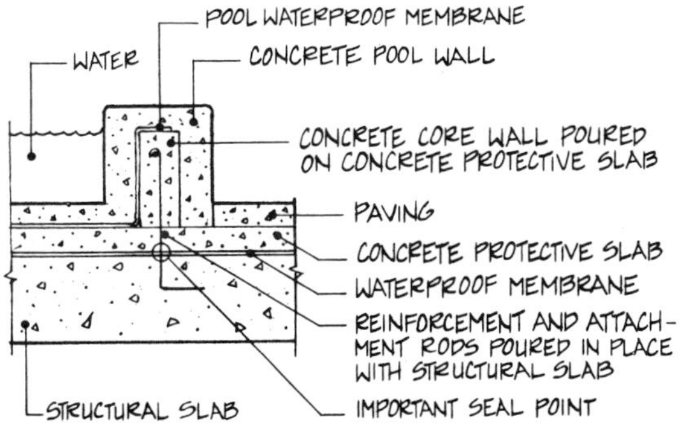
POOL WATERPROOF MEMBRANE
WATER
CONCRETE POOL WALL
CONCRETE CORE WALL POURED ON CONCRETE PROTECTIVE SLAB
PAVING
CONCRETE PROTECTIVE SLAB
WATERPROOF MEMBRANE
REINFORCEMENT AND ATTACHMENT RODS POURED IN PLACE WITH STRUCTURAL SLAB
STRUCTURAL SLAB
IMPORTANT SEAL POINT

Figure 610-33 Pool wall tied to structural slab (alternative 2).

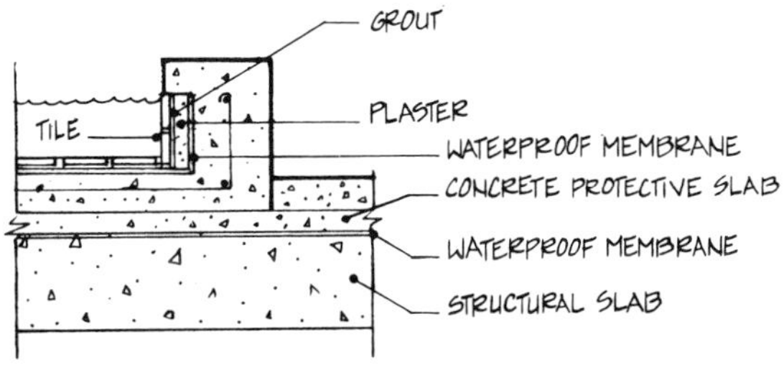
GROUT
PLASTER
TILE
WATERPROOF MEMBRANE
CONCRETE PROTECTIVE SLAB
WATERPROOF MEMBRANE
STRUCTURAL SLAB

Figure 610-34 Pool wall faced with tile.

distribution system should be placed prior to installing the planting medium and/or paving. Electrically operated or optically controlled timing devices are additional conveniences for gardens which are regularly lighted at night.

6.2 Water

A supply of clean water is needed for irrigation, ornamental pools and fountains, the cleaning of roof surfaces, and fire protection. Water pressure for irrigation systems should be provided from a minimum level of 35 psi to a maximum of approximately 70 psi. If this supply is connected to the building's potable water system, then it can also be used for drinking fountains. Water for fire protection can be separate and need not be potable. Irrigation and fountain water supplies must contain suitable backflow prevention devices to guard against contamination of potable water sources.

Provision should be made for indoor locations of lighting and irrigation controllers, electrical panels, pumps, motors, and other mechanical equipment needed for the garden, as well as for gardening tools and supplies.

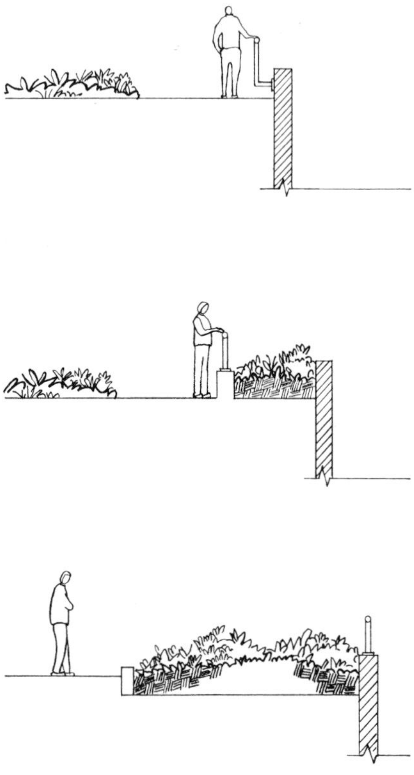

Figure 610-35 Techniques for creating safety barriers.

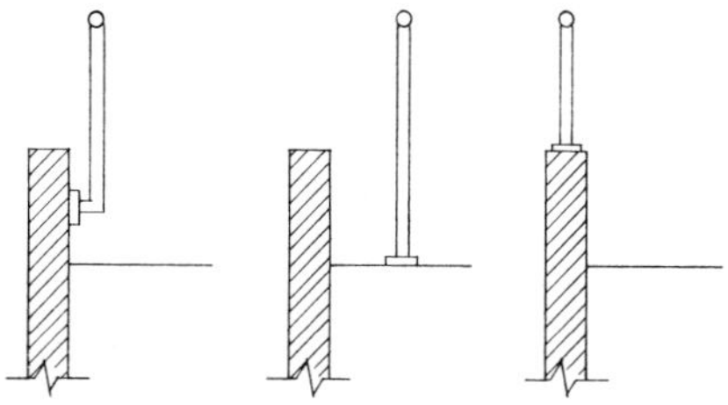

Figure 610-36 Techniques for attaching railings.

7.0 PUBLIC SAFETY AND SECURITY

By virtue of the fact that most roof gardens are several stories above ground level, there is a need to alleviate psychological fears as well as to provide physical barriers for safety. Given limited roof space, it may be necessary to allow users to approach the edge of a roof, but it is generally more appealing to have a space or barrier between the roof edge and the usable areas. Figure 610-35 shows three ways to handle parapet walls.

For those who desire to do so, there should be places where people can gain access to a railing on the roof's parapet in order to look downward as well as horizontally.

The spaces between railings and posts should be closed in with wire fabric, safety plate glass, fiberglass, or other suitable material to prevent easy or accidental penetration by small children, pets, or others. Figure 610-36 shows how guard railings can be attached to the top or roof side of the parapet or set slightly back from the parapet. Higher barriers of opaque or transparent material can be substituted in these same locations for both safety and wind protection.

8.0 MAINTENANCE

Not unlike successful gardens on the ground, most roof gardens require consistent, good maintenance. This includes watering, fertilizing, shearing, pruning, bracing, raking, replanting, sweeping, the removal of debris, the repair and adjustment of irrigation and lighting equipment, and the clearance of obstructions in the drainage system.

8.1 Paving, Fixtures, and Furnishings

Paving, drinking fountains, light fixtures, benches, pools, fountains, decks, walls, fences, steps, ramps, etc., require little, if any, special maintenance not found in gardens on the ground.

Planted areas near pavement edges should be checked every 2 to 3 years to determine whether roots have penetrated under the pavement. Roots growing under paving can tip the paving and as a result change the surface drainage and make the paving unsightly. These roots should be cut to slow down further growth.

8.2 Plant Maintenance

Normal seasonal levels of maintenance are needed all year. Special attention should be given to pruning trees and shrubs in order to maintain a balance between aboveground and underground growth. If this is done regularly, it will not only prolong the life of the plants but will also help prevent the overturning of top-heavy plants due to strong winds. Except in the case of plants used for windbreaks, periodic thinning should be done to allow the wind to pass through the foliage.

It should be kept in mind that because roof gardens need to be well-drained, plants need more frequent feeding and related care. A year after installation, all planted areas should receive a top dressing, approximately ¼ in (6 mm) thick, made up of a mixture similar to the original planting medium. This should be continued annually or adjusted to maintain the original level of the grades and planting mixture.

Failing plants should be replaced as soon as their conditions become obvious. Usually, these plants should be replaced with the same variety unless it can be determined that the particular plant is not hardy in a specific location.

Lastly, maintenance can be simplified if plants are selected for their zonal hardiness, for their resistance to wind and human abuse, for their noninvasive root systems, and for their reliability in not exceeding a specified size. There are few ornamental landscape plants used in the world which will not grow in well-designed roof gardens in their own locality. However, just as designers must carefully choose plants for the specific microclimate, soil, and other habitat conditions found in ground level landscapes, so they also must exercise sound judgment in selecting plants for roof landscapes.

The intent of this section has been to help provide the physical context needed for plants to grow successfully rather than to provide data on the large number of plants that may be suitable from every climatic zone in the world. (Section 550: Plants and Planting, includes some more data that may be useful when selecting and planting plants for roof and deck landscapes.)

REFERENCES

Baker, Maxwell C. *Roofs,* Multi-Science Publisher, Ltd., Montreal, Canada, 1980.

Central Mortgage & Housing Corp., Corp. Staff, and Consultants. *Roof Decks Design Guidelines,* CMHC, Montreal, Canada, 1979.

"Design Guidelines: Roof Garden Series," *Architect's Journal,* A. J. Information Library, London, 1980–1982.

Osmundson, Theodore. "The Changing Technique of Roof Garden Design," *Landscape Architecture Magazine,* Washington, DC, September 1981.

Wirth, Thomas. "Landscape Architecture above Ground," *Conference on Underground Space,* Vol. I (Harvard University, Cambridge, MA, 1976), Pergamon Press, London, 1976. ■

section 620: Interior Landscapes

CREDITS

Contributors:

Jay Graham
Graham Landscape Architecture
Annapolis, Maryland

Gerard Leider
Tropical Plants Rentals
Riverwood, Illinois

Reviewers:

Ellen Carlsen
Creative Plantings
Burtonsville, Maryland

Roger Cheever
City Gardens
Newton, Massachusetts

Nelson Hammer
Earl Flansburgh & Associates, Inc.
Boston, Massachusetts

CONTENTS

1.0 INTRODUCTION

In parts of the world where there are strong seasonal shifts in temperature, the design of interior landscapes requires special considerations with regard to the choice and care of the plant material used. Other aspects of interior landscape design and construction, (i.e., paving materials, landscape furniture, pools and fountains, etc.) are not significantly different than those same elements in the out-of-doors.

A major consideration when planning and designing interior landscapes is the need to create and maintain an artificial climate suitable for plant growth within a building, the primary function of which is to serve people rather than to grow plants.

With minor modifications to the physical conditions within a building, however, it is possible to find many plants, primarily from the tropical regions of the world, that will survive indoors at temperatures and environmental conditions also comfortable for human activity. This section will focus primarily on the physical needs and requirements of plant materials used within interior landscapes.

2.0 PHYSICAL REQUIREMENTS OF PLANTS

Figure 620-1 illustrates the many requirements necessary for satisfactory plant growth indoors.

2.1 Light

Growing plants convert radiant energy (from daylight or electric light sources) into food. Plants use radiant energy of wavelengths in the 400- to 850-nanometer (nm) range. White light, the visible part of the radiant energy spectrum, consists of wavelengths in the 430- to 700-nm range.

Light for plant growth is typically described in terms of intensity, duration, and quality.

Intensity:

Intensity of light is a quantitative figure typically measured in footcandles. One footcandle (fc) equals one lumen per square foot (lm/ft^2). A *lumen* is a specific quantity of light emitted by a light source and a *footcandle* is a quantitative measure of how much light is being received on a surface. (Refer to Section 540: Outdoor Lighting, for more information on definitions and principles of lighting.)

Different plants have varying minimum requirements for light intensity (Table 620-1). Bright daylight is typically about 5000 to 12,000 fc (depending on latitude, season, and time of day), while the average building interior sometimes receives 50 fc or less.

Duration:

While research continues to seek the necessary balance between intensity and duration for optimum plant growth, it is apparent that continuous illumination is not a suitable substitute for less than the minimum required intensity. Plants need periods of rest, each species having evolved unique preferences for particular photoperiods. The *average* photoperiod for plants is 8 to 12 hours of darkness and 12 to 16 hours of light. If only minimum light intensity is provided, optimum light duration must be provided.

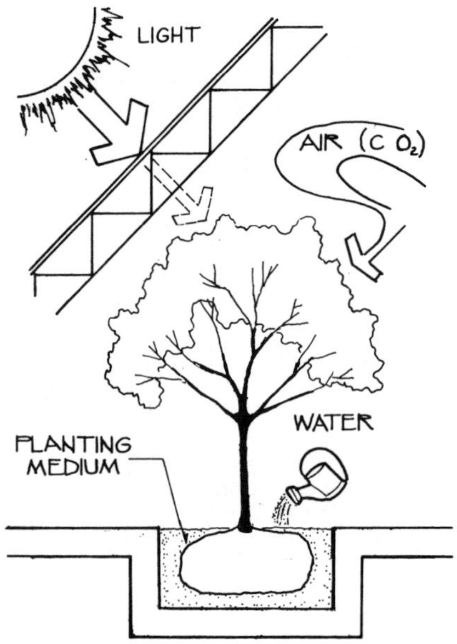
LIGHT
AIR (C O_2)
WATER
PLANTING MEDIUM

Figure 620-1 Physical requirements for interior plants.

Quality:

Light *quality* refers to the *type* of radiant energy available to plants. Figure 620-2 shows that plants use radiant energy primarily from the blue and red ends of the visible spectrum. Most electric light sources are primarily monochromatic and tend to emphasize the yellow-green part of the visible spectrum. Daylight, even in small amounts, can overcome the spectral deficiencies of electric light.

Radiant Energy Calculations:

Table 620-5 (in 5.4 Commonly Used Plants of this section) shows the energy requirements of typical plants. This table is based upon the formula: watts per hour per square meter (Wh/m^2). The use of this formula is explained in a book by Stephen Scrivens and an article by Dr. H. M. Cathey, both of which are listed in the References at the end of this section.

2.2 Temperature, Humidity, and Air Quality

Plant requirements for air typically refer to temperature, relative humidity, and air quality.

Temperature:

Most plants prefer a stable range of temperatures, with a drop of no more than 10 degrees F (5.6 degrees C) from daytime to nighttime temperature, 7 days a week. Tropical region plants generally fall into three categories, each with a preferred range of temperature: cool [40 to 60 degrees F day (4 to 16 degrees C)]; intermediate [50 to 70 degrees F day (10 to 21 degrees C)]; and warm [60 to 85 degrees F day (16 to 29 degrees C)]. Cold temperatures [i.e., 32 degrees F or less (0 degrees C)], even for a short period, can cause permanent damage to foliage. If the temperature of the root ball falls below 50 degrees F (10 degrees C), plant growth will stop, and plants will die if the temperature drops below 30 degrees F (−1 degree C) (Figure 620-3).

Relative Humidity:

Tropical plants prefer a relative humidity of 60 to 90 percent, but most are adaptable to the 35 to 50 percent relative humidity typical of building interiors. This low relative humidity is a better range for disease prevention. If the humidity is ±30 percent or lower, then most plants will require greater amounts of water.

Air Quality:

Plants require carbon dioxide (CO_2) to complete photosynthesis. Air movement helps to maintain ready supplies of CO_2 and to reduce any excessive buildup of heat, but plants can be harmed by hot or cold blasts of air. If the flow of air causes the leaves to move at velocities in excess of 5 fps (1.5 m/s), then the air movement is excessive and is likely to damage the plants. Pollutants in the air, such as cleaning fluids, paints, or petroleum products in quantity, can have a devastating effect on plant foliage, usually turning it black. Most interiors do not have the optimum environmental conditions necessary for plants to regenerate a large amount of damaged foliage.

2.3 Water

The amount of water needed by plants indoors depends upon the physical conditions inherent in a building's design, the time of day, and the season of the year, as well as upon temporary situations in the building. Plants will transpire rapidly in conditions of high light and/or high temperature and/or low humidity, therefore requiring more frequent watering. One of the most important reasons for regular maintenance is to monitor each plant's special need for water. Unsoftened water at a temperature no lower than 60 degrees F (16 degrees C) should be used. Plants should be grouped according to their water requirements. Some plants require that their root balls dry out somewhat, while others require their roots to remain moist or even wet most of the time.

TABLE 620-1
Recommended Lighting Levels

Lighting level	Minimum fc (lx)	Recommended
Low	50 (540)	75–150 (800–1600)
Medium	75–100 (800–1070)	200+ (2150+)
High	200 (2150)	500 (5400)
Very high	500 (5400)	1000 (1100)

2.4 Planting Medium

The planting medium, which may or may not contain any soil, must accomplish three functions:

1. Allow water and nutrients to reach the plant through the roots.

2. Allow oxygen to reach the roots.

3. Anchor and give stability to the plant.

A planting medium should be:

1. Porous
2. Easy to drain
3. Capable of retaining water
4. Sterile
5. Low in soluble salts
6. Lightweight (where needed)

2.5 Space/Volume

It is important to know both the existing and potential height, breadth, and character of each type of plant in order to minimize interference not only between plants but also between them and such architectural features as columns, bulkheads, stairs, and low ceilings (Figure 620-4). With large species of plants, this need for adequate room becomes critical. A plant whose innate form has to be reshaped to accommodate architectural features will usually appear misshapen and incongruous with its interior setting.

2.6 Weight of Plants

The weight of the plants and their planting medium is an important consideration when they are a part of the load calculations for a structural slab or an upper floor planter. The weight of a plant will depend upon its age (caliper), height, head size, and foliage density. The weight of the planting medium varies according to both the material used and the amount of water it contains. A lightweight soil mix is given in Section 610: Roof and Deck Landscapes, and other qualities of the planting medium are covered in Section 810: Soils and Aggregates.

2.7 Acclimatization

Plants being moved from the ideal light conditions of a greenhouse or nursery into a building interior must slowly be acclimatized to the lower light conditions. Without this period of adjustment, most plants will go into shock, stop growing, become weakened, and possibly die. The length of time required to acclimatize a plant depends on the species, the degree of change in light intensity, and the size of the plant. Large trees [10 ft (3 m) or larger] should be allowed at least 3 to 6 months during the growing season to acclimate, and small material [24 in (600 mm) or less] at least 6 to 10 weeks. During this time, the amount of light should be gradually reduced to half the original amount.

2.8 Maintenance

The main purpose of plant maintenance is to meet all the physical requirements of the plants on a continual basis. Specific maintenance tasks include the supplying of water and fertilizer, the control of insects on an as-needed basis, and pruning. The quality of maintenance will be the main determinant in calculating the actual versus the potential life of the plants.

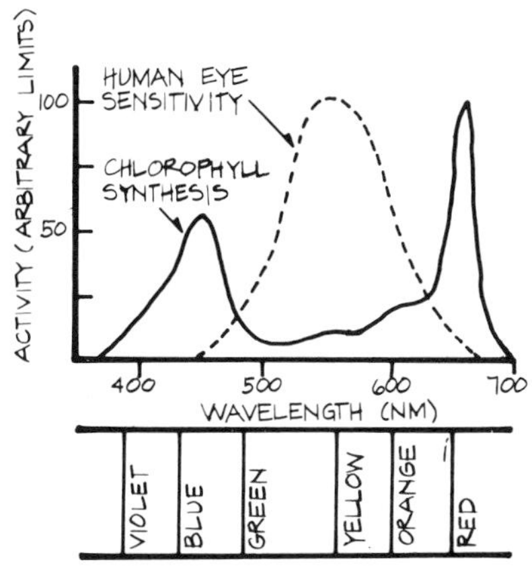
ACTIVITY (ARBITRARY LIMITS)
100
50
HUMAN EYE SENSITIVITY
CHLOROPHYLL SYNTHESIS
400
500
600
700
WAVELENGTH (NM)
VIOLET
BLUE
GREEN
YELLOW
ORANGE
RED

Figure 620-2 Response curves for the manufacture of chlorophyll.

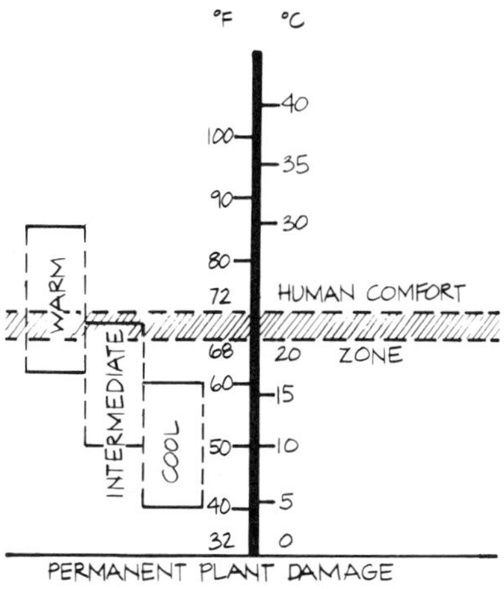
°F
°C
40
100
35
90
30
80
72
HUMAN COMFORT
68
20
ZONE
60
15
50
10
40
5
32
0
WARM
INTERMEDIATE
COOL
PERMANENT PLANT DAMAGE

Figure 620-3 Temperature range of plants.

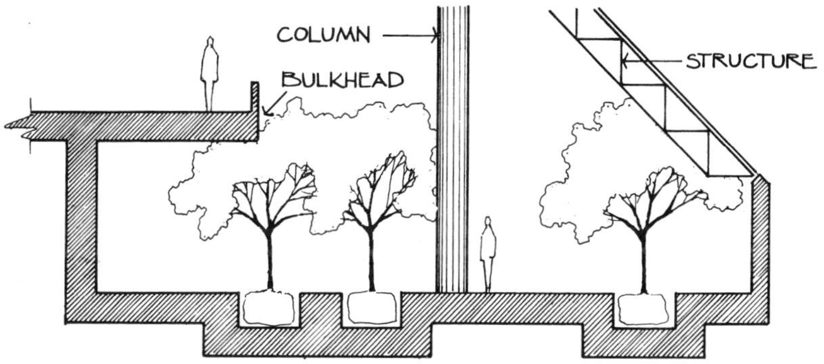
COLUMN
BULKHEAD
STRUCTURE

Figure 620-4 Height and spread of large materials.

3.0 TECHNIQUES AND TECHNOLOGIES TO MEET PHYSICAL REQUIREMENTS

3.1 Light

Light can be provided either from daylight or electric light. Daylight is preferable because it provides a greater spectrum of the radiant energy needed by most plants. However, where daylight is insufficient in quantity or duration (due to the season or the time of day), electric light is often an essential supplementary source.

Daylight:

Daylight refers to the sum of direct sunlight, reflected sunlight, and (on overcast days) skylight. Daylight can be admitted into interior landscapes through windows, clerestories, or skylights.

Windows and Clerestories: Windows and clerestories are only about one-third as efficient in admitting light as are the overhead horizontal openings of skylights (Figures 620-5 and 620-6). Window efficiency is determined by its size, the orientation of the opening, and the type of glazing. In the northern hemisphere, the effective area for plant growth, given a southerly solar orientation, is equal in depth only to the height of the window, assuming that the plants are located at sill height.

Skylights: Skylights have the advantage of encouraging plants to grow upward toward the light (Figure 620-7). If skylights are included as part of the building design for the purpose of providing daylight for interior plants, then there are a number of important considerations for maximizing their effectiveness:

1. *Location:* skylights and plants are more effectively related if they are not aligned in plan but aligned for the angle of the sun to hit the plants.
2. *Orientation:* in the northern hemisphere, north facing skylights are only min-

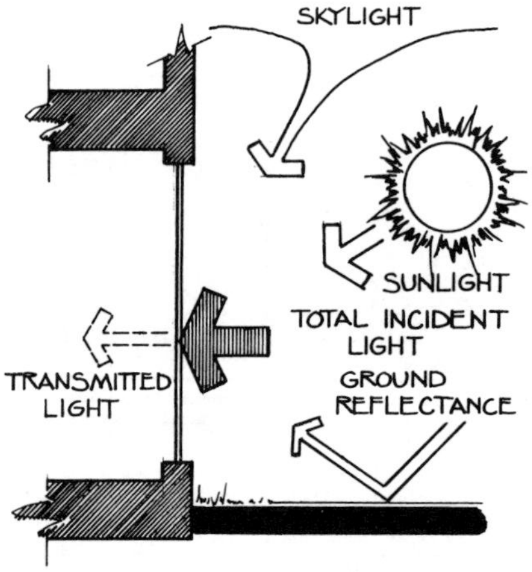
SKYLIGHT
SUNLIGHT
TOTAL INCIDENT LIGHT
TRANSMITTED LIGHT
GROUND REFLECTANCE

Figure 620-5 Daylight through vertical glazing.

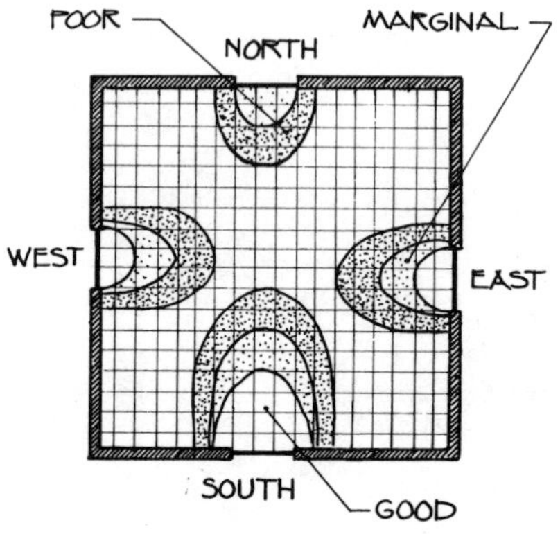
POOR
MARGINAL
NORTH
WEST
EAST
SOUTH
GOOD

Figure 620-6 Effectiveness of daylight through vertical glazing 3 ft wide by 5 ft high (1-ft grid) (northern hemisphere).

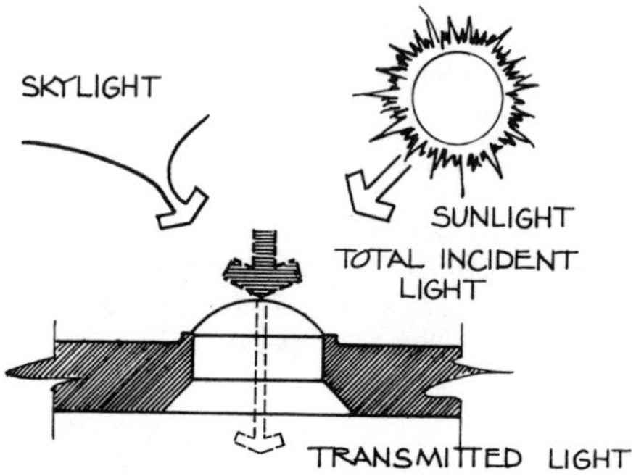
SKYLIGHT
SUNLIGHT
TOTAL INCIDENT LIGHT
TRANSMITTED LIGHT

Figure 620-7 Daylight through skylight.

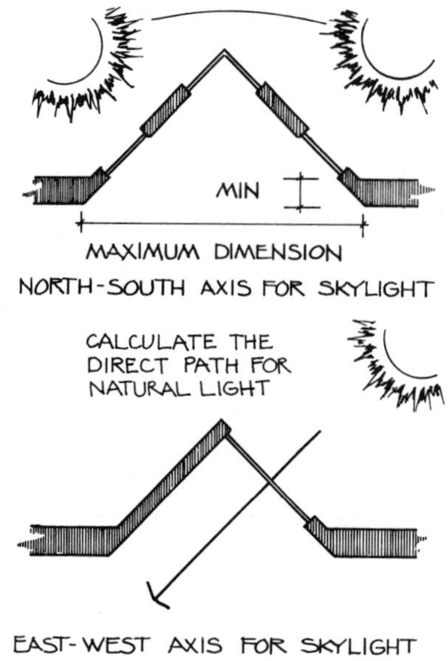
MIN
MAXIMUM DIMENSION
NORTH-SOUTH AXIS FOR SKYLIGHT
CALCULATE THE DIRECT PATH FOR NATURAL LIGHT
EAST-WEST AXIS FOR SKYLIGHT

Figure 620-8 Optimum skylight features.

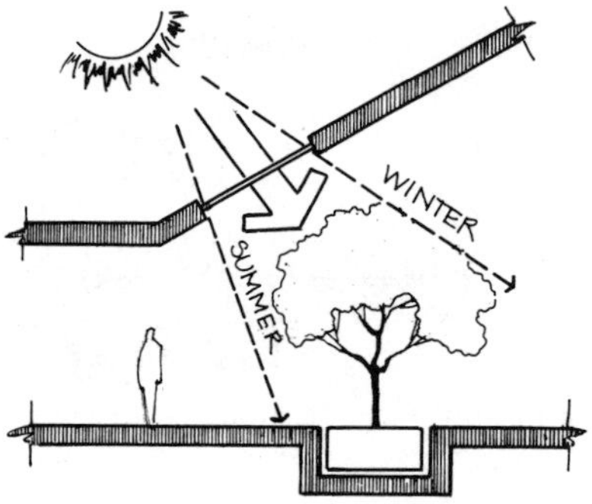
WINTER
SUMMER

Figure 620-9 Placement of skylights.

imally effective. South facing skylights (east-west axis) can provide too much direct light and cause a one-sided plant growth, but they are a good source of reflected light. A mix of east and west facing skylights (north-south axis) provides a better balance of light (Figure 620-8).

3. *Details:* the design of a skylight system that will admit the maximum amount of light possible is as follows:

a. Bulkhead: a minimal distance from ceiling to skylight frame will permit a more direct path for the daylight. Light-colored walls surrounding the bulkhead will increase the amount of reflected light (Figure 620-9).

b. Ceiling opening: if the ceiling opening is larger than the skylight opening, the area influenced by the brightness from the skylight will be extended (Figure 620-8).

Glazing Materials: The glass or plastic used in windows or skylights will have varying properties of light transmittance and reflection. The preconstruction calculations should include daylight figures which take into account the type of glazing material and the amount of light it will transmit. This information is available from all manufacturers of glass and plastic. The range varies from clear glass at 84 percent transmission to double-glazing with bronze tint at 18 percent transmission. (Refer to Section 870: Glass, Plastics, and Fabrics, for more information on the types and properties of glass and plastic for glazing purposes.)

TABLE 620-2
Recommended Light Sources

Distance between light source and plant	Recommended light source
10 ft (3 m) and less	Daylight: vertical glazing, skylights Cool-white flourescent Natural-light fluorescent Mercury lamp, low wattage Incandescent
10–15 ft (3.0–4.6 m)	Daylight: vertical glazing, skylights Quartz–metal halide combination High-pressure sodium lamp (only for plant lighting) Metal halide lamp, phosphor-coated Mercury lamp, deluxe-white Mercury lamp, warm deluxe-white High-pressure sodium (color-rendition a design factor) Quartz-halogen lamp Incandescent
15 ft (4.6 m) and greater	Daylight: vertical glazing, skylights Quartz–metal halide combination High-pressure sodium lamp (only for plant lighting) Metal halide lamp, clear Metal halide lamp, phosphor-coated Mercury lamp, deluxe-white High-pressure sodium (color rendition a design factor) Quartz-halogen lamp Incandescent

TABLE 620-3
Characteristics of Electric Lamps

Characteristics	*Tungsten, halogen, and incandescent*	*Fluorescent*	*Mercury vapor*	*Metal halide*	*High-pressure sodium*	*Low-pressure sodium*
Lumens per watt	6–23	25–100	30–63	68–125	77–140	137–183
Lumens	40–33,600	96–15,000	1200–63,000	12,000–125,000	5400–140,000	4800–33,000
Lumens per watt (%)* maintenance	75–97	75–91	70–86	73–83	90–92	75–90
Wattage range†	6–1500	4–215	40–1000	175–1500	70–1000	35–180
Life†	750–8000	9000–20,000	16,000–24,000+	1500–15,000	20,000–24,000	18,000
Color temperature†	2400–3100	2700–6500	3300–5900	3200–4700	2100	1780
Color rendition†	95–99	55–95	22–52	65–70	21	0
Color breadth of application	Good	Good	Fair	Good	Fair	Poor
Control	Excellent	Poor	Fair	Fair to good	Good	Poor
Initial cost (per lamp)	Low	Moderate	Moderate	High	High	Moderate
Operational cost (power)	High	Moderate	Moderate	Low	Low	Low
Breadth of application	Wide	Wide	Medium	Medium to wide	Narrow	Narrow

* Percentage of output in lumens during life of the bulb.

† Lumens.

Source: Courtesy of GTE Sylvania Lighting Products.

Electric Light:

Normally, electric lighting should be treated only as a supplement to daylight. Electric light has the advantage of being flexible and can therefore achieve good light distribution over plants at optimum footcandle levels. The beamspread of lamps should be considered in the design of lamp spacing. Uplighting will not contribute significantly to plant growth.

Table 620-2 shows the recommended lighting sources for plants. They are listed in order of priority based on plant growth efficiency, color rendition preference, and energy efficiency. Table 620-3 gives data on the characteristics of electric lamps, and Table 620-4 gives information on the suitability of various lamps for plant growth.

TABLE 620-4
Lamp Suitability for Interior Plant Lighting

Types of lamps	*Responses to interior plants*
Incandescent and tungsten halogen	Lamps produce high amounts of infrared energy, which increases the transpiration rate in foliage. They have a high ratio of red to blue energy, which causes long internodes and spindly growth.
Fluorescent	Cool-white and warm-white lamps are deficient in the red and far-red wavelengths. Add 10 to 20% (by wattage) of incandescent lamps to promote more normal growth responses. Standard Gro-Lux and wide spectrum Gro-Lux provide a balance in the red, far-red, and blue regions of the spectrum for optimum plant responses.
Mercury	Of the lamps in the mercury family, bright-white deluxe lamps provide the best light characteristics for plant growth.
Metal halide	Coated metal halide (Metalarc-coated) lamps provide the best light characteristics (red, far-red, and blue wavelengths) of all high-energy discharge (HID) lamps. These are especially suitable for totally enclosed growth areas, such as growthrooms and interior landscapes.
High-pressure sodium (HPS)	These lamps distort colors of ornamental plants because of insufficient blue wavelength emissions. Therefore, they should not be used alone for lighting interior plants. HPS lamps are useful to supplement natural daylight (sunlight).
Low-pressure sodium (LPS)	These lamps are poor sources of light for interior plants because they are monochromatic, emit light in the yellow wavelength, and give poor color renditions.

Source: Adapted from a table prepared by Christos Mpelkas, Plant Pathologist, GTE Sylvania Lighting Products.

3.2 Air

Providing plants with proper aboveground and in-ground temperatures is important and should be considered during the conceptual stage of any building design (Figure 620-10). In temperate climates, the following locations should be avoided:

1. Planting over unheated spaces such as parking garages because root balls need protection from low temperatures

2. Planting near outside doors because drafts are difficult to control

3. Planting immediately adjacent to heating and air-conditioning supply vents because air movement normally exceeds the tolerance of most interior plants

If interior landscape design is studied in both plan and section as well as coordinated with the mechanical systems involved, then such problems as the following can be avoided:

1. Plants located in dead-air corners

2. Plants located against glass walls with no mechanical system to modify extremes in temperature

3. The tops of large plant material or hanging plants located in the poorly conditioned zones near high ceilings and in multistory spaces

3.3 Water

Two methods of watering plants are hand watering and automatic system watering. Many techniques are used that vary and combine these two basic methods.

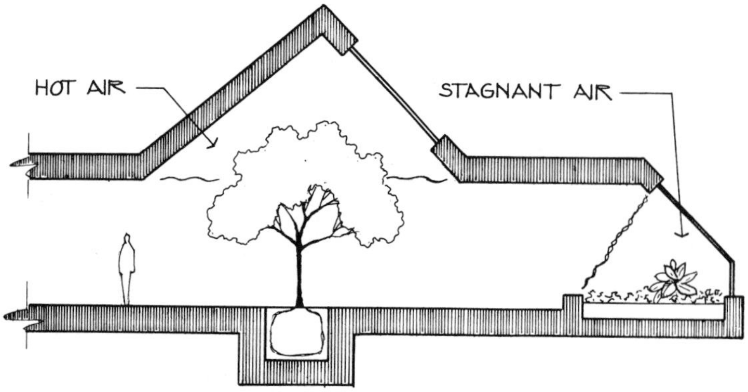
HOT AIR
STAGNANT AIR

Figure 620-10 Air circulation problems.

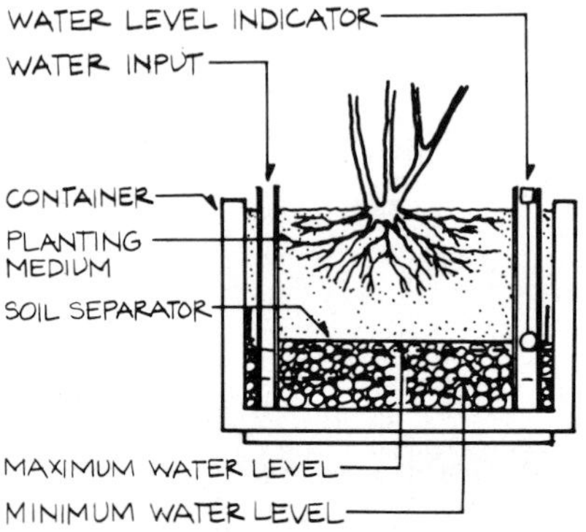
WATER LEVEL INDICATOR
WATER INPUT
CONTAINER
PLANTING MEDIUM
SOIL SEPARATOR
MAXIMUM WATER LEVEL
MINIMUM WATER LEVEL

Figure 620-11 Planter with reservoir.

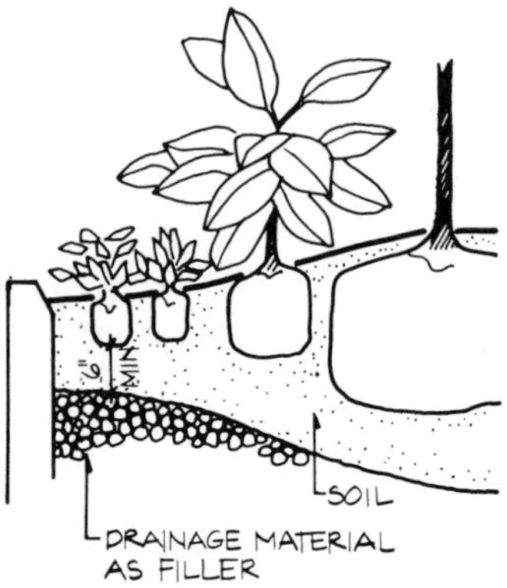
SOIL
DRAINAGE MATERIAL AS FILLER

Figure 620-12 Necessary soil depth.

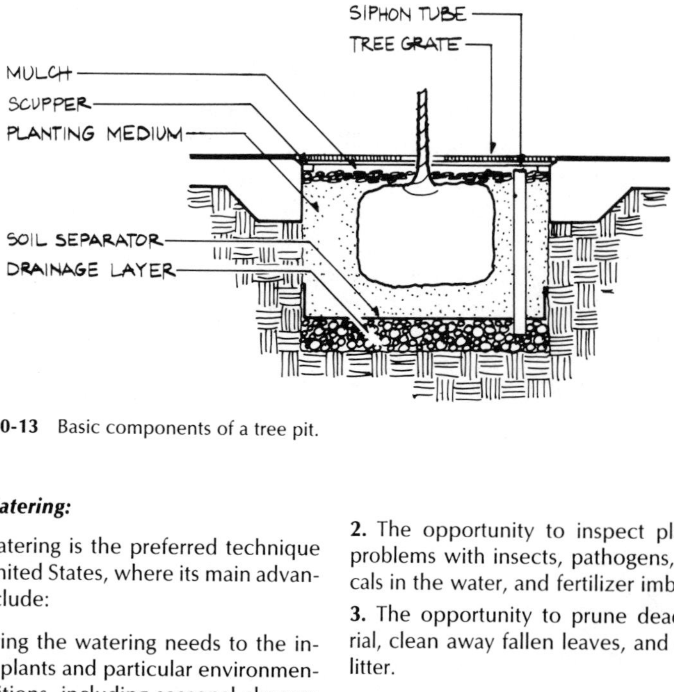
SIPHON TUBE
TREE GRATE
MULCH
SCUPPER
PLANTING MEDIUM
SOIL SEPARATOR
DRAINAGE LAYER

Figure 620-13 Basic components of a tree pit.

Hand Watering:

Hand watering is the preferred technique in the United States, where its main advantages include:

1. Tailoring the watering needs to the individual plants and particular environmental conditions, including seasonal changes in the water requirements of plants (note that many contractors will not guarantee plant health if the plants are watered *automatically*).

2. The opportunity to inspect plants for problems with insects, pathogens, chemicals in the water, and fertilizer imbalance.

3. The opportunity to prune dead material, clean away fallen leaves, and remove litter.

Tools and facilities needed for hand watering include:

1. Hose bibbs or box hydrants convenient for use with 50-ft (15-m) hoses.

2. Access to a sink for a watering cart. The sink should have a threaded hose faucet and at least a 24-in (600-mm) clearance from faucet to sink or floor.

3. A hot-and-cold water mixer faucet.

4. A wand used to water hanging baskets or hard-to-reach ledges.

5. Water carts and watering cans of assorted sizes.

6. Custom-designed equipment for special situations. If such equipment is needed, it would have to be stored in a lockable closet within the building.

Two disadvantages of hand watering are that it is labor-intensive and that all plants need to be accessible.

One variation on hand watering is a system of containers which have their own reservoirs, thus cutting down the number of times that maintenance personnel must water each plant (Figure 620-11). This system has been developed and used in the United Kingdom, where labor costs are a major item in all maintenance contracts.

Automatic Systems:

Most irrigation systems for exterior landscapes are technically possible for interiors but may have one or more of the following disadvantages:

1. The components are prone to vandalism.

2. The system is often ill-suited to the different watering requirements of any multivariety plant palette.

3. The system needs to be monitored for seasonal adjustment and for adjustments required by temporary changes in growing conditions.

The main advantage of an automatic system is that plants in inaccessible locations are often more easily reached. An automatic system may also be advantageous if plants with similar water needs are planted in groups.

3.4 Planting Medium

The ingredients used in a planting mix will depend on their availability, on weight restraints, and on the needs of the particular plants. Soil and soilless mixtures all contain various proportions of the following ingredients and have the indicated weights per cubic foot (cubic meter):

1. *Topsoil:* sandy loam, uniform in composition and free of debris. Weight: 100 lb/ft^3 (45 kg/0.028 m^3).

2. *Peat:* has good water holding capacity, but does not compact readily. Weight: 8 to 10 lb/ft^3 (3.6 to 4.5 kg/0.028 m^3).

3. *Sand:* has poor water holding capacity. Weight: 100 lb/ft^3 (45 kg/0.028 m^3).

4. *Shredded bark:* pine bark is best; hardwood is good. Both have good water holding capacity.

5. *Vermiculite:* a soil additive made of expanded mica. It contains some nutrients and has good water holding capacity. It breaks down under sterilization and therefore cannot be used repeatedly. Weight: 6 to 8 lb/ft^3 (2.7 to 3.6 kg/0.028 m^3).

6. *Perlite:* a soil additive made of siliceous volcanic rock. It contains fluoride, which will damage some plants. It has good porosity and some water holding capacity. Because it does not deteriorate, it can be resterilized and reused. Weight: 6 to 8 lb/ft^3 (2.7 to 3.6 kg/0.028 m^3).

7. *Calcined clay:* a soil additive made of fired clay particles. It retains water and can be reused.

8. *Styrofoam particles:* a soil additive made of plastic. It holds no water, increases the porosity of the mix, and disintegrates under sterilization; therefore, it cannot be reused.

Soil mixtures normally consist of 20 to 30 percent soil and 70 to 80 percent soil additives (see Figure 620-12). Mixtures without soil use variations on the following proportion:

⅓ sand

⅓ shredded bark

⅓ soil additives

3.5 Construction Details

Tree pits and built-in planters for interior plantings have some features that distinguish them from exterior plantings.

1. The need for a tree pit (with sides and a bottom) should be determined after investigation of existing conditions of the soil, underground springs, and draining ability (Figure 620-13).

2. Insulation may be necessary if the tree pit is above an unheated space in temperate climates, such as a parking garage. Heating coils might also be necessary to maintain the root ball temperature above 50 degrees F (10 degrees C).

3. Drains should be included whenever possible and appropriate. A siphon pipe can be used to check the viability of the drain or to check the water retention in the absence of a drain (Figures 620-14 and 620-15).

4. A scupper around each tree pit will serve to catch toxic floor cleansers and waxing liquids.

5. When hose bibbs and electrical junction boxes are included in tree pits or planters, they should be located to the sides, away from where the major plants are located.

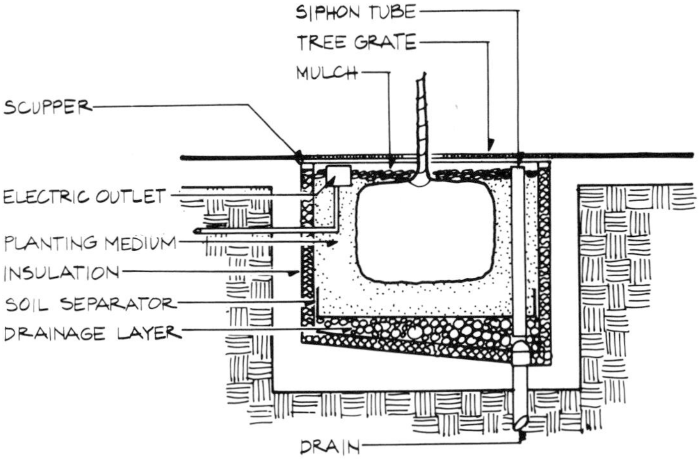
SIPHON TUBE
TREE GRATE
MULCH
SCUPPER
ELECTRIC OUTLET
PLANTING MEDIUM
INSULATION
SOIL SEPARATOR
DRAINAGE LAYER
DRAIN

Figure 620-14 Optional features of a tree pit.

6. Planters should be waterproofed if they are surrounded by a fountain. Water from a fountain may contain chemicals harmful to plants.

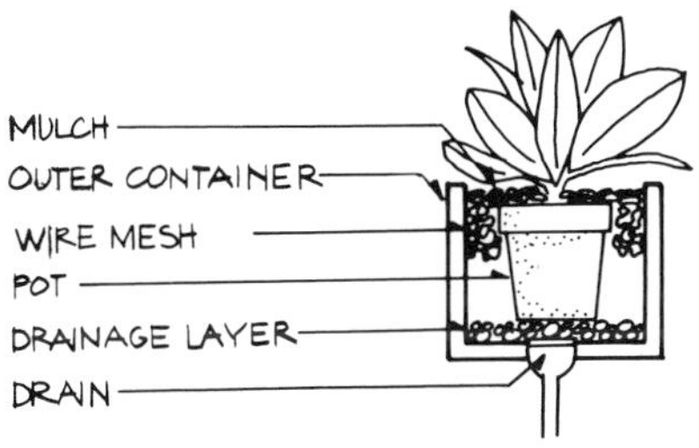
MULCH
OUTER CONTAINER
WIRE MESH
POT
DRAINAGE LAYER
DRAIN

Figure 620-15 Features of built-in planters.

4.0 DESIGN PROCESS

The following considerations and procedure are offered to help guide design work on projects involving the design and construction of interior landscapes. The steps in this procedure focus on problem solving related to the use of plants inside buildings.

1. Review with the client and the design team working on the project the expected role of the interior landscape. Determine whether it is to be a major statement or a background complement to the building.

2. Based upon its role, determine the environmental needs of the interior landscape as early in the design process as possible.

3. Determine the sizes of the largest plants so that sufficient space can be provided without interference from columns, stairs, and similar major elements of the building. The structural engineer needs to know where the major plants will be placed and whether they will be put into tubs sitting on the floor slab or put into pits set into the floor.

4. Plants should be located to minimize unnecessary physical contact with people, but access to all plants for maintenance purposes should be provided.

5. Plants should be selected that will survive under the expected levels of light but will not outgrow their space in a short time. (Note that, in most cases, plants in interior spaces seldom grow much more after they are installed.)

6. All constructed elements, such as built-in planters and watering and drainage systems, should be coordinated with the overall design of the building.

7. If possible, select contractors who have prior experience with interior plantings.

8. Select and tag all large and specimen plant materials far enough ahead of time to allow the plants to be acclimatized in some reliable way before they are installed.

9. All of the interior landscape's environmental systems (lighting, water, air handling, etc.) should be tested and working before any plants are installed. Responsibility for alternative solutions should be established in advance in case any system fails.

10. Maintenance should begin at the time of installation.

11. Access from the outside of a building to interior locations where the planting is being done should be provided. For example, a 200-gal (760-L) plant will require an opening 8 ft (2.4 m) square in order to enter a building. There is also the need for a long-term access route if major plants have to be replaced.

5.0 PLANT PALETTE

5.1 Design Objectives

1. A feeling of transition from exterior space to interior space should be created.

2. A proper sense of scale should be given to large interior spaces.

3. Different functions should be separated physically and visually.

4. Architectural forms should be complemented with plants primarily through contrast in form, texture, and color.

PLATYCERIUM BIFURCATUM
PHYLODENDRON OXYICARDIUM
CISSUS RHOMBIFOLIA
PTYCHOSPERM ELEGANS
FICUS RETUSA NITIDA
BUCIDA BUCERAS
HOWEA FORSTERANA
POLYSCIAS FRUTICOSA
LIRIOPE MUSCARI
AGLAONEMA 'SILVER QUEEN'
SPATHIPYLLUM WALLISII

Figure 620-16 Size comparison of interior plants.

5.2 Character of Interior Plants

Size:

Interior plants can be grouped by the following categories of sizes: groundcovers, small understory, large understory, and trees. Vines and hanging plants are another category. (Refer to 5.4 Commonly Used Plants in this section for height ranges in each of these categories.)

Many plant species can be used in more than one category, depending on their particular size and habit of growth. The height and spread at the time of planting becomes very important because most plants will not continue to grow significantly, once planted indoors, unless given more than their minimum light requirements. Detailed height and spread information is available in the United States from growers through the Associated Landscape Contractors of America (ALCA) guide (see the References at the end of this section). Normal size ranges are shown on the scale in Figure 620-16.

PHOENIX ROEBELENII DOUBLE
FICUS BENJAMINA STANDARD
SPATHIPHYLLUM 'MAUNA LOA' CLUMP
BRACAENA FRAGRANS CANE
BRASSAIA ACTINOPHYLLA MULTI-STEM
BRACAENA MARGINATA SCULPTURED

Figure 620-17 Various growth habits of interior plants.

Growth Habit:

Growth habit refers to the distribution of foliage on a plant and the character of its trunk or trunks. Plants for interior landscapes can be selected that have a wide variety of growth habits from stems or trunks that are single, multiple, straight, or curved (Figure 620-17).

Texture:

Tropical plants are particularly versatile in terms of texture, given their wide range of leaf sizes. The juxtaposition of plants with widely different textures is one of the characteristics associated with creating a tropical appearance (Figure 620-18). Many trunks and stems also give a feeling of texture—from the smooth trunk of the *Ficus* to the coarse trunk of some of the palms.

BRACAENA MARGINATA
SANSEVIERIA TRIFASCIATA
AGLAONEMA 'SILVER QUEEN'
PHILODENDRON OXYCARDIUM
DIEFFENBACHIA 'TROPIC SNOW'
BRASSAIA ARBORICOLA
NEPHROLEPSIS EXALTATA 'BOSTONIENSIS'
PHILODENDRON SELLOUM

Figure 620-18 The textural range of interior plants.

Color:

Flowers are considered the source of color for most plantings, but flowering typically

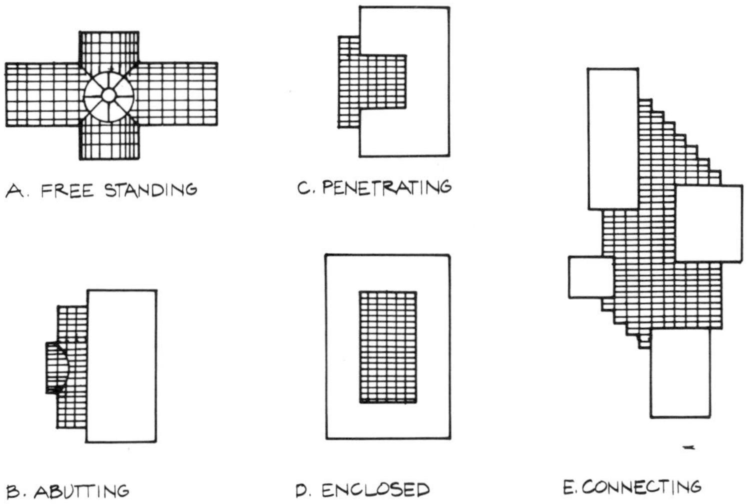
A. FREE STANDING
C. PENETRATING
B. ABUTTING
D. ENCLOSED
E. CONNECTING

Figure 620-19 Building prototypes with interior landscapes.

Figure 620-20 Plants as part of a total interior landscape composition.

requires a high level of light, and plants must be rotated every 3 to 4 weeks. A wide range of colors is available via plant foliage, however, including a range of greens (dark to light), yellow-greens to blue-greens, and variegated varieties (light and dark markings). Color variation is sometimes highlighted, as with texture, by placing plants to emphasize the contrasts.

5.3 Design Suggestions

1. The need for high levels of light, particularly natural light, and the use of glass-enclosed spaces to achieve a transition from exteriors to interiors have resulted in a few common identifiable architectural and interior landscape prototypes (Figure 620-19).

2. Plants should be grouped into massings as a counterbalance to the more dominant architectural forms. Although a matter of subjectivity, most interior planting designs cannot function effectively as part of the overall design unless they are dramatic in quantity, size, and arrangement (Figure 620-20).

3. Regional differences and styles in design can be achieved by selecting plants based on their character, size, and texture, and by the manner in which they are composed. The character of a temperate, tropical, or arid landscape can be replicated through the choice and use of various plants and construction materials. Also, the use of specimen plantings can make a design especially distinctive. The style of planters can also set a tone or establish a particular character.

4. In addition to plants, other landscape elements—such as water features, landforms, and rocks—can be used to help create a variety of landscape effects.

5. Given the relatively low light conditions in typical interior settings [150 fc (1614.6 lx) or less], most interior plants will usually not flower (*Spathiphyllum* is one exception that will flower at 100 fc or greater). For permanent color in the design, therefore, plants grown specifically for their flowers should be used. Flowering plants will need to be changed approximately every 2 to 3 weeks if the flowers are to remain fresh in appearance. A flower selection schedule should be established and coordinated with whatever materials are available locally.

Summary:

1. Creating the proper environment for plants is essential.

2. Light intensity is the most important physical requirement of plants and is usually not adequately present in interior spaces.

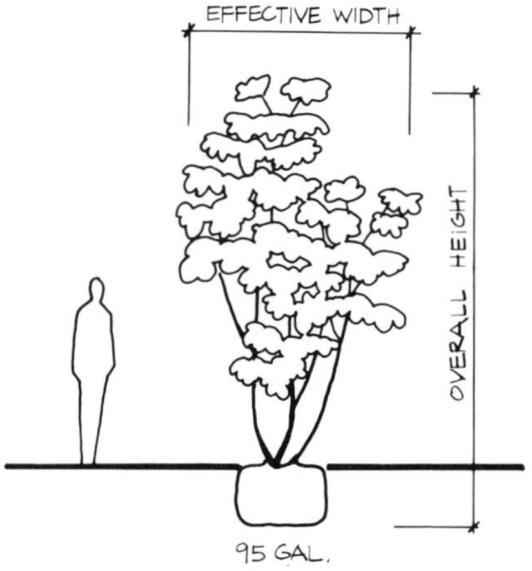
EFFECTIVE WIDTH
OVERALL HEIGHT
95 GAL.

Figure 620-21 *Brassaia actinophylla* (1-ft grid).

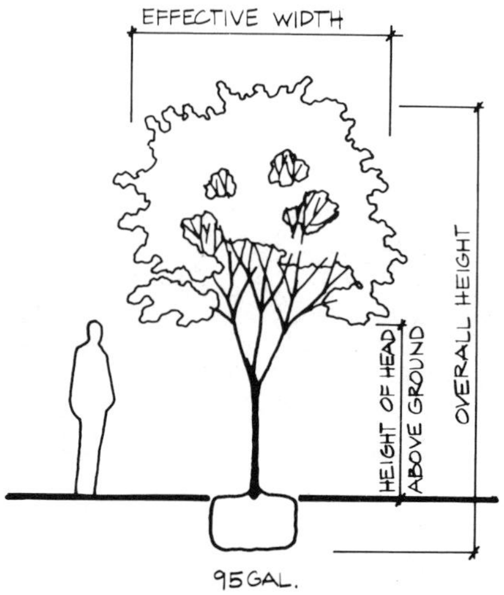
EFFECTIVE WIDTH
HEIGHT OF HEAD ABOVE GROUND
OVERALL HEIGHT
95 GAL.

Figure 620-22 *Ficus benjamina* (standard) (1-ft grid).

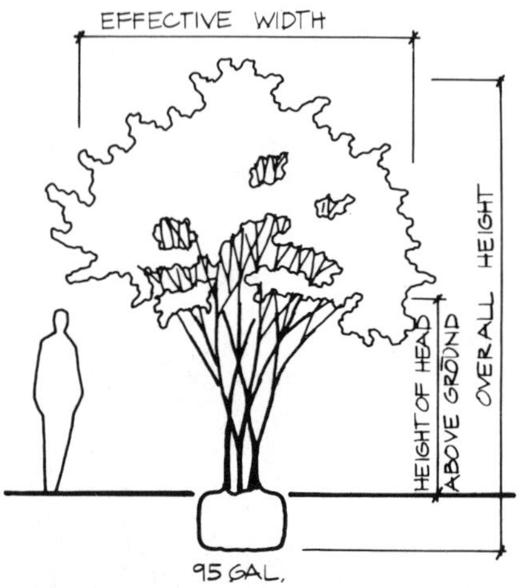
EFFECTIVE WIDTH
HEIGHT OF HEAD ABOVE GROUND
OVERALL HEIGHT
95 GAL.

Figure 620-23 *Ficus benjamina* (multitrunk) (1-ft grid).

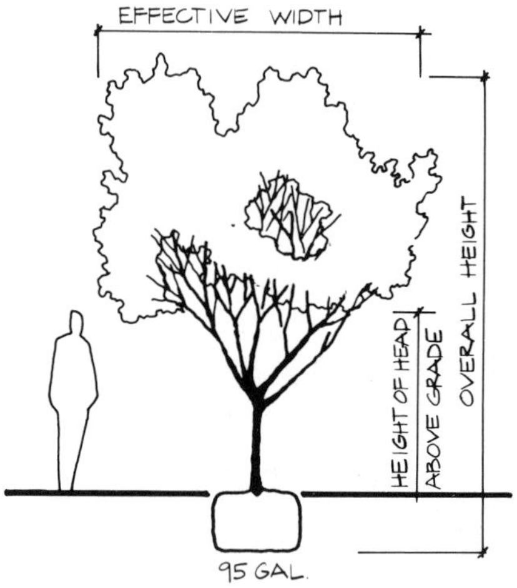
EFFECTIVE WIDTH
HEIGHT OF HEAD ABOVE GRADE
OVERALL HEIGHT
95 GAL.

Figure 620-24 *Ficus retusa nitida* (1-ft grid).

EFFECTIVE WIDTH
HEIGHT OF HEAD ABOVE GROUND
OVERALL HEIGHT
125 GAL.

Figure 620-25 *Phoenix canariensis* (1-ft grid).

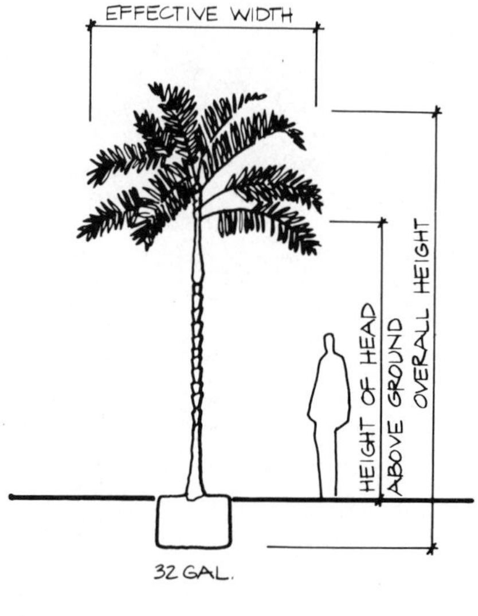
EFFECTIVE WIDTH
HEIGHT OF HEAD ABOVE GROUND
OVERALL HEIGHT
32 GAL.

Figure 620-26 *Ptychosperma elegans* (single) (1-ft grid).

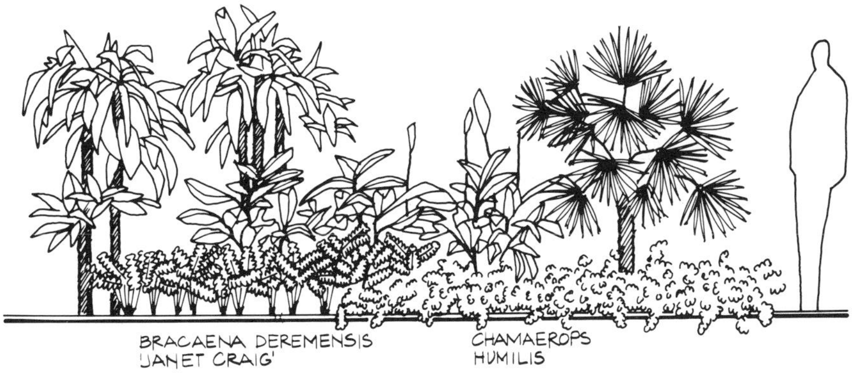
BRACAENA DEREMENSIS
'JANET CRAIG'
CHAMAEROPS
HUMILIS

Figure 620-27 Large understory specimens.

CHAMAEDOREA
ELEGANS
SPATHIPHYLLUM
'MAUNA LOA'
ASPARAGUS
SPRENGERI

Figure 620-28 Small understory specimens.

3. Early involvement in the planning and design of an interior landscape can minimize many potential technical problems.

4. Experimentation with plant species is valid as long as the basic physical requirements are met.

5. Maintenance of a constant climatic condition (24 hours/day, 7 days/week) is critically important.

6. Skillful and continual maintenance, especially of the plants, must be part of the initial program to help ensure the lasting integrity of the design and the survival of the plants.

5.4 Commonly Used Plants

Size Categories:

Interior plants are typically categorized according to the following sizes:

Trees	5 to 25 ft or more (15 to 76 mm)
Large understory	3 to 5 ft (9 to 15 mm)
Small understory	1 to 3 ft (3 to 9 mm)
Groundcover	0 to 1 ft (0 to 3mm)
Vines and hanging plants	Not categorized by size

Plant List:

Figures 620-21 through 620-28 show various plants that have proved to be viable as interior plants and are readily available in North America. Many other species and certainly additional varieties exist that may be as good or better for specific purposes. Designers are urged to keep alert to new plants and to explore new ways to use other familiar plants.

Environmental Conditions:

The number of plants available to the designer increases dramatically as the physical requirements of plants (particularly light) are optimized. Table 620-5 gives information on the range of environmental conditions that various plants require.

REFERENCES

ALCA Guide to Interior Landscaping, Associated Landscape Contractors of America, 1750 Meadow Road, McLean, VA 22102, 1982.

Bednar, Michael J. *The New Atrium,* McGraw-Hill, New York, 1986.

Cathey, H. M. "Rays, The Basis of Light: Indoor Gardening," *Interiorscape,* December 1982.

Furuga, Tok. *Interior Landscaping,* Reston Publication Co., Inc., Reston, VA, 1983.

Gaines, Richard L. *Interior Plantscaping,* Architectural Record Books, New York, 1977.

Graf, Alfred B. *Exotica, Series IV,* Roehrs, East Rutherford, NJ, 1985.

Manaker, George H., *Interior Plantscape,* Prentice-Hall, Englewood Cliffs, NJ, 1981.

Scrivens, Stephen. *Interior Planting in Large Buildings,* The Architectural Press, London, 1980. ■

TABLE 620-5a
Lighting Requirements for Commonly Used Plants—Trees

	Light				*Temperature*			*Moisture*			*Size (Height)*		*Weight*		*Character*			*Use*
Botanical name, common name	*Low, 50 fc*	*Medium, 75–100 fc*	*High, 200 fc*	*Very high, 500 fc*	*Cool, 40–60°*	*Inter-mediate, 50–70°*	*Warm, 62–85°*	*Dry*	*Moist*	*Wet*	*Normal*	*Max., ft*	*Normal*	*Max., lb*	*Broad-leaf*	*Palm*	*Other*	*Large understory*
Aiphanes caryotaefolia, spine palm			o				o		o		5–20	30	2500	6000		o		
Araucaria heterophylla, Norfolk Island pine			o			o			o		3–15	25	1500	5000			o	o
Arecastrum romanzoffianum, queen palm			o				o			o	5–20	30	2500	6000		o		
Beaucarnea recurvata, ponytail palm				o		o		o			2–10	20	1500	2500		o		
Brassaia actinophylla, schefflera				o			o	o			3–20	40	2500	8000			o	o
Bucida buceras, black olive				o							5–10	15	500	1500	o			
Butia capitata jelly palm				o		o			o		5–20	30	2500	6000		o		o
Caryota urens, fishtail palm			o				o			o	5–20	30	2500	6000		o		
Clusia rosea, autograph tree			o				o		o		5–20	30	2500	6000	o			o
Coccoloba uvifera, sea grape			o				o		o		5–15	20	1500	2500	o			
Ficus benjamina, weeping fig			o			o			o		3–20	40	2500	8000	o			o
Ficus benjamina 'Exotica,' Java fig			o			o			o		3–20	40	2500	8000	o			
Ficus elastica 'Decora,' rubber plant			o			o			o		3–20	40	2500	8000	o			o
Ficus lyrata, fiddle leaf fig			o			o			o		3–20	40	2500	8000	o			o
Ficus retusa nitida, Indian laurel			o			o			o		3–20	40	2500	8000	o			o
Livistona chinensis, Chinese fan palm			o			o				o	3–20	30	2500	6000		o		
Phoenix canariensis, Canary Island date			o			o				o	3–20	30	2500	6000		o		
Pytchosperma elegans, solitaire palm			o				o			o	3–20	30	2500	6000		o		
Veitchia Merillii, Christmas palm			o				o			o	3–20	30	2500	6000		o		
Washingtonia robusta, fan palm				o		o			o		3–20	30	2500	6000		o		

TABLE 620-5b
Lighting Requirements for Commonly Used Plants—Large Understory

	Light				*Temperature*			*Moisture*				*Use*
Botanical name, common name	*Low, 50 fc*	*Medium, 75–100 fc*	*High, 200 fc*	*Very high, 500 fc*	*Cool, 40–60°*	*Inter-mediate, 50–70°*	*Warm, 62–85°*	*Dry*	*Moist*	*Wet*	*Size range, ft*	*Small understory*
Brassaia arboricola, Hawaiian schefflera		o					o	o			To 15	o
Caryota mitis, clumping fishtail palm			o				o			o	To 25	
Chamaedorea erumpens, bamboo palm		o					o		o		To 15	
Chamaedorea Seifrizii, reed palm		o					o		o		To 15	
Chamaerops humilis, European fan palm				o		o				o	To 20	
Chrysalidocarpus lutescens, butterfly palm (Areca palm)			o				o			o	To 25	o
Cibotium schiedes, tree fern			o				o		o		To 15	
Cycas circinalis, fern palm			o			o		o			To 12	
Cycas revoluta, sago palm			o			o		o			To 10	
Dicksonia fibrosa, golden tree-fern			o			o				o	To 20	
Dieffenbachia amoena, giant dumbcane		o					o	o			To 6	
Dieffenbachia 'Tropic Snow,' tropic snow dumbcane		o					o	o			To 6	o
Dizygotheca elegantissima, false aralia			o				o		o		To 25	
Dracaena deremensis 'Janet Craig,' Janet Craig dracaena		o					o			o	To 5	o
Dracaena deremensis 'Warneckii,' Warneckii dracaena		o					o			o	To 5	o
Dracaena fragrans 'Massangeana,' corn plant		o					o			o	To 20	o
Dracaena marginata, Madagascar dragon tree		o					o			o	To 20	o
Draecana reflexa angustifolia (Pleomele), Malaysian dracaena		o					o			o	To 20	o
Howeia forsterana, kentia palm		o				o			o		To 15	o
Phoenix roebelenii, dwarf date palm			o			o	o			o	To 12	
Polyscias fruticosa, Ming aralia				o			o		o		To 12	
Rhapsia excelsa, lady palm			o			o				o	To 20	
Spathiphyllum 'Mauna Loa,' Mauna Loa peace lily	o	o					o			o	To 5	o
Yucca elephantipes, spineless yucca				o		o		o			To 20	

TABLE 620-5c
Lighting Requirements for Commonly Used Plants—Small Understory

	Light				*Temperature*			*Moisture*			
Botanical name, common name	*Low, 50 fc*	*Medium, 75–100 fc*	*High, 200 fc*	*Very high, 500 fc*	*Cool, 40–60°*	*Inter-mediate, 50–70°*	*Warm, 62–85°*	*Dry*	*Moist*	*Wet*	*Size range, ft*
Aglaonema commutatum, variegated Chinese evergreen	o						o		o		To 2
Aglaonema 'Fransher,' Fransher evergreen	o						o		o		To 2
Aglaonema 'Malay Beauty' ('Pewter'), pewter aglaonema	o						o		o		To 2
Aglaonema 'Parrot Jungle,' parrot jungle evergreen	o						o		o		To 2
Aglaonema 'Pseudo-bracteatum,' golden evergreen	o						o		o		To 3
Aglaonema 'Silver Queen,' silver queen evergreen	o						o		o		To 2
Asparagus plumosus, fern asparagus			o			o			o		To 2
Asparagus sprengeri, fern asparagus			o			o			o		To 2
Aspidistra elatior, cast-iron plant	o					o			o		To 3
Asplenium nidus, bird's nest fern	o					o				o	To 4
Chamaedorea elegans, Neanthe Bella palm	o						o		o		To 4
Codiaeum × Karen, croton				o			o		o		To 6
Dieffenbachia × Exotica, dumbcane			o				o	o			To 4
Dracaena deremensis 'Janet Craig' Compacta, dwarf Janet Craig dracaena		o					o			o	To 2
Fatsia japonica, Japanese fatsia		o			o				o		To 4
Nephrolepis exaltata 'Bostoniensis,' Boston fern			o			o			o		To 2
Philodendron selloum, saddle-leafed philodendron		o					o		o		To 6
Polypodium aureum 'Mandaianum,' blue hare's-foot-fern			o			o	o		o		To 3
Polyscias balfouriana, Balfour aralia				o			o		o		To 12
Sansevieria trifasciata laurentii, snake plant	o	o	o	o			o	o	o		To 4
Spathiphyllum 'Clevelandii,' Cleveland peace lily	o	o					o			o	To 3
Spathiphyllum wallisii, white flag	o	o					o			o	To 1
Spathiphyllum 'Mauna Loa Supreme,' Mauna Loa peace lily supreme	o	o					o			o	To 2
Zamia furfuracea, Jamaica sago tree		o				o	o		o		To 5

TABLE 620-5d
Lighting Requirements for Commonly Used Plants—Groundcover, Vines, and Hanging Plants

	Light				*Temperature*			*Moisture*			*Use*			
Botanical name, common name	*Low, 50 fc*	*Medium, 75–100 fc*	*High, 200 fc*	*Very high, 500 fc*	*Cool, 40–60°*	*Inter-mediate, 50–70°*	*Warm, 62–85°*	*Dry*	*Moist*	*Wet*	*Ground cover*	*Vine*	*Hanging*	*Size range, ft*
Anansa comosus variegatus, variegated pineapple				o			o		o		o			To 2
Asparagus plumosum, fern asparagus			o			o			o				o	To 3
Asparagus sprengeri, fern asparagus			o			o			o				o	To 3
Chlorophytum comosum 'Variegatum,' variegated spider plant		o				o			o		o		o	To 2
Cissus antarctica, kangaroo vine		o				o	o	o	o			o	o	To 3
Cissus rhombifolia 'Mandaiana,' grape ivy		o				o	o	o	o		o		o	To 3
Cissus rhombifolia 'Ellen Danica,' oakleaf grape ivy		o				o	o	o	o		o		o	To 3
Crytomium falcatum, holly fern	o					o			o		o			To 2
Epipremnum aureum, golden Pothos	o						o		o		o	o	o	To 3
Fatshedera lizei, 'Pia,' aralia ivy				o	o	o			o			o		To 3
Ficus pumila, creeping fig		o					o		o			o		To 2
Hedera canariensis, Algerian ivy				o	o	o			o		o	o		To 3
Hedera helix, English ivy				o	o	o			o		o	o		To 1
Hoya carnosa, Indian rope plant			o			o		o				o		To 3
Liriope muscari, monkey grass			o		o	o			o		o			To 1
Maranta leuconeura carolinae Kerchoviana, prayer plant			o				o		o		o			To ¾
Monstera deliciosa, Mexican breadfruit			o				o		o		o	o		To 3
Neoregelia carolinae 'Tricolor,' tricolor bromeliad			o				o		o		o			To 1
Nephrolepis exaltata 'Bostoniensis,' Boston fern			o			o			o				o	To 2
Philodendron oxycardium, heartleaf philodendron		o					o		o			o		To 3
Philodendron panduraeforme, fiddleleaf philodendron		o										o		To 2
Platycerium bifurcatum, staghorn fern			o			o	o		o				o	To 3
Sanseveria trifasciata 'Hahnii,' bird's nest snake plant	o	o	o	o		o	o				o			To ½
Stephanotis floribunda, Madagascar jasmine		o					o		o			o		To 3
Syngonium podophyllum 'Noack White,' Noack White nephthytis		o					o		o		o		o	To 2
Tradescantia fluminensis, wandering Jew		o				o		o						To ½

section 630: Historic Landscapes

CREDITS

Section Editor:

Albert Fein, Ph.D.
Professor of History and Urban Studies
Long Island University
Brooklyn, New York

Contributors:

Robert R. Harvey, Professor
Department of Landscape Architecture
College of Design, Iowa State University
Ames, Iowa

Susan Buggey
Chief, Historical Services—Prairie and Northern Region, Parks Canada
Winnipeg, Manitoba, Canada

Reviewers:

John J. Stewart
Commonwealth Historic Resource Management, Ltd.
Perth, Ontario, Canada

Anthony Walmsley
Walmsley and Company, Inc.,
New York, New York
Department of Landscape Architecture and Regional Planning
Philadelphia, Pennsylvania

David C. Streatfield
Department of Landscape Architecture
University of Washington
Seattle, Washington

CONTENTS

1.0 INTRODUCTION

1.1 Definition of Historic Landscapes

Historic landscapes are, most simply, the landscapes of the past. They comprise the physical evidence of human presence on the land. Their survival into the present represents a continuity of past and present which permits an understanding, an appreciation, and a stability of our fundamental environment. Their continued survival demands a knowledgeable stewardship committed to conservation.

Historic landscapes focus on the cultural landscape, upon human contribution to the existing character of the land. They do not normally include natural or wilderness landscapes. They encompass both urban and rural environments, falling along a continuum between the exclusively urban and the completely rural (Table 630-1). What distinguishes historic landscapes from other designed landscapes is that their essential character was created in the past. They reflect the distinctive tastes, technologies, and needs of various periods in the past, which themselves vary from period to period, region to region, and district to district. The most acceptable comprehensive definition of a historic landscape to date states that

> the historic landscape includes gardens which can be ranked with the most notable works of artistic creativity, and also more mundane gardens, such as those used for vegetables and cut flowers, and even those simple and informal plantings which characterize a modest rural house. Within a historic district or town, historic landscape can also be the collective setting of structures, including fences and street furniture, as well as paving patterns and public commons and squares. In a broader sense, it can be any evidence of the way in which man regulates and relates to the land, such as the cultivated fields surrounding a plantation house; it can even include natural areas which men have set aside for recreation and inspiration (by Dr. Ernest Connolly).

That which is *historic* exists in a continuum with the modern, the latter constantly receding into the past and becoming part of it. The historic is defined by its distinctiveness and its significance in identifying

TABLE 630-1
Types of Historic Landscapes

Types	*Examples*
	Urban
Parks	Prospect Park, Brooklyn, New York
Squares	King Square, St. John, New Brunswick
Commons	Boston Common, Boston, Massachusetts
Botanical gardens and arboreta	Morton Arboretum, Chicago, Illinois Missouri Botanic Garden, St. Louis, Missouri
Grounds of public buildings	U.S. Capitol, Washington, D.C.
Grounds of commercial buildings	Rockefeller Center, New York City
Grounds of industrial buildings	National Historic District, Lowell, Massachusetts
Grounds of institutions	Iowa State University, Ames, Iowa
Grounds of private residences	Villa Vizcaya, Dade County, Florida Dumbarton Oaks, Washington, D.C.
Cemeteries	Mount Hope, Rochester, New York Mount Auburn, Massachusetts
Recreation grounds	Royal Montreal Golf Club, Montreal, Quebec
Parkways	The Riverway, Boston, Massachusetts
Waterfronts	Mystic Seaport, Connecticut
Reclaimed industrial sites	Butchart Gardens, Victoria, British Columbia
Monuments	Mount Rushmore, South Dakota
	Rural
Farms	Wheeler Farm, Lincoln, Massachusetts
Industrial developments	Mauch Chunk (Jim Thorpe), Pennslyvania
Mining areas	Klondike Goldfields, Yukon
Parks	Yosemite National Park, California; Banff National Park, Alberta
Country residences	Mount Vernon, Virginia
Coastal areas	St. John's, Newfoundland
Recreational areas	Niagara Falls, New York and Ontario
Villages	New Harmony, Indiana; Brookfield, Vermont
Ranches	Grant-Kohrs Ranch, Montana
Agricultural districts	Ebey's Landing, Washington
Trails	Lewis and Clark, Pacific northwest
Battlefields	Batoche, Saskatchewan; Gettysburg, Pennsylvania
Site of historical event	Kitty Hawk, North Carolina

that which is past, rather than necessarily by its age or chronological date.

Landscapes may be typical or unique. Their historical importance as landscapes derives from the degree of their *typicality* (Table 630-2) or their *uniqueness* (Table 630-3) on a local, regional, national, and world scale. The measurement of the importance of a landscape cannot be absolutely fixed. It is determined by the purpose of the measurement (e.g., local conservation district versus national landmark status), by the standards appropriate to the purpose (e.g., general character retained versus historical authenticity of major features), and by the relative weighting of factors in accordance with the purpose (e.g., selection of plant materials in a botanic garden versus land use in an agricultural district). Table 630-4 lists various objectives relevant to historic landscape preservation.

Because historic landscapes are so widely varied, the emphasis of this Section 630 is on those issues and processes necessary to the carrying out of a landscape preservation project. Guidelines and ideas on how to approach historic landscapes are suggested, but this section cannot provide a fixed practice for such a broad, new area of landscape architectural practice.

TABLE 630-2
Historical Importance of a Landscape

Typicality	*High*	*Medium*	*Low*	*None*
Land assembly	_____	_____	_____	_____
Land use	_____	_____	_____	_____
Topographical treatment	_____	_____	_____	_____
Spatial relationships	_____	_____	_____	_____
Circulation patterns	_____	_____	_____	_____
Selection of plant materials	_____	_____	_____	_____
Disposition of plant materials	_____	_____	_____	_____
Types of structures	_____	_____	_____	_____
Siting of structures	_____	_____	_____	_____
Ornamental features	_____	_____	_____	_____
Functional systems	_____	_____	_____	_____
Aesthetic quality	_____	_____	_____	_____
Place in oeuvre of designer	_____	_____	_____	_____

TABLE 630-3
Historical Importance of a Landscape

Uniqueness	*High*	*Medium*	*Low*	*None*
Aesthetic quality	_____	_____	_____	_____
Technical innovation	_____	_____	_____	_____
Historical associations	_____	_____	_____	_____
Distinctive variation from norms	_____	_____	_____	_____
Integrity	_____	_____	_____	_____
Place in oeuvre of designer	_____	_____	_____	_____

TABLE 630-4
Historic Landscape Objectives

1. To preserve the aesthetic character of a property or area
   a. To emphasize continuity of past and present
   b. To complement a historic structure
   c. To arrest the decline of the character of the environment
   d. To interpret the life of an historical person, event, or place
2. To conserve resources
   a. To save trees, shrubs, and other plant materials
   b. To extend the life of site features
   c. To repair and rehabilitate items no longer produced
   d. To reduce maintenance
3. To facilitate environmental education
   a. To illustrate the tastes, processes, and technologies of the past
   b. To evaluate the applicability of the technologies of the past to the present
4. To accommodate the needs of a changing urban, suburban, or rural settlement

1.2 Approaches to Historic Landscapes

Historic landscapes present a number of development options. Preservation assumes recognition of the significance of existing landscapes, whether the significance be cultural, aesthetic, or functional. Preservation recognizes the past investments of capital, labor, and materials in creating the existing urban and rural fabric as well as the responsibility for ensuring its continuance in the future in a sound and useful form. All preservation options require the retention and protection of historic fabric. They differ in the degree of intervention involved and in the extent of their concern for accurate representation of the historic past (Table 630-5). These factors are usually a function of the historic significance of the site or area and of its intended use.

Many historic landscapes encompass various past elements not all belonging to the same period. Most often they include features introduced at certain times in the past, and thus represent the evolution of the site. If a site is to be treated as a museum, those elements which belong to the restoration period or the period of interpretation are essential, and those that do not fit that period may have to be replaced by more appropriate elements to conform to the purity of the museum approach. Accurate historical information about specific period details is essential to such restoration, and if it is not available, restoration should not be attempted. If the site is to be treated, at the opposite end of the spectrum, as preservation, it will emphasize the continuum of development which incorporates features of various periods within an evolving landscape. The latter approach will usually make some sacrifice in aesthetic quality, and more in historical integrity, in order to convey the historical message that past landscapes are not static environments. Landscapes of appropriate ambience but lacking in historical authenticity should not be considered as historic landscapes. Table 630-6 lists various criteria for restoration decision making.

TABLE 630-5
Approaches to Historic Landscapes

Approach	*Definition*	*Implications*
Preservation	To maintain site essentially as it is, neither upgrading nor permitting deterioration, e.g., Dumbarton Oaks, Washington, D.C.	▪ Low intervention—protection of historical fabric without destruction ▪ Only possible where site condition permits such low intervention ▪ Undiscriminating record of site evolution
Conservation	To actively intervene to prevent further deterioration of site or site elements	▪ Protection of historical fabric, sometimes involving partial destruction and replacement ▪ Application of scientific testing and technology
Rehabilitation	To upgrade to modern standards while recognizing and retaining historical character	▪ Limited historical research to ensure recognition of significant elements ▪ Modern and historic elements must be integrated sensitively ▪ May involve a high degree of intervention and the resulting loss of historical fabric
Restoration	To put back what was once there as accurately as possible, e.g., Stourhead, England	▪ Necessitates extensive historical research and accuracy ▪ Archaeological investigation is needed ▪ Usually necessitates a high degree of intervention, e.g., removal ▪ Construction and design: replacement
Reconstruction	To recreate what was there in the past but exists no longer, e.g., Governor's Garden, Williamsburg, Virginia	▪ Necessitates extensive historical and archaeological research to obtain accuracy ▪ Reproduction of design, elements, and artifacts is necessary ▪ Appropriateness to museum site must be considered
Reconstitution	To put in what would be appropriate to period, scale, use, and so forth, e.g., Upper Canada Village, Morrisburg, Ontario	▪ Broad historical research is needed to establish character and pattern to be reproduced

1.3 Historical Overview

This section does not provide a detailed overview of historic landscape styles and character. Such information can be gleaned from various histories of landscape architecture, gardens, and human/land relationships. The objective here is to draw attention to the fact that very different styles have predominated in different periods, even within the four centuries since the first settlements were established in North America. Each style has definable features and details which give it distinctive character. Figures 630-1 through 630-8 illustrate the evolution and great diversity of residential landscape styles through various historical periods.

Comprehensive understanding of these stylistic trends is limited by the availability of documentation and of surviving authentic examples for study. The difficulty of obtaining documentation increases the further back in time the landscape historian must go. For the twentieth and late nineteenth centuries, abundant photographic and documentary sources may exist. For the early and mid-nineteenth centuries, artistic views and a more sporadic literature afford a less reliable and less comprehensive understanding of landscape treatment. Before 1800 it is necessary to turn to earlier European sources for the design inspirations used in the new world. This also recognizes the increased extent of adaptation of European styles to North America.

2.0 PROJECT ORGANIZATION

Recognizing the interdisciplinary nature of landscape preservation is fundamental to project organization. At the minimum, projects require historical knowledge, landscape analysis, planning, design skills, and construction. They may also demand specialized experience in botany, ecology, archaeology, engineering, architecture, land survey, photography, and interpretation.

The first step—before major decisions are taken, schedules set, or commitments made—is to assess existing and available resources in light of multidisciplinary approaches and requirements. Essential to this assessment is a careful examination of

TABLE 630-6
Criteria for Restoration Decision Making

Factors	*Evaluative considerations*	*Implications*
Historical significance	▪ Relative importance of historical significance and uniqueness; e.g., Mount Vernon, Monticello, and the Plains of Abraham	▪ Support for preservation may relate directly to historical associations ▪ Restoration period is defined by the inclusive period of historical association where significance dominates
Extant historic resources	▪ Number and type of major features belonging to the period of historical association; ▪ Historical integrity of surviving resources	▪ Low correlation of major resources to period of association precludes restoration and suggests reconstruction for historical unity ▪ Low integrity implies heavy intervention and high restoration costs
Condition of historical resources	▪ Structural condition ▪ Condition of plant material	▪ Condition determines the degree of intervention necessary and the extent of reconstruction or replacement necessary for coherent restoration
Selection of restoration period	▪ Importance of historical association ▪ Extent of existing resources ▪ Integrity of extant resources ▪ Relation of existing resources to historical association ▪ Condition of extant resources ▪ Historical information available for authentic period restoration	▪ Assigned weight of evaluative factors ▪ Ideally, resources relate to period of historical association and possess integrity to that period ▪ Resources may postdate period of historical association but possess integrity and/or significance in terms of period of construction, which justifies their retention despite chronological incongruity ▪ Resources may belong primarily to a period which postdates that of historical association and may possess little inherent historical significance, in which case more appropriate replacement may be reasonably assessed

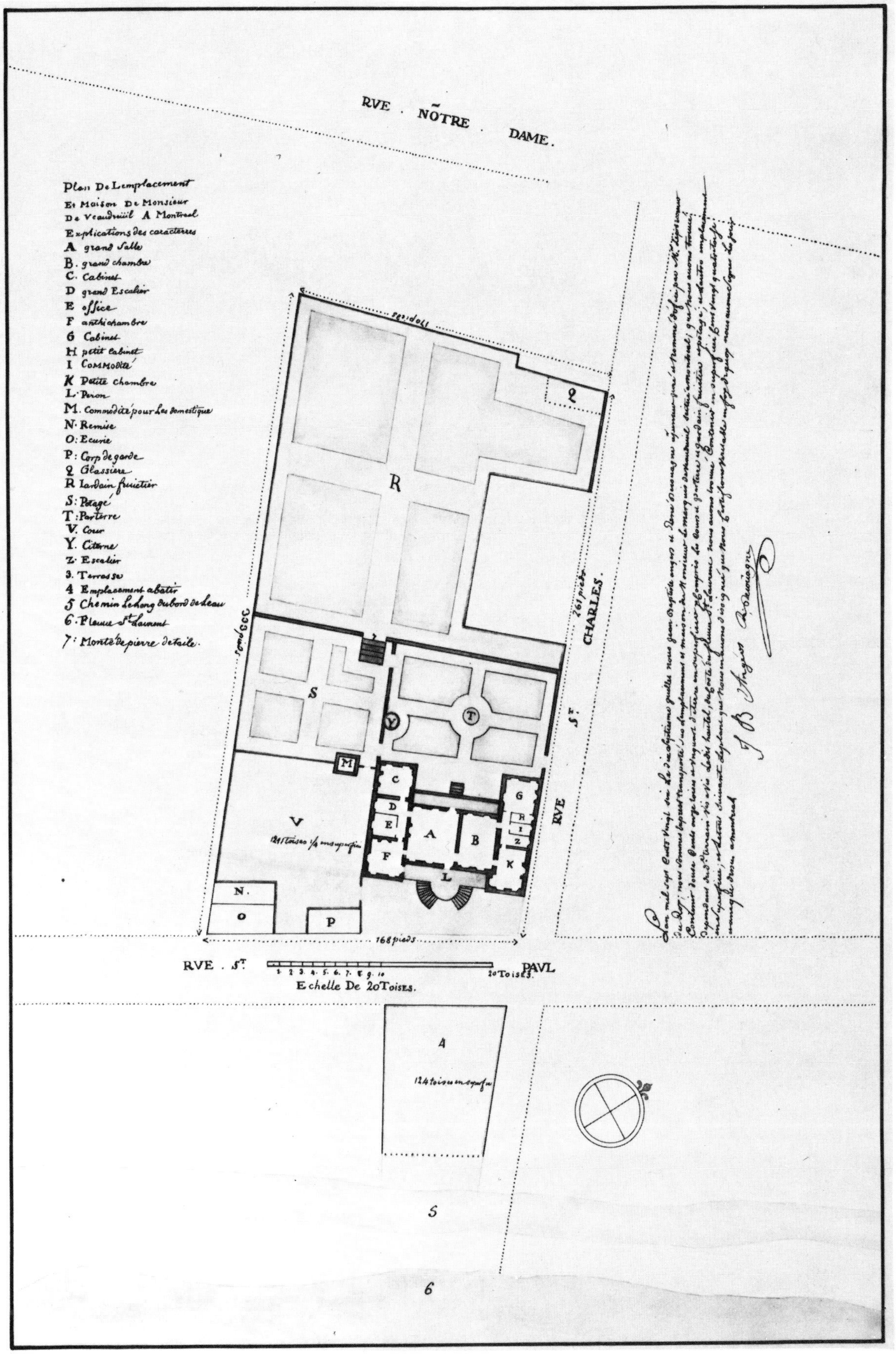
RVE . NOTRE DAME .
Plan De Lemplacement
Et Maison De Monsieur
De Veaudreüil A Montreal
Explications des caracteres
A grand Salle
B. grand chambre
C. Cabinet
D grand Escalier
E office
F antichambre
G Cabinet
H petit cabinet
I Commodité
K Petite chambre
L. Peron
M. Commodité pour les domestique
N. Remise
O: Ecurie
P: Corp de garde
Q Glassiere
R Iardin fruictier
S: Potagé
T: Parterre
V. Cour
Y. Citerne
Z. Escalier
3. Terrasse
4 Emplacement abatir
5 Chemin Le long du bord de leau
6 Fleuve St Laurent
7: Montée de pierre de taile
RVE ST CHARLES.
261 pieds
168 pieds
RVE . ST PAVL
Echelle De 20 Toises.

Figure 630-1 Plan of Vaudreuil's Garden, Montreal, 1726. This figure illustrates the influence of European landscape styles being transferred to the North American continent during the eighteenth century.

Distant Scenery near Stafford.

p, Slope of hill, descending from the back of the belt. *w*, Portion of a more distant ridge. *y y*, Thorn hedges. *z z*, Single thorn trees.

Same View as proposed to be altered.

a, Steep rocky bank. *b*, Patches of furze. *c*, Conical hill, rising in front of the more distant ridge *d*.

Figure 630-2 Scenery near Stafford, England, Showing Alterations Proposed by J. C. Loudon in the Nineteenth Century. This figure illustrates the planting design style advocated by Loudon. Loudon and other European authors influenced North American landscape designers during the nineteenth century.

Figure 630-3 View of the Grounds at Blithewood, Dutchess County, New York, A.J. Downing, 1840. The frontispiece of A.J. Downing's *Treatise on the Theory and Practice of Landscape Gardening, Adapted to North America,* 2d ed., 1840, is used to represent the turning away from the more rigid geometry of the early eighteenth century by the mid-nineteenth century.

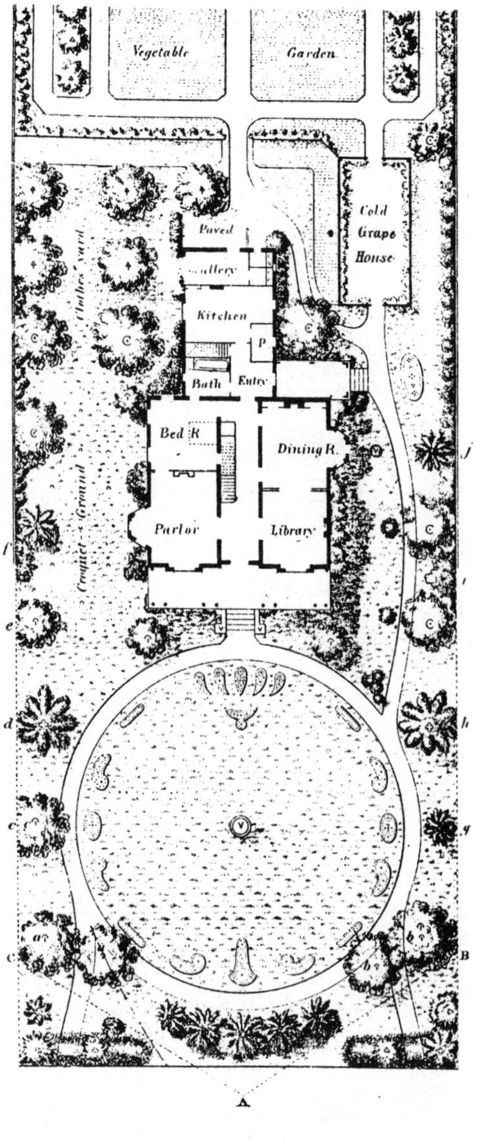
Vegetable
Garden
Cold
Grape
House
Paved
Kitchen
P
Bath
Entry
Bed R
Dining R.
Parlor
Library
A
B

Figure 630-4 Residential Plan from Frank N. Scott's Beautifying Suburban Home Grounds, 1886. This plan from Scott's 1886 publication shows the introduction of the carpet bedding and ribbon plantings which became popular during the Victorian period. The planting design has evolved into a collection of plants, with little concern for structuring outdoor spaces.

KEY TO PLANTING PLAN

A property 75 feet x 150 feet, providing space for flower and Rose garden, tea house, pool and garage. Entrance to the garage is arranged with two cement tracks, with turf between.

Key No.	*Quan.*	*Variety*	*Common Name*
1	9	Juniperus virginiana	Red Cedar
2	16	Roses. Hybrid Tea (Standards)	
3	125	Hybrid Tea Roses	Everblooming Roses
4	350	Ligustrum ovalifolium	California Privet
5	3	Spiræa Van Houttei	Drooping Spiræa
		Lonicera Morrowi { Key Nos.—6 9 22 28 38 63 / No. Plants-5 6 5 5 3 3 }	Bush Honeysuckle
7	1	Magnolia acuminata	Cucumber Tree
8	5	Viburnum Opulus sterilis	Snowball
10	10	Buddleia Veitchiana	Butterfly Plant
11	3	Biota orientalis conspicua	Columnar Chinese Arborvita
12	10	Desmodium japonicum	Purple Bush Clover
13	6	Hydrangea quercifolia	Oak-leaved Hydrangea
14	5	Forsythia suspensa	Drooping Golden Bell
15	1	Red Siberian Crab	Crab Apple
16	14	Dianthus barbatus	Sweet William
		Berberis Thunbergii { Key Nos.—17 18 31 64 / No. Plants- 9 9 5 7 }	Japanese Barberry
19	6	Deutzia Lemoinei	Lemoine's Deutzia
20	8	Phlox W. C. Egan	Hardy Phlox
21	10	Iris Silver King	White Flag
23	8	Rose Pink Baby Rambler	Everblooming Rose
24	12	Rose White Baby Rambler	Everblooming Rose
25	6	Rose Hermosa	Everblooming Rose
26	8	Rose Pink Baby Rambler	Everblooming Rose
27	5	Rosa rugosa	Japanese Rose
29	3	Lonicera fragrantissima	Early Honeysuckle
30	8	Phlox Miss Lingard	Early Phlox
32	5	Juniperus Sabina	Savin Juniper
33	3	Taxus cuspidata	Japanese Yew
34	1	Larix europæa	European Larch
35	1	Cornus florida rubra	Pink Dogwood
36	2	Buxus arborescens (Globe)	Globe-shaped Box
37	4	Taxus cuspidata	Japanese Yew
39	1	Magnolia conspicua	White Magnolia
40	15	Hypericum Moserianum	St. John's Wort
41	5	Forsythia suspensa	Drooping Golden Bell
42	9	Abelia grandiflora	Hybrid Abelia
42½	7	Hydrangea radiata	Silver-leaved Hydrangea
43	8	Xanthorriza apiifolia	Yellow Root
44	6	Spiræa Thunbergii	Snow Garland
44½	4	Syringa vulgaris	Lilac
45	1	Apple, Grimes' Golden	
46	5	Philadelphus coronarius	Mock Orange
47	9	Spiræa Margaritæ	Pink Spiræa
48	3	Juniperus virginiana glauca	Blue Cedar
49	1	Liquidambar styraciflua	Sweet Gum
50	5	Hydrangea paniculata	Late Hydrangea
51	9	Œnothera missouriensis	Evening Primrose
52	10	Iris Blue Boy	German Flag
53	9	Chrysanthemum St. Illoria	Pink Chrysanthemum
54	6	Pæonia Van Houttei	Crimson Peony
55	6	Funkia cærulea	Plantain Lily
56	6	Phlox Diadem	Hardy Phlox
57	3	Pæonia festiva maxima	White Peony
58	7	Delphinium chinense	Chinese Larkspur
59	10	Iris pumila aurea	Dwarf Flag
60	8	Spiræa Thunbergii	Show Garland
61	5	Pyrus Maulei	Pink Japanese Quince
62	1	Juniperus Cannarti	Pyramidal Cedar
65	9	Phlox Eugene Danzanvilliers	Lilac Phlox
66	12	Iris aurea	Yellow Flag
67	6	Pæonia grandiflora	Pink Peony
68	12	Iris pallida dalmatica	Lavender Flag
69	8	Chrysanthemum Julia Lagravère	Red Chrysanthemum
70		Annuals and Perennials	
71	1	Populus fastigiata	Lombardy Poplar

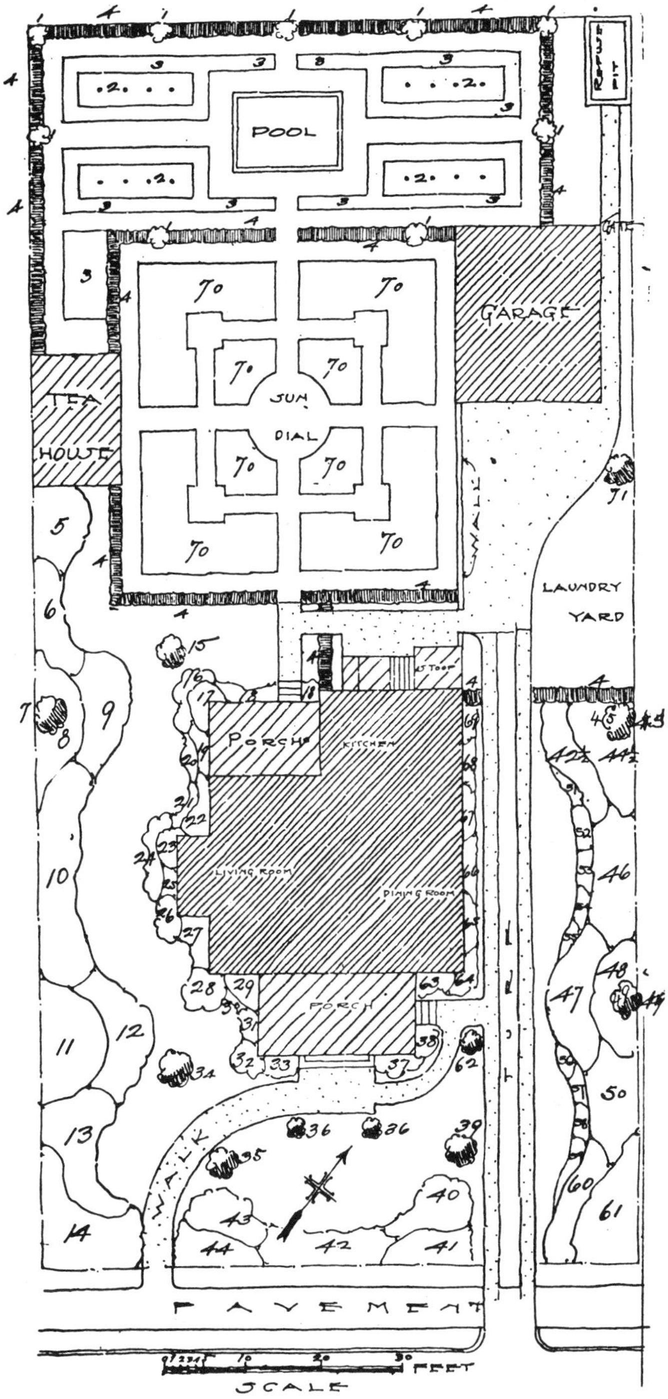
POOL
GARAGE
TEA HOUSE
SUN DIAL
PORCH
KITCHEN
LIVING ROOM
DINING ROOM
PORCH
LAUNDRY YARD
WALK
PAVEMENT
FEET
SCALE

Figure 630-5 Planting Plan from Robert B. Cridland's Practical Landscape Gardening, c. 1918. By the early twentieth century, residential landscape design had evolved to more structured planting design, which represented a return to regular geometry.

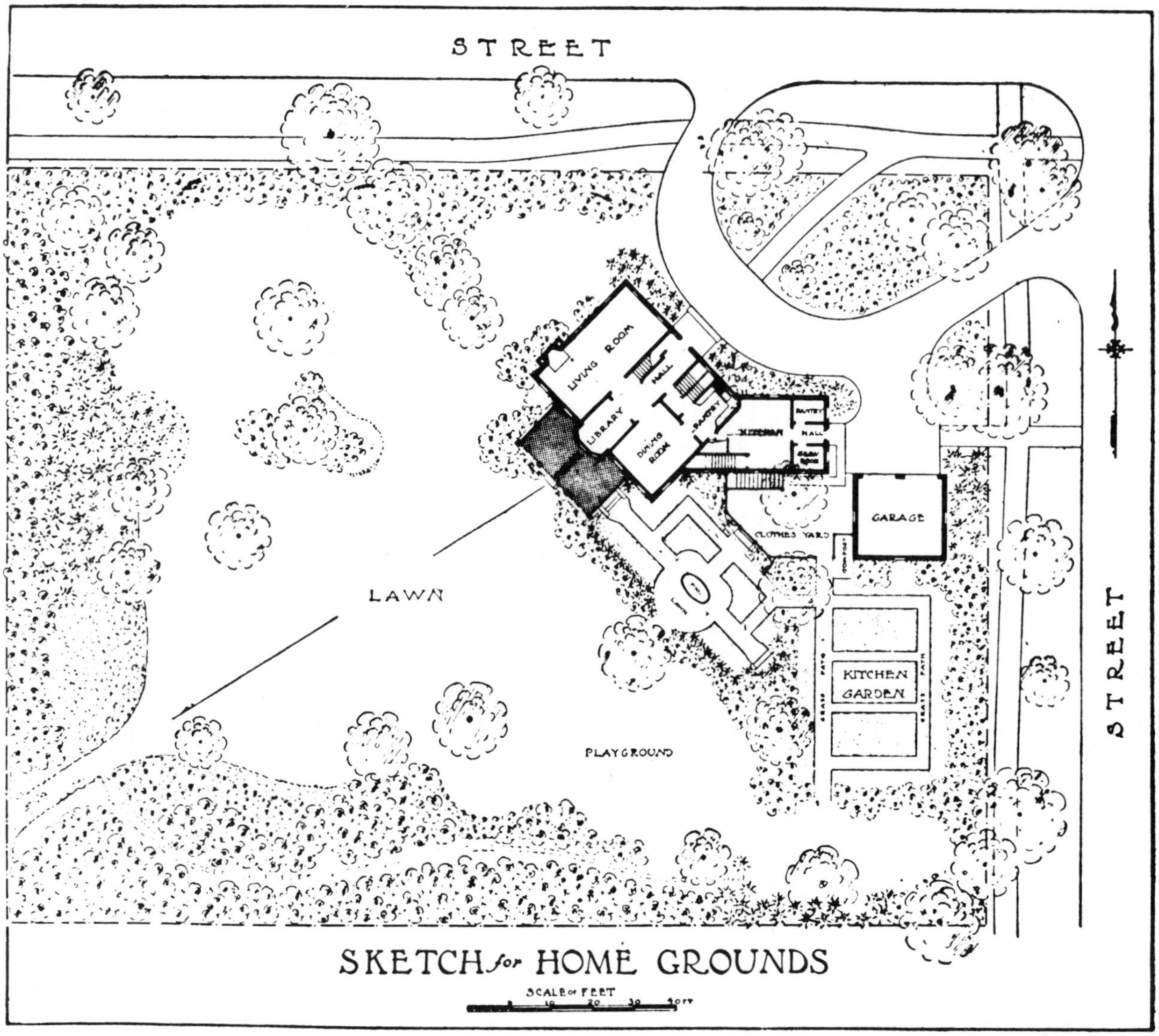
STREET
STREET
LIVING ROOM
HALL
LIBRARY
DINING ROOM
PANTRY
KITCHEN
HALL
GARAGE
CLOTHES YARD
LAWN
PLAYGROUND
KITCHEN GARDEN
SKETCH for HOME GROUNDS
SCALE of FEET
10
20
30
40 FT

Figure 630-6 Sketch for Home Grounds by O.C. Simonds, c 1920. The figure illustrates stronger control of outdoor space—through the use of plant material and multiple layers of plants—by a renowned landscape architect in the early twentieth century.

1. Vanhoutte Spirea
   Spiraea vanhouttei
2. Japanese Barberry
   Berberis thunbergi
3. Snowhill Hydrangea
   Hydrangea arborescens grandiflora
4. Virginal Mockorange
   Philadelphus virginale

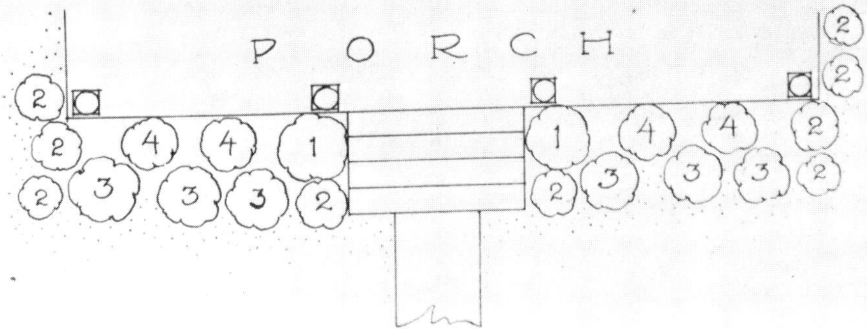
PORCH
2
2
2
2
4
4
1
1
4
4
2
2
2
3
3
3
2
2
3
3
3
2

Figure 630-7 Shrub Planting to Hide Bare Porch Foundations, c. 1927. The ubiquitous foundation planting which often garnishes Victorian as well as twentieth-century residences is included to represent vernacular landscapes and landscapes designed by non-landscape architects. The character of a landscape can be quite variable even within the same time period.

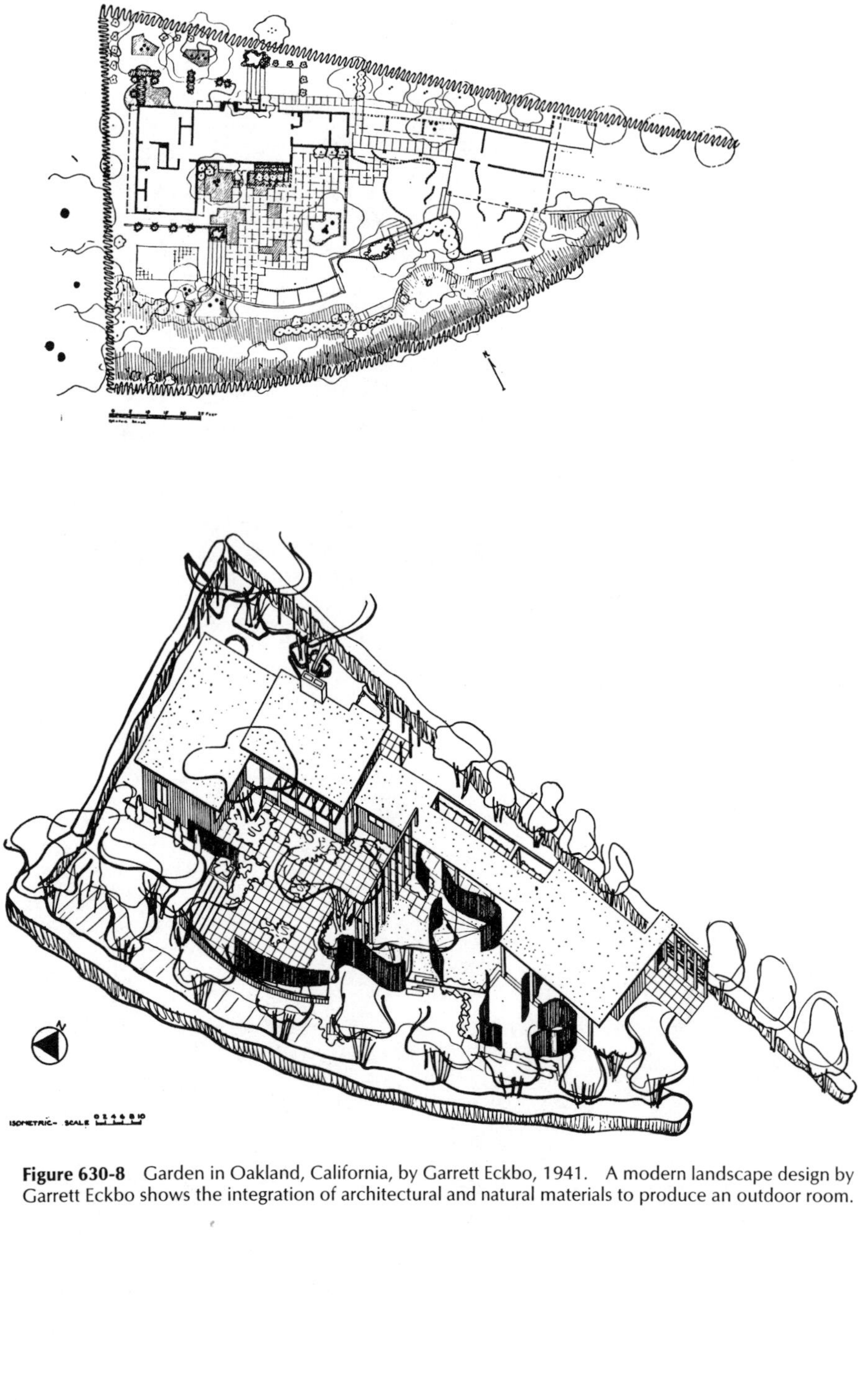

Figure 630-8 Garden in Oakland, California, by Garrett Eckbo, 1941. A modern landscape design by Garrett Eckbo shows the integration of architectural and natural materials to produce an outdoor room.

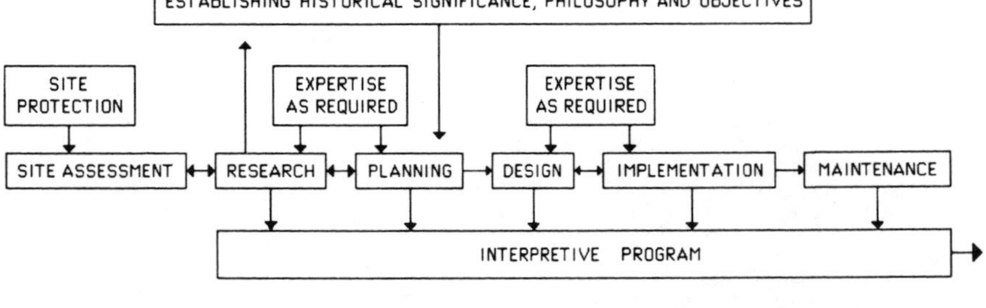
ESTABLISHING HISTORICAL SIGNIFICANCE, PHILOSOPHY AND OBJECTIVES
SITE PROTECTION
EXPERTISE AS REQUIRED
EXPERTISE AS REQUIRED
SITE ASSESSMENT
RESEARCH
PLANNING
DESIGN
IMPLEMENTATION
MAINTENANCE
INTERPRETIVE PROGRAM

Figure 630-9 Flowchart of project organization. *(Drawn by Robert R. Harvey.)*

the total project area (Figure 630-9) and an analysis of the existing site conditions (Table 630-7 and Figure 630-10). These investigations determine the initial questions for research (3.1 Research in this section).

Research establishes the historical significance of the site broadly and in detail. Research information, integrated with site assessment (2.2 Analysis of Existing Conditions in this section) and planning data (4.1 Legislative Tools and 4.2 Planning and Funding Tools in this section), makes feasible the definition of a project philosophy and the determination of realistic objectives. Continuing research and analysis are required to answer questions raised during the course of the project's progress. Interdisciplinary expertise may be necessary to respond to specific problems.

Research makes possible the definition of options and the identification of a best plan (see 4.3 The Planning Process in this section). The selected plan not only sets the direction for the design development but any additional research, planning, maintenance, and the preparation of the interpretative program must all be related to this plan. It is essential to recognize the fundamental role that the historic elements of a site have in the development of the design for a historic site. The basic task is to meld all of these considerations into the evolving best plan.

Because many of the elements in a historic landscape are dynamic, a maintenance plan is an essential part of a preservation project. Without such a plan, the distinctive character, plant material, and transitory features could be lost by the passage of time.

2.1 Flowchart of Project Organization

Figure 630-9 shows the major process and sequencing typical in the organization of a project.

2.2 Analysis of Existing Conditions

Table 630-7 provides a checklist for site analysis of existing conditions; it identifies the areas in which information should be recorded in order to ensure that the data necessary to carry out the projects are collected. Figure 630-10 shows an example of a tree evaluation plan.

3.0 HISTORIC FABRIC

The identification, evaluation, and preservation of historic fabric are fundamental aspects of the treatment of the historic landscape. *Historic fabric* may be defined as all the physical features which contributed at some time in the past to the character of the site. They are most often thought of as comprising buildings and artifacts, but they also encompass landforms, water features, and plant material. It is important, therefore, to recognize that the historic fabric of landscapes includes dynamic processes and elements. This fact necessitates both an assessment of the changes that have taken place over time and a provision for changes that will take place in the future.

It is essential to recognize again the interdisciplinary nature of the research required to understand the historic landscape, to document its evolution, and to explain its current features. The information for this understanding is derived from historical research, from detailed site inventory analysis, and from archaeology. The findings from all these processes must be assessed in close relation to one another and the inconsistencies among them addressed by further investigation where warranted. The integration of these data is critical to successful preservation projects.

3.1 Research

Historic landscape treatments are dependent upon information about the nature of the site or area in the past. The purpose of research is to obtain available data about this evolution and, using this information, to set the site within its historical context culturally, aesthetically, and technologically. The planning and design decisions must incorporate these aspects of prior existence if they are not to be destructive of the historical nature of the site. Research is the sine qua non of the preservation process.

Research is not only an information gathering process but also a problem solving process (Table 630-8). Research problems need careful identification in light of project scale, scope, and objectives (Table 630-9). A diverse range of sources may provide information pertinent to this problem solving process (Table 630-10). Table 630-11 describes various photographic techniques. Research is a dynamic process. As it is carried out, specific questions to be answered are continually refined and redefined in light of information found and not found. As well, the research problems to be resolved are regularly being reshaped in light of understanding gleaned from analysis of the information available and the knowledge gaps.

The extent and depth of research required are determined by the intended treatment of the site and the desired degree of historical accuracy (see Table 630-5). Because of the time-consuming nature of research, it is necessary to begin research well in advance of planning commitments and design development. Complex sites or projects demanding a high degree of historical accuracy require the

TABLE 630-7
Checklist for Site Examination

Site environs:
- Geographic
- Cultural
- Legal
- Social

Site:
- Location
- Size
- Legal status
- Compatibility with environs
- Extent of visual influence
- Views in
- Views out
- Spatial qualities

Topography of site:
- Original
- Imposed changes
- Observable problems
- Soil
- Siting
- Water
    - Lakes
    - Streams
    - Ponds
    - Foundations
    - Wells

Off-site circulation:
- Air
- Railroad
- Freeway
- Arterials
- Pedestrian
- Equestrian

On-site circulation:
- Existing
- Evidences of previous
- Inconsistencies in evidence
- Roads
- Drives
- Paths
- Enclosures
- Fences
- Walls
- Surface materials

Utilities:
- Gas
- Water
- Electricity
- Telephone
- Drainage
    - Storm
    - Sanitary

Plant material (as-found record)

Species	*Location*	*Age*	*Condition*
1			
2			
3			
4			

Architectural features

	Types	*Style and age*	*Location*	*Condition*
Principal building				
Other buildings				
Fences				
Furniture				

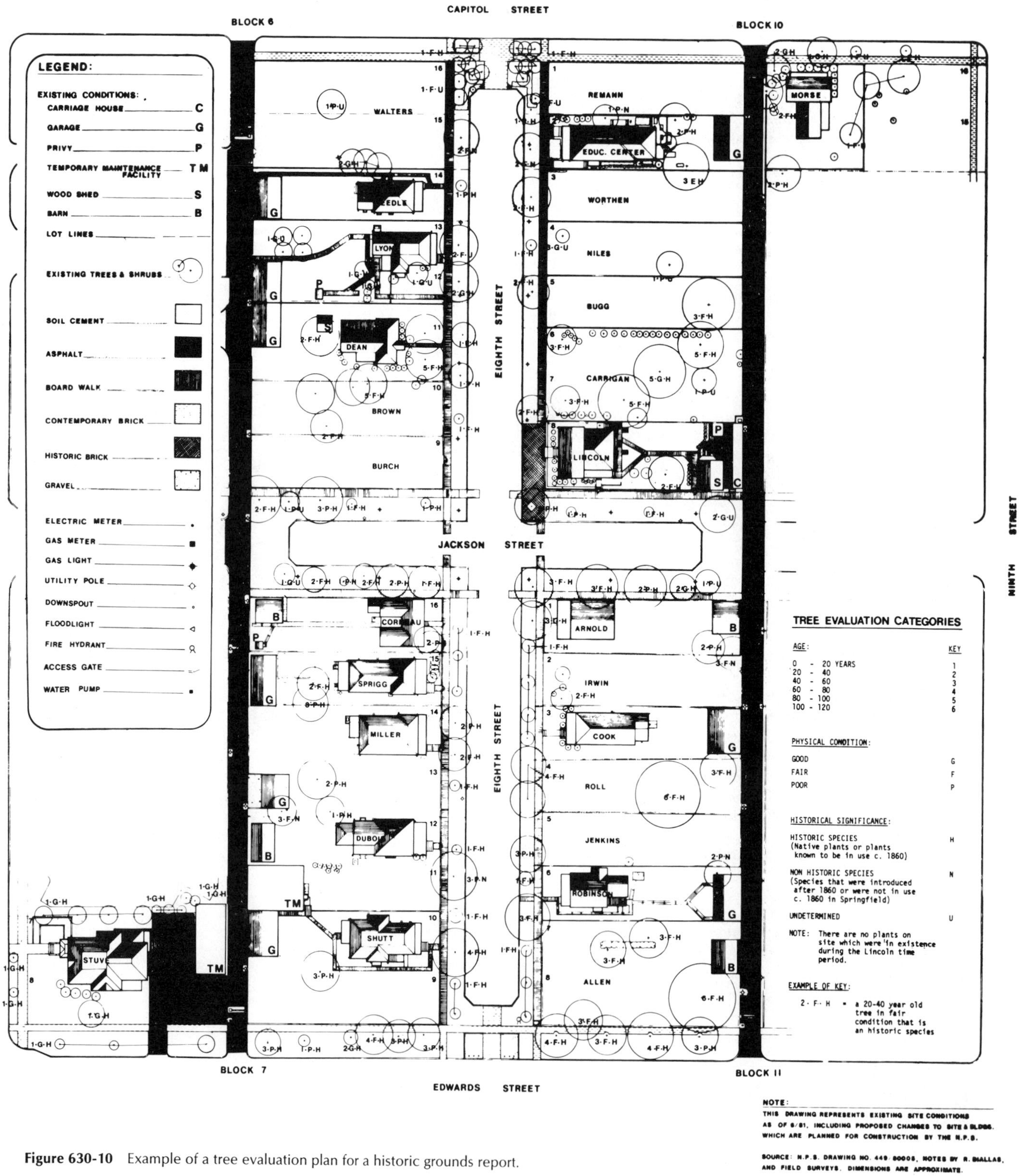
CAPITOL STREET
BLOCK 6
BLOCK 10
LEGEND:
EXISTING CONDITIONS:
CARRIAGE HOUSE C
GARAGE G
PRIVY P
TEMPORARY MAINTENANCE FACILITY TM
WOOD SHED S
BARN B
LOT LINES
EXISTING TREES & SHRUBS
SOIL CEMENT
ASPHALT
BOARD WALK
CONTEMPORARY BRICK
HISTORIC BRICK
GRAVEL
ELECTRIC METER
GAS METER
GAS LIGHT
UTILITY POLE
DOWNSPOUT
FLOODLIGHT
FIRE HYDRANT
ACCESS GATE
WATER PUMP
WALTERS
REMANN
EDUC. CENTER
MORSE
WORTHEN
NILES
LYON
BUGG
DEAN
CARRIGAN
BROWN
BURCH
LINCOLN
EIGHTH STREET
JACKSON STREET
SEVENTH STREET
NINTH STREET
CORNEAU
ARNOLD
SPRIGG
IRWIN
MILLER
COOK
ROLL
DUBOIS
JENKINS
ROBINSON
SHUTT
ALLEN
STUVE
TREE EVALUATION CATEGORIES
AGE: KEY
0 - 20 YEARS 1
20 - 40 2
40 - 60 3
60 - 80 4
80 - 100 5
100 - 120 6
PHYSICAL CONDITION:
GOOD G
FAIR F
POOR P
HISTORICAL SIGNIFICANCE:
HISTORIC SPECIES (Native plants or plants known to be in use c. 1860) H
NON HISTORIC SPECIES (Species that were introduced after 1860 or were not in use c. 1860 in Springfield) N
UNDETERMINED U
NOTE: There are no plants on site which were in existence during the Lincoln time period.
EXAMPLE OF KEY:
2 - F - H = a 20-40 year old tree in fair condition that is an historic species
BLOCK 7
BLOCK 11
EDWARDS STREET
NOTE:
THIS DRAWING REPRESENTS EXISTING SITE CONDITIONS AS OF 8/81, INCLUDING PROPOSED CHANGES TO SITE & BLDGS. WHICH ARE PLANNED FOR CONSTRUCTION BY THE N.P.S.
SOURCE: N.P.S. DRAWING NO. 449-80003, NOTES BY R. BIALLAS, AND FIELD SURVEYS. DIMENSIONS ARE APPROXIMATE.

Figure 630-10 Example of a tree evaluation plan for a historic grounds report.

TABLE 630-8
Research Plan

1. Identify research problems.*
2. Locate relevant sources of information.†
3. Examine sources and evaluate their reliability.
4. Analyze and assess information obtained.
5. Identify information gaps.
6. Seek sources to fill gaps, and repeat numbers 3 and 4.
7. Collate research data with information obtained from site analysis (inventory, as-found recording, archaeology).
8. Resolve conflicts.
9. Repeat numbers 1 to 8 as required.
10. Apply research in planning and design development.

* See Table 630.9.

† See Table 630-10.

TABLE 630-9
Research Problem Identification

1. Define purpose of research.
2. Establish nature of site before development.
3. Identify character of original development (in as much detail as required).
4. Identify character of subsequent changes (in as much detail as required).
5. Date subsequent changes.
6. Establish periods and aspects of historical significance (associations, aesthetics, technology, etc.).
7. Resolve questions posed by site analysis.

TABLE 630-10
Research Sources

A. Selected bibliographies
   1. Blanche Henrey, *British Botanical and Horticultural Literature before 1800,* 3 vols., Oxford University Press, London, 1975.
   2. *Catalog of the Avery Memorial Architectural Library of Columbia University,* 2d ed., G. K. Hall, Boston, 1968.
   3. *Catalog of the Library of the Graduate School of Design Harvard University,* G. K. Hall, Boston, 1968.
   4. *The National Union Catalog of the Library of Congress.*
   5. *American Architectural Books* (microfilm), Research Publications Inc., New Haven.
   6. *Avery Index to Architectural Periodicals,* G. K. Hall, Boston, 1973, 1975, 1979.
   7. *Art Index,* Wilson, New York.

B. Primary sources
   1. Government records
      a. Surveys
      b. Ordinances and bylaws
      c. Property records: grants, deeds, permits, assessments
      d. Census
      e. Court records
      f. Records and reports of government operations
   2. Public records
      a. Directories: city, regional, business
      b. Newspapers, periodicals
      c. Reports of nongovernmental organizations
      d. Promotional literature, including catalogs
      e. Contemporary studies
   3. Private records
      a. Diaries, journals, letters of clients, travelers, contemporaries
      b. Business records: client, practitioner
   4. Oral evidence
      a. Interviews with those associated with site
      b. Folk memory and oral tradition

C. Secondary sources
   1. Landscape literature, general works (general background works give historical patterns):
      a. Geographies
      b. Garden histories
      c. Urban histories
      d. Agricultural histories
      e. General histories of period
   2. Local histories (background works for specific areas; give local historical information):
      a. Regional
      b. State and county
      c. Municipal
      d. Family
   3. Biographies (information about landscape designers, landscape gardeners, plantsmen):
      a. Designers
      b. Prominent figures associated
   4. Journal articles
      a. *Annals of the American Association of Geographers*
      b. *Bulletin of the Association for Preservation Technology*
      c. *Garden History*
      d. *Journal of Garden History*
      e. *Journal of Cultural Geography*
      f. *Landscape*
      g. *Landscape Architecture*
      h. *Landscape Journal*
      i. *Old-House Journal*
      j. *Living Historical Farms Bulletin*

D. Iconographic sources
   1. Historic plans (subject to inaccuracies):
      a. Town plans and plats
      b. District plans
      c. Insurance atlases
      d. Site plans
      e. Design and contract drawings
   2. Topographic views (Not photographic; must be evaluated for reliability):
      a. Drawings and sketches
      b. Engravings
      c. County atlases
      d. Paintings
      e. Birds' eye views
   3. Photographs (subject to reversal, distortion, cropping, and manipulation):
      a. Public collections
         (1) Archives
         (2) Botanical and horticultural societies
         (3) City, county, and state historical societies
         (4) City, county, and state libraries
         (5) Universities and colleges
      b. Private collections
         (1) Individuals
         (2) Corporations

TABLE 630-11
Photographic Techniques

	Period photos	*Chronological contrast*	*Reverse perspective analysis*	*Rectified photography*	*Aerial photography, low oblique and high altitude*	*Infrared photography*
Types of information	▪ Detailed data about landscape elements in the past ▪ Overview of site environs	▪ Detailed data about landscape elements on site at different times ▪ Current site record from same orientation as period photos	▪ Alignments, dimensions, elevations of structures derived by application of science (theory?) of perspective to photos	▪ High-level clarity and detail of complex subject ▪ Similar detail of the past through stereopticon views ▪ Three-dimensional record	▪ Dated photos covering large areas which are retrievable in government surveys ▪ Patterns of layout and design from overhead perspective: e.g., roads and field patterns (high altitude) ▪ Minor variations in undulations of ground surface and in levels of development and compactness (low oblique)	▪ Usually aerial ▪ Measure of heat rather than light radiation ▪ Location of archaeological deposits if site undisturbed ▪ Vegetation condition, distribution, and species (possible patterns) ▪ Moisture and dampness in structures
Problems	▪ Locating old photos of site ▪ Recognizing site in large scale or unidentified photos ▪ Photos often not reliably dated ▪ Dating often necessarily based on circumstantial evidence	▪ Sufficient number of reliably dated photos covering the whole site rarely available; analysis therefore usually partial	▪ Not very useful for determining curvilinear lines such as topographic changes and ground plane because of tendency of photography to flatten surface modeling. ▪ Elements required for establishing vertical and horizontal scales and for locating reference points for horizontal control.	▪ Stereopticon views not available for most sites ▪ Expensive equipment and trained personnel required		▪ Requires repetition in varying moisture and temperature conditions for best success
Application	▪ Amalgam of several photos of different dates and sections of site can provide fairly complete visual record. ▪ Provide detail not available from other sources ▪ Photo enlargement or enhancement to obtain greater detail	▪ Chronology of landscape development can be established if sufficient photo record is available. ▪ Changes over time (e.g., objects added, deleted, or moved; rate of maturity of plant material; seasonal variations)	▪ Provide data required for elements to be reconstructed	▪ Convertible to plotting and line drawing ▪ Data input for preparation of maps, plans, surveys ▪ Substitute for measured drawings	▪ Enlargements can provide detail at single site level ▪ Analysis of broad areas, e.g., rural districts ▪ Map and survey preparation ▪ Chronological contrasts	▪ Plant condition maps ▪ Vegetation analysis through species identification and changes over time ▪ Archaeological investigation ▪ Identification of conservation problems

services of a historian experienced in the study of the built environment.

Examples of Iconographic Sources: Figures 630-11 through 630-16 illustrate various sources from which historical information can be derived.

3.2 Inventory

The purpose of an inventory is to take stock of existing resources in terms of their availability, condition, and significance. Data are compiled in a standardized form across the unit, whether it be a region, district, or single site. (See Figures 630-17 and 630-18.) This compilation is essential to site assessment, preservation planning, and design development.

The scale and detail of an inventory are determined by project needs: the intended use, the degree of intervention anticipated, and the perceived necessity for recognizing historical accuracy within the unit. Table 630-12 identifies a number of types of inventory relevant to historic landscapes and indicates their applicability to various kinds of units. Like historical research, an inventory involves a dynamic process in which additional information leads to reassessment of existing conclusions and to the need for further data.

3.3 Archaeology

The site itself can often provide further information, both above ground and below ground, if specific evidences of age and past occupation are sought from it. These include vegetative contrasts gleaned from detailed plant inventories, ecological transects from small-scale intensive vegetative investigation, path traces, and fence lines, as well as artifacts from subsurface excavation, tree ages from dendrochronology, and plant species from pollen analysis (Table 630-13). All of the above are specific techniques which are most appropriately applied to answering specific problems. Figures 630-19 through 630-21 illustrate the kinds of information that can be obtained through various techniques.

3.4 Protection

Once the historic fabric has been identified by existing evidence, research, inventory, or archaeology, steps should be taken to ensure its protection through the course of development and during the final design and implementation stages. The development process itself poses a number of threats to the historic fabric, as do modern codes and lack of funds. Table 630-14 identifies some potential threats and appropriate ameliorative actions.

Existing plant materials pose unique problems during site restoration. They constitute a resource which requires careful evaluation and stringent protection; otherwise, a major site element may inad-

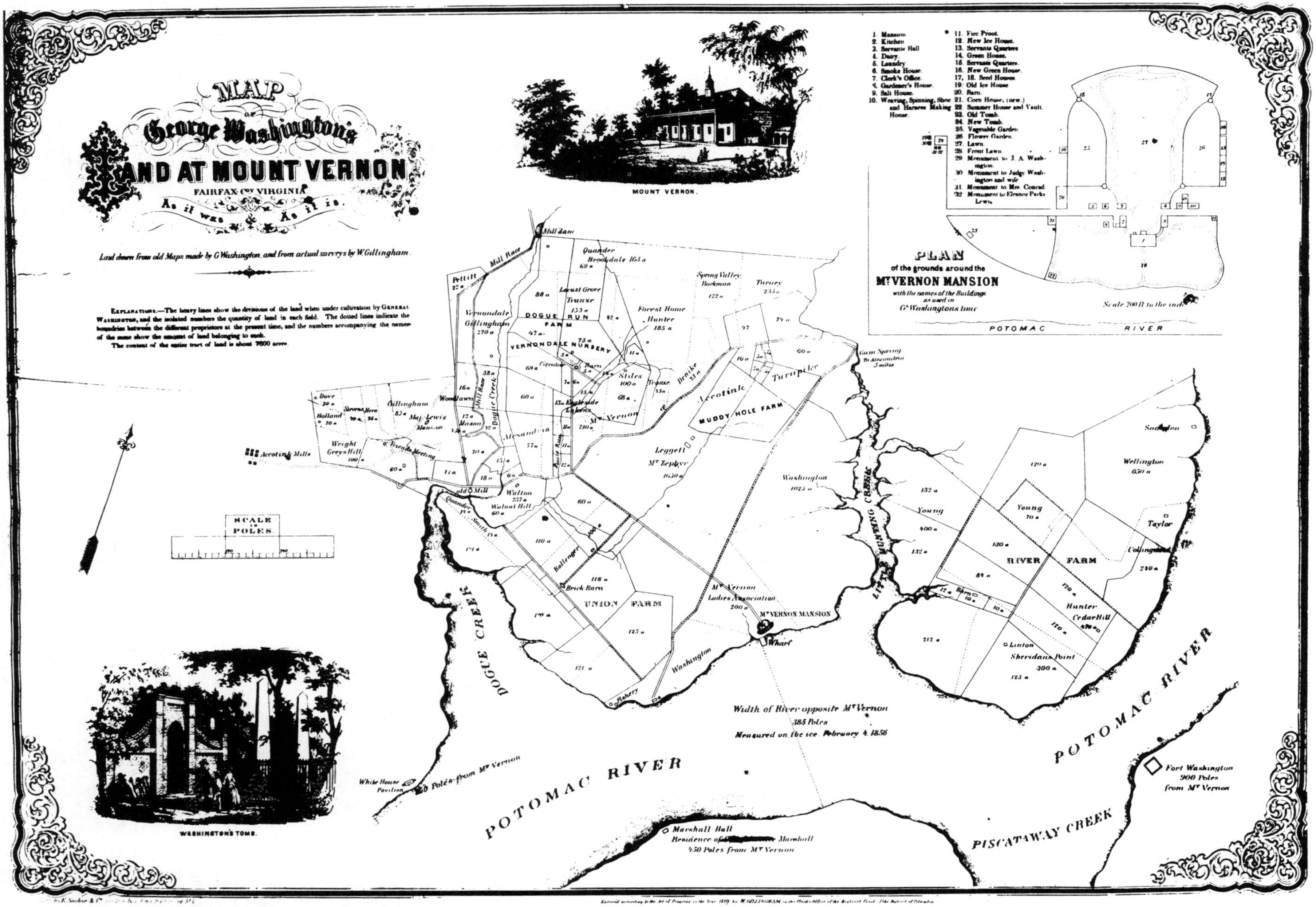
MAP
of
George Washington's
LAND AT MOUNT VERNON
FAIRFAX Cty VIRGINIA
As it was As it is.
Laid down from old Maps made by G Washington, and from actual surveys by W. Gillingham.
EXPLANATIONS.—The heavy lines show the divisions of the land when under cultivation by GENERAL WASHINGTON, and the isolated numbers the quantity of land in each field. The dotted lines indicate the boundries between the different proprietors at the present time, and the numbers accompanying the names of the same show the amount of land belonging to each.
The content of the entire tract of land is about 7600 acres.
MOUNT VERNON.
WASHINGTON'S TOMB.
SCALE in POLES.
1. Mansion
2. Kitchen
3. Servants Hall
4. Dairy.
5. Laundry
6. Smoke House.
7. Clerk's Office.
8. Gardener's House.
9. Salt House.
10. Weaving, Spinning, Shoe and Harness Making House.
11. Fire Proof.
12. New Ice House.
13. Servants Quarters
14. Green House.
15. Servants Quarters.
16. New Green House.
17, 18. Seed Houses.
19. Old Ice House
20. Barn.
21. Corn House, (new.)
22. Summer House and Vault.
23. Old Tomb.
24. New Tomb.
25. Vegetable Garden
26. Flower Garden.
27. Lawn.
28. Front Lawn
29. Monument to J. A. Washington.
30. Monument to Judge Washington and wife
31. Monument to Mrs. Conrad.
32. Monument to Eleanor Parke Lewis.
PLAN
of the grounds around the
MT VERNON MANSION
with the names of the Buildings as used in G. Washingtons time
Scale 200 ft to the inch
POTOMAC RIVER
Mill dam
Mill Race
Pettit
Quander
Brookdale 163 a
Vernondale
Gillingham
270 a
DOGUE RUN FARM
VERNONDALE NURSERY
Locust Grove
Truaxe
Forest Home
Hunter
185 a
Spring Valley
Buckman
Turney
Woodlawn
Gillingham
Dove
Holland
Wright
Greys Hill
Accotink Mills
Friends Meeting
Mason
Dogue Creek
Alexandria
Stiles
100 a
Englewide
Mt Vernon
Accotink
MUDDY HOLE FARM
Turnpike
Leggett
Mt Zephyr
1650 a
Washington
1025 a
Gum Spring
Old Mill
Walton
Walnut Hill
Ballenger
Brick Barn
UNION FARM
Mt Vernon
Ladies Association
200 a
MT VERNON MANSION
Wharf
Washington
Fishery
DOGUE CREEK
LITTLE HUNTING CREEK
Young
400 a
Young
70 a
RIVER FARM
Hunter
CedarHill
Linton
Sheridans Point
300 a
Wellington
650 a
Taylor
Collingwood
Width of River opposite Mt Vernon
385 Poles
Measured on the ice February 4 1856
White House
Pavilion
20 Poles from Mt Vernon
POTOMAC RIVER
Marshall Hall
450 Poles from Mt Vernon
POTOMAC RIVER
PISCATAWAY CREEK
Fort Washington
900 Poles
from Mt Vernon

Figure 630-11 Example of an iconographic source: The William Gillingham map of Mount Vernon of 1859.

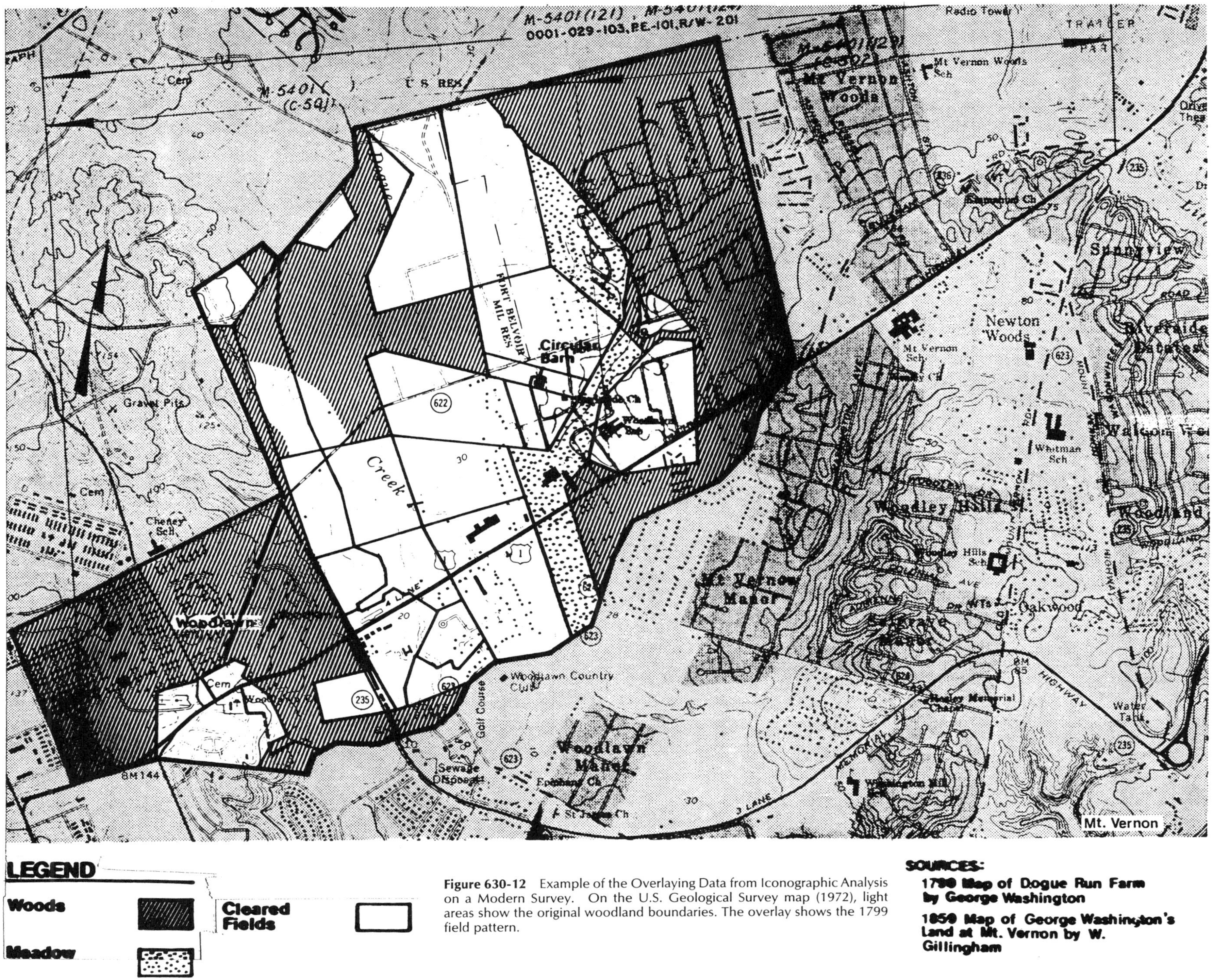
M-5401(121)
0001-029-103,PE-101,R/W-201
Radio Tower
U S RES
M 5401 (C-541)
Mt Vernon Woods
Mt Vernon Woods Sch
Newton Woods
Mt Vernon Sch
Whitman Sch
Sunnyview
Dogue
Creek
FORT BELVOIR MIL RES
Circular Barn
Gravel Pits
Cem
Cheney Sch
Woodlawn
Woodley Hills Sch
Oakwood
Mt Vernon Manor
Woodlawn Country Club
Golf Course
Sewage Disposal
Woodlawn Manor
St James Ch
Water Tank
HIGHWAY
Mt. Vernon
LEGEND
Woods
Meadow
Cleared Fields

Figure 630-12 Example of the Overlaying Data from Iconographic Analysis on a Modern Survey. On the U.S. Geological Survey map (1972), light areas show the original woodland boundaries. The overlay shows the 1799 field pattern.

SOURCES:

1799 Map of Dogue Run Farm by George Washington

1859 Map of George Washington's Land at Mt. Vernon by W. Gillingham

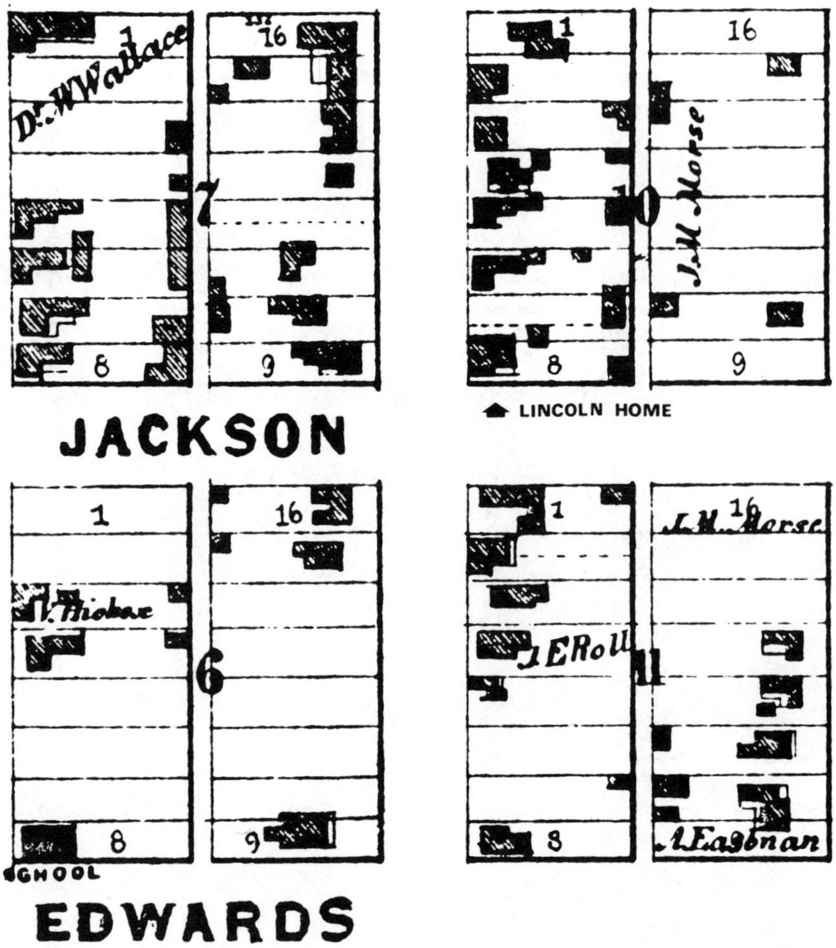
LINCOLN HOME
JACKSON
EDWARDS

Figure 630-13 Example of a town plan which contains site data—a map of the city of Springfield Illinois, 1854.

STREET
STREET
LINCOLN HOME
EDWARDS
STREET
MARKET
JACKSON

Figure 630-14 Example of a bird's-eye view which contains historical site data—bird's-eye view of Springfield, Illinois, by Augustus Koch, c. 1872.

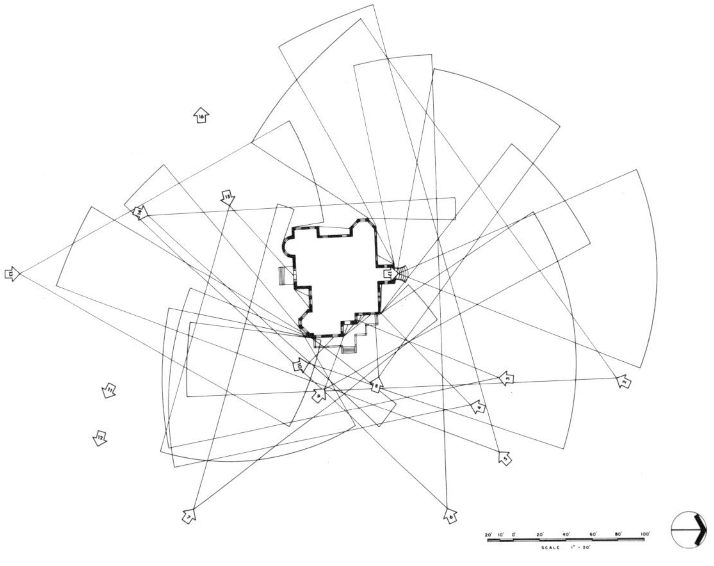
SCALE 1" = 20'

Figure 630-15 Projection of photographic coverage for reverse perspective analysis to reconstruct the historic landscape plan at Terrace Hill, Des Moines, Iowa.

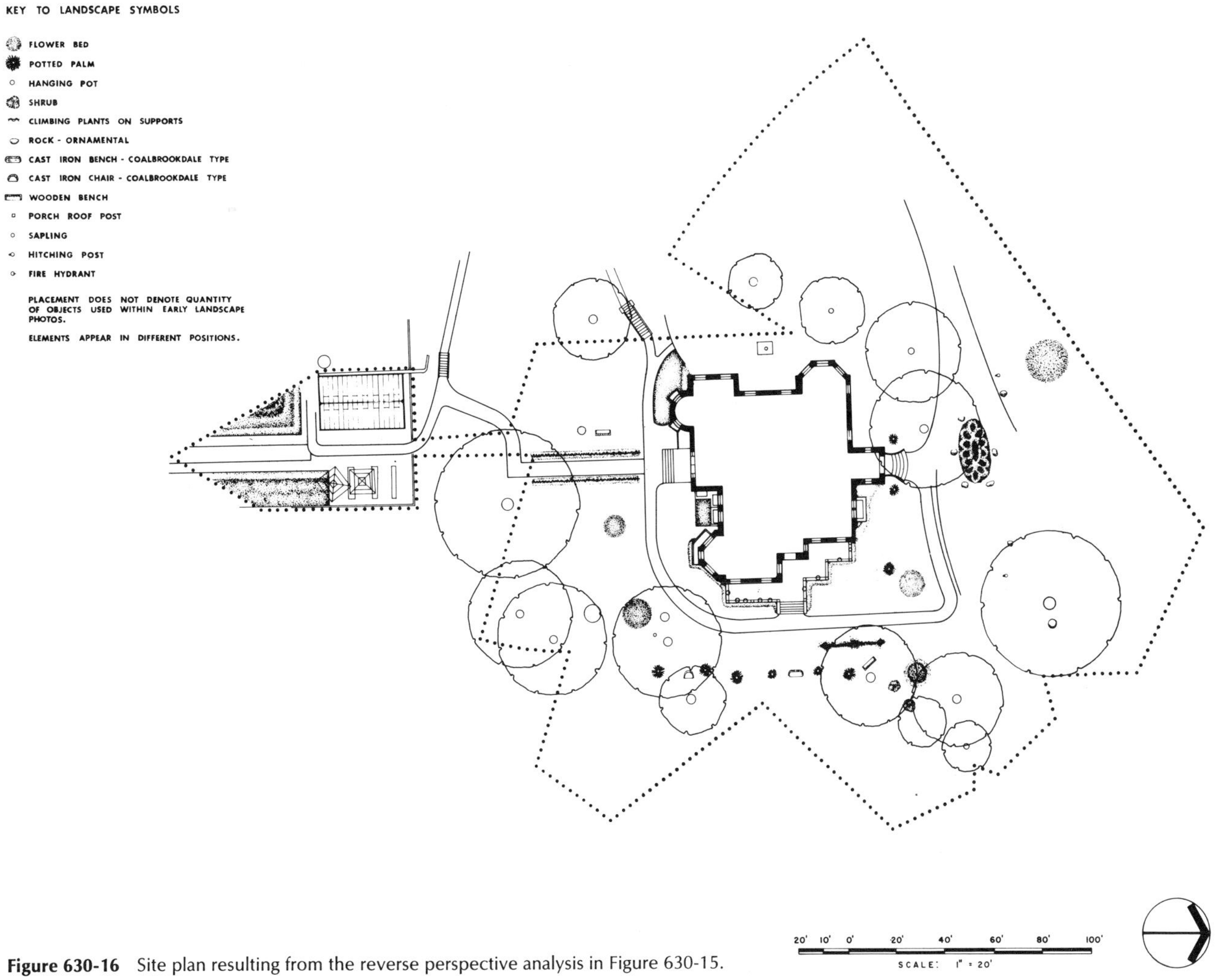
KEY TO LANDSCAPE SYMBOLS
FLOWER BED
POTTED PALM
HANGING POT
SHRUB
CLIMBING PLANTS ON SUPPORTS
ROCK - ORNAMENTAL
CAST IRON BENCH - COALBROOKDALE TYPE
CAST IRON CHAIR - COALBROOKDALE TYPE
WOODEN BENCH
PORCH ROOF POST
SAPLING
HITCHING POST
FIRE HYDRANT
PLACEMENT DOES NOT DENOTE QUANTITY OF OBJECTS USED WITHIN EARLY LANDSCAPE PHOTOS.
ELEMENTS APPEAR IN DIFFERENT POSITIONS.
20' 10' 0' 20' 40' 60' 80' 100'
SCALE: 1" = 20'

Figure 630-16 Site plan resulting from the reverse perspective analysis in Figure 630-15.

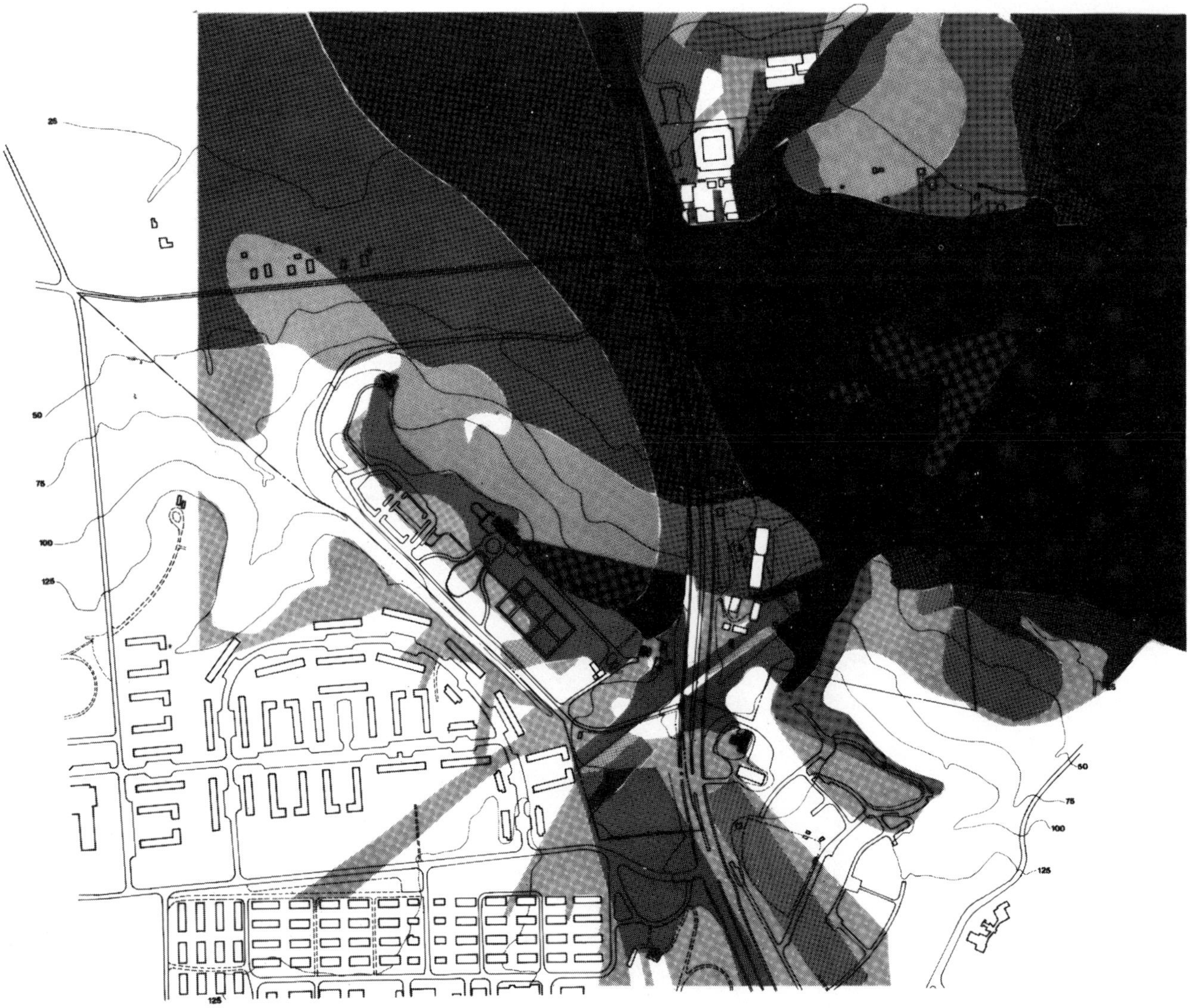
25
50
75
100
125

Figure 630-17 Composite of a "Seen Area Analysis" for the Woodlawn Plantation. The darker the shaded area, the higher the visual impact of the area on the four historic structures analyzed.

Figure 630-18 Example of "Seen Area Analysis" for a Historic District. This example illustrates the areas which potentially can be seen from the roads, the river, and the town. The darker tone indicates a zone potentially visible from all three observation points.

TABLE 630-12
Inventory

Inventory type	*Purpose and information sought*	*Circumstances appropriate to use*	*Applications*
Seen-area studies	▪ To predict what can be seen from particular sight points within the site	▪ Large open space(s) ▪ Topographic diversity ▪ Reasonable facility to implement changes ▪ Rural environments where objective is retention of landscape character ▪ Museum site where objective is historical integrity	▪ To facilitate control of visual intrusion upon historical fabric (protect visual environment) ▪ To identify areas suitable for modern uses without visual intrusion ▪ To identify buffer zones and scenic easement areas ▪ To identify boundaries of easements or zoning districts
Land use maps	▪ To establish the past and existing land uses of a site ▪ Historic land uses ▪ Existing land uses	▪ Areas where land use is observably heterogeneous ▪ Areas where land use is changing ▪ Urban areas where changes in land use are most frequent and where pressures for change are likely to be greatest	▪ To understand historic environment ▪ To identify existing land uses incompatible with the historic environment ▪ To identify compatible and/or appropriate land uses for the purposes of zoning ▪ To identify trends in land use in vicinity of historic area
Vegetation	▪ To identify the nature, species (native and introduced), location, distribution, age, size and/or condition of plant material on site ▪ To identify environmental factors affecting plant material: e.g., pollution, change in water table, intensification of surface winds, vandalism, effects of night lighting ▪ To check and update information available in existing local, state, or federal inventories	▪ Urban areas where environmental stress on plant material is likely to be greatest ▪ Site where plant material constitutes recognized aspect of significance ▪ Rural areas where large scale vegetative patterns are closely tied to land use ▪ Museum sites where complete and accurate site documentation is required for restoration or interpretive purposes	▪ To identify plant material which is botanically, ecologically, aesthetically and/or historically significant ▪ To identify plant material requiring protection or replacement during site development
Architectural features (excluding principal building)	▪ To identify and categorize existing architectural features of site ▪ To identify evidences of architectural features no longer extant ▪ Building types/structural types ▪ Other structures: e.g., fences, pergolas ▪ Styles ▪ Materials ▪ Condition	▪ Site where architectural features constitute a recognized aspect of signficance	▪ To identify architectural features requiring stabilization, preservation, reconstruction, etc., during site development ▪ To identify expertise required from architectural and conservation specialists ▪ To discern patterns of dispersion through computer mapping ▪ To show a relationship to architectural landscape

TABLE 630-13
Archaeological Fieldwork Techniques

Technique	*Definition*	*Evidences sought*	*Circumstances appropriate to use*	*Limitations*
Landscape archaeology Ecological transects	■ Surface examination for evidences of past occupation and activity ■ Small-scale intimate record of vegetative material	■ Vegetative contrasts ■ Vegetation (materials and distribution) ■ Drip lines ■ Road alignments ■ Fence lines ■ Hedge rows ■ Field patterns ■ Visual traces	■ Relatively undisturbed site, especially undisturbed vegetative cover ■ Prior to further disturbance ■ Scale of site sufficient to reach generalizations ■ Requirement for total documentation	■ Dependence on arbitrary survival of materials ■ Survivals may not be chronologically contemporaneous in the past ■ Obliteration of earlier evidence by later development
Traditional archaeology, salvage archaeology, remote sensing, trench tests, site excavation	■ Subsurface examination in accordance with established field practices	■ Post molds ■ Foundations ■ Paths (layout and materials) ■ Land use ■ Wells, cisterns ■ Artifacts ■ Plant material remnants	■ Probability of traceable elements ■ Absence of other reliance evidence ■ Undisturbed subsurface ■ Prediction from comparable sites ■ Salvage: urgent resource assessment prior to development	■ Difficulty of correlating strata with known history of the site ■ Often expensive and time-consuming in relation to returns
Dendrochronology	■ Dating of tree age by measurement of tree rings taken from core sample	■ Number of rings ■ Thickness of rings	■ Absence of information from less destructive techniques (e.g., comparative sample, sonar, documentary records) ■ Necessity for absolute accuracy as opposed to estimated dating of a particular specimen	■ Risk of introducing disease by core boring
Pollen analysis	■ Microscopic analysis of pollen grains retrieved from an archaeological dig	■ Datable samples of distinguishable pollen	■ Site possesses long chronological record	■ Difficulty in identifying whether pollen derives from plants on site or was introduced ■ Samples have to be taken from datable horizons in the stratigraphy

Field boundaries: *circa* 1700 (*redrawn from ms by Thomas Norton*)

Hedges: 1945 (*drawn from aerial photograph*)

Field boundaries: ***circa*** **1835 (*redrawn from Tithe Apportionment Map*)**

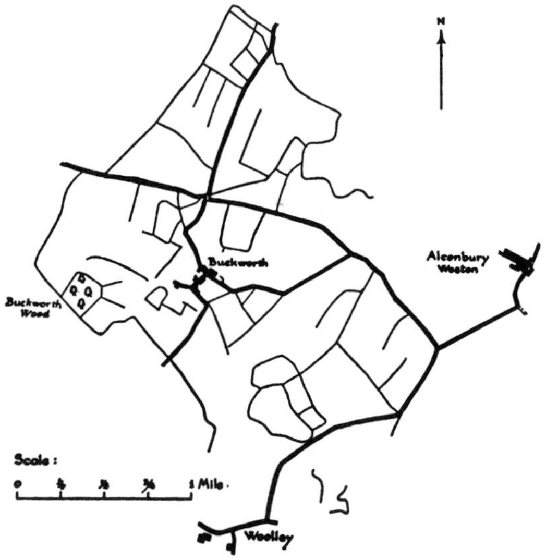
N
Buckworth
Alconbury
Weston
Buckworth
Wood
Scale :
1 Mile.
Woolley

Hedges: 1963 (*drawn from aerial photograph*)

Figure 630-19 Example of surface or landscape archaeology—field boundary and hedge mapping in Buckworth, Huntingdonshire, England, by W.G. Hoskins.

Figure 630-20 *(Right)* Example of landscape archaeology fieldwork techniques.

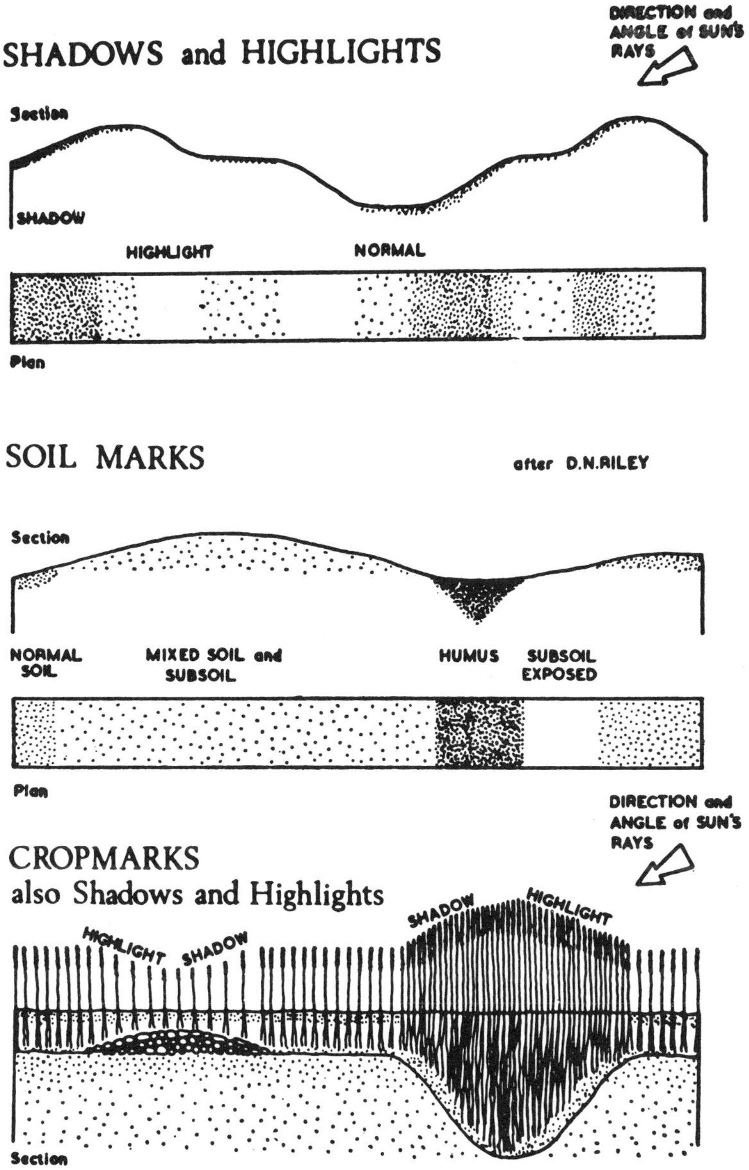
SHADOWS and HIGHLIGHTS
DIRECTION and ANGLE of SUN'S RAYS
Section
SHADOW
HIGHLIGHT
NORMAL
Plan
SOIL MARKS
after D.N.RILEY
Section
NORMAL SOIL
MIXED SOIL and SUBSOIL
HUMUS
SUBSOIL EXPOSED
Plan
DIRECTION and ANGLE of SUN'S RAYS
CROPMARKS
also Shadows and Highlights
SHADOW
HIGHLIGHT
HIGHLIGHT
SHADOW
Section

Figure 630-21 *(Below)* Example of the Type of Information That Might Be Obtained by Traditional Archaeological Methods on a Historic Site, by Hume. Illustration shows rim profiles of flowerpots excavated in Williamsburg, Virginia. The dates are those on which the pots were discarded.

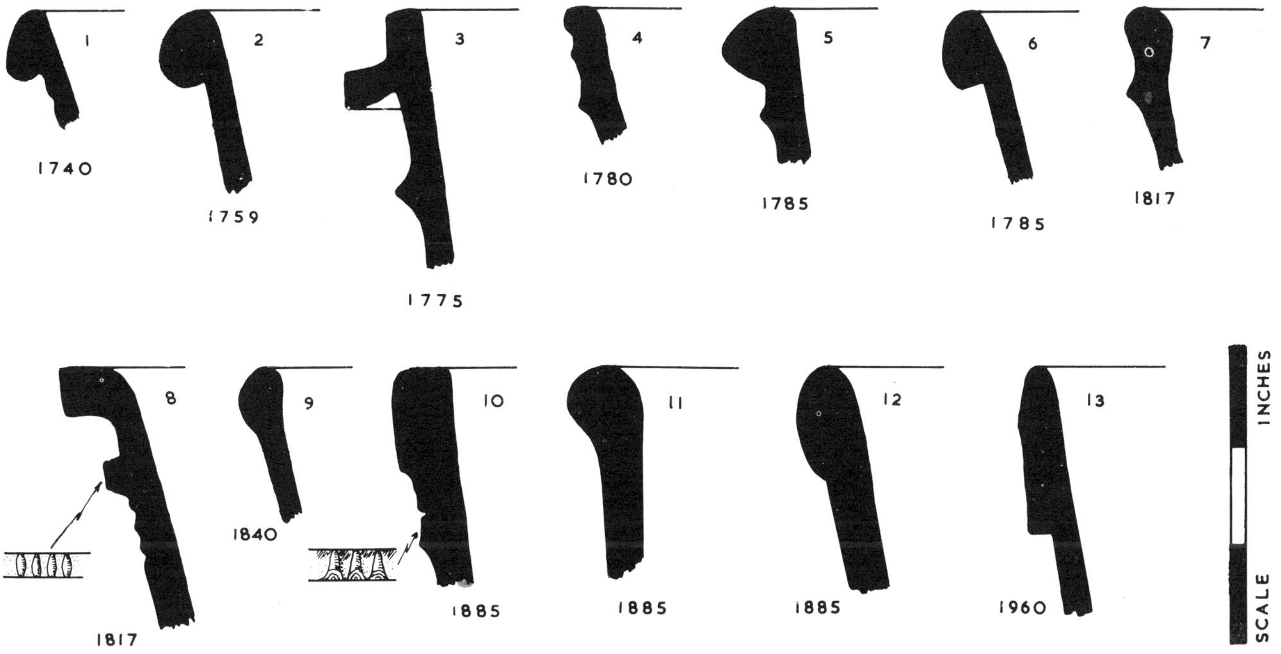
1
1740
2
1759
3
1775
4
1780
5
1785
6
1785
7
1817
8
1817
9
1840
10
1885
11
1885
12
1885
13
1960
SCALE INCHES

TABLE 630-14
Protection of Historic Fabric

Activity or requirement	*Threat*	*Ameliorative action*
Site cleanup	■ Inadvertent removal of evidence of landscape features and character	■ Detailed investigation and inventory prior to cleanup ■ Monitoring
Construction access	■ Damage or destruction of landscape features such as unique surfaces, plant materials	■ Detailed inventory in advance of equipment entering site to identify potential dangers
Architectural restoration	■ Construction disturbance around building obliterates evidence of landscape features	■ Detailed landscape inventory and necessary protective action in construction area prior to start of construction ■ Restricted area of activity
New architectural construction or landscape construction	■ Construction processes damage or destroy plant materials	■ Removal or protection in situ of plant materials prior to construction ■ Restricted area of activity
Modern codes and standards	■ Materials, grades, dimensions specified might be inconsistent with historical patterns	■ Examination of alternatives, e.g., design ■ Camouflage
Handicap access	■ Failure to integrate access into historical aesthetic	■ Alternative location ■ More sensitive design
Donations and gifts	■ Acquisition of inappropriate or irrelevant materials	■ Effective site planning, including clear definition of interpretive program ■ Advice and assistance to donors in finding appropriate repository for articles

TABLE 630-15
Plant Inventory

		Historical significance						*Physical condition**		
Species	*Location*	*Estimated age*	*Source of plant material*	*Original to restoration period*	*Appropriate to restoration period*	*Historical evidence of use on site*	*Historical evidence of use in vicinity*	*Good*	*Fair*	*Poor*

* See Table 630-16.

TABLE 630-16
Rating Guide for Condition of Plant Material

Good	*Fair*	*Poor*
Plant basically in stable condition No serious structural disease or other problems Requires only routine maintenance to sustain in good condition	Structural disease or other damage at an intermediate level which adversely affects appearance or growth conditions Requires immediate treatment to prevent further deterioration	One or more severe problems which cannot be adequately treated with routine maintenance Should be scheduled for removal

TABLE 630-17
Preservation Tools—Legislation

Tool	*Characteristics*	*Application*
Heritage designation: historic sites	■ Municipal, state or provincial, federal levels ■ Compensation available in some instances ■ Identifying and/or restraining powers ■ Process definition, e.g., advisory board ■ Interim controls while designation in process in some legislation	■ Sites representative of past environments ■ Environs of older buildings ■ Sites with significant historical associations, e.g., people, events, activities ■ Archaeological sites; e.g., National Register of Historic Places (U.S.), National Landmarks (U.S.), National Historic Sites (Canada)
Heritage designation: historic districts	■ Defined boundaries ■ Design guidelines ■ Economic stimulus frequently implicit ■ Special quality of place larger than individual sites	■ Areas where individual sites sometimes not of great significance but where unity, integrity, and age prevail: e.g., main streets, warehouse districts, ethnic communities, residential areas, rural communities like Green Springs or Virginia Historic District
Agricultural land protection	■ Primarily provincial or state level ■ Objective to keep land in agricultural production ■ Tax incentives and disincentives based on differential assessment ■ Agricultural districting ■ Purchase or transfer of development rights	■ Land in agricultural use in those states and provinces where applicable, e.g., New York (1971), Quebec (1978) ■ Agricultural districts, e.g., New York, California
Development regulation	■ Legal control on land use ■ Defined evaluation criteria ■ Permit process usual	■ Land affected by development proposals, e.g., Vermont Act 250 and Niagara Escarpment Planning and Development Act (1973)
Environmental impact assessment	■ Legal requirement for assessment in specific circumstances ■ Study of significant impacts ■ Examination of options ■ Inclusion of all points of view, including public ■ Opportunity for citizen challenge in United States	■ Federal actions or federally funded projects in United States significantly affecting quality of human environment—see National Environmental Policy Act (1970) ■ Major development projects in other areas in United States and Canada where legislation exists ■ Environmental Impact Statement (U.S.) Environmental Assessment Review Process (Canada)

vertently be impaired or destroyed. Necessary protective measures include:

1. A complete inventory of the plant species extant on the site

2. An appraisal of the historical significance of the inventoried plant material

3. A detailed assessment of the physical condition of the plant material (Tables 630-15 and 630-16)

This information can be most effectively presented in the form of an evaluation map which illustrates historical significance as well as physical condition. When dating plant material, incremental core borings should not be used, as they can introduce disease into the tree. A knowledgeable botanist can date trees without the risks imposed by core boring.

4.0 PLANNING AND PRESERVATION

A number of legislative, planning, and funding tools can facilitate landscape preservation. Many of the provisions are enabling rather than mandatory, and they vary widely from area to area, whether the jurisdictions be federal, state/provincial, or municipal. Few mechanisms, except land acquisition and subsequent ownership by a preservation organization, are sufficient in themselves to ensure permanent protection, but a combination of various means can more effectively provide long-term conservation. Most tools assume implicitly that *heritage* is defined in terms of buildings, archaeological sites, and places significant because of their historical associations. Neither designed nor broad cultural landscapes are usually mentioned explicitly in the legislation, regulations, procedures, and criteria; on the other hand, the definitions rarely exclude landscapes from their application.

Preservation tools can serve both immediate and long-range purposes. The successful application of such measures as heritage designation, environmental impact assessment, zoning, and easements can protect landscapes from imminent destruction by thwarting impending development. Public involvement through advocacy and citizens' groups may be crucial in these approaches. In the long term, amendments in legislative provisions and comprehensive plans, covenants, endowments, and revolving funds may be necessary for permanent protection and preservation.

4.1 Legislative Tools

Table 630-17 describes a number of legislative tools typically employed in historic preservation of landscapes.

4.2 Planning and Funding Tools

Tables 630-18 through 630-20 describe additional tools available to facilitate historic landscape preservation.

4.3 The Planning Process

A historic landscape project is not simply a variant application of a standard planning model. The general stages of the planning process (data collection, analysis, options, evaluation of alternative plans, and selection of the best plan) may certainly be applied; however, it is essential to recognize that the determinants are not primarily the preferences and constraints of contemporary design projects. Rather, the determinants are the historic features and character of the site. The historical data, not the planning model, shape the outcome.

Data collection is described in detail in 2.2, 3.1, 3.2, 3.3, 4.1, and 4.2 of this section. The analysis focuses upon assessing the validity and limitations of the information available. As has already been shown, data collection and analysis are interactive processes.

The purpose of the analysis is to determine as completely as possible the character of the landscape in the past—e.g.,

TABLE 630-18
Preservation Tools—Planning

Tool	*Characteristics*	*Application*
Community comprehensive plan	▪ Regional or municipal scale ▪ Legal requirement in many states and provinces	▪ Land use controls ▪ Development controls ▪ Heritage conservation ▪ Plan amendments
Preservation bylaws and ordinances	▪ Local application	▪ Standards of maintenance ▪ Provision of fences ▪ Design guidelines, e.g., setbacks, screening ▪ Regulation of signs ▪ Protection of vegetation ▪ Historic districts
Public involvement	▪ Citizen committee action ▪ Commission review processes ▪ Advocacy planning ▪ Public participation programs	▪ Expression of public preference ▪ Review of proposed activity
Site master plan	▪ Definition of implementation ▪ Integrated approach to site	▪ Immediate development plans ▪ Long-range commitments

TABLE 630-19
Preservation Tools—Other Land-Use Controls

Tool	*Characteristics*	*Application*
Zoning	▪ Defined acceptable uses in specified areas ▪ Protection of cultural and aesthetic resources in some instances ▪ Funding in specified circumstances	▪ Large-lot zones, cluster zones, planned unit development ▪ Urban and renewal service districts ▪ Historic districts ▪ Coastal zones ▪ Agricultural zones ▪ Critical protection areas
Scenic or conservation easements	▪ Interest or right in land that is less than fee-simple interest ▪ Preservation rights, often in exchange for tax benefits ▪ Considerations of nature, manner, conditions, timing, donee ▪ Term of perpetual application	▪ Protection of existing design detail, vegetation, undeveloped use, pastoral quality, etc., of property ▪ Provision of buffer zones, visual character, e.g., Green Springs, Virginia Historic District; Piscataway National Park, Maryland; Waterford, Loudoun County, Virginia
Restrictive covenant	▪ Contract binding two parties to mutual obligations	▪ Future transfer of first right of refusal of property to designated individual or body ▪ Prohibition on destruction or deterioration of specified features ▪ Negative commitment: e.g., not permitted to build on site

TABLE 630-20
Preservation Tools—Funding

Tool	*Characteristics*	*Application*
Grant	▪ Grant-in-aid; cost-sharing agreement; matching grant; technical assistance, usually provided by governmental authorities responsible for heritage conservation ▪ Prior heritage designation often required	▪ Eligible properties where it may cover feasibility, design, and/or construction costs ▪ Operation costs normally excluded: e.g., HCRS, Maymont Park, Richmond
Endowment	▪ Funds given to provide income through investment return for specific purpose ▪ Usually private and institutional sources	▪ Future maintenance ▪ Operations
Revolving fund	▪ Funds reused by recouping initial investment and reinvesting in subsequent, sequential projects	▪ Properties where revenue generated either through operations (admission, sales) or through resale of property

its historical significance, its original state, its initial development, and its subsequent evolution (emphasizing significant changes) up to the present.

The presentation of options usually indicates (1) the periods identified by major changes in the character of the site and/or (2) the varying degrees of proposed intervention upon the fabric of the site. The preferred option, or *best plan,* is determined by such factors as available historical data from research, site investigation and archaeology, technical expertise, funding and budget, legislative and planning constraints, and the project objectives.

If detailed historical information about the past landscape is not available, restoration and reconstruction are not viable options. If technical expertise about historic processes, plant material, features, and practice is not available, restoration, reconstruction, and conservation are not feasible options. Decisions regarding the best plan must be made in light of these factors.

5.0 DESIGN DEVELOPMENT

5.1 Existing Landscape Elements

Design development is one of the most important phases in the implementation of a preservation/restoration project. At this point, the results of research, the philosophy of preservation, the existing site conditions, and the modern site requirements are all integrated to produce a plan for implementation. The skill with which these elements are put together will greatly influence the ultimate success of the project. If the research phase has been carried out poorly, forgotten, or discarded, the final plan will be, at best, a poor cartoon of the earlier landscape. If the project lacks a coherent philosophy, it could suffer from inconsistency, ambiguity, and lack of focus.

Existing site conditions play an extremely important role in what can be accomplished reasonably with regard to restoring a historic site. For instance, it is seldom feasible or justifiable to restore a historic landscape when all of the earlier features (plant materials, grading, or elements of human construction) have been lost. This is true despite the fact that historic plans and photographs of the period may be available.

Grades:

The site contours, or grades, are essential character-bestowing elements in all landscapes. For this reason, particular attention should be devoted to protecting, retaining, and restoring all existing grades that have been authenticated during research. There are several activities that can take place on a site during restoration that can inflict damage to the character and aesthetic qualities of a historic site. For instance, repair of foundations of structures or the introduction of underground utilities (water, sewer, and telephone and electric lines) could cause a radical change in the grading, unless careful records are kept of the original lines. There are also present-day building and safety codes related to access for the handicapped or for emergency vehicles (fire, etc.), which may force some change in the "historic" grading. Only careful documentation of the original grades and clever restorative and/or adaptive techniques can help protect the overall qualities.

Topographic Features:

Working in concert with the subtle grade changes of the site are its more pronounced topographic features. These may often be the genius loci of the site—the hill, ridge, and rock formation for which it was initially selected.

Topographic features should be carefully assessed for their overall significance in relation to the site's original historical context. If the original site contained an important topographic feature or features, these landforms should be conserved and/or restored. For example, if significant ridges and escarpments exist, it would be undesirable to dissect them with modern road cuts; other routes should be chosen if at all feasible.

Vistas to adjacent landforms, such as nearby hills or distant mountains, may have been intentionally developed in the original site design; to allow these vistas to be closed by uncontrolled vegetative growth or the introduction of modern structures is not appropriate to the historic site. An example of good vegetative management can be cited at Stourhead, Wiltshire, England. The site is under the control of the National Trust of England, which maintains the historically significant interrelationship between the valley rim above and the valley floor below (with its lake and architectural structures) by studied management of the vegetation which clothes the valley's summit and slopes. All vegetative modifications are managed in relation to documented historical precedents, which obviously have to take into consideration random acts of nature, such as windfalls.

The critical content of topographic features relating to a historic site can also be grasped by hypothesizing how the superb integration of Frank Lloyd Wright's *Falling Water* at Bear Run, Pennsylvania would be affected if, for some unimaginable reason, the entire run were diverted away from the Kaufman residence, leaving it standing on a rock escarpment instead of a waterfall.

Landforms off-site are as important as those within the property boundary. The historically significant view between George Washington's *Mount Vernon,* on the banks of the Potomac, and *Woodlawn,* situated on a distant ridge, could be destroyed if the vista was not protected by easement or zoning from multistory architectural development rising above the forest's canopy.

Water Features:

Water features on a historic site should be protected, analyzed, and, if necessary, restored.

The historic configuration of a shoreline may have been consciously designed. The degree to which silting has taken place, the amount of intrusion of aquatic vegetation, and the historical appropriateness of detailing in shoreline protection, impoundment structures, and drainage structures should be assessed. Has broken concrete been dumped into an area where active shoreline erosion is taking place? If a shoreline was stabilized with wooden pilings, have they rotted away, or if it was stabilized with dry-laid stonework, has this been undercut by wave action and fallen into the water?

Existing water features have often been subjected to dramatic changes; storms, floods, and even droughts can play havoc with waterbodies, just as they do with vegetation. Concurrently, existing water features have doubtless been subjected to almost imperceptible (and usually undocumented) evolutionary changes, which generally do not occur to as great a degree in architectural structures. Because of the nature of hydrological action over time, some water features in the site may have suffered decidedly more than others. For example, the process of downgrading has perhaps been more dynamic and more perpetually active on some features than it has on others.

Therefore, it is essential that all data concerning the evolutionary processes which have occurred in the water feature be considered when making recommendations for remedial action. It is of course pointless to replace a detail that was originally ill-conceived with the same detail, only to have it fail again; however, this should not be considered a license to alter the aesthetic character of the feature in arriving at a better solution to the problem. The development of a satisfactory design solution calls for the integration of the original design detail with the potential solution—to the point that the effect is not appreciably modified. Any modification to the original feature should be interpreted as such.

Plant Materials:

The most difficult decision of the design development phase can be the choice of an acceptable philosophy regarding the integration of existing plant materials on a property. The extent, arrangement, and nature of the vegetation on a historic site may have changed over time. Plant material will certainly have been modified to a greater or lesser extent through many artificial and natural actions. Existing trees and shrubs may be greatly overgrown, thus destroying the intent of the original design. The *Exedra* at Chiswick House, near London, England offers a good example. A drawing by the initial designer, William Kent, shows the cedars of Lebanon bordering each side of the alleé as small, bushy, upright forms, not as the gigantic picturesque trees that currently exist. The overgrown plantings along the main axis of Hampton Court provide another good example; they are now considered too valuable historically to remove.

The main issue that surrounds such plantings is whether the designer's original intent is more significant than the overgrown but historic plant material. In many cases, those with direct responsibility for the historic site are reluctant to rip out existing material in order to replant the original design. At *Ham House* in England, however, the archaeological traces and documentation of more recent landscapes were passed over and a seventeenth century landscape based on iconographic sources was completely replanted by the National Trust to return the grounds to the period complementary to the original construction of the house.

Another important factor regarding existing historic plant material is its availability in the nursery trade. Many older plant varieties are no longer available, although a surprising number are, if the right sources are located. The absence of earlier plant varieties will influence design development in two principal ways. The original material may contrast markedly with the newer plant varieties, or the plant may no longer exist even in new modern varieties. For these reasons, it may be necessary to stage the propagation of earlier varieties for later replanting. Existing plant materials also have to be evaluated for potential replanting. Similarly, original plant material may be diseased and therefore cannot be retained or reused. If the material can be obtained from a nursery, it can be replaced. If not, the substitution of a similar plant material will have to suffice. For example, the American elm *(Ulmus americana)* might be replaced by a hackberry

(Celtis occidentalis) carefully selected for its *vase-shaped* branching characteristics.

Structures and Accessories:

Essential to nearly all landscapes created for one's use and enjoyment are a wide variety of architectural and structural elements plus additional accessories. It may be these elements that give the landscape those unique qualities which establish the particular period to which it belongs.

The aesthetic contribution of existing structures and accessories to the restoration should be evaluated, and they should be carefully conserved and/or restored in accordance with the philosophical objectives guiding the preservation work. Appropriate treatment of the structures and accessories involved typically requires professional expertise in the conservation of historic materials such as masonry, wood, metals, paints, and plaster. Despite the often substantial expense, they should not be sacrificed since they constitute an important artifact in the preservation plan and subsequent design. The structures to remain on-site should also be protected in the design development from improper and inappropriate alterations. If new uses need to be found for them, these should be sympathetic and compatible. The introduction of new or reconstructed elements is a more appropriate way of solving the demands of modern user and code requirements than is the compromise of historic structures.

Existing structures and accessories may have been brought to the site as part of an additive process which has taken place over a number of years and during different stylistic periods. Each period is *historic* in its own right, and careful consideration should be given to how each relates to the total interpretation of the site. It may seem inappropriate to retain 1890s structures in a landscape being restored to the 1860s, but if removing them all would leave a bare site just because the project objectives require it to be reconstructed to the 1860s, then it would be prudent to reexamine both the objectives and the preservation philosophy to see if they have not been drawn too tightly.

In dealing with all elements of the historic landscape (whether grades, topographic features, plant materials, or accessories), it is best to keep in mind that situation ethics may be required. Each particular case has to be evaluated and judged on its own merit. No *cookbook* solutions are likely to exist on the historic site. Each situation will demand its own unique solution to its particular problems.

5.2 New Landscape Elements

To adapt historic sites successfully to modern use, it is often necessary to add new landscape elements. Their introduction will vary on at least two levels. The first level is determined by the *intended use* of the site. For instance, a museum site will demand and allow fewer new elements than a site slated for a high degree of adaptive reuse. The second level of variability is established by the *integrity* of the site, the extent to which it has remained unaltered over time. A site that requires extensive reconstruction to fulfill its purpose will need many new elements; these will of course be introduced on the basis of careful research and documentation.

New landscape elements may have modern functions and may never even have existed in earlier periods. Other new elements may be entirely reconstructed components that attempt to duplicate landscape ingredients present at earlier periods but subsequently lost. In the case of modern functions, the problem of design development is to introduce new elements with as much empathy for the historic parts as possible without perpetuating a hoax by creating something that appears to belong to the period but could never have existed. If a known but no longer existing element has to be replaced, the missing element should be replaced with a new one as identical to the original as possible. In many instances, modern technology can be used to duplicate earlier technologies. The designer will have to decide between the desired aesthetic and the technology available to produce the best design solution possible within modern constraints. This will require a level of expertise not always part of traditional landscape architectural training, for the designer will have to understand well the historic construction techniques and methods of detailing, such as joinery, tool marks, nail types, lumber dimensions, mortar mixes, masonry techniques, and paint colors.

Grades:

When introducing new grades or reestablishing earlier site grades on a historic site, a knowledge of the grading aesthetic practiced in the restoration period is necessary. This information may be gained from early photographs, iconographic sources, archaeological examinations, and period literature. The main problem in the design development phase is how to meet modern codes for access and circulation successfully without creating a totally modern aesthetic. This may not always be possible to accomplish, but it should at least be attempted. If grades do have to be flattened or altered on the existing site, the entire grading plan should be reexamined to determine where new grades have to blend with the earlier ones in order to minimize the visual impact of the modern grades.

Topographic Features:

Although it is improbable that major new topographic features will be introduced on a historic site, the potential does exist. A good example of such intervention occurs at *Longwood Gardens,* Kennett Square, Pennsylvania, where a huge earth berm was erected to separate a large car park visually from the historic *Du Pont Estate.* When a new topographic feature such as this is the best design solution, it must be well integrated either with the existing topographic features or, conversely, in contrast with its surroundings. The decision to integrate (camouflage) or to accent (contrast) is again one that has to be rationalized within the objectives and preservation philosophy of the project.

Obviously, site size and topographic diversity also play a major role in determining what is possible. If the site is level and has little of the topographic diversity that would allow an integration of earthworks to conceal a bisecting road, then a better solution could be to depress the road (as in Olmsted's solution to the crosstown traffic in Central Park) or to tunnel beneath the site (as in the solution to modern traffic demands crossing the historic district in Colonial Williamsburg).

Water Features:

In all probability, new water features will not be introduced to the site except in an attempt to reconstruct a water feature of an earlier period. Solutions to the problems surrounding design development of water features will thus depend upon adequate documentation of the earlier feature and a precise technical knowledge of its construction detailing. Here again, it may be possible to use modern construction techniques better suited to modern requirements for a low level of maintenance, but the end result should possess the aesthetic of the documented original. Shoreline details, cascades, impoundment structures, and diversions should all carry the aesthetic of the earlier works.

It is possible that new drainage structures may be necessary on a historic site as a result of off-site considerations. Historic sites are often located in regions that have recently undergone intense urbanization and that have increased amounts of runoff crossing the site. Modern landscape design solutions may be necessary to handle the increased runoff. If additional drainage structures are required, they should be introduced in such a way as to integrate well with the original system's aesthetic. It would be preferable, however, to control or intercept the runoff before it enters the site.

Plant Materials:

New plant materials may be introduced to the historic site for a variety of reasons. Analysis and documentation may show that many areas of earlier planting have been altered, destroyed, or simply died out. It then becomes necessary to reestablish these areas as accurately as the documentary evidence and the available plant materials allow. Modern site requirements may also have introduced new functions within the site that need to be screened from view. Finally, the surroundings adjacent to the site may have evolved over time in such a way as to require the use of peripheral plantings on-site to minimize undesirable views of off-site features.

Whether the new plantings are replacements for documented plantings or are newly designed areas to provide essential screening, the plant species chosen should be as correct for the restoration period as is possible in light of the documentation and the availability of early species. All modern planting layouts that are added to remedy visual incongruities should be executed by a designer well-versed in the planting design styles of the particular date being interpreted. The added plantings should have the same species and stylistic attributes as the historic plantings so as to integrate well with the historic material, but they should always be interpreted as modern plantings which have a modern function. The public should not be deceived into believing that these plantings are historic or have been replanted based on documentary evidence.

Structures and Accessories:

Structures and accessories probably comprise the majority of new and modern components to be introduced onto a historic site.

New structures and accessories are often required to adapt a historic site to modern-day requirements of visitation or adaptive reuse. Types of structures which might be required to facilitate modern use include parking areas, visitor facilities, restrooms, additional walks and drives, informational markers, security systems, fire protection systems, increased lighting, access for those who are handicapped, and mechanical equipment such as air-conditioning units. Since such modern structures and accessories frequently have no precedents in earlier periods of the historic landscape, their compatibility with the historic environment often presents difficult problems. They are considerably more complicated on a small site than if ample acreage is available to separate the new from the historic.

External air-conditioning units and increased security lighting are types of new components which will probably require camouflaging. Elements such as fire plugs, although not present during the historic period being presented, may be required in order to protect the resource. And in order to fulfill their intended function, they cannot be hidden; hence, a philosophic decision has to be made as to whether to use a modern fire plug or one from an early period in the development of the fire plug. This type of decision will have to be made for all new elements introduced to the historic site.

Particular attention should be paid to the aesthetics of all new components to be added. They should be empathetic with the period being preserved. If, for example, it is a goal not to reconstruct missing elements, then new parts can still be designed in such a way as to suggest another time period rather than being blatantly modern. A new bench or seat to increase the seating capacity does not have to be of the ubiquitous wood slot variety to make the statement that it does not date from the eighteenth or nineteenth century and has been introduced. The same can be said of visitor facilities. They do not have to be a high-style contemporary design to accomplish their purpose, nor should they in all probability be replicas of the architecture of the period without careful consideration of what this does to the interpretation of the site in the mind of the visitor.

All decisions relevant to new structures being introduced to the historic site should be carefully considered during the design development phase—the purpose being to evaluate the necessity of the new structures, their integration with the existing historic fabric, and their aesthetic characteristics.

5.3 Maintenance Program

Historic landscapes require continuous maintenance to ensure that their historic character is retained. Every landscape rehabilitation or restoration project therefore requires a maintenance plan. That plan should be prepared as part of the project and should incorporate the varying tasks, frequencies, and levels of maintenance which the several aspects of the site will require.

Historic landscape *maintenance* may be defined as all those ongoing activities necessary to prolong the life of the historic landscape. The primary objective is to make the historic fabric last as long as possible. This is accomplished by sustaining the form and character of the landscape essentially as it exists and by minimizing deterioration to the greatest extent possible. An additional objective is to maintain the landscape in the most historic, attractive, functional, safe, clean, and convenient manner for the visitors as possible.

Maintenance priorities and levels will vary with the type of landscape and the intensity of its use (Table 630-21). The maintenance requirements arising from these two factors should be established in the form of a soundly developed and clearly presented manual (Table 630-22): "The maintenance manual should form the basis for the entire maintenance program. The work involved in preparation of this document (which is considerable) is an important exercise, because it forces someone to make a careful examination of the . . . grounds and to think about each mainte-

TABLE 630-21
Historic Landscape Maintenance Assessment Categories (including some examples of options for each category)

				Work frequencies				
					Repetitive or ongoing actions			
Landscape type	*Use intensity*	*Philosophy governing maintenance*	*Maintenance class*	*Initial and single-occurrence actions*	*Policing*	*Routine*	*Periodic*	*Special*
Grassland	Low	Retain in natural state	Minor	Reestablish areas	Frequent	None	None	Seldom
Natural forest	Medium	Maintain as modern landscape	Routine	Relocation	Seldom	Low	Low	Medium
Ornamental garden	High	Maintain to protect historic fabric	No intervention	Rehabilitation	Moderate	Medium	Medium	Low
Lawn	Medium to high	Retain in seminatural state	Intensive	Redesign		High	High	

nance task" (Chambers). The manual must make clear the intentions, directions, and expectations of the maintenance plan. A survey of the landscape and of the maintenance tasks associated with it form the data base from which the landscape practice is defined (Table 630-23). This may include an operations calendar designating the approximate dates for various maintenance operations. A calendar serves as a useful guide for planning seasonal work, ensuring regular scheduling, and accomplishing both routine and periodic maintenance. Among the categories for maintenance are:

Vegetation: grassed areas, ground covers, shrubs, trees, annuals and perennials

Architectural elements: buildings, walls, steps, surfaces, fences and gates, seats and benches, recreation equipment, and garden accessories

Utilities: irrigation systems, drainage systems, water systems, electrical systems

TABLE 630-22
Maintenance Manual—Table of Contents

1. Philosophy of maintenance
   a. Goals and objectives
   b. General guidelines
   c. Directions (by landscape type)
   d. Acceptable standards
2. Landscape practice
   a. Survey of materials and facilities
   b. Maintenance tasks required
   c. Methods*
   d. Procedures*
3. Budget and labor
   a. Service costs
   b. Staff job descriptions
   c. Work-order forms

* Stated in simple terms and illustrated by diagrams.

While the development of a maintenance plan is essential to the preservation and treatment of the historic landscape, it is equally critical that the maintenance plan be adequately and continuously budgeted. Budgets must be drawn with the recognition that proper maintenance of the landscape requires considerable knowledge, skill, and good judgment and that adequate funding is required to secure and retain qualified personnel.

The landscape design must be drawn with recognition of the inherent costs of its maintenance implications, and the maintenance plan must comprehend fully the maintenance requirements of the site design. Shortcuts in design which are made for apparent savings in the project budget can sometimes lead to far greater maintenance expenditures in future annual operating budgets. All new design should be undertaken in close consultation with the maintenance staff to avoid serious errors from the standpoint of efficient maintenance.

The maintenance plan requires not only development and implementation but also an evaluation of its effectiveness. Even the most carefully worked out plan will require adjustment in light of practical application. Task definitions should be fine-tuned in terms of actual requirements (based upon on-site experience), and the allocation of duties should be assessed periodically in order to ensure the most efficient use of skills, equipment, and labor. The use of work order forms will provide a systematic record from which a more accurate prediction of tasks and work hours can be formulated. The prenumbered forms, when completed, contain a description of the task performed, the tools and equipment required, the dates of issue and completion, and the number of work hours spent. From this data base an average range of time necessary for the performance can be measured and, if necessary, adjusted.

Maintenance practices of a modern type as well as of a type representing the site's historical period may be appropriate. Contemporary timesaving and laborsaving techniques may be used to create historic effects; they should not be applied to achieve contemporary landscape effects which may be incompatible with the historic character of the site. Alternatively, or in addition, period maintenance techniques appropriate to the period and character of the site may be used as part of an interpretative program serving the dual purposes of education and site care.

Historic landscapes require continuous maintenance of various types, intensities, and frequencies. A carefully developed maintenance plan, adequately funded and routinely evaluated, can provide for the most efficient operation in light of the elemental requirements that the historic resource be protected and conserved for its enjoyment in both the present and the future.

REFERENCES

Association for Preservation Technology *Bulletin* 9, no. 3, 1977; 9, no. 4, 1979; 15, no. 9, 1983.
These issues are devoted exclusively to historic landscape preservation, including research, site investigation, inventories; other issues include historic landscape items.

Borchers, Perry E. *Photogrammetric Recording of Cultural Resources,* National Park Service, Washington, DC, c. 1976.
The standard work on the subject.

Brown, W. Morton III, and Gary L. Hume. *The Secretary of the Interior's Standards for Historic Preservation Projects with Guidelines for Applying the Standards,* U.S. Department of the Interior, Washington, DC, 1983.

TABLE 630-23
Sample Landscape Maintenance Survey

Grassed areas	*Work frequency*	*Task size (amount or area)*	*Tools/materials required*	*Approximate hours required*
Fertilizing and soil conditioning				
Aerating				
Cutting, clipping, removal				
Edging				
Insect and disease control				
Leaf removal				
Seeding, sodding				
Watering				
Weed control				

Required basis for evaluation of proposals for assistance from the Historic Preservation Fund grant and for federal advice to other programs.

Chambers, J. Henry. *Cyclical Maintenance for Historic Buildings,* U.S. Department of the Interior, Washington, DC, 1976.

Principles and practices of maintenance which can be adapted to maintenance of landscapes.

Favretti, Rudy J., and Joy Putnam Favretti. *Landscapes and Gardens for Historic Buildings.* American Association for State and Local History, Nashville, TN, 1978.

A handbook for reproducing and creating authentic landscape settings. Only available handbook consolidating techniques for restoring past landscapes, including plant lists and sources of plant material.

Kalman, Harold. *The Evaluation of Historic Buildings,* Parks Canada, Ottawa, 1979.

A brief explanation of principles and practices applicable to the inventory of historic buildings. Many of the concepts are applicable to landscape assessments.

Landscape Architecture, May 1976, January 1981.

Issues devoted to garden and landscape preservation, including pollen analysis, plant documentation, archaeology, photogrammetry, easements, and managing historic landscapes.

McGuire, Diane Kostial (ed.). *Beatrix Ferrand's Plant Book for Dumbarton Oaks,* Dumbarton Oaks, Washington, DC, 1980.

The landscape architect's guide to planting and maintaining the site, 1941–1947.

Melnick, Robert Z. *Cultural Landscapes: Rural Historic Districts in the National Park Service,* U.S. Department of the Interior, Washington, DC, 1984.

A manual to provide tools for the park manager to identify and manage significant rural landscapes.

Melnick, Robert Z. *Cultural and Historic Landscapes: A Selected Bibliography,* Vance Bibliographies, Monticello, IL, 1980.

A wide-ranging identification of documentary sources on the landscape.

Newton, Norman T. *Design on the Land: the Development of Landscape Architecture,* Belknap Press of the Harvard University Press, Cambridge, MA, 1971.

Classic history of landscape architecture in North America.

Starke, Barry W. *Maymont Park—The Italian Garden Richmond, Virginia Using HCRS Grant-in-Aid Funds for Landscape Restoration,* U.S. Department of the Interior, Washington, DC, 1980.

Preservation case study emphasizing the importance of thorough planning for preservation work.

Stipe, Robert E. (ed.). *New Directions in Rural Preservation,* U.S. Department of the Interior, Washington, DC, 1980.

Series of essays on handling various aspects of preserving rural America, including legislation, funding, and related issues.

Whyte, William H. *The Last Landscape,* Doubleday, Garden City, NY, 1968.

Issues, principles, and environmental aspects of landscape treatments. ■

section 640: Disturbed Landscapes

<u>**CREDITS**</u>

Contributor:

Herbert R. Schaal
EDAW, Inc.
Fort Collins, Colorado

Reviewers:

Dr. William Berg
Southern Plains Range Research Station (USDA)
Woodward, Oklahoma

Bernard Slick
N.E. Forest Experiment Station
Surface Mined Reclamation Research
Forest Science Laboratory
Berea, Kentucky

Timothy Smith
Sa Bell's Hillside Gardens
Lakewood, Colorado

<u>**CONTENTS**</u>

1.0 INTRODUCTION

A *disturbed landscape* is any portion of land surface that has been drastically altered and is not in an attractive, stable, or productive condition. Disturbed lands are extremely vulnerable to erosion, and they may have surfaces unsuitable for plant growth because of compaction, steepness, stoniness, infertility, phytotoxic chemicals, acidity, alkalinity, or instability. Floods, fire, volcanic eruption, agriculture, mining, highway construction, overuse, and land development are examples of natural events and human activities which create disturbed landscapes.

1.1 Problem of Erosion

The impact of a particular land disturbance is rarely limited to the altered site. Soil erosion is inevitable on disturbed landscapes and will significantly affect downstream waters. The U.S. Environmental Protection Agency (EPA) reports that sediment yields from areas undergoing construction are 20 to 40,000 times greater than from undisturbed woodlands. Each year in the United States, 4 billion tons (3600 billion kg) of soil erode from the land. The resulting sediment adversely affects recreational areas, aquatic life, and domestic water supplies.

Soils develop slowly through complex organic and inorganic processes. One hundred years are required for the formation of 1 in (25 mm) of topsoil in typical subhumid regions. In arid regions and high-altitude areas, where natural processes are much slower than in humid regions, 1000 years may be required. Topsoil is clearly a most valuable and limited natural resource which has to be managed with great care and responsibility.

In response to this increasing environmental awareness, important legislation has been drafted to help control the problems of erosion and water pollution. The U.S. federal government passed the National Environmental Policy Act in 1969 and later passed Public Law (PL) 92-500, an amendment to the Federal Water Pollution Control Act Amendments of 1972. This amendment encourages states to establish regulations to control nonpoint sources of water pollutants. Public Law (PL) 95-87, the Surface Mining Control and Reclamation Act of 1977, created the Office of Surface Mining. These two acts set out a variety of specific requirements, but their common goal is to limit erosion and return the landscape to a stable and productive condition.

Section 640 describes general principles and methods of reclamation useful in accomplishing that goal.

2.0 RECLAMATION PROCESS

Although the basic reclamation process is the same for both existing and proposed landscape disturbances, there are several significant advantages to planning the reclamation prior to the disturbance. Prior planning can limit both on- and off-site impacts, make the operations and use of equipment more efficient, speed up the reclamation process, provide better reclamation conditions, and significantly reduce the costs.

The following steps are essential:

1. Establishing objectives

2. Determining factors that may influence methods of reclamation

3. Selecting appropriate methods of reclamation and materials and developing a plan

2.1 Establishing Objectives

Meeting Government Standards:

The standards established in the United States (and in many other countries) by federal, state, and local governments provide the basis for many reclamation objectives. The standards typically require such measures as returning the ground surface to approximately its original contour, reestablishing vegetative cover to control erosion at a degree equal to predisturbance levels, and covering all acid-forming and other toxic materials. Additional objectives are derived from the land use goals for the disturbed area.

Economic and Social Objectives:

Determining potential uses for any given site may be made by:

1. Identifying uses for which there may be a demand or a need

2. Analyzing proposed uses to confirm the degree of demand or need through a market analysis

3. Analyzing the site to determine engineering and environmental feasibilities

4. Analyzing costs and benefits to determine the return on investment and the social, environmental, and economic consequences of development

5. Creatively applying principles of landscape architecture to achieve efficiencies, maximize benefits, and minimize adverse environmental impacts

6. Organizing public meetings to solicit input from the community

Environmental Objectives:

In addition to economic and social objectives, consideration should be given to such environmental factors as:

1. Water quality

2. Air quality

3. Aesthetics

4. Wildlife

5. Adjacent areas

6. Long-range productivity

Evaluation of Objectives:

Objectives should be specific and quantifiable. They must be realistic and matched to acceptable risks and reasonable costs. For example, it is possible to:

1. Determine the amount of erosion which will occur on a disturbed site during certain high-precipitation events.

2. Determine the frequency of these events and establish the risk for any given year.

3. Determine the loss and damage which would result from the event.

4. Design features to mitigate erosion and siltation from the event.

5. Determine the cost of mitigation measures and compare these with anticipated damages and projected benefits.

If the costs exceed the damages or benefits, then the project and its objectives should be reexamined.

2.2 Factors Influencing Methods of Reclamation

The key to successful reclamation begins with a basic knowledge of the site and the nature of the disturbance.

There are many site factors that influence the various methods of reclamation, including: (1) existing soil characteristics, (2) existing vegetation, (3) annual and seasonal precipitation, (4) temperature extremes, (5) evapotranspiration rate, (6) wind, (7) growing period, (8) slope, (9) aspect, (10) elevation, (11) drainage patterns, and (12) animal, insect, and human behavior patterns.

This section will primarily address the first two of these factors because of their critical importance in all reclamation projects. The other factors, however, could prove to be of equal or even greater importance in some circumstances, depending on the region and its climatic characteristics, etc.

It is often the interaction of these factors that is most critical when working with disturbed sites. One or more of these factors may be in an extreme condition; e.g., the soil might be extremely dry or extremely wet, very high in acidity, very low in organic materials, and part of a steep, unstable slope.

In most parts of the world and on most projects, the two fundamental aspects of reestablishing a disturbed landscape are: (1) to provide a viable growing medium (soils, water, suitable slopes, etc.) and (2) to select or encourage appropriate vegetation.

Soil Characteristics:

Soil Mapping: The Soil Conservation Service (SCS) in the United States (or its equivalent in other countries) has general soil maps for most areas. Most of this mapping is considered reconnaissance level, or Order 3, mapping. Order 3 mapping refers to map scales of 1:12,000 to 1:250,000 or smaller with minimum delineations on the order of 10 acres (4 ha). Order 2 mapping refers to scales of 1:12,000 to 1:31,680 with minimum delineations of 1.5 to 10 acres (0.6 to 4 ha). Order 1 mapping refers to scales of less than 1:12,000 and is used for mapping complex areas or where there is a scarcity of topsoil.

Soil Testing: Soil tests provide the fundamental information needed to select measures for establishing vegetation. Important soil characteristics which can be identified by field observation include: horizon thickness, lithology, color, texture, structure, coarse fragments, consistency, hardness, root distribution, presence of lime, presence of soluble salts, and kinds of vegetation. Lab analysis determines: texture, dispersion, weatherability, water retention capacity, saturation percentage, hydraulic conductivity, nutrient content, trace elements, and pH (if pH is greater than 7 or less than 6, additional tests are run for salinity, sodicity, or acidity, respectively). Lab tests for toxicity determine the presence of elements such as boron, molybdenum, selenium, aluminum, iron pyrite, and manganese.

In mining, borehole data is invaluable in determining the amount and character of soil materials. When the mine plan and the reclamation plan are integrated, the most efficient use of equipment and operations results.

Table 640-1 provides data on soil suitability for salvage and reclamation use. *Suitability,* as used in this table, refers to the qualities and properties of natural soils or to soil materials that chemically and physically provide the necessary water and nutrient supply for the top growth and root development of plants. The ratings are indicators of the potential quality of natural soil profiles, certain soil horizons, or the underlying parent material, disregarding nutrient levels.

TABLE 640-1
Soil Material Suitability for Salvage and Reclamation Use

	*Levels of suitability**			
Major parameters	*Good*	*Fair*	*Poor*	*Unsuitable*
USDA soil texture	Fine sandy loam, very fine sandy loam, loam, silt loam, sandy loam	Clay loam, sandy clay loam, silty clay loam	Sandy, loamy sand, sandy clay, silty clay, clay	Clay-textured soils with more than 60% clay
Salinity, mmho/cm	<3	3–6	6–9	> 9
Alkalinity (exchangeable sodium percentage, ESP)	<4	4–8	8–12	>12
Concentration of toxic or undesirable elements; i.e., boron, selenium, arsenic, % lime, etc.	Very low	Low	Moderate	High
Soil pH	6.1–7.8	5.1–6.1 7.9–8.4	4.5–5.0 8.5–9.0	<4.5 >9.1
Additional parameters to be evaluated				
Moist consistency	Very friable, friable	Loose, firm	Very firm, extremely firm	
Coarse fragments, % by volume	0–10	10–20	20–35	>35
Available water-retention capacity, in/in	>0–16	0.08–0.16	<0.8	
Permeability, in/hr	0.6–6.0	0.2–0.6	<0.2 or > 6.0	
Organic matter, %	>1.5	0.5–1.5	<0.5	
Soil structure	Granular, crumb	Platy, blocky, prismatic	Massive, single grain	

* Ratings may be raised one class if soil amendments or management practices can be applied to overcome the limitations.

Source: From USDA Forest Service, "User Guide to Soils: Mining and Reclamation in the West," General Technical Report INT-68, Intermountain Forest and Range Experiment Station.

Vegetation:

Another critical factor influencing methods of reclamation is the selection and/or encouragement of appropriate vegetation. Listed below are typical conditions most often considered *unfavorable* for establishing vegetation on a disturbed landscape.

1. Soil materials on very steep, droughty, or unstable slopes

2. Shallow or stony soils with too little silt, clay, and humus to serve as reservoirs for plant nutrients and soil moisture

3. Strongly acid, strongly alkaline, or high-salt soils

4. Soil materials containing reactive pyrite (FeS_2), which oxidizes to form sulfuric acid (H_2SO_4)

5. Soils with toxic materials such as soluble copper, aluminum, or manganese

6. Soils very low in available nitrogen and phosphorus

7. Wet and ponded soils

8. Very high rainfall or very low and uncertain rainfall

9. Active frost heaving

10. Absence of essential *Rhizobium* (legume) bacteria and mycorrhizal fungi and other beneficial microorganisms

The U.S. SCS soil surveys contain vegetation data for various site types. Additional site descriptions provide a detailed breakdown by species and include other relevant data. Where difficult or unprecedented soil conditions exist, on-site test plots should be specified to determine the response of selected plants to proposed reclamation techniques.

Other Considerations:

The U.S. Weather Service (and similar agencies in other countries) publish climatological data, and U.S. Geological Survey maps provide data needed to determine slope, aspect, elevation, and drainage patterns. Information on animals, insects, and human behavior patterns may be obtained through the SCS, state fish and game departments, local universities, local governments, and knowledgeable area residents.

2.3 Selecting Appropriate Methods of Reclamation and Materials and Developing a Plan

The actual methods used to reclaim disturbed landscapes will vary somewhat from region to region, depending on the many differences involved between basic site factors. The overall reclamation process, however, remains the same and includes the following elements:

1. Protection of soil, water quality, and adjacent undisturbed areas

2. Landshaping and stratigraphy

3. Surface conditioning

4. Planting

5. Establishment and maintenance of vegetation

Each of these elements is covered separately and in more detail in 3.0 of this section.

3.0 METHODS OF RECLAMATION

3.1 Protection of Soil, Water Quality, and Adjacent Undisturbed Areas

Principles and basic measures of controlling and limiting the effect of disturbances include:

1. Carefully limiting the size of disturbances during construction by indicating them on the plans and by using barricades and boundary markers on-site

2. Correcting unstable conditions by removing problem areas and by constructing walls

3. Protecting disturbed surfaces from erosion as soon as possible by covering, mulching, and seeding

4. Keeping storm runoff velocities low by roughening surfaces and by constructing check dams

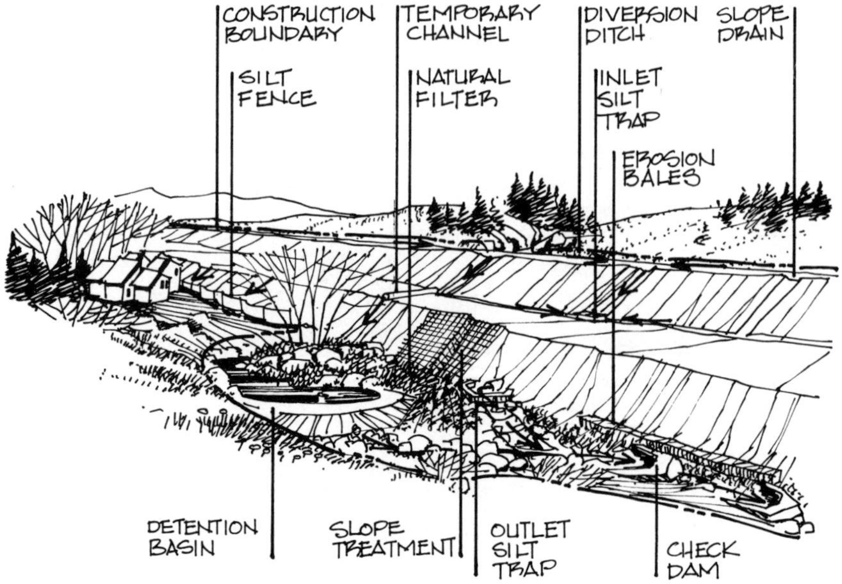
CONSTRUCTION BOUNDARY
TEMPORARY CHANNEL
DIVERSION DITCH
SLOPE DRAIN
SILT FENCE
NATURAL FILTER
INLET SILT TRAP
EROSION BALES
DETENTION BASIN
SLOPE TREATMENT
OUTLET SILT TRAP
CHECK DAM

Figure 640-1 Methods of limiting disturbance to site.

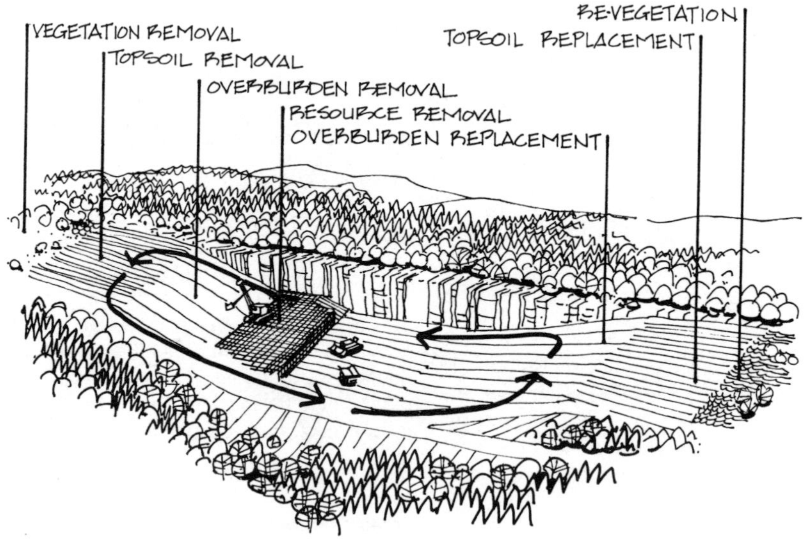
VEGETATION REMOVAL
TOPSOIL REMOVAL
OVERBURDEN REMOVAL
RESOURCE REMOVAL
OVERBURDEN REPLACEMENT
TOPSOIL REPLACEMENT
RE-VEGETATION

Figure 640-2 Soil haulback method.

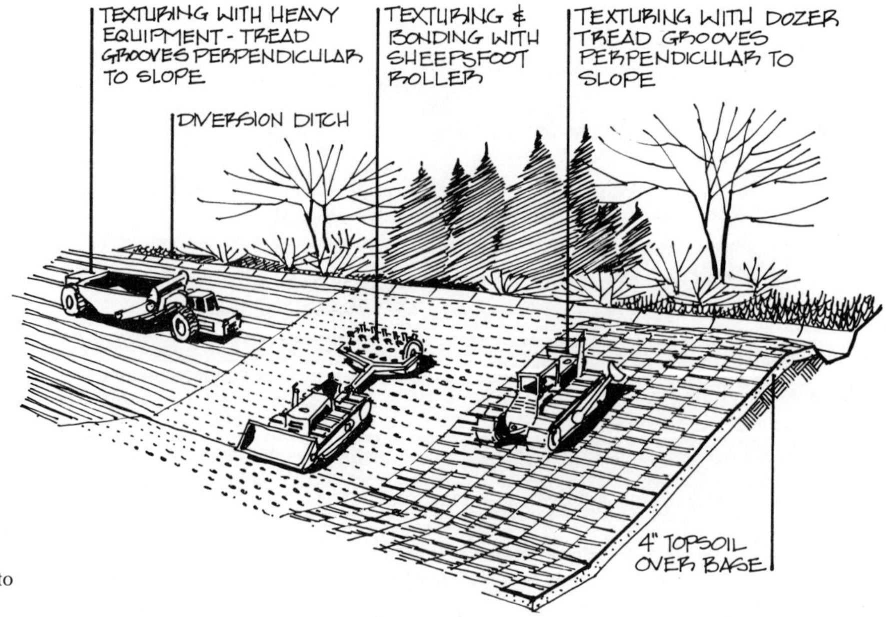
TEXTURING WITH HEAVY EQUIPMENT - TREAD GROOVES PERPENDICULAR TO SLOPE
TEXTURING & BONDING WITH SHEEPSFOOT ROLLER
TEXTURING WITH DOZER TREAD GROOVES PERPENDICULAR TO SLOPE
DIVERSION DITCH
4" TOPSOIL OVER BASE

Figure 640-3 Methods of roughening slopes to slow runoff.

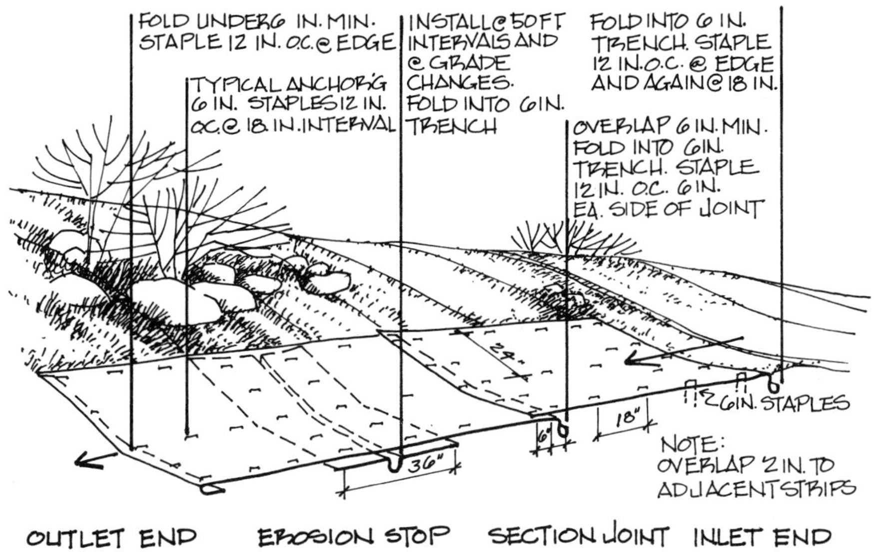
FOLD UNDER 6 IN. MIN.
STAPLE 12 IN. O.C. @ EDGE
INSTALL @ 50 FT
INTERVALS AND
@ GRADE
CHANGES.
FOLD INTO 6 IN.
TRENCH
FOLD INTO 6 IN.
TRENCH. STAPLE
12 IN. O.C. @ EDGE
AND AGAIN @ 18 IN.
TYPICAL ANCHORING
6 IN. STAPLES 12 IN.
O.C. @ 18 IN. INTERVAL
OVERLAP 6 IN. MIN.
FOLD INTO 6 IN.
TRENCH. STAPLE
12 IN. O.C. 6 IN.
EA. SIDE OF JOINT
24"
6 IN. STAPLES
18"
6"
36"
NOTE:
OVERLAP 2 IN. TO
ADJACENT STRIPS
OUTLET END
EROSION STOP
SECTION JOINT
INLET END

Figure 640-4 Methods of installing jute in drainage way.

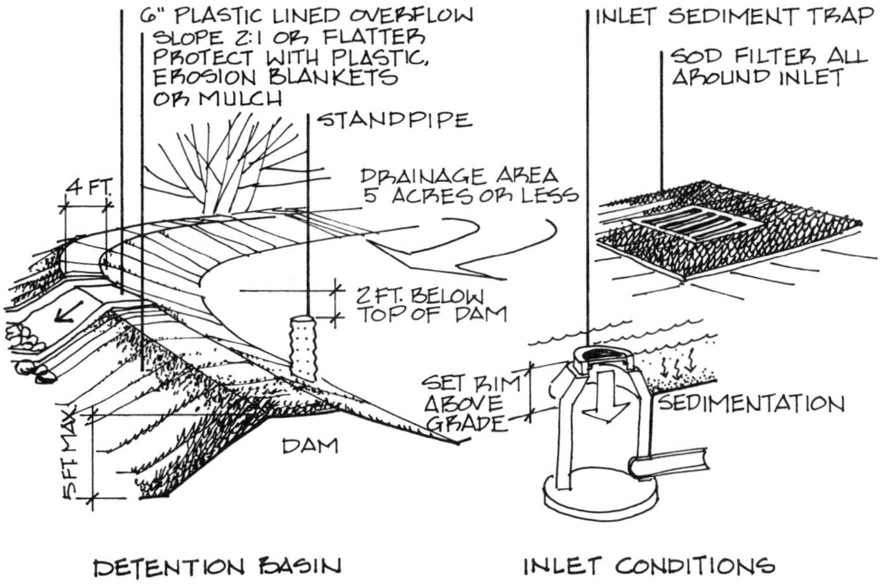
6" PLASTIC LINED OVERFLOW
SLOPE 2:1 OR FLATTER
PROTECT WITH PLASTIC,
EROSION BLANKETS
OR MULCH
STANDPIPE
INLET SEDIMENT TRAP
SOD FILTER ALL
AROUND INLET
4 FT.
DRAINAGE AREA
5 ACRES OR LESS
2 FT. BELOW
TOP OF DAM
SET RIM
ABOVE
GRADE
SEDIMENTATION
DAM
5 FT. MAX.
DETENTION BASIN
INLET CONDITIONS

Figure 640-5 Sediment trapping methods.

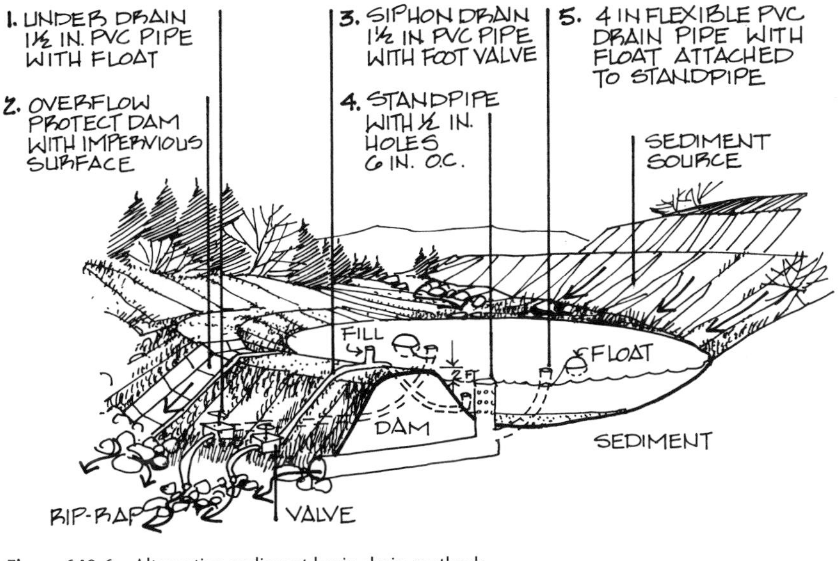
1. UNDER DRAIN
1½ IN. PVC PIPE
WITH FLOAT
2. OVERFLOW
PROTECT DAM
WITH IMPERVIOUS
SURFACE
3. SIPHON DRAIN
1½ IN. PVC PIPE
WITH FOOT VALVE
4. STANDPIPE
WITH ½ IN.
HOLES
6 IN. O.C.
5. 4 IN FLEXIBLE PVC
DRAIN PIPE WITH
FLOAT ATTACHED
TO STANDPIPE
SEDIMENT
SOURCE
FILL
FLOAT
2 FT.
DAM
SEDIMENT
RIP-RAP
VALVE

Figure 640-6 Alternative sediment basin drain methods.

5. Protecting disturbed surfaces from storm runoff by constructing diversion ditches, dikes, and conduits

6. Retaining sediment on-site by constructing sediment ponds, silt fences, and filter boxes, and by using chemical flocculents

Figures 640-1 through 640-10 illustrate various ways to limit erosion on disturbed landscapes. Table 640-2 is a checklist of sediment control measures.

3.2 Landshaping and Stratigraphy

Landshaping:

The aesthetic character of landshaping is largely dependent upon the proposed land use objectives, but care should be taken to create reasonable slopes. The steeper the disturbed slope, the more difficult it is to reclaim. A general rule of thumb is that as the percent of slope doubles, soil loss increases 2.6 times, and as the length of slope doubles, soil loss increases 3 times. Slopes 3:1 or steeper call for special reclamation measures. In most of these cases, no topsoil is present and compaction is inordinately high.

Figures 640-11 through 640-14 illustrate several considerations and treatments related to reclamation of slopes.

Stratigraphy:

Stratigraphy refers to the layering of subsurface materials. The characteristics of the subsurface structure will have a significant impact on stability, on water holding capacity, and on the effect of buried toxic materials. Toxic materials should be placed as deep as possible in locations unaffected by groundwater. In the United States, Public Law (PL) 95-87 requires a minimum of 4 ft (1.2 m) of soil cover over acid-generating materials.

The amount of a plant growth medium necessary to establish a stable vegetative community is 18 to 24 in (450 to 600 mm). This depth is needed to serve as a reservoir, making water available to plants during periods of low precipitation. When the materials below this medium are too porous to retain water, an artificial moisture barrier (plastic, asphalt, or similar material) can be placed between the strata.

3.3 Surface Conditioning

Surface conditioning is concerned with the chemical and physical nature of the top several inches (centimeters) of growth medium.

Topsoil:

Topsoil is the preferred growing medium. The cost of topsoil removal, stockpiling,

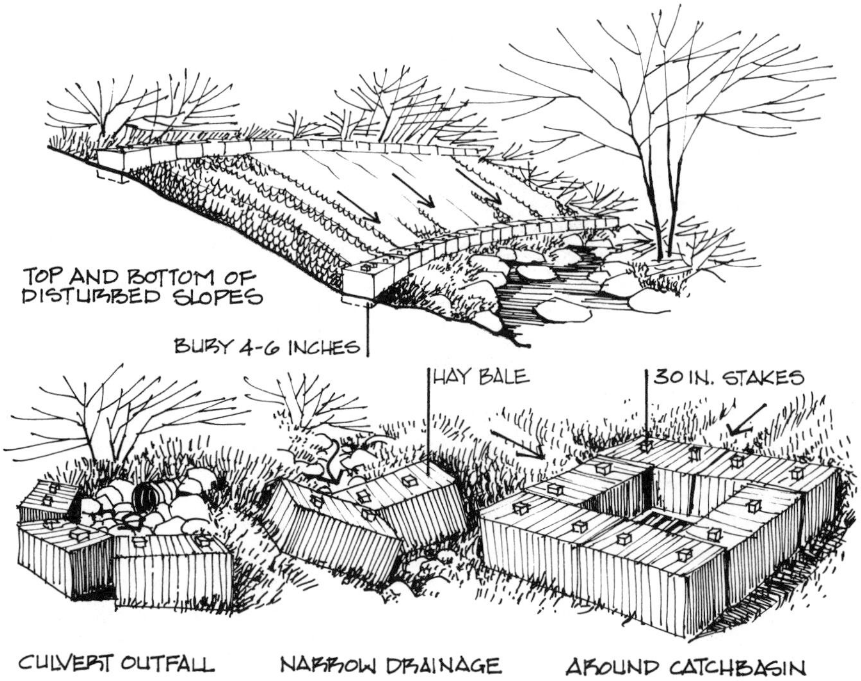
TOP AND BOTTOM OF DISTURBED SLOPES
BURY 4-6 INCHES
HAY BALE
30 IN. STAKES
CULVERT OUTFALL
NARROW DRAINAGE
AROUND CATCHBASIN

Figure 640-7 Sediment control methods using erosion bales.

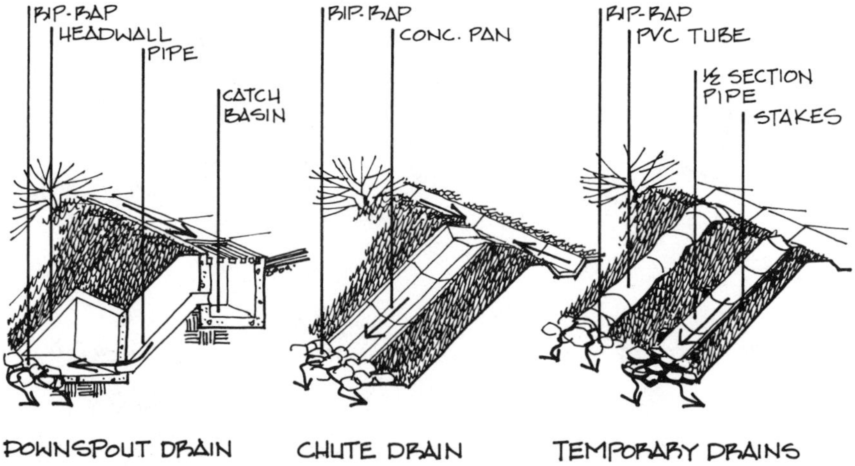
RIP-RAP
HEADWALL
PIPE
CATCH BASIN
RIP-RAP
CONC. PAN
RIP-RAP
PVC TUBE
½ SECTION PIPE
STAKES
DOWNSPOUT DRAIN
CHUTE DRAIN
TEMPORARY DRAINS

Figure 640-8 Slope drain methods.

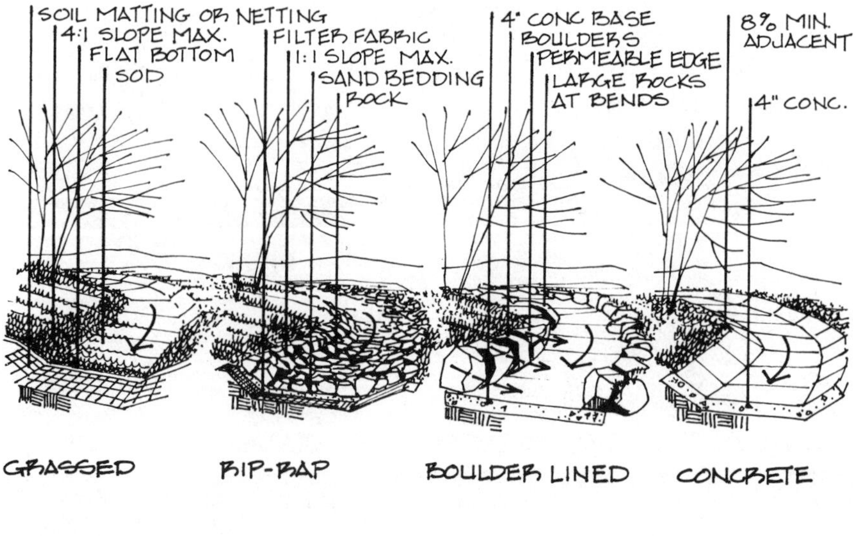
SOIL MATTING OR NETTING
4:1 SLOPE MAX.
FLAT BOTTOM
SOD
FILTER FABRIC
1:1 SLOPE MAX.
SAND BEDDING
ROCK
4" CONC BASE
BOULDERS
PERMEABLE EDGE
LARGE ROCKS AT BENDS
8% MIN. ADJACENT
4" CONC.
GRASSED
RIP-RAP
BOULDER LINED
CONCRETE

Figure 640-9 Drainage channel methods.

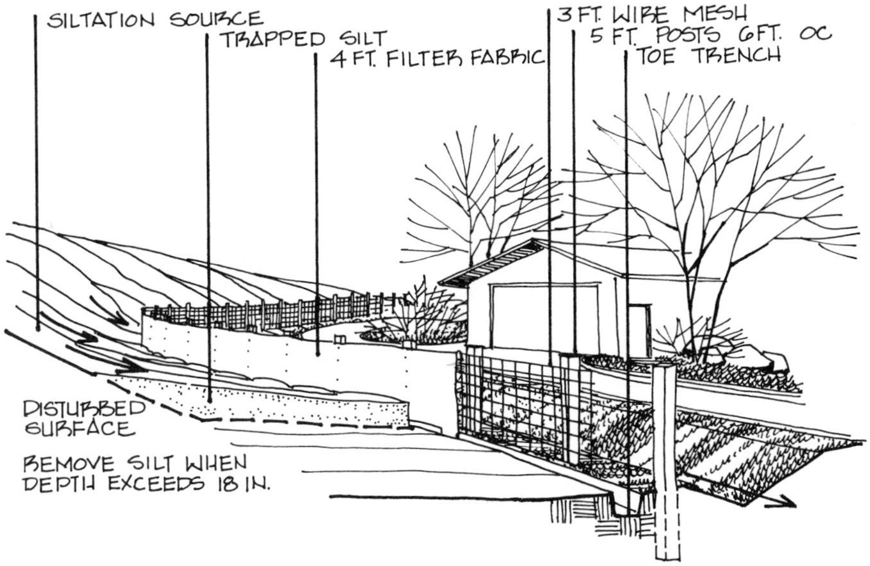
SILTATION SOURCE
TRAPPED SILT
4 FT. FILTER FABRIC
3 FT. WIRE MESH
5 FT. POSTS 6FT. OC
TOE TRENCH
DISTURBED SURFACE
REMOVE SILT WHEN DEPTH EXCEEDS 18 IN.

Figure 640-10 Filter fence method for trapping silt.

TABLE 640-2
Sediment Control Checklist

	Construction operation															
Control measures prior to or concurrent with construction	*Clearing and grubbing*	*Culverts*	*Channel changes*	*Structures*	*Pier construction*	*Stream crossings*	*Temporary roads*	*Excavation*	*Borrow*	*Wasting*	*Embankment*	*Subgrade*	*Base course*	*Paving*	*Perimeter areas*	*Landscaping*
Sediment basins																
Check dams																
Filter barriers																
Diversion dikes and ditches																
Berms																
Slope drains																
Seeding, mulching, and netting																
Mulching																
Sodding																
Ditch paving																
Slope paving																
Riprap																
Other																

Source: Modified from the Colorado Department of Highways, *I-70 in a Mountain Environment—Vail Pass, Colorado,* Denver, Colorado.

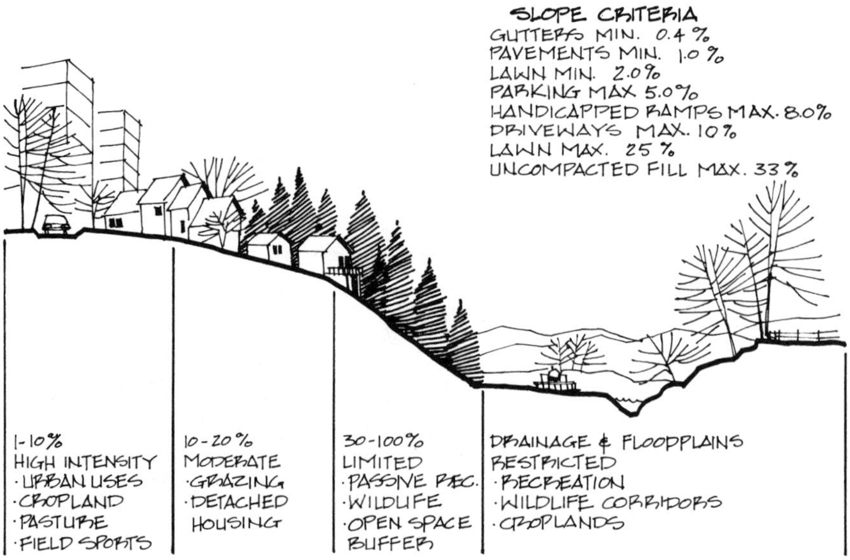
SLOPE CRITERIA
GUTTERS MIN. 0.4 %
PAVEMENTS MIN. 1.0 %
LAWN MIN. 2.0%
PARKING MAX 5.0%
HANDICAPPED RAMPS MAX. 8.0%
DRIVEWAYS MAX. 10%
LAWN MAX. 25 %
UNCOMPACTED FILL MAX. 33%
1-10%
HIGH INTENSITY
·URBAN USES
·CROPLAND
·PASTURE
·FIELD SPORTS
10-20%
MODERATE
·GRAZING
·DETACHED
HOUSING
30-100%
LIMITED
·PASSIVE REC.
·WILDLIFE
·OPEN SPACE
BUFFER
DRAINAGE & FLOODPLAINS
RESTRICTED
·RECREATION
·WILDLIFE CORRIDORS
·CROPLANDS

Figure 640-11 Appropriate land use related to slope.

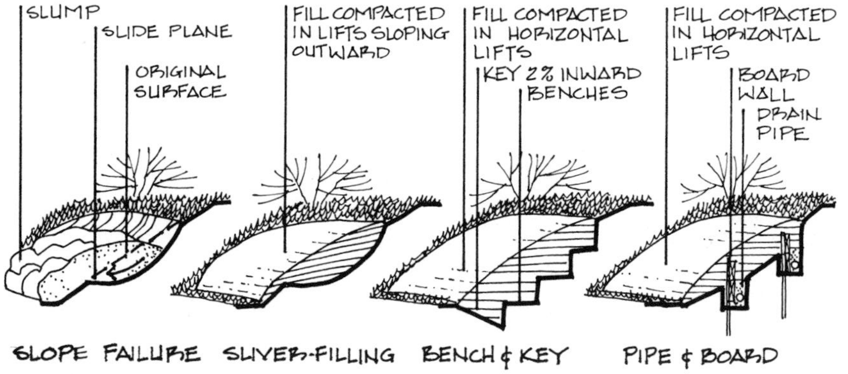
SLUMP
SLIDE PLANE
ORIGINAL
SURFACE
FILL COMPACTED
IN LIFTS SLOPING
OUTWARD
FILL COMPACTED
IN HORIZONTAL
LIFTS
KEY 2% INWARD
BENCHES
FILL COMPACTED
IN HORIZONTAL
LIFTS
BOARD
WALL
DRAIN
PIPE
SLOPE FAILURE
SLIVER-FILLING
BENCH & KEY
PIPE & BOARD

Figure 640-12 Slope failure repair methods.

GOUGING
DOZERBASINS
CHISELING

Figure 640-13 Surface-roughening methods of concentrating precipitation.

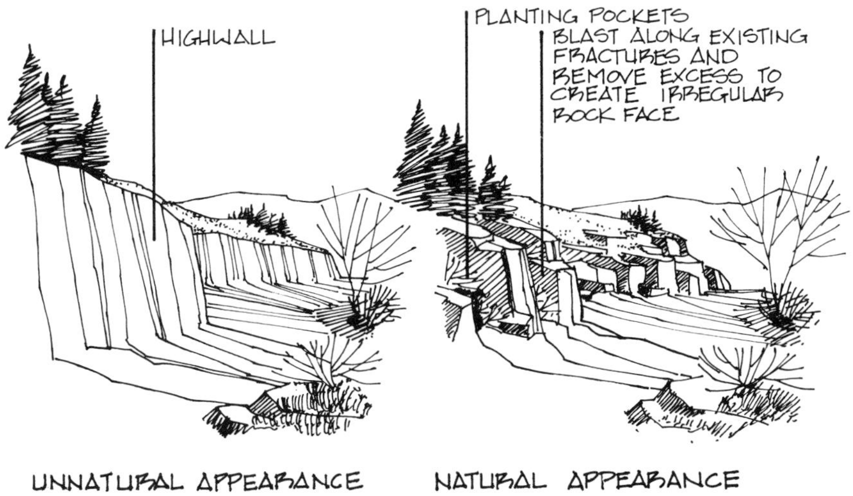
HIGHWALL
PLANTING POCKETS
BLAST ALONG EXISTING FRACTURES AND REMOVE EXCESS TO CREATE IRREGULAR ROCK FACE
UNNATURAL APPEARANCE
NATURAL APPEARANCE

Figure 640-14 Methods of naturalizing highwalls and rock cuts.

and replacement is typically less than changing the chemical and physical properties of subsoil to make it suitable as a plant growing medium. Research has shown that neither the age nor the depth of a stockpile will significantly affect the quality of the soil as a growing medium. However, freshly moved topsoil is easier to spread and is an excellent source of viable native seed and other plant propagules. Older stockpiles, if not properly managed, can be a source of undesirable plants.

Unlike subsoil or mining spoils, topsoil contains important soil fauna and bacteria which are active in maintaining aeration, water infiltration, and root penetration and in transforming minerals into forms useful to plants. Moist, well-aerated, warm soils containing organic matter provide the best conditions for this biological activity.

Stabilizing Topsoil:

It is difficult to create a good bond between topsoil and subsoil or to stabilize topsoil thicknesses of more than 3 to 4 in (75 to 100 mm) on slopes greater than 3:1. Stabilization of the topsoil on such slopes is typically accomplished by using a sheepsfoot roller or by ribbing on contour.

Improving Water Retention Capacity:

Soil materials which have little capacity to retain water can be improved by adding organic matter, such as treated sewage sludge, manure, or compost. Sewage sludge is good because it contains nutrients and trace elements essential to plant growth. Application rates are determined by testing for concentrations of various chemicals in order to prevent excess nitrogen from polluting ground or surface waters, and to prevent a buildup of toxic trace elements. A USDA Forest Service publication entitled *A Guide for Revegetating Coal Mine Soils in the Eastern United States* suggests the following rates of application:

1. Barnyard manure and composted garbage at 15 to 30 tons/acre (34,000 to 68,000 kg/ha)

2. Air-dried leaves at 2 to 4 tons/acre (4550 to 9070 kg/ha)

3. Sewage sludge and effluent at volumes equivalent to 20 to 50 tons/acre (45,000 to 113,000 kg/ha) of dry matter

Any one of a family of gel-like chemical products called *supermoisturizers* can also be used to improve the water retention capacity of dry soils. When mixed into soil, these products act like tiny sponges, expanding many times their original volume and holding water for use by plants. As they have a useful life of only several months, these products are used only to help establish plants.

Modifying Acidic Soils:

High acidity results from the oxidation of minerals like sulfides. Soil materials which are acidic can be modified by adding lime (Table 640-3). The SMP buffer pH test is used for mine spoils to determine lime application rates. Lime should be applied as far in advance of seeding as possible and as deeply as possible, at least to the depth that the materials are exposed to the air during the conditioning process. In addition to correcting low pH, lime will:

1. Improve the physical condition of soil.

2. Add calcium to the soil.

3. Accelerate the decomposition of organic matter, releasing nitrogen.

4. Increase fertilizer efficiency.

5. Increase nutrient availability.

6. Decrease toxicity of aluminum and ferric ions as well as decrease the availability of heavy metals such as lead, mercury, and cadmium.

The approximate amount of lime that should be applied to adjust spoil pH is shown in Figure 640-15.

Modifying Saline Soils:

Saline soils can be modified by leaching excess soluble salts through the soil (Figure 640-16). This can be done by adding organic matter or other such material to improve the infiltration quality of the soil, and by irrigating with low-salt water. Sodic and saline-sodic soils are a different matter, as water alone will not leach out excess exchangeable sodium. The modification procedure involves replacing sodium by another cation and then leaching, initially with salty water. Gypsum is commonly used for this purpose. The gypsum requirement (GR) to reclaim sodic soil is calculated as follows: GR = 1.72 (Na_x), in tons/acre (kg/ha) of gypsum. Na_x is in milliequivalents of exchangeable sodium to be replaced by calcium. Other materials used for this purpose are sulfuric acid, sulfur, lime-sulfur, and iron sulfate.

Applying Fertilizers:

Soil materials low in nutrients can be improved by applying fertilizer. Sufficient nitrogen is usually available in topsoil for plant establishment, while subsoils and geologic materials are usually deficient. Nitrogen is more of a limiting factor in plant productivity than it is in the establishment of plants. Although nitrogen is needed the first season on some sites, its application is most beneficial during the second growing season. Since nitrogen is water soluble, its effect is immediate but short-term. Applications before the desired perennial materials are established will favor annual

TABLE 640-3
Forms of Lime

Type	*Characteristic*
Ground limestone (calcium carbonate)	■ Insoluble in water but soluble in acid ■ Long-range effect (mix at least 10-in deep)
Burnt lime (calcium oxide) and hydrated lime (calcium hydroxide)	■ Very soluble in water ■ Immediate but short-range effect

weeds instead. It is common practice to apply additional nitrogen at the time of mulching to make up for the short-term depletion of available nitrogen by microorganisms when mulch is added. The amount of nitrogen used for 2 tons/acre (4550 kg/ha) of straw is 50 to 60 lb (23 to 27 kg). In the long term, legumes are an important factor in sustaining sufficient nitrogen levels and should be considered in the plant mix.

Unlike nitrogen deficiencies, phosphorus deficiencies will limit and even prevent seedling establishment. On soil materials which test low in phosphorus, 100 lb/acre (112 kg/ha) of P_2O_5 are applied to coarse-textured soil, and 200 lb/acre (228 kg/ha) are applied on fine-textured soils. Since phosphorus is not mobile in the soil, it is important to mix it into the rooting medium.

Seedbed Preparation:

At a minimum, the physical condition of the surface material must be developed into a good seedbed. A good seedbed has the following properties:

1. Firm, but not compacted, under the seeding depth

2. Relatively loose above the seeding depth to allow seed penetration and cover

3. Free of weeds

4. Capable of holding moisture

Favorable physical conditions are typically developed through cultivation by ripping or plowing compacted materials, then disking and harrowing (Figure 640-17). If the surface is partially vegetated and inhibiting erosion, it may be desirable not to cultivate. In such areas, allow existing plants to remain, or use herbicides to eliminate weeds, and deep-furrow the seed directly into the soil. Roughening the surface with pockets, gouges, and furrows slows runoff, checks erosion, and in dry areas provides for the accumulation and retention of snow and rain (see Figure 640-13).

Mulches:

Mulches are helpful in creating favorable surface conditions for plant establishment by:

1. Inhibiting wind and water erosion

2. Facilitating water infiltration

3. Inhibiting evaporation, and thereby reducing the upward movement of salts

4. Moderating soil temperatures

5. Adding desirable propagules to the seedbed when it is comprised of fresh native materials

6. Adding beneficial microorganisms to the soil

In more humid climates, seeding, fertilizing, and mulching are commonly done in one operation hydraulically. In such climates, wood fiber at ¾ ton/acre (1700 kg/ha) is used. In arid climates it is important to place seed beneath the soil surface, and mulch is applied as a separate operation. The most common practice is to apply hay or straw at 1½ to 2 tons/acre (3400 to 4500 kg/ha). The straw is crimped into the surface with a disk-type packer. On slopes greater than 3:1 or in high-wind areas, mulch is anchored with special equipment, nets, and tackifiers such as:

1. Asphalt emulsion at 1200 gal/acre (11,350 L/ha)

2. Resin emulsion in water at 600 gal/acre (5700 L/ha)

3. Latex emulsion at the manufacturer's recommendations

4. Soil binders at the manufacturer's recommendations

5. Wood fiber hydromulch at 750 lb/acre (850 kg/ha)

Mulch may also be integrated into erosion control blankets or mats made of jute, paper, excelsior, or plastic.

Other types of mulch include:

1. Woodchips, pole peelings, and shredded bark or woodchips at 20 tons/acre (45,350 kg/ha)

2. Shredded native grasses and brush at 1½ to 2 tons/acre (3400 to 4500 kg/ha)

3. Manure or dried sewage sludge at 5 to 15 tons/acre (11,340 to 34,000 kg/ha)

4. Rocks and gravel at 1 to 2 in (25 to 50 mm) deep [135 tons/acre = 1 in deep (306,000 kg/ha = 25 mm deep)]

5. Plastic films

3.4 Planting

The selection of plant materials is dependent upon land use objectives and various site factors.

Temporary Erosion Control Plantings:

Temporary erosion control plantings are selected for their ability to establish a quick cover. If these temporary plants are undesirable in the long run, then they can be prevented from going to seed and may be readily eliminated or succeeded by permanent plantings when grown under the nurse crop concept. Commonly used plants for temporary erosion control include annual grasses such as annual ryegrass, barley field brome, oats, winter rye, wheat, sorghums, and millets.

Permanent Plantings:

It is essential that species which are intended to be permanent should be well-adapted to the site; that is, they should be able to reproduce and sustain their popu-

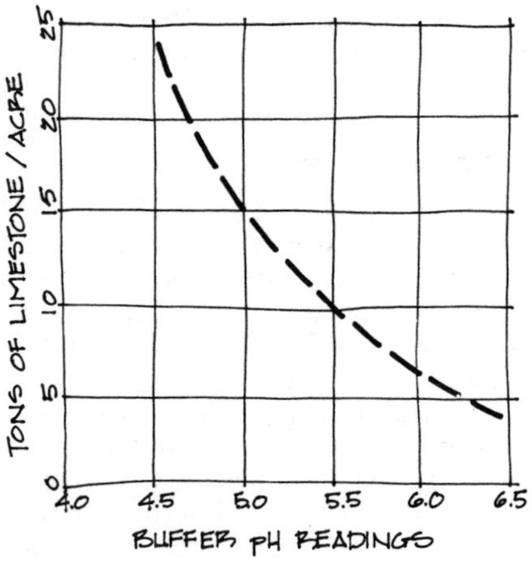
TONS OF LIMESTONE / ACRE
0
5
10
15
20
25
4.0
4.5
5.0
5.5
6.0
6.5
BUFFER pH READINGS

Figure 640-15 Approximate limestone application rates required to adjust spoil to pH 6.4 for buffer pH readings.

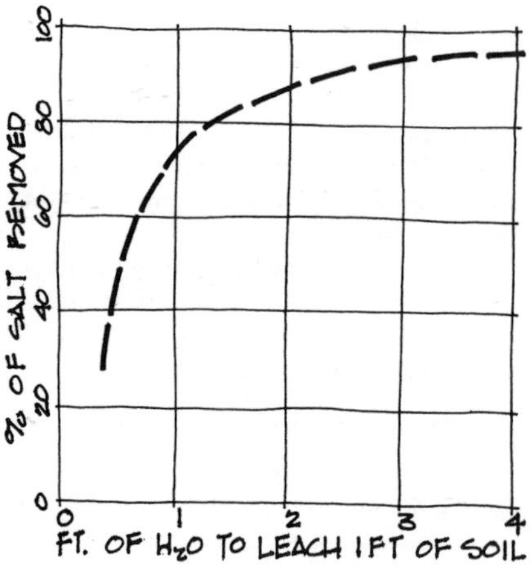
% OF SALT REMOVED
0
20
40
60
80
100
0
1
2
3
4
FT. OF H2O TO LEACH 1 FT OF SOIL

Figure 640-16 Amount of water required to leach salt from saline soil.

lations for a substantial period of time. A process of ecological succession can be promoted by using a wide variety of plant materials, thus facilitating gradual changes in the communities of plants. Nurse crops or pioneer plantings may be required for selected sites to make microclimatic conditions more favorable for latter-stage species. This is particularly important on sites with severely constraining conditions and on those at high elevations. Pioneer tree species unable to reproduce under their own canopy include aspen, bristlecone pine, limber pine, and lodgepole pine. Eventually, these species are either rejuvenated by disturbance or succeeded by species like spruce and fir.

In natural settings, a visual blending of disturbed and undisturbed areas is achieved by selection of new plant materials similar in size, form, texture, and color to those in adjacent undisturbed areas. Most erosion control grasses are selected for their sod forming characteristics. Deep rooting plants are best for slopes.

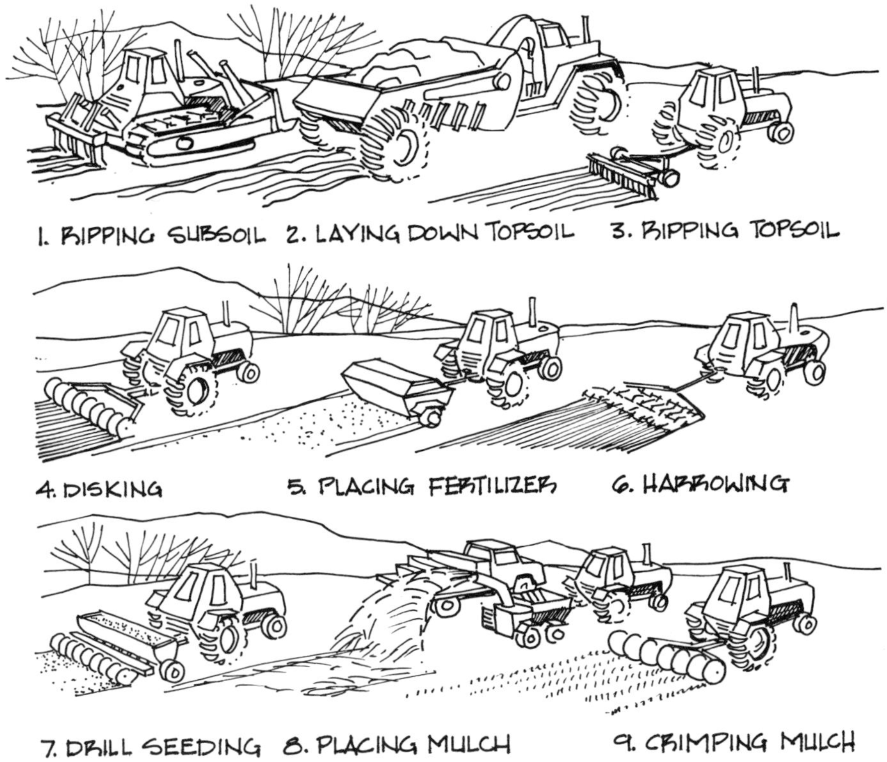
1. RIPPING SUBSOIL
2. LAYING DOWN TOPSOIL
3. RIPPING TOPSOIL
4. DISKING
5. PLACING FERTILIZER
6. HARROWING
7. DRILL SEEDING
8. PLACING MULCH
9. CRIMPING MULCH

Figure 640-17 Methods of surface conditioning.

Selecting Plant Material:

Sources of technical assistance on selecting plant materials for reclamation of disturbed landscapes include:

1. Universities and their extension services.

2. U.S. Soil Conservation Service offices.

3. U.S. Surface Environment and Mining publications.

4. U.S. Soil Conservation Service plant materials centers. (These centers are located throughout the United States and have been set up for the development of forage and erosion control plants.)

5. PIN (Plant Information Network). This network is a computer-based data bank for information on native and naturalized vascular plants of several western states in the United States. PIN information is a service of the U.S. Department of Interior's Fish and Wildlife Service, Western Energy Land Use Team, located at Fort Collins, Colorado.

Acquiring Plant Material:

Plant material can be obtained from one or more of the following sources (the SCS and U.S. Forest Service distribute lists):

1. The predisturbance vegetation and topsoil

2. Existing vegetation collected from the area

3. State nurseries

4. Commercial native plant nurseries

5. Commercial seed suppliers

6. U.S. SCS plant materials centers

7. U.S. Forest Service nurseries

8. Small private seed collectors

Native Regrowth:

A method proved effective for establishing native vegetation on steep slopes is described in an article entitled "The Native Regrowth Method for Steep Slopes," *Landscape Architecture,* January 1979, by Wayne Tyson. This method, using predisturbance vegetation and topsoil, recommends the following steps:

1. Crush or shred low vegetation on the site and remove it with 4 to 6 in (100 to 150 mm) of topsoil.

2. Stockpile the soil/mulch mixture, keeping the surface moist to preserve inherent moisture.

3. Spread the soil mulch evenly over a moist, roughened subgrade. On steep slopes, do not exceed a soil/mulch layer of 4 in (100 mm), and bond it to the subgrade with a sheepsfoot roller.

Nursery Stock:

Collected trees and shrubs are transplanted during their dormant season. Sods and shrub pads are readily transplanted by use of front-end loaders. Containerized materials may be planted during any part of the growing season, provided that ample water is available (Figure 640-18).

TUBELETS 2-3 IN. DIA BY 12 IN. CONSTR. OF VARIOUS PAPER PRODUCTS. DEPTH ALLOWS DEEP ROOT GROWTH
PATENTED PLASTIC 'TUBE PAK'
STYROFOAM MULTIPLE PLANT CONTAINER DIVISIONS 12 IN DEEP

Figure 640-18 Methods of containerizing reclamation plants.

Some nurseries specializing in reclamation plants have developed specialized mini-containers for seedling stock. Actual planting methods follow standard nursery practices. Basins are constructed around plants and are either covered with plastic or mulched to trap and retain moisture and to reduce competition by weeds.

Seeding Methods:

Seed from the area to be disturbed or from nearby areas may be collected by using combines, bumper hoppers, or various hand methods (Figure 640-19). Cleaning and sorting of seed is necessary only for commercial operations. When legumes are used, the seed is typically inoculated with nitrogen-fixing bacteria. The ideal time to collect seed is under dry conditions just before the seeds begin to disperse naturally, which is usually 6 to 8 weeks after blooming. The seed should be spread out and allowed to dry thoroughly for 1 to 2 weeks immediately after collection. Store seeds in dry, ventilated locations. Fabric containers are better than plastic bags.

Seed is planted by broadcasting, hydroseeding, or drilling (Figure 640-20). Broadcasting requires at least twice as much seed as drilling, and poorer sites need more seed than favorable sites. Seeding rates are based on the number of individual plants (PLS) desired per square foot (converted to pounds of seed per area). The formula for calculating the seeding rate is as follows: 43,560 × PLS desired per square foot ÷ Seeds per pound × purity × germination = Planting rate of commercial seeds in pounds per acre.

In arid areas, it is important to drill the seed ¼ to 1 in (6 to 25 mm) under the surface to prevent germinating seeds from drying out. It is important that the seedbed be firm; otherwise, its moisture holding capacity will be reduced. Rolling before and/or after seed placement is beneficial.

Broadcasting is the least expensive and fastest seeding method; it is not so dependent upon surface conditions and it has the advantage of handling uncleaned seed. Broadcasting can also be accomplished aerially. Broadcast seeding may be effective in arid areas under the following conditions:

1. On loose soil where sloughing will cover the seed

2. Following plowing or disking

3. Ahead of mechanical treatment providing seed coverage

4. In deep ashes after burns

5. Under deciduous trees prior to leaf fall

HAND COLLECTION
SMALL COMBINE
VACUUM
BUMPER HOPPER

Figure 640-19 Seed collecting methods.

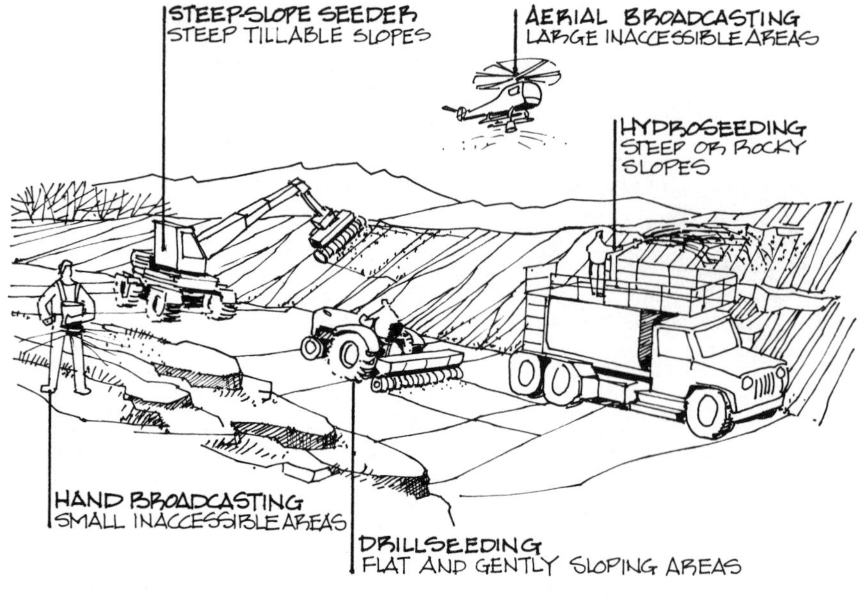
STEEP-SLOPE SEEDER
STEEP TILLABLE SLOPES
AERIAL BROADCASTING
LARGE INACCESSIBLE AREAS
HYDROSEEDING
STEEP OR ROCKY SLOPES
HAND BROADCASTING
SMALL INACCESSIBLE AREAS
DRILLSEEDING
FLAT AND GENTLY SLOPING AREAS

Figure 640-20 Seeding methods and applications.

Planting Schedules:

In general, the best season to plant is just prior to the season that receives the most dependable precipitation, usually in North America spring or fall. Cover can be established during any part of the growing period when moisture is available and by proper selection of species. Perennial grasses that grow in cool seasons usually do better when planted in the fall; legumes and woody plants do better when planted in the spring; some annuals can be successful when planted in mid to late summer. In critical areas, clear plastic may be used as a temporary way to increase seed germination. This material helps preserve soil moisture and will increase early and late season soil temperatures, but it requires careful management to prevent excessive temperatures in some areas. Table 640-4 lists grass species recommended for use in landscape reclamation (*Weeds, Trees and Turf,* July 1979).

3.5 Establishment and Maintenance of Vegetation

Figures 640-21 through 640-26 illustrate a variety of techniques for transplanting, watering, and protecting vegetation.

Once plant materials are established, the following management practices can help achieve desired densities and relatively stable conditions:

1. Supplemental watering (particularly important for trees and shrubs in arid areas)

2. Periodic fertilization to increase plant vigor

3. Mowing or burning to favor perennials

4. Fencing, screening, and the use of chemical repellents (Table 640-5) and poisons for pest control

5. Providing roosts and rockpiles to encourage natural predator control

REFERENCES

Colorado Department of Highways. *I-70 in a Mountain Environment,* Federal Highway Administration, Washington, DC, 1978.

Cook, Wayne C., Robert M. Hyde, and Phillip L. Sims. *Revegetation Guidelines for Surface Mined Areas,* Colorado State University/Range Science Department, Fort Collins, CO, 1974.

Gray, Donald H., and Andrew T. Elsier. *Biotechnical Slope Protection and Erosion Control,* Van Nostrand Reinhold, New York, 1982.

TABLE 640-4
Grasses for Landscape Reclamation*

Species	Scientific name	Variety	Eastern to midwestern states	Midwest to western states	Species availability	Seeds per lb, in 1000's
Drought-tolerant bunchgrass						
Beardless wheatgrass	*Agropyron inerme*	Whitmar		X	A	142
Big bluegrass	*Poa ampla*	Sherman		X	A	900
Bluebunch wheatgrass	*Agropyron spicatum*		X	X	L	117
Hard fescue	*Festuca ovina, variety duriuscula*	Durar	X	X	A	565
Indian ricegrass	*Oryzopsis hymenoides*			X	L	188
Needle and thread	*Stipa comata*			X	L	123
Russian wildrye	*Elymus junceus*	Sawki		X	A	175
Sand dropseed	*Sporobolus cryptandrus*		X	X	L	5,000
Siberian wheatgrass	*Agropyron sibiticum*			X	A	206
Slender wheatgrass	*Agropyron trachycaulum*		X	X	A	160
Weeping lovegrass	*Eragrostis curvula*		X(W)	X	A	1,500
Sheep fescue	*Festuca ovina*		X	X	A	565
Drought-tolerant sod-forming grasses						
Canada bluegrass	*Poa Compressa*	Rubens	X	X	A	2,495
Tall fescue	*Festuca arundinacea*		X		A	227
Creeping red fescue	*Festuca rubra*			X	A	615
Pubescent wheatgrass	*Agropyron trichophorum*	Greenleaf or		X	A	90
		Topar	X	X	A	
Streambank wheatgrass	*Agropyron riparium*	Sodar		X	A	170
Intermediate wheatgrass	*Agropyron intermedium*	Oahe		X	A	93
Thickpike wheatgrass	*Agropyron dasystachyum*			X	L	186
Western wheatgrass	*Agropyron smithii*		X	X	A	126
Bermudagrass	*Cynodon dactylon*		X(W)	X	A	1,787
Timothy	*Phleum pratense*		X	X	A	1,230
Kentucky bluegrass	*Poa pratensis*		X	X	A	2,150
Sand stabilizing plants						
Prairie sandreed	*Calamovilla longifolia*			X	L	274
Switchgrass	*Panicum virgatum*		X	X	A	389
Sand bluestem	*Andropogon hallii*			X	L	113
Indian ricegrass	*Oryzopsis hymenoides*			X	L	188
Needle and thread	*Stipa comata*			X	L	123
Sand lovegrass	*Eragrostis trichodes*			X	A	1,300
Beachgrass	*Ammophila spp.*		X		NA	114
Blowout grass	*Redfieldia flexuosa*		(W)	X	L	263
Sandhill muhly	*Muhlenbergia pungens*		(W)	X	L	614
Acid-tolerant grasses						
Canada bluegrass	*Poa Compressa*	Rubens	X	X	A	2,495
Perennial ryegrass	*Lolium perenne*		X	X	A	247
Colonial bentgrass	*Agrostis tenuis*	Highland	X	X	A	8,723
Creeping bentgrass	*Agrostis palustris*		X	X	A	7,800
Creeping foxtail	*Alopecurus arundinaceus*	Garrison	X	X	A	400
Hard fescue	*Festuca ovina, variety duriuscula*	Durar	X	X	A	565
Bermudagrass	*Cynodon dactylon*		X(W)	X	A	1,787
Meadow foxtail	*Alopecurus pratensis*		X	X	A	580
Red fescue	*Festuca rubra*		X	X	A	615
Redtop	*Agrostis alba*		X	X	A	4,990
Switchgrass	*Panicum virgatum*		X(W)	X	A	389
Weeping lovegrass	*Eragrostis curvula*		X(W)	X	A	1,500
Akaline-tolerant grasses						
Alkali sacaton	*Sporobolus airoides*			X	A	1,750
Bermudagrass	*Cynodon dactylon*		X(W)	X	A	1,787
Foxtail barley	*Hordeum jubatum*		X	X	A	352
Perennial ryegrass	*Lolium perenne*		X	X	A	247
Streambank wheatgrass	*Agropyron riparium*	Sodar	X	X	A	170
Tall wheatgrass	*Agropyron elongatum*	Alkar	X	X	A	79
Western wheatgrass	*Agropyron smithii*		X	X	A	126
Alkali cordgrass	*Spartina gracilis*			X	NA	224
Basin wildrye	*Elymus Cinereus*			X	NA	95
Canada wildrye	*Elymus canadensis*		X	X	NA	106
Saltgrass	*Distichlis stricta*		(W)	X	NA	83
Russian wildrye	*Elymus junceus*	Sawki		X	A	175
Crested wheatgrass	*Agropyron desertorum*			X	A	175
Alkali grass	*Puccinellia lemmoni*	Lemmons		X	A	2,100
Slender wheatgrass	*Agropyron trachycaulum*					160

(continued)

Table 640-4 *(Continued)*

Species	Scientific name	Variety	Eastern to midwestern states	Midwest to western states	Species availability	Seeds per lb, in 1000's
Grasses and legumes tolerant of moist soils						
Alsike clover	*Trifolium hybridum*		X	X	A	680
Alkali cordgrass	*Spartina gracilis*			X	A	224
Reed canarygrass	*Phalaris arundinacea*		X	X	A	506
Colonial bentgrass	*Agrostis tenuis*	Highland	X	X	A	8,723
Creeping bentgrass	*Agrostis palustris*		X	X	A	7,800
Poa trivialis	*Poa trivialis*	Sabre	X		A	2,540
Creeping foxtail	*Alopecurius arundinaceus*	Garrison	X	X	A	400
Meadow foxtail	*Alopecurus pratensis*		X	X	A	580
Perennial ryegrass	*Lolium perenne*		X	X	A	247
Legumes						
Crown vetch	*Coronilla varia*	Penngift	X	X	A	110
Birdfoot treefoil	*Lotus corniculatus*	Empire	X	X	A	407
Sericea lespedeza	*Lespedeza cuneata*		X	X	A	350
White clover	*Trifolium repens*		X	X	A	850
Alsike clover	*Trifolium hybridum*					680

* Codes are as follows: an X indicates presence of species in a given area, A indicates commercially available, L indicates limited availability, NA indicates not commercially available, and W indicates a warm-season grass best adapted to the southern states, or similar climate.

Source: Adapted from "Reclamation Grass Selection Depends on Combinations, Cost," *Weeds, Trees, and Turf,* July 1979.

BACKHOE
TREESPADE
FRONTEND LOADER

Figure 640-21 Shrub and tree collection methods using equipment.

CONNECT'G STOLON
CUT
DRY SOIL
PLANT 2nd ROOT DEEP IN DAMP SOIL
EXISTING CONDITION
REMOVE & PRUNE TOP
TRANSPLANT

Figure 640-22 Methods of transplanting stoloniferous plants in arid areas.

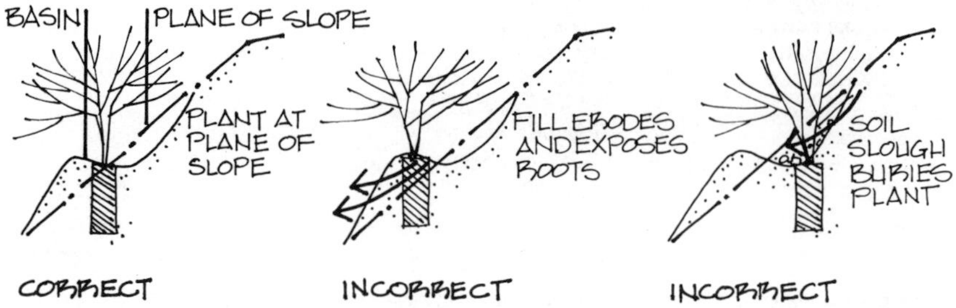

BASIN
PLANE OF SLOPE
PLANT AT PLANE OF SLOPE
FILL ERODES AND EXPOSES ROOTS
SOIL SLOUGH BURIES PLANT
CORRECT
INCORRECT
INCORRECT

Figure 640-23 Correct slope-planting method.

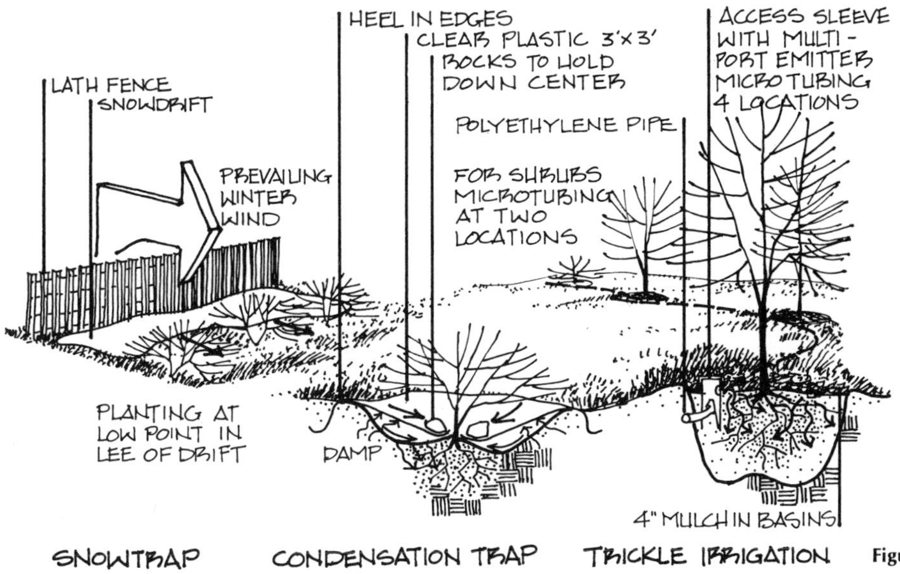
HEEL IN EDGES
CLEAR PLASTIC 3'x3'
ROCKS TO HOLD DOWN CENTER
ACCESS SLEEVE WITH MULTI-PORT EMITTER MICROTUBING 4 LOCATIONS
LATH FENCE
SNOWDRIFT
POLYETHYLENE PIPE
PREVAILING WINTER WIND
FOR SHRUBS MICROTUBING AT TWO LOCATIONS
PLANTING AT LOW POINT IN LEE OF DRIFT
DAMP
4" MULCH IN BASINS
SNOWTRAP
CONDENSATION TRAP
TRICKLE IRRIGATION

Figure 640-24 Methods of increasing water.

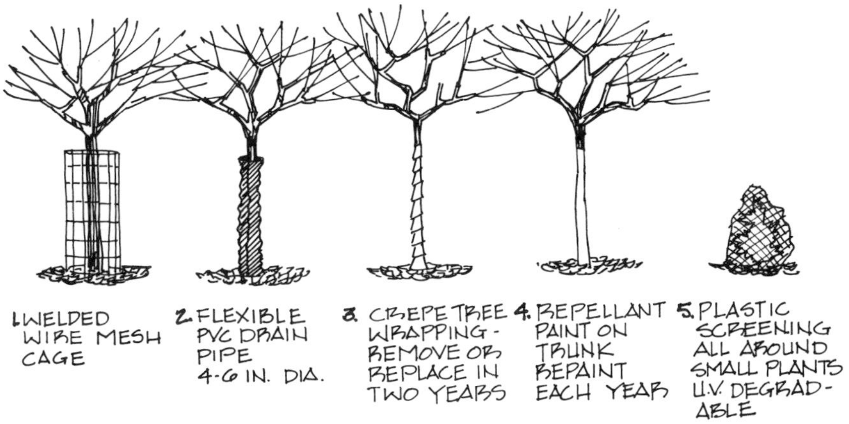
1. WELDED WIRE MESH CAGE
2. FLEXIBLE PVC DRAIN PIPE 4-6 IN. DIA.
3. CREPE TREE WRAPPING - REMOVE OR REPLACE IN TWO YEARS
4. REPELLANT PAINT ON TRUNK REPAINT EACH YEAR
5. PLASTIC SCREENING ALL AROUND SMALL PLANTS U.V. DEGRAD-ABLE

Figure 640-25 Methods of protecting plants from pests.

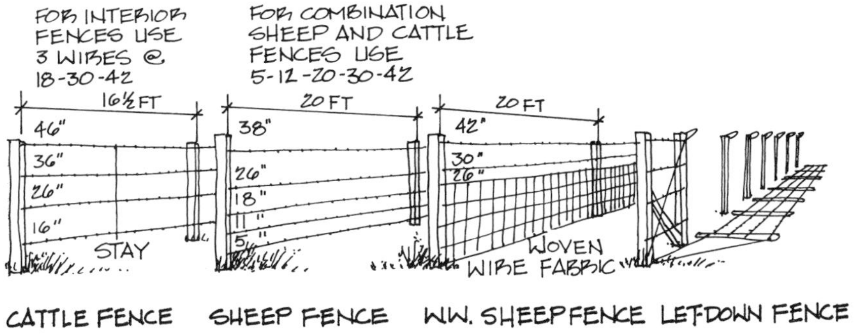
FOR INTERIOR FENCES USE 3 WIRES @ 18-30-42
FOR COMBINATION SHEEP AND CATTLE FENCES USE 5-12-20-30-42
16½ FT
20 FT
20 FT
46"
36"
26"
16"
STAY
38"
26"
18"
11"
5"
42"
30"
26"
WOVEN WIRE FABRIC
CATTLE FENCE
SHEEP FENCE
W.W. SHEEPFENCE
LET-DOWN FENCE

Figure 640-26 Range fencing methods.

Grim, Elmore C., and Ronald D. Hill. *Environmental Protection in Surface Mining of Coal,* U.S. Environmental Protection Agency, Cincinnati, OH, 1974.

Simpson, Dave. *Selective Spoil Handling: An Operator's View,* Adequate Reclamation of Mined Lands Symposium, Billings, MT, 1980.

USDA Forest Service. *User Guide to Vegetation-Mining and Reclamation in the West,* U.S. Department of Agriculture, Ogden, UT, 1979.

Willard, Beatrice E. *High-Elevation Reclamation Nuts and Bolts,* High Altitude Revegetation Workshop 2, Fort Collins, CO, 1976. ■

TABLE 640-5
Common Animal Repellents

Compound	*Animals repelled*
Tetramethylthiuram	Rodents and deer
Bone tar oil	Carnivores
9, 10 anthraquinone	Birds
4, aminopyridine	Birds
0, 0-dimethyl-0-4-methylthio-m-tolyl phosphorothioate	Birds
3-chloro-p-toluidine hydrochloride	Birds

Source: From USDA Forest Service, "User Guide to Vegetation: Mining and Reclamation in the West," General Technical Report INT-64, Intermountain Range and Experiment Station.

section 660: Sound Control

CREDITS

Contributors:

Walter Kehm
E. D. A. Collaborative, Inc.
Toronto, Ontario
Canada

Phillip Ellis
Wimpey Laboratories, Ltd.
Hayes, Middlesex
England

Reviewers:

J. R. Wear
Ministry of Transportation and Communications
Province of Ontario
Downsview, Ontario
Canada

Robert Armstrong
Federal Highway Administration
Washington, D.C.

Robert Newman
Christopher Menge
Bolt Beranek and Newman Inc.
Cambridge, Massachusetts

CONTENTS

1.0 INTRODUCTION

This section provides design and planning guidelines for the reduction or elimination of unwanted sound in the landscape. Because sound control is a very large subject, the amount of technical information presented here is necessarily limited. However, sources of additional information are listed under References at the end of this section. Regulations and standards for noise abatement and acoustical planning are not common, but an investigation of local ordinances is nevertheless essential when one is involved in any land use planning project.

The science of sound control in the landscape involves much more than the simple quantification of data. The quality of sound may be as important as the quantity of sound. Some sounds can have profound psychological effects on people. For example, the constant drone of cars on a highway is rarely as offensive as the squealing of brakes at an intersection. Masking unwanted sound (by falling water, for instance) is a technique which can mitigate noise disturbance by modifying the quality of the sound received by the ear.

1.1 Basic Approaches to Sound Control

Two approaches to sound control in the landscape include *acoustical planning,* where potential noise problems are minimized during design stages, prior to any construction, and *retrofitting,* where noise problems are mitigated by alteration to existing developments.

Acoustical Planning (Preplanning):

Where acoustical planning is possible, setbacks and other methods can be employed to minimize sound transmissions. Acoustical planning should be part of any land use planning project, especially with such major projects as airports, highways, and railroads. Acoustical models should be developed and tested to assess the planning implications both on and off the property.

Acoustical planning is more desirable than retrofitting, because as potential noise problems are identified, cost-saving mitigative measures can be taken to reduce noise levels to acceptable standards while at the same time designing a physical landscape with improved visual qualities. This can be achieved, for instance, through grading concepts that retain significant natural landforms and existing vegetation, as well as incorporate noise buffer mounds where necessary. Preplanning can accommodate public and private interests by reducing noise to acceptable levels, while retaining landscapes of high quality.

Retrofitting:

Acoustical planning principles can also be effectively applied to existing development, but the aesthetic results are often unattractive. Establishing adequate rights-of-way or buffer zones is difficult, typically including architectural barriers or walls. Capital construction and eventual maintenance costs can become limiting factors.

1.2 Acoustic Variables

Three acoustic variables to address when attempting to minimize noise problems in the landscape are: (1) the source of the sound, (2) the path and distance of the sound transmission, and (3) the receiver of the sound.

Source of the Sound:

Most noise can be modified by acoustical treatment at its source; however, this is often not as economically feasible as control of noise by various landscape planning techniques.

Path and Distance of Sound Transmission:

The path and the distance of sound transmission constitute an important variable in any strategy of noise reduction. A valley or a downwind site, for instance, can make any development located in these areas more susceptible to noise. Valleys and ravines can exacerbate conditions by channelizing sound waves. Such topographic conditions can present problems when intensively used highways or railways cross a valley, for instance. Analyses of topographic and climatic factors are required to assess the directions of sound transmission.

Receiver of the Sound:

People who are accustomed to quiet landscapes are significantly less tolerant of noise than people accustomed to suburban or urban environments. Masking of noise can sometimes be accomplished by introducing pleasant sounds, such as the sound of flowing water or rustling leaves.

2.0 PHYSICS OF SOUND

2.1 Nature of Sound Waves

Sound waves are generated by any pulsation or vibration of a source. The surrounding air is disturbed, thereby causing pressure changes which can be heard. The greater the change in pressure, the louder the sound.

The rate of repetition of these sound waves is referred to as *frequency.* It is measured in cycles per second or units of hertz (Hz). The normal audible range for humans is 20 to 20,000 Hz.

2.2 Sound Pressures and Decibels

Although the human ear acts like a sound filter by discriminating against some frequencies and giving preference to others, the range of sound pressure which the human ear can detect is relatively broad. Given this broad range, the measurement of sound is made more convenient by use of a logarithmic scale called the *decibel* (dB) scale.

To simulate human hearing, a sound measuring instrument is equipped with an electronic *A*-weighting filter which corresponds to human detection of sound. Sound pressure levels measured with the *A*-weighting filter switched on are given in dB(*A*).

Table 660-1 lists typical sound levels of everyday occurrences.

TABLE 660-1
Typical Sound Levels of Everyday Occurrences

Occurrence	*Sound level, dB(A)*
Weakest sound that can be heard (threshold of hearing)	0
Inside broadcast studio	20
Rural area at night	25
Whispered conversation at 2 m (6 ft)	30
Library	35
Residential area during daytime	
Rural	40
Suburban	50
Suburban, adjacent to airport	60
Conversation at 1 m (3 ft)	60
City center	65
Major roads (adjacent property ±20 m (65 ft) inside)	
Township road	50
Highway	60
Freeway (12-lane)	75
Diesel truck at 15 m (50 ft)	90
Noisy metal-working shop	100
Impulsive pile driving at 10 m (32 ft)	110
Jet taking off at 50 m (165 ft)	120
Pain begins	>120

3.0 NOISE

3.1 Definition and Sources of Noise

Under all circumstances, any unwanted, unpleasant, loud, or harsh sound is referred to as *noise.*

Table 660-2 summarizes a noise survey carried out in London, England. This survey and more recent studies confirm that vehicular traffic is the major source of urban noise.

3.2 Psychological Response to Noise

Although the acceptability of the type and level of noise is highly subjective, noise often disturbs people by interfering with communication, sleep, and other everyday activities. Noise can also cause physical discomfort and, if intense enough, can cause damage to hearing. People are usually annoyed more by high-frequency sound than by low-frequency sound, by certain tonal qualities (e.g., whines, hisses, or squeals), by impulsive sound (e.g., bangs and clanks), and by intermittent sound. Any frequent or continuous exposure to noise can lead to a reduction of human efficiency by a deterioration of physical and emotional well-being.

3.3 Units of Noise Measurement

The *A*-weighted sound level [db(*A*)] is typically used to measure sound levels in environmental studies. It is good practice to state the mode of measurement used when referring to noise levels measured with a meter (i.e., *slow, fast,* or *peak*). Three noise descriptions are: L_{eq}, L_{dn}, and L_n.

L_{eq} *(Equivalent Noise Level):*

Even though noise levels may be fluctuating continuously, a single-figure dB(*A*) measurement will only refer to noise levels at a particular point in time. To use a single, or *equivalent,* level which has the same effect on human ears, the *average* sound energy of the fluctuating noise is calculated. This is termed the *equivalent energy concept,* and the single-figure level, measured in units of dB(*A*), is called the *equivalent noise level,* or L_{eq}. L_{eq} can be determined over any time period and is usually expressed in brackets, e.g., L_{eq} (1 hour). Instruments are commercially available which measure L_{eq} directly.

L_{dn} *(Day-Night Equivalent Noise Level):*

The day-night equivalent noise level L_{dn} is a noise unit which is obtained by combining the equivalent energy level for the daytime period (07:00 to 22:00 hours) with the equivalent energy level for nighttime (22:00 to 07:00 hours). Because noise at night is more disturbing and more annoying than noise during the day, a weighting factor of 10 is applied to the nighttime noise.

L_n:

The noise level L_n refers to that level which is exceeded for *n* percent of the measurement time period. L_n is used to provide statistical information about a fluctuating noise signal. Some representative examples of L_n are L_{10} (peak), L_{50}, and L_{90} (ambient).

TABLE 660-2
Noise Survey (London, early 1960s)

Source of noise	Percentage of persons questioned who were disturbed by noise: When home	When outdoors	When at work
Street traffic	36	20	7
Aircraft	9	4	1
Railway	5	1	4
Industry and buildings	4	—	4
Internal noises at home	4	—	—
Noise from neighbors	6	—	—
Children	9	3	—
Adults (talking)	10	2	2
Radio and television	7	1	1
Bells and sirens	3	1	1
Pets	3	—	—

4.0 NOISE ESTIMATIONS AND CALCULATIONS

To assess the potential impact of noise from a proposed major facility such as a new highway or airport expansion, noise levels must be predicted. Common sources of noise and characteristics from which calculations can be made are described below.

4.1 Traffic Noise

Noise generated by traffic depends on:

1. Volume
2. Mix (e.g., cars and trucks)
3. Speed
4. Road characteristics (e.g., gradient and surface)

Noise propagated to a receiver depends on:

1. Distance from traffic
2. Type of ground
3. Height of receiver
4. Amount of shielding
5. Height of source

The easiest way to incorporate all these variables in any calculation is by use of a computer, especially if a large number of positions along a road have to be considered. Several calculation methods are available. A guide which gives detailed instructions for both a manual and a computer method of noise prediction has been produced in Alberta, Canada. The L_{eq} nomograph shown in Figure 660-1 can be used to illustrate a simple example as follows:

1. A straight line is drawn from the starting point through 60 mph on the auto speed scale to the turn line.
2. A second straight line is drawn from this turning point to the point on the volume scale indicating 5000 vehicles per hour. The intersection of this straight line with the pivot line is boxed.
3. A third straight line is drawn from this box to the 500-ft point on the distance scale.
4. The intersection of this line with the L_{eq} scale gives the predicted L_{eq} at the observer: 65 dB(*A*).

This method can be repeated for both medium and heavy trucks, and the resultant of all three values is obtained by using the dB additions method shown in Table 660-3.

A completed calculation of noise prediction involves additional calculations which take into account road and noise propagation characteristics. A comprehensive traffic noise study typically involves calculating the L_{eq} for both the day and night periods and then combining them to obtain the L_{dn}.

4.2 Train Noise

The L_{eq} nomograph used for traffic noise can also be used for train noise prediction (Figure 660-1). Adjustments to the basic calculated level have to be made for such factors as the existence of welded tracks or whether or not the railway crosses a steel structure (i.e., an overpass).

4.3 Aircraft Noise

Aircraft noise predictions are usually represented by a set of noise contours for areas surrounding the airport. Several

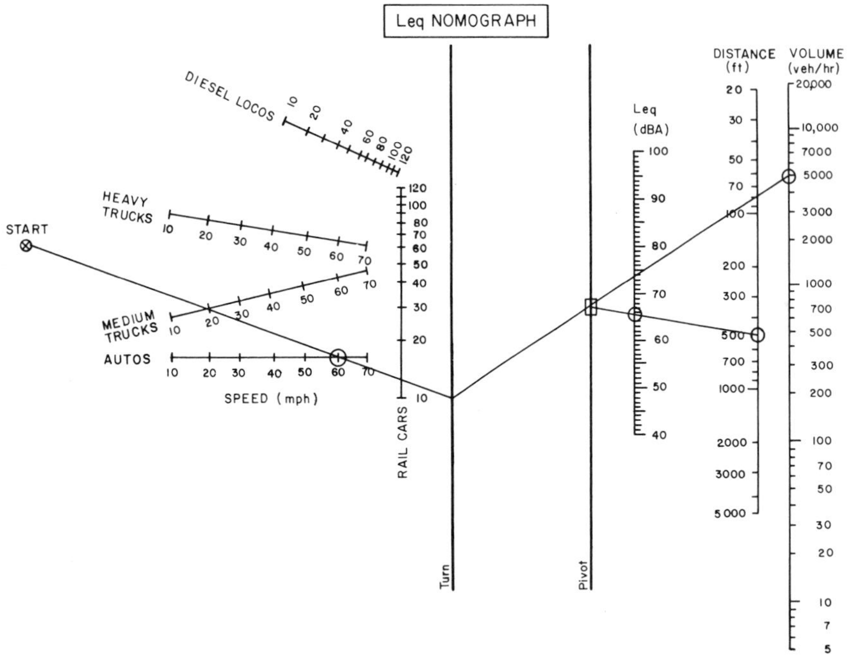
Leq NOMOGRAPH
DIESEL LOCOS
HEAVY TRUCKS
START
MEDIUM TRUCKS
AUTOS
SPEED (mph)
RAIL CARS
Turn
Pivot
Leq (dBA)
DISTANCE (ft)
VOLUME (veh/hr)

Figure 660-1 L_{eq} Nomograph. This nomograph can be used to predict noise levels of vehicular traffic. The L_{eq} scale gives the predicted L_{eq} at the observer.

TABLE 660-3
Calculating Differences between Decibel Levels

Difference between the two levels, dB	*Addition to higher level, dB*
0	3
1	3
2	2
3	2
4	1
5	1
6	1
7	1
8	1
9	1
10	0

Example: 50 dB + 50 dB + 50 dB + 60 dB

53 dB 60 dB

61 dB

methods for rating aircraft noise exposure have been developed, including:

NEF	noise exposure forecast
NNI	noise and number index
CNR	composite noise rating
L_{dn}	day-night sound level

The first three of these are similar because they combine many factors into a single number evaluation. The formulas require information about the types of aircraft using the airport, the number of movements, and the amount of noise generated, measured in terms of *effective perceived noise decibels* (EPN dB).

The L_{dn} method of aircraft noise annoyance assessment has recently been adopted in the United States. This is the same unit as described in 3.3 Units of Noise Measurement in this section.

4.4 Industrial Noise

Industrial installations generate noise from a wide variety of sources, such as fans, blowers, transformers, heating and ventilating systems, and reciprocating or turbine engines. Methods for estimating noise emission and for controlling noise are therefore varied. For a useful description of various methods, refer to Harris in the References at the end of this section.

5.0 NOISE CONTROL STANDARDS

Noise control legislation in North America can be found at federal, provincial/state, and local levels. Regulations commonly deal with the following:

1. Transportation
2. Source emission (maximum levels)
3. Nuisance
4. Zoning
5. Recreational areas

5.1 Acceptable Sound Levels in Residential and Recreational Environments

Table 660-4 shows maximum acceptable levels of road and rail traffic noise for residential environments and outdoor recreational areas, as recommended by the Canadian Central Mortgage and Housing Corporation (CMHC). (Note that this is the recommendation of only one authority.)

5.2 Noise Rating

The International Standards Organization document ISO 1996 (1971) shows how to assess the following:

1. The acceptability of a noise level
2. The setting of noise limits
3. Appropriate noise criteria

The ISO document uses a basic criterion of 35 to 45 dB(*A*) for residential purposes. Corrections to this are applied for different times of the day and for different community zones. In order to establish the acceptability of a measured noise level (called the *rating level*), this criterion is used for comparative purposes.

5.3 Sound Level Zoning and Land Use Planning

Sound level zoning, or acoustical planning, refers to the separation between the source of noise and the receivers of that noise (usually in residential areas). Such planning is accomplished by categorizing various land uses in a developing community, and then prescribing design noise levels not to be exceeded in any particular area. In this manner, sensitive buildings such as schools, churches, and hospitals can be separated from industrial areas and traffic noise. In established communities, however, acoustical planning is usually a difficult concept to implement. Certain types of activity and development have to be restricted, prohibited, or confined to certain areas to meet planning requirements. Of current interest is the retrofitting of highways with noise barriers to reduce noise levels in surrounding residential areas.

In most cases, local, state, or federal governments have noise control standards for various types of land use. For example, the CMHC recognizes three different categories of noise level (L_{eq}/24 hours) at the building facade and applies the following recommended policy to new residential development (Figure 660-2):

1. In the lower noise zone, where the noise level is between 45 and 55 dB (Figure 660-2), new housing construction meeting Canada's National Housing Act

Residential Standards is considered to have sufficient sound insulation.

2. In the intermediate noise zone, between 55 and 75 dB (Figure 660-2), housing shall be denied financing under the National Housing Act unless special and adequate sound insulation is provided.

3. In the upper noise zone, where the level exceeds 75 dB (Figure 660-2), financing for housing shall be denied under the National Housing Act.

The Canadian Ministry of Transport has implemented the guidelines shown in Table 660-5 for assessing likely community reaction to noise created by aircraft.

6.0 CONTROL OF NOISE—OUTDOORS

Measures to control noise can be divided into three categories, each of which can be addressed in a noise control strategy. These are:

1. Source of the sound

2. Path and distance of the sound transmission

3. Receiver of the sound

6.1 Source of the Sound

Noise can be reduced at the source either by architecture or equipment modification. In some instances the amount of noise generated is so great that it is rarely cost-effective or feasible to abate the noise at the source. In such cases a combination of other acoustical control measures may be required.

6.2 Path and Distance of the Sound Transmission

Noise can be attenuated by increasing the distance between the source and the receiver and/or by introducing noise screening.

At sufficient distances, all noise sources can be considered a point source. Thus, the sound level at a receiver can be calculated by the following equation:

$$L_p = L_w - (20 \log R) - 8$$

where L_p = sound level at receiver, dB(*A*)
L_w = sound level of source, dB(*A*) (If the noise is caused by a machine, the value of L_w can sometimes be obtained from the manufacturer.)
R = distance between source and receiver, (ft) (A useful criterion for a *sufficient distance* is that *R* should be greater than the sum of the three principle dimensions of the source. At distances less than this, the equation is unreliable.)

Figure 660-3 shows how the sound level given by the above equation can be obtained graphically.

Example (Figure 660-3): Given a welding machine with a sound level of 110 dB(*A*), the sound level 50 m (164 ft) away is determined. The graph shows that, at

TABLE 660-4
Acceptable Noise Levels for Residential and Outdoor Recreation Environments

Environment	*Noise level,* L_{eq}*(24 h)*
Bedrooms	35
Living, dining, recreation rooms	40
Kitchens, bathrooms, hallways, utility rooms	45
Outdoor recreation areas	55

Source: Courtesy of Canadian Mortgage and Housing Corporation.

UNACCEPTABLE
Noise exposure so severe that sound insulation costs would be prohibitive, and outdoor environment would be excessively noisy.

75 dB --------------------------------------

NORMALLY UNACCEPTABLE
Noise exposure is significantly more severe. Indoor conditions unacceptable unless adequate sound insulation is provided. Outdoor recreation space may have to be sheltered.

NOISE LEVEL AT BUILDING FACADE

55 dB --------------------------------------

NORMALLY ACCEPTABLE
Noise exposure may cause some concern but construction complying with "Residential Standards"* should provide acceptable indoor conditions.

45 dB --------------------------------------

ACCEPTABLE
Noise exposure both indoors and outdoors is obtrusive.

* Referring to Canadian Central Mortgage and Housing Corporation standards.

Figure 660-2 Noise Levels at Building Facade. This chart shows noise standards developed by the Canada Mortgage and Housing Corporation for evaluation of proposed residential development within its jurisdiction. *(Canada Mortgage and Housing Corporation, Ottawa, Canada, 1979)*

TABLE 660-5
Community Reaction to Aircraft Noise

Noise exposure forecast (NEF)	*Community response prediction*
> 40	Repeated and vigorous individual complaints are likely. Concerned group and legal action might be expected.
35–40	Individual complaints may be vigorous. Group action and appeals to authorities might result.
30–35	Sporadic to repeated individual complaints. Group action is possible.
< 30	Sporadic complaints may occur. Noise may interfere occasionally with resident's activities.

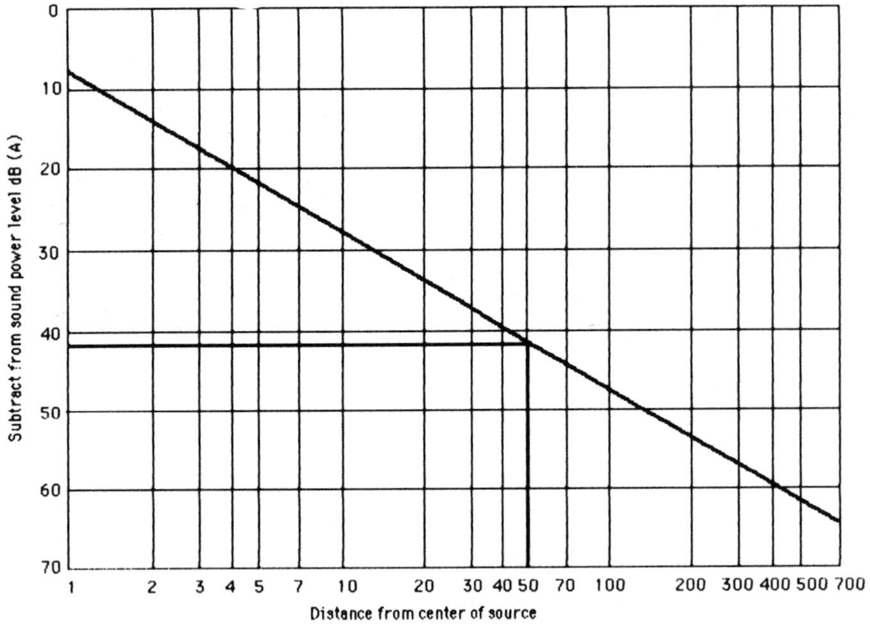
Subtract from sound power level dB (A)
0
10
20
30
40
50
60
70
1
2
3
4
5
7
10
20
30
40
50
70
100
200
300
400
500
700
Distance from center of source

Figure 660-3 Effect of Distance from a Line Source. This chart shows the amount to be subtracted from a sound power level at the source in order to determine the sound level at some distance. Note that sound levels determined with this graph are unreliable if at distances less than three major dimensions from the source, and if the source radiates sound in a marked directional manner.

distance, 42 dB(*A*) can be subtracted from the sound level at the source [110 dB(*A*)], resulting in a sound level at the receiver of 68 dB(*A*).

Effect of Distance from a Point Source:

Referring to the above example, note that each time the distance is doubled, the sound level falls off by 6 dB(*A*). Therefore, if the distance away from the same welding machine were increased to 100 m (300 ft), the sound level would be 62 dB(*A*).

Effect of Distance from a Line Source:

For line sources such as trains or continuous traffic, the sound level will decay by 3 dB(*A*) per doubling of distance, up to a distance of about half the length of the line source.

Other Effects (Point and Line Sources):

The dependence on distance given above is for propagation of noise over hard ground (such as pavement), or for an elevated source or receiver over soft ground (such as a grassy field or a garden). The decay rate over soft ground, when both source and receiver are less than 2 m (6 ft) above the ground, is increased by 1½ dB per doubling of distance. Sound levels and attenuation over a distance may also vary substantially according to wind, air turbulence, and temperature. These effects are difficult to predict.

6.3 Sound Barriers

The degree of attenuation provided by a noise barrier is mainly a function of (1) the diffraction angle α through which the sound path must be bent in order to get from source to receiver and (2) the frequency of the sound source (Figure 660-4).

Five main factors that influence the acoustic effectiveness of a barrier are: (1) distance (offset), (2) height, (3) continuity, (4) length, and (5) mass.

An additional factor influencing the acoustic effectiveness of a barrier is the sound absorption capability of the barrier, i.e., the degree to which it minimizes reflection of sound.

Distance (Placement of Barrier):

A sound barrier should be erected as close as possible to either the noise source or the receiving position in order to maximize the diffraction angle (Figure 660-5).

Height of Barrier:

The minimum height of the barrier should be such that the line of sight between source and receiver is interrupted (Figure 660-6).

Continuity of Barrier:

No gaps or holes should be present in a noise barrier. It must be effectively airtight (Figure 660-7).

Length of Barrier:

As a guideline, the length of a noise barrier should be at least 1 to 2 times the distance between the barrier and the protected structure to minimize sound diffraction around the ends of the barrier (Figure 660-8).

Physical Mass of a Barrier (Material):

To minimize sound passing through a barrier, it should have a surface weight, or mass, of at least 6 to 12 kg/m^2. A noise level reduction of 10 to 15 dB(*A*) is possible with such a barrier; however, a reduction of 5 to 10 dB(*A*) is considered to be more cost-effective.

6.4 Earth Berms

The careful design and situation of earth berms can be an effective way of reducing noise from traffic or construction operations. Berms can either be temporary or remain as a permanent feature of the landscape (Figures 660-9 and 660-10). The slope of a berm depends on the type of surface treatment or maintenance involved. For instance, a mowed grass berm is easier to maintain if graded to a slope of 3:1 or less.

6.5 Barrier Walls and Earth Berms

Barrier walls can be used separately or in combination with earth berms to minimize noise levels (Figure 660-11).

6.6 Vegetation

The type of ground surface over which sound travels does have a substantial effect on sound attenuation, particularly when traveling over large distances. Areas covered with grass or other types of groundcover are more absorptive than hard, paved surfaces, which tend to reflect the sound. Taller plantings, such as hedges or shallow *screen plantings* (even though they may completely block the view of the noise source), will not significantly reduce actual noise levels. However, dense plantings of trees with an understory of shrubs can result in a reduction of 3 to 5 dB(*A*) per 100 ft (30 m) of depth from the sound source (Figure 660-12).

The primary value of vegetation in connection with sound control in the landscape is for its aesthetic and psychological appeal. Perhaps the most important value of planting is to make barrier walls, berms, and other sound control devices seem less visually intrusive in the landscape.

6.7 Building Layout and Site Selection

Specially constructed noise barriers are expensive, but fortunately are not the only

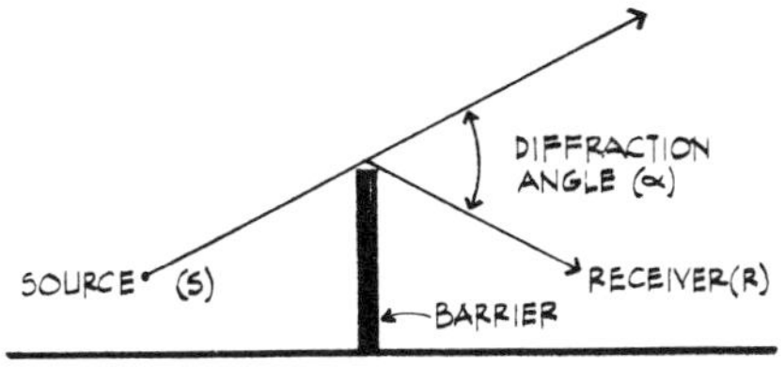
DIFFRACTION ANGLE (α)
SOURCE (S)
RECEIVER (R)
BARRIER

Figure 660-4 Sound level attenuation as a function of diffraction angle.

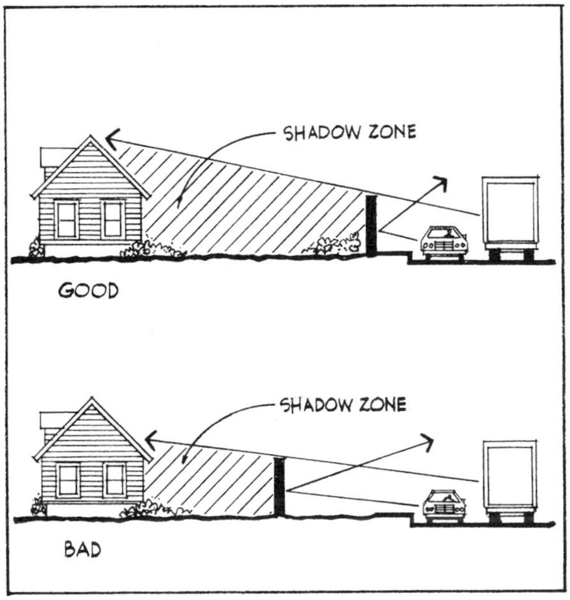
SHADOW ZONE
GOOD
SHADOW ZONE
BAD

Figure 660-5 *Distance as a Variable Influencing the Effectiveness of a Noise Barrier.* Barriers should be placed to maximize the diffraction angle.

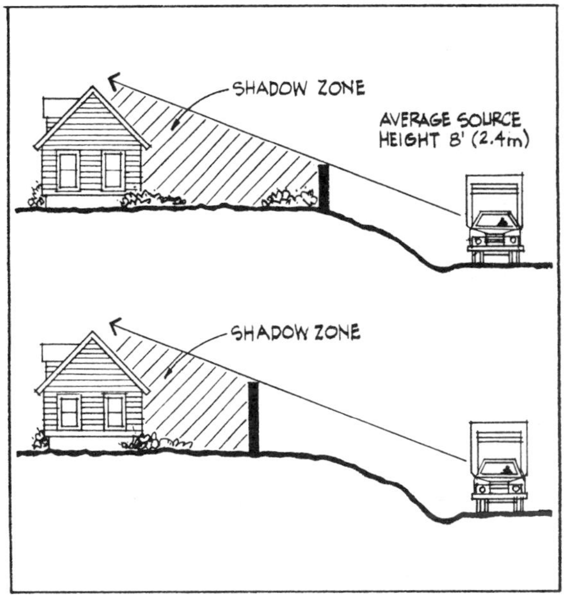
SHADOW ZONE
AVERAGE SOURCE HEIGHT 8' (2.4m)
SHADOW ZONE

Figure 660-6 *Height as a Variable Influencing the Effectiveness of a Noise Barrier.* Barriers should be placed to interrupt lines of sight.

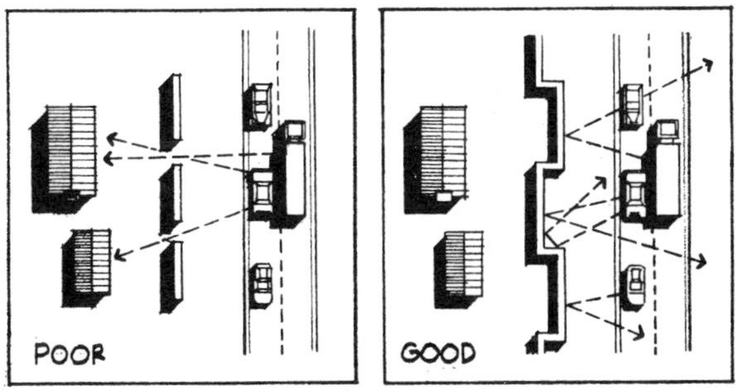
POOR
GOOD

Figure 660-7 *Continuity as a Variable Influencing the Effectiveness of a Noise Barrier.* Barriers should be solid rather than perforated.

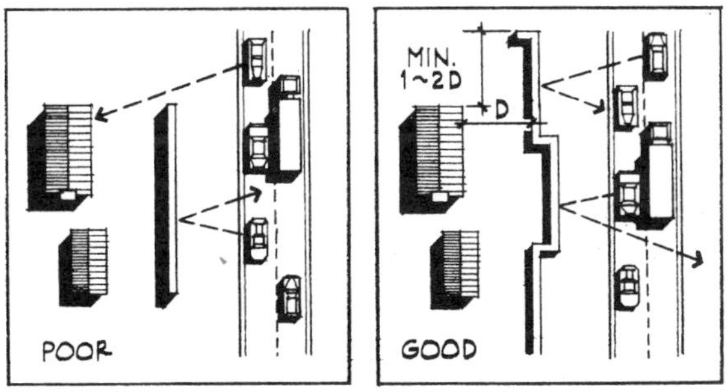
POOR
MIN. 1~2D
D
GOOD

Figure 660-8 *Length as a Variable Influencing the Effectiveness of a Noise Barrier.* Barriers should extend beyond the protected structure to minimize sound diffraction around the ends of the barrier.

means available for noise control. Other means available include:

1. The use of existing or proposed buildings to shield others that are more sensitive
2. The use of natural or constructed landscape features (hills and valleys, earth berms, etc.)
3. The optimization of other site planning or design criteria (discussed in 7.0, which follows)

7.0 DESIGN PRINCIPLES

7.1 Design Criteria

The three most important criteria for noise barrier design are acoustic effectiveness, economic feasibility, and visual attractiveness. Acoustic criteria include the site planning objectives, the choice of barrier material, and the quality of construction. Economic criteria include the cost of materials and labor, implementation ease, and operating and maintenance costs. Visual criteria include environmentally acceptable alternatives for highway users as well as for people who have to live near the barriers.

The design of noise barriers should incorporate both the functional requirements and the aesthetic preferences of all who are affected. In the case of a highway,

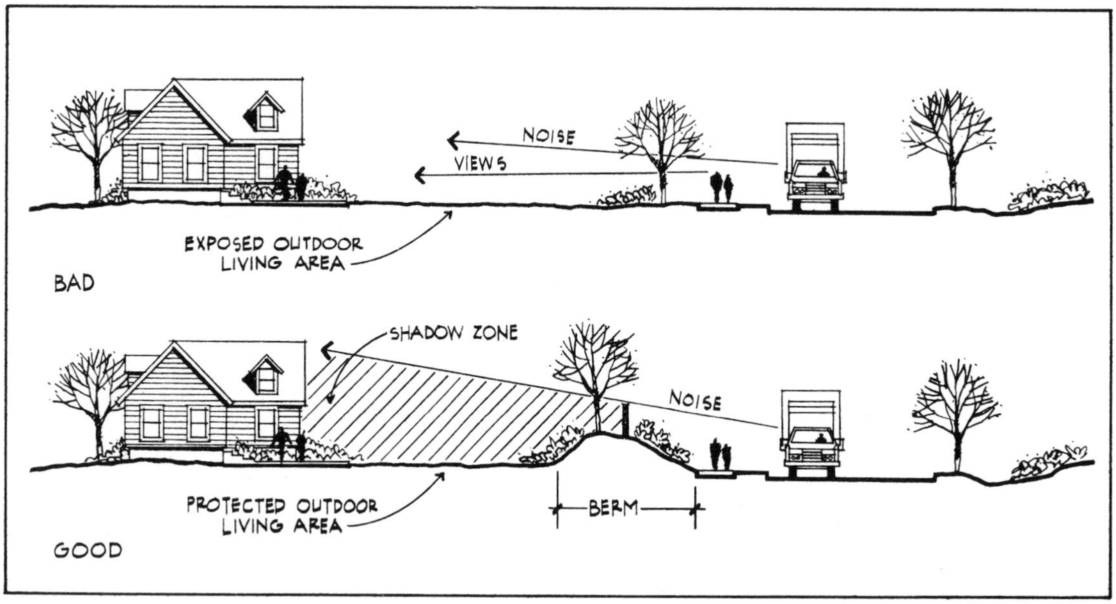
NOISE
VIEWS
EXPOSED OUTDOOR LIVING AREA
BAD
SHADOW ZONE
NOISE
PROTECTED OUTDOOR LIVING AREA
BERM
GOOD

Figure 660-9 *Earth Berms for Noise Control.* Earth berms and walls can help control wind and noise. Plantings can provide psychological relief from noise and also help to control wind.

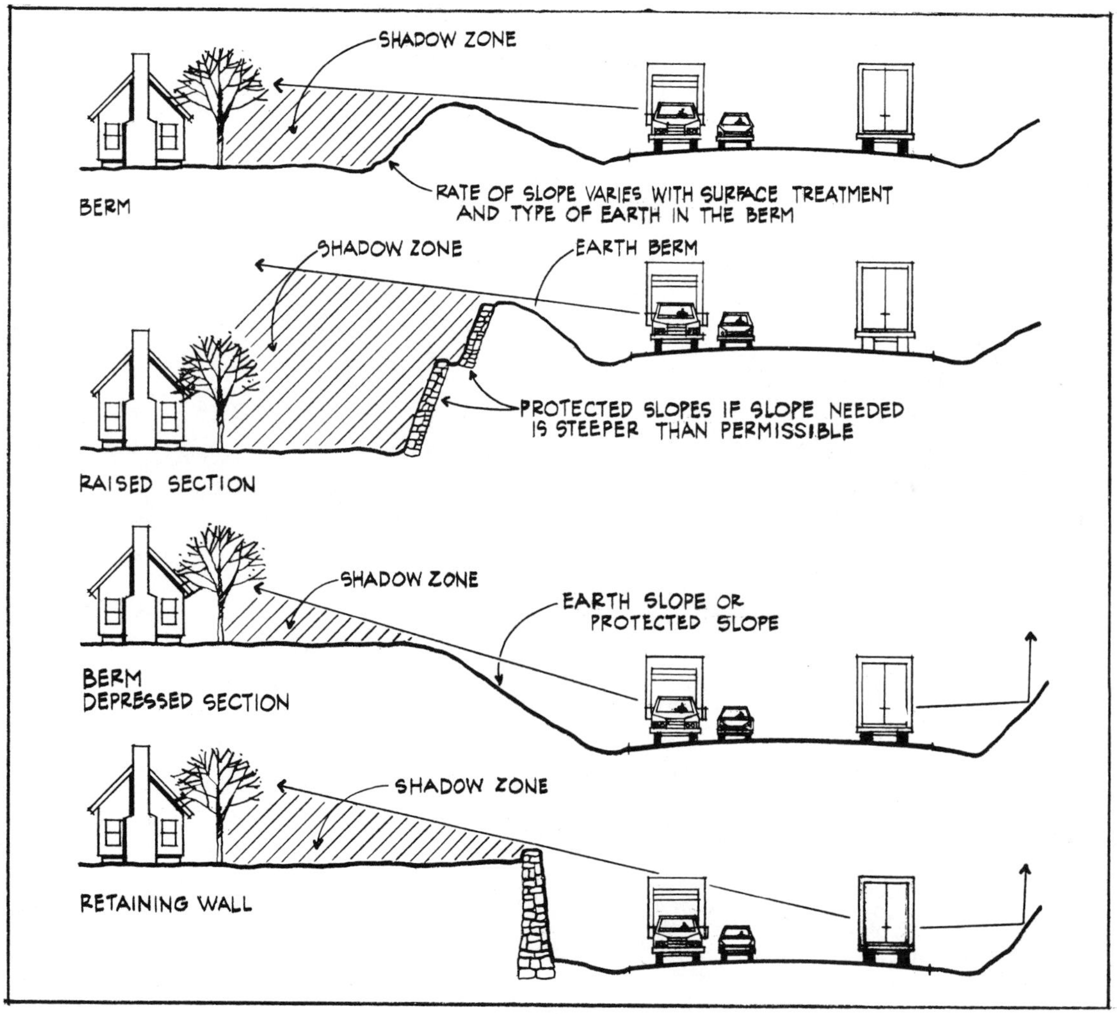
SHADOW ZONE
RATE OF SLOPE VARIES WITH SURFACE TREATMENT AND TYPE OF EARTH IN THE BERM
BERM
SHADOW ZONE
EARTH BERM
PROTECTED SLOPES IF SLOPE NEEDED IS STEEPER THAN PERMISSIBLE
RAISED SECTION
SHADOW ZONE
EARTH SLOPE OR PROTECTED SLOPE
BERM
DEPRESSED SECTION
SHADOW ZONE
RETAINING WALL

Figure 660-10 *Earth Berms for Noise Control.* Various types of embankments can be used to maximize diffraction angles.

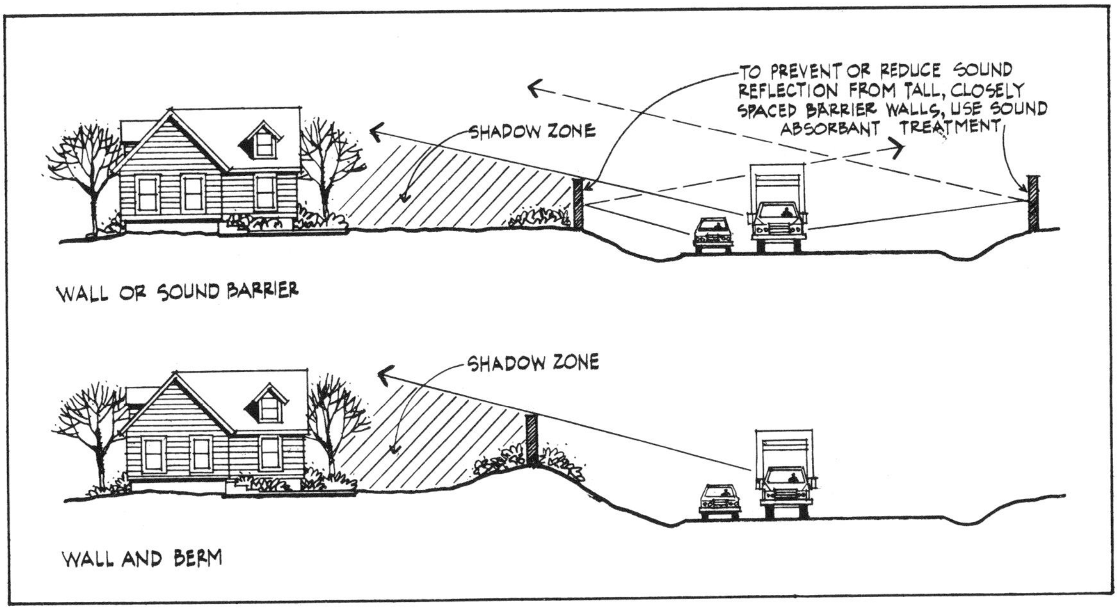
TO PREVENT OR REDUCE SOUND REFLECTION FROM TALL, CLOSELY SPACED BARRIER WALLS, USE SOUND ABSORBANT TREATMENT
SHADOW ZONE
WALL OR SOUND BARRIER
SHADOW ZONE
WALL AND BERM

Figure 660-11 Barrier wall or combination of wall and berm.

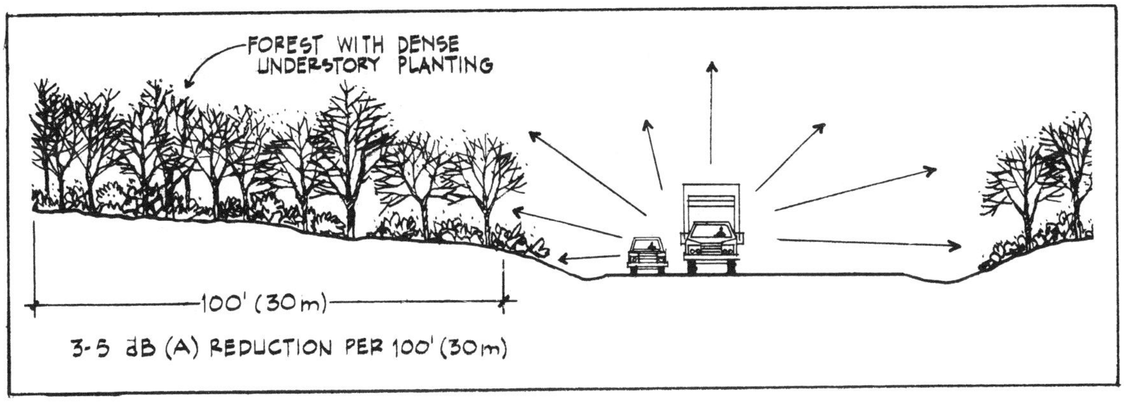
FOREST WITH DENSE UNDERSTORY PLANTING
100' (30 m)
3-5 dB (A) REDUCTION PER 100' (30 m)

Figure 660-12 *Vegetation as a Noise Barrier.* Vegetation will not significantly reduce sound levels unless plantings are dense and 100 ft (30 m) deep or greater.

for instance, both the actual users of the highway as well as the users of adjacent lands are factors to consider. Design criteria are not limited to aesthetic concerns alone but should also address a set of program objectives established for the roadway, taking into account the views to both natural and built surroundings. Noise barriers can aid driver orientation and decision making and provide sequential visual experiences. They should integrate well with the existing landscape and promote feelings of security and comfort for both drivers and passengers.

7.2 Aesthetic Issues

Noise barriers along highway corridors should be seen as elements which define and enclose linear space. Visual perception in these corridors will be influenced by travel speed, light, spatial quality, location, physical distances, roadway characteristics, and viewing height, all modified by the basic design elements of planes, mass, and texture.

Planes:

Planes are an important element in noise barrier design. In highway design, for instance, where minimal rights-of-way exist, barriers can provoke feelings of excessive enclosure or give a monotonous appearance. In such circumstances, it is necessary to create variety and interest in the design of the barriers and related landscape by changing the textures, choosing different materials, using color, and articulating the forms (Figure 660-13).

Mass:

Mass refers to the form and shape of a barrier. Massive, unrelieved forms can sometimes arouse uncomfortable feelings of claustrophobia or insecurity (Figure 660-14).

The apparent mass of a noise barrier can be minimized by means of stepped wall sections, staggered alignments, plantings, shadow lines or reveals, color variation, articulation of form, and integration with landform (Figure 660-15).

Texture:

Texture is a visual, surficial quality referring to the extent of detail of a material or design (Figure 660-16). Increased speed of travel, angle of vision, and distance from

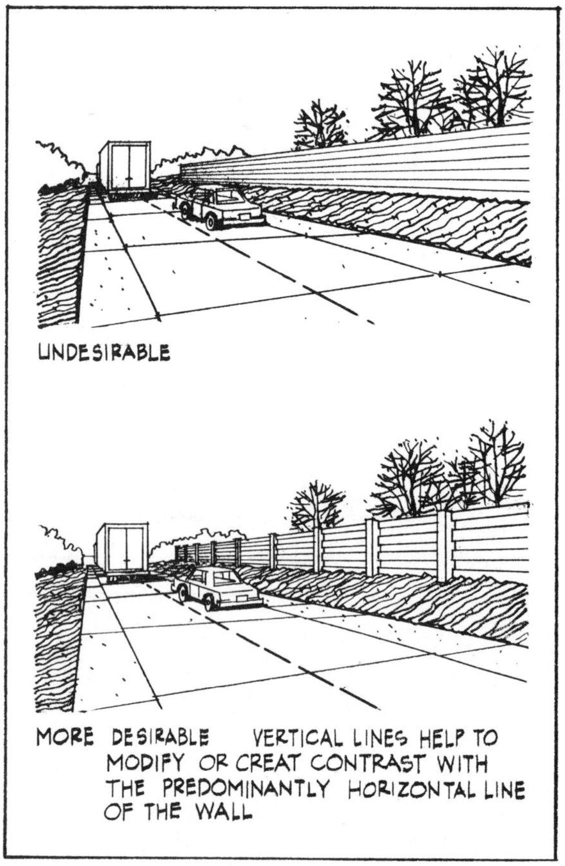
UNDESIRABLE
MORE DESIRABLE
VERTICAL LINES HELP TO MODIFY OR CREAT CONTRAST WITH THE PREDOMINANTLY HORIZONTAL LINE OF THE WALL

Figure 660-13 *The Apparent Height of a Wall.* A combination of vertical and horizontal lines in a wall (i.e., articulation and texture rather than a monolithic mass) can reduce the apparent height of the wall.

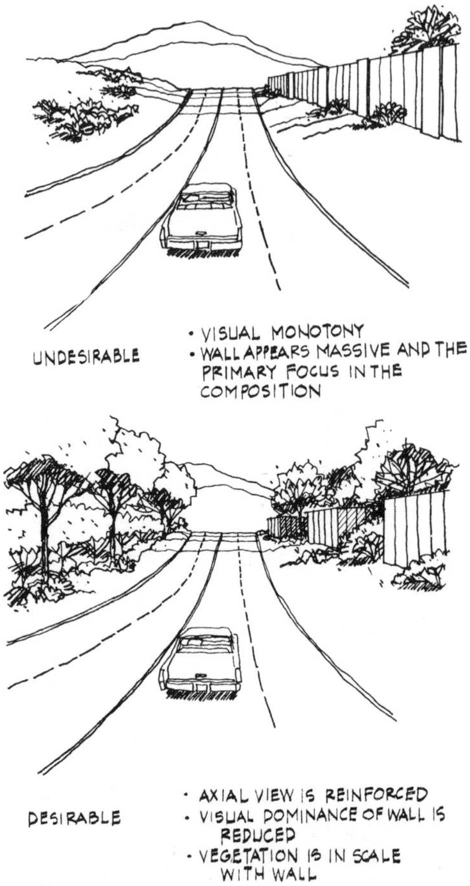
UNDESIRABLE
• VISUAL MONOTONY
• WALL APPEARS MASSIVE AND THE PRIMARY FOCUS IN THE COMPOSITION
DESIRABLE
• AXIAL VIEW IS REINFORCED
• VISUAL DOMINANCE OF WALL IS REDUCED
• VEGETATION IS IN SCALE WITH WALL

Figure 660-15 *Visual Diversity along Highways.* Wall design and plantings can be composed to provide interesting visual sequences along highway corridors. Scale is important.

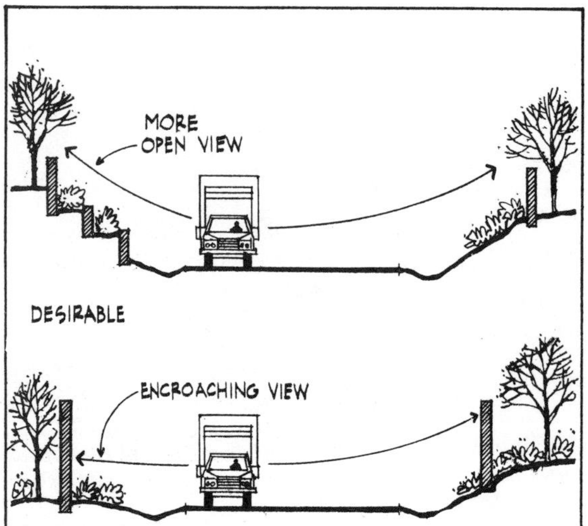
MORE OPEN VIEW
DESIRABLE
ENCROACHING VIEW
UNDESIRABLE

Figure 660-14 *Stepped-Back Wall.* A wall which steps back can open up the view for the motorist and provide psychological relief from feelings of tight enclosure.

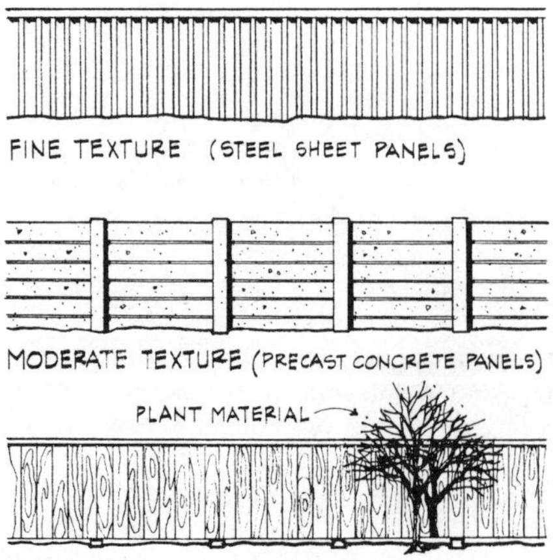
FINE TEXTURE (STEEL SHEET PANELS)
MODERATE TEXTURE (PRECAST CONCRETE PANELS)
PLANT MATERIAL
ROUGH TEXTURE (WOOD WALL)

Figure 660-16 *Wall Texture.* Fine-textured walls are often monotonous, and may cause problems of reflective glare.

an object all tend to decrease the apparent degree of texture. Surfaces that are relatively smooth (i.e., fine-textured) not only cause undesirable reflections of light and sound but also promote monotony in the landscape (Figure 660-17).

8.0 DESIGN APPLICATION (CASE STUDIES)

To illustrate the application of noise abatement techniques and design principles, four case studies are presented below. All four cases are assumed to be based upon preplanned sites.

8.1 Recreational Development (Example Problem)

Description:

A major highway is proposed on the periphery of a proposed recreational park. Prior to development, it is necessary to assess the likely impact of traffic noise on the park (Figure 660-18).

Procedure:

1. Existing L_{eq} ambient noise levels at 12 positions in the park are measured at morning, evening, and night (Figure 660-19).

2. Projected traffic volumes for the proposed highway are obtained and used to predict traffic noise levels at various distances throughout the park.

3. The existing and predicted noise levels are compared, and an impact category is assigned to each of the 12 positions in the park according to Table 660-6.

4. An analysis of park program components is completed to assess plan relationships and sensitivity to noise.

5. A conceptual land use plan is prepared. The plan includes consideration of future noise levels for each program element, utilization of existing and proposed vegetation for noise buffering [100-ft (30-m) minimum], and placement of the least noise-sensitive facilities in the noisiest zones (e.g., parking lot, park building, and active recreational areas).

8.2 Residential Development (Example Problem)

Description:

A housing development is proposed next to an existing major highway. A noise limit of L_{dn} 60 dB(*A*) at the facades of the nearest houses is required (Figure 660-20).

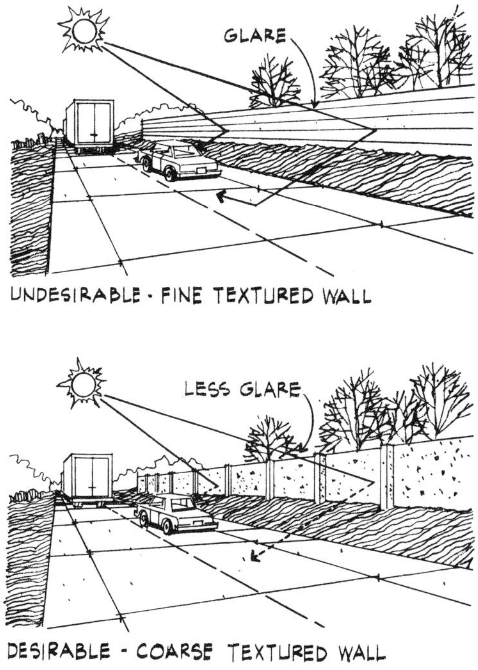
GLARE
UNDESIRABLE - FINE TEXTURED WALL
LESS GLARE
DESIRABLE - COARSE TEXTURED WALL

Figure 660-17 *Coarse-Textured Walls Minimize Reflective Glare and Provide Visual Diversity along Highways.* Plantings can also be used to minimize glare and enhance visual diversity.

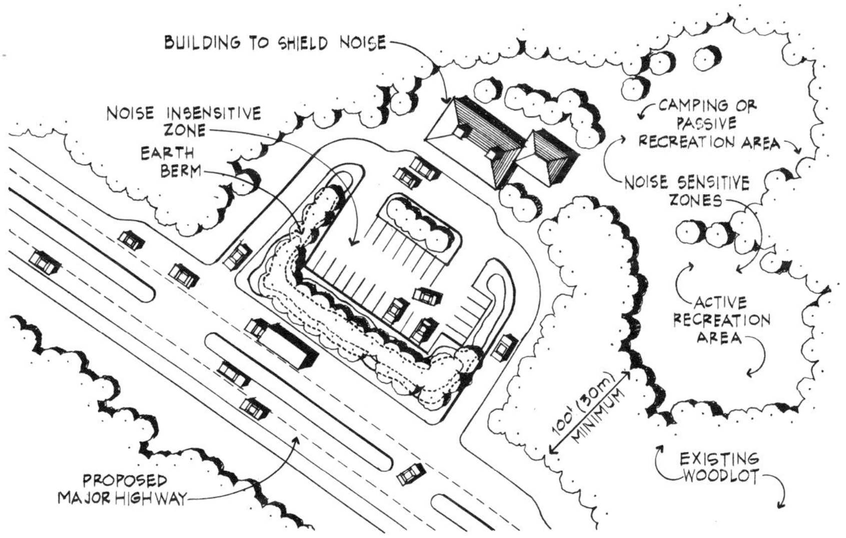
BUILDING TO SHIELD NOISE
NOISE INSENSITIVE ZONE
EARTH BERM
CAMPING OR PASSIVE RECREATION AREA
NOISE SENSITIVE ZONES
ACTIVE RECREATION AREA
100' (30m) MINIMUM
EXISTING WOODLOT
PROPOSED MAJOR HIGHWAY

Figure 660-18 *Acoustical Site Planning (Example Problem).* In this example, the noise-insensitive area (parking lot) is used as a buffer zone between the highway and the recreational areas.

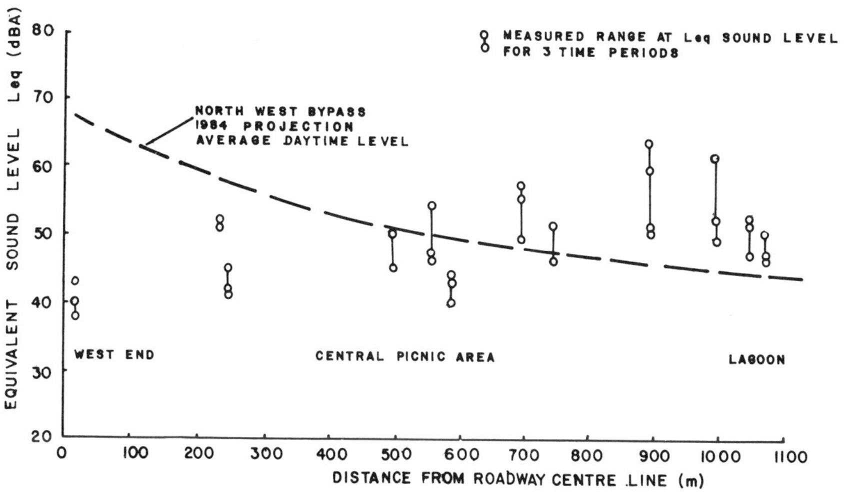
EQUIVALENT SOUND LEVEL Leq (dBA)
MEASURED RANGE AT Leq SOUND LEVEL FOR 3 TIME PERIODS
NORTH WEST BYPASS 1984 PROJECTION AVERAGE DAYTIME LEVEL
WEST END
CENTRAL PICNIC AREA
LAGOON
80
70
60
50
40
30
20
0
100
200
300
400
500
600
700
800
900
1000
1100
DISTANCE FROM ROADWAY CENTRE LINE (m)

Figure 660-19 Existing L_{eq} Ambient Noise Levels (Example Problem). Noise levels are measured at twelve different places in the park. Small circles refer to morning, evening, and nightime readings.

TABLE 660-6
Assessment of Community Response to Various Noise Levels

Intruding noise, L_{eq}, minus existing ambient L_{eq}	*Impact category*	*Estimated community response description*
−5	None	No observed reaction
0	Little	Sporadic complaints
+5	Medium	Widespread complaints
+10	Strong	Threats of community action
Greater than +10	Very strong	Vigorous community action

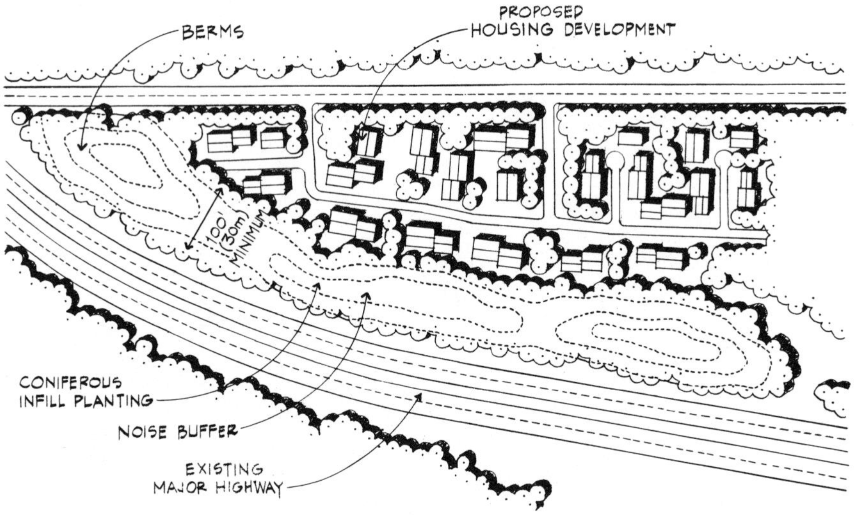
BERMS
PROPOSED
HOUSING DEVELOPMENT
100' (30m) MINIMUM
CONIFEROUS
INFILL PLANTING
NOISE BUFFER
EXISTING
MAJOR HIGHWAY

Figure 660-20 *Acoustical Site Planning (Example Problem).* In this example, a greenbelt is used as a noise buffer between the major highway and the proposed residential development.

Procedure:

1. Computer predictions show that with no noise screening, traffic noise levels would be 8 dB(*A*) above the limit.

2. The relative ground heights of the housing lots and the roadway vary along the length of the development. Sections are taken along this length and the height and position of berms and/or barrier walls are tested (Figure 660-21).

3. In the final design of the site plan, an earth berm solution is chosen. Care is given to its layout and form in order to minimize monotonous elevations and to ensure that slopes can be easily maintained. A variety of shrub and tree species is recommended to enhance the visual quality of the berm.

In the overall site plan of the community, the concern for sound control results in the integration of open space with the noise berm; this includes a pedestrian walkway, playground areas, and infill buffer planting. Housing units are laid out in clusters to maximize open space and to minimize the undesirable visual effects of a long, continuous facade. The buildings are used as shielding elements, and the spaces within the clusters are oriented away from noise sources to prevent a reverberation of sound within the spaces.

8.3 Industrial Development: Open-Pit Mine (Example Problem)

Description:

The development and operation of an open-pit coal mine is proposed in an area

TABLE 660-7
Noise Level Data at Site for Various Phases of Mining (Example Problem)

	Plant				*Noise-level data*	
		Power				
Phase	*Type*	*hp*	*kW*	*Number*	*At 10-m (32-ft) distance*	*Sound power level*
Initial ground clearance	Dozer	282	210	2	86	114
	Dump truck	416	310	2	81	109
	Excavator	101	75	2	80	108
	Loader	101	75	2	79	107
Overburden removal	Excavator					
	Electric	268	200	2	75	103
	Diesel	268	200	1	85	113
	Dump truck	416	310	18	81	109
	Grader	188	140	1	80	108
	Rock drill	—	—	1	90	118
	Hydraulic breaker	—	—	1	85	113
Coal extraction	Excavator					
	Electric	268	200	2	75	103
	Diesel	268	200	1	85	113
	Loader	268	200	1	85	113
	Dump truck	416	310	3	81	109
Waste-tip dressing	Dozer	282	210	2–3	86	114
	Grader	188	140	1	80	108

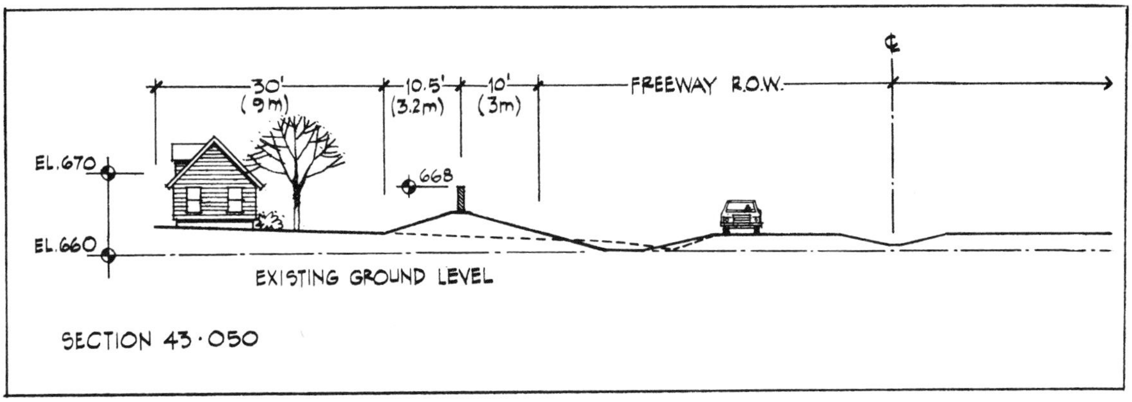
30' (9m)
10.5' (3.2m)
10' (3m)
FREEWAY R.O.W.
EL.670
668
EL.660
EXISTING GROUND LEVEL
SECTION 43·050

Figure 660-21 *Berm Height Design (Example Problem).* Elevations are taken of all pertinent elements to determine whether or not diffraction angles are adequate, etc.

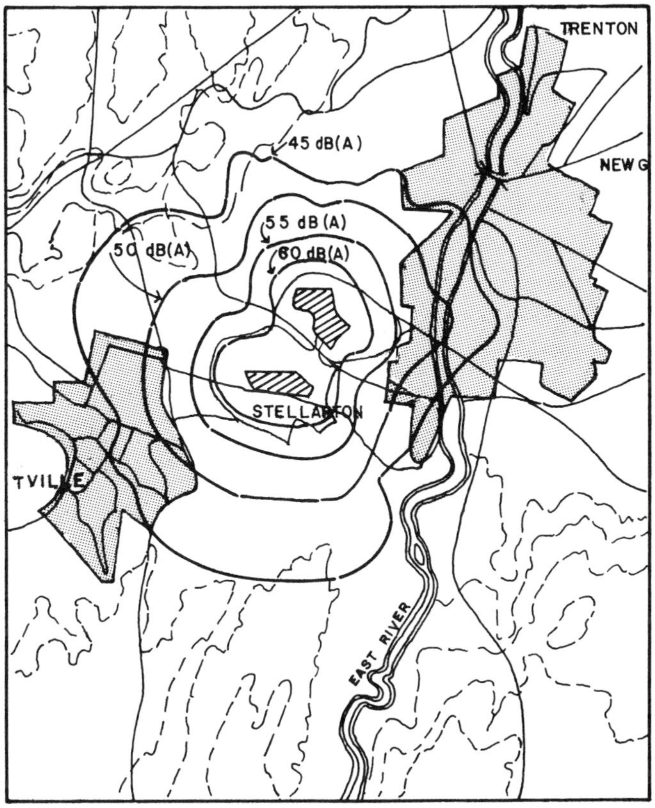
TRENTON
45 dB(A)
NEW G
55 dB(A)
50 dB(A)
60 dB(A)
STELLARTON
TVILLE
EAST RIVER

Figure 660-22 *Mine Location and Predicted Noise Contours (Example Problem).* Contours show what noise levels can be expected at any location in the community.

close to existing residential areas. Noise levels from earthmoving, blasting, transportation, and coal processing are a major concern.

Procedure:

1. A baseline survey is undertaken to measure existing L_{eq} ambient noise levels at 10 selected locations in the vicinity of the proposed mine.

2. Noise level data for each type of equipment to be used during the various phases of mining are compiled in Table 660-7. These data are then plotted on the community map to produce noise contours of the noise levels that can be expected at any place in the community (Figure 660-22).

3. Groups of dwellings where noise intrusion is expected to be a problem are identified.

4. Various methods of noise control are recommended, depending on the extent of expected intrusion. These include:

- **a.** Choice of quieter equipment
- **b.** Design of noise berms or other sound control structures where appropriate
- **c.** Acoustic insulation of certain dwellings
- **d.** Restriction of some mining operations to certain hours of the day
- **e.** Choice of transportation routes to minimize the extent of truck use in or near residential areas

8.4 Industrial Development: Steel Plant (Example Problem)

Description:

A steel mill is proposed adjacent to existing public recreational areas and a small rural community. Noise levels during the construction phase and afterwards from the operation of either blast or electric reduction furnaces are of great concern to the community and the regulating agencies (Figure 660-23).

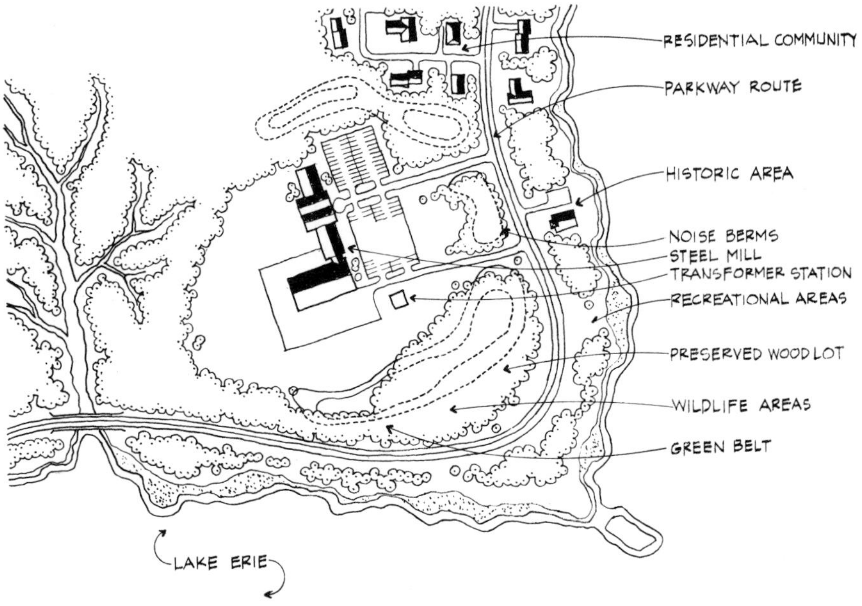
RESIDENTIAL COMMUNITY
PARKWAY ROUTE
HISTORIC AREA
NOISE BERMS
STEEL MILL
TRANSFORMER STATION
RECREATIONAL AREAS
PRESERVED WOOD LOT
WILDLIFE AREAS
GREEN BELT
LAKE ERIE

Figure 660-23 *Preplanning of Grading (Example Problem).* In this example, a greenbelt with noise berms buffers sensitive areas from industrial noise and visual intrusion, and also blends in integrally with existing public open space.

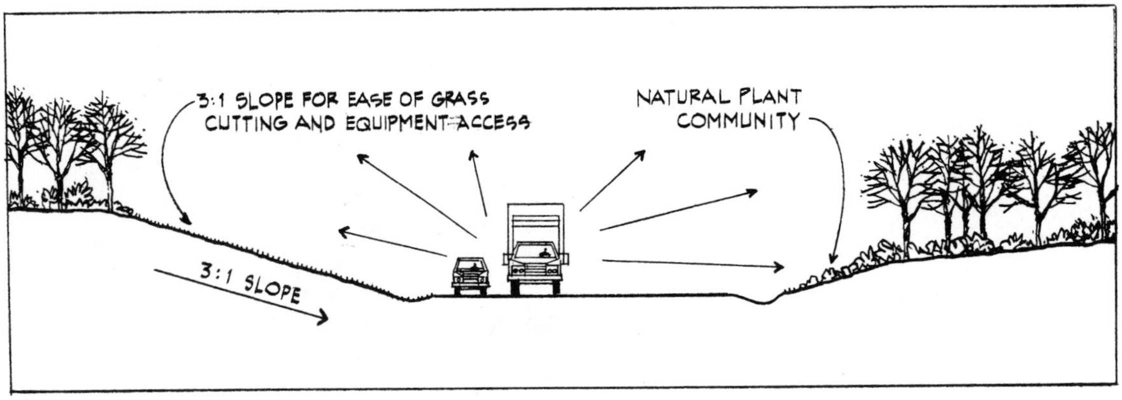
3:1 SLOPE FOR EASE OF GRASS CUTTING AND EQUIPMENT ACCESS
NATURAL PLANT COMMUNITY
3:1 SLOPE

Figure 660-24 *Low-Maintenance Ground Covers for Earth Berms.* Long-term, self-maintaining plant communities can be used as low-maintenance ground covers for earth berms.

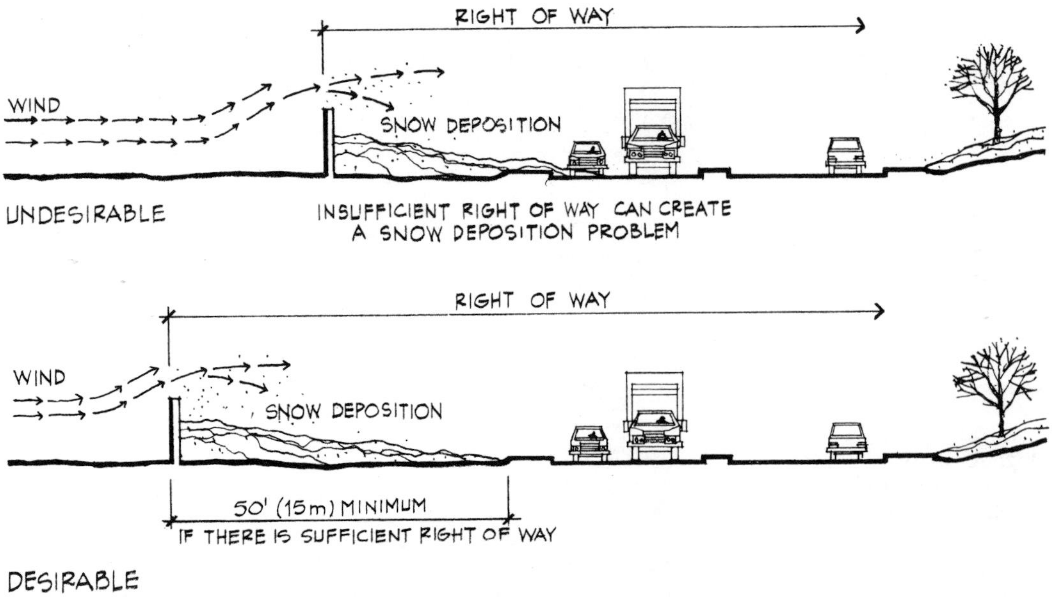
RIGHT OF WAY
WIND
SNOW DEPOSITION
UNDESIRABLE
INSUFFICIENT RIGHT OF WAY CAN CREATE A SNOW DEPOSITION PROBLEM
RIGHT OF WAY
WIND
SNOW DEPOSITION
50' (15m) MINIMUM
IF THERE IS SUFFICIENT RIGHT OF WAY
DESIRABLE

Figure 660-25 *Noise Barriers and Snow Deposition.* Rights-of-way should be established where possible to allow for accumulations of snow.

Procedure:

1. A baseline survey is undertaken to measure existing L_{eq} ambient noise levels at selected locations within the existing recreational and residential areas.

2. Noise level data for the proposed blast and electric arc furnaces are collected.

3. A generalized site master plan evaluation is prepared to assess the most desirable location for the proposed furnaces.

4. After establishing the most feasible site locations, calculations of noise levels at the property line are made to determine where the levels would exceed 55 dB(*A*).

5. For those areas where noise levels would exceed 55 dB(*A*), recommendations are prepared to reduce the noise by the preservation of woodlot stands and/or the design of earth berms, etc.

6. Overall grading plans for the site are integrated with the requirements for earth berms to minimize construction costs.

7. A parkway belt is created to separate the construction and plant traffic from the recreational and residential areas.

The integration of noise berm design with a comprehensive master plan for the steel plant leads to the creation of a greenbelt area, which is constructed for the advantage of the public with little additional cost to the owner.

9.0 MAINTENANCE CONSIDERATIONS

A major concern in the design of acoustical barriers is the long-term maintenance involved. Ease of access, intrusion on adjacent property owners, durability of materials, minimum cost, ease of replacement, and visual appearances are the major considerations. Initial least-cost options may, in fact, have the highest cost when considering the implications of long-term maintenance.

9.1 Earth Berms

The development of earth berms as noise barriers requires the manipulation of landforms and the stabilization of the soil. The manipulation of landforms involves careful consideration of the surrounding grading and drainage conditions. New grading should blend into existing landscape as much as possible. Slopes should not exceed 3:1 for ease of grass cutting and equipment access. Groundcovers other than grass may be used; they usually require less maintenance, although weed control can be a major problem, especially in municipalities which have weed control legislation.

Recently, there has been an increased use of various groundcovers, shrubs, and trees in an attempt to provide a long-term, self-maintaining natural plant community, although the initial maintenance requirements can be higher (Figure 660-24).

9.2 Barrier Walls

The maintenance implications of noise barrier walls include such basic consideratins as access to both sides of the barriers and access to possible cutoff land. Design complexity, quality control during construction, and the choice of materials to minimize damage and abuse are factors that will affect long-term maintenance costs. As with berms, the location and alignment of noise barriers require study in order to prevent or reduce problems of snow drifting across roadways and walks, etc. (Figure 660-25).

REFERENCES

Acoustics Technology in Land Use Planning, vol. 1: *Analysis of Noise Impact,* and vol. 2: *Road Traffic Noise Tables.* Ontario Ministry of the Environment, Ottawa, Ontario, Canada, November 1978.

Assessment of Noise with Respect to Community Response, International Organization for Standardization ISO Recommendations R1996, 1971.

The Audible Landscape: A Manual for Highway Noise and Land Use, report for U.S. Department of Transportation, November 1974.

Barry, T. M., and J. A. Reagan. *FHWA Highway Traffic Noise Prediction Model,* U.S. Federal Highway Administration Report FHWA-RD-77-108, December 1978.

A Description of the CNR and NEF Systems for Estimating Aircraft Noise Annoyance, Canadian Air Transportation Administration Report R-71-20, Ottawa, Ontario, Canada, 1971.

Federal Aviation Administration. *Airport-Land Use Compatibility Planning,* U.S. Department of Transportation Advisory Circular, no. 15015050-6, U.S. Government Printing Office, Washington, DC, December 1977.

A Guide to Visual Quality in Noise Barrier Design, report for U.S. Department of Transportation, December 1976.

Harris, Cyril M. (ed.). *Handbook of Noise Control,* 2d ed., McGraw-Hill, 1979.

New Housing and Airport Noise (metric ed.), Central Mortgage and Housing Corporation, Ottawa, Ontario, Canada, March 1978.

Road and Rail Noise—Effects on Housing. Central Mortgage and Housing Corporation, Ottawa, Ontario, Canada.

Savienman, H. J., J. T. Nelson, and G. P. Wilson. *Handbook of Urban Rail Noise and Vibration Control,* U.S. Department of Transportation Report DOT-TSC-UMTA-81-72, NTIS, Springfield, VA, February 1982.

U.S. Department of Labor, *Noise Control, A Guide for Workers and Employers,* OSHA, Office of Information, 1980. ■

section 710: Water Supply

CREDITS

Contributor:

Daniel Bubly, P.E., L.A., A.I.C.P.
Bubly Associates, Inc.
Sharon, Massachusetts

Graphics:

Joseph C. Cloud
(using a MacIntosh computer)

Reviewer:

Robert T. Ferrari, P.E.
Ferrari-Atwood Engineering, Inc.
Providence, Rhode Island

CONTENTS

1.0 INTRODUCTION

Piped water supplies are ordinarily used for:

1. Potable water for homes, schools, industries, etc.

2. Fire fighting

3. Nonagricultural irrigation (lawns and gardens)

In many cases, all three uses are supplied by a single system of piping, although there are cases where all three are supplied by separate systems.

2.0 STANDARDS AND CRITERIA

2.1 Water Quality

Water intended for human consumption must meet extensive physical, chemical, and biological standards for quality and reliability. These standards include color, taste, and transparency as well as freedom from bacteria and chemicals related to human or industrial wastes.

Specific water quality standards are published in the United States by individual state and federal agencies, but there are variations between states and counties and these standards do change with time. Some existing public water supplies do not meet all the standards to which they are subject because (1) most of these standards are very conservative and (2) some are not related to public health or safety but rather to aesthetic qualities of water (e.g., the ease of use in washing machines).

2.2 Water Quantity

The amount of water used in various parts of the world varies with regional legal, and political traditions. For instance, in the northeastern United States the average water use is about 75 gal (285 L) per capita per day in rural areas, and 150 gal (570 L) per capita per day in metropolitan areas. This is a region (1) where the English common-law tradition limits the right to water to nonconsumptive uses (use and return to stream), (2) where little water is used for irrigation, and (3) where water supply systems are funded entirely with local fees and taxes. In metropolitan areas of the southwest, where the Spanish law tradition grants preemptive rights to water on a first-come–first-established basis, average (publicly supplied) water use is about 350 gal (1325 L) per capita per day.

Tables 710-1 and 710-2 illustrate the specific water requirements for various land uses and the rates of flow for various plumbing fixtures.

TABLE 710-1
Planning Guide for Water Use

Types of establishments	*Gallons per day*
Airports (per passenger)	3–5
Apartments, multiple family (per resident)	60
Bathhouses (per bather)	10
Camps:	
Construction, semipermanent (per worker)	50
Day with no meals served (per camper)	15
Luxury (per camper)	100–150
Resorts, day and night, with limited plumbing (per camper)	50
Tourist with central bath and toilet facilities (per person)	35
Cottages with seasonal occupancy (per resident)	50
Courts, tourist with individual bath units (per person)	50
Clubs:	
Country (per resident member)	100
Country (per nonresident member present)	25
Dwellings:	
Boardinghouses (per boarder)	50
Additional kitchen requirements for nonresident boarders	10
Luxury (per person)	100–150
Multiple-family apartments (per resident)	40
Rooming houses (per resident)	60
Single-family houses (per resident)	50–75
Estates (per resident)	100–150
Factories (gallons per person per shift)	15–35
Highway rest area (per person)	5
Hotels with private baths (two persons per room)	60
Hotels without private baths (per person)	50
Institutions other than hospitals (per person)	75–125
Hospitals (per bed)	250–400
Laundries, self-serviced (gallons per washing, i.e., per customer)	50
Motels with bath, toilet, and kitchen facilities (per bed space)	50
With bed and toilet (per bed space)	40
Parks:	
Overnight with flush toilets (per camper)	25
Trailers with individual bath units, no sewer connection (per trailer)	25
Trailers with individual baths, connected to sewer (per person)	50
Picnic:	
With bathhouses, showers, and flush toilets (per picnicker)	20
With toilet facilities only (gallon per picnicker)	10
Restaurants with toilet facilities (per patron)	7–10
Without toilet facilities (per patron)	2.5–3
With bars and cocktail lounge (additional quantity per patron)	2
Schools:	
Boarding (per pupil)	75–100
Day, with cafeteria, gymnasiums, and showers (per pupil)	25
Day, with cafeteria but no gymnasiums or showers (per pupil)	20
Day, without cafeteria, gymnasiums, or showers (per pupil)	15
Service stations (per vehicle)	10
Stores (per toilet room)	400
Swimming pools (per swimmer)	10
Theaters:	
Drive-in (per car space)	5
Movie (per auditorium seat)	5
Workers:	
Construction (per person per shift)	50
Day (school or offices per person per shift)	15

Source: EPA, *Manual of Water Supply Systems,* U.S. Government Printing Office, Washington, D.C., 1973.

2.3 Fire Fighting Requirements

For fire fighting, the amount of water that should be immediately available—particularly the rate at which it should be capable of being delivered to any building or group of buildings—is a function of the size, density, and value of the building or group of buildings.

Successful fire fighting depends more on the speed with which coolant (water, typically) can be applied to a fire rather than the total amount of water available. The key to success is the speed with which fire fighting equipment can get onto the site and the rate at which water can be applied.

To minimize damage, it is essential to apply coolant to the fire before any room is fully involved. This is usually done either with hand-held chemical extinguishers or with water carried to the site by fire trucks. These trucks typically have 500- to 1000-gal (1900- to 3800-L) water tanks and a *booster* hose coiled on a spool for immediate use.

Once a room or building is fully involved, larger amounts of water are necessary for control. In low-density residential areas, the ability to supply at least three full-size fire hose streams [500 to 750 gpm (1900 to 2840 Lpm)] is recommended. Figure 710-1 shows the size of the mains and the length of the runs for a typical water pressure of 60 psi (413.7 Pa).

For large building complexes or denser urban development, conflagration control becomes the key consideration. The recommended design includes delivery rates of 2500 gpm (9500 Lpm) or more, with reserves of over 150,000 gal (570,000 L). To meet these goals in rural or suburban areas without excessive investment in very large diameter water mains, which are costly, adequate reserves of water should be provided as close as conveniently possible to the highly valued buildings.

This reserve usually takes the form of elevated tanks or standpipes linked to the water supply system with large-diameter or redundant mains from the standpipes to the vicinity of the highly valued development (Figure 710-2).

Alternative water reserves for conflagration control could be provided by surface impoundments located close to the highly valued buildings. Such surface supplies would have to be placed (1) so that fire trucks can park immediately adjacent to the impoundment [less than 20 ft (6 m) away] and (2) so that all parts of the buildings can be reached with not more than 600 ft (180 m) of hose. Alternatively, a separate water main and hydrant system can be provided to increase the effectiveness of the impoundment. Figure 710-3 shows a classical application of this principle.

Proper site design for fire fighting includes:

1. Direct, easily perceived, all-weather vehicular access to each building, to each hydrant, and, where appropriate, to each surface water impoundment

2. Control of the massing of any development with firebreaks or fire walls to reduce the possibility of conflagration

3. Site layout that allows fire hoses to be run to all sides of each building

In areas prone to brushfires, site design should include control of flammable vegetation around or near buildings, including the use of pavements, mowed lawns, irrigated plantings, and the avoidance of flammable shrubs (cedar, pine, spruce, etc.).

Hydrants should be laid out so that at

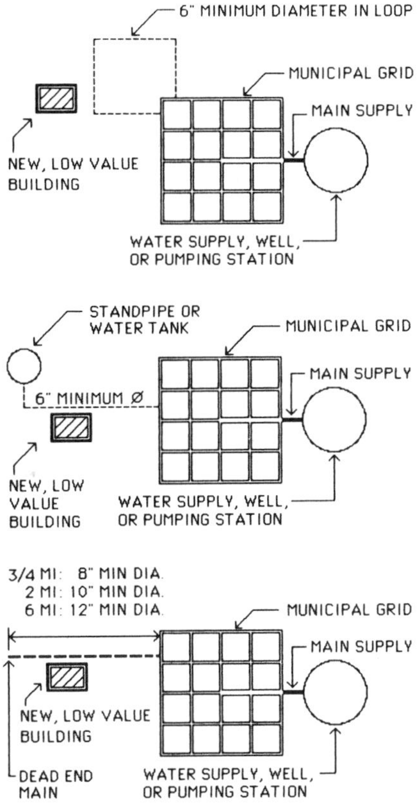
6" MINIMUM DIAMETER IN LOOP
MUNICIPAL GRID
MAIN SUPPLY
NEW, LOW VALUE BUILDING
WATER SUPPLY, WELL, OR PUMPING STATION
STANDPIPE OR WATER TANK
MUNICIPAL GRID
MAIN SUPPLY
6" MINIMUM Ø
NEW, LOW VALUE BUILDING
WATER SUPPLY, WELL, OR PUMPING STATION
3/4 MI: 8" MIN DIA.
2 MI: 10" MIN DIA.
6 MI: 12" MIN DIA.
MUNICIPAL GRID
MAIN SUPPLY
NEW, LOW VALUE BUILDING
DEAD END MAIN
WATER SUPPLY, WELL, OR PUMPING STATION

Figure 710-1 Water supply system configuration for fire fighting.

TABLE 710-2
Rates of Flow for Certain Plumbing, Household, and Farm Fixtures

Location	*Flow pressure, pounds per square inch (psi)**	*Flow rate, gallons per minute (gpm)*
Ordinary basin faucet	8	2.0
Self-closing basin faucet	8	2.5
Sink faucet, ⅜-in	8	4.5
Sink faucet, ½-in	8	4.5
Bathtub faucet	8	6.0
Laundry tub faucet, ½-in	8	5.0
Shower	8	5.0
Ball-cock for closet	8	3.0
Flush valve for closet	15	15–40†
Flushometer valve for urinal	15	15.0
Garden hose (50-ft, ¾-in sill cock)	30	5.0
Garden hose (50-ft, ⅝-in outlet)	15	3.33
Drinking fountains	15	0.75
Fire hose 1½-in, ½-in nozzle	30	40.0

* Flow pressure is the pressure in the supply near the faucet or water outlet while the faucet or water outlet is wide open and flowing.

† Wide range is due to variation in design and type of closet flush valves.

Source: EPA, *Manual of Water Supply Systems,* U.S. Government Printing Office, Washington, D.C., 1973.

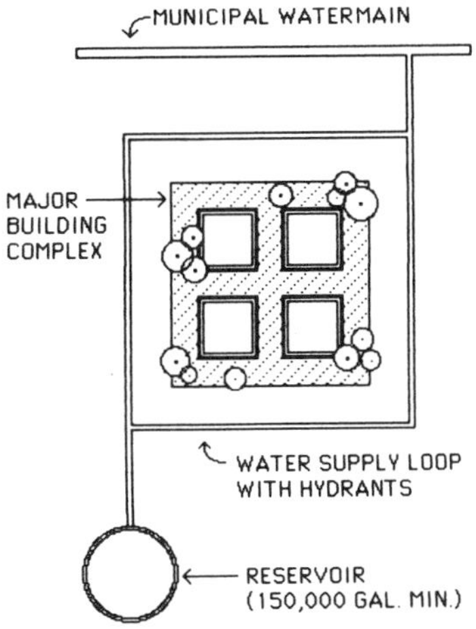
MUNICIPAL WATERMAIN
MAJOR BUILDING COMPLEX
WATER SUPPLY LOOP WITH HYDRANTS
RESERVOIR (150,000 GAL. MIN.)

Figure 710-2 Firefighting water supply system configuration for highly valued development.

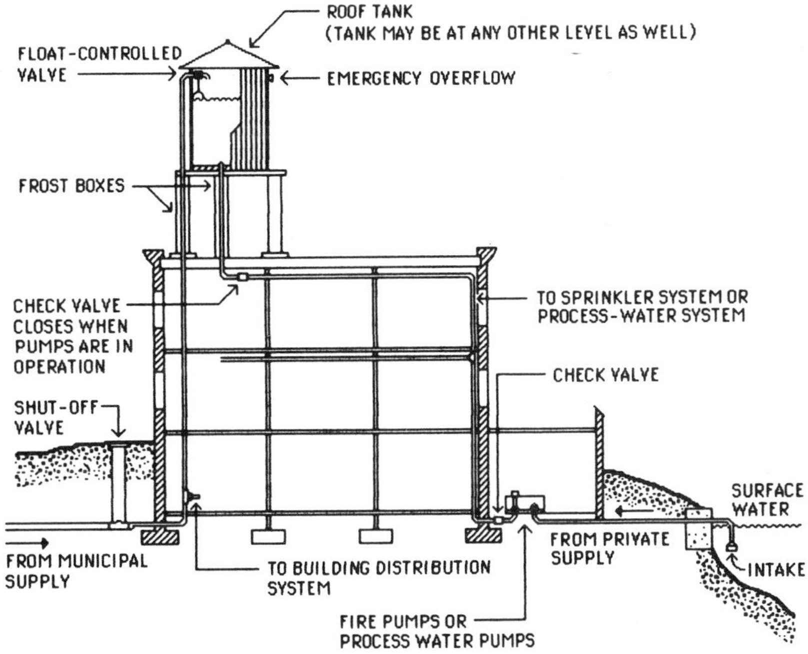
ROOF TANK
(TANK MAY BE AT ANY OTHER LEVEL AS WELL)
FLOAT-CONTROLLED VALVE
EMERGENCY OVERFLOW
FROST BOXES
CHECK VALVE CLOSES WHEN PUMPS ARE IN OPERATION
TO SPRINKLER SYSTEM OR PROCESS-WATER SYSTEM
CHECK VALVE
SHUT-OFF VALVE
SURFACE WATER
FROM MUNICIPAL SUPPLY
TO BUILDING DISTRIBUTION SYSTEM
FROM PRIVATE SUPPLY
INTAKE
FIRE PUMPS OR PROCESS WATER PUMPS

Figure 710-3 Private water supply for fire fighting.

least two are within 500 to 600 ft (150 to 180 m) of every building, with a larger number within that distance of any major building or congested area.

2.4 Nonagricultural Irrigation

Piped water supply systems are often used for nonagricultural irrigation. Normally, most communities regulate the time and condition of its use and design the supply system to handle an unrestricted flow. While the total volume of water used for such purposes in most areas is small compared to potable use, the peak rate of flow in suburban neighborhoods on the afternoon of hot summer days can be greater than the flow required for fire fighting. Unless the distribution system has been specifically designed for it, this peak demand will substantially reduce the ability of the system to deliver water to fires at the necessary rates, both during the peak hours and for several hours thereafter.

Since the use of water for nonagricultural irrigation is essentially an aesthetic or recreational concern, its provision cannot be considered essential to public health, safety, or welfare. Options include: (1) restrictions on the use of water, either prohibiting irrigation entirely or limiting it to hours of low water demand; (2) provision of automatic irrigation systems that operate at off-peak hours only; or (3) development of alternative water sources for irrigation. It must be recognized that waters diverted from ponds, streams, or groundwater, if drawn from sources of limited storage capacity, can have significant adverse effects both on the ponds and streams from which such water is drawn and on downstream waterbodies as well.

3.0 SOURCES OF WATER

3.1 General

Alternative sources of potable water for any building project include: (1) public water supply systems, (2) on-site wells of various kinds, and (3) surface reservoirs and ponds. Selection of the source depends on location and project size. In arid areas, public systems that draw their water from distant sources may be the only alternative. In more humid regions, especially away from urbanized areas, on-site sources may be the only alternative. In general, public sources, where available, will be the least costly and complex, and their use will often be mandated by local officials. Selection of the type of on-site source will depend on geologic opportunity.

3.2 Low-Yield Systems

For small projects requiring only a limited water supply, there are several possible sources, including wells, springs, cisterns, and surface impoundments (or catchments). The choice of system generally depends on regional geohydrologic conditions, with wells (where they are feasible) usually being the most cost-effective alternative.

Wells:

In most areas where annual rainfall exceeds evapotranspiration, sufficient moisture is retained in the soil to make low-yield wells feasible. Figure 710-4 shows the areas in the United States where adequate soil moisture can be expected, and Figure 710-5 shows principal aquifers. Note that the aquifer map (Figure 710-5) shows only those aquifers that can be expected to produce at least 50 gpm (190 Lpm) per well, a yield sufficient to support a community of 1000 people. If lesser aquifers were included on the map, including those capable of supplying enough water for a single dwelling unit, then virtually the entire area where rainfall exceeds evapotranspiration would be indicated.

Many of these lesser aquifers are in areas that, upon casual examination, would not appear promising. In glaciated regions of the northeastern United States, for example, wells are commonly drilled into areas that have a thin mantle of compact glacial till overlying hard, seemingly impermeable rock in order to draw water from fractures in the upper 200 ft (60 m) of the bedrock. For specific information on the feasibility and cost of a low-yield well in any locality, contact local well contractors, local public health officials, or state or federal geologists. Table 710-3 shows a summary of the kinds of wells that have been used under various geological conditions.

Cisterns:

In areas where there is insufficient soil or fractured rock to retain enough water for wells, where the water table is inaccessible, or where the groundwater is contaminated, but where there is sufficient rainfall, potable water may be supplied by catching the rainfall on a controlled, impermeable surface and storing it in a cistern or covered reservoir. A typical installation would include a building roof to provide the

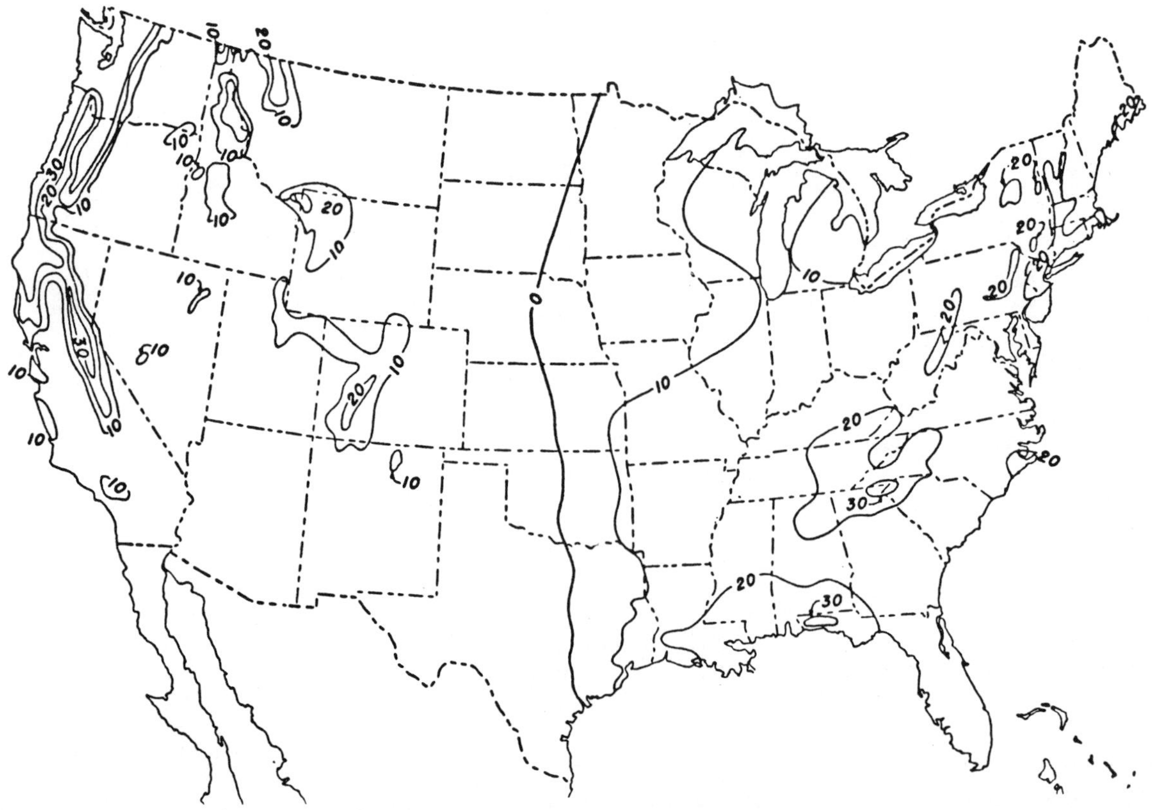
0
10
20
30

Figure 710-4 Areas of the United States where rainfall exceeds evapotranspiration (inches). Note that west of the zero line there is generally no annual excess except in mountain areas and in the Pacific Northwest.

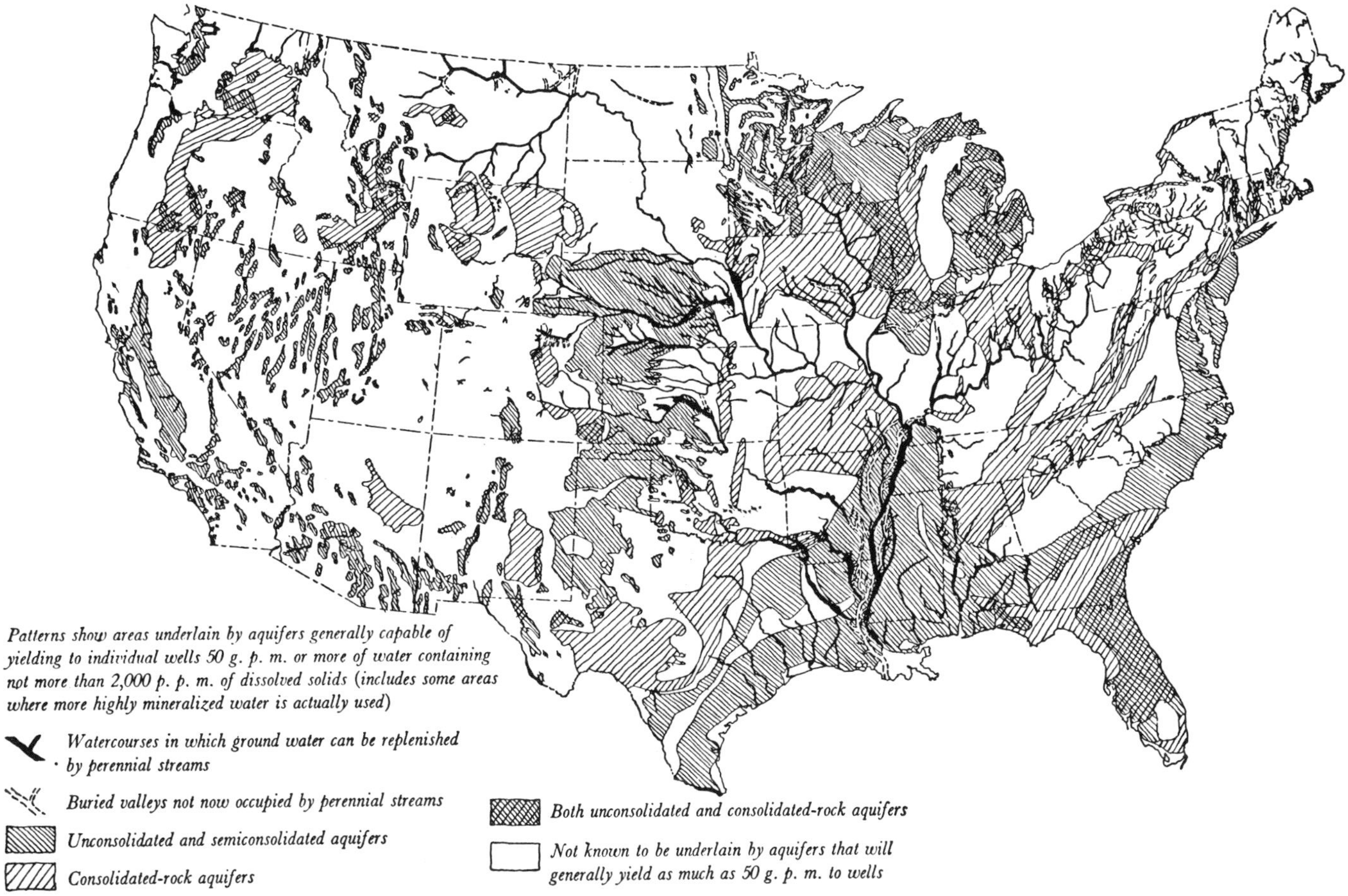
Patterns show areas underlain by aquifers generally capable of yielding to individual wells 50 g. p. m. or more of water containing not more than 2,000 p. p. m. of dissolved solids (includes some areas where more highly mineralized water is actually used)
Watercourses in which ground water can be replenished by perennial streams
Buried valleys not now occupied by perennial streams
Unconsolidated and semiconsolidated aquifers
Consolidated-rock aquifers
Both unconsolidated and consolidated-rock aquifers
Not known to be underlain by aquifers that will generally yield as much as 50 g. p. m. to wells

Figure 710-5 Principal aquifers of the United States.

TABLE 710-3
Suitability of Well Construction Methods for Different Geological Conditions*

				Drilled			
					Rotary		
Characteristics	*Dug*	*Bored*	*Driven*	*Percussion*	*Hydraulic*	*Air*	*Jetted*
Range of practical depths (general order of magnitude)	0–50 ft	0–100 ft	0–50 ft	0–1000 ft	0–1000 ft	0–750 ft	0–100 ft
Diameter	3–20 ft	2–30 in	1¼–2 in	4–18 in	4–24 in	4–10 in	2–12 in
Type of geologic formation:							
Clay	Yes	Yes	Yes	Yes	Yes	No	Yes
Silt	Yes	Yes	Yes	Yes	Yes	No	Yes
Sand	Yes	Yes	Yes	Yes	Yes	No	Yes
Gravel	Yes	Yes	Fine	Yes	Yes	No	¼-in pea gravel
Cemented gravel	Yes	No	No	Yes	Yes	No	No
Boulders	Yes	Yes, if less than well diameter	No	Yes, when in firm bedding	Difficult	No	No
Sandstone	Yes, if soft and/or fractured	Yes, if soft and/or fractured	Thin layers only	Yes	Yes	Yes	No
Limestone	Yes, if soft and/or fractured	Yes, if soft and/or fractured	No	Yes	Yes	Yes	No
Dense igneous rock	No	No	No	Yes	Yes	Yes	No

* The ranges of values in this table are based upon general conditions. They may be exceeded for specific areas or conditions.

Source: EPA, *Manual of Water Supply Systems,* U.S. Government Printing Office, Washington, D.C., 1973.

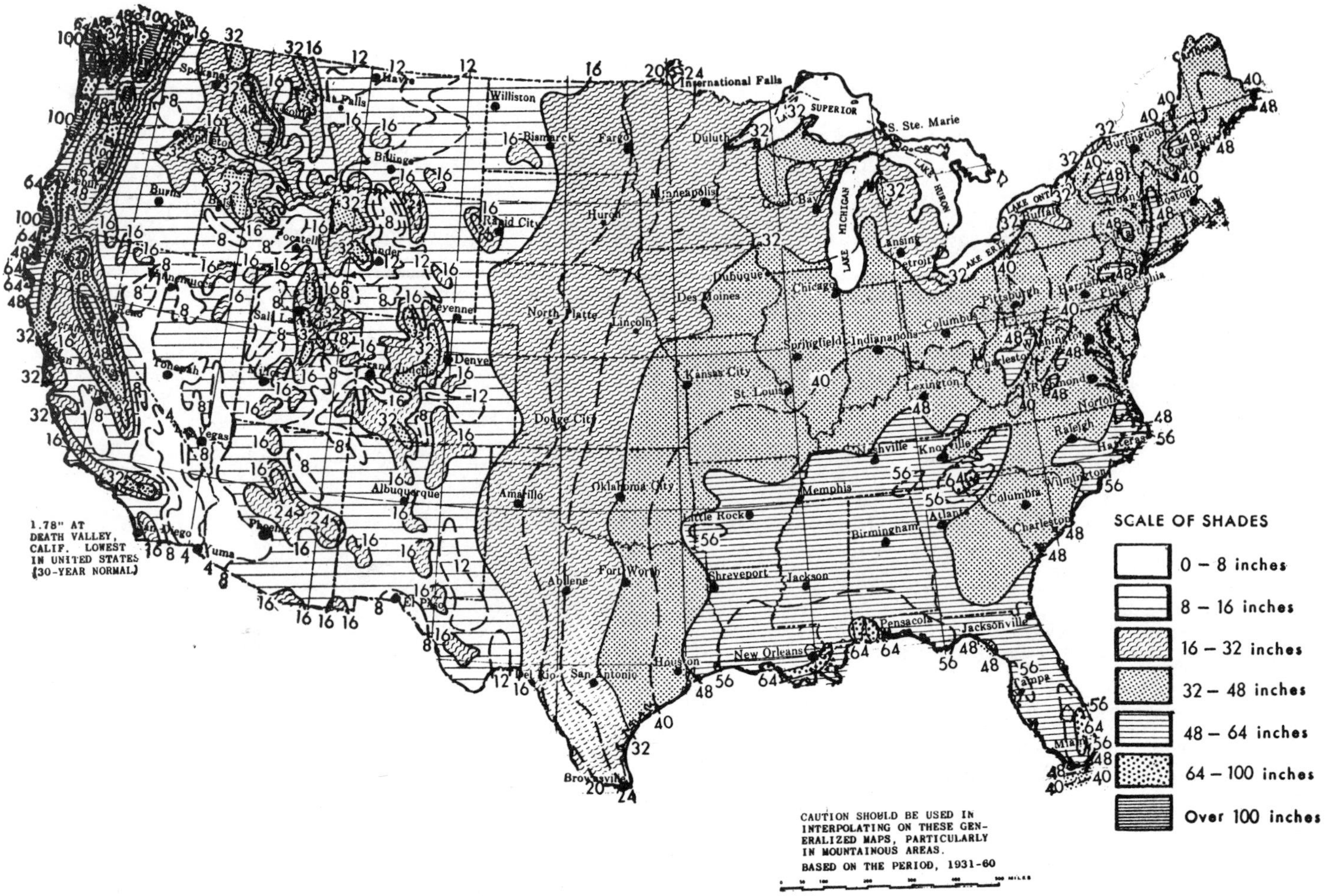
1.78" AT DEATH VALLEY, CALIF. LOWEST IN UNITED STATES (30-YEAR NORMAL)
SCALE OF SHADES
0 – 8 inches
8 – 16 inches
16 – 32 inches
32 – 48 inches
48 – 64 inches
64 – 100 inches
Over 100 inches
CAUTION SHOULD BE USED IN INTERPOLATING ON THESE GENERALIZED MAPS, PARTICULARLY IN MOUNTAINOUS AREAS.
BASED ON THE PERIOD, 1931-60

Figure 710-6 Mean annual precipitation in the United States.

catchment area, some form of pretreatment system (to keep debris, leaves, insects, bird droppings, etc., out of the cistern), the cistern itself (a large reinforced concrete or masonry tank), a water pump, and some form of final treatment or disinfection (chlorination) system.

The catchment area necessary to yield 100 gal (380 L) of water per day, assuming 75 percent capture and a dry year, would be 2000 ft^2 for 60 in of mean rainfall per year (185 m^2 for 1525 mm), 3000 ft^2 for 40 in (280 m^2 for 1015 mm), and 6000 ft^2 for 20 in (560 m^2 for 510 mm). Figure 710-6 shows mean annual rainfall figures for the United States.

The cistern volume required is a function of the distribution of rainfall through the year. In areas with rainfall limited to only one season, a very large storage capacity—about 30,000 gal (a volume 10 ft × 15 ft × 30 ft), or 115,000 L (a volume 3 m × 5 m × 9 m)—will be required per 100 gal (380 L) of water use per day. In regions with rainfall distributed throughout the year, only a fraction of this—perhaps 20 to 25 percent—would be required. Figure 710-7 shows the seasonal distribution of rainfall for the United States.

Figure 710-8 shows a typical cistern design with a simple pretreatment device shown between the roof drain downspout and the cistern. The cistern itself must be structurally designed to withstand the hydrostatic pressure inherent in liquid containers (as in swimming pools). The pretreatment system shown is intended only to screen coarse debris and to divert the dust-laden *first flush* away from the cistern. Final treatment of the water would be performed between the cistern and the user and should include filtration and chlorination.

Figure 710-9 shows a very old type of cistern and pretreatment system used in dry areas of the Mediterranean to capture rainwater that fell in village or palace courtyards. The surface runoff would infiltrate to the system all around the perimeter of the cistern's apron and be filtered through sand fill to the cistern's water level. Storage includes both the cistern itself and the saturated sands (percent water in total volume = about 40 percent). This construction requires no reinforcing and relatively little cement.

Surface Catchments:

In areas where groundwater is not available and where rainfall is not well-distributed throughout the year, individual water collection and storage may be possible if the runoff from a large enough area can be intercepted and impounded. Figure 710-10 shows the drainage area in acres required to supply 1 acre-foot (1233.5 m^3) [326,000 gal (1,304,000 L), or enough for the domestic use of two to three dwelling units] of water for various parts of the United States, or for similar areas in other parts of the world. This drainage area should be clean (preferably grassed) and free of all livestock uses or other sources of pollution.

The reservoir should be no less than 8 ft (2.4 m) deep at its maximum and should be large enough to store at least 1 year's average runoff from its tributary watershed. Figure 710-11 shows a plan and section of a typical storage pond.

Treatment should include filtration and disinfection (chlorination). Filtration could be by slow, sand filtration in a treatment facility constructed of concrete built on-site for the purpose, or by pressure sand filtration or diatomaceous filtration in a prefabricated metal or plastic package system. For detailed information on treatment systems and disinfection available in any locality, consult local health officials, equipment suppliers, and the U.S. Soil Conservation Service or a similar agency outside the United States.

3.3 High-Yield Wells

For larger projects, such as a large institution or a new town, a larger well or surface reservoir may be required. The design of either system will require specialized engineering and/or hydrogeologic expertise. In the northeastern United States and southeastern Canada, wells can be expected to be less costly and require less (if any) water treatment, if they are geologically feasible. The feasibility of high-yield wells is highly dependent on local conditions, with yields ranging from 50,000 to 1 million gal (190,000 to 3,800,000 L) per well per day. Well sites with good yield potential can be very valuable, and they should be carefully considered in planning any large land area. Unfortunately, local water supply officials usually lack the funds, foresight, and capability to protect good well sites from development for other uses.

In the glaciated northeastern United States, good sites for high-yield wells include coarse outwash plains, ice channel fillings along valleys, river terraces, kame fields, and similar surficial deposits. Shallow aquifers are often characterized on their surface by xerophytic species such as pitch pine *(Pinus rigida).*

Development of high-yield wells should take into account:

1. State well protection requirements
2. The character and land use history of the tributary area

When used for *public* water supplies, high-yield wells are often required to be protected by a buffer zone on which most other land uses are prohibited. Such zones can be several hundred feet wide [e.g., in Massachusetts (in the United States) a 400-ft (120-m) radius is required].

3.4 Surface Water Supplies

Surface water supplies include:

1. Uncontrolled run-of-river systems (as in St. Louis and New Orleans)
2. Main stream, multipurpose dams (e.g., Hoover Dam/Lake Mead)
3. Special-purpose reservoirs built on tributary streams (e.g., Massachusetts Quabbin and a multiplicity of small reservoirs throughout the northeastern United States)
4. Natural ponds and lakes with clean waters (e.g., Lake Michigan)

Water drawn from run-of-river and main stream, multipurpose dams requires extensive treatment before use, including clarification, filtration, and chlorination, with constant quality control.

Water drawn from tributary reservoirs and from clean ponds and lakes can be used with relatively little pretreatment, depending on the specific case and on state standards.

For information on surface water quality, consult state and other water quality agencies. In the United States, surface waters are generally classified by state as Class A, suitable for drinking with little or no treatment; Class B, suitable for drinking with treatment; and Class C or lower, not suitable for drinking.

4.0 CONSTRAINTS ON WELL DEVELOPMENT

The development of high-yield wells can lower water tables significantly and draw water from considerable distances. The planning of a high-yield well should include consideration of the following development constraints:

1. Proximity to seawater and the possibility of salt intrusion
2. Proximity to organic deposits (swamps, marshes, etc.)
3. Possible urban land use conflicts
4. Possible industrial and waste disposal contamination

4.1 Proximity to Seawater

Figure 710-12 shows the typical relationship of fresh groundwater to brackish groundwater in ideally homogeneous soils in seacoast conditions. Note that the fresh water, in effect, floats on top of the salt water because of its lower specific gravity.

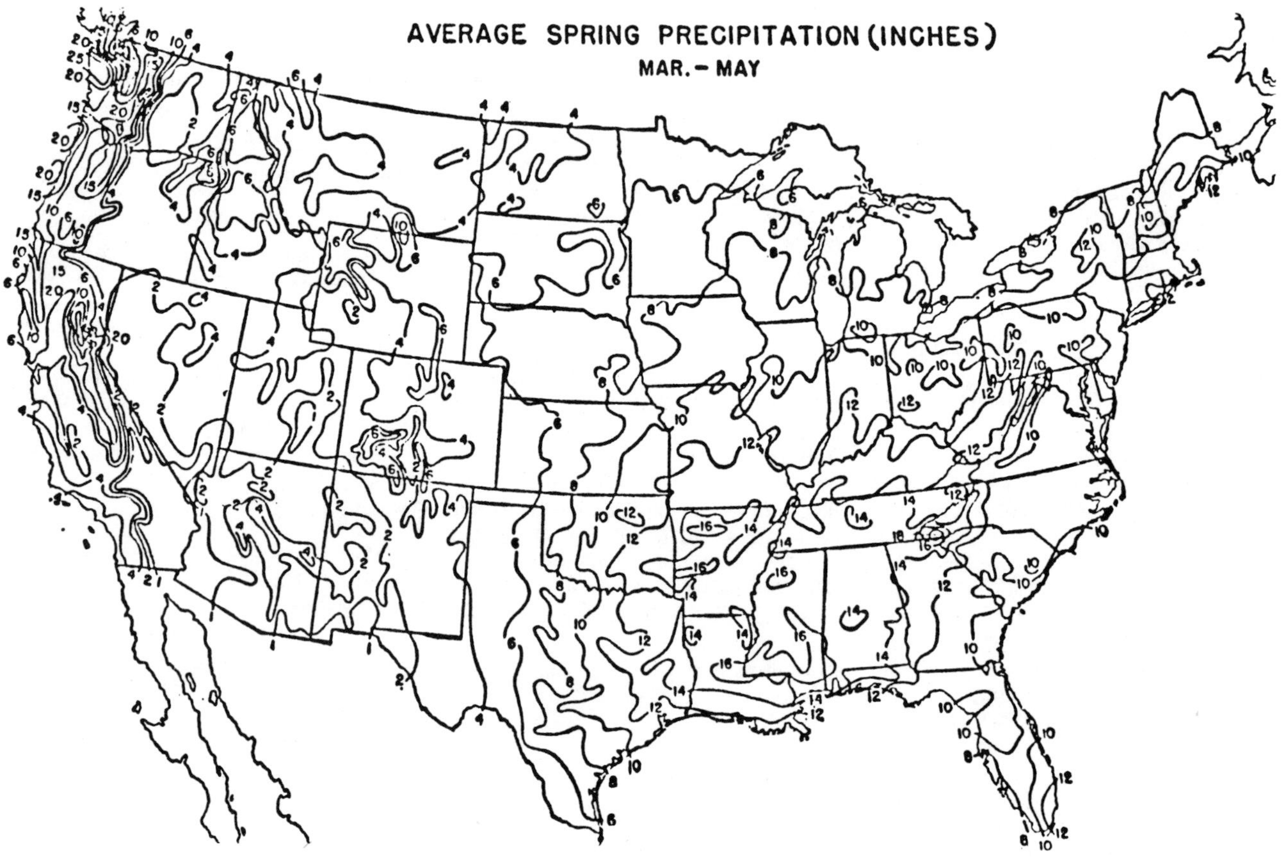
AVERAGE SPRING PRECIPITATION (INCHES)
MAR. – MAY

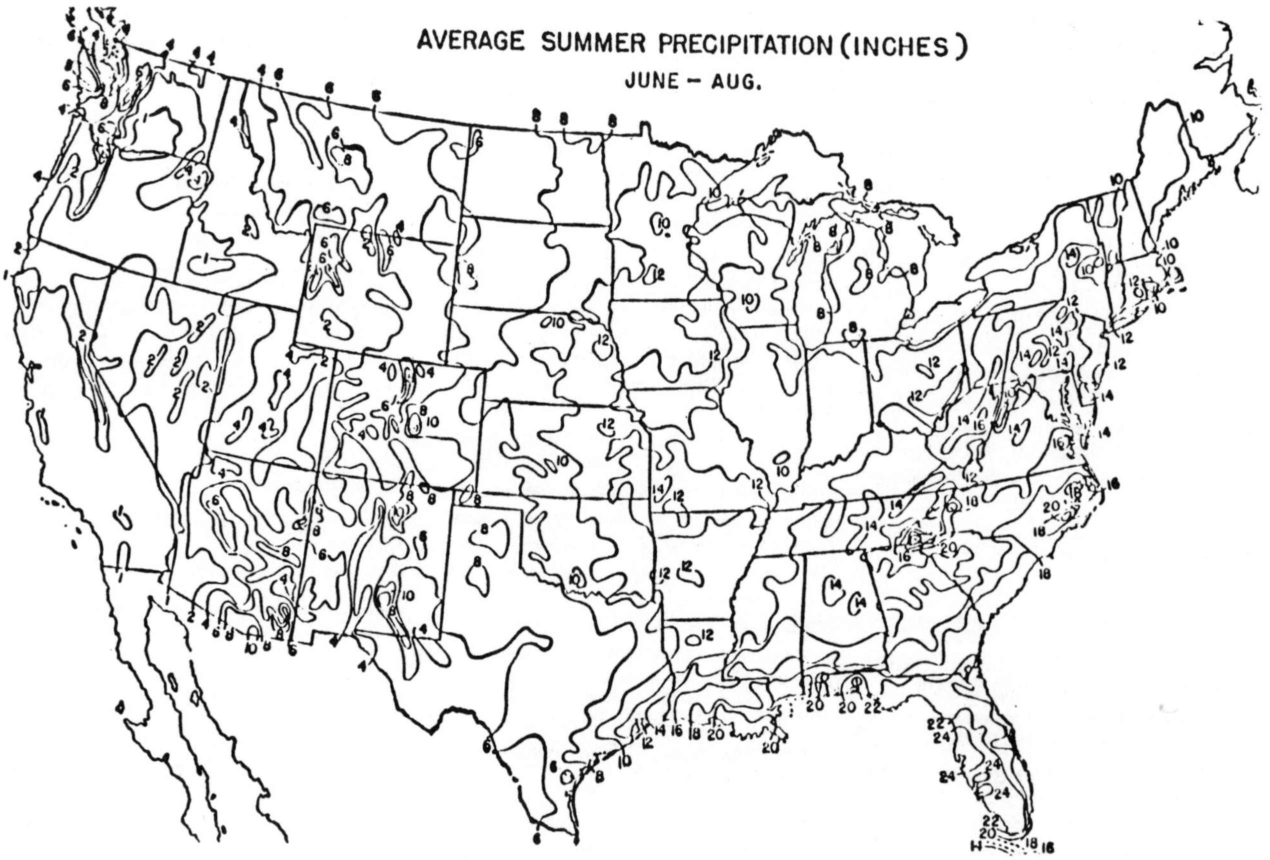
AVERAGE SUMMER PRECIPITATION (INCHES)
JUNE – AUG.

Figure 710-7 Seasonal rainfall distribution in the United States.

AVERAGE FALL PRECIPITATION (INCHES)

SEPT. – NOV.

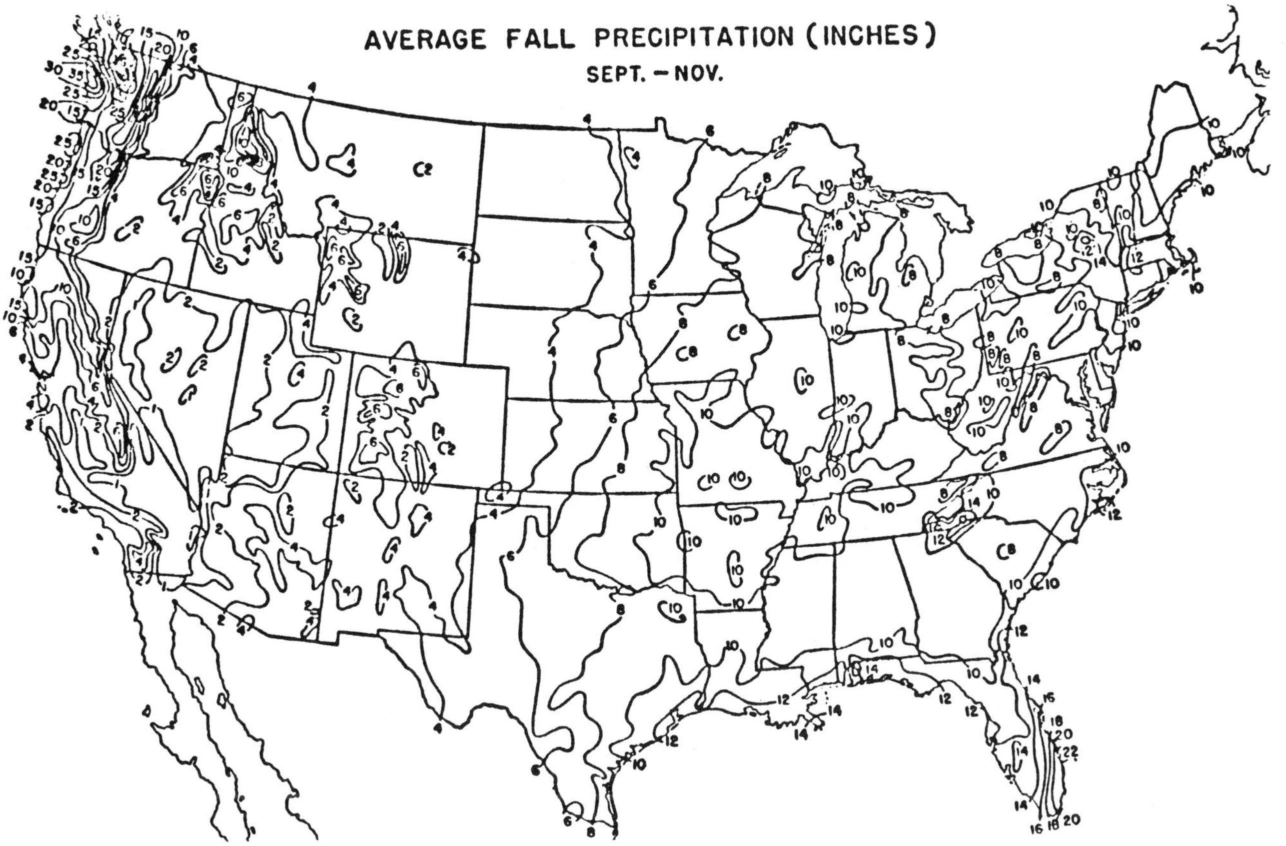

AVERAGE WINTER PRECIPITATION (INCHES)

DEC. – FEB.

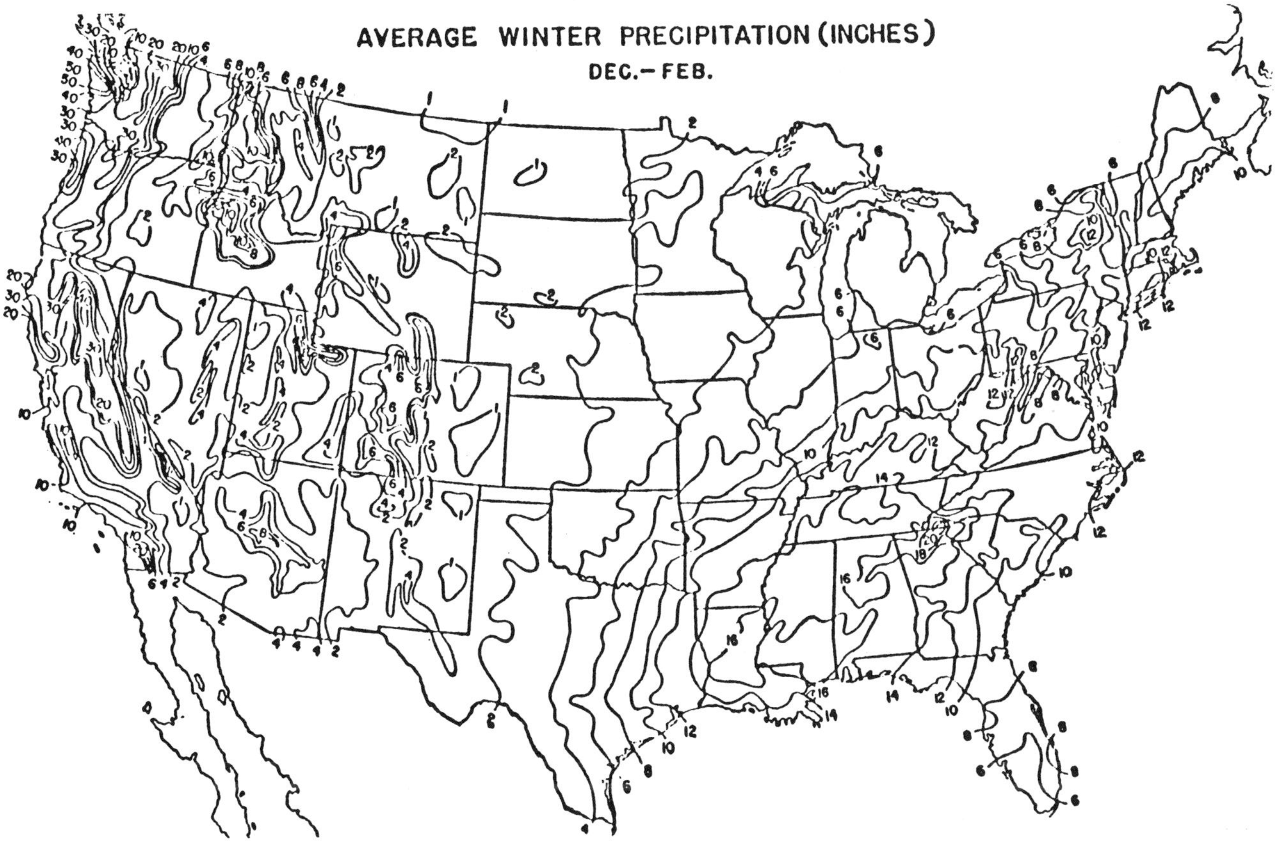

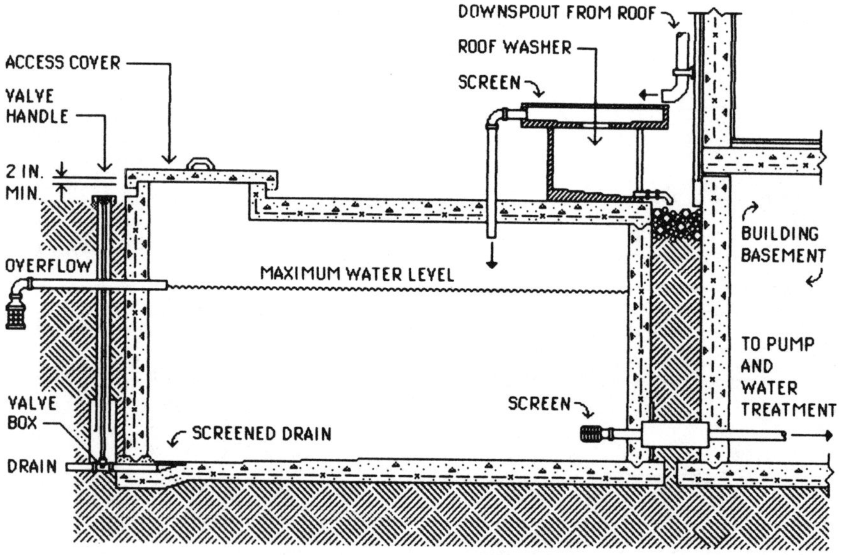
DOWNSPOUT FROM ROOF
ROOF WASHER
SCREEN
ACCESS COVER
VALVE HANDLE
2 IN. MIN.
OVERFLOW
MAXIMUM WATER LEVEL
BUILDING BASEMENT
TO PUMP AND WATER TREATMENT
SCREEN
VALVE BOX
SCREENED DRAIN
DRAIN

Figure 710-8 Typical cistern design.

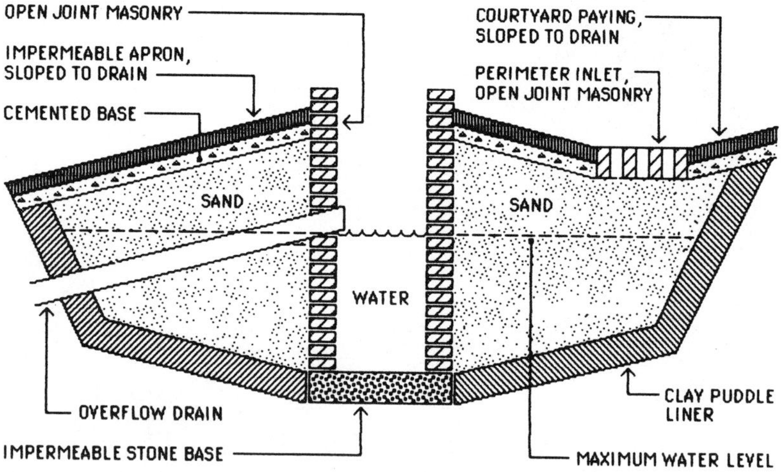
OPEN JOINT MASONRY
IMPERMEABLE APRON, SLOPED TO DRAIN
CEMENTED BASE
COURTYARD PAVING, SLOPED TO DRAIN
PERIMETER INLET, OPEN JOINT MASONRY
SAND
SAND
WATER
OVERFLOW DRAIN
CLAY PUDDLE LINER
IMPERMEABLE STONE BASE
MAXIMUM WATER LEVEL

Figure 710-9 Ancient Mediterranean cistern.

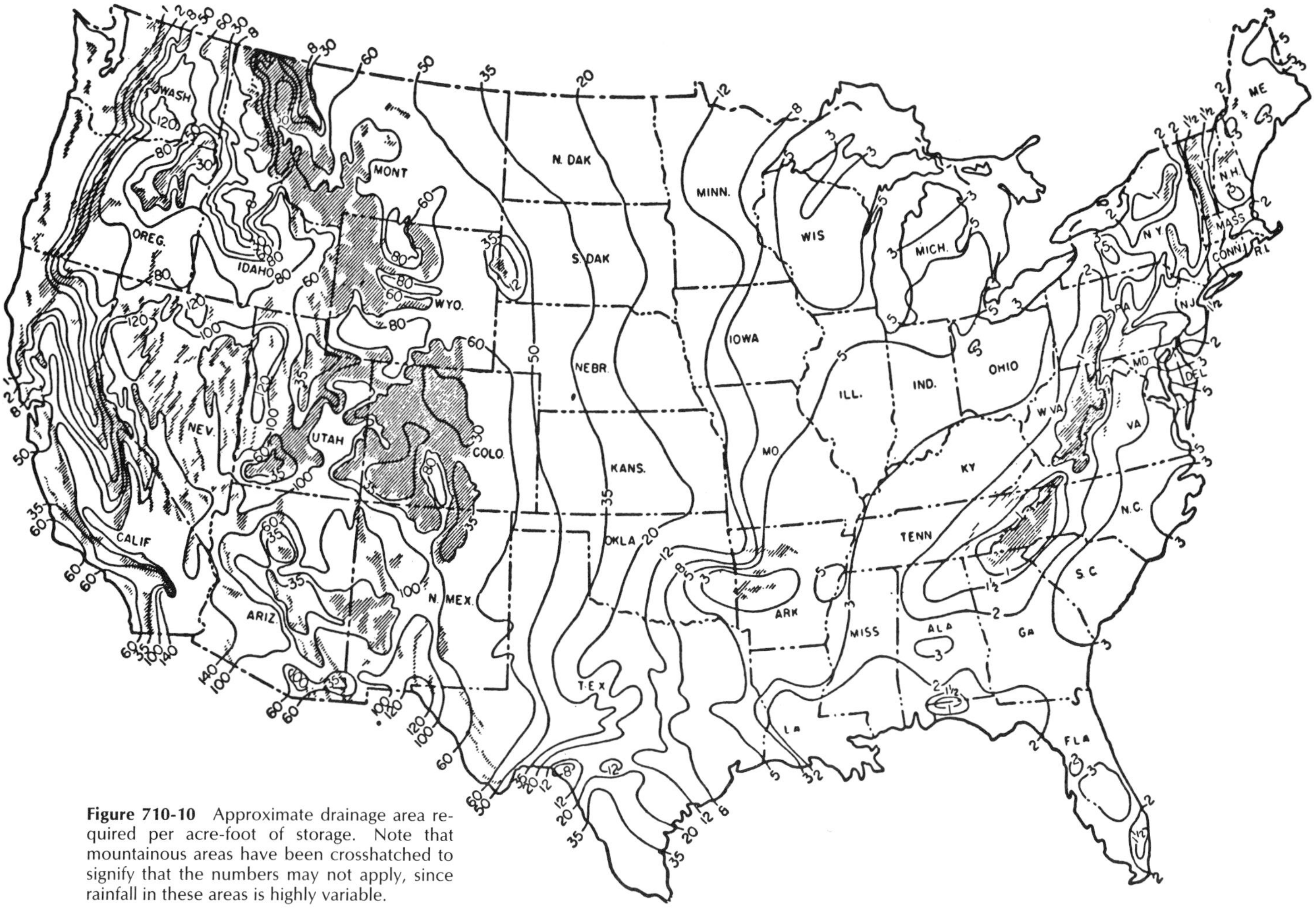

WASH
OREG.
IDAHO
MONT
WYO.
CALIF
NEV.
UTAH
COLO.
ARIZ
N. MEX.
N. DAK
S. DAK
NEBR.
KANS.
OKLA
TEX
MINN.
IOWA
MO.
ARK
LA
WIS
MICH.
ILL.
IND.
OHIO
KY
TENN
MISS
ALA
GA
FLA
S.C
N.C.
VA
W VA
MD
DEL
PA
NJ
N Y
CONN
R I
MASS
N H
VT
ME

Figure 710-10 Approximate drainage area required per acre-foot of storage. Note that mountainous areas have been crosshatched to signify that the numbers may not apply, since rainfall in these areas is highly variable.

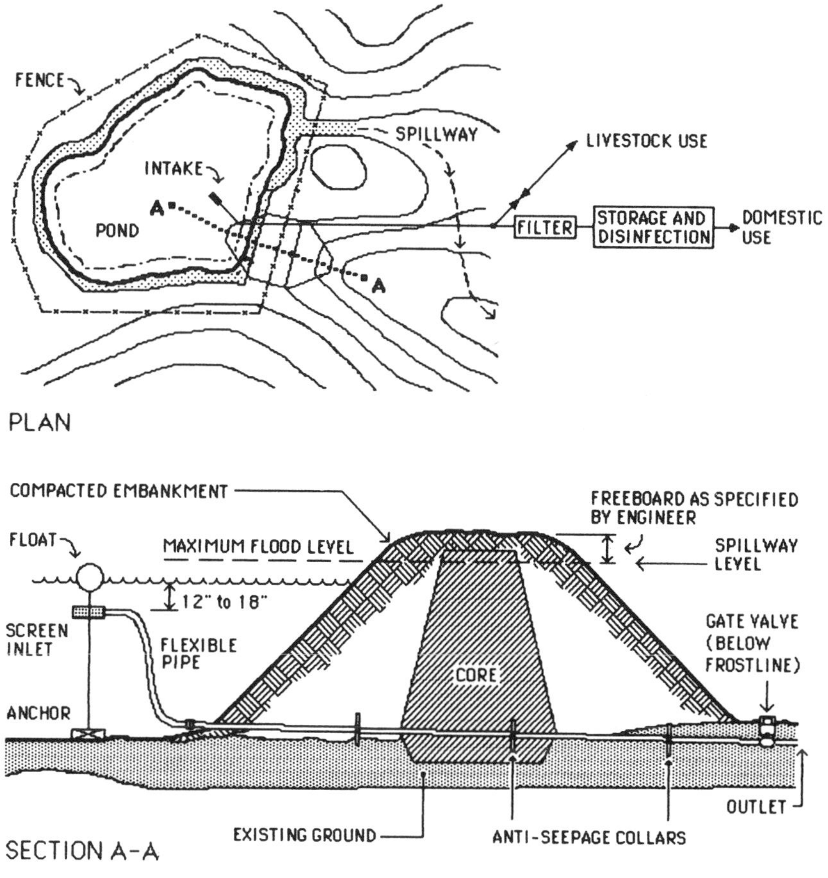

FENCE
SPILLWAY
LIVESTOCK USE
INTAKE
A
POND
FILTER
STORAGE AND DISINFECTION
DOMESTIC USE
A
PLAN
COMPACTED EMBANKMENT
FREEBOARD AS SPECIFIED BY ENGINEER
FLOAT
MAXIMUM FLOOD LEVEL
SPILLWAY LEVEL
12" to 18"
SCREEN INLET
FLEXIBLE PIPE
CORE
GATE VALVE (BELOW FROSTLINE)
ANCHOR
OUTLET
EXISTING GROUND
ANTI-SEEPAGE COLLARS
SECTION A-A

Figure 710-11 Storage pond.

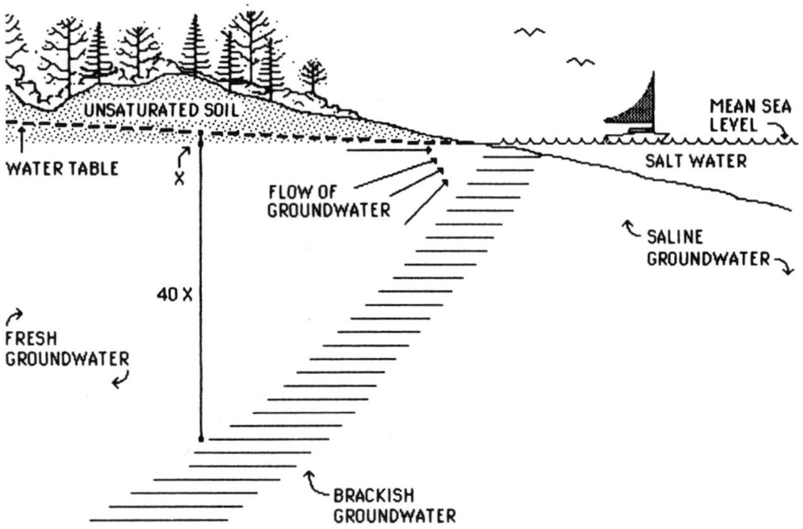
UNSATURATED SOIL
MEAN SEA LEVEL
WATER TABLE
X
SALT WATER
FLOW OF GROUNDWATER
SALINE GROUNDWATER
40 X
FRESH GROUNDWATER
BRACKISH GROUNDWATER

Figure 710-12 Groundwater environment at seacoast.

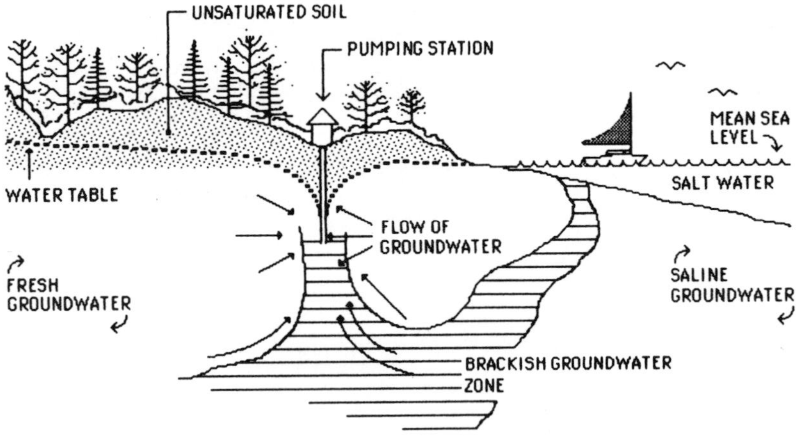
UNSATURATED SOIL
PUMPING STATION
MEAN SEA LEVEL
WATER TABLE
SALT WATER
FLOW OF GROUNDWATER
FRESH GROUNDWATER
SALINE GROUNDWATER
BRACKISH GROUNDWATER
ZONE

Figure 710-13 Effect of well drawdown below mean sea level on groundwater flow.

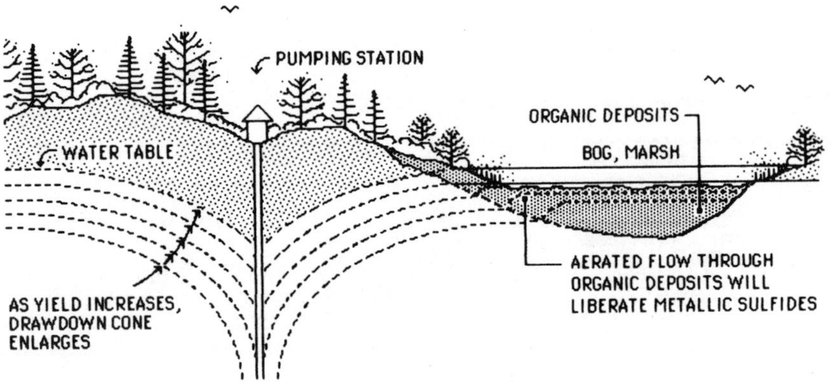
PUMPING STATION
ORGANIC DEPOSITS
WATER TABLE
BOG, MARSH
AERATED FLOW THROUGH ORGANIC DEPOSITS WILL LIBERATE METALLIC SULFIDES
AS YIELD INCREASES, DRAWDOWN CONE ENLARGES

Figure 710-14 Effects of well drawdown on metallic sulfides in organic deposits.

Figure 710-13 shows the effect of lowering the water table with a well. The area of the cone of the depression will be such that the annual yield of the well will equal the annual surplus of rainfall over runoff and evapotranspiration for the area of the cone, and the depth of the cone will be whatever is necessary to provide a steep enough gradient to move the water to the well. The more permeable the soil, the flatter the cone. The greater the yield, the larger the cone in all dimensions.

In a seacoast condition, if too high an annual volume is withdrawn, so that the water table falls to mean sea level, brackish water will enter the well, ruining it for water supply purposes.

4.2 Proximity to Organic Deposits

Figure 710-14 shows a typical high-yield well installation in the northeastern United States. Both the organic deposits and the unconsolidated aquifer lie along a valley. A specific problem is that organic deposits tend to be concentrators of metallic sulfides (bog iron) by the decomposition of organic detritus. These sulfides are stable only as long as they are surrounded by water devoid of dissolved oxygen. Fortunately, these organic deposits also tend to be relatively impermeable; as a result, the cone of depression at nearby wells will deform, drawing a relatively small proportion of the well's total flow from the organic deposit.

However, if too high an annual volume of water is withdrawn from such a well, waters bearing oxygen will both dissolve the metallic sulfides and increase the permeability of the deposit, significantly increasing the iron and/or manganese content of the well, ruining it for water supply purposes. (*Resting* the well, allowing anaerobic conditions to reestablish themselves in the organic deposits, will often restore the *status quo ante*.)

4.3 Land Use Density and Waste Disposal

The urbanized use of land and the potable use of the waters underlying it are compatible, subject to the following conditions:

1. The wastewater is disposed of through leaching systems that do not intersect or penetrate the water table.

2. The land use density is not excessive.

3. The past land uses of the recharge area did not involve the use, storage, shipment, or disposal of chemicals.

Relationship between Sewage Leaching Systems and the Water Table:

All modern sanitary codes in the United States require at least 2 ft (0.6 m) of free percolation between the bottom of any infiltration device (cesspool, leaching bed, leaching trench, leaching pit, etc.) and the water table. This percolation is essential to the effective control of pathogens and the oxidation of wastes.

Unfortunately, in the last century no such restrictions existed, and in fact the texts of the period recommended that cesspools and leaching pits be dug down into the water table. Furthermore, in many older neighborhoods where the cesspools were not deliberately dug deeply, the advent of public water supplies led to the conversion of the old dug wells to cesspools. The result is that no well should be developed in an area where the well's cone of depression would include any significant number of old buildings, unless site specific analyses demonstrate that no problem exists.

Density of Development:

Although proper on-site wastewater disposal will eliminate or destroy most water contaminants, it does increase significantly the nitrate concentration of the groundwater. The denser the development, the higher the concentration, but higher rainfall spread over the entire year will lower the concentration. As a general measure of the acceptable level of concentration for any region, densities of 1 to 2 dwelling units per acre are considered an upper limit in the United States (where the excess of rainfall over evapotranspiration is 20 in (510 mm) per year). Where the excess of rainfall is less, the density would also be less. Table 710-4 shows the lot sizes required for adequate dilution of on-site sewage disposal nitrates in the underlying groundwater for various parts of the United States, assuming highly permeable soils and rapid infiltration of rainwater.

4.4 Industrial and Waste Contamination

Regarding past land uses, both new and old industries use an enormous variety of chemicals whose effects on human health are insufficiently understood and whose effects were totally misunderstood in the past. Many of these chemicals are quite stable in the soil and may, as a result of ion interaction with soil particles, move at rates much slower than the normally slow rates of groundwater flow. As a result, it is prudent to assume that any area ever used for industrial purposes, including processing, chemical storage, shipping, or waste disposal, should not be included in the recharge cone of any potable water supply well, unless site specific analyses prove otherwise.

TABLE 710-4
Required Lot Sizes for Inches of Excess Rainfall over Evapotranspiration

Excess rainfall, in	*Lot size, ft²/d.u.**
5	120,000
10	60,000
20	30,000
30	22,500
40	15,000

*Ft² per dwelling unit.

5.0 GROUNDWATER FLOW ANALYSIS

Determining patterns of groundwater flow is similar to determining patterns of surface flow. First a contour map of the upper surface of the groundwater (i.e., the water table) is constructed, and then the pattern of flow through the ground is considered as though it were a surface flow across the water-table contours. Like surface water, the flows will be perpendicular to the lines of equal potential (contours), and again like surface water, the flows will be faster where the contours are closer together, adjusting for the permeability of the soil (like the coefficient of roughness on surface flow).

To construct a water-table contour map:

1. Plot all known water-table elevations on ponds, streams, swamps, wells, etc.

2. Assume that the water table is lower than the ground surface at all low spots where no surface water is evident, and that the two surfaces coincide wherever there is a pond or wet spot, unless there is solid evidence to the contrary.

3. In regions where *rainfall exceeds evaporation* (i.e., humid regions), assume that the water table is higher than adjoining streams (Figure 710-15, top). In regions where *evapotranspiration exceeds rainfall* (i.e., arid regions), assume that the water table is lower than adjoining streams (Figure 710-15, bottom).

4. Interpolate the contours in the same manner in which ground surface topography is interpolated. (Check that the groundwater surface is not higher than the ground surface.)

Obviously, where there are ample exposures of water on the surface, the groundwater surface will be close to the ground surface and there will be little doubt as to the depth and slope of the groundwater surface. In places where there is little surface water, the water table is likely to be well down and not much can be deduced about it.

In highly permeable soils, where groundwater can move easily, the water-table surfaces are likely to be quite flat and only minimally reflect the shape of the ground surface, but in less permeable soils the water table is more likely to reflect the contour of the ground surface (Figure 710-16). The groundwater contours in valleys can be expected to assume the same V form as the surface contours, where there is a stream in the valley. However, where there is no surface stream and impermeable strata are well down, the groundwater surface is not likely to be influenced by the surface topography at all.

Interpretation of a groundwater contour map is similar to interpretation of surface topography. In general, flows are perpendicular to contours, so that it is reasonably possible to delineate groundwater watersheds of ponds, streams, and estuaries and to forecast the directional movement of contaminants.

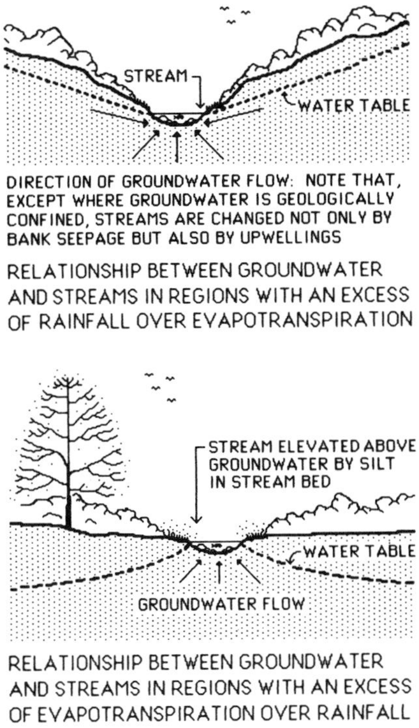
STREAM
WATER TABLE
DIRECTION OF GROUNDWATER FLOW: NOTE THAT, EXCEPT WHERE GROUNDWATER IS GEOLOGICALLY CONFINED, STREAMS ARE CHANGED NOT ONLY BY BANK SEEPAGE BUT ALSO BY UPWELLINGS
RELATIONSHIP BETWEEN GROUNDWATER AND STREAMS IN REGIONS WITH AN EXCESS OF RAINFALL OVER EVAPOTRANSPIRATION
STREAM ELEVATED ABOVE GROUNDWATER BY SILT IN STREAM BED
WATER TABLE
GROUNDWATER FLOW
RELATIONSHIP BETWEEN GROUNDWATER AND STREAMS IN REGIONS WITH AN EXCESS OF EVAPOTRANSPIRATION OVER RAINFALL

Figure 710-15 Relationship between groundwater and streams.

6.0 WELL RECHARGE AREA ANALYSIS

To determine the area from which a high-yield well will draw its water, a cone of depression must be drawn into the groundwater surface. Figure 710-17 shows a cross section through a hypothetical well in uniformly permeable sands with a flat water table (an improbable situation). Fig-

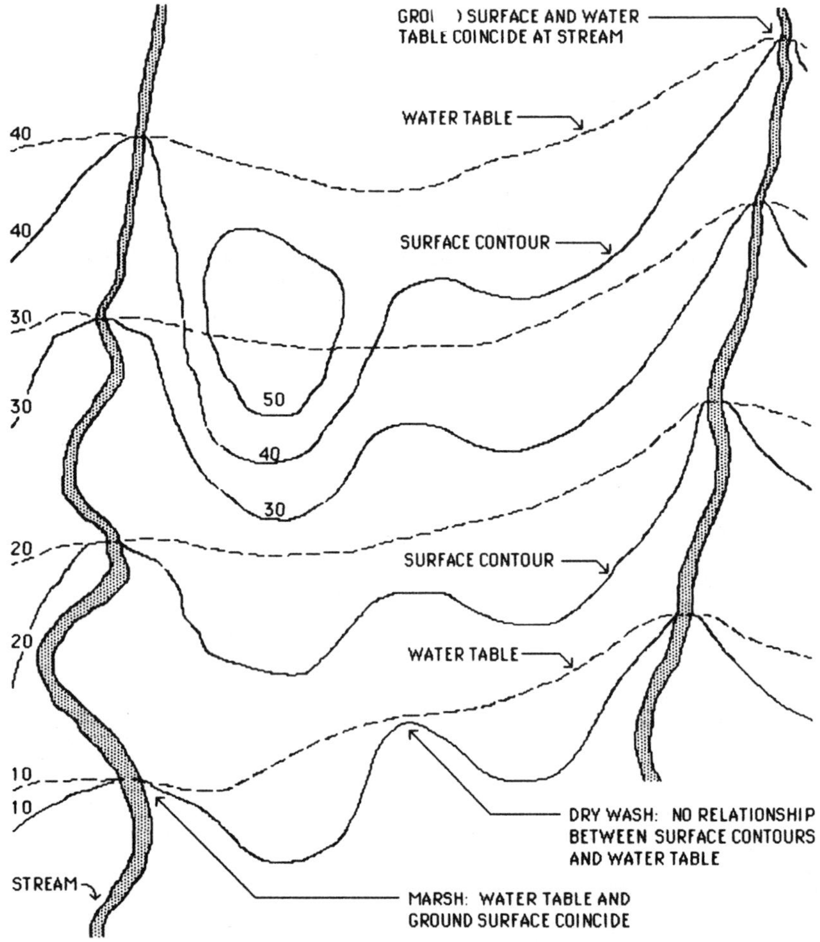
GROI) SURFACE AND WATER TABLE COINCIDE AT STREAM
WATER TABLE
SURFACE CONTOUR
SURFACE CONTOUR
WATER TABLE
DRY WASH: NO RELATIONSHIP BETWEEN SURFACE CONTOURS AND WATER TABLE
MARSH: WATER TABLE AND GROUND SURFACE COINCIDE
STREAM
40
40
30
30
50
40
30
20
20
10
10

Figure 710-16 Relationship of groundwater and water table in unconsolidated and unconfined aquifers in regions where rainfall exceeds evaporation.

ure 710-18 shows the same cone in an oblique view. Figure 710-19 is the same situation as Figure 710-17 but with a uniformly sloping water table (a somewhat more realistic assumption, but still only theoretical). Figure 710-20 is an oblique view of Figure 710-19. Note that the plan view of the cone is no longer circular but oval. Figure 710-21 is the same situation as Figure 710-20 but as a contoured surface viewed as a horizontal map. Figure 710-22 is similar to 710-21 but is drawn on a three-dimensionally curved groundwater surface in a relatively shallow aquifer, the kind of groundwater surface likely to be found in a complex outwash or kame plain.

Where aquifers are deep, it is essential to assume that groundwater flow is laminar. Figure 710-23 shows a section through a deep but homogeneous aquifer. The groundwater does not mix but remains stratified.

Figure 710-24 shows the effect of this laminar flow on water movement to a well in the upper portion of an aquifer. Note that groundwater from distant recharge areas can pass entirely under a low-yield well. The larger the well, the larger its recharge area and the deeper its draw on the ground.

Figure 710-25 shows the effects of small and large wells on the same aquifer. Note

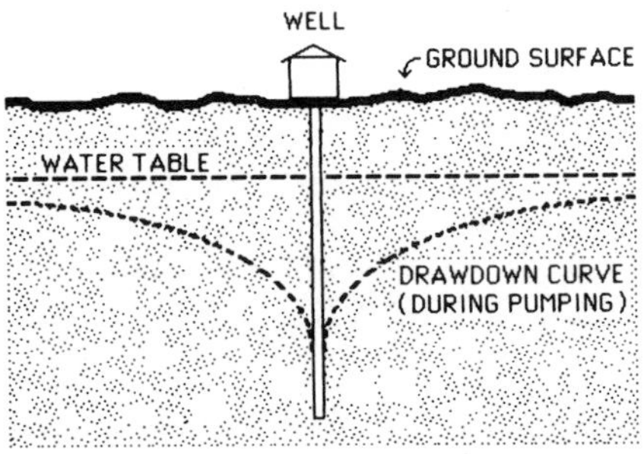
WELL
GROUND SURFACE
WATER TABLE
DRAWDOWN CURVE
(DURING PUMPING)

Figure 710-17 Drawdown cone in uniformly permeable sands and a flat water table. Note that the drawdown curve is not a simple cone but is hyperbolic.

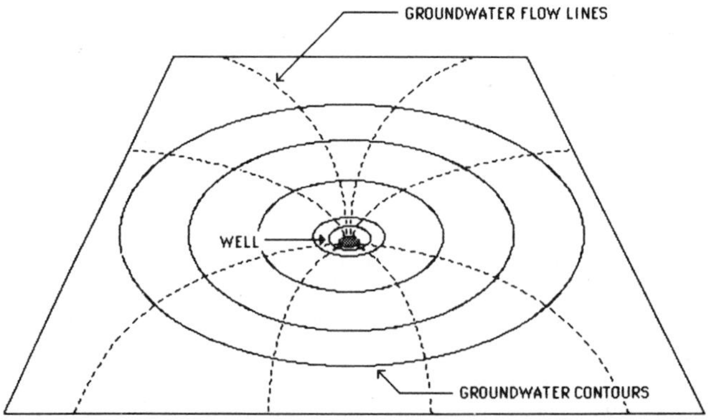
GROUNDWATER FLOW LINES
WELL
GROUNDWATER CONTOURS

Figure 710-18 Oblique view of Figure 710-17. Note that the intersection of the drawdown cone and the water table is circular.

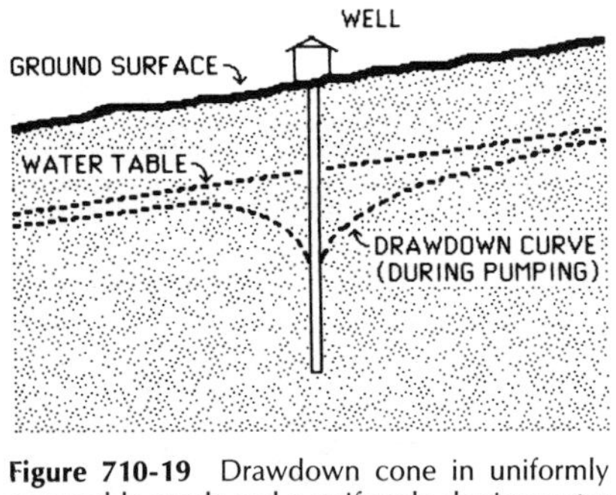
WELL
GROUND SURFACE
WATER TABLE
DRAWDOWN CURVE
(DURING PUMPING)

Figure 710-19 Drawdown cone in uniformly permeable sands and a uniformly sloping water table.

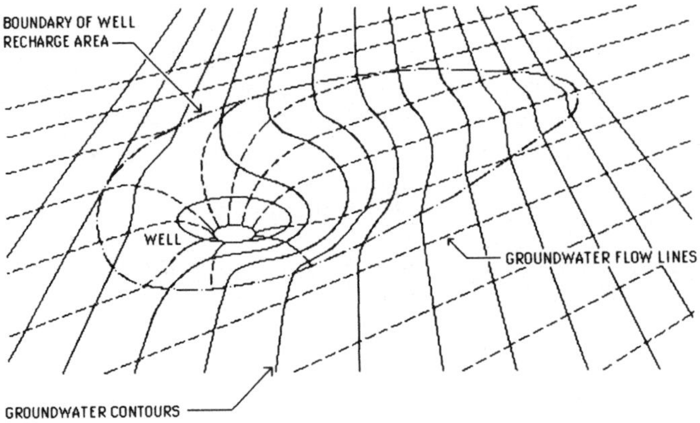
BOUNDARY OF WELL
RECHARGE AREA
WELL
GROUNDWATER FLOW LINES
GROUNDWATER CONTOURS

Figure 710-20 Oblique view of Figure 710-19.

that aquifers that have been satisfactorily serving low-yield wells cannot be assumed to be suitable for high-yield wells.

7.0 RESERVOIR DESIGN CONSIDERATIONS

Site selection criteria for a water supply reservoir should include:

1. A watershed large enough to yield an adequate water supply

2. An impoundment volume large enough for adequate, long-term water storage

3. Suitable soil conditions (i.e., the less permeable, the better)

4. A topographic form capable of being shaped into a reservoir at reasonable cost (minimum regrading)

5. A watershed free of contaminants

6. A reservoir site free of excessive organic materials

7.1 Size of Watershed

Per capita potable water use in the United States varies from under 150 gal (570 L) per day in the northeast to over 350 gal (1325 L) per day in the southwest (where extensive irrigation takes place). In periods of drought in the northeast, with restrictions on lawn irrigation, automobile washing, etc., water use can be reduced by 50 percent. Such drought restrictions on use are normal and widespread in the rural northeast.

The annual gross yield of a watershed, assuming a very large, long-term storage volume, could reach the average annual rainfall for the watershed less the watershed's evapotranspiration and the reservoir's evaporation and leakage. (Figure

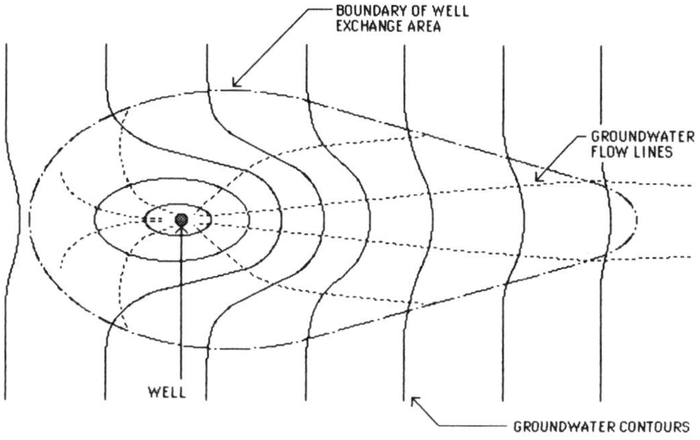
BOUNDARY OF WELL EXCHANGE AREA
GROUNDWATER FLOW LINES
WELL
GROUNDWATER CONTOURS

Figure 710-21 Plan view of Figure 710-19. The contour lines are lines of uniform, constant elevation; the dashed lines show the direction of slope and water flow.

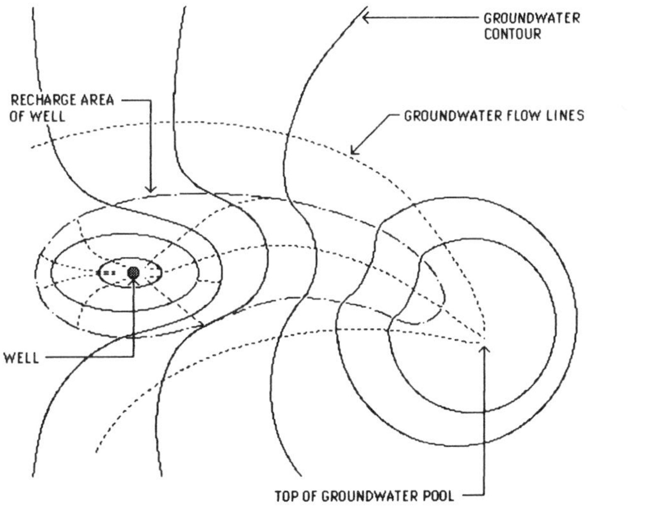
GROUNDWATER CONTOUR
RECHARGE AREA OF WELL
GROUNDWATER FLOW LINES
WELL
TOP OF GROUNDWATER POOL

Figure 710-22 Drawdown cone in uniformly permeable sands and a three-dimensionally curved groundwater surface.

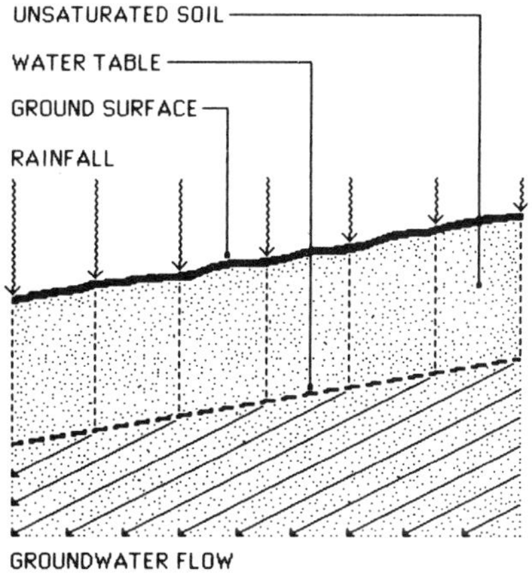
UNSATURATED SOIL
WATER TABLE
GROUND SURFACE
RAINFALL
GROUNDWATER FLOW

Figure 710-23 Longitudinal section through homogeneous aquifer, showing laminar flow in ground.

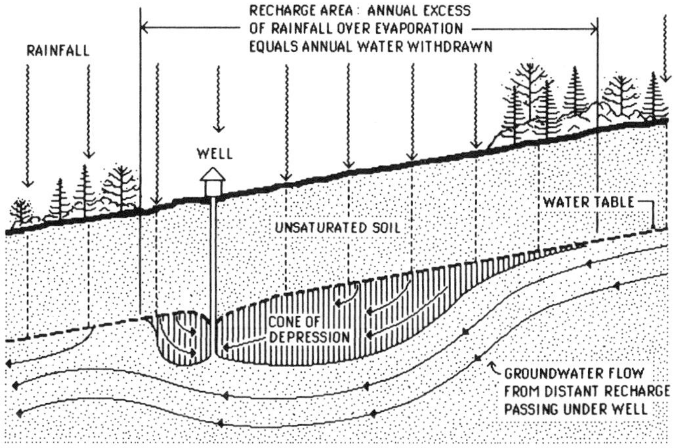
RECHARGE AREA: ANNUAL EXCESS OF RAINFALL OVER EVAPORATION EQUALS ANNUAL WATER WITHDRAWN
RAINFALL
WELL
WATER TABLE
UNSATURATED SOIL
CONE OF DEPRESSION
GROUNDWATER FLOW FROM DISTANT RECHARGE PASSING UNDER WELL

Figure 710-24 Longitudinal section showing flows passing under well.

710-26 shows the average annual runoff per square mile for the United States.) However, to provide that much storage is likely to be very costly. The most cost-effective use of a stream is likely to be achieved with an amount of storage equal to 1 year's average annual runoff (the *critical point* on Hazen's yield-storage curve). At this level of storage, the gross annual safe yield would be equal to the gross runoff of a typical drought year (about one-half that of an average rainfall year).

With no storage, the safe yield of any stream would fall to a fraction of its lowest summer flows. For most streams, this is a very small amount.

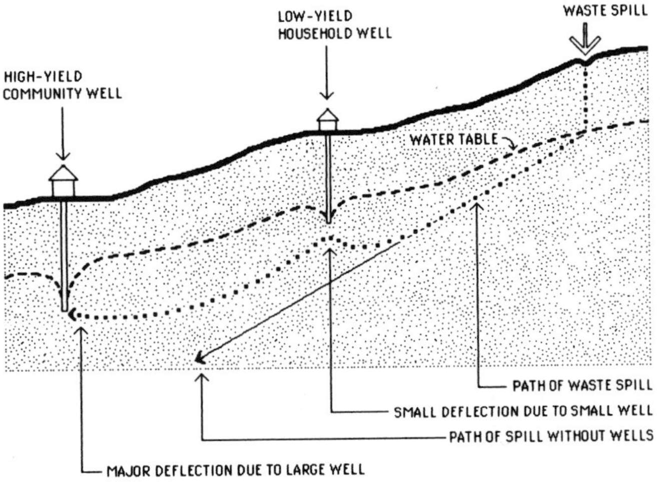
LOW-YIELD HOUSEHOLD WELL
WASTE SPILL
HIGH-YIELD COMMUNITY WELL
WATER TABLE
PATH OF WASTE SPILL
SMALL DEFLECTION DUE TO SMALL WELL
PATH OF SPILL WITHOUT WELLS
MAJOR DEFLECTION DUE TO LARGE WELL

Figure 710-25 Effects of well size on groundwater flow.

7.2 Size of Reservoir

The size of a reservoir with respect to its watershed size determines both the safe yield of the system and the quality of the water. The minimum size of a reservoir to be used for potable water should be at least equal to 1 year's annual average runoff from its tributary watershed in order to achieve good water quality (without extensive treatment), although a somewhat larger volume (e.g., 1½ years' runoff) would be better. A small reservoir (i.e., one that stored much less than 1 year's runoff) would unlikely have very clear water because of suspended colloidal materials; a larger reservoir, if it were low in phosphates, would be likely to have much clearer water.

7.3 Shape and Depth of Reservoir

Much concern has arisen in times past about the shape and depth of reservoirs, based on the belief that shallow water encouraged the growth of aquatic weeds, imparting a foul taste to the water. Several

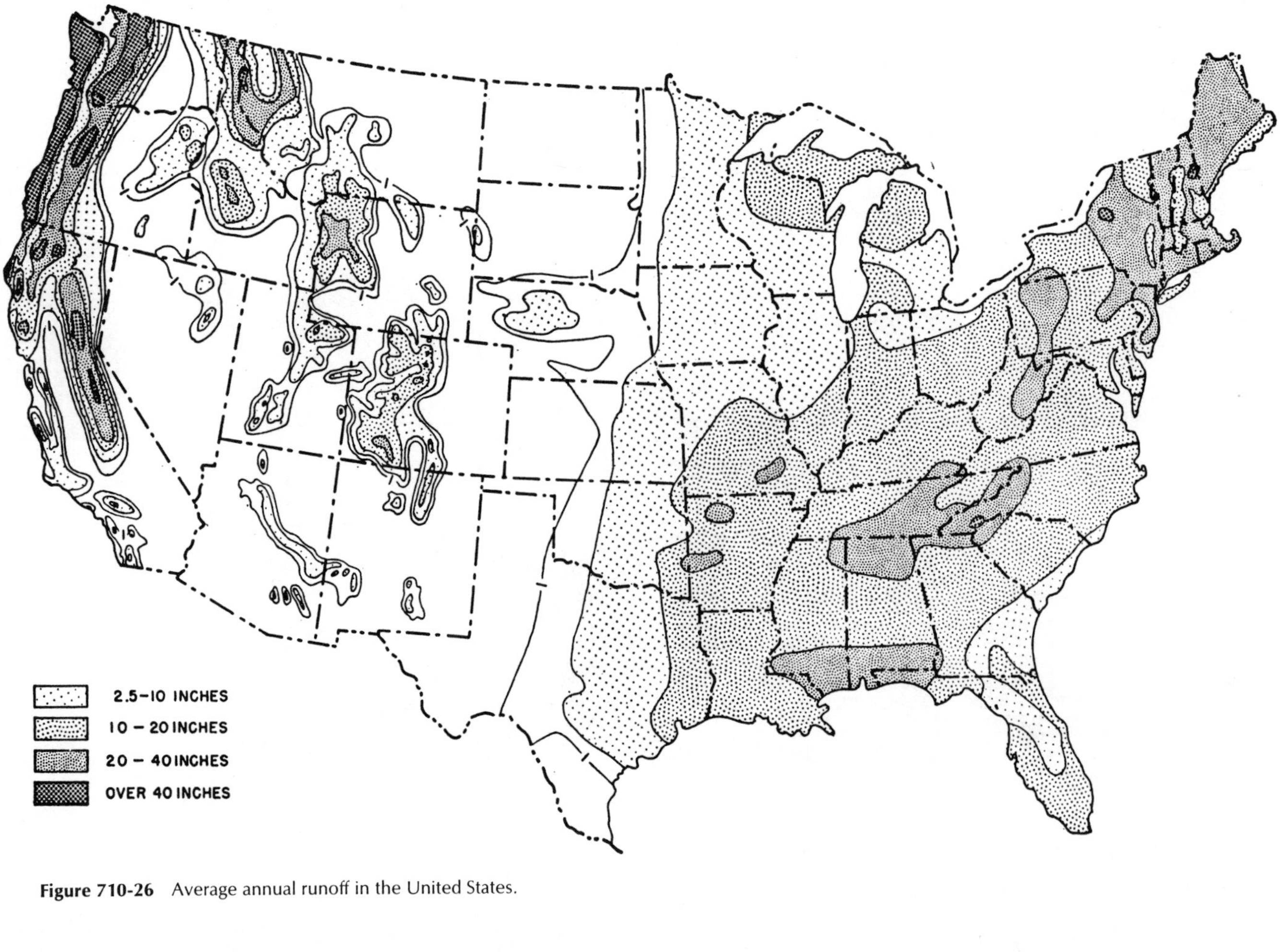
2.5–10 INCHES
10 – 20 INCHES
20 – 40 INCHES
OVER 40 INCHES

Figure 710-26 Average annual runoff in the United States.

major reservoirs were built on this premise in the 1890s with dredged-and-filled bathtublike edges. These reservoirs have not all been successful, and a few (as at Hopkinton and Ashland, Massachusetts) have never been regularly used for water supply. Some minimum depth is essential to the natural semiannual thermal and chemical stratification and turnover required to settle organic detritus and other suspended materials, but any pond large enough to contain at least 1 year's flowthrough is likely to be adequately deep. In general, the deeper the pond, the clearer the water, all else being equal.

7.4 Watershed Characteristics

Watershed characteristics for potable water reservoirs include: (1) freedom from past industrial and waste disposal uses, (2) freedom from geologic sources of phosphorus, and (3) freedom from urbanization-related sources of phosphorus.

A search should be made for industrial and waste disposal activities in the past, and suspicious sites should then be investigated with test wells and chemical sampling. Many early industries used large amounts of toxic substances for a variety of purposes and no potentially contaminated site should be accepted without testing, regardless of the kind of industry.

Geologically occurring phosphates can support enough algae to make untreated water unacceptable for drinking. Surface water at the reservoir site should be chemically tested for its phosphate content. Levels above 15 parts per billion (ppb) may be high enough to rule out a successful surface water supply without algae controls. Samples should be collected in acid-washed bottles available from an analytical testing laboratory that does water testing. Samples should be collected without disturbing bottom sediments. Guidance on sampling techniques should be requested from an analytical laboratory.

Urbanization-related phosphate enrichment appears to be a result of atmospheric phosphate dust falling onto dry roofs and pavements and then being washed into drains and streams. (Phosphate dust, which falls onto moist soil, will be adsorbed by the soil particles and become insoluble. Phosphate fertilizers tend to be adsorbed even more rapidly.)

Conventional approaches to surface drainage, even if buffered with retention basins to control flood peaks and sediments, will sweep the more soluble (and more damaging) surface phosphates into streams and reservoirs too quickly for them to be adsorbed by soil particles. The better control of soluble phosphate can be achieved by restricting the amount of land development within a watershed, restraining the use of impermeable surfaces, and/or by design of the drainage for maximum on-site soil infiltration. (Refer to Section 730: Stormwater Management and Water Resources Protection, for more information.)

7.5 Dam Location

Dams for water supply can be located either on the stream from which they will draw their water or at some other convenient location. Any reservoir site, to be economical, should take advantage of natural topographic containment, but this is not always essential. It is more important that the underlying materials be relatively impermeable so that seepage waters will not undermine the structure. Since many stream bottoms are alluvium or outwash sand, off-stream reservoirs are sometimes used with water pumped from the supply stream to the storage reservoir during spring flow peaks. The same concerns apply to off-stream reservoirs as to on-stream reservoirs, i.e., water quality, control of urbanization, and adequate volume of storage (more than 1 year). (Refer to Section 420: Small Dams, for more information about the selection of dam sites and the types of dams that can be used for water supply.)

7.6 Water Treatment

Surface water will generally require some form of treatment under state law. Treat-

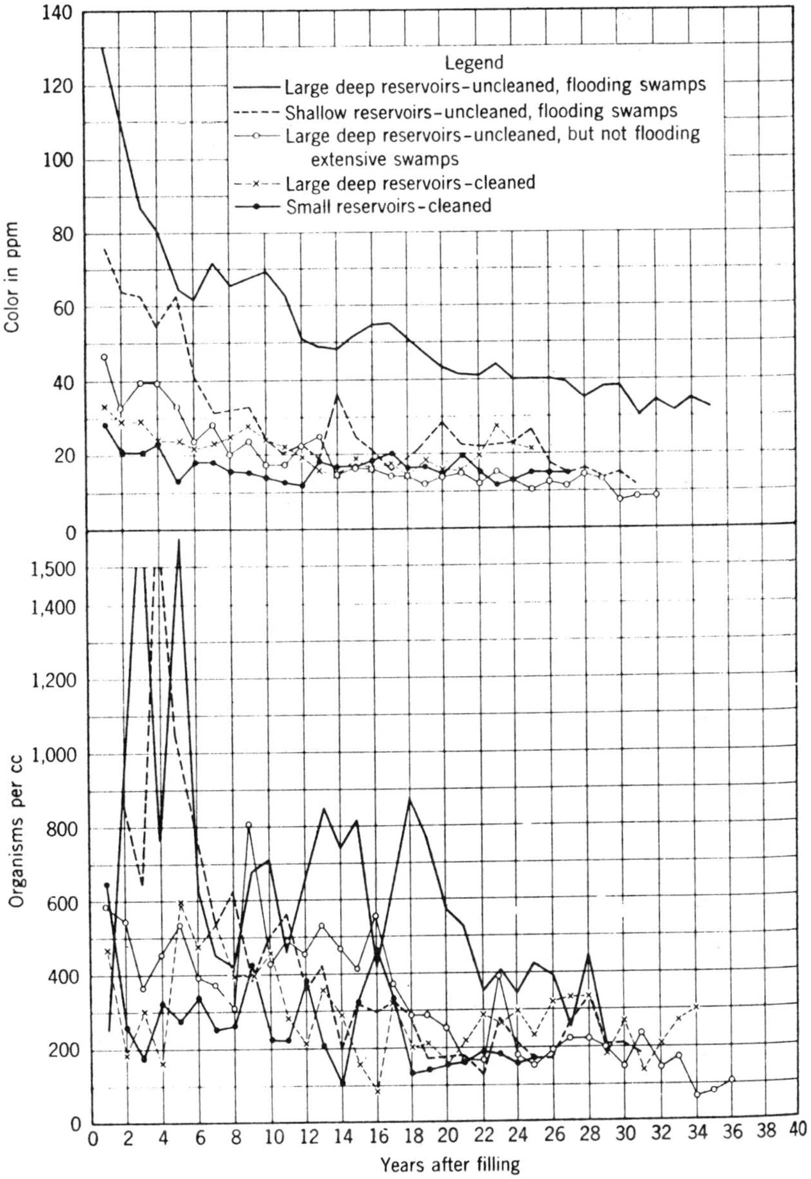
Legend
Large deep reservoirs-uncleaned, flooding swamps
Shallow reservoirs-uncleaned, flooding swamps
Large deep reservoirs-uncleaned, but not flooding extensive swamps
Large deep reservoirs-cleaned
Small reservoirs-cleaned
Color in ppm
Organisms per cc
Years after filling
0
20
40
60
80
100
120
140
200
400
600
800
1,000
1,200
1,400
1,500
0 2 4 6 8 10 12 14 16 18 20 22 24 26 28 30 32 34 36 38 40

Figure 710-27 Color and Algae in Water Supply Reservoirs. This graph shows progressive reduction in color and algae in impounding reservoirs subsequent to their filling.

ment is likely to include chlorination and pH adjustment, and it may also include fluoridation and/or filtration, depending on raw water characteristics.

7.7 Site Preparation

To achieve high water quality in a short period of time, the reservoir bottom should be stripped of all debris, organic deposits, and topsoil. For water supplies not needed for immediate use (future growth a decade or more away), this step can sometimes be eliminated (Figure 710-27).

7.8 Consultants

The services of a geotechnical engineer should be retained for the design of dams and dikes; the services of a sanitary engineer should be retained for water testing and for the design of pumping stations and water treatment equipment; and the services of a hydrologist should be retained to ensure that spillways are adequate to protect the dam from flood damage.

REFERENCES

Clark, J. W., W. Viessman, Jr., and M. J. Hammer. *Water Supply and Pollution Control,* 3d ed., Harper and Row, New York, 1977.

Salvato, Joseph A. *Environmental Engineering and Sanitation,* 3d ed., Wiley, New York, 1982.

U.S. Department of Agriculture, Soil Conservation Service, *Engineering Field Manual,* U.S. Government Printing Office, Washington, DC.

U.S. Department of Agriculture, Soil Conservation Service, *SCS National Engineering Handbook: Hydrology-Section 4,* August 1972.

U.S. Department of Agriculture. *The Yearbook of Agriculture, 1955, Water,* U.S. Government Printing Office, Washington, DC, 1955.

U.S. Department of Commerce, Environmental Science Services Administration, *Climate Atlas of the United States,* National Climate Center, Asheville, NC, 1984.

U.S. Department of the Interior, Geological Survey. *The National Atlas of the United States of America,* Washington, DC, 1970.

U.S. Environmental Protection Agency, Office of Water Programs, Water Supply Division. *Manual of Water Supply Systems,* U.S. Government Printing Office, Washington, DC, 1973. ■

section 720: Sewage Disposal

CREDITS

Contributor:

Daniel Bubly, P.E., L.A., A.I.C.P.
Bubly Associates, Inc.
Sharon, Massachusetts

Graphics:

Gary M. Fishbeck, using a MacIntosh computer

Reviewer:

Robert F. Ferrari, P.E.
Ferrari-Atwood Engineering, Inc.
Providence, Rhode Island

CONTENTS

1.0 INTRODUCTION

Some form of sewage disposal is necessary in most building or land development projects for the disposal of domestic waterborne wastes. Such wastes are either piped off-site to a municipal sewer system or are treated and disposed of on-site. Proper design for the treatment and disposal of domestic waterborne wastes is essential for the protection of public health, safety, and welfare.

1.1 Types of Sewage Systems

The type of sewage disposal system chosen for the development of any tract of land will influence the pattern and density of that development. The sewerage for any project can include:

1. Simple, economical systems for the safe, environmentally sound disposal of wastewater

2. More complex and costly systems for overcoming the limits of poorly drained or impermeable soils on sites that have good locations or other valuable aspects

3. More complex and costly systems for increasing the density of development on a site (Figure 720-1)

1.2 On-Site Disposal

It is expected that the use of on-site disposal will increase as urban development spreads outward beyond the extent of existing sewage collection systems and as existing public treatment plants run out of reserve capacity.

Some developments, particularly industrial use, will require special on-site systems for wastes that cannot be discharged to municipal sewer systems or that cannot be disposed of through on-site systems designed for domestic or human wastes. Site designers should be aware: (1) that many industrial wastes require special treatment

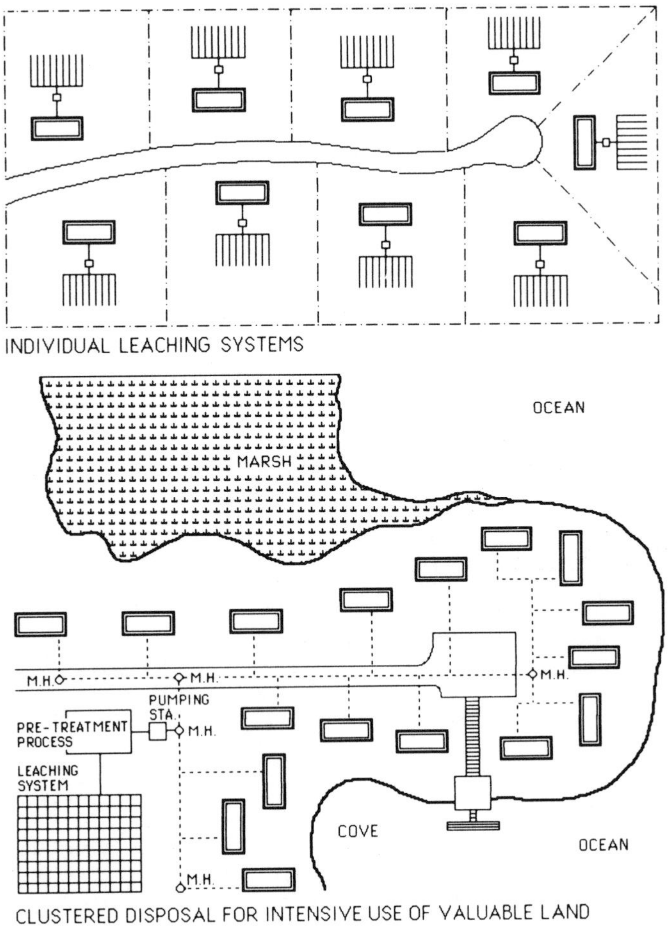
INDIVIDUAL LEACHING SYSTEMS
OCEAN
MARSH
M.H.
PUMPING STA.
PRE-TREATMENT PROCESS
LEACHING SYSTEM
COVE
OCEAN
CLUSTERED DISPOSAL FOR INTENSIVE USE OF VALUABLE LAND

Figure 720-1 Alternative land use and alternative on-site disposal.

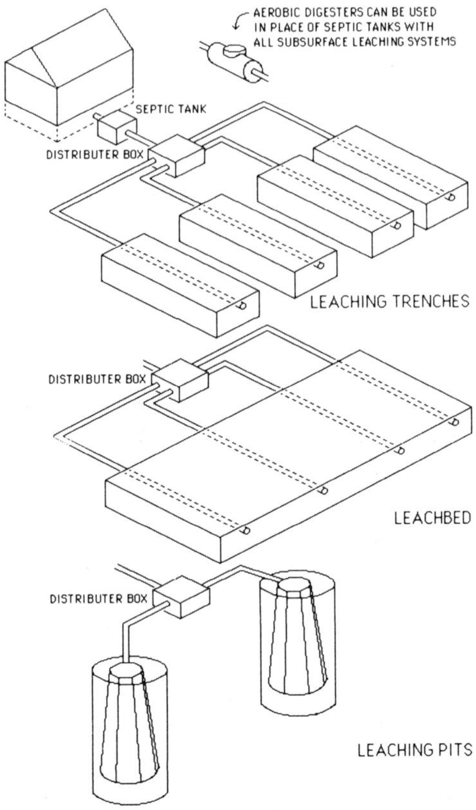
AEROBIC DIGESTERS CAN BE USED IN PLACE OF SEPTIC TANKS WITH ALL SUBSURFACE LEACHING SYSTEMS
SEPTIC TANK
DISTRIBUTER BOX
LEACHING TRENCHES
DISTRIBUTER BOX
LEACHBED
DISTRIBUTER BOX
LEACHING PITS

Figure 720-2 Types of Subsurface Leaching Systems. Septic tanks or aerobic digesters can be used with any of these three systems.

(designed by specialists in the specific industry) and (2) that for such industrial wastes, after removal of hazardous compounds, the treated effluent may be disposed of by ordinary on-site leaching or by discharge to a municipal sewer.

2.0 DESCRIPTION OF SEWAGE SYSTEM PROCESSES

Effective sewage disposal includes physical disposal of the sewage into the environment without adverse health, odor, aesthetic, or nutrient (fertilization) effects.

All currently permissible sewage disposal systems include some method for separation of solids from wastewater, for disposal of the solids, for oxidation of putrescible substances dissolved in the wastewater, for destruction of pathogens, and ultimately for discharge of the resulting effluent to the ground, to a waterbody, or to the atmosphere.

At a typical modern large-scale municipal treatment plant, the solids are physically skimmed off the top and bottom of the wastewater stream and either incinerated or landfilled, the wastewater is actively aerated to remove most of the dissolved putrescibles and suspended organic solids, and the resulting effluent is dosed with chlorine and discharged to a river or large body of water.

For a small on-site system, the processes would include the digestion of solids into liquids and gases, the oxidation of dissolved putrescibles, the destruction of pathogens by biologically active filtration, and the discharge of effluent, preferably to the ground or, alternatively, to a waterbody or to the atmosphere.

The average amount of domestic sewage disposed in the United States is about 65 gal (245 L) per capita per day. About one-third of domestic sewage is toilet waste; one-third, laundry waste; and one-third, drainage from sinks and tubs.

3.0 SYSTEM ALTERNATIVES

Alternative methods of sewage disposal on a tract of land include: (1) discharge to a municipal sewer system and (2) various kinds of on-site disposal systems. Selection of the method depends on location, geohydrologic conditions, and density of development.

In general, connection to an existing municipal system will be the least complex method. In addition, where such connections are available, they are often mandated by local officials. (Note that this may not be the least costly or the most environmentally desirable alternative.)

Considerations for on-site disposal include the following alternatives:

1. For overall system configuration:
   - **a.** Small individual systems scattered over the site
   - **b.** Large clustered or community systems concentrated at one or a few points on the site
2. For ultimate wastewater disposal:
   - **a.** Soil leaching with subsurface effluent application
   - **b.** Soil leaching with surface effluent application
   - **c.** Evapotranspiration
   - **d.** Surface water discharge
3. For processing before disposal:
   - **a.** Simple anaerobic (septic) digestion of solids
   - **b.** Oxidation

4. Miscellaneous variants:
   a. *Clivus multrum* and other composting systems
   b. High-tech mechanical systems
   c. Holding tanks
   d. Cesspools

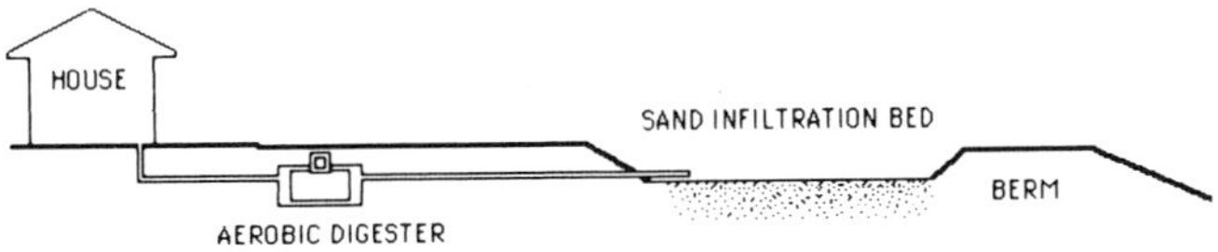
HOUSE
SAND INFILTRATION BED
BERM
AEROBIC DIGESTER

Figure 720-3 Aerobic digester with surface infiltration bed.

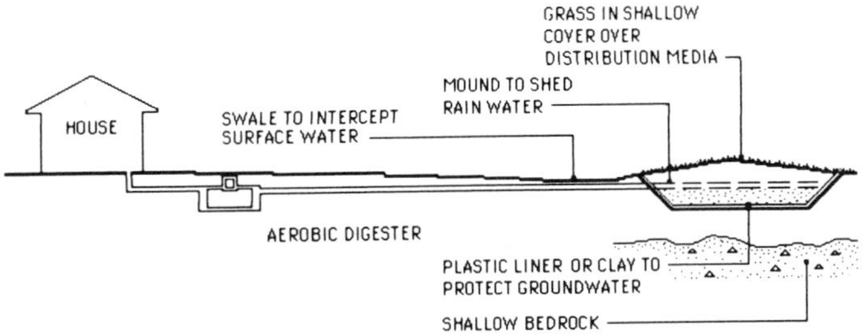
GRASS IN SHALLOW COVER OVER DISTRIBUTION MEDIA
MOUND TO SHED RAIN WATER
HOUSE
SWALE TO INTERCEPT SURFACE WATER
AEROBIC DIGESTER
PLASTIC LINER OR CLAY TO PROTECT GROUNDWATER
SHALLOW BEDROCK

Figure 720-4 Aerobic digester with evapotranspiration system.

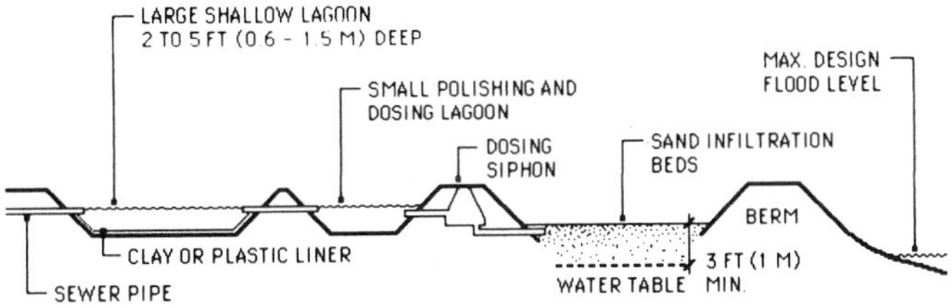
LARGE SHALLOW LAGOON 2 TO 5 FT (0.6 - 1.5 M) DEEP
MAX. DESIGN FLOOD LEVEL
SMALL POLISHING AND DOSING LAGOON
DOSING SIPHON
SAND INFILTRATION BEDS
BERM
CLAY OR PLASTIC LINER
3 FT (1 M) MIN.
SEWER PIPE
WATER TABLE

Figure 720-5 Unaerated lagoon system (schematic section).

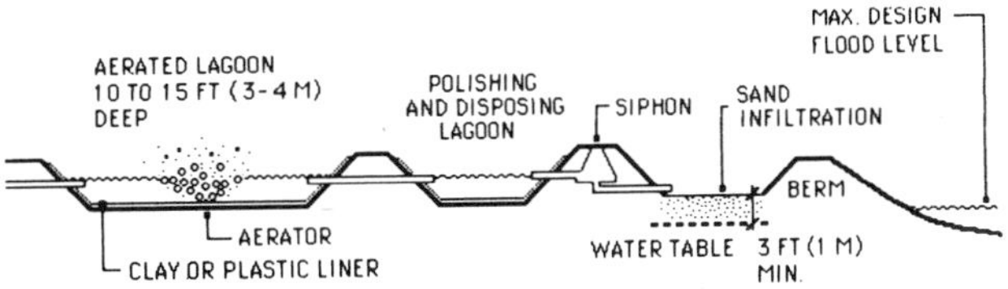
MAX. DESIGN FLOOD LEVEL
AERATED LAGOON 10 TO 15 FT (3-4 M) DEEP
POLISHING AND DISPOSING LAGOON
SIPHON
SAND INFILTRATION
BERM
AERATOR
CLAY OR PLASTIC LINER
WATER TABLE
3 FT (1 M) MIN.

Figure 720-6 Aerated lagoon system (schematic section).

3.1 System Components

Small Individual Systems:

Specific small individual systems include:

1. Septic tanks combined with any of a variety of subsurface leaching systems (leaching trenches, leaching beds, leaching pits, etc.). All septic systems are limited to subsurface effluent disposal because of the odor inherent to septic effluent (Figure 720-2).
2. Aerobic digesters with subsurface leaching systems can also be used with a variety of leaching system configurations (Figure 720-2).
3. Aerobic digesters with surface infiltration beds (Figure 720-3).
4. Aerobic digesters with evapotranspiration disposal systems (Figure 720-4).
5. Composting toilets for human wastes and garbage, combined with an appropriate disposal system for wash waters.
6. Cesspools.

Large Cluster Systems:

Specific large cluster systems include:

1. Large septic tanks with subsurface leaching systems
2. Large aerobic digesters (often called *package plants*) with surface infiltration beds
3. Large aerobic digesters with evapotranspiration disposal of effluent
4. Unaerated lagoons with overflow disposal to surface infiltration beds (Figure 720-5)
5. Aerated lagoons with overflow disposal to surface infiltration beds (Figure 720-6)

3.2 System Configuration

Regarding the selection of the overall system configuration (i.e., individual systems versus cluster systems), the designer should consider:

1. Costs
2. Density of development
3. Site suitability
4. Local governmental regulations and policies

Costs:

Regarding costs, any type of individual on-site approach (where acceptable) is likely to be much less expensive than a cluster system, often by a ratio of 10:1. The major economy of individual systems is the elimination of pipelines, pumping stations, and manholes between individual buildings and the cluster disposal site.

Density of Development:

Regarding the density of development, individual on-site disposal (with systems large enough to be relied on for trouble-free long-term service) limits the development density to about 5 dwelling units (du) per acre (0.4 ha) for single detached housing, and to about 12 du per acre (0.4 ha) for three-story apartment buildings (Figures 720-7 and 720-8).

Community disposal systems could raise the density of such development somewhat, but a separate land allocation for the community system would be required; consequently, the overall dwelling density might not be significantly higher.

Site Suitability:

Regarding the suitability of sites, individual on-site disposal can be accommodated only if adequate permeability and depth to groundwater exist.

3.3 Additional Factors

Regarding the selection of ultimate wastewater disposal alternatives, whether to groundwater, surface water, or the atmosphere, the designer should consider:

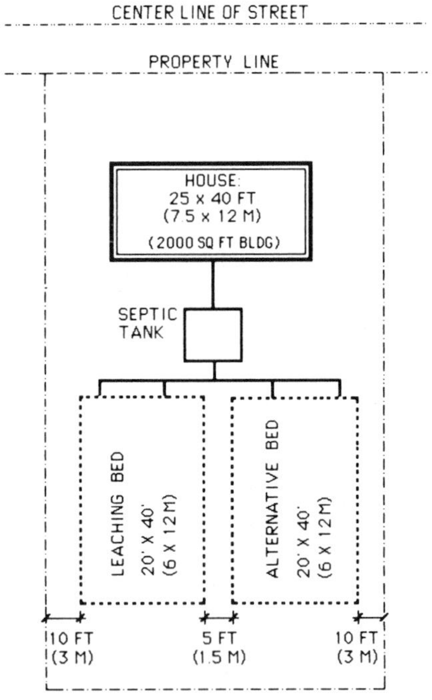
CENTER LINE OF STREET
PROPERTY LINE
HOUSE:
25 x 40 FT
(7.5 x 12 M)
(2000 SQ FT BLDG)
SEPTIC
TANK
LEACHING BED
20' X 40'
(6 X 12 M)
ALTERNATIVE BED
20' X 40'
(6 X 12 M)
10 FT
(3 M)
5 FT
(1.5 M)
10 FT
(3 M)

Note: 3 bedrooms @ 130 gallons per bedroom per day
or
6 people @ 65 gallons per capita per day @ 1/2 gallon per square foot per day = 780 square feet per leaching bed.

Figure 720-7 Single-home densities attainable with on-site disposal.

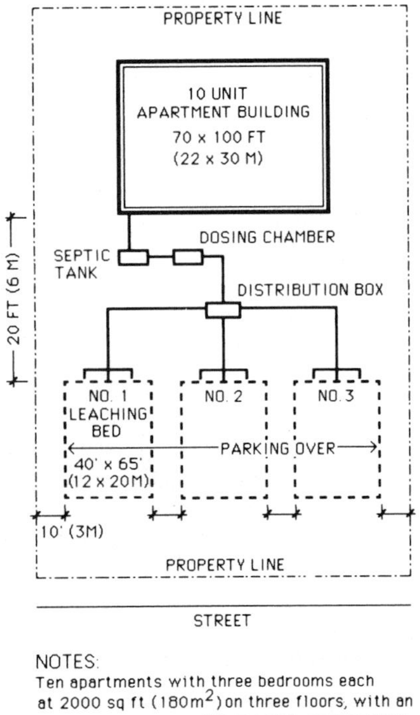
PROPERTY LINE
10 UNIT
APARTMENT BUILDING
70 x 100 FT
(22 x 30 M)
DOSING CHAMBER
SEPTIC
TANK
DISTRIBUTION BOX
20 FT (6 M)
NO. 1
LEACHING
BED
NO. 2
NO. 3
PARKING OVER
40' x 65'
(12 x 20M)
10' (3M)
PROPERTY LINE
STREET

NOTES:
Ten apartments with three bedrooms each at 2000 sq ft (180m²) on three floors, with an average occupancy of four people per dwelling unit (d.u.) and consumption of 65 gal (245 L) per capita per day (i.e., 2,600 gal (9,900 L) per day)

1. Provide a minimum of 1 sq ft of leaching area for each 0.5 gal (1.9 L) (i.e., 5,200 sq ft (468 m²).
2. Install three leaching beds so that two can be used immediately and one can be kept in reserve.

Figure 720-8 Apartment densities attainable with on-site disposal.

1. Site conditions
2. Costs
3. Local governmental regulations and policies
4. Impacts on water quality

Filtration through Soil:

Overall, the most effective, economical, and environmentally safe method for disposing of wastewater (and simultaneously oxidizing its putrescibles and ammonia, destroying its pathogens, and immobilizing its phosphates) is the slow filtration of the wastewater through soil. The soil bacteria, at the interface of the wastewater distribution system and the soil, multiply and form a gelatinous, organic slime which holds the wastewater and allows it to filter slowly into the soil. As the wastewater passes through the slime, soil bacteria digest the putrescibles, pathogens, ammonia, and organic phosphates. The resulting filtered effluent is clean, odor-free, and nearly suitable for drinking except for its significantly high nitrate content and its moderately high salt content.

For low-density developments, depending on regional hydrologic characteristics (see Section 710: Water Supply), the resulting nitrate concentration from scattered small systems will usually not affect the potable quality of underground water. For large systems or for high-density developments, the chemical effects on groundwater should be examined and evaluated on a case-by-case basis.

Removal of Nitrates:

The removal of nitrates is inherently difficult, costly, and experimental at this time. At Lake Tahoe, in the western United States, effluent from the community treatment plant is air-stripped of ammonia (the chemical antecedent of the nitrates in filtered effluent) and requires complex mechanical and chemical processes. Elsewhere, nitrate removal has been achieved biologically by using spray irrigation, shallow ponds and marshes, or, after filtration, an additional stage of anaerobic digestion.

The alternative that uses spray irrigation requires a large land area, winter storage of effluent in cold climates, and energy for pumping. It can increase the sodium content of the groundwater beyond acceptable levels, and its acceptability for use on crops appears to depend on whether the effluent has been previously filtered. (Tests of spray irrigation to date have been limited primarily to unfiltered effluent.)

Shallow pond or marsh denitrification alternatives require ideal site conditions—such as a large, preexisting marsh or swamp that can be used without diminishing other environmental values.

The anaerobic decomposition alternative is more costly, requires the collection of the filtered effluent, and is not well understood technically.

Soil Modification:

In some cases, where soils are not suitable for slow infiltration, they can be modified. If they are too permeable (too coarse) to support a biogenic slime, finer soil can be placed along the bottom and sides of leaching beds, but this cannot be done as conveniently when trenches or pits are used (Figure 720-9).

Where the soil stratum is too shallow to groundwater or too impermeable, earth fill can be brought in to correct the inadequacy. This method can be very costly, especially if suitable fill is not available on or near the site.

To mitigate the costs of extensive earth fill, where fill is necessary, it is sometimes feasible to upgrade the quality of the wastewater effluent applied to the soil, reducing its nutrient value to soil bacteria. Such improved treatment would reduce the density of the biogenic slimes produced in the soil and so reduce the size of the leaching area required. In general, the better the processed effluent, the smaller the leaching area required. With septic tank effluent, the maximum long-term loading appears to be about ½ gal/ft² (0.19 L/m²) per day. With effluent from more effective processing, as in a lagoon system, loading rates up to 5 gal/ft² (1.76 L/m²) per day are possible.

In more extreme cases, where the soil itself is insufficiently permeable to accept the filtered effluent, sewage can be disposed of by some form of evapotranspiration system or by discharge to surface waters. In desert areas, simple evaporation off the surface of a lagoon is possible. In warm, wetter climates, grasses can transpire large amounts of water during the growing season; using this approach may only be feasible for campgrounds, parks, or summer resort developments. For either direct evaporation or for transpiration, sewage processing would require some form of aeration, both to control odor (for evaporation ponds) and to prevent root rot (for transpiration systems).

Before effluent can be discharged to surface water, local public health regulations normally require a detailed analysis of and an impact statement on downstream water resources, a consideration of all other alternatives beforehand, and a compelling case made for developing the specific site in the manner proposed.

3.4 Solids Removal/Digestion Systems

Regarding the selection of alternative systems for the removal and/or digestion of solids, consideration should be given to:

1. Costs
2. Site adaptability
3. Local government regulations and policies

The alternatives include septic systems, various forms of aerobic processors or digestion, and several hybrid systems.

Septic Systems:

In terms of cost, septic systems are usually the least-expensive small systems, having no machinery, no energy inputs, and no requirements for security, regular maintenance, or frequent inspection.

In terms of site adaptability, simple septic systems can only be used in areas where subsurface effluent disposal is practical, i.e., where there is sufficient soil permeability [¾ to 1 in (2 to 3 cm) per day]. Where the depth to groundwater is inadequate, the soil surface must be built up with fill material so as to provide adequate depth for percolation through the soil without saturating it and to provide enough cover over the leaching system to control odors.

Aerobic Systems:

Aerobic systems ordinarily require the same site conditions as septic systems, but their odor-free effluent can be applied to a surface infiltration bed, usually at much higher rates of application, thus reducing both the size of the leaching facility and the costs per square foot. However, this practice is not readily approved by local health officials except under unusual circumstances, since aerobic systems require systematic maintenance and the exposed effluent can transmit a variety of pathogens and parasites.

Aerobic processing of sewage can be accomplished either in some form of energy-intensive and mechanically complex package plant, usually prefabricated, or in one of two kinds of lagoons.

Package Plants: The package plant appears to have special applicability where space and site conditions are constrained. Package plants are miniature versions of municipal sewage treatment plants and, as such, have as their primary functions: (1) the settling of solids and (2) the conversion of dissolved organics into settleable solids. When operating properly, they produce effluent that can be applied to infiltration beds at quantities up to 5 gal/ft^2 (18.9 L) per day (10 times the loading rate of septic tank effluent). However, since these devices generally have no provision for automatic, systematic removal of the accumulated solids, they are subject to solids overloads, the washing of solids into leaching systems, and mechanical breakdown unless they are pumped out once or twice a year.

If not adequately sized and carefully maintained, package plants perform no better than septic tanks and require equally large leaching systems.

Passive Lagoons: Passive lagoons, or *stabilization* ponds, are large shallow ponds [2 to 5 ft (0.6 to 1.5 m) deep] aerated by natural processes (sun and wind) through their extensive upper surface. They are commonly used in very rural areas where adequate space is available and where they can be sited far enough away from people to minimize the odor nuisance of their twice-a-year thermal turnovers (which bring odorous bottom sediments to the surface).

Aerated Lagoons: Aerated lagoons are deeper and smaller than passive lagoons and use sufficient mechanical aeration to preclude thermal stratification and the resulting twice-a-year thermal turnovers. These types of lagoons have been used on sites that are large enough for passive lagoons but are too close to abutting land uses that require positive odor control. The water in these lagoons is mixed and aerated by small streams of air that are pumped through weighted plastic tubes by relatively small compressors.

3.5 Other Sewage Disposal Alternatives

Miscellaneous alternatives are usually limited to sites where either the disposal of normal amounts of wastewater or a supply of adequate amounts of water are not feasible. These include composting toilets, high-technology recirculating systems, and holding tanks.

Composting Toilets:

At one extreme, such limited sites have been dealt with by a combination of simple actions—such as using an old-fashioned pit toilet (or outhouse) or a composting toilet (an inside outhouse), taking laundry out to a commercial facility, and not using garbage grinders. Under such conditions, water use and wastewater generation in a residence can be reduced about 75 percent, pathogens can be kept out of the wastewater stream, and wastewater treatment facilities can be kept small and simple. However, it should be noted that both local permits and mortgages for such facilities are difficult if not impossible to obtain.

Recirculating Systems:

At the other extreme, systems have been developed that allow normal washing, flushing, etc., without normal water supplies or normal wastewater discharges; the systems accomplish this by recycling and treating washwater within the building, and then using the filtered washwater for toilet flushing, etc. These systems are very costly and complex, and they require unusual amounts of space within the buildings.

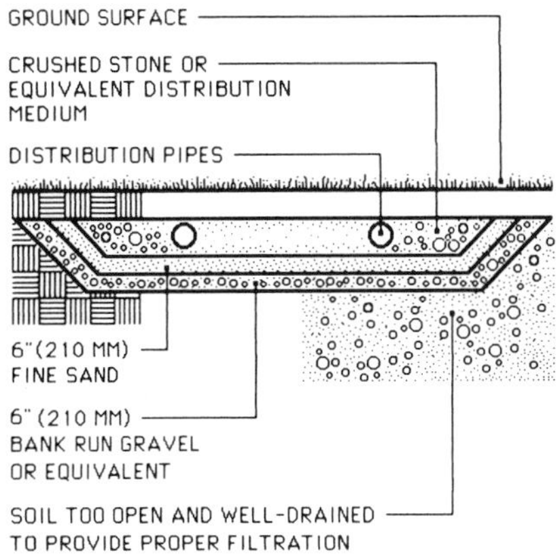
GROUND SURFACE
CRUSHED STONE OR EQUIVALENT DISTRIBUTION MEDIUM
DISTRIBUTION PIPES
6" (210 MM) FINE SAND
6" (210 MM) BANK RUN GRAVEL OR EQUIVALENT
SOIL TOO OPEN AND WELL-DRAINED TO PROVIDE PROPER FILTRATION

Figure 720-9 Leaching bed in excessively drained soils (schematic section).

Holding Tanks:

For severely constrained sites where no discharge to the environment can be permitted, wastes can be drained to a holding tank [of up to 5000 gal (19,000 L)] for periodic pumping or, for larger water users, drained directly to a tank truck.

3.6 Cesspools

Cesspools are a very low cost but effective disposal technique for very small systems [up to 100 or 150 gal (375 or 575 L) per cesspool per day] or for systems with intermittent use. They require suitable soils and a water table at least 10 ft (3 m) deep. They combine, at their center, the anaerobic digestion process of the septic tank and, around their vertical perimeter, the filtering process of the leaching pit (Figure 710-10).

Their only disadvantage is that, like any other soil infiltration mechanism (leaching bed, leaching field, leaching trench, leaching pit, etc.), they will contaminate groundwater with pathogens, unoxidized putrescibles, ammonia, and organic phosphates unless there is an adequate zone of unsaturated soil between the bottom of the infiltration mechanism and the groundwater. This unsaturated soil is essential for the formation of a biologically active filter and for the oxidation of effluents. (In the nineteenth century it was noted that if cesspools were dug down into saturated soils, the cesspools would have a high infiltrative capacity as a result, and so, where

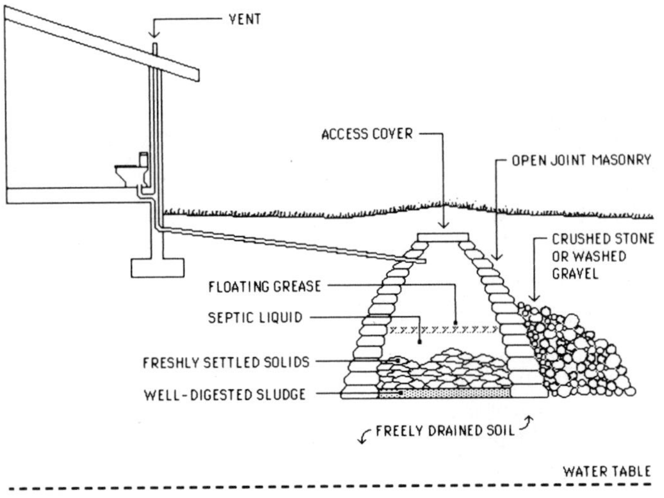
VENT
ACCESS COVER
OPEN JOINT MASONRY
CRUSHED STONE
OR WASHED
GRAVEL
FLOATING GREASE
SEPTIC LIQUID
FRESHLY SETTLED SOLIDS
WELL-DIGESTED SLUDGE
FREELY DRAINED SOIL
WATER TABLE

Figure 720-10 Typical cesspool system.

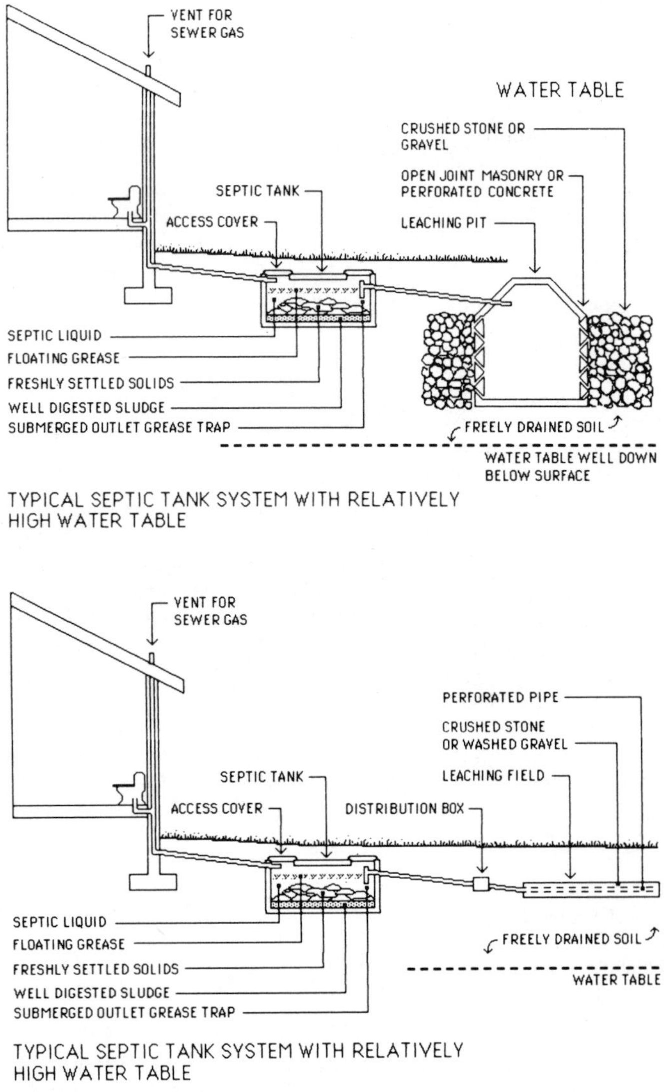
VENT FOR
SEWER GAS
WATER TABLE
CRUSHED STONE OR
GRAVEL
OPEN JOINT MASONRY OR
PERFORATED CONCRETE
SEPTIC TANK
ACCESS COVER
LEACHING PIT
SEPTIC LIQUID
FLOATING GREASE
FRESHLY SETTLED SOLIDS
WELL DIGESTED SLUDGE
SUBMERGED OUTLET GREASE TRAP
FREELY DRAINED SOIL
WATER TABLE WELL DOWN
BELOW SURFACE
TYPICAL SEPTIC TANK SYSTEM WITH RELATIVELY
HIGH WATER TABLE
VENT FOR
SEWER GAS
PERFORATED PIPE
CRUSHED STONE
OR WASHED GRAVEL
SEPTIC TANK
LEACHING FIELD
ACCESS COVER
DISTRIBUTION BOX
SEPTIC LIQUID
FLOATING GREASE
FRESHLY SETTLED SOLIDS
WELL DIGESTED SLUDGE
SUBMERGED OUTLET GREASE TRAP
FREELY DRAINED SOIL
WATER TABLE
TYPICAL SEPTIC TANK SYSTEM WITH RELATIVELY
HIGH WATER TABLE

Figure 720-11 Typical septic tank installation.

possible, most new systems were deliberately extended down into groundwater. This approach caused disease and eventually earned a bad reputation for all cesspools.)

4.0 DESIGN OF SEPTIC TANKS AND LEACHING SYSTEMS

4.1 Applications

Septic tanks and leaching fields are the most economical, adaptable, trouble-free, and generaly accepted form of treatment and disposal suitable for small and medium-size sewage disposal systems, i.e., up to about 15,000 gal (57,000 L) per day. They can be adapted to a great range of sites, including slowly permeable silts and relatively high water tables.

Figure 720-11 shows a section through a typical installation. The key siting requirement for any soil disposal system is an adequate depth of unsaturated soil between the effluent leaching device and the water table. State and local requirements vary, 3 to 4 ft (1 to 1.2 m) being typical. Note that the system can have very little slope, as little as 6 in (150 mm) across the length of the system.

For sites with higher water tables, many jurisdictions will allow septic tank effluent to be pumped to a mounded leaching field (Figure 720-12). Where the underlying soils are permeable (even though they are saturated), this is an acceptable approach. Where the underlying soils are not permeable (rock or clay), there is likely to be seepage at the toe of the mound, a condition unacceptable in most jurisdictions.

For sites with lower water tables, particularly where the land slopes steeply, some jurisdictions will allow the use of leaching pits in place of leaching trenches or leaching beds (Figure 720-13).

In areas where leaching pits are not allowed, or where a hillside site is underlain with impermeable materials, shallow leaching trenches are possible, but they must be designed to prevent a tilted distribution box (or distribution tee) from directing too much flow to any one trench. Figure 720-14 shows two suitable layouts for such conditions. Note that the leaching trenches are horizontal, following the contours, and that each trench is loaded with the overflow from higher ones. No distribution box is used.

4.2 Theory

Primary Functions:

Septic tanks are baffled containers that serve three primary functions: They (1) trap grease and floating solids on the top of

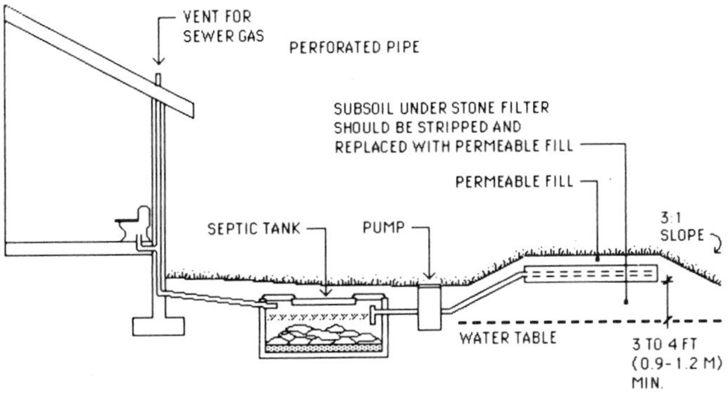
VENT FOR
SEWER GAS
PERFORATED PIPE
SUBSOIL UNDER STONE FILTER
SHOULD BE STRIPPED AND
REPLACED WITH PERMEABLE FILL
PERMEABLE FILL
SEPTIC TANK
PUMP
3:1
SLOPE
WATER TABLE
3 TO 4 FT
(0.9-1.2 M)
MIN.

Figure 720-12 Mounded leaching field system.

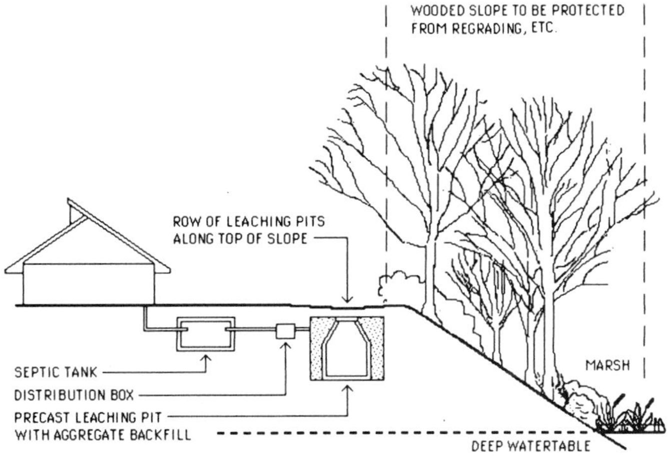
WOODED SLOPE TO BE PROTECTED
FROM REGRADING, ETC.
ROW OF LEACHING PITS
ALONG TOP OF SLOPE
SEPTIC TANK
DISTRIBUTION BOX
PRECAST LEACHING PIT
WITH AGGREGATE BACKFILL
MARSH
DEEP WATERTABLE

Figure 720-13 Typical leaching pit system.

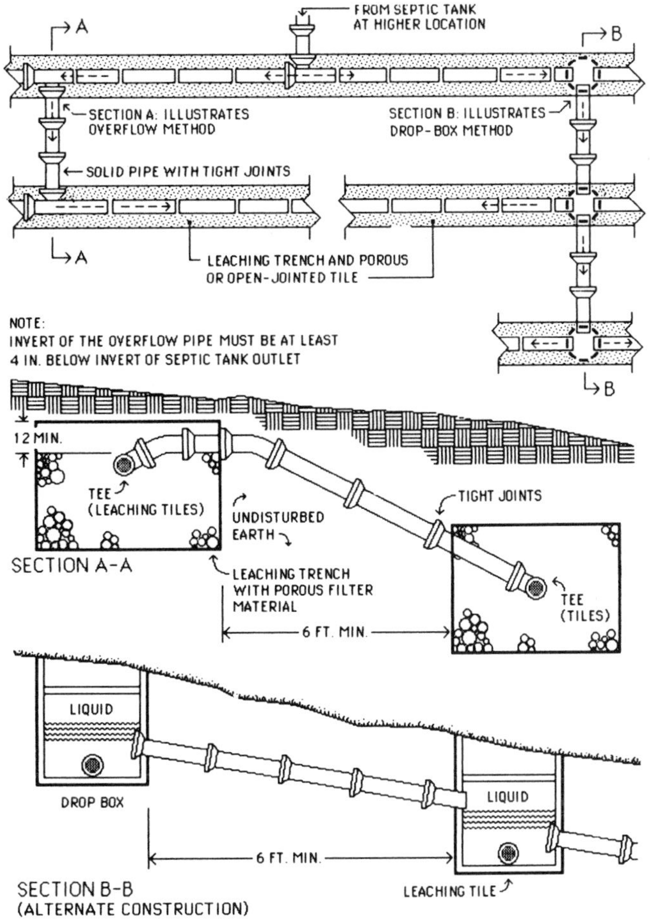
FROM SEPTIC TANK
AT HIGHER LOCATION
A
B
SECTION A: ILLUSTRATES
OVERFLOW METHOD
SECTION B: ILLUSTRATES
DROP-BOX METHOD
SOLID PIPE WITH TIGHT JOINTS
LEACHING TRENCH AND POROUS
OR OPEN-JOINTED TILE
NOTE:
INVERT OF THE OVERFLOW PIPE MUST BE AT LEAST
4 IN. BELOW INVERT OF SEPTIC TANK OUTLET
12 MIN.
TEE
(LEACHING TILES)
UNDISTURBED
EARTH
TIGHT JOINTS
SECTION A-A
LEACHING TRENCH
WITH POROUS FILTER
MATERIAL
TEE
(TILES)
6 FT. MIN.
LIQUID
DROP BOX
LIQUID
6 FT. MIN.
SECTION B-B
(ALTERNATE CONSTRUCTION)
LEACHING TILE

Figure 720-14 Leaching Trenches on Shallow Hillside. Differing ground slopes over subsurface disposal field may require the use of various combinations of fittings.

sewage flows, (2) allow most heavy solids (including paper products and laundry lint) to settle out of the sewage flows to the tank bottom, and (3) permit bacterial decomposition of putrescible solids into simple soluble compounds for disposal with the effluent waters. They also precipitate some inorganic chemicals out of the liquid, convert some organic materials into methane gas (which vents off through the inflow sewer to the house plumbing stack), and destroy some pathogens. However, none of these latter effects is important to the overall waste disposal objective.

The effluent from the septic tank is rich in dissolved putrescible organics, ammonia, organic phosphates, suspended organic particles, and pathogens and is offensively odorous. When this effluent is applied to unsaturated soil (or to a sand filter), it stimulates the growth of a bacterial slime on the soil particles. This slime acts as a very effective filter, physically trapping the suspended particles and biologically digesting putrescible organics and ammonia. The slime also destroys pathogens and odors, and it converts the organic phosphates into inorganic phosphates, a form which can either precipitate out of solution or adsorb to soil particles.

The resulting filtered effluent is relatively harmless except for (1) its higher concentrations of nitrates and (2) an occasional, localized death of the bacterial slime, which permits small, short-lived breakthroughs of untreated effluent. Protection against these occasional breakthroughs is usually provided by setting the leaching facilities back some 50 or 100 ft (15 or 30 m) from wells and surface waters, and protection against the nitrate contamination of drinking water is provided by limiting the density of development. (Refer to Section 710: Water Supply, for more information.)

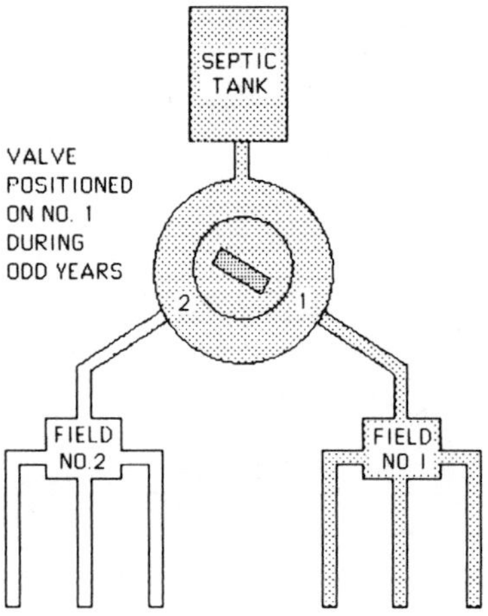
SEPTIC TANK
VALVE POSITIONED ON NO. 1 DURING ODD YEARS
2
1
FIELD NO.2
FIELD NO I

Figure 720-15 Alternating leaching systems.

Maintenance:

The maintenance of septic tanks is limited to (1) infrequent pumping of the septic tank to remove accumulated nondegradable solids (sand, paper, laundry lint, etc.) and (2) *resting* of the leaching facility.

Recommendations for frequency of septic tank pumping vary, the need being a function of the tank's size and its usage. The need for pumping should be accommodated in the design and location of a septic tank. Local boards of health in the United States require that septic tank locations be clearly marked and be accessible to pump trucks. Beyond this, it is important to recognize the following considerations regarding pump trucks:

1. Most pump trucks carry hoses only 70 to 100 ft (20 to 30 m) long, although some carry hoses up to 200 ft (60 m) long.

2. Although most pump trucks cannot pump septic tanks whose tops are more than 10 ft (3 m) below the elevation of the

TABLE 720-1
Quantities of Sewage Flows

Type of establishment	*Gallons per person per day (unless otherwise noted)*
Airports (per passenger)	5
Apartments, multiple-family (per resident)	60
Bathhouses and swimming pools	10
Camps:	
Campground with central comfort stations	35
With flush toilets, no showers	25
Construction camps (semipermanent)	50
Day camps (no meals served)	15
Resort camps (night and day) with limited plumbing	50
Luxury camps	100
Cottages and small dwellings with seasonal occupancy	50
Country clubs (per resident member)	100
Country clubs (per nonresident member present)	25
Dwellings:	
Boarding houses	50
Additional for nonresident boarders	10
Luxury residences and estates	150
Multiple-family dwellings (apartments)	60
Rooming houses	40
Single-family dwellings	75
Factories (gallons per person, per shift, exclusive of industrial wastes)	35
Hospitals (per bed space)	250+
Hotels with private baths (two persons per room)	60
Hotels without private baths	50
Institutions other than hospitals (per bed space)	125
Laundries, self-service (gallons per wash, i.e., per customer)	50
Mobile home parks (per space)	250
Motels with bath, toilet, and kitchen wastes (per bed space)	50
Motels (per bed space)	40
Picnic parks (toilet wastes only, per picnicker)	5
Picnic parks with bathhouses, showers, and flush toilets	10
Restaurants (toilet and kitchen wastes per person)	10
Restaurants (kitchen wastes per meal served)	3
Restaurants, additional for bars and cocktail lounges	2
Schools:	
Boarding	100
Day, without gyms, cafeterias, or showers	15
Day, with gyms, cafeteria, and showers	25
Day, with cafeteria, but without gyms or showers	20
Service stations (per vehicle served)	10
Swimming pools and bathhouses	10
Theaters:	
Movie (per auditorium seat)	5
Drive-in (per car space)	5
Travel trailer parks without individual water and sewer hookups (per space)	50
Travel trailer parks with individual water and sewer hookups (per space)	100
Workers:	
Construction (at semipermanent camps)	50
Days, at schools and offices (per shift)	15

truck, some special pump trucks can lift up to 30 ft (9 m). As a general rule the shorter the hose, the higher the lift. Check with local experts to confirm what standards are recommended for a specific project.

The need to *rest* a leaching facility periodically has been well documented in recent years but is usually not provided for in leaching facility design. Its basis is that the long-term continuous loading of septic tank effluent onto soil or sand will result in a gradual filling of the soil pores with ferrous sulfide particles and perhaps also with cellulose fibers (from paper and laundry lint) and grease. Taking a leaching facility off-line and allowing it to rest for a few months will allow the clogging materials to decay by natural processes.

In order to take a leaching facility off-line (except for seasonal uses), a second, alternate leaching facility should be available. However, since the original leaching facility will function well for 20 years in this regard, it is not necessary to build a second leaching facility until the need becomes apparent. Proper site design would in most cases require: (1) layout for two parallel systems, (2) initial construction of only one, and (3) provision for access of construction equipment to the second site.

Figure 720-15 shows the overall layout of a septic tank/leaching field facility with parallel fields and a switching valve.

NOTE OF CAUTION: Most codes, especially for larger systems, require alternating leaching facilities fed by alternating dosing siphons. Where required, they must be used, but they do not provide the long-term resting required for removal of soil clogging and are not a substitute for the second leaching facility recommended herein. For long-term on-site system viability, a parallel system for long-term alternation will still be necessary.

4.3 Sizing and Details: Septic Tanks

Sizing:

Septic tanks are ordinarily sized to hold 1 to 2 days' average sewage flow, the larger ratio for smaller buildings such as houses, and the smaller ratio for larger systems. Local code requirements vary, but the specific size is not crucial. In general, larger tanks will likely require less frequent pumping.

Table 720-1 shows estimated sewage flows for various generators. For specific flows in any locality, check local codes.

Design Details:

Regarding the design of the tank, shape and size are relatively unimportant. Figure 720-16 shows a typical 1000-gal (3785-L) tank made by a precast concrete products company. Essential characteristics include:

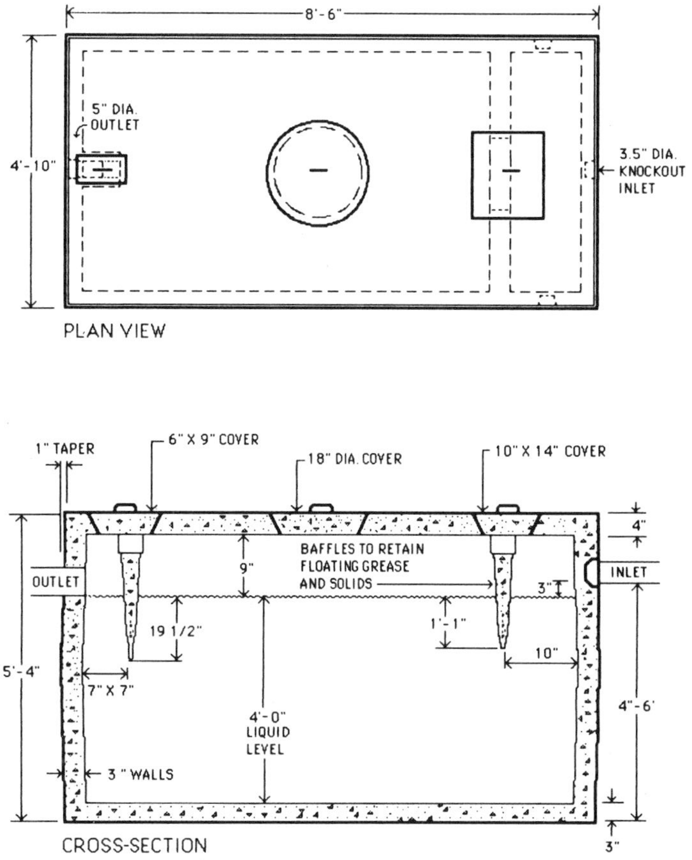
8'-6"
4'-10"
5" DIA. OUTLET
3.5" DIA. KNOCKOUT INLET
PLAN VIEW
1" TAPER
6" X 9" COVER
18" DIA. COVER
10" X 14" COVER
OUTLET
INLET
BAFFLES TO RETAIN FLOATING GREASE AND SOLIDS
9"
4"
3"
1'-1"
19 1/2"
10"
5'-4"
7" X 7"
4'-0" LIQUID LEVEL
4'-6'
3 " WALLS
3"
CROSS-SECTION

Figure 720-16 Typical precast septic tank (1000 gal).

1. A relatively deep shape to allow solids and greases to separate vertically
2. A deeply baffled outlet to draw liquids from mid-depth
3. A baffled inlet to keep grease from plugging the inlet
4. Positive drop for the influent, also to prevent plugging of the inlet
5. Access holes for clearing clogs from the inlet and outlet
6. Access for the pumping of bottom sediments
7. Through ventilation to allow gas flows from the leaching field to vent off through the building vent stack

Figure 720-17 shows a typical 15,000-gal (56,775-L) tank. It has the same essential features as the 1000-gal (3785-L) tank, but it uses pipe tees instead of concrete inlet and outlet baffles, and it can be supplied with an intermediate baffle to provide a settling, or clarification, tank at its outlet end. For details and specifications in any locality, contact local precast concrete products suppliers.

4.4 Sizing and Details: Leaching Facilities

Sizing:

Leaching facilities are ordinarily sized to expected sewage flows and soil permeabilities. Local codes give instruction on techniques for measuring soil permeability and for sizing leaching facilities. Each jurisdiction has its own method, and local codes usually must be satisfied or exceeded.

The typical procedure is to dig one (or more) small-diameter holes [4 to 12 in (100 to 300 mm)] to the depth of the proposed leaching system, fill the hole with 1 ft (0.3 m) of water, keep the water level stable for a specified period of time, and then measure the vertical drop of the water surface in the hole during another specified period of time (typically 30 minutes). The rate of fall, called the *percolation rate* (or *perc rate*), is then entered in a table provided by the code which specifies a corresponding size of leaching facility in terms of square feet (square meters) of leaching area per gallon (per liter) of wastewater or per bedroom. This number is then used to size the bottom area of the leaching trenches or beds, or the combination of vertical and

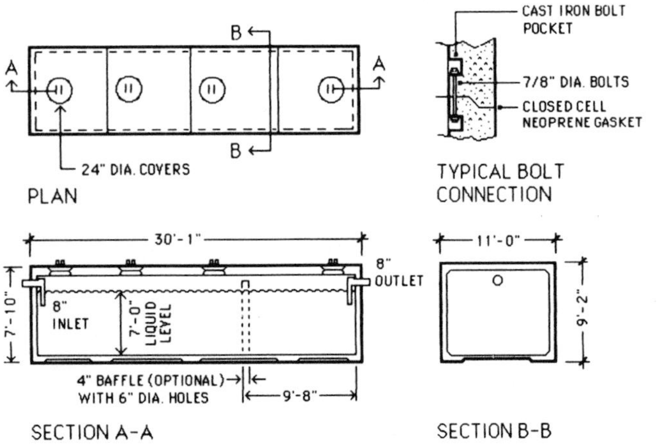
CAST IRON BOLT POCKET
7/8" DIA. BOLTS
CLOSED CELL NEOPRENE GASKET
24" DIA. COVERS
PLAN
TYPICAL BOLT CONNECTION
30'-1"
11'-0"
8" OUTLET
8" INLET
7'-0" LIQUID LEVEL
7'-10"
9'-2"
4" BAFFLE (OPTIONAL) WITH 6" DIA. HOLES
9'-8"
SECTION A-A
SECTION B-B

Figure 720-17 Typical precast septic tank (15,000 gal).

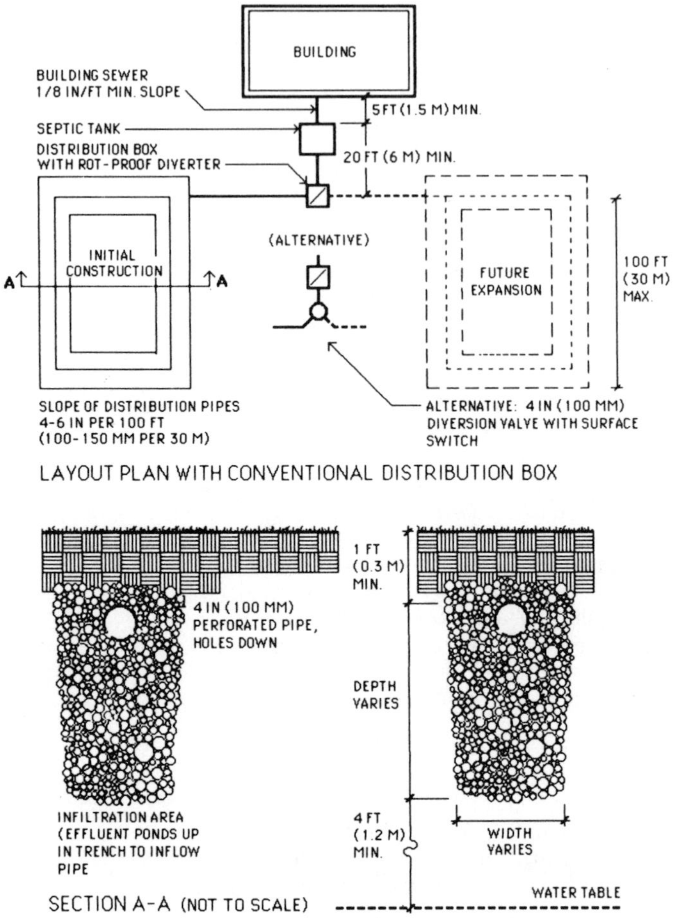
BUILDING
BUILDING SEWER
1/8 IN/FT MIN. SLOPE
5FT (1.5 M) MIN.
SEPTIC TANK
DISTRIBUTION BOX WITH ROT-PROOF DIVERTER
20 FT (6 M) MIN.
INITIAL CONSTRUCTION
(ALTERNATIVE)
FUTURE EXPANSION
100 FT (30 M) MAX.
SLOPE OF DISTRIBUTION PIPES 4-6 IN PER 100 FT (100-150 MM PER 30 M)
ALTERNATIVE: 4 IN (100 MM) DIVERSION VALVE WITH SURFACE SWITCH
LAYOUT PLAN WITH CONVENTIONAL DISTRIBUTION BOX
1 FT (0.3 M) MIN.
4 IN (100 MM) PERFORATED PIPE, HOLES DOWN
DEPTH VARIES
INFILTRATION AREA (EFFLUENT PONDS UP IN TRENCH TO INFLOW PIPE
4 FT (1.2 M) MIN.
WIDTH VARIES
WATER TABLE
SECTION A-A (NOT TO SCALE)

Figure 720-18 Key Elements of a Leaching Trench System. In *Section A*, the distance between trenches should be 3W (3 times the width of the trench), or 2D (2 times the depth of the trench), whichever is greater. The distance between the pipe and the top of the trench should be 2 in.

horizontal surfaces of the trenches up to the inverts of the distribution pipes, or some other parameter (e.g., 100 percent of the vertical surfaces plus 50 percent of the bottom surface), as specified by code.

It must be recognized that many (or most) of these requirements have little or no basis either in scientific analysis of leaching system hydraulics or in experience with what actually has worked historically in the field. Consequently, a design that meets the local code is no guarantee that the system will perform satisfactorily.

Key points the designer should note:

1. Except for the finest-grained soils (i.e., clayey silt and clays), it is the permeability of the bacterial slimes generated in the soil by the sewage itself, not the permeability of the soils, that limits effluent absorption.

2. Percolation tests yield results in inches (centimeters) of infiltration per hour, but the permeability of the bacterial slime is in fractions of an inch (millimeters) per day. As a result, most codes use a *factor of safety* of about 100 to compensate.

3. In the United States, leaching systems designed according to inadequate codes often are not loaded at the maximum flow rates possible from the buildings they serve; i.e., a three-bedroom dwelling unit that could serve five, six, or seven people usually serves only three people. At three people per dwelling unit, typical code-designed leaching systems suffice; at six people per unit, the same design fails.

4. Effluent does not percolate into the soil at the rate at which it is applied; instead, it ponds up, filling the coarse distribution media until the rate of infiltration matches the rate of effluent application.

5. The maximum steady-state long-term absorption capacity of the bacterial slime in a leaching facility for ordinary septic tank effluent is about ½ gal/ft^2 (0.19 L/m^2) per day regardless of whether the infiltrative surface is vertical or horizontal.

6. The permeability of the slime appears to be inversely proportional to the nutrient concentration of the effluent; thus, a vigorous water conservation program without a corresponding reduction in organic loading will have no long-term benefit. (It will appear to work for 2 to 3 months.)

Figure 720-18 shows the key characteristics of a leaching trench system. The system includes both an initial leaching area and space for future construction of an alternative leaching area. Each should be sized for application of not more than ½ gal/ft^2 (0.19 L/m^2) per day, measured over the entire trench surface below the invert.

TABLE 720-2
Typical Setback Requirements

	Horizontal distance, ft				
Component of system	*Well or suction line*	*Water supply line pressure*	*Stream*	*Dwelling*	*Property line*
Building sewer	50	10	50	—	—
Septic tank	50	10	50	5	10
Disposal field and seepage	100	25	50	20	5
Seepage pit	100	50	50	20	10
Cesspool	150	50	50	20	15

Note: This table refers to minimum distances between components of sewage disposal systems.

Design Details:

The distribution of the septic tank effluent can be either by a *distribution box* or by pipe tees. The distribution box is traditional, and although it has been found to offer no advantage in studies by the U.S. Federal Housing Administration, it is more likely to be accepted by conservative public officials. The distribution box can be converted into a diversion device between parallel leaching systems by inserting a simple board (of rot-proof material) diagonally into the box and changing its position as needed. A plastic diversion valve, a newer and neater device, can be used for the same purpose.

The layout of the system can take whatever form fits the site, but a plan that looks rational and orderly (symmetrical, etc.) is more likely to be approved. Table 720-2 shows typical setback requirements for various parts of the system. These vary from code to code.

4.5 Grease Traps

For restaurants and other food preparation areas, a separate grease trap between kitchen drains (those without garbage grinders) and septic tanks is often required. The design of a grease trap is identical to the design of a septic tank except that its outlet pipe is placed much lower in the tank to provide maximum volume for the grease.

Figure 720-19 shows a typical precast 1000-gal (3785-L) trap. The trap size is 125 gal (473 L) per 50 patrons (U.S. Public Health Service).

4.6 Dosing Chambers

For large systems, many codes require that septic tank effluent not be allowed to trickle into the leaching facility at the rate at which it is displaced from the septic tank by new inflows, but that it instead be collected in a dosing chamber for slug discharge to the leaching facility via one or two automatic siphons every 3 or 4 hours. It is claimed that this procedure results in a more even distribution of effluent within the leaching facility and that it allows the system to *rest,* i.e., allows the soil to reaerate between doses.

Unfortunately, none of this is true in most cases, since in a typical leaching facility the effluent ponds up, creating a more or less constant underground pool that extends full-time across the full width and length of the facility.

Where leaching is to be accomplished in several separate leaching facilities at more than one level, dosing siphons and distribution boxes can be used advantageously to balance the loading of the various parts. Figure 720-20 shows a typical precast dosing chamber. Note that the chamber is designed to provide a maximum of volume with a minimum of head loss. The siphons themselves have no moving parts.

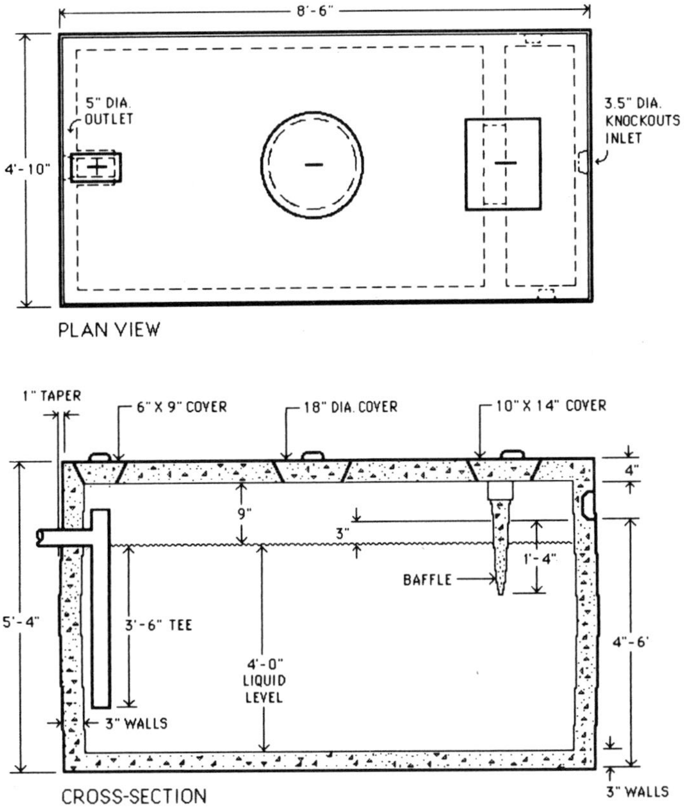
8'-6"
4'-10"
5" DIA. OUTLET
3.5" DIA. KNOCKOUTS INLET
PLAN VIEW
1" TAPER
6" X 9" COVER
18" DIA. COVER
10" X 14" COVER
4"
9"
3"
1'-4"
BAFFLE
5'-4"
3'-6" TEE
4'-0" LIQUID LEVEL
4'-6'
3" WALLS
CROSS-SECTION
3" WALLS

Figure 720-19 Typical precast grease trap (1000 gal).

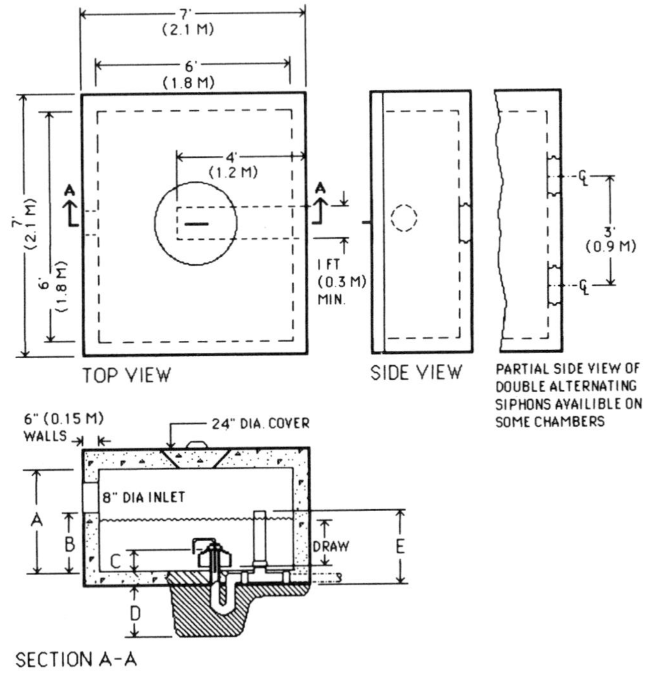
7' (2.1 M)
6' (1.8 M)
4' (1.2 M)
A
A
1 FT (0.3 M) MIN.
7' (2.1 M)
6' (1.8 M)
3' (0.9 M)
TOP VIEW
SIDE VIEW
PARTIAL SIDE VIEW OF DOUBLE ALTERNATING SIPHONS AVAILIBLE ON SOME CHAMBERS
6" (0.15 M) WALLS
24" DIA. COVER
8" DIA INLET
A
B
C
D
DRAW
E
SECTION A-A

SIPHON	GALLONS	DRAW	A	B	C	D	E
3" (.075M)	290	13" (.325 M)	29" (.725 M)	19" (.475 M)	7 1/4" (.18 M)	15" (.375 M)	23" (.575 M)
4" (.10 M)	380	17" (.425 M)	33" (.825 M)	23" (.575 M)	11 3/4" (.29 M)	18" (.45 M)	28" (.70 M)
5" (.125 M)	515	23" (.625 M)	39" (.975 M)	29" (.725 M)	9 1/2" (.24 M)	29" (.725 M)	36" (.90 M)

Figure 720-20 Typical precast dosing chamber.

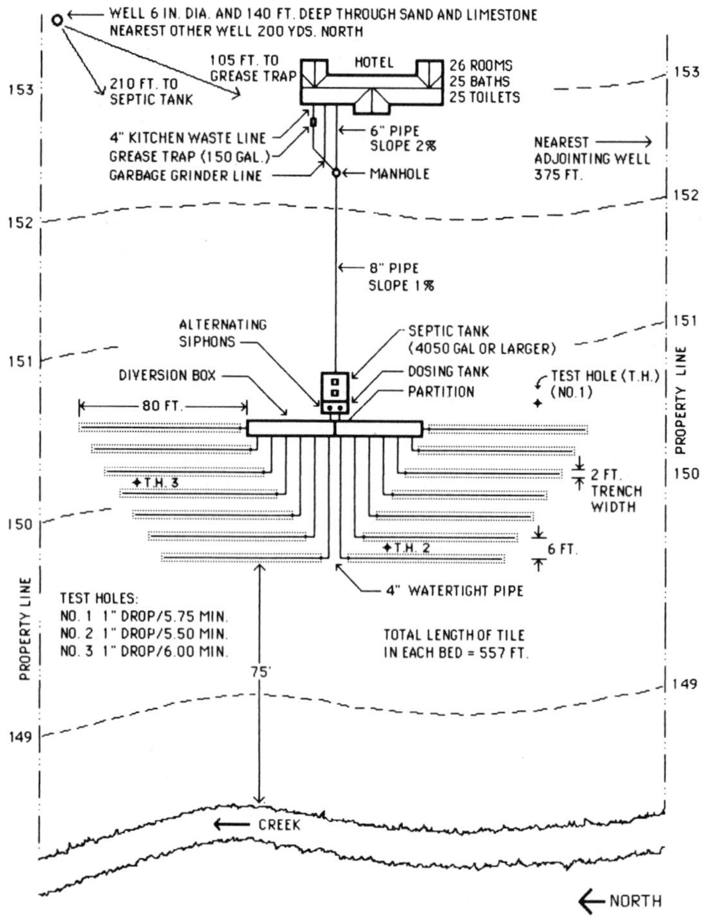
WELL 6 IN. DIA. AND 140 FT. DEEP THROUGH SAND AND LIMESTONE
NEAREST OTHER WELL 200 YDS. NORTH
105 FT. TO GREASE TRAP
HOTEL
26 ROOMS
25 BATHS
25 TOILETS
210 FT. TO SEPTIC TANK
153
4" KITCHEN WASTE LINE
GREASE TRAP (150 GAL.)
GARBAGE GRINDER LINE
6" PIPE SLOPE 2%
MANHOLE
NEAREST ADJOINTING WELL 375 FT.
152
8" PIPE SLOPE 1%
ALTERNATING SIPHONS
SEPTIC TANK (4050 GAL OR LARGER)
151
DIVERSION BOX
DOSING TANK
PARTITION
TEST HOLE (T.H.) (NO. 1)
80 FT.
PROPERTY LINE
T.H. 3
2 FT. TRENCH WIDTH
150
T.H. 2
6 FT.
4" WATERTIGHT PIPE
TEST HOLES:
NO. 1 1" DROP/5.75 MIN.
NO. 2 1" DROP/5.50 MIN.
NO. 3 1" DROP/6.00 MIN.
TOTAL LENGTH OF TILE IN EACH BED = 557 FT.
75'
149
CREEK
NORTH

Figure 720-21 Principal elements of a large leaching system.

Figure 720-21 shows a plan of the principal elements of a large system.

4.7 Relationship of On-Site Systems to Trees and Paving

Trees:

Regarding the relationship of disposal systems to trees, note that the effluent in and near the leaching facilities, the septic tank, and the pipelines between are anaerobic and hence not attractive to most plant roots, with the possible exception of such trees as larch, willow, and alder. The sewer pipe between the building and the septic tank is not anaerobic, however, and can be invaded and clogged by roots. Consequently, except for the building sewer, no special care need be given to the relationship between trees and septic on-site sewage facilities.

Paving:

Regarding the relationship between disposal facilities and paving, some codes prohibit leaching facilities under pavements, others permit them if the leaching fields' distribution pipes are vented, and still others have no restrictions. For heavy traffic, pipes should either be adequately covered with roadbase material [e.g., 2 ft (0.6 m)] or be made of crush-proof materials (cast iron or precast concrete, etc.).

Vents, where required, are typically vertical 4-in (100-mm) cast-iron pipes affixed to tees on the outer ends of the leaching pipes, topped with 180-degree bends, and protected from traffic by a cluster of bollards or other traffic control devices.

5.0 AEROBIC SYSTEMS WITH SURFACE INFILTRATION

5.1 Application

As septic tank/subsurface disposal systems get larger, their costs and space requirements increase proportionately, with little economy of scale. At some point over 15,000 gal (56,775 L) per day, other approaches become competitive. These approaches include not only the settlement and digestion of the suspended solids in the wastewater before its application to the leaching fields, but also the removal of dissolved organic compounds by biological processes.

The resulting effluent can contain as little as 10 percent of the bacterial nutrients of septic tank effluent and thus can be applied to the soil at several times the rate practical for septic tank effluent. Furthermore, because these alternate processes are aerobic rather than septic, their effluent normally and theoretically is odor-free and thus can be applied to surface infiltration beds as well as to subsurface filters. Alternatives suitable for smaller communities include lagoons or stabilization ponds and package plants.

5.2 Lagoons

The most economical and most trouble-free of these alternatives are the various forms of lagoons. Basically, the lagoon is a shallow pond [2 to 5 ft (0.6 to 1.5 m) deep], open to the sun and wind, used to retain sewage for about a month. Like the septic tank, it relies entirely on natural processes and, with favorable topography, on gravity flow. The solids settle to the bottom and decompose anaerobically (as in a septic tank), but their odor is contained and absorbed by the overlying aerated water. The mineral nutrients released in the decomposition, together with the sun shining on the pond's surface, support a vigorous growth of algae. The algae produce oxygen; this, along with the oxygen absorbed by the pond's surface, keeps the upper layers of the pond fresh and odor-free.

The effluent from the stabilization pond is siphoned off the top to a polishing lagoon (about 1 day's flow) and then dosed onto sand filters at rates up to 2½ gal/ft^2 (0.95 L/m^2) per day.

This system, like septic systems, requires almost no management or maintenance. It must be fenced, however, since it has surface ponds and sewage on the ground surface in various stages of beneficiation. The ponds do have to be drained and cleaned (like septic tanks) at infrequent intervals (up to 20 years) and the leaching beds do need to be alternated and rested, if and when they show signs of clogging.

Unlike septic tanks with subsurface filters, the land used for lagoon systems and surface infiltration cannot be used for other purposes.

In regions where winter freezing does not occur, unaerated lagoons are usually odor-free, but in areas where freezing does occur there will be serious odor generated during the twice-a-year thermal turnovers of the ponds.

To control these turnovers and their resulting odors, each lagoon can be very gently mixed with a low-energy aerator (a small air compressor and a weighted polyethylene tube run into the lagoon to generate columns of bubbles). This mixing not only effectively controls the odors but allows the pond to be deepened to 10 or 15 ft (3 to 4.5 m), further reducing space requirements.

The aerated lagoon system is in all other respects similar to the passive lagoon.

Figure 720-22 shows the overall space requirements for septic leaching and aerated leaching systems for housing clusters of various sizes. Note that septic systems are quite competitive at the lower end of the range, especially since their space requirements are subsurface.

Figure 720-23 shows a schematic aerated lagoon system. The aerated lagoon is divided into two or more ponds so that half of the system can be drained and cleaned when the need arises. On favorable topography it can be designed to work hydraulically, with no pumps. The only inputs to the system are the sewage itself and compressed air.

Actual design configurations of lagoons vary. Advantage should be made of existing topography where possible; since there is no mechanical equipment to be incorporated other than the compressed-air lines, the ponds and beds can be any shape desired.

The lagoon can usually be built of locally available or on-site materials. Lagoons can be contained by seeded earthen berms of clayey or silty soils. If sited so that the lagoon bottoms are a minimum of 3 to 4 ft (1 to 1.2 m) above the local water table, no serious groundwater contamination is likely after the lagoons have been in use for a period of time. Natural processes will tend to seal the soil with organic slimes.

5.3 Package Plants

Package plants, or prefabricated secondary sewage treatment plants, can accomplish the same effluent quality as lagoons, usually in less space, and within a building if desired. These systems are mechanically complex, require constant energy inputs, and must be regularly and competently maintained. In addition, the U.S. Environmental Protection Agency has recommended that they be pumped once or twice a year to remove accumulating biomass. If not pumped, the biomass can overload the equipment or wash out into the infiltration beds. Contact a manufacturer's representative for specific details.

In some jurisdictions, package plants are either not allowed or must have oversized infiltration beds to accommodate the washed out biomass.

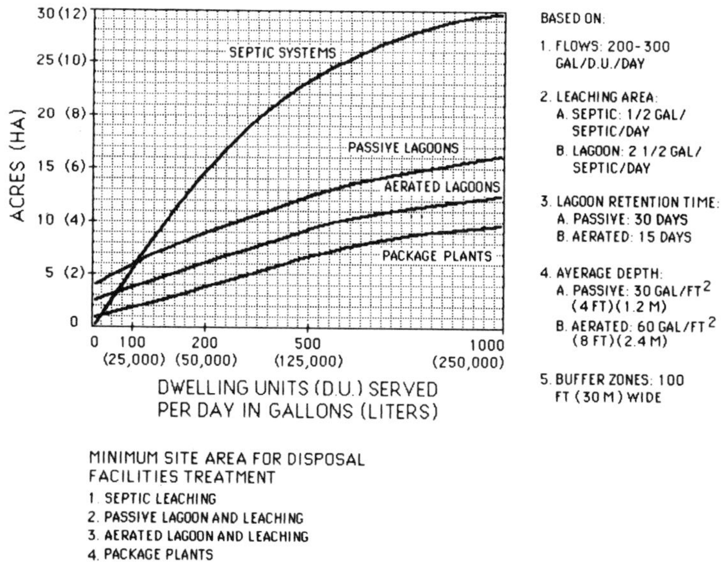
ACRES (HA)
30 (12)
25 (10)
20 (8)
15 (6)
10 (4)
5 (2)
0
SEPTIC SYSTEMS
PASSIVE LAGOONS
AERATED LAGOONS
PACKAGE PLANTS
0 100 200 500 1000
(25,000) (50,000) (125,000) (250,000)
DWELLING UNITS (D.U.) SERVED
PER DAY IN GALLONS (LITERS)
BASED ON:
1. FLOWS: 200-300 GAL/D.U./DAY
2. LEACHING AREA:
A. SEPTIC: 1/2 GAL/SEPTIC/DAY
B. LAGOON: 2 1/2 GAL/SEPTIC/DAY
3. LAGOON RETENTION TIME:
A. PASSIVE: 30 DAYS
B. AERATED: 15 DAYS
4. AVERAGE DEPTH:
A. PASSIVE: 30 GAL/FT2 (4 FT)(1.2 M)
B. AERATED: 60 GAL/FT2 (8 FT)(2.4 M)
5. BUFFER ZONES: 100 FT (30 M) WIDE
MINIMUM SITE AREA FOR DISPOSAL FACILITIES TREATMENT
1. SEPTIC LEACHING
2. PASSIVE LAGOON AND LEACHING
3. AERATED LAGOON AND LEACHING
4. PACKAGE PLANTS

Figure 720-22 Minimum site area required for disposal facilities.

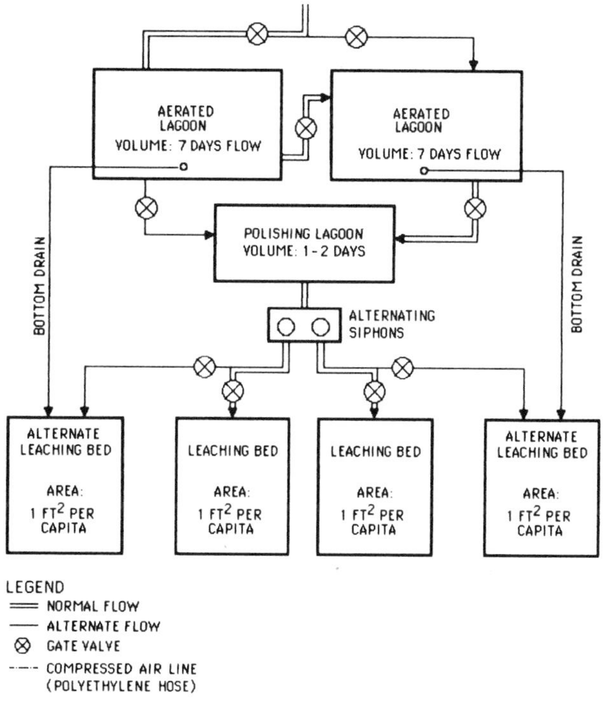
AERATED LAGOON
VOLUME: 7 DAYS FLOW
AERATED LAGOON
VOLUME: 7 DAYS FLOW
POLISHING LAGOON
VOLUME: 1-2 DAYS
ALTERNATING SIPHONS
BOTTOM DRAIN
BOTTOM DRAIN
ALTERNATE LEACHING BED
AREA: 1 FT2 PER CAPITA
LEACHING BED
AREA: 1 FT2 PER CAPITA
LEACHING BED
AREA: 1 FT2 PER CAPITA
ALTERNATE LEACHING BED
AREA: 1 FT2 PER CAPITA
LEGEND
NORMAL FLOW
ALTERNATE FLOW
GATE VALVE
COMPRESSED AIR LINE (POLYETHYLENE HOSE)

Figure 720-23 Typical aerated lagoon system (schematic diagram).

5.4 Subsurface Leaching

Aerobic systems of any kind can be used with subsurface leaching beds, and the leaching beds can be smaller than those used for septic tank effluent. These subsurface beds would be identical to those used with septic systems, with the exception of size.

6.0 AEROBIC SYSTEMS WITH EVAPOTRANSPIRATION SYSTEMS

For sites with limited absorptive capacity where the usage is limited to the growing season, it is possible to dispose of a high proportion of wastewater by evapotranspiration. This approach has been used for summer resorts and as a seasonal alternative to discharge into streams.

NOTE: Streams in various regions have seasonal variations in the quantities of flow. For instance, streams in the eastern United States have the lowest ability to dilute wastewater at the height of the growing season.

For evapotranspiration to work, the effluent must be well aerated so that plant roots will readily take up the liquid. As a consequence, evapotranspiration is not feasible with effluent from septic systems, but it can work with any aerobic effluent. The effluent can be applied by a number of methods, including subirrigation, surface flooding, and spray irrigation.

For subirrigation, the system would be similar to a shallow trench infiltration system for septic effluent, but it should be constructed as close to the ground surface as possible. Like the subsurface disposal of septic effluent, the subirrigation method does not pose any hazards to surface use of the land.

For surface flooding or spray irrigation, consideration must be given to the potential pathogenic hazards of the unfiltered effluent. The areas used for surface irrigation are not normally available for other uses, at least during the seasons in which they are used for wastewater disposal. Crops that might be grown on the land are not normally used for human food. Compatible land uses and crops include game habitat and hunting grounds, forest products, and forage crops for horses.

The application rates for any evapotranspiration system are a function of temperature, hours of sunshine, wind velocity and duration, rainfall, etc. All these vary considerably with the location and the season; thus, any evapotranspiration system will require careful custom design to the specific case.

7.0 AEROBIC SYSTEMS WITH SURFACE WATER DISCHARGE

The discharge of sewage to surface waters, whether treated or untreated, is an ancient practice which has been widely used because of its low cost and ease of accomplishment. As long as the total discharge was small and scattered and the volume of the receiving waters large, it was considered acceptable.

However, as the discharges increased in size and in number, their impacts grew. In an attempt to reverse this trend, the art and science of sanitary engineering was invented and various forms of sewage treatment were developed. Various treatment techniques applied to large volumes of municipal sewage, usually on limited sites in congested urban waterfront areas, have done much to ameliorate the adverse effects of the water discharges, but these techniques are far from perfect. Indeed, almost no municipal treatment plant approaches the overall treatment effectiveness (or low cost) of the common backyard leaching field.

In most areas of the United States, in order to obtain permits for discharging sewage effluent directly into surface waters from new developments, the designer must demonstrate that there are no feasible alternatives—including *no action* (either foregoing the project or siting it elsewhere)— and that the treatment process will produce no significant environmentally adverse impacts on the receiving waters (including the biochemical effects of chlorine or other disinfectants). The degree and type of treatment for the effluent will depend in large part on the character of the receiving waters, but the designer of a new project should anticipate much more extensive treatment than that usually applied at a municipal treatment plant.

For land development planning purposes, space should be provided for some form of digestion (a package plant or an aerated lagoon), for a sand filter, and for some form of denitrification for the filtered effluent—perhaps a second lagoon, shallow and weedy, 2 to 3 ft (0.6 to 1 m) deep, or surface flooding across an existing marsh—before discharge to surface waters.

REFERENCES

Bouma, J., et al. *Soil Absorption of Septic Tank Effluent,* Information Circular 20, University of Wisconsin, Soil Survey Division, Madison, WI, 1972.

Bubly, Daniel (ed.). *Draft Environmental Impact Statement, Wastewater Collection and Treatment Facilities, Sandwich, Massachusetts,* U.S. Environmental Protection Agency, Region I, Boston, MA, September 1981.

Kropf, F. W., R. Laak, and K. A. Healey. "Equilibrium Operation of Subsurface Absorption Systems," *Journal of Water Pollution Control Federation,* September 1977.

Salvato, Joseph A. *Environmental Engineering and Sanitation,* 3d ed., Wiley, New York, 1982.

U.S. Department of Health, Education, and Welfare, Public Health Service. *Manual of Septic Tank Practice,* U.S. Government Printing Office, Washington, DC, 1972. ■

section 730: Stormwater Management and Water Resources Protection

CREDITS

Contributor:

Daniel Bubly, P.E., L.A., A.I.C.P.
Bubly Associates, Inc.
Sharon, Massachusetts

Graphics:

Gary M. Fishbeck, using a MacIntosh computer

Reviewer:

Robert F. Ferrari, P.E.
Ferrari-Atwood Engineering, Inc.
Providence, Rhode Island

CONTENTS

1.0 INTRODUCTION

The alteration of any landscape caused by the simple regrading of land, by increasing the extent of impervious paving, or by altering natural drainage systems can lead to a series of downstream environmental changes, including:

1. Flooding

2. Erosion of stream profiles and undermining of stream banks

3. Sedimentation

4. Turbidity in downstream waterbodies

5. Algae blooms and loss of water quality in downstream waterbodies

6. Loss or adverse alteration of the habitat of aquatic biota

2.0 DESIGN CRITERIA

Proper management of stormwater includes a design that will:

1. Control flooding on-site

2. Control flooding downstream

3. Limit erosion on-site

4. Limit erosion downstream

5. Control sedimentation

6. Limit turbidity of runoff waters

7. Limit adverse impacts on aquatic biota

3.0 EFFECTS OF GRADING

3.1 Erosion and Sedimentation

Regrading of land, including the removal of existing vegetative cover and pavement, is likely to lead to the erosion and transport in runoff waters of a variety of materials, including coarse, settleable soil particles, finer, suspended soil particles, and phosphates. Phosphate is an important plant nutrient with a serious potential for creating nuisance conditions.

The coarser soil particles, when moving along with the runoff waters, can abrade stream inverts, increasing invert erosion, and, when carried into stream reaches with lower velocities, can settle out, choking existing channels, filling waterways and waterbodies, raising stream profiles, and causing local flooding.

3.2 Sedimentation Control

Coarse soil particles are relatively easy to control by using wide strips of grass or other types of vegetation to intercept sheet runoff, by using straw or hay bales as temporary traps in drainage swales, or by using permanent retention and sediment basins constructed to regulate stormwater runoff from the site. Any significant slowing of the runoff waters will cause most coarse particles to settle out.

The finer soil particles, in contrast, tend to pass through temporary straw or hay traps and stormwater retention basins, with little removal of suspended material. These particles can be very damaging to downstream biota, often clogging their breathing apparatus and suffocating them. In addition, these suspended materials cause turbidity of water in downstream ponds and lakes, thereby impairing their aesthetic qualities, especially for drinking and swimming. Turbidity can also interfere with the rescue of swimmers faced with possible drowning. In some jurisdictions, the use of

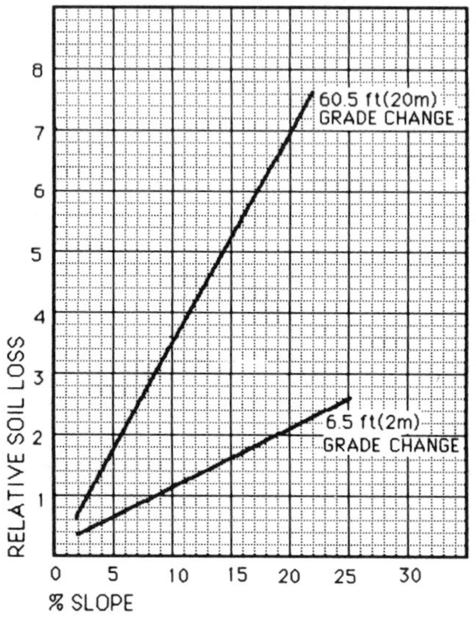
60.5 ft(20m) GRADE CHANGE
6.5 ft(2m) GRADE CHANGE
RELATIVE SOIL LOSS
% SLOPE

Figure 730-1 Relationship between slope steepness and soil loss.

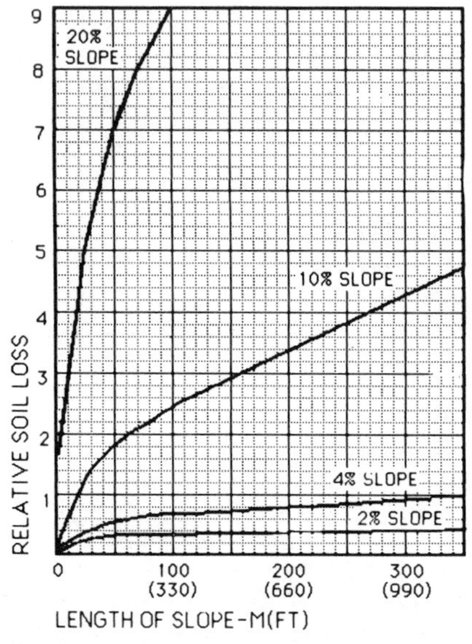
20% SLOPE
10% SLOPE
4% SLOPE
2% SLOPE
RELATIVE SOIL LOSS
LENGTH OF SLOPE-M(FT)

Figure 730-2 Relationship between slope length and soil loss.

waterbodies for public swimming is regulated according to the transparency of the water; generally, a minimum transparency of 4 ft (1.2 m) is required.

The only practical controls of these fine particles are:

1. Prevention of the erosion in the first place

2. Restricting grading in the watersheds of swimming ponds to the autumn and winter seasons only

3. Chemical flocculation and sedimentation of waters withdrawn for water supply use

3.3 Erosion Control

Erosion control techniques include: (1) restricting the steepness of unprotected slopes and (2) paving, sodding, or mulching all graded areas, especially steep slopes.

Steepness of Slopes:

Steep slopes, especially those consisting of fine-grained soils, need to be restricted. Figure 730-1 shows the relationship between slope steepness and soil loss for a 6.5-ft (2-m) and a 60.5-ft (20-m) grade change. (Note the direct relationship between steepness and soil loss.)

Effects of Slope Length:

Figure 730-2 shows the relationship between slope length and soil loss for various slope steepnesses. Note that on flatter slopes the length of slope is not significant after the first 97.5 to 130.0 ft (30 to 40 m), but that on steeper slopes the soil loss continues to rise dramatically as the slope lengthens. The implications of these two figures taken together is that even though flatter slopes, when used without retaining walls, will result in a greater area of land being disturbed, they can be expected to cause less erosion.

Mulching, Paving, and Sodding:

Table 730-1 shows the comparative effectiveness of various surface treatments. Coarse sands, crushed rock, and gravels (similar to those used as roadbase material) are very effective in limiting erosion, especially of fine particles.

3.4 Control of Phosphates

Phosphates that are carried off construction sites with soil are likely to consist almost entirely of particles with low solubility. As a general rule, they will have little effect other than as soil particles unless they are allowed to settle in shallow water [less than 3 ft (1 m)] where rooted aquatic plants can dissolve them. In such locations, phosphates will encourage lush vegetative growth, thereby blocking stream flow, depleting oxygen, and causing noxious odors in the water when the plants die, decay, and contribute detritus to the downstream waters.

The same management techniques used for control of erosion and sedimentation (as shown in Table 730-1) can be used for control of soil phosphates.

4.0 HYDRAULIC EFFECTS OF INCREASED PAVING AND IMPROVED DRAINAGE

The paving of land and the improvement of its drainage can be expected to increase both the volume and velocity of stormwater runoff, with a number of related adverse environmental effects.

4.1 Runoff

The peak volume and velocity of runoff in a storm of any given probability of recurrence is a function of the area of the site, soil permeability, and the speed at which the runoff from the entire site can concentrate at any point in the drainage system.

Development of any site will usually reduce the permeability of the land and reduce the time in which runoff is concentrated. The effect of the decrease in permeability will be limited more or less in proportion to the increase in the area paved or roofed over—but the effect of change in the concentration time, even if it is the result of a relatively small amount of paved, piped, or concentrated drainage, can be dramatic. The net effect is that even a small amount of development on a site, with naturally permeable soils and poorly developed drainage ways, will dramatically increase runoff and its impacts, even if the proposed development has an efficient drainage system. These impacts would not only include increases in the depth and width of downstream floodplains, but perhaps more importantly would include changes in the velocity of downstream flow during and after storms. This increase in the velocity of downstream flow will:

1. Make the waters uninhabitable to some of the stream's existing biota, each species of which has adapted to a range of velocities that occur within a particular reach

2. Scour and erode previously deposited bottom sediments:

- **a.** Sometimes releasing toxic materials (heavy metals) naturally accumulated in the sediments over the years
- **b.** Undermining stream banks, leading

to erosion and collapse of their vegetative cover

c. Redepositing scoured sediments further downstream, choking previously established channels and burying downstream biota

4.2 Control

Control of the harmful effects of runoff described above include:

1. Minimizing the use of paved gutters or drainage pipes and maximizing the use of vegetated drainage swales, etc.

2. Retarding stormwater runoff via various water impoundment techniques so that peak runoff for frequent storms (10-year or less recurrence probability) will be no greater after development than before

3. Providing maximum opportunity for rainwaters to infiltrate the soil

Refer to Section 330: Site Drainage, for specific information on the design of water retention or detention systems.

5.0 EFFECTS ON WATER QUALITY DUE TO INCREASED PAVING AND IMPROVED DRAINAGE

Testing of stormwater runoff from streets, parking lots, and roof drains indicates that runoff water is normally heavily laden with a variety of contaminants that usually have severe adverse impacts on downstream surface waters. In extreme cases, contaminated runoff has resulted in the closing of recreational ponds to swimming, the destruction of fishery resources, the production of botulism poisoning in wildlife, and salmonella poisoning in humans.

5.1 Types of Contaminants

The sources of contaminants are complex. They include airborne fallout from industrial air pollution, bird and animal wastes, leaves, lawn clippings and other organic detritus, motor vehicle lubricants, tire abrasions, wind and water erosion of soil, detergents, and pesticides.

In general, the contamination is greatest in highly urbanized areas, with the lowest levels of contaminants found in runoff from pastures and lawns.

Specific contaminants of concern include phosphates and nitrates, hydrocarbons, putrescible organics (expressed as BOD_5), lead, zinc, copper, and nickel. The phosphates and nitrates can cause a substantial growth of algae in waterbodies. The putrescible organics, by contributing to the depletion of oxygen levels in receiving waters, can kill fish and cause odors.

TABLE 730-1

Effectiveness of Various Surface Materials for Controlling Erosion*

Type	*Tonnes/ha*	*Slope (%)*	*C*
Cropland, pasture, or woodland			
Continuous fallow tilled up and down slope			1.00
Shortly after seeding or harvesting†			0.3–0.8
For crops during main part of growing season			
Corn‡			0.1–0.3
Wheat‡			0.05–0.15
Cotton‡			0.4
Soybeans‡			0.2–0.3
Meadow‡			0.01–0.02
For permanent pasture, idle land, unmanaged woodland			
Ground cover 95–100%			
As grass			0.003
As weeds			0.01
Ground cover 80%			
As grass			0.01
As weeds			0.04
Ground cover 60%			
As grass			0.04
As weeds			0.09
For managed woodland			
Tree canopy of			
75–100%			0.001
40–75%			0.002–0.004
20–40%			0.003–0.01
Urban or construction sites			
No mulch or seeding		All	1.00
Straw or hay tied down by anchoring	2.25	<5	0.2
and tracking equipment used on slope	2.25	6–10	0.2
	3.4	<5	0.12
	3.4	6–10	0.12
	4.5	<5	0.06
	4.5	6–10	0.06
	4.5	11–15	0.07
	4.5	16–20	0.11
	4.5	21–25	0.14
Crushed stone	300	<15	0.05
	300	16–20	0.05
	300	21–33	0.05
	540	<20	0.02
	540	21–33	0.02
Wood chips	15	<15	0.08
	15	16–20	0.08
	27	<15	0.05
	27	16–20	0.05
	56	<15	0.02
	56	16–20	0.02
	56	21–33	0.02
Asphalt emulsion, 12m³/ha			0.03
Temporary seeding with grain or fast-growing grass with:			
No mulch			0.70§ 0.10¶
Straw	2.25		0.20§ 0.07¶
Straw	3.4		0.12§ 0.05¶
Stone	300		0.05§ 0.05¶
Stone	540		0.02§ 0.02¶
Wood chips	15		0.08§ 0.05¶
Wood chips	27		0.05§ 0.02§
Wood chips	56		0.02§ 0.02¶
Sod			0.01§ 0.01¶

* The smaller the number the more effective is the surface material for erosion control.

† Depends on root and residue density.

‡ Depends on yield.

§ During first six weeks of growth.

¶ After the sixth week of growth.

Source: Adapted from Vladimir Novotny and Gordon Chesters, *Handbook of Nonpoint Pollution Sources and Management*, Van Nostrand Reinhold, New York, 1981.

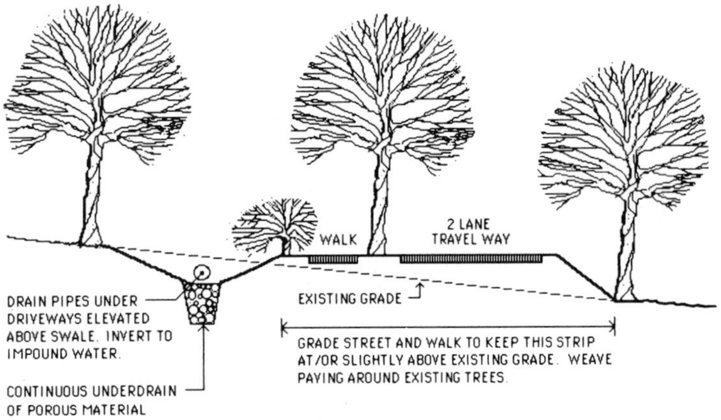
2 LANE
TRAVEL WAY
WALK
DRAIN PIPES UNDER DRIVEWAYS ELEVATED ABOVE SWALE. INVERT TO IMPOUND WATER.
EXISTING GRADE
GRADE STREET AND WALK TO KEEP THIS STRIP AT/OR SLIGHTLY ABOVE EXISTING GRADE. WEAVE PAVING AROUND EXISTING TREES.
CONTINUOUS UNDERDRAIN OF POROUS MATERIAL

Figure 730-3 Controlling pavement runoff (section).

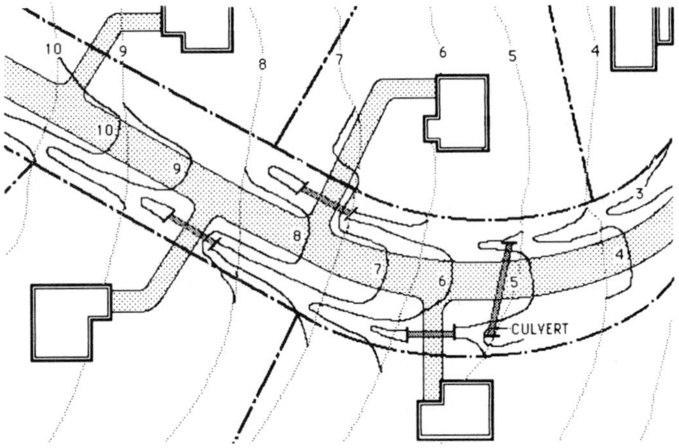
CULVERT

Figure 730-4 Controlling pavement runoff (plan).

stormwater retention system, or below the surface, using the gravel base of parking lots and other lightly loaded pavements as a distribution system).

Selection of an alternative depends on site conditions. Routing stormwater runoff around waterbodies of concern may not be feasible in some cases.

Pavement Runoff:

Designing pavements so that dust will blow or wash off into vegetated areas is not difficult if: (1) adequate landscaped areas are provided, (2) drainage is channeled via vegetated surface swales rather than by pipe, (3) pavements are not curbed, and (4) pavement cross slopes are adequate to move drainage water off the pavement into the adjoining vegetation.

Figure 730-3 shows a cross section through a residential street designed to these criteria. Note that this approach sometimes requires more land than a typical curbed street with piped storm drainage, but it costs much less, retains stormwater as an integral part of the design (rather than an add-on), and helps limit downstream pollution. Figure 730-4 shows the cross section applied to a hypothetical subdivision street.

The lead, zinc, copper, and nickel can degrade water supplies below acceptable drinking standards.

5.2 Controlling Contamination

For the most part, these contaminants cannot be effectively removed from the runoff water by simple settlement, contrary to some claims. In the case of phosphates (the single most important cause of surface water degradation), simple sedimentation removes relatively insoluble phosphate particles that normally have little or no effect on receiving waters. Settlement does not remove the dissolved phosphates responsible for algae blooms, the most severe problem.

Alternatives for control of these specific stormwater pollutants include:

1. Routing the surface drainage from paved areas around, rather than into, swimming ponds and water supply reservoirs.

2. Designing pavements to shed the stormwater and its pollutants to surrounding vegetated areas rather than to gutters. (Most contaminants, particularly soluble phosphates, are effectively adsorbed by soil.)

3. Filtering runoff waters through sand filters (either on the surface, as part of a

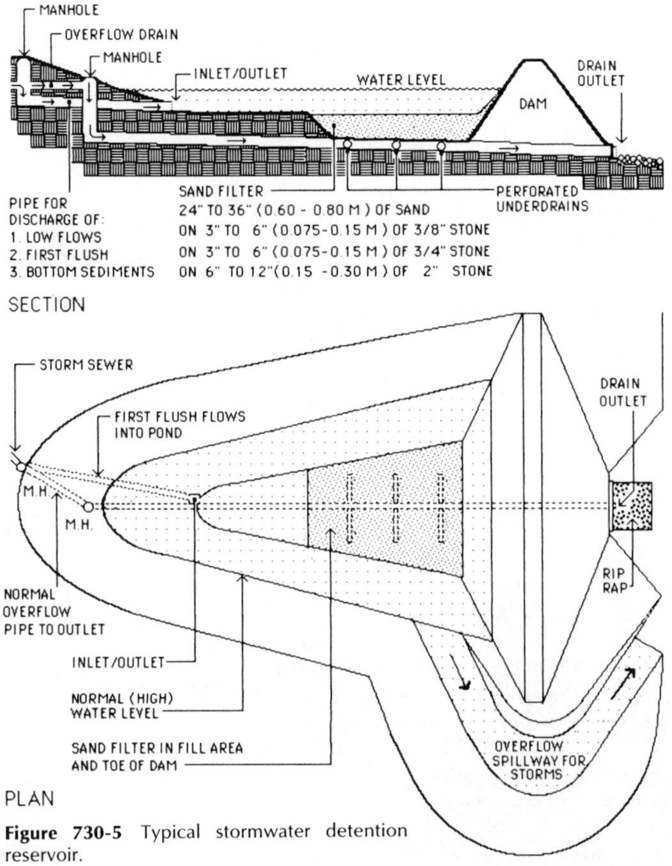
MANHOLE
OVERFLOW DRAIN
MANHOLE
INLET/OUTLET
WATER LEVEL
DAM
DRAIN OUTLET
SAND FILTER
24" TO 36" (0.60 - 0.80 M) OF SAND
ON 3" TO 6" (0.075-0.15 M) OF 3/8" STONE
ON 3" TO 6" (0.075-0.15 M) OF 3/4" STONE
ON 6" TO 12"(0.15 -0.30 M) OF 2" STONE
PERFORATED UNDERDRAINS
PIPE FOR DISCHARGE OF:
1. LOW FLOWS
2. FIRST FLUSH
3. BOTTOM SEDIMENTS
SECTION
STORM SEWER
FIRST FLUSH FLOWS INTO POND
M.H.
M.H.
DRAIN OUTLET
RIP RAP
NORMAL OVERFLOW PIPE TO OUTLET
INLET/OUTLET
NORMAL (HIGH) WATER LEVEL
SAND FILTER IN FILL AREA AND TOE OF DAM
OVERFLOW SPILLWAY FOR STORMS
PLAN

Figure 730-5 Typical stormwater detention reservoir.

Conventional Stormwater Detention:

As an *add-on* alternative to water quality protection, Figure 730-5 shows a plan and section through a conventional stormwater detention reservoir which has been modified to include a sand filter instead of a conventional outfall and to prevent *first-flush* drainage from being washed out by subsequent flows.

Sand filtration is effective in: (1) precipitating and/or adsorbing phosphates and toxic metals and (2) oxidizing putrescibles and hydrocarbons. The inlet works are designed to allow sustained flows to bypass the retention basin after the normal water level is achieved, without washing the dirtier first-flush water out of the basin.

The intermittent loading of the filter, with no flow between storms, will allow organic materials (including cellulose) to degrade between storms. Since a majority of runoff in most areas occurs in small but frequent storms and since the short-duration or low-intensity storm runoffs from pavements are likely to be relatively more contaminated than larger storm runoffs, most of the runoff and an even higher proportion of the contaminants are likely to be treated.

Sand filters of this type can handle some 1 to 5 million gal per acre of surface per day, or 3 to 15 acre-ft (3700.5 to 18,502.5 m^3) of water per acre (4046.9 m^2) per day.

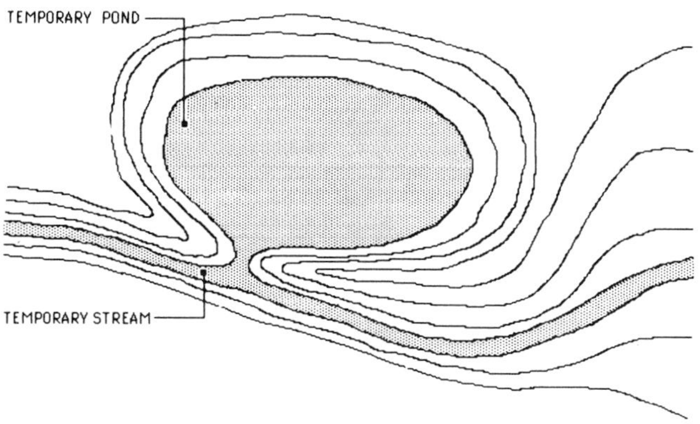
TEMPORARY POND
TEMPORARY STREAM

Figure 730-6 Stormwater detention reservoir.

Alternative Stormwater Detention:

Figures 730-6 and 730-7 are variations of the same concept shown in Figure 730-5 but with a biomorphic form and surface swales instead of piped drainage. As in Figure 730-5, the drainage ways are designed to intercept the first flush and heavy sediments but to bypass other runoff.

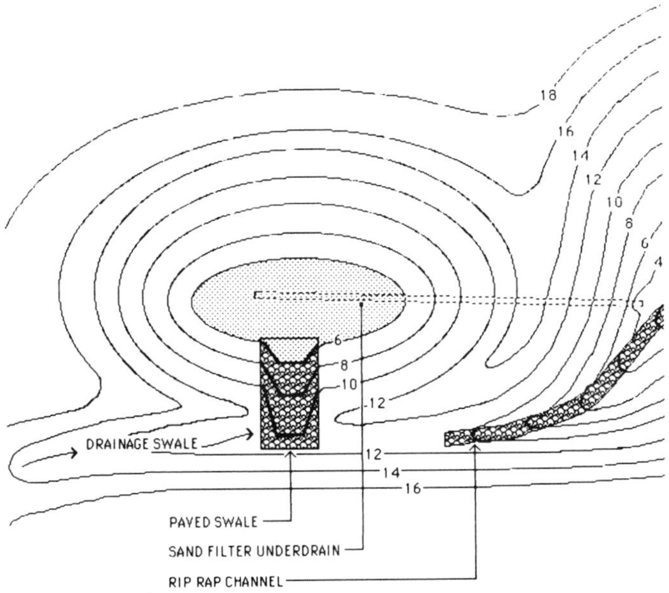
18
16
14
12
10
8
6
4
DRAINAGE SWALE
6
8
10
12
12
14
16
PAVED SWALE
SAND FILTER UNDERDRAIN
RIP RAP CHANNEL

Figure 730-7 Stormwater detention reservoir.

An alternative approach to filtering pavement runoff is to use the soil and porous subbase under the pavement as a filter. A 12-in (300-mm) gravel or other type of porous base under a pavement has sufficient void space to hold 1 to 2½ in (25 to 65 mm) of water, and the underlying soils, if permeable by nature and properly underdrained, can absorb well over 1 ft (0.3 m) of water per day.

The principal problems of the use of pavement bases for water storage and of subbases for filtration include: (1) control of clogging of the inlets to the pavement base material with fine sediments and (2) drainage of the subbase.

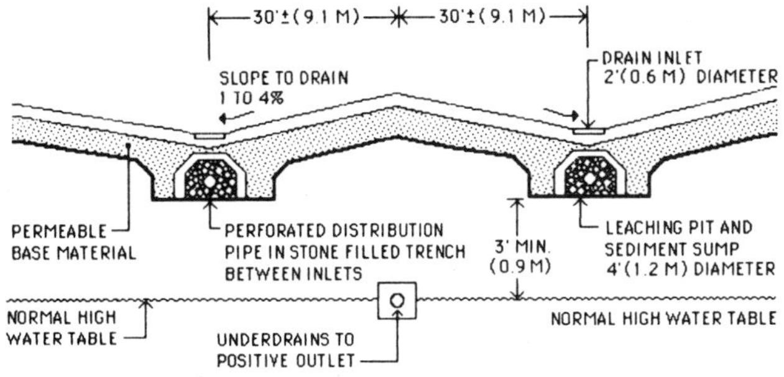
30'±(9.1 M)
30'±(9.1 M)
SLOPE TO DRAIN
1 TO 4%
DRAIN INLET
2'(0.6 M) DIAMETER
PERMEABLE
BASE MATERIAL
PERFORATED DISTRIBUTION
PIPE IN STONE FILLED TRENCH
BETWEEN INLETS
3' MIN.
(0.9 M)
LEACHING PIT AND
SEDIMENT SUMP
4'(1.2 M) DIAMETER
NORMAL HIGH
WATER TABLE
UNDERDRAINS TO
POSITIVE OUTLET
NORMAL HIGH WATER TABLE

Figure 730-8 Stormwater control for parking lot.

Figure 730-8 shows a section through a parking lot with shallow leaching pits 4 ft (1.2 m) in diameter used as sediment traps (to be cleaned with catch basin cleaning equipment) and with conventional underdrains used to control groundwater levels. To ensure adequate treatment of runoff and to prevent pollution of the underlying groundwater with putrescible dissolved organics and ammonia, it is essential that the water table be at least 3 ft (1 m) below the leaching pit or sumps.

Other alternatives can be used to accomplish subpavement leaching, such as surface swales with french drains (trenches filled with washed or broken stone) to facilitate the entry of runoff water into the pavement base. Consideration should be given to the need for periodic replacement of the stone, because sediments and organic debris fill the voids.

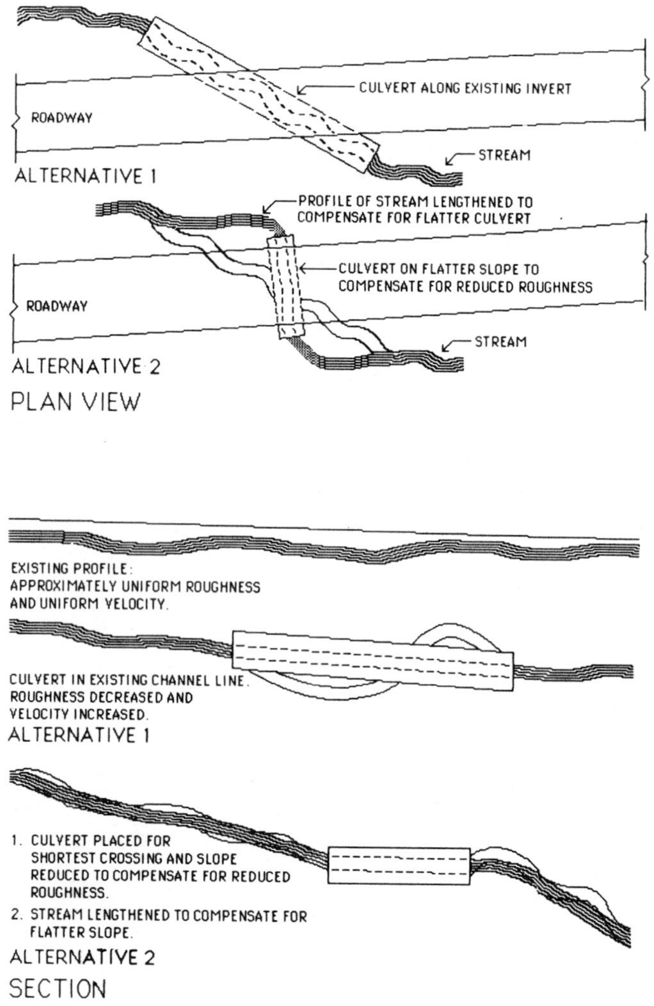
CULVERT ALONG EXISTING INVERT
ROADWAY
STREAM
ALTERNATIVE 1
PROFILE OF STREAM LENGTHENED TO COMPENSATE FOR FLATTER CULVERT
CULVERT ON FLATTER SLOPE TO COMPENSATE FOR REDUCED ROUGHNESS
ROADWAY
STREAM
ALTERNATIVE 2
PLAN VIEW
EXISTING PROFILE: APPROXIMATELY UNIFORM ROUGHNESS AND UNIFORM VELOCITY.
CULVERT IN EXISTING CHANNEL LINE. ROUGHNESS DECREASED AND VELOCITY INCREASED.
ALTERNATIVE 1
1. CULVERT PLACED FOR SHORTEST CROSSING AND SLOPE REDUCED TO COMPENSATE FOR REDUCED ROUGHNESS.
2. STREAM LENGTHENED TO COMPENSATE FOR FLATTER SLOPE.
ALTERNATIVE 2
SECTION

Figure 730-9 Stream relocation and culvert crossings.

6.0 STREAM RELOCATION AND CULVERT CROSSINGS

The development of land often requires the relocation of minor streams, the installation of culverts, and the impounding of stormwater runoff. All these changes adversely impact the streams' biotic systems and in many jurisdictions are closely regulated by law.

6.1 Important Considerations

A key consideration in the alteration of streams is preserving the physical characteristics of the water, i.e., its velocity, depth, aeration, exposure to sunlight, etc. Natural stream systems tend to grade from rapid, turbulent flow at their headwaters to slow, smooth flow near their mouths, with long stretches of homogeneous water. Each reach of the stream supports biota adapted to the velocity, turbulence, depth, and length of the reach.

6.2 Ecological Impact of Stream Alteration

Alteration of the stream, such as breaking any long reach into two shorter ones, can have an adverse impact on its biota. Using an existing stream valley as a stormwater impoundment or replacing a section of natural stream invert with a smooth culvert will also result in adverse ecological effects.

6.3 Minimizing Detrimental Effects

To avoid adverse ecological impacts, stormwater impoundments should be sited off existing streams with culverts placed to minimize the effects of their smoothness on stream velocities. Figure 730-9 illustrates a typical culvert crossing and an ecologically more acceptable alternative. Note that the design that appears to have the greatest change in plan (Alternative 2) has the smallest change in water habitat character.

REFERENCES

Munson, Albe E. *Construction Design for Landscape Architects,* McGraw-Hill, New York, 1974.

Novotny, Vladimir, and Gordon Chesters. *Handbook of Nonpoint Pollution Sources and Management,* Van Nostrand Reinhold, New York, 1981.

Wanielista, M. P., Y. A. Yousef, and J. S. Taylor. *Stormwater Management to Improve Lake Water Quality,* National Technical Information Service, (Order no. PB82-227711), 5285 Port Royal Road, Springfield, VA, 1982.

Whipple, William, et al. *Stormwater Management in Urbanizing Areas,* Prentice-Hall, Englewood Cliffs, NJ, 1983. ■

section 740: Recreational Water Bodies

CREDITS

Contributor:

Daniel Bubly, P.E., L.A., A.I.C.P.
Bubly Associates, Inc.
Sharon, Massachusetts

Computer Graphics:

Gary M. Fishbeck

Reviewer:

Robert F. Ferrari, P.E.
Ferrari-Atwood Engineering, Inc.
Providence, Rhode Island

Contents

1.0 INTRODUCTION

Impounded surface waters are often valued for:

1. Swimming and related recreation
2. Wildlife habitat
3. Aesthetic (i.e., visual) reasons

Principal concerns in the design of recreational water bodies are control of (a) water quality, (b) water level fluctuation, and (c) edge treatment. Each of these concerns should be addressed and specifically incorporated into the plans and designs for recreational water bodies. Unless the water body is large enough to establish zones, it is often not feasible to incorporate several recreational functions into one area. For instance, swimming and boating do not mix.

Impoundments designed primarily for power and flood control tend to have short periods of water detention, i.e., their annual flowthrough is larger than their storage capacity, hence their retained water tends to be turbid and tactilely unattractive. On the other hand, impoundments designed for water storage (i.e., water supply and large-scale irrigation) tend to have long periods of retention, and therefore their water is more transparent and tactilely more attractive.

Similarly, reservoirs that are small with respect to the amount of water drawn from them may have wider variations of water levels. This makes the shorelines more difficult to use for recreational purposes and may affect the aesthetic values during certain seasons. Large reservoirs tend to have more stable water levels with respect to their slower rates of withdrawal and, therefore, are more suitable for recreational uses.

Note that daily flowthrough, a key parameter in the design of mechanically filtered swimming pools, is not appropriate to determine for ponds and lakes. They typically have far more water per swimmer than the typical large public swimming pool.

2.0 EVALUATIVE CRITERIA FOR RECREATIONAL WATER BODIES

Waters for recreational use must meet various standards of quality, appearance, and ease of maintenance.

2.1 Water Quality

1. In a public health sense, fresh water used for swimming should approach the quality standards used for drinking waters.

2. In an aesthetic sense, swimming waters should be as transparent as possible, including being free from algae, weeds, organic detritus, and suspended silts and clays.

3. In a public safety sense, intensively used swimming waters should have sufficient transparency to facilitate rescue of drowning victims.

4. For wildlife habitat and scenic values, any water quality except the most seriously polluted will be appropriate. A diversity of water body characteristics (i.e., quality, depth, temperature, and form) will support the greatest number of species.

2.2 Water Levels

1. For swimming uses, water control systems should be designed so that levels can be maintained during dry summer seasons, or so that access to the water can be maintained when water levels fall.

2. For aesthetic (i.e., nonswimming) reasons, water bodies that are expected to lose a major portion of their water during the summer should be shaped as a shallow basin to support a vegetative cover (i.e., marsh, shrub swamp, etc.) to avoid revealing a muddy edge or bottom.

2.3 Side Slopes

1. The action of waves will eventually erode any pond embankment to a wave-cut beach (except those heavily armored with stone, concrete, or metal). The eventual slope of the beach will depend on the texture of the soil involved. For instance, coarse sand will form an approximate 10 percent slope, and finer sands a 5 percent slope. The vertical extent of the erosion will approximate the height of waves generated on the pond. Wave height is a function of pond size, its wind exposure, and other factors, including the size of boats and the relative exposure of the particular reach of shoreline.

Figure 740-1 shows the form of a wave-cut beach, with 1-ft waves and a stable water level, on a 5:1 slope in coarse sand. Note the steep drop that can form just below the beach. On a steeper average slope, say 3:1, or in fine sand, the drop would be over 3 ft (1 m) deep and could constitute a safety hazard for swimmers, especially children.

2. Alternative shoreline treatments include riprap, stone armor, and various types of walls. In each, consideration should be given to the human usage of the surrounding area, including ways to escape if anyone happens to fall into the water.

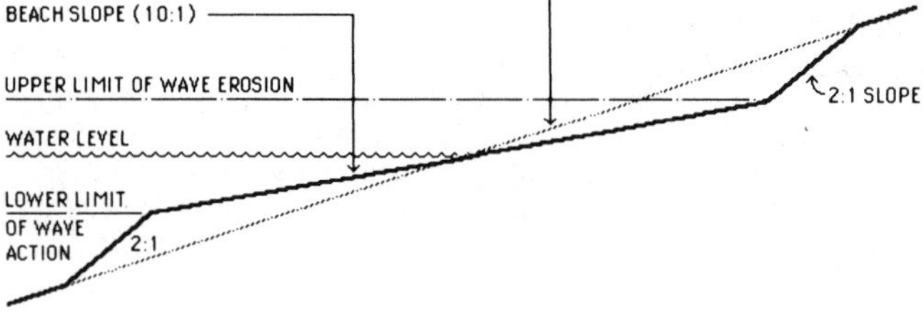
EXISTING SLOPE (5:1)
BEACH SLOPE (10:1)
UPPER LIMIT OF WAVE EROSION
WATER LEVEL
LOWER LIMIT OF WAVE ACTION
2:1
2:1 SLOPE

Figure 740-1 Wave-cut beach form on erodible shore.

3.0 SWIMMING WATERS

3.1 General

Two common alternatives for swimming include:

1. Swimming pools with:
   a. Filtration to remove suspended materials
   b. Algicides to control algae
   c. Chlorination to control bacteria
2. Ponds and lakes with:
   a. Long storage times to settle suspended materials
   b. Control of algae by controlling watershed land use and drainage
   c. Control of bacteria and viruses by natural processes (e.g., maintaining natural biota, including predators)

The selection of an alternative for swimming depends on the purpose of the project, the necessary size of the water body, and the particular amenities of the site. For small swimming areas, filtered, chemically treated swimming pools are usually the most appropriate, and they can be built almost anywhere. For larger facilities, ponds or lakes are likely to be the most appropriate, but their feasibility is a function of hydrologic, geologic, and topographic opportunities.

3.2 Swimming Pools

For small residential swimming pools, a variety of design alternatives are possible, ranging from prefabricated aboveground plastic-lined metal containers to in-the-ground concrete structures, all connected by some means to the necessary filtering equipment. For specific design information in any locality, local swimming pool supply houses or contractors should be contacted and their offerings adapted to specific site conditions.

For larger swimming pools, those for institutional or public use, specialized professional engineering of the structural containment and mechanical systems will usually be necessary to optimize effectiveness and costs.

3.3 Ponds and Lakes

High-quality water for swimming can be found in naturally clean, existing ponds and lakes or in ponds and lakes specifically designed to control suspended sediments and nutrient inputs. (Refer to Section 730: Stormwater Management and Water Resources Protection, for information on the control of suspended sediments and nutrients inputs.)

3.4 Stream Impoundments

Site Selection:

General design considerations for swimming impoundments on streams include:

1. Suitable soil conditions on the bottom (i.e., the less permeable, the better)
2. A topographic form capable of being shaped into a pond at reasonable cost (minimum regrading)
3. A site free of excessive organic materials
4. An adequate water supply
5. A watershed free of contaminants
6. An impoundment volume large enough for long-term water storage

A large watershed is in most cases neither necessary nor desirable since, except for the initial filling of the pond, only enough additional water to compensate for leakage and evaporation is needed. (Refer to Section 330: Site Drainage, for information on the calculation of runoff quantities.)

Water Supply:

Figure 740-2 shows the average dry year rainfall, less evaporation, for the United States. Note that in many areas the dry year rainfall exceeds the evaporation, so that if the impoundment had no leakage, no watershed beyond the water body itself would be necessary. However, since leakage will occur and since the reservoir must be filled initially, some tributary area will be necessary. A professional geohydrologist should be consulted to estimate leakage. (Refer to Section 710: Water Supply, for more information.)

Figure 740-3 shows the size of tributary area required to produce a given volume of makeup water to replace likely water losses. Note that even in areas that are relatively dry (except for very dry deserts), enough runoff water can be gathered during the rainy season if the watershed is carefully selected.

Water Quality:

To meet water quality standards desirable for swimming:

1. The site of the impoundment should be stripped of all organic material (i.e., vegetation, topsoil, peat, etc.).

2. The retention time of the water in the impoundment should be greater than 1 year (i.e., the volume of the reservoir divided by the annual rainfall runoff to it should be greater than 1).

3. Suspended sediments and limiting plant nutrients (phosphates) must be rigorously excluded.

4. The reservoir should be suitably shaped to allow natural pond clarification processes to occur.

Reservoir Form:

Naturally clear ponds will result from a number of mechanisms that contribute to water quality, including:

1. Adequate depth, typically over 10 ft (3 m), to allow thermal stratification of the water and seasonal turnovers. This process leads to the seasonal formation of a natural ferrous sulfate floc, which traps and removes suspended particles that would otherwise be too fine to settle of their own weight. Note that the depth need not occur over the entire pond bottom but can be limited to a single large hole (probably near the dam). (Refer to Section 420: Small Dams, for information on the design and construction of small dams.)

2. Adequate shoal water, less than 3 to 5 ft (1 to 1.5 m) deep, away from swimming areas and close to inflows to the pond. This will allow rooted aquatic vegetation to establish itself and absorb plant nutrients, thereby partially denying the nutrients to

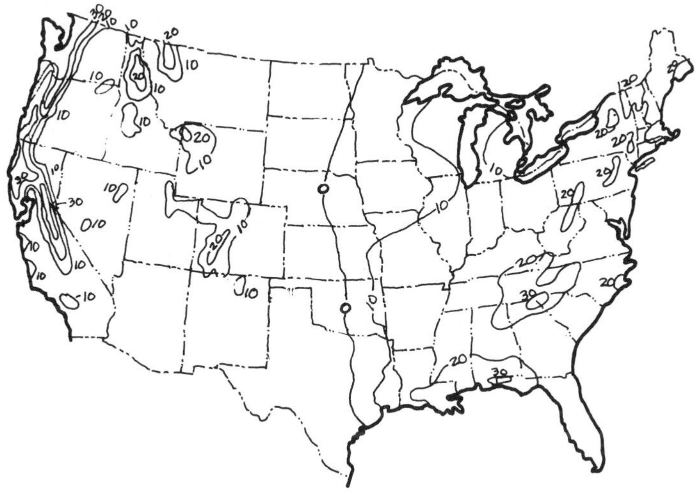

Figure 740-2 Average dry year rainfall less lake evaporation.

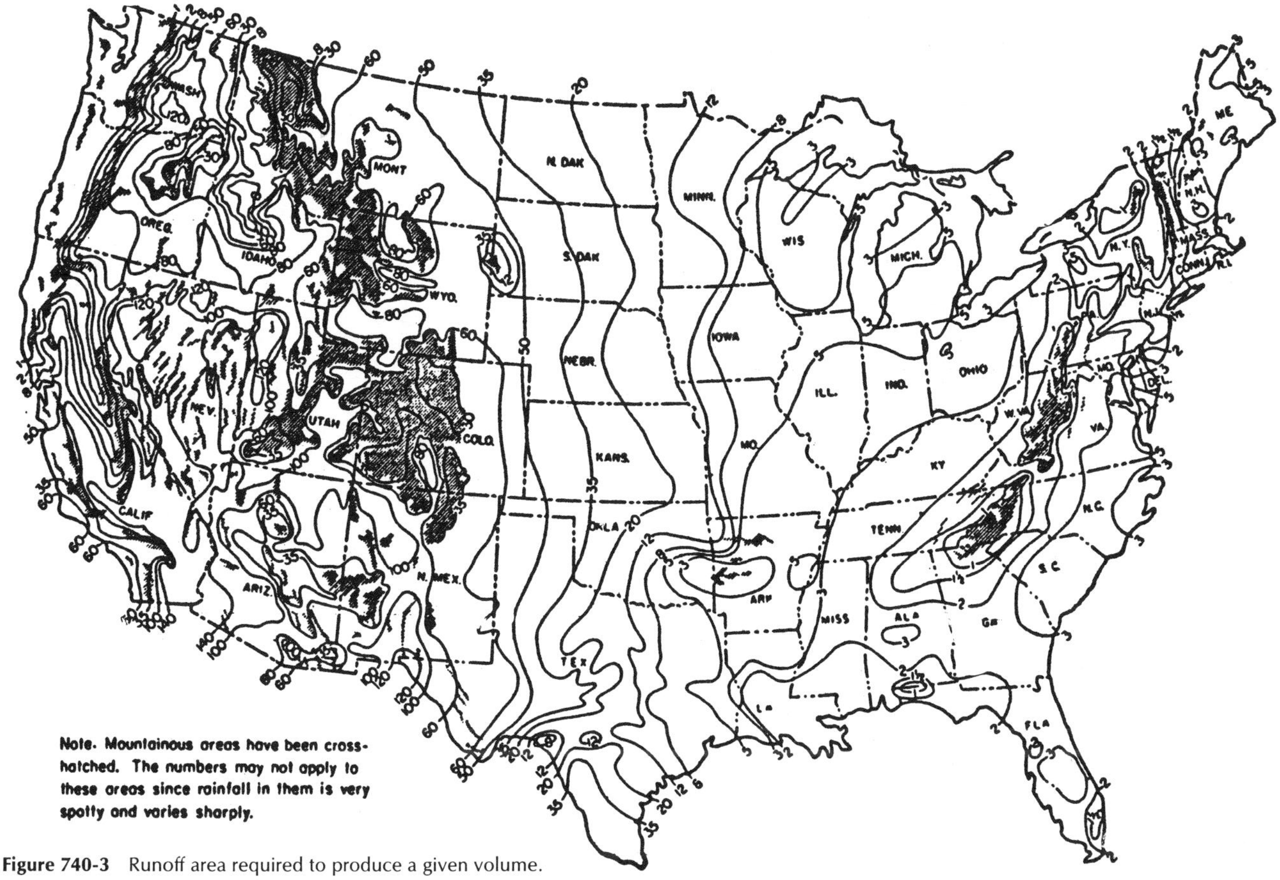
Note. Mountainous areas have been cross-hatched. The numbers may not apply to these areas since rainfall in them is very spotty and varies sharply.

Figure 740-3 Runoff area required to produce a given volume.

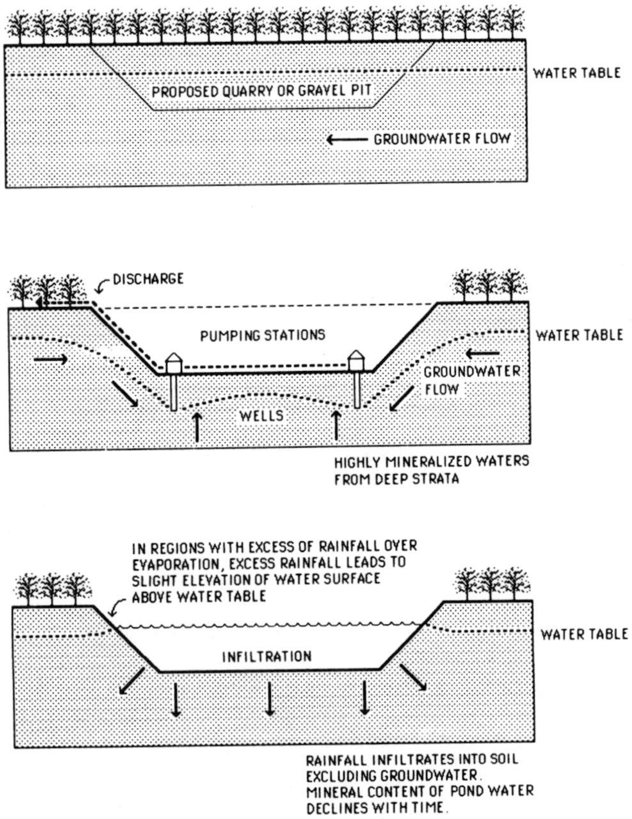
WATER TABLE
PROPOSED QUARRY OR GRAVEL PIT
GROUNDWATER FLOW
DISCHARGE
PUMPING STATIONS
WATER TABLE
GROUNDWATER FLOW
WELLS
HIGHLY MINERALIZED WATERS FROM DEEP STRATA
IN REGIONS WITH EXCESS OF RAINFALL OVER EVAPORATION, EXCESS RAINFALL LEADS TO SLIGHT ELEVATION OF WATER SURFACE ABOVE WATER TABLE
WATER TABLE
INFILTRATION
RAINFALL INFILTRATES INTO SOIL EXCLUDING GROUNDWATER. MINERAL CONTENT OF POND WATER DECLINES WITH TIME.

Figure 740-4 Hydrologic progression in permeable soils with a flat water table.

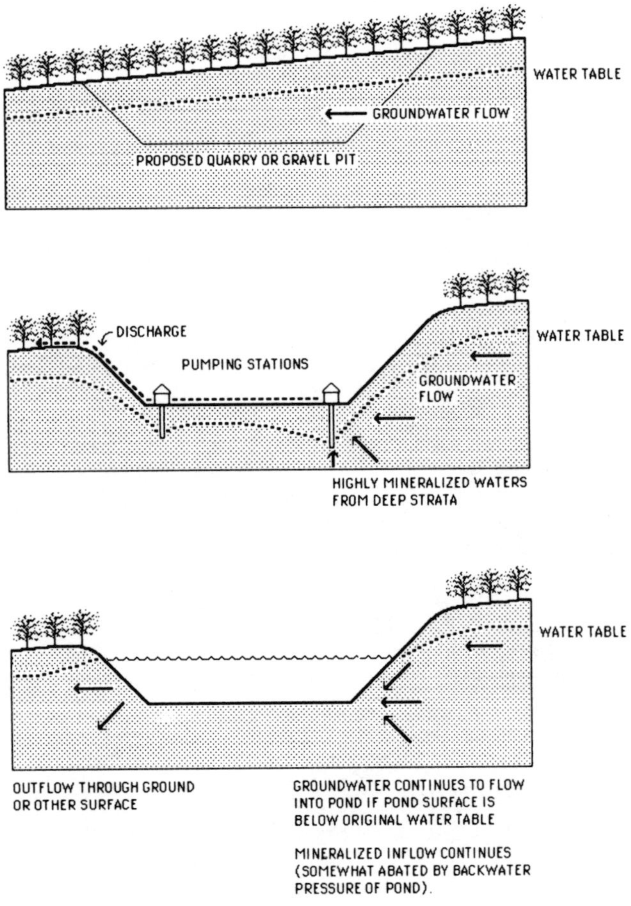
WATER TABLE
GROUNDWATER FLOW
PROPOSED QUARRY OR GRAVEL PIT
DISCHARGE
PUMPING STATIONS
WATER TABLE
GROUNDWATER FLOW
HIGHLY MINERALIZED WATERS FROM DEEP STRATA
WATER TABLE
OUTFLOW THROUGH GROUND OR OTHER SURFACE
GROUNDWATER CONTINUES TO FLOW INTO POND IF POND SURFACE IS BELOW ORIGINAL WATER TABLE
MINERALIZED INFLOW CONTINUES (SOMEWHAT ABATED BY BACKWATER PRESSURE OF POND).

Figure 740-5 Hydrologic progression in permeable soils with a sloping water table.

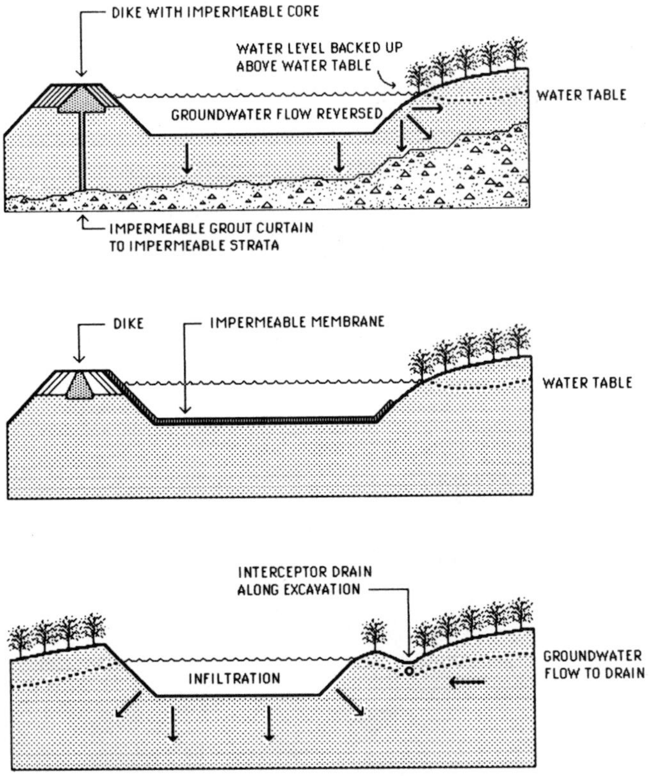
DIKE WITH IMPERMEABLE CORE
WATER LEVEL BACKED UP ABOVE WATER TABLE
WATER TABLE
GROUNDWATER FLOW REVERSED
IMPERMEABLE GROUT CURTAIN TO IMPERMEABLE STRATA
DIKE
IMPERMEABLE MEMBRANE
WATER TABLE
INTERCEPTOR DRAIN ALONG EXCAVATION
INFILTRATION
GROUNDWATER FLOW TO DRAIN

Figure 740-6 Correction strategies if pond surface is below original water table.

algae. Over time, this vegetation can be expected to occur through natural processes, but it can also be introduced artificially.

Watershed Considerations:

The watershed of a swimming pond need not be much larger than what is necessary to provide adequate makeup water for leakage and evaporation in a dry year, and it should not be large enough to yield more runoff in a wet year to drop the reservoir's storage ratio below 1. If this happens, it tends to create problems of increased sediment.

Equally important, the nutrient intake (especially phosphates) of the watershed must be carefully controlled to inhibit eutrophication. Common sources of phosphates are geologic in origin (i.e., springs, seeps, and geohydrologic upwellings) and urban in origin (runoff from roofs, pavements, etc.).

To control urban runoff, a development's drainage that would normally flow into the pond should either be filtered in some way or diverted around the pond by ditch or culvert, including diversion of the entire inflow stream if necessary.

To control geologic phosphate sources, the surface streams that flow into the impoundment should be tested. If they are phosphate-enriched (more than 15 parts per billion), they should be excluded or an alternative site should be found.

Construction of Small Dams:

Where a small dam or dike is needed tc help retain water, several considerations regarding the location, design, and construction of the dam are important. Sectior 420: Small Dams, discusses these and pro vides information on the design and con struction of several types of dams.

3.5 Excavated Ponds

General:

Ponds are sometimes feasible in borrow pit excavations and quarries. Their suitability for swimming is partially a function of their water quality and partially a function of safety (i.e., their form and depth). The latter can often be improved by grading.

Water Supply and Quality:

Ponds in borrow pits or quarries are usually fed by a mixture of rainwater, runoff, and groundwater. If the runoff and groundwater are bacterially clean and low in phosphates (i.e., less than 15 parts per billion), the pond is likely to be attractive to swimmers regardless of the source of the water. However, where the runoff or groundwater is a problem either geologically or because of improper disposal of wastes in the region, the monitoring and control of runoff and groundwater flow into the pond is essential to the pond's acceptability.

Surface runoff can be controlled by ditching and culverting, but groundwater flows must be controlled by the design of the excavation in order to achieve a hydrostatic balance between rainwater and groundwater that excludes the unwanted groundwater.

Figure 740-4 shows the hydrologic progression that would occur in the development of a borrow pit in readily permeable soils in an area with a flat or nearly flat water table. Note that the natural processes in regions with an excess of rainfall over evaporation (average year, not just dry year) will normally result in a clean, transparent water body.

Excavation in an area with a sloping water table, however, will not produce the same effect unless carefully designed. Figure 740-5 shows a similar progression with a sloping water table.

In the case illustrated, with the resulting pond lower than the water table, groundwater will continue to flow in, and if the groundwater contains phosphates from any source, the pond is likely to become eutrophic. Correction of this condition is possible. Figure 740-6 shows several possible correction strategies, all costly.

REFERENCES

Cowen, W. F., and G. F. Lee. "Phosphorus Availability in Particulate Materials Transported by Urban Runoff," *Journal of the Water Pollution Control Federation,* vol. 48, no. 3, March 1976.

Novotny, Vladimir, and Gordon Chesters. *Handbook of Nonpoint Pollution Sources and Management,* Van Nostrand Reinhold, New York, 1981.

Wanielista, M. P., Y. A. Yousef, and J. S. Taylor. *Stormwater Management to Improve Lake Water Quality,* National Technical Information Service (order no. PB82-227711), 5285 Port Royal Road, Springfield, VA, 1982.

Whipple, William, et al. *Stormwater Management in Urbanizing Areas,* Prentice-Hall, Englewood Cliffs, NJ, 1983. ■

section 750: Irrigation

CREDITS

Contributor:

Erich O. Wittig
The Toro Company
Riverside, California

Advisors/Reviewers:

Ken Killian
Killian Design Group, Inc.
Howard, Illinois

Jeffrey D. Brauer
Golfscapes, Inc.
Dallas, Texas

Richard Lakutis
The Architects Collaborative, Inc.
Cambridge, Massachusetts

Stephen W. Smith
EDAW, Inc.
Fort Collins, Colorado

John Hooper
Hooper Engineering, Ltd.
Palintine, Illinois

Michael Holland
Sasaki Associates, Inc.
Watertown, Massachusetts

CONTENTS

1.0 INTRODUCTION

1.1 General

Irrigation is sometimes necessary to keep landscapes at an optimum functional or aesthetical peak. Although all geographic areas receive rainfall sufficient to sustain indigenous plant materials growing under natural conditions, situations involving introduced species, or species growing under less-than-ideal conditions, often require some form of irrigation to maintain healthy plant growth.

This section focuses on various types of irrigation systems and on means for selecting the most economical system for any given situation.

1.2 Important Considerations

Plant Growth Requirements:

The quantity of water necessary for healthy plant growth must be determined in order to design an irrigation system of highest efficiency. If growth conditions are less than ideal, supplemental water may be necessary to overcome incidences of plant stress.

Some plantings may require irrigation during construction processes, or during and after transplantation until established. A controlled application of water will greatly improve the germination rate in seeded areas and will enable seedlings to develop to maturity. Turfgrass is used most often in nonnative environments, and even though some varieties are drought-tolerant, a regular schedule of water is necessary to maintain a green, healthy turf.

Conservation of Water:

Conservation of water is an important ecological issue. Along with water depletion, common problems include saltwater intrusion and land subsidence. The rising cost of water requires efficient use and management of all water resources.

Automatic sprinkler systems are designed to increase the efficiency of landscape water usage. Efficiency is accomplished by first determining which plant materials require irrigation and how much water is required, and then designing irrigation systems which apply that water with a minimum of wastage.

Effluent water is being used in many areas as a conservation measure, with considerable success. (Refer to 2.4 Effluent Water in this section for more information.)

2.0 WATER SOURCES

2.1 Municipal Water

Most landscape projects use potable water provided by the local water district.

Research necessary at the outset of an irrigation project includes:

1. The possibility of an alternative source of water that would be more cost-effective on a long-term basis.

2. A determination of existing static pressure in municipal lines (including high and low times), of the size of the main line in closest proximity to the project site, and of any local codes that may be pertinent to the installation of an irrigation system.

3. Investigation into municipal water and sewer rates, based on water meter readings. Separate water meters for the irrigation system may exclude owners from paying a sewer surcharge.

2.2 Lakes, Ponds, Reservoirs, Streams, and Rivers

Natural bodies of water can be used very effectively, depending on the *riparian rights* of that water.

Design considerations include:

1. Pump capabilities and the power (usually electric) required to operate the pump.

2. The quality of water at different seasons during usage (filtration must usually be provided).

3. The possibility of having to transport water from one source to a holding pond or reservoir (depending on the water requirements). This is especially common in golf course applications, where even potable city water is used on occasion to maintain water levels in a body of water that is ultimately used for irrigation.

2.3 Wells

High water tables are a good source of irrigation water, even for small installations.

Design considerations include:

1. The amount of water available, i.e., how much consistent flow is realized (sometimes water is available, but replenishment is not achieved at a rate adequate for the system's demand).

2. The amount of sand particles pumped with the water. Sprinkler heads with small orifices in the nozzle may have to be avoided.

2.4 Effluent Water

Definitions:

Effluent water (also referred to as recycled water, gray water, sewage effluent, wastewater, and recycled sewage) is basically liquid sewage from a municipal sewage plant or industrial plant which has been

TABLE 750-1
Rainfall and Evapotranspiration Data (Example)

Massachusetts	*Jan.*	*Feb.*	*Mar.*	*Apr.*	*May*	*June*	*July*	*Aug.*	*Sept.*	*Oct.*	*Nov.*	*Dec.*	*Total*
Western (Pittsfield)													
RF	3.39	2.69	3.56	3.90	4.00	3.96	4.41	3.73	4.43	3.25	4.06	3.41	44.79
EVT	0.00	0.00	0.46	1.51	3.33	4.78	5.77	4.93	3.05	1.61	0.58	0.00	26.02
DIFF	3.39	2.69	3.10	2.39	0.67	−0.82	−1.36	−1.20	1.38	1.64	3.48	3.41	18.77
Central (Springfield)													
RF	3.86	3.10	4.09	3.84	3.58	3.71	3.60	3.79	3.95	3.23	4.14	3.60	44.49
EVT	0.00	0.00	0.67	1.79	3.66	5.30	6.38	5.50	3.55	1.89	0.76	0.00	29.50
DIFF	3.86	3.10	3.42	2.05	−0.08	−1.59	−2.78	−1.71	0.40	1.34	3.38	3.60	14.99
Coastal (Boston)													
RF	4.04	3.37	4.19	3.86	3.23	3.17	2.85	3.85	3.64	3.33	4.11	3.73	43.37
EVT	0.00	0.00	0.73	1.71	3.37	4.95	6.18	5.48	3.58	2.05	0.87	0.30	29.22
DIFF	4.04	3.37	3.46	2.15	−0.14	−1.78	−3.33	−1.63	0.06	1.28	3.24	3.43	14.15

Note: RF—rainfall, EVT—evapotranspiration rate, DIFF—the average amount of water needed to be added per month to sustain healthy turf.

treated and is ready for disposal. Effluent water is more than 99 percent pure water and by recent federal legislation is treated in a manner similar to drinking water.

In the United States, the vast majority of effluent water is pumped into rivers or streams (eventually to end up in the ocean), although some is currently used in agriculture to irrigate field crops. Many industrial plants are using their own effluent to irrigate their grounds, and a number of golf courses have begun to use effluent water for irrigation. Some new communities have begun to build networks of pipe (separate from potable water and sewage lines) for carrying effluent water. In such communities, effluent water would not be affected by the possibility of rationing.

Most states in the United States do not bar the use of effluent to irrigate turfgrasses. Not only can the use of effluent be a real aid to turfgrass maintenance, but it can serve to replenish groundwater resources. Turfgrass will effectively remove most of the impurities in effluent, and percolation through the soil will remove the remainder.

Acquisition:

Both municipal and industrial sewage treatment plants can supply effluent water for use in irrigation. The facilities should be relatively close to the site requiring irrigation, since piping long distances is usually cost-prohibitive. Facilities will provide effluent in volumes ranging from a few thousand gallons to several million gallons or liters per day.

Analysis:

Effluent water available from any source should be analyzed for its suitability as irrigation water. Not all effluent can be used on turfgrasses, for instance. Chemicals that exist in the potable water supply of a municipality will exist in even greater concentrations in its effluent water (sometimes at a level toxic to plants); chemicals such as boron and sodium are especially important to monitor. The salt levels may not be toxic, but a means may have to be provided to prevent the problem of salt buildup.

The levels of nitrogen, phosphorus, and potassium found in most effluent are often high enough that users may only have to use one-fourth as much fertilizer as without effluent water, or sometimes none at all.

Permits and Regulations:

When effluent water is used for irrigation, permits have to be secured from appropriate authorities. Pollution control agencies will be involved, as well as county health departments.

Public Attention:

It is best not to keep information from anyone who has a right to know about what is being done. There is no reason to be secretive about using effluent for landscape irrigation purposes, but public attention will nevertheless be drawn to practices that seem potentially harmful.

Assessing Water Requirements:

Before an agreement can be signed with a municipal agency or industrial treatment plant to accept effluent for irrigation, the amount of water required to irrigate the site must be accurately calculated. Overcommitments are as problematic as undercommitments.

3.0 DESIGN CRITERIA

3.1 Climatic Conditions

Rainfall:

The amount of annual rainfall in a given area will determine the selection of plant materials as well as the type of irrigation system most appropriate in that area. The U.S. Weather Service keeps annual rainfall data for the entire United States but such data alone will not determine whether or not an irrigation system is necessary in any particular region.

Six major factors determine the need to apply water in quantities greater than annual precipitation. These are: (1) the length of the growing season, (2) the rainfall or precipitation rate (during the growing season), (3) the evaporation rate, (4) the type of soil present, (5) the transpiration rate of the plants to be irrigated, and (6) the water requirements of the plant materials. In this regard, the factor of greatest importance is the *water deficit,* i.e., the difference during the growing season between natural precipitation and the amount of water required for satisfactory growth.

Rainfall and evapotranspiration data for the United States, Canada, and other parts of the world are readily available. In the United States, local offices of the U.S. Weather Service can provide rainfall data. Data on evapotranspiration are available in a report by Marvin E. Jensen (ed.), *Consumptive Use of Water and Irrigation Water Requirements* (cited in the References at the end of this section).

Table 750-1 is an example of rainfall and evapotranspiration data for the state of Massachusetts.

Wind:

Wind will disrupt the uniform distribution of water from a conventional irrigation system, causing areas not intended to be watered to be irrigated and causing areas intended to be watered to develop dry spots. Timers should be set to irrigate when the wind speeds are minimal, such as in the early morning hours. In addition, sprinkler head spacing, arc, and location can be designed to compensate for prevailing winds. Sprinkler heads with lower trajectories and larger orifice sizes can also be used.

Windy areas also have a greater evaporation rate than do similar areas that are not windy and thus may require more water.

3.2 Soil Characteristics

The percolation rate is an important characteristic influencing the design of conventional irrigation systems, and capillary action becomes important when lateral movement of water is required (as in drip systems and furrow flooding). In drip irrigation, the area of soil wetness is commonly referred to as the *onion* since a soil profile in a loam soil will produce a wet area shaped like an onion. A sandy soil will produce a shape similar to a carrot.

With a conventional sprinkler system, the main objective is to apply water at a rate that the soil can accept, without causing runoff. A typical soil will accept about ⅓ in (8 mm) of water per hour before runoff occurs. Some sprinkler systems have a precipitation rate as high as 4 in (100 mm) per hour. Station timing can be adjusted according to the percolation rate of the soil and the precipitation rate of the sprinkler. Often, a repeat cycle or additional watering cycles of shorter duration must be planned in order to prevent runoff.

Precipitation rates for sprinklers in inches per hour (in/h) or milliliters per hour (mlh) can be calculated by using the three formulas below. The first two formulas apply only to systems using matched precipitation heads (i.e., a quarter-circle head emits exactly one-quarter that of a full circle head).

Precipitation rate formulas (in/h or mlh): For triangle-spaced sprinklers with matched full-circle heads:

$$\text{in/h} = \frac{\text{GPM} \times 96.3^{*}}{(\text{spacing})^2}$$

$$\left[\text{mlh} = \frac{\text{liters} \times 60}{(\text{spacing})^2 \times 0.866}\right]$$

*96.3 is a constant based on the fact that l gal = 231 in^3 and there are 144 in^2/ft^2; thus, 231/144 = 1.604 in/(ft^2) (gpm), and 1.604 × 60 minutes = 96.3 in/(ft^2) (hour).

For square-spaced sprinklers with matched full-circle heads:

$$\text{in/h} = \frac{\text{GPM} \times 96.3\,^{*}}{(\text{spacing})^2}$$

$$\left[\text{mlh} = \frac{\text{liters} \times 60}{(\text{spacing})^2}\right]$$

For sprinkler heads that are not matched and for layouts with irregular spacing of sprinkler heads, an *average precipitation rate* can be determined by using the following formula:

$$\text{in/h} = \frac{\text{total gpm of heads within a zone} \times 96.3^{*}}{\text{square feet of the zone}}$$

$$\left[\frac{\text{mlh} = \text{liters} \times 60}{\text{meters}^2}\right]$$

With drip irrigation systems, it is important to determine the extent of the root zone to be irrigated and then to design the *onion* to envelop that zone. In areas of infrequent rainfall, where the primary source of water is the drip system, the roots will seek that onion. Where irrigation is supplemental, the designs are more critical because the roots are more dispersed. Sandy soils may require the use of more emitters and shorter watering cycles.

3.3 Plant Materials

A knowledge of plant materials is invaluable when designing irrigation systems. All plants have special requirements which have to be met if optimum health and physical appearance are to be maintained. For instance, roses are subject to powdery mildew, rust, and other diseases if subjected to water on their leaves (as are a host of other plants), and plants like camellias, azaleas, and rhododendrons prefer to be (and look their best when) watered from an overhead system.

3.4 Available Watering Time

Available watering time is usually a concern only when designing large projects, such as golf courses. After the water requirements and the number of hours available to water have been determined, the pump size can be determined (or the size of the main line if connecting to the municipal water). The more sprinklers that are on at any given time, the greater the water demand will be and the larger the water source required.

Early morning hours are usually the best time to water because wind speeds are typically low, evaporation is at a minimum, and plant leaves do not remain wet for long periods of time.

*96.3 is a constant based on the fact that l gal = 231 in^3 and there are 144 in^2/ft^2; thus, 231/144 = 1.604 in/(ft^2) (gpm), and 1.604 × 60 minutes = 96.3 in/(ft^2) (hour).

3.5 Property Size and Shape

In landscape projects, the shapes of the areas to be irrigated seldom lend themselves to an exact equilateral triangular spacing of sprinklers (as is recommended by sprinkler manufacturers). Most small system designs tend to use square spacing unless the area is a free-form or irregular shape. Large areas like athletic fields, however, are typically designed for triangular spacing.

3.6 Location of Buildings, Trees, and Other Fixed Objects

Fixed objects have to be accounted for in the design of sprinkler systems and should be marked on a plot plan at the outset of the project. Sprinklers should not spray directly into a tree or shrub at close range because of possible harm to the plant and because a void results on the opposite side of the disrupting object. Buildings located within the sprinkler pattern cause a wasting of water, create saturated areas on the ground, and may cause brick and other types of masonry to effloresce (become powdery), and cause unsightly discoloration.

Concern should also be given to walkways and property lines. Some walkway systems are sufficiently complex that the most efficient design will simply ignore the walkways and include these areas as part of the pattern. This often allows the use of larger rotating heads instead of spray heads. However, the use of the walkway and local codes may preclude such efficiency. The likelihood of surprised or annoyed pedestrians is also a consideration.

If overthrow of water will occur on neighboring property, the owners should be contacted before proceeding with the design.

3.7 Elevation Changes

Any site with significant elevation differences will require the use of a topographic map. Pressure in pounds per square inch (psi) or kilopascal (kPa) is an important factor in an irrigation system. Each foot of elevation change brings a corresponding change in pressure of 0.433 psi (2.986 kPa). It is important that the sprinkler pressure recommended by the manufacturer be realized. Too little pressure will alter the pattern and create dry spots and will sometimes prevent a rotating head from rotating. Excessive pressure will cause such atomization that much of the water will be lost to the atmosphere.

Another problem associated with significant changes in elevation is low-head drainage; that is, when a valve is turned off, the sprinkler at the lowest elevation in that system will continue to drain until all pipes located higher than that head are void of water. This may necessitate the use of check valves or the selection of heads with built-in check valves. On large turfgrass projects, another solution may be to design valve-in-heads, i.e., heads with an automatic valve built into the unit or valve under head.

On landscape projects with built-up berms, similar considerations are important. Berms are sometimes built from an outside source of soil which may differ, in terms of drainage characteristics, from existing on-site soils. Berms will also drain faster than level ground because of slope. Berms are often irrigated by a separate station, or, alternatively, system layouts are designed so that berms will receive more water. Careful attention should also be given to the actual location of the sprinklers and the plant materials. For example, sprinklers placed at the bottom edge of a mound can cut into the base of plants located higher up on the mound.

3.8 Economic Considerations

The costs of an irrigation system are difficult to determine until a design and a set of specifications have been completed. The costs also vary significantly from one geographic area to another. On a price-per-square-foot basis, large turf areas cost considerably less to irrigate than do areas consisting of smaller mixed plantings. Installation techniques and maintenance problems also have to be considered. Proper hydraulic engineering will prevent costly problems later in the life of a system.

The long-term maintenance expense of an irrigation system is an important consideration. For example, the initial cost of a pop-up sprinkler head may exceed that of a stationary head, but in a lawn area the savings are rapidly lost to additional maintenance expenses. Vandalism is also an issue especially with systems that include exposed components.

4.0 TYPES OF IRRIGATION

4.1 Sprinkler Irrigation Systems

Sprinkler irrigation systems refer to those with sprinkler heads. Because these systems are so widely used, they are given detailed coverage in 6.0 Hydraulics Engineering and 7.0 Sprinkler Irrigation Systems later in this section.

4.2 Quick-Coupler Systems

Often referred to as a *snap-valve system* or *manual system,* a *quick coupler* is a valve which is opened when a quick-coupler key is inserted (Figure 750-1). As the key is rotated, an increase in water volume is realized, much as when turning the handle on a hose bibb. A hose or sprinkler head can be attached to the key to distribute the water as required. Even on totally automatic system designs, quick couplers are often dispersed throughout the design to provide additional water access for maintenance purposes. On golf course and other large turfgrass projects, quick couplers are spaced at appropriate intervals to accommodate large rotary heads. For reasons of water economy and lack of control, however, the use of quick couplers on large turfgrass projects is declining in favor of a fully automatic sprinkler system.

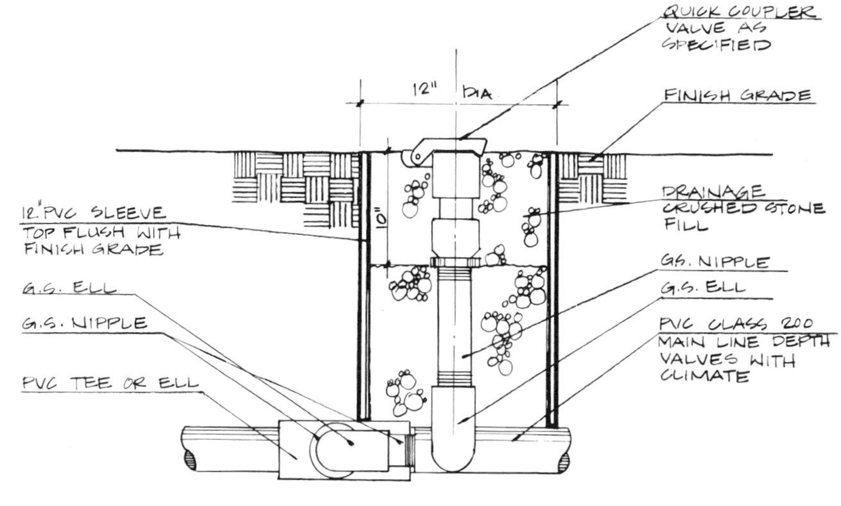
QUICK COUPLER VALVE AS SPECIFIED
12" DIA
FINISH GRADE
10"
12" PVC SLEEVE TOP FLUSH WITH FINISH GRADE
DRAINAGE CRUSHED STONE FILL
GS. NIPPLE
G.S. ELL
G.S. ELL
G.S. NIPPLE
PVC CLASS 200 MAIN LINE DEPTH VALVES WITH CLIMATE
PVC TEE OR ELL

Figure 750-1 Quick-coupler valve.

4.3 Drip/Trickle Systems

Although drip systems are most applicable to types of agriculture in which the plant material is of the same variety, with uniform size and spacing, they are increasingly being designed into landscape projects because of their efficiency. The orifices of a drip system are small, however, and can sometimes become clogged if the system is improperly designed for the purpose intended.

The primary element of a drip system is the emitter, of which several types are available (Figure 750-2). Some emit droplets of water, while others (referred to as *aerosol* emitters) emit minute streams of water. Generally, emitters fall into one of two categories: compensating emitters and noncompensating emitters. Noncompensating emitters will release a set amount of water at a given pressure (determined by graphs provided by the manufacturer); greater pressures emit more water, and lower pressures emit less water. Friction loss and elevation changes have to be carefully determined when using noncompensating emitters.

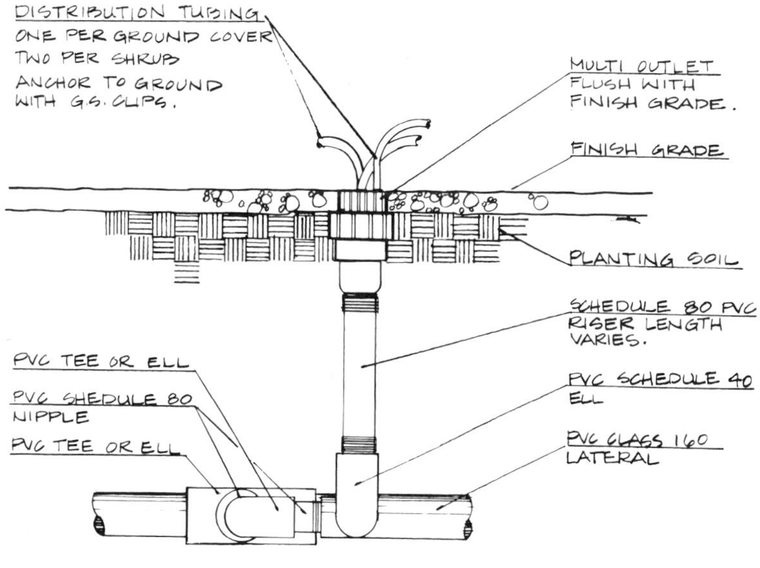
DISTRIBUTION TUBING ONE PER GROUND COVER TWO PER SHRUB ANCHOR TO GROUND WITH G.S. CLIPS.
MULTI OUTLET FLUSH WITH FINISH GRADE.
FINISH GRADE
PLANTING SOIL
SCHEDULE 80 PVC RISER LENGTH VARIES.
PVC TEE OR ELL
PVC SCHEDULE 40 ELL
PVC SHEDULE 80 NIPPLE
PVC TEE OR ELL
PVC CLASS 160 LATERAL

Figure 750-2 Typical drip emitter.

For maximum efficiency in water use, all systems with long pipe runs or significant elevation changes are best designed with pressure compensating emitters. These are designed to compensate for pressure differences and will emit a predetermined amount of water through each emitter at a uniform rate within a particular pressure range.

Since clogging is sometimes a problem with drip irrigation systems, special attention should be given to filtration design. When the water source for an irrigation system is potable or otherwise clean and free of visible particulates, screen filters are usually adequate to protect the system from any pipe breaks upstream. Exceptions occur in some areas when diatomaceous skeletal remains occur in the form of a slime during certain seasons (usually late summer and fall).

Diatomaceous slime will accumulate rapidly around the screen filter, causing flow loss downstream (flow loss is often an indicator of a dirty filter). As pressure builds up at the filter, slimy debris is forced through the screen and eventually clogs the emitters. Similar problems with slimy material exist if the pipe is not absolutely opaque (i.e., is subjected to sunlight) because algae can grow on the internal walls of the pipe and eventually break free. Algal growth can be eliminated by specifying quality opaque drip hose and by burying all other pipe. When slimy matter is encountered in the source water, a sand filter should be used. For small systems in which a sand filter would not be economically practical, the maintenance schedule should include frequent filter cleaning.

Filters should be located throughout larger drip systems so that a pipe break near the beginning of the system will not contaminate the entire system. Ideally, the system should be buried, yet accessible. Figures 750-3 through 750-7 show typical installations of both single- and multi-outlet emitters.

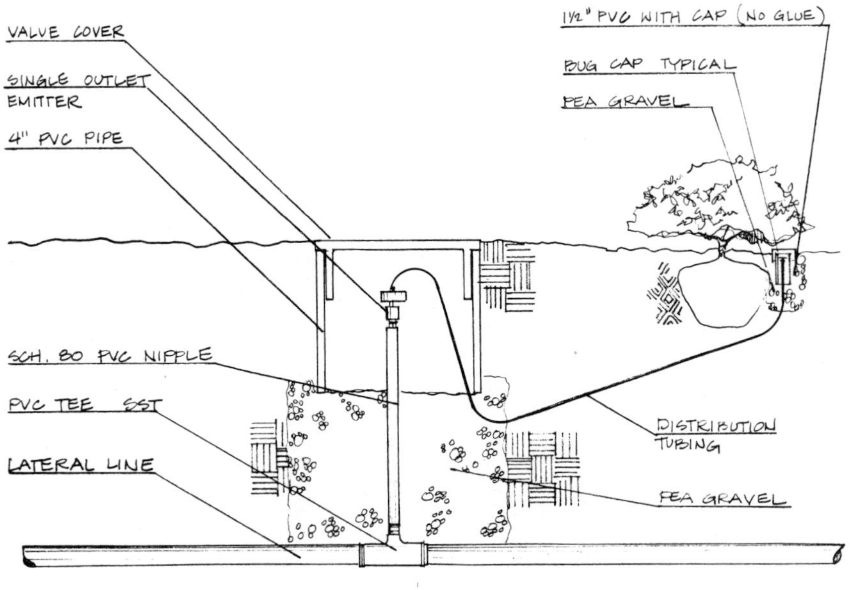
VALVE COVER
SINGLE OUTLET EMITTER
4" PVC PIPE
SCH. 80 PVC NIPPLE
PVC TEE SST
LATERAL LINE
1½" PVC WITH CAP (NO GLUE)
BUG CAP TYPICAL
PEA GRAVEL
DISTRIBUTION TUBING
PEA GRAVEL

Figure 750-3 Single-outlet emitter installation (lateral line).

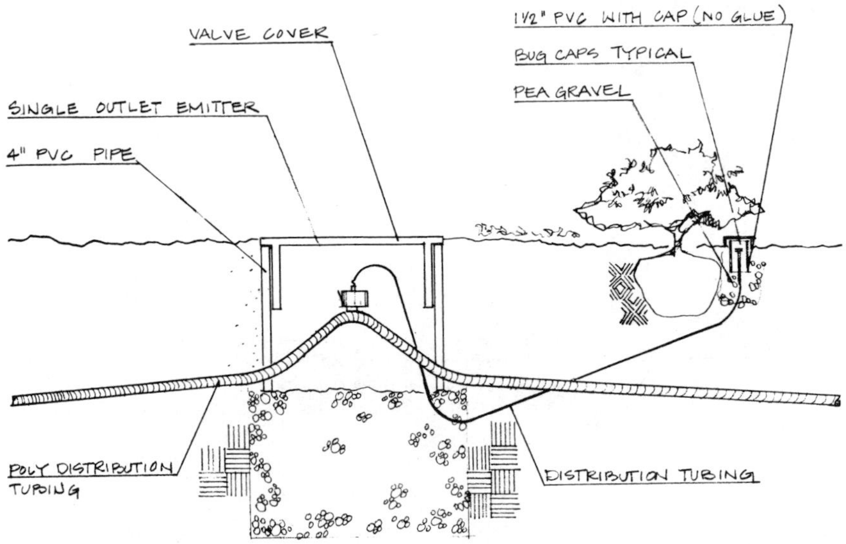
VALVE COVER
SINGLE OUTLET EMITTER
4" PVC PIPE
1½" PVC WITH CAP (NO GLUE)
BUG CAPS TYPICAL
PEA GRAVEL
POLY DISTRIBUTION TUBING
DISTRIBUTION TUBING

Figure 750-4 Single-outlet emitter installation (polyvinyl tubing).

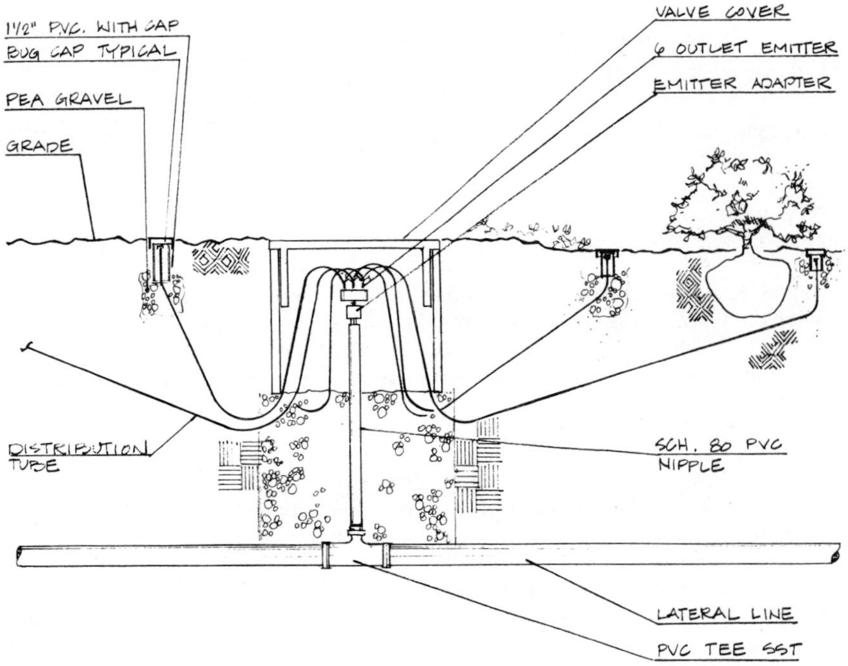
1½" PVC. WITH CAP
BUG CAP TYPICAL
PEA GRAVEL
GRADE
VALVE COVER
6 OUTLET EMITTER
EMITTER ADAPTER
DISTRIBUTION TUBE
SCH. 80 PVC NIPPLE
LATERAL LINE
PVC TEE SST

Figure 750-5 Multiple-outlet emitter installation (lateral line). Future distribution tubes can be installed but not connected.

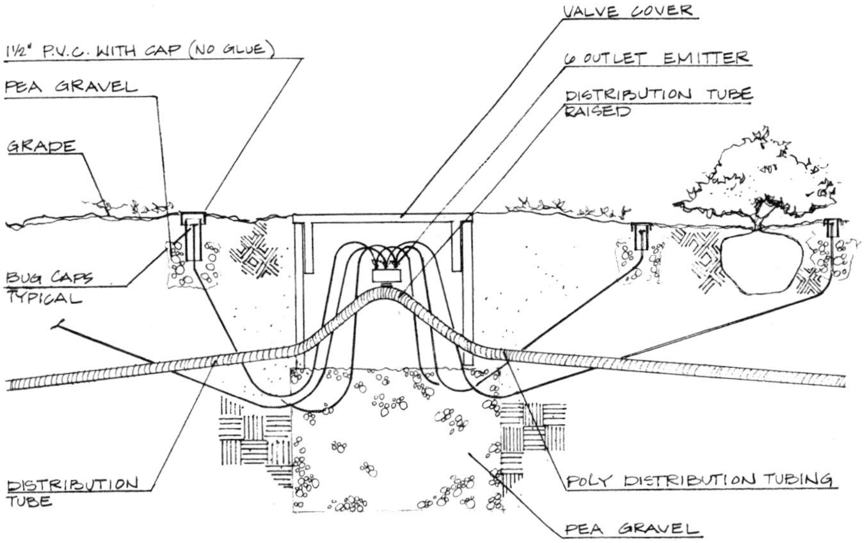
VALVE COVER
1½" P.V.C. WITH CAP (NO GLUE)
6 OUTLET EMITTER
PEA GRAVEL
DISTRIBUTION TUBE RAISED
GRADE
BUG CAPS TYPICAL
DISTRIBUTION TUBE
POLY DISTRIBUTION TUBING
PEA GRAVEL

Figure 750-6 Multiple-outlet emitter installation (polyvinyl tubing).

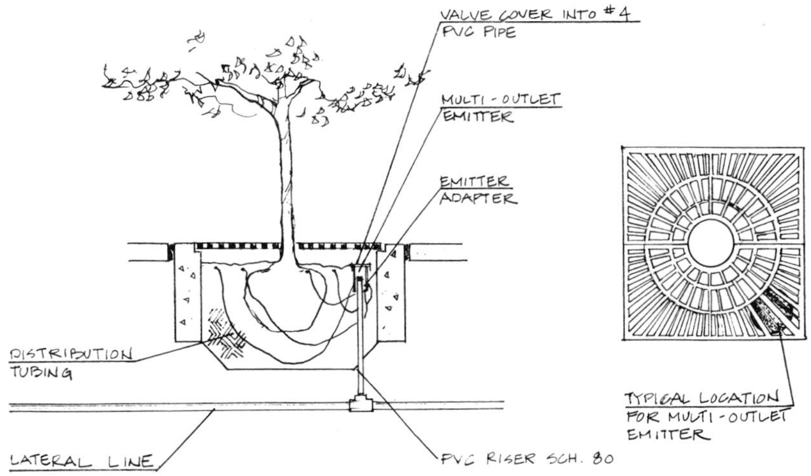
VALVE COVER INTO #4 PVC PIPE
MULTI - OUTLET EMITTER
EMITTER ADAPTER
DISTRIBUTION TUBING
TYPICAL LOCATION FOR MULTI - OUTLET EMITTER
LATERAL LINE
PVC RISER SCH. 80

Figure 750-7 Typical emitter installation for trees with tree grates.

5.0 APPLICATION AND DESIGN

5.1 Golf Course Irrigation

Specialized systems for golf course irrigation often provide functions beyond that of satisfying the water requirements of turfgrasses, although that is their primary function. For instance, there can be provided a syringe cycle, which is a sprinkle cycle that is operated from the central control for only a few minutes, rather than the full irrigation cycle. Syringe cycles are used to provide earlier play schedules by eliminating dew or frost from tees and greens. During hot afternoons, a short syringe cycle will add humidity to the air, which can reduce stress on turfgrasses.

The desire for greens and fairways that are closely cropped—as well as the traffic from golf carts, heavy mowing equipment, and golfers—places unusual stress on the turfgrasses of most golf courses. Turfgrasses must be kept in a healthy, turgid state if they are to remain resilient to such use. Although designing the irrigation system for golf courses is not difficult, it is an extensive procedure and does require a good understanding of pumps and special design techniques. Consultation with irrigation specialists, golf course architects, and manufacturers of irrigation equipment is recommended.

5.2 Interior Plantings

Interior plantings often have special irrigation requirements that are best accomplished manually. A quick coupler or a hose bib can be located at each planted area in order to avoid extensive dragging of hose line. The type of irrigation employed for interior plantings will largely depend on the plant materials involved and the microclimatic conditions present. Some planting designs require nozzles that fog an area (to increase the humidity level), and some require sprays to keep plant leaves clean. Some are best watered by drip systems so that an appropriate amount of water is delivered to each plant.

5.3 Athletic Fields

The components of irrigation systems for athletic fields must be as inconspicuous as possible, because anything that projects above ground will become both a safety hazard and subject to vandalism. Sprinkler heads with a low profile are preferable. Several types of heads are available that are designed especially for athletic fields.

Since athletic fields are standard in measurement, most sprinkler manufacturers have typical designs available on request. Most manufacturers also have heads with rubber covers, or have rubber cover kits available.

5.4 Other Applications

Sprinkler systems are available that are specially designed for dust control, including some for use during construction and some for clay tennis courts, etc.

6.0 HYDRAULICS ENGINEERING

In all piped irrigation systems, designs will include calculations for hydraulic pressure (measured in psi or kPa), velocity (measured in fps or m/s), and flow (measured in gpm or mlh).

6.1 Sprinkler Water Requirement

Sprinklers are designed by manufacturers to emit a specific amount of water (gpm or mlh) at a specific pressure (psi or kPa). These data will vary by type of head and between manufacturers. Most manufacturers will list a range of pressures for a particular head, with the corresponding gallons (ml) and radius of throw at each pressure listed.

Velocity is a relevant quotient not in terms of feet per second (m/s), but rather in terms of radius of throw. This will determine the spacing of the sprinkler heads. Sprinkler charts will show that the pressure (psi), flowrate (gpm), and radius of throw are all relative to one another. As one value increases, the other two will also increase. However, this relationship will not hold true in pressure ranges that exceed the chart, since excess atomization caused by excess pressure will actually decrease the radius of throw. Conversely, a pressure which is less than that listed in a manufacturer's chart will distort the distribution pattern to a point at which it is no longer functional. In the case of rotating heads, some may not rotate.

The ideal working pressure of a particular sprinkler head, if not specifically listed by the manufacturer, will usually fall near the middle to high end of the pressures listed. The results achieved at this middle to high end psi are a maximum radius, an ideal water breakup, and a uniform rotation for the rotating heads.

6.2 Pipe Sizing

In any irrigation system, the sizing and routing of pipe should be done in a matter which is most economical during installation, yet which is also durable to the extent that unnecessary long-term maintenance and repair will be avoided. The particular sprinkler heads selected, the nozzle sizes, and the number of heads running together determine the required flowrate (gpm or mlh).

The static pressure in a system must be greater than the sprinkler head requirement, since a certain amount of pressure is always lost to friction (unless there is downhill elevation change or a booster pump which will increase pressure). The friction loss varies with the length of pipe, the type of pipe, the pipe size, and the quantity and speed at which the water is moving through the pipe. Pipe fittings also contribute to friction loss, especially fittings (such as 90-degree elbows) that cause a major change in water direction. This is normally significant; however, it should be noted that some pipe friction-loss charts account for an average number of fittings in a system (Table 750-2). When working on small areas that require many fittings, additional friction loss should be calculated by using a *fitting friction-loss chart.* These are normally included as part of the data supplied with various manufacturers' charts for pipe friction loss and are not included here.

The velocity of water in a system is perhaps the most overlooked aspect of pipe sizing. Although a system with excess velocities will still function, problems of surge pressure and water hammer can be minimized by keeping the velocities throughout the pipe at 5 fps (1.52 m/s) or less. This ultimately results in less maintenance and less chance of pipe breakage. When compensating for excess pressures due to high static pressure at the source or to large downhill elevation changes, pipe velocities should continue to be designed at 5 fps (1.52 m/s) or less. Excess pressures should be controlled by devices such as pressure regulators and pressure regulating valves and by adjusting the flow control of a valve.

6.3 Valve Sizing

Most automatic valves withstand velocities well in excess of 5 fps (1.52 m/s), and most actually function better with greater differentials between the inlet and outlet pressures (i.e., a friction loss through the valve must occur in order for most automatic valves to operate). The main concern when sizing valves is to determine how much pressure (friction loss) can be lost while still achieving the desired working pressure at the last sprinkler head. It is relatively common to use a valve smaller than the downstream pipe (which may be larger to keep the pipe velocities under 5 fps or 1.52 m/s).

Valve sizes should be designed so that the flow rates fall toward the middle of the manufacturer's friction-loss chart for a particular valve size. This will usually give the best performance, efficiency, and economy.

6.4 Flow and Friction Loss through Other System Components

All system components that have water flowing through them will have some friction loss. If the point of connection is a potable water supply with a meter, the friction loss through the meter must be calculated, along with the pipe friction loss from the street to the meter. From the point of connection, the friction loss must be calculated through the following: the main line, the valves, and the backflow or antisiphon device; any manual gate, globe, or ball valves in the line; and other special components, such as filters or chemical injecters. Friction-loss charts are provided by component manufacturers and will vary from one manufacturer to another. Unless velocity data are given for each component, they can be treated as if they were valves, in that for a given size, a specific friction loss will be realized at any flow.

6.5 Control Wire and Control Tubing Sizing

Just as friction losses occur in pipe, voltage drops occur through electrical wire. If a current is increased by starting several valves on one station, the voltage drop will increase. The number of valves that can be operated on one station depend on the size of the transformer and the inrush amperage requirement of the solenoid (valve) (Table 750-3). This information should be furnished by the manufacturer.

Wire no smaller than No. 14 gauge UF (direct burial) should be used in irrigation systems, not because a smaller-gauge wire is inadequate, but because smaller-gauge wire is more easily kinked or broken during installation. Smaller gauges are also more susceptible to nicks and scrapes because of a thinner insulation jacket. A 0.25-ampere inrush solenoid and a No. 14 gauge wire are ideal for a run of 7500 ft (2300 m). A run of 2500 ft (760 m) could be achieved with a solenoid requiring a 0.847-ampere inrush.

For runs longer than 7500 ft (2300 m), wire gauges larger than No. 14 must be used. In large systems with controllers far away from the power source, or in central/satellite systems (described in 7.3 Controllers of this section), the wire must be correctly sized from the source to the controller as well as from the controller to the solenoid (valve). The manufacturer should indicate the amperage requirements for valves and control satellites or should supply charts or formulas for determining the most efficient wire size at various points throughout the project.

In a hydraulic system, ¼-in (6.5-mm) tubing is the standard-size line used to control valves. The length from the con-

TABLE 750-2
Friction-Loss Table for Pipe (PVC 1120–1220 Class 160 in)*

		Loss per pipe length noted, psi§										
GPM†	*Velocity‡*	*5*	*10*	*20*	*30*	*40*	*50*	*60*	*70*	*80*	*90*	*100*
		½-in pipe, 0.720-in-inside diameter										
1	0.8	0.01	0.02	0.04	0.06	0.08	0.10	0.12	0.14	0.16	0.18	0.20
2	1.6	0.04	0.07	0.15	0.22	0.30	0.37	0.44	0.52	0.59	0.67	0.74
3	2.4	0.08	0.16	0.31	0.47	0.62	0.78	0.94	1.09	1.25	1.40	1.56
4	3.2	0.13	0.27	0.54	0.80	1.07	1.34	1.61	1.88	2.14	2.41	2.68
5	4.0	0.20	0.40	0.81	1.21	1.62	2.02	2.42	2.83	3.23	3.64	4.04
6	4.8	0.29	0.58	1.15	1.73	2.30	2.88	3.46	4.03	4.61	5.18	5.76
7	5.6	0.38	0.77	1.53	2.30	3.06	3.83	4.60	5.36	6.13	6.89	7.66
8	6.4	0.49	0.98	1.96	2.93	3.91	4.89	5.87	6.85	7.82	8.80	9.78
		¾-in pipe, 0.930-in inside diameter										
2	0.9	0.01	0.02	0.04	0.07	0.09	0.11	0.13	0.15	0.18	0.20	0.22
4	1.9	0.04	0.08	0.16	0.23	0.31	0.39	0.47	0.55	0.63	0.70	0.78
6	2.8	0.09	0.17	0.34	0.50	0.66	0.83	1.00	1.16	1.34	1.49	1.66
8	3.8	0.14	0.28	0.56	0.85	1.14	1.42	1.70	1.99	2.27	2.56	2.84
10	4.7	0.22	0.43	0.86	1.29	1.72	2.15	2.58	3.01	3.45	3.87	4.30
12	5.7	0.30	0.60	1.20	1.80	2.40	3.00	3.60	4.20	4.80	5.40	6.00
14	6.6	0.40	0.80	1.60	2.40	3.20	4.00	4.80	5.60	6.40	7.20	8.00
		1-in pipe, 1.195-in inside diameter										
6	1.7	0.03	0.05	0.10	0.15	0.20	0.24	0.29	0.34	0.39	0.44	0.48
8	2.3	0.04	0.08	0.16	0.25	0.34	0.42	0.50	0.59	0.67	0.76	0.84
10	2.9	0.07	0.13	0.26	0.38	0.50	0.63	0.76	0.88	1.02	1.13	1.26
12	3.4	0.09	0.18	0.36	0.53	0.71	0.89	1.07	1.25	1.43	1.60	1.78
14	4.0	0.12	0.24	0.48	0.71	0.94	1.18	1.42	1.65	1.89	2.12	2.36
16	4.5	0.15	0.30	0.60	0.91	1.21	1.52	1.82	2.12	2.43	2.73	3.04
18	5.1	0.19	0.38	0.76	1.13	1.50	1.88	2.26	2.63	3.01	3.38	3.76
20	5.7	0.23	0.46	0.92	1.37	1.82	2.28	2.74	3.19	3.65	4.10	4.56
22	6.3	0.28	0.55	1.10	1.65	2.20	2.75	3.30	3.85	4.40	4.95	5.50
24	6.8	0.38	0.65	1.30	1.94	2.58	3.23	3.88	4.52	5.23	5.81	6.46

* Name of pipe and its pressure grouping. The C value constant used in determining friction losses, based on relative smoothness of the interior of the pipe is 150.

† Gallons per minute flow is given in equal increments with logical increment spacing to satisfy most designer needs.

‡ Velocity of water through pipe. In no instance are friction losses given where the velocity exceeds 7 fps as this should be the extreme limit of velocity in design.

§ Friction loss of water through pipe in increments of 10 ft up to 100 ft with an additional column for 5 ft. This enables rapid selection of loss in all length pipe runs.

troller to the valves should not exceed 1000 ft (300 m).

7.0 SPRINKLER IRRIGATION SYSTEM (DESIGN PROCEDURE)

7.1 Sprinkler Head Selection and Layout

Sprinkler head selection and layout is the most difficult aspect of sprinkler irrigation system design. Seldom will an area lend itself perfectly to a particular grid spacing, whether triangular or square, and seldom is an area free of objects such as trees, walkways, and buildings.

The first step in the selection and layout of sprinkler heads is to divide the area to be irrigated into zones that have similar water requirements, e.g., lawn areas, shrub areas, and different exposures to the sun. Where possible, the use of large-radius heads should be considered first, since their use will progressively decrease the cost of the system on a square-foot basis. Triangular spacing is more efficient than square spacing, although many areas lend themselves to square spacing (such as the small rectangular areas typical of most residential and small commercial projects).

The most important objective when laying out sprinklers is the even distribution of water. Sprinklers that produce different precipitation rates should not be used in the same zone. Sprinkler-to-sprinkler dimensions should be based on manufacturer's recommendations, with deviations for wind velocity. Spacing for triangular and square patterns varies with brand and model.

When designing with single-row spacing through the center of an area, only about two-thirds of the radius will give effective coverage. Consequently, single-row spacing should only be used in special circumstances.

Many spray heads have matched precipitation rates, allowing quarter-circle heads to be used on the same line as half- and full-circle heads. However, rotary heads may not be matched; consequently, water distribution with rotary heads must be balanced by using a smaller nozzle size for particular heads in relation to full-circle heads on the same line. When the nozzle size is decreased, the radius also decreases and must be accounted for in the design. Under such circumstances, it is best to isolate heads with similar arcs in one zone and to balance the zones at the controller; for example, full-head zones would be programmed to water 4 times as long as quarter-head zones.

Flood and stream bubblers are often used to water small shrub areas and to

TABLE 750-3
Maximum Controller to Solenoid Wire Length, Ft

Copper wire size		Maximum number of solenoids activated simultaneously by controller															
		1								2							
		Controller output voltage (VAC)															
Control	*Common*	*21*	*22*	*23*	*24*	*25*	*26*	*27*	*28*	*21*	*22*	*23*	*24*	*25*	*26*	*27*	*28*
18	18	225	450	667	890	1112	1335	1557	1780	112	222	333	445	556	667	779	890
18	16	273	546	819	1092	1366	1639	1912	2185	137	273	409	546	683	819	956	1092
16	16	354	707	1061	1415	1768	2122	2476	2829	177	353	530	707	884	1061	1238	1415
16	14	431	861	1292	1723	2153	2584	3015	3446	216	430	646	861	1007	1292	1507	1723
14	14	550	1101	1651	2202	2753	3303	3854	4404	276	550	826	1101	1376*	1652	1927	2202
14	12	677	1353	2029	2706	3382	4058	4735	5411	338	676	1014	1353	1691	2029	2367	2706
14	10	789	1578	2367	3156	3946	4735	5524	6313	394	789	1183	1578	1973	2367	2762	3156
12	12	877	1753	2630	3507	4384	5261	6138	7014	439	877	1315	1754	2192	2630	3069	3507

Notes
- Divide distance in feet by 3.28 to convert to meters.
- Table is based on solenoid consumption of 8.5VA (0.35 amp).
- Wire sizes smaller than no. 14 (first four rows) may not carry the UL listing for direct burial application.
- *Example: A controller is activating two solenoids simultaneously and the output is 25 VAC. Using 14-14 wires, the maximum run is 1376 ft (419 m).

water plants that prefer dry foliage (Figure 750-11). Bubblers emit water at a much faster rate than the soil can absorb it and are used only to flood an area rapidly. Bubblers do not work well on sloping ground. Pressure-compensating bubblers should be used in areas with potential pressure fluctuations or high pressures.

Several features of sprinkler heads are commonly available which require consideration by the designer:

1. Stationary heads versus pop-up heads (if pop-up, how high?)
2. Filtration
3. Ease of maintenance
4. Guarantee
5. Type of material (brass, plastic, stainless steel, etc.)
6. Positive retraction for pop-ups
7. Angle of trajectory
8. Exposed surface area
9. Speed of rotation
10. Distribution curve
11. Adjustment (arc and radius)
12. Built-in check valve to prevent low-head drainage
13. Vandal resistance
14. Gear, impact, cam, or ball drives
15. Pressure compensation

Figures 750-8 through 750-11 show typical examples of various types of conventional sprinklers.

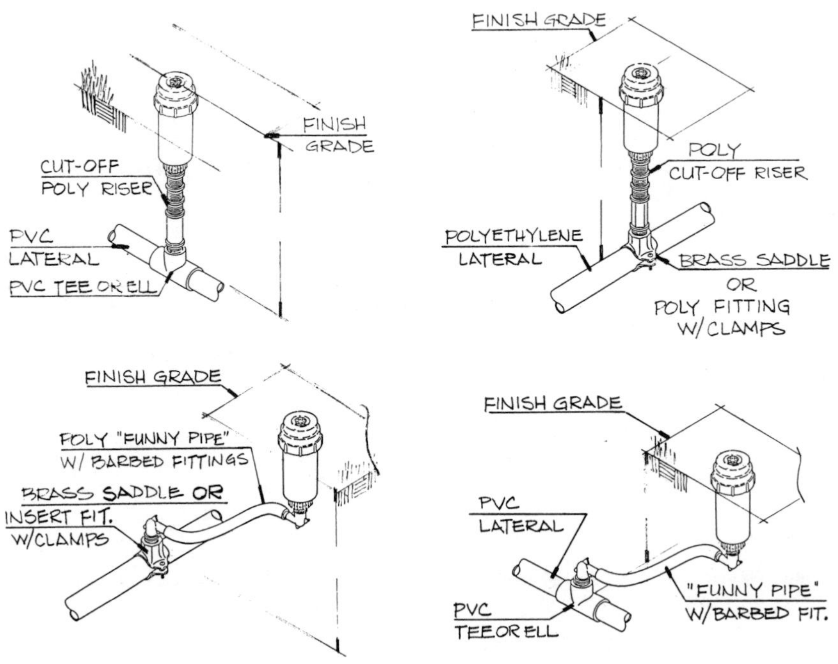
FINISH GRADE
CUT-OFF
POLY RISER
PVC
LATERAL
PVC TEE OR ELL
FINISH GRADE
POLY
CUT-OFF RISER
POLYETHYLENE
LATERAL
BRASS SADDLE
OR
POLY FITTING
W/CLAMPS
FINISH GRADE
POLY "FUNNY PIPE"
W/ BARBED FITTINGS
BRASS SADDLE OR
INSERT FIT.
W/CLAMPS
FINISH GRADE
PVC
LATERAL
"FUNNY PIPE"
W/BARBED FIT.
PVC
TEE OR ELL

Figure 750-8 Typical pop-up spray head assemblies.

7.2 Control Systems

Manual Systems:

Manual systems require an individual to open and close a valve by hand. Since

3							
21	22	23	24	25	26	27	28
74	148	222	297	371	445	519	593
91	182	273	364	455	546	637	728
117	235	353	471	589	707	825	943
143	287	430	574	718	861	1005	1148
183	367	550	734	918	1101	1285	1468
226	451	676	902	1127	1353	1578	1804
263	526	789	1052	1315	1578	1841	2104
293	584	877	1169	1461	1754	2046	2338

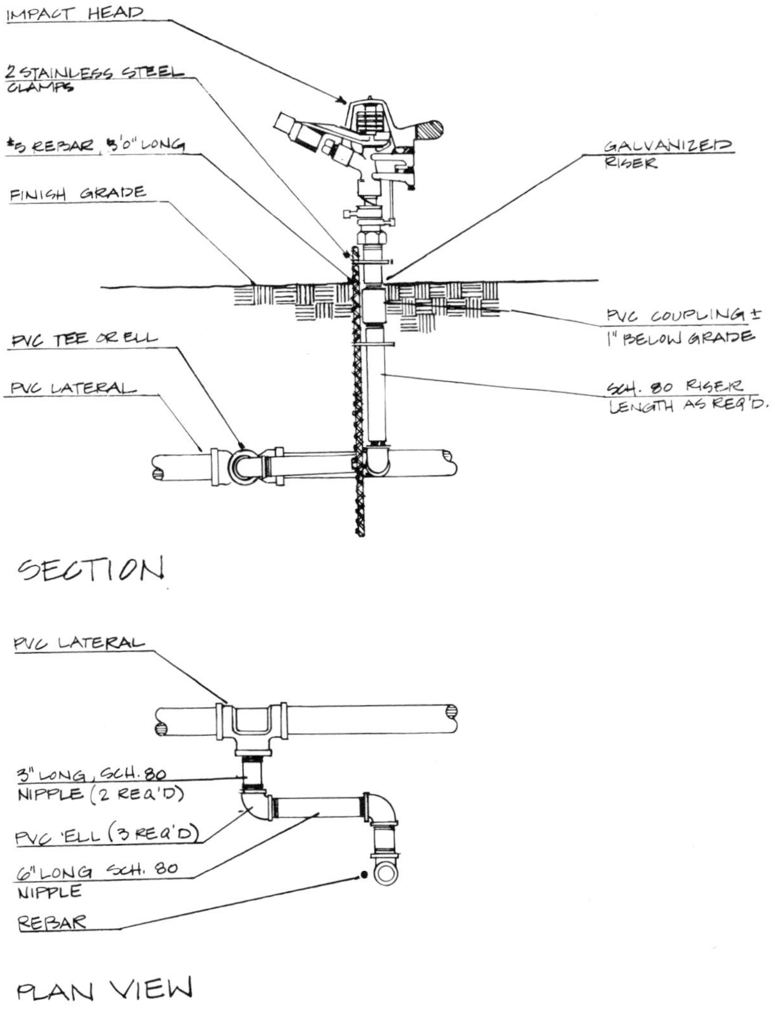
IMPACT HEAD
2 STAINLESS STEEL CLAMPS
#5 REBAR, 5'0" LONG
FINISH GRADE
GALVANIZED RISER
PVC COUPLING ± 1" BELOW GRADE
PVC TEE OR ELL
PVC LATERAL
SCH. 80 RISER LENGTH AS REQ'D.
SECTION
PVC LATERAL
3" LONG, SCH. 80 NIPPLE (2 REQ'D)
PVC 'ELL (3 REQ'D)
6" LONG SCH. 80 NIPPLE
REBAR
PLAN VIEW

Figure 750-9 Typical impact head assembly.

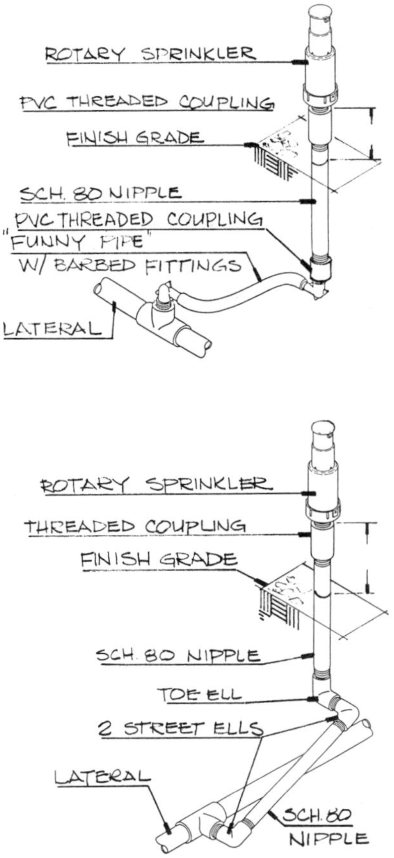
ROTARY SPRINKLER
PVC THREADED COUPLING
FINISH GRADE
SCH. 80 NIPPLE
PVC THREADED COUPLING
"FUNNY PIPE"
W/ BARBED FITTINGS
LATERAL
ROTARY SPRINKLER
THREADED COUPLING
FINISH GRADE
SCH. 80 NIPPLE
TOE ELL
2 STREET ELLS
LATERAL
SCH. 80 NIPPLE

Figure 750-10 Typical shrub head assemblies.

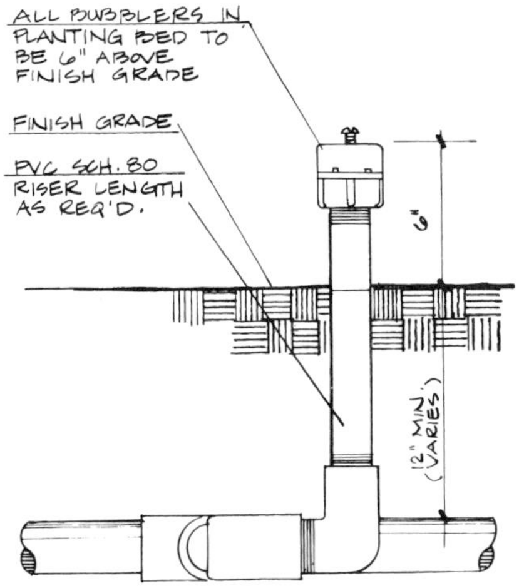
ALL BUBBLERS IN PLANTING BED TO BE 6" ABOVE FINISH GRADE
FINISH GRADE
PVC SCH. 80 RISER LENGTH AS REQ'D.
6"
12" MIN. (VARIES)

Figure 750-11 Typical bubbler assembly.

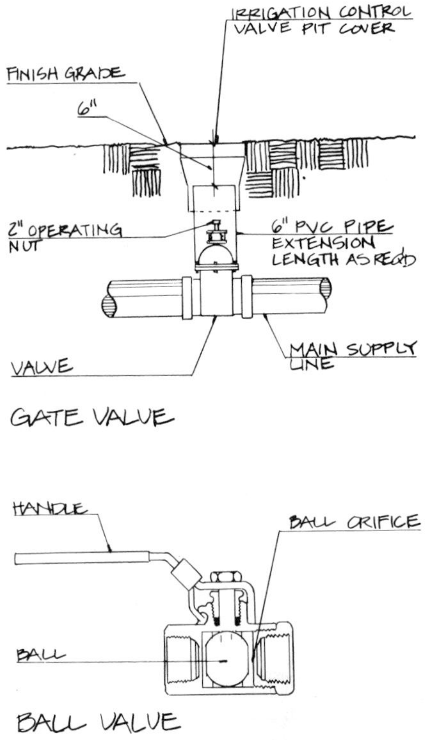
IRRIGATION CONTROL VALVE PIT COVER
FINISH GRADE
6"
2" OPERATING NUT
6" PVC PIPE EXTENSION LENGTH AS REQ'D
VALVE
MAIN SUPPLY LINE
GATE VALVE
HANDLE
BALL ORIFICE
BALL
BALL VALVE

Figure 750-12 Typical gate-valve and ball-valve assemblies. Soil around control-valve pit assembly must be compacted to same density as adjacent undisturbed soil. Note that the lever arm will require a larger valve box.

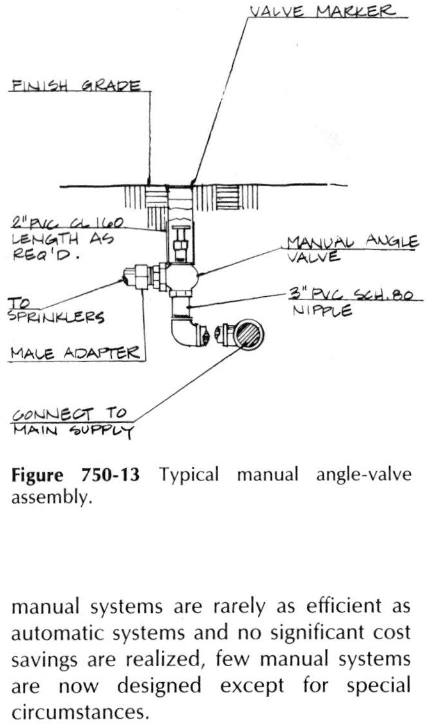
VALVE MARKER
FINISH GRADE
2" PVC CL 160 LENGTH AS REQ'D.
MANUAL ANGLE VALVE
3" PVC SCH. 80 NIPPLE
TO SPRINKLERS
MALE ADAPTER
CONNECT TO MAIN SUPPLY

Figure 750-13 Typical manual angle-valve assembly.

manual systems are rarely as efficient as automatic systems and no significant cost savings are realized, few manual systems are now designed except for special circumstances.

Automatic Systems:

In theory, automatic systems are much more efficient than manual systems since optimal water requirements can be satisifed by programming a controller. Controllers can send signals to the valves in two ways: electrically through wires or hydraulically through control tubing (see Figures 750-15 and 750-16). Most areas of the world predominantly use electricity, although there are exceptions. For reasons of availability, electrical systems do not include thermohydraulic systems, and hydraulic systems do not include normally closed hydraulic systems. (These are control systems once available in whole product, but now available only for replacement.)

Electrical systems: The advantages of electrical systems inlcude:

1. Faster response time
2. Longer runs between controller and valve
3. Ease of use with new solid-state controllers
4. Unaffected by elevation
5. Normally closed system (if a control wire is severed, the valve will remain closed)

The disadvantages of electrical systems include:

1. Susceptible to lightning damage
2. Susceptible to dirty water clogging the orifices which allow the valve to open and close (through the use of contamination-resistant valves which have two noncontinual bleed-through orifices that make operation less susceptible to dirty water).

7.3 Controllers

Controllers are programmed to determine when to water, how long to water, and the time(s) of day to begin watering. Many optional features are available for controllers. Generally, the more features a controller has, the more complicated the programming becomes.

On large projects, a *central/satellite system* is often used. A central controller sends signals to satellite controllers regarding the day and starting time(s) to water, with only the station's run time set at the satellite. These systems are also available with many features to satisfy specific requirements.

7.4 Valves

Manual Valves:

Gate valves are used as emergency shutoff valves or as isolation valves and are not designed for regular use (Figure 750-12). Since there is no rubber seat or washer, frequent usage will create wear and cause the valve to leak. Gate valves are used mainly because they have almost no friction loss.

Ball valves are similar to gate valves in that little friction loss exists. However, ball valves are advantageous in that frequent usage is less apt to cause leakage. Ball valves are increasingly being used in place of gate valves (Figure 750-12).

Globe or angle valves are used in manual systems where the valve is used regularly (Figure 750-13). Like a hose bibb, a *globe valve* has a replaceable rubber washer. Globe valves are not used as isolation valves since there is considerably more friction loss than with a ball or gate valve. An *angle valve* is simply a globe valve whose inlet is at the bottom of the valve with an exit at the side. Less friction loss occurs with an angle valve than with a straight globe valve. Often, an angle valve will be connected to an atmospheric vacuum breaker as one unit. Local codes will dictate such an installation, but it is usually 6 in (150 mm) above the highest outlet.

Automatic drain valves are special valves which are sometimes used in geographic regions with freezing climates (Figure 750-14). Such valves drain the water in the line each time the system is shut off. In heavy soils, however, this can create a problem of excessive wetness during seasons when the system is in use. To be effective, automatic drain valves should be located at all the system low points. The best method for eliminating water in the lines is physically to blow out the system with an air compressor before heavy frosts occur.

Gas cocks are special valves often used by manufacturers of backflow devices and pressure vacuum breakers for testing purposes. They are also occasionally used on lateral lines on hilly sites to reduce excess pressure on long downhill runs.

Check valves are used on hilly sites to prevent low-head drainage.

Automatic Valves:

Electric valves are activated by an electric current sent from a controller (Figure 750-15). Although electric current is involved, hydraulic forces actually open and close the valve. Inside the valve is a diaphragm (or piston) which moves up or down to open or close the valve. The diaphragm (or piston) is designed to have a greater surface area on the upper chamber than on the lower area which rests on the valve seat. A small orifice connects the upper and lower portions of the valve so that pressure is equalized between the two. The greater surface area of the top portion creates a mechanical advantage and causes the valve to close. Another, larger orifice connects the upper chamber and the downstream portion of the valve. A solenoid-activated plunger sits over this orifice; when the solenoid is activated by electricity, an electromagnetic field is cre-

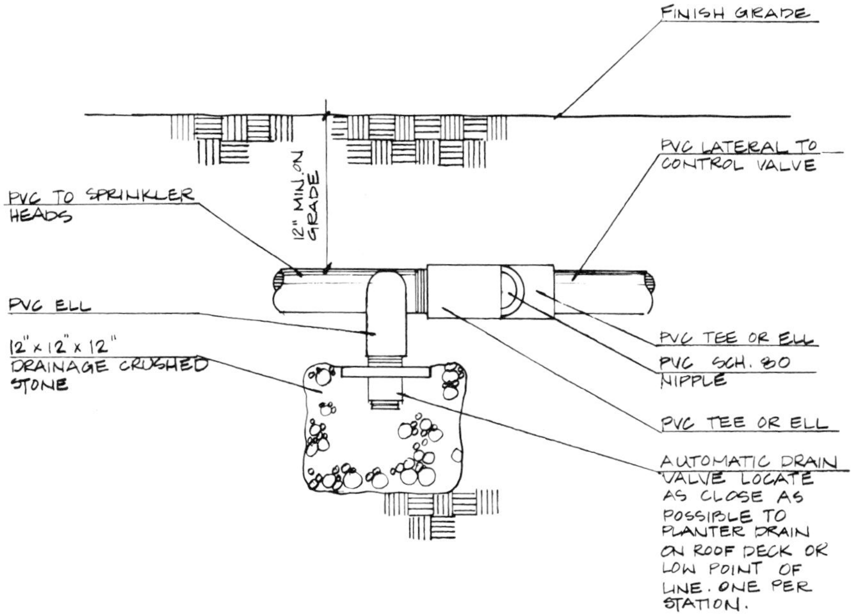
FINISH GRADE
PVC LATERAL TO CONTROL VALVE
PVC TO SPRINKLER HEADS
12" MIN. ON GRADE
PVC ELL
12" x 12" x 12" DRAINAGE CRUSHED STONE
PVC TEE OR ELL
PVC SCH. 80 NIPPLE
PVC TEE OR ELL
AUTOMATIC DRAIN VALVE LOCATE AS CLOSE AS POSSIBLE TO PLANTER DRAIN ON ROOF DECK OR LOW POINT OF LINE. ONE PER STATION.

Figure 750-14 Typical automatic drain valve assembly.

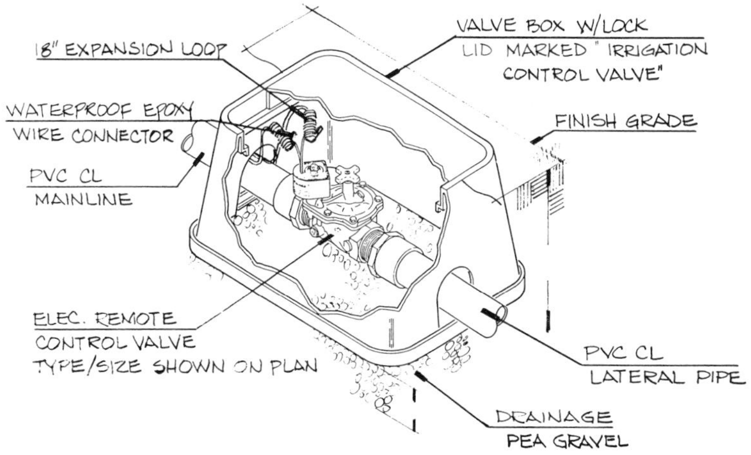
18" EXPANSION LOOP
VALVE BOX W/LOCK
LID MARKED "IRRIGATION CONTROL VALVE"
WATERPROOF EPOXY WIRE CONNECTOR
FINISH GRADE
PVC CL MAINLINE
ELEC. REMOTE CONTROL VALVE TYPE/SIZE SHOWN ON PLAN
PVC CL LATERAL PIPE
DRAINAGE PEA GRAVEL

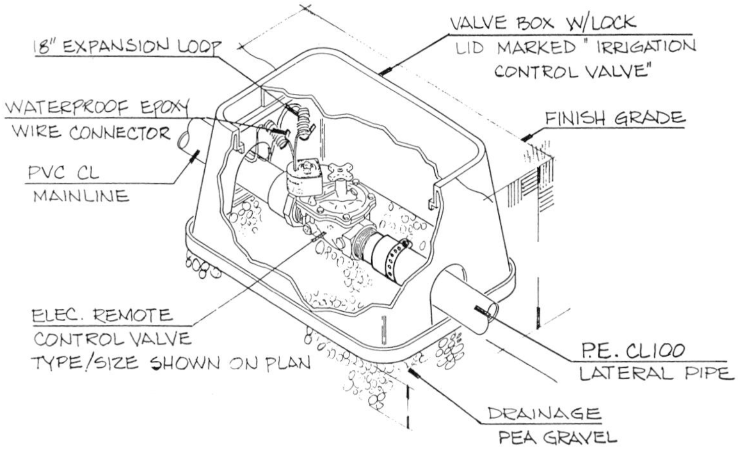
18" EXPANSION LOOP
VALVE BOX W/LOCK
LID MARKED "IRRIGATION CONTROL VALVE"
WATERPROOF EPOXY WIRE CONNECTOR
FINISH GRADE
PVC CL MAINLINE
ELEC. REMOTE CONTROL VALVE TYPE/SIZE SHOWN ON PLAN
P.E. CL100 LATERAL PIPE
DRAINAGE PEA GRAVEL

Figure 750-15 Electric remote control valve assembly.

ated within it which lifts the plunger off the orifice. Water is forced through the orifice faster than it can enter through the smaller orifice, and the diaphragm (or piston) is pushed up to open the valve. During operation, a steady stream of water is passing through both orifices.

Electric valves are subject to clogging by dirty water even though a filter is usually installed on the intake orifice (or a metering pin through the orifice) to clean the orifice each time the valve opens or closes. In some systems the solenoid plunger controls both orifices, thereby eliminating the constant stream of water passing through the orifice while the valve is on. However, an electric valve is still using system water to open and close.

Hydraulic valves are normally operated by water other than the irrigation water (Figure 750-16). Therefore, there is no small orifice to clog. The diaphragm (or piston) still has a greater surface area in the upper chamber and uses the same mechanical advantage to shut the valve. However, the water used to control the valve comes from another source, possibly a clean potable supply, whereas the irrigation water may originate from an algae-laden pond.

The water used for the control system should be clean and under the same or greater pressure than the system water pressure. Since only a few tablespoonsful of water are used each time a valve is activated, the cost of potable water is not a factor, whereas it would be if potable water were used for the system. Because there is no orifice to clog with irrigation water, normally open hydraulic valves are the best to use with dirty water.

7.5 Pipe

Polyvinyl Chloride (PVC) Pipe:

PVC pipe has become the standard in the irrigation industry for several reasons:

1. Excellent flow characteristics
2. Relatively lightweight (easy to work with)
3. Not subject to corrosion
4. Relatively inexpensive
5. Uses external solvent weld fittings
6. Flexibility
7. Durability

PVC is available via two different designations: schedule pipe or class pipe. *Schedule PVC pipe* (e.g., SCH40 and SCH80) means that the wall thickness is the same as in steel pipe at the same schedule and pipe size. In the design of irrigation systems, schedule pipe is used primarily for precut threaded nipples for sprinkler risers in shrub beds. *Class PVC pipe* is customarily designated for other parts of the irrigation system because class pipe is designated by pressure ratings (such as CL160, CL200, and CL315).

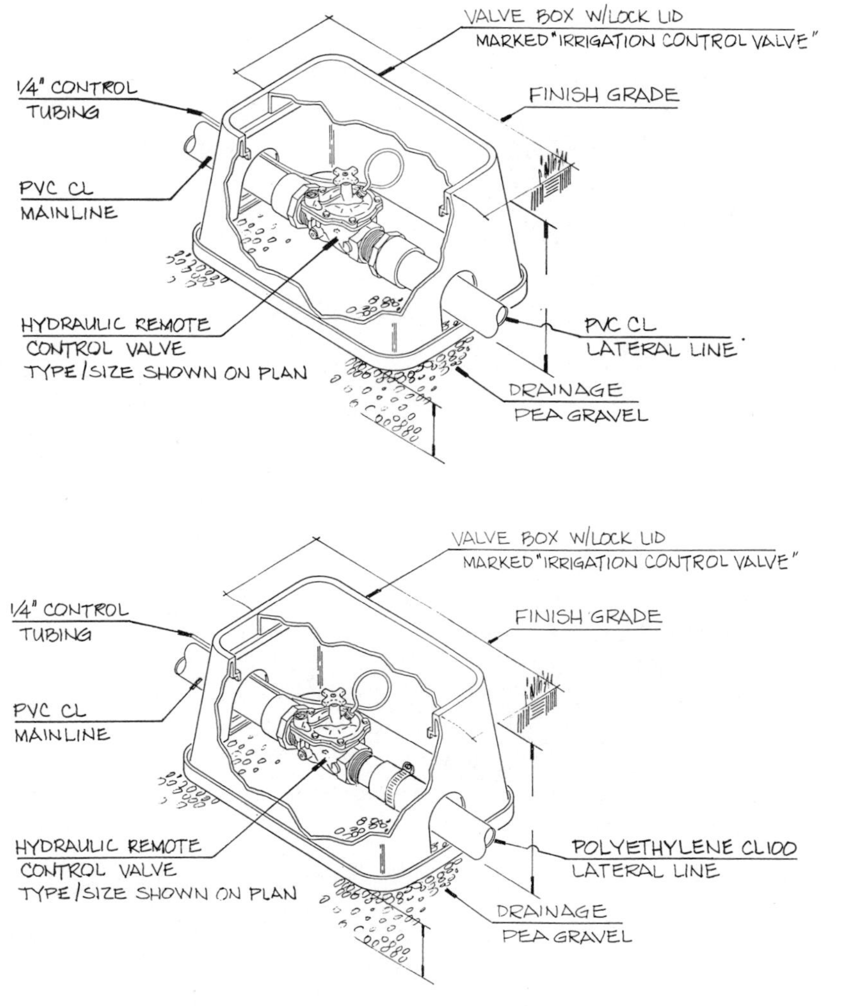
VALVE BOX W/LOCK LID
MARKED "IRRIGATION CONTROL VALVE"
1/4" CONTROL TUBING
FINISH GRADE
PVC CL MAINLINE
HYDRAULIC REMOTE CONTROL VALVE TYPE/SIZE SHOWN ON PLAN
PVC CL LATERAL LINE
DRAINAGE PEA GRAVEL
VALVE BOX W/LOCK LID
MARKED "IRRIGATION CONTROL VALVE"
1/4" CONTROL TUBING
FINISH GRADE
PVC CL MAINLINE
HYDRAULIC REMOTE CONTROL VALVE TYPE/SIZE SHOWN ON PLAN
POLYETHYLENE CL100 LATERAL LINE
DRAINAGE PEA GRAVEL

Figure 750-16 Hydraulic remote control valve assembly.

Polyethylene (PE) Pipe:

Polyethylene pipe is widely used because it is easily pulled into the ground with a vibrating plow (i.e., it is very flexible). In cold climates, polyethylene pipe is often used instead of PVC for lateral lines since it is not nearly as subject to damage from freezing.

The most common classes of polyethylene pipe used are CL80 and CL100; although CL120 is sometimes available, connecting the fittings to CL120 is difficult. Polyethylene pipe uses internal, barbed fittings which must be secured by stainless-steel clamps or other tightening devices. Because of the internal fittings, the flow characteristics of polyethylene pipe are not as good as PVC.

Copper Pipe:

Type K copper pipe is used most commonly for irrigation purposes and has the thickest wall of all copper pipe sizes. Type L and Type M copper pipe are also used occasionally.

Copper is commonly used in situations where the pipe will be exposed to sunlight, such as when mounting a vacuum breaker or as a riser for shrub heads.

Galvanized Steel Pipe:

Since galvanized steel pipe is highly susceptible to deterioration caused by minerals in the water, it is seldom used except as risers for shrub heads and in areas with a high potential for vandalism.

Asbestos Cement (AC) Pipe:

Because asbestos cement pipe is difficult to install and not practical, it is seldom used except to repair existing systems.

Cast-Iron Pipe:

Cast-iron pipe is used around pumping stations where pipe is subject to thrust. The connections are flanged and fastened with bolts.

Thrust blocks are used to distribute pressures evenly to firm ground along the trench wall. They should be built in wedge form, with the widest area along the solid trench wall. A standard mix would consist of 1 part portland cement, 2 parts washed sand, and 5 parts washed gravel (Figure 750-17).

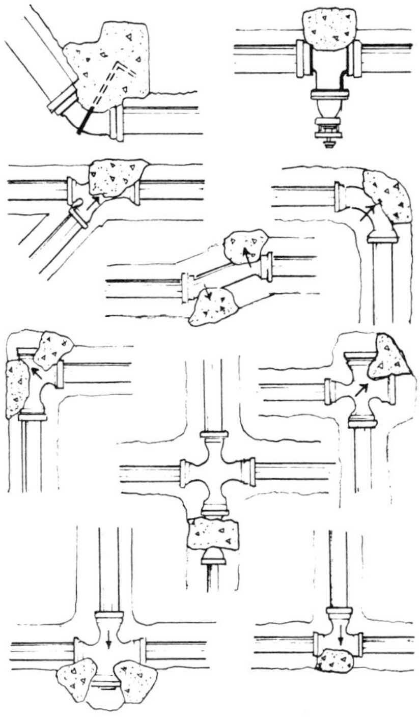

Figure 750-17 Thrust blocks for cast-iron pipe.

Concrete Pipe:

Concrete pipe is used primarily by water districts for city mainlines.

7.6 Backflow Preventors

As a consequence of the federal Clean Water Act, backflow preventors must be installed when working with potable water to protect the potable supply from a cross connection. Legally, irrigation systems are considered to be a high hazard. In most cases, local ordinances will dictate the type of backflow preventor to be installed.

Backflow preventors are categorized into one of two distinct types: antisiphon devices and back-pressure devices.

Antisiphon Devices:

Atmospheric Vacuum Breaker (AVB): Atmospheric vacuum breakers must be mounted downstream of any valve and be positioned in 6 in (150 mm) above the highest outlet (Figure 750-18). An AVB has a float which seals against a seat under pressure but which will drop down by gravity when the pressure ceases, thereby allowing air to enter the line and break any vacuum hold downstream.

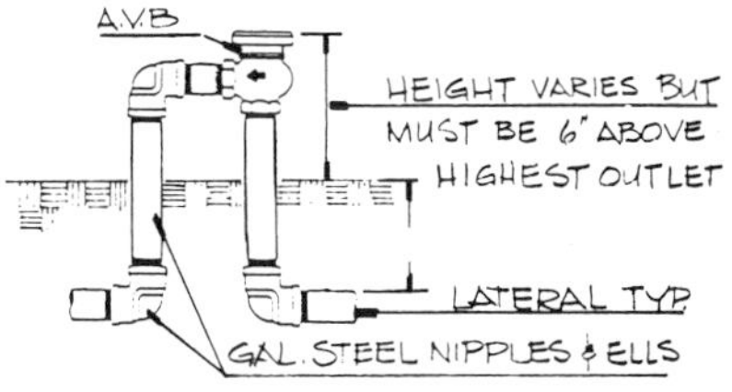
A.V.B.
HEIGHT VARIES BUT MUST BE 6" ABOVE HIGHEST OUTLET
LATERAL TYP.
GAL. STEEL NIPPLES & ELLS

Figure 750-18 Typical atmospheric vacuum breaker.

Pressure Vacuum Breaker (PVB): The only functional difference between an AVB and a PVB is a small spring that assists the force of gravity in getting the float to drop down after pressure has been removed (Figure 750-19). Also, gate or ball valves and test cocks are added so that the unit can be tested for reliability. Pressure vacuum breakers may be mounted upstream of valves, and they are usually preferable to atmospheric vacuum breakers because only one per source is necessary. Pressure vacuum breakers must be mounted at least 12 in (300 mm), but less than 30 in (755 mm), above the highest outlet.

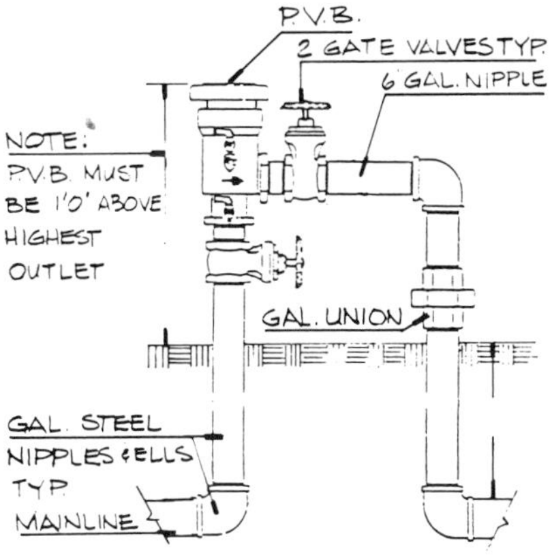
P.V.B.
2 GATE VALVES TYP.
6" GAL. NIPPLE
NOTE: P.V.B. MUST BE 1'0" ABOVE HIGHEST OUTLET
GAL. UNION
GAL. STEEL NIPPLES & ELLS TYP.
MAINLINE

Figure 750-19 Typical pressure vacuum breaker.

Back-Pressure Devices:

Double Check Valves: Double check valves are not approved for high-hazard situations, yet some local codes allow their

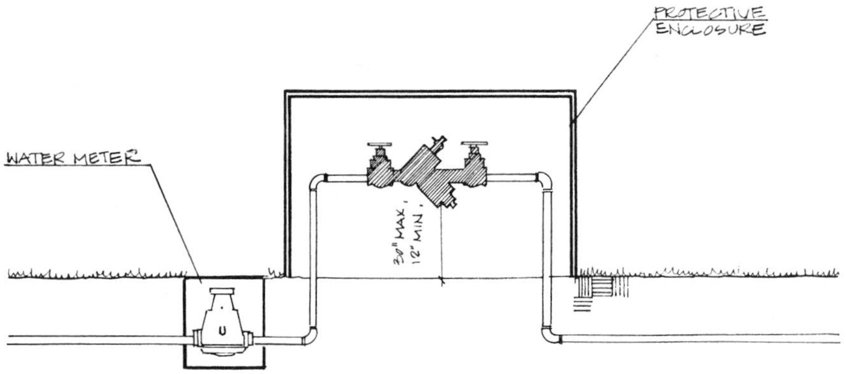
PROTECTIVE ENCLOSURE
WATER METER
30" MAX. 12" MIN.

Figure 750-20 Typical double check backflow preventor.

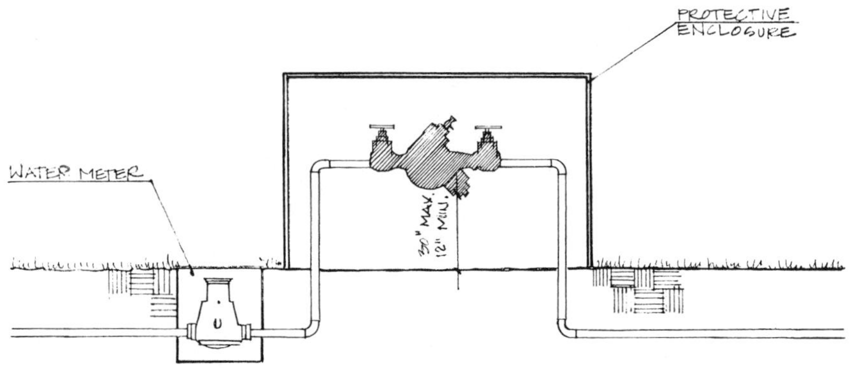
PROTECTIVE ENCLOSURE
WATER METER
30" MAX. 12" MIN.

Figure 750-21 Typical reduced-pressure backflow preventor.

use in irrigation (Figure 750-20). Check valves allow water to flow in one direction only. The second check valve is simply a safety feature in case the first check valve fails. Double check backflow devices do not have to be mounted above the highest outlet but should be accessible for testing purposes.

Reduced-Pressure Backflow Device (RP): Reduced-pressure devices are approved for high-hazard situations and are generally accepted as the surest safeguard against backflow for irrigation purposes (Figure 750-21). Reduced-pressure devices are also the most expensive and have the greatest friction loss of all backflow devices.

Like double check valves, reduced-pressure devices have two check valves, but the first valve has a stronger spring than the second in order to create a pressure differential between the two check valves. Should pressure ever vary from that desired between the two valves, a pressure-relief valve will open and dump the water to the atmosphere. Nothing should be connected to the relief valve.

To prevent flooding of a basement or area where the reduced-pressure device is located, an air gap should exist between the check valve and drain line to permit the water to flow to a drain. Reduced-pressure devices should not be located in a pit or in any area that might be submerged in water. Since these devices are meant to be checked annually by a certified tester, they should remain accessible.

7.7 Supplementary Equipment

Water Meters:

Although water meters are not used in irrigation systems per se, they are of concern to the designer because the meter, the static pressure, and the feed line from the street to the meter will ultimately determine how much water is available for the irrigation system. The friction loss through the meter must also be calculated when totaling all friction losses.

The amount of water available for an irrigation system is determined by taking a static pressure reading, noting the meter size, and noting the size and type of pipe coming into the meter. The following three criteria are then addressed; the most critical of the three [i.e., the smallest gpm figure] will determine the available water:

1. Seventy-five percent of the safe flow of the meter chart should not be exceeded. (Use the meter chart.)

2. The pressure loss through the meter should never exceed 10 percent of the static pressure. (Use the meter chart.)

3. The water in the service line should not exceed 5 fps (1.52 mls) though it is sometimes necessary to exceed this due to flow limitations of small service lines and the needs of the sprinkler system. It may be prudent to specify a new service line if the existing line supplies insufficient water due to size or mineral buildup.

Pumps:

If an existing pump is to be the water source for an irrigation system, the manufacturer, horsepower, and model must be noted, and a pump curve must be located so that the pressure and flowrate (gpm or l/s) can be identified (Figure 750-22 and Table 750-4). The type of pump to use depends on the number of hours per day available for irrigation; a pump that will satisfy this requirement during the most critical time of the year should be used. Before the system is actually designed, a calculation has to be made to determine the precipitation rate of the sprinkler heads intended and the number of hours per week that watering is required. This will determine the approximate number of zones to be irrigated and the average size of each zone. The flowrate of an average-size zone plus 10 percent will provide enough information to determine tentatively the pump size necessary. When the design is finished, an exact pump size can be determined.

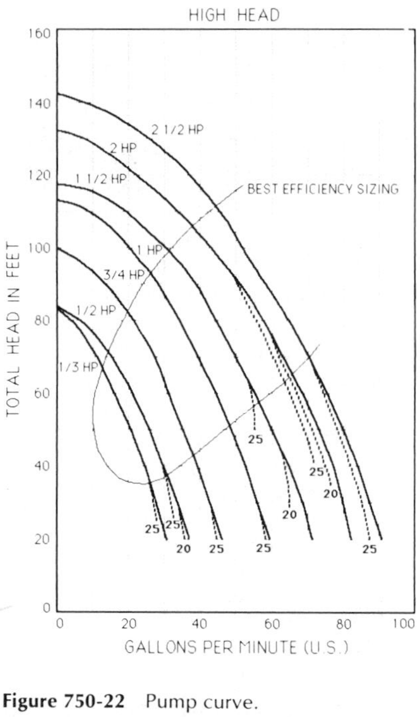
HIGH HEAD
TOTAL HEAD IN FEET
GALLONS PER MINUTE (U.S.)
2 1/2 HP
2 HP
1 1/2 HP
1 HP
3/4 HP
1/2 HP
1/3 HP
BEST EFFICIENCY SIZING
0
20
40
60
80
100
120
140
160
25
20

Figure 750-22 Pump curve.

In general terms, a pump operates by spinning its motor-driven impeller so that a pressure *less* than atmospheric pressure is created at the eye of the impeller, whereby the atmospheric pressure exerted upon a body of water outside of the pump forces the water up into the pump's suction line. For this to work, the impeller must be submerged in water (i.e., primed) and the suction line must be filled. Unless it is a self-priming pump, a pump will not work if it loses water in the suction line (i.e., loses prime); a self-priming pump has a reservoir in its volute case (impeller housing) so that prime cannot be lost even if water does not remain in the suction line. Usually, a foot valve is installed at the base of the suction line to prevent losing prime.

Because impellers do not create a perfect vacuum and because atmospheric pressure at sea level is about 32 ft (9.5 m) of water, no pump will function if placed 32 ft (9.5 m) above water level. Centrifugal pumps should be placed as close to water level as possible for maximum efficiency. Efficiency curves on a pump chart refer to the *net positive suction head* (NPSH); in reality, this is seldom over 18 to 20 ft (5.4 to 6.0 m). If the water is much deeper (as in a well), a vertical turbine pump is used (which has a long shaft and an impeller or a series of impellers attached at the end of the shaft); the shaft runs down the well casing and the impeller lies in the water. Pumps always have an easier time *pushing* water than *sucking* it.

In regard to pumps, pressure is usually expressed in terms of *foot head* (FH), which is multiplied by 0.433 to convert to psi or kPa.

Designers confronted with large uphill elevation changes or insufficient static pressure often use centrifugal pumps as booster pumps. The pressure at a given flowrate (gpm) on the pump curve can be added to the existing pressure to arrive at the new boosted pressure. Since a booster pump does not create water, the flowrate will remain the same.

TABLE 750-4
Pump Graph: High Head

	Discharge pressure		*Dynamic suction lift, gallons per minute*				
Hp	*Psi*	*Feet head*	*5 ft*	*10 ft*	*15 ft*	*20 ft*	*25 ft*
	20	46.2	47	45	43	40	38
1	30	69.3	36	33	31	27	23
	40	92.4	21	16	10	—	—
	20	46.2	58	56	54	51	48
1½	30	69.3	47	44	41	38	34
	40	92.4	31	27	21	12	—
	20	46.2	71	68	66	62	60
2	30	69.3	61	57	55	51	47
	40	92.4	45	40	36	31	26
	50	115.5	22	15	—	—	—
	20	46.2	78	76	73	71	68
2½	30	69.3	67	64	61	58	54
	40	92.4	52	48	44	40	36
	50	115.5	33	28	22	15	—

Pressure Regulators:

When the static pressure is greater than necessary for the sprinkler heads of a system, a pressure regulator can be used to lower the pressure. If the pressure is excessive only in certain areas (due to elevation or to the use of heads requiring low pressure), a pressure regulating valve can also be used to remedy the situation. Pressure regulators will convert a high pressure to a lower set pressure and regulate it regardless of any fluctuations that may occur on the high-pressure side of the system.

Valve Boxes:

Valves should not be buried below ground except under special circumstances. Valve boxes are designed to house irrigation valves and should remain accessible for ease of maintenance (see Figure 750-15). Boxes are available in a variety of materials, and some have locking devices for added security.

Pipe Sleeves/Chases:

Whenever possible, pipe sleeves (chases) should be installed under sidewalks, roadways, parking lots, etc., for ease of system installation and later maintenance. Pipe sleeves should be four pipe sizes larger than the pipe that will run through the sleeve.

Chemical Injection Devices:

Injection devices are used to inject fertilizer or other chemicals into the sprinkler system. Such devices are either flow-regulated (venturi principle) or physically injected by a pump. The effectiveness of an injection system is directly related to the efficiency of the sprinkler system. For this reason, these devices are most effective with drip irrigation systems.

8.0 DRIP IRRIGATION (DESIGN PROCEDURE)

8.1 Calculations

In drip irrigation, it is important to determine the amount of water that each plant will use and then to select the number and flow sizes of the emitters that will apply the water within a specified period of time. An important rule of thumb regarding drip irrigation design is to *always design water applications so that at least 50 percent of the plant root zone will be wet.*

Water Requirement of Plants:

A formula for determining the daily water requirement of a plant in gallons (liters) per day (gpd or mlh) is:

$$\text{Water requirement of plant (gpd) of mlh} = \frac{0.623 \times \text{canopy area} \times \text{potential use (inches per day)} \times \text{plant factor}}{\text{irrigation efficiency}}$$

Canopy area refers to the square-foot area or plan-view size) of the plant. To calculate the area, square the diameter of the canopy and multiply by 0.7854. For example, a tree with a canopy diameter of 10 ft (3 m) will have an area of 78.54 ft^2 (0.94 m^2).

Potential use factor, also referred to as the *climate factor* or the *potential evapotranspiration rate* (PET), refers to the amount of water required by the plant for healthy growth (depending on climate) in inches (centimeters) per day (Table 750-5).

Plant factor refers to the water requirements of plants. Plants are classified according to their resistance to stress (Table 750-6).

Irrigation efficiency refers to the ability of an irrigation system to deliver water to plants without evaporation or other means of water loss (Table 750-7).

Example of calculation for determining the daily water requirement of a plant: Given a tree with a 15-ft (4.6-m) canopy diameter in a moderate climate,

TABLE 750-5
Climatic Factors Related to Water Use

Climate type	*Average peak temperature, °F*	*Humidity*	*Potential use, in/day*
Very cool	50°–60°	Humid	0.10
Cool	70°–80°	Medium–humid	0.20
Moderate	80°–90°	Medium–humid	0.25
Hot	90°–100°	Medium–humid	0.30
High desert	90°–100°	Dry	0.35
Low desert	100°+	Dry	0.40

TABLE 750-6
Plant Factor (Resistance to Stress)

Plant factor	*Types of plants*
1.0	Evergreens, fruit trees, small shrubs, vines, perennials, and lush ground cover
0.70	Newly planted native plants in semiarid and arid regions; ornamental or shade trees and shrubs native to more humid areas
0.40	Established plants native to the area

TABLE 750-7
Irrigation Efficiency

Climate	*Factor*
Hot, dry, and high-desert	0.85
Moderate and hot	0.90
Cool and very cool	0.95

TABLE 750-8
Emitter Sizes, Numbers, and Operating Times (Example)

Soil type	*Emitter number*	×	*Emitter type, gph*	×	*Operating time, hr*	=	*Gph*
Clay	2	×	1	×	15	=	30
Moderate	2	×	2	×	7.5	=	30
Sandy	5	×	2	×	3	=	30

TABLE 750-9
Irrigation Duration for Plants in Containers (Min)

Container size, gal	*Emitter flow size, Gph*	*Soil type*			
		Sandy	*Medium*	*Heavy*	*Potting*
1	0.5	3	5	11	2
2	0.5	6	10	25	5
5	1.0	8	15	30	6
15	1.0	25	40	90	20
25	1.0	40	75	150	30

TABLE 750-10
Frequency for Plants in Containers (days)

Climate	*Soil type*			
	Sandy	*Medium*	*Heavy*	*Potting*
Very cool	2	3	8	2
Cool	1½	2	6	1
Moderate	1½	2	6	1
Hot	1	2	5	1
High-desert	1	1½	4	1
Low-desert	1	1	3	1

SANDY SOIL
20 SQ FT.
MEDIUM SOIL
60 SQ FT.
HEAVY SOIL
120 SQ. FT.

Figure 750-23 Soil wetting areas based on soil type.

$$\text{GPD} = \frac{0.623 \times (152 \times 0.7854) \times 0.25 \times 1.0}{0.90}$$

$$= 30.5$$

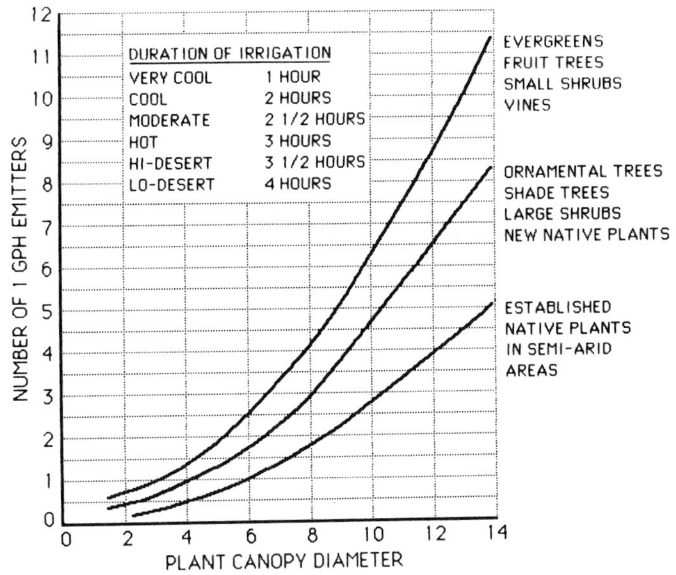
DURATION OF IRRIGATION
VERY COOL 1 HOUR
COOL 2 HOURS
MODERATE 2 1/2 HOURS
HOT 3 HOURS
HI-DESERT 3 1/2 HOURS
LO-DESERT 4 HOURS
EVERGREENS
FRUIT TREES
SMALL SHRUBS
VINES
ORNAMENTAL TREES
SHADE TREES
LARGE SHRUBS
NEW NATIVE PLANTS
ESTABLISHED
NATIVE PLANTS
IN SEMI-ARID
AREAS
NUMBER OF 1 GPH EMITTERS
PLANT CANOPY DIAMETER
0
1
2
3
4
5
6
7
8
9
10
11
12
14

Figure 750-24 Simplified drip design.

Determining the Number of Emitters:

Figure 750-23 shows the shape and square footage (meters) of typical soil wetting areas as a function of soil type. Generally speaking, heavy soils have a larger, shallower bulb than sandy soils, which have a narrower, longer bulb.

The following formula is used to determine the number of emitters required for any plant:

$$\text{Number of emitters} = \frac{\text{50 percent canopy area, ft}^2\ (\text{m}^2)}{\text{soil wetted area, ft}^2\ (\text{m}^2)}$$

Fractional values for the number of emitters should be rounded up to the next highest positive integer (as illustrated in the following example).

Example of calculation for determining the number of emitters required: Given a tree with a 15-ft (4.6-m) canopy diameter, where the canopy area is 176.7 ft² (1900 m²):

For a sandy (i.e., well-drained) soil;

$$\text{Number of emitters} = \frac{88.3\ \text{ft}^2\ (949.5\ \text{m}^2)}{20\ \text{ft}^2\ (215.1\ \text{m}^2)}$$

$$= 4.4\ (47.3\ \text{m}^2) \approx 5\ (54\ \text{m}^2)$$

For a moderately well-drained soil;

$$\text{Number of emitters} = \frac{88.3\ \text{ft}^2\ (949.5\ \text{m}^2)}{60\ \text{ft}^2\ (645.2\ \text{m}^2)}$$

$$= 1.5\ (16.1\ \text{m}^2) \approx 2\ (2.15\ \text{cm}^2)$$

For a heavy (i.e., poorly drained) soil;

$$\text{Number of emitters} = \frac{88.3\ \text{ft}^2\ (949.5\ \text{m}^2)}{120\ \text{ft}^2\ (1290.3\ \text{m}^2)}$$

$$= 0.54\ (.0006\ \text{cm}) \approx 1\ (.001)$$

Determining the Flowrate:

The following formula can be used to calculate the flowrate and length of time to operate each emitter:

GPD = number of emitters

× emitter flowrate

× duration of irrigation

The tree in a moderately well-drained soil will require two 2-gph (0.002-l/s) emitters for a period of 7.5 hours. A sandy soil will require five 2-gph (0.002-l/s) emitters for a period of 3 hours. Clay soils are a special case because one 2-gph (0.002-l/s) emitter could cause runoff; one solution might be to use two 1-gph (0.001-l/s) emitters for a period of 15 hours.

The duration of irrigation can be reduced by adding more emitters. In the tree example used, ten 1-gph (0.001-l/s) emitters would satisfy the water requirements in 3 hours of running time (Table 750-8).

8.2 Design Procedure

The following procedure can be used to design and lay out drip irrigation systems for small commercial and residential projects. This procedure and the guidelines listed below are based upon the warmest part of the season, with irrigation occurring every day. Depending on the soil conditions, the exposure, and seasonal change, the frequency of irrigation may have to be altered.

Procedure:

1. Make an accurate map of the area.

2. Locate all plant materials and indicate their plant classifications and canopy sizes.

3. Based on the map of the area, select the correct number of emitters required for each plant.

4. On the map, lay out the emitter locations to determine the fittings and various accuracies required.

Important Considerations:

The following guidelines will help simplify the hydraulics of small irrigation systems:

1. The lateral lengths should not exceed 200 ft (60 m).

2. The flow should not exceed 200 gph (3.33 gpm or 758 l/h).

3. The maximum working pressure should be 40 psi (276 kPa) [pressures over this amount should be regulated].

4. The line used should be ½-in (13-mm) PVC or polyethylene tubing.

Figure 750-24 provides a simplified means to design a drip irrigation system. Table 750-9 provides the duration of drip irrigation (in minutes) for plants growing in containers. Table 750-10 provides information on the frequency of watering required for plants growing in containers.

REFERENCES

Jensen, Marvin E. *Consumptive Use of Water & Irrigation Water Requirements,* American Society of Civil Engineers, New York, 1973.

Pair, Claude (ed.). *Irrigation,* Sprinkler Association, Kimberly, ID, 1983.

Sarsfield, A. C. Chett. *ABC of Lawn Sprinkler Systems,* Irrigation Technical Services, Lafayette, CA, 1966.

Watkins, James A. *Turf Irrigation Manual,* Telsco/Weathermatic, Dallas, TX, 1978.

Young, Virgil E. *Sprinkler Irrigation Systems* (3d ed.), Craftsman Press, Tacoma, WA, 1976. ■

section 810: Soils and Aggregates

CREDITS

Section Editor: Charles W. Harris
Technical Writer: Tobias Dayman
Research Assistant: Krisan Osterby-Benson

Reviewers:

Douglas S. Way
Ohio State University
Department of Landscape Architecture
Columbus, Ohio

Neil Cavanaugh, P.E.
Bradford Saivetz & Associates, Inc.
Braintree, MA

Robert N. Pine, P.E.
Pine & Swallow Associates
West Acton, Massachusetts

CONTENTS

1.0 INTRODUCTION

1.1 General

Physical and chemical properties of soils are important site determinants influencing the spatial allocation of land uses, the design and construction of structures, and the selection and installation of plant materials.

Certain properties of soils can be readily deduced from knowledge of soil type, while others can only be determined by careful field and/or laboratory testing. The particular properties of a soil that are important to a proposed development depend on the type of development proposed.

1.2 Soils

The term *soil* is defined in various ways, depending on the purpose for which it is defined. Consequently, several different soil classification systems have evolved for various purposes. The most common classification systems are described in 2.0 Soil Classification Systems in this section.

Soil Profile:

In the process of natural formation, soil layers (i.e., *horizons*) develop with characteristically different textures, mineral contents, and chemical makeup. A *soil profile* refers to a vertical section of these horizons, and a taxonomy has been developed to designate each horizon and zones within each horizon. The extent to which a profile becomes well-developed is largely a consequence of climate, humid climates producing more developed profiles than do arid climates. A typical profile in a humid climate has a well-developed A-, B-, C-, and sometimes D-horizon. Figure 810-1 illustrates a hypothetical soil profile, showing all major soil horizons.

1.3 Aggregates

In landscape construction, the term *aggregate* typically refers to crushed rock or gravel rather than to the aggregation of soil particles. Information on the choice of an aggregate for specific purposes (foundations, road construction, etc.) is presented in 5.0 Aggregates of this section. Information on aggregates for the mixing of asphaltic concrete or concrete is covered in Sections 820: Asphalt, and 830: Concrete, respectively.

2.0 SOIL CLASSIFICATION SYSTEMS

A number of soil classification systems have been developed for various pur-

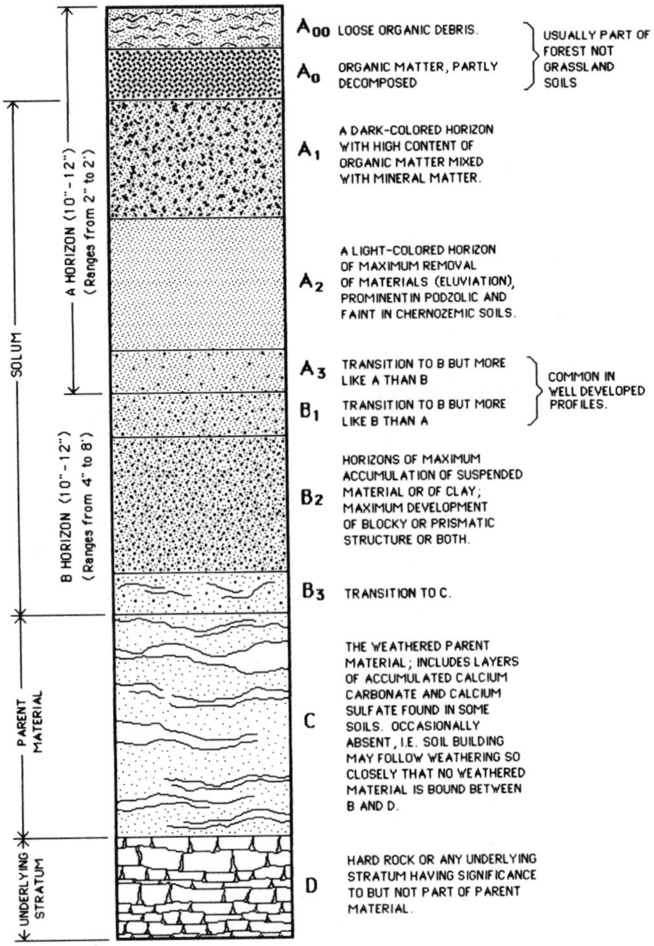
A_{00} LOOSE ORGANIC DEBRIS.
A_0 ORGANIC MATTER, PARTLY DECOMPOSED
USUALLY PART OF FOREST NOT GRASSLAND SOILS
A_1 A DARK-COLORED HORIZON WITH HIGH CONTENT OF ORGANIC MATTER MIXED WITH MINERAL MATTER.
A_2 A LIGHT-COLORED HORIZON OF MAXIMUM REMOVAL OF MATERIALS (ELUVIATION), PROMINENT IN PODZOLIC AND FAINT IN CHERNOZEMIC SOILS.
A_3 TRANSITION TO B BUT MORE LIKE A THAN B
B_1 TRANSITION TO B BUT MORE LIKE B THAN A
COMMON IN WELL DEVELOPED PROFILES.
B_2 HORIZONS OF MAXIMUM ACCUMULATION OF SUSPENDED MATERIAL OR OF CLAY; MAXIMUM DEVELOPMENT OF BLOCKY OR PRISMATIC STRUCTURE OR BOTH.
B_3 TRANSITION TO C.
C THE WEATHERED PARENT MATERIAL; INCLUDES LAYERS OF ACCUMULATED CALCIUM CARBONATE AND CALCIUM SULFATE FOUND IN SOME SOILS. OCCASIONALLY ABSENT, I.E. SOIL BUILDING MAY FOLLOW WEATHERING SO CLOSELY THAT NO WEATHERED MATERIAL IS BOUND BETWEEN B AND D.
D HARD ROCK OR ANY UNDERLYING STRATUM HAVING SIGNIFICANCE TO BUT NOT PART OF PARENT MATERIAL.
SOLUM
A HORIZON (10" - 12") (Ranges from 2" to 2')
B HORIZON (10" - 12") (Ranges from 4" to 8')
PARENT MATERIAL
UNDERLYING STRATUM

Master horizons and subordinate symbols for horizons of soil profiles

Master horizons	
01	Organic undecomposed horizon
02	Organic decomposed horizon
A1	Organic accumulation in mineral soil horizon
A2	Leached bleached horizon (eluviated)
A3	Transition horizon to B
AB	Transition horizon between A and B – more like A in upper part
A and B	A2 with less than 50% of horizon occupied by spots of B
AC	Transition horizon, not dominated by either A or C
B and A	B with less than 50% of horizon occupied by spots of A2
B	Horizon with accumulation of clay, iron, cations, humus; residual concentration of clay; coatings; or alterations of original material forming clay and structure
B1	Transition horizon more like B than A
B2	Maximum expression of B horizon
B3	Transitional horizon to C or R
C	Altered material from which A and B horizons are presumed to be formed
R	Consolidated bedrock
Subordinate symbols	
b	Buried horizon
ca	Calcium in horizon
cs	Gypsum in horizon
cn	Concretions in horizon
f	Frozen horizon
g	Gleyed horizon
h	Humus in horizon
ir	Iron accumulation in horizon
m	Cemented horizon
p	Plowed horizon
sa	Salt accumulation in horizon
si	Silica cemented horizon
t	Clay accumulation in horizon
x	Fragipan horizon
II, III, IV	Lithologic discontinuities
A'2, B'2	Second sequence in bisequal soil

Figure 810-1 Hypothetical soil profile showing all major soil horizons. Note that no one soil has all of these profiles.

poses. The four most commonly used soil classification systems are described below, and their relevance to landscape planning and design is explained. Table 810-1 illustrates the differences between these systems in terms of soil texture and their relationship to standard ASTM sieve sizes.

2.1 The New Soil Taxonomy (World Seventh Approximation)

The New Soil Taxonomy lists ten basic soil orders based primarily on climate, parent material, and vegetation (Table 810-2). This classification system provides a framework within which the United States Department of Agriculture Soil Conservation Service (USDA system) operates.

2.2 The USDA System

The United States Department of Agriculture Soil Conservation Service has developed a soil classification system which evaluates and classifies soils in terms of their agricultural suitability. In the continental United States, only about one-half of the country has been mapped. Urbanized areas are not mapped. Newer surveys are now superimposed on aerial photographs and are supplemented with information applicable to land uses other than agriculture.

In the USDA system, information on soils is limited to depths of about 3 ft (1 m). Consequently, such data cannot be used to solve problems requiring soil information at greater depths.

Figure 810-2 shows the USDA soil textural triangle, and Table 810-3 lists common terms used in the USDA classification system.

2.3 The AASHTO System

The American Association of State Highway Transportation Officials (AASHTO) has developed a soil classification system based on engineering properties of soils and their suitability for highway construction (Table 810-4). Soils are classified into seven groups (A-1 through A-7) based on laboratory determination of particle size distribution, liquid limit, and plasticity index. Soils are evaluated within each group by a *group index* value which is calculated from an empirical formula. Group classification and group index values determine the relative quality of soils for their suitability in embankments, subgrades, bases, and subbases. Soils are divided into two major groups: (1) granular materials, which pass less than 35 percent of materials through a No. 200 sieve, and (2) silt-clay materials, which pass more than 35 percent of the material through a No. 200 sieve.

TABLE 810-1
Soil Particle Size Classification

Particle size, mm	*Sieve sizes*	*Unified Soil Classification**	*U.S. Department of Agriculture Soil Classification*	*American Association of State Highway Officials Soil Classification*	*American Society for Testing and Materials Soil Classification*
0.001			Clay	Colloids	Colloids
0.002					
0.003				Clay	Clay
0.004					
0.006		Fines (silt or clay)			
0.008					
0.01			Silt		
0.02				Silt	Silt
0.03					
0.04					
	270				
0.06			Very fine sand		
0.08	200				
0.1	140				
0.2		Fine sand	Fine sand	Fine sand	Fine sand
0.3	60				
0.4			Medium sand		
0.6	40				
0.8			Coarse sand		
1.0	20	Medium sand	Very coarse sand	Coarse sand	Coarse sand
2.0	10				
3.0					
4.0		Coarse sand	Fine gravel	Fine gravel	
	4				
6.0					
8.0		Fine gravel			
10	½″				
	¾″			Medium gravel	Gravel
20					
30		Coarse gravel	Coarse gravel		
40				Coarse gravel	
60	3″				
80		Cobbles	Cobbles	Boulders	

*Corps of Engineers, Department of the Army, and Bureau of Reclamation.
Source: Douglas S. Way, *Terrain Analysis: A Guide to Site Selection Using Aerial Photographic Interpretation,* 2d ed., Douglas S. Way, Columbus, Ohio, 1978.

TABLE 810-2
The New Soil Taxonomy (World Seventh Approximation)

Soil order	*Climatic range*	*Natural vegetation*	*Parent materials*	*Horizon development*	*Drainage*	*Colors*
Entisol	All climates, arid to humid, tropical to polar	Highly variable. Forests, grass, desert, tidal marsh	Primarily free-draining alluvium and aeolian, and low-activity clays	None, except perhaps for a thin A horizon	Good; slopes not significant	Not significant
Vertisols	Subhumid to arid with wet and dry seasons, or arid areas subject to flooding	Grasses and woody shrubs	High-activity clays, shrinking when dry, swelling when wet, with montmorillonite common	B horizon commonly absent	Poor; slopes flat to gentle	Black, gray, brown
Inceptisols	Humid, from arctic to tropical	Mostly forests, occasionally grasslands	Young soils from residuum, loess, glacial till. Soils moist.	One or more formed without significant illuviation or eluviation. A horizon very organic	Slopes flat to moderately steep	Light to dark
Aridsols	Arid to semiarid	Sparse grasses and other desert vegetation	Generally alluvium	Poor horizon development and very little organic matter. Soil rich in lime, gypsum, or sodium chloride. Caliche common	Slopes flat to gentle	Light to red
Mollisols	Alpine to tropical; with cool, dry seasons, and hot, moist seasons	Grasses, sedges, hardwood forests	Variable: loess, alluvium, till, residuum	Distinct horizons. Highly organic A layer. B and C horizons may have secondary lime accumulations	Flat to slight slopes and poor drainage	Medium to dark colors
Spodosol	Humid regions, alpine to tropical	Coniferous forest, savannah, or rain forest	Usually siliceous, granular, and not very clayey	B horizon illuviated with organic matter, iron and aluminum oxides	Good	Black, brown, reddish
Alfisols	Cool humid to subhumid with seasonal rainfall	Deciduous forest, some tall grasslands	Variable, but generally young; alluvium, till, loess, or coastal plain. Calcareous in cool, humid climates	Thin, highly organic A horizon. B horizon illuviated with clay, organic matter, and iron oxide	Poor. Flat to gentle slopes	Black, brown, reddish
Ultisols	Humid	Forest, savannah, marsh, or swamp	Old and strongly weathered residuum or coastal plain	Thin A horizon with some humus over illuviated B horizon. Approaching a lateritic soil	Poor to fair. Slopes moderate to steep	Variable and often mottled with gray, yellow, and red
Oxisols	Tropics and subtropics with wet and dry seasons	Forest to savannah	Lateritic soils primarily from basic rock residuum	Little organic soil development. Clay content high but formation porous. Concentrations of iron and aluminum at various depths	Good	Reds, browns
Histosols	Moist to wet	Swamp, marsh, and bog	Organic materials	None visible	Very poor	Gray to black

Source: Roy E. Hunt, *Geotechnical Engineering Investigation Manual,* McGraw-Hill, New York, 1984. [Original source: U.S. Soil Conservation Service, *Soil Classification: A Comprehensive System (7th Approximation),* Washington, D.C., 1960.]

TABLE 810-3
Common Terms of the USDA Soil Classification System

General terms	Basic soil-textural class names
Sandy soils, coarse-textured soils	Sands, loamy sands
Loamy soils	
Moderately coarse-textured soils	Sandy loam, fine sandy loam
Medium-textured soils	Very fine sandy loam, loam, silt loam, silt
Moderately fine-textured soils	Clay loam, sandy clay loam, silty clay loam
Clayey soils, fine-textured soils	Sandy clay, silty clay, clay

Source: U.S. Department of Agriculture, *Soil Taxonomy,* Washington, D.C., 1975.

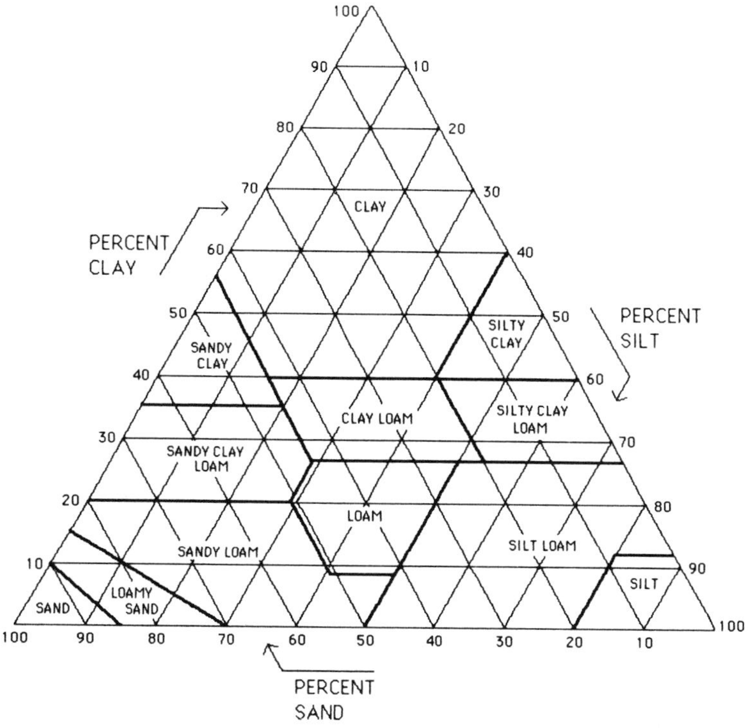
PERCENT CLAY
PERCENT SILT
PERCENT SAND
CLAY
SANDY CLAY
SILTY CLAY
CLAY LOAM
SILTY CLAY LOAM
SANDY CLAY LOAM
LOAM
SANDY LOAM
SILT LOAM
SILT
LOAMY SAND
SAND
100
90
80
70
60
50
40
30
20
10

Figure 810-2 USDA soil textural triangle.

TABLE 810-4
AASHTO Soil Classification System and General Ratings

General classification	*Granular materials**							*Silt-clay materials†*			
Group classification‡	*A-1*		*A-3*	*A-2*				*A-4*	*A-5*	*A-6*	*A-7*
	A-1-a	*A-1-b*		*A-2-4*	*A-2-5*	*A-2-6*	*A-2-7*				*A-7-5§ A-7-6¶*
Sieve analysis: Percent passing											
No. 10	50 max.	—	—	—	—	—	—	—	—	—	—
No. 40	30 max.	50 max.	51 min.	—	—	—	—	—	—	—	—
No. 200	15 max.	25 max.	10 max.	35 max.	35 max.	35 max.	35 max.	36 min.	36 min.	36 min.	36 min.
Characteristics of fraction passing No. 40 sieve											
Liquid limit	—	—	—	40 max.	41 min.	40 max.	41 min.	40 max.	41 min.	40 max.	41 max.
Plasticity index	6 max.	6 max.	Nonplastic	10 max.	10 max.	11 min.	11 min.	10 max.	10 max.	11 min.	11 min.
Group index	0	0	0	0	0	4 max.	4 max.	8 max.	12 max.	16 max.	20 max.
Usual types of significant constituent materials	Stone fragments: gravel and sand		Fine sand	Silty or clayey gravel and sand				Silty soils		Clayey soils	
General rating as subgrade	← Excellent to good →							← Fair to poor →		← Very poor →	

*35% or less passing through a No. 200 sieve.
†More than 35% passing through a No. 200 sieve.
‡Placing A-3 before A-2 is necessary in the left-to-right elimination process and does not indicate superiority of A-3 over A-2.
§Plasticity index of A-7-5 subgroup is equal to or less than the liquid limit minus 30.
¶Plasticity index of A-7-6 subgroup is greater than liquid limit minus 30.
Source: Douglas S. Way, *Terrain Analysis: A Guide to Site Selection Using Aerial Photographic Interpretation,* 2d ed., Douglas S. Way, Columbus, Ohio, 1978.

TABLE 810-5
Soil Types and Their Properties (Unified Soil Classification System)

Division	*Symbols* Letter	Color	*Soil description*	*Value as a foundation material**	*Frost action*	*Drainage*
Gravel and gravelly soils	GW	Red	Well-graded gravel, or gravel-sand mixture, little or no fines	Excellent	None	Excellent
	GP	Red	Poorly graded gravel, or gravel-sand mixtures, little or no fines	Good	None	Excellent
	GM	Yellow	Silty gravels, gravel-sand-silt mixtures	Good	Slight	Poor
	GC	Yellow	Clayey-gravels, gravel-clay-sand mixtures	Good	Slight	Poor
Sand and sandy soils	SW	Red	Well-graded sands, or gravelly sands, little or no fines	Good	None	Excellent
	SP	Red	Poorly graded sands, or gravelly sands, little or no fines	Fair	None	Excellent
	SM	Yellow	Silty sands, sand-silt mixtures	Fair	Slight	Fair
	SC	Yellow	Clayey sands, sand-clay mixtures	Fair	Medium	Poor
Silts and clays LL <50†	ML	Green	Inorganic silts, rock flour, silty or clayey fine sands, or clayey silts with slight plasticity	Fair	Very high	Poor
	CL	Green	Inorganic clays of low to medium plasticity, gravelly clays, silty clays, lean clays	Fair	Medium	Impervious
	OL	Green	Organic silt-clays of low plasticity	Poor	High	Impervious
Silts and clays LL >50	MH	Blue	Inorganic silts, micaceous or diatomaceous fine sandy or silty soils, elastic silts	Poor	Very high	Poor
	CH	Blue	Inorganic clays of high plasticity, fat clays	Very poor	Medium	Impervious
	OH	Blue	Organic clays of medium to high plasticity, organic silts	Very poor	Medium	Impervious
Highly organic soils	Pt	Orange	Peat and other highly organic soils	Not suitable	Slight	Poor

* Consult soil engineers and local building codes for allowable soil-bearing capacities.

† LL indicates liquid limit.

Source: Adapted from Charles G. Ramsey and Harold R. Sleeper, *Architectural Graphic Standards,* 7th ed., Robert T. Packard (ed.), Wiley, New York, 1981.

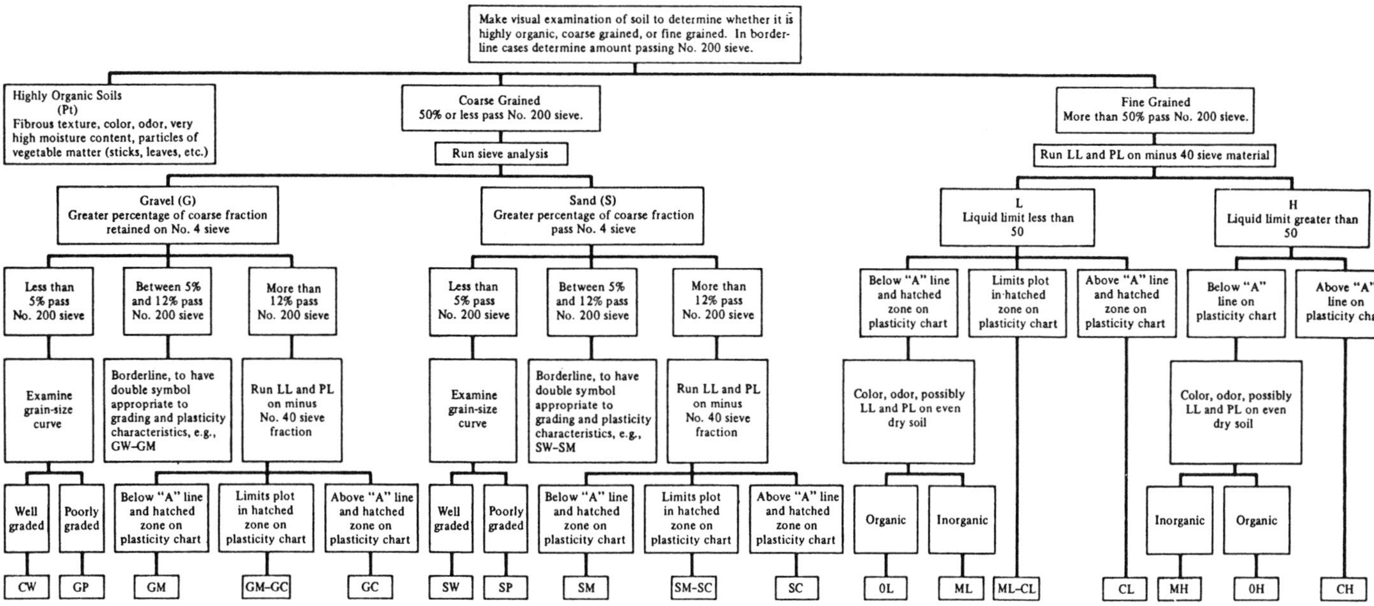
Make visual examination of soil to determine whether it is highly organic, coarse grained, or fine grained. In borderline cases determine amount passing No. 200 sieve.
Highly Organic Soils (Pt) Fibrous texture, color, odor, very high moisture content, particles of vegetable matter (sticks, leaves, etc.)
Coarse Grained 50% or less pass No. 200 sieve.
Fine Grained More than 50% pass No. 200 sieve.
Run sieve analysis
Run LL and PL on minus 40 sieve material
Gravel (G) Greater percentage of coarse fraction retained on No. 4 sieve
Sand (S) Greater percentage of coarse fraction pass No. 4 sieve
L Liquid limit less than 50
H Liquid limit greater than 50
Less than 5% pass No. 200 sieve
Between 5% and 12% pass No. 200 sieve
More than 12% pass No. 200 sieve
Below "A" line and hatched zone on plasticity chart
Limits plot in hatched zone on plasticity chart
Above "A" line and hatched zone on plasticity chart
Below "A" line on plasticity chart
Above "A" line on plasticity chart
Examine grain-size curve
Borderline, to have double symbol appropriate to grading and plasticity characteristics, e.g., GW-GM
Run LL and PL on minus No. 40 sieve fraction
Borderline, to have double symbol appropriate to grading and plasticity characteristics, e.g., SW-SM
Color, odor, possibly LL and PL on even dry soil
Well graded
Poorly graded
Organic
Inorganic
CW
GP
GM
GM-GC
GC
SW
SP
SM
SM-SC
SC
OL
ML
ML-CL
CL
MH
OH
CH

Figure 810-3 Classification procedure for the unified system.

2.4 The Unified System

The Unified Soil Classification System divides soils into three basic categories: (1) coarse-grained soils, (2) fine-grained soils, and (3) organic soils (Table 810-5). Coarse-grained soils pass less than 50 percent fines through a No. 200 sieve, and fine-grained soils pass more than 50 percent fines through a No. 200 sieve. Organic soils are identified by visual examination. Soil divisions are further delineated by 15 soil groups based on liquid limit, major soil textural fraction, and relative gradation.

The unified system was devised mainly for highway engineering purposes. Figure 810-3 shows how specific classifications are determined.

TABLE 810-6
Classification of Soils by Origin

Type	*Origin*
Residual	Rock weathered in place—wacke, laterite, podzols, residual sands, clays, and gravels
Cumulose	Organic accumulations—peat, muck, swamp soils, muskeg, humus, bog soils
Transported:	
Glacial	Moraines, eskers, drumlins, kames—till, drift, boulder clay, glacial sands, and gravels
Alluvial	Flood plains, deltas, bars—sedimentary clays and silts, alluvial sands and gravels
Aeolian	Wind-borne deposits—blow sands, dune sands, loess, adobe
Colluvial	Gravity deposits—cliff debris, talus, avalanches, masses of rock waste
Volcanic	Volcanic deposits—Dakota bentonite, volclay, volcanic ash, lava
Fill	Synthetic deposits—ranging from waste and rubbish to built embankments

Source: Adapted from Elwyn E. Seelye, *Design: Data Book for Civil Engineers,* 3d ed., Wiley, New York, 1945; and from the Portland Cement Association, *Soil Cement Laboratory Handbook,* Skokie, Ill.

2.5 Classification of Soil by Origin

Soils can be classified either as *residual soils* (formed in place through weathering of bedrock and disintegration of organic matter) or as *transported soils* (materials that have been moved from another place by glaciation, wind, water, or gravity). Table 810-6 indicates a classification of soils according to their origin.

3.0 SOILS AND SITE ENGINEERING

The properties of soils relevant to site engineering are as follows: *Colloidal content* basically refers to the amount of clay particles in a soil sample. A high clay content limits the permeability of the soil and can adversely affect the ability of plants to absorb dissolved nutrients in solution. Some clays (e.g., montmorillonite clays) have great absorptive capacity, meaning that they swell enormously when wet and shrink and crack when dry.

Capillarity refers to the upward movement of water above the water table as a function of fine soil texture. Clay and silt soils have higher capillarity than coarse-textured soils (Table 810-7).

Permeability refers to the ability of a soil to transmit water downward by the force of gravity (Table 810-8). Permeability is a function of pore space and varies with void ratio, grain size and distribution, structure, degree of cementation, degree of saturation, and degree of compaction. Coarse-grained soils are typically more permeable than fine-grained soils. Percolation tests measure the permeability of a soil for use as a septic leaching field.

Elasticity refers to the ability of soil to return to its original shape after being deformed by a load. Conversely, it refers to the compactability of a soil. In landscape construction, the relative elasticity of soils on a site may determine where heavy equipment can be moved or allowed to travel, to avoid undesirable compaction of soils.

Plasticity refers to the ability of soil to be deformed under pressure without cracking or crumbling and to maintain a deformed shape after pressure is released. Plastic deformation is an important factor in road

TABLE 810-7
Capillary Action in Various Soil Types*

Capillary rise			*Saturation zone*	
Ft	*M*	*Soil type*	*Ft*	*M*
>8	2.4	Clay	>5	1.5
>8	2.4	Silt	>5	1.5
3–8	1–2.4	Fine sand	1–5	0.3–1.5
1–3	0.3–1	Coarse sand	0–1	0–0.3
0	0	Gravel	0	0

* Water rises in most soils by capillary action. Clays and silts may become fully saturated to almost 6 ft (2 m) above a water table, and some water may rise more than 11 ft (3.4 m). Note that coarse sand may allow a rise up to 3 ft (1 m). No capillarity results in coarse gravel.

Source: Adapted with permission from Harold B. Olin, John L. Schmidt, and Walter H. Lewis, *Construction: Principles, Materials, and Methods,* U.S. League of Savings Institutions, Chicago, 1983.

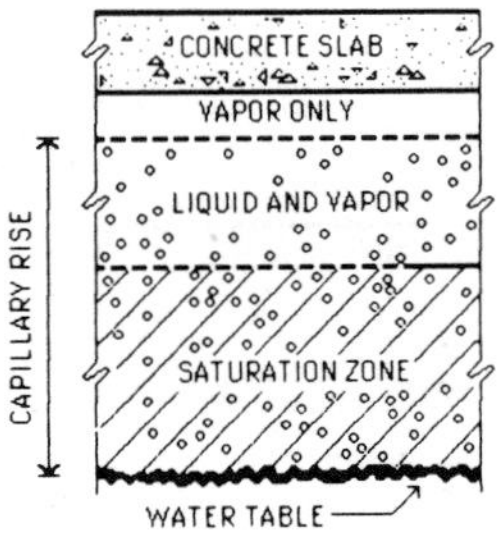
CONCRETE SLAB
VAPOR ONLY
LIQUID AND VAPOR
SATURATION ZONE
CAPILLARY RISE
WATER TABLE

TABLE 810-8
Permeability and Drainage Characteristics of Various Soil Types

Soil type	*Approximate coefficient of permeability* k, *cm per sec*	*Drainage characteristic*
Clean gravel	5–10	Good
Clean coarse sand	0.4–3	Good
Clean medium sand	0.05–0.15	Good
Clean fine sand	0.004–0.02	Good
Silty sand and gravel	10^{-5}–0.01	Poor to good
Silty sand	10^{-5}–10^{-4}	Poor
Sandy clay	10^{-6}–10^{-5}	Poor
Silty clay	10^{-6}	Poor
Clay	10^{-7}	Poor
Colloidal clay	10^{-9}	Poor

Source: Frederick S. Merritt, *Standard Handbook for Civil Engineers,* 3d ed., McGraw-Hill, New York, 1983.

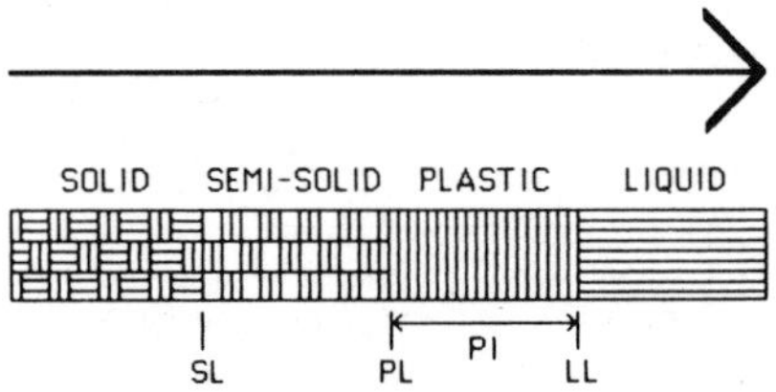
SOLID
SEMI-SOLID
PLASTIC
LIQUID
SL
PL
PI
LL

Figure 810-4 States of fine-soil consistency. As water content increases, soils become increasingly fluid. *PI* refers to the *plastic index, PL* to the *plastic limit, LL* to the *liquid limit,* and *SL* to the *shrinkage limit.*

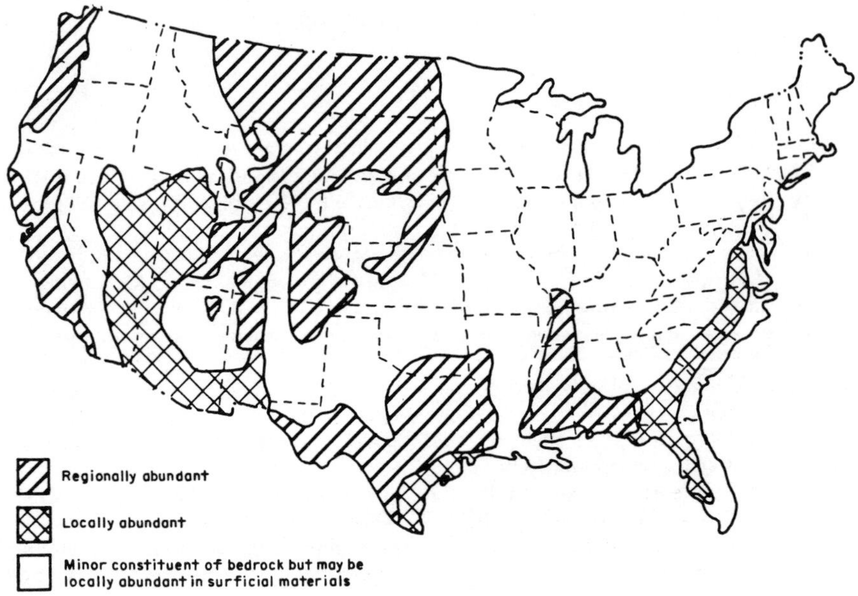
Regionally abundant
Locally abundant
Minor constituent of bedrock but may be locally abundant in surficial materials

Figure 810-5 Areas of expansive soils in the United States. Expansive soils are most widespread in areas labeled regionally abundant, but many locations in these areas will have no expansive soils. In the unshaded portions of the map, some expansive soils may be found, but not in major regional concentrations.

and foundation work and is more significant under increasingly greater loads. Given a sufficiently large load, a soil mass can fail in shear. *Liquid limit* refers to the moisture content at which a soil passes from a liquid to a plastic state as moisture is removed. *Plastic limit* refers to the moisture content at which soil passes from a plastic to a semisolid state as water is removed. *Plasticity index* refers to liquid limit minus plastic limit (Figure 810-4).

Shrinkage and swell (volume change) refers to the buildup and release of capillary tensile stresses within soil pore water. Volume changes are most profound among *expansive soils*. Figure 810-5 shows the general distribution of expansive soils in the United States. (Refer to Section 255: Natural Hazards: Expansive Soils, for more information on expansive soils and their implications in site planning, design, and engineering.)

Frost susceptibility refers to the relative susceptibility of a soil to frost heave when moisture in the soil becomes frozen. Fine-grained soils exhibit a greater tendency to heave under cold temperatures than do coarse-grained soils. The likelihood of heaving is dependent upon: (1) freezing temperatures in the soil, (2) a water table close to the frost line, and (3) soil characteristics favoring rapid upward movement of capillary water (i.e., clays and silts). Preventative action against frost heave includes such measures as the removal of the fine-grained material and its replacement with a non-frost-susceptible subbase and base (typically gravel or rock fill), the intentional lowering of water tables, and the installation of some form of insulation above the frost-susceptible material (Figures 810-6 through 810-8).

Cohesion refers to the ability of a soil sample to bind together when moderately dry. Cohesionless soils (like beach sand, for instance) are easy to excavate, but vertical side slopes cannot be maintained without support.

Compressibility refers to the measured volume change of soil as a result of changed soil structure and the expulsion of water. *Compaction* refers to the densification process through the compaction and expulsion of air. In landscape construction, soils often have to be compacted to prescribed *densities* to meet predetermined performance criteria. Proper compaction of soils is best accomplished when soils are of fairly specific moisture contents, depending on the type of soil to be compacted.

Table 810-9 describes a number of compaction techniques for soils, and Figure 810-9 shows optimum moisture contents for compaction of various soil types.

Bearing Strength refers to the ability of a soil to bear a load without failure; it de-

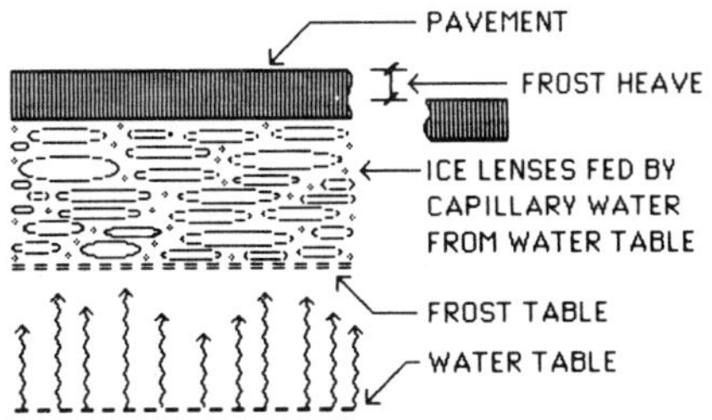
PAVEMENT
FROST HEAVE
ICE LENSES FED BY CAPILLARY WATER FROM WATER TABLE
FROST TABLE
WATER TABLE

Figure 810-6 Dynamics of frost heave. Frost heave is caused by ice lenses forming beneath the pavement structure.

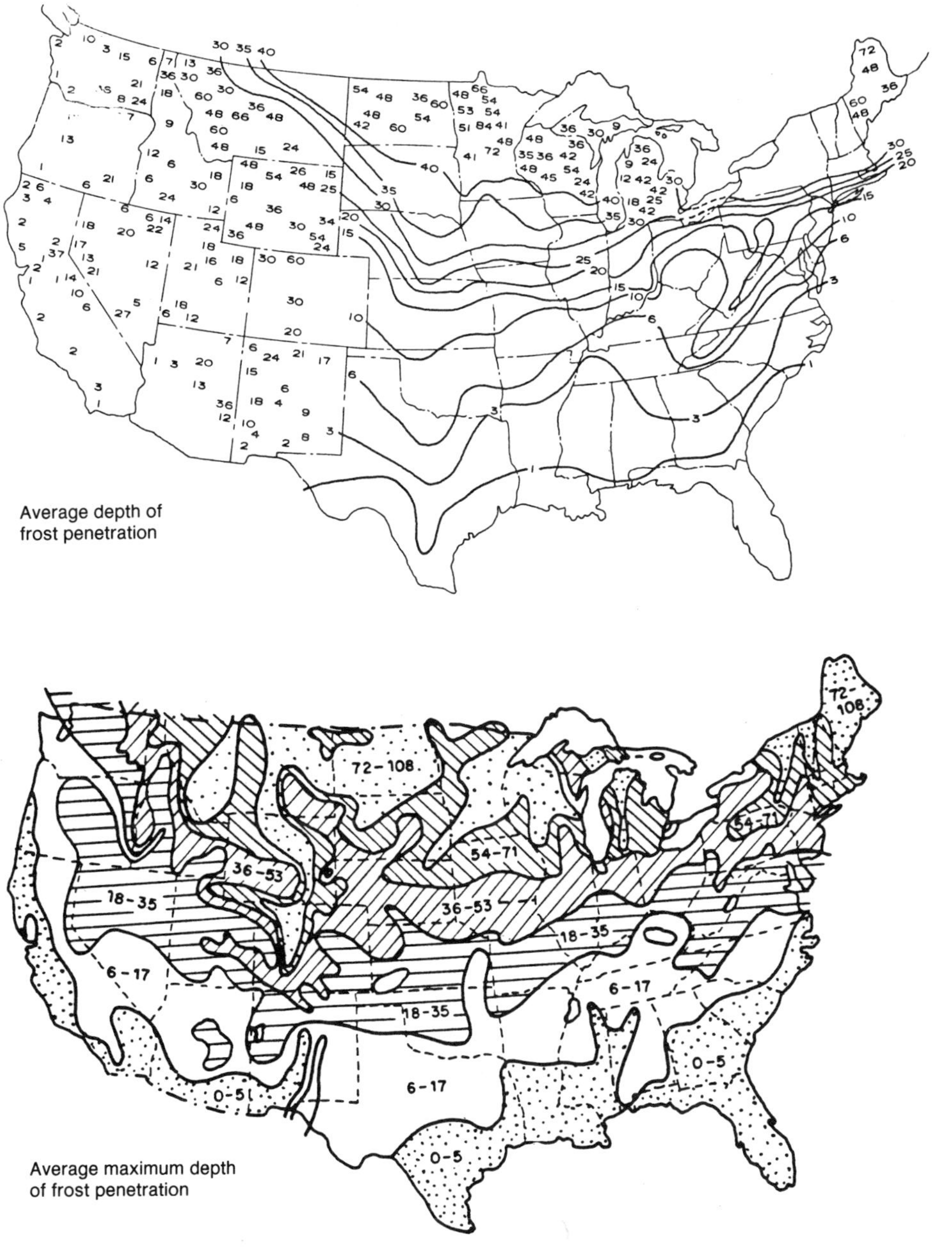
Average depth of frost penetration
Average maximum depth of frost penetration
72-108
54-71
36-53
18-35
6-17
0-5

Figure 810-7 Depths of frost penetration in the United States (inches). Note that depths of frost penetration can vary from these averages in specific geographical locations, especially in areas of significant topographic change. Always check local sources for more precise averages.

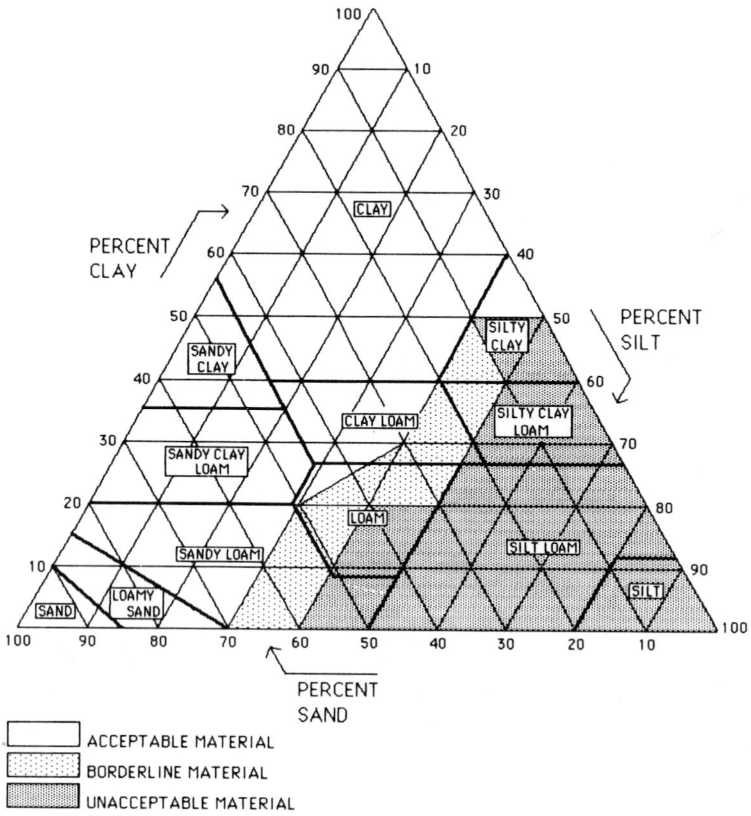
PERCENT CLAY
PERCENT SILT
PERCENT SAND
CLAY
SILTY CLAY
SANDY CLAY
SILTY CLAY LOAM
CLAY LOAM
SANDY CLAY LOAM
LOAM
SILT LOAM
SANDY LOAM
LOAMY SAND
SAND
SILT
ACCEPTABLE MATERIAL
BORDERLINE MATERIAL
UNACCEPTABLE MATERIAL

Figure 810-8 Soils most susceptible to frost heave.

TABLE 810-9
Compaction Techniques for Soils

General soil types	*Compaction technique of fill*	*Compaction technique of natural formation*
Cohesionless soil (sand and gravel)	Compaction is best when soil is vibrated and rolled. Rolling with saturated soil is possible, but rapid permeability makes continued saturation difficult.	Vibration by pile driving, vibrofloation, or dynamite
Moderately cohesive soils (sand and silt)	Compacted in thin layers at optimum moisture content. Pneumatic rollers work best on slightly cohesive soils, gravel and silt soils, sandy soils, and nonplastic silt soils. Sheepsfoot rollers are better on plastic silt and clay soils.	Pile driving above water table. Must lower water table and use pile driving to compact lower levels
Cohesive soils (clay and clay silt)	Soils should be compacted in thin layers at optimum moisture content. Pneumatic rollers work best on slightly cohesive soils, gravel and silt soils, sandy soils, and nonplastic silt soils. Sheepsfoot rollers are better on plastic silt and clay soils.	Clays, organic material, and loose silts are best compacted by surcharging, i.e., by covering the area with sufficient amounts of fill (weight) to a desired degree of settlement

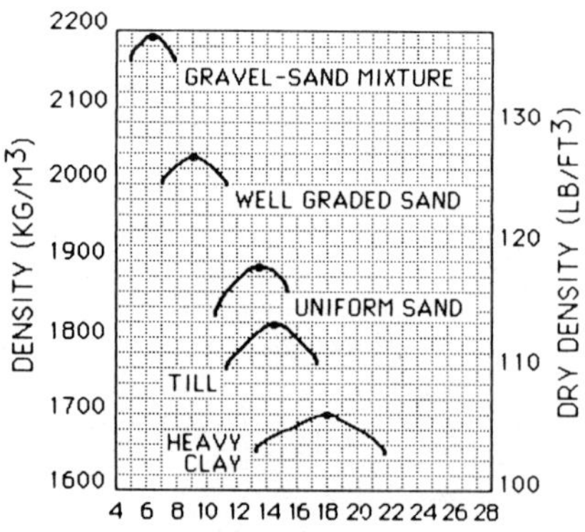
DENSITY (KG/M³)
DRY DENSITY (LB/FT³)
GRAVEL-SAND MIXTURE
WELL GRADED SAND
UNIFORM SAND
TILL
HEAVY CLAY

Figure 810-9 Optimum moisture contents (compaction curves) for various soil types (percent). High point on curve denotes optimum moisture content for particular soil type.

pends both upon internal friction between soil particles and upon cohesion. Bearing strength is affected by changes in water content, rate and time of loading, and confining pressure. Soils compacted at optimal moisture content typically exhibit greater shear strengths than do wet soils. Approximate *bearing strengths* of various types of soils are shown in Table 810-10.

Erodibility of a soil refers to the extent to which a soil mass can withstand the forces of wind or water erosion. Figure 810-10 shows degrees of erodibility for various types of soils. (Refer to Section 253: Natural Hazards: Landslides and Snow Avalanches, for information on processes of mass wasting or landslides attributable to various soil conditions.)

TABLE 810-10
Presumed Bearing Capacity of Various Types of Soil

Soil types	*U.S. tons/ft²*	*Metric tons/m²*
Well-graded, well-compacted clayey sands and gravels	10	120
Gravels and gravelly sands, ranging from loose to well-compacted	4–8	45–95
Coarse sands, from loose to well-compacted	2–4	25–45
Fine, silty, or clayey sands, not well-graded, from loose to well-compacted	1.5–3	20–35
Homogeneous, nonplastic, inorganic clays, from soft to very stiff	0.5–4	5–45
Inorganic, nonplastic silts, from soft to very stiff	0.5–3	5–35

Source: Kevin Lynch and Gary Hack, *Site Planning,* 3d ed., MIT Press, Cambridge, Mass., 1984.

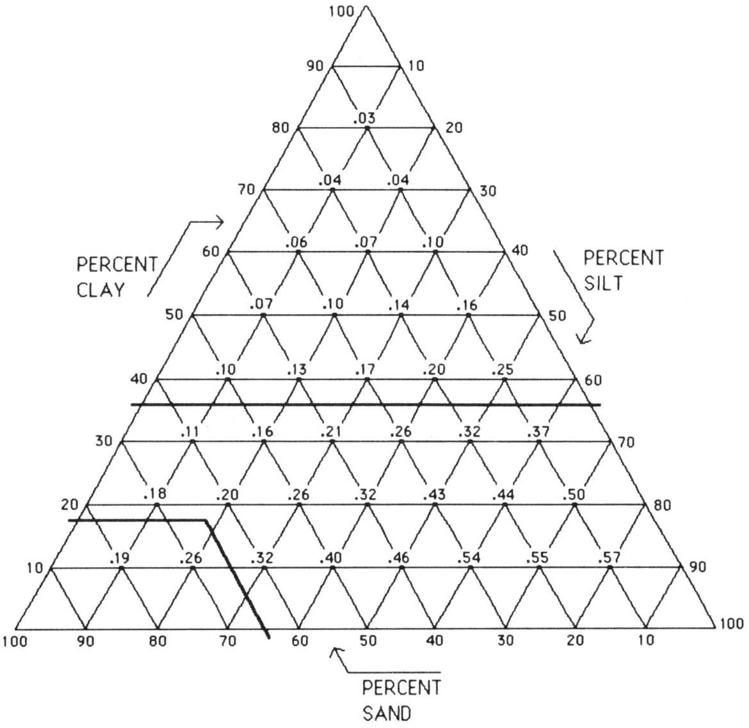
PERCENT CLAY
PERCENT SILT
PERCENT SAND
100
90
80
70
60
50
40
30
20
10
.03
.04 .04
.06 .07 .10
.07 .10 .14 .16
.10 .13 .17 .20 .25
.11 .16 .21 .26 .32 .37
.18 .20 .26 .32 .43 .44 .50
.19 .26 .32 .40 .46 .54 .55 .57

Figure 810-10 Soil erodibility factor (*K*). USDA textural triangle with plotted *K* values to show relationships between sizes of mineral particles and soil erodibility.

4.0 SOILS AND HORTICULTURAL APPLICATIONS

4.1 Properties of Soils Relevant to Horticulture

Available Moisture and Adequate Drainage:

The existence of soil moisture does not ensure that water will be available to plants (Figure 810-11). Ideally, the ratio of air space to water in the soil should be 1:1. Plants begin to wilt at the point at which the remaining soil moisture is held in tension by hygroscopic forces.

Soil pH:

Soil pH refers to the relative acidity or alkalinity of a soil. It is an important determinant in the selection of plant materials because of its effect on nutrient availability (Table 810-11 and Figure 810-12). The pH values are expressed as the logarithm of the reciprocal of the hydrogen ion concentration in the soil; they range from 1 to 10, with 7 being neutral. Values below 7 indicate acidity, while higher values indicate alkalinity. Because all plants have specific tolerances for soil acidity or alkalinity, the pH tolerances for all proposed plant materials must be known before specifying or modifying soils for particular landscape projects.

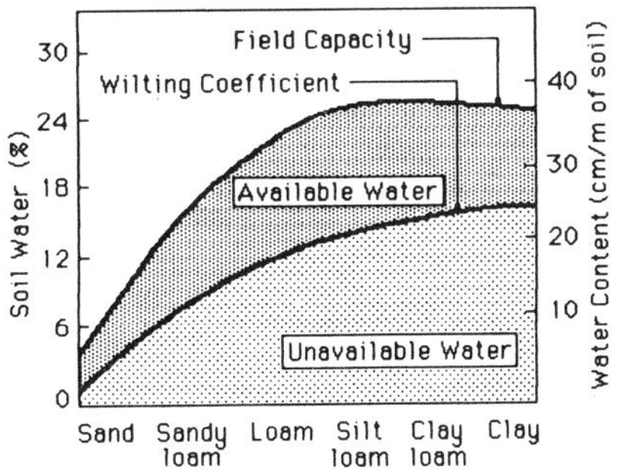
Field Capacity
Wilting Coefficient
Available Water
Unavailable Water
Soil Water (%)
0
6
12
18
24
30
Water Content (cm/m of soil)
10
20
30
40
Sand
Sandy loam
Loam
Silt loam
Clay loam
Clay

Figure 810-11 Water availability in soils (for plant growth). This chart shows the general relationship between soil moisture characteristics and soil texture. Note that the wilting coefficient increases as soil texture becomes coarser. These are representative curves. Individual soils would likely have values different than those shown.

4.2 Soils and Planting

Table 810-12 shows the relative suitability of various soils as a medium for healthy plant growth. Table 810-13 illustrates the relationship of soil texture to other soi characteristics.

TABLE 810-11
Terms for Various pH Levels

Characteristics	*pH*
Extremely acid	Below 4.5
Very strongly acid	4.5–5.0
Strongly acid	5.1–5.5
Medium acid	5.6–6.0
Slightly acid	6.1–6.5
Neutral*	6.6–7.3
Mildly alkaline	7.4–7.8
Moderately alkaline	7.9–8.4
Strongly alkaline	8.5–9.0
Very strongly alkaline	9.1 and higher

* Strict neutrality is pH 7.0, but in field work those soils between pH 6.6 and 7.3 are considered neutral.

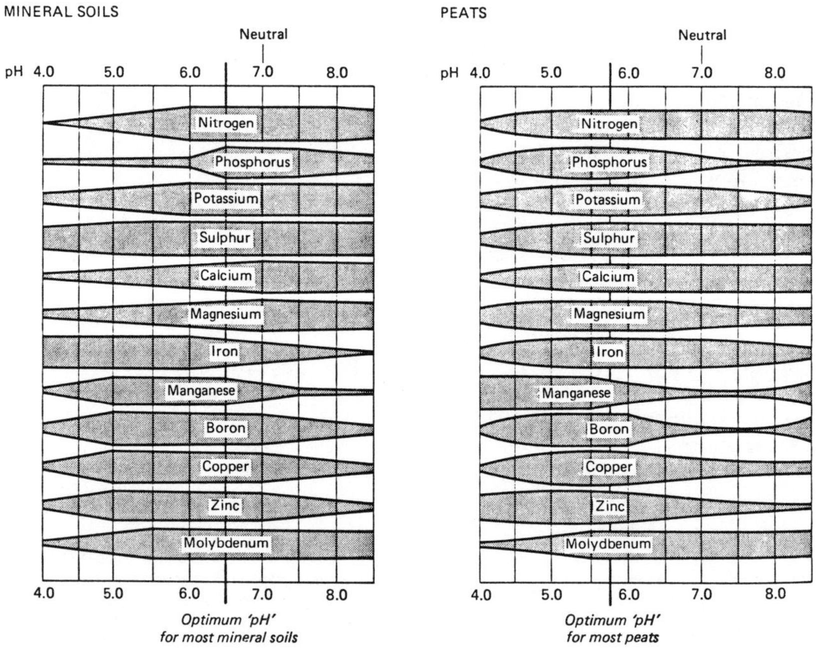
MINERAL SOILS
Neutral
pH 4.0 5.0 6.0 7.0 8.0
Nitrogen
Phosphorus
Potassium
Sulphur
Calcium
Magnesium
Iron
Manganese
Boron
Copper
Zinc
Molybdenum
4.0 5.0 6.0 7.0 8.0
Optimum 'pH' for most mineral soils
PEATS
Neutral
pH 4.0 5.0 6.0 7.0 8.0
Nitrogen
Phosphorus
Potassium
Sulphur
Calcium
Magnesium
Iron
Manganese
Boron
Copper
Zinc
Molybdenum
4.0 5.0 6.0 7.0 8.0
Optimum 'pH' for most peats

Figure 810-12 pH levels and nutrient availability. These graphs illustrate the effect of soil pH on nutrient availability. The growing media should be kept at a pH level at which all essential nutrients are available for the plantings. For most plants, the optimum pH level is 6.5 in mineral soils and 5.8 in peats.

TABLE 810-12
Relative Suitability of Various Soils for Healthy Plant Growth

	Soil suitability rating		
Item affecting use	*Good*	*Moderate*	*Poor*
Soil drainage class	Well and moderately well-drained	Somewhat poorly drained	Poorly and very poorly drained
Moist consistence	Very friable, friable	Loose, firm	Very firm, extremely firm
Textures*	vfsl, fsl, l, sil, sl	cl, scl, sicl, sc	s, c, sic
Thickness of soil (above hard layer, water table, or bedrock)	>30 in	20–30 in	<20 in
Coarse fragments (volume)	<8%	8–15%	>15%
Slope	<8%	8–15%	>15%

Key:
Vfsl—very fine sandy loam
Fsl—fine sandy loam
L—loam
Sil—silt loam
Sl—sandy loam
Cl—clay loam
Scl—sandy clay loam
Sicl—silty clay loam
Sc—sand/clay mixture
S—sand
C—clay
Sic—silt/clay mixture

TABLE 810-13
Relationship of Soil Texture to Other Soil Characteristics

Characteristic	*Sand*	*Loam*	*Silt Loam*	*Clay*
Identification	Loose	Cohesive	Shows fingerprints	Shiny streak
Permeability	Excessive	Good	Fair	Fair to poor
Available water	Low	Medium	High	High to medium
Tillability	Easy	Easy	Moderate	Difficult
Runoff potential	Low	Low to medium	High	Medium to high
Nutrient storage capacity	Low	Medium	Medium	High
Compactability	Low	Medium	Medium to high	High
Suitability	High	High	High to medium	Low
Susceptibility to problems of insufficient aeration	Low	Medium	Medium	High

Source: Phillip J. Craul, *Urban Forest Soils,* School of Forestry, State University of New York, Syracuse, N.Y. (From workbook for conference on Urban Forest Soils, sponsored by U.S. Forest Service, U.S. National Park Service, 1982.)

TABLE 810-14
Compressive Strength of Common Rock Types Used as Aggregates

Rock type	*Approximate strength range, MPa*
Quartzite	423–124
Basalt	377–201
Schist	297–91
Granite	257–115
Limestone	241–93
Gneiss	235–94
Sandstone	240–94

4.3 Soils and Urban Plantings

Planted areas in urban environments (primarily paved areas near streets and heavy pedestrian traffic) often have problems of compaction, limited nutrient availability, and pollution from poisonous elements. One of the most severe is compaction of soils which results in retarded water infiltration, increased runoff, inhibited gas exchange, an oxygen deficient environment, a reduction in valuable soil organisms, severely inhibited root growth, and increased thermal conductivity. Soils for all urban plantings require special preparation to ensure the long-term healthy growth of plant materials.

5.0 AGGREGATES

Aggregates refer to granular materials, including sand, gravel, and crushed stone, as well as lightweight manufactured materials such as slag, vermiculite, and pumice. Aggregates are used in the mixing of concretes, mortars, asphaltic concretes, mastics, and plasters. Untreated, aggregates are commonly used as a subbase, base, or surface material for walkways and roads. Other uses include material for setting brick and stone, playground material, use as mulch, slope and shore protection, use in water recharge techniques, and use as filtration material in sewage and water treatments.

5.1 Classification of Aggregates

The quality of an aggregate is a measure of its strength, toughness, hardness, durability, resistance to freeze/thaw, surface characteristics, and chemical stability. Desirable characteristics vary depending on the purpose for which the aggregate will be used.

Cleanliness, soundness, strength, and gradation are important properties in aggregate for most of the purposes it will be used. Aggregates are considered clean if they are free of excess clay, silt, mica, organic matter, chemical salts, and coated grains. An aggregate is physically sound if it remains dimensionally stable under temperature or moisture change and resists weathering without decomposition. If exposed aggregate is to be used, it may be necessary to conduct abrasion tests to determine its durability as part of the wearing surface. Typically, strength is not empirically measured; reliance is placed on the performance of existing structures, i.e., precedence, for evidence of adequate strength (Table 810-14).

Aggregates are graded by size through progressively smaller sieves and are commonly combined in certain proportions to produce aggregate mixtures. The aggregate composition is defined by the percentage of the total sample (by weight) that passes through each sieve. Grading is controlled by the producer and can be adjusted to meet the grading requirements of project specifications.

TABLE 810-15
Common Loose Aggregates Used for Walkways

Material	*Color*	*Physical properties*	*Considerations*
Gravel:			
Pea gravel	Salmon, buff, off-white	Round-shaped (small)	Used for residential terraces and walks
Gravel	Varies with region	Dries quickly; washes easily; excellent base and margin for stepping stones, tile, or concrete paving	Easy to maintain by raking; stands up best when used as a topping over a more permanent bed
Crushed stone:			
Granite chips ($\frac{1}{16}$–1 in)		Angular shape; compacts well; particles interlock	Stays in place longer than rounded materials; can be manufactured with smooth edges; provides stable surface
Decomposed granite		Compacts solidly when dampened and rolled	Similar to redrock; wears better; costs ± ⅓ more
Colored rock	Pink, red, others	Small fragments make impervious bedding advisable	Not as economical as other gravels; some colored rocks only available locally
Dolomite	Stark white	Discolors easily	Requires extra care; not expensive; used best in small areas
Redrock		Compacts solidly when dampened and rolled; provides clean, hard, surface; surface breaks down into dust over time	Available under other names
Crushed brick	Venetian red (intense)	Fragments break up and wear down; stable base required	Good accent to planting; not suitable in areas with heavy traffic; expensive (10 times the cost of redrock)
Smelting byproducts:			
Chert		Medium to lightweight; compacts; crowns and rolls easily; soft, crunchy surface	
Red blaes		Medium to lightweight; porous; holds water	
Leca	Similar to pea gravel	Lightweight; absorbs water	Excellent for roof landscapes

5.2 Common Applications and Important Considerations

Aggregates are used for a wide variety of purposes in landscape construction, ranging from use as a foundation material to use in finished surfaces for walkways, driveways, and parking areas. Two of the most common uses of loose aggregate are for walkways and gravel roads. Other common uses of aggregate are discussed comprehensively in other sections of this handbook.

Pedestrian Walkways:

In regions where aggregate materials are readily available, aggregate walkways are inexpensive and easy to install (Table 810-15). Aggregates can be used to supplement existing paving, to pave secondary areas such as walkways and terraces, or as a temporary treatment.

The inherent disadvantages of loose aggregate may discourage its use under certain circumstances. For instance, aggregate walkways may be difficult to walk on, and they require periodic maintenance and replenishment. Chemical treatment or plastic liners are sometimes used to control unwanted vegetative growth. (Refer to Section 440: Surfacing and Paving, and Division 900: Details and Devices, for more information.)

Gravel Roads and Parking Areas:

Gravel, crushed stone, and other types of aggregates are used for finished surfaces of roads, driveways,and parking areas.

Important qualities of a good untreated gravel, crushed stone, or other types of aggregate surface are:

1. The ability to withstand abrasion from pedestrian and/or vehicular traffic. This can be achieved by using a well-graded coarse aggregate (retained by a No. 10 sieve) combined with sand or similar fine aggregates to create a tight water-resistant surface and an interlocking of aggregates to resist shear forces.

2. The ability to support loads (pedestrian and/or vehicular) with little or no deformation. This can be achieved by adding some type of binding material, such as clay.

3. The ability to drain off surface water to prevent excess infiltration into the subgrade.

4. The ability to allow some upward movement of subsurface moisture to help maintain a desirable moisture level in the paving.

AGENCIES AND ORGANIZATIONS

American Association of State Highway and Transportation Officials (AASHTO)
Washington, D.C.

American Society of Nurserymen
Washington, D.C.

American Society for Testing and Materials (ASTM)
Philadelphia, Pennsylvania

Ecological Services Laboratory (Urban Soils Research)
National Park Service
Washington, D.C.

National Crushed Stone Association
Washington, D.C.

National Sand and Gravel Association
Washington, D.C.

U.S. Soil Conservation Service
Department of Agriculture
Washington, D.C.

REFERENCES

Hunt, Roy E. *Geotechnical Engineering Investigation Manual.* McGraw-Hill, New York, 1984.

Schroeder, W. L. *Soils in Construction,* 3d ed., Wiley, New York, 1984.

Seelye, Elwin E. *Design: Data Book for Civil Engineers,* 3d ed., Wiley, New York, 1960.

U.S. Department of the Interior, Bureau of Land Reclamation. *Earth Manual: A Guide to the Use of Soils as Foundations and as Construction Materials for Hydraulic Structures,* 2d ed., 1974.

Way, Douglas S. *Terrain Analysis: A Guide to Site Selection Using Aerial Photographic Interpretation,* 2d ed., Van Nostrand Reinhold, New York, 1978. ■

section 820: Asphalt

CREDITS

Section Editor: Charles W. Harris
Technical Writer: Tobias Dayman, *with extensive professional advice and assistance from Robert H. Joubert of the Asphalt Institute*

Reviewers:

Robert Joubert
The Asphalt Institute
Lawrence, Massachusetts

C. J. Owen, Jr., P.E.
Wayland, Massachusetts

CONTENTS

1.0 INTRODUCTION

1.1 Definitions

Technically, the term *asphalt* refers only to asphalt cement, the basic cementitious material that is eventually mixed with aggregate to form pavements. In common usage, however, the terms *asphalt, asphalt pavement, asphalt concrete,* and *bituminous concrete* refer to the many available mixtures of asphalt and aggregate that form pavements. The most common type of asphalt-aggregate mixture is *asphalt concrete* (also known as *hot-mix*). Asphalt concrete is a combination of heated asphalt cement and a heated aggregate mix that is applied to the surface of a base or subgrade, thoroughly compacted, and then allowed to cool.

1.2 Uses of Asphalt

This section focuses exclusively on asphalt pavement design, although asphalt cement is also commonly used as a sealant and as an adhesive (mastic).

The American Society for Testing and Materials (ASTM) and the American Association of State Highway and Transportation Officials (AASHTO) have established specifications on the manufacture and use of asphalt cement, asphalt cement products, and asphalt concrete mixtures commonly used in the United States. These specifications will serve as a guide for data shown in this section.

Since the availability of materials and the methods of construction vary between regions in the United States, every state or major governmental unit has established a set of standard specifications that serve as a guide to the production of quality asphalt pavements within its jurisdiction. Such local standards and practices should always be consulted for the appropriate application of materials.

2.0 ASPHALT CEMENT

2.1 Important Properties of Asphalt Cement

Thermoplasticity:

Asphalt cement is an adhesive, thermoplastic substance that will deform under load, liquify with increasing temperature, and solidify with decreasing temperature. It is for this reason that asphalt concrete pavements are referred to as *flexible* pavements.

Viscosity and Grades:

During processing, asphalt cement is refined into various viscous grades, each grade intended for specific purposes. Generally, the more viscous (i.e., harder) the material, the greater are its stiffening (i.e., strength) capabilities. Asphalt cement is graded by any of three different methods in the United States and Canada, all three of which grade the asphalt according to degree of *hardness,* or viscosity (Table 820-1). Table 820-2 lists various asphalts appropriate for roads, depending on climatic conditions.

TABLE 820-1
Asphalt Cement Grading Systems

*Grading system**	*Grades†* Hard, or thicker ⟷ Soft, or thinner	*Remarks*
Penetration graded	40–50 60–70 85–100 120–150 200–300	Older system that measures needle penetration. Asphalt is sampled at 77°F (25°C). Still in use in Canada and in some states.
Viscosity graded	AC-40 AC-30 AC-20 AC-10 AC-5 AC-2.5	Newer system introduced in 1972. Scientifically measures viscosity of the asphalt at 140°F (60°C). Most states use this system.
Viscosity graded on aged residue (AR)	AR-160 AR-20 AR-40 AR-80 AR-10	A variation of the more standard viscosity graded system. Measures asphalt after simulated aging. Used in several western states.

* Consult local highway departments for criteria of local grading systems. Local criteria are often slight modifications of the above specifications, altered to suit local conditions.

† The hard-soft scale is used to indicate relative hardness within each grading system and not as a comparison of hardness from one grading system to another. The grades toward the harder, or thicker, end of the spectrum tend to be used in heavier traffic conditions or warmer climates. Cooler climates or lighter loads utilize grades toward the softer end of the spectrum.

Weathering:

The oxidation of the surface and the evaporation of lighter hydrocarbons (volatilization) causes asphalt to lose its plasticity permanently and to become brittle with age. High quality in the initial construction and timely maintenance treatments keep weathering to a minimum.

Insolvency:

Asphalt is resistant to the chemical effects of water and of most salts, acids, and alkalies, but petroleum-based materials, such as gasoline and oil-based paints, will dissolve asphalt if applied in concentrated amounts. Tar sealers are used on asphalt surfaces where concentrated spillage is expected.

Color:

Asphalt is naturally black, but certain proprietary products or paving processes can alter that color. (Refer to 7.3 Colored Asphalt Pavements in this section for more information.)

TABLE 820-2
Temperature and Recommended Asphalt Cement Grades for Roads

Temperature condition	*Asphalt grades**	
Cold, mean annual air temperature ≤7°C (45°F)†	AC-5 AR-2000 120–150 penetration	AC-10 AR-4000 85–100 penetration
Warm, mean annual air temperature between 7°C (45°F) and 24°C (75°F)	AC-10 AR-4000 85–100 penetration	AC-20 AR-8000 60–70 penetration
Hot, mean annual air temperature (≥24°C (75°F)†	AC-20 AR-8000 60–70 penetration	AC-40 AR-16000 40–50 penetration

* The above recommendations serve only as a guide. Consult local practices and standards to determine local specifications.

† Severely cold temperatures may require very soft asphalts to minimize cracking. In very hot climates, an asphalt mixture should be designed to resist rutting and to maintain stiffness.

Source: The Asphalt Institute, *Thickness Design: Asphalt Pavements for Highways and Streets,* MS-1, College Park, Md.

2.2 Liquid Asphalts

Liquid asphalts are classified in two families: emulsified asphalt and cutback asphalt. Asphalt cement sometimes needs to be liquified by one of these two means so that the material can be used at ambient rather than higher temperatures. Although most pavements are made of hot asphalt cement because it cures faster and has greater assured strength, the use of a liquid asphalt is sometimes more appropriate, as in the case of surface treatments or of projects far removed from a hot-mix plant, for instance. The curing time for a liquid asphalt pavement is longer than it is for a hot-mix pavement because the curing must rely on the evaporation of a solvent or water rather than on the cooling of the asphalt cement.

Emulsified Asphalt:

Emulsified asphalt refers to asphalt cement that has been emulsified with water and a small amount of emulsifying agent (Table 820-3).

Cutback Asphalt:

Cutback asphalt refers to asphalt cement that has been diluted with a selected petroleum solvent. The more volatile distillates evaporate more quickly, resulting in faster curing times. The degree of viscosity depends upon the grade of the asphalt cement, the volatility of the solvent, and the proportion of the solvent to asphalt cement (Table 820-4).

In recent years, the use of cutback asphalts has been reduced in order to conserve petroleum and minimize the amount of volatiles released into the atmosphere. Check with local pollution control agencies and local practices for regulations on its use.

2.3 Selection Criteria

Various tasks require specific asphalt cements or liquid asphalts. Table 820-5 lists various types and grades of asphalt cement and their appropriate uses. In all cases, local standards and practices should be consulted.

3.0 AGGREGATE FOR ASPHALT PAVEMENTS

The aggregate used in asphalt pavements must consist of an appropriate gradation and possess certain specific properties if it is to produce a strong, durable, skid-resistant pavement. Local standards and practices often reflect readily available aggregate materials and gradations that have proved most suitable and economical to use in that area.

3.1 Sizes of Aggregate for Asphalt Pavements

Aggregate is typically classified according to size. The various sizes are mixed in certain proportions (i.e., gradations) for eventual use in an asphalt-aggregate mixture (e.g., asphalt concrete). (Refer to 3.2 Aggregate Gradations in this section for more information.)

Fine Aggregate:

Fine aggregate refers to aggregates that pass the No. 8 (2.36-mm) sieve. *Mineral dust* refers to the portion of fine aggregate that passes the No. 200 (0.075-mm) sieve, and *mineral filler* refers to that portion of fine aggregate that passes the No. 30 (0.60-mm) sieve. Mineral dust and mineral filler are typically used in precise percentages to fill voids of coarse aggregate to produce a cohesive, dense, watertight asphalt concrete mixture.

Coarse Aggregate:

Coarse aggregate refers to aggregates retained on the No. 8 (2.36-mm) sieve. The interlocking and friction of coarse aggregates provide the major stability function in a pavement.

Macadam Aggregate:

Macadam aggregate refers to coarse aggregates of uniform size, nominally sized between 1½ to 2½ in (38 to 62 mm), usually of crushed stone, slag, or gravel. Such aggregate was typically used in macadam construction. Macadam construction has been rarely used since 1965.

3.2 Aggregate Gradations

Aggregate gradations contain a selected range of aggregate sizes in desired proportions. *Maximum particle size* or *maximum stone size* is the smallest sieve which 100 percent of the aggregates will pass, and *nominal maximum size* is the largest sieve that retains any of the aggregates, but generally not more than 10 percent of the larger-size aggregates.

Asphalt mixtures are commonly referred to by their nominal maximum size (refer-

TABLE 820-3
Emulsified Asphalts

Category	*Grade**	*Available viscosities†*
Anionic (negatively charged asphalt gobules)‡	Rapid setting	RS-1, RS-2
	Medium setting	MS-1, HFMS-1, MS-2, HFMS-2, MS-2h, HFMS-2h, HFMS-2s
	Slow setting	SS-1, SS-2
Cationic (positively charged asphalt gobules)‡	Rapid setting	CRS-1, CRS-2
	Medium setting	CMS-2, CMS-2h
	Slow setting	CSS-1, CSS-1h

* All emulsified asphalts are a mixture of asphalt cement base, water, and an emulsifying agent. With different emulsifying agents, various grades, based upon setting time, can be manufactured.

† The 1 indicates a thinner, or less viscous, material than those noted by a 2. An "h" or "s" refers to the hardness or softness of the asphalt cement base material. The prefix "HF" refers to properties of the residual asphalt cement that have been altered by proprietary additives to yield high values on the standard ASTM Method of Test D139 Float Test, indicating that the residual asphalt cement can withstand slightly higher pressures and loads in the test than standard unaltered cement.

‡ Anionic emulsified asphalts work more effectively in pavements with an aggregate that has an electropositive charge (such as limestones). Cationic emulsified asphalts work more effectively with aggregates that have an electronegative charge (such as silicon aggregates).

TABLE 820-4
Cutback Asphalts

			Available viscosities†‡				
*Grade**	*Base material*	*Solvent*	*Thick* ⟵				⟶ *Thin*
Rapid-curing (RC)‡	Asphalt cement	Highly volatile gasoline or naptha	RC-3000	RC-800	RC-250	RC-70	—
Medium-curing (MC)‡	Asphalt cement	Medium volatile kerosene	MC-3000	MC-800	MC-250	MC-70	MC-30
Slow-curing (SC) (road oils)‡	Asphalt cement	Slow volatile oils	SC-3000	SC-800	SC-250	SC-70	—

* These grades are based upon rates of curing (time for evaporation of solvent).

† A viscosity of 30 flows at room temperature. A viscosity of 3000 hardly flows at room temperature and may require heating to be used.

‡ Air pollution controls often exist regarding the use of cutback asphalts because of volatiles released into the atmosphere. Consult local pollution control agencies and local practices for applicable regulations.

TABLE 820-5
Guide for Uses of Asphalt

Type of construction	Asphalt cements														
	Viscosity graded original					*Viscosity graded residue*					*Penetration graded*				
	AC-40	*AC-20*	*AC-10*	*AC-5*	*AC-2.5*	*AR-16000*	*AR-8000*	*AR-4000*	*AR-2000*	*AR-1000*	*40–50*	*60–70*	*85–100*	*120–150*	*200–300*
Asphalt-aggregate mixtures															
Asphalt concrete and hot-laid plant mix															
Pavement base and surfaces															
Highways	X	X	X	X	X[7]	X	X	X	X	X[7]	X	X	X	X	X[7]
Airports		X	X	X			X	X				X	X	X	
Parking areas	X	X	X			X	X	X			X	X	X		
Driveways		X	X				X	X				X	X		
Curbs		X					X					X			
Industrial floors	X	X				X	X				X	X			
Blocks	X					X					X				
Groins	X	X				X	X				X	X			
Dam facings	X	X				X	X				X	X			
Canal and reservoir linings	X	X				X	X				X	X			
Cold-laid plant mix[10]															
Pavement base and surfaces															
Open-graded aggregate															
Well-graded aggregate															
Patching, immediate use															
Patching, stockpile															
Mixed in place (road mix)[10]															
Pavement base and surfaces															
Open-graded aggregate															
Well-graded aggregate															
Sand					X									X	
Sandy soil					X									X	
Patching, immediate use															
Patching, stockpile															
Recycling															
Hot mix			X	X	X			X	X	X			X	X	X
Cold mix[10]					X					X					X
Asphalt-aggregate applications															
Surface treatments															
Single surface treatment				X	X									X	X
Multiple surface treatment				X	X									X	X
Aggregate seal				X	X				X					X	X
Sand seal															
Slurry seal															
Asphalt applications															
Surface treatment															
Fog seal															
Prime coat															
Tack coat															
Dust laying															
Mulch															
Membrane															
Canal and reservoir linings	X										X				
Embankment envelopes	X	X				X	X				X	X			
Crack filling															
Asphalt pavements															
Portland cement concrete pavements	X[4]					X[4]					X[4]				

[1] Mixed-in prime only.

[2] Diluted with water.

[3] Slurry mix.

[4] Rubber asphalt compounds.

[5] Diluted with water by the manufacturer.

[6] MS-2 only.

[7] For use in cold climates.

[8] Before using MC's for spray applications (other than prime coats), check with local pollution control agency.

Emulsified asphalts[9]														*Cutback asphalts*[11]								
Anionic								*Cationic*						*Medium curing (MC)*[8]					*Slow curing (SC)*			
RS-1	*RS-2*	*MS-1, HFMS-1*	*MS-2, HFMS-2*	*MS-2h, HFMS-2h*	*HFMS-2s*	*SS-1*	*SS-1h*	*CRS-1*	*CRS-2*	*CMS-2*	*CMS-2h*	*CSS-1*	*CSS-1h*	*30*	*70*	*250*	*800*	*3000*	*70*	*250*	*800*	*3000*
			X	X						X	X											
					X	X	X					X	X			X	X	X		X	X	X
						X	X					X	X			X	X				X	
																X	X			X	X	
			X	X						X	X						X	X			X	X
					X	X	X					X	X			X	X			X	X	
					X	X	X					X	X		X	X	X					
					X	X	X					X	X			X	X					
					X	X	X					X	X			X	X				X	
																X	X			X	X	
			X	X	X	X	X			X	X	X	X									
X	X							X	X													
X	X							X	X													
X	X	X						X	X													
X	X	X						X	X													
						X	X					X	X									
		X[5]				X[2]	X[2]					X[2]	X[2]									
			X[1,6]			X[1]	X[1]			X[1]		X[1]	X[1]	X	X	X						
X		X[5]				X[2]	X[2]	X				X[2]	X[2]									
						X[2]	X[2]					X[2]	X[2]	X	X	X			X	X		
						X[2]	X[2]															
						X[3]	X[3]					X[3]	X[3]									

[9] Emulsified asphalts shown are AASHTO and ASTM grades and may not include all grades produced in all geographical areas.

[10] Evaluation of emulsified asphalt-aggregate system required to determine the proper grade of emulsified asphalt to use.

[11] Use of rapid cure (RC) asphalts is not shown on this chart since their use is becoming rare and is discouraged for energy and environmental reasons. Use of emulsified asphalts is encouraged instead.

Source: The Asphalt Institute.

ring to the aggregate contained therein). Four common aggregate gradations are: (1) fine-graded, (2) coarse-graded, (3) dense- or well-graded, and (4) open-graded.

Fine-Graded Aggregate:

Fine-graded aggregate refers to a continuous grading of sizes with a predominance of fine aggregates. Such a gradation produces a surface of finer texture and less road noise than would a gradation with a predominance of coarse aggregates.

Coarse-Graded Aggregate:

Coarse-graded aggregate refers to a continuous grading of sizes with a predominance of coarse aggregates. Such a gradation produces a more stable pavement, coarser surface texture, and more road noise.

Dense-Graded (Well-Graded) Aggregate:

Dense-graded aggregate refers to a grading of a wide range of sizes resulting in an asphalt aggregate mixture with a controlled void content. Pavements with such a gradation are very watertight, highly stable, and durable.

Open-Graded Aggregate:

Open-graded aggregate contains little or no mineral filler, thereby resulting in larger void spaces. Individual aggregates are interlocking and usually very jagged, thus producing a pavement with good strength, rough texture, and high permeability.

Table 820-6 shows coarse aggregate gradations used for highway construction. When used singly or in combination, such gradations are also suitable for asphalt mixes. The proportional distributions shown in the table can be altered to suit job requirements and local conditions. Because of their perviousness, they are restricted to special applications that accommodate the special mix design and drainage needs of this type of paving mixture.

3.3 Selection Criteria

Table 820-7 shows four important criteria to consider when assessing the value of a particular aggregate for use in an asphalt pavement. Each criterion is described below.

TABLE 820-6
Coarse Aggregate Gradations for Highway Construction

Gradation size number	Nominal size of gradation, square openings	*Sieve size (square openings)*														
		100 mm (4 in)	*90 mm (3½ in)*	*75 mm (3 in)*	*63 mm (2½ in)*	*50 mm (2 in)*	*38.1 mm (1½ in)*	*25.0 mm (1 in)*	*19.0 mm (¾ in)*	*12.5 mm (½ in)*	*9.5 mm (⅜ in)*	*4.75 mm (No. 4)*	*2.36 mm (No. 8)*	*1.18 mm (No. 16)*	*300 μm (No. 50)*	*150 μm (No. 100)*
1	90–38.1 mm (3½–1½ in)	100	90–100		25–60		0–15		0–5							
2	63–38.1 mm (2½–1½ in)			100	90–100	35–70	0–15		0–5							
24	63–19.0 mm (2½–¾ in)			100	90–100		25–60		0–10	0–5						
3	50–25.0 mm (2–1 in)				100	90–100	35–70	0–15		0–5						
357	50–4.75 mm (2 in–No. 4)				100	95–100		35–70		10–30		0–5				
4	38.1–19.0 mm (1½–¾ in)					100	90–100		20–55	0–15		0–5				
467	38.1–4.75 mm (1½ in–No. 4)					100	95–100		35–70		10–30	0–5				
5	25.0–12.5 mm (1–½ in)						100	90–100	20–55	0–10	0–5					
56	25.0–9.5 mm (1–⅜ in)						100	90–100	40–75	15–35	0–15	0–5				
57	25.0–4.75 mm (1 in–No. 4)						100	95–100		25–60		0–10	0–5			
6	19.0–9.5 mm (¾–⅜ in)							100	90–100	20–55	0–15	0–5				
67	19.0–4.75 mm (¾ in–No. 4)							100	90–100		20–55	0–10	0–5			
68	19.0–2.36 mm (¾ in–No. 8)							100	90–100		30–65	5–25	0–10	0–5		
7	12.5–4.75 mm (½ in–No. 4)								100	90–100	40–70	0–15	0–5			
78	12.5–2.36 mm (½ in–No. 8)								100	90–100	40–75	5–25	0–10	0–5		
8	9.5–2.36 mm (⅜ in–No. 8)									100	85–100	10–30	0–10	0–5		
89	9.5–1.18 mm (⅜ in–No. 16)									100	90–100	20–55	5–30	0–10	0–5	
9	4.75–1.18 mm (No. 4–No. 16)										100	85–100	10–40	0–10	0–5	
10	4.75 mm (No. 4–0*)										100	85–100				10–30

* Screenings—Note that some of these gradations are suitable for use in a selected asphalt-concrete mixture (Refer to Table 820-8). For granular bases and granular surface courses, refer to Table 820-11 and 4.4 of this section.

Source: AASHTO M43 and ASTM 448.

1. *Hardness (Toughness):* refers to the ability of the aggregate to withstand loads and wear.

2. *Resistance to Stripping:* hydrophilic *(water loving)* aggregates, usually acidic, tend to strip away from the asphalt bond, reducing the stability and skid resistance of the pavement. Antistripping compounds may have to be added to various asphalt mixtures to permit the use of some hydrophilic aggregates. Check local practice.

3. *Surface Texture:* a rough surface texture aids in bonding and making the pavement more stable and resistant to abrasion and skidding.

4. *Crushed Shape:* cubic, angular, crushed shapes interlock and give the pavement more strength than do smooth, rounded aggregates.

In addition to these four criteria, a few other criteria must be considered when selecting an aggregate for an asphalt concrete mixture:

1. The larger the size of aggregates in a gradation, the greater will be the strength and durability of the pavement.

2. Gradations with larger aggregates result in a rougher pavement (or surface texture) than do gradations with finer aggregate.

3. The larger the aggregates, the greater will be the road noise generated by vehicular traffic (but always less than concrete pavements).

4. The maximum particle size of an aggregate gradation should never be more than half (preferably less) the thickness of the asphalt concrete layer of which it is a part (see Table 820-8).

5. The color of a weathered asphalt pavement is also a function of the color of the larger aggregates. Darker gray tones are achieved by increasing the amounts of sand and filler.

TABLE 820-7
Properties of Various Aggregate Types for Asphalt Pavements

	Hardness, toughness	*Resistance to stripping*	*Surface texture*	*Crushed shape*
Igneous				
Granite	Fair	Fair	Fair	Fair
Syenite	Good	Fair	Fair	Fair
Diorite	Good	Fair	Fair	Good
Basalt (trap rock)	Good	Good	Good	Good
Diabase (trap rock)	Good	Good	Good	Good
Gabbro (trap rock)	Good	Good	Good	Good
Sedimentary				
Limestone, dolomite	Poor	Good	Good	Fair
Sandstone	Fair	Good	Good	Good
Chert	Good	Fair	Poor	Good
Shale	Poor	Poor	Fair	Fair
Metamorphic				
Gneiss	Fair	Fair	Good	Good
Schist	Fair	Fair	Good	Fair
Slate	Good	Fair	Fair	Fair
Quartzite	Good	Fair	Good	Good
Marble	Poor	Good	Fair	Fair
Serpentine	Good	Fair	Fair	Fair

Source: W. A. Cordon, *Properties, Evaluation and Control of Engineering Materials,* McGraw-Hill, New York, 1979.

4.0 ASPHALT PAVING MIXTURES

4.1 Asphalt Concrete

Asphalt concrete, the most widely used asphalt paving mixture, consists of a dense-graded aggregate heated to approximately 300 degrees F (150 degrees C), which is then mixed (at a plant) with asphalt cement heated to a temperature of 275 degrees F (135 degrees C). The heated mixture is taken to the site, placed either by paving machines or by hand, compacted to achieve maximum density, and allowed to cool. Asphalt concrete is typically applied in compacted thicknesses ranging from ¾ in (20 mm) to more than 1 ft (300 mm). The thickness of any layer of asphalt concrete should always be at least twice the nominal maximum size (or maximum particle size) of the aggregate.

Table 820-8 shows the composition of various asphalt concrete mixtures. Refer to subsections later in this section for definitions and descriptions of the various courses in an asphalt pavement.

A finished asphalt concrete pavement should contain 2 to 7 percent voids (air) by volume to allow for expansion of the pavement and to allow for compaction of the aggregate over the life of the pavement. Too high a void content (over 8 percent) can lead to reduced durability and generally is caused by insufficient compaction.

4.2 Surface Treatments

Surface treatments refer to special asphalt-aggregate applications laid in less than 1-in (25-mm) thicknesses on existing or new pavement. Surface treatments are used for color coating, sealing, improving skid resistance, or prolonging the service life of a fair to good pavement surface.

The application of a surface treatment involves spraying heated asphalt cement (emulsified or cutback asphalt) onto a surface, followed by the desired aggregate. The application is then rolled, thereby forcing the asphalt and aggregate to firmly set together. Some surface treatments do not use aggregate, and some have the aggregate and asphalt premixed.

Various surface treatments are described in Table 820-9 and illustrated in Figure 820-1.

Table 820-10 provides information on the quantities of asphalt and aggregate necessary for single surface treatments and

TABLE 820-8
Composition of Asphalt Mixtures[a]

Sieve size	*Asphalt concrete*[b,c,d,e,f]					*Sand asphalt*[g]	*Sheet asphalt*[g,h]
	Mix designation and nominal maximum size of aggregate[i]						
	1½ in (37.5 mm)	1 in (25.0 mm)	¾ in (19.0 mm)	½ in (12.5 mm)	⅜ in (9.5 mm)	No. 4 (4.75 mm)	No. 16[h] (1.18 mm)
	Typical pavement courses for corresponding mix designation						
	Base courses[j]		*Intermediate or binder courses*[j]	*Surface courses*[j]			
	Grading of total aggregate (coarse plus fine, plus filler if required) Amounts finer than each laboratory sieve (square opening), weight percent[f]						
2 in (50 mm)	100	—	—	—	—	—	—
1½ in (37.5 mm)	90 to 100	100	—	—	—	—	—
1 in (25.0 mm)	—	90 to 100	100	—	—	—	—
¾ in (19.0 mm)	56 to 80	—	90 to 100	100	—	—	—
½ in (12.5 mm)	—	56 to 80	—	90 to 100	100	—	—
⅜ in (9.5 mm)	—	—	56 to 80	—	90 to 100	100	—
No. 4 (4.75 mm)	23 to 53	29 to 59	35 to 65	44 to 74	55 to 85	80 to 100	100
No. 8 (2.36 mm)[k]	15 to 41	19 to 45	23 to 49	28 to 58	32 to 67	65 to 100	95 to 100
No. 16 (1.18 mm)	—	—	—	—	—	40 to 80	85 to 100
No. 30 (600 μm)	—	—	—	—	—	20 to 65	70 to 95
No. 50 (300 μm)	4 to 16	5 to 17	5 to 19	5 to 21	7 to 23	7 to 40	45 to 75
No. 100 (150 μm)	—	—	—	—	—	3 to 20	20 to 40
No. 200 (75 μm)[l]	0 to 6	1 to 7	2 to 8	2 to 10	2 to 10	2 to 10	9 to 20
	Asphalt cement, weight percent of total mixture[f,m,n]						
	3 to 8	3 to 9	4 to 10	4 to 11	5 to 12	6 to 12	8 to 12
	Suggested coarse aggregate sizes, number[o]						
	4 and 67 or 4 and 68	5 and 7 or 57	67 or 68 or 6 and 8	7 or 78	8		

[a] Consult local standards and practices for composition mixes and durabilities at local construction sites. These figures serve as a guide only.

[b] Typical life expectancy is about 20 years, at which time resurfacing operations would be needed. Durability based upon a number of factors, including traffic, environment, maintenance, climate, materials, and construction of pavement.

[c] The larger the maximum stone size, the louder the traffic noise will be.

[d] Color of normal pavements (after initial wear) is a function of the color of the larger aggregate. Darker tones are achieved by increasing amounts of finer sand and filler.

[e] Mixtures with coarse aggregate have rougher finished surface texture than mixtures with fine aggregate.

[f] The unit of measures for asphalt concrete is tons. Commonly, a square yard of asphalt concrete pavement one inch thick weighs .055 tons (110 lbs). In some instances, the specific gravity of the aggregate may be higher or lower than normal, thereby altering this figure accordingly. For most jobs up to 1 to 2 acres in size, the figure mentioned is adequate. Consult local practices and standards.

[g] Sheet and sand asphalt have finer texture. However, these mixtures lack the larger aggregate that tend to produce stable, dense, strong pavements. Where stability and fine texture are important factors, utilize the more common ⅜-in nominal mix designation.

[h] Sheet asphalt produces a clean, relatively noiseless surface that has been used in many areas for decades. The relatively higher asphalt content and increasing amounts of finer mineral dust causes mixture to be somewhat more expensive to produce. An excess in asphalt could produce an unstable surface, bleed asphalt to surface, or be slick when wet. Sheet asphalt scuffs more easily than coarser mixtures.

[i] The thickness of any compacted pavement layer should be at least twice the nominal maximum size or maximum stone size (whichever term is used).

[j] Asphalt pavement courses typically used for the corresponding asphalt concrete nominal mix designations. Surface courses typically are ⅜-in and ½-in mix designation reserved for surface courses where heavier duty is expected. See note i above.

[k] In considering the total grading characteristics of an asphalt paving mixture, the amount passing the 2.36 mm (No. 8) sieve is a significant and convenient field control point between fine and coarse aggregate. Gradings approaching the maximum amount permitted to pass the 2.36-mm sieve will result in pavement surfaces having comparatively fine texture, while gradings approaching the minimum amount passing the 2.36-mm sieve will result in surfaces with comparatively coarse texture.

[l] The materials passing the 75-μm (No. 200) sieve may consist of fine particles of the aggregates or mineral filler, or both. It shall be free of organic matter and clay particles and have a plasticity index not greater than 4 when tested in accordance with ASTM Method D 423 and ASTM Method D 424.

[m] The quantity of asphalt cement is given in terms of weight percent of the total mixture. The wide difference in the specific gravity of various aggregates, as well as a considerable difference in absorption, results in a comparatively wide range in the limiting amount of asphalt cement specified. The amount of asphalt required for a given mixture should be determined by appropriate laboratory testing or on the basis of past experience with similar mixtures, or by a combination of both.

[n] Table 820-5 lists asphalt cement grades appropriate for certain pavements.

[o] Refer to Table 820-6 for coarse aggregate gradations.

Source: Adapted from ASTM Designation 3515, *Standard Specifications for Hot-Mix, Hot-Laid Bituminous Paving Mixtures.*

TABLE 820-9
Surface Treatment Types and Characteristics

Surface treatment type	*Intended uses*	*Constituent materials*	*Remarks*[a,b,c]
Prime coat[d] (Fig. 820-1)	To waterproof and provide some structural strength to untreated gravel base by penetration	Heavy application of dilute or thin liquid asphalt of low viscosity to gravel base	Penetrates gravel road surface ½ in, more or less. Saturates gravel base so subsequent surface treatments will not be absorbed. Not intended to be applied to paved surfaces. Applied on aggregate bases when asphalt pavements are less than 3 in thick.
Dust palliative[d] (Fig. 820-2)	To reduce road dust produced by wind or moving vehicles	Best slow-curing cutback asphalt or diluted (4:9 with water) slow-setting emulsified asphalt, medium-curing asphalt or medium-setting emulsified asphalt	Penetrates surface about ½ in binding particles together. Light applications are typical (about 0.2 gal/yd^2). Consult local practices and standards. Medium-curing and medium-setting asphalts typically become brittle and crack, thus their use is limited. Slow-curing cutback asphalts endure longest.
Fog seal[d] (Fig. 820-3)	To seal and fill very small cracks and voids in open-graded pavements	Slow-setting emulsified asphalt diluted with water	Apply only on coarse-textured surface so fog can be absorbed into surface. Do not use on dense smooth surfaces or slickness will result. Over-applications produce a slippery surface.
Slurry seal,[d] (Fig. 820-4)	To seal previously paved surfaces and fill cracks in old pavements that otherwise are in good condition	Slow-setting emulsified asphalt, fine aggregate, mineral filler, and water	Provides smooth, tight surface. Most often handled by specialty contractor.
Sand seals[d,f] (Fig. 820-5)	To fill fine cracks and to seal existing pavement	Low viscosity or moderately diluted asphalt with sand aggregate	Very low-cost sealing treatment as done by local labor, material, and/or contract. Generally restricted to low-volume rural road maintenance. Rarely used in commercial applications.
Single-surface treatment[c,f] (chip, seal, or aggregate seal) (Fig. 820-6)	To seal and waterproof, provide a wearing course, increase skid resistance, or provide color over other pavement.	Liquid asphalt followed by uniform-sized aggregate, ⅜ to ½ in most common, sometimes $\frac{3}{16}$ to $\frac{5}{16}$ in	Moderate cost sealing and surface rejuvenation. Difficult to apply in small areas such as parking lots. More common for roads.
Multiple surface treatment[e,f] (Fig. 820-7)	To seal and provide wearing course over other pavements	Two or more surface treatments applied on top of one another	Aggregate sizes vary as maximum-sized aggregate of successive treatment is usually one-half of the previous one. Difficult to apply in small areas such as parking lots. More common for roads.

[a] Consult local sources for standards and practices for specific construction jobs.

[b] Use of liquid asphalts necessitates a period of airing time during which pavement is unusable. Failure to take precautions during application results in tracking and improperly sealed pavement.

[c] Because of thinness, average life expectancies for surface treatments range from 3 to 8 years, based on factors such as traffic, climate, environment, and quality of original pavement. Consult local practices and standards for expected durabilities at local job sites.

[d] Applied from a prepared mixture.

[e] Applied by placing the liquid asphalt on the desired surface first, then covering with a layer of aggregate particles. Compaction forces the aggregate down, mixing with the asphalt.

[f] Refer to Table 820-5 for information on surface treatments and specific liquid asphalt grades and viscosities. Refer to Table 820-10 for the asphalts and Table 820-11 for the aggregates used in these surface treatments.

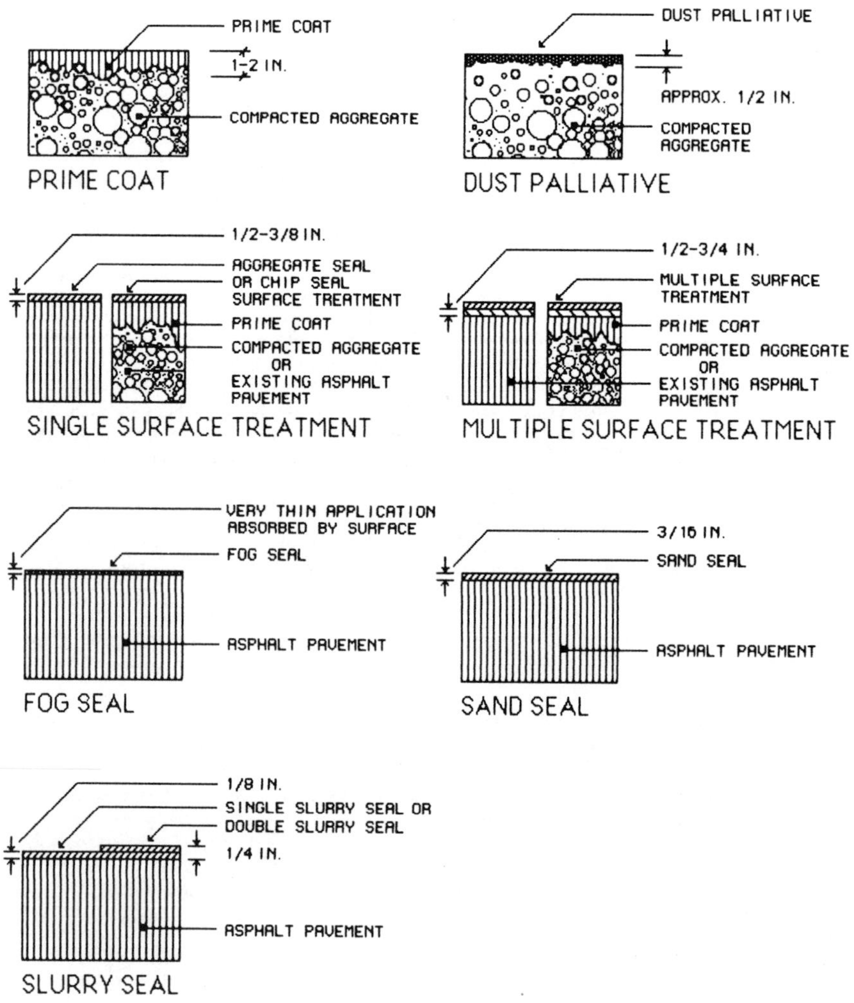
PRIME COAT
1–2 IN.
COMPACTED AGGREGATE
PRIME COAT
DUST PALLIATIVE
APPROX. 1/2 IN.
COMPACTED AGGREGATE
DUST PALLIATIVE
1/2–3/8 IN.
AGGREGATE SEAL OR CHIP SEAL SURFACE TREATMENT
PRIME COAT
COMPACTED AGGREGATE OR EXISTING ASPHALT PAVEMENT
SINGLE SURFACE TREATMENT
1/2–3/4 IN.
MULTIPLE SURFACE TREATMENT
PRIME COAT
COMPACTED AGGREGATE OR EXISTING ASPHALT PAVEMENT
MULTIPLE SURFACE TREATMENT
VERY THIN APPLICATION ABSORBED BY SURFACE
FOG SEAL
ASPHALT PAVEMENT
FOG SEAL
3/16 IN.
SAND SEAL
ASPHALT PAVEMENT
SAND SEAL
1/8 IN.
SINGLE SLURRY SEAL OR DOUBLE SLURRY SEAL
1/4 IN.
ASPHALT PAVEMENT
SLURRY SEAL

Figure 820-1 Typical asphalt surface treatments.

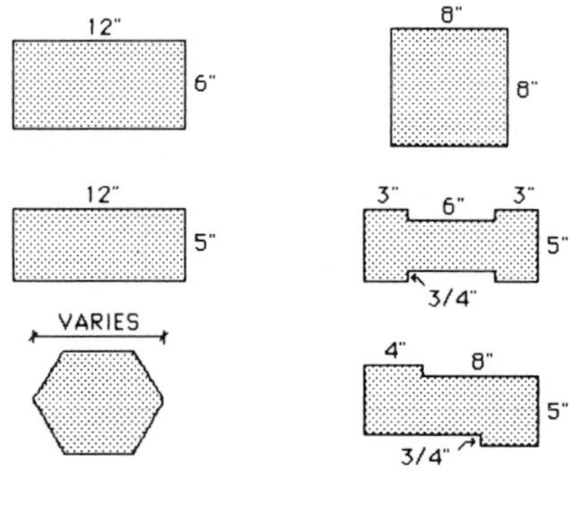
12"
6"
8"
8"
12"
5"
3"
6"
3"
5"
3/4"
VARIES
4"
8"
5"
3/4"

Figure 820-2 Typical shapes of asphalt blocks.

seal coats. Table 820-11 provides information on aggregate gradations appropriate for surface treatments. Surface treatments are intended to extend pavement life but do not increase its structural strength.

4.3 Asphalt Paving Blocks

Premolded asphalt blocks are often used for pedestrian paving and some vehicular paving. The precise mixture of asphalt, aggregate, and rock dust varies in manufacture to suit specific uses. Smooth surfaces are available as well as exposed aggregate finishes in colors of black, brown, gray, and tan. After placement, the aggregate may be further exposed and given a weathered effect by sandblasting. If blocks will be sandblasted, they all should be manufactured with the same aggregate to avoid varied color tints in the pavement.

Table 820-12 shows thicknesses and typical applications of asphalt paving blocks. Figure 820-2 shows a few standard shapes that are commercially available. Special orders are also possible. Block pavements require base and subbase courses and typically require some type of edging for containment. Information on construction specifications and the availability of particular thicknesses, shapes, and colors can be acquired from the manufacturer.

4.4 Asphalt-Treated Granular Base Courses

Granular materials unsuitable for base courses (e.g., because of poor interlocking ability) can be treated with an asphalt cement to produce a stabilized base course (i.e., bituminous stabilization). Although this is used less commonly than aggregate or asphalt base courses, a suitable base at less cost is possible in some locations.

Other methods of base stabilization, including cement stabilization and lime stabilization, are sometimes more appropriate than asphalt-treated base courses in some situations. The economics and performance record of cement stabilization should be checked in each location. The Asphalt Institute does not recommend such base stabilization. Asphalt surfacings, when placed on a cement-treated base, should be expected to form the same shrinkage or crack patterns as is common to most cement-treated materials.

4.5 Less-Common Mixtures

Commercially available asphalt paving mixtures less commonly used than those just described (in subsection 4.4) are shown in Table 820-13.

TABLE 820-10
Quantities of Asphalt and Aggregate for Single Surface Treatments and Seal Coats*

Line	*Nominal size of aggregate*	*Quantity of aggregate kg/m² (lb/yd²)*†‡	*Quantity of asphalt, L/m² (gal/yd²)*†¶	*Type and grade of asphalt*
1	19.0–9.5 mm (¾–⅜ in)	22–27 (40–50)	1.6–2.0 (0.35–0.45) 1.8–2.3 (0.40–0.50)	Asphalt cement§ RS-2, CRS-2
2	12.5–4.75 mm (½ in–No. 4)	14–16 (25–30)	0.9–1.4 (0.20–0.30) 1.4–2.0 (0.30–0.45)	Asphalt cement§ RS-1, RS-2, CRS-1, CRS-2
3	9.5–2.36 mm (⅜ in–No. 8)	11–14 (20–25)	0.7–1.1 (0.15–0.25) 0.9–1.6 (0.20–0.35)	Asphalt cement§ RS-1, RS-2, CRS-1, CRS-2
4	6.3–1.18 mm (¼ in–No. 16)	8–11 (15–20)	0.7–0.9 (0.15–0.20)	RS-1, MS-1, CRS-1, HFMS-1
5	Sand	5–8 (10–15)	0.5–0.7 (0.10–0.15)	RS-1, CRS-1, MS-1, HFMS-1

* These quantities of asphalt cover the average range of conditions that include primed granular bases and old pavement surfaces. The quantities and types of materials may be varied according to local conditions and experience.

† The lower application rates of asphalt shown in the above table should be used for aggregate having gradations on the fine side of the specified limits. The higher application rates should be used for aggregate having gradations on the coarse side of the specified limits.

‡ The weight of aggregate shown in the table is based on aggregate with a specific gravity of 2.65. In case the specific gravity of the aggregate used is lower than 2.55 or higher than 2.75, the amount shown in the table above should be multiplied by the ratio that the bulk specific gravity of the aggregate used bears to 2.65.

§ AC-2.5, AC-5; AR-1000, AR-2000; 200/300 pen., 120/150 pen. (Note: In some areas persistent difficulty in retaining aggregate has been experienced with 200–300 penetration asphalt cements. Where this has occurred, the use of 200–300 penetration asphalt is not recommended.)

¶ It is important to adjust the asphalt content for the condition of the road, increasing it if the road is absorbent, badly cracked, or coarse, and decreasing it if the road is "fat" with flushed asphalt.

Corrections for Surface Conditions

Texture	*Gal/yd²*
Black, flushed asphalt	−0.01 to −0.06
Smooth, nonporous	0.00
Absorbent	
Slightly porous, oxidized	+0.03
Slightly pocked, porous, oxidized	+0.06
Badly pocked, porous, oxidized	+0.09

TABLE 820-11
Gradations of Aggregates for Surface Treatments:* Sizes of Coarse Aggregates

Sieve size (square opening)	*Nominal size square openings*†				
	¾ to ⅜	*½ to No. 4*	*⅜ to No. 8*	*¼ to No. 16*	*Sand*
	Percentage passing by weight				
1	100				
¾	90–100	100			
½	20–55	90–100	100		
⅜	0–15	40–70	85–100	100	100
¼				90–100	
No. 4	0–5	0–15	10–30	60–85	95–100
No. 8		0–5	0–10	0–25	
No. 16			0–5	0–5	45–70
No. 50					5–25
No. 100					0–10
No. 200				0–2	0–2

* Refer to Table 820-10 for information on aggregate gradations used in surface treatments.

† In inches unless otherwise indicated.

Source: The Asphalt Institute, *Asphalt Surface Treatments—Specifications,* ES-11, February, 1982.

TABLE 820-12
Recommended Thickness of Asphalt Blocks for Typical Applications*

Typical applications	*Thickness of unit recommended, in*
Traffic aisles and loading platforms	1½ or 2
Piers and docks	1½ or 2
Roof decks—parking or storage	1½
Roof decks and balconies—recreational	1¼ or 1½
Airport, hangars, runways, aprons	1½, 2, or 2½
Ramps and bridge approaches	2½ or 3
Streets, roads, bridges, viaducts	2½ or 3
Waterproofing protection courses	1¼
Estate, residential, and institutional driveways	2, hexagonal or rectangular
Walks, courts, plazas, and terraces	2, hexagonal or rectangular

* Check local practices and standards, manufacturers' specifications, or a civil engineer to more accurately determine proper thickness for particular jobs.

Source: Adapted from The Asphalt Institute, *The Asphalt Handbook*, 1965.

5.0 PRINCIPLES OF ASPHALT PAVEMENT DESIGN

5.1 Typical Pavement Sections and Definitions

Asphalt pavements typically consist of a combination of layered asphalt-aggregate mixtures placed either directly on a subgrade or improved subgrade, or on an aggregate base over a subgrade or improved subgrade, or on an existing pavement made of concrete, brick, or stone. Figure 820-3 shows several *typical* pavement profiles, each designed for specific purposes (depending on expected loads, local standards, etc.).

5.2 Pavement Functions

The *subgrade* under an asphalt-aggregate mixture ultimately carries all loads. The structural functions of a pavement are (1) to support the wheel on the pavement surface and (2) to transfer and spread the load to the subgrade without overtaxing either the strength of the subgrade or the internal strength of the pavement itself. The *aggregate* of the various pavement layers sup-

TABLE 820-13
Less Common Asphalt Paving Mixtures*

Asphalt mixture type	*Intended use*	*Constituent† materials*	*Remarks*
Cold laid plant mixes Cold mixes Emulsified asphalt Emulsified sand asphalt Emulsified sheet asphalt	For immediate patching or stockpiling. Use on sites far-removed from asphalt concrete plant, base, or surface courses.	Different mix designations available composed of liquid asphalts and various aggregate gradations in a plant-prepared mixture. Aggregate options include open and dense-graded gradations. A prepared and compacted subgrade	Placed by paving machines at ambient temperatures and compacted. Requires a period of time for water or solvents to evaporate. Care is needed to ensure proper curing for desired strength. Fully cured strength 20 to 30% less than asphalt concrete. Deficiencies in strength typically remedied by using thicker layers.
Road mixes mixed in place Cold laid road mixes	For base and surface courses. Immediate patching or stockpiling. Use on surfaces far-removed from hot-mix plant.	Liquid asphalt or asphalt cement, open or dense-graded aggregate, sand or sandy soil	Mixed in traveling plant or by graders manipulating layers of asphalt material and aggregate. Not as precise as plant mixing. Additional surface treatments may be added to seal surface or provide wearing coat.
Open-graded mixes	Typically as an overlay or nonskid surface (sometimes called friction course) on continuous flow, high-speed highway traffic surfaces	Asphalt cements or emulsified asphalts. Open-graded aggregate, often tougher than other aggregate mixes; high degree of interlocking necessary	As an overlay, has coarse appearance and temporarily absorbs water from light rains in pavement's porous structure. Better resists transferral of reflection cracks of pavement underneath than other mixes. Typically, not used for residential streets and parking lots.
Penetration macadam	Base courses or surface courses of roads	Macadam aggregate nominally sized at 1½ to 2½ in; asphalt cement or emulsified asphalt, seal coat, and compacted and prepared subgrade	Larger aggregate compacted onto prepared subgrade covered with asphalt material that seeps and penetrates into aggregate. Covered by smaller aggregate and then entire material compacted. Seal coat applied to surface. Application requires experienced labor to produce smooth riding surface. Rarely used today.

* Consult local practices and state specifications or an engineer for materials and application guidelines.

† See Table 820-5 for specific asphalt types of these mixtures.

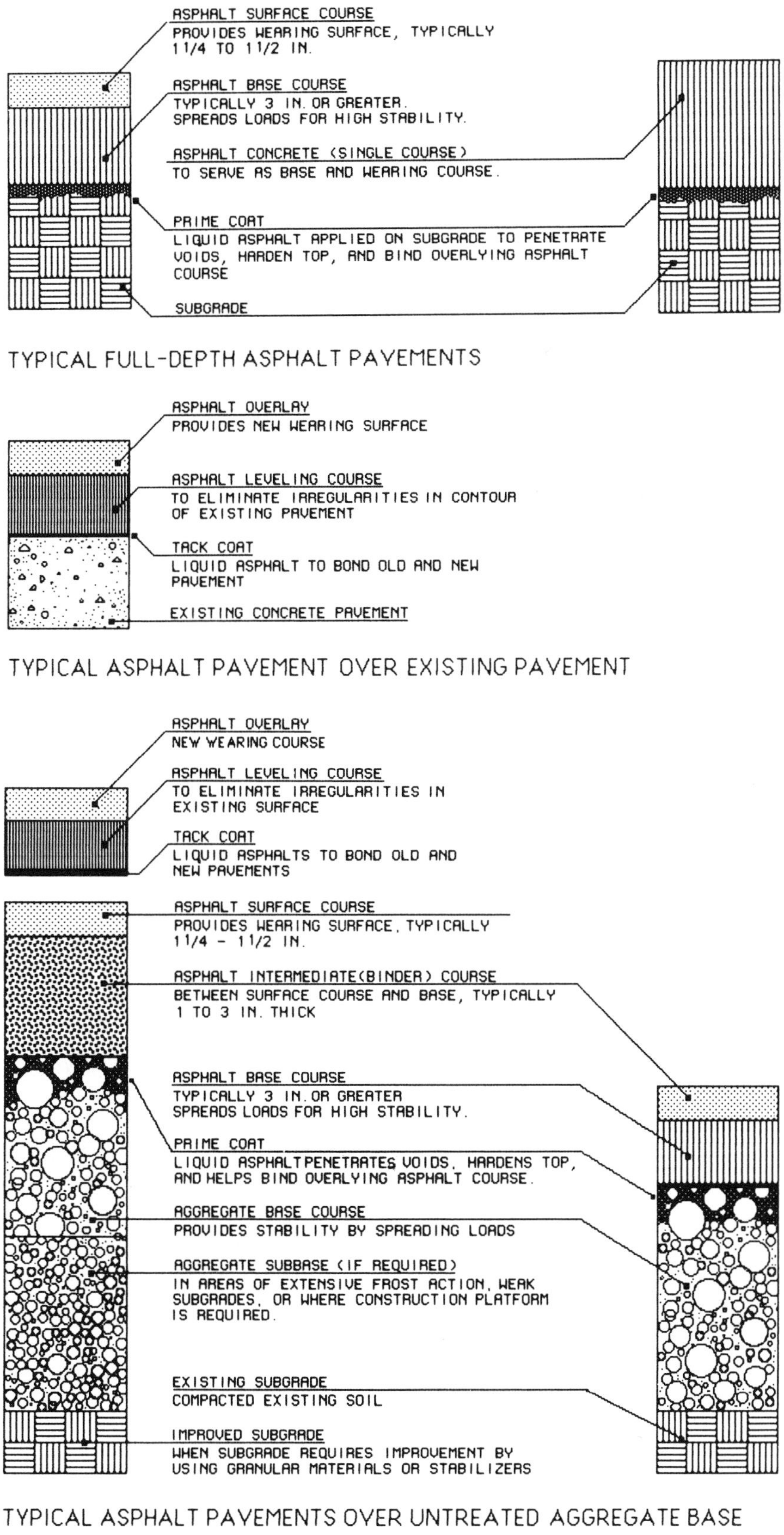
ASPHALT SURFACE COURSE
PROVIDES WEARING SURFACE, TYPICALLY 1 1/4 TO 1 1/2 IN.
ASPHALT BASE COURSE
TYPICALLY 3 IN. OR GREATER. SPREADS LOADS FOR HIGH STABILITY.
ASPHALT CONCRETE (SINGLE COURSE)
TO SERVE AS BASE AND WEARING COURSE.
PRIME COAT
LIQUID ASPHALT APPLIED ON SUBGRADE TO PENETRATE VOIDS, HARDEN TOP, AND BIND OVERLYING ASPHALT COURSE
SUBGRADE
TYPICAL FULL-DEPTH ASPHALT PAVEMENTS
ASPHALT OVERLAY
PROVIDES NEW WEARING SURFACE
ASPHALT LEVELING COURSE
TO ELIMINATE IRREGULARITIES IN CONTOUR OF EXISTING PAVEMENT
TACK COAT
LIQUID ASPHALT TO BOND OLD AND NEW PAVEMENT
EXISTING CONCRETE PAVEMENT
TYPICAL ASPHALT PAVEMENT OVER EXISTING PAVEMENT
ASPHALT OVERLAY
NEW WEARING COURSE
ASPHALT LEVELING COURSE
TO ELIMINATE IRREGULARITIES IN EXISTING SURFACE
TACK COAT
LIQUID ASPHALTS TO BOND OLD AND NEW PAVEMENTS
ASPHALT SURFACE COURSE
PROVIDES WEARING SURFACE, TYPICALLY 1 1/4 - 1 1/2 IN.
ASPHALT INTERMEDIATE(BINDER) COURSE
BETWEEN SURFACE COURSE AND BASE, TYPICALLY 1 TO 3 IN. THICK
ASPHALT BASE COURSE
TYPICALLY 3 IN. OR GREATER SPREADS LOADS FOR HIGH STABILITY.
PRIME COAT
LIQUID ASPHALT PENETRATES VOIDS, HARDENS TOP, AND HELPS BIND OVERLYING ASPHALT COURSE.
AGGREGATE BASE COURSE
PROVIDES STABILITY BY SPREADING LOADS
AGGREGATE SUBBASE (IF REQUIRED)
IN AREAS OF EXTENSIVE FROST ACTION, WEAK SUBGRADES, OR WHERE CONSTRUCTION PLATFORM IS REQUIRED.
EXISTING SUBGRADE
COMPACTED EXISTING SOIL
IMPROVED SUBGRADE
WHEN SUBGRADE REQUIRES IMPROVEMENT BY USING GRANULAR MATERIALS OR STABILIZERS
TYPICAL ASPHALT PAVEMENTS OVER UNTREATED AGGREGATE BASE

Figure 820-3 Typical asphalt pavement sections. These sections show various courses of materials typically used in asphalt pavement construction. The actual pavement design used, including dimensional specifications, will depend on load, subgrade, materials, climate, and local practices. Prime coats are generally not used on pavements thicker than 3 to 4 in (75 to 100 mm) over aggregate, and are rarely used in full-depth pavements. Asphalt pavements over existing concrete, brick, or stone require special overlay construction techniques not covered in this handbook.

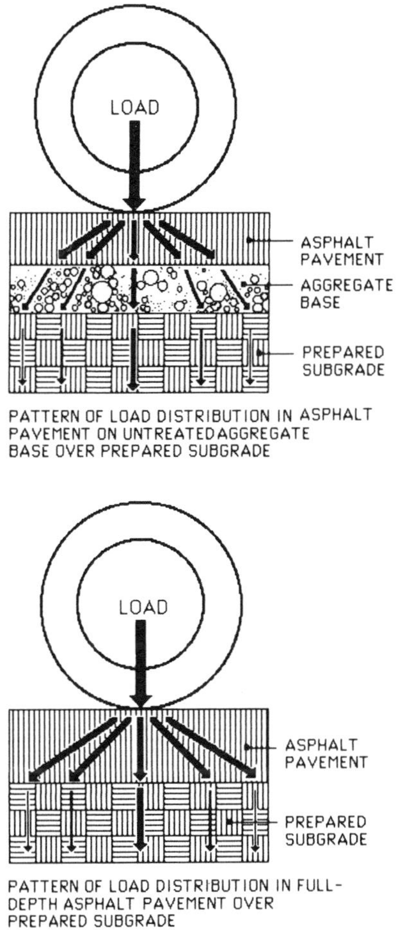
LOAD
ASPHALT PAVEMENT
AGGREGATE BASE
PREPARED SUBGRADE
PATTERN OF LOAD DISTRIBUTION IN ASPHALT PAVEMENT ON UNTREATEDAGGREGATE BASE OVER PREPARED SUBGRADE
LOAD
ASPHALT PAVEMENT
PREPARED SUBGRADE
PATTERN OF LOAD DISTRIBUTION IN FULL-DEPTH ASPHALT PAVEMENT OVER PREPARED SUBGRADE

Figure 820-4 Load distribution in asphalt pavements. Stronger materials spread loads more widely than do weaker materials. Pavement and aggregate thicknesses depend on the strength of the subgrade. Subgrades that are less likely to fail under load require less thickness in overlying pavement.

ports the loads imposed on it while the *asphalt cement* waterproofs and helps to bind everything together (Figure 820-4). The watertightness prevents moisture from entering and weakening the subgrade. For heavier loads and weaker subgrades, more and/or thicker layers of asphalt mixtures and/or base and subbase aggregate are required to distribute the loads and to prevent pavement failure. The top surface needs to be smooth, skid-resistant, and resistant to wear, distortion, and deterioration by weathering and by deicing chemicals.

5.3 Basics of Pavement Construction

Asphalt pavement design tends to be an empirical (or experience-based) technology derived from local practices and materials. The information on pavement construction contained in this section is a summary of what is required to produce a conservative design that performs well and requires little or no maintenance for approximately 20 years. Designs that vary significantly from the ones suggested herein should be used where local experience has demonstrated that an equal or satisfactory performance is assured.

NOTE: Where *ranges* are shown in the following design recommendations, a precise figure for the respective layer's thickness should be based upon local practice and standards, or, if such data are not known, the *higher* pavement design value should be used.

The *minimum* total thickness of the combined asphalt concrete layers in a pavement designed to carry very light loads (e.g., playgrounds and walkways) is 3 in (75 mm). However, most landscape design requires a minimum of at least 4 in (100 mm). With higher loads and/or weaker subgrades, a thicker minimum is required.

In the United States, the subgrade and base supporting capacities for flexible pavements are typically measured by the California bearing ratio (CBR). Some states utilize the *R*-value test, while others determine subgrade strength based on soil classification or other less-common soil strength tests. None of these are discussed further here but some are covered in more detail in Section 810: Soils and Aggregates.

All subgrades for pavements must be stable, relatively free of frost, and designed to minimize possible heaving due to frost. All subgrade layers require adequate compaction to ensure maximum strength and bearing potential. Good drainage is essential, and subgrades must be kept in a reasonably dry condition such that localized poor drainage does not affect their strength.

Types of Pavement Construction:

The two basic types of pavement construction commonly used in the United States are: (1) full-depth design and (2) aggregate base design.

Full-Depth Design: Full-depth design is quite commonly used today. It refers to an asphalt concrete or other asphalt-aggregate mixture that is placed directly on a subgrade without an aggregate base (see Figure 820-3).

The subgrade should be finished to uniform grade and compacted at or near optimum moisture level. Full-depth pavements *can* be used in frost zones but should not be used on highly frost-susceptible subgrades. The existence of unusually wet, plastic soil requires drying out the subgrade or replacing the problem soil with 4 in (100 mm) or more of untreated, coarse aggregate material. Since the suitability of this type of pavement design varies with soils and degree of frost penetration, check local practice when in doubt.

Aggregate Base Design: Aggregate base design refers to an asphalt concrete or other asphalt-aggregate mixture that is placed on an untreated aggregate base over a prepared subgrade (see Figure 820-3). This type of construction is most appropriate in areas where heavy frost exists or where soils are highly susceptible to frost action.

The prepared base and subbase aggregate layer minimizes frost heave and helps distribute the imposed loads, thus allowing the installation of slightly less thick layers of asphalt concrete or asphalt-aggregate mixtures than are necessary in full-depth design. Untreated aggregate base and subbase should be compacted at or near optimum moisture levels.

TABLE 820-14
Traffic Classifications for Roads

Traffic class	*Type of street or highway*	*Approximate range—number of heavy trucks expected during design period*†*	*EAL‡*
I	■ Parking lots, driveways ■ Light traffic, residential streets ■ Light traffic, farm roads	≤7000	5×10^3
II	■ Residential streets ■ Rural farm and residential roads	7000–15,000¶	10^4
III	■ Urban minor collector streets ■ Rural minor collector roads	70,000–150,000¶	10^5
IV§	■ Urban minor arterial and light industrial streets ■ Rural major collector and minor arterial highways	700,000–1,500,000	10^6
V§	■ Urban freeways, expressways, and other principal arterial highways ■ Rural interstate and other principal arterial highways ■ Urban interstate highways ■ Some industrial roads	>2,000,000	3×10^6

* "Heavy trucks" refers to two-axle, six-tire trucks or larger, as well as to trucks with heavy-duty, wide-based tires.

† "Design period" refers to the number of years from the initial application of traffic to the first planned major resurfacing or overlay.

‡ "EAL" is the equivalent number of 80k N (18,000 lb) single-axle loads. The equivalent is the effect on the pavement of any combination of axle loads of varying magnitude that equals 18,000 lb (80 k N).

§ Thickness determination with increasing loads becomes very complex. Whenever possible, consult the Asphalt Institute's manual MS-1, *Thickness Design—Asphalt Pavements for Highways and Streets,* to determine proper procedures and recommendations for classes IV and higher. For reasons of complexity, pavement thicknesses of class V will not be discussed. In these cases, consult with a civil engineer.

¶ When the value of truck use is between two class values, proportionately alter the thickness of the finished pavement (see Design Example B in the text).

Source: Adapted from The Asphalt Institute, *Asphalt Pavement Thickness and Design,* IS-181, November 1981.

Expected Pavement Life:

Asphalt concrete pavements, properly constructed, typically require surface maintenance or resurfacing overlays about every 20 years. The durability of the pavement depends upon many factors, including traffic volume, quality of construction, frequency of maintenance, severity of climate, and the quality of the materials involved.

6.0 THICKNESS DESIGN OF ASPHALT PAVEMENTS FOR TYPICAL USES

6.1 Roads

Design Factors:

The thickness of asphalt concrete pavements for roads depends on three factors:

1. *Traffic weight and number of vehicles:* the heavier and/or more numerous the load, the thicker the pavement required.

2. *Subgrade support:* weaker subgrades require thicker and/or more layers of asphalt concrete or aggregate.

3. *Materials in the pavement structure:* hot-mix asphalt concrete results in more strength than cold mixes. An aggregate base distributes loads better than does a subgrade alone.

Thickness Design Procedure:

The following design procedure is recommended for roads in the United States by The Asphalt Institute. Local practices and standards should be investigated, as local conditions may suggest modification of this procedure somewhat.

1. *Classify the traffic:* select the appropriate traffic classification shown in Table 820-14.

2. *Classify the subgrade:* determine the proper subgrade classification based on the criteria in Table 820-15. Consult a civil engineer to confirm the proper classification.

3. *Determine the optimum asphalt concrete specifications:* use the specifications of the governing authority responsible for asphalt pavement specifications. If these are not available, determine the optimum asphalt cement and aggregate combination, considering the proposed load and subgrade. (This procedure is described in The Asphalt Institute's publication, *Model Construction Specifications for Asphalt Concrete and Other Plant-Mix Types.*)

Any untreated aggregate incorporated in the design should comply with *Graded Aggregate Material for Bases and Subbases for Highways and Airports* (ASTM D2940). The aggregate should meet those requirements listed in Table 820-16.

The bases and subbases should be compacted at optimum moisture content, plus or minus 1.5 percentage points, to achieve a minimum density of 100 percent maximum laboratory density. The subgrade should be compacted at or near optimum moisture content to achieve maximum density.

4. *Determine the thickness:* Tables 820-14 through 820-17 list the thickness requirements for a *full-depth* asphalt concrete pavement. Tables 820-18 through 820-20 show thickness requirements for an asphalt concrete pavement over an untreated aggregate base.

Design Examples:

Two design examples are included here to clarify the procedure given above.

Example A: (rural minor collector road):

1. A rural minor collector road is expected to average 10 heavy trucks per day over a 20-year design period. The total number of heavy trucks will be 10 × 365 × 20 = 73,000. Traffic Class III is indicated (Table 820-14).

TABLE 820-15
Subgrade Classifications for Roads

Subgrade class	*CBR**†	*Resilient modulus, MPa (psi)**†	*R-value**†	*Remarks*
Poor	3	30 (4500)	6	Poor subgrade soils become quite soft and plastic when wet. Included are those soils having appreciable amounts of clay and fine silt. The coarser silts and sandy loams also may exhibit poor bearing properties in areas where frost penetration into the subgrade is a factor.
Medium	8	80 (12,000)	20	Medium subgrade soils retain a moderate degree of firmness under adverse moisture conditions. Included are such soils as loams, silty sands, and sand gravels containing moderate amounts of clay and fine silt.
Good to excellent	17	170 (25,000)	43	Good subgrade soils retain a substantial amount of their load-supporting capacity when wet. Included are the clean sands and sand gravels and soils free of detrimental amounts of plastic materials. Excellent subgrade soils are unaffected by moisture or frost. They include clean and sharp sands and gravels, particularly those that are well-graded.

* The following are specifications for the soil-testing procedures used. California Bearing Ratio (CBR): ASTM Method D 1883 (AASHTO Method T 193), compact samples according to ASTM Method D 155 T (AASHTO Method T 180), Method B or D. Resistance value (R-value): ASTM Method D 2844 (AASHTO Method T 190). Resilient modulus: approximately computed from CBR by equation

$$Mr(\text{MPa}) = 10.342\ \text{CBR or}$$
$$Mr(\text{psi}) = 1500\ \text{CBR}$$

or from R-value by equation

$$Mr(\text{MPa}) = 7.963 + 3.826\ (\text{R-value}) \text{ or}$$
$$Mr(\text{psi}) = 1155 + 555\ (\text{R-value})$$

Resilient modulus is approximated by these equations when the expected figure is 207 MPa (30,000 psi) or less. Such an approximation is useful in soils classified as CL, CH, ML, SC, SM, and SP (Unified Soil Classification, ASTM D 2487). With other soils, resilient modulus needs to be determined by laboratory testing. The resilient modulus used here and these approximations are not the same as the dynamic modulus test now being used by some agencies. The latter tends to give lower *Mr* results. For a more complete discussion, consult with a civil engineer or refer to the Asphalt Institute's *Soils Manual* (MS-10).

† The designer is cautioned to determine that estimated soil strength is accurate and conforms to the above specifications before utilizing the table.

Source: Adapted from The Asphalt Institute, *Asphalt Pavement Thickness and Design,* IS-181, November 1981.

TABLE 820-16
Untreated Aggregate Base and Subbase Quality Requirements for Asphalt Roads*†

Test	Test requirements‡ Subbase	Base
CBR, minimum or	20	80
R-value, minimum	55	78
Liquid limit, maximum	25	25
Plasticity index, maximum, or	6	Nonplastic
Sand equivalent, minimum	25	35
Passing No. 200 sieve, maximum	12	7

* All bases and subbases should be compacted at optimum moisture content, plus or minus 1.5 percentage points, to achieve a minimum of 100% maximum laboratory density as established by ASTM Method Test D 1557, Method D (or AASHTO Method T 180).

† These requirements apply to all untreated aggregate used in this pavement design. Such aggregate should comply with *Graded Aggregate Material for Bases or Subbase for Highways and Airports,* ASTM specification D2940.

‡ The upper 6 in (150 mm) of untreated aggregate should meet the requirements for base material. Material below this may meet subbase requirements.

Source: Adapted from The Asphalt Institute, *Asphalt Pavement Thickness and Design,* IS-181, November 1981.

TABLE 820-17
Asphalt Concrete Thickness for Roads—Full-Depth Design[a,b,c]

Subgrade class[d]	Pavement section	Traffic classification[e] I	II	III	IV
		Full-depth asphalt concrete, in (mm)			
Poor	Asphalt concrete surface	1.0 (25)	1.0 (25)	1.5 (40)	2.0 (50)
	Asphalt concrete base	3.5 (85)	4.0 (95)	5.5 (140)	8.0 (205)
	Total:	4.5 (110)	5.0 (120)	7.0 (180)	10.0 (255)
Medium	Asphalt concrete surface[f]	1.0 (25)	1.0 (25)	1.5 (40)	2.0 (50)
	Asphalt concrete base	3.0 (75)	3.0 (75)	3.5 (85)	6.0 (155)
	Total:	4.0 (100)[g]	4.0 (100)[g]	5.0 (125)	8.0 (205)
Good to excellent	Asphalt concrete surface[f]	1.0 (25)	1.0 (25)	1.5 (40)	2.0 (50)
	Asphalt concrete base	3.0 (75)	3.0 (75)	2.5 (60)	4.0 (105)
	Total:	4.0 (100)[g]	4.0 (100)[g]	4.0 (100)[g]	6.0 (155)

[a] Consult local standards and practices for all pavements. Such specifications supercede those mentioned here.

[b] See Table 820-13 for typical asphalt mixtures. The thickness of any asphalt concrete layer should be at least twice either the nominal maximum size mix designation or the maximum particle size of the mix (whichever term is used).

[c] Use full-depth pavements where highly frost-susceptible soils or heavy frost is not a problem. Otherwise, use asphalt concrete over an aggregate base.

[d] See Table 820-15.

[e] See Table 820-14.

[f] Minimum recommended thickness of asphalt concrete surface.

[g] Minimum recommended design.

Source: Adapted from The Asphalt Institute, *Asphalt Pavement Thickness and Design,* 1S-181, November 1981.

TABLE 820-18

Pavement Thickness for Roads over Poor Subgrades—Asphalt Concrete on Aggregate Base[a,b,c,d]

Pavement section/various aggregate base thicknesses	Traffic classification[a]			
	I	*II*	*III*	*IV*
	Thickness in inches (mm)			
4-in				
Asphalt concrete surface	1.0 (25)	1.0 (25)	1.5 (40)	2.0 (50)
Asphalt concrete base	2.5 (65)	3.0 (80)	5.0 (120)	8.0 (200)
Untreated aggregate base[e]	4.0 (100)	4.0 (100)	4.0 (100)	4.0 (100)
Total:	7.5 (190)	8.0 (205)	10.5 (260)	14.0 (350)
6-in				
Asphalt concrete surface	1.0 (25)	1.0 (25)	1.5 (40)	2.0 (50)
Asphalt concrete base	2.0 (55)	3.0 (75)	4.5 (120)	7.5 (190)
Untreated aggregate base[e]	6.0 (150)	6.0 (150)	6.0 (150)	6.0 (150)
Total:	9.0 (230)	10.0 (250)[f]	12.0 (310)	15.5 (390)
8-in				
Asphalt concrete surface	1.0 (25)	1.0 (25)	1.5 (40)	2.0 (50)
Asphalt concrete base	2.0 (50)	3.0 (75)	4.0 (105)	7.0 (185)
Untreated aggregate base[e]	8.0 (200)	8.0 (200)	8.0 (200)	8.0 (200)
Total:	11.0 (275)[f]	12.0 (300)[f]	13.5 (345)	17.0 (435)
10-in				
Asphalt concrete surface	1.0 (25)	1.0 (25)	1.5 (40)	2.0 (50)
Asphalt concrete base	2.0 (50)	3.0 (75)	3.5 (90)	7.0 (175)
Untreated aggregate base[e]	10.0 (250)	10.0 (250)	10.0 (250)	10.0 (250)
Total:	13.0 (325)[f]	14.0 (350)[f]	15.0 (380)	19.0 (475)
12-in				
Asphalt concrete surface	1.0 (25)	1.0 (25)	1.5 (40)	2.0 (50)
Asphalt concrete base	2.0 (50)	3.0 (75)	3.0 (85)	6.0 (160)
Untreated aggregate base[e]	12.0 (300)	12.0 (300)	12.0 (300)	12.0 (300)
Total:	15.0 (375)[f]	16.0 (400)[f]	16.5 (425)	20.0 (510)
18-in				
Asphalt concrete surface	1.0 (25)	1.0 (25)	1.5 (40)	2.0 (50)
Asphalt concrete base	2.0 (50)	3.0 (75)	2.5 (60)	5.5 (135)
Untreated aggregate base[e]	18.0 (450)	18.0 (450)	18.0 (450)	18.0 (450)
Total:	21.0 (525)[f]	22.0 (550)[f]	22.0 (550)[f]	25.5 (635)

[a] See Table 820-14.

[b] Depth of untreated aggregate base is dependent upon depth necessary to mitigate frost action. Local practice typically defines required depths. For aggregate bases greater than 18 in, consult with a civil engineer.

[c] Refer to Table 820-13 for typical asphalt mixtures. The thickness of any asphalt concrete layer should be at least twice either the nominal maximum size mix designation or the maximum particle size (whichever term is used).

[d] Consult local standards and practices for all pavements. Such specifications may supercede those mentioned herein if they provide the same service life of these designs.

[e] The top 6 in of untreated aggregate should meet base course quality requirements. Subbase quality requirements may be used below 6 in.

[f] Minimum thicknesses of asphalt concrete over untreated aggregate base and subbase apply to these designs as follows: for traffic class I, 3.0 in (75 mm); for traffic class II, 4.0 in (100 mm); for traffic class III, 4.0 in (100 mm); and for traffic class IV, 5.0 in (125 mm).

Source: Adapted from The Asphalt Institute, *Asphalt Pavement Thickness and Design,* 1S-181, November 1981.

TABLE 820-19
Pavement Thickness for Roads over Medium Subgrades—Asphalt Concrete on Aggregate Base[a,b,c,d]

Pavement section/various aggregate base thicknesses	*Traffic classification*[a]			
	I	*II*	*III*	*IV*
	Thickness in inches (mm)			
4 in				
Asphalt concrete surface	1.0 (25)	1.0 (25)	1.5 (40)	2.0 (50)
Asphalt concrete base	2.0 (50)	3.0 (75)	2.5 (60)	5.0 (130)
Untreated aggregate base[e]	4.0 (100)	4.0 (100)	4.0 (100)	4.0 (100)
Total:	7.0 (175)	8.0 (200)[f]	8.0 (200)[f]	11.0 (280)
6 in				
Asphalt concrete surface	1.0 (25)	1.0 (25)	1.5 (40)	2.0 (50)
Asphalt concrete base	2.0 (50)	3.0 (75)	2.5 (60)	4.5 (115)
Untreated aggregate base[e]	6.0 (150)	6.0 (150)	6.0 (150)	6.0 (150)
Total:	9.0 (225)[f]	10.0 (250)[f]	10.0 (250)[f]	12.5 (315)
8 in				
Asphalt concrete surface	1.0 (25)	1.0 (25)	1.5 (40)	2.0 (50)
Asphalt concrete base	2.0 (50)	3.0 (75)	2.5 (60)	4.0 (110)
Untreated aggregate base[e]	8.0 (200)	8.0 (200)	8.0 (200)	8.0 (200)
Total:	11.0 (275)[f]	12.0 (300)[f]	12.0 (300)[f]	14.0 (360)
10 in				
Asphalt concrete surface	1.0 (25)	1.0 (25)	1.5 (40)	2.0 (50)
Asphalt concrete base	2.0 (50)	3.0 (75)	2.5 (60)	3.5 (95)
Untreated aggregate base[e]	10.0 (250)	10.0 (250)	10.0 (250)	10.0 (250)
Total:	13.0 (325)[f]	14.0 (350)[f]	14.0 (350)[f]	15.5 (395)
12 in				
Asphalt concrete surface	1.0 (25)	1.0 (25)	1.5 (40)	2.0 (50)
Asphalt concrete base	2.0 (50)	3.0 (75)	2.5 (60)	3.5 (90)
Untreated aggregate base[e]	12.0 (300)	12.0 (300)	12.0 (300)	12.0 (300)
Total:	15.0 (375)[f]	16.0 (400)[f]	16.0 (400)[f]	17.5 (440)
18 in				
Asphalt concrete surface	1.0 (25)	1.0 (25)	1.5 (40)	2.0 (50)
Asphalt concrete base	2.0 (50)	3.0 (75)	2.5 (60)	3.0 (85)
Untreated aggregate base[e]	18.0 (450)	18.0 (450)	18.0 (450)	18.0 (450)
Total:	21.0 (525)[f]	22.0 (550)[f]	22.0 (550)[f]	23.0 (585)

[a] See Table 820-14.

[b] Depth of untreated aggregate base is dependent upon depth necessary to mitigate frost action. Local practice typically defines required depth. For aggregate bases greater than 18 in, consult with a civil engineer.

[c] Refer to Table 820-13 for typical asphalt mixtures. The thickness of any asphalt concrete layer should be at least twice either the nominal maximum size mix designation or the maximum particle size (whichever term is used).

[d] Consult local standards and practices for all pavements. Such specifications supercede those mentioned here.

[e] The top 6 in of untreated aggregate should meet base course quality requirements. Subbase quality requirements may be used below 6 in.

[f] Minimum recommended thicknesses of asphalt concrete over untreated aggregate base and subbase apply to these designs as follows: for traffic class I, 3.0 in (75 mm); for traffic class II, 4.0 in (100 mm); for traffic class III, 4.0 in (100 mm); and for traffic class IV, 5.0 in (125 mm).

Source: Adapted from The Asphalt Institute, *Asphalt Pavement Thickness and Design,* 1S-181, November 1981.

TABLE 820-20

Pavement Thickness for Roads over Good to Excellent Subgrades—Asphalt Concrete on Aggregate Base[a,b,c,d]

Pavement section/various aggregate base thicknesses	Traffic classification[a]			
	I	*II*	*III*	*IV*
	Thickness in inches (mm)			
4 in				
Asphalt concrete surface	1.0 (25)	1.0 (25)	1.5 (40)	2.0 (50)
Asphalt concrete base	2.0 (50)	3.0 (75)	2.5 (60)	3.0 (75)
Untreated aggregate base	4.0 (100)	4.0 (100)	4.0 (100)	4.0 (100)
Total:	7.0 (175)[f]	8.0 (200)[f]	8.0 (200)[f]	9.0 (225)[f]
6 in				
Asphalt concrete surface	1.0 (25)	1.0 (25)	1.5 (40)	2.0 (50)
Asphalt concrete base	2.0 (50)	3.0 (75)	2.5 (60)	3.0 (75)
Untreated aggregate base	6.0 (150)	6.0 (150)	6.0 (150)	6.0 (150)
Total:	9.0 (225)[f]	10.0 (250)[f]	10.0 (250)[f]	11.0 (275)[f]
8 in				
Asphalt concrete surface	1.0 (25)	1.0 (25)	1.5 (40)	2.0 (50)
Asphalt concrete base	2.0 (50)	3.0 (75)	2.5 (60)	3.0 (75)
Untreated aggregate base	8.0 (200)	8.0 (200)	8.0 (200)	8.0 (200)
Total:	11.0 (275)[f]	12.0 (300)[f]	12.0 (300)[f]	13.0 (325)[f]
10 in				
Asphalt concrete surface	1.0 (25)	1.0 (25)	1.5 (40)	2.0 (50)
Asphalt concrete base	2.0 (50)	3.0 (75)	2.5 (60)	3.0 (75)
Untreated aggregate base	10.0 (250)	10.0 (250)	10.0 (250)	10.0 (250)
Total:	13.0 (325)[f]	14.0 (350)[f]	14.0 (350)[f]	15.0 (375)[f]
12 in				
Asphalt concrete surface	1.0 (25)	1.0 (25)	1.5 (40)	2.0 (50)
Asphalt concrete base	2.0 (50)	3.0 (75)	2.5 (60)	3.0 (75)
Untreated aggregate base	12.0 (300)	12.0 (300)	12.0 (300)	12.0 (300)
Total:	15.0 (375)[f]	16.0 (400)[f]	16.0 (400)[f]	17.0 (425)[f]
18 in				
Asphalt concrete surface	1.0 (25)	1.0 (25)	1.5 (40)	2.0 (50)
Asphalt concrete base	2.0 (50)	3.0 (75)	2.5 (60)	3.0 (75)
Untreated aggregate base	18.0 (450)	18.0 (450)	18.0 (450)	18.0 (450)
Total:	21.0 (525)[f]	22.0 (550)[f]	22.0 (550)[f]	23.0 (575)[f]

[a] See Table 820-14.

[b] Depth of untreated aggregate base is dependent upon depth necessary to mitigate frost action. Local practice typically defines required depth. For aggregate bases greater than 18 in, consult with a civil engineer.

[c] Refer to Table 820-13 for typical asphalt mixtures. The thickness of any asphalt concrete layer should be at least twice either the nominal maximum size mix designation or the maximum particle size (whichever term is used).

[d] Consult local standards and practices for all pavements. Such specifications supercede those mentioned here.

[e] The top 6 in of untreated aggregate should meet base course quality requirements. Subbase quality requirements may be used below 6 in.

[f] Minimum recommended thicknesses of asphalt concrete over untreated aggregate base and subbase apply to these designs as follows: for traffic class I, 3.0 in (75 mm); for traffic class II, 4.0 in (100 mm); for traffic class III, 4.0 in (100 mm); and for traffic class IV, 5.0 in (125 mm).

Source: Adapted from The Asphalt Institute, *Asphalt Pavement Thickness and Design,* 1S-181, November 1981.

2. From past experience and CBR test data, the subgrade is expected to have a CBR between 8 and 10. A *medium* subgrade soil classification is indicated (Table 820-15). Confirm the findings with an engineering study.

3. Two alternative pavements are considered: full-depth asphalt concrete (Table 820-17) and asphalt concrete over a 6-in (150-mm) untreated aggregate base (Table 820-19).

4. The final thicknesses for each pavement type are computed below:

Pavement layer	*Full-depth design*	*Asphalt concrete on untreated aggregate base*
Asphalt concrete surface, in	1.5 (3.8 mm)	1.5 (3.8 mm)
Asphalt concrete base, in	3.5 (9.0 mm)	2.5 (6.4 mm)
Untreated aggregate base, in		6.0 (15.0 mm)
Total thickness	5.0 (12.7mm)	10.0 (25.4 mm)

Example B: (interpolation between traffic classifications):

1. A minor arterial street is estimated to average 70 heavy trucks per day over a 20-year period. The total number of heavy trucks will be 70 × 365 × 20 = 511,000. This falls between Traffic Classes III and IV (Table 820-14).

2. Old soil-test records indicate that the design CBR value in the area was 7. This falls in the medium subgrade soil classification (Table 820-15). Confirm the findings with an engineering study.

3. Full-depth asphalt concrete has been selected for the pavement structure (Table 820-17).

4. Because the total number of heavy trucks (511,000) falls between Traffic Classes III and IV, a number (thickness) between 5.0 and 8.0 must be determined by interpolation.

Interpolation (from Table 820-17):

Traffic Class IV = 8.0 in (20.32 mm) total thickness

Traffic Class III = 5.0 in (12.7 mm) total thickness

Difference = 3.0 in (7.6 mm)

Let *x* equal that amount of thickness needed to be added to 5 in to produce a total adequate thickness for 511,000 trucks. The number 511,000 falls between 150,000 (Class III) and 700,000 (Class IV). Thus,

$$\frac{x}{3.0} = \frac{511{,}000 - 150{,}000}{700{,}000 - 150{,}000} = \frac{361{,}000}{550{,}000} = 2.0 \text{ in}$$

Therefore, the total design thickness necessary will be:

2.0 + 5.0 = 7.0 in

This 2-in additional thickness should be accounted for (added to) in the asphalt concrete *base course* rather than in the *surface course* (see Table 820-17).

Note that the thickness of the asphalt concrete *surface course* (in cases of interpolation between traffic classifications) should be the *thicker* value of the two traffic classes (i.e., 2 instead of 1.5 in. in Table 820-17).

Final thickness design: Therefore, the thickness design should be:

TABLE 820-21
Thickness Design for Driveways and Passenger Car Parking Areas (No Trucks)

		Soft clay soils, plastic when wet	*Average clay loam soils, not plastic*	*Gravel or sandy soils, well-drained*
	*Full-depth asphalt concrete**			
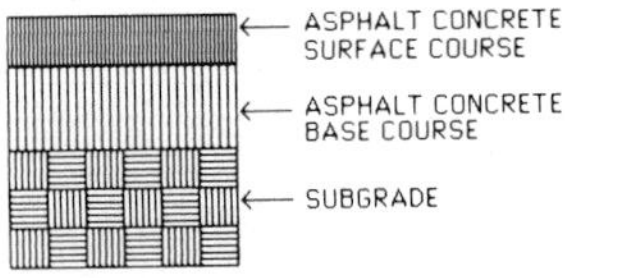	Surface course, in	1	1	1
	Base course, in	4–5†	3–4†	2–3†
	Total thickness, in	5–6	4–5	3–4
	*Asphalt concrete and aggregate base**‡			
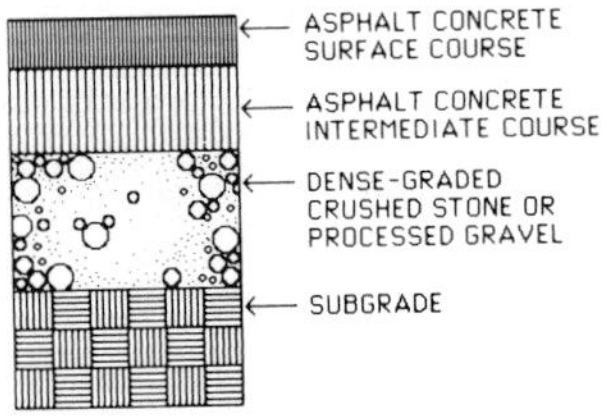	Surface course, in	1	1	1
	Intermediate course, in	2	2	2
	Gravel, in	6–8§	4–6§	2–4§
	Total thickness, in	9–11	7–9	5–7

ASPHALT CONCRETE SURFACE COURSE
ASPHALT CONCRETE BASE COURSE
SUBGRADE

ASPHALT CONCRETE SURFACE COURSE
ASPHALT CONCRETE INTERMEDIATE COURSE
DENSE-GRADED CRUSHED STONE OR PROCESSED GRAVEL
SUBGRADE

* See Table 820-8 for typical mixture specifications. The thickness of any asphalt concrete layer should be at least twice either the nominal maximum size mix designation or the maximum particle size of the mix. Local standards and practices supercede those mentioned here and should be consulted for all pavements.

† Where ranges in asphalt concrete thicknesses are shown, consult local practice and standards for a precise value. If such knowledge is not available, assume the higher value and consult a civil engineer.

‡ Utilize full-depth pavements where frost-susceptible soils or heavy frost is not a problem.

§ Aggregate base course depth varies depending on strength of subgrade soil and depth of frost. Check with local practices for safety and applicable standards.

Source: Adapted from The Asphalt Institute, The *Asphalt Handbook,* March 1970.

Asphalt concrete surface = 2.0 in

Asphalt concrete base = 5.0 in

Total thickness = 7.0 in

6.2 Driveways and Parking Areas

Thickness Design Tables:

Table 820-21 can be used to determine pavement thickness for driveways and passenger car parking areas (no trucks), and Table 820-22 can be used to determine pavement thickness for heavy truck parking areas. For parking areas used by higher volumes of heavy trucks, such as truck stops or truck terminals, the design recommendations outlined in 6.1 Roads of this section can be used.

Considerations:

Dolly wheels of a parked truck trailer will indent asphalt surfaces unless planks are placed under each wheel or a concrete pad installed. Although grease or oil drippings from vehicles will not dissolve asphalt, concentrated amounts of gasoline will dissolve asphalt. Protection can be provided by a tar emulsion sealer (which is not dissolved by gasoline) or by substituting an alternative pavement material.

6.3 Bicycle, Pedestrian, and Golf Cart Paths

Bikepaths and Walkways:

Bikepaths and walkways utilize a total asphalt concrete thickness of 3 to 4 in (75 to 100 mm) in a full-depth or untreated aggregate base design (Figure 820-5). Local practices should be followed where applicable.

Golf Cart Paths:

Golf cart paths require a softer surface to minimize golf shoe spike wear. Although the overall construction is similar to bikepaths and walkways, the surface course should be a sand-asphalt mixture with an asphalt content slightly higher than for normal highway paving (Figure 820-5). Alternatively, an open-graded mix may be used as a surface course. Local practices should be followed where applicable.

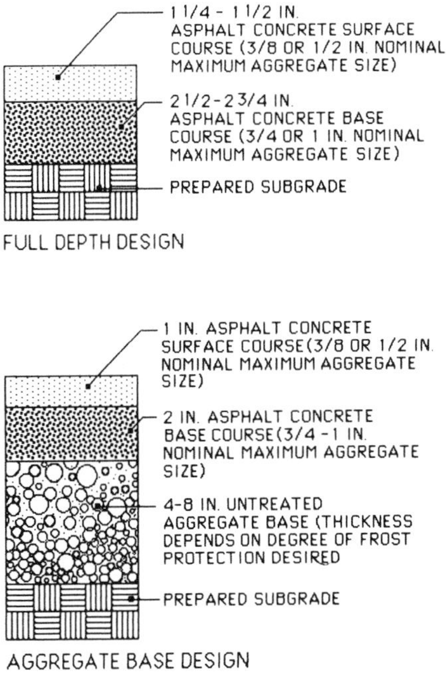
1 1/4 - 1 1/2 IN. ASPHALT CONCRETE SURFACE COURSE (3/8 OR 1/2 IN. NOMINAL MAXIMUM AGGREGATE SIZE)
2 1/2 - 2 3/4 IN. ASPHALT CONCRETE BASE COURSE (3/4 OR 1 IN. NOMINAL MAXIMUM AGGREGATE SIZE)
PREPARED SUBGRADE
FULL DEPTH DESIGN
1 IN. ASPHALT CONCRETE SURFACE COURSE (3/8 OR 1/2 IN. NOMINAL MAXIMUM AGGREGATE SIZE)
2 IN. ASPHALT CONCRETE BASE COURSE (3/4 - 1 IN. NOMINAL MAXIMUM AGGREGATE SIZE)
4-8 IN. UNTREATED AGGREGATE BASE (THICKNESS DEPENDS ON DEGREE OF FROST PROTECTION DESIRED
PREPARED SUBGRADE
AGGREGATE BASE DESIGN

Figure 820-5 Typical design for walkways, bicycle trails, and golf cart paths. Golf cart paths require a surface course of a sand-asphalt mixture with an asphalt content slightly higher than for normal roadway pavements. Refer to Table 820-8 for information on asphalt-concrete mixtures.

TABLE 820-22
Thickness Design for Parking Areas for Heavy Trucks and Service Stations*

		Soft clay soils, plastic when wet	*Average clay loam soils, not plastic*	*Gravel or sandy soils, well-drained*
	Full-depth asphalt concrete†			
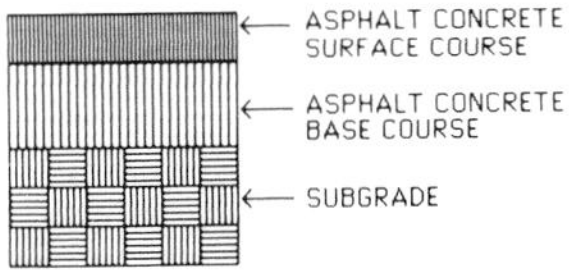 ASPHALT CONCRETE SURFACE COURSE ASPHALT CONCRETE BASE COURSE SUBGRADE	Surface course, in	1.5	1.5	1.5
	Base course, in	6–8‡	5–6‡	3–6‡
	Total thickness, in	7.5–9.5	6.5–7.5	4.5–6.5
	Asphalt concrete and aggregate base†·§			
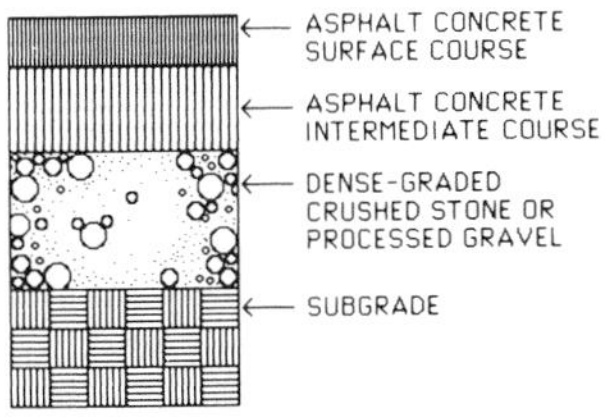 ASPHALT CONCRETE SURFACE COURSE ASPHALT CONCRETE INTERMEDIATE COURSE DENSE-GRADED CRUSHED STONE OR PROCESSED GRAVEL SUBGRADE	Surface course, in	1.5	1.5	1.5
	Intermediate course, in	3	3	3
	Gravel, in	6–10¶	5–8¶	3–6¶
	Total thickness, in	10.5–14.5	9.5–12.5	7.5–10.5

* For areas affected by higher volumes of heavy trucks (such as terminals), the recommendations outlines in 6.1 of this section should be followed.

† See Table 820-8 for typical mixture specifications. The thickness of any asphalt concrete layer should be at least twice either the nominal maximum size mix designation or the maximum particle size of the mix. Local standards and practices supercede those mentioned here and should be consulted for all pavements.

‡ Where ranges in asphalt concrete thicknesses are shown, consult local practice and standards for a precise value. If such knowledge is not available, assume the higher value and consult a civil engineer.

§ Utilize full-depth pavements where frost-susceptible soils or heavy frost is not a problem.

¶ Aggregate base course depth varies depending on strength of subgrade soil and depth of frost. Check with local practices for safety and applicable standards.

Source: Adapted from The Asphalt Institute, The *Asphalt Handbook,* March 1970.

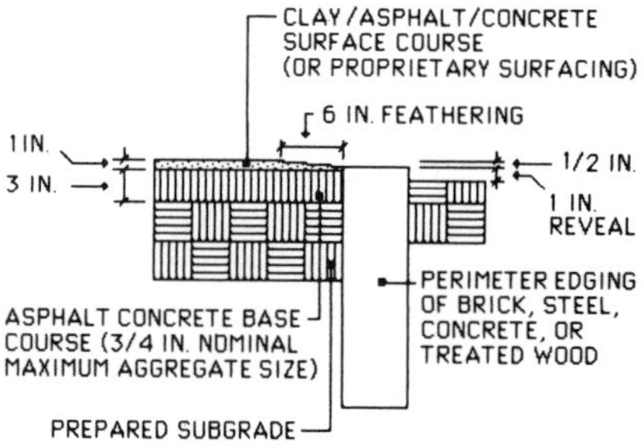
CLAY/ASPHALT/CONCRETE SURFACE COURSE (OR PROPRIETARY SURFACING)
6 IN. FEATHERING
1 IN.
3 IN.
1/2 IN.
1 IN. REVEAL
PERIMETER EDGING OF BRICK, STEEL, CONCRETE, OR TREATED WOOD
ASPHALT CONCRETE BASE COURSE (3/4 IN. NOMINAL MAXIMUM AGGREGATE SIZE)
PREPARED SUBGRADE

Figure 820-6 Tennis courts and perimeter edging. Consult manufacturer's specifications for information on pavement construction and detailing when using proprietary surfaces. Refer to Table 820-8 for information on asphalt-concrete mixtures. Refer to Division 900: Details and Devices, for additional edging details.

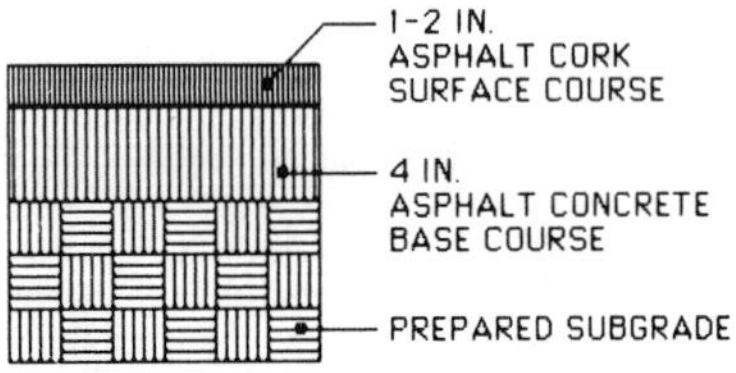
1-2 IN. ASPHALT CORK SURFACE COURSE
4 IN. ASPHALT CONCRETE BASE COURSE
PREPARED SUBGRADE

Figure 820-7 Typical asphalt cork surface course. Recreational asphalt pavement courses often consist of proprietary products. Consult manufacturer's specifications for information on construction details.

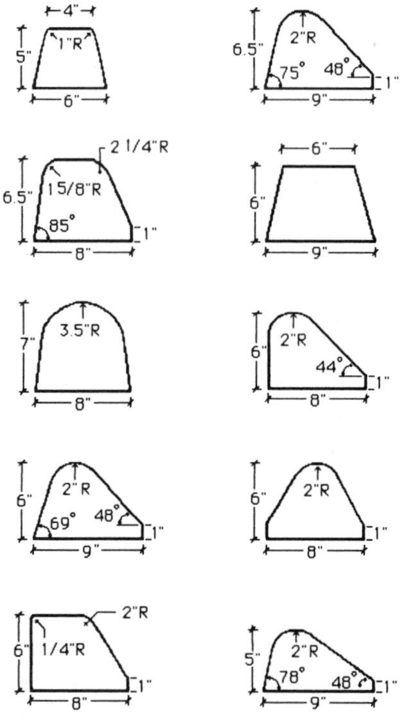
4"
1"R
5"
6"
6.5"
2"R
75°
48°
1"
9"
2 1/4"R
15/8"R
6.5"
85°
1"
8"
6"
6"
9"
7"
3.5"R
8"
6"
2"R
44°
1"
8"
6"
2"R
69°
48°
1"
9"
6"
2"R
1"
8"
2"R
6"
1/4"R
1"
8"
5"
2"R
78°
48°
1"
9"

Figure 820-8 Typical shapes for asphalt curbs.

6.4 Tennis Courts

Tennis court surfaces require a high degree of smoothness with a maximum irregularity of ⅛ in (3 mm) over a 10-ft (3-m) distance. This can be achieved with an asphalt concrete base of ¾ in (20 mm) of nominal maximum size designation covered either with sand-asphalt for the surface course or with proprietary surfacing (Figure 820-6). The base course is 3 in (75 mm) and the surface course is 1 in (25 mm), creating a minimal total thickness of 4 in (100 mm). For more specific thickness design information, especially under various soil and environmental conditions, refer to Table 820-21. If a proprietary mixture is used, follow the manufacturer's recommendation for the surface course and, if mentioned, for the base course as well. Perimeter edging is usually necessary to prevent edge failures.

If sand-asphalt is used, a latex paint of minimum thickness should be used no sooner than 30 days after construction. If a color finish has been applied, lines should be painted with a compatible material. Traffic, oil, alkyd, or solvent-vehicle-type paints should not be used.

6.5 Playgrounds and Recreational Areas

Thickness designs for playgrounds and other recreational areas should be the same as those used for tennis courts (see Figure 820-6).

Asphalt concrete can serve as a base for proprietary products such as sealers, color coats, resilient surface coatings, and artificial turf. The asphalt concrete base can be molded on a prepared subgrade to produce any desired gradient. Erosional undermining of pavement edges should be prevented.

If proprietary surfacing materials are used, consult the manufacturer's recommendations for pavement specifications.

Combining a small percentage of cork with asphalt cement, sharp coarse sand, and limestone dust produces a resilient playground surface (Figure 820-7); the cork granules should have a maximum diameter size of ¼ in (6.5 mm). Other ingredients may also be used, such as vermiculite and rubber. Many such surfaces are proprietary products, and the manufacturer's specifications should be carefully followed.

7.0 MISCELLANEOUS

7.1 Asphalt Curbs and Gutters

Asphalt Curbs:

Asphalt concrete curbs are available in various shapes (Figure 820-8). Although not affected by snow- and ice-melting chemicals, asphalt curbs can be sheared off when struck by heavy loads or deformed when subjected to pressure or abrasion. Curbs should be back-filled with a solid granular material or well-compacted soil. Asphalt curbs are set by a curbing machine at an average rate of 2000 ft (610 m) per day and must be installed on top of a solid, impervious pavement that will not erode or fail (Figure 820-9). Curbs are made of specially proportioned asphalt-aggregate mixtures (Table 820-23).

Asphalt concrete berms are an alternative to curbs (Figure 820-10).

Asphalt Gutters:

Asphalt gutters can be formed in a variety of cross sections and are placed mostly by hand or on occasion (for special large projects) by a small paving machine, specially adapted to fit a particular job (Figure 820-11).

7.2 Asphalt Underlayments

Asphalt concrete is often used as an underlayment for surface courses, including brick, stone block, and recreational proprietary products. In principle, the surface material can provide a good wearing surface but may or may not contribute to the overall pavement strength that is necessary to *distribute* the loads. The underlayment must therefore fulfill the remaining strength requirements. Consequently, the manufacturer's specifications for the surface product should be consulted to ascertain the strength of the material and thus determine the appropriate design for an underlayment.

7.3 Colored Asphalt Pavements

Over time, as the asphalt film wears off the surface of a pavement, the pavement will weather to a grayish tone and reveal the color of the aggregate, especially its larger particles. Asphalt mixtures with higher amounts of finer sand and filler produce darker-toned surfaces. The dark color helps hide grease drippings, accelerates melting of snow, and provides a good background for line striping.

Methods of Coloring:

1. Paints and applied coatings are typically used on tennis courts, pools, playgrounds, and bikeways. Only paints designed for use on asphalt pavements should be used, and these are typically sprayed on. The paint and proprietary surface manufacturer's recommendations should be carefully followed. Oil-based paints dissolve asphalt and should not be used.

2. Colored stone chips can be embedded in a single or a multiple surface treatment

TABLE 820-23
Curb Mixture Specification

Sieve size	*Passing, percent by weight**‡
19 mm (¾ in)	100
12.5 mm (½ in)	85–100
4.75 mm (No. 4)	65–80
2.36 mm (No. 8)	50–65
300 μm (No. 50)	18–30
75 μm (No. 200)	5–15
Asphalt content: AC-20 (AR-8000, 60–70 pen)	6.0–9.0 percent by weight of total mix†

* Mineral aggregate should be crushed stone, crushed gravel, crushed slag, natural or manufactured sand, or a combination of these materials. At least 50% by weight of the combined aggregate, other than naturally occurring rough-textured aggregate, should consist of crushed pieces.

† The asphalt content range includes a 0.5–1.0% increase over surface paving mix of same gradation to facilitate compaction and increase durability. The upper limit may need to be raised when slag or other absorptive aggregates are used.

‡ Other gradings may be used if they have a history of satisfactory performance. Consult local standards and practices.

Source: Adapted from The Asphalt Institute, *Construction Specifications for Asphalt Curbs and Gutters,* 4th ed., SS-3, March 1978.

procedure. This procedure may require much handwork and should only be done by competent specialists. Precautionary measures are necessary to protect nearby objects from the splatter of the spray applicator. This method provides a very coarse surface texture.

3. Asphalt concrete can be composed of selected colored aggregate that is produced on a large-enough scale from a known quarry. The asphalt film will wear off, exposing the colored aggregate. Larger maximum-size stones [¾ in (20 mm)] reveal more color but create a coarser surface texture. Smaller maximum-size stones [⅜ in (10 mm)] are standard.

4. Asphalt block pavements with exposed colored aggregate are commercially available. (Refer to 7.3 Selection Criteria in this section.)

AGENCIES AND ORGANIZATIONS

The Asphalt Institute
College Park, Maryland
(Regional offices throughout the United States and some other countries)

Federal Highway Administration
Department of Transportation
Washington, D.C.

National Asphalt Pavement Association
Riverdale, Maryland
(In the United States, many affiliated state pavement associations also exist.)

State Highway Departments

REFERENCES

Oglesby, Clarkson H., and R. Gary Hicks. *Highway Engineering,* 4th ed., Wiley, New York, 1982.

Asphalt Institute Documents

The Asphalt Institute in College Park, MD, publishes a number of documents on many aspects and uses of asphalt paving, including:

Asphalt in Pavement Maintenance (MS-16).

Asphalt Overlays for Highway and Street Rehabilitation (MS-17).

Model Construction Specifications for Asphalt Concrete and Other Plant-Mix Types (SS-1).

Soils Manual (MS-10).

Thickness Design—Asphalt Pavements for Highways and Streets (MS-1). ■

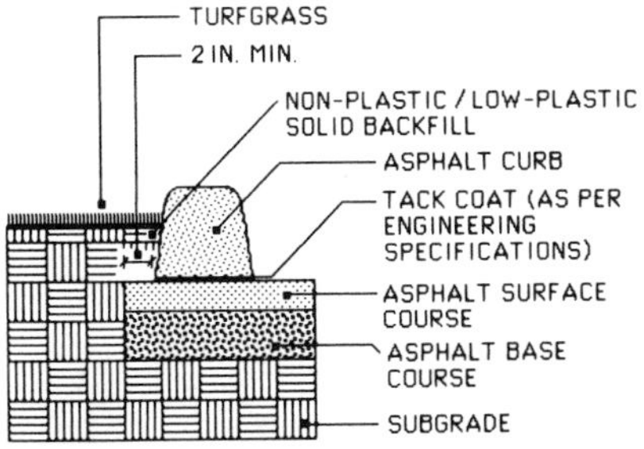

TURFGRASS
2 IN. MIN.
NON-PLASTIC / LOW-PLASTIC SOLID BACKFILL
ASPHALT CURB
TACK COAT (AS PER ENGINEERING SPECIFICATIONS)
ASPHALT SURFACE COURSE
ASPHALT BASE COURSE
SUBGRADE

Figure 820-9 Typical bituminous curb and parking lot edge.

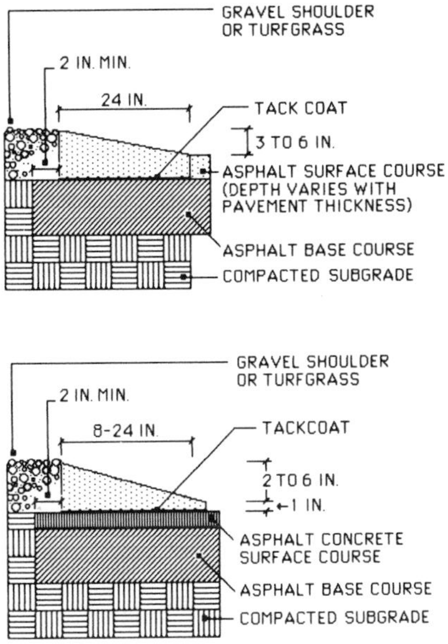

GRAVEL SHOULDER OR TURFGRASS
2 IN. MIN.
24 IN.
TACK COAT
3 TO 6 IN.
ASPHALT SURFACE COURSE (DEPTH VARIES WITH PAVEMENT THICKNESS)
ASPHALT BASE COURSE
COMPACTED SUBGRADE
GRAVEL SHOULDER OR TURFGRASS
2 IN. MIN.
8-24 IN.
TACKCOAT
2 TO 6 IN.
1 IN.
ASPHALT CONCRETE SURFACE COURSE
ASPHALT BASE COURSE
COMPACTED SUBGRADE

Figure 820-10 Typical asphalt concrete berms. Widths, slopes, and overall dimensions vary. Increasing speeds and higher traffic volumes typically use wider berms and flatter slopes.

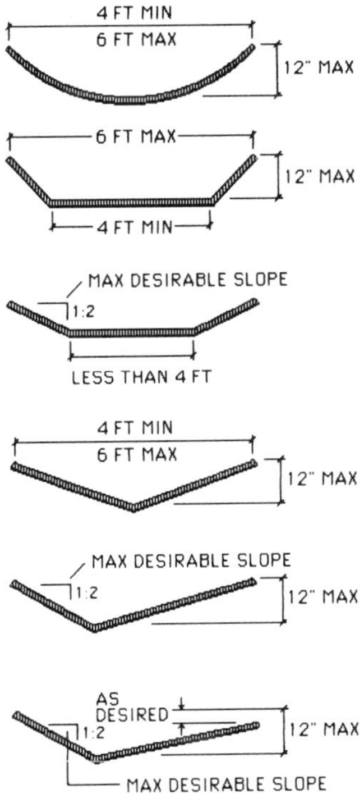

4 FT MIN
6 FT MAX
12" MAX
6 FT MAX
12" MAX
4 FT MIN
MAX DESIRABLE SLOPE
1:2
LESS THAN 4 FT
4 FT MIN
6 FT MAX
12" MAX
MAX DESIRABLE SLOPE
1:2
12" MAX
AS DESIRED
1:2
12" MAX
MAX DESIRABLE SLOPE

Figure 820-11 Typical shapes of asphalt gutters.

section 830: Concrete

CREDITS

Section Editor: Charles W. Harris

Reviewers:

Ronald Chiaramonte
The Architect's Collaborative, Inc.
Cambridge, Massachusetts

Paul L. DiBona
Sasaki Associates, Inc.
Watertown, Massachusetts

Robert Fager
Sasaki Associates, Inc.
Watertown, Massachusetts

William Panarese
Portland Cement Association
Skokie, Illinois

Herman G. Protze, President
Herman G. Protze, Inc.
Materials Technologists
Newton Highlands, Massachusetts

Daniel Sieben
Bomanite Corporation
Palo Alto, California

CONTENTS

1.0 INTRODUCTION

1.1 General Description

Concrete is a mixture of aggregate, portland cement, water, and sometimes special admixtures. As a material, concrete is used for a variety of purposes in landscape design and construction. Its most outstanding qualities are strength, durability, stability, availability, adaptability, and, in most cases, its relatively low cost in terms of construction and lifetime maintenance.

The Romans used concrete for a variety of purposes, ranging from filling (or *hearting*) walls faced with stones or bricks to helping build domes and vaults. After the fall of the Roman empire, the use of concrete was forgotten for several hundred years. The invention of portland cement is widely credited to Joseph Aspdin, an English mason. He obtained a patent on it in 1824, naming it *portland cement* because it resembled a limestone quarried on the Isle of Portland. Reinforced concrete was invented in 1868. Twenty years later prestressed concrete was invented but did not come into extensive use until after 1919.

1.2 Selection Considerations

Below is a list of the advantages and disadvantages of concrete as a construction material.

Advantages of Concrete:

1. Adaptable to a variety of forms and shapes

2. High compressive strength

3. Durable nonresilient surface

4. Available in a wide choice of types for special needs

5. Many colors, finishes, and textures available

6. Low maintenance cost

7. Resistant to damage by freeze/thaw processes and deicing chemicals when air-entrained and properly mixed

Disadvantages of Concrete:

1. Requires formwork in most applications.

2. Has low resiliency or tensile strength unless reinforced.

3. Requires contraction and construction joints.

4. Special materials and/or finishing techniques are needed for making permanent-colored concrete with uniform tones.

5. May cause glare from sun or strong artificial lights, particularly if the surface is trowel-finished.

2.0 CONCRETE

2.1 Properties of Concrete

The properties of concrete are determined by any one of the following several factors: (1) the quality of all constituents, including the type of cement used, the soundness of the aggregates used, the relative proportion of coarse and fine aggregate, the ratio of water to cement, and the type and amount of any chemicals, admixtures, and other compounds added to the mix; and (2) the skills used in placing, consolidating, finishing, and curing the concrete.

Five major parameters to consider when producing finished concrete are described below.

Strength:

Strength is usually the first consideration for all concretes except for lightweight or insulating concretes. Nearly all the desirable properties of concrete increase as the ratio of water to cement decreases. Although the hydration process of the cement paste actually requires little water, the resulting stiff mixtures of concrete would be difficult to mix, place, and consolidate (vibrate, etc.); therefore, additional water is required to produce the necessary workability. (Refer to 7.1 Mixing, Placing, and Testing in this section and to Table 830-2 for more information.)

Resistance to Freeze/Thaw and Deicing Chemicals (Durability):

Resistance to freeze/thaw and deicing chemicals can be increased by the use of an *air-entraining agent* (i.e., an air-entraining admixture). Admixtures may reduce, or enhance somewhat, the potential strength of the concrete mix. (Refer to 5.0 Admixtures for Concrete in this section for more information.)

Resistance to Abrasion and Wear:

Resistance to abrasion and wear can be increased if the concrete mix contains well-graded strong aggregate and is well-consolidated when placed. For some purposes, special aggregate and finishes may be required. On-site finishing procedures are extremely critical for achieving abrasion resistance.

Reduction of Water Penetration:

Reduction of water penetration can be achieved by four means: (1) by keeping the water/cement ratio to less than 0.50 by weight, (2) by carefully treating all joints and cracks to prevent leaks, (3) by adding chemicals and admixtures to the concrete mix to reduce water penetration, and (4) by applying a waterproof surface seal or compound. Adding certain chemicals and admixtures to reduce water penetration often requires adding more mixing water, which may increase the permeability of the concrete.

Control of Setting Time for Concrete:

Control of the setting time for concrete is often needed in order (1) to reduce the setting time when temperatures are low enough to cause the water in the mix to freeze, (2) to increase the time for working concrete during very hot weather, and (3) to control *bleeding,* or the movement of water to the surface of freshly placed concrete. Such bleeding creates an increased surface water/cement ratio, thereby causing a weak surface layer and surface cracks (i.e., crazing). Normal bleeding will be a problem if finishing (floating, troweling, etc.) is performed while bleed water is on the surface.

2.2 Methods of Placement

Three basic methods for placing concrete include:

1. Formed and molded (cast in place or precast)

2. Sprayed or air-blown (shotcrete)

3. Mixed in place (such as soil cement, or a special technique called dry-casting)

This section covers in detail only the most commonly used of these three methods of placement, the formed and molded method. If the reader is considering the use of some other method of placement, such as one of the other two listed, then other technical books on that particular method should be consulted. Readers are urged to not overlook the possible advantages of one of these other methods. For instance, sprayed concrete can be applied to very complex horizontal and vertical surfaces, including hyperbolic forms. It can also be applied in relatively thin cross sections and will attain a very high density and strength. Sprayed concrete is widely used for constructing swimming pools and other sculptured elements within the landscape and for repairing deteriorating structures.

Mixed-in-place concrete has been used for a long time to create low-cost stabilized surfaces. This typically involves mixing dry cement into the existing soil or surface materials, adding water, and then remixing and compacting.

A relatively old technique called *dry-casting* has recently been revived and is coming into increased use today. The ingredients for the concrete are mixed dry, placed in forms, and tamped. If decorative textures, patterns, or designs are desired, they are tooled into the dry surface. Water is then infused through the casting to hydrate the concrete. No floating or hand troweling is necessary; therefore, no time constraint exists on getting the surface finished.

It is claimed that this approach results in: (1) about half the curing time of conventional plastic-mixed concrete, (2) development of at least the same 4000 psi (26,680 kPa) as regular concrete [often achieving strengths of 6000 to 12,000 psi (40,020 to 80,040 kPa)], and (3) concrete having the same resistance to freezing and deicing chemicals as air-entrained concrete.

2.3 Types of Concrete

There are many types of concrete that can be mixed for various applications. The most frequently used types are listed in Table 830-1. Each type has special properties that should be understood before a selection is made. Typical uses are also listed in the table.

3.0 CEMENT

3.1 Properties of Cement

Process of Hydration:

Cements used to make concrete are products of a hydration process; therefore, when cements are mixed with water, a chemical reaction occurs which results in hardening of the cement.

Heat of Dehydration:

Heat is released during the hydration process between the cement and water. The amount of heat released increases with the type of cement, the mass of the concrete, and/or higher ambient temperatures.

Development of Strength:

Twenty-eight days has been arbitrarily selected as the time required for most normal types of cement paste to develop full compressive strength. Typically, this strength continues to increase, to a moderate degree, as long as there is moisture to sustain the process of hydration. Table 830-2 shows the approximate relative strengths of concrete as affected by type of cement.

3.2 Types of Cement

All portland cements are made from lime, silica, alumina, and gypsum. Gypsum is used to slow the setting time of the concrete. Five major types of portland cement are commonly used and classified both in the United States and Canada. In the United States, all cement should meet the American Society for Testing and Materials (ASTM) standards for portland cement, and in Canada the cements should meet the Canadian Standards Association (CSA) standards. These are listed and briefly described in Table 830-3. Additionally, other types of cement are specially formulated for certain purposes (Table 830-3).

TABLE 830-1
Types of Concrete

Type	*Description*	*Typical uses*
Normal weight	Weight of coarse aggregate used determines type; weight of aggregate: 135–165 lb/ft^3	
Lightweight—Structural	Weight of coarse aggregate used determines type; weight of aggregate: 85–115 lb/ft^3	Loadbearing and exterior walls, structural floors, prestressed concrete
Lightweight—Insulating	Weight of coarse aggregate used determines type; weight of aggregate: 15–90 lb/ft^3	Partitions and panel walls, decks, casing of structural steel, roof fill
Heavyweight	Weight of coarse aggregate determines type; weight of aggregate: 130–290 lb/ft^3	Walls of spaces containing radioactive materials; sometimes as counterweight
Cellular	Air or gas bubbles, suspended in mortar, characterize type; small amounts or no coarse aggregate provided	Where top insulating properties are required
Gap-graded	Omission of intermediate sizes of coarse aggregate characterizes type	Where aggregate is to be exposed; as insulating concrete, especially when lightweight aggregate and/or sand is not available or desirable; as inexpensive concrete for foundations
Shotcrete or gunite	Method of placement characterizes type; pneumatic equipment, using dry or wet method employed	Wherever construction without formwork is very desirable, as in complex forms (shells, domes, swimming pools)
Preplaced	Method of Placement characterizes type; coarse aggregate is placed dry, then mortar is pumped into it	Special forms and surfaces; e.g., exposed aggregate finishes on cast-in-place concrete columns
Pumped	Method of conveying plastic concrete for placement characterizes type	When concrete is to be placed high above grade or in formwork of complex shape
Ferrocement	Mix, method of placement, and reinforcement provided characterize type; mortar with large amount of light gauge reinforcing is used	Containers; e.g., bins, boat hulls, and other thin, complex shapes
Fiber	Addition of short fibers to mix characterizes type; where prevention of cracking is important; e.g., in highways and bridges, especially for pavement overlays	
Nailing	Nail-holding strength characterizes type; has high insulating value	

Source: Sweet's Selection Data: Cement and Concrete, McGraw-Hill, New York, 1979.

4.0 AGGREGATE FOR CONCRETE

As shown in Figure 830-1, the aggregate used to make concrete performs several different functions. It typically constitutes 60 to 75 percent of the volume of most types of normal concrete. The most common types of aggregate used in making concrete are sand, gravel, and crushed stone. Aggregate is classified as *fine* if the particles are smaller than ¼ in (0.65 mm), or *coarse* if larger than ¼ in (0.65 mm) in diameter. Both the quality and the cost of the concrete are affected by the type of aggregate used in the mixture. Often, the choice of an aggregate is based on its local availability. This can give a special indigenous quality to the concrete mix if the aggregate is exposed in the final finishing process.

TABLE 830-2
Approximate Relative Strength of Concrete as Affected by Type of Cement

Type of portland cement		*Compression strength; percent of strength of Type I or normal portland cement concrete*			
ASTM	*CSA*	*1 day*	*7 days*	*28 days*	*3 months*
I	Normal	100	100	100	100
II	Moderate	75	85	90	100
III	High-early-strength	190	120	110	100
IV	Low-heat	55	55	75	100
V	Sulfate-resisting	65	75	85	100

Source: Portland Cement Association, *Design and Control of Concrete Mixtures,* 11th ed., Skokie, Ill., 1968.

TABLE 830-3
Types of Portland Cement

ASTM (C150)	*CSA (A5)*	*Description*
Type I, IA*	Normal	This type of cement is used when the special properties of other types of cement are not needed. Uses include road and walk paving, bridges, culverts, masonry units, etc. Also used when light, buff-colored architectural concrete is desired for cosmetic reasons.
Type II, IIA*	Moderate	This type of cement generates less heat during hydration than Type I. It is more resistant to damage by freeze and thaw processes and sulfate attack but not as resistant as Type V. It is recommended for use in concrete exposed to salt water. Used where considerable masses of concrete are required, such as heavy retaining walls, abutments, etc.
Type III, IIIA*	High-early-strength	This type of cement is used when high strengths are needed within a week or less. This type permits (a) earlier removal of forms, (b) earlier use of the concrete installation, (c) shortest period of protection from low temperatures, and (d) shortest curing periods.
Type IV	Low-heat of hydration	This special type of cement is used when large masses of concrete (e.g., large gravity dams) would otherwise build up high temperatures during the hydration process.
Type V	Sulfate-resisting	This special type of cement is used when the concrete will be exposed to severe sulfate action in soil and/or groundwater (as found in some areas of the southwestern United States).
White Portland Cement (ASTM C150 and C175)		This cement is white rather than gray and is used primarily to produce decorative finishes and whenever white, colored concrete, or mortar is desired.
Portland-Pozzolan Cements (four types include IP, IP-A, P, and P-A)*		These cements are used when making large concrete structures such as bridge piers and dams. The cement contains a pozzolan material (15 to 40% by weight) which makes the concrete harden and gain strength at a slower rate than concrete made with Type I cement, thereby resulting in a concrete of greater durability.
Masonry Cements* (ASTM C91, CSA A8)		These cements are used to make mortar for use in masonry construction. They should not be used to make concrete. Masonry cements contain mixtures of portland cement, lime, air-entraining additives, and other materials selected to improve workability, plasticity, and water retention.

* The letter "A" in types IA, IIA, and IIIA cements, and in IP-A and P-A cements, refers to air-entraining portland cement which produces a more durable concrete that is more resistant to severe frost action and/or to the effects of salt or other chemicals used for snow and ice removal. Some types of air-entraining cements are not always available, but normally such cement should cost no more than the corresponding ASTM C150 type. Types IA, IIA, and IIIA cements are self-air-entraining and are not recommended. Use of air-entraining additives to concrete containing regular Types I, II, or III cements provides better control of air and resistance to freezing and thawing.

Source: Adapted from the American Concrete Association, *Slabs on Grade,* Detroit, Mich., 1982.

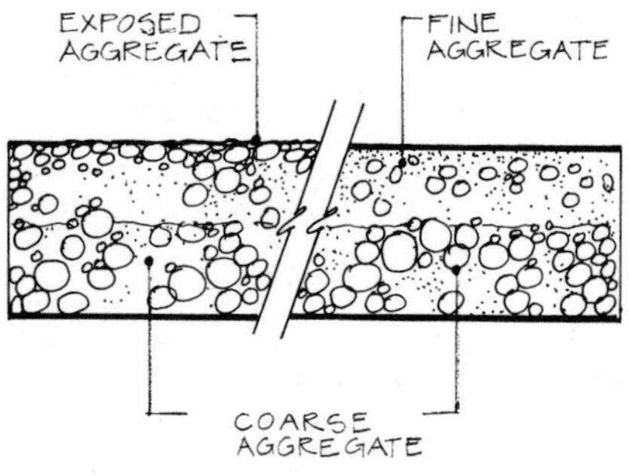
EXPOSED AGGREGATE
FINE AGGREGATE
COARSE AGGREGATE

Figure 830-1 Aggregate for Concrete. Aggregate should be obtained from reliable suppliers and should meet requirements of standard specifications for concrete aggregate, ASTM C33 (or equivalent in other countries, e.g., CSA standards in Canada.)

TABLE 830-4
Types and Properties of Aggregate for Concrete

Type of rock	*Mechanical strength*	*Durability*	*Chemical stability*	*Surface characteristics*	*Presence of undersirable impurities*
Igneous					
Granite, syenite, diorite	Good	Good	Good	Good	Possible
Felsite	Good	Good	Questionable	Fair	Possible
Basalt, diabase, gabbro	Good	Good	Good	Good	Seldom
Peridotite	Good	Fair	Questionable	Good	Possible
Sedimentary					
Limestone, dolomite	Good	Fair	Fair	Good	Possible
Sandstone	Fair	Fair	Good	Good	Seldom
Graywackes	Good	Fair	Good	Good	Seldom
Chert	Good	Poor	Poor	Fair	Likely
Conglomerate, breccia	Fair	Fair	Good	Good	Seldom
Shale	Poor	Poor	Fair	Good	Possible
Argillites	Poor	Poor	Fair	Poor	Possible
Phyllites	Fair	Fair	Fair	Poor	Possible
Metamorphic					
Gneiss, schist	Good	Good	Good	Good	Seldom
Quartzite	Good	Good	Good	Good	Seldom
Highly granulated quartzite	Fair	Good	Good	Fair	Seldom
Marble	Fair	Good	Good	Good	Possible
Serpentinite	Fair	Fair	Good	Fair to poor	Possible
Amphibolite	Good	Good	Good	Good	Seldom
Slate	Good	Good	Good	Poor	Seldom

Source: W. A. Gordon, "Field Experience Using Water-Reducers in Ready Mixed Concrete," ASTM Spec. Tech. Pub., 1960.

4.1 Types of Aggregate

There is wide variation in the types of aggregate used in construction, since each has particular advantages and disadvantages for any one purpose. Table 830-4 lists types and properties of aggregate particularly suitable for use in concrete mixtures. (Refer to Section 810: Soils and Aggregates, for a general discussion of aggregate.)

4.2 Selection of Aggregate

Selection of an aggregate should be based on the following criteria:

1. Resistance to abrasion if in a wearing surface

2. Performance record under conditions of similar use

3. Resistance to pop-outs or spalls caused by freezing or chemicals

4. Range of aggregate sizes needed for the required mix

5. Unit weight of the aggregate when used for lightweight concrete on rooftop gardens, plazas, decks, etc.

In addition, both the size and shape of the aggregate used in a concrete mixture are major variables affecting concrete properties (see Figure 830-1). The following rules of thumb should be considered:

1. The size of aggregate should not exceed: (a) one-fifth the dimension of nonreinforced elements, (b) three-fourths the clear spacing between reinforcing bars and/or forms, and (c) one-third the depth of slabs. Use of the largest-size aggregate practical will generally reduce shrinkage and cracking of concrete.

2. Use of a proper mix of both large (coarse) and small (fine) aggregates will reduce the amount of necessary water in the mix.

3. The shape of aggregate is also an important factor. Generally, rough angular aggregate (such as crushed stone) will provide a better bond for the cement paste. Rough angular aggregates will not necessarily result in a concrete of greater tensile and compressive strength than smooth, rounded aggregate (e.g., pebbles) because the angular aggregate requires more water in concrete and thereby somewhat reduces the ultimate strength of the concrete. With quality materials, both types of aggregate concrete exhibit equal strength. Elongated or flat aggregate should be avoided or limited to no more than 15 percent of the total aggregate by weight.

5.0 ADMIXTURES FOR CONCRETE

5.1 Purposes of Admixtures

All substances that are added before or during the mixing of the concrete are referred to as *admixtures*. They are used to enhance one or more properties of the resulting concrete. Admixtures are often used for the following reasons:

1. To improve the workability of the concrete mixture by minimizing the separation of coarse and fine aggregate while it is being cast and/or worked

2. To reduce the water requirement of concrete significantly and thereby increase its strength

3. To entrain air in the mixture and thereby improve the concrete's durability and resistance to freeze/thaw damage, and its resistance to scaling caused by deicing chemicals

4. To accelerate or retard the hardening or setting of concrete

5. To increase the flowability of concrete to aid in placement

Before specifying an admixture, the following should be determined: (1) whether the admixture will be compatible with the cement, aggregate, and any other admixtures that may be used; (2) whether the admixture will affect the workability, setting time, shrinkage, strength, and/or permeability of the concrete; and (3) whether the admixture will actually produce the desired results.

5.2 Types of Admixtures

Some of the more-common types of ad-

TABLE 830-5
Types of Admixtures

Types	*Description*
Air-entraining	Improves the concrete's resistance to freeze and thaw damage as well as to scaling due to deicing chemicals.
Water-reducing	Reduces the amount of water required for a given consistency of mix, and may affect the setting time. Some will increase drying shrinkage. May entrain some air.
Set-accelerating	Used to accelerate the set of concrete resulting in higher early strength. Some will increase dry shrinkage of the concrete during curing.
Set-retarding	Used to decelerate the set of concrete which results in lower early strength.
Pozzolans	Used to reduce the amount of cement required in a concrete mix. Improves workability. Strength is enhanced at later ages; heat of hydration is reduced.
Superplasticizers	Allows use of a much lower water to cement ratio in a concrete mixture. Can produce a more flowable concrete so that it can be pumped to the area of placement.

mixtures used in concrete and their effect on the concrete are listed in Table 830-5.

6.0 WATER

6.1 Water Quality

The water used to make concrete should be clean and free of oils, alkalies, acids, organic materials, and other deleterious substances. Water containing high concentrations of sulfates or salts should also be avoided. Potable water is normally satisfactory for use in concrete.

6.2 Water Quantity

The quantity of water needed for a mixture is always measured in relative proportion to the amount of cement used. Note that an increase in the amount of water to cement will always result in concrete with less strength. Table 830-6 lists typical

TABLE 830-6
ACI Recommended Maximum Permissible Water to Cement Ratios for Different Types of Structures and Degrees of Exposure*

	Exposure conditions†					
	Severe wide range in temperature or frequent alternations of freezing and thawing (air-entrained concrete only)			*Mild temperature rarely below freezing, or rainy, or arid*		
		At water line or within range of fluctuating water level or spray			*At water line or within range of fluctuating water level or spray*	
Type of structures	*In air*	*In fresh water*	*In seawater or in contact with sulfates‡*	*In air*	*In fresh water*	*In seawater or in contact with sulfates‡*
Thin sections such as reinforced piles and pipe	0.49	0.44	0.40	0.53	0.49	0.40
Bridge decks	0.44	0.44	0.40	0.49	0.49	0.44
Thin sections such as railings, curbs, sills, ledges, ornamental or architectural concrete, and all sections with less than 1-in concrete cover over reinforcement	0.49	—	—	0.53	0.49	—
Moderate sections, such as retaining walls, abutments, piers, girders, beams	0.53	0.49	0.44	§	0.53	0.44
Exterior portions of heavy (mass) sections	0.58	0.49	0.44	§	0.53	0.44
Concrete deposited by tremie under water	—	0.44	0.44	—	0.44	0.44
Concrete slabs laid on the ground	0.53	—	—	§	—	—
Pavements	0.49	—	—	0.53	—	—
Concrete protected from the weather, interiors of buildings, concrete below ground	‡	—	—	§	—	—
Concrete which will later be protected by enclosure or backfill but which may be exposed to freezing and thawing for several years before such protection is offered	0.53	—	—	§	—	—

*Adapted from Recommended Practice for Selecting Proportions for Concrete (ACI 613-54).

† Air-entrained concrete should be used under all conditions involving severe exposure and may be used under mild exposure conditions to improve workability of the mixture.

‡ Soil or groundwater containing sulfate concentrations of more than 0.2%. For moderate sulfate resistance, the tricalcium aluminate content of the cement should be limited to 8%, and for high sulfate resistance, to 5%. CSA Sulfate-Resisting cement limits tricalcium aluminate to 4%. At equal cement contents, air-entrained concrete is significantly more resistant to sulfate attack than non-air-entrained concrete.

§ Water-to-cement ratio should be selected on the basis of strength and workability requirements, but minimum cement content should not be less than 470 lb/yd^3.

Source: Portland Cement Association, *Design and Control of Concrete Mixtures,* 11th ed., Skokie, Illinois, 1968.

water/cement ratios for various concrete construction applications.

7.0 PREPARATION AND PLACEMENT OF CONCRETE

7.1 Mixing, Placing, and Testing

Mixing and Placing Concrete:

All concrete should be mixed until all the ingredients form a homogeneous mass. There are many aspects to the procedure of mixing, but the subject can only be briefly discussed here. Most of these are considered part of the normal operating procedures of suppliers of ready-mixed or site-mixed concrete.

If ready-mixed concrete is available from local suppliers, then on-site mixing is seldom justified except on special projects such as large dams. Ready-mixed concrete should be delivered and placed within 90 minutes after cement has been added to the mixture. If concrete is less than 90 minutes old and has started to stiffen or dry out before it has been placed, it may still be used but only if it can be completely consolidated into forms. Adding water to the concrete to make the mixture more workable (retempering) is not considered ideal, but ASTM C94 (standard for ready-mixed concrete) does allow *one* retempering to bring the mix up to design slump requirements.

Testing Concrete:

A number of concrete control tests are performed by inspection personnel, some of which are conducted while the concrete is fresh, and others while the concrete is in a hardened state. Some government authorities require certification by inspection personnel. Three common tests are described below.

SLUMP TEST: The slump test determines the relative consistency among batches of concrete of the same design by measuring the amount of slump for a given-size cone of concrete (Figure 830-2 and Table 830-7). Changes in slump typically reflect changes in the amount of water in the mix, but they may also indicate changes in air content, sand content, aggregate gradation, temperature or hydration, and setting. Slump for concrete that will be placed using vibrators can be one-half to one-third of that required for hand-placed concrete.

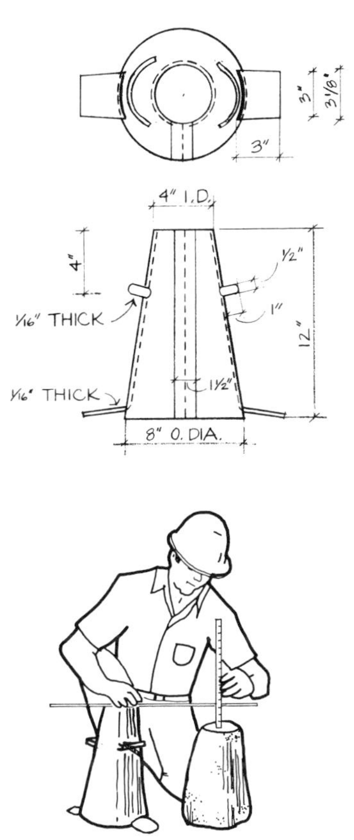
3"
3 1/8"
3"
4" I.D.
4"
1/2"
1/16" THICK
1"
12"
1/16" THICK
1 1/2"
8" O. DIA.

Figure 830-2 Slump Test (ASTM C143). Slump cones are made of metal and are 12 in high, with a 4-in-diameter opening at the top and an 8-in-diameter opening at the bottom. The cone is filled with concrete in three layers of equal volume, and each layer is rodded 25 times with a steel tamping rod. After the cone is filled and the top surface is smoothed, the slump cone is slowly lifted vertically and the subsidence (slump) is measured.

(A) FILL THE OPEN-TOP CUP WITH MORTAR FROM THE CONCRETE BEING CAREFUL TO AVOID ANY PIECES OF GRAVEL OR ROCK.
(B) INSERT THE STOPPER (WHICH CONTAINS THE CUP) INTO THE GLASS TUBE.
(C) FILL THE GLASS TUBE WITH ALCOHOL TO THE ZERO MARK.
(D) SHAKE THE TUBE (THUMB OVER THE OPEN END) UNTIL THE MORTAR IS MIXED WITH THE ALCOHOL.
(E) THE DROP IN LEVEL OF THE ALCOHOL IS A MEASURE OF THE AIR CONTENT.

Figure 830-3 Air Content Test. The *air indicator test* is the simplest of the many tests that can be used to estimate air content in fresh concrete.

TABLE 830-7
Recommended Slumps for Various Types of Concrete Construction

	Slump, in	
Concrete construction	*Maximum**	*Minimum*
Reinforced foundation walls and footings	3	1
Plain footings, caissons, and substructure walls	3	1
Beams and reinforced walls	4	1
Building columns	4	1
Pavements and slabs	3	1
Mass concrete	2	1

* May be increased 1 in for consolidation by hand methods such as rodding and spading.

Source: C. G. Ramsey and H. R. Sleeper, *Architectural Graphic Standards,* 7th ed., Robert T. Packard (ed.), Wiley, New York, 1981.

AIR CONTENT TEST: The air-content test determines the air entrainment at the time of use, thereby allowing an opportunity to adjust the mixture, if necessary, by adding more air entraining agent. An insufficient amount of air results in a concrete with poor resistance to freeze/thaw damage, and too much air results in a lower-strength concrete. Any one of several air content tests can be performed, the easiest of which is performed with an *air indicator* (Figure 830-3).

CYLINDER TEST: The cylinder test is used to determine the compressive strength of

Figure 830-4 Cylinder Test (ASTM C31). Cardboard or steel molds are filled with fresh concrete in three equal layers, and each layer is rodded 25 times with a ⅝-in-diameter tamping rod. Cylinders are labeled and covered with a plate or plastic bag.

cured concrete (Figure 830-4). This test involves putting concrete into a cylindrical mold 6 in (152 mm) in diameter and 12 in (305 mm) high. After the concrete has cured, the concrete cylinder is prepared and put into a special testing machine and subjected to increasing pressure until it fails. The point of failure is recorded as the concrete's strength in *pounds per square inch* or *grams per square centimeter.* Typically, cylinder tests are conducted at 7 days and 28 days following placement.

Codes and Regulations:

Most communities or local government authorities have adopted codes and regulations which require approvals or permits before any kind of construction can begin in their jurisdiction. These regulations are especially important when a project is located on public land or when it involves public health and safety.

Site Preparation for Use of Concrete:

The use of any type of concrete in the landscape requires a thorough understanding of both soil and drainage data. Except in extremely dry, very stable soils, nearly all landscape-related uses of concrete require construction of an appropriate granular subbase over a prepared (compacted) subgrade. Construction details involving the use of concrete are shown in several sections of this handbook, including Division 900: Details and Devices.

Subgrade preparation is one of the most important steps in the process of constructing any kind of concrete structure on grade. The subgrade should be uniformly compacted, moist, and free of organic matter and expansive clays. Soft or muddy areas should be excavated, filled with soil similar to the abutting subgrade (or with a granular material such as sand, gravel, or crushed stone) and then compacted to the required density. The subbase material between the subgrade and the concrete can be composed of a variety of granular materials as long as it is free-draining, durable, and capable of being compacted. (Refer to Section 810: Soils and Aggregates, for more information on soils and the use of various types of aggregate in landscape construction.)

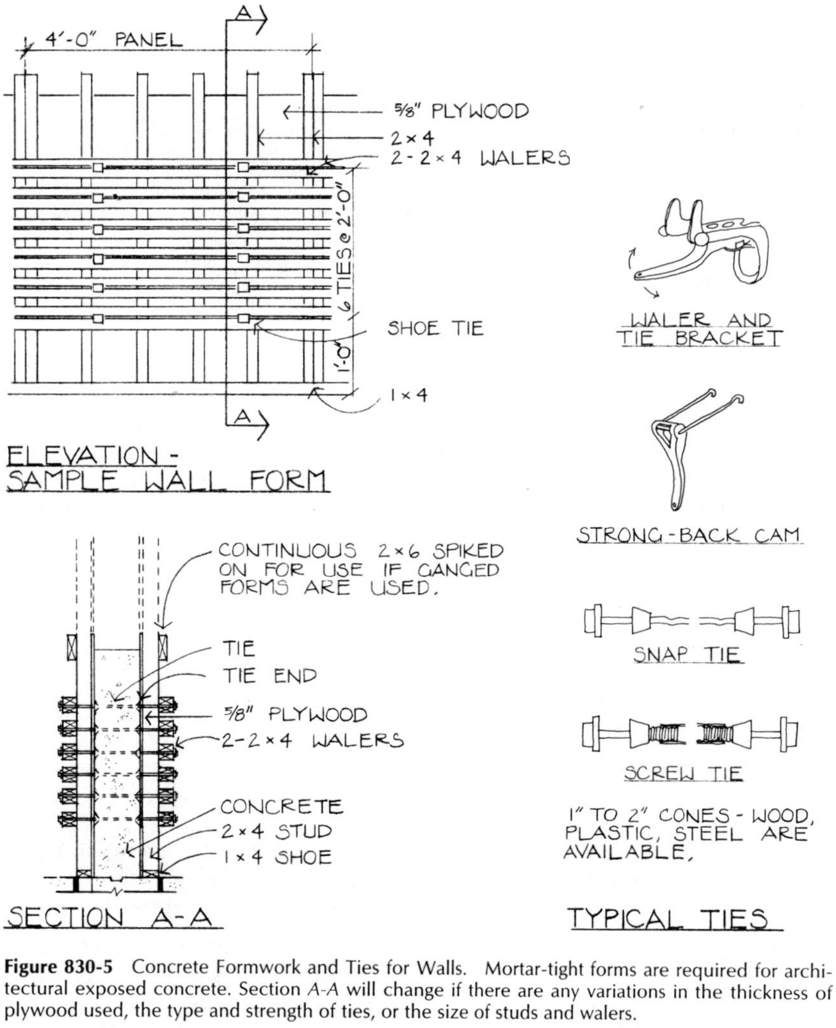
A
4'-0" PANEL
5/8" PLYWOOD
2 × 4
2 - 2 × 4 WALERS
6 TIES @ 2'-0"
1'-0"
SHOE TIE
1 × 4
A
ELEVATION - SAMPLE WALL FORM
CONTINUOUS 2 × 6 SPIKED ON FOR USE IF GANGED FORMS ARE USED.
TIE
TIE END
5/8" PLYWOOD
2-2 × 4 WALERS
CONCRETE
2 × 4 STUD
1 × 4 SHOE
SECTION A-A
WALER AND TIE BRACKET
STRONG-BACK CAM
SNAP TIE
SCREW TIE
1" TO 2" CONES - WOOD, PLASTIC, STEEL ARE AVAILABLE.
TYPICAL TIES

Figure 830-5 Concrete Formwork and Ties for Walls. Mortar-tight forms are required for architectural exposed concrete. Section *A-A* will change if there are any variations in the thickness of plywood used, the type and strength of ties, or the size of studs and walers.

7.2 Formwork for Concrete

Basic Function:

Formwork for concrete provides a container and supports the concrete when it is being placed and while it is setting. The shape of a completed concrete structure is limited only by the designer's imagination and the practical constraints of making the formwork. Typically, a designer will determine the configuration of a completed work, while a contractor or builder will be responsible for the actual strength design of the forms.

Formwork is sometimes used only once and then discarded or is reused many times, depending on the type of formwork. In some cases the formwork is left in place as either a concealed or exposed part of the final design (referred to as a *deadform*).

Various types of materials are used for formwork. Many are modular and have accompanying connection hardware (Figure 830-5). Special types of hardware are often used in formwork construction, some being patented products that provide quick and easy release of forms for multiple use on a site.

Table 830-8 shows types and possible uses of formwork and materials.

Curved formwork for the construction of walks, drives, walls, etc., can be made from thin plywood [¼ to ½ in (6.5 to 13 mm)], hardboard, or sheet metal or made by saw-kerfing thicker lumber (Figure 830-6).

Slip forms are used where continuous pouring is an advantage. This is seldom the

TABLE 830-8
Types and Uses of Formwork

Type	*Uses*	*Remarks*
Lumber	Form framing, form facing, shoring and bracing, edge forms (columns, beams, etc.)	
Plywood	Form facing	
Hardboard	Form facing	
Steel	Form framing, form facing, shoring and bracing, prefabricated forms, edge forms (columns, beams, etc.)	Patented prefabricated forms available, such as waffle slabs, joists, columns
Aluminum	Form framing, form facing, edge forms (columns, beams, etc.)	Light weight; facilitates handling
Fiberglass	Form facing, form liners, prefabricated forms	May be bonded to plywood or other form facings for a smoother patterned surface
Laminated fiber	Column forms, voids in concrete	Created to reduce weight of structure and provide passage for ductwork, raceways, etc.
Corrugated paper	Voids in slabs	See note
Metal decks	Floor framing, roof framing	May provide raceways for power and telephone; may be selected for composite action with concrete

Note: Form liners: (1) sandblasted Douglas fir or long-leaf yellow pine dressed one side away from the concrete surface; (2) flexible steel strip formwork adapted to curbed surfaces (Schwellmer System); (3) resin-coated, striated, or sandblasted plywood; (4) rubber mats; (5) thermoplastic sheets with high glass or texture laid over stone, for example; (6) formed plastics; (7) plaster of Paris molds for sculptured work; (8) clay (sculpturing and staining concrete); (9) hardboard (screen side); (10) standard steel forms; (11) wood boarding and reversed battens; (12) square-edged lumber dressed on one side; (13) resawn wood boards. Release agents: (1) oils, petroleum-based, used on wood, concrete, and steel forms; (2) soft scrubs; (3) talcum; (4) whitewash used on wood with tannin in conjunction with oils; (5) calcium stearate powder; (6) silicones used on steel forms; (7) plastics used on wood forms; (8) lacquers used on plywood and plaster forms; (9) resins used on plywood forms; (10) sodium silicate; (11) membrane used over any form; (12) grease used on plaster forms; (13) epoxy resin plastic used on plywood.

Source: Adapted from *Sweet's Selection Data: Cement and Concrete,* McGraw-Hill, New York, 1979; also C. G. Ramsey and H. R. Sleeper, *Architectural Graphic Standards,* 7th ed., Robert T. Packard, (ed.), Wiley, New York, 1981.

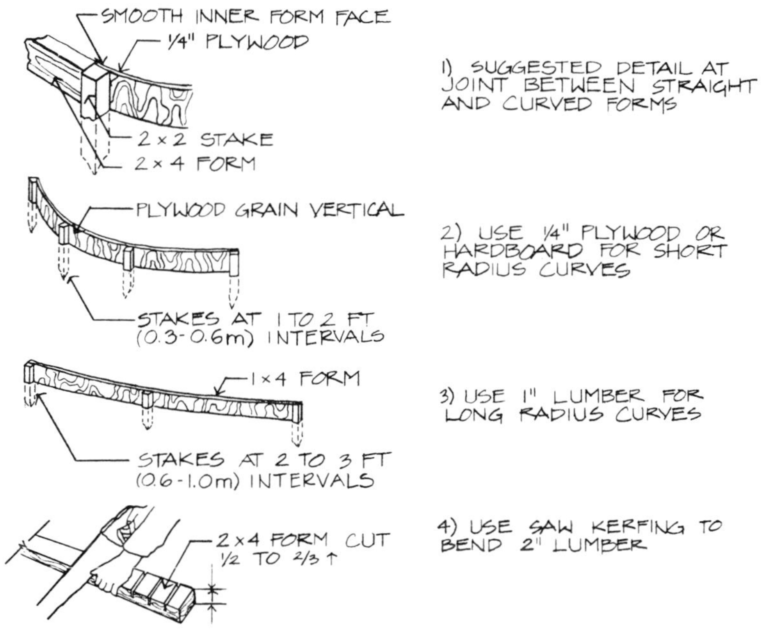
SMOOTH INNER FORM FACE
1/4" PLYWOOD
2 × 2 STAKE
2 × 4 FORM
1) SUGGESTED DETAIL AT JOINT BETWEEN STRAIGHT AND CURVED FORMS
PLYWOOD GRAIN VERTICAL
STAKES AT 1 TO 2 FT (0.3-0.6m) INTERVALS
2) USE 1/4" PLYWOOD OR HARDBOARD FOR SHORT RADIUS CURVES
1 × 4 FORM
STAKES AT 2 TO 3 FT (0.6-1.0m) INTERVALS
3) USE 1" LUMBER FOR LONG RADIUS CURVES
2 × 4 FORM CUT 1/2 TO 2/3
4) USE SAW KERFING TO BEND 2" LUMBER

Figure 830-6 Details for Making Curved Formwork.

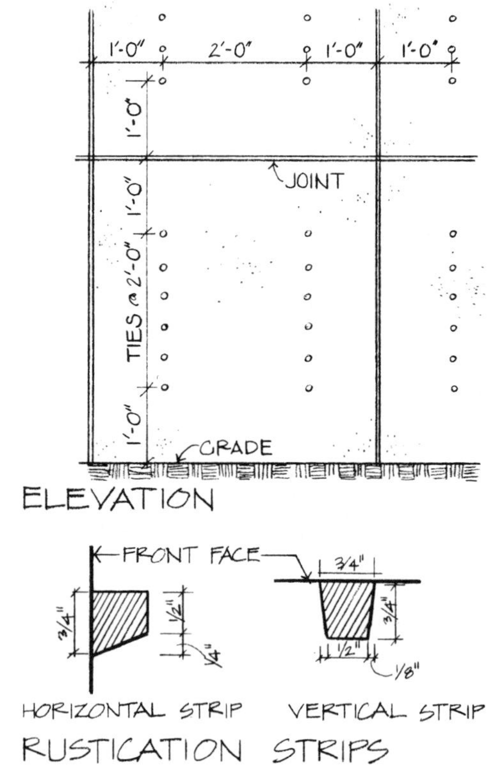
1'-0"
2'-0"
1'-0"
1'-0"
1'-0"
JOINT
1'-0"
TIES @ 2'-0"
1'-0"
GRADE
ELEVATION
FRONT FACE
3/4"
1/2"
1/4"
1/2"
1/8"
HORIZONTAL STRIP
VERTICAL STRIP
RUSTICATION STRIPS

Figure 830-7 Exposed Concrete with Rustication Strips. Tie holes should be placed in a systematic pattern for aesthetic reasons.

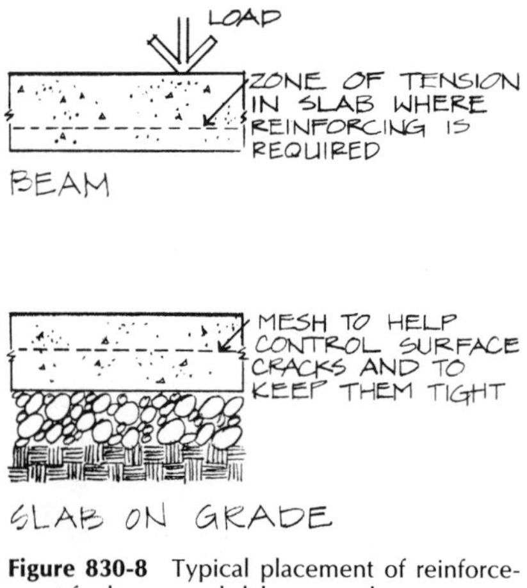
LOAD
ZONE OF TENSION IN SLAB WHERE REINFORCING IS REQUIRED
BEAM
MESH TO HELP CONTROL SURFACE CRACKS AND TO KEEP THEM TIGHT
SLAB ON GRADE

Figure 830-8 Typical placement of reinforcement for beams and slabs on-grade.

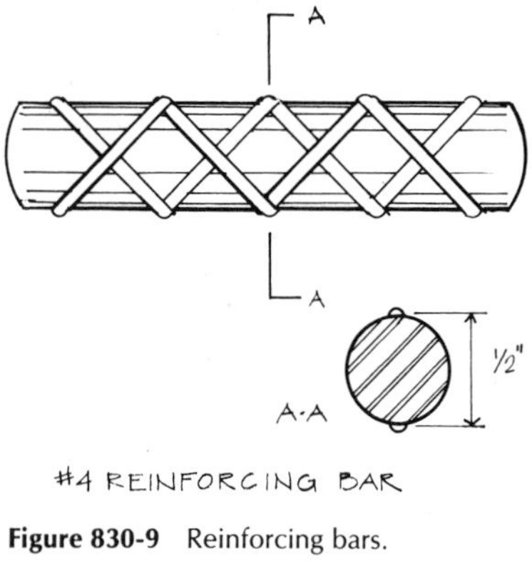
A
A
1/2"
A-A
#4 REINFORCING BAR

Figure 830-9 Reinforcing bars.

case with regard to site construction. One U.S. company has a machine that uses the slip-form technique to form small concrete curbs and gutters up to 40 in (1 m) wide. It can turn a radius as tight as 25 in (0.6 m) and a cul-de-sac as tight as 11½ ft (3.5 m).

Pattern Making:

Various patterns can be created in the surface of finished concrete by adding wood or plastic strips, special plastic liners, or small cones or other shapes to the faces of forms (Figure 830-7). *Form liners* made of plastic, rubber, or other materials can be placed between the form's face and the concrete to provide special finishes, textures, and patterns. The variety of standard or specially made patterns, textures, and even relief sculpture is infinite. (Refer to 7.6 Finishing Concrete, in this section and to Table 830-13 for more information.)

7.3 Reinforcement of Concrete

Placement of Reinforcement:

Reinforcement is used to give concrete structures and slabs greater tensile strength and also to control cracking. Figure 830-8 shows the typical placement of steel or wire mesh reinforcement within a simple concrete slab.

Types of Reinforcement:

Two types of reinforcement commonly used in landscape-related concrete are welded wire fabric and reinforcing bars. Plastic, glass, or steel fibers are also used as secondary reinforcement in concrete mixes.

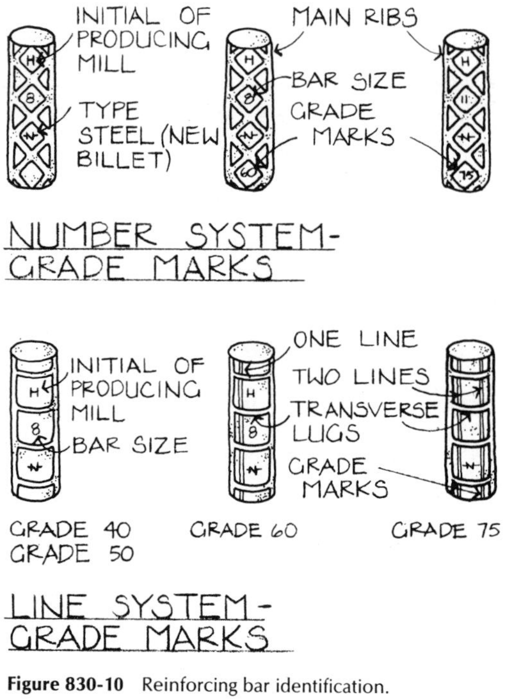
INITIAL OF PRODUCING MILL
MAIN RIBS
BAR SIZE
TYPE STEEL (NEW BILLET)
GRADE MARKS
NUMBER SYSTEM-GRADE MARKS
INITIAL OF PRODUCING MILL
BAR SIZE
ONE LINE
TWO LINES
TRANSVERSE LUGS
GRADE MARKS
GRADE 40
GRADE 50
GRADE 60
GRADE 75
LINE SYSTEM-GRADE MARKS

Figure 830-10 Reinforcing bar identification.

Welded Wire Fabric (WWF): Welded wire fabric, also called *mesh,* consists of electrically welded grids of steel wire with or without galvanized coating or epoxy treatment. Mesh is typically available from manufacturers in rolls or flat sheets. Various gauges of wire and grid spacing are available. WWF sizes are referred to by a system of four numbers, such as: 6 × 6 × W1.4 × W1.4. The first number is the longitudinal spacing of the wires, and the second number is the transverse spacing. The third and fourth numbers indicate the wire sizes. Table 830-9 shows common styles of welded wire fabric.

Reinforcing Bars: Reinforcing bars are also available with or without galvanized or epoxy coatings. Reinforcing bars have irregularities or embossments called *deformations* which keep the bars from slipping within the concrete (Figure 830-9). The bar size is indicated by a number which, when multiplied by ⅛ in (3 mm), gives the nominal diameter of the bar in inches; for example, a No. 4 bar has an area equal to a bar of ½-in (13-mm) diameter. (Reformations are counted in the total cross-sectional area in Table 830-10.)

Figure 830-10 shows reinforcing bar identification, and Table 830-11 shows reinforcing steel grades and strengths. The minimum thickness of concrete needed to cover metal reinforcement is shown in Table 830-12.

Steel reinforcing can be galvanized or coated with paints, plastic, or epoxy coatings, etc. Some type of coating is essential where high corrosion is a factor, such as for bridges, waterfront seawalls, docks, and similar structures. Plastic-coated bars are often used in joints subject to movement.

Secondary Reinforcement: Plastic or glass fibers can be added to a concrete mix at the ready-mix plant or at the job site to create three-dimensional secondary reinforcement and to act as moderate inhibitors of cracks. They are lightweight, noncorrosive, and inert to alkali attack. They can be used for precast as well as cast-in-place concrete. Each manufacturer of this product has slightly different requirements for effective use. Most specifications call for 1½ lb of fiber per cubic yard (0.884 kg/m^3) of concrete. Some manufacturers make their fiber in lengths from ¾ to 2½ in (20 to 65 mm) to meet the needs of concrete with different sizes of aggregate.

Steel fibers are also available for use when the concrete will not be exposed to the elements.

TABLE 830-9
Common Stock Styles of Welded Wire Fabric

New designation		*Old designation*		*Steel area per ft*				*Approximate weight per 100 ft²*	
				Longitudinal		*Transverse*			
Spacing, in	*Cross-sectional area, in²/100*	*Spacing, in*	*Wire gauge, AS&W*	*in*	*cm*	*in*	*cm*	*lb*	*kg*
				Rolls					
6 × 6	W1.4 × W1.4	6 × 6	10 × 10	0.028	0.071	0.028	0.071	21	9.53
6 × 6	W2.0 × W2.0	6 × 6	8 × 8*	0.040	0.102	0.040	0.102	29	13.15
6 × 6	W2.9 × W2.9	6 × 6	6 × 6	0.058	0.147	0.058	0.147	42	19.05
6 × 6	W4.0 × W4.0	6 × 6	4 × 4	0.080	0.203	0.080	0.203	58	26.31
4 × 4	W1.4 × W1.4	4 × 4	10 × 10	0.042	0.107	0.042	0.107	31	14.06
4 × 4	W2.0 × W2.0	4 × 4	8 × 8*	0.060	0.152	0.060	0.152	43	19.50
4 × 4	W2.9 × W2.9	4 × 4	6 × 6	0.087	0.221	0.087	0.221	62	28.12
4 × 4	W4.0 × W4.0	4 × 4	4 × 4	0.120	0.305	0.120	0.305	85	38.56
				Sheets					
6 × 6	W2.9 × W2.9	6 × 6	6 × 6	0.058	0.147	0.058	0.147	42	19.05
6 × 6	W4.0 × W4.0	6 × 6	4 × 4	0.080	0.203	0.080	0.203	58	26.31
6 × 6	W5.5 × W5.5	6 × 6	2 × 2†	0.110	0.279	0.110	0.279	80	36.29
4 × 4	W4.0 × W4.0	4 × 4	4 × 4	0.120	0.305	0.120	0.305	85	38.56

* Exact W-number size for 8 gauge is W2.1.
† Exact W-number size for 2 gauge is W5.4.
Source: Wire Reinforcement Institute, Washington, D. C., 1963.

TABLE 830-10
ASTM Standard Reinforcing Bar Sizes—Nominal Diameter

Bar size designation	*Weight per foot*		*Diameter*		*Cross-sectional area squared*	
	lb	*kg*	*in*	*cm*	*in*	*cm*
3	0.376	0.171	0.375	0.953	0.11	0.71
4	0.668	0.303	0.500	1.270	0.20	1.29
5	1.043	0.473	0.625	1.588	0.31	2.00
6	1.502	0.681	0.750	1.905	0.44	2.84
7	2.044	0.927	0.875	2.223	0.60	3.87
8	2.670	1.211	1.000	2.540	0.79	5.10
9	3.400	1.542	1.128	2.865	1.00	6.45
10	4.303	1.952	1.270	3.226	1.27	8.19
11	5.313	2.410	1.410	3.581	1.56	10.07
14	7.650	3.470	1.693	4.300	2.25	14.52
18	13.600	6.169	2.257	5.733	4.00	25.81

Source: C. G. Ramsey and H. R. Sleeper, *Architectural Graphic Standards,* 7th ed., Robert T. Packard (ed.) Wiley, New York, 1981.

TABLE 830-11
Reinforcing Steel Grades and Strengths

Deformed billet	*Minimum yield point or yield strength (psi)*	*Tensile strength (psi)*
ASTM A 615		
Grade 40	40,000	70,000
Grade 50	50,000	90,000
Grade 60	60,000	90,000
Rail steel		
ASTM A 616		
Grade 50	50,000	80,000
Grade 60	60,000	90,000
Axly steel		
ASTM A 617		
Grade 40	40,000	70,000
Grade 60	50,000	90,000
Deformed wire		
ASTM A 496		
Welded fabric	70,000	80,000
Cold drawn		
ASTM A 82		
Welded fabric		
< W 1.2	56,000	70,000
Size ≥W 1.2	65,000	75,000

Source: C. G. Ramsey and H. R. Sleeper, *Architectural Graphic Standards,* 7th ed., Robert T. Packard (ed.), Wiley, New York, 1981.

TABLE 830-12
Minimum Cover of Concrete over Reinforcement

Location and use		*Minimum cover, in*
Against ground without forms		3
Exposed to weather or ground but placed in forms	Greater than ⅝-in-diameter bars	2
	Less than ⅝-in-diameter bars	1½
Slabs and walls (no exposure)		¾
Beams, girders, columns (no exposure)		1½

Source: Harold B. Olin, John L. Schmidt, and Walter H. Lewis, *Construction: Principles, Materials & Methods,* U.S. League of Savings Institutions, Chicago, 1983.

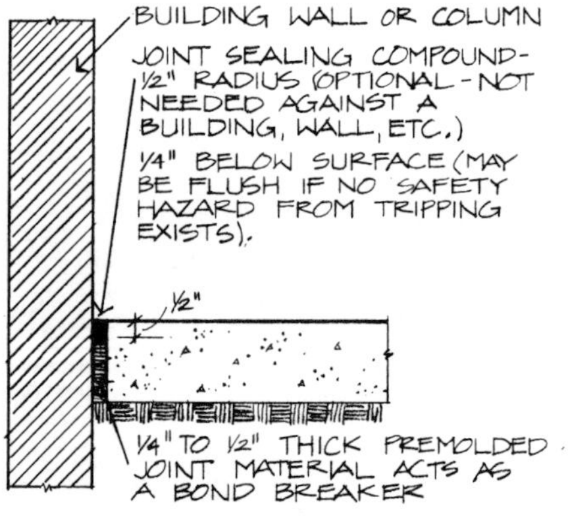
BUILDING WALL OR COLUMN
JOINT SEALING COMPOUND-
1/2" RADIUS (OPTIONAL - NOT NEEDED AGAINST A BUILDING, WALL, ETC.)
1/4" BELOW SURFACE (MAY BE FLUSH IF NO SAFETY HAZARD FROM TRIPPING EXISTS).
1/2"
1/4" TO 1/2" THICK PREMOLDED JOINT MATERIAL ACTS AS A BOND BREAKER

Figure 830-11 Isolation joints.

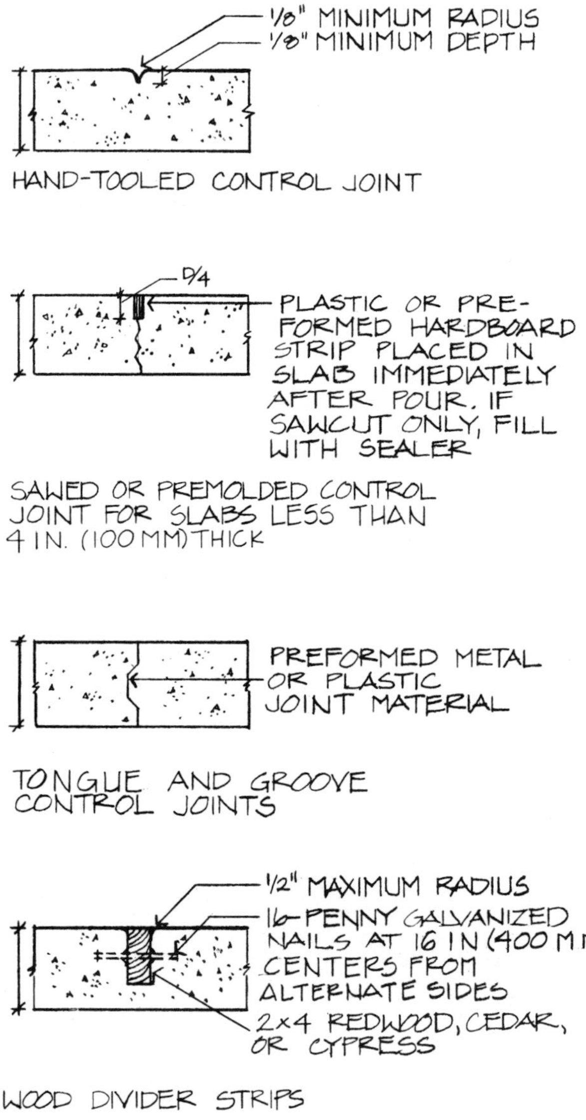
1/8" MINIMUM RADIUS
1/8" MINIMUM DEPTH
HAND-TOOLED CONTROL JOINT
D/4
PLASTIC OR PRE-FORMED HARDBOARD STRIP PLACED IN SLAB IMMEDIATELY AFTER POUR. IF SAWCUT ONLY, FILL WITH SEALER
SAWED OR PREMOLDED CONTROL JOINT FOR SLABS LESS THAN 4 IN. (100 MM) THICK
PREFORMED METAL OR PLASTIC JOINT MATERIAL
TONGUE AND GROOVE CONTROL JOINTS
1/2" MAXIMUM RADIUS
16-PENNY GALVANIZED NAILS AT 16 IN (400 MM) CENTERS FROM ALTERNATE SIDES
2x4 REDWOOD, CEDAR, OR CYPRESS
WOOD DIVIDER STRIPS

Figure 830-12 Types of control joints.

7.4 Placing and Consolidating Concrete

Once the subgrade is compacted and moistened, the forms erected, and the reinforcing steel set in place, the concreting can begin. Both the subgrade and all forms must be moistened to prevent extraction of water from the concrete. Forms should also be treated with a nonstaining release agent for easier removal.

In slab construction, the placement of fresh concrete should begin along the perimeter of one end, with each successive batch placed against previously placed concrete. Concrete should not be moved into position *horizontally,* for segregation between the mortar and coarse aggregate will result.

In wall construction, the placement should begin at both ends and then progress from each end toward the center. The concrete should be placed in horizontal layers of uniform thickness, with each layer thoroughly consolidated before placement of the next layer. The layers should be 6 to 20 in (150 to 500 mm) thick for reinforced members, and 15 to 20 in (380 to 500 mm) thick for mass work. Concrete moved horizontally into position should be kept to an absolute minimum to prevent segregation.

The consolidation of concrete is accomplished either by hand tools or by vibrators. Concrete mixes (slumps) that will be consolidated by vibration should be considerably stiffer than those intended for consolidation by hand tools. The proportion of fine aggregate used in a concrete mix can also be reduced significantly if vibrators are used.

Various types of vibrators include immersion-type (internal) vibrators, form vibrators, and vibrating screeds. Hand methods include the use of spades or puddling sticks or of various types of tampers.

7.5 Joints, Locations, and Fillers

Purpose of Joints:

Joints are needed in most types of concrete construction to minimize or control the possibly damaging effects of expansion and contraction in the concrete due to temperature variations and the presence of moisture. Concrete contracts after the curing period as a result of drying, and it will also expand or contract with variations in temperature. Contraction due to the curing process is most dramatic during the first few months, but it may continue for a year or more.

Types of Joints:

Three types of joints typically used in concrete construction include:

1. *Isolation, or expansion, joints:* these joints extend the full depth of the concrete and provide for lateral movement between slabs or other fixed structures, such as buildings or retaining walls, steps, and posts.

2. *Control, or contraction, joints:* these joints are designed to restrict the cracking of the concrete to predetermined locations. Joints should be tooled or sawn to a depth of at least one-third the thickness of

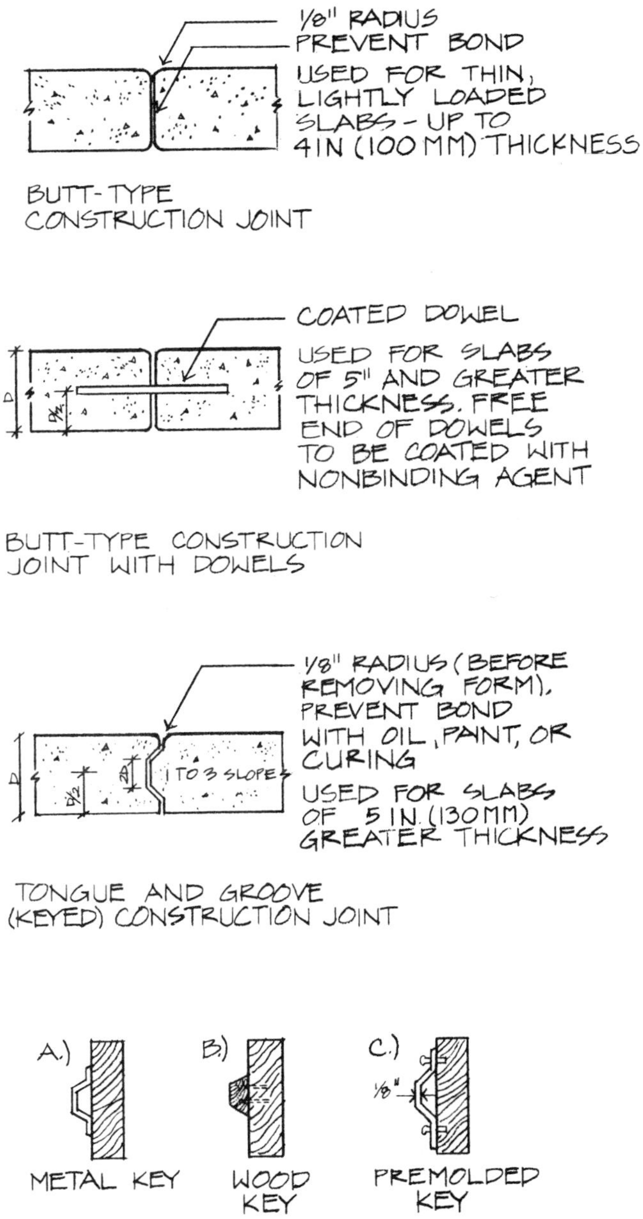
1/8" RADIUS
PREVENT BOND
USED FOR THIN, LIGHTLY LOADED SLABS - UP TO 4 IN (100 MM) THICKNESS
BUTT-TYPE CONSTRUCTION JOINT
COATED DOWEL
USED FOR SLABS OF 5" AND GREATER THICKNESS. FREE END OF DOWELS TO BE COATED WITH NONBINDING AGENT
BUTT-TYPE CONSTRUCTION JOINT WITH DOWELS
1/8" RADIUS (BEFORE REMOVING FORM). PREVENT BOND WITH OIL, PAINT, OR CURING
1 TO 3 SLOPE
USED FOR SLABS OF 5 IN. (130 MM) GREATER THICKNESS
TONGUE AND GROOVE (KEYED) CONSTRUCTION JOINT
A.)
B.)
C.)
1/8"
METAL KEY
WOOD KEY
PREMOLDED KEY

Figure 830-13 Types of construction joints.

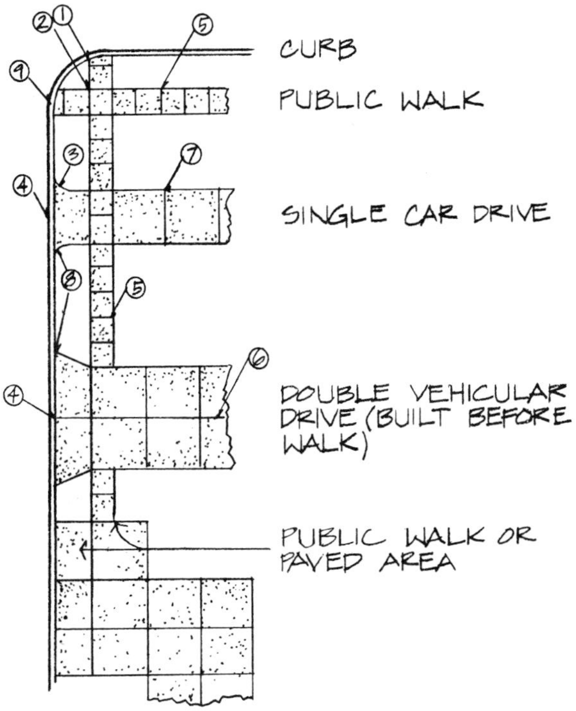
CURB
PUBLIC WALK
SINGLE CAR DRIVE
DOUBLE VEHICULAR DRIVE (BUILT BEFORE WALK)
PUBLIC WALK OR PAVED AREA

ISOLATION JOINT:
① BETWEEN WALK AND CURB
② WHERE WALKS MEET
③ BETWEEN WALK AND DRIVE
④ BETWEEN DRIVE AND DROPPED OR ROLLED CURB
⑤ ISOLATION OR CONTROL JOINTS IN WALKS SHOULD FORM SQUARE PANELS
⑥ LONGITUDINAL CONTROL JOINT DOWN CENTER OF DOUBLE VEHICULAR DRIVE
⑦ CONTROL JOINTS IN DRIVES AND PAVED AREAS AT 10 FT (3 M) INTERVALS
⑧ RADIUS OR FLARE AT DRIVE ENTRANCE
⑨ HANDICAPPED ACCESS RAMP (AS REQUIRED)

Figure 830-14 Location of joints.

the concrete. If tooled, this is done during the finishing of the concrete surface. If sawn, this is done when the surface of the concrete is firm enough not to be damaged by the sawing process, normally 12 to 24 hours after finishing; if this is delayed too long, the concrete may crack before it is sawn or may start cracking just ahead of the saw. Note that saw cutting is ineffective unless *all* of the reinforcing is also cut, and slip dowels should be used between adjacent concrete.

3. *Construction joints:* these joints provide places where casting of concrete can be stopped. They may contain tie bars, slip dowels, and/or keyways for load transfer.

Figures 830-11 through 830-13 show ways to create and treat all three types of joints.

Location of Joints:

The locations of joints in concrete walks, drives, large paved terraces, etc., are shown in Figure 830-14. For walks and drives, the control joints should be spaced at intervals about equal to their widths. Ideally, concrete slabs 4 in (100 mm) thick or more should have control joints about 8 to 10 ft (2.5 to 3 m) apart, but never more than 20 ft (6 m) apart in any direction. Where possible, these panels should be approximately square. If spaced wider than 10 to 12 ft (3 to 3.5 m), then control joints down the center should be used. Panels with acute-angled corners should be avoided, as these corners tend to break off and initiate cracking. Control joints should be continuous, not staggered or offset. The spacing of control joints should be related to the slab's thickness and the expected shrinkage of the concrete. The wetness of the mix and the maximum size of the aggregate will influence this. Refer to Table 830-13 for suggested spacing of control joints.

TABLE 830-13
Spacing of Control Joints*

Slab thickness, in	*Less than ¾-in aggregate spacing, ft*	*Larger than ¾-in aggregate spacing, ft*	*Slump less than 4-in spacing, ft*
5	10	13	15
6	12	15	18
7	14	18	21
8	16	20	24
9	18	23	27
10	20	25	30

* Given spacings also apply to the distance from control joints to parallel isolation joints or parallel construction joints. Spacings greater than 15 ft (5 m) show a marked loss in effectiveness of aggregate interlock to provide load transfer across the joint.

Source: Portland Cement Association, *Concrete Floors on Ground,* 2d ed., Skokie, Ill., 1983.

Joint Fillers:

Typically, all joints except control joints are filled with some special material and usually sealed. Some of these materials are manufactured and come preformed, ready to install prior to the placing of the concrete. Others are installed or applied after the concrete has been placed. Three of the most common types of joint fillers are:

1. *Fiber filler:* these are boards or strips made with or without asphalt impregnation. Those without asphalt normally require a joint sealant to keep out moisture.

2. *Wood dividers:* these are made of pressure-treated or decay-resistant wood left in the concrete after it has been cast.

3. *Plastics, rubber, cork, or metal:* these materials are also used to fill and seal joints. They are available in a wide variety of forms, from simple strips to complex shapes.

Several other types of materials can be used as joint fillers, including *closed cell* polyurethane, sponge or regular rubber, cork, special plastics, and metal expansion-joint systems. The reader is urged to investigate the range of types and determine what is best for a particular purpose. Joint sealants are used to prevent joint filler material from bleeding or being squeezed up, to keep out sand and other debris, and, in climates where freezing occurs, to help keep water out of the joints. Some joint sealants are available in a variety of colors. The sealant must be compatible with the joint filler material, the concrete, and other materials in contact. Bacher rods or bond breaking materials may be recommended between the joint filler and sealant to prevent three-sided adhesion of sealant.

In climates where freezing and thawing occurs, it is desirable to caulk or seal control joints in concrete slabs, especially if they have been saw-cut.

Extra-wide, or *open,* joints can be filled with a variety of materials, such as sand or different types of aggregate, brick, natural or cut stone, or even wood (Figure 830-15). In some cases, these extrawide expansion or control joints can be left open as a part of the overall design for a paved area, low seat, wall, etc. However, extrawide joints in paved areas can be hazardous to pedestrians, especially to elderly and handicapped people. (Refer to Section 240: Access and Egress: Outdoor Standards, for more information.)

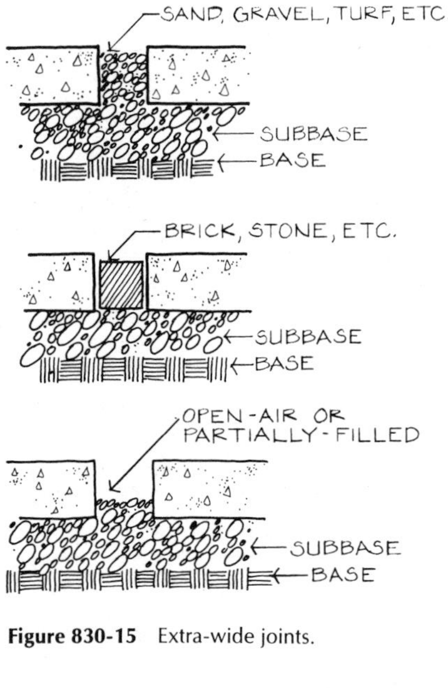
SAND, GRAVEL, TURF, ETC.
SUBBASE
BASE
BRICK, STONE, ETC.
SUBBASE
BASE
OPEN-AIR OR PARTIALLY-FILLED
SUBBASE
BASE

Figure 830-15 Extra-wide joints.

7.6 Finishing Concrete

Surface Finishing:

Finishing concrete involves a number of steps, including: screeding, floating, troweling, brooming, edging, and jointing. Floating and troweling can begin as soon as, but not before, the concrete starts to stiffen. The acceptable time period depends on the wind, temperature, relative humidity, and type of concrete used. Finishing should not begin until bleed water (which is often present on the surface of the new concrete) has been reabsorbed by the concrete.

Concrete surfaces can be finished in either of two ways:

1. For precast elements or for vertical surfaces, such as the exposed faces of retaining or freestanding concrete walls, the formwork itself can be used to give different patterns to the surface via strips of wood, metal, or plastic or via rubber liners.

2. For horizontal surfaces, such as paved walks, there are several different ways to finish the concrete.

Types of Finishes:

Table 830-14 shows several common types of concrete finishes. Some are quite simple and widely known by all who use and install concrete. Others are used less frequently or only in special cases.

Two of the most common types of concrete finishes are:

1. *Floated finish* is used when concrete has been placed, consolidated, struck off, leveled, and when the water sheen has disappeared and the surface has stiffened enough to permit floating. Floating can be done with a hand float, blade power trowel equiped with float shoes, or with a powered trowel disc float. During and after the first floating, the evenness of the surface should be checked with a 10-ft straightedge applied to no less than two different angles. When the surface has met the desired slope tolerance, the slab should be refloated immediately to a uniform sandy texture.

2. *Troweled finish* is used after the surface has been float finished as described above. Typically, the surface is first power troweled to make it smooth. Then, when it has hardened enough to cause a ringing sound when the trowel is moved over the surface, a hand trowel is used to make the surface free of trowel marks and uniform in texture and appearance.

Special finish types commonly used in landscape construction are described below.

Colored Concrete: Coloring can be achieved in any of three different ways.

1. *Color pigments* can be added as an integral additive to the concrete by either a one- or two-course method. The one-course method involves mixing special pigments into the concrete mix before it is placed. White cement is best for the lightest colors, but common Type I buff cement is used most frequently. The two-course method involves a first course of regular concrete, whose surface is left rough, and then a top or finish course of ½ to 1 in (12 to 25 mm) of colored concrete.

2. The *dry-shake method* consists of sprinkling special dry pigments on the surface of the newly cast concrete after it has had a

TABLE 830-14
Types of Concrete Finishes

Category	Finish	Color	Forms	Critical details
		Casting processes		
	Remains as is after form removal[1]	Cement first influence, fine aggregate second influence	Wide range of options[1]	Slump = 2½–3½ in; joinery of forms; proper release agent; point form joints to avoid marks
		Abrasive processes		
Brush blast	Uniform scour cleaning	Cement and fine aggregate have equal influence	All smooth	Scouring after 7 days; slump = 2½–3½ in
Light blast[2]	Sandblast to expose fine and some coarse aggregate	Fine aggregate primary, coarse aggregate and cement secondary	All smooth	10% more coarse aggregate; slump = 2½–3½ in; blasting between 7 and 45 days
Medium exposed aggregate[2]	Sandblasted to expose coarse aggregate	Coarse aggregate	All smooth	Higher than normal coarse aggregate; slump = 2–3 in; blast before 7 days
Heavy exposed aggregate[2]	Sandblasted to expose coarse aggregate; 80% viable	Coarse aggregate	All smooth	Special mix coarse aggregate; slump = 0–2 in; blast within 24 hr; use high frequency vibrator
		Chemical processes		
Retardation of surface set	Chemicals expose aggregate	Coarse aggregate and cement	Glass fiber best and all smooth	Grade of chemical determines depth of etch; Stripping scheduled to prevent long drying period between stripping and washoff
Hardeners and coatings[3]	Aggregate can be adhered to surface			
		Mechanical processes		
Surface fracturing, scaling, bush hammering, jack hammering, tooling[4]	Varied	Cement; fine and coarse aggregate	Textured	Aggregate particles ⅜ in for scaling and tooling; aggregate particles
		Combination processes		
	Striated/abrasive blasted/irregular pattern; corrugated/abrasive; vertical rusticated/abrasive blasted; reeded and bush hammered; reeded and hammered	The shallower the surface, the more influence aggregate fines and cement have	Wood or rubber strips, corrugated sheet metal, glass fiber, or asbestos cement	Depends on type of finish desired; wood flute kerfed and nailed loosely

[1] Form liners—rubber mats, plastic panels, wood boards (unfinished sheathing lumber or tongue-and-groove lumber), plywood, wood siding, and wood strips: used for walls and wall panels; secured to surfaces, either horizontal or vertical, against which concrete is poured; joints between plastic panels may have to be specially treated (Among other ways, the grain of the wood in plywood can be exposed by wire-brushing or sandblasting or in other ways)

Form liners—plaster-of-paris forms, wood forms, molded fiberglass forms: also used for walls and panels; repetitive elements used to allow multiple use of formwork. Wood forms may be protected with sprayed-on fiberglass

Dimpled: used for wall panels; size of aggregate bed against which concrete is cast and thickness of plastic film covering will influence pattern

[2] Exposed aggregate—marble chips, crushed rock, glass fragments, flagstone, gravel: Used for walls and wall panels, walks and terraces; large-size aggregates and flagstone are generally used when panels are cast exposed face down; aggregate transfer is used in vertically cast wall panels

Exposed aggregate—ground or polished: used for floors, floor tile, and stair treads, and for wall-facing panels; a surface sealer is recommended for floors, floor tile, and stair treads, not recommended for outdoor paving if pavement can become wet from rainfall or other sources of water

[3] Hardeners include liquid ones for sealing surfaces of poorly finished concrete paving in order to prevent dusting. Penetrating surface coatings are for waterproofing vertical surfaces. Film-forming and clear or pigmented surface coatings are for waterproofing and sealing horizontal and vertical surfaces.

[4] Types of mechanical processes include:

- Rubbing, grinding, acid etching, soundblasting, and bushhammering for removing imperfections on exposed concrete surfaces after forms are stripped. Surface texture will be changed to varying degrees depending on process used.
- Screeding or strike-off for surfaces not exposed to weather, wear, or view, e.g., footings and top surfaces of base course in two-course construction. May be floated to correct irregularities and level the surface.
- Float, trowel, or broomed swirl for horizontal surfaces, such as walks, ramps, and terraces, where slip-resistance is required and appearance is important.
- Burlap drag for large surfaces, such as pavements and driveways, where slip-resistance is required and appearance is of secondary importance.
- Steel-troweled for horizontal surfaces exposed to wear, such as residential, commercial, and light industrial floors.
- Shake-on aggregate steel-troweled for horizontal surfaces, such as heavy industrial and warehouse floors, that are exposed to severe wear.
- Travertine for walks and terraces. The finish coat is of white cement and yellow pigment is generally added.
- Rock salt for walks and terraces; not recommended in freeze-thaw climates.
- Stamped pattern for walks and terraces; many varieties of stamping tools are available.

Source: C. G. Ramsey and H. R. Sleeper, *Architectural Graphic Standards*, 7th ed., Robert T. Packard ed., Wiley, New York, 1981.

TABLE 830-15
(a) Coloring Agents for Concrete; (b) Color Ranges and Sources

Color	*Ingredients*
White	White portland cement, white sand
Buff	Buff portland cement, small quantity of black iron oxide, magnesium black, Germantown lampblack
Brown	Burnt umber, brown iron oxide, yellow oxide of iron to obtain modification
Yellow	Yellow oxide of iron
Buff	Yellow ochre, yellow oxide of iron, red oxide of iron may be used in small quantity
Cream	Small quantity of yellow oxide of iron
Pink	Small quantity of red oxide of iron
Rose	Red oxide of iron
Green	Chromium oxide, yellow oxide of iron may be added
Blue	Phthalocyanine blue
Black	Powdered carbon black

(a)

Sources	*Colors*	*Comments*
Iron oxides (natural)	Brown, yellow, red, and black are combined to make a range of colors	This is the most commonly used source of color for concrete. It has good color retention and does not affect the life of the concrete.
Lamp black and carbon black	Grays and blacks	This has poor retention of color.
Synthetic iron oxides	Same range of colors as above	Some of the richest shades are possible

(b)

Source: Adapted from American Concrete Institute, *Slabs on Concrete,*Detroit, 1982.

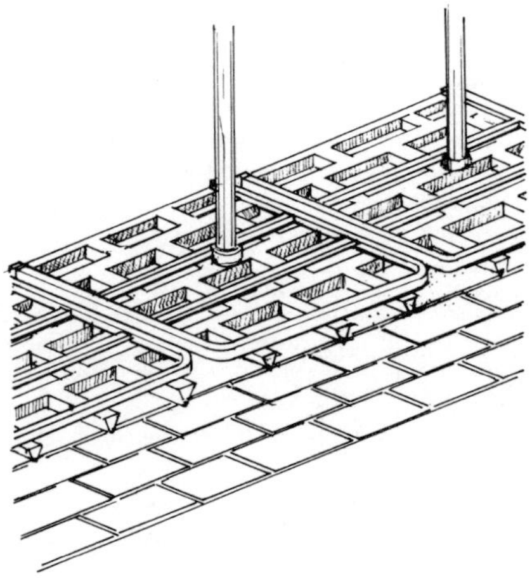

Figure 830-16 Imprinting or Pattern Stamping Tool. Laborers step from pad to pad, stamping the design to a depth of about 1 in (25 mm).

preliminary floating, edging, and grooving. This technique requires the skill of a professional cement finisher to achieve uniform colors. Sometimes special effects can be achieved by adding color pigment to the mix, and then after the concrete is poured the dry-shake method is used. The dry-shake method allows a wider range of dark and/or more intense colors.

3. *Stains* and *paints* are typically used only when an existing slab of concrete has to be colored. Paints wear off and have to be reapplied over time, whereas stains or dyes penetrate into the surface. It is difficult to achieve uniform colors with some stains. Most stains eventually fade in sunlight.

The selection of a proper curing method is important when curing colored concrete. Waterproof paper or plastic sheets should not be used because they will cause discoloration. In most cases, a better solution involves the application of a wax-based curing compound that is clear or the exact same color as the colorant. It is difficult to steel-trowel the surface of colored concrete without causing variations or discolorations.

Table 830-15 lists the range of colors and agents used to make colored concrete.

Exposed Aggregate Finishes: Exposed aggregate finishes are widely used because they offer a wide range of colors and textures as well as provide resistance to slipping and heavy wear. Three methods most often used to create an exposed aggregate finish include:

1. The *one-course,* or *integral, method* involves a single cast of concrete. The mix must contain a very high proportion of coarse to fine aggregate. The coarse aggregate to be left exposed should be of uniform size, specially selected for durability, and of contrasting color to the concrete paste. The concrete is finished in the usual way via floating, etc., until it begins to set; then the aggregate is ready for exposure by hosing or acid washing and brushing (or later by grinding, as with terrazzo). A surface retarding agent is sometimes applied, to better control the time of exposure.

2. The *two-course method* involves a base course of conventional concrete, over which is promptly placed a ½- to 1-in (12- to 25-mm) concrete topping with special aggregate. The same technique of finishing and exposing the aggregate is used in the two-course method as is used in the one-course method.

3. The *seeding method* involves sprinkling specially selected aggregate over a freshly placed and rough-finished or screeded concrete base and pounding it into the surface while floating the concrete. This method requires much more working time, but a special retardant can be used to provide the extra time needed to perform this method. This method requires skilled labor to achieve uniformity of appearance.

The use of ground or polished terrazzo for exterior paving is not recommended because of the danger of pedestrians slipping on it whenever it becomes wet. A rustic terrazzo, similar to exposed aggregate concrete, is possible via terrazzo contractors.

Special Nonslip Finishes: These finishes for concrete can be achieved by hand-tooling with floats, trowels, or brooms or by dry-shaking abrasive grains onto the surface. The two most widely used abrasives are silicon carbide and aluminum oxide. Such abrasives are applied in the same way as the dry-shake method for coloring concrete.

Patterned or Stamped Finishes: These finishes can be produced on freshly placed concrete surfaces through the use of special imprinting tools (Figure 830-16). Typically, these methods are used for horizontal surfaces, but they can be used for precast tilt-up walls, etc., if cast faceup outside. These patterns can be achieved on the surface of any fresh concrete, whether that of a monolithic slab or a thin topcoat of concrete [with a minimum thickness of ½ to 3 in (15 to 75 m)] over an existing slab of concrete.

The fresh concrete is screeded to the proper grade, wood-floated, colored (if not premixed with color), and then imprinted with tools used to create the desired patterns.

Several companies in the United States make the imprinting tools, and a few have developed trademarked techniques for installation. The imprinting tools are either open-faced, with only the pattern part touching the concrete, or solid-faced, with total contact made with the fresh concrete. Rubber-faced steel rollers are also used for texturing concrete surfaces. A range of typical patterns is shown in Figure 830-17.

Finishing Tools:

To achieve a desired finish on concrete, a designer will often indicate which tool should be used. Table 830-16 describes typical concrete finishing tools and illustrates a *generic* example of each major type.

Edging:

Edging the concrete produces rounded edges that prevent chipping or other damage when forms are removed. Also, edging helps compact and harden the surface concrete next to the form, where floats and trowels are normally less effective. Edging may have to be done several times during the finishing operation to produce a clean, smooth, uniform edge.

CAUTION: If retarder is used for exposed aggregate finishes, then edging is not feasible because the retarder will affect the edging (i.e., a smooth edge cannot be created).

7.7 Curing

The durability of concrete continues to improve significantly up to 28 days and for several months beyond, as long as (1) moisture is present and (2) temperatures are favorable. Concrete should be protected from rapid drying and from freezing temperatures particularly during the first week after it is placed and finished. Several methods and materials are used to achieve proper curing (Table 830-17). These are described below.

Moisture Control:

Four of the most common methods for retaining the moisture in concrete for proper curing are:

1. *Wet covering:* this involves placing burlap or other moisture-retaining fabric over the wet concrete and keeping it wet. The use of coverings that may stain the concrete surface should be avoided.

2. *Waterproof paper or plastic sheets:* these can be used to prevent rapid loss of moisture from the concrete. The edges of materials must be lapped or sealed, and if exposed to wind, secured in place. Surfaces should be wetted before being covered.

3. *Sprinkling or ponding of water:* this is very effective but often expensive and difficult to supervise. Ponding requires sand or earth berms which have to be removed later and may leave stains.

4. *Curing compounds:* these can be used to help sustain curing after removal of the forms or protective coverings. Some curing compounds should not be used when waterproofing, sealers, glazers, or other thin set type coatings are to be added later because they are not compatible with coating compounds. Both materials should be compatible, or an acid solution should be used to remove the curing compound before applying the waterproofing or coating compound.

Temperature Control:

Favorable temperatures for curing are those about 50 degrees F (10 degrees C) and below 75 degrees F (24 degrees C). Temperature affects the rate of setting of concrete as follows:

95 degrees F (35 degrees C)	1 hour or less
70 degrees F (21 degrees C)	2 hours or less
50 degrees F (10 degrees C)	3 hours or more
35 degrees F (2 degrees C)	5 hours or more

At low temperatures, slightly less water is needed to create a workable mix.

Protection against freezing in cold weather should be provided during placing and for at least 7 days and sometimes up to 2 weeks after placement. This can be accomplished in several ways, e.g., by covering the concrete with plastic sheets and using portable heaters or insulating blankets, by steam curing, or by special mixes such as Type III high early strength cement, a low water/cement ratio, or accelerator-type admixtures. Fresh concrete that freezes before it has sufficiently cured may have to be replaced, but strength may sometimes be restored by proper curing after a *single* freeze-up.

7.8 Sealers and Glazers

Special compounds are sometimes used to seal or glaze new or old concrete. They are typically used to provide a waterproof sealer which prevents or reduces moisture and chloride penetration. Some are also used to bring out natural colors in the aggregate or the colors of the concrete. Most of these sealers and glazers have an epoxy or acrylic base.

Various manufacturers have their own types and associated trade names for these sealers and glazers. Three common types include:

1. *Sealer and curing compound:* this compound is suitable for use on concrete surfaces and has a low-viscosity two-component epoxy sealer. It can be applied on damp concrete or used on fresh concrete as a nonfugitive curing compound which will provide continuous protection.

2. *Glazer-sealer:* this is a compound that brings out the natural color of slate, brick, stone, and concrete. It is recommended for exterior paved surfaces and walls.

3. *Deck coating:* this is a two-coat sealer for concrete slabs and decks which reportedly allows water vapor to evaporate but blocks penetration of moisture and chlorides. The first coat of oligomeric alkoxysilane chemically bonds to the substrate, penetrating the concrete surface about ¼ in (6 mm). The second coat cures to a breathing film that reduces water absorp-

TABLE 830-16
Concrete Finishing Tools

Tool	*Description*	*Illustration*
Straight-edge (screeds): Wood (6–16 ft long) Magnesium (6–14 ft long) Vibrating straightedges (up to 80-ft spans)	Used to strike off concrete to the required elevation	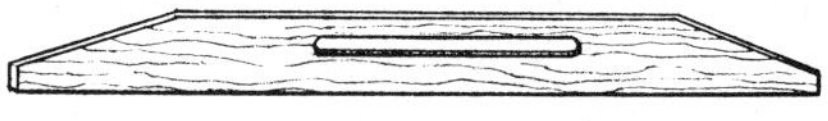
Tampers (jitterbug): Flat grill Roller grill Power compactors (subgrades and subbases)	Used to push down coarse aggregates to just below the surface. Used only on very stiff concrete mixtures immediately after striking off the surface (straightedging)	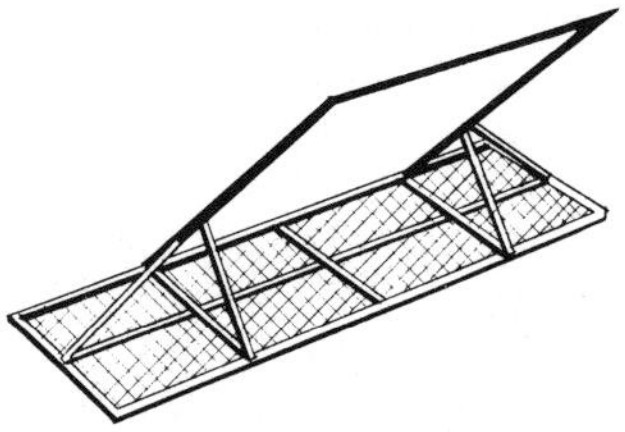
Bull floats: Wood (42–60 in wide) Magnesium (42–60 in wide)	Used to smooth the surface following straightedging (to get rid of high and low spots). Generally, wood bull floats perform better except on air-entrained and lightweight concretes	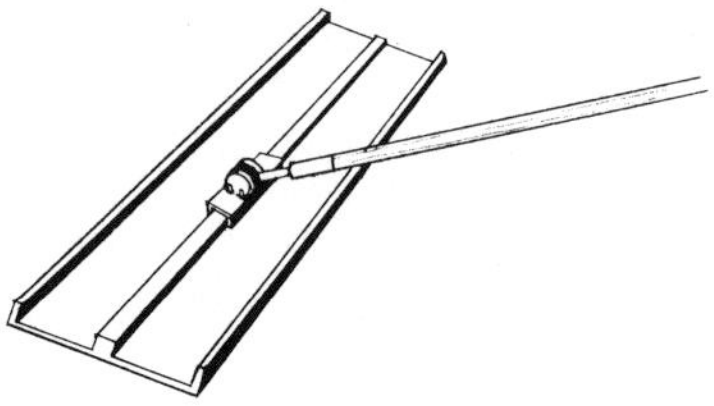
Darbies: Short darbies (wood or magnesium) Long-handled darbies (wood or magnesium)	Used for the same purpose as bull floats (to get rid of high and low spots)	 (a) (b) (a) *Short-handled, and* (b) *long-handled darbies.*
Floats: Wood Magnesium Power floats (rotary)	Used to make surfaces true. Wood floats are best for non-air-entrained concrete and for high-slump concrete. Magnesium is used for low-slump, air-entrained, and lightweight concretes	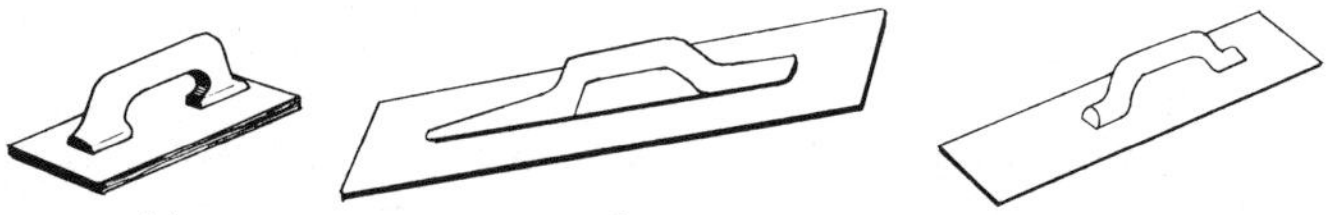 (a) (b) (c) (a) *Small wood float;* (b) *large magnesium float;* (c) *small magnesium float.*
Trowels: Spring steel (various sizes) Power trowelers (rotary)	Makes the surface hard and dense. Done after floating	
Fresno: Spring steel	A long-handled trowel, used as a trowel, not a bull float, where speed of troweling is important	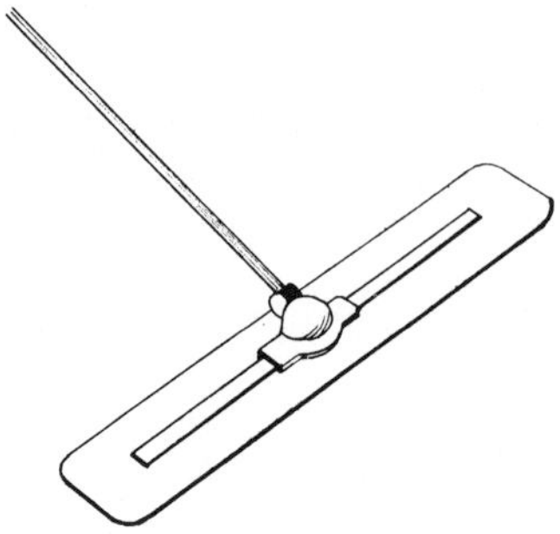

Source: American Concrete Association, *Slabs on Grade,* Detroit, 1982.

TABLE 830-16
Concrete Finishing Tools

Tool	*Description*	*Illustration*
Edging Tools: Short edgers Long edgers Corner tools Walking edgers	Used to round off edges so they are less likely to chip. Done after the slab has been bull floated and darbied	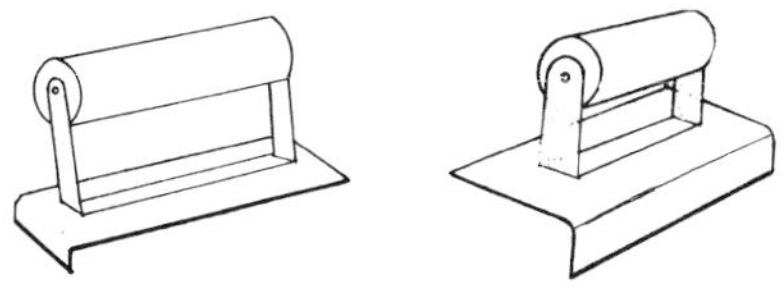 (*a*) (*b*) *A shorter edger (a) is used on curves, while the longer edger (b) is used on straight runs.*
Jointers (Groovers):	Used to make contraction joints in slabs, about one-fourth the thickness of the slab	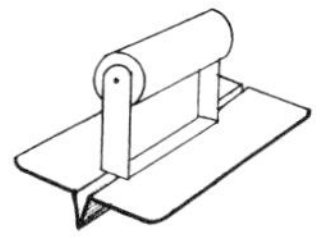
Special tools: Tools to spread concrete: Square-nose shovel Concrete rake Come-along Tools to texture the surface: Wire comb texture broom (for nonslip surfaces, 3–5 ft wide) Shallow groovers ("cheaters")		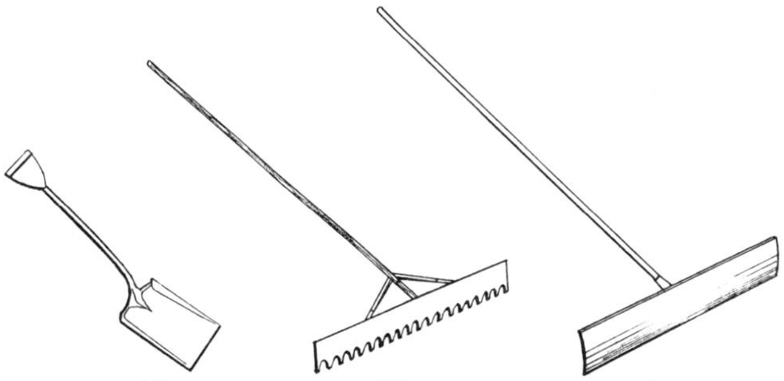 (*a*) (*b*) (*c*) *(a) A no. 2 square-nose shovel gives good leverage for moving concrete; (b) a concrete rake (not a garden rake) can be used with stiff concrete; (c) a come-along is wide enough to minimize segregation of the aggregates from the paste.*
Vibrators: Internal vibrators External vibrators Form vibrators Surface vibrators (vibrating screeds)	Used to consolidate concrete.	
Power Floats and Trowels: "Pony" trowels Heavy disk-type floats ("Kelly float") Large riding machines	Used for both floating and troweling. Kelly floats are used to compact and float heavy-duty floor toppings made with very low-slump concrete.	

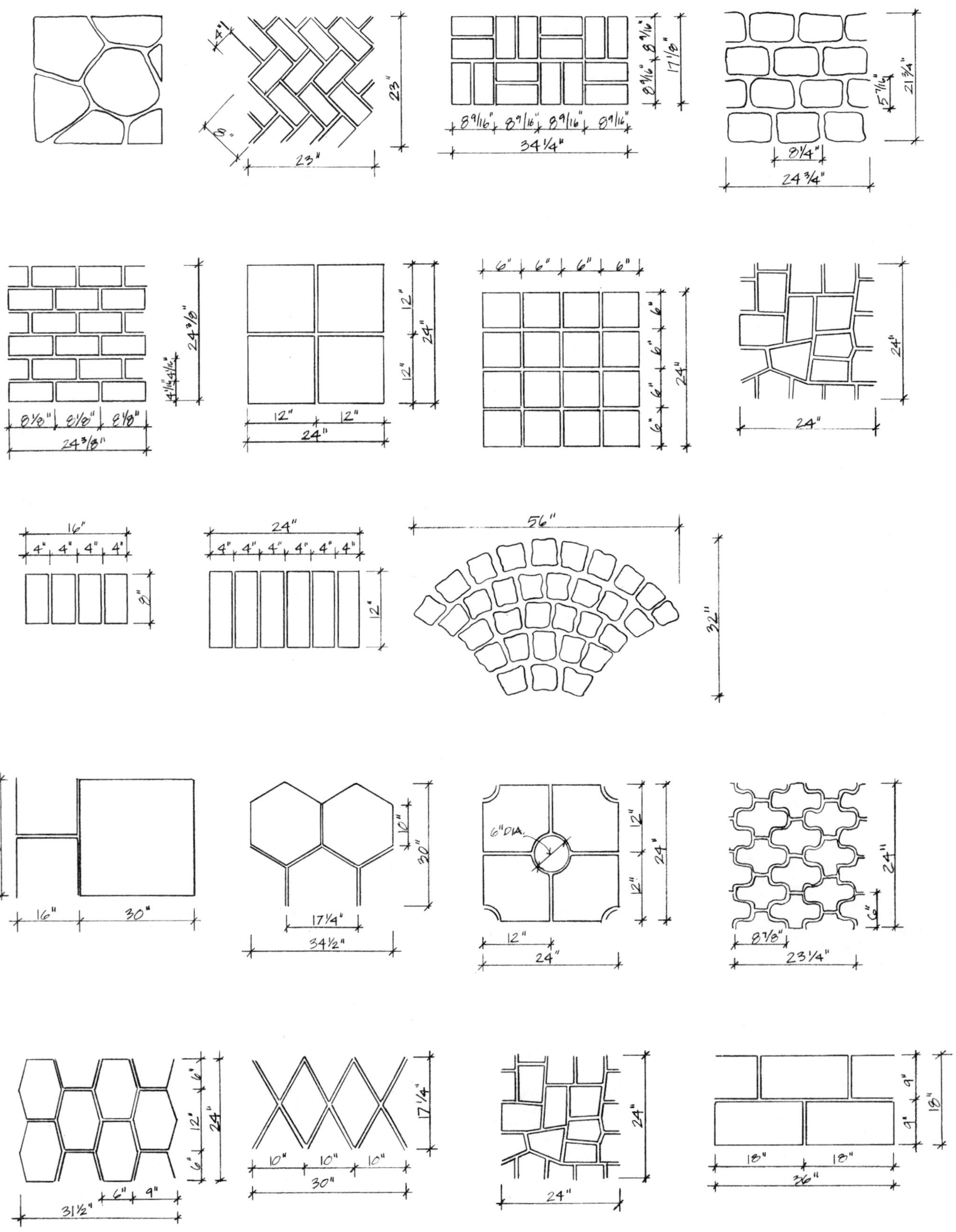
4"
8"
23"
23"
8 9/16"
8 9/16"
8 9/16"
8 9/16"
34 1/4"
8 9/16"
8 9/16"
8"
17 1/8"
5 7/16"
21 3/4"
8 1/4"
24 3/4"
8 1/8"
8 1/8"
8 1/8"
24 3/8"
24 3/8"
12"
12"
12"
12"
24"
24"
6"
6"
6"
6"
24"
24"
24"
16"
4"
4"
4"
4"
8"
24"
4"
4"
4"
4"
4"
4"
12"
56"
32"
30"
16"
30"
10"
30"
17 1/4"
34 1/2"
6" DIA.
12"
12"
24"
12"
24"
24"
6"
8 7/8"
23 1/4"
6"
12"
6"
24"
31 1/2"
6"
9"
17 1/4"
10"
10"
10"
30"
24"
24"
9"
9"
18"
18"
18"
36"

Figure 830-17 Typical Stamped Patterns for Concrete. Crack control and an attractive appearance are obtained by orienting bond lines across the short dimension of the pavement for cobblestone and all running bond patterns. Dimensions are centerline to centerline. Drawings are not in scale with each other.

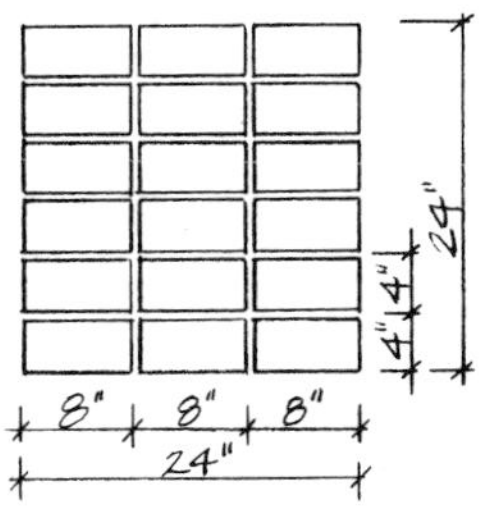
8"
8"
8"
24"
4"
4"
24"

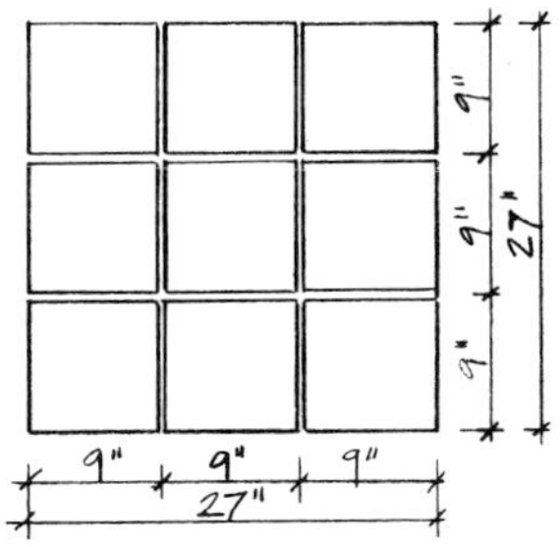
9"
9"
9"
27"
9"
9"
9"
27"

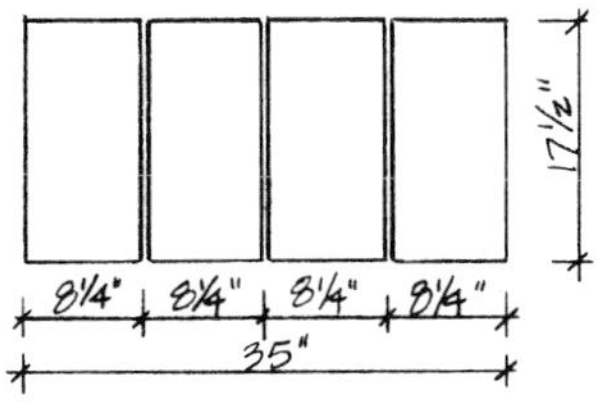
8¼"
8¼"
8¼"
8¼"
35"
17½"

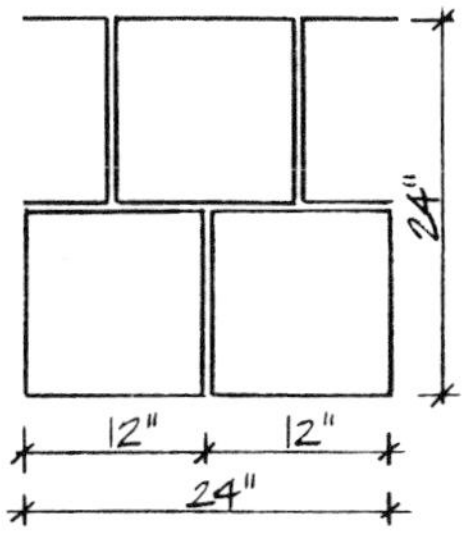
12"
12"
24"
24"

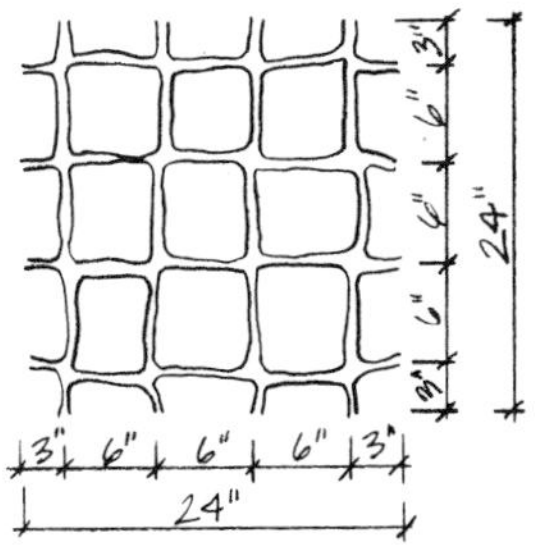
3"
6"
6"
6"
3"
24"
3"
6"
6"
6"
3"
24"

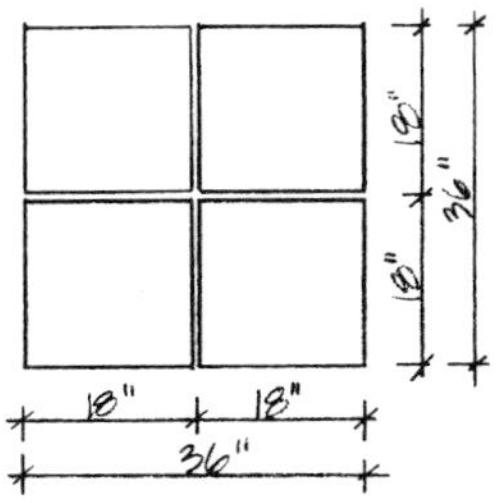
18"
18"
36"
18"
18"
36"

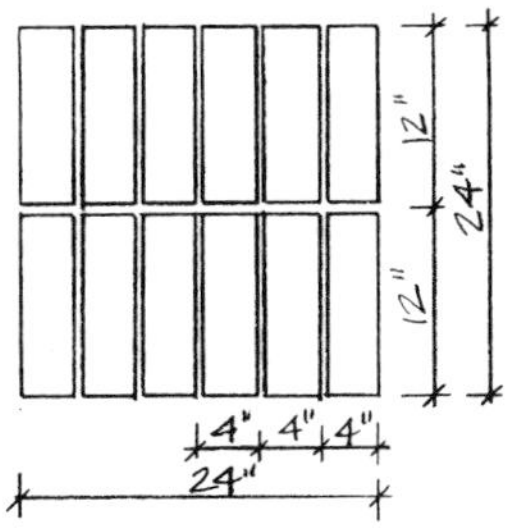
4"
4"
4"
24"
12"
12"
24"

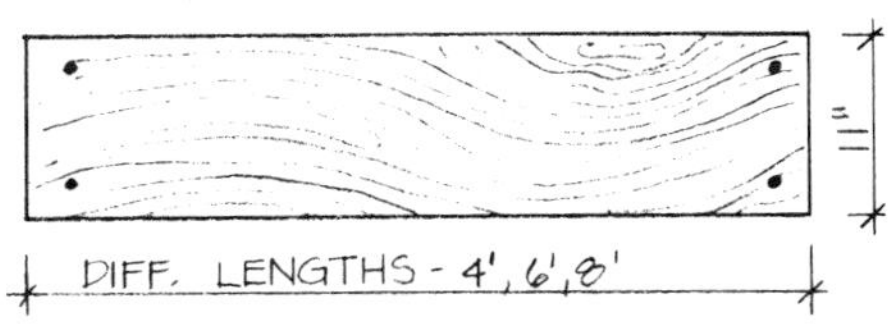
11"
DIFF. LENGTHS - 4', 6', 8'

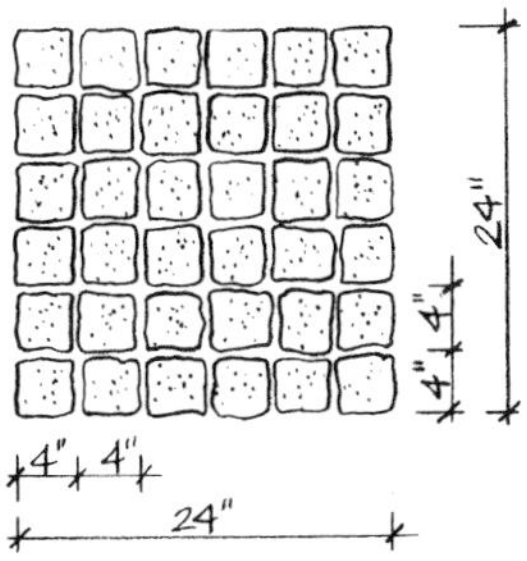
4"
4"
24"
4"
4"
24"

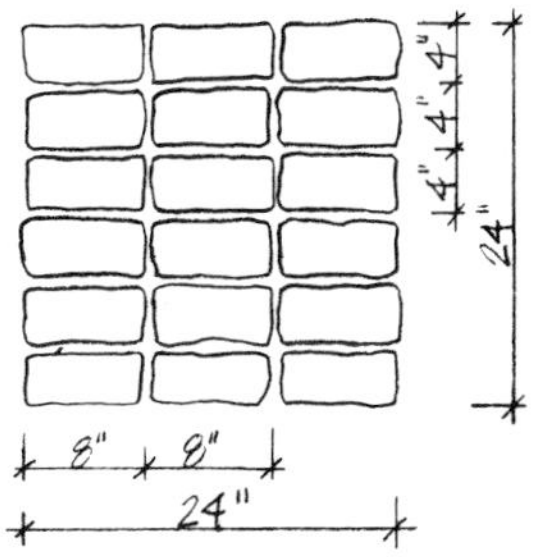
8"
8"
24"
4"
4"
4"
24"

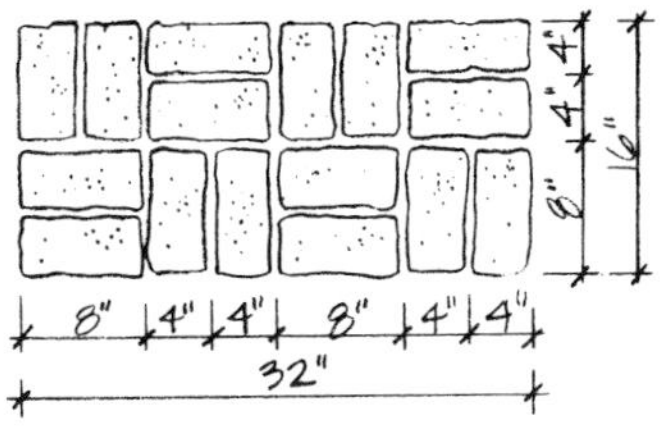
8"
4"
4"
8"
4"
4"
32"
4"
4"
6"
8"

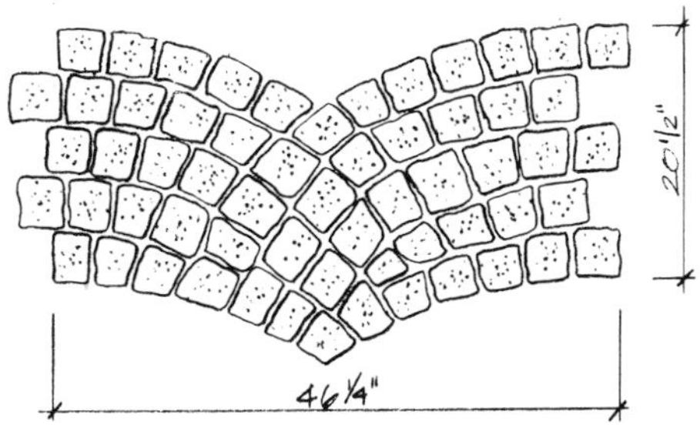
20½"
46¼"

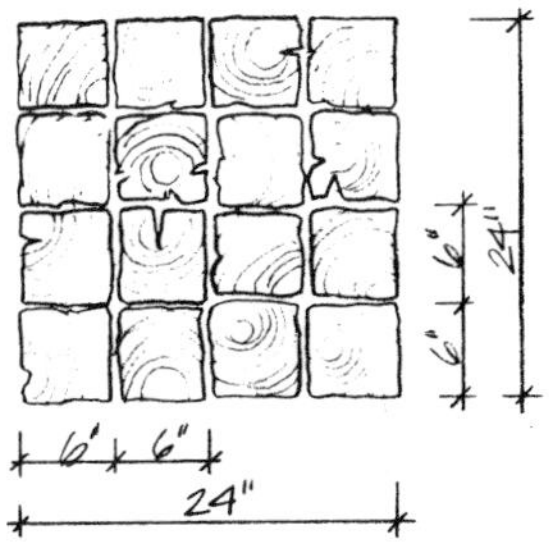
6"
6"
24"
6"
6"
24"

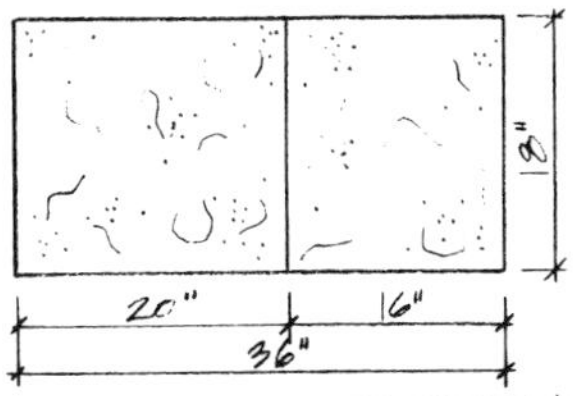
20"
16"
36"
18"

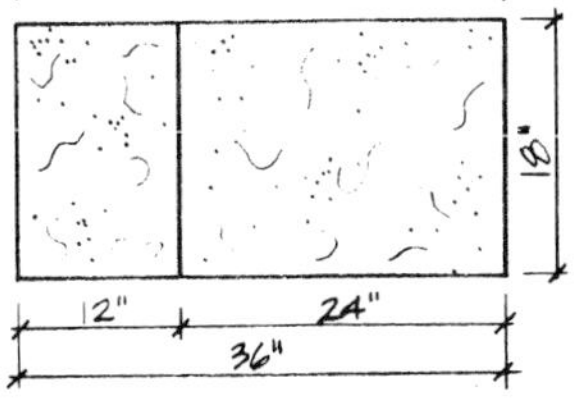
12"
24"
36"
18"

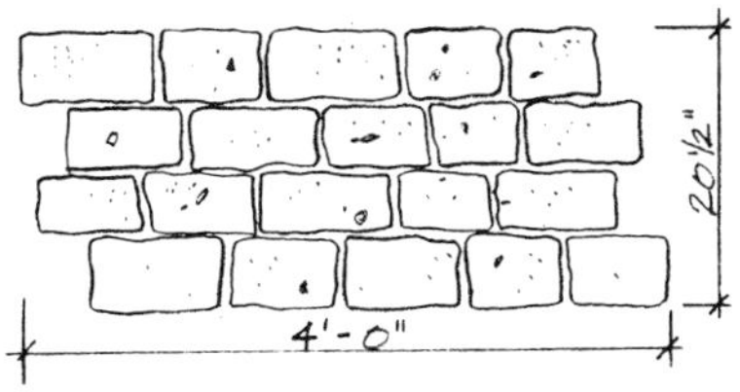
20½"
4'-0"

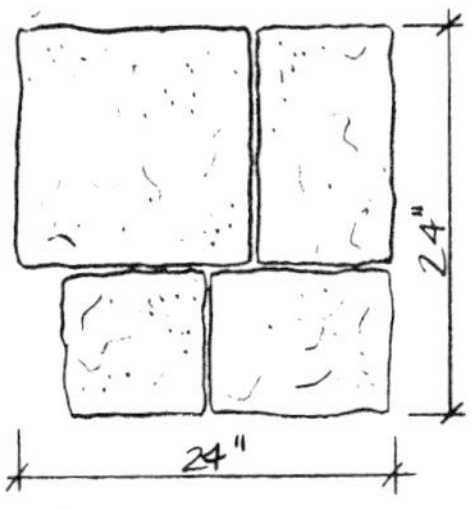
24"
24"

TABLE 830-17
Curing Materials and Techniques

Type	*Uses*	*Remarks*
Water ponding: with sand or earth dykes to contain water	For all horizontal surfaces, such as: pavements, walks, floors, horizontally cast panels	This will also maintain uniform temperature in concrete.
Continuous sprinkling	For horizontal and vertical surfaces: pavements, walks, floors, walls, cement plaster, stucco	Use fine spray through nozzles or soil-soaker hose.
Wet coverings: burlap, cotton mats	For horizontal and curved surfaces: pavements, walks, floors, shell roofs, horizontally cast panels	Wet sand, earth, straw, or hay could also be used.
Waterproof paper	For horizontal surfaces: pavements, walks, floors, horizontally cast panels	Should conform to ASTM C171.
Plastic sheets	For horizontal surfaces and complex shapes: pavements, walks, floors, shell roofs, horizontally cast panels	Should conform to ASTM C171.
Forms left in place	For vertical surfaces	Must be kep wet using spray or soil soaker hose.
Steam curing	For: cast-in-place, plant cast units	Enclosure for items to be cured is required.
Curing compounds: clear, white pigmented, light-gray pigmented, black	For all horizontal and vertical surfaces	Should conform to ASTM C 309.

Source: Sweet's Selection Data: Cement and Concrete, McGraw-Hill, New York, 1979.

tion but permits escape of water vapor. It is resistant to deterioration from ultraviolet light and will not turn a yellow color. It should not be applied until the concrete has thoroughly dried.

7.9 Weathering Indexes in the United States

Figure 830-18 shows *weathering indexes* for the United States, which are determined by computing the product of the average number of freezing-cycle days and the average annual amount of winter rainfall, defined as follows:

A *freezing-cycle day* is any day during which the air temperature passes either above or below 32 degrees F (0 degrees C). The average number of freezing-cycle days in a year may be taken to equal the difference between the mean number of days during which the minimum temperature was 32 degrees F (0 degrees C) or below and the mean number of days during which the maximum temperature was 32 degrees F (0 degrees C) or below.

Winter rainfall is the sum, in inches (or centimeters), of the mean monthly corrected precipitation (rainfall) occurring during the period between, and including, the normal date of the first killing frost in the fall and the normal date of the last killing frost in the spring. The winter rainfall for any period is equal to the total precipitation less one-tenth of the total fall of snow, sleet, and hail. Rainfall for a portion of a month is prorated.

7.10 Restoration and Repair of Concrete

Restoration and repair of concrete involves the following procedure:

1. Removal of all damaged and spalling concrete and cleaning of existing concrete of loose material and dust.

2. Concrete is mixed in small amounts. Aggregate is left out, or individual pieces are hand-placed.

3. After cleaning, the damaged area is saturated with water and a neat cement slurry or bonding agent is applied to the entire base and to the water used in the patch mix. Mortar mix should comprise 1 to 1.5 parts of cement to concrete sand by weight or volume and be mixed damp (crumbly dry) to the touch.

4. The new concrete is finished to match the existing adjacent surfaces.

5. The concrete is moisture-cured to prevent shrinkage and cracking.

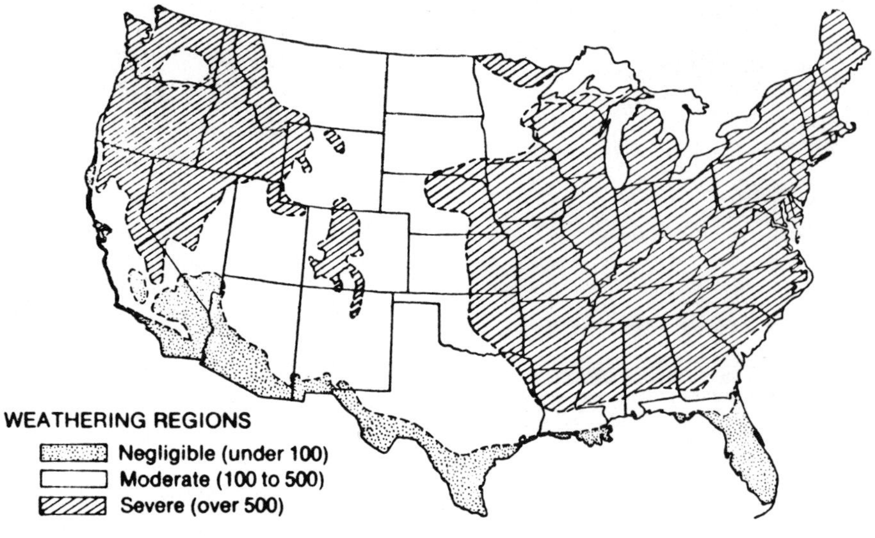
WEATHERING REGIONS
Negligible (under 100)
Moderate (100 to 500)
Severe (over 500)

Figure 830-18 Weathering Indexes in the United States. This index shows general areas where concrete is subject to severe, moderate, and negligible weathering. Data needed to determine the weathering index for any locality in the United States may be found or estimated from tables of local climatological data, published by the U.S. Weather Bureau, U.S. Department of Commerce, Washington, D.C.

GLOSSARY*

Accelerator: An admixture added to concrete to hasten its set and increase the rate of strength gain (the opposite of retarder).

Admixture: A material (other than portland cement, water, or aggregate) added to concrete to alter its properties (i.e., accelerators, retarders, air entraining agents).

Aggregate: Normally, a hard, inert material mixed with cement and water to form concrete.

Bag (of cement): A quantity of cement that weighs 94 lb in the United States and 50 kg in most other countries using the metric system.

Bleeding: The appearance of excess water rising to the surface shortly after the placing of concrete.

Cement: A binding agent (i.e., *glue*) capable of uniting dissimilar materials into a composite whole.

*Glossary adapted from Portland Cement Association.

Concrete: A composite material made of cement, water, aggregates, and sometimes special admixtures.

Consistency: The uniformity of mixes or batches as measured by the slump test.

Crazing: Numerous fine hair cracks in the surface of a newly hardened slab.

Dusting: The appearance of a powdery material at the surface of a hardened concrete slab, probably caused by an improperly moist cure.

Formwork: A structure erected to temporarily contain the concrete during its placing and initial hardening.

Graded aggregate: Aggregate containing graduated particle sizes from the finest fine aggregate size to the maximum size of coarse aggregate.

Graded sand: A sand containing uniformly graduated particle sizes from very fine up to ¼ in (6 mm).

Grout: A fluid mixture of cement, water, and sand of casting consistency.

Heat of hydration: Heat created during the hardening process of concrete.

Hydration: The chemical reaction of water and cement that produces a hardened concrete.

Hydraulic cement: A cement that can set or harden while under water.

Inert: Having inactive chemical properties.

Monolithic concrete: Concrete placed in one continuous cast without joints.

Neat cement: A mixture of cement and water (no aggregate).

Placing: The act of putting concrete in position (sometimes incorrectly referred to as *pouring*).

Plastic concrete: Easily molded concrete that will change its form slowly only if the mold is removed.

Precast concrete: Concrete components which are cast and cured off-site or in a factory before being placed into their final position.

Prestressed concrete: Concrete subjected to compressive forces by the prestretching (or stressing) of reinforcing bars or cables within, thereby developing greater strength, stiffness, and crack resistance in the concrete.

Puddling: The compacting or consolidating of concrete with a spade, rod, or other tool.

Ready-mixed concrete: Concrete mixed at a central plant or in trucks enroute to the job and delivered ready for placement.

Reinforcing: Steel placed in concrete to take tensile stresses.

Retarder: An admixture added to concrete to retard its set.

Scaling: The breaking away of the hardened concrete surface of the slab [to a depth of about $\frac{1}{16}$ to $\frac{3}{16}$ in (1.6 to 4.8 mm)], usually occurring at an early age of the slab.

Scoring: The partial cutting of concrete to control shrinkage and cracking. Also used to denote the roughening of a base slab to develop mechanical bond with a finish slab, etc.

Segregation: A separation of the heavier coarse aggregate from the mortar or of the water from the other ingredients of a concrete mix during handling or placing.

Shrinkage: A decrease in initial volume due to the removal of moisture from fresh concrete. May also refer to a decrease in volume due to subsequent decreases in temperature or moisture content.

Spalls: The fragments of concrete dislodged from the surface of concrete.

Subbase: A layer of material, aggregate, or coarse-graded concrete between the subgrade (soil, etc.) and the top course of the paving.

Subgrade: The compacted fill or earth surface upon which subbase is placed.

Swale: A low, flat depression to drain off storm water.

Water/cement ratio: The amount of water (gallons or liters) used per sack of cement in making concrete, often expressed as a pure number ratio, such as *pound of water per pound of cement.* It is an index to strength, durability, watertightness, and workability.

Workability: The relative ease or difficulty with which concrete can be placed and worked into its final position within forms, around reinforcing, etc.

AGENCIES AND ORGANIZATIONS

Industry Associations (United States)

American Concrete Institute (ACI)
Detroit, Michigan

Concrete Reinforcing Steel Institute (CRSI)
National Headquarters
Chicago, Illinois

Concrete Sawing and Drilling Association (CSDA)
Los Angeles, California

National Crushed Stone Association (NCSA)
Washington, D.C.

National Precast Concrete Association (NPCA)
Indianapolis, Indiana

National Ready-Mixed Concrete Association (NRMCA)
Silver Spring, Maryland

National Sand and Gravel Association (NSGA)
Silver Spring, Maryland

Portland Cement Association (PCA)
Skokie, Illinois

Wire Reinforcement Institute (WRI)
McLean, Virginia

Institutes and Agencies

Construction Specifications Institute (CSI)
Washington, D.C.

National Bureau of Standards (NBS)
U.S. Department of Commerce
Washington, D.C.

National Institute of Building Sciences (NIBS)
Washington, D.C.

National Technical Information Service (NTIS)
U.S. Department of Commerce
Springfield, Virginia

U.S. Department of Energy (DOE)
Energy Research and Development Administration
Washington, D.C.

REFERENCES

General

Gage, Michael. *Guide to Exposed Concrete Finishes,* The Architectural Press, London.

McGraw-Hill Information Systems. *Sweet's Selection Data: Cement and Concrete,* McGraw-Hill, New York, annual.

Olin, Harold, John L. Schmidt, and Walter H. Lewis. *Construction: Principles, Materials and Methods,* 3d ed., The Institute of Financial Education, Chicago, 1975.

Portland Cement Association. *Basic Concrete Construction Practices,* Wiley, New York, 1975.

Waddell, Joseph J. *Concrete Construction Handbook,* 2d ed., McGraw-Hill, New York, 1974.

Wilson, J. Gilchrist. *Exposed Concrete Finishes,* Wiley, New York.

Publications by Trade Associations

American Concrete Institute (ACI):
- *Manual of Concrete Practice*

Concrete Sawing and Drilling Association (CSDA):
- *Concrete Sawing—What Choice Joints*

National Crushed Stone Association (NCSA):
- *Quality Concrete With Crushed Stone Aggregate*

Portland Cement Association (PCA):
- *Admixtures for Concrete*
- *Aggregates for Concrete*
- *Design of Concrete Mixtures*
- *Exploring Color and Texture*
- *Exposed Aggregate Concrete* (very good)
- *Exposed Aggregate Finishes for Slabs*
- *Factors Influencing Joint and Sealant Designs for Concrete Pavements*
- *Guidelines for Outdoor Concrete Flatwork*
- *Jobsite Precast Concrete Panels—Textures, Patterns, and Designs*
- *Textured Finishes for Slabs*
- *Patterned Finishes for Slabs*
- *Bushhammering of Concrete Surfaces*

Wire Reinforcement Institute (WRI):
- *Welded Wire Fabric* ■

section 840: Masonry

CREDITS

Section Editor: Charles W. Harris
Technical Writer: David Clough

Research Assistants:

Tobias Dayman
Krisan Osterby-Benson

Reviewers:

David Clough
Sasaki Associates, Inc.
Watertown, Massachusetts

Richard Lakutis
The Architect's Collaborative, Inc.
Cambridge, Massachusetts

Robert J. Beiner, P.E.
Director of Engineering
International Masonry Institute
Washington, D.C.

Hugh MacDonald
Brick Institute of America
Reston, Virginia

CONTENTS

1.0 INTRODUCTION

Clay, concrete, and stone masonry products are used extensively in landscape construction for both aesthetic and structural reasons. Their modular characteristics, texture, and color, as well as their properties of durability, compressive strength, and resistance to moisture, allow them to be used in a wide range of applications.

2.0 CLAY MASONRY

2.1 General

Classification of Clay Masonry Units:

Clay masonry is typically classified into three groups: solid masonry units, hollow masonry units, and architectural terra-cotta. Individual products within these groups are further classified by size, grade, type, color, and texture.

Solid Masonry Units (Brick): A masonry unit is classified as solid if the void area does not exceed 25 percent of the total cross-sectional area of the unit. An exception is hollow brick (ASTM C652) whose void area does not exceed 40 percent of the total cross-sectional area of the unit. Solid masonry units typically include building brick (ASTM C62), facing brick (ASTM C216), ceramic glazed facing brick (ASTM C126), hollow brick (ASTM C652), and paving brick (ASTM C902).

Hollow Masonry Units (Tile): A masonry unit is classified as hollow if the void area exceeds 40 percent of the total cross-sectional area of the unit. Hollow clay masonry units typically include structural clay tile and structural clay facing tile.

Architectural Terra-Cotta (Ceramic Veneer): Terra-cotta refers to the larger custom ceramic veneer products used for interior walls, exterior walls, and ornamentation. Other surficial clay tiles (i.e., ceramic floor tile, ceramic wall tile, and mosaic tile) are not discussed in this section.

Properties of Clay Masonry Units:

The characteristics of the raw clay material as well as the manufacturing process itself will determine the properties of finished clay masonry units. Table 840-1 shows basic properties of clay masonry units. Descriptions of each of these properties follow.

Compressive Strength (Table 840-1): The maximum stress to which a unit can be loaded perpendicularly to the bedding plane varies from 700 to 20,000 psi. Bricks can be classified by compressive strength when such values are above those used in the graded classification.

Water Absorption (Table 840-1): The *initial rate of absorption* (IRA) or *suction* affects the bond between brick and mortar where 20 gpm/30 in^2 develops peak strength. Units with rates greater than 30 gpm/30 in^2 have too rapid an IRA and should be wetted thoroughly 3 to 24 hours before placement. The *absorption (percent)* is the amount of water absorbed by the unit. A lower percentage indicates less water absorption and contributes to better weathering characteristics in exposed, exterior conditions.

Durability (Table 840-1): The combined factors of compressive strength and absorption constitute a measure of durability. The durability of brick is also reflected in its susceptibility to weathering, which is expressed by various grades (see Tables 840-4 through 840-7). Weathering, primarily caused by alternate freezing and thawing in the presence of moisture, varies by climatic regions (Figure 840-1). Resistance to abrasion and staining, particularly important when using paving brick, is demonstrated by the denser hard-burned brick that exhibits low absorption. Local practices should be investigated to ascertain more precisely the impact of weathering on various grades of brick.

TABLE 840-1
Basic Properties of Clay Masonry

	*Properties and test methods**				
	Compressive strength, psi	*Modulus of rupture, psi†*	*Water absorption, %*	*Density, pcf*	*Material specifications*
		Clay—solid masonry units (brick)‡			
Building and facing					ASTM C62-84 (building brick)
Grade SW	3000		17		ASTM C216-84 (facing brick)
Grade MW	2500		22		
Grade NW	1500				
Glazed facing	3000				ASTM C126-82
Paving					ASTM (902-79a)
Grade SX	8000		8		
Grade MX	3000		14		
Grade NX	3000		no limit		
Hollow					ASTM C652-81
Grade SW	3000		17		
Grade MW	2500		22		
		Hollow masonry units (tile)			
Load-bearing wall tile					ASTM C34-62 (reapproved 1975)
Type LBX	1400		18	52	
Type LB	1000		25	52	
Facing tile					ASTM C212-60 (reapproved 1981)
Standard	1400		7	48	
Special duty	2500		13	48	
Sand lime brick					ASTM C73-75
Grade SW	4500	650	7–10		
Grade MW	2500	450	7–10		

* For methods of testing clay brick, see ASTM C67-83.
† Modulus of rupture is a measure of flexural strength.
‡ Density, pcf = 103–145.
Source: Sweet's Selection Data: Stone and Masonry, McGraw-Hill, New York, 1979.

Texture, Colors, and Finishes: Commonly specified brick textures include *smooth, matte, rugs, barks, stippled, sandmold, waterstruck,* and *sandstruck.* Commonly available clay masonry colors include buff, cream, purple, maroon, black, pearl gray, and various shades of red. Use of glazes or special kiln techniques can produce an infinite range of color options. Finishes commonly applied to clay masonry units include:

1. *Smooth finish:* formed by the die in manufacturing
2. *Scored finish:* grooved as it comes from the die in order to increase bonding
3. *Combed finish:* altered by parallel grooving after manufacture for texture or to increase bonding
4. *Roughened finish:* surface entirely roughened by wire cutting or other means for texture or to increase bonding
5. *Clear glaze:* transparent coating fused to surface
6. *Nonlustrous glaze:* transparent coating with a matte finish
7. *Ceramic color glaze:* solid or mottled with gloss or matte finish; wide range of colors
8. *Polychrome finish:* two or more colors applied and burned separately

Size Variation: Shrinkage in clays varies from 4.5 to 15 percent during the process of drying and firing and increases with higher temperatures. Some variation between dark and light units is inevitable. Therefore, industry specifications include tolerances in size and color.

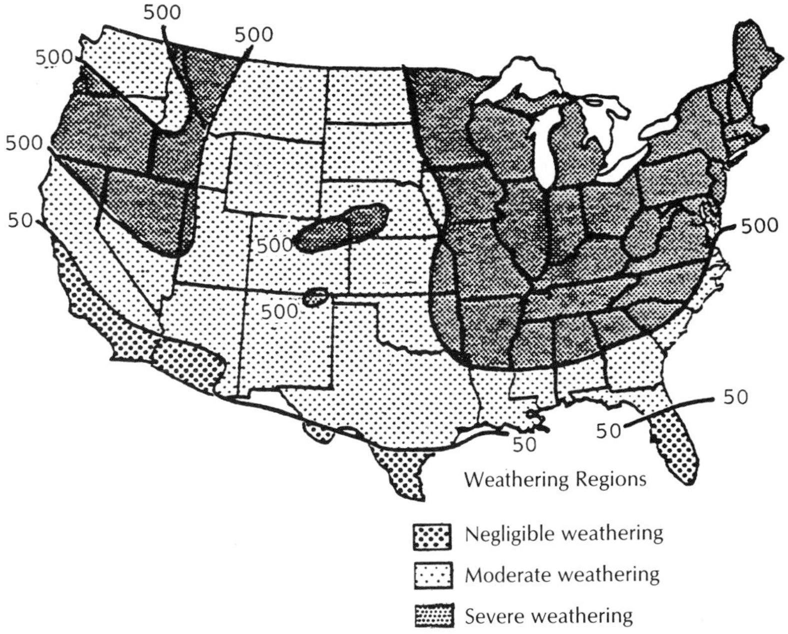
500
500
500
500
50
500
500
500
50
50
50
Weathering Regions
Negligible weathering
Moderate weathering
Severe weathering

Figure 840-1 Regions of weathering in the United States.

2.2 Brick

Standard formats and dimensions have been established for each category of brick.

Units are classified by grades and/or types, based on durability and type of use.

Building Brick (ASTM C62):

Building (common) brick is the standard clay masonry unit used in brick masonry construction. Most sizes conform to a module based upon 4 in (Table 840-2). A few brick types do not conform to such a module (Table 840-3); these *three-inch* bricks (referring to bed depth) are often referred to by various trade names, such as *Kingsize* or *Jumbo.* Nonmodular brick was originally developed as a veneer unit but is often used to construct cavity and grouted walls. Formats and dimensions for building brick are given in Tables 840-2 and 840-3. The grading system used for building brick is given in Table 840-4.

Facing Brick (ASTM C216):

Facing brick is manufactured with stringent tolerances for size, warpage, chippage, and color and is used where an exposed brick face is desired. The dimensions of facing brick are the same as for building brick (see Table 840-2). Table 840-5 shows the grading system used for facing brick. Ceramic glazed facing brick is also available and conforms to different ASTM specifications (Table 840-6).

Hollow Brick (ASTM C652):

Hollow bricks, with a void area up to 40 percent, produce a larger brick unit for the same weight of a building or facing brick. More rapid construction becomes possible with larger units. In principle, building brick can be substituted by hollow brick, but the design of any hollow brick wall must conform to accepted hollow brick wall construction. Formats and dimensions for hollow brick are given in Figure 840-2. Table 840-7 shows the grading system used for hollow brick.

Pedestrian and Light Traffic Paving Brick (ASTM C902):

Paving brick is manufactured with high compressive strength and low absorption, thereby constituting a durable brick material suitable for paving. Formats and dimensions for paving brick are given in Table 840-8. Table 840-9 shows the grading system used for paving brick.

2.3 Tile

Tile is typically classified into two categories: structural clay tile and structural clay facing tile. Both types of tile can be either

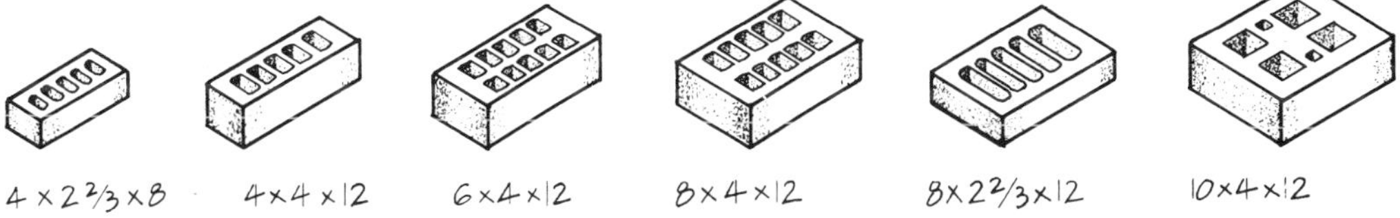
4 x 2 2/3 x 8
4 x 4 x 12
6 x 4 x 12
8 x 4 x 12
8 x 2 2/3 x 12
10 x 4 x 12

Figure 840-2 Standard sizes and shapes of hollow bricks.

TABLE 840-2
Sizes of Modular Brick*†

Unit designation		Nominal dimensions, in‡			Joint thickness, in	Manufactured dimensions, in			Modular coursing, in
		T	*H*	*L*		*T*	*H*	*L*	
Standard modular	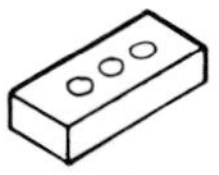	4 (10.16)	2⅔ (6.77)	8 (20.32)	⅜ (0.95) ½ (1.27)	3⅝ (9.21) 3½ (8.89)	2¼ (5.72) 2¼ (5.72)	7⅝ (19.37) 7½ (19.05)	3C = 8 (20.32)
Engineer		4 (10.16)	3⅕ (8.13)	8 (20.32)	⅜ (0.95) ½ (1.27)	3⅝ (9.21) 3½ (8.89)	2 13/16 (7.15) 2 11/16 (6.83)	7⅝ (19.37) 7½ (19.05)	5C = 16 (40.64)
Economy 8 or jumbo closure	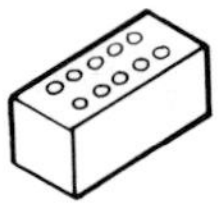	4 (10.16)	4 (10.16)	8 (20.32)	⅜ (0.95) ½ (1.27)	3⅝ (9.21) 3½ (8.89)	3⅝ (9.21) 3½ (8.89)	7⅝ (19.37) 7½ (19.05)	1C = 4 (10.16)
Double		4 (10.16)	5⅓ (13.55)	8 (20.32)	⅜ (0.95) ½ (1.27)	3⅝ (9.21) 3½ (8.89)	4 15/16 (12.55) 4 13/16 (12.23)	7⅝ (19.37) 7½ (19.05)	3C = 16 (40.64)
Roman	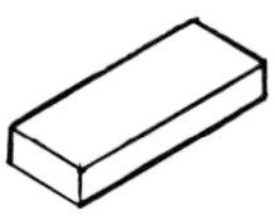	4 (10.16)	2 (5.08)	12 (30.50)	⅜ (0.95) ½ (1.27)	3⅝ (9.21) 3½ (8.89)	1⅝ (4.13) 1½ (3.81)	11⅝ (29.55) 11½ (29.23)	2C = 4 (10.16)
Norman	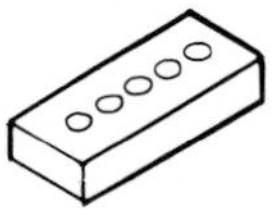	4 (10.16)	2⅔ (6.77)	12 (30.50)	⅜ (0.95) ½ (1.27)	3⅝ (9.21) 3½ (8.89)	2¼ (5.72) 2¼ (5.72)	11⅝ (29.55) 11½ (29.23)	3C = 8 (20.32)
Norwegian	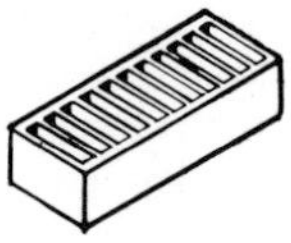	4 (10.16)	3⅕ (8.13)	12 (30.50)	⅜ (0.95) ½ (1.27)	3⅝ (9.21) 3½ (8.89)	2 13/16 (7.15) 2 11/16 (6.83)	11⅝ (29.55) 11½ (29.23)	5C = 16 (40.64)

* Although the coring types shown are typical for solid units, they do not necessarily apply to the specific types of units with which they are shown above. Types will vary between manufacturers. Values shown in parentheses are metric dimensions.

† Available as solid units conforming to ASTM C 216 (facing brick) or ASTM C 62 (building brick), or, in a number of cases, as hollow brick conforming to ASTM C 652.

‡ Nominal dimensions refer to the manufactured width of a unit plus the width of a mortared joint.

§ Reg. U.S. Patent Office, SCPI (BIA).

Source: Adapted from Jot Carpenter (ed.), *Handbook of Landscape Architectural Construction,* The Landscape Architecture Foundation, McLean, Virginia, 1976. p. 640.

Unit designation		Nominal dimensions, in‡			Joint thickness, in	Manufactured dimensions, in			Modular coursing, in
		T	H	L		T	H	L	
Economy 12 or jumbo utility	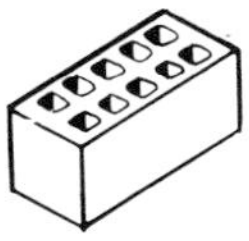	4 (10.16)	4 (10.16)	12 (30.50)	⅜ (0.95) ½ (1.27)	3⅝ (9.21) 3½ (8.89)	3⅝ (9.21) 3½ (8.89)	11⅝ (29.55) 11½ (29.23)	1C = 4 (10.16)
Triple	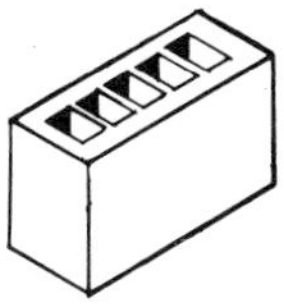	4 (10.16)	5⅓ (13.55)	12 (30.50)	⅜ (0.95) ½ (1.27)	3⅝ (9.21) 3½ (8.89)	4 15/16 (12.55) 4 13/16 (12.23)	11⅝ (29.55) 11½ (29.23)	3C = 16 (40.64)
SCR brick§	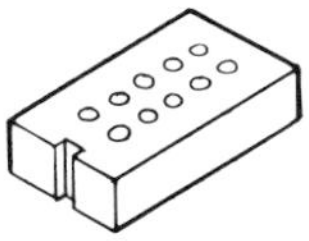	6 (15.24)	2⅔ (6.77)	12 (30.50)	⅜ (0.95) ½ (1.27)	5⅝ (14.29) 5½ (13.97)	2¼ (5.72) 2¼ (5.72)	11⅝ (29.55) 11½ (29.23)	3C = 8 (20.32)
6-in Norwegian	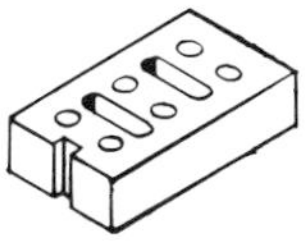	6 (15.24)	3⅕ (8.13)	12 (30.50)	⅜ (0.95) ½ (1.27)	5⅝ (14.29) 5½ (13.97)	2 13/16 (7.15) 2 11/16 (6.83)	11⅝ (29.55) 11½ (29.23)	5C = 16 (40.64)
6-in jumbo	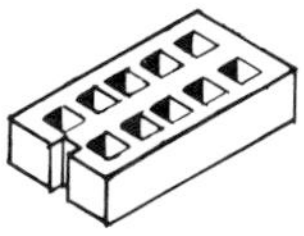	6 (15.24)	4 (10.16)	12 (30.50)	⅜ (0.95) ½ (1.27)	5⅝ (14.29) 5½ (13.97)	3⅝ (9.21) 3½ (8.89)	11⅝ (29.55) 11½ (29.23)	1C = 4 (10.16)
8-in jumbo	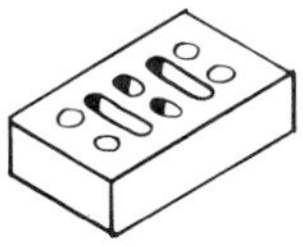	8 (20.32)	4 (10.16)	12 (30.50)	⅜ (0.95) ½ (1.27)	7⅝ (19.37) 7½ (19.05)	3⅝ (9.21) 3½ (8.89)	11⅝ (29.55) 11½ (29.23)	1C = 4 (10.16)

TABLE 840-3
Sizes of Nonmodular Brick*

Unit designation		Manufactured size, in (cm)		
		T	H	L
3-in	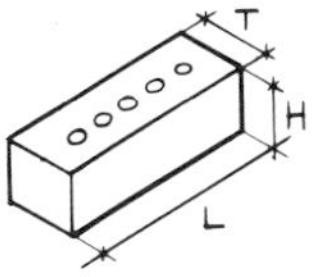T H L	3 (7.62) 3 (7.62)	2⅝ (6.67) 2¾ (6.99)	9⅝ (24.45) 9¾ (24.77)
Standard	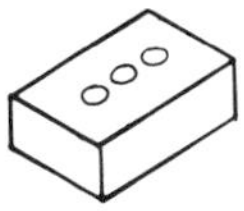	3¾ (9.53)	2¼ (5.72)	8 (20.32)
Oversize	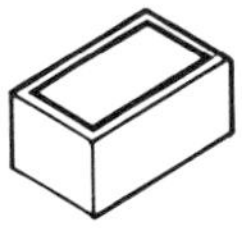	3¾ (9.53)	2¾ (6.99)	8 (20.32)

* Sizes shown in this table are those most commonly produced under the designation "kingsize." Other sizes of 3-in brick are produced under other designations. The manufactured thickness of standard or oversize nonmodular brick will vary from 3½ to 3¾ in. Therefore, if other than a running bond is desired, the designer should check with the manufacturer of the brick selected.

Source: Adapted from Jot Carpenter (ed.), *Handbook of Landscape Architectural Construction,* The Landscape Architecture Foundation, McLean, Virginia, 1976.

TABLE 840-4
Grades of Building (Common) Brick (ASTM C62)

*Grades**	*Use*
Severe weather (SW)	For foundations or other structures below grade or in contact with earth, especially when subjected to freezing temperatures
Medium weather (MW)	For exterior walls and other exposed masonry above grade
No weather (NW)	For all interior masonry or use as backup

* Based on durability.

Source: Adapted with permission from Harold B. Olin, John L. Schmidt, and Walter H. Lewis, *Construction: Principles, Materials, and Methods,* U.S. League of Savings Institutions, Chicago, 1983.

TABLE 840-5
Grades of Facing Brick (ASTM C216)

*Grade**	*Use*
Severe weather (SW)	For masonry in contact with earth, especially when subject to freezing temperatures
Medium weather (MW)	For exterior walls and other exposed masonry above grade

* Based on durability.

Source: Adapted with permission from Harold B. Olin, John L. Schmidt, and Walter H. Lewis, *Construction: Principles, Materials, and Methods,* U.S. League of Savings Institutions, Chicago, 1983.

TABLE 840-6
Grades and Types of Ceramic Glazed Facing Brick (ASTM C126)

Grade	*Use*
Select (S)	For masonry with narrow mortar joints (¼ in)
Ground-edge (G)	For masonry where face dimension variation must be very small
Type	*Use*
I*	For masonry where only one finished face will be exposed
II†	For masonry where two opposite finished faces will be exposed

* Single-face units.

† Two-face units.

Source: Adapted with permission from Harold B. Olin, John L. Schmidt, and Walter H. Lewis, *Construction: Principles, Materials, and Methods,* U.S. League of Savings Institutions, Chicago, 1983.

TABLE 840-7
Grades of Hollow Brick (ASTM C652-81)

*Grade**	*Use*
Severe weather (SW)	For use where high and uniform resistance to freezing is desired or where unit is expected to be saturated with water when frozen
Medium weather (MW)	For use where moderate and nonuniform resistance to freezing is desired or where unit is not expected to be saturated with water when frozen

* Based on durability.

Source: Adapted from ASTM, Designation C652, Philadelphia, Pennsylvania, as reprinted in Brick Institute of America, "ASTM Standard Specifications for Brick and Applicable Testing Methods for Units and BIA Standard Specification for Portland Cement—Lime Mortar for Brick Masonry, BIA Designation MI-72", July, 1981.

TABLE 840-8
Sizes of Brick Paver Units*

Face dimensions (actual size)				
Width, in	*Length, in*	*Thickness, in*	*Paver face area, (in²)*	*Paver units, per ft²*
4	8	The unit thickness of brick pavers varies. The most popular thicknesses are 2¼ and 1⅝. The range of thickness is generally from ¾–2½.	32.0	4.5
3¾	8		30.0	4.8
3⅝	7⅝		27.6	5.2
3⅞	8¼		32.0	4.5
3⅞	7¾		30.0	4.8
3¾	7½		28.2	5.1
3¾	7¾		29.1	5.0
3⅝	11⅝		42.1	3.4
3⅝	8		29.0	5.0
3⅝	11¾		42.6	3.4
3 9/16	8		28.5	5.1
3½	7¾		27.1	5.3
3½	7½		26.3	5.5
3⅜	7½		25.3	5.7
4	4		16.0	9.0
6	6		36.0	4.0
7⅝	7⅝		58.1	2.5
7¾	7¾		60.1	2.4
8	8		64.0	2.3
8	16		128.0	1.1
12	12		144.0	1.0
16	16		256.0	0.6
6	6 hexagon		31.2	4.6
8	8 hexagon		55.4	2.6
12	12 hexagon		124.7	1.2

* This table does not include provisions for waste. Allow at least 5% for waste and breakage. Also, it is not a complete list but does provide those sizes most commonly available. Consult manufacturers for availability of sizes and colors.

Source: Brick Institute of America, "Brick Floors and Pavements, Part II," Technical Note 14A, 1975.

TABLE 840-9
Grades and Types of Paving Brick (ASTM C902-79a)

*Grade**	*Use*
Sx	For use where brick is expected to be frozen while saturated with water
Mx	For exterior use where resistance to freezing is not a factor
Nx	For interior use and when a sealer or coating will be applied to prevent infiltration of dirt
Type†	*Use*
I	For use when exposed to extensive abrasion, such as in driveways and entranceways
II	For use when intermediate levels of traffic are expected, such as in walkways, etc.
III	For use when low levels of traffic are expected, such as in patios, terraces, etc.

* Based on durability.

† Based on traffic.

Source: Adapted from ASTM, Designation C902, Philadelphia, Pa., as reprinted in Brick Institute of America, "ASTM Standard Specifications for Brick and Applicable Testing Methods for Units and BIA Standard Specification for Portland Cement—Lime Mortar for Brick Masonry, BIA Designation MI-72," July 1981.

TABLE 840-10
Standard Sizes and Shapes of Structural Clay Tile

	Width, in	*Height, in*	*Thickness, in*
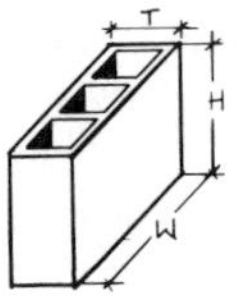	12	12	4
	12	12	6
	12	12	8
	12	12	10
	12	12	12
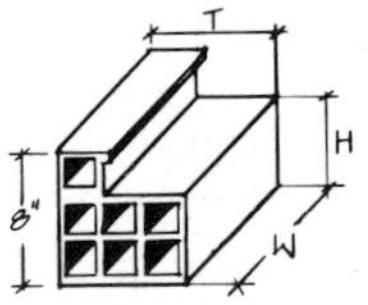	12	5⅓	8
	12	5⅓	12
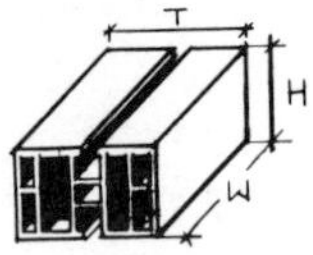	12	5⅓	8
	12	6⅔	8
	12	8	12
	12	11	8
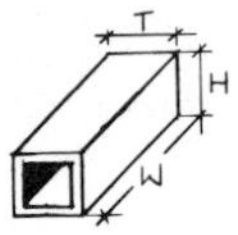	12	5⅓	4
	12	5⅓	8
	12	5⅓	10
	12	8	10
	16	5⅓	10
	16	8	10
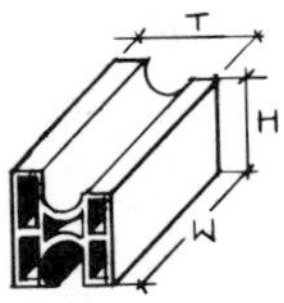	12	6⅔	6
	12	6⅔	8
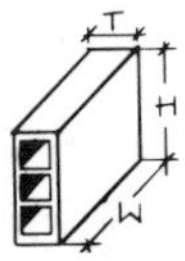	8	8	4
	12	8	4
	12	11	4
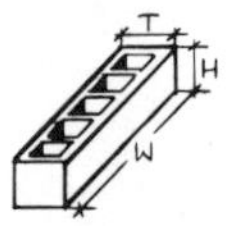	12	5⅓	4
	12	5⅓	8
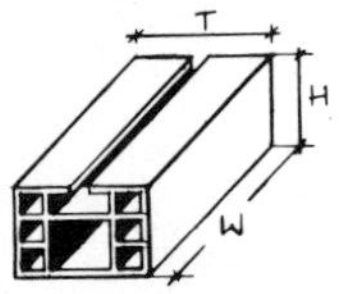	12	8	8
	12	8	12
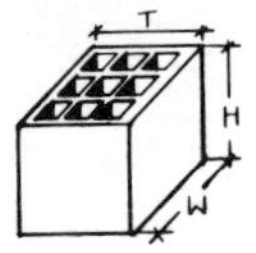	8	8	8

Source: Caleb Hornbostel, *Construction Materials,* Wiley, New York, 1981.

side construction (*horizontal cell*), designed to be laid with the cells in a horizontal plane, or *end construction* (*vertical cell*), designed to be laid with the cells in a vertical plane.

Structural Clay Tile (ASTM C34 and C56):

This tile is used in the structure of a wall where none of the faces is intended as a finished wall surface. Both load-bearing units (ASTM C34) and non-load-bearing units (ASTM C56) are available. Specifications for these units are based on structural properties, including durability and strength. Standard formats and dimensions are given in Table 840-10. Table 840-11 shows the grading system used for both load-bearing and non-load-bearing tile.

Structural Clay Facing Tile (ASTM C126 and C212):

This tile is used in the structure of a wall where a face is intended as a finished wall surface. Both glazed units (ASTM C126) and unglazed units (ASTM C212) are available. Specifications for these units are based on appearance, color, and texture. Standard formats and dimensions are given in Table 840-12, and special formats and dimensions are given in Table 840-13. Table 840-14 shows the grading system used for both unglazed and glazed facing tile.

2.4 Architectural Terra-Cotta (Ceramic Veneer)

Terra-cotta is used as an exterior veneer. Modern ceramic veneer refers to a machine-made product shaped by extruding plastic clay through dies (Table 840-15). Handmade terra-cotta is molded or pressed. Both are custom-made products, available in a wide variety of colors and manufactured to conform to job specifications. Figure 840-5 shows both handmade and machine-made standard shapes and sizes of architectural terra-cotta.

2.5 Brick Unit Positions

Specific terms are given to brick units, depending on their position in a wall structure (Figure 840-3).

2.6 Jointing

Joints that exhibit the highest degree of watertightness are those that are compressed and tooled, thereby forcing the mortar tightly into the joint. Joints that are made with a small shelf on the lower edge should be avoided, as should joints with protruding mortar, because they tend to collect water and are less impermeable (Figure 840-4). Figure 840-5 describes the

TABLE 840-11
Grades of Structural Clay Tile

*Grade**	*Use*
	Load-bearing tile (ASTM C34)
LBX	For masonry exposed to weather or earth and for direct application of stucco.
LB	For masonry not exposed to frost action or earth. May be used in exposed masonry if protected with a facing of 3 in or more of other masonry material.
	Non-load-bearing tile (ASTM C56)
NB	For use in non-load-bearing walls, etc.

* Based on durability.

Source: Adapted with permission from Harold B. Olin, John L. Schmidt, and Walter H. Lewis, *Construction: Principles, Materials, and Methods,* U.S. League of Savings Institutions, Chicago, 1983.

TABLE 840-12
Standard Sizes and Shapes of Load-Bearing Structural Clay Facing Tile*

	Width, in	*Height, in*	*Thickness, in*
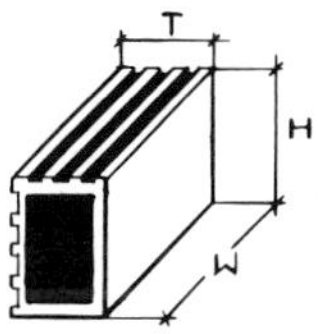 T H W	7¾	3¾	3¾
	7¾	3¾	7¾
	7¾	5 1/16	3¾
	7¾	5 1/16	7¾
	11¾	3¾	3¾
	11¾	3¾	7¾
	11¾	5 1/16	3¾
	11¾	5 1/16	7¾
	15¾	7¾	3¾
	15¾	7¾	5¾
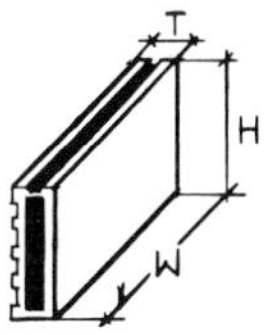 T H W	7¾	3¾	1¾
	7¾	5 1/16	1¾
	11¾	3¾	1¾
	11¾	5 1/16	1¾
	15¾	7¾	1¾
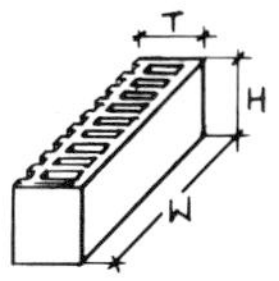 T H W	7¾	3¾	3¾
	7¾	5 1/16	3¾
	11¾	3¾	3¾
	11¾	5 1/16	3¾
Stretchers scored or unscored			
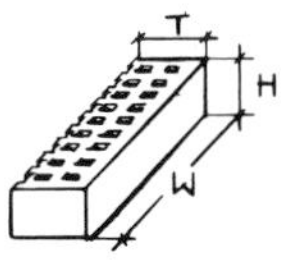 T H W	7¾	2⅝	3¾
	11¾	2⅝	3¾
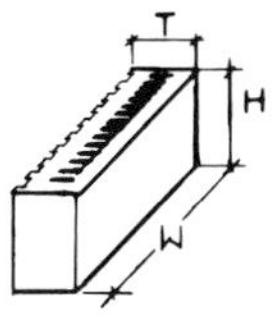 T H W	7¾	3¾	1¾
	7¾	5 1/16	1¾
	11¾	3¾	1¾
	11¾	5 1/16	1¾
Soaps scored or unscored			
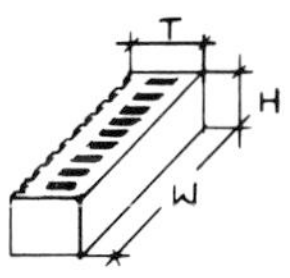 T H W	7¾	2⅝	1¾
	11¾	2⅝	1¾

* Dimensions do not account for mortar joints.

Source: Caleb Hornbostel, *Construction Materials,* Wiley, New York, 1981.

TABLE 840-13
Special Shapes and Sizes of Load-Bearing Structural Clay Facing Tile Other Than Stretchers and Soaps*

	Width, in	*Height, in*	*Thickness, in*
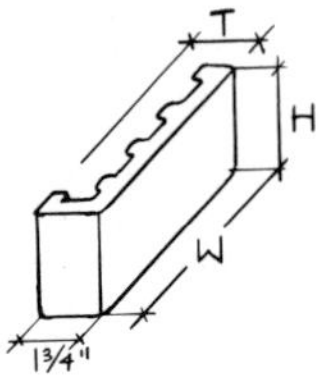 T H W 1¾"	7¾	2⅜	1¾
	7¾	2⅜	3¾
	7¾	5 1/16	1¾
	7¾	5 1/16	3¾
	7¾	7¾	1¾
	7¾	7¾	3¾
	11¾	3¾	1¾
	11¾	5 1/16	3¾
	11¾	7¾	1¾
	11¾	11¾	3¾
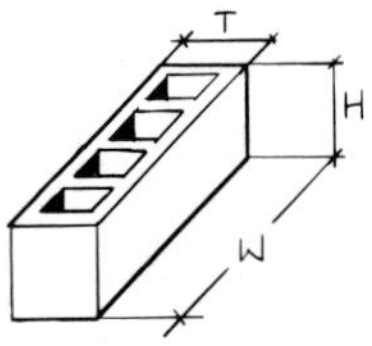 T H W	7¾	2⅜	3¾
	7¾	5 1/16	3¾
	7¾	7¾	3¾
	11¾	3¾	3¾
	11¾	5 1/16	3¾
	11¾	7¾	3¾
	11¾	11¾	3¾
External corners			
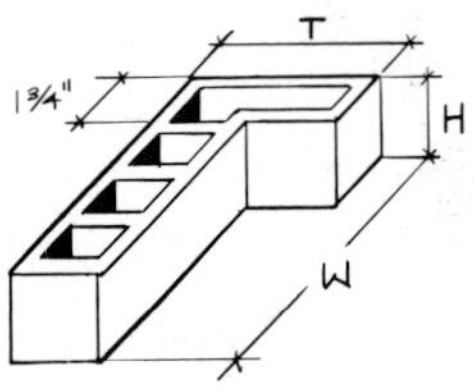 T 1¾" H W	6	2⅜	3¾
	6	5 1/16	3¾
	8	3¾	3¾
	8	5 1/16	3¾
	10	7¾	3¾
Internal corner			
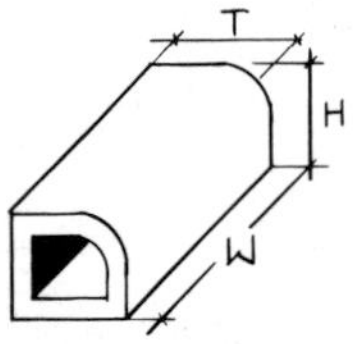 T H W	7¾	2⅜	3¾
	7¾	5 1/16	3¾
	7¾	7¾	3¾
	11¾	3¾	3¾
	11¾	5 1/16	3¾
	11¾	7¾	3¾
	11¾	11¾	3¾
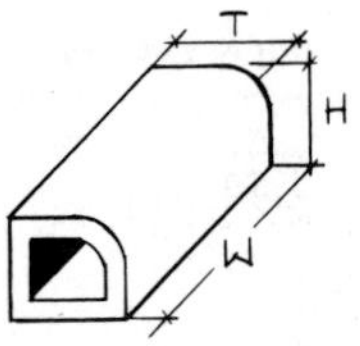 T H W	5¾	5 1/16	7¾
	5¾	5 1/6	11¾
	5¾	7¾	11¾
	7¾	5 1/16	7¾
	7¾	5 1/6	11¾
	7¾	7¾	11¾
	15¾	7¾	3¾
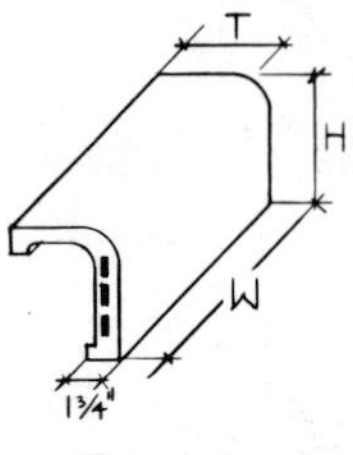 T H W 1¾"	7¾	5 1/16	1¾
	7¾	5 1/16	3¾
	7¾	7¾	1¾
	7¾	7¾	3¾
	11¾	3¾	1¾
	11¾	3¾	3¾
	11¾	5 1/16	1¾
	11¾	5 1/16	3¾
	11¾	11¾	1¾
Cap pieces	11¾	11¾	3¾
	15¾	7¾	1¾
	15¾	7¾	3¾

	Width, in	Height, in	Thickness, in
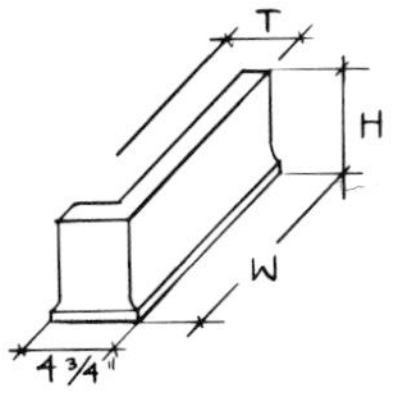	8¾	5 13/16	3¾
	8¾	8½	3¾
	10¾	4½	3¾
	10¾	5 13/16	3¾
	12¾	8½	3¾
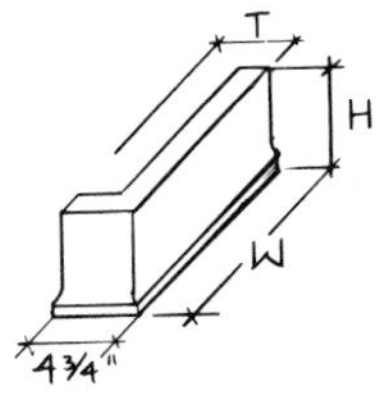	4½	9¾	3¾
	5 13/16	7¾	3¾
	5 13/16	9¾	3¾
	8½	7¾	3¾
	8½	11¾	3¾
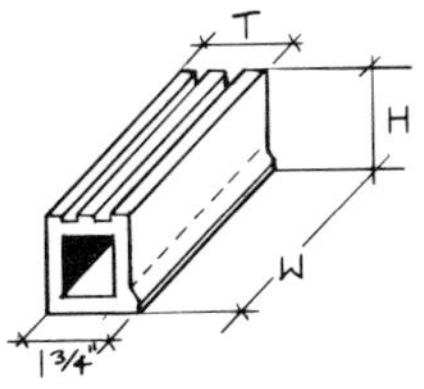	7¾	5 13/16	1¾
	7¾	5 13/16	3¾
	7¾	8½	1¾
	7¾	8½	3¾
	11¾	4½	1¾
	11¾	4½	3¾
	11¾	5 13/16	1¾
	11¾	5 13/16	3¾
Cove bases	11¾	8½	1¾
	11¾	8½	3¾
	15¾	8½	1¾
	15¾	8½	3¾
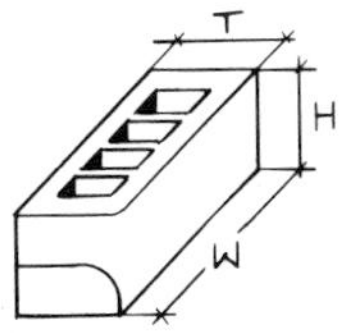	7¾	7¾	3¾
	7¾	5 1/16	3¾
	7¾	10⅜	3¾
Wall end			
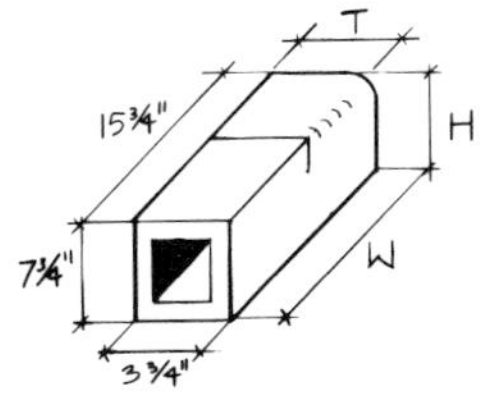	7¾	2⅜	3¾
	7¾	5 1/16	3¾
	11¾	3¾	3¾
	11¾	5 1/16	3¾
	11¾	7¾	3¾
Sill			
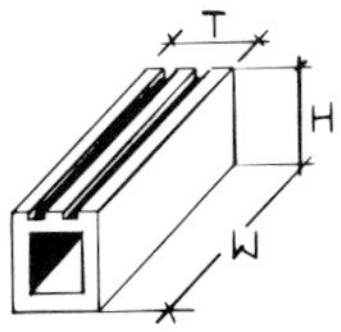	7¾	2⅜	3¾
	7¾	5 1/16	3¾
	7¾	7¾	3¾
	11¾	3¾	3¾
	11¾	5 1/16	3¾
	11¾	7¾	3¾
	11¾	11¾	3¾
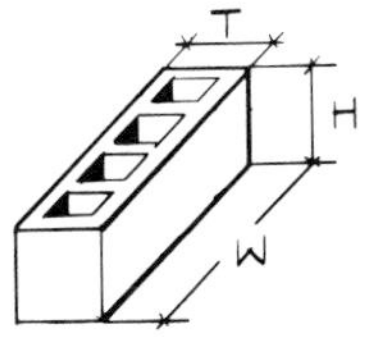	7¾	2⅜	3¾
	7¾	5 1/16	3¾
	7¾	7¾	3¾
	11¾	3¾	3¾
	11¾	5 1/16	3¾
	11¾	7¾	3¾
	11¾	11¾	3¾
Mitres			

* Dimensions do not account for mortar joints.

Source: Caleb Hornbostel, *Construction Materials,* Wiley, New York, 1981.

TABLE 840-14
Grades of Structural Clay Facing Tile

Grade/type	*Use*
	Unglazed tile
Standard	Exterior and interior walls
Special duty	Composed of heavier shells and webs for walls of greater impact. Moisture resistance as well as higher lateral and compressive leads than standard grade
	Glazed tile (ASTM C126)
Select (S)	For masonry with narrow mortar joints (¼ in)
Ground-edge (G)	For masonry where face dimension variation must be very small
Type I*	For masonry where only one finished face will be exposed
Type II†	For masonry where two opposite finished faces will be exposed

* Single-face units.

† Two-faced units.

Source: Robert R. Schneider and Walter L. Dickey, *Reinforced Masonry Design*, Prentice-Hall, Englewood Cliffs, New Jersey, 1980; and adapted with permission from Harold B. Olin, John L. Schmidt, and Walter H. Lewis, *Construction: Principles, Materials, and Methods*, U.S. League of Savings Institutions, Chicago, 1983.

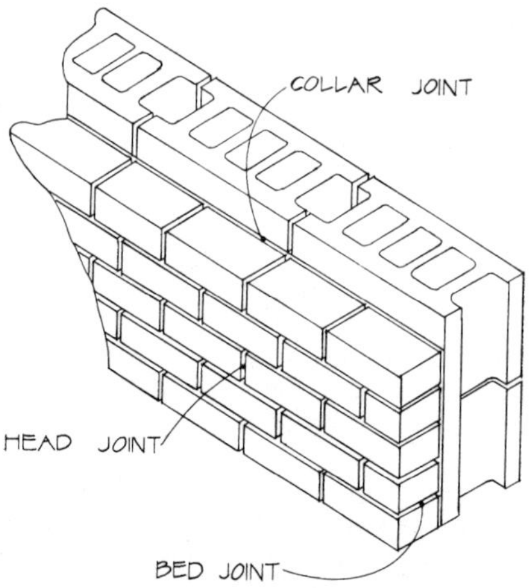
COLLAR JOINT
HEAD JOINT
BED JOINT

Figure 840-5 Terms applied to mortar joints in wall construction.

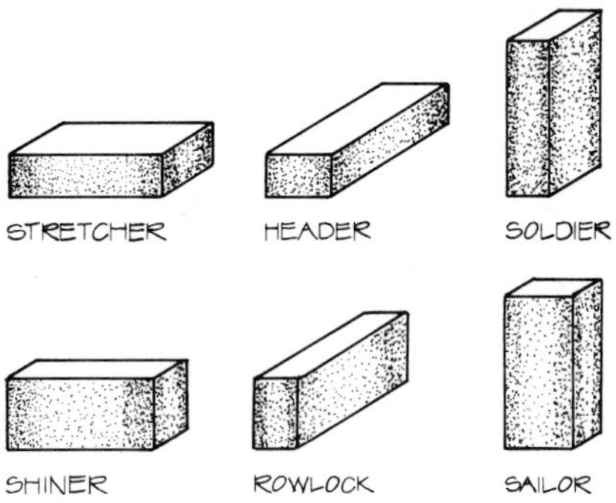
STRETCHER
HEADER
SOLDIER
SHINER
ROWLOCK
SAILOR

Figure 840-3 Terms applied to brick unit positions.

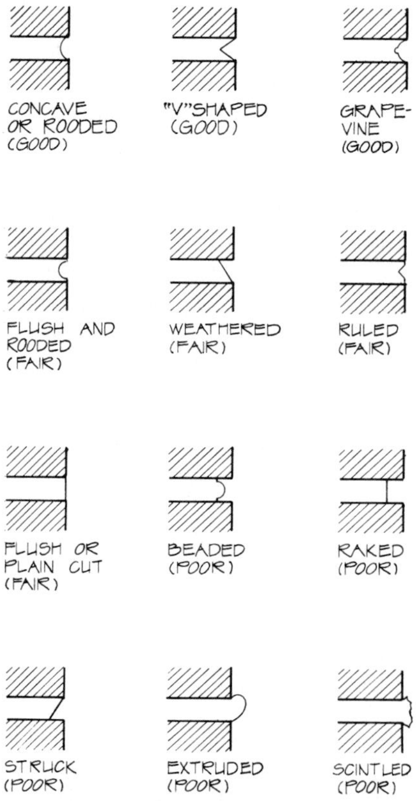
CONCAVE OR ROODED (GOOD)
"V"SHAPED (GOOD)
GRAPE-VINE (GOOD)
FLUSH AND ROODED (FAIR)
WEATHERED (FAIR)
RULED (FAIR)
FLUSH OR PLAIN CUT (FAIR)
BEADED (POOR)
RAKED (POOR)
STRUCK (POOR)
EXTRUDED (POOR)
SCINTLED (POOR)

Figure 840-4 Types of joints (and weatherability).

TABLE 840-15
Standard Shapes and Sizes of Architectural Terra-Cotta*

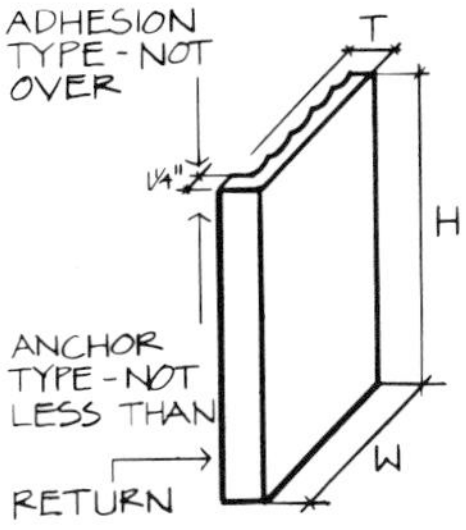
ADHESION TYPE - NOT OVER
T
1/4"
H
ANCHOR TYPE - NOT LESS THAN
RETURN
W

Machine-made extruded terra-cotta	*Width*	*Height*	*Thickness*
Return	5¾ in	2 ft 0 in	3½ in
	7¾ in	2 ft 0 in	3½ in
	11¾ in	2 ft 0 in	3½ in
	1 ft 2¾ in	2 ft 2 in	3½ in
	1 ft 3¾ in	2 ft 2 in	3½ in
	1 ft 5¾ in	2 ft 2 in	3½ in

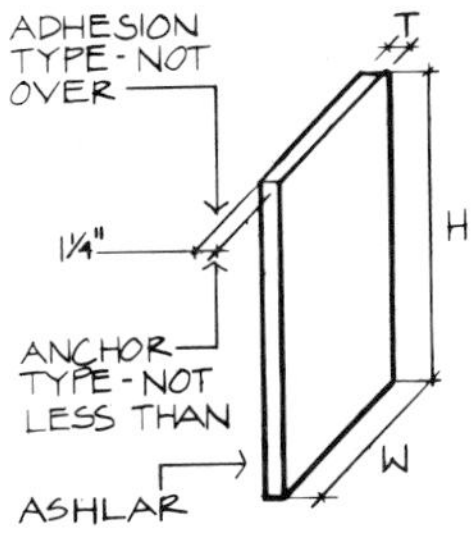
ADHESION TYPE - NOT OVER
T
1¼"
H
ANCHOR TYPE - NOT LESS THAN
ASHLAR
W

Machine-made extruded terra-cotta	*Width*	*Height*	*Thickness*
Ashlar	5¾ in	2 ft 0 in	1¼ in
	7¾ in	2 ft 0 in	1¼ in
	11¾ in	2 ft 0 in	1¼ in
	1 ft 2¾ in	2 ft 2 in	1¼ in
	1 ft 3¾ in	2 ft 2 in	1¼ in
	1 ft 5¾ in	2 ft 2 in	1¼ in

Handmade terra-cotta thickness and web dimensions

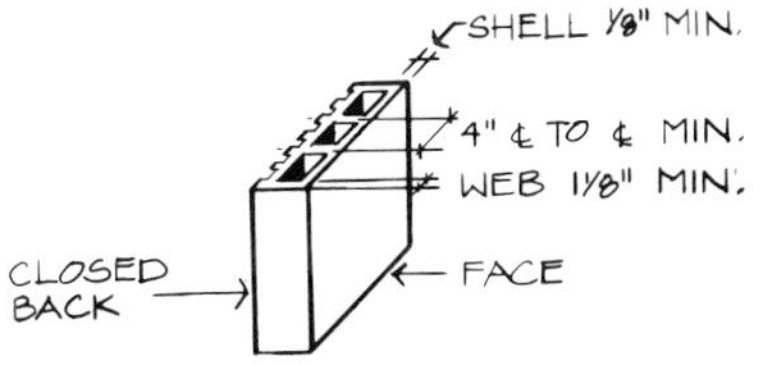
SHELL 1⅛" MIN.
4" ℄ TO ℄ MIN.
WEB 1⅛" MIN.
CLOSED BACK
FACE

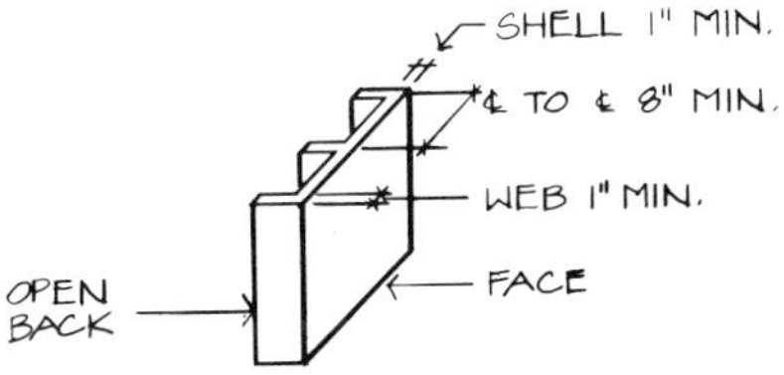
SHELL 1" MIN.
℄ TO ℄ 8" MIN.
WEB 1" MIN.
OPEN BACK
FACE

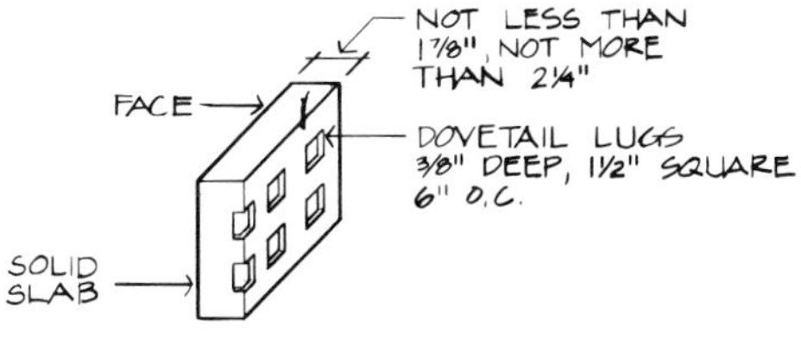
NOT LESS THAN 1⅞", NOT MORE THAN 2¼"
FACE
DOVETAIL LUGS ⅜" DEEP, 1½" SQUARE 6" O.C.
SOLID SLAB

* In adhesion types any one dimension is not to be greater than 30 in, and maximum outer face area is limited to 540 in^2. Anchor type veneers can possess larger dimensions and superficial area.

Source: Caleb Hornbostel, *Construction Materials,* Wiley, New York, 1981.

various terms applied to joints in the construction of brick walls.

2.7 Typical Uses of Clay Masonry Units

Typical uses of clay masonry products are outlined in Table 840-16.

3.0 CONCRETE MASONRY

3.1 General

Classification of Concrete Masonry Units:

Molded concrete masonry units are typically classified into three groups: concrete brick (solid), concrete block (solid and hollow), and special units.

Grades: All load-bearing concrete masonry units are classified into one of two grades (ASTM). Grades are further classified by type. Units classified as *grade N* are suitable for general use, such as for exterior walls, for below- or aboveground work that may be exposed to moisture penetration or the weather, and for interior and backup walls. Units classified as *grade S* are limited to use above-grade, in exterior walls with weather protective coatings, and in walls not exposed to the weather.

Types: *Type* refers to load-bearing and non-load-bearing units manufactured to ASTM specified limits of moisture content. *Type I* units are available in grades N-I and S-I. These are restrictive in terms of maximum moisture content and potential shrinkage. Units not restricted to moisture content are designated *type II*. These are available in grades N-II and S-II.

Properties of Concrete Masonry Units:

The physical properties of concrete masonry units are determined by the properties of the hardened cement paste and the type and gradation of aggregate used in their manufacture. Table 840-17 shows basic properties of concrete masonry units made of different aggregates. ASTM specifications also establish standards for strength and water absorption (Table 840-18). Descriptions of each of these properties follow.

Compressive Strength: Measured by the amount of stress placed perpendicularly to the loading plane, based on gross bearing area, including core spaces.

TABLE 840-16
Typical Uses of Clay Masonry Units

Material	*Walls, function*				*Non-load-bearing*	*Facing*
	Retaining	*Foundation*	*Reinforced*	*Load-bearing*		*Exterior*
			Clay			
Brick						
Building	•	•	•	•	•	
Face-unglazed	•	•	•	•	•	•
Face-glazed			•	•	•	•
Hollow-unglazed	•	•	•	•	•	•
Hollow-glazed	•		•	•	•	•
Thin veneer*						
Prefab panels			•	•		•
			Tile			
Structural clay, wall			•	•	•	•
Structural clay, facing					•	
Terra cotta						
			Sand-lime brick, silicate			
			•	•	•	

* Use of this veneer does not relate to type of wall or its function.

Source: Sweet's Selection Data: Stone and Masonry, McGraw-Hill, New York, 1979.

TABLE 840-17
Properties of Concrete Block Made of Different Aggregates

Aggregate, (Graded: ⅜ to 0 in)						
Type	*Density (air-dry), lb/ft³*	*Weight, lb/ft³ of concrete*	*Weight, 8 in × 8 in × 16 in unit*	*Compressive strength (gross area), psi**	*Water absorption, lb/ft³ of concrete*	*Thermal expansion coefficient, (per °F) × 10⁻⁶*
			Normal weight			
Sand and gravel	130–145	135	40	1200–1800	7–10	5.0
Limestone	120–140	135	40	1100–1800	8–12	5.0
Air-cooled slag	100–125	120	35	1100–1500	9–13	4.6
			Lightweight			
Expanded shale	75–90	85	25	1000–1500	12–15	4.5
Expanded slag	80–105	95	28	700–1200	12–16	4.0
Cinders	80–105	95	28	700–1000	12–18	4.5
Pumice	60–85	75	22	700–900	13–19	4.0
Scoria	75–100	95	28	700–1200	12–16	4.0

* Multiply these values by 1.80 to obtain approximate corresponding values of strength of the concrete strength of unit on net area.

Source: Adapted with permission from Harold B. Olin, John L. Schmidt, and Walter H. Lewis, *Construction: Principles, Materials, and Methods,* U.S. League of Savings Institutions, Chicago, 1983.

Water Absorption: A measure of the density (pores and pore structure) of concrete. Water absorption varies for hollow concrete block in the following way:

1. Four to five pounds per cubic foot (pcf) for the heaviest sand and gravel units
2. Nearly 20 pcf for very porous lightweight aggregate units

All units intended for exposed, exterior walls should have low water absorption properties, and mortar joints should be tooled for watertightness.

Volume Changes (Thermal Expansion Coefficient): Volume changes are due in part to changes in temperature, which primarily affects the aggregate used. Volume changes are more often due to changes in moisture (i.e., units expand when wet and contract when dry). This problem arises when improperly cured units are used, but it can be reduced by using high-pressure steam curing in the manufacturing process and by adjusting the moisture content of the unit in response to the relative humidity at the job site.

Texture: Textures range from very smooth to rough and uneven. Open surface textures help to absorb sound.

Color: A wide range of colors is possible by mixing pure mineral oxide pigments with the concrete before molding it into various units.

3.2 Concrete Block

Concrete block is manufactured in three classes: solid load-bearing units, hollow load-bearing units, and hollow non-load-bearing units.

Solid Load-Bearing Units:

Solid load-bearing units (ASTM C145) refer to those units with at least 75 percent net area in cross section. Figure 840-6 gives formats and dimensions of solid load-bearing masonry units.

Hollow Load-Bearing Units:

Hollow load-bearing units (ASTM C90) refer to hollow units whose face shell and web thickness conform to specific dimensions (as shown in Table 840-19). A nominal modular dimension of 8 in × 8 in × 16 in (200 mm × 200 mm × 400 mm) is produced with ⅜-in (9.5-mm) mortar joints. Half-length and half-height units are also available. Figure 840-7 shows standard formats and dimensions of hollow load-bearing concrete units.

TABLE 840-18
Compression Strength and Water Absorption Properties of Various Concrete Masonry Units

	Compression strength (lb/in.²), gross area		*Water absorption (max. lb/ft³), average of three units*		
			Oven-dry weight, lb/ft³		
Type of masonry unit	*Average of three units*	*Individual*	*Over 125*	*105–125*	*105 or less*
Hollow load-bearing units (ASTM C90)					
Grades N-I, N-II	1000	800	13	15*	18
S-I, S-II	700	600			20†
Solid load-bearing units (ASTM C145)					
Grades N-I, N-II	1800	1500	13	15*	18
S-I, S-II	1200	1000			20†
Concrete building brick (C55) (ASTM C55)					
Grades N-I, N-II	3500*	3000*	10	13	15
S-I, S-II	2500*	2000*	13	15	18
Hollow non-load-bearing unit (ASTM C 129)					
Types I, II	600	500			

* Concrete brick tested flatwise.

† This figure applies to lightweight units weighing less than 85 lb/ft³.

Source: Robert R. Schneider and Walter L. Dickey, *Reinforced Masonry Design,* Prentice-Hall, Englewood Cliffs, New Jersey, 1980.

TABLE 840-19
Minimum Thickness of Block Face Shell and Webs for Hollow Load-Bearing Concrete Units

	Web thickness		
Nominal width of units, in	*FST, minimum in**	*Webs, minimum in**	*Equivalent web thickness, minimum in/lin. ft†*
3 and 4	¾	¾	1⅝
6	1	1	2¼
8	1¼	1	2¼
10	1⅜ 1¼‡	1⅛	2½
12	1½ 1¼‡	1⅛	2½

* Average of measurements on three units taken at the thinnest point.

† Sum of the measured thickness of all webs in the unit, multiplied by 12 and divided by the length of the unit.

‡ This face-shell thickness (FST) is applicable where allowable design load is reduced in proportion to the reduction in thickness from the basic face-shell thickness shown.

Source: Robert R. Schneider and Walter L. Dickey, *Reinforced Masonry Design,* Prentice-Hall, Englewood Cliffs, New Jersey, 1980, p. 70.

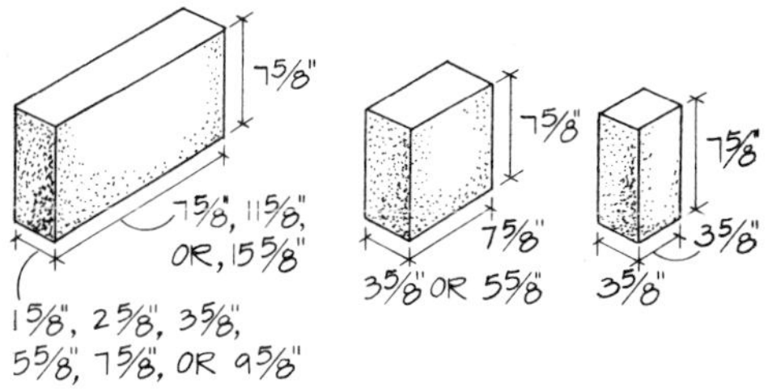
7⅝"
7⅝", 11⅝",
OR, 15⅝"
1⅝", 2⅝", 3⅝",
5⅝", 7⅝", OR 9⅝"
7⅝"
7⅝"
3⅝" OR 5⅝"
7⅝
3⅝"
3⅝"

Figure 840-6 Standard shapes and sizes of solid load-bearing concrete masonry units.

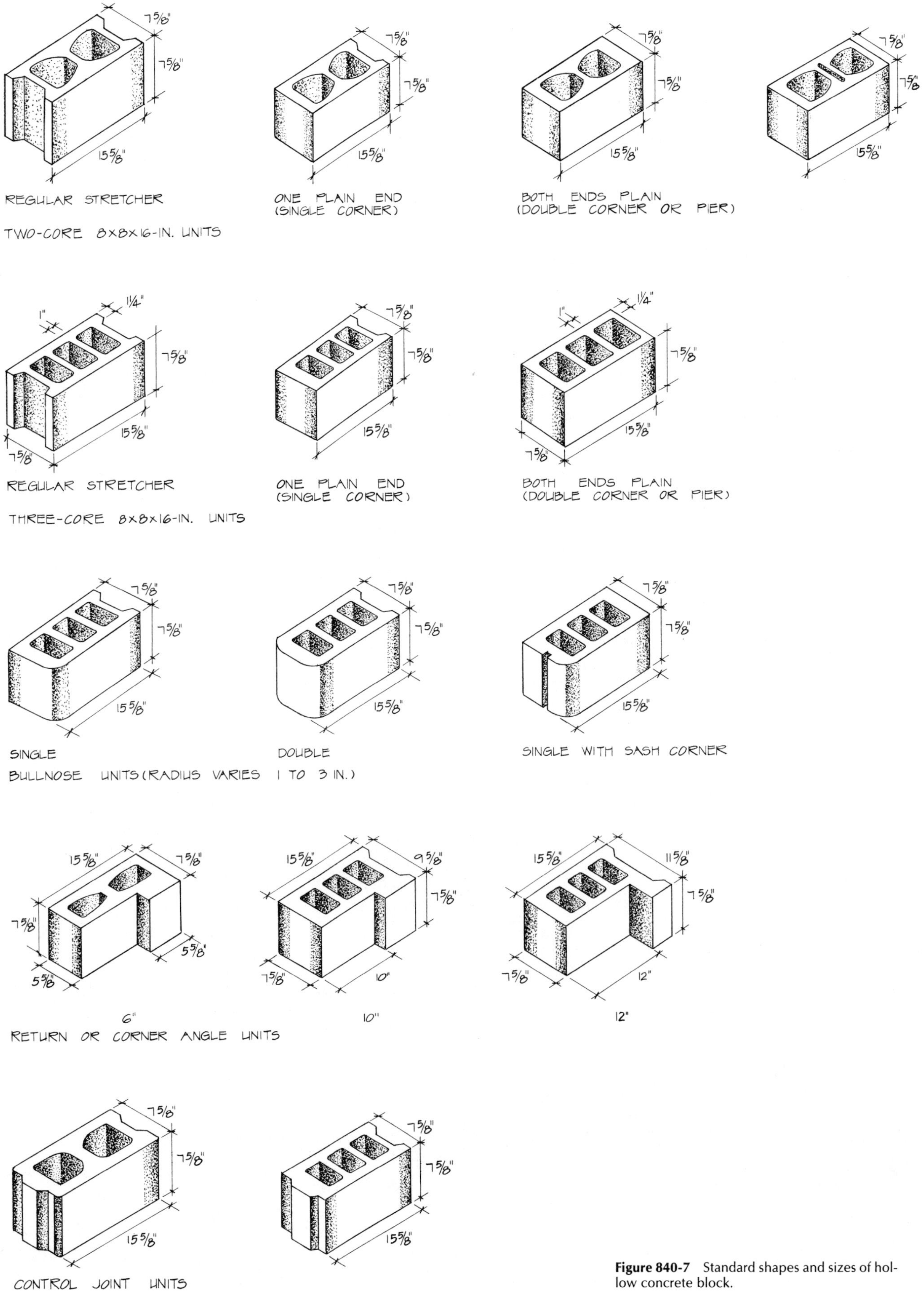
REGULAR STRETCHER
ONE PLAIN END (SINGLE CORNER)
BOTH ENDS PLAIN (DOUBLE CORNER OR PIER)
TWO-CORE 8x8x16-IN. UNITS
REGULAR STRETCHER
ONE PLAIN END (SINGLE CORNER)
BOTH ENDS PLAIN (DOUBLE CORNER OR PIER)
THREE-CORE 8x8x16-IN. UNITS
SINGLE
DOUBLE
SINGLE WITH SASH CORNER
BULLNOSE UNITS (RADIUS VARIES 1 TO 3 IN.)
6"
10"
12"
RETURN OR CORNER ANGLE UNITS
CONTROL JOINT UNITS

Figure 840-7 Standard shapes and sizes of hollow concrete block.

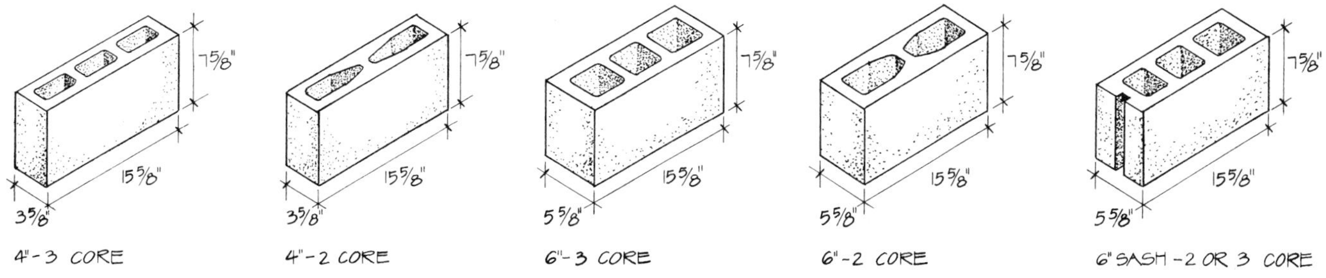
4"-3 CORE
4"-2 CORE
6"-3 CORE
6"-2 CORE
6" SASH -2 OR 3 CORE

Figure 840-8 Standard shapes and sizes of hollow non-load-bearing concrete units (partition units).

Hollow Non-Load-Bearing Units:

Hollow non-load-bearing units (ASTM C129) refer to hollow units whose dimensions are less than the ASTM specifications given in Table 840-19. The typical face shell thickness is ½ in (12.5) mm). Nominal dimensions allow for a joint of ¼ in (6.4 mm) or ⅜ in (9.5 mm), depending upon the actual dimensions of the unit. Figure 840-8 shows standard formats and dimensions of non-load-bearing hollow concrete units. Half-length and half-height units are also available.

Special Units:

Split-face blocks are solid or hollow units that are split lengthwise to produce a rough texture. Units are laid with the split face exposed. Figure 840-9 shows standard formats and dimensions of split-face blocks.

Faced blocks are units with ceramic glazed, plastic, polished, or ground faces. The facing is produced during a separate operation after the blocks are produced.

Decorative blocks are manufactured in different forms with beveled face-shell recesses that produce decorative effects on wall surfaces (Figure 840-10). Figure 840-11 shows various types of screen wall units.

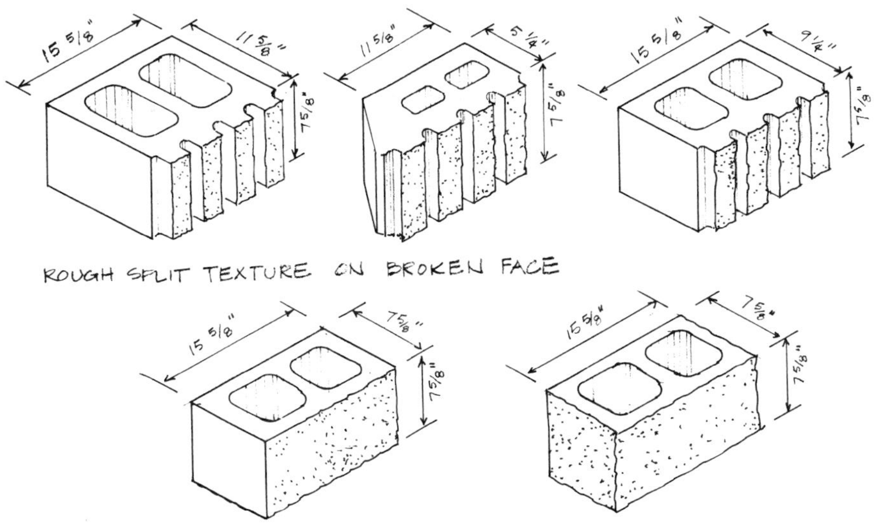
ROUGH SPLIT TEXTURE ON BROKEN FACE

Figure 840-9 Standard shapes and sizes of split-face blocks.

3.3 Concrete Brick (Solid)

Concrete building brick (ASTM C55) is manufactured as a solid unit with or without a shallow depression called a *frog* (Figure 840-12). The frog reduces the weight of the brick and produces a better mechanical bond when laid in mortar. Modular dimensions typically are 4 in (100 mm) in width and 8 in (200 mm) in length, allowing for ⅜-in (9.5-mm) mortar joints.

Slump bricks and blocks are irregularly faced units which vary considerably in height, surface texture, and general appearance (Figure 840-13). A unique irregular wall surface is attained by using slump brick and block.

3.4 Concrete Pavers

Concrete pavers are units of concrete of various shapes and sizes used for paving (Figure 840-14). These pavers possess low absorption and high compressive strength characteristics (Table 840-20) in order to resist breakage from freeze/thaw cycles and to withstand loading from pedestrian and light vehicular traffic. Dimensional tolerances in units of the same pattern must fall within 1⁄16 in (1.6 mm) of the approved unit pattern standard because a proper fit is necessary for the proper transfer of loads through a pavement surface.

Commonly used colors of concrete pavers are red, gray, and brown. Other colors include blues, greens, and other bright colors, but these tend to fade with age. Beveled edges help to hide irregularities in surface and to prevent sucking of sand from joints.

Figure 840-14 shows typical formats and dimensions of concrete pavers, some of which are advertised as *interlocking* pavers. Figure 840-15 shows two types of *grid paving* that allow vegetative growth to occur in the interstitial spaces.

3.5 Jointing

The typical joints and weathertightness principles of brick masonry jointing (2.6 Jointing in this section) are also applicable to joints used in concrete masonry construction.

3.6 Typical Uses of Concrete Masonry Units

Typical uses for concrete masonry units are outlined in Table 840-21.

4.0 STONE MASONRY

4.1 General

Classification of Stone Masonry Units:

Stone is commonly referred to by various names.

1. *Fieldstone:* naturally fractured and weathered masses of varying shapes and sizes.

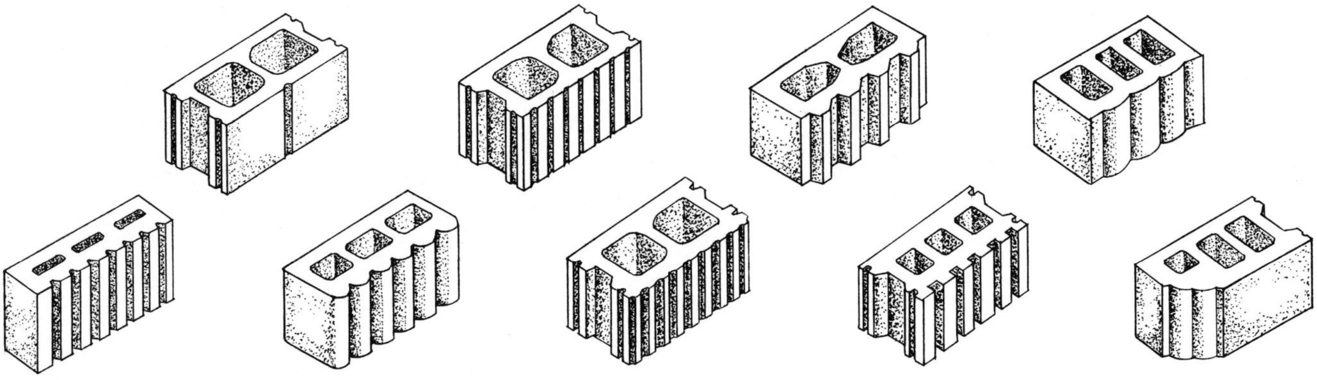

SCORED, RIBBED, AND FLUTED FACES

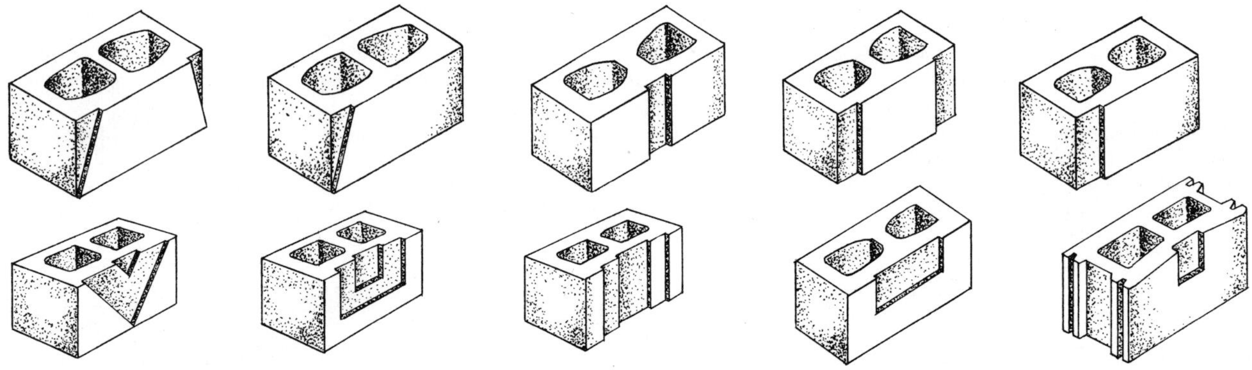

RECESSED FACES

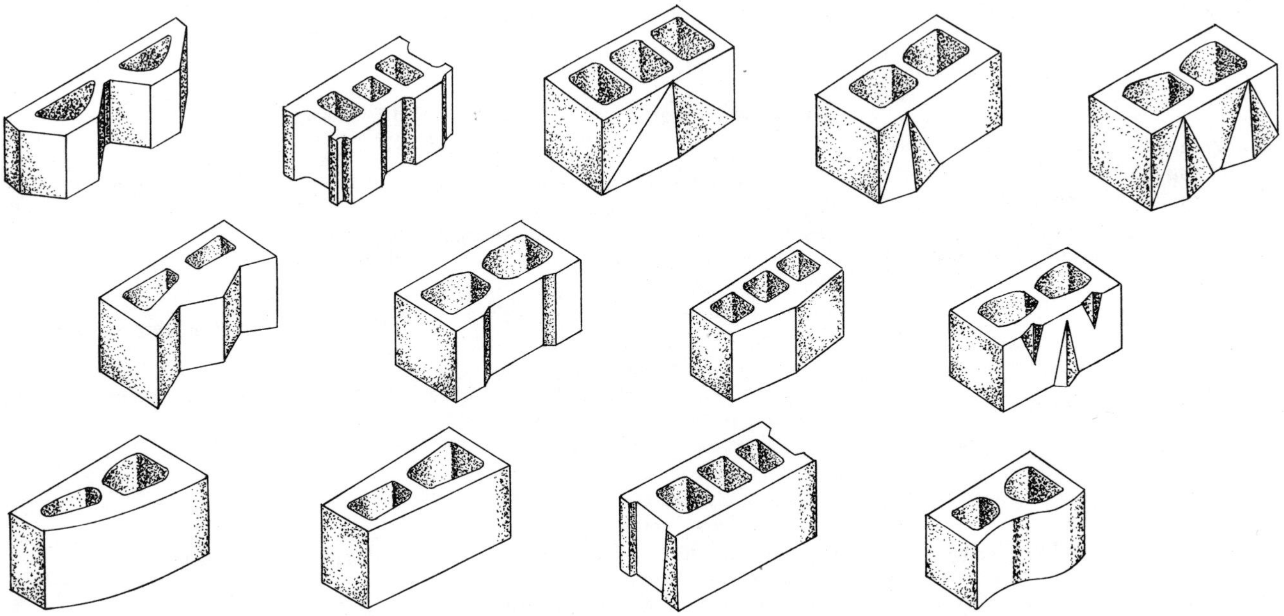

BASKET WEAVE TAPER BLOCK BEVEL SIDING SERPENTINE

ANGULAR AND CURVED FACES

Figure 840-10 Standard shapes of decorative blocks.

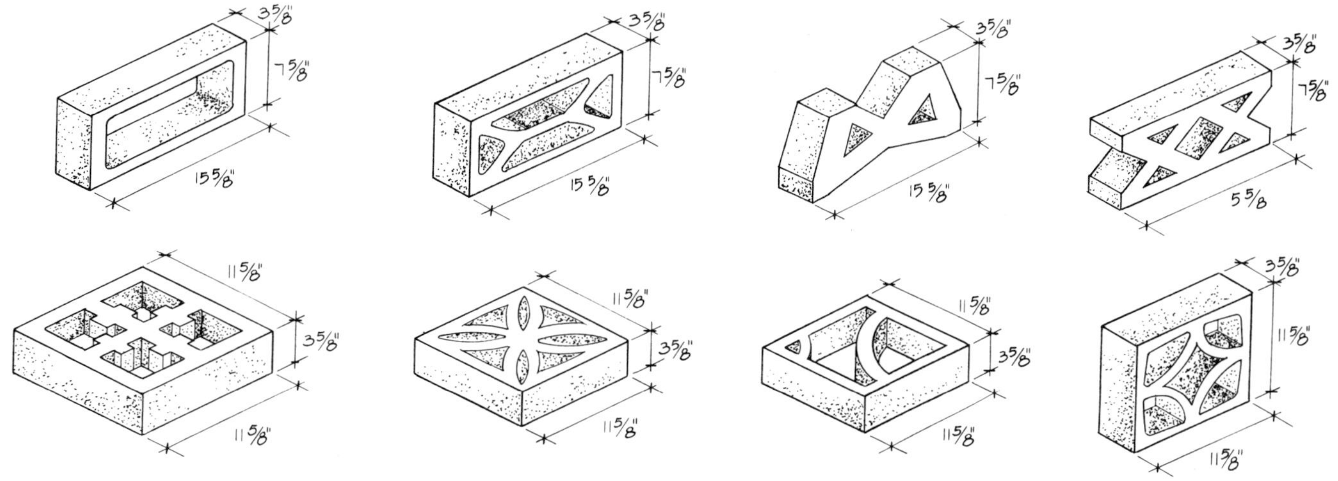
3 5/8"
7 5/8"
15 5/8"
5 5/8
11 5/8"

Figure 840-11 Standard shapes and sizes of screen wall units.

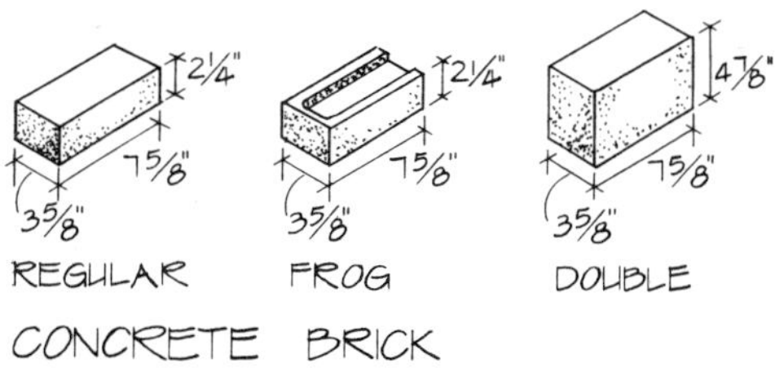
2 1/4"
7 5/8"
3 5/8"
4 7/8"
REGULAR
FROG
DOUBLE
CONCRETE BRICK

Figure 840-12 Standard sizes and shapes of concrete building brick.

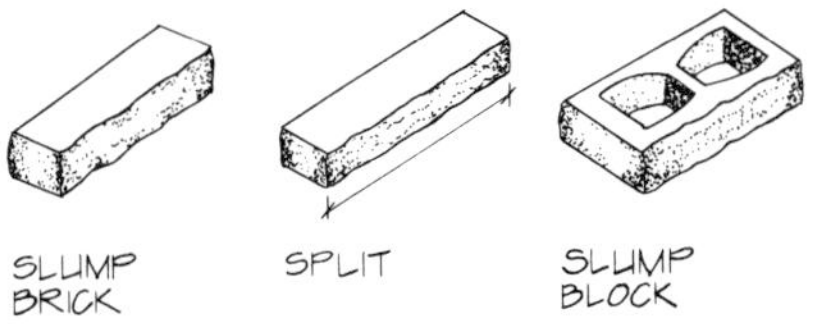
SLUMP
BRICK
SPLIT
SLUMP
BLOCK

Figure 840-13 Standard shapes and sizes of slump brick and block.

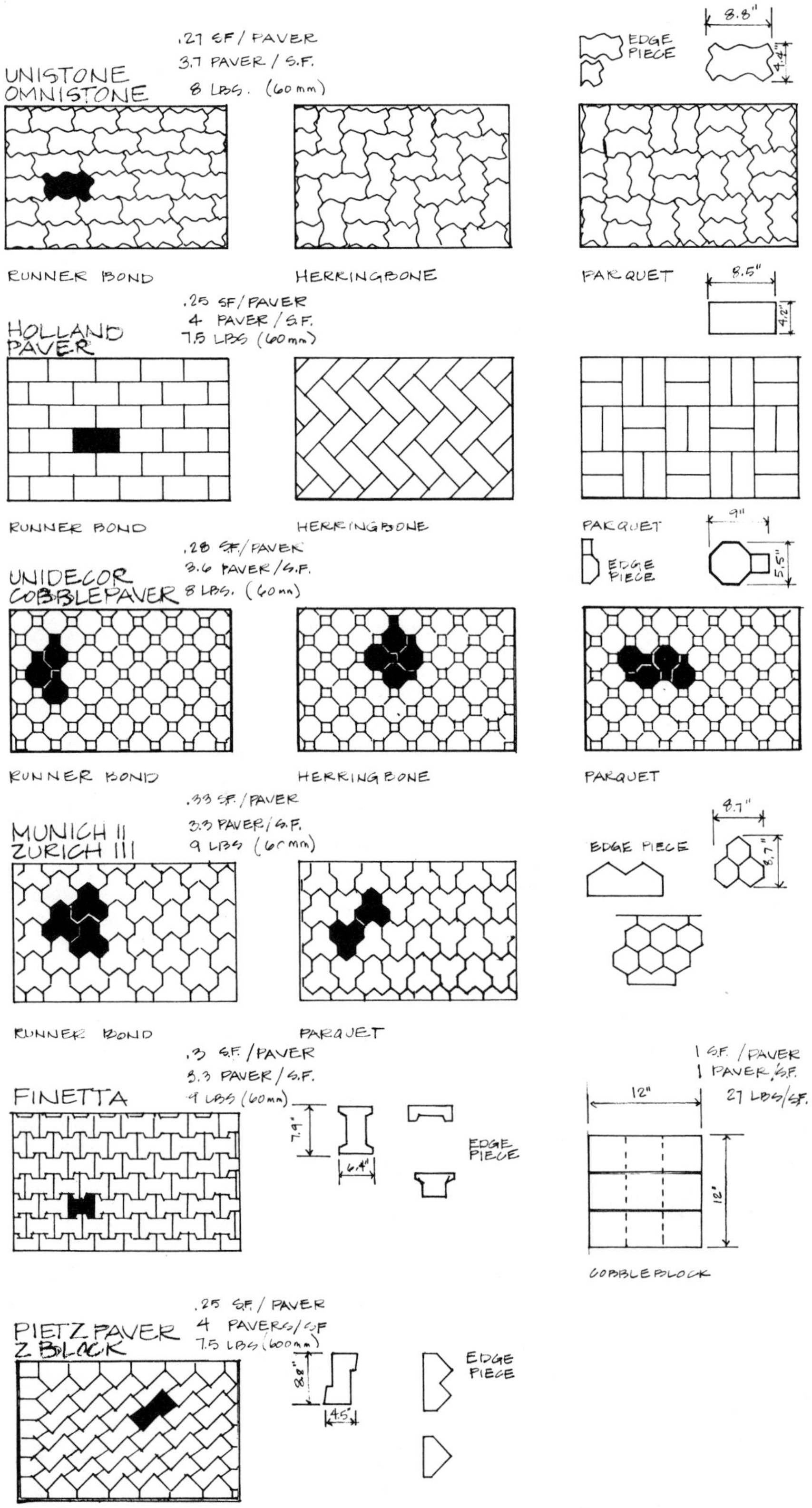
UNISTONE
OMNISTONE
.27 SF / PAVER
3.7 PAVER / S.F.
8 LBS. (60 mm)
EDGE PIECE
8.8"
4.4"
RUNNER BOND
HERRINGBONE
PARQUET
HOLLAND PAVER
.25 SF / PAVER
4 PAVER / S.F.
7.5 LBS (60 mm)
8.5"
4.2"
RUNNER BOND
HERRINGBONE
PARQUET
UNIDECOR COBBLEPAVER
.28 SF / PAVER
3.6 PAVER / S.F.
8 LBS. (60 mm)
EDGE PIECE
9"
5.5"
RUNNER BOND
HERRINGBONE
PARQUET
MUNICH II
ZURICH III
.33 SF / PAVER
3.3 PAVER / S.F.
9 LBS (60 mm)
EDGE PIECE
8.7"
RUNNER BOND
PARQUET
FINETTA
.3 SF / PAVER
3.3 PAVER / S.F.
9 LBS (60 mm)
7.9"
6.4"
EDGE PIECE
1 S.F. / PAVER
1 PAVER / S.F.
27 LBS / S.F.
12"
12"
COBBLEBLOCK
PIETZ PAVER
Z BLOCK
.25 SF / PAVER
4 PAVERS / SF
7.5 LBS (60 mm)
8.8"
4.5"
EDGE PIECE

Figure 840-14 Typical Concrete Pavers. Typical thicknesses include 2⅜ in, 3⅛ in, and 4 in. Manufacturers should be consulted for other shapes and sizes, specifications for installation, and product specifications.

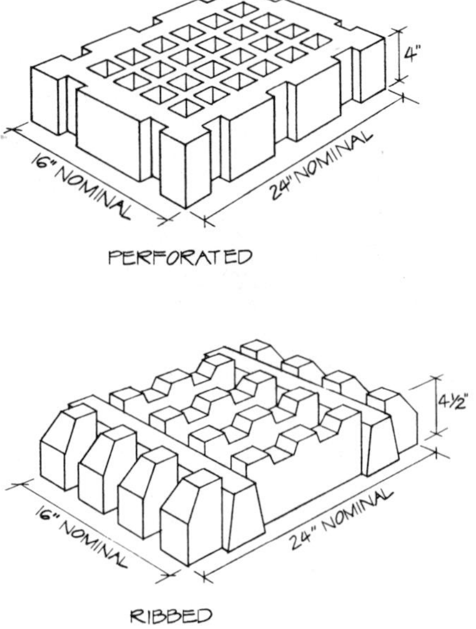
4"
16" NOMINAL
24" NOMINAL
PERFORATED
4½"
16" NOMINAL
24" NOMINAL
RIBBED

Figure 840-15 Grid or grass-filled blocks.

2. *Rubble stone:* irregular stone fragments with at least one good face, from quarrying operations. Usually within dimensions of 1 ft × 2 ft (0.3 m × 0.6 m).

3. *Dimension stone (cut stone, ashlar):* cut at the quarry or mill to specified dimensions and finished. Ashlar is a smaller rectangular dimension stone with flat faces and sawn edges.

4. *Monumental stone:* either rough or finished; used for monuments, gravestones, etc.

5. *Flagstone:* flat thin stones [1 to 2 in (25 to 50 mm) thick], irregular or cut to dimension. Used for paving, flooring, etc.

6. *Crushed and broken stone:* graded and sized. Crushed stone usually varies from ¼ to 2¼ in (6 to 54 mm) in diameter and consists of one type of rock. Used alone or as an aggregate in concrete or asphalt.

7. *Stone dust or powder:* graded particles from a crushing process [¼ in (6 mm) and less]. Commonly used as a surfacing or as a bedding material for pavers, etc.

Properties of Stone Masonry Units:

Important physical properties of common stone types are outlined in Table 840-22.

TABLE 840-20
Specifications for Concrete Pavers (ASTM 938-82)

Average compressive strength, psi	*Minimum compressive strength of individual unit, psi*	*Average absorption (increase in block weight after immersion)*	*Absorption of individual unit (increase in block weight after immersion)*
8000	7200	Not greater than 5%	Not greater than 7%

Source: American Society for Testing and Materials, *Annual Book of ASTM Standards,* Philadelphia, Pennsylvania, 1983.

TABLE 840-21
Typical Uses of Concrete Masonry Units

	Walls, function				
Concrete	*Retaining*	*Foundation*	*Reinforced*	*Load-bearing*	*Non-load-bearing*
Brick					
Common	•	•	•	•	•
Face	•		•	•	•
Block					
Solid	•	•	•	•	
Hollow load-bearing	•	•	•	•	
Hollow non-load-bearing					•
Screen					•
Glazed			•	•	•
Prefab panels				•	•

Source: Sweet's Selection Data: Stone and Masonry, McGraw-Hill, New York, 1979.

TABLE 840-22
Important Properties of Common Stone Types

	Properties						
	Absorption by weight, maximum, %[a]	*Density, minimum lb/ft³[a]*	*Compressive strength, minimum, psi[b]*	*Compressive strength, minimum, psi[c]*	*Modulus of rupture, minimum, psi[d]*	*Abrasion resistance, minimum Ha[e,f]*	*ASTM Specifications*
Granite, all grades	0.4	160	19,000	20,000–36,000	1500	NA[g]	ASTM C615-80 Standard Specification for Granite Building Stone
Limestone							
Category I—low density	12	110	1,800	2,600	400		ASTM C568-79 Standard Specification for Limestone Building Stone
Category II—medium density	7.5	135	4,000	to	500	10	
Category III—high density	3	160	8,000	20,000	1000		
Marble							
Group A	0.75	144		8,000		10	ASTM C503-79 Standard Specification for Marble Building Stone
		to	7,500	to	1000		
Groups B, C, and D		175		23,000			
Sandstone							
Standard—sandstone	20	140	2,000	3,000	300		ASTM C616-80 Standard Specification for Sandstone Building Stone
Quartzite—quartzitic sandstone	3	150	10,000	to	1000	8	
Bluestone—quartzite	1	160	20,000	20,000	2000		
Slate—structural							
Exterior	0.25			10,000	9000		ASTM C629-80 Standard Specification for Slate Building Stone
		NA		to	across grain	8	
Interior	0.45			15,000	7200 along grain		

[a] When tested in accordance with ASTM C97.

[b] Range when tested in accordance with ASTM C170.

[c] Common range of available stones.

[d] Range when tested in accordance with ASTM C99, except for slate, which is tested in accordance with ASTM C120.

[e] Ha refers to the abrasive hardness value which is the reciprocal of the volume of material abraded multiplied by 10.

[f] When tested in accordance with ASTM C241.

[g] Not available or not established in cited ASTM Standard Specifications.

Source: Sweet's Selection Data: Stone and Masonry, McGraw-Hill, New York, 1979.

TABLE 840-23
Common Types of Stone Used in Construction

Common name	Type of stone	Characteristics: Texture	Appearance	Color
Black granite (traprock)	Igneous	Fine to coarse-grained, polished	Generally uniform	Black
Bluestone	Sedimentary	Smooth to rough	Uniform	Blue-gray
Granite	Igneous	Fine to coarse-grained, polished	Generally uniform; some colors have spots, veins, and variations in grain	Wide range of colors; white and black
Limestone	Sedimentary	Fine-grained	Uniform in color	Buff-gray
Marble	Metamorphic	Fine-grained, polished	Uniform or with wide variations of veining and colors	Wide range of colors; white and black
Sandstone	Sedimentary	Rough	Generally uniform	White, gray, yellow, brown, red
Slate	Metamorphic	Smooth to rough	Generally uniform	Blue, gray, green, reddish
Soapstone	Metamorphic	Smooth to rough	Generally uniform	Gray, green, blue
Travertine	Sedimentary	Smooth to rough, also polished	Irregularly shaped pores	Gray, white, buff

Source: Caleb Hornbostel, *Construction Materials,* John Wiley & Sons, New York, 1981.

TABLE 840-24
Grades and Dimensions of Masonry Units

	Rubble, chunk		*Ashlar*			*Panels**		*Flags, pavers**	
	Thickness range, in	*Face dimensions (S.F.) average range*	*Thickness range, in*	*Face dimensions range*	*Rise range, in*	*Thickness range, in*	*Face dimensions, common limits, ft†*	*Thickness range, in*	*Maximum face area (S.F.) range*
Granite, all grades	1/4–1 1/2	1/2–2	4–12	1/2–10 ft²	4–13, 1 1/2 in increments	1 1/4–4 and over	4 × 10	1 3/4–3	4–16
Limestone Category I—low density Category II—medium density Category III—high density	1/2–4	1–5	3 1/2–6	Length: 10–36 in	2 3/16 4 7/8 7 1/2 11 1/2 2 1/4* 5 7 3/4	7/8 2 1/4 3	5 × 14	1 3/4 2 1/2	1–6
Marble Group A‡ Groups B, C, and D§	1/4–3	1/2–4	1/2–2		2 1/2 5 7 3/4	1/2–2	6 × 7	7/8 to 1	1–2
Sandstone Standard—sandstone	1 1/2–5		4	Height: 3/4–14 in Length: 8–48 in		2 1/4–4		1 1/2–3	1–4
Quartzite—quartzitic sandstone		1–4					4 × 10		
Bluestone—quartzite	1–4		4–12		2 1/4, 5, 7 3/4	1 1/2–2		5/8–2	1–10
Slate—structural Exterior and interior						1–1 1/2	4 × 8	1/4–2	Over 4

* Sizes and thicknesses shown are only indicative of some of the sizes and thicknesses generally used and do not imply size and/or thickness limitations. Intended use and size will generally dictate minimum thickness. In all instances consult industry associations or individual manufacturers before making final decisions.

† Larger sizes may be available.

‡ Uniform and good working quality; exterior or interior use.

§ Grades with increasing amounts of faults and more uncertain working quality; mainly for interior use.

Source: Sweet's Selection Data: Stone and Masonry, McGraw-Hill, New York, 1979.

4.2 Common Types of Stone

Table 840-23 lists various types and characteristics of building stone commonly used in construction. Formats, dimensions, grades, and typical finishes for each type are described below.

Granite:

Granite is a hard, strong, durable, impervious, igneous rock with a fine-, medium-, or coarse-grained appearance. Granite is very difficult to finish and the costs can be high. Typical uses include building veneer and stone, pavers, curbing, crushed stone, and granite dust. Grades and dimensions of granite masonry units are given in Table 840-24.

Limestone:

Limestone is composed of particles of calcium carbonate and magnesium carbonate naturally cemented by silica, iron oxide, or lime carbonate. The properties of limestone are highly variable, depending on the type of cementing agent. Limestone is chemically reactive and should not be used in areas of industrial fumes, smoke, or acids, in areas where hard impacts may occur, or in places where oil and grease may contact and readily soil the limestone. Typical uses include building veneer, ashlar or flagstone walls, pavers, crushed aggregate, and limestone dust. Grades and dimensions of limestone masonry units are given in Table 840-24.

Marble:

Marble is metamorphosed limestone that can be polished but is relatively expensive. Grades range from a uniform material with a minimal number of defects and variations (grade A) to grades with increasing numbers of defects, flaws, and working difficulties (grades B, C, and D). Despite the flaws, grade D often has the most beautiful colors. Marble is chemically reactive and should not be used in areas of industrial fumes, acids, or air pollution or where severe weather can be expected. Typical uses include veneer, monumental marble, and crushed marble. Grades and dimensions of marble masonry units are given in Table 840-24.

Sandstone:

Sandstone is composed of sand that has been naturally cemented together. Strength and workability characteristics vary, depending on the cementing agent. The gritty surface of sandstone serves well as a nonslip walking surface. Typical uses include panels, pavers, cut stone, and rubble. Grades and dimensions of sandstone masonry units are given in Table 840-24.

Slate:

Slate is metamorphosed shale that cleaves easily into thin slabs. The material is strong and durable, with high tensile strength, and is typically available in colors of red, purple, green, black, and gray. Typical uses are flagstones for paving or walls, and roofing slate. Grades and dimensions of slate masonry units are given in Table 840-24.

4.3 Common Finishes for Stone Masonry Units

Table 840-25 describes typical finishes and their general availability for various stone masonry units. Note that fine or polished stone surfaces may be slick when wet. Table 840-26 lists the colors of various building stones commonly available.

4.4 Typical Uses of Stone Masonry Units

Typical uses for various stone types are outlined in Table 840-27.

5.0 GLASS BLOCK MASONRY

5.1 General

Classification of Glass Block Units:

Glass block is available both as a solid unit and in hollow core types, including single-cavity and double-cavity. Units can be used for vertical walls or screens as well as for floors, decks, and skylights.

Properties of Glass Block Units:

Glass block units allow reduction of heat transmission, unique surface texture, and transmission of light, but not a clear view. Table 840-28 gives compressive strength and light transmission values for various glass blocks. Consult the manufacturer's specifications for limitations regarding the maximum size that a glass block panel can be constructed.

5.2 Dimensions of Glass Block Units

Single-Cavity Units:

Single-cavity units are the basic glass block unit and are useful where light transmission or diffusion, solar gain reduction, or decorative effect is desired (see Table 840-29).

Double-Cavity Units:

Double-cavity units are typically a single-cavity block with an insert for increased glare and/or heat transmission control (see Table 840-29).

Solid Units:

Solid units are useful where light transmission, strength, and acoustic decibel reduction are desired. Solid units are recommended for use in public areas where vandalism may be a problem. (Table 840-29).

5.3 Installation

Figure 840-16 illustrates the typical method of construction for glass block walls.

6.0 RELATED MATERIALS

6.1 Mortar

Mortar is produced by mixing cementitious materials, clean well-graded sand, and water. Basic functions of mortar are to:

1. Bond units together

2. Compensate for size variation in masonry units

3. Allow use of metal ties and reinforcing as an integral part of the wall

4. Provide color or texture for aesthetic reasons

Types of Mortar and Their Uses:

Mortars are produced in various types, each composed of a unique combination of ingredients and used for a specific masonry task (Table 840-30).

Sand Gradation Limits for Mortar:

Sand has to be mixed according to specific gradation requirements to produce a mortar with smooth workability and proper strength (Table 840-31).

Plastic Properties:

While wet, mortar contains the following important plastic properties:

1. *Workability:* a uniform, cohesive, and usable consistency; resistant to segregation

2. *Water retention:* prevents loss of plasticity and bleeding

3. *Initial flow:* indicates the flow of mortar and is required to be 130 to 150 percent of the flow after suction

4. *Flow after suction:* indicates the flow of mortar after loss of water due to contact with an absorbent masonry unit

TABLE 840-25
Types and Availability of Stone Finishes

Types of stone finishes			
Type of finish	*How made*	*Appearance*	*Major use*
Broached	Produced by planing; the planer cuts out smooth valleys with a rough surface between valleys	Rough-ribbed texture with smooth valleys	Cut stone, panels, and preassembled units
Carborundum	Cut by Carborundum-type planer	Very smooth finish	Cut stone, molded stone surfaces, and preassembled units
Chat-sawed	By using a coarse abrasive during gang sawing	A coarse, pebbled surface	Cut stone, panels, preassembled units, and ashlar
Hand-tooled	By hand with various types of tools	Various types of finishes having handmade appearance	Confined to small, important areas because of cost
Honed	Machine-rubbed with find sand and water	Superfine, smooth finish	Cut stone, molded stone surfaces, and preassembled units
Machine-tooled or tooled	Cut by machine in only one direction, by hand in the other direction	Two, four, six, and eight parallel concave or convex grooves to the inch (25.4 mm)	Types of ashlar only
Plucked	By rough-planing the surface and breaking or plucking out small particles	Rough texture	Cut stone, molded stone surfaces, and preassembled units
Rock-faced	Sawed top and bottom; exposed face, a natural split dressed by machine	Rough, irregular texture	Types of ashlar only
Rusticated	Rustication done by machine, but surfaces that cannot be made by machine are done by hand	Extra deep joint effect	Types of ashlar; cut stone, and preassembled units
Sand-sawed	Gang saw only; no other finishing work	Granular surface containing saw marks, moderately smooth	Types of ashlar only
Shot-sawed	Gang saw, using steel shot for abrasive	Medium-rough pebbled surface to a surface with irregular, rough, parallel lines; brown tones obtained from rust stains from ground steel shot	Types of ashlar only
Smooth machine	By planers	Relatively smooth with a certain amount of texture	Cut stone, molded stone, and preassembled units
Split-faced	Sawed top and bottom; exposed face a natural split when stone is broken	Rough, irregular texture	Types of ashlar only
Textured Light	Cut by machine	Light textures, varying from slight texture to various vertical ribbing, minimum thickness 3½ in (63.5 mm)	Cut stone, panels, and preassembled units
Medium	Cut by machine in one direction	Various types and combinations of vertical ribbing, minimum thickness 3½ in (63.5 mm)	Cut stone, panels, and preassembled units
Rough	Cut by machine in one direction	Various types and combinations of vertical ribbing, minimum thickness 4 in (101.6 mm)	Cut stone, panels, and preassembled units
Thermal	Flame covers surface	Varies depending on grain of stone	Cut stone, panels, paving
Wet-rubbed	Machine-rubbed with fine sand and water	Smooth finish	Cut stone, molded stone, and preassembled units

	Availability of finishes								
Type of stone	*Honed*	*Polished*	*Rubbed*	*Sand-blasted*	*Sawed*	*Split-face*	*Textured*	*Thermal*	*Tooled*
Granite									
Building	•	•	•	•	•	•	•		•
Veneer	•	•	•	•	•		•	•	•
Masonry					•	•	•		•
Limestone*									
Oolitic									
Select	•		•	•	•	•	•		•
Standard	•		•	•	•	•	•		•
Rustic				•	•	•	•		•
Variegated					•	•	•		•
Dolomitic	•		•	•	•	•	•		•
Travertine	•	•	•						
Marble									
Group A	•	•	•						
Group B	•	•	•						
Group C	•	•							
Group D	•	•							
Sandstone†									
Standard					•	•			•
Quartzitic			•		•	•			
Quartzite			•		•	•			
Bluestone	•		•		•	•		•	
Slate									
Structural	•	•	•			•			
Roofing						•			
Specialty stones									
Serpentine	•	•		•	•				
Soapstone	•				•	•			
Expanded stone									
Reconstituted stone	•	•							
Simulated stone‡	•								

* Select, standard, and rustic come in colors of buff or gray and vary depending on grain coarseness. Variegated contains mixture of buff and gray colors as well as grain sizes.

† Certain OSHA regulations have limited the types of finishes available for sandstone; check local availability.

‡ Commonly imitates appearance of variegated rubble stone walls.

Source: Adapted from Caleb Hornbostel, *Construction Materials,* Wiley, New York, 1981; and *Sweet's Selection Data: Stone and Masonry,* McGraw-Hill, New York, 1979.

TABLE 840-26
Colors of Building Stone[a]

	Color ranges																	
			Gray				*Red*					*Brown*						
	White	*Cream*	*Light*	*Medium*	*Dark*	*Black*	*Light*	*Medium*	*Dark*	*Pink*	*Yellow*	*Light*	*Medium*	*Dark*	*Green*	*Blue*	*Blue-grey*	*Purple*
Granite																		
Building	•	•	•	•		•	•	•	•	•		•	•	•	•	•	•	
Veneer	•	•	•	•		•	•	•	•	•		•	•	•	•	•	•	
Masonry	•	•	•	•		•	•	•	•	•		•	•	•	•	•	•	
Limestone																		
Oolitic[b]																		
Select	•	•	•									•	•					
Standard	•	•	•									•	•					
Rustic	•	•	•									•	•					
Variegated[c]				•	•												•	
Dolomitic	•	•	•		•					•		•	•	•			•	
Travertine[d]	•	•										•						
Marble																		
Group A[e]	•	•	•	•	•	•				•		•					•	
Group B[f]		•					•	•		•	•	•					•	
Group C							•	•	•	•				•	•		•	
Group D						•			•	•		•	•	•	•			
Sandstone[g]																		
Standard	•	•				•				•		•	•	•			•	•
Quartzitic	•	•				•				•		•	•				•	
Quartzite	•	•	•	•	•	•				•		•	•		•	•	•	
Bluestone					•											•	•	
Slate																		
Structural					•	•			•						•	•	•	•
Roofing					•	•			•						•	•	•	•
Specialty stones																		
Serpentine					•				•	•		•	•	•	•			
Soapstone			•	•	•												•	
Expanded stone		•	•	•	•	•						•						
Reconstituted stone	•	•	•	•	•	•	•	•	•	•	•	•	•	•	•	•	•	•
Simulated stone[h]	•																	

[a] Color classifications are generalized and may not be identical for all stone types. Colors are dependent on mineral deposits at quarries; not all are available at all quarries.

[b] Appearance grades for oolitic limestone obtained from Indiana Limestone Institute. Oolitic limestone available also from other sources.

[c] Travertine.

[d] Travertine is also classified as marble.

[e] Only group A marble suitable for exterior use.

[f] The most colorful and interesting marbles are in groups B, C, and D.

[g] Certain OSHA regulations have limited the types of finishes available for sandstone; check local availability.

[h] Commonly imitates appearance of variegated rubble stone walls; colors of simulated stone depend on choice of aggregate and epoxy matrix.

Source: Sweet's Selection Data: Stone and Masonry, McGraw-Hill, New York, 1979.

TABLE 840-27
Typical Uses of Stone Masonry Units

	Walls				*Paving and floors*							*Miscellaneous*					
	Retaining	*Other landscape*	*Building*	*Exterior-facing*	*Chips, roofs, and landscape*	*Pebble paving*	*Blocks*	*Flags*	*Slabs*	*Treads, platforms*	*Curbs, coping*	*Aggregate*	*Worktops*	*Ecclesiastical*	*Sculpture*	*Hearths*	*Standard reference specifications*
Granite																	
Building	•	•	•	•	•	•	•	•	•	•	•	•	•	•	•	•	ASTM C615
Veneer	•	•	•	•				•	•	•	•		•	•		•	
Masonry	•			•			•				•						
Limestone																	
Oolitic																	
Category I (low density)			•	•	•	•		•	•	•		•		•	•		ASTM C568
Category II (medium density)		•	•	•	•	•	•		•	•	•	•		•	•		
Category III (high density)	•	•	•	•	•	•	•	•	•	•	•	•		•			
Dolomitic																	
Category I (low density)		•	•	•	•	•				•		•		•	•		
Category II (medium density)		•	•	•	•	•	•	•	•	•	•	•		•	•		
Category III (high density)	•	•	•	•	•	•	•	•	•	•	•	•		•			
Travertine			•	•					•	•				•			
Marble																	
Group A	•	•	•	•					•	•			•	•	•	•	ASTM C503
Group B, C and D			•		•				•	•			•	•	•	•	
Sandstone																	
Standard					•			•									
Quartzitic		•		•													
Quartzite				•				•	•	•		•					
Bluestone		•		•			•	•	•	•	•		•			•	
Slate																	
Structural			•	•				•	•	•			•	•		•	ASTM C629, structural slate
Roofing																	ASTM C406, roofing slate
Specialty stones																	
Serpentine				•					•	•			•			•	
Soapstone									•				•			•	
Lava				•	•	•										•	
Expanded stone																	
Shale					•							•					
Slate					•							•					
Obsidian		•	•	•													
Reconstituted		•	•	•				•		•			•				
Simulated		•		•													

Source: Sweet's Selection Data: Stone & Masonry, McGraw-Hill Information Systems Company, New York, 1979.

TABLE 840-28
Properties of Glass Block Units

	Compressive strength	*Approximate weight (ABS)*	*Light transmission, %*	*Recommended panel size*
Single capacity	400–600	20 psf (4 in) 15 psf (3 in)	20–75	250 ft^2 (4 in) 150 ft^2 (3 in)
Double capacity	400–600	20 psf (4 in) 15 psf (3 in)	28–43	250 ft^2 (4 in) 150 ft^2 (3 in)
Solid	80,000	6 (5 × 5 × 2⅝) 15 (8 × 8 × 3) 6 (3 × 8 × 3¾)	80	Consult manufacturer

Source: Adapted from *Sweet's Selection Data: Glass and Glazing,* McGraw-Hill, New York, 1979.

TABLE 840-29
Dimensions of Glass Block Units

	Type of unit	*Nominal sizes available, in* 4-in thick	*Nominal sizes available, in* 3-in thick
	Single cavity		
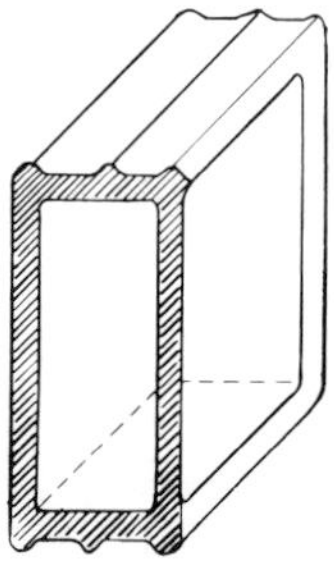 Section through single-cavity clear glass block	Clear	6 × 6 8 × 8 12 × 12	6 × 6 3 × 6 8 × 8 4 × 8 12 × 12 4 × 12 6 × 8
	Clear with reflective coating	8 × 8 12 × 12	Not available
	Light-diffusing patterned	8 × 8 12 × 12	Not available
	Decorative patterned (two-way fluted, semiclear, etc.)	6 × 6 3 × 6 8 × 8 4 × 8 12 × 12 4 × 12	6 × 6 3 × 6 8 × 8 4 × 8 12 × 12 4 × 12 6 × 8
	Double cavity		
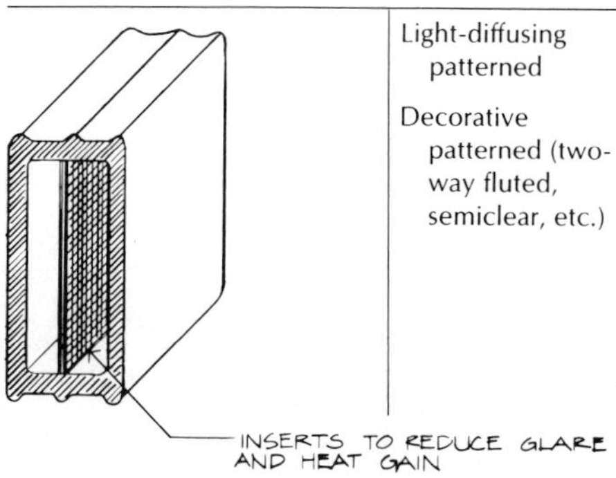 INSERTS TO REDUCE GLARE AND HEAT GAIN Section through double-cavity unit Inserts to reduce glare and heat gain	Light-diffusing patterned	8 × 12 12 × 12	Not available
	Decorative patterned (two-way fluted, semiclear, etc.)	6 × 6 3 × 6 8 × 8 4 × 8 12 × 12 4 × 12	Not available
	Solid unit		
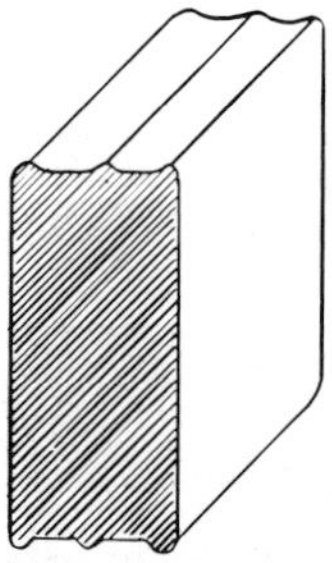 Section through solid block	Clear	5 × 5 × 2⅝ 8 × 8 × 3 3 × 8 × 3¾ round: 6½ diameter × 2	

Source: Adapted from *Sweet's Selection Data: Glass and Glazing,* McGraw-Hill, New York, 1979.

TABLE 840-30
Types of Mortar and Their Uses

Type of mortar	Variations	*Proportions of constituents (parts)* Cement, Portland cement, or blast furnace slag cement	Masonry cement	Hydrated lime	Lime putty	Sand as aggregate	Major uses
M	(1) (2)	1 1	1 —	¼ —		Not less than 2¼ and not more than 3 times the sum of the volume of cement and lime used	Heavy-loaded and below-grade masonry subjected to rigorous exposure. Best for durability and compressive strength
S	(1) (2)	½ 1	1 —	— Over ¼ to ½			Load-bearing partitions and above-grade masonry subjected to severe exposure. Good for tensile bond and lateral strength
N	(1) (2)	— 1	1 —	— Over ½ to 1¼			Load-bearing partitions and above-grade masonry subjected to less severe exposure
O	(1) (2)	— 1	1 —	— Over 1½ to 2½			Interior masonry and above-grade, lightly loaded bearing masonry subjected to exposure in mild climate (above freezing temperature)
Lime		—	—	1 of either hydrated lime or lime putty		3	Interior non-load-bearing work where shrinkage is not important
Nonstaining cement		Nonstaining Portland, 1	—	⅕ of the cement and sand	—	3	Limestone, marble, ceramic veneer, glazed brick, and block masonry work
Nonstaining cement lime		Nonstaining Portland, ½	—	½	—	3	Cut stone and marble, and where nonstaining mortar is required
Nonstaining waterproof cement		Nonstaining waterproof Portland, 1	—	⅕	—	3	Where waterproofing is required (caps, copings, sills, etc.)
Gypsum		Neat-setting unfibered gypsum (retarded 4-hr set), 1	—	—	—	3	Gypsum blocks, decking, etc.
Pointing	(1)	Nonstaining Portland, 1	—	Sufficient amount to make as stiff a mixture as can be worked		2 white	Stonework facing
	(2)	White nonstaining	—	—	1	3	Stonework facing
Grout	(1)	Portland nonstaining, 1; Portland, 1	—	—	—	1	Stone or brick facing; setting bearing plates and railings
	(2)	Portland cement or blended cement, 1	—	0–$\frac{1}{10}$	—	2¼ to 3 times the sum of the volumes of cementitious materials	
Coarse grout	(3)	Portland cement or blended cement, 1	—	0–$\frac{1}{10}$	—	Coarse aggregate 1 to 2 times the sum of the volumes of cementitious materials. Note: coarse aggregate contains fine aggregate plus coarse aggregate	

Source: Adapted from Caleb Hornbostel, *Construction Materials,* Wiley, New York, 1981.

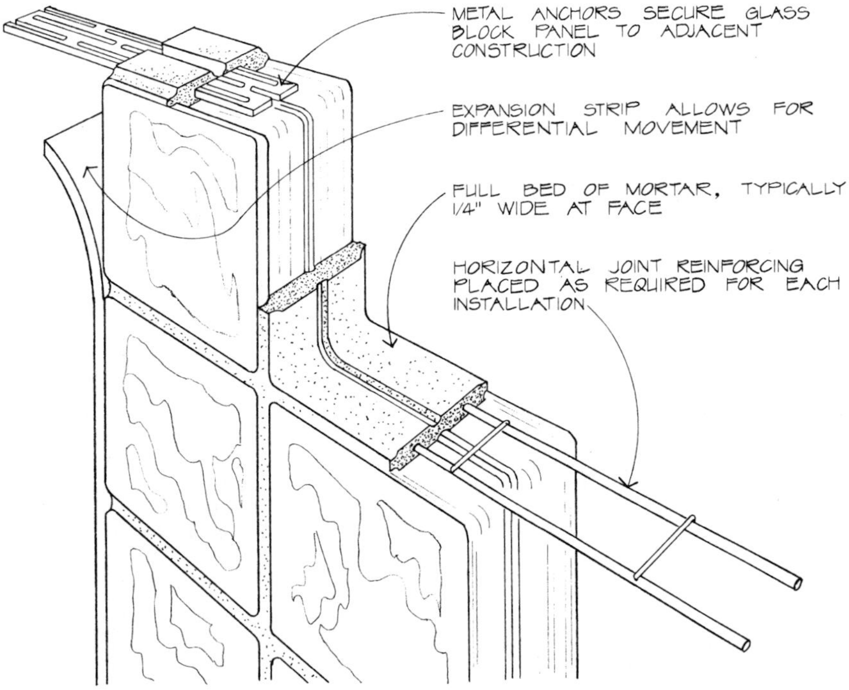
METAL ANCHORS SECURE GLASS BLOCK PANEL TO ADJACENT CONSTRUCTION
EXPANSION STRIP ALLOWS FOR DIFFERENTIAL MOVEMENT
FULL BED OF MORTAR, TYPICALLY 1/4" WIDE AT FACE
HORIZONTAL JOINT REINFORCING PLACED AS REQUIRED FOR EACH INSTALLATION

Figure 840-16 Construction detail for glass block wall.

TABLE 840-31
Recommended Sand Gradation Limits of Aggregate for Masonry Mortar

	Percent passing	
Sieve size	*Natural sand*	*Manufactured sand*
No. 4	100	100
No. 8	95–100	95–100
No. 16	70–100	70–100
No. 30	40–75	40–75
No. 50	10–35	20–40
No. 100	2–15	10–25
No. 200	—	0–10

Source: Adapted from Jot Carpenter (ed.), *Handbook of Landscape Architectural Construction,* The Landscape Architectural Foundation, McLean, Virginia, 1976; and The American Society for Testing and Materials, *Annual Book of ASTM Standards,* Philadelphia, Pennsylvania, 1983.

Hardened Properties:

Once hardened, mortar needs to possess the following properties to provide a strong, watertight, durable wall:

1. *Bond strength:* this is the most important property of hardened mortar and is affected as follows:

a. As the air content is increased, the bond strength decreases.

b. As the flow increases, the bond strength increases.

c. As the lapsed time between the spreading of mortar and the laying of units increases, the bond strength decreases.

2. *Compressive strength:* depends upon the amount of portland cement in the mix.

3. *Volume change:* influences the amount of water penetration through walls and is dependent upon good materials, workmanship, and design.

4. *Rate of hardening:* the speed at which mortar develops resistance to indentation and crushing. A consistent rate of hardening allows tooling of the joints at the same degree of hardness to obtain uniform joint finishes.

Color Additives:

Mortar is colored either by the use of colored aggregate or by pigments. Pigments must be fine enough to disperse thoroughly, impart the desired color, and not react with the mortar ingredients. Iron, manganese oxides, chromium oxides, carbon black, and ultramarine blue may be used successfully. The use of organic colors, such as Prussian blue, cadmium, lithopone, zinc chromate, and lead chromate should be avoided. The maximum permissible quantities of metallic oxide pigments are typically 10 to 15 percent of the cement content by weight. Carbon black should be limited to 2 to 3 percent of the cement content by weight.

6.2 Types of Reinforcement

The types of reinforcement used in masonry construction include wire reinforcement, wall ties, anchors, dowels, and reinforcing bars. Table 840-32 shows typical configurations of wire reinforcement. (Reinforcing bars are described in more detail in Section 830: Concrete.) For masonry reinforcement, the spacing and sizes of the masonry units need to be determined in order to select the proper reinforcement.

The metal products should be corrosion-resistant to avoid deterioration and staining. Heavily galvanized or asphalt-coated steel as well as stainless-steel devices are available. Care must be exercised

TABLE 840-32
Types of Wire Reinforcement

Type and use	*Ladder configurations*	*Truss configurations*
Two-wire ■ Horizontal reinforcement of single wythe wall ■ Continuous rigid tie for composite or cavity walls ■ Reinforcement of stacked bond walls	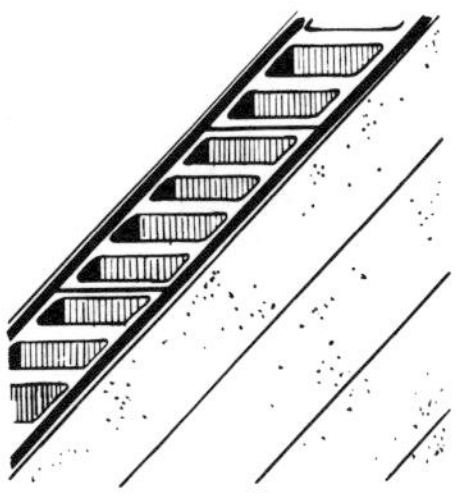	
Three-wire ■ Horizontal reinforcement of one wythe of composite or cavity wall where rigid anchorage of second wythe is required ■ Continuous rigid tie system for cavity and/or composite walls	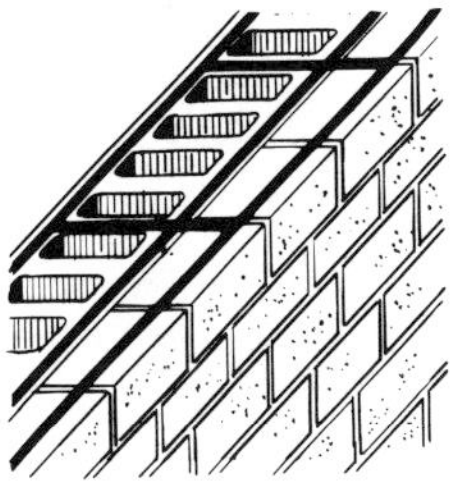	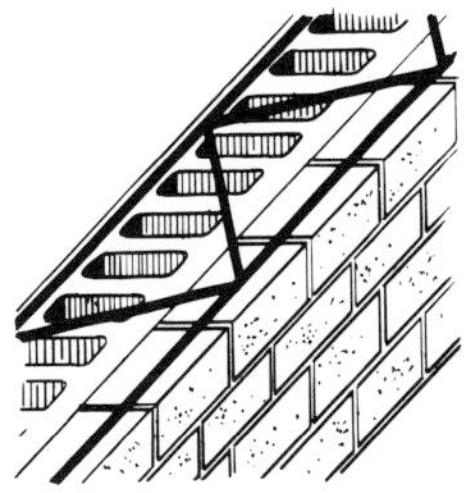
Four-wire ■ Horizontal reinforcement of each wythe of a composite or cavity wall where rigid anchorage of second wythe is required ■ Reinforced masonry walls in heavy seismic zones	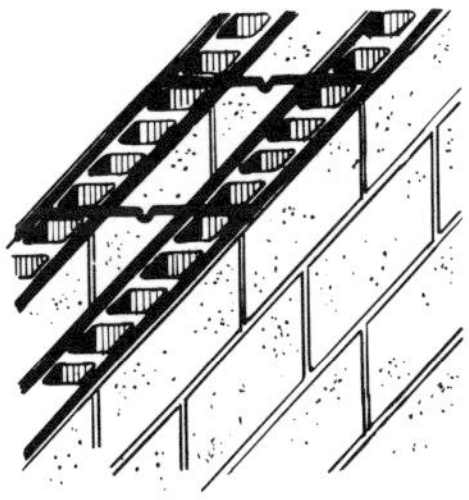	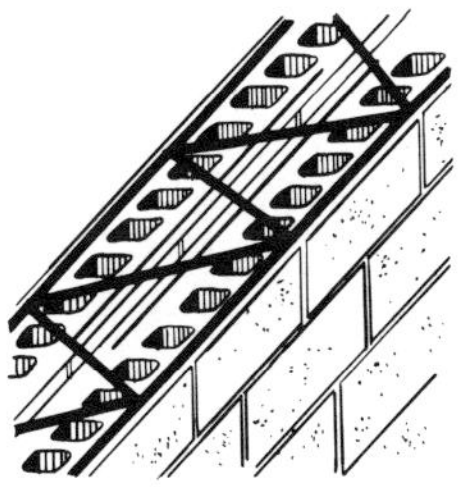
Tab ■ Horizontal reinforcement of one wythe of composite or cavity wall where flexible anchorage of second wythe is required	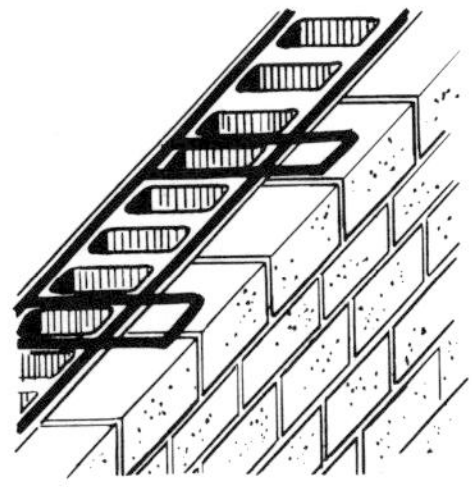	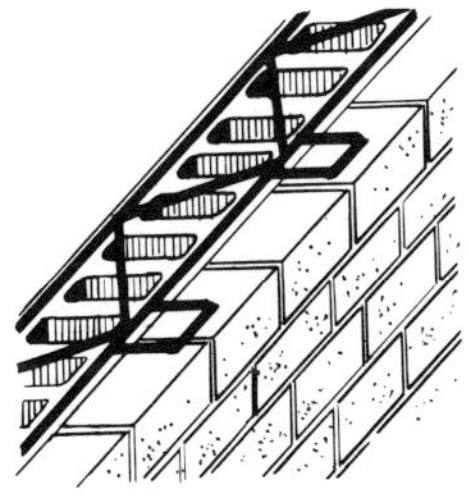
Adjustable ■ Horizontal reinforcement of one wythe of a composite or cavity wall where adjustment of tie to second wythe is required		

Notes: 1. Actual width of joint reinforcing is 2 in less than nominal wall width. 2. Different designs are available from various manufacturers. 3. Reinforcing is typically available for wall thicknesses of 3, 4, 6, 8, 10, 12, 13, 14 and 16 in.

Source: Sweet's Selection Data: Stone and Masonry, McGraw-Hill, New York, 1979.

TABLE 840-33
Common Materials Used for Cleaning Masonry

	Surfaces								Problems							Application notes	Remarks
													Environmental Hazard				
	Porous	Hard	Soft	Decorated/carved	Rough	Smooth	Polished	Light colored	Dark colored	Erosion and abrasion	Cause other stains	Damage other materials	Low	Medium	High		▪ Mortar and joints should be in good condition. ▪ Cleaning should occur only after all restoration is complete. ▪ Make sample cleaning tests. ▪ Protect against possible damage to adjacent materials, environment.
Water																	
Low pressure		•	•			•	•	•	•		•	•				▪ Gentle, safe to surface ▪ Not effective for heavy staining	▪ Generally safest and least expensive type of method ▪ Do not use in cold weather. ▪ Chemical salts present in masonry may react with water and form stains. ▪ Provide for disposal of water.
Medium-high pressure		•				•	•	•	•		•			•		▪ Pressure can cause damage ▪ Generates large volume of water	
Steam		•	•	•	•	•	•	•	•					•		▪ Generally cleans most structures. Especially good on rough surfaces and buildings with varied surfaces.	
Chemical																	
Acids		•				•			•		•	•			•	▪ Don't use on high-lime-content stones and mortars, or on lightcolored, glazed, or polished masonry.	▪ Generally contain water in base mixture and in rinse ▪ Can create all of the problems of plain water as well as: Discoloration Damage to plant and animal life Damage to adjacent materials, e.g., metals, glass
Cleansers, detergents	•				•	•			•		•			•		▪ Many common household cleansers can be used.	
Proprietary compounds		•	•													▪ Consult manufacturer's literature for specific product recommended for various masonry types.	
Steam and chemicals		•	•	•	•	•	•	•	•			•		•		▪ Takes off heavy applied stains that simple steam cleaning won't remove	
Mechanical																	
Sand blasting		•			•			•	•	•		•			•	▪ Don't use on polished surfaces or detailed carvings. ▪ Choice available as to type of abrasive and amount of pressure	▪ Generally better for heavier staining ▪ Potentially damaging due to: Dust Surface erosion and need to preserve or weatherproof masonry Abrasion of adjacent surfaces
Sanding discs, grinders		•			•					•		•			•	▪ Removes outer surface. Don't use on polished or carved surfaces.	
Wet sand		•								•		•				▪ Less abrasive than blasting or grinding ▪ Eliminates dust	
Wet aggregate		•	•		•	•		•	•			•		•		▪ Contains a silica-free friable aggregate to lessen abrasion	

Source: Sweet's Selection Data: Stone and Masonry, McGraw-Hill, New York,1979.

TABLE 840-34
Standard Methods of Stain Removal

	Water			*Chemical*				*Mechanical*				*Hand*		*Remarks*
	Low pressure	*High pressure*	*Steam*	*Acid*	*Detergents, cleaners*	*Proprietary compounds*	*Chemicals with steam*	*Sanding discs, grinders*	*Wet sand*	*Wet aggregate*	*Sand blasting*	*Dry brush*	*Chisel*	■ Test masonry before cleaning. ■ Chemical methods use H_2O often in mixture and always in rinse. ■ With acid, do entire surface to keep color uniform.
Dirt, smoke Pollutants	•	•	•	•	•	•	•	•	•	•	•			■ See chart on general cleaning for evaluation
Oil, tar					•	•	•							
Efflorescence (Bloom)	•			•	•	•						•		■ Dilute HCL acid used. Rinse with H_2O. Do not use on light-colored, soft, sandy brick.
Green stains Vanadium	•				•	•								■ May appear after cleaning with acid to remove efflorescence
Brown stains Manganese				•		•								
White bleed $CaCo_3$		•				•			•					
Rust				•	•	•								
Paint Graffiti						•	•	•	•	•	•	•		■ Fresh paint removed with prop. compound. Old paint requires mechanical method or steam with chemicals.
Organic stains Plant growth, foods, etc.				•	•	•	•							■ Most removed with bleach or oxalic acid. See NCMA-43.
Mortar spatter												•	•	
Unknown stains				•										■ Test for organic material with sulfuric acid.

Source: Sweet's Selection Data: Stone and Masonry, McGraw-Hill, New York, 1979.

when selecting metals for anchors so as to avoid galvanic action.

7.0 CLEANING MASONRY

The appropriateness of using various processes to clean masonry depends upon the nature and surface of the material, as well as upon the inherent cleaning action of each particular process (Table 840-33). The nature of particular stains can warrant the use of specific cleaning processes (Table 840-34). Sandblasting is a process that should never be used to clean masonry, for masonry that is sandblasted is subject to rapid deterioration.

GLOSSARY

Backup: The part of the masonry wall behind the exterior facing.

Batter: The process of recessing or sloping a wall back in successive courses; the opposite of corbel.

Bond: *Structural bond* refers to tying a masonry wall together by lapping units one over another or by connecting them with metal ties. *Tensile bond* refers to adhesion between the mortar and masonry units or their reinforcement. *Pattern bond* refers to patterns formed by the exposed faces of units.

Corbel: A shelf or ledge formed by projecting successive courses of masonry out from the face of the wall.

Efflorescence: A white powdery substance composed of soluble salts carried to the wall surface by the movement and consequent evaporation of water.

Parging: The application of mortar to the face or back of a masonry, sometimes called *back-plastering.*

Pointing: Troweling mortar into a joint after the masonry unit is laid.

Toothing: Projecting brick or block in alternate courses to provide for a bond with the adjoining masonry that will be laid later.

Tuck pointing: Involves refilling mortar joints that have been cut or have fallen out of existing masonry.

INDUSTRY ASSOCIATIONS AND AGENCIES

Associations

Association for Preservation Technology (APT)
Ottawa, Ontario, Canada

Brick Institute of America (BIA)
Reston, Virginia

Building Stone Institute (BSI)
New York, New York

Facing Tile Institute (FTI)
Washington, D.C.

International Masonry Institute (IMI)
Washington, D.C.

National Concrete Masonry Association (NCMA)
Herndon, Virginia

National Crushed Stone Association (NCSA)
Washington, D.C.

National Sand and Gravel Association (NSGA)
Silver Spring, Maryland

National Terrazzo and Mosaic Association (NTMA)
Leesburg, Virginia

Institutes and Agencies

American National Standards Institute (ANSI)
New York, New York

Construction Specifications Institute (CSI)
Washington, D.C.

National Bureau of Standards (NBS)
Washington, D.C.

REFERENCES

Callender, John H. (ed.). *Time-Saver Standards for Architectural Design Data,* 6th ed., McGraw-Hill, New York, 1982.

Hornbostel, Caleb, D.P.L.G., R.A. *Construction Materials,* Wiley, New York, 1981.

McGraw-Hill Information Systems. *Sweet's Selection Data: Cement and Concrete,* McGraw-Hill, New York, annual.

Principles of Clay Masonry Construction, Brick Institute of America, Washington, DC.

Ramsey/Sleeper, *Architectural Graphic Standards,* 7th ed., Robert Packard (ed.). Wiley, New York, 1981.

Randall, Frank A., Jr., and William C. Panarese. *Concrete Masonry Handbook for Architects, Engineers, Builders,* Portland Cement Association, Skokie, IL, 1976. ■

section 850: Wood

CREDITS

Section Editor: Charles W. Harris
Technical Writer: Tobias Dayman
Research Assistant: Krisan Osterby-Benson

Reviewers:

Robert Fager
Sasaki Associates, Inc.
Watertown, Massachusetts

Laurence Zuelke
The Architects Collaborative, Inc.
Cambridge, Massachusetts

CONTENTS

1.0 INTRODUCTION

1.1 General

This section provides basic information on lumber and the proper use of wood in outdoor environments, focusing primarily on softwoods because of their inherent resistance to decay out-of-doors. It does not include information on techniques of construction.

Other sections, such as 460: Wood Decks and Boardwalks, and 470: Pedestrian Bridges, focus on issues of design and specific techniques of construction when using wood as a material. Section 460: Wood Decks and Boardwalks, includes further information on lumber, as well as tables and formulas for sizing load-bearing members. Sections 460: Wood Decks and Boardwalks, and 860: Metals, include information on hardware and fasteners used in wood construction.

1.2 Important Properties of Wood

Certain properties of wood are important to understand before selecting a wood material for any given purpose.

Moisture Content:

Moisture Content (MC) refers to the amount of water contained in a wood member and is usually expressed as a percentage relative to the weight of oven-dried wood (at 0 percent MC). Unseasoned (i.e., *green*) wood has a very high moisture content that is lowered during the process of seasoning, either by air drying or by kiln drying.

Lumber is typically seasoned to a moisture content of about 15 to 19 percent, which improves the strength of the wood member; reduces shrinkage, checking, and warpage in service; provides less susceptibility to fungal attack; and improves the ability of the wood member to receive pressure preservative treatments.

Kiln-dried lumber refers to wood that has been dried in a kiln under controlled heat and temperature to achieve a desired moisture content. Such seasoning is intended for appearance grades of lumber where dimensional stability is important. The term *kiln-dried* stamped on individual wood members is always accompanied by a moisture content percentage. Typical industry standards are 6 to 12 percent in finish lumber and a maximum of 15 to 19 percent in common yard lumber.

Air-dried lumber refers to wood that has been dried by simple exposure to the atmosphere. Most lumber is air-dried. The moisture content of lumber completely air-dried is typically 12 to 15 percent, although in arid regions it may be as low as 6 percent and in humid regions as high as 24 percent. A complete air drying of large timbers is usually impractical. Some shrinkage after installation should be expected.

At the time of surfacing, lumber up to 5 in thick is graded and marked by its moisture content according to the folowing conventions:

1. *S-GRN* means that the lumber has a moisture content greater than 19 percent.

2. *S-DRY* means that the lumber has a maximum moisture content of 19 percent.

3. *MC15* or *KD* (used by some grading agencies) means that the lumber has a maximum moisture content of 15 percent.

Equilibrium moisture content refers to the moisture content that a wood member will attain in service as affected by the atmospheric conditions in which it is situated. Specification of a moisture content level in lumber stock should be as near as possible to the moisture content the lumber will attain in service. The use of wood in arid regions may require lumber with slightly lower moisture contents to prevent further drying and warpage of the wood in service (see Table 850-12).

Weight:

The unit weight of various woods depends both on the species and on the moisture content of the individual piece. The unit weight of individual pieces within a wood species can also vary somewhat from the average as a result of their varying growth rates and of the percentage of heartwood to sapwood. The unit weight of a material is important for calculating dead loads and for calculating imposed loads on roof decks and the like. The unit weight of wood is a rough indicator of its relative strength, with higher values implying greater strengths. Refer to Table 850-12 for the specific values of various species.

Strength:

The ability of a wood member to resist loading depends on the inherent strength of the wood species, its orientation in the structure, and the cross-sectional dimension of the member. The inherent strength of a wood is expressed in a variety of ways, each of which is described below. Design values for various softwood species are given in Tables 850-10 and 850-11.

Tensile strength (Ft) refers to the ability of a wood member to resist loads that are *stretching* the member, and it typically refers to stresses imposed parallel to the grain. Tensile strength is reduced by the presence of knots, splits, and checks in the member. The tensile strength of wood perpendicular to the grain is very low.

Compressive strength refers to the ability of a wood member to resist loads that are *crushing* the wood member. Compressive strengths parallel to the grain (Fc) are 2 to 5 times greater than compressive forces perpendicular to the grain (Fc ⊥). The former is applicable to vertical load-bearing members, while the latter is applicable to horizontal load-bearing members.

Extreme fiber stress in bending (Fb) refers to the ability of a horizontal load-bearing member to carry maximum load in bending without causing the fibers at the utmost top of the member (those most in compressive action) or those at the utmost bottom of the member (those most in tension) to fail. Single-member Fb values refer to loads borne by an individual member, while repetitive Fb values refer to instances where three or more load-bearing members, spaced no more than 24 in (610 mm) apart, are joined by load distributing elements. Fb values are used in load-bearing calculations to determine the sizing of horizontal members.

Modulus of elasticity (*E*) is a measure of stiffness in a wood member; it refers to the ability of the member to resist deflection. *E* is a ratio of the amount by which a material will deflect in proportion to an applied load. *E* values are used in load-bearing calculations to determine the sizing of horizontal members, based on deflection.

Horizontal shear strength refers to the ability of wood fibers at the top half of a

TABLE 850-1
Regional Classifications and Organizations

Species covered by grading rules	*Name of grading authority*
Bald cypress, eastern red cedar	National Hardwood Lumber Association (NHLA) Memphis, Tennessee
Balsam fir, eastern white pine, red pine, eastern hemlock, black spruce, white spruce, red spruce, pitch pine, tamarack, jack pine, northern white cedar	Northeastern Lumber Manufacturer's Association Falmouth, Maine
Bigtooth aspen, quaking aspen, eastern white pine, red pine, jack pine, black spruce, white spruce, red spruce, balsam fir, eastern hemlock, tamarack	Northern Hardwood and Pine Manufacturers' Association (NHPMA) Green Bay, Wisconsin
Western red cedar (shingles and shakes)	Red Cedar Shingle and Handsplit Shake Bureau (RCSHSB) Bellevue, Washington
Redwood	Redwood Inspection Service Mill Valley, California
Bald cypress	Southern Cypress Manufacturers' Association (SCMA) Memphis, Tennessee
Longleaf pine, slash pine, shortleaf pine, loblolly pine, Virginia pine, pond pine, pitch pine	Southern Pine Inspection Bureau (SPIB) Pensacola, Florida
Douglas fir, western hemlock, western red cedar, incense cedar, Port Orford cedar, Alaska cedar, western true firs, mountain hemlock, Sitka spruce	West Coast Lumber Inspection Bureau (WCLIB) Portland, Oregon
Ponderosa pine, western white pine, Douglas fir, sugar pine, western true firs, western larch, Englemann spruce, incense cedar, western hemlock, lodgepole pine, western red cedar, mountain hemlock, red alder	Western Wood Products Association (WWPA) Portland, Oregon
Coast Sitka spruce, Douglas fir, Larch (north), eastern white pine (north), western white pine	National Lumber Grades Authority (NLGA) Vancouver, British Colombia, Canada

Source: U.S. Forest Products Laboratory, *Wood Engineering Handbook,* Prentice-Hall, Englewood Cliffs, New Jersey, 1974.

bending member (that part in compression) to resist shearing horizontally from the fibers in the bottom half of a bending member (that part in tension). Horizontal shear is most likely to occur along the neutral axis of a member (i.e., the horizontal plane running the length of a member approximately two-thirds of the way down from the top of the member). The installation of bolts is avoided along this plane.

Appearance:

Color, figure patterns, grain, and defects in the wood influence the aesthetic value of a piece of lumber. However, in most landscape construction, these qualities of appearance are usually less important than they are in interior applications. In most cases, wood used out-of-doors is either allowed to weather naturally or is preserved, thereby changing its natural appearance to some extent.

Color typically refers to the color of the heartwood in a species, since the sapwood of all species is light in color (virtually white). Heartwood is darker than sapwood and ranges in color from nearly white to deep reddish brown, depending on the species. Refer to Table 850-9 for a description of several wood species.

Figure refers to the pattern of tree ring growth as a consequence of sawing the log. Depending on whether the log is plain-sawn or quartersawn, various species exhibit either conspicuous or nonconspicuous growth rings. Refer to Table 850-9 for descriptions of the figure in various species as a consequence of both sawing methods.

Grain is an ambiguous term generally referring to the density of wood growth in a log or piece of lumber. Annual rings that are close together (with small pores) are referred to as being *close-grained,* whereas widely spaced rings (with large pores) are referred to as being *coarse-grained.* Coarse-grained woods more readily accept stains and other preservatives and more readily hold paints and surface sealers than do close-grained woods.

The term *grain* is also used to refer to the direction of fibers in a piece of lumber, this direction being a consequence either of the tree's natural growth or of sawing the log. For maximum strength, the fibers in a piece of lumber should be parallel (or nearly so) to the edge of the member; any *cross-grain* in a piece of lumber adversely affects the strength of the member, which should be carefully examined before being used in a load-bearing situation.

Defects in a piece of lumber affect both the strength of the member and its appearance. Defects are caused either by natural growth in the tree or by manufacturing (i.e., sawing and surfacing) operations. Refer to Figures 850-4 through 850-8 for descriptions of various types of defects in lumber.

Insect and Decay Resistance:

A variety of insect species can degrade wood, termites by far being the most destructive. Marine borers are a problem in marine environments. The range of termite infestation in the United States is shown in Figure 850-16.

Because termites require moist soil conditions, antitermite construction techniques, termite shields, chemically treated soils and timbers, and termite-resistant wood species can minimize the problem. Termite-resistant wood species include redwood, bald cypress (tidewater red), and eastern red cedar.

Fungi—in the form of mold, stains, dry rot, and soft rot—also can seriously degrade wood if not controlled. Resistance to decay is improved by restricting the moisture content of new wood and of wood in place to 20 percent or less. Dry rot is avoided if moisture contents are kept to 30 percent or less. Wood that is completely and continuously submerged in water will not rot.

Some softwood species are inherently resistant to attack from insects and fungi. The heartwood of any wood species is typically more resistant than its sapwood. Maximum resistance to attack from insects and fungi, without chemical preservation, can be achieved by specifying all heartwood lumber from a resistant species like California redwood *(Sequoia sempervirens)* or bald cypress *(Taxodium distichum).*

Pressure-treated wood should be used where a member will be embedded in moist ground, especially when used for the support of permanent structures. Paints and stains can provide increased insect and decay resistance. Refer to Table 850-5 for more information on decay-resistant species.

The construction plans should detail how to join the wood members so as to minimize the trapping of moisture.

Weatherability:

Weathering generally refers to the ability of a wood to resist cupping, warping, and checking as well as to the aesthetic effects of weathering on the wood's color. Checking is most evident in coarse-grained woods and plain-sawn boards. Warping is most evident in plain-sawn boards. Cupping is most evident in dense woods and in boards which are much wider than they are thick. To minimize cupping, boards should be used whose width is no more than 8 times their thickness, and boards used as a decking material should be laid bark-side up.

Exposed (i.e., untreated) woods characteristically turn various shades of gray with various degrees of sheen, depending on the species. Weathered appearances are sometimes desired, are predictable, and can be arrested at any stage in the process by the application of sealers or other types of preservative. Refer to Tables 850-6 and 850-7 for information on the weathering characteristics of various softwood species.

2.0 LUMBER CLASSIFICATION

2.1 Regional Grading Authorities

In the United States, a number of regional grading authorities have established standards of sizes, properties, and design stress values for particular woods grown in their jurisdiction, based on guidelines established by the American Lumber Standards Committee *(PS 20-70 American Softwood Lumber Standards).* The terminology on sizes and their associated grading hierarchies generally agree from one authority to another, although slight variations do occur. Softwood species in the United States and the respective grading authorities are shown in Table 850-1.

2.2 Regional Production

Because various wood species are produced in different regions of the United States, certain species are preferred in each region because of their availability and consequent lower costs (Figure 850-1 and Table 850-2).

2.3 Sawing and Surfacing

Sawing:

The method used to saw lumber from a log affects the appearance and wearability of the wood member. Two types of sawn lumber are plain-sawn (producing *flat-grained* boards) and quartersawn (producing *edge-* or *vertical-grained* boards).

Plain-sawn lumber is made by sawing directly across the entire log (Figure 850-2). Members are produced that are relatively inexpensive, have conspicuous growth rings and figure patterns, and are less affected in strength by knots. Shrinkage and swelling are more evident in the width than in the thickness, and plain-sawn boards tend easily to develop checks and surface splits during seasoning.

Quartersawn lumber is cut from a quarter section of log (Figure 850-2). Members are more expensive to produce than by plain-sawing, figure patterns peculiar to the radial pattern are conspicuously displayed, and members will shrink and swell

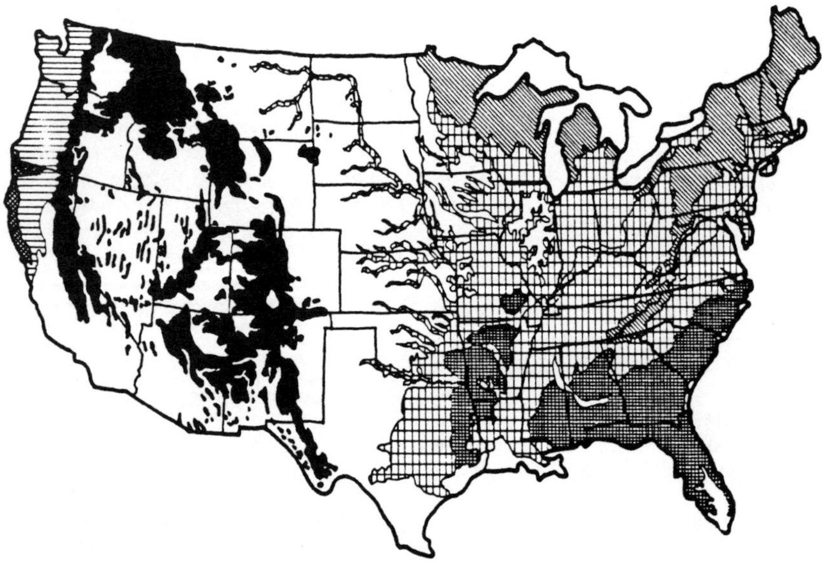
SOFTWOODS
WEST COAST REGION
Douglas fir west coast hemlock western red cedar Sitka spruce
REDWOOD REGION
redwood Douglas fir
WESTERN PINE REGION
ponderosa pine Idaho white pine Douglas fir white fir sugar pine inland red cedar western larch Engelmann spruce lodgepole pine incense cedar
NORTHERN FORESTS
northern white pine eastern spruce jack pine aspen northern hemlock
SOUTHERN PINE REGION
loblolly pine slash pine shortleaf pine longleaf pine cypress
HARDWOODS
NORTHERN FORESTS
maple birch beech ash black-cherry
CENTRAL AND SOUTHERN HARDWOOD FORESTS
oaks yellow poplar gum hickory black walnut basswood

Figure 850-1 Areas of timber growth in the United States.

TABLE 850-2
Lumber and Locations of Growth

Type of wood and location	*Type of wood and location*	*Type of wood and location*
Cypress, bald From Delaware to Florida along the Atlantic coastal plain, along the Gulf coast, and up the Mississippi Valley to Indiana Fir, Douglas From the Rocky Mountains to the Pacific coast and from Mexico to central British Columbia Fir, true eastern New England, New York, Pennsylvania, and the Great Lakes states Fir, true western From the Rocky Mountains to the Pacific coast Hemlock, eastern From New England along the Appalachian Mountains to Alabama and Georgia and the Great Lakes states Hemlock, western Pacific coast of Oregon and Washington, Rocky Mountains north to Canada and Alaska Cedar, incense California, Oregon, and Nevada Larch, western Montana, Idaho, Oregon, and Washington	Pine, eastern white From Maine along the Appalachian Mountains to Georgia and the Great Lakes states Pine, lodge pole (knotty) Rocky Mountains and Pacific coast to Alaska Pine, pitch Maine and northern New York, south to Tennessee and Georgia Pine, pond New Jersey to Florida Pine, ponderosa From Arizona and New Mexico to South Dakota and westward to the Pacific coast mountains Pine, red New England states, New York, Pennsylvania, and the Great Lakes states Pine, southern yellow New York and New Jersey, southward to Florida, westward to Texas and Oklahoma, and north to the Ohio Valley and Missouri Pine, sugar From the Pacific coast and Cascade Mountains of Oregon along coast ranges and Sierra Nevada of California	Pine, western white Western Montana, northern Idaho, Washington, Oregon, and California Cedar, Port Orford Pacific coast from Coos Bay, Oregon, south to California; extends only 40 miles inland Cedar, red, eastern Eastern half of the United States except Maine, Florida, and small area along Gulf coast Cedar, red, western Pacific coast north to Alaska; also in Idaho and Montana Redwood In the Sierra Nevada of California Spruce, eastern Great Lakes states, New England and the Appalachian Mountains Spruce, Engelmann High elevations of the Rocky Mountains Spruce, Sitka Northwestern coast of the United States from California to Alaska Tamarack From Maine to Minnesota

Source: Adapted from Caleb Hornbostel, *Construction Materials,* Wiley, New York, 1978.

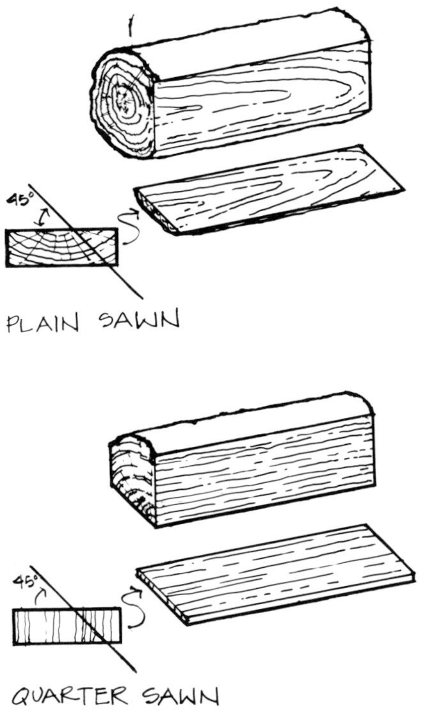
45°
PLAIN SAWN
45°
QUARTER SAWN

Figure 850-2 Methods of Sawing. Lumber sawed so that the annual rings form an angle of 45 degrees or less with the wide face of the piece is called *plain-sawed* or *flat-grained* lumber. *Quartersawn, edge-grained,* or *vertical-grained* lumber refers to boards in which the annual rings are at an angle of 45 degrees or more.

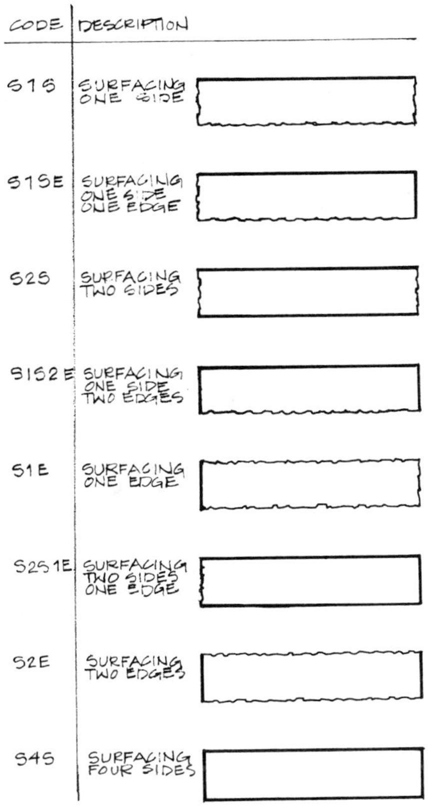
CODE
DESCRIPTION
S1S
SURFACING ONE SIDE
S1SE
SURFACING ONE SIDE ONE EDGE
S2S
SURFACING TWO SIDES
S1S2E
SURFACING ONE SIDE TWO EDGES
S1E
SURFACING ONE EDGE
S2S1E
SURFACING TWO SIDES ONE EDGE
S2E
SURFACING TWO EDGES
S4S
SURFACING FOUR SIDES

Figure 850-3 Surface finishing.

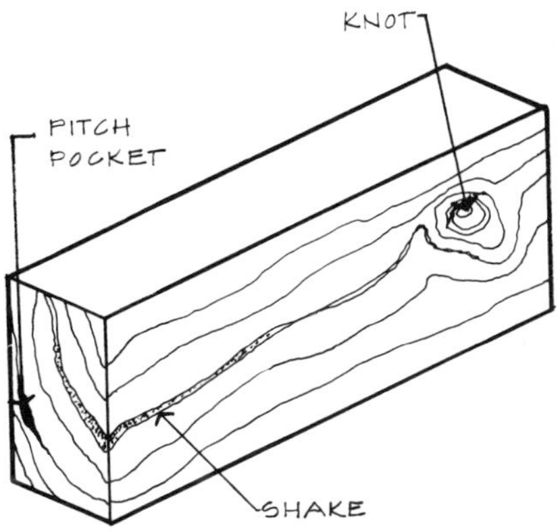
KNOT
PITCH POCKET
SHAKE

Figure 850-4 Natural Defects. *Pitch pockets* are openings containing resin. Their number, size, and location do not significantly affect strength if kept within established guidelines. *Shakes* are separations along the grain which can affect shear strength if they are significant. *Knots* refer to the growth of tree limbs and can affect both the appearance of a wood member and its strength. Reduction in strength is found acceptable within certain established limits.

less in width than in thickness. Edge-grained lumber wears more evenly, twists and cups less, and has less tendency to develop surface checks and splits during seasoning and in service.

Surfacing:

The surfacing of a wood member influences its appearance and determines its actual cross-sectional dimensions.

Rough lumber refers to lumber that has been sawed, edged, and trimmed but not surfaced by planing. *Dressed* (i.e., *surfaced*) lumber refers to lumber that has been surfaced by a planing machine to achieve smooth surfaces and uniform dimensions. Figure 850-3 illustrates the designations that indicate the various combinations of dressed faces.

2.4 Lumber Grading Methods

The grading rules established by each of the regional grading authorities are based on detailed criteria which classify the wide range of lumber qualities obtained from the log. The grades are based on *quality-reducing* characteristics (defects) that adversely affect the appearance, strength, durability, or utility of the wood member.

Visually Graded Lumber:

Most lumber is visually graded by trained inspectors who classify the pieces into one of a number of categories according to specific criteria. Criteria for evaluation include slope of grain, natural and manufacturing defects, and the number, tightness, and location of knots. Allowable working stresses for each grading category are assumed. (Refer to 5.0 Design Values in this section for specifications on visually graded lumber.)

Defects: Natural defects refer to natural processes in timber growth that adversely affect the appearance or strength and consequent grading of the wood member (Figure 850-4).

Manufacturing defects refer to faults due to improper seasoning, sawing, and surfacing operations that adversely affect the appearance or strength and consequent grading of the wood member (Figures 850-5 through 850-8).

Improper sawing may produce *cross-grain* that diminishes the strength of a wood member. This condition occurs when either the fibers and/or the grain in a piece of wood are not parallel to the edges (Figure 850-7). Cross-grained lumber should be avoided because it is more susceptible to warpage, end shrinkage, rough faces, torn or lifted grain, and structural weakness.

Grading systems have been established that correspond with standard stock sizes of lumber (see Table 850-3). Structural grades in a few species (e.g., Douglas fir and southern pine) have additional grade requirements based on density and growth ring count.

Machine Stress-Rated Lumber:

Lumber 2 in thick or less may be machine stress-rated at the sawmill in order to standardize and guarantee the load-bearing capacity of each piece. As the piece leaves the machine, a stamped impression is

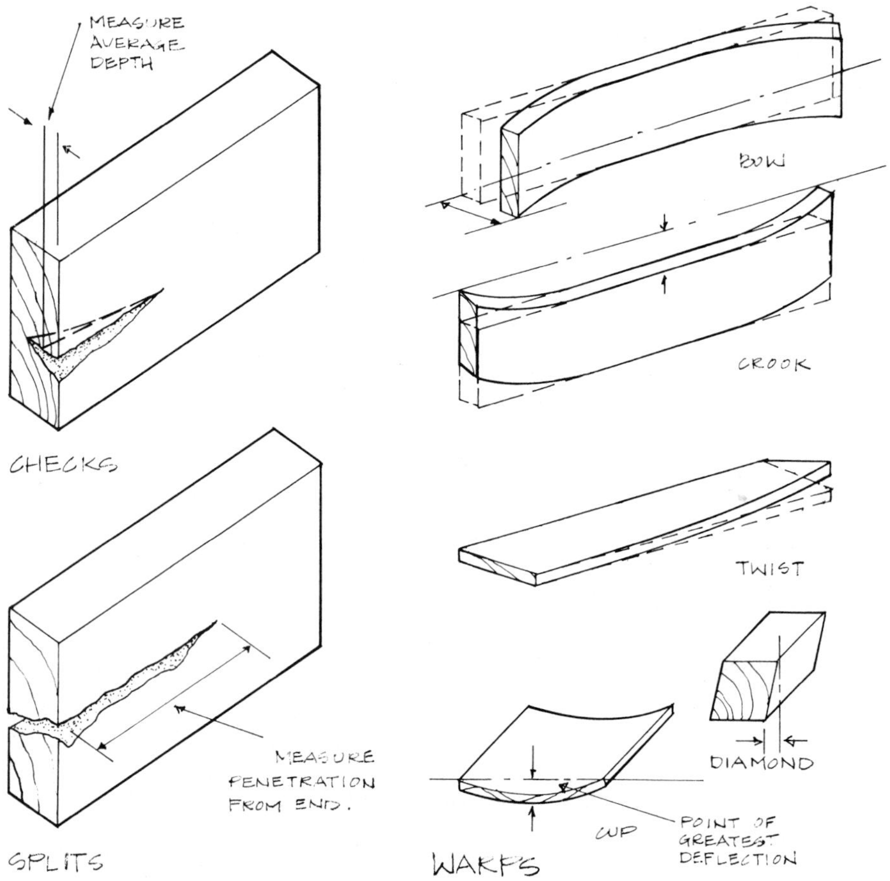
MEASURE AVERAGE DEPTH
CHECKS
BOW
CROOK
TWIST
DIAMOND
MEASURE PENETRATION FROM END.
SPLITS
CUP
POINT OF GREATEST DEFLECTION
WARPS

Figure 850-5 Defects Due to Seasoning. *Checks* are separations across the grain due to seasoning. *Splits* are lengthwise separations through the entire piece. *Warp* is any deviation from a true or plane surface, including bowing, crooking, twisting, cupping, or combinations of each.

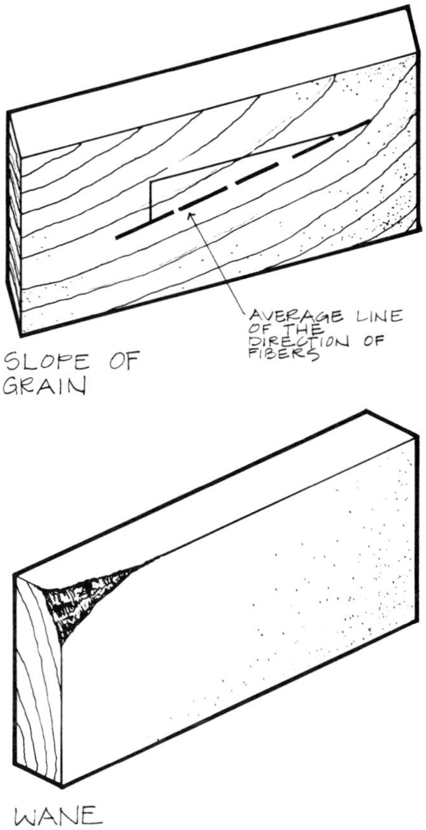

AVERAGE LINE OF THE DIRECTION OF FIBERS
SLOPE OF GRAIN
WANE

Figure 850-6 Defects Due to Sawing. *Slope of grain* refers to the angle of the grain relative to the member's edge. The greater the slope, the weaker the member. *Wane* refers to an absence of wood, or the presence of bark.

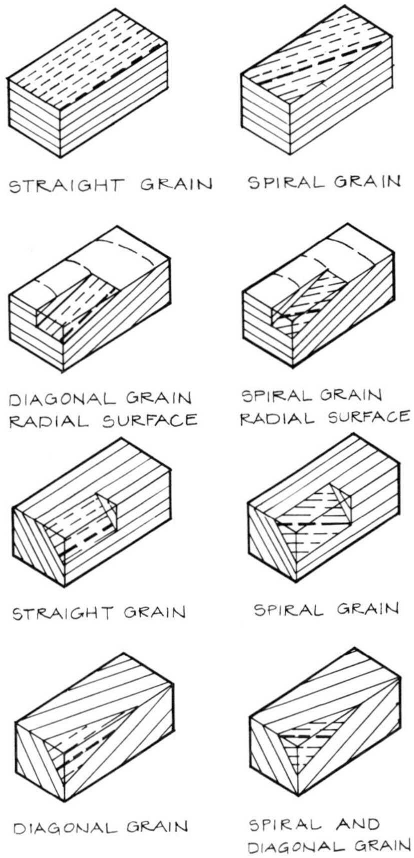

STRAIGHT GRAIN
SPIRAL GRAIN
DIAGONAL GRAIN RADIAL SURFACE
SPIRAL GRAIN RADIAL SURFACE
STRAIGHT GRAIN
SPIRAL GRAIN
DIAGONAL GRAIN
SPIRAL AND DIAGONAL GRAIN

Figure 850-7 Defects Due to Cross-Grain. Cross-grain is a *slope of grain* defect caused by aberrant growth of the tree or by improper sawing, and results in a weaker piece of lumber than straight grain. Straight-grained lumber is strongest and has fibers oriented parallel to the longitudinal axis of the piece (shown with bold dashed line).

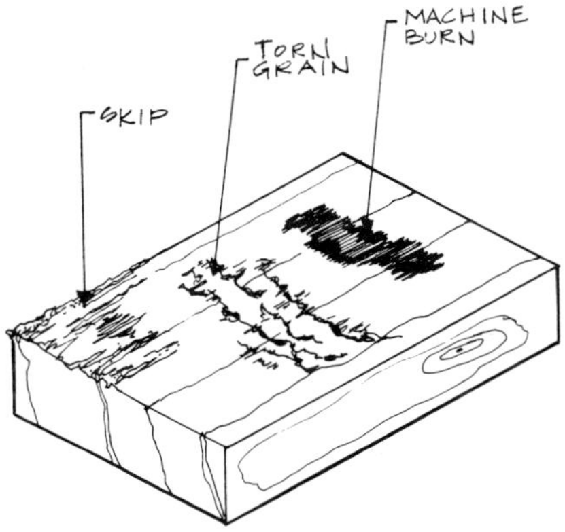

MACHINE BURN
TORN GRAIN
SKIP

Figure 850-8 Defects Due to Surfacing. *Machine burn* is the darkening of wood due to overheating by machine knives or rollers when pieces are stopped in the machine. *Torn grain* is a roughened area caused by the machine tearing out bits of wood in the dressing. *Skip* is an area on a piece that fails to surface smoothly as it passes through the planer.

TABLE 850-3
Yard Lumber Sizes and Grading

Type of yard lumber	Common sizes*						Common stock			Available grades and comments
	Thicknesses			Face widths						
		Minimum dressed			Minimum dressed					
	Nominal	Dry	Green	Nominal	Dry	Green	Specific stock	Nominal thickness	Nominal width	
Boards: generally 1-in thick, greater than or equal to 2-in wide				2	1½	1 9/16	Sheathing, siding, flooring, paneling	1 in	2 in or more	Select: good appearance; used where natural or painted finish is desired ■ B & B (B and better): highest grade for exterior finish, trim, paneling, siding, flooring, and moulding ■ C Select: less quality and cost than B & B ■ D Select: less quality and cost than C Select Common: for general construction and utility ■ No. 1 Common (highest common grade) ■ No. 2 Common ■ No. 3 Common ■ No. 4 Common ■ No. 5 Common (lowest grade)
				3	2½	2 9/16				
				4	3½	3 9/16				
				5	4½	4⅝				
	1	¾	25/32	6	5½	5⅝	Siding	Thickness expressed as dimensions of butt edge		
				7	6½	6⅝				
	1¼	1	1 1/32	8	7¼	7½				
				9	8¼	8½				
	1½	1¼	1 9/32	10	9¼	9½	Moulding and trim	Thickness expressed as size at thickest and widest points		
				11	10¼	10½				
				12	11¼	11½				
				14	13¼	13½				
				16	15¼	15½				
Dimension: 2–4 in thick, greater than or equal to 2-in wide				2	1½	1 9/16	Light framing (not stress-graded)	2–4 in	2–4 in	For uses not demanding high strength, such as blocking and plates ■ Construction: low in bending strength ■ Standard: less strength than construction grade ■ Utility: very low in bending strength
				3	2½	2 9/16				
				4	3½	3 9/16				
	2	1½	1 9/16	5	4½	4⅝				
	2½	2	2 1/16	6	5½	5⅝				
	3	2½	2 9/16	8	7¼	7½				
	3½	3	3 1/16	10	9¼	9½				
				12	11¼	11½				
				14	13¼	13½	Structural light framing	2–4 in	2–4 in	For engineering uses, especially when greater strength in bending is needed ■ Select Structural: highest bending strength† ■ No. 1: less strength than select structural grade ■ No. 2: less strength than No. 1 grade ■ No. 3: lowest bending strength of structural light framing pieces
				16	15¼	15½				
				2	1½	1 9/16				
				3	2½	2 9/16				
				4	3½	3 9/16				
				5	4½	4⅝				
	4	3½	3 9/16	6	5½	5⅝				
	4½	4	4 1/16	8	7¼	7½				
				10	9¼	9½				
				12	11¼	11¼				
				14		13½	Studs (always	2–4 in	2–6 in	For use in walls

* Nominal and minimum dressed sizes of lumber products are shown in inches.

† Select means high quality, not necessarily guaranteed to be a good surface for painting and finishing.

‡ Timbers are sawn and surfaced in green condition.

Source: Adapted from Caleb Hornbostel, *Construction Materials,* Wiley, New York, 1978.

Type of yard lumber	Common sizes*						Common stock			Available grades and comments
	Thicknesses			Face widths			Specific stock	Nominal thickness	Nominal width	
	Nominal	Minimum dressed: Dry	Minimum dressed: Green	Nominal	Minimum dressed: Dry	Minimum dressed: Green				
				16		15½	in lengths of 10 ft or less			▪ Studs: only one grade available, comparable to structural light framing No. 3
							Structural joists and planks	2–4 in	5 in and wider	Joists are loaded on narrow edge; planks are loaded on wide side. Structural joists and planks are stress-graded for engineering purposes. ▪ Select Structural: highest bending strength† ▪ No. 1: less bending strength than Select ▪ No. 2: less bending strength than No. 1 ▪ No. 3: lowest bending strength of structural joists and planks
							Appearance framing	2–4 in	4–12 in	For use as light framing, joist, or plank-measured pieces where moderately high strength and good appearance are desired. ▪ Appearance grade: only grade offered
							Decking	2–4 in	4–12 in	For decking or planking. Moisture typically limited to 15% MC (moisture content). Members typically used with tongue-and-groove pattern. Faces finished to provide plain, grooved, or striated surfaces and rounded or V edges. ▪ Select decking: greater strength than commercial decking† ▪ Commercial decking: less strength than select decking
Timbers: greater than 5-in thick and greater than 5-in wide‡	5 6 8 10 12 14 16	4½ 5½ 7¼ 9¼ 11½ 13¼ 15¼	4⅝ 5⅝ 7½ 9½ 11½ 13½ 15½	5 6 8 10 12 14 16	4½ 5½ 7¼ 9¼ 11¼ 13¼ 14¼	4⅝ 5⅝ 7½ 9½ 11½ 11½ 15½	Post and timbers Beams and stringers	5 in and thicker	5 in and wider but not more than 2 in greater than thickness	For posts; lower bending strengths than beams. ▪ Select structural: greater strength than No. 1† ▪ No. 1: less strength than select structural grade. For beams and stringers; slightly higher bending strength than posts. ▪ Select structural: greater strength than No. 1.† ▪ No. 1: less strength than Select Structural grade.

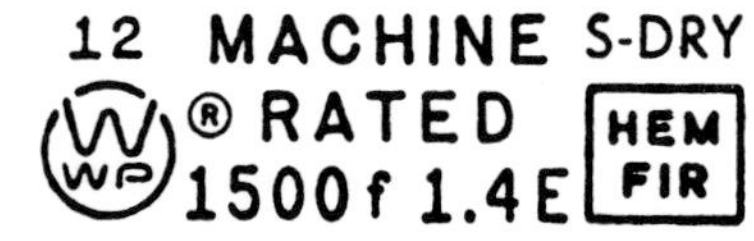
12 MACHINE S-DRY
® RATED
1500f 1.4E
HEM
FIR
WP

Figure 850-9 Stamp for machine stress-graded lumber.

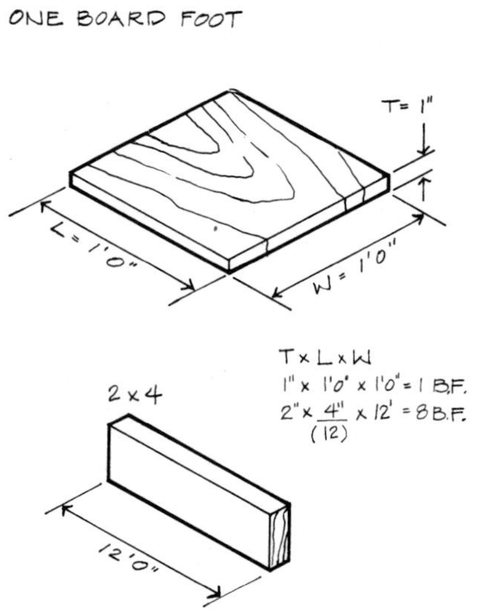
ONE BOARD FOOT
T= 1"
L = 1'0"
W = 1'0"
T x L x W
1" x 1'0" x 1'0" = 1 B.F.
2" x 4"/(12) x 12' = 8 B.F.
2x4
12'0"

Figure 850-10 Board Foot Calculations. Board measure is computed using nominal dimensions. The smallest value used in computations is 1 in.

made which specifies values for *fiber stress in bending* (stamped as *f*) and *modulus of elasticity* (stamped as *E*) (Figure 850-9). (Refer to 5.0 Design Values in this section for specifications on machine stress-rated lumber.)

3.0 STANDARD LUMBER DIMENSIONS

3.1 Nominal Sizing

Cross-sectional lumber specifications typically refer to the *nominal* size of a piece, i.e., the size before shrinkage and planing, rather than to the actual size. Actual dressed dimensions are smaller than nominal dimensions. Dimensions of length are nearly exact because shrinkage longitudinal to the grain is negligible.

3.2 Yard Lumber Sizes and Grading

Yard lumber refers to standard construction lumber, as opposed to worked lumber and special wood products. All yard lumber is grouped into one of three categories: *boards, dimension lumber,* and *timbers* (Table 850-3). The nomenclature and sizing for this classification system are fairly standard and are recognized by most regional grading authorities, although minor variations may occur.

Redwood lumber is graded according to a unique classification system, as shown in Table 850-4.

3.3 Methods for Specifying Sizes and Quantities of Lumber

The size and quantity of lumber is specified by one of four methods:

1. *Board measure:* *foot board measure* or *board measure* (BDM or BD FT) refers to volumes of lumber of a stock of nominal thickness and width. *Board measure* is typically used when specifying boards (Figure 850-10).

2. *Lineal feet:* occasionally, boards are ordered by the *lineal foot* (or *running foot*) (Lf or Lft) of a stock of nominal thickness and width.

3. *Nominal size and length:* yard stock is often ordered by numbers of specific pieces. Lengths of yard lumber typically range from 6 to 24 ft in 2-ft increments. Some lumber mills will cut lengths to exact specifications upon request.

4. *Areas to be covered:* shakes and shingles are ordered according to an area to be covered. One square unit (i.e., *one square*) covers 100 ft^2 (9.3 m^2) of area when laid with a normally exposed coursing width.

4.0 CHARACTERISTICS OF VARIOUS SOFTWOODS

The characteristics of various softwoods, including decay resistance, weathering, ease of keeping painted, color, and figure, are described in Tables 850-5 through 850-9.

TABLE 850-4
Redwood Grades

Grade characteristics	*Description*
Clear, all heart	Top quality; one face completely free of defects; opposite face may have no more than two pin knots regardless of board size; excellent stability; usually kiln-dried; more expensive
Clear	High-quality finish lumber similar to *clear, all heart* but may contain sapwood, some small knots, and medium surface checks; usually kiln dried; more expensive
Select heart	All sound heartwood; available in surfaced or unsurfaced condition; usually not kiln dried; knots permitted
Construction heart*	An economical, all-purpose grade; good choice for posts, decks, and smaller garden projects; usually not kiln dried; all heartwood and small knots; available unseasoned; shrinkage to be expected
Select	Very similar to *select heart* but used where termites and decay are not problems; contains sapwood
Construction common*	A good all-purpose material but for above-grade constructions; contains sapwood; knots permitted; available unseasoned; shrinkage to be expected
Merchantable*	Contains larger and looser knots and more imperfections than other grades; heartwood and sapwood are included in this grade, so some pieces are good for ground contact projects; available unseasoned; shrinkage to be expected

* Often designated as garden grades.

Source: Adapted from R. J. Christoforo ed., *Wood Projects for the Garden,* Ortho Books, Chevron Chemical Company, San Francisco, 1976.

TABLE 850-5
Relative Decay Resistance of Various Softwoods

Resistant or very resistant	*Moderately resistant*	*Slightly or nonresistant*
Bald cypress, old growth*	Bald cypress, young growth*	Pines (other than long leaf, slash, and eastern white)‡
Cedars	Douglas fir	Spruces
Cypress, Arizona	Honey locust‡	True firs, western and eastern
Junipers	Larch, western	Yellow poplar
Locust, black†	Pine, eastern white*	
Osage orange†	Southern pine:	
Redwood	Longleaf*	
Sassafras	Slash*	
Yew, Pacific†	Tamarack	

* The southern and eastern pines and bald cypress are now largely second growth with a large proportion of sapwood. Consequently, substantial quantities of heartwood lumber of these species are not available.

† These woods have exceptionally high decay resistance.

‡ These species or certain species within the group have higher decay resistance than most woods in this grouping.

Source: Adapted from U.S. Forest Products Laboratory, *Wood Engineering Handbook,* Prentice-Hall, Englewood Cliffs, New Jersey, 1974.

TABLE 850-6
Effects of Weathering on Various Softwoods

Woods (softwoods)	*Weathering*	
	*Resistance to cupping**	*Conspicuousness of checking†*
Cedar:		
Alaska	1	1
California incense	—	—
Port Orford	—	1
Western red cedar	1	1
White	1	—
Cypress	1	1
Redwood	1	1
Pine:		
Eastern white	2	2
Sugar	2	2
Western white	2	2
Ponderosa	2	2
Fir, commercial white	2	2
Hemlock	2	2
Spruce	2	2
Douglas fir (lumber and plywood)	2	2
Larch	2	2
Lauan (plywood)	2	2
Pine:		
Norway	2	2
Southern (lumber and plywood)	2	2
Tamarack	2	2

* 1 = best, 4 = worst. † 1 = least, 2 = most.

Source: Adapted from U.S. Forest Products Laboratory, *Wood Engineering Handbook,* Prentice-Hall, Englewood Cliffs, New Jersey, 1974.

TABLE 850-7
Color Effects of Weathering on Various Softwoods

Type of Wood	*Changes to light gray color with silvery sheen*	*Changes to light gray color with moderate sheen*	*Changes to dark gray color with little or no sheen*
Evergreen (softwood)	Bald cypress	Hemlock:	Douglas fir
	Cedar:	Eastern	Fir:
	Alaska	Western	Commercial
	Port Orford	Pine:	White
		Eastern white	Larch:
		Ponderosa	Western
		Sugar	Pine:
		Western white	Southern yellow
		Spruce:	Cedar:
		Eastern	Western red
		Sitka	Redwood

Source: Adapted from Caleb Hornbostel, *Construction Materials,* John Wiley, New York, 1978.

TABLE 850-8
Characteristics of Woods for Painting

Softwoods	*Suitability for paint**
Cedar:	
Alaska	I
California incense	I
Port Orford	I
Western red cedar	I
White	I
Cypress	I
Redwood	I
Products overlaid with resin-treated paper	I
Pine:	
Eastern white	II
Sugar	II
Western white	II
Ponderosa	III
Fir, commercial white	III
Hemlock	III
Spruce	III
Douglas fir (lumber and plywood)	IV
Larch	IV
Lauan (plywood)	IV
Pine:	
Norway	IV
Southern (lumber and plywood)	IV
Tamarack	IV

* I = easiest to maintain; V = most exacting.

Source: Adapted from U.S. Forest Products Laboratory, *Wood Engineering Handbook,* Prentice-Hall, Englewood Cliffs, New Jersey, 1974.

TABLE 850-9
Color and Figure Characteristics of Various Softwoods

Species	Color of dry heartwood*	Type of figure in	
		Plain-sawed lumber or rotary-cut veneer	*Quartersawed lumber or quarter-sliced veneer*
Bald cypress	Light yellowish brown to reddish brown	Conspicuous irregular growth ring	Distinct, not conspicuous, growth-ring stripe
Cedar:			
Alaska	Yellow	Faint growth ring	None
Atlantic white	Light brown with reddish tinge	Distinct, not conspicuous, growth ring	None
Eastern red	Brick red to deep reddish brown	Occasionally streaks of white sapwood alternating with heartwood	Occasionally streaks of white sapwood alternating with heartwood
Incense	Reddish brown	Faint growth ring	Faint growth-ring stripe
Northern white	Light to dark brown	Faint growth ring	Faint growth-ring stripe
Port Orford	Light yellow to pale brown	Faint growth ring	None
Western red	Reddish brown	Distinct, not conspicuous, growth ring	Faint growth-ring stripe
Douglas fir	Orange red to red; sometimes yellow	Conspicuous growth ring	Distinct, not conspicuous, growth-ring stripe
Fir:			
Balsam	Nearly white	Distinct, not conspicuous, growth ring	Faint growth-ring stripe
White	Nearly white to pale reddish brown	Conspicuous growth ring	Distinct, not conspicuous, growth-ring stripe
Hemlock:			
Eastern	Light reddish brown	Distinct, not conspicuous, growth ring	Faint growth-ring stripe
Western	Light reddish brown	Distinct, not conspicuous, growth ring	Faint growth-ring stripe
Larch, western	Russet to reddish brown	Conspicuous growth ring	Distinct, not conspicuous, growth-ring stripe
Pine:			
Eastern white	Cream to light reddish brown	Faint growth ring	None
Lodgepole	Light reddish brown	Distinct, not conspicuous, growth ring; faint pocked appearance	None
Ponderosa	Orange to reddish brown	Distinct, not conspicuous, growth ring	Faint growth-ring stripe
Red	Orange to reddish brown	Distinct, not conspicuous, growth ring	Faint growth-ring stripe
Southern:			
longleaf, loblolly, shortleaf, and slash	Orange to reddish brown	Conspicuous growth ring	Distinct, not conspicuous, growth-ring stripe
Sugar	Light creamy brown	Faint growth ring	None
Western white	Cream to light reddish brown	Faint growth ring	None
Redwood	Cherry to deep reddish brown	Distinct, not conspicuous, growth ring; occasionally wavy and burl	Faint growth-ring stripe; occasionally wavy and burl
Spruce:			
Black, Engelmann, Red, White	Nearly white	Faint growth ring	None
Sitka	Light reddish brown	Distinct, not conspicuous, growth ring	Faint growth-ring stripe
Tamarack	Russet brown	Conspicuous growth ring	Distinct, not conspicuous, growth ring

* The sapwood of all species is light in color or virtually white unless discolored by fungus or chemical stains.

Source: Adapted from U.S. Forest Products Laboratory, *Wood Engineering Handbook,* Prentice-Hall, Englewood Cliffs, New Jersey, 1974.

5.0 DESIGN VALUES (TABLES)

Design values for common softwoods are given in Tables 850-10 through 850-13. Additional tables are given in Section 460: Wood Decks and Boardwalks.

5.1 Machine Stress-Graded Structural Lumber

Design values for machine-graded lumber are given in Table 850-10.

5.2 Equilibrium Moisture Contents

The equilibrium moisture contents of lumber pieces are determined by the temperature and humidity of the environment in which the lumber is situated (Table 850-11).

5.3 Unit Weights

The unit weights of wood depend on the species as well as on the moisture content at the time of measurement. Table 850-12 lists the unit weights for common softwood species.

6.0 SPECIAL PRODUCTS

6.1 Plywood

Plywood refers to sheet lumber that is manufactured by bonding together several layers of wood veneer under high pressure with a waterproof or water-resistant adhesive (Figure 850-11). A solid lumber or fire-resistant mineral core may also be incorporated. Plywood is manufactured for both indoor and outdoor applications and is typically available in 4 × 8 ft sheets.

Plywood panels are manufactured from a variety of wood species and can be made up of more than one kind of wood. Species that make up the various veneers are grouped according to stiffness and strength into one of the five groups, as established by the National Bureau of Standards (Product Standard PS 1). Group 1 species produce panels with the least strength and stiffness.

Construction plywood is used in exterior applications. It is manufactured primarily from softwoods, although hardwoods are sometimes used. *Decorative construction and industrial hardwood* is a type of plywood used in interior applications only.

Properties:

Apart from the characteristics of the veneer used, the most important properties of plywood are the result of its cross-laminated construction. Properties that are important to construction include durability, bending strength and stiffness, and shear resistance.

Durability refers to the ability of a plywood to remain intact over time. The glueline used to bond veneers is as durable as the wood itself, enabling the material to be exposed out-of-doors without delaminating. Checking occurs less than in common lumber. Paints or stains can protect against weathering or chalking. Preservatives are required in areas of high decay or termite hazard.

Bending strength and stiffness refers to the strength and stiffness of plywood in its plane, a property that makes it suitable as a bracing material. The grain of the face should be placed perpendicularly to the support members. The minimum recommended thickness for a bracing support is 5⁄16 in (8 mm).

Shear resistance refers to the ability of plywood to distribute loads applied perpendicularly to its face without shearing. Plywood has a great ability to bear loads from nails and can be securely nailed as near as ¼ in (6.5 mm) to its edge.

Grades:

All plywood falls into one of two categories: (1) *appearance grades,* which are based mainly on the appearance of the outer plies, and (2) *engineered grades,* which are based mainly on properties of strength. Veneer grades for both categories are described in Table 850-13.

The grades within each of these two general categories include both interior and exterior plywood types that refer to the exposure capability of the panel.

Exterior (waterproof) types incorporate Grade C veneer or better throughout the panel. Exterior plywoods retain their glue bond when repeatedly wetted and dried and are manufactured for permanent outdoor exposure.

Interior (water-resistant) plywoods incorporate all grades of veneer. Three separate levels of adhesive durability permit interior plywood to be exposed for different periods of time until it has been totally protected:

1. Plywood bonded with *interior* glue, for no exposure to the elements during construction

2. Plywood bonded with *intermediate* glue, for use where moderate delays in protection are expected or where, in temporary delays, material may be exposed to water or high humidity

3. Plywood bonded with *exterior* glue, for use where long delays or humid exposure

TABLE 850-10
Design Values for Machine Stress-Rated Structural Lumber[a,b]

Grade designation	Grading rules agency (See notes h–j)	Size classification	Design values (lb/in²)[c]: Extreme fiber in bending, F_b[d]: Single member uses	Repetitive member uses	Tension parallel to grain, F_t	Compression parallel to grain, F_c	Modulus of elasticity, E
900f-1.0E	j	Machine-rated lumber, 2-in thick or less, all widths	900	1050	350	725	1,000,000
1200f-1.2E	h,i,j		1200	1400	650	950	1,200,000
1350f-1.3E	i		1350	1550	750	1100	1,300,000
1450f-1.3E	h,j		1450	1650	800	1150	1,300,000
1500f-1.4E	h,i,j		1500	1750	900	1200	1,400,000
1650f-1.5E	h,i,j		1650	1900	1020	1320	1,500,000
1800f-1.6E	h,i,j		1800	2050	1175	1450	1,600,000
1950f-1.7E	h,i		1950	2250	1375	1550	1,700,000
2100f-1.8E	h,i,j		2100	2400	1575	1700	1,800,000
2250f-1.9E	h,i		2250	2600	1750	1800	1,900,000
2400f-2.0E	h,i,j		2400	2750	1925	1925	2,000,000
2550f-2.1E	h,i		2550	2950	2050	2050	2,100,000
2700f-2.2E	h,i,j		2700	3100	2150	2150	2,200,000
2850f-2.3E	i		2850	3300	2300	2300	2,300,000
3000f-2.4E	h,i		3000	3450	2400	2400	2,400,000
3150f-2.5E	i		3150	3600	2500	2500	2,500,000
3300f-2.6E	i		3300	3800	2650	2650	2,600,000
900f-1.0E	h,i,j	See note j	900	1050	350	725	1,000,000
900f-1.2E	h,i,j		900	1050	350	725	1,200,000
1200f-1.5E	h,i,j		1200	1400	600	950	1,500,000
1350f-1.8E	h,i		1350	1550	750	1075	1,800,000
1500f-1.8E	j		1500	1750	900	1200	1,800,000
1800f-2.1E	h,i,j		1800	2050	1175	1450	2,100,000

[a] Stresses apply at 19% maximum moisture content.

[b] Design values listed are for normal loading conditions (see notes below) and other provisions in the national design specification. For adjustments of tabulated values, see Note d.

[c] Design values for horizontal shear F_v (DRY) and compression perpendicular to grain F_{c1} (DRY) are:

	Cedar* (WWPA/ WCLIB)	Douglas fir, larch (WWPA/ WCLIB/ NLGA)	Douglas fir, south (WWPA)	Engelmann spruce (WWPA)	Hemlock, fir (WWPA/WCLIB/ NLGA)	Mixed species (WCLIB)	Pine (WWPA)	Southern pine (SPIB)	Spruce, pine, fir (NLGA)	Western hemlock (WWPA/WCLIB)
Horizontal shear F_v (DRY)	75	95	90	70	75	70	70	90	70	90
Compression perpendicular to grain F_{c1} (DRY)	265	385	335	195	245	190	190	405	265	280

* Cedar includes incense or western red cedar. Pine includes Idaho white pine, lodgepole pine, ponderosa pine, or sugar pine.

[d] Tabulated extreme fiber values in bending values F_b are applicable to lumber loaded on edge. When loaded flat, these values may be increased by multiplying by the following factors:

Nominal width (in)	3	4	5	6	8	10	12	14
Factor	1.06	1.10	1.12	1.15	1.19	1.22	1.25	1.28

[e] Grading rules agencies listed include the following:
Northeastern Lumber Manufacturers Association, Incorporated (NELMA)
Northern Hardwood and Pine Manufacturers Association, Incorporated (NHPMA)
National Lumber Grades Authority (Canada) (NLGA)
Redwood Inspection Service (RIS)
Southern Pine Inspection Bureau (SPIB)
West Coast Lumber Inspection Bureau (WCLIB)
Western Wood Products Association (WWPA)
The design values are applicable to lumber that will be used under dry conditions. For 2- to 4-in thick lumber, the DRY surfaced size should be used in member design.
The design values for surfaced dry or surfaced green lumber may be multiplied by the following factors (for southern pine use tabulated design values without adjustment:

Thickness of lumber	*Moisture content (MC)*	*Extreme fiber in bending in* F_b	*Tension parallel to grain* F_t	*Horizontal shear* F_v	*Compression perpendicular to grain* F_c	*Compression parallel to grain* F_c	*Modulus of elasticity* E
2-4 in	15% maximum	1.08	1.08	1.05	1.00	1.17	1.05
2-4 in	19% and above	0.86	0.84	0.97	0.67	0.70	0.97
5 in	19% and above	1.00	1.00	1.00	0.67	0.91	1.00

[f] National Lumber Grades Authority grading rules.

[g] Southern Pine Inspection Bureau grading rules.

[h] West Coast Lumber Inspection Bureau grading rules.

[i] Western Wood Products Association grading rules.

[j] Size classifications for these grades are:
NLGA—machine rated lumber; 2-in thick or less; all widths
SPIB—machine rated lumber; 2-in thick or less; all widths
WCLIB—machine rated joists; 2-in thick or less; 6 inches and wider
WWPA—machine rated lumber; 2-in thick or less; all widths

Source: Adapted from C. G. Ramsey and H. R. Sleeper, *Architectural Graphic Standards,* 7th ed., John T. Packard (ed.), Wiley, New York, 1981, as prepared by the National Forest Products Association, *Design Values for Wood Construction,* Washington, D.C.

TABLE 850-11
Equilibrium Moisture Contents for Wood in Various Environments

Temperature (dry-bulb) °F	Relative humidity, %																			
	5	10	15	20	25	30	35	40	45	50	55	60	65	70	75	80	85	90	95	98
30	1.4	2.6	3.7	4.6	5.5	6.3	7.1	7.9	8.7	9.5	10.4	11.3	12.4	13.5	14.9	16.5	18.5	21.0	24.3	26.9
40	1.4	2.6	3.7	4.6	5.5	6.3	7.1	7.9	8.7	9.5	10.4	11.3	12.3	13.5	14.9	16.5	18.5	21.0	24.3	26.9
50	1.4	2.6	3.6	4.6	5.5	6.3	7.1	7.9	8.7	9.5	10.3	11.2	12.3	13.4	14.8	16.4	18.4	20.9	24.3	26.9
60	1.3	2.5	3.6	4.6	5.4	6.2	7.0	7.8	8.6	9.4	10.2	11.1	12.1	13.3	14.6	16.2	18.2	20.7	24.1	26.8
70	1.3	2.5	3.5	4.5	5.4	6.2	6.9	7.7	8.5	9.2	10.1	11.0	12.0	13.1	14.4	16.0	17.9	20.5	23.9	26.6
80	1.3	2.4	3.5	4.4	5.3	6.1	6.8	7.6	8.3	9.1	9.9	10.8	11.7	12.9	14.2	15.7	17.7	20.2	23.6	26.3
90	1.2	2.3	3.4	4.3	5.1	5.9	6.7	7.4	8.1	8.9	9.7	10.5	11.5	12.6	13.9	15.4	17.3	19.8	23.3	26.0
100	1.2	2.3	3.3	4.2	5.0	5.8	6.5	7.2	7.9	8.7	9.5	10.3	11.2	12.3	13.6	15.1	17.0	19.5	22.9	25.6
110	1.1	2.2	3.2	4.0	4.9	5.6	6.3	7.0	7.7	8.4	9.2	10.0	11.0	12.0	13.2	14.7	16.6	19.1	22.4	25.2
120	1.1	2.1	3.0	3.9	4.7	5.4	6.1	6.8	7.5	8.2	8.9	9.7	10.6	11.7	12.9	14.4	16.2	18.6	22.0	24.7
130	1.0	2.0	2.9	3.7	4.5	5.2	5.9	6.6	7.2	7.9	8.7	9.4	10.3	11.3	12.5	14.0	15.8	18.2	21.5	24.2
140	.9	1.9	2.8	3.6	4.3	5.0	5.7	6.3	7.0	7.7	8.4	9.1	10.0	11.0	12.1	13.6	15.3	17.7	21.0	23.7
150	.9	1.8	2.6	3.4	4.1	4.8	5.5	6.1	6.7	7.4	8.1	8.8	9.7	10.6	11.8	13.1	14.9	17.2	20.4	23.1
160	.8	1.6	2.4	3.2	3.9	4.6	5.2	5.8	6.4	7.1	7.8	8.5	9.3	10.3	11.4	12.7	14.4	16.7	19.9	22.5
170	.7	1.5	2.3	3.0	3.7	4.3	4.9	5.6	6.2	6.8	7.4	8.2	9.0	9.9	11.0	12.3	14.0	16.2	19.3	21.9
180	.7	1.4	2.1	2.8	3.5	4.1	4.7	5.3	5.9	6.5	7.1	7.8	8.6	9.5	10.5	11.8	13.5	15.7	18.7	21.3
190	.6	1.3	1.9	2.6	3.2	3.8	4.4	5.0	5.5	6.1	6.8	7.5	8.2	9.1	10.1	11.4	13.0	15.1	18.1	20.7
200	.5	1.1	1.7	2.4	3.0	3.5	4.1	4.6	5.2	5.8	6.4	7.1	7.8	8.7	9.7	10.9	12.5	14.6	17.5	20.0
210	.5	1.0	1.6	2.1	2.7	3.2	3.8	4.3	4.9	5.4	6.0	6.7	7.4	8.3	9.2	10.4	12.0	14.0	16.9	19.3

Source: U.S. Forest Products Laboratory, *Wood Engineering Handbook,* Prentice-Hall, Englewood Cliffs, New Jersey, 1974.

TABLE 850-12
Unit Weights of Various Softwoods

	Weight			
	Moisture content, 15%		*Moisture content, 8%*	
Softwoods	*lb/ft*^{3}	*kg/m*^{3}	*lb/ft*^{3}	*kg/m*^{3}
Cedar, Alaska	31.6	506.23	30.4	487.01
Cypress, bald	32.6	522.25	31.4	503.03
Fir, Douglas	30.5–34.3	488.61–549.49	29.2–33.1	467.78–530.26
Fir, true eastern	26.9	430.94	26.4	422.93
Fir, true western	26.7–28.3	427.73–453.37	25.8–27.2	413.32–435.74
Hemlock, eastern	29.0	464.58	28.0	448.56
Hemlock, western	29.6	474.19	28.7	459.77
Cedar, incense	25.5	408.51	24.2	387.68
Larch, western	39.4	613.19	38.2	611.96
Pine, eastern white	25.4	406.91	24.2	387.68
Pine, lodgepole (knotty pine)	29.2	467.78	28.2	451.76
Pine, pitch	34.9	551.09	33.8	541.48
Pine, pond	38.7	619.97	37.5	600.75
Pine, ponderosa	28.6	618.37	27.5	440.55
Pine, red	31.4	503.03	30.4	487.01
Pine, southern yellow	41.6–43.9	666.43–703.28	40.3–42.6	645.61–682.45
	35.7–36.3	571.91–581.53	34.6–25.3	554.29–565.51
Pine, sugar	26.0	416.52	24.0	384.48
Pine, western white	28.0	448.56	27.1	434.14
Cedar, Port Orford	30.1	482.20	28.9	462.98
Cedar, red eastern	33.5	536.67	32.2	515.84
Cedar, red western	23.4	347.87	22.4	358.85
Redwood	28.6	458.17	27.4	438.94
Spruce, eastern	29.4–28.4	470.99–459.97	28.7–27.2	459.77–435.74
Spruce, Engelmann	24.1	386.08	23.2	371.66
Spruce, Sitka	28.1	450.16	27.1	434.14
Tamarack	37.6	602.35	36.3	480.53

Source: Adapted from U.S. Forest Products Laboratory, *Wood Engineering Handbook,* Prentice-Hall, Englewood Cliffs, New Jersey, 1974.

TABLE 850-13
Typical Exterior Grades and Uses of Plywood

Grade[b]	*Common uses*	*Veneer*[a]			*Thickness, in*										
		Face	*Middle*	*Back*	1/4	5/16	11/32	3/8	15/32	1/2	19/32	5/8	23/32	3/4	1 1/8
		Appearance[b, c, d]													
A-A EXT-APA[f]	Use where both sides are visible	A	C	A	o		o	o	o	o	o	o	o	o	
A-B EXT-APA[f]	Use where view of one side is less important	A	C	B	o		o	o	o	o	o	o	o	o	
A-C EXT-APA[f]	Use where only one side is visible	A	C	C	o		o	o	o	o	o	o	o	o	
B-B EXT-APA[f]	Utility panel with two solid faces	B	C	B	o		o	o	o	o	o	o	o	o	
B-C EXT-APA[f]	Utility panel. Also used as base for exterior coatings on walls and roofs	B	C	C	o		o	o	o	o	o	o	o	o	
HDO-EXT-APA[f]	High density overlay plywood has a hard, semiopaque resin fiber overlay on both faces. Abrasion resistant. Use for concrete forms, cabinets, and counter tops	A B	C C plugged	A B		o		o		o		o		o	
MDO-EXT-APA[f]	Medium-density overlay with smooth resin fiber overlay on one or two faces. Recommended for siding and other outdoor applications. Ideal base for paint	B	C	B C		o	o	o	o	o	o	o	o	o	
303 Siding EXT-APA[h]	Special surface treatment such as V-groove, channel groove, striated, brushed, rough sawn	[g]	C	C			o	o	o	o	o	o			
T1-11 Ext-APA[h]	Special 303 panels have grooves 1/4-in deep, 3/8-in wide, normally spaced 4 or 8 in o.c. Other spacing optional. Edges shiplapped. Available unsanded, textured, and medium-density overlay	A B C	C	C							o	o			

[a] N = smooth surface "natural" finish veneer. Select, all heartwood, or all sapwood. Free of open defects. Allows not more than six repairs, wood only, per 4 × 8 panel. Made parallel to grain and well-matched for grain and color.

A = smooth, paintable. Not more than 18 neatly made repairs, boat, sled, or router type, and parallel to grain, permitted. May be used for natural finish in less demanding applications.

B = solid surface. Shims, circular repair plugs, and tight knots to 1 in across grain permitted. Some minor splits permitted.

C plugged = improved C veneer with splits limited to 1/8-in width and knotholes and borer holes limited to 1/4 × 1/2 in. Admits some broken grain. Synthetic repairs permitted.

C = tight knots to 1 1/2 in. Knotholes to 1 in across grain and some to 1 1/2 in if total width of knots and knotholes is within specified limits. Synthetic or wood repairs. Discoloration and sanding defects that do not impair strength permitted. Limited splits allowed. Stitching permitted.

D = Knots and knotholes to 2 1/2 in width across grain and 1/2 in larger within specified limits. Limited splits are permitted. Stitching permitted. Limited to interior grades of plywood.

[b] Available in group 1, 2, 3, 4, or 5 unless otherwise noted.

[c] Sanded on both sides except where decorative or other surfaces specified.

Grade[b]	Common uses	Veneer[a]			Thickness, in										
		Face	Middle	Back	¼	5/16	11/32	3/8	15/32	½	19/32	5/8	23/32	¾	1 1/8
Plyron EXT-APA	Hardboard faces both sides, tempered, smooth, or screened	HB	C	HB						o		o		o	
Marine EXT-APA	Made only with Douglas fir or Western larch. Special solid-jointed core construction. Subject to special limitations on core gaps and number of face repairs. Also available with HDO or MDO faces.	A B	B	A B	o			o		o		o		o	
	Engineered[d]														
C-C EXT-APA[j]	Unsanded grade with waterproof bond	C	C	C		o		o	o	o	o	o	o	o	o
Structural I C-C EXT-APA	For engineered applications in construction and industry where full exterior type panels are required. Unsanded. See Note f for species group requirement	C	C	C		o		o	o	o	o	o	o	o	o
Structural II C-C EXT-APA Underlayment C-C plugged EXT-APA C-C plugged EXT-APA[b,f]	For underlayment or combination subfloor underlayment under resilient floor coverings where severe moisture conditions exist, as in balcony decks. Use for tile backing in atmosphere-controlled rooms. Touch-sanded and tongue-and-groove	C plugged	C	C	o	o	o	o		o	o	o	o	o	o
B-B Plyform Class I and Class II EXT-APA[e]	Concrete form grades with high reuse factor. Sanded on both sides. Mill oiled unless otherwise specified. Special restrictions on species. Also available in HDO.	B	C	B				o		o	o	o	o	o	o

[d] Standard 4 × 8 panel sizes; other sizes available.

[e] Also available in Structural I.

[f] Also available in Structural I (all plies limited to group 1 species) and Structural II (all plies limited to group 1, 2, or 3 species).

[g] C or better for five plies; C plugged or better for three-ply panels.

[h] Stud spacing is shown on trademark stamp.

[i] Made only in woods of certain species to conform to APA specifications.

[j] Made in many different species combinations. Specify by span rating.

Source: Adapted from the American Plywood Association, *Guide to Grades and Specifications,* Tacoma, Washington, 1986.

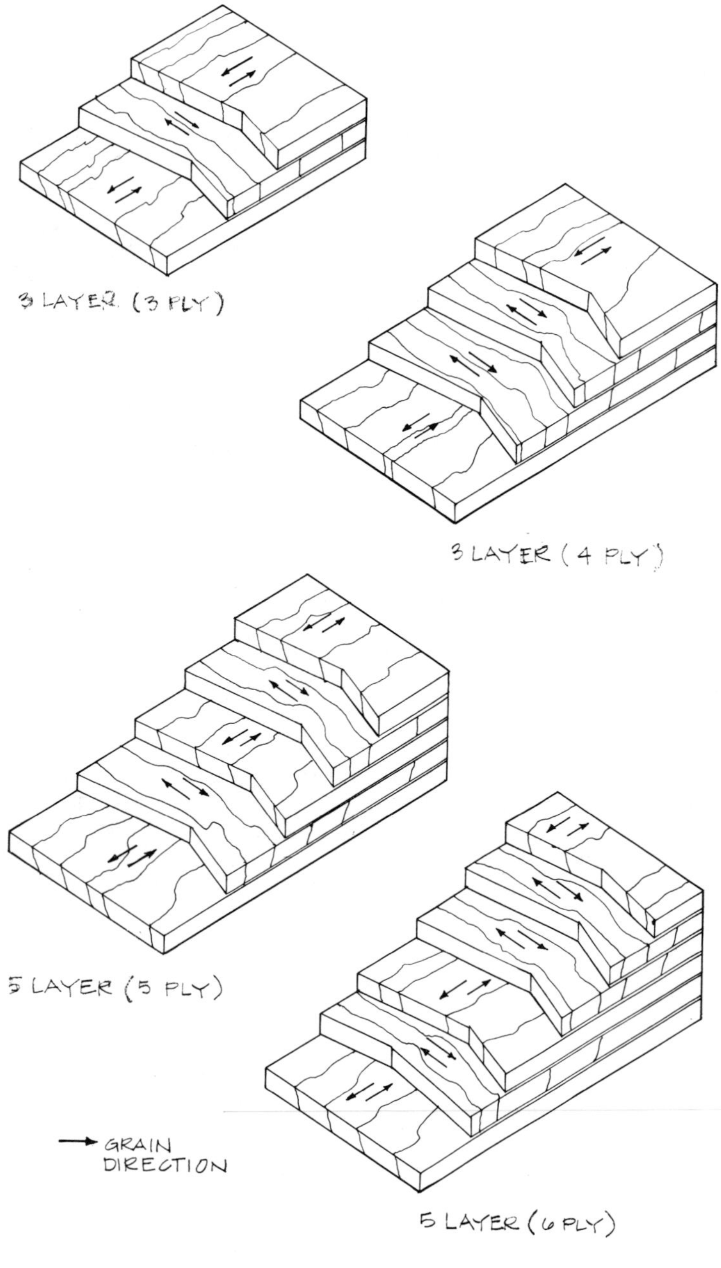
3 LAYER (3 PLY)
3 LAYER (4 PLY)
5 LAYER (5 PLY)
5 LAYER (6 PLY)
GRAIN DIRECTION

Figure 850-11 Plywood Construction. Typical three- and five-layer construction with parallel-laminated crossbands in the 4- and 6-ply panels.

TABLE 850-14
Appearance Grades of Plywood (Exterior Type)[a,g]

Grade designation[b]	Description and most common uses	Veneer grade: Face	Veneer grade: Back	Veneer grade: Inner plies	Most common thicknesses, in[c]									
A-A EXT-APA	Use where appearance of both sides is important. Fences, built-ins, signs, boats, cabinets, commercial refrigerators, shipping containers, tote boxes, tanks, and ducts.[d]	A	A	C	1/4		11/32	3/8	15/32	1/2	19/32	5/8	23/32	3/4
A-B EXT-APA	Use where the appearance of one side is less important.[d]	A	B	C	1/4		11/32	3/8	15/32	1/2	19/32	5/8	23/32	3/4
A-C EXT-APA	Use where the appearance of only one side is important. Soffits, fences, structural uses, boxcar and truck lining, farm buildings, tanks, trays, and commercial refrigerators.[d]	A	C	C	1/4		11/32	3/8	15/32	1/2	19/32	5/8	23/32	3/4
B-B EXT-APA	Utility panel with solid faces.[d]	B	B	C	1/4		11/32	3/8	15/32	1/2	19/32	5/8	23/32	3/4
B-C EXT-APA	Utility panel for farm service and work buildings, boxcar and truck lining, containers, tanks, agricultural equipment. Also as base for exterior coatings for walls, roofs.[d]	B	C	C	1/4		11/32	3/8	15/32	1/2	19/32	5/8	23/32	3/4
HDO EXT-APA	High density overlay (HDO) plywood. Has a hard, semiopaque resin-fiber overlay, both faces. Abrasion-resistant. For concrete forms, cabinets, counter tops, signs and tanks.[d]	A or B	A or B	C or C (plugged)				3/8		1/2		5/8		3/4
MDO EXT-APA	Medium density overlay (MDO) with smooth, opaque, resin-fiber overlay, one or both panel faces. Highly recommended for siding and other outdoor applications, built-ins, signs, and displays. Ideal base for paint.[d]	B	B or C	C		5/16		3/8	15/32	1/2	19/32	5/8	23/32	3/4
303 Siding EXT-APA	Proprietary plywood products for exterior siding, fencing, etc. Special surface treatment such as V-groove, channel groove, striated, brushed, rough-sawn. 4-ft × 9-ft and 4-ft × 10-ft panels available.[f]	[e]	C	C			11/32	3/8		1/2	19/32	5/8		
T 1-11 EXT-APA	Special 303 panel having grooves 1/4 in deep, 3/8 in wide, spaced 4 in or 8 in o.c. Other spacing optional. Edges shiplapped. Available unsanded, textured, and MDO. 4-ft × 9-ft and 4-ft × 10-ft panels available[f]	C or btr.	C	C							19/32	5/8		
MARINE EXT-APA	Ideal for boat hulls. Made only with Douglas fir or western larch. Special solid jointed core construction. Subject to special limitations on core gaps and number of face repairs. Also available with HDO or MDO faces.	A or B	A or B	B	1/4			3/8		1/2		5/8		3/4

[a] Sanded both sides except where decorative or other surfaces specified.

[b] Available in Group 1, 2, 3, 4, or 5 unless otherwise noted.

[c] Sandard 4 × 8 panel sizes, other sizes available.

[d] Also available in Structural I (all plies limited to Group 1 species) and Structural II (all plies limited to Group 1, 2, or 3 species)

[e] C or better for 5 plies. C plugged or better for 3-ply panels.

[f] Stud spacing is shown on grade stamp.

[g] For strength properties of appearance grades, refer to "Plywood Design Specification," form Y510, American Plywood Association.

Source: American Plywood Association, *Guide to Grades and Specifications,* Tacoma, Washington, 1986.

TABLE 850-15
Engineered Grades of Plywood

Grade designation	*Description and most common uses*	*Veneer grade: Face*	*Veneer grade: Back*	*Veneer grade: Inner plies*	*Most common thicknesses, in*[c]
			Interior type		
C-D INT-APA	For wall and roof sheathing, subflooring, and industrial uses such as pallets. Commonly available with exterior glue. Specify exterior glue for better durability in somewhat longer construction delays and for treated wood foundations.[b,i]	C	D	D	5/16, 3/8, 7/16, 15/32, 1/2, 19/32, 5/8, 23/32, 3/4, 7/8
Structural I C-D INT-APA and Structural II C-D INT-APA	Unsanded structural grades where plywood strength properties are of maximum importance: structural diaphragms, box beams, gusset plates; stressed-skin panels, containers, and pallet bins. Made only with exterior glue.	C[f]	D[f]	D[f]	5/16, 3/8, 7/16, 15/32, 1/2, 19/32, 5/8, 23/32, 3/4, 7/8
Underlayment INT-APA	For underlayment or combination subfloor underlayment under resilient floor coverings, carpeting. Specify exterior glue where moisture may be present, such as bathrooms and utility rooms, or if construction may be delayed, as in site-built floors. Touch-sanded. Also available in tongue-and-groove.[b,c,h]	C[k]	D	C[g], D	1/4, 5/16, 11/32, 3/8, 15/32, 1/2, 19/32, 5/8, 23/32, 3/4
C-D Plugged INT-APA	For built-ins, wall and ceiling tile backing, cable reels, walkways, separator boards. Not a substitute for underlayment as it lacks underlayment's indentation resistance. Touch-sanded.[b,c,h]	C[k]	D	D	5/16, 3/8, 1/2, 19/32, 5/8, 23/32, 3/4
2-4-1 INT-APA	Combination subfloor underlayment. Use 2-4-1 with exterior glue in areas subject to moisture or if construction may be delayed, as in site-built floors. Unsanded or touch-sanded as specified.[b,e,j]	C[k]	D	C, D	1 1/8 in
			Exterior type		
C-C EXT-APA	Unsanded grade with waterproof bond for subflooring and roof decking, siding on service and farm buildings, crating, pallets, pallet bins, and cable reels.	C	C	C	5/16, 3/8, 7/16, 15/32, 1/2, 19/32, 5/8, 23/32, 3/4
Structural I C-C EXT-APA and Structural II C-C EXT-APA	For engineered applications in construction and industry where full exterior type panels are required. Unsanded. See h for species group requirements.	C	C	C	5/16, 3/8, 7/16, 15/32, 1/2, 19/32, 5/8, 23/32, 3/4
Underlayment C-C plugged EXT-APA C-C Plugged EXT-APA	For underlayment or combination subfloor–underlayment under resilient floor coverings where severe moisture conditions may be present, as in balcony decks. Use for tile backing where severe moisture conditions exist. For refrigerated or controlled atmosphere rooms, pallets, fruit pallet bins, reusable cargo containers, tanks, and boxcar and truck floors and linings. Touch-sanded. Also available in tongue-and-groove.[c,h]	C[k]	C	C[g]	1/4, 5/16, 11/32, 3/8, 7/16, 15/32, 1/2, 19/32, 5/8, 23/32, 3/4
B-B Plyform Class I and Class II EXT-APA	Concrete form grades with high reuse factor. Sanded on both sides. Mill-oiled unless otherwise specified. Special restrictions on species. Also available in HDO.[d]	B	B	C	19/32, 5/8, 23/32, 3/4

[a] Panels are standard 4-ft × 8-ft size. Other sizes available.

[b] Also made with exterior glue.

[c] Available in Group 1, 2, 3, 4, or 5.

[d] Also available in Structural I.

[e] Made only in woods of certain species to conform to APA specifications.

[f] Special improved grade for structural panels.

[g] Special construction to resist indentation from concentrated loads.

[h] Also available in Structural I (all plies limited to Group 1 species) and Structural II (all plies limited to Group 1, 2, or 3 species).

[i] Made in many different species combinations. Specify by Identification Index.

[j] Can be special-ordered in Exterior type for porches and patio decks, roof overhangs, and exterior balconies.

[k] Plugged.

Source: American Plywood Association, *Guide to Grades and Specifications,* Tacoma, Washington, 1986.

of similar magnitude is expected before protection.

Appearance Grades: The grade designation is based primarily on the appearance and quality of the facing veneer as well as on the species groups of the component layers. The grade of a plywood is indicated on the piece by two letters describing the face and the back veneer (Table 850-14). Panels are sanded smooth on both sides for appearance and balanced construction. Decorative surfaces are also available.

Engineered Grades: These grades are developed for wall sheathing, roof sheathing, subflooring, and underlayment to ensure a suitable base for overlying materials (Table 850-15). Engineered plywood requires stiffness and strength, nail holding ability, durability, dimensional stability, and resistance to puncture and impact.

Identification index numbers are based on the species group, thickness, bending strength, and stiffness of the face and back plies of the panel (Table 850-16).

TABLE 850-16
Guide to Span Ratings for Engineered Grades of Plywood*

Thickness, in	*C-D INT-APA C-C EXT-APA*		
	Group 1 and structural I	*Group 2† or 3 and structural II†,§*	*Group 4‡*
5/16	20/0	16/0	12/0
3/8	24/0	20/0	16/0
1/2	32/16	24/0	24/0
5/8	40/20	32/16	30/12§
3/4	48/24	40/20	32/16§
7/8	—	48/24	40/20

* "Span rating" is designated by two numbers separated by a slash, where the first number represents the maximum recommended support spacing when the sheet is used as roof sheathing, and the second number represents the maximum recommended support spacing when the sheet is used as subflooring.

† Panels with Group 2 outer plies and special thickness and construction requirements or Structural II panels with Group 1 faces may carry the span rating numbers shown for Group 1 panels.

‡ Panels made with Group 4 outer plies may carry the span rating numbers shown for Group 3 panels when they conform to special thickness and construction requirements detailed in PS 1.

§ Check local availability.

Source: American Plywood Association, *Guide to Grades and Specifications,* Tacoma, Washington, 1986.

6.2 Particleboard

Particleboard is sheet lumber consisting of wood chips or sawdust glued together under heat and pressure to form 4 × 8 ft panels. *Waferboard* is composed of wafers of wood that roughly measure several inches square individually and that have been glued, heated, and pressed into a 4- × 8-ft panel.

Particleboard is a uniform material produced with various uniform surface textures, some of which can easily be painted or finished. The binder and additives chosen determine the strength, abrasion resistance, fire resistance, and durability of the panel. Particleboard is weak in tension perpendicularly to the face. The screw or nail holding ability may be poor in some particleboards.

Particleboard is dimensionally stable and warp-resistant. Its stability depends upon the density of the compressed particles and the type of glues used. Common uses of particleboard include sheathing, underlayment, and siding. Grades of particleboard suitable for exterior use are shown in Table 850-17. The thicknesses range from ⅛ to 2 in, in increments of 1/16 or ⅛ in.

TABLE 850-17
Exterior Grade Particleboards

Grade	*Density, lb/ft3*
2-H-1	High: 50 and over
2-H-2	High: 50 and over
2-M-1	Medium: 37–50
2-M-2	Medium: 37–50
2-M-3	Medium: 37–50
2-M-W*	Medium: 37–50
2-M-F†	Medium: 37–50

* W indicates that this product is made from wafers.

† F indicates that this product is made from flakes.

Source: National Particleboard Association, *Particleboard, the Versatile Product of the 1980s,* 1982.

6.3 Wood Shingles and Shakes

Shingles:

Most wood shingles are produced from western red cedar, although eastern white cedar, tidewater cypress, and California redwood are also available. Shingles are sawn from blocks of wood to produce smooth faces. Surfaces can be sawn smooth or later grooved (striated by ma-

TABLE 850-18
Grades, Types, and Sizes of Red Cedar Shingles*

Grade	Type, in	Bundles or cartons per square† No.	Weight, lb	Description
No. 1, Blue label	24 (Royals) 18 (Perfections) 16 (XXXXX)	4 bundles 4 bundles 4 bundles	192 158 144	The premium grade of shingles for roofs and sidewalls. These shingles are 100% heartwood, 100% clear, and 100% edge-grain.
No. 2, Red label	24 (Royals) 18 (Perfections) 16 (XXXXX)	4 bundles 4 bundles 4 bundles	192 158 144	A good grade for most applications. Not less than 10 in clear on 16-in shingles, 11 in clear on 18-in shingles, and 16 in clear on 24-in shingles. Flat grain and limited sapwood are permitted.
No. 3, Black label	24 (Royals) 18 (Perfections) 16 (XXXXX)	4 bundles 4 bundles 4 bundles	192 158 144	A utility grade for economy applications and secondary buildings. Guaranteed 6 in clear on 16-in and 18-in shingles, 10 in clear on 24-in shingles.
No. 4, Undercoursing	18 (Perfections) 16 (XXXXX)	2 bundles 2 bundles	60 60	A low grade for undercoursing on double-coursed sidewall applications.
No. 1 or No. 2, Rebutted-and-rejointed	18 (Perfections) 16 (XXXXX)	1 carton 1 carton	60 60	Same specifications as No. 1 and No. 2 grades above but machine-trimmed for exactly parallel edges with butts sawn at precise right angles. Used for sidewall application where tightly fitting joints between shingles are desired. Also available with smooth sanded face.
No. 1, Machine-grooved	18 (Perfections) 16 (XXXXX)	1 carton 1 carton	60 60	Same specifications as No. 1 and No. 2 grades above; these shingles are used at maximum weather exposures and are always applied as the outer course of double-coursed sidewalls.
No. 1 or No. 2, Dimension	24 (Royals) 18 (Perfections) 16 (XXXXX)	4 bundles 4 bundles 4 bundles	192 158 144	Same specifications as No. 1 and No. 2 grades above, except they are cut to specific uniform widths and may have butts trimmed to special shapes.
No. 1 or No. 2, Hip-and-ridge	18 (Perfections) 16 (XXXXX)			Same specifications as No. 1 and No. 2 grades above; factory-cut, mitered, and assembled units produced for a 6-in-12 slope and adjust to fit slopes between 4 in 12 and 8 in 12.

* Redwood, white cedar, and cypress shingles are also available. Grades and types will vary.

† Nearly all manufacturers pack four bundles to cover 100 ft^2. When used at maximum exposures, undercoursing, rebutted-and-rejointed, and machine-grooved shingles typically are packed to cover 100 ft^2 when used at maximum exposure.

Source: Adapted with permission from Harold B. Olin, John L. Schmidt, and Walter H. Lewis, *Construction: Principles, Materials, and Methods,* U.S. League of Savings Institutions, Chicago, 1983.

TABLE 850-19
Types and Sizes of Red Cedar Shakes

Grade	Length and thickness, in	Bundles, per square*	Weight, lb per square	Description
No. 1, Hand-split and resawn	18 × ½ to ¾ 18 × ¾ to 1¼ 24 × ⅜	4 5 4	220 250 260	These shakes have split faces and sawn backs. Cedar blanks or boards are split from logs and then run diagonally through a bandsaw to produce two tapered shakes from each.
	24 × ½ to ¾ 24 × ¾ to 1¼ 32 × ¾ to 1¼	4 5 6	280 350 450	
No. 1, Tapersplit	24 × ½ to ⅝	4	260	Produced largely by hand, using a sharp-bladed steel froe and a wooden mallet. The natural shingle-like taper is achieved by reversing the block, end-for-end, with each split.
No. 1, Straight-split (barn)	18 × ⅜ (true edge) 18 × ⅜ 24 × ⅜	4 5 5	200 200 260	Produced in the same manner as taper-split shakes except that by splitting from the same end of the block, the shapes acquire the same thickness throughout.
No. 1, Starter finish	15 × ½ to 1¼	—	—	These shakes are used as the starting or underlay course at the eaves and as the final course at the ridge.
No. 1, Hip and ridge	18 × ½ to 1¼ 24 × ½ to 1¼	—	—	Factory cut, mitered, and assembled units are produced for a 6 in 12 slope; they adjust to fit slopes between 4 in 12 and 8 in 12.

* Generally represents the number of bundles required to cover 100 ft^2 when used for roof construction at the maximum recommended weather exposure.

Source: Adapted with permission from Harold B. Olin, John L. Schmidt, and Walter H. Lewis, *Construction: Principles, Materials, and Methods,* U.S. League of Savings Institutions, Chicago, 1983.

chine). Special shapes are sometimes available (Figure 850-12).

Available Sizes: Shingles are produced in random or specified widths (i.e., *dimension* shingles). Random widths range from a minimum of 3 in to a maximum of 14 in, and dimension shingles are either 5 or 6 in wide. All are available in three standard lengths (Table 850-18). Standard thicknesses of shingles are described as 4/2, 5/2¼, and 5/2 (four shingles to 2 in of butt thickness, five shingles to 2¼ of butt thickness, and five shingles to 2 in of butt thickness).

Grades: Grades for western red cedar shingles are shown in Table 850-18. Grades for northern white cedar are Extra, Clear, 2nd Clear, Clear Wall, and Utility. Grades for bald cypress are No. 1, Bests, Primas, Economy, and Clippers. Grades for redwood shingles are No. 1, No. 2 VG, and No. 2 MG.

The No. 1 grade for all species of wood is all clear, all heartwood, and all quartersawn. The lower grades are quartersawn or plain-sawn, have heartwood and sapwood, and have increasing degrees of imperfections.

Shakes:

Shakes refer to *hand-split* shingles; they have rough, split faces and either sawn or split backs (Figure 850-13). Most shakes are split by machine. All shakes are manufactured from western red cedar.

Three types of shakes are:

1. *Taper-split* shakes have a uniform texture and 100 percent edge-grain. Preferred for siding.
2. *Straight-split* shakes have a uniform texture and 100 percent edge-grain. Preferred for siding.
3. *Hand-split and resawn* shakes have heavy butt lines, a rugged appearance, and 50 to 100 percent edge-grain. Preferred for roofing.

Available Sizes: Shakes are manufactured in random widths (minimum of 4 in) and in lengths of 18 and 24 in, although 32-in shakes are sometimes available (Table 850-19). A *starter-finish* course of 15 in is also available. Shake thicknesses range from ⅜ to 1¼ in.

Grades: All cedar shakes are graded No. 1 and are 100 percent heartwood, free of both bark and sapwood (Table 850-19). Shakes are graded from the best face.

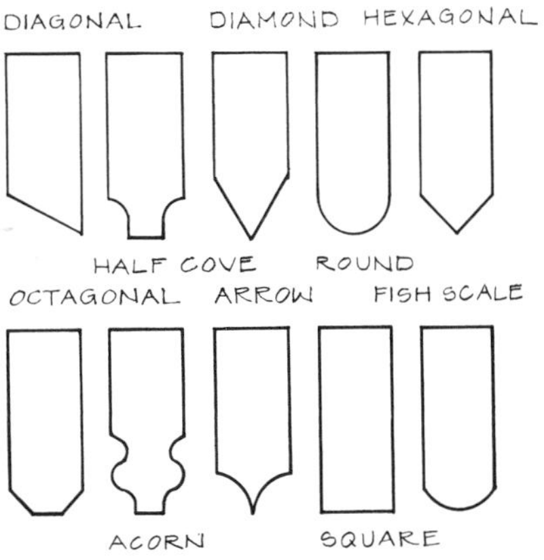
DIAGONAL
DIAMOND
HEXAGONAL
HALF COVE
ROUND
OCTAGONAL
ARROW
FISH SCALE
ACORN
SQUARE

Figure 850-12 Fancy Butt Red Cedar Shingles. Fancy butt shingles are 5 in wide and 7½ in long, custom-produced to individual orders.

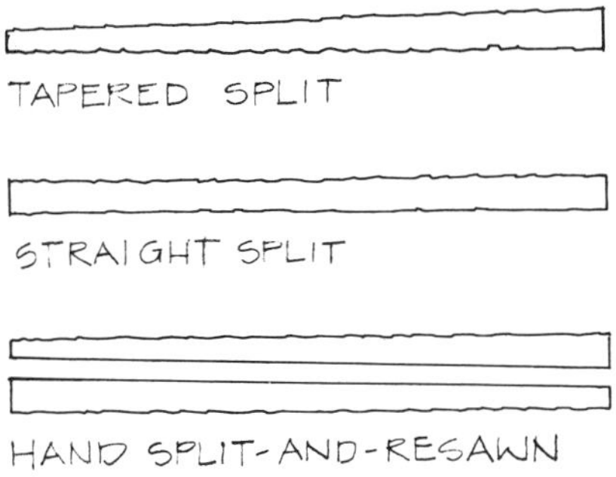
TAPERED SPLIT
STRAIGHT SPLIT
HAND SPLIT-AND-RESAWN

Figure 850-13 Types of wood shakes.

TABLE 850-20
Appearance Grades for Glue-Laminated Beams

	Appearance grades†		
*Grading criteria**	*Premium‡*	*Architectural‡*	*Industrial‡*
Characteristics and requirements for appearance	Used where the finest appearance is demanded. In exposed surfaces, knotholes and other voids shall be replaced with clear wood inserts or a neutral colored filler. Inserts shall be selected with a similarity of color and grain to the adjacent wood. The wide face of exposed laminates shall be selected for appearance free of loose knots or voids and with a similarity of color and grain of the laminations at end and edge joints. Knot size is limited to 20% of the net face width of the lamination. No more than two maximum knots shall occur in a 6-ft (1.829-m) length. Exposed surfaces shall be surfaced smooth, misses not permitted. The corners of the wide face of exposed laminations in the final member shall be eased.	Used where appearance is an important requirement. In exposed surfaces knotholes and other voids in excess of ¾ in (19.05 mm) shall be replaced with clear wood inserts or filler. The wide face of exposed laminations shall be free of loose knots and open knotholes. The material shall be selected for similarity of color and grain of the laminations at end and edge joints. Exposed surfaces shall be surfaced smooth. The corners of the wide face of exposed laminations in the final member shall be eased.	Used where appearance is not of primary importance. Inserts and wood fillers are not required. The wide face of exposed laminations shall be free from loose knots and open knotholes, and shall be surfaced on two sides only, an occasional miss being permitted along individual laminations.

* Unless otherwise specified, laminated timber truss members shall be industrial grade or better, except that the wide face of exposed laminates is permitted to have loose knots and open knotholes.

† When opaque finishes are specified, similarity of color and grain is not required.

‡ In all grades the laminations may possess the natural growth characteristics of the lumber grades.

Source: Caleb Hornbostel, *Construction Materials,* John Wiley, New York, 1978.

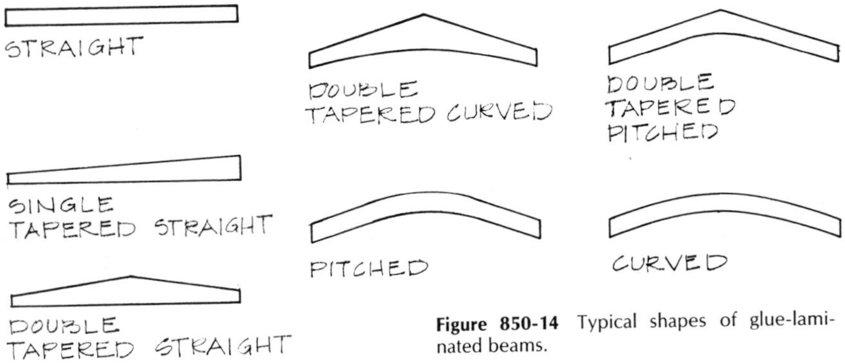
STRAIGHT
DOUBLE TAPERED CURVED
DOUBLE TAPERED PITCHED
SINGLE TAPERED STRAIGHT
PITCHED
CURVED
DOUBLE TAPERED STRAIGHT

Figure 850-14 Typical shapes of glue-laminated beams.

TABLE 850-21
Typical Sizes of Glue-Laminated Beams*†

Nominal, in	*Net finished, in (mm)*
3	2 ¼ (57)
4	3 ⅛ (79)
6	5 ⅛ (130)
8	6 ¾ (171)
10	8 ¾ (222)
12	10 ¾ (273)
14	12 ¼ (311)
16	14 ¼ (362)

* Special widths are available for particular jobs. Depths and spans vary in size as constructed to match the needs of a particular job.

† Standard widths.

Source: C. G. Ramsey and H. R. Sleeper, *Architectural Graphic Standards,* 7th ed., Robert T. Packard ed., New York, Wiley, 1981.

TABLE 850-22
Creosote* Wood Preservatives

Type of preservative	*Composition*	*Advantages*	*Disadvantages*
Coal-tar creosote	Black or brownish oil made from distilling coal tar	High toxicity to wood-destroying organisms; insolubility in water; low volatility; ease of application; permanence and depth of penetration can be determined	Dark brown color, cannot be painted; strong, unpleasant odor; easily ignited when first applied
Crystal-free coal-tar creosote	Coal-tar creosote from which some crystal-forming materials have been removed	Same advantages as coal-tar creosote; can be brushed and sprayed on more easily	Same disadvantages as coal-tar creosote
Anthracene oils	Coal-tar distillates of higher specific gravity and higher boiling ranges than coal-tar creosote	Same advantages as coal-tar creosote, plus less loss through evaporation during heating for application	Same disadvantages as coal-tar creosote
Creosotes derived from wood, oil, and water gas	Creosotes distilled from wood, oil, and water gas	Same advantages as coal-tar creosote	Less effective than coal-tar creosote
Creosote solutions	Mixture of coal tar or petroleum oils and 50–80 % by volume of coal-tar creosote	Same advantages as coal-tar creosote; less expensive	Less effective than coal-tar creosote

* Creosote may be hazardous to human health if exposure is not limited or prevented.

Source: Caleb Hornbostel, *Construction Materials,* Wiley, New York, 1978.

6.4 Glue-Laminated Beams

General:

Glue-laminated beams *(glulams)* refer to large structural members composed of pieces of lumber that have been placed with the grain running longitudinally, glued with adhesive, laminated, and, if specified, bent into various shapes (Figure 850-14). Such members are adaptable to construction needs and offer a variety of shapes, sizes, and strengths.

Their strengths are greater than lumber due to their increasing member size as well as to selectively using strong laminates on the outer layers where the stress is greatest.

Lumber species commonly used in the manufacture of glue-laminated beams include Douglas fir, larch, hemlock or fir, redwood, and southern yellow pine.

Glue-laminated beams for exterior applications require certain adhesives and preservative impregnation. If the site is particularly humid, all-heartwood construction may be warranted.

A beam's surface appearance will reflect the characteristics and grade of its lumber components. Glue-laminated timbers are produced in one of three grades that specify the appearance of the timber (Table 850-20). Structural properties and design values are not affected. A *rough-sawn* surface can be specified instead of a grade.

Available Sizes:

Commercially available sizes of glue-laminated beams are indicated in Table 850-21, although other sizes are available. Heights can vary and have been as high as 10 ft (3 m). Lengths vary as the task demands and have been as long as 130 ft (40 m).

7.0 PROTECTIVE TREATMENTS

Selection of a protective treatment for wood depends on the purpose of protection and the extent of protection required.

Figures 850-15 and 850-16 show regions in the United States where precautions against decay and termites are necessary.

7.1 Types of Preservatives

Wood preservatives are classified as either oilborne or waterborne preservatives. Creosote is an oilborne preservative with such widespread use that it is often talked about as a separate category. Creosote, however, has been proved to be a carcinogenic substance that is now restricted in several states and municipalities. Its use should be avoided whenever possible.

Creosote:

Creosote is a distillate of coal tar that is highly toxic to both plant and animal life, but it has been widely used because of its effectiveness as a wood preservative, especially in demanding situations such as those typical of marine environments. In addition to its toxic nature, creosote has the disadvantages of being odorous, flammable, and unsightly (turning wood black), as well as being incompatible with most paints and finishes (Table 850-22). Creosote has been proved to be an unreasonable risk to public health, and its use has been restricted in certain areas and under various circumstances. Effective protection can last as long as 30 to 60 years.

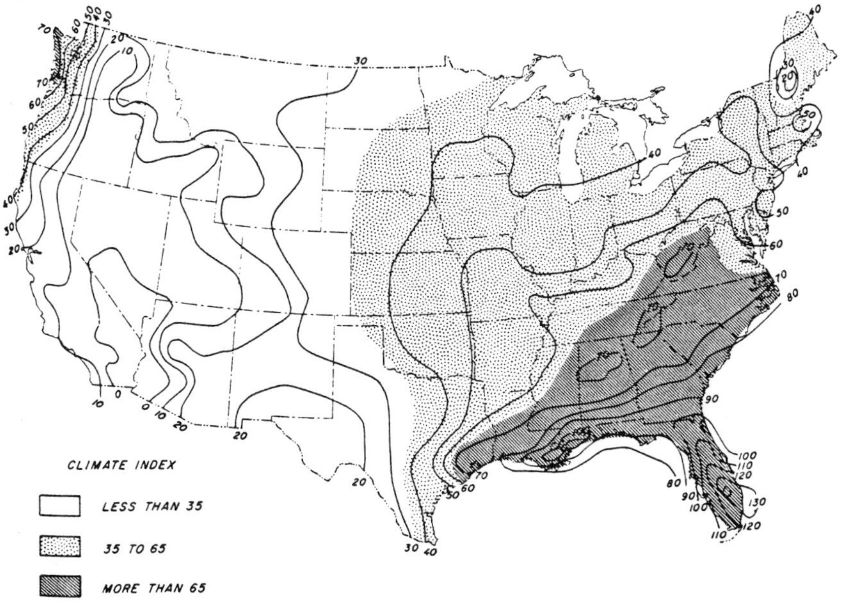
CLIMATE INDEX
LESS THAN 35
35 TO 65
MORE THAN 65

Figure 850-15 Levels of Decay Potential in the United States. Zones illustrate levels of decay potential for wood in aboveground service. Darker tones indicate increased potential for decay. Regions are determined based on rainfall and temperature data.

Oilborne Preservatives:

Oilborne preservatives, the most commonly used of which is pentachlorophenol, are not quite as effective as creosote compounds but are suitable for all but the most demanding situations (Table 850-23). Their disadvantages include toxicity and discoloration of wood (turning it brown), but they are relatively odor-free and can be painted over if they are applied using liquified petroleum gas (LPG) rather than a heavier oil as a base. Water-repellent preservatives are used to treat wood prior to painting.

Waterborne Preservatives:

Waterborne preservatives are salts which have the advantage of being clean, odorless, and paintable (Table 850-24). Wood is typically stained a light tint of green.

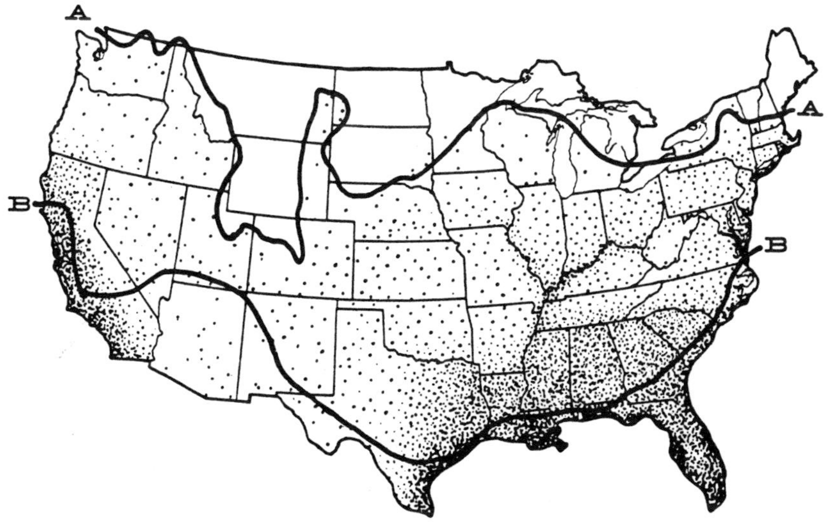
A
A
B
B

Figure 850-16 Extent of Termite Infestation in the United States. Zones illustrate general relative hazard of termite infestation. Subterranean termites have been found as far north as line A-A. Line B-B shows the northern limit of nonsubterranean termites.

7.2 Fire Retardants

Fire retardants can reduce the rate at which a fire can spread and the amount of smoke produced during the fire. The fire hazard classification of wood can be reduced for safety and/or insurance reasons. Wood is easily painted after treatment. Fire retardants are produced for both indoor and outdoor use.

7.3 Methods of Application

The effectiveness of a particular preservative depends to some extent on the manner in which it is applied to the wood.

Brushing and Spraying:

Brushing or spraying a preservative relies on capillary action for penetration and is effective to depths of a few millimeters into the wood. The process is adequate for most situations.

Dipping:

Dipping wood members into a solution for approximately 3 minutes also relies on capillary action for penetration. Dipping is more effective than brushing or spraying because checks and cracks are completely filled with preservative. *Soaking* refers to dipping for less than 1 day in a preservative bath, while *steeping* refers to immersion for more than 1 day in a waterborne preservative. Soaking, and especially steeping, are very effective means of protection.

Double-diffusion refers to the steeping of a wood member in one bath for a few days and then a second bath for an additional few days, resulting in considerable penetration of the preservative.

Thermal Processes:

Greater penetration and retention of a wood preservative can be achieved by immersing wood members in a hot chemical bath and then in a cold chemical bath.

TABLE 850-23
Oilborne Preservatives*

Type of preservative	*Composition*	*Advantages*	*Disadvantages*
Pentachlorophenol	Mixture of petroleum oils and 5% of pentachlorophenol, also 2% penta in creosote Pena mixture comes mixed with either light oil, heavy oil, or liquified petroleum, gas (LPG). Mixtures penetrate into wood leaving penta deeply inbedded. LPG evaporates rapidly after applying and leaves wood clean to touch.	High protection against decay fungi and termites; can be painted; no unpleasant odor; less easily ignited than coal-tar creosotes (fire hazard compares to that of untreated wood if volatile solvents are used and allowed to evaporate)	May alter color if dark-colored petroleum oils are used; provides less protection against marine borers
Copper naphthenate	Mixture of petroleum oils and 0.3–0.5% copper metal equivalent (5–30% copper naphthenate)		Gives wood greenish or dark color and provides less protection against marine borers than creosote
Water-repellent preservatives†	Mineral spirits and 10–25% maximum of nonvolative matter including the preservatives; preservatives shall be not less than 5% pentachlorophenol; copper naphthenate varies from 1–2%	Retards moisture changes in wood; good protection against decay and insects	Cannot be used in contact with ground or areas where continual dampness can occur unless preservative is thoroughly applied (water repellent has little value)

* Some of the above wood preservatives may be hazardous to human health if exposure is not limited or prevented.

† Not less than 0.045% copper 8 quinolinolate for areas where foodstuffs will be in contact with treated woods.

Source: Caleb Hornbostel, *Construction Materials,* Wiley, New York, 1978.

TABLE 850-24
Waterborne Wood Preservatives*

Type of preservative	*Composition*			*Advantages*	*Disadvantages*
Acid copper chromate† (Celcure)	31.8% copper oxide and 68.2% chromic acid; copper sulfate, potassium dichromate, or sodium dichromate may be substituted for copper oxide			Good protection against insects and decay; can be painted; no objectionable odor; impregnated with 0.5 lb/ft^3 (8.10 kg/m^3); resistant to marine borer attack	Wood can be in contact with ground or water, but degree of impregnation depends on use of wood
	Parts by weight				
Chromated copper arsenate:	Chromium trioxide	Copper oxide	Arsenic pentoxide		
Type I† (Erdalith, Greensalt, Tanalith, and CCA)	61	17	22	Excellent protection against decay, fungi, and termites; good resistance to marine borer attack when only *Limnoria* and *Terdeo* borers are present	Wood can be in contact with ground; used in salt water when only *Limnoria* and *Terdeo* borers are present
Type II† (Boliden, K33)	35.3	19.6	45.1	Good protection against decay and insect attack; can be painted; no objectionable odor	Can be in contact with ground or water
Type III† (Wolman, CCA)	47	19	34		
	The following substitutions are permitted: sodium or potassium dichromate for chromium trioxide; copper sulfate, basic copper carbonate, or copper trioxide for copper oxide; and arsenic acid or sodium arsenate for arsenic pentoxide				
Chromated zinc chloride	80% zinc oxide and 20% chromium trioxide; the following substitutions are permitted: zinc chloride for zinc oxide and sodium dichromate for chromium trioxide			Moderately effective in contact with ground; good protection under somewhat drier conditions	Should not be used in contact with ground or water because it has some leaching action
Chromated zinc chloride (FR)‡	80% chromated zinc chloride, 10% boric acid, and 10% ammonium sulfate			Retention of 1½–3 lb/ft^3 (24.03–48.06 kg/m^3) provides protection from decay and insect attack and has good fire-retardant characteristics	
Ammonical copper arsenite† (Chemonite)	49.8% copper oxide, 50.2% arsenic pentoxide, 1.7% acetic acid; the following substitutions are permitted: copper hydroxide for copper oxide, and arsenic trioxide for arsenic pentoxide			Good protection against decay and termite attack; protection against marine environment, provided pholad-type borers are not present	Wood can be in contact with ground or water, but degree of impregnation and high retention of preservatives depend on end use of wood
Chromated zinc arsenate†	20% arsenic acid, 21% sodium arsenate, 10% sodium dichromate, and 43% zinc sulfate			Good protection against decay and termites; can be painted; no objectionable odor	Wood can be in contact with ground but not water
Fluor chrome Arsenate phenol† (Wolman salts. Osmosalts)	22% fluoride, 37% chromium trioxide, 25% arsenic pentoxide, and 10% dinitrophenol; the following substitutions are permitted: sodium pentachlorophenate for dinitrophenol; sodium or potassium fluoride for fluoride, sodium chromate or dichromate for chromium trioxide, and sodium arsenate for arsenic pentoxide			Good protection against decay, fungi, and insects in above-ground wood construction, and moderate protection when in contact with ground	Wood cannot be used in contact with ground or water when good protection is required
Zinc metal arsenite	60 parts arsenious acid and 40 parts zinc oxide with sufficient acetic acid to maintain preservations in solution			Good protection against decay and insects; can be painted; no objectionable odor	Wood can be used in contact with ground but generally not recommended for contact with water

* Some of these wood preservatives may be hazardous to human health if exposure is not limited or prevented.

† Many of these preservatives are trademark products covered by patents and should not be used without the specific consent of the patentee.

‡ Designation for fire retardant.

Source: Caleb Hornbostel, *Construction Materials*, Wiley, New York, 1978.

TABLE 850-25
Summary of Wood Preservative Treatments[a]

Industry standard	*Uses*	*Description*
	Pressure treatment: waterborne solutions[b]	
AWPB LP-2—Softwood lumber, timber, and plywood, pressure-treated with waterborne preservatives for above-ground use	All construction uses (framing lumber, sheathing, siding, and trim) where wood should be protected from moderate decay hazard and insect attack.	
AWPB LP-22—Softwood lumber, timber, and plywood, pressure-treated with waterborne preservative for ground-contact use	All construction uses when exposed to severe insect attack and decay hazard. Also where wood is used in contact with the ground such as fence posts, steps, decks, etc.	Treated wood is clean, bright, and odorless; it is readily painted and glued with most adhesives.
AWPB-FDN—Softwood lumber, timber and plywood, pressure-treated with waterborne preservatives for ground-contact use	All parts of wood foundation systems for residential and light construction placed directly in the ground	The preservative is permanently fixed in the wood and will not leach out when exposed to weather.
AWPA C-23 Residential and commercial building poles, pressure-treated with waterborne preservatives	Poles for use in ground contact as a building foundation and column support against both lateral and vertical forces	
	Pressure treatment: oilborne solutions (pentachlorophenol)[c]	
AWPB LP-3—Softwood lumber, timber, and plywood, pressure-treated with light petroleum solvent-penta solution for aboveground use	All construction uses (framing lumber, sheathing, siding, and trim) where wood should be protected from moderate decay hazard and insect attack	
AWPB LP-33—Softwood lumber, timber, and plywood, pressure-treated with light petroleum solvent-penta solution for ground-contact use	All construction uses where exposed to severe insect attack and decay hazard. Also where wood is used in contact with the ground such as fence posts, steps, decks, etc.	Treated wood is clean, bright, and relatively odorless; it is paintable and can be glued with special adhesives.
AWPB LP-4—Softwood lumber, timber, and plywood, pressure-treated with volatile petroleum solvent (LPG)-penta solution for aboveground use	All construction uses (framing lumber, sheathing, siding, and trim) where wood should be protected from moderate decay hazard and insect attack.	Suitable for indoor and outdoor use.
AWPB LP-44—Softwood lumber, timber and plywood, pressure-treated with volatile petroleum solvent (LPG)-penta solution for ground-contact use	All construction uses where exposed to severe insect attack and decay hazard. Also where wood is used in contact with the ground such as fence posts, steps, decks, etc.	All petroleum solvent must be evaporated before painting and to eliminate odor.
AWPB CP-33—Residential and commercial building poles, pressure-treated with pentachlorophenol in light hydrocarbon solvent	Poles for use in ground contact as a building foundation and column support against both lateral and vertical forces	

[a] Some of the above wood preservatives may be hazardous to human health if exposure is not limited or prevented.

[b] Treated wood can be painted and glued, after redrying; not recommended for hardwoods.

[c] Suitable for treatment of hardwoods as well as softwoods; not recommended for marine use.

[d] Suitable for marine use; generally not paintable and retains odor for long periods; finish materials may be stained by contact with treated wood.

Industry standard	Uses	Description
	Pressure treatment: oilborne solutions (pantachlorophenol)[c]	
AWPB CP-44—Residential and commercial building poles, pressure-treated with pentachlorophenol in volatile petroleum solvent (LPG)	Poles for use in ground contact as a building foundation and column support against both lateral and vertical forces	
AWPA LP-7—Softwood lumber, timber, and plywood, pressure-treated with solvent-penta for aboveground use	Farm buildings, fences, bridges, etc. Good for outdoor applications because of good weathering characteristics	
AWPA C-23—Softwood lumber, timber, and plywood, pressure-treated with solvent-penta for ground use	All construction uses where exposed to severe insect attack and decay hazard. Also where wood is used in contact with the ground as in fence posts, steps, decks, etc.	Treated wood varies from light to dark brown, surface slightly oily; odor of oil and penta remain for several months after treatment.[e]
AWPA C-23—Residential and commercial building poles, pressure-treated with pentachlorophenol	Poles for use in ground contact as a building foundation and column support against both lateral and vertical forces	
AWPA C-23—Residential and commercial building poles, pressure-treated with creosote and creosote solutions	Creosote poles are widely used for pole-platform construction. They are suitable for residential pole-frame construction, but their use should be generally limited to those exterior poles that do not pass through enclosed, living space.	Creosoted poles range from dark brown to black, blending well with earth colors and natural surroundings. Because their surfaces are oily, painting is difficult at best and a characteristic smoky odor is detectable for some time following treatment.
	Pressure treatment: creosote and creosote solutions[d]	
AWPB LP-5—Softwood lumber, timber, and plywood, pressure-treated with creosote or creosote coal-tar solutions for aboveground use	Farm buildings, fences, bridges, etc. Good for outdoor applications because of good weathering characteristics. Suitable for marine use (wharfs, docks, etc.)	Treated wood varies from dark brown to black, surface oily, and creosote odor remains for many months after treatment.[f]
AWPB LP-55—Softwood lumber, timber, and plywood, pressure-treated with creosote or creosote coal-tar solutions for ground-contact use	All construction uses when exposed to severe insect attack and decay hazard. Also where wood is used in contact with the ground as in fence posts, steps, decks, etc. Suitable for marine use.	
	Nonpressure treatment: oilborne, water-repellent preservative solution	
NWMA IS-4—Water-repellent preservative, nonpressure treatment for millwork	Exterior millwork: precut window, door, and trim components	Clear, odorless, and easily painted[f]

[e] Generally not paintable; should not be used for subflooring or in contact with materials subject to staining (plaster, wallboard, etc.); retains odor for a long period when enclosed in a structure.

[f] Should not be used in contact with the ground or for conditions of severe insect attack and decay hazard.

Source: Adapted with permission from Harold B. Olin, John L. Schmidt, and Walter H. Lewis, *Construction: Principles, Materials, and Methods,* U.S. League of Savings Institutions, Chicago, 1983.

Such processes are warranted in instances where dipping alone would be inadequate.

Pressure Treatments:

Pressure treatments rely on differences in atmospheric pressure to force preservatives into wood tissue farther than would otherwise be possible. The *full-cell* process involves the vacuum removal of air out of the wood member, followed by forced entry of preservative into the tissue, resulting in high levels of retention. This process is often used for members that will be in contact with moist ground and for members used in marine environments.

The *empty-cell* process involves the forced entry of preservative into the wood tissue without prior vacuum air removal. Penetration is uniform and deep and leaves the wood surface drier than the full-cell process. The empty-cell process is suitable for the application of oilborne preservatives.

Penetration by pressure treatments will be complete in sapwoods but only partial in heartwoods due to the higher density of the wood. Pressure treatments are often effective for 30 to 60 years.

7.4 Selection Criteria

The proper selection of a preservative and a means of application depends on the type and situation of the wood members in question. Table 850-25 summarizes common wood preservatives used for various situations.

AGENCIES AND ORGANIZATIONS

National Bureau of Standards (NBS)
U.S. Department of Commerce
Washington, D.C.

National Technical Information Service (NTIS)
U.S. Department of Commerce
Springfield, Virginia

American Institute of Timber Construction (AITC)
Englewood, Colorado

American Plywood Association (APA)
Tacoma, Washington

American Wood Preservers Institute (AWPI)
McLean, Virginia

National Forest Products Association (NFPA)
Washington, D.C.

National Hardwood Lumber Association (NHLA)
Memphis, Tennessee

National Lumber Grades Authority (NLGA)
Vancouver, British Columbia, Canada

National Particleboard Association (NPA)
Silver Spring, Maryland

Northeastern Lumber Manufacturer's Association, Inc. (NELMA)
Falmouth, Maine

Northern Hardwood and Pine Manufacturers Association (NHPMA)
Green Bay, Wisconsin

Red Cedar Shingle and Handsplit Shake Bureau (RCSHSB)
Bellevue, Washington

Redwood Inspection Service (RIS)
Mill Valley, California

Southern Cypress Manufacturers Association (SCMA)
Memphis, Tennessee

Southern Pine Inspection Bureau (SPIB)
Pensacola, Florida

West Coast Lumber Inspection Bureau (WCLIB)
Portland, Oregon

Western Wood Products Association (WWPA)
Portland, Oregon

REFERENCES

American Lumber Standards Committee, National Bureau of Standards. *PS 20-70 American Softwood Lumber Standards,* U.S. Government Printing Office, Washington, DC, 1970 (or latest edition).

American Plywood Association. *PS 1-74 Construction and Industrial Plywood,* Tacoma, WA, 1974 (or latest edition).

Canada Standards Association. *Standard Grading Rules for Canadian Lumber,* National Lumber Grades Authority, Vancouver, British Columbia, (see latest edition).

U.S. Forest Products Laboratory. *Wood Engineering Handbook,* Prentice-Hall, Englewood Cliffs, NJ, 1982 (or latest edition). ■

section 860: Metals

CREDITS

Section Editor: Charles W. Harris
Technical Writer: Tobias Dayman, with extensive professional advice and assistance from David Mittlestadt

Reviewers:

David Mittlestadt
Sasaki Associates, Inc.
Watertown, Massachusetts

Laurence Zuelke
The Architect's Collaborative, Inc.
Cambridge, Massachusetts

CONTENTS

1.0 INTRODUCTION

1.1 General

Metal is an important construction material, the use of which requires an understanding of various types, their physical properties, and various construction techniques. The technology is complex, and consultation with a structural engineer is important whenever issues of bearing strength, durability, codes, or issues of safety are involved. Optimal use of the material is a primary objective.

1.2 Important Considerations

Galvanic Corrosion:

Galvanic corrosion is a process that can occur when two different metals are in physical contact with one another. The more anodic of the two metals corrodes, and its material is deposited on the more cathodic (more noble) metal when a solution (such as water) is present. The solution conducts electricity between the two metals.

Typically, the solution is water in the form of moisture condensation, and contaminants within the water act as the electrolyte. The corrosion potential increases in industrial, nonarid, and seacoast areas because of increased contaminants and/or moisture. The galvanic predisposition of several metals and metal alloys is shown in Table 860-1.

Galvanic corrosion is controlled by:

1. Using similar metals in the galvanic series

2. Using sacrificial anode coatings that purposely corrode, thereby leaving another desired anode nearby untouched or the cathode continually protected (e.g., zinc with a galvanized coating sacrificially corrodes to any exposed iron, leaving deposits, and thereby forming a layer that continues to protect the iron)

3. Providing a barrier, such as paint or a bituminous coating, to inhibit exposure to moisture

4. Installing a surface metal cladding (with galvanic potential similar to the expected conditions) onto a base metal that, if exposed, would otherwise be anodic or cathodic

5. Applying a paint or primer that either chemically changes the surface of the metal or includes an alkaline chemical that greatly reduces the rate of galvanic action to an acceptable level

Chemical Corrosion:

Chemical corrosion refers to the dissolving of a metal by chemical reaction with another gas or liquid, such as sulfuric acid. Particular metal types react differently to the many chemicals common to various environments. Proper selection of a metal for both its corrosion characteristics and its proper use in construction is essential.

Finishes, Protection, and Appearance:

Metal products can be finished to provide a variety of colors, textures, patterns, and degrees of reflectivity as well as to provide greater protection against abrasion and corrosion and/or to prepare the surface for applied coatings. Metal finishing can involve very complex processes. Consultation with fabricators, trade associations, and local practices is necessary for a comprehensive understanding of the subject.

Metal finishes are categorized according to the basic process by which they are applied. Certain finishing processes are suitable only for certain kinds of metals. Basic finishes for metals include:

1. *Mechanical finishes,* which include grinding, polishing, buffing, rubbing, or sandblasting. Various textures and degrees of reflectivity can be produced.

2. *Chemical finishes,* which refer to the reaction of a chemical and a metal surface to produce desired colors, textures, and/or corrosion resistance. Chemical finishes are commonly used on nonferrous metals and typically include conversion coatings and etches.

3. *Anodized finishes,* which are produced by placing a material in an acid solution through which passes an electric current; this alters the outer surface of the metal to create an integral corrosion-resistant layer. Clear, translucent, or opaque finishes in a variety of colors are available. Anodized finishes are used almost exclusively on aluminum.

4. *Applied coatings,* which refer to the process of adding materials to the surface of a metal to provide color, corrosion resistance, and/or protection against abrasion. Such coatings include paints, enamels, plastic films, galvanizing, and cladding. Some plastic coatings are proprietary products not covered by established standards of performance. Selections should be based on a full knowledge of benefits and limitations.

Manufacturing and Fastening:

A knowledge of the various stages in the manufacturing of metal products is helpful in the selection of a metal for any particular purpose.

Initially, metals are formulated in a *mill,* and afterwards undergo *fabrication* to produce objects in desired shapes. Fabrication processes include rolling, extruding, casting, drawing, and forging. Certain metals and/or desired shapes are limited to certain fabrication processes. Some finishes are produced during the fabricating process.

Fabricated metals can, if required, undergo a secondary *forming* operation whereby mechanical processes further shape the product for a particular purpose. Forming processes include bending, brake forming (pressing into shapes), spinning, embossing, blanking (cutting to achieve an outline), perforating, and piercing.

Thermal treatments are applied to metals to alter their strength, hardness, machinability, ductility, and cold-forming characteristics during the secondary forming stage. Many types of thermal treatments are available, the most common of which are tempering, quenching, and annealing. Some finish appearances are produced as a result of forming processes.

Metals that have been fabricated, formed, and/or finished may need continued work as part of their being fastened on-site in a specific situation. Typical fastening techniques include welding (molten temperatures with or without a metal filler), brazing [nonferrous filler that melts above 800 degrees F (427 degrees C)], soldering [seals without strength, using tin or a lead-based filler that melts below 500 degrees F (260 degrees C)], riveting, bolting, and screwing. Not all metals can be fastened in all of these ways. Finishes on certain metals may be limited to particular fastening techniques if marring of the surface is a concern. Specialists should be consulted when fastening metals in order to determine the suitability of a fastening technique in any particular situation.

2.0 METALS USED IN CONSTRUCTION

2.1 Aluminum

Aluminum is a lightweight, corrosion-resistant metal (one-third the weight of iron) that reflects light and heat and displays a moderately high degree of thermal expansion. It can be manufactured in a wide variety of shapes and is easily fastened by bolting, riveting, and welding. Some alloys are very strong and are used for structural purposes. Corrosion is controlled by an oxide that naturally forms on the surface of the metal, thereby preventing further oxidation of the metal beneath. The oxide layers will be thicker if the material is located in industrial, marine, or other highly corrosive environments. Some aluminum alloys display less corrosion resistance than does pure aluminum. Increased surface protection is achieved by increasing the film thickness either by anodizing, applying a paint, or cladding a more corrosion-resistant material (such as pure aluminum, zinc alloys, or magnesium silicide) onto a stronger corrosion-susceptible aluminum-alloy substrate.

Aluminum is subject to chemical attack from alkalies, hydrochloric acid, and, to a lesser degree, diluted acids. Typical corrosive situations occur when it is used with lime mortar, high alkaline concrete, or masonry where wet conditions are expected. These can be corrected by applying bituminous or zinc chromate prime on metal. Corrosion can also occur when using aluminum with green or damp wood, but this too can be corrected by applying paint or using wood treated with preservatives not containing acid.

Aluminum Alloys:

Pure aluminum is soft and highly corrosion-resistant. The addition of alloying element(s) can enhance desired properties of strength, machinability, impact resistance, and maleability, but it typically lessens resistance to corrosion. A nomenclature system used in the United States, devised by the Aluminum Association, categorizes both casting and wrought aluminum and its alloys based upon the major alloying element(s) used, as indicated by the first digit of the aluminum numeric (Table 860-2). In countries other than the United States, one of several different nomenclature systems is used that describes the same alloys.

Casting alloys are those that are cast in their intended form. *Wrought alloys* are those produced by mechanically shaping cast aluminum ingots. Aluminum alloys are often tempered to improve their strength, stability, and/or workability.

Finishes for Aluminum:

As an alternative to the natural formation of an oxide layer on exposed aluminum (which inhibits further corrosion), finishes can be applied (prior to the development of the oxide layer) to improve the corrosion or abrasion resistance, to alter the sur-

TABLE 860-1
Galvanic Series of Metals*

1. Aluminum
2. Zinc
3. Steel
4. Iron
5. Nickel
6. Tin
7. Lead
8. Copper
9. Stainless steel

* When any two metals on the list are in contact with one another in the presence of moisture, the lower one will be corroded. The further apart on the list, the more rapid and extensive will be the galvanic corrosion. This series is meant only as a guide to illustrate relative susceptibilities to galvanic corrosion.

TABLE 860-2
Common Aluminum Alloys

Casting nomenclature and product	*Wrought nomenclature and product*	*Major alloying element*	*Remarks and typical uses*
1xx.x	1xxx	Aluminum (at least 99% pure)	Corrosion resistance and workability are excellent. Used in small quantities. Slight amounts of silicon and iron increase strength but decrease corrosion resistance. Non-heat-treatable alloy
	1100-H16		Sheet, ducts
2xx.x	2xxx	Copper	Series displays strength and hardness but ductility and workability are decreased. Corrosion resistance often less; thus typically clad. Heat-treatable alloy
214			Fittings and railings
	2014-T6		Structural members
	2017-T4		Screws
	2024-T4		Screws and rivets
3xx.x	3xxx	Manganese	Series for general purposes as alloy displays moderate strength with ductility, workability, corrosion resistance, and brightness almost that of pure aluminum. Commercial 3003 anodizes very well. Non-heat-treatable alloy
356.0-T6			Hardware, railings, supports
	3003-O		Concealed and exposed flashing
	3003-H18		Hardware
4xxx.x	4xxx	Silicon	Series exhibits best corrosion resistance of the aluminum alloys. Good for marine, heavily weathered, and heavy chemical environments. Non-heat-treatable alloy
B443.0-F			Casting or sand casting. Used for panels, hardware, lettering, grilles, posts, sculpure
5xx.x	5xxx	Magnesium	Series displays higher tensile strengths and resistance to fatigue. Have excellent corrosion resistance in many environments, including seacoast atmospheres and saltwater. Does not cut or work as clean as other alloys. Non-heat-treatable alloy
514.0-F			Lettering, posts
	5050-O		Hardware
6xx.x	6xxx	Magnesium–silicon	Somewhat less strength than 2xxx series, but displays better corrosion resistance and workability. Heat-treatable alloy.
	6061-T13		Pipe railings. Excellent fusion weldability properties
	6061-T6		Structural member, gratings, treads, steps, floor, and angle flanges. Excellent fusion weldability characteristics
	6061-T913		Nails
	6063-T4		Poles for flagpoles or lamps
	6063-T42		Exposed flashing
	6063-T5		Door and window frames, railings, thresholds, exposed flashing, hardware bars, rods, tubes
	6063-T6		Structural members, nails, corrugated sheets
7xx.x	7xxx	Magnesium–zinc	Series displays strongest properties of aluminum alloys. Highest yield strength. More difficult to work with and more expensive. Heat-treatable alloy
	7075-T6		Structural members

TABLE 860-3
Finishes for Aluminum

Type of finish	*Designation**	*Description*	*Remarks*
		Mechanical	
As fabricated	M10 M11 M12 M1X	Unspecified Specular as fabricated (bright finish) Nonspecular as fabricated (dull finish) Other	Used where appearance is not important; can be discolored when welded
Buffed	M20 M21 M22 M2X	Unspecified Smooth specular (mirrorlike finish) Specular Other	Used where bright finish is desired (entrance doors and hardware); avoid using on broad flat surfaces where "oil canning" is objectionable
Directional textured	M30 M31 M32 M33 M34 M35 M3X	Unspecified Fine satin Medium satin Coarse satin Hand-rubbed Brushed Other	Use where smooth satin sheen of limited reflectivity is desired; easy to restore after welding
Nondirectional textured	M40 M41 M42 M43 M44 M45 M46 M47 M4X	Unspecified Extra fine matte Fine matte Medium matte Coarse matte Fine shot blast Medium shot blast Coarse shot blast Other	Used primarily for castings in architectural use; produced by blasting (sand, beads, shot, etc.)
Patterned		Embossed and coined patterns and textures	Available in light gauge sheet; patterns can be highlighted by polishing.
		Chemical	
Nonetched cleaned	C10 C11 C12 C1X	Unspecified Degreased Inhibited chemical cleaned Other	Used to clean in preparation for other finishes
Etched	C20 C21 C22 C23 C2X	Unspecified Fine matte Medium matte Coarse matte Other	Typically used for surfaces to be anodized, although finish can be clear lacquer; can be used to produce patterns in the metal surface

* The complete designation must be preceded by AA—signifying Aluminum Association.

† *Impregnated* color coatings are available in many colors. Not all colors are suitable for exterior use. Gold is the most colorfast.

Integral color coatings offer a range of colors from bronze to gray to black. Some colors can be obtained only with certain alloys. Colorfastness is excellent. Typically, these colors are applied by a proprietary process.

face texture or color, or to prepare a surface for a subsequent finish coating (Table 860-3).

Mechanical Finishes: Mechanical finishes should not be applied to aluminum-clad surfaces because such finishes will damage the integrity of the cladding (Table 860-3).

Chemical Finishes: Chemical finishes are often used to provide intermediate finishes for surface cleaning, to produce a matte texture or a bright finish, or to prepare the surface for painting or another finish (Table 860-3).

Anodized Finishes: Surface textures are not affected by the anodizing process. Because the colors typically vary slightly from piece to piece, designers should investigate aesthetic compatibility. Anodized coatings require a sealer to provide resistance to staining and to ensure greater durability of color. Flash welding is suitable for exposed areas, but arc welding should be limited to concealed surfaces. Acid materials should be avoided when cleaning or maintaining anodized surfaces.

Designers should specify the precise thickness, density, and proper sealing of an anodized product to ensure that the anodizing process (a proprietary product) is performed to desired intentions (Table 860-3).

Applied Coatings: Aluminum cladding and plastic films are commonly applied to aluminum. Plastic films are durable and fade-resistant and demonstrate excellent

Type of finish	*Designation**	*Description*	*Remarks*
		Chemical	
Brightened	C30	Unspecified	Limited architectural use; avoid use in large surfaces (fascias, spandrel panels, etc.); appropriate for window frames
	C31	Highly specular (mirror bright)	
	C32	Diffuse bright	
	C3X	Other	
Chemical conversion coatings†	C40	Unspecified	Used to improve adhesion of surfaces for painting, and can be used as final finish; most methods are proprietary.
	C41	Acid chromate-fluoride (clear to yellowish color)	
	C42	Acid chromate-fluoride-phosphate (clear to greenish color)	
	C43	Alkaline chromate (gray color)	
	C4X	Other	
		Anodized	
Architectural class II (0.4 to 0.7 mil coating)	A31	Clear (natural) coating	Thickness of coating ranges from 0.4 to 0.7 mils. For interiors not subject to excessive wear and for exteriors that are regularly maintained. Sulfuric acid (clear) process: thick-thin coats
	A32	Coating with integral color	
	A33	Coating with impregnated color	
	A34	Coating with electrolytically deposited color	
	A3X	Other	
Architectural class I (0.7 mil and greater anodic coating)	A41	Clear (natural) coating	Thickness of coating must be at least 0.7 mils. For interiors with normal wear and exteriors receiving no regular maintenance
	A42	Coating with integral color	
	A43	Coating with impregnated color	
	A44	Coating with electrolytically deposited color	
	A4X	Other	
		Applied coatings	
Laminated: three types of plastic films		Polyvinyl chloride: range of colors Polyvinyl fluoride:: limited color range, medium gloss, smooth surface Acrylic: clear by nature but can be pigmented	Resistant to thermal expansion; highly durable; excellent color retention and weatherability; can be applied in one operation; recommended for interiors and exterior metal work

Electrolytically deposited color coatings are available in a range of colors from light bronze to black. Of all anodized coatings, colors that are electrolytically deposited are the least susceptible to sunlight and other types of weathering.

Source: Adapted from *Sweet's Selection Data: Metals,* McGraw-Hill, New York, 1978; and adapted with permission from Harold B. Olin, John L. Schmidt, and Walter H. Lewis, *Construction: Principles, Materials, and Methods,* U.S. League of Savings Institutions, Chicago, 1983.

weatherability (Table 860-3). Typical films include polyvinyl chloride (wide range of colors), polyvinyl fluoride (smooth surface, medium gloss, but limited color range), and acrylics (clear and colored).

2.2 Copper

Copper is a malleable, ductile, reddish-brown metal that is resistant to corrosion and easily welded, brazed, or soldered. It easily conducts heat and is a superb conductor of electricity. When combined with certain alloying elements, copper can be made sufficiently strong for some construction work.

The natural oxidation of copper causes the formation of a bluish-green *patina* on the surface of the material. Copper carbonate forms in the presence of water, while copper sulfate forms in the presence of a sulfurous atmosphere. Copper is susceptible to attack from alkalies and most common acids, especially in areas where sulfur is present.

Copper Alloys:

In the United States, the Copper Development Association has established a nomenclature system for copper and copper alloys (Table 860-4), of which the following are found in the construction industry:

1. *Coppers:* contain a minimum of 99.3 percent copper.

2. *High-copper alloys:* if wrought, contain 96.0 and 99.3 percent copper, and if cast, contain 94.0 to 99.3 percent copper.

TABLE 860-4
Copper and Copper Alloys

Alloys	Remarks	Color			Typical uses	Fabrication							
		Unexposed	Initial weathering	Final weathered		Machinability*	Brazenability†	Solderability†	Weldability: Oxyacetylene†	Weldability: Cas shielded arc†	Weldability: Coated metal arc†	Weldability: Resistance (spot)†	Weldability: Resistance (seam)†
Wrought alloys													
Copper													
110 99.99 copper	Copper (110) and high copper alloy (122) are corrosion resistant and best for wire.	Salmon-red	Reddish brown	Gray-green patina	Gutters, flashing, screens, nails, tacks	20	B	A	D	C	D	D	D
122 99.99 copper		Salmon-red	Reddish brown	Gray-green patina	Tube, sheet, plate, welding	20	A	A	B	A	D	D	D
Architectural bronze and common brasses													
220 Commercial bronze	Plain brasses have a high percentage of zinc, hardened by cold-working; less expensive than high copper alloys. Red brass is excellent to resist corrosion. Cartridge brass has good combination of strength and durability.	Red-gold	Brown	Gray-green patina	Grills, screws, rivets, hardware	20	A	A	B	B	D	D	D
230 Red brass		Reddish yellow	Chocolate brown	Gray-green patina	Trim, weatherstripping, fasteners	30	A	A	B	B	C	D	D
260 Cartridge brass		Yellow	Usually protected from weathering to preserve color		Grills, rivets, screws, miscellaneous hardware	30	A	A	B	C	B	D	D
280 Muntz metal		Reddish yellow	Red brown	Gray brown	Sheet and stripping trim large nuts and bolts	40	A	A	B	C	B	D	D
314 Leaded commercial bronze					Screws and miscellaneous rough hardware	80	B	A	D	D	D	D	D
320* Leaded red brass	Leaded brass has improved machinability but cannot be cold-worked as easily.	Reddish yellow	Chocolate brown	Gray-green patina		30	A	A	B	B	C	D	D
350 Medium leaded brass					Finish hardware	70	B	A	D	D	D	D	D
377 Forging brass		Reddish yellow	Russet brown	Dark brown	Forging	80	B	A	D	D	D	D	D
385 Architectural bronze		Reddish yellow	Russet brown	Dark brown	Architectural extrusions and hardware	90	B	A	D	D	D	D	D
Nickel silver and silicon bronze													
651 Silicon bronze	Silicon bronzes have higher tensile strength and good corrosion resistance.	Reddish old gold	Russet brown	Finely mottled dark gray-brown	Hardware	30	A	A	B	A	C	A	B
655 Silicon bronze		Reddish old gold	Russet brown	Finely mottled dark gray-brown	Hardware	30	A	B	B	A	C	A	A
745 Nickel-silver	Nickel-silvers: copper-zinc-nickel formulations. Lead, if added, improves machinability. Easily hot-worked and fabricated into intricate parts	Warm silver	Gray-brown	Finely mottled gray-green	Rivets, screws, fasteners, hardware	20	A	A	B	C	D	B	C
774 Nickel-silver		Warm silver	Gray-brown	Finely mottled gray-green	Typically for extrusions	—	—	—	—	—	—	—	—
796 Leaded nickel silver		Warm silver	Gray-brown	Finely mottled gray-green	Typically for extrusions	50	A	A	B	D	D	B	B
Cast alloys													
Architectural bronze and common brasses													
834 Similar to 220	See appropriate remarks above.	Red-gold	Brown	Gray-green patina		60	A	A	C	C	D	—	—
836 Similar to 230		Reddish yellow	Chocolate brown	Gray-green patina		84	B	A	D	D	C	—	—
852 Similar to 260		Yellow	Usually protected from weathering to preserve color			80	C	A	C	D	D	—	—
853 Similar to 260		Yellow				30	A	A	B	B	D	—	—
855 Similar to 260		Yellow				80	C	B	D	D	D	—	—
857 Similar to 260		Yellow				80	C	B	D	D	D	—	—
875 Similar to 651 and 635		Reddish old gold	Russet brown	Finely mottled gray-green		50	C	C	C	C	D	—	—
Nickel-silver													
973 Composition similar to nickel-silver		Warm silver	Gray-brown	Finely mottled gray-green		70	A	A	D	D	D	—	—

* 0-100 scale of increasing ease.

† A = excellent; B = good; C = fair; D = not recommended.

Source: Adapted from *Sweet's Selection Data: Metals,* McGraw-Hill, New York, 1978.

TABLE 860-5
Finishes for Copper

Finishes	*Appearance, pattern, and color*	*Remarks*
	Mechanical	
"As fabricated"—originally imparted by a rolling, extrusion, or casting process	Hot-rolled and heat-treated products have dull finish. Cold-rolled surfaces have brighter finish	Do not use where appearance is important.
Buffed	Available in specular and smooth specular finish	Used mostly for hardware; high reflectivity; avoid use on wide, flat surfaces.
Directional textured	Satin sheen in fine, medium, or coarse texture (also in hand-rubbed or brushed finishes)	Limited reflectivity
Nondirectional textured	Available in fine, medium, or coarse matte finishes	Primarily used for hardware, castings; "se" is restricted to metal at least ¼ in thick.
Patterned	Embossed and coined patterns and textures	Minimal marring in service; elimination of distorted reflections; pattern can be highlighted by polishing; increased sheet stiffness
	Chemical	
Nonetch cleaning	Removes oil, grease, soil, etc., from the surface of the metal	Used to clean surfaces in preparation for other finishes via degreasing or chemical cleaning
Matte finishes	Matte, textured surface	Tend not to be used on copper alloys; used mainly on bronzes
Bright-dipped	Smooth, bright	Limited architectural uses; used mostly as a surface preparation for plating or painting
Conversion coating	Statuary bronze finishes can be toned, which will vary from a light golden color to black. Sulfide treatments produce statuary brown colors. Selenide treatments provide deep colors.	Most important finish for copper alloys; used primarily to alter color and provide final finish; duplicates weathering effects from 1–12 yr; types include treatments which produce (a) patinas or verde antiques, (b) statuary or oxidized colors; statuary treatment has better color uniformity; statuary finish is difficult to produce and maintain and requires periodic rubbing with oil.
	Applied	
Laminated coatings	Clear film (bonded polyvinyl fluoride)	Chemically inert; mechanically strong; resists impact, abrasion, weathering
Oils and waxes	Rich luster and depth of color	Primarily used for maintenance purposes on site

Source: Adapted from *Sweet's Selection Data: Metals,* McGraw-Hill, New York, 1978.

3. *Brasses:* zinc is the main alloying element.

4. *Bronze:* the alloying elements(s) are other than zinc or lead, or the alloying elements are predominant over the zinc.

5. *Nickel silvers:* alloys that have a mixture of copper, nickel, and zinc.

Finishes for Copper:

Coppers, brasses, bronzes, nickel silvers, and silicon bronzes have integral colors, patinas, and surface textures that can be altered by mechanical or chemical means in a variety of ways (Table 860-5).

Mechanical Finishes: Mechanical finishes for copper produce surfaces ranging from a natural to a bright or reflective appearance (Table 860-5). Marring is much more noticeable on specular or mirrorlike finishes.

Chemical Finishes: Chemicals are used on coppers to clean the surface, to provide a matte or smooth bright finish, to age the surface artificially, or to preserve surface color (Table 860-5).

Applied Coatings: Applied coatings (clear films) are often used on copper to protect the copper from abrasion and to preserve its color (Table 860-5).

2.3 Iron

Pure iron is a tough, malleable, soft metal that readily oxidizes in air. Iron is the base metal of cast iron, wrought iron, and steel.

Cast Iron:

Cast iron is distinguished from wrought iron or steel by containing more than 2 percent carbon. A major advantage of cast iron is that it can be poured into forms of various shapes to produce objects for specific purposes. Cast iron exhibits good compressive strength and is relatively inexpensive, but it has poor tensile strength. Alloys in special castings can enhance certain properties—such as increased corrosion resistance, heat resistance, strength, machinability, and hardness. If corrosion is to be minimized, cast iron should be alloyed with a corrosion-resistant alloy or be protected by either a galvanized, plated, or asphalt surface coating.

Typical uses of cast iron include piping and fittings, pavement opening frames and

TABLE 860-6
Types of Iron Used in Construction

Types	*Remarks*
Gray cast iron	Gray color when broken; soft and tough; easily machinable
Malleable cast iron	Light gray color when broken, strong and tough, easily machined; more ductile with increased breakage resistance as compared to gray cast iron
Wrought iron	Soft, resistant to corrosion and fatigue, easily machined and worked; resistant to progressive corrosion

Source: Adapted from Caleb Hornbostel, *Construction Materials,* Wiley, New York, 1978.

TABLE 860-7
Carbon Steel (a) Classes, (b) Common Designated Steels

Class	*Percentage of carbon*
Soft	0.20
Mild	0.15-0.25
Medium	0.25-0.45
Hard	0.45-0.85
Spring	0.85-1.15

(a)

Common designated steels	
ASTM	AISI
ASTM A373	
	10XX
A283	
	11XX
Merchant quality: A 663 bars	
	12XX
A 675 bars	
	15XX
ASTM A36	

(b)

Source: Adapted with permission from Harold B. Olin, John L. Schmidt, and Walter H. Lewis, *Construction: Principles, Materials, and Methods,* U.S. League of Savings Institutions, Chicago, 1983.

covers, gratings, ornamental ironwork, custom-made objects, and hardware. The two types of cast iron typically used in construction are *gray* and *malleable* (Table 860-6).

Wrought Iron:

Wrought iron is distinguished from cast iron by a smaller carbon content (less than 0.1 percent), which makes the material softer, more malleable, easily machined and welded, and resistant to continued corrosion and fatigue (Table 860-6). Basic forms include bars, sheets, plates, pipes, and special shapes. Applications include ornamental ironwork, railings, fences, furniture, grilles, and screens.

2.4 Steel

Steels are combinations of iron, carbon, and other alloying elements characterized by unusual properties of strength.

Carbon Steels:

The most common form of steel is carbon steel, which consists of iron, carbon (up to 2 percent), manganese, silicon, and copper. Increasing amounts of carbon improve the strength, reduce the ductility, and decrease the melting point of steel. Carbon contents from 0.05 to 0.08 percent increase abrasion resistance, strength, and hardness but decrease the toughness, ductility, machinability, and impact resistance. Carbon steels exhibit poor corrosion resistance but can be improved by incorporating copper as an alloying element or by specifying a galvanized or other protective finish.

A number of nomenclature systems designate carbon steels. ASTM designates common architectural structural steels (Table 860-7). The American Iron and Steel Institute (AISI) has established a system based upon constituents. A Unified Numbering System (UNS) was established in 1975 as a comprehensive nomenclature system that combines the two former systems.

Carbon steels are available in both wrought and cast products, although advances in technology may enable the manufacturing of extruded products in the near future. Wrought uses include structural steel, reinforcing rods, sheet and strip, mesh and wire cloth, ornamental metal, and hardware.

Finishes for Carbon Steel: Chemical finishes are used to clean the surface without otherwise affecting it and to prepare the surface for applied coatings. Common finishes for carbon steel are described in Table 860-8.

Alloy Steels:

Alloy steels consist of one or more alloying elements in amounts sufficient to impart unique properties unattainable in carbon steels. The numerical system developed by the AISI to designate types of alloy steels is based upon constituents, while ASTM designations are based on performance criteria.

Due to high production costs, the use of alloy steels in architectural applications is limited.

High-Strength Low-Alloy Steels (Weathering Steels):

High-strength low-alloy steels are alloy steels that contain less than 1 percent of any alloying element and exhibit properties of high strength, stiffness, ductility, and excellent resistance to corrosion (Table 860-9). Such steels are most useful where a high degree of strength with low weight and/or corrosion resistance is required (e.g., bridges). Weathering steels can be worked by gas cutting, punching, riveting, welding, and hot and cold forming. Typical forms include plate, sheet, bar, tube, pipe, wire, and structural shapes.

Within a period of 18 months to 3 years, a protective oxide film forms on surfaces that have been openly exposed to the atmosphere. Surfaces must be fully exposed to atmospheric changes in moisture and drying and not be located under debris or puddles. If the material cannot be fully exposed to complete natural dry/wet cycles, the surfaces must be painted. During the oxide forming period, any moisture dripping from the steel will stain surrounding surfaces, especially porous ones. The color of exposed steel begins as a red-orange rust and eventually turns to a purple-brown, brown-black, or blue-black color. The colors remain a light shade in nonindustrial environments and remain even lighter in rural areas.

The use of weathering steels should be avoided in corrosive industrial atmospheres, marine environments, and those situations where the metal may be in constant contact with water (soil moisture, groundwater, etc.).

Stainless Steels:

Stainless steels are ferrous steels with a chromium content of at least 12 percent and additional amounts of nickel, manganese, or molybdenum (Table 860-10). Stainless steels exhibit a high degree of permanence, high resistance to corrosion, high strength, high rates of thermal expansion, low rates of thermal conductivity, and surfaces that are relatively bright. The initial costs are relatively high, but the long-term maintenance costs are minimal.

TABLE 860-8
Finishes for Carbon Steel

Finishes	*Appearance, pattern, and color*	*Remarks*
	Mechanical	
As fabricated (mill finishes)	Hot-rolled: tight mill scale and rust powder	Improper preparation could prevent complete adhesion and provide focal points for corrosion. Mill scale and rust powder must be removed.
	Cold-rolled: may be extremely smooth; must be degreased before painting	Must be cleaned and possibly roughened for extremely smooth surfaces
Cleaning methods	Removal of mill scale, corrosion products, and dirt	Methods to remove mill scale, dirt, etc.: hand cleaning (for spot cleaning), power tool cleaning (for heavy stock), shot- and sand-blasting (provides most suitable surface for painting), flame cleaning (for heavy stock)
Pattern	Various embossed patterns	
	Chemical	
Cleaned only	Clean mill finish surface	Methods: pickling (removes dirt, rust, mill scale), vapor degreasing (removes oil and grease), alkaline cleaning (removes oil and grease)
Conversion coatings	Fine matte surface texture; usually slate gray	Acid phosphate solutions are generally used to prepare the surface for paint and other coatings; usually proprietary
	Applied	
Zinc (galvanizing) G90	Gray crystalline	For normal use, steel sheets use 0.90 oz/ft^2 of zinc coating
Lightweight	Gray crystalline; fine matte finish	Coatings less than 0.1 oz/ft^2 of sheet require painting.
After fabrication	Gray crystalline	Used with a variety of small and large fabricated shapes for critical exposures (aggressive industrial atmospheres). Standard galvanized coating, applied after fabrication, lasts up to 25 years.
		Zinc coatings will burn off during welding operations but can be restored. Heavier coatings last longer.
Aluminum (aluminizing) Type 2	Weathers like aluminum	Provides excellent corrosion resistance; not recommended for use at temperatures above 900°F; wide acceptance in many building applications
Porcelain enamel	Wide range of colors and textures, from low gloss (semimatte) to dull (full matte)	Color uniformity from part to part excellent; bonded by fusion at 800°F or higher; resists chemical stains; nonporous; highly durable
Laminated	Polyvinyl chloride plastic films (grained embossed); polyvinyl flouride plastic films (medium gloss, smooth surface); acrylic films (clear but usually pigmented)	Good resistance to thermal expansion; durable and weather-resistant for exterior use; can be applied in one operation; excellent color retention; recommended for exterior metal work

Source: Adapted from *Sweet's Selection Data: Metals,* McGraw-Hill, New York, 1978.

TABLE 860-9
Corrosion Resistance of Some High-Strength, Low-Alloy Steels

Type of steel	*ASTM specification*	*Approximate corrosion resistance relative to carbon steel*
High-strength, low-alloy, structural Mn-V steel	A 441	2 times
High-strength, low-alloy, structural steel	A 242	5–8 times (Type I)
High-strength, low-alloy, structural steel	A 588	4 times
High-strength, low-alloy, sheet steel	A 606	
	Type 2	2 times
	Type 4	4 times

Source: Adapted with permission from Harold B. Olin, John L. Schmidt, and Walter H. Lewis, *Construction: Principles, Materials, and Methods,* U.S. League of Savings Institutions, Chicago, 1983; C. G. Ramsey and H. R. Sleeper, *Architectural Graphic Standards,* 7th ed., Robert T. Packard, ed., Wiley, New York, 1981; and Frederick S. Merritt, *Building Design and Construction Handbook,* McGraw-Hill, New York.

TABLE 860-10
Stainless Steels

Grain structure	*Type*	*Corrosion resistance*	*Welding, combining*	*Remarks*
Austentic (hardenable by cold-working; nonmagnetic, high ductility; with care, it can be fusion and resistance welded)	201	Excellent even at high temperatures. Compared to other stainless steels, more susceptible to deoxidizing by sulfur gases.	Fusion and resistance welding	Exterior work: same as 301 but stronger and harder
	202	Excellent even at high temperatures compared to other stainless steels, more susceptible to deoxidizing by sulphur gases.	Fusion and resistance welding	Exterior work: similar to 302
	301	Excellent except when in contact directly with salt spray or seawater	Fusion and resistance welding and good cold-forming	Exterior flashings: sometimes used as a structural member when cold-worked.
	302	Excellent except when in contact directly with salt spray or seawater	Fusion and resistance welding	Exterior work: often interchangable with 304
	304	Excellent except when in direct contact with salt spray or seawater	Fusion and resistance welding	Exterior work: often interchangable with 302; more machinable
	305	Excellent		Bolts, screws, nuts, and fasteners
	361	Best of stainless steels. Suitable in salt spray, seawater, and many chemical environments	Fusion and resistance welding	Exterior use, salt spray environments, and industrial areas
Ferritic (chromium content, at 12–27%; does not respond to heat treatment; can be welded but joint must not be subject to bending stress or shock)	430	Very good corrosion resistance	Fusion and resistance welded, but joint should not be exposed to shock or bending stress	Exterior use, sometimes for gutters, downspouts, trim, and column covers
Martinsitic (hardened by heat treatment; can be cold-formed or hot-forged and cooled slowly to prevent cracking)	410	Moderate. Avoid in industrial, marine, salt, and seawater environments.	Easily welded but needs to be followed by annealing or tempering to reestablish ductility	Bolts, screws, nuts, fasteners. Suitable where hardness, strength, and resistance to abrasion are necessary.

Resistance to corrosion is achieved by natural oxidation of the exposed surface (chromium oxide film), which protects the metal beneath. However, the oxide layer and the metal beneath is corroded in atmospheres containing chloride (seacoast environments, etc.).

Surface oils or dirt can inhibit exposure to oxygen and result in corrosion of the steel. Stainless steel will not corrode when placed in concrete masonry and its wash will not stain nearby materials. It can, however, be stained from the washes of other materials.

Stainless steels used in construction are first categorized by grain structure and subsequently according to the alloying elements therein, these combinations producing types of steel with unique properties (Table 860-10). Some types can be tempered for greater strength and hardness. The standard tempers, in terms of increasing strength and hardness, are *¼-hard, ½-hard, ¾-hard,* and *full-hard* (i.e., *½-hard* implies that the steel is half as hard as it can be, and *full-hard* means that it is tempered to the point of maximum hardness).

If welding of stainless steel is required, the manufacturer of the product should be contacted to determine which welding techniques are appropriate.

Given stainless steel's high rate of thermal expansion, expansion joints are often necessary to avoid a warping of panels.

Finishes for Stainless Steels: Stainless steels can be finished by mechanical or chemical means or by applied finishes (Table 860-11). Fabricators carry a wide variety of finish types.

2.5 Nickel

Nickel is a silvery metal that is strong, tough, and highly resistant to corrosion from both alkalies and acids, with the exception of nitric acid. Nickel can be welded, brazed, soldered, easily worked, and polished by a variety of methods. As an alloying element, nickel will impart strength, corrosion resistance, ductility, toughness, hardness, electrical resistance, and expansion control, even when the alloyed material has been exposed to high temperatures. Nickel is typically a high-cost alloy, but it is economical under conditions where maintenance would otherwise be expensive.

Typical nickel commercial products include:

Nickel plating: a layer of off-white-colored nickel is often applied to metals for a particular finish or for improved corrosion resistance. Finishes can be matte, satin, or bright polish. Nickel plating will tarnish in sulfuric atmospheres, resulting in the exposure of substrate metal. Nickel is galvanically compatible with many metals.

Monel: *Monel* is a trade name for an alloy consisting of 61.5 percent nickel, 31.5 percent copper, and other elements, including silicon, iron, and manganese. The material is bright, with a silver-white color, and strong; it has good resistance to fatigue and fatigue cracking; it is very rigid, relatively low in thermal expansion, and corrosion-resistant to many materials, including acids and salt water. Monel can be welded or soldered with acid fluxes. Typical forms include tube, sheet, strip, wire, rod, bar, and plate.

TABLE 860-11
Finishes for Stainless Steel

Finishes	*Appearance, pattern, and color*	*Remarks*
	Mechanical	
Standard mill finish	No. 1: dull	Used for concealed applications
Sheet-rolled	No. 2D: dull, nonreflective	Used when appearance is not important
	No. 2B: bright, moderately reflective finish	General purpose finish; used when appearance is not important
	Bright annealed: bright, highly reflective finish	Used when appearance is not important
Polished finish	No. 3: coarser than No. 4	Used as an intermediate, polished finish
	No. 4: bright machine-polished finish with grain	Most frequently used finish for architectural applications
	No. 6: dull, satin finish	Used when a high luster is undesirable and to contrast with brighter finishes
	No. 7: bright, highly reflective finish	Gaining acceptance in architectural work
	No. 8: Bright, "mirror" finish	Used for applications such as mirrors and reflectors
Patterned	Embossed and coined patterns and textures	Provides more stiffness to sheet; reduces optical distortion; available in light gauge sheet; patterns can be highlighted by polishing.
	Chemical	
Conversion coatings	Light to dark bronze; bluish hue to dark brown or brown-black	Acquired by controlled oxidation; excellent resistance to abrasion, humidity, corrosion, soiling, and oxidation; acquired by controlled heat-treating
	Applied	
Proprietary	Variety of forms	Used when appearance is not critical
Porcelain enamel	Essentially glass applied in translucent colors with metallic luster seen through glaze	Used at times for color and visual contrast; more durable but somewhat less elastic than organic coatings
Metallic	Copper and terne	

Notes: Most of the stainless steel used architecturally is in the form of sheet or strip. Unpolished No. 2D and 3B, proprietary finishes and bright rolled finishes cannot be matched in a fabricator shop. For fabricated products, use only if appearance is not critical. For large flat areas, use nonreflective matte, textured, patterned, or contoured finishes. For welded assemblies, use blendable finishes (No. 4).

Source: Adapted from *Sweet's Selection Data: Metals,* McGraw-Hill, New York, 1978.

3.0 METAL STOCK

In addition to designations for type, shape, and size, many kinds of metal stock (whether in the form of sheets, strips, wire, tubing, rivets, or screws) are typically specified according to thickness. The term *gauge* refers to the thickness (or cross-sectional dimension) of a material, but references can be misleading because the exact dimensions for identical gauge size differ between various standard gauging systems (Table 860-12). Different industries and sometimes different products within a particular industry may use more than one gauging system. Designers should be wary of these differences and should specify products in decimal inches or millimeters to indicate clearly the desired size, if such precision is important.

3.1 Bars, Flats, Squares, and Rounds

Bars, flats, squares, and rounds refer to solid stock, typically available in lengths of 12, 16, or 20 ft. Weight is calculated in terms of linear feet (Tables 860-13 through 860-17).

3.2 Tees

Tables 860-18 through 860-23 list commonly available sizes of tees in aluminum, bronze, and steel.

3.3 Zees

Tables 860-24 through 860-25 list commonly available sizes of zees in aluminum and steel.

3.4 Angles

Angle stock is manufactured either with equal legs or unequal legs (Tables 860-26 through 860-29). They are manufactured with square or rounded corners, and with either square or rounded inside radii, in aluminum, bronze, steel, and stainless steel.

3.5 Channels

Channel stock is manufactured either with square or rounded corners and inside radii in aluminum, bronze, steel, and stainless steel. Commonly available sizes are shown in Tables 860-30 through 860-34.

3.6 Aluminum I Beams

Specifications for structural aluminum I beams following American Standard and Aluminum Association standards are shown in Table 860-35. Aluminum Association standards for I beams specify less thickness in noncritical areas.

3.7 Aluminum H Beams

Commonly available sizes of aluminum H beams, incorporating a wide flange, are shown in Table 860-36.

3.8 Steel W Shapes

Steel W shapes are manufactured in a wider range of sizes than are other structural shapes (Table 860-37). The depth dimension varies slightly for each nominal size according to the thickness and strength of the flange.

3.9 Steel S Shapes

Steel S shapes are similar to W shapes. However, S shapes have rounded flanges and a more-restricted range of commonly available sizes (Table 860-38).

3.10 Steel M Shapes

Steel M shapes are a wide-flange steel shape with different combinations of depth, width, and thickness than other shapes (Table 860-39).

3.11 Steel HP Shapes

Steel HP shapes are manufactured with the

TABLE 860-12
Standard Gauges

GAUGE NO.	US STD. REVISED — For hot and cold rolled steel sheets.		UNITED STATES STANDARD (USS) — For stainless steel and monel metal sheets.		AMERICAN STEEL WIRE OR WASHBURN & MOEN (W & M) — For iron and steel wire.		BROWN AND SHARP (B & S) OR AMERICAN WIRE (AW) — For aluminum, copper, brass, bronze, and nickel silver sheets, strips, and wire. Small sizes in copper and brass tubing.		BIRMINGHAM WIRE (BWG) OR STUBS IRON WIRE — For hot and cold rolled steel strips. Rivets, spring steel, and flat steel wire. Steel, aluminum, bronze, monel stainless, and large size copper and brass tubing.		MACHINE AND WOOD SCREWS — For machine screws and ferrous and nonferrous wood screws.		GAUGE NO.
	DECIMAL	FRACTION	DECIMAL	FRACTION	DECIMAL	FRACTION	DECIMAL	FRACTION	DECIMAL		DECIMAL	FRACTION	
000	.3750"	3/8"	.3750"	3/8"	.3625"	23/64"	.4096"	13/32"+	.425"	27/64"+	GRAPHIC SIZES DO NOT APPLY TO THIS COLUMN		000
00	.3437"	11/32"	.3437"	11/32"	.3310"	21/64"+	.3648"	23/64"+	.380"	3/8"+			00
0	.3125"	5/16"	.3125"	5/16"	.3065"	5/16"−	.3249"	21/64"−	.340"	11/32"−	.060"	1/16"	0
1	.2812"	9/32"	.2812"	9/32"	.2830"	9/32"	.2893"	19/64"−	.300"	19/64"+	.073"	5/64"−	1
2	.2656"	17/64"	.2656"	17/64"	.2625"	17/64"−	.2576"	1/4"+	.284"	9/32"+	.086"	3/32"−	2
3	.2391"	15/64"+	.2500"	1/4"	.2437"	1/4"−	.2294"	15/64"−	.259"	17/64"−	.099"	3/32"+	3
4	.2242"	7/32"+	.2344"	15/64"	.2253"	7/32"+	.2043"	13/64"+	.238"	15/64"+	.112"	7/64"+	4
5	.2092"	13/64"+	.2187"	7/32"	.2070"	13/64"+	.1819"	3/16"−	.220"	7/32"+	.125"	1/8"	5
6	.1943"	3/16"+	.2031"	13/64"	.1920"	3/16"+	.1620"	5/32"+	.203"	13/64"	.138"	9/64"−	6
7	.1793"	11/64"+	.1875"	3/16"	.1770"	11/64"+	.1443"	9/64"+	.180"	3/16"−	.151"	5/32"−	7
8	.1644"	11/64"−	.1719"	11/64"	.1620"	5/32"+	.1285"	1/8"+	.165"	11/64"−	.164"	11/64"−	8
9	.1495"	5/32"−	.1562"	5/32"	.1483"	9/64"+	.1144"	7/64"+	.148"	9/64"+	.177"	11/64"+	9
10	.1345"	9/64"−	.1406"	9/64"	.1350"	9/64"−	.1019"	7/64"−	.134"	9/64"−	.190"	3/16"+	10
11	.1196"	1/8"−	.1250"	1/8"	.1205"	1/8"−	.0907"	3/32"−	.120"	1/8"−	.203"	13/64"	11
12	.1046"	7/64"−	.1094"	7/64"	.1055"	7/64"−	.0808"	5/64"+	.109"	7/64"	.216"	7/32"−	12
13	.0897"	3/32"−	.0938"	3/32"	.0915"	3/32"−	.0719"	5/64"−	.095"	3/32"+	–	–	13
14	.0747"	5/64"−	.0781"	5/64"	.0800"	5/64"+	.064"	1/16"+	.083"	5/64"+	.242"	1/4"−	14
15	.0673"	1/16"+	.0703"	5/64"−	.0720"	5/64"−	.0571"	1/16"−	.072"	5/64"−	–	–	15
16	.0598"	1/16"−	.0625"	1/16"	.0625"	1/16"	.0508"	3/64"+	.065"	1/16"+	.268"	17/64"+	16
17	.0538"	3/64"+	.0562"	1/16"−	.0540"	3/64"+	.0453"	3/64"−	.058"	1/16"−	–	–	17
18	.0478"	3/64"+	.0500"	3/64"+	.0475"	3/64"+	.0403"	3/64"−	.049"	3/64"+	.294"	19/64"	18
19	.0418"	3/64"−	.0437"	3/64"−	.0410"	3/64"−	.0359"	1/32"+	.042"	3/64"−	–	–	19
20	.0359"	1/32"+	.0375"	1/32"+	.0348"	1/32"+	.0320"	1/32"+	.035"	1/32"+	.320"	5/16"+	20
21	.0329"	1/32"+	.0344"	1/32"+	.0318"	1/32"+	.0285"	1/32"	.032"	1/32"+	–	–	21
22	.0299"	1/32"−	.0312"	1/32"	.0286"	1/32"−	.0253"	1/32"−	.028"	1/32"−	–	–	22
23	.0269"	1/32"−	.0281"	1/32"−	.0258"	1/32"−	.0226"	1/64"+	.025"	1/32"−	–	–	23
24	.0239"	1/32"−	.0250"	1/32"−	.0230"	1/64"+	.0201"	1/64"+	.022"	1/64"+	.372"	3/8"−	24
25	.0209"	1/64"+	.0219"	1/64"+	.0204"	1/64"+	.0179"	1/64"+	.020"	1/64"+	–	–	25
26	.0179"	1/64"+	.0187"	1/64"+	.0181"	1/64"+	.0159"	1/64"+	.018"	1/64"+	–	–	26
27	.0164"	1/64"+	.0172"	1/64"+	.0173"	1/64"+	.0142"	1/64"−	.016"	1/64"+	–	–	27
28	.0149"	1/64"−	.0156"	1/64"	.0162"	1/64"+	.0126"	1/64"−	.014"	1/64"−	–	–	28
29	.0135"	1/64"−	.0141"	1/64"−	.0150"	1/64"−	.0113"	1/64"−	.013"	1/64"−	–	–	29
30	.0120"	1/64"−	.0125"	1/64"−	.0140"	1/64"−	.0100"	1/64"−	.012"	1/64"−	.450"	29/64"	30

Note: Fractional data are provided for reference purposes. Thicknesses should be specified in decimal inches.

Source: Adapted from C. G. Ramsey and H. R. Sleeper, *Architectural Graphic Standards,* 7th ed., Robert T. Packard, ed., Wiley, New York, 1981.

TABLE 860-13
Aluminum Bars (Round Corners, 20-Ft Lengths)

Size (in)	*Corner radius (in)*
1 1/4 × 1 1/4	3/32
1/2 × 2	1/4
3/4 × 2 1/2	3/16
3/4 × 3	1/8
1 1/4 × 2 3/4	3/32

Source: Adapted from Theodore D. Walker, *Site Design and Construction Detailing,* 2d ed., PDA Publishers, Mesa, Arizona, 1986.

TABLE 860-14
Aluminum, Bronze, and Stainless Steel Flats

Size (in)	*Aluminum**	*Bronze**	*Stainless steel†*	*Size (in)*	*Aluminum**	*Bronze**	*Stainless steel†*
1/8 × 1/2	x	x		3/8 × 1/2	x	x	
1/8 × 5/8	x	x		3/8 × 5/8	x	x	
1/8 × 3/4	x	x		3/8 × 3/4	x	x	x
1/8 × 1	x	x		3/8 × 1	x	x	x
1/8 × 1 1/8	x			3/8 × 1 1/4	x	x	x
1/8 × 1 1/4	x	x		3/8 × 1 1/2	x	x	x
1/8 × 1 1/2	x	x		3/8 × 1 3/4	x		
1/8 × 1 3/4	x			3/8 × 2	x	x	x
1/8 × 2	x	x		3/8 × 2 1/2	x	x	x
1/8 × 2 1/2	x			3/8 × 3	x	x	x
1/8 × 3	x	x		3/8 × 3 1/2	x		
1/8 × 3 1/2	x			3/8 × 4	x	x	x
1/8 × 4	x			1/2 × 3/4	x	x	x
1/8 × 5	x			1/2 × 1	x	x	x
3/16 × 1/2	x	x	x	1/2 × 1 1/4	x	x	x
3/16 × 5/8		x		1/2 × 1 1/2	x	x	x
3/16 × 3/4	x	x		1/2 × 1 3/4	x		
3/16 × 1	x	x	x	1/2 × 2	x	x	x
3/16 × 1 1/4	x	x	x	1/2 × 2 1/2	x	x	x
3/16 × 1 1/2	x	x	x	1/2 × 3	x	x	x
3/16 × 1 3/4	x			1/2 × 3 1/2	x		
3/16 × 2	x	x	x	1/2 × 4	x		
3/16 × 2 1/2	x	x		5/8 × 1	x		
3/16 × 3	x	x	x	5/8 × 1 1/4	x		
3/16 × 3 1/2		x		5/8 × 1 1/2	x		
3/16 × 4	x	x		5/8 × 2	x		
1/4 × 3/8		x		5/8 × 3	x		
1/4 × 1/2	x	x		3/4 × 1	x	x	x
1/4 × 5/8	x	x		3/4 × 1 1/4	x		
1/4 × 3/4	x	x	x	3/4 × 1 1/2	x	x	x
1/4 × 1	x	x	x	3/4 × 1 3/4	x		
1/4 × 1 1/4	x	x	x	3/4 × 2	x	x	x
1/4 × 1 1/2	x	x	x	3/4 × 2 1/2	x		
1/4 × 1 3/4	x			3/4 × 3	x		
1/4 × 2	x	x	x	3/4 × 3 1/2	x		
1/4 × 2 1/2	x	x	x	3/4 × 4	x		
1/4 × 3	x	x	x	1 × 1 1/4	x		
1/4 × 3 1/2	x			1 × 1 1/2	x		x
1/4 × 4	x	x		1 × 1 3/4	x		
1/4 × 5	x			1 × 2	x		
1/4 × 6	x			1 × 2 1/2	x		
5/16 × 1	x			1 × 3	x		
5/16 × 1 1/4	x			1 × 3 1/2	x		
5/16 × 1 1/2	x			1 × 4	x		
5/16 × 2	x						

* 16 ft lengths.

† 12 and 16 ft lengths.

Source: Adapted from Theodore D. Walker, *Site Design and Construction Detailing,* 2d ed., PDA Publishers, Mesa, Arizona, 1986.

TABLE 860-15
Aluminum, Bronze, and Stainless-Steel Squares

Size (in)	*Aluminum**	*Bronze**	*Stainless Steel†*
¼ × ¼	x	x	
5/16 × 5/16	x	x	
⅜ × ⅜	x	x	
½ × ½	x	x	x
⅝ × ⅝	x	x	x
¾ × ¾	x	x	x
1 × 1	x	x	x
1¼ × 1¼	x	x	x
1½ × 1½	x	x	
1¾ × 1¾	x		
2 × 2	x		

* 16 ft lengths

† 12 and 16 ft lengths

Source: Adapted from Theodore D. Walker, *Site Design and Construction Detailing,* 2d ed., PDA Publishers, Mesa, Arizona, 1986.

TABLE 860-16
Aluminum, Bronze, and Stainless-Steel Rounds

Diameter (in)	*Aluminum**	*Bronze†*	*Stainless steel†*
3/16	x		
⅜	x	x	
½	x	x	x
9/16			x
⅝	x	x	x
¾	x	x	x
⅞	x	x	x
1	x	x	x
1⅛	x		
1¼	x	x	
1½	x	x	
2	x	x	

* 6 and 16 ft lengths

† 12 and 16 ft lengths

Source: Adapted from Theodore D. Walker, *Site Design and Construction Detailing,* 2d ed., PDA Publishers, Mesa, Arizona, 1986.

TABLE 860-17
Steel Half Rounds (20-Ft Lengths)

Size (in)
½ × ¼
⅝ × 5/16
1¼ × ⅝

Source: Adapted from Theodore D. Walker, *Site Design and Construction Detailing,* 2d ed., PDA Publishers, Mesa, Arizona, 1986.

TABLE 860-18
Aluminum Structural Tees

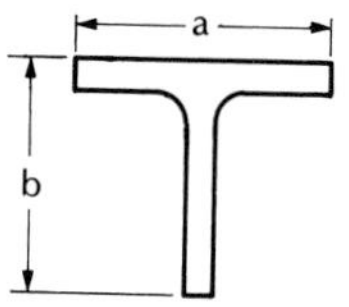
a
b

Shape	*Size*		
	Flange (a), in	*Stem (b), in*	*Thickness (t), in*
	1	1	⅛
	1½	1¼	⅛
	1½	1¼	3/16
	1½	1½	3/16
	1½	1½	¼
	1½	2	3/16
	2*	2	¼
	2	2	5/16
	2¼*	2¼	¼
	2½	1¼	3/16
	2½*	2½	5/16
	2½	3	5/16
	3	2½	5/16
	3*	3	⅜
	4	2	⅜
	4	3	5/16
	4*	4	⅜
	4	5	⅜
	4	5	½
	4½	3	5/16
	5	3	⅜

* Standard shapes normally available from warehouse stocks.

Source: The Aluminum Association, *Engineering Data for Aluminum Structures,* New York, 1986.

TABLE 860-19
Bronze Tees (20-Ft Lengths)

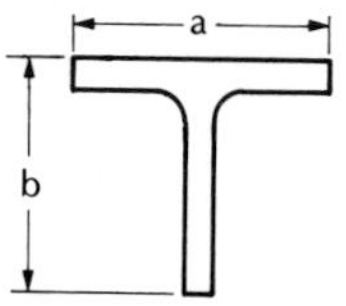
a
b

	Width (a), in	*Depth (b), in*	*Thickness (t), in*
	¾	¾	⅛
	1	1	⅛
	1½	1½	⅛
	1½	1½	3/16
	2	2	3/16

Source: Adapted from Theodore D. Walker, *Site Design and Construction Detailing,* 2d ed., PDA Publishers, Mesa, Arizona, 1986.

TABLE 860-20
Steel Structural Tees

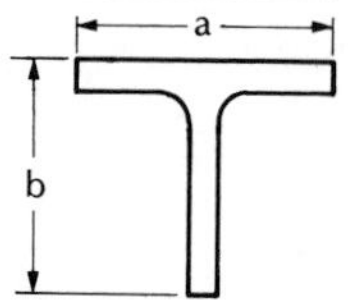
a
b

Shape	*Width (a), in*	*Depth (b), in*
	3	2½
	3	3
	4	3
	4	4
	5	3½

Source: Adapted from American Institute of Steel Construction, *Manual on Steel Construction,* Chicago, 1980.

TABLE 860-21
Structural Steel Tees Cut from "S" Shapes

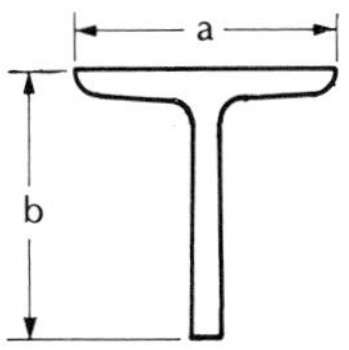
a
b

Shape	*Designation*	*Width (a), in*	*Depth (b), in*
	ST6 X 17.5	5.078	6.00
	X 15.9	5.000	6.00
	ST5 X 17.5	4.944	5.00
	X 12.7	4.661	5.00
	ST4 X 11.5	4.171	4.00
	X 9.2	4.001	4.00

Source: Adapted from American Institute of Steel Construction, *Manual on Steel Construction,* Chicago, 1980.

TABLE 860-22
Structural Steel Tees Cut from "W" Shapes*

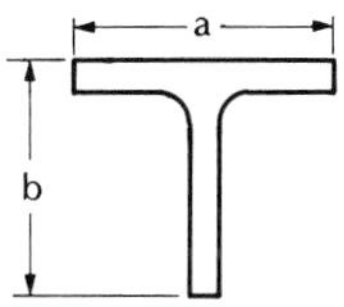
a
b

Shape	*Designation*	*Depth (b), in*	*Flange (a), in*
	WT6 X 11	6.155	4.030
	X 9.5	6.080	4.005
	X 8	5.995	3.990
	X 7	5.955	3.970
	WT5 X 9.5	5.120	4.020
	X 8.5	5.055	4.010
	X 7.5	4.995	4.000
	X 6	4.935	3.960
	WT4 X 7.5	4.055	4.015
	X 6.5	3.995	4.000
	X 5	3.945	3.940

* Most commonly used sizes shown here.

Source: Adapted from American Institute of Steel Construction, *Manual on Steel Construction,* Chicago, 1980.

TABLE 860-23
Stainless Steel Tees

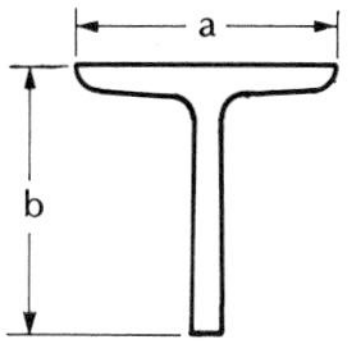
a
b

	Size		
Shape	*Flange (a), in*	*Stem (b), in*	*Thickness (t), in*
	1¼	1¼	3/16
	1½	1½	3/16
	2	2	¼
	2½	2½	¼
	2½	2½	⅜
	1½	1	3/16
	1¼	2	3/16
	1½	2⅜	3/16
	1	1¼	¼
	2	1¼	¼
	2½	1½	¼
	1½	2	¼
	2½	3	⅜
	3½	4	5/16

Source: Caleb Hornbostel, *Construction Materials,* Wiley, New York, 1978.

TABLE 860-24
Aluminum Structural Zees

Shape	Nominal depth (b), in	Width (a), in	Thickness (t), in
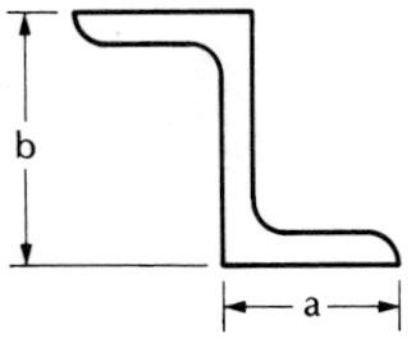b a	1 3/4	1 3/4	3/16
	2	1 1/4	3/16
	2 3/8	1 1/4	3/16
	3*	2 11/16	1/4
	3*	2 11/16	3/8
	4*	3 1/16	1/4
	4*	3 1/8	5/16
	4*	3 3/16	3/8
	4	3 1/16	7/16
	4	3 3/16	9/16
	5	3 1/4	5/16
	5*	3 5/16	3/8
	5*	3 1/4	1/2
	6	3 5/8	11/16

* Standard shapes normally available from warehouse stocks.

Source: Adapted from The Aluminum Association, *Engineering Data for Aluminum Structures,* New York, 1986.

TABLE 860-25
Steel Structural Zees

Shape	Size, in		
	(b)	(a)	(c)
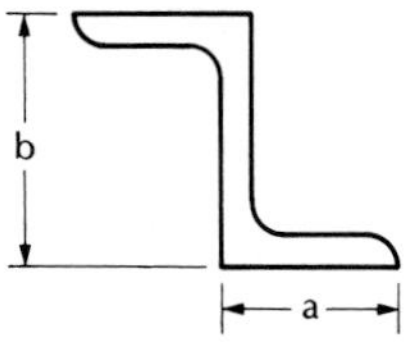b a	3	2 11/16	2 11/16
	4	3 1/16	3 1/16
	4 1/16	3 1/8	3 1/8
	4 1/8	3 3/16	3 3/16
	5	3 1/4	3 1/4
	5 1/16	3 5/16	3 5/16
	6	3 1/2	3 1/2

Source: Adapted from American Institute of Steel Construction, *Manual on Steel Construction,* Chicago, 1980.

TABLE 860-26
Aluminum Angles

Shape	Size, in	Size, in	Size, in
	Equal legs, square corners		
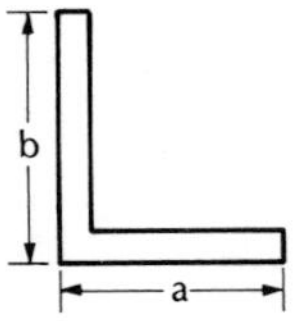b a	1/2	1 1/8	2
	1/2	1 1/4	2
	5/8	1 1/4	2 1/2
	3/4	1 1/2	3
	3/4	1 1/2	3
	1	1 1/2	3 1/2
	1	1 3/4	4
	1	2	
	Unequal legs, square corners		
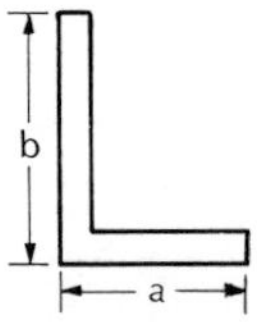b a	3/4 × 3/8	2 × 3/4	3 1/2 × 2
	1 × 1/2	2 × 1	3 1/2 × 2 1/2
	1 × 3/4	2 × 1	3 1/2 × 3
	1 1/4 × 1/2	2 × 1 1/2	4 × 2
	1 1/2 × 1/2	2 1/2 × 1	4 × 3
	1 1/2 × 3/4	2 1/2 × 1 1/2	5 × 3
	1 1/2 × 1	2 1/2 × 2	5 × 4
	1 3/4 × 1	3 × 1	5 1/4 × 2 1/4
	1 3/4 × 1 1/2	3 × 2	
	2 × 1/2	3 1/2 × 1 1/4	
	Equal legs, rounded corners		
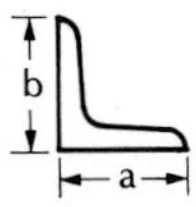b a	3/4	2	5
	1	2 1/2	6
	1 1/4	3	8
	1 1/2	3 1/2	
	1 3/4	4	
	Unequal legs, rounded corners		
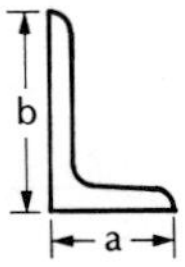b a	3/4 × 1 1/4	2 × 2 1/2	3 × 5
	3/4 × 1 1/2	2 × 3	3 1/2 × 5
	1 × 1 1/2	2 1/2 × 3	3 1/2 × 6
	1 1/4 × 1 1/2	2 1/2 × 3 1/2	4 × 6
	1 1/4 × 1 3/4	3 × 3 1/2	6 × 8
	1 1/2 × 2	3 × 4	
	1 1/2 × 2 1/2	3 1/2 × 4	

Source: Adapted from The Aluminum Association, *Engineering Data for Aluminum Structures,* New York, 1986.

TABLE 860-27
Bronze Angles

Shape	*Size, in*	*Size, in*	*Size, in*
	Equal legs		
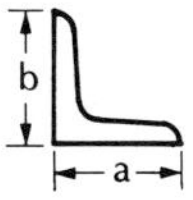 b a	½	1⅛	2½
	⅝	1¼	3
	¾	1½	
	1	2	
	Unequal legs		
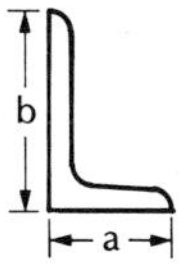 b a	¾ × ⅜	1¼ × ¾	2 × 1
	1 × ½	1½ × ¾	3 × 2
	1 × ¾	1½ × 1	4 × 2½

Source: Adapted from Theodore D. Walker, *Site Design and Construction Detailing,* 2d ed., PDA Publishers, Mesa, Arizona, 1986.

TABLE 860-28
Steel Angles

Shape	*Size, in*	*Size, in*	*Size, in*
	Equal legs, rounded corners		
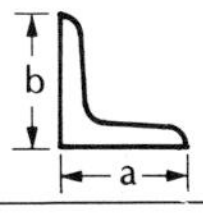 b a	1	2	4
	1¼	2½	5
	1½	3	6
	1¾	3½	8
	Unequal legs, rounded corners		
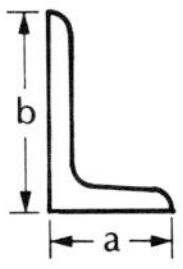 b a	1¾ × 1¼	3½ × 2½	6 × 4
	2 × 1¼	3½ × 3	7 × 4
	2 × 1½	4 × 3	8 × 4
	2½ × 1½	4 × 3½	8 × 6
	2½ × 2	5 × 3	9 × 4
	3 × 2	5 × 3½	
	3 × 2½	6 × 3½	

Source: Adapted from American Institute of Steel Construction, *Manual on Steel Construction,* Chicago, 1980.

TABLE 860-29
Stainless Steel Angles

Shape	*Size, in*	*Size, in*	*Size, in*
	Equal legs, cold-rolled		
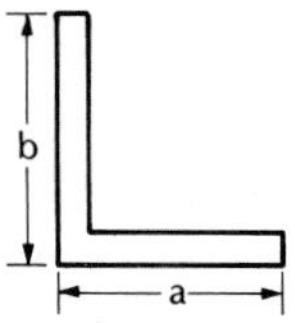 b a	½ ⅝ ¾	1 1¼ 1½	2
	Unequal legs, cold-rolled		
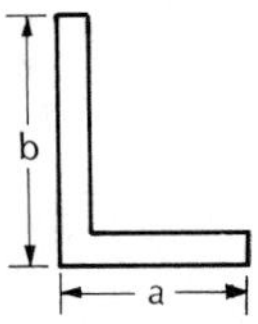 b a	1 × ⅝ 1¾ × ¾	1½ × 1 2 × 1	
	Equal legs, extruded		
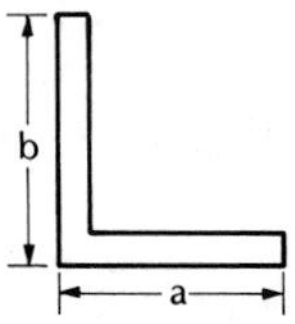 b a	1 1¼ 1½	1¾ 2 2½	3 3½
	Unequal legs, extruded		
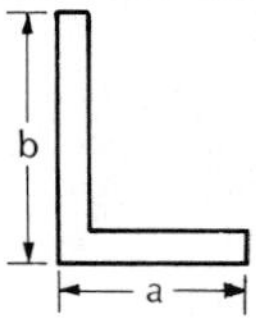 b a	2 × 1 2 × 1½ 2½ × 1¼ 2½ × 1½ 2½ × 2	3 × 1 3 × 1½ 3 × 2 3½ × 1½ 3½ × 2½	3½ × 3 4 × 3

Source: Adapted from Caleb Hornbostel, *Construction Materials,* Wiley, New York, 1978.

TABLE 860-30
Aluminum Channels

Shape	*Size, in*	*Size, in*	*Size, in*
	Channels, square corners		
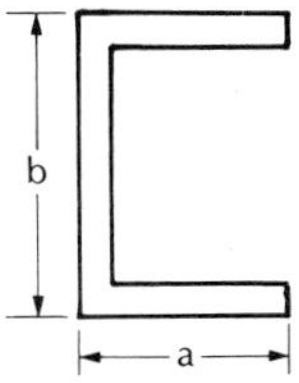	⅜ × ⅜	1¼ × ¾	2½ × ¾
	½ × ⅜	1¼ × 1¼	2½ × 1½
	½ × ½	1½ × ½	2½ × 2½
	½ × ¾	1½ × ⅝	3 × ½
	⅝ × ⅝	1½ × ¾	3 × 1
	⅝ × 1	1½ × 1	3 × 2
	¾ × ⅜	1½ × 1½	3 × 3
	¾ × ½	1¾ × ½	4 × 1½
	¾ × ¾	1¾ × ¾	4½ × 2
	1 × 1½	1¾ × 1	5 × 2
	1 × ¾	2 × ½	
	1 × 1	2 × 1	
	1¼ × ½	2 × 2	
	1¼ × ⅝	2¼ × ⅞	
	Channels, rounded corners		
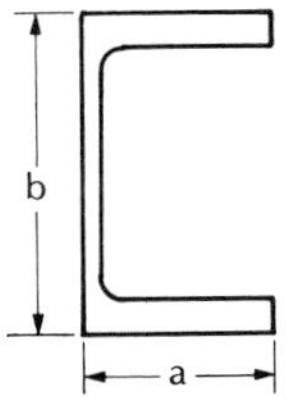	2 × 1	5 × 2¾	9 × 3¼
	2 × 1¼	6 × 2½	9 × 4
	3 × 1½	6 × 3¼	10 × 3½
	3 × 1¾	7 × 2¾	10 × 4¼
	4 × 2	7 × 3½	12 × 4
	4 × 2¼	8 × 3	12 × 5
	5 × 2¼	8 × 3¾	
	Channels		
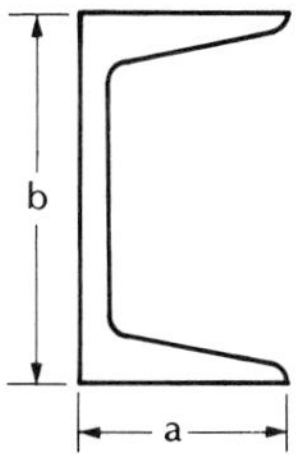	3 × 1.410	6 × 1.945	9 × 2.430
	3 × 1.498	6 × 2.034	9 × 2.648
	3 × 1.596	6 × 2.157	10 × 2.600
	4 × 1.580	7 × 2.110	10 × 2.886
	4 × 1.647	7 × 2.194	12 × 2.960
	4 × 1.720	7 × 2.299	12 × 3.047
	5 × 1.750	8 × 2.290	12 × 3.170
	5 × 1.885	8 × 2.343	15 × 3.400
	5 × 2.032	8 × 2.435	15 × 3.716
	6 × 1.920	8 × 2.527	

Source: Adapted from The Aluminum Association, *Engineering Data for Aluminum Structures,* New York, 1986.

TABLE 860-31
Bronze Channels

Shape	*Size, in*	*Size, in*	*Size, in*
		Equal sides	
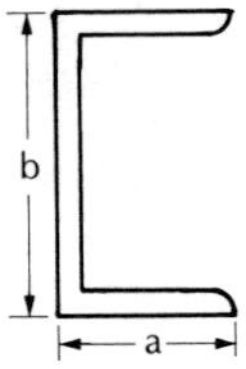b a	½ ¾	1 1¼	1½
		Unequal sides	
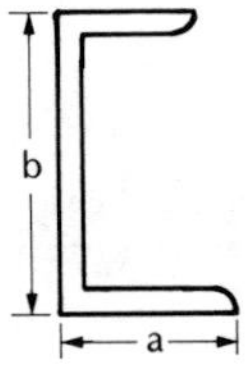b a	¾ × ⅜ 1 × ½ 1 × ¾ 1¼ × ½	1¼ × ⅝ 1½ × ½ 1½ × ⅝ 1½ × 1	2 × ¾ 2¼ × ⅞ 2½ × 1

Source: Adapted from Theodore D. Walker, *Site Design and Construction Detailing,* 2d ed., PDA Publishers, Mesa, Arizona, 1986.

TABLE 860-32
Steel Channels, Cold-Rolled

Shape	*Size, in*	*Size, in*	*Size, in*
	Equal sides, square corners		
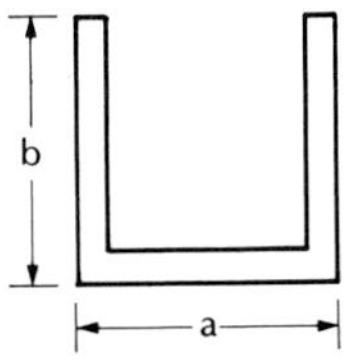b a	½ ¾	1 1¼	1½ 2
	Unequal sides, square corners		
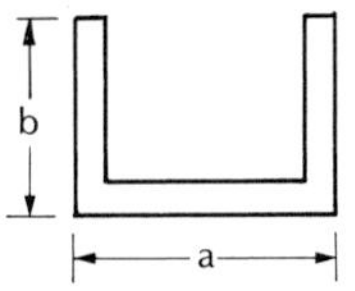b a	1 × 1½ 1½ × 1¾	1 × 2 2 3/16 × 2⅜	
	Channels—bar size		
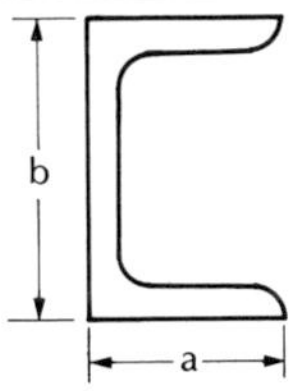b a	¾ × 5/16 ¾ × ⅜ ⅞ × ⅜ ⅞ × 7/16 1 × ⅜ 1 × ½ 1⅛ × 9/16	1¼ × ½ 1½ × ½ 1½ × 9/16 1½ × ¾ 1½ × 1½ 1¾ × ½ 2 × ½	2 × 9/16 2 × ⅝ 2 × 1 2½ × ⅝
	Channels with designations		
	Designation	(a)	(b)
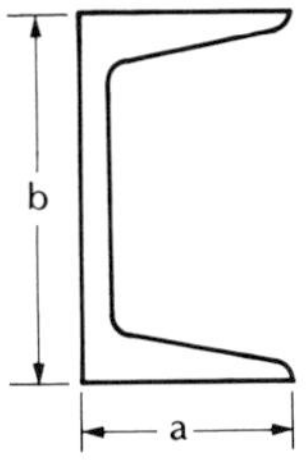b a	C6 × 8.2 × 10.5 × 13 C10 × 15.3 × 20 × 25 × 30 C12 × 20.7 × 25 × 30	6 6 6 10 10 10 10 12 12 12	1⅞ 2 2⅛ 2⅝ 2¾ 2⅞ 3 3 3 3⅛

Source: Adapted from Theodore D. Walker, *Site Design and Construction Detailing,* 2d ed., PDA Publishers, Mesa, Arizona, 1986; and C. G. Ramsey and H. R. Sleeper, *Architectural Graphic Standards,* 7th ed., Robert T. Packard, ed., Wiley, New York, 1981.

TABLE 860-33
Stainless Steel Channels

Shape	*Size, in*	*Size, in*	*Size, in*
	Equal sides, cold-rolled		
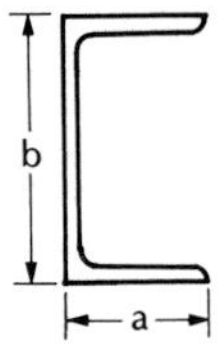 b a	½ ¾	1 1¼	1½ 2
	Unequal sides, cold-rolled		
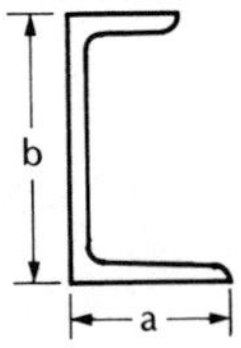 b a	⅝ × 5/16 ¾ × ⅜	1½ × 1 1¾ × 1⅛	2 × 1 2⅜ × 2 3/16
	Unequal sides, extruded		
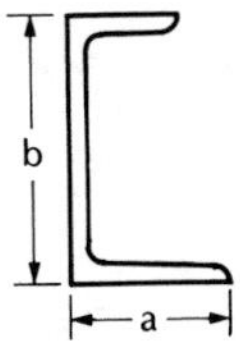 b a	1 × ½ 1¼ × 1 1½ × ½	2 × ¾ 2½ × ⅝ 3 × 1⅜	4 × 1¾

Source: Adapted from Caleb Hornbostel, *Construction Materials,* Wiley, New York, 1978.

TABLE 860-34
Miscellaneous Channels

Shape	*Designation*	*Width (a), in*	*Depth (b), in*
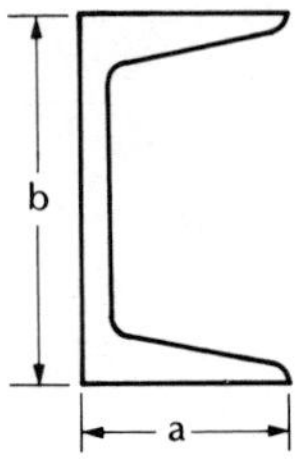 b a	MC8 × 8.5 MC12 × 10.6	8 12	1⅞ 1½

Source: Adapted from American Institute of Steel Construction, *Manual on Steel Construction,* Chicago, 1980.

TABLE 860-35
Aluminum Structural I- Beams*

Shape	I- Beam, in		
	American Standard		
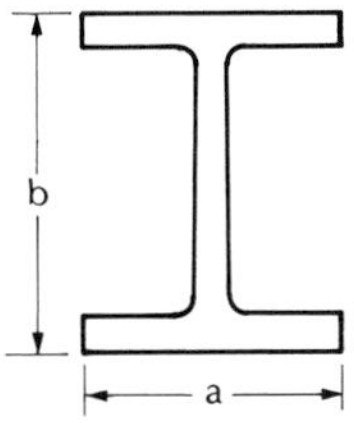 b a	3 × 2.330	5 × 3.000	7 × 3.755
	3 × 2.509	5 × 3.284	8 × 4.000
	4 × 2.660	6 × 3.330	8 × 4.262
	4 × 2.796	6 × 3.443	10 × 4.660
			12 × 5.00
	Aluminum Association Standard		
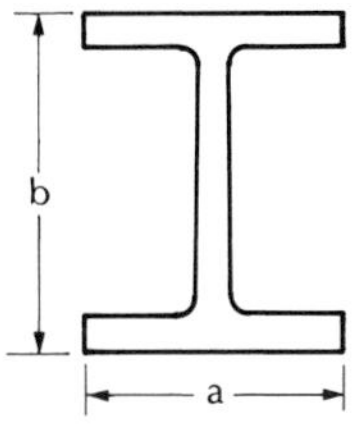 b a	3 × 2½	6 × 4	9 × 5½
	4 × 3	7 × 4½	10 × 6
	5 × 3½	8 × 5	12 × 7

* Structural shapes in this table range in web thickness from 0.17 to 0.687 in; flange thickness from 0.257 to 0.653 in; unit weights from 1.96 to 17.28 lb/ft^2.

Source: Adapted from The Aluminum Association, *Engineering Data for Aluminum Structures,* 2d ed., New York, 1986.

TABLE 860-36
Aluminum H- Beams, Structural Wide-Flange

Shape	*Nominal dimensions (in)*		
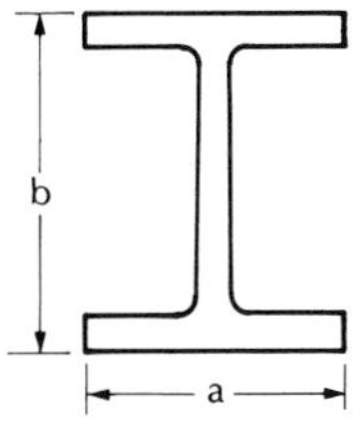 b a	2 × 2	6 × 4	8 × 8
	2½ × 2	6 × 6	10 × 5¾
	4 × 4	8 × 5¼	
	5 × 5	8 × 6½	

Source: Adapted from The Aluminum Association, *Engineering Data for Aluminum Structures,* 2d ed., New York, 1986.

TABLE 860-37
Steel "W" Shapes*

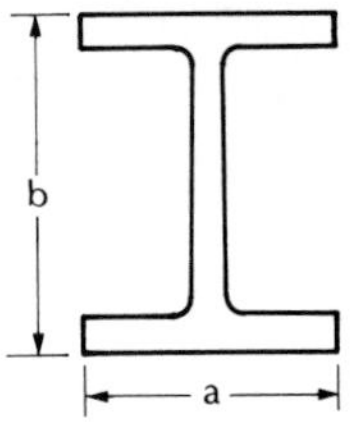
b
a

Shape	*I- Beams from W shapes, in*		
	Designation	*Depth (b)*	*Width (a)*
	W8 × 13	8	4
	W12 × 16	12	4
	W14 × 43	13⅝	8
	W14 × 53	13⅞	8
	W14 × 68	14	10
	W14 × 90	14	14½
	W14 × 159	15	15⅝
	W14 × 257	16⅜	16
	W14 × 500	19⅝	17
	W16 × 40	16	7

* Sizes shown here are those within the range typically used for structural columns.

Source: Adapted from American Institute of Steel Construction, *Manual on Steel Construction*, Chicago, 1980.

TABLE 860-38
Steel "S" Shapes

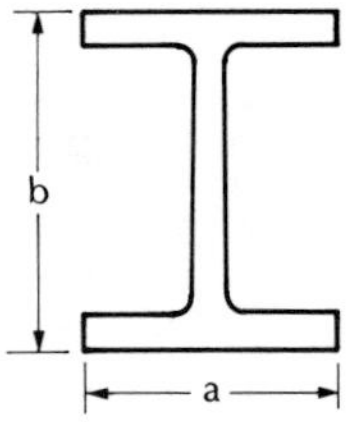
b
a

Shape	*S shapes, in*		
	Designation	*Depth (b)*	*Width (a)*
	S3 × 7.5	3	2½
	S4 × 9.5	4	2¾
	S5 × 14.75	5	3¼
	S6 × 17.25	6	3⅝
	S7 × 20.0	7	3⅞
	S8 × 23	8	4⅛
	S10 × 35	10	5
	S12 × 35	12	5½
	S12 × 50	12	5½
	S15 × 50	15	5⅝
	S18 × 70	18	6¼
	S20 × 75	20	6⅜
	S20 × 95	20	7¼
	S24 × 100	24	7¼
	S24 × 120	24	8

Source: Adapted from American Institute of Steel Construction, *Manual on Steel Construction*, Chicago, 1980.

TABLE 860-39
Steel "M" Shapes*

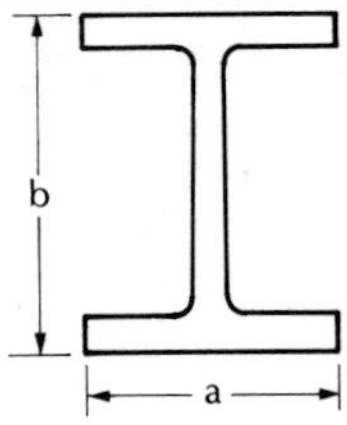
b
a

Shape	*M shapes, in*		
	Designation	*Depth (b)*	*Width (a)*
	M4 × 13	4	4
	M5 × 18.9	5	5
	M6 × 22.5	6	6
	M7 × 5.5	7	2⅛
	M8 × 32.6	8	8
	M10 × 9	10	2¾
	M12 × 11.8	12	3⅛
	M14 × 17.2	14	4

* Selected typical range.

Source: Adapted from American Institute of Steel Construction, *Manual on Steel Construction*, Chicago, 1980.

depth and width dimensions nearly equal and come in heavier weights than other shapes (Table 860-40). They are primarily used for piles.

3.12 Stainless-Steel I Beams

Table 860-41 lists commonly available sizes of stainless-steel I beams.

3.13 Pipe and Tubing

Pipe and *tubing* refer to hollow tubular metals with round, square, or rectangular cross sections.

Various cross sections of pipe and tubing are available in aluminum, brass, steel, and stainless steel (Tables 860-42 through 860-52). Steel pipe is produced in welded or seamless formats and can be used for structural purposes. Galvanized steel pipe is sometimes used for water transport.

Pipe is sized by a number of different systems, including:

Schedule rating: an older pipe sizing system, *schedule rating* refers to consistency in the thickness of the pipe wall (for strength and threading).

Iron pipe size (IPS): a system based on the consistency of the pipe's inner diameter (ID). Its purpose is to facilitate the threading and joining of the pipe.

Outside dimension (OD): a system based on the outside dimension of the pipe.

Class rating: a system that rates the pipe by the utmost working pressure at which it can operate with a high degree of safety. Wall thicknesses are sometimes too thin for threading, so the pipe is often slip-ringed or welded instead.

Type: a system that rates copper pipe and tubing based on proportions between pipe diameter and wall thickness. Type L is suitable for average conditions, and type K is better suited to heavier use conditions.

3.14 Wire (Stainless-Steel)

Sizes and important characteristics of stainless-steel wire commonly used in construction are listed in Table 860-53. A variety of finishes are available to minimize corrosion.

4.0 COMMON METAL PRODUCTS

All fasteners and base metals should be checked for galvanic compatibility.

4.1 Nails, Screws, and Bolts

Nails:

Nails commonly used in construction are shown in Tables 860-55 and 860-56. Ma-

TABLE 860-40
Steel "HP" Shapes

	HP shapes, in		
Shape	*Designation*	*Depth (b)*	*Width (a)*
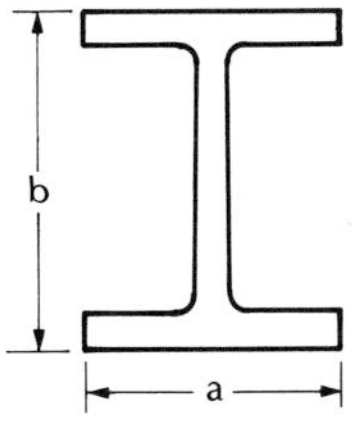	HP8 × 36	8	8⅛
	HP10 × 57	10	10¼
	HP12 × 74	12⅛	12¼
	HP14 × 102	14	14¾

Source: Adapted from American Institute of Steel Construction, *Manual on Steel Construction*, Chicago, 1980.

TABLE 860-41
Stainless Steel I- Beams, Extruded

Shape	*Size, in*	*Size, in*	*Size, in*
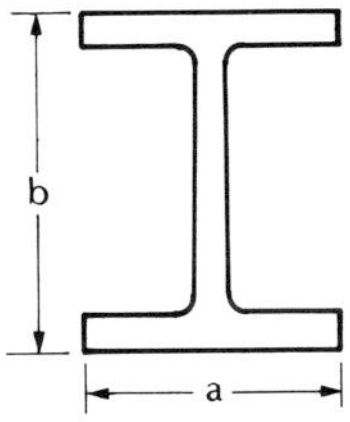	1½ × 1	2½ × 1½	4 × 2¾
	2 × 1¼	3 × 2⅜	

Source: Adapted from Caleb Hornbostel, *Construction Materials*, Wiley, New York, 1978.

TABLE 860-42
Aluminum Pipe

Shape	*Size (diameter), in*	*Schedule number*	*Outside diameter, in*
	1	5-160	1.315
	1¼	5-160	1.660
	1½	5-160	1.900
	2	5-160	2.375
	2½	5-160	2.875
	3	5-160	3.500
	3½	5-80	4.000
	4	5-160	4.500
	5	5-100	5.536
	6	5-160	6.625

Source: Adapted from Caleb Hornbostel, *Construction Materials*, Wiley, New York, 1978.

TABLE 860-43
Steel Pipe

	Size (nominal inside diameter), in		
Shape	*Standard*	*Extra strong*	*Double extra strong*
	2.067	1.939	1.503
	2.69	2.323	1.771
	3.068	2.900	2.300
	3.48	3.364	2.728
	4.026	3.826	3.152
	5.047	4.813	4.063
	6.065	5.761	4.897

Source: Adapted from American Institute of Steel Construction, *Manual on Steel Construction*, Chicago, 1980.

TABLE 860-44
Stainless Steel Pipe: Nominal Pipe Sizes

Shape	*Sizes, in*	*Sizes, in*	*Sizes, in*
	½ × 0.84	2 × 2.375	5 × 5.563
	¾ × 1.050	2½ × 2.875	6 × 6.625
	1 × 1.315	3 × 3.5	8 × 8.625
	1¼ × 1.660	3½ × 4.0	10 × 10.750
	1½ × 1.900	4 × 4.5	12 × 12.750

Source: Adapted from Caleb Hornbostel, *Construction Materials,* Wiley, New York, 1978.

TABLE 860-45
Square Aluminum Tubing

Shape	*Sizes, in*	*Sizes, in*	*Sizes, in*
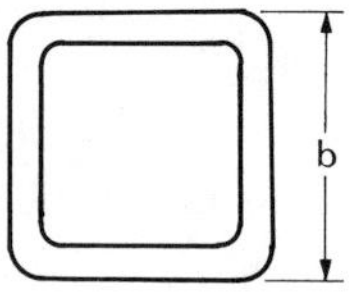	½	1	1¾
	⅝	1¼	2
	¾	1½	2½
			3
			4

Source: Adapted from Theodore D. Walker, *Site Design and Construction Detailing,* 2d ed., PDA Publishers, Mesa, Arizona, 1986.

TABLE 860-46
Square Red Brass Tubing

Shape	*Sizes, in*	*Sizes, in*	*Sizes, in*
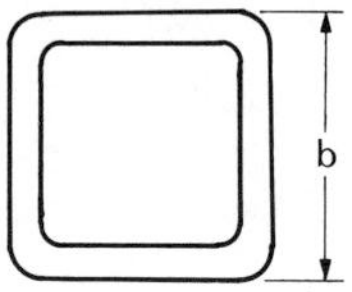	½	1	2
	⅝	1¼	2½
	¾	1½	3
	⅞	1¾	

Source: Adapted from Theodore D. Walker, *Site Design and Construction Detailing,* 2d ed., PDA Publishers, Mesa, Arizona, 1986.

TABLE 860-47
Square Steel Tubing

Shape	*Sizes, in*	*Sizes, in*	*Sizes, in*
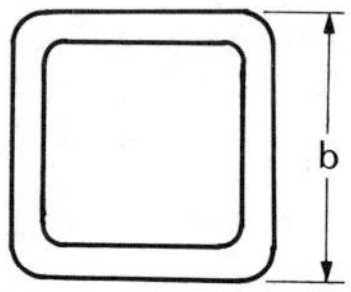	1	2	4
	1⅛	2½	5
	1¼	3	6
	1½	3½	

Source: Adapted from Theodore D. Walker, *Site Design and Construction Detailing,* 2d ed., PDA Publishers, Mesa, Arizona, 1986.

TABLE 860-48
Square Stainless Steel Tubing, Rounded Corners

Shape	*Sizes, in*	*Sizes, in*	*Sizes, in*
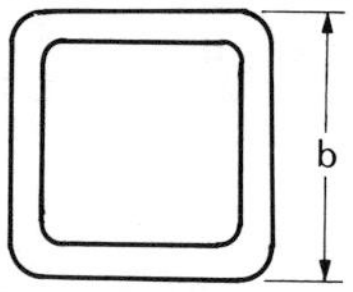	1	1½	2½
	1⅛	1¾	2⅝
	1¼	2	3
	1⅜	2¼	3½
			4

Source: Adapted from Caleb Hornbostel, *Construction Materials,* Wiley, New York, 1978.

TABLE 860-49
Rectangular Aluminum Tubing

Shape	Sizes, in	Sizes, in	Sizes, in
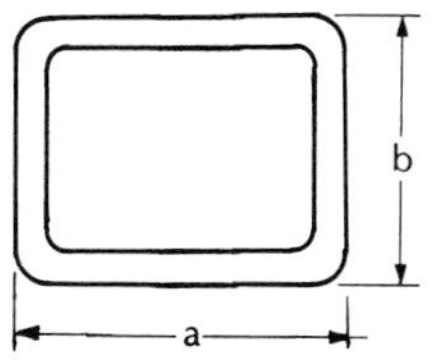b a	1 × 1½	1½ × 2½	2 × 3
	1 × 2	1½ × 6	2 × 4
	1 × 3	1¾ × 2¼	2 × 5
	1¼ × 2½	1¾ × 3	2 × 6
	1¼ × 3	1¾ × 4½	3 × 5
	1½ × 2	1¾ × 5	3 × 6

Source: Adapted from Theodore D. Walker, *Site Design and Construction Detailing,* 2d ed., PDA Publishers, Mesa, Arizona, 1986.

TABLE 860-50
Rectangular Red Brass Tubing

Shape	Sizes, in	Sizes, in	Sizes, in
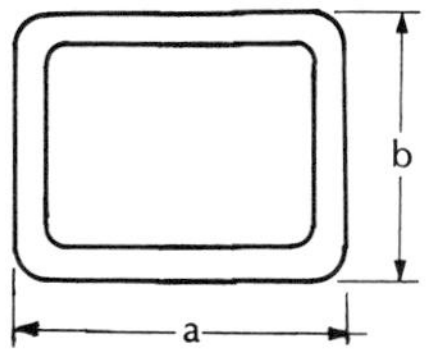b a	1 × ½	2½ × 1¼	3 × 2
	1½ × ½	3 × 1	4 × 1¾
	1½ × ¾	3 × 1¼	4½ × 1¾
	1½ × 1	3 × 1½	
	2 × 1	3 × 1¾	

Source: Adapted from Theodore D. Walker, *Site Design and Construction Detailing,* 2d ed., PDA Publishers, Mesa, Arizona, 1986.

TABLE 860-51
Rectangular Steel Tubing

Shape	Sizes, in	Sizes, in	Sizes, in
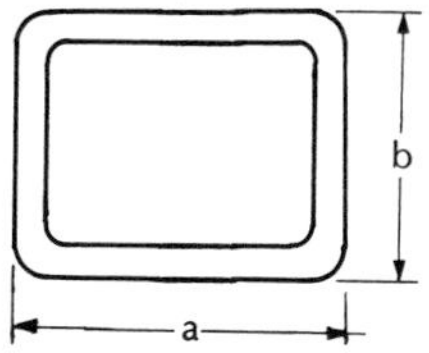b a	2 × 4	3 × 4	4 × 6
	2 × 6	3 × 5	4 × 8
	2 × 12	3 × 6	4 × 12

Source: Adapted from Theodore D. Walker *Site Design and Construction Detailing,* 2d ed., PDA Publishers, Mesa, Arizona, 1986.

TABLE 860-52
Rectangular Stainless Steel Tubing

Shape	Sizes, in	Sizes, in	Sizes, in
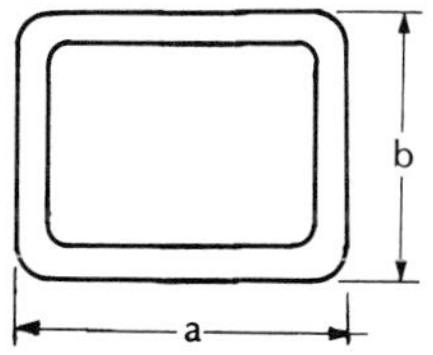b a	1 × 1⅛	1¼ × 1¾	2½ × 3
	1 × 1¼	1¼ × 2	2½ × 4
	1 × 1½	1¼ × 3	2½ × 5
	1 × 1¾	1¼ × 3½	3 × 3½
	1 × 2	1¼ × 4	3 × 4
	1 × 2½	2 × 3	3 × 5
	1 × 3	2 × 4	
	1 × 3½	2 × 5	

Source: Adapted from Caleb Hornbostel, *Construction Materials,* Wiley, New York, 1978.

TABLE 860-53
Stainless-Steel Wire*

Type of wire	*Type of stainless*	*Tensile strength, lb-ft/in^2*	*Major uses*
Cold-drawn	302, 430	90,000–100,000	Nuts, bolts, screws, rivets, and similar products
Weaving	302	70,000–150,000	Wire mesh and cloth
Rope	302	140,000–355,100	Tension members and wire rope

* When obtained in coils, typical sizes range from 0.003 to 0.5 in diameter. When obtained in straight or cut units, typical sizes include 0.03 in and greater.

Source: Adapted from Caleb Hornbostel, *Construction Materials,* Wiley, New York, 1978.

TABLE 860-54
Cable (Braided Wire)

Nominal diameter, in	*Weight, lb/ft*	*Nominal diameter, in*	*Weight, lb/ft*				
3/8	0.24	1 1/2	3.82	13/16	1.10	2 3/4	12.74
7/16	0.32	1 5/8	4.51	7/8	1.28	3	15.11
1/2	0.42	1 3/4	5.24	15/16	1.47	3 1/4	18.00
9/16	0.53	1 7/8	6.03	1	1.67	3 1/2	21.00
5/8	0.65	2	6.85	1 1/8	2.11	3 3/4	24.00
11/16	0.79	2 1/4	8.66	1 1/4	2.64	4	27.00
3/4	0.95	2 1/2	10.60	1 3/8	3.21		

Source: Adapted from Caleb Hornbostel, *Construction Materials,* Wiley, New York, 1978.

TABLE 860-55
Common and Joist Hanger Nails

Common Nails

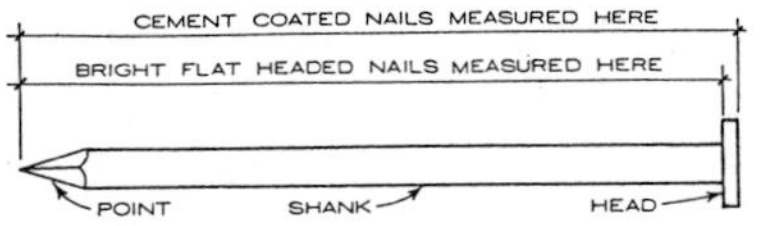
CEMENT COATED NAILS MEASURED HERE
BRIGHT FLAT HEADED NAILS MEASURED HERE
POINT
SHANK
HEAD

Length, in	*Penny, d*	*Gauge, #*	*Diameter of head, in*	*Number per pound*
1	2	15	11/64	847
1 1/4	3	14	13/64	543
1 1/2	4	12 1/2	1/4	296
1 3/4	5	12 1/2	1/4	254
2	6	11 1/2	17/64	167
2 1/4	7	11 1/2	17/64	150
2 1/2	8	10 1/4	9/32	101
2 3/4	9	10 1/4	9/32	92
3	10	9	5/16	66
3 1/4	12	9	5/16	66
3 1/2	16	8	11/32	47
4	20	6	13/32	30
4 1/2	30	5	7/16	23
5	40	4	15/32	17
5 1/2	50	3	1/2	14
6	60	2	17/32	11

Joist hanger nails

Length, in	*Penny, d*	*Gauge, #*	*Notes*
1 1/4	8	11	Joist hanger nails are shorter than common nails of the same gauge or penny.
1 1/2	10	9	
2 1/2	16	8	
1 3/4	20	(0.192)	Annular ring
2 1/2	1/8-in diameter	(0.250)	Annular ring
2 1/8	20	(0.192)	Annular ring

Source: Adapted from C. G. Ramsey and H. R. Sleeper, *Architectural Graphic Standards,* 7th ed., Robert T. Packard, ed., Wiley, New York, 1981.

terials include zinc, brass, Monel, copper, aluminum, iron or steel, stainless steel, copper-bearing steel, and muntz metal. Coatings include tin, copper, cement, brass-plated, zinc, nickel, chrome, cadmium, acid-etched, and parkerized.

A nail's diameter, length, shape, and surface affect its holding power. For the United States, refer to National Fire Protection Association publications for more information.

Joint hanger nails are not equivalent to common nails because of their length and should not be considered a substitute unless the shorter length is specified in load tables.

Wood Screws and Lag Bolts:

Wood screws commonly used in construction are shown in Table 860-57. Wood screws are not often used in landscape construction but do find occasional application. They are never used in instances where bearing strength is an issue, but rather for decorative assemblies, small planter boxes, light trellises, and the like. Wood screws should extend three-fourths of the way into the second piece of wood. Pilot holes are sometimes drilled to prevent splitting of the wood, especially near edges or with harder woods.

Lag bolts are typically installed with a large washer under the head to prevent mashing of the wood and consequent loss of holding power. The center-hole diameters of washers should match the bolt or screw to ensure maximum strength of the fastening. Pilot holes are always drilled to facilitate easier installation of the bolt and to prevent splitting of the wood.

Screws and Bolts:

Metal screws are used primarily to fasten metals together, but they can be used in place of bolts to fasten small wood members together. If used to fasten wood members together, washers are typically used at both ends, unless the screw heads are of the flat or oval variety. If used to fasten metals, metal screws should be matched in terms of metal type to the metals being fastened in order to avoid galvanic corrosion.

Machine bolts require a large washer under both head and nut if used to fasten wood members together. Carriage bolts require a square hole in a metal plate to prevent the bolt from turning. The round head has the advantage of being snag-free and provides a clean appearance.

Screws and bolts commonly used in landscape construction are shown in Table 860-58. To avoid the hazard of protruding ends, the length should be only that which is necessary.

TABLE 860-56
Miscellaneous Nails

		Size		
Nail types	*Materials*	*Length (l), in*	*Penny (d)*	*Gauge (#)*
Cement or concrete nail  o d also flathead cs	Smooth, bright, oil-quenched	½–3	8–30	10–5
Common brad  lnf	Bright or cement-coated; cupped head available	1–6	2–60	15–2
Common nail  f d	Steel, plain or zinc-coated	1–6	2–60	15–2
Double-headed nail 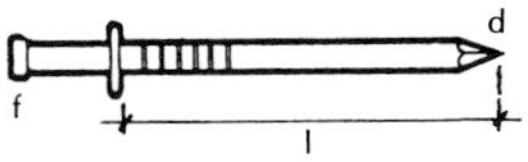 d f l	Bright, cement-coated, and made in several designs	1¾–4½	6	11½
Fence nail  f o	Smooth, bright, cement-coated	1¾–4	8	10
Finishing nail  lnf d	Smooth wire; cupped head available	1–4	2–20	15
Hinge nail 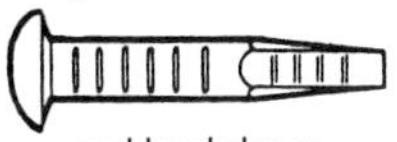 oval head also cs	Smooth, bright, or annealed	1½–4 (3/16–¼)	—	—
Masonry nail  f	High carbon steel, heated and tempered	½–4	10–18	9–7
Roofing nail 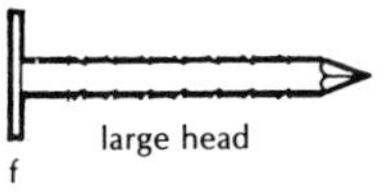 large head f	Barbed, bright, or zinc-coated; neoprene washer optional	¾–2½	4–16	8–12
Shingle nail  f d	Smooth, bright, zinc; cement-coated; light and heavy aluminum	2½–3	4	12
Siding nail  f d	Steel, zinc-coated (used for fences, gates, etc.)	2½–3	6	11
Slating nail 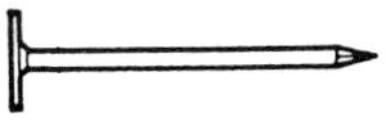 f	Zinc-coated, bright cement-coated, or copper-clad	1–2	several	several
Round wire spike 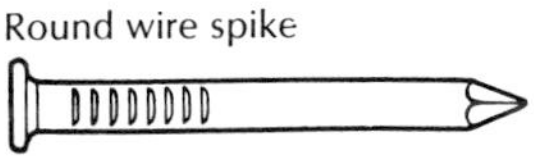 f or ocs d	Smooth, bright, or zinc-coated (also in lengths up to 12–16 in)	3–6	(⅜″)–20	(⅜″)–6

Source: Adapted from C. G. Ramsey and H. R. Sleeper, *Architectural Graphic Standards,* 7th ed., Robert T. Packard, ed., Wiley, New York, 1981.

TABLE 860-57
Wood Screws and Lag Bolts*

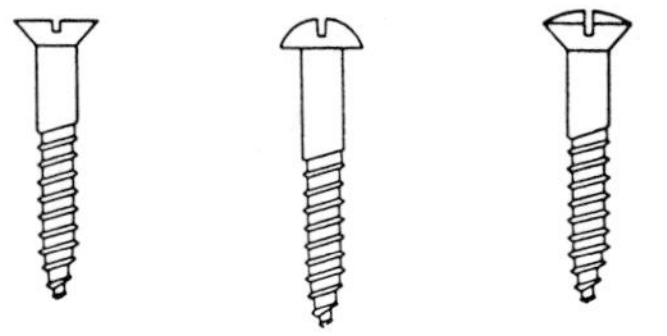
FLAT HEAD
ROUND HEAD
OVAL HEAD

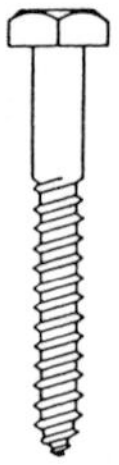

Wood screws			*Lag bolts*		
Diameter	*Decimal equivalent, in*	*Length, in*	*Diameter*	*Decimal equivalent, in*	*Length, in*
0	0.063	¼–⅜	¼	0.250	1–6
1	0.073	¼–½	5/16	0.313	1–10
2	0.086	¼–¾	⅜	0.375	1–12
3	0.099	¼–1	7/16	0.438	1–12
4	0.112	¼–1½	½	0.500	1–12
5	0.125	⅜–1½	⅝	0.625	1½–16
6	0.138	⅜–2½	¾	0.750	1½–16
7	0.151	⅜–2½	⅞	0.875	2–16
8	0.164	⅜–3	1	1.000	2–16
9	0.177	½–3			
10	0.190	½–3½			
11	0.203	⅝–3½			
12	0.216	⅝–4			
14	0.242	¾–5			
16	0.268	1–5			
18	0.294	1¼–5			
20	0.320	1½–5			
24	0.372	3–5			

* American Standard sizes by the American Bolt, Nut, and Rivet Manufacturers. Many screws are available in aluminum, brass, copper, stainless steel, monel, and bronze.

† Length intervals: ⅛-in increments up to 1 in, ¼-in increments from 1¼ to 3 in, and ½-in increments from 3½ to 5 in.

Source: Adapted from C. G. Ramsey and H. R. Sleeper, *Architectural Graphic Standards*, 7th ed., Robert T. Packard, ed., Wiley, New York, 1981.

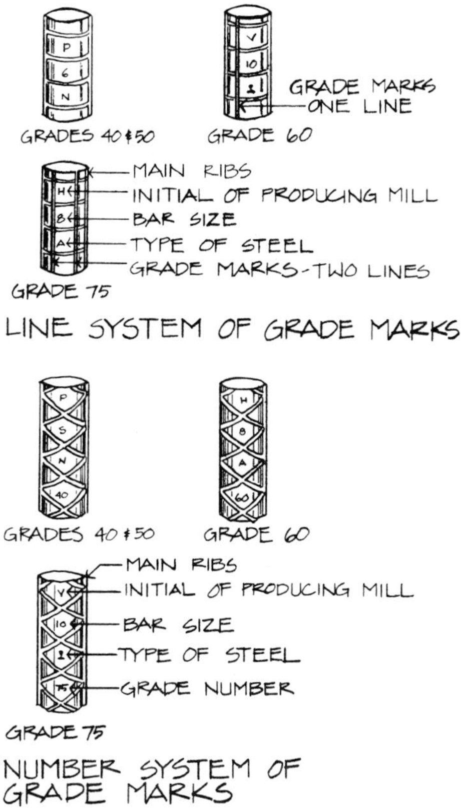
GRADE MARKS
ONE LINE
GRADES 40 & 50
GRADE 60
MAIN RIBS
INITIAL OF PRODUCING MILL
BAR SIZE
TYPE OF STEEL
GRADE MARKS - TWO LINES
GRADE 75
LINE SYSTEM OF GRADE MARKS
GRADES 40 & 50
GRADE 60
MAIN RIBS
INITIAL OF PRODUCING MILL
BAR SIZE
TYPE OF STEEL
GRADE NUMBER
GRADE 75
NUMBER SYSTEM OF GRADE MARKS

Figure 860-1 Reinforcement bar markings. *N* refers to *new billet*, *A* refers to *axle*, and ⊥ refers to *rail*. Grade mark lines must be continued for at least five deformation spaces on the bar. Bar identifications and grade mark numbers may read horizontally (90 degrees to those shown above).

4.2 Concrete Reinforcing Bars

Reinforcing bars are manufactured out of carbon steel (Figure 860-1 and Table 860-59). Bars can be specified to receive an epoxy coating for use under conditions of high corrosion potential.

4.3 Welded Wire Fabric

Welded wire fabric is manufactured from carbon steels. It is currently specified according to a revised means of designation (Table 860-60).

4.4 Cable (Braided Wire)

Specifications for cable refer to a size such as $a \times b$ (where *a* refers to the number of wires in a strand and *b* to the number of strands in a cable) (Figure 860-2). Table 860-54 shows nominal diameters commonly available. Various zinc coatings are available to minimize corrosion. Class A coatings refer to *normal* protection against corrosion, Class B to *intermediate* protection, and Class C to *highest* protection.

TABLE 860-58
(*a*) Cap Screws and Bolts, (*b*) Nuts and Set Screws, (*c*) Machine Screws and Stove Bolts

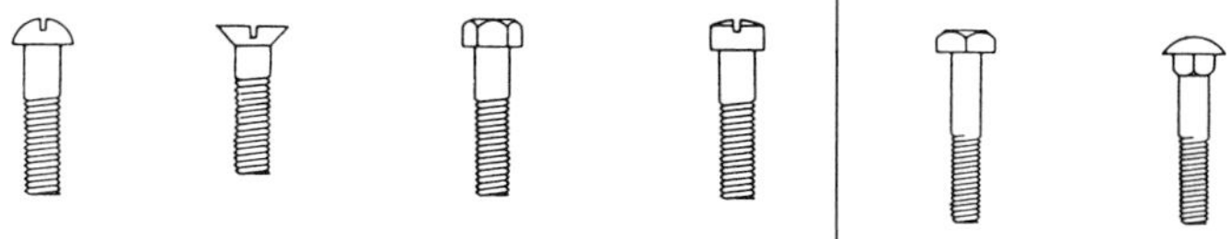

	Cap screws: length, in				*Bolts: length, in*	
Screw diameter	*Button head*	*Flat head*	*Hexagon head*	*Fillister head*	*Machine bolt*	*Carriage bolt*
1/4	1/2–2 1/4	1/2–2 1/4	1/2–3 1/2	3/4–3	1/2–8	3/4–8
5/16	1/2–2 3/4	1/2–2 3/4	1/2–3 1/2	3/4–3 3/4	1/2–8	3/4–8
3/8	5/8–3	5/8–3	1/2–4	3/4–3 1/2	3/4–12	3/4–12
7/16	3/4–3	3/4–3	3/4–4	3/4–3 3/4	3/4–12	1–12
1/2	3/4–4	3/4–4	3/4–4 1/2	3/4–4	3/4–24	1–20
9/16	1–4	1–4	1–4 1/2	1–4	1–30	1–20
5/8	1–4	1–4	1–5	1 1/4–4 1/2	1–30	1–20
3/4	1–4	1–4	1 1/4–5	1 1/2–4 1/2	1–30	1–20
7/8	—	—	2–6	1 3/4–5	1 1/2–30	—
1	—	—	2–6	2–5	1 1/2–30	—

Nuts		*Set screws*			
Square nut	*Hexagon nut*	*Square head diameter*	*Length*	*Headless diameter*	*Length*
Nuts are available for all screws and bolts		1/4–1	1/2–5	‡(4)–1/2	1/2–5

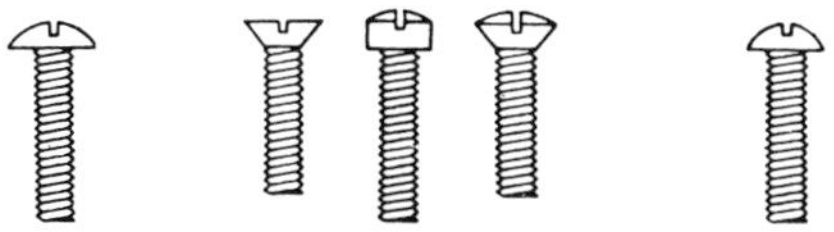

Machine screws and stove bolts: length, in				
Stove bolt diameter	*Machine screw diameter*	*Round head*	*Flat head, fillister head, oval head*	*Oven head*
—	2	1/8–7/8	1/8–7/8	—
—	3	1/8–7/8	1/8–7/8	—
—	4	1/8–1 1/2	1/8–1 1/2	—
—	4	1/8–1 1/2	1/8–1 1/2	1/8–3/4
1/8	5	1/8–2	1/8–2	3/8–2
—	6	1/8–2	1/8–2	1/8–1
5/32	8	3/16–3	3/16–3	3/16–2
3/16	10	3/16–6	3/16–3	1/4–6
—	12	3/4–3	1/4–3	
1/4	1/4	5/16–6	5/16–3	3/8–6
5/16	5/16	3/8–6	3/8–3	3/4–6
3/8	3/8	1/2–5	1/2–3	3/4–6
1/2	1/2	1–4	—	—

* Stove bolts have wider tolerances than machine screws.

† Length intervals: 1/16-in increments up to 1/2 in, 1/8-in increments from 5/8 to 1 1/4 in, 1/4-in increments from 1 1/2 to 3 1/2 in, and 1/2-in increments from 3 1/2 to 5 in.

‡ Size 4 screw to 1/2-in diameter.

Source: Adapted from C. G. Ramsey and H. R. Sleeper, *Architectural Graphic Standards,* 7th ed., Robert T. Packard, ed., Wiley, New York, 1981.

TABLE 860-59
ASTM Standard Steel Reinforcing Bars (Nominal Diameter)

Bar size designation*	Diameter, in	Weight, lb
#3	0.375	0.376
#4	0.500	0.668
#5	0.625	1.043
#6	0.750	1.502
#7	0.875	2.044
#8	1.000	2.670
#9	1.128	3.400
#10	1.270	4.303
#11	1.410	5.313
#14	1.693	7.650
#18	2.257	13.600

* Bar numbers are based on the number of ⅛ in included in the normal diameter of the bar.

Source: Adapted from Wire Reinforcement Institute, McLean, Virginia, 1963.

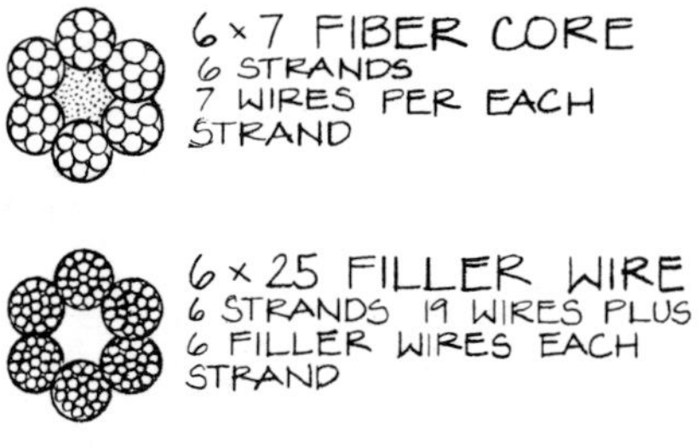
6×7 FIBER CORE
6 STRANDS
7 WIRES PER EACH STRAND
6×25 FILLER WIRE
6 STRANDS 19 WIRES PLUS
6 FILLER WIRES EACH STRAND

Figure 860-2 Cable (braided wire).

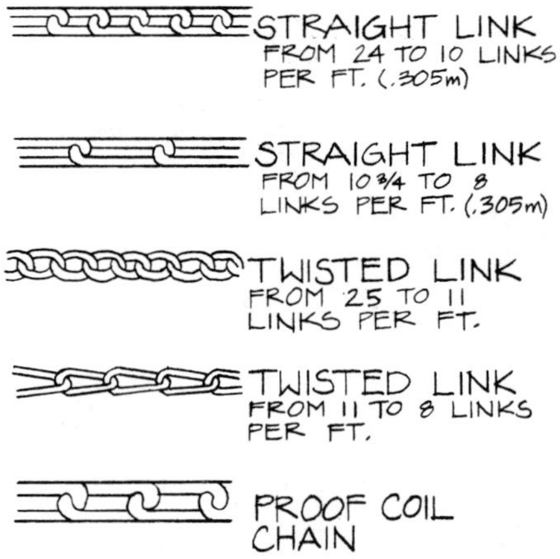
STRAIGHT LINK
FROM 24 TO 10 LINKS PER FT. (.305m)
STRAIGHT LINK
FROM 10 3/4 TO 8 LINKS PER FT. (.305m)
TWISTED LINK
FROM 25 TO 11 LINKS PER FT.
TWISTED LINK
FROM 11 TO 8 LINKS PER FT.
PROOF COIL CHAIN

Figure 860-3 Common types of chain.

Consultation with an engineer is advisable to ensure proper selection of cable whenever strength is an important consideration.

4.5 Chain

Metal chain is produced in a variety of styles, sizes, and strengths (Figure 860-3). Chains intended for loading or safety situations should be carefully selected for adequate strength. Products are typically referred to by the number of links per foot, weight per 100 ft, and tensile strength.

TABLE 860-60
Welded Wire Fabric (Common Stock)

New designation[1]	Old designation	Steel area/ft	
Spacing—cross sectional area, in—in²/100	Spacing—wire gauge, in—AS&W	Longitudinal, in	Transverse, in
	Rolls[2,3,4]		
6 × 6—W1.4 × W1.4[5]	6 × 6—10 × 10	0.028	0.028
6 × 6—W2.0 × W2.0[5]	6 × 6—8 × 8[6]	0.040	0.040
6 × 6—W2.9 × W2.9[5]	6 × 6—6 × 6	0.058	0.058
6 × 6—W4.0 × W4.0	6 × 6—4 × 4	0.080	0.080
4 × 4—W1.4 × W1.4	4 × 4—10 × 10	0.042	0.042
4 × 4—W2.0 × W2.0	4 × 4—8 × 8[6]	0.060	0.060
4 × 4—W2.9 × W2.9	4 × 4—6 × 6	0.087	0.087
4 × 4—W4.0 × W4.0	4 × 4—4 × 4	0.120	0.120
	Sheets[3,4]		
6 × 6—W2.9 × W2.9	6 × 6—6 × 6	0.058	0.058
6 × 6—W4.0 × W4.0	6 × 6—4 × 4	0.080	0.080
6 × 6—W5.5 × W5.5[7]	6 × 6—2 × 2[8]	0.110	0.110
4 × 4—W4.0 × W4.0	4 × 4—4 × 4	0.120	0.120

[1] Method of designating:

WWF 6 × 12 − W16 × W26
WWF 6 in = longitudinal wire spacing
12 in = transverse wire spacing
W16 = longitudinal wire size
W26 = transverse wire size

[2] Welded mesh comes in rolls: 150-, 200-, and 300-ft lengths.

[3] Widths vary from 56 to 72 inches in 2-inch increments and from 84 to 96 inches in 3- and 4-inch increments.

[4] Tensile strength: 70,000–80,000 psi.

[5] Most commonly used sizes.

[6] Exact W-number size for 8 gauge is W2.1.

[7] No. 2 gauge and larger comes only in sheets.

[8] Exact W-number size for 2 gauge is W5.4.

Source: Adapted from Wire Reinforcement Institute, McLean, Virginia, 1963.

AGENCIES AND ORGANIZATIONS

The Aluminum Association
Washington, D.C.

The Copper Development Association, Inc.
Greenwich, Connecticut

The American Society for Testing and Materials (ASTM)
Philadelphia, Pennsylvania

American Iron and Steel Institute (AISI)
Washington, D.C.

National Fire Protection Association
Quincy, Massachusetts

REFERENCES

Aluminum Association. *Aluminum Standards and Data,* Washington, DC.

American Iron and Steel Institute. *Steel Products Limits,* Washington, DC.

American Society for Metals. *Metals Handbook,* Metals Park, OH.

American Society for Testing and Materials (ASTM). *Standards,* Philadelphia, published annually.

American Welding Society. *The Welding Handbook,* Miami, FL. ■

section 870: Glass, Plastics, and Fabrics

CREDITS

Section Editor: Charles W. Harris

Technical Writers:

Tobias Dayman
Krisan Osterby-Benson

Computer Graphics:

Do Kyong Kim

Reviewers:

Neil Dean
Sasaki Associates, Inc.
Watertown, Massachusetts

Gretchen Artig
Industrial Fabrics Association International (IFAI)
St. Paul, Minnesota

Albert Dietz
Department of Architecture
Massachusetts Institute of Technology
Cambridge, Massachusetts

John Lawrence
Society of the Plastics Industry
New York, New York

Donn Harter
Special Consultant to National Glass Association
Bellflower, California

CONTENTS

1.0 INTRODUCTION

This section describes three groups of materials: glass, plastics, and fabrics. Although the use of these materials in landscape development is not as widespread as some other materials, they do have properties which warrant their consideration in certain design applications.

2.0 GLASS

Glass is a unique material with properties useful in a variety of applications. Inappropriate use of glass, however, can produce hazardous situations. Safety glazing products, i.e., fully tempered or laminated glass, are typically required for hazardous locations, such as glass doors, as well as for all glass within 12 in (300 mm) of a door.

To determine code requirements for the application of glass products, the Consumer Product Safety Commission (CPSC) standards, local regulations, and specifications of the regional building code agency should be consulted. In the United States, such building code agencies are either the Building Officials and Code Administrators International (BOCA), the International Conference of Building Officials (ICBO), or the Southern Building Code Congress, International (SBCCI).

2.1 Properties of Glass

Optical Properties:

Visible light transmittance varies from 85 to 90 percent in clear commercial glass to 21 to 75 percent in tinted glasses, depending on color and thickness. Reflective-coated glasses may transmit only 8 to 50 percent of visible light, depending on the coating. Metallic coating produces a true mirror, allowing no visible light transmittance. Table 870-1 lists transmittance values for various types of flat glass.

Fidelity refers to freedom from distortion. Distortion is caused by variations in glass thickness.

Mechanical Properties:

Compression rarely damages glass, but stretching, bending, or impacts will cause breakage. The compressive strength of glass block makes it useful in a variety of applications.

Chemical Properties:

Glass is inert, durable, nonporous, nonabsorptive, and resistant to weathering and corrosion. It can be acid-etched for greater obscurity.

Thermal Properties:

Insulating glass, reflective-coated glass, and tinted glass greatly reduce heat gain by absorbing solar energy. These glasses expand and contract more than clear glass.

When two types of glass or a glass and another material are joined together, the expansion rates of the materials must be closely matched to minimize stress differentials and consequent breakage.

2.2 Basic Types and Sizes

Flat Glass:

Basic types of flat, commercial glass include sheet, float, and plate. Plate glass is rarely used today because of its high cost. Any of these types can be made clear or tinted, or surfaced with a variety of finishes. They can also be strengthened by either heat or chemical treatments. Table 870-1 provides information on various types and sizes of flat glass.

Glass Block:

Glass block can be laid in the same manner as any type of masonry construction. Glass block will allow light transmission but not a clear view. Table 870-2 gives information on various types, sizes, and construction properties of glass block.

2.3 Special Types of Flat Glass

Patterned Glass:

Patterned glass refers to glass that has a linear or geometric pattern pressed onto one or both sides of the glass to obscure vision. Acid etching or sandblasting will also create greater obscurity. Patterned glass is available in a wide range of textures and patterns, primarily in thicknesses of ⅛ in (3 mm) and 7/32 in (5 mm). Table 870-3 provides information on types and sizes.

Wired Glass:

Plate glass and certain kinds of patterned glass can be made with wire mesh or parallel wires rolled into the center of the glass thickness to hold the glass together under low levels of impact or excessive heat. Wired glass is generally produced in ¼-in (6-mm) thickness only. Table 870-4 provides information on types and sizes.

Composite Glass:

Composite glass is made by combining two or more layers of glass into a single unit. Two types of composite glass are (1) laminated and (2) insulating. Insulating glass is seldom used in landscape construction.

Laminated glass consists of two or more layers of annealed or tempered glass with interlayers of polyvinyl butyral plastic sandwiched between them (Table 870-5). The thickness of the glass *layers* may range from 3/32-in (3-mm) sheet glass to ⅞-in (22-mm) plate or float glass. The glass surfaces which are to be bonded to the plastic may not be patterned or irregular.

When laminated glass is broken, glass fragments adhere safely to the plastic interlayer and do not evacuate the opening. All varieties of laminated glass are considered safety glazing materials.

Bullet-resistant glass is a laminated glass typically available in thicknesses up to 2 in (50 mm). Greater thicknesses up to 7 in (180 mm) are available on special order (Table 870-5).

Burglar-resistant glass is a laminated glass which typically consists of two layers of ⅛-in (3-mm) glass with a 0.060- to 0.090-in (1.6- to 2.3-mm) plastic interlayer (Table 870-5). Greater thicknesses and layers are available in some instances.

Acoustical glass reduces sound transmission in the frequency ranges of 250 to 4000 hertz (Hz), characteristic of speech, radio, and television (Table 870-5).

Heat-Treated Glass:

Heat-treated glass is classified as either *fully tempered* or *heat-strengthened.* Exact sizes must be specified when ordering either type of glass, because the glass cannot be cut, drilled, or notched after the heat treatment.

Fully Tempered Glass: Any glass ⅛ in (3 mm) or thicker may be fully tempered, ex-

TABLE 870-1
Flat Glass Types and Sizes

Product	Quality	Thickness, in	Maximum area*	Weight, lb/ft^2	Visible light transmission, %
Float glass (heavy sheet)	AA, A, B†	3/16	84 × 120 in	2.50	90
		7/32	84 × 120 in	2.85	89
Float glass	Silvering‡	¼	50 ft^2	3.28	89
	Mirror	¼	75 ft^2	3.28	89
	Glazing	⅛	74 × 120 in	1.64	90
		¼	120 × 180 in	3.28	89
	Glazing	5/16	120 × 180 in	4.10	88
		⅜	120 × 180 in	4.92	88
		½	120 × 180 in	6.56	86
		⅝	120 × 180 in	8.20	84
		¾	120 × 180 in	9.85	83
		1	—§	13.13	80
Rough plate	Polished, one side	17/64	58 × 120 in	3.28	88
	Rough, both sides	9/32	124 × 240 in	3.70	88

* Maximum area varies according to producer. Larger sizes may be available from some producers.

† Federal specification DD-G-451c: AA for highest grade work, A for superior glazing, BB for general glazing.

‡ Silvering quality is free from defects. Mirror quality also suitable for mirrors and other demanding applications. Glazing quality is for ordinary glazing purposes.

§ Available from some producers, subject to factory operations.

Source: Adapted with permission from Harold B. Olin, J. L. Schmidt, and W. H. Lewis, *Construction: Principles, Materials, and Methods,* U.S. League of Savings Institutions, Chicago, 1983.

TABLE 870-2
Glass Block

	*Nominal sizes available**		*Approximate weight (lb)*	*Compressive strength (psi)*	*Maximum recommended panel size*	*Light transmission, %*	*Remarks†*
	4-in thick	*3-in thick*					
			Single cavity				
Clear	6 × 6 8 × 8 12 × 12	6 × 6 3 × 6 8 × 8 4 × 8 12 × 12 4 × 12 6 × 8	Installed	400–600	Exterior: consult manufacturer	75	Corner pieces 6 × 6 size only. Consult manufacturer for minimum radius for curved construction.
Clear with reflective coating	8 × 8 12 × 12	Not available	20 psf (4 in)	400–600		5–20	Gold, bronze, or gray coating on one or both sides (for solar heat gain control).
Light-diffusing patterned	8 × 8 12 × 12	Not available	15 psf (3 in)	400–600	Interior: $144\ ft^2$ 25 ft high	39	Provides maximum quantity of diffused light (for glare control, privacy).
Decorative patterned (two-way fluted, semi-clear, etc.)	6 × 6 3 × 6 8 × 8 4 × 8 12 × 12 4 × 12	6 × 6 3 × 6 8 × 8 4 × 8 12 × 12 4 × 12 6 × 8	Consult manufacturer for individual block weights	400–600		20–75	Consult manufacturer for specific patterns.
			Double cavity				
Light diffusing patterned	8 × 12 12 × 12	Not available	Same as single cavity	400–600	Same as single cavity	28	Double cavity formed by fibrous glass insert; white or colors (for glare and heat transmission control).
Decorative patterned (two-way fluted, semiclear, etc.)	6 × 6 3 × 6 8 × 8 4 × 8 12 × 12 4 × 12	Not available	Same as single cavity	400–600	Same as single cavity	43	Consult manufacturer for specific patterns (for heat transmission control).
			Solid				
Clear	5 × 5 × $2\frac{5}{8}$ 8 × 8 × 3 3 × 8 × $3\frac{3}{4}$ Round: $6\frac{1}{2}$ diameter × 2		6 15 6 —	80,000	Consult manufacturer	80	Consult manufacturer for information concerning anchors, stiffeners, expansion strips, mortars, reinforcement, etc., for all block types.

* Check with manufacturers for exact dimensions, especially solid block.
† Mortar joints for glass block construction are typically $\frac{1}{4}$ in (6 mm).
Source: Sweet's *Building Product Selection Data,* McGraw-Hill, New York, 1984.

cept for wired glass or patterned glass with deep patterns. Tempering increases the strength of glass 4½ times that of annealed glass. Fully tempered glass is considered a safety glazing material because, when fractured, it breaks into relatively small, harmless particles. Its use is typically required by state or local codes in public and some residential construction.

Heat-Strengthened Glass: Heat-strengthened glass is similar to fully tempered glass, but it has only a partial heat temper and is therefore only twice as strong as ordinary annealed glass of the same thickness. It is not considered a safety glazing material. Any type of glass that can be tempered can be heat-strengthened.

Tinted Glass:

Sheet and float glass can be tinted. Gray and bronze are most commonly available. Tinted glasses are generally produced in thicknesses up to ½ in (13 mm) and in glazing quality only. Green-tinted glass is generally available in thicknesses up to ¼ in (6 mm) only. Equal thicknesses of gray-, bronze-, and green-tinted glass all absorb the same percentage of solar energy. Tinted glasses offer a wide range of visible light transmittance (21 to 75 percent), depending both upon the thickness and the color of the glass (Tables 870-6 and 870-7).

Because of its heat-absorbing character-

TABLE 870-3
Patterned Glass Types and Sizes

Product	*Type*	*Thickness, in*	*Maximum area, in**	*Weight, lb/ft²*	*Visible light transmission, %*
Patterned glass	Floral				
	Hammered	⅛	60 × 132	1.60–2.10	80–90
	Stippled				
	Granular				
	Ribbed				
	Fluted	7/32	60 × 132	2.40–3.00	80–90
	Striped†				

* Maximum area varies according to producer; larger sizes may be available from some producers.

† These are just a few of the most common patterns available; many patterns are patented and made by one producer only.

Source: Adapted with permission from Harold B. Olin, J. L. Schmidt, and W. H. Lewis, *Construction: Principles, Materials, and Methods,* U.S. League of Savings Institutions, Chicago, 1983.

TABLE 870-4
Wired Glass Types and Sizes

Product	*Type*	*Thickness, in*	*Maximum area, in**	*Weight, lb/ft²*	*Visible light transmission, %*
Wired glass	Polished (square or diamond mesh)	¼	60 × 144	3.50	80–85
	Patterned (square or diamond mesh)	¼	60 × 144	3.50	80–85
	Parallel wired*	7/32	54 × 120	2.82	80–85
		¼	60 × 144	3.50	80–85
		⅜	60 × 144	4.45	80–85

* This type of wired glass does not carry Underwriter's Laboratory, Inc. fire-retardant rating; it is used mainly for decorative partitions.

Source: Adapted with permission from Harold B. Olin, J. L. Schmidt, and W. H. Lewis, *Construction: Principles, Materials, and Methods,* U.S. League of Savings Institutions, Chicago, 1983.

TABLE 870-5
Laminated Glass Types and Sizes

Product	*Glass type*	*Plastic interlayer, in*	*Thickness, in*	*Maximum area**	*Weight lb/ft²*
Laminated glass	SS/SS sheet†	.015–.030	13/64	48 × 80 in	2.45
	Lam/Lam sheet†	.015–.030	15/64	48 × 100 in	2.90
	DS/DS sheet†	.015–.030	¼	48 × 100 in	3.30
	2 lites ⅛ in plate or float	.015–.030	¼	72 × 120 in	3.30
	2 lites heavy plate or float	.015–.030	⅜	72 × 120 in	4.80
			½	72 × 120 in	6.35
			⅝	72 × 120 in	8.00
			¾	72 × 120 in	9.70
			⅞	72 × 120 in	11.40
			1	72 × 120 in	12.95
Burglar-resistant‡	2 lites ⅛ in plate or float	.060–.090	5/16	60 × 120 in	3.50
Bullet-resistant‡	At least 4 lites of plate or float	At least 3 plies of .015	1 3/16	40 ft²	15.50
			1 9/16	30 ft²	20.00
			1¾	25 ft²	23.00
			2	22 ft²	26.20
Acoustical‡	2 lites of plate or float	One or more plies of .045			
STC-36§			9/32	60 × 120 in	3.40
STC-40			½	60 × 120 in	6.36
STC-43			¾	60 × 120 in	9.74

* Maximum area varies according to producer. Larger sizes may be available from some producers.

† Lam indicates 7/64 in sheet glass; SS, 3/32 in sheet; DS, ⅛ in sheet.

‡ Burglar, bullet-resistant, and acoustical glass specifications are determined by local code and various industrial associations. The list above is not complete. The glass type, plastic interlayer, and thickness dimensions shown above are minimal suggestions. The maximum area and weight serves as a guide.

§ Refers to Sound Transmission Class ratings.

Source: Adapted with permission from Harold B. Olin, J. L. Schmidt, and W. H. Lewis, *Construction: Principles, Materials, and Methods,* U.S. League of Savings Institutions, Chicago, 1983.

TABLE 870-6
Tinted Glass Types and Sizes

Product	Quality	Thickness, in	Maximum area, in*	Weight, lb/ft^2	Visible light transmission, %	Solar energy transmission, %†
Bronze—float	Glazing	3/16	120 × 180	2.54	56	52
		1/4	120 × 180	3.28	50	46
		3/8	120 × 180	4.92	37	33
		1/2	120 × 180	6.56	27	24
Gray—float	Glazing	3/16	120 × 180	2.54	50	52
		1/4	120 × 180	3.28	43	46
		3/8	120 × 180	4.92	29	33
		1/2	120 × 180	6.56	20	24
Green—float	Glazing	3/16	110 × 120	2.45	79	55
		1/4	120 × 180	3.28	75	47

* Maximum area varies according to producer; larger sizes may be available.

† Transmission values vary slightly from one producer to another.

Source: Adapted with permission from Harold B. Olin, J. L. Schmidt, and W. H. Lewis, *Construction: Principles, Materials, and Methods,* U.S. League of Savings Institutions, Chicago, 1983.

TABLE 870-7
Additives for Coloring Glass

Additive	% in glass	Color produced
Cadmium sulfide	0.03–0.1	Yellow
Cadmium sulfoselenide	0.03–0.1	Ruby and orange
Carbon and sulfur compounds		Amber
Chromium oxide	0.05–0.2	Green to yellow-green
Cobalt oxide	0.001–0.1	Blue
Copper	0.03–0.1	Ruby
Copper oxide	0.2–2.0	Blue-green
Ferric oxide	Up to 4.0	Yellow-green
Ferrous oxide		Blue-green
Gold	0.01–0.03	Ruby
Iron oxide and manganese oxide	1.0–2.0 2.0–4.0	Amber
Manganese oxide	0.5–3.0	Pink-purple
Neodymium oxide	Up to 2.0	Pink
Nickel oxide	0.05–0.5	Brown and purple
Selenides		Amber
Selenium		Bronze
Uranium oxide	0.1–1.0	Yellow with green fluorescence

Source: Adapted with permission from Harold B. Olin, J. L. Schmidt, and W. H. Lewis, *Construction: Principles, Materials, and Methods,* U.S. League of Savings Institutions, Chicago, 1983.

istics, special precautions should be taken when using tinted glass to avoid damage to the edges and consequent breakage from thermal stresses.

2.4 Surface Finishes

Etching:

Acid etching can produce varying degrees of transparency in glass, from a semipolished, translucent quality to a nearly opaque, frosted appearance. Etching reduces the strength of glass.

Sandblasting:

The translucent finish obtained by this method is usually rougher than that obtained by etching. Sandblasting can reduce the strength of glass by as much as 50 percent.

Enameling:

Glass can be coated with vitreous enamels in translucent and solid colors fired at high temperatures. The firing process also partially tempers the glass.

Silvering:

Most mirrors are manufactured by direct deposit of silver on the glass by a spray technique. The silvering can then be protectively coated with shellac, varnish, or paint. Large commercial mirrors are made from float glass.

Reflective Coatings:

A thin reflective coating, applied either to one surface of a single sheet of glass or to an inside surface of a laminated or insulating glass, is used primarily to control the transmission of solar energy into buildings. Under appropriate lighting conditions, reflective-coated glass can become a type of one-way mirror, permitting vision only to the side with the greater amount of light.

3.0 PLASTICS

3.1 Properties of Plastics

General:

Plastics have become important materials in construction primarily because of their unusually wide range of properties. These include moisture and corrosion resistance, toughness, malleability, and lightness in weight. Various plastics offer different advantages, thus providing potential solutions to a multitude of design problems.

Plastics are typically categorized into two basic groups as a function of their response to heat. *Thermoplastics* soften with exposure to heat and harden when cooled (like candle wax). This process can be repeated any number of times. *Thermosets,* after their initial cooling and hardening, are permanently set; repeated exposure to heat will only cause chemical decomposition.

Properties Important in Construction:

Tensile Strength: Most plastics are similar to wood in terms of tensile strength—with the exception of laminates and reinforced plastics, a few of which exceed the strength of steel, especially on a strength-to-weight basis (Table 870-8). Fiberglass-reinforced plastics (FRPs) have the highest tensile strengths.

Stiffness: In construction, stiffness is often more important than strength. Thermosets are slightly stiffer than thermoplastics, and reinforced plastics are the stiffest of all. Most are roughly comparable to wood, although the stiffness of some high-performance composites approaches that of aluminum or steel.

TABLE 870-8
Selected Properties of Plastics

Plastic	*Tensile strength lb/in²*	*Compressive strength lb/in²*	*Impact strength ft-lb/in notch*	*Resistance to heat, continuous, °F*	*Effect of sunlight*	*Clarity*	*Machining qualities*
Acrylonitrile-butadiene-styrene (ABS)	4000–8000	7000–22,000	1.0–10	140–230	None to slight yellowing	Translucent to opaque	Good to excellent
Acrylic (PMMA)	7000–11,000	11,000–19,000	0.3–0.5	140–200	None	Excellent to opaque	Fair to excellent
Cellulosics, (CA, CAB, CAP, CN, CP, EC)	2000–9000	2000–36,000	0.4–8.5	115–220	Slight to discoloration, embrittlement	Transparent to opaque	Good to excellent
Epoxies (EP)	4000–30,000	1000–40,000	0.2–10	200–550	None to slight	Transparent to opaque	Poor to excellent
Fluoroplastics, (FEP, PCTFE, PTFE, PVF)	2000–7000	1700–10,000	3.0 to no break	300–550	None to slight bleaching	Transparent to opaque	Excellent
Melamine-formaldehyde (MF)	5000–13,000	20,000–45,000	0.24–6	210–400	Slight to darkening	Translucent to opaque	Fair to good
Nylon polyamide (PA)	7000–35,000	6700–24,000	1.0–5.5	175–400	Slight discoloration	Translucent to opaque	Fair to excellent
Phenol-formaldehyde/ phenolics (PF)	3000–18,000	10,000–70,000	0.2–18	200–550	Darkens	Transparent to opaque	Poor to good
Polycarbonate (PC)	8000–20,000	12,500–19,000	1.2–17.5	250–275	Slight color change	Transparent to opaque	Fair to excellent
Polyesters	800–50,000	12,000–50,000	0.2–16.0	250–450	None to slight yellowing, embrittlement	Transparent to opaque	Poor to excellent
Polyethylene (PE)	1000–5500	— to 5500	0.5–2.0 to no break	180–275	Unprotected crazes fast, weather resistance available	Transparent to opaque	Fair to excellent
Polypropylene (PP)	2900–9000	3700–8000	0.5–20.0	190–320	Unprotected crazes fast, weather resistance available	Transparent to opaque	Fair to good
Polystyrene (PS, SAN, SBP, SRP)	1500–20,000	4000–22,000	0.25–11.0	140–220	Slight yellowing	Excellent to opaque	Fair to good
Silicones (SI)	800–35,000	100–18,000	— to 15	400–>600	None to slight	Clear to opaque	Fair to good
Urea-formaldehyde (UF)	5500–13,000	25,000–45,000	0.25–0.40	170	Pastels, gray	Transparent to opaque	Fair
Urethanes (UP)	175–10,000	20,000	5 to flexible	190–250	None to yellowing	Clear to opaque	Fair to excellent
Vinyls (PVAc, PVAl, PVB, PVC, PVCAc, PVFM)	500–9000	1000–22,000	0.4–20 (impact strength varies with type and amount of plasticizer)	120–210	Slight	Transparent to opaque	Poor to excellent

Source: Albert G. H. Dietz, *Plastics for Architects and Builders,* The MIT Press, Cambridge, Mass., 1969.

TABLE 870-9
Types of Plastics

Thermoplastics	
Acrylics (PMMA)	Common trade names in the United States include Lucite and Plexiglas. They are transparent, break-resistant, and weather-resistant. They scratch easily and soften at 200°F (90°C). Uses include skylights and roof domes, glazing, lighting fixtures, clear or corrugated sheets for roofing, films or sheets bonded to wood or metal for exterior finishes, and molded pieces of hardware.
Acrylonitrile-Butadiene-Styrene (ABS)	Copolymers noted for toughness, chemical resistance, nonbrittleness at low temperatures, rigidity, and tensile strength. Typically used for piping and pipe fittings; water and gas supply lines for drain, waste, and vent systems.
Cellulosics (CA, CAB, CAP, CN, CP, EC)	Transparent (cellulose acetate) but optical properties are not as good as acrylics. Remarkably tough and withstand rough handling, but not all are suited for prolonged outdoor exposure. Primarily used in photographic film and recording tape, but also for piping and pipe fittings, outdoor-lighting fixtures, and handrailings.
Fluorocarbons (FEP, PCTFE, PTFE, PVF)	Very inert, high thermal stability (450 to 500°F) (230 to 260°C) and excellent resistance to chemical attack. Used in piping for highly corrosive chemicals at high temperatures; for low friction slider pads to permit movement in steam lines; and as nonstick linings for pots and pans (Teflon).
Nylon/polyamide (PA)	A common name for a group of plastics called polyamides. Molded nylons are tough, with high strength, good chemical resistance, and good shear resistance, but not good weather resistance. Nylon fabric uses include sails, parachutes, and air-supported structures.
Polyethylene (PE)	Waxy, chemically inert, flexible at low temperatures, and good water or vapor barrier, but untreated polyethylene deteriorates in sunlight. Used for vapor barriers in building construction, wire and cable insulation, and for certain types of piping (e.g., cold water, gas, and chemicals). Not suitable for conditions involving high temperatures or extremely corrosive chemicals.
Polystyrene (PS, SAN, SBP, SRP)	Brittle, weathers poorly, and begins to soften at about 212°F (100°C). It is transparent, has a wide range of colors, and is water-resistant. Used for lighting fixtures and various molded pieces of hardware. Expanded (foamed) polystyrene is used in construction for insulation, as well as for core material in the manufacture of doors and sandwich panels.
Vinyls (PVAc, PVA1, PVB, PVC, PVCAc, PVFM)	Have a wide range of properties ranging from flexible film to rigid pipe. Most possess good strength and toughness, fair chemical resistance, and low water absorption. They do not perform well at high temperatures, and some may soften at 130°F (55°C), but some are suitable for outdoor exposure (e.g., polyvinyl chloride). Used to produce sheet and tile flooring; gutters and downspouts; moldings; clapboards and siding; window frames; piping and drainage systems. In sheet form it is used for facings in sandwich construction and is bonded to wood or metal for exterior building finishes, doors, and window frames.
Thermosets	
Epoxy (EP)	Remarkable adhesive strength, chemical resistance, and water resistance. Used for bonding metal, glass, masonry, and other plastics; in coating compounds and adhesives; and as protective coatings. Also can be mixed with mineral aggregate or plastic chips to produce terrazzo.
Melamine-Formaldehyde/Urea-Formaldehyde (MF, UF)	Both are classified as amino plastics and have similar properties: hard, relatively dimensionally stable, and available in a wide color range. Melamine is mainly used in high-pressure laminates for countertops and cabinet finishes, as adhesives for plywood, and as a protective treatment for fabrics and paper.
Phenol-Formaldehyde/Phenolics (PF)	Low-cost plastic limited to dark colors, strong, and both electrical- and heat-resistant. Pure phenolics are brittle and hard, but mixing with fillers improves their impact resistance. In molded form, they are used for electrical parts and hardware items. As foamed insulation, they are used as the core for sandwich panels and around piping and ducts. Resins are used to form high-pressure laminations.
Silicones (SI)	Stable compounds of high corrosion resistance, electrical resistance, a wide service range of temperatures (−80 to 500°F) (−60 to 260°C), and resistance to weathering. Applied to masonry as a water-repellent, sealant, and retardant to weathering.
Urethane/Polyurethane (UP)	Used primarily as low-density foams for either soft, flexible, open-cell types or tough, rigid, closed-cell types. Resistant to heat, chemicals, and fire (when properly formulated, but smoke may be severe). Uses include building insulation and as the core material in sandwich panels. Flexible urethane foams are used for cushions, upholstery, and padding.
Composites	
	Simple one-component plastics sometimes do not have all the properties necessary for specific applications. Plastics are often combined with other materials to produce a product with properties not inherent in the individual materials themselves. Three principal types of composite plastic products include laminates, reinforced plastics, and sandwiches.

Toughness: Toughness is generally expressed in terms of the ability to resist impact. Plastics (and different formulations of the same plastic) can vary widely in impact strength.

Hardness: Plastics scratch more easily than glass or steel, but their resistance to wear (e.g., as bearings) may be superior to steel. Their resistance to indentation is usually better than that of commonly used wood species across the grain, but some soft plastics are easily indented.

Expansion and Contraction: Thermal expansion is characteristically high in plastics. Thermosets expand less than thermoplastics. Reinforced plastics and laminates expand the least amount and are more nearly comparable to aluminum. Expansion joints are necessary when materials of widely different expansion rates are joined.

Corrosion Resistance: Plastics vary in their resistance to attack by chemical reagents. Generally speaking, a plastic can be found to resist any common chemical. Fluorocarbons are the most inert and are susceptible to attack by only the most powerful reagents. Other plastics are susceptible to only selective action by particular chemicals.

3.2 Basic Types of Plastics

Many kinds of plastics are commercially available for a variety of purposes. Table 870-9 describes those commonly used in the construction industry.

TABLE 870-10
Sheet Plastic Types and Sizes*†

KEY:

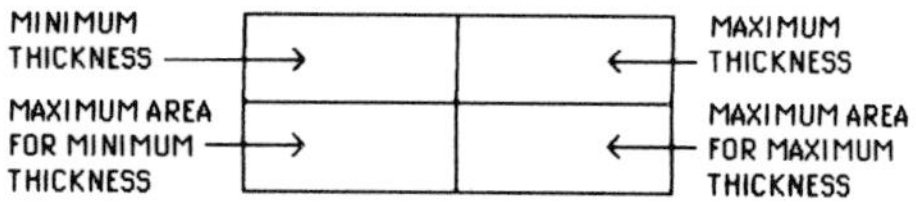
MINIMUM THICKNESS
MAXIMUM AREA FOR MINIMUM THICKNESS
MAXIMUM THICKNESS
MAXIMUM AREA FOR MAXIMUM THICKNESS

Plastic type	*Clear*		*Tinted*		*Reflective coated*	*Opaque ceramic frit*	*Patterned*	
Acrylic, sheet	0.060 24 × 36	4½ 120 × 144	Same as clear		Same as clear	Available in some colors		
Polycarbonate, sheet	3/32 72 × 96	½ 96 × 96	0.06 36 × 48	¼ 120 × 144		Available in some colors	0.125	0.250 72 × 96
Acrylic polycarbonate, double-skin	⅛ 48 × 96	58 48 × 144+	Same as clear					
Acrylic polycarbonate, laminates	1 48 × 96	1¼	Same as clear					
Reinforced	3/32 44 × 96	3/16	Same as clear					

* Maximum sizes are available from one or more manufacturers; larger sizes and/or additional material variants may be available on request. Larger sizes may be approved by UL on special request.

† Strength values given are average and for short-term loading; they may vary from manufacturer to manufacturer and from product to product; check with manufacturer also for long-term and cyclic loads.

Source: Sweet's Division, *Building Product Selection Data,* McGraw-Hill, New York, 1984.

TABLE 870-11
Corrugated Plastic Sheeting Types and Sizes

Type		*Slope, minimum, in/ft*	*Maximum span, in**	*Width*	*Length*	*Weight or thickness, oz/ft²*	*Exposure or lap*	*General notes*
Corrugated fiberglass, reinforced plastic	1¼-in corrugations, ¼-in deep	3	40–22	26 in (maximum 50 in)	4–39 ft	5, 6, 8	1, 1½, or 2 corrugation side lap. 6-in minimum end lap	Self-tapping screws, drive screws and nails. All with neoprene washers
	2½-in corrugations, ½-in deep		65–32	26 in (maximum 50 in)	4–39 ft	4, 5, 6, 8, 10, 12		(a) Weight: approximately 40 lb/ft²
	4.2-in corrugations, 1 1/16-in deep		72–50	42 in; 50⅝ in	4–39 ft	5–12		(b) Color and texture: many colors translucent to opaque, smooth or pebble finish
	2.67-in corrugations, ⅞-in deep		70–42	50 in	4–39 ft	5–12		(c) Fastener: self-tapping screws. Drive screws and nails with neoprene washers
	5-V crimp, 1-in deep		65–32	26 in	4–39 ft	5–8		
	5.3-V crimp, 1-in deep		84–60	41⅝ in; 45 in	4–39 ft	5–12		
Corrugated plastic, nonreinforced plastic	2.67-in corrugations, 9/16-in deep	1	70–42	50½ in	8, 10, 12, 15, 20 ft	5–8	1 corrugation side lap. 8-in minimum end lap	

* For 15–40 lb/ft².

Source: C. G. Ramsey and H. R. Sleeper, *Architectural Graphic Standards,* 7th ed., Robert T. Packard ed., Wiley, New York, 1981.

TABLE 870-12
Schedule 80 Rigid PVC Pipe Sizes

Nominal pipe size, in	½	¾	1	1¼	1½	2	2½	3	4
Actual inside diameter	.546	.742	.957	1.278	1.500	1.939	2.323	2.900	3.826
Actual outside diameter	.840	1.050	1.315	1.660	1.900	2.375	2.875	3.500	4.50

Source: Theodore D. Walker, *Site Design and Construction Detailing,* 2d ed., PDA Publishers, Mesa, Arizona, 1986.

TABLE 870-13
125 PSI Flexible Polyethylene Tubing Sizes

Nominal pipe size, in	½	¾	1	1¼	1½	2
Actual inside diameter	.622	.824	1.049	1.380	1.610	2.067
Actual outside diameter	.711	.942	1.199	1.577	1.840	2.364

Source: Theodore D. Walker, *Site Design and Construction Detailing,* 2d ed., PDA Publishers, Mesa, Arizona, 1986.

3.3 Available Formats and Sizes

Plastic products are available in a variety of formats and sizes. Tables 870-10 through 870-13 give commonly available sizes and important characteristics.

Sheet Plastic:

The availability of sheet plastic varies between manufacturers. Special orders are sometimes possible (Table 870-10).

Corrugated Plastic Sheeting:

Corrugated sheeting made of fiberglass or nonreinforced plastic are typically used in roofing applications. These products are often rated for strength, fire resistance, and other characteristics (Table 870-11).

Rigid Plastic Pipe:

Plastic pipe is commonly used in drainage and irrigation applications (Table 870-12).

Flexible Tubing:

Flexible tubing is commonly used to protect underground wires and in irrigation applications (Table 870-13).

4.0 FABRICS

4.1 General Description

Fabrics can be used in a variety of ways outdoors, both in aboveground applications (e.g., tensile structures, decorative banners, fences, and canopies) and in-ground applications (e.g., to separate materials, provide reinforcement, control drainage, control erosion, and serve as construction forms). (Refer to Section 880: Geotextiles, for comprehensive information on the use of fabrics in ground engineering applications.)

The selection of a fabric for any particular purpose depends on those properties that are required of the fabric. In part, the selection should depend on precedent in other similar field projects; this is mainly because professionally oriented literature and test results on the use of fibers and fabrics in outdoor applications are not widely available.

Durability is a major constraint regarding the use of fabrics in outdoor applications. Periodic replacement or repair is a major consideration in their use.

4.2 Basic Elements of Fabric Construction

Fabrics can be engineered for specific tasks. The basic elements are fibers which are spun into yarns which are in turn woven or combined by nonwoven processes into fabrics.

Woven Fabrics:

Woven fabrics are made by weaving lengthwise yarns (warp yarns) with crosswise filling yarns (weft yarns). Basic weaves include the *plain* weave (one up and one over), the stronger *twill* weave, and the *smooth satin* weave. The term *count* refers to the number of yarns per inch (millimeter) of fabric. A higher count refers to a tighter weave and implies greater strength, longer durability, decreased porosity, and less chance of shrinkage and of pulling apart at the seams.

Nonwoven Fabrics:

Nonwoven fabrics are fabrics that have textile fibers or yarns bonded together by resins, by other bonding agents, or by mechanical means to form a smooth, uniform mat. The concept of warp and weft yarns does not apply to unwoven fabrics. Many landscape construction fabrics are nonwoven.

Finishes:

Any fabric can be chemically or mechanically finished in a variety of ways to enhance or impart certain desirable properties. However, excessive amounts of surface treatment may make a material too heavy or too costly for a particular application. Table 870-14 describes various surface treatments available.

4.3 Types of Fabric for Outdoor Use

Canvas:

Canvas is a dense fabric of cotton yarns in a plain or a basket weave, and its standard treatments today include mildew resistants and water repellents (not waterproofing). It is light, strong, abrasion-resistant, and durable. Canvas is basically white but can be dyed in a variety of colors.

Resistance to Mildew and Sunlight: Treatments for mildew resistance, ultraviolet light resistance, and antiflammability are available for canvas. Local codes should be checked for antiflammability requirements.

Water-Repellent Qualities: Stretched untouched canvas sheds water and does not allow water to penetrate, but if touched, the fabric will leak at the point of contact. Canvas can shrink, but special treatments are available to minimize this problem.

Types of Canvas: Canvas for outdoor use is available in two basic types, *drill* and *duck*. Drill is a twill weave and the lighter fabric; it weighs 7 to 8 oz per linear yard of cloth 31 in wide (8 to 9 oz/yd²).

The more common canvas product, commonly referred to as *army duck* in the United States, is a basket weave that can be used in heavy-duty applications. Army

TABLE 870-14
Surface Treatments for Fabrics

Surface treatment (finish)	*Description*
Bleaching, dyeing, and scoring	Bleaching whitens fabric. Scoring removes oils, waxes, dirt, and sizing. Dyeing colors fabric.
Preshrinking	Promotes dimensional stability in cotton and rayon fabrics. Most cotton canvas today is preshrunk.
Heat setting	Promotes dimensional stability in nylon and polyester, or other thermoplastic fibers
Mildew and rot resistants	Help prevent development of mildew in cottons and rayons. Treatment is ineffective if material is in constant contact with water. Mildew growth is accentuated in heated environments. Necessary for most fabrics used outdoors
Waterproofing and water repellents	Make the fabric repel water (pores not fully closed) or stop inflow of water (pores closed completely)
Flame retardants	Minimize flammability of fabrics. Local building codes sometimes require such treatment.
Light degradation retardant and antioxidants	Minimize degradation of fabric from sunlight and other environmental factors.

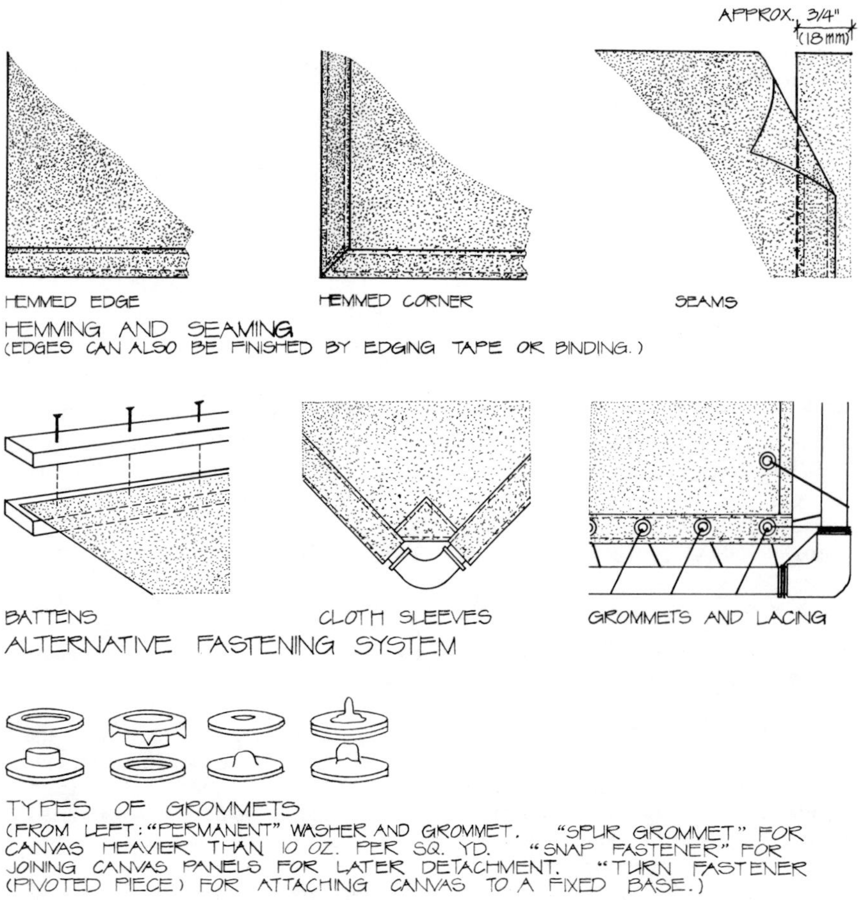
APPROX. 3/4" (18mm)
HEMMED EDGE
HEMMED CORNER
SEAMS
HEMMING AND SEAMING
(EDGES CAN ALSO BE FINISHED BY EDGING TAPE OR BINDING.)
BATTENS
CLOTH SLEEVES
GROMMETS AND LACING
ALTERNATIVE FASTENING SYSTEM
TYPES OF GROMMETS
(FROM LEFT: "PERMANENT" WASHER AND GROMMET. "SPUR GROMMET" FOR CANVAS HEAVIER THAN 10 OZ. PER SQ. YD. "SNAP FASTENER" FOR JOINING CANVAS PANELS FOR LATER DETACHMENT. "TURN FASTENER (PIVOTED PIECE) FOR ATTACHING CANVAS TO A FIXED BASE.)

Figure 870-1 Canvas hemming and fastening techniques.

duck is available in weights from 11.5 to 20.5 oz/yd^2. *Painted army duck* is a fabric consisting of acrylic paint on cotton fabric. The acrylic coating will rub off when subjected to abrasion. The surface of the fabric is dull, with a visibly linenlike texture. The fabric's dimensional stability is very good.

Various techniques have been developed for hemming, seaming, and fastening canvas materials (Figure 870-1).

Vinyl-Coated Cotton:

Vinyl-coated cotton is a fabric consisting of a vinyl coating on a woven cotton base fabric. Its surface is shiny, with little or no texture. Its dimensional stability is very good.

Acrylics:

Acrylic fabric consists of woven spun acrylic yarns. It has a woven texture and relatively good dimensional stability. Some shrinkage may occur in cold weather and some stretching in hot weather. Its mildew resistance is very good.

Nylons and Polyesters:

Nylons are high-strength fabrics, durable and tear-resistant, with high softening temperatures and good chemical resistance. Although they are resistant to abrasion, they are susceptible to deterioration by ultraviolet light; however, treatments are available to minimize the problem.

Mesh fabrics are available; they are primarily used for tennis courts. Mesh fabric is available by the square measure, in one weight only, and may be treated with various colorants. Nylon rope is also available in various sizes and colors.

Polyesters exhibit poor resistance to abrasion and are sensitive to ultraviolet light, but their properties vary widely between different formulations. Additives are available to reduce degradation by ultraviolet light.

Vinyl-Laminated Polyester:

Vinyl-laminated polyester is a trilayered fabric commonly used in tensile structures (Figure 870-2). The top and bottom layers are vinyl, and the middle layer is woven polyester. The surface has a matte finish with a slight woven or linenlike texture. Its dimensional stability is very good, and its mildew resistance is exceptional.

The use of such fabrics as vinyl-laminated polyesters and fiberglass fabrics has become widespread in the manufacture of tensile structures. Figure 870-2 shows representative examples of tensile forms commonly used in the landscape.

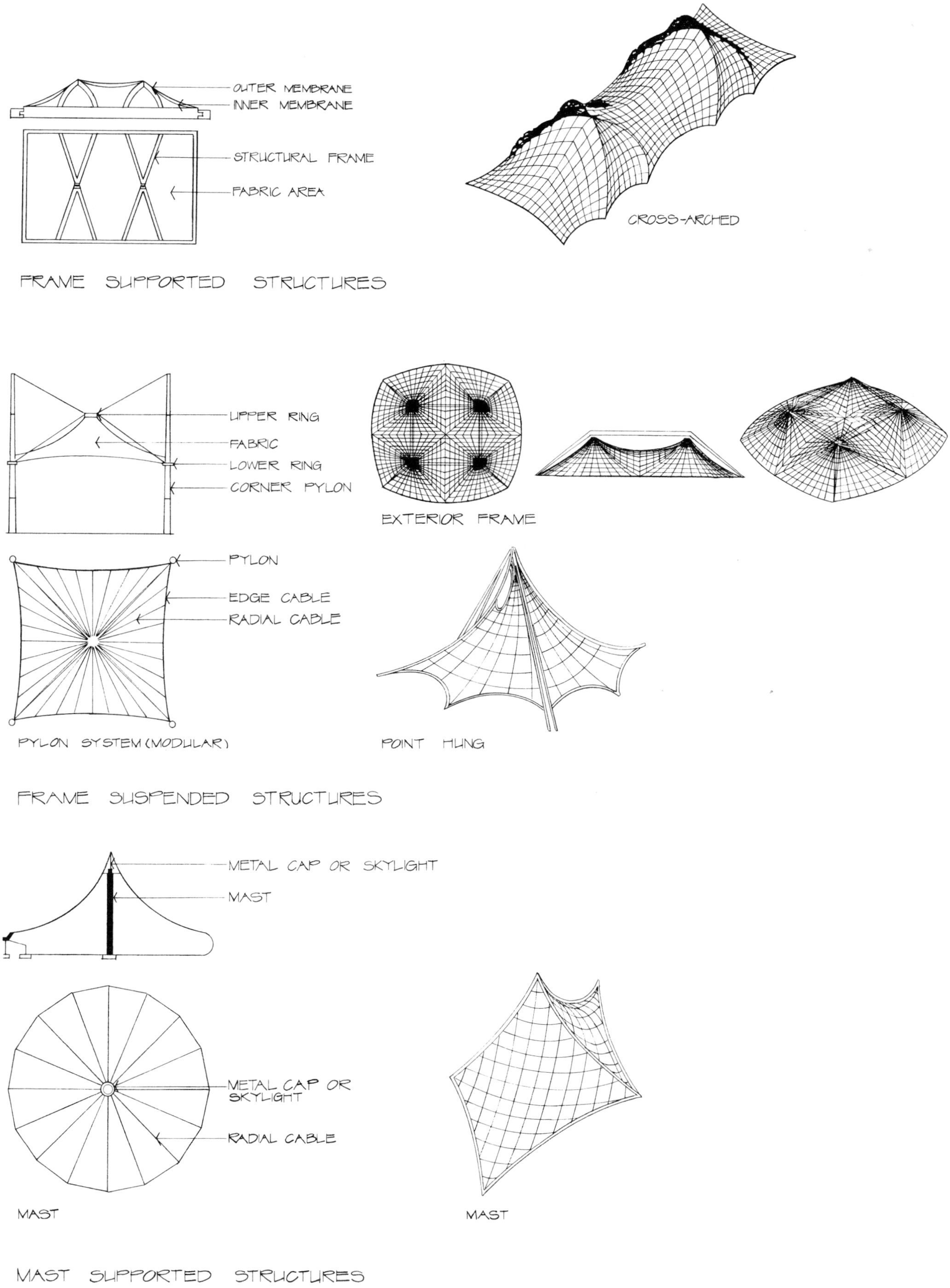
OUTER MEMBRANE
INNER MEMBRANE
STRUCTURAL FRAME
FABRIC AREA
CROSS-ARCHED
FRAME SUPPORTED STRUCTURES
UPPER RING
FABRIC
LOWER RING
CORNER PYLON
EXTERIOR FRAME
PYLON
EDGE CABLE
RADIAL CABLE
PYLON SYSTEM (MODULAR)
POINT HUNG
FRAME SUSPENDED STRUCTURES
METAL CAP OR SKYLIGHT
MAST
METAL CAP OR SKYLIGHT
RADIAL CABLE
MAST
MAST
MAST SUPPORTED STRUCTURES

Figure 870-2 Typical Tensile Structures. Suspension systems can be of tube plastic or metal. Anchors can be points or continuous fastening. Structures are typically open at sides but can be enclosed. Scale of designs can vary significantly.

AGENCIES AND ORGANIZATIONS

GENERAL

Government Agencies

Consumer Product Safety Commission (CPSC)
Bethesda, Maryland (or nearest regional office)

National Bureau of Standards (NBS)
U.S. Department of Commerce
Standards Development Services Section
Washington, D.C.

Private Institutes and Agencies

American National Standards Institute (ANSI)
New York, New York

American Society for Testing and Materials (ASTM)
Philadelphia, Pennsylvania

Construction Specifications Institute (CSI)
Washington, D.C.

GLASS

Building Officials and Code Administrators International (BOCA)
Country Club Hills, Illinois

Flat Glass Marketing Association (FGMA)
Topeka, Kansas

International Conference of Building Officials (ICBO)
Whittier, California

National Glass Association (NGA)
McLean, Virginia
(21 regional groups)

Southern Building Code Congress, International (SBCCI)
Birmingham, Alabama

Stained Glass Association of America (SGAA)
Fairfax, Virginia

PLASTICS

National Association of Plastic Fabricators (NAPF)
Washington, D.C.

Society of the Plastics Industry (SPI)
New York, New York

FABRICS

American Textile Manufacturers Institute, Inc.
Charlotte, North Carolina

Industrial Fabrics Association International (IFAI)
St. Paul, Minnesota

Man-Made Fiber Products Association, Inc.
Washington, D.C.

REFERENCES

Glass and Plastics

Dietz, Albert G. H. *Plastics for Architects and Builders,* MIT Press, Cambridge, MA, 1969.

Knofer, Diebert. *Corrosion of Building Materials,* Van Nostrand Reinhold, New York, 1975.

Olin, Harold B., John L. Schmidt, and Walter H. Lewis. *Construction Principles, Materials, and Methods,* The Institute for Financial Education and Interstate Printers and Publishers, Chicago, 1975.

Fabrics

Koerner, Robert M., and Joseph P. Welsh. *Construction and Geotechnical Engineering Using Synthetic Fabrics,* Wiley, New York, 1980.

McGraw-Hill Information Systems. *Sweet's Selection Data: Building Products Selection Data,* McGraw-Hill, New York, 1984.

Wingate, Isabel B., and June F. Mohler. *Textile Fabrics and Their Selection,* Prentice-Hall, Englewood Cliffs, NJ, 1984. ■

section 880: Geotextiles

CREDITS

Contributor:

Thomas & Heather Ryan
Sasaki Associates, Inc.
Watertown, Massachusetts

Reviewer:

Christopher J. Stohr, Associate Geologist
Engineering Geology Division
State Geological Survey
Champaign, Illinois

CONTENTS

1.0 INTRODUCTION

Geotextiles are a group of relatively new products that refer to woven or nonwoven fabric mats used in earth construction. Although geotextile products are relatively new, the idea of using mats to modify the earth for construction is very old. The ancient Romans used reed mats to stabilize roadbeds over soft ground. In the United States, the city of New York has used marsh hay to keep planting soil out of gravel drainage layers in tree pits for many years, and in the 1920s the South Carolina Highway Department was successful in their experiments using asphalt-treated cotton as a reinforcement in roadways.

Not until the 1950s, however, were weather-resistant synthetic fabrics designed for specific site engineering applications. For the first time, a plastic filter cloth was used by a U.S. company in place of a graded aggregate drainage system. Since that time, the use of geotextiles has greatly expanded. The first noteworthy U.S. publication on the use of geotextiles was published in 1961, with several other significant papers following in the late 1960s and early 1970s. In recent years, papers have been given at the First and at the Second International Conference on Geotextiles, held in 1977 and 1982, respectively.

2.0 BASIC FUNCTIONS OF GEOTEXTILES

The physical characteristics of a geotextile determine its value for an intended application. For example, some fabrics (or portions thereof) deteriorate over time—a trait desirable for short-term erosion control, while others resist deterioration—a trait desirable for soil separation and drainage applications. Common functions are described below.

2.1 Separation

A major use of geotextiles is to separate materials. Subsoil can be prevented from migrating into roadway base aggregate or railroad ballast, and different zones of material (i.e., clay, drain rock, etc.) can be kept separate in earth dams. Drain rock can be kept unclogged in planters, and retaining wall backfill can be kept separate from adjacent soil. The function of separation often coincides with other functions, such as filtration and reinforcement.

2.2 Reinforcement

Geotextiles can be used to reinforce subsoil beneath structures. They can also be used between layers of pavement to control reflected cracking and other failures. Geotextiles can be laid over soft, compressible subsoils and under an aggregate base for both drainage and added strength in roadways and other structures. Fabrics can also be used in turf to increase the durability of playing fields.

2.3 Filtration (Drainage)

Geotextiles can be used as a filter material in many drainage applications. Fabric is used to filter fine soil particles out of coarser stone drainage media in underdrains, at the base of planters, behind retaining walls, etc. They can also be used to wrap perforated pipe or other drainage media to prevent intrusion of fine soil particles into the drainage medium.

2.4 Erosion Control

Geotextiles have been used effectively to reduce soil erosion by reducing the velocity of surface runoff waters. Fabrics for this purpose can be made of durable artificial fibers offering a long life, or natural fibers that deteriorate over time, or a combination of the two.

Erosion along coastlines or along waterways can be minimized by using a permeable fabric covered by heavy aggregate (the fabric traps soil particles while allowing water to move through it).

Fabric fences can also be used as windbreaks to reduce wind erosion.

2.5 Formwork

Fabrics can be used as flexible concrete formwork. The fabric can be placed in difficult-to-get-at places and *inflated* with concrete or grout. The permeability of the fabric allows air or water to escape from the form as the concrete fills the cavity between the layers of fabric.

3.0 GEOTEXTILE MATERIALS

Geotextiles are composed of various fibers that are either woven or bonded together to form fabric.

3.1 Fibers

Basic Types of Fibers:

The main fibers used in geotextiles are polypropylene, polyester, polyvinyl chloride, nylon, polyethylene, fiberglass, and natural fibers such as jute.

Properties of Fibers:

The type of fiber used in the manufacture of a geotextile determines the fabric's overall strength and resistance to various environmental weathering agents (i.e., biological attack, chemical reaction, temperature, abrasion, and ultraviolet light) (Table 880-1).

3.2 Basic Types of Fabrics

Woven Fabrics:

Woven fibers are bound together into yarns, and the yarns are interlaced to form a weave (Figure 880-1). This rectangular structure gives woven fabrics their characteristic strength and extensibility (stretch). Parallel to the warp and weft, the fabric is the weakest and stretches the least, while it is the strongest and stretches the most at 45 degrees to the warp and weft (Figure 880-2).

The number of yarns per area is the count of the fabric, and the count helps determine the porosity, weight, thickness, and extensibility of the fabric. The finish (if any) applied to the surface of the fabric can modify its properties.

Nonwoven Fabrics:

Nonwoven fabrics consist of continuous filaments or cut fibers bound together in a

TABLE 880-1
Properties of Various Geotextile Fibers

	Fibers					
Property	*Nylon 66*	*Nylon 6*	*Polyethylene*	*Polypropylene*	*Polyvinyl chloride*	*Jute*
Fiber properties:						
Tenacity, g/denier (approx.)	8	8	4.5	8	1.8	—
Extension at break, % (approx.)	15	17	25	18	25	—
Specific gravity	1.14	1.14	0.94	0.91	1.69	1.5
Melting point, °C	250	215	120	165	—	—
Maximum operating temperature, °C (approx.)	90	Below 65	55	90	—	Below 65
Resistance to:*						
Fungus	3	3	4	3	3	1
Insects	2	2	4	2	3	1
Vermin	2	2	4	2	3	1
Mineral acids	2	2	4	4	3	1
Alkalis	3	3	4	4	3	1
Dry heat	2	2	2	2	2	2
Moist heat	3	3	2	2	2	2
Oxidizing agents	2	2	1	3	—	—
Abrasion	4	4	3	3	4	3
Ultraviolet light	3	3	1	3	4	1

* Poor 1; fair 2; good 3; excellent 4.

Source: Extracted from a paper by E. W. Cannon, *Civil Engineering*, March 1976.

random manner by mechanical entanglement, chemical bonding, or thermal bonding. Many geotextiles are then needle-punched to improve their permeability.

Nonwoven fabrics tend to be equally strong and extensible in all directions and to have an evenly distributed range of pore sizes over the entire fabric (Figure 880-2).

4.0 PROPERTIES OF GEOTEXTILES

4.1 Physical Properties

Thickness and porosity are the two physical properties of geotextiles most important in landscape applications. (Refer to Section 870: Glass, Plastics, and Fabrics, for more information on the physical properties of fabrics.)

Thickness:

As the thickness of a fabric increases (particularly a nonwoven fabric), the overall strength of the fabric increases, but it has proportionately less permeability. Thicker nonwoven fabrics (three-dimensional fabrics or felts) are much stronger than thinner fabrics (two-dimensional fabrics) but can become clogged internally by soil particles.

Porosity:

The permeability of a fabric is related to its *porosity,* the size of the openings in the fabric (Figure 880-3). Porosity is expressed as equivalent opening size (EOS) and corresponds to the closest U.S. standard sieve size (i.e., a fabric with an EOS of 200 has openings equivalent to a No. 200 sieve).

4.2 Mechanical Properties

Elongation, grab strength, and burst pressure are three mechanical properties of geotextiles most important in landscape applications. (Refer to Section 870: Glass, Plastics, and Fabrics, for more information on the mechanical properties of fabrics.)

Elongation:

Elongation is the percent increase in overall length the fabric attains when it is extended.

Grab Strength:

The grab strength is the measure of force in pounds (kilograms) required to pull a fabric apart.

TABLE 880-2
Recommendations for Fabric Overlap

CBR of soil	*Overlap, %*
20	10
15	12
10	14
8	15
6	18
4	22
2	25

Source: E. I duPont de Nemours, "A Method for Constructing Aggregate Bases Using 'Typer' Spunbonded Polypropylene," unpublished report, Wilmington, Delaware.

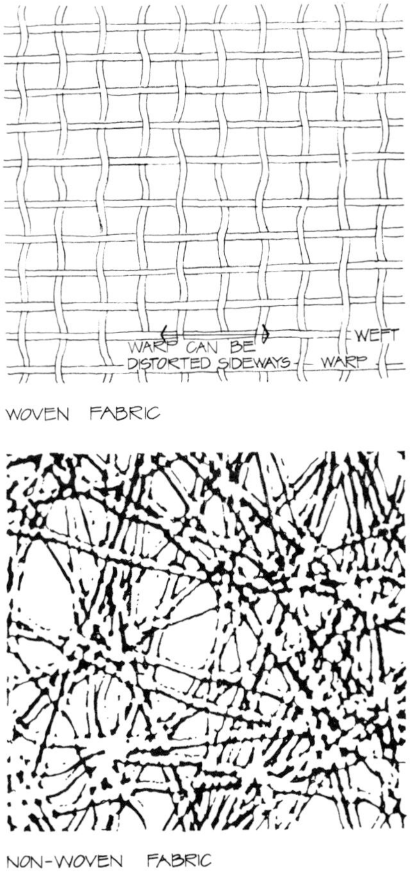
WARP CAN BE DISTORTED SIDEWAYS
WEFT
WARP
WOVEN FABRIC
NON-WOVEN FABRIC

Figure 880-1 Basic Types of Fabrics. Woven fabrics consist of yarns that have been woven together, whereas nonwoven fabrics consist of filaments randomly bound together by mechanical, chemical, or thermal means.

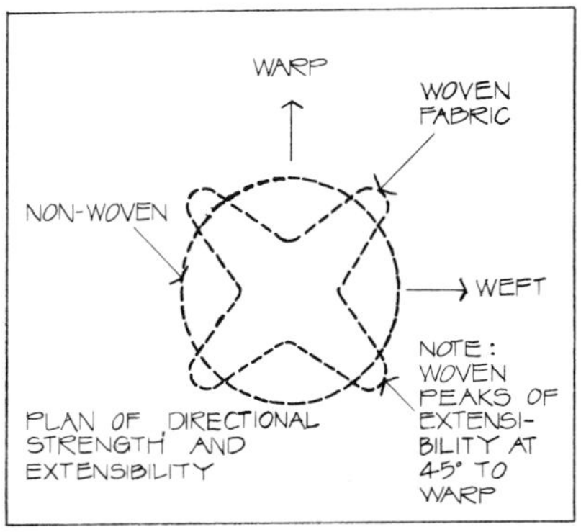
WARP
WOVEN FABRIC
NON-WOVEN
WEFT
NOTE: WOVEN PEAKS OF EXTENSIBILITY AT 45° TO WARP
PLAN OF DIRECTIONAL STRENGTH AND EXTENSIBILITY

Figure 880-2 Strength and Extensibility of Fabrics. Nonwoven fabrics are equally strong and extensible in all directions, whereas woven fabrics are strongest and most extensible at an angle of 45 degrees to the warp and weft.

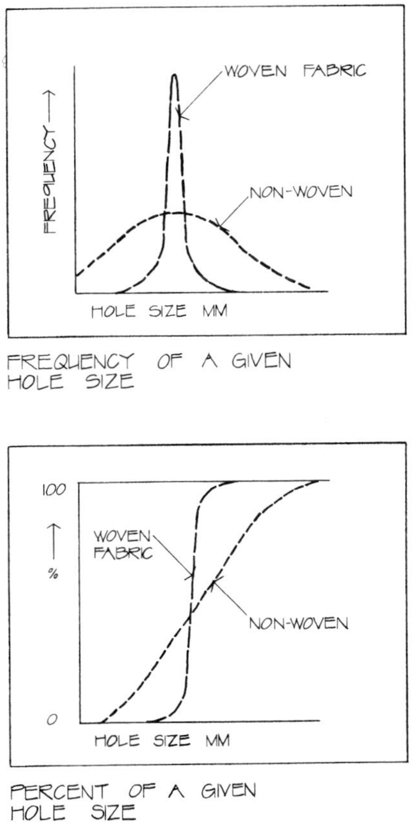
WOVEN FABRIC
FREQUENCY
NON-WOVEN
HOLE SIZE MM
FREQUENCY OF A GIVEN HOLE SIZE
100
%
0
WOVEN FABRIC
NON-WOVEN
HOLE SIZE MM
PERCENT OF A GIVEN HOLE SIZE

Figure 880-3 Porosity of Fabrics. Nonwoven fabrics have a variety of pore sizes, while woven fabrics have consistently sized pores.

Burst Pressure:

Burst pressure is the amount of pressure required to burst a section of fabric.

5.0 CRITERIA FOR SELECTION

The following characteristics of geotextiles are typically considered when assessing their value for a particular application:

1. The filtering and piping characteristics of a fabric (e.g., the ability of the fabric to filter without clogging).

2. The permeability *K* of a fabric (e.g., important in drainage applications).

3. The pore size (EOS) of a fabric (e.g., important in drainage and separation applications).

4. The moisture absorption properties of a fabric (e.g., important in irrigation applications. Natural fibers tend to absorb more water than synthetics).

5. The chemical resistance of a fabric (e.g., resistance to chemical fertilizers and organic soils).

6. The ultraviolet resistance of a fabric (e.g., important if fabric will be exposed to sunlight in part or in full).

7. The tensile strength and extensibility of a fabric (e.g., important if the fabric is to hold together or remain in place under the force of gravity on a steep slope, or to conform to uneven terrain).

8. The impact and abrasion resistance of a fabric (e.g., important if an aggregate will be installed over the fabric).

9. The thickness of a fabric (e.g., the thickness will affect the permeability and extensibility of the fabric).

10. The effect of on-site versus brought-in soils on a fabric (e.g., the soil beneath a fabric may be different both chemically and texturally from the soil above).

11. The soil holding ability of a fabric (e.g., important on steep slopes and areas subject to considerable runoff).

6.0 SITE APPLICATIONS

6.1 Separation

Roadway or Railroad Bed:

A geotextile placed between the subgrade and aggregate subbase will maintain the required design thickness of a bed by preventing the subgrade from migrating or pumping into the subbase (Figure 880-4).

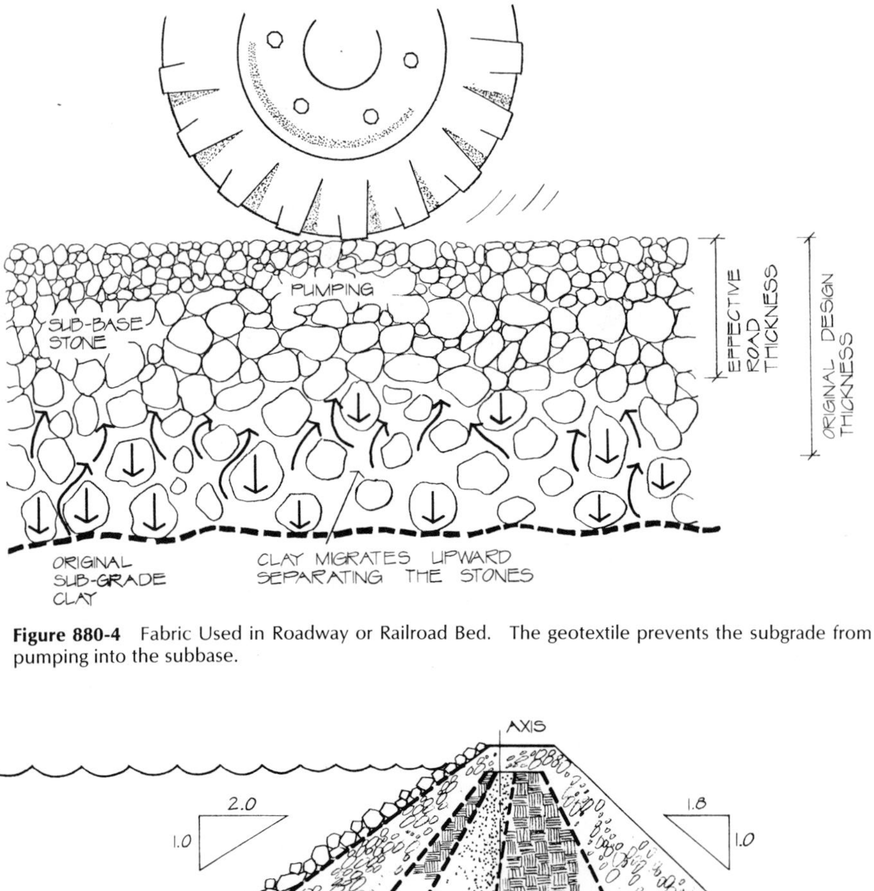
PUMPING
SUB-BASE STONE
EFFECTIVE ROAD THICKNESS
ORIGINAL DESIGN THICKNESS
ORIGINAL SUB-GRADE CLAY
CLAY MIGRATES UPWARD SEPARATING THE STONES

Figure 880-4 Fabric Used in Roadway or Railroad Bed. The geotextile prevents the subgrade from pumping into the subbase.

Earth Dam Design:

Modern earth dam designs utilize many different zones of materials that are separated by geotextiles to maintain their individual functions (Figure 880-5).

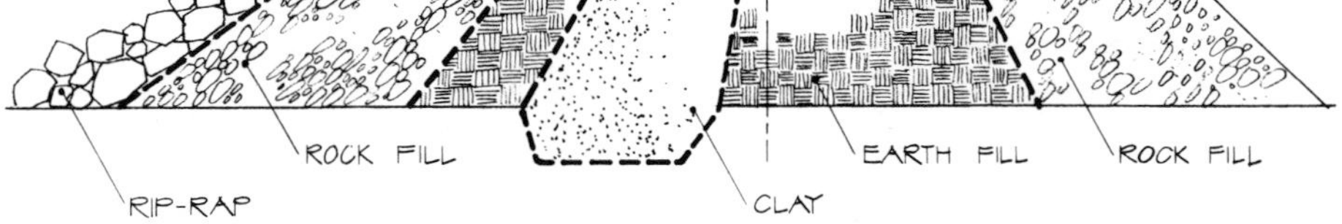
AXIS
2.0
1.0
1.8
1.0
ROCK FILL
EARTH FILL
ROCK FILL
RIP-RAP
CLAY

Figure 880-5 Fabric Used in Zoned Earthfill Dam. Geotextiles are used to separate the various zones of materials, thereby improving their individual functions.

Drainage Medium Separation in Planters:

The drainage medium can be kept separate from the planting soil by the use of a geotextile in planters or in planted areas over a structure (Figure 880-6).

6.2 Reinforcement

Paving:

Geotextiles can be used to prevent cracks in old pavements from being reflected in new pavement overlays. Fabrics are installed with a tack coat over the old pavement. The fabric bridges over the cracks and its strength supports the imposed loads, thereby protecting the overlying surface course (Figure 880-7).

Retaining Wall Support:

Geotextile tiebacks are used to anchor retaining wall facing units, utilizing the weight of the ground behind the wall to hold the wall's facing units (Figure 880-8).

Roadways:

Compressible fabrics can reduce the amount of aggregate base material needed in a roadway construction. The separation of materials also extends the life of a roadway by maintaining proper drainage (Figure 880-9).

The ability of soil to resist a load is measured by the California bearing ratio (CBR). By adding a fabric to the soil, the effective CBR can be functionally increased and the amount of aggregate required for a roadbed can be reduced (Figure 880-10).

Since rolls of fabric are available in limited widths, fabric must be overlapped, fused, or sewn together to function as a continuous mat. Typical overlaps range form 12 to 60 in (0.3 to 1.5 m), depending on the nature of the soil, the fabric, the degree of loading, and the thickness of the cover material. Table 880-2 gives recommendations for overlap based on the CBR of the soil.

Turf Areas:

Three-dimensional geotextiles, such as *Enkamat,* have been used to reinforce turf areas. Such fabrics have sufficient structural integrity to distribute the load of light vehicles or heavy play directly to the subgrade so that turfgrass can grow, free from problems of compaction or abrasion. Such geotextiles are installed either by spreading fine topsoil over the fabric, followed by seeding, or by spreading sod over the fabric and rolling the sod to ensure proper full contact with the earth.

SOIL
FABRIC
AGGREGATE
WATER PROOF MEMBRANE
CONCRETE
DRAIN

Figure 880-6 Fabric Used in Roof Garden Planter. The geotextile keeps the drainage material separate from the planting soil.

6.3 Filtration

Fabrics are used to prevent small soil particles from entering aggregate layers in a base. In a traditional french drain, filtering is accomplished by using layers of graded aggregate outside of a coarse aggregate zone. The key to a successful filter is for the filter to have openings that are large enough to allow movement of water and small enough to prevent piping (fine particles of soil passing through the fabric and entering the drainage zone). The physical properties of a soil determine the range of the filter sizes needed to achieve proper drainage.

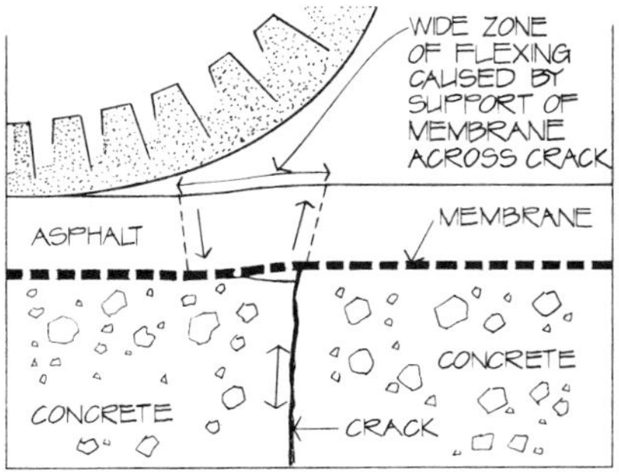
WIDE ZONE OF FLEXING CAUSED BY SUPPORT OF MEMBRANE ACROSS CRACK
ASPHALT
MEMBRANE
CONCRETE
CONCRETE
CRACK

Figure 880-7 Fabric Used to Inhibit Cracking of Pavement. The fabric bridges over cracks in the underlying pavement, thereby preventing the cracks from being reflected in the overlying surface course.

Permeability:

The permeability K of a soil (i.e., K soil) is the factor which determines the minimum permeability of the geotextiles that can be used. In theory, a given fabric *will not* inhibit soil drainage if the following equation is satisfied:

$K \text{ (fabric)} > 0.1 \ (K \text{ soil})$

In other words, in theory, a fabric *will not* inhibit soil drainage if the fabric's permeability is greater than one-tenth the permeability of the soil with which it is used.

Practically speaking, however, it is generally recommended that the minimum permeability of a geotextile used should be *greater than or equal to* the permeability of the soil. The minimum can be up to 5 times the permeability of the soil if the fabric used retains fine particles of soil as a result of electrochemical forces.

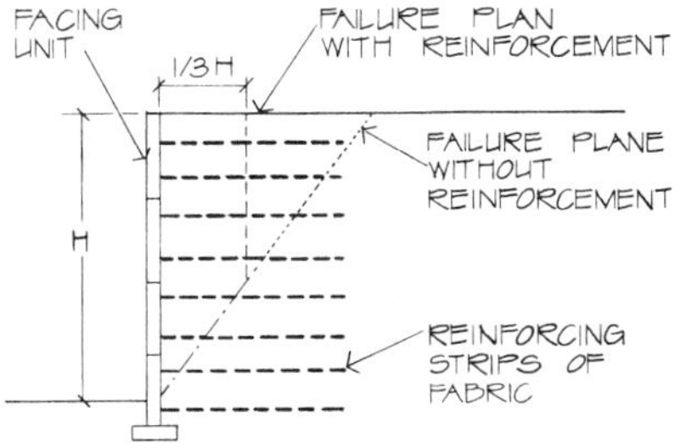
FACING UNIT
FAILURE PLAN WITH REINFORCEMENT
1/3 H
FAILURE PLANE WITHOUT REINFORCEMENT
H
REINFORCING STRIPS OF FABRIC

Figure 880-8 Fabric Used as a Deadman in a Retaining Wall. Geotextiles function in the same way as other forms of deadmen to anchor the retaining wall into the hillside.

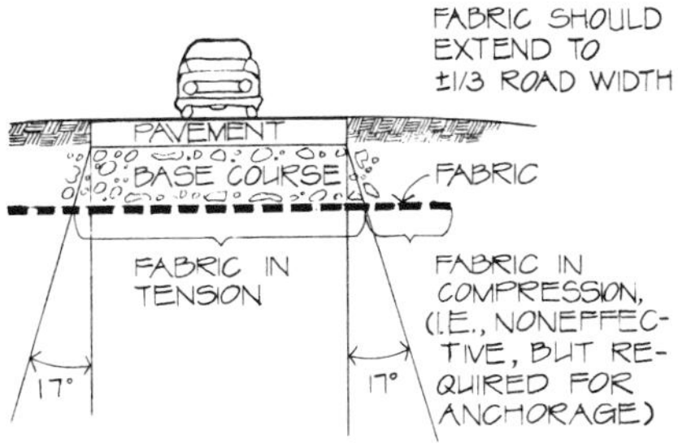
FABRIC SHOULD EXTEND TO ±1/3 ROAD WIDTH
PAVEMENT
BASE COURSE
FABRIC
FABRIC IN TENSION
FABRIC IN COMPRESSION, (I.E., NONEFFECTIVE, BUT REQUIRED FOR ANCHORAGE)
17°
17°

Figure 880-9 Fabric Used in Roadway Construction. The fabric separates the base course from the underlying subbase, thereby reducing the amount of base material required under the roadway. The fabric also helps maintain proper drainage of the base course.

Protection against Piping:

Piping refers to the process of fine particles of soil passing through a fabric rather than being retained. To prevent piping (and the consequent clogging of drainage media), the opening size of a fabric must be small enough to stop the passage of these fine soil particles (but still large enough to allow water to drain) (Figure 880-11).

The maximum equivalent opening size (EOS) of a geotextile refers to the maximum opening size that a fabric can have and still prevent piping of fine soil particles (of a given size). To find out the maximum EOS appropriate for a given soil, the composition of the soil must be analyzed for

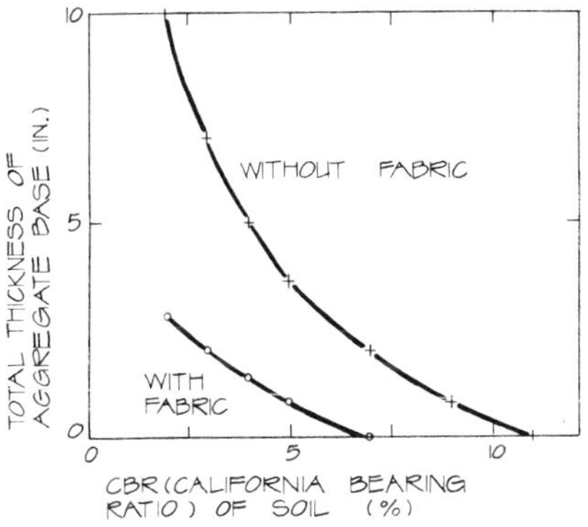
TOTAL THICKNESS OF AGGREGATE BASE (IN.)
10
5
0
WITHOUT FABRIC
WITH FABRIC
0
5
10
CBR (CALIFORNIA BEARING RATIO) OF SOIL (%)

Figure 880-10 The Effect of Fabric on the Bearing Capacity of a Road Base. Recent studies show that geotextiles can significantly improve the bearing capacity of soils with a low CBR, thereby reducing the necessary thickness of the base material.

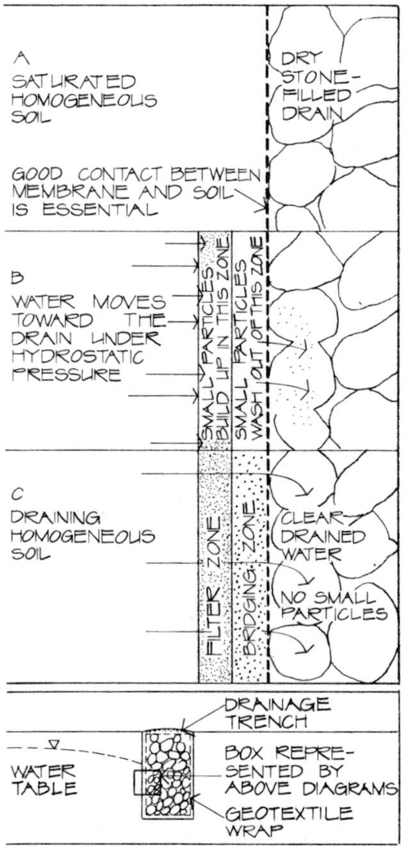
A
SATURATED
HOMOGENEOUS
SOIL
DRY
STONE-
FILLED
DRAIN
GOOD CONTACT BETWEEN
MEMBRANE AND SOIL
IS ESSENTIAL
B
WATER MOVES
TOWARD THE
DRAIN UNDER
HYDROSTATIC
PRESSURE
SMALL PARTICLES
BUILD UP IN THIS ZONE
SMALL PARTICLES
WASH OUT OF THIS ZONE
C
DRAINING
HOMOGENEOUS
SOIL
CLEAR
DRAINED
WATER
NO SMALL
PARTICLES
FILTER ZONE
BRIDGING ZONE
DRAINAGE
TRENCH
WATER
TABLE
BOX REPRE-
SENTED BY
ABOVE DIAGRAMS
GEOTEXTILE
WRAP

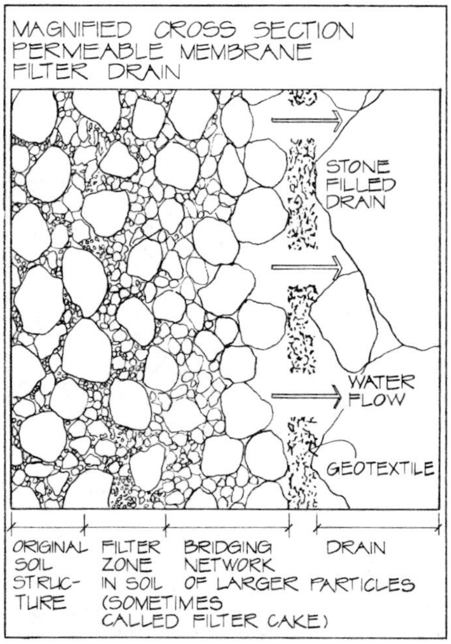
MAGNIFIED CROSS SECTION
PERMEABLE MEMBRANE
FILTER DRAIN
STONE
FILLED
DRAIN
WATER
FLOW
GEOTEXTILE
ORIGINAL SOIL STRUC-TURE
FILTER ZONE IN SOIL
BRIDGING NETWORK OF LARGER PARTICLES (SOMETIMES CALLED FILTER CAKE)
DRAIN

Figure 880-11 Fabric Used to Prevent Clogging of Drainage Media. This illustration shows the development of the *cake* of fine soil materials that builds up behind a fabric. This cake acts as the filtering mechanism that prevents piping of fine soil materials into a drainage medium.

the size distribution of the smallest soil particles.

The criterion established by the U.S. Corps of Engineers to determine the maximum EOS for a given situation states that if a fabric is to prevent piping, the EOS of the fabric must be *less than* twice the opening or sieve size that will allow 85 percent of the soil to pass through it (D_{85} soil). The following condition must be satisfied:

$$\frac{\text{EOS fabric}}{D_{85}\text{ soil}} < 2$$

This formula was developed for granular soils containing 50 percent or less silt (No. 200 sieve size) by weight. For soils containing more than 50 percent silt, the U.S. Corps of Engineers recommends the following formula:

$$\frac{\text{EOS fabric}}{D_{85}\text{ soil}} < 1$$

To reduce clogging, a minimum EOS of 100 or a minimum open area of 4 percent is recommended.

There has been a disagreement among professionals regarding minimum guidelines for the use of geotextiles in landscape applications. Few experimental installations exist where a fabric's performance has been measured, and comprehensive guidelines have not been well developed. However, current research has shown that fabrics with differing EOS and *K* ratings can perform very similarly. This is because the fabric itself at some time after installation no longer functions as the primary filtering mechanism; rather, the *cake* of fine soil particles that builds up adjacent to the fabric assumes the role of the filtering mechanism. The fabric then merely acts as a permeable constraint (Figure 880-11).

6.4 Erosion Control

Protection against Water Erosion:

Fabrics can be used to protect the soil against erosion from overland runoff, either permanently or temporarily, while still allowing vegetation to germinate and grow. When selecting a fabric, care should be taken to select materials that will be biodegradable for a vegetative solution, or if a permanent nonvegetative installation is desired, to select fabrics that are resistant to abrasion, ultraviolet rays, etc.

If a fabric is to be placed in a situation where an upward gradient may exist (i.e., upward movement of water through a fabric), care must be taken to specify a fabric that will not clog from upward movement of fine soil particles.

If aggregate or ballast is to be placed over a fabric, the fabric should be strong enough to withstand dumping of the aggregate from trucks without tearing the fabric. The fabric should be anchored in place by wire staples, the ends of the fabric buried, and/or the fabric covered with ballast.

If a fabric will frequently or constantly be exposed to water, a nonbiodegradable variety should be specified. At the toe of an embankment, for instance, a shallow trench should be dug and the fabric secured in it by use of staples, pins, or ballast (Figure 880-12). The fabric is then secured up the entire embankment. At the top of the embankment the fabric must be secured to prevent surface water from undermining the fabric. After the fabric is in place, a layer of fine aggregate is placed over the entire surface and then covered by coarser aggregate. This process helps protect the membrane from damage when the coarser aggregate is installed.

Protection against Wind Erosion:

Fabric *fences,* similar to those used for sediment traps (Figure 880-13), can be used to reduce wind-caused soil erosion.

Sediment Traps:

Preassembled fences (made of fabric with integral support and posts) can be used to trap sediment. These fences are located downslope from open excavations, etc., to trap waterborne silts and clays. They are installed by rolling out a fabric and driving posts into the ground. The bottom of the fence is buried in the ground to prevent runoff from undermining the fence (Figure 880-13). Similarly, these fences can be used to reduce water turbidity (cloudiness or pollution) when dredging or excavating waterbodies or shorelines.

6.5 Formwork

Fabrics can be used as formwork in either mat or tube forms. Two sheets of fabric are joined together at various points and then inflated with concrete or grout in a manner similar to inflating an air mattress. These concrete or grout mats are used to stabilize embankments and to fill in voids beneath large structures set on irregular surfaces (Figure 880-14). Tubes of fabric can be used to set concrete or grout in difficult-to-get-at places, such as when underpinning bridge supports (Figure 880-15) and encasing piers in concrete (Figure 880-16). The flexibility of the fabric allows for easy placement of the formwork and allows

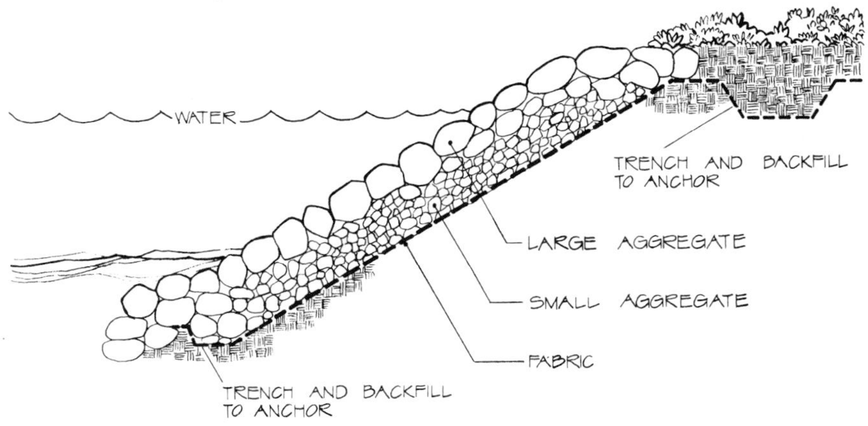
WATER
TRENCH AND BACKFILL TO ANCHOR
LARGE AGGREGATE
SMALL AGGREGATE
FABRIC
TRENCH AND BACKFILL TO ANCHOR

Figure 880-12 Fabric used for shoreline erosion control.

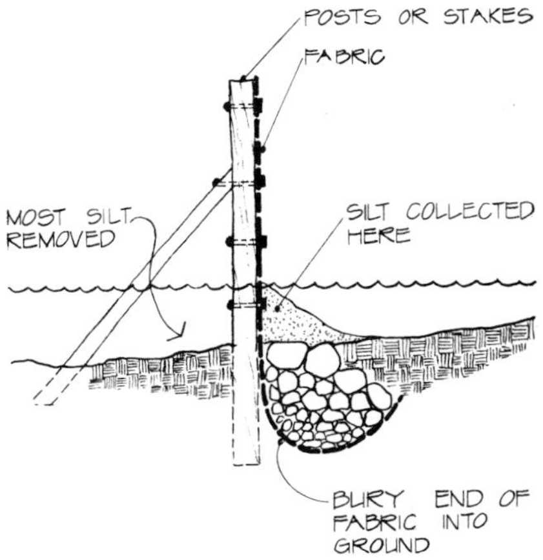
POSTS OR STAKES
FABRIC
MOST SILT REMOVED
SILT COLLECTED HERE
BURY END OF FABRIC INTO GROUND

Figure 880-13 Fabric used to help control sediment in a stream.

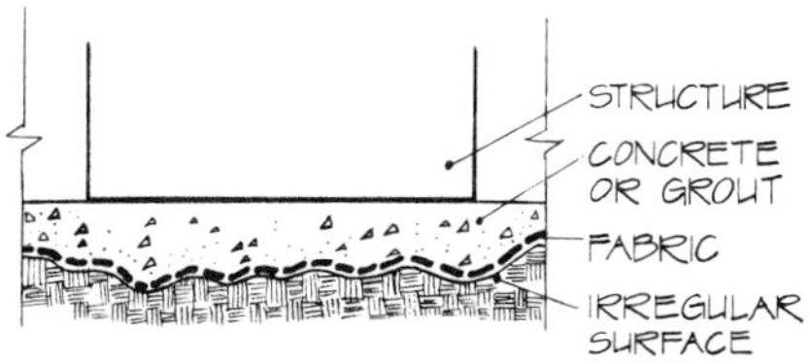
STRUCTURE
CONCRETE OR GROUT
FABRIC
IRREGULAR SURFACE

Figure 880-14 Fabric formwork for structures on irregular surfaces.

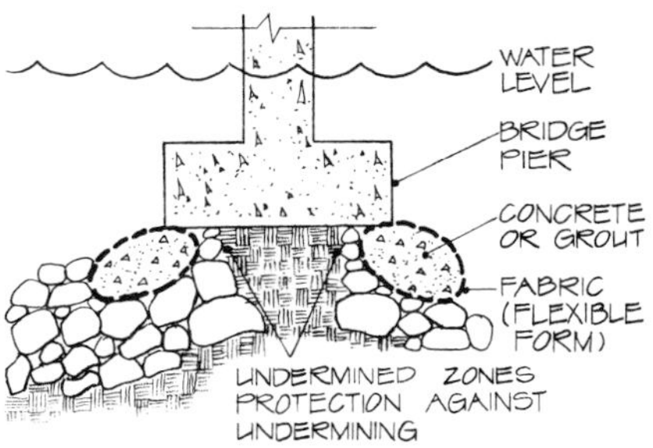
WATER LEVEL
BRIDGE PIER
CONCRETE OR GROUT
FABRIC (FLEXIBLE FORM)
UNDERMINED ZONES
PROTECTION AGAINST UNDERMINING

Figure 880-15 Fabric Formwork Used to Install Concrete under a Bridge Support to Prevent Undermining. The fabric formwork is in the shape of a *donut* which, when filled with concrete, protects the foundation on all sides.

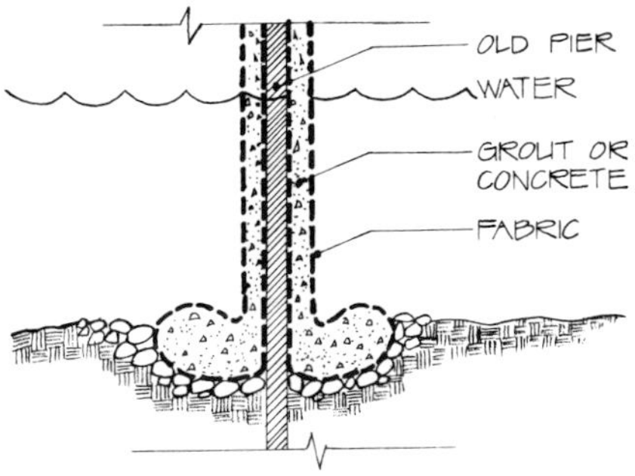
OLD PIER
WATER
GROUT OR CONCRETE
FABRIC

Figure 880-16 Fabric Used for Pier Encasement. The fabric is in the shape of a *sleeve* which, when filled with concrete, encases the deteriorating pier.

water and/or air to escape when the concrete or grout is injected into the tube.

Tubes or mats can also be filled with soil (rather like oversized sandbags) for inexpensive dams or retaining walls and/or shoreline protection.

REFERENCES

"Erosion Control: Devices, Methods and Practices," *Highway and Heavy Construction,* September 1978.

Giroud, J. P. *Filter Criteria for Geotextiles,* paper presented at the Second International Conference on Geotextiles, Las Vegas, NV, August 1982.

Kellner, L., R. J. Bally, and S. Matei. *Some Aspects Concerning Retaining Capacity of Geotextiles,* paper presented at the Second International Conference on Geotextiles, Las Vegas, NV, August 1982.

Koerner, Robert M., and Joseph P. Welsh. *Construction and Geotechnical Engineering Using Synthetic Fabrics,* Wiley, New York, 1980.

Rankilor, P. R. *Membranes in Ground Engineering,* Wiley, New York, 1981.

"Spreading Out to Cover a Host of Jobs," *Engineering News-Record,* September 24, 1981.

"State-of-the-Art-Report Construction Fabrics,' *Engineering News-Record,* August 1981.

"State-of-the-Art-Report Fabrics Weave Their Way Into Construction," *Highway and Heavy Construction,* February 1978.

Steward, J., R. Williamson, and J. Mohney. *Guidelines for Use of Fabrics in Construction and Maintenance of Low-Volume Roads,* Report FHWA-TS-78-205, Federal Highway Administration, Offices of Research and Development, Washington, DC, 1978.

Available from National Technical Information Service, Springfield, VA.

Tan, H. H., and R. D. Weimar, with Y. H. Chen, P. M. Demery, and D. B. Simons. *Hydraulic Function and Performance of Various Geotextiles in Drainage and Related Applications,* paper presented at the Second International Conference on Geotextiles, Las Vegas, NV, August 1982. ■

900

Details and Devices

INTRODUCTION

Division 900: Details and Devices has been prepared to provide a range of details and devices that go beyond those shown within specific sections elsewhere in this handbook. In most of the topical sections the reader is shown only a few generic types of details and devices related to that topic. Where appropriate and possible, some of the variety of alternatives for one detail, such as paving, is shown under a heading contained within Division 900.

Division 900 contains ten sections, or categories. Each section has one or more subsections showing a range of details and/or devices.

This is not intended to be a comprehensive source of details and devices. Most of the ones included here have been adapted after examining many variations taken from several sources. In some cases they are considered "standard" and may be widely used. In other cases, they may be considered "special" and will be used only rarely. Considerable effort has been made to recognize that climate and other factors might require some adjustment to the data shown. Readers are urged to cross-check the appropriateness of each item before using it beyond the preliminary planning and design-development stages. Local standards and requirements are expected to override any data shown here or the reader has to seek permission to override such local requirements. Sometimes, being able to demonstrate that such a detail or device is widely used elsewhere may support efforts to introduce new details or devices into a local scene where they have not been used or thought acceptable in the past. The reader is urged to remain creative and innovative in the use or adaptation of all details and devices. A direct copy of some of these details or from any other source may not be appropriate for a specific use or site.

The material contained in Division 900 is the creative work of the several people listed below. Much of the original material and preliminary development of the details and devices was done by Chien-Cheng Wu. He assembled the initial material as part of a master's thesis when he was a graduate student at the University of California, Berkeley, in 1981. Since then he has started work on a book of landscape construction details that he hopes to publish in the near future.

CREDITS

Division Editors: Nicholas T. Dines and Gary M. Fishbeck

Technical Coordinator and Detailer: Chien-Cheng Wu, *Anthony Guzzardo & Associates, San Francisco, California*

Computer Graphic Coordination and Production:

Gary M. Fishbeck, Assistant Editor
Thomas Oslund
Joseph Cloud
Nancy Green
All graphics were drawn using the MacPaint program on the Apple/Macintosh computer and were then laser printed.

section 910: Paving

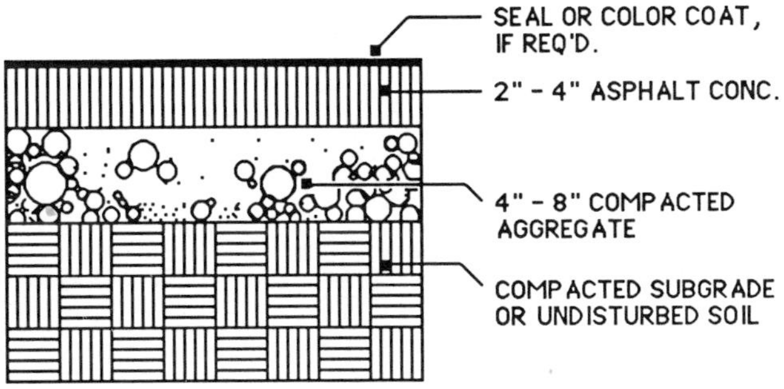

SEAL OR COLOR COAT, IF REQ'D.
2" - 4" ASPHALT CONC.
4" - 8" COMPACTED AGGREGATE
COMPACTED SUBGRADE OR UNDISTURBED SOIL

Figure 910-1 Asphalt concrete paving on aggregate base. Suitable for pedestrian walks, bikeways, running tracks, tennis courts, residential driveways, and automobile parking lots.

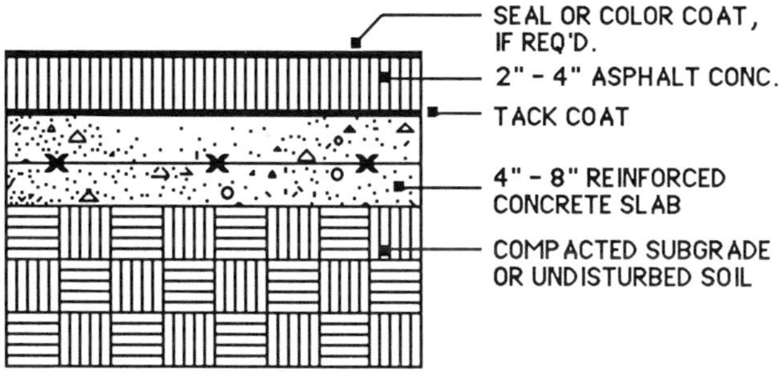

SEAL OR COLOR COAT, IF REQ'D.
2" - 4" ASPHALT CONC.
TACK COAT
4" - 8" REINFORCED CONCRETE SLAB
COMPACTED SUBGRADE OR UNDISTURBED SOIL

Figure 910-2 Asphalt concrete paving on concrete base. The thickness of the layers depends on expected traffic loads and bearing properties of the subgrade.

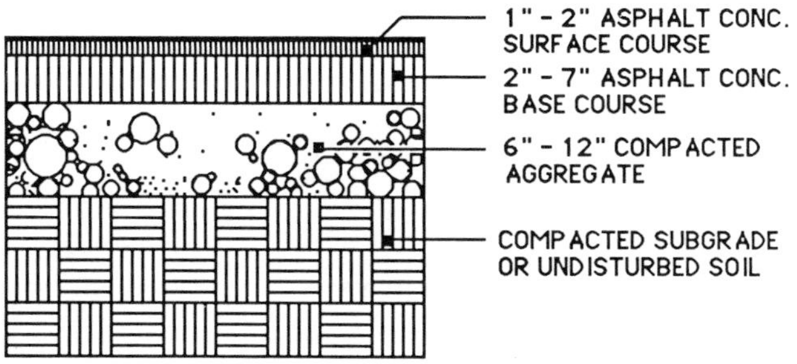

1" - 2" ASPHALT CONC. SURFACE COURSE
2" - 7" ASPHALT CONC. BASE COURSE
6" - 12" COMPACTED AGGREGATE
COMPACTED SUBGRADE OR UNDISTURBED SOIL

Figure 910-3 Asphalt concrete paving for heavy traffic. Suitable for streets and highways. Thickness of the asphalt layers depends on expected traffic loads and bearing properties of the subgrade.

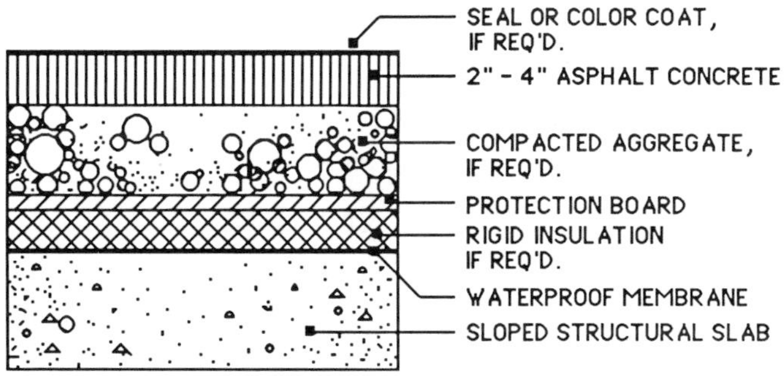

SEAL OR COLOR COAT, IF REQ'D.
2" - 4" ASPHALT CONCRETE
COMPACTED AGGREGATE, IF REQ'D.
PROTECTION BOARD
RIGID INSULATION IF REQ'D.
WATERPROOF MEMBRANE
SLOPED STRUCTURAL SLAB

Figure 910-4 Asphalt concrete paving (on structure). Suitable for rooftop pavements.

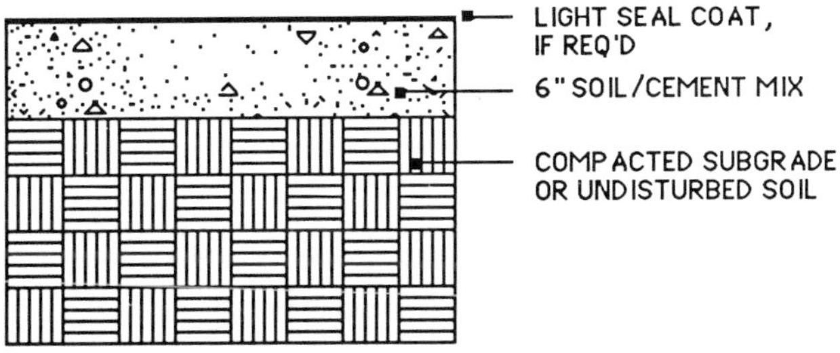

LIGHT SEAL COAT, IF REQ'D
6" SOIL/CEMENT MIX
COMPACTED SUBGRADE OR UNDISTURBED SOIL

Figure 910-5 Soil cement paving. Soil cement is a mixture of on-site soil and cement. It is porous, inexpensive, and commonly used over granular soils for light traffic areas.

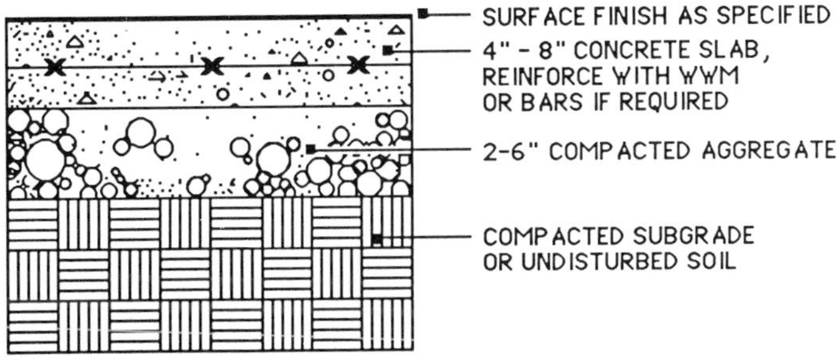

SURFACE FINISH AS SPECIFIED
4" - 8" CONCRETE SLAB, REINFORCE WITH WWM OR BARS IF REQUIRED
2-6" COMPACTED AGGREGATE
COMPACTED SUBGRADE OR UNDISTURBED SOIL

Figure 910-6 Reinforced concrete paving. Reinforced concrete paving is suitable for medium- to high-traffic areas. Use reinforcing bars only in heavy load areas. Provide expansion joints 25′-0″ on center maximum.

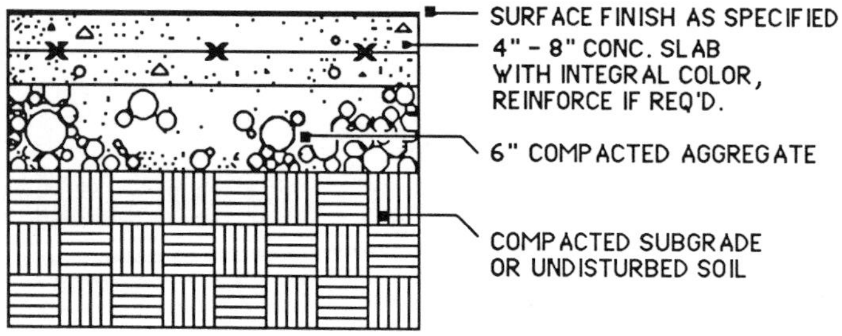
SURFACE FINISH AS SPECIFIED
4" - 8" CONC. SLAB WITH INTEGRAL COLOR, REINFORCE IF REQ'D.
6" COMPACTED AGGREGATE
COMPACTED SUBGRADE OR UNDISTURBED SOIL

Figure 910-7 Colored concrete paving (integral).

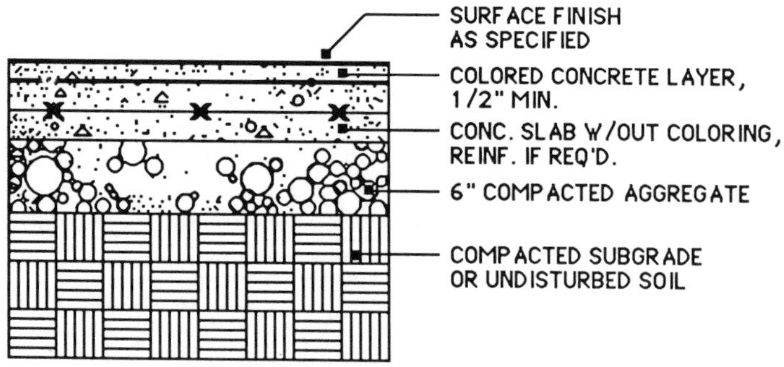
SURFACE FINISH AS SPECIFIED
COLORED CONCRETE LAYER, 1/2" MIN.
CONC. SLAB W/OUT COLORING, REINF. IF REQ'D.
6" COMPACTED AGGREGATE
COMPACTED SUBGRADE OR UNDISTURBED SOIL

Figure 910-8 Colored concrete paving (surficial).

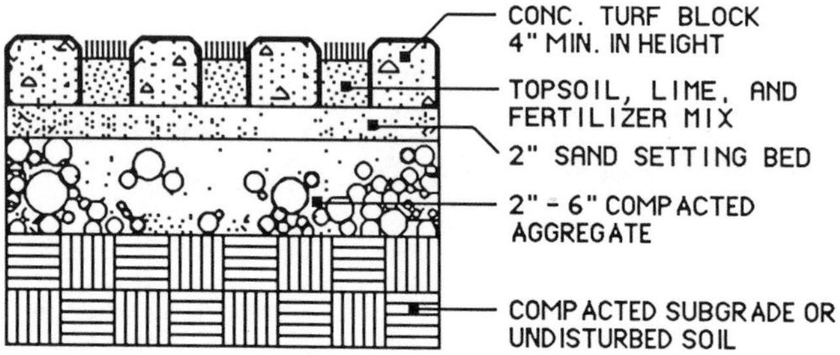
CONC. TURF BLOCK 4" MIN. IN HEIGHT
TOPSOIL, LIME, AND FERTILIZER MIX
2" SAND SETTING BED
2" - 6" COMPACTED AGGREGATE
COMPACTED SUBGRADE OR UNDISTURBED SOIL

Figure 910-9 Concrete paving (on structure). Suitable for rooftop landscape use.

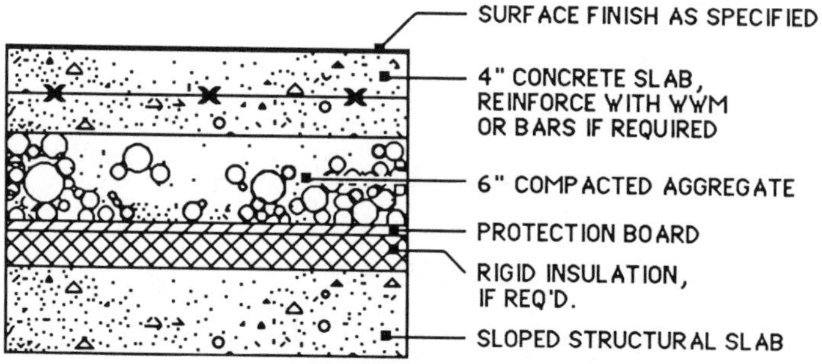
SURFACE FINISH AS SPECIFIED
4" CONCRETE SLAB, REINFORCE WITH WWM OR BARS IF REQUIRED
6" COMPACTED AGGREGATE
PROTECTION BOARD
RIGID INSULATION, IF REQ'D.
SLOPED STRUCTURAL SLAB

Figure 910-10 Concrete turfblock paving. Turfblock paving is commonly used where turfgrass is desired but light or infrequent traffic is involved. It can be used to stabilize steep slopes, streambanks, and lakeshore embankments. Irrigation may be necessary in drier climates.

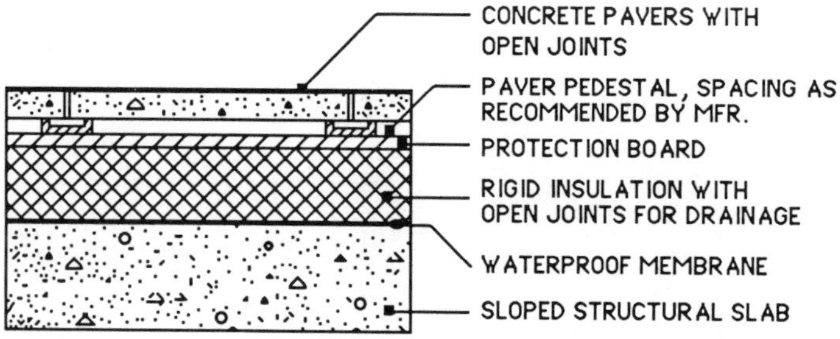
CONCRETE PAVERS WITH OPEN JOINTS
PAVER PEDESTAL, SPACING AS RECOMMENDED BY MFR.
PROTECTION BOARD
RIGID INSULATION WITH OPEN JOINTS FOR DRAINAGE
WATERPROOF MEMBRANE
SLOPED STRUCTURAL SLAB

Figure 910-11 Concrete pavers (on structure).

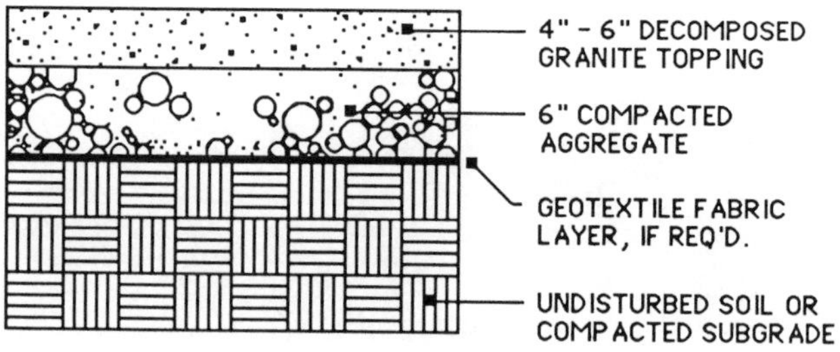
4" - 6" DECOMPOSED GRANITE TOPPING
6" COMPACTED AGGREGATE
GEOTEXTILE FABRIC LAYER, IF REQ'D.
UNDISTURBED SOIL OR COMPACTED SUBGRADE

Figure 910-12 Decomposed granite paving.

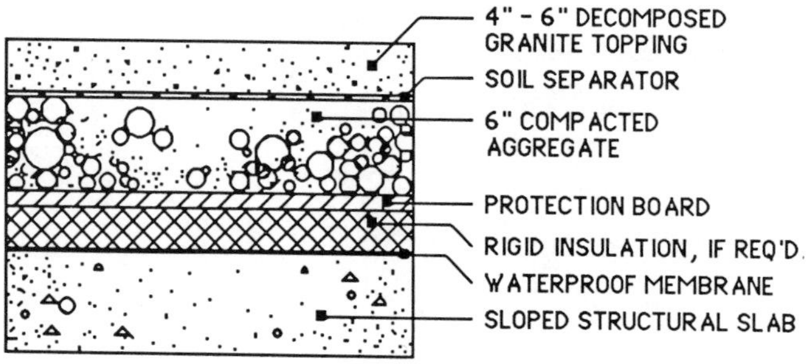
4" - 6" DECOMPOSED GRANITE TOPPING
SOIL SEPARATOR
6" COMPACTED AGGREGATE
PROTECTION BOARD
RIGID INSULATION, IF REQ'D.
WATERPROOF MEMBRANE
SLOPED STRUCTURAL SLAB

Figure 910-13 Decomposed granite paving (on structure). Color and texture is variable.

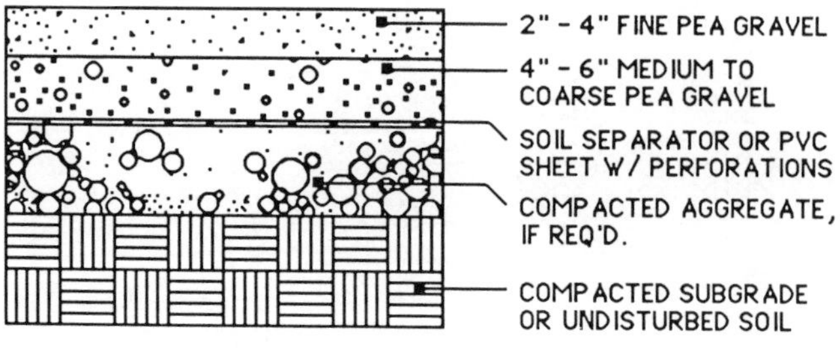
2" - 4" FINE PEA GRAVEL
4" - 6" MEDIUM TO COARSE PEA GRAVEL
SOIL SEPARATOR OR PVC SHEET W/ PERFORATIONS
COMPACTED AGGREGATE, IF REQ'D.
COMPACTED SUBGRADE OR UNDISTURBED SOIL

Figure 910-14 Pea gravel.

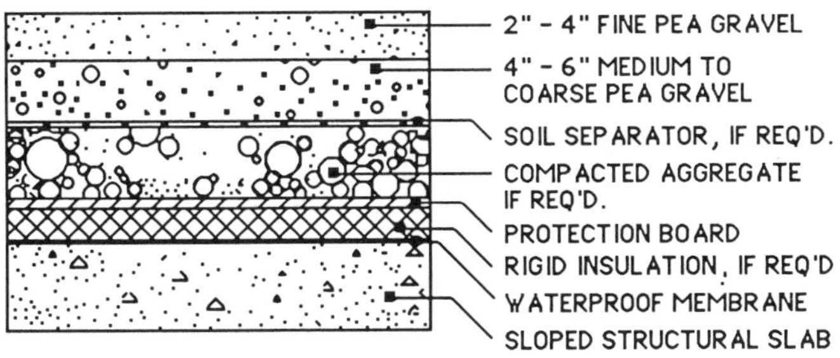
2" - 4" FINE PEA GRAVEL
4" - 6" MEDIUM TO COARSE PEA GRAVEL
SOIL SEPARATOR, IF REQ'D.
COMPACTED AGGREGATE IF REQ'D.
PROTECTION BOARD
RIGID INSULATION, IF REQ'D
WATERPROOF MEMBRANE
SLOPED STRUCTURAL SLAB

Figure 910-15 Pea gravel (on structure).

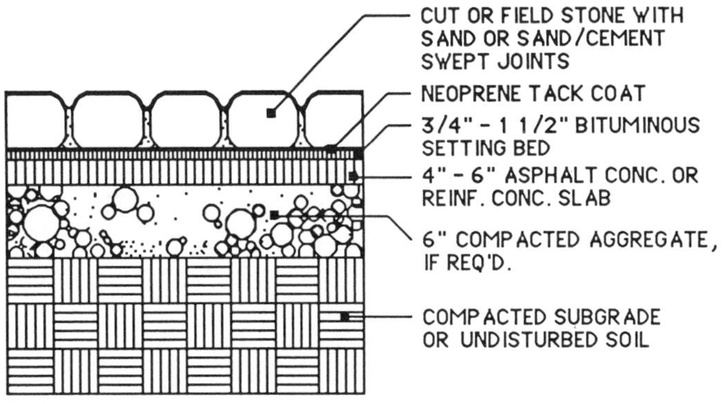
CUT OR FIELD STONE WITH SAND OR SAND/CEMENT SWEPT JOINTS
NEOPRENE TACK COAT
3/4" - 1 1/2" BITUMINOUS SETTING BED
4" - 6" ASPHALT CONC. OR REINF. CONC. SLAB
6" COMPACTED AGGREGATE, IF REQ'D.
COMPACTED SUBGRADE OR UNDISTURBED SOIL

Figure 910-16 Stone pavers on sand setting bed. Provide aggregate layer only in area of high traffic or expansive soils.

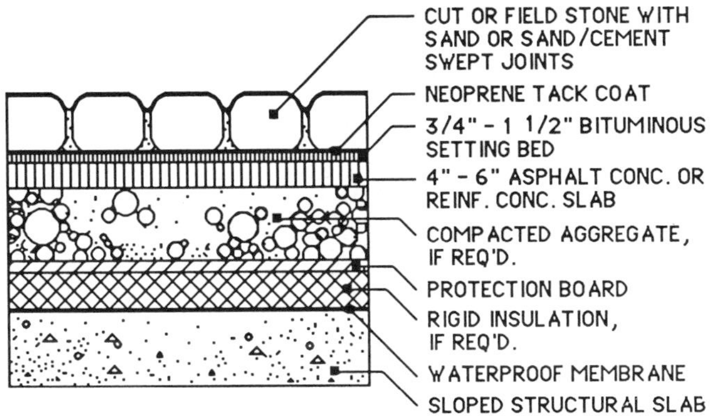
CUT OR FIELD STONE WITH SAND OR SAND/CEMENT SWEPT JOINTS
NEOPRENE TACK COAT
3/4" - 1 1/2" BITUMINOUS SETTING BED
4" - 6" ASPHALT CONC. OR REINF. CONC. SLAB
COMPACTED AGGREGATE, IF REQ'D.
PROTECTION BOARD
RIGID INSULATION, IF REQ'D.
WATERPROOF MEMBRANE
SLOPED STRUCTURAL SLAB

Figure 910-17 Stone pavers on sand setting bed (on structure).

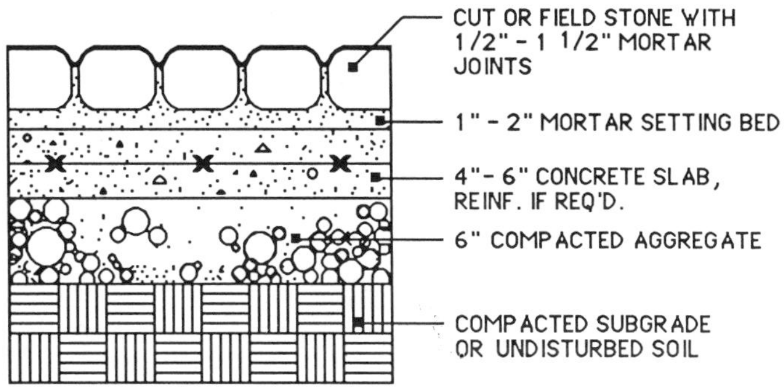
CUT OR FIELD STONE WITH 1/2" - 1 1/2" MORTAR JOINTS
1" - 2" MORTAR SETTING BED
4"- 6" CONCRETE SLAB, REINF. IF REQ'D.
6" COMPACTED AGGREGATE
COMPACTED SUBGRADE OR UNDISTURBED SOIL

Figure 910-18 Stone pavers on bituminous setting bed.

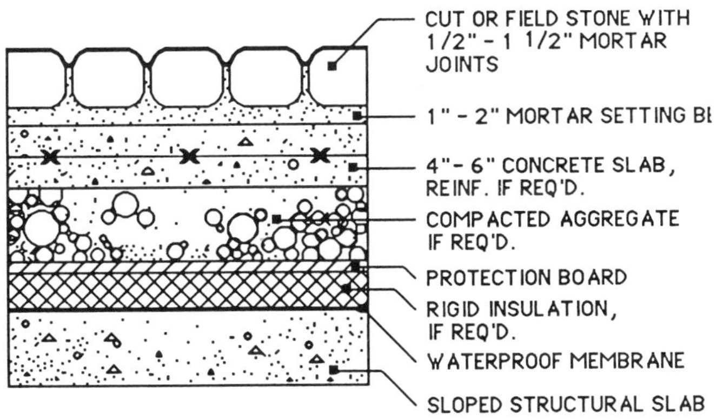
CUT OR FIELD STONE WITH 1/2" - 1 1/2" MORTAR JOINTS
1" - 2" MORTAR SETTING B
4"- 6" CONCRETE SLAB, REINF. IF REQ'D.
COMPACTED AGGREGATE IF REQ'D.
PROTECTION BOARD
RIGID INSULATION, IF REQ'D.
WATERPROOF MEMBRANE
SLOPED STRUCTURAL SLAB

Figure 910-19 Stone pavers on bituminous setting bed (on structure).

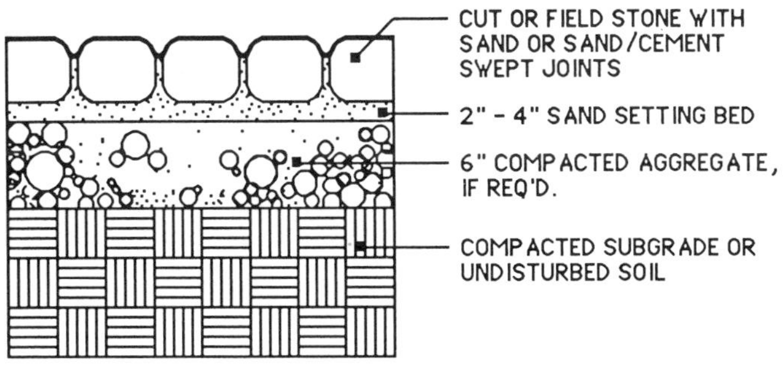
CUT OR FIELD STONE WITH SAND OR SAND/CEMENT SWEPT JOINTS
2" - 4" SAND SETTING BED
6" COMPACTED AGGREGATE, IF REQ'D.
COMPACTED SUBGRADE OR UNDISTURBED SOIL

Figure 910-20 Stone pavers on mortar setting bed.

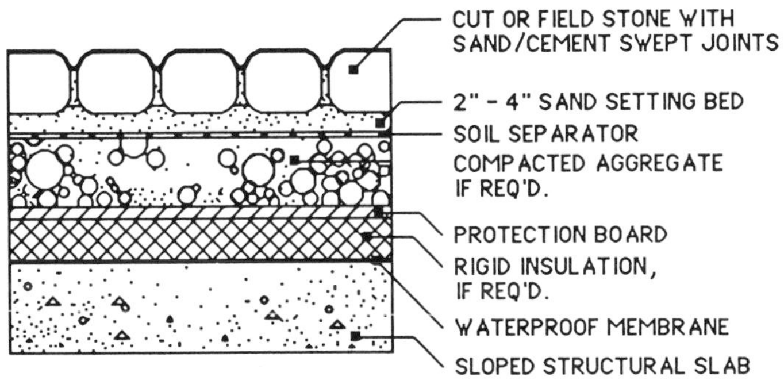
CUT OR FIELD STONE WITH SAND/CEMENT SWEPT JOINTS
2" - 4" SAND SETTING BED
SOIL SEPARATOR
COMPACTED AGGREGATE IF REQ'D.
PROTECTION BOARD
RIGID INSULATION, IF REQ'D.
WATERPROOF MEMBRANE
SLOPED STRUCTURAL SLAB

Figure 910-21 Stone pavers on mortar setting bed (on structure).

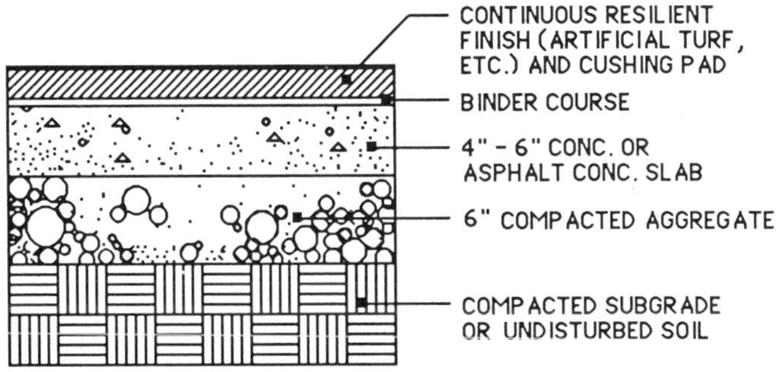
CONTINUOUS RESILIENT FINISH (ARTIFICIAL TURF, ETC.) AND CUSHING PAD
BINDER COURSE
4" - 6" CONC. OR ASPHALT CONC. SLAB
6" COMPACTED AGGREGATE
COMPACTED SUBGRADE OR UNDISTURBED SOIL

Figure 910-22 Synthetic turf (continuous mat).

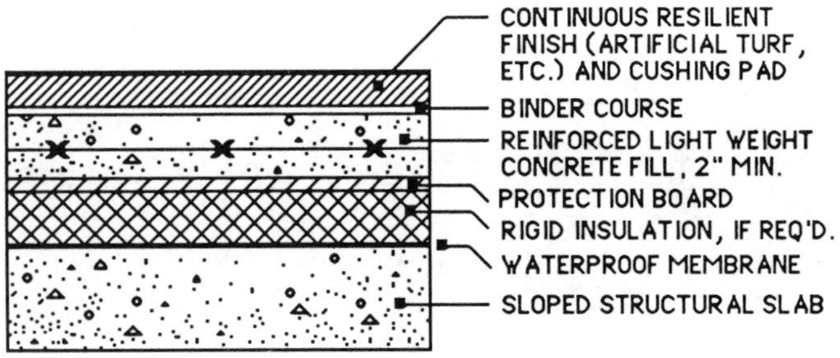
CONTINUOUS RESILIENT FINISH (ARTIFICIAL TURF, ETC.) AND CUSHING PAD
BINDER COURSE
REINFORCED LIGHT WEIGHT CONCRETE FILL, 2" MIN.
PROTECTION BOARD
RIGID INSULATION, IF REQ'D.
WATERPROOF MEMBRANE
SLOPED STRUCTURAL SLAB

Figure 910-23 Synthetic turf (continuous mat on structure).

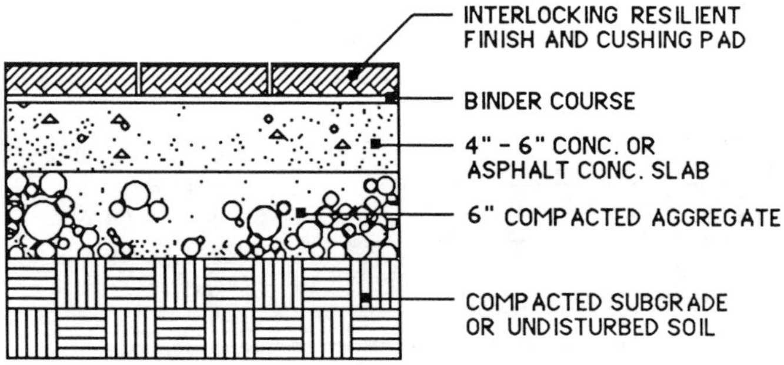
INTERLOCKING RESILIENT FINISH AND CUSHING PAD
BINDER COURSE
4" - 6" CONC. OR ASPHALT CONC. SLAB
6" COMPACTED AGGREGATE
COMPACTED SUBGRADE OR UNDISTURBED SOIL

Figure 910-24 Synthetic turf (interlocking mat). Interlocking mats require an edge retainer and are removable.

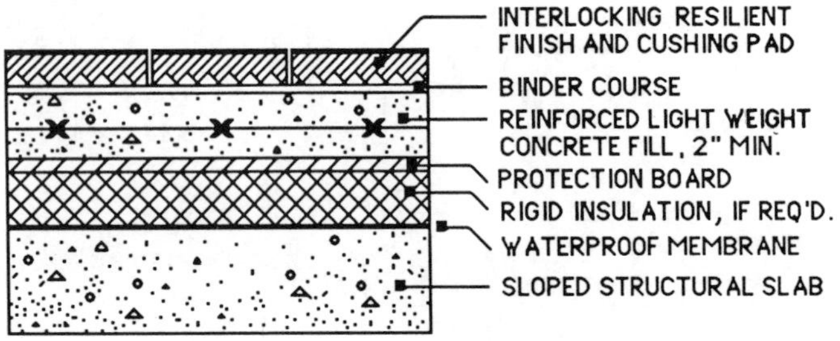
INTERLOCKING RESILIENT FINISH AND CUSHING PAD
BINDER COURSE
REINFORCED LIGHT WEIGHT CONCRETE FILL, 2" MIN.
PROTECTION BOARD
RIGID INSULATION, IF REQ'D.
WATERPROOF MEMBRANE
SLOPED STRUCTURAL SLAB

Figure 910-25 Synthetic turf (interlocking mat on structure).

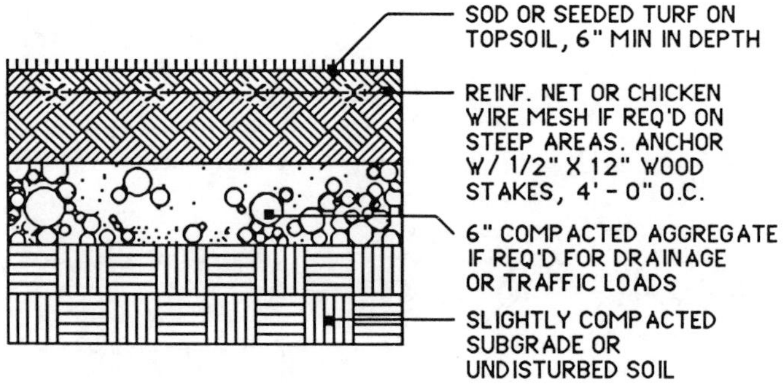
SOD OR SEEDED TURF ON TOPSOIL, 6" MIN IN DEPTH
REINF. NET OR CHICKEN WIRE MESH IF REQ'D ON STEEP AREAS. ANCHOR W/ 1/2" X 12" WOOD STAKES, 4' - 0" O.C.
6" COMPACTED AGGREGATE IF REQ'D FOR DRAINAGE OR TRAFFIC LOADS
SLIGHTLY COMPACTED SUBGRADE OR UNDISTURBED SOIL

Figure 910-26 Natural turf.

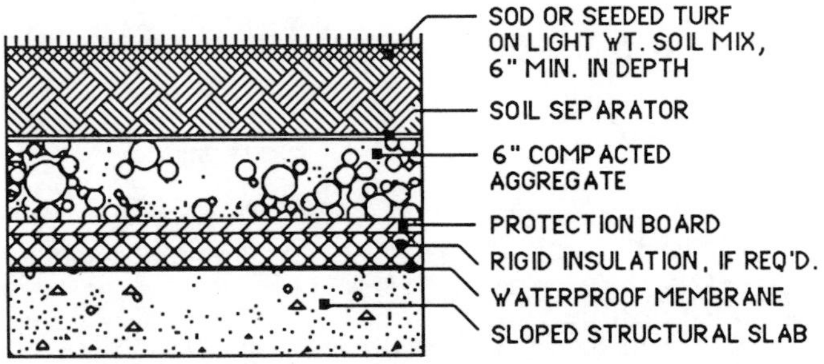
SOD OR SEEDED TURF ON LIGHT WT. SOIL MIX, 6" MIN. IN DEPTH
SOIL SEPARATOR
6" COMPACTED AGGREGATE
PROTECTION BOARD
RIGID INSULATION, IF REQ'D.
WATERPROOF MEMBRANE
SLOPED STRUCTURAL SLAB

Figure 910-27 Natural turf (on structure).

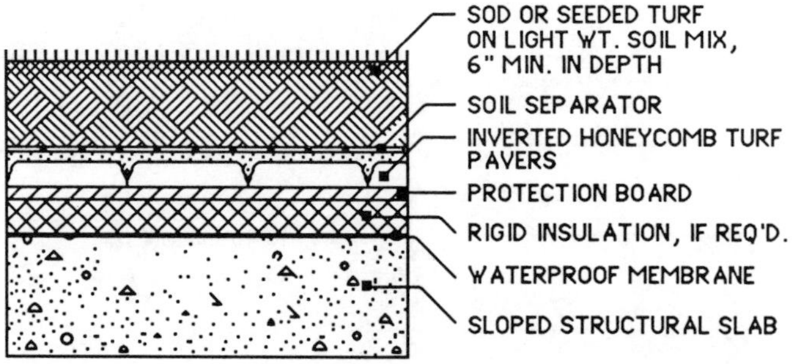
SOD OR SEEDED TURF ON LIGHT WT. SOIL MIX, 6" MIN. IN DEPTH
SOIL SEPARATOR
INVERTED HONEYCOMB TURF PAVERS
PROTECTION BOARD
RIGID INSULATION, IF REQ'D.
WATERPROOF MEMBRANE
SLOPED STRUCTURAL SLAB

Figure 910-28 Natural turf over honeycomb pavers (on structure). If weight is a concern, honeycomb pavers can be inverted and installed with a high-density styrofoam fill.

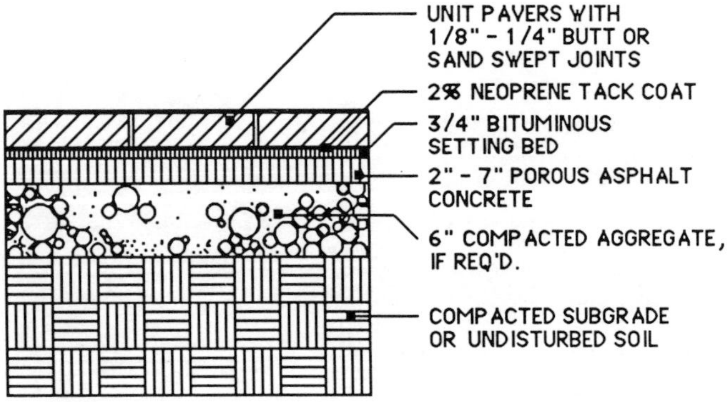
UNIT PAVERS WITH 1/8" - 1/4" BUTT OR SAND SWEPT JOINTS
2% NEOPRENE TACK COAT
3/4" BITUMINOUS SETTING BED
2" - 7" POROUS ASPHALT CONCRETE
6" COMPACTED AGGREGATE, IF REQ'D.
COMPACTED SUBGRADE OR UNDISTURBED SOIL

Figure 910-29 Unit pavers on sand setting bed.

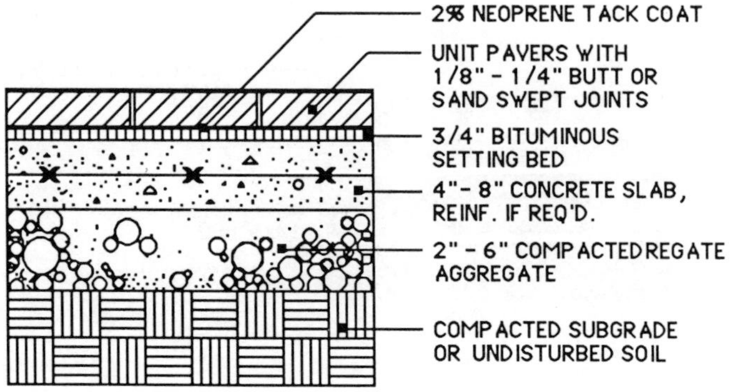
2% NEOPRENE TACK COAT
UNIT PAVERS WITH 1/8" - 1/4" BUTT OR SAND SWEPT JOINTS
3/4" BITUMINOUS SETTING BED
4"- 8" CONCRETE SLAB, REINF. IF REQ'D.
2" - 6" COMPACTEDREGATE AGGREGATE
COMPACTED SUBGRADE OR UNDISTURBED SOIL

Figure 910-30 Unit pavers on sand setting bed (on sloped structural slab).

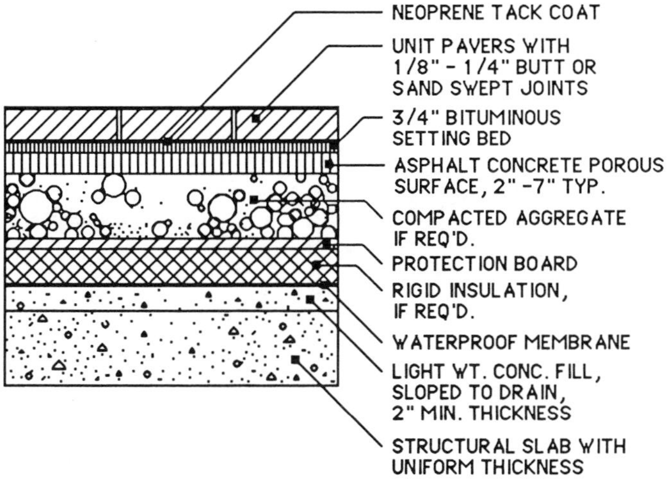
NEOPRENE TACK COAT
UNIT PAVERS WITH 1/8" - 1/4" BUTT OR SAND SWEPT JOINTS
3/4" BITUMINOUS SETTING BED
ASPHALT CONCRETE POROUS SURFACE, 2" -7" TYP.
COMPACTED AGGREGATE IF REQ'D.
PROTECTION BOARD
RIGID INSULATION, IF REQ'D.
WATERPROOF MEMBRANE
LIGHT WT. CONC. FILL, SLOPED TO DRAIN, 2" MIN. THICKNESS
STRUCTURAL SLAB WITH UNIFORM THICKNESS

Figure 910-31 Unit pavers on sand setting bed (on structural slab with sloped concrete fill).

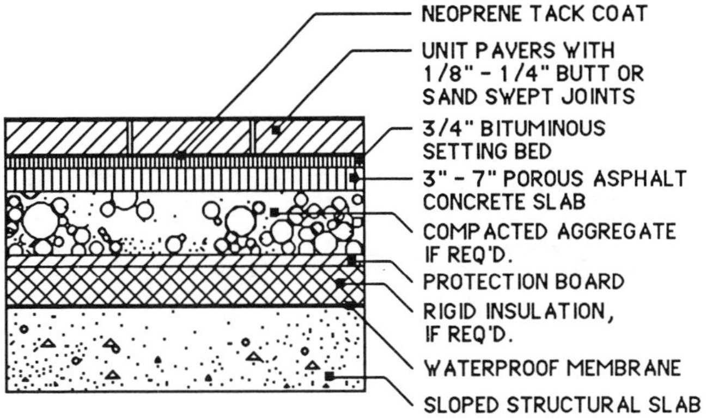
NEOPRENE TACK COAT
UNIT PAVERS WITH 1/8" - 1/4" BUTT OR SAND SWEPT JOINTS
3/4" BITUMINOUS SETTING BED
3" - 7" POROUS ASPHALT CONCRETE SLAB
COMPACTED AGGREGATE IF REQ'D.
PROTECTION BOARD
RIGID INSULATION, IF REQ'D.
WATERPROOF MEMBRANE
SLOPED STRUCTURAL SLAB

Figure 910-32 Unit pavers on bituminous setting bed.

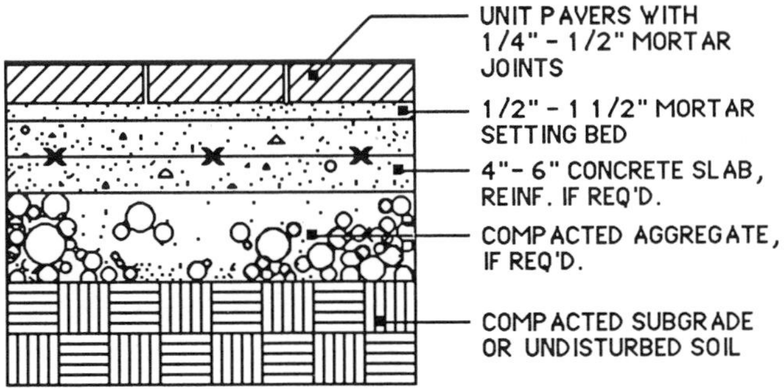
UNIT PAVERS WITH 1/4" - 1/2" MORTAR JOINTS
1/2" - 1 1/2" MORTAR SETTING BED
4"- 6" CONCRETE SLAB, REINF. IF REQ'D.
COMPACTED AGGREGATE, IF REQ'D.
COMPACTED SUBGRADE OR UNDISTURBED SOIL

Figure 910-33 Unit pavers on bituminous setting bed (on concrete slab).

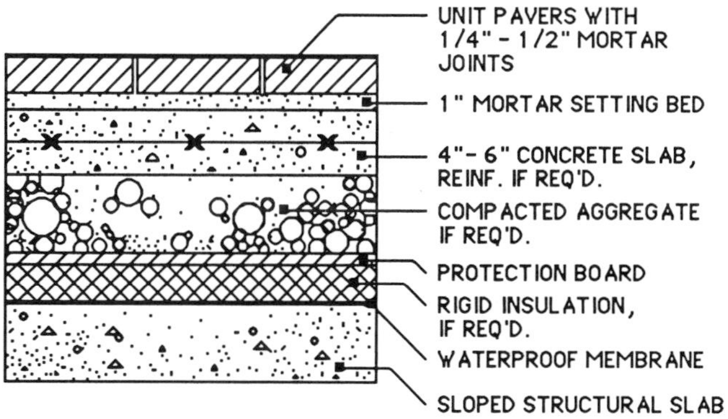
UNIT PAVERS WITH 1/4" - 1/2" MORTAR JOINTS
1" MORTAR SETTING BED
4"- 6" CONCRETE SLAB, REINF. IF REQ'D.
COMPACTED AGGREGATE IF REQ'D.
PROTECTION BOARD
RIGID INSULATION, IF REQ'D.
WATERPROOF MEMBRANE
SLOPED STRUCTURAL SLAB

Figure 910-34 Unit pavers on bituminous setting bed (on structure).

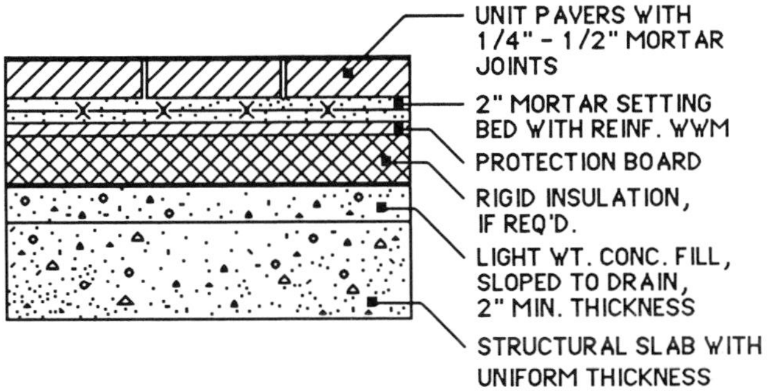
UNIT PAVERS WITH 1/4" - 1/2" MORTAR JOINTS
2" MORTAR SETTING BED WITH REINF. WWM
PROTECTION BOARD
RIGID INSULATION, IF REQ'D.
LIGHT WT. CONC. FILL, SLOPED TO DRAIN, 2" MIN. THICKNESS
STRUCTURAL SLAB WITH UNIFORM THICKNESS

Figure 910-35 Unit pavers on bituminous setting bed (on structure).

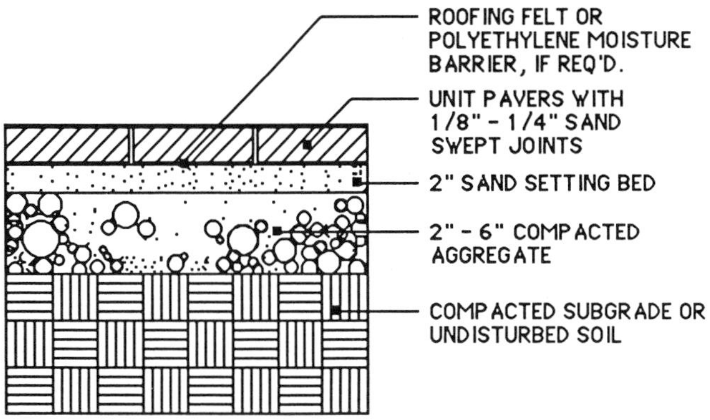
ROOFING FELT OR POLYETHYLENE MOISTURE BARRIER, IF REQ'D.
UNIT PAVERS WITH 1/8" - 1/4" SAND SWEPT JOINTS
2" SAND SETTING BED
2" - 6" COMPACTED AGGREGATE
COMPACTED SUBGRADE OR UNDISTURBED SOIL

Figure 910-36 Unit pavers on mortar setting bed.

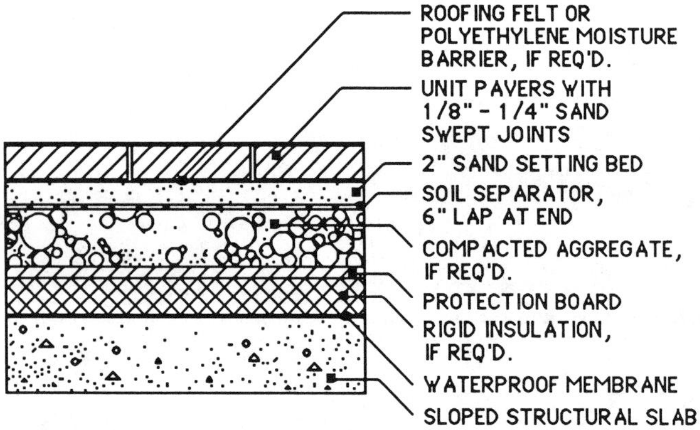
ROOFING FELT OR POLYETHYLENE MOISTURE BARRIER, IF REQ'D.
UNIT PAVERS WITH 1/8" - 1/4" SAND SWEPT JOINTS
2" SAND SETTING BED
SOIL SEPARATOR, 6" LAP AT END
COMPACTED AGGREGATE, IF REQ'D.
PROTECTION BOARD
RIGID INSULATION, IF REQ'D.
WATERPROOF MEMBRANE
SLOPED STRUCTURAL SLAB

Figure 910-37 Unit pavers on mortar setting bed (on sloped structural slab).

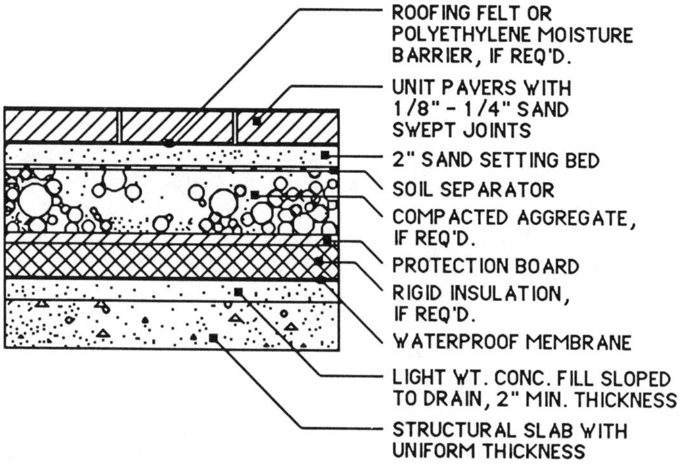
ROOFING FELT OR POLYETHYLENE MOISTURE BARRIER, IF REQ'D.
UNIT PAVERS WITH 1/8" - 1/4" SAND SWEPT JOINTS
2" SAND SETTING BED
SOIL SEPARATOR
COMPACTED AGGREGATE, IF REQ'D.
PROTECTION BOARD
RIGID INSULATION, IF REQ'D.
WATERPROOF MEMBRANE
LIGHT WT. CONC. FILL SLOPED TO DRAIN, 2" MIN. THICKNESS
STRUCTURAL SLAB WITH UNIFORM THICKNESS

Figure 910-38 Unit pavers on mortar setting bed (on structural slab with sloped concrete fill).

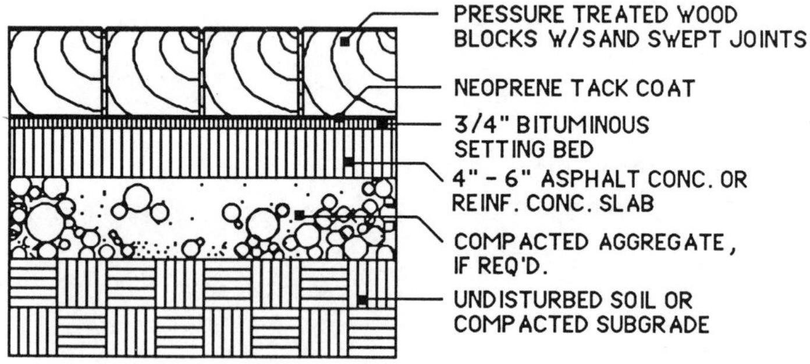
PRESSURE TREATED WOOD BLOCKS W/SAND SWEPT JOINTS
NEOPRENE TACK COAT
3/4" BITUMINOUS SETTING BED
4" - 6" ASPHALT CONC. OR REINF. CONC. SLAB
COMPACTED AGGREGATE, IF REQ'D.
UNDISTURBED SOIL OR COMPACTED SUBGRADE

Figure 910-39 Wood blocks on sand setting bed.

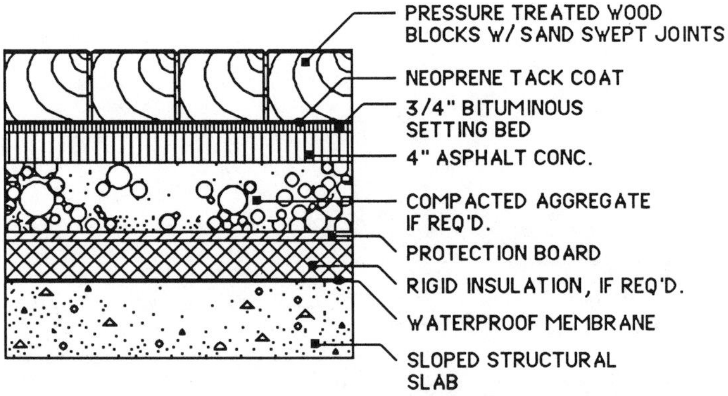
PRESSURE TREATED WOOD BLOCKS W/ SAND SWEPT JOINTS
NEOPRENE TACK COAT
3/4" BITUMINOUS SETTING BED
4" ASPHALT CONC.
COMPACTED AGGREGATE IF REQ'D.
PROTECTION BOARD
RIGID INSULATION, IF REQ'D.
WATERPROOF MEMBRANE
SLOPED STRUCTURAL SLAB

Figure 910-40 Wood blocks on sand setting bed (on structure).

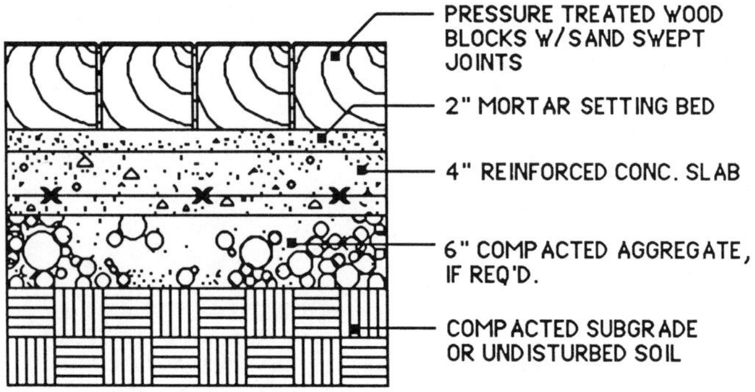
PRESSURE TREATED WOOD BLOCKS W/SAND SWEPT JOINTS
2" MORTAR SETTING BED
4" REINFORCED CONC. SLAB
6" COMPACTED AGGREGATE, IF REQ'D.
COMPACTED SUBGRADE OR UNDISTURBED SOIL

Figure 910-41 Wood blocks on bituminous setting bed (on structure).

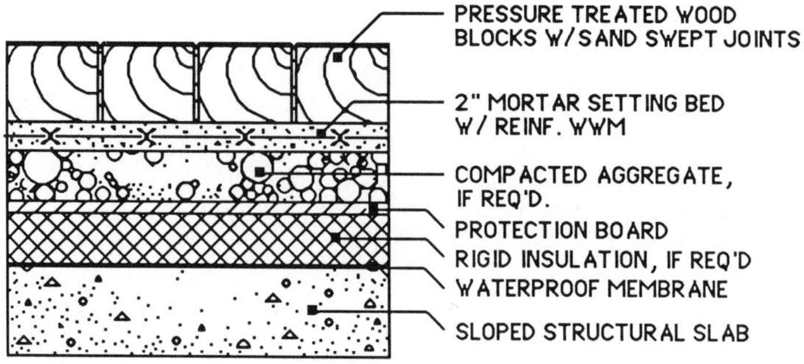
PRESSURE TREATED WOOD BLOCKS W/SAND SWEPT JOINTS
2" MORTAR SETTING BED W/ REINF. WWM
COMPACTED AGGREGATE, IF REQ'D.
PROTECTION BOARD
RIGID INSULATION, IF REQ'D
WATERPROOF MEMBRANE
SLOPED STRUCTURAL SLAB

Figure 910-42 Wood blocks on bituminous setting bed (on structure).

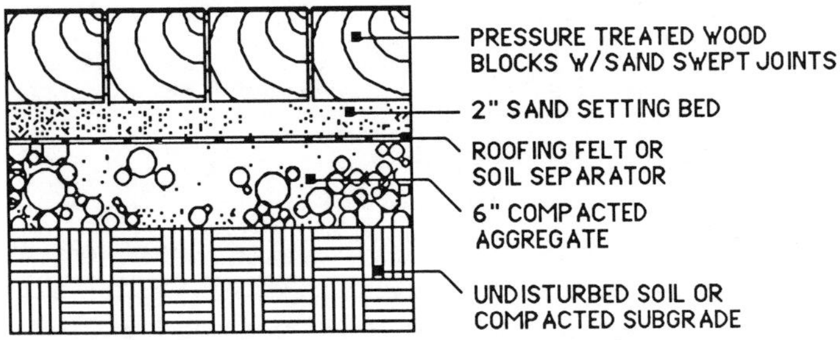
PRESSURE TREATED WOOD BLOCKS W/SAND SWEPT JOINTS
2" SAND SETTING BED
ROOFING FELT OR SOIL SEPARATOR
6" COMPACTED AGGREGATE
UNDISTURBED SOIL OR COMPACTED SUBGRADE

Figure 910-43 Wood blocks on mortar setting bed.

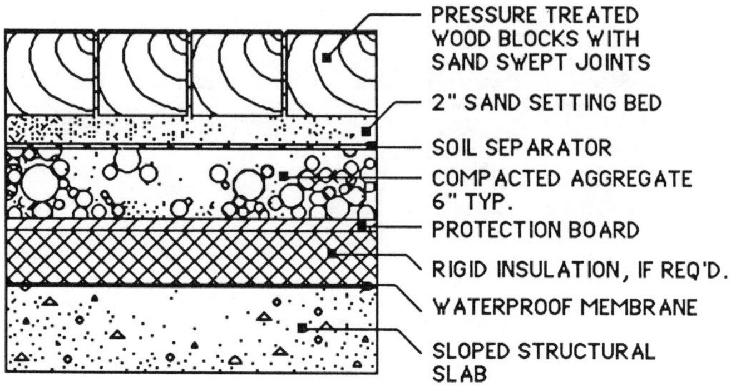
PRESSURE TREATED WOOD BLOCKS WITH SAND SWEPT JOINTS
2" SAND SETTING BED
SOIL SEPARATOR
COMPACTED AGGREGATE 6" TYP.
PROTECTION BOARD
RIGID INSULATION, IF REQ'D.
WATERPROOF MEMBRANE
SLOPED STRUCTURAL SLAB

Figure 910-44 Wood blocks on mortar setting bed (on structure).

section 911: Paving Joints

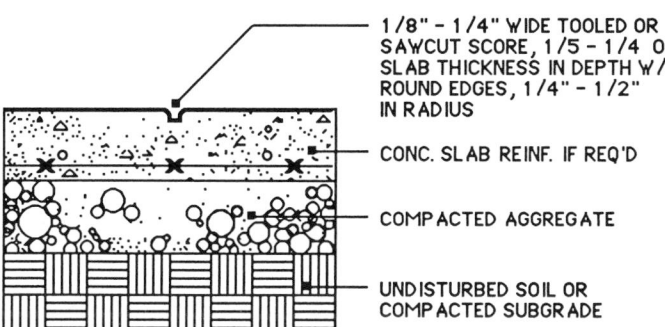

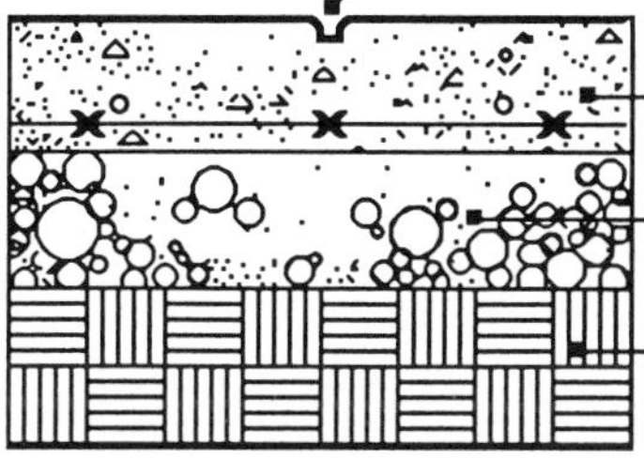
1/8" - 1/4" WIDE TOOLED OR SAWCUT SCORE, 1/5 - 1/4 OF SLAB THICKNESS IN DEPTH W/ ROUND EDGES, 1/4" - 1/2" IN RADIUS
CONC. SLAB REINF. IF REQ'D
COMPACTED AGGREGATE
UNDISTURBED SOIL OR COMPACTED SUBGRADE

Figure 911-1 Paving control joint (on grade).

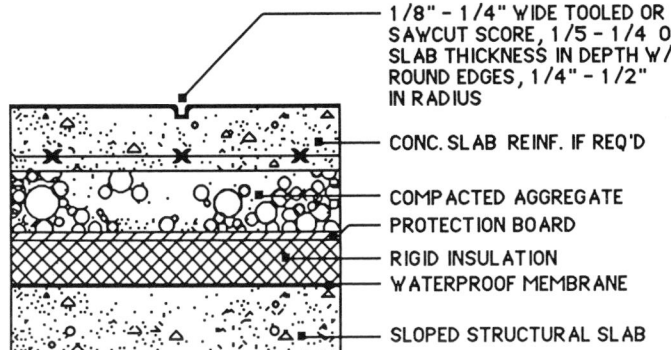

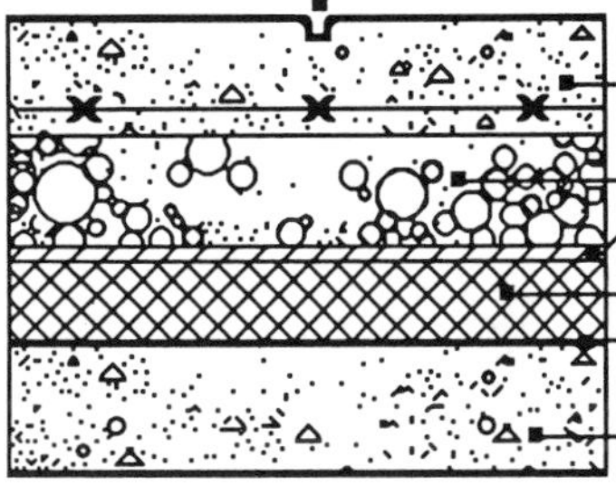
1/8" - 1/4" WIDE TOOLED OR SAWCUT SCORE, 1/5 - 1/4 OF SLAB THICKNESS IN DEPTH W/ ROUND EDGES, 1/4" - 1/2" IN RADIUS
CONC. SLAB REINF. IF REQ'D
COMPACTED AGGREGATE
PROTECTION BOARD
RIGID INSULATION
WATERPROOF MEMBRANE
SLOPED STRUCTURAL SLAB

Figure 911-2 Paving control joint (on structure).

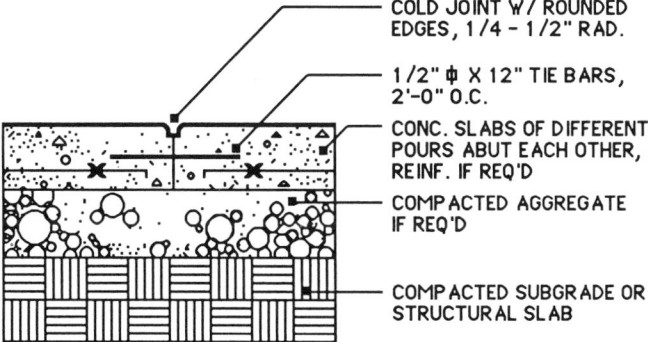

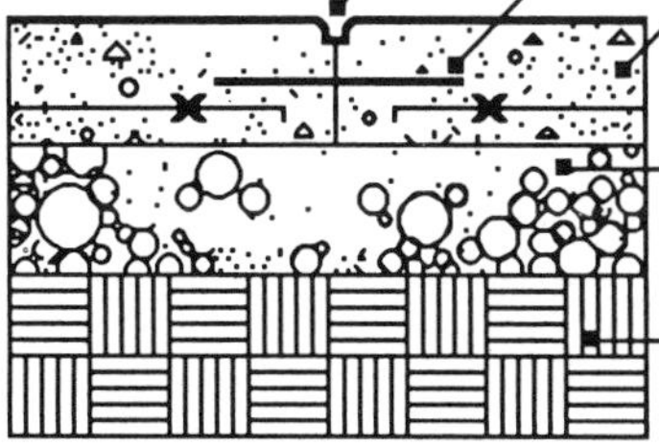
COLD JOINT W/ ROUNDED EDGES, 1/4 - 1/2" RAD.
1/2" ɸ X 12" TIE BARS, 2'-0" O.C.
CONC. SLABS OF DIFFERENT POURS ABUT EACH OTHER, REINF. IF REQ'D
COMPACTED AGGREGATE IF REQ'D
COMPACTED SUBGRADE OR STRUCTURAL SLAB

Figure 911-3 Cold joint or butt joint (on grade, monolithic).

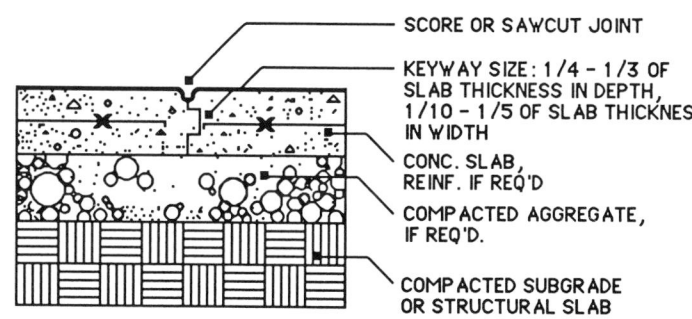

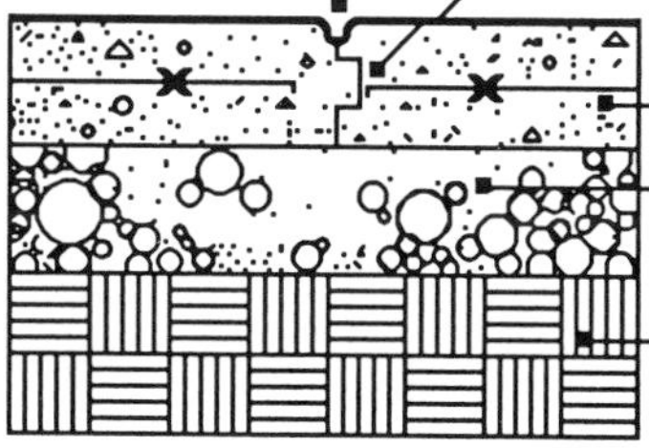
SCORE OR SAWCUT JOINT
KEYWAY SIZE: 1/4 - 1/3 OF SLAB THICKNESS IN DEPTH, 1/10 - 1/5 OF SLAB THICKNESS IN WIDTH
CONC. SLAB, REINF. IF REQ'D
COMPACTED AGGREGATE, IF REQ'D.
COMPACTED SUBGRADE OR STRUCTURAL SLAB

Figure 911-4 Keyed control joint (on grade or structure, monolithic).

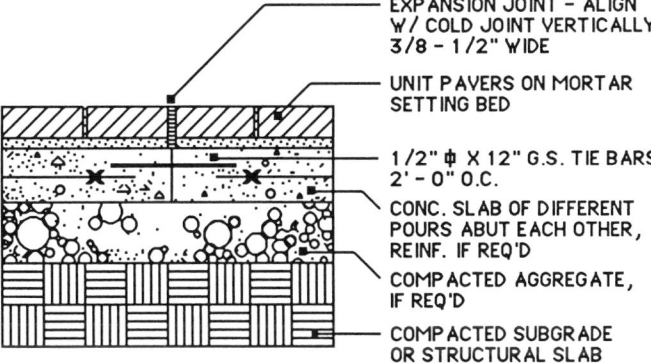

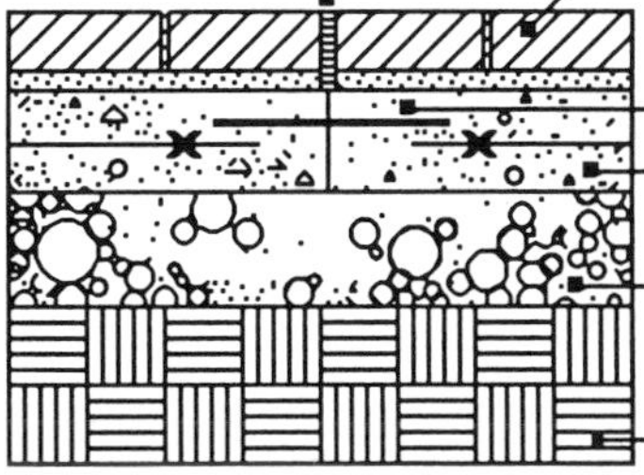
EXPANSION JOINT - ALIGN W/ COLD JOINT VERTICALLY, 3/8 - 1/2" WIDE
UNIT PAVERS ON MORTAR SETTING BED
1/2" ɸ X 12" G.S. TIE BARS, 2' - 0" O.C.
CONC. SLAB OF DIFFERENT POURS ABUT EACH OTHER, REINF. IF REQ'D
COMPACTED AGGREGATE, IF REQ'D
COMPACTED SUBGRADE OR STRUCTURAL SLAB

Figure 911-5 Cold control joint in sandwiched paving (on grade or structure).

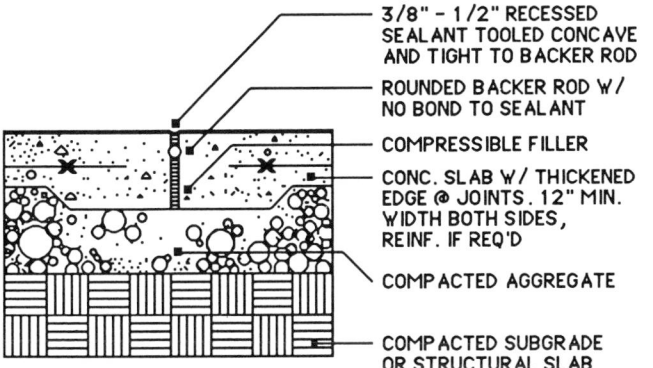

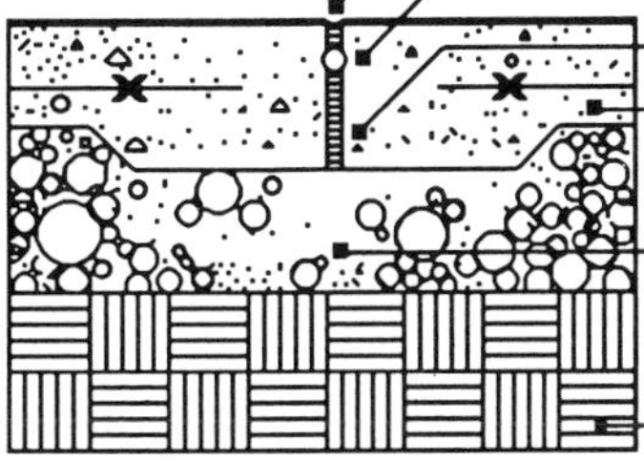
3/8" - 1/2" RECESSED SEALANT TOOLED CONCAVE AND TIGHT TO BACKER ROD
ROUNDED BACKER ROD W/ NO BOND TO SEALANT
COMPRESSIBLE FILLER
CONC. SLAB W/ THICKENED EDGE @ JOINTS. 12" MIN. WIDTH BOTH SIDES, REINF. IF REQ'D
COMPACTED AGGREGATE
COMPACTED SUBGRADE OR STRUCTURAL SLAB

Figure 911-6 Expansion joint with thickened edge (on grade or structure). Use of this joint is limited to pavements on structure or those limited to light traffic loads. Spacing of expansion joints depends on the local climate, the material used, and the desired visual effect.

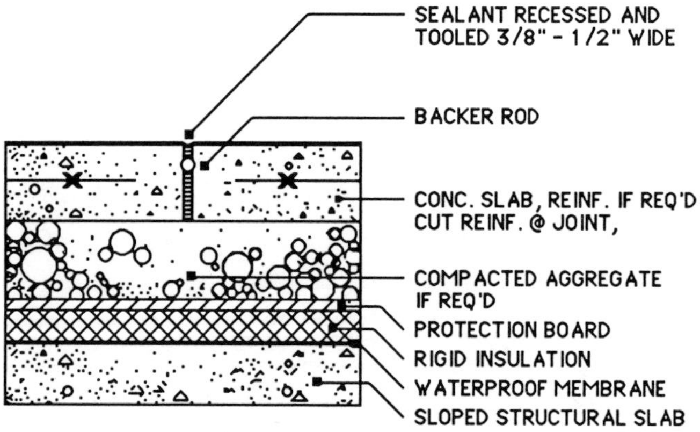
SEALANT RECESSED AND TOOLED 3/8" - 1/2" WIDE
BACKER ROD
CONC. SLAB, REINF. IF REQ'D CUT REINF. @ JOINT,
COMPACTED AGGREGATE IF REQ'D
PROTECTION BOARD
RIGID INSULATION
WATERPROOF MEMBRANE
SLOPED STRUCTURAL SLAB

Figure 911-7 Cold expansion joint (on structure, monolithic).

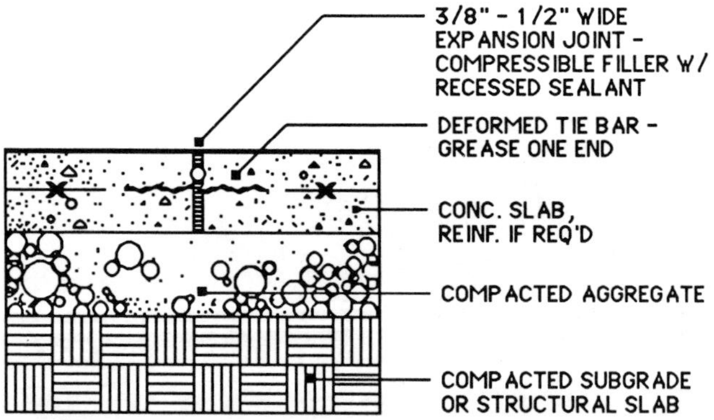
3/8" - 1/2" WIDE EXPANSION JOINT - COMPRESSIBLE FILLER W/ RECESSED SEALANT
DEFORMED TIE BAR - GREASE ONE END
CONC. SLAB, REINF. IF REQ'D
COMPACTED AGGREGATE
COMPACTED SUBGRADE OR STRUCTURAL SLAB

Figure 911-8 Expansion joint in monolithic paving with deformed tie bar (on grade or structure). The size and spacing of tie bars depends on expected traffic loads but are typically ½″ diameter by 30″ at 2′-0″ o.c. Spacing of joints depends on the local climate, the material used, and desired visual effect.

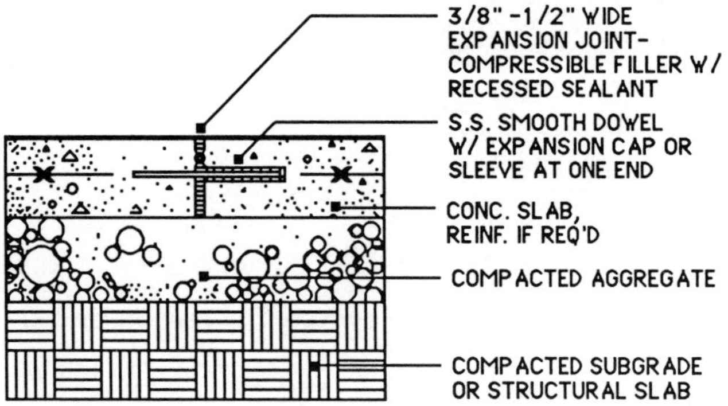
3/8" -1/2" WIDE EXPANSION JOINT- COMPRESSIBLE FILLER W/ RECESSED SEALANT
S.S. SMOOTH DOWEL W/ EXPANSION CAP OR SLEEVE AT ONE END
CONC. SLAB, REINF. IF REQ'D
COMPACTED AGGREGATE
COMPACTED SUBGRADE OR STRUCTURAL SLAB

Figure 911-9 Expansion joint in monolithic paving with smooth schedules (tie bar and dowel schedules). The size and spacing of the dowels depend on traffic loading but are typically ½″ diameter by 30″ at 2′-0″ o.c. Spacing of the joints depends on the local climate, materials used, and desired visual effect.

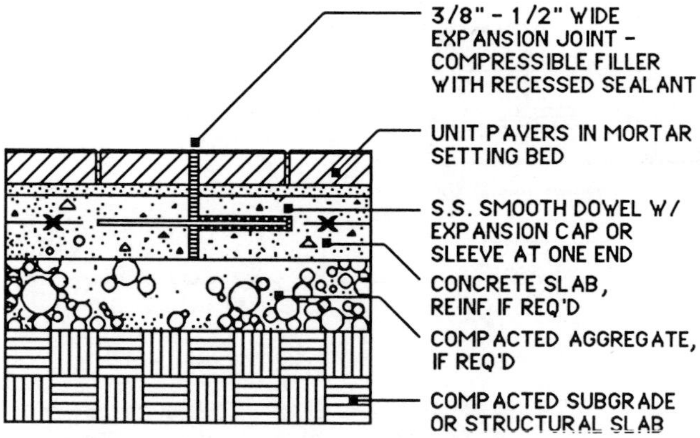
3/8" - 1/2" WIDE EXPANSION JOINT - COMPRESSIBLE FILLER WITH RECESSED SEALANT
UNIT PAVERS IN MORTAR SETTING BED
S.S. SMOOTH DOWEL W/ EXPANSION CAP OR SLEEVE AT ONE END
CONCRETE SLAB, REINF. IF REQ'D
COMPACTED AGGREGATE, IF REQ'D
COMPACTED SUBGRADE OR STRUCTURAL SLAB

Figure 911-10 Expansion joint in sandwiched paving (on grade or structure). The expansion joint can be omitted if the unit pavers are set on a bituminous setting bed with butt joints. Size and spacing of dowels depends on traffic loading but typically is ½″ by 30″ at 2′-0″ o.c. Spacing of expansion joints depends on the local climate, materials used, and desired visual effect.

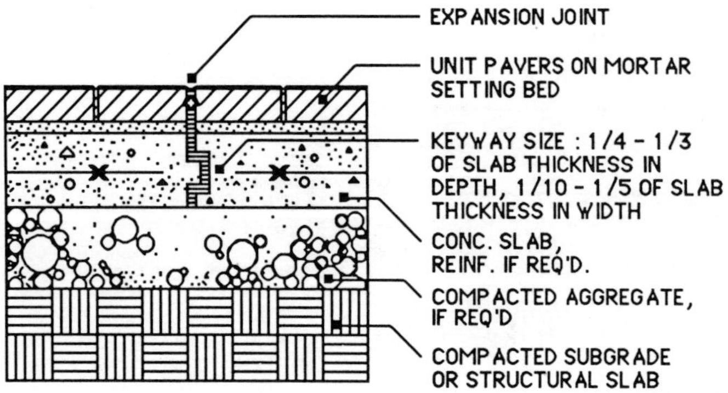
EXPANSION JOINT
UNIT PAVERS ON MORTAR SETTING BED
KEYWAY SIZE : 1/4 - 1/3 OF SLAB THICKNESS IN DEPTH, 1/10 - 1/5 OF SLAB THICKNESS IN WIDTH
CONC. SLAB, REINF. IF REQ'D.
COMPACTED AGGREGATE, IF REQ'D
COMPACTED SUBGRADE OR STRUCTURAL SLAB

Figure 911-11 Keyed expansion joint in sandwiched paving (on grade or structure).

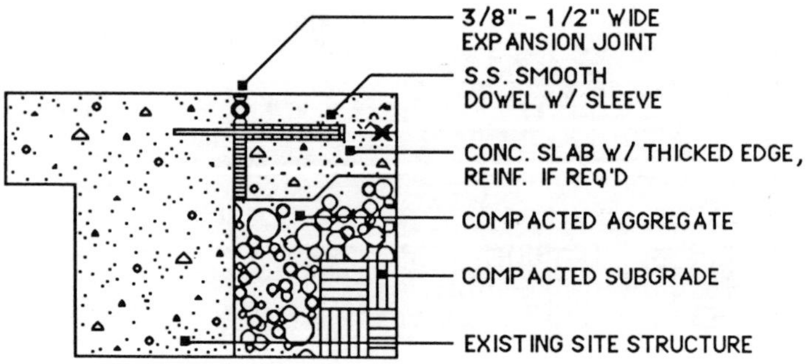
3/8" - 1/2" WIDE EXPANSION JOINT
S.S. SMOOTH DOWEL W/ SLEEVE
CONC. SLAB W/ THICKED EDGE, REINF. IF REQ'D
COMPACTED AGGREGATE
COMPACTED SUBGRADE
EXISTING SITE STRUCTURE

Figure 911-12 Expansion joint between paving and existing site structure.

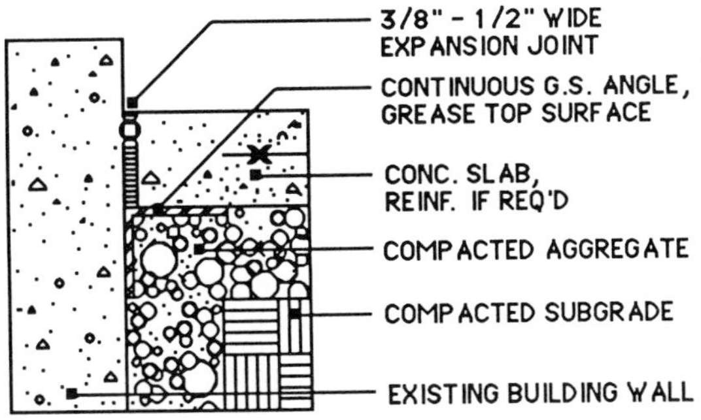
3/8" - 1/2" WIDE EXPANSION JOINT
CONTINUOUS G.S. ANGLE, GREASE TOP SURFACE
CONC. SLAB, REINF. IF REQ'D
COMPACTED AGGREGATE
COMPACTED SUBGRADE
EXISTING BUILDING WALL

Figure 911-13 Expansion joint between paving and existing building wall.

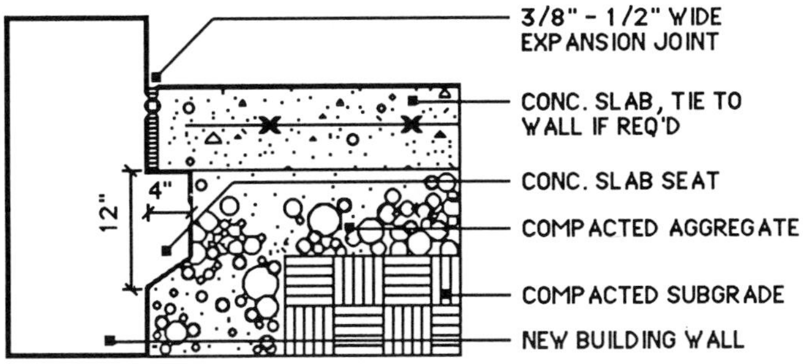
3/8" - 1/2" WIDE EXPANSION JOINT
CONC. SLAB, TIE TO WALL IF REQ'D
CONC. SLAB SEAT
COMPACTED AGGREGATE
COMPACTED SUBGRADE
NEW BUILDING WALL
12"
4"

Figure 911-14 Expansion joint between paving and new building wall.

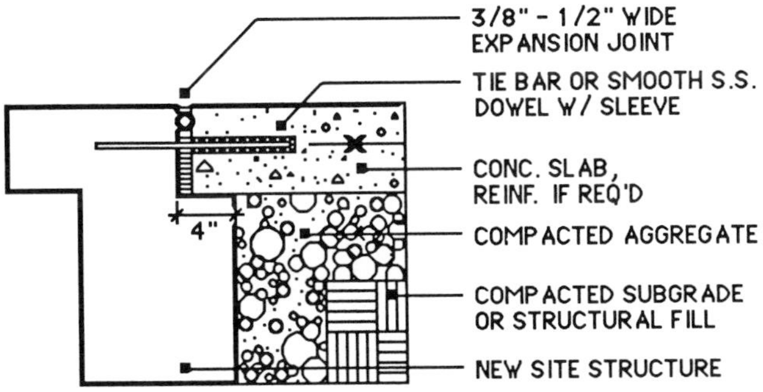
3/8" - 1/2" WIDE EXPANSION JOINT
TIE BAR OR SMOOTH S.S. DOWEL W/ SLEEVE
CONC. SLAB, REINF. IF REQ'D
COMPACTED AGGREGATE
COMPACTED SUBGRADE OR STRUCTURAL FILL
NEW SITE STRUCTURE
4"

Figure 911-15 Expansion joint between paving and new site structure.

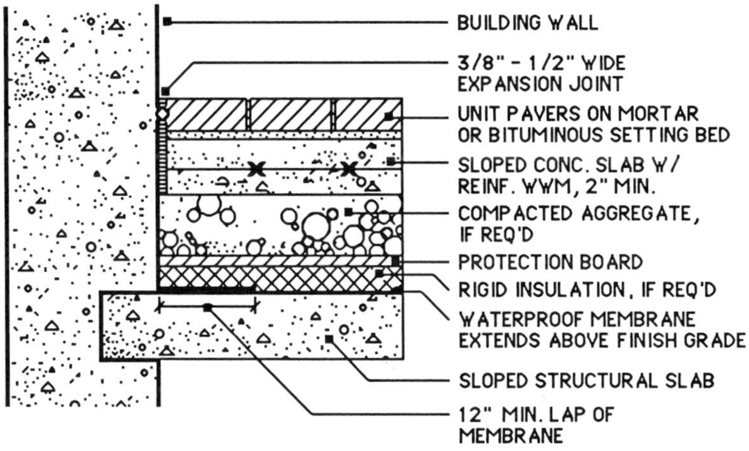
BUILDING WALL
3/8" - 1/2" WIDE EXPANSION JOINT
UNIT PAVERS ON MORTAR OR BITUMINOUS SETTING BED
SLOPED CONC. SLAB W/ REINF. WWM, 2" MIN.
COMPACTED AGGREGATE, IF REQ'D
PROTECTION BOARD
RIGID INSULATION, IF REQ'D
WATERPROOF MEMBRANE EXTENDS ABOVE FINISH GRADE
SLOPED STRUCTURAL SLAB
12" MIN. LAP OF MEMBRANE

Figure 911-16 Expansion joint between paving and building wall (on structure).

section 912: Edges

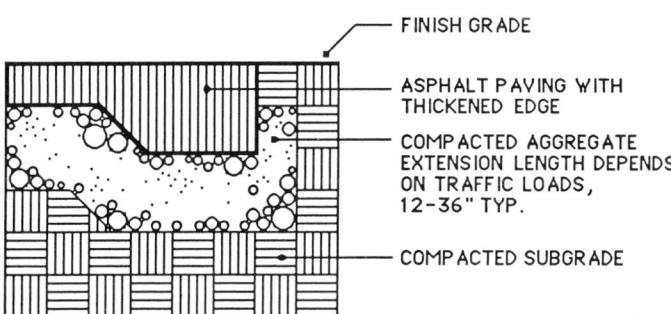

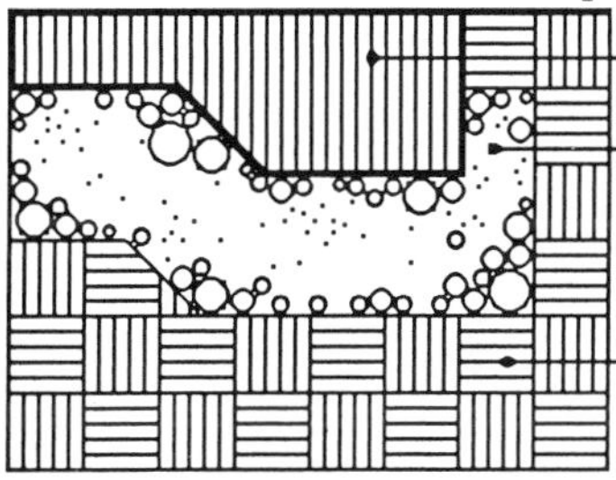

FINISH GRADE
ASPHALT PAVING WITH THICKENED EDGE
COMPACTED AGGREGATE EXTENSION LENGTH DEPENDS ON TRAFFIC LOADS, 12-36" TYP.
COMPACTED SUBGRADE

Figure 912-1 Asphalt paving with thickened edge.

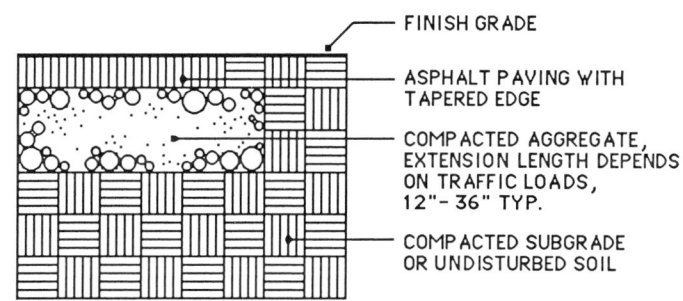

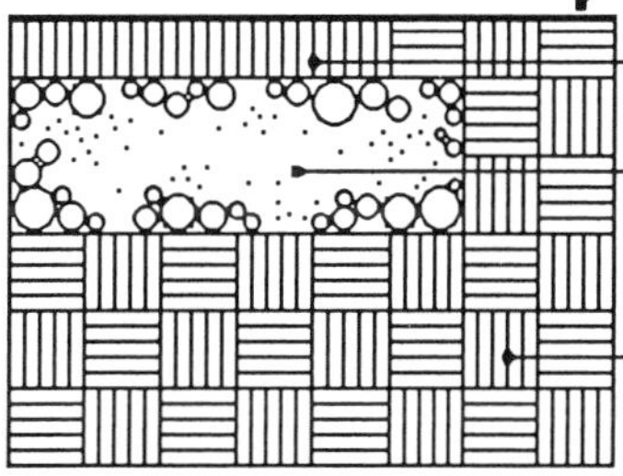

FINISH GRADE
ASPHALT PAVING WITH TAPERED EDGE
COMPACTED AGGREGATE, EXTENSION LENGTH DEPENDS ON TRAFFIC LOADS, 12"- 36" TYP.
COMPACTED SUBGRADE OR UNDISTURBED SOIL

Figure 912-2 Asphalt paving with tapered edge.

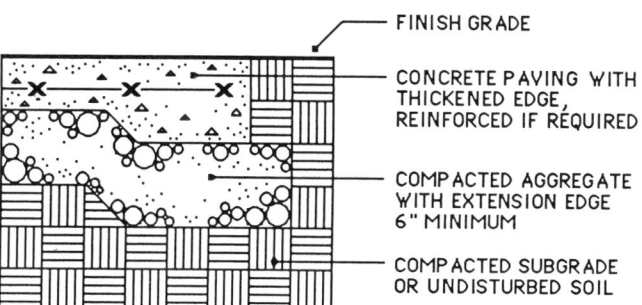

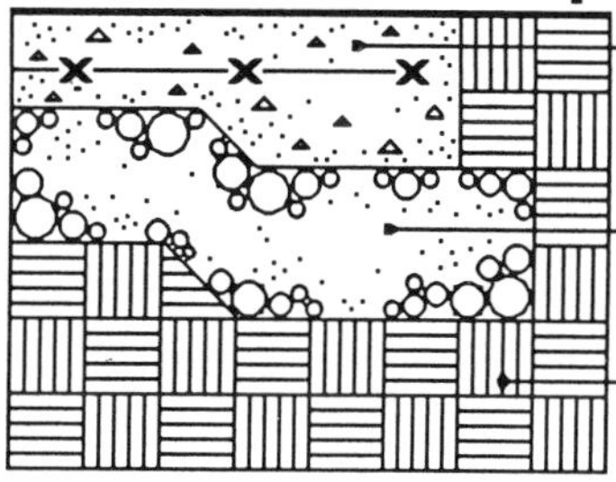

FINISH GRADE
CONCRETE PAVING WITH THICKENED EDGE, REINFORCED IF REQUIRED
COMPACTED AGGREGATE WITH EXTENSION EDGE 6" MINIMUM
COMPACTED SUBGRADE OR UNDISTURBED SOIL

Figure 912-3 Concrete paving with thickened edge.

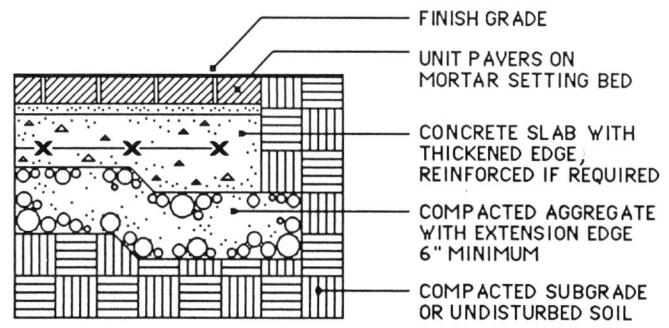

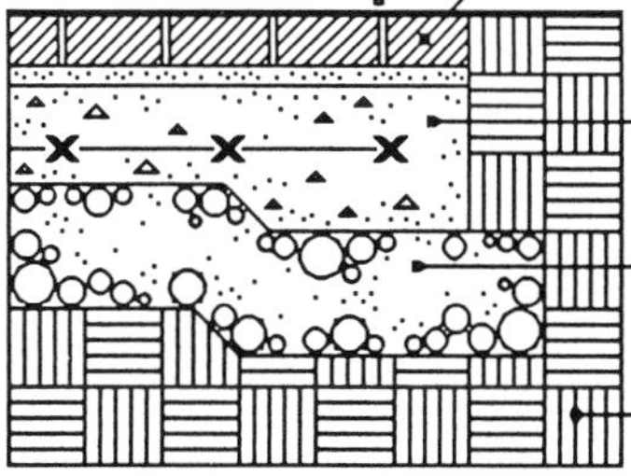

FINISH GRADE
UNIT PAVERS ON MORTAR SETTING BED
CONCRETE SLAB WITH THICKENED EDGE, REINFORCED IF REQUIRED
COMPACTED AGGREGATE WITH EXTENSION EDGE 6" MINIMUM
COMPACTED SUBGRADE OR UNDISTURBED SOIL

Figure 912-4 Unit pavers on concrete slab with thickened edge.

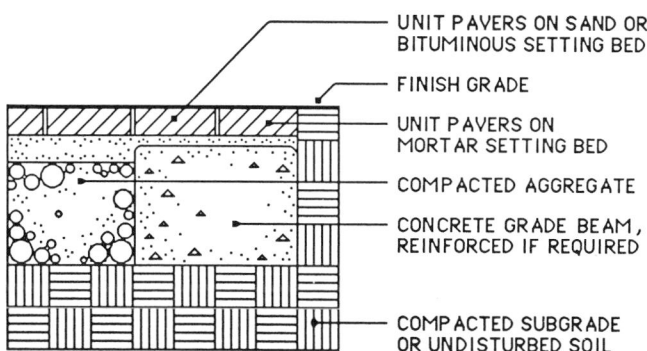

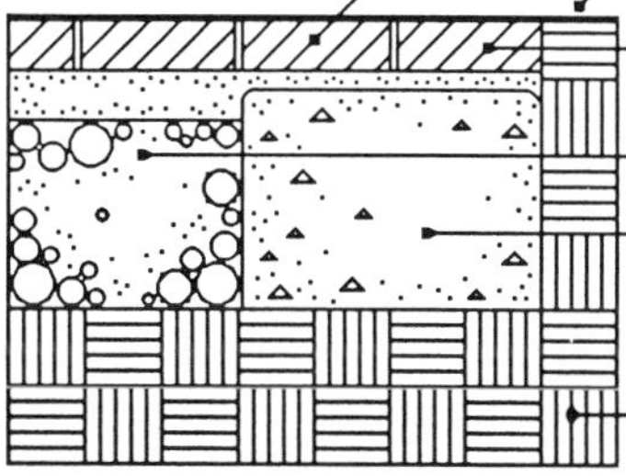

UNIT PAVERS ON SAND OR BITUMINOUS SETTING BED
FINISH GRADE
UNIT PAVERS ON MORTAR SETTING BED
COMPACTED AGGREGATE
CONCRETE GRADE BEAM, REINFORCED IF REQUIRED
COMPACTED SUBGRADE OR UNDISTURBED SOIL

Figure 912-5 Unit pavers on concrete grade beam.

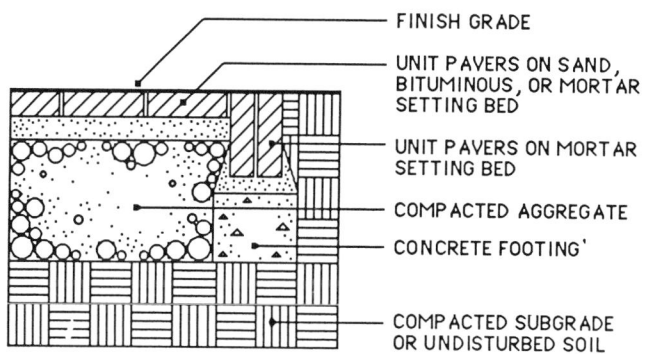

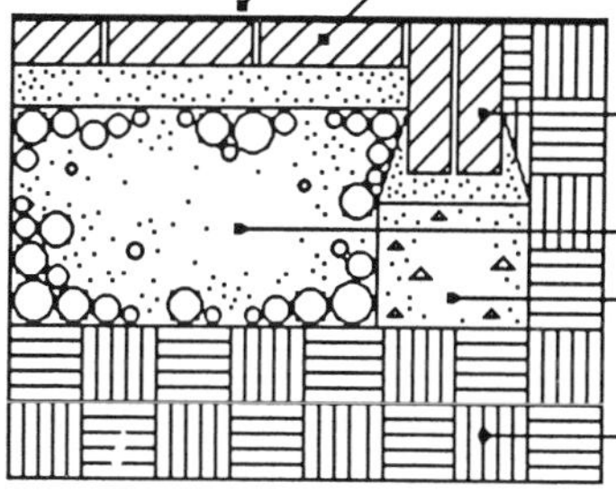

FINISH GRADE
UNIT PAVERS ON SAND, BITUMINOUS, OR MORTAR SETTING BED
UNIT PAVERS ON MORTAR SETTING BED
COMPACTED AGGREGATE
CONCRETE FOOTING'
COMPACTED SUBGRADE OR UNDISTURBED SOIL

Figure 912-6 Unit pavers on concrete footing (vertical).

section 913: Dividers

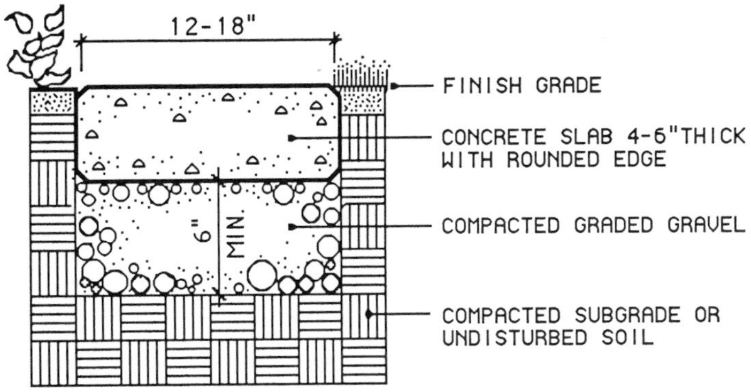

12-18"
6" MIN.
FINISH GRADE
CONCRETE SLAB 4-6"THICK WITH ROUNDED EDGE
COMPACTED GRADED GRAVEL
COMPACTED SUBGRADE OR UNDISTURBED SOIL

Figure 913-1 Concrete mowing strip. Provide expansion joints 20 ft 0 in on center, typically.

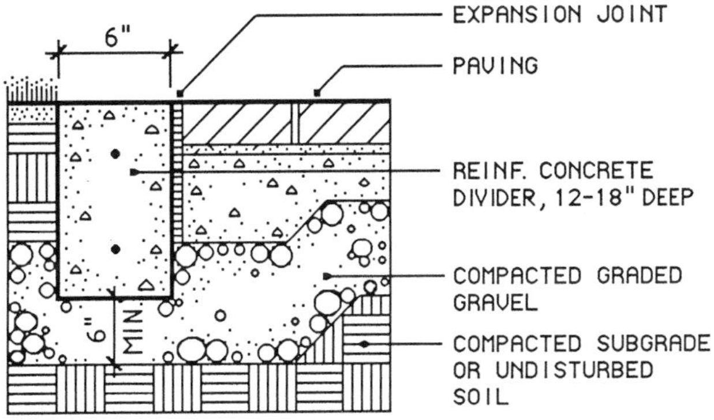

6"
6" MIN.
EXPANSION JOINT
PAVING
REINF. CONCRETE DIVIDER, 12-18" DEEP
COMPACTED GRADED GRAVEL
COMPACTED SUBGRADE OR UNDISTURBED SOIL

Figure 913-2 Concrete band. Provide expansion joints 20 ft 0 in on center, typically.

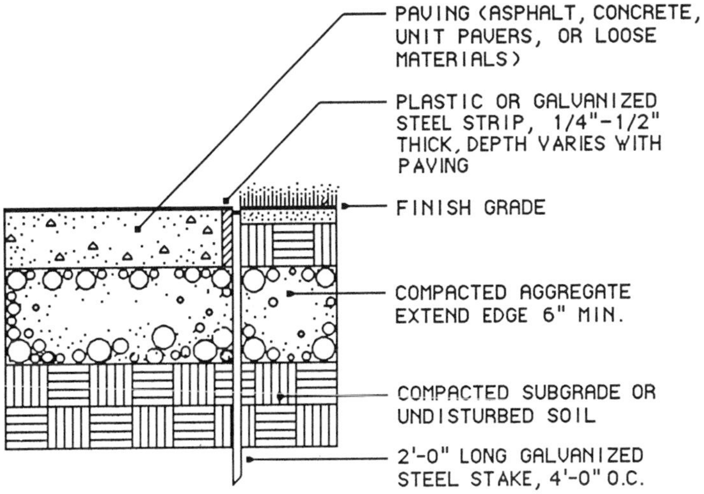

PAVING (ASPHALT, CONCRETE, UNIT PAVERS, OR LOOSE MATERIALS)
PLASTIC OR GALVANIZED STEEL STRIP, 1/4"-1/2" THICK, DEPTH VARIES WITH PAVING
FINISH GRADE
COMPACTED AGGREGATE EXTEND EDGE 6" MIN.
COMPACTED SUBGRADE OR UNDISTURBED SOIL
2'-0" LONG GALVANIZED STEEL STAKE, 4'-0" O.C.

Figure 913-3 Metal or plastic strips.

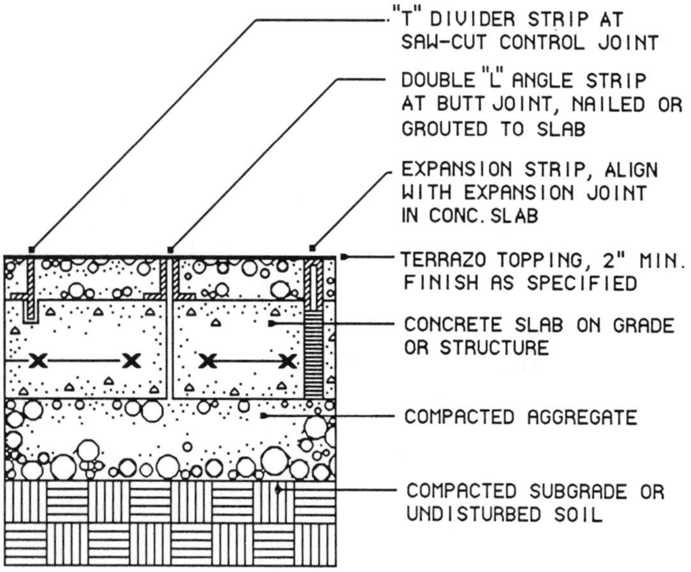
"T" DIVIDER STRIP AT SAW-CUT CONTROL JOINT
DOUBLE "L" ANGLE STRIP AT BUTT JOINT, NAILED OR GROUTED TO SLAB
EXPANSION STRIP, ALIGN WITH EXPANSION JOINT IN CONC. SLAB
TERRAZO TOPPING, 2" MIN. FINISH AS SPECIFIED
CONCRETE SLAB ON GRADE OR STRUCTURE
COMPACTED AGGREGATE
COMPACTED SUBGRADE OR UNDISTURBED SOIL

Figure 913-4 Metal or palstice strips in terrazzo paving. The metal divider strips should be 16 ft 0 in on center, maximum.

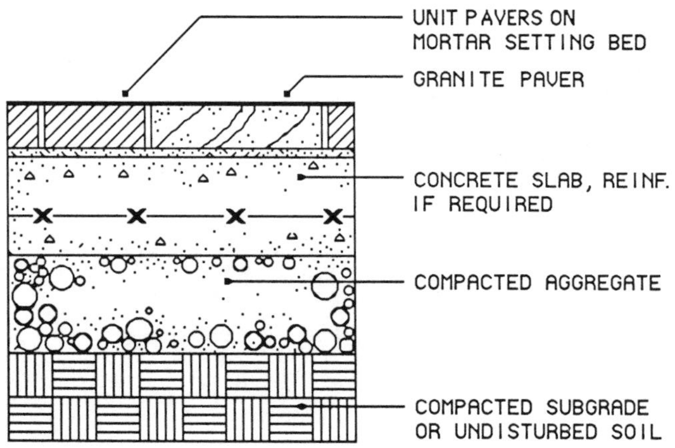
UNIT PAVERS ON MORTAR SETTING BED
GRANITE PAVER
CONCRETE SLAB, REINF. IF REQUIRED
COMPACTED AGGREGATE
COMPACTED SUBGRADE OR UNDISTURBED SOIL

Figure 913-5 Brick paving with granite band.

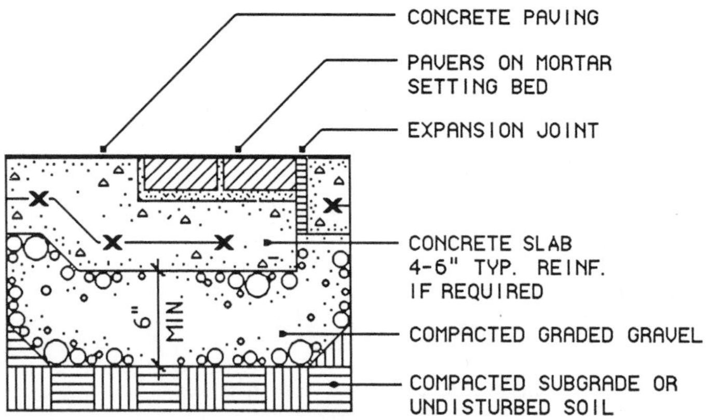
CONCRETE PAVING
PAVERS ON MORTAR SETTING BED
EXPANSION JOINT
CONCRETE SLAB 4-6" TYP. REINF. IF REQUIRED
6" MIN.
COMPACTED GRADED GRAVEL
COMPACTED SUBGRADE OR UNDISTURBED SOIL

Figure 913-6 Concrete paving with brick or precast pavers.

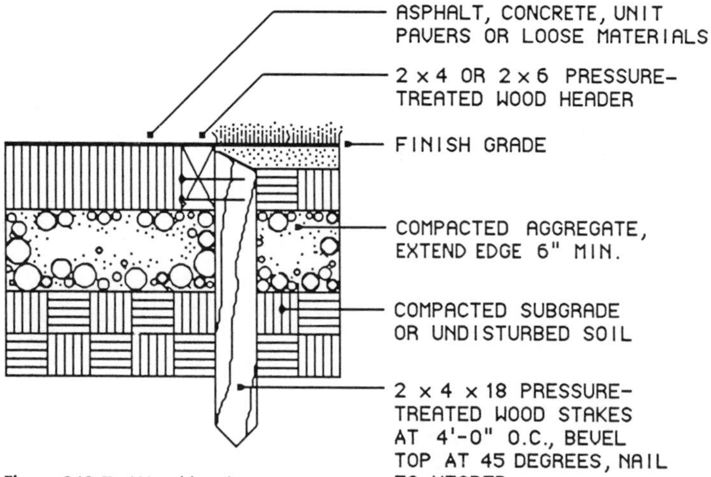
ASPHALT, CONCRETE, UNIT PAVERS OR LOOSE MATERIALS
2 x 4 OR 2 x 6 PRESSURE-TREATED WOOD HEADER
FINISH GRADE
COMPACTED AGGREGATE, EXTEND EDGE 6" MIN.
COMPACTED SUBGRADE OR UNDISTURBED SOIL
2 x 4 x 18 PRESSURE-TREATED WOOD STAKES AT 4'-0" O.C., BEVEL TOP AT 45 DEGREES, NAIL TO HEADER

Figure 913-7 Wood header.

section 914: Curbs

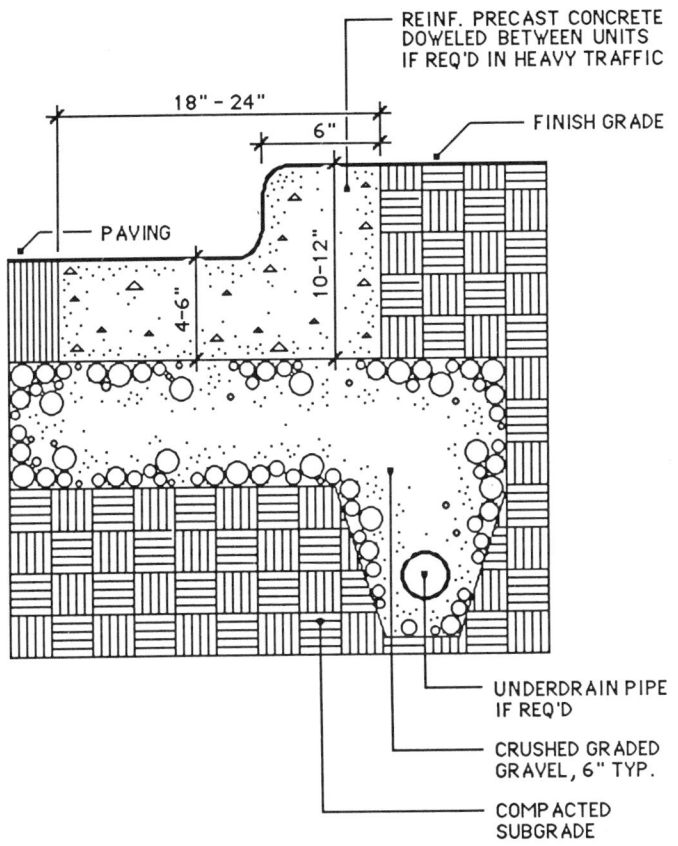

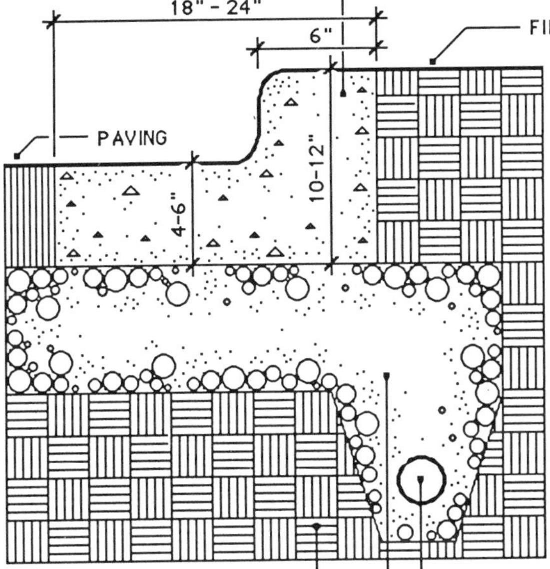

REINF. PRECAST CONCRETE DOWELED BETWEEN UNITS IF REQ'D IN HEAVY TRAFFIC
18" - 24"
6"
FINISH GRADE
PAVING
4-6"
10-12"
UNDERDRAIN PIPE IF REQ'D
CRUSHED GRADED GRAVEL, 6" TYP.
COMPACTED SUBGRADE

Figure 914-1 Combined curb and gutter. Many precast and poured concrete forms are available.

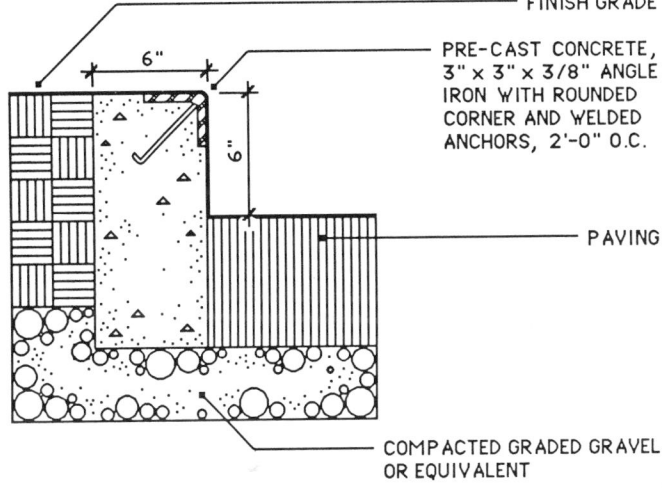

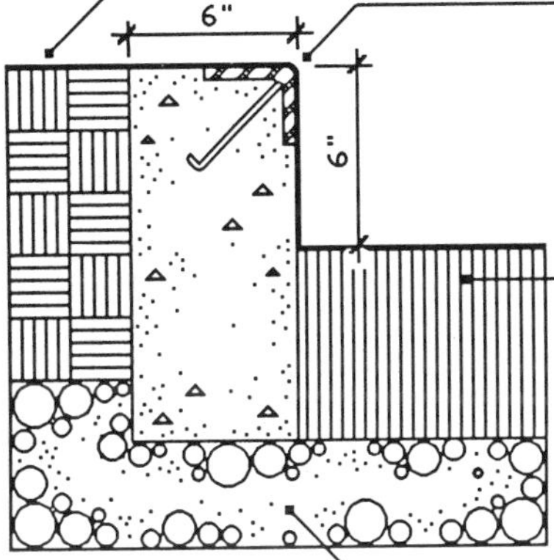

FINISH GRADE
6"
PRE-CAST CONCRETE, 3" x 3" x 3/8" ANGLE IRON WITH ROUNDED CORNER AND WELDED ANCHORS, 2'-0" O.C.
6"
PAVING
COMPACTED GRADED GRAVEL OR EQUIVALENT

Figure 914-2 Concrete curb with steel guard at edge.

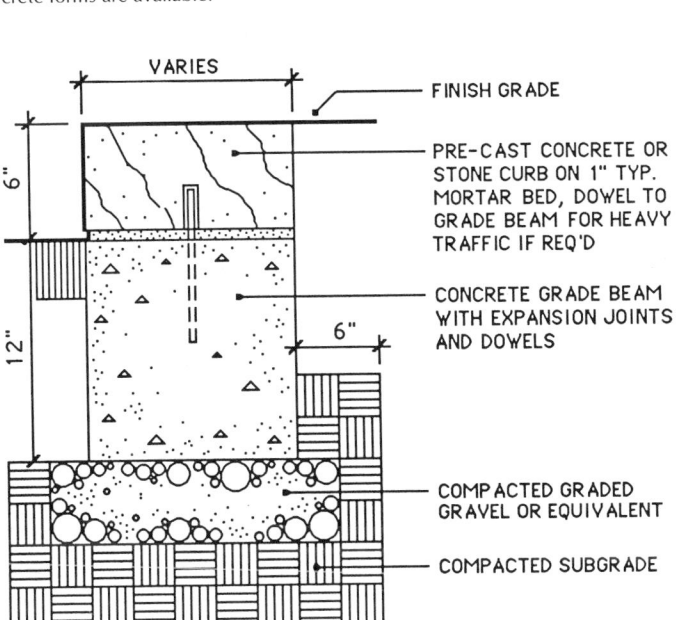

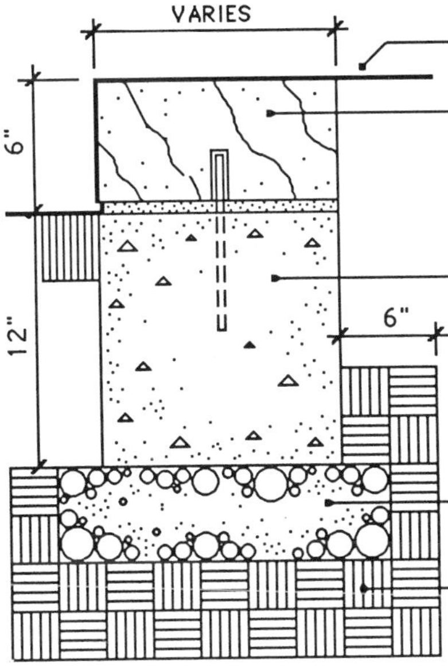

VARIES
FINISH GRADE
6"
PRE-CAST CONCRETE OR STONE CURB ON 1" TYP. MORTAR BED, DOWEL TO GRADE BEAM FOR HEAVY TRAFFIC IF REQ'D
CONCRETE GRADE BEAM WITH EXPANSION JOINTS AND DOWELS
12"
6"
COMPACTED GRADED GRAVEL OR EQUIVALENT
COMPACTED SUBGRADE

Figure 914-3 Poured concrete or stone curb.

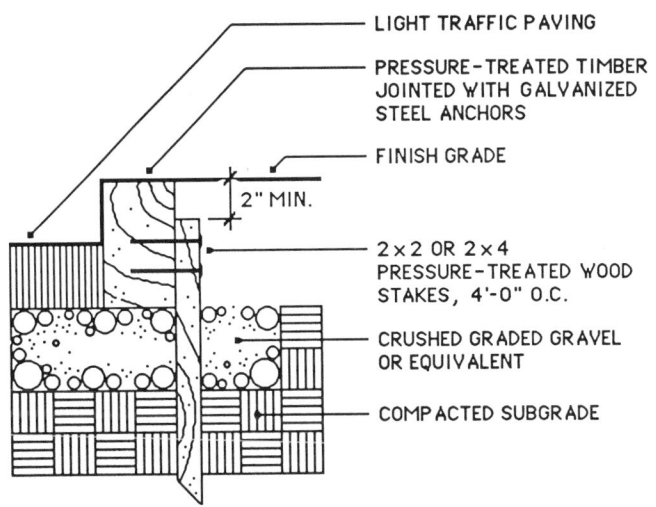

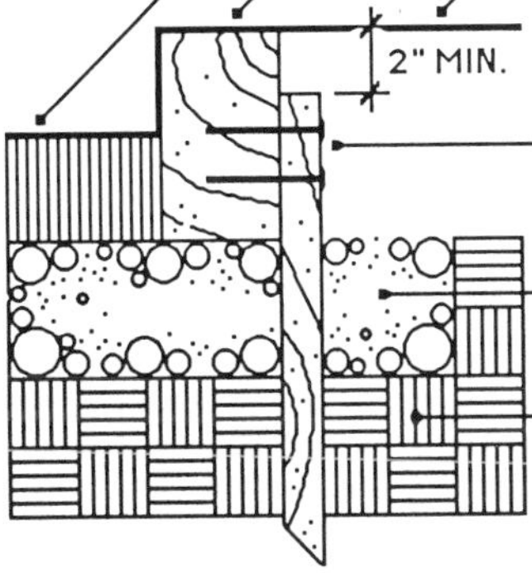

LIGHT TRAFFIC PAVING
PRESSURE-TREATED TIMBER JOINTED WITH GALVANIZED STEEL ANCHORS
FINISH GRADE
2" MIN.
2×2 OR 2×4 PRESSURE-TREATED WOOD STAKES, 4'-0" O.C.
CRUSHED GRADED GRAVEL OR EQUIVALENT
COMPACTED SUBGRADE

Figure 914-4 Wood curb. As an alternative to the wood stakes, ¾-in × 24-in galvanized steel anchor bolts or pins may be used.

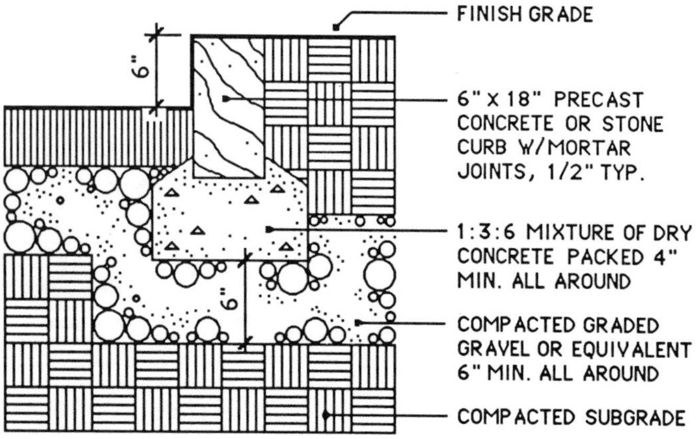
6"
FINISH GRADE
6" X 18" PRECAST CONCRETE OR STONE CURB W/MORTAR JOINTS, 1/2" TYP.
1:3:6 MIXTURE OF DRY CONCRETE PACKED 4" MIN. ALL AROUND
6"
COMPACTED GRADED GRAVEL OR EQUIVALENT 6" MIN. ALL AROUND
COMPACTED SUBGRADE

Figure 914-5 Precast concrete or stone curb (vertical).

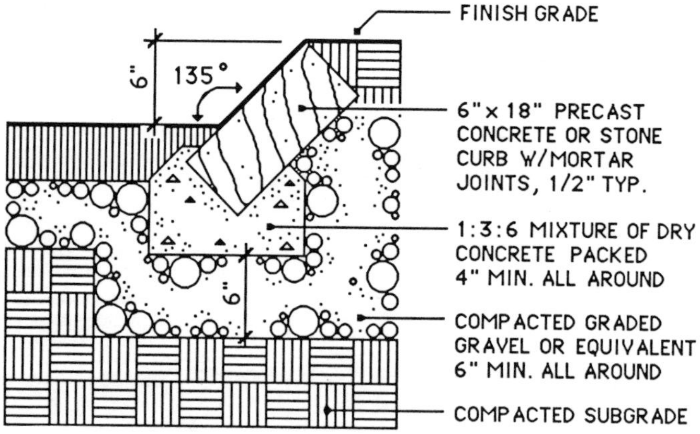
6"
135°
FINISH GRADE
6" x 18" PRECAST CONCRETE OR STONE CURB W/MORTAR JOINTS, 1/2" TYP.
1:3:6 MIXTURE OF DRY CONCRETE PACKED 4" MIN. ALL AROUND
6"
COMPACTED GRADED GRAVEL OR EQUIVALENT 6" MIN. ALL AROUND
COMPACTED SUBGRADE

Figure 914-6 Precast concrete or stone curb (sloped).

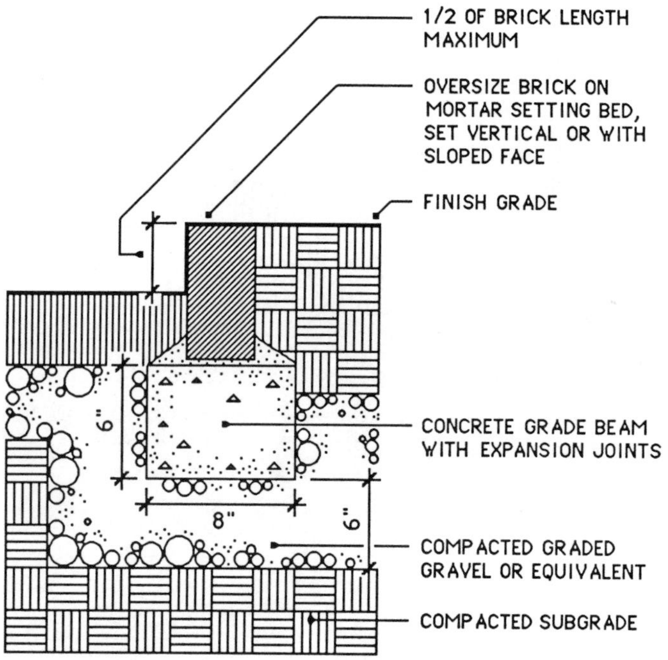
1/2 OF BRICK LENGTH MAXIMUM
OVERSIZE BRICK ON MORTAR SETTING BED, SET VERTICAL OR WITH SLOPED FACE
FINISH GRADE
6"
CONCRETE GRADE BEAM WITH EXPANSION JOINTS
8"
6"
COMPACTED GRADED GRAVEL OR EQUIVALENT
COMPACTED SUBGRADE

Figure 914-7 Brick curb (vertical). This detail is commonly used along pedestrian walkways.

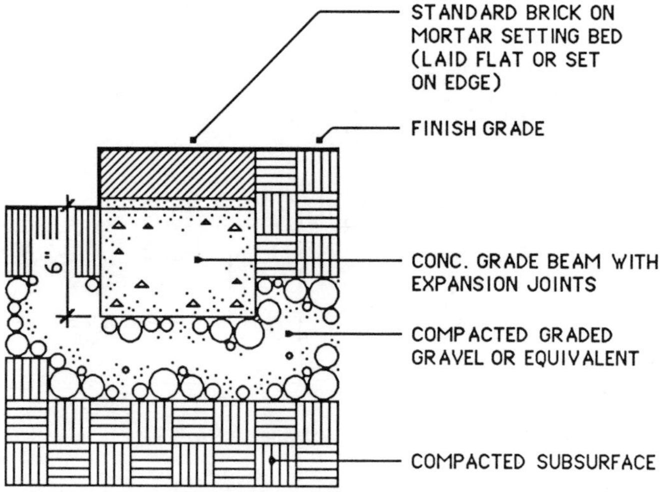
STANDARD BRICK ON MORTAR SETTING BED (LAID FLAT OR SET ON EDGE)
FINISH GRADE
6"
CONC. GRADE BEAM WITH EXPANSION JOINTS
COMPACTED GRADED GRAVEL OR EQUIVALENT
COMPACTED SUBSURFACE

Figure 914-8 Brick curb (horizontal).

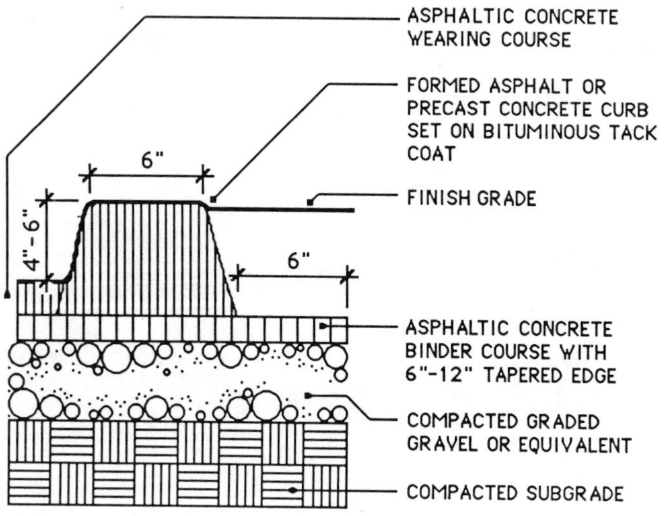
ASPHALTIC CONCRETE WEARING COURSE
FORMED ASPHALT OR PRECAST CONCRETE CURB SET ON BITUMINOUS TACK COAT
6"
FINISH GRADE
4"-6"
6"
ASPHALTIC CONCRETE BINDER COURSE WITH 6"-12" TAPERED EDGE
COMPACTED GRADED GRAVEL OR EQUIVALENT
COMPACTED SUBGRADE

Figure 914-9 Extruded curb. This detail is commonly used along light traffic drives and along parking lot edges.

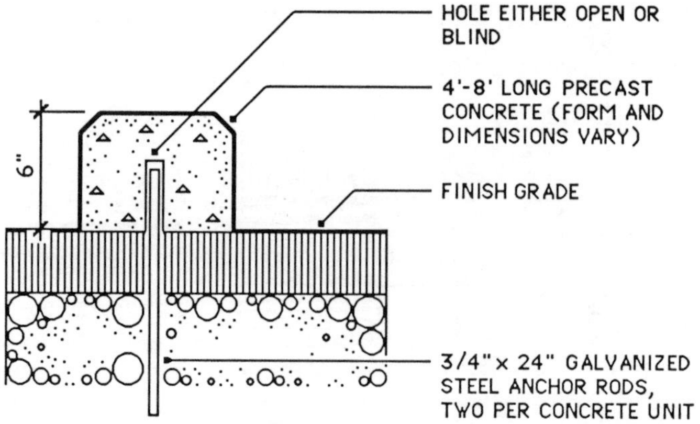
HOLE EITHER OPEN OR BLIND
4'-8' LONG PRECAST CONCRETE (FORM AND DIMENSIONS VARY)
6"
FINISH GRADE
3/4" x 24" GALVANIZED STEEL ANCHOR RODS, TWO PER CONCRETE UNIT

Figure 914-10 Concrete wheel stop. If the finish grade is a paved surface, the concrete wheel stop can be glued to it with an appropriate epoxy adhesive.

section 920: Steps

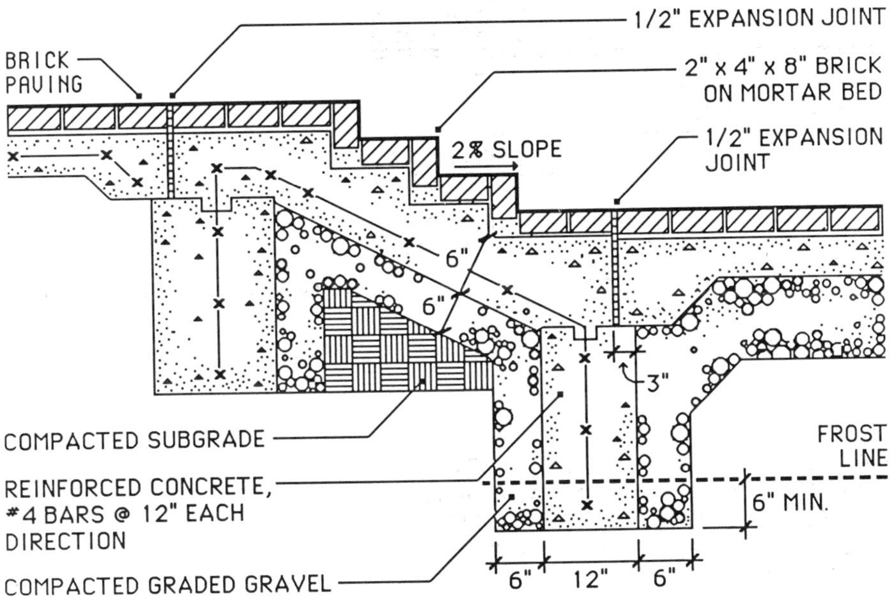

BRICK PAVING
1/2" EXPANSION JOINT
2" x 4" x 8" BRICK ON MORTAR BED
2% SLOPE
1/2" EXPANSION JOINT
6"
6"
3"
FROST LINE
6" MIN.
COMPACTED SUBGRADE
REINFORCED CONCRETE, #4 BARS @ 12" EACH DIRECTION
COMPACTED GRADED GRAVEL
6"
12"
6"

Figure 920-1 Brick veneered steps. Footing depth varies with frostline (12-in minimum, typically).

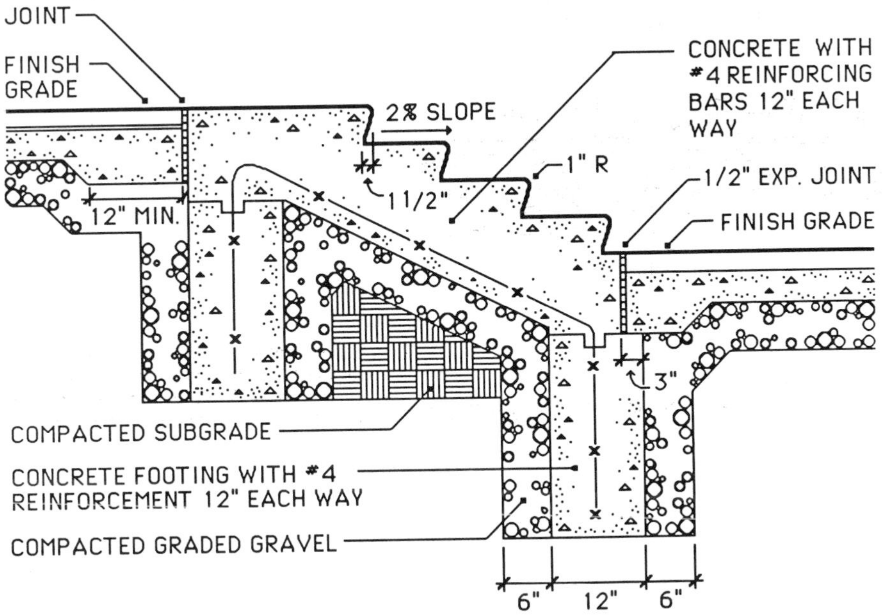

1/2" EXPANSION JOINT
FINISH GRADE
2% SLOPE
CONCRETE WITH #4 REINFORCING BARS 12" EACH WAY
1" R
1 1/2"
12" MIN.
1/2" EXP. JOINT
FINISH GRADE
3"
COMPACTED SUBGRADE
CONCRETE FOOTING WITH #4 REINFORCEMENT 12" EACH WAY
COMPACTED GRADED GRAVEL
6"
12"
6"

Figure 920-2 Concrete steps. Footing depth varies with frostline (12-in minimum, typically).

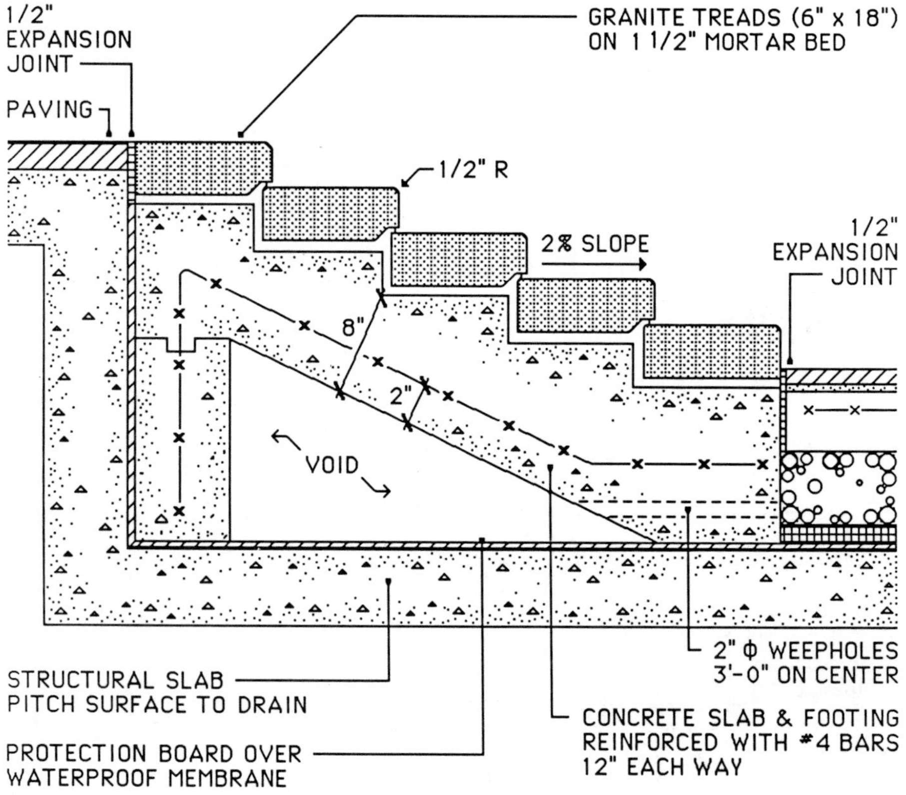
1/2" EXPANSION JOINT
PAVING
GRANITE TREADS (6" x 18") ON 1 1/2" MORTAR BED
1/2" R
2% SLOPE
1/2" EXPANSION JOINT
8"
2"
VOID
2" Φ WEEPHOLES 3'-0" ON CENTER
STRUCTURAL SLAB PITCH SURFACE TO DRAIN
CONCRETE SLAB & FOOTING REINFORCED WITH #4 BARS 12" EACH WAY
PROTECTION BOARD OVER WATERPROOF MEMBRANE

Figure 920-3 Granite steps on structure.

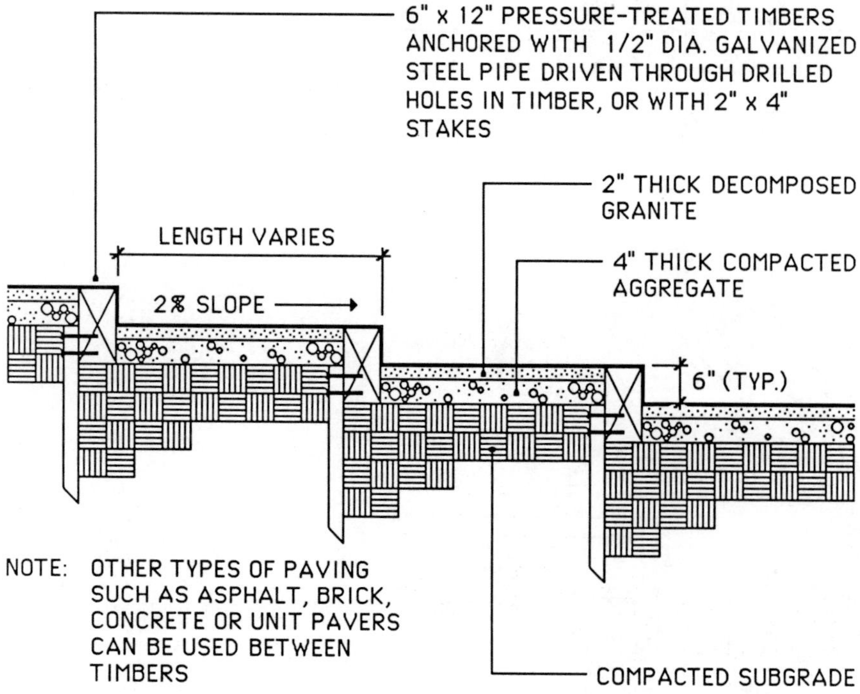
6" x 12" PRESSURE-TREATED TIMBERS ANCHORED WITH 1/2" DIA. GALVANIZED STEEL PIPE DRIVEN THROUGH DRILLED HOLES IN TIMBER, OR WITH 2" x 4" STAKES
2" THICK DECOMPOSED GRANITE
LENGTH VARIES
4" THICK COMPACTED AGGREGATE
2% SLOPE
6" (TYP.)
NOTE: OTHER TYPES OF PAVING SUCH AS ASPHALT, BRICK, CONCRETE OR UNIT PAVERS CAN BE USED BETWEEN TIMBERS
COMPACTED SUBGRADE

Figure 920-4 Wood/decomposed granite steps. Note that other types of paving such as asphalt, brick, concrete, or unit pavers can be used between timbers.

section 931: Seatwalls

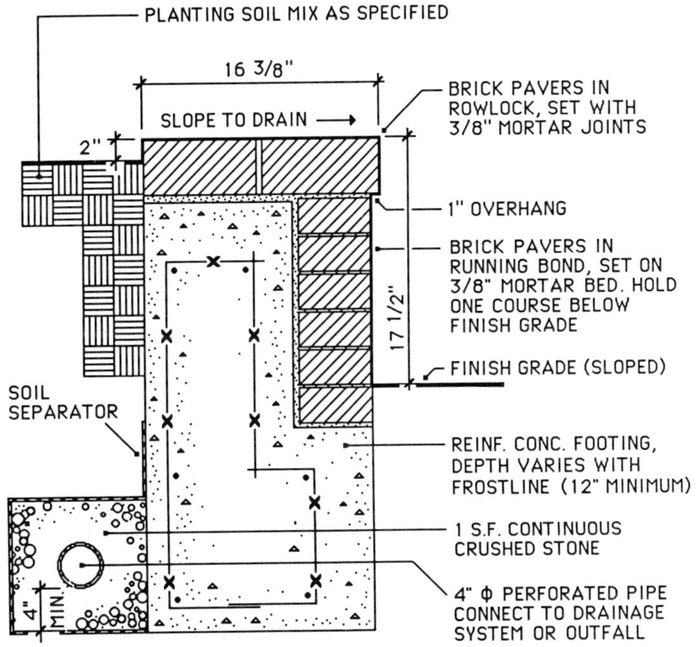

PLANTING SOIL MIX AS SPECIFIED
16 3/8"
SLOPE TO DRAIN
2"
BRICK PAVERS IN ROWLOCK, SET WITH 3/8" MORTAR JOINTS
1" OVERHANG
BRICK PAVERS IN RUNNING BOND, SET ON 3/8" MORTAR BED. HOLD ONE COURSE BELOW FINISH GRADE
17 1/2"
FINISH GRADE (SLOPED)
SOIL SEPARATOR
REINF. CONC. FOOTING, DEPTH VARIES WITH FROSTLINE (12" MINIMUM)
1 S.F. CONTINUOUS CRUSHED STONE
4" Φ PERFORATED PIPE CONNECT TO DRAINAGE SYSTEM OR OUTFALL
4" MIN.

Figure 931-1 Brick-veneered seatwall with drain tiles.

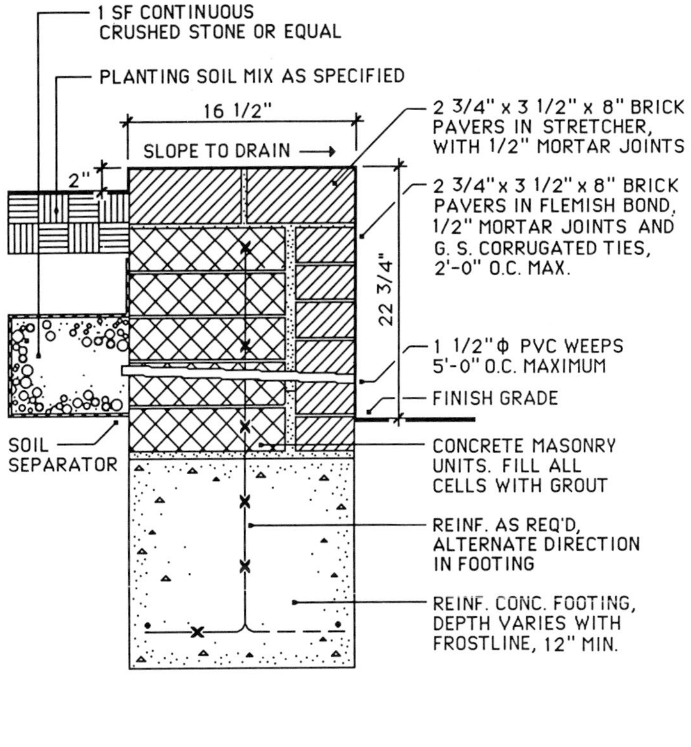

1 SF CONTINUOUS CRUSHED STONE OR EQUAL
PLANTING SOIL MIX AS SPECIFIED
16 1/2"
SLOPE TO DRAIN
2"
2 3/4" x 3 1/2" x 8" BRICK PAVERS IN STRETCHER, WITH 1/2" MORTAR JOINTS
2 3/4" x 3 1/2" x 8" BRICK PAVERS IN FLEMISH BOND, 1/2" MORTAR JOINTS AND G. S. CORRUGATED TIES, 2'-0" O.C. MAX.
22 3/4"
1 1/2" Φ PVC WEEPS 5'-0" O.C. MAXIMUM
FINISH GRADE
SOIL SEPARATOR
CONCRETE MASONRY UNITS. FILL ALL CELLS WITH GROUT
REINF. AS REQ'D, ALTERNATE DIRECTION IN FOOTING
REINF. CONC. FOOTING, DEPTH VARIES WITH FROSTLINE, 12" MIN.

Figure 931-2 Brick-veneered seatwall with weep holes.

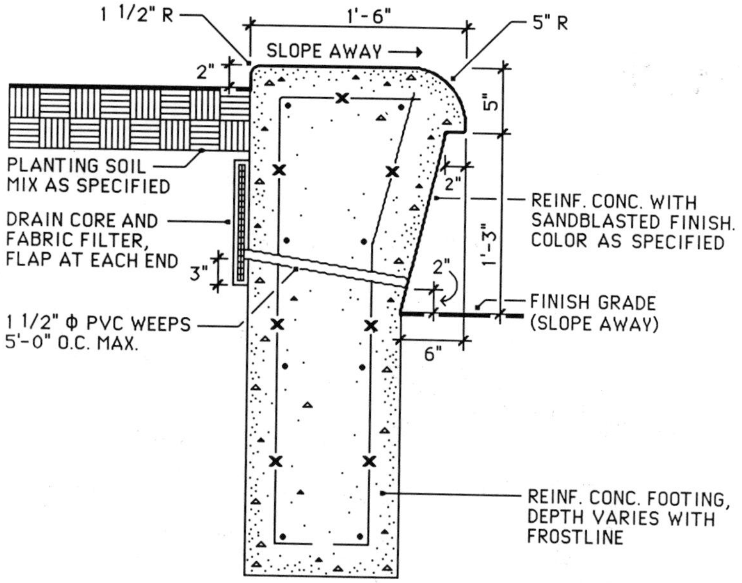
1 1/2" R
1'-6"
5" R
SLOPE AWAY
2"
5"
PLANTING SOIL MIX AS SPECIFIED
2"
DRAIN CORE AND FABRIC FILTER, FLAP AT EACH END
REINF. CONC. WITH SANDBLASTED FINISH. COLOR AS SPECIFIED
1'-3"
3"
2"
FINISH GRADE (SLOPE AWAY)
1 1/2" Φ PVC WEEPS 5'-0" O.C. MAX.
6"
REINF. CONC. FOOTING, DEPTH VARIES WITH FROSTLINE

Figure 931-3 Concrete seatwall.

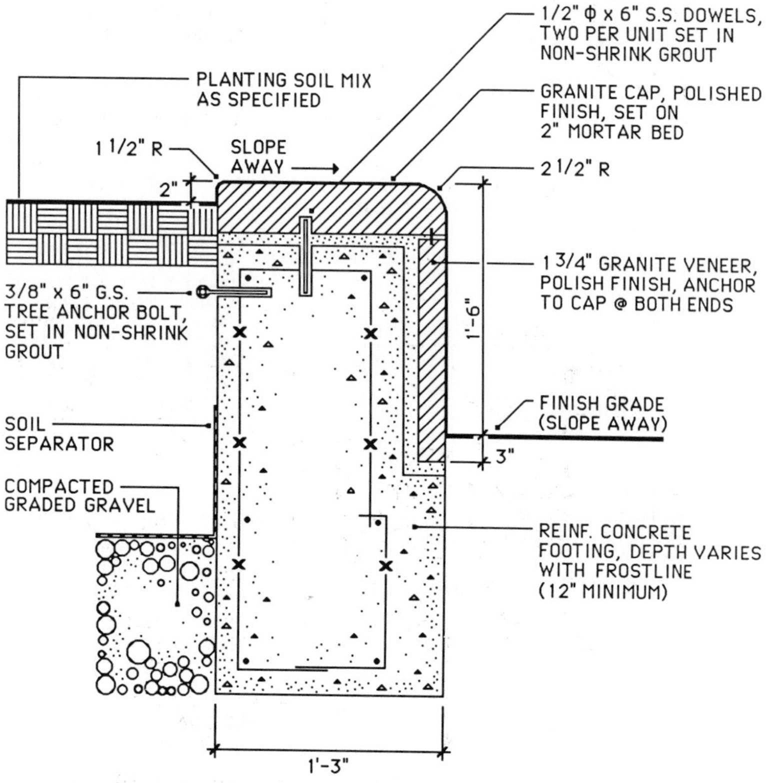
1/2" Φ x 6" S.S. DOWELS, TWO PER UNIT SET IN NON-SHRINK GROUT
PLANTING SOIL MIX AS SPECIFIED
GRANITE CAP, POLISHED FINISH, SET ON 2" MORTAR BED
1 1/2" R
SLOPE AWAY
2 1/2" R
2"
3/8" x 6" G.S. TREE ANCHOR BOLT, SET IN NON-SHRINK GROUT
1 3/4" GRANITE VENEER, POLISH FINISH, ANCHOR TO CAP @ BOTH ENDS
1'-6"
SOIL SEPARATOR
FINISH GRADE (SLOPE AWAY)
3"
COMPACTED GRADED GRAVEL
REINF. CONCRETE FOOTING, DEPTH VARIES WITH FROSTLINE (12" MINIMUM)
1'-3"

Figure 931-4 Granite-veneered seatwall.

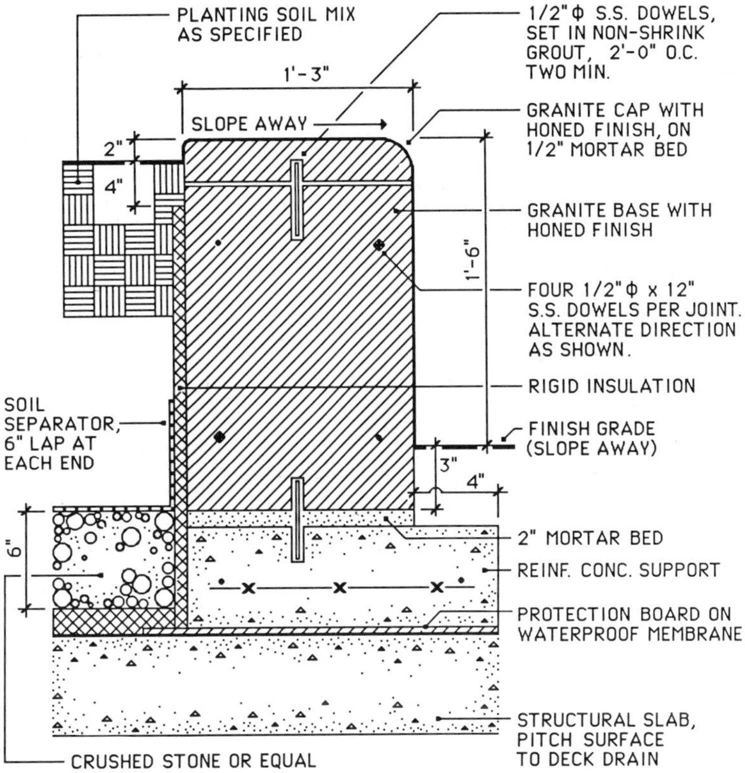
PLANTING SOIL MIX AS SPECIFIED
1'-3"
SLOPE AWAY
2"
4"
1/2" ϕ S.S. DOWELS, SET IN NON-SHRINK GROUT, 2'-0" O.C. TWO MIN.
GRANITE CAP WITH HONED FINISH, ON 1/2" MORTAR BED
GRANITE BASE WITH HONED FINISH
1'-6"
FOUR 1/2" ϕ x 12" S.S. DOWELS PER JOINT. ALTERNATE DIRECTION AS SHOWN.
RIGID INSULATION
SOIL SEPARATOR, 6" LAP AT EACH END
FINISH GRADE (SLOPE AWAY)
3"
4"
6"
2" MORTAR BED
REINF. CONC. SUPPORT
PROTECTION BOARD ON WATERPROOF MEMBRANE
STRUCTURAL SLAB, PITCH SURFACE TO DECK DRAIN
CRUSHED STONE OR EQUAL

Figure 931-5 Granite seatwall on structure.

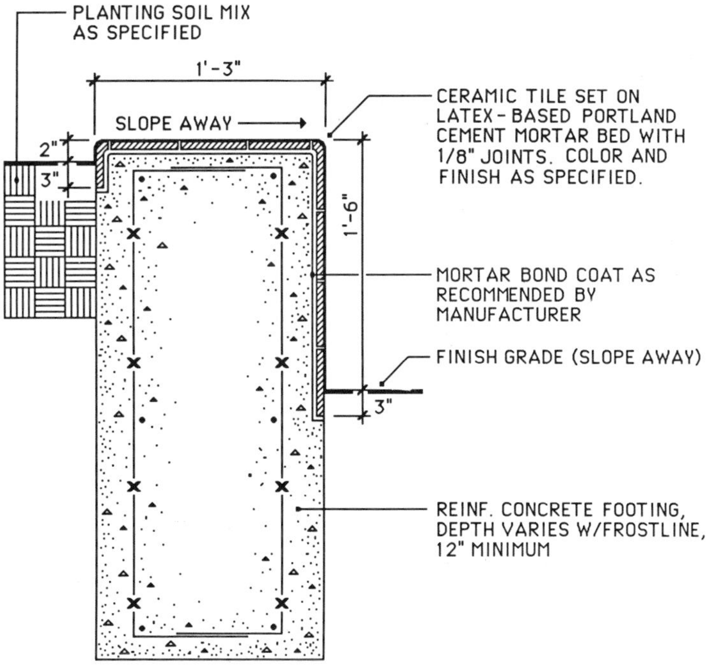
PLANTING SOIL MIX AS SPECIFIED
1'-3"
SLOPE AWAY
2"
3"
CERAMIC TILE SET ON LATEX-BASED PORTLAND CEMENT MORTAR BED WITH 1/8" JOINTS. COLOR AND FINISH AS SPECIFIED.
1'-6"
MORTAR BOND COAT AS RECOMMENDED BY MANUFACTURER
FINISH GRADE (SLOPE AWAY)
3"
REINF. CONCRETE FOOTING, DEPTH VARIES W/FROSTLINE, 12" MINIMUM

Figure 931-6 Ceramic tile seatwall.

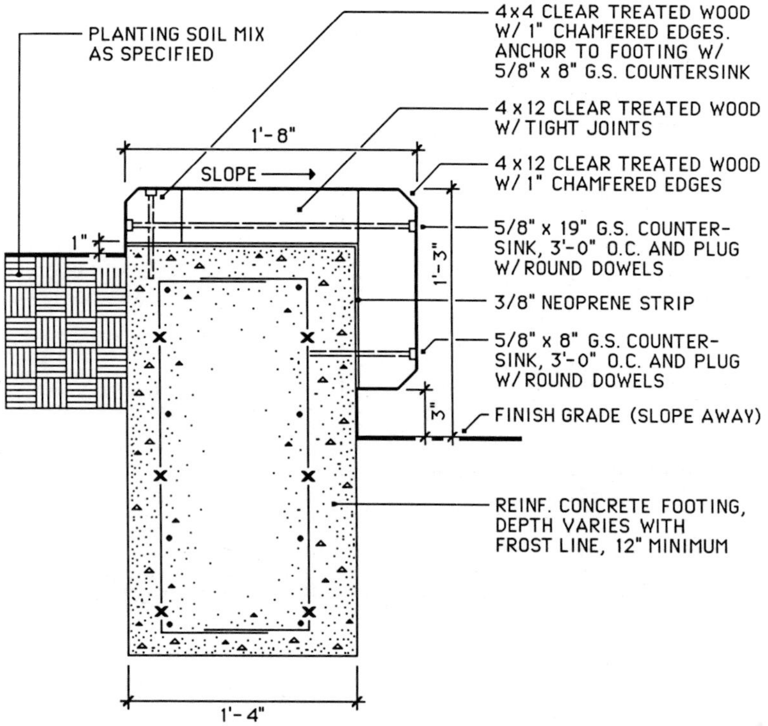
PLANTING SOIL MIX AS SPECIFIED
4x4 CLEAR TREATED WOOD W/ 1" CHAMFERED EDGES. ANCHOR TO FOOTING W/ 5/8" x 8" G.S. COUNTERSINK
4 x 12 CLEAR TREATED WOOD W/ TIGHT JOINTS
4 x 12 CLEAR TREATED WOOD W/ 1" CHAMFERED EDGES
1'-8"
SLOPE
1"
1'-3"
5/8" x 19" G.S. COUNTER-SINK, 3'-0" O.C. AND PLUG W/ ROUND DOWELS
3/8" NEOPRENE STRIP
5/8" x 8" G.S. COUNTER-SINK, 3'-0" O.C. AND PLUG W/ ROUND DOWELS
3"
FINISH GRADE (SLOPE AWAY)
REINF. CONCRETE FOOTING, DEPTH VARIES WITH FROST LINE, 12" MINIMUM
1'- 4"

Figure 931-7 Wood-veneered seatwall.

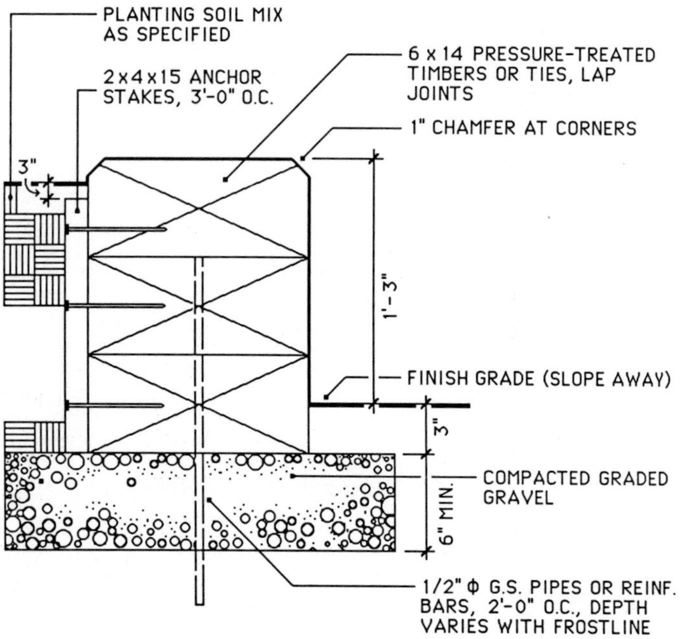
PLANTING SOIL MIX AS SPECIFIED
2x4x15 ANCHOR STAKES, 3'-0" O.C.
6 x 14 PRESSURE-TREATED TIMBERS OR TIES, LAP JOINTS
1" CHAMFER AT CORNERS
3"
1'-3"
FINISH GRADE (SLOPE AWAY)
3"
COMPACTED GRADED GRAVEL
6" MIN.
1/2" Φ G.S. PIPES OR REINF. BARS, 2'-0" O.C., DEPTH VARIES WITH FROSTLINE

Figure 931-8 Wood seatwall.

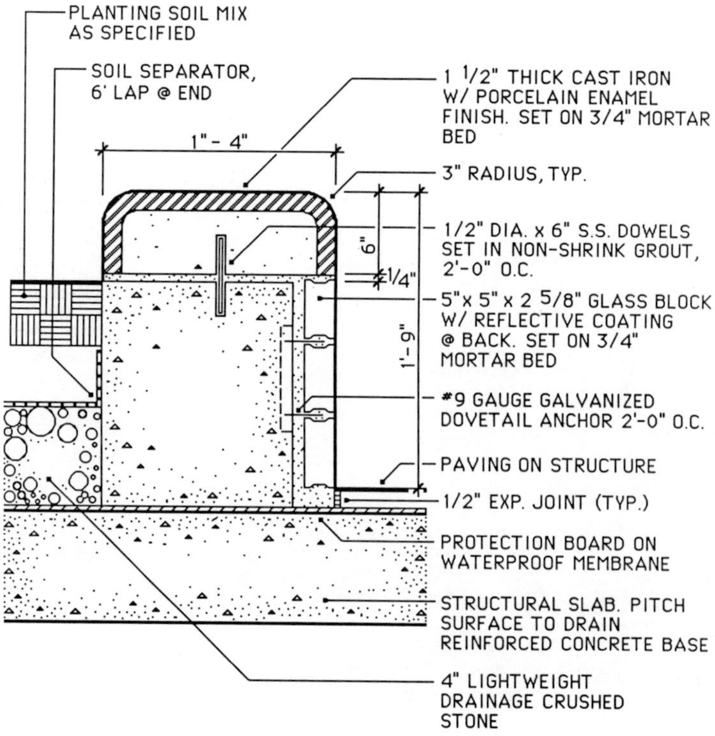
PLANTING SOIL MIX AS SPECIFIED
SOIL SEPARATOR, 6' LAP @ END
1 1/2" THICK CAST IRON W/ PORCELAIN ENAMEL FINISH. SET ON 3/4" MORTAR BED
1"- 4"
3" RADIUS, TYP.
6"
1/2" DIA. x 6" S.S. DOWELS SET IN NON-SHRINK GROUT, 2'-0" O.C.
1/4"
5"x 5" x 2 5/8" GLASS BLOCK W/ REFLECTIVE COATING @ BACK. SET ON 3/4" MORTAR BED
1'-9"
#9 GAUGE GALVANIZED DOVETAIL ANCHOR 2'-0" O.C.
PAVING ON STRUCTURE
1/2" EXP. JOINT (TYP.)
PROTECTION BOARD ON WATERPROOF MEMBRANE
STRUCTURAL SLAB. PITCH SURFACE TO DRAIN REINFORCED CONCRETE BASE
4" LIGHTWEIGHT DRAINAGE CRUSHED STONE

Figure 931-9 Glass block-veneered seatwall with porcelain cap.

section 950: Planting

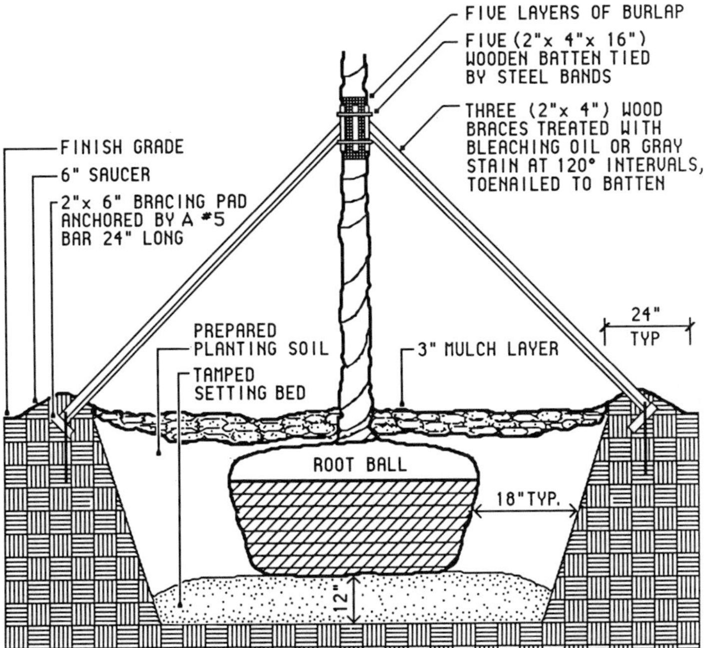
FIVE LAYERS OF BURLAP
FIVE (2"x 4"x 16") WOODEN BATTEN TIED BY STEEL BANDS
THREE (2"x 4") WOOD BRACES TREATED WITH BLEACHING OIL OR GRAY STAIN AT 120° INTERVALS, TOENAILED TO BATTEN
FINISH GRADE
6" SAUCER
2"x 6" BRACING PAD ANCHORED BY A #5 BAR 24" LONG
24" TYP
PREPARED PLANTING SOIL
3" MULCH LAYER
TAMPED SETTING BED
ROOT BALL
18"TYP.
12"

Figure 950-1 Tree planting with braces. Height of batten shall be located in relation to the height of the tree trunk (1:2 ratio minimum).

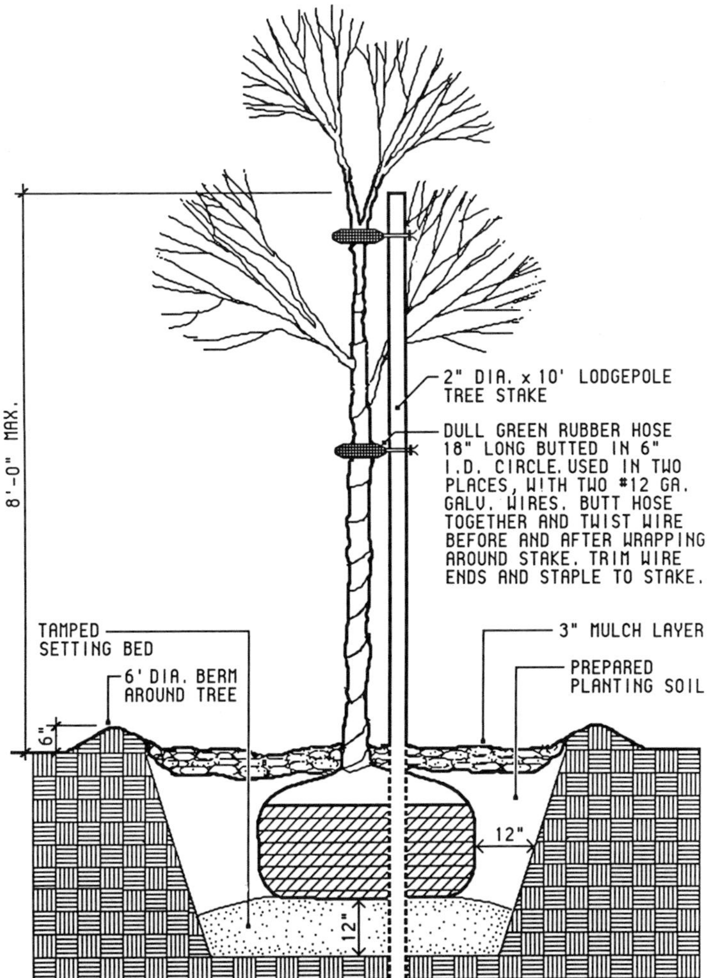
8'-0" MAX.
2" DIA. x 10' LODGEPOLE TREE STAKE
DULL GREEN RUBBER HOSE 18" LONG BUTTED IN 6" I.D. CIRCLE. USED IN TWO PLACES, WITH TWO #12 GA. GALV. WIRES. BUTT HOSE TOGETHER AND TWIST WIRE BEFORE AND AFTER WRAPPING AROUND STAKE. TRIM WIRE ENDS AND STAPLE TO STAKE.
TAMPED SETTING BED
3" MULCH LAYER
6' DIA. BERM AROUND TREE
PREPARED PLANTING SOIL
6"
12"
12"

Figure 950-2 Tree planting with stake. Set stake on windward side and remove after six months. Set crown of root ball 1½ inch ± below surrounding grade. Single staking is used where wind is minimal and predominantly from one direction.

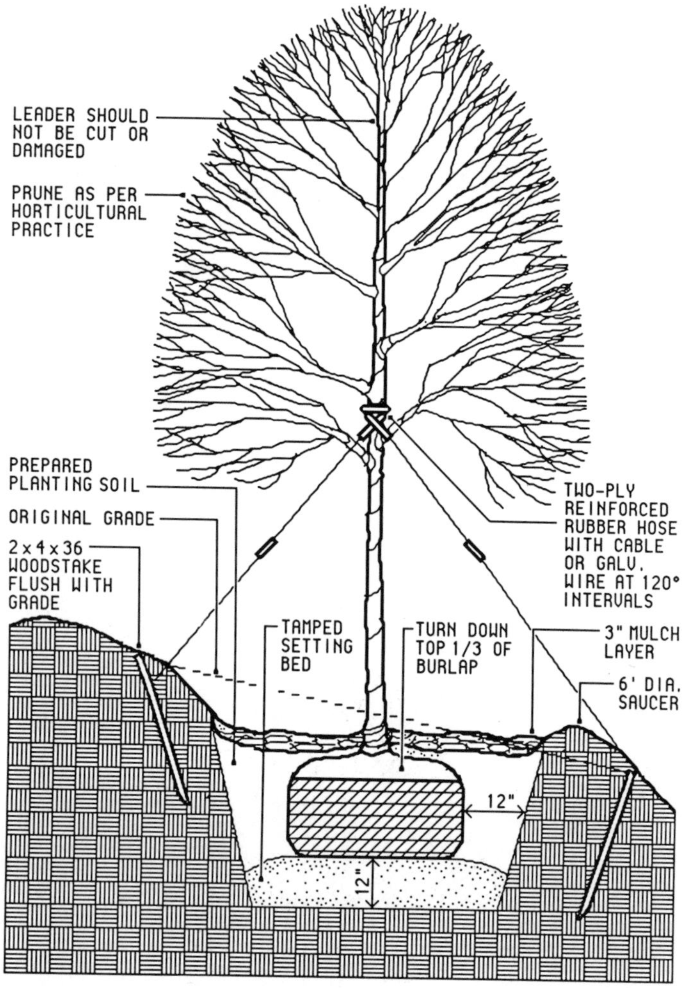
LEADER SHOULD NOT BE CUT OR DAMAGED
PRUNE AS PER HORTICULTURAL PRACTICE
PREPARED PLANTING SOIL
ORIGINAL GRADE
2 x 4 x 36 WOODSTAKE FLUSH WITH GRADE
TAMPED SETTING BED
TURN DOWN TOP 1/3 OF BURLAP
TWO-PLY REINFORCED RUBBER HOSE WITH CABLE OR GALV. WIRE AT 120° INTERVALS
3" MULCH LAYER
6' DIA. SAUCER
12"
12"

Figure 950-3 Tree planting with guys on slope. Install two of the three stakes and guy wires on the uphill side of the tree. Use guying on specimen and evergreen trees in low-density pedestrian traffic areas only.

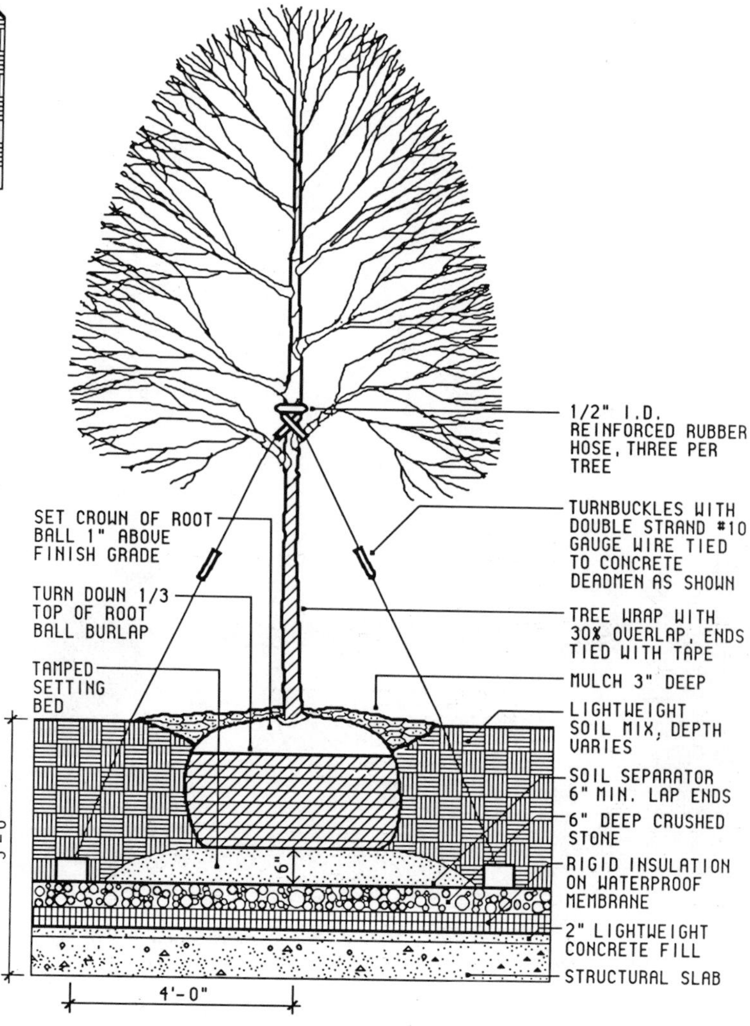
1/2" I.D. REINFORCED RUBBER HOSE, THREE PER TREE
SET CROWN OF ROOT BALL 1" ABOVE FINISH GRADE
TURNBUCKLES WITH DOUBLE STRAND #10 GAUGE WIRE TIED TO CONCRETE DEADMEN AS SHOWN
TURN DOWN 1/3 TOP OF ROOT BALL BURLAP
TREE WRAP WITH 30% OVERLAP, ENDS TIED WITH TAPE
TAMPED SETTING BED
MULCH 3" DEEP
LIGHTWEIGHT SOIL MIX, DEPTH VARIES
SOIL SEPARATOR 6" MIN. LAP ENDS
6" DEEP CRUSHED STONE
RIGID INSULATION ON WATERPROOF MEMBRANE
2" LIGHTWEIGHT CONCRETE FILL
STRUCTURAL SLAB
3'-0"
6"
4'-0"

Figure 950-4 Tree planting with guy wires on structure. To restrain growth of tree or for temporary plantings, trees and shrubs are planted with nursery containers (PVC or clay).

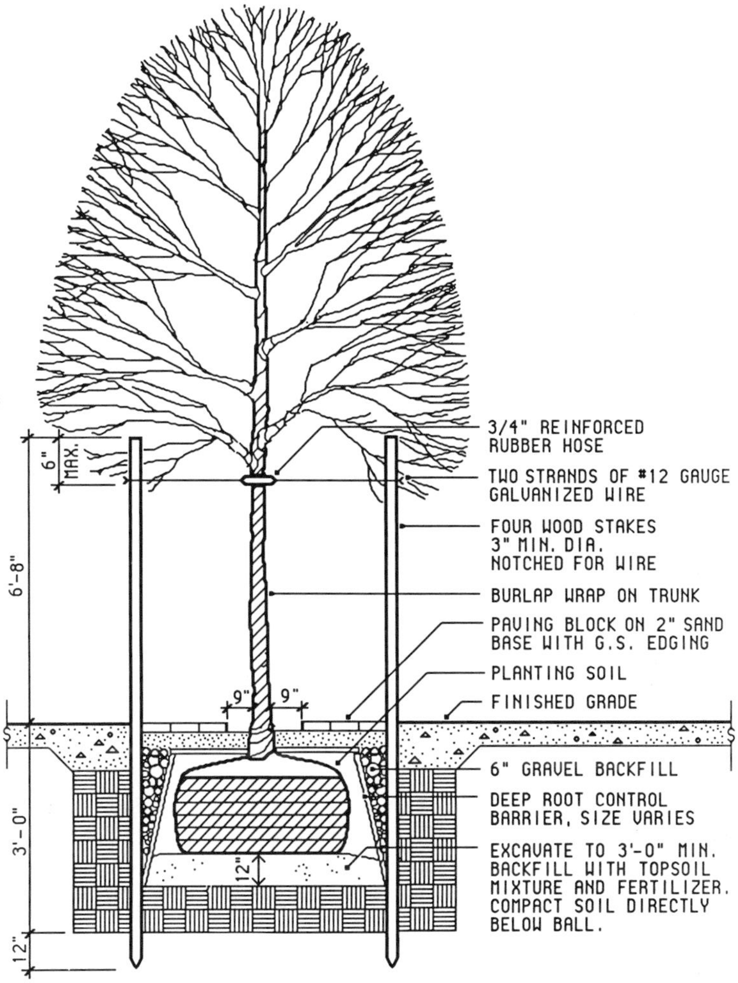
3/4" REINFORCED RUBBER HOSE
TWO STRANDS OF #12 GAUGE GALVANIZED WIRE
FOUR WOOD STAKES 3" MIN. DIA. NOTCHED FOR WIRE
BURLAP WRAP ON TRUNK
PAVING BLOCK ON 2" SAND BASE WITH G.S. EDGING
PLANTING SOIL
FINISHED GRADE
6" GRAVEL BACKFILL
DEEP ROOT CONTROL BARRIER, SIZE VARIES
EXCAVATE TO 3'-0" MIN. BACKFILL WITH TOPSOIL MIXTURE AND FERTILIZER. COMPACT SOIL DIRECTLY BELOW BALL.
6"
MAX. 1'
6'-8"
9"
9"
3'-0"
12"
12"

Figure 950-5 Tree planting with deep root control barrier. Specify this method of planting for trees with shallow root systems planted in paved areas.

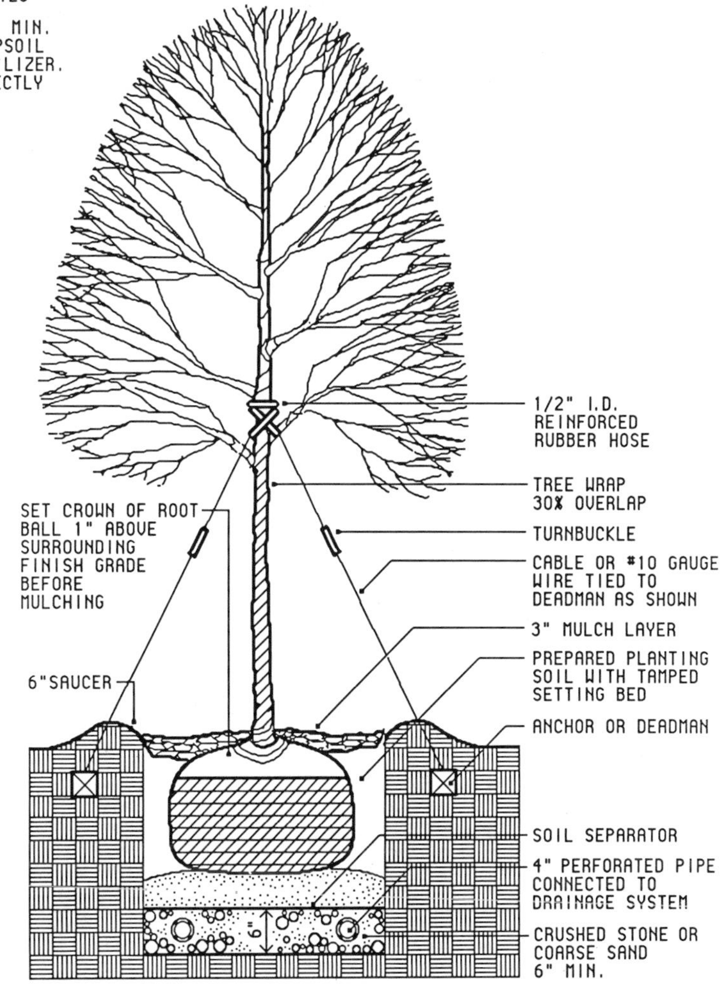
1/2" I.D. REINFORCED RUBBER HOSE
TREE WRAP 30% OVERLAP
TURNBUCKLE
CABLE OR #10 GAUGE WIRE TIED TO DEADMAN AS SHOWN
3" MULCH LAYER
PREPARED PLANTING SOIL WITH TAMPED SETTING BED
ANCHOR OR DEADMAN
SOIL SEPARATOR
4" PERFORATED PIPE CONNECTED TO DRAINAGE SYSTEM
CRUSHED STONE OR COARSE SAND 6" MIN.
SET CROWN OF ROOT BALL 1" ABOVE SURROUNDING FINISH GRADE BEFORE MULCHING
6"SAUCER
6"

Figure 950-6 Tree planting in clayey soil.

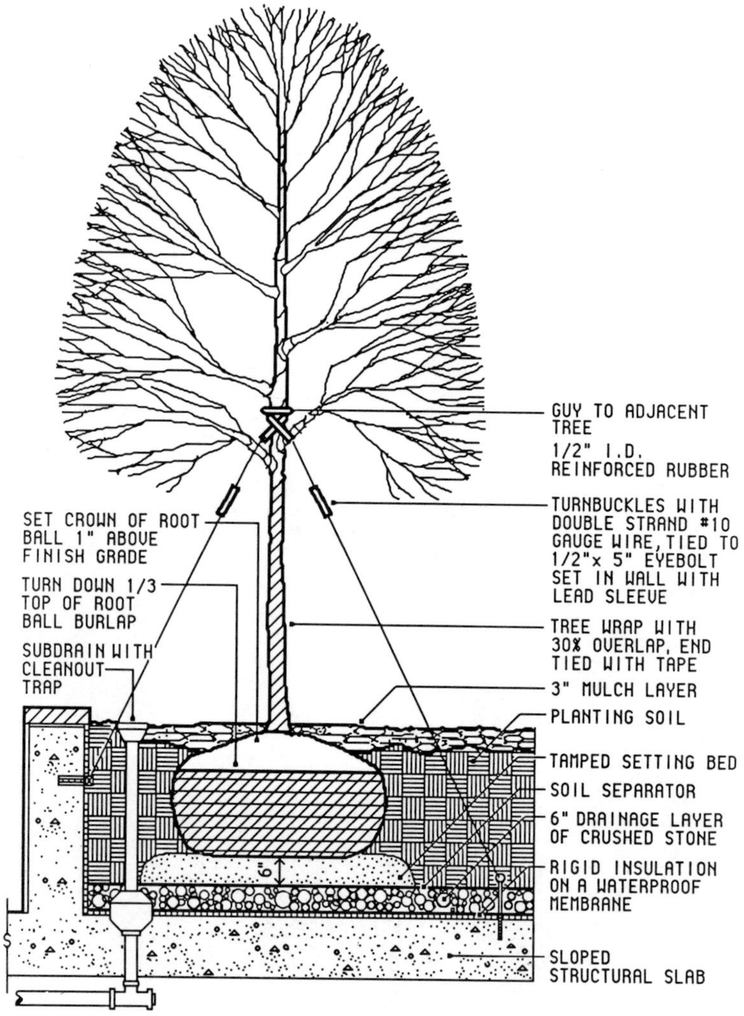
GUY TO ADJACENT TREE
1/2" I.D. REINFORCED RUBBER
TURNBUCKLES WITH DOUBLE STRAND #10 GAUGE WIRE, TIED TO 1/2"x 5" EYEBOLT SET IN WALL WITH LEAD SLEEVE
SET CROWN OF ROOT BALL 1" ABOVE FINISH GRADE
TURN DOWN 1/3 TOP OF ROOT BALL BURLAP
SUBDRAIN WITH CLEANOUT TRAP
TREE WRAP WITH 30% OVERLAP, END TIED WITH TAPE
3" MULCH LAYER
PLANTING SOIL
TAMPED SETTING BED
SOIL SEPARATOR
6" DRAINAGE LAYER OF CRUSHED STONE
6"
RIGID INSULATION ON A WATERPROOF MEMBRANE
SLOPED STRUCTURAL SLAB

Figure 950-7 Tree planting in raised container on structure.

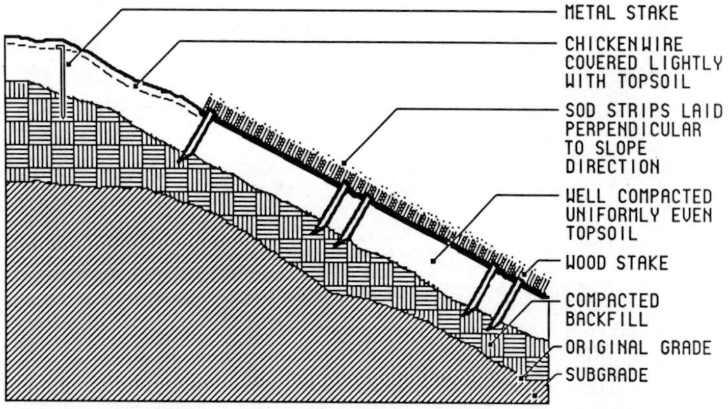
METAL STAKE
CHICKENWIRE COVERED LIGHTLY WITH TOPSOIL
SOD STRIPS LAID PERPENDICULAR TO SLOPE DIRECTION
WELL COMPACTED UNIFORMLY EVEN TOPSOIL
WOOD STAKE
COMPACTED BACKFILL
ORIGINAL GRADE
SUBGRADE

Figure 950-8 Sodding on slope. Lay sod in rows perpendicular to direction of slope, with staggered butt joints. Provide close contact between soil and sod by light rolling. Water immediately after installation. Prevent trespassing on sodded slopes for at least four weeks after installation. Remove wooden sod stakes six weeks after installation.

section 960: Lighting

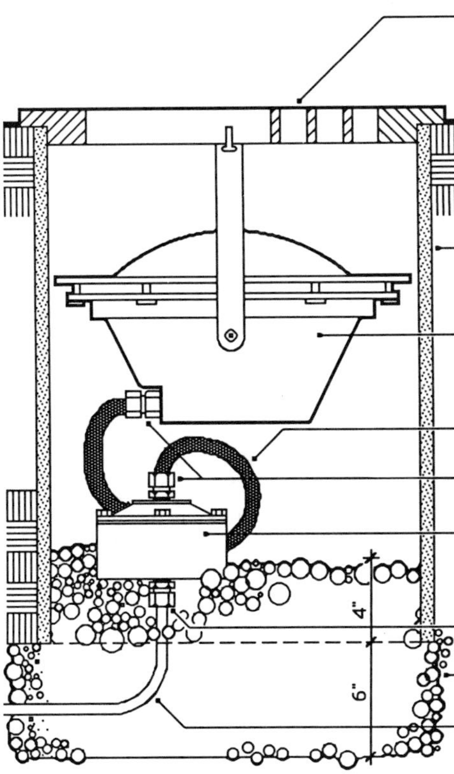

CAST ALUM. LOUVER GUARD SECURED TO WELL W/ S.S. SCREWS
FINISH GRADE
12" I.D. TRANSITE PIPE, 18" LONG, PAINT INSIDE MATTE BLACK
CAST ALUM., ADJUSTABLE WEATHERPROOF LAMP-HOLDER WITH INVERTED ALUM. STRAP YOKE
#16/3 TYPE STANDARD CORD, 5 FT. MIN. LENGTH
WATERTIGHT CORD SEAL BUSHING
GALV. CAST IRON BURIABLE J-BOX. ENCAPSULATE SPLICES AND POT THOROUGHLY
ALS WATERTIGHT CONNECTOR
CRUSHED STONE
TYP. ALS CABLE, PVC JACKETED
4"
6"

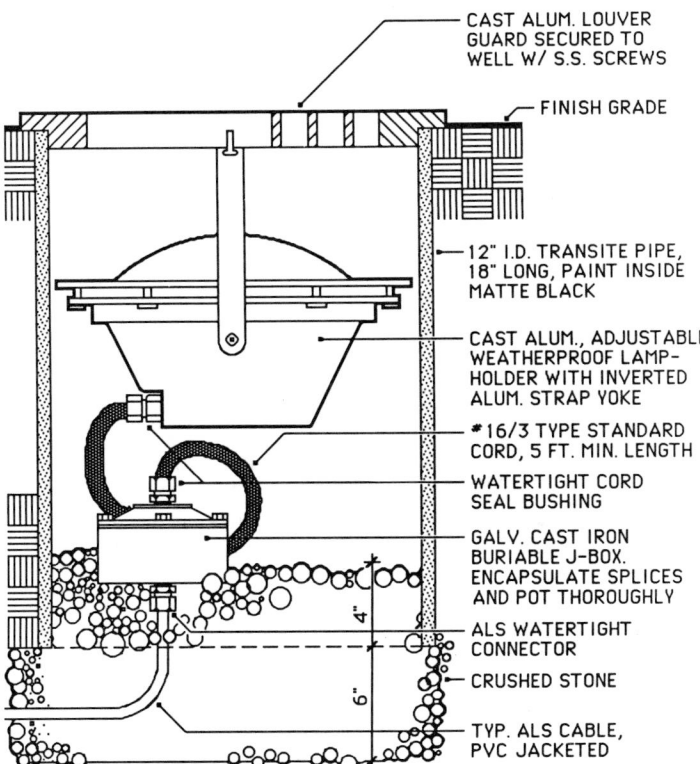

Figure 960-1 Up light (below grade).

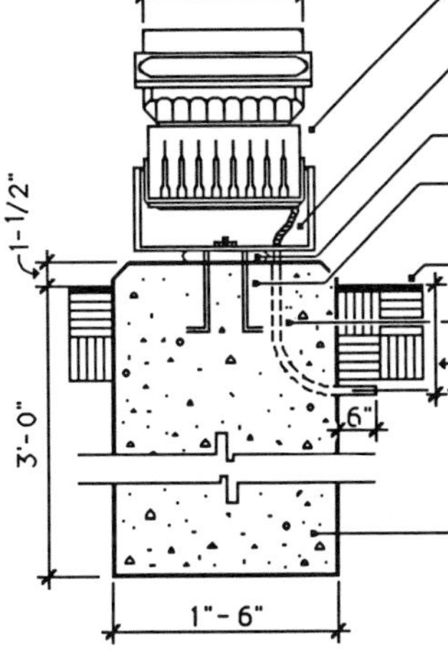

1'- 2"
1-1/2"
3'- 0"
6"
1"- 6"
LIGHT FIXTURE W/LOUVER AS SPECIFIED
3/4" L.T.F.M. CONDUIT TO ALLOW 90° VERTICAL ROTATION
MOUNTING PLATE
FOUR 3/8" DIA. X 6" LONG S.S. VANDAL RESISTANT EXP. BOLTS
FINISH GRADE
3/4" DIA. G.S. CONDUIT
2' MIN. DEPTH
3 #12 FLEXIBLE CABLE TYPE U.S.E.
REINF. CONC. FOUNDATION W/ 3/4" CHAMFERED TOP, DEPTH VARIES W/ FROST LINE

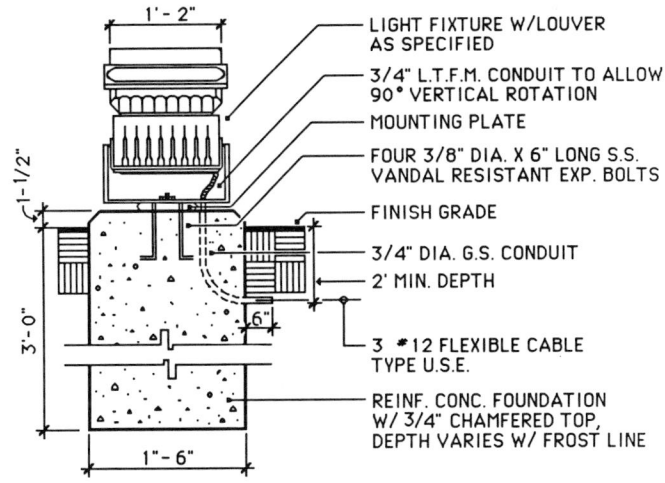

Figure 960-2 Up light (above grade).

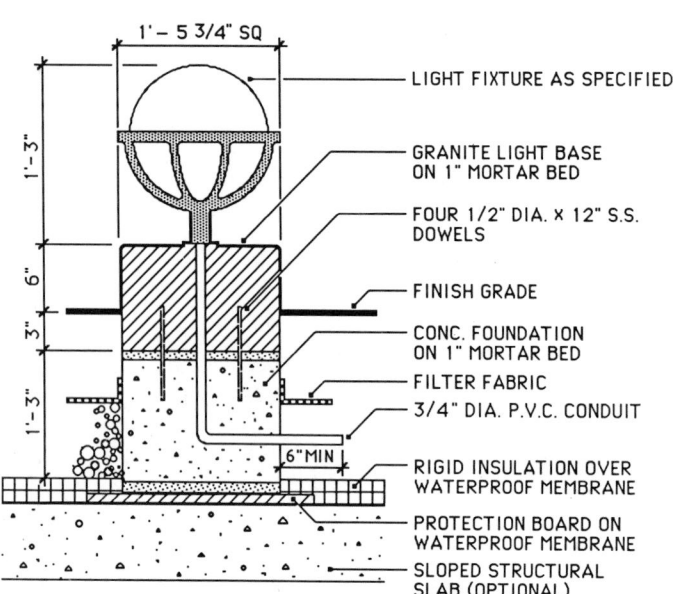

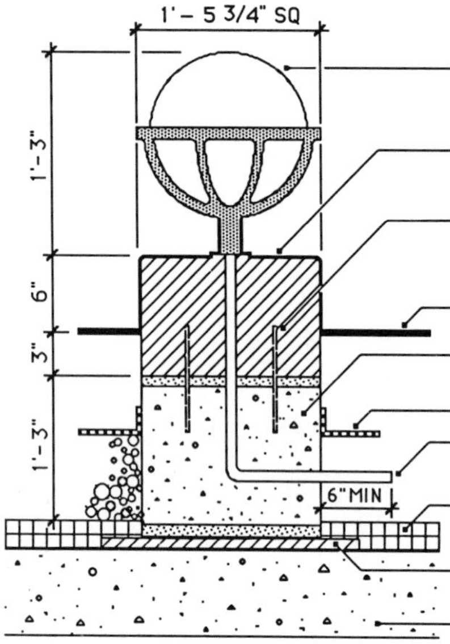
1'– 5 3/4" SQ
1'-3"
6"
3"
1'-3"
6" MIN
LIGHT FIXTURE AS SPECIFIED
GRANITE LIGHT BASE ON 1" MORTAR BED
FOUR 1/2" DIA. x 12" S.S. DOWELS
FINISH GRADE
CONC. FOUNDATION ON 1" MORTAR BED
FILTER FABRIC
3/4" DIA. P.V.C. CONDUIT
RIGID INSULATION OVER WATERPROOF MEMBRANE
PROTECTION BOARD ON WATERPROOF MEMBRANE
SLOPED STRUCTURAL SLAB (OPTIONAL)

Figure 960-3 Area light (on structure).

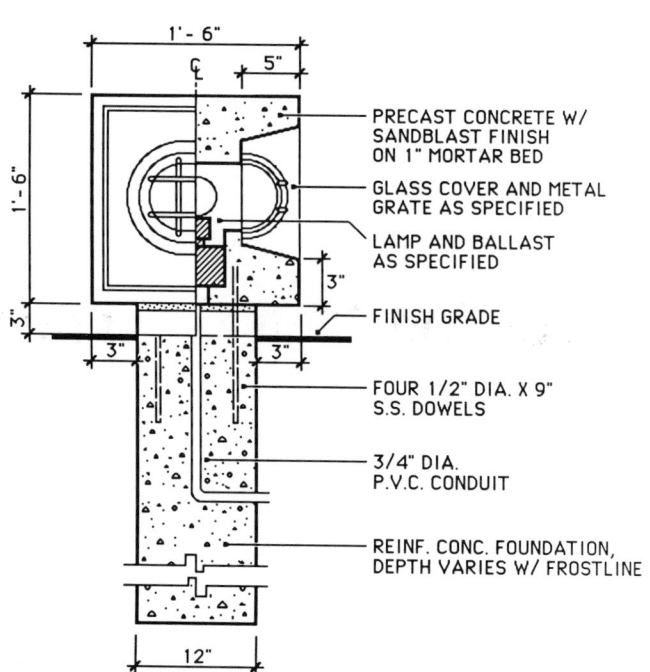

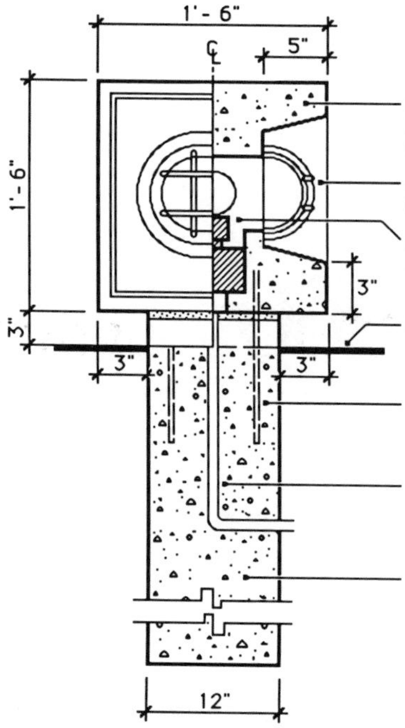
1'- 6"
5"
1'-6"
3"
3"
3"
3"
12"
PRECAST CONCRETE W/ SANDBLAST FINISH ON 1" MORTAR BED
GLASS COVER AND METAL GRATE AS SPECIFIED
LAMP AND BALLAST AS SPECIFIED
FINISH GRADE
FOUR 1/2" DIA. X 9" S.S. DOWELS
3/4" DIA. P.V.C. CONDUIT
REINF. CONC. FOUNDATION, DEPTH VARIES W/ FROSTLINE

Figure 960-4 Area light (on grade).

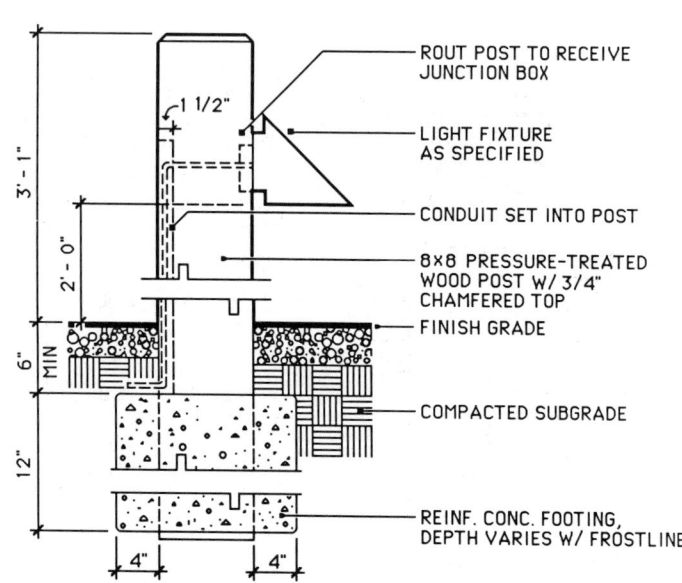

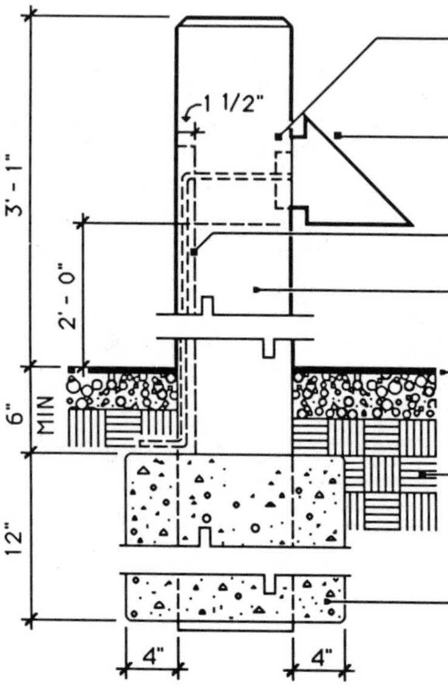
3'- 1"
1 1/2"
2'- 0"
6" MIN
12"
4"
4"
ROUT POST TO RECEIVE JUNCTION BOX
LIGHT FIXTURE AS SPECIFIED
CONDUIT SET INTO POST
8x8 PRESSURE-TREATED WOOD POST W/ 3/4" CHAMFERED TOP
FINISH GRADE
COMPACTED SUBGRADE
REINF. CONC. FOOTING, DEPTH VARIES W/ FROSTLINE

Figure 960-5 Wood bollard light.

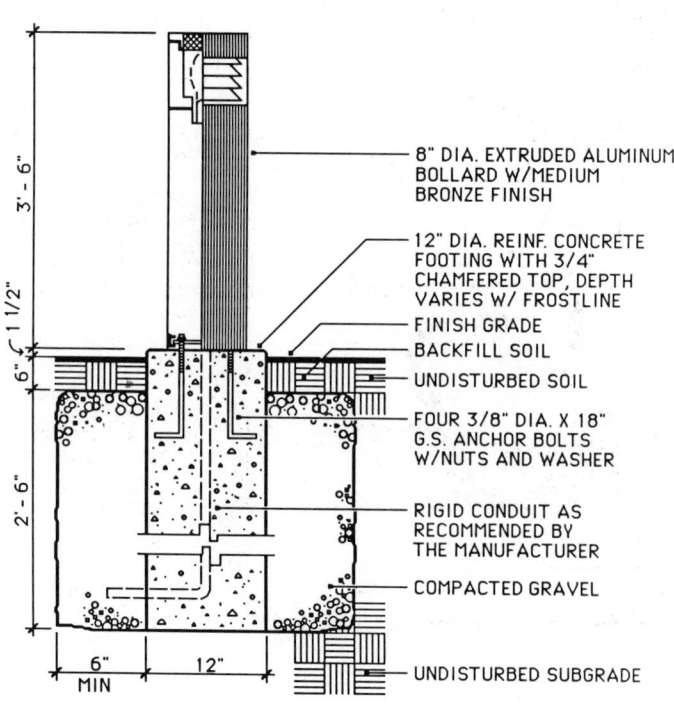

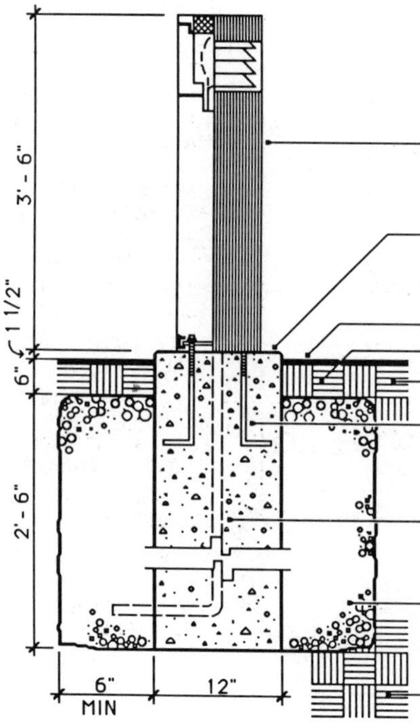
3'- 6"
1 1/2"
6"
2'- 6"
6" MIN
12"
8" DIA. EXTRUDED ALUMINUM BOLLARD W/MEDIUM BRONZE FINISH
12" DIA. REINF. CONCRETE FOOTING WITH 3/4" CHAMFERED TOP, DEPTH VARIES W/ FROSTLINE
FINISH GRADE
BACKFILL SOIL
UNDISTURBED SOIL
FOUR 3/8" DIA. X 18" G.S. ANCHOR BOLTS W/NUTS AND WASHER
RIGID CONDUIT AS RECOMMENDED BY THE MANUFACTURER
COMPACTED GRAVEL
UNDISTURBED SUBGRADE

Figure 960-6 Metal bollard light.

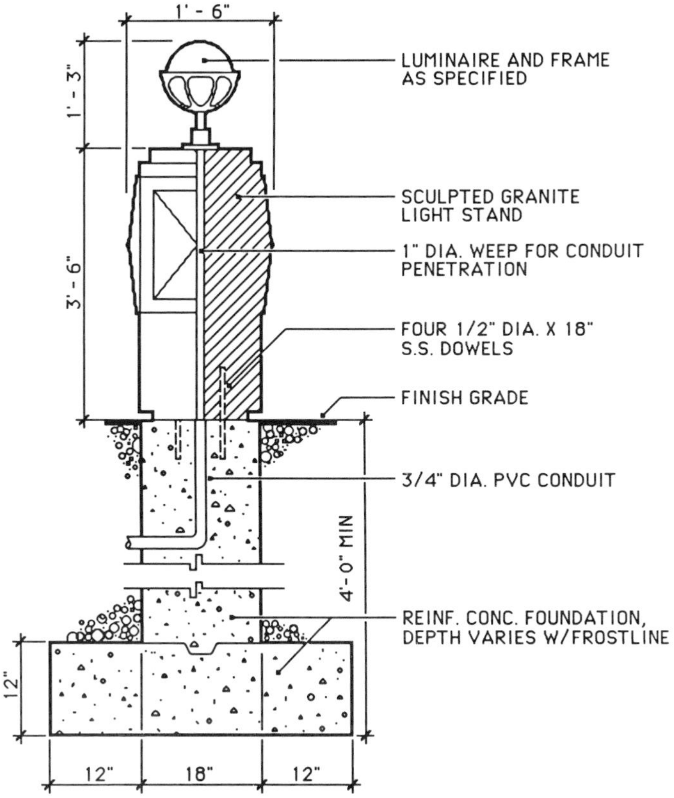
1' - 6"
1' - 3"
3' - 6"
LUMINAIRE AND FRAME AS SPECIFIED
SCULPTED GRANITE LIGHT STAND
1" DIA. WEEP FOR CONDUIT PENETRATION
FOUR 1/2" DIA. X 18" S.S. DOWELS
FINISH GRADE
3/4" DIA. PVC CONDUIT
4'-0" MIN
REINF. CONC. FOUNDATION, DEPTH VARIES W/FROSTLINE
12"
12"
18"
12"

Figure 960-7 Light standard with sculpted granite stand.

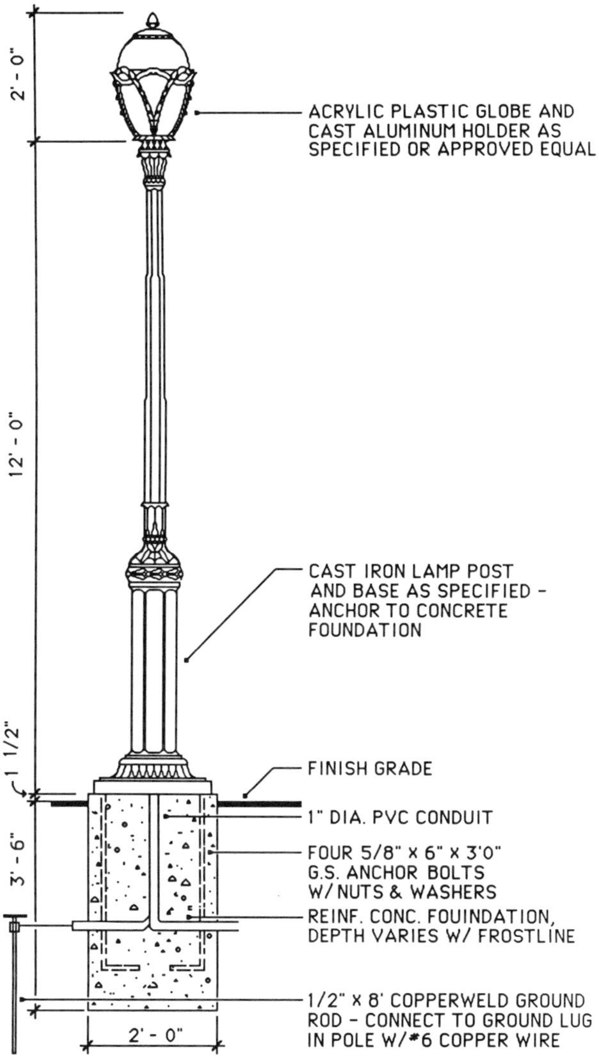
2' - 0"
12' - 0"
1 1/2"
3' - 6"
2' - 0"
ACRYLIC PLASTIC GLOBE AND CAST ALUMINUM HOLDER AS SPECIFIED OR APPROVED EQUAL
CAST IRON LAMP POST AND BASE AS SPECIFIED - ANCHOR TO CONCRETE FOUNDATION
FINISH GRADE
1" DIA. PVC CONDUIT
FOUR 5/8" x 6" x 3'0" G.S. ANCHOR BOLTS W/ NUTS & WASHERS
REINF. CONC. FOUINDATION, DEPTH VARIES W/ FROSTLINE
1/2" x 8' COPPERWELD GROUND ROD - CONNECT TO GROUND LUG IN POLE W/#6 COPPER WIRE

Figure 960-8 Typical historic walkway light.

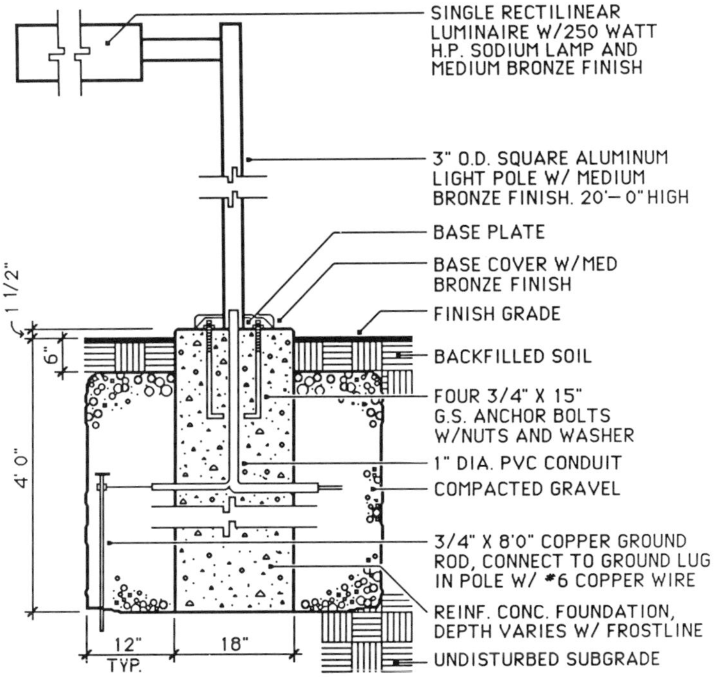
SINGLE RECTILINEAR LUMINAIRE W/250 WATT H.P. SODIUM LAMP AND MEDIUM BRONZE FINISH
3" O.D. SQUARE ALUMINUM LIGHT POLE W/ MEDIUM BRONZE FINISH. 20'– 0" HIGH
BASE PLATE
BASE COVER W/MED BRONZE FINISH
FINISH GRADE
BACKFILLED SOIL
FOUR 3/4" X 15" G.S. ANCHOR BOLTS W/NUTS AND WASHER
1" DIA. PVC CONDUIT
COMPACTED GRAVEL
3/4" X 8'0" COPPER GROUND ROD, CONNECT TO GROUND LUG IN POLE W/ #6 COPPER WIRE
REINF. CONC. FOUNDATION, DEPTH VARIES W/ FROSTLINE
UNDISTURBED SUBGRADE
1 1/2"
6"
4' 0"
12" TYP.
18"

Figure 960-9 Typical cutoff light.

Illustration Source Notes

Figure 210-1 Courtesy of Henry Dreyfuss Associates, New York, New York; from C. G. Ramsey and H. R. Sleeper, *Architectural Graphic Standards,* 7th ed., Robert T. Packard (ed.), Copyright © 1980, John Wiley & Sons, Inc, New York.

Figure 210-2 Ibid. (adapted).

Figure 210-3 Adapted from C. G. Ramsey and H. R. Sleeper, *Architectural Graphic Standards,* 7th ed., Robert T. Packard (ed.), Copyright © 1980, John Wiley & Sons, Inc., New York.

Figure 210-4 Ibid. (adapted); and from John H. Callendar, *Time-Saver Standards for Architecture,* McGraw-Hill, New York, 1974.

Figure 210-6 Motor Vehicle Manufacturers' Association, *Parking Dimensions: 1983 Model Passenger Cars,* Motor Vehicle Manufacturers' Association, Detroit, 1983.

Figure 210-7 Op cit., Ramsey and Sleeper (adapted).

Figure 210-8 Ibid. (adapted).

Figure 210-9 Ibid. (adapted).

Figure 210-10 Ibid. (adapted).

Figure 210-11 Ibid. (adapted).

Figure 210-12 Ibid. (adapted).

Figure 210-13 Ibid. (adapted).

Figure 210-14 Ibid. (adapted).

Figure 210-15 Ibid. (adapted).

Figure 210-16 Ibid. (adapted).

Figure 210-17 Ibid. (adapted).

Figure 210-18 Ibid. (adapted).

Figure 210-19 Ibid. (adapted).

Figure 210-20 Ibid.

Figure 210-21 Ibid.

Figure 210-22 Ibid.

Figure 210-23 Ibid. (adapted).

Figure 210-24 Kevin Lynch and Gary Hack, Site Planning, 3d ed., MIT Press, Cambridge, Massachusetts, 1984.

Figure 210-25 Ibid.

Figure 210-26 Ibid.

Figure 210-27 Ibid.

Figure 210-28 William A. Mann, *Space and Time in Landscape Architectural History,* Landscape Architecture Foundation, Washington, D.C., 1981.

Figure 210-28 Ibid.

Figure 210-29 Ibid.

Figure 210-30 Ibid.

Figure 210-31 Ibid.

Figure 210-32 Ibid.

Figure 240-2 American National Standards Institute.

Figure 240-3 Ibid.

Figure 240-5 Ibid.

Figure 240-22 Ibid.

Figure 240-23 U.S. Department of Transportation.

Figure 240-25 Minnesota Department of Natural Resources.

Figure 252-1 Adapted from W. W. Hays (ed.), "Facing Geologic and Hydrologic Hazards," U.S. Geological Survey Professional Paper 1240-B, U.S. Government Printing Office, Washington, D.C., 1981.

Figure 252-2 After M. Brarazangi and J. Dorman, "World Seismicity Map," Seismological Society of America, Bulletin No. 59, pp. 369–380, 1969.

Figure 252-3 Gary B. Griggs and John A. Gilchrist, *The Earth and Land Use Planning,* Duxbury Press, North Scituate, Massachusetts, 1977.

Figure 252-4 B. A. Bolt et al., *Geological Hazards,* Springer-Verlag, New York, 1975 (After *California Geology,* November 1971).

Figure 252-5 M. E. Blair and W. E. Spangle, "Seismic Safety and Land Use Planning (selected examples from California)," U.S. Geological Survey Professional Paper 941-B, U.S. Government Printing Office, Washington, D.C., 1979.

Figure 252-6 John E. Costa and Victor R. Baker, *Surficial Geology: Building with the Earth,* Copyright © 1981 John Wiley & Sons, Reprinted by permission of John Wiley & Sons.

Figure 252-7 D. R. Nicholas and J. M. Buchanan-Banks, "Seismic Hazards and Land Use Planning," U.S. Geological Survey Circular 690, U.S. Government Printing Office, Washington, D.C., 1974.

Figure 252-8 Ibid.

Figure 252-9 From E. E. Brabb (ed.), "Progress on Seismic Zonation in the San Francisco Bay Region," U.S. Geological Survey Circular 807, U.S. Government Printing Office, Washington, D.C., 1979.

Figure 252-10 Op cit., Hays.

Figure 252-11 G. C. Brown and A. E. Mussett, *The Inaccessible Earth,* Allen and Unwin, London, 1981.

Figure 252-12 Op cit., Hays.

Figure 252-13 After H. B. Seed and I. M. Idriss, "Simplified Procedure for Evaluating Soil Liquefaction Potential," *Journal of Soil Mechanics and Foundation Division*, ASCE97, SM9, 1249–1273, September 1971.

Figure 252-14 Shannon and Wilson, "Soil Behavior Under Earthquake Loading Conditions," from *State of Art Evaluation for U.S.*, Atomic Energy Commission, January 1972.

Figure 252-15 Op cit., Blair and Spangle.

Figure 252-16 Ibid.

Figure 252-17 Op cit., Costa and Baker.

Figure 252-18 E. E. Botsai et al., *Architects and Earthquakes,* AIA Research Corporation, Washington, D.C., 1977.

Figure 252-19 Ibid.

Figure 252-20 Ibid.

Figure 252-21 Ibid.

Figure 252-22 Ibid.

Figure 252-23 Ibid.

Figure 252-24 D. J. Dowrick, *Earthquake Resistant Design,* John Wiley & Sons, Chicester, England, 1977.

Figure 253-1 D. J. Varnes, "Slope Movement Types and Processes." in *Landslides: Analysis and Control,* R. L. Schuster and R. J. Krizek, eds., Transportation Research Board, Report 176 NAS–NRC, Washington, D.C. pp.12–33, 1978.

Figure 253-2 Rodbruch-Hall et al., Miscellaneous Field Studies Map MF-771, "Landslide Overview, Coterminous United States," U.S. Geological Survey, 1978.

Figure 253-3 Adapted from Hugo M. Schiechtl, *Bioengineering for Land Reclamation and Conservation,* University of Alberta Press, 1980.

Figure 253-4 James E. Hough and Associates, Inc.

Figure 253-5 Donald H. Gray and Andrew T. Leiser, *Biotechnical Slope Protection and Erosion Control,* Van Nostrand Reinhold, New York, 1982. (After Amin Moto. *Erosion and Sediment Control Handbook,* WPA 44013–7–003, Department of Conservation, State of California, 1978.

Figure 253-6 Adapted from Douglas R. Piteau and F. Lionel Peckover, *Landslides: Analysis and Control,* Special Report 176, Transportation Research Board, National Academy of Sciences, Washington, D.C., 1978.

Figure 253-7 Op cit., James E. Hough and Associates, Inc.

Figure 253-8 Ibid.

Figure 253-9 Op cit., Piteau and Peckover.

Figure 253-10 Ibid.

Figure 253-11 Op cit., Schiechtl.

Figure 253-12 Op cit., James E. Hough and Associates, Inc.

Figure 253-13 Ibid.

Figure 253-14 Ibid.

Figure 253-15 *Newsweek,* February 15, 1982, drawing by Ib Ohlsson.

Figure 253-16 From J. D. Ives and Misha Plam, "Avalanche Hazard Mapping and Zoning Problems in the Rocky Mountains with Examples from Colorado, USA," Reproduced courtesy of the authors and the International Glaciological Society from the *Journal of Glaciology,* vol. 26, no. 94, p. 370, 1980.

Figure 253-17 J. D. Ives, A. I. Meares, P. E. Carrarra, and M. J. Vovis, "Natural Hazards in Mountain Colorado," *Annals of the Association of American Geographers,* vol. 66, no. 1, 1976.

Figure 253-18 Op cit., Griggs and Gilchrist.

Figure 253-19 Op cit., Schiechtl.

Figure 254-1 A. N. Strahler, *Physical Geography,* 3d ed., Wiley, New York, 1969.

Figure 254-2 U.S. Geological Survey, Professional Paper 1240-B.

Figure 254-3 Ibid.

Figure 254-4 David Leveson, *Geology and the Urban Environment,* Oxford University Press, New York, 1980.

Figure 254-5 U.S. Geological Survey, Professional Paper 1240-B.

Figure 254-6 Op cit., Griggs and Gilchrist.

Figure 254-7 Forty-sixth annual meeting, Transportation Research Board, Washington, D.C.

Figure 254-8 M. J. Bradshaw et al, *The Earth's Changing Surface,* Hodder and Stoughton, London, 1978 (After USGS pamphlet 'Permafrost,' 1973).

Figure 254-9 U.S. Geological Survey, Professional Paper 648, 1969.

Figure 255-1 Russell O. Utgard, *Geology in the Urban Environment,* Burgess, Minneapolis, 1978.

Figure 255-2 Ernest L. Buckley, *Construction Materials, Methods, and Estimating,* Arlington Research Institute, Arlington, Texas, October 1978, p. 24.

Figure 255-3 B. A. Kantey, "Some Secrets to Building Structures on Expansive Soils," *Civil Engineering,* ASCE, December 1980, p. 53.

Figure 255-4 Ibid.

Figure 255-5 Op cit., modified from U.S. Geological Survey, Professional Paper 1240-B.

Figure 255-6 A. B. A. Brink, T. C. Partridge, and A. A. B. Williams, *Soil Survey for Engineering,* Oxford University Press, New York, 1982.

Figure 255-7 *Proceedings of the Second International Research and Engineering Conference on Expansive Clay Soils,* Texas A & M University, 1969.

Figure 255-9 Ibid.

Figure 255-10 K. A. Godfrey, Jr., "Expansive and Shrinking Soils—Building Design Problems Being Attacked," *Civil Engineering,* ASCE, October 1978.

Figure 255-11 Voidco, Inc., Dallas, Texas.

Figure 255-12 Ibid.

Figure 255-13 Op cit., *Proceedings of the Second International Conference on Expansive Clay Soils.*

Figure 255-14 Ibid.

Figure 255-15 Op cit., Buckley, p. 25.

Figure 320-10 Parker and MacGuire, *Simplified Site Engineering for Architects and Builders,* Wiley, New York, 1952 Copyright © and reprinted by permission of John Wiley & Sons, Inc.

Figure 320-13 Ibid.

Figure 320-24 Jot D. Carpenter (ed.), *Handbook of Landscape Architectural Construction,* The Landscape Architecture Foundation, Washington, D.C., 1976.

Figure 320-25 Ibid.

Figure 320-26 Ibid.

Figure 320-40 Ibid.

Figure 320-41 Ibid.

Figure 320-42 Ibid.

Figure 320-43 Ibid.

Figure 320-65 Adapted from *Michigan Soil Erosion and Sedimentation Control Guidebook,* Michigan Department of Natural Resources.

Figure 320-66 Adapted from Arnold Weddle, *Techniques of Landscape Architecture,* Heinemann, London, 1979.

Figure 320-67 Ibid.

Figure 320-77 Adapted from Richard K. Untermann, *Grade Easy,* ASLA Foundation, Washington, D.C., 1974.

Figure 320-78 Adapted from Albe E. Munson, *Construction Design for Landscape Architects,* McGraw-Hill, New York, 1974.

Figure 330-1 H. H. Lamb, *Climate: Present, Past, and Future,* Methuen and Co., 1975.

Figure 330-4 J. Toby Tourbier and Richard Westmacott, *Water Resources Protection Technology,* The Urban Land Institute, Washington, D.C., 1981.

Figure 330-5 Ibid.

Figure 330-10 Ibid.

Figure 330-11 Ibid.

Figure 330-12 Courtesy of Mackintosh and Lamba, University of Pennsylvania, 1981.

Figure 330-13 Op cit., Tourbier and Westmacott.

Figure 330-14 Ibid.

Figure 330-15 Ibid.

Figure 330-16 Courtesy of Beaver and Bratt, University of Pennsylvania, 1981.

Figure 330-18 USDA Soil Conservation Service, *Guidelines for Soil and Water Conservation in Urbanizing Areas of Massachusetts,* 1975.

Figure 330-19 Courtesy of Schooley Caldwell Associates, Inc.

Figure 330-20 Reprinted by permission from Harlow C. Landphair and Fred Klatt, Jr., *Landscape Architecture Construction,* Copyright 1979, Elsevier Science Publishing Co., Inc., North Holland, New York, 1979.

Figure 330-21 Ibid.

Figure 330-22 Ibid.

Figure 330-23 Beckett, Jackson, Reuder, Inc., *Michigan Soil Erosion and Sedimentation Control Guidebook,* Michigan Department of Natural Resources.

Figure 330-24 Op cit., Landphair and Klatt.

Figure 330-25 K. H. Beauchamp, "Structures for Soil and Water Conservation Purposes," Engineering Field Manual, Soil Conservation Service, Lincoln NE.

Figure 330-27 Soil Conservation Service TR-55, 1986, or Dunne and Leopold, *Water in Environmental Planning,* 1978. Originally from Hershfield, 1961, data from U.S. Weather Bureau.

Figure 330-28 SCS TR 55, 1986 (210-VI, TR 55, 2d ed., June 1986.

Figure 330-34 Op cit., Carpenter.

Figure 330-35 Op cit., Landphair and Klatt.

Figure 330-36 Op cit., Seelye.

Figure 330-37 *Handbook of Steel Drainage and Construction Products.* American Iron and Steel Institute, Washington D.C. 1983.

Figure 330-38 Op cit., Landphair and Klatt.

Figure 330-39 Ibid.

Figure 330-40 Ibid.

Figure 340-5 FHWA, 1979

Figure 340-6 Adapted from John J. Fruin, "Pedestrian Planning and Design," *Elevator World*, New York, 1988 (by Federal Highway Administration, November 1978, Report FHA-Rd-79, vol. 32.

Figure 340-7 Ibid.

Figure 340-10 Op cit., Lynch and Hack.

Figure 340-11 Adapted from Edward T. Hall, *The Hidden Dimension*, Doubleday, Garden City, New York, 1969 (reprinted by permission of the publisher).

Figure 340-20 Ibid.

Figure 340-21 Ibid.

Figure 341-6 AASHTO, *Guide for the Development of New Bicycle Facilities*, 1981.

Figure 341-7 Ibid.

Figure 341-8 Ibid.

Figure 410-1 Op cit., Ramsey and Sleeper.

Figure 420-1 Adapted from U.S. Department of the Interior, Bureau of Reclamation, *Design of Small Dams*, 2d ed., U.S. Government Printing Office, Washington, D.C., 1973.

Figure 420-2 Ibid.

Figure 420-3 Ibid.

Figure 420-4 Ibid.

Figure 420-5 Ibid.

Figure 420-6 Ibid.

Figure 420-8 Ibid.

Figure 420-11 Ibid.

Figure 420-13 Ibid.

Figure 420-16 Ibid.

Figure 420-20 Ibid.

Figure 420-21 Ibid.

Figure 420-22 Ibid.

Figure 420-23 U.S. Department of Agriculture, Soil Conservation Service, *Agriculture Handbook No. 590*, "Ponds—Planning, Design, Construction," June 1982.

Figure 420-24 Adapted from Elwyn E. Seelye, *Design: Data Book for Civil Engineers*, vol. 1, Wiley, New York, 1960; and Eudell G. Whitten, Civil Engineer, *Reference Transactions American Fisheries Societies*, Dr. George A. Rownsefell (ed.).

Figure 420-25 Adapted from the American Iron and Steel Institute, *Handbook of Steel Drainage and Highway Construction Products*, 2d ed., Washington, D.C., 1983 (designed by the U.S. Soil Conservation Service).

Figure 440-4 Op cit., Seelye.

Figure 440-7 Courtesy of Royston, Hanamoto, Alley, and Abey.

Figure 450-3 Op cit., Carpenter (adapted).

Figure 450-7 Ibid.

Figure 450-20 Ibid.

Figure 450-36 Ibid.

Figure 450-37 Ibid.

Figure 450-38 Ibid.

Figure 470-1 Countryside Commission for Scotland, *Footbridges in the Countryside*, Perth, 1981 (prepared by Reiach Hall Blyth Partnership).

Figure 470-2 Ibid.

Figure 470-3 Ibid.

Figure 470-4 Ibid.

Figure 470-5 Ibid.

Figure 470-6 Ibid.

Figure 470-7 Ibid.

Figure 470-8 Ibid.

Figure 470-9 Ibid.

Figure 470-10 Ibid.

Figure 470-11 Ibid.

Figure 470-12 Ibid.

Figure 470-13 Ibid.

Figure 470-14 Ibid.

Figure 470-15 Ibid.

Figure 470-16 Ibid.

Figure 470-17 Ibid.

Figure 470-18 Ibid.

Figure 470-23 Ibid.

Figure 470-24 Ibid.

Figure 470-25 Ibid.

Figure 470-26 American Association of State Highway and Transportation Officials (AASHTO), *Standards for Highway Bridges,* Washington, D.C., 1977.

Figure 470-27 Op cit., Countryside Commission for Scotland.

Figure 470-28 Ibid.

Figure 470-29 Ibid.

Figure 470-30 Ibid.

Figure 470-31 Ibid.

Figure 470-32 Ibid.

Figure 470-33 Ibid.

Figure 470-34 Ibid.

Figure 470-35 Ibid.

Figure 470-36 Ibid.

Figure 470-37 Ibid.

Figure 470-38 C. R. Thomas and T. F. Hickerson, *Culverts and Small Bridges for Country Roads in North Carolina,* North Carolina Geological and Economic Survey, Raleigh, North Carolina, 1912.

Figure 470-39 Op cit., Countryside Commission for Scotland.

Figure 520-36 Courtesy of Ernie Ralston, ASLA.

Figure 520-38 Adapted from "Design," National Park Service and the National Park and Recreation Association.

Figure 520-46 Adapted from Department of the Army, *Planning and Design of Outdoor Recreation Facilities,* U.S. Government Printing Office, Washington, D.C., 1975.

Figure 520-48 Op cit., National Park Service and National Park and Recreation Association, "Design."

Figure 520-49 Ibid.

Figure 520-51 Departments of the Army, Navy, and Air Force, *Planning and Design of Outdoor Sports Facilities,* U.S. Government Printing Office, Washington, D.C., 1975.

Figure 520-52 Ibid.

Figure 520-54 Op cit., National Park Service and the National Park and Recreation Association, "Design."

Figure 520-55 Ibid.

Figure 630-2 J. C. Loudon, *The Villa Gardener,* 2d ed., Mrs. Loudon (ed.). Wm. S. Orr & Co., London, 1850, p. 387.

Figure 630-3 A. J. Downing, *A Treatise on the Theory and Practice of Landscape Gardening, Adapted to North America,* 2d ed., Wiley and Putnam, New York, 1840 (Frontispiece).

Figure 630-4 Frank J. Scott, *The Art of Beautifying Suburban Home Grounds of Small Extent,* John B. Alden, New York, 1886, Plate XX, p. 208.

Figure 630-5 Robert B. Cridland, *Practical Landscape Gardening,* A. T. De La Mare, 1925.

Figure 630-6 Ossian C. Simonds, *Landscape Gardening,* Macmillan, New York, 1920.

Figure 630-7 Leonard H. Johnson, *Foundation Planting,* A. T. De La Mare, New York, 1927, p. 89.

Figure 630-8 Garrett Eckbo, *Landscape for Living,* F. W. Dodge Corporation, *Architectural Record,* 1950, Figure 16.

Figure 630-9 Drawn by Robert R. Harvey.

Figure 630-10 Robert R. Harvey and Associates, *Historic Grounds Report and Landscape Plan, Lincoln Home National Historic Site, Springfield, Illinois,* U.S. Department of the Interior, National Park Service, Ames, Iowa, April 1982, Figure V1-2, p. 147.

Figure 630-11 Wehner, Nowysz, Pattschull, and Pfiffner, *Woodlawn Pope—Leighey House Comprehensive Development Plan,* The National Trust for Historic Preservation, Iowa City, January 1981, Figure 8, p. 37.

Figure 630-12 Ibid.

Figure 630-13 Op cit., Robert R. Harvey and Associates, p. 21.

Figure 630-14 Ibid., p. 28.

Figure 630-15 Robert T. Harvey, *Terrace Hill Preliminary Site Investigation,* Ames, Iowa, 1976.

Figure 630-16 Ibid.

Figure 630-17 Op cit., Wehner, Nowysz, Pattschull, and Piffner, Figure 33, p. 81.

Figure 630-18 Robert R. Harvey, *Heritage at Risk: A Study of the Historic and Scenic Potential along the Des Moines River from Keosauqua to Framington,* Van Buren County, Iowa, Area XV Regional Planning Commission, Ames, Iowa, July 1979, Figure 31, p. 50.

Figure 630-19 W. G. Hoskins, *Fieldwork in Local History,* Faber and Faber, London, 1967, pp. 120–121.

Figure 630-20 Michael Anston and Rowley Trevor, *Landscape Archaeology,* David and Charles, London, 1974, Figure 18, p. 78.

Figure 630-21 Audrey Noel Hume, *Archaeology and the Colonial Gardener,* Colonial Williamsburg Archaeological Series, No. 7, Colonial Williamsburg Foundation, Williamsburg, Virginia, 1974, Figure 26, p. 44.

Figure 640-3 Modified from *Michigan Soil Erosion and Sedimentation Control Guidebook,* Michigan Department of Natural Resources.

Figure 640-4 Modified from *Erosion and Sediment Control Handbook for Urban Areas,* U.S. Soil Conservation Service, Morgantown, West Virginia, 1975.

Figure 640-6 Modified from *Erosion Control Manual,* Colorado Department of Highways, 1978.

Figure 640-12 Modified from Lou Nelson and Julie Opell Klym, "Slopes Erosion Control—Part II," *Western Landscaping News,* November 1979.

Figure 640-15 Modified from R. I. Barnhisel, *Lime and Fertilizer Recommendations for Reclamation of Surface-Mined Spoils,* AGR 40.

Figure 640-16 Modified from J. D. Rhoades, "Drainage for Salinity Control," *Drainage for Agriculture,* No. 17 in the Agronomy Series, J. V. Schilfgaarde (ed.), American Society of Agronomy, Inc., Madison, Wisconsin, 1974.

Figure 640-22 Modified from Richard L. Hodder, "Planting Methods and Equipment," a paper presented at a workshop entitled *Reclamation of Western Surface-Mined Lands,* 1976.

Figure 640-23 Modified from Dr. Dennis Hansen, *Reclamation Planting of Disturbed Sites,* Native Plants, Inc., Salt Lake City, Utah, 1982.

Figure 640-26 Modified from John F. Valentine, *Range Development and Improvements,* Brigham Young University Press, Provo, Utah, 1982.

Figure 660-1 L_{eq} Nomograph. This nomograph can be used to predict noise levels of vehicular traffic. The L_{eq} scale gives the predicted L_{eq} at the observer.

Figure 660-2 Canada Mortgage and Housing Corporation, Ottawa, Canada, 1979.

Figure 660-19 Existing L_{eq} Ambient Noise Levels (Example Problem). Noise levels are measured at twelve different places in the park. Small circles refer to morning, evening, and nightime readings.

Figure 710-3 G. M. Fair, J. C. Geyer, and D. A. Okun, *Water and Wastewater Engineering,* Wiley, New York, vol. 1, 1966; vol. 2, 1968 (Copyright © and used with permission of publisher).

Figure 710-4 Reproduced with permission from G. E. Meinzer, *Physics of the Earth,* vol. 9, *Hydrology,* McGraw-Hill, New York, 1942.

Figure 710-5 U.S. Department of Agriculture, "Water," *The Yearbook of Agriculture, 1955,* U.S. Government Printing Office, Washington, D. C., 1955.

Figure 710-6 Adapted from National Weather Service, *Climates of the U.S.,* U.S. Department of Commerce, Washington, D.C., 1974.

Figure 710-7 Ray K. Linsley, Jr., Max A. Kohler, and Joseph L. Paulhus, *Applied Hydrology,* McGraw-Hill, New York, 1949 (originally from the U.S. Weather Bureau for the period 1899–1939).

Figure 710-8 U.S. Environmental Protection Agency, *Manual of Water Supply Systems,* U.S. Government Printing Office, Washington, D.C., 1973.

Figure 710-10 U.S. Department of Agriculture, SCS, *Engineering Field Manual,* U.S. Government Printing Office, Washington, D.C., July, 1974.

Figure 710-11 Op cit., U.S. Environmental Protection Agency.

Figure 710-17 Op cit., Fair, Geyer, and Okun.

Figure 710-26 V. T. Chow (ed.), *Handbook of Applied Hydrology,* McGraw-Hill, New York, 1964.

Figure 710-27 Whipple, Fair, and Whipple, *Microcsopy of Drinking Water,* 4th ed., Wiley, New York, 1927 (Copyright © and used with permission of the publisher).

Figure 740-2 Op cit., Seelye.

Figure 740-3 Herbert L. Nichols, Jr., *Moving the Earth,* Van Nostrand Reinhold, Princeton, New Jersey, 1955.

Figure 750-3 Army Corps of Engineers.

Figure 750-4 Ibid.

Figure 750-5 Ibid.

Figure 750-6 Ibid.

Figure 750-7 Ibid.

Figure 750-20 Febco Company.

Figure 750-21 Ibid.

Figure 810-1 Douglas S. Way, *Terrain Analysis: A Guide to Site Selection Using Aerial Photographic Interpretation,* 2d ed., Douglas S. Way, Columbus, Ohio, 1978 (original source: *Yearbook of Agriculture,* 1957); and Gerald W. Olson, *Soils and the Environment: A Guide to Soil Surveys and Their Applications,* Chapman and Hall, New York, 1981.

Figure 810-2 Nyle C. Brady, *The Nature and Properties of Soils,* 8th ed., Macmillan, New York, 1974.

Figure 810-3 Harold N. Atkins, *Highway Materials, Soils, and Concretes,* Reston Publishing Company, Reston, Virginia, 1980, p. 27.

Figure 810-4 W. L. Schroeder, *Soils in Construction,* 2d ed., Wiley, New York, 1980.

Figure 810-5 Op cit., Godfrey.

Figure 810-7 U.S. Department of Commerce Weather Bureau; Highway Research Board, "Frost Action in Roads and Airfields," National Academy of Sciences-National Research Council, Washington, D.C., 1952.

Figure 810-8 The Asphalt Institute, *Drainage of Asphalt Pavement Structures,* Soil Manual SM10, College Park, Maryland, 1969.

Figure 810-9 Op cit., Atkins.

Figure 810-10 P. M. Ahn. "A Note on the Apparent Effect of Soil Texture on Soil Erodibility as Deduced from the Wischmeier Monograph," in Technical Newsletter #1, December 1978, Rome, Italy, Food and Agricultural Organization of the United Nations.

Figure 810-11 Op cit., Brady.

Figure 810-12 C. R. Adams, K. M. Bamford, and M. P. Early, *Principles of Horticulture,* Heinemann, London, 1984.

Figure 820-2 Op cit., Carpenter.

Figure 820-6 Adapted from "Full-Depth Asphalt Tennis Courts," The Asphalt Institute, 1974.

Figure 820-8 "Construction Specifications for Curbs and Gutters," The Asphalt Institute, 1978.

Figure 820-10 Adapted from *Massachusetts Department of Public Works Standards,* 1966.

Figure 820-11 Op cit., "Construction Specifications for Curbs and Gutters."

Figure 830-2 American Concrete Institute, "Slabs on Grade," Detroit, 1982.

Figure 830-3 Ibid.

Figure 830-4 Ibid.

Figure 830-5 Op cit., Ramsey and Sleeper.

Figure 830-6 Portland Cement Association, *Cement Mason's Guide,* Skokie, Illinois, 1973.

Figure 830-7 Op cit., Ramsey and Sleeper.

Figure 830-10 Ibid.

Figure 830-11 Ibid.

Figure 830-12 Op cit., Carpenter.

Figure 830-13 Ibid.

Figure 830-14 Ibid.; also The Portland Cement Association, *Design and Control of Concrete Mixtures,* 12th ed., Skokie, Illinois, 1979.

Figure 830-16 Bomanite Corporation, Palo Alto, California.

Figure 830-18 NAHB Research Foundation, *Residential Concrete,* National Association of Home Builders of the United States, Washington, D.C., 1983.

Figure 840-1 American Society for Testing and Materials, "Designation C 216-81 and C 62-81," Philadelphia, 1981, as reprinted in *ASTM Standard Specifications for Brick and Applicable Testing Methods for Units;* and *BIA Standard Specification for Portland Cement—Lime Mortar for Brick Masonry,* BIA Designation MI-72, Brick Institute of America, July 1981.

Figure 840-2 Op cit., Carpenter.

Figure 840-3 Ibid.

Figure 840-4 "Brick Masonry Cavity Wall Construction," Technical Note 21c, Brick Institute of America.

Figure 840-5 Op cit., Ramsey and Sleeper.

Figure 840-6 Frank A. Randall, Jr. and William C. Panarese, *Concrete Masonry Handbook,* Portland Cement Association, 1976.

Figure 840-7 Ibid.

Figure 840-8 Op cit., Hornbostel; Op cit., Randall and Panarese.

Figure 840-9 Op cit., Randall and Panarese; also Robert R. Schneider and Walter L. Dickey, *Reinforced Masonry Design,* Prentice Hall, Englewood Cliffs, New Jersey, 1980.

Figure 840-10 Op cit., Randall and Panarese

Figure 840-11 Harold B. Olin, John L. Schmidt, and Walter H. Lewis, *Construction: Principles, Materials, and Methods,* the Institute for Financial Education and Interstate Printers and Publishers, Chicago, 1983.

Figure 840-12 Ibid.

Figure 840-13 Ibid.

Figure 840-14 The American Society of Landscape Architects, *Landscape Architecture Magazine,* July 1982.

Figure 840-15 Max Alth, *Masonry—A Homeowner's Bible,* Doubleday, Garden City, New York, 1982.

Figure 840-16 Op cit., Ramsey and Sleeper.

Figure 840-17 Op cit., Olin et al.

Figure 840-31 Op cit., Carpenter.

Figure 850-1 Op cit., Olin et al.

Figure 850-2 Ibid.

Figure 850-4 Ibid.

Figure 850-5 Ibid.

Figure 850-6 Ibid.

Figure 850-7 U.S. Forest Products Laboratory, *Wood Engineering Handbook,* Prentice Hall, Englewood Cliffs, New Jersey, 1974.

Figure 850-8 Op cit., Olin et al.

Figure 850-9 Ibid.

Figure 850-10 Ibid.

Figure 850-11 American Plywood Association, "Plywood Design Specifications," 1976.

Figure 850-12 Op cit., Ramsey and Sleeper.

Figure 850-13 Op cit., Olin et al.

Figure 850-14 Op cit., Ramsey and Sleeper.

Figure 850-15 T. C. Scheffer and A. F. Verall, *Principles for Protecting Wood from Decay,* U.S. Forest Products Laboratory, Madison, Wisconsin, 1973.

Figure 850-16 Op cit., Olin et al.

Figure 860-1 Op cit., Hornbostel.

Figure 860-3 Ibid.

Figure 870-2 "Architectural Fiberglas Fabric Structures," Owens-Corning Fiberglas Corporation; and "Helios Soft Shell Structures," Helios Industries.

Figure 880-2 P. R. Rankilor, *Membranes in Ground Engineering,* Wiley, New York, 1981.

Figure 880-3 Ibid.

Figure 880-4 Ibid.

Figure 880-9 Robert M. Koerner and Joseph P. Welsh, *Construction and Geotechnical Engineering Using Synthetic Fabrics,* Wiley, New York, 1980.

Figure 880-10 Ibid.

Figure 880-11 Op cit., Rankilor.

Figure 880-14 Op cit., Koerner and Welsh.

Index